8 CLASSIC AMERICAN NOVELS

DAVID MADDEN
Louisiana State University

HBJ

Harcourt Brace Jovanovich, Publishers
San Diego New York Chicago Austin Washington, D.C.
London Sydney Tokyo Toronto

Cover art and woodcuts by Janine Muelchi.

ISBN: 0-15-520926-4

Printed in the United States of America

PREFACE

Eight Classic American Novels draws together in a single volume eight novels that are acknowledged American masterpieces. Extensive research, including a survey of teachers of American literature, revealed that the American novels included here are the ones most often taught in college literature courses. For that reason, this collection can meet a variety of course needs: (1) as a supplement to the standard American literature anthologies; (2) in introduction to literature courses; (3) in junior, senior, and graduate courses in American literature; and (4) in courses on the novel as a form.

Instructional material has been kept to a minimum. Biographical notes appear as headnotes to each novel. Further Readings for each novel appear at the back of the book. Some Elements for Discussion and Writing are a unique feature. Each list of elements offers handy, practical references to the principal characters and themes, motifs and symbols, and other key elements for discussion and writing.

I would like to thank my colleagues who prepared the lists: John Allison, Eastern Illinois University; J. Bainard Cowan, Louisiana State University; Daniel M. Fogel, Louisiana State University; J. Gerald Kennedy, Louisiana State University; Robert Merrill, University of Nevada, Reno; Scott F. Stoddart, Mount St. Clare College; and Warren Walker, Texas Tech University. Peggy Bach gave me valuable advice and encouragement. For advice on choices for and the usefulness of this collection, I would also like to acknowledge: Carolyn Becker, James Babin, Deborah Fox, Steve Kitzman, Miriam Phelps, Rich Howard, Sue Crider, Elizabeth Cooper, Jeff Caphew, Cheryl Hurley, and Ross Willis.

David Madden

CONTENTS

DETAILED CONTENTS

MARK TWAIN 715

THE ADVENTURES OF HUCKLEBERRY FINN 719

STEPHEN CRANE 884

THE RED BADGE OF COURAGE 887

KATE CHOPIN 963

THE AWAKENING 965

JAMES FENIMORE COOPER (1789–1851)

James Fenimore Cooper created a character who is perhaps as world famous as Don Quixote and Hamlet—Natty Bumppo. Also called Leather-Stocking, the Daniel Boone-like hunter on the American frontier is the mythic embodiment of democratic individualism in action. Over eighteen years of his literary career, during which he wrote 33 novels and many works of nonfiction, Cooper produced five novels revolving around Natty Bumppo, calling him by various names. He did not plan a quintet; The Leather-Stocking Tales evolved as Cooper witnessed the evolution of America. One way to appreciate *The Last of the Mohicans* is to keep in mind the astonishing richness and variety of Cooper's raw material and his various roles as an active American citizen and as the author of many different kinds of books, several of which were innovative. Simultaneously depicting the past and the present, with a vision of the future, Cooper idealized and criticized America's ongoing experiment with democracy. His passionate convictions endowed all his work with great force and energy.

Cooper was born September 15, 1789, in Burlington, New Jersey. A year later his family moved to Cooperstown at the foot of Lake Otsego in upstate New York. His father, author of *Guide in the Wilderness* (1810), had founded the town in 1786. Growing up in a family of landed aristocrats, Cooper observed the incipient decline of American frontier values. After two years at Yale, he went to sea for four years. When he returned in 1811, Cooper married Susan Augusta De Lancey, of a prominent Tory family. He then pursued agricultural, political, religious, military, cultural, and domestic activities in Westchester County and Cooperstown.

Cooper's literary career, like that of most early American writers, began with an imitation not only of the method but also of the content of British literature. *Precaution* (1820) is a tedious satire of English high society reminiscent of Jane Austen. Cooper's second novel was modelled after the historical romances of Sir Walter Scott, but in its use of legendary revolutionary heroes, *The Spy* (1821) was the first genuinely American novel, earning Cooper world-wide fame.

During the next four years, Cooper lived the life of a literary celebrity in New York City, but his visionary imagination was drawn to the frontier past. Having discovered his identity as an American writer using American materials, he produced the first Leather-Stocking tale, *The Pioneers* (1823). Readers first meet Natty

Bumppo when he is already about 70 years old. In 1793, around the time Cooper's hometown was first settled, Natty Bumppo moves across the Alleghenies to escape the corrupting ways of civilization, and his life-long friend Chief Chingachgook dies. Drawing next on personal experience and making use of the American folk-hero John Paul Jones, Cooper wrote one of the first great sea novels, *The Pilot* (1824). Over the next two decades, he produced four more sea novels. After writing another novel of the revolution, *Lionel Lincoln* (1825), Cooper at 35 imagines Natty Bumppo at age forty in 1757, involved, with Chief Chingachgook, in a typical action adventure pattern of chase, capture, and escape in *The Last of the Mohicans* (1826). With this sixth, and most famous novel, Cooper provided good reason to be called The American Scott and The Father of the American Novel.

While living abroad from 1826 to 1833, as American Consul at Lyon, France, among other roles, Cooper wrote nonfiction works that defended America against her foreign critics, made important contributions to the literature of travel, and put Scott's historical romance pattern to new use in his creation of three satires of European feudalism (1831–1833). But soon after he began his tenure as a critical observer of the Old World, Cooper returned to Natty Bumppo, now almost 90 years old in the year 1804, dying of old age on the Great Plains among white and Indian friends. Some readers consider *The Prairie* (1827) the most enduring of the five tales.

Back in New York City in 1833, Cooper measured America with a perspective enhanced by years in Europe, but still shaped by his vision of the frontier past. In 1836, he returned to his hometown, Cooperstown, the site personally emblematic of the frontier. What he observed compelled him to become in life and in literature one of the country's most severe critics of her failure to realize her potential, seen best perhaps in *The American Democrat*, *Homeward Bound*, and *Home As Found*, all three published in 1838. Involved in protracted lawsuits over land and literary libel, Cooper lost the affection of his reading public, while the reputation of his novels grew.

Cooper's announced retirement from writing did not last long. His abiding intention to depict American ideals, as he conceived them, prompted him to produce the monumental *History of the Navy of the United States* (1839). Then he returned again to the frontier in *The Pathfinder; or The Inland Sea* (1840). Natty Bumppo is forty years old, the scene is a small outpost on Lake Ontario, and his companion is again Chief Chingachgook. A year later the last of the Leather-Stocking tales appeared. In *The Deerslayer; or The First War Path*, Natty Bumppo is a young man, reared among the Delaware Indians, during the years 1740–1745, a time of war with the Huron Indians. Written last, it is the first in the chronology of Natty Bumppo's life; second is *The Last of the Mohicans*; then come *The Pathfinder*, *The Pioneer*, and *The Prairie*.

In the last decade of his life, Cooper wrote 13 novels. The socio-political family trilogy, *The Little-Page Manuscripts*, about the Anti-Rent Wars, and the first American utopian novel, *The Crater* (1847), are examples of his steady flow of innovation. Cooper died September 14, 1851, at age 62.

Within the framework of romantic historical fiction, Cooper presented American political, religious, and moral ideals in action. Both his life and his literature are characterized by a dual vision: romantic and realistic, celebratory and critical. Using the very stuff of American experience, and mainly because of his masterwork The Leather-Stocking Tales, Cooper became known as the American Homer. He was more highly esteemed abroad, especially in France, where Balzac admired him, than at home, ironically for the mythic dimension of his tales of the hunter allied with his Indian warrior friends. Individualistic in his life, Cooper created vigorously individualistic heroes, most of whom are outsiders embodying ideal and enduring aspects of the American character shaped by the American landscape.

Washington Irving and William Cullen Bryant "had helped to create an art for America," wrote Robert E. Spiller, an early Cooper scholar, "but Cooper took the first strong step toward an American art." Criticized for his sometimes turgid style and his reliance on Scott's historical romance formula, Cooper is praised for having both reflected and criticized his time in a massive body of work. But the scope of his symbolic vision has not yet been fully appreciated. One may do well to begin with *The Last of the Mohicans*.

THE LAST OF THE MOHICANS

James Fenimore Cooper

CHAPTER I

Mine ear is open and my heart prepared:
The worst is worldly loss thou canst unfold.
Say, is my kingdom lost?

SHAKESPEARE, *King Richard II.*, III. 11. 93.

It was a feature peculiar to the colonial wars of North America, that the toils and dangers of the wilderness were to be encountered before the adverse hosts could meet. A wide and apparently an impervious boundary of forests severed the possessions of the hostile provinces of France and England. The hardy colonist, and the trained European who fought at his side, frequently expended months in struggling against the rapids of the streams, or in effecting the rugged passes of the mountains, in quest of an opportunity to exhibit their courage in a more martial conflict. But, emulating the patience and self-denial of the practiced native warriors, they learned to overcome every difficulty; and it would seem that, in time, there was no recess of the woods so dark, nor any secret place so lonely, that it might claim exemption from the inroads of those who had pledged their blood to satiate their vengeance, or to uphold the cold and selfish policy of the distant monarchs of Europe.

Perhaps no district throughout the wide extent of the intermediate frontiers can furnish a livelier picture of the cruelty and fierceness of the savage warfare of those periods than the country which lies between the head waters of the Hudson and the adjacent lakes.

The facilities which nature had there offered to the march of the combatants were too obvious to be neglected. The lengthened sheet of the Champlain stretched from the frontiers of Canada, deep within the borders of the neighboring province of New York, forming a natural passage across half the distance that the French were compelled to master in order to strike their enemies. Near its southern termination, it received the contributions of another lake, whose waters were so limpid as to have been exclusively selected by the Jesuit missionaries to perform the typical purification of baptism, and to obtain for it the title of lake "du Saint Sacrement." The less zealous English thought they conferred a sufficient honor on its unsullied fountains, when they bestowed the name of their reigning prince, the second of the house of Hanover. The two united to rob the untutored possessors of its wooded scenery of their native right to perpetuate its original appellation of "Horican."[1]

Winding its way among countless islands, and imbedded in mountains, the "holy lake" extended a dozen leagues still further to the south. With the high plain that there interposed itself to the further passage of the water, commenced a portage of as many miles, which conducted the adventurer to the banks of the Hudson, at a point where, with the usual obstructions of the rapids, or rifts, as they were then termed in the language of the country, the river became navigable to the tide.

While, in the pursuit of their daring plans of annoyance, the restless enterprise of the French even attempted the distant and difficult gorges of the Alleghany, it may easily be imagined that their proverbial acuteness would not overlook the natural advantages of the district we have just described. It became, emphatically, the bloody arena, in which most of the battles for the mastery of the colonies were contested. Forts were erected at the different points that commanded the facilities of the route, and were taken and retaken, razed and rebuilt, as victory alighted on the hostile banners. While the husbandman shrank back from the dangerous passes, within the safer boundaries of the more ancient settlements, armies larger than those that had often disposed of the sceptres of the mother countries were seen to bury themselves in these forests, whence they rarely returned but in skeleton bands, that were haggard with care, or dejected by defeat. Though the arts of peace were unknown to this fatal region, its forests were alive with men; its shades and glens rang with the sounds of martial music, and the echoes of its mountains threw back the laugh, or repeated the wanton cry, of many a gallant and reckless youth, as he hurried by them, in the noontide of his spirits, to slumber in a long night of forgetfulness.

It was in this scene of strife and bloodshed that the incidents we shall attempt to relate occurred, during the third year of the war which England and France last waged for the possession of a country that neither was destined to retain.

The imbecility of her military leaders abroad, and the fatal want of energy in her councils at home, had lowered the character of Great Britain from the proud elevation on which it had been placed by the talents and enterprise of her former warriors and statesmen. No longer dreaded by her enemies, her servants were fast losing the confidence of self-respect. In this mortifying abasement, the colonists, though innocent of her imbecility, and too humble to be the agents of her blunders, were but the natural participators.

They had recently seen a chosen army from that country, which, reverencing as a mother, they had blindly believed invincible—an army led by a chief who had

---

[1]As each nation of the Indians had either its language or its dialect, they usually gave different names to the same places, though nearly all of their appellations were descriptive of the object. Thus, a literal translation of the name of this beautiful sheet of water, used by the tribe that dwelt on its banks, would be "The Tail of the Lake." Lake George, as it is vulgarly, and now indeed legally called, forms a sort of tail to Lake Champlain, when viewed on the map. Hence the name. [J.F.C.]

been selected from a crowd of trained warriors, for his rare military endowments, disgracefully routed by a handful of French and Indians, and only saved from annihilation by the coolness and spirit of a Virginian boy, whose riper fame has since diffused itself, with the steady influence of moral truth, to the uttermost confines of Christendom.[2] A wide frontier had been laid naked by this unexpected disaster, and more substantial evils were preceded by a thousand fanciful and imaginary dangers. The alarmed colonists believed that the yells of the savages mingled with every fitful gust of wind that issued from the interminable forests of the west. The terrific character of their merciless enemies increased immeasurably the natural horrors of warfare. Numberless recent massacres were still vivid in their recollections; nor was there any ear in the provinces so deaf as not to have drunk in with avidity the narrative of some fearful tale of midnight murder, in which the natives of the forests were the principal and barbarous actors. As the credulous and excited traveller related the hazardous chances of the wilderness, the blood of the timid curdled with terror, and mothers cast anxious glances even at those children which slumbered within the security of the largest towns. In short, the magnifying influence of fear began to set at naught the calculations of reason, and to render those who should have remembered their manhood, the slaves of the basest of passions. Even the most confident and the stoutest hearts began to think the issue of the contest was becoming doubtful; and that abject class was hourly increasing in numbers, who thought they foresaw all the possessions of the English crown in America subdued by their Christian foes, or laid waste by the inroads of their relentless allies.

When, therefore, intelligence was received at the fort which covered the southern termination of the portage between the Hudson and the lakes, that Montcalm had been seen moving up the Champlain, with an army "numerous as the leaves on the trees," its truth was admitted with more of the craven reluctance of fear than with the stern joy that a warrior should feel, in finding an enemy within reach of his blow. The news had been brought, towards the decline of a day in midsummer, by an Indian runner, who also bore an urgent request from Munro, the commander of a work on the shore of the "holy lake," for a speedy and powerful reinforcement. It has already been mentioned that the distance between these two posts was less than five leagues. The rude path, which originally formed their line of communication, had been widened for the passage of wagons; so that the distance which had been travelled by the son of the forest in two hours might easily be effected by a detachment of troops, with their necessary baggage, between the rising and setting of a summer sun. The loyal servants of the British crown had given to one of these forest fastnesses the name of William Henry, and to the other that of Fort Edward; calling each after a favorite prince of the reigning family. The veteran Scotchman just named held the first, with a regiment of regulars and a few provincials; a force really by far too small to make head against the formidable power that Montcalm was leading to the foot of his earthen mounds. At the latter, however, lay General Webb, who commanded the armies of the king in the northern provinces, with a body of more than five thousand men. By uniting the several

[2]Washington: who, after uselessly admonishing the European general [Braddock] of the danger into which he was heedlessly running, saved the remnants of the British army, on this occasion, by his decision and courage. The reputation earned by Washington in this battle was the principal cause of his being selected to command the American armies at a later day. It is a circumstance worthy of observation, that, while all America rang with his well merited reputation, his name does not occur in any European account of the battle; at least, the author has searched for it without success. In this manner does the mother country absorb even the fame, under that system of rule. [J.F.C.]

detachments of his command, this officer might have arrayed nearly double that number of combatants against the enterprising Frenchman, who had ventured so far from his reinforcements, with an army but little superior in numbers.

But under the influence of their degraded fortunes, both officers and men appeared better disposed to await the approach of their formidable antagonists, within their works, than to resist the progress of their march, by emulating the successful example of the French at Fort du Quesne, and striking a blow on their advance.

After the first surprise of the intelligence had a little abated, a rumor was spread through the entrenched camp, which stretched along the margin of the Hudson, forming a chain of outworks to the body of the fort itself, that a chosen detachment of fifteen hundred men was to depart, with the dawn, for William Henry, the post at the northern extremity of the portage. That which at first was only rumor soon became certainty, as orders passed from the quarters of the commander-in-chief to the several corps he had selected for this service, to prepare for their speedy departure. All doubt as to the intention of Webb now vanished, and an hour or two of hurried footsteps and anxious faces succeeded. The novice in the military art flew from point to point, retarding his own preparations by the excess of his violent and somewhat distempered zeal; while the more practiced veteran made his arrangements with a deliberation that scorned every appearance of haste; though his sober lineaments and anxious eye sufficiently betrayed that he had no very strong professional relish for the as yet untried and dreaded warfare of the wilderness. At length the sun set in a flood of glory, behind the distant western hills, and as darkness drew its veil around the secluded spot the sounds of preparation diminished; the last light finally disappeared from the log cabin of some officer; the trees cast their deeper shadows over the mounds and the rippling stream, and a silence soon pervaded the camp, as deep as that which reigned in the vast forest by which it was environed.

According to the orders of the preceding night, the heavy sleep of the army was broken by the rolling of the warning drums, whose rattling echoes were heard issuing, on the damp morning air, out of every vista of the woods, just as day began to draw the shaggy outlines of some tall pines of the vicinity on the opening brightness of a soft and cloudless eastern sky. In an instant the whole camp was in motion; the meanest soldier arousing from his lair to witness the departure of his comrades, and to share in the excitement and incidents of the hour. The simple array of the chosen band was soon completed. While the regular and trained hirelings of the king marched with haughtiness to the right of the line, the less pretending colonists took their humbler position on its left, with a docility that long practice had rendered easy. The scouts departed; strong guards preceded and followed the lumbering vehicles that bore the baggage; and before the gray light of morning was mellowed by the rays of the sun, the main body of the combatants wheeled into column, and left the encampment with a show of high military bearing, that served to drown the slumbering apprehensions of many a novice, who was now about to make his first essay in arms. While in view of their admiring comrades, the same proud front and ordered array was observed, until the notes of their fifes growing fainter in the distance, the forest at length appeared to swallow up the living mass which had slowly entered its bosom.

The deepest sounds of the retiring and invisible column had ceased to be borne on the breeze to the listeners, and the latest straggler had already disappeared in pursuit; but there still remained the signs of another departure, before a log cabin of unusual size and accommodations, in front of which those sentinels paced their rounds, who were known to guard the person of the English general. At this spot were gathered some half dozen horses, caparisoned in a manner which showed that two, at least, were destined to bear the persons of females, of a rank that it was not usual to meet so far in the wilds of the country. A third wore the trappings and arms of an officer of the staff; while the rest, from the plainness of the housings, and the travelling mails with which they were encumbered, were evidently fitted for the reception of as many menials, who were, seemingly, already awaiting the pleasure of those they served. At a respectful distance from this unusual show were gathered divers groups of curious idlers; some admiring the blood and bone of the high-mettled military charger, and others gazing at the preparations, with the dull wonder of vulgar curiosity. There was one man, however, who, by his countenance and actions, formed a marked exception to those who composed the latter class of spectators, being neither idle, nor seemingly very ignorant.

The person of this individual was to the last degree ungainly, without being in any particular manner deformed. He had all the bones and joints of other men, without any of their proportions. Erect, his stature surpassed that of his fellows; though, seated, he appeared reduced within the ordinary limits of the race. The same contrariety in his members seemed to exist throughout the whole man. His head was large; his shoulders narrow, his arms long and dangling; while his hands were small, if not delicate. His legs and thighs were thin, nearly to emaciation, but of extraordinary length; and his knees would have been considered tremendous, had they not been outdone by the broader foundations on which this false superstructure of blended human orders was so profanely reared. The ill-assorted and injudicious attire of the individual only served to render his awkwardness more conspicuous. A sky-blue coat, with short and broad skirts and low cape, exposed a long thin neck, and longer and thinner legs, to the worst animadversions of the evil disposed. His nether garment was of yellow nankeen, closely fitted to the shape, and tied at his bunches of knees by large knots of white ribbon, a good deal sullied by use. Clouded cotton stockings, and shoes, on one of the latter of which was a plated spur, completed the costume of the lower extremity of this figure, no curve or angle of which was concealed, but, on the other hand, studiously exhibited, through the vanity or simplicity of its owner. From beneath the flap of an enormous pocket of a soiled vest of embossed silk, heavily ornamented with tarnished silver lace, projected an instrument, which, from being seen in such martial company, might have been easily mistaken for some mischievous and unknown implement of war. Small as it was, this uncommon engine had excited the curiosity of most of the Europeans in the camp, though several of the provincials were seen to handle it, not only without fear, but with the utmost familiarity. A large, civil cocked hat, like those worn by clergymen within the last thirty years, surmounted the whole, furnishing dignity to a good-natured and somewhat vacant countenance, that apparently needed such artificial aid, to support the gravity of some high and extraordinary trust.

While the common herd stood aloof, in deference to the quarters of Webb, the figure we have described stalked into the centre of the domestics, freely expressing his censures or commendations on the merits of the horses, as by chance they displeased or satisfied his judgment.

"This beast, I rather conclude, friend, is not of home raising, but is from foreign lands, or perhaps from the little island itself over the blue water?" he said, in a voice as remarkable for the softness and sweetness of its tones, as was his person for its rare proportions: "I may speak of these things, and be no braggart; for I have been down at both havens; that which is situate at the mouth of Thames, and is named after the capital of Old England, and that which is called 'Haven,' with the addition of the word 'New;' and have seen the snows and brigantines collecting their droves, like the gathering to the ark, being outward bound to the Island of Jamaica, for the purpose of barter and traffic in four-footed animals; but never before have I beheld a beast which verified the true Scripture war-horse like this: 'He paweth in the valley, and rejoiceth in his strength: he goeth on to meet the armed men. He saith among the trumpets, Ha, ha; and he smelleth the battle afar off, the thunder of the captains, and the shouting.' It would seem that the stock of the horse of Israel has descended to our own time; would it not, friend?"

Receiving no reply to this extraordinary appeal, which in truth, as it was delivered with the vigor of full and sonorous tones, merited some sort of notice, he who had thus sung forth the language of the holy book turned to the silent figure to whom he had unwittingly addressed himself, and found a new and more powerful subject of admiration in the object that encountered his gaze. His eyes fell on the still, upright, and rigid form of the "Indian runner," who had borne to the camp the unwelcome tidings of the preceding evening. Although in a state of perfect repose, and apparently disregarding, with characteristic stoicism, the excitement and bustle around him, there was a sullen fierceness mingled with the quiet of the savage, that was likely to arrest the attention of much more experienced eyes than those which now scanned him, in unconcealed amazement. The native bore both the tomahawk and knife of his tribe; and yet his appearance was not altogether that of a warrior. On the contrary, there was an air of neglect about his person, like that which might have proceeded from great and recent exertion, which he had not yet found leisure to repair. The colors of the war-paint had blended in dark confusion about his fierce countenance, and rendered his swarthy lineaments still more savage and repulsive than if art had attempted an effect which had been thus produced by chance. His eye, alone, which glistened like a fiery star amid lowering clouds, was to be seen in its state of native wildness. For a single instant, his searching and yet wary glance met the wondering look of the other, and then changing its direction, partly in cunning, and partly in disdain, it remained fixed, as if penetrating the distant air.

It is impossible to say what unlooked-for remark this short and silent communication, between two such singular men, might have elicited from the white man, had not his active curiosity been again drawn to other objects. A general movement amongst the domestics, and a low sound of gentle voices, announced the approach of those whose presence alone was wanted to enable the cavalcade to move. The simple admirer of the war-horse instantly fell back to a low, gaunt, switch-tailed mare, that was unconsciously gleaning the faded herbage of the camp nigh by; where, leaning with one elbow on the blanket that concealed an apology for a saddle, he became a spectator of the departure, while a foal was quietly making its morning repast, on the opposite side of the same animal.

A young man, in the dress of an officer, conducted to their steeds two females, who, as it was apparent by their dresses, were prepared to encounter the fatigues of a journey in the woods. One, and she was the most juvenile in her appearance, though both were young, permitted glimpses of her dazzling complexion, fair golden hair, and bright blue eyes, to be caught, as she artlessly suffered the morning air to blow aside the green veil which descended low from her beaver. The flush which still lingered above the pines in the western sky was not more bright nor delicate than the bloom on her cheek; nor was the opening day more cheering than the animated smile which she bestowed on the youth, as he assisted her into the saddle. The other, who appeared to share equally in the attentions of the young officer, concealed her charms from the gaze of the soldiery with a care that seemed better fitted to the experience of four or five additional years. It could be seen, however, that her person, though moulded with the same exquisite proportions, of which none of the graces were lost by the travelling dress she wore, was rather fuller and more mature than that of her companion.

No sooner were these females seated, than their attendant sprang lightly into the saddle of the war-horse, when the whole three bowed to Webb, who, in courtesy, awaited their parting on the threshold of his cabin, and turning their horses' heads, they proceeded at a slow amble, followed by their train, towards the northern entrance of the encampment. As they traversed that short distance, not a voice was heard amongst them; but a slight exclamation proceeded from the younger of the females, as the Indian runner glided by her, unexpectedly, and led the way along the military road in her front. Though this sudden and startling movement of the Indian produced no sound from the other, in the surprise her veil also was allowed to open its folds, and betrayed an indescribable look of pity, admiration, and horror, as her dark eye followed the easy motions of the savage. The tresses of this lady were shining and black, like the plumage of the raven. Her complexion was not brown, but it rather appeared charged with the color of the rich blood, that seemed ready to burst its bounds. And yet there was neither coarseness nor want of shadowing in a countenance that was exquisitely regular and dignified, and surpassingly beautiful. She smiled, as if in pity at her own momentary forgetfulness, discovering by the act a row of teeth that would have shamed the purest ivory; when, replacing the veil, she bowed her face, and rode in silence, like one whose thoughts were abstracted from the scene around her.

CHAPTER II

Sola, sola! wo ha, ho! sola, sola!
SHAKESPEARE, *Merchant of Venice,* V. i. 39.

While one of the lovely beings we have so cursorily presented to the reader was thus lost in thought, the other quickly recovered from the alarm which induced the exclamation, and, laughing at her own weakness, she inquired of the youth who rode by her side,—

"Are such spectres frequent in the woods, Heyward; or is this sight an especial entertainment ordered on our behalf? If the latter, gratitude must close our mouths; but if the former, both Cora and I shall have need to draw largely on that stock of hereditary courage which we boast, even before we are made to encounter the redoubtable Montcalm."

"Yon Indian is a 'runner' of the army; and, after the fashion of his people, he may become accounted a hero," returned the officer. "He has volunteered to guide us to the lake, by a path but little known, sooner than if we followed the tardy movements of the column: and, by consequence, more agreeably."

"I like him not," said the lady, shuddering, partly in assumed, yet more in real terror. "You know him, Duncan, or you would not trust yourself so freely to his keeping?"

"Say, rather, Alice, that I would not trust you. I do know him, or he would not have my confidence, and least of all at this moment. He is said to be a Canadian too; and yet he served with our friends the Mohawks, who, as you know, are one of the six allied nations.[3] He was brought amongst us, as I have heard, by some strange accident in which your father was interested, and in which the savage was rigidly dealt by—but I forget the idle tale; it is enough, that he is now our friend."

"If he has been my father's enemy, I like him still less!" exclaimed the now really anxious girl. "Will you not speak to him, Major Heyward, that I may hear his tones? Foolish though it may be, you have often heard me avow my faith in the tones of the human voice!"

"It would be in vain; and answered, most probably, by an ejaculation. Though he may understand it, he affects, like most of his people, to be ignorant of the English; and least of all will he condescend to speak it, now that war demands the utmost exercise of his dignity. But he stops; the private path by which we are to journey is doubtless at hand."

The conjecture of Major Heyward was true. When they reached the spot where the Indian stood, pointing into the thicket that fringed the military road, a narrow and blind path, which might with some little inconvenience receive one person at a time, became visible.

"Here, then, lies our way," said the young man, in a low voice. "Manifest no distrust, or you may invite the danger you appear to apprehend."

"Cora, what think you?" asked the reluctant fair one. "If we journey with the troops, though we may find their presence irksome, shall we not feel better assurance of our safety?"

"Being little accustomed to the practices of the savages, Alice, you mistake the place of real danger," said Heyward. "If enemies have reached the portage at all, a thing by no means probable, as our scouts are abroad, they will surely be found skirting the column, where scalps abound the most. The route of the detachment is known, while ours, having been determined within the hour, must still be secret."

"Should we distrust the man because his manners are not our manners, and that his skin is dark?" coldly asked Cora.

Alice hesitated no longer; but giving her Narraganset[4] a smart cut of the whip, she was the first to dash aside the slight branches of the bushes, and to follow the runner along the dark and tangled pathway. The young man regarded the last speaker in open admiration, and even permitted her fairer though certainly not more beautiful companion to proceed unattended, while he sedulously opened the way himself for the passage of her who has been called Cora. It would seem that

---

[3]There existed for a long time a confederation among the Indian tribes which occupied the northwestern part of the colony of New York, which was at first known as the "Five Nations." At a later day it admitted another tribe, when the appellation was changed to that of the "Six Nations." The original confederation consisted of the Mohawks, Oneidas, the Senecas, the Cayugas, and the Onondagoes. The sixth tribe was the Tuscaroras. There are remnants of all these people still living on lands secured to them by the State; but they are daily disappearing, either by deaths or by removals to scenes more congenial to their habits. In a short time there will be no remains of these extraordinary people, in those regions in which they dwelt for centuries, but their names. The State of New York has counties named after all of them but the Mohawks and the Tuscaroras. The second river of that State is called the Mohawk. [J.F.C.]

[4]In the state of Rhode Island there is a bay called Narraganset, so named after a powerful tribe of Indians, which formerly dwelt on its banks. Accident, or one of those unaccountable freaks which nature sometimes plays in the animal world, gave rise to a breed of horses which were once well known in America by the name of the Narragansets. They were small, commonly of the color called sorrel in America, and distinguished by their habit of pacing. Horses of this race were, and are still, in much request as saddle horses, on account of their hardiness and the ease of their movements. As they were also sure of foot, the Narragansets were greatly sought for by females who were obliged to travel over the roots and holes in the "new countries." [J.F.C.]

the domestics had been previously instructed; for, instead of penetrating the thicket, they followed the route of the column; a measure which Heyward stated had been dictated by the sagacity of their guide, in order to diminish the marks of their trail, if, haply, the Canadian savages should be lurking so far in advance of their army. For many minutes the intricacy of the route admitted of no further dialogue; after which they emerged from the broad border of underbrush which grew along the line of the highway, and entered under the high but dark arches of the forest. Here their progress was less interrupted; and the instant the guide perceived that the females could command their steeds, he moved on, at a pace between a trot and a walk, and at a rate which kept the sure-footed and peculiar animals they rode, at a fast yet easy amble. The youth had turned to speak to the dark-eyed Cora, when the distant sound of horses' hoofs, clattering over the roots of the broken way in his rear, caused him to check his charger; and, as his companions drew their reins at the same instant, the whole party came to a halt, in order to obtain an explanation of the unlooked-for interruption.

In a few moments a colt was seen gliding, like a fallow deer, amongst the straight trunks of the pines; and, in another instant, the person of the ungainly man, described in the preceding chapter, came into view, with as much rapidity as he could excite his meagre beast to endure without coming to an open rupture. Until now this personage had escaped the observation of the travellers. If he possessed the power to arrest any wandering eye when exhibiting the glories of his altitude on foot, his equestrian graces were still more likely to attract attention. Notwithstanding a constant application of his one armed heel to the flanks of the mare, the most confirmed gait that he could establish was a Canterbury gallop with the hind legs, in which those more forward assisted for doubtful moments, though generally content to maintain a loping trot. Perhaps the rapidity of the changes from one of these paces to the other created an optical illusion, which might thus magnify the powers of the beast; for it is certain that Heyward, who possessed a true eye for the merits of a horse, was unable, with his utmost ingenuity, to decide by what sort of movement his pursuer worked his sinuous way on his footsteps with such persevering hardihood.

The industry and movements of the rider were not less remarkable than those of the ridden. At each change in the evolutions of the latter, the former raised his tall person in the stirrups; producing, in this manner, by the undue elongation of his legs, such sudden growths and diminishings of the stature, as baffled every conjecture that might be made as to his dimensions. If to this be added the fact that, in consequence of the *ex parte* application of the spur, one side of the mare appeared to journey faster than the other; and that the aggrieved flank was resolutely indicated by unremitted flourishes of a bushy tail, we finish the picture of both horse and man.

The frown which had gathered around the handsome, open, and manly brow of Heyward, gradually relaxed, and his lips curled into a slight smile, as he regarded the stranger. Alice made no very powerful effort to control her merriment; and even the dark, thoughtful eye of Cora lighted with a humor that, it would seem, the habit, rather than the nature of its mistress repressed.

"Seek you any here?" demanded Heyward, when the other had arrived sufficiently nigh to abate his speed; "I trust you are no messenger of evil tidings?"

"Even so," replied the stranger, making diligent use of his triangular castor, to produce a circulation in the close air of the woods, and leaving his hearers in doubt to which of the young man's questions he responded; when, however, he had cooled his face, and recovered his breath, he continued, "I hear you are riding to William Henry; as I am journeying thitherward myself, I concluded good company would seem consistent to the wishes of both parties."

"You appear to possess the privilege of a casting vote," returned Heyward: "we are three, whilst you have consulted no one but yourself."

"Even so. The first point to be obtained is to know one's own mind. Once sure of that, and where women are concerned it is not easy, the next is, to act up to the decision. I have endeavored to do both, and here I am."

"If you journey to the lake, you have mistaken your route," said Heyward haughtily; "the highway thither is at least half a mile behind you."

"Even so," returned the stranger, nothing daunted by this cold reception; "I have tarried at 'Edward' a week, and I should be dumb not to have inquired the road I was to journey; and if dumb there would be an end to my calling." After simpering in a small way, like one whose modesty prohibited a more open expression of his admiration of a witticism that was perfectly unintelligible to his hearers, he continued, "It is not prudent for any one of my profession to be too familiar with those he has to instruct; for which reason I follow not the line of the army; besides which, I conclude that a gentleman of your character has the best judgment in matters of wayfaring; I have therefore decided to join company, in order that the ride may be made agreeable, and partake of social communion."

"A most arbitrary, if not a hasty decision!" exclaimed Heyward, undecided whether to give vent to his growing anger, or to laugh in the other's face. "But you speak of instruction, and of a profession; are you an adjunct to the provincial corps, as a master of the noble science of defense and offense; or, perhaps, you are one who draws lines and angles, under the pretense of expounding the mathematics?"

The stranger regarded his interrogator a moment, in wonder; and then, losing every mark of self-satisfaction in an expression of solemn humility, he answered:—

"Of offense I hope there is none, to either party: of defense, I make none—by God's good mercy, having committed no palpable sin since last entreating his pardoning grace. I understand not your allusions about lines and angles; and I leave expounding to those who have been called and set apart for that holy office. I lay claim to no higher gift than a small insight into the glorious art of petitioning and thanksgiving, as practiced in psalmody."

"The man is, most manifestly, a disciple of Apollo," cried the amused Alice, "and I take him under my own especial protection. Nay, throw aside that frown, Heyward, and, in pity to my longing ears, suffer him to journey in our train. Besides," she added in a low and hurried voice, casting a glance at the distant Cora, who slowly followed the footsteps of their silent but sullen guide, "it may be a friend added to our strength, in time of need."

"Think you, Alice, that I would trust those I love by this secret path, did I imagine such need could happen?"

"Nay, nay, I think not of it now; but this strange man amuses me; and if he 'hath music in his soul,' let us not churlishly reject his company." She pointed persuasively along the path with her riding-whip, while their eyes met in a look which the young man lingered a moment to prolong; then yielding to her gentle influence, he clapped his spurs into his charger, and in a few bounds was again at the side of Cora.

"I am glad to encounter thee, friend," continued the maiden, waving her hand to the stranger to proceed, as she urged her Narraganset to renew its amble.

"Partial relatives have almost persuaded me that I am not entirely worthless in a duet myself; and we may enliven our wayfaring by indulging in our favorite pursuit. It might be of signal advantage to one, ignorant as I, to hear the opinions and experience of a master in the art."

"It is refreshing both to the spirits and to the body to indulge in psalmody, in befitting seasons," returned the master of song, unhesitatingly complying with her intimation to follow; "and nothing would relieve the mind more than such a consoling communion. But four parts are altogether necessary to the perfection of melody. You have all the manifestations of a soft and rich treble; I can, by especial aid, carry a full tenor to the highest letter; but we lack counter and bass! Yon officer of the king, who hesitated to admit me to his company, might fill the latter, if one may judge from the intonations of his voice in common dialogue."

"Judge not too rashly from hasty and deceptive appearances," said the lady, smiling; "though Major Heyward can assume such deep notes on occasion, believe me, his natural tones are better fitted for a mellow tenor than the bass you heard."

"Is he, then, much practiced in the art of psalmody?" demanded her simple companion.

Alice felt disposed to laugh, though she succeeded in suppressing her merriment, ere she answered,—

"I apprehend that he is rather addicted to profane song. The chances of a soldier's life are but little fitted for the encouragement of more sober inclinations."

"Man's voice is given to him, like his other talents, to be used, and not to be abused. None can say they have ever known me neglect my gifts! I am thankful that, though my boyhood may be said to have been set apart, like the youth of the royal David, for the purposes of music, no syllable of rude verse has ever profaned my lips."

"You have, then, limited your efforts to sacred song?"

"Even so. As the psalms of David exceed all other language, so does the psalmody that has been fitted to them by the divines and sages of the land surpass all vain poetry. Happily, I may say that I utter nothing but the thoughts and the wishes of the King of Israel himself; for though the times may call for some slight changes, yet does this version which we use in the colonies of New England so much exceed all other versions, that, by its richness, its exactness, and its spiritual simplicity, it approacheth, as near as may be, to the great work of the inspired writer. I never abide in any place, sleeping or waking, without an example of this gifted work. 'T is the six-and-twentieth edition, promulgated at Boston, Anno Domini 1744; and is entitled, 'The Psalms, Hymns, and Spiritual Songs of the Old and New Testaments; faithfully translated into English Metre, for the Use, Edification, and Comfort of the Saints, in Public and Private, especially in New England.'"

During this eulogism on the rare production of his native poets, the stranger had drawn the book from his pocket, and, fitting a pair of iron-rimmed spectacles to his nose, opened the volume with a care and veneration suited to its sacred purposes. Then, without circumlocution or apology, first pronouncing the word "Standish," and placing the unknown engine, already described, to his mouth, from which he drew a high, shrill sound, that was followed by an octave below, from his own voice, he commenced singing the following words, in full, sweet, and melodious tones, that set the music, the poetry, and even the uneasy motion of his ill-trained beast at defiance:—

"How good it is, O see,
   And how it pleaseth well,
Together, e'en in unity,
   For brethren so to dwell.
It's like the choice ointment,
   From the head to the beard did go:
Down Aaron's beard, that downward went,
   His garment's skirts unto."

The delivery of these skillful rhymes was accompanied, on the part of the stranger, by a regular rise and fall of his right hand, which terminated at the descent, by suffering the fingers to dwell a moment on the leaves of the little volume; and on the ascent, by such a flourish of the member as none but the initiated may ever hope to imitate. It would seem that long practice had rendered this manual accompaniment necessary; for it did not cease until the preposition which the poet had selected for the close of his verse had been duly delivered like a word of two syllables.

Such an innovation on the silence and retirement of the forest could not fail to enlist the ears of those who journeyed at so short a distance in advance. The Indian muttered a few words in broken English to Heyward, who, in his turn, spoke to the stranger; at once interrupting, and, for the time, closing his musical efforts.

"Though we are not in danger, common prudence would teach us to journey through this wilderness in as quiet a manner as possible. You will, then, pardon me, Alice, should I diminish your enjoyments by requesting this gentleman to postpone his chant until a safer opportunity."

"You will diminish them, indeed," returned the arch girl, "for never did I hear a more unworthy conjunction of execution and language, than that to which I have been listening; and I was far gone in a learned inquiry into the causes of such an unfitness between sound and sense, when you broke the charm of my musings by that bass of yours, Duncan!"

"I know not what you call my bass," said Heyward, piqued at her remark, "but I know that your safety, and that of Cora, is far dearer to me than could be any orchestra of Handel's music." He paused and turned his head quickly towards a thicket, and then bent his eyes suspiciously on their guide, who continued his steady pace, in undisturbed gravity. The young man smiled to himself, for he believed he had mistaken some shining berry of the woods for the glistening eyeballs of a prowling savage, and he rode forward, continuing the conversation which had been interrupted by the passing thought.

Major Heyward was mistaken only in suffering his youthful and generous pride to suppress his active watchfulness. The cavalcade had not long passed, before the branches of the bushes that formed the thicket were cautiously moved asunder, and a human visage, as fiercely wild as savage art and unbridled passions could make it, peered out on the retiring footsteps of the travellers. A gleam of exultation shot across the darkly painted lineaments of the inhabitant of the forest, as he traced the route of his intended victims, who rode unconsciously onward; the light and graceful forms of the females waving among the trees, in the curvatures of their path, followed at each bend by the manly figure of Heyward, until finally, the shapeless person of the singing-master was concealed behind the numberless trunks of trees, that rose, in dark lines, in the intermediate space.

CHAPTER III

Before these fields were shorn and tilled,
Full to the brim our rivers flowed;
The melody of waters filled
The fresh and boundless wood;
And torrents dashed, and rivulets played,
And fountains spouted in the shade.
BRYANT, *An Indian at the Burial-Place of his Fathers.*

Leaving the unsuspecting Heyward and his confiding companions to penetrate still deeper into a forest that contained such treacherous inmates, we must use an author's privilege, and shift the scene a few miles to the westward of the place where we have last seen them.

On that day, two men were lingering on the banks of a small but rapid stream, within an hour's journey of the encampment of Webb, like those who awaited the appearance of an absent person, or the approach of some expected event. The vast canopy of woods spread itself to the margin of the river, overhanging the water, and shadowing its dark current with a deeper hue. The rays of the sun were beginning to grow less fierce, and the intense heat of the day was lessened, as the cooler vapors of the springs and fountains rose above their leafy beds, and rested in the atmosphere. Still that breathing silence, which marks the drowsy sultriness of an American landscape in July, pervaded the secluded spot, interrupted only by the low voices of the men, the occasional and lazy tap of a woodpecker, the discordant cry of some gaudy jay, or a swelling on the ear, from the dull roar of a distant waterfall.

These feeble and broken sounds were, however, too familiar to the foresters, to draw their attention from the more interesting matter of their dialogue. While one of these loiterers showed the red skin and wild accoutrements of a native of the woods, the other exhibited, through the mask of his rude and nearly savage equipments, the brighter, though sun-burnt and long-faded complexion of one who might claim descent from a European parentage. The former was seated on the end of a mossy log, in a posture that permitted him to heighten the effect of his earnest language, by the calm but expressive gestures of an Indian engaged in debate. His body, which was nearly naked, presented a terrific emblem of death, drawn in intermingled colors of white and black. His closely shaved head, on which no other hair than the well known and chivalrous scalping tuft[5] was preserved, was without ornament of any kind, with the exception of a solitary eagle's plume, that crossed his crown, and depended over the left shoulder. A tomahawk and scalping-knife, of English manufacture, were in his girdle; while a short military rifle, of that sort with which the policy of the whites armed their savage allies, lay carelessly across his bare and sinewy knee. The expanded chest, full formed limbs, and grave countenance of this warrior, would denote that he

---

[5]The North American warrior caused the hair to be plucked from his whole body; a small tuft, only, was left on the crown of his head, in order that his enemy might avail himself of it, in wrenching off the scalp in the event of his fall. The scalp was the only admissible trophy of victory. Thus, it was deemed more important to obtain the scalp than to kill the man. Some tribes lay great stress on the honor of striking a dead body. These practices have nearly disappeared among the Indians of the Atlantic States. [J.F.C.]

had reached the vigor of his days, though no symptoms of decay appeared to have yet weakened his manhood.

The frame of the white man, judging by such parts as were not concealed by his clothes, was like that of one who had known hardships and exertion from his earliest youth. His person, though muscular, was rather attenuated than full; but every nerve and muscle appeared strung and indurated by unremitted exposure and toil. He wore a hunting-shirt of forest green, fringed with faded yellow,[6] and a summer cap of skins which had been shorn of their fur. He also bore a knife in a girdle of wampum, like that which confined the scanty garments of the Indian, but no tomahawk. His moccasins were ornamented after the gay fashion of the natives, while the only part of his under dress which appeared below the hunting-frock, was a pair of buckskin leggings, that laced at the sides, and which were gartered above the knees with the sinews of a deer. A pouch and horn completed his personal accoutrements, though a rifle of great length,[7] which the theory of the more ingenious whites had taught them was the most dangerous of all fire-arms, leaned against a neighboring sapling. The eye of the hunter, or scout, whichever he might be, was small, quick, keen, and restless, roving while he spoke, on every side of him, as if in quest of game, or distrusting the sudden approach of some lurking enemy. Notwithstanding the symptoms of habitual suspicion, his countenance was not only without guile, but at the moment at which he is introduced, it was charged with an expression of sturdy honesty.

"Even your traditions make the case in my favor, Chingachgook," he said, speaking in the tongue which was known to all the natives who formerly inhabited the country between the Hudson and the Potomac, and of which we shall give a free translation for the benefit of the reader; endeavoring, at the same time, to preserve some of the peculiarities, both of the individual and of the language. "Your fathers came from the setting sun, crossed the big river,[8] fought the people of the country, and took the land; and mine come from the red sky of the morning, over the salt lake, and did their work much after the fashion that had been set them by yours; then let God judge the matter between us, and friends spare their words!"

"My fathers fought with the naked red-man!" returned the Indian sternly, in the same language. "Is there no difference, Hawkeye, between the stone-headed arrow of the warrior, and the leaden bullet with which you kill?"

"There is reason in an Indian, though nature has made him with a red skin!" said the white man, shaking his head like one on whom such an appeal to his justice was not thrown away. For a moment he appeared to be conscious of having the worst of the argument, then, rallying again, he answered the objection of his antagonist in the best manner his limited information would allow: "I am no scholar, and I care not who knows it; but judging from what I have seen, at deer chases and squirrel hunts, of the sparks below, I should think a rifle in the hands of their grandfathers was not so dangerous as a hickory bow and a good flint-head might be, if drawn with Indian judgment, and sent by an Indian eye."

---

[6]The hunting-shirt is a picturesque smock-frock, being shorter, and ornamented with fringes and tassels. The colors are intended to imitate the hues of the wood, with a view to concealment. Many corps of American riflemen have been thus attired; and the dress is one of the most striking of modern times. The hunting-shirt is frequently white. [J.F.C.]

[7]The rifle of the army is short; that of the hunter is always long. [J.F.C.]

[8]The Mississippi. The scout alludes to a tradition which is very popular among the tribes of the Atlantic States. Evidence of their Asiatic origin is deduced from the circumstances, though great uncertainty hangs over the whole history of the Indians. [J.F.C.]

"You have the story told by your fathers," returned the other, coldly waving his hand. "What say your old men? do they tell the young warriors that the pale-faces met the red-men, painted for war and armed with the stone hatchet and wooden gun?"

"I am not a prejudiced man, nor one who vaunts himself on his natural privileges, though the worst enemy I have on earth, and he is an Iroquois, daren't deny that I am genuine white," the scout replied, surveying, with secret satisfaction, the faded color of his bony and sinewy hand; "and I am willing to own that my people have many ways of which, as an honest man, I can't approve. It is one of their customs to write in books what they have done and seen, instead of telling them in their villages, where the lie can be given to the face of a cowardly boaster, and the brave soldier can call on his comrades to witness for the truth of his words. In consequence of this bad fashion, a man who is too conscientious to misspend his days among the women, in learning the names of black marks, may never hear of the deeds of his fathers, nor feel a pride in striving to outdo them. For myself, I conclude the Bumppos could shoot, for I have a natural turn with a rifle, which must have been handed down from generation to generation, as, our holy commandments tell us, all good and evil gifts are bestowed; though I should be loth to answer for other people in such a matter. But every story has its two sides; so I ask you, Chingachgook, what passed, according to the traditions of the red-men, when our fathers first met?"

A silence of a minute succeeded, during which the Indian sat mute; then, full of the dignity of his office, he commenced his brief tale, with a solemnity that served to heighten its appearance of truth.

"Listen, Hawkeye, and your ear shall drink no lie. 'T is what my fathers have said, and what the Mohicans have done." He hesitated a single instant, and bending a cautious glance towards his companion, he continued, in a manner that was divided between interrogation and assertion, "Does not this stream at our feet run towards the summer, until its waters grow salt, and the current flows upward?"

"It can't be denied that your traditions tell you true in both these matters," said the white man; "for I have been there, and have seen them; though, why water, which is so sweet in the shade, should become bitter in the sun, is an alteration for which I have never been able to account."

"And the current!" demanded the Indian, who expected his reply with that sort of interest that a man feels in the confirmation of testimony at which he marvels even while he respects it; "the fathers of Chingachgook have not lied!"

"The holy Bible is not more true, and that is the truest thing in nature. They call this up-stream current the tide, which is a thing soon explained, and clear enough. Six hours the waters run in, and six hours they run out, and the reason is this: when there is higher water in the sea than in the river, they run in, until the river gets to be highest, and then it runs out again."

"The waters in the woods, and on the great lakes, run downward until they lie like my hand," said the Indian, stretching the limb horizontally before him, "and then they run no more."

"No honest man will deny it," said the scout, a little nettled at the implied distrust of his explanation of the mystery of the tides; "and I grant that it is true on the small scale, and where the land is level. But everything depends on what scale you look at things. Now, on the small scale, the 'arth is level; but on the large scale it is round. In this manner, pools and ponds, and even the great fresh-water lakes, may be stagnant, as you and I both know they are, having seen them; but when you come to spread water over a great tract, like the sea, where the earth is round, how in reason can the water be quiet? You might as well expect the river to lie still on the brink of those black rocks a mile above us, though your own ears tell you that it is tumbling over them at this very moment!"

If unsatisfied by the philosophy of his companion, the Indian was far too dignified to betray his unbelief. He listened like one who was convinced, and resumed his narrative in his former solemn manner.

"We came from the place where the sun is hid at night, over great plains where the buffaloes live, until we reached the big river. There we fought the Alligewi, till the ground was red with their blood. From the banks of the big river to the shores of the salt lake, there was none to meet us. The Maquas followed at a distance. We said the country should be ours from the place where the water runs up no longer on this stream, to a river twenty suns' journey toward the summer. The land we had taken like warriors, we kept like men. We drove the Maquas into the woods with the bears. They only tasted salt at the licks; they drew no fish from the great lake; we threw them the bones."

"All this I have heard and believe," said the white man, observing that the Indian paused; "but it was long before the English came into the country."

"A pine grew then where this chestnut now stands. The first pale-faces who came among us spoke no English. They came in a large canoe, when my fathers had buried the tomahawk with the red-men around them. Then, Hawkeye," he continued, betraying his deep emotion only by permitting his voice to fall to those low, gutteral tones, which render his language, as spoken at times, so very musical; "then, Hawkeye, we were one people, and we were happy. The salt lake gave us its fish, the wood its deer, and the air its birds. We took wives who bore us children; we worshipped the Great Spirit; and we kept the Maquas beyond the sound of our songs of triumph!"

"Know you anything of your own family at that time?" demanded the white. "But you are a just man, for an Indian! and, as I suppose you hold their gifts, your fathers must have been brave warriors, and wise men at the council fire."

"My tribe is the grandfather of nations, but I am an unmixed man. The blood of chiefs is in my veins, where it must stay forever. The Dutch landed, and gave my people the fire-water; they drank until the heavens and the earth seemed to meet, and they foolishly thought they had found the Great Spirit. Then they parted with their land. Foot by foot, they were driven back from the shores, until I, that am a chief and a Sagamore, have never seen the sun shine but through the trees, and have never visited the graves of my fathers!"

"Graves bring solemn feelings over the mind," returned the scout, a good deal touched at the calm suffering of his companion; "and they often aid a man in his good intentions; though, for myself, I expect to leave my own bones unburied, to bleach in the woods, or to be torn asunder by the wolves. But where are to be found those of your race who came to their kin in the Delaware country, so many summers since?"

"Where are the blossoms of those summers!—fallen, one by one: so all of my family departed, each in his turn, to the land of spirits. I am on the hill-top, and must go down into the valley; and when Uncas follows in my footsteps, there will no longer be any of the blood of the Sagamores, for my boy is the last of the Mohicans."

"Uncas is here!" said another voice, in the same soft, guttural tones, near his elbow; "who speaks to Uncas?"

The white man loosened his knife in his leathern sheath, and made an involuntary movement of the hand towards his rifle, at this sudden interruption; but the Indian sat composed, and without turning his head at the unexpected sounds.

At the next instant, a youthful warrior passed between them, with a noiseless step, and seated himself on the bank of the rapid stream. No exclamation of surprise escaped the father, nor was any question asked, or reply given, for several mintues; each appearing to await the moment when he might speak, without betraying womanish curiosity or childish impatience. The white man seemed to take counsel from their customs, and, relinquishing his grasp of the rifle, he also remained silent and reserved. At length Chingachgook turned his eyes slowly towards his son, and demanded,—

"Do the Maquas dare to leave the print of their moccasins in these woods?"

"I have been on their trail," replied the young Indian, "and know that they number as many as the fingers of my two hands; but they lie hid like cowards."

"The thieves are out-lying for scalps and plunder!" said the white man, whom we shall call Hawkeye, after the manner of his companions. "That busy Frenchman, Montcalm, will send his spies into our very camp, but he will know what road we travel!"

"'T is enough!" returned the father, glancing his eye towards the setting sun; "they shall be driven like deer from their bushes. Hawkeye, let us eat to-night, and show the Maquas that we are men to-morrow."

"I am as ready to do the one as the other; but to fight the Iroquois 't is necessary to find the skulkers; and to eat, 't is necessary to get the game—talk of the devil and he will come; there is a pair of the biggest antlers I have seen this season, moving the bushes below the hill! Now, Uncas," he continued in a half whisper, and laughing with a kind of inward sound, like one who had learnt to be watchful, "I will bet my charger three times full of powder, against a foot of wampum, that I take him atwix the eyes, and nearer to the right than to the left."

"It cannot be!" said the young Indian, springing to his feet with youthful eagerness; "all but the tips of his horns are hid!"

"He 's a boy!" said the white man, shaking his head while he spoke, and addressing the father. "Does he think when a hunter sees a part of the creatur', he can't tell where the rest of him should be!"

Adjusting his rifle, he was about to make an exhibition of that skill on which he so much valued himself, when the warrior struck up the piece with his hand, saying,—

"Hawkeye! will you fight the Maquas?"

"These Indians know the nature of the woods, as it might be by instinct!" returned the scout, dropping his rifle, and turning away like a man who was convinced of his error. "I must leave the buck to your arrow, Uncas, or we may kill a deer for them thieves, the Iroquois, to eat."

The instant the father seconded this intimation by an expressive gesture of the hand, Uncas threw himself on the ground, and approached the animal with wary movements. When within a few yards of the cover, he fitted an arrow to his bow with the utmost care, while the antlers moved, as if their owner snuffed an enemy in the tainted air. In another moment the twang of the cord was heard, a white streak was seen glancing into the bushes, and the wounded buck plunged from the cover, to the very feet of his hidden enemy. Avoiding the horns of the infuriated animal, Uncas darted to his side, and passed his knife across the throat, when bounding to the edge of the river it fell, dyeing the waters with its blood.

"'T was done with Indian skill," said the scout, laughing inwardly, but with vast satisfaction; "and 't was a pretty sight to behold! Though an arrow is a near shot, and needs a knife to finish the work."

"Hugh!" ejaculated his companion, turning quickly, like a hound who scented game.

"By the Lord, there is a drove of them!" exclaimed the scout, whose eyes began to glisten with the ardor of his usual occupation; "if they come within range of a bullet I will drop one, though the whole Six Nations should be lurking within sound! What do you hear, Chingachgook? for to my ears the woods are dumb."

"There is but one deer, and he is dead," said the Indian, bending his body till his ear nearly touched the earth. "I hear the sounds of feet!"

"Perhaps the wolves have driven the buck to shelter, and are following on his trail."

"No. The horses of white men are coming!" returned the other, raising himself with dignity, and resuming his seat on the log with his former composure. "Hawkeye, they are your brothers; speak to them."

"That will I, and in English that the king need n't be ashamed to answer," returned the hunter, speaking in the language of which he boasted; "but I see nothing, nor do I hear the sounds of man or beast; 't is strange that an Indian should understand white sounds better than a man who, his very enemies will own, has no cross in his blood, although he may have lived with the red-skins long enough to be suspected! Ha! there goes something like the cracking of a dry stick, too—now I hear the bushes move—yes, yes, there is a trampling that I mistook for the falls—and—but here they come themselves; God keep them from the Iroquois!"

CHAPTER IV

Well, go thy way: thou shalt not from this grove
Till I torment thee for this injury.

SHAKESPEARE, *Midsummer Night's Dream*, II. i. 147.

The words were still in the mouth of the scout, when the leader of the party whose approaching footsteps had caught the vigilant ear of the Indian came openly into view. A beaten path, such as those made by the periodical passage of the deer, wound through a little glen at no great distance, and struck the river at the point where the white man and his red companions had posted themselves. Along this track the travellers, who had produced a surprise so unusual in the depths of the forest, advanced slowly towards the hunter, who was in front of his associates, in readiness to receive them.

"Who comes?" demanded the scout, throwing his rifle carelessly across his left arm, and keeping the fore-finger of his right hand on the trigger, though he avoided all appearance of menace in the act. "Who comes hither, among the beasts and dangers of the wilderness?"

"Believers in religion, and friends to the law and to the king," returned he who rode foremost. "Men who have journeyed since the rising sun, in the shades of this forest, without nourishment, and are sadly tired of their wayfaring."

"You are, then, lost," interrupted the hunter, "and have found how helpless 't is not to know whether to take the right hand or the left?"

"Even so; sucking babes are not more dependent on those who guide them than we who are of larger growth, and who may now be said to possess the stature without the knowledge of men. Know you the distance to a post of the crown called William Henry?"

"Hoot!" shouted the scout, who did not spare his open laughter, though, instantly checking the dangerous sounds, he indulged his merriment at less risk of being overheard by any lurking enemies. "You are as much off the scent as a hound would be, with Horican atwixt him and the deer! William Henry, man! if you are friends to the king, and have business with the army, your better way would be to follow the river down to Edward, and lay the matter before Webb, who tarries there, instead of pushing into the defiles and driving this saucy Frenchman back across Champlain, into his den again."

Before the stranger could make any reply to this unexpected proposition, another horseman dashed the bushes aside, and leaped his charger into the pathway, in front of his companion.

"What, then, may be our distance from Fort Edward?" demanded a new speaker; "the place you advise us to seek we left this morning, and our destination is the head of the lake."

"Then you must have lost your eyesight afore losing your way, for the road across the portage is cut to a good two rods, and is as grand a path, I calculate, as any that runs into London, or even before the palace of the king himself."

"We will not dispute concerning the excellence of the passage," returned Heyward, smiling; for, as the reader has anticipated, it was he. "It is enough, for the present, that we trusted to an Indian guide to take us by a nearer, though blinder path, and that we are deceived in his knowledge. In plain words, we know not where we are."

"An Indian lost in the woods!" said the scout, shaking his head doubtingly; "when the sun is scorching the tree tops, and the water-courses are full; when the moss on every beech he sees will tell him in which quarter the north star will shine at night! The woods are full of deer paths which run to the streams and licks, places well known to everybody; nor have the geese done their flight to the Canada waters altogether! 'T is strange that an Indian should be lost atwixt Horican and the bend in the river. Is he a Mohawk?"

"Not by birth, though adopted in that tribe; I think his birthplace was farther north, and he is one of those you call a Huron."

"Hugh!" exclaimed the two companions of the scout, who had continued, until this part of the dialogue, seated immovable, and apparently indifferent to what passed, but who now sprang to their feet with an activity and interest that had evidently got the better of their reserve, by surprise.

"A Huron!" repeated the sturdy scout, once more shaking his head in open distrust; "they are a thievish race, nor do I care by whom they are adopted; you can never make anything of them but skulks and vagabonds. Since you trusted yourself to the care of one of that nation, I only wonder that you have not fallen in with more."

"Of that there is little danger, since William Henry is so many miles in our front. You forget that I have told you our guide is now a Mohawk, and that he serves with our forces as a friend."

"And I tell you that he who is born a Mingo will die a Mingo," returned the other, positively. "A Mohawk! No, give me a Delaware or a Mohican for honesty; and when they will fight, which they won't all do, having suffered their cunning enemies, the Maquas, to make them women,—but when they will fight at all, look to a Delaware, or a Mohican, for a warrior!"

"Enough of this," said Heyward, impatiently; "I wish not to inquire into the character of a man that I know, and to whom you must be a stranger. You have not yet answered my question; what is our distance from the main army at Edward?"

"It seems that may depend on who is your guide. One would think such a horse as that might get over a good deal of ground atwixt sun-up and sun-down."

"I wish no contention of idle words with you, friend," said Heyward, curbing his dissatisfied manner, and speaking in a more gentle voice; "if you will tell me the distance to Fort Edward, and conduct me thither, your labor shall not go without its reward."

"And in so doing, how know I that I don't guide an enemy, and a spy of Montcalm, to the works of the army? It is not every man who can speak the English tongue that is an honest subject."

"If you serve with the troops, of whom I judge you to be a scout, you should know of such a regiment of the king as the 60th."

"The 60th! you can tell me little of the Royal Americans that I don't know, though I do wear a hunting-shirt instead of a scarlet jacket."

"Well, then, among other things you may know the name of its major?"

"Its major!" interrupted the hunter, elevating his body like one who was proud of his trust. "If there is a man in the country who knows Major Effingham, he stands before you."

"It is a corps which has many majors; the gentleman you name is the senior, but I speak of the junior of them all; he who commands the companies in garrison at William Henry."

"Yes, yes, I have heard that a young gentleman of vast riches, from one of the provinces far south, has got the place. He is over young, too, to hold such rank, and to be put above men whose heads are beginning to bleach; and yet they say he is a soldier in his knowledge, and a gallant gentleman!"

"Whatever he may be, or however he may be qualified for his rank, he now speaks to you, and of course can be no enemy to dread."

The scout regarded Heyward in surprise, and then lifting his cap, he answered in a tone less confident than before, though still expressing doubt,—

"I have heard a party was to leave the encampment this morning, for the lake shore?"

"You have heard the truth; but I preferred a nearer route, trusting to the knowledge of the Indian I mentioned."

"And he deceived you, and then deserted?"

"Neither, as I believe; certainly not the latter, for he is to be found in the rear."

"I should like to look at the creatur'; if it is a true Iroquois I can tell him by his knavish look, and by his paint," said the scout, stepping past the charger of Heyward, and entering the path behind the mare of the singing-master, whose foal had taken advantage of the halt to exact the maternal contribution. After shoving aside the bushes, and proceeding a few paces, he encountered the females, who awaited the result of the conference with anxiety, and not entirely without apprehension. Behind these, the runner leaned against a tree, where he stood the close examination of the scout with an air unmoved, though with a look so dark and savage, that it might in itself excite fear. Satisfied with his scrutiny, the hunter soon left him. As he repassed the females, he paused a moment to gaze upon their beauty, answering to the smile and nod of Alice with a look of open pleasure.

Thence he went to the side of the motherly animal, and spending a minute in a fruitless inquiry into the character of her rider, he shook his head and returned to Heyward.

"A Mingo is a Mingo, and God having made him so, neither the Mohawks nor any other tribe can alter him," he said, when he had regained his former position. "If we were alone, and you would leave that noble horse at the mercy of the wolves to-night, I could show you the way to Edward, myself, within an hour, for it lies only about an hour's journey hence; but with such ladies in your company 't is impossible!"

"And why? they are fatigued, but they are quite equal to a ride of a few more miles."

"'T is a natural impossibility!" repeated the scout; "I would n't walk a mile in these woods after night gets into them, in company with that runner, for the best rifle in the colonies. They are full of outlying Iroquois, and your mongrel Mohawk knows where to find them too well to be my companion."

"Think you so?" said Heyward, leaning forward in the saddle and dropping his voice nearly to a whisper; "I confess I have not been without my own suspicions, though I have endeavored to conceal them, and affected a confidence I have not always felt, on account of my companions. It was because I suspected him that I would follow no longer; making him, as you see, follow me."

"I knew he was one of the cheats as soon as I laid eyes on him!" returned the scout, placing a finger on his nose, in sign of caution. "The thief is leaning against the foot of the sugar sapling, that you can see over them bushes; his right leg is in a line with the bark of the tree, and," tapping his rifle, "I can take him from where I stand, between the ankle and the knee, with a single shot, putting an end to his tramping through the woods, for at least a month to come. If I should go back to him, the cunning varmint would suspect something, and be dodging through the trees like a frightened deer."

"It will not do. He may be innocent, and I dislike the act. Though, if I felt confident of his treachery—"

"'T is a safe thing to calculate on the knavery of an Iroquois," said the scout, throwing his rifle forward, by a sort of instinctive movement.

"Hold!" interrupted Heyward, "it will not do—we must think of some other scheme; and yet, I have much reason to believe the rascal has deceived me."

The hunter, who had already abandoned his intention of maiming the runner, mused a moment, and then made a gesture, which instantly brought his two red companions to his side. They spoke together earnestly in the Delaware language, though in an undertone; and by the gestures of the white man, which were frequently directed towards the top of the sapling, it was evident he pointed out the situation of their hidden enemy. His companions were not long in comprehending his wishes, and laying aside their fire-arms, they parted, taking opposite sides of the path, and burying themselves in the thicket, with such cautious movements, that their steps were inaudible.

"Now, go you back," said the hunter, speaking again to Heyward, "and hold the imp in talk; these Mohicans here will take him without breaking his paint."

"Nay," said Heyward, proudly, "I will seize him myself."

"Hist! what could you do, mounted, against an Indian in the bushes?"

"I will dismount."

"And, think you, when he saw one of your feet out of the stirrup, he would wait for the other to be free? Whoever comes into the woods to deal with the natives must use Indian fashions, if he would wish to prosper in his undertakings. Go, then, talk openly to the miscreant, and seem to believe him the truest friend you have on 'arth."

Heyward prepared to comply, though with strong disgust at the nature of the office he was compelled to execute. Each moment, however, pressed upon him a conviction of the critical situation in which he had suffered his invaluable trust to be involved through his own confidence. The sun had already disappeared, and the woods, suddenly deprived of his light,[9] were assuming a dusky hue, which keenly reminded him that the hour the savage usually chose for his most barbarous and remorseless acts of vengeance or hostility was speedily drawing near. Stimulated by apprehension, he left the scout, who immediately entered into a loud conversation with the stranger that had so unceremoniously enlisted himself in the party of travellers that morning. In passing his gentler companions Heyward uttered a few words of encouragement, and was pleased to find that, though fatigued with the exercise of the day, they appeared to entertain no suspicion that their present embarrassment was other than the result of accident. Giving them reason to believe he was merely employed in a consultation concerning the future route, he spurred his charger, and drew the reins again, when the animal had carried him within a few yards of the place where the sullen runner still stood, leaning against the tree.

"You may see, Magua," he said, endeavoring to assume an air of freedom and confidence, "that the night is closing around us, and yet we are no nearer to William Henry than when we left the encampment of Webb with the rising sun. You have missed the way, nor have I been more fortunate. But happily we have fallen in with a hunter, he whom you hear talking to the singer, that is acquainted with the deer-paths and by-ways of the woods, and who promises to lead us to a place where we may rest securely till the morning."

The Indian riveted his glowing eyes on Heyward as he asked, in his imperfect English, "Is he alone?"

"Alone!" hesitatingly answered Heyward, to whom deception was too new to be assumed without embarrassment. "Oh! not alone, surely, Magua, for you know that we are with him."

"Then Le Renard Subtil will go," returned the runner, coolly raising his little wallet from the place where it had lain at his feet; "and the pale-faces will see none but their own color."

"Go! Whom call you Le Renard?"

"'T is the name his Canada fathers have given to Magua," returned the runner, with an air that manifested his pride at the distinction. "Night is the same as day to Le Subtil, when Munro waits for him."

"And what account will Le Renard give the chief of William Henry concerning his daughters? Will he dare to tell the hotblooded Scotsman that his children are left without a guide, though Magua promised to be one?"

"Though the gray head has a loud voice, and a long arm, Le Renard will not hear him, or feel him, in the woods."

"But what will the Mohawks say? They will make him petticoats, and bid him stay in the wigwam with the women, for he is no longer to be trusted with the business of a man."

[9]The scene of this tale was in the 42d degree of latitude, where the twilight is never of long continuance. [J.F.C.]

"Le Subtil knows the path to the great lakes, and he can find the bones of his fathers," was the answer of the unmoved runner.

"Enough, Magua," said Heyward; "are we not friends? Why should there be bitter words between us? Munro has promised you a gift for your services when performed, and I shall be your debtor for another. Rest your weary limbs, then, and open your wallet to eat. We have a few moments to spare; let us not waste them in talk like wrangling women. When the ladies are refreshed we will proceed."

"The pale-faces make themselves dogs to their women," muttered the Indian, in his native language, "and when they want to eat, their warriors must lay aside the tomahawk to feed their laziness."

"What say you, Renard?"

"Le Subtil says it is good."

The Indian then fastened his eyes keenly on the open countenance of Heyward, but meeting his glance, he turned them quickly away, and seating himself deliberately on the ground, he drew forth the remnant of some former repast, and began to eat, though not without first bending his looks slowly and cautiously around him.

"This is well," continued Heyward; "and le Renard will have strength and sight to find the path in the morning;" he paused, for sounds like the snapping of a dried stick, and the rustling of leaves, rose from the adjacent bushes, but recollecting himself instantly, he continued,—"we must be moving before the sun is seen, or Montcalm may lie in our path, and shut us out from the fortress."

The hand of Magua dropped from his mouth to his side, and though his eyes were fastened on the ground, his head was turned aside, his nostrils expanded, and his ears seemed even to stand more erect than usual, giving to him the appearance of a statue that was made to represent intense attention.

Heyward, who watched his movements with a vigilant eye, carelessly extricated one of his feet from the stirrup, while he passed a hand towards the bear-skin covering of his holsters. Every effort to detect the point most regarded by the runner was completely frustrated by the tremulous glances of his organs, which seemed not to rest a single instant on any particular object, and which, at the same time, could be hardly said to move. While he hesitated how to proceed, Le Subtil cautiously raised himself to his feet, though with a motion so slow and guarded that not the slightest noise was produced by the change. Heyward felt it had now become incumbent on him to act. Throwing his leg over the saddle, he dismounted, with a determination to advance and seize his treacherous companion, trusting the result to his own manhood. In order, however, to prevent unnecessary alarm, he still preserved an air of calmness and friendship.

"Le Renard Subtil does not eat," he said, using the appellation he had found most flattering to the vanity of the Indian. "His corn is not well parched, and it seems dry. Let me examine; perhaps something may be found among my own provisions that will help his appetite."

Magua held out the wallet to the proffer of the other. He even suffered their hands to meet, without betraying the least emotion, or varying his riveted attitude of attention. But when he felt the fingers of Heyward moving gently along his own naked arm, he struck up the limb of the young man, and, uttering a piercing cry as he darted beneath it, plunged at a single bound into the opposite thicket. At the next instant the form of Chingachgook appeared from the bushes, looking like a spectre in its paint, and glided across the path in swift pursuit. Next followed the shout of Uncas, when the woods were lighted by a sudden flash, that was accompanied by the sharp report of the hunter's rifle.

CHAPTER V

In such a night
Did Thisbe fearfully o'ertrip the dew,
And saw the lion's shadow ere himself.
SHAKESPEARE, *Merchant of Venice,* V. i. 7.

The suddenness of the flight of his guide, and the wild cries of the pursuers, caused Heyward to remain fixed, for a few moments, in inactive surprise. Then recollecting the importance of securing the fugitive, he dashed aside the surrounding bushes, and pressed eagerly forward to lend his aid in the chase. Before he had, however, proceeded a hundred yards, he met the three foresters already returning from their unsuccessful pursuit.

"Why so soon disheartened!" he exclaimed; "the scoundrel must be concealed behind some of these trees, and may yet be secured. We are not safe while he goes at large."

"Would you set a cloud to chase the wind?" returned the disappointed scout; "I heard the imp, brushing over the dry leaves, like a black snake, and blinking a glimpse of him, just over ag'in yon big pine, I pulled as it might be on the scent; but 't would n't do! and yet for a reasoning aim, if anybody but myself had touched the trigger, I should call it a quick sight; and I may be accounted to have experience in these matters, and one who ought to know. Look at this sumach; its leaves are red, though everybody knows the fruit is in the yellow blossom, in the month of July!"

"'T is the blood of Le Subtil! he is hurt, and may yet fall!"

"No, no," returned the scout, in decided approbation of this opinion, "I rubbed the bark off a limb, perhaps, but the creature leaped the longer for it. A rifle bullet acts on a running animal, when it barks him, much the same as one of your spurs on a horse; that is, it quickens motion, and puts life into the flesh, instead of taking it away. But when it cuts the ragged hole, after a bound or two, there is, commonly, a stagnation of further leaping, be it Indian or be it deer!"

"We are four able bodies, to one wounded man!"

"Is life grievous to you?" interrupted the scout. "Yonder red devil would draw you within swing of the tomahawks of his comrades, before you were heated in the chase. It was an unthoughtful act in a man who has so often slept with the warwhoop ringing in the air, to let off his piece within sound of an ambushment! But then it was a natural temptation! 't was very natural! Come, friends, let us move our station, and in such a fashion, too, as will throw the cunning of a Mingo on a wrong scent, or our scalps will be drying in the wind in front of Montcalm's marquee, ag'in this hour to-morrow."

This appalling declaration, which the scout uttered with the cool assurance of a man who fully comprehended, while he did not fear to face the danger, served to remind Heyward of the importance of the charge with which he himself had been intrusted. Glancing his eyes around, with a vain effort to pierce the gloom that was thickening beneath the leafy arches of the forest, he felt as if, cut off from human aid, his unresisting companions would soon lie at the entire mercy of those barbarous enemies, who, like beasts of prey, only waited till the gathering darkness might render their blows more fatally certain. His awakened imagination, deluded by the deceptive light, converted each waving bush, or the fragment of some fallen tree, into human forms, and twenty times he fancied he could distinguish the horrid visages of his lurking foes, peering from their hiding-places, in never-ceasing watchfulness of the movements of his party. Looking upward, he found that the thin fleecy clouds, which evening had painted on the blue sky, were already losing their faintest tints of rose-color, while the imbedded stream, which glided past the spot where he stood, was to be traced only by the dark boundary of its wooded banks.

"What is to be done?" he said, feeling the utter helplessness of doubt in such a pressing strait; "desert me not, for God's sake! remain to defend those I escort, and freely name your own reward!"

His companions, who conversed apart in the language of their tribe, heeded not this sudden and earnest appeal. Though their dialogue was maintained in low and cautious sounds, but little above a whisper, Heyward, who now approached, could easily distinguish the earnest tones of the younger warrior from the more deliberate speeches of his seniors. It was evident that they debated on the propriety of some measure that nearly concerned the welfare of the travellers. Yielding to his powerful interest in the subject, and impatient of a delay that seemed fraught with so much additional danger, Heyward drew still nigher to the dusky group, with an intention of making his offers of compensation more definite, when the white man, motioning, with his hand, as if he conceded the disputed point, turned away, saying in a sort of soliloquy, and in the English tongue,—

"Uncas is right! it would not be the act of men to leave such harmless things to their fate, even though it breaks up the harboring place forever. If you would save these tender blossoms from the fangs of the worst of sarpents, gentleman, you have neither time to lose nor resolution to throw away!"

"How can such a wish be doubted! have I not already offered—"

"Offer your prayers to Him who can give us wisdom to circumvent the cunning of the devils who fill these woods," calmly interrupted the scout, "but spare your offers of money, which neither you may live to realize, nor I to profit by. These Mohicans and I will do what man's thoughts can invent, to keep such flowers, which, though so sweet, were never made for the wilderness, from harm, and that without hope of any other recompense but such as God always gives to upright dealings. First, you must promise two things, both in your own name and for your friends, or without serving you, we shall only injure ourselves!"

"Name them."

"The one is, to be still as these sleeping woods, let what will happen; and the other is, to keep the place where we shall take you, forever a secret from all mortal men."

"I will do my utmost to see both these conditions fulfilled."

"Then follow, for we are losing moments that are as precious as the heart's blood to a stricken deer!"

Heyward could distinguish the impatient gesture of the scout, through the increasing shadows of the evening, and he moved in his footsteps, swiftly, towards the place where he had left the remainder of his party. When they rejoined the expecting and anxious females, he briefly acquainted them with the conditions of their new guide, and with the necessity that existed for their hushing every apprehension, in instant and serious exertions. Although his alarming communication was not received without much secret terror by the listeners, his earnest and impressive manner, aided perhaps by the nature of the danger, succeeded in bracing their nerves to undergo some unlooked-for and unusual trial. Silently, and without a moment's delay, they permitted him to assist them from their saddles, when they descended quickly to the water's edge, where the scout had collected the rest of the party, more by the agency of expressive gestures than by any use of words.

"What to do with these dumb creatures!" muttered the white man, on whom the sole control of their future movements appeared to devolve; "it would be time lost to cut their throats, and cast them into the river; and to leave them here, would be to tell the Mingoes that they have not far to seek to find their owners!"

"Then give them their bridles, and let them range the woods," Heyward ventured to suggest.

"No; it would be better to mislead the imps, and make them believe they must equal a horse's speed to run down their chase. Aye, aye, that will blind their fire-balls of eyes! Chingach—Hist! what stirs the bush?"

"The colt."

"That colt, at least, must die," muttered the scout, grasping at the mane of the nimble beast, which easily eluded his hand; "Uncas, your arrows!"

"Hold!" exclaimed the proprietor of the condemned animal, aloud, without regard to the whispering tones used by the others; "spare the foal of Miriam! it is the comely offspring of a faithful dam, and would willingly injure naught."

"When men struggle for the single life God has given them," said the scout sternly, "even their own kind seem no more than the beasts of the wood. If you speak again, I shall leave you to the mercy of the Maquas! Draw to your arrow's head, Uncas; we have no time for second blows."

The low, muttering sounds of his threatening voice were still audible, when the wounded foal, first rearing on its hinder legs, plunged forward to its knees. It was met by Chingachgook, whose knife passed across its throat quicker than thought, and then precipitating the motions of the struggling victim, he dashed it into the river, down whose stream it glided away, gasping audibly for breath with its ebbing life. This deed of apparent cruelty, but of real necessity, fell upon the spirits of the travellers like a terrific warning of the peril in which they stood, heightened as it was by the calm though steady resolution of the actors in the scene. The sisters shuddered and clung closer to each other, while Heyward instinctively laid his hand on one of the pistols he had just drawn from their holsters, as he placed himself between his charge and those dense shadows that seemed to draw an impenetrable veil before the bosom of the forest.

The Indians, however, hesitated not a moment, but taking the bridles, they led the frightened and reluctant horses into the bed of the river.

At a short distance from the shore they turned, and were soon concealed by the projection of the bank, under the brow of which they moved, in a direction opposite to the course of the waters. In the mean time, the scout drew a canoe of bark from its place of concealment beneath some low bushes, whose branches were waving with the eddies of the current, into which he silently motioned for the females to enter. They complied without hesitation, though many a fearful and anxious glance was thrown behind them, towards the thickening gloom, which now lay like a dark barrier along the margin of the stream.

So soon as Cora and Alice were seated, the scout, without regarding the element, directed Heyward to support one side of the frail vessel, and posting himself at the other, they bore it up against the stream, followed by the dejected owner of the dead foal. In this manner they proceeded, for many rods, in a silence that was only interrupted by the rippling of the water, as its eddies played around them, or the low dash made by their own cautious footsteps. Heyward yielded the guidance of the canoe implicitly to the scout, who approached or receded from the shore, to avoid the fragments of rocks, or deeper parts of the river, with a readiness that showed his knowledge of the route they held. Occasionally he would stop; and in the midst of a breathing stillness, that the dull but increasing roar of the waterfall only served to render more impressive, he would listen with painful intenseness, to catch any sounds that might arise from the slumbering forest. When assured that all was still, and unable to detect, even by the aid of his practiced senses, any sign of his approaching foes, he would deliberately resume his slow and guarded progress. At length they reached a point in the river where the roving eye of Heyward became riveted on a cluster of black objects, collected at a spot where the high bank threw a deeper shadow than usual on the dark waters. Hesitating to advance, he pointed out the place to the attention of his companion.

"Aye," returned the composed scout, "the Indians have hid the beasts with the judgment of natives! water leaves no trail, and an owl's eyes would be blinded by the darkness of such a hole."

The whole party was soon reunited, and another consultation was held between the scout and his new comrades, during which, they whose fates depended on the faith and ingenuity of these unknown foresters had a little leisure to observe their situation more minutely.

The river was confined between high and cragged rocks, one of which impended above the spot where the canoe rested. As these, again, were surmounted by tall trees, which appeared to totter on the brows of the precipice, it gave the stream the appearance of running through a deep and narrow dell. All beneath the fantastic limbs and ragged tree tops, which were, here and there, dimly painted against the starry zenith, lay alike in shadowed obscurity. Behind them, the curvature of the banks soon bounded the view, by the same dark and wooded outline; but in front, and apparently at no great distance, the water seemed piled against the heavens, whence it tumbled into caverns, out of which issued those sullen sounds that had loaded the evening atmosphere. It seemed, in truth, to be a spot devoted to seclusion, and the sisters imbibed a soothing impression of security, as they gazed upon its romantic, though not unappalling beauties. A general movement among their conductors, however, soon recalled them from a contemplation of the wild charms that night had assisted to lend the place, to a painful sense of their real peril.

The horses had been secured to some scattering shrubs that grew in the fissures of the rocks, where, standing in the water, they were left to pass the night. The scout directed Heyward and his disconsolate fellow-travellers to seat themselves in the forward end of the canoe, and took possession of the other himself, as erect and steady as if he floated in a vessel of much firmer materials. The Indians warily retraced their steps towards the place they had left, when the scout, placing his pole against a rock, by a powerful shove, sent his frail bark directly into the centre of the turbulent stream. For many minutes the struggle between the light bubble in which they floated, and the swift current, was severe and doubtful. Forbidden to stir even a hand, and almost afraid to breathe, lest they should expose the frail fabric to the fury of the stream, the passengers watched the glancing waters in feverish suspense. Twenty times they thought the whirling eddies were sweeping them to destruction, when the master-hand of their pilot would bring the bows of the canoe to stem the rapid. A long, a vigorous, and, as it appeared to the females, a desperate effort, closed the struggle. Just as Alice veiled her eyes in horror, under the impression that they were about to be swept within the vortex at the foot of the cataract, the canoe floated, stationary, at the side of a flat rock, that lay on a level with the water.

"Where are we? and what is next to be done?" demanded Heyward, perceiving that the exertions of the scout had ceased.

"You are at the foot of Glenn's," returned the other, speaking aloud, without fear of consequences, within the roar of the cataract; "and the next thing is to make a steady landing, lest the canoe upset, and you should go down again the hard road we have travelled, faster than you came up; 't is a hard rift to stem, when the river is a little swelled; and five is an unnatural number to keep dry, in the hurry-skurry, with a little birchen bark and gum. There, go you all on the rock, and I will bring up the Mohicans with the venison. A man had better sleep without his scalp, than famish in the midst of plenty."

His passengers gladly complied with these directions. As the last foot touched the rock, the canoe whirled from its station, when the tall form of the scout was seen, for an instant, gliding above the waters, before it disappeared in the impenetrable darkness that rested on the bed of the river. Left by their guide, the travellers remained a few minutes in helpless ignorance, afraid even to move along the broken rocks, lest a false step should precipitate them down some one of the many deep and roaring caverns, into which the water seemed to tumble on every side of them. Their suspense, however, was soon relieved; for aided by the skill of the natives, the canoe shot back into the eddy, and floated again at the side of the low rock before they thought the scout had even time to rejoin his companions.

"We are now fortified, garrisoned, and provisioned," cried Heyward, cheerfully, "and may set Montcalm and his allies at defiance. How, now, my vigilant sentinel, can you see anything of those you called the Iroquois, on the main land?"

"I call them Iroquois, because to me every native, who speaks a foreign tongue, is accounted an enemy, though he may pretend to serve the king! If Webb wants faith and honesty in an Indian, let him bring out the tribes of the Delawares, and send these greedy and lying Mohawks and Oneidas, with their six nations of varlets, where in nature they belong, among the French!"

"We should then exchange a warlike for a useless friend! I have heard that the Delawares have laid aside the hatchet, and are content to be called women!"

"Aye, shame on the Hollanders[10] and Iroquois, who circumvented them by their deviltries into such a treaty! But I have known them for twenty years, and I call him liar, that says cowardly blood runs in the veins of a Delaware. You have driven their tribes from the seashore, and would now believe what their enemies say, that you may sleep at night upon an easy pillow. No, no; to me, every Indian who speaks a foreign tongue is an Iroquois, whether the castle[11] of his tribe be in Canada, or be in York."

Heyward, perceiving that the stubborn adherence of the scout to the cause of his friends the Delawares or Mohicans, for they were branches of the same numerous people, was likely to prolong a useless discussion, changed the subject.

"Treaty or no treaty, I know full well that your two companions are brave and cautious warriors! have they heard or seen anything of our enemies?"

---

[10]The reader will remember that New York was originally a colony of the Dutch. [J.F.C.]

[11]The principal villages of the Indians are still called "castles" by the whites of New York. "Oneida castle" is no more than a scattered hamlet; but the name is in general use. [J.F.C.]

"An Indian is a mortal to be felt afore he is seen," returned the scout, ascending the rock, and throwing the deer carelessly down. "I trust to other signs than such as come in at the eye, when I am outlying on the trail of the Mingoes."

"Do your ears tell you that they have traced our retreat?"

"I should be sorry to think they had, though this is a spot that stout courage might hold for a smart skrimmage. I will not deny, however, but the horses cowered when I passed them, as though they scented the wolves; and a wolf is a beast that is apt to hover about an Indian ambush, craving the offals of the deer the savages kill."

You forget the buck at your feet! or, may we not owe their visit to the dead colt? Ha! what noise is that?"

"Poor Miriam!" murmered the stranger; "thy foal was foreordained to become a prey to ravenous beasts!" Then, suddenly lifting up his voice, amid the eternal din of the waters, he sang aloud,—

"First born of Egypt smite did He,
Of mankind, and of beast also;
O Egypt! wonders sent 'midst thee,
On Pharoah and his servants too!"

"The death of the colt sits heavy on the heart of its owner," said the scout; "but it's a good sign to see a man account upon his dumb friends. He has the religion of the matter, in believing what is to happen will happen; and with such a consolation, it won't be long afore he submits to the rationality of killing a four-footed beast, to save the lives of human men. It may be as you say," he continued, reverting to the purport of Heyward's last remark; "and the greater the reason why we should cut our steaks, and let the carcass drive down the stream, or we shall have the pack howling along the cliffs, begrudging every mouthful we swallow. Besides, though the Delaware tongue is the same as a book to the Iroquois, the cunning varlets are quick enough at understanding the reason of a wolf's howl."

The scout, whilst making his remarks, was busied in collecting certain necessary implements; as he concluded, he moved silently by the group of travellers, accompanied by the Mohicans, who seemed to comprehend his intentions with instinctive readiness, when the whole three disappeared in succession, seeming to vanish against the dark face of a perpendicular rock, that rose to the height of a few yards within as many feet of the water's edge.

CHAPTER VI

Those strains that once did sweet in Zion glide,
He wales a portion with judicious care;
And "Let us worship God," he says, with solemn air.
BURNS, *The Cotter's Saturday Night.*

Heyward and his female companions witnessed this mysterious movement with secret uneasiness; for, though the conduct of the white man had hitherto been above reproach, his rude equipments, blunt address, and strong antipathies, together with the character of his silent associates, were all causes for exciting distrust in minds that had been so recently alarmed by Indian treachery.

The stranger alone disregarded the passing incidents. He seated himself on a projection of the rocks, whence he gave no other signs of consciousness than by the struggles of his spirit; as manifested in frequent and heavy sighs. Smothered voices were next heard, as though men called to each other in the bowels of the earth, when a sudden light flashed upon those without, and laid bare the much-prized secret of the place.

At the further extremity of a narrow, deep cavern in the rock, whose length appeared much extended by the perspective and the nature of the light by which it was seen, was seated the scout, holding a blazing knot of pine. The strong glare of the fire fell full upon his sturdy, weather-beaten countenance and forest attire, lending an air of romantic wildness to the aspect of an individual who, seen by the sober light of day, would have exhibited the peculiarities of a man remarkable for the strangeness of his dress, the iron-like inflexibility of his frame, and the singular compound of quick, vigilant sagacity, and of exquisite simplicity, that by turns usurped the possession of his muscular features. At a little distance in advance stood Uncas, his whole person thrown powerfully into view. The travellers anxiously regarded the upright, flexible figure of the young Mohican, graceful and unrestrained in the attitudes and movements of nature. Though his person was more than usually screened by a green and fringed hunting-shirt, like that of the white man, there was no concealment to his dark, glancing, fearless eye, alike terrible and calm; the bold outline of his high, haughty features, pure in their native red; or to the dignified elevation of his receding forehead, together with all the finest proportions of a noble head, bared to the generous scalping tuft. It was the first opportunity possessed by Duncan and his companions to view the marked lineaments of either of their Indian attendants, and each individual of the party felt relieved from a burden of doubt, as the proud and determined, though wild expression of the features of the young warrior forced itself on their notice. They felt it might be a being partially benighted in the vale of ignorance, but it could not be one who would willingly devote his rich natural gifts to the purposes of wanton treachery. The ingenuous Alice gazed at his free air and proud carriage, as she would have looked upon some precious relic of the Grecian chisel, to which life had been imparted by the intervention of a miracle; while Heyward, though accustomed to see the perfection of form which abounds among the uncorrupted natives, openly expressed his admiration at such an unblemished specimen of the noblest proportions of man.

"I could sleep in peace," whispered Alice, in reply, "with such a fearless and generous looking youth for my sentinel. Surely, Duncan, those cruel murderers, those terrific scenes of torture, of which we read and hear so much, are never acted in the presence of such as he!"

"This, certainly, is a rare and brilliant instance of those natural qualities in which these peculiar people are said to excel," he answered. "I agree with you, Alice, in thinking that such a front and eye were formed rather to intimidate than to deceive; but let us not practice a deception upon ourselves, by expecting any other exhibition of what we esteem virtue than according to the fashion of a savage. As bright examples of great qualities are but too uncommon among Christians, so are they singular and solitary with the Indians; though, for the honor of our common nature, neither are incapable of producing them. Let us then hope that this Mohican may not disappoint our wishes, but prove what his looks assert him to be, a brave and constant friend."

"Now Major Heyward speaks as Major Heyward should," said Cora; "who, that looks at this creature of nature, remembers the shade of his skin!"

A short, and apparently an embarrassed silence succeeded this remark, which was interrupted by the scout calling to them, aloud, to enter.

"This fire begins to show too bright a flame," he continued, as they complied, "and might light the Mingoes to our undoing. Uncas, drop the blanket, and show the knaves its dark side. This is not such a supper as a major of the Royal Americans has a right to expect, but I 've known stout detachments of the corps glad to eat their venison raw, and without a relish too.[12] Here, you see, we have plenty of salt, and can make a quick broil. There 's fresh sassafras boughs for the ladies to sit on, which may not be as proud as their my-hog-guinea chairs, but which sends up a sweeter flavor than the skin of any hog can do, be it of Guinea, or be it of any other land. Come, friend, don't be mournful for the colt; 't was an innocent thing, and had not seen much hardship. Its death will save the creature many a sore back and weary foot!"

Uncas did as the other had directed, and when the voice of Hawkeye ceased, the roar of the cataract sounded like the rumbling of distant thunder.

"Are we quite safe in this cavern?" demanded Heyward. "Is there no danger of surprise? A single armed man, at its entrance, would hold us at his mercy."

A spectral-looking figure stalked from out the darkness behind the scout, and seizing a blazing brand, held it towards the further extremity of their place of retreat. Alice uttered a faint shriek, and even Cora rose to her feet, as this appalling object moved into the light; but a single word from Heyward calmed them, with the assurance it was only their attendant, Chingachgook, who, lifting another blanket, discovered that the cavern had two outlets. Then, holding the brand, he crossed a deep, narrow chasm in the rocks, which ran at right angles with the passage they were in, but which, unlike that, was open to the heavens, and entered another cave, answering to the description of the first, in every essential particular.

"Such old foxes as Chingachgook and myself are not often caught in a burrow with one hole," said Hawkeye, laughing; "you can easily see the cunning of the place—the rock is black limestone, which everybody knows is soft; it makes no uncomfortable pillow, where brush and pine wood is scarce; well, the fall was once a few yards below us, and I dare to say was, in its time, as regular and as handsome a sheet of water as any along the Hudson. But old age is a great injury to good looks, as these sweet young ladies have yet to l'arn! The place is sadly changed! These rocks are full of cracks, and in some places they are softer than at othersome, and the water has worked out deep hollows for itself, until it has fallen back, aye, some hundred feet, breaking here and wearing there, until the falls have neither shape nor consistency."

"In what part of them are we?" asked Heyward.

"Why, we are nigh the spot that Providence first placed them at, but where, it seems, they were too rebellious to stay. The rock proved softer on each side of us, and so they left the centre of the river bare and dry, first working out these two little holes for us to hide in."

"We are then on an island?"

"Aye! there are the falls on two sides of us, and the river above and below. If you had daylight, it would be worth the trouble to step up on the height of this rock,

[12]In vulgar parlance the condiments of a repast are called by the American "a relish," substituting the thing for its effect. These provincial terms are frequently put in the mouths of the speakers, according to their several conditions in life. Most of them are of local use, and others quite peculiar to the particular class of men to which the character belongs. In the present instance, the scout uses the word with immediate reference to the "salt," with which his own party was so fortunate as to be provided. [J.F.C.]

and look at the perversity of the water. It falls by no rule at all; sometimes it leaps, sometimes it tumbles; there, it skips; here, it shoots; in one place 't is white as snow, and in another 't is green as grass; hereabouts it pitches into deep hollows that rumble and quake the 'arth; and thereaway it ripples and sings like a brook, fashioning whirlpools and gulleys in the old stone, as if 't was no harder than trodden clay. The whole design of the river seems disconcerted. First it runs smoothly, as if meaning to go down the descent as things were ordered; then it angles about and faces the shores; nor are there places wanting where it looks backward, as if unwilling to leave the wilderness, to mingle with the salt! Aye, lady, the fine cobweb-looking cloth you wear at your throat is coarse, and like a fish net, to little spots I can show you, where the river fabricates all sorts of images, as if, having broke loose from order, it would try its hand at everything. And yet what does it amount to? After the water has been suffered to have its will, for a time, like a headstrong man, it is gathered together by the hand that made it, and a few rods below you may see it all, flowing steadily towards the sea, as was foreordained from the first foundation of the 'arth!"

While his auditors received a cheering assurance of the security of their place of concealment, from this untutored description of Glenn's,[13] they were much inclined to judge differently from Hawkeye, of its wild beauties. But they were not in a situation to suffer their thoughts to dwell on the charms of natural objects; and, as the scout had not found it necessary to cease his culinary labors while he spoke, unless to point out, with a broken fork, the direction of some particularly obnoxious point in the rebellious stream, they now suffered their attention to be drawn to the necessary, though more vulgar consideration of their supper.

The repast, which was greatly aided by the addition of a few delicacies that Heyward had the precaution to bring with him when they left their horses, was exceedingly refreshing to the wearied party. Uncas acted as attendant to the females, performing all the little offices within his power, with a mixture of dignity and anxious grace, that served to amuse Heyward, who well knew that it was an utter innovation on the Indian customs, which forbid their warriors to descend to any menial employment, especially in favor of their women. As the rites of hospitality were, however, considered sacred among them, this little departure from the dignity of manhood excited no audible comment. Had there been one there sufficiently disengaged to become a close observer, he might have fancied that the services of the young chief were not entirely impartial; that while he tendered to Alice the gourd of sweet water, and the venison in a trencher, neatly carved from the knot of the pepperidge, with sufficient courtesy, in performing the same offices to her sister his dark eye lingered on her rich, speaking countenance. Once or twice he was compelled to speak, to command the attention of those he served. In such cases, he made use of English, broken and imperfect, but sufficiently intelligible, and which he rendered so mild and musical, by his deep,[14] guttural voice, that it never failed to cause both ladies to look up in admiration and astonishment. In

[13]Glenn's Falls are on the Hudson, some forty or fifty miles above the head of tide, or the place where that river becomes navigable for sloops. The description of this picturesque and remarkable little cataract, as given by the scout, is sufficiently correct, though the application of the water to the uses of civilized life has materially injured its beauties. The rocky island and the two caverns are well known to every traveller, since the former sustains a pier of a bridge, which is now thrown across the river, immediately above the fall. In explanation of the taste of Hawkeye, it should be remembered that men always prize that most which is least enjoyed. Thus, in a new country, the woods and other objects, which in an old country would be maintained at great cost, are got rid of, simply with a view of "improving," as it is called. [J.F.C.]

[14]The meaning of Indian words is much governed by the emphasis and tones. [J.F.C.]

the course of these civilities, a few sentences were exchanged, that served to establish the appearance of an amicable intercourse between the parties.

In the mean while, the gravity of Chingachgook remained immovable. He had seated himself more within the circle of light, where the frequent uneasy glances of his guests were better enabled to separate the natural expression of his face from the artificial terrors of the war-paint. They found a strong resemblance between father and son, with the difference that might be expected from age and hardships. The fierceness of his countenance now seemed to slumber, and in its place was to be seen the quiet, vacant composure, which distinguishes an Indian warrior, when his faculties are not required for any of the greater purposes of his existence. It was, however, easy to be seen, by the occasional gleams that shot across his swarthy visage, that it was only necessary to arouse his passions, in order to give full effect to the terrific device which he had adopted to intimidate his enemies. On the other hand, the quick, roving eye of the scout seldom rested. He ate and drank with an appetite that no sense of danger could disturb, but his vigilance seemed never to desert him. Twenty times the gourd or the venison was suspended before his lips, while his head was turned aside, as though he listened to some distant and distrusted sounds—a movement that never failed to recall his guests from regarding the novelties of their situation, to a recollection of the alarming reasons that had driven them to seek it. As these frequent pauses were never followed by any remark, the momentary uneasiness they created quickly passed away, and for a time was forgotten.

"Come, friend," said Hawkeye, drawing out a keg from beneath a cover of leaves, towards the close of the repast, and addressing the stranger, who sat at his elbow doing great justice to his culinary skill, "try a little spruce; 't will wash away all thoughts of the colt, and quicken the life in your bosom. I drink to our better friendship, hoping that a little horseflesh may leave no heart-burnings atween us. How do you name yourself?"

"Gamut—David Gamut," returned the singing-master, preparing to wash down his sorrows in a powerful draught of the woodman's high-flavored and well-laced compound.

"A very good name, and, I dare say, handed down from honest forefathers. I 'm an admirator of names, though the Christian fashions fall far below savage customs in this particular. The biggest coward I ever knew was called Lyon; and his wife, Patience, would scold you out of hearing in less time than a hunted deer would run a rod. With an Indian 't is a matter of conscience; what he calls himself, he generally is—not that Chingachgook, which signifies Big Sarpent, is really a snake, big or little; but that he understands the windings and turnings of human natur', and is silent, and strikes his enemies when they least expect him. What may be your calling?"

"I am an unworthy instructor in the art of psalmody."

"Anan!"

"I teach singing to the youths of the Connecticut levy."

"You might be better employed. The young hounds go laughing and singing too much already through the woods, when they ought not to breathe louder than a fox in his cover. Can you use the smooth bore, or handle the rifle?"

"Praised be God, I have never had occasion to meddle with murderous implements!"

"Perhaps you understand the compass, and lay down the water-courses and mountains of the wilderness on paper, in order that they who follow may find places by their given names?"

"I practice no such employment."

"You have a pair of legs that might make a long path seem short! you journey sometimes, I fancy, with tidings for the general."

"Never; I follow no other than my own high vocation, which is instruction in sacred music!"

"'T is a strange calling!" muttered Hawkeye, with an inward laugh, "to go through life, like a cat-bird, mocking all the ups and downs that may happen to come out of other men's throats. Well, friend, I suppose it is your gift, and must n't be denied any more than if 't was shooting, or some other better inclination. Let us hear what you can do in that way; 't will be a friendly manner of saying good-night, for 't is time that these ladies should be getting strength for a hard and a long push, in the pride of the morning, afore the Maquas are stirring!"

"With joyful pleasure do I consent," said David, adjusting his iron-rimmed spectacles, and producing his beloved little volume, which he immediately tendered to Alice. "What can be more fitting and consolatory, than to offer up evening praise, after a day of such exceeding jeopardy!"

Alice smiled; but regarding Heyward, she blushed and hesitated.

"Indulge yourself," he whispered: "ought not the suggestion of the worthy namesake of the Psalmist to have its weight at such a moment?"

Encouraged by his opinion, Alice did what her pious inclinations and her keen relish for gentle sounds had before so strongly urged. The book was opened at a hymn not ill adapted to their situation, and in which the poet, no longer goaded by his desire to excel the inspired king of Israel, had discovered some chastened and respectable powers. Cora betrayed a disposition to support her sister, and the sacred song proceeded, after the indispensable preliminaries of the pitch-pipe and the tune had been duly attended to by the methodical David.

The air was solemn and slow. At times it rose to the fullest compass of the rich voices of the females, who hung over their little book in holy excitement, and again it sank so low that the rushing of the waters ran through their melody, like a hollow accompaniment. The natural taste and true ear of David governed and modified the sounds to suit the confined cavern, every crevice and cranny of which was filled with the thrilling notes of their flexible voices. The Indians riveted their eyes on the rocks, and listened with an attention that seemed to turn them into stone. But the scout, who had placed his chin in his hand, with an expression of cold indifference, gradually suffered his rigid features to relax, until, as verse succeeded verse, he felt his iron nature subdued, while his recollection was carried back to boyhood, when his ears had been accustomed to listen to similar sounds of praise, in the settlements of the colony. His roving eyes began to moisten, and before the hymn was ended, scalding tears rolled out of fountains that had long seemed dry, and followed each other down those cheeks, that had oftener felt the storms of heaven than any testimonials of weakness. The singers were dwelling on one of those low, dying chords, which the ear devours with such greedy rapture, as if conscious that it is about to lose them, when a cry, that seemed neither human nor earthly, rose in the outward air, penetrating not only the recesses of the cavern, but to the inmost hearts of all who heard it. It was followed by a stillness apparently as deep as if the waters had been checked in their furious progress, at such a horrid and unusual interruption.

"What is it?" murmured Alice, after a few moments of terrible suspense.

"What is it?" repeated Heyward aloud.

Neither Hawkeye nor the Indians made any reply. They listened, as if expecting the sound would be repeated, with a manner that expressed their own astonishment. At length they spoke together earnestly, in the Delaware language, when Uncas, passing by the inner and most concealed aperture, cautiously left the cavern. When he had gone, the scout first spoke in English.

"What it is, or what it is not, none here can tell; though two of us have ranged the woods for more than thirty years! I did believe there was no cry that Indian or beast could make, that my ears had not heard; but this has proved that I was only a vain and conceited mortal!"

"Was it not, then, the shout the warriors make when they wish to intimidate their enemies?" asked Cora, who stood drawing her veil about her person, with a calmness to which her agitated sister was a stranger.

"No, no; this was bad, and shocking, and had a sort of unhuman sound; but when you once hear the war-whoop, you will never mistake it for anything else! Well, Uncas!" speaking in Delaware to the young chief as he reëntered, "what see you? do our lights shine through the blankets?"

The answer was short, and apparently decided, being given in the same tongue.

"There is nothing to be seen without," continued Hawkeye, shaking his head in discontent; "and our hiding-place is still in darkness! Pass into the other cave, you that need it, and seek for sleep; we must be afoot long before the sun, and make the most of our time to get to Edward, while the Mingoes are taking their morning nap."

Cora set the example of compliance, with a steadiness that taught the more timid Alice the necessity of obedience. Before leaving the place, however, she whispered a request to Duncan that he would follow. Uncas raised the blanket for their passage, and as the sisters turned to thank him for this act of attention, they saw the scout seated again before the dying embers, with his face resting on his hands, in a manner which showed how deeply he brooded on the unaccountable interruption which had broken up their evening devotions.

Heyward took with him a blazing knot, which threw a dim light through the narrow vista of their new apartment. Placing it in a favorable position, he joined the females, who now found themselves alone with him for the first time since they had left the friendly ramparts of Fort Edward.

"Leave us not, Duncan," said Alice; "we cannot sleep in such a place as this, with that horrid cry still ringing in our ears!"

"First let us examine into the security of your fortress," he answered, "and then we will speak of rest."

He approached the further end of the cavern, to an outlet which, like the others, was concealed by blankets, and removing the thick screen, breathed the fresh and reviving air from the cataract. One arm of the river flowed through a deep, narrow ravine, which its current had worn in the soft rock, directly beneath his feet, forming an effectual defense, as he believed, against any danger from that quarter; the water, a few rods above them, plunging, glancing, and sweeping along, in its most violent and broken manner.

"Nature has made an impenetrable barrier on this side," he continued, pointing down the perpendicular declivity into the dark current, before he dropped the blanket; "and as you know that good men and true are on guard in front, I see no reason why the advice of our honest host should be disregarded. I am certain Cora will join me in saying that sleep is necessary to you both."

"Cora may submit to the justice of your opinion, though she cannot put it in practice," returned the elder sister, who had placed herself by the side of Alice, on a couch of sassafras; "there would be other causes to chase away sleep, though we had been spared the shock of this mysterious noise. Ask yourself, Heyward, can daughters forget the anxiety a father must endure, whose children lodge, he knows not where or how, in such a wilderness, and in the midst of so many perils?"

"He is a soldier, and knows how to estimate the chances of the woods."

"He is a father, and cannot deny his nature."

"How kind has he ever been to all my follies! and how tender and indulgent to all my wishes!" sobbed Alice. "We have been selfish, sister, in urging our visit at such hazard!"

"I may have been rash in pressing his consent in a moment of much embarrassment, but I would have proved to him, that however others might neglect him in his strait, his children at least were faithful!"

"When he heard of your arrival at Edward," said Heyward, kindly, "there was a powerful struggle in his bosom between fear and love; though the latter, heightened, if possible, by so long a separation, quickly prevailed. 'It is the spirit of my noble-minded Cora that leads them, Duncan,' he said, 'and I will not balk it. Would to God, that he who holds the honor of our royal master in his guardianship would show but half her firmness!'"

"And did he not speak of me, Heyward?" demanded Alice, with jealous affection. "Surely, he forgot not altogether his little Elsie!"

"That were impossible," returned the young man; "he called you by a thousand endearing epithets, that I may not presume to use, but to the justice of which I can warmly testify. Once, indeed, he said—"

Duncan ceased speaking; for while his eyes were riveted on those of Alice, who had turned towards him with the eagerness of filial affection, to catch his words, the same strong, horrid cry, as before, filled the air, and rendered him mute. A long, breathless silence succeeded, during which each looked at the others in fearful expectation of hearing the sound repeated. At length the blanket was slowly raised, and the scout stood in the aperture with a countenance whose firmness evidently began to give way, before a mystery that seemed to threaten some danger, against which all his cunning and experience might prove of no avail.

CHAPTER VII

They do not sleep.
On yonder cliffs, a grisly band,
I see them sit.
GRAY, *The Bard.*

"'T would be neglecting a warning that is given for our good, to lie hid any longer," said Hawkeye, "when such sounds are raised in the forest! The gentle ones may keep close, but the Mohicans and I will watch upon the rock, where I suppose a major of the 60th would wish to keep us company."

"Is then our danger so pressing?" asked Cora.

"He who makes strange sounds, and gives them out for man's information, alone knows our danger. I should think myself wicked, unto rebellion against his will, was I to burrow with such warnings in the air! Even the weak soul who passes his days in singing is stirred by the cry, and, as he says, is 'ready to go forth to the battle.' If 't were only a battle, it would be a thing understood by us all, and easily managed; but I have heard that when such shrieks are atween heaven and 'arth, it betokens another sort of warfare!"

"If all our reasons for fear, my friend, are confined to such as proceed from supernatural causes, we have but little occasion to be alarmed," continued the undisturbed Cora; "are you certain that our enemies have not invented some new and ingenious method to strike us with terror, that their conquest may become more easy?"

"Lady," returned the scout, solemnly, "I have listened to all the sounds of the woods for thirty years, as a man will listen whose life and death depend on the quickness of his ears. There is no whine of the panther, no whistle of the cat-bird, nor any invention of the devilish Mingoes, that can cheat me! I have heard the forest moan like mortal men in their affliction; often and again have I listened to the wind playing its music in the branches of the girdled trees; and I have heard the lightning cracking in the air like the snapping of blazing brush, as it spitted forth sparks and forked flames; but never have I thought that I heard more than the pleasure of Him who sported with the things of his hand. But neither the Mohicans, nor I, who am a white man without a cross, can explain the cry just heard. We therefore believe it a sign given for our good."

"It is extraordinary!" said Heyward, taking his pistols from the place where he had laid them on entering; "be it a sign of peace or a signal of war, it must be looked to. Lead the way, my friend; I follow."

On issuing from their place of confinement, the whole party instantly experienced a grateful renovation of spirits, by exchanging the pent air of the hiding-place for the cool and invigorating atmosphere which played around the whirlpools and pitches of the cataract. A heavy evening breeze swept along the surface of the river, and seemed to drive the roar of the falls into the recesses of their own caverns, whence it issued heavily and constant, like thunder rumbling beyond the distant hills. The moon had risen, and its light was already glancing here and there on the waters above them; but the extremity of the rock where they stood still lay in shadow. With the exception of the sounds produced by the rushing waters, and an occasional breathing of the air, as it murmured past them in fitful currents, the scene was as still as night and solitude could make it. In vain were the eyes of each individual bent along the opposite shores, in quest of some signs of life that might explain the nature of the interruption they had heard. Their anxious and eager looks were baffled by the deceptive light, or rested only on naked rocks, and straight and immovable trees.

"Here is nothing to be seen but the gloom and quiet of a lovely evening," whispered Duncan; "how much should we prize such a scene, and all this breathing solitude, at any other moment, Cora! Fancy yourselves in security, and what now, perhaps, increases your terror, may be made conducive to enjoyment—"

"Listen!" interrupted Alice.

The caution was unnecessary. Once more the same sound arose, as if from the bed of the river, and having broken out of the narrow bounds of the cliffs, was heard undulating through the forest, in distant and dying cadences. "Can any here give a name to such a cry?" demanded Hawkeye, when the last echo was lost in the woods; "if so, let him speak; for myself, I judge it not to belong to 'arth!"

"Here, then, is one who can undeceive you," said Duncan; "I know the sound full well, for often have I heard it on the field of battle, and in situations which are frequent in a soldier's life. 'T is the horrid shriek that a horse will give in his agony;

oftener drawn from him in pain, though sometimes in terror. My charger is either a prey to the beasts of the forest, or he sees his danger, without the power to avoid it. The sound might deceive me in the cavern, but in the open air I know it too well to be wrong."

The scout and his companions listened to this simple explanation with the interest of men who imbibe new ideas at the same time that they get rid of old ones, which had proved disagreeable inmates. The two latter uttered their usual and expressive exclamation, "Hugh!" as the truth first glanced upon their minds, while the former, after a short musing pause, took upon himself to reply.

"I cannot deny your words," he said; "for I am little skilled in horses, though born where they abound. The wolves must be hovering above their heads on the bank, and the timorsome creatures are calling on man for help, in the best manner they are able. Uncas"—he spoke in Delaware—"Uncas, drop down in the canoe, and whirl a brand among the pack; or fear may do what the wolves can't get at to perform, and leave us without horses in the morning, when we shall have so much need to journey swiftly!"

The young native had already descended to the water, to comply, when a long howl was raised on the edge of the river, and was borne swiftly off into the depths of the forest, as though the beasts, of their own accord, were abandoning their prey in sudden terror. Uncas, with instinctive quickness, receded, and the three foresters held another of their low, earnest conferences.

"We have been like hunters who have lost the points of the heavens, and from whom the sun has been hid for days," said Hawkeye, turning away from his companions; "now we begin again to know the signs of our course, and the paths are cleared from briers! Seat yourselves in the shade which the moon throws from younder beech—'t is thicker than that of the pines—and let us wait for that which the Lord may choose to send next. Let all your conversation be in whispers; though it would be better, and perhaps, in the end, wiser, if each one held discourse with his own thoughts, for a time."

The manner of the scout was seriously impressive, though no longer distinguished by any signs of unmanly apprehension. It was evident that his momentary weakness had vanished with the explanation of a mystery which his own experience had not served to fathom; and, though he now felt all the realities of their actual condition, that he was prepared to meet them with the energy of his hardy nature. This feeling seemed also common to the natives, who placed themselves in positions which commanded a full view of both shores, while their own persons were effectually concealed from observation. In such circumstances, common prudence dictated that Heyward and his companions should imitate a caution that proceeded from so intelligent a source. The young man drew a pile of the sassafras from the cave, and placing it in the chasm which separated the two caverns, it was occupied by the sisters, who were thus protected by the rocks from any missiles, while their anxiety was relieved by the assurance that no danger could approach without a warning. Heyward himself was posted at hand, so near that he might communicate with his companions without raising his voice to a dangerous elevation, while David, in imitation of the woodsmen, bestowed his person in such a manner among the fissures of the rocks, that his ungainly limbs were no longer offensive to the eye.

In this manner, hours passed by without further interruption. The moon reached the zenith, and shed its mild light perpendicularly on the lovely sight of the sisters slumbering peacefully in each other's arms. Duncan cast the wide shawl of Cora before a spectacle he so much loved to contemplate, and then suffered his own head to seek a pillow on the rock. David began to utter sounds that would have shocked his delicate organs in more wakeful moments; in short, all but Hawkeye and the Mohicans lost every idea of consciousness, in uncontrollable drowsiness. But the watchfulness, of these vigilant protectors neither tired nor slumbered. Immovable as that rock of which each appeared to form a part, they lay, with their eyes roving, without intermission, along the dark margin of trees that bounded the adjacent shores of the narrow stream. Not a sound escaped them; the most subtle examination could not have told they breathed. It was evident that this excess of caution proceeded from an experience that no subtlety on the part of their enemies could deceive. It was, however, continued without any apparent consequences, until the moon had set, and a pale streak above the tree-tops, at the bend of the river a little below, announced the approach of day.

Then, for the first time, Hawkeye was seen to stir. He crawled along the rock, and shook Duncan from his heavy slumbers.

"Now is the time to journey," he whispered; "awake the gentle ones, and be ready to get into the canoe when I bring it to the landing-place."

"Have you had a quiet night?" said Heyward; "for myself, I believe sleep has got the better of my vigilance."

"All is yet still as midnight. Be silent, but be quick."

By this time Duncan was thoroughly awake, and he immediately lifted the shawl from the sleeping females. The motion caused Cora to raise her hand as if to repulse him, while Alice murmured, in her soft, gentle voice, "No, no, dear father, we were not deserted; Duncan was with us!"

"Yes, sweet innocence," whispered the youth; "Duncan is here, and while life continues or danger remains, he will never quit thee. Cora! Alice! awake! The hour has come to move!"

A loud shriek from the younger of the sisters, and the form of the other standing upright before him, in bewildered horror, was the unexpected answer he received. While the words were still on the lips of Heyward, there had arisen such a tumult of yells and cries as served to drive the swift currents of his own blood back from its bounding course into the fountains of his heart. It seemed, for near a minute, as if the demons of hell had possessed themselves of the air about them, and were venting their savage humors in barbarous sounds. The cries came from no particular direction, though it was evident they filled the woods, and as the appalled listeners easily imagined, the caverns of the falls, the rocks, the bed of the river, and the upper air. David raised his tall person in the midst of the infernal din, with a hand on either ear, exclaiming, "Whence comes this discord? Has hell broke loose, that man should utter sounds like these?"

The bright flashes and the quick reports of a dozen rifles, from the opposite banks of the stream, followed this incautious exposure of his person, and left the unfortunate singing-master senseless on that rock where he had been so long slumbering. The Mohicans boldly sent back the intimidating yell of their enemies, who raised a shout of savage triumph at the fall of Gamut. The flash of rifles was then quick and close between them, but either party was too well skilled to leave even a limb exposed to the hostile aim. Duncan listened with intense anxiety for the strokes of the paddle, believing that flight was now their only refuge. The river glanced by with its ordinary velocity, but the canoe was nowhere to be seen on its dark waters. He had just fancied they were cruelly deserted by the scout, as a stream of flame issued from the rock beneath him, and a fierce yell, blended with a shriek of agony, announced that the messenger of death, sent from the fatal weapon of Hawkeye, had found a victim. At this slight repulse the assailants instantly withdrew, and gradually the place became as still as before the sudden tumult.

Duncan seized the favorable moment to spring to the body of Gamut, which he bore within the shelter of the narrow chasm that protected the sisters. In another minute the whole party was collected in this spot of comparative safety.

"The poor fellow has saved his scalp," said Hawkeye, coolly passing his hand over the head of David; "but he is a proof that a man may be born with too long a tongue! 'T was downright madness to show six feet of flesh and blood, on a naked rock, to the raging savages. I only wonder he has escaped with life."

"Is he not dead?" demanded Cora, in a voice whose husky tones showed how powerfully natural horror struggled with her assumed firmness. "Can we do aught to assist the wretched man?"

"No, no! the life is in his heart yet, and after he has slept awhile he will come to himself, and be a wiser man for it, till the hour of his real time shall come," returned Hawkeye, casting another oblique glance at the insensible body, while he filled his charger with admirable nicety. "Carry him in, Uncas, and lay him on the sassafras. The longer his nap lasts the better it will be for him, as I doubt whether he can find a proper cover for such a shape on these rocks; and singing won't do any good with the Iroquois."

"You believe, then, the attack will be renewed?" asked Heyward.

"Do I expect a hungry wolf will satisfy his craving with a mouthful? They have lost a man, and 't is their fashion, when they meet a loss, and fail in the surprise, to fall back; but we shall have them on again, with new expedients to circumvent us, and master our scalps. Our main hope," he continued, raising his rugged countenance, across which a shade of anxiety just then passed like a darkening cloud, "will be to keep the rock until Munro can send a party to our help! God send it may be soon, and under a leader that knows the Indian customs!"

"You hear our probable fortunes, Cora," said Duncan, "and you know we have everything to hope from the anxiety and experience of your father. Come, then, with Alice, into this cavern, where you, at least, will be safe from the murderous rifles of our enemies, and where you may bestow a care suited to your gentle natures on our unfortunate comrade."

The sisters followed him into the outer cave, where David was beginning, by his sighs, to give symptoms of returning consciousness; and then commending the wounded man to their attention, he immediately prepared to leave them.

"Duncan!" said the tremulous voice of Cora, when he had reached the mouth of the cavern. He turned, and beheld the speaker, whose color had changed to a deadly paleness, and whose lip quivered, gazing after him, with an expression of interest which immediately recalled him to her side. "Remember, Duncan, how necessary your safety is to our own—how you bear a father's sacred trust—how much depends on your discretion and care—in short," she added, while the telltale blood stole over her features, crimsoning her very temples, "how very deservedly dear you are to all of the name of Munro."

"If anything could add to my own base love of life," said Heyward, suffering his unconscious eyes to wander to the youthful form of the silent Alice, "it would be so kind an assurance. As major of the 60th, our honest host will tell you I must take my share of the fray; but our task will be easy; it is merely to keep these bloodhounds at bay for a few hours."

Without waiting for reply, he tore himself from the presence of the sisters, and joined the scout and his companions, who still lay within the protection of the little chasm between the two caves.

"I tell you, Uncas," said the former, as Heyward joined them, "you are wasteful of your powder, and the kick of the rifle disconcerts your aim! Little powder, light lead, and a long arm, seldom fail of bringing the death screech from a Mingo! At least, such has been my experience with the creatur's. Come, friends; let us to our covers, for no man can tell when or where a Maqua[15] will strike his blow."

The Indians silently repaired to their appointed stations, which were fissures in the rocks, whence they could command the approaches to the foot of the falls. In the centre of the little island, a few short and stunted pines had found root, forming a thicket, into which Hawkeye darted with the swiftness of a deer, followed by the active Duncan. Here they secured themselves, as well as circumstances would permit, among the shrubs and fragments of stone that were scattered about the place. Above them was a bare, rounded rock, on each side of which the water played its gambols, and plunged into the abysses beneath, in the manner already described. As the day had now dawned, the opposite shores no longer presented a confused outline, but they were able to look into the woods, and distinguish objects beneath the canopy of gloomy pines.

A long and anxious watch succeeded, but without any further evidences of a renewed attack; and Duncan began to hope that their fire had proved more fatal than was supposed, and that their enemies had been effectually repulsed. When he ventured to utter this impression to his companion, it was met by Hawkeye with an incredulous shake of the head.

"You know not the nature of a Maqua, if you think he is so easily beaten back without a scalp!" he answered. "If there was one of the imps yelling this morning, there were forty! and they know our number and quality too well to give up the chase so soon. Hist! look into the water above, just where it breaks over the rocks. I am no mortal, if the risky devils have n't swam down upon the very pitch, and, as bad luck would have it, they have hit the head of the island. Hist! man, keep close! or the hair will be off your crown in the turning of a knife!"

Heyward lifted his head from the cover, and beheld what he justly considered a prodigy of rashness and skill. The river had worn away the edge of the soft rock in such a manner as to render its first pitch less abrupt and perpendicular than is usual at waterfalls. With no other guide than the ripple of the stream where it met the head of the island, a party of their insatiable foes had ventured into the current, and swam down upon this point, knowing the ready access it would give, if successful, to their intended victims. As Hawkeye ceased speaking, four human heads could be seen peering above a few logs of driftwood that had lodged on these naked rocks, and which had probably suggested the idea of the practicability of the hazardous undertaking. At the next moment, a fifth form was seen floating over the green edge of the fall, a little from the line of the island. The savage struggled

---

[15]Mingo was the Delaware term for the Five Nations. Maquas was the name given them by the Dutch. The French, from their first intercourse with them, called them Iroquois. [J.F.C.]

powerfully to gain the point of safety, and, favored by the glancing water, he was already stretching forth an arm to meet the grasp of his companions, when he shot away again with the whirling current, appeared to rise into the air, with uplifted arms and starting eyeballs, and fell, with a sullen plunge, into that deep and yawning abyss over which he hovered. A single, wild, despairing shriek rose from the cavern, and all was hushed again, as the grave.

The first generous impulse of Duncan was to rush to the rescue of the hapless wretch; but he felt himself bound to the spot by the iron grasp of the immovable scout.

"Would ye bring certain death upon us, by telling the Mingoes where we lie?" demanded Hawkeye, sternly; "'t is a charge of powder saved, and ammunition is as precious now as breath to a worried deer! Freshen the priming of your pistols—the mist of the falls is apt to dampen the brimstone—and stand firm for a close struggle, while I fire on their rush."

He placed a finger in his mouth, and drew a long, shrill whistle, which was answered from the rocks that were guarded by the Mohicans. Duncan caught glimpses of heads above the scattered driftwood, as this signal rose on the air, but they disappeared again as suddenly as they had glanced upon his sight. A low, rustling sound next drew his attention behind him, and turning his head, he beheld Uncas within a few feet, creeping to his side. Hawkeye spoke to him in Delaware, when the young chief took his position with singular caution and undisturbed coolness. To Heyward this was a moment of feverish and impatient suspense; though the scout saw fit to select it as a fit occasion to read a lecture to his more youthful associates on the art of using firearms with discretion.

"Of all we'pons," he commenced, "the long-barreled, truegrooved, soft-metaled rifle is the most dangerous in skillful hands, though it wants a strong arm, a quick eye, and great judgment in charging, to put forth all its beauties. The gunsmiths can have but little insight into their trade, when they make their fowling-pieces and short horsemen's—"

He was interrupted by the low but expressive "Hugh!" of Uncas.

"I see them, boy, I see them!" continued Hawkeye; "they are gathering for the rush, or they would keep their dingy backs below the logs. Well, let them," he added, examining his flint; "the leading man certainly comes on to his death, though it should be Montcalm himself!"

At that moment the woods were filled with another burst of cries, and at the signal four savages sprang from the cover of the drift-wood. Heyward felt a burning desire to rush forward to meet them, so intense was the delirious anxiety of the moment; but he was restrained by the deliberate examples of the scout and Uncas. When their foes who leaped over the black rock that divided them, with long bounds, uttering the wildest yells, were within a few rods, the rifle of Hawkeye slowly rose among the shrubs, and poured out its fatal contents. The foremost Indian bounded like a stricken deer, and fell headlong among the clefts of the island.

"Now, Uncas!" cried the scout, drawing his long knife, while his quick eyes began to flash with ardor, "take the last of the screeching imps; of the other two we are sartain!"

He was obeyed; and but two enemies remained to be overcome. Heyward had given one of his pistols to Hawkeye, and together they rushed down a little declivity towards their foes; they discharged their weapons at the same instant, and equally without success.

"I know'd it! and I said it!" muttered the scout, whirling the despised little implement over the falls with bitter disdain. "Come on, ye bloody-minded hell-hounds! ye meet a man without a cross!"

The words were barely uttered, when he encountered a savage of gigantic stature, and of the fiercest mien. At the same moment, Duncan found himself engaged with the other, in a similar contest of hand to hand. With ready skill, Hawkeye and his antagonist each grasped that uplifted arm of the other which held the dangerous knife. For near a minute they stood looking one another in the eye, and gradually exerting the power of their muscles for the mastery. At length, the toughened sinews of the white man prevailed over the less practiced limbs of the native. The arm of the latter slowly gave way before the increasing force of the scout, who, suddenly wresting his armed hand from the grasp of the foe, drove the sharp weapon through his naked bosom to the heart. In the mean time Heyward had been pressed in a more deadly struggle. His slight sword was snapped in the first encounter. As he was destitute of any other means of defense, his safety now depended entirely on bodily strength and resolution. Though deficient in neither of these qualities, he had met an enemy every way his equal. Happily, he soon succeeded in disarming his adversary, whose knife fell on the rock at their feet; and from this moment it became a fierce struggle, who should cast the other over the dizzy height into a neighboring cavern of the falls. Every successive struggle brought them nearer to the verge, where Duncan perceived the final and conquering effort must be made. Each of the combatants threw all his energies into that effort, and the result was, that both tottered on the brink of the precipice. Heyward felt the grasp of the other at his throat, and saw the grim smile the savage gave, under the revengeful hope that he hurried his enemy to a fate similar to his own, as he felt his body slowly yielding to a resistless power, and the young man experienced the passing agony of such a moment in all its horrors. At that instant of extreme danger, a dark hand and glancing knife appeared before him; the Indian released his hold, as the blood flowed freely from around the severed tendons of the wrist; and while Duncan was drawn backward by the saving arm of Uncas, his charmed eyes were still riveted on the fierce and disappointed countenance of his foe, who fell sullenly and disappointed down the irrecoverable precipice.

"To cover! to cover!" cried Hawkeye, who just then had dispatched the enemy; "to cover, for your lives! the work is but half ended!"

The young Mohican gave a shout of triumph, and, followed by Duncan, he glided up the acclivity they had descended to the combat, and sought the friendly shelter of the rocks and shrubs.

CHAPTER VIII

They linger yet,
Avengers of their native land.
GRAY, *The Bard.*

The warning call of the scout was not uttered without occasion. During the occurrence of the deadly encounter just related, the roar of the falls was unbroken by any human sound whatever. It would seem that interest in the result had kept the natives on the opposite shores in breathless suspense, while the quick evolutions and swift changes in the positions of the combatants effectually prevented a fire that might prove dangerous alike to friend and enemy. But the moment the struggle was decided, a yell arose as fierce and savage as wild and revengeful passions could throw into the air. It was followed by the swift flashes of the rifles, which sent their leaden messengers across the rock in volleys, as though the assailants would pour out their impotent fury on the insensible scene of the fatal contest.

A steady, though deliberate return was made from the rifle of Chingachgook, who had maintained his post throughout the fray with unmoved resolution. When the triumphant shout of Uncas was borne to his ears, the gratified father raised his voice in a single responsive cry, after which his busy piece alone proved that he still guarded his pass with unwearied diligence. In this manner many minutes flew by with the swiftness of thought: the rifles of the assailants speaking, at times, in rattling volleys, and at others, in occasional, scattering shots. Though the rock, the trees, and the shrubs were cut and torn in a hundred places around the besieged, their cover was so close, and so rigidly maintained, that as yet David had been the only sufferer in their little band.

"Let them burn their powder," said the deliberate scout, while bullet after bullet whizzed by the place where he securely lay; "there will be a fine gathering of lead when it is over, and I fancy the imps will tire of the sport, afore these old stones cry out for mercy! Uncas, boy, you waste the kernels by overcharging: and a kicking rifle never carries a true bullet. I told you to take that loping miscreant under the line of white paint; now, if your bullet went a hair's breadth, it went two inches above it. The life lies low in a Mingo, and humanity teaches us to make a quick end of the sarpents."

A quiet smile lighted the haughty features of the young Mohican, betraying his knowledge of the English language, as well as of the other's meaning; but he suffered it to pass away without vindication or reply.

"I cannot permit you to accuse Uncas of want of judgment or of skill," said Duncan: "he saved my life in the coolest and readiest manner, and he has made a friend who never will require to be reminded of the debt he owes."

Uncas partly raised his body, and offered his hand to the grasp of Heyward. During this act of friendship, the two young men exchanged looks of intelligence which caused Duncan to forget the character and condition of his wild associate. In the mean while, Hawkeye, who looked on this burst of youthful feeling with a cool but kind regard, made the following reply:—

"Life is an obligation which friends often owe each other in the wilderness. I dare say I may have served Uncas some such turn myself before now; and I very well remember that he has stood between me and death five different times: three times from the Mingoes, once in crossing Horican, and—"

"That bullet was better aimed than common!" exclaimed Duncan, involuntarily shrinking from a shot which struck the rock at his side with a smart rebound.

Hawkeye laid his hand on the shapeless metal, and shook his head, as he examined it, saying, "Falling lead is never flattened! had it come from the clouds this might have happened!"

But the rifle of Uncas was deliberately raised towards the heavens, directing the eyes of his companions to a point where the mystery was immediately explained. A ragged oak grew on the right bank of the river, nearly opposite to their position, which, seeking the freedom of the open space, had inclined so far forward, that its upper branches overhung that arm of the stream which flowed nearest to its own shore. Among the topmost leaves, which scantily concealed the gnarled and stunted limbs, a savage was nestled, partly concealed by the trunk of the tree, and partly exposed, as though looking down upon them to ascertain the effect produced by his treacherous aim.

"These devils will scale heaven to circumvent us to our ruin," said Hawkeye; "keep him in play, boy, until I can bring 'Killdeer' to bear, when we will try his metal on each side of the tree at once."

Uncas delayed his fire until the scout uttered the word. The rifles flashed, the leaves and bark of the oak flew into the air, and were scattered by the wind, but the Indian answered their assault by a taunting laugh, sending down upon them another bullet in return, that struck the cap of Hawkeye from his head. Once more the savage yells burst out of the woods, and the leaden hail whistled above the heads of the besieged, as if to confine them to a place where they might become easy victims to the enterprise of the warrior who had mounted the tree.

"This must be looked to!" said the scout, glancing about him with an anxious eye. "Uncas, call up your father; we have need of all our we'pons to bring the cunning varment from his roost."

The signal was instantly given; and, before Hawkeye had reloaded his rifle, they were joined by Chingachgook. When his son pointed out to the experienced warrior the situation of their dangerous enemy, the usual exclamatory "Hugh!" burst from his lips; after which, no further expression of surprise or alarm was suffered to escape him. Hawkeye and the Mohicans conversed earnestly together in Delaware for a few moments, when each quietly took his post, in order to execute the plan they had speedily devised.

The warrior in the oak had maintained a quick, though ineffectual fire, from the moment of his discovery. But his aim was interrupted by the vigilance of his enemies, whose rifles instantaneously bore on any part of his person that was left exposed. Still his bullets fell in the centre of the crouching party. The clothes of Heyward, which rendered him peculiarly conspicuous, were repeatedly cut, and once blood was drawn from a slight wound in his arm.

At length, emboldened by the long and patient watchfulness of his enemies, the Huron attempted a better and more fatal aim. The quick eyes of the Mohicans caught the dark line of his lower limbs incautiously exposed through the thin foliage, a few inches from the trunk of the tree. Their rifles made a common report, when, sinking on his wounded limb, part of the body of the savage came into view. Swift as thought, Hawkeye seized the advantage, and discharged his fatal weapon into the top of the oak. The leaves were unusually agitated; the dangerous rifle fell from its commanding elevation, and after a few moments of vain struggling, the form of the savage was seen swinging in the wind, while he still grasped a ragged and naked branch of the tree, with hands clenched in desperation.

"Give him—in pity give him the contents of another rifle!" cried Duncan, turning away his eyes in horror from the spectacle of a fellow-creature in such awful jeopardy.

"Not a karnel!" exclaimed the obdurate Hawkeye; "his death is certain, and we have no powder to spare, for Indian fights sometimes last for days; 't is their scalps or ours!—and God, who made us, has put into our natures the craving to keep the skin on the head!"

Against this stern and unyielding morality, supported as it was by such visible policy, there was no appeal. From that moment the yells in the forest once more ceased, the fire was suffered to decline, and all eyes, those of friends as well as enemies, became fixed on the hopeless condition of the wretch who was dangling between heaven and earth. The body yielded to the currents of air, and though no murmur or groan escaped the victim, there were instants when he grimly faced his foes, and the anguish of cold despair might be traced, through the intervening distance, in possession of his swarthy lineaments. Three several times the scout raised his piece in mercy, and as often prudence getting the better of his intention, it was again silently lowered. At length one hand of the Huron lost its hold and dropped exhausted to his side. A desperate and fruitless struggle to recover the branch succeeded, and then the savage was seen for a fleeting instant, grasping wildly at the empty air. The lightning is not quicker than was the flame from the rifle of Hawkeye; the limbs of the victim trembled and contracted, the head fell to the bosom, and the body parted the foaming water like lead, when the element closed above it, in its ceaseless velocity, and every vestige of the unhappy Huron was lost forever.

No shout of triumph succeeded this important advantage, but even the Mohicans gazed at each other in silent horror. A single yell burst from the woods, and all was again still. Hawkeye, who alone appeared to reason on the occasion, shook his head at his own momentary weakness, even uttering his self-disapprobation aloud.

"'T was the last charge in my horn, and the last bullet in my pouch, and 't was the act of a boy!" he said; "what mattered it whether he struck the rock living or dead! feeling would soon be over. Uncas, lad, go down to the canoe, and bring up the big horn; it is all the powder we have left, and we shall need it to the last grain, or I am ignorant of the Mingo nature."

The young Mohican complied, leaving the scout turning over the useless contents of his pouch, and shaking the empty horn with renewed discontent. From this unsatisfactory examination, however, he was soon called by a loud and piercing exclamation from Uncas, that sounded, even to the unpracticed ears of Duncan, as the signal of some new and unexpected calamity. Every thought filled with apprehension for the precious treasure he had concealed in the cavern, the young man started to his feet, totally regardless of the hazard he incurred by such an exposure. As if actuated by a common impulse, his movement was imitated by his companions, and, together, they rushed down the pass to the friendly chasm, with a rapidity that rendered the scattering fire of their enemies perfectly harmless. The unwonted cry had brought the sisters, together with the wounded David, from their place of refuge; and the whole party, at a single glance, was made acquainted with the nature of the disaster that had disturbed even the practiced stoicism of their youthful Indian protector.

At a short distance from the rock, their little bark was to be seen floating across the eddy, towards the swift current of the river, in a manner which proved that its course was directed by some hidden agent. The instant this unwelcome sight caught the eye of the scout, his rifle was leveled as by instinct, but the barrel gave no answer to the bright sparks of the flint.

"'T is too late, 't is too late!" Hawkeye exclaimed, dropping the useless piece in bitter disappointment; "the miscreant has struck to the rapid; and had we powder, it could hardly send the lead swifter than he now goes!"

The adventurous Huron raised his head above the shelter of the canoe, and while it glided swiftly down the stream, he waved his hand, and gave forth the shout, which was the known signal of success. His cry was answered by a yell and a laugh from the woods, as tauntingly exulting as if fifty demons were uttering their blasphemies at the fall of some Christian soul.

"Well may you laugh, ye children of the devil!" said the scout, seating himself on a projection of the rock, and suffering his gun to fall neglected at his feet, "for the three quickest and truest rifles in these woods are no better than so many stalks of mullein, or the last year's horns of a buck!"

"What is to be done?" demanded Duncan, losing the first feeling of disappointment in a more manly desire for exertion; "what will become of us?"

Hawkeye made no other reply than by passing his finger around the crown of his head, in a manner so significant, that none who witnessed the action could mistake its meaning.

"Surely, surely, our case is not so desperate!" exclaimed the youth; "the Hurons are not here; we may make good the caverns; we may oppose their landing."

"With what?" coolly demanded the scout. "The arrows of Uncas, or such tears as women shed! No, no; you are young, and rich, and have friends, and at such an age I know it is hard to die! But," glancing his eyes at the Mohicans, "let us remember we are men without a cross, and let us teach these natives of the forest that white blood can run as freely as red, when the appointed hour is come."

Duncan turned quickly in the direction indicated by the other's eyes, and read a confirmation of his worst apprehensions in the conduct of the Indians. Chingachgook, placing himself in a dignified posture on another fragment of the rock, had already laid aside his knife and tomahawk, and was in the act of taking the eagle's plume from his head, and smoothing the solitary tuft of hair in readiness to perform its last and revolting office. His countenance was composed, though thoughtful, while his dark gleaming eyes were gradually losing the fierceness of the combat in an expression better suited to the change he expected momentarily to undergo.

"Our case is not, cannot be so hopeless!" said Duncan; "even at this very moment succor may be at hand. I see no enemies! they have sickened of a struggle in which they risk so much with so little prospect of gain!"

"It may be a minute, or it may be an hour, afore the wily sarpents steal upon us, and it is quite in natur' for them to be lying within hearing at this very moment," said Hawkeye; "but come they will, and in such a fashion as will leave us nothing to hope! Chingachgook"—he spoke in Delaware—"my brother, we have fought our last battle together, and the Maquas will triumph in the death of the sage man of the Mohicans, and of the pale-face whose eyes can make night as day, and level the clouds to the mists of the springs!"

"Let the Mingo women go weep over their slain!" returned the Indian, with characteristic pride and unmoved firmness; "the Great Snake of the Mohicans has coiled himself in their wigwams, and has poisoned their triumph with the wailings of children, whose fathers have not returned! Eleven warriors lie hid from the graves of their tribes since the snows have melted, and none will tell where to find them when the tongue of Chingachgook shall be silent! Let them draw the sharpest knife, and whirl the swiftest tomahawk, for their bitterest enemy is in their hands. Uncas, topmost branch of a noble trunk, call on the cowards to hasten or their hearts will soften, and they will change to women!"

"They look among the fishes for their dead!" returned the low, soft voice of the youthful chieftain; "the Hurons float with the slimy eels! They drop from the oaks like the fruit that is ready to be eaten! and the Delawares laugh!"

"Aye, aye," muttered the scout, who had listened to this peculiar burst of the natives with deep attention; "they have warmed their Indian feelings, and they'll soon provoke the Maquas to give them a speedy end. As for me, who am of the whole blood of the whites, it is befitting that I should die as becomes my color, with no words of scoffing in my mouth, and without bitterness at the heart!"

"Why die at all!" said Cora, advancing from the place where natural horror had, until this moment, held her riveted to the rock; "the path is open on every side; fly, then, to the woods, and call on God for succor. Go, brave men, we owe you too much already; let us no longer involve you in our hapless fortunes!"

"You but little know the craft of the Iroquois, lady, if you judge they have left the path open to the woods!" returned Hawkeye, who, however, immediately added in his simplicity, "the down stream current, it is certain, might soon sweep us beyond the reach of their rifles or the sounds of their voices."

"Then try the river. Why linger to add to the number of the victims of our merciless enemies?"

"Why," repeated the scout, looking about him proudly, "because it is better for a man to die at peace with himself than to live haunted by an evil conscience! What answer could we give Munro, when he asked us where and how we left his children?"

"Go to him, and say that you left them with a message to hasten to their aid," returned Cora, advancing nigher to the scout, in her generous ardor; "that the Hurons bear them into the northern wilds, but that by vigilance and speed they may yet be rescued; and if, after all, it should please heaven that his assistance come too late, bear to him," she continued, her voice gradually lowering, until it seemed nearly choked, "the love, the blessings, the final prayers of his daughters, and bid him not mourn their early fate, but to look forward with humble confidence to the Christian's goal to meet his children."

The hard, weather-beaten features of the scout began to work, and when she had ended, he dropped his chin to his hand, like a man musing profoundly on the nature of the proposal.

"There is reason in her words!" at length broke from his compressed and trembling lips; "aye, and they bear the spirit of Christianity; what might be right and proper in a red-skin, may be sinful in a man who has not even a cross in blood to plead for his ignorance. Chingachgook! Uncas! hear you the talk of the dark-eyed woman!"

He now spoke in Delaware to his companions, and his address, though calm and deliberate, seemed very decided. The elder Mohican heard him with deep gravity, and appeared to ponder on his words, as though he felt the importance of their import. After a moment of hesitation, he waved his hand in assent, and uttered the English word "Good!" with the peculiar emphasis of his people. Then, replacing his knife and tomahawk in his girdle, the warrior moved silently to the edge of the rock which was most concealed from the banks of the river. Here he paused a moment, pointed significantly to the woods below, and saying a few words in his own language, as if indicating his intended route, he dropped into the water, and sank from before the eyes of the witnesses of his movements.

The scout delayed his departure to speak to the generous girl, whose breathing became lighter as she saw the success of her remonstrance.

"Wisdom is sometimes given to the young, as well as to the old," he said; "and what you have spoken is wise, not to call it by a better word. If you are led into the woods, that is, such of you as may be spared for a while, break the twigs on the bushes as you pass, and make the marks of your trail as broad as you can, when, if mortal eyes can see them, depend on having a friend who will follow to the ends of 'arth afore he desarts you."

He gave Cora an affectionate shake of the hand, lifted his rifle, and after regarding it a moment with melancholy solicitude, laid it carefully aside, and descended to the place where Chingachgook had just disappeared. For an instant he hung suspended by the rock; and looking about him, with a countenance of peculiar care, he added bitterly, "Had the powder held out, this disgrace could never have befallen!" then, loosening his hold, the water closed above his head, and he also became lost to view.

All eyes were now turned on Uncas, who stood leaning against the ragged rock, in immovable composure. After waiting a short time, Cora pointed down the river, and said:—

"Your friends have not been seen, and are now, most probably, in safety; is it not time for you to follow?"

"Uncas will stay," the young Mohican calmly answered in English.

"To increase the horror of our capture, and to diminish the chances of our release! Go, generous young man," Cora continued, lowering her eyes under the gaze of the Mohican, and perhaps, with an intuitive consciousness of her power; "go to my father, as I have said, and be the most confidential of my messengers. Tell him to trust you with the means to buy the freedom of his daughters. Go! 't is my wish, 't is my prayer, that you will go!"

The settled, calm look of the young chief changed to an expression of gloom, but he no longer hesitated. With a noiseless step he crossed the rock, and dropped into the troubled stream. Hardly a breath was drawn by those he left behind, until they caught a glimpse of his head emerging for air, far down the current, when he again sank, and was seen no more.

These sudden and apparently successful experiments had all taken place in a few minutes of that time which had now become so precious. After the last look at Uncas, Cora turned, and, with a quivering lip, addressed herself to Heyward:—

"I have heard of your boasted skill in the water, too, Duncan," she said; "follow, then, the wise example set you by these simple and faithful beings."

"Is such the faith that Cora Munro would exact from her protector?" said the young man, smiling mournfully, but with bitterness.

"This is not the time for idle subtleties and false opinions," she answered; "but a moment when every duty should be equally considered. To us you can be of no further service here, but your precious life may be saved for other and nearer friends."

He made no reply, though his eyes fell wistfully on the beautiful form of Alice, who was clinging to his arm with the dependency of an infant.

"Consider," continued Cora, after a pause, during which she seemed to struggle with a pang even more acute than any that her fears had excited, "that the worst to us can be but death; a tribute that all must pay at the good time of God's appointment."

"There are evils worse than death," said Duncan, speaking hoarsely, and as if fretful at her importunity, "but which the presence of one who would die in your behalf may avert."

Cora ceased her entreaties; and, veiling her face in her shawl, drew the nearly insensible Alice after her into the deepest recess of the inner cavern.

CHAPTER IX

Be gay securely;
Dispel, my fair, with smiles, the tim'rous clouds,
That hand on thy clear brow.
Death of Agrippina.

The sudden and almost magical change, from the stirring incidents of the combat to the stillness that now reigned around him, acted on the heated imagination of Heyward like some exciting dream. While all the images and events he had witnessed remained deeply impressed on his memory, he felt a difficulty in persuading himself of their truth. Still ignorant of the fate of those who had trusted to the aid of the swift current, he at first listened intently for any signal, or sounds of alarm, which might announce the good or evil fortune of their hazardous undertaking. His attention was, however, bestowed in vain; for, with the disappearance of Uncas, every sign of the adventurers had been lost, leaving him in total uncertainty of their fate.

In a moment of such painful doubt, Duncan did not hesitate to look about him, without consulting that protection from the rocks which just before had been so necessary to his safety. Every effort, however, to detect the least evidence of the approach of their hidden enemies, was as fruitless as the inquiry after his late companions. The wooded banks of the river seemed again deserted by everything possessing animal life. The uproar which had so lately echoed through the vaults of the forest was gone, leaving the rush of the waters to swell and sink on the currents of the air, in the unmingled sweetness of nature. A fish-hawk, which, secure on the topmost branches of a dead pine, had been a distant spectator of the fray, now stooped from his high and ragged perch, and soared, in wide sweeps, above his prey; while a jay, whose noisy voice had been stilled by the hoarser cries of the savages, ventured again to open his discordant throat, as though once more in undisturbed possession of his wild domains. Duncan caught from these natural accompaniments of the solitary scene a glimmering of hope; and he began to rally his faculties to renewed exertions, with something like a reviving confidence of success.

"The Hurons are not to be seen," he said, addressing David, who had by no means recovered from the effects of the stunning blow he had received; "let us conceal ourselves in the cavern, and trust the rest to Providence."

"I remember to have united with two comely maidens, in lifting up our voices in praise and thanksgiving," returned the bewildered singing-master; "since which time I have been visited by a heavy judgment for my sins. I have been mocked with the likeness of sleep, while sounds of discord have rent my ears, such as might manifest the fullness of time, and that nature had forgotten her harmony."

"Poor fellow! thine own period was, in truth, near its accomplishment! But arouse, and come with me; I will lead you where all other sounds but those of your own psalmody shall be excluded."

"There is melody in the fall of the cataract, and the rushing of many waters is sweet to the senses!" said David, pressing his hand confusedly on his brow. "Is not the air yet filled with shrieks and cries, as though the departed spirits of the damned—"

"Not now, not now," interrupted the impatient Heyward, "they have ceased; and they who raised them, I trust in God they are gone too! everything but the water is still and at peace; in, then, where you may create those sounds you love so well to hear."

David smiled sadly, though not without a momentary gleam of pleasure, at this allusion to his beloved vocation. He no longer hesitated to be led to a spot which promised such unalloyed gratification to his wearied senses; and, leaning on the arm of his companion, he entered the narrow mouth of the cave. Duncan seized a pile of the sassafras, which he drew before the passage, studiously concealing every appearance of an aperture. Within this fragile barrier he arranged the blankets abandoned by the foresters, darkening the inner extremity of the cavern, while its outer received a chastened light from the narrow ravine, through which one arm of the river rushed, to form the junction with its sister branch, a few rods below.

"I like not that principle of the natives, which teaches them to submit without a struggle, in emergencies that appear desperate," he said, while busied in this employment; "our own maxim, which says, 'while life remains there is hope,' is more consoling, and better suited to a soldier's temperament. To you, Cora, I will urge no words of idle encouragement; your own fortitude and undisturbed reason will teach you all that may become your sex; but cannot we dry the tears of that trembling weeper on your bosom?"

"I am calmer, Duncan," said Alice, raising herself from the arms of her sister, and forcing an appearance of composure through her tears; "much calmer, now. Surely, in this hidden spot we are safe, we are secret, free from injury; we will hope everything from those generous men who have risked so much already in our behalf."

"Now does our gentle Alice speak like a daughter of Munro!" said Heyward, pausing to press her hand as he passed towards the outer entrance of the cavern. "With two such examples of courage before him, a man would be ashamed to prove other than a hero." He then seated himself in the centre of the cavern, grasping his remaining pistol with a hand convulsively clenched, while his contracted and frowning eye announced the sullen desperation of his purpose. "The Hurons, if they come, may not gain our position so easily as they think," he lowly muttered; and dropping his head back against the rock, he seemed to await the result in patience, though his gaze was unceasingly bent on the open avenue to their place of retreat.

With the last sound of his voice, a deep, a long, and almost breathless silence succeeded. The fresh air of the morning had penetrated the recess, and its influence was gradually felt on the spirits of its inmates. As minute after minute passed by, leaving them in undisturbed security, the insinuating feeling of hope was gradually gaining possession of every bosom, though each one felt reluctant to give utterance to expectations that the next moment might so fearfully destroy.

David alone formed an exception to these varying emotions. A gleam of light from the opening crossed his wan countenance, and fell upon the pages of the little volume, whose leaves he was again occupied in turning, as if searching for some song more fitted to their condition than any that had yet met his eye. He was, most probably, acting all this time under a confused recollection of the promised consolation of Duncan. At length, it would seem, his patient industry found its reward; for, without explanation or apology, he pronounced aloud the words "Isle of Wight," drew a long, sweet sound from his pitch-pipe, and then ran through the preliminary modulations of the air, whose name he had just mentioned, with the sweeter tones of his own musical voice.

"May not this prove dangerous?" asked Cora, glancing her dark eye at Major Heyward.

"Poor fellow! his voice is too feeble to be heard amid the din of the falls," was the answer; "besides, the cavern will prove his friend. Let him indulge his passion, since it may be done without hazard."

"Isle of Wight!" repeated David, looking about him with that dignity with which he had long been wont to silence the whispering echoes of his school; "'t is a brave tune, and set to solemn words; let it be sung with meet respect!"

After allowing a moment of stillness to enforce his discipline, the voice of the singer was heard, in low, murmuring syllables, gradually stealing on the ear, until it filled the narrow vault with sounds rendered trebly thrilling by the feeble and tremulous utterance produced by his debility. The melody, which no weakness could destroy, gradually wrought its sweet influence on the senses of those who heard it. It even prevailed over the miserable travesty of the song of David which the singer had selected from a volume of similar effusions, and caused the sense to be forgotten in the insinuating harmony of the sounds. Alice unconsciously dried her tears, and bent her melting eyes on the pallid features of Gamut, with an expression of chastened delight that she neither affected nor wished to conceal. Cora bestowed an approving smile on the pious efforts of the namesake of the Jewish prince, and Heyward soon turned his steady, stern look from the outlet of the cavern, to fasten it, with a milder character, on the face of David, or to meet the wandering beams which at moments strayed from the humid eyes of Alice. The open sympathy of the listeners stirred the spirit of the votary of music, whose voice regained its richness and volume, without losing that touching softness which proved its secret charm. Exerting his renovated powers to their utmost, he was yet filling the arches of the cave with long and full tones, when a yell burst into the air without, that instantly stilled his pious strains, choking his voice suddenly, as though his heart had literally bounded into the passage of his throat.

"We are lost!" exclaimed Alice, throwing herself into the arms of Cora.

"Not yet, not yet," returned the agitated but undaunted Heyward; "the sound came from the centre of the island, and it has been produced by the sight of their dead companions. We are not yet discovered, and there is still hope."

Faint and almost despairing as was the prospect of escape, the words of Duncan were not thrown away, for it awakened the powers of the sisters in such a manner that they awaited the result in silence. A second yell soon followed the first, when a rush of voices was heard pouring down the island, from its upper to its lower extremity, until they reached the naked rock above the caverns, where, after a shout of savage triumph, the air continued full of horrible cries and screams, such as man alone can utter, and he only when in a state of the fiercest barbarity.

The sounds quickly spread around them in every direction. Some called to their fellows from the water's edge, and were answered from the heights above. Cries were heard in the startling vicinity of the chasm between the two caves, which mingled with hoarser yells that arose out of the abyss of the deep ravine. In short, so rapidly had the savage sounds diffused themselves over the barren rock, that it was not difficult for the anxious listeners to imagine they could be heard beneath, as in truth they were above and on every side of them.

In the midst of this tumult, a triumphant yell was raised within a few yards of the hidden entrance to the cave. Heyward abandoned every hope, with the belief it was the signal that they were discovered. Again the impression passed away, as he heard the voices collect near the spot where the white man had so reluctantly abandoned his rifle. Amid the jargon of the Indian dialects that he now plainly heard, it was easy to distinguish not only words, but sentences, in the patois of the Canadas. A burst of voices had shouted simultaneously, "La Longue Carabine!" causing the opposite woods to reëcho with a name which, Heyward well remembered, had been given by his enemies to a celebrated hunter and scout of the English camp, and who, he now learnt for the first time, had been his late companion.

"La Longue Carabine! La Longue Carabine!" passed from mouth to mouth, until the whole band appeared to be collected around a trophy which would seem to announce the death of its formidable owner. After a vociferous consultation, which was, at times, deafened by bursts of savage joy, they again separated, filling the air with the name of a foe whose body, Heyward could collect from their expressions, they hoped to find concealed in some crevice of the island.

"Now," he whispered to the trembling sisters, "now is the moment of uncertainty! if our place of retreat escape this scrutiny, we are still safe! In every event, we are assured, by what has fallen from our enemies, that our friends have escaped, and in two short hours we may look for succor from Webb."

There were now a few minutes of fearful stillness, during which Heyward well knew that the savages conducted their search with greater vigilance and method. More than once he could distinguish their footsteps, as they brushed the sassafras, causing the faded leaves to rustle, and the branches to snap. At length, the pile yielded a little, a corner of a blanket fell, and a faint ray of light gleamed into the inner part of the cave. Cora folded Alice to her bosom in agony, and Duncan sprang to his feet. A shout was at that moment heard, as if issuing from the centre of the rock, announcing that the neighboring cavern had at length been entered. In a minute, the number and loudness of the voices indicated that the whole party was collected in and around that secret place.

As the inner passages to the two caves were so close to each other, Duncan, believing that escape was no longer possible, passed David and the sisters, to place himself between the latter and the first onset of the terrible meeting. Grown desperate by his situation, he drew nigh the slight barrier which separated him only by a few feet from his relentless pursuers, and placing his face to the casual opening, he even looked out, with a sort of desperate indifference, on their movements.

Within reach of his arm was the brawny shoulder of a gigantic Indian, whose deep and authoritative voice appeared to give directions to the proceedings of his fellows. Beyond him again, Duncan could look into the vault opposite, which was filled with savages, upturning and rifling the humble furniture of the scout. The wound of David had dyed the leaves of sassafras with a color that the natives well knew was anticipating the season. Over this sign of their success, they set up a howl, like an opening from so many hounds who had recovered a lost trail. After this yell of victory, they tore up the fragrant bed of the cavern, and bore the branches into the chasm, scattering the boughs, as if they suspected them of concealing the person of the man they had so long hated and feared. One fierce and wild-looking warrior approached the chief, bearing a load of the brush, and pointing, exultingly, to the deep red stains with which it was sprinkled, uttered his joy in Indian yells, whose meaning Heyward was only enabled to comprehend by the frequent repetition of the name of "La Longue Carabine!" When his triumph had ceased, he cast the brush on the slight heap that Duncan had made before the entrance of the second cavern, and closed the view. His example was soon followed by others, who, as they drew the branches from the cave of the scout, threw them into one pile, adding, unconsciously, to the security of those they sought. The very slightness of the defense was its chief merit, for no one thought of disturbing a mass of brush, which all of them believed, in that moment of hurry and confusion, had been accidentally raised by the hands of their own party.

As the blankets yielded before the outward pressure, and the branches settled in the fissure of the rock by their own weight, forming a compact body, Duncan once more breathed freely. With a light step, and lighter heart, he returned to the centre of the cave, and took the place he had left, where he could command a view of the opening next the river. While he was in the act of making this movement, the Indians, as if changing their purpose by a common impulse, broke away from the chasm in a body, and were heard rushing up the island again, towards the point whence they had originally descended. Here another wailing cry betrayed that they were again collected around the bodies of their dead comrades.

Duncan now ventured to look at his companions; for, during the most critical moments of their danger, he had been apprehensive that the anxiety of his countenance might communicate some additional alarm to those who were so little able to sustain it.

"They are gone, Cora!" he whispered; "Alice, they are returned whence they came, and we are saved! To Heaven, that has alone delivered us from the grasp of so merciless an enemy, be all the praise!"

"Then to Heaven will I return my thanks!" exclaimed the younger sister, rising from the encircling arms of Cora, and casting herself with enthusiastic gratitude on the naked rock; "to that Heaven who has spared the tears of a gray-headed father; has saved the lives of those I so much love—"

Both Heyward and the more tempered Cora witnessed the act of involuntary emotion with powerful sympathy, the former secretly believing that piety had never worn a form so lovely as it had now assumed in the youthful person of Alice. Her eyes were radiant with the glow of grateful feelings; the flush of her beauty was again seated on her cheeks, and her whole soul seemed ready and anxious to pour out its thanksgivings, through the medium of her eloquent features. But when her lips moved, the words they should have uttered appeared frozen by some new and sudden chill. Her bloom gave place to the paleness of death; her soft and melting eyes grew hard, and seemed contracting with horror; while those hands which she had raised, clasped in each other, towards heaven, dropped in horizontal lines before her, the fingers pointed forward in convulsed motion. Heyward turned, the instant she gave a direction to his suspicions, and, peering just above the ledge which formed the threshold of the open outlet of the cavern, he beheld the malignant, fierce, and savage features of Le Renard Subtil.

In that moment of surprise, the self-possession of Heyward did not desert him. He observed by the vacant expression of the Indian's countenance, that his eye, accustomed to the open air, had not yet been able to penetrate the dusky light which pervaded the depth of the cavern. He had even thought of retreating beyond a curvature in the natural wall, which might still conceal him and his companions, when, by the sudden gleam of intelligence that shot across the features of the savage, he saw it was too late, and that they were betrayed.

The look of exultation and brutal triumph which announced this terrible truth was irresistibly irritating. Forgetful of everything but the impulses of his hot blood, Duncan leveled his pistol and fired. The report of the weapon made the cavern bellow like an eruption from a volcano; and when the smoke it vomited had been driven away before the current of air which issued from the ravine, the place so lately occupied by the features of his treacherous guide was vacant. Rushing to the outlet, Heyward caught a glimpse of his dark figure, stealing around a low and narrow ledge, which soon hid him entirely from sight.

Among the savages, a frightful stillness succeeded the explosion, which had just been heard bursting from the bowels of the rock. But when Le Renard raised his voice in a long and intelligible whoop, it was answered by a spontaneous yell from the mouth of every Indian within hearing of the sound. The clamorous noises again rushed down the island; and before Duncan had time to recover from the shock, his feeble barrier of brush was scattered to the winds, the cavern was entered at both its extremities, and he and his companions were dragged from their shelter and borne into the day, where they stood surrounded by the whole band of the triumphant Hurons.

CHAPTER X

I fear we shall outsleep the coming morn
As much as we this night have overwatched.

SHAKESPEARE, *Midsummer Night's Dream,* V. i. 372.

The instant the shock of this sudden misfortune had abated, Duncan began to make his observations on the appearance and proceedings of their captors. Contrary to the usages of the natives in the wantonness of their success, they had respected not only the persons of the trembling sisters, but his own. The rich ornaments of his military attire had indeed been repeatedly handled by different individuals of the tribe with eyes expressing a savage longing to possess the baubles; but before the customary violence could be resorted to, a mandate in the authoritative voice of the large warrior already mentioned stayed the uplifted hand, and convinced Heyward that they were to be reserved for some object of particular moment.

While, however, these manifestations of weakness were exhibited by the young and vain of the party, the more experienced warriors continued their search throughout both caverns, with an activity that denoted they were far from being satisfied with those fruits of their conquest which had already been brought to light. Unable to discover any new victim, these diligent workers of vengeance soon approached their male prisoners, pronouncing the name of "La Longue Carabine," with a fierceness that could not easily be mistaken. Duncan affected not to comprehend the meaning of their repeated and violent interrogatories, while his companion was spared the effort of a similar deception by his ignorance of French. Wearied, at length, by their importunities, and apprehensive of irritating his captors by too stubborn a silence, the former looked about him in quest of Magua, who might interpret his answers to questions which were at each moment becoming more earnest and threatening.

The conduct of this savage had formed a solitary exception to that of all his fellows. While the others were busily occupied in seeking to gratify their childish passion for finery, by plundering even the miserable effects of the scout, or had been searching, with such bloodthirsty vengeance in their looks, for their absent owner, Le Renard had stood at a little distance from the prisoners, with a demeanor so quiet and satisfied as to betray that he had already effected the grand purpose of his treachery. When the eyes of Heyward first met those of his recent guide, he turned them away in horror at the sinister though calm look he encountered. Conquering his disgust, however, he was able, with an averted face, to address his successful enemy.

"Le Renard Subtil is too much of a warrior," said the reluctant Heyward, "to refuse telling an unarmed man what his conquerors say."

"They ask for the hunter who knows the paths through the woods," returned Magua, in his broken English, laying his hand, at the same time, with a ferocious smile, on the bundle of leaves with which a wound on his own shoulder was bandaged. "La Longue Carabine! his rifle is good, and his eye never shut; but, like the short gun of the white chief, it is nothing against the life of Le Subtil!"

"Le Renard is too brave to remember the hurts received in war, or the hands that gave them!"

"Was it war, when the tired Indian rested at the sugar-tree to taste his corn? who filled the bushes with creeping enemies? who drew the knife? whose tongue was peace, while his heart was colored with blood? Did Magua say that the hatchet was out of the ground, and that his hand had dug it up?"

As Duncan dared not retort upon his accuser by reminding him of his own premeditated treachery, and disdained to deprecate his resentment by any words of apology, he remained silent. Magua seemed also content to rest the controversy as well as all further communication there, for he resumed the leaning attitude against the rock, from which, in momentary energy, he had arisen. But the cry of "La Longue Carabine" was renewed the instant the impatient savages perceived that the short dialogue was ended.

"You hear," said Magua, with stubborn indifference; "the red Hurons call for the life of 'The Long Rifle,' or they will have the blood of them that keep him hid!"

"He is gone—escaped; he is far beyond their reach."

Renard smiled with cold contempt, as he answered,—

"When the white man dies, he thinks he is at peace; but the red-men know how to torture even the ghosts of their enemies. Where is his body? Let the Hurons see his scalp!"

"He is not dead, but escaped."

Magua shook his head incredulously.

"Is he a bird, to spread his wings; or is he a fish, to swim without air! The white chief reads in his books, and he believes the Hurons are fools!"

"Though no fish, 'The Long Rifle' can swim. He floated down the stream when the powder was all burnt, and when the eyes of the Hurons were behind a cloud."

"And why did the white chief stay?" demanded the still incredulous Indian. "Is he a stone that goes to the bottom, or does the scalp burn his head?"

"That I am not a stone, your dead comrade, who fell into the falls, might answer, were the life still in him," said the provoked young man, using, in his anger, that boastful language which was most likely to excite the admiration of an Indian. "The white man thinks none but cowards desert their women."

Magua muttered a few words, inaudibly, between his teeth, before he continued aloud,—

"Can the Delawares swim, too, as well as crawl in the bushes? Where is 'Le Gros Serpent'?"

Duncan, who perceived by the use of these Canadian appellations, that his late companions were much better known to his enemies than to himself, answered reluctantly, "He also is gone down with the water."

"'Le Cerf Agile' is not here?"

"I know not whom you call 'The Nimble Deer,'" said Duncan, gladly profiting by any excuse to create delay.

"Uncas," returned Magua, pronouncing the Delaware name with even greater difficulty than he spoke his English words. "'Bounding Elk' is what the white man says, when he calls to the young Mohican."

"Here is some confusion in names between us, Le Renard," said Duncan, hoping to provoke a discussion. "Daim is the French for deer, and cerf for stag; élan is the true term, when one would speak of an elk."

"Yes," muttered the Indian, in his native tongue; "the palefaces are prattling women! they have two words for each thing, while a red-skin will make the sound of his voice speak for him." Then changing his language, he continued, adhering to the imperfect nomenclature of his provincial instructors. "The deer is swift, but weak; the elk is swift, but strong; and the son of 'Le Serpent' is 'Le Cerf Agile.' Has he leaped the river to the woods?"

"If you mean the younger Delaware, he too is gone down with the water."

As there was nothing improbable to an Indian in the manner of the escape, Magua admitted the truth of what he had heard, with a readiness that afforded additional evidence how little he would prize such worthless captives. With his companions, however, the feeling was manifestly different.

The Hurons had awaited the result of this short dialogue with characteristic patience, and with a silence that increased until there was a general stillness in the band. When Heyward ceased to speak, they turned their eyes, as one man, on Magua, demanding, in this expressive manner, an explanation of what had been said. Their interpreter pointed to the river, and made them acquainted with the result, as much by the action as by the few words he uttered. When the fact was generally understood, the savages raised a frightful yell, which declared the extent of their disappointment. Some ran furiously to the water's edge, beating the air with frantic gestures, while others spat upon the element, to resent the supposed treason it had committed against their acknowledged right as conquerors. A few, and they not the least powerful and terrific of the band, threw lowering looks, in which the fiercest passion was only tempered by habitual self-command, at those captives who still remained in their power; while one or two even gave vent to their malignant feelings by the most menacing gestures, against which neither the sex nor the beauty of the sisters was any protection. The young soldier made a desperate, but fruitless effort, to spring to the side of Alice, when he saw the dark hand of a savage twisted in the rich tresses which were flowing in volumes over her shoulders, while a knife was passed around the head from which they fell, as if to denote the horrid manner in which it was about to be robbed of its beautiful ornament. But his hands were bound; and at the first movement he made, he felt the grasp of the powerful Indian who directed the band, pressing his shoulder like a vise. Immediately conscious how unavailing any struggle against such an overwhelming force must prove, he submitted to his fate, encouraging his gentle companions by a few low and tender assurances that the natives seldom failed to threaten more than they performed.

But, while Duncan resorted to these words of consolation to quiet the apprehensions of the sisters, he was not so weak as to deceive himself. He well knew that the authority of an Indian chief was so little conventional, that it was oftener maintained by physical superiority than by any moral supremacy he might possess. The danger was, therefore, magnified exactly in proportion to the number of the savage spirits by which they were surrounded. The most positive mandate from him who seemed the acknowledged leader was liable to be violated at each moment, by any rash hand that might choose to sacrifice a victim to the manes of some dead friend or relative. While, therefore, he sustained an outward appearance of calmness and fortitude, his heart leaped into his throat, whenever any of their fierce captors drew nearer than common to the helpless sisters, or fastened one of their sullen wandering looks on those fragile forms which were so little able to resist the slightest assault.

His apprehensions were, however, greatly relieved, when he saw that the leader had summoned his warriors to himself in council. Their deliberations were short, and it would seem, by the silence of most of the party, the decision unanimous. By the frequency with which the few speakers pointed in the direction of the encampment of Webb, it was apparent they dreaded the approach of danger from that quarter. This consideration probably hastened their determination, and quickened the subsequent movements.

During this short conference, Heyward, finding a respite from his greatest fears, had leisure to admire the cautious manner in which the Hurons had made their approaches, even after hostilities had ceased.

It has already been stated that the upper half of the island was a naked rock, and destitute of any other defenses than a few scattered logs of driftwood. They had selected this point to make their descent, having borne the canoe through the wood around the cataract for that purpose. Placing their arms in the little vessel, a dozen men clinging to its sides had trusted themselves to the direction of the canoe, which was controlled by two of the most skillful warriors, in attitudes that enabled them to command a view of the dangerous passage. Favored by this arrangement, they touched the head of the island at that point which had proved so fatal to their first adventurers, but with the advantages of superior numbers, and the possession of fire-arms. That such had been the manner of their descent was rendered quite apparent to Duncan; for they now bore the light bark from the upper end of the rock, and placed it in the water, near the mouth of the outer cavern. As soon as this change was made, the leader made signs to the prisoners to descend and enter.

As resistance was impossible, and remonstrance useless, Heyward set the example of submission, by leading the way into the canoe, where he was soon seated with the sisters and the still wondering David. Notwithstanding the Hurons were necessarily ignorant of the little channels among the eddies and rapids of the stream, they knew the common signs of such a navigation too well to commit any material blunder. When the pilot chosen for the task of guiding the canoe had taken his station, the whole band plunged again into the river, the vessel glided down the current, and in a few moments the captives found themselves on the south bank of the stream, nearly opposite to the point where they had struck it the preceding evening.

Here was held another short but earnest consultation, during which the horses, to whose panic their owners ascribed their heaviest misfortune, were led from the cover of the woods, and brought to the sheltered spot. The band now divided. The great chief so often mentioned, mounting the charger of Heyward, led the way directly across the river, followed by most of his people, and disappeared in the woods, leaving the prisoners in charge of six savages, at whose head was Le Renard Subtil. Duncan witnessed all their movements with renewed uneasiness.

He had been fond of believing, from the uncommon forbearance of the savages, that he was reserved as a prisoner to be delivered to Montcalm. As the thoughts of those who are in misery seldom slumber, and the invention is never more lively than when it is stimulated by hope, however feeble and remote, he had even imagined that the parental feelings of Munro were to be made instrumental in seducing him from his duty to the king. For though the French commander bore a high character for courage and enterprise, he was also thought to be expert in those political practices which do not always respect the nicer obligations of morality, and which so generally disgraced the European diplomacy of that period.

All those busy and ingenious speculations were now annihilated by the conduct of his captors. That portion of the band who had followed the huge warrior took the route towards the foot of the Horican, and no other expectation was left for himself and his companions than that they were to be retained as hopeless captives by their savage conquerors. Anxious to know the worst, and willing, in such an emergency, to try the potency of gold, he overcame his reluctance to speak to Magua. Addressing himself to his former guide, who had now assumed the authority and manner of one who was to direct the future movements of the party, he said, in tones as friendly and confiding as he could assume,—

"I would speak to Magua what is fit only for so great a chief to hear."

The Indian turned his eyes on the young soldier scornfully, as he answered,—

"Speak; trees have no ears!"

"But the red Hurons are not deaf; and counsel that is fit for the great men of a nation would make the young warriors drunk. If Magua will not listen, the officer of the king knows how to be silent."

The savage spoke carelessly to his comrades, who were busied, after their awkward manner, in preparing the horses for the reception of the sisters, and moved a little to one side, whither, by a cautious gesture, he induced Heyward to follow.

"Now speak," he said; "if the words are such as Magua should hear."

"Le Renard Subtil has proved himself worthy of the honorable name given to him by his Canada fathers," commenced Heyward; "I see his wisdom, and all that he has done for us, and shall remember it, when the hour to reward him arrives. Yes! Renard has proved that he is not only a great chief in council, but one who knows how to deceive his enemies!"

"What has Renard done?" coldly demanded the Indian.

"What! has he not seen that the woods were filled with outlying parties of the enemies, and that the Serpent could not steal through them without being seen? Then, did he not lose his path to blind the eyes of the Hurons? Did he not pretend to go back to his tribe, who had treated him ill, and driven him from their wigwams like a dog? And, when we saw what he wished to do, did we not aid him, by making a false face, that the Hurons might think the white man believed that his friend was his enemy? Is not all this true? And when Le Subtil had shut the eyes and stopped the ears of his nation by his wisdom, did they not forget that they had once done him wrong, and forced him to flee to the Mohawks? And did they not leave him on the south side of the river, with their prisoners, while they have gone foolishly on the north? Does not Renard mean to turn like a fox on his footsteps, and to carry to the rich and gray-headed Scotchman his daughters? Yes, Magua, I see it all, and I have already been thinking how so much wisdom and honesty should be repaid. First, the chief of William Henry will give as a great chief should for such a service. The medal[16] of Magua will no longer be of tin, but of beaten gold; his horn will run over with powder; dollars will be as plenty in his pouch as pebbles on the shore of Horican; and the deer will lick his hand, for they will know it to be vain to fly from the rifle he will carry! As for myself, I know not how to exceed the gratitude of the Scotchman, but I—yes, I will—"

"What will the young chief who comes from towards the sun give?" demanded the Huron, observing that Heyward hesitated in his desire to end the enumeration of benefits with that which might form the climax of an Indian's wishes.

"He will make the fire-water from the Islands in the salt lake flow before the wigwam of Magua, until the heart of the Indian shall be lighter than the feathers of the humming-bird, and his breath sweeter than the wild honeysuckle."

Le Renard had listened gravely as Heyward slowly proceeded in this subtle speech. When the young man mentioned the artifice he supposed the Indian to have practiced on his own nation, the countenance of the listener was veiled in an expression of cautious gravity. At the allusion to the injury which Duncan affected to believe had driven the Huron from his native tribe, a gleam of such ungovernable ferocity flashed from the other's eyes, as induced the adventurous speaker to believe he had struck the proper chord. And by the time he reached the part where he so artfully blended the thirst of vengeance with the desire of gain, he had, at least, obtained a command of the deepest attention of the savage. The question put by Le Renard had been calm, and with all the dignity of an Indian; but it was quite apparent, by the thoughtful expression of the listener's countenance, that the answer was most cunningly devised. The Huron mused a few moments, and then laying his hand on the rude bandages of his wounded shoulder, he said, with some energy,—

"Do friends make such marks?"

"Would 'La Longue Carabine' cut one so light on an enemy?"

"Do the Delawares crawl upon those they love like snakes, twisting themselves to strike?"

"Would 'Le Gros Serpent' have been heard by the ears of one he wished to be deaf?"

"Does the white chief burn his powder in the faces of his brothers?"

"Does he ever miss his aim, when seriously bent to kill?" returned Duncan, smiling with well acted sincerity.

Another long and deliberate pause succeeded these sententious questions and ready replies. Duncan saw that the Indian hesitated. In order to complete his victory, he was in the act of recommencing the enumeration of the rewards, when Magua made an expressive gesture and said—

"Enough; Le Renard is a wise chief, and what he does will be seen. Go, and keep the mouth shut. When Magua speaks, it will be the time to answer."

Heyward, perceiving that the eyes of his companion were warily fastened on the rest of the band, fell back immediately, in order to avoid the appearance of any suspicious confederacy with their leader. Magua approached the horses, and affected to be well pleased with the diligence and ingenuity of his comrades. He then signed to Heyward to assist the sisters into the saddles, for he seldom deigned to use the English tongue, unless urged by some motive of more than usual moment.

---

[16]It has long been a practice with the whites to conciliate the important men of the Indians by presenting medals, which are worn in the place of their own rude ornaments. Those given by the English generally bear the impression of the reigning king, and those given by the Americans that of the President. [J.F.C.]

There was no longer any plausible pretext for delay; and Duncan was obliged, however reluctantly, to comply. As he performed this office, he whispered his reviving hopes in the ears of the trembling females, who, through dread of encountering the savage countenances of their captors, seldom raised their eyes from the ground. The mare of David had been taken with the followers of the large chief; in consequence, its owner, as well as Duncan, was compelled to journey on foot. The latter did not, however, so much regret this circumstance, as it might enable him to retard the speed of the party; for he still turned his longing looks in the direction of Fort Edward, in the vain expectation of catching some sound from that quarter of the forest, which might denote the approach of succor.

When all were prepared, Magua made the signal to proceed, advancing in front to lead the party in person. Next followed David, who was gradually coming to a true sense of his condition, as the effects of the wound became less and less apparent. The sisters rode in his rear, with Heyward at their side, while the Indians flanked the party, and brought up the close of the march, with a caution that seemed never to tire.

In this manner they proceeded in uninterrupted silence, except when Heyward addressed some solitary word of comfort to the females, or David gave vent to the moaning of his spirit, in piteous exclamations, which he intended should express the humility of resignation. Their direction lay towards the south, and in a course nearly opposite to the road to William Henry. Notwithstanding this apparent adherence in Magua to the original determination of his conquerors, Heyward could not believe his tempting bait was so soon forgotten; and he knew the windings of an Indian path too well to suppose that its apparent course led directly to its object, when artifice was at all necessary. Mile after mile was, however, passed through the boundless woods, in this painful manner, without any prospect of a termination to their journey. Heyward watched the sun, as he darted his meridian rays through the branches of the trees, and pined for the moment when the policy of Magua should change their route to one more favorable to his hopes. Sometimes he fancied the wary savage, despairing of passing the army of Montcalm in safety, was holding his way towards a well-known border settlement, where a distinguished officer of the crown, and a favored friend of the Six Nations, held his large possessions, as well as his usual residence. To be delivered into the hands of Sir William Johnson was far preferable to being led into the wilds of Canada; but in order to effect even the former, it would be necessary to traverse the forest for many weary leagues, each step of which was carrying him further from the scene of the war, and, consequently, from the post, not only of honor, but of duty.

Cora alone remembered the parting injunctions of the scout, and whenever an opportunity offered, she stretched forth her arm to bend aside the twigs that met her hands. But the vigilance of the Indians rendered this act of precaution both difficult and dangerous. She was often defeated in her purpose, by encountering their watchful eyes, when it became necessary to feign an alarm she did not feel, and occupy the limb by some gesture of feminine apprehension. Once, and once only, was she completely successful; when she broke down the bough of a large sumach, and, by a sudden thought, let her glove fall at the same instant. This sign, intended for those that might follow, was observed by one of her conductors, who restored the glove, broke the remaining branches of the bush in such a manner that it appeared to proceed from the struggling of some beast in its branches, and then laid his hand on his tomahawk, with a look so significant that it put an effectual end to these stolen memorials of their passage.

As there were horses, to leave the prints of their footsteps, in both bands of the Indians, this interruption cut off any probable hopes of assistance being conveyed through the means of their trail.

Heyward would have ventured a remonstrance, had there been anything encouraging in the gloomy reserve of Magua. But the savage, during all this time, seldom turned to look at his followers, and never spoke. With the sun for his only guide, or aided by such blind marks as are only known to the sagacity of a native, he held his way along the barrens of pine, through occasional little fertile vales, across brooks and rivulets, and over undulating hills, with the accuracy of instinct, and nearly with the directness of a bird. He never seemed to hesitate. Whether the path was hardly distinguishable, whether it disappeared, or whether it lay beaten and plain before him, made no sensible difference in his speed or certainty. It seemed as if fatigue could not affect him. Whenever the eyes of the wearied travellers rose from the decayed leaves over which they trod, his dark form was to be seen glancing among the stems of the trees in front, his head immovably fastened in a forward position, with the light plume on his crest fluttering in a current of air made solely by the swiftness of his own motion.

But all this diligence and speed were not without an object. After crossing a low vale, through which a gushing brook meandered, he suddenly ascended a hill, so steep and difficult of ascent that the sisters were compelled to alight, in order to follow. When the summit was gained, they found themselves on a level spot, but thinly covered with trees, under one of which Magua had thrown his dark form, as if willing and ready to seek that rest which was so much needed by the whole party.

CHAPTER XI

Cursed be my tribe
If I forgive him.
SHAKESPEARE, *The Merchant of Venice,* I. iii. 52.

The Indian had selected, for this desirable purpose, one of those steep, pyramidal hills which bear a strong resemblance to artificial mounds, and which so frequently occur in the valleys of America. The one in question was high and precipitous; its top flattened, as usual; but with one of its sides more than ordinarily irregular. It possessed no other apparent advantage, for a resting-place, than in its elevation and form, which might render defense easy, and surprise nearly impossible. As Heyward, however, no longer expected that rescue which time and distance now rendered so improbable, he regarded these little peculiarities with an eye devoid of interest, devoting himself entirely to the comfort and condolence of his feebler companions. The Narragansets were suffered to browse on the branches of the trees and shrubs that were thinly scattered over the summit of the hill, while the remains of their provisions were spread under the shade of a beech, that stretched its horizontal limbs like a canopy above them.

Notwithstanding the swiftness of their flight, one of the Indians had found an opportunity to strike a straggling fawn with an arrow, and had borne the more preferable fragments of the victim, patiently on his shoulders, to the stopping-place. Without any aid from the science of cookery, he was immediately employed, in common with his fellows, in gorging himself with this digestible sustenance. Magua alone sat apart, without participating in the revolting meal, and apparently buried in the deepest thought.

This abstinence, so remarkable in an Indian, when he possessed the means of satisfying hunger, at length attracted the notice of Heyward. The young man willingly believed that the Huron deliberated on the most eligible manner of eluding the vigilance of his associates. With a view to assist his plans, by any suggestion of his own, and to strengthen the temptation, he left the beech, and straggled, as if without an object, to the spot where Le Renard was seated.

"Has not Magua kept the sun in his face long enough to escape all danger from the Canadians?" he asked, as though no longer doubtful of the good intelligence established between them; "and will not the chief of William Henry be better pleased to see his daughters before another night may have hardened his heart to their loss, to make him less liberal in his reward?"

"Do the pale-faces love their children less in the morning than at night?" asked the Indian coldly.

"By no means," returned Heyward, anxious to recall his error, if he had made one; "the white man may, and does often, forget the burial-place of his fathers; he sometimes ceases to remember those he should love, and has promised to cherish; but the affection of a parent for his child is never permitted to die."

"And is the heart of the white-headed chief soft, and will he think of the babes that his squaws have given him? He is hard to his warriors, and his eyes are made of stone!"

"He is severe to the idle and wicked, but to the sober and deserving he is a leader both just and humane. I have known many fond and tender parents, but never have I seen a man whose heart was softer towards his child. You have seen the gray-head in front of his warriors, Magua; but I have seen his eyes swimming in water, when he spoke of those children who are now in your power!"

Heyward paused, for he knew not how to construe the remarkable expression that gleamed across the swarthy features of the attentive Indian. At first it seemed as if the remembrance of the promised reward grew vivid in his mind, while he listened to the sources of parental feeling which were to assure its possession; but as Duncan proceeded, the expression of joy became so fiercely malignant, that it was impossible not to apprehend it proceeded from some passion more sinister than avarice.

"Go," said the Huron, suppressing the alarming exhibition in an instant, in a death-like calmness of countenance; "go to the dark-haired daughter, and say, Magua waits to speak. The father will remember what the child promises."

Duncan, who interpreted this speech to express a wish for some additional pledge that the promised gifts should not be withheld, slowly and reluctantly repaired to the place where the sisters were now resting from their fatigue, to communicate its purport to Cora.

"You understand the nature of an Indian's wishes," he concluded, as he led her towards the place where she was expected, "and must be prodigal of your offers of powder and blankets. Ardent spirits are, however, the most prized by such as he; nor would it be amiss to add some boon from your own hand, with that grace you so well know how to practice. Remember, Cora, that on your presence of mind and ingenuity even your life, as well as that of Alice, may in some measure depend."

"Heyward, and yours!"

"Mine is of little moment; it is already sold to my king, and is a prize to be seized by any enemy who may possess the power. I have no father to expect me, and but few friends to lament a fate which I have courted with the unsatiable longings of youth after distinction. But hush! we approach the Indian. Magua, the lady with whom you wish to speak is here."

The Indian rose slowly from his seat, and stood for near a minute silent and motionless. He then signed with his hand for Heyward to retire, saying coldly,—

"When the Huron talks to the women, his tribe shut their ears."

Duncan still lingering, as if refusing to comply, Cora said, with a calm smile,—

"You hear, Heyward, and delicacy at least should urge you to retire. Go to Alice, and comfort her with our reviving prospects."

She waited until he had departed, and then turning to the native, with the dignity of her sex in her voice and manner, she added, "What would Le Renard say to the daughter of Munro?"

"Listen," said the Indian, laying his hand firmly upon her arm, as if willing to draw her utmost attention to his words; a movement that Cora as firmly but quietly repulsed, by extricating the limb from his grasp: "Magua was born a chief and a warrior among the red Hurons of the lakes; he saw the suns of twenty summers make the snows of twenty winters run off in the streams before he saw a pale-face; and he was happy! Then his Canada fathers came into the woods, and taught him to drink the fire-water, and he became a rascal. The Hurons drove him from the graves of his fathers, as they would chase the hunted buffalo. He ran down the shores of the lakes, and followed their outlet to the 'city of cannon.' There he hunted and fished, till the people chased him again through the woods into the arms of his enemies. The chief, who was born a Huron, was at last a warrior among the Mohawks!"

"Something like this I had heard before," said Cora, observing that he paused to suppress those passions which began to burn with too bright a flame, as he recalled the recollection of his supposed injuries.

"Was it the fault of Le Renard that his head was not made of rock? Who gave him the fire-water? who made him a villain? 'T was the pale-faces, the people of your own color."

"And am I answerable that thoughtless and unprincipled men exist, whose shades of countenance may resemble mine?" Cora calmly demanded of the excited savage.

"No; Magua is a man, and not a fool; such as you never open their lips to the burning stream: the Great Spirit has given you wisdom!"

"What then have I to do, or say, in the matter of your misfortunes, not to say of your errors?"

"Listen," repeated the Indian, resuming his earnest attitude; "when his English and French fathers dug up the hatchet, Le Renard struck the war-post of the Mohawks, and went out against his own nation. The pale-faces have driven the redskins from their hunting grounds, and now when they fight, a white man leads the way. The old chief at Horican, your father, was the great captain of our war-party. He said to the Mohawks do this, and do that, and he was minded. He made a law, that if an Indian swallowed the fire-water, and came into the cloth wigwams of his warriors, it should not be forgotten. Magua foolishly opened his mouth, and the hot liquor led him into the cabin of Munro. What did the gray-head? let his daughter say."

"He forgot not his words, and did justice, by punishing the offender," said the undaunted daughter.

"Justice!" repeated the Indian, casting an oblique glance of the most ferocious expression at her unyielding countenance; "is it justice to make evil, and then punish for it? Magua was not himself; it was the fire-water that spoke and acted for him! but Munro did not believe it. The Huron chief was tied up before all the pale-faced warriors, and whipped like a dog."

Cora remained silent, for she knew not how to palliate this imprudent severity on the part of her father, in a manner to suit the comprehension of an Indian.

"See!" continued Magua, tearing aside the slight calico that very imperfectly concealed his painted breast; "here are scars given by knives and bullets—of these a warrior may boast before his nation; but the gray-head has left marks on the back of the Huron chief, that he must hide, like a squaw, under this painted cloth of the whites."

"I had thought," resumed Cora, "that an Indian warrior was patient, and that his spirit felt not, and knew not, the pain his body suffered."

"When the Chippewas tied Magua to the stake, and cut this gash," said the other, laying his finger on a deep scar, "the Huron laughed in their faces, and told them, Women struck so light! His spirit was then in the clouds! But when he felt the blows of Munro, his spirit lay under the birch. The spirit of a Huron is never drunk; it remembers forever!"

"But it may be appeased. If my father has done you this injustice, show him how an Indian can forgive an injury, and take back his daughters. You have heard from Major Heyward—"

Magua shook his head, forbidding the repetition of offers he so much despised.

"What would you have?" continued Cora, after a most painful pause, while the conviction forced itself on her mind that the too sanguine and generous Duncan had been cruelly deceived by the cunning of the savage.

"What a Huron loves—good for good; bad for bad!"

"You would then revenge the injury inflicted by Munro on his helpless daughters. Would it not be more like a man to go before his face, and take the satisfaction of a warrior?"

"The arms of the pale-faces are long, and their knives sharp!" returned the savage, with a malignant laugh; "why should Le Renard go among the muskets of his warriors, when he holds the spirit of the gray-head in his hand?"

"Name your intention, Magua," said Cora, struggling with herself to speak with steady calmness. "Is it to lead us prisoners to the woods, or do you contemplate even some greater evil? Is there no reward, no means of palliating the injury, and of softening your heart? At least, release my gentle sister, and pour out all your malice on me. Purchase wealth by her safety, and satisfy your revenge with a single victim. The loss of both his daughters might bring the aged man to his grave, and where would then be the satisfaction of Le Renard?"

"Listen," said the Indian again. "The light eyes can go back to the Horican, and tell the old chief what has been done, if the dark-haired woman will swear by the Great Spirit of her fathers to tell no lie."

"What must I promise?" demanded Cora, still maintaining a secret ascendency over the fierce native, by the collected and feminine dignity of her presence.

"When Magua left his people, his wife was given to another chief; he has now made friends with the Hurons, and will go back to the graves of his tribe, on the shores of the great lake. Let the daughter of the English chief follow, and live in his wigwam forever."

However revolting a proposal of such a character might prove to Cora, she retained, notwithstanding her powerful disgust, sufficient self-command to reply, without betraying the weakness.

"And what pleasure would Magua find in sharing his cabin with a wife he did not love; one who would be of a nation and color different than his own? It would be better to take the gold of Munro, and buy the heart of some Huron maid with his gifts."

The Indian made no reply for near a minute, but bent his fierce looks on the countenance of Cora in such wavering glances that her eyes sank with shame, under an impression that, for the first time, they had encountered an expression that no chaste female might endure. While she was shrinking within herself, in dread of having her ears wounded by some proposal still more shocking than the last, the voice of Magua answered, in its tones of deepest malignancy—

"When the blows scorched the back of the Huron, he would know where to find a woman to feel the smart. The daughter of Munro would draw his water, hoe his corn, and cook his venison. The body of the gray-head would sleep among his cannon, but his heart would lie within reach of the knife of Le Subtil."

"Monster! well dost thou deserve thy treacherous name!" cried Cora, in an ungovernable burst of filial indignation. "None but a fiend could meditate such a vengeance! But thou overratest thy power! You shall find it is, in truth, the heart of Munro you hold, and that it will defy your utmost malice!"

The Indian answered this bold defiance by a ghastly smile, that showed an unaltered purpose, while he motioned her away, as if to close the conference forever. Cora, already regretting her precipitation, was obliged to comply; for Magua instantly left the spot, and approached his gluttonous comrades. Heyward flew to the side of the agitated female, and demanded the result of a dialogue that he had watched at a distance with so much interest. But unwilling to alarm the fears of Alice, she evaded a direct reply, betraying only by her countenance her utter want of success, and keeping her anxious looks fastened on the slightest movements of their captors. To the reiterated and earnest questions of her sister, concerning their probable destination, she made no other answer than by pointing towards the dark group, with an agitation she could not control, and murmuring, as she folded Alice to her bosom—

"There, there; read our fortunes in their faces; we shall see; we shall see!"

The action, and the choked utterance of Cora, spoke more impressively than any words, and quickly drew the attention of her companions on that spot where her own was riveted with an intenseness that nothing but the importance of the stake could create.

When Magua reached the cluster of lolling savages, who, gorged with their disgusting meal, lay stretched on the earth in brutal indulgence, he commenced speaking with the dignity of an Indian chief. The first syllables he uttered had the effect to cause his listeners to raise themselves in attitudes of respectful attention. As the Huron used his native language, the prisoners, notwithstanding the caution of the natives had kept them within the swing of their tomahawks, could only conjecture the substance of his harangue, from the nature of those significant gestures with which an Indian always illustrates his eloquence.

At first, the language, as well as the action of Magua, appeared calm and deliberative. When he had succeeded in sufficiently awakening the attention of his comrades, Heyward fancied, by his pointing so frequently toward the direction of the great lakes, that he spoke of the land of their fathers, and of their distant tribe. Frequent indications of applause escaped the listeners, who, as they uttered the expressive "Hugh!" looked at each other in commendation of the speaker. Le Renard was too skillful to neglect his advantage. He now spoke of the long and painful route by which they had left those spacious grounds and happy villages, to come and battle against the enemies of their Canadian fathers. He enumerated the warriors of the party; their several merits; their frequent services to the nation; their wounds, and the number of scalps they had taken. Whenever he alluded to any present (and the subtle Indian neglected none), the dark countenance of the flattered individual gleamed with exultation, nor did he even hesitate to assert the truth of the words, by gestures of applause and confirmation. Then the voice of the speaker fell, and lost the loud, animated tones of triumph with which he had enumerated their deeds of success and victory. He described the cataract of Glenn's; the impregnable position of its rocky island, with its caverns and its numerous rapids and whirlpools; he named the name of "La Longue Carabine," and paused until the forest beneath them had sent up the last echo of a loud and long yell, with which the hated appellation was received. He pointed toward the youthful military captive, and described the death of a favorite warrior, who had been precipitated into the deep ravine by his hand. He not only mentioned the fate of him who, hanging between heaven and earth, had presented such a spectacle of horror to the whole band, but he acted anew the terrors of his situation, his resolution and his death, on the branches of a sapling; and, finally, he rapidly recounted the manner in which each of their friends had fallen, never failing to touch upon their courage and their most acknowledged virtues. When this recital of events was ended, his voice once more changed, and became plaintive, and even musical, in its low guttural sounds. He now spoke of the wives and children of the slain; their destitution; their misery, both physical and moral; their distance; and, at last, of their unavenged wrongs. Then suddenly lifting his voice to a pitch of terrific energy, he concluded, by demanding,—

"Are the Hurons dogs to bear this? Who shall say to the wife of Menowgua that the fishes have his scalp, and that his nation have not taken revenge! Who will dare meet the mother of Wassawattimie, that scornful woman, with his hands clean! What shall be said to the old men when they ask us for scalps, and we have not a hair from a white head to give them! The women will point their fingers at us. There is a dark spot on the names of the Hurons, and it must be hid in blood!"

His voice was no longer audible in the burst of rage which now broke into the air, as if the wood, instead of containing so small a band, was filled with the nation. During the foregoing address the progress of the speaker was too plainly read by those most interested in his success, through the medium of the countenances of the men he addressed. They had answered his melancholy and mourning by sympathy and sorrow; his assertions, by gestures of confirmation; and his boastings, with the exultation of savages. When he spoke of courage, their looks were firm and responsive; when he alluded to their injuries, their eyes kindled with fury; when he mentioned the taunts of the women, they dropped their heads in shame; but when he pointed out their means of vengeance, he struck a chord which never failed to thrill in the breast of an Indian. With the first intimation that it was within their reach, the whole band sprang upon their feet as one man; giving utterance to their rage in the most frantic cries, They rushed upon their prisoners in a body with drawn knives and uplifted tomahawks. Heyward threw himself between the sisters and the foremost, whom he grappled with a desperate strength that for a moment checked his violence. This unexpected resistance gave Magua time to interpose, and with rapid enunciation and animated gesture, he drew the attention of the band again to himself. In that language he knew so well how to assume, he diverted his comrades from their instant purpose, and invited them to prolong the misery of their victims. His proposal was received with acclamations, and executed with the swiftness of thought.

Two powerful warriors cast themselves on Heyward, while another was occupied in securing the less active singing-master. Neither of the captives, however, submitted without a desperate though fruitless struggle. Even David hurled his assailant to the earth; nor was Heyward secured until the victory over his companion enabled the Indians to direct their united force to that object. He was then bound and fastened to the body of the sapling on whose branches Magua had acted the pantomime of the falling Huron. When the young soldier regained his recollection, he had the painful certainty before his eyes that a common fate was intended for the whole party. On his right was Cora, in a durance similar to his own, pale and agitated, but with an eye whose steady look still read the proceedings of their enemies. On his left, the withes which bound her to a pine performed that office for Alice which her trembling limbs refused, and alone kept her fragile form from sinking. Her hands were clasped before her in prayer, but instead of looking upwards towards that power which alone could rescue them, her unconscious looks wandered to the countenance of Duncan with infantile dependency. David had contended, and the novelty of the circumstance held him silent, in deliberation on the propriety of the unusual occurrence.

The vengeance of the Hurons had now taken a new direction, and they prepared to execute it with that barbarous ingenuity with which they were familiarized by the practice of centuries. Some sought knots, to raise the blazing pile; one was riving the splinters of pine, in order to pierce the flesh of their captives with the burning fragments; and others bent the tops of two saplings to the earth; in order to suspend Heyward by the arms between the recoiling branches. But the vengeance of Magua sought a deeper and a more malignant enjoyment.

While the less refined monsters of the band prepared, before the eyes of those who were to suffer, these well known and vulgar means of torture, he approached Cora, and pointed out, with the most malign expression of countenance, the speedy fate that awaited her:—

"Ha!" he added, "what says the daughter of Munro? Her head is too good to find a pillow in the wigwam of Le Renard; will she like it better when it rolls about this hill, a plaything for the wolves? Her bosom cannot nurse the children of a Huron; she will see it spit upon by Indians!"

"What means the monster!" demanded the astonished Heyward.

"Nothing!" was the firm reply. "He is a savage, a barbarous and ignorant savage, and knows not what he does. Let us find leisure, with our dying breath, to ask for him penitence and pardon."

"Pardon!" echoed the fierce Huron, mistaking, in his anger, the meaning of her words; "the memory of an Indian is longer than the arm of the pale-faces; his mercy shorter than their justice! Say; shall I send the yellow hair to her father, and will you follow Magua to the great lakes, to carry his water, and feed him with corn?"

Cora beckoned him away, with an emotion of disgust she could not control.

"Leave me," she said, with a solemnity that for a moment checked the barbarity of the Indian; "you mingle bitterness in my prayers; you stand between me and my God!"

The slight impression produced on the savage was, however, soon forgotten, and he continued pointing, with taunting irony, towards Alice.

"Look! the child weeps! She is young to die! Send her to Munro, to comb his gray hairs, and keep life in the heart of the old man."

Cora could not resist the desire to look upon her youthful sister, in whose eyes she met an imploring glance, that betrayed the longings of nature.

"What says he, dearest Cora?" asked the trembling voice of Alice. "Did he speak of sending me to our father?"

For many moments the elder sister looked upon the younger, with a countenance that wavered with powerful and contending emotions. At length she spoke, though her tones had lost their rich and calm fullness, in an expression of tenderness that seemed maternal.

"Alice," she said, "the Huron offers us both life, nay, more than both; he offers to restore Duncan, our invaluable Duncan, as well as you, to our friends—to our father—to our heartstricken, childless father, if I will bow down this rebellious stubborn pride of mine, and consent—"

Her voice became choked, and clasping her hands, she looked upward, as if seeking, in her agony, intelligence from a wisdom that was infinite.

"Say on," cried Alice; "to what, dearest Cora? Oh, that the proffer were made to me! to save you, to cheer our aged father, to restore Duncan, how cheerfully could I die!"

"Die!" repeated Cora, with a calmer and a firmer voice, "that were easy! Perhaps the alternative may not be less so. He would have me," she continued, her accents sinking under a deep consciousness of the degradation of the proposal, "follow him to the wilderness; go to the habitations of the Hurons; to remain there; in short to become his wife! Speak, then, Alice; child of my affections! sister of my love! And you, too, Major Heyward, aid my weak reason with your counsel. Is life to be purchased by such a sacrifice? Will you, Alice, receive it at my hands at such a price? And *you,* Duncan, guide me; control me between you; for I am wholly yours."

"Would I!" echoed the indignant and astonished youth. "Cora! Cora! you jest with our misery! Name not the horrid alternative again; the thought itself is worse than a thousand deaths."

"That such would be *your* answer, I well knew!" exclaimed Cora, her cheeks flushing, and her dark eyes once more sparkling with the lingering emotions of a woman. "What says my Alice? for her will I submit without another murmur."

Although both Heyward and Cora listened with painful suspense and the deepest attention, no sounds were heard in reply. It appeared as if the delicate and sensitive form of Alice would shrink into itself, as she listened to this proposal. Her arms had fallen lengthwise before her, the fingers moving in slight convulsions; her head dropped upon her bosom, and her whole person seemed suspended against the tree, looking like some beautiful emblem of the wounded delicacy of her sex, devoid of animation, and yet keenly conscious. In a few moments, however, her head began to move slowly, in a sign of deep, unconquerable disapprobation.

"No, no, no; better that we die as we have lived, together!"

"Then die!" shouted Magua, hurling his tomahawk with violence at the unresisting speaker, and gnashing his teeth with a rage that could no longer be bridled, at this sudden exhibition of firmness in the one he believed the weakest of the party. The axe cleaved the air in front of Heyward, and cutting some of the flowing ringlets of Alice, quivered in the tree above her head. The sight maddened Duncan to desperation. Collecting all his energies in one effort, he snapped the twigs which bound him and rushed upon another savage, who was preparing with loud yells, and a more deliberate aim, to repeat the blow. They encountered, grappled, and fell to the earth together. The naked body of his antagonist afforded Heyward no means of holding his adversary, who glided from his grasp, and rose again with one knee on his chest, pressing him down with the weight of a giant. Duncan already saw the knife gleaming in the air, when a whistling sound swept past him, and was rather accompanied, than followed, by the sharp crack of a rifle. He felt his breast relieved from the load it had endured; he saw the savage expression of his adversary's countenance change to a look of vacant wildness when the Indian fell dead on the faded leaves by his side.

CHAPTER XII

Clo.—*I am gone, sir,*
And anon, sir,
I'll be with you again.
Shakespeare, *Twelfth Night,* IV. ii. 131.

The Hurons stood aghast at this sudden visitation of death on one of their band. But, as they regarded the fatal accuracy of an aim which had dared to immolate an enemy at so much hazard to a friend, the name of "La Longue Carabine" burst simultaneously from every lip, and was succeeded by a wild and a sort of plaintive howl. The cry was answered by a loud shout from a little thicket, where the incautious party had piled their arms; and at the next moment, Hawkeye, too eager to load the rifle he had regained, was seen advancing upon them, brandishing the clubbed weapon, and cutting the air with wide and powerful sweeps. Bold and rapid as was the progress of the scout, it was exceeded by that of a light and vigorous form which, bounding past him, leaped, with incredible activity and daring, into the very centre of the Hurons, where it stood, whirling a tomahawk, and flourishing a glittering knife, with fearful menaces, in front of Cora. Quicker than the thoughts could follow these unexpected and audacious movements, an image, armed in the emblematic panoply of death, glided before their eyes, and assumed a threatening attitude at the other's side. The savage tormentors recoiled before these warlike intruders, and uttered, as they appeared in such quick succession, the often repeated and peculiar exclamation of surprise, followed by the well known and dreaded appellations of—

"Le Cerf Agile! Le Gros Serpent!"

But the wary and vigilant leader of the Hurons was not so easily disconcerted. Casting his keen eyes around the little plain, he comprehended the nature of the assault at a glance, and encouraging his followers by his voice as well as by his example, he unsheathed his long and dangerous knife, and rushed with a loud whoop upon the expecting Chingachgook. It was the signal for a general combat. Neither party had fire-arms, and the contest was to be decided in the deadliest manner; hand to hand, with weapons of offense, and none of defense.

Uncas answered the whoop, and leaping on an enemy, with a single, well directed blow of his tomahawk, cleft him to the brain. Heyward tore the weapon of Magua from the sapling, and rushed eagerly toward the fray. As the combatants were now equal in number, each singled an opponent from the adverse band. The rush and blows passed with the fury of a whirlwind, and the swiftness of lightning. Hawkeye soon got another enemy within reach of his arm, and with one sweep of his formidable weapon he beat down the slight and inartificial defenses of his antagonist, crushing him to the earth with the blow. Heyward ventured to hurl the tomahawk he had seized, too ardent to await the moment of closing. It struck the Indian he had selected on the forehead, and checked for an instant his onward rush. Encouraged by this slight advantage, the impetuous young man continued his onset, and sprang upon his enemy with naked hands. A single instant was enough to assure him of the rashness of the measure, for he immediately found himself fully engaged, with all his activity and courage, in endeavoring to ward the desperate thrusts made with the knife of the Huron. Unable longer to foil an enemy so alert and vigilant, he threw his arms about him, and succeeded in pinning the limbs of the other to his side, with an iron grasp, but one that was far too exhausting to himself to continue long. In this extremity he heard a voice near him, shouting—

"Extarminate the varlets! no quarter to an accursed Mingo!"

At the next moment, the breech of Hawkeye's rifle fell on the naked head of his adversary, whose muscles appeared to wither under the shock, as he sank from the arms of Duncan, flexible and motionless.

When Uncas had brained his first antagonist, he turned, like a hungry lion, to seek another. The fifth and only Huron disengaged at the first onset had paused a moment, and then seeing that all around him were employed in the deadly strife, he had sought, with hellish vengeance, to complete the baffled work of revenge. Raising a shout of triumph, he sprang towards the defenseless Cora, sending his keen axe, as the dreadful precursor of his approach. The tomahawk grazed her shoulder, and cutting the withes which bound her to the tree, left the maiden at liberty to fly. She eluded the grasp of the savage, and reckless of her own safety, threw herself on the bosom of Alice, striving with convulsed and ill-directed fingers, to tear asunder the twigs which confined the person of her sister. Any other than a monster would have relented at such an act of generous devotion to the best and purest affection; but the breast of the Huron was a stranger to sympathy. Seizing Cora by the rich tresses which fell in confusion about her form, he tore her from her frantic hold, and bowed her down with brutal violence to her knees. The savage drew the flowing curls through his hand, and raising them on high with an outstretched arm, he passed the knife around the exquisitely moulded head of his victim, with a taunting and exulting laugh. But he purchased this moment of fierce gratification with the loss of the fatal opportunity. It was just then the sight caught the eye of Uncas. Bounding from his footsteps he appeared for an instant darting through the air, and descending in a ball he fell on the chest of his enemy, driving him many yards from the spot, headlong and prostrate. The violence of the exertion cast the young Mohican at his side. They arose together, fought, and bled, each in his turn. But the conflict was soon decided; the tomahawk of Heyward and the rifle of Hawkeye descended on the skull of the Huron, at the same moment that the knife of Uncas reached his heart.

The battle was now entirely terminated, with the exception of the protracted struggle between Le Renard Subtil and Le Gros Serpent. Well did these barbarous warriors prove that they deserved those significant names which had been bestowed for deeds in former wars. When they engaged, some little time was lost in eluding the quick and vigorous thrusts which had been aimed at their lives.

Suddenly darting on each other, they closed, and came to the earth, twisted together like twining serpents, in pliant and subtle folds. At the moment when the victors found themselves unoccupied, the spot where these experienced and desperate combatants lay, could only be distinguished by a cloud of dust and leaves which moved from the centre of the little plain towards its boundary, as if raised by the passage of a whirlwind. Urged by the different motives of filial affection, friendship, and gratitude, Heyward and his companions rushed with one accord to the place, encircling the little canopy of dust which hung above the warriors. In vain did Uncas dart around the cloud, with a wish to strike his knife into the heart of his father's foe; the threatening rifle of Hawkeye was raised and suspended in vain, while Duncan endeavored to seized the limbs of the Huron with hands that appeared to have lost their power. Covered, as they were, with dust and blood, the swift evolutions of the combatants seemed to incorporate their bodies into one. The death-like looking figure of the Mohican, and the dark form of the Huron, gleamed before their eyes in such quick and confused succession, that the friends of the former knew not where nor when to plant the succoring blow. It is true there were short and fleeting moments when the fiery eyes of Magua were seen glittering, like the fabled organs of the basilisk, through the dusty wreath by which he was enveloped, and he read by those short and deadly glances the fate of the combat in the presence of his enemies; ere, however, any hostile hand could descend on his devoted head, its place was filled by the scowling visage of Chingachgook. In this manner the scene of the combat was removed from the centre of the little plain to its verge. The Mohican now found an opportunity to make a powerful thrust with his knife; Magua suddenly relinquished his grasp, and fell backward without motion, and seemingly without life. His adversary leaped on his feet, making the arches of the forest ring with the sounds of triumph.

"Well done for the Delawares! victory to the Mohican!" cried Hawkeye, once more elevating the butt of the long and fatal rifle; "a finishing blow from a man without a cross will never tell against his honor, nor rob him of his right to the scalp."

But at the very moment when the dangerous weapon was in the act of descending, the subtle Huron rolled swiftly from beneath the danger, over the edge of the precipice, and, falling on his feet, was seen leaping with a single bound into the centre of a thicket of low bushes, which clung along its sides. The Delawares, who had believed their enemy dead, uttered their exclamation of surprise, and were following with speed and clamor, like hounds in open view of the deer, when a shrill and peculiar cry from the scout instantly changed their purpose, and recalled them to the summit of the hill.

"'T was like himself," cried the inveterate forester, whose prejudices contributed so largely to veil his natural sense of justice in all matters which concerned the Mingoes; "a lying and deceitful varlet he is. An honest Delaware now, being fairly vanquished, would have lain still, and been knocked on the head, but these knavish Maquas cling to life like so many cats-o'-the-mountain. Let him go—let him go; 't is but one man, and he without rifle or bow, many a long mile from his French commerades; and, like a rattler that has lost his fangs, he can do no farther mischief, until such time as he, and we too, may leave the prints of our moccasins over a long reach of sandy plain. See, Uncas," he added, in Delaware, "your father is flaying the scalps already. It may be well to go round and feel the vagabonds that are left, or we may have another of them loping through the woods, and screeching like a jay that has been winged."

So saying, the honest, but implacable scout made the circuit of the dead, into whose senseless bosoms he thrust his long knife, with as much coolness as though they had been so many brute carcasses. He had, however, been anticipated by the elder Mohican, who had already torn the emblems of victory from the unresisting heads of the slain.

But Uncas, denying his habits, we had almost said his nature, flew with instinctive delicacy, accompanied by Heyward, to the assistance of the females, and quickly releasing Alice, placed her in the arms of Cora. We shall not attempt to describe the gratitude to the Almighty Disposer of events which glowed in the bosoms of the sisters, who were thus unexpectedly restored to life and to each other. Their thanksgivings were deep and silent; the offerings of their gentle spirits, burning brightest and purest on the secret altars of their hearts; and their renovated and more earthly feelings exhibiting themselves in long and fervent, though speechless caresses. As Alice rose from her knees, where she had sunk by the side of Cora, she threw herself on the bosom of the latter, and sobbed aloud the name of their aged father, while her soft, dove-like eyes sparkled with the rays of hope.

"We are saved! we are saved!" she murmured; "to return to the arms of our dear, dear father, and his heart will not be broken with grief. And you too, Cora, my sister; my more than sister, my mother; you too are spared. And Duncan," she added, looking round upon the youth with a smile of ineffable innocence, "even our own brave and noble Duncan has escaped without a hurt."

To these ardent and nearly incoherent words Cora made no other answer than by straining the youthful speaker to her heart, as she bent over her, in melting tenderness. The manhood of Heyward felt no shame in dropping tears over this spectacle of affectionate rapture; and Uncas stood, fresh and blood-stained from the combat, a calm, and, apparently, an unmoved looker-on, it is true, but with eyes that had already lost their fierceness, and were beaming with a sympathy that elevated him far above the intelligence, and advanced him probably centuries before the practices of his nation.

During this display of emotions so natural in their situation, Hawkeye, whose vigilant distrust had satisfied itself that the Hurons, who disfigured the heavenly scene, no longer possessed the power to interrupt its harmony, approached David, and liberated him from the bonds he had, until that moment, endured with the most exemplary patience.

"There," exclaimed the scout, casting the last withe behind him, "you are once more master of your own limbs, though you seem not to use them with much greater judgment than that in which they were first fashioned. If advice from one who is not older than yourself, but who, having lived most of his time in the wilderness, may be said to have experienced beyond his years, will give no offense, you are welcome to my thoughts; and these are, to part with the little tooting instrument in your jacket to the first fool you meet with, and buy some useful we'pon with the money, if it be only the barrel of a horseman's pistol. By industry and care, you might thus come to some prefarment; for by this time, I should think, your eyes would plainly tell you that a carrion crow is a better bird than a mocking thresher. The one will, at least, remove foul sights from before the face of man, while the other is only good to brew disturbances in the woods, by cheating the ears of all that hear them."

"Arms and the clarion for the battle, but the song of thanksgiving to the victory!" answered the liberated David. "Friend," he added, thrusting forth his lean, delicate hand towards Hawkeye, in kindness, while his eyes twinkled and grew moist, "I thank thee that the hairs of my head still grow where they were first rooted by Providence; for, though those of other men may be more glossy and curling, I have ever found mine own well suited to the brain they shelter. That I did not join myself to the battle was less owing to disinclination, than to the bonds of the heathen. Valiant and skillful hast thou proved thyself in the conflict, and I hereby thank thee, before proceeding to discharge other and more important duties, because thou hast proved thyself well worthy of a Christian's praise."

"The thing is but a trifle, and what you may often see, if you tarry long among us," returned the scout, a good deal softened towards the man of song, by this unequivocal expression of gratitude. "I have got back my old companion, Killdeer," he added, striking his hand on the breech of his rifle; "and that in itself is a victory. These Iroquois are cunning, but they outwitted themselves when they placed their fire-arms out of reach; and had Uncas or his father been gifted with only their common Indian patience, we should have come in upon the knaves with three bullets instead of one, and that would have made a finish of the whole pack; yon loping varlet, as well as his commerades. But 't was all fore-ordered, and for the best."

"Thou sayest well," returned David, "and hast caught the true spirit of Christianity. He that is to be saved will be saved, and he that is predestined to be damned will be damned. This is the doctrine of truth, and most consoling and refreshing it is to the true believer."

The scout, who by this time was seated, examining into the state of his rifle with a species of parental assiduity, now looked up at the other in a displeasure that he did not affect to conceal, roughly interrupting further speech.

"Doctrine or no doctrine," said the sturdy woodsman, "'t is the belief of knaves, and the curse of an honest man. I can credit that yonder Huron was to fall by my hand, for with my own eyes I have seen it; but nothing short of being a witness will cause me to think he has met with any reward, or that Chingachgook, there, will be condemned at the final day."

"You have no warranty for such an audacious doctrine, nor any covenant to support it," cried David, who was deeply tinctured with the subtle distinctions which, in his time, and more especially in his province, had been drawn around the beautiful simplicity of revelation, by endeavoring to penetrate the awful mystery of the divine nature, supplying faith by self-sufficiency, and, by consequence, involving those who reasoned from such human dogmas in absurdities and doubt; "your temple is reared on the sands, and the first tempest will wash away its foundation. I demand your authorities for such an uncharitable assertion (like other advocates of a system, David was not always accurate in his use of terms). Name chapter and verse; in which of the holy books do you find language to support you?"

"Book!" repeated Hawkeye, with singular and ill-concealed disdain; "do you take me for a whimpering boy at the apron-string of one of your old gals; and this good rifle on my knee for the feather of a goose's wing, my ox's horn for a bottle of ink, and my leathern pouch for a cross-barred handkercher to carry my dinner? Book! what have such as I, who am a warrior of the wilderness, though a man without a cross, to do with books? I never read but in one, and the words that are written there are too simple and too plain to need much schooling; though I may boast that of forty long and hard-working years."

"What call you the volume?" said David, misconceiving the other's meaning.

"'T is open before your eyes," returned the scout; "and he who owns it is not a niggard of its use. I have heard it said that there are men who read in books to convince themselves there is a God. I know not but man may so deform his works in the settlement, as to leave that which is so clear in the wilderness a matter of doubt among traders and priests. If any such there be, and he will follow me from sun to sun, through the windings of the forest, he shall see enough to teach him that he is a fool, and that the greatest of his folly lies in striving to rise to the level of One he can never equal, be it in goodness, or be it in power."

The instant David discovered that he battled with a disputant who imbibed his faith from the lights of nature, eschewing all subtleties of doctrine, he willingly abandoned a controversy from which he believed neither profit nor credit was to be derived. While the scout was speaking, he had also seated himself, and producing the ready little volume and the iron-rimmed spectacles, he prepared to discharge a duty which nothing but the unexpected assault he had received in his orthodoxy could have so long suspended. He was, in truth, a minstrel of the western continent—of a much later day, certainly, than those gifted bards who formerly sang the profane renown of baron and prince, but after the spirit of his own age and country; and he was now prepared to exercise the cunning of his craft in celebration of, or rather in thanksgiving for, the recent victory. He waited patiently for Hawkeye to cease, then lifting his eyes, together with his voice, he said aloud,—

"I invite you, friends, to join in praise for this signal deliverance from the hands of barbarians and infidels, to the comfortable and solemn tones of the tune called 'Northampton.'"

He next named the page and verse where the rhymes selected were to be found, and applied the pitch-pipe to his lips, with the decent gravity that he had been wont to use in the temple. This time he was, however, without any accompaniment, for the sisters were just then pouring out those tender effusions of affection which have been already alluded to. Nothing deterred by the smallness of his audience, which, in truth, consisted only of the discontented scout, he raised his voice, commencing and ending the sacred song without accident or interruption of any kind.

Hawkeye listened, while he coolly adjusted his flint and reloaded his rifle; but the sounds, wanting the extraneous assistance of scene and sympathy, failed to awaken his slumbering emotions. Never minstrel, or by whatever more suitable name David should be known, drew upon his talents in the presence of more insensible auditors; though considering the singleness and sincerity of his motive, it is probable that no bard of profane song ever uttered notes that ascended so near to that throne where all homage and praise is due. The scout shook his head, and muttering some unintelligible words, among which "throat" and "Iroquois," were alone audible, he walked away, to collect, and to examine into, the state of the captured arsenal of the Hurons. In this office he was now joined by Chingachgook, who found his own, as well as the rifle of his son, among the arms. Even Heyward and David were furnished with weapons; nor was ammunition wanting to render them all effectual.

When the foresters had made their selection, and distributed their prizes, the scout announced that the hour had arrived when it was necessary to move. By this time the song of Gamut had ceased, and the sisters had learned to still the exhibition of their emotions. Aided by Duncan and the younger Mohican, the two latter descended the precipitous sides of that hill which they had so lately ascended under so very different auspices, and whose summit had so nearly proved the scene of their massacre. At the foot, they found the Narragansets browsing the herbage of the bushes; and having mounted, they followed the movements of a guide who, in the most deadly straits, had so often proved himself their friend. The journey was, however, short. Hawkeye, leaving the blind path that the Hurons had followed, turned short to his right, and entering the thicket, he crossed a babbling brook, and halted in a narrow dell, under the shade of a few water elms. Their distance from the base of the fatal hill was but a few rods, and the steeds had been serviceable only in crossing the shallow stream.

The scout and the Indians appeared to be familiar with the sequestered place where they now were; for, leaning their rifles against the trees, they commenced throwing aside the dried leaves, and opening the blue clay, out of which a clear and sparkling spring of bright, glancing water quickly bubbled. The white man then looked about him, as though seeking for some object which was not to be found as readily as he expected:—

"Them careless imps, the Mohawks, with their Tuscarora and Onandaga brethren, have been here slaking their thirst," he muttered, "and the vagabonds have thrown away the gourd! This is the way with benefits, when they are bestowed on such disremembering hounds! Here has the Lord laid his hand, in the midst of the howling wilderness, for their good, and raised a fountain of water from the bowels of the 'arth, that might laugh at the richest shop of apothecary's ware in all the colonies; and see! the knaves have trodden in the clay, and deformed the cleanliness of the place, as though they were brute beasts, instead of human men."

Uncas silently extended towards him the desired gourd, which the spleen of Hawkeye had hitherto prevented him from observing, on a branch of an elm. Filling it with water, he retired a short distance, to a place where the ground was more firm and dry; here he coolly seated himself, and after taking a long, and, apparently, a grateful draught, he commenced a very strict examination of the fragments of food left by the Hurons, which had hung in a wallet on his arm.

"Thank you, lad!" he continued, returning the empty gourd to Uncas; "now we will see how these rampaging Hurons lived, when outlying in ambushments. Look at this! The varlets know the better pieces of the deer; and one would think they might carve and roast a saddle, equal to the best cook in the land! But everything is raw, for the Iroquois are thorough savages. Uncas, take my steel and kindle a fire; a mouthful of a tender broil will give natur' a helping hand, after so long a trail."

Heyward, perceiving that their guides now set about their repast in sober earnest, assisted the ladies to alight, and placed himself at their side, not unwilling to enjoy a few moments of grateful rest, after the bloody scene he had just gone through. While the culinary process was in hand, curiosity induced him to inquire into the circumstances which had led to their timely and unexpected rescue.

"How is it that we see you so soon, my generous friend," he asked, "and without aid from the garrison of Edward?"

"Had we gone to the bend in the river, we might have been in time to rake the leaves over your bodies, but too late to have saved your scalps," coolly answered the scout. "No, no; instead of throwing away strength and opportunity by crossing to the fort, we lay by, under the bank of the Hudson, waiting to watch the movements of the Hurons."

"You were, then, witnesses of all that passed?"

"Not of all; for Indian sight is too keen to be easily cheated, and we kept close. A difficult matter it was, too, to keep this Mohican boy snug in the ambushment. Ah! Uncas, Uncas, your behavior was more like that of a curious woman than of a warrior on his scent."

Uncas permitted his eyes to turn for an instant on the sturdy countenance of the speaker, but he neither spoke nor gave any indication of repentance. On the contrary, Heyward thought the manner of the young Mohican was disdainful, if not a little fierce, and that he suppressed passions that were ready to explode, as much in compliment to the listeners, as from the deference he usually paid to his white associate.

"You saw our capture?" Heyward next demanded.

"We heard it," was the significant answer. "An Indian yell is plain language to men who have passed their days in the woods. But when you landed, we were driven to crawl, like sarpents, beneath the leaves; and then we lost sight of you entirely, until we placed eyes on you again, trussed to the trees, and ready bound for an Indian massacre."

"Our rescue was the deed of Providence. It was nearly a miracle that you did not mistake the path, for the Hurons divided, and each band had its horses."

"Aye! there we were thrown off the scent, and might, indeed, have lost the trail, had it not been for Uncas; we took the path, however, that led into the wilderness; for we judged, and judged rightly, that the savages would hold that course with their prisoners. But when we had followed it for many miles, without finding a single twig broken, as I had advised, my mind misgave me; especially as all the footsteps had the prints of moccasins."

"Our captors had the precaution to see us shod like themselves," said Duncan, raising a foot, and exhibiting the buckskin he wore.

"Aye! 't was judgmatical, and like themselves: though we were too expart to be thrown from a trail by so common an invention."

"To what, then, are we indebted for our safety?"

"To what, as a white man who has no taint of Indian blood, I should be ashamed to own; to the judgment of the young Mohican, in matters which I should know better than he, but which I can now hardly believe to be true, though my own eyes tell me it is so."

"'T is extraordinary! will you not name the reason?"

"Uncas was bold enough to say that the beasts ridden by the gentle ones," continued Hawkeye, glancing his eyes, not without curious interest, on the fillies of the ladies, "planted the legs of one side on the ground at the same time, which is contrary to the movements of all trotting four-footed animals of my knowledge, except the bear. And yet here are horses that always journey in this manner, as my own eyes have seen, and as their trail has shown for twenty long miles."

"'T is the merit of the animal! They come from the shores of Narraganset Bay, in the small province of Providence Plantations, and are celebrated for their hardihood, and the ease of this peculiar movement; though other horses are not unfrequently trained to the same."

"It may be—it may be," said Hawkeye, who had listened with singular attention to this explanation; "though I am a man who has the full blood of the whites, my judgment in deer and beaver is greater than in beasts of burden. Major Effingham has many noble chargers, but I have never seen one travel after such a sideling gait."

"True; for he would value the animals for very different properties. Still is this a breed highly esteemed, and, as you witness, much honored with the burdens it is often destined to bear."

The Mohicans had suspended their operations about the glimmering fire, to listen; and when Duncan had done, they looked at each other significantly, the father uttering the never-failing exclamation of surprise. The scout ruminated, like a man digesting his newly acquired knowledge, and once more stole a curious glance at the horses.

"I dare to say there are even stranger sights to be seen in the settlements!" he said, at length; "natur' is sadly abused by man, when he once gets the mastery. But, go sideling or go straight, Uncas had seen the movement, and their trail led us on to the broken bush. The outer branch, near the prints of one of the horses, was bent upward, as a lady breaks a flower from its stem, but all the rest were ragged and broken down, as if the strong hand of a man had been tearing them! So I concluded that the cunning varments had seen the twig bent, and had torn the rest, to make us believe a buck had been feeling the boughs with his antlers."

"I do believe your sagacity did not deceive you; for some such thing occurred!"

"That was easy to see," added the scout, in no degree conscious of having exhibited any extraordinary sagacity; "and a very different matter it was from a waddling horse! It then struck me the Mingoes would push for this spring, for the knaves well know the vartue of its waters!"

"Is it, then, so famous?" demanded Heyward, examining, with a more curious eye, the secluded dell, with its bubbling fountain, surrounded, as it was, by earth of a deep dingy brown.

"Few red-skins, who travel south and east of the great lakes, but have heard of its qualities. Will you taste for yourself?"

Heyward took the gourd, and, after swallowing a little of the water, threw it aside with grimaces of discontent. The scout laughed in his silent but heartfelt manner, and shook his head with vast satisfaction.

"Ah! you want the flavor that one gets by habit; the time was when I liked it as little as yourself; but I have come to my taste, and I now crave it, as a deer does the licks.[17] Your high spiced wines are not better liked than a red-skin relishes this water; especially when his natur' is ailing. But Uncas has made his fire, and it is time we think of eating, for our journey is long, and all before us."

Interrupting the dialogue by this abrupt transition, the scout had instant recourse to the fragments of food which had escaped the voracity of the Hurons. A very summary process completed the simple cookery, when he and the Mohicans commenced their humble meal, with the silence and characteristic diligence of men who ate in order to enable themselves to endure great and unremitting toil.

When this necessary, and, happily, grateful duty had been performed, each of the foresters stooped and took a long and parting draught at that solitary and silent spring,[18] around which and its sister fountains, within fifty years, the wealth, beauty, and talents of a hemisphere were to assemble in throngs, in pursuit of

---

[17]Many of the animals of the American forests resort to those spots where salt springs are found. These are called "licks" or "salt licks," in the language of the country, from the circumstance that the quadruped is often obliged to lick the earth, in order to obtain the saline particles. These licks are great places of resort with the hunters, who waylay their game near the paths that lead to them. [J.F.C.]

[18]The scene of the foregoing incidents is on the spot where the village of Ballston now stands, one of the two principal watering places of America. [J.F.C.]

health and pleasure. Then Hawkeye announced his determination to proceed. The sisters resumed their saddles; Duncan and David grasped their rifles, and followed on their footsteps; the scout leading the advance, and the Mohicans bringing up the rear. The whole party moved swiftly through the narrow path, towards the north, leaving the healing waters to mingle unheeded with the adjacent brook, and the bodies of the dead to fester on the neighboring mount, without the rites of sepulture; a fate but too common to the warriors of the woods to excite either commiseration or comment.

CHAPTER XIII

I'll seek a readier path.
PARNELL, *A Night-Piece on Death.*

The route taken by Hawkeye lay across those sandy plains, relieved by occasional valleys and swells of land, which had been traversed by their party on the morning of the same day, with the baffled Magua for their guide. The sun had now fallen low towards the distant mountains; and as their journey lay through the interminable forest, the heat was no longer oppressive. Their progress, in consequence, was proportionate; and long before the twilight gathered about them, they had made good many toilsome miles on their return.

The hunter, like the savage whose place he filled, seemed to select among the blind signs of their wild route with a species of instinct, seldom abating his speed, and never pausing to deliberate. A rapid and oblique glance at the moss on the trees, with an occasional upward gaze towards the setting sun, or a steady but passing look at the direction of the numerous watercourses, through which he waded, were sufficient to determine his path and remove his greatest difficulties. In the mean time, the forest began to change its hues, losing that lively green which had embellished its arches, in the graver light which is the usual precursor of the close of day.

While the eyes of the sisters were endeavoring to catch glimpses, through the trees, of the flood of golden glory which formed a glittering halo around the sun, tingeing here and there with ruby streaks, or bordering with narrow edgings of shining yellow, a mass of clouds that lay piled at no great distance above the western hills, Hawkeye turned suddenly, and, pointing upwards towards the gorgeous heavens, he spoke.

"Yonder is the signal given to man to seek his food and natural rest," he said; "better and wiser would it be, if he could understand the signs of nature, and take a lesson from the fowls of the air and the beasts of the fields! Our night, however, will soon be over; for, with the moon, we must be up and moving again. I remember to have fou't the Maquas, hereaways, in the first war in which I ever drew blood from man; and we threw up a work of blocks, to keep the ravenous varments from handling our scalps. If my marks do not fail me, we shall find the place a few rods further to our left."

Without waiting for an assent, or, indeed, for any reply, the sturdy hunter moved boldly into a dense thicket of young chestnuts, shoving aside the branches of the exuberant shoots which nearly covered the ground, like a man who expected, at each step, to discover some object he had formerly known. The recollection of the scout did not deceive him. After penetrating through the brush, matted as it was with briers, for a few hundred feet, he entered an open space, that surrounded a low, green hillock, which was crowned by the decayed block-house in question. This rude and neglected building was one of those deserted works, which, having been thrown up on an emergency, had been abandoned with the disappearance of danger, and was now quietly crumbling in the solitude of the forest, neglected, and nearly forgotten, like the circumstances which had caused it to be reared. Such memorials of the passage and struggles of man are yet frequent throughout the broad barrier of wilderness which once separated the hostile provinces, and form a species of ruins that are intimately associated with the recollections of colonial history, and which are in appropriate keeping with the gloomy character of the surrounding scenery.[19] The roof of bark had long since fallen and mingled with the soil, but the huge logs of pine, which had been hastily thrown together, still preserved their relative positions, though one angle of the work had given way under pressure, and threatened a speedy downfall to the remainder of the rustic edifice. While Heyward and his companions hesitated to approach a building so decayed, Hawkeye and the Indians entered within the low walls, not only without fear, but with obvious interest. While the former surveyed the ruins, both internally and externally, with the curiosity of one whose recollections were reviving at each moment, Chingachgook related to his son, in the language of the Delawares, and with the pride of a conqueror, the brief history of the skirmish which had been fought, in his youth, in that secluded spot. A strain of melancholy, however, blended with his triumph, rendering his voice, as usual, soft and musical.

In the mean time, the sisters gladly dismounted, and prepared to enjoy their halt in the coolness of the evening, and in a security which they believed nothing but the beasts of the forest could invade.

"Would not our resting-place have been more retired, my worthy friend," demanded the more vigilant Duncan, perceiving that the scout had already finished his short survey, "had we chosen a spot less known, and one more rarely visited than this?"

"Few live who know the block-house was ever raised," was the slow and musing answer; "'t is not often that books are made and narratives written, of such a skrimmage as was here fou't atween the Mohicans and the Mohawks, in a war of their own waging. I was then a younker, and went out with the Delawares, because I know'd they were a scandalized and wronged race. Forty days and forty nights did the imps crave our blood around this pile of logs, which I designed and partly reared, being, as you'll remember, no Indian myself, but a man without a cross. The Delawares lent themselves to the work, and we made it good, ten to

---

[19]Some years since, the writer was shooting in the vicinity of the ruins of Fort Oswego, which stands on the shores of Lake Ontario. His game was deer, and his chase a forest that stretched with little interruption, fifty miles inland. Unexpectedly he came upon six or eight ladders lying in the woods within a short distance of each other. They were rudely made, and much decayed. Wondering what could have assembled so many of these instruments in such a place, he sought an old man who resided near for the explanation.

During the war of 1776, Fort Oswego was held by the British. An expedition had been sent two hundred miles through the wilderness to surprise the fort. It appears that the Americans, on reaching the spot named, which was within a mile or two of the fort, first learned that they were expected, and in great danger of being cut off. They threw away their scaling-ladders, and made a rapid retreat. These ladders had lain unmolested thirty years, in the spot where they had thus been cast. [J.F.C.]

twenty, until our numbers were nearly equal, and then we sallied out upon the hounds and not a man of them ever got back to tell the fate of his party. Yes, yes; I was then young, and new to the sight of blood; and not relishing the thought that creatures who had spirits like myself should lay on the naked ground, to be torn asunder by beasts, or to bleach in the rains, I buried the dead with my own hands, under that very little hillock where you have placed yourselves; and no bad seat does it make neither, though it be raised by the bones of mortal men."

Heyward and the sisters arose, on the instant, from the grassy sepulchre; nor could the two latter, notwithstanding the terrific scenes they had so recently passed through, entirely suppress an emotion of natural horror, when they found themselves in such familiar contact with the grave of the dead Mohawks. The gray light, the gloomy little area of dark grass, surrounded by its border of brush, beyond which the pines rose, in breathing silence, apparently, into the very clouds, and the deathlike stillness of the vast forest, were all in unison to deepen such a sensation.

"They are gone, and they are harmless," continued Hawkeye, waving his hand, with a melancholy smile, at their manifest alarm: "they'll never shout the war-whoop nor strike a blow with the tomahawk again! And of all those who aided in placing them where they lie, Chingachgook and I only are living! The brothers and family of the Mohican formed our war party; and you see before you all that are now left of his race."

The eyes of the listeners involuntarily sought the forms of the Indians, with a compassionate interest in their desolate fortune. Their dark persons were still to be seen within the shadows of the block-house, the son listening to the relation of his father with that sort of intenseness which would be created by a narrative that redounded so much to the honor of those whose names he had long revered for their courage and savage virtues.

"I had thought the Delawares a pacific people," said Duncan, "and that they never waged war in person; trusting the defense of their lands to those very Mohawks that you slew!"

"'T is true in part," returned the scout, "and yet, at the bottom, 't is a wicked lie. Such a treaty was made in ages gone by, through the deviltries of the Dutchers, who wished to disarm the natives that had the best right to the country where they had settled themselves. The Mohicans, though a part of the same nation, having to deal with the English, never entered into the silly bargain, but kept to their manhood; as in truth did the Delawares, when their eyes were opened to their folly. You see before you a chief of the great Mohican Sagamores! Once his family could chase their deer over tracts of country wider than that which belongs to the Albany Patteroon, without crossing brook or hill that was not their own; but what is left to their descendant! He may find his six feet of earth when God chooses, and keep it in peace, perhaps, if he has a friend who will take the pains to sink his head so low that the ploughshares cannot reach it!"

"Enough!" said Heyward, apprehensive that the subject might lead to a discussion that would interrupt that harmony so necessary to the preservation of his fair companions: "we have journeyed far, and few among us are blessed with forms like that of yours, which seems to know neither fatigue nor weakness."

"The sinews and bones of a man carry me through it all," said the hunter, surveying his muscular limbs with a simplicity that betrayed the honest pleasure the compliment afforded him: "there are larger and heavier men to be found in the settlements, but you might travel many days in a city before you could meet one able to walk fifty miles without stopping to take breath, or who has kept the hounds within hearing during a chase of hours. However, as flesh and blood are not always the same, it is quite reasonable to suppose that the gentle ones are willing to rest, after all they have seen and done this day. Uncas, clear out the spring, while your father and I make a cover for their tender heads of these chestnut shoots, and a bed of grass and leaves."

The dialogue ceased, while the hunter and his companions busied themselves in preparations for the comfort and protection of those they guided. A spring, which many long years before had induced the natives to select the place for their temporary fortification, was soon cleared of leaves, and a fountain of crystal gushed from the bed, diffusing its waters over the verdant hillock. A corner of the building was then roofed in such a manner as to exclude the heavy dew of the climate, and piles of sweet shrubs and dried leaves were laid beneath it for the sisters to repose on.

While the diligent woodsmen were employed in this manner, Cora and Alice partook of that refreshment which duty required much more than inclination prompted them to accept. They then retired within the walls, and first offering up their thanksgivings for past mercies, and petitioning for a continuance of the Divine favor throughout the coming night, they laid their tender forms on the fragrant couch, and in spite of recollections and forebodings, soon sank into those slumbers which nature so imperiously demanded, and which were sweetened by hopes for the morrow. Duncan had prepared himself to pass the night in watchfulness near them, just without the ruin, but the scout, perceiving his intention, pointed towards Chingachgook, as he coolly disposed his own person on the grass, and said—

"The eyes of a white man are too heavy and too blind for such a watch as this! The Mohican will be our sentinel, therefore let us sleep."

"I proved myself a sluggard on my post during the past night," said Heyward, "and have less need of repose than you, who did more credit to the character of a soldier. Let all the party seek their rest, then, while I hold the guard."

"If we lay among the white tents of the 60th, and in front of an enemy like the French, I could not ask for a better watchman," returned the scout; "but in the darkness and among the signs of the wilderness your judgment would be like the folly of a child, and your vigilance thrown away. Do then, like Uncas and myself, sleep, and sleep in safety."

Heyward perceived, in truth, that the younger Indian had thrown his form on the side of the hillock while they were talking, like one who sought to make the most of the time allotted to rest, and that his example had been followed by David, whose voice literally "clove to his jaws," with the fever of his wound, heightened, as it was, by their toilsome march. Unwilling to prolong a useless discussion, the young man affected to comply, by posting his back against the logs of the blockhouse, in a half-recumbent posture, though resolutely determined, in his own mind, not to close an eye until he had delivered his precious charge into the arms of Munro himself. Hawkeye, believing he had prevailed, soon fell asleep, and a silence as deep as the solitude in which they had found it, pervaded the retired spot.

For many minutes Duncan succeeded in keeping his senses on the alert, and alive to every moaning sound that arose from the forest. His vision became more acute as the shades of evening settled on the place; and even after the stars were glimmering above his head, he was able to distinguish the recumbent forms of his companions, as they lay stretched on the grass, and to note the person of Chingachgook, who sat upright and motionless as one of the trees which formed the dark barrier on every side. He still heard the gentle breathings of the sisters, who lay within a few feet of him, and not a leaf was ruffled by the passing air, of which his ear did not detect the whispering sound. At length, however, the mournful notes of a whippoorwill became blended with the moanings of an owl; his heavy eyes occasionally sought the bright rays of the stars, and then he fancied he saw them through the fallen lids. At instants of momentary wakefulness he mistook a bush for his associate sentinel; his head next sank upon his shoulder, which, in its turn, sought the support of the ground; and finally his whole person became relaxed and pliant, and the young man sank into a deep sleep, dreaming that he was a knight of ancient chivalry, holding his midnight vigils before the tent of a recaptured princess, whose favor he did not despair of gaining, by such a proof of devotion and watchfulness.

How long the tired Duncan lay in this insensible state he never knew himself, but his slumbering visions had been long lost in total forgetfulness, when he was awakened by a light tap on the shoulder. Aroused by this signal, slight as it was, he sprang upon his feet with a confused recollection of the self-imposed duty he had assumed with the commencement of the night.

"Who comes?" he demanded, feeling for his sword at the place where it was usually suspended. "Speak! friend or enemy?"

"Friend," replied the low voice of Chingachgook; who, pointing upwards at the luminary which was shedding its mild light through the opening in the trees, directly in their bivouac, immediately added, in his rude English, "moon comes, and white man's fort far—far off; time to move, when sleep shuts both eyes of the Frenchman!"

"You say true! call up your friends, and bridle the horses, while I prepare my own companions for the march!"

"We are awake, Duncan," said the soft, silvery tones of Alice within the building, "and ready to travel very fast after so refreshing a sleep; but you have watched through the tedious night in our behalf, after having endured so much fatigue the livelong day!"

"Say, rather, I would have watched, but my treacherous eyes betrayed me; twice have I proved myself unfit for the trust I bear."

"Nay, Duncan, deny it not," interrupted the smiling Alice, issuing from the shadows of the building into the light of the moon, in all the loveliness of her freshened beauty; "I know you to be a heedless one, when self is the object of your care, and but too vigilant in favor of others. Can we not tarry here a little longer, while you find the rest you need? Cheerfully, most cheerfully, will Cora and I keep the vigils, while you, and all these brave men, endeavor to snatch a little sleep!"

"If shame could cure me of my drowsiness, I should never close an eye again," said the uneasy youth, gazing at the ingenuous countenance of Alice, where, however, in its sweet solicitude, he read nothing to confirm his half awakened suspicion. "It is but too true, that after leading you into danger by my heedlessness, I have not even the merit of guarding your pillows as should become a soldier."

"No one but Duncan himself should accuse Duncan of such a weakness. Go, then, and sleep; believe me, neither of us, weak girls as we are, will betray our watch."

The young man was relieved from the awkwardness of making any further protestations of his own demerits, by an exclamation from Chingachgook, and the attitude of riveted attention assumed by his son.

"The Mohicans hear an enemy!" whispered Hawkeye, who, by this time, in common with the whole party, was awake and stirring. "They scent danger in the wind!"

"God forbid!" exclaimed Heyward. "Surely we have had enough of bloodshed!"

While he spoke, however, the young soldier seized his rifle, and, advancing towards the front, prepared to atone for his venial remissness, by freely exposing his life in defense of those he attended.

"'T is some creature of the forest prowling around us in quest of food," he said, in a whisper, as soon as the low, and apparently distant sounds, which had startled the Mohicans, reached his own ears.

"Hist!" returned the attentive scout; "'t is man; even I can now tell his tread, poor as my senses are when compared to an Indian's! That scampering Huron has fallen in with one of Montcalm's outlying parties, and they have struck upon our trail. I should n't like, myself, to spill more human blood in this spot," he added, looking around with anxiety in his features, at the dim objects by which he was surrounded; "but what must be, must! Lead the horses into the block-house, Uncas; and, friends, do you follow to the same shelter. Poor and old as it is, it offers a cover, and has rung with the crack of a rifle afore to-night!"

He was instantly obeyed, the Mohicans leading the Narragansets within the ruin, whither the whole party repaired with the most guarded silence.

The sounds of approaching footsteps were now too distinctly audible to leave any doubts as to the nature of the interruption. They were soon mingled with voices calling to each other in an Indian dialect, which the hunter, in a whisper, affirmed to Heyward was the language of the Hurons. When the party reached the point where the horses had entered the thicket which surrounded the block-house, they were evidently at fault, having lost those marks which, until that moment, had directed their pursuit.

It would seem by the voices that twenty men were soon collected at that one spot, mingling their different opinions and advice in noisy clamor.

"The knaves know our weakness," whispered Hawkeye, who stood by the side of Heyward, in deep shade, looking through an opening in the logs, "or they would n't indulge their idleness in such a squaw's march. Listen to the reptiles! each man among them seems to have two tongues, and but a single leg."

Duncan, brave as he was in the combat, could not, in such a moment of painful suspense, make any reply to the cool and characteristic remark of the scout. He only grasped his rifle more firmly, and fastened his eyes upon the narrow opening, through which he gazed upon the moonlight view with increasing anxiety. The deeper tones of one who spoke as having authority were next heard, amid a silence that denoted the respect with which his orders, or rather advice, was received. After which, by the rustling of leaves, and cracking of dried twigs, it was apparent the savages were separating in pursuit of the lost trail. Fortunately for the pursued, the light of the moon, while it shed a flood of mild lustre upon the little area around the ruin, was not sufficiently strong to penetrate the deep arches of the forest, where the objects still lay in deceptive shadow. The search proved fruitless; for so short and sudden had been the passage from the faint path the travellers had journeyed into the thicket, that every trace of their footsteps was lost in the obscurity of the woods.

It was not long, however, before the restless savages were heard beating the brush, and gradually approaching the inner edge of that dense border of young chestnuts which encircled the little area.

"They are coming," muttered Heyward, endeavoring to thrust his rifle through the chink in the logs; "let us fire on their approach."

"Keep everything in the shade," returned the scout; "the snapping of a flint, or even the smell of a single karnel of the brimstone, would bring the hungry varlets upon us in a body. Should it please God that we must give battle for the scalps, trust to the experience of men who know the ways of the savages, and who are not often backward when the war-whoop is howled."

Duncan cast his eyes behind him, and saw that the trembling sisters were cowering in the far corner of the building, while the Mohicans stood in the shadow, like two upright posts, ready, and apparently willing, to strike when the blow should be needed. Curbing his impatience, he again looked out upon the area, and awaited the result in silence. At that instant the thicket opened, and a tall and armed Huron advanced a few paces into the open space. As he gazed upon the silent block-house, the moon fell upon his swarthy countenance, and betrayed its surprise and curiosity. He made the exclamation which usually accompanies the former emotion in an Indian, and, calling in a low voice, soon drew a companion to his side.

These children of the woods stood together for several moments pointing at the crumbling edifice, and conversing in the unintelligible language of their tribe. They then approached, though with slow and cautious steps, pausing every instant to look at the building, like startled deer, whose curiosity struggled powerfully with their awakened apprehensions for the mastery. The foot of one of them suddenly rested on the mound, and he stooped to examine its nature. At this moment, Heyward observed that the scout loosened his knife in its sheath, and lowered the muzzle of his rifle. Imitating these movements, the young man prepared himself for the struggle, which now seemed inevitable.

The savages were so near that the least motion in one of the horses, or even a breath louder than common, would have betrayed the fugitives. But, in discovering the character of the mound, the attention of the Hurons appeared directed to a different object. They spoke together, and the sounds of their voices were low and solemn, as if influenced by a reverence that was deeply blended with awe. Then they drew warily back, keeping their eyes riveted on the ruin, as if they expected to see the apparitions of the dead issue from its silent walls, until having reached the boundary of the area, they moved slowly into the thicket, and disappeared.

Hawkeye dropped the breech of his rifle to the earth, and drawing a long, free breath, exclaimed in an audible whisper,—

"Aye! they respect the dead, and it has this time saved their own lives, and, it may be, the lives of better men too."

Heyward lent his attention for a single moment to his companion, but without replying he again turned towards those who just then interested him more. He heard the two Hurons leave the bushes, and it was soon plain that all the pursuers were gathered about them, in deep attention to their report. After a few minutes of earnest and solemn dialogue, altogether different from the noisy clamor with which they had first collected about the spot, the sounds grew fainter and more distant, and finally were lost in the depths of the forest.

Hawkeye waited until a signal from the listening Chingachgook assured him that every sound from the retiring party was completely swallowed by the distance, when he motioned to Heyward to lead forth the horses, and to assist the sisters into their saddles. The instant this was done, they issued through the broken gateway, and stealing out by a direction opposite to the one by which they had entered, they quitted the spot, the sisters casting furtive glances at the silent grave and crumbling ruin, as they left the soft light of the moon, to bury themselves in the gloom of the woods.

CHAPTER XIV

Watch.—Qui est là?
Puc.—Paisans, pauvres gens de France.
SHAKESPEARE, *King Henry VI.*, First Part, III. ii. 14.

During the rapid movement from the block-house, and until the party was deeply buried in the forest, each individual was too much interested in the escape to hazard a word even in whispers. The scout resumed his post in the advance, though his steps, after he had thrown a safe distance between himself and his enemies, were more deliberate than in their previous march, in consequence of his utter ignorance of the localities of the surrounding woods. More than once he halted to consult with his confederates, the Mohicans, pointing upwards at the moon, and examining the barks of the trees with care. In these brief pauses Heyward and the sisters listened, with senses rendered doubly acute by the danger, to detect any symptoms which might announce the proximity of their foes. At such moments it seemed as if a vast range of country lay buried in eternal sleep; not the least sound arising from the forest, unless it was the distant and scarcely audible rippling of a water-course. Birds, beasts, and man appeared to slumber alike, if, indeed, any of the latter were to be found in that wide tract of wilderness. But the sounds of the rivulet, feeble and murmuring as they were, relieved the guides at once from no trifling embarrassment, and towards it they immediately held their way.

When the banks of the little stream were gained, Hawkeye made another halt; and, taking the moccasins from his feet, he invited Heyward and Gamut to follow his example. He then entered the water, and for near an hour they travelled in the bed of the brook, leaving no trail. The moon had already sunk into an immense pile of black clouds, which lay impending above the western horizon, when they issued from the low and devious water-course to rise again to the light and level of the sandy but wooded plain. Here the scout seemed to be once more at home, for he held on his way with the certainty and diligence of a man who moved in the security of his own knowledge. The path soon became more uneven, and the travellers could plainly perceive that the mountains drew nigher to them on each hand, and that they were, in truth, about entering one of their gorges. Suddenly Hawkeye made a pause, and waiting until he was joined by the whole party, he spoke, though in tones so low and cautious that they added to the solemnity of his words, in the quiet and darkness of the place.

"It is easy to know the pathways and to find the licks and water-courses of the wilderness," he said; "but who that saw this spot could venture to say that a mighty army was at rest among yonder silent trees and barren mountains?"

"We are then at no great distance from William Henry?" said Heyward, advancing nigher to the scout.

"It is yet a long and weary path, and when and where to strike it, is now our greatest difficulty. See," he said, pointing through the trees towards a spot where a little basin of water reflected the stars from its placid bosom, "here is the 'bloody pond;' and I am on ground that I have not only often travelled, but over which I have fou't the enemy from the rising to the setting sun."

"Ha! that sheet of dull and dreary water, then, is the sepulchre of the brave men who fell in the contest. I have heard it named, but never have I stood on its banks before."

"Three battles did we make with the Dutch-Frenchman[20] in a day," continued Hawkeye, pursuing the train of his own thoughts rather than replying to the remark of Duncan. "He met us hard by, in our outward march to ambush his advance, and scattered us, like driven deer, through the defile, to the shores of Horican. Then we rallied behind our fallen trees, and made head against him, under Sir William—who was made Sir William for that very deed; and well did we pay him for the disgrace of the morning! Hundreds of Frenchmen saw the sun that day for the last time; and even their leader, Dieskau himself, fell into our hands, so cut and torn with the lead that he has gone back to his own country, unfit for further acts in war."

"'T was a noble repulse!" exclaimed Heyward, in the heat of his youthful ardor; "the fame of it reached us early, in our southern army."

"Aye! but it did not end there. I was sent by Major Effingham, at Sir William's own bidding, to outflank the French, and carry the tidings of their disaster across the portage to the fort on the Hudson. Just here-away, where you see the trees rise into a mountain swell, I met a party coming down to our aid, and I led them where the enemy were taking their meal, little dreaming that they had not finished the bloody work of the day."

"And you surprised them?"

"If death can be a surprise to men who are thinking only of the cravings of their appetites. We gave them but little breathing time, for they had borne hard upon us in the fight of the morning, and there were few in our party who had not lost friend or relative by their hands. When all was over, the dead, and some say the dying, were cast into that little pond. These eyes have seen its waters colored with blood, as natural water never yet flowed from the bowels of the 'arth."

"It was a convenient, and, I trust, will prove a peaceful grave for a soldier. You have, then, seen much service on this frontier?"

"I!" said the scout, erecting his tall person with an air of military pride; "there are not many echoes among these hills that have n't rung with the crack of my rifle, nor is there the space of a square mile atwixt Horican and the river that Killdeer hasn't dropped a living body on, be it an enemy or be it a brute beast. As for the grave, there, being as quiet as you mention, it is another matter. There are them in the camp who say and think man, to lie still, should not be buried while the breath is in the body; and certain it is that in the hurry of that evening the doctors had but little time to say who was living and who was dead. Hist! see you nothing walking on the shore of the pond?"

"'T is not probable that any are as houseless as ourselves in this dreary forest."

"Such as he may care but little for house or shelter, and night dew can never wet a body that passes its days in the water," returned the scout, grasping the shoulder of Heyward with such convulsive strength as to make the young soldier painfully

---

[20]Baron Dieskau, a German, in the service of France. A few years previously to the period of the tale, this officer was defeated by Sir William Johnson of Johnstown, New York, on the shores of Lake George. [J.F.C.]

sensible how much superstitious terror had got the mastery of a man usually so dauntless.

"By heaven! there is a human form, and it approaches! Stand to your arms, my friends; for we know not whom we encounter."

"Qui vive?" demanded a stern, quick voice, which sounded like a challenge from another world, issuing out of that solitary and solemn place.

"What says it?" whispered the scout; "it speaks neither Indian nor English!"

"Qui vive?" repeated the same voice, which was quickly followed by the rattling of arms and a menacing attitude.

"France!" cried Heyward, advancing from the shadow of the trees to the shore of the pond, within a few yards of the sentinel.

"D'où venez-vous—où allez-vous, d'aussi bonne heure?" demanded the grenadier, in the language and with the accent of a man from old France.

"Je viens de la découverte, et je vais me coucher."

"Etes-vous officier du roi?"

"Sans doute, mon camarade; me prends-tu pour un provincial? Je suis capitaine de chasseurs (Heyward well knew that the other was of a regiment in the line); j'ai ici, avec moi, les filles du commandant de la fortification. Aha! tu en as entendu parler! je les ai fait prisonnières près de l'autre forte, et je les conduis au général."

"Ma foi! mesdames; j'en suis faché pour vous," exclaimed the young soldier, touching his cap with grace; "mais—fortune de guerre! vous trouverez notre général un brave homme, et bien poli avec les dames."

"C'est le caractère des gens de guerre," said Cora, with admirable self-possession. "Adieu, mon ami; je vous souhaiterais un devoir plus agéable à remplir."

The soldier made a low and humble acknowledgment for her civility; and Heyward adding a "Bonne nuit, mon camarade," they moved deliberately forward, leaving the sentinel pacing the banks of the silent pond, little suspecting an enemy of so much effrontery, and humming to himself those words, which were recalled to his mind by the sight of women, and perhaps by recollections of his own distant and beautiful France—

"Vive le vin, vive l'amour," etc., etc.

"'T is well you understood the knave!" whispered the scout, when they had gained a little distance from the place, and letting his rifle fall into the hollow of his arm again; "I soon saw that he was one of them uneasy Frenchers; and well for him it was that his speech was friendly and his wishes kind, or a place might have been found for his bones amongst those of his countrymen."

He was interrupted by a long and heavy groan which arose from the little basin, as though, in truth, the spirits of the departed lingered about their watery sepulchre.

"Surely it was of flesh!" continued the scout; "no spirit could handle its arms so steadily!"

"It *was* of flesh; but whether the poor fellow still belongs to this world may well be doubted," said Heyward, glancing his eyes around him, and missing Chingachgook from their little band. Another groan, more faint than the former, was succeeded by a heavy and sullen plunge into the water, and all was as still again as if the borders of the dreary pool had never been awakened from the silence of creation. While they yet hesitated in uncertainty, the form of the Indian was seen gliding out of the thicket. As the chief rejoined them, with one hand he attached the reeking scalp of the unfortunate young Frenchman to his girdle, and with the other he replaced the knife and tomahawk that had drunk his blood. He then took his wonted station, with the air of a man who believed he had done a deed of merit.

The scout dropped one end of his rifle to the earth, and leaning his hands on the other, he stood musing in profound silence. Then shaking his head in a mournful manner, he muttered,—

"'T would have been a cruel and an unhuman act for a white-skin; but 't is the gift and natur' of an Indian, and I suppose it should not be denied. I could wish, though, it had befallen an accursed Mingo, rather than that gay young boy from the old countries."

"Enough!" said Heyward, apprehensive the unconscious sisters might comprehend the nature of the detention, and conquering his disgust by a train of reflections very much like that of the hunter; "'t is done; and though better it were left undone, cannot be amended. You see we are, too obviously, within the sentinels of the enemy; what course do you propose to follow?"

"Yes," said Hawkeye, rousing himself again, "'t is as you say, too late to harbor further thoughts about it. Aye, the French have gathered around the fort in good earnest, and we have a delicate needle to thread in passing them."

"And but little time to do it in," added Heyward, glancing his eyes upwards, towards the bank of vapor that concealed the setting moon.

"And little time to do it in!" repeated the scout. "The thing may be done in two fashions, by the help of Providence, without which it may not be done at all."

"Name them quickly, for time presses."

"One would be to dismount the gentle ones, and let their beasts range the plain; by sending the Mohicans in front, we might then cut a lane through their sentries, and enter the fort over the dead bodies."

"It will not do—it will not do!" interrupted the generous Heyward; "a soldier might force his way in this manner, but never with such a convoy."

"'T would be, indeed, a bloody path for such tender feet to wade in," returned the equally reluctant scout; "but I thought it befitting my manhood to name it. We must then turn on our trail and get without the line of their lookouts, when we will bend short to the west, and enter the mountains, where I can hide you so that all the devil's hounds in Montcalm's pay would be thrown off the scent, for months to come."

"Let it be done, and that instantly."

Further words were unnecessary; for Hawkeye, merely uttering the mandate to "follow," moved along the route by which they had just entered their present critical and even dangerous situation. Their progress, like their late dialogue, was guarded, and without noise; for none knew at what moment a passing patrol, or a crouching picket of the enemy, might rise upon their path. As they held their silent way along the margin of the pond, again Heyward and the scout stole furtive glances at its appalling dreariness. They looked in vain for the form they had so recently seen stalking along its silent shores, while a low and regular wash of the little waves, by announcing that the waters were not yet subsided, furnished a frightful memorial of the deed of blood they had just witnessed. Like all that passing and gloomy scene, the low basin, however, quickly melted in the darkness, and became blended with the mass of black objects in the rear of the travellers.

Hawkeye soon deviated from the line of their retreat, and striking off towards the mountains which form the western boundary of the narrow plain, he led his followers, with swift steps, deep within the shadows that were cast from their high and broken summits. The route was now painful, lying over ground ragged with rocks, and intersected ravines, and their progress proportionately slow. Bleak and black hills lay on every side of them, compensating in some degree for the additional toil of the march, by the sense of security they imparted. At length the party began slowly to rise a steep and rugged ascent, by a path that curiously wound among rocks and trees, avoiding the one, and supported by the other, in a manner that showed it had been devised by men long practiced in the arts of the wilderness. As they gradually rose from the level of the valleys, the thick darkness which usually precedes the approach of day began to disperse, and objects were seen in the plain and palpable colors with which they had been gifted by nature. When they issued from the stunted woods which clung to the barren sides of the mountain, upon a flat and mossy rock that formed its summit, they met the morning, as it came blushing above the green pines of a hill that lay on the opposite side of the valley of the Horican.

The scout now told the sisters to dismount; and taking the bridles from the mouths, and the saddles off the backs of the jaded beasts, he turned them loose, to glean a scanty subsistence among the shrubs and meagre herbage of that elevated region.

"Go," he said, "and seek your food where natur' gives it you; and beware that you become not food to ravenous wolves yourselves among these hills."

"Have we no further need of them?" demanded Heyward.

"See, and judge with your own eyes," said the scout, advancing towards the eastern brow of the mountain, whither he beckoned for the whole party to follow; "if it was as easy to look into the heart of man as it is to spy out the nakedness of Montcalm's camp from this spot, hypocrites would grow scarce, and the cunning of a Mingo might prove a losing game, compared to the honesty of a Delaware."

When the travellers reached the verge of the precipice, they saw at a glance the truth of the scout's declaration, and the admirable foresight with which he had led them to their commanding station.

The mountain on which they stood, elevated, perhaps, a thousand feet in the air, was a high cone that rose a little in advance of that range which stretches for miles along the western shores of the lake, until meeting its sister piles, beyond the water, it ran off towards the Canadas in confused and broken masses of rock, thinly sprinkled with evergreens. Immediately at the feet of the party, the southern shore of the Horican swept in a broad semicircle, from mountain to mountain, marking a wide strand, that soon rose into an uneven and somewhat elevated plain. To the north, stretched the limpid and, as it appeared from that dizzy height, the narrow sheet of the "holy lake," indented with numberless bays, embellished by fantastic headlands, and dotted with countless islands. At the distance of a few leagues, the bed of the waters became lost among mountains, or was wrapped in the masses of vapor that came slowly rolling along their bosom, before a light morning air. But a narrow opening between the crests of the hills pointed out the passage by which they found their way still further north, to spread their pure and ample sheets again, before pouring out their tribute into the distant Champlain. To the south stretched the defile, or rather broken plain, so often mentioned. For several miles in this direction, the mountains appeared reluctant to yield their dominion, but within reach of the eye they diverged, and finally melted into the level and sandy lands, across which we have accompanied our adventurers in their double journey. Along both ranges of hills, which bounded the opposite sides of the lake and valley, clouds of light vapor were rising in spiral wreaths from the uninhabited woods, looking like the smokes of hidden cottages; or rolled lazily down the declivities, to mingle with the fogs of the lower land. A single, solitary, snow-white cloud floated above the valley, and marked the spot beneath which lay the silent pool of the "bloody pond."

Directly on the shore of the lake, and nearer to its western than to its eastern margin, lay the extensive earthen ramparts and low buildings of William Henry. Two of the sweeping bastions appeared to rest on the water which washed their bases, while a deep ditch and extensive morasses guarded its other sides and angles. The land had been cleared of wood for a reasonable distance around the work, but every other part of the scene lay in the green livery of nature, except where the limpid water mellowed the view, or the bold rocks thrust their black and naked heads above the undulating outline of the mountain ranges. In its front might be seen the scattered sentinels, who held a weary watch against their numerous foes; and within the walls themselves, the travellers looked down upon men still drowsy with a night of vigilance. Towards the southeast, but in immediate contact with the fort, was an entrenched camp, posted on a rocky eminence, that would have been far more eligible for the work itself, in which Hawkeye pointed out the presence of those auxiliary regiments that had so recently left the Hudson in their company. From the woods, a little further to the south, rose numerous dark and lurid smokes, that were easily to be distinguished from the purer exhalations of the springs, and which the scout also showed to Heyward, as evidences that the enemy lay in force in that direction.

But the spectacle which most concerned the young soldier was on the western bank of the lake, though quite near to its southern termination. On a strip of land, which appeared, from his stand, too narrow to contain such an army, but which, in truth, extended many hundreds of yards from the shores of the Horican to the base of the mountain, were to be seen the white tents and military engines of an encampment of ten thousand men. Batteries were already thrown up in their front, and even while the spectators above them were looking down, with such different emotions, on a scene which lay like a map beneath their feet, the roar of artillery rose from the valley, and passed off in thundering echoes along the eastern hills.

"Morning is just touching them below," said the deliberate and musing scout, "and the watchers have a mind to wake up the sleepers by the sound of cannon. We are a few hours too late! Montcalm has already filled the woods with his accursed Iroquois."

"The place is, indeed, invested," returned Duncan, "but is there no expedient by which we may enter? capture in the works would be far preferable to falling again into the hands of roving Indians."

"See!" exclaimed the scout, unconsciously directing the attention of Cora to the quarters of her own father, "how that shot has made the stones fly from the side of the commandant's house! Aye! these Frenchers will pull it to pieces faster than it was put together, solid and thick though it be."

"Heyward, I sicken at the sight of danger that I cannot share," said the undaunted but anxious daughter. "Let us go to Montcalm and demand admission; he dare not deny a child the boon."

"You would scarce find the tent of the Frenchman with the hair on your head," said the blunt scout. "If I had but one of the thousand boats which lie empty along that shore, it might be done. Ha! here will soon be an end of the firing, for yonder comes a fog that will turn day to night, and make an Indian arrow more dangerous than a moulded cannon. Now, if you are equal to the work, and will follow, I will make a push; for I long to get down into that camp, if it be only to scatter some Mingo dogs that I see lurking in the skirts of yonder thicket of birch."

"We are equal," said Cora, firmly: "on such an errand we will follow to any danger."

The scout turned to her with a smile of honest and cordial approbation, as he answered,—

"I would I had a thousand men, of brawny limbs and quick eyes, that feared death as little as you! I'd send them jabbering Frenchers back into their den again afore the week was ended, howling like so many fettered hounds or hungry wolves. But stir," he added, turning from her to the rest of the party, "the fog comes rolling down so fast, we shall have but just the time to meet it on the plain, and use it as a cover. Remember, if any accident should befall me to keep the air blowing on your left cheeks—or rather, follow the Mohicans; they'd scent their way, be it in day or be it at night."

He then waved his hand for them to follow, and threw himself down the steep declivity, with free but careful footsteps. Heyward assisted the sisters to descend, and in a few minutes they were all far down a mountain whose sides they had climbed with so much toil and pain.

The direction taken by Hawkeye soon brought the travellers to the level of the plain, nearly opposite to a sally-port in the western curtain of the fort, which lay, itself, at the distance of about half a mile from the point where he halted to allow Duncan to come up with his charge. In their eagerness, and favored by the nature of the ground, they had anticipated the fog, which was rolling heavily down the lake, and it became necessary to pause, until the mists had wrapped the camp of the enemy in their fleecy mantle. The Mohicans profited by the delay, to steal out of the woods, and to make a survey of surrounding objects. They were followed at a little distance by the scout, with a view to profit early by their report, and to obtain some faint knowledge for himself of the more immediate localities.

In a very few moments he returned, his face reddened with vexation, while he muttered his disappointment in words of no very gentle import.

"Here has the cunning Frenchman been posting a picket directly in our path," he said; "red-skins and whites; and we shall be as likely to fall into their midst as to pass them in the fog!"

"Cannot we make a circuit to avoid the danger," asked Heyward, "and come into our path again when it is passed?"

"Who that once bends from the line of his march in a fog can tell when or how to turn to find it again! The mists of Horican are not like the curls from a peace-pipe, or the smoke which settles above a mosquito fire."

He was yet speaking, when a crashing sound was heard, and a cannon-ball entered the thicket, striking the body of a sapling and rebounding to the earth, its force being much expended by previous resistance. The Indians followed instantly like busy attendants on the terrible messenger, and Uncas commenced speaking earnestly and with much action in the Delaware tongue.

"It may be so, lad," muttered the scout, when he had ended; "for desperate fevers are not to be treated like a toothache. Come, then, the fog is shutting in."

"Stop!" cried Heyward; "first explain your expectations."

"'T is soon done, and a small hope it is; but it is better than nothing. This shot that you see," added the scout, kicking the harmless iron with his foot, "has ploughed the 'arth in its road from the fort, and we shall hunt for the furrow it has made when all other signs may fail. No more words, but follow, or the fog may leave us in the middle of our path, a mark for both armies to shoot at."

Heyward perceiving that, in fact, a crisis had arrived, when acts were more required than words, placed himself between the sisters, and drew them swiftly forward, keeping the dim figure of their leader in his eye. It was soon apparent that Hawkeye had not magnified the power of the fog, for before they had proceeded twenty yards it was difficult for the different individuals of the party to distinguish each other in the vapor.

They had made their little circuit to the left, and were already inclining again towards the right, having, as Heyward thought, got over nearly half the distance to the friendly works, when his ears were saluted with the fierce summons, apparently within twenty feet of them, of—

"Qui va là?"

"Push on!" whispered the scout, once more bending to the left.

"Push on!" repeated Heyward; when the summons was renewed by a dozen voices, each of which seemed charged with menace.

"C'est moi," cried Duncan, dragging, rather than leading those he supported, swiftly onward.

"Bête!—qui?—moi!"

"Ami de la France."

"Tu m'as plus l'air d'un *ennemi* de la France; arrête! ou pardieu je te ferai ami du diable. Non! feu, camarades, feu!"

The order was instantly obeyed, and the fog was stirred by the explosion of fifty muskets. Happily, the aim was bad, and the bullets cut the air in a direction a little different from that taken by the fugitives; though still so nigh them, that to the unpracticed ears of David and the two females, it appeared as if they whistled within a few inches of the organs. The outcry was renewed, and the order, not only to fire again, but to pursue, was too plainly audible. When Heyward briefly explained the meaning of the words they heard, Hawkeye halted, and spoke with quick decision and great firmness.

"Let us deliver our fire," he said; "they will believe it a sortie, and give way, or they will wait for reënforcements."

The scheme was well conceived, but failed in its effect. The instant the French heard the pieces, it seemed as if the plain was alive with men, muskets rattling along its whole extent, from the shores of the lake to the furthest boundary of the woods.

"We shall draw their entire army upon us, and bring on a general assault," said Duncan; "lead on, my friend, for your own life, and ours."

The scout seemed willing to comply; but, in the hurry of the moment, and in the change of position, he had lost the direction. In vain he turned either cheek towards the light air; they felt equally cool. In this dilemma, Uncas lighted on the furrow of the cannon-ball, where it had cut the ground in three adjacent ant-hills.

"Give me the range!" said Hawkeye, bending to catch a glimpse of the direction, and then instantly moving onward.

Cries, oaths, voices calling to each other, and the reports of muskets, were now quick and incessant, and, apparently, on every side of them. Suddenly, a strong glare of light flashed across the scene, the fog rolled upwards in thick wreaths, and several cannon belched across the plain, and the roar was thrown heavily back from the bellowing echoes of the mountain.

"'T is from the fort!" exclaimed Hawkeye, turning short on his tracks; "and we, like stricken fools, were rushing to the woods, under the very knives of the Maquas."

The instant their mistake was rectified, the whole party retraced the error with the utmost diligence. Duncan willingly relinquished the support of Cora to the arm of Uncas, and Cora as readily accepted the welcome assistance. Men, hot and angry in pursuit, were evidently on their footsteps, and each instant threatened their capture, if not their destruction.

"Point de quartier aux coquins!" cried an eager pursuer, who seemed to direct the operations of the enemy.

"Stand firm, and be ready, my gallant 60ths!" suddenly exclaimed a voice above them; "wait to see the enemy; fire low, and sweep the glacis."

"Father! father!" exclaimed a piercing cry from out the mist; "it is I! Alice! thy own Elsie! spare, oh! save your daughters!"

"Hold!" shouted the former speaker, in the awful tones of parental agony, the sound reaching even to the woods, and rolling back in solemn echo. "'T is she! God has restored me my children! Throw open the sally-port; to the field, 60ths, to the field; pull not a trigger, lest ye kill my lambs! Drive off these dogs of France with your steel."

Duncan heard the grating of the rusty hinges, and darting to the spot, directed by the sound, he met a long line of dark-red warriors, passing swiftly towards the glacis. He knew them for his own battalion of the royal Americans, and flying to their head, soon swept every trace of his pursuers from before the works.

For an instant, Cora and Alice had stood trembling and bewildered by this unexpected desertion; but, before either had leisure for speech or even thought, an officer of gigantic frame, whose locks were bleached with years and service, but whose air of military grandeur had been rather softened than destroyed by time, rushed out of the body of the mist, and folded them to his bosom, while large scalding tears rolled down his pale and wrinkled cheeks, and he exclaimed, in the peculiar accent of Scotland,—

"For this I thank thee, Lord! Let danger come as it will, thy servant is now prepared!"

CHAPTER XV

Then go we in, to know his embassy;
Which I could with a ready guess declare,
Before the Frenchman speak a word of it.
SHAKESPEARE, *King Henry V.*, I. i. 95.

A few succeeding days were passed amid the privations, the uproar, and the dangers of the siege, which was vigorously pressed by a power against whose approaches Munro possessed no competent means of resistance. It appeared as if Webb, with his army, which lay slumbering on the banks of the Hudson, had utterly forgotten the straits to which his countrymen were reduced. Montcalm had filled the woods of the portage with his savages, every yell and whoop from whom rang through the British encampment, chilling the hearts of men who were already but too much disposed to magnify the danger.

Not so, however, with the besieged. Animated by the words, and stimulated by the examples, of their leaders, they had found their courage, and maintained their ancient reputation, with a zeal that did justice to the stern character of their commander. As if satisfied with the toil of marching through the wilderness to encounter his enemy, the French general, though of approved skill, had neglected to seize the adjacent mountains; whence the besieged might have been exterminated with impunity, and which, in the more modern warfare of the country, would not have been neglected for a single hour. This sort of contempt for eminences, or rather dread of the labor of ascending them, might have been termed the besetting weakness of the warfare of the period. It originated in the simplicity of the Indian contests, in which, from the nature of the combats, and the density of the forests, fortresses were rare, and artillery next to useless. The carelessness engendered by these usages descended even to the war of the Revolution, and lost the States the important fortress of Ticonderoga, opening a way for the army of Burgoyne into what was then the bosom of the country. We look back at this ignorance, or infatuation, whichever it may be called, with wonder, knowing that the neglect of an eminence, whose difficulties, like those of Mount Defiance, have been so greatly exaggerated, would at the present time prove fatal to the reputation of the engineer who had planned the works at their base, or to that of the general whose lot it was to defend them.

The tourist, the valetudinarian, or the amateur of the beauties of nature, who, in the train of his four-in-hand, now rolls through the scenes we have attempted to describe, in quest of information, health, or pleasure, or floats steadily towards his object on those artificial waters which have sprung up under the administration of a statesman[21] who has dared to stake his political character on the hazardous issue, is not to suppose that his ancestors traversed those hills, or struggled with the same currents, with equal facility. The transportation of a single heavy gun was often considered equal to a victory gained; if, happily, the difficulties of the passage had not so far separated it from its necessary concomitant, the ammunition, as to render it no more than a useless tube of unweildy iron.

The evils of this state of things pressed heavily on the fortunes of the resolute Scotsman who now defended William Henry. Though his adversary neglected the hills, he had planted his batteries with judgment on the plain, and caused them to be served with vigor and skill. Against this assault, the besieged could only oppose the imperfect and hasty preparations of a fortress in the wilderness.

It was in the afternoon of the fifth day of the siege, and the fourth of his own service in it, that Major Heyward profited by a parley that had just been beaten, by repairing to the ramparts of one of the water bastions, to breathe the cool air from the lake, and to take a survey of the progress of the siege. He was alone, if the solitary sentinel who paced the mound be excepted; for the artillerists had hastened also to profit by the temporary suspension of their arduous duties. The evening was delightfully calm, and the light air from the limpid water fresh and soothing. It seemed as if, with the termination to the roar of artillery and the plunging of shot, nature had also seized the moment to assume her mildest and most captivating form. The sun poured down his parting glory on the scene, without the oppression of those fierce rays that belong to the climate and the season. The mountains looked green, and fresh, and lovely; tempered with the milder light, or softened in shadow, as thin vapors floated between them and the sun. The numerous islands rested on the bosom of the Horican, some low and sunken, as if imbedded in the waters, and others appearing to hover above the element, in little

---

[21]Evidently the late De Witt Clinton, who died governor of New York in 1828. [J.F.C.]

hillocks of green velvet, among which the fishermen of the beleaguering army peacefully rowed their skiffs, or floated at rest on the glassy mirror, in quiet pursuit of their employment.

The scene was at once animated and still. All that pertained to nature was sweet, or simply grand; while those parts which depended on the temper and movements of man were lively and playful.

Two little spotless flags were abroad, the one on a salient angle of the fort, and the other on the advanced battery of the besiegers; emblems of the truce which existed, not only to the acts, but it would seem, also, to the enmity of the combatants.

Behind these, again, swung, heavily opening and closing in silken folds, the rival standards of England and France.

A hundred gay and thoughtless young Frenchmen were drawing a net to the pebbly beach, within dangerous proximity to the sullen but silent cannon of the fort, while the eastern mountain was sending back the loud shouts and gay merriment that attended their sport. Some were rushing eagerly to enjoy the aquatic games of the lake, and others were already toiling their way up the neighboring hills, with the restless curiosity of their nation. To all these sports and pursuits, those of the enemy who watched the besieged, and the besieged themselves, were, however, merely the idle, though sympathizing spectators. Here and there a picket had indeed raised a song, or mingled in a dance, which had drawn the dusky savages around them, from their lairs in the forest. In short, everything wore rather the appearance of a day of pleasure, than of an hour stolen from the dangers and toil of a bloody and vindictive warfare.

Duncan had stood in a musing attitude, contemplating this scene a few minutes, when his eyes were directed to the glacis in front of the sallyport already mentioned, by the sounds of approaching footsteps. He walked to an angle of the bastion, and beheld the scout advancing, under the custody of a French officer, to the body of the fort. The countenance of Hawkeye was haggard and careworn, and his air dejected, as though he felt the deepest degradation at having fallen into the power of his enemies. He was without his favorite weapon, and his arms were even bound behind him with thongs, made of the skin of a deer. The arrival of flags, to cover the messengers of summons, had occurred so often of late, that when Heyward first threw his careless glance on this group, he expected to see another of the officers of the enemy, charged with a similar office; but the instant he recognized the tall person, and still sturdy, though downcast features of his friend, the woodsman, he started with surprise, and turned to descend from the bastion into the bosom of the work.

The sounds of other voices, however, caught his attention, and for a moment caused him to forget his purpose. At the inner angle of the mound he met the sisters, walking along the parapet, in search, like himself, of air and relief from confinement. They had not met from that painful moment when he deserted them on the plain only to assure their safety. He had parted from them worn with care, and jaded with fatigue; he now saw them refreshed and blooming, though timid and anxious. Under such an inducement, it will cause no surprise that the young man lost sight, for a time, of other objects in order to address them. He was, however, anticipated by the voice of the ingenuous and youthful Alice.

"Ah! thou truant! thou recreant knight! he who abandons his damsels in the very lists!" she cried; "here have we been days, nay, ages, expecting you at our feet, imploring mercy and forgetfulness of your craven backsliding, or, I should rather say, backrunning—for verily you fled in a manner that no stricken deer, as our worthy friend the scout would say, could equal!"

"You know that Alice means our thanks and our blessings," added the graver and more thoughtful Cora. "In truth, we have a little wondered why you should so rigidly absent yourself from a place where the gratitude of the daughters might receive the support of a parent's thanks."

"Your father himself could tell you, that though absent from your presence, I have not been altogether forgetful of your safety," returned the young man; "the mastery of yonder village of huts," pointing to the neighboring entrenched camp, "has been keenly disputed; and he who holds it is sure to be possessed of this fort, and that which it contains. My days and my nights have all been passed there since we separated, because I thought that duty called me thither. But," he added with an air of chagrin, which he endeavored, though unsuccessfully, to conceal, "had I been aware that what I then believed a soldier's conduct could so be construed, shame would have been added to the list of reasons."

"Heyward!—Duncan!" exclaimed Alice, bending forward to read his half-averted countenance, until a lock of her golden hair rested on her flushed cheek, and nearly concealed the tear that had started to her eye; "did I think this idle tongue of mine had pained you, I would silence it forever. Cora can say, if Cora would, how justly we have prized your services, and how deep—I had almost said, how fervent—is our gratitude."

"And will Cora attest the truth of this?" cried Duncan, suffering the cloud to be chased from his countenance by a smile of open pleasure. "What says our graver sister? Will she find an excuse for the neglect of the knight in the duty of a soldier?"

Cora made no immediate answer, but turned her face towards the water, as if looking on the sheet of the Horican. When she did bend her dark eyes on the young man, they were yet filled with an expression of anguish that at once drove every thought but that of kind solicitude from his mind.

"You are not well, dearest Miss Munro!" he exclaimed; "we have trifled while you are in suffering."

"'T is nothing," she answered, refusing his offered support with feminine reserve. "That I cannot see the sunny side of the picture of life, like this artless but ardent enthusiast," she added, laying her hand lightly, but affectionately, on the arm of her sister, "is the penalty of experience, and, perhaps, the misfortune of my nature. See," she continued, as if determined to shake off infirmity, in a sense of duty; "look around you, Major Heyward, and tell me what a prospect is this for the daughter of a soldier whose greatest happiness is his honor and his military renown."

"Neither ought nor shall be tarnished by circumstances over which he has had no control," Duncan warmly replied. "But your words recall me to my own duty. I go now to your gallant father, to hear his determination in matters of the last moment to the defense. God bless you in every fortune, noble—Cora—I may and must call you." She frankly gave him her hand, though her lips quivered, and her cheeks gradually became of an ashy paleness. "In every fortune, I know you will be an ornament and honor to your sex. Alice, adieu"—his tone changed from admiration to tenderness—"adieu, Alice; we shall soon meet again; as conquerors, I trust, and amid rejoicings!"

Without waiting for an answer from either, the young man threw himself down the grassy steps of the bastion, and moving rapidly across the parade, he was quickly in the presence of their father. Munro was pacing his narrow apartment with a disturbed air and gigantic strides as Duncan entered.

"You have anticipated my wishes, Major Heyward," he said; "I was about to request this favor."

"I am sorry to see, sir, that the messenger I so warmly recommended has returned in custody of the French! I hope there is no reason to distrust his fidelity?"

"The fidelity of 'The Long Rifle' is well known to me," returned Munro, "and is above suspicion; though his usual good fortune seems, at last, to have failed. Montcalm has got him, and with the accursed politeness of his nation, he has sent him in with a doleful tale, of 'knowing how I valued the fellow, he could not think of retaining him.' A jesuitical way, that, Major Duncan Heyward, of telling a man of his misfortunes!"

"But the general and his succor?"

"Did ye look to the south as ye entered, and could ye not see them?" said the old soldier, laughing bitterly. "Hoot! hoot! you're an impatient boy, sir, and cannot give the gentlemen leisure for their march!"

"They are coming, then? The scout has said as much?"

"When? and by what path? for the dunce has omitted to tell me this. There is a letter, it would seem, too; and that is the only agreeable part of the matter. For the customary attentions of your Marquis of Montcalm—I warrant me, Duncan, that he of Lothian would buy a dozen such marquisates—but, if the news of the letter were bad, the gentility of this French monsieur would certainly compel him to let us know it."

"He keeps the letter, then, while he releases the messenger?"

"Aye, that does he, and all for the sake of what you call your 'bonhommie.' I would venture, if the truth was known, the fellow's grandfather taught the noble science of dancing."

"But what says the scout? he has eyes and ears, and a tongue: what verbal report does he make?"

"Oh, sir, he is not wanting in natural organs, and he is free to tell all that he has seen and heard. The whole amount is this: there is a fort of his majesty's on the banks of the Hudson, called Edward, in honor of his gracious highness of York, you'll know; and it is well filled with armed men, as such a work should be."

"But was there no movement, no signs of any intention to advance to our relief?"

"There were the morning and evening parades; and when one of the provincial loons—you'll know, Duncan, you're half a Scotsman yourself—when one of them dropped his powder over his porretch, if it touched the coals, it just burnt!" Then suddenly changing his bitter, ironical manner, to one more grave and thoughtful, he continued; "and yet there might, and must be, something in that letter which it would be well to know!"

"Our decision should be speedy," said Duncan, gladly availing himself of this change of humor, to press the more important objects of their interview; "I cannot conceal from you sir, that the camp will not be much longer tenable; and I am sorry to add, that things appear no better in the fort; more than half the guns are bursted."

"And how should it be otherwise? Some were fished from the bottom of the lake; some have been rusting in the woods since the discovery of the country; and some were never guns at all—mere privateersmen's playthings! Do you think, sir, you can have Woolwich Warren in the midst of a wilderness, three thousand miles from Great Britain?"

"The walls are crumbling about our ears, and provisions begin to fail us," continued Heyward, without regarding this new burst of indignation; "even the men show signs of discontent and alarm."

"Major Heyward," said Munro, turning to his youthful associate with the dignity of his years and superior rank; "I should have served his majesty for half a century, and earned these gray hairs, in vain, were I ignorant of all you say, and of the pressing nature of our circumstances; still, there is everything due to the honor of the king's arms and something to ourselves. While there is hope of succor, this fortress will I defend, though it be to be done with pebbles gathered on the lake shore. It is a sight of the letter, therefore, that we want, that we may know the intentions of the man the Earl of Loudon has left among us as his substitute.

"And can I be of service in the matter?"

"Sir, you can; the Marquis of Montcalm has, in addition to his other civilities, invited me to a personal interview between the works and his own camp; in order, as he says, to impart some additional information. Now, I think it would not be wise to show any undue solicitude to meet him, and I would employ you, an officer of rank, as my substitute; for it would but ill comport with the honor of Scotland to let it be said one of her gentlemen was outdone in civility by a native of any other country on earth."

Without assuming the supererogatory task of entering into a discussion of the comparative merits of national courtesy, Duncan cheerfully assented to supply the place of the veteran in the approaching interview. A long and confidential communication now succeeded, during which the young man received some additional insight into his duty, from the experience and native acuteness of his commander, and then the former took his leave.

As Duncan could only act as the representative of the commandant of the fort, the ceremonies which should have accompanied a meeting between the heads of the adverse forces were of course dispensed with. The truce still existed, and with a roll and beat of the drum, and covered by a little white flag, Duncan left the sally-port, within ten minutes after his instructions were ended. He was received by the French officer in advance with the usual formalities, and immediately accompanied to a distant marquee of the renowned soldier who led the forces of France.

The general of the enemy received the youthful messenger, surrounded by his principal officers, and by a swarthy band of the native chiefs, who had followed him to the field, with the warriors of their several tribes. Heyward paused short, when, in glancing his eyes rapidly over the dark group of the latter, he beheld the malignant countenance of Magua, regarding him with the calm but sullen attention which marked the expression of that subtle savage. A slight exclamation of surprise even burst from the lips of the young man; but instantly recollecting his errand, and the presence in which he stood, he suppressed every appearance of emotion, and turned to the hostile leader, who had already advanced a step to receive him.

The Marquis of Montcalm was, at the period of which we write, in the flower of his age, and, it may be added, in the zenith of his fortunes. But, even in that enviable situation, he was affable, and distinguished as much for his attention to the forms of courtesy, as for that chivalrous courage which, only two short years afterwards, induced him to throw away his life on the plains of Abraham. Duncan, in turning his eyes from the malign expression of Magua, suffered them to rest with pleasure on the smiling and polished features, and the noble military air, of the French general.

"Monsieur," said the latter, "j'ai beaucoup de plaisir à—bah!—où est cet interprête?"

"Je crois, monsieur, qu'il ne sera pas nécessaire," Heyward modestly replied; "je parle un peu Français."

"Ah! j'en suis bien aise," said Montcalm, taking Duncan familiarly by the arm, and leading him deep into the marquee, a little out of ear-shot; "je déteste ce fripons-là; on ne sait jamais sur quel pié on est avec eux. Eh, bien! monsieur," he continued, still speaking in French; "though I should have been proud of receiving your commandant, I am very happy that he has seen proper to employ an officer so distinguished, and who, I am sure, is so amiable, as yourself."

Duncan bowed low, pleased with the compliment, in spite of a most heroic determination to suffer no artifice to allure him into forgetfulness of the interest of his prince; and Montcalm, after a pause of a moment, as if to collect his thoughts, proceeded,—

"Your commandant is a brave man, and well qualified to repel my assault. Mais, monsieur, is it not time to begin to take more counsel of humanity, and less of your courage? The one as strongly characterizes the hero as the other."

"We consider the qualities as inseparable," returned Duncan, smiling; "but while we find in the vigor of your excellency every motive to stimulate the one, we can, as yet, see no particular call for the exercise of the other."

Montcalm, in his turn, slightly bowed, but it was with the air of a man too practiced to remember the language of flattery. After musing a moment, he added,—

"It is possible my glasses have deceived me, and that your works resist our cannon better than I had supposed. You know our force?"

"Our accounts vary," said Duncan, carelessly; "the highest, however, has not exceeded twenty thousand men."

The Frenchman bit his lip, and fastened his eyes keenly on the other as if to read his thoughts; then, with a readiness peculiar to himself, he continued, as if assenting to the truth of an enumeration which quite doubled his army,—

"It is a poor compliment to the vigilance of us soldiers, monsieur, that, do what we will, we never can conceal our numbers. If it were to be done at all, one would believe it might succeed in these woods. Though you think it too soon to listen to the calls of humanity," he added, smiling archly, "I may be permitted to believe that gallantry is not forgotten by one so young as yourself. The daughters of the commandant, I learn, have passed into the fort since it was invested?"

"It is true, monsieur; but, so far from weakening our efforts, they set us an example of courage in their own fortitude. Were nothing but resolution necessary to repel so accomplished a soldier as M. de Montcalm, I would gladly trust the defense of William Henry to the elder of those ladies."

"We have a wise ordinance in our Salique laws, which says, 'The crown of France shall never degrade the lance to the distaff,'" said Montcalm dryly, and with a little hauteur; but instantly adding, with his former frank and easy air, "as all the nobler qualities are hereditary, I can easily credit you; though, as I said before, courage has its limits, and humanity must not be forgotten. I trust, monsieur, you come authorized to treat for the surrender of the place?"

"Has your excellency found our defense so feeble as to believe the measure necessary?"

"I should be sorry to have the defense protracted in such a manner as to irritate my red friends there," continued Montcalm, glancing his eyes at the group of grave and attentive Indians, without attending to the other's question; "I find it difficult, even now, to limit them to the usages of war."

Heyward was silent; for a painful recollection of the dangers he had so recently escaped came over his mind, and recalled the images of those defenseless beings who had shared in all his sufferings.

"Ces messieurs-là," said Montcalm, following up on the advantage which he conceived he had gained, "are most formidable when baffled: and it is unnecessary to tell you with what difficulty they are restrained in their anger. Eh bien, monsieur! shall we speak of the terms?"

"I fear your excellency has been deceived as to the strength of William Henry, and the resources of its garrison!"

"I have not sat down before Quebec, but an earthen work, that is defended by twenty-three hundred gallant men," was the laconic reply.

"Our mounds are earthen, certainly—nor are they seated on the rocks of Cape Diamond; but they stand on the shore which proved so destructive to Dieskau and his army. There is also a powerful force within a few hours' march of us, which we account upon as part of our means."

"Some six or eight thousand men," returned Montcalm, with much apparent indifference, "whom their leader wisely judges to be safer in their works than in the field."

It was now Heyward's turn to bite his lip with vexation, as the other so coolly alluded to a force which the young man knew to be overrated. Both mused a little while in silence, when Montcalm renewed the conversation, in a way that showed he believed the visit of his guest was solely to propose terms of capitulation. On the other hand, Heyward began to throw sundry inducements in the way of the French general, to betray the discoveries he had made through the intercepted letter. The artifice of neither, however, succeeded; and after a protracted and fruitless interview, Duncan took his leave, favorably impressed with an opinion of the courtesy and talents of the enemy's captain, but as ignorant of what he came to learn as when he arrived. Montcalm followed him as far as the entrance to the marquee, renewing his invitations to the commandant of the fort to give him an immediate meeting in the open ground, between the two armies.

There they separated, and Duncan returned to the advanced post of the French, accompanied as before; whence he instantly proceeded to the fort, and to the quarters of his own commander.

CHAPTER XVI

Edgar.—*Before you fight the battle, ope this letter.*
SHAKESPEARE, *King Lear,* V. i. 40.

Major Heyward found Munro attended only by his daughters. Alice sat upon his knee, parting the gray hairs on the forehead of the old man with her delicate fingers; and, whenever he affected to frown on her trifling, appeasing his assumed anger by pressing her ruby lips fondly on his wrinkled brow. Cora was seated nigh them, a calm and amused looker-on; regarding the wayward movements of her more youthful sister with that species of maternal fondness which characterized her love for Alice. Not only the dangers through which they had passed, but those which still impended above them, appeared to be momentarily forgotten, in the soothing indulgence of such a family meeting. It seemed as if they had profited by the short truce, to devote an instant to the purest and best affections: the daughters forgetting their fears, and the veteran his cares, in the security of the moment. Of this scene, Duncan, who in his eagerness to report his arrival had entered unannounced, stood many moments an unobserved and a delighted spectator. But the quick and dancing eyes of Alice soon caught a glimpse of his figure reflected from a glass, and she sprang blushing from her father's knee, exclaiming aloud,—

"Major Heyward!"

"What of the lad?" demanded her father; "I have sent him to crack a little with the Frenchman. Ha! sir, you are young, and you're nimble! Away with you, ye baggage; as if there were not troubles enough for a soldier, without having his camp filled with such prattling hussies as yourself!"

Alice laughingly followed her sister, who instantly led the way from an apartment where she perceived their presence was no longer desirable. Munro, instead of demanding the result of the young man's mission, paced the room for a few moments, with his hands behind his back, and his head inclinded towards the floor, like a man lost in thought. At length he raised his eyes, glistening with a father's fondness, and exclaimed,—

"They are a pair of excellent girls, Heyward, and such as any one may boast of."

"You are not now to learn my opinion of your daughters, Colonel Munro."

"True, lad, true," interrupted the impatient old man; "you were about opening your mind more fully on that matter the day you got in; but I did not think it becoming in an old soldier to be talking of nuptial blessings and wedding jokes when the enemies of his king were likely to be unbidden guests at the feast! But I was wrong, Duncan, boy, I was wrong there; and I am now ready to hear what you have to say."

"Notwithstanding the pleasure your assurance gives me, dear sir, I have, just now, a message from Montcalm—"

"Let the Frenchman and all his host go to the devil, sir!" exclaimed the hasty veteran. "He is not yet master of William Henry, nor shall he ever be, provided Webb proves himself the man he should. No, sir! thank Heaven, we are not yet in such a strait that it can be said Munro is too much pressed to discharge the little domestic duties of his own family. Your mother was the only child of my bosom friend, Duncan; and I'll just give you a hearing, though all the knights of St. Louis were in a body at the sally-port, with the French saint at their head, craving to speak a word under favor. A pretty degree of knighthood, sir, is that which can be bought with sugar-hogsheads! and then your two-penny marquisates! The thistle is the order for dignity and antiquity; the veritable 'nemo me impune lacessit' of chivalry! Ye had ancestors in that degree, Duncan, and they were an ornament to the nobles of Scotland."

Heyward, who perceived that his superior took a malicious pleasure in exhibiting his contempt for the message of the French general, was fain to humor a spleen that he knew would be short-lived; he therefore replied with as much indifference as he could assume on such a subject,—

"My request, as you know, sir, went so far as to presume to the honor of being your son."

"Aye, boy, you found words to make yourself very plainly comprehended. but, let me ask ye, sir, have you been as intelligible to the girl?"

"On my honor, no," exclaimed Duncan, warmly; "there would have been an abuse of a confided trust, had I taken advantage of my situation for such a purpose."

"Your notions are those of a gentleman, Major Heyward, and well enough in their place. But Cora Munro is a maiden too discreet, and of a mind too elevated and improved, to need the guardianship even of a father."

"Cora!"

"Aye—Cora! we are talking of your pretensions to Miss Munro, are we not, sir?"

"I—I—I was not conscious of having mentioned her name," said Duncan, stammering.

"And to marry whom, then, did you wish my consent, Major Heyward?" demanded the old soldier, erecting himself in the dignity of offended feeling.

"You have another, and not less lovely child."

"Alice!" exclaimed the father, in an astonishment equal to that with which Duncan had just repeated the name of her sister.

"Such was the direction of my wishes, sir."

The young man awaited in silence the result of the extraordinary effect produced by a communication which, as it now appeared, was so unexpected. For several minutes Munro paced the chamber with long and rapid strides, his rigid features working convulsively, and every faculty seemingly absorbed in the musings of his own mind. At length, he paused directly in front of Heyward, and riveting his eyes upon those of the other, he said with a lip that quivered violently,—

"Duncan Heyward, I have loved you for the sake of him whose blood is in your veins; I have loved you for your own good qualities; and I have loved you, because I thought you would contribute to the happiness of my child. But all this love would turn to hatred, were I assured that what I so much apprehend is true."

"God forbid that any act or thought of mine should lead to such a change!" exclaimed the young man, whose eye never quailed under the penetrating look it encountered. Without adverting to the impossibility of the other's comprehending those feelings which were hid in his own bosom, Munro suffered himself to be appeased by the unaltered countenance he met, and with a voice sensibly softened, he continued,—

"You would be my son, Duncan, and you're ignorant of the history of the man you wish to call your father. Sit ye down, young man, and I will open to you the wounds of a seared heart, in as few words as may be suitable."

By this time, the message of Montcalm was as much forgotten by him who bore it as by the man for whose ears it was intended. Each drew a chair, and while the veteran communed a few moments with his own thoughts, apparently in sadness, the youth suppressed his impatience in a look and attitude of respectful attention. At length the former spoke.

"You'll know, already, Major Heyward, that my family was both ancient and honorable," commenced the Scotsman; "though it might not altogether be endowed with that amount of wealth that should correspond with its degree. I was, may be, such an one as yourself when I plighted my faith to Alice Graham, the only child of a neighboring laird of some estate. But the connection was disagreeable to her father, on more accounts than my poverty. I did therefore what an honest man should—restored the maiden her troth, and departed the country in the service of my king. I had seen many regions, and had shed much blood in different lands, before duty called me to the islands of the West Indies. There it was my lot to form a connection with one who in time became my wife, and the mother of Cora. She was the daughter of a gentleman of those isles, by a lady whose misfortune it was, if you will," said the old man proudly, "to be descended, remotely, from that unfortunate class who are so basely enslaved to administer to the wants of a luxurious people. Aye, sir, that is a curse entailed on Scotland by her unnatural union with a foreign and trading people. But could I find a man among them who would dare to reflect on my child, he should feel the weight of a father's anger! Ha! Major Heyward, you are yourself born at the south, where these unfortunate beings are considered of a race inferior to your own."

"'T is most unfortunately true, sir," said Duncan, unable any longer to prevent his eyes from sinking to the floor in embarrassment.

"And you cast it on my child as a reproach! You scorn to mingle the blood of the Heywards with one so degraded—lovely and virtuous though she be?" fiercely demanded the jealous parent.

"Heaven protect me from a prejudice so unworthy of my reason!" returned Duncan, at the same time conscious of such a feeling, and that as deeply rooted as if it had been ingrafted in his nature. "The sweetness, the beauty, the witchery of your younger daughter, Colonel Munro, might explain my motives, without imputing to me this injustice."

"Ye are right, sir," returned the old man, again changing his tones to those of gentleness, or rather softness; "the girl is the image of what her mother was at her years, and before she had become acquainted with grief. When death deprived me of my wife I returned to Scotland, enriched by the marriage; and would you think it, Duncan! the suffering angel had remained in the heartless state of celibacy twenty long years, and that for the sake of a man who could forget her! She did more, sir; she overlooked my want of faith, and all difficulties being now removed, she took me for her husband."

"And became the mother of Alice?" exclaimed Duncan, with an eagerness that might have proved dangerous at a moment when the thoughts of Munro were less occupied than at present.

"She did, indeed," said the old man, "and dearly did she pay for the blessing she bestowed. But she is a saint in heaven, sir; and it ill becomes one whose foot rests on the grave to mourn a lot so blessed. I had her but a single year, though; a short term of happiness for one who had seen her youth fade in hopeless pining."

There was something so commanding in the distress of the old man, that Heyward did not dare to venture a syllable of consolation. Munro sat utterly unconscious of the other's presence, his features exposed and working with the anguish of his regrets, while heavy tears fell from his eyes, and rolled unheeded from his cheeks to the floor. At length he moved, as if suddenly recovering his recollection; when he arose, and taking a single turn across the room, he approached his companion with an air of military grandeur, and demanded,—

"Have you not, Major Heyward, some communication that I should hear from the Marquis de Montcalm?"

Duncan started, in his turn, and immediately commenced, in an embarrassed voice, the half-forgotten message. It is unnecessary to dwell upon the evasive, though polite manner with which the French general had eluded every attempt of Heyward to worm from him the purport of the communication he had proposed making, or on the decided, though still polished message by which he now gave his enemy to understand that unless he chose to receive it in person, he should not receive it at all. As Munro listened to the detail of Duncan, the excited feelings of the father gradually gave way before the obligations of his station, and when the other was done, he saw before him nothing but the veteran, swelling with the wounded feelings of a soldier.

"You have said enough, Major Heyward!" exclaimed the angry old man; "enough to make a volume of commentary on French civility. Here has this gentleman invited me to a conference, and when I send him a capable substitute, for ye 're all that, Duncan, though your years are but few, he answers me with a riddle."

"He may have thought less favorably of the substitute, my dear sir; and you will remember that the invitation, which he now repeats, was to the commandant of the works, and not to his second."

"Well, sir, is not a substitute clothed with all the power and dignity of him who grants the commission? He wishes to confer with Munro! Faith, sir, I have much inclination to indulge the man, if it should only be to let him behold the firm countenance we maintain in spite of his numbers and his summons. There might be no bad policy in such a stroke, young man."

Duncan, who believed it of the last importance that they should speedily come at the contents of the letter borne by the scout, gladly encouraged this idea.

"Without doubt, he could gather no confidence by witnessing our indifference," he said.

"You never said truer word. I could wish, sir, that he would visit the works in open day, and in the form of a storming party: that is the least failing method of proving the countenance of an enemy, and would be far preferable to the battering system he has chosen. The beauty and manliness of warfare has been much deformed, Major Heyward, by the arts of your Monsieur Vauban. Our ancestors were far above such scientific cowardice!"

"It may be very true, sir; but we are now obliged to repel art by art. What is your pleasure in the matter of the interview?"

"I will meet the Frenchman, and that without fear or delay; promptly, sir, as becomes a servant of my royal master. Go, Major Heyward, and give them a flourish of the music; and send out a messenger to let them know who is coming. We will follow with a small guard, for such respect is due to one who holds the honor of his king in keeping; and harkee, Duncan," he added, in a half whisper, though they were alone, "it may be prudent to have some aid at hand, in case there should be treachery at the bottom of it all."

The young man availed himself of this order to quit the apartment; and, as the day was fast coming to a close, he hastened, without delay, to make the necessary arrangements. A very few minutes only were necessary to parade a few files, and to dispatch an orderly with a flag to announce the approach of the commandant of the fort. When Duncan had done both these, he led the guard to the sally-port, near which he found his superior ready, waiting his appearance. As soon as the usual ceremonials of a military departure were observed, the veteran and his more youthful companion left the fortress, attended by the escort.

They had proceeded only a hundred yards from the works, when the little array which attended the French general to the conference was seen issuing from the hollow way which formed the bed of a brook that ran between the batteries of the besiegers and the fort. From the moment that Munro left his own works to appear in front of his enemies, his air had been grand, and his step and countenance highly military. The instant he caught a glimpse of the white plume that waved in the hat of Montcalm, his eye lighted, and age no longer appeared to possess any influence over his vast and still muscular person.

"Speak to the boys to be watchful, sir," he said, in an undertone, to Duncan; "and to look well to their flints and steel, for one is never safe with a servant of these Louis's; at the same time, we will show them the front of men in deep security. Ye 'll understand me, Major Heyward!"

He was interrupted by the clamor of a drum from the approaching Frenchmen, which was immediately answered, when each party pushed an orderly in advance, bearing a white flag, and the wary Scotsman halted, with his guard close at his back. As soon as this slight salutation had passed, Montcalm moved towards them with a quick but graceful step, baring his head to the veteran, and dropping his spotless plume nearly to the earth in courtesy. If the air of Munro was more commanding and manly, it wanted both the ease and insinuating polish of that of the Frenchman. Neither spoke for a few moments, each regarding the other with curious and interested eyes. Then, as became his superior rank and the nature of the interview, Montcalm broke the silence. After uttering the usual words of greeting, he turned to Duncan, and continued, with a smile of recognition, speaking always in French,—

"I am rejoiced, monsieur, that you have given us the pleasure of your company on this occasion. There will be no necessity to employ an ordinary interpreter; for, in your hands, I feel the same security as if I spoke your language myself."

Duncan acknowledged the compliment, when Montcalm, turning to his guard, which, in imitation of that of their enemies, pressed close upon him, continued,—

"En arrière, mes enfans—il fait chaud—retirez-vous un peu."

Before Major Heyward would imitate this proof of confidence, he glanced his eyes around the plain, and beheld with uneasiness the numerous dusky groups of savages, who looked out from the margin of the surrounding woods, curious spectators of the interview.

"Monsieur de Montcalm will readily acknowledge the difference in our situation," he said, with some embarrassment, pointing at the same time towards those dangerous foes, who were to be seen in almost every direction.

"Were we to dismiss our guard, we should stand here at the mercy of our enemies."

"Monsieur, you have the plighted faith of 'un gentilhomme Français,' for your safety," returned Montcalm, laying his hand impressively on his heart; "it should suffice."

"It shall. Fall back," Duncan added to the officer who led the escort; "fall back, sir, beyond hearing, and wait for orders."

Munro witnessed this movement with manifest uneasiness; nor did he fail to demand an instant explanation.

"Is it not in our interest, sir, to betray no distrust?" retorted Duncan. "Monsieur de Montcalm pledges his word for our safety, and I have ordered the men to withdraw a little, in order to prove how much we depend on his assurance."

"It may be all right, sir, but I have no overweening reliance on the faith of these marquesses, or marquis, as they call themselves. Their patents of nobility are too common to be certain that they bear the seal of true honor."

"You forget, dear sir, that we confer with an officer, distinguished alike in Europe and America, for his deeds. From a soldier of his reputation we can have nothing to apprehend."

The old man made a gesture of resignation, though his rigid features still betrayed his obstinate adherence to a distrust which he derived from a sort of hereditary contempt of his enemy, rather than from any present signs which might warrant so uncharitable a feeling. Montcalm waited patiently until this little dialogue in demi-voice was ended, when he drew nigher, and opened the subject of their conference.

"I have solicited this interview from your superior, monsieur," he said, "because I believe he will allow himself to be persuaded that he has already done everything which is necessary for the honor of his prince, and will now listen to the admonitions of humanity. I will forever bear testimony that his resistance has been gallant, and was continued as long as there was hope."

When this opening was translated to Munro, he answered with dignity, but with sufficient courtesy,—

"However I may prize such testimony from Monsieur Montcalm, it will be more valuable when it shall be better merited."

The French general smiled, as Duncan gave him the purport of this reply, and observed,—

"What is now so freely accorded to approved courage, may be refused to useless obstinacy. Monsieur would wish to see my camp, and witness, for himself, our numbers, and the impossibility of his resisting them with success?"

"I know that the King of France is well served," returned the unmoved Scotsman, as soon as Duncan ended his translation; "but my own royal master has as many and as faithful troops."

"Though not at hand, fortunately for us," said Montcalm, without waiting, in his ardor, for the interpreter. "There is a destiny in war to which a brave man knows how to submit with the same courage that he faces his foes."

"Had I been conscious that Monsieur Montcalm was master of the English, I should have spared myself the trouble of so awkward a translation," said the vexed Duncan, dryly; remembering instantly his recent by-play with Munro.

"Your pardon, monsieur," rejoined the Frenchman, suffering a slight color to appear on his dark cheek. "There is a vast difference between understanding and speaking a foreign tongue; you will, therefore, please to assist me still." Then, after a short pause, he added, "These hills afford us every opportunity of reconnoitering your works, messieurs, and I am possibly as well acquainted with their weak condition as you can be yourselves."

"Ask the French general if his glasses can reach to the Hudson," said Munro, proudly; "and if he knows when and where to expect the army of Webb."

"Let General Webb be his own interpreter," returned the politic Montcalm, suddenly extending an open letter towards Munro, as he spoke; "you will there learn, monsieur, that his movements are not likely to prove embarrassing to my army."

The veteran seized the offered paper, without waiting for Duncan to translate the speech, and with an eagerness that betrayed how important he deemed its contents. As his eye passed hastily over the words, his countenance changed from its look of military pride to one of deep chagrin: his lip began to quiver; and, suffering the paper to fall from his hand, his head dropped upon his chest, like that of a man whose hopes were withered at a single blow. Duncan caught the letter from the ground, and, without apology for the liberty he took, he read at a glance its cruel purport. Their common superior, so far from encouraging them to resist, advised a speedy surrender, urging in the plainest language, as a reason, the utter impossibility of his sending a single man to their rescue.

"Here is no deception!" exclaimed Duncan, examining the billet both inside and out; "this is the signature of Webb, and must be the captured letter."

"The man has betrayed me!" Munro at length bitterly exclaimed: "he has brought dishonor to the door of one where disgrace was never before known to dwell, and shame has he heaped heavily on my gray hairs."

"Say not so," cried Duncan; "we are yet masters of the fort, and of our honor. Let us then sell our lives at such a rate as shall make our enemies believe the purchase too dear."

"Boy, I thank thee," exclaimed the old man, rousing himself from his stupor; "you have, for once, reminded Munro of his duty. We will go back, and dig our graves behind those ramparts."

"Messieurs," said Montcalm, advancing towards them a step, in generous interest, "you little know Louis de Saint Véran, if you believe him capable of profiting by this letter to humble brave men, or to build up a dishonest reputation for himself. Listen to my terms before you leave me."

"What says the Frenchman?" demanded the veteran, sternly; "does he make a merit of having captured a scout, with a note from headquarters? Sir, he had better raise this siege, to go and sit down before Edward if he wishes to frighten his enemy with words."

Duncan explained the other's meaning.

"Monsieur de Montcalm, we will hear you," the veteran added, more calmly, as Duncan ended.

"To retain the fort is now impossible," said his liberal enemy; "it is necessary to the interests of my master that it should be destroyed; but, as for yourselves, and your brave comrades, there is no privilege dear to a soldier that shall be denied."

"Our colors?" demanded Heyward.

"Carry them to England, and show them to your king."

"Our arms?"

"Keep them; none can use them better."

"Our march; the surrender of the place?"

"Shall all be done in a way most honorable to yourselves."

Duncan now turned to explain these proposals to his commander, who heard him with amazement, and a sensibility that was deeply touched by so unusual and unexpected generosity.

"Go you, Duncan," he said; "go with this marquess, as indeed marquess he should be; go to his marquee and arrange it all. I have lived to see two things in my old age, that never did I expect to behold. An Englishman afraid to support a friend, and a Frenchman too honest to profit by his advantage."

So saying, the veteran again dropped his head to his chest, and returned slowly towards the fort, exhibiting, by the dejection of his air, to the anxious garrison, a harbinger of evil tidings.

From the shock of this unexected blow the haughty feelings of Munro never recovered; but from that moment there commenced a change in his determined character, which accompanied him to a speedy grave. Duncan remained to settle the terms of the capitulation. He was seen to reënter the works during the first watches of the night, and, immediately after a private conference with the commandant, to leave them again. It was then openly announced that hostilities must cease—Munro having signed a treaty by which the place was to be yielded to the enemy, with the morning; the garrison to retain their arms, their colors, and their baggage, and consequently, according to military opinion, their honor.

CHAPTER XVII

Weave we the woof. The thread is spun.
The web is wove. The work is done.
GRAY, *The Bard.*

The hostile armies which lay in the wilds of the Horican passed the night of the ninth of August, 1757, much in the manner they would had they encountered on the fairest field of Europe. While the conquered were still, sullen, and dejected, the victors triumphed. But there are limits alike to grief and joy; and long before the watches of morning came, the stillness of those boundless woods was only broken by a gay call from some exulting young Frenchman of the advanced pickets, or a menacing challenge from the fort, which sternly forbade the approach of any hostile footsteps before the stipulated moment. Even these occasional threatening sounds ceased to be heard in that dull hour which precedes the day, at which period a listener might have sought in vain any evidence of the presence of those armed powers that then slumbered on the shores of the "holy lake."

It was during these moments of deep silence that the canvas which concealed the entrance to a spacious marquee in the French encampment was shoved aside, and a man issued from beneath the drapery into the open air. He was enveloped in a cloak that might have been intended as a protection from the chilling damps of the woods, but which served equally well as a mantle, to conceal his person. He was permitted to pass the grenadier, who watched over the slumbers of the French commander, without interruption, the man making the usual salute which betokens military deference, as the other passed swiftly through the little city of tents, in the direction of William Henry. Whenever this unknown individual encountered one of the numberless sentinels who crossed his path, his answer was prompt, and as it appeared satisfactory; for he was uniformly allowed to proceed, without further interrogation.

With the exception of such repeated, but brief interruptions, he had moved silently from the centre of the camp to its most advanced outposts, when he drew nigh the soldier who held his watch nearest to the works of the enemy. As he approached he was received with the usual challenge,—

"Qui vive?"

"France," was the reply.

"Le mot d'ordre?"

"La victoire," said the other, drawing so nigh as to be heard in a loud whisper.

"C'est bien," returned the sentinel, throwing his musket from the charge to his shoulder; "vous vous promenez bien matin, monsieur!"

"Il est nécessaire d'être vigilant, mon enfant," the other observed, dropping a fold of his cloak, and looking the soldier close in the face, as he passed him, still continuing his way towards the British fortification. The man started; his arms rattled heavily, as he threw them forward, in the lowest and most respectful salute; and when he had again recovered his piece, he turned to walk his post, muttering between his teeth,—

"Il faut être vigilant, en vérité! Je crois que nous avons là, un caporal qui ne dort jamais!"

The officer proceeded, without affecting to hear the words which escaped the sentinel in his surprise; nor did he again pause until he had reached the low strand, and in a somewhat dangerous vicinity to the western water bastion of the fort. The light of an obscure moon was just sufficient to render objects, though dim, perceptible in their outlines. He therefore took the precaution to place himself against the trunk of a tree, where he leaned for many minutes, and seemed to contemplate the dark and silent mounds of the English works in profound attention. His gaze at the ramparts was not that of a curious or idle spectator; but his looks wandered from point to point, denoting his knowledge of military usages, and betraying that his search was not unaccompanied by distrust. At length he appeared satisfied; and having cast his eyes impatiently upward towards the summit of the eastern mountain, as if anticipating the approach of the morning, he was in the act of turning on his footsteps, when a light sound on the nearest angle of the bastion caught his ear, and induced him to remain.

Just then a figure was seen to approach the edge of the rampart, where it stood, apparently contemplating in its turn the distant tents of the French encampment. Its head was then turned towards the east, as though equally anxious for the appearance of light, when the form leaned against the mound, and seemed to gaze upon the glassy expanse of the waters, which, like a submarine firmament, glittered with its thousand mimic stars. The melancholy air, the hour, together with the vast frame of the man who thus leaned, in musing, against the English ramparts, left no doubt as to his person, in the mind of the observant spectator. Delicacy, no less than prudence, now urged him to retire; and he had moved cautiously round the body of the tree for that purpose, when another sound drew his attention, and once more arrested his footsteps. It was a low and almost inaudible movement of the water, and was succeeded by a grating of pebbles one against the other. In a moment he saw a dark form rise, as it were out of the lake, and steal without further noise to the land, within a few feet of the place where he himself stood. A rifle next slowly rose between his eyes and the watery mirror; but before it could be discharged his own hand was on the lock.

"Hugh!" exclaimed the savage, whose treacherous aim was so singularly and so unexpectedly interrupted.

Without making any reply, the French officer laid his hand on the shoulder of the Indian, and led him in profound silence to a distance from the spot where their subsequent dialogue might have proved dangerous, and where it seemed that one of them, at least, sought a victim. Then, throwing open his cloak, so as to expose his uniform and the cross of St. Louis which was suspended at his breast, Montcalm sternly demanded,—

"What means this? Does not my son know that the hatchet is buried between the English and his Canadian Father?"

"What can the Hurons do?" returned the savage, speaking also, though imperfectly, in the French language. "Not a warrior has a scalp, and the pale-faces make friends!"

"Ha! Le Renard Subtil! Methinks this is an excess of zeal for a friend who was so late an enemy! How many suns have set since Le Renard struck the war-post of the English?"

"Where is that sun!" demanded the sullen savage. "Behind the hill; and it is dark and cold. But when he comes again, it will be bright and warm. Le Subtil is the sun of his tribe. There have been clouds, and many mountains between him and his nation; but now he shines, and it is a clear sky!"

"That Le Renard has power with his people, I well know," said Montcalm; "for yesterday he hunted for their scalps, and to-day they hear him at the council fire."

"Magua is a great chief."

"Let him prove it, by teaching his nation how to conduct itself towards our new friends."

"Why did the chief of the Canadas bring his young men into the woods, and fire his cannon at the earthen house?" demanded the subtle Indian.

"To subdue it. My master owns the land, and your father was ordered to drive off these English squatters. They have consented to go, and now he calls them enemies no longer."

"'T is well. Magua took the hatchet to color it with blood. It is now bright; when it is red, it shall be buried."

"But Magua is pledged not to sully the lilies of France. The enemies of the great king across the salt lake are his enemies; his friends, the friends of the Hurons."

"Friends!" repeated the Indian, in scorn. "Let his father give Magua a hand."

Montcalm, who felt that his influence over the warlike tribes he had gathered was to be maintained by concession rather than by power, complied reluctantly with the other's request. The savage placed the finger of the French commander on a deep scar in his bosom, and then exultingly demanded,—

"Does my father know that?"

"What warrior does not? 't is where a leaden bullet has cut."

"And this?" continued the Indian, who had turned his naked back to the other, his body being without its usual calico mantle.

"This!—my son has been sadly injured, here; who has done this?"

"Magua slept hard in the English wigwams, and the sticks have left their mark," returned the savage, with a hollow laugh, which did not conceal the fierce temper that nearly choked him. Then recollecting himself, with sudden and native dignity, he added, "Go; teach your young men, it is peace. Le Renard Subtil knows how to speak to a Huron warrior."

Without deigning to bestow further words, or to wait for any answer, the savage cast his rifle into the hollow of his arm, and moved silently through the encampment towards the woods where his own tribe was known to lie. Every few yards as he proceeded he was challenged by the sentinels; but he stalked sullenly onward, utterly disregarding the summons of the soldiers, who only spared his life because they knew the air and tread no less than the obstinate daring of an Indian.

Montcalm lingered long and melancholy on the strand, where he had been left by his companion, brooding deeply on the temper which his ungovernable ally had just discovered. Already had his fair fame been tarnished by one horrid scene, and in circumstances fearfully resembling those under which he now found himself. As he mused he became keenly sensible of the deep responsibility they assume who disregard the means to attain their end, and of all the danger of setting in motion an engine which it exceeds human power to control. Then shaking off a train of reflections that he accounted a weakness in such a moment of triumph, he retraced his steps towards his tent, giving the order, as he passed, to make the signal that should arouse the army from its slumbers.

The first tap of the French drums was echoed from the bosom of the fort, and presently the valley was filled with the strains of martial music, rising long, thrilling, and lively above the rattling accompaniment. The horns of the victors sounded merry and cheerful flourishes, until the last laggard of the camp was at his post; but the instant the British fifes had blown their shrill signal, they became mute. In the mean time the day had dawned, and when the line of the French army was ready to receive its general, the rays of a brilliant sun were glancing along the glittering array. Then that success, which was already so well known, was officially announced; the favored band who were selected to guard the gates of the fort were detailed, and defiled before their chief; the signal of their approach was given, and all the usual preparations for a change of masters were ordered and executed directly under the guns of the contested works.

A very different scene presented itself within the lines of the Anglo-American army. As soon as the warning signal was given, it exhibited all the signs of a hurried and forced departure. The sullen soldiers shouldered their empty tubes and fell into their places, like men whose blood had been heated by the past contest, and who only desired the opportunity to revenge an indignity which was still wounding to their pride, concealed as it was under all the observances of military etiquette. Women and children ran from place to place, some bearing the scanty remnants of their baggage, and others searching in the ranks for those countenances they looked up to for protection.

Munro appeared among his silent troops firm but dejected. It was evident that the unexpected blow had struck deep into his heart, though he struggled to sustain his misfortune with the port of a man.

Duncan was touched at the quiet and impressive exhibition of his grief. He had discharged his own duty, and he now pressed to the side of the old man, to know in what particular he might serve him.

"My daughters," was the brief but expressive reply.

"Good heavens! are not arrangements already made for their convenience?"

"To-day I am only a soldier, Major Heyward," said the veteran. "All that you see here, claim alike to be my children."

Duncan had heard enough. Without losing one of those moments which had now become so precious, he flew towards the quarters of Munro, in quest of the sisters. He found them on the threshold of the low edifice, already prepared to depart, and surrounded by a clamorous and weeping assemblage of their own sex, that had gathered about the place, with a sort of instinctive consciousness that it was the point most likely to be protected. Though the cheeks of Cora were pale, and her countenance anxious, she had lost none of her firmness; but the eyes of Alice were inflamed, and betrayed how long and bitterly she had wept. They both, however, received the young man with undisguised pleasure; the former, for a novelty, being the first to speak.

"The fort is lost," she said, with a melancholy smile; "though our good name, I trust, remains."

"'T is brighter than ever. But, dearest Miss Munro, it is time to think less of others, and to make some provision for yourself. Military usage,—pride,—that pride on which you so much value yourself, demands that your father and I should for a little while continue with the troops. Then where to seek a proper protector for you against the confusion and chances of such a scene?"

"None is necessary," returned Cora; "who will dare to injure or insult the daughter of such a father, at a time like this?"

"I would not leave you alone," continued the youth, looking about him in a hurried manner, "for the command of the best regiment in the pay of the king. Remember, our Alice is not gifted with all your firmness, and God only knows the terror she might endure."

"You may be right," Cora replied, smiling again, but far more sadly than before. "Listen! chance has already sent us a friend when he is most needed."

Duncan did listen, and on the instant comprehended her meaning. The low and serious sounds of the sacred music so well known to the eastern provinces caught his ear, and instantly drew him to an apartment in an adjacent building, which had already been deserted by its customary tenants. There he found David, pouring out his pious feelings through the only medium in which he ever indulged. Duncan waited until, by the cessation of the movement of the hand, he believed the strain was ended, when, by touching his shoulder, he drew the attention of the other to himself, and in a few words explained his wishes.

"Even so," replied the single-minded disciple of the King of Israel, when the young man had ended; "I have found much that is comely and melodious in the maidens, and it is fitting that we who have consorted in so much peril should abide together in peace. I will attend them, when I have completed my morning praise, to which nothing is now wanting but the doxology. Wilt thou bear a part, friend? The metre is common, and the tune 'Southwell.'"

Then, extending the little volume, and giving the pitch of the air anew with considerate attention, David recommenced and finished his strains, with a fixedness of manner that it was not easy to interrupt. Heyward was fain to wait until the verse was ended; when, seeing David relieving himself from the spectacles, and replacing the book, he continued,—

"It will be your duty to see that none dare to approach the ladies with any rude intention, or to offer insult or taunt at the misfortune of their brave father. In this task you will be seconded by the domestics of their household."

"Even so."

"It is possible that the Indians and stragglers of the enemy may intrude, in which case you will remind them of the terms of the capitulation, and threaten to report their conduct to Montcalm. A word will suffice."

"If not, I have that here which shall," returned David, exhibiting his book, with an air in which meekness and confidence were singularly blended. "Here are words which, uttered, or rather thundered, with proper emphasis, and in measured time, shall quiet the most unruly temper:—

"'Why rage the heathen furiously!'"—

"Enough," said Heyward, interrupting the burst of his musical invocation: "we understand each other; it is time that we should now assume our respective duties."

Gamut cheerfully assented, and together they sought the females. Cora received her new and somewhat extraordinary protector courteously at least; and even the pallid features of Alice lighted again with some of their native archness as she thanked Heyward for his care. Duncan took occasion to assure them he had done the best that circumstances permitted, and, as he believed, quite enough for the security of their feelings; of danger there was none. He then spoke gladly of his intentions to rejoin them the moment he had led the advance a few miles towards the Hudson, and immediately took his leave.

By this time the signal of departure had been given, and the head of the English column was in motion. The sisters started at the sound, and glancing their eyes around, they saw the white uniforms of the French grenadiers, who had already taken possession of the gates of the fort. At that moment, an enormous cloud seemed to pass suddenly above their heads, and looking upward, they discovered that they stood beneath the wide folds of the standard of France.

"Let us go," said Cora; "this is no longer a fit place for the children of an English officer."

Alice clung to the arm of her sister, and together they left the parade, accompanied by the moving throng that surrounded them.

As they passed the gates, the French officers, who had learned their rank, bowed often and low, forbearing, however, to intrude those attentions which they saw, with peculiar tact, might not be agreeable. As every vehicle and each beast of burden was occupied by the sick and wounded, Cora had decided to endure the fatigues of a foot march, rather than interfere with their comforts. Indeed, many a maimed and feeble soldier was compelled to drag his exhausted limbs in the rear of the columns, for the want of the necessary means of conveyance in that wilderness. The whole, however, was in motion; the weak and wounded, groaning, and in suffering; their comrades, silent and sullen; and the women and children in terror, they knew not of what.

As the confused and timid throng left the protecting mounds of the fort, and issued on the open plain, the whole scene was at once presented to their eyes. At a little distance on the right, and somewhat in the rear, the French army stood to their arms, Montcalm having collected his parties, so soon as his guards had possession of the works. They were attentive but silent observers of the proceedings of the vanquished, failing in none of the stipulated military honors, and offering no taunt or insult, in their success, to their less fortunate foes. Living masses of the English, to the amount in the whole of near three thousand, were moving slowly across the plain, towards the common centre, and gradually approached each other, as they converged to the point of their march, a vista cut through the lofty trees, where the road to the Hudson entered the forest. Along the sweeping borders of the woods hung a dark cloud of savages, eyeing the passage of their enemies, and hovering, at a distance, like vultures, who were only kept from swooping on their prey, by the presence and restraint of a superior army. A few had straggled among the conquered columns, where they stalked in sullen discontent; attentive, though, as yet, passive observers of the moving multitude.

The advance, with Heyward at its head, had already reached the defile, and was slowly disappearing, when the attention of Cora was drawn to a collection of stragglers, by the sounds of contention. A truant provincial was paying the forfeit of his disobedience, by being plundered of those very effects which had caused him to desert his place in the ranks. The man was of powerful frame, and too avaricious to part with his goods without a struggle. Individuals from either party interfered, the one side to prevent, and the other to aid in the robbery. Voices grew loud and angry, and a hundred savages appeared, as it were by magic, where a dozen only had been seen a minute before. It was then that Cora saw the form of Magua gliding among his countrymen, and speaking with his fatal and artful eloquence. The mass of women and children stopped, and hovered together like alarmed and fluttering birds. But the cupidity of the Indian was soon gratified, and the different bodies again moved slowly onward.

The savages now fell back, and seemed content to let their enemies advance without further molestation. But as the female crowd approached them, the gaudy colors of a shawl attracted the eyes of a wild and untutored Huron. He advanced to seize it, without the least hesitation. The woman, more in terror than through love of the ornament, wrapped her child in the coveted article, and folded both more closely to her bosom. Cora was in the act of speaking, with an intent to advise the woman to abandon the trifle, when the savage relinquished his hold of the shawl, and tore the screaming infant from her arms. Abandoning everything to the greedy grasp of those around her, the mother darted, with distraction in her mien, to reclaim her child. The Indian smiled grimly, and extended one hand, in sign of a willingness to exchange, while with the other, he flourished the babe over his head, holding it by the feet as if to enhance the value of the ransom.

"Here—here—there—all—any—everything!" exclaimed the breathless woman; tearing the lighter articles of dress from her person, with ill-directed and trembling fingers; "take all, but give me my babe!"

The savage spurned the worthless rags, and perceiving that the shawl had already become a prize to another, his bantering but sullen smile changing to a gleam of ferocity, he dashed the head of the infant against a rock, and cast its quivering remains to her very feet. For an instant, the mother stood, like a statue of despair, looking wildly down at the unseemly object, which had so lately nestled in her bosom and smiled in her face; and then she raised her eyes and countenance towards heaven, as if calling on God to curse the perpetrator of the foul deed. She was spared the sin of such a prayer; for, maddened at his disappointment, and excited at the sight of blood, the Huron mercifully drove his tomahawk into her own brain. The mother sank under the blow, and fell, grasping at her child, in death, with the same engrossing love that had caused her to cherish it when living.

At that dangerous moment Magua placed his hands to his mouth, and raised the fatal and appalling whoop. The scattered Indians started at the well-known cry, as coursers bound at the signal to quit the goal; and, directly, there arose such a yell along the plain, and through the arches of the wood, as seldom burst from human lips before. They who heard it listened with a curdling horror at the heart, little inferior to that dread which may be expected to attend the blasts of the final summons.

More than two thousand raving savages broke from the forest at the signal, and threw themselves across the fatal plain with instinctive alacrity. We shall not dwell on the revolting horrors that succeeded. Death was everywhere, and in his most terrific and disgusting aspects. Resistance only served to inflame the murderers, who inflicted their furious blows long after their victims were beyond the power of their resentment. The flow of blood might be likened to the outbreaking of a torrent; and as the natives became heated and maddened by the sight, many among them even kneeled to the earth, and drank freely, exultingly, hellishly, of the crimson tide.

The trained bodies of the troops threw themselves quickly into solid masses, endeavoring to awe their assailants by the imposing appearance of a military front. The experiment in some measure succeeded, though far too many suffered their unloaded muskets to be torn from their hands, in the vain hope of appeasing the savages.

In such a scene none had leisure to note the fleeting moments. It might have been ten minutes (it seemed an age), that the sisters had stood riveted to one spot, horror-stricken, and nearly helpless. When the first blow was struck, their screaming companions had pressed upon them in a body, rendering flight impossible; and now that fear or death had scattered most, if not all, from around them, they saw no avenue open, but such as conducted to the tomahawks of their foes. On every side arose shrieks, groans, exhortations, and curses. At this moment, Alice caught a glimpse of the vast form of her father, moving rapidly across the plain, in the direction of the French army. He was, in truth, proceeding to Montcalm, fearless of every danger, to claim the tardy escort for which he had before conditioned.

Fifty glittering axes and barbed spears were offered unheeded at his life, but the savages respected his rank and calmness, even in their fury. The dangerous weapons were brushed aside by the still nervous arm of the veteran, or fell of themselves, after menacing an act that it would seem no one had courage to perform. Fortunately, the vindictive Magua was searching for his victim in the very band the veteran had just quitted.

"Father—father—we are here!" shrieked Alice, as he passed, at no great distance, without appearing to heed them. "Come to us, father, or we die!"

The cry was repeated, and in terms and tones that might have melted a heart of stone, but it was unanswered. Once, indeed, the old man appeared to catch the sounds, for he paused and listened; but Alice had dropped senseless on the earth, and Cora had sunk at her side, hovering in untiring tenderness over her lifeless form. Munro shook his head in disappointment, and proceeded, bent on the high duty of his station.

"Lady," said Gamut, who, helpless and useless as he was, had not yet dreamed of deserting his trust, "it is the jubilee of the devils, and this is not a meet place for Christians to tarry in. Let us up and fly."

"Go," said Cora, still gazing at her unconscious sister, "save thyself. To me thou canst not be of further use."

David comprehended the unyielding character of her resolution, by the simple but expressive gesture that accompanied her words. He gazed, for a moment, at the dusky forms that were acting their hellish rites on every side of him, and his tall person grew more erect, while his chest heaved, and every feature swelled, and seemed to speak with the power of the feelings by which he was governed.

"If the Jewish boy might tame the evil spirit of Saul by the sound of his harp, and the words of sacred song, it may not be amiss," he said, "to try the potency of music here."

Then raising his voice to its highest tones, he poured out a strain so powerful as to be heard even amid the din of that bloody field. More than one savage rushed towards them, thinking to rifle the unprotected sisters of their attire, and bear away their scalps; but when they found this strange and unmoved figure riveted to his post, they paused to listen. Astonishment soon changed to admiration, and they passed on to other and less courageous victims, openly expressing their satisfaction at the firmness with which the white warrior sang his death song. Encouraged and deluded by his success, David exerted all his powers to extend what he believed so holy an influence. The unwonted sounds caught the ears of a distant savage, who flew raging from group to group like one who, scorning to touch the vulgar herd, hunted for some victim more worthy of his renown. It was Magua, who uttered a yell of pleasure when he beheld his ancient prisoners again at his mercy.

"Come," he said, laying his soiled hands on the dress of Cora, "the wigwam of the Huron is still open. Is it not better than this place?"

"Away!" cried Cora, veiling her eyes from his revolting aspect.

The Indian laughed tauntingly, as he held up his reeking hand, and answered, "It is red, but it comes from white veins!"

"Monster! there is blood, oceans of blood, upon thy soul: thy spirit has moved this scene."

"Magua is a great chief!" returned the exulting savage; "will the dark hair go to his tribe?"

"Never! strike, if thou wilt, and complete thy revenge."

He hesitated a moment; and then catching the light and senseless form of Alice in his arms, the subtle Indian moved swiftly across the plain towards the woods.

"Hold!" shrieked Cora, following wildly on his footsteps: "release the child! wretch! what is 't you do?"

But Magua was deaf to her voice; or rather he knew his power, and was determined to maintain it.

"Stay—lady—stay," called Gamut, after the unconscious Cora. "The holy charm is beginning to be felt, and soon shalt thou see this horrid tumult stilled."

Perceiving that, in his turn, he was unheeded, the faithful David followed the distracted sister, raising his voice again in sacred song, and sweeping the air to the measure, with his long arm, in diligent accompaniment. In this manner they traversed the plain, through the flying, the wounded, and the dead. The fierce Huron was at any time sufficient for himself and the victim that he bore; though Cora would have fallen, more than once, under the blows of her savage enemies, but for the extraordinary being who stalked in her rear, and who now appeared to the astonished natives gifted with the protecting spirit of madness.

Magua, who knew how to avoid the more pressing dangers, and also to elude pursuit, entered the woods through a low ravine, where he quickly found the Narragansets, which the travellers had abandoned so shortly before, awaiting his appearance, in custody of a savage as fierce and as malign in his expression as himself. Laying Alice on one of the horses, he made a sign to Cora to mount the other.

Notwithstanding the horror excited by the presence of her captor, there was a present relief in escaping from the bloody scene enacting on the plain, to which Cora could not be altogether insensible. She took her seat, and held forth her arms for her sister, with an air of entreaty and love that even the Huron could not deny. Placing Alice, then, on the same animal with Cora, he seized the bridle, and commenced his route by plunging deeper into the forest. David, perceiving that he was left alone, utterly disregarded as a subject too worthless even to destroy, threw his long limb across the saddle of the beast they had deserted, and made such progress in the pursuit as the difficulties of the path permitted.

They soon began to ascend; but as the motion had a tendency to revive the dormant faculties of her sister, the attention of Cora was too much divided between the tenderest solicitude in her behalf, and in listening to the cries which were still too audible on the plain, to note the direction in which they journeyed. When, however, they gained the flattened surface of the mountain-top, and approached the eastern precipice, she recognized the spot to which she had once before been led under the more friendly auspices of the scout. Here Magua suffered them to dismount; and, notwithstanding their own captivity, the curiosity which seems inseparable from horror induced them to gaze at the sickening sight below.

The cruel work was still unchecked. On every side the captured were flying before their relentless persecutors, while the armed columns of the Christian king stood fast in an apathy which has never been explained, and which has left an immovable blot on the otherwise fair escutcheon of their leader. Nor was the sword of death stayed until cupidity got the mastery of revenge. Then, indeed, the shrieks of the wounded and the yells of their murderers grew less frequent, until finally the cries of horror were lost to their ear, or were drowned in the loud, long, and piercing whoops of the triumphant savages.

CHAPTER XVIII

Why, any thing:
An honorable murderer, if you will;
For nought I did in hate, but all in honor.
SHAKESPEARE, *Othello,* V. ii. 293.

The bloody and inhuman scene rather incidentally mentioned than described in the preceding chapter, is conspicuous in the pages of colonial history, by the merited title of "The Massacre of William Henry." It so far deepened the stain which a previous and very similar event had left upon the reputation of the French commander, that it was not entirely erased by his early and glorious death. It is now becoming obscured by time; and thousands, who know that Montcalm died like a hero on the plains of Abraham, have yet to learn how much he was deficient in that moral courage without which no man can be truly great. Pages might be written to prove, from this illustrious example, the defects of human excellence; to show how easy it is for generous sentiments, high courtesy, and chivalrous courage, to lose their influence beneath the chilling blight of selfishness, and to exhibit to the world a man who was great in all the minor attributes of character, but who was found wanting when it became necessary to prove how much principle is superior to policy. But the task would exceed our prerogatives; and, as history, like love, is so apt to surround her heroes with an atmosphere of imaginary brightness, it is probable that Louis de Saint Véran will be viewed by posterity only as the gallant defender of his country, while his cruel apathy on the shores of the Oswego and of the Horican will be forgotten. Deeply regretting this weakness on the part of a sister muse, we shall at once retire from her sacred precincts, within the proper limits of our own humble vocation.

The third day from the capture of the fort was drawing to a close, but the business of the narrative must still detain the reader on the shores of the "holy lake." When last seen, the environs of the works were filled with violence and uproar. They were now possessed by stillness and death. The blood-stained conquerors had departed; and their camp, which had so lately rung with the merry rejoicings of a victorious army, lay a silent and deserted city of huts. The fortress was a smouldering ruin; charred rafters, fragments of exploded artillery, and rent masonwork, covering its earthen mounds in confused disorder.

A frightful change had also occurred in the season. The sun had hid its warmth behind an impenetrable mass of vapor, and hundreds of human forms, which had blackened beneath the fierce heats of August, were stiffening in their deformity, before the blasts of a premature November. The curling and spotless mists, which had been seen sailing above the hills towards the north, were now returning in an interminable dusky sheet, that was urged along by the fury of a tempest. The crowded mirror of the Horican was gone; and in its place the green and angry waters lashed the shores, as if indignantly casting back its impurities to the polluted strand. Still the clear fountain retained a portion of its charmed influence, but it reflected only the sombre gloom that fell from the impending heavens. That humid and congenial atmosphere which commonly adorned the view, veiling its harshness and softening its asperities, had disappeared, and the northern air poured across the waste of water so harsh and unmingled that nothing was left to be conjectured by the eye, or fashioned by the fancy.

The fiercer element had cropped the verdure of the plain, which looked as though it were scathed by the consuming lightning. But here and there a dark green tuft rose in the midst of the desolation; the earliest fruits of a soil that had been fattened with human blood. The whole landscape, which, seen by a favoring light and in a genial temperature, had been found so lovely, appeared now like some pictured allegory of life, in which objects were arrayed in their harshest but truest colors, and without the relief of any shadowing.

The solitary and arid blades of grass arose from the passing gusts fearfully perceptible; the bold and rocky mountains were too distinct in their barrenness, and the eye even sought relief, in vain, by attempting to pierce the illimitable void of heaven, which was shut to its gaze by the dusky sheet of ragged and driving vapor.

The wind blew unequally; sometimes sweeping heavily along the ground, seeming to whisper its moanings in the cold ears of the dead, then rising in a shrill and mournful whistling, it entered the forest with a rush that filled the air with the leaves and branches it scattered in its path. Amid the unnatural shower, a few hungry ravens struggled with the gale; but no sooner was the green ocean of woods, which stretched beneath them, passed, than they gladly stooped, at random, to their hideous banquet.

In short, it was a scene of wildness and desolation; and it appeared as if all who had profanely entered it had been stricken, at a blow, by the relentless arm of death. But the prohibition had ceased; and for the first time since the perpetrators of those foul deeds which had assisted to disfigure the scene were gone, living human beings had now presumed to approach the place.

About an hour before the setting of the sun, on the day already mentioned, the forms of five men might have been seen issuing from the narrow vista of trees, where the path to the Hudson entered the forest, and advancing in the direction of the ruined works. At first their progress was slow and guarded, as though they entered with reluctance amid the horrors of the spot, or dreaded the renewal of its frightful incidents. A light figure preceded the rest of the party, with the caution and activity of a native; ascending every hillock to reconnoitre, and indicating, by gestures, to his companions, the route he deemed it most prudent to pursue. Nor were those in the rear wanting in every caution and foresight known to forest warfare. One among them, he also was an Indian, moved a little on one flank, and watched the margin of the woods, with eyes long accustomed to read the smallest sign of danger. The remaining three were white, though clad in vestments adapted, both in quality and color, to their present hazardous pursuit,—that of hanging on the skirts of the retiring army in the wilderness.

The effect produced by the appalling sights that constantly arose in their path to the lake shore were as different as the characters of the respective individuals who composed the party. The youth in front threw serious but furtive glances at the mangled victims, as he stepped lightly across the plain, afraid to exhibit his feelings, and yet too inexperienced to quell entirely their sudden and powerful influence. His red associate, however, was superior to such a weakness. He passed the groups of dead with a steadiness of purpose, and an eye so calm, that nothing but long and inveterate practice could enable him to maintain. The sensations produced in the minds of even the white men were different, though uniformly sorrowful. One, whose gray locks and furrowed lineaments, blending with a martial air and tread, betrayed, in spite of the disguise of a woodsman's dress, a man long experienced in scenes of war, was not ashamed to groan aloud, whenever a spectacle of more than usual horror came under his view. The young man at his elbow shuddered, but seemed to suppress his feelings in tenderness to his companion. Of them all, the straggler who brought up the rear appeared alone to betray his real thoughts, without fear of observation or dread of consequences. He gazed at the most appalling sight with eyes and muscles that knew not how to waver, but with execrations so bitter and deep as to denote how much he denounced the crime of his enemies.

The reader will perceive at once, in these respective characters, the Mohicans, and their white friend, the scout; together with Munro and Heyward. It was, in truth, the father in quest of his children, attended by the youth who felt so deep a stake in their happiness, and those brave and trusty foresters, who had already proved their skill and fidelity through the trying scenes related.

When Uncas, who moved in front, had reached the centre of the plain, he raised a cry that drew his companions in a body to the spot. The young warrior had halted over a group of females who lay in a cluster, a confused mass of dead. Notwithstanding the revolting horror of the exhibition, Munro and Heyward flew towards the festering heap, endeavoring, with a love that no unseemliness could extinguish, to discover whether any vestiges of those they sought were to be seen among the tattered and many-colored garments. The father and the lover found instant relief in the search; though each was condemned again to experience the misery of an uncertainty that was hardly less insupportable than the most revolting truth. They were standing silent and thoughtful, around the melancholy pile, when the scout approached. Eyeing the sad spectacle with an angry countenance, the sturdy woodsman, for the first time since entering the plain, spoke intelligibly and aloud:—

"I have been on many a shocking field, and have followed a trail of blood for weary miles," he said, "but never have I found that hand of the devil so plain as it is here to be seen! Revenge is an Indian feeling, and all who know me know that there is no cross in my veins; but this much will I say—here, in the face of heaven, and with the power of the Lord so manifest in this howling wilderness,—that should these Frenchers ever trust themselves again within the range of a ragged bullet, there is one rifle shall play its part, so long as flint will fire or powder burn! I leave the tomahawk and knife to such as have a natural gift to use them. What say you, Chingachgook," he added in Delaware; "shall the Hurons boast of this to their women when the deep snows come?"

A gleam of resentment flashed across the dark lineaments of the Mohican chief; he loosened his knife in his sheath, and then turning calmly from the sight, his countenance settled into a repose as deep as if he never knew the instigation of passion.

"Montcalm! Montcalm!" continued the deeply resentful and less self-restrained scout; "they say a time must come, when all the deeds done in the flesh will be seen at a single look; and that by eyes cleared from mortal infirmities. Woe betide the wretch who is born to behold this plain, with the judgment hanging about his soul! Ha—as I am a man of white blood, yonder lies a red-skin, without the hair of his head where nature rooted it! Look to him, Delaware; it may be one of your missing people; and he should have burial like a stout warrior. I see it in your eye, Sagamore: a Huron pays for this, afore the fall winds have blown away the scent of the blood!"

Chingachgook approached the mutilated form, and turning it over, he found the distinguishing marks of one of those six allied tribes, or nations, as they were called, who, while they fought in the English ranks, were so deadly hostile to his own people. Spurning the loathsome object with his foot, he turned from it with the same indifference he would have quitted a brute carcass. The scout comprehended the action, and very deliberately pursued his own way, continuing, however, his denunciations against the French commander in the same resentful strain.

"Nothing but vast wisdom and onlimited power should dare to sweep off men in multitudes," he added; "for it is only the one that can know the necessity of the judgment; and what is there, short of the other, than can replace the creatures of the Lord? I hold it a sin to kill the second buck afore the first is eaten, unless a march in the front, or an ambushment, be contemplated. It is a different matter with a few warriors in open and rugged fight, for 't is their gift to die with the rifle or the tomahawk in hand; according as their natures may happen to be, white or red. Uncas, come this way, lad, and let the ravens settle upon the Mingo. I know, from often seeing it, that they have a craving for the flesh of an Oneida; and it is as well to let the bird follow the gift of its natural appetite."

"Hugh!" exclaimed the young Mohican, rising on the extremities of his feet, and gazing intently in his front, frightening the raven to some other prey, by the sound and the action.

"What is it, boy?" whispered the scout, lowering his tall form into a crouching attitude, like a panther about to take his leap; "God send it be a tardy Frencher, skulking for plunder. I do believe Killdeer would take an oncommon range to-day!"

Uncas, without making any reply, bounded away from the spot, and in the next instant he was seen tearing from a bush, and waving in triumph, a fragment of the green riding-veil of Cora. The movement, the exhibition, and the cry, which again burst from the lips of the young Mohican, instantly drew the whole party about him.

"My child!" said Munro, speaking quick and wildly; "give me my child!"

"Uncas will try," was the short and touching answer. The simple but meaning assurance was lost on the father, who seized the piece of gauze, and crushed it in his hand, while his eyes roamed fearfully among the bushes, as if he equally dreaded and hoped for the secrets they might reveal.

"Here are no dead," said Heyward; "the storm seems not to have passed this way."

"That 's manifest; and clearer than the heavens above our heads," returned the undisturbed scout; "but either she, or they that have robbed her, have passed the bush; for I remember the rag she wore to hide a face that all did love to look upon. Uncas, you are right; the dark-hair has been here, and she has fled like a frightened fawn, to the wood; none who could fly would remain to be murdered. Let us search for the marks she left; for to Indian eyes, I sometimes think even a humming-bird leaves his trail in the air."

The young Mohican darted away at the suggestion, and the scout had hardly done speaking, before the former raised a cry of success from the margin of the forest. On reaching the spot, the anxious party perceived another portion of the veil fluttering on the lower branch of a beech.

"Softly, softly," said the scout, extending his long rifle in front of the eager Heyward; "we now know our work, but the beauty of the trail must not be deformed. A step too soon may give us hours of trouble. We have them though, that much is beyond denial."

"Bless ye, bless ye, worthy man!" exlaimed Munro, "whither, then, have they fled, and where are my babes?"

"The path they have taken depends on many chances. If they have gone alone, they are quite as likely to move in a circle as straight, and they may be within a dozen miles of us; but if the Hurons, or any of the French Indians, have laid hands on them, 't is probable they are now near the borders of the Canadas. But what matters that?" continued the deliberate scout, observing the powerful anxiety and disappointment the listeners exhibited; "here are the Mohicans and I on one end of the trail, and, rely on it, we find the other, though they should be a hundred leagues asunder! Gently, gently, Uncas, you are as impatient as a man in the settlements; you forget that light feet leave but faint marks!"

"Hugh!" exclaimed Chingachgook, who had been occupied in examining an opening that had been evidently made through the low underbush, which skirted the forest; and who now stood erect, as he pointed downwards, in the attitude and with the air of a man who beheld a disgusting serpent.

"Here is the palpable impression of the footstep of a man," cried Heyward, bending over the indicated spot; "he has trod in the margin of this pool, and the mark cannot be mistaken. They are captives."

"Better so than left to starve in the wilderness," returned the scout; "and they will leave a wider trail. I would wager fifty beaver skins against as many flints, that the Mohicans and I enter their wigwams within the month! Stoop to it, Uncas, and try what you can make of the moccasin; for moccasin it plainly is, and no shoe."

The young Mohican bent over the track, and removing the scattered leaves from around the place, he examined it with much of that sort of scrutiny that a money-dealer, in these days of pecuniary doubts, would bestow on a suspected due-bill. At length he arose from his knees, satisfied with the result of the examination.

"Well, boy," demanded the attentive scout, "what does it say? Can you make anything of the tell-tale?"

"Le Renard Subtil!"

"Ha! that rampaging devil again! there never will be an end of his loping till Killdeer has said a friendly word to him."

Heyward reluctantly admitted the truth of this intelligence, and now expressed rather his hopes than his doubts by saying,—

"One moccasin is so much like another, it is probable there is some mistake."

"One moccasin like another! you may as well say that one foot is like another; though we all know that some are long, and others short; some broad, and others narrow; some with high, and some with low insteps; some in-toed, and some out. One moccasin is no more like another than one book is like another; though they who can read in one are seldom able to tell the marks of the other. Which is all ordered for the best, giving to every man his natural advantages. Let me get down to it, Uncas; neither book nor moccasin is the worse for having two opinions, instead of one." The scout stooped to the task, and instantly added, "You are right, boy; here is the patch we saw so often in the other chase. And the fellow will drink when he can get an opportunity; your drinking Indian always learns to walk with a wider toe than the natural savage, it being the gift of a drunkard to straddle, whether of white or red skin. 'T is just the length and breadth, too! look at it, Sagamore; you measured the prints more than once, when we hunted the varments from Glenn's to the health-springs."

Chingachgook complied; and after finishing his short examination, he arose, and with a quiet demeanor, he merely pronounced the word—

"Magua!"

"Aye, 't is a settled thing; here then have passed the dark-hair and Magua."

"And not Alice?" demanded Heyward.

"Of her we have not yet seen the signs," returned the scout, looking closely around at the trees, the bushes, and the ground. "What have we there? Uncas, bring hither the thing you see dangling from yonder thorn-bush."

When the Indian had complied, the scout received the prize, and holding it on high, he laughed in his silent but heartfelt manner.

"'T is the tooting we'pon of the singer! now we shall have a trail a priest might travel," he said. "Uncas, look for the marks of a shoe that is long enough to uphold six feet two of tottering human flesh. I begin to have some hopes of the fellow, since he has given up squalling to follow some better trade."

"At least, he has been faithful to his trust," said Heyward; "and Cora and Alice are not without a friend."

"Yes," said Hawkeye, dropping his rifle, and leaning on it with an air of visible contempt, "he will do their singing. Can he slay a buck for their dinner, journey by the moss on the beeches, or cut the throat of a Huron? If not, the first cat-bird[22] he meets is the cleverest of the two. Well, boy, any signs of such a foundation?"

"Here is something like the footstep of one who has worn a shoe; can it be that of our friend?"

"Touch the leaves lightly, or you'll disconsart the formation. That! that is the print of a foot, but 't is the dark-hair's; and small it is, too, for one of such a noble height and grand appearance. The singer would cover it with his heel."

"Where! let me look on the footsteps of my child," said Munro, shoving the bushes aside, and bending fondly over the nearly obliterated impression. Though the tread which had left the mark had been light and rapid, it was still plainly visible. The aged soldier examined it with eyes that grew dim as he gazed; nor did he rise from his stooping posture until Heyward saw that he had watered the trace of his daughter's passage with a scalding tear. Willing to divert a distress which threatened each moment to break through the restraint of appearances, by giving the veteran something to do, the young man said to the scout,—

"As we now possess these infallible signs, let us commence our march. A moment, at such a time, will appear an age to the captives."

"It is not the swiftest leaping deer that gives the longest chase," returned Hawkeye, without moving his eyes from the different marks that had come under his view; "we know that the rampaging Huron has passed,—and the dark hair,—and the singer,—but where is she of the yellow locks and blue eyes? Though little, and far from being as bold as her sister, she is fair to the view, and pleasant in discourse. Has she no friend, that none care for her?"

"God forbid she should ever want hundreds! Are we not now in her pursuit? for one, I will never cease the search till she be found."

"In that case we may have to journey by different paths; for here she has not passed, light and little as her footstep would be."

---

[22]The powers of the American mocking-bird are generally known. But the true mocking-bird is not found so far north as the State of New York, where it has, however, two substitutes of inferior excellence: the cat-bird, so often named by the scout, and the bird vulgarly called ground-thresher. Either of these two last birds is superior to the nightingale, or the lark, though, in general, the American birds are less musical than those of Europe. [J.F.C.]

Heyward drew back, all his ardor to proceed seeming to vanish on the instant. Without attending to this sudden change in the other's humor, the scout, after musing a moment, continued,—

"There is no woman in this wilderness could leave such a print as that, but the dark-hair or her sister. We know that the first has been here, but where are the signs of the other? Let us push deeper on the trail, and if nothing offers, we must go back to the plain and strike another scent. Move on, Uncas, and keep your eyes on the dried leaves. I will watch the bushes, while your father shall run with a low nose to the ground. Move on, friends; the sun is getting behind the hills."

"Is there nothing that I can do?" demanded the anxious Heyward.

"You!" repeated the scout, who, with his red friends, was already advancing in the order he had prescribed; "yes, you can keep in our rear, and be careful not to cross the trail."

Before they had proceeded many rods, the Indians stopped, and appeared to gaze at some signs on the earth, with more than their usual keenness. Both father and son spoke quick and loud, now looking at the object of their mutual admiration, and now regarding each other with the most unequivocal pleasure.

"They have found the little foot!" exclaimed the scout, moving forward, without attending further to his own portion of the duty. "What have we here! An ambushment has been planted in the spot! No, by the truest rifle on the frontiers, here have been them one-sided horses again! Now the whole secret is out, and all is plain as the north star at midnight. Yes, here they have mounted. There the beasts have been bound to a sapling, in waiting; and yonder runs the broad path away to the north, in full sweep for the Canadas."

"But still there are no signs of Alice,—of the younger Miss Munro," said Duncan.

"Unless the shining bauble Uncas has just lifted from the ground should prove one. Pass it this way, lad, that we may look at it."

Heyward instantly knew it for a trinket that Alice was fond of wearing, and which he recollected, with the tenacious memory of a lover, to have seen, on the fatal morning of the massacre, dangling from the fair neck of his mistress. He seized the highly prized jewel; and as he proclaimed the fact, it vanished from the eyes of the wondering scout, who in vain looked for it on the ground, long after it was warmly pressed against the beating heart of Duncan.

"Pshaw!" said the disappointed Hawkeye, ceasing to rake the leaves with the breech of his rifle; "'t is a certain sign of age, when the sight begins to weaken. Such a glittering gewgaw, and not to be seen! Well, well, I can squint along a clouded barrel yet, and that is enough to settle all disputes between me and the Mingoes. I should like to find the thing too, if it were only to carry it to the right owner, and that would be bringing the two ends of what I call a long trail together,—for by this time the broad St. Lawrence, or, perhaps, the Great Lakes themselves, are atwixt us."

"So much the more reason why we should not delay our march," returned Heyward; "let us proceed."

"Young blood and hot blood, they say, are much the same thing. We are not about to start on a squirrel hunt, or to drive a deer into the Horican, but to outlie for days and nights, and to stretch across a wilderness where the feet of men seldom go, and where no bookish knowledge would carry you through harmless. An Indian never starts on such an expedition without smoking over his council fire; and though a man of white blood, I honor their customs in this particular, seeing that they are deliberate and wise. We will therefore go back, and light our fire to-night in the ruins of the old fort, and in the morning we shall be fresh, and ready to undertake our work like men, and not like babbling women or eager boys."

Heyward saw, by the manner of the scout, that altercation would be useless. Munro had again sunk into that sort of apathy which had beset him since his late overwhelming misfortunes, and from which he was apparently to be roused only by some new and powerful excitement. Making a merit of necessity, the young man took the veteran by the arm, and followed in the footsteps of the Indians and the scout, who had already begun to retrace the path which conducted them to the plain.

CHAPTER XIX

Salarino.—*Why, I am sure, if he forfeit, thou wilt not take his flesh: what's that good for?*
Shylock.—*To bait fish withal: if it will feed nothing else, it will feed my revenge.*

SHAKESPEARE, *Merchant of Venice,* III. i. 53.

The shades of evening had come to increase the dreariness of the place, when the party entered the ruins of William Henry. The scout and his companions immediately made their preparations to pass the night there, but with an earnestness and sobriety of demeanor that betrayed how much the unusual horrors they had just witnessed worked on even their practiced feelings. A few fragments of rafters were reared against a blackened wall; and when Uncas had covered them slightly with brush, the temporary accommodations were deemed sufficient. The young Indian pointed towards his rude hut, when his labor was ended; and Heyward, who understood the meaning of the silent gesture, gently urged Munro to enter. Leaving the bereaved old man alone with his sorrows, Duncan immediately returned into the open air, too much excited himself to seek the repose he had recommended to his veteran friend.

While Hawkeye and the Indians lighted their fire, and took their evening's repast, a frugal meal of dried bear's meat, the young man paid a visit to that curtain of the dilapidated fort which looked out on the sheet of the Horican. The wind had fallen, and the waves were already rolling on the sandy beach beneath him in a more regular and tempered succession. The clouds, as if tired of their furious chase, were breaking asunder, the heavier volumes gathering in black masses about the horizon, while the lighter scud still hurried above the water, or eddied among the tops of the mountains, like broken flights of birds hovering around their roosts. Here and there a red and fiery star struggled through the drifting vapor, furnishing a lurid gleam of brightness to the dull aspect of the heavens. Within the bosom of the encircling hills, an impenetrable darkness had already settled; and the plain lay like a vast and deserted charnelhouse, without omen or whisper to disturb the slumbers of its numerous and hapless tenants.

Of this scene, so chillingly in accordance with the past, Duncan stood for many minutes a rapt observer. His eyes wandered from the bosom of the mound, where the foresters were seated around their glimmering fire, to the fainter light which still lingered in the skies, and then rested long and anxiously on the embodied gloom which lay like a dreary void on that side of him where the dead reposed. He soon fancied that inexplicable sounds arose from the place, though so indistinct and stolen as to render not only their nature but even their existence uncertain.

Ashamed of his apprehensions, the young man turned towards the water, and strove to divert his attention to the mimic stars that dimly glimmered on its moving surface. Still, his too conscious ears performed their ungrateful duty, as if to warn him of some lurking danger. At length a swift trampling seemed, quite audibly, to rush athwart the darkness. Unable any longer to quiet his uneasiness, Duncan spoke in a low voice to the scout, requesting him to ascend the mound to the place where he stood. Hawkeye threw his rifle across an arm, and complied, but with an air so unmoved and calm as to prove how much he counted on the security of their position.

"Listen!" said Duncan, when the other placed himself deliberately at his elbow; "there are suppressed noises on the plain, which may show that Montcalm has not yet entirely deserted his conquest."

"Then ears are better than eyes," said the undisturbed scout, who, having just deposited a portion of a bear between his grinders, spoke thick and slow, like one whose mouth was doubly occupied. "I myself saw him caged in Ty, with all his host; for your Frenchers, when they have done a clever thing, like to get back, and have a dance or a merry-making with the women over their success."

"I know not. An Indian seldom sleeps in war, and plunder may keep a Huron here after his tribe has departed. It would be well to extinguish the fire, and have a watch—listen! you hear the noise I mean!"

"An Indian more rarely lurks about the graves. Though ready to slay, and not over-regardful of the means, he is commonly content with the scalp, unless when blood is hot, and temper up; but after the spirit is once fairly gone, he forgets his enmity, and is willing to let the dead find their natural rest. Speaking of spirits, Major, are you of opinion that the heaven of a red-skin and of us whites will be one and the same?"

"No doubt—no doubt. I thought I heard it again! or was it the rustling of the leaves in the top of the beech?"

"For my own part," continued Hawkeye, turning his face, for a moment, in the direction indicated by Heyward, but with a vacant and careless manner, "I believe that paradise is ordained for happiness; and that men will be indulged in it according to their dispositions and gifts. I therefore judge that a red-skin is not far from the truth when he believes he is to find them glorious hunting-grounds of which his traditions tell; nor, for that matter, do I think it would be any disparagement to a man without a cross to pass his time"—

"You hear it again?" interrupted Duncan.

"Aye, aye; when food is scarce, and when food is plenty, a wolf grows bold," said the unmoved scout. "There would be picking, too, among the skins of the devils, if there was light and time for the sport. But, concerning the life that is to come, Major: I have heard preachers say, in the settlements, that heaven was a place of rest. Now men's minds differ as to their ideas of enjoyment. For myself, and I say it with reverence to the ordering of Providence, it would be no great indulgence to be kept shut up in those mansions of which they preach, having a natural longing for motion and the chase."

Duncan, who was now made to understand the nature of the noises he had heard, answered, with more attention to the subject which the humor of the scout had chosen for discussion, by saying,—

"It is difficult to account for the feelings that may attend the last great change."

"It would be a change, indeed, for a man who has passed his days in the open air," returned the single-minded scout; "and who has so often broken his fast on the head waters of the Hudson, to sleep within sound of the roaring Mohawk. But it is a comfort to know we serve a merciful Master, though we do it each after his fashion, and with great tracts of wilderness atween us—what goes there?"

"Is it not the rushing of the wolves you have mentioned?"

Hawkeye slowly shook his head, and beckoned for Duncan to follow him to a spot to which the glare from the fire did not extend. When he had taken this precaution, the scout placed himself in an attitude of intense attention, and listened long and keenly for a repetition of the low sound that had so unexpectedly startled him. His vigilance, however, seemed exercised in vain; for after a fruitless pause he whispered to Duncan,—

"We must give a call to Uncas. The boy has Indian senses, and may hear what is hid from us; for being a white-skin, I will not deny my nature."

The young Mohican, who was conversing in a low voice with his father, started as he heard the moaning of an owl, and springing on his feet he looked towards the black mounds, as if seeking the place whence the sounds proceeded. The scout repeated the call, and in a few moments Duncan saw the figure of Uncas stealing cautiously along the rampart, to the spot where they stood.

Hawkeye explained his wishes in a very few words, which were spoken in the Delaware tongue. So soon as Uncas was in possession of the reason why he was summoned, he threw himself flat on the turf, where, to the eyes of Duncan, he appeared to lie quiet and motionless. Surprised at the immovable attitude of the young warrior, and curious to observe the manner in which he employed his faculties to obtain the desired information, Heyward advanced a few steps, and bent over the dark object on which he had kept his eyes riveted. Then it was he discovered that the form of Uncas had vanished, and that he beheld only the dark outline of an inequality in the embankment.

"What has become of the Mohican?" he demanded of the scout, stepping back in amazement; "it was here that I saw him fall, and I could have sworn that here he yet remained."

"Hist! speak lower; for we know not what ears are open, and the Mingoes are a quick-witted breed. As for Uncas, he is out on the plain, and the Maquas, if any such are about us, will find their equal."

"You think that Montcalm has not called off all his Indians? Let us give the alarm to our companions, that we may stand to our arms. Here are five of us, who are not unused to meet an enemy."

"Not a word to either, as you value life. Look at the Sagamore, how like a grand Indian chief he sits by the fire. If there are any skulkers out in the darkness, they will never discover, by his countenance, that we suspect danger at hand."

"But they may discover him, and it will prove his death. His person can be too plainly seen by the light of that fire, and he will become the first and most certain victim."

"It is undeniable that now you speak the truth," returned the scout, betraying more anxiety than was usual; "yet what can be done? A single suspicious look might bring on an attack before we are ready to receive it. He knows, by the call I gave to Uncas, that we have struck a scent: I will tell him that we are on the trail of the Mingoes; his Indian nature will teach him how to act."

The scout applied his fingers to his mouth, and raised a low hissing sound, that caused Duncan, at first, to start aside, believing that he heard a serpent. The head of Chingachgook was resting on a hand, as he sat musing by himself; but the moment he heard the warning of the animal whose name he bore, it arose to an upright position, and his dark eyes glanced swiftly and keenly on every side of him. With this sudden and perhaps involuntary movement, every appearance of surprise or alarm ended. His rifle lay untouched, and apparently unnoticed, within reach of his hand. The tomahawk that he had loosened in his belt for the sake of ease, was even suffered to fall from its usual situation to the ground, and his form seemed to sink, like that of a man whose nerves and sinews were suffered to relax for the purpose of rest. Cunningly resuming his former position, though with a change of hands, as if the movement had been made merely to relieve the limb, the native awaited the result with a calmness and fortitude that none but an Indian warrior would have known how to exercise.

But Heyward saw that while to a less instructed eye the Mohican chief appeared to slumber, his nostrils were expanded, his head was turned a little to one side, as if to assist the organs of hearing, and that his quick and rapid glances ran incessantly over every object within the power of his vision.

"See the noble fellow!" whispered Hawkeye, pressing the arm of Heyward; "he knows that a look or a motion might disconsart our schemes, and put us at the mercy of them imps"—

He was interrupted by the flash and report of a rifle. The air was filled with sparks of fire, around that spot where the eyes of Heyward were still fastened with admiration and wonder. A second look told him that Chingachgook had disappeared in the confusion. In the meantime, the scout had thrown forward his rifle, like one prepared for service, and awaited impatiently the moment when an enemy might rise to view. But with the solitary and fruitless attempt made on the life of Chingachgook, the attack appeared to have terminated. Once or twice the listeners thought they could distinguish the distant rustling of bushes, as bodies of some unknown description rushed through them; nor was it long before Hawkeye pointed out the "scampering of the wolves," as they fled precipitately before the passage of some intruder on their proper domains. After an impatient and breathless pause, a plunge was heard in the water, and it was immediately followed by the report of another rifle.

"There goes Uncas!" said the scout: "the boy bears a smart piece! I know its crack, as well as a father knows the language of his child, for I carried the gun myself until a better offered."

"What can this mean?" demanded Duncan: "we are watched, and, as it would seem, marked for destruction."

"Yonder scattered brand can witness that no good was intended, and this Indian will testify that no harm has been done," returned the scout, dropping his rifle across his arm again, and following Chingachgook, who just then reappeared within the circle of light, into the bosom of the works. "How is it, Sagamore? Are the Mingoes upon us in earnest, or is it only one of those reptiles who hang upon the skirts of a war party, to scalp the dead, go in, and make their boast among the squaws of the valiant deeds done on the pale-faces?"

Chingachgook very quietly resumed his seat; nor did he make any reply, until after he had examined the firebrand which had been struck by the bullet, that had nearly proved fatal to himself. After which, he was content to reply, holding a single finger up to view, with the English monosyllable,—

"One."

"I thought as much," returned Hawkeye, seating himself; "and as he had got the cover of the lake afore Uncas pulled upon him, it is more than probable the knave will sing his lies about some great ambushment, in which he was outlying on the trail of two Mohicans and a white hunter—for the officers can be considered as little better than idlers in such a skrimmage. Well, let him—let him. There are always some honest men in every nation, though heaven knows, too, that they are scarce among the Maquas, to look down an upstart when he brags ag'in the face of reason. The varlet sent his lead within whistle of your ears, Sagamore."

Chingachgook turned a calm and incurious eye towards the place where the ball had struck, and then resumed his former attitude, with a composure that could not be disturbed by so trifling an incident. Just then Uncas glided into the circle, and seated himself at the fire, with the same appearance of indifference as was maintained by his father.

Of these several movements Heyward was a deeply interested and wondering observer. It appeared to him as though the foresters had some secret means of intelligence, which had escaped the vigilance of his own faculties. In place of that eager and garrulous narration with which a white youth would have endeavored to communicate, and perhaps exaggerate, that which had passed out in the darkness of the plain, the young warrior was seemingly content to let his deeds speak for themselves. It was, in fact, neither the moment nor the occasion for an Indian to boast of his exploits; and it is probable that had Heyward neglected to inquire, not another syllable would, just then, have been uttered on the subject.

"What has become of our enemy, Uncas?" demanded Duncan: "we heard your rifle, and hoped you had not fired in vain."

The young chief removed a fold of his hunting shirt, and quietly exposed the fatal tuft of hair, which he bore as the symbol of victory. Chingachgook laid his hand on the scalp, and considered it for a moment with deep attention. Then dropping it, with disgust depicted on his strong features, he ejaculated,—

"Oneida!"

"Oneida!" repeated the scout, who was fast losing his interest in the scene, in an apathy nearly assimilated to that of his red associates, but who now advanced with uncommon earnestness to regard the bloody badge. "By the Lord, if the Oneidas are outlying upon the trail, we shall be flanked by devils on every side of us! Now, to white eyes there is no difference between this bit of skin and that of any other Indian, and yet the Sagamore declares it came from the poll of a Mingo; nay, he even names the tribe of the poor devil with as much ease as if the scalp was the leaf of a book, and each hair a letter. What right have Christian whites to boast of their learning, when a savage can read a language that would prove too much for the wisest of them all! What say *you*, lad; of what people was the knave?"

Uncas raised his eyes to the face of the scout, and answered, in his soft voice,—

"Oneida."

"Oneida, again! when one Indian makes a declaration it is commonly true; but when he is supported by his people, set it down as gospel!"

"The poor fellow has mistaken us for French," said Heyward; "or he would not have attempted the life of a friend."

"He mistake a Mohican in his paint for a Huron! You would be as likely to mistake the white-coated grenadiers of Montcalm for the scarlet jackets of the 'Royal Americans,'" returned the scout. "No, no, the sarpent knew his errand; nor was there any great mistake in the matter, for there is but little love atween a Delaware and a Mingo, let their tribes go out to fight for whom they may, in a white quarrel. For that matter, though the Oneidas do serve his sacred Majesty, who is my own sovereign lord and master, I should not have deliberated long about letting off Killdeer at the imp myself had luck thrown him in my way."

"That would have been an abuse of our treaties, and unworthy of your character."

"When a man consorts much with a people," continued Hawkeye, "if they are honest and he no knave, love will grow up atwixt them. It is true that white cunning has managed to throw the tribes into great confusion, as respects friends and enemies; so that the Hurons and the Oneidas, who speak the same tongue, or what may be called the same, take each other's scalps, and the Delawares are divided among themselves; a few hanging about their great council fire on their own river, and fighting on the same side with the Mingoes, while the greater part are in the Canadas, out of natural enmity to the Maquas—thus throwing everything into disorder, and destroying all the harmony of warfare. Yet a red natur' is not likely to alter with every shift of policy; so that the love atwixt a Mohican and a Mingo is much like the regard between a white man and a sarpent."

"I regret to hear it; for I had believed those natives who dwelt within our boundaries had found us too just and liberal, not to identify themselves fully with our quarrels."

"Why, I believe it is natur' to give a preference to one's own quarrels before those of strangers. Now, for myself, I do love justice; and therefore I will not say I hate a Mingo, for that may be unsuitable to my color and my religion, though I will just repeat, it may have been owing to the night that Killdeer had no hand in the death of this skulking Oneida."

Then, as if satisfied with the force of his own reasons, whatever might be their effect on the opinions of the other disputant, the honest but implacable woodsman turned from the fire, content to let the controversy slumber. Heyward withdrew to the rampart, too uneasy and too little accustomed to the warfare of the woods to remain at ease under the possibility of such insidious attacks. Not so, however, with the scout and the Mohicans. Those acute and long practiced senses, whose powers so often exceed the limits of all ordinary credulity, after having detected the danger, had enabled them to ascertain its magnitude and duration. Not one of the three appeared in the least to doubt their perfect security, as was indicated by the preparations that were soon made to sit in council over their future proceedings.

The confusion of nations, and even of tribes, to which Hawkeye alluded, existed at that period in the fullest force. The great tie of language, and, of course, of a common origin, was severed in many places; and it was one of its consequences, that the Delaware and the Mingo (as the people of the Six Nations were called) were found fighting in the same ranks, while the latter sought the scalp of the Huron, though believed to be the root of his own stock. The Delawares were even divided among themselves. Though love for the soil which had belonged to his ancestors kept the Sagamore of the Mohicans with a small band of followers who were serving at Edward, under the banners of the English king, by far the largest portion of his nation were known to be in the field as allies of Montcalm. The reader probably knows, if enough has not already been gleaned from this narrative, that the Delaware, or Lenape, claimed to be the progenitors of that numerous people who once were masters of most of the Eastern and Northern States of America, of whom the community of the Mohicans was an ancient and highly honored member.

It was, of course, with a perfect understanding of the minute and intricate interests which had armed friend against friend, and brought natural enemies to combat by each other's side, that the scout and his companions now disposed themselves to deliberate on the measures that were to govern their future movements, amid so many jarring and savage races of men. Duncan knew enough of Indian customs to understand the reason that the fire was replenished, and why the warriors, not excepting Hawkeye, took their seats within the curl of its smoke with so much gravity and decorum. Placing himself at an angle of the works, where he might be a spectator of the scene within, while he kept a watchful eye against any danger from without, he awaited the result with as much patience as he could summon.

After a short and impressive pause, Chingachgook lighted a pipe whose bowl was curiously carved in one of the soft stones of the country, and whose stem was a tube of wood, and commenced smoking. When he had inhaled enough of the fragrance of the soothing weed, he passed the instrument into the hands of the scout. In this manner the pipe had made its rounds three several times, amid the most profound silence, before either of the party opened his lips. Then the Sagamore, as the oldest and highest in rank, in a few calm and dignified words proposed the subject for deliberation. He was answered by the scout, and Chingachgook rejoined when the other objected to his opinions. But the youthful Uncas continued a silent and respectful listener, until Hawkeye, in complaisance, demanded his opinion. Heyward gathered from the manners of the different speakers that the father and son espoused one side of a disputed question, while the white man maintained the other. The contest gradually grew warmer, until it was quite evident the feelings of the speakers began to be somewhat enlisted in the debate.

Notwithstanding the increasing warmth of the amicable contest, the most decorous Christian assembly, not even excepting those in which its reverend ministers are collected, might have learned a wholesome lesson of moderation from the forbearance and courtesy of the disputants. The words of Uncas were received with the same deep attention as those which fell from the maturer wisdom of his father; and so far from manifesting any impatience, neither spoke in reply, until a few moments of silent meditation were, seemingly, bestowed in deliberating on what had already been said.

The language of the Mohicans was accompanied by gestures so direct and natural, that Heyward had but little difficulty in following the thread of their argument. On the other hand, the scout was obscure; because, from the lingering pride of color, he rather affected the cold and artificial manner which characterizes all classes of Anglo-Americans, when unexcited. By the frequency with which the Indians described the marks of a forest trail, it was evident they urged a pursuit by land, while the repeated sweep of Hawkeye's arm towards the Horican denoted that he was for a passage across its waters.

The latter was, to every appearance, fast losing ground, and the point was about to be decided against him, when he arose to his feet, and shaking off his apathy, he suddenly assumed the manner of an Indian, and adopted all the arts of native eloquence. Elevating an arm, he pointed out the track of the sun, repeating the gesture for every day that was necessary to accomplish their object. Then he delineated a long and painful path, amid rocks and water-courses. The age and weakness of the slumbering and unconscious Munro were indicated by signs too palpable to be mistaken. Duncan perceived that even his own powers were spoken lightly of, as the scout extended his palm, and mentioned him by the appellation of the "Open Hand,"—a name his liberality had purchased of all the friendly tribes. Then came a representation of the light and graceful movements of a canoe, set in forcible contrast to the tottering steps of one enfeebled and tired. He concluded by pointing to the scalp of the Oneida, and apparently urging the necessity of their departing speedily, and in a manner that should leave no trail.

The Mohicans listened gravely, and with countenances that reflected the sentiments of the speaker. Conviction gradually wrought its influence, and towards the close of Hawkeye's speech, his sentences were accompanied by the customary exclamation of commendation. In short, Uncas and his father became converts to his way of thinking, abandoning their own previously expressed opinions with a liberality and candor that, had they been the representatives of some great and civilized people, would have infallibly worked their political ruin, by destroying forever their reputation for consistency.

The instant the matter in discussion was decided, the debate, and everything connected with it, except the result, appeared to be forgotten. Hawkeye, without looking round to read his triumph in applauding eyes, very composedly stretched his tall frame before the dying embers, and closed his own organs for sleep.

Left now in a measure to themselves, the Mohicans, whose time had been so much devoted to the interests of others, seized the moment to devote some attention to themselves. Casting off, at once, the grave and austere demeanor of an Indian chief, Chingachgook commenced speaking to his son in the soft and playful tones of affection. Uncas gladly met the familiar air of his father; and before the hard breathing of the scout announced that he slept, a complete change was effected in the manner of his two associates.

It is impossible to describe the music of their language, while thus engaged in laughter and endearments, in such a way as to render it intelligible to those whose ears have never listened to its melody. The compass of their voices, particularly that of the youth, was wonderful,—extending from the deepest bass to tones that were even feminine in softness. The eyes of the father followed the plastic and ingenious movements of the son with open delight, and he never failed to smile in reply to the other's contagious, but low laughter. While under the influence of these gentle and natural feelings, no trace of ferocity was to be seen in the softened features of the Sagamore. His figured panoply of death looked more like a disguise assumed in mockery, than a fierce annunciation of a desire to carry destruction in his footsteps.

After an hour passed in the indulgence of their better feelings, Chingachgook abruptly announced his desire to sleep, by wrapping his head in his blanket, and stretching his form on the naked earth. The merriment of Uncas instantly ceased; and carefully raking the coals in such a manner that they should impart their warmth to his father's feet, the youth sought his own pillow among the ruins of the place.

Imbibing renewed confidence from the security of these experienced foresters, Heyward soon imitated their example; and long before the night had turned, they who lay in the bosom of the ruined work seemed to slumber as heavily as the unconscious multitude whose bones were already beginning to bleach on the surrounding plain.

CHAPTER XX

Land of Albania! let me bend mine eyes
On thee, thou rugged nurse of savage men!
BYRON, *Childe Harold,* Canto II. xxxviii.

The heavens were still studded with stars when Hawkeye came to arouse the sleepers. Casting aside their cloaks, Munro and Heyward were on their feet while the woodsman was still making his low calls, at the entrance of the rude shelter where they had passed the night. When they issued from beneath its concealment, they found the scout awaiting their appearance nigh by, and the only salutation between them was the significant gesture for silence, made by their sagacious leader.

"Think over your prayers," he whispered, as they approached him; "for He to whom you make them knows all tongues; that of the heart, as well as those of the mouth. But speak not a syllable; it is rare for a white voice to pitch itself properly in the woods, as we have seen by the example of that miserable devil, the singer. Come," he continued, turning towards a curtain of the works; "let us get into the ditch on this side, and be regardful to step on the stones and fragments of wood as you go."

His companions complied, though to two of them the reasons of this extraordinary precaution were yet a mystery. When they were in the low cavity that surrounded the earthen fort on three sides, they found the passage nearly choked by the ruins. With care and patience, however, they succeeded in clambering after the scout, until they reached the sandy shore of the Horican.

"That's a trail that nothing but a nose can follow," said the satisfied scout, looking back along their difficult way; "grass is a treacherous carpet for a flying party to tread on, but wood and stone take no imprint from a moccasin. Had you worn your armed boots, there might, indeed, have been something to fear; but with the deerskin suitably prepared, a man may trust himself, generally, on rocks with safety. Shove in the canoe nigher to the land, Uncas; this sand will take a stamp as easily as the butter of the Jarmans on the Mohawk. Softly, lad, softly; it must not touch the beach, or the knaves will know by what road we have left the place."

The young man observed the precaution; and the scout, laying a board from the ruins to the canoe, made a sign for the two officers to enter. When this was done, everything was studiously restored to its former disorder; and then Hawkeye succeeded in reaching his little birchen vessel without leaving behind him any of those marks which he appeared so much to dread. Heyward was silent, until the Indians had cautiously paddled the canoe some distance from the fort, and within the broad and dark shadow that fell from the eastern mountain on the glassy surface of the lake; then he demanded,—

"What need have we for this stolen and hurried departure?"

"If the blood of an Oneida could stain such a sheet of pure water as this we float on," returned the scout, "your two eyes would answer your own question. Have you forgotten the skulking reptyle that Uncas slew?"

"By no means. But he was said to be alone, and dead men give no cause for fear."

"Aye, he was alone in his deviltry! but an Indian whose tribe counts so many warriors need seldom fear his blood will run without the death-shriek coming speedily from some of his enemies."

"But our presence—the authority of Colonel Munro—would prove a sufficient protection against the anger of our allies, especially in a case where the wretch so well merited his fate. I trust in Heaven you have not deviated a single foot from the direct line of our course, with so slight a reason!"

"Do you think the bullet of that varlet's rifle would have turned aside, though his sacred Majesty the King had stood in its path?" returned the stubborn scout. "Why did not the grand Frencher, he who is captain-general of the Canadas, bury the tomahawks of the Hurons, if a word from a white can work so strongly on the natur' of an Indian?"

The reply of Heyward was interrupted by a groan from Munro; but after he had paused a moment, in deference to the sorrow of his aged friend, he resumed the subject.

"The Marquis of Montcalm can only settle that error with his God," said the young man solemnly.

"Aye, aye; now there is reason in your words, for they are bottomed on religion and honesty. There is a vast difference between throwing a regiment of white coats atwixt the tribes and the prisoners, and coaxing an angry savage to forget he carries a knife and a rifle, with words that must begin with calling him your son. No, no," continued the scout, looking back at the dim shore of William Henry, which was now fast receding, and laughing in his own silent but heartfelt manner; "I have put a trail of water atween us; and unless the imps can make friends with the fishes, and hear who has paddled across their basin this fine morning, we shall throw the length of the Horican behind us before they have made up their minds which path to take."

"With foes in front, and foes in our rear, our journey is like to be one of danger."

"Danger!" repeated Hawkeye, calmly; "no, not absolutely of danger; for, with vigilant ears and quick eyes, we can manage to keep a few hours ahead of the knaves; or, if we must try the rifle, there are three of us who understand its gifts as well as any you can name on the borders. No, not of danger; but that we shall have what you may call a brisk push of it, is probable; and it may happen, a brush, a skrimmage, or some such divarsion, but always where covers are good, and ammunition abundant."

It is possible that Heyward's estimate of danger differed in some degree from that of the scout, for, instead of replying, he now sat in silence, while the canoe glided over several miles of water. Just as the day dawned, they entered the narrows of the lake,[23] and stole swiftly and cautiously among their numberless little islands. It was by this road that Montcalm had retired with his army, and the adventurers knew not but he had left some of his Indians in ambush, to protect the rear of his forces, and collect the stragglers. They therefore approached the passage with the customary silence of their guarded habits.

Chingachgook laid aside his paddle; while Uncas and the scout urged the light vessel through crooked and intricate channels, where every foot that they advanced exposed them to the danger of some sudden rising on their progress. The eyes of the Sagamore moved warily from islet to islet and copse to copse as the canoe proceeded; and when a clearer sheet of water permitted, his keen vision was bent along the bald rocks and impending forests that frowned upon the narrow strait.

Heyward, who was a doubly interested spectator, as well from the beauties of the place as from the apprehensions natural to his situation, was just believing that

---

[23]The beauties of Lake George are well known to every American tourist. In the height of the mountains which surround it, and in artificial accessories, it is inferior to the finest of the Swiss and Italian lakes, while in outline and purity of water it is fully their equal, and in the number and disposition of its isles and islets much superior to them all together. There are said to be some hundreds of islands in a sheet of water less than thirty miles long. The narrows which connect what may be called, in truth, two lakes, are crowded with islands to such a degree as to leave passages between them frequently of only a few feet in width. The lake itself varies in breadth from one to three miles.

The State of New York is remarkable for the number and beauty of its lakes. One of its frontiers lies on the vast sheet of Ontario, while Champlain stretches nearly a hundred miles along another. Oneida, Cayuga, Canandaigua, Seneca, and George, are all lakes of thirty miles in length, while those of a size smaller are without number. On most of these lakes there are now beautiful villages, and on many of them are steamboats. [J.F.C.]

he had permitted the latter to be excited without sufficient reason, when the paddle ceased moving, in obedience to a signal from Chingachgook.

"Hugh!" exclaimed Uncas, nearly at the moment that the light tap his father had made on the side of the canoe notified them of the vicinity of danger.

"What now?" asked the scout; "the lake is as smooth as if the winds had never blown, and I can see along its sheet for miles; there is not so much as the black head of a loon dotting the water."

The Indian gravely raised his paddle, and pointed in the direction in which his own steady look was riveted. Duncan's eyes followed the motion. A few rods in their front lay another of the low wooded islets, but it appeared as calm and peaceful as if its solitude had never been disturbed by the foot of man.

"I see nothing," he said, "but land and water; and a lovely scene it is."

"Hist!" interrupted the scout. "Aye, Sagamore, there is always a reason for what you do. 'T is but a shade and yet it is not natural. You see the mist, Major, that is rising above the island; you can't call it a fog, for it is more like a streak of thin cloud—"

"It is vapor from the water."

"That a child could tell. But what is the edging of blacker smoke that hangs along its lower side, and which you may trace down into the thicket of hazel? 'T is from a fire; but one that, in my judgment, has been suffered to burn low."

"Let us then push for the place, and relieve our doubts," said the impatient Duncan; "the party must be small that can lie on such a bit of land."

"If you judge Indian cunning by the rules you find in books, or by white sagacity, they will lead you astray, if not to your death," returned Hawkeye, examining the signs of the place with that acuteness which distinguished him. "If I may be permitted to speak in this matter, it will be to say that we have but two things to choose between: the one is to return, and give up all thoughts of following the Hurons—"

"Never!" exclaimed Heyward, in a voice far too loud for their circumstances.

"Well, well," continued Hawkeye, making a hasty sign to repress his impatience; "I am much of your mind myself, though I thought it becoming my experience to tell the whole. We must then make a push, and, if the Indians or Frenchers are in the narrows, run the guantlet through these toppling mountains. Is there reason in my words, Sagamore?"

The Indian made no other answer than by dropping his paddle into the water, and urging forward the canoe. As he held the office of directing its course, his resolution was sufficiently indicated by the movement. The whole party now plied their paddles vigorously, and in a very few moments they had reached a point whence they might command an entire view of the northern shore of the island, the side that had hitherto been concealed.

"There they are, by all the truth of signs," whispered the scout; "two canoes and a smoke. The knaves have n't yet got their eyes out of the mist, or we should hear the accursed whoop. Together friends! we are leaving them, and are already nearly out of whistle of a bullet."

The well known crack of a rifle, whose ball came skipping along the placid surface of the strait, and a shrill yell from the island, interrupted his speech, and announced that their passage was discovered. In another instant several savages were seen rushing into the canoes, which were soon dancing over the water, in pursuit. These fearful precursors of a coming struggle produced no change in the countenances and movements of his three guides, so far as Duncan could discover, except that the strokes of their paddles were longer and more in unison, and caused the little bark to spring forward like a creature possessing life and volition.

"Hold them there, Sagamore," said Hawkeye, looking coolly backward over his left shoulder, while he still plied his paddle; "keep them just there. Them Hurons have never a piece in their nation that will execute at this distance; but Killdeer has a barrel on which a man may calculate."

The scout, having ascertained that the Mohicans were sufficient of themselves to maintain the requisite distance, deliberately laid aside his paddle, and raised the fatal rifle. Three several times he brought the piece to his shoulder, and when his companions were expecting its report, he as often lowered it to request the Indians would permit their enemies to approach a little nigher. At length his acurate and fastidious eye seemed satisfied, and throwing out his left arm on the barrel, he was slowly elevating the muzzle, when an exclamation from Uncas, who sat in the bow, once more caused him to suspend the shot.

"What now, lad?" demanded Hawkeye; "you saved a Huron from the death-shriek by that word; have you reason for what you do?"

Uncas pointed towards the rocky shore a little in their front, whence another war canoe was darting directly across their course. It was too obvious now that their situation was imminently perilous, to need the aid of language to confirm it. The scout laid aside his rifle, and resumed the paddle, while Chingachgook inclined the bows of the canoe a little towards the western shore, in order to increase the distance between them and this new enemy. In the mean time they were reminded of the presence of those who pressed upon their rear, by wild and exulting shouts. The stirring scene awakened even Munro from his apathy.

"Let us make for the rocks on the main," he said, with the mien of a tired soldier, "and give battle to the savages. God forbid that I, or those attached to me and mine, should ever trust again to the faith of any servant of the Louis's!"

"He who wishes to prosper in Indian warfare," returned the scout, "must not be too proud to learn from the wit of a native. Lay her more along the land, Sagamore; we are doubling on the varlets, and perhaps they may try to strike our trail on the long calculation."

Hawkeye was not mistaken; for when the Hurons found their course was likely to throw them behind their chase, they rendered it less direct, until, by gradually bearing more and more obliquely, the two canoes were, ere long, gliding on parallel lines, within two hundred yards of each other. It now became entirely a trial of speed. So rapid was the progress of the light vessels, that the lake curled in their front, in miniature waves, and their motion became undulating by its own velocity. It was, perhaps, owing to this circumstance, in addition to the necessity of keeping every hand employed at the paddles, that the Hurons had not immediate recourse to their fire-arms. The exertions of the fugitives were too severe to continue long, and the pursuers had the advantage of numbers. Duncan observed, with uneasiness, that the scout began to look anxiously about him, as if searching for some further means of assisting their flight.

"Edge her a little more from the sun, Sagamore," said the stubborn woodsman; "I see the knaves are sparing a man to the rifle. A single broken bone might lose us our scalps. Edge more from the sun and we will put the island between us."

The expedient was not without its use. A long, low island lay at a little distance before them, and as they closed with it, the chasing canoe was compelled to take a side opposite to that on which the pursued passed. The scout and his companions did not neglect this advantage. But the instant they were hid from observation by the bushes, they redoubled efforts that before had seemed prodigious. The two canoes came round the last low point like two coursers at the top of their speed, the fugitives taking the lead. This change had brought them nigher to each other, however, while it altered their relative positions.

"You showed knowledge in the shaping of birchen bark, Uncas, when you chose this from among the Huron canoes," said the scout, smiling, apparently more in satisfaction at their superiority in the race, than from that prospect of final escape which now began to open a little upon them. "The imps have put all their strength again at the paddles, and we are to struggle for our scalps with bits of flattened wood, instead of clouded barrels and true eyes. A long stroke, and together, friends."

"They are preparing for a shot," said Heyward; "and as we are in a line with them, it can scarcely fail."

"Get you then into the bottom of the canoe," returned the scout; "you and the colonel; it will be so much taken from the size of the mark."

Heyward smiled, as he answered,—

"It would be but an ill example for the highest in rank to dodge while the warriors were under fire!"

"Lord! Lord! That is now a white man's courage!" exclaimed the scout; "and like too many of his notions, not to be maintained by reason. Do you think the Sagamore, or Uncas, or even I, who am a man without a cross, would deliberate about finding a cover in the skrimmage, when an open body would do no good? For what have the Frenchers reared up their Quebec, if fighting is always to be done in the clearings?"

"All that you say is very true, my friend," replied Heyward; "still, our customs must prevent us from doing as you wish."

A volley from the Hurons interrupted the discourse, and as the bullets whistled about them, Duncan saw the head of Uncas turned, looking back at himself and Munro. Notwithstanding the nearness of the enemy, and his own great personal danger, the countenance of the young warrior expressed no other emotion, as the former was compelled to think, than amazement at finding men willing to encounter so useless an exposure. Chingachgook was probably better acquainted with the notions of white men, for he did not even cast a glance aside from the riveted look his eye maintained on the object by which he governed their course. A ball soon struck the light and polished paddle from the hands of the chief, and drove it through the air, far in the advance. A shout arose from the Hurons, who seized the opportunity to fire another volley. Uncas described an arc in the water with his own blade, and as the canoe passed swiftly on, Chingachgook recovered his paddle, and flourishing it on high, he gave the war-whoop of the Mohicans, and then lent his strength and skill again to the important task.

The clamorous sounds of "Le Gros Serpent!" "La Longue Carabine!" "Le Cerf Agile!" burst at once from the canoes behind, and seemed to give new zeal to the pursuers. The scout seized Killdeer in his left hand, and elevating it above his head, he shook it in triumph at his enemies. The savages answered the insult with a yell, and immediately another volley succeeded. The bullets pattered along the lake, and one even pierced the bark of their little vessel. No perceptible emotion could be discovered in the Mohicans during this critical moment, their rigid features expressed neither hope nor alarm; but the scout again turned his head, and laughing in his own silent manner, he said to Heyward,—

"The knaves love to hear the sounds of their pieces; but the eye is not to be found among the Mingoes that can calculate a true range in a dancing canoe! You see the dumb devils have taken off a man to charge, and by the smallest measurement that can be allowed, we move three feet to their two!"

Duncan, who was not altogether as easy under this nice estimate of distances as his companions, was glad to find, however, that owing to their superior dexterity, and the diversion among their enemies, they were very sensibly obtaining the advantage. The Hurons soon fired again, and a bullet struck the blade of Hawkeye's paddle without injury.

"That will do," said the scout, examining the slight indentation with a curious eye; "it would not have cut the skin of an infant, much less of men who, like us, have been blown upon by the heavens in their anger. Now, Major, if you will try to use this piece of flattened wood, I'll let Killdeer take a part in the conversation."

Heyward seized the paddle, and applied himself to the work with an eagerness that supplied the place of skill, while Hawkeye was engaged in inspecting the priming of his rifle. The latter then took a swift aim, and fired. The Huron in the bows of the leading canoe had risen with a similar object, and he now fell backward, suffering his gun to escape from his hands into the water. In an instant, however, he recovered his feet, though his gestures were wild and bewildered. At the same moment his companions suspended their efforts, and the chasing canoes clustered together, and became stationary. Chingachgook and Uncas profited by the interval to regain their wind, though Duncan continued to work with the most persevering industry. The father and son now cast calm but inquiring glances at each other, to learn if either had sustained any injury by the fire; for both well knew that no cry or exclamation would, in such a moment of necessity, have been permitted to betray the accident. A few large drops of blood were trickling down the shoulder of the Sagamore, who, when he perceived that the eyes of Uncas dwelt too long on the sight, raised some water in the hollow of his hand, and, washing off the stain, was content to manifest in this simple manner the slightness of the injury.

"Softly, softly, Major," said the scout, who by this time had reloaded his rifle; "we are a little too far already for a rifle to put forth its beauties, and you see yonder imps are holding a council. Let them come up within striking distance—my eye may well be trusted in such a matter—and I will trail the varlets the length of the Horican, guaranteeing that not a shot of theirs shall, at the worst, more than break the skin, while Killdeer shall touch the life twice in three times."

"We forget our errand," returned the diligent Duncan. "For God's sake let us profit by this advantage, and increase our distance from the enemy."

"Give me my children," said Munro hoarsely; "trifle no longer with a father's agony, but restore me my babes."

Long and habitual deference to the mandates of his superiors had taught the scout the virute of obedience. Throwing a last and lingering glance at the distant canoes, he laid aside his rifle, and, relieving the wearied Duncan, resumed the paddle, which he wielded with sinews that never tired. His efforts were seconded by those of the Mohicans, and a very few minutes served to place such a sheet of water between them and their enemies that Heyward once more breathed freely.

The lake now began to expand, and their route lay along a wide reach, that was lined, as before, by high and ragged mountains. But the islands were few, and easily avoided. The strokes of the paddles grew more measured and regular, while they who plied them continued their labor, after the close and deadly chase from which they had just relieved themselves, with as much coolness as though their speed had been tried in sport, rather than under such pressing, nay, almost desperate circumstances.

Instead of following the western shore, whither their errand led them, the wary Mohican inclined his course more towards those hills behind which Montcalm was known to have led his army into the formidable fortress of Ticonderoga. As the Hurons, to every appearance, had abandoned the pursuit, there was no apparent reason for this excess of caution. It was, however, maintained for hours, until they had reached a bay, nigh the northern termination of the lake. Here the canoe was driven upon the beach, and the whole party landed. Hawkeye and Heyward ascended an adjacent bluff, where the former, after considering the expanse of water beneath him, pointed out to the latter a small black object, hovering under a headland, at the distance of several miles.

"Do you see it?" demanded the scout. "Now, what would you account that spot, were you left alone to white experience to find your way through this wilderness?"

"But for its distance and its magnitude, I should suppose it a bird. Can it be a living object?"

"'T is a canoe of good birchen bark, and paddled by fierce and crafty Mingoes. Though Providence has lent to those who inhabit the woods eyes that would be needless to men in the settlements, where there are inventions to assist the sight, yet no human organs can see all the dangers which at this moment circumvent us. These varlets pretend to be bent chiefly on their sun-down meal, but the moment it is dark they will be on our trail, as true as hounds on the scent. We must throw them off, or our pursuit of Le Renard Subtil may be given up. These lakes are useful at times, especially when the game takes the water," continued the scout, gazing about him with a countenance of concern; "but they give no cover, except it be to the fishes. God knows what the country would be, if the settlements should ever spread far from the two rivers. Both hunting and war would lose their beauty."

"Let us not delay a moment, without some good and obvious cause."

"I little like that smoke, which you may see worming up along the rock above the canoe," interrupted the abstracted scout. "My life on it, other's eyes than ours see it, and know its meaning. Well, words will not mend the matter, and it is time that we were doing."

Hawkeye moved away from the lookout, and descended, musing profoundly, to the shore. He communicated the result of his observations to his companions, in Delaware, and a short and earnest consultation succeeded. When it terminated, the three instantly set about executing their new resolutions.

The canoe was lifted from the water, and borne on the shoulders of the party. They proceeded into the wood, making as broad and obvious a trail as possible. They soon reached a watercourse, which they crossed, and continued onward, until they came to an extensive and naked rock. At this point, where their footsteps might be expected to be no longer visible, they retraced their route to the brook, walking backwards, with the utmost care. They now followed the bed of the little stream to the lake, into which they immediately launched their canoe again. A low point concealed them from the headland, and the margin of the lake was fringed for some distance with dense and overhanging bushes. Under the cover of these natural advantages, they toiled their way, with patient industry, until the scout pronounced that he believed it would be safe once more to land.

The halt continued until evening rendered objects indistinct and uncertain to the eye. Then they resumed their route, and, favored by the darkness, pushed silently and vigorously towards the western shore. Although the rugged outline of mountain, to which they were steering, presented no distinctive marks to the eyes of Duncan, the Mohican entered the little haven he had selected with the confidence and accuracy of an experienced pilot.

The boat was again lifted and borne into the woods, where it was carefully concealed under a pile of brush. The adventurers assumed their arms and packs, and the scout announced to Munro and Heyward that he and the Indians were at last in readiness to proceed.

CHAPTER XXI

If you find a man there, he shall die a flea's death.
SHAKESPEARE, *Merry Wives of Windsor,* IV. ii. 158.

The party had landed on the border of a region that is, even to this day, less known to the inhabitants of the States, than the deserts of Arabia or the steppes of Tartary. It was the sterile and rugged district which separates the tributaries of Champlain from those of the Hudson, the Mohawk, and the St. Lawrence. Since the period of our tale, the active spirit of the country has surrounded it with a belt of rich and thriving settlements, though none but the hunter or the savage is ever known, even now, to penetrate its wild recesses.

As Hawkeye and the Mohicans had, however, often traversed the mountains and valleys of this vast wilderness, they did not hesitate to plunge into its depths, with the freedom of men accustomed to its privations and difficulties. For many hours the travellers toiled on their laborious way, guided by a star, or following the direction of some water-course, until the scout called a halt, and holding a short consultation with the Indians, they lighted their fire, and made the usual preparations to pass the remainder of the night where they then were.

Imitating the example, and emulating the confidence, of their more experienced associates, Munro and Duncan slept without fear, if not without uneasiness. The dews were suffered to exhale, and the sun had dispersed the mists, and was shedding a strong and clear light in the forest, when the travellers resumed their journey.

After proceeding a few miles, the progress of Hawkeye, who led the advance, became more deliberate and watchful. He often stopped to examine the trees; nor did he cross a rivulet without attentively considering the quantity, the velocity, and the color of its waters. Distrusting his own judgment, his appeals to the opinion of Chingachgook were frequent and earnest. During one of these conferences, Heyward observed that Uncas stood a patient and silent, though, as he imagined, an interested listener. He was strongly tempted to address the young chief, and demand his opinion of their progress; but the calm and dignified demeanor of the native induced him to believe that, like himself, the other was wholly dependent on the sagacity and intelligence of the seniors of the party. At last, the scout spoke in English, and at once explained the embarrassment of their situation.

"When I found that the home path of the Hurons runs north," he said, "it did not need the judgment of many long years to tell that they would follow the valleys, and keep atween the waters of the Hudson and the Horican, until they might strike the springs of the Canada streams, which would lead them into the heart of the country of the Frenchers. Yet here are we, within a short range of the Scaroon, and not a sign of a trail have we crossed! Human natur' is weak, and it is possible we may not have taken the proper scent."

"Heaven protect us from such an error!" exclaimed Duncan. "Let us retrace our steps, and examine as we go, with keener eyes. Has Uncas no counsel to offer in such a strait?"

The young Mohican cast a glance at his father, but maintaining his quiet and reserved mien, he continued silent. Chingachgook had caught the look, and motioning with his hand, he bade him speak. The moment this permission was accorded, the countenance of Uncas changed from its grave composure to a gleam of intelligence and joy. Bounding forward like a deer, he sprang up the side of a little acclivity, a few rods in advance, and stood, exultingly, over a spot of fresh earth, that looked as though it had been recently upturned by the passage of some heavy animal. The eyes of the whole party followed the unexpected movement, and read their success in the air of triumph that the youth assumed.

"'T is the trail!" exclaimed the scout, advancing to the spot; "the lad is quick of sight and keen of wit for his years."

"'T is extraordinary that he should have withheld his knowledge so long," muttered Duncan, at his elbow.

"It would have been more wonderful had he spoken without a bidding. No, no; your young white, who gathers his learning from books and can measure what he knows by the page, may conceit that his knowledge, like his legs, outruns that of his father; but where experience is the master, the scholar is made to know the value of years, and respects them accordingly."

"See!" said Uncas, pointing north and south, at the evident marks of the broad trail on either side of him: "the dark-hair has gone towards the frost."

"Hound never ran on a more beautiful scent," responded the scout, dashing forward, at once, on the indicated route; "we are favored, greatly favored, and can follow with high noses. Aye, here are both your waddling beasts: this Huron travels like a white general. The fellow is stricken with a judgment, and is mad! Look sharp for wheels, Sagamore," he continued, looking back, and laughing in his newly awakened satisfaction; "we shall soon have the fool journeying in a coach, and that with three of the best pair of eyes on the borders in his rear."

The spirits of the scout, and the astonishing success of the chase, in which a circuitous distance of more than forty miles had been passed, did not fail to impart a portion of hope to the whole party. Their advance was rapid, and made with as much confidence as a traveller would proceed along a wide highway. If a rock, or a rivulet, or a bit of earth harder than common, severed the links of the clue they followed, the true eye of the scout recovered them at a distance, and seldom rendered the delay of a single moment necessary. Their progress was much facilitated by the certainty that Magua had found it necessary to journey through the valleys; a circumstance which rendered the general direction of the route sure. Nor had the Huron entirely neglected the arts uniformly practiced by the natives when retiring in front of an enemy. False trails and sudden turnings were frequent, wherever a brook, or the formation of the ground, rendered them feasible; but his pursuers were rarely deceived, and never failed to detect their error before they had lost either time or distance on the deceptive track.

By the middle of the afternoon they had passed the Scaroon, and were following the route of the declining sun. After descending an eminence to a low bottom, through which a swift stream glided, they suddenly came to a place where the party of Le Renard had made a halt. Extinguished brands were lying around a spring, the offals of a deer were scattered about the place, and the trees bore evident marks of having been browsed by the horses. At this little distance, Heyward discovered, and contemplated with tender emotion, the small bower under which he was fain to believe that Cora and Alice had reposed. But while the earth was trodden, and the footsteps of both men and beasts were so plainly visible around the place, the trail appeared to have suddenly ended.

It was easy to follow the tracks of the Narragansets, but they seemed only to have wandered without guides, or any other object than the pursuit of food. At length Uncas, who, with his father, had endeavored to trace the route of the horses, came upon a sign of their presence that was quite recent. Before following the clue, he communicated his success to his companions; and while the latter were consulting on the circumstance, the youth reappeared, leading the two fillies, with their saddles broken, and the housing soiled, as though they had been permitted to run at will for several days.

"What should this prove?" said Duncan, turning pale, and glancing his eyes around him, as if he feared the brush and leaves were about to give up some horrid secret.

"That our march is come to a quick end, and that we are in an enemy's country," returned the scout. "Had the knave been pressed, and the gentle ones wanted horses to keep up with the party, he might have taken their scalps; but without an enemy at his heels, and with such rugged beasts as these, he would not hurt a hair of their heads. I know your thoughts, and shame be it to our color that you have reason for them; but he who thinks that even a Mingo would ill-treat a woman, unless it be to tomahawk her, knows nothing of Indian natur', or the laws of the woods. No, no; I have heard that the French Indians had come into these hills, to hunt the moose, and we are getting within scent of their camp. Why should they not? the morning and evening guns of Ty may be heard any day among these mountains; for the Frenchers are running a new line atween the provinces of the King and the Canadas. It is true that the horses are here, but the Hurons are gone; let us then hunt for the path by which they departed."

Hawkeye and the Mohicans now applied themselves to their task in good earnest. A circle of a few hundred feet in circumference was drawn, and each of the party took a segment for his portion. The examination, however, resulted in no discovery. The impressions of footsteps were numerous, but they all appeared like those of men who had wandered about the spot without any design to quit it. Again the scout and his companions made the circuit of the halting-place, each slowly following the other, until they assembled in the centre once more, no wiser than when they started.

"Such cunning is not without its deviltry," exclaimed Hawkeye, when he met the disappointed looks of his assistants.

"We must get down to it, Sagamore, beginning at the spring, and going over the ground by inches. The Huron shall never brag in his tribe that he has a foot which leaves no print."

Setting the example himself, the scout engaged in the scrutiny with renewed zeal. Not a leaf was left unturned. The sticks were removed, and the stones lifted; for Indian cunning was known frequently to adopt these objects as covers, laboring with the utmost patience and industry, to conceal each footstep as they proceeded. Still no discovery was made. At length Uncas, whose activity had enabled him to achieve his portion of the task the soonest, raked the earth across the turbid little rill which ran from the spring, and diverted its course into another channel. So soon as its narrow bed below the dam was dry, he stooped over it with keen and curious eyes. A cry of exultation immediately announced the success of the young warrior. The whole party crowded to the spot where Uncas pointed out the impression of a moccasin in the moist alluvion.

"The lad will be an honor to his people," said Hawkeye, regarding the trail with as much admiration as a naturalist would expend on the tusk of a mammoth or the rib of a mastodon; "aye, and a thorn in the sides of the Hurons. Yet that is not the footstep of an Indian! the weight is too much on the heel, and the toes are squared, as though one of the French dancers had been in, pigeon-winging his tribe! Run back, Uncas, and bring me the size of the singer's foot. You will find a beautiful print of it just opposite yon rock, agin the hillside."

While the youth was engaged in this commission, the scout and Chingachgook were attentively considering the impressions. The measurements agreed, and the former unhesitatingly pronounced that the footstep was that of David, who had once more been made to exchange his shoes for moccasins.

"I can now read the whole of it, as plainly as if I had seen the arts of Le Subtil," he added; "the singer, being a man whose gifts lay chiefly in his throat and feet, was made to go first, and the others have trod in his steps, imitating their formation."

"But," cried Duncan, "I see no signs of—"

"The gentle ones," interrupted the scout; "the varlet has found a way to carry them, until he supposed he had thrown any followers off the scent. My life on it, we see their pretty little feet again, before many rods go by."

The whole party now proceeded, following the course of the rill, keeping anxious eyes on the regular impressions. The water soon flowed into its bed again, but watching the ground on either side, the foresters pursued their way, content with knowing that the trail lay beneath. More than half a mile was passed, before the rill rippled close around the base of an extensive and dry rock. Here they paused to make sure that the Hurons had not quitted the water.

It was fortunate they did so. For the quick and active Uncas soon found the impression of a foot on a bunch of moss, where it would seem an Indian had inadvertently trodden. Pursuing the direction given by this discovery, he entered the neighboring thicket, and struck the trail, as fresh and obvious as it had been before they reached the spring. Another shout announced the good fortune of the youth to his companions, and at once terminated the search.

"Aye, it has been planned with Indian judgment," said the scout, when the party was assembled around the place, "and would have blinded white eyes."

"Shall we proceed?" demanded Heyward.

"Softly, softly: we know our path; but it is good to examine the formation of things. This is my schooling, Major; and if one neglects the book, there is little chance of learning from the open hand of Providence. All is plain but one thing, which is the manner that the knave contrived to get the gentle ones along the blind trail. Even a Huron would be too proud to let their tender feet touch the water."

"Will this assist in explaining the difficulty?" said Heyward, pointing towards the fragments of a sort of handbarrow, that had been rudely constructed of boughs, and bound together with withes, and which now seemed carelessly cast aside as useless.

"'T is explained!" cried the delighted Hawkeye. "If them varlets have passed a minute, they have spent hours in striving to fabricate a lying end to their trail! Well, I 've known them waste a day in the same manner, to as little purpose. Here we have three pairs of moccasins, and two of little feet. It is amazing that any mortal beings can journey on limbs so small! Pass me the thong of buckskin, Uncas, and let me take the length of this foot. By the Lord, it is no longer than a child's, and yet the maidens are tall and comely. That Providence is partial in its gifts, for its own wise reasons, the best and most contented of us must allow."

"The tender limbs of my daughters are unequal to these hardships," said Munro, looking at the light footsteps of his children, with a parent's love: "we shall find their fainting forms in this desert."

"Of that there is little cause of fear," returned the scout, slowly shaking his head: "this is a firm and straight, though a light step, and not over long. See, the heel has hardly touched the ground; and there the dark-hair has made a little jump, from root to root. No, no; my knowledge for it, neither of them was nigh fainting, here-away. Now, the singer was beginning to be foot-sore and leg-weary, as is plain by his trail. There, you see, he slipped; here he has traveled wide, and tottered; and there, again, it looks as though he journeyed on snowshoes. Aye, aye, a man who uses his throat altogether, can hardly give his legs a proper training."

From such undeniable testimony did the practiced woodsman arrive at the truth, with nearly as much certainty and precision as if he had been a witness of all those events which his ingenuity so easily elucidated. Cheered by these assurances, and satisfied by a reasoning that was so obvious, while it was so simple, the party resumed its course, after making a short halt to take a hurried repast.

When the meal was ended, the scout cast a glance upwards at the setting sun, and pushed forward with a rapidity which compelled Heyward and the still vigorous Munro to exert all their muscles to equal. Their route now lay along the bottom which has already been mentioned. As the Hurons had made no further efforts to conceal their footsteps, the progress of the pursuers was no longer delayed by uncertainty. Before an hour had elapsed, however, the speed of Hawk-eye sensibly abated, and his head, instead of maintaining its former direct and forward look, began to turn suspiciously from side to side, as if he were conscious of approaching danger. He soon stopped again, and waited for the whole party to come up.

"I scent the Hurons," he said, speaking to the Mohicans; "yonder is open sky, through the tree-tops, and we are getting too nigh their encampment. Sagamore, you will take the hillside, to the right; Uncas will bend along the brook to the left, while I will try the trail. If anything should happen, the call will be three croaks of a crow. I saw one of the birds fanning himself in the air, just beyond the dead oak—another sign that we are touching an encampment."

The Indians departed their several ways without reply, while Hawkeye cautiously proceeded with the two gentlemen. Heyward soon pressed to the side of their guide, eager to catch an early glimpse of those enemies he had pursued with so much toil and anxiety. His companion told him to steal to the edge of the wood, which, as usual, was fringed with a thicket, and wait his coming, for he wished to examine certain suspicious signs a little on one side. Duncan obeyed, and soon found himself in a situation to command a view which he found as extraordinary as it was novel.

The trees of many acres had been felled, and the glow of a mild summer's evening had fallen on the clearing, in beautiful contrast to the gray light of the forest. A short distance from the place where Duncan stood, the stream had seemingly expanded into a little lake, covering most of the low land, from mountain to mountain. The water fell out of this wide basin in a cataract so regular and gentle that it appeared rather to be the work of human hands, than fashioned by nature. A hundred earthen dwellings stood on the margin of the lake, and even in its water, as though the latter had overflowed its usual banks. Their rounded roofs, admirably moulded for defense against the weather, denoted more of industry and foresight than the natives were wont to bestow on their regular habitations, much less on those they occupied for the temporary purposes of hunting and war. In short, the whole village or town, whichever it might be termed, possessed more of method and neatness of execution than the white men had been accustomed to believe belonged, ordinarily, to the Indian habits. It appeared, however, to be deserted. At least, so thought Duncan for many minutes; but at length, he fancied he discovered several human forms advancing towards him on all fours, and apparently dragging in their train some heavy, and he was quick to apprehend, some formidable engine. Just then a few dark looking heads gleamed out of the dwellings, and the place seemed suddenly alive with beings, which, however, glided from cover to cover so swiftly as to allow no opportunity of examining their humors or pursuits. Alarmed at these suspicious and inexplicable movements, he was about to attempt the signal of the crows, when the rustling of leaves at hand drew his eyes in another direction.

The young man started, and recoiled a few paces instinctively, when he found himself within a hundred yards of a stranger Indian. Recovering his recollection on the instant, instead of sounding an alarm, which might prove fatal to himself, he remained stationary, an attentive observer of the other's motions.

An instant of calm observation served to assure Duncan that he was undiscovered. The native, like himself, seemed occupied in considering the low dwellings of the village, and the stolen movements of its inhabitants. It was impossible to discover the expression of his features, through the grotesque mask of paint under which they were concealed; though Duncan fancied it was rather melancholy than savage. His head was shaved, as usual, with the exception of the crown, from whose tuft three or four faded feathers from a hawk's wing were loosely dangling. A ragged calico mantle half encircled his body, while his nether garment was composed of an ordinary shirt, the sleeves of which were made to perform the office that is usually executed by a much more commodious arrangement. His legs were bare, and sadly cut and torn by briers. The feet were, however, covered with a pair of good deer-skin moccasins. Altogether, the appearance of the individual was forlorn and miserable.

Duncan was still curiously observing the person of his neighbor, when the scout stole silently and cautiously to his side.

"You see we have reached their settlement or encampment," whispered the young man; "and here is one of the savages himself, in a very embarrassing position for our further movements."

Hawkeye started, and dropped his rifle, when, directed by the finger of his companion, the stranger came under his view. Then lowering the dangerous muzzle, he stretched forward his long neck, as if to assist a scrutiny that was already intensely keen.

"The imp is not a Huron," he said, "nor of any of the Canada tribes; and yet you see, by his clothes, the knave has been plundering a white. Aye, Montcalm has raked the woods for his inroad, and a whooping, murdering set of varlets has he gathered together. Can you see where he has put his rifle or his bow?"

"He appears to have no arms; nor does he seem to be viciously inclined. Unless he communicate the alarm to his fellows, who, as you see, are dodging about the water, we have but little to fear from him."

The scout turned to Heyward, and regarded him a moment with unconcealed amazement. Then opening wide his mouth, he indulged in unrestrained and heartfelt laughter, though in that silent and peculiar manner which danger had so long taught him to practice.

Repeating the words, "Fellows who are dodging about the water!" he added, "so much for schooling and passing a boyhood in the settlements! The knave has long legs, though, and shall not be trusted. Do you keep him under your rifle while I creep in behind, through the bush, and take him alive. Fire on no account."

Heyward had already permitted his companion to bury part of his person in the thicket, when, stretching forth an arm, he arrested him, in order to ask,—

"If I see you in danger, may I not risk a shot?"

Hawkeye regarded him a moment, like one who knew not how to take the question; then nodding his head, he answered, still laughing, though inaudibly,—

"Fire a whole platoon, Major."

In the next moment he was concealed by the leaves. Duncan waited several minutes in feverish impatience, before he caught another glimpse of the scout. Then he reappeared, creeping along the earth, from which his dress was hardly distinguishable, directly in the rear of his intended captive. Having reached within a few yards of the latter, he arose to his feet, silently and slowly. At that instant, several loud blows were struck on the water, and Duncan turned his eyes just in time to perceive that a hundred dark forms were plunging, in a body, into the troubled little sheet. Grasping his rifle, his looks were again bent on the Indian near him. Instead of taking the alarm, the unconscious savage stretched forward his neck, as if he also watched the movements about the gloomy lake, with a sort of silly curiosity. In the mean time, the uplifted hand of Hawkeye was above him. But, without any apparent reason, it was withdrawn, and its owner indulged in another long, though still silent, fit of merriment. When the peculiar and hearty laughter of Hawkeye was ended, instead of grasping his victim by the throat, he tapped him lightly on the shoulder, and exclaimed aloud,—

"How now, friend! have you a mind to teach the beavers to sing?"

"Even so," was the ready answer. "It would seem that the Being that gave them power to improve his gifts so well, would not deny them voices to proclaim his praise."

CHAPTER XXII

> Bottom.—*Are we all met?*
> Quince.—*Pat—pat; and here 's a marvelous convenient place for our rehearsal.*
>
> SHAKESPEARE, *Midsummer Night's Dream,* III. i. 5.

The reader may better imagine, than we describe, the surprise of Heyward. His lurking Indians were suddenly converted into four-footed beasts; his lake into a beaver pond; his cataract into a dam, constructed by those industrious and ingenious quadrupeds; and a suspected enemy into his tried friend, David Gamut, the master of psalmody. The presence of the latter created so many unexpected hopes relative to the sisters that, without a moment's hesitation, the young man broke out of his ambush, and sprang forward to join the two principal actors in the scene.

The merriment of Hawkeye was not easily appeased. Without ceremony, and with a rough hand, he twirled the supple Gamut around on his heel, and more than once affirmed that the Hurons had done themselves great credit in the fashion of his costume. Then seizing the hand of the other, he squeezed it with a grip that brought the tears into the eyes of the placid David, and wished him joy of his new condition.

"You were about opening your throat-practysings among the beavers, were ye?" he said. "The cunning devils know half the trade already, for they beat the time with their tails, as you heard just now; and in good time it was too, or Killdeer might have sounded the first note among them. I have known greater fools, who could read and write, than an experienced old beaver: but as for squalling, the animals are born dumb! What think you of such a song as this?"

David shut his sensitive ears, and even Heyward, apprised as he was of the nature of the cry, looked upwards in quest of the bird, as the cawing of a crow rang in the air about them.

"See!" continued the laughing scout, as he pointed towards the remainder of the party, who, in obedience to the signal, were already approaching; "this is music which has its natural virtues; it brings two good rifles to my elbow, to say nothing of the knives and tomahawks. But we see that you are safe; now tell us what has become of the maidens."

"They are captives of the heathen," said David; "and though greatly troubled in spirit, enjoying comfort and safety in the body."

"Both?" demanded the breathless Heyward.

"Even so. Though our wayfaring has been sore and our sustenance scanty, we have had little other cause for complaint, except the violence done our feelings by being thus led in captivity into a far land."

"Bless ye for these very words!" exclaimed the trembling Munro; "I shall then receive my babes, spotless and angel-like, as I lost them!"

"I know not that their delivery is at hand," returned the doubting David; "the leader of these savages is possessed of an evil spirit that no power short of Omnipotence can tame. I have tried him sleeping and waking, but neither sounds nor language seem to touch his soul."

"Where is the knave?" bluntly interrupted the scout.

"He hunts the moose to-day, with his young men; and tomorrow, as I hear, they pass further into these forests, and nigher to the borders of Canada. The elder maiden is conveyed to a neighboring people, whose lodges are situate beyond yonder black pinnacle of rock; while the younger is detained among the women of the Hurons, whose dwellings are but two short miles hence, on a table-land, where the fire has done the office of the axe, and prepared the place for their reception."

"Alice, my gentle Alice!" murmured Heyward; "she has lost the consolation of her sister's presence!"

"Even so. But so far as praise and thanksgiving in psalmody can temper the spirit in affliction, she has not suffered."

"Has she then a heart for music?"

"Of the graver and more solemn character; though it must be acknowledged that, in spite of all my endeavors, the maiden oftener weeps than she smiles. At such moments I forbear to press the holy songs; but there are many sweet and comfortable periods of satisfactory communication, when the ears of the savages are astounded with the upliftings of our voices."

"And why are you permitted to go at large, unwatched?"

David composed his features into what he intended should express an air of modest humility, before he meekly replied,—

"Little be the praise to such a worm as I. But, though the power of psalmody was suspended in the terrible business of that field of blood through which we passed, it has recovered its influence even over the souls of the heathen, and I am suffered to go and come at will."

The scout laughed, and tapping his own forehead significantly, he perhaps explained the singular indulgence more satisfactorily when he said,—

"The Indians never harm a non-composser. But why, when the path lay open before your eyes, did you not strike back on your own trail (it is not so blind as that which a squirrel would make), and bring in the tidings to Edward?"

The scout, remembering only his own sturdy and iron nature, had probably exacted a task that David, under no circumstances could have performed. But, without entirely losing the meekness of his air, the latter was content to answer,—

"Though my soul would rejoice to visit the habitations of Christendom once more, my feet would rather follow the tender spirits intrusted to my keeping, even into the idolatrous province of the Jesuits, than take one step backward while they pined in captivity and sorrow."

Though the figurative language of David was not very intelligible, the sincere and steady expression of his eye, and the glow on his honest countenance, were not easily mistaken. Uncas pressed closer to his side, and regarded the speaker with a look of commendation, while his father expressed his satisfaction by the ordinary pithy exclamation of approbation. The scout shook his head as he rejoined,—

"The Lord never intended that the man should place all his endeavors in his throat, to the neglect of other and better gifts! But he has fallen into the hands of some silly woman, when he should have been gathering his education under a blue sky, among the beauties of the forest. Here, friend; I did intend to kindle a fire with this tooting whistle of thine; but as you value the thing, take it, and blow your best on it!"

Gamut received his pitch-pipe with as strong an expression of pleasure as he believed compatible with the grave functions he exercised. After essaying its virtues repeatedly, in contrast with his own voice, and satisfying himself that none of its melody was lost, he made a very serious demonstration towards achieving a few stanzas of one of the longest effusions in the little volume so often mentioned.

Heyward, however, hastily interrupted his pious purpose, by continuing questions concerning the past and present condition of his fellow-captives, and in a manner more methodical than had been permitted by his feelings in the opening of their interview. David, though he regarded his treasure with longing eyes, was constrained to answer: especially as the venerable father took a part in the interrogatories, with an interest too imposing to be denied. Nor did the scout fail to throw in a pertinent inquiry, whenever a fitting occasion presented. In this manner, though with frequent interruptions, which were filled with certain threatening sounds from the recovered instrument, the pursuers were put in possession of such leading circumstances as were likely to prove useful in accomplishing their great and engrossing object—the recovery of the sisters. The narrative of David was simple, and the facts but few.

Magua had waited on the mountain until a safe moment to retire presented itself, when he had descended, and taken the route along the western side of the Horican, in the direction of the Canadas. As the subtle Huron was familiar with the paths, and well knew there was no immediate danger of pursuit, their progress had been moderate, and far from fatiguing. It appeared from the unembellished statement of David, that his own presence had been rather endured than desired; though even Magua had not been entirely exempt from that veneration with which the Indians regard those whom the Great Spirit has visited in their intellects. At night, the utmost care had been taken of the captives, both to prevent injury from the damps of the woods, and to guard against an escape. At the spring, the horses were turned loose, as has been seen; and notwithstanding the remoteness and length of their trail, the artifices already named were resorted to, in order to cut off every clue to their place of retreat. On their arrival at the encampment of his people, Magua, in obedience to a policy seldom departed from, separated his prisoners. Cora had been sent to a tribe that temporarily occupied an adjacent valley, though David was far too ignorant of the customs and history of the natives, to be able to declare anything satisfactory concerning their name or character. He only knew that they had not engaged in the late expedition against William Henry; that, like the Hurons themselves, they were allies of Montcalm; and that they maintained an amicable, though a watchful intercourse with the warlike and savage people whom chance had, for a time, brought in such close and disagreeable contact with themselves.

The Mohicans and the scout listened to his interrupted and imperfect narrative, with an interest that obviously increased as he proceeded; and it was while attempting to explain the pursuits of the community in which Cora was detained, that the latter abruptly demanded,—

"Did you see the fashion of their knives? were they of English or French formation?"

"My thoughts were bent on no such vanities, but rather mingled in consolation with those of the maidens."

"The time may come when you will not consider the knife of a savage such a despisable vanity," returned the scout, with a strong expression of contempt for the other's dullness. "Had they held their corn-feast—or can you say anything of the totems of the tribe?"

"Of corn, we had many and plentiful feasts; for the grain, being in the milk, is both sweet to the mouth and comfortable to the stomach. Of totem, I know not the meaning; but if it appertaineth in any wise to the art of Indian music, it need not be inquired after at their hands. They never join their voices in praise, and it would seem that they are among the profanest of the idolatrous."

"Therein you belie the nature of an Indian. Even the Mingo adores but the true and living God. 'T is a wicked fabrication of the whites, and I say it to the shame of my color, that would make the warrior bow down before images of his own creation. It is true, they endeavor to make truces with the wicked one,—as who would not with an enemy he cannot conquer!—but they look up for favor and assistance to the Great and Good Spirit only."

"It may be so," said David; "but I have seen strange and fantastic images drawn in their paint, of which their admiration and care savored of a spiritual pride; especially one, and that, too, a foul and loathsome object."

"Was it a sarpent?" quickly demanded the scout.

"Much the same. It was in the likeness of an abject and creeping tortoise."

"Hugh!" exclaimed both the attentive Mohicans in a breath; while the scout shook his head with the air of one who had made an important, but by no means a pleasing discovery. Then the father spoke, in the language of the Delawares, and with a calmness and dignity that instantly arrested the attention even of those to whom his words were unintelligible. His gestures were impressive, and at times energetic. Once he lifted his arm on high; and as it descended, the action threw aside the folds of his light mantle, a finger resting on his breast, as if he would enforce his meaning by the attitude. Duncan's eyes followed the movement, and he perceived that the animal just mentioned was beautifully, though faintly, worked in a blue tint, on the swarthy breast of the chief. All that he had ever heard of the violent separation of the vast tribes of the Delawares rushed across his mind, and he awaited the proper moment to speak, with a suspense that was rendered nearly intolerable, by his interest in the stake. His wish, however, was anticipated by the scout, who turned from his red friend, saying,—

"We have found that which may be good or evil to us, as Heaven disposes. The Sagamore is of the high blood of the Delawares, and is the great chief of their Tortoises! That some of this stock are among the people of whom the singer tells us, is plain, by his words; and had he but spent half the breath in prudent questions, that he has blown away in making a trumpet of his throat, we might have known how many warriors they numbered. It is, altogether, a dangerous path we move in; for a friend whose face is turned from you often bears a bloodier mind than the enemy who seeks your scalp."

"Explain," said Duncan.

"'T is a long and melancholy tradition, and one I little like to think of; for it is not to be denied that the evil has been mainly done by men with white skins. But it has ended in turning the tomahawk of brother against brother, and brought the Mingo and the Delaware to travel in the same path."

"You then suspect it is a portion of that people among whom Cora resides?"

The scout nodded his head in assent, though he seemed anxious to waive the further discussion of a subject that appeared painful. The impatient Duncan now made several hasty and desperate propositions to attempt the release of the sisters. Munro seemed to shake off his apathy, and listened to the wild schemes of the young man with a deference that his gray hairs and reverend years should have denied. But the scout, after suffering the ardor of the lover to expend itself a little, found means to convince him of the folly of precipitation, in a matter that would require their coolest judgment and utmost fortitude.

"It would be well," he added, "to let this man go in again, as usual, and for him to tarry in the lodges, giving notice to the gentle ones of our approach, until we call him out, by signal, to consult. You know the cry of a crow, friend, from the whistle of the whip-poor-will?"

"'T is a pleasing bird," returned David, "and has a soft and melancholy note! though the time is rather quick and ill-measured."

"He speaks of the wish-ton-wish," said the scout: "well, since you like his whistle, it shall be your signal. Remember, then, when you hear the whip-poor-will's call three times repeated, you are to come into the bushes where the bird might be supposed—"

"Stop," interrupted Heyward; "I will accompany him."

"You!" exclaimed the astonished Hawkeye; "are you tired of seeing the sun rise and set?"

"David is a living proof that the Hurons can be merciful."

"Aye, but David can use his throat as no man in his senses would pervart the gift."

"I too can play the madman, the fool, the hero; in short, any or everything to rescue her I love. Name your objections no longer: I am resolved."

Hawkeye regarded the young man a moment in speechless amazement. But Duncan, who, in deference to the other's skill and services, had hitherto submitted somewhat implicitly to his dictation, now assumed the superior, with a manner that was not easily resisted. He waved his hand, in sign of his dislike to all remonstrance, and then, in more tempered language, he continued,—

"You have the means of disguise; change me; paint me too, if you will; in short, alter me to anything—a fool."

"It is not for one like me to say that he who is already formed by so powerful a hand as Providence, stands in need of a change," muttered the discontented scout. "When you send your parties abroad in war, you find it prudent at least to arrange the marks and places of encampment, in order that they who fight on your side may know when and where to expect a friend."

"Listen," interrupted Duncan; "you have heard from this faithful follower of the captives, that the Indians are of two tribes, if not of different nations. With one, whom you think to be a branch of the Delawares, is she you call the 'dark-hair;' the other and younger of the ladies is undeniably with our declared enemies, the Hurons. It becomes my youth and rank to attempt the latter adventure. While you, therefore, are negotiating with your friends for the release of one of the sisters, I will effect that of the other, or die."

The awakened spirit of the young soldier gleamed in his eyes, and his form became imposing under its influence. Hawkeye, though too much accustomed to Indian artifices not to foresee the danger of the experiment, knew not well how to combat this sudden resolution.

Perhaps there was something in the proposal that suited his own hardy nature, and that secret love of desperate adventure which had increased with his experience, until hazard and danger had become, in some measure, necessary to the enjoyment of his existence. Instead of continuing to oppose the scheme of Duncan, his humor suddenly altered, and he lent himself to its execution.

"Come," he said, with a good-humored smile; "the buck that will take to the water must be headed, and not followed. Chingachgook has as many different paints as the engineer officer's wife, who takes down natur' on scraps of paper, making the mountains look like cocks of rusty hay, and placing the blue sky in reach of your hand. The Sagamore can use them too. Seat yourself on the log; and my life on it, he can soon make a natural fool of you, and that well to your liking."

Duncan complied, and the Mohican, who had been an attentive listener to the discourse, readily undertook the office. Long practiced in all the subtle arts of his race, he drew with great dexterity and quickness the fantastic shadow that the natives were accustomed to consider as the evidence of a friendly and jocular disposition. Every line that could possibly be interpreted into a secret inclination for war was carefully avoided; while, on the other hand, he studied those conceits that might be construed into amity.

In short, he entirely sacrificed every appearance of the warrior to the masquerade of a buffoon. Such exhibitions were not uncommon among the Indians; and as Duncan was already sufficiently disguised in his dress, there certainly did exist some reason for believing that, with his knowledge of French, he might pass for a juggler from Ticonderoga, straggling among the allied and friendly tribes.

When he was thought to be sufficiently painted, the scout gave him much friendly advice; concerted signals, and appointed the place where they should meet, in the event of mutual success. The parting between Munro and his young friend was more melancholy; still, the former submitted to the separation with an indifference that his warm and honest nature would never have permitted in a more healthful state of mind. The scout led Heyward aside, and acquainted him with his intention to leave the veteran in some safe encampment, in charge of

Chingachgook, while he and Uncas pursued their inquiries among the people they had reason to believe were Delawares. Then renewing his cautions and advice, he concluded by saying, with a solemnity and warmth of feeling with which Duncan was deeply touched,—

"And now God bless you! You have shown a spirit that I like; for it is the gift of youth, more especially one of warm blood and a stout heart. But believe the warning of a man who has reason to know all he says to be true. You will have occasion for your best manhood, and for a sharper wit than what is to be gathered in books, afore you outdo the cunning or get the better of the courage of a Mingo. God bless you! if the Hurons master your scalp, rely on the promise of one who has two stout warriors to back him. They shall pay for their victory, with a life for every hair it holds. I say, young gentleman, may Providence bless your undertaking, which is altogether for good; and remember, that to outwit the knaves it is lawful to practice things that may not be naturally the gift of a white skin."

Duncan shook his worthy and reluctant associate warmly by the hand, once more recommended his aged friend to his care, and returning his good wishes, he motioned to David to proceed. Hawkeye gazed after the high-spirited and adventurous young man for several moments, in open admiration; then shaking his head doubtingly, he turned, and led his own division of the party into the concealment of the forest.

The route taken by Duncan and David lay directly across the clearing of the beavers, and along the margin of their pond.

When the former found himself alone with one so simple, and so little qualified to render any assistance in desperate emergencies, he first began to be sensible of the difficulties of the task he had undertaken. The fading light increased the gloominess of the bleak and savage wilderness that stretched so far on every side of him; and there was even a fearful character in the stillness of those little huts, that he knew were so abundantly peopled. It struck him, as he gazed at the admirable structures and the wonderful precautions of their sagacious inmates, that even the brutes of these vast wilds were possessed of an instinct nearly commensurate with his own reason; and he could not reflect, without anxiety, on the unequal contest that he had so rashly courted. Then came the glowing image of Alice; her distress; her actual danger; and all the peril of his situation was forgotten. Cheering David, he moved on with the light and vigorous step of youth and enterprise.

After making nearly a semicircle around the pond, they diverged from the water-course, and began to ascend to the level of a slight elevation in that bottom land over which they journeyed. Within half an hour they gained the margin of another opening that bore all the signs of having been also made by the beavers, and which those sagacious animals had probably been induced by some accident to abandon, for the more eligible position they now occupied. A very natural sensation caused Duncan to hesitate a moment, unwilling to leave the cover of their bushy path, as a man pauses to collect his energies before he essays any hazardous experiment, in which he is secretly conscious they will all be needed. He profited by the halt, to gather such information as might be obtained from his short and hasty glances.

On the opposite side of the clearing, and near the point where the brook tumbled over some rocks, from a still higher level, some fifty or sixty lodges, rudely fabricated of logs, brush, and earth intermingled, were to be discovered. They were arranged without any order, and seemed to be constructed with very little attention to neatness or beauty. Indeed, so very inferior were they in the two latter particulars to the village Duncan had just seen, that he began to expect a second surprise, no less astonishing than the former. This expectation was in no degree diminished when, by the doubtful twilight, he beheld twenty or thirty forms rising alternately from the cover of the tall, coarse grass, in front of the lodges, and then sinking again from the sight, as it were to burrow in the earth. By the sudden and hasty glimpses that he caught of these figures, they seemed more like dark glancing spectres, or some other unearthly beings, than creatures fashioned with the ordinary and vulgar materials of flesh and blood. A gaunt, naked form was seen, for a single instant, tossing its arms wildly in the air, and then the spot it had filled was vacant; the figure appearing suddenly in some other and distant place, or being succeeded by another, possessing the same mysterious character. David, observing that his companion lingered, pursued the direction of his gaze, and in some measure recalled the recollection of Heyward, by speaking.

"There is much fruitful soil uncultivated here," he said; "and I may add, without the sinful leaven of self-commendation, that since my short sojourn in these heathenish abodes, much good seed has been scattered by the wayside."

"The tribes are fonder of the chase than of the arts of men and labor," returned the unconscious Duncan, still gazing at the objects of his wonder.

"It is rather joy than labor to the spirit, to lift up the voice in praise; but sadly do these boys abuse their gifts. Rarely have I found any of their age, on whom nature has so freely bestowed the elements of psalmody; and surely, surely, there are none who neglect them more. Three nights have I now tarried here, and three several times have I assembled the urchins to join in sacred song; and as often have they responded to my efforts with whoopings and howlings that have chilled my soul!"

"Of whom speak you?"

"Of those children of the devil, who waste the precious moments in yonder idle antics. Ah! the wholesome restraint of discipline is but little known among this self-abandoned people. In a country of birches, a rod is never seen; and it ought not to appear a marvel in my eyes, that the choicest blessings of Providence are wasted in such cries as these."

David closed his ears against the juvenile pack, whose yell just then rang shrilly through the forest; and Duncan, suffering his lip to curl, as in mockery of his own superstition, said firmly,—

"We will proceed."

Without removing the safeguards from his ears, the master of song complied, and together they pursued their way towards what David was sometimes wont to call "the tents of the Philistines."

CHAPTER XXIII

But though the beast of game
The privilege of chase may claim;
Though space and law the stag we lend
Ere hound we slip, or bow we bend;
Who ever recked, where, how, or when
The prowling fox was trapped or slain?

SCOTT, *Lady of the Lake*, CANTO IV. XXX.

It is unusual to find an encampment of the natives, like those of the more instructed whites, guarded by the presence of armed men. Well informed of the approach of every danger while it is yet at a distance, the Indian generally rests secure under his knowledge of the signs of the forest, and the long and difficult paths that separate him from those he has most reason to dread. But the enemy who, by any lucky concurrence of accidents, has found means to elude the vigilance of the scouts, will seldom meet with sentinels nearer home to sound the alarm. In addition to this general usage, the tribes friendly to the French knew too well the weight of the blow that had just been struck, to apprehend any immediate danger from the hostile nations that were tributary to the crown of Britain.

When Duncan and David, therefore, found themselves in the centre of the children, who played the antics already mentioned, it was without the least previous intimation of their approach. But so soon as they were observed, the whole of the juvenile pack raised, by common consent, a shrill and warning whoop; and then sank, as it were, by magic, from before the sight of their visitors. The naked, tawny bodies of the crouching urchins blended so nicely, at that hour, with the withered herbage, that at first it seemed as if the earth had in truth swallowed up their forms; though when surprise permitted Duncan to bend his look more curiously about the spot, he found it everywhere met by dark, quick, and rolling eye-balls.

Gathering no encouragement from this startling presage of the nature of the scrutiny he was likely to undergo from the more mature judgments of the men, there was an instant when the young soldier would have retreated. It was, however, too late to appear to hesitate. The cry of the children had drawn a dozen warriors to the door of the nearest lodge, where they stood clustered in a dark and savage group, gravely awaiting the nearer approach of those who had unexpectedly come among them.

David, in some measure familiarized to the scene, led the way with a steadiness that no slight obstacle was likely to disconcert, into this very building. It was the principal edifice of the village, though roughly constructed of the bark and branches of trees; being the lodge in which the tribe held its councils and public meetings during their temporary residence on the borders of the English province. Duncan found it difficult to assume the necessary appearance of unconcern, as he brushed the dark and powerful frames of the savages who thronged its threshold; but, conscious that his existence depended on his presence of mind, he trusted to the discretion of his companion, whose footsteps he closely followed, endeavoring, as he proceeded, to rally his thoughts for the occasion. His blood curdled when he found himself in absolute contact with such fierce and implacable enemies; but he so far mastered his feelings as to pursue his way into the centre of the lodge, with an exterior that did not betray the weakness. Imitating the example of the deliberate Gamut, he drew a bundle of fragrant brush from beneath a pile that filled a corner of the hut, and seated himself in silence.

So soon as their visitor had passed, the observant warriors fell back from the entrance, and arranging themselves about him, they seemed patiently to await the moment when it might comport with the dignity of the stranger to speak. By far the greater number stood leaning, in lazy, lounging attitudes, against the upright posts that supported the crazy building, while three or four of the oldest and most distinguished of the chiefs placed themselves on the earth a little more in advance.

A flaring torch was burning in the place, and sent its red glare from face to face and figure to figure, as it waved in the currents of air. Duncan profited by its light to read the probable character of his reception, in the countenances of his hosts. But his ingenuity availed him little, against the cold artifices of the people he had encountered. The chiefs in front scarce cast a glance at his person, keeping their eyes on the ground, with an air that might have been intended for respect, but which it was quite easy to construe into distrust. The men in shadow were less reserved. Duncan soon detected their searching, but stolen looks, which, in truth, scanned his person and attire inch by inch; leaving no emotion of the countenance, no gesture, no line of the paint, nor even the fashion of a garment, unheeded, and without comment.

At length one whose hair was beginning to be sprinkled with gray, but whose sinewy limbs and firm tread announced that he was still equal to the duties of manhood, advanced out of the gloom of a corner, whither he had probably posted himself to make his observations unseen, and spoke. He used the language of the Wyandots, or Hurons; his words were consequently unintelligible to Heyward, though they seemed, by the gestures that accompanied them, to be uttered more in courtesy than anger. The latter shook his head, and made a gesture indicative of his inability to reply.

"Do none of my brothers speak the French or the English?" he said, in the former language, looking about him from countenance to countenance, in hopes of finding a nod of assent.

Though more than one had turned, as if to catch the meaning of his words, they remained unanswered.

"I should be grieved to think," continued Duncan, speaking slowly and using the simplest French of which he was the master, "to believe that none of this wise and brave nation understand the language that the 'Grand Monarque' uses when he talks to his children. His heart would be heavy did he believe his red warriors paid him so little respect!"

A long and grave pause succeeded, during which no movement of a limb, nor any expression of an eye betrayed the impression produced by his remark. Duncan, who knew that silence was a virtue among his hosts, gladly had recourse to the custom, in order to arrange his ideas. At length the same warrior who had before addressed him replied, by dryly demanding, in the language of the Canadas,—

"When our Great Father speaks to his people, is it with the tongue of a Huron?"

"He knows no difference in his children, whether the color of the skin be red, or black, or white," returned Duncan, evasively; "though chiefly is he satisfied with the brave Hurons."

"In what manner will he speak," demanded the wary chief, "when the runners count to him the scalps which five nights ago grew on the heads of the Yengeese?"

"They were his enemies," said Duncan, shuddering involuntarily; "and doubtless he will say, It is good; my Hurons are very gallant."

"Our Canada father does not think it. Instead of looking forward to reward his Indians, his eyes are turned backward. He sees the dead Yengeese, but no Huron. What can this mean?"

"A great chief, like him, has more thoughts than tongues. He looks to see that no enemies are on his trail."

"The canoe of a dead warrior will not float on the Horican," returned the savage gloomily. "His ears are open to the Delawares, who are not our friends, and they fill them with lies."

"It cannot be. See; he has bid me, who am a man that knows the art of healing, to go to his children, the red Hurons of the great lakes, and ask if any are sick!"

Another silence succeeded this annunciation of the character Duncan had assumed. Every eye was simultaneously bent on his person, as if to inquire into the truth or falsehood of the declaration, with an intelligence and keenness that caused the subject of their scrutiny to tremble for the result. He was, however, relieved again by the former speaker.

"Do the cunning men of the Canadas paint their skins?" the Huron coldly continued; "we have heard them boast that their faces were pale."

"When an Indian chief comes among his white fathers," returned Duncan, with great steadiness, "he lays aside his buffalo robe, to carry the shirt that is offered him. My brothers have given me paint, and I wear it."

A low murmur of applause announced that the compliment to the tribe was favorably received. The elderly chief made a gesture of commendation, which was answered by most of his companions, who each threw forth a hand, and uttered a brief exclamation of pleasure. Duncan began to breathe more freely, believing that the weight of his examination was past; and as he had already prepared a simple and probable tale to support his pretended occupation, his hopes of ultimate success grew brighter.

After a silence of a few moments, as if adjusting his thoughts, in order to make a suitable answer to the declaration their guest had just given, another warrior arose, and placed himself in an attitude to speak. While his lips were yet in the act of parting, a low but fearful sound arose from the forest, and was immediately succeeded by a high, shrill yell, that was drawn out, until it equaled the longest and most plaintive howl of the wolf. The sudden and terrible interruption caused Duncan to start from his seat, unconscious of everything but the effect produced by so frightful a cry. At the same moment, the warriors glided in a body from the lodge, and the outer air was filled with loud shouts, that nearly drowned those awful sounds, which were still ringing beneath the arches of the woods. Unable to command himself any longer, the youth broke from the place, and presently stood in the centre of a disorderly throng, that included nearly everything having life, within the limits of the encampment. Men, women, and children; the aged, the infirm, the active, and the strong, were alike abroad; some exclaiming aloud, others clapping their hands with a joy that seemed frantic, and all expressing their savage pleasure in some unexpected event. Though astounded, at first, by the uproar, Heyward was soon enabled to find its solution by the scene that followed.

There yet lingered sufficient light in the heavens to exhibit those bright openings among the tree-tops, where different paths left the clearing to enter the depths of the wilderness. Beneath one of them, a line of warriors issued from the woods, and advanced slowly towards the dwellings. One in front bore a short pole, on which, as it afterwards appeared, were suspended several human scalps. The startling sounds that Duncan had heard were what the whites have not inappropriately called the "death-halloo;" and each repetition of the cry was intended to announce to the tribe the fate of an enemy. Thus far the knowledge of Heyward assisted him in the explanation; and as he now knew that the interruption was caused by the unlooked-for return of a successful war-party, every disagreeable sensation was quieted in inward congratulation, for the opportune relief and insignificance it conferred on himself.

When at the distance of a few hundred feet from the lodges, the newly arrived warriors halted. Their plaintive and terrific cry, which was intended to represent equally the wailings of the dead and the triumph of the victors, had entirely ceased. One of their number now called aloud, in words that were far from appalling, though not more intelligible to those for whose ears they were intended, than their expressive yells. It would be difficult to convey a suitable idea of the savage ecstacy with which the news thus imparted was received. The whole encampment, in a moment, became a scene of the most violent bustle and commotion. The warriors drew their knives, and flourishing them, they arranged themselves in two lines, forming a lane that extended from the war-party to the lodges. The squaws seized clubs, axes, or whatever weapon of offense first offered itself to their hands, and rushed eagerly to act their part in the cruel game that was at hand. Even the children would not be excluded; but boys, little able to wield the instruments, tore the tomahawks from the belts of their fathers, and stole into the ranks, apt imitators of the savage traits exhibited by their parents.

Large piles of brush lay scattered about the clearing, and a wary and aged squaw was occupied in firing as many as might serve to light the coming exhibition. As the flame arose, its power exceeded that of the parting day, and assisted to render objects at the same time more distinct and more hideous. The whole scene formed a striking picture, whose frame was composed of the dark and tall border of pines. The warriors just arrived were the most distant figures. A little in advance stood two men, who were apparently selected from the rest, as the principal actors in what was to follow. The light was not strong enough to render their features distinct, though it was quite evident that they were governed by very different emotions. While one stood erect and firm, prepared to meet his fate like a hero, the other bowed his head, as if palsied by terror or stricken with shame. The high-spirited Duncan felt a powerful impulse of admiration and pity towards the former, though no opportunity could offer to exhibit his generous emotions. He watched his slightest movement, however, with eager eyes; and as he traced the fine outline of his admirably proportioned and active frame, he endeavored to persuade himself that if the powers of man, seconded by such noble resolution, could bear one harmless through so severe a trial, the youthful captive before him might hope for success in the hazardous race he was about to run. Insensibly the young man drew nigher to the swarthy lines of the Hurons, and scarcely breathed, so intense became his interest in the spectacle. Just then the signal yell was given, and the momentary quiet which had preceded it was broken by a burst of cries that far exceeded any before heard. The most abject of the two victims continued motionless; but the other bounded from the place at the cry, with the activity and swiftness of a deer. Instead of rushing through the hostile lines, as had been expected, he just entered the dangerous defile, and before time was given for a single blow, turned short, and leaping the heads of a row of children, he gained at once the exterior and safer side of the formidable array. The artifice was answered by a hundred voices raised in imprecations; and the whole of the excited multitude broke from their order, and spread themselves about the place in wild confusion.

A dozen blazing piles now shed their lurid brightness on the place, which resembled some unhallowed and supernatural arena, in which malicious demons had assembled to act their bloody and lawless rites. The forms in the background looked like unearthly beings, gliding before the eye, and cleaving the air with frantic and unmeaning gestures; while the savage passions of such as passed the flames were rendered fearfully distinct by the gleams that shot athwart their inflamed visages.

It will easily be understood, that amid such a concourse of vindictive enemies, no breathing time was allowed the fugitive. There was a single moment when it seemed as if he would have reached the forest, but the whole body of his captors threw themselves before him, and drove him back into the centre of his relentless persecutors. Turning like a headed deer, he shot, with the swiftness of an arrow, through a pillar of forked flame, and passing the whole multitude harmless, he appeared on the opposite side of the clearing. Here too he was met and turned by a few of the older and more subtle of the Hurons. Once more he tried the throng, as if seeking safety in its blindness, and then several moments succeeded, during which Duncan believed the active and courageous young stranger was lost.

Nothing could be distinguished but a dark mass of human forms tossed and involved in inextricable confusion. Arms, gleaming knives, and formidable clubs appeared above them, but the blows were evidently given at random. The awful effect was heightened by the piercing shrieks of the women and the fierce yells of the warriors. Now and then Duncan caught a glimpse of a light form cleaving the air in some desperate bound, and he rather hoped than believed that the captive yet retained the command of his astonishing powers of activity. Suddenly the multitude rolled backward, and approached the spot where he himself stood. The heavy body in the rear pressed upon the women and children in front, and bore them to the earth. The stranger reappeared in the confusion. Human power could not, however, much longer endure so severe a trial. Of this the captive seemed conscious. Profiting by the momentary opening, he darted from among the warriors, and made a desperate, and what seemed to Duncan a final effort to gain the wood. As if aware that no danger was to be apprehended from the young soldier, the fugitive nearly brushed his person in his flight. A tall and powerful Huron, who had husbanded his forces, pressed close upon his heels, and with an uplifed arm menaced a fatal blow. Duncan thrust forth a foot, and the shock precipitated the eager savage headlong, many feet in advance of his intended victim. Thought itself is not quicker than was the motion with which the latter profited by the advantage; he turned, gleamed like a meteor again before the eyes of Duncan, and at the next moment, when the latter recovered his recollection, and gazed around in quest of the captive, he saw him quietly leaning against a small painted post, which stood before the door of the principal lodge.

Apprehensive that the part he had taken in the escape might prove fatal to himself, Duncan left the place without delay. He followed the crowd, which drew nigh the lodges, gloomy and sullen, like any other multitude that had been disappointed in an execution. Curiosity, or perhaps a better feeling, induced him to approach the stranger. He found him standing with one arm cast about the protecting post, and breathing thick and hard, after his exertions, but disdaining to permit a single sign of suffering to escape. His person was now protected by immemorial and sacred usage, until the tribe in council had deliberated and determined on his fate. It was not difficult, however, to foretell the result, if any presage could be drawn from the feelings of those who crowded the place.

There was no term of abuse to the Huron vocabulary that the disappointed women did not lavishly expend on the successful stranger. They flouted at his efforts, and told him, with bitter scoffs, that his feet were better than his hands; and that he merited wings, while he knew not the use of an arrow or a knife. To all this the captive made no reply, but was content to preserve an attitude in which dignity was singularly blended with disdain. Exasperated as much by his composure as by his good-fortune, their words became unintelligible, and were succeeded by shrill, piercing yells. Just then the crafty squaw, who had taken the necessary precaution to fire the piles, made her way through the throng, and cleared a place for herself in front of the captive. The squalid and withered person of this hag might well have obtained for her the character of possessing more than human cunning. Throwing back her light vestment, she stretched forth her long skinny arm, in derision, and using the language of the Lenape, as more intelligible to the subject of her gibes, she commenced aloud,—

"Look you, Delaware!" she said, snapping her fingers in his face; "your nation is a race of women, and the hoe is better fitted to your hands than the gun. Your squaws are the mothers of deer; but if a bear, or a wild cat, or a serpent were born among you, ye would flee. The Huron girls shall make you petticoats, and we will find you a husband."

A burst of savage laughter succeeded this attack, during which the soft and musical merriment of the younger females strangely chimed with the cracked voice of their older and more malignant companion. But the stranger was superior to all their efforts. His head was immovable; nor did he betray the slightest consciousness that any were present, except when his haughty eye rolled towards the dusky forms of the warriors, who stalked in the background, silent and sullen observers of the scene.

Infuriated at the self-command of the captive, the woman placed her arms akimbo, and throwing herself into a posture of defiance, she broke out anew, in a torrent of words that no art of ours could commit successfully to paper. Her breath was, however, expended in vain; for, although distinguished in her nation as a proficient in the art of abuse, she was permitted to work herself into such a fury as actually to foam at the mouth, without causing a muscle to vibrate in the motionless figure of the stranger. The effect of his indifference began to extend itself to the other spectators; and a youngster, who was just quitting the condition of a boy, to enter the state of manhood, attempted to assist the termagant, by flourishing his tomahawk before their victim, and adding his empty boasts to the taunts of the woman. Then, indeed, the captive turned his face towards the light, and looked down on the stripling with an expression that was superior to contempt. At the next moment he resumed his quiet and reclining attitude against the post. But the change of posture had permitted Duncan to exchange glances with the firm and piercing eyes of Uncas.

Breathless with amazement, and heavily oppressed with the critical situation of his friend, Heyward recoiled before the look, trembling lest its meaning might, in some unknown manner, hasten the prisoner's fate. There was not, however, any instant cause for such an apprehension. Just then a warrior forced his way into the exasperated crowd. Motioning the women and children aside with a stern gesture, he took Uncas by the arm, and led him towards the door of the council lodge. Thither all the chiefs, and most of the distinguished warriors, followed; among whom the anxious Heyward found means to enter without attracting any dangerous attention to himself.

A few minutes were consumed in disposing of those present in a manner suitable to their rank and influence in the tribe. An order very similar to that adopted in the preceding interview was observed; the aged and superior chiefs occupying the area of the spacious apartment, within the powerful light of a glaring torch, while their juniors and inferiors were arranged in the background, presenting a dark outline of swarthy and marked visages. In the very centre of the lodge, immediately under an opening that admitted the twinkling light of one or two stars, stood Uncas, calm, elevated, and collected. His high and haughty carriage was not lost on his captors, who often bent their looks on his person, with eyes which, while they lost none of their inflexibility of purpose, plainly betrayed their admiration of the stranger's daring.

The case was different with the individual whom Duncan had observed to stand forth with his friend, previously to the desperate trial of speed; and who, instead of joining in the chase, had remained throughout its turbulent uproar, like a cringing statue, expressive of shame and disgrace. Though not a hand had been extended to greet him, nor yet an eye had condescended to watch his movements, he had also entered the lodge, as though impelled by a fate to whose decrees he submitted, seemingly, without a struggle. Heyward profited by the first opportunity to gaze in his face, secretly apprehensive he might find the features of another acquaintance; but they proved to be those of a stranger, and, what was still more inexplicable, of one who bore all the distinctive marks of a Huron warrior. Instead of mingling with his tribe, however, he sat apart, a solitary being in a multitude, his form shrinking into a crouching and abject attitude, as if anxious to fill as little space as possible. When each individual had taken his proper station, and silence reigned in the place, the gray-haired chief already introduced to the reader, spoke aloud, in the language of the Lenni Lenape.

"Delaware," he said, "though one of a nation of women, you have proved yourself a man. I would give you food; but he who eats with a Huron should become his friend. Rest in peace till the morning sun, when our last words shall be spoken."

"Seven nights, and as many summer days, have I fasted on the trail of the Hurons," Uncas coldly replied; "the children of the Lenape know how to travel the path of the just without lingering to eat."

"Two of my young men are in pursuit of your companion." resumed the other, without appearing to regard the boast of his captive; "when they get back, then will our wise men say to you 'live' or 'die.'"

"Has a Huron no ears?" scornfully exclaimed Uncas; "twice, since he has been your prisoner, has the Delaware heard a gun that he knows. Your young men will never come back!"

A short and sullen pause succeeded this bold assertion. Duncan, who understood the Mohican to allude to the fatal rifle of the scout, bent forward in earnest observation of the effect it might produce on the conquerors; but the chief was content with simply retorting,—

"If the Lenape are so skillful, why is one of their braves warriors here?"

"He followed in the steps of a flying coward, and fell into a snare. The cunning beaver may be caught."

As Uncas thus replied, he pointed with his finger towards the solitary Huron, but without deigning to bestow any other notice on so unworthy an object. The words of the answer and the air of the speaker produced a strong sensation among his auditors. Every eye rolled sullenly towards the individual indicated by the simple gesture, and a low threatening murmur passed through the crowd. The ominous sounds reached the outer door, and the women and children pressing into the throng, no gap had been left, between shoulder and shoulder, that was not now filled with the dark lineaments of some eager and curious human countenance.

In the mean time, the more aged chiefs, in the centre, communed with each other in short and broken sentences. Not a word was uttered that did not convey the meaning of the speaker, in the simplest and most energetic form. Again, a long and deeply solemn pause took place. It was known, by all present, to be the grave precursor of a weighty and important judgment. They who composed the outer circle of faces were on tiptoe to gaze; and even the culprit for an instant forgot his shame in a deeper emotion, and exposed his abject features, in order to cast an anxious and troubled glance at the dark assemblage of chiefs. The silence was finally broken by the aged warrior so often named. He arose from the earth, and moving past the immovable form of Uncas, placed himself in a dignified attitude before the offender. At that moment, the withered squaw already mentioned moved into the circle, in a slow, sideling sort of a dance, holding the torch, and muttering the indistinct words of what might have been a species of incantation. Though her presence was altogether an intrusion, it was unheeded.

Approaching Uncas, she held the blazing brand in such a manner as to cast its red glare on his person, and to expose the slightest emotion of his countenance. The Mohican maintained his firm and haughty attitude; and his eye, so far from deigning to meet her inquisitive look, dwelt steadily on the distance, as though it penetrated the obstacles which impeded the view, and looked into futurity. Satisfied with her examination, she left him, with a slight expression of pleasure, and proceeded to practice the same trying experiment on her delinquent countryman.

The young Huron was in his war paint, and very little of a finely moulded form was concealed by his attire. The light rendered every limb and joint discernible, and Duncan turned away in horror when he saw that they were writhing in irrepressible agony. The woman was commencing a low and plaintive howl at the sad and shameful spectacle, when the chief put forth his hand and gently pushed her aside.

"Reed-that-bends," he said, addressing the young culprit by name, and in his proper language, "though the Great Spirit has made you pleasant to the eyes, it would have been better that you had not been born. Your tongue is loud in the village, but in battle it is still. None of my young men strike the tomahawk deeper into the war-post—none of them so lightly on the Yengeese. The enemy know the shape of your back, but they have never seen the color of your eyes. Three times have they called on you to come, and as often did you forget to answer. Your name will never be mentioned again in your tribe—it is already forgotten."

As the chief slowly uttered these words, pausing impressively between each sentence, the culprit raised his face, in deference to the other's rank and years. Shame, horror, and pride struggled in its lineaments. His eye, which was contracted with inward anguish, gleamed on the persons of those whose breath was his fame; and the latter emotion for an instant predominated. He arose to his feet, and baring his bosom, looked steadily on the keen, glittering knife, that was already upheld by his inexorable judge. As the weapon passed slowly into his heart he even smiled, as if in joy at having found death less dreadful than he had anticipated, and fell heavily on his face, at the feet of the rigid and unyielding form of Uncas.

The squaw gave a loud and plaintive yell, dashed the torch to the earth, and buried everything in darkness. The whole shuddering group of spectators glided from the lodge, like troubled sprites; and Duncan thought that he and the yet throbbing body of the victim of an Indian judgment had now become its only tenants.

CHAPTER XXIV

Thus spoke the sage: the kings without delay
Dissolve the council, and their chief obey.
POPE'S *Iliad.*

A single moment served to convince the youth that he was mistaken. A hand was laid with a powerful pressure on his arm, and the low voice of Uncas muttered in his ears,—

"The Hurons are dogs. The sight of a coward's blood can never make a warrior tremble. The 'Gray Head' and the Sagamore are safe, and the rifle of Hawkeye is not asleep. Go,—Uncas and the 'Open Hand' are now strangers. It is enough."

Heyward would gladly have heard more, but a gentle push from his friend urged him towards the door, and admonished him of the danger that might attend the discovery of their intercourse. Slowly and reluctantly yielding to the necessity, he quitted the place, and mingled with the throng that hovered nigh. The dying fires in the clearing cast a dim and uncertain light on the dusky figures that were silently stalking to and fro; and occasionally a brighter gleam than common glanced into the lodge, and exhibited the figure of Uncas still maintaining its upright attitude near the dead body of the Huron.

A knot of warriors soon entered the place again, and reissuing, they bore the senseless remains into the adjacent woods. After this termination of the scene, Duncan wandered among the lodges, unquestioned and unnoticed, endeavoring to find some trace of her in whose behalf he incurred the risk he ran. In the present temper of the tribe, it would have been easy to have fled and rejoined his companions, had such a wish crossed his mind. But, in addition to the never-ceasing anxiety on account of Alice, a fresher, though feebler interest in the fate of Uncas assisted to chain him to the spot. He continued, therefore, to stray from hut to hut, looking into each only to encounter additional disappointment, until he had made the entire circuit of the village. Abandoning a species of inquiry that proved so fruitless, he retraced his steps to the council lodge, resolved to seek and question David, in order to put an end to his doubts.

On reaching the building which had proved alike the seat of judgment and the place of execution, the young man found that the excitement had already subsided. The warriors had reassembled, and were now calmly smoking, while they conversed gravely on the chief incidents of their recent expedition to the head of the Horican. Though the return of Duncan was likely to remind them of his character, and the suspicious circumstances of his visit, it produced no visible sensation. So far, the terrible scene that had just occurred proved favorable to his views, and he required no other prompter than his own feelings to convince him of the expediency of profiting by so unexpected an advantage.

Without seeming to hesitate, he walked into the lodge, and took his seat with a gravity that accorded admirably with the deportment of his hosts. A hasty but searching glance sufficed to tell him that, though Uncas still remained where he had left him, David had not reappeared. No other restraint was imposed on the former than the watchful looks of a young Huron, who had placed himself at hand; though an armed warrior leaned against the post that formed one side of the narrow doorway. In every other respect, the captive seemed at liberty; still he was excluded from all participation in the discourse, and possessed much more of the air of some finely moulded statue than a man having life and volition.

Heyward had too recently witnessed a frightful instance of the prompt punishments of the people into whose hands he had fallen, to hazard an exposure by any officious boldness. He would greatly have preferred silence and meditation to speech, when a discovery of his real condition might prove so instantly fatal. Unfortunately for this prudent resolution, his entertainers appeared otherwise disposed. He had not long occupied the seat wisely taken a little in the shade, when another of the elder warriors, who spoke the French language, addressed him:—

"My Canada father does not forget his children," said the chief; "I thank him. An evil spirit lives in the wife of one of my young men. Can the cunning stranger frighten him away?"

Heyward possessed some knowledge of the mummery practiced among the Indians, in the cases of such supposed visitations. He saw, at a glance, that the circumstance might possibly be improved to further his own ends. It would therefore have been difficult, just then, to have uttered a proposal that would have given him more satisfaction. Aware of the necessity of preserving the dignity of his imaginary character, however, he repressed his feelings, and answered with suitable mystery,—

"Spirits differ; some yield to the power of wisdom, while others are too strong."

"My brother is a great medicine," said the cunning savage; "he will try?"

A gesture of assent was the answer. The Huron was content with the assurance, and resuming his pipe, he awaited the proper moment to move. The impatient Heyward, inwardly execrating the cold customs of the savages, which required such sacrifices to appearance, was fain to assume an air of indifference, equal to that maintained by the chief, who was, in truth a near relative of the afflicted woman. The minutes lingered, and the delay had seemed an hour to the adventurer in empiricism, when the Huron laid aside his pipe, and drew his robe across his breast, as if about to lead the way to the lodge of the invalid. Just then a warrior of powerful frame darkened the door, and stalking silently among the attentive group, he seated himself on one end of the low pile of brush which sustained Duncan. The latter cast an impatient look at his neighbor, and felt his flesh creep with uncontrolled horror when he found himself in actual contact with Magua.

The sudden return of this artful and dreaded chief caused a delay in the departure of the Huron. Several pipes, that had been extinguished, were lighted again; while the new-comer, without speaking a word drew his tomahawk from his girdle, and filling the bowl on its head, began to inhale the vapors of the weed through the hollow handle, with as much indifference as if he had not been absent two weary days on a long and toilsome hunt. Ten minutes, which appeared as many ages to Duncan, might have passed in this manner; and the warriors were fairly enveloped in a cloud of white smoke before any of them spoke.

"Welcome!" one at length uttered; "has my friend found the moose?"

"The young men stagger under their burdens," returned Magua. "Let 'Reed-that-bends' go to the hunting path; he will meet them."

A deep and awful silence succeeded the utterance of the forbidden name. Each pipe dropped from the lips of its owner as though all had inhaled an impurity at the same instant. The smoke wreathed above their heads in little eddies, and curling in a spiral form, it ascended swiftly through the opening in the roof of the lodge, leaving the place beneath clear of its fumes, and each dark visage distinctly visible. The looks of most of the warriors were riveted on the earth; though a few of the younger and less gifted of the party suffered their wild and glaring eye-balls to roll in the direction of a white-headed savage, who sat between two of the most venerated chiefs of the tribe. There was nothing in the air or attire of this Indian that would seem to entitle him to such a distinction. The former was rather depressed, than remarkable for the bearing of the natives; and the latter was such as was commonly worn by the ordinary men of the nation. Like most around him, for more than a minute his look too was on the ground; but, trusting his eyes at length to steal a glance aside, he perceived that he was becoming an object of general attention. Then he arose and lifted his voice in the general silence.

"It was a lie," he said; "I had no son. He who was called by that name is forgotten; his blood was pale, and it came not from the veins of a Huron; the wicked Chippewas cheated my squaw. The Great Spirit has said, that the family of Wiss-entush should end; he is happy who knows that the evil of his race dies with himself. I have done."

The speaker, who was the father of the recreant young Indian, looked round and about him, as if seeking commendation of his stoicism in the eyes of his auditors. But the stern customs of his people had made too severe an exaction of the feeble old man. The expression of his eye contradicted his figurative and boastful language, while every muscle in his wrinkled visage was working with anguish. Standing a single minute to enjoy his bitter triumph, he turned away, as if sickening at the gaze of men, and veiling his face in his blanket, he walked from the lodge with the noiseless step of an Indian, seeking, in the privacy of his own abode, the sympathy of one like himself, aged, forlorn, and childless.

The Indians, who believe in the hereditary transmission of virtues and defects in character, suffered him to depart in silence. Then, with an elevation of breeding that many in a more cultivated state of society might profitably emulate, one of the chiefs drew the attention of the young men from the weakness they had just witnessed, by saying, in a cheerful voice, addressing himself in courtesy to Magua, as the newest comer,—

"The Delawares have been like bears after the honey-pots, prowling around my village. But who has ever found a Huron asleep?"

The darkness of the impending cloud which precedes a burst of thunder was not blacker than the brow of Magua as he exclaimed,—

"The Delawares of the Lakes!"

"Not so. They who wear the petticoats of squaws, on their own river. One of them has been passing the tribe."

"Did my young men take his scalp?"

"His legs were good, though his arm is better for the hoe than the tomahawk," returned the other, pointing to the immovable form of Uncas.

Instead of manifesting any womanish curiosity to feast his eyes with the sight of a captive from a people he was known to have so much reason to hate, Magua continued to smoke, with the meditative air that he usually maintained, when there was no immediate call on his cunning or his eloquence. Although secretly amazed at the facts communicated by the speech of the aged father, he permitted himself to ask no questions, reserving his inquiries for a more suitable moment. It was only after a sufficient interval that he shook the ashes from his pipe, replaced the tomahawk, tightened his girdle, and arose, casting for the first time a glance in the direction of the prisoner, who stood a little behind him. The wary though seemingly abstracted Uncas caught a glimpse of the movement and turning suddenly to the light, their looks met. Near a minute these two bold and untamed spirits stood regarding one another steadily in the eye, neither quailing in the least before the fierce gaze he encountered. The form of Uncas dilated, and his nostrils opened like those of a tiger at bay; but so rigid and unyielding was his posture, that he might easily have been converted by the imagination into an exquisite and faultless representation of the warlike deity of his tribe. The lineaments of the quivering features of Magua proved more ductile; his countenance gradually lost its character of defiance in an expression of ferocious joy, and heaving a breath from the very bottom of his chest, he pronounced aloud the formidable name of—

"Le Cerf Agile!"

Each warrior sprang upon his feet at the utterance of the well known appellation, and there was a short period during which the stoical constancy of the natives was completely conquered by surprise. The hated and yet respected name was repeated as by one voice, carrying the sound even beyond the limits of the lodge. The women and children, who lingered around the entrance, took up the words in an echo, which was succeeded by another shrill and plaintive howl. The latter was not yet ended, when the sensation among the men had entirely abated. Each one in presence seated himself, as though ashamed of his precipitation; but it was many minutes before their meaning eyes ceased to roll towards their captive, in curious examination of a warrior who had so often proved his prowess on the best and proudest of their nation. Uncas enjoyed his victory, but was content with merely exhibiting his triumph by a quiet smile—an emblem of scorn which belongs to all time and every nation.

Magua caught the expression, and raising his arm, he shook it at the captive, the light silver ornaments attached to his bracelet rattling with the trembling agitation of the limb, as, in a tone of vengeance, he exclaimed, in English,—

"Mohican, you die!"

"The healing waters will never bring the dead Hurons to life," returned Uncas, in the music of the Delawares; "the tumbling river washes their bones; their men are squaws; their women owls. Go! call together the Huron dogs, that they may look upon a warrior. My nostrils are offended; they scent the blood of a coward."

The latter allusion struck deep, and the injury rankled. Many of the Hurons understood the strange tongue in which the captive spoke, among which number was Magua. This cunning savage beheld, and instantly profited by his advantage. Dropping the light robe of skin from his shoulder, he stretched forth his arm, and commenced a burst of his dangerous and artful eloquence. However much his influence among his people had been impaired by his occasional and besetting weakness, as well as by his desertion of the tribe, his courage and his fame as an orator were undeniable. He never spoke without auditors, and rarely without making converts to his opinions. On the present occasion, his native powers were stimulated by the thirst of revenge.

He again recounted the events of the attack on the island at Glenn's, the death of his associates, and the escape of their most formidable enemies. Then he described the nature and position of the mount whither he had led such captives as had fallen into their hands. Of his own bloody intentions towards the maidens, and of his baffled malice he made no mention, but passed rapidly on to the surprise of the party by 'La Longue Carabine,' and its fatal termination. Here he paused, and looked about him, in affected veneration for the departed, but, in truth, to note the effect of his opening narrative. As usual, every eye was riveted on his face. Each dusky figure seemed a breathing statue, so motionless was the posture, so intense the attention of the individual.

Then Magua dropped his voice, which had hitherto been clear, strong, and elevated, and touched upon the merits of the dead. No quality that was likely to command the sympathy of an Indian escaped his notice. One had never been known to follow the chase in vain; another had been indefatigable on the trail of their enemies. This was brave, that generous. In short, he so managed his allusions, that in a nation which was composed of so few families, he contrived to strike every chord that might find, in its turn, some breast in which to vibrate.

"Are the bones of my young men," he concluded, "in the burial-place of the Hurons? You know they are not. Their spirits are gone towards the setting sun, and are already crossing the great waters, to the happy hunting-grounds. But they departed without food, without guns or knives, without moccasins, naked and poor as they were born. Shall this be? Are their souls to enter the land of the just like hungry Iroquois or unmanly Delawares; or shall they meet their friends with arms in their hands and robes on their backs? What will our fathers think the tribes of the Wyandots have become? They will look on their children with a dark eye, and say, Go! a Chippewa has come hither with the name of a Huron. Brothers, we must not forget the dead; a red-skin never ceases to remember. We will load the back of this Mohican until he staggers under our bounty, and dispatch him after my young men. They call to us for aid, though our ears are not open; they say, Forget us not. When they see the spirit of this Mohican toiling after them with his burden, they will know we are of that mind. Then will they go on happy; and our children will say, 'So did our fathers to their friends, so must we do to them.' What is a Yengee? we have slain many, but the earth is still pale. A stain on the name of a Huron can only be hid by blood that comes from the veins of an Indian. Let this Delaware die."

The effect of such an harangue, delivered in the nervous language and with the emphatic manner of a Huron orator, could scarcely be mistaken. Magua had so artfully blended the natural sympathies with the religious superstition of his auditors, that their minds, already prepared by custom to sacrifice a victim to the manes of their countrymen, lost every vestige of humanity in a wish for revenge. One warrior in particular, a man of wild and ferocious mien, had been conspicuous for the attention he had given to the words of the speaker. His countenance had changed with each passing emotion, until it settled into a look of deadly malice. As Magua ended he arose, and uttering the yell of a demon, his polished little axe was seen glancing in the torch-light as he whirled it above his head. The motion and the cry were too sudden for words to interrupt his bloody intention. It appeared as if a bright gleam shot from his hand, which was crossed at the same moment by a dark and powerful line. The former was the tomahawk in its passage; the latter the arm that Magua darted forward to divert its aim. The quick and ready motion of the chief was not entirely too late. The keen weapon cut the war-plume from the scalping tuft of Uncas, and passed through the frail wall of the lodge as though it were hurled from some formidable engine.

Duncan had seen the threatening action, and sprang upon his feet, with a heart which, while it leaped into his throat, swelled with the most generous resolution in behalf of his friend. A glance told him that the blow had failed, and terror changed to admiration. Uncas stood still, looking his enemy in the eye with features that seemed superior to emotion. Marble could not be colder, calmer, or steadier than the countenance he put upon this sudden and vindictive attack. Then, as if pitying a want of skill which had proved so fortunate to himself, he smiled, and muttered a few words of contempt in his own tongue.

"No!" said Magua, after satisfying himself of the safety of the captive; "the sun must shine on his shame; the squaws must see his flesh tremble, or our revenge will be like the play of boys. Go! take him where there is silence; let us see if a Delaware can sleep at night, and in the morning die."

The young men whose duty it was to guard the prisoner instantly passed their ligaments of bark across his arms, and led him from the lodge, amid a profound and ominous silence. It was only as the figure of Uncas stood in the opening of the door that his firm step hesitated. There he turned, and, in the sweeping and haughty glance that he threw around the circle of his enemies, Duncan caught a look which he was glad to construe into an expression that he was not entirely deserted by hope.

Magua was content with his success, or too much occupied with his secret purposes to push his inquiries any further. Shaking his mantle, and folding it on his bosom, he also quitted the place, without pursuing a subject which might have proved so fatal to the individual at his elbow. Notwithstanding his rising resentment, his natural firmness, and his anxiety in behalf of Uncas, Heyward felt sensibly relieved by the absence of so dangerous and so subtle a foe. The excitement produced by the speech gradually subsided. The warriors resumed their seats, and clouds of smoke once more filled the lodge. For near half an hour, not a syllable was uttered, or scarcely a look cast aside; a grave and meditative silence being the ordinary succession to every scene of violence and commotion amongst those beings, who were alike so impetuous and yet so self-restrained.

When the chief who had solicited the aid of Duncan finished his pipe, he made a final and successful movement towards departing. A motion of a finger was the intimation he gave the supposed physician to follow; and passing through the clouds of smoke, Duncan was glad, on more accounts than one, to be able at last to breathe the pure air of a cool and refreshing summer evening.

Instead of pursuing his way among those lodges where Heyward had already made his unsuccessful search, his companion turned aside, and proceeded directly towards the base of an adjacent mountain, which overhung the temporary village. A thicket of brush skirted its foot, and it became necessary to proceed through a crooked and narrow path. The boys had resumed their sports in the clearing, and were enacting a mimic chase to the post among themselves. In order to render their games as like the reality as possible, one of the boldest of their number had conveyed a few brands into some piles of tree-tops that had hitherto escaped the burning. The blaze of one of these fires lighted the way of the chief and Duncan, and gave a character of additional wildness to the rude scenery. At a little distance from a bald rock, and directly in its front, they entered a grassy opening, which they prepared to cross. Just then fresh fuel was added to the fire, and a powerful light penetrated even to that distant spot. It fell upon the white surface of the mountain, and was reflected downwards upon a dark and mysterious-looking being that arose, unexpectedly, in their path.

The Indian paused, as if doubtful whether to proceed, and permitted his companion to approach his side. A large black ball, which at first seemed stationary, now began to move in a manner that to the latter was inexplicable. Again the fire brightened, and its glare fell more distinctly on the object. Then even Duncan knew it, by its restless and sideling attitudes, which kept the upper part of its form in constant motion, while the animal itself appeared seated, to be a bear. Though it growled loudly and fiercely, and there were instants when its glistening eye-balls might be seen, it gave no other indications of hostility. The Huron, at least, seemed assured that the intentions of this singular intruder were peaceable, for after giving it an attentive examination, he quietly pursued his course.

Duncan, who knew that the animal was often domesticated among the Indians, followed the example of his companion, believing that some favorite of the tribe had found its way into the thicket, in search of food. They passed it unmolested. Though obliged to come nearly in contact with the monster, the Huron, who had at first so warily determined the character of his strange visitor, was now content with proceeding without wasting a moment in further examination; but Heyward was unable to prevent his eyes from looking backward, in salutary watchfulness against attacks in the rear. His uneasiness was in no degree diminished when he perceived the beast rolling along their path, and following their footsteps. He would have spoken, but the Indian at that moment shoved aside a door of bark, and entered a cavern in the bosom of the mountain.

Profiting by so easy a method of retreat, Duncan stepped after him, and was gladly closing the slight cover to the opening, when he felt it drawn from his hand by the beast, whose shaggy form immediately darkened the passage. They were now in a straight and long gallery, in a chasm of the rocks, where retreat without encountering the animal was impossible. Making the best of the circumstances, the young man pressed forward, keeping as close as possible to his conductor. The bear growled frequently at his heels, and once or twice its enormous paws were laid on his person, as if disposed to prevent his further passage into the den.

How long the nerves of Heyward would have sustained him in this extraordinary situation, it might be difficult to decide; for, happily, he soon found relief. A glimmer of light had constantly been in their front, and they now arrived at the place whence it proceeded.

A large cavity in the rock had been rudely fitted to answer the purposes of many apartments. The subdivisions were simple but ingenious, being composed of stone, sticks, and bark, intermingled. Openings above admitted the light by day, and at night fires and torches supplied the place of the sun. Hither the Hurons had brought most of their valuables, especially those which more particularly pertained to the nation; and hither, as it now appeared, the sick woman, who was believed to be the victim of supernatural power, had been transported also, under an impression that her tormentor would find more difficulty in making his assaults through walls of stone than through the leafy coverings of the lodges. The apartment into which Duncan and his guide first entered, had been exclusively devoted to her accommodation. The latter approached her bedside, which was surrounded by females, in the centre of whom Heyward was surprised to find his missing friend David.

A single look was sufficient to apprise the pretended leech that the invalid was far beyond his powers of healing. She lay in a sort of paralysis, indifferent to the objects which crowded before her sight, and happily unconscious of suffering. Heyward was far from regretting that his mummeries were to be performed on one who was much too ill to take an interest in their failure or success. The slight qualm of conscience which had been excited by the intended deception was instantly appeased, and he began to collect his thoughts, in order to enact his part with suitable spirit, when he found he was about to be anticipated in his skill by an attempt to prove the power of music.

Gamut, who had stood prepared to pour forth his spirit in song when the visitors entered, after delaying a moment, drew a strain from his pipe, and commenced a hymn that might have worked a miracle, had faith in its efficacy been of much avail. He was allowed to proceed to the close, the Indians respecting his imaginary infirmity, and Duncan too glad of the delay to hazard the slightest interruption. As the dying cadence of his strains was falling on the ears of the latter, he started aside at hearing them repeated behind him, in a voice half human and half sepulchral. Looking around, he beheld the shaggy monster seated on end in a shadow of the cavern, where, while his restless body swung in the uneasy manner of the animal, it repeated, in a sort of low growl, sounds, if not words, which bore some slight resemblance to the melody of the singer.

The effect of so strange an echo on David may better be imagined than described. His eyes opened as if he doubted their truth; and his voice became instantly mute in excess of wonder. A deep-laid scheme, of communicating some important intelligence to Heyward, was driven from his recollection by an emotion which very nearly resembled fear, but which he was fain to believe was admiration. Under its influence, he exclaimed aloud, "She expects you, she is at hand;" and precipitately left the cavern.

CHAPTER XXV

> Snug.—*Have you the lion's part written? Pray you, if it be, give it me, for I am slow of study.*
>
> Quince.—*You may do it extempore, for it is nothing but roaring.*
>
> SHAKESPEARE, *Midsummer Night's Dream,* I. ii. 68.

There was a strange blending of the ridiculous with that which was solemn in this scene. The beast still continued its rolling, and apparently untiring movements, though its ludicrous attempt to imitate the melody of David ceased the instant the latter abandoned the field. The words of Gamut were, as has been seen, in his native tongue; and to Duncan they seemed pregnant with some hidden meaning, though nothing present assisted him in discovering the object of their allusion. A speedy end was, however, put to every conjecture on the subject, by the manner of the chief, who advanced to the bedside of the invalid, and beckoned away the whole group of female attendants that had clustered there to witness the skill of the stranger. He was implicitly, though reluctantly, obeyed; and when the low echo which rang along the hollow natural gallery, from the distant closing door, had ceased, pointing towards his insensible daughter, he said,—

"Now let my brother show his power."

Thus unequivocally called on to exercise the functions of his assumed character, Heyward was apprehensive that the smallest delay might prove dangerous. Endeavoring then to collect his ideas, he prepared to perform that species of incantation, and those uncouth rites, under which the Indian conjurers are accustomed to conceal their ignorance and impotency. It is more than probable that, in the disordered state of his thoughts, he would soon have fallen into some suspicious, if not fatal error, had not his incipient attempts been interrupted by a fierce growl from the quadruped. Three several times did he renew his efforts to proceed, and as often was he met by the same unaccountable opposition, each interruption seeming more savage and threatening than the preceding.

"The cunning ones are jealous," said the Huron; "I go. Brother, the woman is the wife of one of my bravest young men; deal justly by her. Peace!" he added, beckoning to the discontented beast to be quiet; "I go."

The chief was as good as his word, and Duncan now found himself alone in that wild and desolate abode, with the helpless invalid and the fierce and dangerous brute. The latter listened to the movements of the Indian with that air of sagacity that a bear is known to possess, until another echo announced that he had also left the cavern, when it turned and came waddling up to Duncan, before whom it seated itself, in its natural attitude, erect like a man. The youth looked anxiously about him for some weapon, with which he might make a resistance against the attack he now seriously expected.

It seemed, however, as if the humor of the animal had suddenly changed. Instead of continuing its discontented growls, or manifesting any further signs of anger, the whole of its shaggy body shook violently, as if agitated by some strange internal convulsion. The huge and unwieldy talons pawed stupidly about the grinning muzzle, and while Heyward kept his eyes riveted on its movements with jealous watchfulness, the grim head fell on one side, and in its place appeared the honest, sturdy countenance of the scout, who was indulging, from the bottom of his soul, in his own peculiar expression of merriment.

"Hist!" said the wary woodsman, interrupting Heyward's exclamation of surprise; "the varlets are about the place, and any sounds that are not natural to witchcraft would bring them back upon us in a body."

"Tell me the meaning of this masquerade; and why you have attempted so desperate an adventure?"

"Ah! reason and calculation are often outdone by accident," returned the scout. "But as a story should always commence at the beginning, I will tell you the whole in order. After we parted I placed the commandant and the Sagamore in an old beaver lodge, where they are safer from the Hurons than they would be in the garrison of Edward; for your high northwest Indians, not having as yet got the traders among them, continue to venerate the beaver. After which Uncas and I pushed for the other encampment, as was agreed; have you seen the lad?"

"To my great grief! he is captive, and condemned to die at the rising of the sun."

"I had misgivings that such would be his fate," resumed the scout, in a less confident and joyous tone. But soon regaining his naturally firm voice, he continued: "His bad fortune is the true reason of my being here, for it would never do to abandon such a boy to the Hurons. A rare time the knaves would have of it, could they tie 'The Bounding Elk' and 'The Long Carabine,' as they call me, to the same stake! Though why they have given me such a name I never knew, there being as little likeness between the gifts of Killdeer and the performance of one of your real Canada carabynes, as there is between the natur' of a pipe-stone and a flint!"

"Keep to your tale," said the impatient Heyward; "we know not at what moment the Hurons may return."

"No fear of them. A conjurer must have his time, like a straggling priest in the settlements. We are as safe from interruption as a missionary would be at the beginning of a two hours' discourse. Well, Uncas and I fell in with a return party of the varlets; the lad was much too forward for a scout; nay, for that matter, being of hot blood, he was not so much to blame; and, after all, one of the Hurons proved a coward, and in fleeing led him into an ambushment."

"And dearly has he paid for the weakness!"

The scout significantly passed his hand across his own throat, and nodded, as if he said, "I comprehend your meaning." After which he continued, in a more audible though scarcely more intelligible language,—

"After the loss of the boy I turned upon the Hurons, as you may judge. There have been skrimmages atween one or two of their outlyers and myself; but that is neither here nor there. So, after I had shot the imps, I got in pretty nigh to the lodges without further commotion. Then what should luck do in my favor, but lead me to the very spot where one of the most famous conjurers of the tribe was dressing himself, as I well knew, for some great battle with Satan—though why should I call that luck, which it now seems was an especial ordering of Providence! So a judgmatical rap over the head stiffened the lying imposter for a time, and leaving him a bit of walnut for his supper, to prevent an uproar, and stringing him up atween two saplings, I made free with his finery, and took the part of the bear on myself, in order that the operations might proceed."

"And admirably did you enact the character; the animal itself might have been shamed by the representation."

"Lord, Major," returned the flattered woodsman, "I should be but a poor scholar for one who has studied so long in the wilderness, did I not know how to set forth the movements and natur' of such a beast. Had it been now a catamount, or even a full-sized panther, I would have embellished a performance for you worth regarding. But it is no such marvelous feat to exhibit the feats of so dull a beast; though, for that matter too, a bear may be over-acted. Yes, yes; it is not every imitator that knows natur' may be outdone easier than she is equaled. But all our work is yet before us: where is the gentle one?"

"Heaven knows; I have examined every lodge in the village, without discovering the slightest trace of her presence in the tribe."

"You heard what the singer said, as he left us, 'She is at hand, and expects you'?"

"I have been compelled to believe he alluded to this unhappy woman."

"The simpleton was frightened, and blundered through his message; but he had a deeper meaning. Here are walls enough to separate the whole settlement. A bear ought to climb; therefore will I take a look above them. There may be honey-pots hid in these rocks, and I am a beast, you know, that has a hankering for the sweets."

The scout looked behind him, laughing at his own conceit, while he clambered up the partition, imitating, as he went, the clumsy motions of the beast he represented; but the instant the summit was gained he made a gesture for silence, and slid down with the utmost precipitation.

"She is here," he whispered, "and by that door you will find her. I would have spoken a word of comfort to the afflicted soul; but the sight of such a monster might upset her reason. Though for that matter, Major, you are none of the most inviting yourself in your paint."

Duncan, who had already sprung eagerly forward, drew instantly back on hearing these discouraging words.

"Am I, then, so very revolting?" he demanded, with an air of chagrin.

"You might not startle a wolf, or turn the Royal Americans from a charge; but I have seen the time when you had a better-favored look; your streaked countenances are not ill-judged of by the squaws, but young women of white blood give the preference to their own color. See," he added, pointing to a place where the water trickled from a rock, forming a little crystal spring before it found an issue through the adjacent crevices; "you may easily get rid of the Sagamore's daub, and when you come back I will try my hand at a new embellishment. It 's as common for a conjurer to alter his paint as for a buck in the settlements to change his finery."

The deliberate woodsman had little occasion to hunt for arguments to enforce his advice. He was yet speaking when Duncan availed himself of the water. In a moment every frightful or offensive mark was obliterated, and the youth appeared again in the lineaments with which he had been gifted by nature. Thus prepared for an interview with his mistress, he took a hasty leave of his companion, and disappeared through the indicated passage. The scout witnessed his departure with complacency, nodding his head after him, and muttering his good wishes; after which he very coolly set about an examination of the state of the larder, among the Hurons—the cavern, among other purposes, being used as a receptacle for the fruits of their hunts.

Duncan had no other guide than a distant glimmering light, which served, however, the office of a polar star to the lover. By its aid he was enabled to enter the haven of his hopes, which was merely another apartment of the cavern, that had been solely appropriated to the safe-keeping of so important a prisoner as a daughter of the commandant of William Henry. It was profusely strewed with the plunder of that unlucky fortress. In the midst of this confusion he found her he sought, pale, anxious, and terrified, but lovely. David had prepared her for such a visit.

"Duncan!" she exclaimed, in a voice that seemed to tremble at the sounds created by itself.

"Alice!" he answered, leaping carelessly among trunks, boxes, arms, and furniture, until he stood at her side.

"I knew that you would never desert me," she said, looking up with a momentary glow on her otherwise dejected countenance. "But you are alone! grateful as it is to be thus remembered, I could wish to think you are not entirely alone."

Duncan, observing that she trembled in a manner which betrayed her inability to stand, gently induced her to be seated, while he recounted those leading incidents which it has been our task to record. Alice listened with breathless interest; and though the young man touched lightly on the sorrows of the stricken father, taking care, however, not to wound the self-love of his auditor, the tears ran as freely down the cheeks of the daughter as though she had never wept before. The soothing tenderness of Duncan, however, soon quieted the first burst of her emotions, and she then heard him to the close with undivided attention, if not with composure.

"And now, Alice," he added, "you will see how much is still expected of you. By the assistance of our experienced and invaluable friend, the scout, we may find our way from this savage people, but you will have to exert your utmost fortitude. Remember that you fly to the arms of your venerable parent, and how much his happiness, as well as your own, depends on those exertions."

"Can I do otherwise for a father who has done so much for me?"

"And for me too," continued the youth, gently pressing the hand he held in both his own.

The look of innocence and surprise which he received in return convinced Duncan of the necessity of being more explicit.

"This is neither the place nor the occasion to detain you with selfish wishes," he added; "but what heart loaded like mine would not wish to cast its burden? They say misery is the closest of all ties; our common suffering in your behalf left but little to be explained between your father and myself."

"And dearest Cora, Duncan; surely Cora was not forgotten?"

"Not forgotten! no; regretted, as woman was seldom mourned before. Your venerable father knew no difference between his children; but I—Alice, you will not be offended when I say, that to me her worth was in a degree obscured—"

"Then you knew not the merit of my sisiter," said Alice, withdrawing her hand; "of you she ever speaks as of one who is her dearest friend."

"I would gladly believe her such," returned Duncan, hastily; "I could wish her to be even more; but with you, Alice, I have the permission of your father to aspire to a still nearer and dearer tie."

Alice trembled violently, and there was an instant during which she bent her face aside, yielding to the emotions common to her sex; but they quickly passed away, leaving her mistress of her deportment, if not of her affections.

"Heyward," she said, looking him full in the face with a touching expression of innocence and dependency, "give me the sacred presence and the holy sanction of that parent before you urge me further."

"Though more I should not, less I could not say," the youth was about to answer, when he was interrupted by a light tap on his shoulder. Starting to his feet, he turned, and, confronting the intruder, his looks fell on the dark form and malignant visage of Magua. The deep guttural laugh of the savage sounded, at such a moment, to Duncan like the hellish taunt of a demon. Had he pursued the sudden and fierce impulse of the instant, he would have cast himself on the Huron, and committed their fortunes to the issue of a deadly struggle. But, without arms of any description, ignorant of what succor his subtle enemy could command, and charged with the safety of one who was just then dearer than ever to his heart, he no sooner entertained than he abandoned the desperate intention.

"What is your purpose?" said Alice, meekly folding her arms on her bosom, and struggling to conceal an agony of apprehension in behalf of Heyward, in the usual cold and distant manner with which she received the visits of her captor.

The exulting Indian had resumed his austere countenance, though he drew warily back before the menacing glance of the young man's fiery eye. He regarded both his captives for a moment with a steady look, and then stepping aside, he dropped a log of wood across a door different from that by which Duncan had entered. The latter now comprehended the manner of his surprise, and believing himself irretrievably lost, he drew Alice to his bosom, and stood prepared to meet a fate which he hardly regretted, since it was to be suffered in such company. But Magua meditated no immediate violence. His first measures were very evidently taken to secure his new captive; nor did he even bestow a second glance at the motionless forms in the centre of the cavern, until he had completely cut off every hope of retreat through the private outlet he had himself used. He was watched in all his movements by Heyward, who, however, remained firm, still folding the fragile form of Alice to his heart, at once too proud and too hopeless to ask favor of an enemy so often foiled. When Magua had effected his object he approached his prisoners, and said in English,—

"The pale-faces trap the cunning beavers; but the red-skins know how to take the Yengeese."

"Huron, do your worst!" exclaimed the excited Heyward, forgetful that a double stake was involved in his life; "you and your vengeance are alike despised."

"Will the white man speak these words at the stake?" asked Magua; manifesting, at the same time, how little faith he had in the other's resolution by the sneer that accompanied his words.

"Here; singly to your face, or in the presence of your nation."

"Le Renard Subtil is a great chief!" returned the Indian; "he will go and bring his young men, to see how bravely a pale-face can laugh at the tortures."

He turned away while speaking, and was about to leave the place through the avenue by which Duncan had approached, when a growl caught his ear, and caused him to hesitate. The figure of the bear appeared in the door, where it sat, rolling from side to side in its customary restlessness. Magua, like the father of the sick woman, eyed it keenly for a moment, as if to ascertain its character. He was far above the more vulgar superstitions of his tribe, and so soon as he recognized the well-known attire of the conjurer, he prepared to pass it in cool contempt. But a louder and more threatening growl caused him again to pause. Then he seemed as if suddenly resolved to trifle no longer, and moved resolutely forward. The mimic animal, which had advanced a little, retired slowly in his front, until it arrived again at the pass, when rearing on its hinder legs it beat the air with its paws, in the manner practiced by its brutal prototype.

"Fool!" exclaimed the chief, in Huron, "go play with the children and squaws; leave men to their wisdom."

He once more endeavored to pass the supposed empiric, scorning even the parade of threatening to use the knife, or tomahawk, that was pendent from his belt. Suddenly the beast extended its arms, or rather legs, and inclosed him in a grasp that might have vied with the far-famed power of the "bear's hug" itself. Heyward had watched the whole procedure, on the part of Hawkeye, with breathless interest. At first he relinquished his hold of Alice; then he caught up a thong of buckskin, which had been used around some bundle, and when he beheld his enemy with his two arms pinned to his side by the iron muscles of the scout, he rushed upon him, and effectually secured them there. Arms, legs, and feet were encircled in twenty folds of the thong, in less time than we have taken to record the circumstance. When the formidable Huron was completely pinioned, the scout released his hold, and Duncan laid his enemy on his back, utterly helpless.

Throughout the whole of this sudden and extraordinary operation, Magua, though he had struggled violently, until assured he was in the hands of one whose nerves were far better strung than his own, had not uttered the slightest exclamation. But when Hawkeye, by way of making a summary explanation of his conduct, removed the shaggy jaws of the beast, and exposed his own rugged and earnest countenance to the gaze of the Huron, the philosophy of the latter was so far mastered as to permit him to utter the never-failing,—

"Hugh!"

"Aye! you've found your tongue," said his undisturbed conqueror; "now, in order that you shall not use it to our ruin, I must make free to stop your mouth."

As there was no time to be lost, the scout immediately set about effecting so necessary a precaution; and when he had gagged the Indian, his enemy might safely have been considered as "hors de combat."

"By what place did the imp enter?" asked the industrious scout, when his work was ended. "Not a soul has passed my way since you left me."

Duncan pointed out the door by which Magua had come, and which now presented too many obstacles to a quick retreat.

"Bring on the gentle one then," continued his friend; "we must make a push for the woods by the other outlet."

"'T is impossible!" said Duncan; "fear has overcome her, and she is helpless. Alice! my sweet, my own Alice, arouse yourself; now is the moment to fly. 'T is in vain! she hears, but is unable to follow. Go, noble and worthy friend; save yourself, and leave me to my fate!"

"Every trail has its end, and every calamity brings its lesson!" returned the scout. "There, wrap her in them Indian cloths. Conceal all of her little form. Nay, that foot has no fellow in the wilderness; it will betray her. All, every part. Now take her in your arms, and follow. Leave the rest to me."

Duncan, as may be gathered from the words of his companion, was eagerly obeying; and as the other finished speaking, he took the light person of Alice in his arms, and followed on the footsteps of the scout. They found the sick woman as they had left her, still alone, and passed swiftly on, by the natural gallery, to the place of entrance.

As they approached the little door of bark, a murmur of voices without announced that the friends and relatives of the invalid were gathered about the place, patiently awaiting a summons to reënter.

"If I open my lips to speak," Hawkeye whispered, "my English, which is the genuine tongue of a white-skin, will tell the varlets that an enemy is among them. You must give 'em your jargon, Major; and say that we have shut the evil spirit in the cave, and are taking the woman to the woods in order to find strengthening roots. Practyse all your cunning, for it is a lawful undertaking."

The door opened a little, as if one without was listening to the proceedings within, and compelled the scout to cease his directions. A fierce growl repelled the eavesdropper, and then the scout boldly threw open the covering of bark, and left the place, enacting the character of the bear as he proceeded. Duncan kept close at his heels, and soon found himself in the centre of a cluster of twenty anxious relatives and friends.

The crowd fell back a little, and permitted the father, and one who appeared to be the husband of the woman, to approach.

"Has my brother driven away the evil spirit?" demanded the former. "What has he in his arms?"

"Thy child," returned Duncan, gravely; "the disease has gone out of her; it is shut up in the rocks. I take the woman to a distance, where I will strengthen her against any further attacks. She shall be in the wigwam of the young man when the sun comes again."

When the father had translated the meaning of the stranger's words into the Huron language, a suppressed murmur announced the satisfaction with which this intelligence was received. The chief himself waved his hand for Duncan to proceed, saying aloud, in a firm voice, and with a lofty manner,—

"Go; I am a man, and I will enter the rock and fight the wicked one."

Heyward had gladly obeyed, and was already past the little group, when these startling words arrested him.

"Is my brother mad?" he exclaimed; "is he cruel! He will meet the disease, and it will enter him; or he will drive out the disease, and it will chase his daughter into the woods. No; let my children wait without, and if the spirit appears beat him down with clubs. He is cunning, and will bury himself in the mountain, when he sees how many are ready to fight him."

This singular warning had the desired effect. Instead of entering the cavern, the father and husband drew their tomahawks, and posted themselves in readiness to deal their vengeance on the imaginary tormentor of their sick relative, while the women and children broke branches from the bushes, or seized fragments of the rock, with a similar intention. At this favorable moment the counterfeit conjurers disappeared.

Hawkeye, at the same time that he had presumed so far on the nature of the Indian superstitions, was not ignorant that they were rather tolerated than relied on by the wisest of the chiefs. He well knew the value of time in the present emergency. Whatever might be the extent of the self-delusion of his enemies, and however it had tended to assist his schemes, the slightest cause of suspicion, acting on the subtle nature of an Indian, would be likely to prove fatal. Taking the path, therefore, that was most likely to avoid observation, he rather skirted than entered the village. The warriors were still to be seen in the distance, by the fading light of the fires, stalking from lodge to lodge. But the children had abandoned their sports for their beds of skins, and the quiet of night was already beginning to prevail over the turbulence and excitement of so busy and important an evening.

Alice revived under the renovating influence of the open air, and as her physical rather than her mental powers had been the subject of weakness, she stood in no need of any explanation of that which had occurred.

"Now let me make an effort to walk," she said, when they had entered the forest, blushing, though unseen, that she had not been sooner able to quit the arms of Duncan; "I am indeed restored."

"Nay, Alice, you are yet too weak."

The maiden struggled gently to release herself, and Heyward was compelled to part with his precious burden. The representative of the bear had certainly been an entire stranger to the delicious emotions of the lover while his arms encircled his mistress; and he was, perhaps, a stranger also to the nature of that feeling of ingenuous shame that oppressed the trembling Alice. But when he found himself at a suitable distance from the lodges he made a halt, and spoke on a subject of which he was thoroughly the master.

"This path will lead you to the brook," he said; "follow its northern bank until you come to a fall; mount the hill on your right, and you will see the fires of the other people. There you must go and demand protection; if they are true Delawares, you will be safe. A distant flight with that gentle one, just now, is impossible. The Hurons would follow up our trail, and master our scalps, before we had got a dozen miles. Go, and Providence be with you."

"And you!" demanded Heyward, in surprise; "surely we part not here?"

"The Hurons hold the pride of the Delawares; the last of the high blood of the Mohicans is in their power," returned the scout; "I go to see what can be done in his favor. Had they mastered your scalp, Major, a knave should have fallen for every hair it held, as I promised; but if the young Sagamore is to be led to the stake, the Indians shall see also how a man without a cross can die."

Not in the least offended with the decided preference that the sturdy woodsman gave to one who might, in some degree, be called the child of his adoption, Duncan still continued to urge such reasons against so desperate an effort as presented themselves. He was aided by Alice, who mingled her entreaties with those of Heyward that he would abandon a resolution that promised so much danger, with so little hope of success. Their eloquence and ingenuity were expended in vain. The scout heard them attentively, but impatiently, and finally closed the discussion, by answering, in a tone that instantly silenced Alice, while it told Heyward how fruitless any further remonstrances would be,—

"I have heard," he said, "that there is a feeling in youth which binds man to woman closer than the father is tied to the son. It may be so. I have seldom been where women of my color dwell; but such may be the gifts of nature in the settlements. You have risked life, and all that is dear to you, to bring off this gentle one, and I suppose that some such disposition is at the bottom of it all. As for me, I taught the lad the real character of a rifle; and well has he paid me for it. I have fou't at his side in many a bloody skrimmage; and so long as I could hear the crack of his piece in one ear, and that of the Sagamore in the other, I knew no enemy was on my back. Winters and summers, nights and days, have we roved the wilderness in company, eating of the same dish, one sleeping while the other watched; and afore it shall be said that Uncas was taken to the torment, and I at hand—There is but a single ruler of us all, whatever may be the color of the skin; and Him I call to witness, that before the Mohican boy shall perish for the want of a friend, good faith shall depart the 'arth, and Killdeer become as harmless as the tooting we'pon of the singer!"

Duncan released his hold on the arm of the scout, who turned, and steadily retraced his steps towards the lodges. After pausing a moment to gaze at his retiring form, the successful and yet sorrowful Heyward, and Alice, took their way together towards the distant village of the Delawares.

CHAPTER XXVI

Bottom.—*Let me play the lion too.*
SHAKESPEARE, *Midsummer Night's Dream,* I. ii. 72.

Notwithstanding the high resolution of Hawkeye, he fully comprehended all the difficulties and dangers he was about to incur. In his return to the camp, his acute and practiced intellects were intently engaged in devising means to counteract a watchfulness and suspicion on the part of his enemies, that he knew were in no degree inferior to his own. Nothing but the color of his skin had saved the lives of Magua and the conjurer, who would have been the first victims sacrificed to his own security, had not the scout believed such an act, however congenial it might be to the nature of an Indian, utterly unworthy of one who boasted a descent from men that knew no cross of blood. Accordingly, he trusted to the withes and ligaments with which he had bound his captives, and pursued his way directly towards the centre of the lodges.

As he approached the buildings, his steps became more deliberate, and his vigilant eye suffered no sign, whether friendly or hostile, to escape him. A neglected hut was a little in advance of the others, and appeared as if it had been deserted when half completed—most probably on account of failing in some of the more important requisites, such as wood or water. A faint light glimmered through its cracks, however, and announced that, notwithstanding its imperfect structure, it was not without a tenant. Thither, then, the scout proceeded, like a prudent general, who was about to feel the advanced positions of his enemy, before he hazarded the main attack.

Throwing himself into a suitable posture for the beast he represented, Hawkeye crawled to a little opening, where he might command a view of the interior. It proved to be the abiding-place of David Gamut. Hither the faithful singing-master had now brought himself, together with all his sorrows, his apprehensions, and his meek dependence on the protection of Providence. At the precise moment when his ungainly person came under the observation of the scout, in the manner just mentioned, the woodsman himself, though in his assumed character, was the subject of the solitary being's profoundest reflections.

However implicit the faith of David was in the performance of ancient miracles, he eschewed the belief of any direct supernatural agency in the management of modern morality. In other words, while he had implicit faith in the ability of Balaam's ass to speak, he was somewhat skeptical on the subject of a bear's singing; and yet he had been assured of the latter, on the testimony of his own exquisite organs. There was something in his air and manner that betrayed to the scout the utter confusion of the state of his mind. He was seated on a pile of brush, a few twigs from which occasionally fed his low fire, with his head leaning on his arm, in a posture of melancholy musing. The costume of the votary of music had undergone no other alteration from that so lately described, except that he had covered his bald head with the triangular beaver, which had not proved sufficiently alluring to excite the cupidity of any of his captors.

The ingenious Hawkeye, who recalled the hasty manner in which the other had abandoned his post at the bedside of the sick woman, was not without his suspicions concerning the subject of so much solemn deliberation. First making the circuit of the hut, and ascertaining that it stood quite alone, and that the character of its inmate was likely to protect it from visitors, he ventured through its low door, into the very presence of Gamut. The position of the latter brought the fire between them; and when Hawkeye had seated himself on end, near a minute elapsed, during which the two remained regarding each other without speaking. The suddenness and the nature of the surprise had nearly proved too much for—we will not say the philosophy—but for the faith and resolution of David. He fumbled for his pitch-pipe, and arose with a confused intention of attempting a musical exorcism.

"Dark and mysterious monster!" he exclaimed, while with trembling hands he disposed of his auxiliary eyes, and sought his never-failing resource in trouble, the gifted version of the Psalms; "I know not your nature nor intents; but if aught you meditate against the person and rights of one of the humblest servants of the temple, listen to the inspired language of the youth of Israel, and repent."

The bear shook his shaggy sides, and then a well-known voice replied, "Put up the tooting we'pon, and teach your throat modesty. Five words of plain and comprehendible English are worth, just now, an hour of squalling."

"What art thou!" demanded David, utterly disqualified to pursue his original intention, and nearly gasping for breath.

"A man like yourself; and one whose blood is as little tainted by the cross of a bear, or an Indian, as your own. Have you so soon forgotten from whom you received the foolish instrument you hold in your hand?"

"Can these things be?" returned David, breathing more freely, as the truth began to dawn upon him. "I have found many marvels during my sojourn with the heathen, but surely nothing to excel this!"

"Come, come," returned Hawkeye, uncasing his honest countenance, the better to assure the wavering confidence of his companion; "you may see a skin which, if it be not as white as one of the gentle ones, has no tinge of red to it that the winds of the heaven and the sun have not bestowed. Now let us to business."

"First tell me of the maiden, and of the youth who so bravely sought her," interrupted David.

"Aye, they are happily freed from the tomahawks of these varlets. But can you put me on the scent of Uncas?"

"The young man is in bondage, and much I fear his death is decreed. I greatly mourn that one so well disposed should die in his ignorance, and I have sought a goodly hymn—"

"Can you lead me to him?"

"The task will not be difficult," returned David, hesitating; "though I greatly fear your presence would rather increase than mitigate his unhappy fortunes."

"No more words, but lead on," returned Hawkeye, concealing his face again, and setting the example in his own person, by instantly quitting the lodge.

As they proceeded, the scout ascertained that his companion found access to Uncas under privilege of his imaginary infirmity, aided by the favor he had acquired with one of the guards, who, in consequence of speaking a little English, had been selected by David as the subject of a religious conversion. How far the Huron comprehended the intentions of his new friend may well be doubted; but as exclusive attention is as flattering to a savage as to a more civilized individual, it had produced the effect we have mentioned. It is unnecessary to repeat the shrewd manner with which the scout extracted these particulars from the simple David; neither shall we dwell in his place on the nature of the instructions he delivered, when completely master of all the necessary facts, as the whole will be sufficiently explained to the reader in the course of the narrative.

The lodge in which Uncas was confined was in the very centre of the village, and in a situation, perhaps, more difficult than any other to approach, or leave, wihout observation. But it was not the policy of Hawkeye to affect the least concealment. Presuming on his disguise, and his ability to sustain the character he had assumed, he took the most plain and direct route to the place. The hour, however, afforded him some little of that protection which he appeared so much to despise. The boys were already buried in sleep, and all the women, and most of the warriors, had retired to their lodges for the night. Four or five of the latter only lingered about the door of the prison of Uncas, wary but close observers of the manner of their captive.

At the sight of Gamut, accompanied by one in the well-known masquerade of their most distinguished conjurer, they readily made way for them both. Still they betrayed no intention to depart. On the other hand, they were evidently disposed to remain bound to the place by an additional interest in the mysterious mummeries that they of course expected from such a visit.

From the total inability of the scout to address the Hurons in their own language, he was compelled to trust the conversation entirely to David. Notwithstanding the simplicity of the latter, he did ample justice to the instructions he had received, more than fulfilling the strongest hopes of his teacher.

"The Delawares are women!" he exclaimed, addressing himself to the savage who had a slight understanding of the language in which he spoke; "the Yengeese, my foolish countrymen, have told them to take up the tomahawk, and strike their fathers in the Canadas, and they have forgotten their sex. Does my brother wish to hear Le Cerf Agile ask for his petticoats, and see him weep before the Hurons, at the stake?"

The exclamation "Hugh!" delivered in a strong tone of assent, announced the gratification the savage would receive in witnessing such an exhibition of weakness in an enemy so long hated and so much feared.

"Then let him step aside, and the cunning man will blow upon the dog! Tell it to my brothers."

The Huron explained the meaning of David to his fellows, who, in their turn, listened to the project with that sort of satisfaction that their untamed spirits might be expected to find in such a refinement in cruelty. They drew back a little from the entrance, and motioned to the supposed conjurer to enter. But the bear, instead of obeying, maintained the seat it had taken, and growled.

"The cunning man is afraid that his breath will blow upon his brothers, and take away their courage too," continued David, improving the hint he received; "they must stand further off."

The Hurons, who would have deemed such a misfortune the heaviest calamity that could befall them, fell back in a body, taking a position where they were out of earshot, though at the same time they could command a view of the entrance to the lodge. Then, as if satisfied of their safety, the scout left his position, and slowly entered the place. It was silent and gloomy, being tenanted solely by the captive, and lighted by the dying embers of a fire, which had been used for the purposes of cookery.

Uncas occupied a distant corner, in a reclining attitude, being rigidly bound, both hands and feet, by strong and painful withes. When the frightful object first presented itself to the young Mohican, he did not deign to bestow a single glance on the animal. The scout, who had left David at the door, to ascertain they were not observed, thought it prudent to preserve his disguise until assured of their privacy. Instead of speaking, therefore, he exerted himself to enact one of the antics of the animal he represented. The young Mohican, who at first believed his enemies had sent in a real beast to torment him, and try his nerves, detected, in those performances that to Heyward had appeared so accurate, certain blemishes that at once betrayed the counterfeit. Had Hawkeye been aware of the low estimation in which the more skillful Uncas held his representations, he would probably have prolonged the entertainment a little in pique. But the scornful expression of the young man's eye admitted of so many constructions, that the worthy scout was spared the mortification of such a discovery. As soon, therefore, as David gave the preconcerted signal, a low hissing sound was heard in the lodge in place of the fierce growlings of the bear.

Uncas had cast his body back against the wall of the hut, and closed his eyes, as if willing to exclude so contemptible and disagreeable an object from his sight. But the moment the noise of the serpent was heard, he arose, and cast his looks on each side of him, bending his head low, and turning it inquiringly in every direction, until his keen eye rested on the shaggy monster, where it remained riveted, as though fixed by the power of a charm. Again the same sounds were repeated, evidently proceeding from the mouth of the beast. Once more the eyes of the youth roamed over the interior of the lodge, and returning to their former resting-place, he uttered, in a deep suppressed voice,—

"Hawkeye!"

"Cut his bands," said Hawkeye to David, who just then approached them.

The singer did as he was ordered, and Uncas found his limbs released. At the same moment the dried skin of the animal rattled, and presently the scout arose to his feet, in proper person. The Mohican appeared to comprehend the nature of the attempt his friend had made, intuitively; neither tongue nor feature betraying another symptom of surprise. When Hawkeye had cast his shaggy vestment, which was done by simply loosing certain thongs of skin, he drew a long glittering knife, and put it in the hands of Uncas.

"The red Hurons are without," he said; "let us be ready."

At the same time he laid his finger significantly on another similar weapon, both being the fruits of his prowess among their enemies during the evening.

"We will go," said Uncas.

"Whither?"

"To the Tortoises; they are the children of my grand-fathers."

"Aye, lad," said the scout in English—a language he was apt to use when a little abstracted in mind; "the same blood runs in your veins, I believe; but time and distance has a little changed its color. What shall we do with the Mingoes at the door? They count six, and this singer is as good as nothing."

"The Hurons are boasters," said Uncas scornfully; "their totem is a moose, and they run like snails. The Delawares are children of the tortoise, and they outstrip the deer."

"Aye, lad, there is truth in what you say; and I doubt not, on a rush, you would pass the whole nation; and, in a straight race of two miles, would be in, and get your breath again, afore a knave of them all was within hearing of the other village. But the gift of a white man lies more in his arms than in his legs. As for myself, I can brain a Huron as well as a better man; but when it comes to a race, the knaves would prove too much for me."

Uncas, who had already approached the door, in readiness to lead the way, now recoiled, and placed himself once more in the bottom of the lodge. But Hawkeye, who was too much occupied with his own thoughts to note the movement, continued speaking more to himself than to his companion.

"After all," he said, "it is unreasonable to keep one man in bondage to the gifts of another. So, Uncas, you had better take the leap, while I will put on the skin again, and trust to cunning for want of speed."

The young Mohican made no reply, but quietly folded his arms, and leaned his body against one of the upright posts that supported the wall of the hut.

"Well," said the scout, looking up at him, "why do you tarry? There will be time enough for me, as the knaves will give chase to you at first."

"Uncas will stay," was the calm reply.

"For what?"

"To fight with his father's brother, and die with the friend of the Delawares."

"Aye, lad," returned Hawkeye, squeezing the hand of Uncas between his own iron fingers; "'t would have been more like a Mingo than a Mohican had you left me. But I thought I would make the offer, seeing that youth commonly loves life. Well, what can't be done by main courage, in war, must be done by circumvention. Put on the skin; I doubt not you can play the bear nearly as well as myself."

Whatever might have been the private opinion of Uncas of their respective abilities in this particular, his grave countenance manifested no opinion of his own superiority. He silently and expeditiously encased himself in the covering of the beast, and then awaited such other movements as his more aged companion saw fit to dictate.

"Now, friend," said Hawkeye, addressing David, "an exchange of garments will be a great convenience to you, inasmuch as you are but little accustomed to the make-shifts of the wilderness. Here, take my hunting shirt and cap, and give me your blanket and hat. You must trust me with the book and spectacles, as well as the tooter, too; if we ever meet again, in better times, you shall have all back again, with many thanks into the bargain."

David parted with the several articles named with a readiness that would have done great credit to his liberality, had he not certainly profited, in many particulars, by the exchange. Hawkeye was not long in assuming his borrowed garments; and when his restless eyes were hid behind the glasses, and his head was surmounted by the triangular beaver, as their statures were not dissimilar, he might readily have passed for the singer by starlight. As soon as these dispositions were made, the scout turned to David, and gave him his parting instructions.

"Are you much given to cowardice?" he bluntly asked, by way of obtaining a suitable understanding of the whole case before he ventured a prescription.

"My pursuits are peaceful, and my temper, I humbly trust, is greatly given to mercy and love," returned David, a little nettled at so direct an attack on his manhood; "but there are none who can say that I have ever forgotten my faith in the Lord, even in the greatest straits."

"Your chiefest danger will be at the moment when the savages find out that they have been deceived. If you are not then knocked in the head, your being a non-composser will protect you; and you'll then have good reason to expect to die in your bed. If you stay, it must be to sit down here in the shadow, and take the part of Uncas, until such times as the cunning of the Indians discover the cheat, when, as I have already said, your time of trial will come. So choose for yourself,—to make a rush or tarry here."

"Even so," said David, firmly; "I will abide in the place of the Delaware. Bravely and generously has he battled in my behalf; and this, and more, will I dare in his service."

"You have spoken as a man, and like one who, under wiser schooling, would have been brought to better things. Hold your head down, and draw in your legs;

their formation might tell the truth too early. Keep silent as long as may be; and it would be wise, when you do speak, to break out suddenly in one of your shoutings, which will serve to remind the Indians that you are not altogether as responsible as men should be. If, however, they take your scalp, as I trust and believe they will not, depend on it, Uncas and I will not forget the deed, but revenge it as becomes true warriors and trusty friends."

"Hold!" said David, perceiving that with this assurance they were about to leave him; "I am an unworthy and humble follower of One who taught not the damnable principle of revenge. Should I fall, therefore, seek no victims to my manes, but rather forgive my destroyers; and if you remember them at all, let it be in prayers for the enlightening of their minds, and for their eternal welfare."

The scout hesitated, and appeared to muse.

"There is a principle in that," he said, "different from the law of the woods; and yet it is fair and noble to reflect upon." Then, heaving a heavy sigh, probably among the last he ever drew in pining for a condition he had so long abandoned, he added. "It is what I would wish to practice myself, as one without a cross of blood, though it is not always easy to deal with an Indian as you would with a fellow-Christian. God bless you, friend; I do believe your scent is not greatly wrong, when the matter is duly considered, and keeping eternity before the eyes, though much depends on the natural gifts and the force of temptation."

So saying, the scout returned and shook David cordially by the hand; after which act of friendship he immediately left the lodge, attended by the new representative of the beast.

The instant Hawkeye found himself under the observation of the Hurons, he drew up his tall form in the rigid manner of David, threw out his arm in the act of keeping time, and commenced what he intended for an imitation of his psalmody. Happily for the success of this delicate adventure, he had to deal with ears but little practiced in the concord of sweet sounds, or the miserable effort would infallibly have been detected. It was necessary to pass within a dangerous proximity of the dark group of the savages, and the voice of the scout grew louder as they drew nigher. When at the nearest point, the Huron who spoke the English thrust out an arm, and stopped the supposed singing-master.

"The Delaware dog!" he said, leaning forward, and peering through the dim light to catch the expression of the other's features; "is he afraid? will the Hurons hear his groans?"

A growl so exceedingly fierce and natural proceeded from the beast, that the young Indian released his hold and started aside, as if to assure himself that it was not a veritable bear, and no counterfeit, that was rolling before him. Hawkeye, who feared his voice would betray him to his subtle enemies, gladly profited by the interruption, to break out anew in such a burst of musical expression as would probably, in a more refined state of society, have been termed "a grand crash." Among his actual auditors, however, it merely gave him an additional claim to that respect which they never withhold from such as are believed to be the subjects of mental alienation. The little knot of Indians drew back in a body, and suffered, as they thought, the conjurer and his inspired assistant to proceed.

It required no common exercise of fortitude in Uncas and the scout, to continue the dignified and deliberate pace they had assumed in passing the lodges; especially as they immediately perceived that curiosity had so far mastered fear as to induce the watchers to approach the hut, in order to witness the effect of the incantations. The least injudicious or impatient movement on the part of David might betray them, and time was absolutely necessary to insure the safety of the scout. The loud noise the latter conceived it politic to continue drew many curious gazers to the doors of the different huts as they passed; and once or twice a dark-looking warrior stepped across their path, led to the act by superstition, or watchfulness. They were not, however, interrupted; the darkness of the hour, and the boldness of the attempt, proving their principal friends.

The adventurers had got clear of the village, and were now swiftly approaching the shelter of the woods, when a loud and long cry arose from the lodge where Uncas had been confined. The Mohican started on his feet, and shook his shaggy covering as though the animal he counterfeited was about to make some desperate effort.

"Hold!" said the scout, grasping his friend by the shoulder, "let them yell again! 'T was nothing but wonderment."

He had no occasion to delay, for at the next instant a burst of cries filled the outer air, and ran along the whole extent of the village. Uncas cast his skin, and stepped forth in his own beautiful proportions. Hawkeye tapped him lightly on the shoulder, and glided ahead.

"Now let the devils strike our scent!" said the scout, tearing two rifles, with all their attendant accoutrements, from beneath a bush, and flourishing Killdeer as he handed Uncas his weapon; "two, at least, will find it to their deaths."

Then throwing their pieces to a low trail, like sportsmen in readiness for their game, they dashed forward, and were soon buried in the sombre darkness of the forest.

CHAPTER XXVII

Antony.—*I shall remember:*
When Cæsar says, "Do this," *it is performed.*
SHAKESPEARE, *Julius Cæsar*, I. ii. 9.

The impatience of the savages who lingered about the prison of Uncas, as has been seen, had overcome their dread of the conjurer's breath. They stole cautiously, and with beating hearts, to a crevice, through which the faint light of the fire was glimmering. For several minutes they mistook the form of David for that of their prisoner; but the very accident which Hawkeye had foreseen occurred. Tired of keeping the extremities of his long person so near together, the singer gradually suffered the lower limbs to extend themselves, until one of his misshapen feet actually came in contact with and shoved aside the embers of the fire. At first the Hurons believed the Delaware had been thus deformed by witchcraft. But when David, unconscious of being observed, turned his head, and exposed his simple, mild countenance, in place of the haughty lineaments of their prisoner, it would have exceeded the credulity of even a native to have doubted any longer. They rushed together into the lodge, and laying their hands, with but little ceremony, on their captive, immediately detected the imposition. Then arose the cry first heard by the fugitives. It was succeeded by the most frantic and angry demonstrations of vengeance. David, however firm in his determination to cover the retreat of his friends, was compelled to believe that his own final hour had come. Deprived of his book and his pipe, he was fain to trust to a memory that rarely failed him on such subjects; and breaking forth in a loud and impassioned strain, he endeavored to soothe his passage into the other world, by singing the opening verse of a funeral anthem. The Indians were seasonably reminded of his infirmity, and rushing into the open air, they aroused the village in the manner described.

A native warrior fights as he sleeps, without the protection of anything defensive. The sounds of the alarm were, therefore, hardly uttered, before two hundred men were afoot, and ready for the battle or the chase, as either might be required. The escape was soon known; and the whole tribe crowded, in a body, around the council lodge, impatiently awaiting the instruction of their chiefs. In such a sudden demand on their wisdom, the presence of the cunning Magua could scarcely fail of being needed. His name was mentioned, and all looked round in wonder that he did not appear. Messengers were then dispatched to his lodge, requiring his presence.

In the mean time, some of the swiftest and most discreet of the young men were ordered to make the circuit of the clearing, under cover of the woods, in order to ascertain that their suspected neighbors, the Delawares, designed no mischief. Women and children ran to and fro; and, in short, the whole encampment exhibited another scene of wild and savage confusion. Gradually, however, these symptoms of disorder diminished; and in a few minutes the oldest and most distinguished chiefs were assembled in the lodge, in grave consultation.

The clamor of many voices soon announced that a party approached, who might be expected to communicate some intelligence that would explain the mystery of the novel surpise. The crowd without gave way, and several warriors entered the place, bringing with them the hapless conjurer, who had been left so long by the scout in duresse.

Notwithstanding this man was held in very unequal estimation among the Hurons, some believing implicitly in his power, and others deeming him an impostor, he was now listened to by all with the deepest attention. When his brief story was ended, the father of the sick woman stepped forth, and, in a few pithy expressions, related, in his turn, what he knew. These two narratives gave a proper direction to the subsequent inquiries, which were now made with the characteristic cunning of savages.

Instead of rushing in a confused and disorderly throng to the cavern, ten of the wisest and firmest among the chiefs were selected to prosecute the investigation. As no time was to be lost, the instant the choice was made the individuals appointed rose in a body, and left the place without speaking. On reaching the entrance, the younger men in advance made way for their seniors; and the whole proceeded along the low, dark gallery, with the firmness of warriors ready to devote themselves to the public good, though, at the same time, secretly doubting the nature of the power with which they were about to contend.

The outer apartment of the cavern was silent and gloomy. The woman lay in her usual place and posture, though there were those present who affirmed that they had seen her borne to the woods, by the supposed "medicine of the white men." Such a direct and palpable contradiction of the tale related by the father caused all eyes to be turned on him. Chafed by the silent imputation, and inwardly troubled by so unaccountable a circumstance, the chief advanced to the side of the bed, and stooping, cast an incredulous look at the features, as if distrusting their reality. His daughter was dead.

The unerring feeling of nature for a moment prevailed, and the old warrior hid his eyes in sorrow. Then recovering his self-possession, he faced his companions, and pointing towards the corpse, he said, in the language of his people,—

"The wife of my young man has left us! the Great Spirit is angry with his children."

The mournful intelligence was received in solemn silence. After a short pause, one of the elder Indians was about to speak, when a dark-looking object was seen rolling out of an adjoining apartment, into the very centre of the room where they stood. Ignorant of the nature of the beings they had to deal with, the whole party drew back a little, and gazed in admiration, until the object fronted the light, and rising on end, exhibited the distorted, but still fierce and sullen features of Magua. The discovery was succeeded by a general exclamation of amazement.

As soon, however, as the true situation of the chief was understood, several ready knives appeared, and his limbs and tongue were quickly released. The Huron arose, and shook himself like a lion quitting his lair. Not a word escaped him, though his hand played convulsively with the handle of his knife, while his lowering eyes scanned the whole party, as if they sought an object suited to the first burst of his vengeance.

It was happy for Uncas and the scout, and even David, that they were all beyond the reach of his arm at such a moment; for assuredly no refinement in cruelty would then have deferred their deaths, in opposition to the promptings of the fierce temper that nearly choked him. Meeting everywhere faces that he knew as friends, the savage grated his teeth together like rasps of iron, and swallowed his passion for want of a victim on whom to vent it. This exhibition of anger was noted by all present; and, from an apprehension of exasperating a temper that was already chafed nearly to madness, several minutes were suffered to pass before another word was uttered. When, however, suitable time had elapsed, the oldest of the party spoke.

"My friend has found an enemy," he said. "Is he nigh, that the Hurons may take revenge?"

"Let the Delaware die!" exclaimed Magua, in a voice of thunder.

Another long and expressive silence was observed, and was broken, as before, with due precaution, by the same individual.

"The Mohican is swift of foot, and leaps far," he said; "but my young men are on his trail."

"Is he gone?" demanded Magua, in tones so deep and guttural that they seemed to proceed from his inmost chest.

"An evil spirit has been among us, and the Delaware has blinded our eyes."

"An evil spirit!" repeated the other, mockingly; "'t is the spirit that has taken the lives of so many Hurons: the spirit that slew my young men at 'the tumbling river;' that took their scalps at the 'healing spring;' and who has now bound the arms of Le Renard Subtil!"

"Of whom does my friend speak?"

"Of the dog who carries the heart and cunning of a Huron under a pale skin—La Longue Carabine."

The pronunciation of so terrible a name produced the usual effect among his auditors. But when time was given for reflection, and the warriors remembered that their formidable and daring enemy had even been in the bosom of their encampment, working injury, fearful rage took the place of wonder, and all those fierce passions with which the bosom of Magua had just been struggling were suddenly transferred to his companions. Some among them gnashed their teeth in anger, others vented their feelings in yells, and some, again, beat the air as frantically as if the object of their resentment were suffering under their blows. But this sudden outbreaking of temper as quickly subsided in the still and sullen restraint they most affected, in their moments of inaction.

Magua, who had in his turn found leisure for reflection, now changed his manner, and assumed the air of one who knew how to think and act with a dignity worthy of so grave a subject.

"Let us go to my people," he said; "they wait for us."

His companions consented in silence, and the whole of the savage party left the cavern and returned to the council lodge. When they were seated, all eyes turned on Magua, who understood, from such an indication, that, by common consent, they had devolved the duty of relating what had passed on him. He arose, and told his tale without duplicity or reservation. The whole deception practiced by both Duncan and Hawkeye was, of course, laid naked; and no room was found even for the most superstitious of the tribe any longer to affix a doubt on the character of the occurrences. It was but too apparent that they had been insultingly, shamefully, disgracefully deceived. When he had ended, and resumed his seat, the collected tribe—for his auditors, in substance, included all the fighting men of the party—sat regarding each other like men astonished equally at the audacity and the success of their enemies. The next consideration, however, was the means and opportunities for revenge.

Additional pursuers were sent on the trail of the fugitives; and then the chiefs applied themselves, in earnest, to the business of consultation. Many different expedients were proposed by the elder warriors, in succession, to all of which Magua was a silent and respectful listener. That subtle savage had recovered his artifice and self-command, and now proceeded towards his object with his customary caution and skill. It was only when each one disposed to speak had uttered his sentiments, that he prepared to advance his own opinions. They were given with additional weight from the circumstance that some of the runners had already returned, and reported that their enemies had been traced so far as to leave no doubt of their having sought safety in the neighboring camp of their suspected allies, the Delawares. With the advantage of possessing this important intelligence, the chief warily laid his plans before his fellows, and, as might have been anticipated from his eloquence and cunning, they were adopted without a dissenting voice. They were, briefly, as follows, both in opinions and in motives.

It has been already stated that, in obedience to a policy rarely departed from, the sisters were separated so soon as they reached the Huron village. Magua had early discovered that in retaining the person of Alice, he possessed the most effectual check on Cora. When they parted, therefore, he kept the former within reach of his hand, consigning the one he most valued to the keeping of their allies. The arrangement was understood to be merely temporary, and was made as much with a view to flatter his neighbors as in obedience to the invariable rule of Indian policy.

While goaded incessantly by those revengeful impulses that in a savage seldom slumber, the chief was still attentive to his more permanent personal interests. The follies and disloyalty committed in his youth were to be expiated by a long and painful penance, ere he could be restored to the full enjoyment of the confidence of his ancient people; and without confidence there could be no authority in an Indian tribe. In this delicate and arduous situation, the crafty native had neglected no means of increasing his influence; and one of the happiest of his expedients had been the success with which he had cultivated the favor of their powerful and dangerous neighbors. The result of his experiment had answered all the expectations of his policy; for the Hurons were in no degree exempt from that governing principle of nature, which induces man to value his gifts precisely in the degree that they are appreciated by others.

But, while he was making this ostensible sacrifice to general considerations, Magua never lost sight of his individual motives. The latter had been frustrated by the unlooked-for events which had placed all his prisoners beyond his control; and he now found himself reduced to the necessity of suing for favors to those whom it had so lately been his policy to oblige.

Several of the chiefs had proposed deep and treacherous schemes to surprise the Delawares, and, by gaining possession of their camp, to recover their prisoners by the same blow; for all agreed that their honor, their interests, and the peace and happiness of their dead countrymen, imperiously required them speedily to immolate some victims to their revenge. But plans so dangerous to attempt, and of such doubtful issue, Magua found little difficulty in defeating. He exposed their risk and fallacy with his usual skill; and it was only after he had removed every impediment, in the shape of opposing advice, that he ventured to propose his own projects.

He commenced by flattering the self-love of his auditors; a never-failing method of commanding attention. When he had enumerated the many different occasions on which the Hurons had exhibited their courage and prowess, in the punishment of insults, he digressed in a high encomium on the virtue of wisdom. He painted the quality, as forming the great point of difference between the beaver and other brutes; between brutes and men; and finally between the Hurons, in particular, and the rest of the human race. After he had sufficiently extolled the property of discretion, he undertook to exhibit in what manner its use was applicable to the present situation of their tribe. On the one hand, he said, was their great pale father, the governor of the Canadas, who had looked upon his children with a hard eye since their tomahawks had been so red; on the other, a people as numerous as themselves, who spoke a different language, possessed different interests, and loved them not, and who would be glad of any pretense to bring them in disgrace with the great white chief. Then he spoke of their necessities; of the gifts they had a right to expect for their past services; of their distance from their proper hunting-grounds and native villages; and of the necessity of consulting prudence more, and inclination less, in so critical circumstances. When he perceived that, while the old men applauded his moderation, many of the fiercest and most distinguished of the warriors listened to these politic plans with lowering looks, he cunningly led them back to the subject which they most loved. He spoke openly of the fruits of their wisdom, which he boldly pronounced would be a complete and final triumph over their enemies. He even darkly hinted that their success might be extended, with proper caution, in such a manner as to include the destruction of all whom they had reason to hate. In short, he so blended the warlike with the artful, the obvious with the obscure, as to flatter the propensities of both parties, and to leave to each subject of hope, while neither could say it clearly comprehended his intentions.

The orator, or the politician, who can produce such a state of things, is commonly popular with his contemporaries, however he may be treated by posterity. All perceived that more was meant than was uttered, and each one believed that the hidden meaning was precisely such as his own faculties enabled him to understand, or his own wishes led him to anticipate.

In this happy state of things, it is not surprising that the management of Magua prevailed. The tribe consented to act with deliberation, and with one voice they committed the direction of the whole affair to the government of the chief who had suggested such wise and intelligible expedients.

Magua had now attained one great object of all his cunning and enterprise. The ground he had lost in the favor of his people was completely regained, and he found himself even placed at the head of affairs. He was, in truth, their ruler; and so long as he could maintain his popularity, no monarch could be more despotic, especially while the tribe continued in a hostile country. Throwing off, therefore, the appearance of consultation, he assumed the grave air of authority necessary to support the dignity of his office.

Runners were dispatched for intelligence in different directions; spies were ordered to approach and feel the encampment of the Delawares; the warriors were dismissed to their lodges, with an intimation that their services would soon be needed; and the women and children were ordered to retire, with a warning that it was their province to be silent. When these several arrangements were made, Magua passed through the village, stopping here and there to pay a visit where he thought his presence might be flattering to the individual. He confirmed his friends in their confidence, fixed the wavering, and gratified all. Then he sought his own lodge. The wife the Huron chief had abandoned, when he was chased from among his people, was dead. Children he had none; and he now occupied a hut without companion of any sort. It was, in fact, the dilapidated and solitary structure in which David had been discovered, and whom he had tolerated in his presence, on those few occasions when they met, with the contemptuous indifference of a haughty superiority.

Hither, then, Magua retired, when his labors of policy were ended. While others slept, however, he neither knew nor sought repose. Had there been one sufficiently curious to have watched the movements of the newly elected chief, he would have seen him seated in a corner of his lodge, musing on the subject of his future plans, from the hour of his retirement to the time he had appointed for the warriors to assemble again. Occasionally the air breathed through the crevices of the hut, and the low flames that fluttered about the embers of the fire threw their wavering light on the person of the sullen recluse. At such moments it would not have been difficult to have fancied the dusky savage the Prince of Darkness, brooding on his own fancied wrongs and plotting evil.

Long before the day dawned, however, warrior after warrior entered the solitary hut of Magua, until they had collected to the number of twenty. Each bore his rifle, and all the other accoutrements of war, though the paint was uniformly peaceful. The entrance of these fierce-looking beings was unnoticed; some seating themselves in the shadows of the place, and others standing like motionless statues, until the whole of the designated band was collected.

Then Magua arose and gave the signal to proceed, marching himself in advance. They followed their leader singly, and in that well-known order which has obtained the distinguishing appellation of "Indian file." Unlike other men engaged in the spirit-stirring business of war, they stole from their camp unostentatiously and unobserved, resembling a band of gliding spectres more than warriors seeking the bubble reputation by deeds of desperate daring.

Instead of taking the path which led directly towards the camp of the Delawares, Magua led his party for some distance down the windings of the stream, and along the little artificial lake of the beavers. The day began to dawn as they entered the clearing which had been formed by those sagacious and industrious animals. Though Magua, who had resumed his ancient garb, bore the outline of a fox on the dressed skin which formed his robe, there was one chief of his party who carried the beaver as his peculiar symbol, or "totem." There would have been a species of profanity in the omission, had this man passed so powerful a community of his fancied kindred, without bestowing some evidence of his regard. Accordingly, he paused, and spoke in words as kind and friendly as if he were addressing more intelligent beings. He called the animals his cousins, and reminded them that his protecting influence was the reason they remained unharmed, while so many avaricious traders were prompting the Indians to take their lives. He promised a continuance of his favors, and admonished them to be grateful. After which, he spoke of the expedition in which he was himself engaged, and intimated, though with sufficient delicacy and circumlocution, the expediency of bestowing on their relative a portion of that wisdom for which they were so renowned.[24]

During the utterance of this extraordinary address, the companions of the speaker were as grave and as attentive to his language as though they were all equally impressed with its propriety. Once or twice black objects were seen rising to the surface of the water, and the Huron expressed pleasure, conceiving that his words were not bestowed in vain. Just as he had ended his address, the head of a large beaver was thrust from the door of a lodge whose earthen walls had been much injured, and which the party had believed, from its situation, to be uninhabited. Such an extraordinary sign of confidence was received by the orator as a highly favorable omen; and though the animal retreated a little precipitately, he was lavish of his thanks and commendations.

When Magua thought sufficient time had been lost in gratifying the family affection of the warrior, he again made the signal to proceed. As the Indians moved away in a body, and with a step that would have been inaudible to the ears of any common man, the same venerable-looking beaver once more ventured his head from its cover. Had any of the Hurons turned to look behind them, they would have seen the animal watching their movements with an interest and sagacity that might easily have been mistaken for reason. Indeed, so very distinct and intelligible were the devices of the quadruped, that even the most experienced observer would have been at a loss to account for its actions, until the moment when the party entered the forest, when the whole would have been explained by seeing the entire animal issue from the lodge, uncasing, by the act, the grave features of Chingachgook from his mask of fur.

CHAPTER XXVIII

Brief, I pray you; for you see, 't is a busy time with me.
SHAKESPEARE, *Much Ado about Nothing*, III, v. 5.

The tribe, or rather half tribe, of Delawares, which has been so often mentioned, and whose present place of encampment was so nigh the temporary village of the Hurons, could assemble about an equal number of warriors with the latter people. Like their neighbors, they had followed Montcalm into the territories of

---

[24]These harangues of the beasts are frequent among the Indians. They often address their victims in this way, reproaching them for cowardice, or commending their resolution, as they may happen to exhibit fortitude or the reverse in suffering. [J.F.C.]

the English crown, and were making heavy and serious inroads on the hunting-grounds of the Mohawks; though they had seen fit, with the mysterious reserve so common among the natives, to withhold their assistance at the moment when it was most required. The French had accounted for this unexpected defection on the part of their ally in various ways. It was the prevalent opinion, however, that they had been influenced by veneration for the ancient treaty, that had once made them dependent on the Six Nations for military protection, and now rendered them reluctant to encounter their former masters. As for the tribe itself, it had been content to announce to Montcalm, through his emissaries, with Indian brevity, that their hatchets were dull, and time was necessary to sharpen them. The politic captain of the Canadas had deemed it wiser to submit to entertain a passive friend, than by any acts of ill-judged severity to convert him into an open enemy.

On that morning when Magua led his silent party from the settlement of the beavers into the forest, in the manner described, the sun rose upon the Delaware encampment as if it had suddenly burst upon a busy people, actively employed in all the customary avocations of high noon. The women ran from lodge to lodge, some engaged in preparing their morning's meal, a few earnestly bent on seeking the comforts necessary to their habits, but more pausing to exchange hasty and whispered sentences with their friends. The warriors were lounging in groups, musing more than they conversed; and when a few words were uttered, speaking like men who deeply weighed their opinions. The instruments of the chase were to be seen in abundance among the lodges; but none departed. Here and there a warrior was examining his arms, with an attention that is rarely bestowed on the implements, when no other enemy than the beasts of the forest is expected to be encountered. And occasionally, the eyes of a whole group were turned simultaneously towards a large and silent lodge in the centre of the village, as if it contained the subject of their common thoughts.

During the existence of this scene, a man suddenly appeared at the furthest extremity of a platform of rock which formed the level of the village. He was without arms, and his paint tended rather to soften than increase the natural sternness of his austere countenance. When in full view of the Delawares he stopped, and made a gesture of amity, by throwing his arm upward towards heaven, and then letting it fall impressively on his breast. The inhabitants of the village answered his salute by a low murmur of welcome, and encouraged him to advance by similar indications of friendship. Fortified by these assurances, the dark figure left the brow of the natural rocky terrace, where it had stood a moment, drawn in a strong outline against the blushing morning sky, and moved with dignity into the very centre of the huts. As he approached, nothing was audible but the rattling of the light silver ornaments that loaded his arms and neck, and the tinkling of the little bells that fringed his deerskin moccasins. He made, as he advanced, many courteous signs of greeting to the men he passed, neglecting to notice the women, however, like one who deemed their favor, in the present enterprise, of no importance. When he had reached the group in which it was evident, by the haughtiness of their common mien, that the principal chiefs were collected, the stranger paused, and then the Delawares saw that the active and erect form that stood before them was that of the well-known Huron chief, Le Renard Subtil.

His reception was grave, silent, and wary. The warriors in front stepped aside, opening the way to their most approved orator by the action; one who spoke all those languages that were cultivated among the northern aborigines.

"The wise Huron is welcome," said the Delaware, in the language of the Maquas; "he is come to eat his 'succotash,'[25] with his brothers of the lakes."

"He is come," repeated Magua, bending his head with the dignity of an Eastern prince.

The chief extended his arm, and taking the other by the wrist, they once more exchanged friendly salutations. Then the Delaware invited his guest to enter his own lodge, and share his morning meal. The invitation was accepted; and the two warriors, attended by three or four of the old men, walked calmly away, leaving the rest of the tribe devoured by a desire to understand the reasons of so unusual a visit, and yet not betraying the least impatience by sign or word.

During the short and frugal repast that followed, the conversation was extremely circumspect, and related entirely to the events of the hunt, in which Magua had so lately been engaged. It would have been impossible for the most finished breeding to wear more of the appearance of considering the visit as a thing of course, than did his hosts, notwithstanding every individual present was perfectly aware that it must be connected with some secret object, and that probably of importance to themselves. When the appetites of the whole were appeased, the squaws removed the trenchers and gourds, and the two parties began to prepare themselves for a subtle trial of their wits.

"Is the face of my great Canada father turned again towards his Huron children?" demanded the orator of the Delawares.

"When was it ever otherwise?" returned Magua. "He calls my people 'most beloved.'"

The Delaware gravely bowed his acquiescence to what he knew to be false, and continued,—

"The tomahawks of your young men have been very red."

"It is so; but they are now bright and dull; for the Yengeese are dead, and the Delawares are our neighbors."

The other acknowledged the pacific compliment by a gesture of the hand, and remained silent. Then Magua, as if recalled to such a recollection, by the allusion to the massacre, demanded,—

"Does my prisoner give trouble to my brothers?"

"She is welcome."

"The path between the Hurons and the Delawares is short, and it is open; let her be sent to my squaws, if she gives trouble to my brother."

"She is welcome," returned the chief of the latter nation, still more emphatically.

The baffled Magua continued silent several minutes, apparently indifferent, however, to the repulse he had received in this his opening effort to regain possession of Cora.

"Do my young men leave the Delawares room on the mountains for their hunts?" he at length continued.

"The Lenape are rulers of their own hills," returned the other, a little haughtily.

"It is well. Justice is the master of a red-skin! Why should they brighten their tomahawks, and sharpen their knives against each other? Are not the pale-faces thicker than the swallows in the season of flowers?"

---

[25]A dish composed of cracked corn and beans. It is much used also by the whites. By corn is meant maize. [J.F.C.]

"Good!" exclaimed two or three of his auditors at the same time.

Magua waited a little, to permit his words to soften the feelings of the Delawares, before he added,—

"Have there not been strange moccasins in the woods? Have not my brothers scented the feet of white men?"

"Let my Canada father come," returned the other evasively; "his children are ready to see him."

"When the great chief comes, it is to smoke with the Indians in their wigwams. The Hurons say, too, he is welcome. But the Yengeese have long arms, and legs that never tire! My young men dreamed they had seen the trail of the Yengeese nigh the village of the Delawares!"

"They will not find the Lenape asleep."

"It is well. The warrior whose eye is open can see his enemy," said Magua, once more shifting his ground, when he found himself unable to penetrate the caution of his companion. "I have brought gifts to my brother. His nation would not go on the war-path, because they did not think it well; but their friends have remembered where they lived."

When he had thus announced his liberal intention, the crafty chief arose, and gravely spread his presents before the dazzled eyes of his hosts. They consisted principally of trinkets of little value, plundered from the slaughtered females of William Henry. In the division of the baubles the cunning Huron discovered no less art than in their selection. While he bestowed those of greater value on the two most distinguished warriors, one of whom was his host, he seasoned his offerings to their inferiors with such well-timed and apposite compliments, as left them no grounds of complaint. In short, the whole ceremony contained such a happy blending of the profitable with the flattering, that it was not difficult for the donor immediately to read the effect of a generosity so aptly mingled with praise, in the eyes of those he addressed.

This well-judged and politic stroke on the part of Magua was not without instantaneous results. The Delawares lost their gravity in a much more cordial expression; and the host, in particular, after contemplating his own liberal share of the spoil for some moments with peculiar gratification, repeated with strong emphasis, the words,—

"My brother is a wise chief. He is welcome."

"The Hurons love their friends the Delawares," returned Magua. "Why should they not? they are colored by the same sun, and their just men will hunt in the same grounds after death. The red-skins should be friends, and look with open eyes on the white men. Has not my brother scented spies in the woods?"

The Delaware whose name in English signified "Hard Heart," an appellation that the French had translated into "Le Cœur-dur," forgot that obduracy of purpose which had probably obtained him so significant a title. His countenance grew very sensibly less stern, and he now deigned to answer more directly.

"There have been strange moccasins about my camp. They have been tracked into my lodges."

"Did my brother beat out the dogs?" asked Magua, without adverting in any manner to the former equivocation of the chief.

"It would not do. The stranger is always welcome to the children of the Lenape."

"The stranger, but not the spy."

"Would the Yengeese send their women as spies? Did not the Huron chief say he took women in the battle?"

"He told no lie. The Yengeese have sent out their scouts. They have been in my wigwams, but they found there no one to say welcome. Then they fled to the Delawares—for, they say, the Delawares are our friends; their minds are turned from their Canada father."

This insinuation was a home thrust, and one that in a more advanced state of society would have entitled Magua to the reputation of a skillful diplomatist. The recent defection of the tribe had, as they well knew themselves, subjected the Delawares to much reproach among their French allies; and they were now made to feel that their future actions were to be regarded with jealousy and distrust. There was no deep insight into causes and effects necessary to foresee that such a situation of things was likely to prove highly prejudicial to their future movements. Their distant villages, their hunting-grounds, and hundreds of their women and children, together with a material part of their physical force, were actually within the limits of the French territory. Accordingly, this alarming annunciation was received, as Magua intended, with manifest disapprobation, if not with alarm.

"Let my father look in my face," said Le Cœur-dur; "he will see no change. It is true, my young men did not go out on the war-path; they had dreams for not doing so. But they love and venerate the great white chief."

"Will he think so when he hears that his greatest enemy is fed in the camp of his children? When he is told a bloody Yengee smokes at your fire? That the pale-face who has slain so many of his friends goes in and out among the Delawares? Go! my great Canada father is not a fool!"

"Where is the Yengee that the Delawares fear?" returned the other; "who has slain my young men? who is the mortal enemy of my Great Father!"

"La Longue Carabine."

The Delaware warriors started at the well known name, betraying, by their amazement, that they now learnt, for the first time, one so famous among the Indian allies of France was within their power.

"What does my brother mean?" demanded Le Cœur-dur, in a tone that, by its wonder, far exceeded the usual apathy of his race.

"A Huron never lies!" returned Magua coldly, leaning his head against the side of the lodge, and drawing his slight robe across his tawny breast. "Let the Delawares count their prisoners; they will find one whose skin is neither red nor pale."

A long and musing pause succeeded. The chief consulted apart with his companions, and messengers were dispatched to collect certain others of the most distinguished men of the tribe.

As warrior after warrior dropped in, they were each made acquainted, in turn, with the important intelligence that Magua had just communicated. The air of surprise, and the usual low, deep, guttural exclamation, were common to them all. The news spread from mouth to mouth, until the whole encampment became powerfully agitated. The women suspended their labors, to catch such syllables as unguardedly fell from the lips of the consulting warriors. The boys deserted their sports, and walking fearlessly among their fathers, looked up in curious admiration, as they heard the brief exclamations of wonder they so freely expressed at the temerity of their hated foe. In short, every occupation was abandoned for the time, and all other pursuits seemed discarded, in order that the tribe might freely indulge, after their own peculiar manner, in an open expression of feeling.

When the excitement had a little abated, the old men disposed themselves seriously to consider that which it became the honor and safety of their tribe to perform, under circumstances of so much delicacy and embarrassment. During all these movements, and in the midst of the general commotion, Magua had not only maintained his seat, but the very attitude he had originally taken, against the side of the lodge, where he continued as immovable, and, apparently, as unconcerned, as if he had no interest in the result. Not a single indication of the future intentions of his hosts, however, escaped his vigilant eyes. With his consummate knowledge of the nature of the people with whom he had to deal, he anticipated every measure on which they decided; and it might almost be said, that, in many instances, he knew their intentions, even before they became known to themselves.

The council of the Delawares was short. When it was ended, a general bustle announced that it was to be immediately succeeded by a solemn and formal assemblage of the nation. As such meetings were rare, and only called on occasions of the last importance, the subtle Huron, who still sat apart, a wily and dark observer of the proceedings, now knew that all his projects must be brought to their final issue. He, therefore, left the lodge, and walked silently forth to the place, in front of the encampment, whither the warriors were already beginning to collect.

It might have been half an hour before each individual, including even the women and children, was in his place. The delay had been created by the grave preparations that were deemed necessary to so solemn and unusual a conference. But when the sun was seen climbing above the tops of that mountain, against whose bosom the Delawares had constructed their encampment, most were seated; and as his bright rays darted from behind the outline of trees that fringed the eminence, they fell upon as grave, as attentive, and as deeply interested a multitude, as was probably ever before lighted by his morning beams. Its number somewhat exceeded a thousand souls.

In a collection of so serious savages, there is never to be found any impatient aspirant after premature distinction, standing ready to move his auditors to some hasty, and, perhaps, injudicious discussion, in order that his own reputation may be the gainer. An act of so much precipitancy and presumption would seal the downfall of precocious intellect forever. It rested solely with the oldest and most experienced of the men to lay the subject of the conference before the people. Until such a one chose to make some movement, no needs in arms, no natural gifts, nor any renown as an orator, would have justified the slightest interruption. On the present occasion, the aged warrior whose privilege it was to speak, was silent, seemingly oppressed with the magnitude of his subject. The delay had already continued long beyond the usual deliberative pause that always precedes a conference; but no sign of impatience or surprise escaped even the youngest boy. Occasionally, an eye was raised from the earth, where the looks of most were riveted, and strayed towards a particular lodge, that was, however, in no manner distinguished from those around it, except in the peculiar care that had been taken to protect it against the assaults of the weather.

At length, one of those low murmurs that are so apt to disturb a multitude, was heard, and the whole nation arose to their feet by a common impulse. At that instant the door of the lodge in question opened, and three men, issuing from it, slowly approached the place of consultation. They were all aged, even beyond that period to which the oldest present had reached; but one in the centre, who leaned on his companions for support, had numbered an amount of years to which the human race is seldom permitted to attain. His frame, which had once been tall and erect, like the cedar, was now bending under the pressure of more than a century. The elastic, light step of an Indian was gone, and in its place he was compelled to toil his tardy way over the ground, inch by inch. His dark, wrinkled countenance was in singular and wild contrast with the long white locks which floated on his shoulders, in such thickness, as to announce that generations had probably passed away since they had last been shorn.

The dress of this patriarch—for such, considering his vast age, in conjunction with his affinity and influence with his people, he might very properly be termed—was rich and imposing, though strictly after the simple fashions of the tribe. His robe was of the finest skins, which had been deprived of their fur in order to admit of a hieroglyphical representation of various deeds in arms, done in former ages. His bosom was loaded with medals, some in massive silver, and one or two even in gold, the gifts of various Christian potentates during the long period of his life. He also wore armlets, and cinctures above the ankles, of the latter precious metal. His head, on the whole of which the hair had been permitted to grow, the pursuits of war having so long been abandoned, was encircled by a sort of plated diadem, which, in its turn, bore lesser and more glittering ornaments, that sparkled amid the glossy hues of three drooping ostrich feathers, dyed a deep black, in touching contrast to the color of his snow-white locks. His tomahawk was nearly hid in silver, and the handle of his knife shone like a horn of solid gold.

So soon as the first hum of emotion and pleasure which the sudden appearance of this venerated individual created had a little subsided, the name of "Tamenund"[26] was whispered from mouth to mouth. Magua had often heard the fame of this wise and just Delaware; a reputation that even proceeded so far as to bestow on him the rare gift of holding secret communion with the Great Spirit, and which has since transmitted his name, with some slight alteration, to the white usurpers of his ancient territory, as the imaginary tutelar saint of a vast empire. The Huron chief, therefore, stepped eagerly out a little from the throng, to a spot whence he might catch a nearer glimpse of the features of the man, whose decision was likely to produce so deep an influence on his own fortunes.

The eyes of the old man were closed, as though the organs were wearied with having so long witnessed the selfish workings of the human passions. The color of his skin differed from that of most around him, being richer and darker, the latter hue having been produced by certain delicate and mazy lines of complicated and yet beautiful figures, which had been traced over most of his person by the operation of tattooing. Notwithstanding the position of the Huron, he passed the observant and silent Magua without notice, and leaning on his two venerable supporters proceeded to the high place of the multitude, where he seated himself in the centre of his nation, with the dignity of a monarch and the air of a father.

Nothing could surpass the reverence and affection with which this unexpected visit from one who belonged rather to another world than to this, was received by his people. After a suitable and decent pause, the principal chiefs arose; and approaching the patriarch, they placed his hands reverently on their heads, seem-

---

[26]The Americans sometimes call their tutelar saint Tamenay, a corruption of the name of the renowned chief here introduced. There are many traditions which speak of the character and power of Tamenund. [J.F.C.]

ing to entreat a blessing. The younger men were content with touching his robe, or even drawing nigh his person, in order to breathe in the atmosphere of one so aged, so just, and so valiant. None but the most distinguished among the youthful warriors even presumed so far as to perform the latter ceremony; the great mass of the multitude deeming it a sufficient happiness to look upon a form so deeply venerated, and so well beloved. When these acts of affection and respect were performed, the chiefs drew back again to their several places, and silence reigned in the whole encampment.

After a short delay, a few of the young men, to whom instructions had been whispered by one of the aged attendants of Tamenund, arose, left the crowd, and entered the lodge which has already been noted as the object of so much attention throughout that morning. In a few minutes they reappeared, escorting the individuals who had caused all these solemn preparations towards the seat of judgment. The crowd opened in a lane; and when the party had reentered, it closed in again, forming a large and dense belt of human bodies, arranged in an open circle.

CHAPTER XXIX

The assembly seated, rising o'er the rest,
Achilles thus the king of men addressed.
POPE'S *Iliad.*

Cora stood foremost among the prisoners, entwining her arms in those of Alice, in the tenderness of sisterly love. Notwithstanding the fearful and menacing array of savages on every side of her, no apprehension on her own account could prevent the noble-minded maiden from keeping her eyes fastened on the pale and anxious features of the trembling Alice. Close at their side stood Heyward, with an interest in both, that, at such a moment of intense uncertainty, scarcely knew a preponderance in favor of her whom he most loved. Hawkeye had placed himself a little in the rear, with a deference to the superior rank of his companions, that no similarity in the state of their present fortunes could induce him to forget. Uncas was not there.

When perfect silence was again restored, and after the usual long, impressive pause, one of the two aged chiefs who sat at the side of the patriarch arose, and demanded aloud, in very intelligible English,—

"Which of my prisoners is La Longue Carabine?"

Neither Duncan nor the scout answered. The former, however, glanced his eyes around the dark and silent assembly, and recoiled a pace, when they fell on the malignant visage of Magua. He saw, at once, that this wily savage had some secret agency in their present arraignment before the nation, and determined to throw every possible impediment in the way of the execution of his sinister plans. He had witnessed one instance of the summary punishments of the Indians, and now dreaded that his companion was to be selected for a second. In this dilemma, with little or no time for reflection, he suddenly determined to cloak his invaluable friend, at any or every hazard to himself. Before he had time, however, to speak, the question was repeated in a louder voice, and with a clearer utterance.

"Give us arms," the young man haughtily replied, "and place us in yonder woods. Our deeds shall speak for us!"

"This is the warrior whose name has filled our ears!" returned the chief, regarding Heyward with that sort of curious interest which seems inseparable from man, when first beholding one of his fellows to whom merit or accident, virtue or crime, has given notoriety. "What has brought the white man into the camp of the Delawares?"

"My necessities. I come for food, shelter, and friends."

"It cannot be. The woods are full of game. The head of a warrior needs no other shelter than a sky without clouds; and the Delawares are the enemies, and not the friends, of the Yengeese. Go! the mouth has spoken, while the heart said nothing."

Duncan, a little at a loss in what manner to proceed, remained silent; but the scout, who had listened attentively to all that passed, now advanced steadily to the front.

"That I did not answer to the call for La Longue Carabine, was not owing either to shame or fear," he said; "for neither one nor the other is the gift of an honest man. But I do not admit the right of the Mingoes to bestow a name on one whose friends have been mindful of his gifts, in this particular; especially as their title is a lie, 'Killdeer' being a grooved barrel and no carabyne. I am the man, however, that got the name of Nathaniel from my kin; the compliment of Hawkeye from the Delawares, who live on their own river; and whom the Iroquois have presumed to style the 'Long Rifle,' without any warranty from him who is most concerned in the matter."

The eyes of all present, which had hitherto been gravely scanning the person of Duncan, were now turned, on the instant, towards the upright iron frame of this new pretender to the distinguished appellation. It was in no degree remarkable that there should be found two who were willing to claim so great an honor, for impostors, though rare, were not unknown amongst the natives; but it was altogether material to the just and severe intentions of the Delawares, that there should be no mistake in the matter. Some of their old men consulted together in private, and then, as it would seem, they determined to interrogate their visitor on the subject.

"My brother has said that a snake crept into my camp," said the chief to Magua; "which is he?"

The Huron pointed to the scout.

"Will a wise Delaware believe the barking of a wolf?" exclaimed Duncan, still more confirmed in the evil intentions of his ancient enemy: "a dog never lies, but when was a wolf known to speak the truth?"

The eyes of Magua flashed fire; but, suddenly recollecting the necessity of maintaining his presence of mind, he turned away in silent disdain, well assured that the sagacity of the Indians would not fail to extract the real merits of the point in controversy. He was not deceived; for, after another short consultation, the wary Delaware turned to him again, and expressed the determination of the chiefs, though in the most considerate language.

"My brother has been called a liar," he said, "and his friends are angry. They will show that he has spoken the truth. Give my prisoners guns, and let them prove which is the man."

Magua affected to consider the expedient, which he well knew proceeded from distrust of himself, as a compliment, and made a gesture of acquiescence, well content that his veracity should be supported by so skillful a marksman as the scout. The weapons were instantly placed in the hands of the friendly opponents, and they were bid to fire, over the heads of the seated multitude, at an earthen vessel, which lay, by accident, on a stump, some fifty yards from the place where they stood.

Heyward smiled to himself at the idea of a competition with the scout, though he determined to persevere in the deception, until apprised of the real designs of Magua. Raising his rifle with the utmost care, and renewing his aim three several times, he fired. The bullet cut the wood within a few inches of the vessel; and a general exclamation of satisfaction announced that the shot was considered a proof of great skill in the use of the weapon. Even Hawkeye nodded his head, as if he would say, it was better than he had expected. But, instead of manifesting an intention to contend with the successful marksman, he stood leaning on his rifle for more than a minute, like a man who was completely buried in thought. From this reverie he was, however, awakened by one of the young Indians who had furnished the arms, and who now touched his shoulder, saying, in exceedingly broken English,—

"Can the paleface beat it?"

"Yes, Huron!" exclaimed the scout, raising the short rifle in his right hand, and shaking it at Magua, with as much apparent ease as if it were a reed; "yes, Huron, I could strike you now, and no power of earth could prevent the deed! The soaring hawk is not more certain of the dove than I am this moment of you, did I choose to send a bullet to your heart! Why should I not? Why!—because the gifts of my color forbid it, and I might draw down evil on tender and innocent heads. If you know such a being as God, thank Him, therefore, in your inward soul; for you have reason!"

The flushed countenance, angry eye, and swelling figure of the scout, produced a sensation of secret awe in all that heard him. The Delawares held their breath in expectation; but Magua himself, even while he distrusted the forbearance of his enemy, remained immovable and calm, where he stood wedged in by the crowd, as one who grew to the spot.

"Beat it," repeated the young Delaware at the elbow of the scout.

"Beat what, fool!—what!" exclaimed Hawkeye, still flourishing the weapon angrily above his head, though his eye no longer sought the person of Magua.

"If the white man is the warrior he pretends," said the aged chief, "let him strike nigher to the mark."

The scout laughed aloud—a noise that produced the startling effect of an unnatural sound on Heyward; then dropping the piece, heavily, into his extended left hand, it was discharged, apparently by the shock, driving the fragments of the vessel into the air and scattering them on every side. Almost at the same instant, the rattling sound of the rifle was heard, as he suffered it to fall, contemptuously, to the earth.

The first impression of so strange a scene was engrossing admiration. Then a low, but increasing murmur, ran through the multitude, and finally swelled into sounds that denoted a lively opposition in the sentiments of the spectators. While some openly testified their satisfaction at so unexampled dexterity, by far the larger portion of the tribe were inclined to believe the success of the shot was the result of accident. Heyward was not slow to confirm an opinion that was so favorable to his own pretensions.

"It was chance!" he exclaimed; "none can shoot without an aim!"

"Chance!" echoed the excited woodsman, who was now stubbornly bent on maintaining his identity at every hazard, and on whom the secret hints of Heyward to acquiesce in the deception were entirely lost. "Does yonder lying Huron, too, think it chance? Give him another gun, and place us face to face, without cover or dodge, and let Providence, and our own eyes, decide the matter atween us! I do not make the offer to you, Major; for our blood is of color, and we serve the same master."

"That the Huron is a liar, is very evident," returned Heyward, coolly; "you have yourself heard him assert you to be La Longue Carabine."

It were impossible to say what violent assertion the stubborn Hawkeye would have next made, in his headlong wish to vindicate his identity, had not the aged Delaware once more interposed.

"The hawk which comes from the clouds can return when he will," he said; "give them the guns."

This time the scout seized the rifle with avidity; nor had Magua, though he watched the movement of the marksman with jealous eyes, any further cause for apprehension.

"Now let it be proved, in the face of this tribe of Delawares, which is the better man," cried the scout, tapping the butt of his piece with that finger which had pulled so many fatal triggers. "You see the gourd hanging against yonder tree, Major; if you are a marksman fit for the borders, let me see you break its shell!"

Duncan noted the object, and prepared himself to renew the trial. The gourd was one of the usual little vessels used by the Indians, and it was suspended from a dead branch of a small pine, by a thong of deer-skin, at the full distance of a hundred yards. So strangely compounded is the feeling of self-love, that the young soldier, while he knew the utter worthlessness of the suffrages of his savage umpires, forgot the sudden motives of the contest in a wish to excel. It has been seen, already, that his skill was far from being contemptible, and he now resolved to put forth its nicest qualities. Had his life depended on the issue, the aim of Duncan could not have been more deliberate or guarded. He fired; and three or four young Indians, who sprang forward at the report, announced with a shout, that the ball was in the tree, a very little on one side of the proper object. The warriors uttered a common ejaculation of pleasure, and then turned their eyes inquiringly on the movements of his rival.

"It may do for the Royal Americans!" said Hawkeye, laughing once more in his own silent, heartfelt manner; "but had my gun often turned so much from the true line, many a marten, whose skin is now in a lady's muff, would still be in the woods; aye, and many a bloody Mingo, who has departed to his final account, would be acting his deviltries at this very day, atween the provinces. I hope the squaw who owns the gourd has more of them in her wigwam, for this will never hold water again!"

The scout had shook his priming, and cocked his piece, while speaking; and, as he ended, he threw back a foot, and slowly raised the muzzle from the earth: the motion was steady, uniform, and in one direction. When on a perfect level, it remained for a single moment, without tremor or variation, as though both man and rifle were carved in stone. During that stationary instant, it poured forth its contents, in a bright, glancing sheet of flame. Again the young Indians bounded forward; but their hurried search and disappointed looks announced that no traces of the bullet were to be seen.

"Go!" said the old chief to the scout, in a tone of strong disgust; "thou art a wolf in the skin of a dog. I will talk to the 'Long Rifle' of the Yengeese."

"Ah! had I that piece which furnished the name you use, I would obligate myself to cut the thong, and drop the gourd without breaking it!" returned Hawkeye, perfectly undisturbed by the other's manner. "Fools, if you would find the bullet of a sharpshooter of these woods, you must look *in* the object and not around it!"

The Indian youths instantly comprehended his meaning—for this time he spoke in the Delaware tongue—and tearing the gourd from the tree, they held it on high with an exulting shout, displaying a hole in its bottom, which had been cut by the bullet, after passing through the usual orifice in the centre of its upper side. At this unexpected exhibition, a loud and vehement expression of pleasure burst from the mouth of every warrior present. It decided the question, and effectually established Hawkeye in the possession of his dangerous reputation. Those curious and admiring eyes which had been turned again on Heyward, were finally directed to the weather-beaten form of the scout, who immediately became the principal object of attention to the simple and unsophisticated beings by whom he was surrounded. When the sudden and noisy commotion had a little subsided, the aged chief resumed his examination.

"Why did you wish to stop my ears?" he said, addressing Duncan; "are the Delawares fools, that they could not know the young panther from the cat?"

"They will yet find the Huron a singing-bird," said Duncan, endeavoring to adopt the figurative language of the natives.

"It is good. We will know who can shut the ears of men. Brother," added the chief, turning his eyes on Magua, "the Delawares listen."

Thus singled, and directly called on to declare his object, the Huron arose; and advancing with great deliberation and dignity into the very centre of the circle, where he stood confronted to the prisoners, he placed himself in an attitude to speak. Before opening his mouth, however, he bent his eyes slowly along the whole living boundary of earnest faces, as if to temper his expressions to the capacities of his audience. On Hawkeye he cast a glance of respectful enmity; on Duncan, a look of inextinguishable hatred; the shrinking figure of Alice he scarcely deigned to notice; but when his glance met the firm, commanding, and yet lovely form of Cora, his eye lingered a moment, with an expression that it might have been difficult to define. Then, filled with his own dark intentions, he spoke in the language of the Canadas, a tongue that he well knew was comprehended by most of his auditors.

"The Spirit that made men colored them differently," commenced the subtle Huron. "Some are blacker than the sluggish bear. These He said should be slaves; and He ordered them to work forever, like the beaver. You may hear them groan, when the south wind blows, louder than the lowing buffaloes, along the shores of the great salt lake, where the big canoes come and go with them in droves. Some He made with faces paler than the ermine of the forests: and these He ordered to be traders; dogs to their women, and wolves to their slaves. He gave this people the nature of the pigeon; wings that never tire; young, more plentiful than the leaves on the trees, and appetites to devour the earth. He gave them tongues like the false call of the wild-cat; hearts like rabbits; the cunning of the hog (but none of the fox), and arms longer than the legs of the moose. With his tongue, he stops the ears of the Indians; his heart teaches him to pay warriors to fight his battles; his cunning tells him how to get together the goods of the earth; and his arms inclose the land from the shores of the salt-water to the islands of the great lake. His gluttony makes him sick. God gave him enough, and yet he wants all. Such are the pale-faces.

"Some the Great Spirit made with skins brighter and redder than yonder sun," continued Magua, pointing impressively upwards to the lurid luminary, which was struggling through the misty atmosphere of the horizon; "and these did He fashion to his own mind. He gave them this island as He had made it, covered with trees, and filled with game. The wind made their clearings; the sun and rains ripened their fruits; and the snows came to tell them to be thankful. What need had they of roads to journey by! They saw through the hills! When the beavers worked, they lay in the shade, and looked on. The winds cooled them in summer; in winter, skins kept them warm. If they fought among themselves, it was to prove that they were men. They were brave; they were just; they were happy."

Here the speaker paused, and again looked around him, to discover if his legend had touched the sympathies of his listeners. He met everywhere with eyes riveted on his own, heads erect, and nostrils expanded, as if each individual present felt himself able and willing, singly, to redress the wrongs of his race.

"If the Great Spirit gave different tongues to his red children," he continued, in a low, still, melancholy voice, "it was that all animals might understand them. Some He placed among the snows, with their cousin the bear. Some He placed near the setting sun on the road to the happy hunting-grounds. Some on the lands around the great fresh waters; but to His greatest, and most beloved, He gave the sands of the salt lake. Do my brothers know the name of this favored people?"

"It was the Lenape!" exclaimed twenty eager voices, in a breath.

"It was the Lenni Lenape," returned Magua, affecting to bend his head in reverence to their former greatness. "It was the tribes of the Lenape! The sun rose from water that was salt, and set in water that was sweet, and never hid himself from their eyes. But why should I, a Huron of the woods, tell a wise people their own traditions? Why remind them of their injuries; their ancient greatness; their deeds; their glory; their happiness,—their losses; their defeats; their misery? Is there not one among them who has seen it all, and who knows it to be true? I have done. My tongue is still, for my heart is of lead. I listen."

As the voice of the speaker suddenly ceased, every face and all eyes turned, by a common movement, towards the venerable Tamenund. From the moment that he took his seat, until the present instant, the lips of the patriarch had not severed, and scarcely a sign of life had escaped him. He sat bent in feebleness, and apparently unconscious of the presence he was in, during the whole of that opening scene, in which the skill of the scout had been so clearly established. At the nicely graduated sound of Magua's voice, however, he betrayed some evidence of consciousness, and once or twice he even raised his head, as if to listen. But when the crafty Huron spoke of his nation by name, the eyelids of the old man raised themselves, and he looked out upon the multitude with that sort of dull, unmeaning expression which might be supposed to belong to the countenance of a spectre. Then he made an effort to rise, and being upheld by his supporters, he gained his feet, in a posture commanding by its dignity, while he tottered with weakness.

"Who calls upon the children of the Lenape!" he said, in a deep, guttural voice, that was rendered awfully audible by the breathless silence of the multitude: "who speaks of things gone! Does not the egg become a worm—the worm a fly, and perish? Why tell the Delawares of good that is past? Better thank the Manitou for that which remains."

"It is a Wyandot," said Magua, stepping nigher to the rude platform on which the other stood; "a friend of Tamenund."

"A friend!" repeated the sage, on whose brow a dark frown settled, imparting a portion of that severity which had rendered his eye so terrible in middle age. "Are the Mingoes rulers of the earth? What brings a Huron here?"

"Justice. His prisoners are with his brothers, and he comes for his own."

Tamenund turned his head towards one of his supporters, and listened to the short explanation the man gave. Then facing the applicant, he regarded him a moment with deep attention; after which he said, in a low and reluctant voice,—

"Justice is the law of the great Manitou. My children, give the stranger food. Then, Huron, take thine own and depart."

On the delivery of this solemn judgment, the patriarch seated himself, and closed his eyes again, as if better pleased with the images of his own ripened experience than with the visible objects of the world. Against such a decree there was no Delaware sufficiently hardy to murmur, much less oppose himself. The words were barely uttered when four or five of the younger warriors, stepping behind Heyward and the scout, passed thongs so dexterously and rapidly around their arms, as to hold them both in instant bondage. The former was too much engrossed with his precious and nearly insensible burden, to be aware of their intentions before they were executed; and the latter, who considered even the hostile tribes of the Delawares a superior race of beings, submitted without resistance. Perhaps, however, the manner of the scout would not have been so passive, had he fully comprehended the language in which the preceding dialogue had been conducted.

Magua cast a look of triumph around the whole assembly before he proceeded to the execution of his purpose. Perceiving that the men were unable to offer any resistance, he turned his looks on her he valued most. Cora met his gaze with an eye so calm and firm, that his resolution wavered. Then recollecting his former artifice, he raised Alice from the arms of the warrior against whom she leaned, and beckoning Heyward to follow, he motioned for the encircling crowd to open. But Cora, instead of obeying the impulse he had expected, rushed to the feet of the patriarch, and raising her voice, exclaimed aloud,—

"Just and venerable Delaware, on thy wisdom and power we lean for mercy! Be deaf to yonder artful and remorseless monster, who poisons thy ears with falsehoods to feed his thirst for blood. Thou that hast lived long, and that hast seen the evil of the world, should know how to temper its calamities to the miserable."

The eyes of the old man opened heavily, and he once more looked upwards at the multitude. As the piercing tones of the supplicant swelled on his ears, they moved slowly in the direction of her person, and finally settled there in a steady gaze. Cora had cast herself to her knees; and, with hands clenched in each other and pressed upon her bosom, she remained like a beauteous and breathing model of her sex, looking up in his faded, but majestic countenance, with a species of holy reverence. Gradually the expression of Tamenund's features changed, and losing their vacancy in admiration, they lighted with a portion of that intelligence which a century before had been wont to communicate his youthful fire to the extensive bands of the Delawares. Rising without assistance, and seemingly without an effort, he demanded, in a voice that startled its auditors by its firmness,—

"What art thou?"

"A woman. One of a hated race, if thou wilt—a Yengee. But one who has never harmed thee, and who cannot harm thy people, if she would; who asks for succor."

"Tell me, my children," continued the patriarch, hoarsely, motioning to those around him, though his eyes still dwelt upon the kneeling form of Cora, "where have the Delawares camped?"

"In the mountains of the Iroquois, beyond the clear springs of the Horican."

"Many parching summers are come and gone," continued the sage, "since I drank of the water of my own rivers. The children of Miquon[27] are the justest white men; but they were thirsty, and they took it to themselves. Do they follow us so far?"

"We follow none; we covet nothing," answered Cora. "Captives against our wills have we been brought amongst you; and we ask but permission to depart to our own in peace. Art thou not Tamenund—the father, the judge, I had almost said, the prophet—of this people?"

"I am Tamenund of many days."

"'T is now some seven years that one of thy people was at the mercy of a white chief on the borders of this province. He claimed to be of the blood of the good and just Tamenund. 'Go,' said the white man, 'for thy parent's sake thou art free.' Dost thou remember the name of that English warrior?"

"I remember, that when a laughing boy," returned the patriarch, with the peculiar recollection of vast age, "I stood upon the sands of the sea-shore, and saw a big canoe, with wings whiter than the swan's, and wider than many eagles, come from the rising sun."

"Nay, nay; I speak not of a time so very distant, but of favor shown to thy kindred by one of mine, within the memory of thy youngest warrior."

"Was it when the Yengeese and the Dutchmanne fought for the hunting-grounds of the Delawares? Then Tamenund was a chief, and first laid aside the bow for the lightning of the palefaces—"

"Nor yet then," interrupted Cora, "by many ages; I speak of a thing of yesterday. Surely, surely, you forget it not."

"It was but yesterday," rejoined the aged man, with touching pathos, "that the children of the Lenape were masters of the world. The fishes of the salt lake, the birds, the beasts, and the Mengwe of the woods owned them for Sagamores."

Cora bowed her head in disappointment, and, for a bitter moment, struggled with her chagrin. Then elevating her rich features and beaming eyes, she continued, in tones scarcely less penetrating than the unearthly voice of the patriarch himself,—

"Tell me, is Tamenund a father?"

The old man looked down upon her from his elevated stand, with a benignant smile on his wasted countenance, and then casting his eyes slowly over the whole assemblage, he answered,—

"Of a nation."

"For myself I ask nothing. Like thee and thine, venerable chief," she continued, pressing her hands convulsively on her heart, and suffering her head to droop until her burning cheeks were nearly concealed in the maze of dark glossy tresses that fell in disorder upon her shoulders, "the curse of my ancestors has fallen heavily on their child. But yonder is one who has never known the weight of Heaven's displeasure until now. She is the daughter of an old and failing man, whose days

---

[27]William Penn was termed Miquon by the Delawares, and, as he never used violence or injustice in his dealings with them, his reputation for probity passed into a proverb. The American is justly proud of the origin of his nation, which is perhaps unequaled in the history of the world; but the Pennsylvanian and Jerseyman have more reason to value themselves in their ancestors than the natives of any other State, since no wrong was ever done the original owners of the soil. [J.F.C.]

are near their close. She has many, very many, to love her, and delight in her; and she is too good, much too precious, to become the victim of that villain."

"I know that the pale-faces are a proud and hungry race. I know that they claim not only to have the earth, but that the meanest of their color is better than the Sachems of the redman. The dogs and crows of their tribes," continued the earnest old chieftain, without heeding the wounded spirit of his listener, whose head was nearly crushed to the earth in shame, as he proceeded, "would bark and caw before they would take a woman to their wigwams whose blood was not of the color of snow. But let them not boast before the face of the Manitou too loud. They entered the land at the rising, and may yet go off at the setting sun. I have often seen the locusts strip the leaves from the trees, but the season of blossoms has always come again."

"It is so," said Cora, drawing a long breath, as if reviving from a trance, raising her face, and shaking back her shining veil, with a kindling eye, that contradicted the death-like paleness of her countenance; "but why—it is not permitted us to inquire. There is yet one of thine own people who has not been brought before thee; before thou lettest the Huron depart in triumph, hear him speak."

Observing Tamenund to look about him doubtingly, one of his companions said,—

"It is a snake—a red-skin in the pay of the Yengeese. We keep him for the torture."

"Let him come," returned the sage.

Then Tamenund once more sank into his seat, and a silence so deep prevailed, while the young men prepared to obey his simple mandate, that the leaves, which fluttered in the draught of the light morning air, were distinctly heard rustling in the surrounding forest.

CHAPTER XXX

If you deny me, fie upon your law!
There is no force in the decrees of Venice.
I stand for judgment: answer; shall I have it?
SHAKESPEARE, *Merchant of Venice,* IV. i.

The silence continued unbroken by human sounds for many anxious minutes. Then the waving multitude opened and shut again, and Uncas stood in the living circle. All those eyes, which had been curiously studying the lineaments of the sage, as the source of their own intelligence, turned on the instant, and were now bent in secret admiration on the erect, agile, and faultless person of the captive. But neither the presence in which he found himself, nor the exclusive attention that he attracted, in any manner disturbed the self-possession of the young Mohican. He cast a deliberate and observing look on every side of him, meeting the settled expression of hostility that lowered in the visages of the chiefs, with the same calmness as the curious gaze of the attentive children. But when, last in his haughty scrutiny, the person of Tamenund came under his glance, his eye became fixed, as though all other objects were already forgotten. Then advancing with a slow and noiseless step up the area, he placed himself immediately before the footstool of the sage. Here he stood unnoted, though keenly observant himself, until one of the chiefs apprised the latter of his presence.

"With what tongue does the prisoner speak to the Manitou?" demanded the patriarch, without unclosing his eyes.

"Like his fathers," Uncas replied; "with the tongue of a Delaware."

At this sudden and unexpected annunciation, a low, fierce yell ran through the multitude, that might not inaptly be compared to the growl of the lion, as his choler is first awakened—a fearful omen of the weight of his future anger. The effect was eqully strong on the sage, though differently exhibited. He passed a hand before his eyes, as if to exclude the least evidence of so shameful a spectacle, while he repeated, in his low, guttural tones, the words he had just heard.

"A Delaware! I have lived to see the tribes of the Lenape driven from their council fires, and scattered, like broken herds of deer, among the hills of the Iroquois! I have seen the hatchets of a strange people sweep woods from the valleys, that the winds of heaven had spared! The beasts that run on the mountains, and the birds that fly above the trees, have I seen living in the wigwams of men; but never before have I found a Delaware so base as to creep, like a poisonous serpent, into the camps of his nation."

"The singing-birds have opened their bills," returned Uncas, in the softest notes of his own musical voice; "and Tamenund has heard their song."

The sage started, and bent his head aside, as if to catch the fleeting sounds of some passing melody.

"Does Tamenund dream?" he exclaimed. "What voice is at his ear? Have the winters gone backward? Will summer come again to the children of the Lenape?"

A solemn and respectful silence succeeded this incoherent burst from the lips of the Delaware prophet. His people readily construed his unintelligible language into one of those mysterious conferences he was believed to hold so frequently with a superior intelligence, and they awaited the issue of the revelation in awe. After a patient pause, however, one of the aged men, perceiving that the sage had lost the recollection of the subject before them, ventured to remind him again of the presence of the prisoner.

"The false Delaware trembles lest he should hear the words of Tamenund," he said. "'T is a hound that howls, when the Yengeese show him a trail."

"And ye," returned Uncas, looking sternly around him "are dogs that whine, when the Frenchman casts ye the offals of his deer!"

Twenty knives gleamed in the air, and as many warriors sprang to their feet, at this biting, and perhaps merited retort; but a motion from one of the chiefs suppressed the outbreaking of their tempers, and restored the appearance of quiet. The task might probably have been more difficult, had not a movement made by Tamenund indicated that he was again about to speak.

"Delaware!" resumed the sage, "little art thou worthy of thy name. My people have not seen a bright sun in many winters; and the warrior who deserts his tribe when hid in clouds is doubly a traitor. The law of the Manitou is just. It is so; while the rivers run and the mountains stand, while the blossoms come and go on the trees, it must be so. He is thine, my children; deal justly by him."

Not a limb was moved, nor was a breath drawn louder and longer than common, until the closing syllable of this final decree had passed the lips of Tamenund. Then a cry of vengeance burst at once, as it might be, from the united lips of the nation; a frightful augury of their ruthless intentions. In the midst of these prolonged and savage yells, a chief proclaimed, in a high voice, that the captive was condemned to endure the dreadful trial of torture by fire. The circle broke its order, and screams of delight mingled with the bustle and tumult of preparation. Heyward struggled madly with his captors; the anxious eyes of Hawkeye began to look around him, with an expression of peculiar earnestness; and Cora again threw herself at the feet of the patriarch, once more a suppliant for mercy.

Throughout the whole of these trying moments, Uncas had alone preserved his serenity. He looked on the preparations with a steady eye, and when the tormentors came to seize him, he met them with a firm and upright attitude. One among them, if possible, more fierce and savage than his fellows, seized the hunting-shirt of the young warrior, and at a single effort tore it from his body. Then, with a yell of frantic pleasure, he leaped towards his unresisting victim, and prepared to lead him to the stake. But, at that moment, when he appeared most a stranger to the feelings of humanity, the purpose of the savage was arrested as suddenly as if a supernatural agency had interposed in the behalf of Uncas. The eyeballs of the Delaware seemed to start from their sockets; his mouth opened, and his whole form became frozen in an attitude of amazement. Raising his hand with a slow and regulated motion, he pointed with a finger to the bosom of the captive. His companions crowded about him in wonder, and every eye was, like his own, fastened intently on the figure of a small tortoise, beautifully tattooed on the breast of the prisoner, in a bright blue tint.

For a single instant Uncas enjoyed his triumph, smiling calmly on the scene. Then motioning the crowd away with a high and haughty sweep of his arm, he advanced in front of the nation with the air of a king, and spoke in a voice louder than the murmur of admiration that ran through the multitude.

"Men of the Lenni Lenape!" he said, "my race upholds the earth! Your feeble tribe stands on my shell! What fire that a Delaware can light would burn the child of my fathers?" he added, pointing proudly to the simple blazonry on his skin; "the blood that came from such a stock would smother your flames! My race is the grandfather of nations!"

"Who art thou?" demanded Tamenund, rising at the startling tones he heard, more than at any meaning conveyed by the language of the prisoner.

"Uncas, the son of Chingachgook," answered the captive modestly, turning from the nation, and bending his head in reverence to the other's character and years; "a son of the great Unamis."

"The hour of Tamenund is nigh!" exclaimed the sage; "the day is come, at last, to the night! I thank the Manitou, that one is here to fill my place at the council-fire. Uncas, the child of Uncas, is found! Let the eyes of a dying eagle gaze on the rising sun."

The youth stepped lightly, but proudly, on the platform, where he became visible to the whole agitated and wondering multitude. Tamenund held him long at the length of his arm, and read every turn in the fine lineaments of his countenance, with the untiring gaze of one who recalled days of happiness.

"Is Tamenund a boy?" at length the bewildered prophet exclaimed. "Have I dreamt of so many snows—that my people were scattered like floating sands—of Yengeese, more plenty than the leaves on the trees! The arrow of Tamenund would not frighten the fawn; his arm is withered like the branch of a dead oak; the snail would be swifter in the race; yet is Uncas before him as they went to battle against the pale-faces! Uncas, the panther of his tribe, the eldest son of the Lenape, the wisest Sagamore of the Mohicans! Tell me, ye Delawares, has Tamenund been a sleeper for a hundred winters?"

The calm and deep silence which succeeded these words, sufficiently announced the awful reverence with which his people received the communication of the patriarch. None dared to answer, though all listened in breathless expectation of what might follow. Uncas, however, looking in his face with the fondness and veneration of a favored child, presumed on his own high and acknowledged rank, to reply.

"Four warriors of his race have lived, and died," he said, "since the friend of Tamenund led his people in battle. The blood of the turtle has been in many chiefs, but all have gone back into the earth from whence they came except Chingachgook and his son."

"It is true—it is true," returned the sage—a flash of recollection destroying all his pleasing fancies, and restoring him at once to a consciousness of the true history of his nation. "Our wise men have often said that two warriors of the unchanged race were in the hills of the Yengeese; why have their seats at the council-fires of the Delawares been so long empty?"

At these words the young man raised his head, which he had kept bowed a little, in reverence; and lifting his voice so as to be heard by the multitude, as if to explain at once and forever the policy of his family, he said aloud,—

"Once we slept where we could hear the salt lake speak in its anger. Then we were rulers and Sagamores over the land. But when a pale-face was seen on every brook, we followed the deer back to the river of our nation. The Delawares were gone. Few warriors of them all stayed to drink of the stream they loved. Then said my fathers, 'Here will we hunt. The waters of the river go into the salt lake. If we go towards the setting sun, we shall find streams that run into the great lakes of sweet water; there would a Mohican die, like fishes of the sea, in the clear springs. When the Manitou is ready, and shall say "Come," we will follow the river to the sea, and take our own again.' Such, Delawares, is the belief of the children of the Turtle. Our eyes are on the rising, and not towards the setting sun. We know whence he comes, but we know not whither he goes. It is enough."

The men of the Lenape listened to his words with all the respect that superstition could lend, finding a secret charm even in the figurative language with which the young Sagamore imparted his ideas. Uncas himself watched the effect of his brief explanation with intelligent eyes, and gradually dropped the air of authority he had assumed, as he perceived that his auditors were content. Then permitting his looks to wander over the silent throng that crowded around the elevated seat of Tamenund, he first perceived Hawkeye in his bonds. Stepping eagerly from his stand, he made way for himself to the side of his friend; and cutting his thongs with a quick and angry stroke of his own knife, he motioned to the crowd to divide. The Indians silently obeyed, and once more they stood ranged in their circle, as before his appearance among them. Uncas took the scout by the hand, and led him to the feet of the patriarch.

"Father," he said, "look at this pale-face; a just man, and the friend of the Delawares."

"Is he a son of Miquon?"

"Not so; a warrior known to the Yengeese, and feared by the Maquas."

"What name has he gained by his deeds?"

"We call him Hawkeye," Uncas replied, using the Delaware phrase; "for his sight never fails. The Mingoes know him better by the death he gives their warriors; with them he is 'The Long Rifle.'"

"La Longue Carabine!" exclaimed Tamenund, opening his eyes, and regarding the scout sternly. "My son has not done well to call him friend."

"I call him so who proves himself such," returned the young chief, with great calmness, but with a steady mien. "If Uncas is welcome among the Delawares, then is Hawkeye with his friends."

"The pale-face has slain my young men; his name is great for the blows he has struck the Lenape."

"If a Mingo has whispered that much in the ear of the Delaware, he has only shown that he is a singing-bird," said the scout, who now believed that it was time to vindicate himself from such offensive charges, and who spoke in the tongue of the man he addressed, modifying his Indian figures, however, with his own peculiar notions. "That I have slain the Maquas I am not the man to deny, even at their own council-fires; but that, knowingly, my hand has ever harmed a Delaware, is opposed to the reason of my gifts, which is friendly to them, and all that belongs to their nation."

A low exclamation of applause passed among the warriors, who exchanged looks with each other like men that first began to perceive their error.

"Where is the Huron?" demanded Tamenund. "Has he stopped my ears?"

Magua, whose feelings during that scene in which Uncas had triumphed may be much better imagined than described, answered to the call by stepping boldly in front of the patriarch.

"The just Tamenund," he said, "will not keep what a Huron has lent."

"Tell me, son of my brother," returned the sage, avoiding the dark countenance of Le Subtil, and turning gladly to the more ingenuous features of Uncas, "has the stranger a conqueror's right over you?"

"He has none. The panther may get into snares set by the women; but he is strong, and knows how to leap through them."

"La Longue Carabine?"

"Laughs at the Mingoes. Go, Huron, ask your squaws the color of a bear."

"The stranger and the white maiden that came into my camp together?"

"Should journey on an open path."

"And the woman that Huron left with my warriors?"

Uncas made no reply.

"And the woman that the Mingo has brought into my camp," repeated Tamenund, gravely.

"She is mine," cried Magua, shaking his hand in triumph at Uncas. "Mohican, you know that she is mine."

"My son is silent," said Tamenund, endeavoring to read the expression of the face that the youth turned from him in sorrow.

"It is so," was the low answer.

A short and impressive pause succeeded, during which it was very apparent with what reluctance the multitude admitted the justice of the Mingo's claim. At length the sage, on whom alone the decision depended, said, in a firm voice,—

"Huron, depart."

"As he came, just Tamenund," demanded the wily Magua, "or with hands filled with the faith of the Delawares? The wigwam of Le Renard Subtil is empty. Make him strong with his own."

The aged man mused with himself for a time; and then bending his head towards one of his venerable companions, he asked,—

"Are my ears open?"

"It is true."

"Is this Mingo a chief?"

"The first in his nation."

"Girl, what wouldst thou? A great warrior takes thee to wife. Go! thy race will not end."

"Better, a thousand times, it should," exclaimed the horror-struck Cora, "than meet with such a degradation!"

"Huron, her mind is in the tents of her fathers. An unwilling maiden makes an unhappy wigwam."

"She speaks with the tongue of her people," returned Magua, regarding his victim with a look of bitter irony. "She is of a race of traders, and will bargain for a bright look. Let Tamenund speak the words."

"Take you the wampum, and our love."

"Nothing hence but what Magua brought hither."

"Then depart with thine own. The Great Manitou forbids that a Delaware should be unjust."

Magua advanced, and seized his captive strongly by the arm; the Delawares fell back, in silence; and Cora, as if conscious that remonstrance would be useless, prepared to submit to her fate without resistance.

"Hold, hold!" cried Duncan, springing forward; "Huron, have mercy! her ransom shall make thee richer than any of thy people were ever yet known to be."

"Magua is a red-skin; he wants not the beads of the palefaces."

"Gold, silver, powder, lead—all that a warrior needs shall be in thy wigwam; all that becomes the greatest chief."

"Le Subtil is very strong," cried Magua, violently shaking the hand which grasped the unresisting arm of Cora; "he has his revenge!"

"Mighty ruler of providence!" exclaimed Heyward, clasping his hands together in agony, "can this be suffered? To you, just Tamenund, I appeal for mercy."

"The words of the Delaware are said," returned the sage, closing his eyes, and dropping back into his seat, alike wearied with his mental and his bodily exertion. "Men speak not twice."

"That a chief should not misspend his time in unsaying what has once been spoken, is wise and reasonable," said Hawkeye, motioning to Duncan to be silent; "but it is also prudent in every warrior to consider well before he strikes his tomahawk into the head of his prisoner. Huron, I love you not; nor can I say that any Mingo has ever received much favor at my hands. It is fair to conclude that, if this war does not soon end, many more of your warriors will meet me in the woods. Put it to your judgment, then, whether you would prefer taking such a prisoner as that into your encampment, or one like myself, who am a man that it would greatly rejoice your nation to see with naked hands."

"Will 'The Long Rifle' give his life for the woman?" demanded Magua, hesitatingly; for he had already made a motion towards quitting the place with his victim.

"No, no; I have not said so much as that," returned Hawkeye, drawing back with suitable discretion, when he noted the eagerness with which Magua listened to his proposal. "It would be an unequal exchange, to give a warrior, in the prime of his age and usefulness, for the best woman on the frontiers. I might consent to go into winter quarters, now—at least six weeks afore the leaves will turn—on condition you will release the maiden."

Magua shook his head, and made an impatient sign for the crowd to open.

"Well, then," added the scout, with the musing air of a man who had not half made up his mind, "I will throw Killdeer into the bargain. Take the word of an experienced hunter, the piece has not its equal atween the provinces."

Magua still disdained to reply, continuing his efforts to disperse the crowd.

"Perhaps," added the scout, losing his dissembled coolness, exactly in proportion as the other manifested an indifference to the exchange, "if I should condition to teach your young men the real virtue of the we'pon, it would smooth the little differences in our judgments."

Le Renard fiercely ordered the Delawares, who still lingered in an impenetrable belt around him, in hopes he would listen to the amicable proposal, to open his path, threatening, by the glance of his eye, another appeal to the infallible justice of their "prophet."

"What is ordered must sooner or later arrive," continued Hawkeye, turning with a sad and humbled look to Uncas. "The varlet knows his advantage, and will keep it! God bless you, boy; you have found friends among your natural kin and I hope they will prove as true as some you have met who had no Indian cross. As for me, sooner or later, I must die; it is therefore fortunate there are but few to make my death-howl. After all, it is likely the imps would have managed to master my scalp, so a day or two will make no great difference in the everlasting reckoning of time. God bless you," added the rugged woodsman, bending his head aside and then instantly changing its direction again, with a wistful look towards the youth; "I loved both you and your father, Uncas, though our skins are not altogether of a color, and our gifts are somewhat different. Tell the Sagamore I never lost sight of him in my greatest trouble; and, as for you, think of me sometimes when on a lucky trail; and depend on it, boy, whether there be one heaven or two, there is a path in the other world by which honest men may come together again. You'll find the rifle in the place we hid it; take it, and keep it for my sake; and harkee, lad, as your natural gifts don't deny you the use of vengeance, use it a little freely on the Mingoes; it may unburden grief at my loss, and ease your mind. Huron, I accept your offer; release the woman. I am your prisoner!"

A suppressed, but still distinct murmur of approbation, ran through the crowd at this generous proposition; even the fiercest among the Delaware warriors manifesting pleasure at the manliness of the intended sacrifice. Magua paused, and for an anxious moment, it might be said, he doubted; then casting his eyes on Cora, with an expression in which ferocity and admiration were strangely mingled, his purpose became fixed forever.

He intimated his contempt of the offer with a backward motion of his head, and said, in a steady and settled voice,—

"Le Renard Subtil is a great chief; he has but one mind. Come," he added, laying his hand too familiarly on the shoulder of his captive to urge her onward; "a Huron is no tattler; we will go."

The maiden drew back in lofty womanly reserve, and her dark eye kindled, while the rich blood shot, like the passing brightness of the sun, into her very temples, at the indignity.

"I am your prisoner, and at a fitting time shall be ready to follow, even to my death. But violence is unnecessary," she coldly said, and, immediately turning to

Hawkeye, added, "Generous hunter! from my soul I thank you. Your offer is vain, neither could it be accepted; but still you may serve me, even more than in your noble intention. Look at that drooping, humbled child! Abandon her not until you leave her in the habitations of civilized men. I will not say," wringing the hard hand of the scout, "that her father will reward you—for such as you are above the rewards of men—but he will thank you, and bless you. And, believe me, the blessing of a just and aged man has virtue in the sight of Heaven. Would to God, I could hear one from his lips at this awful moment!" Her voice became choked, and, for an instant, she was silent; then advancing a step nigher to Duncan, who was supporting her unconscious sister, she continued, in more subdued tones, but in which feeling and the habits of her sex maintained a fearful struggle,—"I need not tell you to cherish the treasure you will possess. You love her, Heyward; that would conceal a thousand faults, though she had them. She is kind, gentle, sweet, good, as mortal may be. There is not a blemish in mind or person at which the proudest of you all would sicken. She is fair—Oh, how surpassingly fair!" laying her own beautiful, but less brilliant hand, in melancholy affection on the alabaster forehead of Alice, and parting the golden hair which clustered about her brows; "and yet her soul is pure and spotless as her skin! I could say much—more, perhaps, than cooler reason would approve; but I will spare you and myself—" Her voice became inaudible, and her face was bent over the form of her sister. After a long and burning kiss, she arose, and with features of the hue of death, but without even a tear in her feverish eye, she turned away, and added, to the savage, with all her former elevation of manner, "Now, sir, if it be your pleasure, I will follow."

"Aye, go," cried Duncan, placing Alice in the arms of an Indian girl; "go, Magua, go. These Delawares have their laws, which forbid them to detain you; but I—I have no such obligation. Go, malignant monster—why do you delay?"

It would be difficult to describe the expression with which Magua listened to this threat to follow. There was at first a fierce and manifest display of joy, and then it was instantly subdued in a look of cunning coldness.

"The woods are open," he was content with answering. "'The Open Hand' can come."

"Hold," cried Hawkeye, seizing Duncan by the arm, and detaining him by violence; "you know not the craft of the imp. He would lead you to an ambushment, and your death—"

"Huron," interrupted Uncas, who, submissive to the stern customs of his people, had been an attentive and grave listener to all that passed; "Huron, the justice of the Delawares comes from the Manitou. Look at the sun. He is now in the upper branches of the hemlock. Your path is short and open. When he is seen above the trees, there will be men on your trail."

"I hear a crow!" exclaimed Magua, with a taunting laugh. "Go!" he added, shaking his hand at the crowd, which had slowly opened to admit his passage, "where are the petticoats of the Delawares? Let them send their arrows and their guns to the Wyandots; they shall have venison to eat and corn to hoe. Dogs, rabbits, thieves—I spit on you!"

His parting gibes were listened to in a dead, boding silence, and, with these biting words in his mouth, the triumphant Magua passed unmolested into the forest, followed by his passive captive, and protected by the inviolable laws of Indian hospitality.

CHAPTER XXXI

Fluellen.—*Kill the poys and the luggage! 't is expressly against the law of arms: 't is as arrant a piece of knavery, mark you now, as can be offered in the world.*

SHAKESPEARE, *King Henry V.*, IV. vii.

So long as their enemy and his victim continued in sight, the multitude remained motionless as beings charmed to the place by some power that was friendly to the Huron; but the instant he disappeared, it became tossed and agitated by fierce and powerful passion. Uncas maintained his elevated stand, keeping his eyes on the form of Cora, until the colors of her dress were blended with the foliage of the forest; when he descended, and moving silently through the throng, he disappeared in that lodge from which he had so recently issued. A few of the graver and more attentive warriors, who caught the gleams of anger that shot from the eyes of the young chief in passing, followed him to the place he had selected for his meditations. After which Tamenund and Alice were removed, and the women and children were ordered to disperse. During the momentous hour that succeeded, the encampment resembled a hive of troubled bees, who only awaited the appearance and example of their leader to take some distant and momentous flight.

A young warrior at length issued from the lodge of Uncas; and moving deliberately, with a sort of grave march, towards a dwarf pine that grew in the crevices of the rocky terrace, he tore the bark from its body, and then returned whence he came without speaking. He was soon followed by another, who stripped the sapling of its branches, leaving it a naked and blazed[28] trunk. A third colored the post with stripes of a dark red paint; all which indications of a hostile design in the leaders of the nation were received by the men without in a gloomy and ominous silence. Finally, the Mohican himself reappeared, divested of all his attire except his girdle and leggings, and with one half of his fine features hid under a cloud of threatening black.

Uncas moved with a slow and dignified tread towards the post, which he immediately commenced encircling with a measured step, not unlike an ancient dance, raising his voice, at the same time, in the wild and irregular chant of his war-song. The notes were in the extremes of human sounds; being sometimes melancholy and exquisitely plaintive, even rivaling the melody of birds—and then, by sudden and startling transitions, causing the auditors to tremble by their depth and energy. The words were few and often repeated, proceeding gradually from a sort of invocation, or hymn to the Deity, to an intimation of the warrior's object, and terminating as they commenced with an acknowledgement of his own dependence on the Great Spirit. If it were possible to translate the comprehensive and melodious language in which he spoke, the ode might read something like the following:—

"Manitou! Manitou! Manitou!
Thou art great, thou art good, thou art wise:
Manitou! Manitou!
Thou art just.

---

[28]A tree which has been partially or entirely stripped of its bark is said, in the language of the country, to be "blazed." The term is strictly English; for a horse is said to be blazed when it has a white mark. [J.F.C.]

"In the heavens, in the clouds, O, I see
Many spots—many dark, many red:
In the heavens, O, I see
Many clouds.

"In the woods, in the air, O, I hear
The whoop, the long yell, and the cry:
In the woods, O, I hear
The loud whoop!

"Manitou! Manitou! Manitou!
I am weak—thou art strong; I am slow;
Manitou! Manitou!
Give me aid."

At the end of what might be called each verse he made a pause, by raising a note louder and longer than common, that was peculiarly suited to the sentiment just expressed. The first close was solemn, and intended to convey the idea of veneration; the second descriptive, bordering on the alarming; and the third was the well known and terrific war-whoop, which burst from the lips of the young warrior, like a combination of all the frightful sounds of battle. The last was like the first, humble and imploring. Three times did he repeat this song, and as often did he encircle the post in his dance.

At the close of the first turn, a grave and highly esteemed chief of the Lenape followed his example, singing words of his own, however, to music of a similar character. Warrior after warrior enlisted in the dance, until all of any renown and authority were numbered in its mazes. The spectacle now became wildly terrific; the fierce-looking and menacing visages of the chiefs receiving additional power from the appalling strains in which they mingled their guttural tones. Just then Uncas struck his tomahawk deep into the post, and raised his voice in a shout, which might be termed his own battle-cry. The act announced that he had assumed the chief authority in the intended expedition.

It was a signal that awakened all the slumbering passions of the nation. A hundred youths, who had hiterto been restrained by the diffidence of their years, rushed in a frantic body on the fancied emblem of their enemy, and severed it asunder, splinter by splinter, until nothing remained of the trunk but its roots in the earth. During this moment of tumult, the most ruthless deeds of war were performed on the fragments of the tree, with as much apparent ferocity as if they were the living victims of their cruelty. Some were scalped; some received the keen and trembling axe; and others suffered by thrusts from the fatal knife. In short, the manifestations of zeal and fierce delight were so great and unequivocal, that the expedition was declared to be a war of the nation.

The instant Uncas had struck the blow, he moved out of the circle, and cast his eyes up to the sun, which was just gaining the point, when the truce with Magua was to end. The fact was soon announced by a significant gesture accompanied by a corresponding cry; and the whole of the excited multitude abandoned their mimic warfare, with shrill yells of pleasure, to prepare for the more hazardous experiment of the reality.

The whole face of the encampment was instantly changed. The warriors, who were already armed and painted, became as still as if they were incapable of any uncommon burst of emotion. On the other hand, the women broke out of the lodges, with the songs of joy and those of lamentation, so strangely mingled, that it might have been difficult to have said which passion preponderated. None, however, were idle. Some bore their choicest articles, others their young, and some their aged and infirm, into the forest, which spread itself like a verdant carpet of bright green against the side of the mountain. Thither Tamenund also retired, with calm composure, after a short and touching interview with Uncas; from whom the sage separated with the reluctance that a parent would quit a long lost and just recovered child. In the mean time, Duncan saw Alice to a place of safety, and then sought the scout, with a countenance that denoted how eagerly he also panted for the approaching contest.

But Hawkeye was too much accustomed to the war-song and the enlistments of the natives, to betray any interest in the passing scene. He merely cast an occasional look at the number and quality of the warriors, who, from time to time, signified their readiness to accompany Uncas to the field. In this particular he was soon satisfied; for, as has been already seen, the power of the young chief quickly embraced every fighting man in the nation. After this material point was so satisfactorily decided, he dispatched an Indian boy in quest of Killdeer and the rifle of Uncas, to the place where they had deposited the weapons on approaching the camp of the Delawares; a measure of double policy, inasmuch as it protected the arms from their own fate, if detained as prisoners, and gave them the advantage of appearing among the strangers rather as sufferers than as men provided with the means of defense and subsistence. In selecting another to perform the office of reclaiming his highly prized rifle, the scout had lost sight of none of his habitual caution. He knew that Magua had not come unattended, and he also knew that Huron spies watched the movements of their new enemies, along the whole boundary of the woods. It would, therefore, have been fatal to himself to have attempted the experiment; a warrior would have fared no better; but the danger of a boy would not be likely to commence until after his object was discovered. When Heyward joined him, the scout was coolly awaiting the result of this experiment.

The boy, who had been well instructed, and was sufficiently crafty, proceeded, with a bosom that was swelling with the pride of such a confidence, and all the hopes of young ambition, carelessly across the clearing to the wood, which he entered at a point at some little distance from the place where the guns were secreted. The instant, however, he was concealed by the foliage of the bushes, his dusky form was to be seen gliding, like that of a serpent, towards the desired treasure. He was successful; and in another moment he appeared flying across the narrow opening that skirted the base of the terrace on which the village stood, with the velocity of an arrow, and bearing a prize in each hand. He had actually gained the crags, and was leaping up their sides with incredible activity, when a shot from the woods showed how accurate had been the judgment of the scout. The boy answered it with a feeble but contemptuous shout; and immediately a second bullet was sent after him from another part of the cover. At the next instant he appeared on the level above, elevating his guns in triumph, while he moved with the air of a conqueror towards the renowned hunter who had honored him by so glorious a commission.

Notwithstanding the lively interest Hawkeye had taken in the fate of his messenger, he received Killdeer with a satisfaction that, momentarily, drove all other recollections from his mind. After examining the piece with an intelligent eye, and opening and shutting the pan some ten or fifteen times, and trying sundry other equally important experiments on the lock, he turned to the boy, and demanded with great manifestations of kindness, if he was hurt. The urchin looked proudly up in his face, but made no reply.

"Ah! I see, lad, the knaves have barked your arm!" added the scout, taking up the limb of the patient sufferer, across which a deep flesh wound had been made by one of the bullets; "but a little bruised alder will act like a charm. In the mean time I will wrap it in a badge of wampum! You have commenced the business of a warrior early, my brave boy, and are likely to bear a plenty of honorable scars to your grave. I know many young men that have taken scalps who cannot show such a mark as this. Go!" having bound up the arm; "you will be a chief!"

The lad departed, prouder of his flowing blood than the vainest courtier could be of his blushing ribbon; and stalked among the fellows of his age, an object of general admiration and envy.

But in a moment of so many serious and important duties, this single act of juvenile fortitude did not attract the general notice and commendation it would have received under milder auspices. It had, however, served to apprise the Delawares of the position and the intentions of their enemies. Accordingly a party of adventurers, better suited to the task than the weak though spirited boy, was ordered to dislodge the skulkers. The duty was soon performed; for most of the Hurons retired of themselves when they found they had been discovered. The Delawares followed to a sufficient distance from their own encampment, and then halted for orders, apprehensive of being led into an ambush. As both parties secreted themselves, the woods were again as still and quiet as a mild summer morning and deep solitude could render them.

The calm but still impatient Uncas now collected his chiefs, and divided his power. He presented Hawkeye as a warrior, often tried, and always found deserving of confidence. When he found his friend met with a favorable reception, he bestowed on him the command of twenty men, like himself, active, skillful, and resolute. He gave the Delawares to understand the rank of Heyward among the troops of the Yengeese, and then tendered to him a trust of equal authority. But Duncan declined the charge, professing his readiness to serve as a volunteer by the side of the scout. After this disposition, the young Mohican appointed various native chiefs to fill the different situations of responsibility, and the time pressing, he gave forth the word to march. He was cheerfully, but silently, obeyed by more than two hundred men.

Their entrance into the forest was perfectly unmolested; nor did they encounter any living objects, that could either give the alarm, or furnish the intelligence they needed, until they came upon the lairs of their own scouts. Here a halt was ordered, and the chiefs were assembled to hold a "whispering council."

At this meeting divers plans of operation were suggested, though none of a character to meet the wishes of their ardent leader. Had Uncas followed the promptings of his own inclinations, he would have led his followers to the charge without a moment's delay, and put the conflict to the hazard of an instant issue; but such a course would have been in opposition to all the received practices and opinions of his countrymen. He was, therefore, fain to adopt a caution that in the present temper of his mind he execrated, and to listen to advice at which his fiery spirit chafed, under the vivid recollection of Cora's danger and Magua's insolence.

After an unsatisfactory conference of many minutes, a solitary individual was seen advancing from the side of the enemy, with such apparent haste, as to induce the belief he might be a messenger charged with pacific overtures. When within a hundred yards, however, of the cover behind which the Delaware council had assembled, the stranger hestitated, appeared uncertain what course to take, and finally halted. All eyes were now turned on Uncas, as if seeking directions how to proceed.

"Hawkeye," said the young chief, in a low voice, "he must never speak to the Hurons again."

"His time has come," said the laconic scout, thrusting the long barrel of his rifle through the leaves, and taking his deliberate and fatal aim. But, instead of pulling the trigger, he lowered the muzzle again, and indulged himself in a fit of his peculiar mirth. "I took the imp for a Mingo, as I'm a miserable sinner!" he said; "but when my eye ranged along his ribs for a place to get the bullet in—would you think it, Uncas?—I saw the musicianer's blower; and so, after all, it is the man they call Gamut, whose death can profit no one, and whose life, if his tongue can do anything but sing, may be made serviceable to our own ends. If sounds have not lost their virtue, I'll soon have a discourse with the honest fellow, and that in a voice he'll find more agreeable than the speech of Killdeer."

So saying, Hawkeye laid aside his rifle; and crawling through the bushes until within hearing of David, he attempted to repeat the musical effort, which had conducted himself, with so much safety and *éclat*, through the Huron encampment. The exquisite organs of Gamut could not readily be deceived (and, to say the truth, it would have been difficult for any other than Hawkeye to produce a similar noise), and consequently, having once before heard the sounds, he now knew whence they proceeded. The poor fellow appeared relieved from a state of great embarrassment; for pursuing the direction of the voice—a task that to him was not much less arduous than it would have been to have gone up in the face of a battery—he soon discovered the hidden songster.

"I wonder what the Hurons will think of that!" said the scout, laughing, as he took his companion by the arm, and urged him towards the rear. "If the knaves lie within ear-shot, they will say there are two non-compossers instead of one! But here we are safe," he added, pointing to Uncas and his associates. "Now give us the history of the Mingo inventions in natural English, and without any ups and downs of voice."

David gazed about him, at the fierce and wild-looking chiefs, in mute wonder; but assured by the presence of faces that he knew, he soon rallied his faculties so far as to make an intelligent reply.

"The heathen are abroad in goodly numbers," said David, "and, I fear, with evil intent. There has been much howling and ungodly revelry, together with such sounds as it is profanity to utter, in their habitations within the past hour; so much so, in truth, that I have fled to the Delawares in search of peace."

"Your ears might not have profited much by the exchange, had you been quicker of foot," returned the scout a little dryly. "But let that be as it may; where are the Hurons?"

"They lie hid in the forest, between this spot and their village, in such force, that prudence would teach you instantly to return."

Uncas cast a glance along the range of trees which concealed his own band and mentioned the name of—

"Magua?"

"Is among them. He brought in the maiden that had sojourned with the Delawares, and leaving her in the cave, has put himself, like a raging wolf, at the head of his savages. I know not what has troubled his spirit so greatly!"

"He has left her, you say, in the cave!" interrupted Heyward; "'t is well that we know its situation! May not something be done for her instant relief?"

Uncas looked earnestly at the scout, before he asked,—

"What says Hawkeye?"

"Give me my twenty rifles, and I will turn to the right, along the stream; and passing by the huts of the beaver, will join the Sagamore and the colonel. You shall then hear the whoop from that quarter; with this wind one may easily send it a mile. Then, Uncas, do you drive in their front; when they come within range of our pieces, we will give them a blow that, I pledge the good name of an old frontiersman, shall make their line bend like an ashen bow. After which, we will carry their village, and take the woman from the cave; when the affair may be finished with the tribe, according to a white man's battle, by a blow and a victory; or, in the Indian fashion, with dodge and cover. There may be no great learning, Major, in this plan, but with courage and patience it can all be done."

"I like it much," cried Duncan, who saw that the release of Cora was the primary object in the mind of the scout; "I like it much. Let it be instantly attempted."

After a short conference, the plan was matured, and rendered more intelligible to the several parties; the different signals were appointed, and the chiefs separated, each to his allotted station.

CHAPTER XXXII

But plagues shall spread, and funeral fires increase,
Till the great king, without a ransom paid,
To her own Chrysa send the black-eyed maid.
POPE'S *Iliad.*

During the time Uncas was making this disposition of his forces, the woods were as still, and, with the exception of those who had met in council, apparently as much untenanted, as when they came fresh from the hands of their Almighty Creator. The eye could range in every direction through the long and shadowed vistas of the trees; but nowhere was any object to be seen that did not properly belong to the peaceful and slumbering scenery. Here and there a bird was heard fluttering among the branches of the beeches, and occasionally a squirrel dropped a nut, drawing the startled looks of the party, for a moment, to the place; but the instant the casual interruption ceased, the passing air was heard murmuring above their heads, along that verdant and undulating surface of forest which spread itself unbroken, unless by stream or lake, over such a vast region of country. Across the tract of wilderness which lay between the Delawares and the village of their enemies, it seemed as if the foot of man had never trodden, so breathing and deep was the silence in which it lay. But Hawkeye, whose duty led him foremost in the adventure, knew the character of those with whom he was about to contend too well to trust the treacherous quiet.

When he saw his little band collected, the scout threw Killdeer into the hollow of his arm, and making a silent signal that he would be followed, he led them many rods towards the rear, into the bed of a little brook which they had crossed in advancing. Here he halted, and after waiting for the whole of his grave and attentive warriors to close about him, he spoke in Delaware, demanding,—

"Do any of my young men know whither this run will lead us?"

A Delaware stretched forth a hand, with the two fingers separated, and indicating the manner in which they were joined at the root, he answered,—

"Before the sun could go his own length, the little water will be in the big." Then he added, pointing in the direction of the place he mentioned, "The two make enough for the beavers."

"I thought as much," returned the scout, glancing his eye upwards at the opening in the tree-tops, "from the course it takes, and the bearings of the mountains. Men, we will keep within the cover of its banks till we scent the Hurons."

His companions gave the usual brief exclamation of assent, but perceiving that their leader was about to lead the way in person, one or two made signs that all was not as it should be. Hawkeye, who comprehended their meaning glances, turned, and perceived that his party had been followed thus far by the singing-master.

"Do you know, friend," asked the scout gravely, and perhaps with a little of the pride of conscious deserving in his manner, "that this is a band of rangers chosen for the most desperate service, and put under the command of one who, though another might say it with a better face, will not be apt to leave them idle. It may not be five, it cannot be thirty minutes before we tread on the body of a Huron, living or dead."

"Though not admonished of your intentions in words," returned David, whose face was a little flushed, and whose ordinarily quiet and unmeaning eyes glimmered with an expression of unusual fire, "your men have reminded me of the children of Jacob going out to battle against the Shechemites, for wickedly aspiring to wedlock with a woman of a race that was favored of the Lord. Now, I have journeyed far, and sojourned much in good and evil with the maiden ye seek; and though not a man of war, with my loins girded and my sword sharpened, yet would I gladly strike a blow in her behalf."

The scout hesitated, as if weighing the chances of such a strange enlistment in his mind before he answered,—

"You know not the use of any we'pon. You carry no rifle; and believe me, what the Mingoes take they will freely give again."

"Though not a vaunting and bloodily disposed Goliath," returned David, drawing a sling from beneath his parti-colored and uncouth attire, "I have not forgotten the example of the Jewish boy. With this ancient instrument of war have I practiced much in my youth, and peradventure the skill has not entirely departed from me."

"Aye!" said Hawkeye, considering the deer-skin thong and apron, with a cold and discouraging eye; "the thing might do its work among arrows, or even knives; but these Mengwe have been furnished by the Frenchers with a good grooved barrel a man. However, it seems to be your gift to go unharmed amid fire; and as you have hitherto been favored—Major, you have left your rifle at a cock; a single shot before the time would be just twenty scalps lost to no purpose—singer, you can follow; we may find use for you in the shoutings."

"I thank you, friend," returned David, supplying himself, like his royal namesake, from among the pebbles of the brook; "though not given to the desire to kill, had you sent me away my spirit would have been troubled."

"Remember," added the scout, tapping his own head significantly on that spot where Gamut was yet sore, "we come to fight, and not to musickate. Until the general whoop is given, nothing speaks but the rifle."

David nodded, as much as to signify his acquiescence with the terms; and then Hawkeye, casting another observant glance over his followers, made the signal to proceed.

Their route lay, for the distance of a mile, along the bed of the water-course. Though protected from any great danger of observation by the precipitous banks, and the thick shrubbery which skirted the stream, no precaution known to an Indian attack was neglected. A warrior rather crawled than walked on each flank, so as to catch occasional glimpses into the forest; and every few minutes the band came to a halt, and listened for hostile sounds, with an acuteness of organs that would be scarcely conceivable to a man in a less natural state. Their march was, however, unmolested, and they reached the point where the lesser stream was lost in the greater, without the smallest evidence that their progress had been noted. Here the scout again halted, to consult the signs of the forest.

"We are likely to have a good day for a fight," he said, in English, addressing Heyward, and glancing his eye upwards at the clouds, which began to move in broad sheets across the firmament; "a bright sun and a glittering barrel are no friends to true sight. Everything is favorable; they have the wind, which will bring down their noises and their smoke too, no little matter in itself; whereas with us it will be first a shot and then a clear view. But here is an end of our cover; the beavers have had the range of this stream for hundreds of years, and what atween their food and their dams, there is, as you see, many a girdled stub, but few living trees."

Hawkeye had, in truth, in these few words, given no bad description of the prospect that now lay in their front. The brook was irregular in its width, sometimes shooting through narrow fissures in the rocks, and at others spreading over acres of bottom land, forming little areas that might be termed ponds. Everywhere along its banks were the mouldering relics of dead trees, in all the stages of decay, from those that groaned on their tottering trunks to such as had recently been robbed of those rugged coats that so mysteriously contain their principle of life. A few long, low, and moss-covered piles were scattered among them, like the memorials of a former and long-departed generation.

All these minute particulars were noted by the scout, with a gravity and interest that they probably had never before attracted. He knew that the Huron encampment lay a short half mile up the brook; and, with the characteristic anxiety of one who dreaded a hidden danger, he was greatly troubled at not finding the smallest trace of the presence of his enemy. Once or twice he felt induced to give the order for a rush, and to attempt the village by surprise, but his experience quickly admonished him of the danger of so useless an experiment. Then he listened intently, and with painful uncertainty, for the sounds of hostility in the quarter where Uncas was left; but nothing was audible except the sighing of the wind, that began to sweep over the bosom of the forest in gusts which threatened a tempest. At length, yielding rather to his unusual impatience than taking counsel from his knowledge, he determined to bring matters to an issue, by unmasking his force, and proceeding cautiously, but steadily, up the stream.

The scout had stood, while making his observations, sheltered by a brake, and his companions still lay in the bed of the ravine, through which the smaller stream debouched; but on hearing his low, though intelligible signal, the whole party stole up the bank, like so many dark spectres, and silently arranged themselves around him. Pointing in the direction he wished to proceed, Hawkeye advanced, the band breaking off in single files, and following so accurately in his footsteps, as to leave it, if we except Heyward and David, the trail of but a single man.

The party was, however, scarcely uncovered before a volley from a dozen rifles was heard in their rear; and a Delaware leaping high into the air, like a wounded deer, fell at his whole length, perfectly dead.

"Ah! I feared some deviltry like this!" exclaimed the scout, in English; adding, with the quickness of thought, in his adopted tongue, "To cover, men, and charge!"

The band dispersed at the word, and before Heyward had well recovered from his surprise, he found himself standing alone with David. Luckily, the Hurons had already fallen back, and he was safe from their fire. But this state of things was evidently to be of short continuance; for the scout set the example of pressing on their retreat, by discharging his rifle, and darting from tree to tree as his enemy slowly yielded ground.

It would seem that the assault had been made by a very small party of the Hurons, which, however, continued to increase in numbers, as it retired on its friends, until the return fire was very nearly, if not quite, equal to that maintained by the advancing Delawares. Heyward threw himself among the combatants, and imitating the necessary caution of his companions, he made quick discharges with his own rifle. The contest now grew warm and stationary. Few were injured, as both parties kept their bodies as much protected as possible by the trees; never, indeed, exposing any part of their persons except in the act of taking aim. But the chances were gradually growing unfavorable to Hawkeye and his band. The quick-sighted scout perceived his danger, without knowing how to remedy it. He saw it was more dangerous to retreat than to maintain his ground; while he found his enemy throwing out men on his flank, which rendered the task of keeping themselves covered so very difficult to the Delawares, as nearly to silence their fire. At this embarrassing moment, when they began to think the whole of the hostile tribe was gradually encircling them, they heard the yell of combatants, and the rattling of arms, echoing under the arches of the wood, at the place where Uncas was posted; a bottom which, in a manner, lay beneath the ground on which Hawkeye and his party were contending.

The effects of this attack were instantaneous, and to the scout and his friends greatly relieving. It would seem that, while his own surprise had been anticipated, and had consequently failed, the enemy, in their turn, having been deceived in its object and in his numbers, had left too small a force to resist the impetuous onset of the young Mohican. This fact was doubly apparent, by the rapid manner in which the battle in the forest rolled upwards towards the village, and by an instant falling off in the number of their assailants, who rushed to assist in maintaining the front, and, as it now proved to be, the principal point of defense.

Animating his followers by his voice and his own example, Hawkeye then gave the word to bear down upon their foes. The charge, in that rude species of warfare, consisted merely in pushing from cover to cover, nigher to the enemy; and in this manœuvre he was instantly and successfully obeyed. The Hurons were compelled to withdraw, and the scene of the contest rapidly changed from the more open ground on which it had commenced, to a spot where the assailed found a thicket to rest upon. Here the struggle was protracted, arduous, and seemingly of doubtful issue; the Delawares, though none of them fell, beginning to bleed freely, in consequence of the disadvantage at which they were held.

In this crisis, Hawkeye found means to get behind the same tree as that which served for a cover to Heyward; most of his own combatants being within call, a little on his right, where they maintained rapid, though fruitless, discharges on their sheltered enemies.

"You are a young man, Major," said the scout, dropping the butt of Killdeer to the earth, and leaning on the barrel, a little fatigued with his previous industry; "and it may be your gift to lead armies, at some future day, agin these imps, the Mingoes. You may here see the philosophy of an Indian fight. It consists, mainly, in a ready hand, a quick eye, and a good cover. Now, if you had a company of the Royal Americans here, in what manner would you set them to work in this business?"

"The bayonet would make a road."

"Aye, there is white reason in what you say; but a man must ask himself, in this wilderness, how many lives he can spare. No—horse,"[29] continued the scout, shaking his head, like one who mused; "horse, I am ashamed to say, must, sooner or later, decide these skrimmages. The brutes are better than men, and to horse must we come at last. Put a shodden hoof on the moccasin of a red-skin; and if his rifle be once emptied, he will never stop to load it again."

"This is a subject that might better be discussed at another time," returned Heyward; "shall we charge?"

"I see no contradiction to the gifts of any man, in passing his breathing spells in useful reflections," the scout replied. "As to a rush, I little relish such a measure; for a scalp or two must be thrown away in the attempt. And yet," he added, bending his head aside, to catch the sounds of the distant combat, "if we are to be of use to Uncas, these knaves in our front must be got rid of!"

Then turning, with a prompt and decided air, he called aloud to his Indians, in their own language. His words were answered by a shout; and, at a given signal, each warrior made a swift movement around his particular tree. The sight of so many dark bodies, glancing before their eyes at the same instant, drew a hasty, and consequently an ineffectual fire from the Hurons. Without stopping to breathe, the Delawares leaped in long bounds towards the wood, like so many panthers springing upon their prey. Hawkeye was in front, brandishing his terrible rifle, and animating his followers by his example. A few of the older and more cunning Hurons, who had not been deceived by the artifice which had been practiced to draw their fire, now made a close and deadly discharge of their pieces, and justified the apprehensions of the scout, by felling three of his foremost warriors. But the shock was insufficient to repel the impetus of the charge. The Delawares broke into the cover with the ferocity of their natures, and swept away every trace of resistance by the fury of the onset.

The combat endured only for an instant, hand to hand, and then the assailed yielded ground rapidly, until they reached the opposite margin of the thicket, where they clung to the cover, with the sort of obstinacy that is so often witnessed in hunted brutes. At this critical moment, when the success of the struggle was again becoming doubtful, the crack of a rifle was heard behind the Hurons, and a

---

[29]The American forest admits of the passage of horse, there being little underbrush and few tangled brakes. The plan of Hawkeye is the one which has always proved the most successful in the battles between the whites and the Indians. Wayne, in his celebrated campaign on the Miami, received the fire of his enemies in line; and then causing his dragoons to wheel round his flanks, the Indians were driven from their covers before they had time to load. One of the most conspicuous of the chiefs who fought in the battle of Miami assured the writer that the red-men could not fight the warriors with "long knives and leather-stockings;" meaning the dragoons with their sabres and boots. [J.F.C.]

bullet came whizzing from among some beaver lodges, which were situated in the clearing, in their rear, and was followed by the fierce and appalling yell of the war-whoop.

"There speaks the Sagamore!" shouted Hawkeye, answering the cry with his own stentorian voice; "we have them now in face and back!"

The effect on the Hurons was instantaneous. Discouraged by an assault from a quarter that left them no opportunity for cover, their warriors uttered a common yell of disappointment, and breaking off in a body, they spread themselves across the opening, heedless of every consideration but flight. Many fell, in making the experiment, under the bullets and the blows of the pursuing Delawares.

We shall not pause to detail the meeting between the scout and Chingachgook, or the more touching interview that Duncan held with Munro. A few brief and hurried words served to explain the state of things to both parties; and then Hawkeye, pointing out the Sagamore to his band, resigned the chief authority into the hands of the Mohican chief. Chingachgook assumed the station to which his birth and experience gave him so distinguished a claim, with the grave dignity that always gives force to the mandates of a native warrior. Following the footsteps of the scout, he led the party back through the thicket, his men scalping the fallen Hurons, and secreting the bodies of their own dead as they proceeded, until they gained a point where the former was content to make a halt.

The warriors, who had breathed themselves freely in the preceding struggle, were now posted on a bit of level ground, sprinkled with trees in sufficient numbers to conceal them. The land fell away rather precipitately in front, and beneath their eyes stretched, for several miles, a narrow, dark, and wooded vale. It was through this dense and dark forest that Uncas was still contending with the main body of the Hurons.

The Mohican and his friends advanced to the brow of the hill, and listened, with practiced ears, to the sounds of the combat. A few birds hovered over the leafy bosom of the valley, frightened from their secluded nests; and here and there a light vapory cloud, which seemed already blending with the atmosphere, arose above the trees, and indicated some spot where the struggle had been fierce and stationary.

"The fight is coming up the ascent," said Duncan, pointing in the direction of a new explosion of fire-arms; "we are too much in the centre of their line to be effective."

"They will incline into the hollow, where the cover is thicker," said the scout, "and that will leave us well on their flank. Go, Sagamore; you will hardly be in time to give the whoop, and lead on the young men. I will fight this skrimmage with warriors of my own color. You know me, Mohican; not a Huron of them all shall cross the swell, into your rear, without the notice of Killdeer."

The Indian chief paused another moment to consider the signs of the contest, which was now rolling rapidly up the ascent, a certain evidence that the Delawares triumphed; nor did he actually quit the place until admonished of the proximity of his friends, as well as enemies, by the bullets of the former, which began to patter among the dried leaves on the ground, like the bits of falling hail which precede the bursting of the tempest. Hawkeye and his three companions withdrew a few paces to a shelter, and awaited the issue with calmness, that nothing but great practice could impart in such a scene.

It was not long before the reports of the rifles began to lose the echoes of the woods, and to sound like weapons discharged in the open air. Then a warrior appeared, here and there, driven to the skirts of the forest, and rallying as he entered the clearing, as at the place where the final stand was to be made. These were soon joined by others, until a long line of swarthy figures was to be seen clinging to the cover with the obstinacy of desperation. Heyward began to grow impatient, and turned his eyes anxiously in the direction of Chingachgook. The chief was seated on a rock, with nothing visible but his calm visage, considering the spectacle with an eye as deliberate as if he were posted there merely to view the struggle.

"The time is come for the Delaware to strike!" said Duncan.

"Not so, not so," returned the scout; "when he scents his friends, he will let them know that he is here. See, see; the knaves are getting in that clump of pines, like bees settling after their flight. By the Lord, a squaw might put a bullet into the centre of such a knot of dark skins."

At that instant the whoop was given, and a dozen Hurons fell by a discharge from Chingachgook and his band. The shout that followed was answered by a single war-cry from the forest, and a yell passed through the air that sounded as if a thousand throats were united in a common effort. The Hurons staggered, deserting the centre of their line, and Uncas issued from the forest through the opening they left, at the head of a hundred warriors.

Waving his hands right and left, the young chief pointed out the enemy to his followers, who separated in pursuit. The war now divided, both wings of the broken Hurons seeking protection in the woods again, hotly pressed by the victorious warriors of the Lenape. A minute might have passed, but the sounds were already receding in different directions, and gradually losing their distinctness beneath the echoing arches of the woods. One little knot of Hurons, however, had disdained to seek a cover, and were retiring, like lions at bay, slowly and sullenly up the acclivity which Chingachgook and his band had just deserted, to mingle more closely in the fray. Magua was conspicuous in this party, both by his fierce and savage mien, and by the air of haughty authority he yet maintained.

In his eagerness to expedite the pursuit, Uncas had left himself nearly alone; but the moment his eye caught the figure of Le Subtil, every other consideration was forgotten. Raising his cry of battle, which recalled some six or seven warriors, and reckless of the disparity of their numbers, he rushed upon his enemy. Le Renard, who watched the movement, paused to receive him with secret joy. But at the moment when he thought the rashness of his impetuous young assailant had left him at his mercy, another shout was given, and "La Longue Carabine" was seen rushing to the rescue, attended by all his white associates. The Huron instantly turned, and commenced a rapid retreat up the ascent.

There was no time for greetings or congratulations; for Uncas, though unconscious of the presence of his friends, continued the pursuit with the velocity of the wind. In vain Hawkeye called to him to respect the covers; the young Mohican braved the dangerous fire of his enemies and soon compelled them to a flight as swift as his own headlong speed. It was fortunate that the race was of short continuance, and that the white men were much favored by their position, or the Delaware would soon have outstripped all his companions, and fallen a victim to his own temerity. But ere such a calamity could happen, the pursuers and pursued entered the Wyandot village, within striking distance of each other.

Excited by the presence of their dwellings, and tired of the chase, the Hurons now made a stand, and fought around their council-lodge with the fury of despair. The onset and the issue were like the passage and destruction of a whirlwind. The tomahawk of Uncas, the blows of Hawkeye, and even the still nervous arm of Munro, were all busy for that passing moment, and the ground was quickly strewed with their enemies. Still Magua, though daring and much exposed, escaped from every effort against his life, with that sort of fabled protection that was made to overlook the fortunes of favored heroes in the legends of ancient poetry. Raising a yell that spoke volumes of anger and disappointment, the subtle chief, when he saw his comrades fallen, darted away from the place, attended by his two only surviving friends, leaving the Delawares engaged in stripping the dead of the bloody trophies of their victory.

But Uncas, who had vainly sought him in the mêlée, bounded forward in pursuit; Hawkeye, Heyward, and David still pressing on his footsteps. The utmost that the scout could effect was to keep the muzzle of his rifle a little in advance of his friend, to whom, however, it answered every purpose of a charmed shield. Once Magua appeared disposed to make another and a final effort to revenge his losses; but, abandoning his intention as soon as demonstrated, he leaped into a thicket of bushes, through which he was followed by his enemies, and suddenly entered the mouth of the cave already known to the reader. Hawkeye, who had only forborne to fire in tenderness to Uncas, raised a shout of success, and proclaimed aloud that now they were certain of their game. The pursuers dashed into the long and narrow entrance, in time to catch a glimpse of the retreating forms of the Hurons. Their passage through the natural galleries and subterraneous apartments of the cavern was preceded by the shrieks and cries of hundreds of women and children. The place, seen by its dim and uncertain light, appeared like the shades of the infernal regions, across which unhappy ghosts and savage demons were flitting in multitudes.

Still Uncas kept his eye on Magua, as if life to him possessed but a single object. Heyward and the scout still pressed on his rear, actuated, though possibly in a less degree, by a common feeling. But their way was becoming intricate, in those dark and gloomy passages, and the glimpses of the retiring warriors less distinct and frequent; and for a moment the trace was believed to be lost, when a white robe was seen fluttering in the further extremity of a passage that seemed to lead up the mountain.

"'T is Cora!" exclaimed Heyward, in a voice in which horror and delight were wildly mingled.

"Cora! Cora!" echoed Uncas, bounding forward like a deer.

"'T is the maiden!" shouted the scout. "Courage, lady; we come!—we come!"

The chase was renewed with a diligence rendered tenfold encouraging by this glimpse of the captive. But the way was rugged, broken, and in spots nearly impassable. Uncas abandoned his rifle, and leaped forward with headlong precipitation. Heyward rashly imitated his example, though both were, a moment afterwards, admonished of its madness, by hearing the bellowing of a piece that the Hurons found time to discharge down the passage in the rocks, the bullet from which even gave the young Mohican a slight wound.

"We must close!" said the scout, passing his friends by a desperate leap; "the knaves will pick us all off at this distance; and see, they hold the maiden so as to shield themselves!"

Though his words were unheeded, or rather unheard, his example was followed by his companions, who, by incredible exertions, got near enough to the fugitives to perceive that Cora was borne along between the two warriors, while Magua prescribed the direction and manner of their flight. At this moment the forms of all four were strongly drawn against an opening in the sky, and they disappeared. Nearly frantic with disappointment, Uncas and Heyward increased efforts that already seemed superhuman, and they issued from the cavern on the side of the mountain in time to note the route of the pursued. The course lay up the ascent, and still continued hazardous and laborious.

Encumbered by his rifle, and, perhaps, not sustained by so deep an interest in the captive as his companions, the scout suffered the latter to precede him a little, Uncas, in his turn, taking the lead of Heyward. In this manner, rocks, precipices, and difficulties were surmounted in an incredibly short space, that at another time, and under other circumstances, would have been deemed almost insuperable. But the impetuous young men were rewarded by finding that, encumbered with Cora, the Hurons were losing ground in the race.

"Stay, dog of the Wyandots!" exclaimed Uncas, shaking his bright tomahawk at Magua; "a Delaware girl calls stay!"

"I will go no further," cried Cora, stopping unexpectedly on a ledge of rocks, that overhung a deep precipice, at no great distance from the summit of the mountain. "Kill me if thou wilt, detestable Huron; I will go no further."

The supporters of the maiden raised their ready tomahawks with the impious joy that fiends are thought to take in mischief, but Magua stayed the uplifted arms. The Huron chief, after casting the weapons he had wrested from his companions over the rock, drew his knife, and turned to his captive, with a look in which conflicting passions fiercely contended.

"Woman," he said, "choose; the wigwam or the knife of Le Subtil!"

Cora regarded him not, but dropping on her knees, she raised her eyes and stretched her arms towards heaven, saying, in a meek and yet confiding voice,—

"I am thine! do with me as thou seest best!"

"Woman," repeated Magua, hoarsely, and endeavoring in vain to catch a glance from her serene and beaming eye, "choose!"

But Cora neither heard nor heeded his demand. The form of the Huron trembled in every fibre, and he raised his arm on high, but dropped it again with a bewildered air, like one who doubted. Once more he struggled with himself and lifted the keen weapon again; but just then a piercing cry was heard above them, and Uncas appeared, leaping frantically, from a fearful height, upon the ledge. Magua recoiled a step; and one of his assistants, profiting by the chance, sheathed his own knife in the bosom of Cora.

The Huron sprang like a tiger on his offending and already retreating countryman, but the falling form of Uncas separated the unnatural combatants. Diverted from his object by this interruption, and maddened by the murder he had just witnessed, Magua buried his weapon in the back of the prostrate Delaware, uttering an unearthly shout as he committed the dastardly deed. But Uncas arose from the blow, as the wounded panther turns upon his foe, and struck the murderer of Cora to his feet, by an effort in which the last of his failing strength was expended. Then, with a stern and steady look, he turned to Le Subtil, and indicated by the expression of his eye all that he would do, had not the power deserted him. The latter seized the nerveless arm of the unresisting Delaware, and passed his knife into his bosom three several times, before his victim, still keeping his gaze riveted on his enemy with a look of inextinguishable scorn, fell dead at his feet.

"Mercy! mercy! Huron," cried Heyward, from above, in tones nearly choked by horror; "give mercy, and thou shalt receive it!"

Whirling the bloody knife up at the imploring youth, the victorius Magua uttered a cry so fierce, so wild, and yet so joyous, that it conveyed the sounds of savage triumph to the ears of those who fought in the valley, a thousand feet below. He was answered by a burst from the lips of the scout, whose tall person was just then seen moving swiftly towards him, along those dangerous crags, with steps as bold and reckless as if he possessed the power to move in air. But when the hunter reached the scene of the ruthless massacre, the ledge was tenanted only by the dead.

His keen eye took a single look at the victims, and then shot its glances over the difficulties of the ascent in his front. A form stood at the brow of the mountain, on the very edge of the giddy height, with uplifted arms, in an awful attitude of menace. Without stopping to consider his person, the rifle of Hawkeye was raised; but a rock, which fell on the head of one of the fugitives below exposed the indignant and glowing countenance of the honest Gamut. Then Magua issued from a crevice, and stepping with calm indifference over the body of the last of his associates, he leaped a wide fissure, and ascended the rocks at a point where the arm of David could not reach him. A single bound would carry him to the brow of the precipice, and assure his safety. Before taking the leap, however, the Huron paused, and shaking his hand at the scout, he shouted,—

"The pale-faces are dogs! the Delawares women! Magua leaves them on the rocks, for the crows!"

Laughing hoarsely, he made a desperate leap, and fell short of his mark, though his hands grasped a shrub on the verge of the height. The form of Hawkeye had crouched like a beast about to take its spring, and his frame trembled so violently with eagerness, that the muzzle of the half-raised rifle played like a leaf fluttering in the wind. Without exhausting himself with fruitless efforts, the cunning Magua suffered his body to drop to the length of his arms, and found a fragment for his feet to rest on. Then summoning all his powers, he renewed the attempt, and so far succeeded as to draw his knees on the edge of the mountain. It was now, when the body of his enemy was most collected together, that the agitated weapon of the scout was drawn to his shoulder. The surrounding rocks themselves were not steadier than the piece became, for the single instant that it poured out its contents. The arms of the Huron relaxed, and his body fell back a little, while his knees still kept their position. Turning a relentless look on his enemy, he shook a hand in grim defiance. But his hold loosened, and his dark person was seen cutting the air with its head downwards, for a fleeting instant, until it glided past the fringe of shrubbery which clung to the mountain, in its rapid flight to destruction.

CHAPTER XXXIII

They fought, like brave men, long and well;
They piled that ground with Moslem slain,
They conquered—but Bozzaris fell,
Bleeding at every vein.
His few surviving comrades saw
His smile when rang their proud hurrah,
And the red field was won;
Then saw in death his eyelids close
Calmly, as to a night's repose,
Like flowers at set of sun.

FITZ-GREENE HALLECK, *Marco Bozzaris.*

The sun found the Lenape, on the succeeding day, a nation of mourners. The sounds of the battle were over, and they had fed fat their ancient grudge, and had avenged their recent quarrel with the Mengwe, by the destruction of a whole community. The black and murky atmosphere that floated around the spot where the Hurons had encamped, sufficiently announced, of itself, the fate of that wandering tribe; while hundreds of ravens, that struggled above the bleak summits of the mountains, or swept, in noisy flocks, across the wide ranges of the woods, furnished a frightful direction to the scene of the combat. In short, any eye, at all practiced in the signs of a frontier warfare, might easily have traced all those unerring evidences of the ruthless results which attend an Indian vengeance.

Still, the sun rose on the Lenape a nation of mourners. No shouts of success, no songs of triumph, were heard, in rejoicings for their victory. The latest straggler had returned from his fell employment, only to strip himself of the terrific emblems of his bloody calling, and to join in the lamentations of his countrymen, as a stricken people. Pride and exultation were supplanted by humility, and the fiercest of human passions was already succeeded by the most profound and unequivocal demonstrations of grief.

The lodges were deserted; but a broad belt of earnest faces encircled a spot in their vicinity, whither everything possessing life had repaired, and where all were now collected, in deep and awful silence. Though beings of every rank and age, of both sexes, and of all pursuits, had united to form this breathing wall of bodies, they were influenced by a single emotion. Each eye was riveted on the centre of that ring, which contained the objects of so much, and of so common, an interest.

Six Delaware girls, with their long, dark, flowing tresses falling loosely across their bosoms, stood apart, and only gave proofs of their existence as they occasionally strewed sweet-scented herbs and forest flowers on a litter of fragrant plants, that, under a pall of Indian robes, supported all that now remained of the ardent, high-souled, and generous Cora. Her form was concealed in many wrappers of the same simple manufacture, and her face was shut forever from the gaze of men. At her feet was seated the desolate Munro. His aged head was bowed nearly to the earth, in compelled submission to the stroke of Providence; but a hidden anguish struggled about his furrowed brow, that was only partially concealed by the careless locks of gray that had fallen, neglected, on his temples. Gamut stood at his side, his meek head bared to the rays of the sun, while his eyes, wandering and concerned, seemed to be equally divided between that little volume which contained so many quaint but holy maxims, and the being in whose behalf his soul yearned to administer consolation. Heyward was also nigh, supporting himself against a tree, and endeavoring to keep down those sudden risings of sorrow that it required his utmost manhood to subdue.

But sad and melancholy as this group may easily be imagined, it was far less touching than another, that occupied the opposite space of the same area. Seated as in life, with his form and limbs arranged in grave and decent composure, Uncas appeared, arrayed in the most gorgeous ornaments that the wealth of the tribe could furnish. Rich plumes nodded above his head; wampum, gorgets, bracelets, and medals adorned his person in profusion; though his dull eye and vacant lineaments too strongly contradicted the idle tale of pride they would convey.

Directly in front of the corpse Chingachgook was placed, without arms, paint, or adornment of any sort, except the bright blue blazonry of his race, that was indelibly impressed on his naked bosom. During the long period that the tribe had been thus collected, the Mohican warrior had kept a steady, anxious look on the cold and senseless countenance of his son. So riveted and intense had been that gaze, and so changeless his attitude, that a stranger might not have told the living from the dead, but for the occasional gleamings of a troubled spirit that shot athwart the dark visage of one, and the death-like calm that had forever settled on the lineaments of the other.

The scout was hard by, leaning in a pensive posture on his own fatal and avenging weapon; while Tamenund, supported by the elders of his nation, occupied a high place at hand, whence he might look down on the mute and sorrowful assemblage of his people.

Just within the inner edge of the circle stood a soldier, in the military attire of a strange nation; and without it was his warhorse, in the centre of a collection of mounted domestics, seemingly in readiness to undertake some distant journey. The vestments of the stranger announced him to be one who held a responsible situation near the person of the captain of the Canadas; and who, as it would now seem, finding his errand of peace frustrated by the fierce impetuosity of his allies, was content to become a silent and sad spectator of the fruits of a contest that he had arrived too late to anticipate.

The day was drawing to the close of its first quarter, and yet had the multitude maintained its breathing stillness since its dawn. No sound louder than a stifled sob had been heard among them, nor had even a limb been moved throughout that long and painful period, except to perform the simple and touching offerings that were made, from time to time, in commemoration of the dead. The patience and forbearance of Indian fortitude could alone support such an appearance of abstraction as seemed now to have turned each dark and motionless figure into stone.

At length, the sage of the Delawares stretched forth an arm, and leaning on the shoulders of his attendants, he arose with an air as feeble as if another age had already intervened between the man who had met his nation the preceding day, and him who now tottered on his elevated stand.

"Men of the Lenape!" he said, in hollow tones that sounded like a voice charged with some prophetic mission; "the face of the Manitou is behind a cloud! his eye is turned from you; his ears are shut; his tongue gives no answer. You see Him not; yet his judgments are before you. Let your hearts be open and your spirits tell no lie. Men of the Lenape! the face of the Manitou is behind a cloud."

As this simple and yet terrible annunciation stole on the ears of the multitude, a stillness as deep and awful succeeded as if the venerated spirit they worshipped had uttered the words without the aid of human organs; and even the inanimate Uncas appeared a being of life, compared with the humbled and submissive throng by whom he was surrounded. As the immediate effect, however, gradually passed away, a low murmur of voices commenced a sort of chant in honor of the dead. The sounds were those of females, and were thrillingly soft and wailing. The words were connected by no regular continuation, but as one ceased another took up the eulogy, or lamentation, whichever it might be called, and gave vent to her emotions in such language as was suggested by her feelings and the occasion. At intervals the speaker was interrupted by general and loud bursts of sorrow, during which the girls around the bier of Cora plucked the plants and flowers blindly from her body, as if bewildered with grief. But, in the milder moments of their plaint, these emblems of purity and sweetness were cast back to their places, with every sign of tenderness and regret. Though rendered less connected by many and general interruptions and outbreakings, a translation of their language would have contained a regular descant, which, in substance, might have proved to possess a train of consecutive ideas.

A girl, selected for the task by her rank and qualifications, commenced by modest allusions to the qualities of the deceased warrior, embellishing her expressions with those oriental images that the Indians have probably brought with them from the extremes of the other continent, and which form of themselves a link to connect the ancient histories of the two worlds. She called him the "panther of his tribe;" and described him as one whose moccasin left no trail on the dews; whose bound was like the leap of the young fawn; whose eye was brighter than a star in the dark night; and whose voice, in battle, was loud as the thunder of the Manitou. She reminded him of the mother who bore him, and dwelt forcibly on the happiness she must feel in possessing such a son. She bade him tell her, when they met in the world of spirits, that the Delaware girls had shed tears above the grave of her child, and had called her blessed.

Then they who succeeded, changing their tones to a milder and still more tender strain, alluded, with the delicacy and sensitiveness of women, to the stranger maiden, who had left the upper earth at a time so near his own departure as to render the will of the Great Spirit too manifest to be disregarded. They admonished him to be kind to her, and to have consideration for her ignorance of those arts which were so necessary to the comfort of a warrior like himself. They dwelt upon her matchless beauty, and on her noble resolution, without the taint of envy, and as angels may be thought to delight in a superior excellence; adding, that these endowments should prove more than equivalent for any little imperfections in her education.

After which, others again, in due succession, spoke to the maiden herself, in the low, soft language of tenderness and love. They exhorted her to be of cheerful mind, and to fear nothing for her future welfare. A hunter would be her companion who knew how to provide for her smallest wants; and a warrior was at her side who was able to protect her against every danger. They promised that her path should be pleasant, and her burden light. They cautioned her against unavailing regrets for the friends of her youth, and the scenes where her fathers had dwelt; assuring her that the "blessed hunting-grounds of the Lenape" contained vales as pleasant, streams as pure, and flowers as sweet, as the "heaven of the pale-faces." They advised her to be attentive to the wants of her companion, and never to forget the distinction which the Manitou had so wisely established between them. Then, in a wild burst of their chant, they sang with united voices the temper of the Mohican's mind. They pronounced him noble, manly and generous; all that became a warrior, and all that a maid might love. Clothing their ideas in the most remote and subtle images, they betrayed that in the short period of their intercourse they had discovered, with the intuitive perception of their sex, the truant disposition of his inclinations. The Delaware girls had found no favor in his eyes! He was of a race that had once been lords on the shores of the salt lake, and his wishes had led him back to a people who dwelt about the graves of his fathers. Why should not such a predilection be encouraged? That she was of a blood purer and richer than the rest of her nation, any eye might have seen; that she was equal to the dangers and daring of a life in the woods, her conduct had proved; and now, they added, the "wise one of the earth" had transplanted her to a place where she would find congenial spirits, and might be forever happy.

Then, with another transition in voice and subject, allusions were made to the virgin who wept in the adjacent lodge. They compared her to flakes of snow; as pure, as white, as brilliant, and as liable to melt in the fierce heats of summer, or congeal in the frosts of winter. They doubted not that she was lovely in the eyes of the young chief, whose skin and whose sorrow seemed so like her own; but, though far from expressing such a preference, it was evident they deemed her less excellent than the maid they mourned. Still they denied her no meed her rare charms might properly claim. Her ringlets were compared to the exuberant tendrils of the vine, her eye to the blue vault of the heavens, and the most spotless cloud, with its glowing flush of the sun, was admitted to be less attractive than her bloom.

During these and similar songs nothing was audible but the murmurs of the music; relieved, as it was, or rather rendered terrible, by those occasional bursts of grief which might be called its choruses. The Delawares themselves listened like charmed men; and it was very apparent, by the variations of their speaking countenances, how deep and true was their sympathy. Even David was not reluctant to lend his ears to the tones of voices so sweet; and long ere the chant was ended, his gaze announced that his soul was enthralled.

The scout, to whom alone, of all the white men, the words were intelligible, suffered himself to be a little aroused from his meditative posture, and bent his face aside, to catch their meaning, as the girls proceeded. But when they spoke of the future prospects of Cora and Uncas, he shook his head, like one who knew the error of their simple creed, and resuming his reclining attitude, he maintained it until the ceremony—if that might be called a ceremony, in which feeling was so deeply imbued—was finished. Happily for the self-command of both Heyward and Munro, they knew not the meaning of the wild sounds they heard.

Chingachgook was a solitary exception to the interest manifested by the native part of the audience. His look never changed throughout the whole of the scene, nor did a muscle move in his rigid countenance, even at the wildest or the most pathetic parts of the lamentation. The cold and senseless remains of his son was all to him, and every other sense but that of sight seemed frozen, in order that his eyes might take their final gaze at those lineaments he had so long loved, and which were now about to be closed forever from his view.

In this stage of the funeral obsequies, a warrior much renowned for deeds in arms, and more especially for services in the recent combat, a man of stern and grave demeanor, advanced slowly from the crowd, and placed himself nigh the person of the dead.

"Why hast thou left us, pride of the Wapanachki?" he said, addressing himself to the dull ears of Uncas, as if the empty clay retained the faculties of the animated man; "thy time has been like that of the sun when in the trees; thy glory brighter than his light at noonday. Thou art gone, youthful warrior, but a hundred Wyandots are clearing the briers from thy path to the world of spirits. Who that saw thee in battle would believe that thou couldst die? Who before thee has even shown Uttawa the way into the fight? Thy feet were like the wings of eagles; thine arm heavier than falling branches from the pine; and thy voice like the Manitou when he speaks in the clouds. The tongue of Uttawa is weak," he added, looking about him with a melancholy gaze, "and his heart exceeding heavy. Pride of the Wapanachki, why hast thou left us?"

He was succeeded by others, in due order, until most of the high and gifted men of the nation had sung or spoken their tribute of praise over the manes of the deceased chief. When each had ended, another deep and breathing silence reigned in all the place.

Then a low, deep sound was heard, like the suppressed accompaniment of distant music, rising just high enough on the air to be audible, and yet so indistinctly as to leave its character, and the place whence it proceeded, alike matters of conjecture. It was, however, succeeded by another and another strain, each in a higher key, until they grew on the ear, first in long drawn and often repeated interjections, and finally in words. The lips of Chingachgook had so far parted as to announce that it was the monody of the father. Though not an eye was turned towards him, nor the smallest sign of impatience exhibited, it was apparent, by the manner in which the multitude elevated their heads to listen, that they drank in the sounds with an intenseness of attention that none but Tamenund himself had ever before commanded. But they listened in vain. The strains rose just so loud as to become intelligible, and then grew fainter and more trembling, until they finally sank on the ear, as if borne away by a passing breath of wind. The lips of the Sagamore closed, and he remained silent in his seat, looking, with his riveted eye and motionless form, like some creature that had been turned from the Almighty hand with the form but without the spirit of a man. The Delawares, who knew by these symptoms that the mind of their friend was not prepared for so mighty an effort of fortitude, relaxed in their attention; and, with an innate delicacy, seemed to bestow all their thoughts on the obsequies of the stranger maiden.

A signal was given, by one of the elder chiefs, to the women who crowded that part of the circle near which the body of Cora lay. Obedient to the sign, the girls raised the bier to the elevation of their heads, and advanced with slow and regulated steps, chanting, as they proceeded, another wailing song in praise of the deceased. Gamut, who had been a close observer of rites he deemed so heathenish, now bent his head over the shoulder of the unconscious father, whispering,—

"They move with the remains of thy child; shall we not follow, and see them interred with Christian burial?"

Munro started, as if the last trumpet had sounded in his ear, and bestowing one anxious and hurried glance around him, he arose and followed in the simple train, with the mien of a soldier, but bearing the full burden of a parent's suffering. His friends pressed around him with a sorrow that was too strong to be termed sympathy—even the young Frenchman joining in the procession, with the air of a man who was sensibly touched at the early and melancholy fate of one so lovely. But when the last and humblest female of the tribe had joined in the wild, and yet ordered array, the men of the Lenape contracted their circle, and formed again around the person of Uncas, as silent, as grave, and as motionless as before.

The place which had been chosen for the grave of Cora was a little knoll, where a cluster of young and healthful pines had taken root, forming of themselves a melancholy and appropriate shade over the spot. On reaching it the girls deposited their burden, and continued for many minutes waiting, with characteristic patience, and native timidity, for some evidence that they whose feelings were most concerned were content with the arrangement. At length the scout, who alone understoood their habits, said, in their own language,—

"My daughters have done well; the white men thank them."

Satisfied with this testimony in their favor, the girls proceeded to deposit the body in a shell, ingeniously, and not inelegantly, fabricated of the bark of the birch; after which they lowered it into its dark and final abode. The ceremony of covering the remains, and concealing the marks of the fresh earth, by leaves and other natural and customary objects, was conducted with the same simple and silent forms. But when the labors of the kind beings who had performed these sad and friendly offices were so far completed, they hesitated, in a way to show that they knew not how much further they might proceed. It was in this stage of the rites that the scout again addressed them:—

"My young women have done enough," he said; "the spirit of a pale-face has no need of food or raiment, their gifts being according to the heaven of their color. I see," he added, glancing an eye at David, who was preparing his book in a manner that indicated an intention to lead the way in sacred song, "that one who better knows the Christian fashions is about to speak."

The females stood modestly aside, and, from having been the principal actors in the scene, they now became the meek and attentive observers of that which followed. During the time David was occupied in pouring out the pious feelings of his spirit in this manner, not a sign of surprise, nor a look of impatience, escaped them. They listened like those who knew the meaning of the strange words, and appeared as if they felt the mingled emotions of sorrow, hope, and resignation, they were intended to convey.

Excited by the scene he had just witnessed, and perhaps influenced by his own secret emotions, the master of song exceeded his usual efforts. His full, rich voice was not found to suffer by a comparison with the soft tones of the girls; and his more modulated strains possessed, at least for the ears of those to whom they were peculiarly addressed, the additional power of intelligence. He ended the anthem, as he had commenced it, in the midst of a grave and solemn stillness.

When, however, the closing cadence had fallen on the ears of his auditors, the secret, timorous glances of the eyes, and the general and yet subdued movement of the assemblage, betrayed that something was expected from the father of the deceased. Munro seemed sensible that the time was come for him to exert what is, perhaps, the greatest effort of which human nature is capable. He bared his gray locks, and looked around the timid and quiet throng by which he was encircled with a firm and collected countenance. Then motioning with his hand for the scout to listen, he said,—

"Say to these kind and gentle females, that a heartbroken and failing man returns them his thanks. Tell them that the Being we all worship, under different names, will be mindful of their charity; and that the time shall not be distant when we may assemble around his throne without distinction of sex, or rank, or color."

The scout listened to the tremulous voice in which the veteran delivered these words, and shook his head slowly when they were ended, as one who doubted their efficacy.

"To tell them this," he said, "would be to tell them that the snows come not in the winter, or that the sun shines fiercest when the trees are stripped of their leaves."

Then turning to the women, he made such a communication of the other's gratitude as he deemed most suited to the capacities of his listeners. The head of Munro had already sunk upon his chest, and he was again fast relapsing into melancholy, when the young Frenchman before named ventured to touch him lightly on the elbow. As soon as he had gained the attention of the mourning old man, he pointed towards a group of young Indians, who approached with a light but closely covered litter, and then pointed upwards towards the sun.

"I understand you, sir," returned Munro, with a voice of forced firmness; "I understand you. It is the will of Heaven, and I submit. Cora, my child! if the prayers of a heartbroken father could avail thee now, how blessed shouldst thou be! Come, gentlemen," he added, looking about him with an air of lofty composure, though the anguish that quivered in his faded countenance was far too powerful to be concealed, "our duty here is ended; let us depart."

Heyward gladly obeyed a summons that took them from a spot where, each instant, he felt his self-control was about to desert him. While his companions were mounting, however, he found time to press the hand of the scout, and to repeat the terms of an engagement they had made, to meet again within the posts of the British army. Then gladly throwing himself into the saddle, he spurred his charger to the side of the litter, whence low and stifled sobs alone announced the presence of Alice. In this manner, the head of Munro again dropping on his bosom, with Heyward and David following in sorrowing silence, and attended by the aide of Montcalm with his guard, all the white men, with the exception of Hawkeye, passed from before the eyes of the Delawares, and were soon buried in the vast forests of that region.

But the tie which, through their common calamity, had united the feelings of these simple dwellers in the woods with the strangers who had thus transiently visited them, was not so easily broken. Years passed away before the traditionary tale of the white maiden, and of the young warrior of the Mohicans, ceased to beguile the long nights and tedious marches, or to animate their youthful and brave with a desire for vengeance. Neither were the secondary actors in these momentous incidents forgotten. Through the medium of the scout, who served for years afterwards as a link between them and civilized life, they learned, in answer to their inquiries, that the "Gray Head" was speedily gathered to his fathers—borne down, as was erroneously believed, by his military misfortunes; and that the "Open Hand" had conveyed his surviving daughter far into the settlements of the "pale-faces," where her tears had at last ceased to flow, and had been succeeded by the bright smiles which were better suited to her joyous nature.

But these were events of a time later than that which concerns our tale. Deserted by all of his color, Hawkeye returned to the spot where his own sympathies led him with a force that no ideal bond of union could bestow. He was just in time to catch a parting look of the features of Uncas, whom the Delawares were already inclosing in his last vestments of skins. They paused to permit the longing and lingering gaze of the sturdy woodsman, and when it was ended, the body was enveloped, never to be unclosed again. Then came a procession like the other, and the whole nation was collected about the temporary grave of the chief—temporary, because it was proper that, at some future day, his bones should rest among those of his own people.

The movement, like the feeling, had been simultaneous and general. The same grave expression of grief, the same rigid silence, and the same deference to the principal mourner, were observed around the place of interment as have been already described. The body was deposited in an attitude of repose, facing the rising sun, with the implements of war and of the chase at hand, in readiness for the final journey. An opening was left in the shell, by which it was protected from the soil, for the spirit to communicate with its earthly tenement, when necessary; and the whole was concealed from the instinct and protected from the ravages of the beasts of prey, with an ingenuity peculiar to the natives. The manual rites then ceased, and all present reverted to the more spiritual part of the ceremonies.

Chingachgook became once more the object of the common attention. He had not yet spoken, and something consolatory and instructive was expected from so renowned a chief on an occasion of such interest. Conscious of the wishes of the people, the stern and self-restrained warrior raised his face, which had latterly been buried in his robe, and looked about him with a steady eye. His firmly compressed and expressive lips then severed, and for the first time during the long ceremonies his voice was distinctly audible.

"Why do my brothers mourn?" he said, regarding the dark race of dejected warriors by whom he was environed; "why do my daughters weep? that a young man has gone to the happy hunting-grounds; that a chief has filled his time with honor! He was good; he was dutiful; he was brave. Who can deny it? The Manitou had need of such a warrior, and He has called him away. As for me, the son and the father of Uncas, I am a blazed pine, in a clearing of the pale-faces. My race has gone from the shores of the salt lake, and the hills of the Delawares. But who can say that the Serpent of his tribe has forgotten his wisdom? I am alone"—

"No, no," cried Hawkeye, who had been gazing with a yearning look at the rigid features of his friend, with something like his own self-command, but whose philosophy could endure no longer; "no, Sagamore, not alone. The gifts of our colors may be different, but God has so placed us as to journey in the same path. I have no kin, and I may also say, like you, no people. He was your son, and a red-skin by nature; and it may be that your blood was nearer—but if ever I forget the lad who has so often fou't at my side in war, and slept at my side in peace, may He who made us all, whatever may be our color or our gifts, forget me! The boy has left us for a time; but, Sagamore, you are not alone."

Chingachgook grasped the hand that, in the warmth of feeling, the scout had stretched across the fresh earth, and in that attitude of friendship these two sturdy and intrepid woodsmen bowed their heads together, while scalding tears fell to their feet, watering the grave of Uncas like drops of falling rain.

In the midst of the awful stillness with which such a burst of feeling, coming, as it did, from the two most renowned warriors of that region, was received, Tamenund lifted his voice to disperse the multitude.

"It is enough," he said. "Go, children of the Lenape, the anger of the Manitou is not done. Why should Tamenund stay? The pale-faces are masters of the earth, and the time of the red-men has not yet come again. My day has been too long. In the morning I saw the sons of Unamis happy and strong; and yet, before the night has come, have I lived to see the last warrior of the wise race of the Mohicans."

NATHANIEL HAWTHORNE
(1804–1864)

Nathaniel Hawthorne was a product of, and an exile from, the Puritan New England village where he was born on Independence Day, 1804. In spirit, Hawthorne never left Salem, scene of his two greatest novels, *The Scarlet Letter* and *The House of the Seven Gables*. But in reality, Hawthorne moved around continuously, living in a number of Massachusetts and New Hampshire villages and in Europe. Because of his criticism of Puritan morality, and because he was the first American novelist to think of himself as an artist, Hawthorne was alienated from his ancestry and from contemporary society. The conflict between his desire to be an active member of a community and his disdain for the prejudices and injustices in the community was reflected throughout Hawthorne's life and art.

Hawthorne's Puritan ancestors arrived in Massachusetts in 1630. One of them was a high-ranking official who persecuted Quakers. Another was a judge who presided over the Salem witch trials and executions in 1692. Hawthorne's father was a sea captain who died of fever in Surinam when Nathaniel, an only son, was four. His mother then became a recluse. Like her, Hawthorne led a solitary life. After graduating from Bowdoin College in Maine, he stayed alone in Salem, reading, meditating, and writing, from 1825 to 1837. All his life, Hawthorne brooded upon the nature of the relation of the individual to society. In 1841, he even joined a communal living venture at Brook Farm. But that lasted less than a year.

In 1842, Hawthorne married Sophia Peabody, of the famous Salem family. From 1842 to 1845, they rented "Old Manse," the home of Emerson's ancestors in Concord. Hawthorne came to believe that the isolated individual who fails to connect with his community is damned. His tranquil domesticity with Sophia enabled him to connect with ordinary life. But the family life he designed competed with the life of the imagination he had cultivated during his years of seclusion.

Hawthorne spent the rest of his years going back and forth between trying to lead a public life and being a recluse. In 1839, he worked in the Boston Custom House. Then, in 1846, he worked in the Salem Custom House. By 1850, he again felt the need for privacy, so the Hawthornes moved to a farmhouse near Lenox in the Berkshires. Herman Melville lived nearby and they became friends. Melville even dedicated *Moby Dick* to Hawthorne. In 1852, Hawthorne bought "The Wayside," in Concord.

In 1853, Hawthorne went back to public life. For five years, he served as U.S. Consul at Liverpool, England. He spent a year in Rome and in Florence, where he began *The Marble Faun*. When he returned to "The Wayside," his physical and artistic decline was already underway.

Hawthorne was a major figure in the American Renaissance of art and expression. Appearing in the half-decade of 1850–1855 were: Emerson's *Representative Men*; Thoreau's *Walden*; Whitman's *Leaves of Grass*; Melville's *Moby Dick* and *Pierre*; and Hawthorne's *The Scarlet Letter* and *The House of the Seven Gables*. At his burial in Sleepy Hollow Cemetery at Concord, the year before the Civil War ended, Hawthorne's pallbearers were Longfellow, Lowell, Alcott, Holmes, and Emerson, all leaders of the New England Renaissance.

His first novel, *Fanshawe: A Tale* (1828), shows that Hawthorne, like Cooper, started out under the influence of Sir Walter Scott's historical romances. But Hawthorne realized the novel's faults and destroyed as many copies as he could. He spoke of his next two books as parables, fantasies, moralized legends, "allegories of the heart," and "Tales of My Native Land." *Twice Told Tales* (1837) and *Mosses from an Old Manse* (1846) show Hawthorne's preoccupation with certain themes, such as the isolated individual's damnation, the power of the imagination, the conflict between good and evil, and the role of the artist. Hawthorne wrote about the supernatural, the mysterious, the marvelous, even the miraculous. Some of his stories are historical, some satirical, while others are enchanting and delightfully curious. These two and his five later collections exhibit affinities with the tales of Washington Irving and Edgar Allen Poe, and some anticipate Kafka.

Having achieved success late in life, Hawthorne was 46 when his masterpiece, *The Scarlet Letter*, appeared in 1850. It was hailed as the best of many novels set in Puritan New England. It is the first American novel to be regarded as a fine work of art, a judgment that has never wavered. In the novel, Hawthorne employs a forceful coherence of character contrasts, plot, structure, symbolic and allegorical elements, and an omniscient narrative voice, as if it were a dramatized meditation.

Hawthorne called his works of long fiction "romances," as opposed to novels. Novels "aim at a very minute fidelity . . . to the probable and ordinary course of man's everyday existence," while romances express "the truth of the human heart" (his word for the psyche). Hawthorne believed romances described circumstances created by an author's imagination, rather than what the factual world dictates. His temperament predisposed him to see signs, symbols, emblems, and allegorical possibilities everywhere he looked. To him, real things had ideal or symbolic forms that he wanted to free from the literal, to show that "the spiritual life is a reality." His romances exhibit both traditional allegory and an early use of modern symbolism to conjure clear projections of psychological realities. Hawthorne also felt that psychological equipoise was possible only if a person understood and accepted the nature of good and evil, and the effects of a belief in sin and redemption.

As an almost obsessed student of New England history, Hawthorne was always aware of the effects of the past in the present. *The House of the Seven Gables* (1851) is a dramatization of the way the sins of fathers ruin the lives of children. It may have reminded Hawthorne's readers of Charles Brockden Brown's *Wieland; or, the Transformation, An American Tale* (1798); readers today may see affinities with Faulkner's *Absalom, Absalom!*

The Blithesdale Romance (1852) is a relatively minor work, a somewhat satirical treatment of Hawthorne's participation in communal living. Hawthorne's last major work, *The Marble Faun, or The Romance of Monte Beni* (1860), did not appear until eight years later. It was first published in England under the title *Transformation*. Set in contemporary Rome, it is an allegory of the problem of evil as experienced by two young Americans and two Italians.

Hawthorne died profoundly frustrated by the realization that in three abortive romances (unfinished at his death), his imagination and artistry were failing him, and that he was only reworking old plots, themes, allegories, and symbols.

cf. James

THE SCARLET LETTER

Nathaniel Hawthorne

The Custom-House

INTRODUCTORY TO "THE SCARLET LETTER"

It is a little remarkable, that—though disinclined to talk overmuch of myself and my affairs at the fireside, and to my personal friends—an autobiographical impulse should twice in my life have taken possession of me, in addressing the public. The first time was three or four years since, when I favored the reader—inexcusably, and for no earthly reason, that either the indulgent reader or the intrusive author could imagine—with a description of my way of life in the deep quietude of an Old Manse. And now—because, beyond my deserts, I was happy enough to find a listener or two on the former occasion—I again seize the public by the button, and talk of my three years' experience in a Custom-House. The example of the famous "P. P., Clerk of this Parish," was never more faithfully followed. The truth seems to be, however, that, when he casts his leaves forth upon the wind, the author addresses, not the many who will fling aside his volume, or never take it up, but the few who will understand him, better than most of his schoolmates and lifemates. Some authors, indeed, do far more than this, and indulge themselves in such confidential depths of revelation as could fittingly be addressed, only and exclusively, to the one heart and mind of perfect sympathy; as if the printed book, thrown at large on the wide world, were certain to find out the divided segment of the writer's own nature, and complete his circle of existence by bringing him into communion with it. It is scarcely decorous, however, to speak all, even where we speak impersonally. But—as thoughts are frozen and utterance benumbed, unless the speaker stand in some true relation with his audience—it may be pardonable to imagine that a friend, a kind and apprehensive, though not the closest friend, is listening to our talk; and then, a native reserve being thawed by this genial consciousness, we may prate of the circumstances that lie around us, and even of ourself, but still keep the inmost Me behind its veil. To this extent and within these limits, an author, methinks, may be autobiographical, without violating either the reader's rights or his own.

It will be seen, likewise, that this Custom-House sketch has a certain propriety, of a kind always recognized in literature, as explaining how a large portion of the following pages came into my possession, and as offering proofs of the authenticity of a narrative therein contained. This, in fact,—a desire to put myself in my true position as editor, or very little more, of the most prolix among the tales that make up my volume,—this, and no other, is my true reason for assuming a personal relation with the public. In accomplishing the main purpose, it has appeared allowable, by a few extra touches, to give a faint representation of a mode of life not heretofore described, together with some of the characters that move in it, among whom the author happened to make one.

In my native town of Salem, at the head of what, half a century ago, in the days of old King Derby, was a bustling wharf,—but which is now burdened with decayed wooden warehouses, and exhibits few or no symptoms of commercial life; except, perhaps, a bark or brig, half-way down its melancholy length, discharging hides; or, nearer at hand, a Nova Scotia schooner, pitching out her cargo of firewood,—at the head, I say, of this dilapidated wharf, which the tide often overflows, and along which, at the base and in the rear of the row of buildings, the track of many languid years is seen in a border of unthrifty grass,—here, with a view from its front windows adown this not very enlivening prospect, and thence across the harbour, stands a spacious edifice of brick. From the loftiest point of its roof, during precisely three and a half hours of each forenoon, floats or droops, in breeze or calm, the banner of the republic; but with the thirteen stripes turned vertically, instead of horizontally, and thus indicating that a civil, and not a military post of Uncle Sam's government, is here established. Its front is ornamented with a portico of half a dozen wooden pillars, supporting a balcony, beneath which a flight of wide granite steps descends towards the street. Over the entrance hovers an enormous specimen of the American eagle, with outspread wings, a shield before her breast, and, if I recollect aright, a bunch of intermingled thunderbolts and barbed arrows in each claw. With the customary infirmity of temper that characterizes this unhappy fowl, she appears, by the fierceness of her beak and eye and the general truculency of her attitude, to threaten mischief to the inoffensive community; and especially to warn all citizens, careful of their safety, against intruding on the premises which she overshadows with her wings. Nevertheless, vixenly as she looks, many people are seeking, at this very moment, to shelter themselves under the wing of the federal eagle; imagining, I presume, that her bosom has all the softness and snugness of an eider-down pillow. But she has no great tenderness, even in her best of moods, and, sooner or later,—oftener soon than late,—is apt to fling off her nestlings with a scratch of her claw, a dab of her beak, or a rankling wound from her barbed arrows.

The pavement round about the above-described edifice—which we may as well name at once as the Custom-House of the port—has grass enough growing in its chinks to show that it has not, of late days, been worn by any multitudinous resort of business. In some months of the year, however, there often chances a forenoon when affairs move onward with a livelier tread. Such occasions might remind the elderly citizen of that period, before the last war with England, when Salem was a port by itself; not scorned, as she is now, by her own merchants and ship-owners, who permit her wharves to crumble to ruin, while their ventures go to swell, needlessly and imperceptibly, the mighty flood of commerce at New York or Boston. On some such morning, when three or four vessels happen to have arrived at once,—usually from Africa or South America,—or to be on the verge of their departure thitherward, there is a sound of frequent feet, passing briskly up and down the granite steps. Here, before his own wife has greeted him, you may greet the sea-flushed ship-master, just in port, with his vessel's papers under his arm in a tarnished tin box. Here, too, comes his owner, cheerful or sombre, gracious or in the sulks, accordingly as his scheme of the now accomplished voyage has been realized in merchandise that will readily be turned to gold, or has buried him under a bulk of incommodities, such as nobody will care to rid him of. Here, likewise,—the germ of the wrinkle-browed, grizzly-bearded, careworn merchant,—we have the smart young clerk, who gets the taste of traffic as a wolf-cub does of blood, and already sends adventures in his master's ships, when he had better be sailing mimic boats upon a millpond. Another figure in the scene is the outward-bound sailor, in quest of a protection; or the recently arrived one, pale and feeble, seeking a passport to the hospital. Nor must we forget the captains of the rusty little schooners that bring firewood from the British provinces; a rough-looking set of tarpaulins, without the alertness of the Yankee aspect, but contributing an item of no slight importance to our decaying trade.

Cluster all these individuals together, as they sometimes were, with other miscellaneous ones to diversify the group, and, for the time being, it made the Custom-House a stirring scene. More frequently, however, on ascending the steps, you would discern—in the entry, if it were summer time, or in their appropriate rooms, if wintry or inclement weather—a row of venerable figures, sitting in old-fashioned chairs, which were tipped on their hind legs back against the wall. Oftentimes they were asleep, but occasionally might be heard talking together, in voices between speech and a snore, and with that lack of energy that distinguishes the occupants of alms-houses, and all other human beings who depend for subsistence on charity, on monopolized labor, or any thing else but their own independent exertions. These old gentlemen—seated, like Matthew, at the receipt of custom, but not very liable to be summoned thence, like him, for apostolic errands—were Custom-House officers.

Furthermore, on the left hand as you enter the front door, is a certain room or office, about fifteen feet square, and of a lofty height; with two of its arched windows commanding a view of the aforesaid dilapidated wharf, and the third looking across a narrow lane, and along a portion of Derby Street. All three give glimpses of the shops of grocers, block-makers, slop-sellers, and ship-chandlers; around the doors of which are generally to be seen, laughing and gossiping, clusters of old salts, and such other wharf-rats as haunt the Wapping of a seaport. The room itself is cobwebbed, and dingy with old paint; its floor is strewn with gray sand, in a fashion that has elsewhere fallen into long disuse; and it is easy to conclude, from the general slovenliness of the place, that this is a sanctuary into which womankind, with her tools of magic, the broom and mop, has very infrequent access. In the way of furniture, there is a stove with a voluminous funnel; an old pine desk, with a three-legged stool beside it; two or three wooden-bottom chairs, exceedingly decrepit and infirm; and,—not to forget the library,—on some shelves, a score or two of volumes of the Acts of Congress, and a bulky Digest of the Revenue Laws. A tin pipe ascends through the ceiling, and forms a medium of vocal communication with other parts of the edifice. And here, some six months ago,—pacing from corner to corner, or lounging on the longlegged stool, with his elbow on the desk, and his eyes wandering up and down the columns of the morning newspaper,—you might have recognized, honored reader, the same individual who welcomed you into his cheery little study, where the sunshine glimmered so pleasantly through the willow branches, on the western side of the Old Manse. But now, should you go thither to seek him, you would inquire in vain for the Loco-foco Surveyor. The besom of reform has swept him out of office; and a worthier successor wears his dignity and pockets his emoluments.

This old town of Salem—my native place, though I have dwelt much away from it, both in boyhood and maturer years—possesses, or did possess, a hold on my affections, the force of which I have never realized during my seasons of actual residence here. Indeed, so far as its physical aspect is concerned, with its flat, unvaried surface, covered chiefly with wooden houses, few or none of which pretend to architectural beauty,—its irregularity, which is neither picturesque nor quaint, but only tame,—its long and lazy street, lounging wearisomely through the whole extent of the peninsula, with Gallows Hill and New Guinea at one end, and a view of the alms-house at the other,—such being the features of my native town, it would be quite as reasonable to form a sentimental attachment to a disarranged checkerboard. And yet, though invariably happiest elsewhere, there is within me a feeling for old Salem, which, in lack of a better phrase, I must be content to call affection. The sentiment is probably assignable to the deep and aged roots which my family has struck into the soil. It is now nearly two centuries and a quarter since the original Briton, the earliest emigrant of my name, made his appearance in the wild and forest-bordered settlement, which has since become a city. And here his descendants have been born and died, and have mingled their earthy substance with the soil; until no small portion of it must necessarily be akin to the mortal frame wherewith, for a little while, I walk the streets. In part, therefore, the attachment which I speak of is the mere sensuous sympathy of dust for dust. Few of my countrymen can know what it is; nor, as frequent transplantation is perhaps better for the stock, need they consider it desirable to know.

But the sentiment has likewise its moral quality. The figure of that first ancestor, invested by family tradition with a dim and dusky grandeur, was present to my boyish imagination, as far back as I can remember. It still haunts me, and induces a sort of home-feeling with the past, which I scarcely claim in reference to the present phase of the town. I seem to have a stronger claim to a residence here on account of this grave, bearded, sable-cloaked, and steeple-crowned progenitor,—who came so early, with his Bible and his sword, and trode the unworn street with such a stately port, and made so large a figure, as a man of war and peace,—a stronger claim than for myself, whose name is seldom heard and my face hardly known. He was a soldier, legislator, judge; he was a ruler in the Church; he had all the Puritanic traits, both good and evil. He was likewise a bitter persecutor; as witness the Quakers, who have remembered him in their histories, and relate an incident of his hard severity towards a woman of their sect, which will last longer, it is to be feared, than any record of his better deeds, although these were many. His son, too, inherited the persecuting spirit, and made himself so conspicuous in the martyrdom of the witches, that their blood may fairly be said to have left a stain upon him. So deep a stain, indeed, that his old dry bones, in the Charter

Street burial-ground, must still retain it, if they have not crumbled utterly to dust! I know not whether these ancestors of mine bethought themselves to repent, and ask pardon of Heaven for their cruelties; or whether they are now groaning under the heavy consequences of them, in another state of being. At all events, I, the present writer, as their representative, hereby take shame upon myself for their sakes, and pray that any curse incurred by them—as I have heard, and as the dreary and unprosperous condition of the race, for many a long year back, would argue to exist—may be now and henceforth removed.

Doubtless, however, either of these stern and black-browed Puritans would have thought it quite a sufficient retribution for his sins, that, after so long a lapse of years, the old trunk of the family tree, with so much venerable moss upon it, should have borne, as its topmost bough, an idler like myself. No aim, that I have ever cherished, would they recognize as laudable; no success of mine—if my life, beyond its domestic scope, had ever been brightened by success—would they deem otherwise than worthless, if not positively disgraceful. "What is he?" murmurs one gray shadow of my forefathers to the other. "A writer of story-books! What kind of a business in life,—what mode of glorifying God, or being serviceable to mankind in his day and generation,—may that be? Why, the degenerate fellow might as well have been a fiddler!" Such are the compliments bandied between my greatgrandsires and myself, across the gulf of time! And yet, let them scorn me as they will, strong traits of their nature have intertwined themselves with mine.

Planted deep, in the town's earliest infancy and childhood, by these two earnest and energetic men, the race has ever since subsisted here; always, too, in respectability; never, so far as I have known, disgraced by a single unworthy member; but seldom or never, on the other hand, after the first two generations, performing any memorable deed, or so much as putting forward a claim to public notice. Gradually, they have sunk almost out of sight; as old houses, here and there about the streets, get covered half-way to the eaves by the accumulation of new soil. From father to son, for above a hundred years, they followed the sea; a gray-headed shipmaster, in each generation, retiring from the quarter-deck to the homestead, while a boy of fourteen took the hereditary place before the mast, confronting the salt spray and the gale, which had blustered against his sire and grandsire. The boy, also, in due time, passed from the forecastle to the cabin, spent a tempestuous manhood, and returned from his world-wanderings, to grow old, and die, and mingle his dust with the natal earth. This long connection of a family with one spot, as its place of birth and burial, creates a kindred between the human being and the locality, quite independent of any charm in the scenery or moral circumstances that surround him. It is not love, but instinct. The new inhabitant—who came himself from a foreign land, or whose father or grandfather came—has little claim to be called a Salemite; he has no conception of the oyster-like tenacity with which an old settler, over whom his third century is creeping, clings to the spot where his successive generations have been imbedded. It is no matter that the place is joyless for him; that he is weary of the old wooden houses, the mud and dust, the dead level of site and sentiment, the chill east wind, and the chillest of social atmospheres;—all these, and whatever faults besides he may see or imagine, are nothing to the purpose. The spell survives, and just as powerfully as if the natal spot were an earthly paradise. So has it been in my case. I felt it almost as a destiny to make Salem my home; so that the mould of features and cast of character which had all along been familiar here—ever, as one representative of the race lay down in his grave, another assuming, as it were, his sentry-march along the Main Street—might still in my little day be seen and recognized in the old town. Nevertheless, this very sentiment is an evidence that the connection, which has become an unhealthy one, should at last be severed. Human nature will not flourish, any more than a potato, if it be planted and replanted, for too long a series of generations, in the same worn-out soil. My children have had other birthplaces, and, so far as their fortunes may be within my control, shall strike their roots into unaccustomed earth.

On emerging from the Old Manse, it was chiefly this strange, indolent, unjoyous attachment for my native town, that brought me to fill a place in Uncle Sam's brick edifice, when I might as well, or better, have gone somewhere else. My doom was on me. It was not the first time, nor the second, that I had gone away,—as it seemed, permanently,—but yet returned, like the bad half-penny; or as if Salem were for me the inevitable centre of the universe. So, one fine morning, I ascended the flight of granite steps, with the President's commission in my pocket, and was introduced to the corps of gentlemen who were to aid me in my weighty responsibility, as chief executive officer of the Custom-House.

I doubt greatly—or rather, I do not doubt at all—whether any public functionary of the United States, either in the civil or military line, has ever had such a patriarchal body of veterans under his orders as myself. The whereabouts of the Oldest Inhabitant was at once settled, when I looked at them. For upwards of twenty years before this epoch, the independent position of the Collector had kept the Salem Custom-House out of the whirlpool of political vicissitude, which makes the tenure of office generally so fragile. A soldier,—New England's most distinguished soldier,—he stood firmly on the pedestal of his gallant services; and, himself secure in the wise liberality of the successive administrations through which he had held office, he had been the safety of his subordinates in many an hour of danger and heartquake. General Miller was radically conservative; a man over whose kindly nature habit had no slight influence; attaching himself strongly to familiar faces, and with difficulty moved to change, even when change might have brought unquestionable improvement. Thus, on taking charge of my department, I found few but aged men. They were ancient sea-captains, for the most part, who, after being tost on every sea, and standing up sturdily against life's tempestuous blast, had finally drifted into this quiet nook; where, with little to disturb them, except the periodical terrors of a Presidential election, they one and all acquired a new lease of existence. Though by no means less liable than their fellow-men to age and infirmity, they had evidently some talisman or other that kept death at bay. Two or three of their number, as I was assured, being gouty and rheumatic, or perhaps bed-ridden, never dreamed of making their appearance at the Custom-House, during a large part of the year; but, after a torpid winter, would creep out into the warm sunshine of May or June, go lazily about what they termed duty, and, at their own leisure and convenience, betake themselves to bed again. I must plead guilty to the charge of abbreviating the official breath of more than one of these venerable servants of the republic. They were allowed, on my representation, to rest from their arduous labors, and soon afterwards—as if their sole principle of life had been zeal for their country's service; as I verily believe it was—withdrew to a better world. It is a pious consolation to me, that, through my interference, a sufficient space was allowed them for repentance of the evil and corrupt practices, into which, as a matter of course, every Custom-House officer must be supposed to fall. Neither the front nor the back entrance of the Custom-House opens on the road to Paradise.

The greater part of my officers were Whigs. It was well for their venerable brotherhood, that the new Surveyor was not a politician, and, though a faithful Democrat in principle, neither received nor held his office with any reference to political services. Had it been otherwise,—had an active politician been put into this influential post, to assume the easy task of making head against a Whig Collector, whose infirmities withheld him from the personal administration of his office,—hardly a man of the old corps would have drawn the breath of official life, within a month after the exterminating angel had come up the Custom-House steps. According to the received code in such matters, it would have been nothing short of duty, in a politician, to bring every one of those white heads under the axe of the guillotine. It was plain enough to discern, that the old fellows dreaded some such discourtesy at my hands. It pained, and at the same time amused me, to behold the terrors that attended my advent; to see a furrowed cheek, weather-beaten by half a century of storm, turn ashy pale at the glance of so harmless an individual as myself; to detect, as one or another addressed me, the tremor of a voice, which, in long-past days, had been wont to bellow through a speaking-trumpet, hoarsely enough to frighten Boreas himself to silence. They knew, these excellent old persons, that, by all established rule,—and, as regarded some of them, weighed by their own lack of efficiency for business,—they ought to have given place to younger men, more orthodox in politics, and altogether fitter than themselves to serve our common Uncle. I knew it too, but could never quite find in my heart to act upon the knowledge. Much and deservedly to my own discredit, therefore, and considerably to the detriment of my official conscience, they continued, during my incumbency, to creep about the wharves, and loiter up and down the Custom-House steps. They spent a good deal of time, also, asleep in their accustomed corners, with their chairs tilted back against the wall; awaking, however, once or twice in a forenoon, to bore one another with the several thousandth repetition of old sea-stories, and mouldy jokes, that had grown to be pass-words and countersigns among them.

The discovery was soon made, I imagine, that the new Surveyor had no great harm in him. So, with lightsome hearts, and the happy consciousness of being usefully employed,—in their own behalf, at least, if not for our beloved country,—these good old gentlemen went through the various formalities of office. Sagaciously, under their spectacles, did they peep into the holds of vessels! Mighty was their fuss about little matters, and marvellous, sometimes, the obtuseness that allowed greater ones to slip between their fingers! Whenever such a mischance occurred,—when a wagon-load of valuable merchandise had been smuggled ashore, at noonday, perhaps, and directly beneath their unsuspicious noses,—nothing could exceed the vigilance and alacrity with which they proceeded to lock, and double-lock, and secure with tape and sealing-wax, all the avenues of the delinquent vessel. Instead of a reprimand for their previous negligence, the case seemed rather to require an eulogium on their praiseworthy caution, after the mischief had happened; a grateful recognition of the promptitude of their zeal, the moment that there was no longer any remedy!

Unless people are more than commonly disagreeable, it is my foolish habit to contract a kindness for them. The better part of my companion's character, if it have a better part, is that which usually comes uppermost in my regard, and forms the type whereby I recognize the man. As most of these old Custom-House officers had good traits, and as my position in reference to them, being paternal and protective, was favorable to the growth of friendly sentiments, I soon grew to like them all. It was pleasant, in the summer forenoons,—when the fervent heat, that almost liquefied the rest of the human family, merely communicated a genial warmth to their half-torpid systems,—it was pleasant to hear them chatting in the back entry, a row of them all tipped against the wall, as usual; while the frozen witticisms of past generations were thawed out, and came bubbling with laughter from their lips. Externally, the jollity of aged men has much in common with the mirth of children; the intellect, any more than a deep sense of humor, has little to do with the matter; it is, with both, a gleam that plays upon the surface, and imparts a sunny and cheery aspect alike to the green branch, and gray, mouldering trunk. In one case, however, it is real sunshine; in the other, it more resembles the phosphorescent glow of decaying wood.

It would be sad injustice, the reader must understand, to represent all my excellent old friends as in their dotage. In the first place, my coadjutors were not invariably old; there were men among them in their strength and prime, of marked ability and energy, and altogether superior to the sluggish and dependent mode of life on which their evil stars had cast them. Then, moreover, the white locks of age were sometimes found to be the thatch of an intellectual tenement in good repair. But, as respects the majority of my corps of veterans, there will be no wrong done, if I characterize them generally as a set of wearisome old souls, who had gathered nothing worth preservation from their varied experience of life. They seemed to have flung away all the golden grain of practical wisdom, which they had enjoyed so many opportunities of harvesting, and most carefully to have stored their memories with the husks. They spoke with far more interest and unction of their morning's breakfast, or yesterday's, today's, or to-morrow's dinner, than of the shipwreck of forty or fifty years ago, and all the world's wonders which they had witnessed with their youthful eyes.

The father of the Custom-House—the patriarch, not only of this little squad of officials, but, I am bold to say, of the respectable body of tide-waiters all over the United States—was a certain permanent Inspector. He might truly be termed a legitimate son of the revenue system, dyed in the wool, or rather, born in the purple; since his sire, a Revolutionary colonel, and formerly collector of the port, had created an office for him, and appointed him to fill it, at a period of the early ages which few living men can now remember. This Inspector, when I first knew him, was a man of four-score years, or thereabouts, and certainly one of the most wonderful specimens of winter-green that you would be likely to discover in a lifetime's search. With his florid cheek, his compact figure, smartly arrayed in a bright-buttoned blue coat, his brisk and vigorous step, and his hale and hearty aspect, altogether, he seemed—not young, indeed—but a kind of new contrivance of Mother Nature in the shape of man, whom age and infirmity had no business to touch. His voice and laugh, which perpetually reëchoed through the Custom-House, had nothing of the tremulous quaver and cackle of an old man's utterance; they came strutting out of his lungs, like the crow of a cock, or the blast of a clarion. Looking at him merely as an animal,—and there was very little else to look at,—he was a most satisfactory object, from the thorough healthfulness and wholesomeness of his system, and his capacity, at that extreme age, to enjoy all, or nearly all, the delights which he had ever aimed at, or conceived of. The careless security of his life in the Custom-House, on a regular income, and with but slight and infrequent apprehensions of removal, had no doubt contributed to make time pass lightly over him. The original and more potent causes, however, lay in the rare perfection of his animal nature, the moderate proportion of intellect, and the very trifling admixture of moral and spiritual ingredients; these latter qualities, indeed, being in barely enough measure to keep the old gentleman from walking on all-fours. He possessed no power of thought, no depth of feeling, no troublesome sensibilities; nothing, in short, but a few commonplace instincts, which, aided by the cheerful temper that grew inevitably out of his physical well-being, did duty very respectably, and to general acceptance, in lieu of a heart. He had been the husband of three wives, all long since dead; the father of twenty children, most of whom, at every age of childhood or maturity, had likewise returned to dust. Here, one would suppose, might have been sorrow enough to imbue the sunniest disposition, through and through, with a sable tinge. Not so with our old Inspector! One brief sigh sufficed to carry off the entire burden of these dismal reminiscences. The next moment, he was as ready for sport as any unbreeched infant; far readier than the Collector's junior clerk, who, at nineteen years, was much the elder and graver man of the two.

I used to watch and study this patriarchal personage with, I think, livelier curiosity than any other form of humanity there presented to my notice. He was, in truth, a rare phenomenon; so perfect in one point of view; so shallow, so delusive, so impalpable, such an absolute nonentity, in every other. My conclusion was that he had no soul, no heart, no mind; nothing, as I have already said, but instincts; and yet, withal, so cunningly had the few materials of his character been put together, that there was no painful perception of deficiency, but, on my part, an entire contentment with what I found in him. It might be difficult—and it was so—to conceive how he should exist hereafter, so earthy and sensuous did he seem; but surely his existence here, admitting that it was to terminate with his last breath, had been not unkindly given; with no higher moral responsibilities than the beasts of the field, but with a larger scope of enjoyment than theirs, and with all their blessed immunity from the dreariness and duskiness of age.

One point, in which he had vastly the advantage over his four-footed brethren, was his ability to recollect the good dinners which it had made no small portion of the happiness of his life to eat. His gourmandism was a highly agreeable trait; and to hear him talk of roast-meat was as appetizing as a pickle or an oyster. As he possessed no higher attribute, and neither sacrificed nor vitiated any spiritual endowment by devoting all his energies and ingenuities to subserve the delight and profit of his maw, it always pleased and satisfied me to hear him expatiate on fish, poultry, and butcher's meat, and the most eligible methods of preparing them for the table. His reminiscences of good cheer, however ancient the date of the actual banquet, seemed to bring the savor of pig or turkey under one's very nostrils. There were flavors on his palate, that had lingered there not less than sixty or seventy years, and were still apparently as fresh as that of the muttonchop which he had just devoured for his breakfast. I have heard him smack his lips over dinners, every guest at which, except himself, had long been food for worms. It was marvellous to observe how the ghosts of bygone meals were continually rising up before him; not in anger or retribution, but as if grateful for his former appreciation, and seeking to reduplicate an endless series of enjoyment, at once shadowy and sensual. A tenderloin of beef, a hind-quarter of veal, a sparerib of pork, a particular chicken, or a remarkably praiseworthy turkey, which had perhaps adorned his board in the days of the elder Adams, would be remembered; while all the subsequent experience of our race, and all the events that brightened or darkened his individual career, had gone over him with as little permanent effect as the passing breeze. The chief tragic event of the old man's life, so far as I could judge, was his mishap with a certain goose, which lived and died some twenty or forty years ago; a goose of most promising figure, but which, at table, proved so inveterately tough that the carving-knife would make no impression on its carcass; and it could only be divided with an axe and handsaw.

But it is time to quit this sketch; on which, however, I should be glad to dwell at considerably more length, because, of all men whom I have ever known, this individual was fittest to be a Custom-House officer. Most persons, owing to causes which I may not have space to hint at, suffer moral detriment from this peculiar mode of life. The old Inspector was incapable of it, and, were he to continue in office to the end of time, would be just as good as he was then, and sit down to dinner with just as good an appetite.

There is one likeness, without which my gallery of Custom-House portraits would be strangely incomplete; but which my comparatively few opportunities for observation enable me to sketch only in the merest outline. It is that of the Collector, our gallant old General, who, after his brilliant military service, subsequently to which he had ruled over a wild Western territory, had come hither, twenty years before, to spend the decline of his varied and honorable life. The brave soldier had already numbered, nearly or quite, his threescore years and ten, and was pursuing the remainder of his earthly march, burdened with infirmities which even the martial music of his own spirit-stirring recollections could do little towards lightening. The step was palsied now, that had been foremost in the charge. It was only with the assistance of a servant, and by leaning his hand heavily on the iron balustrade, that he could slowly and painfully ascend the Custom-House steps, and, with a toilsome progress across the floor, attain his customary chair beside the fireplace. There he used to sit, gazing with a somewhat dim serenity of aspect at the figures that came and went; amid the rustle of papers, the administering of oaths, the discussion of business, and the casual talk of the office; all which sounds and circumstances seemed but indistinctly to impress his senses, and hardly to make their way into his inner sphere of contemplation. His countenance, in this repose, was mild and kindly. If his notice was sought, an expression of courtesy and interest gleamed out upon his features; proving that there was light within him, and that it was only the outward medium of the intellectual lamp that obstructed the rays in their passage. The closer you penetrated to the substance of his mind, the sounder it appeared. When no longer called upon to speak, or listen, either of which operations cost him an evident effort, his face would briefly subside into its former not uncheerful quietude. It was not painful to behold this look; for, though dim, it had not the imbecility of decaying age. The framework of his nature, originally strong and massive, was not yet crumbled into ruin.

To observe and define his character, however, under such disadvantages, was as difficult a task as to trace out and build up anew, in imagination, an old fortress, like Ticonderoga, from a view of its gray and broken ruins. Here and there, perchance, the walls may remain almost complete; but elsewhere may be only a shapeless mound, cumbrous with its very strength, and overgrown, through long years of peace and neglect, with grass and alien weeds.

Nevertheless, looking at the old warrior with affection,—for, slight as was the communication between us, my feeling towards him, like that of all bipeds and quadrupeds who knew him, might not improperly be termed so,—I could discern the main points of his portrait. It was marked with the noble and heroic qualities which showed it to be not by a mere accident, but of good right, that he had won a distinguished name. His spirit could never, I conceive, have been characterized by an uneasy activity; it must, at any period of his life, have required an impulse to set him in motion; but, once stirred up, with obstacles to overcome, and an adequate object to be attained, it was not in the man to give out or fail. The heat that had formerly pervaded his nature, and which was not yet extinct, was never of the kind that flashes and flickers in a blaze, but, rather, a deep, red glow, as of iron in a furnace. Weight, solidity, firmness; this was the expression of his repose, even in such decay as had crept untimely over him, at the period of which I speak. But I could imagine, even then, that, under some excitement which should go deeply into his consciousness,—roused by a trumpet-peal, loud enough to awaken all of his energies that were not dead, but only slumbering,—he was yet capable of flinging off his infirmities like a sick man's gown, dropping the staff of age to seize a battle-sword, and starting up once more a warrior. And, in so intense a moment, his demeanour would have still been calm. Such an exhibition, however, was but to be pictured in fancy; not to be anticipated, nor desired. What I saw in him—as evidently as the indestructible ramparts of Old Ticonderoga, already cited as the most appropriate simile—were the features of stubborn and ponderous endurance, which might well have amounted to obstinacy in his earlier days; of integrity, that, like most of his other endowments, lay in a somewhat heavy mass, and was just as unmalleable and unmanageable as a ton of iron ore; and of benevolence, which, fiercely as he led the bayonets on at Chippewa or Fort Erie, I take to be of quite as genuine a stamp as what actuates any or all the polemical philanthropists of the age. He had slain men with his own hand, for aught I know;—certainly, they had fallen, like blades of grass at the sweep of the scythe, before the charge to which his spirit imparted its triumphant energy;—but, be that as it might, there was never in his heart so much cruelty as would have brushed the down off a butterfly's wing. I have not known the man, to whose innate kindliness I would more confidently make an appeal.

Many characteristics—and those, too, which contribute not the least forcibly to impart resemblance in a sketch—must have vanished, or been obscured, before I met the General. All merely graceful attributes are usually the most evanescent; nor does Nature adorn the human ruin with blossoms of new beauty, that have their roots and proper nutriment only in the chinks and crevices of decay, as she sows wallflowers over the ruined fortress of Ticonderoga. Still, even in respect of grace and beauty, there were points well worth noting. A ray of humor, now and then, would make its way through the veil of dim obstruction, and glimmer pleasantly upon our faces. A trait of native elegance, seldom seen in the masculine character after childhood or early youth, was shown in the General's fondness for the sight and fragrance of flowers. An old soldier might be supposed to prize only the bloody laurel on his brow; but here was one, who seemed to have a young girl's appreciation of the floral tribe.

There, beside the fireplace, the brave old General used to sit; while the Surveyor—though seldom, when it could be avoided, taking upon himself the difficult task of engaging him in conversation—was fond of standing at a distance, and watching his quiet and almost slumberous countenance. He seemed away from us, although we saw him but a few yards off; remote, though we passed close beside his chair; unattainable, though we might have stretched forth our hands and touched his own. It might be, that he lived a more real life within his thoughts, than amid the unappropriate environment of the Collector's office. The evolutions of the parade; the tumult of the battle; the flourish of old, heroic music, heard thirty years before;—such scenes and sounds, perhaps, were all alive before his intellectual sense. Meanwhile, the merchants and ship-masters, the spruce clerks, and uncouth sailors, entered and departed; the bustle of this commercial and Custom-House life kept up its little murmur round about him; and neither with the men nor their affairs did the General appear to sustain the most distant relation. He was as much out of place as an old sword—now rusty, but which had flashed once in the battle's front, and showed still a bright gleam along its blade—would have been, among the inkstands, paper-folders, and mahogany rulers, on the Deputy Collector's desk.

There was one thing that much aided me in renewing and re-creating the stalwart soldier of the Niagara frontier,—the man of true and simple energy. It was the recollection of those memorable words of his,—"I'll try, Sir!"—spoken on the very verge of a desperate and heroic enterprise, and breathing the soul and spirit of New England hardihood, comprehending all perils, and encountering all. If, in our country, valor were rewarded by heraldic honor, this phrase—which it seems so easy to speak, but which only he, with such a task of danger and glory before him, has ever spoken—would be the best and fittest of all mottoes for the General's shield of arms.

It contributes greatly towards a man's moral and intellectual health, to be brought into habits of companionship with individuals unlike himself, who care little for his pursuits, and whose sphere and abilities he must go out of himself to appreciate. The accidents of my life have often afforded me this advantage, but never with more fulness and variety than during my continuance in office. There was one man, especially, the observation of whose character gave me a new idea of talent. His gifts were emphatically those of a man of business; prompt, acute, clear-minded; with an eye that saw through all perplexities, and a faculty of arrangement that made them vanish, as by the waving of an enchanter's wand. Bred up from boyhood in the Custom-House, it was his proper field of activity; and the many intricacies of business, so harassing to the interloper, presented themselves before him with the regularity of a perfectly comprehended system. In my contemplation, he stood as the ideal of his class. He was, indeed, the Custom-House in himself; or, at all events, the main-spring that kept its variously revolving wheels in motion; for, in an institution like this, where its officers are appointed to subserve their own profit and convenience, and seldom with a leading reference to their fitness for the duty to be performed, they must perforce seek elsewhere the dexterity which is not in them. Thus, by an inevitable necessity, as a magnet attracts steel-filings, so did our man of business draw to himself the difficulties which everybody met with. With an easy condescension, and kind of forbearance towards our stupidity,—which, to his order of mind, must have seemed little short of crime,—would he forthwith, by the merest touch of his finger, make the incomprehensible as clear as daylight. The merchants valued him not less than we, his esoteric friends. His integrity was perfect; it was a law of nature with him, rather than a choice or a principle; nor can it be otherwise than the main condition of an intellect so remarkably clear and accurate as his, to be honest and regular in the administration of affairs. A stain on his conscience, as to any thing that came within the range of his vocation, would trouble such a man very much in the same way, though to a far greater degree, than an error in the balance of an account, or an ink-blot on the fair page of a book of record. Here, in a word,—and it is a rare instance in my life,—I had met with a person thoroughly adapted to the situation which he held.

Such were some of the people with whom I now found myself connected. I took it in good part at the hands of Providence, that I was thrown into a position so little akin to my past habits; and set myself seriously to gather from it whatever profit was to be had. After my fellowship of toil and impracticable schemes, with the dreamy brethren of Brook Farm; after living for three years within the subtile influence of an intellect like Emerson's; after those wild, free days on the Assabeth, indulging fantastic speculations beside our fire of fallen boughs, with Ellery Channing; after talking with Thoreau about pine-trees and Indian relics, in his hermitage at Walden; after growing fastidious by sympathy with the classic refinement of Hillard's culture; after becoming imbued with poetic sentiment at Longellow's hearth-stone;—it was time, at length, that I should exercise other faculties of my nature, and nourish myself with food for which I had hitherto had little appetite. Even the old Inspector was desirable, as a change of diet, to a man who had known Alcott. I looked upon it as an evidence, in some measure, of a system naturally well balanced, and lacking no essential part of a thorough organization, that, with such associates to remember, I could mingle at once with men of altogether different qualities, and never murmur at the change.

Literature, its exertions and objects, were now of little moment in my regard. I cared not, at this period, for books; they were apart from me. Nature,—except it were human nature,—the nature that is developed in earth and sky, was, in one sense, hidden from me; and all the imaginative delight, wherewith it had been spiritualized, passed away out of my mind. A gift, a faculty, if it had not departed, was suspended and inanimate within me. There would have been something sad, unutterably dreary, in all this, had I not been conscious that it lay at my own option to recall whatever was valuable in the past. It might be true, indeed, that this was a life which could not, with impunity, be lived too long; else, it might make me permanently other than I had been, without transforming me into any shape which it would be worth my while to take. But I never considered it as other than a transitory life. There was always a prophetic instinct, a low whisper in my ear, that, within no long period, and whenever a new change of custom should be essential to my good, a change would come.

Meanwhile, there I was, a Surveyor of the Revenue, and, so far as I have been able to understand, as good a Surveyor as need be. A man of thought, fancy, and sensibility, (had he ten times the Surveyor's proportion of those qualities,) may, at any time, be a man of affairs, if he will only choose to give himself the trouble. My fellow-officers, and the merchants and sea-captains with whom my official duties brought me into any manner of connection, viewed me in no other light, and probably knew me in no other character. None of them, I presume, had ever read a page of my inditing, or would have cared a fig the more for me, if they had read them all; nor would it have mended the matter, in the least, had those same unprofitable pages been written with a pen like that of Burns or of Chaucer, each of whom was a Custom-House officer in his day, as well as I. It is a good lesson—though it may often be a hard one—for a man who has dreamed of literary fame, and of making for himself a rank among the world's dignitaries by such means, to step aside out of the narrow circle in which his claims are recognized, and to find how utterly devoid of significance, beyond that circle, is all that he achieves, and all he aims at. I know not that I especially needed the lesson, either in the way of warning or rebuke; but, at any rate, I learned it thoroughly; nor, it gives me pleasure to reflect, did the truth, as it came home to my perception, ever cost me a pang, or require to be thrown off in a sigh. In the way of literary talk, it is true, the Naval Officer—an excellent fellow, who came into office with me, and went out only a little later—would often engage me in a discussion about one of the other of his favorite topics, Napoleon or Shakespeare. The Collector's junior clerk, too,—a young gentleman who, it was whispered, occasionally covered a sheet of Uncle Sam's letter-paper with what, (at the distance of a few yards,) looked very much like poetry,—used now and then to speak to me of books, as matters with which I might possibly be conversant. This was my all of lettered intercourse; and it was quite sufficient for my necessities.

No longer seeking nor caring that my name should be blazoned abroad on title-pages, I smiled to think that it had now another kind of vogue. The Custom-House marker imprinted it, with a stencil and black paint, on pepper-bags, and baskets of anatto, and cigar-boxes, and bales of all kinds of dutiable merchandise, in testimony that these commodities had paid the impost, and gone regularly through the office. Borne on such queer vehicle of fame, a knowledge of my existence, so far as a name conveys it, was carried where it had never been before, and, I hope, will never go again.

But the past was not dead. Once in a great while, the thoughts, that had seemed so vital and so active, yet had been put to rest so quietly, revived again. One of the most remarkable occasions, when the habit of bygone days awoke in me, was that which brings it within the law of literary propriety to offer the public the sketch which I am now writing.

In the second story of the Custom-House, there is a large room, in which the brick-work and naked rafters have never been covered with panelling and plaster. The edifice—originally projected on a scale adapted to the old commercial enterprise of the port, and with an idea of subsequent prosperity destined never to be realized—contains far more space than its occupants know what to do with. This airy hall, therefore, over the Collector's apartments, remains unfinished to this day, and, in spite of the aged cobwebs that festoon its dusky beams, appears still to await the labor of the carpenter and mason. At one end of the room, in a recess, were a number of barrels, piled one upon another, containing bundles of official documents. Large quantities of similar rubbish lay lumbering the floor. It was sorrowful to think how many days, and weeks, and months, and years of toil, had been wasted on these musty papers, which were now only an encumbrance on earth, and were hidden away in this forgotten corner, never more to be glanced at by human eyes. But, then, what reams of other manuscripts—filled, not with the dulness of official formalities, but with the thought of inventive brains and the rich effusion of deep hearts—had gone equally to oblivion; and that, moreover, without serving a purpose in their day, as these heaped up papers had, and—saddest of all—without purchasing for their writers the comfortable livelihood which the clerks of the Custom-House had gained by these worthless scratchings of the pen! Yet not altogether worthless, perhaps, as materials of local history. Here, no doubt, statistics of the former commerce of Salem might be discovered, and memorials of her princely merchants,—old King Derby,—old Billy Gray,—old Simon Forrester,—and many another magnate in his day; whose powdered head, however, was scarcely in the tomb, before his mountain-pile of wealth began to dwindle. The founders of the greater part of the families which now compose the aristocracy of Salem might here be traced, from the petty and obscure beginnings of their traffic, at periods generally much posterior to the Revolution, upward to what their children look upon as long-established rank.

Prior to the Revolution, there is a dearth of records; the earlier documents and archives of the Custom-House having, probably, been carried off to Halifax, when all the King's officials accompanied the British army in its flight from Boston. It has often been a matter of regret with me; for, going back, perhaps, to the days of the Protectorate, those papers must have contained many references to forgotten or remembered men, and to antique customs, which would have affected me with the same pleasure as when I used to pick up Indian arrow-heads in the field near the Old Manse.

But, one idle and rainy day, it was my fortune to make a discovery of some little interest. Poking and burrowing into the heaped-up rubbish in the corner; unfolding one and another document, and reading the names of vessels that had long ago foundered at sea or rotted at the wharves, and those of merchants, never heard of now on 'Change, nor very readily decipherable on their mossy tombstones; glancing at such matters with the saddened, weary, half-reluctant interest which we bestow on the corpse of dead activity,—and exerting my fancy, sluggish with little use, to raise up from these dry bones an image of the old town's brighter aspect, when India was a new region, and only Salem knew the way thither,—I chanced to lay my hand on a small package, carefully done up in a piece of ancient yellow parchment. This envelope had the air of an official record of some period long past, when clerks engrossed their stiff and formal chirography on more substantial materials than at present. There was something about it that quickened an instinctive curiosity, and made me undo the faded red tape, that tied up the package, with the sense that a treasure would here be brought to light. Unbending the rigid folds of the parchment cover, I found it to be a commission, under the hand and seal of Governor Shirley, in favor of one Jonathan Pue, as Surveyor of his Majesty's Customs for the port of Salem, in the Province of Massachusetts Bay. I remembered to have read (probably in Felt's Annals) a notice of the decease of Mr. Surveyor Pue, about fourscore years ago; and likewise, in a newspaper of recent times, an account of the digging up of his remains in the little grave-yard of St. Peter's Church, during the renewal of that edifice. Nothing, if I rightly call to mind, was left of my respected predecessor, save an imperfect skeleton, and some fragments of apparel, and a wig of majestic frizzle; which, unlike the head that it once adorned, was in very satisfactory preservation. But, on examining the papers which the parchment commission served to envelop, I found more traces of Mr. Pue's mental part, and the internal operations of his head, than the frizzled wig had contained of the venerable skull itself.

They were documents, in short, not official, but of a private nature, or, at least, written in his private capacity, and apparently with his own hand. I could account for their being included in the heap of Custom-House lumber only by the fact, that Mr. Pue's death had happened suddenly; and that these papers, which he probably kept in his official desk, had never come to the knowledge of his heirs, or were supposed to relate to the business of the revenue. On the transfer of the archives to Halifax, this package, proving to be of no public concern, was left behind, and had remained ever since unopened.

The ancient Surveyor—being little molested, I suppose, at that early day, with business pertaining to his office—seems to have devoted some of his many leisure hours to researches as a local antiquarian, and other inquisitions of a similar nature. These supplied material for petty activity to a mind that would otherwise have been eaten up with rust. A portion of his facts, by and by, did me good service in the preparation of the article entitled "MAIN STREET," included in the present volume. The remainder may perhaps be applied to purposes equally valuable, hereafter; or not impossibly may be worked up, so far as they go, into a regular history of Salem, should my veneration for the natal soil ever impel me to so pious a task. Meanwhile, they shall be at the command of any gentleman, inclined, and competent, to take the unprofitable labor off my hands. As a final disposition, I contemplate depositing them with the Essex Historical Society.

But the object that most drew my attention, in the mysterious package, was a certain affair of fine red cloth, much worn and faded. There were traces about it of gold embroidery, which, however, was greatly frayed and defaced; so that none, or very little, of the glitter was left. It had been wrought, as was easy to perceive, with wonderful skill of needlework; and the stitch (as I am assured by ladies conversant with such mysteries) gives evidence of a now forgotten art, not to be recovered even by the process of picking out the threads. This rag of scarlet cloth,—for time, and wear, and a sacrilegious moth, had reduced it to little other than a rag,—on careful examination, assumed the shape of a letter. It was the capital letter A. By an accurate measurement, each limb proved to be precisely three inches and a quarter in length. It had been intended, there could be no doubt, as an ornamental article of dress; but how it was to be worn, or what rank, honor, and dignity, in by-past times, were signified by it, was a riddle which (so evanescent are the fashions of the world in these particulars) I saw little hope of solving. And yet it strangely interested me. My eyes fastened themselves upon the old scarlet letter, and would not be turned aside. Certainly, there was some deep meaning in it, most worthy of interpretation, and which, as it were, streamed forth from the mystic symbol, subtly communicating itself to my sensibilities, but evading the analysis of my mind.

While thus perplexed,—and cogitating, among other hypotheses, whether the letter might not have been one of those decorations which the white men used to contrive, in order to take the eyes of Indians,—I happened to place it on my breast. It seemed to me,—the reader may smile, but must not doubt my word,—it seemed to me, then, that I experienced a sensation not altogether physical, yet almost so, as of burning heat; and as if the letter were not of red cloth, but red-hot iron. I shuddered, and involuntarily let it fall upon the floor.

In the absorbing contemplation of the scarlet letter, I had hitherto neglected to examine a small roll of dingy paper, around which it had been twisted. This I now opened, and had the satisfaction to find, recorded by the old Surveyor's pen, a reasonably complete explanation of the whole affair. There were several foolscap sheets, containing many particulars respecting the life and conversation of one Hester Prynne, who appeared to have been rather a noteworthy personage in the view of our ancestors. She had flourished during a period between the early days of Massachusetts and the close of the seventeenth century. Aged persons, alive in the time of Mr. Surveyor Pue, and from whose oral testimony he had made up his narrative, remembered her, in their youth, as a very old, but not decrepit woman, of a stately and solemn aspect. It had been her habit, from an almost immemorial date, to go about the country as a kind of voluntary nurse, and doing whatever miscellaneous good she might; taking upon herself, likewise, to give advice in all matters, especially those of the heart; by which means, as a person of such propensities inevitably must, she gained from many people the reverence due to an angel, but, I should imagine, was looked upon by others as an intruder and a nuisance. Prying farther into the manuscript, I found the record of other doings and sufferings of this singular woman, for most of which the reader is referred to the story entitled "THE SCARLET LETTER"; and it should be borne carefully in mind, that the main facts of that story are authorized and authenticated by the document of Mr. Surveyor Pue. The original papers, together with the scarlet letter itself,—a most curious relic,—are still in my possession, and shall be freely exhibited to whomsoever, induced by the great interest of the narrative, may desire a sight of them. I must not be understood as affirming, that, in the dressing up of the tale, and imagining the motives and modes of passion that influenced the characters who figure in it, I have invariably confined myself within the limits of the old Surveyor's half a dozen sheets of foolscap. On the contrary, I have allowed myself, as to such points, nearly or altogether as much license as if the facts had been entirely of my own invention. What I contend for is the authenticity of the outline.

This incident recalled my mind, in some degree, to its old track. There seemed to be here the groundwork of a tale. It impressed me as if the ancient Surveyor, in his garb of a hundred years gone by, and wearing his immortal wig,—which was buried with him, but did not perish in the grave,—had met me in the deserted chamber of the Custom-House. In his port was the dignity of one who had borne his Majesty's commission, and who was therefore illuminated by a ray of the splendor that shone so dazzlingly about the throne. How unlike, alas! the hang-dog look of a republican official, who, as the servant of the people, feels himself less than the least, and below the lowest, of his masters. With his own ghostly hand, the obscurely seen, but majestic, figure had imparted to me the scarlet symbol, and the little roll of explanatory manuscript. With his own ghostly voice, he had exhorted me, on the sacred consideration of my filial duty and reverence towards him,—who might reasonably regard himself as my official ancestor,—to bring his mouldy and moth-eaten lucubrations before the public. "Do this," said the ghost of Mr. Surveyor Pue, emphatically nodding the head that looked so imposing within its memorable wig, "do this, and the profit shall be all your own! You will shortly need it; for it is not in your days as it was in mine, when a man's office was a life-lease, and oftentimes an heirloom. But, I charge you, in this matter of old Mistress Prynne, give to your predecessor's memory the credit which will be rightfully its due!" And I said to the ghost of Mr. Surveyor Pue,—"I will!"

On Hester Prynne's story, therefore, I bestowed much thought. It was the subject of my meditations for many an hour, while pacing to and fro across my room, or traversing, with a hundredfold repetition, the long extent from the front-door of the Custom-House to the side-entrance, and back again. Great were the weariness and annoyance of the old Inspector and the Weighters and Gaugers, whose slumbers were disturbed by the unmercifully lengthened tramp of my passing and returning footsteps. Remembering their own former habits, they used to say that the Surveyor was walking the quarter-deck. They probably fancied that my sole object—and, indeed, the sole object for which a sane man could ever put himself into voluntary motion—was, to get an appetite for dinner. And to say the truth, an appetite, sharpened by the east-wind that generally blew along the passage, was the only valuable result of so much indefatigable exercise. So little adapted is the atmosphere of a Custom-House to the delicate harvest of fancy and sensibility, that, had I remained there through ten Presidencies yet to come, I doubt whether the tale of "The Scarlet Letter" would ever have been brought before the public eye. My imagination was a tarnished mirror. It would not reflect, or only with miserable dimness, the figures with which I did my best to people it. The characters of the narrative would not be warmed and rendered malleable, by any heat that I could kindle at my intellectual forge. They would take neither the glow of passion nor the tenderness of sentiment, but retained all the rigidity of dead corpses, and stared me in the face with a fixed and ghastly grin of contemptuous defiance. "What have you do to with us?" that expression seemed to say. "The little power you might once have possessed over the tribe of unrealities is gone! You have bartered it for a pittance of the public gold. Go, then, and earn your wages!" In short, the almost torpid creatures of my own fancy twitted me with imbecility, and not without fair occasion.

It was not merely during the three hours and a half which Uncle Sam claimed as his share of my daily life, that this wretched numbness held possession of me. It went with me on my sea-shore walks and rambles into the country, whenever—which was seldom and reluctantly—I bestirred myself to seek that invigorating charm of Nature, which used to give me such freshness and activity of thought, the moment that I stepped across the threshold of the Old Manse. The same torpor, as regarded the capacity for intellectual effort, accompanied me home, and weighed upon me in the chamber which I most absurdly termed my study. Nor did it quit me, when, late at night, I sat in the deserted parlour, lighted only by the glimmering coal-fire and the moon, striving to picture forth imaginary scenes, which, the next day, might flow out on the brightening page in many-hued description.

If the imaginative faculty refused to act at such an hour, it might well be deemed a hopeless case. Moonlight, in a familiar room, falling so white upon the carpet, and showing all its figures so distinctly,—making every object so minutely visible, yet so unlike a morning or noontide visibility,—is a medium the most suitable for a romance-writer to get acquainted with his illusive guests. There is the little domestic scenery of the well-known apartment; the chairs, with each its separate individuality; the centre-table, sustaining a workbasket, a volume or two, and an extinguished lamp; the sofa; the book-case; the picture on the wall;—all these details, so completely seen, are so spiritualized by the unusual light, that they seem to lose their actual substance, and become things of intellect. Nothing is too small or too trifling to undergo this change, and acquire dignity thereby. A child's shoe; the doll, seated in her little wicker carriage; the hobby-horse;—whatever, in a word, has been used or played with, during the day, is now invested with a quality of strangeness and remoteness, though still almost as vividly present as by daylight. Thus, therefore, the floor of our familiar room has become a neutral territory, somewhere between the real world and fairy-land, where the Actual and the Imaginary may meet, and each imbue itself with the nature of the other. Ghosts might enter here, without affrighting us. It would be too much in keeping with the scene to excite surprise, were we to look about us and discover a form, beloved, but gone hence, now sitting quietly in a streak of this magic moonshine, with an aspect that would make us doubt whether it had returned from afar, or had never once stirred from our fireside.

The somewhat dim coal-fire has an essential influence in producing the effect which I would describe. It throws its unobtrusive tinge throughout the room, with a faint ruddiness upon the walls and ceiling, and a reflected gleam from the polish of the furniture. This warmer light mingles itself with the cold spirituality of the moonbeams, and communicates, as it were, a heart and sensibilities of human tenderness to the forms which fancy summons up. It converts them from snow-images into men and women. Glancing at the looking-glass, we behold—deep within its haunted verge—the smouldering glow of the half-extinguished anthracite, the white moonbeams on the floor, and a repetition of all the gleam and shadow of the picture, with one remove farther from the actual, and nearer to the imaginative. Then, at such an hour, and with this scene before him, if a man, sitting all alone, cannot dream strange things, and make them look like truth, he need never try to write romances.

But, for myself, during the whole of my Custom-House experience, moonlight and sunshine, and the glow of firelight, were just alike in my regard; and neither of them was of one whit more avail than the twinkle of a tallow-candle. An entire class of susceptibilities, and a gift connected with them,—of no great richness or value, but the best I had,—was gone from me.

It is my belief, however, that, had I attempted a different order of composition, my faculties would not have been found so pointless and inefficacious. I might, for instance, have contented myself with writing out the narratives of a veteran shipmaster, one of the Inspectors, whom I should be most ungrateful not to mention; since scarcely a day passed that he did not stir me to laughter and admiration by his marvellous gifts as a story-teller. Could I have preserved the picturesque force of his style, and the humorous coloring which nature taught him how to throw over his descriptions, the result, I honestly believe, would have been something new in literature. Or I might readily have found a more serious task. It was a folly, with the materiality of this daily life pressing so intrusively upon me, to attempt to fling myself back into another age; or to insist on creating the semblance of a world out of airy matter, when, at every moment, the impalpable beauty of my soap-bubble was broken by the rude contact of some actual circumstance. The wiser effort would have been, to diffuse thought and imagination through the opaque substance of to-day, and thus to make it a bright transparency; to spiritualize the burden that began to weigh so heavily; to seek, resolutely, the true and indestructible value that lay hidden in the petty and wearisome incidents, and ordinary characters, with which I was now conversant. The fault was mine. The page of life that was spread out before me seemed dull and commonplace, only because I had not fathomed its deeper import. A better book than I shall ever write was there; leaf after leaf presenting itself to me, just as it was written out by the reality of the flitting hour, and vanishing as fast as written, only because my brain wanted the insight and my hand the cunning to transcribe it. At some future day, it may be, I shall remember a few scattered fragments and broken paragraphs, and write them down, and find the letters turn to gold upon the page.

These perceptions have come too late. At the instant, I was only conscious that what would have been a pleasure once was now a hopeless toil. There was no occasion to make much moan about this state of affairs. I had ceased to be a writer of tolerably poor tales and essays, and had become a tolerably good Surveyor of the Customs. That was all. But, nevertheless, it is any thing but agreeable to be haunted by a suspicion that one's intellect is dwindling away; or exhaling, without your consciousness, like ether out of a phial; so that, at every glance, you find a smaller and less volatile residuum. Of the fact, there could be no doubt; and, examining myself and others, I was led to conclusions in reference to the effect of public office on the character, not very favorable to the mode of life in question. In some other form, perhaps, I may hereafter develop these effects. Suffice it here to say, that a Custom-House officer, of long continuance, can hardly be a very praiseworthy or respectable personage, for many reasons; one of them, the tenure by which he holds his situation, and another, the very nature of his business, which—though, I trust, an honest one—is of such a sort that he does not share in the united effort of mankind.

An effect—which I believe to be observable, more or less, in every individual who has occupied the position—is, that, while he leans on the mighty arm of the Republic, his own proper strength departs from him. He loses, in an extent proportioned to the weakness or force of his original nature, the capability of self-support. If he possess an unusual share of native energy, or the enervating magic of place do not operate too long upon him, his forfeited powers may be redeemable. The ejected officer—fortunate in the unkindly shove that sends him forth betimes, to struggle amid a struggling world—may return to himself, and become all that he has ever been. But this seldom happens. He usually keeps his ground just long enough for his own ruin, and is then thrust out, with sinews all unstrung, to totter along the difficult footpath of life as he best may. Conscious of his own infirmity,—that his tempered steel and elasticity are lost,—he for ever afterwards looks wistfully about him in quest of support external to himself. His pervading and continual hope—a hallucination, which, in the face of all discouragment, and making light of impossibilities, haunts him while he lives, and, I fancy, like the convulsive throes of the cholera, torments him for a brief space after death—is, that, finally, and in no long time, by some happy coincidence of circumstances, he shall be restored to office. This faith, more than any thing else, steals the pith and availability out of whatever enterprise he may dream of undertaking. Why should he toil and moil, and be at so much trouble to pick himself up out of the mud, when, in a little while hence, the strong arm of his Uncle will raise and support him? Why should he work for his living here, or go to dig gold in California, when he is so soon to be made happy, at monthly intervals, with a little pile of glittering coin out of his Uncle's pocket? It is sadly curious to observe how slight a taste of office suffices to infect a poor fellow with this singular disease. Uncle Sam's gold—meaning no disrespect to the worthy old gentleman—has, in this respect, a quality of enchantment like that of the Devil's wages. Whoever touches it should look well to himself, or he may find the bargain to go hard against him, involving, if not his soul, yet many of its better attributes; its sturdy force, its courage and constancy, its truth, its self-reliance, and all that gives the emphasis to manly character.

Here was a fine prospect in the distance! Not that the Surveyor brought the lesson home to himself, or admitted that he could be so utterly undone, either by continuance in office, or ejectment. Yet my reflections were not the most comfortable. I began to grow melancholy and restless; continually prying into my mind, to discover which of its poor properties were gone, and what degree of detriment had already accrued to the remainder. I endeavoured to calculate how much longer I could stay in the Custom-House, and yet go forth a man. To confess the truth, it was my greatest apprehension,—as it would never be a measure of policy to turn out so quiet an individual as myself, and it being hardly in the nature of a public officer to resign,—it was my chief trouble, therefore, that I was likely to grow gray and decrepit in the Surveyorship, and become much such another animal as the old Inspector. Might it not, in the tedious lapse of official life that lay before me, finally be with me as it was with this venerable friend,—to make the dinner-hour the nucleus of the day, and to spend the rest of it, as an old dog spends it, asleep in the sunshine or the shade? A dreary look-forward this, for a man who felt it to be the best definition of happiness to live throughout the whole range of his faculties and sensibilities! But, all this while, I was giving myself very unnecessary alarm. Providence had meditated better things for me than I could possibly imagine for myself.

A remarkable event of the third year of my Surveyorship—to adopt the tone of "P. P."—was the election of General Taylor to the Presidency. It is essential, in order to form a complete estimate of the advantages of official life, to view the incumbent at the in-coming of a hostile administration. His position is then one of the most singularly irksome, and, in every contingency, disagreeable, that a wretched mortal can possibly occupy; with seldom an alternative of good, on either hand, although what presents itself to him as the worst event may very probably be the best. But it is a strange experience, to a man of pride and sensibility, to know that his interests are within the control of individuals who neither love nor understand him, and by whom, since one or the other must needs happen, he would rather be injured than obliged. Strange, too, for one who has kept his calmness throughout the contest, to observe the bloodthirstiness that is developed in the hour of triumph, and to be conscious that he is himself among its objects! There are few uglier traits of human nature than this tendency—which I now witness in men no worse than their neighbours—to grow cruel, merely because they possessed the power of inflicting harm. If the guillotine, as applied to office-holders, were a literal fact, instead of one of the most apt of metaphors, it is my sincere belief, that the active members of the victorious party were sufficiently excited to have chopped off all our heads, and have thanked Heaven for the opportunity! It appears to me—who have been a calm and curious observer, as well in victory as defeat—that this fierce and bitter spirit of malice and revenge has never distinguished the many triumphs of my own party as it now did that of the Whigs. The Democrats take the offices, as a general rule, because they need them, and because the practice of many years has made it the law of political warfare, which, unless a different system be proclaimed, it were weakness and cowardice to murmur at. But the long habit of victory has made them generous. They know how to spare, when they see occasion; and when they strike, the axe may be sharp, indeed, but its edge is seldom poisoned with ill-will; nor is it their custom ignominiously to kick the head which they have just struck off.

In short, unpleasant as was my predicament, at best, I saw much reason to congratulate myself that I was on the losing side, rather than the triumphant one. If, heretofore, I had been none of the warmest of partisans, I began now, at this season of peril and adversity, to be pretty acutely sensible with which party my predilections lay; nor was it without something like regret and shame, that, according to a reasonable calculation of chances, I saw my own prospect of retaining office to be better than those of my Democratic brethren. But who can see an inch into futurity, beyond his nose? My own head was the first that fell!

The moment when a man's head drops off is seldom or never, I am inclined to think, precisely the most agreeable of his life. Nevertheless, like the greater part of our misfortunes, even so serious a contingency brings its remedy and consolation with it, if the sufferer will but make the best, rather than the worst, of the accident which has befallen him. In my particular case, the consolatory topics were close at hand, and, indeed, had suggested themselves to my meditations a considerable time before it was requisite to use them. In view of my previous weariness of office, and vague thoughts of resignation, my fortune somewhat resembled that of a person who should entertain an idea of committing suicide, and, altogether beyond his hopes, meet with the good hap to be murdered. In the Custom-House, as before in the Old Manse, I had spent three years; a term long enough to rest a weary brain; long enough to break off old intellectual habits, and make room for new ones; long enough, and too long, to have lived in an unnatural state, doing what was really of no advantage nor delight to any human being, and withholding myself from toil that would, at least, have stilled an unquiet impulse in me. Then, moreover, as regarded his unceremonious ejectment, the late Surveyor was not altogether ill-pleased to be recognized by the Whigs as an enemy; since his inactivity in political affairs,—his tendency to roam, at will, in that broad and quiet field where all mankind may meet, rather than confine himself to those narrow paths where brethren of the same household must diverge from one another,—had sometimes made it questionable with his brother Democrats whether he was a friend. Now, after he had won the crown of martyrdom, (though with no longer a head to wear it on,) the point might be looked upon as settled. Finally, little heroic as he was, it seemed more decorous to be overthrown in the downfall of the party with which he had been content to stand, than to remain a forlorn survivor, when so many worthier men were falling; and, at last, after subsisting for four years on the mercy of a hostile administration, to be compelled then to define his position anew, and claim the yet more humiliating mercy of a friendly one.

Meanwhile, the press had taken up my affair, and kept me, for a week or two, careering through the public prints, in my decapitated state, like Irving's Headless Horseman; ghastly and grim, and longing to be buried, as a politically dead man ought. So much for my figurative self. The real human being, all this time, with his head safely on his shoulders, had brought himself to the comfortable conclusion, that every thing was for the best; and, making an investment in ink, paper, and steel-pens, had opened his long-disused writing-desk, and was again a literary man.

Now it was, that the lucubrations of my ancient predecessor, Mr. Surveyor Pue, came into play. Rusty through long idleness, some little space was requisite before my intellectual machinery could be brought to work upon the tale, with an effect in any degree satisfactory. Even yet, though my thoughts were ultimately much absorbed in the task, it wears, to my eye, a stern and sombre aspect; too much ungladdened by genial sunshine; too little relieved by the tender and familiar influences which soften almost every scene of nature and real life, and, undoubtedly, should soften every picture of them. This uncaptivating effect is perhaps due to the period of hardly accomplished revolution, and still seething turmoil, in which the story shaped itself. It is no indication, however, of a lack of cheerfulness in the writer's mind; for he was happier, while straying through the gloom of these sunless fantasies, than at any time since he had quitted the Old Manse. Some of the briefer articles, which contribute to make up the volume, have likewise been written since my involuntary withdrawal from the toils and honors of public life, and the remainder are gleaned from annuals and magazines, of such antique date that they have gone round the circle, and come back to novelty again.* Keeping up the metaphor of the political guillotine, the whole may be considered as the POSTHUMOUS PAPERS OF A DECAPITATED SURVEYOR; and the sketch which I am now bringing to a close, if too autobiographical for a modest person to publish in his lifetime, will readily be excused in a gentleman who writes from beyond the grave. Peace be with all the world! My blessing on my friends! My forgiveness to my enemies! For I am in the realm of quiet!

---

*At the time of writing this article, the author intended to publish, along with "The Scarlet Letter," several shorter tales and sketches. These it has been thought advisable to defer. [This footnote appears in all editions.]

The life of the Custom-House lies like a dream behind me. The old Inspector,—who, by the by, I regret to say, was overthrown and killed by a horse, some time ago; else he would certainly have lived for ever,—he, and all those other venerable personages who sat with him at the receipt of custom, are but shadows in my view; white-headed and wrinkled images, which my fancy used to sport with, and has now flung aside for ever. The merchants,—Pingree, Phillips, Shepard, Upton, Kimball, Bertram, Hunt,—these, and many other names, which had such a classic familiarity for my ear six months ago,—these men of traffic, who seemed to occupy so important a position in the world,—how little time has it required to disconnect me from them all, not merely in act, but recollection! It is with an effort that I recall the figures and appellations of these few. Soon, likewise, my old native town will loom upon me through the haze of memory, a mist brooding over and around it; as if it were no portion of the real earth, but an overgrown village in cloud-land, with only imaginary inhabitants to people its wooden houses, and walk its homely lanes, and the unpicturesque prolixity of its main street. Henceforth, it ceases to be a reality of my life. I am a citizen of somewhere else. My good townspeople will not much regret me; for—though it has been as dear an object as any, in my literary efforts, to be of some importance in their eyes, and to win myself a pleasant memory in this abode and burial-place of so many of my forefathers—there has never been, for me, the genial atmosphere which a literary man requires, in order to ripen the best harvest of his mind. I shall do better amongst other faces; and these familiar ones, it need hardly be said, will do just as well without me.

It may be, however,—O, transporting and triumphant thought!—that the great-grandchildren of the present race may sometimes think kindly of the scribbler of bygone days, when the antiquary of days to come, among the sites memorable in the town's history, shall point out the locality of THE TOWN-PUMP!

THE SCARLET LETTER

CHAPTER I

THE PRISON-DOOR

A throng of bearded men, in sad-colored garments and gray, steeple-crowned hats, intermixed with women, some wearing hoods, and others bareheaded, was assembled in front of a wooden edifice, the door of which was heavily timbered with oak, and studded with iron spikes.

The founders of a new colony, whatever Utopia of human virtue and happiness they might originally project, have invariably recognized it among their earliest practical necessities to allot a portion of the virgin soil as a cemetery, and another portion as the site of a prison. In accordance with this rule, it may safely be assumed that the forefathers of Boston had built the first prison-house, somewhere in the vicinity of Cornhill, almost as seasonably as they marked out the first burial-ground, on Isaac Johnson's lot, and round about his grave, which subsequently became the nucleus of all the congregated sepulchres in the old church-yard of King's Chapel. Certain it is, that, some fifteen or twenty years after the settlement of the town, the wooden jail was already marked with weather-stains and other indications of age, which gave a yet darker aspect to its beetle-browed and gloomy front. The rust on the ponderous iron-work of its oaken door looked more antique than any thing else in the new world. Like all that pertains to crime, it seemed never to have known a youthful era. Before this ugly edifice, and between it and the wheel-track of the street, was a grassplot, much overgrown with burdock, pig-weed, apple-peru, and such unsightly vegetation, which evidently found something congenial in the soil that had so early borne the black flower of civilized society, a prison. But, on one side of the portal, and rooted almost at the threshold, was a wild rosebush, covered, in this month of June, with its delicate gems, which might be imagined to offer their fragrance and fragile beauty to the prisoner as he went in, and to the condemned criminal as he came forth to his doom, in token that the deep heart of Nature could pity and be kind to him.

This rose-bush, by a strange chance, has been kept alive in history; but whether it had merely survived out of the stern old wilderness, so long after the fall of the gigantic pines and oaks that originally overshadowed it,—or whether, as there is fair authority for believing, it had sprung up under the footsteps of the sainted Ann Hutchinson, as she entered the prison-door,—we shall not take upon us to determine. Finding it so directly on the threshold of our narrative, which is now about to issue from that inauspicious portal, we could hardly do otherwise than pluck one of its flowers and present it to the reader. It may serve, let us hope, to symbolize some sweet moral blossom, that may be found along the track, or relieve the darkening close of a tale of human frailty and sorrow.

CHAPTER II

THE MARKET-PLACE

The grass-plot before the jail, in Prison Lane, on a certain summer morning, not less than two centuries ago, was occupied by a pretty large number of the inhabitants of Boston; all with their eyes intently fastened on the iron-clamped oaken door. Amongst any other population, or at a later period in the history of New England, the grim rigidity that petrified the bearded physiognomies of these good people would have augured some awful business in hand. It could have betokened nothing short of the anticipated execution of some noted culprit, on whom the sentence of a legal tribunal had but confirmed the verdict of public sentiment. But, in that early severity of the Puritan character, an inference of this kind could not so indubitably be drawn. It might be that a sluggish bond-servant, or an undutiful child, whom his parents had given over to the civil authority, was to be corrected at the whipping-post. It might be, that an Antinomian, a Quaker, or other heterodox religionist, was to be scourged out of the town, or an idle and vagrant Indian, whom the white man's fire-water had made riotous about the streets, was to be driven with stripes into the shadow of the forest. It might be, too, that a witch, like old Mistress Hibbins, the bitter-tempered widow of the magistrate, was to die upon the gallows. In either case, there was very much the same solemnity of demeanour on the part of the spectators; as befitted a people amongst whom religion and law were almost identical, and in whose character both were so thoroughly interfused, that the mildest and the severest acts of public discipline were alike made venerable and awful. Meagre, indeed, and cold, was the sympathy that a transgressor might look for, from such by-standers, at the scaffold. On the other hand, a penalty which, in our days, would infer a degree of mocking infamy and ridicule, might then be invested with almost as stern a dignity as the punishment of death itself.

It was a circumstance to be noted, on the summer morning when our story begins its course, that the women, of whom there were several in the crowd, appeared to take a peculiar interest in whatever penal infliction might be expected to ensue. The age had not so much refinement, that any sense of impropriety restrained the wearers of petticoat and farthingale from stepping forth into the public ways, and wedging their not unsubstantial persons, if occasion were, into the throng nearest to the scaffold at an execution. Morally, as well as materially, there was a coarser fibre in those wives and maidens of old English birth and breeding, than in their fair descendants, separated from them by a series of six or seven generations; for, throughout that chain of ancestry, every successive mother has transmitted to her child a fainter bloom, a more delicate and briefer beauty, and a slighter physical frame, if not a character of less force and solidity, than her own. The women, who were now standing about the prison-door, stood within less than half a century of the period when the man-like Elizabeth had been the not altogether unsuitable representative of the sex. They were her countrywomen; and the beef and ale of their native land, with a moral diet not a whit more refined, entered largely into their composition. The bright morning sun, therefore, shone on broad shoulders and well-developed busts, and on round and ruddy cheeks, that had ripened in the far-off island, and had hardly yet grown paler or thinner in the atmosphere of New England. There was, moreover, a boldness and rotundity of speech among these matrons, as most of them seemed to be, that would startle us at the present day, whether in respect to its purport or its volume of tone.

"Goodwives," said a hard-featured dame of fifty, "I'll tell ye a piece of my mind. It would be greatly for the public behoof, if we women, being of mature age and church-members in good repute, should have the handling of such malefactresses as this Hester Prynne. What think ye, gossips? If the hussy stood up for judgment before us five, that are now here in a knot together, would she come off with such a sentence as the worshipful magistrates have awarded? Marry, I trow not!"

"People say," said another, "that the Reverend Master Dimmesdale, her godly pastor, takes it very grievously to heart that such a scandal should have come upon his congregation."

"The magistrates are God-fearing gentlemen, but merciful overmuch,—that is a truth," added a third autumnal matron. "At the very least, they should have put the brand of a hot iron on Hester Prynne's forehead. Madam Hester would have winced at that, I warrant me. But she,—the naughty baggage,—little will she care what they put upon the bodice of her gown! Why, look you, she may cover it with a brooch, or such like heathenish adornment, and so walk the streets as brave as ever!"

"Ah, but," interposed, more softly, a young wife, holding a child by the hand, "let her cover the mark as she will, the pang of it will be always in her heart."

"What do we talk of marks and brands, whether on the bodice of her gown, or the flesh of her forehead?" cried another female, the ugliest as well as the most pitiless of these self-constituted judges. "This woman has brought shame upon us all, and ought to die. Is there not law for it? Truly there is, both in the Scripture and the statute-book. Then let the magistrates, who have made it of no effect, thank themselves if their own wives and daughters go astray!"

"Mercy on us, goodwife," exclaimed a man in the crowd, "is there no virtue in woman, save what springs from a wholesome fear of the gallows? That is the hardest word yet! Hush, now, gossips; for the lock is turning in the prison-door, and here comes Mistress Prynne herself."

The door of the jail being flung open from within, there appeared, in the first place, like a black shadow emerging into the sunshine, the grim and grisly presence of the town-beadle, with a sword by his side and his staff of office in his hand. This personage prefigured and represented in his aspect the whole dismal severity of the Puritanic code of law, which it was his business to administer in its final and closest application to the offender. Stretching forth the official staff in his left hand, he laid his right upon the shoulder of a young woman, whom he thus drew forward; until, on the threshold of the prison-door, she repelled him, by an action marked with natural dignity and force of character, and stepped into the open air, as if by her own free-will. She bore in her arms a child, a baby of some three months old, who winked and turned aside its little face from the too vivid light of day; because its existence, heretofore, had brought it acquainted only with the gray twilight of a dungeon, or other darksome apartment of the prison.

When the young woman—the mother of this child—stood fully revealed before the crowd, it seemed to be her first impulse to clasp the infant closely to her bosom; not so much by an impulse of motherly affection, as that she might thereby conceal a certain token, which was wrought or fastened into her dress. In a moment, however, wisely judging that one token of her shame would but poorly serve to hide another, she took the baby on her arm, and, with a burning blush, and yet a haughty smile, and a glance that would not be abashed, looked around at her townspeople and neighbours. On the breast of her gown, in fine red cloth, surrounded with an elaborate embroidery and fantastic flourishes of gold thread, appeared the letter A. It was so artistically done, and with so much fertility and gorgeous luxuriance of fancy, that it had all the effect of a last and fitting decoration to the apparel which she wore; and which was of a splendor in accordance with the taste of the age, but greatly beyond what was allowed by the sumptuary regulations of the colony.

The young woman was tall, with a figure of perfect elegance, on a large scale. She had dark and abundant hair, so glossy that it threw off the sunshine with a gleam, and a face which, besides being beautiful from regularity of feature and richness of complexion, had the impressiveness belonging to a marked brow and deep black eyes. She was lady-like, too, after the manner of the feminine gentility of those days; characterized by a certain state and dignity, rather than by the delicate, evanescent, and indescribable grace, which is now recognized as its indication. And never had Hester Prynne appeared more lady-like, in the antique interpretation of the term, than as she issued from the prison. Those who had before known her, and had expected to behold her dimmed and obscured by a disastrous cloud, were astonished, and even startled, to perceive how her beauty shone out, and made a halo of the misfortune and ignominy in which she was enveloped. It may be true, that, to a sensitive observer, there was something exquisitely painful in it. Her attire, which, indeed, she had wrought for the occasion, in prison, and had modelled much after her own fancy, seemed to express the attitude of her spirit, the desperate recklessness of her mood, by its wild and picturesque peculiarity. But the point which drew all eyes, and, as it were, transfigured the wearer,—so that both men and women, who had been familiarly acquainted with Hester Prynne, were now impressed as if they beheld her for the first time,—was that SCARLET LETTER, so fantastically embroidered and illuminated upon her bosom. It had the effect of a spell, taking her out of the ordinary relations with humanity, and inclosing her in a sphere by herself.

"She hath good skill at her needle, that's certain," remarked one of the female spectators; "but did ever a woman, before this brazen hussy, contrive such a way of showing it! Why, gossips, what is it but to laugh in the faces of our godly magistrates, and make a pride out of what they, worthy gentlemen, meant for a punishment?"

"It were well," muttered the most iron-visaged of the old dames, "if we stripped Madam Hester's rich gown off her dainty shoulders; and as for the red letter, which she hath stitched so curiously, I'll bestow a rag of mine own rheumatic flannel, to make a fitter one!"

"O, peace, neighbours, peace!" whispered their youngest companion. "Do not let her hear you! Not a stitch in that embroidered letter, but she has felt it in her heart."

The grim beadle now made a gesture with his staff.

"Make way, good people, make way, in the King's name," cried he. "Open a passage; and, I promise ye, Mistress Prynne shall be set where man, woman, and child may have a fair sight of her brave apparel, from this time till an hour past meridian. A blessing on the righteous Colony of the Massachusetts, where iniquity is dragged out into the sunshine! Come along, Madam Hester, and show your scarlet letter in the market-place!"

A lane was forthwith opened through the crowd of spectators. Preceded by the beadle, and attended by an irregular procession of stern-browed men and unkindly-visaged women, Hester Prynne set forth towards the place appointed for her punishment. A crowd of eager and curious schoolboys, understanding little of the matter in hand, except that it gave them a half-holiday, ran before her progress, turning their heads continually to stare into her face, and at the winking baby in her arms, and at the ignominious letter on her breast. It was no great distance, in those days, from the prison-door to the market-place. Measured by the prisoner's experience, however, it might be reckoned a journey of some length; for, haughty as her demeanour was, she perchance underwent an agony from every footstep of those that thronged to see her, as if her heart had been flung into the street for them all to spurn and trample upon. In our nature, however, there is a provision, alike marvellous and merciful, that the sufferer should never know the intensity of what he endures by its present torture, but chiefly by the pang that rankles after it. With almost a serene deportment, therefore, Hester Prynne passed through this portion of her ordeal, and came to a sort of scaffold, at the western extremity of the market-place. It stood nearly beneath the eaves of Boston's earliest church, and appeared to be a fixture there.

In fact, this scaffold constituted a portion of a penal machine, which now, for two or three generations past, has been merely historical and traditionary among us, but was held, in the old time, to be as effectual an agent in the promotion of good citizenship, as ever was the guillotine among the terrorists of France. It was, in short, the platform of the pillory; and above it rose the framework of that instrument of discipline, so fashioned as to confine the human head in its tight grasp, and thus hold it up to the public gaze. The very ideal of ignominy was embodied and made manifest in this contrivance of wood and iron. There can be no outrage, methinks, against our common nature,—whatever be the delinquencies of the individual,—no outrage more flagrant than to forbid the culprit to hide his face for shame; as it was the essence of this punishment to do. In Hester Prynne's instance, however, as not unfrequently in other cases, her sentence bore, that she should stand a certain time upon the platform, but without undergoing that gripe about the neck and confinement of the head, the proneness to which was the most devilish characteristic of this ugly engine. Knowing well her part, she ascended a flight of wooden steps, and was thus displayed to the surrounding multitude, at about the height of a man's shoulders above the street.

Had there been a Papist among the crowd of Puritans, he might have seen in this beautiful woman, so picturesque in her attire and mien, and with the infant at her bosom, an object to remind him of the image of Divine Maternity, which so many illustrious painters have vied with one another to represent; something which should remind him, indeed, but only by contrast, of that sacred image of sinless motherhood, whose infant was to redeem the world. Here, there was the taint of deepest sin in the most sacred quality of human life, working such effect, that the world was only the darker for this woman's beauty, and the more lost for the infant that she had borne.

The scene was not without a mixture of awe, such as must always invest the spectacle of guilt and shame in a fellow-creature, before society shall have grown corrupt enough to smile, instead of shuddering, at it. The witnesses of Hester Prynne's disgrace had not yet passed beyond their simplicity. They were stern enough to look upon her death, had that been the sentence, without a murmur at its severity, but had none of the heartlessness of another social state, which would find only a theme for jest in an exhibition like the present. Even had there been a disposition to turn the matter into ridicule, it must have been repressed and over-powered by the solemn presence of men no less dignified than the Governor, and several of his counsellors, a judge, a general, and the ministers of the town; all of whom sat or stood in a balcony of the meeting-house, looking down upon the platform. When such personages could constitute a part of the spectacle, without risking the majesty or reverence of rank and office, it was safely to be inferred that the infliction of a legal sentence would have an earnest and effectual meaning. Accordingly, the crowd was sombre and grave. The unhappy culprit sustained herself as best a woman might, under the heavy weight of a thousand unrelenting eyes, all fastened upon her, and concentred at her bosom. It was almost intolerable to be borne. Of an impulsive and passionate nature, she had fortified herself to encounter the stings and venomous stabs of public contumely, wreaking itself in every variety of insult; but there was a quality so much more terrible in the solemn mood of the popular mind, that she longed rather to behold all those rigid countenances contorted with scornful merriment, and herself the object. Had a roar of laughter burst from the multitude,—each man, each woman, each little shrill-voiced child, contributing their individual parts,—Hester Prynne might have repaid them all with a bitter and disdainful smile. But, under the leaden infliction which it was her doom to endure, she felt, at moments, as if she must needs shriek out with the full power of her lungs, and cast herself from the scaffold down upon the ground, or else go mad at once.

Yet there were intervals when the whole scene, in which she was the most conspicuous object, seemed to vanish from her eyes, or, at least, glimmered indistinctly before them, like a mass of imperfectly shaped and spectral images. Her mind, and especially her memory, was preternaturally active, and kept bringing up other scenes than this roughly hewn street of a little town, on the edge of the Western wilderness; other faces than were lowering upon her from beneath the brims of those steeple-crowned hats. Reminiscences, the most trifling and immaterial, passages of infancy and school-days, sports, childish quarrels, and the little domestic traits of her maiden years, came swarming back upon her, intermingled with recollections of whatever was gravest in her subsequent life; one picture precisely as vivid as another; as if all were of similar importance, or all alike a play. Possibly, it was an instinctive device of her spirit, to relieve itself, by the exhibition of these phantasmagoric forms, from the cruel weight and hardness of the reality.

Be that as it might, the scaffold of the pillory was a point of view that revealed to Hester Prynne the entire track along which she had been treading, since her happy infancy. Standing on that miserable eminence, she saw again her native village, in Old England, and her paternal home; a decayed house of gray stone, with a poverty-stricken aspect, but retaining a half-obliterated shield of arms over the portal, in token of antique gentility. She saw her father's face, with its bald brow, and reverend white beard, that flowed over the old-fashioned Elizabethan ruff; her mother's, too, with the look of heedful and anxious love which it always wore in her remembrance, and which, even since her death, had so often laid the impediment of a gentle remonstrance in her daughter's pathway. She saw her own face, glowing with girlish beauty, and illuminating all the interior of the dusky mirror in which she had been wont to gaze at it. There she beheld another countenance, of a man well stricken in years, a pale, thin, scholar-like visage, with eyes dim and bleared by the lamp-light that had served them to pore over many ponderous books. Yet those same bleared optics had a strange, penetrating power, when it was their owner's purpose to read the human soul. This figure of the study and the cloister, as Hester Prynne's womanly fancy failed not to recall, was slightly deformed, with the left shoulder a trifle higher than the right. Next rose before her, in memory's picture-gallery, the intricate and narrow thoroughfares, the tall, gray houses, the huge cathedrals, and the public edifices, ancient in date and quaint in architecture, of a Continental city; where a new life had awaited her, still in connection with the misshapen scholar; a new life, but feeding itself on time-worn materials, like a tuft of green moss on a crumbling wall. Lastly, in lieu of these shifting scenes, came back the rude marketplace of the Puritan settlement, with all the townspeople assembled and levelling their stern regards at Hester Prynne,—yes, at herself,—who stood on the scaffold of the pillory, an infant on her arm, and the letter A, in scarlet, fantastically embroidered with gold thread, upon her bosom!

Could it be true? She clutched the child so fiercely to her breast, that it sent forth a cry; she turned her eyes downward at the scarlet letter, and even touched it with her finger, to assure herself that the infant and the shame were real. Yes!—these were her realities,—all else had vanished!

CHAPTER III

The Recognition

From this intense consciousness of being the object of severe and universal observation, the wearer of the scarlet letter was at length relieved by discerning, on the outskirts of the crowd, a figure which irresistibly took possession of her thoughts. An Indian, in his native garb, was standing there; but the red men were not so infrequent visitors of the English settlements, that one of them would have attracted any notice from Hester Prynne, at such a time; much less would he have excluded all other objects and ideas from her mind. By the Indian's side, and evidently sustaining a companionship with him, stood a white man, clad in a strange disarray of civilized and savage costume.

He was small in stature, with a furrowed visage, which, as yet, could hardly be termed aged. There was a remarkable intelligence in his features, as of a person who had so cultivated his mental part that it could not fail to mould the physical to itself, and become manifest by unmistakable tokens. Although, by a seemingly careless arrangement of his heterogeneous garb, he had endeavoured to conceal or abate the peculiarity, it was sufficiently evident to Hester Prynne, that one of this man's shoulders rose higher than the other. Again, at the first instant of perceiving that thin visage, and the slight deformity of the figure, she pressed her infant to her bosom, with so convulsive a force that the poor babe uttered another cry of pain. But the mother did not seem to hear it.

At his arrival in the market-place, and some time before she saw him, the stranger had bent his eyes on Hester Prynne. It was carelessly, at first, like a man chiefly accustomed to look inward, and to whom external matters are of little value and import, unless they bear relation to something within his mind. Very soon, however, his look became keen and penetrative. A writhing horror twisted itself across his features, like a snake gliding swiftly over them, and making one little pause, with all its wreathed intervolutions in open sight. His face darkened with some powerful emotion, which, nevertheless, he so instantaneously controlled by an effort of his will, that, save at a single moment, its expression might have passed for calmness. After a brief space, the convulsion grew almost imperceptible, and finally subsided into the depths of his nature. When he found the eyes of Hester Prynne fastened on his own, and saw that she appeared to recognize him, he slowly and calmly raised his finger, made a gesture with it in the air, and laid it on his lips.

Then, touching the shoulder of a townsman who stood next to him, he addressed him in a formal and courteous manner.

"I pray you, good Sir," said he, "who is this woman?—and wherefore is she here set up to public shame?"

"You must needs be a stranger in this region, friend," answered the townsman, looking curiously at the questioner and his savage companion; "else you would surely have heard of Mistress Hester Prynne, and her evil doings. She hath raised a great scandal, I promise you, in godly Master Dimmesdale's church."

"You say truly," replied the other. "I am a stranger, and have been a wanderer, sorely against my will. I have met with grievous mishaps by sea and land, and have been long held in bonds among the heathen-folk, to the southward; and am now brought hither by this Indian, to be redeemed out of my captivity. Will it please you, therefore, to tell me of Hester Prynne's,—have I her name rightly?—of this woman's offences, and what has brought her to yonder scaffold?"

"Truly, friend, and methinks it must gladden your heart, after your troubles and sojourn in the wilderness," said the townsman, "to find yourself, at length, in a land where iniquity is searched out, and punished in the sight of rulers and people; as here in our godly New England. Yonder woman, Sir, you must know, was the wife of a certain learned man, English by birth, but who had long dwelt in Amsterdam, whence, some good time agone, he was minded to cross over and cast in his lot with us of the Massachusetts. To this purpose, he sent his wife before him, remaining himself to look after some necessary affairs. Marry, good Sir, in some two years, or less, that the woman has been a dweller here in Boston, no tidings have come of this learned gentleman, Master Prynne; and his young wife, look you, being left to her own misguidance—"

"Ah!—aha!—I conceive you," said the stranger, with a bitter smile. "So learned a man as you speak of should have learned this too in his books. And who, by your favor, Sir, may be the father of yonder babe—it is some three or four months old, I should judge—which Mistress Prynne is holding in her arms?"

"Of a truth, friend, that matter remaineth a riddle; and the Daniel who shall expound it is yet a-wanting," answered the townsman. "Madam Hester absolutely refuseth to speak, and the magistrates have laid their heads together in vain. Peradventure the guilty one stands looking on at this sad spectacle, unknown of man, and forgetting that God sees him."

"The learned man," observed the stranger, with another smile, "should come himself to look into the mystery."

"It behooves him well, if he be still in life," responded the townsman. "Now, good Sir, our Massachusetts magistracy, bethinking themselves that this woman is youthful and fair, and doubtless was strongly tempted to her fall;—and that, moreover, as is most likely, her husband may be at the bottom of the sea;—they have not been bold to put in force the extremity of our righteous law against her. The penalty thereof is death. But, in their great mercy and tenderness of heart, they have doomed Mistress Prynne to stand only a space of three hours on the platform of the pillory, and then and thereafter, for the remainder of her natural life, to wear a mark of shame upon her bosom."

"A wise sentence!" remarked the stranger, gravely bowing his head. "Thus she will be a living sermon against sin, until the ignominious letter be engraved upon her tombstone. It irks me, nevertheless, that the partner of her iniquity should not, at least, stand on the scaffold by her side. But he will be known!—he will be known!—he will be known!"

He bowed courteously to the communicative townsman, and, whispering a few words to his Indian attendant, they both made their way through the crowd.

While this passed, Hester Prynne had been standing on her pedestal, still with a fixed gaze towards the stranger; so fixed a gaze, that, at moments of intense absorption, all other objects in the visible world seemed to vanish, leaving only him and her. Such an interview, perhaps, would have been more terrible than even to meet him as she now did, with the hot, midday sun burning down upon her face, and lighting up its shame; with the scarlet token of infamy on her breast; with the sin-born infant in her arms; with a whole people, drawn forth as to a festival, staring at the features that should have been seen only in the quiet gleam of the fireside, in the happy shadow of a home, or beneath a matronly veil, at church. Dreadful as it was, she was conscious of a shelter in the presence of these thousand witnesses. It was better to stand thus, with so many betwixt him and her, than to greet him, face to face, they two alone. She fled for refuge, as it were, to the public exposure, and dreaded the moment when its protection should be withdrawn from her. Involved in these thoughts, she scarcely heard a voice behind her, until it had repeated her name more than once, in a loud and solemn tone, audible to the whole multitude.

"Hearken unto me, Hester Prynne!" said the voice.

It has already been noticed, that directly over the platform on which Hester Prynne stood was a kind of balcony, or open gallery, appended to the meeting-house. It was the place whence proclamations were wont to be made, amidst an assemblage of the magistracy, with all the ceremonial that attended such public observances in those days. Here, to witness the scene which we are describing, sat Governor Bellingham himself, with four sergeants about his chair, bearing halberds, as a guard of honor. He wore a dark feather in his hat, a border of embroidery on his cloak, and a black velvet tunic beneath; a gentleman advanced in years, and with a hard experience written in his wrinkles. He was not ill fitted to be the head and representative of a community, which owned its origin and progress, and its present state of development, not to the impulses of youth, but to the stern and tempered energies of manhood, and the sombre sagacity of age; accomplishing so much, precisely because it imagined and hoped so little. The other eminent characters, by whom the chief ruler was surrounded, were distinguished by a dignity of mien, belonging to a period when the forms of authority were felt to possess the sacredness of divine institutions. They were, doubtless, good men, just, and sage. But, out of the whole human family, it would not have been easy to select the same number of wise and virtuous persons, who should be less capable of sitting in judgment on an erring woman's heart, and disentangling its mesh of good and evil, than the sages of rigid aspect towards whom Hester Prynne now turned her face. She seemed conscious, indeed, that whatever sympathy she might expect lay in the larger and warmer heart of the multitude; for, as she lifted her eyes towards the balcony, the unhappy woman grew pale and trembled.

The voice which had called her attention was that of the revered and famous John Wilson, the eldest clergyman of Boston, a great scholar, like most of his contemporaries in the profession, and withal a man of kind and genial spirit. This last attribute, however, had been less carefully developed than his intellectual gifts, and was, in truth, rather a matter of shame than self-congratulation with him. There he stood, with a border of grizzled locks beneath his skull-cap; while his gray eyes, accustomed to the shaded light of his study, were winking, like those of Hester's infant, in the unadulterated sunshine. He looked like the darkly engraved portraits which we see prefixed to old volumes of sermons; and had no more right than one of those portraits would have, to step forth, as he now did, and meddle with a question of human guilt, passion, and anguish.

"Hester Prynne," said the clergyman, "I have striven with my young brother here, under whose preaching of the word you have been privileged to sit,"—here Mr. Wilson laid his hand on the shoulder of a pale young man beside him,—"I have sought, I say, to persuade this godly youth, that he should deal with you, here in the face of Heaven, and before these wise and upright rulers, and in hearing of all the people, as touching the vileness and blackness of your sin. Knowing your natural temper better than I, he could the better judge what arguments to use, whether of tenderness or terror, such as might prevail over your hardness and obstinacy; insomuch that you should no longer hide the name of him who tempted you to this grievous fall. But he opposes to me, (with a young man's over-softness, albeit wise beyond his years,) that it were wronging the very nature of woman to force her to lay open her heart's secrets in such broad daylight, and in presence of so great a multitude. Truly, as I sought to convince him, the same lay in the commission of the sin, and not in the showing of it forth. What say you to it, once again, brother Dimmesdale? Must it be thou or I that shall deal with this poor sinner's soul?"

There was a murmur among the dignified and reverend occupants of the balcony; and Governor Bellingham gave expression to its purport, speaking in an authoritative voice, although tempered with respect towards the youthful clergyman whom he addressed.

"Good Master Dimmesdale," said he, "the responsibility of this woman's soul lies greatly with you. It behooves you, therefore, to exhort her to repentance, and to confession, as a proof and consequence thereof."

The directness of this appeal drew the eyes of the whole crowd upon the Reverend Mr. Dimmesdale; a young clergyman, who had come from one of the great English universities, bringing all the learning of the age into our wild forestland. His eloquence and religious fervor had already given the earnest of high eminence in his profession. He was a person of very striking aspect, with a white, lofty, and impending brow, large, brown, melancholy eyes, and a mouth which, unless when he forcibly compressed it, was apt to be tremulous, expressing both nervous sensibility and a vast power of self-restraint. Notwithstanding his high native gifts and scholar-like attainments, there was an air about this young minister,—an apprehensive, a startled, a half-frightened look,—as of a being who felt himself quite astray and at a loss in the pathway of human existence, and could only be at ease in some seclusion of his own. Therefore, so far as his duties would permit, he trode in the shadowy by-paths, and thus kept himself simple and childlike; coming forth, when occasion was, with a freshness, and fragrance, and dewy purity of thought, which, as many people said, affected them like the speech of an angel.

Such was the young man whom the Reverend Mr. Wilson and the Governor had introduced so openly to the public notice, bidding him speak, in the hearing of all men, to that mystery of a woman's soul, so sacred even in its pollution. The trying nature of his position drove the blood from his cheek, and made his lips tremulous.

"Speak to the woman, my brother," said Mr. Wilson. "It is of moment to her soul, and therefore, as the worshipful Governor says, momentous to thine own, in whose charge hers is. Exhort her to confess the truth!"

The Reverend Mr. Dimmesdale bent his head, in silent prayer, as it seemed, and then came forward.

"Hester Prynne," said he, leaning over the balcony, and looking down steadfastly into her eyes, "thou hearest what this good man says, and seest the accountability under which I labor. If thou feelest it to be for thy soul's peace, and that thy earthly punishment will thereby be made more effectual to salvation, I charge thee to speak out the name of thy fellow-sinner and fellow-sufferer! Be not silent from any mistaken pity and tenderness for him; for, believe me, Hester, though he were to step down from a high place, and stand there beside thee, on thy pedestal of shame, yet better were it so, than to hide a guilty heart through life. What can thy silence do for him, except it tempt him—yea, compel him, as it were—to add hypocrisy to sin? Heaven hath granted thee an open ignominy, that thereby thou mayest work out an open triumph over the evil within thee, and the sorrow without. Take heed how thou deniest to him—who, perchance, hath not the courage to grasp it for himself—the bitter, but wholesome, cup that is now presented to thy lips!"

The young pastor's voice was tremulously sweet, rich, deep, and broken. The feeling that it so evidently manifested, rather than the direct purport of the words, caused it to vibrate within all hearts, and brought the listeners into one accord of sympathy. Even the poor baby, at Hester's bosom, was affected by the same influence; for it directed its hitherto vacant gaze towards Mr. Dimmesdale, and held up its little arms, with a half pleased, half plaintive murmur. So powerful seemed the minister's appeal, that the people could not believe but that Hester Prynne would speak out the guilty name; or else that the guilty one himself, in whatever high or lowly place he stood, would be drawn forth by an inward and inevitable necessity, and compelled to ascent the scaffold.

Hester shook her head.

"Woman, transgress not beyond the limits of Heaven's mercy!" cried the Reverend Mr. Wilson, more harshly than before. "That little babe hath been gifted with a voice, to second and confirm the counsel which thou hast heard. Speak out the name! That, and thy repentance, may avail to take the scarlet letter off thy breast."

"Never!" replied Hester Prynne, looking, not at Mr. Wilson, but into the deep and troubled eyes of the younger clergyman. "It is too deeply branded. Ye cannot take it off. And would that I might endure his agony, as well as mine!"

"Speak, woman!" said another voice, coldly and sternly, proceeding from the crowd about the scaffold. "Speak; and give your child a father!"

"I will not speak!" answered Hester, turning pale as death, but responding to this voice, which she too surely recognized. "And my child must seek a heavenly Father; she shall never know an earthly one!"

"She will not speak!" murmured Mr. Dimmesdale, who, leaning over the balcony, with his hand upon his heart, had awaited the result of his appeal. He now drew back, with a long respiration. "Wondrous strength and generosity of a woman's heart! She will not speak!"

Discerning the impracticable state of the poor culprit's mind, the elder clergyman, who had carefully prepared himself for the occasion, addressed to the multitude a discourse on sin, in all its branches, but with continual reference to the ignominious letter. So forcibly did he dwell upon this symbol, for the hour or more during which his periods were rolling over the people's heads, that it assumed new terrors in their imagination, and seemed to derive its scarlet hue from the flames of the infernal pit. Hester Prynne, meanwhile, kept her place upon the pedestal of shame, with glazed eyes, and an air of weary indifference. She had borne, that morning, all that nature could endure; and as her temperament was not of the order that escapes from too intense suffering by a swoon, her spirit could only shelter itself beneath a stony crust of insensibility, while the faculties of animal life remained entire. In this state, the voice of the preacher thundered remorselessly, but unavailingly, upon her ears. The infant, during the latter portion of her ordeal, pierced the air with its wailings and screams; she strove to hush it, mechanically, but seemed scarcely to sympathize with its trouble. With the same hard demeanour, she was led back to prison, and vanished from the public gaze within its iron-clamped portal. It was whispered, by those who peered after her, that the scarlet letter threw a lurid gleam along the dark passage-way of the interior.

CHAPTER IV

THE INTERVIEW

After her return to the prison, Hester Prynne was found to be in a state of nervous excitement that demanded constant watchfulness, lest she should perpetrate violence on herself, or do some half-frenzied mischief to the poor babe. As night approached, it proving impossible to quell her insubordination by rebuke or threats of punishment, Master Brackett, the jailer, thought fit to introduce a physician. He described him as a man of skill in all Christian modes of physical science, and likewise familiar with whatever the savage people could teach, in respect to medicinal herbs and roots that grew in the forest. To say the truth, there was much need of professional assistance, not merely for Hester herself, but still more urgently for the child; who, drawing its sustenance from the maternal bosom, seemed to have drank in with it all the turmoil, the anguish, and despair, which pervaded the mother's system. It now writhed in convulsions of pain, and was a forcible type, in its little frame, of the moral agony which Hester Prynne had borne throughout the day.

Closely following the jailer into the dismal apartment, appeared that individual, of singular aspect, whose presence in the crowd had been of such deep interest to the wearer of the scarlet letter. He was lodged in the prison, not as suspected of any offence, but as the most convenient and suitable mode of disposing of him, until the magistrates should have conferred with the Indian sagamores respecting his ransom. His name was announced as Roger Chillingworth. The jailer, after ushering him into the room, remained a moment, marvelling at the comparative quiet that followed his entrance; for Hester Prynne had immediately become as still as death, although the child continued to moan.

"Prithee, friend, leave me alone with my patient," said the practitioner. "Trust me, good jailer, you shall briefly have peace in your house; and, I promise you, Mistress Prynne shall hereafter be more amenable to just authority than you may have found her heretofore."

"Nay, if your worship can accomplish that," answered Master Brackett, "I shall own you for a man of skill indeed! Verily, the woman hath been like a possessed one; and there lacks little, that I should take in hand to drive Satan out of her with stripes."

The stranger had enetered the room with the characteristic quietude of the profession to which he announced himself as belonging. Nor did his demeanour change, when the withdrawal of the prison-keeper left him face to face with the woman, whose absorbed notice of him, in the crowd, had intimated so close a relation between himself and her. His first care was given to the child; whose cries, indeed, as she lay writhing on the trundle-bed, made it of peremptory necessity to postpone all other business to the task of soothing her. He examined the infant carefully, and then proceeded to unclasp a leathern case, which he took from beneath his dress. It appeared to contain certain medical preparations, one of which he mingled with a cup of water.

"My old studies in alchemy," observed he, "and my sojourn, for above a year past, among a people well versed in the kindly properties of simples, have made a better physician of me than many that claim the medical degree. Here, woman! The child is yours,—she is none of mine,—neither will she recognize my voice or aspect as a father's. Administer this draught, therefore, with thine own hand."

Hester repelled the offered medicine, at the same time gazing with strongly marked apprehension into his face.

"Wouldst thou avenge thyself on the innocent babe?" whispered she.

"Foolish woman!" responded the physician, half coldly, half soothingly. "What should ail me to harm this misbegotten and miserable babe? The medicine is potent for good; and were it my child,—yea, mine own, as well as thine!—I could do no better for it."

As she still hesitated, being, in fact, in no reasonable state of mind, he took the infant in his arms, and himself administered the draught. It soon proved its efficacy, and redeemed the leech's pledge. The moans of the little patient subsided; its convulsive tossings gradually ceased; and in a few moments, as is the custom of young children after relief from pain, it sank into a profound and dewy slumber. The physician, as he had a fair right to be termed, next bestowed his attention on the mother. With calm and intent scrutiny, he felt her pulse, looked into her eyes,—a gaze that made her heart shrink and shudder, because so familiar, and yet so strange and cold,—and, finally, satisfied with his investigation, proceeded to mingle another draught.

"I know not Lethe nor Nepenthe," remarked he; "but I have learned many new secrets in the wilderness, and here is one of them,—a recipe that an Indian taught me, in requital of some lessons of my own, that were as old as Paracelsus. Drink it! It may be less soothing than a sinless conscience. That I cannot give thee. But it will calm the swell and heaving of thy passion, like oil thrown on the waves of a tempestuous sea."

He presented the cup to Hester, who received it with a slow, earnest look into his face; not precisely a look of fear, yet full of doubt and questioning, as to what his purposes might be. She looked also at her slumbering child.

"I have thought of death," said she,—"have wished for it,—would even have prayed for it, were it fit that such as I should pray for any thing. Yet, if death be in this cup, I bid thee think again, ere thou beholdest me quaff it. See! It is even now at my lips."

"Drink, then," replied he, still with the same cold composure. "Dost thou know me so little, Hester Prynne? Are my purposes wont to be so shallow? Even if I imagine a scheme of vengeance, what could I do better for my object than to let thee live,—than to give thee medicines against all harm and peril of life,—so that this burning shame may still blaze upon thy bosom?"—As he spoke, he laid his long forefinger on the scarlet letter, which forthwith seemed to scorch into Hester's breast, as if it had been red-hot. He noticed her involuntary gesture, and smiled.—"Live, therefore, and bear about thy doom with thee, in the eyes of men and women,—in the eyes of him whom thou didst call thy husband,—in the eyes of yonder child! And, that thou mayest live, take off this draught."

Without further expostulation or delay, Hester Prynne drained the cup, and, at the motion of the man of skill, seated herself on the bed where the child was sleeping; while he drew the only chair which the room afforded, and took his own seat beside her. She could not but tremble at these preparations; for she felt that—having now done all that humanity, or principle, or, if so it were, a refined cruelty, impelled him to do, for the relief of physical suffering—he was next to treat with her as the man whom she had most deeply and irreparably injured.

"Hester," said he, "I ask not wherefore, nor how, thou hast fallen into the pit, or say rather, thou hast ascended to the pedestal of infamy, on which I found thee. The reason is not far to seek. It was my folly, and thy weakness. I,—a man of thought,—the book-worm of great libraries,—a man already in decay, having given my best years to feed the hungry dream of knowledge,—what had I to do with youth and beauty like thine own! Misshapen from my birth-hour, how could I delude myself with the idea that intellectual gifts might veil physical deformity in a young girl's fantasy! Men call me wise. If sages were ever wise in their own behoof, I might have foreseen all this. I might have known that, as I came out of the vast and dismal forest, and entered this settlement of Christian men, the very first object to meet my eyes would be thyself, Hester Prynne, standing up, a statue of ignominy, before the people. Nay, from the moment when we came down the old church-steps together, a married pair, I might have beheld the bale-fire of that scarlet letter blazing at the end of our path!"

"Thou knowest," said Hester,—for, depressed as she was, she could not endure this last quiet stab at the token of her shame,—"thou knowest that I was frank with thee. I felt no love, nor feigned any."

"True!" replied he. "It was my folly! I have said it. But, up to that epoch of my life, I had lived in vain. The world had been so cheerless! My heart was a habitation large enough for many guests, but lonely and chill, and without a household fire. I longed to kindle one! It seemed not so wild a dream,—old as I was, and sombre as I was, and misshapen as I was,—that the simple bliss, which is scattered far and wide, for all mankind to gather up, might yet be mine. And so, Hester, I drew thee into my heart, into its innermost chamber, and sought to warm thee by the warmth which thy presence made there!"

"I have greatly wronged thee," murmured Hester.

"We have wronged each other," answered he. "Mine was the first wrong, when I betrayed thy budding youth into a false and unnatural relation with my decay. Therefore, as a man who has not thought and philosophized in vain, I seek no vengeance, plot no evil against thee. Between thee and me, the scale hangs fairly balanced. But, Hester, the man lives who has wronged us both! Who is he?"

"Ask me not!" replied Hester Prynne, looking firmly into his face. "That thou shalt never know!"

"Never, sayest thou?" rejoined he, with a smile of dark and self-relying intelligence. "Never know him! Believe me, Hester, there are few things,—whether in the outward world, or, to a certain depth, in the invisible sphere of thought,—few things hidden from the man, who devotes himself earnestly and unreservedly to the solution of a mystery. Thou mayest cover up thy secret from the prying multitude. Thou mayest conceal it, too, from the ministers and magistrates, even as thou didst this day, when they sought to wrench the name out of thy heart, and give thee a partner on thy pedestal. But, as for me, I come to the inquest with other senses than they possess. I shall seek this man, as I have sought truth in books; as I have sought gold in alchemy. There is a sympathy that will make me conscious of him. I shall see him tremble. I shall feel myself shudder, suddenly and unawares. Sooner or later, he must needs be mine!"

The eyes of the wrinkled scholar glowed so intensely upon her, that Hester Prynne clasped her hands over her heart, dreading lest he should read the secret there at once.

"Thou wilt not reveal his name? Not the less he is mine," resumed he, with a look of confidence, as if destiny were at one with him. "He bears no letter of infamy wrought into his garment, as thou dost; but I shall read it on his heart. Yet fear not for him! Think not that I shall interfere with Heaven's own method of retribution, or, to my own loss, betray him to the gripe of human law. Neither do thou imagine that I shall contrive aught against his life, no, nor against his fame; if, as I judge, he be a man of fair repute. Let him live! Let him hide himself in outward honor, if he may! Not the less he shall be mine!"

"Thy acts are like mercy," said Hester, bewildered and appalled. "But thy words interpret thee as a terror!"

"One thing, thou that wast my wife, I would enjoin upon thee," continued the scholar. "Thou has kept the secret of thy paramour. Keep, likewise, mine! There are none in this land that know me. Breathe not, to any human soul, that thou didst ever call me husband! Here, on this wild outskirt of the earth, I shall pitch my tent; for, elsewhere a wanderer, and isolated from human interests, I find here a woman, a man, a child, amongst whom and myself there exist the closest ligaments. No matter whether of love or hate; no matter whether of right or wrong! Thou and thine, Hester Prynne, belong to me. My home is where thou art, and where he is. But betray me not!"

"Wherefore dost thou desire it?" inquired Hester, shrinking, she hardly knew why, from this secret bond. "Why not announce thyself openly, and cast me off at once?"

"It may be," he replied, "because I will not encounter the dishonor that besmirches the husband of a faithless woman. It may be for other reasons. Enough, it is my purpose to live and die unknown. Let, therefore, thy husband be to the world as one already dead, and of whom no tidings shall ever come. Recognize me not, by word, by sign, by look! Breathe not the secret, above all, to the man thou wottest of. Shouldst thou fail me in this, beware! His fame, his position, his life, will be in my hands. Beware!"

"I will keep thy secret, as I have his," said Hester.

"Swear it!" rejoined he.

And she took the oath.

"And now, Mistress Prynne," said old Roger Chillingworth, as he was hereafter to be named, "I leave thee alone; alone with thy infant, and the scarlet letter! How is it, Hester? Doth thy sentence bind thee to wear the token in thy sleep? Art thou not afraid of nightmares and hideous dreams?"

"Why dost thou smile so at me?" inquired Hester, troubled at the expression of his eyes. "Art thou like the Black Man that haunts the forest round about us? Hast thou enticed me into a bond that will prove the ruin of my soul?"

"Not thy soul," he answered, with another smile. "No, not thine!"

CHAPTER V

Hester at Her Needle

Hester Prynne's term of confinement was now at an end. Her prison-door was thrown open, and she came forth into the sunshine, which, falling on all alike, seemed, to her sick and morbid heart, as if meant for no other purpose than to reveal the scarlet letter on her breast. Perhaps there was a more real torture in her first unattended footsteps from the threshold of the prison, than even in the procession and spectacle that have been described, where she was made the common infamy, at which all mankind was summoned to point its finger. Then, she was supported by an unnatural tension of the nerves, and by all the combative energy of her character, which enabled her to convert the scene into a kind of lurid triumph. It was, moreover, a separate and insulated event, to occur but once in her lifetime, and to meet which, therefore, reckless of economy, she might call up the vital strength that would have sufficed for many quiet years. The very law that condemned her—a giant of stern features, but with vigor to support, as well as to annihilate, in his iron arm—had held her up, through the terrible ordeal of her ignominy. But now, with this unattended walk from her prison-door, began the daily custom, and she must either sustain and carry it forward by the ordinary resources of her nature, or sink beneath it. She could no longer borrow from the future, to help her through the present grief. To-morrow would bring its own trial with it; so would the next day, and so would the next; each its own trial, and yet the very same that was now so unutterably grievous to be borne. The days of the far-off future would toil onward, still with the same burden for her to take up, and bear along with her, but never to fling down; for the accumulating days, and added years, would pile up their misery upon the heap of shame. Throughout them all, giving up her individuality, she would become the general symbol at which the preacher and moralist might point, and in which they might vivify and embody their images of woman's frailty and sinful passion. Thus the young and pure would be taught to look at her, with the scarlet letter flaming on her breast,—at her, the child of honorable parents,—at her, the mother of a babe, that would hereafter be a woman,—at her, who had once been innocent,—as the figure, the body, the reality of sin. And over her grave, the infamy that she must carry thither would be her only monument.

It may seem marvellous, that, with the world before her,—kept by no restrictive clause of her condemnation within the limits of the Puritan settlement, so remote and so obscure,—free to return to her birthplace, or to any other European land, and there hide her character and identity under a new exterior, as completely as if emerging into another state of being,—and having also the passes of the dark, inscrutable forest open to her, where the wildness of her nature might assimilate itself with a people whose customs and life were alien from the law that had condemned her,—it may seem marvellous, that this woman should still call that place her home, where, and where only, she must needs be the type of shame. But there is a fatality, a feeling so irresistible and inevitable that it has the force of doom, which almost invariably compels human beings to linger around and haunt, ghost-like, the spot where some great and marked event has given the color to their lifetime; and still the more irresistibly, the darker the tinge that saddens it. Her sin, her ignominy, were the roots which she had struck into the soil. It was as if a new birth, with stronger assimilations than the first, had converted the forest-land, still so uncongenial to every other pilgrim and wanderer, into Hester Prynne's wild and dreary, but life-long home. All other scenes of earth—even that village of rural England, where happy infancy and stainless maidenhood seemed yet to be in her mother's keeping, like garments put off long ago—were foreign to her, in comparison. The chain that bound her here was of iron links, and galling to her inmost soul, but never could be broken.

It might be, too,—doubtless it was so, although she hid the secret from herself, and grew pale whenever it struggled out of her heart, like a serpent from its hole,—it might be that another feeling kept her within the scene and pathway that had been so fatal. There dwelt, there trode the feet of one with whom she deemed herself connected in a union, that, unrecognized on earth, would bring them together before the bar of final judgment, and make that their marriage-altar, for a joint futurity of endless retribution. Over and over again, the tempter of souls had thrust this idea upon Hester's contemplation, and laughed at the passionate and desperate joy with which she seized, and then strove to cast it from her. She barely looked the idea in the face, and hastened to bar it in its dungeon. What she compelled herself to believe,—what, finally, she reasoned upon, as her motive for continuing a resident of New England,—was half a truth, and half a self-delusion. Here, she said to herself, had been the scene of her guilt, and here should be the scene of her earthly punishment; and so, perchance, the torture of her daily shame would at length purge her soul, and work out another purity than that which she had lost; more saint-like, because the result of martyrdom.

Hester Prynne, therefore, did not flee. On the outskirts of the town, within the verge of the peninsula, but not in close vicinity to any other habitation, there was a small thatched cottage. It had been built by an earlier settler, and abandoned, because the soil about it was too sterile for cultivation, while its comparative remoteness put it out of the sphere of that social activity which already marked the habits of the emigrants. It stood on the shore, looking across a basin of the sea at the forest-covered hills, towards the west. A clump of scrubby trees, such as alone grew on the peninsula, did not so much conceal the cottage from view, as seem to denote that here was some object which would fain have been, or at least ought to be, concealed. In this little, lonesome dwelling, with some slender means that she possessed, and by the license of the magistrates, who still kept an inquisitorial watch over her, Hester established herself, with her infant child. A mystic shadow of suspicion immediately attached itself to the spot. Children, too young to comprehend wherefore this woman should be shut out from the sphere of human charities, would creep nigh enough to behold her plying her needle at the cottage-window, or standing in the door-way, or laboring in her little garden, or coming forth along the pathway that led townward; and, discerning the scarlet letter on her breast, would scamper off, with a strange, contagious fear.

Lonely as was Hester's situation, and without a friend on earth who dared to show himself, she, however, incurred no risk of want. She possessed an art that sufficed, even in a land that afforded comparatively little scope for its exercise, to supply food for her thriving infant and herself. It was the art—then, as now, almost the only one within a woman's grasp—of needle-work. She bore on her breast, in the curiously embroidered letter, a specimen of her delicate and imaginative skill, of which the dames of a court might gladly have availed themselves, to add the richer and more spiritual adornment of human ingenuity to their fabrics of silk and gold. Here, indeed, in the sable simplicity that generally characterized the Puritanic modes of dress, there might be an infrequent call for the finer productions of her handiwork. Yet the taste of the age, demanding whatever was elaborate in compositions of this kind, did not fail to extend its influence over our stern progenitors, who had cast behind them so many fashions which it might seem harder to dispense with. Public ceremonies, such as ordinations, the installation of magistrates, and all that could give majesty to the forms in which a new government manifested itself to the people, were, as a matter of policy, marked by a stately and well-conducted ceremonial, and a sombre, but yet a studied magnificence. Deep ruffs, painfully wrought bands, and gorgeously embroidered gloves, were all deemed necessary to the official state of men assuming the reins of power; and were readily allowed to individuals dignified by rank or wealth, even while sumptuary laws forbade these and similar extravagances to the plebeian order. In the array of funerals, too,—whether for the apparel of the dead body, or to typify, by manifold emblematic devices of sable cloth and snowy lawn, the sorrow of the survivors,—there was a frequent and characteristic demand for such labor as Hester Prynne could supply. Baby-linen—for babies then wore robes of state—afforded still another possibility of toil and emolument.

By degree, nor very slowly, her handiwork became what would now be termed the fashion. Whether from commiseration for a woman of so miserable a destiny; or from the morbid curiosity that gives a fictitious value even to common or worthless things; or by whatever other intangible circumstance was then, as now, sufficent to bestow, on some persons, what others might seek in vain; or because Hester really filled a gap which must otherwise have remained vacant; it is certain that she had ready and fairly requited employment for as many hours as she saw fit to occupy with her needle. Vanity, it may be, chose to mortify itself, by putting on, for ceremonials of pomp and state, the garments that had been wrought by her sinful hands. Her needle-work was seen on the ruff of the Governor; military men wore it on their scarfs, and the minister on his band; it decked the baby's little cap; it was shut up, to be mildewed and moulder away, in the coffins of the dead. But it is not recorded that, in a single instance, her skill was called in aid to embroider the white veil which was to cover the pure blushes of a bride. The exception indicated the ever relentless vigor with which society frowned upon her sin.

Hester sought not to acquire any thing beyond a subsistence, of the plainest and most ascetic description, for herself, and a simple abundance for her child. Her own dress was of the coarsest materials and the most sombre hue; with only that one ornament,—the scarlet letter,—which it was her doom to wear. The child's attire, on the other hand, was distinguished by a fanciful, or, we might rather say, a fantastic ingenuity, which served, indeed, to heighten the airy charm that early began to develop itself in the little girl, but which appeared to have also a deeper meaning. We may speak further of it hereafter. Except for that small expenditure in the decoration of her infant, Hester bestowed all her superfluous means in charity, on wretches less miserable than herself, and who not unfrequently insulted the hand that fed them. Much of the time, which she might readily have applied to the better efforts of her art, she employed in making coarse garments for the poor. It is probable that there was an idea of penance in this mode of occupation, and that she offered up a real sacrifice of enjoyment, in devoting so many hours to such rude handiwork. She had in her nature a rich, voluptuous, Oriental characteristic,—a taste for the gorgeously beautiful, which, save in the exquisite productions of her needle, found nothing else, in all the possibilities of her life, to exercise itself upon. Women derive a pleasure, incomprehensible to the other sex, from the delicate toil of the needle. To Hester Prynne it might have been a mode of expressing, and therefore soothing, the passion of her life. Like all other joys, she rejected it as sin. This morbid meddling of conscience with an immaterial matter betokened, it is to be feared, no genuine and steadfast penitence, but something doubtful, something that might be deeply wrong, beneath.

In this manner, Hester Prynne came to have a part to perform in the world. With her native energy of character, and rare capacity, it could not entirely cast her off, although it had set a mark upon her, more intolerable to a woman's heart than that which branded the brow of Cain. In all her intercourse with society, however, there was nothing that made her feel as if she belonged to it. Every gesture, every word, and even the silence of those with whom she came in contact, implied, and often expressed, that she was banished, and as much alone as if she inhabited another sphere, or commuicated with the common nature by other organs and senses than the rest of human kind. She stood apart from mortal interests, yet close beside them, like a ghost that revisits the familiar fireside, and can no longer make itself seen or felt; no more smile with the household joy, nor mourn with the kindred sorrow; or, should it succeed in manifesting its forbidden sympathy, awakening only terror and horrible repugnance. These emotions, in fact, and its bitterest scorn besides, seemed to be the sole portion that she retained in the universal heart. It was not an age of delicacy; and her position, although she understood it well, and was in little danger of forgetting it, was often brought before her vivid self-perception, like a new anguish, by the rudest touch upon the tenderest spot. The poor, as we have already said, whom she sought out to be the objects of her bounty, often reviled the hand that was stretched forth to succor them. Dames of elevated rank, likewise, whose doors she entered in the way of her occupation, were accustomed to distil drops of bitterness into her heart; sometimes through that alchemy of quiet malice, by which women can concoct a subtile poison from ordinary trifles; and sometimes, also, by a coarser expression, that fell upon the sufferer's defenceless breast like a rough blow upon an ulcerated wound. Hester had schooled herself long and well; she never responded to these attacks, save by a flush of crimson that rose irrepressibly over her pale cheek, and again subsided into the depths of her bosom. She was patient,—a martyr, indeed,—but she forbore to pray for her enemies; lest, in spite of her forgiving aspirations, the words of the blessing should stubbornly twist themselves into a curse.

Continually, and in a thousand other ways, did she feel the innumerable throbs of anguish that had been so cunningly contrived for her by the undying, the ever-active sentence of the Puritan tribunal. Clergymen paused in the street to address words of exhortation, that brought a crowd, with its mingled grin and frown, around the poor, sinful woman. If she entered a church, trusting to share the Sabbath smile of the Universal Father, it was often her mishap to find herself the text of the discourse. She grew to have a dread of children; for they had imbibed from their parents a vague idea of something horrible in this dreary woman, gliding silently through the town, with never any companion but one only child. Therefore, first allowing her to pass, they pursued her at a distance with shrill cries, and the utterance of a word that had no distinct purport to their own minds, but was none the less terrible to her, as proceeding from lips that babbled it unconsciously. It seemed to argue so wide a diffusion of her shame, that all nature knew of it; it could have caused her no deeper pang, had the leaves of the trees whispered the dark story among themselves,—had the summer breeze murmured about it,—had the wintry blast shrieked it aloud! Another peculiar torture was felt in the gaze of a new eye. When strangers looked curiously at the scarlet letter,—and none ever failed to do so,—they branded it afresh into Hester's soul; so that, oftentimes, she could scarcely refrain, yet always did refrain, from covering the symbol with her hand. But then, again, an accustomed eye had likewise its own anguish to inflict. Its cool stare of familiarity was intolerable. From first to last, in short, Hester Prynne had always this dreadful agony in feeling a human eye upon the token; the spot never grew callous; it seemed, on the contrary, to grow more sensitive with daily torture.

But sometimes, once in many days, or perchance in many months, she felt an eye—a human eye—upon the ignominious brand, that seemed to give a momentary relief, as if half of her agony were shared. The next instant, back it all rushed again, with still a deeper throb of pain; for, in that brief interval, she had sinned anew. Had Hester sinned alone?

Her imagination was somehow affected, and, had she been of a softer moral and intellectual fibre, would have been still more so, by the strange and solitary anguish of her life. Walking to and fro, with those lonely footsteps, in the little world with which she was outwardly connected, it now and then appeared to Hester,—if altogether fancy, it was nevertheless too potent to be resisted,—she felt or faniced, then, that the scarlet letter had endowed her with a new sense. She shuddered to believe, yet could not help believing, that it gave her a sympathetic knowledge of the hidden sin in other hearts. She was terror-stricken by the revelations that were thus made. What were they? Could they be other than the insidious whispers of the bad angel, who would fain have persuaded the struggling woman, as yet only half his victim, that the outward guise of purity was but a lie, and that, if truth were everywhere to be shown, a scarlet letter would blaze forth on many a bosom besides Hester Prynne's? Or, must she receive those intimations—so obscure, yet so distinct—as truth? In all her miserable experience, there was nothing else so awful and so loathsome as this sense. It perplexed, as well as shocked her, by the irreverent inopportuneness of the occasions that brought it into vivid action. Sometimes, the red infamy upon her breast would give a sympathetic throb, as she passed near a venerable minister or magistrate, the model of piety and justice, to whom that age of antique reverence looked up, as to a mortal man in fellowship with angels. "What evil thing is at hand?" would Hester say to herself. Lifting her reluctant eyes, there would be nothing human within the scope of view, save the form of this eartly saint! Again, a mystic sisterhood would contumaciously assert itself, as she met the sanctified frown of some matron, who, according to the rumor of all tongues, had kept cold snow within her bosom throughout life. That unsunned snow in the matron's bosom, and the burning shame on Hester Prynne's,—what had the two in common? Or, once more, the electric thrill would give her warning,—"Behold, Hester, here is a companion!"—and, looking up, she would detect the eyes of a young maiden glancing at the scarlet letter, shyly and aside, and quickly averted, with a faint, chill crimson in her cheeks; as if her purity were somewhat sullied by that momentary glance. O Fiend, whose talisman was that fatal symbol, wouldst thou leave nothing, whether in youth or age, for this poor sinner to revere?—Such loss of faith is ever one of the saddest results of sin. Be it accepted as a proof that all was not corrupt in this poor victim of her own frailty, and man's hard law, that Hester Prynne yet struggled to believe that no fellow-mortal was guilty like herself.

The vulgar, who, in those dreary old times, were always contributing a grotesque horror to what interested their imaginations, had a story about the scarlet letter which we might readily work up into a terrific legend. They averred, that the symbol was not mere scarlet cloth, tinged in an earthly dye-pot, but was red-hot with infernal fire, and could be seen glowing all alight, whenever Hester Prynne walked abroad in the night-time. And we must needs say, it seared Hester's bosom so deeply, that perhaps there was more truth in the rumor than our modern incredulity may be inclined to admit.

CHAPTER VI

PEARL

We have as yet hardly spoken of the infant; that little creature, whose innocent life had sprung, by the inscrutable decree of Providence, a lovely and immortal flower, out of the rank luxuriance of a guilty passion. How strange it seemed to the sad woman, as she watched the growth, and the beauty that became every day more brilliant, and the intelligence that threw its quivering sunshine over the tiny features of this child! Her Pearl!—For so had Hester called her; not as a name expressive of her aspect, which had nothing of the calm, white, unimpassioned lustre that would be indicated by the comparison. But she named the infant "Pearl," as being of great price,—purchased with all she had,—her mother's only treasure! How strange, indeed! Man had marked this woman's sin by a scarlet letter, which had such potent and disastrous efficacy that no human sympathy could reach her, save it were sinful like herself. God, as a direct consequence of the sin which man thus punished, had given her a lovely child, whose place was on that same dishonored bosom, to connect her parent for ever with the race and descent of mortals, and to be finally a blessed soul in heaven! Yet these thoughts affected Hester Prynne less with hope than apprehension. She knew that her deed had been evil; she could have no faith, therefore, that its result would be for good. Day after day, she looked fearfully into the child's expanding nature; ever dreading to detect some dark and wild peculiarity, that should correspond with the guiltiness to which she owed her being.

Certainly, there was no physical defect. By its perfect shape, its vigor, and its natural dexterity in the use of all its untried limbs, the infant was worthy to have been brought forth in Eden; worthy to have been left there, to be the plaything of the angels, after the world's first parents were driven out. The child had a native grace which does not invariably coexist with faultless beauty; its attire, however simple, always impressed the beholder as if it were the very garb that precisely became it best. But little Pearl was not clad in rustic weeds. Her mother, with a morbid purpose that may be better understood hereafter, had bought the richest tissues that could be procured, and allowed her imaginative faculty its full play in the arrangement and decoration of the dresses which the child wore, before the public eye. So magnificent was the small figure, when thus arrayed, and such was the splendor of Pearl's own proper beauty, shinning through the gorgeous robes which might have extinguished a paler loveliness, that there was an absolute circle of radiance around her, on the darksome cottage-floor. And yet a russet gown, torn and soiled with the child's rude play, made a picture of her just as perfect. Pearl's aspect was imbued with a spell of infinite variety; in this one child there were many children, comprehending the full scope between the wild-flower prettiness of a peasant-baby, and the pomp, in little, of an infant princess. Throughout all, however, there was a trait of passion, a certain depth of hue, which she never lost; and if, in any of her changes, she had grown fainter or paler, she would have ceased to be herself;—it would have been no longer Pearl!

This outward mutability indicated, and did not more than fairly express, the various properties of her inner life. Her nature appeared to possess depth, too, as well as variety; but—or else Hester's fears deceived her—it lacked reference and adaptation to the world into which she was born. The child could not be made amenable to rules. In giving her existence, a great law had been broken; and the result was a being, whose elements were perhaps beautiful and brilliant, but all in disorder; or with an order peculiar to themselves, amidst which the point of variety and arrangement was difficult or impossible to be discovered. Hester could only account for the child's character—and even then, most vaguely and imperfectly—by recalling what she herself had been, during that momentous period while Pearl was imbibing her soul from the spiritual world, and her bodily frame from its material of earth. The mother's impassioned state had been the medium through which were transmitted to the unborn infant the rays of its moral life; and, however white and clear originally, they had taken the deep stains of crimson and gold, the fiery lustre, the black shadow, and the untempered light, of the intervening substance. Above all, the warfare of Hester's spirit, at that epoch, was perpetuated in Pearl. She could recognize her wild, desperate, defiant mood, the flightiness of her temper, and even some of the very cloudshapes of gloom and despondency that had brooded in her heart. They were now illuminated by the morning radiance of a young child's disposition, but, later in the day of earthly existence, might be prolific of the storm and whirlwind.

The discipline of the family, in those days, was of a far more rigid kind than now. The frown, the harsh rebuke, the frequent application of the rod, enjoined by Scriptural authority, were used, not merely in the way of punishment for actual offences, but as a wholesome regimen for the growth and promotion of all childish virtues. Hester Prynne, nevertheless, the lonely mother of this one child, ran little risk of erring on the side of undue severity. Mindful, however, of her own errors and misfortunes, she early sought to impose a tender, but strict, control over the infant immortality that was committed to her charge. But the task was beyond her skill. After testing both smiles and frowns, and proving that neither mode of treatment possessed any calculable influence, Hester was ultimately compelled to stand aside, and permit the child to be swayed by her own impulses. Physical compulsion or restraint was effectual, of course, while it lasted. As to any other kind of discipline, whether addressed to her mind or heart, little Pearl might or might not be within its reach, in accordance with the caprice that ruled the moment. Her mother, while Pearl was yet an infant, grew acquainted with a certain peculiar look, that warned her when it would be labor thrown away to insist, persuade, or plead. It was a look so intelligent, yet inexplicable, so perverse, sometimes so malicious, but generally accompanied by a wild flow of spirits, that Hester could not help questioning, at such moments, whether Pearl was a human child. She seemed rather an airy sprite, which, after playing its fantastic sports for a little while upon the cottage-floor, would flit away with a mocking smile. Whenever that look appeared in her wild, bright, deeply black eyes, it invested her with a strange remoteness and intangibility; it was as if she were hovering in the air and might vanish, like a glimmering light that comes we know not whence, and goes we know not whither. Beholding it, Hester was constrained to rush towards the child,—to pursue the little elf in the flight which she invariably began,—to snatch her to her bosom, with a close pressure and earnest kisses,—not so much from overflowing love, as to assure herself that Pearl was flesh and blood, and not utterly delusive. But Pearl's laugh, when she was caught, though full of merriment and music, made her mother more doubtful than before.

Heart-smitten at this bewildering and baffling spell, that so often came between herself and her sole treasure, whom she had bought so dear, and who was all her world, Hester sometimes burst into passionate tears. Then, perhaps,—for there was no foreseeing how it might affect her,—Pearl would frown, and clench her little fist, and harden her small features into a stern, unsympathizing look of discontent. Not seldom, she would laugh anew, and louder than before, like a thing incapable and unintelligent of human sorrow. Or—but this more rarely happened—she would be convulsed with a rage of grief, and sob out her love for her mother, in broken words, and seem intent on proving that she had a heart, by breaking it. Yet Hester was hardly safe in confiding herself to that gusty tenderness; it passed, as suddenly as it came. Brooding over all these matters, the mother felt like one who has evoked a spirit, but, by some irregularity in the process of conjuration, has failed to win the master-word that should control this new and incomprehensible intelligence. Her only real comfort was when the child lay in the placidity of sleep. Then she was sure of her, and tasted hours of quiet, sad, delicious happiness; until—perhaps with that perverse expression glimmering from beneath her opening lids—little Pearl awoke!

How soon—with what strange rapidity, indeed!—did Pearl arrive at an age that was capable of social intercourse, beyond the mother's ever-ready smile and nonsense-words! And then what a happiness would it have been, could Hester Prynne have heard her clear, bird-like voice mingling with the uproar of other childish voices, and have distinguished and unravelled her own darling's tones, amid all the entangled outcry of a group of sportive children! But this could never be. Pearl was a born outcast of the infantile world. An imp of evil, emblem and product of sin, she had no right among christened infants. Nothing was more remarkable than the instinct, as it seemed, with which the child comprehended her loneliness; the destiny that had drawn an inviolable circle round about her; the whole peculiarity, in short, of her position in respect to other children. Never, since her release from prison, had Hester met the public gaze without her. In all her walks about the town, Pearl, too, was there; first as the babe in arms, and afterwards as the little girl, small companion of her mother, holding a forefinger with her whole grasp, and tripping along at the rate of three or four footsteps to one of Hester's. She saw the children of the settlement, on the grassy margin of the street, or at the domestic thresholds, disporting themselves in such grim fashion as the Puritanic nurture would permit; playing at going to church, perchance; or at scourging Quakers; or taking scalps in a sham-fight with the Indians; or scaring one another with freaks of imitative witchcraft. Pearl saw, and gazed intently, but never sought to make acquaintance. If spoken to, she would not speak again. If the children gathered about her, as they sometimes did, Pearl would grow positively terrible in her puny wrath, snatching up stones to fling at them, with shrill, incoherent exclamations that made her mother tremble, because they had so much the sound of a witch's anathemas in some unknown tongue.

The truth was, that the little Puritans, being of the most intolerant brood that ever lived, had got a vague idea of something outlandish, unearthly, or at variance with ordinary fashions, in the mother and child; and therefore scorned them in their hearts, and not unfrequently reviled them with their tongues. Pearl felt the sentiment, and requited it with the bitterest hatred that can be supposed to rankle in a childish bosom. These outbreaks of a fierce temper had a kind of value, and even comfort, for her mother; because there was at least an intelligible earnestness in the mood, instead of the fitful caprice that so often thwarted her in the child's manifestations. It appalled her, nevertheless, to discern here, again, a shadowy reflection of the evil that had existed in herself. All this enmity and passion had Pearl inherited, by inalienable right, out of Hester's heart. Mother and daughter stood together in the same circle of seclusion from human society; and in the nature of the child seemed to be perpetuated those unquiet elements that had distracted Hester Prynne before Pearl's birth, but had since begun to be soothed away by the softening influences of maternity.

At home, within and around her mother's cottage, Pearl wanted not a wide and various circle of acquaintance. The spell of life went forth from her ever creative spirit, and communicated itself to a thousand objects, as a torch kindles a flame wherever it may be applied. The unlikeliest materials, a stick, a bunch of rags, a flower, were the puppets of Pearl's witchcraft, and, without undergoing any outward change, became spiritually adapted to whatever drama occupied the stage of her inner world. Her one baby-voice served a multitude of imaginary personages, old and young, to talk withal. The pine-trees, aged, black, and solemn, and flinging groans and other melancholy utterances on the breeze, needed little transformation to figure as Puritan elders; the ugliest weeds of the garden were their children, whom Pearl smote down and uprooted, most unmercifully. It was wonderful, the vast variety of forms into which she threw her intellect, with no continuity, indeed, but darting up and dancing, always in a state of preternatural activity,—soon sinking down, as if exhausted by so rapid and feverish a tide of life,—and succeeded by other shapes of a similar wild energy. It was like nothing so much as the phantasmagoric play of the northern lights. In the mere exercise of the fancy, however, and the sportiveness of a growing mind, there might be little more than was observable in other children of bright faculties; except as Pearl, in the dearth of human playmates, was thrown more upon the visionary throng which she created. The singularity lay in the hostile feelings with which the child regarded all these offspring of her own heart and mind. She never created a friend, but seemed always to be sowing broadcast the dragon's teeth, whence sprung a harvest of armed enemies, against whom she rushed to battle. It was inexpressibly sad—then what depth of sorrow to a mother, who felt in her own heart the cause!—to observe, in one so young, this constant recognition of an adverse world, and so fierce a training of the energies that were to make good her cause, in the contest that must ensue.

Gazing at Pearl, Hester Prynne often dropped her work upon her knees, and cried out, with an agony which she would fain have hidden, but which made utterance for itself, betwixt speech and a groan,—"O Father in Heaven,—if Thou art still my Father,—what is this being which I have brought into the world!" And Pearl, overhearing the ejaculation, or aware, through some more subtile channel, of those throbs of anguish, would turn her vivid and beautiful little face upon her mother, smile with sprite-like intelligence, and resume her play.

One peculiarity of the child's deportment remains yet to be told. The very first thing which she had noticed, in her life, was—what?—not the mother's smile, responding to it, as other babies do, by that faint, embryo smile of the little mouth, remembered so doubtfully afterwards, and with such fond discussion whether it were indeed a smile. By no means! But that first object of which Pearl seemed to become aware was—shall we say it?—the scarlet letter on Hester's bosom! One day, as her mother stooped over the cradle, the infant's eyes had been caught by the glimmering of the gold embroidery about the letter; and, putting up her little hand, she grasped at it, smiling, not doubtfully, but with a decided gleam that gave her face the look of a much older child. Then, gasping for breath, did Hester Prynne clutch the fatal token, instinctively endeavouring to tear it away; so infinite was the torture inflicted by the intelligent touch of Pearl's baby-hand. Again, as if her mother's agonized gesture were meant only to make sport for her, did little Pearl look into her eyes, and smile! From that epoch, except when the child was asleep, Hester had never felt a moment's safety; not a moment's calm enjoyment of her. Weeks, it is true, would sometimes elapse, during which Pearl's gaze might never once be fixed upon the scarlet letter; but then, again, it would come at unawares, like the stroke of sudden death, and always with that peculiar smile, and odd expression of the eyes.

Once, this freakish, elvish cast came into the child's eyes, while Hester was looking at her own image in them, as mothers are fond of doing; and, suddenly,—

for women in solitude, and with troubled hearts, are pestered with unaccountable delusions,—she fancied that she beheld, not her own miniature portrait, but another face in the small black mirror of Pearl's eye. It was a face, fiend-like, full of smiling malice, yet bearing the semblance of features that she had known full well, though seldom with a smile, and never with malice, in them. It was as if an evil spirit possessed the child, and had just then peeped forth in mockery. Many a time afterwards had Hester been tortured, though less vividly, by the same illusion.

In the afternoon of a certain summer's day, after Pearl grew big enough to run about, she amused herself with gathering handfuls of wild-flowers, and flinging them, one by one, at her mother's bosom; dancing up and down, like a little elf, whenever she hit the scarlet letter. Hester's first motion had been to cover her bosom with her clasped hands. But, whether from pride or resignation, or a feeling that her penance might best be wrought out by this unutterable pain, she resisted the impulse, and sat erect, pale as death, looking sadly into little Pearl's wild eyes. Still came the battery of flowers, almost invariably hitting the mark, and covering the mother's breast with hurts for which she could find no balm in this world, nor knew how to seek it in another. At last, her shot being all expended, the child stood still and gazed at Hester, with that little, laughing image of a fiend peeping out—or, whether it peeped or no, her mother so imagined it—from the unsearchable abyss of her black eyes.

"Child, what art thou?" cried the mother.

"O, I am your little Pearl!" answered the child.

But, while she said it, Pearl laughed and began to dance up and down, with the humorsome gesticulation of a little imp, whose next freak might be to fly up the chimney.

"Art thou my child, in very truth?" asked Hester.

Nor did she put the question altogether idly, but, for the moment, with a portion of genuine earnestness; for, such was Pearl's wonderful intelligence, that her mother half doubted whether she were not acquainted with the secret spell of her existence, and might not now reveal herself.

"Yes; I am little Pearl!" repeated the child, continuing her antics.

"Thou art not my child! Thou art no Pearl of mine!" said the mother, half playfully; for it was often the case that a sportive impulse came over her, in the midst of her deepest suffering. "Tell me, then, what thou art, and who sent thee hither?"

"Tell me, mother!" said the child, seriously, coming up to Hester, and pressing herself close to her knees. "Do thou tell me!"

"Thy Heavenly Father sent thee!" answered Hester Prynne.

But she said it with a hestitation that did not escape the acuteness of the child. Whether moved only by her ordinary freakishness, or because an evil spirit prompted her, she put up her small forefinger, and touched the scarlet letter.

"He did not send me!" cried she, positively. "I have no Heavenly Father!"

"Hush, Pearl, hush! Thou must not talk so!" answered the mother, suppressing a groan. "He sent us all into this world. He sent even me, thy mother. Then, much more, thee! Or, if not, thou strange and elfish child, whence didst thou come?"

"Tell me! Tell me!" repeated Pearl, no longer seriously, but laughing, and capering about the floor. "It is thou that must tell me!"

But Hester could not resolve the query, being herself in a dismal labyrinth of doubt. She remembered—betwixt a smile and a shudder—the talk of the neighbouring townspeople; who, seeking vainly elsewhere for the child's paternity, and observing some of her odd attributes, had given out that poor little Pearl was a demon offspring; such as, ever since old Catholic times, had occasionally been seen on earth, through the agency of their mothers' sin, and to promote some foul and wicked purpose. Luther, according to the scandal of his monkish enemies, was a brat of that hellish breed; nor was Pearl the only child to whom this inauspicious origin was assigned, among the New England Puritans.

CHAPTER VII

THE GOVERNOR'S HALL

Hester Prynne went, one day, to the mansion of Governor Bellingham, with a pair of gloves, which she had fringed and embroidered to his order and which were to be worn on some great occasion of state; for, though the chances of a popular election had caused this former ruler to descend a step or two from the highest rank, he still held an honorable and influential place among the colonial magistracy.

Another and far more important reason than the delivery of a pair of embroidered gloves impelled Hester, at this time, to seek an interview with a personage of so much power and activity in the affairs of the settlement. It had reached her ears, that there was a design on the part of some of the leading inhabitants, cherishing the more rigid order of principles in religion and government, to deprive her of her child. On the supposition that Pearl, as already hinted, was of demon origin, these good people not unreasonably argued that a Christian interest in the mother's soul required them to remove such a stumbling-block from her path. If the child, on the other hand, were really capable of moral and religious growth, and possessed the elements of ultimate salvation, then, surely, it would enjoy all the fairer prospect of these advantages by being transferred to wiser and better guardianship than Hester Prynne's. Among those who promoted the design, Governor Bellingham was said to be one of the most busy. It may appear singular, and, indeed, not a little ludicrous, that an affair of this kind, which, in later days, would have been referred to no higher jurisdiction than that of the selectmen of the town, should then have been a question publicly discussed, and on which statesmen of eminence took sides. At that epoch of pristine simplicity, however, matters of even slighter public interest, and of far less intrinsic weight than the welfare of Hester and her child, were strangely mixed up with the deliberations of legislators and acts of state. The period was hardly, if at all, earlier than that of our story, when a dispute concerning the right of property in a pig, not only caused a fierce and bitter contest in the legislative body of the colony, but resulted in an important modification of the framework itself of the legislature.

Full of concern, therefore,—but so conscious of her own right, that it seemed scarcely an unequal match between the public, on the one side, and a lonely woman, backed by the sympathies of nature, on the other,—Hester Prynne set forth from her solitary cottage. Little Pearl, of course, was her companion. She was now of an age to run lightly along by her mother's side, and, constantly in motion from morn till sunset, could have accomplished a much longer journey than that before her. Often, nevertheless, more from caprice than necessity, she demanded to be taken up in arms, but was soon as imperious to be set down again, and frisked onward before Hester on the grassy pathway, with many a harmless trip and tumble. We have spoken of Pearl's rich and luxuriant beauty; a beauty that shone with deep and vivid tints; a bright complexion, eyes possessing intensity both of depth and glow, and hair already of a deep, glossy brown, and which, in after years, would be nearly akin to black. There was fire in her and throughout her; she seemed the unpremeditated offshoot of a passionate moment. Her mother, in contriving the child's garb, had allowed the gorgeous tendencies of her imagination their full play; arraying her in a crimson velvet tunic, of a peculiar cut, abundantly embroidered with fantasies and flourishes of gold thread. So much strength of coloring, which must have given a wan and pallid aspect to cheeks of a fainter bloom, was admirably adapted to Pearl's beauty, and made her the very brightest little jet of flame that ever danced upon the earth.

But it was a remarkable attribute of this garb, and, indeed, of the child's whole appearance, that it irresistibly and inevitably reminded the beholder of the token which Hester Prynne was doomed to wear upon her bosom. It was the scarlet letter in another form; the scarlet letter endowed with life! The mother herself—as if the red ignominy were so deeply scorched into her brain, that all her conceptions assumed its form—had carefully wrought out the similitude; lavishing many hours of morbid ingenuity, to create an analogy between the object of her affection, and the emblem of her guilt and torture. But, in truth, Pearl was the one, as well as the other; and only in consequence of that identity had Hester contrived so perfectly to represent the scarlet letter in her appearance.

As the two wayfarers came within the precincts of the town, the children of the Puritans looked up from their play,—or what passed for play with those sombre little urchins,—and spake gravely one to another:—

"Behold, verily, there is the woman of the scarlet letter; and, of a truth, moreover, there is the likeness of the scarlet letter running along by her side! Come, therefore, and let us fling mud at them!"

But Pearl, who was a dauntless child, after frowning, stamping her foot, and shaking her little hand with a variety of threatening gestures, suddenly made a rush at the knot of her enemies, and put them all to flight. She resembled, in her fierce pursuit of them, an infant pestilence,—the scarlet fever, or some such half-fledged angel of judgment,—whose mission was to punish the sins of the rising generation. She screamed and shouted, too, with a terrific volume of sound, which doubtless caused the hearts of the fugitives to quake within them. The victory accomplished, Pearl returned quietly to her mother, and looked up smiling into her face.

Without further adventure, they reached the dwelling of Governor Bellingham. This was a large wooden house, built in a fashion of which there are specimens still extant in the streets of our elder towns; now moss-grown, crumbling to decay, and melancholy at heart with the many sorrowful or joyful occurrences remembered or forgotten, that have happened, and passed away, within their dusky chambers. Then, however, there was the freshness of the passing year on its exterior, and the cheerfulness, gleaming forth from the sunny windows, of a human habitation into which death had never entered. It had indeed a very cheery aspect; the walls being overspread with a kind of stucco, in which fragments of broken glass were plentifully intermixed; so that, when the sunshine fell aslant-wise over the front of the edifice, it glittered and sparkled as if diamonds had been flung against it by the double handful. The brilliancy might have befitted Aladdin's palace, rather than the mansion of a grave old Puritan ruler. It was further decorated with strange and seemingly cabalistic figures and diagrams, suitable to the quaint taste of the age, which had been drawn in the stucco when newly laid on, and had now grown hard and durable, for the admiration of after times.

Pearl, looking at this bright wonder of a house, began to caper and dance, and imperatively required that the whole breadth of sunshine should be stripped off its front, and given her to play with.

"No, my little Pearl!" said her mother. "Thou must gather thine own sunshine. I have none to give thee!"

They approached the door; which was of an arched form, and flanked on each side by a narrow tower or projection of the edifice, in both of which were lattice-windows, with wooden shutters to close over them at need. Lifting the iron hammer that hung at the portal, Hester Prynne gave a summons, which was answered by one of the Governor's bondservants; a free-born Englishman, but now a seven years' slave. During that term he was to be the property of his master, and as much a commodity of bargain and sale as an ox, or a joint-stool. The serf wore the blue coat, which was the customary garb of serving-men at that period, and long before, in the old hereditary halls of England.

"Is the worshipful Governor Bellingham within?" inquired Hester.

"Yea, forsooth," replied the bond-servant, staring with wide-open eyes at the scarlet letter, which, being a new-comer in the country, he had never before seen. "Yea, his honorable worship is within. But he hath a godly minister or two with him, and likewise a leech. Ye may not see his worship now."

"Nevertheless, I will enter," answered Hester Prynne; and the bond-servant, perhaps judging from the decision of her air and the glittering symbol in her bosom, that she was a great lady in the land, offered no opposition.

So the mother and little Pearl were admitted into the hall of entrance. With many variations, suggested by the nature of his building-materials, diversity of climate, and a different mode of social life, Governor Bellingham had planned his new habitation after the residences of gentlemen of fair estate in his native land. Here, then, was a wide and reasonably lofty hall, extending through the whole depth of the house, and forming a medium of general communication, more or less directly, with all the other apartments. At one extremity, this spacious room was lighted by the windows of the two towers, which formed a small recess on either side of the portal. At the other end, though partly muffled by a curtain, it was more powerfully illuminated by one of those embowed hall-windows which we read of in old books, and which was provided with a deep and cushioned seat. Here, on the cushion, lay a folio tome, probably of the Chronicles of England, or other such substantial literature; even as, in our own days, we scatter gilded volumes on the centre-table, to be turned over by the casual guest. The furniture of the hall consisted of some ponderous chairs, the backs of which were elaborately carved with wreaths of oaken flowers; and likewise a table in the same taste; the whole being of the Elizabethan age, or perhaps earlier, and heirlooms, transferred hither from the Governor's paternal home. On the table—in token that the sentiment of old English hospitality had not been left behind—stood a large pewter tankard, at the bottom of which, had Hester or Pearl peeped into it, they might have seen the frothy remnant of a recent draught of ale.

On the wall hung a row of portraits, representing the forefathers of the Bellingham lineage, some with armour on their breasts and others with stately ruffs and robes of peace. All were characterized by the sternness and severity which old portraits so invariably put on; as if they were the ghosts, rather than the pictures, of departed worthies, and were gazing with harsh and intolerant criticism at the pursuits and enjoyments of living men.

At about the centre of the oaken panels, that lined the hall, was suspended a suit of mail, not, like the pictures, an ancestral relic, but of the most modern date; for it had been manufactured by a skillful armorer in London, the same year in which Governor Bellingham came over to New England. There was a steel head-piece, a cuirass, a gorget, and greaves, with a pair of gauntlets and a sword hanging beneath; all, and especially the helmet and breastplate, so highly burnished as to glow with white radiance, and scatter an illumination everywhere about upon the floor. This bright panoply was not meant for mere idle show, but had been worn by the Governor on many a solemn muster and training field, and had glittered, moreover, at the head of a regiment in the Pequod war. For, though bred a lawyer, and accustomed to speak of Bacon, Coke, Noye, and Finch, as his professional associates, the exigencies of this new country had transformed Governor Bellingham into a soldier, as well as a statesman and ruler.

Little Pearl—who was as greatly pleased with the gleaming armour as she had been with the glittering frontispiece of the house—spent some time looking into the polished mirror of the breastplate.

"Mother," cried she, "I see you here. Look! Look!"

Hester looked, by way of humoring the child; and she saw that, owing to the peculiar effect of this convex mirror, the scarlet letter was represented in exaggerated and gigantic proportions, so as to be greatly the most prominent feature of her appearance. In truth, she seemed absolutely hidden behind it. Pearl pointed upward, also, at a similar picture in the headpiece; smiling at her mother, with the elfish intelligence that was so familiar an expression on her small physiognomy. That look of naughty merriment was likewise reflected in the mirror, with so much breadth and intensity of effect, that it made Hester Prynne feel as if it could not be the image of her own child, but of an imp who was seeking to mould itself into Pearl's shape.

"Come along, Pearl!" said she, drawing her away. "Come and look into this fair garden. It may be, we shall see flowers there; more beautiful ones than we find in the woods."

Pearl, accordingly, ran to the bow-window, at the farther end of the hall, and looked along the vista of a garden-walk, carpeted with closely shaven grass, and bordered with some rude and immature attempt at shrubbery. But the proprietor appeared already to have relinquished, as hopeless, the effort to perpetuate on this side of the Atlantic, in a hard soil and amid the close struggle for subsistence, the native English taste for ornamental gardening. Cabbages grew in plain sight; and a pumpkin vine, rooted at some distance, had run across the intervening space, and deposited one of its gigantic products directly beneath the hall-window; as if to warn the Governor that this great lump of vegetable gold was as rich an ornament as New England earth would offer him. There were a few rose-bushes, however, and a number of apple-trees, probably the descendants of those planted by the Reverend Mr. Blackstone, the first settler of the peninsula; that half mythological personage who rides through our early annals, seated on the back of a bull.

Pearl, seeing the rose-bushes, began to cry for a red rose, and would not be pacified.

"Hush, child, hush!" said her mother earnestly. "Do not cry, dear little Pearl! I hear voices in the garden. The Governor is coming, and gentlemen along with him!"

In fact, adown the vista of the garden-avenue, a number of persons were seen approaching towards the house. Pearl, in utter scorn of her mother's attempt to quiet her, gave an eldritch scream, and then became silent; not from any notion of obedience, but because the quick and mobile curiosity of her disposition was excited by the appearance of these new personages.

CHAPTER VIII

THE ELF-CHILD AND THE MINISTER

Governor Bellingham, in a loose gown and easy cap,—such as elderly gentlemen loved to indue themselves with, in their domestic privacy,—walked foremost, and appeared to be showing off his estate, and expatiating on his projected improvements. The wide circumference of an elaborate ruff, beneath his gray beard, in the antiquated fashion of King James's reign, caused his head to look not a little like that of John the Baptist in a charger. The impression made by his aspect, so rigid and severe, and frost-bitten with more than autumnal age, was hardly in keeping with the appliances of worldly enjoyment wherewith he had evidently done his utmost to surround himself. But it is an error to suppose that our grave forefathers—though accustomed to speak and think of human existence as a state merely of trial and warfare, and though unfeignedly prepared to sacrifice goods and life at the behest of duty—made it a matter of conscience to reject such means of comfort, or even luxury, as lay fairly within their grasp. This creed was never taught, for instance, by the venerable pastor, John Wilson, whose beard, white as a snow-drift, was seen over Governor Bellingham's shoulder; while its wearer suggested that pears and peaches might yet be naturalized in the New England climate, and that purple grapes might possibly be compelled to flourish, against the sunny garden-wall. The old clergyman, nurtured at the rich bosom of the English Church, had a long established and legitimate taste for all good and comfortable things; and however stern he might show himself in the pulpit, or in his public reproof of such transgressions as that of Hester Prynne, still, the genial benevolence of his private life had won him warmer affection than was accorded to any of his professional contemporaries.

Behind the Governor and Mr. Wilson came two other guests; one, the Reverend Arthur Dimmesdale, whom the reader may remember, as having taken a brief and reluctant part in the scene of Hester Prynne's disgrace; and, in close companionship with him, old Roger Chillingworth, a person of great skill in physic, who, for two or three years past, had been settled in the town. It was understood that this learned man was the physician as well as friend of the young minister, whose health had severely suffered, of late, by his too unreserved self-sacrifice to the labors and duties of the pastoral relation.

The Governor, in advance of his visitors, ascended one or two steps, and, throwing open the leaves of the great hall window, found himself close to little Pearl. The shadow of the curtain fell on Hester Prynne, and partially concealed her.

"What have we here?" said Governor Bellingham, looking with surprise at the scarlet little figure before him. "I profess, I have never seen the like, since my days of vanity, in old King James's time, when I was wont to esteem it a high favor to be admitted to a court mask! There used to be a swarm of these small apparitions, in holiday-time; and we called them children of the Lord of Misrule. But how gat such a guest into my hall?"

"Ay, indeed!" cried good old Mr. Wilson. "What little bird of scarlet plumage may this be? Methinks I have seen just such figures, when the sun has been shining through a richly painted window, and tracing out the golden and crimson images across the floor. But that was in the old land. Prithee, young one, who art thou, and what has ailed thy mother to bedizen thee in this strange fashion? Art thou a Christian child,—ha? Dost know thy catechism? Or art thou one of those naughty elfs or fairies, whom we thought to have left behind us, with other relics of Papistry, in merry old England?"

"I am mother's child," answered the scarlet vision, "and my name is Pearl!"

"Pearl?—Ruby, rather!—or Coral!—or Red Rose, at the very least, judging from thy hue!" responded the old minister, putting forth his hand in a vain attempt to pat little Pearl on the cheek. "But where is this mother of thine? Ah! I see," he added; and, turning to Governor Bellingham, whispered,—"This is the selfsame child of whom we have held speech together; and behold here the unhappy woman, Hester Prynne, her mother!"

"Sayest thou so?" cried the Governor. "Nay, we might have judged that such a child's mother must needs be a scarlet woman, and a worthy type of her of Babylon! But she comes at a good time; and we will look into this matter forthwith."

Governor Bellingham stepped through the window into the hall, followed by his three guests.

"Hester Prynne," said he, fixing his naturally stern regard on the wearer of the scarlet letter, "there hath been much question concerning thee, of late. The point hath been weightily discussed, whether we, that are of authority and influence, do well discharge our consciences by trusting an immortal soul, such as there is in yonder child, to the guidance of one who hath stumbled and fallen, amid the pitfalls of this world. Speak thou, the child's own mother! Were it not, thinkest thou, for thy little one's temporal and eternal welfare, that she be taken out of thy charge, and clad soberly, and disciplined strictly, and instructed in the truths of heaven and earth? What canst thou do for the child, in this kind?"

"I can teach my little Pearl what I have learned from this!" answered Hester Prynne, laying her finger on the red token.

"Woman, it is thy badge of shame!" replied the stern magistrate. "It is because of the stain which that letter indicates, that we would transfer thy child to other hands."

"Nevertheless," said the mother calmly, though growing more pale, "this badge hath taught me,—it daily teaches me,—it is teaching me at this moment,—lessons whereof my child may be the wiser and better, albeit they can profit nothing to myself."

"We will judge warily," said Bellingham, "and look well what we are about to do. Good Master Wilson, I pray you, examine this Pearl,—since that is her name,—and see whether she hath had such Christian nurture as befits a child of her age."

The old minister seated himself in an arm-chair, and made an effort to draw Pearl betwixt his knees. But the child, unaccustomed to the touch or familiarity of any but her mother, escaped through the open window and stood on the upper step, looking like a wild, tropical bird, of rich plumage, ready to take flight into the upper air. Mr. Wilson, not a little astonished at this outbreak,—for he was a grandfatherly sort of personage, and usually a vast favorite with children,—essayed, however, to proceed with the examination.

"Pearl," said he, with great solemnity, "thou must take heed to instruction, that so, in due season, thou mayest wear in thy bosom the pearl of great price. Canst thou tell me, my child, who made thee?"

Now Pearl knew well enough who made her; for Hester Prynne, the daughter of a pious home, very soon after her talk with the child about her Heavenly Father, had begun to inform her of those truths which the human spirit, at whatever stage of immaturity, imbibes with such eager interest. Pearl, therefore, so large were the attainments of her three years' lifetime, could have borne a fair examination in the New England Primer, or the first column of the Westminster Catechism, although unacquainted with the outward form of either of those celebrated works. But that perversity, which all children have more or less of, and of which little Pearl had a tenfold portion, now, at the most inopportune moment, took thorough possession of her, and closed her lips, or impelled her to speak words amiss. After putting her finger in her mouth, with many ungracious refusals to answer good Mr. Wilson's question, the child finally announced that she had not been made at all, but had been plucked by her mother off the bush of wild roses, that grew by the prison-door.

This fantasy was probably suggested by the near proximity of the Governor's red roses, as Pearl stood outside of the window; together with her recollection of the prison rose-bush, which she had passed in coming hither.

Old Roger Chillingworth, with a smile on his face, whispered something in the young clergyman's ear. Hester Prynne looked at the man of skill, and even then, with her fate hanging in the balance, was startled to perceive what a change had come over his features,—how much uglier they were,—how his dark complexion seemed to have grown duskier, and his figure more misshapen,—since the days when she had familiarly known him. She met his eyes for an instant, but was immediately constrained to give all her attention to the scene now going forward.

"This is awful!" cried the Governor, slowly recovering from the astonishment into which Pearl's response had thrown him. "Here is a child of three years old, and she cannot tell who made her! Without question, she is equally in the dark as to her soul, its present depravity, and future destiny! Methinks, gentlemen, we need inquire no further."

Hester caught hold of Pearl, and drew her forcibly into her arms, confronting the Old Puritan magistrate with almost a fierce expression. Alone in the world, cast off by it, and with this sole treasure to keep her heart alive, she felt that she possessed indefeasible rights against the world, and was ready to defend them to the death.

"God gave me the child!" cried she. "He gave her, in requital of all things else, which ye had taken from me. She is my happiness!—she is my torture, none the less! Pearl keeps me here in life! Pearl punishes me too! See ye not, she is the scarlet letter, only capable of being loved, and so endowed with a million-fold the power of retribution for my sin! Ye shall not take her! I will die first!"

"My poor woman," said the not unkind old minister, "the child shall be well cared for!—far better than thou canst do it."

"God gave her into my keeping," repeated Hester Prynne, raising her voice almost to a shriek. "I will not give her up!"—And here, by a sudden impulse, she turned to the young clergyman, Mr. Dimmesdale, at whom, up to this moment, she had seemed hardly so much as once to direct her eyes.—"Speak thou for me!" cried she. "Thou wast my pastor, and hadst charge of my soul, and knowest me better than these men can. I will not lose the child! Speak for me! Thou knowest,—for thou hast sympathies which these men lack!—thou knowest what is in my heart, and what are a mother's rights, and how much the stronger they are, when that mother has but her child and the scarlet letter! Look thou to it! I will not lose the child! Look to it!"

At this wild and singular appeal, which indicated that Hester Prynne's situation had provoked her to little less than madness, the young minister at once came forward, pale, and holding his hand over his heart, as was his custom whenever his peculiarly nervous temperament was thrown into agitation. He looked now more careworn and emaciated than as we described him at the scene of Hester's public ignominy; and whether it were his failing health, or whatever the cause might be, his large dark eyes had a world of pain in their troubled and melancholy depth.

"There is truth in what she says," began the minister, with a voice sweet, tremulous, but powerful, insomuch that the hall reëchoed, and the hollow armour rang with it,—"truth in what Hester says, and in the feeling which inspires her! God gave her the child, and gave her, too, an instinctive knowlege of its nature and requirements,—both seemingly so peculiar,—which no other mortal being can possess. And, moreover, is there not a quality of awful sacredness in the relation between this mother and this child?"

"Ay!—how is that, good Master Dimmesdale?" interrupted the Governor. "Make that plain, I pray you!"

"It must be even so," resumed the minister. "For, if we deem it otherwise, do we not thereby say that the Heavenly Father, the Creator of all flesh, hath lightly recognized a deed of sin, and made of no account the distinction between unhallowed lust and holy love? This child of its father's guilt and its mother's shame hath come from the hand of God, to work in many ways upon her heart, who pleads so earnestly, and with such bitterness of spirit, the right to keep her. It was meant for a blessing; for the one blessing of her life! It was meant, doubtless, as the mother herself hath told us, for a retribution too; a torture, to be felt at many an unthought of moment; a pang, a sting, an ever-recurring agony in the midst of a troubled joy! Hath she not expressed this thought in the garb of the poor child, so forcibly reminding us of that red symbol which sears her bosom?"

"Well said, again!" cried good Mr. Wilson. "I feared the woman had no better thought than to make a mountebank of her child!"

"Oh, not so!—not so!" continued Mr. Dimmesdale. "She recognizes, believe me, the solemn miracle which God hath wrought, in the existence of that child. And may she feel, too,—what, methinks, is the very truth,—that this boon was meant, above all things else, to keep the mother's soul alive, and to preserve her from blacker depths of sin into which Satan might else have sought to plunge her! Therefore it is good for this poor, sinful woman that she hath an infant immortality, a being capable of eternal joy or sorrow, confided to her care,—to be trained up by her to righteousness,—to remind her, at every moment, of her fall,—but yet to teach her, as it were by the Creator's sacred pledge, that, if she bring the child to heaven, the child also will bring its parent thither! Herein is the sinful mother happier than the sinful father. For Hester Prynne's sake, then, and no less for the poor child's sake, let us leave them as Providence hath seen fit to place them!"

"You speak, my friend, with a strange earnestness," said old Roger Chillingworth, smiling at him.

"And there is weighty import in what my young brother hath spoken," added the Reverend Mr. Wilson. "What say you, worshipful Master Bellingham? Hath he not pleaded well for the poor woman?"

"Indeed hath he," answered the magistrate, "and hath adduced such arguments, that we will even leave the matter as it now stands; so long, at least, as there shall be no further scandal in the woman. Care must be had, nevertheless, to put the child to due and stated examination in the catechism at thy hands or Master Dimmesdale's. Moreover, at a proper season, the tithing-men must take heed that she go both to school and to meeting."

The young minister, on ceasing to speak, had withdrawn a few steps from the group, and stood with his face partially concealed in the heavy folds of the window-curtain; while the shadow of his figure, which the sunlight cast upon the floor, was tremulous with the vehemence of his appeal. Pearl, that wild and flighty little elf, stole softly towards him, and, taking his hand in the grasp of both her own, laid her cheek against it; a caress so tender, and withal so unobtrusive, that her mother, who was looking on, asked herself,—"Is that my Pearl?" Yet she knew that there was love in the child's heart, although it mostly revealed itself in passion, and hardly twice in her lifetime had been softened by such gentleness as now. The minister,—for, save the long-sought regards of woman, nothing is sweeter than these marks of childish preference, accorded spontaneously by a spiritual instinct, and therefore seeming to imply in us something truly worthy to be loved,—the minister looked round, laid his hand on the child's head, hesitated an instant, and then kissed her brow. Little Pearl's unwonted mood of sentiment lasted no longer; she laughed, and went capering down the hall, so airily, that old Mr. Wilson raised a question whether even her tiptoes touched the floor.

"The little baggage hath witchcraft in her, I profess," said he to Mr. Dimmesdale. "She needs no old woman's broomstick to fly withal!"

"A strange child!" remarked old Roger Chillingworth. "It is easy to see the mother's part in her. Would it be beyond a philosopher's research, think ye, gentlemen, to analyze that child's nature, and, from its make and mould, to give a shrewd guess at the father?"

"Nay; it would be sinful, in such a question, to follow the clew of profane philosophy," said Mr. Wilson. "Better to fast and pray upon it; and still better, it may be, to leave the mystery as we find it, unless Providence reveal it of its own accord. Thereby, every good Christian man hath a title to show a father's kindness towards the poor, deserted babe."

The affair being so satisfactorily concluded, Hester Prynne, with Pearl, departed from the house. As they descended the steps, it is averred that the lattice of a chamber-window was thrown open, and forth into the sunny day was thrust the face of Mistress Hibbins, Governor Bellingham's bitter-tempered sister, and the same who, a few years later, was executed as a witch.

"Hist, hist!" said she, while her ill-omened physiognomy seemed to cast a shadow over the cheerful newness of the house. "Wilt thou go with us to-night? There will be a merry company in the forest; and I wellnigh promised the Black Man that comely Hester Prynne should make one."

"Make my excuse to him, so please you!" answered Hester, with a triumphant smile. "I must tarry at home, and keep watch over my little Pearl. Had they taken her from me, I would willingly have gone with thee into the forest, and signed my name in the Black Man's book too, and that with mine own blood!"

"We shall have thee there anon!" said the witch-lady, frowning, as she drew back her head.

But here—if we suppose this interview betwixt Mistress Hibbins and Hester Prynne to be authentic, and not a parable—was already an illustration of the young minister's argument against sundering the relation of a fallen mother to the offspring of her frailty. Even thus early had the child saved her from Satan's snare.

CHAPTER IX

THE LEECH

Under the appellation of Roger Chillingworth, the reader will remember, was hidden another name, which its former wearer had resolved should never more be spoken. It has been related, how, in the crowd that witnessed Hester Prynne's ignominious exposure, stood a man, elderly, travel-worn, who, just emerging from the perilous wilderness, beheld the woman, in whom he hoped to find embodied the warmth and cheerfulness of home, set up as a type of sin before the people. Her matronly fame was trodden under all men's feet. Infamy was babbling around her in the public market-place. For her kindred, should the tidings ever reach them, and for the companions of her unspotted life, there remained nothing but the contagion of her dishonor; which would not fail to be distributed in strict accordance and proportion with the intimacy and sacredness of their previous relationship. Then why—since the choice was with himself—should the individual, whose connection with the fallen woman had been the most intimate and sacred of them all, come forward to vindicate his claim to an inheritance so little desirable? He resolved not to be pilloried beside her on her pedestal of shame. Unknown to all but Hester Prynne, and possessing the lock and key of her silence, he chose to withdraw his name from the roll of mankind, and, as regarded his former ties and interests, to vanish out of life as completely as if he indeed lay at the bottom of the ocean, whither rumor had long ago consigned him. This purpose once effected, new interests would immediately spring up, and likewise a new purpose; dark, it is true, if not guilty, but of force enough to engage the full strength of his faculties.

In pursuance of this resolve, he took up his residence in the Puritan town, as Roger Chillingworth, without other introduction than the learning and intelligence of which he possessed more than a common measure. As his studies, at a previous period of his life, had made him extensively acquainted with the medical science of the day, it was as a physician that he presented himself, and as such was cordially received. Skilful men, of the medical and chirurgical profession, were of rare occurrence in the colony. They seldom, it would appear, partook of the religious zeal that brought other emigrants across the Atlantic. In their researches into the human frame, it may be that the higher and more subtile faculties of such men were materialized, and that they lost the spiritual view of existence amid the intricacies of that wondrous mechanism, which seemed to involve art enough to comprise all of life within itself. At all events, the health of the good town of

Boston, so far as medicine had aught to do with it, had hitherto lain in the guardianship of an aged deacon and apothecary, whose piety and godly deportment were stronger testimonials in his favor, than any that he could have produced in the shape of a diploma. The only surgeon was one who combined the occasional exercise of that noble art with the daily and habitual flourish of a razor. To such a professional body Roger Chillingworth was a brilliant acquisition. He soon manifested his familiarity with the ponderous and imposing machinery of antique physic; in which every remedy contained a multitude of far-fetched and heterogeneous ingredients, as elaborately compounded as if the proposed result had been the Elixir of Life. In his Indian captivity, moreover, he had gained much knowledge of the properties of native herbs and roots; nor did he conceal from his patients, that these simple medicines, Nature's boon to the untutored savage, had quite as large a share of his own confidence as the European pharmacopœia, which so many learned doctors had spent centuries in elaborating.

This learned stranger was exemplary, as regarded at least the outward forms of a religious life, and, early after his arrival, had chosen for his spiritual guide the Reverend Mr. Dimmesdale. The young divine, whose scholar-like renown still lived in Oxford, was considered by his more fervent admirers as little less than a heaven-ordained apostle, destined, should he live and labor for the ordinary term of life, to do as great deeds for the now feeble New England Church, as the early Fathers had achieved for the infancy of the Christian faith. About this period, however, the health of Mr. Dimmesdale had evidently begun to fail. By those best acquainted with his habits, the paleness of the young minister's cheek was accounted for by his too earnest devotion to study, his scrupulous fulfilment of parochial duty, and, more than all, by the fasts and vigils of which he made a frequent practice, in order to keep the grossness of this earthly state from clogging and obscuring his spiritual lamp. Some declared, that, if Mr. Dimmesdale were really going to die, it was cause enough, that the world was not worthy to be any longer trodden by his feet. He himself, on the other hand, with characteristic humility, avowed his belief, that, if Providence should see fit to remove him, it would be because of his own unworthiness to perform its humblest mission here on earth. With all this difference of opinion as to the cause of his decline, there could be no question of the fact. His form grew emaciated; his voice, though still rich and sweet, had a certain melancholy prophecy of decay in it; he was often observed, on any slight alarm or other sudden accident, to put his hand over his heart, with first a flush and then a paleness, indicative of pain.

Such was the young clergyman's condition, and so imminent the prospect that his dawning light would be extinguished, all untimely, when Roger Chillingworth made his advent to the town. His first entry on the scene, few people could tell whence, dropping down, as it were, out of the sky, or starting from the nether earth, had an aspect of mystery, which was easily heightened to the miraculous. He was now known to be a man of skill; it was observed that he gathered herbs, and the blossoms of wild-flowers, and dug up roots and plucked off twigs from the forest-trees, like one acquainted with hidden virtues in what was valueless to common eyes. He was heard to speak of Sir Kenelm Digby, and other famous men,—whose scientific attainments were esteemed hardly less than supernatural,—as having been his correspondents or associates. Why, with such rank in the learned world, had he come hither? What could he, whose sphere was in great cities, be seeking in the wilderness? In answer to this query, a rumor gained ground,—and, however absurd, was entertained by some very sensible people,—that Heaven had wrought an absolute miracle, by transporting an eminent Doctor of Physic, from a German university, bodily through the air, and setting him down at the door of Mr. Dimmesdale's study! Individuals of wiser faith, indeed, who knew that heaven promotes its purposes without aiming at the stage-effect of what is called miraculous interposition, were inclined to see a providential hand in Roger Chillingworth's so opportune arrival.

This idea was countenanced by the strong interest which the physician ever manifested in the young clergyman; he attached himself to him as a parishioner, and sought to win a friendly regard and confidence from his naturally reserved sensibility. He expressed great alarm at his pastor's state of health, but was anxious to attempt the cure, and, if early undertaken, seemed not despondent of a favorable result. The elders, the deacons, the motherly dames, and the young and fair maidens, of Mr. Dimmesdale's flock, were alike importunate that he should make trial of the physician's frankly offered skill. Mr. Dimmesdale gently repelled their entreaties.

"I need no medicine," said he.

But how could the young minister say so, when, with every successive Sabbath, his cheek was paler and thinner, and his voice more tremulous than before,—when it had now become a constant habit, rather than a casual gesture, to press his hand over his heart? Was he weary of his labors? Did he wish to die? These questions were solemnly propounded to Mr. Dimmesdale by the elder ministers of Boston and the deacons of his church, who, to use their own phrase, "dealt with him" on the sin of rejecting the aid which Providence so manifestly held out. He listened in silence, and finally promised to confer with the physician.

"Were it God's will," said the Reverend Mr. Dimmesdale, when, in fulfilment of this pledge, he requested old Roger Chillingworth's professional advice, "I could be well content, that my labors, and my sorrows, and my sins, and my pains, should shortly end with me, and what is earthly of them be buried in my grave, and the spiritual go with me to my eternal state, rather than that you should put your skill to the proof in my behalf."

"Ah," replied Roger Chillingworth, with that quietness which, whether imposed or natural, marked all his deportment, "it is thus that a young clergyman is apt to speak. Youthful men, not having taken a deep root, give up their hold of life so easily! And saintly men, who walk with God on earth, would fain be away, to walk with him on the golden pavements of the New Jerusalem."

"Nay," rejoined the young minister, putting his hand to his heart, with a flush of pain flitting over his brow, "were I worthier to walk there, I could be better content to toil here."

"Good men ever interpret themselves too meanly," said the physician.

In this manner, the mysterious old Roger Chillingworth became the medical adviser of the Reverend Mr. Dimmesdale. As not only the disease interested the physician, but he was strongly moved to look into the character and qualities of the patient, these two men, so different in age, came gradually to spend much time together. For the sake of the minister's health, and to enable the leech to gather plants with healing balm in them, they took long walks on the sea-shore, or in the forest; mingling various talk with the plash and murmur of the waves, and the solemn wind-anthem among the treetops. Often, likewise, one was the guest of the other, in his place of study and retirement. There was a fascination for the minister in the company of the man of science, in whom he recognized an intellectual cultivation of no moderate depth or scope; together with a range and freedom of ideas, that he would have vainly looked for among the members of his own profession. In truth, he was startled, if not shocked, to find this attribute in the physician. Mr. Dimmesdale was a true priest, a true religionist, with the reverential sentiment largely developed, and an order of mind that impelled itself powerfully along the track of a creed, and wore its passage continually deeper with the lapse of time. In no state of society would he have been what is called a man of liberal views; it would always be essential to his peace to feel the pressure of a faith about him, supporting, while it confined him within its iron framework. Not the less, however, though with a tremulous enjoyment, did he feel the occasional relief of looking at the universe through the medium of another kind of intellect than those with which he habitually held converse. It was as if a window were thrown open, admitting a freer atmosphere into the close and stifled study, where his life was wasting itself away, amid lamp-light, or obstructed day-beams, and the musty fragrance, be it sensual, or moral, that exhales from books. But the air was too fresh and chill to be long breathed, with comfort. So the minister, and the physician with him, withdrew again within the limits of what their church defined as orthodox.

Thus Roger Chillingworth scrutinized his patient carefully, both as he saw him in his ordinary life, keeping an accustomed pathway in the range of thoughts familiar to him, and as he appeared when thrown amidst other moral scenery, the novelty of which might call out something new to the surface of his character. He deemed it essential, it would seem, to know the man, before attempting to do him good. Wherever there is a heart and an intellect, the diseases of the physical frame are tinged with the peculiarities of these. In Arthur Dimmesdale, thought and imagination were so active, and sensibility so intense, that the bodily infirmity would be likely to have its ground-work there. So Roger Chillingworth—the man of skill, the kind and friendly physician—strove to go deep into his patient's bosom, delving among his principles, prying into his recollections, and probing every thing with a cautious touch, like a treasure-seeker in a dark cavern. Few secrets can escape an investigator, who has opportunity and license to undertake such a quest, and skill to follow it up. A man burdened with a secret should especially avoid the intimacy of his physician. If the latter possess native sagacity, and a nameless something more,—let us call it intuition; if he show no intrusive egotism, nor disagreeably prominent characteristics of his own; if he have the power, which must be born with him, to bring his mind into such affinity with his patient's, that this last shall unawares have spoken what he imagines himself only to have thought; if such revelations be received without tumult, and acknowledged not so often by an uttered sympathy, as by silence, an inarticulate breath, and here and there a word, to indicate that all is understood; if, to these qualifications of a confidant be joined the advantages afforded by his recognized character as a physician;—then, at some inevitable moment, will the soul of the sufferer be dissolved, and flow forth in a dark, but transparent stream, bringing all its mysteries into the daylight.

Roger Chillingworth possessed all, or most, of the attributes above enumerated. Nevertheless, time went on; a kind of intimacy, as we have said, grew up between these two cultivated minds, which had as wide a field as the whole sphere of human thought and study, to meet upon; they discussed every topic of ethics and religion, of public affairs, and private character; they talked much, on both sides, of matters that seemed personal to themselves; and yet no secret, such as the physician fancied must exist there, ever stole out of the minister's consciousness into his companion's ear. The later had his suspicions, indeed, that even the nature of Mr. Dimmesdale's bodily disease had never fairly been revealed to him. It was a strange reserve!

After a time, at a hint from Roger Chillingworth, the friends of Mr. Dimmesdale effected an arrangement by which the two were lodged in the same house; so that every ebb and flow of the minister's life-tide might pass under the eye of his anxious and attached physician. There was much joy throughout the town, when this greatly desirable object was attained. It was held to be the best possible measure for the young clergyman's welfare; unless, indeed, as often urged by such as felt authorized to do so, he had selected some one of the many blooming damsels, spiritually devoted to him, to become his devoted wife. This latter step, however, there was no present prospect that Arthur Dimmesdale would be prevailed upon to take; he rejected all suggestions of the kind, as if priestly celibacy were one of his articles of church-discipline. Doomed by his own choice, therefore, as Mr. Dimmesdale so evidently was, to eat his unsavory morsel always at another's board, and endure the life-long chill which must be his lot who seeks to warm himself only at another's fireside, it truly seemed that this sagacious, experienced, benevolent, old physician, with his concord of paternal and reverential love for the young pastor, was the very man, of all mankind, to be constantly within reach of his voice.

The new abode of the two friends was with a pious widow, of good social rank, who dwelt in a house covering pretty nearly the site on which the venerable structure of King's Chapel has since been built. It had the grave-yard, originally Isaac Johnson's home-field, on one side, and so was well adapted to call up serious reflections, suited to their respective employments, in both minister and man of physic. The motherly care of the good widow assigned to Mr. Dimmesdale a front apartment, with a sunny exposure, and heavy window-curtains, to create a noontide shadow, when desirable. The walls were hung round with tapestry, said to be from the Gobelin looms, and, at all events, representing the Scriptural story of David and Bathsheba, and Nathan the Prophet, in colors still unfaded, but which made the fair woman of the scene almost as grimly picturesque as the woe-denouncing seer. Here, the pale clergyman piled up his library, rich with parchment-bound folios of the Fathers, and the lore of Rabbis, and monkish erudition, of which the Protestant divines, even while they vilified and decried that class of writers, were yet constrained often to avail themselves. On the other side of the house, old Roger Chillingworth arranged his study and laboratory; not such as a modern man of science would reckon even tolerably complete, but provided with a distilling apparatus, and the means of compounding drugs and chemicals, which the practised alchemist knew well how to turn to purpose. With such commodiousness of situation, these two learned persons sat themselves down, each in his own domain, yet familiarly passing from one apartment to the other, and bestowing a mutual and not incurious inspection into one another's business.

And the Reverend Arthur Dimmesdale's best discerning friends, as we have intimated, very reasonably imagined that the hand of Providence had done all this, for the purpose—besought in so many public, and domestic, and secret prayers—of restoring the young minister to health. But—it must now be said—another portion of the community had latterly begun to take its own view of the relation betwixt Mr. Dimmesdale and the mysterious old physician. When an uninstructed multitude attempts to see with its eyes, it is exceedingly apt to be deceived. When, however, it forms its judgment, as it usually does, on the intuitions of its great and warm heart, the conclusions thus attained are often so profound and so unerring, as to possess the character of truths supernaturally revealed. The people, in the case of which we speak, could justify its prejudice against Roger Chillingworth by no fact or argument worthy of serious refutation. There was an aged handicraftsman, it is true, who had been a citizen of London at the period of Sir Thomas Overbury's murder, now some thirty years agone; he testified to having seen the physician, under some other name, which the narrator of the story had now forgotten, in company with Doctor Forman, the famous old conjurer, who was implicated in the affair of Overbury. Two or three individuals hinted, that the man of skill, during his Indian captivity, had enlarged his medical attainments by joining in the incantations of the savage priests; who were universally acknowledged to be powerful enchanters, often performing seemingly miraculous cures by their skill in the black art. A large number—and many of these were persons of such sober sense and practical observation, that their opinions would have been valuable, in other matters—affirmed that Roger Chillingworth's aspect had undergone a remarkable change while he had dwelt in town, and especially since his abode with Mr. Dimmesdale. At first, his expression had been calm, meditative, scholar-like. Now, there was something ugly and evil in his face, which they had not previously noticed, and which grew still the more obvious to sight, the oftener they looked upon him. According to the vulgar idea, the fire in his laboratory had been brought from the lower regions, and was fed with infernal fuel; and so, as might be expected, his visage was getting sooty with the smoke.

To sum up the matter, it grew to be a widely diffused opinion, that the Reverend Arthur Dimmesdale, like many other personages of especial sanctity, in all ages of the Christian world, was haunted either by Satan himself, or Satan's emissary, in the guise of old Roger Chillingworth. This diabolical agent had the Divine permission, for a season, to burrow into the clergyman's intimacy, and plot against his soul. No sensible man, it was confessed, could doubt on which side the victory would turn. The people looked, with an unshaken hope, to see the minister come forth out of the conflict, transfigured with the glory which he would unquestionably win. Meanwhile, nevertheless, it was sad to think of the perchance mortal agony through which he must struggle towards his triumph.

Alas, to judge from the gloom and terror in the depths of the poor minister's eyes, the battle was a sore one, and the victory any thing but secure!

CHAPTER X

THE LEECH AND HIS PATIENT

Old Roger Chllingworth, throughout life, had been calm in temperament, kindly, though not of warm affections, but ever, and in all his relations with the world, a pure and upright man. He had begun an investigation, as he imagined, with the severe and equal integrity of a judge, desirous only of truth, even as if the question involved no more than the air-drawn lines and figures of a geometrical problem, instead of human passions, and wrongs inflicted on himself. But, as he proceeded, a terrible fascination, a kind of fierce, though still calm, necessity seized the old man within its gripe, and never set him free again, until he had done all its bidding. He now dug into the poor clergyman's heart, like a miner searching for gold; or, rather, like a sexton delving into a grave, possibly in quest of a jewel that had been buried on the dead man's bosom, but likely to find nothing save mortality and corruption. Alas for his own soul, if these were what he sought!

Sometimes, a light glimmered out of the physician's eyes, burning blue and ominous, like the reflection of a furnace, or, let us say, like one of those gleams of ghastly fire that darted from Bunyan's awful doorway in the hill-side, and quivered on the pilgrim's face. The soil where this dark miner was working had perchance shown indications that encouraged him.

"This man," said he, at one such moment, to himself, "pure as they deem him,—all spiritual as he seems,—hath inherited a strong animal nature from his father or his mother. Let us dig a little farther in the direction of this vein!"

Then, after long search into the minister's dim interior, and turning over many precious materials, in the shape of high aspirations for the welfare of his race, warm love of souls, pure sentiments, natural piety, strengthened by thought and study, and illuminated by revelation,—all of which invaluable gold was perhaps no better than rubbish to the seeker,—he would turn back, discouraged, and begin his quest towards another point. He groped along as stealthily, with as cautious a tread, and as wary an outlook, as a thief entering a chamber where a man lies only half asleep,—or, it may be, broad awake,—with purpose to steal the very treasure which this man guards as the apple of his eye. In spite of his premeditated carefulness, the floor would now and then creak; his garments would rustle; the shadow of his presence, in a forbidden proximity, would be thrown across his victim. In other words, Mr. Dimmesdale, whose sensibility of nerve often produced the effect of spiritual intuition, would become vaguely aware that something inimical to his peace had thrust itself into relation with him. But old Roger Chillingworth, too, had perceptions that were almost intuitive; and when the minister threw his startled eyes towards him, there the physician sat; his kind, watchful, sympathizing, but never intrusive friend.

Yet Mr. Dimmesdale would perhaps have seen this individual's character more perfectly, if a certain morbidness, to which sick hearts are liable, had not rendered him suspicious of all mankind. Trusting no man as his friend, he could not recognize his enemy when the latter actually appeared. He therefore still kept up a familiar intercourse with him, daily receiving the old physician in his study; or visiting the laboratory, and, for recreation's sake, watching the processes by which weeds were converted into drugs of potency.

One day, leaning his forehead on his hand, and his elbow on the sill of the open window, that looked towards the graveyard, he talked with Roger Chillingworth, while the old man was examining a bundle of unsightly plants.

"Where," asked he, with a look askance at them,—for it was the clergyman's peculiarity that he seldom, now-a-days, looked straightforth at any object, whether human or inanimate,—"where, my kind doctor, did you gather those herbs, with such a dark, flabby leaf?"

"Even in the grave-yard, here at hand," answered the physician, continuing his employment. "They are new to me. I found them growing on a grave, which bore no tombstone, nor other memorial of the dead man, save these ugly weeds that have taken upon themselves to keep him in remembrance. They grew out of his heart, and typify, it may be, some hideous secret that was buried with him, and which he had done better to confess during his lifetime."

"Perchance," said Mr. Dimmesdale, "he earnestly desired it, but could not."

"And wherefore?" rejoined the physician. "Wherefore not; since all the powers of nature call so earnestly for the confession of sin, that these black weeds have sprung up out of a buried heart, to make manifest an unspoken crime?"

"That, good Sir, is but a fantasy of yours," replied the minister. "There can be, if I forebode aright, no power, short of the Divine mercy, to disclose, whether by uttered words, or by type or emblem, the secrets that may be buried with a human heart. The heart, making itself guilty of such secrets, must perforce hold them, until the day when all hidden things shall be revealed. Nor have I so read or interpreted Holy Writ, as to understand that the disclosure of human thoughts and deeds, then to be made, is intended as a part of the retribution. That, surely, were a shallow view of it. No; these revelations, unless I greatly err, are meant merely to promote the intellectual satisfaction of all intelligent beings, who will stand waiting, on that day, to see the dark problem of this life made plain. A knowledge of men's hearts will be needful to the completest solution of that problem. And I conceive, moreover, that the hearts holding such miserable secrets as you speak of will yield them up, at that last day, not with reluctance, but with a joy unutterable."

"Then why not reveal them here?" asked Roger Chillingworth, glancing quietly aside at the minister. "Why should not the guilty ones sooner avail themselves of this unutterable solace?"

"They mostly do," said the clergyman, griping hard at his breast, as if afflicted with an importunate throb of pain. "Many, many a poor soul hath given its confidence to me, not only on the death-bed, but while strong in life, and fair in reputation. And ever, after such an outpouring, O, what a relief have I witnessed in those sinful brethren! even as in one who at last draws free air, after long stifling with his own polluted breath. How can it be otherwise? Why should a wretched man, guilty, we will say, of murder, prefer to keep the dead corpse buried in his own heart, rather than fling it forth at once, and let the universe take care of it!"

"Yet some men bury their secrets thus," observed the calm physician.

"True; there are such men," answered Mr. Dimmesdale. "But, not to suggest more obvious reasons, it may be that they are kept silent by the very constitution of their nature. Or,—can we not suppose it?—guilty as they may be, retaining, nevertheless, a zeal for God's glory and man's welfare, they shrink from displaying themselves black and filthy in the view of men; because, thenceforward, no good can be achieved by them; no evil of the past be redeemed by better service. So, to their own unutterable torment, they go about among their fellow-creatures, looking pure as newfallen snow; while their hearts are all speckled and spotted with iniquity of which they cannot rid themselves."

"These men deceive themselves," said Roger Chillingworth, with somewhat more emphasis than usual, and making a slight gesture with his forefinger. "They fear to take up the shame that rightfully belongs to them. Their love for man, their zeal for God's service,—these holy impulses may or may not coexist in their hearts with the evil inmates to which their guilt has unbarred the door, and which must needs propagate a hellish breed within them. But, if they seek to glorify God, let them not lift heavenward their unclean hands! If they would serve their fellow-men, let them do it by making manifest the power and reality of conscience, in constraining them to penitential self-abasement! Wouldst thou have me to believe, O wise and pious friend, that a false show can be better—can be more for God's glory, or man's welfare—than God's own truth? Trust me, such men deceive themselves!"

"It may be so," said the young clergyman indifferently, as waiving a discussion that he considered irrelevant or unseasonable. He had a ready faculty, indeed, of escaping from any topic that agitated his too sensitive and nervous temperament.—"But, now, I would ask of my well-skilled physician, whether, in good sooth, he deems me to have profited by his kindly care of this weak frame of mine?"

Before Roger Chillingworth could answer, they heard the clear, wild laughter of a young child's voice, proceeding from the adjacent burial-ground. Looking instinctively from the open window,—for it was summer-time,—the minister beheld Hester Prynne and little Pearl passing along the footpath that traversed the inclosure. Pearl looked as beautiful as the day, but was in one of those moods of perverse merriment which, whenever they occurred, seemed to remove her entirely out of the sphere of sympathy or human contact. She now skipped irreverently from one grave to another; until, coming to the broad, flat, armorial tombstone of a departed worthy,—perhaps of Isaac Johnson himself,—she began to dance upon it. In reply to her mother's command and entreaty that she would behave more decorously, little Pearl paused to gather the prickly burrs from a tall burdock, which grew beside the tomb. Taking a handful of these, she arranged them along the lines of the scarlet letter that decorated the maternal bosom, to which the burrs, as their nature was, tenaciously adhered. Hester did not pluck them off.

Roger Chillingworth had by this time approached the window, and smiled grimly down.

"There is no law, nor reverence for authority, no regard for human ordinances or opinions, right or wrong, mixed up with that child's composition," remarked he, as much to himself as to his companion. "I saw her, the other day, bespatter the Governor himself with water, at the cattle-trough in Spring Lane. What, in Heaven's name, is she? Is the imp altogether evil? Hath she affections? Hath she any discoverable principle of being?"

"None,—save the freedom of a broken law," answered Mr. Dimmesdale, in a quiet way, as if he had been discussing the point within himself. "Whether capable of good, I know not."

The child probably overheard their voices; for, looking up to the window, with a bright, but naughty smile of mirth and intelligence, she threw one of the prickly burrs at the Reverend Mr. Dimmesdale. The sensitive clergyman shrunk, with nervous dread, from the light missile. Detecting his emotion, Pearl clapped her little hands in the most extravagant ecstasy. Hester Prynne, likewise, had involuntarily looked up; and all these four persons, old and young, regarded one another in silence, till the child laughed aloud, and shouted,—"Come away, mother! Come away, or yonder old Black Man will catch you! He hath got hold of the minister already. Come away, mother, or he will catch you! But he cannot catch little Pearl!"

So she drew her mother away, skipping, dancing, and frisking fantastically among the hillocks of the dead people, like a creature that had nothing in common with a bygone and buried generation, nor owned herself akin to it. It was as if she had been made afresh, out of new elements, and must perforce be permitted to live her own life, and be a law unto herself, without her eccentricities being reckoned to her for a crime.

"There goes a woman," resumed Roger Chillingworth, after a pause, "who, be her demerits what they may, hath none of that mystery of hidden sinfulness which you deem so grievous to be borne. Is Hester Prynne the less miserable, think you, for that scarlet letter on her breast?"

"I do verily believe it," answered the clergyman. "Nevertheless, I cannot answer for her. There was a look of pain in her face, which I would gladly have been spared the sight of. But still, methinks, it must needs be better for the sufferer to be free to show his pain, as this poor woman Hester is, than to cover it all up in his heart."

There was another pause; and the physician began anew to examine and arrange the plants which he had gathered.

"You inquired of me, a little time agone," said he, at length, "my judgment as touching your health."

"I did," answered the clergyman, "and would gladly learn it. Speak frankly, I pray you, be it for life or death."

"Freely, then, and plainly," said the physician, still busy with his plants, but keeping a wary eye on Mr. Dimmesdale, "the disorder is a strange one; not so much in itself, nor as outwardly manifested,—in so far, at least, as the symptoms have been laid open to my observation. Looking daily at you, my good Sir, and watching the tokens of your aspect, now for months gone by, I should deem you a man sore sick, it may be, yet not so sick but that an instructed and watchful physician might well hope to cure you. But—I know not what to say—the disease is what I seem to know, yet know it not."

"You speak in riddles, learned Sir," said the pale minister, glancing aside out of the window.

"Then, to speak more plainly," continued the physician, "and I crave pardon, Sir,—should it seem to require pardon,—for this needful plainness of my speech. Let me ask,—as your friend,—as one having charge, under Providence, of your life and physical well-being,—hath all the operation of this disorder been fairly laid open and recounted to me?"

"How can you question it?" asked the minister. "Surely, it were child's play to call in a physician, and then hide the sore!"

"You would tell me, then, that I know all?" said Roger Chillingworth, deliberately, and fixing an eye, bright with intense and concentrated intelligence, on the minister's face. "Be it so! But, again! He to whom only the outward and physical evil is laid open knoweth, oftentimes, but half the evil which he is called upon to cure. A bodily disease, which we look upon as whole and entire within itself, may, after all, be but a symptom of some ailment in the spiritual part. Your pardon, once again, good Sir, if my speech give the shadow of offence. You, Sir, of all men whom I have known, are he whose body is the closest conjoined, and imbued, and identified, so to speak, with the spirit whereof it is the instrument."

"Then I need ask no further," said the clergyman, somewhat hastily rising from his chair. "You deal not, I take it, in medicine for the soul!"

"Thus, a sickness," continued Roger Chillingworth, going on, in an unaltered tone, without heeding the interruption,—but standing up, and confronting the emaciated and white-cheeked minister with his low, dark, and misshapen figure,—"a sickness, a sore place, if we may so call it, in your spirit, hath immediately its appropriate manifestation in your bodily frame. Would you, therefore, that your physician heal the bodily evil? How may this be, unless you first lay open to him the wound or trouble in your soul?"

"No!—not to thee!—not to an earthly physician!" cried Mr. Dimmesdale, passionately, and turning his eyes, full and bright, and with a kind of fierceness, on old Roger Chillingworth. "Not to thee! But, if it be the soul's disease, then do I commit myself to the one Physician of the soul! He, if it stand with his good pleasure, can cure; or he can kill! Let him do with me as, in his justice and wisdom, he shall see good. But who art thou, that meddlest in this matter?—that dares thrust himself between the sufferer and his God?"

With a frantic gesture, he rushed out of the room.

"It is as well to have made this step," said Roger Chillingworth to himself, looking after the minister with a grave smile. "There is nothing lost. We shall be friends again anon. But see, now, how passion takes hold upon this man, and hurrieth him out of himself! As with one passion, so with another! He hath done a wild thing ere now, this pious Master Dimmesdale, in the hot passion of his heart!"

It proved not difficult to reëstablish the intimacy of the two companions, on the same footing and in the same degree as heretofore. The young clergyman, after a few hours of privacy, was sensible that the disorder of his nerves had hurried him into an unseemly outbreak of temper, which there had been nothing in the physician's words to excuse or palliate. He marvelled, indeed, at the violence with which he had thrust back the kind old man, when merely proffering the advice which it was his duty to bestow, and which the minister himself had expressly sought. With these remorseful feelings, he lost no time in making the amplest apologies, and besought his friend still to continue the care, which, if not successful in restoring him to health, had, in all probability, been the means of prolonging his feeble existence to that hour. Roger Chillingworth readily assented, and went on with his medical supervision of the minister; doing his best for him, in all good faith, but always quitting the patient's apartment, at the close of a professional interview, with a mysterious and puzzled smile upon his lips. This expression was invisible in Mr. Dimmesdale's presence, but grew strongly evident as the physician crossed the threshold.

"A rare case!" he muttered. "I must needs look deeper into it. A strange sympathy betwixt soul and body! Were it only for the art's sake, I must search this matter to the bottom!"

It came to pass, not long after the scene above recorded, that the Reverend Mr. Dimmesdale, at noonday, and entirely unawares, fell into a deep, deep slumber, sitting in his chair, with a large black-letter volume open before him on the table. It must have been a work of vast ability in the somniferous school of literature. The profound depth of the minister's repose was the more remarkable; inasmuch as he was one of those persons whose sleep, ordinarily, is as light, as fitful, and as easily scared away, as a small bird hopping on a twig. To such an unwonted remoteness, however, had his spirit now withdrawn into itself, that he stirred not in his chair, when old Roger Chillingworth, without any extraordinary precaution, came into the room. The physician advanced directly in front of his patient, laid his hand upon his bosom, and thrust aside the vestment, that, hitherto, had always covered it even from the professional eye.

Then, indeed, Mr. Dimmesdale shuddered, and slightly stirred.

After a brief pause, the physician turned away.

But with what a wild look of wonder, joy, and horror! With what a ghastly rapture, as it were, too mighty to be expressed only by the eye and features, and therefore bursting forth through the whole ugliness of his figure, and making itself even riotously manifest by the extravagant gestures with which he threw up his arms towards the ceiling, and stamped his foot upon the floor! Had a man seen old Roger Chillingworth, at that moment of his ecstasy, he would have had no need to ask how Satan comports himself, when a precious human soul is lost to heaven, and won into his kingdom.

But what distinguished the physician's ecstasy from Satan's was the trait of wonder in it!

CHAPTER XI

THE INTERIOR OF A HEART

After the incident last described, the intercourse between the clergyman and the physician, though externally the same, was really of another character than it had previously been. The intellect of Roger Chillingworth had now a sufficiently plain path before it. It was not, indeed, precisely that which he had laid out for himself to tread. Calm, gentle, passionless, as he appeared, there was yet, we fear, a quiet depth of malice, hitherto latent, but active now, in this unfortunate old man, which led him to imagine a more intimate revenge than any mortal had ever wreaked upon an enemy. To make himself the one trusted friend, to whom should be confided all the fear, the remorse, the agony, the ineffectual repentance, the backward rush of sinful thoughts, expelled in vain! All that guilty sorrow, hidden from the world, whose great heart would have pitied and forgiven, to be revealed to him, the Pitiless, to him, the Unforgiving! All that dark treasure to be lavished on the very man, to whom nothing else could so adequately pay the debt of vengeance!

The clergyman's shy and sensitive reserve had balked this scheme. Roger Chillingworth, however, was inclined to be hardly, if at all, less satisfied with the aspect of affairs, which Providence—using the avenger and his victim for its own purposes, and, perchance, pardoning, where it seemed most to punish—had substituted for his black devices. A revelation, he could almost say, had been granted to him. It mattered little, for his object, whether celestial, or from what other region. By its aid, in all the subsequent relations betwixt him and Mr. Dimmesdale, not merely the external presence, but the very inmost soul of the latter seemed to be brought out before his eyes, so that he could see and comprehend its every movement. He became, thenceforth, not a spectator only, but a chief actor, in the poor minister's interior world. He could play upon him as he chose. Would he arouse him with a throb of agony? The victim was for ever on the rack; it needed only to know the spring that controlled the engine;—and the physician knew it well! Would he startle him with sudden fear? As at the waving of a magician's wand, uprose a grisly phantom,—uprose a thousand phantoms,—in many shapes, of death, or more awful shame, all flocking round about the clergyman, and pointing with their fingers at his breast!

All this was accomplished with a subtlety so perfect, that the minister, though he had constantly a dim perception of some evil influence watching over him, could never gain a knowledge of its actual nature. True, he looked doubtfully, fearfully,—even, at times, with horror and the bitterness of hatred,—at the deformed figure of the old physician. His gestures, his gait, his grizzled beard, his slightest and most indifferent acts, the very fashion of his garments, were odious in the clergyman's sight; a token, implicitly to be relied on, of a deeper antipathy in the breast of the latter than he was willing to acknowledge to himself. For, as it was impossible to assign a reason for such distrust and abhorrence, so Mr. Dimmesdale, conscious that the poison of one morbid spot was infecting his heart's entire substance, attributed all his presentiments to no other cause. He took himself to task for his bad sympathies in reference to Roger Chillingworth, disregarded the lesson that he should have drawn from them, and did his best to root them out. Unable to accomplish this, he nevertheless, as a matter of principle, continued his habits of social familiarity with the old man, and thus gave him constant opportunities for perfecting the purpose to which—poor, forlorn creature that he was, and more wretched than his victim—the avenger had devoted himself.

While thus suffering under bodily disease, and gnawed and tortured by some black trouble of the soul, and given over to the machinations of his deadliest enemy, the Reverend Mr. Dimmesdale had achieved a brilliant popularity in his sacred office. He won it, indeed, in great part, by his sorrows. His intellectual gifts, his moral perceptions, his power of experiencing and communicating emotion, were kept in a state of preternatural activity by the prick and anguish of his daily life. His fame, though still on its upward slope, already overshadowed the soberer reputations of his fellow-clergymen, eminent as several of them were. There were scholars among them, who had spent more years in acquiring abstruse lore, connected with the divine profession, than Mr. Dimmesdale had lived; and who might well, therefore, be more profoundly versed in such solid and valuable attainments than their youthful brother. There were men, too, of a sturdier texture of mind than his, and endowed with a far greater share of shrewd, hard, iron or granite understanding; which, duly mingled with a fair proportion of doctrinal ingredient, constitutes a highly respectable, efficacious, and unamiable variety of the clerical species. There were others, again, true saintly fathers, whose faculties had been elaborated by weary toil among their books, and by patient thought, and etherealized, moreover, by spiritual communications with the better world, into which their purity of life had almost introduced these holy personages, with their garments of mortality still clinging to them. All that they lacked was the gift that descended upon the chosen disciples, at Pentecost, in tongues of flame; symbolizing, it would seem, not the power of speech in foreign and unknown languages, but that of addressing the whole human brotherhood in the heart's native language. These fathers, otherwise so apostolic, lacked Heaven's last and rarest attestation of their office, the Tongue of Flame. They would have vainly sought—had they ever dreamed of seeking—to express the highest truths through the humblest medium of familiar words and images. Their voices came down, afar and indistinctly, from the upper heights where they habitually dwelt.

Not improbably, it was to this latter class of men that Mr. Dimmesdale, by many of his traits of character, naturally belonged. To their high mountain-peaks of faith and sanctity he would have climbed, had not the tendency been thwarted by the burden, whatever it might be, of crime or anguish, beneath which it was his doom to totter. It kept him down, on a level with the lowest; him, the man of ethereal attributes, whose voice the angels might else have listened to and answered! But this very burden it was, that gave him sympathies so intimate with the sinful brotherhood of mankind; so that his heart vibrated in unison with theirs, and received their pain into itself, and sent its own throb of pain through a thousand other hearts, in gushes of sad, persuasive eloquence. Oftenest persuasive, but sometimes terrible! The people knew not the power that moved them thus. They deemed the young clergyman a miracle of holiness. They fancied him the mouthpiece of Heaven's messages of wisdom, and rebuke, and love. In their eyes, the very ground on which he trod was sanctified. The virgins of his church grew pale around him, victims of a passion so imbued with religious sentiment that they imagined it to be all religion, and brought it openly, in their white bosoms, as their most acceptable sacrifice before the altar. The aged members of his flock, beholding Mr. Dimmesdale's frame so feeble, while they were themselves so rugged in their infirmity, believed that he would go heavenward before them, and enjoined it upon their children, that their old bones should be buried close to their young pastor's holy grave. And, all this time, perchance, when poor Mr. Dimmesdale was thinking of his grave, he questioned with himself whether the grass would ever grow on it, because an accursed thing must there be buried!

It is inconceivable, the agony with which this public veneration tortured him! It was his genuine impulse to adore the truth, and to reckon all things shadow-like, and utterly devoid of weight or value, that had not its divine essence as the life within their life. Then, what was he?—a substance?—or the dimmest of all shadows? He longed to speak out, from his own pulpit, at the full height of his voice, and tell the people what he was. "I, whom you behold in these black garments of the priesthood,—I who ascend the sacred desk, and turn my pale face heavenward, taking upon myself to hold communion, in your behalf, with the Most High Omniscience,—I, in whose daily life you discern the sanctity of Enoch,—I, whose footsteps, as you suppose, leave a gleam along my earthly track, whereby the pilgrims that shall come after me may be guided to the regions of the blest,—I, who have laid the hand of baptism upon your children,—I, who have breathed the parting prayer over your dying friends, to whom the Amen sounded faintly from a world which they had quitted,—I, your pastor, whom you so reverence and trust, am utterly a pollution and a lie!"

More than once, Mr. Dimmesdale had gone into the pulpit, with a purpose never to come down its steps, until he should have spoken words like the above. More than once, he had cleared his throat, and drawn in the long, deep, and tremulous breath, which, when sent forth again, would come burdened with the black secret of his soul. More than once—nay, more than a hundred times—he had actually spoken! Spoken! But how? He had told his hearers that he was altogether vile, a viler companion of the vilest, the worst of sinners, an abomination, a thing of unimaginable iniquity; and that the only wonder was, that they did not see his wretched body shrivelled up before their eyes, by the burning wrath of the Almighty! Could there be plainer speech than this? Would not the people start up in their seats, by a simultaneous impulse, and tear him down out of the pulpit which he defiled? Not so, indeed! They heard it all, and did but reverence him the more. They little guessed what deadly purport lurked in those self-condemning words. "The godly youth!" said they among themselves. "The saint on earth! Alas, if he discern such sinfulness in his own white soul, what horrid spectacle would be behold in thine or mine!" The minister well knew—subtle, but remorseful hypocrite that he was!—the light in which his vague confession would be viewed. He had striven to put a cheat upon himself by making the avowal of a guilty conscience, but had gained only one other sin, and a self-acknowledged shame, without the momentary relief of being self-deceived. He had spoken the very truth, and transformed it into the veriest falsehood. And yet, by the constitution of his nature, he loved the truth, and loathed the lie, as few men ever did. Therefore, above all things else, he loathed his miserable self!

His inward trouble drove him to practices, more in accordance with the old, corrupted faith of Rome, than with the better light of the church in which he had been born and bred. In Mr. Dimmesdale's secret closet, under lock and key, there was a bloody scourge. Oftentimes, this Protestant and Puritan divine had plied it on his own shoulders; laughing bitterly at himself the while, and smiting so much the more pitilessly, because of that bitter laugh. It was his custom, too, as it has been that of many other pious Puritans, to fast,—not, however, like them, in order to purify the body and render it the fitter medium of celestial illumination,—but rigorously, and until his knees trembled beneath him, as an act of penance. He kept vigils, likewise, night after night, sometimes in utter darkness; sometimes with a glimmering lamp; and sometimes, viewing his own face in a looking-glass, by the most powerful light which he could throw upon it. He thus typified the constant introspection wherewith he tortured, but could not purify, himself. In these lengthened vigils, his brain often reeled, and visions seemed to flit before him; perhaps seen doubtfully, and by a faint light of their own, in the remote dimness of the chamber, or more vividly, and close beside him, within the looking-glass. Now it was a herd of diabolic shapes, that grinned and mocked at the pale minister, and beckoned him away with them; now a group of shining angels, who flew upward heavily, as sorrow-laden, but grew more ethereal as they rose. Now came the dead friends of his youth, and his white-bearded father, with a saint-like frown, and his mother, turning her face away as she passed by. Ghost of a mother,—thinnest fantasy of a mother,—methinks she might yet have thrown a pitying glance towards her son! And now, through the chamber which these spectral thoughts had made so ghastly, glided Hester Prynne, leading along little Pearl, in her scarlet garb, and pointing her forefinger, first, at the scarlet letter on her bosom, and then at the clergyman's own breast.

None of these visions ever quite deluded him. At any moment, by an effort of his will, he could discern substances through their misty lack of substance, and convince himself that they were not solid in their nature, like yonder table of carved oak, or that big, square, leathern-bound and brazen-clasped volume of divinity. But, for all that, they were, in one sense, the truest and most substantial things which the poor minister now dealt with. It is the unspeakable misery of a life so false as his, that it steals the pith and substance out of whatever realities there are around us, and which were meant by Heaven to be the spirit's joy and nutriment. To the untrue man, the whole universe is false,—it is impalpable,—it shrinks to nothing within his grasp. And he himself, in so far as he shows himself in a false light, becomes a shadow, or, indeed, ceases to exist. The only truth, that continued to give Mr. Dimmesdale a real existence on this earth, was the anguish in his inmost soul, and the undissembled expression of it in his aspect. Had he once found power to smile, and wear a face of gayety, there would have been no such man!

On one of those ugly nights, which we have faintly hinted at, but forborne to picture forth, the minister started from his chair. A new thought had struck him. There might be a moment's peace in it. Attiring himself with as much care as if it had been for public worship, and precisely in the same manner, he stole softly down the staircase, undid the door, and issued forth.

CHAPTER XII

THE MINISTER'S VIGIL

Walking in the shadow of a dream, as it were, and perhaps actually under the influence of a species of somnambulism, Mr. Dimmesdale reached the spot, where, now so long since, Hester Prynne had lived through her first hour of public ignominy. The same platform or scaffold, black and weather-stained with the storm or sunshine of seven long years, and foot-worn, too, with the tread of many culprits who had since ascended it, remained standing beneath the balcony of the meeting-house. The minister went up the steps.

It was an obscure night of early May. An unvaried pall of cloud muffled the whole expanse of sky from zenith to horizon. If the same multitude which had stood as eyewitnesses while Hester Prynne sustained her punishment could now have been summoned forth, they would have discerned no face above the platform, nor hardly the outline of a human shape, in the dark gray of the midnight. But the town was all asleep. There was no peril of discovery. The minister might stand there, if it so pleased him, until morning should redden in the east, without other risk than that the dank and chill night-air would creep into his frame, and stiffen his joints with rheumatism, and clog his throat with catarrh and cough; thereby defrauding the expectant audience of to-morrow's prayer and sermon. No eye could see him, save that ever-wakeful one which had seen him in his closet, wielding the bloody scourge. Why, then, had he come hither? Was it but the mockery of penitence? A mockery, indeed, but in which his soul trifled with itself! A mockery at which angels blushed and wept, while fiends rejoiced, with jeering laughter! He had been driven hither by the impulse of that Remorse which dogged him everywhere, and whose own sister and closely linked companion was that Cowardice which invariably drew him back, with her tremulous gripe, just when the other impulse had hurried him to the verge of a disclosure. Poor, miserable man! what right had infirmity like his to burden itself with crime? Crime is for the iron-nerved, who have their choice either to endure it, or, if it press too hard, to exert their fierce and savage strength for a good purpose, and fling it off at once! This feeble and most sensitive of spirits could do neither, yet continually did one thing or another, which intertwined, in the same inextricable knot, the agony of heaven-defying guilt and vain repentance.

And thus, while standing on the scaffold, in this vain show of expiation, Mr. Dimmesdale was overcome with a great horror of mind, as if the universe were gazing at a scarlet token on his naked breast, right over his heart. On that spot, in very truth, there was, and there had long been, the gnawing and poisonous tooth of bodily pain. Without any effort of his will, or power to restrain himself, he shrieked aloud; an outcry that went pealing through the night, and was beaten back from one house to another, and reverberated from the hills in the background; as if a company of devils, detecting so much misery and terror in it, had made a plaything of the sound, and were bandying it to and fro.

"It is done!" muttered the minister, covering his face with his hands. "The whole town will awake, and hurry forth, and find me here!"

But it was not so. The shriek had perhaps sounded with a far greater power, to his own startled ears, than it actually possessed. The town did not awake; or, if it did, the drowsy slumberers mistook the cry either for something frightful in a dream, or for the noise of witches; whose voices, at that period, were often heard to pass over the settlements or lonely cottages, as they rode with Satan through the air. The clergyman, therefore, hearing no symptoms of disturbance, uncovered his eyes and looked about him. At one of the chamber-windows of Governor Bellingham's mansion, which stood at some distance, on the line of another steet, he beheld the appearance of the old magistrate himself, with a lamp in his hand, a white night-cap on his head, and a long white gown enveloping his figure. He looked like a ghost, evoked unseasonably from the grave. The cry had evidently startled him. At another window of the same house, moreover, appeared old

Mistress Hibbins, the Governor's sister, also with a lamp, which, even thus far off, revealed the expression of her sour and discontented face. She thrust forth her head from the lattice, and looked anxiously upward. Beyond the shadow of a doubt, this venerable witch-lady had heard Mr. Dimmesdale's outcry, and interpreted it, with its multitudinous echoes and reverberations, as the clamor of the fiends and night-hags, with whom she was well known to make excursions into the forest.

Detecting the gleam of Governor Bellingham's lamp, the old lady quickly extinguished her own, and vanished. Possibly, she went up among the clouds. The minister saw nothing further of her motions. The magistrate, after a wary observation of the darkness—into which, nevertheless, he could see but little farther than he might into a mill-stone—retired from the window.

The minister grew comparatively calm. His eyes, however, were soon greeted by a little, glimmering light, which, at first a long way off, was approaching up the street. It threw a gleam of recognition on here a post, and there a garden-fence, and here a latticed window-pane, and there a pump, with its full trough of water, and here, again, an arched door of oak, with an iron knocker, and a rough log for the door-step. The Reverend Mr. Dimmesdale noted all these minute particulars, even while firmly convinced that the doom of his existence was stealing onward, in the footsteps which he now heard; and that the gleam of the lantern would fall upon him, in a few moments more, and reveal his long-hidden secret. As the light drew nearer, he beheld, within its illuminated circle, his brother clergyman,—or, to speak more accurately, his professional father, as well as highly valued friend,—the Reverend Mr. Wilson; who, as Mr. Dimmesdale now conjectured, had been praying at the bedside of some dying man. And so he had. The good old minister came freshly from the death-chamber of Governor Winthrop, who had passed from earth to heaven within that very hour. And now, surrounded, like the saint-like personages of olden times, with a radiant halo, that glorified him amid this gloomy night of sin,—as if the departed Governor had left him an inheritance of his glory, or as if he had caught upon himself the distant shine of the celestial city, while looking thitherward to see the triumphant pilgrim pass within its gates,—now, in short, good Father Wilson was moving homeward, aiding his footsteps with a lighted lantern! The glimmer of this luminary suggested the above conceits to Mr. Dimmesdale, who smiled,—nay, almost laughed at them,—and then wondered if he were going mad.

As the Reverend Mr. Wilson passed beside the scaffold, closely muffling his Geneva cloak about him with one arm, and holding the lantern before his breast with the other, the minister could hardly restrain himself from speaking.

"A good evening to you, venerable Father Wilson! Come up hither, I pray you, and pass a pleasant hour with me!"

Good heavens! Had Mr. Dimemsdale actually spoken? For one instant, he believed that these words had passed his lips. But they were uttered only within his imagination. The venerable Father Wilson continued to step slowly onward, looking carefully at the muddy pathway before his feet, and never once turning his head towards the guilty platform. When the light of the glimmering lantern had faded quite away, the minister discovered, by the faintness which came over him, that the last few moments had been a crisis of terrible anxiety; although his mind had made an involuntary effort to relieve itself by a kind of lurid playfulness.

Shortly afterwards, the like grisly sense of the humorous again stole in among the solemn phantoms of his thought. He felt his limbs growing stiff with the unaccustomed chilliness of the night, and doubted whether he should be able to descend the steps of the scaffold. Morning would break, and find him there. The neighbourhood would begin to rouse itself. The earliest riser, coming forth in the dim twilight, would perceive a vaguely defined figure aloft on the place of shame; and, half crazed betwixt alarm and curiosity, would go, knocking from door to door, summoning all the people to behold the ghost—as he needs must think it—of some defunct transgressor. A dusky tumult would flap its wings from one house to another. Then—the morning light still waxing stronger—old patriarchs would rise up in great haste, each in his flannel gown, and matronly dames, without pausing to put off their night-gear. The whole tribe of decorous personages, who had never heretofore been seen with a single hair of their heads awry, would start into public view, with the disorder of a nightmare in their aspects. Old Governor Bellingham would come grimly forth, with his King James's ruff fastened askew; and Mistress Hibbins, with some twigs of the forest clinging to her skirts, and looking sourer than ever, as having hardly got a wink of sleep after her night ride; and good Father Wilson, too, after spending half the night at a death-bed, and liking ill to be disturbed, thus early, out of his dreams about the glorified saints. Hither, likewise, would come the elders and deacons of Mr. Dimmesdale's church, and the young virgins who so idolized their minister, and had made a shrine for him in their white bosoms; which, now, by the by, in their hurry and confusion, they would scantly have given themselves time to cover with their kerchiefs. All people, in a word, would come stumbling over their thresholds, and turning up their amazed and horror-stricken visages around the scaffold. Whom would they discern there, with the red eastern light upon his brow? Whom, but the Reverend Arthur Dimmesdale, half frozen to death, overwhelmed with shame, and standing where Hester Prynne had stood!

Carried away by the grotesque horror of this picture, the minister, unawares, and to his own infinite alarm, burst into a great peal of laughter. It was immediately responded to by a light, airy, childish laugh, in which, with a thrill of the heart,—but he knew not whether of exquisite pain, or pleasure as acute,—he recognized the tones of little Pearl.

"Pearl! Little Pearl!" cried he, after a moment's pause; then, suppressing his voice,—"Hester! Hester Prynne! Are you there?"

"Yes; it is Hester Prynne!" she replied, in a tone of surprise; and the minister heard her footsteps approaching from the sidewalk, along which she had been passing.—"It is I, and my little Pearl."

"Whence come you, Hester?" asked the minister. "What sent you hither?"

"I have been watching at a death-bed," answered Hester Prynne;—"at Governor Winthrop's death-bed, and have taken his measure for a robe, and am now going homeward to my dwelling."

"Come up hither, Hester, thou and little Pearl," said the Reverend Mr. Dimmesdale. "Ye have both been here before, but I was not with you. Come up hither once again, and we will stand all three together!"

She silently ascended the steps, and stood on the platform, holding little Pearl by the hand. The minister felt for the child's other hand, and took it. The moment that he did so, there came what seemed a tumultuous rush of new life, other life than his own, pouring like a torrent into his heart, and hurrying through all his veins, as if the mother and the child were communicating their vital warmth to his half-torpid system. The three formed an electric chain.

"Minister!" whispered little Pearl.

"What wouldst thou say, child?" asked Mr. Dimmesdale.

"Wilt thou stand here with mother and me, to-morrow noontide?" inquired Pearl.

"Nay; not so, my little Pearl!" answered the minister; for, with the new energy of the moment, all the dread of public exposure, that had so long been the anguish of his life, had returned upon him; and he was already trembling at the conjunction in which—with a strange joy, nevertheless—he now found himself. "Not so, my child. I shall, indeed, stand with thy mother and thee one other day, but not tomorrow!"

Pearl laughed, and attempted to pull away her hand. But the minister held it fast.

"A moment longer, my child!" said he.

"But wilt thou promise," asked Pearl, "to take my hand, and mother's hand, to-morrow noontide?"

"Not then, Pearl," said the minister, "but another time!"

"And what other time?" persisted the child.

"At the great judgment day!" whispered the minister,—and, strangely enough, the sense that he was a professional teacher of the truth impelled him to answer the child so. "Then, and there, before the judgment-seat, thy mother, and thou, and I, must stand together! But the daylight of this world shall not see our meeting!"

Pearl laughed again.

But, before Mr. Dimmesdale had done speaking, a light gleamed far and wide over the muffled sky. It was doubtless caused by one of those meteors, which the night-watcher may so often observe burning out to waste, in the vacant regions of the atmosphere. So powerful was its radiance, that it thoroughly illuminated the dense medium of cloud betwixt the sky and earth. The great vault brightened, like the dome of an immense lamp. It showed the familiar scene of the street, with the distinctness of mid-day, but also with the awfulness that is always imparted to familiar objects by an unaccustomed light. The wooden houses, with their jutting stories and quaint gable-peaks; the doorsteps and thresholds, with the early grass springing up about them; the garden-plots, black with freshly turned earth; the wheel-track, little worn, and, even in the market-place, margined with green on either side;—all were visible, but with a singularity of aspect that seemed to give another moral interpretation to the things of this world than they had ever borne before. And there stood the minister, with his hand over his heart; and Hester Prynne, with the embroidered letter glimmering on her bosom; and little Pearl, herself a symbol, and the connecting link between those two. They stood in the noon of that strange and solemn splendor, as if it were the light that is to reveal all secrets, and the daybreak that shall unite all who belong to one another.

There was witchcraft in little Pearl's eyes; and her face, as she glanced upward at the minister, wore that naughty smile which made its expression frequently so elvish. She withdrew her hand from Mr. Dimmesdale's, and pointed across the street. But he clasped both his hands over his breast, and cast his eyes towards the zenith.

Nothing was more common, in those days, than to interpret all meteoric appearances, and other natural phenomena, that occurred with less regularity than the rise and set of sun and moon, as so many revelations from a supernatural source. Thus, a blazing spear, a sword of flame, a bow, or a sheaf of arrows, seen in the midnight sky, prefigured Indian warfare. Pestilence was known to have been foreboded by a shower of crimson light. We doubt whether any marked event, for good or evil, ever befell New England, from its settlement down to Revolutionary times, of which the inhabitants had not been previously warned by some spectacle of this nature. Not seldom, it had been seen by multitudes. Oftener, however, its credibility rested on the faith of some lonely eyewitness, who beheld the wonder through the colored, magnifying, and distorting medium of his imagination, and shaped it more distinctly in his after-thought. It was, indeed, a majestic idea, that the destiny of nations should be revealed, in these awful hieroglyphics, on the cope of heaven. A scroll so wide might not be deemed too expansive for Providence to write a people's doom upon. The belief was a favorite one with our forefathers, as betokening that their infant commonwealth was under a celestial guardianship of peculiar intimacy and strictness. But what shall we say, when an individual discovers a revelation, addressed to himself alone, on the same vast sheet of record! In such a case, it could only be the symptom of a highly disordered mental state, when a man, rendered morbidly self-contemplative by long, intense, and secret pain, had extended his egotism over the whole expanse of nature, until the firmament itself should appear no more than a fitting page for his soul's history and fate.

We impute it, therefore, solely to the disease in his own eye and heart, that the minister, looking upward to the zenith, beheld there the appearance of an immense letter,—the letter A,—marked out in lines of dull red light. Not but the meteor may have shown itself at that point, burning duskily through a veil of cloud; but with no such shape as his guilty imagination gave it; or, at least, with so little definiteness, that another's guilt might have seen another symbol in it.

There was a singular circumstance that characterized Mr. Dimmesdale's psychological state, at this moment. All the time that he gazed upward to the zenith, he was, nevertheless, perfectly aware that little Pearl was pointing her finger towards old Roger Chillingworth, who stood at no great distance from the scaffold. The minister appeared to see him, with the same glance that discerned the miraculous letter. To his features, as to all other objects, the meteroric light imparted a new expression; or it might well be that the physician was not careful then, as at all other times, to hide the malevolence with which he looked upon his victim. Certainly, if the meteor kindled up the sky, and disclosed the earth, with an awfulness that admonished Hester Prynne and the clergyman of the day of judgment, then might Roger Chillingworth have passed with them for the arch-fiend, standing there, with a smile and scowl, to claim his own. So vivid was the expression, or so intense the minister's perception of it, that it seemed still to remain painted on the darkness, after the meteor had vanished, with an effect as if the street and all things else were at once annihilated.

"Who is that man, Hester?" gasped Mr. Dimmesdale, overcome with terror. "I shiver at him! Dost thou know the man? I hate him, Hester!"

She remembered her oath, and was silent.

"I tell thee, my soul shivers at him," muttered the minister again. "Who is he? Who is he? Canst thou do nothing for me? I have a nameless horror of the man."

"Minister," said little Pearl, "I can tell thee who he is!"

"Quickly, then, child!" said the minister, bending his ear close to her lips. "Quickly!—and as low as thou canst whisper."

Pearl mumbled something into his ear, that sounded, indeed, like human language, but was only such gibberish as children may be heard amusing themselves with, by the hour together. At all events, if it involved any secret information in regard to old Roger Chillingworth, it was in a tongue unknown to the erudite clergyman, and did but increase the bewilderment of his mind. The elvish child then laughed aloud.

"Dost thou mock me now?" said the minister.

"Thou was not bold!—thou wast not true!" answered the child. "Thou wouldst not promise to take my hand, and mother's hand, to-morrow noontide!"

"Worthy Sir," said the physician, who had now advanced to the foot of the platform. "Pious Master Dimmesdale! can this be you? Well, well, indeed! We men of study, whose heads are in our books, have need to be straitly looked after! We dream in our waking moments, and walk in our sleep. Come, good Sir, and my dear friend, I pray you, let me lead you home!"

"How knewest thou that I was here?" asked the minister, fearfully.

"Verily, and in good faith," answered Roger Chillingworth, "I knew nothing of the matter. I had spent the better part of the night at the bedside of the worshipful Governor Winthrop, doing what my poor skill might to give him ease. He going home to a better world, I, likewise, was on my way homeward, when this strange light shone out. Come with me, I beseech you, Reverend Sir; else you will be poorly able to do Sabbath duty to-morrow. Aha! see now, how they trouble the brain,—these books!—these books! You should study less, good Sir, and take a little pastime; or these night-whimseys will grow upon you!"

"I will go home with you," said Mr. Dimmesdale.

With a chill despondency, like one awaking, all nerveless, from an ugly dream, he yielded himself to the physician, and was led away.

The next day, however, being the Sabbath, he preached a discourse which was held to be the richest and most powerful, and the most replete with heavenly influences, that had ever proceeded from his lips. Souls, it is said, more souls than one, were brought to the truth by the efficacy of that sermon, and vowed within themselves to cherish a holy gratitude towards Mr. Dimmesdale throughout the long hereafter. But, as he came down the pulpit-steps, the gray-bearded sexton met him, holding up a black glove, which the minister recognized as his own.

"It was found," said the sexton, "this morning, on the scaffold, where evil-doers are set up to public shame. Satan dropped it there, I take it, intending a scurrilous jest against your reverence. But, indeed, he was blind and foolish, as he ever and always is. A pure hand needs no glove to cover it!"

"Thank you, my good friend," said the minister gravely, but startled at heart; for, so confused was his remembrance, that he had almost brought himself to look at the events of the past night as visionary. "Yes, it seems to be my glove indeed!"

"And, since Satan saw fit to steal it, your reverence must needs handle him without gloves, henceforward," remarked the old sexton, grimly smiling. "But did your reverence hear of the portent that was seen last night? A great red letter in the sky,—the letter A,—which we interpret to stand for Angel. For, as our good Governor Winthrop was made an angel this past night, it was doubtless held fit that there should be some notice thereof!"

"No," answered the minister, "I had not heard of it."

CHAPTER XIII

ANOTHER VIEW OF HESTER

In her late singular interview with Mr. Dimmesdale, Hester Prynne was shocked at the condition to which she found the clergyman reduced. His nerve seemed absolutely destroyed. His moral force was abased into more than childish weakness. It grovelled helpless on the ground, even while his intellectual faculties retained their pristine strength, or had perhaps acquired a morbid energy, which disease only could have given them. With her knowledge of a train of circumstances hidden from all others, she could readily infer, that, besides the legitimate action of his own conscience, a terrible machinery had been brought to bear, and was still operating, on Mr. Dimmesdale's well-being and repose. Knowing what this poor, fallen man had once been, her whole soul was moved by the shuddering terror with which he had appealed to her,—the outcast woman,—for support against his instinctively discovered enemy. She decided, moreover, that he had a right to her utmost aid. Little accustomed, in her long seclusion from society, to measure her ideas of right and wrong by any standard external to herself, Hester saw—or seemed to see—that there lay a responsibility upon her, in reference to the clergyman, which she owed to no other, nor to the whole world besides. The links that united her to the rest of human kind—links of flowers, or silk, or gold, or whatever the material—had all been broken. Here was the iron link of mutual crime, which neither he nor she could break. Like all other ties, it brought along with it its obligations.

Hester Prynne did not now occupy precisely the same position in which we beheld her during the earliest periods of her ignominy. Years had come, and gone. Pearl was now seven years old. Her mother, with the scarlet letter on her breast, glittering in its fantastic embroidery, had long been a familiar object to the townspeople. As is apt to be the case when a person stands out in any prominence before the community, and, at the same time, interferes neither with public nor individual interests and convenience, a species of general regard had ultimately grown up in reference to Hester Prynne. It is to the credit of human nature, that, except where its selfishness is brought into play, it loves more readily than it hates. Hatred, by a gradual and quiet process, will even be transformed to love, unless the change be impeded by a continually new irritation of the original feeling of hostility. In this matter of Hester Prynne, there was neither irritation nor irksomeness. She never battled with the public, but submitted uncomplainingly to its worst usage; she made no claim upon it, in requital for what she suffered; she did not weigh upon its sympathies. Then, also, the blameless purity of her life, during all these years in which she had been set apart to infamy, was reckoned largely in her favor. With nothing now to lose, in the sight of mankind, and with no hope, and seemingly no wish, of gaining any thing, it could only be a genuine regard for virtue that had brought back the poor wanderer to its paths.

It was perceived, too, that while Hester never put forward even the humblest title to share in the world's privileges,—farther than to breathe the common air, and earn daily bread for little Pearl and herself by the faithful labor of her hands,—she was quick to acknowledge her sisterhood with the race of man, whenever benefits were to be conferred. None so ready as she to give of her little substance to every demand of poverty; even though the bitter-hearted pauper threw back a gibe in requital of the food brought regularly to his door, or the garments wrought for him by the fingers that could have embroidered a monarch's robe. None so self-devoted as Hester, when pestilence stalked through the town. In all seasons of calamity, indeed, whether general or of individuals, the outcast of society at once found her place. She came, not as a guest, but as a rightful inmate, into the household that was darkened by trouble; as if its gloomy twilight were a medium in which she was entitled to hold intercourse with her fellow-creatures. There glimmered the embroidered letter, with comfort in its unearthly ray. Elsewhere the token of sin, it was the taper of the sick-chamber.. It had even thrown its gleam, in the sufferer's hard extremity, across the verge of time. It had shown him where to set his foot, while the light of earth was fast becoming dim, and ere the light of futurity could reach him. In such emergencies, Hester's nature showed itself warm and rich; a well-spring of human tenderness, unfailing to every real demand, and inexhaustible by the largest. Her breast, with its badge of shame, was but the softer pillow for the head that needed one. She was self-ordained a Sister of Mercy; or, we may rather say, the world's heavy hand had so ordained her, when neither the world nor she looked forward to this result. The letter was the symbol of her calling. Such helpfulness was found in her,—so much power to do, and power to sympathize,—that many people refused to interpret the scarlet A by its original signification. They said that it meant Able; so strong was Hester Prynne, with a woman's strength.

It was only the darkened house that could contain her. When sunshine came again, she was not there. Her shadow had faded across the threshold. The helpful inmate had departed, without one backward glance to gather up the meed of gratitude, if any were in the hearts of those whom she had served so zealously. Meeting them in the street, she never raised her head to receive their greeting. If they were resolute to accost her, she laid her finger on the scarlet letter, and passed on. This might be pride, but was so like humility, that it produced all the softening influence of the latter quality on the public mind. The public is despotic in its temper; it is capable of denying common justice, when too strenuously demanded as a right; but quite as frequently it awards more than justice, when the appeal is made, as despots love to have it made, entirely to its generosity. Interpreting Hester Prynne's deportment as an appeal of this nature, society was inclined to show its former victim a more benign countenance than she cared to be favored with, or, perchance, than she deserved.

The rulers, and the wise and learned men of the community, were longer in acknowledging the influence of Hester's good qualities than the people. The prejudices which they shared in common with the latter were fortified in themselves by an iron framework of reasoning, that made it a far tougher labor to expel them. Day by day, nevertheless, their sour and rigid wrinkles were relaxing into something which, in the due course of years, might grow to be an expression of almost benevolence. Thus it was with the men of rank, on whom their eminent position imposed the guardianship of the public morals. Individuals in private life, meanwhile, had quite forgiven Hester Prynne for her frailty; nay, more, they had begun to look upon the scarlet letter as the token, not of that one sin, for which she had borne so long and dreary a penance, but of her many good deeds since. "Do you see that woman with the embroidered badge?" they would say to strangers. "It is our Hester,—the town's own Hester,—who is so kind to the poor, so helpful to the sick, so comfortable to the afflicted!" Then, it is true, the propensity of human nature to tell the very worst of itself, when embodied in the person of another, would constrain them to whisper the black scandal of bygone years. It was none the less a fact, however, that, in the eyes of the very men who spoke thus, the scarlet letter had the effect of the cross on a nun's bosom. It imparted to the wearer a kind of sacredness, which enabled her to walk securely amid all peril. Had she fallen among thieves, it would have kept her safe. It was reported, and believed by many, that an Indian had drawn his arrow against the badge, and that the missile struck it, but fell harmless to the ground.

The effect of the symbol—or rather, of the position in respect to society that was indicated by it—on the mind of Hester Prynne herself, was powerful and peculiar. All the light and graceful foliage of her character had been withered up by this red-hot brand, and had long ago fallen away, leaving a bare and harsh outline, which might have been repulsive, had she possessed friends or companions to be repelled by it. Even the attractiveness of her person had undergone a similar change. It might be partly owing to the studied austerity of her dress, and partly to the lack of demonstration in her manners. It was a sad transformation, too, that her rich and luxuriant hair had either been cut off, or was so completely hidden by a cap, that not a shining lock of it ever once gushed into the sunshine. It was due in part to all these causes, but still more to something else, that there seemed to be no longer any thing in Hester's face for Love to dwell upon; nothing in Hester's form, though majestic and statue-like, that Passion would ever dream of clasping in its embrace; nothing in Hester's bosom, to make it ever again the pillow of Affection. Some attribute had departed from her, the permanence of which had been essential to keep her a woman. Such is frequently the fate, and such the stern development, of the feminine character and person, when the woman has encountered, and lived through, an experience of peculiar severity. If she be all tenderness, she will die. If she survive, the tenderness will either be crushed out of her, or—and the outward semblance is the same—crushed so deeply into her heart that it can never show itself more. The latter is perhaps the truest theory. She who has once been woman, and ceased to be so, might at any moment become a woman again, if there were only the magic touch to effect the transfiguration. We shall see whether Hester Prynne were ever afterwards so touched, and so transfigured.

Much of the marble coldness of Hester's impression was to be attributed to the circumstance that her life had turned, in a great measure, from passion and feeling, to thought. Standing alone in the world,—alone, as to any dependence on society, and with little Pearl to be guided and protected,—alone, and hopeless of retrieving her position, even had she not scorned to consider it desirable,—she cast away the fragments of a broken chain. The world's law was no law for her mind. It was an age in which the human intellect, newly emancipated, had taken a more active and a wider range than for many centuries before. Men of the sword had overthrown nobles and kings. Men bolder than these had overthrown and rearranged—not actually, but within the sphere of theory, which was their most real abode—the whole system of ancient prejudice, wherewith was linked much of ancient principle. Hester Prynne imbibed this spirit. She assumed a freedom of speculation, then common enough on the other side of the Atlantic, but which our forefathers, had they known of it, would have held to be a deadlier crime than that stigmatized by the scarlet letter. In her lonesome cottage, by the sea-shore, thoughts visited her, such as dared to enter no other dwelling in New England; shadowy guests, that would have been as perilous as demons to their entertainer, could they have been seen so much as knocking at her door.

It is remarkable, that persons who speculate the most boldly often conform with the most perfect quietude to the external regulations of society. The thought suffices them, without investing itself in the flesh and blood of action. So it seemed to be with Hester. Yet, had little Pearl never come to her from the spiritual world, it might have been far otherwise. Then, she might have come down to us in history, hand in hand with Ann Hutchinson, as the foundress of a religious sect. She might, in one of her phases, have been a prophetess. She might, and not improbably would, have suffered death from the stern tribunals of the period, for attempting to undermine the foundations of the Puritan establishment. But, in the education of her child, the mother's enthusiasm of thought had something to wreak itself upon. Providence, in the person of this little girl, had assigned to

Hester's charge the germ and blossom of womanhood, to be cherished and developed amid a host of difficulties. Every thing was against her. The world was hostile. The child's own nature had something wrong in it, which continually betokened that she had been born amiss,—the effluence of her mother's lawless passion,—and often impelled Hester to ask, in bitterness of heart, whether it were for ill or good that the poor little creature had been born at all.

Indeed, the same dark question often rose into her mind, with reference to the whole race of womanhood. Was existence worth accepting, even to the happiest among them? As concerned her own individual existence, she had long ago decided in the negative, and dismissed the point as settled. A tendency to speculation, though it may keep woman quiet, as it does man, yet makes her sad. She discerns, it may be, such a hopeless task before her. As a first step, the whole system of society is to be torn down, and built up anew. Then, the very nature of the opposite sex, or its long hereditary habit, which has become like nature, is to be essentially modified, before woman can be allowed to assume what seems a fair and suitable position. Finally, all other difficulties being obviated, woman cannot take advantage of these preliminary reforms, until she herself shall have undergone a still mightier change; in which, perhaps, the ethereal essence, wherein she has her truest life, will be found to have evaporated. A woman never overcomes these problems by any exercise of thought. They are not to be solved, or only in one way. If her heart chance to come uppermost, they vanish. Thus, Hester Prynne, whose heart had lost its regular and healthy throb, wandered without a clew in the dark labyrinth of mind: now turned aside by an insurmountable precipice; now starting back from a deep chasm. There was wild and ghastly scenery all around her, and a home and comfort nowhere. At times, a fearful doubt strove to possess her soul, whether it were not better to send Pearl at once to heaven, and go herself to such futurity as Eternal Justice should provide.

The scarlet letter had not done its office.

Now, however, her interview with the Reverend Mr. Dimmesdale, on the night of his vigil, had given her a new theme of reflection, and held up to her an object that appeared worthy of any exertion and sacrifice for its attainment. She had witnessed the intense misery beneath which the minister struggled, or, to speak more accurately, had ceased to struggle. She saw that he stood on the verge of lunacy, if he had not already stepped across it. It was impossible to doubt, that, whatever painful efficacy there might be in the secret sting of remorse, a deadlier venom had been infused into it by the hand that proffered relief. A secret enemy had been continually by his side, under the semblance of a friend and helper, and had availed himself of the opportunities thus afforded for tampering with the delicate springs of Mr. Dimmesdale's nature. Hester could not but ask herself, whether there had not originally been a defect of truth, courage, and loyalty, on her own part, in allowing the minister to be thrown into a position where so much evil was to be foreboded, and nothing auspicious to be hoped. Her only justification lay in the fact, that she had been able to discern no method of rescuing him from a blacker ruin than had overwhelmed herself, except by acquiescing in Roger Chillingworth's scheme of disguise. Under that impulse, she had made her choice, and had chosen, as it now appeared, the more wretched alternative of the two. She determined to redeem her error, so far as it might yet be possible. Strengthened by years of hard and solemn trial, she felt herself no longer so inadequate to cope with Roger Chillingworth as on that night, abased by sin, and half maddened by the ignominy that was still new, when they had talked together in the prison-chamber.

She had climbed her way, since then, to a higher point. The old man, on the other hand, had brought himself nearer to her level, or perhaps below it, by the revenge which he had stooped for.

In fine, Hester Prynne resolved to meet her former husband, and do what might be in her power for the rescue of the victim on whom he had so evidently set his gripe. The occasion was not long to seek. One afternoon, walking with Pearl in a retired part of the peninsula, she beheld the old physician, with a basket on one arm, and a staff in the other hand, stooping along the ground, in quest of roots and herbs to concoct his medicines withal.

CHAPTER XIV

HESTER AND THE PHYSICIAN

Hester bade little Pearl run down to the margin of the water, and play with the shells and tangled seaweed, until she should have talked awhile with yonder gatherer of herbs. So the child flew away like a bird, and, making bare her small white feet, went pattering along the moist margin of the sea. Here and there, she came to a full stop, and peeped curiously into a pool, left by the retiring tide as a mirror for Pearl to see her face in. Forth peeped at her, out of the pool, with dark, glistening curls around her head, and an elf-smile in her eyes, the image of a little maid, whom Pearl, having no other playmate, invited to take her hand and run a race with her. But the visionary little maid, on her part, beckoned likewise, as if to say,—"This is a better place! Come thou into the pool!" And Pearl, stepping in, mid-leg deep, beheld her own white feet at the bottom; while, out of a still lower depth, came the gleam of a kind of fragmentary smile, floating to and fro in the agitated water.

Meanwhile, her mother had accosted the physician.

"I would speak a word with you," said she,—"a word that concerns us much."

"Aha! And is it Mistress Hester that has a word for old Roger Chillingworth?" answered he, raising himself from his stooping posture. "With all my heart! Why, Mistress, I hear good tidings of you on all hands! No longer ago than yester-eve, a magistrate, a wise and godly man, was discoursing of your affairs, Mistress Hester, and whispered me that there had been question concerning you in the council. It was debated whether or no, with safety to the common weal, yonder scarlet letter might be taken off your bosom. On my life, Hester, I made my entreaty to the worshipful magistrate that it might be done forthwith!"

"It lies not in the pleasure of the magistrates to take off this badge," calmly replied Hester. "Were I worthy to be quit of it, it would fall away of its own nature, or be transformed into something that should speak a different purport."

"Nay, then, wear it, if it suit you better," rejoined he. "A woman must needs follow her own fancy, touching the adornment of her person. The letter is gayly embroidered, and shows right bravely on your bosom!"

All this while, Hester had been looking steadily at the old man, and was shocked, as well as wonder-smitten, to discern what a change had been wrought upon him within the past seven years. It was not so much that he had grown older; for though the traces of advancing life were visible, he bore his age well, and seemed to retain a wiry vigor and alertness. But the former aspect of an intellectual and studious man, calm and quiet, which was what she best remembered in him, had altogether vanished, and been succeeded by an eager, searching, almost fierce, yet carefully guarded look. It seemed to be his wish and purpose to mask this expression with a smile; but the latter played him false, and flickered over his visage so derisively, that the spectator could see his blackness all the better for it. Ever and anon, too, there came a glare of red light out of his eyes; as if the old man's soul were on fire, and kept on smouldering duskily within his breast, until, by some casual puff of passion, it was blown into a momentary flame. This he repressed as speedily as possible, and strove to look as if nothing of the kind had happened.

In a word, old Roger Chillingworth was a striking evidence of man's faculty of transforming himself into a devil, if he will only, for a reasonable space of time, undertake a devil's office. This unhappy person had effected such a transformation by devoting himself, for seven years, to the constant analysis of a heart full of torture, and deriving his enjoyment thence, and adding fuel to those fiery tortures which he analyzed and gloated over.

The scarlet letter burned on Hester Prynne's bosom. Here was another ruin, the responsibility of which came partly home to her.

"What see you in my face," asked the physician, "that you look at it so earnestly?"

"Something that would make me weep, if there were any tears bitter enough for it," answered she. "But let it pass! It is of yonder miserable man that I would speak."

"And what of him?" cried Roger Chillingworth eagerly, as if he loved the topic, and were glad of an opportunity to discuss it with the only person of whom he could make a confidant. "Not to hide the truth, Mistress Hester, my thoughts happen just now to be busy with the gentleman. So speak freely; and I will make answer."

"When we last spake together," said Hester, "now seven years ago, it was your pleasure to extort a promise of secrecy, as touching the former relation betwixt yourself and me. As the life and good fame of yonder man were in your hands, there seemed no choice to me, save to be silent, in accordance with your behest. Yet it was not without heavy misgivings that I thus bound myself; for, having cast off all duty towards other human beings, there remained a duty towards him; and something whispered me that I was betraying it, in pledging myself to keep your counsel. Since that day, no man is so near to him as you. You tread behind his every footstep. You are beside him, sleeping and waking. You search his thoughts. You burrow and rankle in his heart! Your clutch is on his life, and you cause him to die daily a living death; and still he knows you not. In permitting this, I have surely acted a false part by the only man to whom the power was left me to be true!"

"What choice had you?" asked Roger Chillingworth. "My finger, pointed at this man, would have hurled him from his pulpit into a dungeon,—thence, peradventure, to the gallows!"

"It had been better so!" said Hester Prynne.

"What evil have I done the man?" asked Roger Chillingworth again. "I tell thee, Hester Prynne, the richest fee that ever physician earned from monarch could not have bought such care as I have wasted on this miserable priest! But for my aid, his life would have burned away in torments, within the first two years after the perpetration of his crime and thine. For, Hester, his spirit lacked the strength that could have borne up, as thine has, beneath a burden like thy scarlet letter. O, I could reveal a goodly secret! But enough! What art can do, I have exhausted on him. That he now breathes, and creeps about on earth, is owing to me!"

"Better he had died at once!" said Hester Prynne.

"Yea, woman, thou sayest truly!" cried old Roger Chillingworth, letting the lurid fire of his heart blaze out before her eyes. "Better had he died at once! Never did mortal suffer what this man has suffered. And all, all, in the sight of his worst enemy! He has been conscious of me. He has felt an influence dwelling always upon him like a curse. He knew, by some spiritual sense,—for the Creator never made another being so sensitive as this,—he knew that no friendly hand was pulling at his heart-strings, and that an eye was looking curiously into him, which sought only evil, and found it. But he knew not that the eye and hand were mine! With the superstition common to his brotherhood, he fancied himself given over to a fiend, to be tortured with frightful dreams, and desperate thoughts, the sting of remorse, and despair of pardon; as a foretaste of what awaits him beyond the grave. But it was the constant shadow of my presence!—the closest propinquity of the man whom he had most vilely wronged!—and who had grown to exist only by this perpetual poison of the direst revenge! Yea, indeed!—he did not err!—there was a fiend at his elbow! A mortal man, with once a human heart, has become a fiend for his especial torment!"

The unfortunate physician, while uttering these words, lifted his hands with a look of horror, as if he had beheld some frightful shape, which he could not recognize, usurping the place of his own image in a glass. It was one of those moments—which sometimes occur only at the interval of years—when a man's moral aspect is faithfully revealed to his mind's eye. Not improbably, he had never before viewed himself as he did now.

"Hast thou not tortured him enough?" said Hester, noticing the old man's look. "Has he not paid thee all?"

"No!—no!—He has but increased his debt!" answered the physician; and, as he proceeded, his manner lost its fiercer characteristics, and subsided into gloom. "Dost thou remember me, Hester, as I was nine years agone? Even then, I was in the autumn of my days, nor was it the early autumn. But all my life had been made up of earnest, studious, thoughtful, quiet years, bestowed faithfully for the increase of mine own knowledge, and faithfully, too, though this latter object was but casual to the other,—faithfully for the advancement of human welfare. No life had been more peaceful and innocent than mine; few lives so rich with benefits conferred. Dost thou remember me? Was I not, though you might deem me cold, nevertheless a man thoughtful for others, craving little for himself,—kind, true, just, and of constant, if not warm affections? Was I not all this?"

"All this, and more," said Hester.

"And what am I now?" demanded he, looking into her face, and permitting the whole evil within him to be written on his features. "I have already told thee what I am! A fiend! Who made me so?"

"It was myself!" cried Hester, shuddering. "It was I, not less than he. Why hast thou not avenged thyself on me?"

"I have left thee to the scarlet letter," replied Roger Chillingworth. "If that have not avenged me, I can do no more!"

He laid his finger on it, with a smile.

"It has avenged thee!" answered Hester Prynne.

"I judged no less," said the physician. "And now, what wouldst thou with me touching this man?"

"I must reveal the secret," answered Hester, firmly. "He must discern thee in thy true character. What may be the result, I know not. But this long debt of confidence, due from me to him, whose bane and ruin I have been, shall at length be paid. So far as concerns the overthrow or preservation of his fair fame and his earthly state, and perchance his life, he is in thy hands. Nor do I,—whom the scarlet letter has disciplined to truth, though it be the truth of red-hot iron, entering into the soul,—nor do I perceive such advantage in his living any longer a life of ghastly emptiness, that I shall stoop to implore thy mercy. Do with him as thou wilt! There is no good for him,—no good for me,—no good for thee! There is no good for little Pearl! There is no path to guide us out of this dismal maze!"

"Woman, I could wellnigh pity thee!" said Roger Chillingworth, unable to restrain a thrill of admiration too; for there was a quality almost majestic in the despair which she expressed. "Thou hadst great elements. Peradventure, hadst thou met earlier with a better love than mine, this evil had not been. I pity thee, for the good that has been wasted in thy nature!"

"And I thee," answered Hester Prynne, "for the hatred that has transformed a wise and just man to a fiend! Wilt thou yet purge it out of thee, and be once more human? If not for his sake, then doubly for thine own! Forgive, and leave his further retribution to the Power that claims it! I said, but now, that there could be no good event for him, or thee, or me, who are here wandering together in this gloomy maze of evil, and stumbling, at every step, over the guilt wherewith we have strewn our path. It is not so! There might be good for thee, and thee alone, since thou hast been deeply wronged, and hast it at thy will to pardon. Wilt thou give up that only privilege? Wilt thou reject that priceless benefit?"

"Peace, Hester, peace!" replied the old man with gloomy sternness. "It is not granted me to pardon. I have no such power as thou tellest me of. My old faith, long forgotten, comes back to me, and explains all that we do, and all we suffer. By thy first step awry, thou didst plant the germ of evil; but, since that moment, it has all been a dark necessity. Ye that have wronged me are not sinful, save in a kind of typical illusion; neither am I fiend-like, who have snatched a fiend's office from his hands. It is our fate. Let the black flower blossom as it may! Now go thy ways, and deal as thou wilt with yonder man."

He waved his hand, and betook himself again to his employment of gathering herbs.

CHAPTER XV

HESTER AND PEARL

So Roger Chillingworth—a deformed old figure, with a face that haunted men's memories longer than they liked—took leave of Hester Prynne, and went stooping away along the earth. He gathered here and there an herb, or grubbed up a root, and put it into the basket on his arm. His gray beard almost touched the ground, as he crept onward. Hester gazed after him a little while, looking with a half-fantastic curiosity to see whether the tender grass of early spring would not be blighted beneath him, and show the wavering trace of his footsteps, sere and brown, across its cheerful verdure. She wondered what sort of herbs they were, which the old man was so sedulous to gather. Would not the earth, quickened to an evil purpose by the sympathy of his eye, greet him with poisonous shrubs, of species hitherto unknown, that would start up under his fingers? Or might it suffice him, that every wholesome growth should be converted into something deleterious and malignant at his touch? Did the sun, which shone so brightly everywhere else, really fall upon him? Or was there, as it rather seemed, a circle of ominous shadow moving along with his deformity, whichever way he turned himself? And whither was he now going? Would he not suddenly sink into the earth, leaving a barren and blasted spot, where, in due course of time, would be seen deadly nightshade, dogwood, henbane, and whatever else of vegetable wickedness the climate could produce, all flourishing with hideous luxuriance? Or would he spread bat's wings and flee away, looking so much the uglier, the higher he rose towards heaven?

"Be it sin or no," said Hester Prynne bitterly, as she still gazed after him, "I hate the man!"

She upbraided herself for the sentiment, but could not overcome or lessen it. Attempting to do so, she thought of those long-past days, in a distant land, when he used to emerge at eventide from the seclusion of his study, and sit down in the fire-light of their home, and in the light of her nuptial smile. He needed to bask himself in that smile, he said, in order that the chill of so many lonely hours among his books might be taken off the scholar's heart. Such scenes had once appeared not otherwise than happy, but now, as viewed through the dismal medium of her subsequent life, they classed themselves among her ugliest remembrances. She marvelled how such scenes could have been! She marvelled how she could ever have been wrought upon to marry him! She deemed it her crime most to be repented of, that she had ever endured, and reciprocated, the lukewarm grasp of his hand, and had suffered the smile of her lips and eyes to mingle and melt into his own. And it seemed a fouler offence committed by Roger Chillingworth, than any which had since been done him, that, in the time when her heart knew no better, he had persuaded her to fancy herself happy by his side.

"Yes, I hate him!" repeated Hester, more bitterly than before. "He betrayed me! He has done me worse wrong than I did him!"

Let men tremble to win the hand of woman, unless they win along with it the utmost passion of her heart! Else it may be their miserable fortune, as it was Roger Chillingworth's, when some mightier touch than their own may have awakened all her sensibilities, to be reproached even for the calm content, the marble image of happiness, which they will have imposed upon her as the warm reality. But Hester ought long ago to have done with this injustice. What did it betoken? Had seven long years, under the torture of the scarlet letter, inflicted so much of misery, and wrought out no repentance?

The emotions of that brief space, while she stood gazing after the crooked figure of old Roger Chillingworth, threw a dark light on Hester's state of mind, revealing much that she might not otherwise have acknowledged to herself.

He being gone, she summoned back her child.

"Pearl! Little Pearl! Where are you?"

Pearl, whose activity of spirit never flagged, had been at no loss for amusement while her mother talked with the old gatherer of herbs. At first, as already told, she had flirted fancifully with her own image in a pool of water, beckoning the phantom forth, and—as it declined to venture—seeking a passage for herself into its sphere of impalpable earth and unattainable sky. Soon finding, however, that either she or the image was unreal, she turned elsewhere for better pastime. She made little boats out of birch-bark, and freighted them with snail-shells, and sent out more ventures on the mighty deep than any merchant in New England; but the larger part of them foundered near the shore. She seized a live horseshoe by the tail, and made prize of several five-fingers, and laid out a jelly-fish to melt in the warm sun. Then she took up the white foam, that streaked the line of the advancing tide, and threw it upon the breeze, scampering after it with winged footsteps, to catch the great snow-flakes ere they fell. Perceiving a flock of beach-birds, that fed and fluttered along the shore, the naughty child picked up her apron full of pebbles, and creeping from rock to rock after these small sea-fowl, displayed remarkable dexterity in pelting them. One little gray bird, with a white breast, Pearl was almost sure, had been hit by a pebble, and fluttered away with a broken wing. But then the elf-child sighed, and gave up her sport; because it grieved her to have done harm to a little being that was as wild as the seabreeze, or as wild as Pearl herself.

Her final employment was to gather sea-weed, of various kinds, and make herself a scarf, or mantle, and a head-dress, and thus assume the aspect of a little mermaid. She inherited her mother's gift for devising drapery and costume. As the last touch to her mermaid's garb, Pearl took some eel-grass, and imitated, as best she could, on her own bosom, the decoration with which she was so familiar on her mother's. A letter,—the letter A,—but freshly green, instead of scarlet! The child bent her chin upon her breast, and contemplated this device with strange interest; even as if the one only thing for which she had been sent into the world was to make out its hidden import.

"I wonder if mother will ask me what it means!" thought Pearl.

Just then, she heard her mother's voice, and, flitting along as lightly as one of the little sea-birds, appeared before Hester Prynne, dancing, laughing, and pointing her finger to the ornament upon her bosom.

"My little Pearl," said Hester, after a moment's silence, "the green letter, and on thy childish bosom, has no purport. But dost thou know, my child, what this letter means which thy mother is doomed to wear?"

"Yes, mother," said the child. "It is the great letter A. Thou has taught it me in the horn-book."

Hester looked steadily into her little face; but, though there was that singular expression which she had so often remarked in her black eyes, she could not satisfy herself whether Pearl really attached any meaning to the symbol. She felt a morbid desire to ascertain the point.

"Dost thou know, child, wherefore thy mother wears this letter?"

"Truly do I!" answered Pearl, looking brightly into her mother's face. "It is for the same reason that the minister keeps his hand over his heart!"

"And what reason is that?" asked Hester, half smiling at the absurd incongruity of the child's observation; but, on second thoughts, turning pale. "What has the letter to do with any heart, save mine?"

"Nay, mother, I have told all I know," said Pearl, more seriously than she was wont to speak. "Ask yonder old man whom thou hast been talking with! It may be he can tell. But in good earnest now, mother dear, what does this scarlet letter mean?—and why dost thou wear it on thy bosom?—and why does the minister keep his hand over his heart?"

She took her mother's hand in both her own, and gazed into her eyes with an earnestness that was seldom seen in her wild and capricious character. The thought occurred to Hester, that the child might really be seeking to approach her with childlike confidence, and doing what she could, and as intelligently as she knew how, to establish a meeting-point of sympathy. It showed Pearl in an unwonted aspect. Heretofore, the mother, while loving her child with the intensity of a sole affection, had schooled herself to hope for little other return than the waywardness of an April breeze; which spends its time in airy sport, and has its gusts of inexplicable passion, and is petulant in its best of moods, and chills oftener than caresses you, when you take it to your bosom; in requital of which misdemeanours, it will sometimes, of its own vague purpose, kiss your cheek with a kind of doubtful tenderness, and play gently with your hair, and then begone about its other idle business, leaving a dreamy pleasure at your heart. And this, moreover, was a mother's estimate of the child's disposition. Any other observer might have seen few but unamiable traits, and have given them a far darker coloring. But now the idea came strongly into Hester's mind, that Pearl, with her remarkable precocity and acuteness, might already have approached the age when she could be made a friend, and intrusted with as much of her mother's sorrows as could be imparted, without irreverence either to the parent or the child. In the little chaos of Pearl's character, there might be seen emerging—and could have been, from the very first—the steadfast principles of an unflinching courage,—an uncontrollable will,—a sturdy pride, which might be disciplined into self-respect,—and a bitter scorn of many things, which, when examined, might be found to have the taint of falsehood in them. She possessed affections, too, though hitherto acrid and disagreeable, as are the richest flavors of unripe fruit. With all these sterling attributes, thought Hester, the evil which she inherited from her mother must be great indeed, if a noble woman do not grow out of this elfish child.

Pearl's inevitable tendency to hover about the enigma of the scarlet letter seemed an innate quality of her being. From the earliest epoch of her conscious life, she had entered upon this as her appointed mission. Hester had often fancied that Providence had a design of justice and retribution, in endowing the child with this marked propensity; but never, until now, had she bethought herself to ask, whether, linked with that design, there might not likewise be a purpose of mercy and beneficence. If little Pearl were entertained with faith and trust, as a spirit-messenger no less than an earthly child, might it not be her errand to soothe away the sorrow that lay cold in her mother's heart, and converted it into a tomb?—and to help her to overcome the passion, once so wild, and even yet neither dead nor asleep, but only imprisoned within the same tomb-like heart?

Such were some of the thoughts that now stirred in Hester's mind, with as much vivacity of impression as if they had actually been whispered into her ear. And there was little Pearl, all this while, holding her mother's hand in both her own, and turning her face upward, while she put these searching questions, once, and again, and still a third time.

"What does the letter mean, mother?—and why dost thou wear it?—and why does the minister keep his hand over his heart?"

"What shall I say?" thought Hester to herself.—"No! If this be the price of the child's sympathy, I cannot pay it!"

Then she spoke aloud.

"Silly Pearl," said she, "what questions are these? There are many things in this world that a child must not ask about. What know I of the minister's heart? And as for the scarlet letter, I wear it for the sake of its gold thread!"

In all the seven bygone years, Hester Prynne had never before been false to the symbol on her bosom. It may be that it was the talisman of a stern and severe, but yet a guardian spirit, who now forsook her; as recognizing that, in spite of his strict watch over her heart, some new evil had crept into it, or some old one had never been expelled. As for little Pearl, the earnestness soon passed out of her face.

But the child did not see fit to let the matter drop. Two or three times, as her mother and she went homeward, and as often at supper-time, and while Hester was putting her to bed, and once after she seemed to be fairly asleep, Pearl looked up, with mischief gleaming in her black eyes.

"Mother," said she, "what does the scarlet letter mean?"

And the next morning, the first indication the child gave of being awake was by popping up her head from the pillow, and making that other inquiry, which she had so unaccountably connected with her investigations about the scarlet letter:—

"Mother!—Mother!—Why does the minister keep his hand over his heart?"

"Hold thy tongue, naughty child!" answered her mother, with an asperity that she had never permitted to herself before. "Do not tease me; else I shall shut thee into the dark closet!"

CHAPTER XVI

A FOREST WALK

Hester Prynne remained constant in her resolve to make known to Mr. Dimmesdale, at whatever risk of present pain or ulterior consequences, the true character of the man who had crept into his intimacy. For several days, however, she vainly sought an opportunity of addressing him in some of the meditative walks which she knew him to be in the habit of taking, along the shores of the peninsula, or on the wooded hills of the neighbouring country. There would have been no scandal, indeed, nor peril to the holy whiteness of the clergyman's good fame, had she visited him in his own study; where many a penitent, ere now, had confessed sins of perhaps as deep a dye as the one betokened by the scarlet letter. But, partly that she dreaded the secret or undisguised interference of old Roger Chillingworth, and partly that her conscious heart imputed suspicion where none could have been felt, and partly that both the minister and she would need the whole wide world to breathe in, while they talked together,—for all these reasons, Hester never thought of meeting him in any narrower privacy than beneath the open sky.

At last, while attending in a sick-chamber, whither the Reverend Mr. Dimmesdale had been summoned to make a prayer, she learnt that he had gone, the day before, to visit the Apostle Eliot, among his Indian converts. He would probably return, by a certain hour, in the afternoon of the morrow. Betimes, therefore, the next day, Hester took little Pearl,—who was necessarily the companion of all her mother's expeditions, however inconvenient her presence,—and set forth.

The road, after the two wayfarers had crossed from the peninsula to the mainland, was no other than a footpath. It straggled onward into the mystery of the primeval forest. This hemmed it in so narrowly, and stood so black and dense on either side, and disclosed such imperfect glimpses of the sky above, that, to Hester's mind, it imaged not amiss the moral wilderness in which she had so long been wandering. The day was chill and sombre. Overhead was a gray expanse of cloud, slightly stirred, however, by a breeze; so that a gleam of flickering sunshine might now and then be seen at its solitary play along the path. This flitting cheerfulness was always at the farther extremity of some long vista through the forest. The sportive sunlight—feebly sportive, at best, in the predominant pensiveness of the day and scene—withdrew itself as they came nigh, and left the spots where it had danced the drearier, because they had hoped to find them bright.

"Mother," said little Pearl, "the sunshine does not love you. It runs away and hides itself, because it is afraid of something on your bosom. Now, see! There it is, playing, a good way off. Stand you here, and let me run and catch it. I am but a child. It will not flee from me; for I wear nothing on my bosom yet!"

"Nor ever will, my child, I hope," said Hester.

"And why not, mother?" asked Pearl, stopping short, just at the beginning of her race. "Will not it come of its own accord, when I am a woman grown?"

"Run away, child," answered her mother, "and catch the sunshine! It will soon be gone."

Pearl set forth, at a great pace, and, as Hester smiled to perceive, did actually catch the sunshine, and stood laughing in the midst of it, all brightened by its splendor, and scintillating with the vivacity excited by rapid motion. The light lingered about the lonely child, as if glad of such a playmate, until her mother had drawn almost nigh enough to step into the magic circle too.

"It will go now!" said Pearl, shaking her head.

"See!" answered Hester, smiling. "Now I can stretch out my hand, and grasp some of it."

As she attempted to do so, the sunshine vanished; or, to judge from the bright expression that was dancing on Pearl's features, her mother could have fancied that the child had absorbed it into herself, and would give it forth again, with a gleam about her path, as they should plunge into some gloomier shade. There was no other attribute that so much impressed her with a sense of new and untransmitted vigor in Pearl's nature, as this never-failing vivacity of spirits; she had not the disease of sadness, which almost all children, in these latter days, inherit, with the scrofula, from the troubles of their ancestors. Perhaps this too was a disease, and but the reflex of the wild energy with which Hester had fought against her sorrows, before Pearl's birth. It was certainly a doubtful charm, imparting a hard, metallic lustre to the child's character. She wanted—what some people want throughout life—a grief that should deeply touch her, and thus humanize and make her capable of sympathy. But there was time enough yet for little Pearl!

"Come, my child!" said Hester, looking about her, from the spot where Pearl had stood still in the sunshine. "We will sit down a little way within the wood, and rest ourselves."

"I am not aweary, mother," replied the little girl. "But you may sit down, if you will tell me a story meanwhile."

"A story, child!" said Hester. "And about what?"

"O, a story about the Black Man!" answered Pearl, taking hold of her mother's gown, and looking up, half earnestly, half mischievously, into her face. "How he haunts this forest, and carries a book with him,—a big, heavy book, with iron clasps; and how this ugly Black Man offers his book and an iron pen to every body that meets him here among the trees; and they are to write their names with their own blood. And then he sets his mark on their bosoms! Didst thou ever meet the Black Man, mother?"

"And who told you this story, Pearl?" asked her mother, recognizing a common superstition of the period.

"It was the old dame in the chimney-corner, at the house where you watched last night," said the child. "But she fancied me asleep while she was talking of it.

She said that a thousand and a thousand people had met him here, and had written in his book, and have his mark on them. And that ugly-tempered lady, old Mistress Hibbins, was one. And, mother, the old dame said that this scarlet letter was the Black Man's mark on thee, and that it glows like a red flame when thou meetest him at midnight, here in the dark wood. Is it true, mother? And dost thou go to meet him in the night-time?"

"Didst thou ever awake, and find thy mother gone?" asked Hester.

"Not that I remember," said the child. "If thou fearest to leave me in our cottage, thou mightest take me along with thee. I would very gladly go! But, mother, tell me now! Is there such a Black Man? And didst thou ever meet him? And is this his mark?"

"Wilt thou let me be at peace, if I once tell thee?" asked her mother.

"Yes, if thou tellest me all," answered Pearl.

"Once in my life I met the Black Man!" said her mother. "This scarlet letter is his mark!"

Thus conversing, they entered sufficiently deep into the wood to secure themselves from the observation of any casual passenger along the forest-track. Here they sat down on a luxuriant heap of moss; which, at some epoch of the preceding century, had been a gigantic pine, with its roots and trunk in the darksome shade, and its head aloft in the upper atmosphere. It was a little dell where they had seated themselves, with a leaf-strewn bank rising gently on either side, and a brook flowing through the midst, over a bed of fallen and drowned leaves. The trees impending over it had flung down great branches, from time to time, which choked up the current, and compelled it to form eddies and black depths at some points; while, in its swifter and livelier passages, there appeared a channel-way of pebbles, and brown, sparkling sand. Letting the eyes follow along the course of the stream, they could catch the reflected light from its water, at some short distance within the forest, but soon lost all traces of it amid the bewilderment of tree-trunks and underbrush, and here and there a huge rock, covered over with gray lichens. All these giant trees and boulders of granite seemed intent on making a mystery of the course of this small brook; fearing, perhaps, that, with its never-ceasing loquacity, it should whisper tales out of the heart of the old forest whence it flowed, or mirror its revelations on the smooth surface of a pool. Continually, indeed, as it stole onward, the streamlet kept up a babble, kind, quiet, soothing, but melancholy, like the voice of a young child that was spending its infancy without playfulness, and knew not how to be merry among sad acquaintance and events of sombre hue.

"O brook! O foolish and tiresome little brook!" cried Pearl, after listening awhile to its talk. "Why art thou so sad? Pluck up a spirit, and do not be all the time sighing and murmuring!"

But the brook, in the course of its little lifetime among the forest-trees, had gone through so solemn an experience that it could not help talking about it, and seemed to have nothing else to say. Pearl resembled the brook, inasmuch as the current of her life gushed from a well-spring as mysterious, and had flowed through scenes shadowed as heavily with gloom. But, unlike the little stream, she danced and sparkled, and prattled airily along her course.

"What does this sad little brook say, mother?" inquired she.

"If thou hadst a sorrow of thine own, the brook might tell thee of it," answered her mother, "even as it is telling me of mine! But now, Pearl, I hear a footstep along the path, and the noise of one putting aside the branches. I would have thee betake thyself to play, and leave me to speak with him that comes yonder."

"Is it the Black Man?" asked Pearl.

"Wilt thou go and play, child?" repeated her mother. "But do not stray far into the wood. And take heed that thou come at my first call."

"Yes, mother," answered Pearl. "But, if it be the Black Man, wilt thou not let me stay a moment, and look at him, with his big book under his arm?"

"Go, silly child!" said her mother, impatiently. "It is no Black Man! Thou canst see him now through the trees. It is the minister!"

"And so it is!" said the child. "And, mother, he has his hand over his heart! Is it because, when the minister wrote his name in the book, the Black Man set his mark in that place? But why does he not wear it outside his bosom, as thou dost, mother?"

"Go now, child, and thou shalt tease me as thou wilt another time," cried Hester Prynne. "But do not stray far. Keep where thou canst hear the babble of the brook."

The child went singing away, following up the current of the brook, and striving to mingle a more lightsome cadence with its melancholy voice. But the little stream would not be comforted, and still kept telling its unintelligible secret of some very mournful mystery that had happened—or making a prophetic lamentation about something that was yet to happen—within the verge of the dismal forest. So Pearl, who had enough of shadow in her own life, chose to break off all acquaintance with this repining brook. She set herself, therefore, to gathering violets and wood-anemones, and some scarlet columbines that she found growing in the crevices of a high rock.

When her elf-child had departed, Hester Prynne made a step or two towards the track that led through the forest, but still remained under the deep shadow of the trees. She beheld the minister advancing along the path, entirely alone, and leaning on a staff which he had cut by the way-side. He looked haggard and feeble, and betrayed a nerveless despondency in his air, which had never so remarkably characterized him in his walks about the settlement, nor in any other situation where he deemed himself liable to notice. Here it was wofully visible, in this intense seclusion of the forest, which of itself would have been a heavy trial to the spirits. There was a listlessness in his gait; as if he saw no reason for taking one step farther, nor felt any desire to do so, but would have been glad, could he be glad of any thing, to fling himself down at the root of the nearest tree, and lie there passive for evermore. The leaves might bestrew him, and the soil gradually accumulate and form a little hillock over his frame, no matter whether there were life in it or no. Death was too definite an object to be wished for, or avoided.

To Hester's eye, the Reverend Mr. Dimmesdale exhibited no symptom of positive and vivacious suffering, except that, as little Pearl had remarked, he kept his hand over his heart.

CHAPTER XVII

THE PASTOR AND HIS PARISHIONER

Slowly as the minister walked, he had almost gone by, before Hester Prynne could gather voice enough to attract his observation. At length, she succeeded.

"Arthur Dimmesdale!" she said, faintly at first; then louder, but hoarsely. "Arthur Dimmesdale!"

"Who speaks?" answered the minister.

Gathering himself quickly up, he stood more erect, like a man taken by surprise in a mood to which he was reluctant to have witnesses. Throwing his eyes anxiously in the direction of the voice, he indistinctly beheld a form under the trees, clad in garments so sombre, and so little relieved from the gray twilight into which the clouded sky and the heavy foliage had darkened the noontide, that he knew not whether it were a woman or a shadow. It may be, that his pathway through life was haunted thus, by a spectre that had stolen out from among his thoughts.

He made a step nigher, and discovered the scarlet letter.

"Hester! Hester Prynne!" said he. "Is it thou? Art thou in life?"

"Even so!" she answered. "In such life as has been mine these seven years past! And thou, Arthur Dimmesdale, dost thou yet live?"

It was no wonder that they thus questioned one another's actual and bodily existence, and even doubted of their own. So strangely did they meet, in the dim wood, that it was like the first encounter, in the world beyond the grave, of two spirits who had been intimately connected in their former life, but now stood coldly shuddering, in mutual dread; as not yet familiar with their state, nor wonted to the companionship of disembodied beings. Each a ghost, and awestricken at the other ghost! They were awe-stricken likewise at themselves; because the crisis flung back to them their consciousness, and revealed to each heart its history and experience, as life never does, except at such breathless epochs. The soul beheld its features in the mirror of the passing moment. It was with fear, and tremulously, and, as it were, by a slow, reluctant necessity, that Arthur Dimmesdale put forth his hand, chill as death, and touched the chill hand of Hester Prynne. The grasp, cold as it was, took away what was dreariest in the interview. They now felt themselves, at least, inhabitants of the same sphere.

Without a word more spoken,—neither he nor she assuming the guidance, but with an unexpressed consent,—they glided back into the shadow of the woods, whence Hester had emerged, and sat down on the heap of moss where she and Pearl had before been sitting. When they found voice to speak, it was, at first, only to utter remarks and inquiries such as any two acquaintance might have made, about the gloomy sky, the theatening storm, and, next, the health of each. Thus they went onward, not boldly, but step by step, into the themes that were brooding deepest in their hearts. So long estranged by fate and circumstances, they needed something slight and casual to run before, and throw open the doors of intercourse, so that their real thoughts might be led across the threshold.

After a while, the minister fixed his eyes on Hester Prynne's.

"Hester," said he, "hast thou found peace?"

She smiled drearily, looking down upon her bosom.

"Hast thou?" she asked.

"None!—nothing but despair!" he answered. "What else could I look for, being what I am, and leading such a life as mine? Were I an atheist,—a man devoid of conscience.—a wretch with coarse and brutal instincts,—I might have found peace, long ere now. Nay, I never should have lost it! But, as matters stand with my soul, whatever of good capacity there originally was in me, all of God's gifts that were the choicest have become the ministers of spiritual torment. Hester, I am most miserable!"

"The people reverence thee," said Hester. "And surely thou workest good among them! Doth this bring thee no comfort?"

"More misery, Hester!—only the more misery!" answered the clergyman, with a bitter smile. "As concerns the good which I may appear to do, I have no faith in it. It must needs be a delusion. What can a ruined soul, like mine, effect towards the redemption of other souls?—or a polluted soul, towards their purification? And as for the people's reverence, would that it were turned to scorn and hatred! Canst thou deem it, Hester, a consolation, that I must stand up in my pulpit, and meet so many eyes turned upward to my face, as if the light of heaven were beaming from it!—must see my flock hungry for the truth, and listening to my words as if a tongue of Pentecost were speaking!—and then look inward, and discern the black reality of what they idolize? I have laughed, in bitterness and agony of heart, at the contrast between what I seem and what I am! And Satan laughs at it!"

"You wrong yourself in this," said Hester, gently. "You have deeply and sorely repented. Your sin is left behind you, in the days long past. Your present life is not less holy, in very truth, than it seems in people's eyes. Is there no reality in the penitence thus sealed and witnessed by good works? And wherefore should it not bring you peace?"

"No, Hester, no!" replied the clergyman. "There is no substance in it! It is cold and dead, and can do nothing for me! Of penance I have had enough! Of penitence there has been none! Else, I should long ago have thrown off these garments of mock holiness, and have shown myself to mankind as they will see me at the judgment-seat. Happy are you, Hester, that wear the scarlet letter openly upon your bosom! Mine burns in secret! Thou little knowest what a relief it is, after the torment of a seven years' cheat, to look into an eye that recognizes me for what I am! Had I one friend,—or were it my worst enemy!—to whom, when sickened with the praises of all other men, I could daily betake myself, and be known as the vilest of all sinners, methinks my soul might keep itself alive thereby. Even thus much of truth would save me! But, now, it is all falsehood!—all emptiness!—all death!"

Hester Prynne looked into his face, but hesitated to speak. Yet, uttering his long-restrained emotions so vehemently as he did, his words here offered her the very point of circumstances in which to interpose what she came to say. She conquered her fears, and spoke.

"Such a friend as thou hast even now wished for," said she, "with whom to weep over thy sin, thou hast in me, the partner of it!"—Again she hesitated, but brought out the words with an effort.—"Thou hast long had such an enemy, and dwellest with him under the same roof!"

The minister started to his feet, gasping for breath, and clutching at his heart as if he would have torn it out of his bosom.

"Ha! What sayest thou?" cried he. "An enemy! And under mine own roof! What mean you?"

Hester Prynne was now fully sensible of the deep injury for which she was responsible to this unhappy man, in permitting him to lie for so many years, or, indeed, for a single moment, at the mercy of one, whose purposes could not be other than malevolent. The very contiguity of his enemy, beneath whatever mask the latter might conceal himself, was enough to disurb the magnetic sphere of a being so sensitive as Arthur Dimmesdale. There had been a period when Hester was less alive to this consideration; or, perhaps, in the misanthropy of her own trouble, she left the minister to bear what she might picture to herself as a more tolerable doom. But of late, since the night of his vigil, all her sympathies towards him had been both softened and invigorated. She now read his heart more accurately. She doubted not, that the continual presence of Roger Chillingworth,—the secret poison of his malignity, infecting all the air about him,—and his authorized interference, as a physician, with the minister's physical and spiritual infirmities,—that these bad opportunities had been turned to a cruel purpose. By means of them, the sufferer's conscience had been kept in an irritated state, the tendency of which was, not to cure by wholesome pain, but to disorganize and corrupt his spiritual being. Its result, on earth, could hardly fail to be insanity, and hereafter, that eternal alienation from the Good and True, of which madness is perhaps the earthly type.

Such was the ruin to which she had brought the man, once,—nay, why should we not speak it?—still so passionately loved! Hester felt that the sacrifice of the clergyman's good name, and death itself, as she had already told Roger Chillingworth, would have been infinitely preferable to the alternative which she had taken upon herself to choose. And now, rather than have had this grievous wrong to confess, she would gladly have lain down on the forest-leaves, and died there, at Arthur Dimmesdale's feet.

"O Arthur," cried she, "forgive me! In all things else, I have striven to be true! Truth was the one virtue which I might have held fast, and did hold fast through all extremity; save when thy good,—thy life,—thy fame,—were put in question! Then I consented to a deception. But a lie is never good, even though death threaten on the other side! Dost thou not see what I would say? That old man!—the physician!—he whom they call Roger Chillingworth!—he was my husband!"

The minister looked at her, for an instant, with all that violence of passion, which—intermixed, in more shapes than one, with his higher, purer, softer qualities—was, in fact, the portion of him which the Devil claimed, and through which he sought to win the rest. Never was there a blacker or a fiercer frown, than Hester now encountered. For the brief space that it lasted, it was a dark transfiguration. But his character had been so much enfeebled by suffering, that even its lower energies were incapable of more than a temporary struggle. He sank down on the ground, and buried his face in his hands.

"I might have known it!" murmured he. "I did know it! Was not the secret told me in the natural recoil of my heart, at the first sight of him, and as often as I have seen him since? Why did I not understand? O Hester Prynne, thou little, little knowest all the horror of this thing! And the shame!—the indelicacy!—the horrible ugliness of this exposure of a sick and guilty heart to the very eye that would gloat over it! Woman, woman, thou art accountable for this! I cannot forgive thee!"

"Thou shalt forgive me!" cried Hester, flinging herself on the fallen leaves beside him. "Let God punish! Thou shalt forgive!"

With sudden and desperate tenderness, she threw her arms around him, and pressed his head against her bosom; little caring though his cheek rested on the scarlet letter. He would have released himself, but strove in vain to do so. Hester would not set him free, lest he should look her sternly in the face. All the world had frowned on her,—for seven long years had it frowned upon this lonely woman,—and still she bore it all, nor ever once turned away her firm, sad eyes. Heaven, likewise, had frowned upon her, and she had not died. But the frown of this pale, weak, sinful, and sorrow-stricken man was what Hester could not bear, and live!

"Wilt thou yet forgive me?" she repeated, over and over again. "Wilt thou not frown? Wilt thou forgive?"

"I do forgive you, Hester," replied the minister, at length, with a deep utterance out of an abyss of sadness, but no anger. "I freely forgive you now. May God forgive us both! We are not, Hester, the worst sinners in the world. There is one worse than even the polluted priest! That old man's revenge has been blacker than my sin. He has violated, in cold blood, the sanctity of a human heart. Thou and I, Hester, never did so!"

"Never, never!" whispered she. "What we did had a consecration of its own. We felt it so! We said so to each other! Has thou forgotten it?"

"Hush, Hester!" said Arthur Dimmesdale, rising from the ground. "No; I have not forgotten!"

They sat down again, side by side, and hand clasped in hand, on the mossy trunk of the fallen tree. Life had never brought them a gloomier hour; it was the point whither their pathway had so long been tending, and darkening ever, as it stole along;—and yet it inclosed a charm that made them linger upon it, and claim another, and another, and, after all, another moment. The forest was obscure around them, and creaked with a blast that was passing through it. The boughs were tossing heavily above their heads; while one solemn old tree groaned dolefully to another, as if telling the sad story of the pair that sat beneath, or constrained to forebode evil to come.

And yet they lingered. How dreary looked the forest-track that led backward to the settlement, where Hester Prynne must take up again the burden of her ignominy, and the minister the hollow mockery of his good name! So they lingered an instant longer. No golden light had ever been so precious as the gloom of this dark forest. Here, seen only by his eyes, the scarlet letter need not burn into the bosom of the fallen woman! Here, seen only by her eyes, Arthur Dimmesdale, false to God and man, might be, for one moment, true!

He started at a thought that suddenly occurred to him.

"Hester," cried he, "here is a new horror! Roger Chillingworth knows your purpose to reveal his true character. Will he continue, then, to keep our secret? What will now be the course of his revenge?"

"There is a strange secrecy in his nature," replied Hester, thoughtfully; "and it has grown upon him by the hidden practices of his revenge. I deem it not likely that he will betray the secret. He will doubtless seek other means of satiating his dark passion."

"And I!—how am I to live longer, breathing the same air with this deadly enemy?" exclaimed Arthur Dimmesdale, shrinking within himself, and pressing his hand nervously against his heart,—a gesture that had grown involuntary with him. "Think for me, Hester! Thou art strong. Resolve for me!"

"Thou must dwell no longer with this man," said Hester, slowly and firmly. "Thy heart must be no longer under his evil eye!"

"It were far worse than death!" replied the minister. "But how to avoid it? What choice remains to me? Shall I lie down again on these withered leaves, where I cast myself when thou didst tell me what he was? Must I sink down there, and die at once?"

"Alas, what a ruin has befallen thee!" said Hester, with the tears gushing into her eyes. "Wilt thou die for very weakness? There is no other cause!"

"The judgment of God is on me," answered the conscience-stricken priest. "It is too mighty for me to struggle with!"

"Heaven would show mercy," rejoined Hester, "hadst thou but the strength to take advantage of it."

"Be thou strong for me!" answered he. "Advise me what to do."

"Is the world then so narrow?" exclaimed Hester Prynne, fixing her deep eyes on the minister's, and instinctively exercising a magnetic power over a spirit so shattered and subdued, that it could hardly hold itself erect. "Doth the universe lie within the compass of yonder town, which only a little time ago was but a leaf-strewn desert, as lonely as this around us? Whither leads yonder forest-track? Backward to the settlement, thou sayest! Yes; but onward, too! Deeper it goes, and deeper, into the wilderness, less plainly to be seen at every step; until, some few miles hence, the yellow leaves will show no vestige of the white man's tread. There thou art free! So brief a journey would bring thee from a world where thou hast been most wretched, to one where thou mayest still be happy! Is there not shade enough in all this boundless forest to hide thy heart from the gaze of Roger Chillingworth?"

"Yes, Hester; but only under the fallen leaves!" replied the minister, with a sad smile.

"Then there is the broad pathway of the sea!" continued Hester. "It brought thee hither. If thou so choose, it will bear thee back again. In our native land, whether in some remote rural village or in vast London,—or, surely, in Germany, in France, in pleasant Italy,—thou wouldst be beyond his power and knowledge! And what hast thou to do with all these iron men, and their opinions? They have kept thy better part in bondage too long already!"

"It cannot be!" answered the minister, listening as if he were called upon to realize a dream. "I am powerless to go. Wretched and sinful as I am, I have had no other thought than to drag on my earthly existence in the sphere where Providence hath placed me. Lost as my own soul is, I would still do what I may for other human souls! I dare not quit my post, though an unfaithful sentinel, whose sure reward is death and dishonor, when his dreary watch shall come to an end!"

"Thou art crushed under this seven years' weight of misery," replied Hester, fervently resolved to buoy him up with her own energy. "But thou shalt leave it all behind thee! It shall not cumber thy steps, as thou treadest along the forest-path; neither shalt thou freight the ship with it, if thou prefer to cross the sea. Leave this wreck and ruin here where it hath happened! Meddle no more with it! Begin all anew! Hast thou exhausted possibility in the failure of this one trial? Not so! The future is yet full of trial and success. There is happiness to be enjoyed! There is good to be done! Exchange this false life of thine for a true one. Be, if thy spirit summon thee to such a mission, the teacher and apostle of the red men. Or,—as is more thy nature,—be a scholar and a sage among the wisest and the most renowned of the cultivated world. Preach! Write! Act! Do any thing, save to lie down and die! Give up this name of Arthur Dimmesdale, and make thyself another, and a high one, such as thou canst wear without fear or shame. Why shouldst thou tarry so much as one other day in the torments that have so gnawed into thy life!—that have made thee feeble to will and to do!—that will leave thee powerless even to repent! Up, and away!"

"O Hester!" cried Arthur Dimmesdale, in whose eyes a fitful light, kindled by her enthusiasm, flashed up and died away, "thou tellest of running a race to a man whose knees are tottering beneath him! I must die here. There is not the strength or courage left me to venture into the wide, strange, difficult world, alone!"

It was the last expression of the despondency of a broken spirit. He lacked energy to grasp the better fortune that seemed within his reach.

He repeated the word.

"Alone, Hester!"

"Thou shalt not go alone!" answered she, in a deep whisper.

Then, all was spoken!

CHAPTER XVIII

A FLOOD OF SUNSHINE

Arthur Dimmesdale gazed into Hester's face with a look in which hope and joy shone out, indeed, but with fear betwixt them, and a kind of horror at her boldness, who had spoken what he vaguely hinted at, but dared not speak.

But Hester Prynne, with a mind of native courage and activity, and for so long a period not merely estranged, but outlawed, from society, had habituated herself to such latitude of speculation as was altogether foreign to the clergyman. She had wandered, without rule or guidance, in a moral wilderness; as vast, as intricate and shadowy, as the untamed forest, amid the gloom of which they were now holding a colloquy that was to decide their fate. Her intellect and heart had their home, as it were, in desert places, where she roamed as freely as the wild Indian in his woods. For years past she had looked from this estranged point of view at human institutions, and whatever priests or legislators had established; criticizing all with hardly more reverence than the Indian would feel for the clerical band, the judicial robe, the pillory, the gallows, the fireside, or the church. The tendency of her fate and fortunes had been to set her free. The scarlet letter was her passport into regions where other women dared not tread. Shame, Despair, Solitude! These had been her teachers,—stern and wild ones,—and they had made her strong, but taught her much amiss.

The minister, on the other hand, had never gone through an experience calculated to lead him beyond the scope of generally received laws; although, in a single instance, he had so fearfully transgressed one of the most sacred of them. But this had been a sin of passion, not of principle, nor even purpose. Since that wretched epoch, he had watched, with morbid zeal and minuteness, not his acts,—for those it was easy to arrange,—but each breath of emotion, and his every thought. At the head of the social system, as the clergymen of that day stood, he was only the more trammelled by its regulations, its principles, and even its prejudices. As a priest, the framework of his order inevitably hemmed him in. As a man who had once sinned, but who kept his conscience all alive and painfully sensitive by the fretting of an unhealed wound, he might have been supposed safer within the line of virtue, than if he had never sinned at all.

Thus, we seem to see that, as regarded Hester Prynne, the whole seven years of outlaw and ignominy had been little other than a preparation for this very hour. But Arthur Dimmesdale! Were such a man once more to fall, what plea could be urged in extenuation of his crime? None; unless it avail him somewhat, that he was broken down by long and exquisite suffering; that his mind was darkened and confused by the very remorse which harrowed it; that, between fleeing as an avowed criminal, and remaining as a hypocrite, conscience might find it hard to strike the balance; that it was human to avoid the peril of death and infamy, and the inscrutable machinations of an enemy; that, finally, to this poor pilgrim, on his dreary and desert path, faint, sick, miserable, there appeared a glimpse of human affection and sympathy, a new life, and a true one, in exchange for the heavy doom which he was now expiating. And be the stern and sad truth spoken, that the breach which guilt has once made into the human soul is never, in this mortal state, repaired. It may be watched and guarded; so that the enemy shall not force his way again into the citadel, and might even, in his subsequent assaults, select some other avenue, in preference to that where he had formerly succeeded. But there is still the ruined wall, and, near it, the stealthy tread of the foe that would win over again his unforgotten triumph.

The struggle, if there were one, need not be described. Let it suffice, that the clergyman resolved to flee, and not alone.

"If, in all these past seven years," thought he, "I could recall one instant of peace or hope, I would yet endure, for the sake of that earnest of Heaven's mercy. But now,—since I am irrevocably doomed,—wherefore should I not snatch the solace allowed to the condemned culprit before his execution? Or, if this be the path to a better life, as Hester would persuade me, I surely give up no fairer prospect by pursuing it! Neither can I any longer live without her companionship; so powerful is she to sustain,—so tender to soothe! O Thou to whom I dare not lift mine eyes, wilt Thou yet pardon me!"

"Thou wilt go!" said Hester calmly, as he met her glance.

The decision once made, a glow of strange enjoyment threw its flickering brightness over the trouble of his breast. It was the exhilarating effect—upon a prisoner just escaped from the dungeon of his own heart—of breathing the wild, free atmosphere of an unredeemed, unchristianized, lawless region. His spirit rose, as it were, with a bound, and attained a nearer prospect of the sky, than throughout all the misery which had kept him grovelling on the earth. Of a deeply religious temperament, there was inevitably a tinge of the devotional in his mood.

"Do I feel joy again?" cried he, wondering at himself. "Methought the germ of it was dead in me! O Hester, thou art my better angel! I seem to have flung myself—sick, sin-stained, and sorrow-blackened—down upon these forest leaves, and to have risen up all made anew, and with new powers to glorify Him that hath been merciful! This is already the better life! Why did we not find it sooner?"

"Let us not look back," answered Hester Prynne. "The past is gone! Wherefore should we linger upon it now? See! With this symbol, I undo it all, and make it as it had never been!"

So speaking, she undid the clasp that fastened the scarlet letter, and, taking it from her bosom, threw it to a distance among the withered leaves. The mystic token alighted on the hither verge of the stream. With a hand's breadth farther flight it would have fallen into the water, and have given the little brook another woe to carry onward, besides the unintelligible tale which it still kept murmuring about. But there lay the embroidered letter, glittering like a lost jewel, which some ill-fated wanderer might pick up, and thenceforth be haunted by strange phantoms of guilt, sinkings of the heart, and unaccountable misfortune.

The stigma gone, Hester heaved a long, deep sigh, in which the burden of shame and anguish departed from her spirit. O exquisite relief! She had not known the weight, until she felt the freedom! By another impulse, she took off the formal cap that confined her hair; and down it fell upon her shoulders, dark and rich, with at once a shadow and a light in its abundance, and imparting the charm of softness to her features. There played around her mouth, and beamed out of her eyes, a radiant and tender smile, that seemed gushing from the very heart of womanhood. A crimson flush was glowing on her cheek, that had been long so pale. Her sex, her youth, and the whole richness of her beauty, came back from what men call the irrevocable past, and clustered themselves, with her maiden hope, and a happiness before unknown, within the magic circle of this hour. And, as if the gloom of the earth and sky had been but the effluence of these two mortal hearts, it vanished with their sorrow. All at once, as with a sudden smile of heaven, forth burst the sunshine, pouring a very flood into the obscure forest, gladdening each green leaf, transmuting the yellow fallen ones to gold, and gleaming adown the gray trunks of the solemn trees The objects that had made a shadow hitherto, embodied the brightness now. The course of the little brook might be traced by its merry gleam afar into the wood's heart of mystery, which had become a mystery of joy.

Such was the sympathy of Nature—that wild, heathen Nature of the forest, never subjugated by human law, nor illumined by higher truth—with the bliss of these two spirits! Love, whether newly born, or aroused from a deathlike slumber, must always create a sunshine, filling the heart so full of radiance, that it overflows upon the outward world. Had the forest still kept its gloom, it would have been bright in Hester's eyes, and bright in Arthur Dimmesdale's!

Hester looked at him with the thrill of another joy.

"Thou must know Pearl!" said she. "Our little Pearl! Thou hast seen her,—yes, I know it!—but thou wilt see her now with other eyes. She is a strange child! I hardly comprehend her! But thou wilt love her dearly, as I do, and wilt advise me how to deal with her."

"Dost thou think the child will be glad to know me?" asked the minister, somewhat uneasily. "I have long shrunk from children, because they often show a distrust,—a backwardness to be familiar with me. I have even been afraid of little Pearl!"

"Ah, that was sad!" answered the mother. "But she will love thee dearly, and thou her. She is not far off. I will call her! Pearl! Pearl!"

"I see the child," observed the minister. "Yonder she is, standing in a streak of sunshine, a good way off, on the other side of the brook. So thou thinkest the child will love me?"

Hester smiled, and again called to Pearl, who was visible, at some distance, as the minister had described her, like a bright-apparelled vision, in a sunbeam, which fell down upon her through an arch of boughs. The ray quivered to and fro, making her figure dim or distinct,—now like a real child, now like a child's spirit,—as the splendor went and came again. She heard her mother's voice, and approached slowly through the forest.

Pearl had not found the hour pass wearisomely, while her mother sat talking with the clergyman. The great black forest—stern as it showed itself to those who brought the guilt and troubles of the world into its bosom—became the playmate of the lonely infant, as well as it knew how. Sombre as it was, it put on the kindest of its moods to welcome her. It offered her the partridge-berries, the growth of the preceding autumn, but ripening only in the spring, and now red as drops of blood upon the withered leaves. These Pearl gathered, and was pleased with their wild flavor. The small denizens of the wilderness hardly took pains to move out of her path. A partridge, indeed, with a brood of ten behind her, ran forward threateningly, but soon repented of her fierceness, and clucked to her young ones not to be afraid. A pigeon, alone on a low branch, allowed Pearl to come beneath, and uttered a sound as much of greeting as alarm. A squirrel, from the lofty depths of his domestic tree, chattered either in anger or merriment,—for a squirrel is such a choleric and humorous little personage that it is hard to distinguish between his moods,—so he chattered at the child, and flung down a nut upon her head. It was a last year's nut, and already gnawed by his sharp tooth. A fox, startled from his sleep by her light footstep on the leaves, looked inquisitively at Pearl, as doubting whether it were better to steal off, or renew his nap on the same spot. A wolf, it is said,—but here the tale has surely lapsed into the improbable,—came up, and smelt of Pearl's robe, and offered his savage head to be patted by her hand. The truth seems to be, however, that the mother-forest, and these wild things which it nourished, all recognized a kindred wildness in the human child.

And she was gentler here than in the grassy-margined streets of the settlement, or in her mother's cottage. The flowers appeared to know it; and one and another whispered, as she passed, "Adorn thyself with me, thou beautiful child, adorn thyself with me!"—and, to please them, Pearl gathered the violets, and anemones, and columbines, and some twigs of the freshest green, which the old trees held down before her eyes. With these she decorated her hair, and her young waist, and became a nymph-child, or an infant dryad, or whatever else was in closest sympathy with the antique wood. In such guise had Pearl adorned herself, when she heard her mother's voice, and came slowly back.

Slowly; for she saw the clergyman!

CHAPTER XIX

THE CHILD AT THE BROOK-SIDE

"Thou wilt love her dearly," repeated Hester Prynne, as she and the minister sat watching little Pearl. "Dost thou not think her beautiful? And see with what natural skill she has made those simple flowers adorn her! Had she gathered pearls, and diamonds, and rubies, in the wood, they could not have become her better. She is a splendid child! But I know whose brow she has!"

"Dost thou know, Hester," said Arthur Dimmesdale, with an unquiet smile, "that this dear child, tripping about always at thy side, hath caused me many an alarm? Methought—O Hester, what a thought is that, and how terrible to dread it!—that my own features were partly repeated in her face, and so strikingly that the world might see them! But she is mostly thine!"

"No, no! Not mostly!" answered the mother with a tender smile. "A little longer, and thou needest not to be afraid to trace whose child she is. But how strangely beautiful she looks, with those wild flowers in her hair! It is as if one of the fairies, whom we left in our dear old England, had decked her out to meet us."

It was with a feeling which neither of them had ever before experienced, that they sat and watched Pearl's slow advance. In her was visible the tie that united them. She had been offered to the world, these seven years past, as the living hieroglyphic, in which was revealed the secret they so darkly sought to hide,—all written in this symbol,—all plainly manifest,—had there been a prophet or magician skilled to read the character of flame! And Pearl was the oneness of their being. Be the foregone evil what it might, how could they doubt that their earthly lives and future destinies were conjoined, when they beheld at once the material union, and the spiritual idea, in whom they met, and were to dwell immortally together? Thoughts like these—and perhaps other thoughts, which they did not acknowledge or define—threw an awe about the child, as she came onward.

"Let her see nothing strange—no passion nor eagerness—in thy way of accosting her," whispered Hester. "Our Pearl is a fitful and fantastic little elf, sometimes. Especially, she is seldom tolerant of emotion, when she does not fully comprehend the why and wherefore. But the child hath strong affections! She loves me, and will love thee!"

"Thou canst not think," said the minister, glancing aside at Hester Prynne, "how my heart dreads this interview, and yearns for it! But, in truth, as I already told thee, children are not readily won to be familiar with me. They will not climb my knee, nor prattle in my ear, nor answer to my smile; but stand apart, and eye me strangely. Even little babes, when I take them in my arms, weep bitterly. Yet Pearl, twice in her little lifetime, hath been kind to me! The first time,—thou knowest it well! The last was when thou ledst her with thee to the house of yonder stern old Governor."

"And thou didst plead so bravely in her behalf and mine!" answered the mother. "I remember it; and so shall little Pearl. Fear nothing! She may be strange and shy at first, but will soon learn to love thee!"

By this time Pearl had reached the margin of the brook, and stood on the farther side, gazing silently at Hester and the clergyman, who still sat together on the mossy tree-trunk, waiting to receive her. Just where she had paused the brook chanced to form a pool, so smooth and quiet that it reflected a perfect image of her little figure, with all the brilliant picturesqueness of her beauty, in its adornment of flowers and wreathed foliage, but more refined and spiritualized than the reality. This image, so nearly identical with the living Pearl, seemed to communicate somewhat of its own shadowy and intangible quality to the child herself. It was strange, the way in which Pearl stood, looking so steadfastly at them through the dim medium of the forest-gloom; herself, meanwhile, all glorified with a ray of sunshine, that was attracted thitherward as by a certain sympathy. In the brook beneath stood another child,—another and the same,—with likewise its ray of golden light. Hester felt herself, in some indistinct and tantalizing manner, estranged from Pearl; as if the child, in her lonely ramble through the forest, had strayed out of the sphere in which she and her mother dwelt together, and was now vainly seeking to return to it.

There was both truth and error in the impression; the child and mother estranged, but through Hester's fault, not Pearl's. Since the latter rambled from her side, another inmate had been admitted within the circle of the mother's feelings, and so modified the aspect of them all, that Pearl, the returning wanderer, could not find her wonted place, and hardly knew where she was.

"I have a strange fancy," observed the sensitive minister, "that this brook is the boundary between two worlds, and that thou canst never meet thy Pearl again. Or is she an elfish spirit, who, as the legends of our childhood taught us, is forbidden to cross a running stream? Pray hasten her; for this delay has already imparted a tremor to my nerves."

"Come, dearest child!" said Hester encouragingly, and stretching out both her arms. "How slow thou art! When hast thou been so sluggish before now? Here is a friend of mine, who must be thy friend also. Thou wilt have twice as much love, henceforward, as thy mother alone could give thee! Leap across the brook and come to us. Thou canst leap like a young deer!"

Pearl, without responding in any manner to these honeysweet expressions, remained on the other side of the brook. Now she fixed her bright, wild eyes on her mother, now on the minister, and now included them both in the same glance; as if to detect and explain to herself the relation which they bore to one another. For some unaccountable reason, as Arthur Dimmesdale felt the child's eyes upon himself, his hand—with that gesture so habitual as to have become involuntary—stole over his heart. At length, assuming a singular air of authority, Pearl stretched out her hand, with the small forefinger extended, and pointing evidently towards her mother's breast. And beneath, in the mirror of the brook, there was the flower-girdled and sunny image of little Pearl, pointing her small forefinger too.

"Thou strange child, why dost thou not come to me?" exclaimed Hester.

Pearl still pointed with her forefinger; and a frown gathered on her brow; the more impressive from the childish, the almost baby-like aspect of the features that conveyed it. As her mother still kept beckoning to her, and arraying her face in a holiday suit of unaccustomed smiles, the child stamped her foot with a yet more imperious look and gesture. In the brook, again, was the fantastic beauty of the image, with its reflected frown, its pointed finger, and imperious gesture, giving emphasis to the aspect of little Pearl.

"Hasten, Pearl; or I shall be angry with thee!" cried Hester Prynne, who, however inured to such behaviour on the elf-child's part at other seasons, was naturally anxious for a more seemly deportment now. "Leap across the brook, naughty child, and run hither! Else I must come to thee!"

But Pearl, not a whit startled at her mother's threats, any more than mollified by her entreaties, now suddenly burst into a fit of passion, gesticulating violently, and throwing her small figure into the most extravagant contortions. She accompanied this wild outbreak with piercing shrieks, which the woods reverberated on all sides; so that, alone as she was in her childish and unreasonable wrath, it seemed as if a hidden multitude were lending her their sympathy and encouragement. Seen in the brook, once more, was the shadowy wrath of Pearl's image, crowned and girdled with flowers, but stamping its foot, wildly gesticulating, and, in the midst of all, still pointing its small forefinger at Hester's bosom!

"I see what ails the child," whispered Hester to clergyman, and turning pale in spite of a strong effort to conceal her trouble and annoyance. "Children will not abide any, the slightest, change in the accustomed aspect of things that are daily before their eyes. Pearl misses something which she has always seen me wear!"

"I pray you," answered the minister, "if thou hast any means of pacifying the child, do it forthwith! Save it were the cankered wrath of an old witch, like Mistress Hibbins," added he, attempting to smile, "I know nothing that I would not sooner encounter than this passion in a child. In Pearl's young beauty, as in the wrinkled witch, it has a preternatural effect. Pacify her, if thou lovest me!"

Hester turned again towards Pearl, with a crimson blush upon her cheek, a conscious glance aside at the clergyman, and then a heavy sigh; while, even before she had time to speak, the blush yielded to a deadly pallor.

"Pearl," said she, sadly, "look down at thy feet! There!—before thee!—on the hither side of the brook!"

The child turned her eyes to the point indicated; and there lay the scarlet letter, so close upon the margin of the stream, that the gold embroidery was reflected in it.

"Bring it hither!" said Hester.

"Come thou and take it up!" answered Pearl.

"Was ever such a child!" observed Hester aside to the minister. "O, I have much to tell thee about her. But, in very truth, she is right as regards this hateful token. I must bear its torture yet a little longer,—only a few days longer,—until we shall have left this region, and look back hither as to a land which we have dreamed of. The forest cannot hide it! The mid-ocean shall take it from my hand, and swallow it up for ever!"

With these words, she advanced to the margin of the brook, took up the scarlet letter, and fastened it again into her bosom. Hopefully, but a moment ago, as Hester had spoken of drowning it in the deep sea, there was a sense of inevitable doom upon her, as she thus received back this deadly symbol from the hand of fate. She had flung it into infinite space!—she had drawn an hour's free breath!—and here again was the scarlet misery, glittering on the old spot! So it ever is, whether thus typified or no, that an evil deed invests itself with the character of doom. Hester next gathered up the heavy tresses of her hair, and confined them beneath her cap. As if there were a withering spell in the sad letter, her beauty, the warmth and richness of her womanhood, departed, like fading sunshine; and a gray shadow seemed to fall across her.

When the dreary change was wrought, she extended her hand to Pearl.

"Dost thou know thy mother now, child?" asked she, reproachfully, but with a subdued tone. "Wilt thou come across the brook, and own thy mother, now that she has her shame upon her,—now that she is sad?"

"Yes; now I will!" answered the child, bounding across the brook, and clasping Hester in her arms. "Now thou art my mother indeed! And I am thy little Pearl!"

In a mood of tenderness that was not usual with her, she drew down her mother's head, and kissed her brow and both her cheeks. But then—by a kind of necessity that always impelled this child to alloy whatever comfort she might chance to give with a throb of anguish—Pearl put up her mouth, and kissed the scarlet letter too!

"That was not kind!" said Hester. "When thou hast shown me a little love, thou mockest me!"

"Why doth the minister sit yonder?" asked Pearl.

"He waits to welcome thee," replied her mother. "Come thou, and entreat his blessing! He loves thee, my little Pearl, and loves thy mother too. Wilt thou not love him? Come! he longs to greet thee!"

"Doth he love us?" said Pearl, looking up with acute intelligence into her mother's face. "Will he go back with us, hand in hand, we three together, into the town?"

"Not now, dear child," answered Hester. "But in days to come he will walk hand in hand with us. We will have a home and fireside of our own; and thou shalt sit upon his knee; and he will teach thee many things, and love thee dearly. Thou wilt love him; wilt thou not?"

"And will he aways keep his hand over his heart?" inquired Pearl.

"Foolish child, what a question is that!" exclaimed her mother. "Come and ask his blessing!"

But, whether influenced by the jealousy that seems instinctive with every petted child towards a dangerous rival, or from whatever caprice of her freakish nature, Pearl would show no favor to the clergyman. It was only by an exertion of force that her mother brought her up to him, hanging back, and manifesting her reluctance by odd grimaces; of which, ever since her babyhood, she had possessed a singular variety, and could transform her mobile physiognomy into a series of different aspects, with a new mischief in them, each and all. The minister—painfully embarrassed, but hoping that a kiss might prove a talisman to admit him into the child's kindlier regards—bent forward, and impressed one on her brow. Hereupon, Pearl broke away from her mother, and, running to the brook, stooped over it, and bathed her forehead, until the unwelcome kiss was quite washed off, and diffused through a long lapse of the gliding water. She then remained apart, silently watching Hester and the clergyman; while they talked together, and made such arrangements as were suggested by their new position, and the purposes soon to be fulfilled.

And now this fateful interview had come to a close. The dell was to be left a solitude among its dark, old trees, which, with their multitudinous tongues, would whisper long of what had passed there, and no mortal be the wiser. And the melancholy brook would add this other tale to the mystery with which its little heart was already overburdened, and whereof it still kept up a murmuring babble, with not a whit more cheerfulness of tone than for ages heretofore.

CHAPTER XX

THE MINISTER IN A MAZE

As the minister departed, in advance of Hester Prynne and little Pearl, he threw a backward glance; half expecting that he should discover only some faintly traced features or outline of the mother and the child, slowly fading into the twilight of the woods. So great a vicissitude in his life could not at once be received as real. But there was Hester, clad in her gray robe, still standing beside the tree-trunk, which some blast had overthrown a long antiquity ago, and which time had ever since been covering with moss, so that these two fated ones, with earth's heaviest burden on them, might there sit down together, and find a single hour's rest and solace. And there was Pearl, too, lightly dancing from the margin of the brook,—now that the intrusive third person was gone,—and taking her old place by her mother's side. So the minister had not fallen asleep, and dreamed!

In order to free his mind from this indistinctness and duplicity of impression, which vexed it with a strange disquietude, he recalled and more thoroughly defined the plans which Hester and himself had sketched for their departure. It had been determined between them, that the Old World, with its crowds and cities, offered them a more eligible shelter and concealment than the wilds of New England, or all America, with its alternatives of an Indian wigwam, or the few settlements of Europeans, scattered thinly along the seaboard. Not to speak of the clergyman's health, so inadequate to sustain the hardships of a forest life, his native gifts, his culture, and his entire development would secure him a home only in the midst of civilization and refinement; the higher the state, the more delicately adapted to it the man. In furtherance of this choice, it so happened that a ship lay in the harbour; one of those questionable cruisers, frequent at that day, which, without being absolutely outlaws of the deep, yet roamed over its surface with a remarkable irresponsibility of character. This vessel had recently arrived from the Spanish Main, and, within three days' time, would sail for Bristol. Hester Prynne—whose vocation, as a self-enlisted Sister of Charity, had brought her acquainted with the captain and crew—could take upon herself to secure the passage of two individuals and a child, with all the secrecy which circumstances rendered more than desirable.

The minister had inquired of Hester, with no little interest, the precise time at which the vessel might be expected to depart. It would probably be on the fourth day from the present. "That is most fortunate!" he had then said to himself. Now, why the Reverend Mr. Dimmesdale considered it so very fortunate, we hesitate to reveal. Nevertheless,—to hold nothing back from the reader,—it was because, on the third day from the present, he was to preach the Election Sermon; and, as such an occasion formed an honorable epoch in the life of a New England clergyman, he could not have chanced upon a more suitable mode and time of terminating his professional career. "At least, they shall say of me," thought this exemplary man, "that I leave no public duty unperformed, nor ill performed!" Sad, indeed, that an introspection so profound and acute as this poor minister's should be so miserably deceived! We have had, and may still have, worse things to tell of him; but none, we apprehend, so pitiably weak; no evidence, at once so slight and irrefragable, of a subtle disease, that had long since begun to eat into the real substance of his character. No man, for any considerable period, can wear one face to himself, and another to the multitude, without finally getting bewildered as to which may be the true.

The excitement of Mr. Dimmesdale's feelings, as he returned from his interview with Hester, lent him unaccustomed physical energy, and hurried him townward at a rapid pace. The pathway among the woods seemed wilder, more uncouth with its rude natural obstacles, and less trodden by the foot of man, than he remembered it on his outward journey. But he leaped across the plashy places, thrust himself through the clinging underbrush, climbed the ascent, plunged into the hollow, and overcame, in short, all the difficulties of the track, with an unweariable activity that astonished him. He could not but recall how feebly, and with what frequent pauses for breath, he had toiled over the same ground only two days before. As he drew near the town, he took an impression of change from the series of familiar objects that presented themselves. It seemed not yesterday, not one, nor two, but many days, or even years ago, since he had quitted them. There, indeed, was each former trace of the street, as he remembered it, and all the peculiarities of the houses, with the due multitude of gable-peaks, and a weathercock at every point where his memory suggested one. Not the less, however, came this importunately obtrusive sense of change. The same was true as regarded the acquaintances whom he met, and all the well-known shapes of human life, about the little town. They looked neither older nor younger, now; the beards of the aged were no whiter, nor could the creeping babe of yesterday walk on his feet to-day; it was impossible to describe in what respect they differed from the individuals on whom he had so recently bestowed a parting glance; and yet the minister's deepest sense seemed to inform him of their mutability. A similar impression struck him most remarkably, as he passed under the walls of his own church. The edifice had so very strange, and yet so familiar, an aspect, that Mr. Dimmesdale's mind vibrated between two ideas; either that he had seen it only in a dream hitherto, or that he was merely dreaming about it now.

This phenomenon, in the various shapes which it assumed, indicated no external change, but so sudden and important a change in the spectator of the familiar scene, that the intervening space of a single day had operated on his consciousness like the lapse of years. The minister's own will, and Hester's will, and the fate that grew between them, had wrought this transformation. It was the same town as heretofore; but the same minister returned not from the forest. He might have said to the friends who greeted him,—"I am not the man for whom you take me! I left him yonder in the forest, withdrawn into a secret dell, by a mossy tree-trunk, and near a melancholy brook! Go, seek your minister, and see if his emaciated figure, his thin cheek, his white, heavy, pain-wrinkled brow, be not flung down there like a cast-off garment!" His friends, no doubt, would still have insisted with him,—"Thou art thyself the man!"—but the error would have been their own, not his.

Before Mr. Dimmesdale reached home, his inner man gave him other evidences of a revolution in the sphere of thought and feeling. In truth, nothing short of a total change of dynasty and moral code, in that interior kingdom, was adequate to account for the impulses now communicated to the unfortunate and startled minister. At every step he was incited to do some strange, wild, wicked thing or other, with a sense that it would be at once involuntary and intentional; in spite of himself, yet growing out of a profounder self than that which opposed the impulse. For instance, he met one of his own deacons. The good old man addressed him with the paternal affection and patriarchal privilege, which his venerable age, his upright and holy character, and his station in the Church, entitled him to use; and, conjoined with this, the deep, almost worshipping respect, which the minister's professional and private claims alike demanded. Never was there a more beautiful example of how the majesty of age and wisdom may comport with the obeisance and respect enjoined upon it, as from a lower social rank and inferior order of endowment, towards a higher. Now, during a conversation of some two or three moments between the Reverend Mr. Dimmesdale and this excellent and hoary-bearded deacon, it was only by the most careful self-control that the former could refrain from uttering certain blasphemous suggestions that rose into his mind, respecting the communion-supper. He absolutely trembled and turned pale as ashes, lest his tongue should wag itself, in utterance of these horrible matters, and plead his own consent for so doing, without his having fairly given it. And, even with this terror in his heart, he could hardly avoid laughing to imagine how the sanctified old patriarchal deacon would have been petrified by his minister's impiety!

Again, another incident of the same nature. Hurrying along the street, the Reverend Mr. Dimmesdale encountered the eldest female member of his church; a most pious and exemplary old dame; poor, widowed, lonely, and with a heart as full of reminiscences about her dead husband and children, and her dead friends of long ago, as a burial-ground is full of storied grave-stones. Yet all this, which would else have been such heavy sorrow, was made almost a solemn joy to her devout old soul by religious consolations and the truths of Scripture, wherewith she had fed herself continually for more than thirty years. And, since Mr. Dimmesdale had taken her in charge, the good grandam's chief earthly comfort—which, unless it had been likewise a heavenly comfort, could have been none at all—was to meet her pastor, whether casually, or of set purpose, and be refreshed with a word of warm, fragrant, heaven-breathing Gospel truth from his beloved lips into her dulled, but rapturously attentive ear. But, on this occasion, up to the moment of putting his lips to the old woman's ear, Mr. Dimmesdale, as the great enemy of souls would have it, could recall no text of Scripture, nor aught else, except a brief, pithy, and, as it then appeared to him, unanswerable argument against the immortality of the human soul. The instilment thereof into her mind would probably have caused this aged sister to drop down dead, at once, as by the effect of an intensely poisonous infusion. What he really did whisper, the minister could never afterwards recollect. There was, perhaps, a fortunate disorder in his utterance, which failed to impart any distinct idea to the good widow's comprehension, or which Providence interpreted after a method of its own. Assuredly, as the minister looked back, he beheld an expression of divine gratitude and ecstasy that seemed like the shine of the celestial city on her face, so wrinkled and ashy pale.

Again, a third instance. After parting from the old churchmember, he met the youngest sister of them all. It was a maiden newly won—and won by the Reverend Mr. Dimmesdale's own sermon, on the Sabbath after his vigil—to barter the transitory pleasures of the world for the heavenly hope, that was to assume brighter substance as life grew dark around her, and which would gild the utter gloom with final glory. She was fair and pure as a lily that had bloomed in Paradise. The minister knew well that he was himself enshrined within the stainless sanctity of her heart, which hung its snowy curtains about his image, imparting to religion the warmth of love, and to love a religious purity. Satan, that afternoon, had surely led the poor young girl away from her mother's side, and thrown her into the pathway of this sorely tempted, or—shall we not rather say?—this lost and desperate man. As she drew nigh, the arch-fiend whispered him to condense into small compass and drop into her tender bosom a germ of evil that would be sure to blossom darkly soon, and bear black fruit betimes. Such was his sense of power over this virgin soul, trusting him as she did, that the minister felt potent to blight all the field of innocence with but one wicked look, and develop all its opposite with but a word. So—with a mightier struggle than he had yet sustained—he held his Geneva cloak before his face, and hurried onward, making no sign of recognition, and leaving the young sister to digest his rudeness as she might. She ransacked her conscience,—which was full of harmless little matters, like her pocket or her work-bag,—and took herself to task, poor thing, for a thousand imaginary faults; and went about her household duties with swollen eyelids the next morning.

Before the minister had time to celebrate his victory over this last temptation, he was conscious of another impulse, more ludicrous, and almost as horrible. It was,—we blush to tell it,—it was to stop short in the road, and teach some very wicked words to a knot of little Puritan children who were playing here, and had but just begun to talk. Denying himself this freak, as unworthy of his cloth, he met a drunken seaman, one of the ship's crew from the Spanish Main. And, here, since he had so valiantly forborne all other wickedness, poor Mr. Dimmesdale longed, at least, to shake hands with the tarry blackguard, and recreate himself with a few improper jests, such as dissolute sailors so abound with, and a volley of good, round, solid, satisfactory, and heaven-defying oaths! It was not so much a better principle, as partly his natural good taste, and still more his buckramed habit of clerical decorum, that carried him safely through the latter crisis.

"What is it that haunts and tempts me thus?" cried the minister to himself, at length, pausing in the street, and striking his hand against his forehead. "Am I mad? or am I given over utterly to the fiend? Did I make a contract with him in the forest, and sign it with my blood? And does he now summon me to its fulfilment, by suggesting the performance of every wickedness which his most foul imagination can conceive?"

At the moment when the Reverend Mr. Dimmesdale thus communed with himself, and struck his forehead with his hand, old Mistress Hibbins, the reputed witch-lady, is said to have been passing by. She made a very grand appearance; having on a high head-dress, a rich gown of velvet, and a ruff done up with the famous yellow starch, of which Ann Turner, her especial friend, had taught her the secret, before this last good lady had been hanged for Sir Thomas Overbury's murder. Whether the witch had read the minister's thoughts, or no, she came to a full stop, looked shrewdly into his face, smiled craftily, and—though little given to converse with clergymen—began a conversation.

"So, reverend Sir, you have made a visit into the forest," observed the witch-lady, nodding her high head-dress at him. "The next time, I pray you to allow me only a fair warning, and I shall be proud to bear you company. Without taking overmuch upon myself, my good word will go far towards gaining any strange gentleman a fair reception from yonder potentate you wot of!"

"I profess, madam," answered the clergyman, with a grave obeisance, such as the lady's rank demanded, and his own good-breeding made imperative,—"I profess, on my conscience and character, that I am utterly bewildered as touching the purport of your words! I went not into the forest to seek a potentate; neither do I, at any future time, design a visit thither, with a view to gaining the favor of such personage. My one sufficient object was to greet that pious friend of mine, the Apostle Eliot, and rejoice with him over the many precious souls he hath won from heathendom!"

"Ha, ha, ha!" cackled the old witch-lady, still nodding her high head-dress at the minister. "Well, well, we must needs talk thus in the daytime! You carry it off like an old hand! But at midnight, and in the forest, we shall have other talk together!"

She passed on with her aged stateliness, but often turning back her head and smiling at him, like one willing to recognize a secret intimacy of connection.

"Have I then sold myself," thought the minister, "to the fiend whom, if men say true, this yellow-starched and velveted old hag has chosen for her prince and master!"

The wretched minister! He had made a bargain very like it! Tempted by a dream of happiness, he had yielded himself with deliberate choice, as he had never done before, to what he knew was deadly sin. And the infectious poison of that sin had been thus rapidly diffused throughout his moral system. It had stupefied all blessed impulses, and awakened into vivid life the whole brotherhood of bad ones. Scorn, bitterness, unprovoked malignity, gratuitous desire of ill, ridicule of whatever was good and holy, all awoke, to tempt, even while they frightened him. And his encounter with old Mistress Hibbins, if it were a real incident, did but show his sympathy and fellowship with wicked mortals and the world of perverted spirits.

He had by this time reached his dwelling, on the edge of the burial-ground, and, hastening up the stairs, took refuge in his study. The minister was glad to have reached this shelter, without first betraying himself to the world by any of those strange and wicked eccentricities to which he had been continually impelled while passing through the streets. He entered the accustomed room, and looked around him on its books, its windows, its fireplace, and the tapestried comfort of the walls, with the same perception of strangeness that had haunted him throughout his walk from the forest-dell into the town, and thitherward. Here he had studied and written; here, gone through fast and vigil, and come forth half alive; here, striven to pray; here, borne a hundred thousand agonies! There was the Bible, in its rich old Hebrew, with Moses and the Prophets speaking to him, and God's voice through all! There, on the table, with the inky pen beside it, was an unfinished sermon, with a sentence broken in the midst, where his thoughts had ceased to gush out upon the page two days before. He knew that it was himself, the thin and white-cheeked minister, who had done and suffered these things, and written thus far into the Election Sermon! But he seemed to stand apart, and eye this former self with scornful, pitying, but half-envious curiosity. That self was gone! Another man had returned out of the forest; a wiser one; with a knowledge of hidden mysteries which the simplicity of the former never could have reached. A bitter kind of knowledge that!

While occupied with these reflections, a knock came at the door of the study, and the minister said, "Come in!"—not wholly devoid of an idea that he might behold an evil spirit. And so he did! It was old Roger Chillingworth that entered. The minister stood, white and speechless, with one hand on the Hebrew Scriptures, and the other spread upon his breast.

"Welcome home, reverend Sir!" said the physician. "And how found you that godly man, the Apostle Eliot? But methinks, dear Sir, you look pale; as if the travel through the wilderness had been too sore for you. Will not my aid be requisite to put you in heart and strength to preach your Election Sermon?"

"Nay, I think not so," rejoined the Reverend Mr. Dimmesdale. "My journey, and the sight of the holy Apostle yonder, and the free air which I have breathed, have done me good, after so long confinement in my study. I think to need no more of your drugs, my kind physician, good though they be, and administered by a friendly hand."

All this time, Roger Chillingworth was looking at the minister with the grave and intent regard of a physician towards his patient. But, in spite of this outward show, the latter was almost convinced of the old man's knowledge, or, at least, his confident suspicion, with respect to his own interview with Hester Prynne. The physician knew, then, that, in the minister's regard, he was no longer a trusted friend, but his bitterest enemy. So much being known, it would appear natural that a part of it should be expressed. It is singular, however, how long a time often passes before words embody things; and with what security two persons, who choose to avoid a certain subject, may approach its very verge, and retire without disturbing it. Thus, the minister felt no apprehension that Roger Chillingworth would touch, in express words, upon the real position which they sustained towards one another. yet did the physician, in his dark way, creep frightfully near the secret.

"Were it not better," said he, "that you use my poor skill to-night? Verily, dear Sir, we must take pains to make you strong and vigorous for this occasion of the Election discourse. The people look for great things from you; apprehending that another year may come about, and find their pastor gone."

"Yea, to another world," replied the minister, with pious resignation. "Heaven grant it be a better one; for, in good sooth, I hardly think to tarry with my flock through the flitting seasons of another year! But, touching your medicine, kind Sir, in my present frame of body I need it not."

"I joy to hear it," answered the physician. "It may be that my remedies, so long administered in vain, begin now to take due effect. Happy man were I, and well deserving of New England's gratitude, could I achieve this cure!"

"I thank you from my heart, most watchful friend," said the Reverend Mr. Dimmesdale, with a solemn smile. "I thank you, and can but requite your good deeds with my prayers."

"A good man's prayers are golden recompense!" rejoined old Roger Chillingworth, as he took his leave. "Yea, they are the current gold coin of the New Jerusalem, with the King's own mint-mark on them!"

Left alone, the minister summoned a servant of the house, and requested food, which, being set before him, he ate with ravenous appetite. Then, flinging the already written pages of the Election Sermon into the fire, he forthwith began another, which he wrote with such impulsive flow of thought and emotion, that he fancied himself inspired; and only wondered that Heaven should see fit to transmit the grand and solemn music of its oracles through so foul an organ-pipe as he. However, leaving that mystery to solve itself, or go unsolved for ever, he drove his task onward with earnest haste and ecstasy. Thus the night fled away, as if it were a winged steed, and he careering on it; morning came, and peeped blushing through the curtains; and at last sunrise threw a golden beam into the study, and laid it right across the minister's bedazzled eyes. There he was, with the pen still between his fingers, and a vast, immeasurable tract of written space behind him!

CHAPTER XXI

THE NEW ENGLAND HOLIDAY

Betimes in the morning of the day on which the new Governor was to receive his office at the hands of the people, Hester Prynne and little Pearl came into the market-place. It was already thronged with the craftsmen and other plebeian inhabitants of the town, in considerable numbers; among whom, likewise, were many rough figures, whose attire of deer-skins marked them as belonging to some of the forest settlements, which surrounded the little metropolis of the colony.

On this public holiday, as on all other occasions, for seven years past, Hester was clad in a garment of coarse gray cloth. Not more by its hue than by some indescribable peculiarity in its fashion, it had the effect of making her fade personally out of sight and outline; while, again, the scarlet letter brought her back from this twilight indistinctness, and revealed her under the moral aspect of its own illumination. Her face, so long familiar to the townspeople, showed the marble quietude which they were accustomed to behold there. It was like a mask; or rather, like the frozen calmness of a dead woman's features; owing this dreary resemblance to the fact that Hester was actually dead, in respect to any claim of sympathy, and had departed out of the world with which she still seemed to mingle.

It might be, on this one day, that there was an expression unseen before, nor, indeed, vivid enough to be detected now; unless some preternaturally gifted observer should have first read the heart, and have afterwards sought a corresponding development in the countenance and mien. Such a spiritual seer might have conceived, that, after sustaining the gaze of the multitude through seven miserable years as a necessity, a penance, and something which it was a stern religion to endure, she now, for one last time more, encountered it freely and voluntarily, in order to convert what had so long been agony into a kind of triumph. "Look your last on the scarlet letter and its wearer!"—the people's victim and lifelong bond-slave, as they fancied her, might say to them. "Yet a little while, and she will be beyond your reach! A few hours longer, and the deep, mysterious ocean will quench and hide for ever the symbol which ye have caused to burn upon her bosom!" Nor were it an inconsistency too improbable to be assigned to human nature, should we suppose a feeling of regret in Hester's mind, at the moment when she was about to win her freedom from the pain which had been thus deeply incorporated with her being. Might there not be an irresistible desire to quaff a last, long, breathless draught of the cup of wormwood and aloes, with which nearly all her years of womanhood had been perpetually flavored? The wine of life, henceforth to be presented to her lips, must be indeed rich, delicious, and exhilarating, in its chased and golden beaker; or else leave an inevitable and weary languor, after the lees of bitterness wherewith she had been drugged, as with a cordial of intensest potency.

Pearl was decked out with airy gayety. It would have been impossible to guess that this bright and sunny apparition owed its existence to the shape of gloomy gray; or that a fancy, at once so gorgeous and so delicate as must have been requisite to contrive the child's apparel, was the same that had achieved a task perhaps more difficult, in imparting so distinct a peculiarity to Hester's simple robe. The dress, so proper was it to little Pearl, seemed an effluence, or inevitable development and outward manifestation of her character, no more to be separated from her than the many-hued brilliancy from a butterfly's wing, or the painted glory from the leaf of a bright flower. As with these, so with the child; her garb was all of one idea with her nature. On this eventful day, moreover, there was a certain singular inquietude and excitement in her mood, resembling nothing so much as the shimmer of a diamond, that sparkles and flashes with the varied throbbings of the breast on which it is displayed. Children have always a sympathy in the agitations of those connected with them; always, especially, a sense of any trouble or impending revolution, of whatever kind, in domestic circumstances; and therefore Pearl, who was the gem on her mother's unquiet bosom, betrayed, by the very dance of her spirits, the emotions which none could detect in the marble passiveness of Hester's brow.

This effervescence made her flit with a bird-like movement, rather than walk by her mother's side. She broke continually into shouts of a wild, inarticulate, and sometimes piercing music. When they reached the market-place, she became still more restless, on perceiving the stir and bustle that enlivened the spot; for it was usually more like the broad and lonesome green before a village meeting-house, than the centre of a town's business.

"Why, what is this, mother?" cried she. "Wherefore have all the people left their work to-day? Is it a play-day for the whole world? See, there is the blacksmith! He has washed his sooty face, and put on his Sabbath-day clothes, and looks, as if he would gladly be merry, if any kind body would only teach him how! And there is Master Brackett, the old jailer, nodding and smiling at me. Why does he do so, mother?"

"He remembers thee a little babe, my child," answered Hester.

"He should not nod and smile at me, for all that,—the black, grim, ugly-eyed old man!" said Pearl. "He may nod at thee if he will; for thou art clad in gray, and wearest the scarlet letter. But, see, mother, how many faces of strange people, and Indians among them, and sailors! What have they all come to do here in the market-place?"

"They wait to see the procession pass," said Hester. "For the Governor and the magistrates are to go by, and the ministers, and all the great people and good people, with the music, and the soldiers marching before them."

"And will the minister be there?" asked Pearl. "And will he hold out both his hands to me, as when thou ledst me to him from the brook-side?"

"He will be there, child," answered her mother. "But he will not greet thee today; nor must thou greet him."

"What a strange, sad man is he!" said the child, as if speaking partly to herself. "In the dark night-time, he calls us to him, and holds thy hand and mine, as when we stood with him on the scaffold yonder! And in the deep forest, where only the old trees can hear, and the strip of sky see it, he talks with thee, sitting on a heap of moss! And he kisses my forehead, too, so that the little brook would hardly wash it off! But here in the sunny day, and among all the people, he knows us not; nor must we know him! A strange, sad man is he, with his hand always over his heart!"

"Be quiet, Pearl! Thou understandest not these things," said her mother. "Think not now of the minister, but look about thee, and see how cheery is every body's face to-day. The children have come from their schools, and the grown people from their workshops and their fields, on purpose to be happy. For, to-day, a new man is beginning to rule over them; and so—as has been the custom of mankind ever since a nation was first gathered—they make merry and rejoice; as if a good and golden year were at length to pass over the poor old world!"

It was as Hester said, in regard to the unwonted jollity that brightened the faces of the people. Into this festal season of the year—as it already was, and continued to be during the greater part of two centuries—the Puritans compressed whatever mirth and public joy they deemed allowable to human infirmity; thereby so far dispelling the customary cloud, that, for the space of single holiday, they appeared scarcely more grave than most other communities at a period of general affliction.

But we perhaps exaggerate the gray or sable tinge, which undoubtedly characterized the mood and manners of the age. The persons now in the market-place of Boston had not been born to an inheritance of Puritanic gloom. They were native Englishmen, whose fathers had lived in the sunny richness of the Elizabethan epoch; a time when the life of England, viewed as one great mass, would appear to have been as stately, magnificent, and joyous, as the world has ever witnessed. Had they followed their hereditary taste, the New England settlers would have illustrated all events of public importance by bonfires, banquets, pageantries, and processions. Nor would it have been impracticable, in the observance of majestic ceremonies, to combine mirthful recreation with solemnity, and give, as it were, a grotesque and brilliant embroidery to the great robe of state, which a nation, at such festivals, puts on. There was some shadow of an attempt of this kind in the mode of celebrating the day on which the political year of the colony commenced. The dim reflection of a remembered splendor, a colorless and manifold diluted repetition of what they had beheld in proud old London,—we will not say at a royal coronation, but at a Lord Mayor's show,—might be traced in the customs which our forefathers instituted, with reference to the annual installation of magistrates. The fathers and founders of the commonwealth—the statesman, the priest, and the soldier—deemed it a duty then to assume the outward state and majesty, which, in accordance with antique style, was looked upon as the proper garb of public or social eminence. All came forth, to move in procession before the people's eye, and thus impart a needed dignity to the simple framework of a government so newly constructed.

Then, too, the people were countenanced, if not encouraged, in relaxing the severe and close application to their various modes of rugged industry, which, at all other times, seemed of the same piece and material with their religion. Here, it is true, were none of the appliances which popular merriment would so readily have found in the England of Elizabeth's time, or that of James;—no rude shows of a theatrical kind; no minstrel with his harp and legendary ballad, nor gleeman, with an ape dancing to his music; no juggler, with his tricks of mimic witchcraft; no Merry Andrew, to stir up the multitude with jests, perhaps hundreds of years old, but still effective, by their appeals to the very broadest sources of mirthful sympathy. All such professors of the several branches of jocularity would have been sternly repressed, not only by the rigid discipline of law, but by the general sentiment which gives law its vitality. Not the less, however, the great, honest face of the people smiled, grimly, perhaps, but widely too. Nor were sports wanting, such as the colonists had witnessed, and shared in, long ago, at the country fairs and on the village-greens of England; and which it was thought well to keep alive on this new soil, for the sake of the courage and manliness that were essential in them. Wrestling-matches, in the differing fashions of Cornwall and Devonshire, were seen here and there about the marketplace; in one corner, there was a friendly bout at quarterstaff: and—what attracted most interest of all—on the platform of the pillory, already so noted in our pages, two masters of defence were commencing an exhibition with the buckler and broadsword. But, much to the disappointment of the crowd, this latter business was broken off by the interposition of the town beadle, who had no idea of permitting the majesty of the law to be violated by such an abuse of one of its consecrated places.

It may not be too much to affirm, on the whole, (the people being then in the first stages of joyless deportment, and the offspring of sires who had known how to be merry, in their day,) that they would compare favorably, in point of holiday keeping, with their descendants, even at so long an interval as ourselves. Their immediate posterity, the generation next to the early emigrants, wore the blackest shade of Puritanism, and so darkened the national visage with it, that all the subsequent years have not sufficed to clear it up. We have yet to learn again the forgotten art of gayety.

The picture of human life in the market-place, though its general tint was the sad gray, brown, or black of the English emigrants, was yet enlivened by some diversity of hue. A party of Indians—in their savage finery of curiously embroidered deer-skin robes, wampum-belts, red and yellow ochre, and feathers, and armed with the bow and arrow and stone-headed spear—stood apart, with countenances of inflexible gravity, beyond what even the Puritan aspect could attain. Nor, wild as were these painted barbarians, were they the wildest feature of the scene. This distinction could most justly be claimed by some mariners,—a part of the crew of the vessel from the Spanish Main,—who had come ashore to see the humors of Election Day. They were rough-looking desperadoes, with sun-blackened faces, and an immensity of beard; their wide, short trousers were confined about the waist by belts, often clasped with a rough plate of gold, and sustaining always a long knife, and, in some instances, a sword. From beneath their broad-brimmed hats of palm-leaf, gleamed eyes which, even in good nature and merriment, had a kind of animal ferocity. They transgressed, without fear or scruple, the rules of behaviour that were binding on all others; smoking tobacco under the beadle's very nose, although each whiff would have cost a townsman a shilling; and quaffing, at their pleasure, draughts of wine or aqua-vitæ from pocket-flasks, which they freely tendered to the gaping crowd around them. It remarkably characterized the incomplete morality of the age, rigid as we call it, that a license was allowed the seafaring class, not merely for their freaks on shore, but for far more desperate deeds on their proper element. The sailor of that day would go near to be arraigned as a pirate in our own. There could be little doubt, for instance, that this very ship's crew, though no unfavorable specimens of the nautical brotherhood, had been guilty, as we should phrase it, of depredations on the Spanish commerce, such as would have perilled all their necks in a modern court of justice.

But the sea, in those old times, heaved, swelled, and foamed very much at its own will, or subject only to the tempestuous wind, with hardly any attempts at regulation by human law. The buccaneer on the wave might relinquish his calling, and become at once, if he chose, a man of probity and piety on land; nor, even in the full career of his reckless life, was he regarded as a personage with whom it was disreputable to traffic, or casually associate. Thus, the Puritan elders, in their black cloaks, starched bands, and steeple-crowned hats, smiled not unbenignantly at the clamor and rude deportment of these jolly seafaring men; and it excited neither surprise nor animadversion when so reputable a citizen as old Roger Chillingworth, the physician, was seen to enter the market-place, in close and familiar talk with the commander of the questionable vessel.

The latter was by far the most showy and gallant figure, so far as apparel went, anywhere to be seen among the multitude. He wore a profusion of ribbons on his garment, and gold lace on his hat, which was also encircled by a gold chain, and surmounted with a feather. There was a sword at his side, and a sword-cut on his forehead, which, by the arrangement of his hair, he seemed anxious rather to display than hide. A landsman could hardly have worn this garb and shown this face, and worn and shown them both with such a galliard air, without undergoing stern question before a magistrate, and probably incurring fine or imprisonment, or perhaps an exhibition in the stocks. As regarded the shipmaster, however, all was looked upon as pertaining to the character, as to a fish his glistening scales.

After parting from the physician, the commander of the Bristol ship strolled idly through the market-place; until, happening to approach the spot where Hester Prynne was standing, he appeared to recognize, and did not hestitate to address her. As was usually the case wherever Hester stood, a small, vacant area—a sort of magic circle—had formed itself about her, into which, though the people were elbowing one another at a little distance, none ventured, or felt disposed to intrude. It was a forcible type of the moral solitude in which the scarlet letter enveloped its fated wearer; partly by her own reserve, and partly by the instinctive, though no longer so unkindly, withdrawal of her fellow-creatures. Now, if never before, it answered a good purpose, by enabling Hester and the seaman to speak together without risk of being overhead; and so changed was Hester Prynne's repute before the public, that the matron in town most eminent for rigid morality could not have held such intercourse with less result of scandal than herself.

"So, mistress," said the mariner, "I must bid the steward make ready one more berth than you bargained for! No fear of scurvy or ship-fever, this voyage! What with the ship's surgeon and this other doctor, our only danger will be from drug or pill; more by token, as there is a lot of apothecary's stuff aboard, which I traded for with a Spanish vessel."

"What mean you?" inquired Hester, startled more than she permitted to appear. "Have you another passenger?"

"Why, know you not," cried the shipmaster, "that this physician here—Chillingworth, he calls himself—is minded to try my cabin-fare with you? Ay, ay, you must have known it; for he tells me he is of your party, and a close friend to the gentleman you spoke of,—he that is in peril from these sour old Puritan rulers!"

"They know each other well, indeed," replied Hester, with a mien of calmness, though in the utmost consternation. "They have long dwelt together."

Nothing further passed between the mariner and Hester Prynne. But, at that instant, she beheld old Roger Chillingworth himself, standing in the remotest corner of the market-place, and smiling on her; a smile which—across the wide and bustling square, and through all the talk and laughter, and various thoughts, moods, and interests of the crowd—conveyed secret and fearful meaning.

CHAPTER XXII

THE PROCESSION

Before Hester Prynne could call together her thoughts, and consider what was practicable to be done in this new and startling aspect of affairs, the sound of military music was heard approaching along a contiguous street. It denoted the advance of the procession of magistrates and citizens, on its way towards the meeting-house; where, in compliance with a custom thus early established, and ever since observed, the Reverend Mr. Dimmesdale was to deliver an Election Sermon.

Soon the head of the procession showed itself, with a slow and stately march, turning a corner, and making its way across the market-place. First came the music. It comprised a variety of instruments, perhaps imperfectly adapted to one another, and played with no great skill, but yet attaining the great object for which the harmony of drum and clarion addresses itself to the multitude,—that of imparting a higher and more heroic air to the scene of life that passes before the eye. Little Pearl at first clapped her hands, but then lost, for an instant, the restless agitation that had kept her in a continual effervescence throughout the morning; she gazed silently, and seemed to be borne upward, like a floating seabird, on the long heaves and swells of sound. But she was brought back to her former mood by the shimmer of the sunshine on the weapons and bright armour of the military company, which followed after the music, and formed the honorary escort of the procession. This body of soldiery—which still sustains a corporate existence, and marches down from past ages with an ancient and honorable fame—was composed of no mercenary materials. Its ranks were filled with gentlemen, who felt the stirrings of martial impulse, and sought to establish a kind of College of Arms, where, as in an association of Knights Templars, they might learn the science, and, so far as peaceful exercise would teach them, the practices of war. The high estimation then placed upon the military character might be seen in the lofty port of each individual member of the company. Some of them, indeed, by their services in the Low Countries and on other fields of European warfare, had fairly won their title to assume the name and pomp of soldiership. The entire array, moreover, clad in burnished steel, and with plumage nodding over their bright morions, had a brilliancy of effect which no modern display can aspire to equal.

And yet the men of civil eminence, who came immediately behind the military escort, were better worth a thoughtful observer's eye. Even in outward demeanour they showed a stamp of majesty that made the warrior's haughty stride look vulgar, if not absurd. It was an age when what we call talent had far less consideration than now, but the massive materials which produce stability and dignity of character a great deal more. The people possessed, by hereditary right, the quality of reverence; which, in their descendants, if it survive at all, exists in smaller proportion, and with a vastly diminished force in the selection and estimate of public men. The change may be for good or ill, and is partly, perhaps, for both. In that old day, the English settler on these rude shores,—having left king, nobles, and all degrees of awful rank behind, while still the faculty and necessity of reverence were strong in him,—bestowed it on the white hair and venerable brow of age; on long-tried integrity; on solid wisdom and sad-colored experience; on endowments of that grave and weighty order, which gives the idea of permanence, and comes under the general definition of respectability. These primitive statesmen, therefore,—Bradstreet, Endicott, Dudley, Bellingham, and their compeers,—who were elevated to power by the early choice of the people, seem to have been not often brilliant, but distinguished by a ponderous sobriety, rather than activity of intellect. They had fortitude and self-reliance, and, in time of difficulty or peril, stood up for the welfare of the state like a line of cliffs against a tempestuous tide. The traits of character here indicated were well represented in the square cast of countenance and large physical development of the new colonial magistrates. So far as a demeanour of natural authority was concerned, the mother country need not have been ashamed to see these foremost men of an actual democracy adopted into the House of Peers, or made the Privy Council of the sovereign.

Next in order to the magistrates came the young and eminently distinguished divine, from whose lips the religious discourse of the anniversary was expected. His was the profession, at that era, in which intellectual ability displayed itself far more than in political life; for—leaving a higher motive out of the question—it offered inducements powerful enough, in the almost worshipping respect of the community, to win the most aspiring ambition into its service. Even political power—as in the case of Increase Mather—was within the grasp of a successful priest.

It was the observation of those who beheld him now, that never, since Mr. Dimmesdale first set his foot on the New England shore, had he exhibited such energy as was seen in the gait and air with which he kept his pace in the procession. There was no feebleness of step, as at other times; his frame was not bent; nor did his hand rest ominously upon his heart. Yet, if the clergyman were rightly viewed, his strength seemed not of the body. It might be spiritual, and imparted to him by angelic ministrations. It might be the exhilaration of that potent cordial which is distilled only in the furnace-glow of earnest and long-continued thought. Or, perchance, his sensitive temperament was invigorated by the loud and piercing music, that swelled heavenward, and uplifted him on its ascending wave. Nevertheless, so abstracted was his look, it might be questioned whether Mr. Dimmesdale even heard the music. There was his body, moving onward, and with an unaccustomed force. But where was his mind? Far and deep in its own region, busying itself, with preternatural activity, to marshal a procession of stately thoughts that were soon to issue thence; and so he saw nothing, heard nothing, knew nothing, of what was around him; but the spiritual element took up the feeble frame, and carried it along, unconscious of the burden, and converting it to spirit like itself. Men of uncommon intellect, who have grown morbid, possess this occasional power of mighty effort, into which they throw the life of many days, and then are lifeless for as many more.

Hester Prynne, gazing steadfastly at the clergyman, felt a dreary influence come over her, but wherefore or whence she knew not; unless that he seemed so remote from her own sphere, and utterly beyond her reach. One glance of recognition, she had imagined, must needs pass between them. She thought of the dim forest, with its little dell of solitude, and love, and anguish, and the mossy tree-trunk, where, sitting hand in hand, they had mingled their sad and passionate talk with the melancholy murmur of the brook. How deeply had they known each other then! And was this the man? She hardly knew him now! He, moving proudly past, enveloped, as it were, in the rich music, with the procession of majestic and venerable fathers; he, so unattainable in his worldly position, and still more so in that far vista of his unsympathizing thoughts, through which she now beheld him! Her spirit sank with the idea that all must have been a delusion, and that, vividly as she had dreamed it, there could be no real bond betwixt the clergyman and herself. And thus much of woman was there in Hester, that she could scarcely forgive him,—least of all now, when the heavy footstep of their approaching Fate might be heard, nearer, nearer, nearer!—for being able so completely to withdraw himself from their mutual world; while she groped darkly, and stretched forth her cold hands, and found him not.

Pearl either saw and responded to her mother's feelings, or herself felt the remoteness and intangibility that had fallen around the minister. While the procession passed, the child was uneasy, fluttering up and down, like a bird on the point of taking flight. When the whole had gone by, she looked up into Hester's face.

"Mother," said she, "was that the same minister that kissed me by the brook?"

"Hold thy peace, dear little Pearl!" whispered her mother. "We must not always talk in the market-place of what happens to us in the forest."

"I could not be sure that it was he; so strange he looked," continued the child. "Else I would have run to him, and bid him kiss me now, before all the people; even as he did yonder among the dark old trees. What would the minister have said, mother? Would he have clapped his hand over his heart, and scowled on me, and bid me begone?"

"What should he say, Pearl," answered Hester, "save that it was no time to kiss, and that kisses are not to be given in the market-place? Well for thee, foolish child, that thou didst not speak to him!"

Another shade of the same sentiment, in reference to Mr. Dimmesdale, was expressed by a person whose eccentricities—or insanity, as we should term it—led her to do what few of the townspeople would have ventured on; to begin a conversation with the wearer of the scarlet letter, in public. It was Mistress Hibbins, who, arrayed in great magnificence, with a triple ruff, a broidered stomacher, a gown of rich velvet, and a gold-headed cane, had come forth to see the procession. As this ancient lady had the renown (which subsequently cost her no less a price than her life) of being a principal actor in all the works of necromancy that were continually going forward, the crowd gave way before her, and seemed to fear the touch of her garment, as if it carried the plague among its gorgeous folds. Seen in conjunction with Hester Prynne,—kindly as so many now felt towards the latter,—the dread inspired by Mistress Hibbins was doubled, and caused a general movement from that part of the market-place in which the two women stood.

"Now, what mortal imagination could conceive it!" whispered the old lady confidentially to Hester. "Yonder divine man! That saint on earth, as the people uphold him to be, and as—I must needs say—he really looks! Who, now, that saw him pass in the procession, would think how little while it is since he went forth out of his study,—chewing a Hebrew text of Scripture in his mouth, I warrant,—to take an airing in the forest! Aha! we know what that means, Hester Prynne! But, truly, forsooth, I find it hard to believe him the same man. Many a church-member saw I, walking behind the music, that has danced in the same measure with me, when Somebody was fiddler, and, it might be, an Indian powwow or a Lapland wizard changing hands with us! That is but a trifle, when a woman knows the world. But this minister! Couldst thou surely tell, Hester, whether he was the same man that encountered thee on the forest-path?"

"Madam, I know not of what you speak," answered Hester Prynne, feeling Mistress Hibbins to be of infirm mind; yet strangely startled and awe-stricken by the confidence with which she affirmed a personal connection between so many persons (herself among them) and the Evil One. "It is not for me to talk lightly of a learned and pious minister of the Word, like the Reverend Mr. Dimmesdale!"

"Fie, woman, fie!" cried the old lady, shaking her finger at Hester. "Dost thou think I have been to the forest so many times, and have yet no skill to judge who else has been there? Yea; though no leaf of the wild garlands, which they wore while they danced, be left in their hair! I know thee, Hester; for I behold the token. We may all see it in the sunshine; and it glows like a red flame in the dark. Thou wearest it openly; so there need be no question about that. But this minister! Let me tell thee in thine ear! When the Black Man sees one of his own servants, signed and sealed, so shy of owning to the bond as is the Reverend Mr. Dimmesdale, he hath a way of ordering matters so that the mark shall be disclosed in open daylight to the eyes of all the world! What is it that the minister seeks to hide, with his hand always over his heart? Ha, Hester Prynne!"

"What is it, good Mistress Hibbins?" eagerly asked little Pearl. "Hast thou seen it?"

"No matter, darling!" responded Mistress Hibbins, making Pearl a profound reverence. "Thou thyself wilt see it, one time or another. They say, child, thou art of the lineage of the Prince of the Air! Wilt thou ride with me, some fine night, to see thy father? Then thou shalt know wherefore the minister keeps his hand over his heart!"

Laughing so shrilly that all the market-place could hear her, the weird old gentlewoman took her departure.

By this time the preliminary prayer had been offered in the meeting-house, and the accents of the Reverend Mr. Dimmesdale were heard commencing his discourse. An irresistible feeling kept Hester near the spot. As the sacred edifice was too much thronged to admit another auditor, she took up her position close beside the scaffold of the pillory. It was in sufficient proximity to bring the whole sermon to her ears, in the shape of an indistinct, but varied, murmur and flow of the minister's very peculiar voice.

This vocal organ was in itself a rich endowment; insomuch that a listener, comprehending nothing of the language in which the preacher spoke, might still have been swayed to and fro by the mere tone and cadence. Like all other music, it breathed passion and pathos, and emotions high or tender, in a tongue native to the human heart, wherever educated. Muffled as the sound was by its passage through the church-walls, Hester Prynne listened with such intentness, and sympathized so intimately, that the sermon had throughout a meaning for her, entirely apart from its indistinguishable words. These, perhaps, if more distinctly heard, might have been only a grosser medium, and have clogged the spiritual sense. Now she caught the low undertone, as of the wind sinking down to repose itself; then ascended with it, as it rose through progressive gradations of sweetness and power, until its volume seemed to envelop her with an atmosphere of awe and solemn grandeur. And yet, majestic as the voice sometimes became, there was for ever in it an essential character of plaintiveness. A loud or low expression of anguish,—the whisper, or the shriek, as it might be conceived, of suffering humanity, that touched a sensibility in every bosom! At times this deep strain of pathos was all that could be heard, and scarcely heard, sighing amid a desolate silence. But even when the minister's voice grew high and commanding,—when it gushed irrepressibly upward,—when it assumed its utmost breadth and power, so overfilling the church as to burst its way through the solid walls, and diffuse itself in the open air,—still, if the auditor listened intently, and for the purpose, he could detect the same cry of pain. What was it? The complaint of a human heart, sorrow-laden, perchance guilty, telling its secret, whether of guilt or sorrow, to the great heart of mankind; beseeching its sympathy or forgiveness,—at every moment,—in each accent,—and never in vain! It was this profound and continual undertone that gave the clergyman his most appropriate power.

During all this time Hester stood, statue-like, at the foot of the scaffold. If the minister's voice had not kept her there, there would nevertheless have been an inevitable magnetism in that spot, whence she dated the first hour of her life of ignominy. There was a sense within her,—too ill-defined to be made a thought, but weighing heavily on her mind,—that her whole orb of life, both before and after, was connected with this spot, as with the one point that gave it unity.

Little Pearl, meanwhile, had quitted her mother's side, and was playing at her own will about the market-place. She made the sombre crowd cheerful by her erratic and glistening ray; even as a bird of bright plumage illuminates a whole tree of dusky foliage by darting to and fro, half seen and half concealed, amid the twilight of the clustering leaves. She had an undulating, but, oftentimes, a sharp and irregular movement. It indicated the restless vivacity of her spirit, which to-day was doubly indefatigable in its tiptoe dance, because it was played upon and vibrated with her mother's disquietude. Whenever Pearl saw any thing to excite her ever active and wandering curiosity, she flew thitherward, and, as we might say, seized upon that man or thing as her own property, so far as she desired it; but without yielding the minutest degree of control over her motions in requital. The Puritans looked on, and, if they smiled, were none the less inclined to pronounce the child a demon offspring, from the indescribable charm of beauty and eccentricity that shone through her little figure, and sparkled with its activity. She ran and looked the wild Indian in the face; and he grew conscious of a nature wilder than his own. Thence, with native audacity, but still with a reserve as characteristic, she flew into the midst of a group of mariners, the swarthy-cheeked wild men of the ocean, as the Indians were of the land; and they gazed wonderingly and admiringly at Pearl, as if a flake of the sea-foam had taken the shape of a little maid, and were gifted with a soul of the sea-fire, that flashes beneath the prow in the night-time.

One of these seafaring men—the shipmaster, indeed, who had spoken to Hester Prynne—was so smitten with Pearl's aspect, that he attempted to lay hands upon her, with purpose to snatch a kiss. Finding it as impossible to touch her as to catch a humming-bird in the air, he took from his hat the gold chain that was twisted about it, and threw it to the child. Pearl immediately twined it around her neck and waist, with such happy skill, that, once seen there, it became a part of her, and it was difficult to imagine her without it.

"Thy mother is yonder woman with the scarlet letter," said the seaman. "Wilt thou carry her a message from me?"

"If the message pleases me I will," answered Pearl.

"Then tell her," rejoined he, "that I spake again with the black-a-visaged, hump-shouldered old doctor, and he engages to bring his friend, the gentleman she wots of, aboard with him. So let thy mother take no thought, save for herself and thee. Wilt thou tell her this, thou witch-baby?"

"Mistress Hibbins says my father is the Prince of the Air!" cried Pearl, with her naughty smile. "If thou callest me that ill name, I shall tell him of thee; and he will chase thy ship with a tempest!"

Pursuing a zigzag course across the market-place, the child returned to her mother, and communicated what the mariner had said. Hester's strong, calm, steadfastly enduring spirit almost sank, at last, on beholding this dark and grim countenance of an inevitable doom, which—at the moment when a passage seemed to open for the minister and herself out of their labyrinth of misery—showed itself, with an unrelenting smile, right in the midst of their path.

With her mind harassed by the terrible perplexity in which the shipmaster's intelligence involved her, she was also subjected to another trial. There were many people present, from the country roundabout, who had often heard of the scarlet letter, and to whom it had been made terrific by a hundred false or exaggerated rumors, but who had never beheld it with their own bodily eyes. These, after exhausting other modes of amusement, now thronged about Hester Prynne with rude and boorish intrusiveness. Unscrupulous as it was, however, it could not bring them nearer than a circuit of several yards. At that distance they accordingly stood, fixed there by the centrifugal force of the repugnance which the mystic symbol inspired. The whole gang of sailors, likewise, observing the press of spectators, and learning the purport of the scarlet letter, came and thrust their sunburnt and desperado-looking faces into the ring. Even the Indians were affected by a sort of cold shadow of the white man's curiosity, and, gliding through the crowd, fastened their snakelike black eyes on Hester's bosom; conceiving, perhaps, that the wearer of this brilliantly embroidered badge must needs be a personage of high dignity among her people. Lastly, the inhabitants of the town (their own interest in this worn-out subject languidly reviving itself, by sympathy with what they saw others feel) lounged idly to the same quarter, and tormented Hester Prynne, perhaps more than all the rest, with their cool, well-acquainted gaze at her familiar shame. Hester saw and recognized the self-same faces of that group of matrons, who had awaited her forthcoming from the prison-door, seven years ago; all save one, the youngest and only compassionate among them, whose burial-robe she had since made. At the final hour, when she was so soon to fling aside the burning letter, it had strangely become the centre of more remark and excitement, and was thus made to sear her breast more painfully than at any time since the first day she put it on.

While Hester stood in that magic circle of ignominy, where the cunning cruelty of her sentence seemed to have fixed her for ever, the admirable preacher was looking down from the sacred pulpit upon an audience, whose very inmost spirits had yielded to his control. The sainted minister in the church! The woman of the scarlet letter in the marketplace! What imagination would have been irreverent enough to surmise that the same scorching stigma was on them both?

CHAPTER XXIII

THE REVELATION OF THE SCARLET LETTER

The eloquent voice, on which the souls of the listening audience had been borne aloft, as on the swelling waves of the sea, at length came to a pause. There was a momentary silence, profound as what should follow the utterance of oracles. Then ensued a murmur and half-hushed tumult; as if the auditors, released from the high spell that had transported them into the region of another's mind, were returning into themselves, with all their awe and wonder still heavy on them. In a moment more, the crowd began to gush forth from the doors of the church. Now that there was an end, they needed other breath, more fit to support the gross and earthly life into which they relapsed, than that atmosphere which the preacher had converted into words of flame, and had burdened with the rich fragrance of his thought.

In the open air their rapture broke into speech. The street and the market-place absolutely babbled, from side to side, with applauses of the minister. His hearers could not rest until they had told one another of what each knew better than he could tell or hear. According to their united testimony, never had man spoken in so wise, so high, and so holy a spirit, as he that spake this day; nor had inspiration ever breathed through mortal lips more evidently than it did through his. Its influence could be seen, as it were, descending upon him, and possessing him, and continually lifting him out of the written discourse that lay before him, and filling him with ideas that must have been as marvellous to himself as to his audience. His subject, it appeared, had been the relation between the Deity and the communities of mankind, with a special reference to the New England which they were here planting in the wilderness. And, as he drew towards the close, a spirit as of prophecy had come upon him, constraining him to its purpose as mightily as the old prophets of Israel were constrained; only with this difference, that, whereas the Jewish seers had denounced judgments and ruin on their country, it was his mission to foretell a high and glorious destiny for the newly gathered people of the Lord. But, throughout it all, and through the whole discourse, there had been a certain deep, sad undertone of pathos, which could not be interpreted otherwise than as the natural regret of one soon to pass away. Yes; their minister whom they so loved—and who so loved them all, that he could not depart heavenward without a sigh—had the foreboding of untimely death upon him, and would soon leave them in their tears! This idea of his transitory stay on earth gave the last emphasis to the effect which the preacher had produced; it was as if an angel, in his passage to the skies, had shaken his bright wings over the people for an instant,—at once a shadow and a splendor,—and had shed down a shower of golden truths upon them.

Thus, there had come to the Reverend Mr. Dimmesdale—as to most men, in their various spheres, though seldom recognized until they see it far behind them—an epoch of life more brilliant and full of triumph than any previous one, or than any which could hereafter be. He stood, at this moment, on the very proudest eminence of superiority, to which the gifts of intellect, rich lore, prevailing eloquence, and a reputation of whitest sanctity, could exalt a clergyman in New England's earliest days, when the professional character was of itself a lofty pedestal. Such was the position which the minister occupied, as he bowed his head forward on the cushions of the pulpit, at the close of his Election Sermon. Meanwhile, Hester Prynne was standing beside the scaffold of the pillory, with the scarlet letter still burning on her breast!

Now was heard again the clangor of the music, and the measured tramp of the military escort, issuing from the church-door. The procession was to be marshalled thence to the town-hall, where a solemn banquet would complete the ceremonies of the day.

Once more, therefore, the train of venerable and majestic fathers was seen moving through a broad pathway of the people, who drew back reverently, on either side, as the Governor and magistrates, the old and wise men, the holy ministers, and all that were eminent and renowned, advanced into the midst of them. When they were fairly in the marketplace, their presence was greeted by a shout. This—though doubtless it might acquire additional force and volume from the childlike loyalty which the age awarded to its rulers—was felt to be an irrepressible outburst of the enthusiasm kindled in the auditors by that high strain of eloquence which was yet reverberating in their ears. Each felt the impulse in himself, and, in the same breath, caught it from his neighbour. Within the church, it had hardly been kept down; beneath the sky, it pealed upward to the zenith. There were human beings enough, and enough of highly wrought and symphonious feeling, to produce that more impressive sound than the organ-tones of the blast, or the thunder, or the roar of the sea; even that mighty swell of many voices, blended into one great voice by the universal impulse which makes likewise one vast heart out of the many. Never, from the soil of New England, had gone up such a shout! Never, on New England soil, had stood the man so honored by his mortal brethren as the preacher!

How fared it with him then? Were there not the brilliant particles of a halo in the air about his head? So etherealized by spirit as he was, and so apotheosized by worshipping admirers, did his footsteps in the procession really tread upon the dust of earth?

As the ranks of military men and civil fathers moved onward, all eyes were turned towards the point where the minister was seen to approach among them. The shout died into a murmur, as one portion of the crowd after another obtained a glimpse of him. How feeble and pale he looked amid all his triumph! The energy—or say, rather, the inspiration which had held him up, until he should have delivered the sacred message that brought its own strength along with it from heaven—was withdrawn, now that it had so faithfully performed its office. The glow, which they had just before beheld burning on his cheek, was extinguished, like a flame that sinks down hopelessly among the late-decaying embers. It seemed hardly the face of a man alive, with such a deathlike hue; it was hardly a man with life in him, that tottered on his path so nervelessly, yet tottered, and did not fall!

One of his clerical brethren,—it was the venerable John Wilson,—observing the state in which Mr. Dimmesdale was left by the retiring wave of intellect and sensibility, stepped forward hastily to offer his support. The minister tremulously, but decidedly, repelled the old man's arm. He still walked onward, if that movement could be so described, which rather resembled the wavering effort of an infant, with its mother's arms in view, outstretched to tempt him forward. And now, almost imperceptible as were the latter steps of his progress, he had come opposite the well-remembered and weather-darkened scaffold, where, long since, with all that dreary lapse of time between, Hester Prynne had encountered the world's ignominious stare. There stood Hester, holding little Pearl by the hand! And there was the scarlet letter on her breast! The minister here made a pause; although the music still played the stately and rejoicing march to which the procession moved. It summoned him onward,—onward to the festival!—but here he made a pause.

Bellingham, for the last few moments, had kept an anxious eye upon him. He now left his own place in the procession, and advanced to give assistance; judging from Mr. Dimmesdale's aspect that he must otherwise inevitably fall. But there was something in the latter's expression that warned back the magistrate, although a man not readily obeying the vague intimations that pass from one spirit to another. The crowd, meanwhile, looked on with awe and wonder. This earthly faintness was, in their view, only another phase of the minister's celestial strength; nor would it have seemed a miracle too high to be wrought for one so holy, had he ascended before their eyes, waxing dimmer and brighter, and fading at last into the light of heaven!

He turned towards the scaffold, and stretched forth his arms.

"Hester," said he, "come hither! Come, my little Pearl!"

It was a ghastly look with which he regarded them; but there was something at once tender and strangely triumphant in it. The child, with the bird-like motion which was one of her characteristics, flew to him, and clasped her arms about his knees. Hester Prynne—slowly, as if impelled by inevitable fate, and against her strongest will—likewise drew near, but paused before she reached him. At this instant old Roger Chillingworth thrust himself through the crowd,—or, perhaps, so dark, disturbed, and evil was his look, he rose up out of some nether region,—to snatch back his victim from what he sought to do! Be that as it might, the old man rushed forward and caught the minister by the arm.

"Madman, hold! What is your purpose?" whispered he. "Wave back that woman! Cast off this child! All shall be well! Do not blacken your fame, and perish in dishonor! I can yet save you! Would you bring infamy on your sacred profession?"

"Ha, tempter! Methinks thou art too late!" answered the minister, encountering his eye, fearfully, but firmly. "Thy power is not what it was! With God's help, I shall escape thee now!"

He again extended his hand to the woman of the scarlet letter.

"Hester Prynne," cried he, with a piercing earnestness, "in the name of Him, so terrible and so merciful, who gives me grace, at this last moment, to do what—for my own heavy sin and miserable agony—I withheld myself from doing seven years ago, come hither now, and twine thy strength about me! Thy strength, Hester; but let it be guided by the will which God hath granted me! This wretched and wronged old man is opposing it with all his might!—with all his own might and the fiend's! Come, Hester, come! Support me up yonder scaffold!"

The crowd was in a tumult. The men of rank and dignity, who stood more immediately around the clergyman, were so taken by surprise, and so perplexed as to the purport of what they saw,—unable to receive the explanation which most readily presented itself, or to imagine any other,—that they remained silent and inactive spectators of the judgment which Providence seemed about to work. They beheld the minister, leaning on Hester's shoulder and supported by her arm around him, approach the scaffold, and ascend its steps; while still the little hand of the sin-born child was clasped in his. Old Roger Chillingworth followed, as one intimately connected with the drama of guilt and sorrow in which they had all been actors, and well entitled, therefore, to be present at its closing scene.

"Hadst thou sought the whole earth over," said he, looking darkly at the clergyman, "there was no one place so secret,—no high place nor lowly place, where thou couldst have escaped me,—save on this very scaffold!"

"Thanks be to Him who hath led me hither!" answered the minister.

Yet he trembled, and turned to Hester with an expression of doubt and anxiety in his eyes, not the less evidently betrayed, that there was a feeble smile upon his lips.

"Is not this better," murmured he, "than what we dreamed of in the forest?"

"I know not! I know not!" she hurriedly replied. "Better? Yea; so we may both die, and little Pearl die with us!"

"For thee and Pearl, be it as God shall order," said the minister; "and God is merciful! Let me now do the will which he hath made plain before my sight. For, Hester, I am a dying man. So let me make haste to take my shame upon me!"

Partly supported by Hester Prynne, and holding one hand of little Pearl's, the Reverend Mr. Dimmesdale turned to the dignified and venerable rulers; to the holy ministers, who were his brethren; to the people, whose great heart was thoroughly appalled, yet overflowing with tearful sympathy, as knowing that some deep life-matter—which, if full of sin, was full of anguish and repentance likewise—was now to be laid open to them. The sun, but little past its meridian, shone down upon the clergyman, and gave a distinctness to his figure, as he stood out from all the earth to put in his plea of guilty at the bar of Eternal Justice.

"People of New England!" cried he, with a voice that rose over them, high, solemn, and majestic,—yet had always a tremor through it, and sometimes a shriek, struggling up out of a fathomless depth of remorse and woe,—"ye, that have loved me!—ye, that have deemed me holy!—behold me here, the one sinner of the world! At last!—at last!—I stand upon the spot where, seven years since, I should have stood; here, with this woman, whose arm, more than the little strength wherewith I have crept hitherward, sustains me, at this dreadful moment, from grovelling down upon my face! Lo, the scarlet letter which Hester wears! Ye have all shuddered at it! Wherever her walk hath been,—wherever, so miserably burdened, she may have hoped to find repose,—it hath cast a lurid gleam of awe and horrible repugnance round about her. But there stood one in the midst of you, at whose brand of sin and infamy ye have not shuddered!"

It seemed, at this point, as if the minister must leave the remainder of his secret undisclosed. But he fought back the bodily weakness,—and, still more, the faintness of heart,—that was striving for the mastery with him. He threw off all assistance, and stepped passionately forward a pace before the woman and the child.

"It was on him!" he continued, with a kind of fierceness; so determined was he to speak out the whole. "God's eye beheld it! The angels were forever pointing at it! The Devil knew it well, and fretted it continually with the touch of his burning finger! But he hid it cunningly from men, and walked among you with the mien of a spirit, mournful, because so pure in a sinful world!—and sad, because he missed his heavenly kindred! Now, at the death-hour, he stands up before you! He bids you look again at Hester's scarlet letter! He tells you, that, with all its mysterious horror, it is but the shadow of what he bears on his own breast, and that even this, his own red stigma, is no more than the type of what has seared his inmost heart! Stand any here that question God's judgment on a sinner? Behold! Behold a dreadful witness of it!"

With a convulsive motion he tore away the ministerial band from before his breast. It was revealed! But it were irreverent to describe that revelation. For an instant the gaze of the horror-stricken multitude was concentred on the ghastly miracle; while the minister stood with a flush of triumph in his face, as one who, in the crisis of acutest pain, had won a victory. Then, down he sank upon the scaffold! Hester partly raised him, and supported his head against her bosom. Old Roger Chillingworth knelt down beside him, with a blank, dull countenance, out of which the life seemed to have departed.

"Thou hast escaped me!" he repeated more than once. "Thou hast escaped me!"

"May God forgive thee!" said the minister. "Thou, too, hast deeply sinned!"

He withdrew his dying eyes from the old man, and fixed them on the woman and the child.

"My little Pearl," said he feebly,—and there was a sweet and gentle smile over his face, as of a spirit sinking into deep repose; nay, now that the burden was removed, it seemed almost as if he would be sportive with the child,—"dear little Pearl, wilt thou kiss me now? Thou wouldst not yonder, in the forest! But now thou wilt?"

Pearl kissed his lips. A spell was broken. The great scene of grief, in which the wild infant bore a part, had developed all her sympathies; and as her tears fell upon her father's cheek, they were the pledge that she would grow up amid human joy and sorrow, nor for ever do battle with the world, but be a woman in it. Towards her mother, too, Pearl's errand as a messenger of anguish was all fulfilled.

"Hester," said the clergyman, "farewell!"

"Shall we not meet again?" whispered she, bending her face down close to his. "Shall we not spend our immortal life together? Surely, surely, we have ransomed one another, with all this woe! Thou lookest far into eternity, with those bright dying eyes! Then tell me what thou seest?"

"Hush, Hester, hush!" said he, with tremulous solemnity. "The law we broke!—the sin here so awfully revealed!—let these alone be in thy thoughts! I fear! I fear! It may be, that, when we forgot our God,—when we violated our reverence each for the other's soul,—it was thenceforth vain to hope that we could meet hereafter, in an everlasting and pure reunion. God knows; and He is merciful! He hath proved his mercy, most of all, in my afflictions. By giving me this burning torture to bear upon my breast! By sending yonder dark and terrible old man, to keep the torture always at red-heat! By bringing me hither, to die this death of triumphant ignominy before the people! Had either of these agonies been wanting, I had been lost for ever! Praised be his name! His will be done! Farewell!"

That final word came forth with the minister's expiring breath. The multitude, silent till then, broke out in a strange, deep voice of awe and wonder, which could not as yet find utterance, save in this murmur that rolled so heavily after the departed spirit.

CHAPTER XXIV

CONCLUSION

After many days, when time sufficed for the people to arrange their thoughts in reference to the foregoing scene, there was more than one account of what had been witnessed on the scaffold.

Most of the spectators testified to having seen, on the breast of the unhappy minister, a SCARLET LETTER—the very semblance of that worn by Hester Prynne—imprinted in the flesh. As regarded its origin, there were various explanations, all of which must necessarily have been conjectural. Some affirmed that the Reverend Mr. Dimmesdale, on the very day when Hester Prynne first wore her ignominious badge, had begun a course of penance,—which he afterwards, in so many futile methods, followed out,—by inflicting a hideous torture on himself. Others contended that the stigma had not been produced until a long time subsequent, when old Roger Chillingworth, being a potent necromancer, had caused it to appear, through the agency of magic and poisonous drugs. Others, again,—and those best able to appreciate the minister's peculiar sensibility, and the wonderful operation of his spirit upon the body,—whispered their belief, that the awful symbol was the effect of the ever active tooth of remorse, gnawing from the inmost heart outwardly, and at last manifesting Heaven's dreadful judgment by the visible presence of the letter. The reader may choose among these theories. We have thrown all the light we could acquire upon the portent, and would gladly, now that it has done its office, erase its deep print out of our own brain; where long meditation has fixed it in very undesirable distinctness.

It is singular, nevertheless, that certain persons, who were spectators of the whole scene, and professed never once to have removed their eyes from the Reverend Mr. Dimmesdale, denied that there was any mark whatever on his breast, more than on a new-born infant's. Neither, by their report, had his dying words acknowledged, nor even remotely implied, any, the slightest connection, on his part, with the guilt for which Hester Prynne had so long worn the scarlet letter. According to these highly respectable witnesses, the minister, conscious that he was dying,—conscious, also, that the reverence of the multitude placed him already among saints and angels,—had desired, by yielding up his breath in the arms of that fallen woman, to express to the world how utterly nugatory is the choicest of man's own righteousness. After exhausting life in his efforts for mankind's spiritual good, he had made the manner of his death a parable, in order to impress on his admirers the mighty and mournful lesson, that, in the view of Infinite Purity, we are sinners all alike. It was to teach them, that the holiest among us has but attained so far above his fellows as to discern more clearly the Mercy which looks down, and repudiate more utterly the phantom of human merit, which would look aspiringly upward. Without disputing a truth so momentous, we must be allowed to consider this version of Mr. Dimmesdale's story as only an instance of that stubborn fidelity with which a man's friends—and especially a clergyman's—will sometimes uphold his character; when proofs, clear as the mid-day sunshine on the scarlet letter, establish him a false and sin-stained creature of the dust.

The authority which we have chiefly followed—a manuscript of old date, drawn up from the verbal testimony of individuals, some of whom had known Hester Prynne, while others had heard the tale from contemporary witnesses—fully confirms the view taken in the foregoing pages. Among many morals which press upon us from the poor minister's miserable experience, we put only this into a sentence:—"Be true! Be true! Be true! Show freely to the world, if not your worst, yet some trait whereby the worst may be inferred!"

Nothing was more remarkable than the change which took place, almost immediately after Mr. Dimmesdale's death, in the appearance and demeanour of the old man known as Roger Chillingworth. All his strength and energy—all his vital and intellectual force—seemed at once to desert him; insomuch that he positively withered up, shrivelled away, and almost vanished from mortal sight, like an uprooted weed that lies wilting in the sun. This unhappy man had made the very principle of his life to consist in the pursuit and systematic exercise of revenge; and when, by its completest triumph and consummation, that evil principle was left with no further material to support it,—when, in short, there was no more devil's work on earth for him to do, it only remained for the unhumanized mortal to betake himself whither his Master would find him tasks enough, and pay him his wages duly. But, to all these shadowy beings, so long our near acquaintances,—as well Roger Chillingworth as his companions,—we would fain be merciful. It is a curious subject of observation and inquiry, whether hatred and love be not the same thing at bottom. Each, in its utmost development, supposes a high degree of intimacy and heart-knowledge; each renders one individual dependent for the food of his affections and spiritual life upon another; each leaves the passionate lover, or the no less passionate hater, forlorn and desolate by the withdrawal of his object.

Philosophically considered, therefore, the two passions seem essentially the same, except that one happens to be seen in a celestial radiance, and the other in a dusky and lurid glow. In the spiritual world, the old physician and the minister—mutual victims as they have been—may, unawares, have found their earthly stock of hatred and antipathy transmuted into golden love.

Leaving this discussion apart, we have a matter of business to communicate to the reader. At old Roger Chillingworth's decease (which took place within the year), and by his last will and testament, of which Governor Bellingham and the Reverend Mr. Wilson were executors, he bequeathed a very considerable amount of property, both here and in England, to little Pearl, the daughter of Hester Prynne.

So Pearl—the elf-child,—the demon offspring, as some people, up to that epoch, persisted in considering her—became the richest heiress of her day, in the New World. Not improbably, this circumstance wrought a very material change in the public estimation; and, had the mother and child remained here, little Pearl, at a marriageable period of life, might have mingled her wild blood with the lineage of the devoutest Puritan among them all. But, in no long time after the physician's death, the wearer of the scarlet letter disappeared, and Pearl along with her. For many years, though a vague report would now and then find its way across the sea,—like a shapeless piece of driftwood tost ashore, with the initials of a name upon it,—yet no tidings of them unquestionably authentic were received. The story of the scarlet letter grew into a legend. Its spell, however, was still potent, and kept the scaffold awful where the poor minister had died, and likewise the cottage by the sea-shore, where Hester Prynne had dwelt. Near this latter spot, one afternoon, some children were at play, when they beheld a tall woman, in a gray robe, approach the cottage-door. In all those years it had never once been opened; but either she unlocked it, or the decaying wood and iron yielded to her hand, or she glided shadow-like through these impediments,—and, at all events, went in.

On the threshold she paused,—turned partly round,—for, perchance, the idea of entering, all alone, and all so changed, the home of so intense a former life, was more dreary and desolate than even she could bear. But her hesitation was only for an instant, though long enough to display a scarlet letter on her breast.

And Hester Prynne had returned, and taken up her long-forsaken shame. But where was little Pearl? If still alive, she must now have been in the flush and bloom of early womanhood. None knew—nor ever learned, with the fulness of perfect certainty—whether the elf-child had gone thus untimely to a maiden grave; or whether her wild, rich nature had been softened and subdued, and made capable of a woman's gentle happiness. But, through the remainder of Hester's life, there were indications that the recluse of the scarlet letter was the object of love and interest with some inhabitant of another land. Letters came, with armorial seals upon them, though of bearings unknown to English heraldry. In the cottage there were articles of comfort and luxury, such as Hester never cared to use, but which only wealth could have purchased, and affection have imagined for her. There were trifles, too, little ornaments, beautiful tokens of a continual remembrance, that must have been wrought by delicate fingers, at the impulse of a fond heart. And, once, Hester was seen embroidering a baby-garment, with such a lavish richness of golden fancy as would have raised a public tumult, had any infant, thus apparelled, been shown to our sober-hued community.

In fine, the gossips of that day believed,—and Mr. Surveyor Pue, who made investigations a century later, believed,—and one of his recent successors in office, moreover, faithfully believes,—that Pearl was not only alive, but married, and happy, and mindful of her mother; and that she would most joyfully have entertained that sad and lonely mother at her fireside.

But there was a more real life for Hester Prynne here, in New England, than in that unknown region where Pearl had found a home. Here had been her sin; here, her sorrow; and here was yet to be her penitence. She had returned, therefore, and resumed,—of her own free will, for not the sternest magistrate of that iron period would have imposed it,—resumed the symbol of which we have related so dark a tale. Never afterwards did it quit her bosom. But, in the lapse of the toilsome, thoughtful, and self-devoted years that made up Hester's life, the scarlet letter ceased to be a stigma which attracted the world's scorn and bitterness, and became a type of something to be sorrowed over, and looked upon with awe, yet with reverence too. And, as Hester Prynne had no selfish ends, nor lived in any measure for her own profit and enjoyment, people brought all their sorrows and perplexities, and besought her counsel, as one who had herself gone through a mighty trouble. Women, more especially,—in the continually recurring trials of wounded, wasted, wronged, misplaced, or erring and sinful passion,—or with the dreary burden of a heart unyielded, because unvalued and unsought,—came to Hester's cottage, demanding why they were so wretched, and what the remedy! Hester comforted and counselled them, as best she might. She assured them, too, of her firm belief, that, at some brighter period, when the world should have grown ripe for it, in Heaven's own time, a new truth would be revealed, in order to establish the whole relation between man and woman on a surer ground of mutual happiness. Earlier in life, Hester had vainly imagined that she herself might be the destined prophetess, but had long since recognized the impossibility that any mission of divine and mysterious truth should be confided to a woman stained with sin, bowed down with shame, or even burdened with a life-long sorrow. The angel and apostle of the coming revelation must be a woman, indeed, but lofty, pure, and beautiful; and wise, moreover, not through dusky grief, but the ethereal medium of joy; and showing how sacred love should make us happy, by the truest test of a life successful to such an end!

So said Hester Prynne, and glanced her sad eyes downward at the scarlet letter. And, after many, many years a new grave was delved, near an old and sunken one, in that burial-ground beside which King's Chapel has since been built. It was near that old and sunken grave, yet with a space between, as if the dust of the two sleepers had no right to mingle. Yet one tombstone served for both. All around, there were monuments carved with armorial bearings; and on this simple slab of slate—as the curious investigator may still discern, and perplex himself with the purport—there appeared the semblance of an engraved escutcheon. It bore a device, a herald's wording of which might serve for a motto and brief description of our now concluded legend; so sombre is it, and relieved only by one ever-glowing point of light gloomier than the shadow:—

"ON A FIELD, SABLE, THE LETTER A, GULES."

THE END.

HERMAN MELVILLE
(1819–1891)

Herman Melville was a descendant of royalty in the Old World and revolutionary heroes in the New World. Wellborn like Cooper, he was more like Hawthorne in the fate of family fortune. Melville's father was a merchant of middle class gentry, but he lost his business and died in 1832, when Melville was thirteen. The early loss of his father furthered Melville's affinity with Hawthorne. Melville and his mother suffered the long humiliation of dependence on her wealthy and influential relatives, the Gansevoorts. To the end, Melville's perspective on life was deeply affected by the decline of his family's status.

Melville's family moved to Albany, New York in 1830. After holding various jobs there, and with only four years formal schooling, Melville struck out to find prosperity. He tried to secure a position as scrivener for a law firm in New York City. Fortunately for American literature, he failed. In 1839, at the age of nineteen, Melville signed on a merchant ship to Liverpool, England. He was at sea for four years. In the following four years, he published five novels based on his experiences as a sailor. *Typee*, the first, made him a great popular success. But by the time the fifth, *Moby Dick*, made its way to the public, Melville was a bitterly obscure writer. Seventy years later, its artistic success was celebrated in that phenomenon of American literary history, the Melville revival.

A vast multinational travel literature, especially sea travel, both nonfiction and fiction, existed, to which James Fenimore Cooper had made innovative contributions, and Richard Henry Dana had recently contributed *Two Years Before the Mast* (1840). *Typee, A Peep at Polynesian Life, During a Four Month's Residence in a Valley of the Marquesas* (1846) had the distinction of being the first modern novel of South Sea adventure, anticipating Somerset Maugham and Joseph Conrad. An immediate popular success, it was Melville's best-known novel for decades. The man who called himself "a pondering man" was notorious as "the man who lived among cannibals." Melville's second novel, *Omoo: A Narrative of Adventures in the South Seas* (1841), recounts his experiences after he escaped from the cannibals, was jailed for mutiny in Tahiti, escaped again, and became a beachcomber. Melville was the archetype of the venturesome young American novelist traveling to exotic places.

His third novel, *Mardi: And a Voyage Thither* (1849), was rejected by the public. The first half satisfied the public appetite for sea adventure, but in the second half,

Melville began to explore elements carried further in *Moby Dick*. It was full of quest symbolism and political allegory, presented in a murky style.

Melville won back his readers with the starkly realistic *Redburn, His First Voyage, Being the Sailor Boy Confessions and Reminiscences of the Son-of-A-Gentleman in the Merchant Service* (1849), based on his first voyage. From Tahiti, Melville had signed on a whaler as a harpooner bound for the Hawaiian Islands. From there, he signed on as a crewman on the American naval frigate *United States* to Boston. That ordeal formed the basis for his fourth novel *White-Jacket, or the World in A-Man-of-War* (1850). This was another episodic adventure story and another popular success, but it also presented a darker side—an expose of inhumane naval discipline. Melville's life of adventure ended at age twenty-five; his fame as a novelist ended at thirty.

In 1847, Melville married Elizabeth Shaw, daughter of a Chief Justice of Massachusetts. They settled in New York City, traveled in Europe in 1849, and in 1850 moved to "Arrowhead," a farm near Pittsfield, Massachusetts. Melville became friends with Hawthorne, fifteen years his senior, who was writing *The House of the Seven Gables*. Melville worked there on *Moby Dick, or The White Whale* (1851), now considered the first literary classic about whaling, and one of the world's great sea novels. It is less like Cooper's writing than like Conrad's. With the earlier *Mardi* and the later *Pierre* (1852), it formed a trilogy.

Moby Dick started out to be another fictional autobiography, an epic romance, containing the best elements of the previous novels. But Melville took it to darker depths, until it became the tragic epic of Captain Ahab's monomaniacal pursuit of the embodiment of evil in nature, the great albino whale. "Call me Ishmael," the narrator, an ordinary young adventurer, begins; he ends with the epilogue from Job: "And I only am escaped alone to tell thee." Here are two major motifs in all of Melville's fiction: the first person narrator, and the compulsion to tell more sedentary men about the symbolic but actual events in which he is a participating witness. Like many American novelists, Melville used facts as a basis for developing myths. Living on a factual level, Ishmael witnesses and is deeply affected by the tragic struggle of a flawed hero to control his destiny in a world of beautiful and terrible natural forces.

Moby Dick is almost as complex and encyclopedic as James Joyce's *Ulysses*. In a style influenced by the Bible, Elizabethan drama, and English poets, Melville successfully mixes allegory, symbolism, satire, vast research on seafaring and whaling, American folklore, religion, and philosophy. *Moby Dick* suffered the same fate with the public as *Mardi* did.

During the next six years, Melville published three more novels and a book of short fiction. The public continued to reject his tragic visions. The charge of immorality was added to obscurity once *Pierre, or the Ambiguities*, came out. It is a philosophical romance with elements of melodrama, which also involves brother-sister incest. Some critics consider Melville's mother's Calvinistic vision of life as having a crucial affect on his own, and she is usually considered to be the model for Pierre's mother. Melville could not win back his early admirers with *Israel Potter: His Fifty Years of Exile* (1855), based on an authentic autobiography, about a Revolutionary War soldier who wanders through London and Paris encountering famous men of his time, ending up as an "unknown soldier." Then came *The Piazza Tales* (1856), which includes three novellas: "Bartleby the Scrivener," "The Encantadas or Enchanted Isles," and "Benito Cereno."

Heavily in debt and on the verge of a nervous breakdown, Melville was rescued by his father-in-law, who financed a trip to Europe and the Holy Land. Melville and his wife returned to the United States in 1857, and settled again in New York City. In that year appeared his last novel, *The Confidence Man, His Masquerade*, ending eleven years of extraordinary productivity on a pessimistic note. The story is about the passengers on a Mississippi steamboat who prove the gullibility of man as each succumbs to a con man. Melville's satirical style anticipates the black humor of the 1960s.

From 1866 to 1885, Melville suffered the drudgery of working as Deputy Inspector of Customs in New York City, a position obtained through his mother's family's influence. With one exception, Melville's work over the twenty-five years preceding his death consists of poetry. *Battle Pieces and Aspects of the War*, now regarded as among the best poems inspired by the madness of the Civil War, appeared in 1866. He published three other volumes of poetry. One of them, *Clarel, A Poem and Pilgrimage in the Holy Land* (1876), is distinguished for its modern verse techniques. When Melville died, on September 28, 1891, at the age of 70, he left behind the manuscript of *Billy Budd, Sailor (An Inside Narrative)*. It was not published until 1924. The story reconciles the moral will of the individual with evil in the universe, and is considered now to be a masterpiece of the novella form.

MOBY DICK

ETYMOLOGY

(SUPPLIED BY A LATE CONSUMPTIVE USHER TO A GRAMMAR SCHOOL)

The pale Usher—threadbare in coat, heart, body, and brain; I see him now. He was ever dusting his old lexicons and grammars, with a queer handkerchief, mockingly embellished with all the gay flags of all the known nations of the world. He loved to dust his old grammars; it somehow mildly reminded him of his mortality.

"While you take in hand to school others, and to teach them by what name a whale-fish is to be called in our tongue, leaving out, through ignorance, the letter H, which almost alone maketh up the signification of the word, you deliver that which is not true."

HACKLUYT.

"WHALE. ★★★ *Sw. and Dan.* hval. *This animal is named from roundness or rolling; for in Dan.* hvalt *is arched or vaulted."* WEBSTER'S DICTIONARY.

"WHALE. ★★★ *It is more immediately from the Dut. and Ger.* Wallen; *a. s.* Walwian, *to roll, to wallow."* RICHARDSON'S DICTIONARY.

הך,	*Hebrew.*
χητος,	*Greek.*
CETUS,	*Latin.*
WHŒL,	*Anglo-Saxon.*
HVALT,	*Danish.*
WAL,	*Dutch.*
HWAL,	*Swedish.*
WHALE,	*Icelandic.*
WHALE,	*English.*
BALEINE,	*French.*
BALLENA,	*Spanish.*
PEKEE-NUEE-NUEE,	*Fegee.*
PEHEE-NUEE-NUEE,	*Erromangoan.*

EXTRACTS

(SUPPLIED BY A SUB-SUB-LIBRARIAN)

It will be seen that this mere painstaking burrower and grubworm of a poor devil of a Sub-Sub appears to have gone through the long Vaticans and street-stalls of the earth, picking up whatever random allusions to whales he could anyways find in any book whatsoever, sacred or profane. Therefore you must not, in every case at least, take the higgledy-piggledy whale statements, however authentic, in these extracts, for veritable gospel cetology. Far from it. As touching the ancient authors generally, as well as the poets here appearing, these extracts are solely valuable or entertaining, as affording a glancing bird's eye view of what has been promiscuously said, thought, fancied, and sung of Leviathan, by many nations and generations, including our own.

So fare thee well, poor devil of a Sub-Sub, whose commentator I am. Thou belongest to that hopeless, sallow tribe which no wine of this world will ever warm; and for whom even Pale Sherry would be too rosy-strong; but with whom one sometimes loves to sit, and feel poor-devilish, too; and grow convivial upon tears; and say to them bluntly, with full eyes and empty glasses, and in not altogether unpleasant sadness—Give it up, Sub-Subs! For by how much the more pains ye take to please the world, by so much the more shall ye for ever go thankless! Would that I could clear out Hampton Court and the Tuileries for ye! But gulp down your tears and hie aloft to the royal-mast with your hearts; for your friends who have gone before are clearing out the seven-storied heavens, and making refugees of long-pampered Gabriel, Michael, and Raphael, against your coming. Here ye strike but splintered hearts together—there, ye shall strike unsplinterable glasses!

"And God created great whales."

GENESIS.

"Leviathan maketh a path to shine after him;
One would think the deep to be hoary."

JOB.

"Now the Lord had prepared a great fish to swallow up Jonah."

JONAH.

"There go the ships; there is that Leviathan whom thou hast made to play therein."

PSALMS.

"In that day, the Lord with his sore, and great, and strong sword, shall punish Leviathan the piercing serpent, even Leviathan that crooked serpent; and he shall slay the dragon that is in the sea."

ISAIAH.

"And what thing soever besides cometh within the chaos of this monster's mouth, be it beast, boat, or stone, down it goes all incontinently that foul great swallow of his, and perisheth in the bottomless gulf of his paunch."

HOLLAND'S PLUTARCH'S MORALS.

"The Indian Sea breedeth the most and the biggest fishes that are: among which the Whales and Whirlpooles called Balæne, take up as much in length as four acres or arpens of land."

HOLLAND'S PLINY.

*"Scarcely had we proceeded two days on the sea, when about sunrise a great many Whales and other monsters of the sea, appeared. Among the former, one was of a most monstrous size. * * * This came towards us, open-mouthed, raising the waves on all sides, and beating the sea before him into a foam."*

TOOKE'S LUCIAN.—"THE TRUE HISTORY."

*"He visited this country also with a view of catching horse-whales, which had bones of very great value for their teeth, of which he brought some to the king. * * * The best whales were catched in his own country; of which some were forty-eight; some fifty yards long. He said that he was one of six who had killed sixty in two days."*

OTHER OR OCTHER'S VERBAL NARRATIVE TAKEN DOWN FROM HIS MOUTH BY KING ALFRED. A.D. 890.

"And whereas all the other things; whether beast or vessel; that enter into the dreadful gulf of this monster's (whale's) mouth, are immediately lost and swallowed up, the sea-gudgeon retires into it in great security, and there sleeps."

MONTAIGNE—APOLOGY FOR RAIMOND SEBOND.

"Let us fly, let us fly! Old Nick take me if it is not Leviathan described by the noble prophet Moses in the life of patient Job." RABELAIS.

"This whale's liver was two cart-loads." STOWE'S ANNALS.

"The great Leviathan that maketh the seas to seethe like boiling pan."

LORD BACON'S VERSION OF THE PSALMS.

"Touching that monstrous bulk of the whale or ork we have received nothing certain. They grow exceeding fat, insomuch that an incredible quantity of oil will be extracted out of one whale." IBID. "HISTORY OF LIFE AND DEATH."

"The sovereignest thing on earth is parmacetti for an inward bruise."

KING HENRY.

"Very like a whale." HAMLET.

"Which to secure, no skill of leach's art
Mote him availle, but to returne againe
To his wound's worker, that with lowly dart,
Dinting his breast, had bred his restless paine,
Like as the wounded whale to shore flies thro' the maine."

THE FAIRIE QUEEN.

"Immense as whales, the motion of whose vast bodies can in a peaceful calm trouble the ocean till it boil." SIR WILLIAM DAVENANT. PREFACE TO GONDIBERT.

"What spermacetti is, men might justly doubt, since the learned Hosmannus in his work of thirty years, saith plainly, Nescio quid sit.*"* SIR T. BROWNE. OF SPERMA CETI AND THE SPERMA CETI WHALE. VIDE HIS V. E.

"Like Spencer's Talus with his modern flail
He threatens ruin with his ponderous tail.

* * *

Their fixed jav'lins in his side he wears,
And on his back a grove of pikes appears."

WALLER'S BATTLE OF THE SUMMER ISLANDS.

"By art is created that great Leviathan, called a Commonwealth or State—(in Latin, Civitas) which is but an artificial man."

OPENING SENTENCE OF HOBBES'S LEVIATHAN.

"Silly Mansoul swallowed it without chewing, as if it had been a sprat in the mouth of a whale."

PILGRIM'S PROGRESS.

"That sea beast
Leviathan, which God of all his works
Created hugest that swim the ocean stream."

PARADISE LOST.

——*"There Leviathan,*
Hugest of living creatures, in the deep
Stretched like a promontory sleeps or swims,
And seems a moving land; and at his gills
Draws in, and at his breath spouts out a sea."

IBID.

"The mighty whales which swim in a sea of water, and have a sea of oil swimming in them."

FULLER'S PROFANE AND HOLY STATE.

"So close behind some promontory lie
The huge Leviathans to attend their prey,
And give no chace, but swallow in the fry,
Which through their gaping jaws mistake the way."

DRYDEN'S ANNUS MIRABILUS.

"While the whale is floating at the stern of the ship, they cut off his head, and tow it with a boat as near the shore as it will come; but it will be aground in twelve or thirteen feet water."

THOMAS EDGE'S TEN VOYAGES TO SPITZBERGEN, IN PURCHASS.

"In their way they saw many whales sporting in the ocean, and in wantonness fuzzing up the water through their pipes and vents, which nature has placed on their shoulders."

SIR T. HERBERT'S VOYAGES INTO ASIA AND AFRICA.—HARRIS COLL.

"Here they saw such huge troops of whales, that they were forced to proceed with a great deal of caution for fear they should run their ship upon them."

SCHOUTEN'S SIXTH CIRCUMNAVIGATION.

"We set sail from the Elbe, wind N. E. in the ship called The Jonas-in-the-Whale. ★★★

Some say the whale can't open his mouth, but that is a fable. ★★★

They frequently climb up the masts to see whether they can see a whale, for the first discoverer has a ducat for his pains. ★★★

I was told of a whale taken near Shetland, that had above a barrel of herrings in his belly. ★★★

One of our harpooners told me that he caught once a whale in Spitzbergen that was white all over."

A VOYAGE TO GREENLAND, A.D. 1671.—HARRIS COLL.

"Several whales have come in upon this coast (Fife). Anno 1652, one eighty feet in length of the whale-bone kind came in, which, (as I was informed) besides a vast quantity of oil, did afford 500 weight of baleen. The jaws of it stand for a gate in the garden of Pitferren."

SIBBALD'S FIFE AND KINROSS.

"Myself have agreed to try whether I can master and kill this Sperma-ceti whale, for I could never hear of any of that sort that was killed by any man, such is his fierceness and swiftness."

RICHARD STRAFFORD'S LETTER FROM THE BERMUDAS.—PHIL. TRANS. A.D. 1668.

"Whales in the sea
God's voice obey."

N. E. PRIMER.

"We saw also abundance of large whales, there being more in those southern seas, as I may say, by a hundred to one; than we have to the northward of us."

CAPTAIN COWLEY'S VOYAGE ROUND THE GLOBE. A.D. 1729.

* * * *"and the breath of the whale is frequently attended with such an insupportable smell, as to bring on a disorder of the brain."*

ULLOA'S SOUTH AMERICA.

"To fifty chosen sylphs of special note,
We trust the important charge, the petticoat.
Oft have we known that seven-fold fence to fail,
Tho' stuffed with hoops and armed with ribs of whale."

RAPE OF THE LOCK.

"If we compare land animals in respect to magnitude, with those that take up their abode in the deep, we shall find they will appear contemptible in the comparison. The whale is doubtless the largest animal in creation."

GOLDSMITH, NAT. HIS.

"If you should write a fable for little fishes, you would make them speak like great whales."

GOLDSMITH TO JOHNSON.

"In the afternoon we saw what was supposed to be a rock, but it was found to be a dead whale, which some Asiatics had killed, and were then towing ashore. They seemed to endeavor to conceal themselves behind the whale, in order to avoid being seen by us."

COOK'S VOYAGES.

"The larger whales, they seldom venture to attack. They stand in so great dread of some of them, that when out at sea they are afraid to mention even their names, and carry dung, lime-stone, juniper-wood, and some other articles of the same nature in their boats, in order to terrify and prevent their too near approach."

UNO VON TROIL'S LETTERS ON BANKS'S AND SOLANDER'S VOYAGE TO ICELAND IN 1772.

"The Spermacetti Whale found by the Nantuckois, is an active, fierce animal, and requires vast address and boldness in the fishermen."

THOMAS JEFFERSON'S WHALE MEMORIAL TO THE FRENCH MINISTER IN 1778.

"And pray, sir, what in the world is equal to it?"

EDMUND BURKE'S REFERENCE IN PARLIAMENT TO THE NANTUCKET WHALE-FISHERY.

"Spain——a great whale stranded on the shores of Europe."

EDMUND BURKE. (SOMEWHERE.)

"A tenth branch of the king's ordinary revenue, said to be grounded on the consideration of his guarding and protecting the seas from pirates and robbers, is the right to royal fish, *which are whale and sturgeon. And these, when either thrown ashore or caught near the coast, are the property of the king."* BLACKSTONE.

"Soon to the sport of death the crews repair:
Rodmond unerring o'er his head suspends
The barbed steel, and every turn attends."

FALCONER'S SHIPWRECK.

"Bright shone the roofs, the domes, the spires,
And rockets blew self driven,
To hang their momentary fire
Around the vault of heaven.

"So fire with water to compare,
The ocean serves on high,
Up-spouted by a whale in air,
To express unwieldy joy."

COWPER, ON THE QUEEN'S VISIT TO LONDON.

"Ten or fifteen gallons of blood are thrown out of the heart at a stroke, with immense velocity." JOHN HUNTER'S ACCOUNT OF THE DISSECTION OF A WHALE. (A SMALL SIZED ONE.)

"The aorta of a whale is larger in the bore than the main pipe of the water-works at London Bridge, and the water roaring in its passage through that pipe is inferior in impetus and velocity to the blood gushing from the whale's heart."

PALEY'S THEOLOGY.

"The whale is a mammiferous animal without hind feet."

BARON CUVIER.

"In 40 degrees south, we saw Spermacetti Whales, but did not take any until the first of May, the sea being then covered with them." COLNETT'S VOYAGE FOR THE PURPOSE OF EXTENDING THE SPERMACETTI WHALE FISHERY.

"In the free element beneath me swam,
Floundered and dived, in play, in chace, in battle,
Fishes of every color, form, and kind;
Which language cannot paint, and mariner
Had never seen; from dread Leviathan
To insect millions peopling every wave:
Gather'd in shoals immense, like floating islands,
Led by mysterious instincts through that waste

And trackless region, though on every side
Assaulted by voracious enemies.
Whales, sharks, and monsters, arm'd in front or jaw,
With swords, saws, spiral horns, or hooked fangs."

MONTGOMERY'S WORLD BEFORE THE FLOOD.

"Io! Pæan! Io! sing,
To the finny people's king.
Not a mightier whale than this
In the vast Atlantic is;
Not a fatter fish than he,
Flounders round the Polar Sea."

CHARLES LAMB'S TRIUMPH OF THE WHALE.

"In the year 1690 some persons were on a high hill observing the whales spouting and sporting with each other, when one observed; there—pointing to the sea—is a green pasture where our children's grand-children will go for bread."

OBED MACY'S HISTORY OF NANTUCKET.

"I build a cottage for Susan and myself and made a gateway in the form of a Gothic Arch, by setting up a whale's jaw bones." HAWTHORNE'S TWICE TOLD TALES.

"She came to bespeak a monument for her first love, who had been killed by a whale in the Pacific ocean, no less than forty years ago." IBID.

"No, Sir, 'tis a Right Whale," answered Tom; "I saw his spout; he threw up a pair of as pretty rainbows as a Christian would wish to look at. He's a raal oil-butt, that fellow!"

COOPER'S PILOT.

"The papers were brought in, and we saw in the Berlin Gazette that whales had been introduced on the stage there." ECKERMANN'S CONVERSATIONS WITH GOETHE.

"My God! Mr. Chace, what is the matter?" I answered, "We have been stove by a whale."

NARRATIVE OF THE SHIPWRECK OF THE WHALE SHIP ESSEX OF NANTUCKET, WHICH WAS ATTACKED AND FINALLY DESTROYED BY A LARGE SPERM WHALE IN THE PACIFIC OCEAN. BY OWEN CHACE OF NANTUCKET, FIRST MATE OF SAID VESSEL. NEW YORK. 1821.

"A mariner sat in the shrouds one night,
The wind was piping free;
Now bright, now dimmed, was the moonlight pale,
And the phospher gleamed in the wake of the whale,
As it floundered in the sea." ELIZABETH OAKES SMITH.

"The quantity of line withdrawn from the different boats engaged in the capture of this one whale, amounted altogether to 10,440 yards or nearly six English miles." * * *

"Sometimes the whale shakes its tremendous tail in the air, which, cracking like a whip, resounds to the distance of three or four miles." SCORESBY.

"Mad with the agonies he endures from these fresh attacks, the infuriated Sperm Whale rolls over and over; he rears his enormous head, and with wide expanded jaws snaps at everything around him; he rushes at the boats with his head; they are propelled before him with vast swiftness, and sometimes utterly destroyed.

★ ★ ★ *"It is a matter of great astonishment that the consideration of the habits of so interesting, and, in a commercial point of view, of so important an animal, (as the Sperm Whale) should have been so entirely neglected, or should have excited so little curiosity among the numerous, and many of them competent observers, that of late years must have possessed the most abundant and the most convenient opportunities of witnessing their habitudes."*

THOMAS BEALE'S HISTORY OF THE SPERM WHALE, 1839.

"The Cachalot" (Sperm Whale) "is not only better armed than the True Whale" (Greenland or Right Whale) "in possessing a formidable weapon at either extremity of its body, but also more frequently displays a disposition to employ these weapons offensively, and in a manner at once so artful, bold, and mischievous, as to lead to its being regarded as the most dangerous to attack of all the known species of the whale tribe."

FREDERICK DEBELL BENNETT'S WHALING VOYAGE ROUND THE GLOBE. 1840.

October 13. "There she blows," was sung out from the mast-head.
"Where away?" demanded the captain.
"Three points off the lee bow, sir."
"Raise up your wheel. Steady!"
"Steady, sir."
"Mast-head ahoy! Do you see that whale now?"
"Ay ay, sir! A shoal of Sperm Whales! There she blows! There she breaches!"
"Sing out! sing out every time!"
*"Ay ay, sir! There she blows! there—there—*thar *she blows—bowes—bo-o-o-s!"*
"How far off?"
"Two miles and a half."
"Thunder and lightning! so near! Call all hands!"

J. ROSS BROWNE'S ETCHINGS OF A WHALING CRUISE. 1846.

"The Whale-ship Globe, on board of which vessel occurred the horrid transactions we are about to relate, belonged to the island of Nantucket."

NARRATIVE OF THE GLOBE MUTINY, BY LAY AND HUSSEY SURVIVORS. A.D. 1828.

"Being once pursued by a whale which he had wounded, he parried the assault for some time with a lance; but the furious monster at length rushed on the boat; himself and comrades only being preserved by leaping into the water when they saw the onset was inevitable."

MISSIONARY JOURNAL OF TYERMAN AND BENNETT.

"Nantucket itself," said Mr. Webster, "is a very striking and peculiar portion of the National interest. There is a population of eight or nine thousand persons, living here in the sea, adding largely every year to the National wealth by the boldest and most persevering industry."

REPORT OF DANIEL WEBSTER'S SPEECH IN THE U. S. SENATE, ON THE APPLICATION FOR THE ERECTION OF A BREAKWATER AT NANTUCKET. 1828.

"The whale fell directly over him, and probably killed him in a moment."

"THE WHALE AND HIS CAPTORS, OR THE WHALEMAN'S ADVENTURES AND THE WHALE'S BIOGRAPHY, GATHERED ON THE HOMEWARD CRUISE OF THE COMMODORE PREBLE." BY REV. HENRY T. CHEEVER.

"If you make the least damn bit of noise," replied Samuel, "I will send you to hell."

LIFE OF SAMUEL COMSTOCK (THE MUTINEER), BY HIS BROTHER, WILLIAM COMSTOCK. ANOTHER VERSION OF THE WHALE-SHIP GLOBE NARRATIVE.

"The voyages of the Dutch and English to the Northern Ocean, in order, if possible, to discover a passage through it to India, though they failed of their main object, laid open the haunts of the whale."

McCULLOCH'S COMMERCIAL DICTIONARY.

"These things are reciprocal; the ball rebounds, only to bound forward again; for now in laying open the haunts of the whale, the whalemen seem to have indirectly hit upon new clews to that same mystic North-West Passage."

FROM "SOMETHING" UNPUBLISHED.

"It is impossible to meet a whale-ship on the ocean without being struck by her near appearance. The vessel under short sail, with look-outs at the mast-heads, eagerly scanning the wide expanse around them, has a totally different air from those engaged in a regular voyage."

CURRENTS AND WHALING. U. S. EX. EX.

"Pedestrians in the vicinity of London and elsewhere may recollect having seen large curved bones set upright in the earth, either to form arches over gateways, or entrances to alcoves, and they may perhaps have been told that these were the ribs of whales."

TALES OF A WHALE VOYAGER TO THE ARCTIC OCEAN.

"It was not till the boats returned from the pursuit of these whales, that the whites saw their ship in bloody possession of the savages enrolled among the crew."

NEWSPAPER ACCOUNT OF THE TAKING AND RETAKING OF THE WHALE-SHIP HOBOMACK.

"It is generally well known that out of the crews of Whaling vessels (American) few ever return in the ships on board of which they departed."

CRUISE IN A WHALE BOAT.

"Suddenly a mighty mass emerged from the water, and shot up perpendicularly into the air. It was the whale."

MIRIAM COFFIN OR THE WHALE FISHERMAN.

"The Whale is harpooned to be sure; but bethink you, how you would manage a powerful unbroken colt, with the mere appliance of a rope tied to the root of his tail."

A CHAPTER ON WHALING IN RIBS AND TRUCKS.

"On one occasion I saw two of these monsters (whales) probably male and female, slowly swimming, one after the other, within less than a stone's throw of the shore" (Terra Del Fuego), "over which the beech tree extended its branches."

DARWIN'S VOYAGE OF A NATURALIST.

"'Stern all!' exclaimed the mate, as upon turning his head, he saw the distended jaws of a large Sperm Whale close to the head of the boat, threatening it with instant destruction;—'Stern all, for your lives!'"

WHARTON THE WHALE KILLER.

"So be cheery, my lads, let your hearts never fail,
While the bold harpooner is striking the whale!"

NANTUCKET SONG.

"Oh, the rare old Whale, mid storm and gale
In his ocean home will be
A giant in might, where might is right,
And King of the boundless sea."

WHALE SONG.

MOBY DICK

OR, THE WHALE

Herman Melville

CHAPTER I

Loomings

Call me Ishmael. Some years ago—never mind how long precisely—having little or no money in my purse, and nothing particular to interest me on shore, I thought I would sail about a little and see the watery part of the world. It is a way I have of driving off the spleen, and regulating the circulation. Whenever I find myself growing grim about the mouth; whenever it is a damp, drizzly November in my soul; whenever I find myself involuntarily pausing before coffin warehouses, and bringing up the rear of every funeral I meet; and especially whenever my hypos get such an upper hand of me, that it requires a strong moral principle to prevent me from deliberately stepping into the street, and methodically knocking people's hats off—then, I account it high time to get to sea as soon as I can. This is my substitute for pistol and ball. With a philosophical flourish Cato throws himself upon his sword; I quietly take to the ship. There is nothing surprising in this. If they but knew it, almost all men in their degree, some time or other, cherish very nearly the same feelings towards the ocean with me.

There now is your insular city of the Manhattoes, belted round by wharves as Indian isles by coral reefs—commerce surrounds it with her surf. Right and left, the streets take you waterward. Its extreme down-town is the Battery, where that noble mole is washed by waves, and cooled by breezes, which a few hours previous were out of sight of land. Look at the crowds of water-gazers there.

Circumambulate the city of a dreamy Sabbath afternoon. Go from Corlears Hook to Coenties Slip, and from thence, by Whitehall, northward. What do you see?—Posted like silent sentinels all around the town, stand thousands upon thousands of mortal men fixed in ocean reveries. Some leaning against the spiles; some seated upon the pier-heads; some looking over the bulwarks of ships from China; some high aloft in the rigging, as if striving to get a still better seaward peep. But these are all landsmen; of week days pent up in lath and plaster—tied to counters, nailed to benches, clinched to desks. How then is this? Are the green fields gone? What do they here?

But look! here come more crowds, pacing straight for the water, and seemingly bound for a dive. Strange! Nothing will content them but the extremest limit of the land; loitering under the shady lee of yonder warehouses will not suffice. No. They must get just as nigh the water as they possibly can without falling in. And there they stand—miles of them—leagues. Inlanders all, they come from lanes and alleys, streets and avenues—north, east, south, and west. Yet here they all unite. Tell me, does the magnetic virtue in the needles of the compasses of all those ships attract them thither?

Once more. Say, you are in the country; in some high land of lakes. Take almost any path you please, and ten to one it carries you down in a dale, and leaves you there by a pool in the stream. There is magic in it. Let the most absent-minded of men be plunged in his deepest reveries—stand that man on his legs, set his feet a-going, and he will infallibly lead you to water, if water there be in all that region. Should you ever be athirst in the great American desert, try this experiment, if your caravan happen to be supplied with a metaphysical professor. Yes, as every one knows, meditation and water are wedded for ever.

But here is an artist. He desires to paint you the dreamiest, shadiest, quietest, most enchanting bit of romantic landscape in all the valley of the Saco. What is the chief element he employs? There stand his trees, each with a hollow trunk, as if a hermit and a crucifix were within; and here sleeps his meadow, and there sleep his cattle; and up from yonder cottage goes a sleepy smoke. Deep into distant woodlands winds a mazy way, reaching to overlapping spurs of mountains bathed in their hill-side blue. But though the picture lies thus tranced, and though this pine-tree shakes down its sighs like leaves upon this shepherd's head, yet all were vain, unless the shepherd's eye were fixed upon the magic stream before him. Go visit the Prairies in June, when for scores on scores of miles you wade knee-deep among Tiger-lilies—what is the one charm wanting?—Water—there is not a drop of water there! Were Niagara but a cataract of sand, would you travel your thousand miles to see it? Why did the poor poet of Tennessee, upon suddenly receiving two handfuls of silver, deliberate whether to buy him a coat, which he sadly needed, or invest his money in a pedestrian trip to Rockaway Beach? Why is almost every robust healthy boy with a robust healthy soul in him, at some time or other crazy to go to sea? Why upon your first voyage as a passenger, did you yourself feel such a mystical vibration, when first told that you and your ship were now out of sight of land? Why did the old Persians hold the sea holy? Why did the Greeks give it a separate deity, and own brother of Jove? Surely all this is not without meaning. And still deeper the meaning of that story of Narcissus, who because he could not grasp the tormenting, mild image he saw in the fountain, plunged into it and was drowned. But that same image, we ourselves see in all rivers and oceans. It is the image of the ungraspable phantom of life; and this is the key to it all.

Now, when I say that I am in the habit of going to sea whenever I begin to grow hazy about the eyes, and begin to be over conscious of my lungs, I do not mean to have it inferred that I ever go to sea as a passenger. For to go as a passenger you must needs have a purse, and a purse is but a rag unless you have something in it.

Besides, passengers get sea-sick—grow quarrelsome—don't sleep of nights—do not enjoy themselves much, as a general thing;—no, I never go as a passenger; nor, though I am something of a salt, do I ever go to sea as a Commodore, or a Captain, or a Cook. I abandon the glory and distinction of such offices to those who like them. For my part, I abominate all honorable respectable toils, trials, and tribulations of every kind whatsoever. It is quite as much as I can do to take care of myself, without taking care of ships, barques, brigs, schooners, and what not. And as for going as cook,—though I confess there is considerable glory in that, a cook being a sort of officer on ship-board—yet, somehow, I never fancied broiling fowls;—though once broiled, judiciously buttered, and judgmatically salted and peppered, there is no one who will speak more respectfully, not to say reverentially, of a broiled fowl than I will. It is out of the idolatrous dotings of the old Egyptians upon broiled ibis and roasted river horse, that you see the mummies of those creatures in their huge bake-houses the pyramids.

No, when I go to sea, I go as a simple sailor, right before the mast, plumb down into the forecastle, aloft there to the royal mast-head. True, they rather order me about some, and make me jump from spar to spar, like a grasshopper in a May meadow. And at first, this sort of thing is unpleasant enough. It touches one's sense of honor, particularly if you come of an old established family in the land, the Van Rensselaers, or Randolphs, or Hardicanutes. And more than all, if just previous to putting your hand into the tar-pot, you have been lording it as a country schoolmaster, making the tallest boys stand in awe of you. The transition is a keen one, I assure you, from a schoolmaster to a sailor, and requires a strong decoction of Seneca and the Stoics to enable you to grin and bear it. But even this wears off in time.

What of it, if some old hunks of a sea-captain orders me to get a broom and sweep down the decks? What does that indignity amount to, weighed, I mean, in the scales of the New Testament? Do you think the archangel Gabriel thinks anything the less of me, because I promptly and respectfully obey that old hunks in that particular instance? Who aint a slave? Tell me that. Well, then, however the old sea-captains may order me about—however they may thump and punch me about, I have the satisfaction of knowing that it is all right; that everybody else is one way or other served in much the same way—either in a physical or metaphysical point of view, that is; and so the universal thump is passed round, and all hands should rub each other's shoulder-blades, and be content.

Again, I always go to sea as a sailor, because they make a point of paying me for my trouble, whereas they never pay passengers a single penny that I ever heard of. On the contrary, passengers themselves must pay. And there is all the difference in the world between paying and being paid. The act of paying is perhaps the most uncomfortable infliction that the two orchard thieves entailed upon us. But *being paid,*—what will compare with it? The urbane activity with which a man receives money is really marvellous, considering that we so earnestly believe money to be the root of all earthly ills, and that on no account can a monied man enter heaven. Ah! how cheerfully we consign ourselves to perdition!

Finally, I always go to sea as a sailor, because of the wholesome exercise and pure air of the forecastle deck. For as in this world, head winds are far more prevalent than winds from astern (that is, if you never violate the Pythagorean maxim), so for the most part the Commodore on the quarter-deck gets his atmosphere at second hand from the sailors on the forecastle. He thinks he breathes it first; but not so. In much the same way do the commonalty lead their leaders in many other things, at the same time that the leaders little suspect it. But wherefore it was that after having repeatedly smelt the sea as a merchant sailor, I should now take it into my head to go on a whaling voyage; this the invisible police officer of the Fates, who has the constant surveillance of me, and secretly dogs me, and influences me in some unaccountable way—he can better answer than any one else. And, doubtless, my going on this whaling voyage, formed part of the grand programme of Providence that was drawn up a long time ago. It came in as a sort of brief interlude and solo between more extensive performances. I take it that this part of the bill must have run something like this:

'Grand Contested Election for the Presidency of the United States.

'WHALING VOYAGE BY ONE ISHMAEL.

'BLOODY BATTLE IN AFFGHANISTAN.'

Though I cannot tell why it was exactly that those stage managers, the Fates, put me down for this shabby part of a whaling voyage, when others were set down for magnificent parts in high tragedies, and short and easy parts in genteel comedies, and jolly parts in farces—though I cannot tell why this was exactly; yet, now that I recall all the circumstances, I think I can see a little into the springs and motives which being cunningly presented to me under various disguises, induced me to set about performing the part I did, besides cajoling me into the delusion that it was a choice resulting from my own unbiased free will and discriminating judgment.

Chief among these motives was the overwhelming idea of the great whale himself. Such a portentous and mysterious monster roused all my curiosity. Then the wild and distant seas where he rolled his island bulk; the undeliverable, nameless perils of the whale; these, with all the attending marvels of a thousand Patagonian sights and sounds, helped to sway me to my wish. With other men, perhaps, such things would not have been inducements; but as for me, I am tormented with an everlasting itch for things remote. I love to sail forbidden seas, and land on barbarous coasts. Not ignoring what is good, I am quick to perceive a horror, and could still be social with it—would they let me—since it is but well to be on friendly terms with all the inmates of the place one lodges in.

By reason of these things, then, the whaling voyage was welcome; the great flood-gates of the wonder-world swung open, and in the wild conceits that swayed me to my purpose, two and two there floated into my inmost soul, endless processions of the whale, and, mid most of them all, one grand hooded phantom, like a snow hill in the air.

CHAPTER II

THE CARPET-BAG

I stuffed a shirt or two into my old carpet-bag, tucked it under my arm, and started for Cape Horn and the Pacific. Quitting the good city of old Manhatto, I duly arrived in New Bedford. It was on a Saturday night in December. Much was I disappointed upon learning that the little packet for Nantucket had already sailed, and that no way of reaching that place would offer, till the following Monday.

As most young candidates for the pains and penalties of whaling stop at this same New Bedford, thence to embark on their voyage, it may as well be related that I, for one, had no idea of so doing. For my mind was made up to sail in no other than a Nantucket craft, because there was a fine, boisterous something about everything connected with that famous old island, which amazingly pleased me. Besides though New Bedford has of late been gradually monopolizing the business of whaling, and though in this matter poor old Nantucket is now much behind her, yet Nantucket was her great original—the Tyre of this Carthage;—the place where the first dead American whale was stranded. Where else but from Nantucket did those aboriginal whalemen, the Red-Men, first sally out in canoes to give chase to the Leviathan? And where but from Nantucket, too, did that first adventurous little sloop put forth, partly laden with imported cobble-stones—so goes the story—to throw at the whales, in order to discover when they were nigh enough to risk a harpoon from the bowsprit?

Now having a night, a day, and still another night following before me in New Bedford, ere I could embark for my destined port, it became a matter of concernment where I was to eat and sleep meanwhile. It was a very dubious-looking, nay, a very dark and dismal night, bitingly cold and cheerless. I knew no one in the place. With anxious grapnels I had sounded my pocket, and only brought up a few pieces of silver,—So, wherever you go, Ishmael, said I to myself, as I stood in the middle of a dreary street shouldering my bag, and comparing the gloom towards the north with the darkness towards the south—wherever in your wisdom you may conclude to lodge for the night, my dear Ishmael, be sure to inquire the price, and don't be too particular.

With halting steps I paced the streets, and passed the sign of 'The Crossed Harpoons'—but it looked too expensive and jolly there. Further on, from the bright red windows of the 'Sword-Fish Inn', there came such fervent rays, that it seemed to have melted the packed snow and ice from before the house, for everywhere else the congealed frost lay ten inches thick in a hard, asphaltic pavement,—rather weary for me, when I struck my foot against the flinty projections, because from hard, remorseless service the soles of my boots were in a most miserable plight. Too expensive and jolly, again thought I, pausing one moment to watch the broad glare in the street, and hear the sounds of the tinkling glasses within. But go on, Ishmael, said I at last; don't you hear? get away from before the door; your patched boots are stopping the way. So on I went. I now by instinct followed the streets that took me waterward, for there, doubtless, were the cheapest, if not the cheeriest inns.

Such dreary streets! blocks of blackness, not houses, on either hand, and here and there a candle, like a candle moving about in a tomb. At this hour of the night, of the last day of the week, that quarter of the town proved all but deserted. But presently I came to a smoky light proceeding from a low, wide building, the door of which stood invitingly open. It had a careless look, as if it were meant for the uses of the public; so, entering, the first thing I did was to stumble over an ash-box in the porch. Ha! thought I, ha, as the flying particles almost choked me, are these ashes from that destroyed city, Gomorrah? But 'The Crossed Harpoons', and 'The Sword-Fish'?—this, then, must needs be the sign of 'The Trap'. However, I picked myself up and hearing a loud voice within, pushed on and opened a second, interior door.

It seemed the great Black Parliament sitting in Tophet. A hundred black faces turned round in their rows to peer; and beyond, a black Angel of Doom was beating a book in a pulpit. It was a negro church; and the preacher's text was about the blackness of darkness, and the weeping and wailing and teeth-gnashing there. Ha, Ishmael, muttered I, backing out, Wretched entertainment at the sign of 'The Trap!'

Moving on, I at last came to a dim sort of out-hanging light not far from the docks, and heard a forlorn creaking in the air; and looking up, saw a swinging sign over the door with a white painting upon it, faintly representing a tall straight jet of misty spray, and these words underneath—'The Spouter-Inn:—Peter Coffin.'

Coffin?—Spouter?—Rather ominous in that particular connexion, thought I. But it is a common name in Nantucket, they say, and I suppose this Peter here is an emigrant from there. As the light looked so dim, and the place, for the time, looked quiet enough, and the dilapidated little wooden house itself looked as if it might have been carted here from the ruins of some burnt district, and as the swinging sign had a poverty-stricken sort of creak to it, I thought that here was the very spot for cheap lodgings, and the best of pea coffee.

It was a queer sort of place—a gable-ended old house, one side palsied as it were, and leaning over sadly. It stood on a sharp bleak corner, where that tempestuous wind Euroclydon kept up a worse howling than ever it did about poor Paul's tossed craft. Euroclydon, nevertheless, is a mighty pleasant zephyr to any one in-doors, with his feet on the hob quietly toasting for bed. 'In judging of that tempestuous wind called Euroclydon,' says an old writer—of whose works I possess the only copy extant—'it maketh a marvellous difference, whether thou lookest out at it from a glass window where the frost is all on the outside, or whether thou observest it from that sashless window, where the frost is on both sides, and of which the wight Death is the only glazier.' True enough, thought I, as this passage occurred to my mind—old black-letter, thou reasonest well. Yes, these eyes are windows, and this body of mine is the house. What a pity they didn't stop up the chinks and the crannies though, and thrust in a little lint here and there. But it's too late to make any improvements now. The universe is finished; the copestone is on, and the chips were carted off a million years ago. Poor Lazarus there, chattering his teeth against the curbstone for his pillow, and shaking off his tatters with his shiverings, he might plug up both ears with rags, and put a corn-cob into his mouth, and yet that would not keep out the tempestuous Euroclydon. Euroclydon! says old Dives, in his red silken wrapper (he had a redder one afterwards)—pooh, pooh! What a fine frosty night; how Orion glitters; what northern lights! Let them talk of their oriental summer climes of everlasting conservatories; give me the privilege of making my own summer with my own coals.

But what thinks Lazarus? Can he warm his blue hands by holding them up to the grand northern lights? Would not Lazarus rather be in Sumatra than here? Would he not far rather lay him down lengthwise along the line of the equator; yea, ye gods! go down to the fiery pit itself, in order to keep out this frost?

Now, that Lazarus should lie stranded there on the curbstone before the door of Dives, this is more wonderful than that an iceberg should be moored to one of the Moluccas. Yet Dives himself, he too lives like a Czar in an ice palace made of frozen sighs, and being a president of a temperance society, he only drinks the tepid tears of orphans.

But no more of this blubbering now, we are going a-whaling, and there is plenty of that yet to come. Let us scrape the ice from our frosted feet, and see what sort of a place this 'Spouter' may be.

CHAPTER III

THE SPOUTER-INN

Entering that gable-ended Spouter-Inn, you found yourself in a wide, low, straggling entry with old-fashioned wainscots, reminding one of the bulwarks of some condemned old craft. On one side hung a very large oil-painting so thoroughly be-smoked, and every way defaced, that in the unequal cross-lights by which you viewed it, it was only by diligent study and a series of systematic visits to it, and careful inquiry of the neighbors, that you could any way arrive at an understanding of its purpose. Such unaccountable masses of shades and shadows, that at first you almost thought some ambitious young artist, in the time of the New England hags, had endeavored to delineate chaos bewitched. But by dint of much and earnest contemplation, and oft repeated ponderings, and especially by throwing open the little window towards the back of the entry, you at last come to the conclusion that such an idea, however wild, might not be altogether unwarranted.

But what most puzzled and confounded you was a long, limber, portentous black mass of something hovering in the centre of the picture over three blue, dim, perpendicular lines floating in a nameless yeast. A boggy, soggy, squitchy picture truly, enough to drive a nervous man distracted. Yet was there a sort of indefinite, half-attained, unimaginable sublimity about it that fairly froze you to it, till you involuntarily took an oath with yourself to find out what that marvellous painting meant. Ever and anon a bright, but, alas, deceptive idea would dart you through.—It's the Black Sea in a midnight gale.—It's the unnatural combat of the four primal elements.—It's a blasted heath.—It's a Hyperborean winter scene.—It's the breaking-up of the ice-bound stream of Time. But at last all these fancies yielded to that one portentous something in the picture's midst. *That* once found out, and all the rest were plain. But stop; does it not bear a faint resemblance to a gigantic fish? even the great leviathan himself?

In fact, the artist's design seemed this: a final theory of my own, partly based upon the aggregated opinions of many aged persons with whom I conversed upon the subject. The picture represents a Cape-Horner in a great hurricane; the half-foundered ship weltering there with its three dismantled masts alone visible; and an exasperated whale, purposing to spring clean over the craft, is in the enormous act of impaling himself upon the three mast-heads.

The opposite wall of this entry was hung all over with a heathenish array of monstrous clubs and spears. Some were thickly set with glittering teeth resembling ivory saws; others were tufted with knots of human hair; and one was sickle-shaped, with a vast handle sweeping round like the segment made in the new-mown grass by a long-armed mower. You shuddered as you gazed, and wondered what monstrous cannibal and savage could ever have gone a death-harvesting with such a hacking, horrifying implement. Mixed with these were rusty old whaling lances and harpoons all broken and deformed. Some were storied weapons. With this once long lance, now wildly elbowed, fifty years ago did Nathan Swain kill fifteen whales between a sunrise and a sunset. And that harpoon—so like a cork-screw now—was flung in Javan seas, and run away with by a whale, years afterward slain off the Cape of Blanco. The original iron entered nigh the tail, and, like a restless needle sojourning in the body of a man, travelled full forty feet, and at last was found imbedded in the hump.

Crossing this dusky entry, and on through yon low-arched way—cut through what in old times must have been a great central chimney with fire-places all round—you enter the public room. A still duskier place is this, with such low ponderous beams above, and such old wrinkled planks beneath, that you would almost fancy you trod some old craft's cockpits, especially of such a howling night, when this corner-anchored old ark rocked so furiously. On one side stood a long, low, shelf-like table covered with cracked glass cases, filled with dusty rarities gathered from this wide world's remotest nooks. Projecting from the further angle of the room stands a dark-looking den—the bar—a rude attempt at a right whale's head. Be that how it may, there stands the vast arched bone of the whale's jaw, so wide, a coach might almost drive beneath it. Within are shabby shelves, ranged round with old decanters, bottles, flasks; and in those jaws of swift destruction, like another cursed Jonah (by which name indeed they called him), bustles a little withered old man, who, for their money, dearly sells the sailors deliriums and death.

Abominable are the tumblers into which he pours his poison. Though true cylinders without—within, the villanous green goggling glasses deceitfully tapered downwards to a cheating bottom. Parallel meridians rudely pecked into the glass, surround these footpads' goblets. Fill to *this* mark, and your charge is but a penny; to *this* a penny more; and so on to the full glass—the Cape Horn measure, which you may gulph down for a shilling.

Upon entering the place I found a number of young seamen gathered about a table, examining by a dim light divers specimens of *skrimshander.* I sought the landlord, and telling him I desired to be accommodated with a room, received for answer that his house was full—not a bed unoccupied. 'But avast,' he added, tapping his forehead, 'you haint no objections to sharing a harpooneer's blanket, have ye? I s'pose you are goin' a whalin', so you'd better get used to that sort of thing.'

I told him that I never liked to sleep two in a bed; that if I should ever do so, it would depend upon who the harpooneer might be, and that if he (the landlord) really had no other place for me, and the harpooneer was not decidedly objectionable, why rather than wander further about a strange town on so bitter a night, I would put up with the half of any decent man's blanket.

'I thought so. All right; take a seat. Supper?—you want supper? Supper'll be ready directly.'

I sat down on an old wooden settle, carved all over like a bench on the Battery. At one end a ruminating tar was still further adorning it with his jack-knife, stooping over and diligently working away at the space between his legs. He was trying his hand at a ship under full sail, but he didn't make much headway, I thought.

At last some four or five of us were summoned to our meal in an adjoining room. It was cold as Iceland—no fire at all—the landlord said he couldn't afford it. Nothing but two dismal tallow candles, each in a winding sheet. We were fain to button up our monkey jackets, and hold to our lips cups of scalding tea with our half frozen fingers. But the fare was of the most substantial kind—not only meat and potatoes, but dumplings; good heavens! dumplings for supper! One young fellow in a green box coat, addressed himself to these dumplings in a most direful manner.

'My boy,' said the landlord, 'you'll have the nightmare to a dead sartainty.'

'Landlord,' I whispered, 'that aint the harpooneer, is it?'

'Oh, no,' said he, looking a sort of diabolically funny, 'the harpooner is a dark complexioned chap. He never eats dumplings, he don't—he eats nothing but steaks, and likes 'em rare.'

'The devil he does,' says I. 'Where is that harpooneer? Is he here?'

'He'll be here afore long,' was the answer.

I could not help it, but I began to feel suspicious of this 'dark complexioned' harpooneer. At any rate, I made up my mind that if it so turned out that we should sleep together, he must undress and get into bed before I did.

Supper over, the company went back to the bar-room, when, knowing not what else to do with myself, I resolved to spend the rest of the evening as a looker on.

Presently a rioting noise was heard without. Starting up, the landlord cried, 'That's the Grampus's crew. I seed her reported in the offing this morning; a three years' voyage, and a full ship. Hurrah, boys; now we'll have the latest news from the Feegees.'

A tramping of sea boots was heard in the entry; the door was flung open, and in rolled a wild set of mariners enough. Enveloped in their shaggy watch coats, and with their heads muffled in woollen comforters, all bedarned and ragged, and their beards stiff with icicles, they seemed an eruption of bears from Labrador. They had just landed from their boat, and this was the first house they entered. No wonder, then, that they made a straight wake for the whale's mouth—the bar—when the wrinkled little old Jonah, there officiating, soon poured them out brimmers all round. One complained of a bad cold in his head, upon which Jonah mixed him a pitch-like potion of gin and molasses, which he swore was a sovereign cure for all colds and catarrhs whatsoever, never mind of how long standing, or whether caught off the coast of Labrador, or on the weather side of an ice-island.

The liquor soon mounted into their heads, as it generally does even with the arrantest topers newly landed from sea, and they began capering about most obstreperously.

I observed, however, that one of them held somewhat aloof, and though he seemed desirous not to spoil the hilarity of his shipmates by his own sober face, yet upon the whole he refrained from making as much noise as the rest. This man interested me at once; and since the sea-gods had ordained that he should soon become my shipmate (though but a sleeping-partner one, so far as this narrative is concerned), I will here venture upon a little description of him. He stood full six feet in height, with noble shoulders, and a chest like a coffer-dam. I have seldom seen such brawn in a man. His face was deeply brown and burnt, making his white teeth dazzling by the contrast; while in the deep shadows of his eyes floated some reminiscences that did not seem to give him much joy. His voice at once announced that he was a Southerner, and from his fine stature, I thought he must be one of those tall mountaineers from the Alleganian Ridge in Virginia. When the revelry of his companions had mounted to its height, this man slipped away unobserved, and I saw no more of him till he became my comrade on the sea. In a few minutes, however, he was missed by his shipmates, and being, it seems, for some reason a huge favorite with them, they raised a cry of 'Bulkington! Bulkington! where's Bulkington?' and darted out of the house in pursuit of him.

It was now about nine o'clock, and the room seeming almost supernaturally quiet after these orgies, I began to congratulate myself upon a little plan that had occurred to me just previous to the entrance of the seamen.

No man prefers to sleep two in a bed. In fact, you would a good deal rather not sleep with your own brother. I don't know how it is, but people like to be private when they are sleeping. And when it comes to sleeping with an unknown stranger, in a strange inn, in a strange town, and that stranger a harpooneer, then your objections indefinitely multiply. Nor was there any earthly reason why I as a sailor should sleep two in a bed, more than anybody else; for sailors no more sleep two in a bed at sea, than bachelor Kings do ashore. To be sure they all sleep together in one apartment, but you have your own hammock, and cover yourself with your own blanket, and sleep in your own skin.

The more I pondered over this harpooneer, the more I abominated the thought of sleeping with him. It was fair to presume that being a harpooneer, his linen or woollen, as the case might be, would not be of the tidiest, certainly none of the finest. I began to twitch all over. Besides, it was getting late, and any decent harpooneer ought to be home and going bedwards. Suppose now, he should tumble in upon me at midnight—how could I tell from what vile hole he had been coming?

'Landlord! I've changed my mind about that harpooneer.—I shan't sleep with him. I'll try the bench here.'

'Just as you please; I'm sorry I cant spare ye a tablecloth for a mattress, and it's a plaguy rough board here'—feeling of the knots and notches. 'But wait a bit, Skrimshander; I've got a carpenter's plane there in the bar—wait, I say, and I'll make ye snug enough.' So saying he procured the plane; and with his old silk handkerchief first dusting the bench, vigorously set to planing away at my bed, the while grinning like an ape. The shavings flew right and left; till at last the plane-iron came bump against an indestructible knot. The landlord was near spraining his wrist, and I told him for heaven's sake to quit—the bed was soft enough to suit me, and I did not know how all the planing in the world could make eider down of a pine plank. So gathering up the shavings with another grin, and throwing them into the great stove in the middle of the room, he went about his business, and left me in a brown study.

I now took the measure of the bench, and found that it was a foot too short; but that could be mended with a chair. But it was a foot too narrow, and the other bench in the room was about four inches higher than the planed one—so there was no yoking them. I then placed the first bench lengthwise along the only clear space against the wall, leaving a little interval between, for my back to settle down in. But I soon found that there came such a draught of cold air over me from under the sill of the window, that this plan would never do at all, especially as another current from the rickety door met the one from the window, and both together formed a series of small whirlwinds in the immediate vicinity of the spot where I had thought to spend the night.

The devil fetch that harpooneer, thought I, but stop, couldn't I steal a march on him—bolt his door inside, and jump into his bed, not to be wakened by the most violent knockings? It seemed no bad idea; but upon second thoughts I dismissed it. For who could tell but what the next morning, so soon as I popped out of the room, the harpooneer might be standing in the entry, all ready to knock me down!

Still, looking around me again, and seeing no possible chance of spending a sufferable night unless in some other person's bed, I began to think that after all I might be cherishing unwarrantable prejudices against this unknown harpooneer. Thinks I, I'll wait awhile; he must be dropping in before long. I'll have a good look at him then, and perhaps we may become jolly good bedfellows after all—there's no telling.

But though the other boarders kept coming in by ones, twos, and threes, and going to bed, yet no sign of my harpooneer.

'Landlord!' said I, 'what sort of a chap is he—does he always keep such late hours?' It was now hard upon twelve o'clock.

The landlord chuckled again with his lean chuckle, and seemed to be mightily tickled at something beyond my comprehension. 'No,' he answered, 'generally he's an airley bird—airley to bed and airley to rise—yes, he's the bird what catches the worm.—But tonight he went out a peddling, you see, and I don't see what on airth keeps him so late, unless, may be, he can't sell his head.'

'Can't sell his head?—What sort of a bamboozling story is this you are telling me?' getting into a towering rage. 'Do you pretend to say, landlord, that this harpooneer is actually engaged this blessed Saturday night, or rather Sunday morning, in peddling his head around this town?'

'That's precisely it,' said the landlord, 'and I told him he couldn't sell it here, the market's overstocked.'

'With what?' shouted I.

'With heads to be sure; ain't there too many heads in the world?'

'I tell you what it is, landlord,' said I, quite calmly, 'you'd better stop spinning that yarn to me—I'm not green.'

'May be not,' taking out a stick and whittling a toothpick, 'but I rayther guess you'll be done *brown* if that ere harpooneer hears you a slanderin' his head.'

'I'll break it for him,' said I, now flying into a passion again at this unaccountable farrago of the landlord's.

'It's broke a'ready,' said he.

'Broke,' said I—'*broke,* do you mean?'

'Sartain, and that's the very reason he can't sell it, I guess.'

'Landlord,' said I, going up to him as cool as Mt. Hecla in a snow storm,—'landlord, stop whittling. You and I must understand one another, and that too without delay. I come to your house and want a bed; you tell me you can only give me half a one; that the other half belongs to a certain harpooneer. And about this harpooneer, whom I have not yet seen, you persist in telling me the most mystifying and exasperating stories, tending to beget in me an uncomfortable feeling towards the man whom you design for my bedfellow—a sort of connexion, landlord, which is an intimate and confidential one in the highest degree. I now demand of you to speak out and tell me who and what this harpooneer is, and whether I shall be in all respects safe to spend the night with him. And in the first place, you will be so good as to unsay that story about selling his head, which if true I take to be good evidence that this harpooneer is stark mad, and I've no idea of sleeping with a madman; and you, sir, *you* I mean, landlord, *you,* sir, by trying to induce me to do so knowingly, would thereby render yourself liable to a criminal prosecution.'

'Wall,' said the landlord, fetching a long breath, 'that's a purty long sarmon for a chap that rips a little now and then. But be easy, be easy, this here harpooneer I have been tellin' you of has just arrived from the south seas, where he bought up a lot of 'balmed New Zealand heads (great curios, you know), and he's sold all on 'em but one, and that one he's trying to sell tonight, cause to-morrow's Sunday, and it would not do to be sellin' human heads about the streets when folks is goin' to churches. He wanted to, last Sunday, but I stopped him just as he was goin' out of the door with four heads strung on a string, for all the airth like a string of inions.'

This account cleared up the otherwise unaccountable mystery, and showed that the landlord, after all, had had no idea of fooling me—but at the same time what could I think of a harpooneer who stayed out of a Saturday night clean into the holy Sabbath, engaged in such a cannibal business as selling the heads of dead idolators?

'Depend upon it, landlord, that harpooneer is a dangerous man.'

'He pays reg'lar,' was the rejoinder. 'But come, it's getting dreadful late, you had better be turning flukes—it's a nice bed: Sal and me slept in that ere bed the night we were spliced. There's plenty room for two to kick about in that bed; it's an almighty big bed that. Why, afore we give it up, Sal used to put our Sam and little Johnny in the foot of it. But I got a dreaming and sprawling about one night, and somehow, Sam got pitched on the floor, and came near breaking his arm. Arter that, Sal said it wouldn't do. Come along here, I'll give ye a glim in a jiffy;' and so saying he lighted a candle and held it towards me, offering to lead the way. But I stood irresolute; when looking at a clock in the corner, he exclaimed, 'I vum it's Sunday—you won't see that harpooneer tonight; he's come to anchor somewhere—come along then; *do* come; *won't* ye come?'

I considered the matter a moment, and then up stairs we went, and I was ushered into a small room, cold as a clam, and furnished, sure enough, with a prodigious bed, almost big enough indeed for any four harpooneers to sleep abreast.

'There,' said the landlord, placing the candle on a crazy old sea chest that did double duty as a wash-stand and centre table; 'there, make yourself comfortable now, and good night to ye.' I turned round from eyeing the bed, but he had disappeared.

Folding back the counterpane, I stooped over the bed. Though none of the most elegant, it yet stood the scrutiny tolerably well. I then glanced round the room; and besides the bedstead and centre table, could see no other furniture belonging to the place, but a rude shelf, the four walls, and a papered fireboard representing a man striking a whale. Of things not properly belonging to the room, there was a hammock lashed up, and thrown upon the floor in one corner; also a large seaman's bag, containing the harpooneers' wardrobe, no doubt in lieu of a land trunk. Likewise, there was a parcel of outlandish bone fish hooks on the shelf over the fire-place, and a tall harpoon standing at the head of the bed.

But what is this on the chest? I took it up, and held it close to the light, and felt it, and smelt it, and tried every way possible to arrive at some satisfactory conclusion concerning it. I can compare it to nothing but a large door mat, ornamented at the edges with little tinkling tags something like the stained porcupine quills round an Indian moccasin. There was a hole or slit in the middle of this mat, as you see the same in South American ponchos. But could it be possible that any sober harpooneer would get into a door mat, and parade the streets of any Christian town in that sort of guise? I put it on, to try it, and it weighed me down like a hamper, being uncommonly shaggy and thick, and I thought a little damp, as though this mysterious harpooneer had been wearing it of a rainy day. I went up in it to a bit of glass stuck against the wall, and I never saw such a sight in my life. I tore myself out of it in such a hurry that I gave myself a kink in the neck.

I sat down on the side of the bed, and commenced thinking about this head-peddling harpooneer, and his door mat. After thinking some time on the bed-side, I got up and took off my monkey jacket, and then stood in the middle of the room thinking. I then took off my coat, and thought a little more in my shirt sleeves. But beginning to feel very cold now, half undressed as I was, and remembering what the landlord said about the harpooneer's not coming home at all that night, it being so very late, I made no more ado, but jumped out of my pantaloons and boots, and then blowing out the light tumbled into bed, and commended myself to the care of heaven.

Whether that mattress was stuffed with corn-cobs or broken crockery, there is no telling, but I rolled about a good deal, and could not sleep for a long time. At last I slid off into a light doze, and had pretty nearly made a good offing towards the land of Nod, when I heard a heavy footfall in the passage, and saw a glimmer of light come into the room from under the door.

Lord save me, thinks I, that must be the harpooneer, the infernal head-peddler. But I lay perfectly still, and resolved not to say a word till spoken to. Holding a light in one hand, and that identical New Zealand head in the other, the stranger entered the room, and without looking towards the bed, placed his candle a good way off from me on the floor in one corner, and then began working away at the knotted cords of the large bag I before spoke of as being in the room. I was all eagerness to see his face, but he kept it averted for some time while employed in unlacing the bag's mouth. This accomplished, however, he turned round—when, good heavens! what a sight! Such a face! It was of a dark, purplish, yellow color, here and there stuck over with large blackish looking squares. Yes, it's just as I thought, he's a terrible bedfellow; he's been in a fight, got dreadfully cut, and here he is, just from the surgeon. But at that moment he chanced to turn his face so towards the light, that I plainly saw they could not be sticking-plasters at all, those black squares on his cheeks. They were stains of some sort or other. At first I knew not what to make of this; but soon an inkling of the truth occurred to me. I remembered a story of a white man—a whaleman too—who, falling among the cannibals, had been tattooed by them. I concluded that this harpooneer, in the course of his distant voyages, must have met with a similar adventure. And what is it, thought I, after all! It's only his outside; a man can be honest in any sort of skin. But then, what to make of his unearthly complexion, that part of it, I mean, lying round about, and completely independent of the squares of tattooing. To be sure, it might be nothing but a good coat of tropical tanning; but I never heard of a hot sun's tanning a white man into a purplish yellow one. However, I had never been in the South Seas; and perhaps the sun there produced these extraordinary effects upon the skin. Now, while all these ideas were passing through me like lightning, this harpooneer never noticed me at all. But, after some difficulty having opened his bag, he commenced fumbling in it, and presently pulled out a sort of tomahawk, and a seal-skin wallet with the hair on. Placing these on the old chest in the middle of the room, he then took the New Zealand head—a ghastly thing enough—and crammed it down into the bag. He now took off his hat—a new beaver hat, when I came nigh singing out with fresh surprise. There was no hair on his head—none to speak of at least—nothing but a small scalp-knot twisted up on his forehead. His bald purplish head now looked for all the world like a mildewed skull. Had not the stranger stood between me and the door, I would have bolted out of it quicker than ever I bolted a dinner.

Even as it was, I thought something of slipping out of the window, but it was the second floor back. I am no coward, but what to make of this head-peddling purple rascal altogether passed my comprehension. Ignorance is the parent of fear, and being completely nonplussed and confounded about the stranger, I confess I was now as much afraid of him as if it was the devil himself who had thus broken into my room at the dead of night. In fact, I was so afraid of him that I was not game enough just then to address him, and demand a satisfactory answer concerning what seemed inexplicable in him.

Meanwhile, he continued the business of undressing, and at last showed his chest and arms. As I live, these covered parts of him were checkered with the same squares as his face; his back, too, was all over the same dark squares; he seemed to have been in a Thirty Years' War, and just escaped from it with a sticking-plaster shirt. Still more, his very legs were marked, as if a parcel of dark green frogs were running up the trunks of young palms. It was now quite plain that he must be some abominable savage or other shipped aboard of a whaleman in the South Seas, and so landed in this Christian country. I quaked to think of it. A peddler of heads too—perhaps the heads of his own brothers. He might take a fancy to mine—heavens! look at that tomahawk!

But there was no time for shuddering, for now the savage went about something that completely fascinated my attention, and convinced me that he must indeed be a heathen. Going to his heavy grego, or wrapall, or dreadnaught, which he had previously hung on a chair, he fumbled in the pockets, and produced at length a curious deformed image with a hunch on its back, and exactly the colour of a three days' old Congo baby. Remembering the embalmed head, at first I almost thought that this black manikin was a real baby preserved in some similar manner. But seeing that it was not at all limber, and that it glistened a good deal like polished ebony, I concluded that it must be nothing but a wooden idol, which indeed it proved to be. For now the savage goes up to the empty fire-place, and removing the papered fire-board, sets up this little hunchbacked image, like a tenpin, between the andirons. The chimney jambs and all the bricks inside were very sooty, so that I thought this fire-place made a very appropriate little shrine or chapel for his Congo idol.

I now screwed my eyes hard towards the half hidden image, feeling but ill at ease meantime—to see what was next to follow. First he takes about a double handful of shavings out of his grego pocket, and places them carefully before the idol; then laying a bit of ship biscuit on top and applying the flame from the lamp, he kindled the shavings into a sacrificial blaze. Presently, after many hasty snatches into the fire, and still hastier withdrawals of his fingers (whereby he seemed to be scorching them badly), he at last succeeded in drawing out the biscuit; then blowing off the heat and ashes a little, he made a polite offer of it to the little negro. But the little devil did not seem to fancy such dry sort of fare at all; he never moved his lips. All these strange antics were accompanied by still stranger guttural noises from the devotee, who seemed to be praying in a sing-song or else singing some pagan psalmody or other, during which his face twitched about in the most unnatural manner. At last extinguishing the fire, he took the idol up very unceremoniously, and bagged it again in his grego pocket as carelessly as if he were a sportsman bagging a dead woodcock.

All these queer proceedings increased my uncomfortableness, and seeing him now exhibiting strong symptoms of concluding his business operations, and jumping into bed with me, I thought it was high time, now or never, before the light was put out, to break the spell in which I had so long been bound.

But the interval I spent in deliberating what to say, was a fatal one. Taking up his tomahawk from the table, he examined the head of it for an instant, and then holding it to the light, with his mouth at the handle, he puffed out great clouds of tobacco smoke. The next moment the light was extinguished, and this wild cannibal, tomahawk between his teeth, sprang into bed with me. I sang out, I could not help it now; and giving a sudden grunt of astonishment he began feeling me.

Stammering out something, I knew not what, I rolled away from him against the wall, and then conjured him, whoever or whatever he might be, to keep quiet, and let me get up and light the lamp again. But his guttural responses satisfied me at once that he but ill comprehended my meaning.

'Who-e debel you?'—he at last said—'you no speak-e, dam-me, I kill-e.' And so saying the lighted tomahawk began flourishing about me in the dark.

'Landlord, for God's sake, Peter Coffin!' shouted I. 'Landlord! Watch! Coffin! Angels! save me!'

'Speak-e! tell-ee me whoo-ee be, or dam-me, I kill-e!' again growled the cannibal, while his horrid flourishings of the tomahawk scattered the hot tobacco ashes about me till I thought my linen would get on fire. But thank heaven at that moment the landlord came into the room light in hand, and leaping from the bed I ran up to him.

'Don't be afraid now,' said he, grinning again. 'Queequeg here wouldn't harm a hair of your head.'

'Stop your grinning,' shouted I, 'and why didn't you tell me that that infernal harpooneer was a cannibal?'

'I though ye know'd it;—didn't I tell ye, he was a peddlin' heads around town?—but turn flukes again and go to sleep. Queequeg, look here—you sabbee me, I sabbee you—this man sleepe you—you sabbee?'—

'Me sabbee plenty' grunted Queequeg, puffing away at his pipe and sitting up in bed.

'You gettee in,' he added, motioning to me with his tomahawk, and throwing the clothes to one side. He really did this in not only a civil but a really kind and charitable way. I stood looking at him a moment. For all his tattooings he was on the whole a clean, comely looking cannibal. What's all this fuss I have been making about, thought I to myself—the man's a human being just as I am: he has just as much reason to fear me, as I have to be afraid of him. Better sleep with a sober cannibal than a drunken Christian.

'Landlord,' said I, 'tell him to stash his tomahawk there, or pipe, or whatever you call it; tell him to stop smoking, in short, and I will turn in with him. But I don't fancy having a man smoking in bed with me. It's dangerous. Besides, I ain't insured.'

This being told to Queequeg, he at once complied, and again politely motioned me to get into bed—rolling over to one side as much as to say— I wont touch a leg of ye.

'Good night, landlord,' said I, 'you may go.'

I turned in, and never slept better in my life.

CHAPTER IV

THE COUNTERPANE

Upon waking next morning about daylight, I found Queequeg's arm thrown over me in the most loving and affectionate manner. You had almost thought I had been his wife. The counterpane was of patchwork, full of odd little parti-colored squares and triangles; and this arm of his tattooed all over with an interminable Cretan labyrinth of a figure, no two parts of which were of one precise shade—owing I suppose to his keeping his arm at sea unmethodically in sun and shade, his shirt sleeves irregularly rolled up at various times—this same arm of his, I say, looked for all the world like a strip of that same patchwork quilt. Indeed, partly lying on it as the arm did when I first awoke, I could hardly tell it from the quilt, they so blended their hues together; and it was only by the sense of weight and pressure that I could tell that Queequeg was hugging me.

My sensations were strange. Let me try to explain them. When I was a child, I well remember a somewhat similar circumstance that befell me; whether it was a reality or a dream, I never could entirely settle. The circumstance was this. I had been cutting up some caper or other—I think it was trying to crawl up the chimney, as I had seen a little sweep do a few days previous; and my stepmother who, somehow or other, was all the time whipping me, or sending me to bed supperless,—my mother dragged me by the legs out of the chimney and packed me off to bed, though it was only two o'clock in the afternoon of the 21st June, the longest day in the year in our hemisphere. I felt dreadfully. But there was no help for it, so up stairs I went to my little room in the third floor, undressed myself as slowly as possible so as to kill time, and with a bitter sigh got between the sheets.

I lay there dismally calculating that sixteen entire hours must elapse before I could hope for a resurrection. Sixteen hours in bed! the small of my back ached to think of it. And it was so light too; the sun shining in at the window, and a great rattling of coaches in the streets, and the sound of gay voices all over the house. I felt worse and worse—at last I got up, dressed, and softly going down in my stockinged feet, sought out my stepmother, and suddenly threw myself at her feet, beseeching her as a particular favor to give me a good slippering for my misbehavior; anything indeed but condemning me to lie abed such an unendurable length of time. But she was the best and most conscientious of stepmothers, and back I had to go to my room. For several hours I lay there broad awake, feeling a great deal worse than I have ever done since, even from the greatest subsequent misfortunes. At last I must have fallen into a troubled nightmare of a doze; and slowly waking from it—half steeped in dreams—I opened my eyes, and the before sun-lit room was now wrapped in outer darkness. Instantly I felt a shock running through all my frame; nothing was to be seen, and nothing was to be heard; but a supernatural hand seemed placed in mine. My arm hung over the counterpane, and the nameless, unimaginable, silent form or phantom, to which the hand belonged, seemed closely seated by my bedside. For what seemed ages piled on ages, I lay there, frozen with the most awful fears, not daring to drag away my hand; yet ever thinking that if I could but stir it one single inch, the horrid spell would be broken. I knew not how this consciousness at last glided away from me; but waking in the morning, I shudderingly remembered it all, and for days and weeks and months afterwards I lost myself in confounding attempts to explain the mystery. Nay, to this very hour, I often puzzle myself with it.

Now, take away the awful fear, and my sensations at feeling the supernatural hand in mine were very similar, in their strangeness, to those which I experienced on waking up and seeing Queequeg's pagan arm thrown round me. But at length all the past night's events soberly recurred, one by one, in fixed reality, and then I lay only alive to the comical predicament. For though I tried to move his arm—unlock his bridegroom clasp—yet, sleeping as he was, he still hugged me tightly, as though naught but death should part us twain. I now strove to rouse him—'Queequeg!'—but his only answer was a snore. I then rolled over, my neck feeling as if it were in a horse-collar; and suddenly felt a slight scratch. Throwing aside the counterpane, there lay the tomahawk sleeping by the savage's side, as if it were a hatchet-faced baby. A pretty pickle, truly, thought I; abed here in a strange house in the broad day, with a cannibal and a tomahawk! 'Queequeg!—in the name of goodness, Queequeg, wake!' At length, by dint of much wriggling, and loud and incessant expostulations upon the unbecomingness of his hugging a fellow male in that matrimonial sort of style, I succeeded in extracting a grunt; and presently, he drew back his arm, shook himself all over like a Newfoundland dog just from the water, and sat up in bed, stiff as a pike-staff, looking at me, and rubbing his eyes as if he did not altogether remember how I came to be there, though a dim consciousness of knowing something about me seemed slowly dawning over him. Meanwhile, I lay quietly eyeing him, having no serious misgivings now, and bent upon narrowly observing so curious a creature. When, at last, his mind seemed made up touching the character of his bedfellow, and he became, as it were, reconciled to the fact; he jumped out upon the floor, and by certain signs and sounds gave me to understand that, if it pleased me, he would dress first and then leave me to dress afterwards, having the whole apartment to myself. Thinks I, Queequeg, under the circumstances, this is a very civilized overture; but, the truth is, these savages have an innate sense of delicacy, say what you will; it is marvellous how essentially polite they are. I pay this particular compliment to Queequeg, because he treated me with so much civility and consideration, while I was guilty of great rudeness; staring at him from the bed, and watching all his toilette motions; for the time my curiosity getting the better of my breeding. Nevertheless, a man like Queequeg you don't see every day, he and his ways were well worth unusual regarding.

He commenced dressing at top by donning his beaver hat, a very tall one, by the by, and then—still minus his trowsers—he hunted up his boots. What under the heavens he did it for, I cannot tell, but his next movement was to crush himself—boots in hand, and hat on—under the bed; when, from sundry violent gaspings and strainings, I inferred he was hard at work booting himself; though by no law of propriety that I ever heard of, is any man required to be private when putting on his boots. But Queequeg, do you see, was a creature in the transition state—neither caterpillar nor butterfly. He was just enough civilized to show off his outlandishness in the strangest possible manner. His education was not yet completed. He was an undergraduate. If he had not been a small degree civilized, he very probably would not have troubled himself with boots at all; but then, if he had not been still a savage, he never would have dreamt of getting under the bed to put them on. At last, he emerged with his hat very much dented and crushed down over his eyes, and began creaking and limping about the room, as if, not being much accustomed to boots, his pair of damp, wrinkled cowhide ones—probably not made to order either—rather pinched and tormented him at the first go off of a bitter cold morning.

Seeing, now, that there were no curtains to the window, and that the street being very narrow, the house opposite commanded a plain view into the room, and observing more and more the indecorous figure that Queequeg made, staving about with little else but his hat and boots on; I begged him as well as I could, to accelerate his toilet somewhat, and particularly to get into his pantaloons as soon as possible. He complied, and then proceeded to wash himself. At that time in the morning any Christian would have washed his face; but Queequeg, to my amazement, contented himself with restricting his ablutions to his chest, arms, and hands. He then donned his waistcoat, and taking up a piece of hard soap on the wash-stand centre-table, dipped it into water and commenced lathering his face. I was watching to see where he kept his razor, when lo and behold, he takes the harpoon from the bed corner, slips out the long wooden stock, unsheathes the head, whets it a little on his boot, and striding up to the bit of mirror against the wall, begins a vigorous scraping, or rather harpooning of his cheeks. Thinks I, Queequeg, this is using Rogers's best cutlery with a vengeance. Afterwards I wondered the less at this operation when I came to know of what fine steel the head of a harpoon is made, and how exceedingly sharp the long straight edges are always kept.

The rest of his toilet was soon achieved, and he proudly marched out of the room, wrapped up in his great pilot monkey jacket, and sporting his harpoon like a marshal's baton.

CHAPTER V

BREAKFAST

I quickly followed suit, and descending into the bar-room accosted the grinning landlord very pleasantly. I cherished no malice towards him, though he had been skylarking with me not a little in the matter of my bedfellow.

However, a good laugh is a mighty good thing, and rather too scarce a good thing; the more's the pity. So, if any one man, in his own proper person, afford stuff for a good joke to anybody, let him not be backward, but let him cheerfully allow himself to spend and be spent in that way. And the man that has anything bountifully laughable about him, be sure there is more in that man than you perhaps think for.

The bar-room was now full of the boarders who had been dropping in the night previous, and whom I had not as yet had a good look at. They were nearly all whalemen; chief mates, and second mates, and third mates, and sea carpenters, and sea coopers, and sea blacksmiths, and harpooneers, and ship keepers; a brown and brawny company, with bosky beards; an unshorn, shaggy set, all wearing monkey jackets for morning gowns.

You could pretty plainly tell how long each one had been ashore. This young fellow's healthy cheek is like a suntoasted pear in hue, and would seem to smell almost as musky; he cannot have been three days landed from his Indian voyage. That man next him looks a few shades lighter; you might say a touch of satin wood is in him. In the complexion of a third still lingers a tropic tawn, but slightly bleached withal; *he* doubtless has tarried whole weeks ashore. But who could show a cheek like Queequeg? which, barred with various tints, seemed like the Andes' western slope, to show forth in one array, contrasting climates, zone by zone.

'Grub, ho!' now cried the landlord, flinging open a door, and in we went to breakfast.

They say that men who have seen the world, thereby become quite at ease in manner, quite self-possessed in company. Not always, though: Ledyard, the great New Englander traveller, and Mungo Park, the Scotch one; of all men, they possessed the least assurance in the parlor. But perhaps the mere crossing of Siberia in a sledge drawn by dogs as Ledyard did, or the taking a long solitary walk on an empty stomach, in the negro heart of Africa, which was the sum of poor Mungo's performances—this kind of travel, I say, may not be the very best mode of attaining a high social polish. Still, for the most part, that sort of thing is to be had anywhere.

These reflections just here are occasioned by the circumstance that after we were all seated at the table, and I was preparing to hear some good stories about whaling; to my no small surprise, nearly every man maintained a profound silence. And not only that, but they looked embarrassed. Yes, here were a set of sea-dogs, many of whom without the slightest bashfulness had boarded great whales on the high seas—entire strangers to them—and duelled them dead without winking; and yet, here they sat at a social breakfast table—all of the same calling, all of kindred tastes—looking round as sheepishly at each other as though they had never been out of sight of some sheepfold among the Green Mountains. A curious sight; these bashful bears, these timid warrior whalemen!

But as for Queequeg—why, Queequeg sat there among them—at the head of the table, too, it so chanced; as cool as an icicle. To be sure I cannot say much for his breeding. His greatest admirer could not have cordially justified his bringing his harpoon into breakfast with him, and using it there without ceremony; reaching over the table with it, to the imminent jeopardy of many heads, and grappling the beefsteaks towards him. But *that* was certainly very coolly done by him, and every one knows that in most people's estimation, to do anything coolly is to do it genteelly.

We will not speak of all Queequeg's peculiarities here; how he eschewed coffee and hot rolls, and applied his undivided attention to beefsteaks, done rare. Enough, that when breakfast was over he withdrew like the rest into the public room, lighted his tomahawk-pipe, and was sitting there quietly digesting and smoking with his inseparable hat on, when I sallied out for a stroll.

CHAPTER VI

THE STREET

If I had been astonished at first catching a glimpse of so outlandish an individual as Queequeg circulating among the polite society of a civilized town, that astonishment soon departed upon taking my first daylight stroll through the streets of New Bedford.

In thoroughfares nigh the docks, any considerable seaport will frequently offer to view the queerest looking nondescripts from foreign parts. Even in Broadway and Chestnut streets, Mediterranean mariners will sometimes jostle the affrighted ladies. Regent street is not unknown to Lascars and Malays; and at Bombay, in the Apollo Green, live Yankees have often scared the natives. But New Bedford beats all Water street and Wapping. In these last-mentioned haunts you see only sailors; but in New Bedford, actual cannibals stand chatting at street corners; savages outright; many of whom yet carry on their bones unholy flesh. It makes a stranger stare.

But, besides the Feegeeans, Tongataboooans, Erromanggoans, Pannangians, and Brighggians, and, besides the wild specimens of the whaling-craft which unheeded reel about the streets, you will see other sights still more curious, certainly more comical. There weekly arrive in this town scores of green Vermonters and New Hampshire men, all athirst for gain and glory in the fishery. They are mostly young, of stalwart frames; fellows who have felled forests, and now seek to drop the axe and snatch the whale-lance. Many are as green as the Green Mountains whence they came. In some things you would think them but a few hours old. Look there! that chap strutting round the corner. He wears a beaver hat and swallow-tailed coat, girdled with a sailor-belt and sheath-knife. Here comes another with a sou'-wester and a bombazine cloak.

No town-bred dandy will compare with a country-bred one—I mean a downright bumpkin dandy—a fellow that, in the dog-days, will mow his two acres in buckskin gloves for fear of tanning his hands. Now when a country dandy like this takes it into his head to make a distinguished reputation, and joins the great whale-fishery, you should see the comical things he does upon reaching the seaport. In bespeaking his sea-outfit, he orders bell-buttons to his waistcoats; straps to his canvas trowsers. Ah, poor Hay-Seed! how bitterly will burst those straps in the first howling gale, when thou art driven, straps, buttons, and all, down the throat of the tempest.

But think not that this famous town has only harpooneers, cannibals, and bumpkins to show her visitors. Not at all. Still New Bedford is a queer place. Had it not been for us whalemen, that tract of land would this day perhaps have been in as howling condition as the coast of Labrador. As it is, parts of her back country are enough to frighten one, they look so bony. The town itself is perhaps the dearest place to live in, in all New England. It is a land of oil, true enough: but not like Canaan; a land, also, of corn and wine. The streets do not run with milk; nor in the spring-time do they pave them with fresh eggs. Yet, in spite of this, nowhere in all America will you find more patrician-like houses, parks and gardens more opulent, than in New Bedford. Whence came they? how planted upon this once scraggy scoria of a country?

Go and gaze upon the iron emblematical harpoons round yonder lofty mansion, and your question will be answered. Yes; all these brave houses and flowery gardens came from the Atlantic, Pacific, and Indian oceans. One and all, they were harpooned and dragged up hither from the bottom of the sea. Can Herr Alexander perform a feat like that?

In New Bedford, fathers, they say, gives whales for dowers to their daughters, and portion off their nieces with a few porpoises a-piece. You must go to New Bedford to see a brilliant wedding; for, they say, they have reservoirs of oil in every house, and every night recklessly burn their lengths in spermaceti candles.

In summer time, the town is sweet to see; full of fine maples—long avenues of green and gold. And in August, high in air, the beautiful and bountiful horse-chestnuts, candelabra-wise, proffer the passer-by their tapering upright cones of congregated blossoms. So omnipotent is art; which in many a district of New Bedford has superinduced bright terraces of flowers upon the barren refuse rocks thrown aside at creation's final day.

And the women of New Bedford, they bloom like their own red roses. But roses only bloom in summer; whereas the fine carnation of their cheeks is perennial as sunlight in the seventh heavens. Elsewhere match that bloom of theirs, ye cannot, save in Salem, where they tell me the young girls breathe such musk, their sailor sweethearts smell them miles off shore, as though they were drawing nigh the odorous Moluccas instead of the Puritanic sands.

CHAPTER VII

THE CHAPEL

In this same New Bedford there stands a Whaleman's Chapel, and few are the moody fishermen, shortly bound for the Indian Ocean or Pacific, who fail to make a Sunday visit to the spot. I am sure that I did not.

Returning from my first morning stroll, I again sallied out upon this special errand. The sky had changed from clear, sunny cold, to driving sleet and mist. Wrapping myself in my shaggy jacket of the cloth called bearskin, I fought my way against the stubborn storm. Entering, I found a small scattered congregation of sailors, and sailors' wives and widows. A muffled silence reigned, only broken at times by the shrieks of the storm. Each silent worshipper seemed purposely sitting apart from the other, as if each silent grief were insular and incommunicable. The chaplain had not yet arrived; and there these silent islands of men and women sat steadfastly eyeing several marble tablets, with black borders, masoned into the wall on either side of the pulpit. Three of them ran something like the following, but I do not pretend to quote:

SACRED
To the Memory
OF
JOHN TALBOT,
Who, at the age of eighteen, was lost overboard,
Near the Isle of Desolation, off Patagonia,
November 1*st*, 1836.
THIS TABLET
Is erected to his Memory
BY HIS SISTER

SACRED
To the Memory
OF
ROBERT LONG, WILLIS ELLERY,
NATHAN COLEMAN, WALTER CANNY,
SETH MACY, AND SAMUEL GLEIG,
Forming one of the boats' crews
OF
THE SHIP ELIZA,
Who were towed out of sight by a Whale,
On the Off-shore Ground in the
PACIFIC,
December 31*st*, 1839.
THIS MARBLE
Is here placed by their surviving
SHIPMATES.

SACRED
To the Memory
OF
The late
CAPTAIN EZEKIEL HARDY,
Who in the bows of his boat was killed by a
Sperm Whale on the coast of Japan,
August 3*d*, 1833.
THIS TABLET
Is erected to his Memory
BY
HIS WIDOW.

Shaking off the sleet from my ice-glazed hat and jacket, I seated myself near the door, and turning sideways was surprised to see Queequeg near me. Affected by the solemnity of the scene, there was a wondering gaze of incredulous curiosity in his countenance. This savage was the only person present who seemed to notice my entrance; because he was the only one who could not read, and, therefore, was not reading those frigid inscriptions on the wall. Whether any of the relatives of the seamen whose names appeared there were now among the congregation, I knew not; but so many are the unrecorded accidents in the fishery, and so plainly did several women present wear the countenance if not the trappings of some unceasing grief, that I feel sure that here before me were assembled those, in whose unhealing hearts the sight of those bleak tablets sympathetically caused the old wounds to bleed afresh.

Oh! ye whose dead lie buried beneath the green grass; who standing among flowers can say—here, *here* lies my beloved, ye know not the desolation that broods in bosoms like these. What bitter blanks in those black-bordered marbles which cover no ashes! What despair in those immovable inscriptions! What deadly voids and unbidden infidelities in the lines that seem to gnaw upon all Faith, and refuse resurrections to the beings who have placelessly perished without a grave. As well might those tablets stand in the cave of Elephanta as here.

In what census of living creatures, the dead of mankind are included; why it is that a universal proverb says of them, that they tell no tales, though containing more secrets than the Goodwin Sands; how it is that to his name who yesterday departed for the other world, we prefix so significant and infidel a word, and yet do not thus entitle him, if he but embarks for the remotest Indies of this living earth; why the Life Insurance Companies pay death-forfeitures upon immortals; in what eternal, unstirring paralysis, and deadly, hopeless trance, yet lies antique Adam who died sixty round centuries ago; how it is that we still refuse to be comforted for those who we nevertheless maintain are dwelling in unspeakable bliss; why all the living so strive to hush all the dead; wherefore but the rumor of a knocking in a tomb will terrify a whole city. All these things are not without their meanings.

But Faith, like a jackal, feeds among the tombs, and even from these dead doubts she gathers her most vital hope.

It needs scarcely to be told, with what feelings, on the eve of a Nantucket voyage, I regarded those marble tablets, and by the murky light of that darkened, doleful day read the fate of the whalemen who had gone before me. Yes, Ishmael, the same fate may be thine. But somehow I grew merry again. Delightful inducements to embark, fine chance for promotion, it seems—aye, a stove boat will make me an immortal by brevet. Yes, there is death in this business of whaling—a speechlessly quick chaotic bundling of a man into Eternity. But what then? Methinks we have hugely mistaken this matter of Life and Death. Methinks that what they call my shadow here on earth is my true substance. Methinks that in looking at things spiritual, we are too much like oysters observing the sun through the water, and thinking that thick water the thinnest of air. Methinks my body is but the lees of my better being. In fact take my body who will, take it I say, it is not me. And therefore three cheers for Nantucket; and come a stove boat and stove body when they will, for stave my soul, Jove himself cannot.

CHAPTER VIII

The Pulpit

I had not been seated very long ere a man of a certain venerable robustness entered; immediately as the storm-pelted door flew back upon admitting him, a quick regardful eyeing of him by all the congregation, sufficiently attested that this fine old man was the chaplain. Yes, it was the famous Father Mapple, so called by the whalemen, among whom he was a very great favorite. He had been a sailor and a harpooneer in his youth, but for many years past had dedicated his life to the ministry. At the time I now write of, Father Mapple was in the hardy winter of a healthy old age; that sort of old age which seems merging into a second flowering youth, for among all the fissures of his wrinkles, there shone certain mild gleams of a newly developing bloom—the spring verdure peeping forth even beneath February's snow. No one having previously heard his history, could for the first time behold Father Mapple without the utmost interest, because there were certain engrafted clerical peculiarities about him, imputable to that adventurous maritime life he had led. When he entered I observed that he carried no umbrella, and certainly had not come in his carriage, for his tarpaulin hat ran down with melting sleet, and his great pilot cloth jacket seemed almost to drag him to the floor with the weight of the water it had absorbed. However, hat and coat and overshoes were one by one removed, and hung up in a little space in an adjacent corner; when, arrayed in a decent suit, he quietly approached the pulpit.

Like most old fashioned pulpits, it was a very lofty one, and since a regular stairs to such a height would, by its long angle with the floor, seriously contract the already small area of the chapel, the architect, it seemed, had acted upon the hint of Father Mapple, and finished the pulpit without a stairs, substituting a perpendicular side ladder, like those used in mounting a ship from a boat at sea. The wife of a whaling captain had provided the chapel with a handsome pair of red worsted man-ropes for this ladder, which, being itself nicely headed, and stained with a mahogany color, the whole contrivance, considering what manner of chapel it was, seemed by no means in bad taste. Halting for an instant at the foot of the ladder, and with both hands grasping the ornamental knobs of the man-ropes, Father Mapple cast a look upwards, and then with a truly sailor-like but still reverential dexterity, hand over hand, mounted the steps as if ascending the main-top of his vessel.

The perpendicular parts of this side ladder, as is usually the case with swinging ones, were of cloth-covered rope, only the rounds were of wood, so that at every step there was a joint. At my first glimpse of the pulpit, it had not escaped me that however convenient for a ship, these joints in the present instance seemed unnecessary. For I was not prepared to see Father Mapple after gaining the height, slowly turn round, and stooping over the pulpit, deliberately drag up the ladder step by step, till the whole was deposited within, leaving him impregnable in his little Quebec.

I pondered some time without fully comprehending the reason for this. Father Mapple enjoyed such a wide reputation for sincerity and sanctity, that I could not suspect him of courting notoriety by any mere tricks of the stage. No, thought I, there must be some sober reason for this thing; furthermore, it must symbolize something unseen. Can it be, then, that by that act of physical isolation, he signifies his spiritual withdrawal for the time, from all outward worldly ties and connexions? Yes, for replenished with the meat and wine of the word, to the faithful man of God, this pulpit, I see, is a self-containing strong-hold—a lofty Ehrenbreitstein, with a perennial well of water within the walls.

But the side ladder was not the only strange feature of the place, borrowed from the chaplain's former sea-farings. Between the marble cenotaphs on either hand of the pulpit, the wall which formed its back was adorned with a large painting representing a gallant ship beating against a terrible storm off a lee coast of black rocks and snowy breakers. But high above the flying scud and dark-rolling clouds, there floated a little isle of sunlight, from which beamed forth an angel's face; and this bright face shed a distinct spot of radiance upon the ship's tossed deck, something like that silver plate now inserted into the Victory's plank where Nelson fell. 'Ah, noble ship,' the angel seemed to say, 'beat on, beat on, thou noble ship, and bear a hardy helm; for lo! the sun is breaking through; the clouds are rolling off—serenest azure is at hand.'

Nor was the pulpit itself without a trace of the same sea-taste that had achieved the ladder and the picture. Its panelled front was in the likeness of a ship's bluff bows, and the Holy Bible rested on a projecting piece of scroll work, fashioned after a ship's fiddle-headed beak.

What could be more full of meaning?—for the pulpit is ever this earth's foremost part; all the rest comes in its rear; the pulpit leads the world. From thence it is the storm of God's quick wrath is first descried, and the bow must bear the earliest brunt. From thence it is the God of breezes fair or foul is first invoked for favorable winds. Yes, the world's a ship on its passage out, and not a voyage complete; and the pulpit is its prow.

CHAPTER IX

The Sermon

Father Mapple rose, and in a mild voice of unassuming authority ordered the scattered people to condense. 'Starboard gangway, there! side away to larboard—larboard gangway to starboard! Midships! midships!'

There was a low rumbling of heavy sea-boots among the benches, and a still slighter shuffling of women's shoes, and all was quiet again, and every eye on the preacher.

He paused a little; then kneeling in the pulpit's bows, folded his large brown hands across his chest, uplifted his closed eyes, and offered a prayer so deeply devout that he seemed kneeling and praying at the bottom of the sea.

This ended, in prolonged solemn tones, like the continual tolling of a bell in a ship that is foundering at sea in a fog—in such tones he commenced reading the following hymn; but changing his manner towards the concluding stanzas, burst forth with a pealing exultation and joy—

The ribs and terrors in the whale,
  Arched over me a dismal gloom,
While all God's sun-lit waves rolled by,
  And lift me deepening down to doom.
I saw the opening maw of hell,
  With endless pains and sorrows there;
Which none but they that feel can tell—
  Oh, I was plunging to despair.

In black distress, I called my God,
  When I could scarce believe him mine,
He bowed his ear to my complaints—
  No more the whale did me confine.

With speed he flew to my relief,
  As on a radiant dolphin borne;
Awful, yet bright, as lightning shone
  The face of my Deliverer God.

My song for ever shall record
  That terrible, that joyful hour;
I give the glory to my God,
  His all the mercy and the power.

Nearly all joined in singing this hymn, which swelled high above the howling of the storm. A brief pause ensued; the preacher slowly turned over the leaves of the Bible, and at last, folding his hand down upon the proper page, said: 'Beloved shipmates, clinch the last verse of the first chapter of Jonah—"And God had prepared a great fish to swallow up Jonah."

'Shipmates, this book, containing only four chapters—four yarns—is one of the smallest strands in the mighty cable of the Scriptures. Yet what depths of the soul does Jonah's deep sea-line sound! what a pregnant lesson to us is this prophet! What a noble thing is that canticle in the fish's belly! How billow-like and boisterously grand! We feel the floods surging over us; we sound with him to the kelpy bottom of the waters; sea-weed and all the slime of the sea is about us! But *what* is this lesson that the book of Jonah teaches? Shipmates, it is a two-stranded lesson; a lesson to us all as sinful men, and a lesson to me as a pilot of the living God. As sinful men, it is a lesson to us all, because it is a story of the sin, hard-heartedness, suddenly awakened fears, the swift punishment, repentance, prayers, and finally the deliverance and joy of Jonah. As with all sinners among men, the sin of this son of Amittai was in his wilful disobedience of the command of God—never mind now what that command was, or how conveyed—which he found a hard command. But all the things that God would have us do are hard for us to do—remember that—and hence, he oftener commands us than endeavors to persuade. And if we obey God, we must disobey ourselves; and it is in this disobeying ourselves, wherein the hardness of obeying God consists.

'With this sin of disobedience in him, Jonah still further flouts at God, by seeking to flee from Him. He thinks that a ship made by men, will carry him into countries where God does not reign, but only the Captains of this earth. He skulks about the wharves of Joppa, and seeks a ship that's bound for Tarshish. There lurks, perhaps, a hitherto unheeded meaning here. By all accounts Tarshish could have been no other city than the modern Cadiz. That's the opinion of learned men. And where is Cadiz, shipmates? Cadiz is in Spain; as far by water, from Joppa, as Jonah could possibly have sailed in those ancient days, when the Atlantic was an almost unknown sea. Because Joppa, the modern Jaffa, shipmates, is on the most easterly coast of the Mediterranean, the Syrian; and Tarshish or Cadiz more than two thousand miles to the westward from that, just outside the Straits of Gibraltar. See ye not then, shipmates, that Jonah sought to flee world-wide from God? Miserable man! Oh! most contemptible and worthy of all scorn; with slouched hat and guilty eye, skulking from his God; prowling among the shipping like a vile burglar hastening to cross the sea. So disordered, self-condemning is his look, that had there been policemen in those days, Jonah, on the mere suspicion of something wrong, had been arrested ere he touched a deck. How plainly he's a fugitive! no baggage, not a hat-box, valise, or carpet-bag,—no friends accompany him to the wharf with their adieux. At last, after much dodging search, he finds the Tarshish ship receiving the last items of her cargo; and as he steps on board to see its Captain in the cabin, all the sailors for the moment desist from hoisting in the goods, to mark the stranger's evil eye. Jonah sees this; but in vain he tries to look all ease and confidence; in vain essays his wretched smile. Strong intuitions of the man assure the mariners he can be no innocent. In their gamesome but still serious way, one whispers to the other—"Jack, he's robbed a widow;" or, "Joe, do you mark him; he's a bigamist;" or, "Harry, lad, I guess he's the adulterer that broke jail in old Gomorrah, or belike, one of the missing murderers from Sodom." Another runs to read the bill that's stuck against the spile upon the wharf to which the ship is moored, offering five hundred gold coins for the apprehension of a parricide, and containing a description of his person. He reads, and looks from Jonah to the bill; while all his sympathetic shipmates now crowd round Jonah, prepared to lay their hands upon him. Frighted Jonah trembles, and summoning all his boldness to his face, only looks so much the more a coward. He will not confess himself suspected; but that itself is strong suspicion. So he makes the best of it; and when the sailors find him not to be the man that is advertised, they let him pass, and he descends into the cabin.

'"Who's there?" cries the Captain at his busy desk, hurriedly making out his papers for the Customs—"Who's there?" Oh! how that harmless question mangles Jonah! For the instant he almost turns to flee again. But he rallies. "I seek a passage in this ship to Tarshish; how soon sail ye, sir?" Thus far the busy Captain had not looked up to Jonah, though the man now stands before him; but no sooner does he hear that hollow voice, than he darts a scrutinizing glance. "We sail with the next coming tide," at last he slowly answered, still intently eyeing him. "No sooner, sir?"—"Soon enough for any honest man that goes a passenger." Ha! Jonah, that's another stab. But he swiftly calls away the Captain from that scent. "I'll sail with ye,"—he says,—"the passage money, how much is that?—I'll pay now." For it is particularly written, shipmates, as if it were a thing not to be overlooked in this history, "that he paid the fare thereof" ere the craft did sail. And taken with the context, this is full of meaning.

'Now Jonah's Captain, shipmates, was one whose discernment detects crime in any, but whose cupidity exposes it only in the penniless. In this world, shipmates, sin that pays its way can travel freely, and without a passport; whereas Virtue, if a pauper, is stopped at all frontiers. So Jonah's Captain prepares to test the length of Jonah's purse, ere he judge him openly. He charges him thrice the usual sum; and it's assented to. Then the Captain knows that Jonah is a fugitive; but at the same time resolves to help a flight that paves its rear with gold. Yet when Jonah fairly takes out his purse, prudent suspicions still molest the Captain. He rings every coin to find a counterfeit. Not a forger, any way, he mutters; and Jonah is put down for his passage. "Point out my state-room, Sir," says Jonah now, "I'm travel-weary; I need sleep." "Thou look'st like it," says the Captain, "there's thy room." Jonah enters, and would lock the door, but the lock contains no key. Hearing him foolishly fumbling there, the Captain laughs lowly to himself, and mutters something about the doors of convicts' cells being never allowed to be locked within. All dressed and dusty as he is, Jonah throws himself into his berth, and finds the little state-room ceiling almost resting on his forehead. The air is close, and Jonah gasps. Then, in that contracted hole, sunk, too, beneath the ship's water-line, Jonah feels the heralding presentiment of that stifling hour, when the whale shall hold him in the smallest of his bowel's wards.

'Screwed at its axis against the side, a swinging lamp slightly oscillates in Jonah's room; and the ship, heeling over towards the wharf with the weight of the last bales received, the lamp, flame and all, though in slight motion, still maintains a permanent obliquity with reference to the room; though, in truth, infallibly straight itself, it but made obvious the false, lying levels among which it hung. The lamp alarms and frightens Jonah; as lying in his berth his tormented eyes roll round the place, and this thus far successful fugitive finds no refuge for his restless glance. But that contradiction in the lamp more and more appals him. The floor, the ceiling, and the side, are all awry. "Oh! so my conscience hangs in me!" he groans, "straight upward, so it burns; but the chambers of my soul are all in crookedness!"

'Like one who after a night of drunken revelry hies to his bed, still reeling, but with conscience yet pricking him, as the plungings of the Roman race-horse but so much the more strike his steel tags into him; as one who in that miserable plight still turns and turns in giddy anguish, praying God for annihilation until the fit be passed; and at last amid the whirl of woe he feels, a deep stupor steals over him, as over the man who bleeds to death, for conscience is the wound, and there's naught to staunch it; so, after sore wrestlings in his berth, Jonah's prodigy of ponderous misery drags him drowning down to sleep.

'And now the time of tide has come; the ship casts off her cables and from the deserted wharf the uncheered ship for Tarshish, all careening, glides to sea. That ship, my friends, was the first of recorded smugglers! the contraband was Jonah. But the sea rebels; he will not bear the wicked burden. A dreadful storm comes on, the ship is like to break. But now when the boatswain calls all hands to lighten her; when boxes, bales, and jars are clattering overboard; when the wind is shrieking, and the men are yelling, and every plank thunders with trampling feet right over Jonah's head; in all this raging tumult, Jonah sleeps his hideous sleep. He sees no black sky and raging sea, feels not the reeling timbers, and little hears he or heeds he the far rush of the mighty whale, which even now with open mouth is cleaving the seas after him. Aye, shipmates, Jonah was gone down into the sides of the ship—a berth in the cabin as I have taken it, and was fast asleep. But the frightened master comes to him, and shrieks in his dead ear, "What meanest thou, O sleeper! arise!" Startled from his lethargy by that direful cry, Jonah staggers to his feet, and stumbling to the deck, grasps a shroud, to look out upon the sea. But at that moment he is sprung upon by a panther billow leaping over the bulwarks. Wave after wave thus leaps into the ship, and finding no speedy vent runs roaring fore and aft, till the mariners come nigh to drowning while yet afloat. And ever, as the white moon shows her affrighted face from the steep gullies in the blackness overhead, aghast Jonah sees the rearing bowsprit pointing high upward, but soon beat downward again towards the tormented deep.

'Terrors upon terrors run shouting through his soul. In all his cringing attitudes, the God-fugitive is now too plainly known. The sailors mark him; more and more certain grow their suspicions of him, and at last, fully to test the truth, by referring the whole matter to high Heaven, they fall to casting lots, to see for whose cause this great tempest was upon them. The lot is Jonah's; that discovered, then how furiously they mob him with their questions. "What is thine occupation? Whence comest thou? Thy country? What people" But mark now, my shipmates, the behavior of poor Jonah. The eager mariners but ask him who he is, and where from; whereas, they not only receive an answer to those questions, but likewise another answer to a question not put by them, but the unsolicited answer is forced from Jonah by the hard hand of God that is upon him.

'"I am a Hebrew," he cries—and then—"I fear the Lord the God of Heaven who hath made the sea and the dry land!" Fear him, O Jonah? Aye, well mightest thou fear the Lord God *then*! Straightway, he now goes on to make a full confession; whereupon the mariners become more and more appalled, but still are pitiful. For when Jonah, not yet supplicating God for mercy, since he but too well knew the darkness of his deserts,—when wretched Jonah cries out to them to take him and cast him forth into the sea, for he knew that for *his* sake this great tempest was upon them; they mercifully turn from him, and seek by other means to save the ship. But all in vain; the indignant gale howls louder; then, with one hand raised invokingly to God, with the other they not unreluctantly lay hold of Jonah.

'And now behold Jonah taken up as an anchor and dropped into the sea; when instantly an oily calmness floats out from the east, and the sea is still, as Jonah carries down the gale with him, leaving smooth water behind. He goes down in the whirling heart of such a masterless commotion that he scarce heeds the moment when he drops seething into the yawning jaws awaiting him; and the whale shoots-to all his ivory teeth, like so many white bolts, upon his prison. Then Jonah prayed unto the Lord out of the fish's belly. But observe his prayer, and learn a weighty lesson. For sinful as he is, Jonah does not weep and wail for direct deliverance. He feels that his dreadful punishment is just. He leaves all his deliverance to God, contenting himself with this, that spite of all his pains and pangs, he will still look towards His holy temple. And here, shipmates, is true and faithful repentance; not clamorous for pardon, but grateful for punishment. And how pleasing to God was this conduct in Jonah, is shown in the eventual deliverance of him from the sea and the whale. Shipmates, I do not place Jonah before you to be copied for his sin but I do place him before you as a model for repentance. Sin not; but if you do, take heed to repent of it like Jonah.'

While he was speaking these words, the howling of the shrieking, slanting storm without seemed to add new power to the preacher, who, when describing Jonah's sea-storm, seemed tossed by a storm himself. His deep chest heaved as with a ground-swell; his tossed arms seemed the warring elements at work; and the thunders that rolled away from off his swarthy brow, and the light leaping from his eye, made all his simple hearers look on him with a quick fear that was strange to them.

There now came a lull in his look as he silently turned over the leaves of the Book once more; and, at last, standing motionless, with closed eyes, for the moment, seemed communing with God and himself.

But again he leaned over towards the people, and bowing his head lowly, with an aspect of the deepest yet manliest humility, he spake these words:

'Shipmates, God has laid but one hand upon you; both his hands press upon me. I have read ye by what murky light may be mine the lesson that Jonah teaches to all sinners; and therefore to ye, and still more to me, for I am a greater sinner than ye. And now how gladly would I come down from this mast-head and sit on the hatches there where you sit, and listen as you listen, while some one of you reads *me* that other and more awful lesson which Jonah teaches to *me,* as a pilot of the living God. How being an anointed pilot-prophet, or speaker of true things, and bidden by the Lord to sound those unwelcome truths in the ears of a wicked Nineveh, Jonah, appalled at the hostility he should raise, fled from his mission, and sought to escape his duty and his God by taking ship at Joppa. But God is everywhere; Tarshish he never reached. As we have seen, God came upon him in the whale, and swallowed him down to living gulfs of doom, and with swift slantings tore him along "into the midst of the seas," where the eddying depths sucked him ten thousand fathoms down, and "the weeds were wrapped about his head," and all the watery world of woe bowled over him. Yet even then beyond the reach of any plummet—"out of the belly of hell"—when the whale grounded upon the ocean's utmost bones, even then, God heard the engulphed, repenting prophet when he cried. Then God spake unto the fish; and from the shuddering cold and blackness of the sea, the whale came breeching up towards the warm and pleasant sun, and all the delights of air and earth; and "vomited out Jonah upon the dry land;" when the word of the Lord came a second time; and Jonah, bruised and beaten—his ears, like two sea-shells, still multitudinously murmuring of the ocean—Jonah did the Almighty's bidding. And what was that, shipmates? To preach the Truth to the face of Falsehood! That was it!

'This, shipmates, this is that other lesson; and woe to that pilot of the living God who slights it. Woe to him whom this world charms from Gospel duty! Woe to him who seeks to pour oil upon the waters when God has brewed them into a gale! Woe to him who seeks to please rather than to appal! Woe to him whose good name is more to him than goodness! Woe to him who, in this world courts not dishonor! Woe to him who would not be true, even though to be false were salvation! Yea, woe to him who, as the great Pilot Paul has it, while preaching to others is himself a castaway!'

He drooped and fell away from himself for a moment; then lifting his face to them again, showed a deep joy in his eyes, as he cried out with a heavenly enthusiasm,—'But oh! shipmates! on the starboard hand of every woe, there is a sure delight; and higher the top of that delight, than the bottom of the woe is deep. Is not the main-truck higher than the kelson is low? Delight is to him—a far, far upward, and inward delight—who against the proud gods and commodores of this earth, ever stands forth his own inexorable self. Delight is to him whose strong arms yet support him, when the ship of this base treacherous world has gone down beneath him. Delight is to him, who gives no quarter in the truth, and kills, burns, and destroys all sin though he pluck it out from under the robes of Senators and Judges. Delight—top-gallant delight is to him, who acknowledges no law or lord, but the Lord his God, and is only a patriot to heaven. Delight is to him, whom all the waves of the billows of the seas of the boisterous mob can never shake from this sure Keel of the Ages. And eternal delight and deliciousness will be his, who coming to lay him down, can say with his final breath—O Father!—chiefly known to me by Thy rod—mortal or immortal, here I die. I have striven to be Thine, more than to be this world's, or mine own. Yet this is nothing; I leave eternity to Thee; for what is man that he should live out the lifetime of his God?'

He said no more, but slowly waving a benediction, covered his face with his hands, and so remained kneeling, till all the people had departed, and he was left alone in the place.

CHAPTER X

A BOSOM FRIEND

Returning to the Spouter-Inn from the Chapel, I found Queequeg there quite alone; he having left the Chapel before the benediction some time. He was sitting on a bench before the fire, with his feet on the stove hearth, and in one hand was holding close up to his face that little negro idol of his; peering hard into its face, and with a jack-knife gently whittling away at its nose, meanwhile humming to himself in his heathenish way.

But being now interrupted, he put up the image; and pretty soon, going to the table, took up a large book there, and placing it on his lap began counting the pages with deliberate regularity; at every fiftieth page—as I fancied—stopping a moment, looking vacantly around him, and giving utterance to a long-drawn gurgling whistle of astonishment. He would then begin again at the next fifty; seeming to commence at number one each time, as though he could not count more than fifty, and it was only by such a large number of fifties being found together, that his astonishment at the multitude of pages was excited.

With much interest I sat watching him. Savage though he was, and hideously marred about the face—at least to my taste—his countenance yet had a something in it which was by no means disagreeable. You cannot hide the soul. Through all his unearthly tattooings, I thought I saw the traces of a simple honest heart; and in his large, deep eyes, fiery black and bold, there seemed tokens of a spirit that would dare a thousand devils. And besides all this, there was a certain lofty bearing about the Pagan, which even his uncouthness could not altogether maim. He looked like a man who had never cringed and never had had a creditor. Whether it was, too, that his head being shaved, his forehead was drawn out in freer and brighter relief, and looked more expansive than it otherwise would, this I will not venture to decide; but certain it was his head was phrenologically an excellent one. It may seem ridiculous, but it reminded me of General Washington's head, as seen in the popular busts of him. It had the same long regularly graded retreating slope from above the brows, which were likewise very projecting, like two long promontories thickly wooded on top. Queequeg was George Washington cannibalistically developed.

Whilst I was thus closely scanning him, half-pretending meanwhile to be looking out at the storm from the casement, he never heeded my presence, never troubled himself with so much as a single glance; but appeared wholly occupied with counting the pages of the marvellous book. Considering how sociably we had been sleeping together the night previous, and especially considering the affectionate arm I had found thrown over me upon waking in the morning, I thought this indifference of his very strange. But savages are strange beings; at times you do not know exactly how to take them. At first they are overawing; their calm self-collectedness of simplicity seems a Socratic wisdom. I had noticed also that Queequeg never consorted at all, or but very little, with the other seamen in the inn. He made no advances whatever; appeared to have no desire to enlarge the circle of his acquaintances. All this struck me as mighty singular; yet, upon second thoughts, there was something almost sublime in it. Here was a man some twenty thousand miles from home, by the way of Cape Horn, that is—which was the only way he could get there—thrown among people as strange to him as though he were in the planet Jupiter; and yet he seemed entirely at his ease; preserving the utmost serenity; content with his own companionship; always equal to himself. Surely this was a touch of fine philosophy; though no doubt he had never heard there was such a thing as that. But, perhaps, to be true philosophers, we mortals should not be conscious of so living or so striving. So soon as I hear that such or such a man gives himself out for a philosopher, I conclude that, like the dyspeptic old woman, he must have 'broken his digester.'

As I sat there in that now lonely room; the fire burning low, in that mild stage when, after its first intensity has warmed the air, it then only glows to be looked at; the evening shades and phantoms gathering round the casements, and peering in upon us silent, solitary twain; the storm booming without in solemn swells; I began to be sensible of strange feelings. I felt a melting in me. No more my splintered heart and maddened hand were turned against the wolfish world. This soothing savage had redeemed it. There he sat, his very indifference speaking a nature in which there lurked no civilized hypocrisies and bland deceits. Wild he was; a very sight of sights to see; yet I began to feel myself mysteriously drawn towards him. And those same things that would have repelled most others, they were the very magnets that thus drew me. I'll try a pagan friend, thought I, since Christian kindness has proved but hollow courtesy. I drew my bench near him, and made some friendly signs and hints, doing my best to talk with him meanwhile. At first he little noticed these advances; but presently, upon my referring to his last night's hospitalities, he made out to ask me whether we were again to be bedfellows. I told him yes; whereat I thought he looked pleased, perhaps a little complimented.

We then turned over the book together, and I endeavored to explain to him the purpose of the printing, and the meaning of the few pictures that were in it. Thus I soon engaged his interest; and from that we went to jabbering the best we could about the various outer sights to be seen in this famous town. Soon I proposed a social smoke; and, producing his pouch and tomahawk, he quietly offered me a puff. And then we sat exchanging puffs from that wild pipe of his, and keeping it regularly passing between us.

If there yet lurked any ice of indifference towards me in the Pagan's breast, this pleasant, genial smoke we had, soon thawed it out, and left us cronies. He seemed to take to me quite as naturally and unbiddenly as I to him; and when our smoke was over, he pressed his forehead against mine, clasped me round the waist, and said that henceforth we were married; meaning, in his country's phrase, that we were bosom friends; he would gladly die for me, if need should be. In a countryman, this sudden flame of friendship would have seemed far too premature, a thing to be much distrusted; but in this simple savage those old rules would not apply.

After supper, and another social chat and smoke, we went to our room together. He made me a present of his embalmed head; took out his enormous tobacco wallet, and groping under the tobacco, drew out some thirty dollars in silver; then spreading them on the table, and mechanically dividing them into two equal portions, pushed one of them towards me, and said it was mine. I was going to remonstrate; but he silenced me by pouring them into my trowsers' pockets. I let them stay. He then went about his evening prayers, took out his idol, and removed the paper fireboard. By certain signs and symptoms, I thought he seemed anxious for me to join him; but well knowing what was to follow, I deliberated a moment whether, in case he invited me, I would comply or otherwise.

I was a good Christian; born and bred in the bosom of the infallible Presbyterian Church. How then could I unite with this wild idolator in worshipping his piece of wood? But what is worship? thought I. Do you suppose now, Ishmael, that the magnanimous God of heaven and earth—pagans and all included—can possibly be jealous of an insignificant bit of black wood? Impossible! But what is worship?—to do the will of God—*that* is worship. And what is the will of God?—to do to my fellow man what I would have my fellow man to do to me—*that* is the will of God. Now, Queequeg is my fellow man. And what do I wish that this Queequeg would do to me? Why, unite with me in my particular Presbyterian form of worship. Consequently, I must then unite with him in his; ergo, I must turn idolator. So I kindled the shavings; helped prop up the innocent little idol;

offered him burnt biscuit with Queequeg; salamed before him twice or thrice; kissed his nose; and that done, we undressed and went to bed, at peace with our own consciences and all the world. But we did not go to sleep without some little chat.

How it is I know not; but there is no place like a bed for confidential disclosures between friends. Man and wife, they say, there open the very bottom of their souls to each other; and some old couples often lie and chat over old times till nearly morning. Thus, then, in our hearts' honeymoon, lay I and Queequeg—a cosy, loving pair.

CHAPTER XI

NIGHTGOWN

We had lain thus in bed, chatting and napping at short intervals, and Queequeg now and then affectionately throwing his brown tattooed legs over mine, and then drawing them back; so entirely sociable and free and easy were we; when, at last, by reason of our confabulations, what little nappishness remained in us altogether departed, and we felt like getting up again, though day-break was yet some way down the future.

Yes, we became very wakeful; so much so that our recumbent position began to grow wearisome, and by little and little we found ourselves sitting up; the clothes well tucked around us, leaning against the head-board with our four knees drawn up close together, and our two noses bending over them, as if our knee-pans were warming-pans. We felt very nice and snug, the more so since it was so chilly out of doors; indeed out of bed-clothes too, seeing that there was no fire in the room. The more so, I say, because truly to enjoy bodily warmth, some small part of you must be cold, for there is no quality in this world that is not what it is merely by contrast. Nothing exists in itself. If you flatter yourself that you are all over comfortable, and have been so a long time, then you cannot be said to be comfortable any more. But if, like Queequeg and me in the bed, the tip of your nose or the crown of your head be slightly chilled, why then, indeed, in the general consciousness you feel most delightfully and unmistakably warm. For this reason a sleeping apartment should never be furnished with a fire, which is one of the luxurious discomforts of the rich. For the height of this sort of deliciousness is to have nothing but the blanket between you and your snugness and the cold of the outer air. Then there you lie like the one warm spark in the heart of an arctic crystal.

We had been sitting in this crouching manner for some time, when all at once I thought I would open my eyes; for when between sheets, whether by day or by night, and whether asleep or awake, I have a way of always keeping my eyes shut, in order the more to concentrate the snugness of being in bed. Because no man can ever feel his own identity aright except his eyes be closed; as if darkness were indeed the proper element of our essences, though light be more congenial to our clayey part. Upon opening my eyes then, and coming out of my own pleasant and self-created darkness into the imposed and coarse outer gloom of the unilluminated twelve-o'clock-at-night, I experienced a disagreeable revulsion. Nor did I at all object to the hint from Queequeg that perhaps it were best to strike a light, seeing that we were so wide awake; and besides he felt a strong desire to have a few quiet puffs from his Tomahawk. Be it said, that though I had felt such a strong repugnance to his smoking in the bed the night before, yet see how elastic our stiff prejudices grow when love once comes to bend them. For now I liked nothing better than to have Queequeg smoking by me, even in bed, because he seemed to be full of such serene household joy then. I no more felt unduly concerned for the landlord's policy of insurance. I was only alive to the condensed confidential comfortableness of sharing a pipe and a blanket with a real friend. With our shaggy jackets drawn about our shoulders, we now passed the Tomahawk from one to the other, till slowly there grew over us a blue hanging tester of smoke, illuminated by the flame of the new-lit lamp.

Whether it was that this undulating tester rolled the savage away to far distant scenes, I know not, but he now spoke of his native island; and, eager to hear his history, I begged him to go on and tell it. He gladly complied. Though at the time I but ill comprehended not a few of his words, yet subsequent disclosures, when I had become more familiar with his broken phraseology, now enable me to present the whole story such as it may prove in the mere skeleton I give.

CHAPTER XII

BIOGRAPHICAL

Queequeg was a native of Kokovoko, an island far away to the West and South. It is not down in any map; true places never are.

When a new-hatched savage running wild about his native woodlands in a grass clout, followed by the nibbling goats, as if he were a green sapling; even then, in Queequeg's ambitious soul, lurked a strong desire to see something more of Christendom than a specimen whaler or two. His father was a High Chief, a King; his uncle a High Priest; and on the maternal side he boasted aunts who were the wives of unconquerable warriors. There was excellent blood in his veins—royal stuff; though sadly vitiated, I fear, by the cannibal propensity he nourished in his untutored youth.

A Sag Harbor ship visited his father's bay, and Queequeg sought a passage to Christian lands. But the ship, having her full complement of seamen, spurned his suit; and not all the King his father's influence could prevail. But Queequeg vowed a vow. Alone in his canoe, he paddled off to a distant strait, which he knew the ship must pass through when she quitted the island. On one side was a coral reef; on the other a low tongue of land, covered with mangrove thickets that grew out into the water. Hiding his canoe, still afloat, among these thickets, with its prow seaward, he sat down in the stern, paddle low in hand; and when the ship was gliding by, like a flash he darted out; gained her side; with one backward dash of his foot capsized and sank his canoe; climbed up the chains; and throwing himself at full length upon the deck, grappled a ring-bolt there, and swore not to let it go, though hacked in pieces.

In vain the captain threatened to throw him overboard; suspended a cutlass over his naked wrists; Queequeg was the son of a King, and Queequeg budged not. Struck by his desperate dauntlessness, and his wild desire to visit Christendom, the captain at last relented, and told him he might make himself at home. But this fine young savage—this sea Prince of Wales, never saw the captain's cabin. They put him down among the sailors, and made a whaleman of him. But like Czar Peter content to toil in the shipyards of foreign cities, Queequeg disdained no seeming ignominy, if thereby he might happily gain the power of enlightening his untutored countrymen. For at bottom—so he told me—he was actuated by a profound desire to learn among the Christians, the arts whereby to make his people still happier than they were; and more than that, still better than they were. But, alas! the practices of whalemen soon convinced him that even Christians could be both miserable and wicked; infinitely more so, than all his father's heathens. Arrived at last in old Sag Harbor; and seeing what the sailors did there; and then going on to Nantucket, and seeing how they spent their wages in *that* place also, poor Queequeg gave it up for lost. Thought he, it's a wicked world in all meridians; I'll die a pagan.

And thus an old idolator at heart, he yet lived among these Christians, wore their clothes, and tried to talk their gibberish. Hence the queer ways about him, though now some time from home.

By hints, I asked him whether he did not propose going back, and having a coronation; since he might now consider his father dead and gone, he being very old and feeble at the last accounts. He answered no, not yet; and added that he was fearful Christianity, or rather Christians, had unfitted him for ascending the pure and undefiled throne of thirty pagan Kings before him. But by and by, he said, he would return,—as soon as he felt himself baptized again. For the nonce, however, he proposed to sail about, and sow his wild oats in all four oceans. They had made a harpooneer of him, and that barbed iron was in lieu of a sceptre now.

I asked him what might be his immediate purpose, touching his future movements. He answered, to go to sea again, in his own vocation. Upon this, I told him that whaling was my own design, and informed him of my intention to sail out of Nantucket, as being the most promising port for an adventurous whaleman to embark from. He at once resolved to accompany me to that island, ship aboard the same vessel, get into the same watch, the same boat, the same mess with me, in short to share my every hap; with both my hands in his, boldly dip into the Potluck of both worlds. To all this I joyously assented; for besides the affection I now felt for Queequeg, he was an experienced harpooneer, and as such, could not fail to be of great usefulness to one, who, like me, was wholly ignorant of the mysteries of whaling, though well acquainted with the sea, as known to merchant seamen.

His story being ended with his pipe's last dying puff, Queequeg embraced me, pressed his forehead against mine, and blowing out the light, we rolled over from each other, this way and that, and very soon were sleeping.

CHAPTER XIII

WHEELBARROW

Next morning, Monday, after disposing of the embalmed head to a barber, for a block, I settled my own and comrade's bill; using, however, my comrade's money. The grinning landlord, as well as the boarders, seemed amazingly tickled at the sudden friendship which had sprung up between me and Queequeg—especially as Peter Coffin's cock and bull stories about him had previously so much alarmed me concerning the very person whom I now companied with.

We borrowed a wheelbarrow, and embarking our things, including my own poor carpet-bag, and Queequeg's canvas sack and hammock, away we went down to the 'Moss,' the little Nantucket packet schooner moored at the wharf. As we were going along the people stared; not at Queequeg so much—for they were used to seeing cannibals like him in their streets,—but at seeing him and me upon such confidential terms. But we heeded them not, going along wheeling the barrow by turns, and Queequeg now and then stopping to adjust the sheath on his harpoon barb. I asked him why he carried such a troublesome thing with him ashore, and whether all whaling ships did not find their own harpoons. To this, in substance, he replied, that though what I hinted was true enough, yet he had a particular affection for his own harpoon, because it was of assured stuff, well tried in many a mortal combat, and deeply intimate with the hearts of whales. In short, like many inland reapers and mowers, who go into the farmers' meadows armed with their own scythes—though in no wise obliged to furnish them—even so Queequeg, for his own private reasons, preferred his own harpoon.

Shifting the barrow from my hand to his, he told me a funny story about the first wheelbarrow he had ever seen. It was in Sag Harbor. The owners of his ship, it seems, had lent him one, in which to carry his heavy chest to his boarding house. Not to seem ignorant about the thing—though in truth he was entirely so, concerning the precise way in which to manage the barrow—Queequeg puts his chest upon it; lashes it fast; and then shoulders the barrow and marches up the wharf. 'Why,' said I, 'Queequeg, you might have known better than that, one would think. Didn't the people laugh?'

Upon this, he told me another story. The people of his island of Kokovoko, it seems, at their wedding feasts express the fragrant water of young cocoanuts into a large stained calabash like a punchbowl; and this punchbowl always forms the great central ornament on the braided mat where the feast is held. Now a certain grand merchant ship once touched at Kokovoko, and its commander—from all accounts, a very stately punctilious gentleman, at least for a sea captain—this commander was invited to the wedding feast of Queequeg's sister, a pretty young princess just turned of ten. Well; when all the wedding guests were assembled at the bride's bamboo cottage, this Captain marches in, and being assigned the post of honor, placed himself over against the punchbowl, and between the High Priest and his majesty the King, Queequeg's father. Grace being said,—for those people have their grace as well as we—though Queequeg told me that unlike us, who at such times look downwards to our platters, they, on the contrary, copying the ducks, glance upwards to the great Giver of all feasts—grace, I say, being said, the High Priest opens the banquet by the immemorial ceremony of the island; that is, dipping his consecrated and consecrating fingers into the bowl before the blessed beverage circulates. Seeing himself placed next the Priest, and noting the ceremony, and thinking himself—being Captain of a ship—as having plain precedence over a mere island King, especially in the King's own house—the Captain coolly proceeds to wash his hands in the punch bowl;—taking it I suppose for a huge fingerglass. 'Now,' said Queequeg, 'what you tink now?—Didn't our people laugh?'

At last, passage paid, and luggage safe, we stood on board the schooner. Hoisting sail, it glided down the Acushnet river. On one side, New Bedford rose in terraces of streets, their ice-covered trees all glittering in the clear, cold air. Huge hills and mountains of casks on casks were piled upon her wharves, and side by side the world-wandering whale ships lay silent and safely moored at last; while from others came a sound of carpenters and coopers, with blended noises of fires and forges to melt the pitch, all betokening that new cruises were on the start; that one most perilous and long voyage ended, only begins a second; and a second ended, only begins a third, and so on, for ever and for aye. Such is the endlessness, yea, the intolerableness of all earthly effort.

Gaining the more open water, the bracing breeze waxed fresh; the little Moss tossed the quick foam from her bows, as a young colt his snortings. How I snuffed that Tartar air—how I spurned that turnpike earth!—that common highway all over dented with the marks of slavish heels and hoofs; and turned me to admire the magnanimity of the sea which will permit no records.

At the same foam-fountain, Queequeg seemed to drink and reel with me. His dusky nostrils swelled apart; he showed his filed and pointed teeth. On, on we flew, and our offing gained, the Moss did homage to the blast; ducked and dived her brows as a slave before the Sultan. Sideways leaning, we sideways darted; every ropeyarn tingling like a wire; the two tall masts buckling like Indian canes in land tornadoes. So full of this reeling scene were we, as we stood by the plunging bowsprit, that for some time we did not notice the jeering glances of the passengers, a lubber-like assembly, who marvelled that two fellow beings should be so companionable; as though a white man were anything more dignified than a whitewashed negro. But there were some boobies and bumpkins there, who, by their intense greenness, must have come from the heart and centre of all verdure. Queequeg caught one of these young saplings mimicking him behind his back. I thought the bumpkin's hour of doom was come. Dropping his harpoon, the brawny savage caught him in his arms, and by an almost miraculous dexterity and strength, sent him high up bodily into the air; then slightly tapping his stern in mid-somerset, the fellow landed with bursting lungs upon his feet, while Queequeg, turning his back upon him, lighted his tomahawk pipe and passed it to me for a puff.

'Capting! Capting!' yelled the bumpkin, running towards that officer; 'Capting, Capting, here's the devil.'

'Hallo, *you* sir,' cried the Captain, a gaunt rib of the sea, stalking up to Queequeg, 'what in thunder do you mean by that? Don't you know you might have killed that chap?'

'What him say?' said Queequeg, as he mildly turned to me.

'He say,' said I, 'that you came near kill-e that man there,' pointing to the still shivering greenhorn.

'Kill-e,' cried Queequeg, twisting his tattooed face into an unearthly expression of disdain, 'ah! him bery small-e fish-e; Queequeg no kill-e so small-e fish-e; Queequeg kill-e big whale!'

'Look you,' roared the Captain, 'I'll kill-e *you,* you cannibal, if you try any more of your tricks aboard here; so mind your eye.'

But it so happened just then, that it was high time for the Captain to mind his own eye. The prodigious strain upon the main-sail had parted the weather-sheet, and the tremendous boom was now flying from side to side, completely sweeping the entire after part of the deck. The poor fellow whom Queequeg had handled so roughly, was swept overboard; all hands were in a panic; and to attempt snatching at the boom to stay it, seemed madness. It flew from right to left, and back again, almost in one ticking of a watch, and every instant seemed on the point of snapping into splinters. Nothing was done, and nothing seemed capable of being done; those on deck rushed towards the bows, and stood eyeing the boom as if it were the lower jaw of an exasperated whale. In the midst of this consternation, Queequeg dropped deftly to his knees, and crawling under the path of the boom, whipped hold of a rope, secured one end to the bulwarks, and then flinging the other like a lasso, caught it round the boom as it swept over his head, and at the next jerk, the spar was that way trapped, and all was safe. The schooner was run into the wind, and while the hands were clearing away the stern boat, Queequeg, stripped to the waist, darted from the side with a long living arc of a leap. For three minutes or more he was seen swimming like a dog, throwing his long arms straight out before him, and by turns revealing his brawny shoulders through the freezing foam. I looked at the grand and glorious fellow, but saw no one to be saved. The greenhorn had gone down. Shooting himself perpendicularly from the water, Queequeg now took an instant's glance around him, and seeming to see just how matters were, dived down and disappeared. A few minutes more, and he rose again, one arm still striking out, and with the other dragging a lifeless form. The boat soon picked them up. The poor bumpkin was restored. All hands voted Queequeg a noble trump; the captain begged his pardon. From that hour I clove to Queequeg like a barnacle; yea, till poor Queequeg took his last long dive.

Was there ever such unconsciousness? He did not seem to think that he at all deserved a medal from the Humane and Magnanimous Societies. He only asked for water—fresh water—something to wipe the brine off; that done, he put on dry clothes, lighted his pipe, and leaning against the bulwarks, and mildly eyeing those around him, seemed to be saying to himself—'It's a mutual, joint-stock world, in all meridians. We cannibals must help these Christians.'

CHAPTER XIV

NANTUCKET

Nothing more happened on the passage worthy the mentioning; so, after a fine run, we safely arrived in Nantucket.

Nantucket! Take out your map and look at it. See what a real corner of the world it occupies; how it stands there, away off shore, more lonely than the Eddystone lighthouse. Look at it—a mere hillock, and elbow of sand; all beach, without a background. There is more sand there than you would use in twenty years as a substitute for blotting paper. Some gamesome wights will tell you that they have to plant weeds there, they don't grow naturally; that they import Canada thistles; that they have to send beyond seas for a spile to stop a leak in an oil cask; that pieces of wood in Nantucket are carried about like bits of the true cross in Rome; that people there plant toadstools before their houses, to get under the shade in summer time; that one blade of grass makes an oasis, three blades in a day's walk a prairie; that they wear quicksand shoes, something like Laplander snowshoes; that they are so shut up, belted about, every way inclosed, surrounded, and made an utter island of by the ocean, that to their very chairs and tables small clams will sometimes be found adhering, as to the backs of sea turtles. But these extravaganzas only show that Nantucket is no Illinois.

Look now at the wondrous traditional story of how this island was settled by the red-men. Thus goes the legend. In olden times an eagle swooped down upon the New England coast, and carried off an infant Indian in his talons. With loud lament the parents saw their child borne out of sight over the wide waters. They resolved to follow in the same direction. Setting out in their canoes, after a perilous passage they discovered the island, and there they found an empty ivory casket,—the poor little Indian's skeleton.

What wonder, then, that these Nantucketers, born on a beach, should take to the sea for a livelihood! They first caught crabs and quohogs in the sand; grown bolder, they waded out with nets for mackerel; more experienced, they pushed off in boats and captured cod; and at last, launching a navy of great ships on the sea, explored this watery world; put an incessant belt of circumnavigations round it; peeped in at Behring's Straits; and in all seasons and all oceans declared everlasting war with the mightiest animated mass that has survived the flood; most monstrous and most mountainous! That Himmalehan, salt-sea Mastodon, clothed with such portentousness of unconscious power, that his very panics are more to be dreaded than his most fearless and malicious assaults!

And thus have these naked Nantucketers, these sea hermits, issuing from their ant-hill in the sea, overrun and conquered the watery world like so many Alexanders; parcelling out among them the Atlantic, Pacific, and Indian oceans, as the three pirate powers did Poland. Let America add Mexico to Texas, and pile Cuba upon Canada; let the English overswarm all India, and hang out their blazing banner from the sun; two thirds of this terraqueous globe are the Nantucketer's. For the sea is his; he owns it, as Emperors own empires; other seamen having but a right of way through it. Merchant ships are but extension bridges; armed ones but floating forts; even pirates and privateers, though following the sea as highwaymen the road, they but plunder other ships, other fragments of the land like themselves, without seeking to draw their living from the bottomless deep itself. The Nantucketer, he alone resides and riots on the sea; he alone, in Bible language, goes down to it in ships; to and fro ploughing it as his own special plantation. *There* is his home; *there* lies his business, which a Noah's flood would not interrupt, though it overwhelmed all the millions in China. He lives on the sea, as prairie cocks in the prairie; he hides among the waves, he climbs them as chamois hunters climb the Alps. For years he knows not the land; so that when he comes to it at last, it smells like another world, more strangely than the moon would to an Earthsman. With the landless gull, that at sunset folds her wings and is rocked to sleep between billows; so at nightfall, the Nantucketer, out of sight of land, furls his sails, and lays him to his rest, while under his very pillow rush herds of walruses and whales.

CHAPTER XV

CHOWDER

It was quite late in the evening when the little Moss came snugly to anchor, and Queequeg and I went ashore; so we could attend to no business that day, at least none but a supper and a bed. The landlord of the Spouter-Inn had recommended us to his cousin Hosea Hussey of the Try Pots, whom he asserted to be the proprietor of one of the best kept hotels in all Nantucket, and moreover he had assured us that cousin Hosea, as he called him, was famous for his chowders. In short, he plainly hinted that we could not possibly do better than try pot-luck at the Try Pots. But the directions he had given us about keeping a yellow warehouse on our starboard hand till we opened a white church to the larboard, and then keeping that on the larboard hand till we made a corner three points to the starboard, and that done, then ask the first man we met where the place was: these crooked directions of his very much puzzled us at first, especially as, at the outset, Queequeg insisted that the yellow warehouse—our first point of departure—must be left on the larboard hand, whereas I had understood Peter Coffin to say it was on the starboard. However, by dint of beating about a little in the dark, and now and then knocking up a peaceable inhabitant to inquire the way, we at last came to something which there was no mistaking.

Two enormous wooden pots painted black, and suspended by asses' ears, swung from the cross-trees of an old top-mast, planted in front of an old doorway. The horns of the crosstrees were sawed off on the other side, so that this old topmast looked not a little like a gallows. Perhaps I was over sensitive to such impressions at the time, but I could not help staring at this gallows with a vague misgiving. A sort of crick was in my neck as I gazed up to the two remaining horns; yes, *two* of them, one for Queequeg, and one for me. It's ominous, thinks I. A Coffin my Innkeeper upon landing in my first whaling port, tombstones staring at me in the whalemen's chapel; and here a gallows! and a pair of prodigious black pots too! Are these last throwing out oblique hints touching Tophet?

I was called from these reflections by the sight of a freckled woman with yellow hair and a yellow gown, standing in the porch of the inn, under a dull red lamp swinging there, that looked much like an injured eye, and carrying on a brisk scolding with a man in a purple woollen shirt.

'Get along with ye,' said she to the man, 'or I'll be combing ye!'

'Come on, Queequeg,' said I, 'all right. There's Mrs Hussey.'

And so it turned out; Mr Hosea Hussey being from home, but leaving Mrs Hussey entirely competent to attend to all his affairs. Upon making known our desires for a supper and a bed, Mrs. Hussey, postponing further scolding for the present, ushered us into a little room, and seating us at a table spread with the relics of a recently concluded repast, turned round to us and said—'Clam or Cod?'

'What's that about Cods, ma'am?' said I, with much politeness.

'Clam or Cod?' she repeated.

'A clam for supper? a cold clam; is *that* what you mean, Mrs Hussey?' says I; 'but that's a rather cold and clammy reception in the winter time, ain't it, Mrs Hussey?'

But being in a great hurry to resume scolding the man in the purple shirt, who was waiting for it in the entry, and seeming to hear nothing but the word 'clam,' Mrs Hussey hurried towards an open door leading to the kitchen, and bawling out 'clam for two,' disappeared.

'Queequeg,' said I, 'do you think that we can make out a supper for us both on one clam?'

However, a warm savory steam from the kitchen served to belie the apparently cheerless prospect before us. But when that smoking chowder came in, the mystery was delightfully explained. Oh, sweet friends! hearken to me. It was made of small juicy clams, scarcely bigger than hazel nuts, mixed with pounded ship biscuit, and salted pork cut up into little flakes; the whole enriched with butter, and plentifully seasoned with pepper and salt. Our appetites being sharpened by the frosty voyage, and in particular, Queequeg seeing his favorite fishing food before him, and the chowder being surpassingly excellent, we despatched it with great expedition: when leaning back a moment and bethinking me of Mrs Hussey's clam and cod announcement, I thought I would try a little experiment. Stepping to the kitchen door, I uttered the word 'cod' with great emphasis, and resumed my seat. In a few moments the savory steam came forth again, but with a different flavor, and in good time a fine cod-chowder was placed before us.

We resumed business; and while plying our spoons in the bowl, thinks I to myself, I wonder now if this here has any effect on the head? What's that stultifying saying about chowder-headed people? 'But look, Queequeg, ain't that a live eel in your bowl? Where's your harpoon?'

Fishiest of all fishy places was the Try Pots, which well deserved its name; for the pots there were always boiling chowders. Chowder for breakfast, and chowder for dinner, and chowder for supper, till you began to look for fish-bones coming through your clothes. The area before the house was paved with clam-shells. Mrs Hussey wore a polished necklace of codfish vertebrae; and Hosea Hussey had his account books bound in superior old shark-skin. There was a fishy flavor to the milk, too, which I could not at all account for, till one morning happening to take a stroll along the beach among some fishermen's boats, I saw Hosea's brindled cow feeding on fish remnants, and marching along the sand with each foot in a cod's decapitated head, looking very slip-shod, I assure ye.

Supper concluded, we received a lamp, and directions from Mrs Hussey concerning the nearest way to bed; but, as Queequeg was about to precede me up the stairs, the lady reached forth her arm, and demanded his harpoon; she allowed no harpoon in her chambers. 'Why not?' said I; 'every true whaleman sleeps with his harpoon—but why not?' 'Because it's dangerous,' says she. 'Ever since young Stiggs coming from that unfort'nt v'y'ge of his, when he was gone four years and a half, with ony three barrels of *ile,* was found dead in my first floor back, with his harpoon in his side; ever since then I allow no boarders to take sich dangerous weepons in their rooms a-night. So, Mr Queequeg' (for she had learned his name), 'I will just take this here iron, and keep it for you till morning. But the chowder; clam or cod tomorrow for breakfast, men?'

'Both,' says I; 'and let's have a couple of smoked herring by way of variety.'

CHAPTER XVI

THE SHIP

In bed we concocted our plans for the morrow. But to my surprise and no small concern, Queequeg now gave me to understand, that he had been diligently consulting Yojo—the name of his black little god—and Yojo had told him two or three times over, and strongly insisted upon it everyway, that instead of our going together among the whaling-fleet in harbor, and in concert selecting our craft; instead of this, I say, Yojo earnestly enjoined that the selection of the ship should rest wholly with me, inasmuch as Yojo purposed befriending us; and, in order to do so, had already pitched upon a vessel, which, if left to myself, I, Ishmael, should infallibly light upon, for all the world as though it had turned out by chance; and in that vessel I must immediately ship myself, for the present irrespective of Queequeg.

I have forgotten to mention that, in many things, Queequeg placed great confidence in the excellence of Yojo's judgment and surprising forecast of things; and cherished Yojo with considerable esteem, as a rather good sort of god, who perhaps meant well enough upon the whole, but in all cases did not succeed in his benevolent designs.

Now, this plan of Queequeg's, or rather Yojo's, touching the selection of our craft; I did not like that plan at all. I had not a little relied upon Queequeg's sagacity to point out the whaler best fitted to carry us and our fortunes securely. But as all my remonstrances produced no effect upon Queequeg, I was obliged to acquiesce; and accordingly prepared to set about this business with a determined rushing sort of energy and vigor, that should quickly settle that trifling little affair. Next morning early, leaving Queequeg shut up with Yojo in our little bedroom—for it seemed that it was some sort of Lent or Ramadan, or day of fasting, humiliation, and prayer with Queequeg and Yojo that day; *how* it was I never could find out, for, though I applied myself to it several times, I never could master his liturgies and XXXIX Articles—leaving Queequeg, then, fasting on his tomahawk pipe, and Yojo warming himself at his sacrificial fire of shavings, I sallied out among the shipping. After much prolonged sauntering and many random inquiries, I learnt that there were three ships up for three-years' voyages—The Devil-Dam, the Tit-bit and the Pequod. *Devil-Dam,* I do not know the origin of; *Tit-bit* is obvious; *Pequod,* you will no doubt remember, was the name of a celebrated tribe of Massachusetts Indians, now extinct as the ancient Medes. I peered and pryed about the Devil-Dam; from her, hopped over to the Tit-bit; and, finally, going on board the Pequod, looked around her for a moment, and then decided that this was the very ship for us.

You may have seen many a quaint craft in your day, for aught I know;—squared-toed luggers; mountainous Japanese junks; butter-box galliots, and what not; but take my word for it, you never saw such a rare old craft as this same rare old Pequod. She was a ship of the old school, rather small if anything; with an old fashioned claw-footed look about her. Long seasoned and weather-stained in the typhoons and calms of all four oceans, her old hull's complexion was darkened like a French grenadier's, who has alike fought in Egypt and Siberia. Her venerable bows looked bearded. Her masts—cut somewhere on the coast of Japan, where her original ones were lost overboard in a gale—her masts stood stiffly up like the spines of the three old kings of Cologne. Her ancient decks were worn and wrinkled, like the pilgrim-worshipped flag-stone in Canterbury Cathedral where Beckett bled. But to all these her old antiquities were added new and marvellous features, pertaining to the wild business that for more than half a century she had followed. Old Captain Peleg, many years her chief-mate, before he commanded another vessel of his own, and now a retired seaman, and one of the principal owners of the Pequod,—this old Peleg, during the term of his chief-mateship, had built upon her original grotesqueness, and inlaid it, all over, with a quaintness both of material and device, unmatched by anything except it be Thorkill-Hake's carved buckler or bedstead. She was apparelled like any barbaric Ethiopian emperor, his neck heavy with pendants of polished ivory. She was a thing of trophies. A cannibal of a craft, tricking herself forth in the chased bones of her enemies. All round, her unpanelled, open bulwarks were garnished like one continuous jaw, with the long sharp teeth of the sperm whale, inserted there for pins, to fasten her old hempen thews and tendons to. Those thews ran not through base blocks of land wood, but deftly travelled over sheaves of sea-ivory. Scorning a turnstile wheel at her reverend helm, she sported there a tiller; and that tiller was in one mass, curiously carved from the long narrow lower jaw of her hereditary foe. The helmsman who steered by that tiller in a tempest, felt like the Tartar, when he holds back his fiery steed by clutching its jaw. A noble craft, but somehow a most melancholy! All noble things are touched with that.

Now when I looked about the quarter-deck, for some one having authority, in order to propose myself as a candidate for the voyage, at first I saw nobody; but I could not well overlook a strange sort of tent, or rather wigwam, pitched a little behind the main-mast. It seemed only a temporary erection used in port. It was of a conical shape, some ten feet high; consisting of the long, huge slabs of limber black bone taken from the middle and highest part of the jaws of the right-whale. Planted with their broad ends on the deck, a circle of these slabs laced together, mutually sloped towards each other, and at the apex united in a tufted point, where the loose hairy fibres waved to and fro like the topknot on some old Pottowottamie Sachem's head. A triangular opening faced towards the bows of the ship, so that the insider commanded a complete view forward.

And half concealed in this queer tenement, I at length found one who by his aspect seemed to have authority; and who, it being noon, and the ship's work suspended, was now enjoying respite from the burden of command. He was seated on an old-fashioned oaken chair, wriggling all over with curious carving; and the bottom of which was formed of a stout interlacing of the same elastic stuff of which the wigwam was constructed.

There was nothing so very particular, perhaps, about the appearance of the elderly man I saw; he was brown and brawny, like most old seamen, and heavily rolled up in blue pilot-cloth, cut in the Quaker style; only there was a fine and almost microscopic net-work of the minutest wrinkles interlacing round his eyes, which must have arisen from his continual sailings in many hard gales, and always looking to windward;—for this causes the muscles about the eyes to become pursed together. Such eye-wrinkles are very effectual in a scowl.

'Is this the Captain of the Pequod?' said I, advancing to the door of the tent.

'Supposing it be the Captain of the Pequod, what dost thou want of him?' he demanded.

'I was thinking of shipping.'

'Thou wast, wast thou? I see thou art no Nantucketer—ever been in a stove boat?'

'No, Sir, I never have.'

'Dost know nothing at all about whaling, I dare say—eh?'

'Nothing, Sir; but I have no doubt I shall soon learn. I've been several voyages in the merchant service, and I think that—'

'Marchant service be damned. Talk not that lingo to me. Dost see that leg?—I'll take that leg away from thy stern, if ever thou talkest of the marchant service to me again. Marchant service indeed! I suppose now ye feel considerable proud of having served in those marchant ships. But flukes! man, what makes thee want to go a whaling, eh?—it looks a little suspicious, don't it, eh?—Hast not been a pirate, has thou?—Didst not rob thy last Captain, didst thou?—Dost not think of murdering the officers when thou gettest to sea?'

I protested my innocence of these things. I saw that under the mask of these half humorous innuendoes, this old seaman, as an insulated Quakerish Nantucketer, was full of his insular prejudices, and rather distrustful of all aliens, unless they hailed from Cape Cod or the Vineyard.

'But what takes thee a-whaling? I want to know that before I think of shipping ye.'

'Well, sir, I want to see what whaling is. I want to see the world.'

'Want to see what whaling is, eh? Have ye clapped eye on Captain Ahab?'

'Who is Captain Ahab, sir?'

'Aye, aye, I thought so. Captain Ahab is the Captain of this ship.'

'I am mistaken then. I thought I was speaking to the Captain himself.'

'Thou art speaking to Captain Peleg—that's who ye are speaking to, young man. It belongs to me and Captain Bildad to see the Pequod fitted out for the voyage, and supplied with all her needs, including crew. We are part owners and agents. But as I was going to say, if thou wantest to know what whaling is, as thou tellest ye do, I can put ye in a way of finding it out before ye bind yourself to it, past backing out. Clap eye on Captain Ahab, young man, and thou wilt find that he has only one leg.'

'What do you mean, sir? Was the other one lost by a whale?'

'Lost by a whale! Young man, come nearer to me: it was devoured, chewed up, crunched by the monstrousest parmacetty that ever chipped a boat!—ah, ah!'

I was a little alarmed by his energy, perhaps also a little touched at the hearty grief in his concluding exclamation, but said as calmly as I could, 'What you say is no doubt true enough, sir; but how could I know there was any peculiar ferocity in that particular whale, though indeed I might have inferred as much from the simple fact of the accident.'

'Look ye now, young man, thy lungs are a sort of soft, d'ye see; thou dost not talk shark a bit. *Sure,* ye've been to sea before now; sure of that?'

'Sir,' said I, 'I thought I told you that I had been four voyages in the merchant—'

'Hard down out of that! Mind what I said about the marchant service—don't aggravate me—I won't have it. But let us understand each other. I have given thee a hint about what whaling is; do ye yet feel inclined for it?'

'I do, sir.'

'Very good. Now, art thou the man to pitch a harpoon down a live whale's throat, and then jump after it? Answer, quick!'

'I am, sir, if it should be positively indispensable to do so; not to be got rid of, that is; which I don't take to be the fact.'

'Good again. Now then, thou not only wantest to go a-whaling, to find out by experience what whaling is, but ye also want to go in order to see the world? Was not that what ye said? I thought so. Well then, just step forward there, and take a peep over the weather-bow, and then back to me and tell me what ye see there.'

For a moment I stood a little puzzled by this curious request, not knowing exactly how to take it, whether humorously or in earnest. But concentrating all his crow's feet into one scowl, Captain Peleg started me on the errand.

Going forward and glancing over the weather bow, I perceived that the ship swinging to her anchor with the flood-tide, was now obliquely pointing towards the open ocean. The prospect was unlimited, but exceedingly monotonous and forbidding; not the slightest variety that I could see.

'Well, what's the report?' said Peleg when I came back; 'what did ye see?'

'Not much,' I replied—'nothing but water; considerable horizon though, and there's a squall coming up, I think.'

'Well, what dost thou think then of seeing the world? Do ye wish to go round Cape Horn to see any more of it, eh? Can't ye see the world where you stand?'

I was a little staggered, but go a-whaling I must, and I would; and the Pequod was as good a ship as any—I thought the best—and all this I now repeated to Peleg. Seeing me so determined, he expressed his willingness to ship me.

'And thou mayest as well sign the papers right off,' he added—'come along with ye.' And so saying, he led the way below deck into the cabin.

Seated on the transom was what seemed to me a most uncommon and surprising figure. It turned out to be Captain Bildad, who along with Captain Peleg was one of the largest owners of the vessel; the other shares, as is sometimes the case in these ports, being held by a crowd of old annuitants; widows, fatherless children, and chancery wards; each owning about the value of a timber head, or a foot of plank, or a nail or two in the ship. People in Nantucket invest their money in whaling vessels, the same way that you do yours in approved state stocks bringing in good interest.

Now, Bildad, like Peleg, and indeed many other Nantucketers, was a Quaker, the island having been originally settled by that sect; and to this day its inhabitants in general retain in an uncommon measure the peculiarities of the Quaker, only variously and anomalously modified by things altogether alien and heterogeneous. For some of these same Quakers are the most sanguinary of all sailors and whale-hunters. They are fighting Quakers; they are Quakers with a vengeance.

So that there are instances among them of men, who, named with Scripture names—a singularly common fashion on the island—and in childhood naturally imbibing the stately dramatic *thee* and *thou* of the Quaker idiom; still, from the audacious, daring, and boundless adventure of their subsequent lives, strangely blend with these unoutgrown peculiarities, a thousand bold dashes of character, not unworthy a Scandinavian sea-king, or a poetical Pagan Roman. And when these things unite in a man of greatly superior natural force, with a globular brain and a ponderous heart; who has also by the stillness and seclusion of many long night-watches in the remotest waters, and beneath constellations never seen here at the north, been led to think untraditionally and independently; receiving all nature's sweet or savage impressions fresh from her own virgin voluntary and confiding breast, and thereby chiefly, but with some help from accidental advantages, to learn a bold and nervous lofty language—that man makes one in a whole nation's census—a mighty pageant creature, formed for noble tragedies. Nor will it at all detract from him, dramatically regarded, if either by birth or other circumstances, he have what seems a half wilful over-ruling morbidness at the bottom of his nature. For all men tragically great are made so through a certain morbidness. Be sure of this, O young ambition, all mortal greatness is but disease. But, as yet we have not to do with such an one, but with quite another; and still a man, who, if indeed peculiar, it only results again from another phase of the Quaker, modified by individual circumstances.

Like Captain Peleg, Captain Bildad was a well-to-do, retired whaleman. But unlike Captain Peleg—who cared not a rush for what are called serious things, and indeed deemed those self-same serious things the veriest of all trifles—Captain Bildad had not only been originally educated according to the strictest sect of Nantucket Quakerism, but all his subsequent ocean life, and the sight of many unclad, lovely island creatures, round the Horn—all that had not moved this native born Quaker one single jot, had not so much as altered one angle of his vest. Still, for all this immutableness, was there some lack of common consistency about worthy Captain Bildad. Though refusing, from conscientious scruples, to bear arms against land invaders, yet himself had illimitably invaded the Atlantic and Pacific; and though a sworn foe to human bloodshed, yet had he in his straight-bodied coat, spilled tuns upon tuns of leviathan gore. How now in the contemplative evening of his days, the pious Bildad reconciled these things in the reminiscence, I do not know; but it did not seem to concern him much, and very probably he had long since come to the sage and sensible conclusion that a man's religion is one thing, and this practical world quite another. This world pays dividends. Rising from a little cabin-boy in short clothes of the drabbest drab, to a harpooneer in a broad shad-bellied waistcoat; from that becoming boat-header, chief-mate, and captain, and finally a ship-owner; Bildad, as I hinted before, had concluded his adventurous career by wholly retiring from active life at the goodly age of sixty, and dedicating his remaining days to the quiet receiving of his well-earned income.

Now Bildad, I am sorry to say, had the reputation of being an incorrigible old hunks, and in his sea-going days, a bitter, hard task-master. They told me in Nantucket, though it certainly seems a curious story, that when he sailed the old Categut whaleman, his crew, upon arriving home, were mostly all carried ashore to the hospital, sore exhausted and worn out. For a pious man, especially for a Quaker, he was certainly rather hard-hearted, to say the least. He never used to swear, though, at his men, they said; but somehow he got an inordinate quantity of cruel, unmitigated hard work out of them. When Bildad was a chief-mate, to have his drab-colored eye intently looking at you, made you feel completely nervous, till you could clutch something—a hammer or a marling-spike, and go to work like mad, at something or other, never mind what. Indolence and idleness perished from before him. His own person was the exact embodiment of his utilitarian character. On his long, gaunt body, he carried no spare flesh, no superfluous beard, his chin having a soft, economical nap to it, like the worn nap of his broad-brimmed hat.

Such, then, was the person that I saw seated on the transom when I followed Captain Peleg down into the cabin. The space between the decks was small; and there, bolt-upright, sat old Bildad, who always sat so, and never leaned, and this to save his coat tails. His broad-brim was placed beside him; his legs were stiffly crossed; his drab vesture was buttoned up to his chin; and spectacles on nose, he seemed absorbed in reading from a ponderous volume.

'Bildad,' cried Captain Peleg, 'at it again, Bildad, eh? Ye have been studying those Scriptures, now, for the last thirty years, to my certain knowledge. How far ye got, Bildad?'

As if long habituated to such profane talk from his old shipmate, Bildad, without noticing his present irreverence, quietly looked up, and seeing me, glanced again inquiringly towards Peleg.

'He says he's our man, Bildad,' said Peleg, 'he wants to ship.'

'Dost thee?' said Bildad, in a hollow tone, and turning round to me.

'I *dost*,' said I unconsciously, he was so intense a Quaker.

'What do ye think of him, Bildad?' said Peleg.

'He'll do,' said Bildad, eyeing me, and then went on spelling away at his book in a mumbling tone quite audible.

I thought him the queerest old Quaker I ever saw, especially as Peleg, his friend and old shipmate, seemed such a blusterer. But I said nothing, only looking round me sharply. Peleg now threw open a chest, and drawing forth the ship's articles, placed pen and ink before him, and seated himself at a little table. I began to think it was high time to settle with myself at what terms I would be willing to engage for the voyage. I was already aware that in the whaling business they paid no wages; but all hands, including the captain, received certain shares of the profits called *lays,* and that these lays were proportioned to the degree of importance pertaining to the respective duties of the ship's company. I was also aware that being a green hand at whaling, my own lay would not be very large; but considering that I was used to the sea, could steer a ship, splice a rope, and all that, I made no doubt that from all I had heard I should be offered at least the 275th lay—that is, the 275th part of the clear net proceeds of the voyage, whatever that might eventually amount to. And though the 275th lay was what they call a rather *long lay,* yet it was better than nothing; and if we had a lucky voyage, might pretty nearly pay for the clothing I would wear out on it, not to speak of my three years' beef and board, for which I would not have to pay one stiver.

It might be thought that this was a poor way to accumulate a princely fortune—and so it was, a very poor way indeed. But I am one of those that never take on about princely fortunes, and am quite content if the world is ready to board and lodge me, while I am putting up at this grim sign of the Thunder Cloud. Upon the whole, I thought that the 275th lay would be about the fair thing, but would not have been surprised had I been offered the 200th, considering I was of a broad-shouldered make.

But one thing, nevertheless, that made me a little distrustful about receiving a generous share of the profits was this: Ashore, I had heard something of both Captain Peleg and his unaccountable old crony Bildad; how that they being the principal proprietors of the Pequod, therefore the other and more inconsiderable and scattered owners, left nearly the whole management of the ship's affairs to these two. And I did not know but what the stingy old Bildad might have a mighty deal to say about shipping hands, especially as I now found him on board the Pequod, quite at home there in the cabin, and reading his Bible as if at his own fireside. Now while Peleg was vainly trying to mend a pen with his jack-knife, old Bildad, to my no small surprise, considering that he was such an interested party in these proceedings; Bildad never heeded us, but went on mumbling to himself out of his book, '"*Lay* not up for yourselves treasures upon earth, where moth—"'

'Well, Captain Bildad,' interrupted Peleg, 'what d'ye say, what lay shall we give this young man?'

'Thou knowest best,' was the sepulchral reply, 'the seven hundred and seventy-seventh wouldn't be too much, would it?—"where moth and rust do corrupt, but *lay*—"'

Lay, indeed, thought I, and such a lay! the seven hundred and seventy-seventh! Well, old Bildad, you are determined that I, for one, shall not *lay* up many *lays* here below, where moth and rust do corrupt. It was an exceedingly *long lay* that, indeed; and though from the magnitude of the figure it might at first deceive a landsman, yet the slightest consideration will show that though seven hundred and seventy-seven is a pretty large number, yet, when you come to make a *teenth* of it, you will then see, I say, that the seven hundred and seventy-seventh part of a farthing is a good deal less than seven hundred and seventy-seven gold doubloons; and so I thought at the time.

'Why, blast your eyes, Bildad,' cried Peleg, 'thou dost not want to swindle this young man! he must have more than that.'

'Seven hundred and seventy-seventh,' again said Bildad, without lifting his eyes; and then went on mumbling—'"for where your treasure is, there will your heart be also."'

'I am going to put him down for the three hundredth,' said Peleg, 'do ye hear that, Bildad! The three hundredth lay, I say.'

Bildad laid down his book, and turning solemnly towards him said, 'Captain Peleg, thou hast a generous heart; but thou must consider the duty thou owest to the other owners of this ship—widows and orphans, many of them—and that if we too abundantly reward the labors of this young man, we may be taking the bread from those widows and those orphans. The seven hundred and seventy-seventh lay, Captain Peleg.'

'Thou Bildad!' roared Peleg, starting up and clattering about the cabin. 'Blast ye, Captain Bildad, if I had followed thy advice in these matters, I would afore now had a conscience to lug about that would be heavy enough to founder the largest ship that ever sailed round Cape Horn.'

'Captain Peleg,' said Bildad steadily, 'thy conscience may be drawing ten inches of water, or ten fathoms, I can't tell; but as thou art still an impenitent man, Captain Peleg, I greatly fear lest thy conscience be but a leaky one; and will in the end sink thee foundering down to the fiery pit, Captain Peleg.'

'Fiery pit! fiery pit! ye insult me, man; past all natural bearing, ye insult me. It's an all-fired outrage to tell any human creature that he's bound to hell. Flukes and flames! Bildad, say that again to me, and start my soul-bolts, but I'll—I'll—yes, I'll swallow a live goat with all his hair and horns on. Out of the cabin, ye canting, drab-colored son of a wooden gun—a straight wake with ye!'

As he thundered out this he made a rush at Bildad, but with a marvellous oblique, sliding celerity, Bildad for that time eluded him.

Alarmed at this terrible outburst between the two principal and responsible owners of the ship, and feeling half a mind to give up all idea of sailing in a vessel so questionably owned and temporarily commanded, I stepped aside from the door to give egress to Bildad, who, I made no doubt, was all eagerness to vanish from before the awakened wrath of Peleg. But to my astonishment, he sat down again on the transom very quietly, and seemed to have not the slightest intention of withdrawing. He seemed quite used to impenitent Peleg and his ways. As for Peleg, after letting off his rage as he had, there seemed no more left in him, and he, too, sat down like a lamb, though he twitched a little as if still nervously agitated. 'Whew!' he whistled at last—'the squall's gone off to leeward, I think. Bildad, thou used to be good at sharpening a lance, mend that pen, will ye. My jack-knife here needs the grindstone. That's he; thank ye, Bildad. Now then, my young man, Ishmael's thy name, didn't ye say? Well then, down ye go here, Ishmael, for the three hundredth lay.'

'Captain Peleg,' said I, 'I have a friend with me who wants to ship too—shall I bring him down tomorrow?'

'To be sure,' said Peleg. 'Fetch him along, and we'll look at him.'

'What lay does *he* want?' groaned Bildad, glancing up from the book in which he had again been burying himself.

'Oh! never thee mind about that, Bildad,' said Peleg. 'Has he ever whaled it any?' turning to me.

'Killed more whales than I can count, Captain Peleg.'

'Well, bring him along then.'

And, after signing the papers, off I went; nothing doubting but that I had done a good morning's work, and that the Pequod was the identical ship that Yojo had provided to carry Queequeg and me round the Cape.

But I had not proceeded far, when I began to bethink me that the captain with whom I was to sail yet remained unseen by me; though, indeed, in many cases, a whale-ship will be completely fitted out, and receive all her crew on board, ere the captain makes himself visible by arriving to take command; for sometimes these voyages are so prolonged, and the shore intervals at home so exceedingly brief, that if the captain have a family, or any absorbing concernment of that sort, he does not trouble himself much about his ship in port, but leaves her to the owners till all is ready for sea. However, it is always as well to have a look at him before irrevocably committing yourself into his hands. Turning back I accosted Captain Peleg, inquiring where Captain Ahab was to be found.

'And what dost thou want of Captain Ahab? It's all right enough; thou art shipped.'

'Yes, but I should like to see him.'

'But I don't think thou wilt be able to at present. I don't know exactly what's the matter with him; but he keeps close inside the house; a sort of sick, and yet he don't look so. In fact, he ain't sick; but no, he isn't well either. Any how, young man, he won't always see me, so I don't suppose he will thee. He's a queer man, Captain Ahab—so some think—but a good one. Oh, thou'lt like him well enough; no fear, no fear. He's a grand, ungodly, god-like man, Captain Ahab; doesn't speak much; but, when he does speak, then you may well listen. Mark ye, be forewarned; Ahab's above the common; Ahab's been in colleges, as well as 'mong the cannibals; been used to deeper wonders than the waves; fixed his fiery lance in mightier, stranger foes than whales. His lance! aye, the keenest and the surest that out of all our isle! Oh! he ain't Captain Bildad; no, and he ain't Captain Peleg; *he's Ahab,* boy; and Ahab of old, thou knowest, was a crowned king!'

'And a very vile one. When that wicked king was slain, the dogs, did they not lick his blood?'

'Come hither to me—hither, hither,' said Peleg, with a significance in his eye that almost startled me. 'Look ye, lad; never say that on board the Pequod. Never say it anywhere. Captain Ahab did not name himself. 'Twas a foolish, ignorant whim of his crazy, widowed mother, who died when he was only a twelvemonth old. And yet the old squaw Tistig, at Gayhead, said that the name would somehow prove prophetic. And, perhaps, other fools like her may tell thee the same. I wish to warn thee. It's a lie. I know Captain Ahab well; I've sailed with him as mate years ago; I know what he is—a good man—not a pious, good man, like Bildad, but a swearing good man—something like me—only there's a good deal more of him. Aye, aye, I know that he was never very jolly; and I know that on the passage home, he was a little out of his mind for a spell; but it was the sharp shooting pains in his bleeding stump that brought that about, as any one might see. I know, too, that ever since he lost his leg last voyage by that accursed whale, he's been a kind of moody—desperate moody, and savage sometimes; but that will all pass off. And once for all, let me tell thee and assure thee, young man, it's better to sail with a moody good captain than a laughing bad one. So good-bye to thee—and wrong not Captain Ahab, because he happens to have a wicked name. Besides, my boy, he has a wife—not three voyages wedded—a sweet, resigned girl. Think of that; by that sweet girl that old man has a child: hold ye then there can be any utter, hopeless harm in Ahab? No, no, my lad; stricken, blasted, if he be, Ahab has his humanities!'

As I walked away, I was full of thoughtfulness; what had been incidentally revealed to me of Captain Ahab, filled me with a certain wild vagueness of painfulness concerning him. And somehow, at the time, I felt a sympathy and a sorrow for him, but for I don't know what, unless it was the cruel loss of his leg. And yet I also felt a strange awe of him; but that sort of awe, which I cannot at all describe, was not exactly awe; I do not know what it was. But I felt it; and it did not disincline me towards him; though I felt impatience at what seemed like mystery in him, so imperfectly as he was known to me then. However, my thoughts were at length carried in other directions, so that for the present dark Ahab slipped my mind.

CHAPTER XVII

THE RAMADAN

As Queequeg's Ramadan, or Fasting and Humiliation, was to continue all day, I did not choose to disturb him till towards night-fall; for I cherish the greatest respect towards everybody's religious obligations, never mind how comical, and could not find it in my heart to undervalue even a congregation of ants worshipping a toad-stool; or those other creatures in certain parts of our earth, who with a degree of footmanism quite unprecedented in other planets, bow down before the torso of a deceased landed proprietor merely on account of the inordinate possessions yet owned and rented in his name.

I say, we good Presbyterian Christians should be charitable in these things, and not fancy ourselves so vastly superior to other mortals, pagans and what not, because of their half-crazy conceits on these subjects. There was Queequeg, now, certainly entertaining the most absurd notions about Yojo and his Ramadan;—but what of that? Queequeg thought he knew what he was about, I suppose; he seemed to be content; and there let him rest. All our arguing with him would not avail; let him be, I say: and Heaven have mercy on us all—Presbyterians and Pagans alike—for we are all somehow dreadfully cracked about the head, and sadly need mending.

Towards evening, when I felt assured that all his performances and rituals must be over, I went up to his room and knocked at the door; but no answer. I tried to open it, but it was fastened inside. 'Queequeg,' said I softly through the key-hole:—all silent. 'I say, Queequeg! why don't you speak? It's I—Ishmael.' But all remained still as before. I began to grow alarmed. I had allowed him such abundant time; I thought he might have had an apoplectic fit. I looked through the key-hole; but the door opening into an odd corner of the room, the key-hole prospect was but a crooked and sinister one. I could only see part of the footboard of the bed and a line of the wall, but nothing more. I was surprised to behold resting against the wall the wooden shaft of Queequeg's harpoon, which the landlady the evening previous had taken from him, before our mounting to the chamber. That's strange, thought I; but at any rate, since the harpoon stands yonder, and he seldom or never goes abroad without it, therefore he must be inside here, and no possible mistake.

'Queequeg!—Queequeg!'—all still. Something must have happened. Apoplexy! I tried to burst open the door; but it stubbornly resisted. Running down stairs, I quickly stated my suspicions to the first person I met—the chambermaid. 'La! La!' she cried, 'I thought something must be the matter. I went to make the bed after breakfast, and the door was locked; and not a mouse to be heard; and it's been just so silent ever since. But I thought, may be, you had both gone off and locked your baggage in for safe keeping. La! La, ma'am!—Mistress! murder! Mrs Hussey! apoplexy!'—and with these cries, she ran towards the kitchen, I following.

Mrs Hussey soon appeared, with a mustard-pot in one hand and a vinegar-cruet in the other, having just broken away from the occupation of attending to the castors, and scolding her little black boy meantime.

'Wood-house!' cried I, 'which way to it? Run for God's sake, and fetch something to pry open the door—the axe!—the axe!—he's had a stroke; depend upon it!'—and so saying I was unmethodically rushing up stairs again empty-handed, when Mrs Hussey interposed the mustard-pot and vinegar-cruet, and the entire castor of her countenance.

'What's the matter with you, young man?'

'Get the axe! For God's sake, run for the doctor, some one, while I pry it open!'

'Look here,' said the landlady, quickly putting down the vinegar-cruet, so as to have one hand free; 'look here; are you talking about prying open any of my doors?'—and with that she seized my arm. 'What's the matter with you? What's the matter with you, shipmate?'

In as calm, but rapid a manner as possible, I gave her to understand the whole case. Unconsciously clapping the vinegar-cruet to one side of her nose, she ruminated for an instant; then exclaimed—'No! I haven't seen it since I put it there.' Running to a little closet under the landing of the stairs, she glanced in, and returning, told me that Queequeg's harpoon was missing. 'He's killed himself,' she cried. 'It's unfort'nate Stiggs done over again—there goes another counterpane—God pity his poor mother!—it will be the ruin of my house. Has the poor lad a sister? Where's that girl?—there, Betty, go to Snarles the Painter, and tell him to paint me a sign, with—"no suicides permitted here, and no smoking in the parlor;"—might as well kill both birds at once. Kill? The Lord be merciful to his ghost! What's that noise there? You, young man, avast there!'

And running up after me, she caught me as I was again trying to force open the door.

'I won't allow it; I won't have my premises spoiled. Go for the locksmith, there's one about a mile from here. But avast!' putting her hand in her side-pocket, 'here's a key that'll fit, I guess; let's see.' And with that, she turned it in the lock; but, alas! Queequeg's supplemental bolt remained unwithdrawn within.

'Have to burst it open,' said I, and was running down the entry a little, for a good start, when the landlady caught at me, again vowing I should not break down her premises; but I tore from her, and with a sudden bodily rush dashed myself full against the mark.

With a prodigious noise the door flew open, and the knob slamming against the wall, sent the plaster to the ceiling; and there, good heavens! there sat Queequeg, altogether cool and self-collected; right in the middle of the room; squatting on his hams, and holding Yojo on top of his head. He looked neither one way nor the other way, but sat like a carved image with scarce a sign of active life.

'Queequeg,' said I, going up to him, 'Queequeg, what's the matter with you?'

'He hain't been a sittin' so all day, has he?' said the landlady.

But all we said, not a word could we drag out of him; I almost felt like pushing him over, so as to change his position, for it was almost intolerable, it seemed so painfully and unnaturally constrained; especially, as in all probability he had been sitting so for upwards of eight or ten hours, going too without his regular meals.

'Mrs Hussey,' said I, 'he's *alive* at all events; so leave us, if you please, and I will see to this strange affair myself.'

Closing the door upon the landlady, I endeavored to prevail upon Queequeg to take a chair; but in vain. There he sat; and all I could do—for all my polite arts and blandishments—he would not move a peg, nor say a single word, nor even look at me, nor notice my presence in any the slightest way.

I wonder, thought I, if this can possibly be a part of his Ramadan; do they fast on their hams that way in his native island? It must be so; yes, it's part of his creed, I suppose; well, then, let him rest; he'll get up sooner or later, no doubt. It can't last for ever, thank God, and his Ramadan only comes once a year; and I don't believe it's very punctual then.

I went down to supper. After sitting a long time listening to the long stories of some sailors who had just come from a plum-pudding voyage, as they called it (that is, a short whaling-voyage in a schooner or brig, confined to the north of the line, in the Atlantic Ocean only); after listening to these plum-puddingers till nearly eleven o'clock, I went up stairs to go to bed, feeling quite sure by this time Queequeg must certainly have brought his Ramadan to a termination. But no; there he was just where I had left him; he had not stirred an inch. I began to grow vexed with him; it seemed so downright senseless and insane to be sitting there all day and half the night on his hams in a cold room, holding a piece of wood on his head.

'For heaven's sake, Queequeg, get up and shake yourself; get up and have some supper. You'll starve; you'll kill yourself, Queequeg.' But not a word did he reply.

Despairing of him, therefore, I determined to go to bed and to sleep; and no doubt, before a great while, he would follow me. But previous to turning in, I took my heavy bearskin jacket, and threw it over him, as it promised to be a very cold night; and he had nothing but his ordinary round jacket on. For some time, do all I would, I could not get into the faintest doze. I had blown out the candle; and the mere thought of Queequeg—not four feet off—sitting there in that uneasy position, stark alone in the cold and dark; this made me really wretched. Think of it; sleeping all night in the same room with a wide awake pagan on his hams in this dreary, unaccountable Ramadan!

But somehow I dropped off at last, and knew nothing more till break of day; when, looking over the bedside, there squatted Queequeg, as if he had been screwed down to the floor. But as soon as the first glimpse of sun entered the window, up he got, with stiff and grating joints, but with a cheerful look; limped towards me where I lay; pressed his forehead again against mine; and said his Ramadan was over.

Now, as I before hinted, I have no objection to any person's religion, be it what it may, so long as that person does not kill or insult any other person, because that other person don't believe it also. But when a man's religion becomes really frantic; when it is a positive torment to him; and, in fine, makes this earth of ours an uncomfortable inn to lodge in; then I think it high time to take that individual aside and argue the point with him.

And just so I now did with Queequeg. 'Queequeg,' said I, 'get into bed now, and lie and listen to me.' I then went on, beginning with the rise and progress of the primitive religions, and coming down to the various religions of the present time, during which time I labored to show Queequeg that all these Lents, Ramadans, and prolonged ham-squattings in cold, cheerless rooms were stark nonsense; bad for the health; useless for the soul; opposed, in short, to the obvious laws of Hygiene and common sense. I told him, too, that he being in other things such an extremely sensible and sagacious savage, it pained me, very badly pained me, to see him now so deplorably foolish about this ridiculous Ramadan of his. Besides, argued I, fasting makes the body cave in; hence the spirit caves in; and all thoughts born of a fast must necessarily be half-starved. This is the reason why most dyspeptic religionists cherish such melancholy notions about their hereafters. In one word, Queequeg, said I, rather digressively; hell is an idea first born on an undigested apple-dumpling; and since then perpetuated through the hereditary dyspepsias nurtured by Ramadans.

I then asked Queequeg whether he himself was ever troubled with dyspepsia; expressing the idea very plainly, so that he could take it in. He said no; only upon one memorable occasion. It was after a great feast given by his father the king, on the gaining of a great battle wherein fifty of the enemy had been killed by about two o'clock in the afternoon, and all cooked and eaten that very evening.

'No more, Queequeg,' said I, shuddering; 'that will do;' for I knew the inferences without his further hinting them. I had seen a sailor who had visited that very island, and he told me that it was the custom, when a great battle had been gained there, to barbecue all the slain in the yard or garden of the victor; and then, one by one, they were placed in great wooden trenchers, and garnished round like a pilau, with breadfruit and cocoanuts; and with some parsley in their mouths, were sent round with the victor's compliments to all his friends, just as though these presents were so many Christmas turkeys.

After all, I do not think that my remarks about religion made much impression upon Queequeg. Because, in the first place, he somehow seemed dull of hearing on that important subject, unless considered from his own point of view; and, in the second place, he did not more than one third understand me, couch my ideas simply as I would; and, finally, he no doubt thought he knew a good deal more about the true religion than I did. He looked at me with a sort of condescending concern and compassion, as though he thought it a great pity that such a sensible young man should be so hopelessly lost to evangelical pagan piety.

At last we rose and dressed; and Queequeg, taking a prodigiously hearty breakfast of chowders of all sorts, so that the landlady should not make much profit by reason of his Ramadan, we sallied out to board the Pequod, sauntering along, and picking our teeth with halibut bones.

CHAPTER XVIII

His Mark

As we were walking down the end of the wharf towards the ship, Queequeg carrying his harpoon, Captain Peleg in his gruff voice loudly hailed us from his wigwam, saying he had not suspected my friend was a cannibal, and furthermore announcing that he let no cannibals on board that craft, unless they previously produced their papers.

'What do you mean by that, Captain Peleg!' said I, now jumping on the bulwarks, and leaving my comrade standing on the wharf.

'I mean,' he replied, 'he must show his papers.'

'Yea,' said Captain Bildad in his hollow voice, sticking his head from behind Peleg's, out of the wigwam. 'He must show that he's converted. Son of darkness,' he added, turning to Queequeg, 'art thou at present in communion with any christian church?'

'Why,' said I, 'he's a member of the First Congregational Church.' Here be it said, that many tattooed savages sailing in Nantucket ships at last come to be converted into the churches.

'First Congregational Church,' cried Bildad, 'what! that worships in Deacon Deuteronomy Coleman's meetinghouse?' and so saying, taking out his spectacles, he rubbed them with his great yellow bandana handkerchief, and putting them on very carefully, came out of the wigwam, and leaning stiffly over the bulwarks, took a good long look at Queequeg.

'How long hath he been a member?' he then said, turning to me; 'not very long, I rather guess, young man.'

'No,' said Peleg, 'and he hasn't been baptized right either, or it would have washed some of that devil's blue off his face.'

'Do tell, now,' cried Bildad, 'is this Philistine a regular member of Deacon Deuteronomy's meeting? I never saw him going there, and I pass it every Lord's day.'

'I don't know anything about Deacon Deuteronomy or his meeting,' said I, 'all I know is, that Queequeg here is a born member of the First Congregational Church. He is a deacon himself, Queequeg is.'

'Young man,' said Bildad sternly, 'thou art skylarking with me—explain thyself, thou young Hittite. What church dost thee mean? answer me.'

Finding myself thus hard pushed, I replied. 'I mean, sir, the same ancient Catholic Church to which you and I, and Captain Peleg there, and Queequeg here, and all of us, and every mother's son and soul of us belong; the great and everlasting First Congregation of this whole worshipping world; we all belong to that; only some of us cherish some queer crotchets noways touching the grand belief; in *that* we all join hands.'

'Splice, thou mean'st *splice* hands,' cried Peleg, drawing nearer. 'Young man, you'd better ship for a missionary, instead of a fore-mast hand; I never heard a better sermon. Deacon Deuteronomy—why Father Mapple himself couldn't beat it, and he's reckoned something. Come aboard, come aboard; never mind about the papers. I say, tell Quohog there—what's that you call him? tell Quohog to step along. By the great anchor, what a harpoon he's got there! looks like good stuff that; and he handles it about right. I say, Quohog, or whatever your name is, did you ever stand in the head of a whale-boat? did you ever strike a fish?'

Without saying a word, Queequeg, in his wild sort of way, jumped upon the bulwarks, from thence into the bows of one of the whale-boats hanging to the side; and then bracing his left knee, and poising his harpoon, cried out in some such way as this:—

'Cap'ain, you see him small drop tar on water dere? You see him? well, spose him one whale eye, well, den!' and taking sharp aim at it, he darted the iron right over old Bildad's broad brim, clean across the ship's decks, and struck the glistening tar spot out of sight.

'Now,' said Queequeg, quietly hauling in the line, 'spos-ee him whale-e eye; why, dad whale dead.'

'Quick, Bildad,' said Peleg, to his partner, who, aghast at the close vicinity of the flying harpoon, had retreated towards the cabin gangway. 'Quick, I say, you

Bildad, and get the ship's papers. We must have Hedgehog there, I mean Quohog, in one of our boats. Look ye, Quohog, we'll give ye the ninetieth lay, and that's more than ever was given a harpooneer yet out of Nantucket.'

So down we went into the cabin, and to my great joy Queequeg was soon enrolled among the same ship's company to which I myself belonged.

When all preliminaries were over and Peleg had got everything ready for signing, he turned to me and said, 'I guess, Quohog there don't know how to write, does he? I say, Quohog, blast ye! dost thou sign thy name or make thy mark?'

But at this question, Queequeg, who had twice or thrice taken part in similar ceremonies, looked no ways abashed; but taking the offered pen, copied upon the paper, in the proper place, an exact counterpart of a queer round figure which was tattooed upon his arm; so that through Captain Peleg's obstinate mistake touching his appellative, it stood something like this:—

Quohog.
his ✠ mark.

Meanwhile Captain Bildad sat earnestly and steadfastly eyeing Queequeg, and at last rising solemnly and fumbling in the huge pockets of his broad-skirted drab coat, took out a bundle of tracts, and selecting one entitled 'The Latter Day Coming; or No Time to Lose,' placed it in Queequeg's hands, and then grasping them and the book with both his, looked earnestly into his eyes, and said, 'Son of darkness, I must do my duty by thee; I am part owner of this ship, and feel concerned for the souls of all its crew; if thou still clingest to thy Pagan ways, which I sadly fear, I beseech thee, remain not for aye a Belial bondsman. Spurn the idol Bell, and the hideous dragon; turn from the wrath to come; mind thine eye, I say; oh! goodness gracious! steer clear of the fiery pit!'

Something of the salt sea yet lingered in old Bildad's language, heterogeneously mixed with Scriptural and domestic phrases.

'Avast there, avast there, Bildad, avast now spoiling our harpooneer,' cried Peleg. 'Pious harpooneers never make good voyagers—it takes the shark out of 'em; no harpooneer is worth a straw who aint pretty sharkish. There was young Nat Swaine, once the bravest boat-header out of all Nantucket and the Vineyard; he joined the meeting, and never came to good. He got so frightened about his plaguy soul, that he shrinked and sheered away from whales, for fear of after-claps in case he got stove and went to Davy Jones.'

'Peleg! Peleg!' said Bildad, lifting his eyes and hands, 'thou thyself, as I myself, hast seen many a perilous time; thou knowest, Peleg, what it is to have the fear of death; how, then, can'st thou prate in this ungodly guise. Thou beliest thine own heart, Peleg. Tell me, when this same Pequod here had her three masts overboard in that typhoon off Japan, that same voyage when thou went mate with Captain Ahab, did'st thou not think of Death and the Judgment then?'

'Hear him, hear him now,' cried Peleg, marching across the cabin, and thrusting his hands far down into his pockets,—'hear him, all of ye. Think of that! When every moment we thought the ship would sink! Death and the Judgment then? What? With all three masts making such an everlasting thundering against the side; and every sea breaking over us, fore and aft. Think of Death and the Judgment then? No! no time to think about Death then. Life was what Captain Ahab and I was thinking of; and how to save all hands—how to rig jury-masts—how to get into the nearest port; that was what I was thinking of.'

Bildad said no more, but buttoning up his coat, stalked on deck, where we followed him. There he stood, very quietly overlooking some sail-makers who were mending a top-sail in the waist. Now and then he stooped to pick up a patch, or save an end of the tarred twine, which otherwise might have been wasted.

CHAPTER XIX

The Prophet

'Shipmates, have ye shipped in that ship?'

Queequeg and I had just left the Pequod, and were sauntering away from the water, for the moment each occupied with his own thoughts, when the above words were put to us by a stranger, who, pausing before us, levelled his massive forefinger at the vessel in question. He was but shabbily apparelled in faded jacket and patched trowsers; a rag of a black handkerchief investing his neck. A confluent small-pox had in all directions flowed over his face, and left it like the complicated ribbed bed of a torrent, when the rushing waters have been dried up.

'Have ye shipped in her?' he repeated.

'You mean the ship Pequod, I suppose,' said I, trying to gain a little more time for an uninterrupted look at him.

'Aye, the Pequod—that ship there,' he said, drawing back his whole arm, and then rapidly shoving it straight out from him, with the fixed bayonet of his pointed finger darted full at the object.

'Yes,' said I, 'we have just signed the articles.'

'Anything down there about your souls?'

'About what?'

'Oh, perhaps you hav'n't got any,' he said quickly. 'No matter though, I know many chaps that hav'n't got any,—good luck to 'em; and they are all the better off for it. A soul's a sort of fifth wheel to a wagon.'

'What are you jabbering about, shipmate?' said I.

'*He's* got enough, though, to make up for all deficiencies of that sort in other chaps,' abruptly said the stranger, placing a nervous emphasis upon the word *he*.

'Queequeg,' said I, 'let's go; this fellow has broken loose from somewhere; he's talking about something and somebody we don't know.'

'Stop!' cried the stranger. 'Ye said true—ye hav'n't seen Old Thunder yet, have ye?'

'Who's Old Thunder?' said I, again riveted with the insane earnestness of his manner.

'Captain Ahab.'

'What! the captain of our ship, the Pequod?'

'Aye, among some of us old sailor chaps, he goes by that name. Ye hav'n't seen him yet, have ye?'

'No, we hav'n't. He's sick they say, but is getting better, and will be all right again before long.'

'All right again before long!' laughed the stranger, with a solemnly derisive sort of laugh. 'Look ye; when Captain Ahab is all right, then this left arm of mine will be all right; not before.'

'What do you know about him?'

'What did they *tell* you about him? Say that!'

'They didn't tell much of anything about him; only I've heard that he's a good whale-hunter, and a good captain to his crew.'

'That's true, that's true—yes, both true enough. But you must jump when he gives an order. Step and growl; growl and go—that's the word with Captain Ahab. But nothing about that thing that happened to him off Cape Horn, long ago, when he lay like dead for three days and nights; nothing about that deadly skrimmage with the Spaniard afore the altar in Santa?—heard nothing about that, eh? Nothing about the silver calabash he spat into? And nothing about his losing his leg last voyage, according to the prophecy? Didn't ye hear a word about them matters and something more, eh? No, I don't think ye did; how could ye? Who knows it? Not all Nantucket, I guess. But hows'ever, mayhap, ye've heard tell about the leg, and how he lost it; aye, ye have heard of that, I dare say. Oh yes, *that* every one knows a'most—I mean they know he's only one leg; and that a parmacetti took the other off.'

'My friend,' said I, 'what all this gibberish of yours is about, I don't know, and I don't much care; for it seems to me that you must be a little damaged in the head. But if you are speaking of Captain Ahab, of that ship there, the Pequod, then let me tell you, that I know all about the loss of his leg.'

'*All* about it, eh—sure you do?—all?'

'Pretty sure.'

With finger pointed and eye levelled at the Pequod, the beggar-like stranger stood a moment, as if in a troubled reverie; then starting a little, turned and said:—'Ye've shipped, have ye? Names down on the papers? Well, well, what's signed, is signed; and what's to be, will be; and then again, perhaps it wont be, after all. Any how, it's all fixed and arranged a'ready; and some sailors or other must go with him I suppose; as well these as any other men, God pity 'em! Morning to ye, shipmates, morning; the ineffable heavens bless ye; I'm sorry I stopped ye.'

'Look here, friend,' said I, 'if you have anything important to tell us, out with it; but if you are only trying to bamboozle us, you are mistaken in your game; that's all I have to say.'

'And it's said very well, and I like to hear a chap talk up that way; you are just the man for him—the likes of ye. Morning to ye, shipmates, morning! Oh! when ye get there, tell 'em I've concluded not to make one of 'em.'

'Ah, my dear fellow, you can't fool us that way—you can't fool us. It is the easiest thing in the world for a man to look as if he had a great secret in him.'

'Morning to ye, shipmates, morning.'

'Morning it is,' said I. 'Come along, Queequeg, let's leave this crazy man. But stop, tell me your name, will you?'

'Elijah.'

Elijah! thought I, and we walked away, both commenting, after each other's fashion, upon this ragged old sailor; and agreed that he was nothing but a humbug, trying to be a bugbear. But we had not gone perhaps above a hundred yards, when chancing to turn a corner, and looking back as I did so, who should be seen but Elijah following us, though at a distance. Somehow, the sight of him struck me so, that I said nothing to Queequeg of his being behind, but passed on with my comrade, anxious to see whether the stranger would turn the same corner that we did. He did; and then it seemed to me that he was dogging us, but with what intent I could not for the life of me imagine. This circumstance, coupled with his ambiguous, half-hinting, half-revealing, shrouded sort of talk, now begat in me all kinds of vague wonderments and half-apprehensions, and all connected with the Pequod; and Captain Ahab; and the leg he had lost; and the Cape Horn fit; and the silver calabash; and what Captain Peleg had said of him, when I left the ship the day previous; and the prediction of the squaw Tistig; and the voyage we had bound ourselves to sail; and a hundred other shadowy things.

I was resolved to satisfy myself whether this ragged Elijah was really dogging us or not, and with that intent crossed the way with Queequeg, and on that side of it retraced our steps. But Elijah passed on, without seeming to notice us. This relieved me; and once more, and finally as it seemed to me, I pronounced him in my heart, a humbug.

CHAPTER XX

ALL ASTIR

A day or two passed, and there was great activity aboard the Pequod. Not only were the old sails being mended, but new sails were coming on board, and bolts of canvas, and coils of rigging; in short, everything betokened that the ship's preparations were hurrying to a close. Captain Peleg seldom or never went ashore, but sat in his wigwam keeping a sharp look-out upon the hands; Bildad did all the purchasing and providing at the stores; and the men employed in the hold and on the rigging were working till long after night-fall.

On the day following Queequeg's signing the articles, word was given at all the inns where the ship's company were stopping, that their chests must be on board before night, for there was no telling how soon the vessel might be sailing. So Queequeg and I got down our traps, resolving, however, to sleep ashore till the last. But it seems they always give very long notice in these cases, and the ship did not sail for several days. But no wonder; there was a good deal to be done, and there is no telling how many things to be thought of, before the Pequod was fully equipped.

Every one knows what a multitude of things—beds, saucepans, knives and forks, shovels and tongs, napkins, nutcrackers, and what not, are indispensable to the business of housekeeping. Just so with whaling, which necessitates a three-years' housekeeping upon the wide ocean, far from all grocers, costermongers, doctors, bakers, and bankers. And though this also holds true of merchant vessels, yet not by any means to the same extent as with whalemen. For besides the great length of the whaling voyage, the numerous articles peculiar to the prosecution of the fishery, and the impossibility of replacing them at the remote harbors usually frequented, it must be remembered, that of all ships, whaling vessels are the most exposed to accidents of all kinds, and especially to the destruction and loss of the very things upon which the success of the voyage most depends. Hence, the spare boats, spare spars, and spare lines and harpoons, and spare everythings, almost, but a spare Captain and duplicate ship.

At the period of our arrival at the Island, the heaviest stowage of the Pequod had been almost completed; comprising her beef, bread, water, fuel, and iron hoops and staves. But, as before hinted, for some time there was a continual fetching and carrying on board of divers odds and ends of things, both large and small.

Chief among those who did this fetching and carrying was Captain Bildad's sister, a lean old lady of a most determined and indefatigable spirit, but withal very kindhearted, who seemed resolved that, if *she* could help it, nothing should be found wanting in the Pequod, after once fairly getting to sea. At one time she would come on board with a jar of pickles for the steward's pantry; another time with a bunch of quills for the chief mate's desk, where he kept his log; a third time with a roll of flannel for the small of some one's rheumatic back. Never did any woman better deserve her name, which was Charity—Aunt Charity, as everybody called her. And like a sister of charity did this charitable Aunt Charity bustle about hither and thither, ready to turn her hand and heart to anything that promised to yield safety, comfort, and consolation to all on board a ship in which her beloved brother Bildad was concerned, and in which she herself owned a score or two of well-saved dollars.

But it was startling to see this excellent hearted Quakeress coming on board, as she did the last day, with a long oil-ladle in one hand, and a still longer whaling lance in the other. Nor was Bildad himself nor Captain Peleg at all backward. As for Bildad, he carried about with him a long list of the articles needed, and at every fresh arrival, down went his mark opposite that article upon the paper. Every once and a while Peleg came hobbling out of his whalebone den, roaring at the men down the hatchways, roaring up to the riggers at the mast-head, and then concluded by roaring back into his wigwam.

During these days of preparation, Queequeg and I often visited the craft, and as often I asked about Captain Ahab, and how he was, and when he was going to come on board his ship. To these questions they would answer, that he was getting better and better, and was expected aboard every day; meantime, the two Captains, Peleg and Bildad, could attend to everything necessary to fit the vessel for the voyage. If I had been downright honest with myself, I would have seen very plainly in my heart that I did but half fancy being committed this way to so long a voyage, without once laying my eyes on the man who was to be the absolute dictator of it, so soon as the ship sailed out upon the open sea. But when a man suspects any wrong, it sometimes happens that if he be already involved in the matter, he insensibly strives to cover up his suspicions even from himself. And much this way it was with me. I said nothing, and tried to think nothing.

At last it was given out that some time next day the ship would certainly sail. So next morning, Queequeg and I took a very early start.

CHAPTER XXI

GOING ABOARD

It was nearly six o'clock, but only grey imperfect misty dawn, when we drew nigh the wharf.

'There are some sailors running ahead there, if I see right,' said I to Queequeg, 'it can't be shadows; she's off by sunrise, I guess; come on!'

'Avast!' cried a voice, whose owner at the same time coming close behind us, laid a hand upon both our shoulders, and then insinuating himself between us, stood stooping forward a little, in the uncertain twilight, strangely peering from Queequeg to me. It was Elijah.

'Going aboard?'

'Hands off, will you,' said I.

'Lookee here,' said Queequeg, shaking himself, 'go 'way!'

'Aint going aboard, then?'

'Yes, we are,' said I, 'but what business is that of yours? Do you know, Mr Elijah, that I consider you a little impertinent?'

'No, no, no; I wasn't aware of that,' said Elijah, slowly and wonderingly looking from me to Queequeg, with the most unaccountable glances.

'Elijah,' said I, 'you will oblige my friend and me by withdrawing. We are going to the Indian and Pacific Oceans, and would prefer not to be detained.'

'Ye be, be ye? Coming back afore breakfast?'

'He's cracked, Queequeg,' said I, 'come on.'

'Holloa!' cried stationary Elijah, hailing us when we had removed a few paces.

'Never mind him,' said I, 'Queequeg, come on.'

But he stole up to us again, and suddenly clapping his hand on my shoulder, said—'Did ye see anything looking like men going towards that ship a while ago?'

Struck by this plain matter-of-fact question, I answered, saying, 'Yes, I thought I did see four or five men; but it was too dim to be sure.'

'Very dim, very dim,' said Elijah. 'Morning to ye.'

Once more we quitted him; but once more he came softly after us; and touching my shoulder again, said, 'See if you can find 'em now, will ye?'

'Find who?'

'Morning to ye! morning to ye!' he rejoined, again moving off. 'Oh! I was going to warn ye against—but never mind, never mind—it's all one, all in the family too;—sharp frost this morning, ain't it? Good bye to ye. Shan't see ye again very soon, I guess; unless it's before the Grand Jury.' And with these cracked words he finally departed, leaving me, for the moment, in no small wonderment at his frantic impudence.

At last, stepping on board the Pequod, we found everything in profound quiet, not a soul moving. The cabin entrance was locked within; the hatches were all on, and lumbered with coils of rigging. Going forward to the forecastle, we found the slide of the scuttle open. Seeing a light, we went down, and found only an old rigger there, wrapped in a tattered pea-jacket. He was thrown at whole length upon two chests, his face downwards and inclosed in his folded arms. The profoundest slumber slept upon him.

'Those sailors we saw, Queequeg, where can they have gone to?' said I, looking dubiously at the sleeper. But it seemed that, when on the wharf, Queequeg had not at all noticed what I now alluded to; hence I would have thought myself to have been optically deceived in that matter, were it not for Elijah's otherwise inexplicable question. But I beat the thing down; and again marking the sleeper, jocularly hinted to Queequeg that perhaps we had best sit up with the body; telling him to establish himself accordingly. He put his hand upon the sleeper's rear, as though feeling if it was soft enough; and then, without more ado, sat quietly down there.

'Gracious! Queequeg, don't sit there,' said I.

'Oh! perry dood seat,' said Queequeg, 'my country way; won't hurt him face.'

'Face!' said I, 'call that his face? very benevolent countenance then; but how hard he breathes, he's heaving himself; get off, Queequeg, you are heavy, it's grinding the face of the poor. Get off, Queequeg! Look, he'll twitch you off soon. I wonder he don't wake.'

Queequeg removed himself to just beyond the head of the sleeper, and lighted his tomahawk pipe. I sat at the feet. We kept the pipe passing over the sleeper, from one to the other. Meanwhile, upon questioning him, in his broken fashion, Queequeg gave me to understand that, in his land, owing to the absence of settees and sofas of all sorts, the king, chiefs, and great people generally, were in the custom of fattening some of the lower orders for ottomans; and to furnish a house comfortably in that respect, you had only to buy up eight or ten lazy fellows, and lay them round in the piers and alcoves. Besides, it was very convenient on an excursion; much better than those garden-chairs which are convertible into walking-sticks; upon occasion, a chief calling his attendant, and desiring him to make a settee of himself under a spreading tree, perhaps in some damp marshy place.

While narrating these things, every time Queequeg received the tomahawk from me, he flourished the hatchet-side of it over the sleeper's head.

'What's that for, Queequeg?'

'Perry easy, kill-e; oh! perry easy!'

He was going on with some wild reminiscences about his tomahawk-pipe, which, it seemed, had in its two uses both brained his foes and soothed his soul, when we were directly attracted to the sleeping rigger. The strong vapor now completely filling the contracted hole, it began to tell upon him. He breathed with a sort of muffledness; then seemed troubled in the nose; then revolved over once or twice; then sat up and rubbed his eyes.

'Holloa!' he breathed at last, 'who be ye smokers?'

'Shipped men,' answered I, 'when does she sail?'

'Aye, aye, ye are going in her, be ye? She sails to-day. The Captain came aboard last night.'

'What Captain?—Ahab?'

'Who but him indeed?'

I was going to ask him some further questions concerning Ahab, when we heard a noise on deck.

'Halloa! Starbuck's astir,' said the rigger. 'He's a lively chief mate, that; good man, and a pious; but all alive now, I must turn to.' And so saying he went on deck, and we followed.

It was now clear sunrise. Soon the crew came on board in twos and threes; the riggers bestirred themselves; the mates were actively engaged; and several of the shore people were busy in bringing various last things on board. Meanwhile Captain Ahab remained invisibly enshrined within his cabin.

CHAPTER XXII

MERRY CHRISTMAS

At length, towards noon, upon the final dismissal of the ship's riggers, and after the Pequod had been hauled out from the wharf, and after the ever-thoughtful Charity had come off in a whaleboat, with her last gift—a night-cap for Stubb, the second mate, her brother-in-law, and a spare Bible for the steward—after all this, the two captains, Peleg and Bildad, issued from the cabin, and turning to the chief mate, Peleg said:

'Now, Mr Starbuck, are you sure everything is right? Captain Ahab is all ready—just spoke to him—nothing more to be got from shore, eh? Well, call all hands, then. Muster 'em aft here—blast 'em!'

'No need of profane words, however great the hurry, Peleg,' said Bildad, 'but away with thee, friend Starbuck, and do our bidding.'

How now! Here upon the very point of starting for the voyage, Captain Peleg and Captain Bildad were going it with a high hand on the quarter-deck, just as if they were to be joint-commanders at sea, as well as to all appearances in port. And, as for Captain Ahab, no sign of him was yet to be seen; only, they said he was in the cabin. But then, the idea was, that his presence was by no means necessary in getting the ship under weigh, and steering her well out to sea. Indeed, as that was not at all his proper business, but the pilot's; and as he was not yet completely recovered—so they said—therefore, Captain Ahab stayed below. And all this seemed natural enough; especially as in the merchant service many captains never show themselves on deck for a considerable time after heaving up the anchor, but remain over the cabin table, having a farewell merry-making with their shore friends, before they quit the ship for good with the pilot.

But there was not much chance to think over the matter, for Captain Peleg was now all alive. He seemed to do most of the talking and commanding, and not Bildad.

'Aft here, ye sons of bachelors,' he cried, as the sailors lingered at the main-mast. 'Mr Starbuck, drive 'em aft.'

'Strike the tent there!'—was the next order. As I hinted before, this whalebone marquee was never pitched except in port; and on board the Pequod, for thirty years, the order to strike the tent was well known to be the next thing to heaving up the anchor.

'Man the capstan! Blood and thunder!—jump!'—was the next command, and the crew sprang for the handspikes.

Now, in getting under weigh, the station generally occupied by the pilot is the forward part of the ship. And here Bildad, who, with Peleg, be it known, in addition to his other offices, was one of the licensed pilots of the port—he being suspected to have got himself made a pilot in order to save the Nantucket pilot-fee to all the ships he was concerned in, for he never piloted any other craft—Bildad, I say, might now be seen actively engaged in looking over the bows for the approaching anchor, and at intervals singing what seemed a dismal stave of psalmody, to cheer the hands at the windlass, who roared forth some sort of a chorus about the girls in Booble Alley, with hearty good will. Nevertheless, not three days previous, Bildad had told them that no profane songs would be allowed on board the Pequod, particularly in getting under weigh; and Charity, his sister, had placed a small choice copy of Watts in each seaman's berth.

Meantime, overseeing the other part of the ship, Captain Peleg ripped and swore astern in the most frightful manner. I almost thought he would sink the ship before the anchor could be got up; involuntarily I paused on my handspike, and told Queequeg to do the same, thinking of the perils we both ran, in starting on the voyage with such a devil for a pilot. I was comforting myself, however with the thought that in pious Bildad might be found some salvation, spite of his seven hundred and seventy-seventh lay; when I felt a sudden sharp poke in my rear, and turning round, was horrified at the apparition of Captain Peleg in the act of withdrawing his leg from my immediate vicinity. That was my first kick.

'Is that the way they heave in the marchant service?' he roared. 'Spring, thou sheep-head; spring, and break thy back-bone! Why don't ye spring, I say, all of ye—spring! Quohag! spring, thou chap with the red whiskers; spring there, Scotch-cap; spring, thou green pants. Spring, I say, all of ye, and spring your eyes out!' And so saying, he moved along the windlass, here and there using his leg very freely, while imperturbable Bildad kept leading off with his psalmody. Thinks I, Captain Peleg must have been drinking something to-day.

At last the anchor was up, the sails were set, and off we glided. It was a short, cold Christmas; and as the short northern day merged into night, we found ourselves almost broad upon the wintry ocean, whose freezing spray cased us in ice, as in polished armor. The long rows of teeth on the bulwarks glistened in the moonlight; and like the white ivory tusks of some huge elephant, vast curving icicles depended from the bows.

Lank Bildad, as pilot, headed the first watch, and ever and anon, as the old craft deep dived into the green seas, and sent the shivering frost all over her, and the winds howled, and the cordage rang, his steady notes were heard,—

'Sweet fields beyond the swelling flood,
Stand dressed in living green.
So to the Jews old Canaan stood,
While Jordan rolled between.'

Never did those sweet words sound more sweetly to me than then. They were full of hope and fruition. Spite of this frigid winter night in the boisterous Atlantic, spite of my wet feet and wetter jacket, there was yet, it then seemed to me, many a pleasant haven in store; and meads and glades so eternally vernal, that the grass shot up by the spring, untrodden, unwilted, remains at midsummer.

At last we gained such an offing, that the two pilots were needed no longer. The stout sail-boat that had accompanied us began ranging alongside.

It was curious and not unpleasing, how Peleg and Bildad were affected at this juncture, especially Captain Bildad. For loath to depart, yet; very loath to leave, for good, a ship bound on so long and perilous a voyage—beyond both stormy Capes; a ship in which some thousands of his hard earned dollars were invested; a ship, in which an old shipmate sailed as captain; a man almost as old as he, once more starting to encounter all the terrors of the pitiless jaw; loath to say good-bye to a thing so every way brimful of every interest to him,—poor old Bildad lingered long; paced the deck with anxious strides; ran down into the cabin to speak another farewell word there; again came on deck, and looked to windward; looked towards the wide and endless waters, only bounded by the far-off unseen Eastern Continents; looked towards the land; looked aloft; looked right and left; looked everywhere and nowhere; and at last, mechanically coiling a rope upon its pin, convulsively grasped stout Peleg by the hand, and holding up a lantern, for a moment stood gazing heroically in his face, as much as to say, 'Nevertheless, friend Peleg, I can stand it; yes, I can.'

As for Peleg himself, he took it more like a philosopher; but for all his philosophy, there was a tear twinkling in his eye, when the lantern came too near. And he, too, did not a little run from cabin to deck—now a word below, and now a word with Starbuck, the chief mate.

But, at last, he turned to his comrade, with a final sort of look about him,—'Captain Bildad—come, old shipmate, we must go. Back the main-yard there!

Boat ahoy! Stand by to come close alongside, now! Careful, careful!—come, Bildad, boy—say your last. Luck to ye, Starbuck—luck to ye, Mr Stubb—luck to ye, Mr Flask—good-bye, and good luck to ye all—and this day three years I'll have a hot supper smoking for ye in old Nantucket. Hurrah and away!'

'God bless ye, and have ye in His holy keeping, men,' murmured old Bildad, almost incoherently. 'I hope ye'll have fine weather now, so that Captain Ahab may soon be moving among ye—a pleasant sun is all he needs, and ye'll have plenty of them in the tropic voyage ye go. Be careful in the hunt, ye mates. Don't stave the boats needlessly, ye harpooneers; good white cedar plank is raised full three per cent within the year. Don't forget your prayers, either. Mr Starbuck, mind that cooper don't waste the spare staves. Oh! the sail-needles are in the green locker! Don't whale it too much a' Lord's days, men; but don't miss a fair chance either, that's rejecting Heaven's good gifts. Have an eye to the molasses tierce, Mr Stubb; it was a little leaky, I thought. If ye touch at the islands, Mr Flask, beware of fornication. Good-bye, good-bye! Don't keep that cheese too long down in the hold, Mr Starbuck; it'll spoil. Be careful with the butter—twenty cents the pound it was, and mind ye, if—'

'Come, come, Captain Bildad; stop palavering,—away!' and with that, Peleg hurried him over the side, and both dropt into the boat.

Ship and boat diverged; the cold, damp night breeze blew between; a screaming gull flew overhead; the two hulls wildly rolled; we gave three heavy-hearted cheers, and blindly plunged like fate into the lone Atlantic.

CHAPTER XXIII

THE LEE SHORE

Some chapters back, one Bulkington was spoken of, a tall, new-landed mariner, encountered in New Bedford at the inn.

When on that shivering winter's night, the Pequod thrust her vindictive bows into the cold malicious waves, who should I see standing at her helm but Bulkington! I looked with sympathetic awe and fearfulness upon the man, who in mid-winter just landed from a four years' dangerous voyage, could so unrestingly push off again for still another tempestuous term. The land seemed scorching to his feet. Wonderfullest things are ever the unmentionable; deep memories yield no epitaphs; this six-inch chapter is the stoneless grave of Bulkington. Let me only say that it fared with him as with the storm-tossed ship, that miserably drives along the leeward land. The port would fain give succor; the port is pitiful; in the port is safety, comfort, hearthstone, supper, warm blankets, friends, all that's kind to our mortalities. But in that gale, the port, the land, is the ship's direst jeopardy; she must fly all hospitality; one touch of land, though it but graze the keel, would make her shudder through and through. With all her might she crowds all sail off shore; in so doing, fights 'gainst the very winds that fain would blow her homeward; seeks all the lashed sea's landlessness again; for refuge's sake forlornly rushing into peril; her only friend her bitterest foe!

Know ye, now, Bulkington? Glimpses do ye seem to see of that mortally intolerable truth; that all deep, earnest thinking is but the intrepid effort of the soul to keep the open independence of her sea; while the wildest winds of heaven and earth conspire to cast her on the treacherous, slavish shore?

But as in landlessness alone resides the highest truth, shoreless, indefinite as God—so, better is it to perish in that howling infinite, than be ingloriously dashed upon the lee, even if that were safety! For worm-like, then, oh! who would craven crawl to land! Terrors of the terrible! is all this agony so vain? Take heart, take heart, O Bulkington! Bear thee grimly, demigod! Up from the spray of thy ocean-perishing—straight up, leaps thy apotheosis!

CHAPTER XXIV

THE ADVOCATE

As Queequeg and I are now fairly embarked in this business of whaling; and as this business of whaling has somehow come to be regarded among landsmen as a rather unpoetical and disreputable pursuit; therefore, I am all anxiety to convince ye, ye landsmen, of the injustice hereby done to us hunters of whales.

In the first place, it may be deemed almost superfluous to establish the fact, that among people at large, the business of whaling is not accounted on a level with what are called the liberal professions. If a stranger were introduced into any miscellaneous metropolitan society, it would but slightly advance the general opinion of his merits, were he presented to the company as a harpooneer, say; and if in emulation of the naval officers he should append the initials S.W.F. (Sperm Whale Fishery) to his visiting card, such a procedure would be deemed pre-eminently presuming and ridiculous.

Doubtless one leading reason why the world declines honoring us whalemen, is this: they think that, at best, our vocation amounts to a butchering sort of business; and that when actively engaged therein, we are surrounded by all manner of defilements. Butchers we are, that is true. But butchers, also, and butchers of the bloodiest badge have been all Martial Commanders whom the world invariably delights to honor. And as for the matter of the alleged uncleanliness of our business, ye shall soon be initiated into certain facts hitherto pretty generally unknown, and which, upon the whole, will triumphantly plant the sperm whaleship at least among the cleanliest things of this tidy earth. But even granting the charge in question to be true; what disordered slippery decks of a whale-ship are comparable to the unspeakable carrion of those battle-fields from which so many soldiers return to drink in all ladies' plaudits? And if the idea of peril so much enhances the popular conceit of the soldier's profession; let me assure ye that many a veteran who has freely marched up to a battery, would quickly recoil at the apparition of the sperm whale's vast tail, fanning into eddies the air over his head. For what are the comprehensible terrors of man compared with the interlinked terrors and wonders of God!

But, though the world scouts at us whale hunters, yet does it unwittingly pay us the profoundest homage; yea an all-abounding adoration! for almost all the tapers, lamps, and candles that burn round the globe, burn, as before so many shrines, to our glory!

But look at this matter in other lights; weigh it in all sorts of scales; see what we whalemen are, and have been.

Why did the Dutch in DeWitt's time have admirals of their whaling fleets? Why did Louis XVI of France, at his own personal expense, fit out whaling ships from Dunkirk, and politely invite to that town some score or two of families from our own island of Nantucket? Why did Britain between the years 1750 and 1788 pay to her whalemen in bounties upwards of £1,000,000? And lastly, how comes it that we whalemen of America now outnumber all the rest of the banded whalemen in the world; sail a navy of upwards of seven hundred vessels; manned by eighteen thousand men; yearly consuming 4,000,000 of dollars; the ships worth, at the time of sailing, $20,000,000; and every year importing into our harbors a well reaped harvest of $7,000,000. How comes all this, if there be not something puissant in whaling?

But this is not the half; look again.

I freely assert, that the cosmopolite philosopher cannot, for his life, point out one single peaceful influence, which within the last sixty years has operated more potentially upon the whole broad world, taken in one aggregate, than the high and mighty business of whaling. One way and another, it has begotten events so remarkable in themselves, and so continuously momentous in their sequential issues, that whaling may well be regarded as that Egyptian mother, who bore offspring themselves pregnant from her womb. It would be a hopeless, endless task to catalogue all these things. Let a handful suffice. For many years past the whaleship has been the pioneer in ferreting out the remotest and least known parts of the earth. She has explored seas and archipelagoes which had no chart, where no Cook or Vancouver had ever sailed. If American and European men-of-war now peacefully ride in once savage harbors, let them fire salutes to the honor and the glory of the whale-ship, which originally showed them the way, and first interpreted between them and the savages. They may celebrate as they will the heroes of Exploring Expeditions, your Cookes, your Krusensterns; but I say that scores of anonymous Captains have sailed out of Nantucket, that were as great, and greater than your Cooke and your Krusenstern. For in their succorless empty-handedness, they, in the heathenish sharked waters, and by the beaches of unrecorded, javelin islands, battled with virgin wonders and terrors that Cooke with all his marines and muskets would not willingly have dared. All that is made such a flourish of in the old South Sea Voyages, those things were but the life-time commonplaces of our heroic Nantucketers. Often, adventures which Vancouver dedicates three chapters to, these men accounted unworthy of being set down in the ship's common log. Ah, the world! Oh, the world!

Until the whale fishery rounded Cape Horn, no commerce but colonial, scarcely any intercourse but colonial, was carried on between Europe and the long line of the opulent Spanish provinces on the Pacific coast. It was the whalemen who first broke through the jealous policy of the Spanish crown, touching those colonies; and, if space permitted, it might be distinctly shown how from those whalemen at last eventuated the liberation of Peru, Chili, and Bolivia from the yoke of Old Spain, and the establishment of the eternal democracy in those parts.

That great America on the other side of the sphere, Australia, was given to the enlightened world by the whalemen. After its first blunder-born discovery by a

Dutchman, all other ships long shunned those shores as pestiferously barbarous; but the whale-ship touched there. The whale-ship is the true mother of that now mighty colony. Moreover, in the infancy of the first Australian settlement, the emigrants were several times saved from starvation by the benevolent biscuit of the whale-ship luckily dropping an anchor in their waters. The uncounted isles of all Polynesia confess the same truth, and do commercial homage to the whale-ship, that cleared the way for the missionary and the merchant, and in many cases carried the primitive missionaries to their first destinations. If that double-bolted land, Japan, is ever to become hospitable, it is the whale-ship alone to whom the credit will be due; for already she is on the threshold.

But if, in the face of all this, you still declare that whaling has no aesthetically noble associations connected with it, then am I ready to shiver fifty lances with you there, and unhorse you with a split helmet every time.

The whale has no famous author, and whaling no famous chronicler, you will say.

The whale no famous author, and whaling no famous chronicler? Who wrote the first account of our Leviathan? Who but mighty Job! And who composed the first narrative of a whaling-voyage? Who, but no less a prince than Alfred the Great, who, with his own royal pen, took down the words from Other, the Norwegian whale-hunter of those times! And who pronounced our glowing eulogy in Parliament? Who, but Edmund Burke!

True enough, but then whalemen themselves are poor devils; they have no good blood in their veins.

No good blood in their veins? They have something better than royal blood there. The grandmother of Benjamin Franklin was Mary Morrel; afterwards, by marriage, Mary Folger, one of the old settlers of Nantucket, and the ancestress to a long line of Folgers and harpooneers—all kith and kin to noble Benjamin—this day darting the barbed iron from one side of the world to the other.

Good again; but then all confess that somehow whaling is not respectable.

Whaling not respectable? Whaling is imperial! By old English statutory law, the whale is declared 'a royal fish.'

Oh, that's only nominal! The whale himself has never figured in any grand imposing way.

The whale never figured in any grand imposing way? In one of the mighty triumphs given to a Roman general upon his entering the world's capital, the bones of a whale, brought all the way from the Syrian coast, were the most conspicuous object in the cymballed procession.

Grant it, since you cite it; but, say what you will, there is no real dignity in whaling.

No dignity in whaling? The dignity of our calling the very heavens attest. Cetus is a constellation in the South! No more! Drive down your hat in presence of the Czar, and take it off to Queequeg! No more! I know a man that, in his lifetime, has taken three hundred and fifty whales. I account that man more honorable than the great captain of antiquity who boasted of taking as many walled towns.

And, as for me, if, by any possibility, there be any as yet undiscovered prime thing in me; if I shall ever deserve any real repute in that small but high hushed world which I might not be unreasonably ambitious of; if hereafter I shall do anything that, upon the whole, a man might rather have done than to have left undone; if, at my death, my executors, or more properly my creditors, find any precious MSS. in my desk, then here I prospectively ascribe all the honor and the glory to whaling; for a whale-ship was my Yale College and my Harvard.

CHAPTER XXV

POSTSCRIPT

In behalf of the dignity of whaling, I would fain advance naught but substantiated facts. But after embattling his facts, an advocate who should wholly suppress a not unreasonable surmise, which might tell eloquently upon his cause—such an advocate, would he not be blameworthy?

It is well known that at the coronation of kings and queens, even modern ones, a certain curious process of seasoning them for their functions is gone through. There is a saltcellar of state, so called, and there may be a caster of state. How they use the salt, precisely—who knows? Certain I am, however, that a king's head is solemnly oiled at his coronation, even as a head of salad. Can it be, though, that they anoint it with a view of making its interior run well, as they anoint machinery? Much might be ruminated here, concerning the essential dignity of this regal process, because in common life we esteem but meanly and contemptibly a fellow who anoints his hair, and palpably smells of that anointing. In truth, a mature man who uses hair-oil, unless medicinally, that man has probably got a quoggy spot in him somewhere. As a general rule, he can't amount to much in his totality.

But the only thing to be considered here, is this—what kind of oil is used at coronations? Certainly it cannot be olive oil, nor macassar oil, nor castor oil, nor bear's oil, nor train oil, nor cod-liver oil. What then can it possibly be, but sperm oil in its unmanufactured, unpolluted state, the sweetest of all oils?

Think of that, ye loyal Britons! we whalemen supply your kings and queens with coronation stuff!

CHAPTER XXVI

KNIGHTS AND SQUIRES

The chief mate of the Pequod was Starbuck, a native of Nantucket, and a Quaker by descent. He was a long, earnest man, and though born on an icy coast, seemed well adapted to endure hot latitudes, his flesh being hard as twice-baked biscuit. Transported to the Indies, his live blood would not spoil like bottled ale. He must have been born in some time of general drought and famine, or upon one of those fast days for which his state is famous. Only some thirty arid summers had he seen; those summers had dried up all his physical superfluousness. But this, his thinness, so to speak, seemed no more the token of wasting anxieties and cares, than it seemed the indication of any bodily blight. It was merely the condensation of the man. He was by no means ill-looking; quite the contrary. His pure tight skin was an excellent fit; and closely wrapped up in it, and embalmed with inner health and strength, like a revivified Egyptian, this Starbuck seemed prepared to endure for long ages to come, and to endure always, as now; for be it Polar snow or torrid sun, like a patent chronometer, his interior vitality was warranted to do well in all climates. Looking into his eyes, you seemed to see there the yet lingering images of those thousand-fold perils he had calmly confronted through life. A staid, steadfast man, whose life for the most part was a telling pantomime of action, and not a tame chapter of sounds. Yet, for all his hardy sobriety and fortitude, there were certain qualities in him which at times affected, and in some cases seemed well nigh to overbalance all the rest. Uncommonly conscientious for a seaman, and endued with a deep natural reverence, the wild watery loneliness of his life did therefore strongly incline him to superstition; but to that sort of superstition, which in some organizations seems rather to spring, somehow, from intelligence than from ignorance. Outward portents and inward presentiments were his. And if at times these things bent the welded iron of his soul, much more did his far-away domestic memories of his young Cape wife and child, tend to bend him still more from the original ruggedness of his nature, and open him still further to those latent influences which, in some honest-hearted men, restrain the gush of dare-devil daring, so often evinced by others in the more perilous vicissitudes of the fishery. 'I will have no man in my boat,' said Starbuck, 'who is not afraid of a whale.' By this, he seemed to mean, not only that the most reliable and useful courage was that which arises from the fair estimation of the encountered peril, but that an utterly fearless man is a far more dangerous comrade than a coward.

'Aye, aye,' said Stubb, the second mate, 'Starbuck, there, is as careful a man as you'll find anywhere in this fishery.' But we shall ere long see what that word 'careful' precisely means when used by a man like Stubb, or almost any other whale hunter.

Starbuck was no crusader after perils; in him courage was not a sentiment; but a thing simply useful to him, and always at hand upon all mortally practical occasions. Besides, he thought, perhaps, that in this business of whaling, courage was one of the great staple outfits of the ship, like her beef and her bread, and not to be foolishly wasted. Wherefore he had no fancy for lowering for whales after sundown; nor for persisting in fighting a fish that too much persisted in fighting him. For, thought Starbuck, I am here in this critical ocean to kill whales for my living, and not to be killed by them for theirs; and that hundreds of men had been so killed Starbuck well knew. What doom was his own father's? Where, in the bottomless deeps, could he find the torn limbs of his brother?

With memories like these in him, and, moreover, given to a certain superstitiousness, as has been said; the courage of this Starbuck which could, nevertheless, still flourish, must indeed have been extreme. But it was not in reasonable nature that a man so organized, and with such terrible experiences and remembrances as he had; it was not in nature that these things should fail in latently engendering an element in him, which, under suitable circumstances, would break out from its confinement, and burn all his courage up. And brave as he might be, it was that sort of bravery chiefly, visible in some intrepid men, which, while generally abiding firm in the conflict with seas, or winds, or whales, or any of the ordinary irrational horrors of the world, yet cannot withstand those more terrific, because more spiritual terrors, which sometimes menace you from the concentrating brow of an enraged and mighty man.

But were the coming narrative to reveal, in any instance, the complete abasement of poor Starbuck's fortitude, scarce might I have the heart to write it; for it is a thing most sorrowful, nay shocking, to expose the fall of valor in the soul. Men may seem detestable as joint stock-companies and nations; knaves, fools, and murderers there may be; men may have mean and meagre faces; but man, in the ideal, is so noble and so sparkling, such a grand and glowing creature, that over any ignominious blemish in him all his fellows should run to throw their costliest robes. That immaculate manliness we feel within ourselves, so far within us, that it remains intact though all the outer character seem gone; bleeds with keenest anguish at the undraped spectacle of a valor-ruined man. Nor can piety itself, at such a shameful sight, completely stifle her upbraidings against the permitting stars. But this august dignity I treat of, is not the dignity of kings and robes, but that abounding dignity which has no robed investiture. Thou shalt see it shining in the arm that wields a pick or drives a spike; that democratic dignity which, on all hands, radiates without end from God; Himself! The great God absolute! The centre and circumference of all democracy! His omnipresence, our divine equality!

If, then, to meanest mariners, and renegades and castaways, I shall hereafter ascribe high qualities, though dark; weave round them tragic graces; if even the most mournful, perchance the most abased, among them all, shall at times lift himself to the exalted mounts; if I shall touch that workman's arm with some ethereal light; if I shall spread a rainbow over his disastrous set of sun; then against all mortal critics bear me out in it, thou just Spirit of Equality, which hast spread one royal mantle of humanity over all my kind! Bear me out in it, thou great democratic God! who didst not refuse to the swart convict, Bunyan, the pale, poetic pearl; Thou who didst clothe with doubly hammered leaves of finest gold, the stumped and paupered arm of old Cervantes; Thou who didst pick up Andrew Jackson from the pebbles; who didst hurl him upon a war-horse; who didst thunder him higher than a throne! Thou who, in all Thy mighty, earthly marchings, ever cullest Thy selectest champions from the kingly commons; bear me out in it, O God!

CHAPTER XXVII

KNIGHTS AND SQUIRES

Stubb was the second mate. He was a native of Cape Cod; and hence, according to local usage, was called a Cape-Cod man. A happy-go-lucky; neither craven nor valiant; taking perils as they came with an indifferent air; and while engaged in the most imminent crisis of the chase, toiling away, calm and collected as a journeyman joiner engaged for the year. Good-humored, easy, and careless, he presided over his whale-boat as if the most deadly encounter were but a dinner, and his crew all invited guests. He was as particular about the comfortable arrangement of his part of the boat, as an old stage-driver is about the snugness of his box. When close to the whale, in the very death-lock of the fight, he handled his unpitying lance coolly and off-handedly, as a whistling tinker his hammer. He would hum over his old rigadig tunes while flank and flank with the most exasperated monster. Long usage had, for this Stubb, converted the jaws of death into an easy chair. What he thought of death itself, there is no telling. Whether he ever thought of it at all, might be a question; but, if he ever did chance to cast his mind that way after a comfortable dinner, no doubt, like a good sailor, he took it to be a sort of call of the watch to tumble aloft, and bestir themselves there, about something which he would find out when he obeyed the order, and not sooner.

What, perhaps, with other things, made Stubb such an easy-going, unfearing man, so cheerily trudging off with the burden of life in a world full of grave peddlers, all bowed to the ground with their packs; what helped to bring about that almost impious good-humor of his; that thing must have been his pipe. For, like his nose, his short, black little pipe was one of the regular features of his face. You would almost as soon have expected him to turn out of his bunk without his nose as without his pipe. He kept a whole row of pipes there ready loaded, stuck in a rack, within easy reach of his hand; and, whenever he turned in, he smoked them all out in succession, lighting one from the other to the end of the chapter; then loading them again to be in readiness anew. For, when Stubb dressed, instead of first putting his legs into his trowsers, he put his pipe into his mouth.

I say this continual smoking must have been one cause, at least, of his peculiar disposition; for every one knows that this earthly air, whether ashore or afloat, is terribly infected with the nameless miseries of the numberless mortals who have died exhaling it; and as in time of the cholera, some people go about with a camphorated handkerchief to their mouths; so, likewise, against all mortal tribulations, Stubb's tobacco smoke might have operated as a sort of disinfecting agent.

The third mate was Flask, a native of Tisbury, in Martha's Vineyard. A short, stout, ruddy young fellow, very pugnacious concerning whales, who somehow seemed to think that the great Leviathans had personally and hereditarily affronted him; and therefore it was a sort of point of honor with him, to destroy them whenever encountered. So utterly lost was he to all sense of reverence for the many marvels of their majestic bulk and mystic ways; and so dead to anything like an apprehension of any possible danger from encountering them; that in his poor opinion, the wondrous whale was but a species of magnified mouse, or at least water-rat, requiring only a little circumvention and some small application of time and trouble in order to kill and boil. This ignorant, unconscious fearlessness of his made him a little waggish in the matter of whales; he followed these fish for the fun of it; and a three years' voyage round Cape Horn was only a jolly joke that lasted that length of time. As a carpenter's nails are divided into wrought nails and cut nails; so mankind may be similarly divided. Little Flask was one of the wrought ones; made to clinch tight and last long. They called him King-Post on board of the Pequod; because, in form, he could be well likened to the short, square timber known by that name in Arctic whalers; and which by the means of many radiating side timbers inserted into it, serves to brace the ship against the icy concussions of those battering seas.

Now these three mates—Starbuck, Stubb, and Flask, were momentous men. They it was who by universal prescription commanded three of the Pequod's boats as headsmen. In that grand order of battle in which Captain Ahab would probably marshal his forces to descend on the whales, these three headsmen were as captains of companies. Or, being armed with their long keen whaling spears, they were as a picked trio of lancers; even as the harpooneers were flingers of javelins.

And since in this famous fishery, each mate or headsman, like a Gothic Knight of old, is always accompanied by his boat-steerer or harpooneer, who in certain conjunctures provides him with a fresh lance, when the former one has been badly twisted, or elbowed in the assault; and moreover, as there generally subsists between the two, a close intimacy and friendliness; it is therefore but meet, that in this place we set down who the Pequod's harpooneers were, and to what headsman each of them belonged.

First of all was Queequeg, whom Starbuck, the chief mate, had selected for his squire. But Queequeg is already known.

Next was Tashtego, an unmixed Indian from Gay Head, the most westerly promontory of Martha's Vineyard, where there still exists the last remnant of a village of red men, which has long supplied the neighboring island of Nantucket with many of her most daring harpooneers. In the fishery, they usually go by the generic name of Gay-Headers. Tashtego's long, lean, sable hair, his high cheek bones, and black rounding eyes—for an Indian, Oriental in their largeness, but Antarctic in their glittering expression—all this sufficiently proclaimed him as inheritor of the unvitiated blood of those proud warrior hunters, who, in quest of the great New England moose, had scoured, bow in hand, the aboriginal forests of the main. But no longer snuffing in the trail of the wild beasts of the woodland, Tashtego now hunted in the wake of the great whales of the sea; the unerring harpoon of the son fitly replacing the infallible arrow of the sires. To look at the tawny brawn of his lithe snaky limbs, you would almost have credited the superstitions of some of the early Puritans, and half believed this wild Indian to be a son of the Prince of the Powers of the Air. Tashtego was Stubb the second mate's squire.

Third among the harpooneers was Daggoo, a gigantic, coal-black negro-savage, with a lion-like tread—an Ahasuerus to behold. Suspended from his ears were two golden hoops, so large that the sailors called them ring-bolts, and would talk of securing the top-sail halyards to them. In his youth Daggoo had voluntarily shipped on board of a whaler, lying in a lonely bay on his native coast. And never having been anywhere in the world but in Africa, Nantucket, and the pagan harbors most frequented by whalemen; and having now led for many years the bold life of the fishery in the ships of owners uncommonly heedful of what manner of men they shipped; Daggoo retained all his barbaric virtues, and erect as a giraffe, moved about the decks in all the pomp of six feet five in his socks. There was a corporeal humility in looking up at him; and a white man standing before him seemed a white flag come to beg truce of a fortress. Curious to tell, this imperial negro, Ahasuerus Daggoo, was the Squire of little Flask, who looked like a chess-man beside him. As for the residue of the Pequod's company, be it said, that at the present day not one in two of the many thousand men before the mast employed in the American whale fishery, are Americans born, though pretty nearly all the officers are. Herein it is the same with the American whale fishery as with the American army and military and merchant navies, and the engineering forces employed in the construction of the American Canals and Railroads. The same, I say, because in all these cases the native American liberally provides the brains, the rest of the world as generously supplying the muscles. No small number of these whaling seamen belong to the Azores, where the outward bound Nantucket whalers frequently touch to augment their crews from the hardy peasants of those rocky shores. In like manner, the Greenland whalers sailing out of Hull or London, put in at the Shetland Islands, to receive the full complement of their crew. Upon the passage homewards, they drop them there again. How it is, there is no telling, but Islanders seem to make the best whalemen. They were nearly all Islanders in the Pequod, *Isolatoes* too, I call such, not acknowledging the common continent of men, but each *Isolato* living on a separate continent of his own. Yet now, federated along one keel, what a set these Isolatoes were! An Anacharsis Clootz deputation from all the isles of the sea, and all the ends of the earth, accompanying Old Ahab in the Pequod to lay the world's grievances before that bar from which not very many of them ever come back. Black Little Pip—he never did—oh, no! he went before. Poor Alabama boy! On the grim Pequod's forecastle, ye shall ere long see him, beating his tambourine; prelusive of the eternal time, when sent for, to the great quarter-deck on high, he was bid strike in with angels, and beat his tambourine in glory; called a coward here, hailed a hero there!

CHAPTER XXVIII

AHAB

For several days after leaving Nantucket, nothing above hatches was seen of Captain Ahab. The mates regularly relieved each other at the watches, and for aught that could be seen to the contrary, they seemed to be the only commanders of the ship; only they sometimes issued from the cabin with orders so sudden and peremptory, that after all it was plain they but commanded vicariously. Yes, their supreme lord and dictator was there, though hitherto unseen by any eyes not permitted to penetrate into the now sacred retreat of the cabin.

Every time I ascended to the deck from my watches below, I instantly gazed aft to mark if any strange face were visible; for my first vague disquietude touching the unknown captain, now in the seclusion of the sea, became almost a perturbation. This was strangely heightened at times by the ragged Elijah's diabolical incoherences uninvitedly recurring to me, with a subtle energy I could not have before conceived of. But poorly could I withstand them, much as in other moods I was almost ready to smile at the solemn whimsicalities of that outlandish prophet of the wharves. But whatever it was of apprehensiveness or uneasiness—to call it so—which I felt, yet whenever I came to look about me in the ship, it seemed against all warranty to cherish such emotions. For though the harpooneers, with the great body of the crew, were a far more barbaric, heathenish, and motley set than any of the tame merchant-ship companies which my previous experiences had made me acquainted with, still I ascribed this—and rightly ascribed it—to the fierce uniqueness of the very nature of that wild Scandinavian vocation in which I had so abandonedly embarked. But it was especially the aspect of the three chief officers of the ship, the mates, which was most forcibly calculated to allay these colorless misgivings, and induce confidence and cheerfulness in every presentment of the voyage. Three better, more likely sea-officers and men, each in his own different way, could not readily be found, and they were every one of them Americans; a Nantucketer, a Vineyarder, a Cape man. Now, it being Christmas when the ship shot from out her harbor, for a space we had biting Polar weather, though all the time running away from it to the southward; and by every degree and minute of latitude which we sailed, gradually leaving that merciless winter, and all its intolerable weather behind us. It was one of those less lowering, but still grey and gloomy enough mornings of the transition, when with a fair wind the ship was rushing through the water with a vindictive sort of leaping and melancholy rapidity, that as I mounted to the deck at the call of the forenoon watch, so soon as I levelled my glance towards the taffrail, foreboding shivers ran over me. Reality outran apprehension; Captain Ahab stood upon his quarterdeck.

There seemed no sign of common bodily illness about him, nor of the recovery from any. He looked like a man cut away from the stake, when the fire has overrunningly wasted all the limbs without consuming them, or taking away one particle from their compacted aged robustness. His whole high, broad form, seemed made of solid bronze, and shaped in an unalterable mould, like Cellini's cast Perseus. Threading its way out from among his grey hairs, and continuing right down one side of his tawny scorched face and neck, till it disappeared in his clothing, you saw a slender rod-like mark, lividly whitish. It resembled that perpendicular seam sometimes made in the straight, lofty trunk of a great tree, when the upper lightning tearingly darts down it, and without wrenching a single twig, peels and grooves out the bark from top to bottom, ere running off into the soil, leaving the tree still greenly alive, but branded. Whether that mark was born with him, or whether it was the scar left by some desperate wound, no one could certainly say. By some tacit consent, throughout the voyage little or no allusion was made to it, especially by the mates. But once Tashtego's senior, an old Gay-Head Indian among the crew, superstitiously asserted that not till he was full forty years old did Ahab become that way branded, and then it came upon him, not in the fury of any mortal fray, but in an elemental strife at sea. Yet, this wild hint seemed inferentially negatived, by what a grey Manxman insinuated, an old sepulchral man, who, having never before sailed out of Nantucket, had never ere this laid eye upon wild Ahab. Nevertheless, the old sea-traditions, the immemorial credulities, popularly invested this old Manxman with preternatural powers of discernment. So that no white sailor seriously contradicted him when he said that if ever Captain Ahab should be tranquilly laid out—which might hardly come to pass, so he muttered—then, whoever should do that last office for the dead, would find a birth-mark on him from crown to sole.

So powerfully did the whole grim aspect of Ahab affect me, and the livid brand which streaked it, that for the first few moments I hardly noted that not a little of this overbearing grimness was owing to the barbaric white leg upon which he partly stood. It had previously come to me that this ivory leg had at sea been fashioned from the polished bone of the sperm whale's jaw. 'Aye, he was dismasted off Japan,' said the old Gay-Head Indian once; 'but like his dismasted craft, he shipped another mast without coming home for it. He has a quiver of 'em.'

I was struck with the singular posture he maintained. Upon each side of the Pequod's quarter deck, and pretty close to the mizen shrouds, there was an auger hole, bored about half an inch or so, into the plank. His bone leg steadied in that hole; one arm elevated, and holding by a shroud; Captain Ahab stood erect, looking straight out beyond the ship's ever-pitching prow. There was an infinity of firmest fortitude, a determinate, unsurrenderable wilfulness, in the fixed and fearless, forward dedication of that glance. Not a word he spoke; nor did his officers say aught to him; though by all their minutest gestures and expressions, they plainly showed the uneasy, if not painful, consciousness of being under a troubled master-eye. And not only that, but moody stricken Ahab stood before them with a crucifixion in his face; in all the nameless regal overbearing dignity of some mighty woe.

Ere long, from his first visit in the air, he withdrew into his cabin. But after that morning, he was every day visible to the crew; either standing in his pivot-hole, or seated upon an ivory stool he had; or heavily walking the deck. As the sky grew less gloomy; indeed, began to grow a little genial, he became still less and less a recluse; as if, when the ship had sailed from home, nothing but the dead wintry bleakness of the sea had then kept him so secluded. And, by and by, it came to pass, that he was almost continually in the air; but, as yet, for all that he said, or perceptibly did, on the at last sunny deck, he seemed as unnecessary there as another mast. But the Pequod was only making a passage now; not regularly cruising; nearly all whaling preparatives needing supervision the mates were fully competent to, so that there was little or nothing, out of himself, to employ or excite Ahab, now; and thus chase away, for that one interval, the clouds that layer upon layer were piled upon his brow, as ever all clouds choose the loftiest peaks to pile themselves upon.

Nevertheless, ere long, the warm, warbling persuasiveness of the pleasant, holiday weather we came to, seemed gradually to charm him from his mood. For, as when the red-cheeked, dancing girls, April and May, trip home to the wintry, misanthropic woods; even the barest, ruggedest, most thunder-cloven old oak will at least send forth some few green sprouts, to welcome such glad-hearted visitants; so Ahab did, in the end, a little respond to the playful allurings of that girlish air. More than once did he put forth the faint blossom of a look, which, in any other man, would have soon flowered out in a smile.

CHAPTER XXIX

Enter Ahab; To Him, Stubb

Some days elapsed, and ice and icebergs all astern, the Pequod now went rolling through the bright Quito spring, which, at sea, almost perpetually reigns on the threshold of the eternal August of the Tropic. The warmly cool, clear, ringing, perfumed, overflowing, redundant days, were as crystal goblets of Persian sherbet, heaped up—flaked up, with rose-water snow. The starred and stately nights seemed haughty dames in jewelled velvets, nursing at home in lonely pride, the memory of their absent conquering Earls, the golden helmeted suns! For sleeping man, 'twas hard to choose between such winsome days and such seducing nights. But all the witcheries of that unwaning weather did not merely lend new spells and potencies to the outward world. Inward they turned upon the soul, especially when the still mild hours of eve came on; then, memory shot her crystals as the clear ice most forms of noiseless twilights. And all these subtle agencies, more and more they wrought on Ahab's texture.

Old age is always wakeful; as if, the longer linked with life, the less man has to do with aught that looks like death. Among sea-commanders, the old greybeards will oftenest leave their berths to visit the night-cloaked deck. It was so with Ahab; only that now, of late, he seemed so much to live in the open air, that truly speaking, his visits were more to the cabin, than from the cabin to the planks. 'It feels like going down into one's tomb,'—he would mutter to himself,—'for an old captain like me to be descending this narrow scuttle, to go to my grave-dug berth.'

So, almost every twenty-four hours, when the watches of the night were set, and the band on deck sentinelled the slumbers of the band below; and when if a rope was to be hauled upon the forecastle, the sailors flung it not rudely down, as by day, but with some cautiousness dropt it to its place, for fear of disturbing their slumbering shipmates; when this sort of steady quietude would begin to prevail, habitually, the silent steersman would watch the cabin-scuttle; and ere long the old man would emerge, griping at the iron banister, to help his crippled way. Some considerating touch of humanity was in him; for at times like these, he usually abstained from patrolling the quarter-deck; because to his wearied mates, seeking repose within six inches of his ivory heel, such would have been the reverberating crack and din of that bony step, that their dreams would have been of the crunching teeth of sharks. But once, the mood was on him too deep for common regardings; and as with heavy, lumber-like pace he was measuring the ship from taffrail to mainmast, Stubb, the odd second mate, came up from below, and with a certain unassured, deprecating humorousness, hinted that if Captain Ahab was pleased to walk the planks, then, no one could say nay; but there might be some way of muffling the noise; hinting something indistinctly and hesitatingly about a globe of tow, and the insertion into it, of the ivory heel. Ah! Stubb, thou did'st not know Ahab then.

'Am I a cannon-ball, Stubb,' said Ahab, 'that thou wouldst wad me that fashion? But go thy ways; I had forgot. Below to thy nightly grave; where such as ye sleep between shrouds, to use ye to the filling one at last.—Down, dog, and kennel!'

Starting at the unforeseen concluding exclamation of the so suddenly scornful old man, Stubb was speechless a moment; then said excitedly, 'I am not used to be spoken to that way, sir; I do but less than half like it, sir.'

'Avast!' gritted Ahab between his set teeth, and violently moving away, as if to avoid some passionate temptation.

'No, sir; not yet,' said Stubb, emboldened, 'I will not tamely be called a dog, sir.'

'Then be called ten times a donkey, and a mule, and an ass, and begone, or I'll clear the world of thee!'

As he said this, Ahab advanced upon him with such overbearing terrors in his aspect, that Stubb involuntarily retreated.

'I was never served so before without giving a hard blow for it,' muttered Stubb, as he found himself descending the cabin-scuttle. 'It's very queer. Stop, Stubb; somehow, now, I don't well know whether to go back and strike him, or—what's that?—down here on my knees and pray for him? Yes, that was the thought coming up in me; but it would be the first time I ever *did* pray. It's queer; very queer; and he's queer too; aye, take him fore and aft, he's about the queerest old man Stubb ever sailed with. How he flashed at me!—his eyes like powder-pans! is he mad? Anyway there's something on his mind, as sure as there must be something on a deck when it cracks. He aint in his bed now, either, more than three hours out of the twenty-four; and he don't sleep then. Didn't that Dough-Boy, the steward, tell me that of a morning he always finds the old man's hammock clothes all rumpled and tumbled, and the sheets down at the foot, and the coverlid almost tied into knots, and the pillow a sort of frightful hot, as though a baked brick had been on it? A hot old man! I guess he's got what some folks ashore call a conscience; it's a kind of Tic-Dolly-row they say—worse nor a toothache. Well, well; I don't know what it is, but the Lord keep me from catching it. He's full of riddles; I wonder what he goes into the after hold for, every night, as Dough-Boy tells me he suspects; what's that for, I should like to know? Who's made appointments with him in the hold? Ain't that queer, now? But there's no telling, it's the old game—Here goes for a snooze. Damn me, it's worth a fellow's while to be born into the world, if only to fall right asleep. And now that I think of it, that's about the first thing babies do, and that's a sort of queer, too. Damn me, but all things are queer, come to think of 'em. But that's against my principles. Think not, is my eleventh commandment; and sleep when you can, is my twelfth—So here goes again. But how's that? didn't he call me a dog? blazes! he called me ten times a donkey, and piled a lot of jackasses on top of *that!* He might as well have kicked me, and done with it. Maybe he *did* kick me, and I didn't observe it, I was so taken all aback with his brow, somehow. It flashed like a bleached bone. What the devil's the matter with me? I don't stand right on my legs. Coming afoul of that old man has a sort of turned me wrong side out. By the Lord, I must have been dreaming, though—How? how? how?—but the only way's to stash it; so here goes to hammock again; and in the morning, I'll see how this plaguey juggling thinks over by day-light.'

CHAPTER XXX

THE PIPE

When Stubb had departed, Ahab stood for a while leaning over the bulwarks; and then, as had been usual with him of late, calling a sailor of the watch, he sent him below for his ivory stool, and also his pipe. Lighting the pipe at the binnacle lamp and planting the stool on the weather side of the deck, he sat and smoked.

In old Norse times, the thrones of the sea-loving Danish kings were fabricated, saith tradition, of the tusks of the narwhale. How could one look at Ahab then, seated on that tripod of bones, without bethinking him of the royalty it symbolized? For a Khan of the plank, and a king of the sea, and a great lord of Leviathans was Ahab.

Some moments passed, during which the thick vapor came from his mouth in quick and constant puffs, which blew back again into his face. 'How now,' he soliloquized at last, withdrawing the tube, 'this smoking no longer soothes. Oh, my pipe! hard must it go with me if thy charm be gone! Here have I been unconsciously toiling, not pleasuring,—aye, and ignorantly smoking to windward all the while; to windward, and with such nervous whiffs, as if, like the dying whale, my final jets were the strongest and fullest of trouble. What business have I with this pipe? This thing that is meant for sereneness, to send up mild white vapors among mild white hairs, not among torn iron-grey locks like mine. I'll smoke no more—'

He tossed the still lighted pipe into the sea. The fire hissed in the waves; the same instant the ship shot by the bubble the sinking pipe made. With slouched hat, Ahab lurchingly paced the planks.

CHAPTER XXXI

QUEEN MAB

Next morning Stubb accosted Flask.

'Such a queer dream, King-Post, I never had. You know the old man's ivory leg, well I dreamed he kicked me with it; and when I tried to kick back, upon my soul, my little man, I kicked my leg right off! And then, presto! Ahab seemed a pyramid, and I, like a blazing fool, kept kicking at it. But what was still more curious, Flask—you know how curious all dreams are—through all this rage that I was in, I somehow seemed to be thinking to myself, that after all, it was not much of an insult, that kick from Ahab. "Why," thinks I, "what's the row! It's not a real leg, only a false leg." And there's a mighty difference between a living thump and a dead thump. That's what makes a blow from the hand, Flask, fifty times more savage to bear than a blow from a cane. The living member—that makes the living insult, my little man. And thinks I to myself all the while, mind, while I was stubbing my silly toes against that cursed pyramid—so confoundedly contradictory was it all, all the while, I say, I was thinking to myself, "what's his leg now, but a cane—a whalebone cane. Yes," thinks I, "it was only a playful cudgelling—in fact, only a whaleboning that he gave me—not a base kick. Besides," thinks I, "look at it once; why, the end of it—the foot part—what a small sort of end it is; whereas, if a broad footed farmer kicked me, *there's* a devilish broad insult. But this insult is whittled down to a point only." But now comes the greatest joke of the dream, Flask. While I was battering away at the pyramid, a sort of badger-haired old merman, with a hump on his back, takes me by the shoulders, and slews me round. "What are you 'bout?" says he. 'Slid! man, but I was frightened. Such a phiz! But, somehow, next moment I was over the fright. "What am I about?" says I at last. "And what business is that of yours, I should like to know, Mr Humpback? Do *you* want a kick?" By the lord, Flask, I had no sooner said that, than he turned round his stern to me, bent over, and dragging up a lot of seaweed he had for a clout—what do you think I saw?—why thunder alive, man, his stern was stuck full of marlinspikes, with the points out. Says I, on second thoughts, "I guess I won't kick you, old fellow." "Wise Stubb," said he, "wise Stubb;" and kept muttering it all the time, a sort of eating of his own gums like a chimney hag. Seeing he wasn't going to stop saying over his "wise Stubb, wise Stubb," I thought I might as well fall to kicking the pyramid again. But I had only just lifted my foot for it, when he roared out, "Stop that kicking!" "Halloa," says I, "what's the matter now, old fellow?" "Look ye here," says he; "let's argue the insult. Captain Ahab kicked ye, didn't he?" "Yes, he did," says I—"right *here* it was." "Very good," says he—"he used his ivory leg, didn't he?" "Yes, he did," says I. "Well then," says he, "wise Stubb, what have you to complain of? Didn't he kick with right good will? it wasn't a common pitch pine leg he kicked with, was it? No, you were kicked by a great man, and with a beautiful ivory leg, Stubb. It's an honor; I consider it an honor. Listen, wise Stubb. In old England the greatest lords think it great glory to be slapped by a queen, and made garter-knights of; but, be *your* boast, Stubb, that ye were kicked by old Ahab, and made a wise man of. Remember what I say; *be* kicked by him; account his kicks honors; and on no account kick back; for you can't help yourself, wise Stubb. Don't you see that pyramid?" With that, he all of a sudden seemed somehow, in some queer fashion, to swim off into the air. I snored; rolled over; and there I was in my hammock! Now, what do you think of that dream, Flask?'

'I don't know; it seems a sort of foolish to me, tho'.'

'May be; may be. But it's made a wise man of me, Flask. D'ye see Ahab standing there, sideways looking over the stern? Well, the best thing you can do, Flask, is to let that old man alone; never speak quick to him, whatever he says. Halloa! what's that he shouts? Hark!'

'Mast-head, there! Look sharp, all of ye! There are whales hereabouts! If ye see a white one, split your lungs for him!'

'What d'ye think of that now, Flask? ain't there a small drop of something queer about that, eh? A white whale—did ye mark that, man? Look ye—there's something special in the wind. Stand by for it, Flask. Ahab has that that's bloody on his mind. But, mum; he comes this way.'

CHAPTER XXXII

CETOLOGY

Already we are boldly launched upon the deep; but soon we shall be lost in its unshored, harborless immensities. Ere that come to pass; ere the Pequod's weedy hull rolls side by side with the barnacled hulls of the leviathan; at the outset it is but well to attend to a matter almost indispensable to a thorough appreciative understanding of the more special leviathanic revelations and allusions of all sorts which are to follow.

It is some systematized exhibition of the whale in his broad genera, that I would now fain put before you. Yet is it no easy task. The classification of the constituents of a chaos, nothing less is here essayed. Listen to what the best and latest authorities have laid down.

'No branch of Zoology is so much involved as that which is entitled Cetology,' says Captain Scoresby, A.D. 1820.

'It is not my intention, were it in my power, to enter into the inquiry as to the true method of dividing the cetacea into groups and families. * * * Utter confusion exists among the historians of this animal' (sperm whale), says Surgeon Beale, A.D. 1839.

'Unfitness to pursue our research in the unfathomable waters.' 'Impenetrable veil covering our knowledge of the cetacea.' 'A field strewn with thorns.' 'All these incomplete indications but serve to torture us naturalists.'

Thus speak of the whale, the great Cuvier, and John Hunter, and Lesson, those lights of zoology and anatomy. Nevertheless, though of real knowledge there be little, yet of books there are a plenty; and so in some small degree, with cetology, or the science of whales. Many are the men, small and great, old and new, landsmen and seamen, who have at large or in little, written of the whale. Run over a few:—The Authors of the Bible; Aristotle; Pliny; Aldrovandi; Sir Thomas Browne; Gesner; Ray; Linnæus; Rondeletius; Willoughby; Green; Artedi; Sibbald; Brisson; Marten; Lacépède; Bonneterre; Desmarest; Baron Cuvier; Frederick Cuvier; John Hunter; Owen; Scoresby; Beale; Bennett; J. Ross Browne; the Author of Miriam Coffin; Olmstead; and the Rev. T. Cheever. But to what ultimate generalizing purpose all these have written, the above cited extracts will show.

Of the names in this list of whale authors, only those following Owen ever saw living whales; and but one of them was a real professional harpooneer and whaleman. I mean Captain Scoresby. On the separate subject of the Greenland or right-whale, he is the best existing authority. But Scoresby knew nothing and says nothing of the great sperm whale, compared with which the Greenland whale is almost unworthy mentioning. And here be it said, that the Greenland whale is an usurper upon the throne of the seas. He is not even by any means the largest of the whales. Yet, owing to the long priority of his claims, and the profound ignorance which, till some seventy years back, invested the then fabulous or utterly unknown sperm-whale, and which ignorance to this present day still reigns in all but some few scientific retreats and whale-ports; this usurpation has been every way complete. Reference to nearly all the leviathanic allusions in the great poets of past days, will satisfy you that the Greenland whale, without one rival, was to them the monarch of the seas. But the time has at last come for a new proclamation. This is Charing Cross; hear ye! good people all,—the Greenland whale is deposed,—the great sperm whale now reigneth!

There are only two books in being which at all pretend to put the living sperm whale before you, and at the same time, in the remotest degree succeed in the attempt. Those books are Beale's and Bennett's; both in their time surgeons to English South-Sea whale-ships, and both exact and reliable men. The original matter touching the sperm whale to be found in their volumes is necessarily small; but so far as it goes, it is of excellent quality, though mostly confined to scientific description. As yet, however, the sperm whale, scientific or poetic, lives not complete in any literature. Far above all other hunted whales, his is an unwritten life.

Now the various species of whales need some sort of popular comprehensive classification, if only an easy outline one for the present, hereafter to be filled in all its departments by subsequent laborers. As no better man advances to take this matter in hand, I hereupon offer my own poor endeavors. I promise nothing complete; because any human thing supposed to be complete, must for that very reason infallibly be faulty. I shall not pretend to a minute anatomical description of the various species, or—in this place at least—to much of any description. My object here is simply to project the draught of a systematization of cetology. I am the architect, not the builder.

But it is a ponderous task; no ordinary letter-sorter in the Post-office is equal to it. To grope down into the bottom of the sea after them; to have one's hands among the unspeakable foundations, ribs, and very pelvis of the world; this is a fearful thing. What am I that I should essay to hook the nose of this leviathan! The awful tauntings in Job might well appal me. 'Will he' (the leviathan) 'make a covenant with thee? Behold the hope of him is vain!' But I have swam through libraries and sailed through oceans; I have had to do with whales with these visible hands; I am in earnest; and I will try. There are some preliminaries to settle.

First: The uncertain, unsettled condition of this science of Cetology is in the very vestibule attested by the fact, that in some quarters it still remains a moot point whether a whale be a fish. In his System of Nature, A.D. 1776, Linnæus declares, 'I hereby separate the whales from the fish.' But of my own knowledge, I know that down to the year 1850, sharks and shad, alewives and herring, against Linnæus's express edict, were still found dividing the possession of the same seas with the Leviathan.

The grounds upon which Linnæus would fain have banished the whales from the waters, he states as follows: 'On account of their warm bilocular heart, their lungs, their movable eyelids, their hollow ears, penem intrantem feminam mammis lactantem,' and finally, 'ex lege naturae jure meritoque.' I submitted all this to my friends Simeon Macey and Charley Coffin, of Nantucket, both messmates of mine in a certain voyage, and they united in the opinion that the reasons set forth were altogether insufficient. Charley profanely hinted they were humbug.

Be it known that, waiving all argument, I take the good old fashioned ground that the whale is a fish, and call upon holy Jonah to back me. This fundamental thing settled, the next point is, in what internal respect does the whale differ from other fish. Above, Linnæus has given you those items. But in brief, they are these: lungs and warm blood; whereas, all other fish are lungless and cold blooded.

Next: how shall we define the whale, by his obvious externals, so as conspicuously to label him for all time to come? To be short, then, a whale is *a spouting fish with a horizontal tail*. There you have him. However contracted, that definition is the result of expanded meditation. A walrus spouts much like a whale, but the walrus is not a fish, because he is amphibious. But the last term of the definition is still more cogent, as coupled with the first. Almost any one must have noticed that all the fish familiar to landsmen have not a flat, but a vertical, or up-and-down tail. Whereas, among spouting fish the tail, though it may be similarly shaped, invariably assumes a horizontal position.

By the above definition of what a whale is, I do by no means exclude from the leviathanic brotherhood any sea creature hitherto identified with the whale by the best informed Nantucketers; nor, on the other hand, link with it any fish hitherto authoritatively regarded as alien.* Hence, all the smaller, spouting, and horizontal tailed fish must be included in this ground-plan of Cetology. Now, then, come the grand divisions of the entire whale host.

First: According to magnitude I divide the whales into three primary BOOKS (subdivisible into CHAPTERS), and these shall comprehend them all, both small and large.

I. The FOLIO WHALE; II. the OCTAVO WHALE; III. the DUODECIMO WHALE.

As the type of the FOLIO I present the *Sperm Whale;* of the OCTAVO, the *Grampus;* of the DUODECIMO, the *Porpoise*.

FOLIOS. Among these I here include the following chapters:—I. The *Sperm Whale;* II. the *Right Whale;* III. the *Fin Back Whale;* IV. the *Hump-backed Whale;* V. the *Razor Back Whale;* VI. the *Sulphur Bottom Whale*.

BOOK I. (*Folio*), CHAPTER I. (*Sperm Whale*).—This whale, among the English of old vaguely known as the Trumpa whale, and the Physeter whale, and the Anvil Headed whale, is the present Cachalot of the French, and the Pottsfich of the Germans, and the Macrocephalus of the Long Words. He is, without doubt, the largest inhabitant of the globe; the most formidable of all whales to encounter; the most majestic in aspect; and lastly, by far the most valuable in commerce; he being the only creature from which that valuable substance, spermaceti, is obtained. All his peculiarities will, in many other places, be enlarged upon. It is chiefly with his name that I now have to do. Philologically considered, it is absurd. Some centuries ago, when the Sperm whale was almost wholly unknown in his own proper individuality, and when his oil was only accidentally obtained from the stranded fish; in those days spermaceti, it would seem, was popularly supposed to be derived from a creature identical with the one then known in England as the Greenland or Right Whale. It was the idea also, that this same spermaceti was that quickening humor of the Greenland Whale which the first syllable of the word literally expresses. In those times, also, spermaceti was exceedingly scarce, not being used for light, but only as an ointment and medicament. It was only to be had from the druggists as you nowadays buy an ounce of rhubarb. When, as I opine, in the course of time, the true nature of spermaceti became known, its original name was still retained by the dealers; no doubt to enhance its value by a notion so strangely significant of its scarcity. And so the appellation must at last have come to be bestowed upon the whale from which this spermaceti was really derived.

BOOK I. (*Folio*), CHAPTER II. (*Right Whale*).—In one respect this is the most venerable of the leviathans, being the one first regularly hunted by man. It yields the article commonly known as whalebone or baleen; and the oil specially known as 'whale oil', an inferior article in commerce. Among the fishermen, he is indiscriminately designated by all the following titles: The Whale; the Greenland

*I am aware that down to the present time, the fish styled Lamatins and Dugongs (Pig-fish and Sow-fish of the Coffins of Nantucket) are included by many naturalists among the whales. But as these pig-fish are a nosy, contemptible set, mostly lurking in the mouths of rivers, and feeding on wet hay, and especially as they do not spout, I deny their credentials as whales; and have presented them with their passports to quit the Kingdom of Cetology.

Whale; the Black Whale; the Great Whale; the True Whale; the Right Whale. There is a deal of obscurity concerning the identity of the species thus multitudinously baptized. What then is the whale, which I include in the second species of my Folios? It is the Great Mysticetus of the English naturalists; the Greenland Whale of the English whalemen; the Baliene Ordinaire of the French whalemen; the Growlands Walfish of the Swedes. It is the whale which for more than two centuries past has been hunted by the Dutch and English in the Arctic seas; it is the whale which the American fishermen have long pursued in the Indian ocean, on the Brazil Banks, on the Nor' West Coast, and various other parts of the world, designated by them Right Whale Cruising Grounds.

Some pretend to see a difference between the Greenland whale of the English and the right whale of the Americans. But they precisely agree in all their grand features; nor has there yet been presented a single determinate fact upon which to ground a radical distinction. It is by endless subdivisions based upon the most inconclusive differences, that some departments of natural history become so repellingly intricate. The right whale will be elsewhere treated of at some length, with reference to elucidating the sperm whale.

BOOK I. (*Folio*), CHAPTER III. (*Fin-Back*).—Under this head I reckon a monster which, by the various names of Fin-Back, Tall-Spout, and Long-John, has been seen almost in every sea and is commonly the whale whose distant jet is so often descried by passengers crossing the Atlantic, in the New York packet-tracks. In the length he attains, and in his baleen, the Fin-back resembles the right whale, but is of a less portly girth, and a lighter color, approaching to olive. His great lips present a cable-like aspect, formed by the intertwisting, slanting folds of large wrinkles. His grand distinguishing feature, the fin, from which he derives his name, is often a conspicuous object. This fin is some three or four feet long, growing vertically from the hinder part of the back, of an angular shape, and with a very sharp pointed end. Even if not the slightest other part of the creature be visible, this isolated fin will, at times, be seen plainly projecting from the surface. When the sea is moderately calm, and slightly marked with spherical ripples, and this gnomon-like fin stands up and casts shadows upon the wrinkled surface, it may well be supposed that the watery circle surrounding it somewhat resembles a dial, with its style and wavy hour-lines graved on it. On that Ahaz-dial the shadow often goes back. The Fin-Back is not gregarious. He seems a whale-hater, as some men are man-haters. Very shy; always going solitary; unexpectedly rising to the surface in the remotest and most sullen waters; his straight and single lofty jet rising like a tall misanthropic spear upon a barren plain; gifted with such wondrous power and velocity in swimming, as to defy all present pursuit from man; this leviathan seems the banished and unconquerable Cain of his race, bearing for his mark that style upon his back. From having the baleen in his mouth, the Fin-Back is sometimes included with the right whale, among a theoretic species denominated *Whalebone whales,* that is, whales with baleen. Of these so called Whalebone whales, there would seem to be several varieties, most of which, however, are little known. Broad-nosed whales and beaked whales; pike-headed whales; bunched whales; under-jawed whales and rostrated whales, are the fishermen's names for a few sorts.

In connexion with this appellative of 'Whalebone whales,' it is of great importance to mention, that however such a nomenclature may be convenient in facilitating allusions to some kind of whales, yet it is in vain to attempt a clear classification of the Leviathan, founded upon either his baleen, or hump, or fin, or teeth; notwithstanding that those marked parts or features very obviously seem better adapted to afford the basis for a regular system of Cetology than any other detached bodily distinctions, which the whale, in his kinds, presents. How then? The baleen, hump, back-fin, and teeth; these are things whose peculiarities are indiscriminately dispersed among all sorts of whales, without any regard to what may be the nature of their structure in other and more essential particulars. Thus, the sperm whale and the humpbacked whale, each has a hump; but there the similitude ceases. Then, this same humpbacked whale and the Greenland whale, each of these has baleen; but there again the similitude ceases. And it is just the same with the other parts above mentioned. In various sorts of whales, they form such irregular combinations; or, in the case of any one of them detached, such an irregular isolation; as utterly to defy all general methodization formed upon such a basis. On this rock every one of the whale-naturalists has split.

But it may possibly be conceived that, in the internal parts of the whale, in his anatomy—there, at least, we shall be able to hit the right classification. Nay; what thing, for example, is there in the Greenland whale's anatomy more striking than his baleen? Yet we have seen that by his baleen it is impossible correctly to classify the Greenland whale. And if you descend into the bowels of the various leviathans, why there you will not find distinctions a fiftieth part as available to the systematizer as those external ones already enumerated. What then remains? nothing but to take hold of the whales bodily, in their entire liberal volume, and boldly sort them that way. And this is the Bibliographical system here adopted; and it is the only one that can possibly succeed, for it alone is practicable. To proceed.

BOOK I. (*Folio*), CHAPTER IV. (*Hump Back*).—This whale is often seen on the northern American coast. He has been frequently captured there, and towed into harbor. He has a great pack on him like a peddler; or you might call him the Elephant and Castle whale. At any rate, the popular name for him does not sufficiently distinguish him, since the sperm whale also has a hump, though a smaller one. His oil is not very valuable. He has baleen. He is the most gamesome and light-hearted of all the whales, making more gay foam and white water generally than any other of them.

BOOK I. (*Folio*), CHAPTER V. (*Razor Back*).—Of this whale little is known but his name. I have seen him at a distance off Cape Horn. Of a retiring nature, he eludes both hunters and philosophers. Though no coward, he has never yet shown any part of him but his back, which rises in a long sharp ridge. Let him go. I know little more of him, nor does anybody else.

BOOK I. (*Folio*), CHAPTER VI. (*Sulphur Bottom*).—Another retiring gentleman, with a brimstone belly, doubtless got by scraping along the Tartarian tiles in some of his profounder divings. He is seldom seen; at least I have never seen him except in the remoter southern seas, and then always at too great a distance to study his countenance. He is never chased; he would run away with rope-walks of line. Prodigies are told of him. Adieu, Sulphur Bottom! I can say nothing more that is true of ye, nor can the oldest Nantucketer.

Thus ends BOOK I. (*Folio*), and now begins BOOK II. (*Octavo*).

OCTAVOES.* These embrace the whales of middling magnitude, among which at present may be numbered:—I., the *Grampus;* II., the *Black Fish;* III., the *Narwhale;* IV., the *Thrasher;* V., the *Killer.*

---

*Why this book of whales is not denominated the Quarto is very plain. Because, while the whales of this order, though smaller than those of the former order, nevertheless retain a proportionate likeness to them in figure, yet the bookbinder's Quarto volume in its diminished form does not preserve the shape of the Folio volume, but the Octavo volume does.

BOOK II. (*Octavo*), CHAPTER I. (*Grampus*).—Though this fish, whose loud sonorous breathing, or rather blowing, has furnished a proverb to landsmen, is so well known a denizen of the deep, yet is he not popularly classed among whales. But possessing all the grand distinctive features of the leviathan, most naturalists, have recognised him for one. He is of moderate octavo size, varying from fifteen to twenty-five feet in length, and of corresponding dimensions round the waist. He swims in herds; he is never regularly hunted, though his oil is considerable in quantity, and pretty good for light. By some fishermen his approach is regarded as premonitory of the advance of the great sperm whale.

BOOK II. (*Octavo*), CHAPTER II. (*Black Fish*).—I give the popular fishermen's names for all these fish, for generally they are the best. Where any name happens to be vague or inexpressive, I shall say so, and suggest another. I do so now, touching the Black Fish, so called, because blackness is the rule among almost all whales. So, call him the Hyena Whale, if you please. His voracity is well known, and from the circumstance that the inner angles of his lips are curved upwards, he carries an everlasting Mephistophelean grin on his face. This whale averages some sixteen or eighteen feet in length. He is found in almost all latitudes. He has a peculiar way of showing his dorsal hooked fin in swimming, which looks something like a Roman nose. When not more profitably employed, the sperm whale hunters sometimes capture the Hyena whale, to keep up the supply of cheap oil for domestic employment—as some frugal housekeepers, in the absence of company, and quite alone by themselves, burn unsavory tallow instead of odorous wax. Though their blubber is very thin, some of these whales will yield you upwards of thirty gallons of oil.

BOOK II. (*Octavo*), CHAPTER III. (*Narwhale*), that is, *Nostril whale*.—Another instance of a curiously named whale, so named I suppose from his peculiar horn being originally mistaken for a peaked nose. The creature is some sixteen feet in length, while its horn averages five feet, though some exceed ten, and even attain to fifteen feet. Strictly speaking, this horn is but a lengthened tusk, growing out from the jaw in a line a little depressed from the horizontal. But it is only found on the sinister side, which has an ill effect, giving its owner something analogous to the aspect of a clumsy left-handed man. What precise purpose this ivory horn or lance answers, it would be hard to say. It does not seem to be used like the blade of the swordfish and bill-fish; though some sailors tell me that the Narwhale employs it for a rake in turning over the bottom of the sea for food. Charley Coffin said it was used for an ice-piercer; for the Narwhale, rising to the surface of the Polar Sea, and finding it sheeted with ice, thrusts his horn up, and so breaks through. But you cannot prove either of these surmises to be correct. My own opinion is, that however this one-sided horn may really be used by the Narwhale—however that may be—it would certainly be very convenient to him for a folder in reading pamphlets. The Narwhale I have heard called the Tusked whale, the Horned whale, and the Unicorn whale. He is certainly a curious example of the Unicornism to be found in almost every kingdom of animated nature. From certain cloistered old authors I have gathered that this same sea-unicorn's horn was in ancient days regarded as the great antidote against poison, and as such, preparations of it brought immense prices. It was also distilled to a volatile salts for fainting ladies, the same way that the horns of the male deer are manufactured into hartshorn. Originally it was in itself accounted an object of great curiosity. Black Letter tells me that Sir Martin Frobisher on his return from that voyage, when Queen Bess did gallantly wave her jewelled hand to him from a window of Greenwich Palace, as his bold ship sailed down the Thames; 'when Sir Martin returned from that voyage,' saith Black Letter, 'on bended knees he presented to her highness a prodigious long horn of the Narwhale, which for a long period after hung in the castle at Windsor.' An Irish author avers that the Earl of Leicester, on bended knees, did likewise present to her highness another horn, pertaining to a land beast of the unicorn nature.

The Narwhale has a very picturesque, leopard-like look, being of a milk-white ground color, dotted with round and oblong spots of black. His oil is very superior, clear and fine; but there is little of it, and he is seldom hunted. He is mostly found in the circumpolar seas.

BOOK II. (*Octavo*), CHAPTER IV. (*Killer*).—Of this whale little is precisely known to the Nantucketer, and nothing at all to the professed naturalist. From what I have seen of him at a distance, I should say that he was about the bigness of a grampus. He is very savage—a sort of Feegee fish. He sometimes takes the great Folio whales by the lip, and hangs there like a leech, till the mighty brute is worried to death. The Killer is never hunted. I never heard what sort of oil he has. Exception might be taken to the name bestowed upon this whale, on the ground of its indistinctness. For we are all killers, on land and on sea; Bonapartes and Sharkes included.

BOOK II. (*Octavo*), CHAPTER V. (*Thrasher*).—This gentleman is famous for his tail, which he uses for a ferule in thrashing his foes. He mounts the Folio whale's back, and as he swims, he works his passage by flogging him; as some schoolmasters get along in the world by a similar process. Still less is known of the Thrasher than of the Killer. Both are outlaws, even in the lawless seas.

Thus ends BOOK II. (*Octavo*), and begins BOOK III. (*Duodecimo*).

DUODECIMOES.—These include the smaller whales. I. The Huzza Porpoise. II. The Algerine Porpoise. III. The Mealy-mouthed Porpoise.

To those who have not chanced specially to study the subject, it may possibly seem strange, that fishes not commonly exceeding four or five feet should be marshalled among WHALES—a word, which, in the popular sense, always conveys an idea of hugeness. But the creatures set down above as Duodecimoes are infallibly whales, by the terms of my definition of what a whale is—i.e. a spouting fish, with a horizontal tail.

BOOK III. (*Duodecimo*). CHAPTER I. (*Huzza Porpoise*).—This is the common porpoise found almost all over the globe. The name is of my own bestowal; for there are more than one sort of porpoises, and something must be done to distinguish them. I call him thus, because he always swims in hilarious shoals, which upon the broad sea keep tossing themselves to heaven like caps in a Fourth-of-July crowd. Their appearance is generally hailed with delight by the mariner. Full of fine spirits, they invariably come from the breezy billows to windward. They are the lads that always live before the wind. They are accounted a lucky omen. If you yourself can withstand three cheers at beholding these vivacious fish, then heaven help ye; the spirit of godly gamesomeness is not in ye. A well-fed, plump Huzza Porpoise will yield you one good gallon of good oil. But the fine and delicate fluid extracted from his jaws is exceedingly valuable. It is in request among jewellers and watchmakers. Sailors put it on their hones. Porpoise meat is good eating, you know. It may never have occurred to you that a porpoise spouts. Indeed, his spout is so small that it is not very readily discernible. But the next time you have a chance, watch him; and you will then see the great Sperm whale himself in miniature.

BOOK III. (*Duodecimo*). CHAPTER II. (*Algerine Porpoise*).—A pirate. Very savage. He is only found, I think, in the Pacific. He is somewhat larger than the Huzza Porpoise, but much of the same general make. Provoke him, and he will buckle to a shark. I have lowered for him many times, but never yet saw him captured.

BOOK III. (*Duodecimo*), CHAPTER III. (*Mealy-mouthed Porpoise*).—The largest kind of Porpoise; and only found in the Pacific, so far as it is known. The only English name, by which he has hitherto been designated, is that of the fishers—Right-Whale Porpoise, from the circumstance that he is chiefly found in the vicinity of that Folio. In shape, he differs in some degree from the Huzza Porpoise, being of a less rotund and jolly girth; indeed, he is of quite a neat and gentleman-like figure. He has no fins on his back (most other porpoises have), he has a lovely tail, and sentimental Indian eyes of a hazel hue. But his mealy-mouth spoils all. Though his entire back down to his side fins is of a deep sable, yet a boundary line, distinct as the mark in a ship's hull, called the 'bright waist,' that line streaks him from stem to stern, with two separate colors, black above and white below. The white comprises part of his head, and the whole of his mouth, which makes him look as if he had just escaped from a felonious visit to a meal-bag. A most mean and mealy aspect! His oil is much like that of the common porpoise.

★ ★ ★ ★ ★ ★ ★

Beyond the DUODECIMO, this system does not proceed, inasmuch as the Porpoise is the smallest of the whales. Above, you have all the Leviathans of note. But there are a rabble of uncertain, fugitive, half-fabulous whales, which, as an American whaleman, I know by reputation, but not personally. I shall enumerate them by their forecastle appellations; for possibly such a list may be valuable to future investigators, who may complete what I have here but begun. If any of the following whales, shall hereafter be caught and marked, then he can readily be incorporated into this System, according to his Folio, Octavo, or Duodecimo magnitude:—The Bottle-Nose Whale; the Junk Whale; the Pudding-Headed Whale; the Cape Whale; the Leading Whale; the Cannon Whale; the Scragg Whale; the Coppered Whale; the Elephant Whale; the Iceberg Whale; the Quog Whale; the Blue Whale; &c. From Icelandic, Dutch and old English authorities, there might be quoted other lists of uncertain whales, blessed with all manner of uncouth names. But I omit them as altogether obsolete; and can hardly help suspecting them for mere sounds, full of Leviathanism, but signifying nothing.

Finally: It was stated at the outset, that this system would not be here, and at once, perfected. You cannot but plainly see that I have kept my word. But I now leave my cetological System standing thus unfinished, even as the great Cathedral of Cologne was left, with the crane still standing upon the top of the uncompleted tower. For small erections may be finished by their first architects; grand ones, true ones, ever leave the copestone to posterity. God keep me from ever completing anything. This whole book is but a draught—nay, but the draught of a draught. Oh, Time, Strength, Cash, and Patience!

CHAPTER XXXIII

THE SPECKSYNDER

Concerning the officers of the whale-craft, this seems as good a place as any to set down a little domestic peculiarity on ship-board, arising from the existence of the harpooneer class of officers, a class unknown of course in any other marine than the whale-fleet.

The large importance attached to the harpooneer's vocation is evinced by the fact, that originally in the old Dutch Fishery, two centuries and more ago, the command of a whale ship was not wholly lodged in the person now called the captain, but was divided between him and an officer called the Specksynder. Literally this word means Fat-Cutter; usage, however, in time made it equivalent to Chief Harpooneer. In those days, the captain's authority was restricted to the navigation and general management of the vessel: while over the whale-hunting department and all its concerns, the Specksynder or Chief Harpooneer reigned supreme. In the British Greenland Fishery, under the corrupted title of Specksioneer, this old Dutch official is still retained, but his former dignity is sadly abridged. At present he ranks simply as senior Harpooneer; and as such, is but one of the captain's more inferior subalterns. Nevertheless, as upon the good conduct of the harpooneers the success of a whaling voyage largely depends, and since in the American Fishery he is not only an important officer in the boat, but under certain circumstances (night watches on a whaling ground) the command of the ship's deck is also his; therefore the grand political maxim of the sea demands, that he should nominally live apart from the men before the mast, and be in some way distinguished as their professional superior; though always, by them, familiarly regarded as their social equal.

Now, the grand distinction drawn between officer and man at sea, is this—the first lives aft, the last forward. Hence, in whale-ships and merchantmen alike, the mates have their quarters with the captain; and so, too, in most of the American whalers the harpooneers are lodged in the after part of the ship. That is to say, they take their meals in the captain's cabin, and sleep in a place indirectly communicating with it.

Though the long period of a Southern whaling voyage (by far the longest of all voyages now or ever made by man), the peculiar perils of it, and the community of interest prevailing among a company, all of whom, high or low, depend for their profits, not upon fixed wages, but upon their common luck, together with their common vigilance, intrepidity, and hard work; though all these things do in some cases tend to beget a less rigorous discipline than in merchantmen generally; yet, never mind how much like an old Mesopotamian family these whalemen may, in some primitive instances, live together; for all that, the punctilious externals, at least, of the quarter-deck are seldom materially relaxed, and in no instance done away. Indeed, many are the Nantucket ships in which you will see the skipper parading his quarter-deck with an elated grandeur not surpassed in any military navy; nay, extorting almost as much homage as if he wore the imperial purple, and not the shabbiest of pilot-cloth.

And though of all men the moody captain of the Pequod was the least given to that sort of shallowest assumption; and though the only homage he ever exacted, was implicit, instantaneous obedience; though he required no man to remove the shoes from his feet ere stepping upon the quarter-deck; and though there were times when, owing to peculiar circumstances connected with events hereafter to be detailed, he addressed them in unusual terms, whether of condescension or *in terrorem*, or otherwise; yet even Captain Ahab was by no means unobservant of the paramount forms and usages of the sea.

Nor, perhaps, will it fail to be eventually perceived, that behind those forms and usages, as it were, he sometimes masked himself; incidentally making use of them for other and more private ends than they were legitimately intended to subserve. That certain sultanism of his brain, which had otherwise in a good degree remained unmanifested; through those forms that same sultanism became incarnate in an irresistible dictatorship. For be a man's intellectual superiority what it will, it can never assume the practical, available supremacy over other men, without the aid of some sort of external arts and entrenchments, always, in themselves, more or less paltry and base. This it is, that for ever keeps God's true princes of the Empire from the world's hustings; and leaves the highest honors that this air can give, to those men who become famous more through their infinite inferiority to the choice hidden handful of the Divine Inert, than through their undoubted superiority over the dead level of the mass. Such large virtue lurks in these small things when extreme political superstitions invest them, that in some royal instances even to idiot imbecility they have imparted potency. But when, as in the case of Nicholas the Czar, the ringed crown of geographical empire encircles an imperial brain; then, the plebeian herds crouch abased before the tremendous centralization. Nor, will the tragic dramatist who would depict mortal indomitableness in its fullest sweep and direst swing, ever forget a hint, incidentally so important in his art, as the one now alluded to.

But Ahab, my Captain, still moves before me in all his Nantucket grimness and shagginess; and in this episode touching Emperors and Kings, I must not conceal that I have only to do with a poor old whale-hunter like him; and, therefore, all outward majestical trappings and housings are denied me. Oh, Ahab! what shall be grand in thee, it must needs be plucked at from the skies, and dived for in the deep, and featured in the unbodied air!

CHAPTER XXXIV

THE CABIN-TABLE

It is noon; and Dough-Boy, the steward, thrusting his pale loaf-of-bread face from the cabin-scuttle, announces dinner to his lord and master; who, sitting in the lee quarter-boat, has just been taking an observation of the sun; and is now mutely reckoning the latitude on the smooth, medallion-shaped tablet, reserved for that daily purpose on the upper part of his ivory leg. From his complete inattention to the tidings, you would think that moody Ahab had not heard his menial. But presently, catching hold of the mizen shrouds, he swings himself to the deck, and in an even, unexhilarated voice, saying, 'Dinner, Mr Starbuck,' disappears into the cabin.

When the last echo of his sultan's step has died away, and Starbuck, the first Emir, has every reason to suppose that he is seated, then Starbuck rouses from his quietude, takes a few turns along the planks, and, after a grave peep into the binnacle, says, with some touch of pleasantness, 'Dinner, Mr Stubb,' and descends the scuttle. The second Emir lounges about the rigging awhile, and then slightly shaking the main brace, to see whether it be all right with that important rope, he likewise takes up the old burden, and with a rapid 'Dinner, Mr Flask,' follows after his predecessors.

But the third Emir, now seeing himself all alone on the quarter-deck, seems to feel relieved from some curious restraint; for, tipping all sorts of knowing winks in all sorts of directions, and kicking off his shoes, he strikes into a sharp but noiseless squall of a hornpipe right over the Grand Turk's head; and then, by a dexterous sleight, pitching his cap into the mizen-top for a shelf, he goes down rollicking, so far at least as he remains visible from the deck, reversing all other processions, by bringing up the rear with music. But ere stepping into the cabin doorway below, he pauses, ships a new face altogether, and, then, independent, hilarious little Flask enters King Ahab's presence, in the character of Abjectus, or the Slave.

It is not the least among the strange things bred by the intense artificialness of sea-usages, that while in the open air of the deck some officers will, upon provocation, bear themselves boldly and defyingly enough towards their commander; yet, ten to one, let those very officers the next moment go down to their customary dinner in that same commander's cabin, and straightway their inoffensive, not to say deprecatory and humble air towards him, as he sits at the head of the table; this is marvellous, sometimes most comical. Wherefore this difference? A problem? Perhaps not. To have been Belshazzar, King of Babylon; and to have been Belshazzar, not haughtily but courteously, therein certainly must have been some touch of mundane grandeur. But he who in the rightly regal and intelligent spirit presides over his own private dinner-table of invited guests, that man's unchallenged power and dominion of individual influence for the time; that man's royalty of state transcends Belshazzar's, for Belshazzar was not the greatest. Who has but once dined his friends, has tasted what it is to be Cæsar. It is a witchery of social czarship which there is no withstanding. Now, if to this consideration you superadd the official supremacy of a ship-master, then, by inference, you will derive the cause of that peculiarity of sea-life just mentioned.

Over his ivory-inlaid table, Ahab presided like a mute, maned sea-lion on the white coral beach, surrounded by his warlike but still deferential cubs. In his own proper turn, each officer waited to be served. They were as little children before Ahab; and yet, in Ahab, there seemed not to lurk the smallest social arrogance. With one mind, their intent eyes all fastened upon the old man's knife, as he carved the chief dish before him. I do not suppose that for the world they would have profaned that moment with the slightest observation, even upon so neutral a topic as the weather. No! And when reaching out his knife and fork, between which the slice of beef was locked, Ahab thereby motioned Starbuck's plate towards him, the mate received his meat as though receiving alms; and cut it tenderly; and a little started if, perchance, the knife grazed against the plate; and chewed it noiselessly; and swallowed it, not without circumspection. For, like the Coronation banquet at Frankfort, where the German Emperor profoundly dines with the seven Imperial Electors, so these cabin meals were somehow solemn meals, eaten in awful silence; and yet at table old Ahab forbade not conversation; only he himself was dumb. What a relief it was to choking Stubb, when a rat made a sudden racket in the hold below. And poor little Flask, he was the youngest son, and little boy of this weary family party. His were the shinbones of the saline beef; his would have been the drumsticks. For Flask to have presumed to help himself, this must have seemed to him tantamount to larceny in the first degree. Had he helped himself at that table, doubtless, never more would he have been able to hold his hand up in this honest world; nevertheless, strange to say, Ahab never forbade him. And had Flask helped himself, the chances were Ahab had never so much as noticed it. Least of all, did Flask presume to help himself to butter. Whether he thought the owners of the ship denied it to him, on account of its clotting his clear, sunny complexion; or whether he deemed that, on so long a voyage in such marketless waters, butter was at a premium, and therefore was not for him, a subaltern; however it was, Flask, alas! was a butterless man!

Another thing. Flask was the last person down at the dinner, and Flask is the first man up. Consider! For hereby Flask's dinner was badly jammed in point of time. Starbuck and Stubb both had the start of him; and yet they also have the privilege of lounging in the rear. If Stubb even, who is but a peg higher than Flask, happens to have but a small appetite, and soon shows symptoms of concluding his repast, then Flask must bestir himself, he will not get more than three mouthfuls that day; for it is against holy usage for Stubb to precede Flask to the deck. Therefore it was that Flask once admitted in private, that ever since he had arisen to the dignity of an officer, from that moment he had never known what it was to be otherwise than hungry, more or less. For what he ate did not so much relieve his hunger, as keep it immortal in him. Peace and satisfaction, thought Flask, have for ever departed from my stomach. I am an officer; but, how I wish I could fist a bit of old-fashioned beef in the forecastle, as I used to when I was before the mast. There's the fruits of promotion now; there's the vanity of glory: there's the insanity of life! Besides, if it were so that any mere sailor of the Pequod had a grudge against Flask in Flask's official capacity, all that sailor had to do, in order to obtain ample vengeance, was to go aft at dinnertime, and get a peep at Flask through the cabin sky-light, sitting silly and dumfoundered before awful Ahab.

Now, Ahab and his three mates formed what may be called the first table in the Pequod's cabin. After their departure, taking place in inverted order to their arrival, the canvas cloth was cleared, or rather was restored to some hurried order by the pallid steward. And then the three harpooneers were bidden to the feast, they being its residuary legatees. They made a sort of temporary servants' hall of the high and mighty cabin.

In strange contrast to the hardly tolerable constraint and nameless invisible domineerings of the captain's table, was the entire care-free license and ease, the almost frantic democracy of those inferior fellows the harpooneers. While their masters, the mates, seemed afraid of the sound of the hinges of their own jaws, the harpooneers chewed their food with such a relish that there was a report to it. They dined like lords; they filled their bellies like Indian ships all day loading with spices. Such portentous appetites had Queequeg and Tashtego, that to fill out the vacancies made by the previous repast, often the pale Dough-Boy was fain to bring on a great baron of salt-junk, seemingly quarried out of the solid ox. And if he were not lively about it, if he did not go with a nimble hop-skip-and-jump, then Tashtego had an ungentlemanly way of accelerating him by darting a fork at his back, harpoonwise. And once Daggoo, seized with a sudden humor, assisted Dough-Boy's memory by snatching him up bodily, and thrusting his head into a great empty wooden trencher, while Tashtego, knife in hand, began laying out the circle preliminary to scalping him. He was naturally a very nervous, shuddering sort of little fellow, this bread-faced steward; the progeny of a bankrupt baker and a hospital nurse. And what with the standing spectacle of the black terrific Ahab, and the periodical tumultuous visitations of these three savages, Dough-Boy's whole life was one continual lip-quiver. Commonly, after seeing the harpooneers furnished with all things they demanded, he would escape from their clutches into his little pantry adjoining, and fearfully peep out at them through the blinds of its door, till all was over.

It was a sight to see Queequeg seated over against Tashtego, opposing his filed teeth to the Indian's: crosswise to them, Daggoo seated on the floor, for a bench would have brought his hearse-plumed head to the low carlines; at every motion of his colossal limbs, making the low cabin framework to shake, as when an African elephant goes passenger in a ship. But for all this, the great negro was wonderfully abstemious, not to say dainty. It seemed hardly possible that by such comparatively small mouthfuls he could keep up the vitality diffused through so broad, baronial, and superb a person. But, doubtless, this noble savage fed strong and drank deep of the abounding element of air; and through his dilated nostrils snuffed in the sublime life of the worlds. Not by beef or by bread, are giants made or nourished. But Queequeg, he had a mortal, barbaric smack of the lip in eating—an ugly sound enough—so much so, that the trembling Dough-Boy almost looked to see whether any marks of teeth lurked in his own lean arms. And when he would hear Tashtego singing out for him to produce himself, that his bones might be picked, the simple-witted Steward all but shattered the crockery hanging round him in the pantry, by his sudden fits of the palsy. Nor did the whetstones which the harpooneers carried in their pockets, for their lances and other weapons; and with which whetstones, at dinner, they would ostentatiously sharpen their knives; that grating sound did not at all tend to tranquillize poor Dough-Boy. How could he forget that in his Island days, Queequeg, for one, must certainly have been guilty of some murderous, convivial indiscretions. Alas! Dough-Boy! hard fares the white waiter who waits upon cannibals. Not a napkin should he carry on his arm, but a buckler. In good time, though, to his great delight, the three salt-sea warriors would rise and depart; to his credulous, fable-mongering ears, all their martial bones jingling in them at every step, like Moorish scimetars in scabbards.

But, though these barbarians dined in the cabin, and nominally lived there; still, being anything but sedentary in their habits, they were scarcely ever in it except at mealtimes, and just before sleeping-time, when they passed through it to their own peculiar quarters.

In this one matter, Ahab seemed no exception to most American whale captains, who, as a set, rather incline to the opinion that by rights the ship's cabin belongs to them; and that it is by courtesy alone that anybody else is, at any time, permitted there. So that, in real truth, the mates and harpooneers of the Pequod might more properly be said to have lived out of the cabin than in it. For when they did enter it, it was something as a street-door enters a house; turning inwards for a moment, only to be turned out the next; and, as a permanent thing, residing in the open air. Nor did they lose much hereby; in the cabin was no companionship; socially, Ahab was inaccessible. Though nominally included in the census of Christendom, he was still an alien to it. He lived in the world, as the last of the Grisly Bears lived in settled Missouri. And as when Spring and Summer had departed, that wild Logan of the woods, burying himself in the hollow of a tree, lived out the winter there, sucking his own paws; so, in his inclement, howling old age, Ahab's soul, shut up in the caved trunk of his body, there fed upon the sullen paws of its gloom!

CHAPTER XXXV

THE MAST-HEAD

It was during the more pleasant weather, that in due rotation with the other seamen my first mast-head came round.

In most American whalemen the mast-heads are manned almost simultaneously with the vessel's leaving her port; even though she may have fifteen thousand miles, and more, to sail ere reaching her proper cruising ground. And if, after a three, four, or five years' voyage she is drawing nigh home with anything empty in her—say, an empty vial even—then, her mast-heads are kept manned to the last; and not till her skysail poles sail in among the spires of the port, does she altogether relinquish the hope of capturing one whale more.

Now, as the business of standing mast-heads, ashore or afloat, is a very ancient and interesting one, let us in some measure expatiate here. I take it, that the earliest standers of mast-heads were the old Egyptians; because, in all my researches, I find none prior to them. For though their progenitors, the builders of Babel, must doubtless, by their tower, have intended to rear the loftiest mast-head in all Asia, or Africa either; yet (ere the final truck was put to it) as that great stone mast of theirs may be said to have gone by the board, in the dread gale of God's wrath; therefore, we cannot give these Babel builders priority over the Egyptians. And that the Egyptians were a nation of mast-head standers, is an assertion based upon the general belief among archæologists, that the first pyramids were founded for astronomical purposes: a theory singularly supported by the peculiar stair-like formation of all four sides of those edifices; whereby, with prodigious long upliftings of their legs, those old astronomers were wont to mount to the apex, and sing out for new stars; even as the look-outs of a modern ship sing out for a sail, or a whale just bearing in sight. In Saint Stylites, the famous Christian hermit of old times, who built him a lofty stone pillar in the desert and spent the whole latter portion of his life on its summit, hoisting his food from the ground with a tackle; in him we have a remarkable instance of a dauntless stander-of-mast-heads; who was not to be driven from his place by fogs or frosts, rain, hail, or sleet; but valiantly facing everything out to the last, literally died at his post. Of modern standers-of-mast-heads we have but a lifeless set; mere stone, iron, and bronze men; who, though well capable of facing out a stiff gale, are still entirely incompetent to the business of singing out upon discovering any strange sight. There is Napoleon; who, upon the top of the column of Vendome, stands with arms folded, some one hundred and fifty feet in the air; careless, now, who rules the decks below; whether Louis Philippe, Louis Blanc, or Louis the Devil. Great Washington, too, stands high aloft on his towering main-mast in Baltimore, and like one of Hercules' pillars, his column marks that point of human grandeur beyond which few mortals will go. Admiral Nelson, also, on a capstan of gun-metal, stands his mast-head in Trafalgar Square; and even when most obscured by that London smoke, token is yet given that a hidden hero is there; for where there is smoke, must be fire. But neither great Washington, nor Napoleon, nor Nelson, will answer a single hail from below, however madly invoked to befriend by their counsels the distracted decks upon which they gaze; however, it may be surmised, that their spirits penetrate through the thick haze of the future, and descry what shoals and what rocks must be shunned.

It may seem unwarrantable to couple in any respect the mast-head standers of the land with those of the sea; but that in truth it is not so, is plainly evinced by an item for which Obed Macy, the sole historian of Nantucket, stands accountable. The worthy Obed tells us, that in the early times of the whale fishery, ere ships were regularly launched in pursuit of the game, the people of that island erected lofty spars along the sea-coast, to which the look-outs ascended by means of nailed cleats, something as fowls go upstairs in a hen-house. A few years ago this same plan was adopted by the Bay whalemen of New Zealand, who, upon descrying the game, gave notice to the ready-manned boats nigh the beach. But this custom has now become obsolete; turn we then to the one proper mast-head, that of a whale-ship at sea.

The three mast-heads are kept manned from sun-rise to sun-set; the seamen taking their regular turns (as at the helm), and relieving each other every two hours. In the serene weather of the tropics it is exceedingly pleasant—the mast-head; nay, to a dreamy meditative man it is delightful. There you stand, a hundred feet above the silent decks, striding along the deep, as if the masts were gigantic stilts, while beneath you and between your legs, as it were, swim the hugest monsters of the sea, even as ships once sailed between the boots of the famous Colossus at old Rhodes. There you stand, lost in the infinite series of the sea, with nothing ruffled but the waves. The tranced ship indolently rolls; the drowsy trade winds blow; everything resolves you into languor. For the most part, in this tropic whaling life, a sublime uneventfulness invests you; you hear no news; read no gazettes; extras with startling accounts of commonplaces never delude you into unnecessary excitements; you hear of no domestic afflictions; bankrupt securities; fall of stocks; are never troubled with the thought of what you shall have for dinner—for all your meals for three years and more are snugly stowed in casks, and your bill of fare is immutable.

In one of those southern whalemen, on a long three or four years' voyage, as often happens, the sum of the various hours you spend at the mast-head would amount to several entire months. And it is much to be deplored that the place to which you devote so considerable a portion of the whole term of your natural life, should be so sadly destitute of anything approaching to a cosy inhabitiveness, or adapted to breed a comfortable localness of feeling, such as pertains to a bed, a hammock, a hearse, a sentry box, a pulpit, a coach, or any other of those small and snug contrivances in which men temporarily isolate themselves. Your most usual point of perch is the head of the t' gallant-mast, where you stand upon two thin parallel sticks (almost peculiar to whalemen) called the t' gallant cross-trees. Here, tossed about by the sea, the beginner feels about as cosy as he would standing on a bull's horns. To be sure, in coolish weather you may carry your house aloft with you, in the shape of a watch-coat; but properly speaking the thickest watch-coat is no more of a house than the unclad body; for as the soul is glued inside of its fleshly tabernacle, and cannot freely move about in it, nor even move out of it, without running great risk of perishing (like an ignorant pilgrim crossing the snowy Alps in winter); so a watch-coat is not so much of a house as it is a mere envelope, or additional skin encasing you. You cannot put a shelf or chest of drawers in your body, and no more can you make a convenient closet of your watch-coat.

Concerning all this, it is much to be deplored that the mast-heads of a southern whale ship are unprovided with those enviable little tents or pulpits, called *crow's-nests,* in which the lookouts of a Greenland whaler are protected from the inclement weather of the frozen seas. In the fireside narrative of Captain Sleet, entitled 'A Voyage among the Icebergs, in quest of the Greenland Whale, and incidentally for the re-discovery of the Lost Icelandic Colonies of Old Greenland;' in this admirable volume, all standers of mast-heads are furnished with a charmingly circumstantial account of the then recently invented *crow's-nest* of the Glacier, which was the name of Captain Sleet's good craft. He called it the *Sleet's crow's-nest,* in honor of himself; he being the original inventor and patentee, and free from all ridiculous false delicacy, and holding that if we call our own children after our own names (we fathers being the original inventors and patentees), so likewise should we denominate after ourselves any other apparatus we may beget. In shape, the Sleet's crow's-nest is something like a large tierce or pipe; it is open above, however, where it is furnished with a movable side-screen to keep to windward of your head in a hard gale. Being fixed on the summit of the mast, you ascent into it through a little trap-hatch in the bottom. On the after side, or side next the stern of the ship, is a comfortable seat, with a locker underneath for umbrellas, comforters, and coats. In front is a leather rack, in which to keep your speaking trumpet, pipe, telescope, and other nautical conveniences. When Captain Sleet in person stood his mast-head in this crow's nest of his, he tells us that he always had a rifle with him (also fixed in the rack), together with a powder flask and shot, for the purpose of popping off the stray narwhales, or vagrant sea unicorns infesting those waters; for you cannot successfully shoot at them from the deck owing to the resistance of the water, but to shoot down upon them is a very different thing. Now, it was plainly a labor of love for Captain Sleet to describe, as he does, all the little detailed conveniences of his crow's-nest; but though he so enlarges upon many of these, and though he treats us to a very scientific account of his experiments in this crow's-nest, with a small compass he kept there for the purpose of counteracting the errors resulting from what is called the 'local attraction' of all binnacle magnets; an error ascribable to the horizontal vicinity of the iron in the ship's planks, and in the Glacier's case, perhaps, to there having been so many broken-down black-smiths among her crew; I say, that though the Captain is very discreet and scientific here, yet, for all his learned 'binnacle deviations,' 'azimuth compass observations,' and 'approximate errors,' he knows very well, Captain Sleet, that he was not so much immersed in those profound magnetic meditations, as to fail being attracted occasionally towards that well replenished little case-bottle, so nicely tucked in on one side of his crow's nest, within easy reach of his hand. Though, upon the whole, I greatly admire and even love the brave, the honest, and learned Captain; yet I take it very ill of him that he should so utterly ignore that case-bottle, seeing what a faithful friend and comforter it must have been, while with mittened fingers and hooded head he was studying the mathematics aloft there in that bird's nest within three or four perches of the pole.

But if we Southern whale-fishers are not so snugly housed aloft as Captain Sleet and his Greenland-men were; yet that disadvantage is greatly counterbalanced by the widely contrasting serenity of those seductive seas in which we South fishers mostly float. For one, I used to lounge up the rigging very leisurely, resting in the top to have a chat with Queequeg, or any one else off duty whom I might find there; then ascending a little way further, and throwing a lazy leg over the top-sail yard, take a preliminary view of the watery pastures, and so at last mount to my ultimate destination.

Let me make a clean breast of it here, and frankly admit that I kept but sorry guard. With the problem of the universe revolving in me, how could I—being left completely to myself at such a thought-engendering altitude,—how could I but lightly hold my obligations to observe all whale-ships' standing orders, 'Keep your weather eye open, and sing out every time.'

And let me in this place movingly admonish you, ye shipowners of Nantucket! Beware of enlisting in your vigilant fisheries any lad with lean brow and hollow eye; given to unseasonable meditativeness; and who offers to ship with the Phædon instead of Bowditch in his head. Beware of such an one, I say: your whales must be seen before they can be killed; and this sunken-eyed young Platonist will tow you ten wakes round the world, and never make you one pint of sperm the richer. Nor are these monitions at all unneeded. For nowadays, the whale-fishery furnishes an asylum for many romantic, melancholy, and absent-minded young men, disgusted with the carking cares of earth, and seeking sentiment in tar and blubber. Childe Harold not unfrequently perches himself upon the mast-head of some luckless disappointed whale-ship, and in moody phrase ejaculates:—

> 'Roll on, thou deep and dark blue ocean, roll!
> Ten thousand blubber-hunters sweep over thee in vain.'

Very often do the captains of such ships take those absent-minded young philosophers to task, upbraiding them with not feeling sufficient 'interest' in the voyage; half-hinting that they are so hopelessly lost to all honorable ambition, as that in their secret souls they would rather not see whales than otherwise. But all in vain; those young Platonists have a notion that their vision is imperfect; they are short-sighted; what use, then, to strain the visual nerve? They have left their opera-glasses at home.

'Why, thou monkey,' said a harpooneer to one of these lads, 'we've been cruising now hard upon three years, and thou hast not raised a whale yet. Whales are scarce as hen's teeth whenever thou art up here.' Perhaps they were; or perhaps there might have been shoals of them in the far horizon; but lulled into such an opium-like listlessness of vacant, unconscious reverie is this absent-minded youth by the blending cadence of waves with thoughts, that at last he loses his identity; takes the mystic ocean at his feet for the visible image of that deep, blue, bottomless soul, pervading mankind and nature; and every strange, half-seen, gliding, beautiful thing that eludes him; every dimly-discovered, uprising fin of some undiscernible form, seems to him the embodiment of those elusive thoughts that only people the soul by continually flitting through it. In this enchanted mood, thy spirit ebbs away to whence it came; becomes diffused through time and space; like Cranmer's sprinkled Pantheistic ashes, forming at last a part of every shore the round globe over.

There is no life in thee, now, except that rocking life imparted by a gently rolling ship; by her, borrowed from the sea; by the sea, from the inscrutable tides of God. But while this sleep, this dream is on ye, move your foot or hand an inch; slip your hold at all; and your identity comes back in horror. Over Descartian vortices you hover. And perhaps, at mid-day, in the fairest weather, with one half-throttled shriek you drop through that transparent air into the summer sea, no more to rise for ever. Heed it well, ye Pantheists!

CHAPTER XXXVI

The Quarter-Deck

(*Enter Ahab: Then, all.*)

It was not a great while after the affair of the pipe, that one morning shortly after breakfast, Ahab, as was his wont, ascended the cabin-gangway to the deck. There most sea-captains usually walk at that hour, as country gentlemen, after the same meal, take a few turns in the garden.

Soon his steady, ivory stride was heard, as to and fro he paced his old rounds, upon planks so familiar to his tread, that they were all over dented, like geological stones, with the peculiar mark of his walk. Did you fixedly gaze, too, upon that ribbed and dented brow; there also, you would see still stranger foot-prints—the foot-prints of his one unsleeping, ever-pacing thought.

But on the occasion in question, those dents looked deeper, even as his nervous step that morning left a deeper mark. And, so full of his thought was Ahab, that at every uniform turn that he made, now at the main-mast and now at the binnacle, you could almost see that thought turn in him as he turned, and pace in him as he paced; so completely possessing him, indeed, that it all but seemed the inward mould of every outer movement.

'D'ye mark him, Flask?' whispered Stubb; 'the chick that's in him pecks the shell. 'Twill soon be out.'

The hours wore on; Ahab now shut up within his cabin; anon, pacing the deck, with the same intense bigotry of purpose in his aspect.

It drew near the close of day. Suddenly he came to a halt by the bulwarks, and inserting his bone leg in the auger-hole there, and with one hand grasping a shroud, he ordered Starbuck to send everybody aft.

'Sir!' said the mate, astonished at an order seldom or never given on ship-board except in some extraordinary case.

'Send everybody aft,' repeated Ahab. 'Mast-heads, there! come down!'

When the entire ship's company were assembled, and with curious and not wholly unapprehensive faces, were eyeing him, for he looked not unlike the weather horizon when a storm is coming up, Ahab, after rapidly glancing over the bulwarks, and then darting his eyes among the crew, started from his standpoint; and as though not a soul were nigh him resumed his heavy turns upon the deck. With bent head and half-slouched hat he continued to pace, unmindful of the wondering whispering among the men; still Stubb cautiously whispered to Flask, that Ahab must have summoned them there for the purpose of witnessing a pedestrian feat. But this did not last long. Vehemently pausing, he cried:—

'What do ye do when ye see a whale, men?'

'Sing out for him!' was the impulsive rejoinder from a score of clubbed voices.

'Good!' cried Ahab, with a wild approval in his tones; observing the hearty animation into which his unexpected question had so magnetically thrown them.

'And what do ye next, men?'

'Lower away, and after him!'

'And what tune is it ye pull to, men?'

'A dead whale or a stove boat!'

More and more strangely and fiercely glad and approving, grew the countenance of the old man at every shout: while the mariners began to gaze curiously at each other, as if marvelling how it was that they themselves became so excited at such seemingly purposeless questions.

But, they were all eagerness again, as Ahab, now half-revolving in his pivot-hole, with one hand reaching high up a shroud, and tightly, almost convulsively grasping it, addressed them thus:—

'All ye mast-headers have before now heard me give orders about a white whale. Look ye! d'ye see this Spanish ounce of gold?'—holding up a broad bright coin to the sun—'it is a sixteen dollar piece, men. D'ye see it? Mr Starbuck, hand me yon top-maul.'

While the mate was getting the hammer, Ahab, without speaking, was slowly rubbing the gold piece against the skirts of his jacket, as if to heighten its lustre, and without using any words was meanwhile lowly humming to himself, producing a sound so strangely muffled and inarticulate that it seemed the mechanical humming of the wheels of his vitality in him.

Receiving the top-maul from Starbuck, he advanced towards the main-mast with the hammer uplifted in one hand, exhibiting the gold with the other, and with a high raised voice exclaiming: 'Whosoever of ye raises me a white-headed whale with a wrinkled brow and a crooked jaw; whosoever of ye raises me that white-headed whale, with three holes punctured in his starboard fluke—look ye, whosoever of ye raises me that same white whale, he shall have this gold ounce, my boys!'

'Huzza! huzza!' cried the seamen, as with swinging tarpaulins they hailed the act of nailing the gold to the mast.

'It's a white whale, I say,' resumed Ahab, as he threw down the top-maul; 'a white whale. Skin your eyes for him, men; look sharp for white water; if ye see but a bubble, sing out.'

All this while Tashtego, Daggoo, and Queequeg had looked on with even more intense interest and surprise than the rest, and at the mention of the wrinkled brow and crooked jaw they had started as if each was separately touched by some specific recollection.

'Captain Ahab,' said Tashtego, 'that white whale must be the same that some call Moby Dick.'

'Moby Dick?' shouted Ahab. 'Do ye know the white whale then, Tash?'

'Does he fan-tail a little curious, sir, before he goes down?' said the Gay-Header deliberately.

'And has he a curious spout, too,' said Daggoo, 'very bushy, even for a parmacetty, and mighty quick, Captain Ahab?'

'And he have one, two, tree—oh! good many iron in him hide, too, Captain,' cried Queequeg disjointedly, 'all twisketee be-twisk, like him—him—' faltering hard for a word, and screwing his hand round and round as though uncorking a bottle—'like him—him—'

'Corkscrew!' cried Ahab, 'aye, Queequeg, the harpoons lie all twisted and wrenched in him; aye, Daggoo, his spout is a big one, like a whole shock of wheat, and white as a pile of our Nantucket wool after the great annual sheep-shearing; aye, Tashtego, and he fan-tails like a split jib in a squall. Death and devils! men, it is Moby Dick ye have seen—Moby Dick—Moby Dick!'

'Captain Ahab,' said Starbuck, who, with Stubb and Flask, had thus far been eyeing his superior with increasing surprise, but at last seemed struck with a thought which somewhat explained all the wonder. 'Captain Ahab, I have heard of Moby Dick—but it was not Moby Dick that took off thy leg?'

'Who told thee that?' cried Ahab; then pausing, 'Aye, Starbuck; aye, my hearties all round; it was Moby Dick that dismasted me; Moby Dick that brought me to this dead stump I stand on now. Aye, aye,' he shouted with a terrific, loud, animal sob, like that of a heart-stricken moose; 'Aye, aye! it was that accursed white whale that razeed me; made a poor pegging lubber of me for ever and a day!' Then tossing both arms, with measureless imprecations he shouted out: 'Aye, aye! and I'll chase him round Good Hope, and round the Horn, and round the Norway Maelstrom, and round perdition's flames before I give him up. And this is what ye have shipped for, men! to chase that white whale on both sides of land, and over all sides of earth, till he spouts black blood and rolls fin out. What say ye, men, will ye splice hands on it, now? I think ye do look brave.'

'Aye, aye!' shouted the harpooneers and seamen, running closer to the excited old man: 'A sharp eye for the White Whale; a sharp lance for Moby Dick!'

'God bless ye,' he seemed to half sob and half shout. 'God bless ye, men. Steward! go draw the great measure of grog. But what's this long face about, Mr Starbuck; wilt thou not chase the white whale? art not game for Moby Dick?'

'I am game for his crooked jaw, and for the jaws of Death too, Captain Ahab, if it fairly comes in the way of the business we follow; but I came here to hunt whales, not my commander's vengeance. How many barrels will thy vengeance yield thee even if thou gettest it, Captain Ahab? it will not fetch thee much in our Nantucket market.'

'Nantucket market! Hoot! But come closer, Starbuck; thou requirest a little lower layer. If money's to be the measurer, man, and the accountants have computed their great counting-house the globe, by girdling it with guineas, one to every three parts of an inch; then, let me tell thee, that my vengeance will fetch a great premium *here*!'

'He smites his chest,' whispered Stubb, 'what's that for? methinks it rings most vast, but hollow.'

'Vengeance on a dumb brute!' cried Starbuck, 'that simply smote thee from blindest instinct! Madness! To be enraged with a dumb thing, Captain Ahab, seems blasphemous.'

'Hark ye yet again,—the little lower layer. All visible objects, man, are but as pasteboard masks. But in each event—in the living act, the undoubted deed—there, some unknown but still reasoning thing puts forth the mouldings of its features from behind the unreasoning mask. If man will strike, strike through the mask! How can the prisoner reach outside except by thrusting through the wall? To me, the white whale is that wall, shoved near to me. Sometimes I think there's naught beyond. But 'tis enough. He tasks me; he heaps me; I see in him outrageous strength, with an inscrutable malice sinewing it. That inscrutable thing is chiefly what I hate; and be the white whale agent, or be the white whale principal, I will wreak that hate upon him. Talk not to me of blasphemy, man; I'd strike the sun if it insulted me. For could the sun do that, then could I do the other; since there is ever a sort of fair play herein, jealousy presiding over all creations. But not my master, man, is even that fair play. Who's over me? Truth hath no confines. Take off thine eye! more intolerable than fiends' glarings is a doltish stare! So, so; thou reddenest and palest; my heat has melted thee to anger-glow. But look ye, Starbuck, what is said in heat, that thing unsays itself. There are men from whom warm words are small indignity. I meant not to incense thee. Let it go. Look! see yonder Turkish cheeks of spotted tawn—living, breathing pictures painted by the sun. The Pagan leopards—the unrecking and unworshipping things, that live; and seek, and give no reasons for the torrid life they feel! The crew, man, the crew! Are they not one and all with Ahab, in this matter of the whale? See Stubb! he laughs! See yonder Chilian! he snorts to think of it. Stand up amid the general hurricane, thy one tost sapling cannot, Starbuck! And what is it? Reckon it. 'Tis but to help strike a fin; no wondrous feat for Starbuck. What is it more? From this one poor hunt, then, the best lance out of all Nantucket, surely he will not hang back, when every foremast-hand has clutched a whetstone? Ah! constrainings seize thee; I see! the billow lifts thee! Speak, but speak!—Aye, aye! thy silence, then, *that* voices thee. (*Aside*) Something shot from my dilated nostrils, he has inhaled it in his lungs. Starbuck now is mine; cannot oppose me now, without rebellion.'

'God keep me!—keep us all!' murmured Starbuck, lowly.

But in his joy at the enchanted, tacit acquiescence of the mate, Ahab did not hear his foreboding invocation; nor yet the low laugh from the hold; nor yet the presaging vibrations of the winds in the cordage; nor yet the hollow flap of the sails against the masts, as for a moment their hearts sank in. For again Starbuck's downcast eyes lighted up with the stubbornness of life; the subterranean laugh died away; the winds blew on; the sails filled out; the ship heaved and rolled as before. Ah, ye admonitions and warnings! why stay ye not when ye come? But rather are ye predictions than warnings, ye shadows! Yet not so much predictions from without, as verifications of the foregoing things within. For with little external to constrain us, the innermost necessities in our being, these still drive us on.

'The measure! the measure!' cried Ahab.

Receiving the brimming pewter, and turning to the harpooneers, he ordered them to produce their weapons. Then ranging them before him near the capstan, with their harpoons in their hands, while his three mates stood at his side with their lances, and the rest of the ship's company formed a circle round the group; he stood for an instant searchingly eyeing every man of his crew. But those wild eyes met his, as the bloodshot eyes of the prairie wolves meet the eye of their leader, ere he rushes on at their head in the trail of the bison; but, alas! only to fall into the hidden snare of the Indian.

'Drink and pass!' he cried, handing the heavy charged flagon to the nearest seaman. 'The crew alone now drink. Round with it, round! Short draughts—long swallows, men; 'tis hot as Satan's hoof. So, so; it goes round excellently. It spiralizes in ye; forks out at the serpent-snapping eye. Well done; almost drained. That way it went, this way it comes. Hand it me—here's a hollow! Men, ye seem the years; so brimming life is gulped and gone. Steward, refill!

'Attend now, my braves. I have mustered ye all round this capstan; and ye mates, flank me with your lances; and ye harpooneers, stand there with your irons; and ye, stout mariners, ring me in, that I may in some sort revive a noble custom of my fishermen fathers before me. O men, you will yet see that—Ha! boy, come back? bad pennies come not sooner. Hand it me. Why, now, this pewter had run brimming again, wert not thou St. Vitus' imp—away, thou ague!

'Advance, ye mates! Cross your lances full before me. Well done! Let me touch the axis.' So saying, with extended arm, he grasped the three level, radiating lances at their crossed centre; while so doing, suddenly and nervously twitched them; meanwhile, glancing intently from Starbuck to Stubb; from Stubb to Flask. It seemed as though, by some nameless, interior volition, he would fain have shocked into them the same fiery emotion accumulated within the Leyden jar of his own magnetic life. The three mates quailed before his strong, sustained, and mystic aspect. Stubb and Flask looked sideways from him; the honest eye of Starbuck fell downright.

'In vain!' cried Ahab; 'but, maybe, 'tis well. For did ye three but once take the full-forced shock, then mine own electric thing, *that* had perhaps expired from out me. Perchance, too, it would have dropped ye dead. Perchance ye need it not. Down lances! And now, ye mates, I do appoint ye three cup-bearers to my three pagan kinsmen there—yon three most honorable gentlemen and noblemen, my valiant harpooneers. Disdain the task? What, when the great Pope washes the feet of beggars, using his tiara for ewer? Oh, my sweet cardinals! your own condescension, *that* shall bend ye to it. I do not order ye; ye will it. Cut your seizings and draw the poles, ye harpooneers!'

Silently obeying the order, the three harpooneers now stood with the detached iron part of their harpoons, some three feet long, held, barbs up, before him.

'Stab me not with that keen steel! Cant them; cant them over! know ye not the goblet end? Turn up the socket! So, so; now, ye cup-bearers, advance. The irons! take them; hold them while I fill!' Forthwith, slowly going from one officer to the other, he brimmed the harpoon sockets with the fiery waters from the pewter.

'Now, three to three, ye stand. Commend the murderous chalices! Bestow them, ye who are now made parties to this indissoluble league. Ha! Starbuck! but the deed is done! Yon ratifying sun now waits to sit upon it. Drink, ye har-

the old Mogul has fixed him, too. I twigged it, knew it; had had the gift, might readily have prophesied it—for when I clapped my eye upon his skull I saw it. Well, Stubb, *wise* Stubb—that's my title—well, Stubb, what of it, Stubb? Here's a carcase. I know not all that may be coming, but be it what it will, I'll go to it laughing. Such a waggish leering as lurks in all your horribles! I feel funny. Fa, la! lirra, skirra! What's my juicy little pear at home doing now? Crying its eyes out?—Giving a party to the last arrived harpooneers, I dare say, gay as a frigate's pennant, and so am I—fa, la! lirra, skirra! Oh—

We'll drink to-night with hearts as light,
To love, as gay and fleeting
As bubbles that swim, on the beaker's brim,
And break on the lips while meeting.

A brave stave that—who calls? Mr. Starbuck? Aye, aye, sir—(*Aside*) he's my superior, he has his too, if I'm not mistaken.—Aye, aye, sir, just through with this job—coming.

CHAPTER XL

MIDNIGHT, FORECASTLE

HARPOONEERS AND SAILORS

(*Foresail rises and discovers the watch standing, lounging, leaning, and lying in various attitudes, all singing in chorus.*)

Farewell and adieu to you, Spanish ladies!
Farewell and adieu to you, ladies of Spain!
Our captain's commanded—

1ST NANTUCKET SAILOR

Oh, boys, don't be sentimental; it's bad for the digestion! Take a tonic, follow me!

(*Sings, and all follow.*)

Our captain stood upon the deck,
A spy-glass in his hand,
A viewing of those gallant whales
That blew at every strand.
Oh, your tubs in your boats, my boys,
And by your braces stand,
And we'll have one of those fine whales,
Hand, boys, over hand!
So, be cheery, my lads! may your hearts never fail!
While the bold harpooneer is striking the whale!

MATE'S VOICE FROM THE QUARTER-DECK

Eight bells there, forward!

2D NANTUCKET SAILOR

Avast the chorus! Eight bells there! d'ye hear, bell-boy? Strike the bell eight, thou Pip! thou blackling! and let me call the watch. I've the sort of mouth for that—the hogshead mouth. So, so, (*thrusts his head down the scuttle,*) Star-bo-l-e-e-n-s, a-h-o-y! Eight bells there below! Tumble up!

DUTCH SAILOR

Grand snoozing to-night, maty; fat night for that. I mark this in our old Mogul's wine; it's quite as deadening to some as filliping to others. We sing; they sleep—aye, lie down there, like ground-tier butts. At 'em again! There, take this copper-pump, and hail 'em through it. Tell 'em to avast dreaming of their lasses. Tell 'em it's the resurrection; they must kiss their last, and come to judgment. That's the way—*that's* it; thy throat ain't spoiled with eating Amsterdam butter.

FRENCH SAILOR

Hist, boys! let's have a jig or two before we ride to anchor in Blanket Bay. What say ye? There comes the other watch. Stand by all legs! Pip! little Pip! hurrah with your tambourine!

PIP

(*Sulky and sleepy.*)

Don't know where it is.

FRENCH SAILOR

Beat thy belly, then, and wag thy ears. Jig it, men, I say; merry's the word; hurrah! Damn me, won't you dance? Form, now, Indian-file, and gallop into the double-shuffle? Throw yourselves! Legs! legs!

ICELAND SAILOR

I don't like your floor, maty; it's too springy to my taste. I'm used to ice-floors. I'm sorry to throw cold water on the subject; but excuse me.

MALTESE SAILOR

Me too; where's your girls? Who but a fool would take his left hand by his right, and say to himself, how d'ye do? Partners! I must have partners!

SICILIAN SAILOR

Aye; girls and a green!—then I'll hop with ye; yea, turn grasshopper!

LONG-ISLAND SAILOR

Well, well, ye sulkies, there's plenty more of us. Hoe corn when you may, say I. All legs go to harvest soon. Ah! here comes the music; now for it!

AZORE SAILOR

(*Ascending, and pitching the tambourine up the scuttle.*)

Here you are, Pip; and there's the windlass-bitts; up you mount! Now, boys!

(*The half of them dance to the tambourine; some go below; some sleep or lie among the coils of rigging. Oaths a-plenty.*)

AZORE SAILOR

(*Dancing.*)

Go it, Pip! Bang it, bell-boy! Rig it, dig it, stig it, quig it, bell-boy! Make fire-flies; break the jinglers!

PIP

Jinglers, you say?—there goes another, dropped off, I pound it so.

CHINA SAILOR

Rattle thy teeth, then, and pound away; make a pagoda of thyself.

FRENCH SAILOR

Merry-mad! Hold up thy hoop, Pip, till I jump through it! Split jibs! tear yourselves!

TASHTEGO

(*Quietly smoking.*)

That's a white man; he calls that fun: humph; I save my sweat.

OLD MANX SAILOR

I wonder whether those jolly lads bethink them of what they are dancing over. I'll dance over your grave, I will—that's the bitterest threat of your night-women, that beat head-winds round corners. O Christ! to think of the green navies and the green-skulled crews! Well, well; belike, the whole world's a ball, as you scholars have it; and so 'tis right to make one ball-room of it. Dance on, lads, you're young; I was once.

3D NANTUCKET SAILOR

Spell oh!—whew! this is worse than pulling after whales in a calm—give us a whiff, Tash.

(*They cease dancing, and gather in clusters. Meantime the sky darkens—the wind rises.*)

LASCAR SAILOR

By Brahma! boys, it'll be douse sail soon. The sky-born, high-tide Ganges turned to wind! Thou showest thy black brow, Seeva!

MALTESE SAILOR

(*Reclining and shaking his cap.*)

It's the waves'—the snow-caps' turn to jig it now. They'll shake their tassels soon. Now would all the waves were women, then I'd go drown, and chassee with them evermore! There's naught so sweet on earth—heaven may not match it!—as those swift glances of warm, wild bosoms in the dance, when the over-arboring arms hide such ripe, bursting grapes.

SICILIAN SAILOR

(*Reclining.*)

Tell me not of it! Hark ye. lad—fleet interlacings of the limbs—lithe swayings—coyings—flutterings! lip! heart! hip! all graze: unceasing touch and go! not taste, observe ye, else come satiety. Eh, Pagan? (*Nudging.*)

TAHITAN SAILOR

(*Reclining on a mat.*)

Hail, holy nakedness of our dancing girls!—the Heeva-Heeva! Ah! low veiled, high palmed Tahiti! I still rest me on thy mat, but the soft soil has slid! I saw thee woven in the wood, my mat! green the first day I brought ye thence; now worn and wilted quite. Ah me!—not thou nor can I bear the change! How then, if so be transplanted to yon sky? Hear I the roaring streams from Pirohitee's peak of spears, when they leap down the crags and drown the villages?—The blast! the blast! Up, spine, and meet it! (*Leaps to his feet.*)

PORTUGUESE SAILOR

How the sea rolls swashing 'gainst the side! Stand by for reefing, hearties! the winds are just crossing swords, pell-mell they'll go lunging presently.

DANISH SAILOR

Crack, crack, old ship! so long as thou crackest, thou holdest! Well done! The mate there holds ye to it stiffly. He's no more afraid than the isle fort at Cattegat, put there to fight the Baltic with storm-lashed guns, on which the sea-salt cakes!

4TH NANTUCKET SAILOR

He has his orders, mind ye that. I heard old Ahab tell him he must always kill a squall, something as they burst a water-spout with a pistol—fire your ship right into it!

ENGLISH SAILOR

Blood! but that old man's a grand old cove! We are the lads to hunt him up his whale!

ALL

Aye! aye!

OLD MANX SAILOR

How the three pines shake! Pines are the hardest sort of tree to live when shifted to any other soil, and here there's none but the crew's cursed clay. Steady, helmsman! steady. This is the sort of weather when brave hearts snap ashore, and keeled hulls split at sea. Our captain has his birthmark; look yonder, boys, there's another in the sky—lurid-like, ye see, all else pitch black.

DAGGOO

What of that? Who's afraid of black's afraid of me! I'm quarried out of it!

SPANISH SAILOR

(*Aside.*) He wants to bully, ah!—the old grudge makes me touchy. (*Advancing.*) Aye, harpooneer, thy race is the undeniable dark side of mankind—devilish dark at that. No offence.

DAGGOO (*grimly*)

None.

ST. JAGO'S SAILOR

That Spaniard's mad or drunk. But that can't be, or else in his one case our old Mogul's fire-waters are somewhat long in working.

5TH NANTUCKET SAILOR

What's that I saw—lightning? Yes.

SPANISH SAILOR

No; Daggoo showing his teeth.

DAGGOO (*springing*)

Swallow thine, mannikin! White skin, white liver!

SPANISH SAILOR (*meeting him*)

Knife thee heartily! big frame, small spirit!

ALL

A row! a row! a row!

TASHTEGO (*with a whiff*)

A row a'low, and a row aloft—Gods and men—both brawlers! Humph!

BELFAST SAILOR

A row! arrah a row! The Virgin be blessed, a row! Plunge in with ye!

ENGLISH SAILOR

Fair play! Snatch the Spaniard's knife! A ring, a ring!

OLD MANX SAILOR

Ready formed. There! the ringed horizon. In that ring Cain struck Abel. Sweet work, right work! No? Why then, God, mad'st thou the ring?

MATE'S VOICE FROM THE QUARTER DECK

Hands by the halyards! in top-gallant sails! Stand by to reef topsails!

ALL

The squall! the squall! jump, my jollies! (*They scatter.*)

PIP (*shrinking under the windlass*)

Jollies? Lord help such jollies! Crish, crash! there goes the jib-stay! Blang-whang! God! Duck lower, Pip, here comes the royal yard! It's worse than being in the whirled woods, the last day of the year! Who'd go climbing after chestnuts now? But there they go, all cursing, and here I don't. Fine prospects to 'em; they're on the road to heaven. Hold on hard! Jimmini, what a squall! But those chaps there are worse yet—they are your white squalls, they. White squalls? white whale, shirr! shirr! Here have I heard all their chat just now, and the white whale—shirr! shirr!—but spoken of once! and only this evening—it makes me jingle all over like my tambourine—that anaconda of an old man swore 'em in to hunt him! Oh, thou big white God aloft there somewhere in yon darkness, have mercy on this small black boy down here; preserve him from all men that have no bowels to feel fear!

* * * * * * *

CHAPTER XLI

MOBY DICK

I, Ishmael, was one of that crew; my shouts had gone up with the rest; my oath had been welded with theirs; and stronger I shouted, and more did I hammer and clinch my oath, because of the dread in my soul. A wild, mystical, sympathetical feeling was in me; Ahab's quenchless feud seemed mine. With greedy ears I learned the history of that murderous monster against whom I and all the others had taken our oaths of violence and revenge.

For some time past, though at intervals only, the unaccompanied, secluded White Whale had haunted those uncivilized seas mostly frequented by the Sperm Whale fishermen. But not all of them knew of his existence; only a few of them, comparatively, had knowingly seen him; while the number who as yet had actually and knowingly given battle to him, was small indeed. For, owing to the large number of whale-cruisers; the disorderly way they were sprinkled over the entire watery circumference, many of them adventurously pushing their quest along solitary latitudes, so as seldom or never for a whole twelvemonth or more on a stretch, to encounter a single news-telling sail of any sort; the inordinate length of each separate voyage; the irregularity of the times of sailing from home; all these, with other circumstances, direct and indirect, long obstructed the spread through the whole world-wide whaling-fleet of the special individualizing tidings concerning Moby Dick. It was hardly to be doubted, that several vessels reported to have encountered, at such or such a time, or on such or such a meridian, a Sperm Whale of uncommon magnitude and malignity, which whale, after doing great mischief to his assailants, had completely escaped them; to some minds it was not an unfair presumption, I say, that the whale in question must have been no other than Moby Dick. Yet as of late the Sperm Whale fishery had been marked by various and not infrequent instances of great ferocity, cunning, and malice in the monster attacked; therefore it was, that those who by accident ignorantly gave battle to Moby Dick; such hunters, perhaps, for the most part, were content to ascribe the peculiar terror he bred, more, as it were, to the perils of the Sperm Whale fishery at large, than to the individual cause. In that way, mostly, the disastrous encounter between Ahab and the whale had hitherto been popularly regarded.

And as for those who, previously hearing of the White Whale, by chance caught sight of him; in the beginning of the thing they had every one of them, almost, as boldly and fearlessly lowered for him, as for any other whale of that species. But at length, such calamities did ensue in these assaults—not restricted to sprained wrists and ancles, broken limbs, or devouring amputations—but fatal to the last degree of fatality; those repeated disastrous repulses, all accumulating and piling their terrors upon Moby Dick; those things had gone far to shake the fortitude of many brave hunters, to whom the story of the White Whale had eventually come.

Nor did wild rumors of all sorts fail to exaggerate, and still the more horrify the true histories of these deadly encounters. For not only do fabulous rumors naturally grow out of the very body of all surprising terrible events,—as the smitten tree gives birth to its fungi; but, in maritime life, far more than in that of terra firma, wild rumors abound, wherever there is any adequate reality for them to cling to. And as the sea surpasses the land in this matter, so the whale fishery surpasses every other sort of maritime life, in the wonderfulness and fearfulness of the rumors which sometimes circulate there. For not only are whalemen as a body unexempt from that ignorance and superstitiousness hereditary to all sailors; but of all sailors, they are by all odds the most directly brought into contact with whatever is appallingly astonishing in the sea; face to face they not only eye its greatest marvels, but, hand to jaw, give battle to them. Alone, in such remotest waters, that though you sailed a thousand miles, and passed a thousand shores, you would not come to any chiselled hearthstone, or aught hospitable beneath that part of the sun; in such latitudes and longitudes, pursuing too such a calling as he does, the whaleman is wrapped by influences all tending to make his fancy pregnant with many a mighty birth.

No wonder, then, that ever gathering volume from the mere transit over the widest watery spaces, the outblown rumors of the White Whale did in the end incorporate with themselves all manner of morbid hints, and half-formed fœtal suggestions of supernatural agencies, which eventually invested Moby Dick with new terrors unborrowed from anything that visibly appears. So that in many cases such a panic did he finally strike, that few who by those rumors, at least, had heard of the White Whale, few of those hunters were willing to encounter the perils of his jaw.

But there were still other and more vital practical influences at work. Not even at the present day has the original prestige of the Sperm Whale, as fearfully distinguished from all other species of the leviathan, died out of the minds of the whalemen as a body. There are those this day among them, who, though intelligent and courageous enough in offering battle to the Greenland or Right whale, would perhaps—either from professional inexperience, or incompetency, or timidity, decline a contest with the Sperm Whale; at any rate, there are plenty of whalemen, especially among those whaling nations not sailing under the American flag, who have never hostilely encountered the Sperm Whale, but whose sole knowledge of the leviathan is restricted to the ignoble monster primitively pursued in the North; seated on their hatches, these men will hearken with a childish fire-side interest and awe, to the wild, strange tales of Southern whaling. Nor is the pre-eminent tremendousness of the great Sperm Whale anywhere more feelingly comprehended, than on board of those prows which stem him.

And as if the now tested reality of his might had in former legendary times thrown its shadow before it; we find some book naturalists—Olassen and Povelson—declaring the Sperm Whale not only to be a consternation to every other creature in the sea, but also to be so incredibly ferocious as continually to be athirst for human blood. Nor even down to so late a time as Cuvier's, were these or almost similar impressions effaced. For in his Natural History, the Baron himself affirms that at sight of the Sperm Whale, all fish (sharks included) are 'struck with the most lively terrors,' and 'often in the precipitancy of their flight dash themselves against the rocks with such violence as to cause instantaneous death.' And however the general experiences in the fishery may amend such reports as these; yet in their full terribleness, even to the bloodthirsty item of Povelson, the superstitious belief in them is, in some vicissitudes of their vocation, revived in the minds of the hunters.

So that overawed by the rumors and portents concerning him, not a few of the fishermen recalled, in reference to Moby Dick, the earlier days of the Sperm Whale fishery, when it was oftentimes hard to induce long practised Right whalemen to embark in the perils of this new and daring warfare; such men protesting that although other leviathans might be hopefully pursued, yet to chase and point lance at such an apparition as the Sperm Whale was not for mortal man. That to attempt it, would be inevitably to be torn into a quick eternity. On this head, there are some remarkable documents that may be consulted.

Nevertheless, some there were, who even in the face of these things were ready to give chase to Moby Dick; and a still greater number who, chancing only to hear of him distantly and vaguely, without the specific details of any certain calamity, and without superstitious accompaniments, were sufficiently hardy not to flee from the battle if offered.

One of the wild suggestings referred to, as at last coming to be linked with the White Whale in the minds of the superstitiously inclined, was the unearthly conceit that Moby Dick was ubiquitous; that he had actually been encountered in opposite latitudes at one and the same instant of time.

Nor, credulous as such minds must have been, was this conceit altogether without some faint show of superstitious probability. For as the secrets of the currents in the seas have never yet been divulged, even to the most erudite research; so the hidden ways of the Sperm Whale when beneath the surface remain, in great part, unaccountable to his pursuers; and from time to time have originated the most curious and contradictory speculations regarding them, especially concerning the mystic modes whereby, after sounding to a great depth, he transports himself with such vast swiftness to the most widely distant points.

It is a thing well known to both American and English whaleships, and as well a thing placed upon authoritative record years ago by Scoresby, that some whales have been captured far north in the Pacific, in whose bodies have been found the barbs of harpoons darted in the Greenland seas. Nor is it to be gainsaid, that in some of these instances it has been declared that the interval of time between the two assaults could not have exceeded very many days. Hence, by inference, it has been believed by some whalemen, that the Nor' West Passage, so long a problem to man, was never a problem to the whale. So that here, in the real living experience of living men, the prodigies related in old times of the inland Strello mountain in Portugal (near whose top there was said to be a lake in which the wrecks of ships floated up to the surface); and that still more wonderful story of the Arethusa fountain near Syracuse (whose waters were believed to have come from the Holy Land by an underground passage); these fabulous narrations are almost fully equalled by the realities of the whaleman.

Forced into familiarity, then, with such prodigies as these; and knowing that after repeated, intrepid assaults, the White Whale had escaped alive; it cannot be much matter of surprise that some whalemen should go still further in their superstitions; declaring Moby Dick not only ubiquitous, but immortal (for immortality is but ubiquity in time); that though groves of spears should be planted in his flanks, he would still swim away unharmed; or if indeed he should ever be made to spout thick blood, such a sight would be but a ghastly deception; for again in unensanguined billows hundreds of leagues away, his unsullied jet would once more be seen.

But even stripped of these supernatural surmisings, there was enough in the earthly make and incontestable character of the monster to strike the imagination with unwonted power. For, it was not so much his uncommon bulk that so much distinguished him from other sperm whales, but, as was elsewhere thrown out—a peculiar snow-white wrinkled forehead, and a high, pyramidical white hump. These were his prominent features; the tokens whereby, even in the limitless, uncharted seas, he revealed his identity, at a long distance, to those who knew him.

The rest of his body was so streaked, and spotted, and marbled with the same shrouded hue, that, in the end, he had gained his distinctive appellation of the White Whale; a name, indeed, literally justified by his vivid aspect, when seen gliding at high noon through a dark blue sea, leaving a milky-way wake of creamy foam, all spangled with golden gleamings.

Nor was it his unwonted magnitude, nor his remarkable hue, nor yet his deformed lower jaw, that so much invested the whale with natural terror, as that unexampled, intelligent malignity which, according to specific accounts, he had over and over again evinced in his assaults. More than all, his treacherous retreats struck more of dismay than perhaps aught else. For, when swimming before his exulting pursuers, with every apparent symptom of alarm, he had several times been known to turn round suddenly, and, bearing down upon them, either stave their boats to splinters, or drive them back in consternation to their ship.

Already several fatalities had attended his chase. But though similar disasters, however little bruited ashore, were by no means unusual in the fishery; yet, in most instances, such seemed the White Whale's infernal aforethought of ferocity, that every dismembering or death that he caused, was not wholly regarded as having been inflicted by an unintelligent agent.

Judge, then, to what pitches of inflamed, distracted fury the minds of his more desperate hunters were impelled, when amid the chips of chewed boats, and the sinking limbs of torn comrades, they swam out of the white curds of the whale's direful wrath into the serene, exasperating sunlight, that smiled on, as if at a birth or a bridal.

His three boats stove around him, and oars and men both whirling in the eddies; one captain, seizing the line-knife from his broken prow, had dashed at the whale, as an Arkansas duellist at his foe, blindly seeking with a six inch blade to reach the fathom-deep life of the whale. That captain was Ahab. And then it was, that suddenly sweeping his sickle-shaped lower jaw beneath him, Moby Dick had reaped away Ahab's leg, as a mower a blade of grass in the field. No turbaned Turk, no hired Venetian or Malay, could have smote him with more seeming malice. Small reason was there to doubt, then, that ever since that almost fatal encounter, Ahab had cherished a wild vindictiveness against the whale, all the more fell for that in his frantic morbidness he at last came to identify with him, not only all his bodily woes, but all his intellectual and spiritual exasperations. The White Whale swam before him as the monomaniac incarnation of all those malicious agencies which some deep men feel eating in them, till they are left living on with half a heart and half a lung. That intangible malignity which has been from the beginning; to whose dominion even the modern Christians ascribe one-half of the worlds; which the ancient Ophites of the east reverenced in their statue devil;—Ahab did not fall down and worship it like them; but deliriously transferring its idea to the abhorred white whale, he pitted himself, all mutilated, against it. All that most maddens and torments; all that stirs up the lees of things; all truth with malice in it; all that cracks the sinews and cakes the brain; all the subtle demonisms of life and thought; all evil, to crazy Ahab, were visibly personified, and made practically assailable in Moby Dick. He piled upon the whale's white hump the sum of all the general rage and hate felt by his whole race from Adam down; and then, as if his chest had been a mortar, he burst his hot heart's shell upon it.

It is not probable that this monomania in him took its instant rise at the precise time of his bodily dismemberment. Then, in darting at the monster, knife in hand, he had but given loose to a sudden, passionate, corporal animosity; and when he received the stroke that tore him, he probably but felt the agonizing bodily laceration, but nothing more. Yet, when by this collision forced to turn towards home, and for long months of days and weeks, Ahab and anguish lay stretched together in one hammock, rounding in mid winter that dreary, howling Patagonian Cape; then it was, that his torn body and gashed soul bled into one another; and so interfusing, made him mad. That it was only then, on the homeward voyage, after the encounter, that the final monomania seized him, seems all but certain from the fact that, at intervals during the passage, he was a raving lunatic; and, though unlimbed of a leg, yet such vital strength yet lurked in his Egyptian chest, and was moreover intensified by his delirium, that his mates were forced to lace him fast, even there, as he sailed, raving in his hammock. In a strait-jacket, he swung to the mad rockings of the gales. And, when running into more sufferable latitudes, the ship, with mild stun' sails spread, floated across the tranquil tropics, and, to all appearances, the old man's delirium seemed left behind him with the Cape Horn swells, and he came forth from his dark den into the blessed light and air; even then, when he bore that firm, collected front, however pale, and issued his calm orders once again; and his mates thanked God the direful madness was now gone; even then, Ahab, in his hidden self, raved on. Human madness is oftentimes a cunning and most feline thing. When you think it fled, it may have but become transfigured into some still subtler form. Ahab's full lunacy subsided not, but deepeningly contracted; like the unabated Hudson, when that noble Northman flows narrowly, but unfathomably through the Highland gorge. But, as in his narrow-flowing monomania, not one jot of Ahab's broad madness had been left behind; so in that broad madness, not one jot of his great natural intellect had perished. That before living agent, now became the living instrument. If such a furious trope may stand, his special lunacy stormed his general sanity, and carried it, and turned all its concentred cannon upon its own mad mark; so that far from having lost his strength, Ahab, to that one end, did now possess a thousand fold more potency than ever he had sanely brought to bear upon any one reasonable object.

This is much; yet Ahab's larger, darker, deeper part remains unhinted. But vain to popularize profundities, and all truth is profound. Winding far down from within the very heart of this spiked Hotel de Cluny where we here stand—however grand and wonderful, now quit it;—and take your way, ye nobler, sadder souls, to those vast Roman halls of Thermes; where far beneath the fantastic towers of man's upper earth, his root of grandeur, his whole awful essence sits in bearded state; an antique buried beneath antiquities, and throned on torsoes! So with a broken throne, the great gods mock that captive king; so like a Caryatid, he patient sits, upholding on his frozen brow the piled entablatures of ages. Wind ye down there, ye prouder, sadder souls! question that proud, sad king! A family likeness! aye, he did beget ye, ye young exiled royalties; and from your grim sire only will the old State-secret come.

Now, in his heart, Ahab had some glimpse of this, namely: all my means are sane, my motive and my object mad. Yet without power to kill, or change, or shun the fact; he likewise knew that to mankind he did long dissemble; in some sort, did still. But that thing of his dissembling, was only subject to his perceptibility, not to his will determinate. Nevertheless, so well did he succeed in that dissembling, that when with ivory leg he stepped ashore at last, no Nantucketer thought him otherwise than but naturally grieved, and that to the quick, with the terrible casualty which had overtaken him.

The report of his undeniable delirium at sea was likewise popularly ascribed to a kindred cause. And so too, all the added moodiness which always afterwards, to the very day of sailing in the Pequod on the present voyage, sat brooding on his brow. Nor is it so very unlikely, that far from distrusting his fitness for another whaling voyage, on account of such dark symptoms, the calculating people of that prudent isle were inclined to harbor the conceit, that for those very reasons he was all the better qualified and set on edge, for a pursuit so full of rage and wildness as the bloody hunt of whales. Gnawed within and scorched without, with the infixed, unrelenting fangs of some incurable idea; such an one, could he be found, would seem the very man to dart his iron and lift his lance against the most appalling of all brutes. Or, if for any reason thought to be corporeally incapacitated for that, yet such an one would seem superlatively competent to cheer and howl on his underlings to the attack. But be all this as it may, certain it is, that with the mad secret of his unabated rage bolted up and keyed in him, Ahab had purposely sailed upon the present voyage with the one only and all-engrossing object of hunting the White Whale. Had any one of his old acquaintances on shore but half dreamed of what was lurking in him then, how soon would their aghast and righteous souls have wrenched the ship from such a fiendish man! They were bent on profitable cruises, the profit to be counted down in dollars from the mint. He was intent on an audacious, immitigable, and supernatural revenge.

Here, then, was this grey-headed, ungodly old man, chasing with curses a Job's whale round the world, at the head of a crew, too, chiefly made up of mongrel renegades, and castaways, and cannibals—morally enfeebled also, by the incompetence of mere unaided virtue or right-mindedness in Starbuck, the invulnerable jollity of indifference and recklessness in Stubb, and the pervading mediocrity in Flask. Such a crew, so officered, seemed specially picked and packed by some infernal fatality to help him to his monomaniac revenge. How it was that they so aboundingly responded to the old man's ire—by what evil magic their souls were possessed, that at times his hate seemed almost theirs; the White Whale as much their insufferable foe as his; how all this came to be—what the White Whale was to them, or how to their unconscious understandings, also, in some dim, unsuspected way, he might have seemed the gliding great demon of the seas of life,—all this to explain, would be to dive deeper than Ishmael can go. The subterranean miner that works in us all, how can one tell whither leads his shaft by the ever shifting, muffled sound of his pick? Who does not feel the irresistible arm drag? What skiff in tow of a seventy-four can stand still? For one, I gave myself up to the abandonment of the time and the place; but while yet all a-rush to encounter the whale, could see naught in that brute but the deadliest ill.

CHAPTER XLII

THE WHITENESS OF THE WHALE

What the white whale was to Ahab, has been hinted; what, at times, he was to me, as yet remains unsaid.

Aside from those more obvious considerations touching Moby Dick, which could not but occasionally awaken in any man's soul some alarm, there was another thought, or rather vague, nameless horror concerning him, which at times by its intensity completely overpowered all the rest; and yet so mystical and well nigh ineffable was it, that I almost despair of putting it in a comprehensible form. It was the whiteness of the whale that above all things appalled me. But how can I hope to explain myself here; and yet, in some dim, random way, explain myself I must, else all these chapters might be naught.

Though in many natural objects, whiteness refiningly enhances beauty, as if imparting some special virtue of its own, as in marbles, japonicas, and pearls; and though various nations have in some way recognised a certain royal pre-eminence in this hue; even the barbaric, grand old kings of Pegu placing the title 'Lord of the White Elephants' above all their other magniloquent ascriptions of dominion; and the modern kings of Siam unfurling the same snow-white quadruped in the royal standard; and the Hanoverian flag bearing the one figure of a snow-white charger; and the great Austrian Empire, Cæsarian heir to overlording Rome, having for the imperial color the same imperial hue; and though this pre-eminence in it applies to the human race itself, giving the white man ideal mastership over every dusky tribe; and though, besides all this, whiteness has been even made significant of gladness, for among the Romans a white stone marked a joyful day; and though in other mortal sympathies and symbolizings, this same hue is made the emblem of many touching, noble things—the innocence of brides, the benignity of age; though among the Red Men of America the giving of the white belt of wampum was the deepest pledge of honor; though in many climes, whiteness typifies the majesty of Justice in the ermine of the Judge, and contributes to the daily state of kings and queens drawn by milk-white steeds; though even in the higher mysteries of the most august religions it has been made the symbol of the divine spotlessness and power; by the Persian fire worshippers, the white forked flame being held the holiest on the altar; and in the Greek mythologies, Great Jove himself being made incarnate in a snow-white bull; and though to the noble Iroquois, the midwinter sacrifice of the sacred White Dog was by far the holiest festival of their theology, that spotless, faithful creature being held the purest envoy they could send to the Great Spirit with the annual tidings of their own fidelity; and though directly from the Latin word for white, all Christian priests derive the name of one part of their sacred vesture, the alb or tunic, worn beneath the cassock; and though among the holy pomps of the Romish faith, white is specially employed in the celebration of the Passion of our Lord; though in the Vision of St. John, white robes are given to the redeemed, and the four-and-twenty elders stand clothed in white before the great white throne, and the Holy One that sitteth there white like wool; yet for all these accumulated associations with whatever is sweet, and honorable, and sublime, there yet lurks an elusive something in the innermost idea of this hue, which strikes more of panic to the soul than that redness which affrights in blood.

This elusive quality it is, which causes the thought of whiteness, when divorced from more kindly associations, and coupled with any object terrible in itself, to heighten that terror to the furthest bounds. Witness the white bear of the poles, and the white shark of the tropics; what but their smooth, flaky whiteness makes them the transcendent horrors they are? That ghastly whiteness it is which imparts such an abhorrent mildness, even more loathsome than terrific, to the dumb gloating of their aspect. So that not the fierce-fanged tiger in his heraldic coat can so stagger courage as the white-shrouded bear or shark.*

Bethink thee of the albatross: whence come those clouds of spiritual wonderment and pale dread, in which that white phantom sails in all imaginations? Not Coleridge first threw that spell; but God's great, unflattering laureate, Nature.†

Most famous in our Western annals and Indian traditions is that of the White Steed of the Prairies; a magnificent milk-white charger, large-eyed, small-headed, bluff-chested, and with the dignity of a thousand monarchs in his lofty, overscorning carriage. He was the elected Xerxes of vast herds of wild horses, whose pastures in those days were only fenced by the Rocky Mountains and the Alleghanies. At their flaming head he westward trooped it like that chosen star which every evening leads on the hosts of light. The flashing cascade of his mane, the curving comet of his tail, invested him with housings more resplendent than gold and silver-beaters could have furnished him. A most imperial and archangelical apparition of that unfallen, western world, which to the eyes of the old trappers and hunters revived the glories of those primeval times when Adam walked majestic as a god, bluff-bowed and fearless as this mighty steed. Whether marching amid his aides and marshals in the van of countless cohorts that endlessly streamed it over the plains, like an Ohio; or whether with his circumambient subjects browsing all

---

*With reference to the Polar bear, it may possibly be urged by him who would fain go still deeper into this matter, that it is not the whiteness, separately regarded, which heightens the intolerable hideousness of that brute; for, analysed, that heightened hideousness, it might be said, only arises from the circumstances, that the irresponsible ferociousness of the creature stands invested in the fleece of celestial innocence and love; and hence, by bringing together two such opposite emotions in our minds, the Polar bear frightens us with so unnatural a contrast. But even assuming all this to be true; yet, were it not for the whiteness, you would not have that intensified terror.

As for the white shark, the white gliding ghostliness of repose in that creature, when beheld in his ordinary moods, strangely tallies with the same quality in the Polar quadruped. This peculiarity is most vividly hit by the French in the name they bestow upon that fish. The Romish mass for the dead begins with 'Requiem eternam' (eternal rest), whence *Requiem* denominating the mass itself, and any other funereal music. Now, in allusion to the white, silent stillness of death in this shark, and the mild deadliness of his habits, the French call him *Requin*.

---

†I remember the first albatross I ever saw. It was during a prolonged gale, in waters hard upon the Antarctic seas. From my forenoon watch below, I ascended to the overclouded deck; and there, dashed upon the main hatches, I saw a regal, feathery thing of unspotted whiteness, and with a hooked, Roman bill sublime. At intervals, it arched forth its vast archangel wings, as if to embrace some holy ark. Wondrous flutterings and throbbings shook it. Though bodily unharmed, it uttered cries, as some king's ghost in supernatural distress. Through its inexpressible, strange eyes, methought I peeped to secrets which took hold of God. As Abraham before the angels, I bowed myself; the white thing was so white, its wings so wide, and in those for ever exiled waters, I had lost the miserable warping memories of traditions and of towns. Long I gazed at that prodigy of plumage. I cannot tell, can only hint, the things that darted through me then. But at last I awoke; and turning, asked a sailor what bird was this. A goney, he replied. Goney! I never had heard that name before; is it conceivable that this glorious thing is utterly unknown to men ashore! never! But some time after, I learned that goney was some seaman's name for albatross. So that by no possibility could Coleridge's wild Rhyme have had aught to do with those mystical impressions which were mine, when I saw that bird upon our deck. For neither had I then read the Rhyme, nor knew the bird to be an albatross. Yet, in saying this, I do but indirectly burnish a little brighter the noble merit of the poem and the poet.

I assert, then, that in the wondrous bodily whiteness of the bird chiefly lurks the secret of the spell; a truth the more evinced in this, that by a solecism of terms there are birds called grey albatrosses; and these I have frequently seen, but never with such emotions as when I beheld the Antarctic fowl.

But how had the mystic thing been caught? Whisper it not, and I will tell; with a treacherous hook and line, as the fowl floated on the sea. At last the Captain made a postman of it; tying a lettered, leathern tally round its neck, with the ship's time and place; and then letting it escape. But I doubt not, that leathern tally, meant for man, was taken off in Heaven, when the white fowl flew to join the wing-folding, the invoking, and adoring cherubim!

around at the horizon, the White Steed gallopingly reviewed them with warm nostrils reddening through his cool milkiness; in whatever aspect he presented himself, always to the bravest Indians he was the object of trembling reverence and awe. Nor can it be questioned from what stands on legendary record of this noble horse, that it was his spiritual whiteness chiefly, which so clothed him with divineness; and that this divineness had that in it which, though commanding worship, at the same time enforced a certain nameless terror.

But there are other instances where this whiteness loses all that accessory and strange glory which invests it in the White Steed and Albatross.

What is it that in the Albino man so peculiarly repels and often shocks the eye, as that sometimes he is loathed by his own kith and kin! It is that whiteness which invests him, a thing expressed by the name he bears. The Albino is as well made as other men—has no substantive deformity—and yet this mere aspect of all-pervading whiteness makes him more strangely hideous than the ugliest abortion. Why should this be so?

Nor, in quite other aspects, does Nature in her least palpable but not the less malicious agencies, fail to enlist among her forces this crowning attribute of the terrible. From its snowy aspect, the gauntleted ghost of the Southern Seas has been denominated the White Squall. Nor, in some historic instances, has the art of human malice omitted so potent an auxiliary. How wildly it heightens the effect of that passage in Froissart, when, masked in the snowy symbol of their faction, the desperate White Hoods of Ghent murder their bailiff in the market-place!

Nor, in some things, does the common, hereditary experience of all mankind fail to bear witness to the supernaturalism of this hue. It cannot well be doubted, that the one visible quality in the aspect of the dead which most appals the gazer, is the marble pallor lingering there; as if indeed that pallor were as much like the badge of consternation in the other world, as of mortal trepidation here. And from that pallor of the dead, we borrow the expressive hue of the shroud in which we wrap them. Nor even in our superstitions do we fail to throw the same snowy mantle round our phantoms; all ghosts rising in a milk-white fog—Yea, while these terrors seize us, let us add, that even the king of terrors, when personified by the evangelist, rides on his pallid horse.

Therefore, in his other moods, symbolise whatever grand or gracious thing he will by whiteness, no man can deny that in its profoundest idealized significance it calls up a peculiar apparition to the soul.

But though without dissent this point be fixed, how is mortal man to account for it? To analyse it, would seem impossible. Can we, then, by the citation of some of those instances wherein this thing of whiteness—though for the time either wholly or in great part stripped of all direct associations calculated to impart to it aught fearful, but, nevertheless, is found to exert over us the same sorcery, however modified;—can we thus hope to light upon some chance clue to conduct us to the hidden cause we seek?

Let us try. But in a matter like this, subtlety appeals to subtlety, and without imagination no man can follow another into these halls. And though, doubtless, some at least of the imaginative impressions about to be presented may have been shared by most men, yet few perhaps were entirely conscious of them at the time, and therefore may not be able to recall them now.

Why to the man of untutored ideality, who happens to be but loosely acquainted with the peculiar character of the day, does the bare mention of Whitsuntide marshal in the fancy such long, dreary, speechless processions of slow-pacing pilgrims, down-cast and hooded with new-fallen snow? Or, to the unread, unsophisticated Protestant of the Middle American States, why does the passing mention of a White Friar or a White Nun, evoke such an eyeless statue in the soul?

Or what is there apart from the traditions of dungeoned warriors and kings (which will not wholly account for it) that makes the White Tower of London tell so much more strongly on the imagination of an untravelled American, than those other storied structures, its neighbors—the Byward Tower, or even the Bloody? And those sublimer towers, the White Mountains of New Hampshire, whence, in peculiar moods, comes that gigantic ghostliness over the soul at the bare mention of that name, while the thought of Virginia's Blue Ridge is full of a soft, dewy, distant dreaminess? Or why, irrespective of all latitudes and longitudes, does the name of the White Sea exert such a spectralness over the fancy, while that of the Yellow Sea lulls us with mortal thoughts of long lacquered mild afternoons on the waves, followed by the gaudiest and yet sleepiest of sunsets? Or, to choose a wholly unsubstantial instance, purely addressed to the fancy, why, in reading the old fairy tales of Central Europe, does 'the tall pale man' of the Hartz forests, whose changeless pallor unrustlingly glides through the green of the groves—why is this phantom more terrible than all the whooping imps of the Blocksburg?

Nor is it, altogether, the remembrance of her cathedral-toppling earthquakes; nor the stampedoes of her frantic seas; nor the tearlessness of arid skies that never rain; nor the sight of her wide field of leaning spires, wrenched cope-stones, and crosses all adroop (like canted yards of anchored fleets); and her suburban avenues of house-walls lying over upon each other, as a tossed pack of cards;—it is not these things alone which make tearless Lima, the strangest, saddest city thou can'st see. For Lima has taken the white veil; and there is a higher horror in this whiteness of her woe. Old as Pizarro, this whiteness keeps her ruins for ever new; admits not the cheerful greenness of complete decay; spreads over her broken ramparts the rigid pallor of an apoplexy that fixes its own distortions.

I know that, to the common apprehension, this phenomenon of whiteness is not confessed to be the prime agent in exaggerating the terror of objects otherwise terrible; nor to the unimaginative mind is there aught of terror in those appearances whose awfulness to another mind almost solely consists in this one phenomenon, especially when exhibited under any form at all approaching to muteness or universality. What I mean by these two statements may perhaps be respectively elucidated by the following examples.

First: The mariner, when drawing nigh the coasts of foreign lands, if by night he hear the roar of breakers, starts to vigilance, and feels just enough of trepidation to sharpen all his faculties; but under precisely similar circumstances, let him be called from his hammock to view his ship sailing through a midnight sea of milky whiteness—as if from encircling headlands shoals of combed white bears were swimming round him, then he feels a silent, superstitious dread; the shrouded phantom of the whitened waters is horrible to him as a real ghost; in vain the lead assures him he is still off soundings; heart and helm they both go down; he never rests till blue water is under him again. Yet where is the mariner who will tell thee, 'Sir, it was not so much the fear of striking hidden rocks, as the fear of that hideous whiteness that so stirred me'?

Second: To the native Indian of Peru, the continual sight of the snow-howdahed Andes conveys naught of dread, except, perhaps, in the mere fancying of the eternal frosted desolateness reigning at such vast altitudes, and the natural conceit of what a fearfulness it would be to lose oneself in such inhuman solitudes. Much the same is it with the backwoodsman of the West, who with comparative indifference views an unbounded prairie sheeted with driven snow, no shadow of tree or twig to break the fixed trance of whiteness. Not so the sailor, beholding the scenery of the Antarctic seas; where at times, by some infernal trick of legerdemain in the powers of frost and air, he, shivering and half shipwrecked, instead of rainbows speaking hope and solace to his misery, views what seems a boundless church-yard grinning upon him with its lean ice monuments and splintered crosses.

But thou sayest, methinks this white-lead chapter about whiteness is but a white flag hung out from a craven soul; thou surrenderest to a hypo, Ishmael.

Tell me, why this strong young colt, foaled in some peaceful valley of Vermont, far removed from all beasts of prey—why is it that upon the sunniest day, if you but shake a fresh buffalo robe behind him, so that he cannot even see it, but only smells its wild animal muskiness—why will he start, snort, and with bursting eyes paw the ground in phrensies of affright? There is no remembrance in him of any gorings of wild creatures in his green northern home, so that the strange muskiness he smells cannot recall to him anything associated with the experience of former perils; for what knows he, this New England colt, of the black bisons of distant Oregon?

No: but here thou beholdest even in a dumb brute, the instinct of the knowledge of the demonism in the world. Though thousands of miles from Oregon, still when he smells that savage musk, the rending, goring bison herds are as present as to the deserted wild foal of the prairies, which this instant they may be trampling into dust.

Thus, then, the muffled rollings of a milky sea; the bleak rustlings of the festooned frosts of mountains; the desolate shiftings of the windrowed snows of prairies; all these, to Ishmael, are as the shaking of that buffalo robe to the frightened colt!

Though neither knows where lie the nameless things of which the mystic sign gives forth such hints; yet with me, as with the colt, somewhere those things must exist. Though in many of its aspects this visible world seems formed in love, the invisible spheres were formed in fright.

But not yet have we solved the incantation of this whiteness, and learned why it appeals with such power to the soul; and more strange and far more portentous—why, as we have seen, it is at once the most meaning symbol of spiritual things, nay, the very veil of the Christian's Deity; and yet should be as it is, the intensifying agent in things the most appalling to mankind.

Is it that by its indefiniteness it shadows forth the heartless voids and immensities of the universe, and thus stabs us from behind with the thought of annihilation, when beholding the white depths of the milky way? Or is it, that as in essence whiteness is not so much a color as the visible absence of color, and at the same time the concrete of all colors; is it for these reasons that there is such a dumb blankness, full of meaning, in a wide landscape of snows—a colorless, all-color of atheism from which we shrink? And when we consider that other theory of the natural philosophers, that all other earthly hues—every stately or lovely emblazoning—the sweet tinges of sunset skies and woods; yea, and the gilded velvets of butterflies, and the butterfly cheeks of young girls; all these are but subtile deceits, not actually inherent in substances, but only laid on from without; so that all deified Nature absolutely paints like the harlot, whose allurements cover nothing but the charnel-house within; and when we proceed further, and consider that the mystical cosmetic which produces every one of her hues, the great principle of light, for ever remains white or colorless in itself, and if operating without medium upon matter, would touch all objects, even tulips and roses, with its own blank tinge—pondering all this, the palsied universe lies before us a leper; and like wilful travellers in Lapland, who refuse to wear colored and coloring glasses upon their eyes, so the wretched infidel gazes himself blind at the monumental white shroud that wraps all the prospect around him. And of all these things the Albino whale was the symbol. Wonder ye then at the fiery hunt?

CHAPTER XLIII

HARK!

'Hist! Did you hear that noise, Cabaco?'

It was the middle-watch: a fair moonlight; the seamen were standing in a cordon, extending from one of the freshwater butts in the waist, to the scuttle-butt near the taffrail. In this manner, they passed the buckets to fill the scuttle-butt. Standing, for the most part, on the hallowed precincts of the quarter-deck, they were careful not to speak or rustle their feet. From hand to hand, the buckets went in the deepest silence, only broken by the occasional flap of a sail, and the steady hum of the unceasingly advancing keel.

It was in the midst of this repose, that Archy, one of the cordon, whose post was near the after-hatches, whispered to his neighbor, a Cholo, the words above.

'Hist! did you hear that noise, Cabaco?'

'Take the bucket, will ye, Archy? what noise d'ye mean?'

'There it is again—under the hatches—don't you hear it—a cough—it sounded like a cough.'

'Cough be damned! Pass along that return bucket.'

'There again—there it is!'—it sounds like two or three sleepers turning over, now!'

'Caramba! have done, shipmate, will ye? It's the three soaked biscuits ye eat for supper turning over inside of ye—nothing else. Look to the bucket!'

'Say what ye will, shipmate; I've sharp ears.'

'Aye, you are the chap, ain't ye, that heard the hum of the old Quakeress's knitting-needles fifty miles at sea from Nantucket; you're the chap.'

'Grin away; we'll see what turns up. Hark ye, Cabaco, there is somebody down in the after-hold that has not yet been seen on deck; and I suspect our old Mogul knows something of it too. I heard Stubb tell Flask, one morning watch, that there was something of that sort in the wind.'

'Tish! the bucket!'

CHAPTER XLIV

THE CHART

Had you followed Captain Ahab down into his cabin after the squall that took place on the night succeeding that wild ratification of his purpose with his crew, you would have seen him go to a locker in the transom, and bringing out a large wrinkled roll of yellowish sea charts, spread them before him on his screwed-down table. Then seating himself before it, you would have seen him intently study the various lines and shadings which there met his eye; and with slow but steady pencil trace additional courses over spaces that before were blank. At intervals, he would refer to piles of old log-books beside him, wherein were set down the seasons and places in which, on various former voyages of various ships, sperm whales had been captured or seen.

While thus employed, the heavy pewter lamp suspended in chains over his head, continually rocked with the motion of the ship, and for ever threw shifting gleams and shadows of lines upon his wrinkled brow, till it almost seemed that while he himself was marking out lines and courses on the wrinkled charts, some invisible pencil was also tracing lines and courses upon the deeply marked chart of his forehead.

But it was not this night in particular that, in the solitude of his cabin, Ahab thus pondered over his charts. Almost every night they were brought out; almost every night some pencil marks were effaced, and others were substituted. For with the charts of all four oceans before him, Ahab was threading a maze of currents and eddies, with a view to the more certain accomplishment of that monomaniac thought of his soul.

Now, to any one not fully acquainted with the ways of the leviathans, it might seem an absurdly hopeless task thus to seek out one solitary creature in the unhooped oceans of this planet. But not so did it seem to Ahab, who knew the sets of all tides and currents; and thereby calculating the driftings of the sperm whale's food; and, also, calling to mind the regular, ascertained seasons for hunting him in particular latitudes; could arrive at reasonable surmises, almost approaching to certainties, concerning the timeliest day to be upon this or that ground in search of his prey.

So assured, indeed, is the fact concerning the periodicalness of the sperm whale's resorting to given waters, that many hunters believe that, could he be closely observed and studied throughout the world; were the logs for one voyage of the entire whale fleet carefully collated, then the migrations of the sperm whale would be found to correspond in invariability to those of the herring-shoals or the flights of swallows. On this hint, attempts have been made to construct elaborate migratory charts of the sperm whale.*

Besides, when making a passage from one feeding-ground to another, the sperm whales, guided by some infallible instinct—say, rather, secret intelligence from the Deity—mostly swim in *veins,* as they are called; containing their way along a given ocean-line with such undeviating exactitude, that no ship ever sailed her course, by any chart, with one tithe of such marvellous precision. Though, in these cases, the direction taken by any one whale be straight as a surveyor's parallel, and though the line of advance be strictly confined to its own unavoidable, straight wake, yet the arbitrary *vein* in which at these times he is said to swim, generally embraces some few miles in width (more or less, as the vein is presumed

---

*Since the above was written, the statement is happily borne out by an official circular, issued by Lieutenant Maury, of the National Observatory, Washington, April 16th, 1851. By that circular, it appears that precisely such a chart is in course of completion; and portions of it are presented in the circular. 'This chart divides the ocean into districts of five degrees of latitude by five degrees of longitude; perpendicularly through each of which districts are twelve columns for the twelve months; and horizontally through each of which districts are three lines; one to show the number of days that have been spent in each month in every district, and the two others to show the number of days in which whales, sperm or right, have been seen.'

to expand or contract); but never exceeds the visual sweep from the whale-ship's mast-heads, when circumspectly gliding along this magic zone. The sum is, that at particular seasons within that breadth and along that path, migrating whales may with great confidence be looked for.

And hence not only at substantiated times, upon well known separate feeding-grounds, could Ahab hope to encounter his prey; but in crossing the widest expanses of water between those grounds he could, by his art, so place and time himself on his way, as even then not to be wholly without prospect of a meeting.

There was a circumstance which at first sight seemed to entangle his delirious but still methodical scheme. But not so in the reality, perhaps. Though the gregarious sperm whales have their regular seasons for particular grounds, yet in general you cannot conclude that the herds which haunted such and such a latitude or longitude this year, say, will turn out to be identically the same with those that were found there the preceding season; though there are peculiar and unquestionable instances where the contrary of this has proved true. In general, the same remark, only within a less wide limit, applies to the solitaries and hermits among the matured, aged sperm whales. So that though Moby Dick had in a former year been seen, for example, on what is called the Seychelle ground in the Indian ocean, or Volcano Bay on the Japanese Coast; yet it did not follow, that were the Pequod to visit either of those spots at any subsequent corresponding season, she would infallibly encounter him there. So, too, with some other feeding grounds, where he had at times revealed himself. But all these seemed only his casual stopping-places and ocean-inns, so to speak, not his places of prolonged abode. And where Ahab's chances of accomplishing his object have hitherto been spoken of, allusion has only been made to whatever way-side, antecedent, extra prospects were his, ere a particular set time or place were attained, when all possibilities would become probabilities, and, as Ahab fondly thought, every possibility the next thing to a certainty. That particular set time and place were conjoined in the one technical phrase—the Season-on-the-Line. For there and then, for several consecutive years, Moby Dick had been periodically descried, lingering in those waters for awhile, as the sun, in its annual round, loiters for a predicted interval in any one sign of the Zodiac. There it was, too, that most of the deadly encounters with the white whale had taken place; there the waves were storied with his deeds; there also was that tragic spot where the monomaniac old man had found the awful motive to his vengeance. But in the cautious comprehensiveness and unloitering vigilance with which Ahab threw his brooding soul into this unfaltering hunt, he would not permit himself to rest all his hopes upon the one crowning fact above mentioned, however flattering it might be to those hopes; nor in the sleeplessness of his vow could he so tranquillize his unquiet heart as to postpone all intervening quest.

Now, the Pequod had sailed from Nantucket at the very beginning of the Season-on-the-Line. No possible endeavor then could enable her commander to make the great passage southwards, double Cape Horn, and then running down sixty degrees of latitude arrive in the equatorial Pacific in time to cruise there. Therefore, he must wait for the next ensuing season. Yet the premature hour of the Pequod's sailing had, perhaps, been correctly selected by Ahab, with a view to this very complexion of things. Because, an interval of three hundred and sixty-five days and nights was before him; an interval which, instead of impatiently enduring ashore, he would spend in a miscellaneous hunt; if by chance the White Whale, spending his vacation in seas far remote from his periodical feeding-grounds, should turn up his wrinkled brow off the Persian Gulf, or in the Bengal Bay, or China Seas, or in any other waters haunted by his race. So that Monsoons, Pampas, Nor-Westers, Harmattans, Trades; any wind but the Levanter and Simoom, might blow Moby Dick into the devious zig-zag world-circle of the Pequod's circumnavigating wake.

But granting all this; yet, regarded discreetly and coolly, seems it not but a mad idea, this; that in the broad boundless ocean, one solitary whale, even if encountered, should be thought capable of individual recognition from his hunter, even as a white-bearded Mufti in the thronged thoroughfares of Constantinople? Yes. For the peculiar snow-white brow of Moby Dick, and his snow-white hump, could not but be unmistakable. And have I not tallied the whale, Ahab would mutter to himself, as after poring over his charts till long after midnight he would throw himself back in reveries—tallied him, and shall he escape? His broad fins are bored, and scalloped out like a lost sheep's ear! And here, his mad mind would run on in a breathless race; till a weariness and faintness of pondering came over him; and in the open air of the deck he would seek to recover his strength. Ah, God! what trances of torments does that man endure who is consumed with one unachieved revengeful desire. He sleeps with clenched hands; and wakes with his own bloody nails in his palms.

Often, when forced from his hammock by exhausting and intolerably vivid dreams of the night, which, resuming his own intense thoughts through the day, carried them on amid a clashing of phrensies, and whirled them round and round in his blazing brain, till the very throbbing of his life-spot became insufferable anguish; and when, as was sometimes the case, these spiritual throes in him heaved his being up from its base, and a chasm seemed opening in him, from which forked flames and lightnings shot up, and accursed fiends beckoned him to leap down among them; when this hell in himself yawned beneath him, a wild cry would be heard through the ship; and with glaring eyes Ahab would burst from his state room, as though escaping from a bed that was on fire. Yet these, perhaps, instead of being the unsuppressable symptoms of some latent weakness, or fright at his own resolve, were but the plainest tokens of its intensity. For, at such times, crazy Ahab, the scheming, unappeasedly steadfast hunter of the white whale; this Ahab that had gone to his hammock, was not the agent that so caused him to burst from it in horror again. The latter was the eternal, living principle or soul in him; and in sleep, being for the time dissociated from the characterizing mind, which at other times employed it for its outer vehicle or agent, it spontaneously sought escape from the scorching contiguity of the frantic thing, of which, for the time, it was no longer an integral. But as the mind does not exist unless leagued with the soul, therefore it must have been that, in Ahab's case, yielding up all his thoughts and fancies to his one supreme purpose; that purpose, by its own sheer inveteracy of will, forced itself against gods and devils into a kind of self-assumed, independent being of its own. Nay, could grimly live and burn, while the common vitality to which it was conjoined, fled horror-stricken from the unbidden and unfathered birth. Therefore, the tormented spirit that glared out of bodily eyes, when what seemed Ahab rushed from his room, was for the time but a vacated thing, a formless somnambulistic being, a ray of living light, to be sure, but without an object to color, and therefore a blankness in itself. God help thee, old man, thy thoughts have created a creature in thee; and he whose intense thinking thus makes him a Prometheus; a vulture feeds upon that heart for ever; that vulture the very creature he creates.

CHAPTER XLV

THE AFFIDAVIT

So far as what there may be of a narrative in this book; and, indeed, as indirectly touching one or two very interesting and curious particulars in the habits of sperm whales, the foregoing chapter, in its earlier part, is as important a one as will be found in this volume; but the leading matter of it requires to be still further and more familiarly enlarged upon, in order to be adequately understood, and moreover to take away any incredulity which a profound ignorance of the entire subject may induce in some minds, as to the natural verity of the main points of this affair.

I care not to perform this part of my task methodically; but shall be content to produce the desired impression by separate citations of items, practically or reliably known to me as a whaleman; and from these citations, I take it—the conclusion aimed at will naturally follow of itself.

First: I have personally known three instances where a whale, after receiving a harpoon, had effected a complete escape; and, after an interval (in one instance of three years), has been again struck by the same hand, and slain; when the two irons, both marked by the same private cypher, have been taken from the body. In the instance where three years intervened between the flinging of the two harpoons; and I think it may have been something more than that; the man who darted them happening, in the interval, to go in a trading ship on a voyage to Africa, went ashore there, joined a discovery party, and penetrated far into the interior, where he travelled for a period of nearly two years, often endangered by serpents, savages, tigers, poisonous miasmas, with all the other common perils incident to wandering in the heart of unknown regions. Meanwhile, the whale he had struck must also have been on its travels; no doubt it had thrice circumnavigated the globe, brushing with its flanks all the coasts of Africa; but to no purpose. This man and this whale again came together, and the one vanquished the other. I say I, myself, have known three instances similar to this; that is in two of them I saw the whales struck; and, upon the second attack, saw the two irons with the respective marks cut in them, afterwards taken from the dead fish. In the three-year instance, it so fell out that I was in the boat both times, first and last, and the last time distinctly recognized a peculiar sort of huge mole under the whale's eye, which I had observed there three years previous. I say three years, but I am pretty sure it was more than that. Here are three instances, then, which I personally know the truth of; but I have heard of many other instances from persons whose veracity in the matter there is no good ground to impeach.

Secondly: It is well known in the Sperm Whale Fishery, however ignorant the world ashore may be of it, that there have been several memorable historical instances where a particular whale in the ocean has been at distant times and places popularly cognisable. Why such a whale became thus marked was not altogether and originally owing to his bodily peculiarities as distinguished from other whales; for however peculiar in that respect any chance whale may be, they soon put an end to his peculiarities by killing him, and boiling him down into a peculiarly valuable oil. No: the reason was this: that from the fatal experiences of the fishery there hung a terrible prestige of perilousness about such a whale as there did about Rinaldo Rinaldini, insomuch that most fishermen were content to recognise by merely touching their tarpaulins when he would be discovered lounging by them on the sea, without seeking to cultivate a more intimate acquaintance. Like some poor devils ashore that happen to know an irascible great man, they make distant unobtrusive salutations to him in the street, lest if they pursued the acquaintance further, they might receive a summary thump for their presumption.

But not only did each of these famous whales enjoy great individual celebrity—nay, you may call it an ocean-wide renown; not only was he famous in life and now is immortal in forecastle stories after death, but he was admitted into all the rights, privileges, and distinctions of a name; had as much a name indeed as Cambyses or Cæsar. Was it not so, O Timor Tom! thou famed leviathan, scarred like an iceberg, who so long did'st lurk in the Oriental straits of that name, whose spout was oft seen from the palmy beach of Ombay? Was it not so, O New Zealand Jack! thou terror of all cruisers that crossed their wakes in the vicinity of the Tattoo Land? Was it not so, O Morquan! King of Japan, whose lofty jet they say at times assumed the semblance of a snow-white cross against the sky? Was it not so, O Don Miguel! thou Chilian whale, marked like an old tortoise with mystic hieroglyphics upon the back! In plain prose, here are four whales as well known to the students of Cetacean History as Marius or Sylla to the classic scholar.

But this is not all. New Zealand Tom and Don Miguel, after at various times creating great havoc among the boats of different vessels, were finally gone in quest of, systematically hunted out, chased and killed by valiant whaling captains, who heaved up their anchors with that express object as much in view, as in setting out through the Narragansett Woods, Captain Butler of old had it in his mind to capture that notorious murderous savage Annawon, the headmost warrior of the Indian King Philip.

I do not know where I can find a better place than just here, to make mention of one or two other things, which to me seem important, as in printed form establishing in all respects the reasonableness of the whole story of the White Whale, more especially the catastrophe. For this is one of those disheartening instances where truth requires full as much bolstering as error. So ignorant are most landsmen of some of the plainest and most palpable wonders of the world, that without some hints touching the plain facts, historical and otherwise, of the fishery, they might scout at Moby Dick as a monstrous fable, or still worse and more detestable, a hideous and intolerable allegory.

First: Though most men have some vague flitting ideas of the general perils of the grand fishery, yet they have nothing like a fixed, vivid conception of those perils, and the frequency with which they recur. One reason perhaps is, that not one in fifty of the actual disasters and deaths by casualties in the fishery, ever finds a public record at home, however transient and immediately forgotten that record. Do you suppose that that poor fellow there, who this moment perhaps caught by the whale-line off the coast of New Guinea, is being carried down to the bottom of the sea by the sounding leviathan—do you suppose that that poor fellow's name will appear in the newspaper obituary you will read to-morrow at your breakfast? No: because the mails are very irregular between here and New Guinea. In fact, did you ever hear what might be called regular news direct or indirect from New Guinea? Yet I tell you that upon one particular voyage which I made to the Pacific, among many others, we spoke thirty different ships, every one of which had had a death by a whale, some of them more than one, and three that had each lost a boat's crew. For God's sake, be economical with your lamps and candles! not a gallon you burn, but at least one drop of man's blood was spilled for it.

Secondly: People ashore have indeed some indefinite idea that a whale is an enormous creature of enormous power; but I have ever found that when narrating to them some specific example of this two-fold enormousness, they have significantly complimented me upon my facetiousness; when, I declare upon my soul, I had no more idea of being facetious than Moses, when he wrote the history of the plagues of Egypt.

But fortunately the special point I here seek can be established upon testimony entirely independent of my own. That point is this: The Sperm Whale is in some cases sufficiently powerful, knowing, and judiciously malicious, as with direct aforethought to stave in, utterly destroy, and sink a large ship; and what is more, the Sperm Whale *has* done it.

First: in the year 1820 the ship Essex, Captain Pollard, of Nantucket, was cruising in the Pacific Ocean. One day she saw spouts, lowered her boats, and gave chase to a shoal of sperm whales. Ere long, several of the whales were wounded; when, suddenly, a very large whale escaping from the boats, issued from the shoal, and bore directly down upon the ship. Dashing his forehead against her hull, he so stove her in, that in less than 'ten minutes' she settled down and fell over. Not a surviving plank of her has been seen since. After the severest exposure, part of the crew reached the land in their boats. Being returned home at last, Captain Pollard once more sailed for the Pacific in command of another ship, but the gods shipwrecked him again upon unknown rocks and breakers; for the second time his ship was utterly lost, and forthwith forswearing the sea, he has never tempted it since. At this day Captain Pollard is a resident of Nantucket. I have seen Owen Chace, who was chief mate of the Essex at the time of the tragedy; I have read his plain and faithful narrative; I have conversed with his son; and all this within a few miles of the scene of the catastrophe.*

Secondly: The ship Union, also of Nantucket, was in the year 1807 totally lost off the Azores by a similar onset, but the authentic particulars of this catastrophe I have never chanced to encounter, though from the whale hunters I have now and then heard casual allusions to it.

Thirdly: Some eighteen or twenty years ago Commodore J—— then commanding an American sloop-of-war of the first class, happened to be dining with a party of whaling captains, on board a Nantucket ship in the harbor of Oahu, Sandwich Islands. Conversation turning upon whales, the Commodore was pleased to be sceptical touching the amazing strength ascribed to them by the professional gentlemen present. He peremptorily denied for example, that any whale could so smite his stout sloop-of-war as to cause her to leak so much as a thimbleful. Very good; but there is more coming. Some weeks after, the Commodore set sail in this impregnable craft for Valparaiso. But he was stopped on the

---

*The following are extracts from Chace's narrative: 'Every fact seemed to warrant me in concluding that it was anything but chance which directed his operations; he made two several attacks upon the ship, at a short interval between them, both of which, according to their direction, were calculated to do us the most injury, by being made ahead, and thereby combining the speed of the two objects for the shock; to effect which, the exact manœuvres which he made were necessary. His aspect was most horrible, and such as indicated resentment and fury. He came directly from the shoal which we had just before entered, and in which we had struck three of his companions, as if fired with revenge for their sufferings.' Again: 'At all events, the whole circumstances taken together, all happening before my own eyes, and producing, at the time, impressions in my mind of decided, calculating mischief, on the part of the whale (many of which impressions I cannot now recall), induce me to be satisfied that I am correct in my opinion.'

Here are his reflections some time after quitting the ship, during a black night in an open boat, when almost despairing of reaching any hospitable shore. 'The dark ocean and swelling waters were nothing; the fears of being swallowed up by some dreadful tempest, or dashed upon hidden rocks, with all the other ordinary subjects of fearful contemplation, seemed scarcely entitled to a moment's thought; the dismal looking wreck, and *the horrid aspect and revenge of the whale,* wholly engrossed my reflections, until day again made its appearance.'

In another place—p. 45,—he speaks of *'the mysterious and mortal attack of the animal.'*

way by a portly sperm whale, that begged a few moments' confidential business with him. That business consisted in fetching the Commodore's craft such a thwack, that with all his pumps going he made straight for the nearest port to heave down and repair. I am not superstitious, but I consider the Commodore's interview with that whale as providential. Was not Saul of Tarsus converted from unbelief by a similar fright? I tell you, the sperm whale will stand no nonsense.

I will now refer you to Langsdorff's Voyages for a little circumstance in point, peculiarly interesting to the writer hereof. Langsdorff, you must know by the way, was attached to the Russian Admiral Krusenstern's famous Discovery Expedition in the beginning of the present century. Captain Langsdorff thus begins his seventeenth chapter.

'By the thirteenth of May our ship was ready to sail, and the next day we were out in the open sea, on our way to Ochotsh. The weather was very clear and fine, but so intolerably cold that we were obliged to keep on our fur clothing. For some days we had very little wind; it was not till the nineteenth that a brisk gale from the northwest sprang up. An uncommon large whale, the body of which was larger than the ship itself, lay almost at the surface of the water, but was not perceived by any one on board till the moment when the ship, which was in full sail, was almost upon him, so that it was impossible to prevent its striking against him. We were thus placed in the most imminent danger, as this gigantic creature, setting up its back, raised the ship three feet at least out of the water. The masts reeled, and the sails fell altogether, while we who were below all sprang instantly upon the deck, concluding that we had struck upon some rock; instead of this we saw the monster sailing off with the utmost gravity and solemnity. Captain D'Wolf applied immediately to the pumps to examine whether or not the vessel had received any damage from the shock, but we found that very happily it had escaped entirely uninjured.'

Now, the Captain D'Wolf here alluded to as commanding the ship in question, is a New Englander, who, after a long life of unusual adventures as a sea-captain, this day resides in the village of Dorchester near Boston. I have the honor of being a nephew of his. I have particularly questioned him concerning this passage in Langsdorff. He substantiates every word. The ship, however, was by no means a large one: a Russian craft built on the Siberian coast, and purchased by my uncle after bartering away the vessel in which he sailed from home.

In that up and down manly book of old-fashioned adventure, so full, too, of honest wonders—the voyage of Lionel Wafer, one of ancient Dampier's old chums—I found a little matter set down so like that just quoted from Langsdorff, that I cannot forbear inserting it here for a corroborative example, if such be needed.

Lionel, it seems, was on his way to 'John Ferdinando,' as he calls the modern Juan Fernandes. 'In our way thither,' he says, 'about four o'clock in the morning, when we were about one hundred and fifty leagues from the Main of America, our ship felt a terrible shock, which put our men in such consternation that they could hardly tell where they were or what to think; but every one began to prepare for death. And, indeed, the shock was so sudden and violent, that we took it for granted the ship had struck against a rock; but when the amazement was a little over, we cast the lead, and sounded, but found no ground. * * * * The suddenness of the shock made the guns leap in their carriages, and several of the men were shaken out of their hammocks. Captain Davis, who lay with his head over a gun, was thrown out of his cabin!' Lionel then goes on to impute the shock to an earthquake, and seems to substantiate the imputation by stating that a great earthquake, somewhere about that time, did actually do great mischief along the Spanish land. But I should not much wonder if, in the darkness of that early hour of the morning, the shock was after all caused by an unseen whale vertically bumping the hull from beneath.

I might proceed with several more examples, one way or another known to me, of the great power and malice at times of the sperm whale. In more than one instance, he has been known, not only to chase the assailing boats back to their ships, but to pursue the ship itself, and long withstand all the lances hurled at him from its decks. The English ship Pusie Hall can tell a story on that head; and, as for his strength, let me say, that there have been examples where the lines attached to a running sperm whale have, in a calm, been transferred to the ship, and secured there; the whale towing her great hull through the water, as a horse walks off with a cart. Again, it is very often observed that, if the sperm whale, once struck, is allowed time to rally, he then acts, not so often with blind rage, as with wilful, deliberate designs of destruction to his pursuers; nor is it without conveying some eloquent indication of his character, that upon being attacked he will frequently open his mouth, and retain it in that dread expansion for several consecutive minutes. But I must be content with only one more and a concluding illustration; a remarkable and most significant one, by which you will not fail to see, that not only is the most marvellous event in this book corroborated by plain facts of the present day, but that these marvels (like all marvels) are mere repetitions of the ages; so that for the millionth time we say amen with Solomon—Verily there is nothing new under the sun.

In the sixth Christian century lived Procopius, a Christian magistrate of Constantinople, in the days when Justinian was Emperor and Belisarius general. As many know, he wrote the history of his own times, a work every way of uncommon value. By the best authorities, he has always been considered a most trustworthy and unexaggerating historian, except in some one or two particulars, not at all affecting the matter presently to be mentioned.

Now, in this history of his, Procopius mentions that, during the term of his prefecture at Constantinople, a great sea-monster was captured in the neighboring Propontis, or Sea of Marmora, after having destroyed vessels at intervals in those waters for a period of more than fifty years. A fact thus set down in substantial history cannot easily be gainsaid. Nor is there any reason it should be. Of what precise species this sea-monster was, is not mentioned. But as he destroyed ships, as well as for other reasons, he must have been a whale; and I am strongly inclined to think a sperm whale. And I will tell you why. For a long time I fancied that the sperm whale had been always unknown in the Mediterranean and the deep waters connecting with it. Even now I am certain that those seas are not, and perhaps never can be, in the present constitution of things, a place for his habitual gregarious resort. But further investigations have recently proved to me, that in modern times there have been isolated instances of the presence of the sperm whale in the Mediterranean. I am told, on good authority, that on the Barbary coast, a Commodore Davis of the British navy found the skeleton of a sperm whale. Now, as a vessel of war readily passes through the Dardanelles, hence a sperm whale could, by the same route, pass out of the Mediterranean into the Propontis.

In the Propontis, as far as I can learn, none of that peculiar substance called *brit* is to be found, the aliment of the right whale. But I have every reason to believe that the food of the sperm whale—squid or cuttle-fish—lurks at the bottom of that sea, because large creatures, but by no means the largest of that sort, have been found at its surface. If, then, you properly put these statements together, and reason upon them a bit, you will clearly perceive that, according to all human reasoning, Procopius's sea-monster, that for half a century stove the ships of a Roman Emperor, must in all probability have been a sperm whale.

CHAPTER XLVI

SURMISES

Though, consumed with the hot fire of his purpose, Ahab in all his thoughts and actions ever had in view the ultimate capture of Moby Dick; though he seemed ready to sacrifice all mortal interests to that one passion; nevertheless it may have been that he was by nature and long habituation far too wedded to a fiery whaleman's way, altogether to abandon the collateral prosecution of the voyage. Or at least if this were otherwise, there were not wanting other motives much more influential with him. It would be refining too much, perhaps, even considering his monomania, to hint that his vindictiveness towards the White Whale might have possibly extended itself in some degree to all sperm whales, and that the more monsters he slew by so much the more he multiplied the chances that each subsequently encountered whale would prove to be the hated one he hunted. But if such an hypothesis be indeed exceptionable, there were still additional considerations which, though not so strictly according with the wildness of his ruling passion, yet were by no means incapable of swaying him.

To accomplish his object Ahab must use tools; and of all tools used in the shadow of the moon, men are most apt to get out of order. He knew, for example, that however magnetic his ascendency in some respects was over Starbuck, yet that ascendency did not cover the complete spiritual man any more than mere corporeal superiority involves intellectual mastership; for to the purely spiritual, the intellectual but stands in a sort of corporeal relation. Starbuck's body and Starbuck's coerced will were Ahab's, so long as Ahab kept his magnet at Starbuck's brain; still he knew that for all this the chief mate, in his soul, abhorred his captain's quest, and could he, would joyfully disintegrate himself from it, or even frustrate it. It might be that a long interval would elapse ere the White Whale was seen. During that long interval Starbuck would ever be apt to fall into open relapses of rebellion against his captain's leadership, unless some ordinary, prudential, circumstantial influences were brought to bear upon him. Not only that, but the subtle insanity of Ahab respecting Moby Dick was noways more significantly manifested than in his superlative sense and shrewdness in foreseeing that, for the present, the hunt should in some way be stripped of that strange imaginative impiousness which naturally invested it; that the full terror of the voyage must be kept withdrawn into the obscure background (for few men's courage is proof against protracted meditation unrelieved by action); that when they stood their long night watches, his officers and men must have some nearer things to think of than Moby Dick. For however eagerly and impetuously the savage crew had hailed the announcement of his quest; yet all sailors of all sorts are more or less capricious and unreliable—they live in the varying outer weather, and they inhale its fickleness—and when retained for any object remote and blank in the pursuit, however promissory of life and passion in the end, it is above all things requisite that temporary interests and employments should intervene and hold them healthily suspended for the final dash.

Nor was Ahab unmindful of another thing. In times of strong emotion mankind disdain all base considerations; but such times are evanescent. The permanent constitutional condition of the manufactured man, thought Ahab, is sordidness. Granting that the White Whale fully incites the hearts of this my savage crew, and playing round their savageness even breeds a certain generous knight-errantism in them, still, while for the love of it they give chase to Moby Dick, they must also have food for their more common, daily appetites. For even the high lifted and chivalric Crusaders of old times were not content to traverse two thousand miles of land to fight for their holy sepulchre, without committing burglaries, picking pockets, and gaining other pious perquisites by the way. Had they been strictly held to their one final and romantic object—that final and romantic object, too many would have turned from in disgust. I will not strip these men, thought Ahab, of all hopes of cash—aye, cash. They may scorn cash now; but let some months go by, and no perspective promise of it to them, and then this same quiescent cash all at once mutinying in them, this same cash would soon cashier Ahab.

Nor was there wanting still another precautionary motive more related to Ahab personally. Having impulsively, it is probable, and perhaps somewhat prematurely revealed the prime but private purpose of the Pequod's voyage, Ahab was now entirely conscious that, in so doing, he had indirectly laid himself open to the unanswerable charge of usurpation; and with perfect impunity, both moral and legal, his crew if so disposed, and to that end competent, could refuse all further obedience to him, and even violently wrest from him the command. From even the barely hinted imputation of usurpation, and the possible consequences of such a suppressed impression gaining ground, Ahab must of course have been most anxious to protect himself. That protection could only consist in his own predominating brain and heart and hand, backed by a heedful, closely calculating attention to every minute atmospheric influence which it was possible for his crew to be subjected to.

For all these reasons then, and others perhaps too analytic to be verbally developed here, Ahab plainly saw that he must still in a good degree continue true to the natural, nominal purpose of the Pequod's voyage; observe all customary usages; and not only that, but force himself to evince all his well known passionate interest in the general pursuit of his profession.

Be all this as it may, his voice was now often heard hailing the three mast-heads and admonishing them to keep a bright look-out, and not omit reporting even a porpoise. This vigilance was not long without reward.

CHAPTER XLVII

THE MAT-MAKER

It was a cloudy, sultry afternoon; the seamen were lazily lounging about the decks, or vacantly gazing over into the lead-colored water. Queequeg and I were mildly employed weaving what is called a sword-mat, for an additional lashing to our boat. So still and subdued and yet somehow preluding was all the scene, and such an incantation of revery lurked in the air, that each silent sailor seemed resolved into his own invisible self.

I was the attendant or page of Queequeg, while busy at the mat. As I kept passing and repassing the filling or woof of marline between the long yarns of the warp, using my own hand for the shuttle, and as Queequeg, standing sideways, ever and anon slid his heavy oaken sword between the threads, and idly looking off upon the water, carelessly and unthinkingly drove home every yarn: I say so strange a dreaminess did there then reign all over the ship and all over the sea, only broken by the intermitting dull sound of the sword, that it seemed as if this were the Loom of Time, and I myself were a shuttle mechanically weaving and weaving away at the Fates. There lay the fixed threads of the warp subject to but one single, ever returning, unchanging vibration, and that vibration merely enough to admit of the crosswise interblending of other threads with its own. This warp seemed necessity; and here, thought I, with my own hand I ply my own shuttle and weave my own destiny into these unalterable threads. Meantime, Queequeg's impulsive, indifferent sword, sometimes hitting the woof slantingly, or crookedly, or strongly, or weakly, as the case might be; and by this difference in the concluding blow producing a corresponding contrast in the final aspect of the completed fabric; this savage's sword, thought I, which thus finally shapes and fashions both warp and woof; this easy, indifferent sword must be chance—aye, chance, free will, and necessity—no wise incompatible—all interweavingly working together. The straight warp of necessity, not to be swerved from its ultimate course—its every alternating vibration, indeed, only tending to that; free will still free to ply her shuttle between given threads; and chance, though restrained in its play within the right lines of necessity, and sideways in its motions directed by free will, though thus prescribed to by both, chance by turns rules either, and has the last featuring blow at events.

* * * * * * *

Thus we were weaving and weaving away when I started at a sound so strange, long drawn, and musically wild and unearthly, that the ball of free will dropped from my hand, and I stood gazing up at the clouds whence that voice dropped like a wing. High aloft in the cross-trees was that mad Gay-Header, Tashtego. His body was reaching eagerly forward, his hand stretched out like a wand, and at brief sudden intervals he continued his cries. To be sure the same sound was that very moment perhaps being heard all over the seas, from hundreds of whalemen's look-outs perched as high in the air; but from few of those lungs could that accustomed old cry have derived such a marvellous cadence as from Tashtego the Indian's.

As he stood hovering over you half suspended in air, so wildly and eagerly peering towards the horizon, you would have thought him some prophet or seer beholding the shadows of Fate, and by those wild cries announcing their coming.

'There she blows! there! there! there! she blows! she blows!'

'Where-away?'

'On the lee-beam, about two miles off! a school of them!'

Instantly all was commotion.

The Sperm Whale blows as a clock ticks, with the same undeviating and reliable uniformity. And thereby whalemen distinguish this fish from other tribes of his genus.

'There go flukes!' was now the cry from Tashtego; and the whales disappeared.

'Quick, steward!' cried Ahab. 'Time! time!'

Dough-Boy hurried below, glanced at the watch, and reported the exact minute to Ahab.

The ship was now kept away from the wind, and she went gently rolling before it. Tashtego reporting that the whales had gone down heading to leeward, we confidently looked to see them again directly in advance of our bows. For that singular craft at times evinced by the Sperm Whale when, sounding with his head in one direction, he nevertheless, while concealed beneath the surface, mills round, and swiftly swims off in the opposite quarter—this deceitfulness of his could not now be in action; for there was no reason to suppose that the fish seen by Tashtego had been in any way alarmed, or indeed knew at all of our vicinity. One of the men selected for shipkeepers—that is, those not appointed to the boats, by this time relieved the Indian at the main-mast head. The sailors at the fore and mizzen had come down; the line tubs were fixed in their places; the cranes were thrust out; the mainyard was backed, and the three boats swung over the sea like three samphire baskets over high cliffs. Outside of the bulwarks their eager crews with one hand clung to the rail, while one foot was expectantly poised on the gunwale. So look the long line of man-of-war's men about to throw themselves on board an enemy's ship.

But at this critical instant a sudden exclamation was heard that took every eye from the whale. With a start all glared at dark Ahab, who was surrounded by five dusky phantoms that seemed fresh formed out of air.

CHAPTER XLVIII

THE FIRST LOWERING

The phantoms, for so they then seemed, were flitting on the other side of the deck, and, with a noiseless celerity, were casting loose the tackles and bands of the boat which swung there. This boat had always been deemed one of the spare boats, though technically called the captain's, on account of its hanging from the starboard quarter. The figure that now stood by its bows was tall and swart, with one white tooth evilly protruding from its steel-like lips. A rumpled Chinese jacket of black cotton funereally invested him, with wide black trowsers of the same dark stuff. But strangely crowning this ebonness was a glistening white plaited turban, the living hair braided and coiled round and round upon his head. Less swart in aspect, the companions of this figure were of that vivid, tiger-yellow complexion peculiar to some of the aboriginal natives of the Manillas;—a race notorious for a certain diabolism of subtilty, and by some honest white mariners supposed to be the paid spies and secret confidential agents on the water of the devil, their lord, whose counting-room they suppose to be elsewhere.

While yet the wondering ship's company were gazing upon these strangers, Ahab cried out to the white-turbaned old man at their head, 'All ready there, Fedallah?'

'Ready,' was the half-hissed reply.

'Lower away then; d'ye hear?' shouting across the deck. 'Lower away there, I say.'

Such was the thunder of his voice, that spite of their amazement the men sprang over the rail; the sheaves whirled round in the blocks; with a wallow, the three boats dropped into the sea; while, with a dexterous, off-handed daring, unknown in any other vocation, the sailors, goat-like, leaped down the rolling ship's side into the tossed boats below.

Hardly had they pulled out from under the ship's lee, when a fourth keel, coming from the windward wide, pulled round under the stern, and showed the five strangers rowing Ahab, who, standing erect in the stern, loudly hailed Starbuck, Stubb, and Flask, to spread themselves widely, so as to cover a large expanse of water. But with all their eyes again riveted upon the swart Fedallah and his crew, the inmates of the other boats obeyed not the command.

'Captain Ahab?—' said Starbuck.

'Spread yourselves,' cried Ahab; 'give way, all four boats. Thou, Flask, pull out more to leeward!'

'Aye, aye, sir,' cheerily cried little King-Post, sweeping round his great steering oar. 'Lay back!' addressing his crew. 'There!—there!—there again! There she blows right ahead, boys!—lay back!—Never heed yonder yellow boys, Archy.'

'Oh, I don't mind 'em, sir,' said Archy; 'I knew it all before now. Didn't I hear 'em in the hold? And didn't I tell Cabaco here of it? What say ye, Cabaco? They are stowaways, Mr Flask.'

'Pull, pull, my fine hearts-alive; pull, my children; pull, my little ones,' drawlingly and soothingly sighed Stubb to his crew, some of whom still showed signs of uneasiness. 'Why don't you break your backbones, my boys? What is it you stare at? Those chaps in yonder boat? Tut! They are only five more hands come to help us—never mind from where—the more the merrier. Pull, then, do pull; never mind the brimstone—devils are good fellows enough. So, so; there you are now; that's the stroke for a thousand pounds; that's the stroke to sweep the stakes! Hurrah for the gold cup of sperm oil, my heroes! Three cheers, men—all hearts alive! Easy, easy; don't be in a hurry—don't be in a hurry. Why don't you snap your oars, you rascals? Bite something, you dogs! So, so, so, then;—softly, softly! That's it—that's it! long and strong. Give way there, give way! The devil fetch ye, ye ragamuffin rapscallions; ye are all asleep. Stop snoring, ye sleepers, and pull. Pull, will ye? pull, can't ye? pull, won't ye? Why in the name of gudgeons and ginger-cakes don't ye pull?—pull and break something! pull, and start your eyes out! Here!' whipping out the sharp knife from his girdle; 'every mother's son of ye draw his knife, and pull with the blade between his teeth. That's it—that's it. Now ye do something; that looks like it, my steel-bits. Start her—start her, my silver-spoons! Start her, marling-spikes!'

Stubb's exordium to his crew is given here at large, because he had rather a peculiar way of talking to them in general, and especially in inculcating the religion of rowing. But you must not suppose from this specimen of his sermonizings that he ever flew into downright passions with his congregation. Not at all; and therein consisted his chief peculiarity. He would say the most terrific things to his crew, in a tone so strangely compounded of fun and fury, and the fury seemed so calculated merely as a spice to the fun, that no oarsman could hear such queer invocations without pulling for dear life, and yet pulling for the mere joke of the thing. Besides he all the time looked so easy and indolent himself, so loungingly managed his steering-oar, and so broadly gaped—open-mouthed at times—that the mere sight of such a yawning commander, by sheer force of contrast, acted like a charm upon the crew. Then again, Stubb was one of those odd sort of humorists, whose jollity is sometimes so curiously ambiguous, as to put all inferiors on their guard in the matter of obeying them.

In obedience to a sign from Ahab, Starbuck was now pulling obliquely across Stubb's bow; and when for a minute or so the two boats were pretty near to each other, Stubb hailed the mate.

'Mr Starbuck! larboard boat there, ahoy! a word with ye, sir, if ye please!'

'Halloa!' returned Starbuck, turning round not a single inch as he spoke; still earnestly but whisperingly urging his crew; his face set like a flint from Stubb's.

'What think ye of those yellow boys, sir!'

'Smuggled on board, somehow, before the ship sailed. (Strong, strong, boys!)' in a whisper to his crew, then speaking out loud again: 'A sad business, Mr Stubb! (seethe her, seethe her, my lads!) but never mind, Mr Stubb, all for the best. Let all your crew pull strong, come what will. (Spring, my men, spring!) There's hogsheads of sperm ahead, Mr Stubb, and that's what ye came for. (Pull, my boys!) Sperm, sperm's the play! This at least is duty; duty and profit hand in hand!'

'Aye, aye, I thought as much,' soliloquized Stubb, when the boats diverged, 'as soon as I clapt eye on 'em, I thought so. Aye, and that's what he went into the after hold for, so often, as Dough-Boy long suspected. They were hidden down there. The White Whale's at the bottom of it. Well, well, so be it! Can't be helped! All right! Give way, men! It ain't the White Whale to-day! Give way!'

Now the advent of these outlandish strangers at such a critical instant as the lowering of the boats from the deck, this had not unreasonably awakened a sort of superstitious amazement in some of the ship's company; but Archy's fancied discovery having some time previous got abroad among them, though indeed not credited then, this had in some small measure prepared them for the event. It took off the extreme edge of their wonder; and so what with all this and Stubb's confident way of accounting for their appearance, they were for the time freed from superstitious surmisings; though the affair still left abundant room for all manner of wild conjectures as to dark Ahab's precise agency in the matter from the beginning. For me, I silently recalled the mysterious shadows I had seen creeping on board the Pequod during the dim Nantucket dawn, as well as the enigmatical hintings of the unaccountable Elijah.

Meantime, Ahab, out of hearing of his officers, having sided the furthest to windward, was still ranging ahead of the other boats; a circumstance bespeaking how potent a crew was pulling him. Those tiger yellow creatures of his seemed all steel and whalebone; like five trip-hammers they rose and fell with regular strokes of strength, which periodically started the boat along the water like a horizontal burst boiler out of a Mississippi steamer. As for Fedallah, who was seen pulling the harpooneer oar, he had thrown aside his black jacket, and displayed his naked chest with the whole part of his body above the gunwale, clearly cut against the alternating depressions of the watery horizon; while at the other end of the boat Ahab, with one arm, like a fencer's, thrown half backward into the air, as if to counterbalance any tendency to trip; Ahab was seen steadily managing his steering oar as in a thousand boat lowerings ere the White Whale had torn him. All at once the out-stretched arm gave a peculiar motion and then remained fixed, while the boat's five oars were seen simultaneously peaked. Boat and crew sat motionless on the sea. Instantly the three spread boats in the rear paused on their way. The whales had irregularly settled bodily down into the blue, thus giving no distantly discernible token of the movement, though from his closer vicinity Ahab had observed it.

'Every man look out along his oar!' cried Starbuck. 'Thou, Queequeg, stand up!'

Nimbly springing up on the triangular raised box in the bow, the savage stood erect there, and with intensely eager eyes gazed off towards the spot where the chase had last been descried. Likewise upon the extreme stern of the boat where it was also triangularly platformed level with the gunwale. Starbuck himself was seen coolly and adroitly balancing himself to the jerking tossings of his chip of a craft, and silently eyeing the vast blue eye of the sea.

Not very far distant Flask's boat was also lying breathlessly still; its commander recklessly standing upon the top of the loggerhead, a stout sort of post rooted in the keel, and rising some two feet above the level of the stern platform. It is used for catching turns with the whale line. Its top is not more spacious than the palm of a man's hand, and standing upon such a base as that, Flask seemed perched at the masthead of some ship which had sunk to all but her trucks. But little King-Post was small and short, and at the same time little King-Post was full of a large and tall ambition, so that this loggerhead stand-point of his did by no means satisfy King-Post.

'I can't see three seas off; tip us up an oar there, and let me on to that.'

Upon this, Daggoo, with either hand upon the gunwale to steady his way, swiftly slid aft, and then erecting himself volunteered his lofty shoulders for a pedestal.

'Good a mast-head as any, sir. Will you mount?'

'That I will, and thank ye very much, my fine fellow; only I wish you fifty feet taller.'

Whereupon planting his feet firmly against two opposite planks of the boat, the gigantic negro, stooping a little, presented his flat palm to Flask's foot, and then putting Flask's hand on his hearse-plumed head and bidding him spring as he himself should toss, with one dexterous fling landed the little man high and dry on his shoulders. And here was Flask now standing, Daggoo with one lifted arm furnishing him with a breast-band to lean against and steady himself by.

At any time it is a strange sight to the tyro to see with what wondrous habitude of unconscious skill the whaleman will maintain an erect posture in his boat, even when pitched about by the most riotously perverse and cross-running seas. Still more strange to see him giddily perched upon the loggerhead itself, under such circumstances. But the sight of little Flask mounted upon gigantic Daggoo was yet more curious; for sustaining himself with a cool, indifferent, easy, unthought of, barbaric majesty, the noble negro to every roll of the sea harmoniously rolled his fine form. On his broad back, flaxen-haired Flask seemed a snow-flake. The bearer looked nobler than the rider. Though, truly, vivacious, tumultuous, ostentatious little Flask would now and then stamp with impatience; but not one added heave did he thereby give to the negro's lordly chest. So have I seen Passion and Vanity stamping the living magnanimous earth, but the earth did not alter her tides and her seasons for that.

Meanwhile Stubb, the second mate, betrayed no such far-gazing solicitudes. The whales might have made one of their regular soundings, not a temporary dive from mere fright; and if that were the case, Stubb, as his wont in such cases, it seems, was resolved to solace the languishing interval with his pipe. He withdrew it from his hatband, where he always wore it aslant like a feather. He loaded it, and rammed home the loading with his thumb-end; but hardly had he ignited his match across the rough sand-paper of his hand, when Tashtego, his harpooneer, whose eyes had been setting to windward like two fixed stars, suddenly dropped like light from his erect attitude to his seat, crying out in a quick phrensy of hurry, 'Down, down all, and give way!—there they are!'

To a landsman, no whale, nor any sign of a herring, would have been visible at that moment; nothing but a troubled bit of greenish white water, and thin scattered puffs of vapor hovering over it, and suffusingly blowing off to leeward, like the confused scud from white rolling billows. The air around suddenly vibrated and tingled, as it were, like the air over intensely heated plates of iron. Beneath this atmospheric waving and curling, and partially beneath a thin layer of water, also, the whales were swimming. Seen in advance of all the other indications, the puffs of vapor they spouted, seemed their forerunning couriers and detached flying outriders.

All four boats were now in keen pursuit of that one spot of troubled water and air. But it bade fair to outstrip them; it flew on and on, as a mass of interblending bubbles borne down a rapid stream from the hills.

'Pull, pull, my good boys,' said Starbuck, in the lowest possible but intensest concentrated whisper to his men; while the sharp fixed glance from his eyes, darted straight ahead of the bow, almost seemed as two visible needles in two unerring binnacle compasses. He did not say much to his crew, though, nor did his crew say anything to him. Only the silence of the boat was at intervals startlingly pierced by one of his peculiar whispers, now harsh with command, now soft with entreaty.

How different the loud little King-Post. 'Sing out and say something, my hearties. Roar and pull, my thunderbolts! Beach me, beach me on their black backs, boys; only do that for me, and I'll sign over to you my Martha's Vineyard plantation, boys; including wife and children, boys. Lay me on—lay me on! O Lord, Lord! but I shall go stark, staring mad: See! see that white water!' And so shouting, he pulled his hat from his head, and stamped up and down on it; then picking it up, flirted it far off upon the sea; and finally fell to rearing and plunging in the boat's stern like a crazed colt from the prairie.

'Look at that chap now,' philosophically drawled Stubb, who, with his unlighted short pipe, mechanically retained between his teeth, at a short distance, followed after—'He's got fits, that Flask has. Fits? yes, give him fits—that's the very word—pitch fits into 'em. Merrily, merrily, hearts-alive. Pudding for supper, you know;—merry's the word. Pull, babes—pull, sucklings—pull, all. But what the devil are you hurrying about? Softly, softly, and steadily, my men. Only pull, and keep pulling; nothing more. Crack all your backbones, and bite your knives in two—that's all. Take it easy—why don't ye take it easy, I say, and burst all your livers and lungs!'

But what it was that inscrutable Ahab said to that tiger-yellow crew of his—these were words best omitted here; for you live under the blessed light of the evangelical land. Only the infidel sharks in the audacious seas may give ear to such words, when, with tornado brow, and eyes of red murder, and foam-glued lips, Ahab leaped after his prey.

Meanwhile, all the boats tore on. The repeated specific allusions of Flask to 'that whale,' as he called the fictitious monster which he declared to be incessantly tantalizing his boat's bow with its tail—these allusions of his were at times so vivid and life-like, that they would cause some one or two of his men to snatch a fearful look over the shoulder. But this was against all rule; for the oarsmen must put out their eyes, and ram a skewer through their necks; usage pronouncing that they must have no organs but ears, and no limbs but arms, in these critical moments.

It was a sight full of quick wonder and awe! The vast swells of the omnipotent sea; the surging, hollow roar they made, as they rolled along the eight gunwales, like gigantic bowls in a boundless bowling-green; the brief suspended agony of the boat, as it would tip for an instant on the knife-like edge of the sharper waves, that almost seemed threatening to cut it in two; the sudden profound dip into the watery glens and hollows; the keen spurrings and goadings to gain the top of the opposite hill; the headlong, sled-like slide down its other side;—all these, with the cries of the headsmen and harpooneers, and the shuddering gasps of the oarsmen, with the wondrous sight of the ivory Pequod bearing down upon her boats with outstretched sails, like a wild hen after her screaming brood;—all this was thrilling. Not the raw recruit, marching from the bosom of his wife into the fever heat of his first battle; not the dead man's ghost encountering the first unknown phantom in the other world;—neither of these can feel stranger and stronger emotions than that man does, who for the first time finds himself pulling into the charmed, churned circle of the hunted sperm whale.

The dancing white water made by the chase was now becoming more and more visible, owing to the increasing darkness of the dun cloud-shadows flung upon the sea. The jets of vapor no longer blended, but tilted everywhere to right and left; the whales seemed separating their wakes. The boats were pulled more apart; Starbuck giving chase to three whales running dead to leeward. Our sail was now set, and, with the still rising wind, we rushed along; the boat going with such madness through the water, that the lee oars could scarcely be worked rapidly enough to escape being torn from the row-locks.

Soon we were running through a suffusing wide veil of mist; neither ship nor boat to be seen.

'Give way, men,' whispered Starbuck, drawing still further aft the sheet of his sail; 'there is time to kill a fish yet before the squall comes. There's white water again!—close to! Spring!'

Soon after, two cries in quick succession on each side of us denoted that the other boats had got fast; but hardly were they overheard, when with a lightning-like hurtling whisper Starbuck said: 'Stand up!' and Queequeg, harpoon in hand, sprang to his feet.

Though not one of the oarsmen was then facing the life and death peril so close to them ahead, yet with their eyes on the intense countenance of the mate in the stern of the boat, they knew that the imminent instant had come; they heard, too, an enormous wallowing sound as of fifty elephants stirring in their litter. Meanwhile the boat was still booming through the mist, the waves curling and hissing around us like the erected crests of enraged serpents.

'That's his hump. *There, there*, give it to him!' whispered Starbuck.

A short rushing sound leaped out of the boat; it was the darted iron of Queequeg. Then all in one welded commotion came an invisible push from astern, while forward the boat seemed striking on a ledge; the sail collapsed and exploded; a gush of scalding vapor shot up near by; something rolled and tumbled like an earthquake beneath us. The whole crew were half suffocated as they were tossed helter-skelter into the white curdling cream of the squall. Squall, whale, and harpoon had all blended together; and the whale, merely grazed by the iron, escaped.

Though completely swamped, the boat was nearly unharmed. Swimming round it we picked up the floating oars, and lashing them across the gunwale, tumbled back to our places. There we sat up to our knees in the sea, the water covering every rib and plank, so that to our downward gazing eyes the suspended craft seemed a coral boat grown up to us from the bottom of the ocean.

The wind increased to a howl; the waves dashed their bucklers together; the whole squall roared, forked, and crackled around us like a white fire upon the prairie, in which, unconsumed, we were burning; immortal in these jaws of death! In vain we hailed the other boats; as well roar to the live coals down the chimney of a flaming furnace as hail those boats in that storm. Meanwhile the driving scud, rack, and mist, grew darker with the shadows of night; no sign of the ship could be seen. The rising sea forbade all attempts to bale out the boat. The oars were useless as propellers, performing now the office of life-preservers. So, cutting the lashing of the waterproof match keg, after many failures Starbuck contrived to ignite the lamp in the lantern; then stretching it on a waif pole, handed it to Queequeg as the standard-bearer of this forlorn hope. There, then, he sat, holding up that imbecile candle in the heart of that almighty forlornness. There, then, he sat, the sign and symbol of a man without faith, hopelessly holding up hope in the midst of despair.

Wet, drenched through, and shivering cold, despairing of ship or boat, we lifted up our eyes as the dawn came on. The mist still spread over the sea, the empty lantern lay crushed in the bottom of the boat. Suddenly Queequeg started to his feet, hollowing his hand to his ear. We all heard a faint creaking, as of ropes and yards hitherto muffled by the storm. The sound came nearer and nearer; the thick mists were dimly parted by a huge, vague form. Affrighted, we all sprang into the sea as the ship at last loomed into view, bearing right down upon us within a distance of not much more than its length.

Floating on the waves we saw the abandoned boat, as for one instant it tossed and gaped beneath the ship's bows like a chip at the base of a cataract; and then the vast hull rolled over it, and it was seen no more till it came up weltering astern. Again we swam for it, were dashed against it by the seas, and were at last taken up and safely landed on board. Ere the squall came close to, the other boats had cut loose from their fish and returned to the ship in good time. The ship had given us up, but was still cruising, if haply it might light upon some token of our perishing,—an oar or a lance pole.

CHAPTER XLIX

THE HYENA

There are certain queer times and occasions in this strange mixed affair we call life when a man takes this whole universe for a vast practical joke, though the wit thereof he but dimly discerns, and more than suspects that the joke is at nobody's expense but his own. However, nothing dispirits, and nothing seems worth while disputing. He bolts down all events, all creeds, and beliefs, and persuasions, all hard things visible and invisible, never mind how knobby; as an ostrich of potent digestion gobbles down bullets and gun flints. And as for small difficulties and worryings, prospects of sudden disaster, peril of life and limb; all these, and death itself, seem to him only sly, good-natured hits, and jolly punches in the side bestowed by the unseen and unaccountable old joker. That odd sort of wayward mood I am speaking of, comes over a man only in some time of extreme tribulation; it comes in the very midst of his earnestness, so that what just before might have seemed to him a thing most momentous, now seems but a part of the general joke. There is nothing like the perils of whaling to breed this free and easy sort of genial, desperado philosophy; and with it I now regarded this whole voyage of the Pequod, and the great White Whale its object.

'Queequeg,' said I, when they had dragged me, the last man, to the deck, and I was still shaking myself in my jacket to fling off the water; 'Queequeg, my fine friend, does this sort of thing often happen?' Without much emotion, though soaked through just like me, he gave me to understand that such things did often happen.

'Mr Stubb,' said I, turning to that worthy, who, buttoned up in his oil-jacket, was now calmly smoking his pipe in the rain; 'Mr Stubb, I think I have heard you say that of all whalemen you ever met, our chief mate, Mr Starbuck, is by far the most careful and prudent. I suppose then, that going plump on a flying whale with your sail set in a foggy squall is the height of a whaleman's discretion?'

'Certain. I've lowered for whales from a leaking ship in a gale off Cape Horn.'

'Mr Flask,' said I, turning to little King-Post, who was standing close by; 'you are experienced in these things, and I am not. Will you tell me whether it is an unalterable law in this fishery, Mr Flask, for an oarsman to break his own back pulling himself back-foremost into death's jaws?'

'Can't you twist that smaller?' said Flask. 'Yes, that's the law. I should like to see a boat's crew backing water up to a whale face foremost. Ha, ha! the whale would give them squint for squint, mind that!'

Here then, from three impartial witnesses, I had a deliberate statement of the entire case. Considering, therefore, that squalls and capsizings in the water and consequent bivouacks on the deep, were matters of common occurrence in this kind of life; considering that at the superlatively critical instant of going on to the whale I must resign my life into the hands of him who steered the boat—oftentimes a fellow who at that very moment is in his impetuousness upon the point of scuttling the craft with his own frantic stampings; considering that the particular disaster to our own particular boat was chiefly to be imputed to Starbuck's driving on to his whale almost in the teeth of a squall, and considering that Starbuck, notwithstanding, was famous for his great heedfulness in the fishery; considering that I belonged to this uncommonly prudent Starbuck's boat; and finally considering in what a devil's chase I was implicated, touching the White Whale: taking all things together, I say, I thought I might as well go below and make a rough draft of my will. 'Queequeg,' said I, 'come along, you shall be my lawyer, executor, and legatee.'

It may seem strange that of all men sailors should be tinkering at their last wills and testaments, but there are no people in the world more fond of that diversion. This was the fourth time in my nautical life that I had done the same thing. After the ceremony was concluded upon the present occasion, I felt all the easier; a stone was rolled away from my heart. Besides, all the days I should now live would be as good as the days that Lazarus lived after his resurrection; a supplementary clean gain of so many months or weeks as the case might be. I survived myself; my death and burial were locked up in my chest. I looked round me tranquilly and contentedly, like a quiet ghost with a clean conscience sitting inside the bars of a snug family vault.

Now then, thought I, unconsciously rolling up the sleeves of my frock, here goes for a cool, collected dive at death and destruction, and the devil fetch the hindmost.

CHAPTER L

AHAB'S BOAT AND CREW. FEDALLAH

'Who would have thought it, Flask!' cried Stubb; 'if I had but one leg you would not catch me in a boat, unless maybe to stop the plug-hole with my timber toe. Oh! he's a wonderful old man!'

'I don't think it so strange, after all, on that account,' said Flask. 'If his leg were off at the hip, now, it would be a different thing. That would disable him; but he has one knee, and good part of the other left, you know.'

'I don't know that, my little man; I never yet saw him kneel.'

* * * * * * *

Among whale-wise people it has often been argued whether, considering the paramount importance of his life to the success of the voyage, it is right for a whaling captain to jeopardize that life in the active perils of the chase. So Tamerlane's soldiers often argued with tears in their eyes, whether that invaluable life of his ought to be carried into the thickest of the fight.

But with Ahab the question assumed a modified aspect. Considering that with two legs man is but a hobbling wight in all times of danger; considering that the pursuit of whales is always under great and extraordinary difficulties; that every individual moment, indeed, then comprises a peril; under these circumstances is it wise for any maimed man to enter a whale-boat in the hunt? As a general thing, the joint-owners of the Pequod must have plainly thought not.

Ahab well knew that although his friends at home would think little of his entering a boat in certain comparatively harmless vicissitudes of the chase, for the sake of being near the scene of action and giving his orders in person, yet for Captain Ahab to have a boat actually apportioned to him as a regular headsman in the hunt—above all for Captain Ahab to be supplied with five extra men, as that same boat's crew, he well knew that such generous conceits never entered the heads of the owners of the Pequod. Therefore he had not solicited a boat's crew from them, nor had he in any way hinted his desires on that head. Nevertheless he had taken private measures of his own touching all that matter. Until Archy's published discovery, the sailors had little foreseen it, though to be sure when, after being a little while out of port, all hands had concluded the customary business of fitting the whaleboats for service; when some time after this Ahab was now and then found bestirring himself in the matter of making thole-pins with his own hands for what was thought to be one of the spare boats, and even solicitously cutting the small wooden skewers, which when the line is running out are pinned over the groove in the bow: when all this was observed in him, and particularly his solicitude in having an extra coat of sheathing in the bottom of the boat, as if to make it better withstand the pointed pressure of his ivory limb; and also the anxiety he evinced in exactly shaping the thigh board, or clumsy cleat, as it is sometimes called, the horizontal piece in the boat's bow for bracing the knee against in darting or stabbing at the whale; when it was observed how often he stood up in that boat with his solitary knee fixed in the semi-circular depression in the cleat, and with the carpenter's chisel gouged out a little here and straightened it a little there; all these things, I say, had awakened much interest and curiosity at the time. But almost everybody supposed that this particular preparative heedfulness in Ahab must only be with a view to the ultimate chase of Moby Dick; for he had already revealed his intention to hunt that mortal monster in person. But such a supposition did by no means involve the remotest suspicion as to any boat's crew being assigned to that boat.

Now, with the subordinate phantoms, what wonder remained soon waned away; for in a whaler wonders soon wane. Besides, now and then such unaccountable odds and ends of strange nations come up from the unknown nooks and ash-holes of the earth to man these floating outlaws of whalers; and the ships themselves often pick up such queer castaway creatures found tossing about the open sea on planks, bits of wreck, oars, whaleboats, canoes, blown-off Japanese junks, and what not; that Beelzebub himself might climb up the side and step down into the cabin to chat with the captain, and it would not create any unsubduable excitement in the forecastle.

But be all this as it may, certain it is that while the subordinate phantoms soon found their place among the crew, though still as it were somehow distinct from them, yet that hair-turbaned Fedallah remained a muffled mystery to the last. Whence he came in a mannerly world like this, by what sort of unaccountable tie he soon evinced himself to be linked with Ahab's peculiar fortunes; nay, so far as to have some sort of a half-hinted influence; Heaven knows, but it might have been even authority over him; all this none knew. But one cannot sustain an indifferent air concerning Fedallah. He was such a creature as civilized, domestic people in the temperate zone only see in their dreams, and that but dimly; but the like of whom now and then glide among the unchanging Asiatic communities, especially the Oriental isles to the east of the continent—those insulated, immemorial, unalterable countries, which even in these modern days still preserve much of the ghostly aboriginalness of earth's primal generations, when the memory of the first man was a distinct recollection, and all men his descendants, unknowing whence he came, eyed each other as real phantoms, and asked of the sun and the moon why they were created and to what end; when though, according to Genesis, the angels indeed consorted with the daughters of men, the devils also, add the uncanonical Rabbins, indulged in mundane amours.

CHAPTER LI

The Spirit-Spout

Days, weeks passed, and under easy sail, the ivory Pequod had slowly swept across four several cruising-grounds; that off the Azores; off the Cape de Verdes; on the Plate (so called), being off the mouth of the Rio de la Plata; and the Carrol Ground, an unstaked, watery locality, southerly from St Helena.

It was while gliding through these latter waters that one serene and moonlight night, when all the waves rolled by like scrolls of silver; and, by their soft, suffusing seethings, made what seemed a silvery silence, not a solitude: on such a silent night a silvery jet was seen far in advance of the white bubbles at the bow. Lit up by the moon, it looked celestial; seemed some plumed and glittering god uprising from the sea. Fedallah first descried this jet. For of these moonlight nights, it was his wont to mount to the main-mast head, and stand a look-out there, with the same precision as if it had been day. And yet, though herds of whales were seen by night, not one whaleman in a hundred would venture a lowering for them. You may think with what emotions, then, the seamen beheld this old Oriental perched aloft at such unusual hours; his turban and the moon, companions in one sky. But when, after spending his uniform interval there for several successive nights without uttering a single sound; when, after all this silence, his unearthly voice was heard announcing that silvery, moon-lit jet, every reclining mariner started to his feet as if some winged spirit had lighted in the rigging, and hailed the mortal crew. 'There she blows!' Had the trump of judgment blown, they could not have quivered more; yet still they felt no terror; rather pleasure. For though it was a most unwonted hour, yet so impressive was the cry, and so deliriously exciting, that almost every soul on board instinctively desired a lowering.

Walking the deck with quick, side-lunging strides, Ahab commanded the t'gallant sails and royals to be set, and every stunsail spread. The best man in the ship must take the helm. Then, with every mast-head manned, the piled-up craft rolled down before the wind. The strange, upheaving, lifting tendency of the taffrail breeze filling the hollows of so many sails, made the buoyant, hovering deck to feel like air beneath the feet; while still she rushed along, as if two antagonistic influences were struggling in her—one to mount direct to heaven, the other to drive yawingly to some horizontal goal. And had you watched Ahab's face that night, you would have thought that in him also two different things were warring. While his one live leg made lively echoes along the deck, every stroke of his dead limb sounded like a coffin-tap. On life and death this old man walked. But though the ship so swiftly sped, and though from every eye, like arrows, the eager glances shot, yet the silvery jet was no more seen that night. Every sailor swore he saw it once, but not a second time.

This midnight-spout had almost grown a forgotten thing, when, some days after, lo! at the same silent hour, it was again announced: again it was descried by all; but upon making sail to overtake it, once more it disappeared as if it had never been. And so it served us night after night, till no one heeded it but to wonder at it. Mysteriously jetted into the clear moonlight, or starlight, as the case might be; disappearing again for one whole day, or two days, or three; and somehow seeming at every distinct repetition to be advancing still further and further in our van, this solitary jet seemed for ever alluring us on.

Nor with the immemorial superstition of their race, and in accordance with the preternaturalness, as it seemed, which in many things invested the Pequod, were there wanting some of the seamen who swore that whenever and wherever descried; at however remote times, or in however far apart latitudes and longitudes, that unnearable spout was cast by one self-same whale; and that whale, Moby Dick. For a time, there reigned, too, a sense of peculiar dread at this flitting apparition, as if it were treacherously beckoning us on and on, in order that the monster might turn round upon us, and rend us at last in the remotest and most savage seas.

These temporary apprehensions, so vague but so awful, derived a wondrous potency from the contrasting serenity of the weather, in which, beneath all its blue blandness, some thought there lurked a devilish charm, as for days and days we voyaged along, through seas so wearily, lonesomely mild, that all space, in repugnance to our vengeful errand, seemed vacating itself of life before our urn-like prow.

But, at last, when turning to the eastward, the Cape winds began howling around us, and we rose and fell upon the long, troubled seas that are there; when the ivory-tusked Pequod sharply bowed to the blast, and gored the dark waves in her madness, till, like showers of silver chips, the foam-flakes flew over her bulwarks; then all this desolate vacuity of life went away, but gave place to sights more dismal than before.

Close to our bows, strange forms in the water darted hither and thither before us; while thick in our rear flew the inscrutable sea-ravens. And every morning, perched on our stays, rows of these birds were seen; and spite of our hootings, for a long time obstinately clung to the hemp, as though they deemed our ship some drifting, uninhabited craft; a thing appointed to desolation, and therefore fit roosting-place for their homeless selves. And heaved and heaved, still unrestingly heaved the black sea, as if its vast tides were a conscience; and the great mundane soul were in anguish and remorse for the long sin and suffering it had bred.

Cape of Good Hope, do they call ye? Rather Cape Tormentoso, as called of yore; for long allured by the perfidious silences that before had attended us, we found ourselves launched into this tormented sea, where guilty beings transformed into those fowls and these fish, seemed condemned to swim on everlastingly without any haven in store, or beat that black air without any horizon. But calm, snow-white, and unvarying; still directing its fountain of feathers to the sky; still beckoning us on from before, the solitary jet would at times be descried.

During all this blackness of the elements, Ahab, though assuming for the time the almost continual command of the drenched and dangerous deck, manifested the gloomiest reserve; and more seldom than ever addressed his mates. In tempestuous times like these, after everything above and aloft has been secured, nothing more can be done but passively to wait the issue of the gale. Then Captain and crew become practical fatalists. So, with his ivory leg inserted into its accustomed hole, and with one hand firmly grasping a shroud, Ahab for hours and hours would stand gazing dead to windward, while an occasional squall of sleet or snow would all but congeal his very eyelashes together. Meantime, the crew driven from the forward part of the ship by the perilous seas that burstingly broke over its bows, stood in a line along the bulwarks in the waist; and the better to guard against the leaping waves, each man had slipped himself into a sort of bowline secured to the rail, in which he swung as in a loosened belt. Few or no words were spoken; and the silent ship, as if manned by painted sailors in wax, day after day tore on through all the swift madness and gladness of the demoniac waves. By night the same muteness of humanity before the shrieks of the ocean prevailed; still in silence the men swung in the bowlines; still wordless Ahab stood up to the blast. Even when wearied nature seemed demanding repose he would not seek that repose in his hammock. Never could Starbuck forget the old man's aspect, when one night going down into the cabin to mark how the barometer stood, he saw him with closed eyes sitting straight in his floor-screwed chair; the rain and half-melted sleet of the storm from which he had some time before emerged, still slowly dripping from the unremoved hat and coat. On the table beside him lay unrolled one of those charts of tides and currents which have previously been spoken of. His lantern swung from his tightly clenched hand. Though the body was erect, the head was thrown back so that the closed eyes were pointed towards the needle of the tell-tale that swung from a beam in the ceiling.*

Terrible old man! thought Starbuck with a shudder, sleeping in this gale, still thou steadfastly eyest thy purpose.

CHAPTER LII

THE ALBATROSS

South-eastward from the Cape, off the distant Crozetts, a good cruising ground for Right Whalemen, a sail loomed ahead, the Goney (Albatross) by name. As she slowly drew nigh, from my lofty perch at the fore-mast-head, I had a good view of that sight so remarkable to a tyro in the far ocean fisheries—a whaler at sea, and long absent from home.

As if the waves had been fullers, this craft was bleached like the skeleton of a stranded walrus. All down her sides, this spectral appearance was traced with long channels of reddened rust, while all her spars and her rigging were like the thick branches of trees furred over with hoar-frost. Only her lower sails were set. A wild sight it was to see her long-bearded look-outs at those three mast-heads. They seemed clad in the skin of beasts, so torn and bepatched the raiment that had survived nearly four years of cruising. Standing in iron hoops nailed to the mast, they swayed and swung over a fathomless sea; and though, when the ship slowly glided close under our stern, we six men in the air came so nigh to each other that we might almost have leaped from the mast-heads of one ship to those of the other; yet, those forlorn-looking fishermen, mildly eyeing us as they passed, said not one word to our own look-outs, while the quarter-deck hail was being heard from below.

'Ship ahoy! Have ye seen the White Whale?'

But as the strange captain, leaning over the pallid bulwarks, was in the act of putting his trumpet to his mouth, it somehow fell from his hand into the sea; and the wind now rising amain, he in vain strove to make himself heard without it. Meantime his ship was still increasing the distance between. While in various silent ways the seamen of the Pequod were evincing their observance of this ominous incident at the first mere mention of the White Whale's name to another ship, Ahab for a moment paused; it almost seemed as though he would have lowered a boat to board the stranger, had not the threatening wind forbade. But taking advantage of his windward position, he again seized his trumpet, and knowing by her aspect that the stranger vessel was a Nantucketer and shortly bound home, he loudly hailed—'Ahoy there! This is the Pequod, bound round the world! Tell them to address all future letters to the Pacific ocean! and this time three years, if I am not at home, tell them to address them to—'

At that moment the two wakes were fairly crossed, and instantly, then, in accordance with their singular ways, shoals of small harmless fish, that for some days before had been placidly swimming by our side, darted away with what seemed shuddering fins, and ranged themselves fore and aft with the stranger's flanks. Though in the course of his continual voyagings Ahab must often before

---

*The cabin-compass is called the tell-tale, because without going to the compass at the helm, the Captain, while below, can inform himself of the course of the ship.

have noticed a similar sight, yet, to any monomaniac man, the veriest trifles capriciously carry meanings.

'Swim away from me, do ye?' murmured Ahab, gazing over into the water. There seemed but little in the words, but the tone conveyed more of deep helpless sadness than the insane old man had ever before evinced. But turning to the steersman, who thus far had been holding the ship in the wind to diminish her headway, he cried out in his old lion voice,—'Up helm! Keep her off round the world!'

Round the world! There is much in that sound to inspire proud feelings; but whereto does all that circumnavigation conduct? Only through numberless perils to the very point whence we started, where those that we left behind secure, were all the time before us.

Were this world an endless plain, and by sailing eastward we could for ever reach new distances, and discover sights more sweet and strange than any Cyclades or Islands of King Solomon, then there were promise in the voyage. But in pursuit of those far mysteries we dream of, or in tormented chase of that demon phantom that, some time or other, swims before all human hearts; while chasing such over this round globe, they either lead us on in barren mazes or midway leave us whelmed.

CHAPTER LIII

The Gam

The ostensible reason why Ahab did not go on aboard of the whaler we had spoken was this: the wind and sea betokened storms. But even had this not been the case, he would not after all, perhaps, have boarded her—judging by his subsequent conduct on similar occasions—if so it had been that, by the process of hailing, he had obtained a negative answer to the question he put. For, as it eventually turned out, he cared not to consort, even for five minutes, with any stranger captain, except he could contribute some of that information he so absorbingly sought. But all this might remain inadequately estimated, were not something said here of the peculiar usages of whaling-vessels when meeting each other in foreign seas, and especially on a common cruising-ground.

If two strangers crossing the Pine Barrens in New York State, or the equally desolate Salisbury Plain in England; if casually encountering each other in such inhospitable wilds, these twain, for the life of them, cannot well avoid a mutual salutation; and stopping for a moment to interchange the news; and, perhaps, sitting down for a while and resting in concert: then, how much more natural that upon the illimitable Pine Barrens and Salisbury Plains of the sea, two whaling vessels descrying each other at the ends of the earth—off lone Fanning's Island, or the far away King's Mills; how much more natural, I say, that under such circumstances these ships should not only interchange hails, but come into still closer, more friendly and sociable contact. And especially would this seem to be a matter of course, in the case of vessels owned in one seaport, and whose captains, officers, and not a few of the men are personally known to each other: and consequently, have all sorts of dear domestic things to talk about.

For the long absent ship, the outward-bounder, perhaps, has letters on board; at any rate, she will be sure to let her have some papers of a date a year or two later than the last one on her blurred and thumb-worn files. And in return for that courtesy, the outward-bound ship would receive the latest whaling intelligence from the cruising-ground to which she may be destined, a thing of the utmost importance to her. And in degree, all this will hold true concerning whaling vessels crossing each other's track on the cruising-ground itself, even though they are equally long absent from home. For one of them may have received a transfer of letters from some third, and now far remote vessel; and some of those letters may be for the people of the ship she now meets. Besides, they would exchange the whaling news, and have an agreeable chat. For not only would they meet with all the sympathies of sailors, but likewise with all the peculiar congenialities arising from a common pursuit and mutually shared privations and perils.

Nor would difference of country make any very essential difference; that is, so long as both parties speak one language, as is the case with Americans and English. Though, to be sure, from the small number of English whalers, such meetings do not very often occur, and when they do occur there is too apt to be a sort of shyness between them; for your Englishman is rather reserved, and your Yankee, he does not fancy that sort of thing in anybody but himself. Besides, the English whalers sometimes affect a kind of metropolitan superiority over the American whalers; regarding the long, lean Nantucketer, with his nondescript provincialisms, as a sort of sea-peasant. But where this superiority in the English whalemen does really consist, it would be hard to say, seeing that the Yankees in one day, collectively, kill more whales than all the English, collectively, in ten years. But this is a harmless little foible in the English whale-hunters, which the Nantucketer does not take much to heart; probably, because he knows that he has a few foibles himself.

So, then, we see that of all ships separately sailing the sea, the whalers have most reason to be sociable—and they are so. Whereas, some merchant ships crossing each other's wake in the mid-Atlantic, will oftentimes pass on without so much as a single word of recognition, mutually cutting each other on the high seas, like a brace of dandies in Broadway; and all the time indulging, perhaps, in finical criticism upon each other's rig. As for Men-of-War, when they chance to meet at sea, they first go through such a string of silly bowings and scrapings, such a ducking of ensigns, that there does not seem to be much right-down hearty good-will and brotherly love about it at all. As touching Slave-ships meeting, why, they are in such a prodigious hurry, they run away from each other as soon as possible. And as for Pirates, when they chance to cross each other's cross-bones, the first hail is—'How many skulls?'—the same way that whalers hail—'How many barrels?' And that question once answered, pirates straightway steer apart, for they are infernal villains on both sides, and don't like to see overmuch of each other's villainous likenesses.

But look at the godly, honest, unostentatious, hospitable, sociable, free-and-easy whaler! What does the whaler do when she meets another whaler in any sort of decent weather? She has a *'Gam,'* a thing so utterly unknown to all other ships that they never heard of the name even; and if by chance they should hear of it, they only grin at it, and repeat gamesome stuff about 'spouters' and 'blubber-boilers,' and such like pretty exclamations. Why it is that all Merchant-seamen, and also all Pirates and Man-of-War's men, and Slave-ship sailors, cherish such a scornful feeling towards Whale-ships; this is a question it would be hard to answer. Because, in the case of pirates, say, I should like to know whether that profession of theirs has any peculiar glory about it. It sometimes ends in uncommon elevation, indeed; but only at the gallows. And besides, when a man is elevated in that odd fashion, he has no proper foundation for his superior altitude. Hence, I conclude, that in boasting himself to be high lifted above a whaleman, in that assertion the pirate has no solid basis to stand on.

But what is a *Gam*? You might wear out your index-finger running up and down the columns of dictionaries, and never find the word. Dr Johnson never attained to that erudition; Noah Webster's ark does not hold it. Nevertheless, this same expressive word has now for many years been in constant use among some fifteen thousand true born Yankees. Certainly , it needs a definition, and should be incorporated into the Lexicon. With that view, let me learnedly define it.

GAM. NOUN—*A social meeting of two (or more) Whale-ships, generally on a cruising-ground; when, after exchanging hails, they exchange visits by boats' crews: the two captains remaining, for the time, on board of one ship, and the two chief mates on the other.*

There is another little item about Gamming which must not be forgotten here. All professions have their own little peculiarities of detail; so has the whale fishery. In a pirate, man-of-war, or slave ship, when the captain is rowed anywhere in his boat, he always sits in the stern sheets on a comfortable, sometimes cushioned seat there, and often steers himself with a pretty little milliner's tiller decorated with gay cords and ribbons. But the whale-boat has no seat astern, no sofa of that sort whatever, and no tiller at all. High times indeed, if whaling captains were wheeled about the water on castors like gouty old aldermen in patent chairs. And as for a tiller, the whale-boat never admits of any such effeminacy; and therefore as in gamming a complete boat's crew must leave the ship, and hence as the boat steerer or harpooneer is of the number, that subordinate is the steersman upon the occasion, and the captain, having no place to sit in, is pulled off to his visit all standing like a pine tree. And often you will notice that being conscious of the eyes of the whole visible world resting on him from the sides of the two ships, this standing captain is all alive to the importance of sustaining his dignity by maintaining his legs. Nor is this any very easy matter; for in his rear is the immense projecting steering oar hitting him now and then in the small of his back, the after-oar reciprocating by rapping his knees in front. He is thus completely wedged before and behind, and can only expand himself sideways by settling down on his stretched legs; but a sudden, violent pitch of the boat will often go far to topple him, because length of foundation is nothing without corresponding breadth. Merely make a spread angle of two poles, and you cannot stand them up. Then, again, it would never do in plain sight of the world's riveted eyes, it would never do, I say, for this straddling captain to be seen steadying himself the slightest particle by catching hold of anything with his hands; indeed, as token of his entire, buoyant self-command, he generally carries his hands in his trowsers' pockets; but perhaps being generally very large, heavy hands, he carries them there for ballast. Nevertheless there have occurred instances, well authenticated ones too, where the captain has been known for an uncommonly critical moment or two, in a sudden squall say—to seize hold of the nearest oarsman's hair, and hold on there like grim death.

CHAPTER LIV

THE TOWN-HO'S STORY

(*As told at the Golden Inn*)

The Cape of Good Hope, and all the watery region round about there, is much like some noted four corners of a great highway, where you meet more travellers than in any other part.

It was not very long after speaking the Goney that another homeward-bound whaleman, the Town-Ho,* was encountered. She was manned almost wholly by Polynesians. In the short gam that ensued she gave us strong news of Moby Dick. To some the general interest in the White Whale was now wildly heightened by a circumstance of the Town-Ho's story, which seemed obscurely to involve with the whale a certain wondrous, inverted visitation of one of those so called judgments of God which at times are said to overtake some men. This latter circumstance, with its own particular accompaniments, forming what may be called the secret part of the tragedy about to be narrated, never reached the ears of Captain Ahab or his mates. For that secret part of the story was unknown to the captain of the Town-Ho himself. It was the private property of three confederate white seamen of that ship, one of whom, it seems, communicated it to Tashtego with Romish injunctions of secresy, but the following night Tashtego rambled in his sleep, and revealed so much of it in that way, that when he was awakened he could not well withhold the rest. Nevertheless, so potent an influence did this thing have on those seamen in the Pequod who came to the full knowledge of it, and by such a strange delicacy, to call it so, were they governed in this matter, that they kept the secret among themselves so that it never transpired abaft the Pequod's main-mast. Interweaving in its proper place this darker thread with the story as publicly narrated on the ship, the whole of this strange affair I now proceed to put on lasting record.

For my humor's sake, I shall preserve the style in which I once narrated it at Lima, to a lounging circle of my Spanish friends, one saint's eve, smoking upon the thick-gilt tiled piazza of the Golden Inn. Of those fine cavaliers, the young Dons, Pedro and Sebastian, were on the closer terms with me; and hence the interluding questions they occasionally put, and which are duly answered at the time.

'Some two years prior to my first learning the events which I am about rehearsing to you, gentlemen, the Town-Ho, Sperm Whaler of Nantucket, was cruising in your Pacific here, not very many days' sail westward from the eaves of this good Golden Inn. She was somewhere to the northward of the Line. One morning upon handling the pumps, according to daily usage, it was observed that she made more water in her hold than common. They supposed a sword-fish had stabbed her, gentlemen. But the captain, having some unusual reason for believing that rare good luck awaited him in those latitudes; and therefore being very adverse to quit them, and the leak not being then considered at all dangerous, though, indeed, they could not find it after searching the hold as low down as was possible in rather heavy weather, the ship still continued her cruisings, the mariners working at the pumps at wide and easy intervals; but no good luck came; more days went by, and not only was the leak yet undiscovered, but it sensibly increased. So much so, that now taking some alarm, the captain, making all sail, stood away for the nearest harbor among the islands, there to have his hull hove out and repaired.

'Though no small passage was before her, yet, if the commonest chance favored, he did not at all fear that his ship would founder by the way, because his pumps were of the best, and being periodically relieved at them, those six-and-thirty men of his could easily keep the ship free; never mind if the leak should double on her. In truth, well nigh the whole of this passage being attended by very prosperous breezes the Town-Ho had all but certainly arrived in perfect safety at her port without the occurrence of the least fatality, had it not been for the brutal

---

*The ancient whale-cry upon first sighting a whale from the mast-head, still used by whalemen in hunting the famous Gallipagos terrapin.

overbearing of Radney, the mate, a Vineyarder, and the bitterly provoked vengeance of Steelkilt, a Lakeman and desperado from Buffalo.'

'Lakeman!—Buffalo! Pray, what is a Lakeman, and where is Buffalo?' said Don Sebastian, rising in his swinging mat of grass.

'On the eastern shore of our Lake Erie, Don; but—I crave your courtesy—may be, you shall soon hear further of all that. Now, gentlemen, in square-sail brigs and three-masted ship, well nigh as large and stout as any that ever sailed out of your old Callao to far Manilla; this Lakeman, in the land-locked heart of our America, had yet been nurtured by all those agrarian freebooting impressions popularly connected with the open ocean. For in their interflowing aggregate, those grand fresh-water seas of ours,—Erie, and Ontario, and Huron, and Superior, and Michigan,—possess an ocean-like expansiveness, with many of the ocean's noblest traits; with many of its rimmed varieties of races and of climes. They contain round archipelagoes of romantic isles, even as the Polynesian waters do; in large part, are shored by two great contrasting nations, as the Atlantic is; they furnish long maritime approaches to our numerous territorial colonies from the East, dotted all round their banks; here and there are frowned upon by batteries, and by the goat-like craggy guns of lofty Mackinaw; they have heard the fleet thunderings of naval victories; at intervals, they yield their beaches to wild barbarians, whose red painted faces flash from out their peltry wigwams; for leagues and leagues are flanked by ancient and unentered forests, where the gaunt pines stand like serried lines of kings in Gothic genealogies; those same woods harboring wild Afric beasts of prey, and silken creatures whose exported furs give robes to Tartar Emperors; they mirror the paved capitals of Buffalo and Cleveland, as well as Winnebago villages; they float alike the full-rigged merchant ship, the armed cruiser of the State, the steamer, and the beech canoe; they are swept by Borean and dismasting blasts as direful as any that lash the salted wave; they know what shipwrecks are, for out of sight of land, however inland, they have drowned full many a midnight ship with all its shrieking crew.

'Thus, gentlemen, though an inlander, Steelkilt was wild-ocean born, and wild-ocean nurtured; as much of an audacious mariner as any. And for Radney, though in his infancy he may have laid him down on the lone Nantucket beach, to nurse at his maternal sea; though in after life he had long followed our austere Atlantic and your contemplative Pacific; yet was he quite as vengeful and full of social quarrel as the backwoods seamen, fresh from the latitudes of buckhorn handled Bowie-knives. Yet was this Nantucketer a man with some good-hearted traits; and this Lakeman, a mariner, who though a sort of devil indeed, might yet by inflexible firmness, only tempered by that common decency of human recognition which is the meanest slave's right; thus treated, this Steelkilt had long been retained harmless and docile. At all events, he had proved so thus far; but Radney was doomed and made mad, and Steelkilt—but, gentlemen, you shall hear.

'It was not more than a day or two at the furthest after pointing her prow for her island haven, that the Town-Ho's leak seemed again increasing, but only so as to require an hour or more at the pumps every day. You must know that in a settled and civilized ocean like our Atlantic, for example, some skippers think little of pumping their whole way across it; though of a still, sleepy night, should the officer of the deck happen to forget his duty in that respect, the probability would be that he and his shipmates would never again remember it, on account of all hands gently subsiding to the bottom. Nor in the solitary and savage seas far from you to the westward, gentlemen, is it altogether unusual for ships to keep clanging at their pump-handles in full chorus even for a voyage of considerable length; that is, if it lie along a tolerably accessible coast, or if any other reasonable retreat is afforded them. It is only when a leaky vessel is in some very out of the way part of those waters, some really landless latitude, that her captain begins to feel a little anxious.

'Much this way had it been with the Town-Ho; so when her leak was found gaining once more, there was in truth some small concern manifested by several of her company; especially by Radney the mate. He commanded the upper sails to be well hoisted, sheeted home anew, and every way expanded to the breeze. Now this Radney, I suppose, was as little of a coward, and as little inclined to any sort of nervous apprehensiveness touching his own person as any fearless, unthinking creature on land or on sea that you can conveniently imagine, gentlemen. Therefore when he betrayed this solicitude about the safety of the ship, some of the seamen declared that it was only on account of his being a part owner in her. So when they were working that evening at the pumps, there was on this head no small gamesomeness slily going on among them, as they stood with their feet continually overflowed by the rippling clear water; clear as any mountain spring, gentlemen—that bubbling from the pumps ran across the deck, and poured itself out in steady spouts at the lee scupper-holes.

'Now, as you well know, it is not seldom the case in this conventional world of ours—watery or otherwise; that when a person placed in command over his fellow-men finds one of them to be very significantly his superior in general pride of manhood, straightway against that man he conceives an unconquerable dislike and bitterness; and if he have a chance he will pull down and pulverise that subaltern's tower, and make a little heap of dust of it. Be this conceit of mine as it may, gentlemen, at all events Steelkilt was a tall and noble animal with a head like a Roman, and a flowing golden beard like the tasseled housings of your last viceroy's snorting charger; and a brain, and a heart, and a soul in him, gentlemen, which had made Steelkilt Charlemagne, had he been born son to Charlemagne's father. But Radney, the mate, was ugly as a mule; yet as hardy, as stubborn, as malicious. He did not love Steelkilt, and Steelkilt knew it.

'Espying the mate drawing near as he was toiling at the pump with the rest, the Lakeman affected not to notice him, but unawed, went on with his gay banterings.

'"Aye, aye, my merry lads, it's a lively leak this; hold a cannikin, one of ye, and let's have a taste. By the Lord, it's worth bottling! I tell ye what, men, old Rad's investment must go for it! he had best cut away his part of the hull and tow it home. The fact is, boys, that sword-fish only began the job; he's come back again with a gang of ship-carpenters, saw-fish, and file-fish, and what not; and the whole posse of 'em are now hard at work cutting and slashing at the bottom; making improvements, I suppose. If old Rad were here now, I'd tell him to jump overboard and scatter 'em. They're playing the devil with his estate, I can tell him. But he's a simple old soul,—Rad, and a beauty too. Boys, they say the rest of his property is invested in looking-glasses. I wonder if he'd give a poor devil like me the model of his nose."

'"Damn your eyes! what's that pump stopping for?" roared Radney, pretending not to have heard the sailor's talk. "Thunder away at it!"

'"Aye, aye, sir," said Steelkilt, merry as a cricket. "Lively, boys, lively, now!" And with that the pump clanged like fifty fire-engines; the men tossed their hats off to it, and ere long that peculiar gasping of the lungs was heard which denotes the fullest tension of life's utmost energies.

'Quitting the pump at last, with the rest of his band, the Lakeman went forward all panting, and sat himself down on the windlass; his face fiery red, his eyes bloodshot, and wiping the profuse sweat from his brow. Now what cozening fiend it was, gentlemen, that possessed Radney to meddle with such a man in that corporeally exasperated state, I know not; but so it happened. Intolerably striding along the deck, the mate commanded him to get a broom and sweep down the planks, and also a shovel, and remove some offensive matters consequent upon allowing a pig to run at large.

'Now, gentlemen, sweeping a ship's deck at sea is a piece of household work which in all times but raging gales is regularly attended to every evening; it has been known to be done in the case of ships actually foundering at the time. Such, gentlemen, is the inflexibility of sea-usages and the instinctive love of neatness in seamen; some of whom would not willingly drown without first washing their faces. But in all vessels this broom business is the prescriptive province of the boys, if boys there be aboard. Besides, it was the stronger men in the Town-Ho that had been divided into gangs, taking turns at the pumps; and being the most athletic seaman of them all, Steelkilt had been regularly assigned captain of one of the gangs; consequently he should have been freed from any trivial business not connected with truly nautical duties, such being the case with his comrades. I mention all these particulars so that you may understand exactly how this affair stood between the two men.

'But there was more than this: the order about the shovel was almost as plainly meant to sting and insult Steelkilt, as though Radney had spat in his face. Any man who has gone sailor in a whale-ship will understand this; and all this and doubtless much more, the Lakeman fully comprehended when the mate uttered his command. But as he sat still for a moment, and as he steadfastly looked into the mate's malignant eye and perceived the stacks of powder-casks heaped up in him and the slow-match silently burning along towards them; as he instinctively saw all this, that strange forbearance and unwillingness to stir up the deeper passionateness in any already ireful being—a repugnance most felt, when felt at all, by really valiant men even when aggrieved—this nameless phantom feeling, gentlemen, stole over Steelkilt.

'Therefore, in his ordinary tone, only a little broken by the bodily exhaustion he was temporarily in, he answered him saying that sweeping the deck was not his business, and he would not do it. And then, without at all alluding to the shovel, he pointed to three lads as the customary sweepers; who, not being billeted at the pumps, had done little or nothing all day. To this, Radney replied with an oath, in a most domineering and outrageous manner unconditionally reiterating his command; meanwhile advancing upon the still seated Lakeman, with an uplifted cooper's club hammer which he had snatched from a cask near by.

'Heated and irritated as he was by his spasmodic toil at the pumps, for all his first nameless feeling of forbearance the sweating Steelkilt could but ill brook this bearing in the mate; but somehow still smothering the conflagration within him, without speaking he remained doggedly rooted to his seat, till at last the incensed Radney shook the hammer within a few inches of his face, furiously commanding him to do his bidding.

'Steelkilt rose, and slowly retreating round the windlass, steadily followed by the mate with his menacing hammer, deliberately repeated his intention not to obey. Seeing, however, that his forbearance had not the slightest effect, by an awful and unspeakable intimation with his twisted hand he warned off the foolish and infatuated man; but it was to no purpose. And in this way the two went once slowly round the windlass; when, resolved at last no longer to retreat, bethinking him that he had now forborne as much as comported with his humor, the Lakeman paused on the hatches and thus spoke to the officer:

'"Mr Radney, I will not obey you. Take that hammer away, or look to yourself." But the predestinated mate coming still closer to him, where the Lakeman stood fixed, now shook the heavy hammer within an inch of his teeth; meanwhile repeating a string of insufferable maledictions. Retreating not the thousandth part of an inch; stabbing him in the eye with the unflinching poniard of his glance, Steelkilt, clenching his right hand behind him and creepingly drawing it back, told his persecutor that if the hammer but grazed his cheek he (Steelkilt) would murder him. But, gentlemen, the fool had been branded for the slaughter by the gods. Immediately the hammer touched the cheek; the next instant the lower jaw of the mate was stove in his head; he fell on the hatch spouting blood like a whale.

'Ere the cry could go aft Steelkilt was shaking one of the backstays leading far aloft to where two of his comrades were standing their mast-heads. They were both Canallers.'

'Canallers!' cried Don Pedro. 'We have seen many whaleships in our harbors, but never heard of your Canallers. Pardon: who and what are they?'

'Canallers, Don, are the boatmen belonging to our grand Erie Canal. You must have heard of it.'

'Nay, Senor; hereabouts in this dull, warm, most lazy, and hereditary land, we know but little of your vigorous North.'

'Aye? Well then, Don, refill my cup. Your chicha's very fine; and ere proceeding further I will tell ye what our Canallers are; for such information may throw side-lights upon my story.

'For three hundred and sixty miles, gentlemen, through the entire breadth of the state of New York; through numerous populous cities and most thriving villages; through long, dismal, uninhabited swamps, and affluent, cultivated fields, unrivalled for fertility; by billiard-room and barroom; through the holy-of-holies of great forests; on Roman arches over Indian rivers; through sun and shade; by happy hearts or broken; through all the wide contrasting scenery of those noble Mohawk counties; and especially, by rows of snow-white chapels, whose spires stand almost like milestones, flows one continual stream of Venetianly corrupt and often lawless life. There's your true Ashantee, gentlemen; there howl your pagans; where you ever find them, next door to you; under the long-flung shadow, and the snug patronizing lee of churches. For by some curious fatality, as it is often noted of your metropolitan freebooters that they ever encamp around the halls of justice, so sinners, gentlemen, most abound in holiest vicinities.'

'Is that a friar passing?' said Don Pedro, looking downwards into the crowded plaza, with humorous concern.

'Well for our northern friend, Dame Isabella's Inquisition wanes in Lima,' laughed Don Sebastian. 'Proceed, Senor.'

'A moment! Pardon!' cried another of the company. 'In the name of all us Limeese, I but desire to express to you, sir sailor, that we have by no means overlooked your delicacy in not substituting present Lima for distant Venice in your corrupt comparison. Oh! do not bow and look surprised; you know the proverb all along this coast—"Corrupt as Lima." It but bears out your saying, too; churches more plentiful than billiard-tables, and for ever open—and "Corrupt as Lima." So, too, Venice; I have been there; the holy city of the blessed evangelist, St Mark!—St Dominic, purge it! Your cup! Thanks: here I refill; now, you pour out again.'

'Freely depicted in his own vocation, gentlemen, the Canaller would make a fine dramatic hero, so abundantly and picturesquely wicked is he. Like Mark Antony, for days and days along his green-turfed, flowery Nile, he indolently floats, openly toying with his red-cheeked Cleopatra, ripening his apricot thigh upon the sunny deck. But ashore, all this effeminacy is dashed. The brigandish guise which the Canaller so proudly sports; his slouched and gaily-ribboned hat betoken his grand features. A terror to the smiling innocence of the villages through which he floats; his swart visage and bold swagger are not unshunned in cities. Once a vagabond on his own canal, I have received good turns from one of these Canallers; I thank him heartily; would fain be not ungrateful; but it is often one of the prime redeeming qualities of your man of violence, that at times he has as stiff an arm to back a poor stranger in a strait, as to plunder a wealthy one. In sum, gentlemen, what the wildness of this canal life is, is emphatically evinced by this; that our wild whale-fishery contains so many of its most finished graduates, and that scarce any race of mankind, except Sydney men, are so much distrusted by our whaling captains. Nor does it at all diminish the curiousness of this matter, that to many thousands of our rural boys and young men born along its line, the probationary life of the Grand Canal furnishes the sole transition between quietly reaping in a Christian corn-field, and recklessly ploughing the waters of the most barbaric seas.'

'I see! I see!' impetuously exclaimed Don Pedro, spilling his chicha upon his silvery ruffles. 'No need to travel! The world's one Lima. I had thought, now, that at your temperate North the generations were cold and holy as the hills.—But the story.'

'I left off, gentlemen, where the Lakeman shook the backstay. Hardly had he done so, when he was surrounded by the three junior mates and the four harpooneers, who all crowded him to the deck. But sliding down the ropes like baleful comets, the two Canallers rushed into the uproar, and sought to drag their man out of it towards the forecastle. Others of the sailors joined with them in this attempt, and a twisted turmoil ensued; while standing out of harm's way, the valiant captain danced up and down with a whale-pike, calling upon his officers to manhandle that atrocious scoundrel, and smoke him along to the quarter-deck. At intervals, he ran close up to the revolving border of the confusion, and prying into the heart of it with his pike, sought to prick out the object of his resentment. But Steelkilt and his desperadoes were too much for them all; they succeeded in gaining the forecastle deck, where, hastily slewing about three or four large casks in a line with the windlass, these sea-Parisians entrenched themselves behind the barricade.'

'"Come out of that, ye pirates!" roared the captain, now menacing them with a pistol in each hand, just brought to him by the steward. "Come out of that, ye cut-throats!"

'Steelkilt leaped on the barricade, and striding up and down there, defied the worst the pistols could do; but gave the captain to understand distinctly, that his (Steelkilt's) death would be the signal for a murderous mutiny on the part of all hands. Fearing in his heart lest this might prove but too true, the captain a little desisted, but still commanded the insurgents instantly to return to their duty.

'"Will you promise not to touch us, if we do?" demanded their ringleader.

'"Turn to! turn to!—I make no promise;—to your duty! Do you want to sink the ship, by knocking off at a time like this? Turn to!" and he once more raised a pistol.

'"Sink the ship?" cried Steelkilt. "Aye, let her sink. Not a man of us turns to, unless you swear not to raise a rope-yarn against us. What say ye, men?" turning to his comrades. A fierce cheer was their response.

'The Lakeman now patrolled the barricade, all the while keeping his eye on the Captain, and jerking out such sentences as these:—"It's not our fault; we didn't want it; I told him to take his hammer away; it was boys' business; he might have known me before this; I told him not to prick the buffalo; I believe I have broken a finger here against his cursed jaw; ain't those mincing knives down in the forecastle there, men? look to those handspikes, my hearties. Captain, by God, look to yourself; say the word; don't be a fool; forget it all; we are ready to turn to; treat us decently, and we're your men; but we won't be flogged."

'"Turn to! I make no promises, turn to, I say!"

'"Look ye, now," cried the Lakeman, flinging out his arm towards him, "there are a few of us here (and I am one of them) who have shipped for the cruise, d'ye see; now as you well know, sir, we can claim our discharge as soon as the anchor is down; so we don't want a row; it's not our interest; we want to be peaceable; we are ready to work, but we won't be flogged."

'"Turn to!" roared the Captain.

'Steelkilt glanced round him a moment, and then said:—"I tell you what it is now, Captain, rather than kill ye, and be hung for such a shabby rascal, we won't lift a hand against ye unless ye attack us; but till you say the word about not flogging us, we don't do a hand's turn."

'"Down into the forecastle then, down with ye, I'll keep ye there till ye're sick of it. Down ye go."

'"Shall we?" cried the ringleader to his men. Most of them were against it; but at length, in obedience to Steelkilt, they preceded him down into their dark den, growlingly disappearing, like bears into a cave.

'As the Lakeman's bare head was just level with the planks, the Captain and his posse leaped the barricade, and rapidly drawing over the slide of the scuttle, planted their group of hands upon it, and loudly called for the steward to bring the heavy brass padlock belonging to the companionway. Then opening the slide a little, the Captain whispered something down the crack, closed it, and turned the key upon them—ten in number—leaving on deck some twenty or more, who thus far had remained neutral.

'All night a wide-awake watch was kept by all the officers, forward and aft, especially about the forecastle scuttle and fore hatchway; at which last place it was feared the insurgents might emerge, after breaking through the bulkhead below. But the hours of darkness passed in peace; the men who still remained at their duty toiling hard at the pumps, whose clinking and clanking at intervals through the dreary night dismally resounded through the ship.

'At sunrise the Captain went forward, and knocking on the deck, summoned the prisoners to work; but with a yell they refused. Water was then lowered down to them, and a couple of handfuls of biscuit were tossed after it; when again turning the key upon them and pocketing it, the Captain returned to the quarter-deck. Twice every day for three days this was repeated; but on the fourth morning a confused wrangling, and then a scuffling was heard, as the customary summons was delivered; and suddenly four men burst up from the forecastle, saying they were ready to turn to. The fetid closeness of the air, and a famishing diet, united perhaps to some fears of ultimate retribution, had constrained them to surrender at discretion. Emboldened by this, the Captain reiterated his demand to the rest, but Steelkilt shouted up to him a terrific hint to stop his babbling and betake himself where he belonged. On the fifth morning three others of the mutineers bolted up into the air from the desperate arms below that sought to restrain them. Only three were left.

'"Better turn to, now?" said the Captain with a heartless jeer.

'"Shut us up again, will ye!" cried Steelkilt.

'"Oh! certainly," said the Captain, and the key clicked.

'It was at this point, gentlemen, that enraged by the defection of seven of his former associates, and stung by the mocking voice that had last hailed him, and maddened by his long entombment in a place as black as the bowels of despair; it was then that Steelkilt proposed to the two Canallers, thus far apparently of one mind with him, to burst out of their hole at the next summoning of the garrison; and armed with their keen mincing knives (long, crescentic, heavy implements with a handle at each end) run amuck from the bowsprit to the taffrail; and if by any devilishness of desperation possible, seize the ship. For himself, he would do this, he said, whether they joined him or not. That was the last night he should spend in that den. But the scheme met with no opposition on the part of the other two; they swore they were ready for that, or for any other mad thing, for anything in short but a surrender. And what was more, they each insisted upon being the first man on deck, when the time to make the rush should come. But to this their leader as fiercely objected, reserving that priority for himself; particularly as his two comrades would not yield, the one to the other, in the matter; and both of them could not be first, for the ladder would but admit one man at a time. And here, gentlemen, the foul play of these miscreants must come out.

'Upon hearing the frantic project of their leader, each in his own separate soul had suddenly lighted, it would seem, upon the same piece of treachery, namely: to be foremost in breaking out, in order to be the first of the three, though the last of the ten, to surrender; and thereby secure whatever small chance of pardon such conduct might merit. But when Steelkilt made known his determination still to lead them to the last, they in some way, by some subtle chemistry of villany, mixed their before secret treacheries together; and when their leader fell into a doze, verbally opened their souls to each other in three sentences; and bound the sleeper with cords, and gagged him with cords; and shrieked out for the Captain at midnight.

'Thinking murder at hand, and smelling in the dark for the blood, he and all his armed mates and harpooneers rushed for the forecastle. In a few minutes the scuttle was opened, and, bound hand and foot, the still struggling ringleader was shoved up into the air by his perfidious allies, who at once claimed the honor of securing a man who had been fully ripe for murder. But all three were collared, and dragged along the deck like dead cattle; and, side by side, were seized up into the mizen rigging, like three quarters of meat, and there they hung till morning. "Damn ye," cried the Captain, pacing to and fro before them, "the vultures would not touch ye, ye villains!"

'At sunrise he summoned all hands; and separating those who had rebelled from those who had taken no part in the mutiny, he told the former that he had a good mind to flog them all round—thought, upon the whole, he would do so—he ought to—justice demanded it; but for the present, considering their timely surrender, he would let them go with a reprimand, which he accordingly administered in the vernacular.

'"But as for you, ye carrion rogues," turning to the three men in the rigging—"for you, I mean to mince ye up for the try-pots;" and, seizing a rope, he applied it with all his might to the backs of the two traitors, till they yelled no more, but lifelessly hung their heads sideways, as the two crucified thieves are drawn.

'"My wrist is sprained with ye!" he cried, at last; "but there is still rope enough left for you, my fine bantam, that wouldn't give up. Take that gag from his mouth, and let us hear what he can say for himself."

'For a moment the exhausted mutineer made a tremulous motion of his cramped jaws, and then painfully twisting round his head, said in a sort of hiss, "What I say is this—and mind it well—if you flog me, I murder you!"

'"Say ye so? then see how ye frighten me"—and the Captain drew off with the rope to strike.

'"Best not," hissed the Lakeman.

'"But I must,"—and the rope was once more drawn back for the stroke.

'Steelkilt here hissed out something, inaudible to all but the Captain; who, to the amazement of all hands, started back, pacing the deck rapidly two or three times, and then suddenly throwing down his rope, said, "I won't do it—let him go—cut him down: d'ye hear?"

'But as the junior mates were hurrying to execute the order, a pale man, with a bandaged head, arrested them—Radney the chief mate. Ever since the blow, he had lain in his berth; but that morning, hearing the tumult on the deck, he had crept out, and thus far had watched the whole scene. Such was the state of his mouth, that he could hardly speak; but mumbling something about *his* being willing and able to do what the captain dared not attempt, he snatched the rope and advanced to his pinioned foe.

'"You are a coward!" hissed the Lakeman.

'"So I am, but take that." The mate was in the very act of striking, when another hiss stayed his uplifted arm. He paused: and then pausing no more, made good his word, spite of Steelkilt's threat, whatever that might have been. The three men were then cut down, all hands were turned to, and, sullenly worked by the moody seamen, the iron pumps clanged as before.

'Just after dark that day, when one watch had retired below, a clamor was heard in the forecastle; and the two trembling traitors running up, besieged the cabin door, saying they durst not consort with the crew. Entreaties, cuffs, and kicks could not drive them back, so at their own instance they were put down in the ship's run for salvation. Still, no sign of mutiny reappeared among the rest. On the contrary, it seemed, that mainly at Steelkilt's instigation, they had resolved to maintain the strictest peacefulness, obey all orders to the last, and, when the ship reached port, desert her in a body. But in order to insure the speediest end to the voyage, they all agreed to another thing—namely, not to sing out for whales, in case any should be discovered. For, spite of her leak, and spite of all her other perils, the Town-Ho still maintained her mast-heads, and her captain was just as willing to lower for a fish that moment, as on the day his craft first struck the cruising ground; and Radney the mate was quite as ready to change his berth for a boat, and with his bandaged mouth seek to gag in death the vital jaw of the whale.

'But though the Lakeman had induced the seamen to adopt this sort of passiveness in their conduct, he kept his own counsel (at least till all was over) concerning his own proper and private revenge upon the man who had stung him in the ventricles of his heart. He was in Radney the chief mate's watch; and as if the infatuated man sought to run more than half way to meet his doom, after the scene at the rigging, he insisted, against the express counsel of the captain, upon resuming the head of his watch at night. Upon this, and one or two other circumstances. Steelkilt systematically built the plan of his revenge.

'During the night, Radney had an unseamanlike way of sitting on the bulwarks of the quarter-deck, and leaning his arm upon the gunwale of the boat which was hoisted up there, a little above the ship's side. In this attitude, it was well known, he sometimes dozed. There was a considerable vacancy between the boat and the ship, and down between this was the sea. Steelkilt calculated his time, and found that his next trick at the helm would come round at two o'clock, in the morning of the third day from that in which he had been betrayed. At his leisure, he employed the interval in braiding something very carefully in his watches below.

'"What are you making there?" said a shipmate.

'"What do you think? what does it look like?"

'"Like a lanyard for your bag; but it's an odd one, seems to me."

'"Yes, rather oddish," said the Lakeman, holding it at arm's length before him; "but I think it will answer. Shipmate, I haven't enough twine,—have you any?"

'But there was none in the forecastle.

'"Then I must get some from old Rad;" and he rose to go aft.

'"You don't mean to go a begging to *him*!" said a sailor.

'"Why not? Do you think he won't do me a turn, when it's to help himself in the end, shipmate?" and going to the mate, he looked at him quietly, and asked him for some twine to mend his hammock. It was given him—neither twine nor lanyard were seen again; but the next night an iron ball, closely netted, partly rolled from the pocket of the Lakeman's monkey jacket, as he was tucking the coat into his hammock for a pillow. Twenty-four hours after, his trick at the silent helm—nigh to the man who was apt to doze over the grave always ready dug to the seaman's hand—that fatal hour was then to come; and in the fore-ordaining soul of Steelkilt, the mate was already stark and stretched as a corpse, with his forehead crushed in.

'But, gentlemen, a fool saved the would-be murderer from the bloody deed he had planned. Yet complete revenge he had, and without being the avenger. For by a mysterious fatality, Heaven itself seemed to step in to take out of his hands into its own the damning thing he would have done.

'It was just between daybreak and sunrise of the morning of the second day, when they were washing down the decks, that a stupid Teneriffe man, drawing water in the main-chains, all at once shouted out, "There she rolls! there she rolls! Jesu! what a whale!" It was Moby Dick.'

'Moby Dick!' cried Don Sebastian; 'St Dominic! Sir sailor, but do whales have christenings? Whom call you Moby Dick?"

'A very white, and famous, and most deadly immortal monster, Don;—but that would be too long a story.'

'How? how?' cried all the young Spaniards, crowding.

'Nay, Dons, Dons—nay, nay! I cannot rehearse that now. Let me get more into the air, Sirs.'

'The chicha; the chicha;' cried Don Pedro; 'our vigorous friend looks faint;—fill up his empty glass!'

'No need, gentlemen; one moment, and I proceed.—Now, gentlemen, so suddenly perceiving the snowy whale within fifty yards of the ship—forgetful of the compact among the crew—in the excitement of the moment, the Teneriffe man had instinctively and involuntarily lifted his voice for the monster, though for some little time past it had been plainly beheld from the three sullen mast-heads. All was now a phrensy. "The White Whale—the White Whale!" was the cry from captain, mates, and harpooneers, who, undeterred by fearful rumors, were all anxious to capture so famous and precious a fish; while the dogged crew eyed askance, and with curses, the appalling beauty of the vast milky mass, that lit up by a horizontal spangling sun, shifted and glistened like a living opal in the blue morning sea. Gentlemen, a strange fatality pervades the whole career of these events, as if verily mapped out before the world itself was charted. The mutineer was the bowsman of the mate, and when fast to a fish, it was his duty to sit next him, while Radney stood up with his lance in the prow, and haul in or slacken the line, at the word of command. Moreover, when the four boats were lowered, the mate's got the start; and none howled more fiercely with delight than did Steelkilt, as he strained at his oar. After a stiff pull, their harpooneer got fast, and, spear in hand, Radney sprang to the bow. He was always a furious man, it seems, in a boat. And now his bandaged cry was, to beach him on the whale's topmost back. Nothing loath, his bowsman hauled him up and up, through a blinding foam that blent two whitenesses together; till of a sudden the boat struck as against a sunken ledge, and keeling over, spilled out the standing mate. That instant, as he fell on the whale's slippery back, the boat righted, and was dashed aside by the swell, while Radney was tossed over into the sea, on the other flank of the whale. He struck out through the spray, and, for an instant, was dimly seen through that veil, wildly seeking to remove himself from the eye of Moby Dick. But the whale rushed round in a sudden maelstrom; seized the swimmer between his jaws; and rearing high up with him, plunged headlong again, and went down.

'Meantime, at the first tap of the boat's bottom, the Lakeman had slackened the line, so as to drop astern from the whirlpool; calmly looking on, he thought his own thoughts. But a sudden, terrific, downward jerking of the boat, quickly brought his knife to the line. He cut it; and the whale was free. But, at some distance, Moby Dick rose again, with some tatters of Radney's red woollen shirt, caught in the teeth that had destroyed him. All four boats gave chase again; but the whale eluded them, and finally wholly disappeared.

'In good time, the Town-Ho reached her port—a savage, solitary place—where no civilized creature resided. There, headed by the Lakeman, all but five or six of the foremastmen deliberately deserted among the palms; eventually, as it turned out, seizing a large double war-canoe of the savages, and setting sail for some other harbor.

'The ship's company being reduced to but a handful, the captain called upon the Islanders to assist him in the laborious business of heaving down the ship to stop the leak. But to such unresting vigilance over their dangerous allies was this small band of whites necessitated, both by night and by day, and so extreme was the hard work they underwent, that upon the vessel being ready again for sea, they were in such a weakened condition that the captain durst not put off with them in so heavy a vessel. After taking counsel with his officers, he anchored the ship as far off shore as possible; loaded and ran out his two cannon from the bows; stacked his muskets on the poop; and warning the Islanders not to approach the ship at their peril, took one man with him, and setting the sail of his best whaleboat, steered straight before the wind for Tahiti, five hundred miles distant, to procure a reinforcement to his crew.

'On the fourth day of the sail, a large canoe was descried, which seemed to have touched at a low isle of corals. He steered away from it; but the savage craft bore down on him; and soon the voice of Steelkilt hailed him to heave to, or he would run him under water. The captain presented a pistol. With one foot on each prow of the yoked war-canoes, the Lakeman laughed him to scorn; assuring him that if the pistol so much as clicked in the lock, he would bury him in bubbles and foam.

'"What do you want of me?" cried the captain.

'"Where are you bound? and for what are you bound?" demanded Steelkilt; "no lies."

'"I am bound to Tahiti for more men."

'"Very good. Let me board you a moment—I come in peace." With that he leaped from the canoe, swam to the boat; and climbing the gunwale, stood face to face with the captain.

'"Cross your arms, sir; throw back your head. Now, repeat after me. As soon as Steelkilt leaves me, I swear to beach this boat on yonder island, and remain there six days. If I do not, may lightning strike me!"

'"A pretty scholar," laughed the Lakeman. "Adios, Senor!" and leaping into the sea, he swam back to his comrades.

'Watching the boat till it was fairly beached, and drawn up to the roots of the cocoa-nut trees, Steelkilt made sail again, and in due time arrived at Tahiti, his own place of destination. There, luck befriended him; two ships were about to sail for France, and were providentially in want of precisely that number of men which the sailor headed. They embarked; and so for ever got the start of their former captain, had he been at all minded to work them legal retribution.

'Some ten days after the French ships sailed, the whale-boat arrived, and the captain was forced to enlist some of the more civilized Tahitians, who had been somewhat used to the sea. Chartering a small native schooner, he returned with them to his vessel; and finding all right there, again resumed his cruisings.

'Where Steelkilt now is, gentlemen, none know; but upon the island of Nantucket, the widow of Radney still turns to the sea which refuses to give up its dead; still in dreams sees the awful white whale that destroyed him.' ★ ★ ★

'Are you through?' said Don Sebastian, quietly.

'I am, Don.'

'Then I entreat you, tell me if to the best of your own convictions, this your story is in substance really true? It is so passing wonderful! Did you get it from an unquestionable source? Bear with me if I seem to press.'

'Also bear with all of us, sir sailor; for we all join in Don Sebastian's suit,' cried the company, with exceeding interest.

'Is there a copy of the Holy Evangelists in the Golden Inn, gentlemen?'

'Nay,' said Don Sebastian; 'but I know a worthy priest near by, who will quickly procure one for me. I go for it; but are you well advised? this may grow too serious.'

'Will you be so good as to bring the priest also, Don?'

'Though there are no Auto-da-Fés in Lima now,' said one of the company to another; 'I fear our sailor friend runs risk of the archiepiscopacy. Let us withdraw more out of the moonlight. I see no need of this.'

'Excuse me for running after you, Don Sebastian; but may I also beg that you will be particular in procuring the largest sized Evangelist you can.'

★ ★ ★ ★ ★ ★ ★

'This is the priest, he brings you the Evangelists,' said Don Sebastian, gravely, returning with a tall and solemn figure.

'Let me remove my hat. Now, venerable priest, further into the light, and hold the Holy Book before me that I may touch it.'

'So help me Heaven, and on my honor, the story I have told ye, gentlemen, is in substance and its great items, true. I know it to be true; it happened on this ball; I trod the ship; I knew the crew; I have seen and talked with Steelkilt since the death of Radney.'

CHAPTER LV

OF THE MONSTROUS PICTURES OF WHALES

I shall ere long paint to you as well as one can without canvas, something like the true form of the whale as he actually appears to the eye of the whaleman when in his own absolute body the whale is moored alongside the whale-ship so that he can be fairly stepped upon there. It may be worth while, therefore, previously to advert to those curious imaginary portraits of him which even down to the present day confidently challenge the faith of the landsman. It is time to set the world right in this matter, by proving such pictures of the whale all wrong.

It may be that the primal source of all those pictorial delusions will be found among the oldest Hindoo, Egyptian, and Grecian sculptures. For ever since those inventive but unscrupulous times when on the marble panellings of temples, the pedestals of statues, and on shields, medallions, cups, and coins, the dolphin was drawn in scales of chain-armor like Saladin's, and a helmeted head like St George's; ever since then has something of the same sort of license prevailed, not only in most popular pictures of the whale, but in many scientific presentations of him.

Now, by all odds, the most ancient extant portrait anyways purporting to the be the whale's, is to be found in the famous cavern-pagoda of Elephanta, in India. The Brahmins maintain that in the almost endless sculptures of that immemorial pagoda, all the trades and pursuits, every conceivable avocation of man, were prefigured ages before any of them actually came into being. No wonder then, that in some sort our noble profession of whaling should have been there shadowed forth. The Hindoo whale referred to, occurs in a separate department of the wall, depicting the incarnation of Vishnu in the form of leviathan, learnedly known as the Matse Avatar. But though this sculpture is half man and half whale, so as only to give the tail of the latter, yet that small section of him is all wrong. It looks more like the tapering tail of an anaconda, than the broad palms of the true whale's majestic flukes.

But go to the old Galleries, and look now at a great Christian painter's portrait of this fish; for he succeeds no better than the antediluvian Hindoo. It is Guido's picture of Perseus rescuing Andromeda from the sea-monster or whale. Where did Guido get the model of such a strange creature as that? Nor does Hogarth, in painting the same scene in his own 'Perseus Descending,' make out one whit better. The huge corpulence of that Hogarthian monster undulates on the surface, scarcely drawing one inch of water. It has a sort of howdah on its back, and its distended tusked mouth into which the billows are rolling, might be taken for the Traitors' Gate leading from the Thames by water into the Tower. Then, there are the Prodromus whales of old Scotch Sibbald, and Jonah's whale, as depicted in the prints of old Bibles and the cuts of old primers. What shall be said of these? As for the book-binder's whale winding like a vine-stalk round the stock of a descending anchor—as stamped and gilded on the backs and title-pages of many books both old and new—that is a very picturesque but purely fabulous creature, imitated, I take it, from the figures on antique vases. Though universally denominated a dolphin, I nevertheless call this book-binder's fish an attempt at a whale; because it was so intended when the device was first introduced. It was introduced by an old Italian publisher somewhere about the 15th century, during the Revival of Learning; and in those days, and even down to a comparatively late period, dolphins were popularly supposed to be a species of the Leviathan.

In the vignettes and other embellishments of some ancient books you will at times meet with very curious touches at the whale, where all manner of spouts, jets d'eau, hot springs and cold, Saratoga and Baden-Baden, come bubbling up from his unexhausted brain. In the title-page of the original edition of the 'Advancement of Learning' you will find some curious whales.

But quitting all these unprofessional attempts, let us glance at those pictures of leviathan purporting to be sober, scientific delineations, by those who know. In old Harris's collection of voyages there are some plates of whales extracted from a Dutch book of voyages, A.D. 1671, entitled 'A Whaling Voyage to Spitzbergen in the ship Jonas in the Whale, Peter Peterson of Friesland, master.' In one of those plates the whales, like great rafts of logs, are represented lying among ice-isles, with white bears running over their living backs. In another plate, the prodigious blunder is made of representing the whale with perpendicular flukes.

Then again, there is an imposing quarto, written by one Captain Colnett, a Post Captain in the English navy, entitled 'A Voyage round Cape Horn into the South Seas, for the purpose of extending the Spermaceti Whale Fisheries.' In this book is an outline purporting to be a 'Picture of a Physeter or Spermaceti whale, drawn by scale from one killed on the coast of Mexico, August, 1793, and hoisted on deck.' I doubt not the captain had this veracious picture taken for the benefit of his marines. To mention but one thing about it, let me say that it has an eye which applied, according to the accompanying scale, to a full grown sperm whale, would make the eye of that whale a bow-window some five feet long. Ah, my gallant captain, why did ye not give us Jonah looking out of that eye!

Nor are the most conscientious compilations of Natural History for the benefit of the young and tender, free from the same heinousness of mistake. Look at that popular work 'Goldsmith's Animated Nature.' In the abridged London edition of 1807, there are plates of an alleged 'whale' and a 'narwhale.' I do not wish to seem inelegant, but this unsightly whale looks much like an amputated sow; and, as for the narwhale, one glimpse at it is enough to amaze one, that in this nineteenth century such a hippogriff could be palmed for genuine upon any intelligent public of schoolboys.

Then, again, in 1825, Bernard Germain, Count de Lacépède, a great naturalist, published a scientific systemized whale book, wherein are several pictures of the different species of the Leviathan. All these are not only incorrect, but the picture of the Mysticetus or Greenland whale (that is to say, the Right whale), even Scoresby, a long experienced man as touching that species, declares not to have its counterpart in nature.

But the placing of the cap-sheaf to all this blundering business was reserved for the scientific Frederick Cuvier, brother to the famous Baron. In 1836 he published a Natural History of Whales, in which he gives what he calls a picture of the Sperm Whale. Before showing that picture to any Nantucketer, you had best provide for your summary retreat from Nantucket. In a word, Frederick Cuvier's Sperm Whale is not a Sperm Whale, but a squash. Of course, he never had the benefit of a whaling voyage (such men seldom have), but whence he derived that picture, who can tell? Perhaps he got it as his scientific predecessor in the same field, Desmarest, got one of his authentic abortions; that is, from a Chinese drawing. And what sort of lively lads with the pencil those Chinese are, many queer cups and saucers inform us.

As for the sign-painters' whales seen in the streets hanging over the shops of oil-dealers, what shall be said of them? They are generally Richard III whales, with dromedary humps, and very savage; breakfasting on three or four sailor tarts, that is whaleboats full of mariners: their deformities floundering in seas of blood and blue paint.

But these manifold mistakes in depicting the whale are not so very surprising after all. Consider! Most of the scientific drawings have been taken from the stranded fish; and these are about as correct as a drawing of a wrecked ship, with broken back, would correctly represent the noble animal itself in all its undashed pride of hull and spars. Though elephants have stood for their full-lengths, the living Leviathan has never yet fairly floated himself for his portrait. The living whale, in his full majesty and significance, is only to be seen at sea in unfathomable waters; and afloat the vast bulk of him is out of sight, like a launched line-of-battle ship; and out of that element it is a thing eternally impossible for mortal man to hoist him bodily into the air, so as to preserve all his mighty swells and undulations. And, not to speak of the highly presumable difference of contour between a young sucking whale and a full-grown Platonian Leviathan; yet, even in the case of one of those young sucking whales hoisted to a ship's deck, such is then the outlandish, eel-like, limbered, varying shape of him, that his precise expression the devil himself could not catch.

But it may be fancied, that from the naked skeleton of the stranded whale, accurate hints may be derived touching his true form. Not at all. For it is one of the more curious things about this Leviathan, that his skeleton gives very little idea of his general shape. Though Jeremy Bentham's skeleton, which hangs for candelabra in the library of one of his executors, correctly conveys the idea of a burly-browed utilitarian old gentleman, with all Jeremy's other leading personal characteristics; yet nothing of this kind could be inferred from any leviathan's articulated bones. In fact, as the great Hunter says, the mere skeleton of the whale bears the same relation to the fully invested and padded animal as the insect does to the chrysalis that so roundingly envelopes it. This peculiarity is strikingly evinced in the head, as in some part of this book will be incidentally shown. It is also very curiously displayed in the side fin, the bones of which almost exactly answer to the bones of the human hand, minus only the thumb. This fin has four regular bone-fingers, the index, middle, ring, and little finger. But all these are permanently lodged in their fleshy covering, as the human fingers in an artificial covering. 'However recklessly the whale may sometimes serve us,' said humorous Stubb one day, 'he can never be truly said to handle us without mittens.'

For all these reasons, then, any way you may look at it, you must needs conclude that the great Leviathan is that one creature in the world which must remain unpainted to the last. True, one portrait may hit the mark much nearer than another, but none can hit it with any very considerable degree of exactness. So there is no earthly way of finding out precisely what the whale really looks like. And the only mode in which you can derive even a tolerable idea of his living contour, is by going a whaling yourself; but by so doing, you run no small risk of being eternally stove and sunk by him. Wherefore, it seems to me you had best not be too fastidious in your curiosity touching this Leviathan.

CHAPTER LVI

Of the Less Erroneous Pictures of Whales, and the True Pictures of Whaling Scenes

In connexion with the monstrous pictures of whales, I am strongly tempted here to enter upon those still more monstrous stories of them which are to be found in certain books, both ancient and modern, especially in Pliny, Purchas, Hackluyt, Harris, Cuvier, &c. But I pass that matter by.

I know of only four published outlines of the great Sperm Whale; Colnett's, Huggins's, Frederick Cuvier's, and Beale's. In the previous chapter Colnett and Cuvier have been referred to. Huggins's is far better than theirs; but, by great odds, Beale's is the best. All Beale's drawings of this whale are good, excepting the middle figure in the picture of three whales in various attitudes, capping his second chapter. His frontispiece, boats attacking Sperm Whales, though no doubt calculated to excite the civil scepticism of some parlor men, is admirably correct and life-like in its general effect. Some of the Sperm Whale drawings in J. Ross Browne are pretty correct in contour; but they are wretchedly engraved. That is not his fault though.

Of the Right Whale, the best outline pictures are in Scoresby; but they are drawn on too small a scale to convey a desirable impression. He has but one picture of whaling scenes, and this is a sad deficiency, because it is by such pictures only, when at all well done, that you can derive anything like a truthful idea of the living whale as seen by his living hunters.

But, taken for all in all, by far the finest, though in some details not the most correct, presentations of whales and whaling scenes to be anywhere found, are two large French engravings, well executed, and taken from paintings by one Garnery. Respectively, they represent attacks on the Sperm and Right Whale. In the first engraving a noble Sperm Whale is depicted in full majesty of might, just risen beneath the boat from the profundities of the ocean, and bearing high in the air upon his back the terrific wreck of the stoven planks. The prow of the boat is partially unbroken, and is drawn just balancing upon the monster's spine; and standing in that prow, for that one single incomputable flash of time, you behold an oarsman, half shrouded by the incensed boiling spout of the whale, and in the act of leaping, as if from a precipice. The action of the whole thing is wonderfully good and true. The half-emptied line-tub floats on the whitened sea; the wooden poles of the spilled harpoons obliquely bob in it; the heads of the swimming crew are scattered about the whale in contrasting expressions of affright; while in the black stormy distance the ship is bearing down upon the scene. Serious fault might be found with the anatomical details of this whale, but let that pass; since, for the life of me, I could not draw so good a one.

In the second engraving, the boat is in the act of drawing alongside the barnacled flank of a large running Right Whale, that rolls his black weedy bulk in the sea like some mossy rock-slide from the Patagonian cliffs. His jets are erect, full, and black like soot; so that from so abounding a smoke in the chimney, you would think there must be a brave supper cooking in the great bowels below. Sea fowls are pecking at the small crabs, shell-fish, and other sea candies and maccaroni, which the Right Whale sometimes carries on his pestilent back. And all the while the thick-lipped leviathan is rushing through the deep, leaving tons of tumultuous white curds in his wake, and causing the slight boat to rock in the swells like a skiff caught nigh the paddle-wheels of an ocean steamer. Thus, the foreground is all raging commotion; but behind, in admirable artistic contrast, is the glassy level of a sea becalmed, the drooping unstarched sails of the powerless ship, and the inert mass of a dead whale, a conquered fortress, with the flag of capture lazily hanging from the whale-pole inserted into his spout-hole.

Who Garnery the painter is, or was, I know not. But my life for it he was either practically conversant with his subject, or else marvellously tutored by some experienced whaleman. The French are the lads for painting action. Go and gaze upon all the paintings of Europe, and where will you find such a gallery of living and breathing commotion on canvas, as in that triumphal hall at Versailles; where the beholder fights his way, pell-mell, through the consecutive great battles of France; where every sword seems a flash of the Northern Lights, and the successive armed kings and Emperors dash by, like a charge of crowned centaurs? Not wholly unworthy of a place in that gallery, are these sea battle-pieces of Garnery.

The natural aptitude of the French for seizing the picturesqueness of things seems to be peculiarly evinced in what paintings and engravings they have of their whaling scenes. With not one tenth of England's experience in the fishery, and not the thousandth part of that of the Americans, they have nevertheless furnished both nations with the only finished sketches at all capable of conveying the real spirit of the whale hunt. For the most part, the English and American whale draughtsmen seem entirely content with presenting the mechanical outline of things, such as the vacant profile of the whale; which, so far as picturesqueness of effect is concerned, is about tantamount to sketching the profile of a pyramid. Even Scoresby, the justly renowned Right whaleman, after giving us a stiff full length of the Greenland whale, and three or four delicate miniatures of narwhales and porpoises, treats us to a series of classical engravings of boat hooks, chopping knives, and grapnels; and with the microscopic diligence of a Leuwenhoeck submits to the inspection of a shivering world ninety-six facsimiles of magnified Arctic snow crystals. I mean no disparagement to the excellent voyager (I honor him for a veteran), but in so important a matter it was certainly an oversight not to have procured for every crystal a sworn affidavit taken before a Greenland Justice of the Peace.

In addition to those fine engravings from Garnery, there are two other French engravings worthy of note, by some one who subscribes himself 'H. Durand.' One of them, though not precisely adapted to our present purpose, nevertheless deserves mention on other accounts. It is a quiet noon-scene among the isles of the Pacific; a French whaler anchored, inshore, in a calm, and lazily taking water on board; the loosened sails of the ship, and the long leaves of the palms in the background, both drooping together in the breezeless air. The effect is very fine, when considered with reference to its presenting the hardy fishermen under one of their few aspects of oriental repose. The other engraving is quite a different affair: the ship hove-to upon the open sea, and in the very heart of the Leviathanic life, with a Right Whale alongside; the vessel (in the act of cutting-in) hove over to the monster as if to a quay; and a boat, hurriedly pushing off from this scene of activity, is about giving chase to whales in the distance. The harpoons and lances lie levelled for use; three oarsmen are just setting the mast in its hole; while from a sudden roll of the sea, the little craft stands half-erect out of the water, like a rearing horse. From the ship, the smoke of the torments of the boiling whale is going up like the smoke over a village of smithies; and to windward, a black cloud, rising up with earnest of squalls and rains, seems to quicken the activity of the excited seamen.

CHAPTER LVII

Of Whales in Paint; In Teeth; In Wood; In Sheet-Iron; In Stone; In Mountains; In Stars

On Tower-hill, as you go down to the London docks, you may have seen a crippled beggar (or *kedger,* as the sailors say) holding a painted board before him, representing the tragic scene in which he lost his leg. There are three whales and three boats; and one of the boats (presumed to contain the missing leg in all its original integrity) is being crunched by the jaws of the foremost whale. Any time these ten years, they tell me, has that man held up that picture, and exhibited that stump to an incredulous world. But the time of his justification has now come. His three whales are as good whales as were ever published in Wapping, at any rate; and his stump as unquestionable a stump as any you will find in the western clearings. But, though for ever mounted on that stump, never a stump-speech does the poor whaleman make; but, with downcast eyes, stands ruefully contemplating his own amputation.

Throughout the Pacific, and also in Nantucket, and New Bedford, and Sag Harbor, you will come across lively sketches of whales and whaling-scenes, graven by the fishermen themselves on Sperm Whale-teeth, or ladies' busks wrought out of the Right Whale-bone, and other like skrimshander articles, as the whalemen call the numerous little ingenious contrivances they elaborately carve out of the rough material, in their hours of ocean leisure. Some of them have little boxes of dentistical-looking implements, specially intended for the skrimshandering business. But, in general, they toil with their jack-knives alone; and, with that almost omnipotent tool of the sailor, they will turn you out anything you please, in the way of a mariner's fancy.

Long exile from Christendom and civilization inevitably restores a man to that condition in which God placed him, *i.e.* what is called savagery. Your true whale-hunter is as much a savage as an Iroquois. I myself am a savage, owning no allegiance but to the King of the Cannibals; and ready at any moment to rebel against him.

Now, one of the peculiar characteristics of the savage in his domestic hours, is his wonderful patience of industry. An ancient Hawaiian war-club or spear-paddle, in its full multiplicity and elaboration of carving, is as great a trophy of human perseverance as a Latin lexicon. For, with but a bit of broken sea-shell or a shark's tooth, that miraculous intricacy of wooden net-work has been achieved; and it has cost steady years of steady application.

As with the Hawaiian savage, so with the white sailor-savage. With the same marvellous patience, and with the same single shark's tooth, of his one poor jack-knife, he will carve you a bit of bone sculpture, not quite as workmanlike, but as close packed in its maziness of design, as the Greek savage, Achilles's shield; and full of barbaric spirit and suggestiveness, as the prints of that fine old Dutch savage, Albert Durer.

Wooden whales, or whales cut in profile out of the small dark slabs of the noble South Sea war-wood, are frequently met with in the forecastles of American whalers. Some of them are done with much accuracy.

At some gable-roofed country houses you will see brass whales hung by the tail for knockers to the road-side door. When the porter is sleepy, the anvil-headed whale would be best. But these knocking whales are seldom remarkable as faithful essays. On the spires of some old-fashioned churches you will see sheet-iron whales placed there for weathercocks; but they are so elevated, and besides that are to all intents and purposes so labelled with *'Hands off!'* you cannot examine them closely enough to decide upon their merit.

In bony, ribby regions of the earth, where at the base of high broken cliffs masses of rock lie strewn in fantastic groupings upon the plain, you will often discover images of the petrified forms of the Leviathan partly merged in grass, which of a windy day breaks against them in a surf of green surges.

Then, again, in mountainous countries where the traveller is continually girdled by amphitheatrical heights; here and there from some lucky point of view you will catch passing glimpses of the profiles of whales defined along the undulating ridges. But you must be a thorough whaleman, to see these sights; and not only that, but if you wish to return to such a sight again, you must be sure and take the exact intersecting latitude and longitude of your first standpoint, else so chance-like are such observations of the hills, that your precise, previous standpoint would require a laborious re-discovery; like the Solomon islands, which still remain incognita, though once high-ruffed Mendanna trod them and old Figuera chronicled them.

Nor when expandingly lifted by your subject, can you fail to trace out great whales in the starry heavens, and boats in pursuit of them; as when long filled with thoughts of war the Eastern nations saw armies locked in battle among the clouds. Thus at the North have I chased Leviathan round and round the Pole with the revolutions of the bright points that first defined him to me. And beneath the effulgent Antarctic skies I have boarded the Argo-Navis, and joined the chase against the starry Cetus far beyond the utmost stretch of Hydrus and the Flying Fish.

With a frigate's anchors for my bridle-bits and fasces of harpoons for spurs, would I could mount that whale and leap the topmost skies, to see whether the fabled heavens with all their countless tents really lie encamped beyond my mortal sight!

CHAPTER LVIII

BRIT

Steering north-eastward from the Corzetts, we fell in with vast meadows of brit, the minute, yellow substance, upon which the Right Whale largely feeds. For leagues and leagues it undulated round us, so that we seemed to be sailing through boundless fields of ripe and golden wheat.

On the second day, numbers of Right Whales were seen, who, secure from the attack of a Sperm Whaler like the Pequod, with open jaws sluggishly swam through the brit, which, adhering to the fringing fibres of that wondrous Venetian blind in their mouths, was in that manner separated from the water that escaped at the lip.

As morning mowers, who side by side slowly and seethingly advance their scythes through the long wet grass of marshy meads; even so these monsters swam, making a strange, grassy, cutting sound; and leaving behind them endless swaths of blue upon the yellow sea.*

But it was only the sound they made as they parted the brit which at all reminded one of mowers. Seen from the mast-heads, especially when they paused and were stationary for a while, their vast black forms looked more like lifeless masses of rock than anything else. And as in the great hunting countries of India, the stranger at a distance will sometimes pass on the plains recumbent elephants without knowing them to be such, taking them for bare, blackened elevations of the soil; even so, often, with him, who for the first time beholds this species of the leviathans of the sea. And even when recognized at last, their immense magnitude renders it very hard really to believe that such bulky masses of overgrowth can possibly be instinct, in all parts, with the same sort of life that lives in a dog or a horse.

Indeed, in other respects, you can hardly regard any creatures of the deep with the same feelings that you do those of the shore. For though some old naturalists have maintained that all creatures of the land are of their kind in the sea; and though taking a broad general view of the thing, this may very well be; yet coming to specialities, where, for example, does the ocean furnish any fish that in disposition answers to the sagacious kindness of the dog? The accursed shark alone can in any generic respect be said to bear comparative analogy to him.

But though, to landsmen in general, the native inhabitants of the seas have ever been regarded with emotions unspeakably unsocial and repelling; though we know the sea to be an everlasting terra incognita, so that Columbus sailed over numberless unknown worlds to discover his one superficial western one; though, by vast odds, the most terrific of all mortal disasters have immemorially and indiscriminately befallen tens and hundreds of thousands of those who have gone upon the waters; though but a moment's consideration will teach, that however baby man may brag of his science and skill, and however much, in a flattering future, that science and skill may augment; yet for ever and for ever, to the crack of doom, the sea will insult and murder him, and pulverize the stateliest, stiffest frigate he can make; nevertheless, by the continual repetition of these very impressions, man has lost that sense of the full awfulness of the sea which aboriginally belongs to it.

The first boat we read of, floated on an ocean, that with Portuguese vengeance had whelmed a whole world without leaving so much as a widow. That same ocean rolls now; that same ocean destroyed the wrecked ships of last year. Yea, foolish mortals, Noah's flood is not yet subsided; two thirds of the fair world it yet covers.

---

*That part of the sea known among whalemen as the 'Brazil Banks' does not bear that name as the Banks of Newfoundland do, because of there being shallows and soundings there, but because of this remarkable meadow-like appearance, caused by the vast drifts of brit continually floating in those latitudes, where the Right Whale is often chased.

Wherein differ the sea and the land, that a miracle upon one is not a miracle upon the other? Preternatural terrors rested upon the Hebrews, when under the feet of Korah and his company the live ground opened and swallowed them up for ever; yet not a modern sun ever sets, but in precisely the same manner the live sea swallows up ships and crews.

But not only is the sea such a foe to man who is an alien to it, but it is also a fiend to its own offspring; worse than the Persian host who murdered his own guests; sparing not the creatures which itself hath spawned. Like a savage tigress that tossing in the jungle overlays her own cubs, so the sea dashes even the mightiest whales against the rocks, and leaves them there side by side with the split wrecks of ships. No mercy, no power but its own controls it. Panting and snorting like a mad battle steed that has lost its rider, the masterless ocean overruns the globe.

Consider the subtleness of the sea; how its most dreaded creatures glide under water, unapparent for the most part, and treacherously hidden beneath the loveliest tints of azure. Consider also the devilish brilliance and beauty of many of its most remorseless tribes, as the dainty embellished shape of many species of sharks. Consider, once more, the universal cannibalism of the sea; all whose creatures prey upon each other, carrying on eternal war since the world began.

Consider all this; and then turn to this green, gentle, and most docile earth; consider them both, the sea and the land; and do you not find a strange analogy to something in yourself? For as this appalling ocean surrounds the verdant land, so in the soul of man there lies one insular Tahiti, full of peace and joy, but encompassed by all the horrors of the half known life. God keep thee! Push not off from that isle, thou canst never return!

CHAPTER LIX

SQUID

Slowly wading through the meadows of brit, the Pequod still held on her way north-eastward towards the island of Java; a gentle air impelling her keel, so that in the surrounding serenity her three tall tapering masts mildly waved to that languid breeze, as three mild palms on a plain. And still, at wide intervals in the silvery night, the lonely, alluring jet would be seen.

But one transparent blue morning, when a stillness almost preternatural spread over the sea, however unattended with any stagnant calm; when the long burnished sun-glade on the waters seemed a golden finger laid across them, enjoining some secrecy; when the slippered waves whispered together as they softly ran on; in this profound hush of the visible sphere a strange spectre was seen by Daggoo from the main-mast-head.

In the distance, a great white mass lazily rose, and rising higher and higher, and disentangling itself from the azure, at last gleamed before our prow like a snow-slide, new slid from the hills. Thus glistening for a moment, as slowly it subsided, and sank. Then once more arose, and silently gleamed. It seemed not a whale; and yet is this Moby Dick? thought Daggoo. Again the phantom went down, but on reappearing once more, with a stiletto-like cry that startled every man from his nod, the negro yelled out—'There! there again! there she breaches! right ahead! The White Whale, the White Whale!'

Upon this, the seamen rushed to the yard-arms, as in swarming-time the bees rush to the boughs. Bare-headed in the sultry sun, Ahab stood on the bowsprit, and with one hand pushed far behind in readiness to wave his orders to the helmsman, cast his eager glance in the direction indicated aloft by the outstretched motionless arm of Daggoo.

Whether the flitting attendance of the one still and solitary jet had gradually worked upon Ahab, so that he was now prepared to connect the ideas of mildness and repose with the first sight of the particular whale he pursued; however this was, or whether his eagerness betrayed him; whichever way it might have been, no sooner did he distinctly perceive the white mass, than with a quick intensity he instantly gave orders for lowering.

The four boats were soon on the water; Ahab's in advance, and all swiftly pulling towards their prey. Soon it went down, and while, with oars suspended, we were awaiting its reappearance, lo! in the same spot where it sank, once more it slowly rose. Almost forgetting for a moment all thoughts of Moby Dick, we now gazed at the most wondrous phenomenon which the secret seas have hitherto revealed to mankind. A vast pulpy mass, furlongs in length and breadth, of a glancing cream-color, lay floating on the water, innumerable long arms radiating from its centre, and curling and twisting like a nest of anacondas, as if blindly to clutch at any hapless object within reach. No perceptible face or front did it have; no conceivable token of either sensation or instinct; but undulated there on the billows, an unearthly, formless, chance-like apparition of life.

As with a low sucking sound it slowly disappeared again, Starbuck still gazing at the agitated waters where it had sunk, with a wild voice exclaimed—'Almost rather had I seen Moby Dick and fought him, than to have seen thee, thou white ghost!'

'What was it, Sir?' said Flask.

'The great live squid, which, they say, few whale-ships ever beheld, and returned to their ports to tell of it.'

But Ahab said nothing; turning his boat, he sailed back to the vessel; the rest as silently following.

Whatever superstitions the sperm whalemen in general have connected with the sight of this object, certain it is, that a glimpse of it being so very unusual, that circumstance has gone far to invest it with portentousness. So rarely is it beheld, that though one and all of them declare it to be the largest animated thing in the ocean, yet very few of them have any but the most vague ideas concerning its true nature and form; notwithstanding, they believe it to furnish to the sperm whale his only food. For though other species of whales find their food above water, and may be seen by man in the act of feeding, the spermaceti whale obtains his whole food in unknown zones below the surface; and only by inference is it that any one can tell of what, precisely, that food consists. At times, when closely pursued, he will disgorge what are supposed to be the detached arms of the squid; some of them thus exhibited exceeding twenty and thirty feet in length. They fancy that the monster to which these arms belonged ordinarily clings by them to the bed of the ocean; and that the sperm whale, unlike other species, is supplied with teeth in order to attack and tear it.

There seems some ground to imagine that the great Kraken of Bishop Pontoppodan may ultimately resolve itself into Squid. The manner in which the Bishop describes it, as alternately rising and sinking, with some other particulars he narrates, in all this the two correspond. But much abatement is necessary with respect to the incredible bulk he assigns it.

By some naturalists who have vaguely heard rumors of the mysterious creature, here spoken of, it is included among the class of cuttle-fish, to which, indeed, in certain external respects it would seem to belong, but only as the Anak of the tribe.

CHAPTER LX

THE LINE

With reference to the whaling scene shortly to be described, as well as for the better understanding of all similar scenes elsewhere presented, I have here to speak of the magical, sometimes horrible whale-line.

The line originally used in the fishery was one of the best hemp, slightly vapored with tar, not impregnated with it, as in the case of ordinary ropes; for while tar, as ordinarily used, makes the hemp more pliable to the rope-maker, and also renders the rope itself more convenient to the sailor for common ship use; yet, not only would the ordinary quantity too much stiffen the whale-line for the close coiling to which it must be subjected; but as most seamen are beginning to learn, tar in general by no means adds to the rope's durability or strength, however much it may give it compactness and gloss.

Of late years the Manilla rope has in the American fishery almost entirely superseded hemp as a material for whale-lines; for, though not so durable as hemp, it is stronger, and far more soft and elastic; and I will add (since there is an aesthetics in all things), is much more handsome and becoming to the boat, than hemp. Hemp is a dusky, dark fellow, a sort of Indian; but Manilla is as a golden-haired Circassian to behold.

The whale line is only two thirds of an inch in thickness. At first sight, you would not think it so strong as it really is. By experiment its one and fifty yarns will each suspend a weight of one hundred and twenty pounds; so that the whole rope will bear a strain nearly equal to three tons. In length, the common sperm whale-line measures something over two hundred fathoms. Towards the stern of the boat it is spirally coiled away in the tub, not like the worm-pipe of a still though, but so as to form one round, cheese-shaped mass of densely bedded 'sheaves', or layers of concentric spiralizations, without any hollow but the 'heart', or minute vertical tube formed at the axis of the cheese. As the least tangle or kink in the coiling would, in running out, infallibly take somebody's arm, leg, or entire body off, the utmost precaution is used in stowing the line in its tub. Some harpooneers will consume almost an entire morning in this business, carrying the line high aloft and then reeving it downwards through a block towards the tub, so as in the act of coiling to free it from all possible wrinkles and twists.

In the English boats two tubs are used instead of one; the same line being continuously coiled in both tubs. There is some advantage in this; because these twin-tubs being so small they fit more readily into the boat, and do not strain it so much; whereas, the American tub, nearly three feet in diameter and of proportionate depth, makes a rather bulky freight for a craft whose planks are but one half-inch in thickness; for the bottom of the whale-boat is like critical ice, which will bear up a considerable distributed weight, but not very much of a concentrated one. When the painted canvas cover is clapped on the American line-tub, the boat looks as if it were pulling off with a prodigious great wedding-cake to present to the whales.

Both ends of the line are exposed; the lower end terminating in an eye-splice or loop coming up from the bottom against the side of the tub, and hanging over its edge completely disengaged from everything. This arrangement of the lower end is necessary on two accounts. First: In order to facilitate the fastening to it of an additional line from a neighboring boat, in case the stricken whale should sound so deep as to threaten to carry off the entire line originally attached to the harpoon. In these instances, the whale of course is shifted like a mug of ale, as it were, from the one boat to the other; though the first boat always hovers at hand to assist its consort. Second: This arrangement is indispensable for common safety's sake; for were the lower end of the line in any way attached to the boat, and were the whale then to run the line out to the end almost in a single, smoking minute as he sometimes does, he would not stop there, for the doomed boat would infallibly be dragged down after him into the profundity of the sea; and in that case no town-crier would ever find her again.

Before lowering the boat for the chase, the upper end of the line is taken aft from the tub, and passing round the loggerhead there, is again carried forward the entire length of the boat, resting crosswise upon the loom or handle of every man's oar, so that it jogs against his wrist in rowing; and also passing between the men, as they alternately sit at the opposite gunwales, to the leaded chocks or grooves in the extreme pointed prow of the boat, where a wooden pin or skewer the size of a common quill, prevents it from slipping out. From the chocks it hangs in a slight festoon over the bows, and is then passed inside the boat again; and some ten or twenty fathoms (called box-line) being coiled upon the box in the bows, it continues its way to the gunwale still a little further aft, and is then attached to the short-warp—rope which is immediately connected with the harpoon; but previous to that connexion, the short-warp goes through sundry mystifications too tedious to detail.

Thus the whale-line folds the whole boat in its complicated coils, twisting and writhing around it in almost every direction. All the oarsmen are involved in its perilous contortions; so that to the timid eye of the landsman, they seem as Indian jugglers, with the deadliest snakes sportively festooning their limbs. Nor can any son of mortal woman, for the first time, seat himself amid those hempen intricacies, and while straining his utmost at the oar, bethink him that at any unknown instant the harpoon may be darted, and all these horrible contortions be put in play like ringed lightnings; he cannot be thus circumstanced without a shudder that makes the very marrow in his bones to quiver in him like a shaken jelly. Yet habit—strange thing! what cannot habit accomplish?—Gayer sallies, more merry mirth, better jokes, and brighter repartees, you never heard over your mahogany, than you will hear over the half-inch white cedar of the whale-boat, when thus hung in hangman's nooses; and, like the six burghers of Calais before King Edward, the six men composing the crew pull into the jaws of death, with a halter around every neck, as you may say.

Perhaps a very little thought will now enable you to account for those repeated whaling disasters—some few of which are casually chronicled—of this man or that man being taken out of the boat by the line, and lost. For, when the line is darting out, to be seated then in the boat, is like being seated in the midst of the manifold whizzings of a steam-engine in full play, when every flying beam, and shaft, and wheel, is grazing you. It is worse; for you cannot sit motionless in the heart of these perils, because the boat is rocking like a cradle, and you are pitched one way and the other, without the slightest warning; and only by a certain self-adjusting buoyancy and simultaneousness of volition and action, can you escape being made a Mazeppa of, and run away with where the all-seeing sun himself could never pierce you out.

Again: as the profound calm which only apparently precedes and prophesies of the storm, is perhaps more awful than the storm itself; for, indeed, the calm is but the wrapper and envelope of the storm; and contains it in itself, as the seemingly harmless rifle holds the fatal powder, and the ball, and the explosion; so the graceful repose of the line, as it silently serpentines about the oarsmen before being brought into actual play—this is a thing which carries more of true terror than any other aspect of this dangerous affair. But why say more? All men live enveloped in whale-lines. All are born with halters round their necks; but it is only when caught in the swift, sudden turn of death, that mortals realize the silent, subtle, ever-present perils of life. And if you be a philosopher, though seated in the whale-boat, you would not at heart feel one whit more of terror, than though seated before your evening fire with a poker, and not a harpoon, by your side.

CHAPTER LXI

STUBB KILLS A WHALE

If to Starbuck the apparition of the Squid was a thing of portents, to Queequeg it was quite a different object.

'When you see him 'quid,' said the savage, honing his harpoon in the bow of his hoisted boat, 'then you quick see him 'parm whale.'

The next day was exceedingly still and sultry, and with nothing special to engage them, the Pequod's crew could hardly resist the spell of sleep induced by such a vacant sea. For this part of the Indian Ocean through which we then were voyaging is not what whalemen call a lively ground; that is, it affords fewer glimpses of porpoises, dolphins, flying-fish, and other vivacious denizens of more stirring waters, than those off the Rio de la Plata, or the in-shore ground off Peru.

It was my turn to stand at the foremast-head; and with my shoulders leaning against the slackened royal shrouds, to and fro I idly swayed in what seemed an enchanted air. No resolution could withstand it; in that dreamy mood losing all consciousness, at last my soul went out of my body; though my body still continued to sway as a pendulum will, long after the power which first moved it is withdrawn.

Ere forgetfulness altogether came over me, I had noticed that the seamen at the main and mizen mast-heads were already drowsy. So that at last all three of us lifelessly swung from the spars, and for every swing that we made there was a nod from below from the slumbering helmsman. The waves, too, nodded their indolent crests; and across the wide trance of the sea, east nodded to west, and the sun over all.

Suddenly bubbles seemed bursting beneath my closed eyes; like vices my hands grasped the shrouds; some invisible, gracious agency preserved me; with a shock I came back to life. And lo! close under our lee, not forty fathoms off, a gigantic Sperm Whale lay rolling in the water like the capsized hull of a frigate, his broad, glossy back, of an Ethiopian hue, glistening in the sun's rays like a mirror. But lazily undulating in the trough of the sea, and ever and anon tranquilly spouting his vapory jet, the whale looked like a portly burgher smoking his pipe of a warm afternoon. But that pipe, poor whale, was thy last. As if struck by some enchanter's wand, the sleepy ship and every sleeper in it all at once started into wakefulness; and more than a score of voices from all parts of the vessel, simultaneously with the three notes from aloft, shouted forth the accustomed cry, as the great fish slowly and regularly spouted the sparkling brine into the air.

'Clear away the boats! Luff!' cried Ahab. And obeying his own order, he dashed the helm down before the helmsman could handle the spokes.

The sudden exclamations of the crew must have alarmed the whale; and ere the boats were down, majestically turning, he swam away to the leeward, but with such a steady tranquillity, and making so few ripples as he swam, that thinking after all he might not as yet be alarmed, Ahab gave orders that not an oar should be used, and no man must speak but in whispers. So seated like Ontario Indians on the gunwales of the boats, we swiftly but silently paddled along; the calm not admitting of the noiseless sails being set. Presently, as we thus glided in chase, the monster perpendicularly flitted his tail forty feet into the air, and then sank out of sight like a tower swallowed up.

'There go flukes!' was the cry, an announcement immediately followed by Stubb's producing his match and igniting his pipe, for now a respite was granted. After the full interval of his sounding had elapsed, the whale rose again, and being now in advance of the smoker's boat, and much nearer to it than to any of the others, Stubb counted upon the honor of the capture. It was obvious, now, that the whale had at length become aware of his pursuers. All silence of cautiousness was therefore no longer of use. Paddles were dropped, and oars came loudly into play. And still puffing at his pipe, Stubb cheered on his crew to the assault.

Yes, a mighty change had come over the fish. All alive to his jeopardy, he was going 'head out'; that part obliquely projecting from the mad yeast which he brewed.*

'Start her, start her, my men! Don't hurry yourselves; take plenty of time—but start her; start her like thunder-claps, that's all,' cried Stubb, spluttering out the smoke as he spoke. 'Start her, now; give 'em the long and strong stroke, Tashtego. Start her, Tash, my boy—start her, all; but keep cool, keep cool—cucumbers is the word—easy, easy—only start her like grim death and grinning devils, and raise the buried dead perpendicular out of their graves, boys—that's all. Start her!'

'Woo-hoo! Wa-hee!' screamed the Gay-Header in reply, raising some old war-whoop to the skies; as every oarsman in the strained boat involuntarily bounced forward with the one tremendous leading stroke which the eager Indian gave.

*It will be seen in some other place of what a very light substance the entire interior of the sperm whale's enormous head consists. Though apparently the most massive, it is by far the most buoyant part about him. So that with ease he elevates it in the air, and invariably does so when going at his utmost speed. Besides, such is the breadth of the upper part of the front of his head, and such the tapering cut-water formation of the lower part, that by obliquely elevating his head, he thereby may be said to transform himself from a bluff-bowed sluggish galliot into a sharp-pointed New York pilot-boat.

But his wild screams were answered by others quite as wild. 'Kee-hee! Kee-hee!' yelled Daggoo, straining forwards and backwards on his seat, like a pacing tiger in his cage.

'Ka-la! Koo-loo!' howled Queequeg, as if smacking his lips over a mouthful of Grenadier's steak. And thus with oars and yells the keels cut the sea. Meanwhile, Stubb retaining his place in the van, still encouraged his men to the onset, all the while puffing the smoke from his mouth. Like desperadoes they tugged and they strained, till the welcome cry was heard—'Stand up, Tashtego!—give it to him!' The harpoon was hurled. 'Stern all!' The oarsmen backed water; the same moment something went hot and hissing along every one of their wrists. It was the magical line. An instant before, Stubb had swiftly caught two additional turns with it round the loggerhead, whence, by reason of its increased rapid circlings, a hempen blue smoke now jetted up and mingled with the steady fumes from his pipe. As the line passed round and round the loggerhead; so also, just before reaching that point, it blisteringly passed through and through both of Stubb's hands, from which the hand-cloths, or squares of quilted canvas sometimes worn at these times, had accidentally dropped. It was like holding an enemy's sharp two-edged sword by the blade, and that enemy all the time striving to wrest it out of your clutch.

'Wet the line! wet the line!' cried Stubb to the tub oarsman (him seated by the tub) who, snatching off his hat, dashed the sea-water into it.* More turns were taken, so that the line began holding its place. The boat now flew through the boiling water like a shark all fins. Stubb and Tashtego here changed places—stem for stern—a staggering business truly in that rocking commotion.

From the vibrating line extending the entire length of the upper part of the boat, and from its now being more tight than a harpstring, you would have thought the craft had two keels—one cleaving the water, the other the air—as the boat churned on through both opposing elements at once. A continual cascade played at the bows; a ceaseless whirling eddy in her wake; and, at the slightest motion from within, even but of a little finger, the vibrating, cracking craft canted over her spasmodic gunwale into the sea. Thus they rushed; each man with might and main clinging to his seat, to prevent being tossed to the foam; and the tall form of Tashtego at the steering oar crouching almost double, in order to bring down his centre of gravity. Whole Atlantics and Pacifics seemed passed as they shot on their way, till at length the whale somewhat slackened his flight.

'Haul in—haul in!' cried Stubb to the bowsman; and, facing round towards the whale, all hands began pulling the boat up to him, while yet the boat was being towed on. Soon ranging up by his flank, Stubb, firmly planting his knee in the clumsy cleat, darted dart after dart into the flying fish; at the word of command, the boat alternately sterning out of the way of the whale's horrible wallow, and then ranging up for another fling.

The red tide now poured from all sides of the monster like brooks down a hill. His tormented body rolled not in brine but in blood, which bubbled and seethed for furlongs behind in their wake. The slanting sun playing upon this crimson pond in the sea, sent back its reflection into every face, so that they all glowed to

*Partly to show the indispensableness of this act, it may here be stated, that, in the old Dutch fishery, a mop was used to dash the running line with water; in many other ships, a wooden piggin, or bailer, is set apart for that purpose. Your hat, however, is the most convenient.

each other like red men. And all the while, jet after jet of white smoke was agonizingly shot from the spiracle of the whale, and vehement puff after puff from the mouth of the excited headsman; as at every dart, hauling in upon his crooked lance (by the line attached to it), Stubb straightened it again and again, by a few rapid blows against the gunwale, then again and again sent it into the whale.

'Pull up—pull up!' he now cried to the bowsman, as the waning whale relaxed in his wrath. 'Pull up—close to!' and the boat ranged along the fish's flank. When reaching far over the bow, Stubb slowly churned his long sharp lance into the fish, and kept it there, carefully churning and churning, as if cautiously seeking to feel after some gold watch that the whale might have swallowed, and which he was fearful of breaking ere he could hook it out. But that gold watch he sought was the innermost life of the fish. And now it is struck; for, starting from his trance into that unspeakable thing called his 'flurry,' the monster horribly wallowed in his blood, overwrapped himself in impenetrable, mad, boiling spray, so that the imperilled craft, instantly dropping astern, had much ado blindly to struggle out from that phrensied twilight into the clear air of the day.

And now abating in his flurry, the whale once more rolled out into view; surging from side to side; spasmodically dilating and contracting his spout-hole, with sharp, cracking, agonized respirations. At last, gush after gush of clotted red gore, as if it had been the purple lees of red wine, shot into the frighted air; and falling back again, ran dripping down his motionless flanks into the sea. His heart had burst!

'He's dead, Mr Stubb,' said Tashtego.

'Yes; both pipes smoked out!' and withdrawing his own from his mouth, Stubb scattered the dead ashes over the water; and, for a moment, stood thoughtfully eyeing the vast corpse he had made.

CHAPTER LXII

The Dart

A word concerning an incident in the last chapter.

According to the invariable usage of the fishery, the whale-boat pushes off from the ship, with the headsman or whale-killer as temporary steersman, and the harpooneer or whale-fastener pulling the foremost oar, the one known as the harpooneer-oar. Now it needs a strong, nervous arm to strike the first iron into the fish; for often, in what is called a long dart, the heavy implement has to be flung to the distance of twenty or thirty feet. But however prolonged and exhausting the chase, the harpooneer is expected to pull his oar meanwhile to the uttermost; indeed, he is expected to set an example of superhuman activity to the rest, not only by incredible rowing, but by repeated loud and intrepid exclamations; and what it is to keep shouting at the top of one's compass, while all the other muscles are strained and half started—what that is none know but those who have tried it. For me, I cannot bawl very heartily and work very recklessly at one and the same time. In this straining, bawling state, then, with his back to the fish, all at once the exhausted harpooneer hears the exulting cry, 'Stand up, and give it to him!' He now has to drop and secure his oar, turn round on his centre half way, seize his harpoon from the crotch, and with what little strength may remain, he essays to pitch it somehow into the whale. No wonder, taking the whole fleet of whalemen in a body, that out of fifty fair chances for a dart, not five are successful; no wonder that so many hapless harpooneers are madly cursed and disrated; no wonder that some of them actually burst their blood-vessels in the boat; no wonder that some sperm whalemen are absent four years with four barrels; no wonder that to many ship owners, whaling is but a losing concern; for it is the harpooneer that makes the voyage, and if you take the breath out of his body how can you expect to find it there when most wanted!

Again, if the dart be successful, then at the second critical instant, that is, when the whale starts to run, the boat-header and harpooneer likewise start to running fore and aft, to the imminent jeopardy of themselves and every one else. It is then they change places; and the headsman, the chief officer of the little craft, takes his proper station in the bows of the boat.

Now, I care not who maintains the contrary, but all this is both foolish and unnecessary. The headsman should stay in the bows from first to last; he should both dart the harpoon and the lance, and no rowing whatever should be expected of him, except under circumstances obvious to any fisherman. I know that this would sometimes involve a slight loss of speed in the chase; but long experience in various whalemen of more than one nation has convinced me that in the vast majority of failures in the fishery, it has not by any means been so much the speed of the whale as the before described exhaustion of the harpooneer that has caused them.

To insure the greatest efficiency in the dart, the harpooneers of this world must start to their feet from out of idleness, and not from out of toil.

CHAPTER LXIII

THE CROTCH

Out of the trunk, the branches grow; out of them, the twigs. So, in productive subjects, grow the chapters.

The crotch alluded to on a previous page deserves independent mention. It is a notched stick of a peculiar form, some two feet in length, which is perpendicularly inserted into the starboard gunwale near the bow, for the purpose of furnishing a rest for the wooden extremity of the harpoon, whose other naked, barbed end slopingly projects from the prow. Thereby the weapon is instantly at hand to its hurler, who snatches it up as readily from its rest as a backwoodsman swings his rifle from the wall. It is customary to have two harpoons reposing in the crotch, respectively called the first and second irons.

But these two harpoons, each by its own cord, are both connected with the line; the object being this: to dart them both, if possible, one instantly after the other into the same whale; so that if, in the coming drag, one should draw out, the other may still retain a hold. It is a doubling of the chances. But it very often happens that owing to the instantaneous, violent, convulsive running of the whale upon receiving the first iron, it becomes impossible for the harpooneer, however lightning-like in his movements, to pitch the second iron into him. Nevertheless, as the second iron is already connected with the line, and the line is running, hence that weapon must, at all events, be anticipatingly tossed out of the boat, somehow and somewhere; else the most terrible jeopardy would involve all hands. Tumbled into the water, it accordingly is in such cases; the spare coils of box line (mentioned in a preceding chapter) making this feat, in most instances, prudently practicable. But this critical act is not always unattended with the saddest and most fatal casualties.

Furthermore: you must know that when the second iron is thrown overboard, it thenceforth becomes a dangling, sharp-edged terror, skittishly curvetting about both boat and whale, entangling the lines, or cutting them, and making a prodigious sensation in all directions. Nor, in general, is it possible to secure it again until the whale is fairly captured and a corpse.

Consider, now, how it must be in the case of four boats all engaging one unusually strong, active, and knowing whale; when owing to these qualities in him, as well as to the thousand concurring accidents of such an audacious enterprise, eight or ten loose second irons may be simultaneously dangling about him. For, of course, each boat is supplied with several harpoons to bend on to the line should the first one be ineffectually darted without recovery. All these particulars are faithfully narrated here, as they will not fail to elucidate several most important, however intricate passages, in scenes hereafter to be painted.

CHAPTER LXIV

Stubb's Supper

Stubb's whale had been killed some distance from the ship. It was a calm; so, forming a tandem of three boats, we commenced the slow business of towing the trophy to the Pequod. And now, as we eighteen men with our thirty-six arms, and one hundred and eighty thumbs and fingers, slowly toiled hour after hour upon that inert, sluggish corpse in the sea; and it seemed hardly to budge at all, except at long intervals; good evidence was hereby furnished of the enormousness of the mass we moved. For, upon the great canal of Hang-Ho, or whatever they call it, in China, four or five laborers on the foot-path will draw a bulky freighted junk at the rate of a mile an hour; but this grand argosy we towed heavily forged along, as if laden with pig-lead in bulk.

Darkness came on; but three lights up and down in the Pequod's main-rigging dimly guided our way; till drawing nearer we saw Ahab dropping one of several more lanterns over the bulwarks. Vacantly eyeing the heaving whale for a moment, he issued the usual orders for securing it for the night, and then handing his lantern to a seaman, went his way into the cabin, and did not come forward again until morning.

Though, in overseeing the pursuit of this whale, Captain Ahab had evinced his customary activity, to call it so; yet now that the creature was dead, some vague dissatisfaction, or impatience, or despair, seemed working in him; as if the sight of that dead body reminded him that Moby Dick was yet to be slain; and though a thousand other whales were brought to his ship, all that would not one jot advance his grand, monomaniac object. Very soon you would have thought from the sound on the Pequod's decks, that all hands were preparing to cast anchor in the deep; for heavy chains are being dragged along the deck, and thrust rattling out of the port-holes. But by those clanking links, the vast corpse itself, not the ship, is to be moored. Tied by the head to the stern, and by the tail to the bows, the whale now lies with its black hull close to the vessel's, and seen through the darkness of the night, which obscured the spars and rigging aloft, the two—ship and whale, seemed yoked together like colossal bullocks, whereof one reclines while the other remains standing.*

If moody Ahab was now all quiescence, at least so far as could be known on deck, Stubb, his second mate, flushed with conquest, betrayed an unusual but still good-natured excitement. Such an unwonted bustle was he in that the staid Starbuck, his official superior, quietly resigned to him for the time the sole management of affairs. One small, helping cause of all this liveliness in Stubb, was soon made strangely manifest. Stubb was a high liver; he was somewhat intemperately fond of the whale as a flavorish thing to his palate.

'A steak, a steak, ere I sleep! You, Daggoo! overboard you go, and cut me one from his small!'

Here be it known, that though these wild fishermen do not, as a general thing, and according to the great military maxim, make the enemy defray the current expenses of the war (at least before realizing the proceeds of the voyage), yet now and then you find some of these Nantucketers who have a genuine relish for that particular part of the Sperm Whale designated by Stubb; comprising the tapering extremity of the body.

About midnight that steak was cut and cooked; and lighted by two lanterns of sperm oil, Stubb stoutly stood up to his spermaceti supper at the capstan-head, as if that capstan were a sideboard. Nor was Stubb the only banqueter on whale's flesh that night. Mingling their mumblings with his own mastication, thousands on thousands of sharks, swarming round the dead leviathan, smackingly feasted on its fatness. The few sleepers below in their bunks were often startled by the sharp slapping of their tails against the hull, within a few inches of the sleepers' hearts. Peering over the side you could just see them (as before you heard them) wallowing in the sullen, black waters, and turning over on their backs as they scooped out huge globular pieces of the whale of the bigness of a human head. This particular feat of the shark seems all but miraculous. How, at such an apparently unassailable surface, they contrive to gouge out such symmetrical mouthfuls, remains a part of the universal problem of all things. The mark they thus leave on the whale, may best be likened to the hollow made by a carpenter in countersinking for a screw.

Though amid all the smoking horror and diabolism of a sea-fight, sharks will be seen longingly gazing up to the ship's decks, like hungry dogs round a table where

*A little item may as well be related here. The strongest and most reliable hold which the ship has upon the whale when moored along-side, is by the flukes or tail; and as from its greater density that part is relatively heavier than any other (excepting the side-fins), its flexibility even in death, causes it to sink low beneath the surface; so that with the hand you cannot get at it from the boat, in order to put the chain round it. But this difficulty is ingeniously overcome: a small, strong line is prepared with a wooden float at its outer end, and a weight in its middle, while the other end is secured to the ship. By adroit management, the wooden float is made to rise on the other side of the mass, so that now having girdled the whale, the chain is readily made to follow suit; and being slipped along the body, is at last locked fast round the smallest part of the tail, at the point of junction with its broad flukes or lobes.

red meat is being carved, ready to bolt down every killed man that is tossed to them; and though, while the valiant butchers over the deck-table are thus cannibally carving each other's live meat with carving-knives all gilded and tasselled, the sharks, also, with their jewel-hilted mouths, are quarrelsomely carving away under the table at the dead meat; and though, were you to turn the whole affair upside down, it would still be pretty much the same thing, that is to say, a shocking sharkish business enough for all parties; and though sharks also are the invariable outriders of all slave ships crossing the Atlantic, systematically trotting alongside, to be handy in case a parcel is to be carried anywhere, or a dead slave to be decently buried; and though one or two other like instances might be set down, touching the set terms, places, and occasions, when sharks do most socially congregate, and most hilariously feast; yet is there no conceivable time or occasion when you will find them in such countless numbers, and in gayer or more jovial spirits, than around a dead sperm whale, moored by night to a whale-ship at sea. If you have never seen that sight, then suspend your decision about the propriety of devil-worship, and the expediency of conciliating the devil.

But, as yet, Stubb heeded not the mumblings of the banquet that was going on so nigh him, no more than the sharks heeded the smacking of his own epicurean lips.

'Cook, cook!—where's that old Fleece?' he cried at length, widening his legs still further, as if to form a more secure base for his supper; and, at the same time, darting his fork into the dish, as if stabbing with his lance; 'cook, you cook!—sail this way, cook!'

The old black, not in any very high glee at having been previously roused from his warm hammock at a most unseasonable hour, came shambling along from his galley, for, like many old blacks, there was something the matter with his knee-pans, which he did not keep well scoured like his other pans; this old Fleece, as they called him, came shuffling and limping along, assisting his step with his tongs, which, after a clumsy fashion, were made of straightened iron hoops; this old Ebony floundered along, and in obedience to the word of command, came to a dead stop on the opposite side of Stubb's sideboard; when, with both hands folded before him, and resting on his two-legged cane, he bowed his arched back still further over, at the same time sideways inclining his head, so as to bring his best ear into play.

'Cook,' said Stubb, rapidly lifting a rather reddish morsel to his mouth, 'don't you think this steak is rather overdone? You've been beating this steak too much, cook; it's too tender. Don't I always say that to be good, a whale-steak must be tough? There are those sharks now over the side, don't you see they prefer it tough and rare? What a shindy they are kicking up! Cook, go and talk to 'em; tell 'em they are welcome to help themselves civilly, and in moderation, but they must keep quiet. Blast me, if I can hear my own voice. Away, cook, and deliver my message. Here, take this lantern,' snatching one from his sideboard; 'now then, go and preach to 'em!'

Sullenly taking the offered lantern, old Fleece limped across the deck to the bulwarks; and then, with one hand dropping his light low over the sea, so as to get a good view of his congregation, with the other hand he solemnly flourished his tongs, and leaning far over the side in a mumbling voice began addressing the sharks, while Stubb, softly crawling behind, overhead all that was said.

'Fellow-critters: I'se ordered here to say dat you must stop dat dam noise dare. You hear? Stop dat dam smackin' ob de lip! Massa Stubb say dat you can fill your dam bellies up to de hatching, but by Gor! you must stop dat dam racket!'

'Cook,' here interposed Stubb, accompanying the word with a sudden slap on the shoulder,—'Cook! why, damn your eyes, you mustn't swear that way when you're preaching. That's no way to convert sinners, Cook!'

'Who dat? Den preach to him yourself,' sullenly turning to go.

'No, Cook; go on, go on.'

'Well, den, Belubed fellow-critters:'—

'Right!' exclaimed Stubb, approvingly, 'coax 'em to it; try that,' and Fleece continued.

'Dough you is all sharks, and by natur wery woracious, yet I zay to you, fellow-critters, dat dat woraciousness—'top dat dam slappin' ob de tail! How you tink to hear, 'spose you keep up such a dam slappin' and bitin' dare?'

'Cook,' cried Stubb, collaring him, 'I wont have that swearing. Talk to 'em gentlemanly.'

Once more the sermon proceeded.

'Your woraciousness, fellow-critters, I don't blame ye so much for; dat is natur, and can't be helped; but to gobern dat wicked natur, dat is de pint. You is sharks, sartin; but if you gobern de shark in you, why den you be angel; for all angel is not'ing more dan de shark well goberned. Now, look here, bred'ren, just try wonst to be cibil, a helping yourselbs from dat whale. Don't be tearin' de blubber out your neighbour's mout, I say. Is not one shark dood right as toder to dat whale? And, by Gor, none on you has de right to dat whale; dat whale belong to some one else. I know some o' you has berry brig mout, brigger dan oders; but den de brig mouts sometimes has de small bellies; so dat de brigness ob de mout is not to swallar wid, but to bite off de blubber for de small fry ob sharks, dat can't get into de scrouge to help demselves.'

'Well done, old Fleece!' cried Stubb, 'that's Christianity; go on.'

'No use goin' on; de dam willains will keep a scrougin' and slappin' each oder, Massa Stubb; dey don't hear one word; no use a-preachin' to such dam g'uttons as you call 'em, till dare bellies is full, and dare bellies is bottomless; and when dey do get 'em full, dey won't hear you den; for den dey sink in de sea, go fast to sleep on de coral, and can't hear not'ing at all, no more, for eber and eber.'

'Upon my soul, I am about of the same opinion; so give the benediction, Fleece, and I'll away to my supper.'

Upon this, Fleece, holding both hands over the fishy mob, raised his shrill voice, and cried—

'Cussed fellow-critters! Kick up de damndest row as ever you can; fill your dam' bellies till dey bust—and den die.'

'Now, cook,' said Stubb, resuming his supper at the capstan; 'Stand just where you stood before, there, over against me, and pay particular attention.'

'All 'dention,' said Fleece, again stooping over upon his tongs in the desired position.

'Well,' said Stubb, helping himself freely meanwhile; 'I shall now go back to the subject of this steak. In the first place, how old are you, cook?'

'What dat do wid de 'teak,' said the old black, testily.

'Silence! How old are you, cook?'

''Bout ninety, dey say,' he gloomily muttered.

'And have you lived in this world hard upon one hundred years, cook, and don't know yet how to cook a whale-steak?' rapidly bolting another mouthful at the last word, so that that morsel seemed a continuation of the question. 'Where were you born, cook?'

‘’Hind de hatchway, in ferry-boat, goin’ ober de Roanoke.’

‘Born in a ferry-boat! That’s queer, too. But I want to know what country you were born in, cook?’

‘Didn’t I say Roanoke country?’ he cried, sharply.

‘No, you didn’t, cook; but I’ll tell you what I’m coming to, cook. You must go home and be born over again; you don’t know how to cook a whale-steak yet.’

‘Bress my soul, if I cook ’noder one,’ he growled, angrily, turning round to depart.

‘Come back, cook;—here, hand me those tongs;—now take that bit of steak there, and tell me if you think that steak cooked as it should be? Take it, I say’—holding the tongs towards him—‘take it, and taste it.’

Faintly smacking his withered lips over it for a moment, the old negro muttered, ‘Best cooked ’teak I eber taste; joosy, berry joosy.’

‘Cook,’ said Stubb, squaring himself once more; ‘do you belong to the church?’

‘Passed one once in Cape-Down,’ said the old man sullenly.

‘And you have once in your life passed a holy church in Cape-Town, where you doubtless overheard a holy parson addressing his hearers as his beloved fellow-creatures, have you, cook! And yet you come here, and tell me such a dreadful lie as you did just now, eh?’ said Stubb. ‘Where do you expect to go to, cook?’

‘Go to bed berry soon,’ he mumbled, half-turning as he spoke.

‘Avast! heave to! I mean when you die, cook. It’s an awful question. Now what’s your answer?’

‘When dis old brack man dies,’ said the negro slowly, changing his whole air and demeanor, ‘he hisself won’t go nowhere; but some bressed angel will come and fetch him.’

‘Fetch him? How? In a coach and four, as they fetched Elijah? And fetch him where?’

‘Up dere,’ said Fleece, holding his tongs straight over his head, and keeping it there very solemnly.

‘So, then, you expect to go up into our main-top, do you, cook, when you are dead? But don’t you know the higher you climb the colder it gets? Main-top, eh?’

‘Didn’t say dat ’tall,’ said Fleece, again in the sulks.

‘You said up there, didn’t you? and now look yourself, and see where your tongs are pointing. But, perhaps you expect to get into heaven by crawling through the lubber’s hole, cook; but, no, cook, you don’t get there, except you go the regular way, round by the rigging. It’s a ticklish business, but must be done, or else it’s no go. But none of us are in heaven yet. Drop your tongs, cook, and hear my orders. Do ye hear? Hold your hat in one hand, and clap t’other a’top of your heart, when I’m giving my orders, cook. What! that your heart, there?—that’s your gizzard! Aloft! aloft!—that’s it—now you have it. Hold it there now, and pay attention.’

‘All ’dention,’ said the old black, with both hands placed as desired, vainly wriggling his grizzled head, as if to get both ears in front at one and the same time.

‘Well then, cook, you see this whale-steak of yours was so very bad, that I have put it out of sight as soon as possible; you see that, don’t you? Well, for the future, when you cook another whale steak for my private table here, the capstan, I’ll tell you what to do so as not to spoil it by overdoing. Hold the steak in one hand, and show a live coal to it with the other; that done, dish it; d’ye hear? And now tomorrow, cook, when we are cutting in the fish, be sure you stand by to get the tops of his fins; have them put in pickle. As for the ends of the flukes, have them soused, cook. There, now ye may go.’

But Fleece had hardly got three paces off, when he was recalled.

'Cook, give me cutlets for supper to-morrow night in the mid-watch. D'ye hear? away you sail, then.—Halloa! stop! make a bow before you go.—Avast heaving again! Whale-balls for breakfast—don't forget.'

'Wish, by gor! whale eat him, 'stead of him eat whale. I'm bressed if he ain't more of shark dan Massa Shark hisself,' muttered the old man, limping away; with which sage ejaculation he went to his hammock.

CHAPTER LXV

THE WHALE AS A DISH

That mortal man should feed upon the creature that feeds his lamp, and, like Stubb, eat him by his own light, as you may say; this seems so outlandish a thing that one must needs go a little into the history and philosophy of it.

It is upon record, that three centuries ago the tongue of the Right Whale was esteemed a great delicacy in France, and commanded large prices there. Also, that in Henry VIIIth's time, a certain cook of the court obtained a handsome reward for inventing an admirable sauce to be eaten with barbacued porpoises, which, you remember, are a species of whale. Porpoises, indeed, are to this day considered fine eating. The meat is made into balls about the size of billiard balls, and being well seasoned and spiced might be taken for turtle-balls or veal balls. The old monks of Dunfermline were very fond of them. They had a great porpoise grant from the crown.

The fact is, that among his hunters at least, the whale would by all hands be considered a noble dish, were there not so much of him; but when you come to sit down before a meat-pie nearly one hundred feet long, it takes away your appetite. Only the most unprejudiced of men like Stubb, nowadays partake of cooked whales; but the Esquimaux are not so fastidious. We all know how they live upon whales, and have rare old vintages of prime old train oil. Zogranda, one of their most famous doctors, recommends strips of blubber for infants, as being exceedingly juicy and nourishing. And this reminds me that certain Englishmen, who long ago were accidentally left in Greenland by a whaling vessel—that these men actually lived for several months on the mouldy scraps of whales which had been left ashore after trying out the blubber. Among the Dutch whalemen these scraps are called 'fritters'; which, indeed, they greatly resemble, being brown and crisp, and smelling something like old Amsterdam housewives' dough-nuts or oly-cooks, when fresh. They have such an eatable look that the most self-denying stranger can hardly keep his hands off.

But what further depreciates the whale as a civilized dish, is his exceeding richness. He is the great prize ox of the sea, too fat to be delicately good. Look at his hump, which would be as fine eating as the buffalo's (which is esteemed a rare dish), were it not such a solid pyramid of fat. But the spermaceti itself, how bland and creamy that is; like the transparent, half-jellied, white meat of a cocoanut in the third month of its growth, yet far too rich to supply a substitute for butter. Nevertheless, many whalemen have a method of absorbing it into some other substance, and then partaking of it. In the long try watches of the night it is a common thing for the seamen to dip their ship-biscuit into the huge oil-pots and let them fry there awhile. Many a good supper have I thus made.

In the case of a small Sperm Whale the brains are accounted a fine dish. The casket of the skull is broken into with an axe, and the two plump, whitish lobes being withdrawn (precisely resembling two large puddings), they are then mixed with flour, and cooked into a most delectable mess, in flavor somewhat resembling calves' heads, which is quite a dish among some epicures; and every one knows that some young bucks among the epicures, by continually dining upon calves' brains, by and by get to have a little brains of their own, so as to be able to tell a calf's head from their own heads; which, indeed, requires uncommon discrimination. And that is the reason why a young buck with an intelligent looking calf's head before him, is somehow one of the saddest sights you can see. The head looks a sort of reproachfully at him, with an 'Et tu Brute!' expression.

It is not, perhaps, entirely because the whale is so excessively unctuous that landsmen seem to regard the eating of him with abhorrence; that appears to result, in some way, from the consideration before mentioned: i.e. that a man should eat a newly murdered thing of the sea, and eat it too by its own light. But no doubt the first man that ever murdered an ox was regarded as a murderer; perhaps he was hung; and if he had been put on his trial by oxen, he certainly would have been; and he certainly deserved it if any murderer does. Go to the meat-market of a Saturday night and see the crowds of live bipeds staring up at the long rows of dead quadrupeds. Does not that sight take a tooth out of the cannibal's jaw? Cannibals? who is not a cannibal? I tell you it will be more tolerable for the Fejee that salted down a lean missionary in his cellar against a coming famine; it will be more tolerable for that provident Fejee, I say, in the day of judgment, than for thee, civilized and enlightened gourmand, who nailest geese to the ground and feastest on their bloated livers in thy paté-de-foie-gras.

But Stubb, he eats the whale by its own light, does he? and that is adding insult to injury, is it? Look at your knifehandle, there, my civilized and enlightened gourmand dining off that roast beef, what is that handle made of?—what but the bones of the brother of the very ox you are eating? And what do you pick your teeth with, after devouring that fat goose? With a feather of the same fowl. And with what quill did the Secretary of the Society for the Suppression of Cruelty to Ganders formally indite his circulars? It is only within the last month or two that that society passed a resolution to patronize nothing but steel pens.

CHAPTER LXVI

THE SHARK MASSACRE

When in the Southern Fishery, a captured Sperm Whale, after long and weary toil, is brought alongside late at night, it is not, as a general thing at least, customary to proceed at once to the business of cutting him in. For that business is an exceedingly laborious one; is not very soon completed; and requires all hands to set about it. Therefore, the common usage is to take in all sail; lash the helm a'lee; and then send every one below to his hammock till daylight, with the reservation that, until that time, anchor-watches shall be kept; that is, two and two, for an hour each couple, the crew in rotation shall mount the deck to see that all goes well.

But sometimes, especially upon the Line in the Pacific, this plan will not answer at all; because such incalculable hosts of sharks gather round the moored carcase, that were he left so for six hours, say, on a stretch, little more than the skeleton would be visible by morning. In most other parts of the ocean, however, where these fish do not so largely abound, their wondrous voracity can be at times considerably diminished, by vigorously stirring them up with sharp whaling-spades, a procedure notwithstanding, which, in some instances, only seems to tickle them into still greater activity. But it was not thus in the present case with the Pequod's sharks; though, to be sure, any man unaccustomed to such sights, to have looked over her side that night, would have almost thought the whole round sea was one huge cheese, and those sharks the maggots in it.

Nevertheless, upon Stubb setting the anchor-watch after his supper was concluded; and when, accordingly, Queequeg and a forecastle seaman came on deck, no small excitement was created among the sharks; for immediately suspending the cutting stages over the side, and lowering three lanterns, so that they cast long gleams of light over the turbid sea, these two mariners, darting their long whaling-spades, kept up an incessant murdering of the sharks,* by striking the keen steel deep into their skulls, seemingly their only vital part. But in the foamy confusion of their mixed and struggling hosts, the marksmen could not always hit their marks; and this brought about new revelations of the incredible ferocity of the foe. They viciously snapped, not only at each other's disembowelments, but like flexible bows, bent round, and bit their own; till those entrails seemed swallowed over and over again by the same mouth, to be oppositely voided by the gaping wound. Nor was this all. It was unsafe to meddle with the corpses and ghosts of these creatures. A sort of generic or Pantheistic vitality seemed to lurk in their very joints and bones, after what might be called the individual life had departed. Killed and hoisted on deck for the sake of his skin, one of these sharks almost took poor Queequeg's hand off, when he tried to shut down the dead lid of his murderous jaw.

'Queequeg no care what god made him shark,' said the savage, agonizingly lifting his hand up and down; 'wedder Fejee god or Nantucket god; but de god wat made shark must be one dam Ingin.'

CHAPTER LXVII

CUTTING IN

It was a Saturday night, and such a Sabbath as followed! Ex officio professors of Sabbath breaking are all whalemen. The ivory Pequod was turned into what seemed a shamble; every sailor a butcher. You would have thought we were offering up ten thousand red oxen to the sea gods.

---

*The whaling-spade used for cutting-in is made of the very best steel; is about the bigness of a man's spread hand; and in general shape, corresponds to the garden implement after which it is named; only its sides are perfectly flat, and its upper end considerably narrower than the lower. This weapon is always kept as sharp as possible; and when being used is occasionally honed, just like a razor. In its socket, a stiff pole, from twenty to thirty feet long, is inserted for a handle.

In the first place, the enormous cutting tackles, among other ponderous things comprising a cluster of blocks generally painted green, and which no single man can possibly lift—this vast bunch of grapes was swayed up to the main-top and firmly lashed to the lower mast-head, the strongest point anywhere above a ship's deck. The end of the hawser-like rope winding through these intricacies, was then conducted to the windlass, and the huge lower block of the tackles was swung over the whale; to this block the great blubber hook, weighing some one hundred pounds, was attached. And now suspended in stages over the side, Starbuck and Stubb, the mates, armed with their long spades, began cutting a hole in the body for the insertion of the hook just above the nearest of the two side-fins. This done, a broad, semicircular line is cut round the hole, the hook is inserted, and the main body of the crew striking up a wild chorus, now commence heaving in one dense crowd at the windlass. When instantly, the entire ship careens over on her side; every bolt in her starts like the nail-heads of an old house in frosty weather; she trembles, quivers, and nods her frighted mast-heads to the sky. More and more she leans over to the whale, while every gasping heave of the windlass is answered by a helping heave from the billows; till at last, a swift, startling snap is heard; with a great swash the ship rolls upwards and backwards from the whale, and the triumphant tackle rises into sight dragging after it the disengaged semicircular end of the first strip of blubber. Now as the blubber envelopes the whale precisely as the rind does an orange, so is it stripped off from the body precisely as an orange is sometimes stripped by spiralizing it. For the strain constantly kept up by the windlass continually keeps the whale rolling over and over in the water, and as the blubber in one strip uniformly peels off along the line called the 'scarf', simultaneously cut by the spades of Starbuck and Stubb, the mates; and just as fast as it is thus peeled off, and indeed by that very act itself, it is all the time being hoisted higher and higher aloft till its upper end grazes the main-top; the men at the windlass then cease heaving, and for a moment or two the prodigious blood-dripping mass sways to and fro as if let down from the sky, and every one present must take good heed to dodge it when it swings, else it may box his ears and pitch him headlong overboard.

One of the attending harpooneers now advances with a long, keen weapon called a boarding-sword, and watching his chance he dexterously slices out a considerable hole in the lower part of the swaying mass. Into this hole, the end of the second alternating great tackle is then hooked so as to retain a hold upon the blubber, in order to prepare for what follows. Whereupon, this accomplished swordsman, warning all hands to stand off, once more makes a scientific dash at the mass, and with a few sidelong, desperate, lunging slicings, severs it completely in twain; so that while the short lower part is still fast, the long upper strip, called a blanket-piece, swings clear, and is all ready for lowering. The heavers forward now resume their song, and while the one tackle is peeling and hoisting a second strip from the whale, the other is slowly slackened away, and down goes the first strip through the main hatchway right beneath, into an unfurnished parlor called the blubber-room. Into this twilight apartment sundry nimble hands keep coiling away the long blanket-piece as if it were a great live mass of plaited serpents. And thus the work proceeds; the two tackles hoisting and lowering simultaneously; both whale and windlass heaving, the heavers singing, the blubber-room gentlemen coiling, the mates scarfing, the ship straining, and all hand swearing occasionally, by way of assuaging the general friction.

CHAPTER LXVIII

THE BLANKET

I have given no small attention to that not unvexed subject, the skin of the whale. I have had controversies about it with experienced whalemen afloat, and learned naturalists ashore. My original opinion remains unchanged; but it is only an opinion.

The question is, what and where is the skin of the whale? Already you know what his blubber is. That blubber is something of the consistence of firm, close-grained beef, but tougher, more elastic and compact, and ranges from eight or ten to twelve and fifteen inches in thickness.

Now, however preposterous it may at first seem to talk of any creature's skin as being of that sort of consistence and thickness, yet in point of fact these are no arguments against such a presumption; because you cannot raise any other dense enveloping layer from the whale's body but that same blubber; and the outermost enveloping layer of any animal, if reasonably dense, what can that be but the skin? True, from the unmarred dead body of the whale, you may scrape off with your hand an infinitely thin, transparent substance, somewhat resembling the thinnest shreds of isinglass, only it is almost as flexible and soft as satin; that is, previous to being dried, when it not only contracts and thickens, but becomes rather hard and brittle. I have several such dried bits, which I use for marks in my whale-books. It is transparent, as I said before; and being laid upon the printed page, I have sometimes pleased myself with fancying it exerted a magnifying influence. At any rate, it is pleasant to read about whales through their own spectacles, as you may say. But what I am driving at here is this. That same infinitely thin, isinglass substance, which, I admit, invests the entire body of the whale, is not so much to be regarded as the skin of the creature, as the skin of the skin, so to speak; for it were simply ridiculous to say, that the proper skin of the tremendous whale is thinner and more tender than the skin of a new-born child. But no more of this.

Assuming the blubber to be the skin of the whale; then, when this skin, as in the case of a very large Sperm Whale, will yield the bulk of one hundred barrels of oil; and, when it is considered that, in quantity, or rather weight, that oil, in its expressed state, is only three fourths, and not the entire substance of the coat; some idea may hence be had of the enormousness of that animated mass, a mere part of whose mere integument yields such a lake of liquid as that. Reckoning ten barrels to the ton, you have ten tons for the net weight of only three quarters of the stuff of the whale's skin.

In life, the visible surface of the Sperm Whale is not the least among the many marvels he presents. Almost invariably it is all over obliquely crossed and re-crossed with numberless straight marks in thick array, something like those in the finest Italian line engravings. But these marks do not seem to be impressed upon the isinglass substance above mentioned, but seem to be seen through it, as if they were engraved upon the body itself. Nor is this all. In some instances, to the quick, observant eye, those linear marks, as in a veritable engraving, but afford the ground for far other delineations. These are hieroglyphical; that is, if you call those mysterious cyphers on the walls of pyramids hieroglyphics, then that is the proper word to use in the present connexion. By my retentive memory of the hieroglyphics upon one Sperm Whale in particular, I was much struck with a plate representing the old Indian characters chiselled on the famous hieroglyphic palisades on the banks of the Upper Mississippi. Like those mystic rocks, too, the mystic-marked whale remains undecipherable. This allusion to the Indian rocks reminds me of another thing. Besides all the other phenomena which the exterior of the Sperm Whale presents, he not seldom displays the back, and more especially his flanks, effaced in great part of the regular linear appearance, by reason of numerous rude scratches, altogether of an irregular, random aspect. I should say that those New England rocks on the sea-coast, which Agassiz imagines to bear the marks of violent scraping contact with vast floating icebergs—I should say, that those rocks must not a little resemble the Sperm Whale in this particular. It also seems to me that such scratches in the whale are probably made by hostile contact with other whales; for I have most remarked them in the large, full-grown bulls of the species.

A word or two more concerning this matter of the skin or blubber of the whale. It has already been said, that it is stript from him in long pieces, called blanket-pieces. Like most sea-terms, this one is very happy and significant. For the whale is indeed wrapt up in his blubber as in a real blanket or counterpane; or, still better, an Indian poncho slipt over his head, and skirting his extremity. It is by reason of this cosy blanketing of his body, that the whale is enabled to keep himself comfortable in all weathers, in all seas, times, and tides. What would become of a Greenland whale, say, in those shuddering, icy seas of the North, if unsupplied with his cosy surtout? True, other fish are found exceedingly brisk in those Hyperborean waters; but these, be it observed, are your cold-blooded, lungless fish, whose very bellies are refrigerators; creatures, that warm themselves under the lee of an iceberg, as a traveller in winter would bask before an inn fire, whereas, like man, the whale has lungs and warm blood. Freeze his blood, and he dies. How wonderful is it then—except after explanation—that this great monster, to whom corporeal warmth is as indispensable as it is to man; how wonderful that he should be found at home, immersed to his lips for life in those Arctic waters! where, when seamen fall overboard, they are sometimes found, months afterwards, perpendicularly frozen into the hearts of fields of ice, as a fly is found glued in amber. But more surprising is it to know, as has been proved by experiment, that the blood of a Polar whale is warmer than that of a Borneo negro in summer.

It does seem to me, that herein we see the rare virtue of a strong individual vitality, and the rare virtue of thick walls, and the rare virtue of interior spaciousness. Oh, man! admire and model thyself after the whale! Do thou, too, remain warm among ice. Do thou, too, live in this world without being of it. Be cool at the equator; keep thy blood fluid at the Pole. Like the great dome of St Peter's, and like the great whale, retain, O man! in all seasons a temperature of thine own.

But how easy and how hopeless to teach these fine things! Of erections, how few are domed like St Peter's! of creatures, how few vast as the whale!

CHAPTER LXIX

THE FUNERAL

'Haul in the chains! Let the carcase go astern!'

The vast tackles have now done their duty. The peeled white body of the beheaded whale flashes like a marble sepulchre; though changed in hue, it has not perceptibly lost anything in bulk. It is still colossal. Slowly it floats more and more away, the water round it torn and splashed by the insatiate sharks, and the air above vexed with rapacious flights of screaming fowls, whose beaks are like so many insulting poniards in the whale. The vast white headless phantom floats further and further from the ship, and every rod that it so floats, what seem square roods of sharks and cubic roods of fowls, augment the murderous din. For hours and hours from the almost stationary ship that hideous sight is seen. Beneath the unclouded and mild azure sky, upon the fair face of the pleasant sea, wafted by the joyous breezes, that great mass of death floats on and on, till lost in infinite perspectives.

There's a most doleful and most mocking funeral! The sea-vultures all in pious mourning, the air-sharks all punctiliously in black or speckled. In life but few of them would have helped the whale, I ween, if peradventure he had needed it; but upon the banquet of his funeral they most piously do pounce. Oh, horrible vulturism of earth! from which not the mightiest whale is free.

Nor is this the end. Desecrated as the body is, a vengeful ghost survives and hovers over it to scare. Espied by some timid man-of-war or blundering discovery-vessel from afar, when the distance obscuring the swarming fowls, nevertheless still shows the white mass floating in the sun, and the white spray heaving high against it; straightway the whale's unharming corpse, with trembling fingers is set down in the log—*shoals, rocks, and breakers hereabouts: beware!* And for years afterwards, perhaps, ships shun the place; leaping over it as silly sheep leap over a vacuum, because their leader originally leaped there when a stick was held. There's your law of precedents; there's your utility of traditions; there's the story of your obstinate survival of old beliefs never bottomed on the earth, and now not even hovering in the air! There's orthodoxy!

Thus, while in life the great whale's body may have been a real terror to his foes, in his death his ghost becomes a powerless panic to a world.

Are you a believer in ghosts, my friend? There are other ghosts than the Cock-Lane one, and far deeper men than Doctor Johnson who believe in them.

CHAPTER LXX

THE SPHYNX

It should not have been omitted that previous to completely stripping the body of the leviathan, he was beheaded. Now, the beheading of the Sperm Whale is a scientific anatomical feat, upon which experienced whale surgeons very much pride themselves: and not without reason.

Consider that the whale has nothing that can properly be called a neck; on the contrary, where his head and body seem to join, there, in that very place, is the thickest part of him. Remember, also, that the surgeon must operate from above, some eight or ten feet intervening between him and his subject, and that subject almost hidden in a discolored, rolling, and oftentimes tumultuous and bursting sea. Bear in mind, too, that under these untoward circumstances he has to cut many feet deep in the flesh; and in that subterraneous manner, without so much as getting one single peep into the ever-contracting gash thus made, he must skilfully steer clear of all adjacent, interdicted parts, and exactly divide the spine at a critical point hard by its insertion into the skull. Do you not marvel, then, at Stubb's boast, that he demanded but ten minutes to behead a sperm whale?

When first severed, the head is dropped astern and held there by a cable till the body is stripped. That done, if it belong to a small whale it is hoisted on deck to be deliberately disposed of. But, with a full grown leviathan this is impossible; for the sperm whale's head embraces nearly one third of his entire bulk, and completely to suspend such a burden as that, even by the immense tackles of a whaler, this were as vain a thing as to attempt weighing a Dutch barn in jewellers' scales.

The Pequod's whale being decapitated and the body stripped, the head was hoisted against the ship's side—about half way out of the sea, so that it might yet in great part be buoyed up by its native element. And there with the strained craft steeply leaning over to it, by reason of the enormous downward drag from the lower mast-head, and every yard-arm on that side projecting like a crane over the waves; there, that blood-dripping head hung to the Pequod's waist like the giant Holofernes's from the girdle of Judith.

When this last task was accomplished it was noon, and the seamen went below to their dinner. Silence reigned over the before tumultuous but now deserted deck. An intense copper calm, like a universal yellow lotus, was more and more unfolding its noiseless measureless leaves upon the sea.

A short space elapsed, and up into this noiselessness came Ahab alone from his cabin. Taking a few turns on the quarter-deck, he paused to gaze over the side, then slowly getting into the main-chains he took Stubb's long spade—still remaining there after the whale's decapitation—and striking it into the lower part of the half-suspended mass, placed its other end crutch-wise under one arm, and so stood leaning over with eyes attentively fixed on this head.

It was a black and hooded head; and hanging there in the midst of so intense a calm, it seemed the Sphynx's in the desert. 'Speak, thou vast and venerable head,' muttered Ahab, 'which, though ungarnished with a beard, yet here and there lookest hoary with mosses; speak, mighty head, and tell us the secret thing that is in thee. Of all divers, thou hast dived the deepest. That head upon which the upper sun now gleams, has moved amid this world's foundations. Where unrecorded names and navies rust, and untold hopes and anchors rot; where in her murderous hold this frigate earth is ballasted with bones of millions of the drowned; there, in that awful water-land, there was thy most familiar home. Thou has been where bell or diver never went; hast slept by many a sailor's side, where sleepless mothers would give their lives to lay them down. Thou saw'st the locked lovers when leaping from their flaming ship; heart to heart they sank beneath the exulting wave; true to each other, when heaven seemed false to them. Thou saw'st the murdered mate when tossed by pirates from the midnight deck; for hours he fell into the deeper midnight of the insatiate maw; and his murderers still sailed on unharmed—while swift lightnings shivered the neighboring ship that would have borne a righteous husband to outstretched, longing arms. O head! thou has seen enough to split the planets and make an infidel of Abraham, and not one syllable is thine!'

'Sail ho!' cried a triumphant voice from the main-mast-head.

'Aye? Well, now, that's cheering,' cried Ahab, suddenly erecting himself, while whole thunder-clouds swept aside from his brow. 'That lively cry upon this deadly calm might almost convert a better man.—Where away?'

'Three points on the starboard bow, sir, and bringing down her breeze to us!'

'Better and better, man. Would now St Paul would come along that way, and to my breezelessness bring his breeze! O Nature, and O soul of man! how far beyond all utterance are your linked analogies! not the smallest atom stirs or lives in matter, but has its cunning duplicate in mind.'

CHAPTER LXXI

THE JEROBOAM'S STORY

Hand in hand, ship and breeze blew on; but the breeze came faster than the ship, and soon the Pequod began to rock.

By and by, through the glass the stranger's boats and manned mast-heads proved her a whale-ship. But as she was so far to windward, and shooting by, apparently making a passage to some other ground, the Pequod could not hope to reach her. So the signal was set to see what response would be made.

Here be it said, that like the vessels of military marines, the ships of the American Whale Fleet have each a private signal; all which signals being collected in a book with the names of the respective vessels attached, every captain is provided with it. Thereby, the whale commanders are enabled to recognise each other upon the ocean, even at considerable distances, and with no small facility.

The Pequod's signal was at last responded to by the stranger's setting her own; which proved the ship to be the Jeroboam of Nantucket. Squaring her yards, she bore down, ranged abeam under the Pequod's lee, and lowered a boat; it soon drew nigh; but, as the side-ladder was being rigged by Starbuck's order to accommodate the visiting captain, the stranger in question waved his hand from his boat's stern in token of that proceeding being entirely unnecessary. It turned out that the Jeroboam had a malignant epidemic on board, and that Mayhew, her captain, was fearful of infecting the Pequod's company. For, though himself and boat's crew remained untainted, and though his ship was half a rifle-shot off, and an incorruptible sea and air rolling and flowing between; yet conscientiously adhering to the timid quarantine of the land, he peremptorily refused to come into direct contact with the Pequod.

But this did by no means prevent all communication. Preserving an interval of some few yards between itself and the ship, the Jeroboam's boat by the occasional use of its oars contrived to keep parallel to the Pequod, as she heavily forged through the sea (for by this time it blew very fresh), with her main-topsail aback; though, indeed, at times by the sudden onset of a large rolling wave, the boat would be pushed some way ahead; but would be soon skilfully brought to her proper bearings again. Subject to this, and other the like interruptions now and then, a conversation was sustained between the two parties; but at intervals not without still another interruption of a very different sort.

Pulling an oar in the Jeroboam's boat, was a man of a singular appearance, even in that wild whaling life where individual notabilities make up all totalities. He was a small, short, youngish man, sprinkled all over his face with freckles, and wearing redundant yellow hair. A long-skirted, cabalistically-cut coat of a faded walnut tinge enveloped him; the overlapping sleeves of which were rolled up on his wrists. A deep, settled, fanatic delirium was in his eyes.

So soon as this figure had been first descried, Stubb had exclaimed—'That's he! that's he!—the long-togged scaramouch the Town-Ho's company told us of!' Stubb here alluded to a strange story told of the Jeroboam, and a certain man among her crew, some time previous when the Pequod spoke the Town-Ho. According to this account and what was subsequently learned, it seemed that the scaramouch in question had gained a wonderful ascendency over almost everybody in the Jeroboam. His story was this:

He had been originally nurtured among the crazy society of Neskyeuna Shakers, where he had been a great prophet; in their cracked, secret meetings having several times descended from heaven by the way of a trap-door, announcing the speedy opening of the seventh vial, which he carried in his vest-pocket; but, which, instead of containing gunpowder, was supposed to be charged with laudanum. A strange, apostolic whim having seized him, he had left Neskyeuna for Nantucket, where, with that cunning peculiar to craziness, he assumed a steady, common sense exterior, and offered himself as a green-hand candidate for the Jeroboam's whaling voyage. They engaged him; but straightway upon the ship's getting out of sight of land, his insanity broke out in a freshet. He announced himself as the archangel Gabriel, and commanded the captain to jump overboard. He published his manifesto, whereby he set himself forth as the deliverer of the isles of the sea and vicar-general of all Oceanica. The unflinching earnestness with which he declared these things;—the dark, daring play of his sleepless, excited imagination, and all the preternatural terrors of real delirium, united to invest this Gabriel in the minds of the majority of the ignorant crew, with an atmosphere of sacredness. Moreover, they were afraid of him. As such a man, however, was not of much practical use in the ship, especially as he refused to work except when he pleased, the incredulous captain would fain have been rid of him; but apprised that that individual's intention was to land him in the first convenient port, the archangel forthwith opened all his seals and vials—devoting the ship and all hands to unconditional perdition, in case this intention was carried out. So strongly did he work upon his disciples among the crew, that at last in a body they went to the captain and told him if Gabriel was sent from the ship, not a man of them would remain. He was therefore forced to relinquish his plan. Nor would they permit Gabriel to be any way maltreated, say or do what he would; so that it came to pass that Gabriel had the complete freedom of the ship. The consequence of all this was, that the archangel cared little or nothing for the captain and mates; and since the epidemic had broken out, he carried a higher hand than ever; declaring that the plague, as he called it, was at his sole command; nor should it be stayed but according to his good pleasure. The sailors, mostly poor devils, cringed, and some of them fawned before him; in obedience to his instructions, sometimes rendering him personal homage, as to a god. Such things may seem incredible; but, however wondrous, they are true. Nor is the history of fanatics half so striking in respect to the measureless self-deception of the fanatic himself, as his measureless power of deceiving and bedevilling so many others. But it is time to return to the Pequod.

'I fear not thy epidemic, man,' said Ahab from the bulwarks, to Captain Mayhew, who stood in the boat's stern; 'come on board.'

But now Gabriel started to his feet.

'Think, think of the fevers, yellow and bilious! Beware of the horrible plague!'

'Gabriel, Gabriel!' cried Captain Mayhew; 'thou must either—' But that instant a headlong wave shot the boat far ahead, and its seethings drowned all speech.

'Hast thou seen the White Whale?' demanded Ahab, when the boat drifted back.

'Think, think of thy whale-boat, stoven and sunk! Beware of the horrible tail!'

'I tell thee again, Gabriel, that—' But again the boat tore ahead as if dragged by fiends. Nothing was said for some moments, while a succession of riotous waves rolled by, which by one of those occasional caprices of the seas were tumbling, not heaving it. Meantime, the hoisted sperm whale's head jogged about very violently, and Gabriel was seen eyeing it with rather more apprehensiveness than his archangel nature seemed to warrant.

When this interlude was over, Captain Mayhew began a dark story concerning Moby Dick; not, however, without frequent interruptions from Gabriel, whenever his name was mentioned, and the crazy sea that seemed leagued with him.

It seemed that the Jeroboam had not long left home, when upon speaking a whale-ship, her people were reliably apprised of the existence of Moby Dick, and the havoc he had made. Greedily sucking in this intelligence, Gabriel solemnly warned the captain against attacking the White Whale, in case the monster should be seen; in his gibbering insanity, pronouncing the White Whale to be no less a being than the Shaker God incarnated; the Shakers receiving the Bible. But when, some year or two afterwards, Moby Dick was fairly sighted from the mast-heads, Macey, the chief mate, burned with ardor to encounter him; and the captain himself being not unwilling to let him have the opportunity, despite all the archangel's denunciations and forewarnings, Macey succeeded in persuading five men to man his boat. With them he pushed off; and, after much weary pulling, and many perilous, unsuccessful onsets, he at last succeeded in getting one iron fast. Meantime, Gabriel, ascending to the main-royal mast-head, was tossing one arm in frantic gestures, and hurling forth prophecies of speedy doom to the sacrilegious assailants of his divinity. Now, while Macey, the mate, was standing up in his boat's bow, and with all the reckless energy of his tribe was venting his wild exclamations upon the whale, and essaying to get a fair chance for his poised lance, lo! a broad white shadow rose from the sea; by its quick, fanning motion, temporarily taking the breath out of the bodies of the oarsmen. Next instant, the luckless mate, so full of furious life, was smitten bodily into the air, and making a long arc in his descent, fell into the sea at the distance of about fifty yards. Not a chip of the boat was harmed, nor a hair of any oarsman's head; but the mate for ever sank.

(It is well to parenthesize here, that of the fatal accidents in the Sperm-Whale Fishery, this kind is perhaps almost as frequent as any. Sometimes, nothing is injured but the man who is thus annihilated; oftener the boat's bow is knocked off, or the thighboard, in which the headsman stands, is torn from its place and accompanies the body. But strangest of all is the circumstance, that in more instances than one, when the body has been recovered, not a single mark of violence is discernible; the man being stark dead.)

The whole calamity, with the falling form of Macey, was plainly descried from the ship. Raising a piercing shriek—'The vial; the vial!' Gabriel called off the terror-stricken crew from the further hunting of the whale. This terrible event clothed the archangel with added influence; because his credulous disciples believed that he had specifically fore-announced it, instead of only making a general prophecy, which any one might have done, and so have chanced to hit one of many marks in the wide margin allowed. He became a nameless terror to the ship.

Mayhew having concluded his narration, Ahab put such questions to him, that the stranger captain could not forbear inquiring whether he intended to hunt the White Whale, if opportunity should offer. To which Ahab answered—'Aye.' Straightway, then, Gabriel once more started to his feet, glaring upon the old man, and vehemently exclaimed, with downward pointed finger—'Think, think of the blasphemer—dead, and down there!—beware of the blasphemer's end!'

Ahab stolidly turned aside; then said to Mayhew, 'Captain, I have just bethought me of my letter-bag; there is a letter for one of thy officers, if I mistake not. Starbuck, look over the bag.'

Every whale-ship takes out a goodly number of letters for various ships, whose delivery to the persons to whom they may be addressed, depends upon the mere chance of encountering them in the four oceans. Thus, most letters never reach their mark; and many are only received after attaining an age of two or three years or more.

Soon Starbuck returned with a letter in his hand. It was sorely tumbled, damp, and covered with a dull, spotted, green mould, in consequence of being kept in a dark locker of the cabin. Of such a letter, Death himself might well have been the post-boy.

'Can'st not read it?' cried Ahab. 'Give it me, man. Aye, aye, it's but a dim scrawl;—what's this?' As he was studying it out, Starbuck took a long cutting-spade pole, and with his knife slightly split the end, to insert the letter there, and in that way, hand it to the boat, without its coming any closer to the ship.

Meantime, Ahab holding the letter, muttered, 'Mr Har—yes, Mr Harry—(a woman's pinny hand,—the man's wife, I'll wager)—Aye—Mr Harry Macey, Ship Jeroboam;—why it's Macey, and he's dead!'

'Poor fellow! poor fellow! and from his wife,' sighed Mayhew; 'but let me have it.'

'Nay, keep it thyself,' cried Gabriel to Ahab; 'thou art soon going that way.'

'Curses throttle thee!' yelled Ahab. 'Captain Mayhew, stand by now to receive it;' and taking the fatal missive from Starbuck's hands, he caught it in the slit of the pole, and reached it over towards the boat. But as he did so, the oarsmen expectantly desisted from rowing; the boat drifted a little towards the ship's stern; so that, as if by magic, the letter suddenly ranged along with Gabriel's eager hand. He clutched it in an instant, seized the boat-knife, and impaling the letter on it, sent it thus loaded back into the ship. It fell at Ahab's feet. Then Gabriel shrieked out to his comrades to give way with their oars, and in that manner the mutinous boat rapidly shot away from the Pequod.

As, after this interlude, the seamen resumed their work upon the jacket of the whale, many strange things were hinted in reference to this wild affair.

CHAPTER LXXII

THE MONKEY-ROPE

In the tumultuous business of cutting-in and attending to a whale, there is much running backwards and forwards among the crew. Now hands are wanted here, and then again hands are wanted there. There is no staying in any one place; for at one and the same time everything has to be done everywhere. It is much the same with him who endeavors the description of the scene. We must now retrace our way a little. It was mentioned that upon first breaking ground in the whale's back, the blubber-hook was inserted into the original hole there cut by the spades of the mates. But how did so clumsy and weighty a mass as that same hook get fixed in that hole? It was inserted there by my particular friend Queequeg, whose duty it was, as harpooneer, to descend upon the monster's back for the special purpose referred to. But in very many cases, circumstances require that the harpooneer shall remain on the whale till the whole flensing or stripping operation is concluded. The whale, be it observed, lies almost entirely submerged, excepting the immediate parts operated upon. So down there, some ten feet below the level of the deck, the poor harpooneer flounders about, half on the whale and half in the water, as the vast mass revolves like a tread-mill beneath him. On the occasion in question, Queequeg figured in the Highland costume—a shirt and socks—in which to my eyes, at least, he appeared to uncommon advantage; and no one had a better chance to observe him, as will presently be seen.

Being the savage's bowsman, that is, the person who pulled the bow-oar in his boat (the second one from forward), it was my cheerful duty to attend upon him while taking that hard-scrabble scramble upon the dead whale's back. You have seen Italian organ-boys holding a dancing-ape by a long cord. Just so, from the ship's steep side, did I hold Queequeg down there in the sea, by what is technically called in the fishery a monkey-rope, attached to a strong strip of canvas belted round his waist.

It was a humorously perilous business for both of us. For, before we proceed further, it must be said that the monkey-rope was fast at both ends; fast to Queequeg's broad canvas belt, and fast to my narrow leather one. So that for better or for worse, we two, for the time, were wedded; and should poor Queequeg sink to rise no more, then both usage and honor demanded, that instead of cutting the cord, it should drag me down in his wake. So, then, an elongated Siamese ligature united us. Queequeg was my own inseparable twin brother; nor could I any way get rid of the dangerous liabilities which the hempen bond entailed.

So strongly and metaphysically did I conceive of my situation then, that while earnestly watching his motions, I seemed distinctly to perceive that my own individuality was now merged in a joint stock company of two: that my free will had received a mortal wound; and that another's mistake or misfortune might plunge innocent me into unmerited disaster and death. Therefore, I saw that here was a sort of interregnum in Providence; for its even-handed equity never could have sanctioned so gross an injustice. And yet still further pondering—while I jerked him now and then from between the whale and the ship, which would threaten to jam him—still further pondering, I say, I saw that this situation of mine was the precise situation of every mortal that breathes; only, in most cases, he, one way or other, has this Siamese connexion with a plurality of other mortals. If your banker breaks, you snap; if your apothecary by mistake sends you poison in your pills, you die. True, you may say that, by exceeding caution, you may possibly escape these and the multitudinous other evil chances of life. But handle Queequeg's monkey-rope heedfully as I would, sometimes he jerked it so, that I came very near sliding overboard. Nor could I possibly forget that, do what I would, I only had the management of one end of it.*

I have hinted that I would often jerk poor Queequeg from between the whale and the ship—where he would occasionally fall, from the incessant rolling and swaying of both. But this was not the only jamming jeopardy he was exposed to.

*The monkey-rope is found in all whalers; but it was only in the Pequod that the monkey and his holder were ever tied together. This improvement upon the original usage was introduced by no less a man than Stubb, in order to afford to the imperilled harpooneer the strongest possible guarantee for the faithfulness and vigilance of his monkey-rope holder.

Unappalled by the massacre made upon them during the night, the sharks now freshly and more keenly allured by the before pent blood which began to flow from the carcase—the rabid creatures swarmed round it like bees in a beehive.

And right in among those sharks was Queequeg; who often pushed them aside with his floundering feet. A thing altogether incredible were it not that attracted by such prey as a dead whale, the otherwise miscellaneously carnivorous shark will seldom touch a man.

Nevertheless, it may well be believed that since they have such a ravenous finger in the pie, it is deemed but wise to look sharp to them. Accordingly, besides the monkey-rope, with which I now and then jerked the poor fellow from too close a vicinity to the maw of what seemed a peculiarly ferocious shark—he was provided with still another protection. Suspended over the side in one of the stages, Tashtego and Daggoo continually flourished over his head a couple of keen whale-spades, wherewith they slaughtered as many sharks as they could reach. This procedure of theirs, to be sure, was very disinterested and benevolent of them. They meant Queequeg's best happiness, I admit; but in their hasty zeal to befriend him, and from the circumstance that both he and the sharks were at times half hidden by the blood-mudded water, those indiscreet spades of theirs would come nearer amputating a leg than a tail. But poor Queequeg, I suppose, straining and gasping there with that great iron hook—poor Queequeg, I suppose, only prayed to his Yojo, and gave up his life into the hands of his gods.

Well, well, my dear comrade and twin-brother, thought I, as I drew in and then slacked off the rope to every swell of the sea—what matters it, after all? Are you not the precious image of each and all of us men in this whaling world? That unsounded ocean you gasp in, is Life; those sharks, your foes; those spades, your friends; and what between sharks and spades you are in a sad pickle and peril, poor lad.

But courage! there is good cheer in store for you, Queequeg. For now, as with blue lips and bloodshot eyes the exhausted savage at last climbs up the chains and stands all dripping and involuntarily trembling over the side; the steward advances, and with a benevolent, consolatory glance hands him—what? Some hot Cogniac? No! hands him, ye gods! hands him a cup of tepid ginger and water!

'Ginger? Do I smell ginger?' suspiciously asked Stubb, coming near. 'Yes, this must be ginger,' peering into the as yet untasted cup. Then standing as if incredulous for a while, he calmly walked towards the astonished steward slowly saying, 'Ginger? ginger? and will you have the goodness to tell me, Mr Dough-Boy, where lies the virtue of ginger? Ginger! is ginger the sort of fuel you use, Dough-Boy, to kindle a fire in this shivering cannibal? Ginger!—what the devil is ginger?—sea-coal?—fire-wood?—lucifer matches?—tinder?—gun-powder?—what the devil is ginger, I say, that you offer this cup to our poor Queequeg here?'

'There is some sneaking Temperance Society movement about this business,' he suddenly added, now approaching Starbuck, who had just come from forward. 'Will you look at that kannakin, sir: smell of it, if you please.' Then watching the mate's countenance, he added: 'The steward, Mr Starbuck, had the face to offer that calomel and jalap to Queequeg, there, this instant off the whale. Is the steward an apothecary, sir? and may I ask whether this is the sort of bellows by which he blows back the breath into a half-drowned man?'

'I trust not,' said Starbuck, 'it is poor stuff enough.'

'Aye, aye, steward,' cried Stubb, 'we'll teach you to drug a harpooneer; none of your apothecary's medicine here; you want to poison us, do ye? You have got out insurances on our lives and want to murder us all, and pocket the proceeds, do ye?'

'It was not me,' cried Dough-Boy, 'it was Aunt Charity that brought the ginger on board; and bade me never give the harpooneers any spirits, but only this ginger-jub—so she called it.'

'Ginger-jub! you gingerly rascal! take that! and run along with ye to the lockers, and get something better. I hope I do no wrong, Mr Starbuck. It is the captain's orders—grog for the harpooneer on a whale.'

'Enough,' replied Starbuck, 'only don't hit him again, but—'

'Oh, I never hurt when I hit, except when I hit a whale or something of that sort; and this fellow's a weazel. What were you about saying, sir?'

'Only this: go down with him, and get what thou wantest thyself.'

When Stubb reappeared, he came with a dark flask in one hand, and a sort of tea-caddy in the other. The first contained strong spirits, and was handed to Queequeg; the second was Aunt Charity's gift, and that was freely given to the waves.

CHAPTER LXXIII

STUBB AND FLASK KILL A RIGHT WHALE; AND THEN HAVE A TALK OVER HIM

It must be borne in mind that all this time we have a Sperm Whale's prodigious head hanging to the Pequod's side. But we must let it continue hanging there a while till we can get a chance to attend to it. For the present other matters press, and the best we can do now for the head, is to pray heaven the tackles may hold.

Now, during the past night and forenoon, the Pequod had gradually drifted into a sea, which, by its occasional patches of yellow brit, gave unusual tokens of the vicinity of Right Whales, a species of the Leviathan that but few supposed to be at this particular time lurking anywhere near. And though all hands commonly disdained the capture of those inferior creatures; and though the Pequod was not commissioned to cruise for them at all, and though she had passed numbers of them near the Crozetts without lowering a boat; yet now that a Sperm Whale had been brought alongside and beheaded, to the surprise of all, the announcement was made that a Right Whale should be captured that day, if opportunity offered.

Nor was this long wanting. Tall spouts were seen to leeward; and two boats, Stubb's and Flask's, were detached in pursuit. Pulling further and further away, they at last became almost invisible to the men at the mast-head. But suddenly in the distance, they saw a great heap of tumultuous white water, and soon after news came from aloft that one or both the boats must be fast. An interval passed and the boats were in plain sight, in the act of being dragged right towards the ship by the towing whale. So close did the monster come to the hull, that at first it seemed as if he meant it malice; but suddenly going down in a maelstrom, within three rods of the planks, he wholly disappeared from view, as if diving under the keel. 'Cut, cut!' was the cry from the ship to the boats, which, for one instant, seemed on the point of being brought with a deadly dash against the vessel's hide. But having plenty of line yet in the tubs, and the whale not sounding very rapidly, they paid out abundance of rope, and at the same time pulled with all their might so as to get ahead of the ship. For a few minutes the struggle was intensely critical; for while they still slacked out the tightened line in one direction, and still plied their oars in another, the contending strain threatened to take them under. But it was only a few feet advance they sought to gain. And they stuck to it till they did gain it; when instantly, a swift tremor was felt running like lightning along the keel, as the strained line, scraping beneath the ship, suddenly rose to view under her bows, snapping and quivering; and so flinging off its drippings, that the drops fell like bits of broken glass on the water, while the whale beyond also rose to sight, and once more the boats were free to fly. But the fagged whale abated his speed, and blindly altering his course, went round the stern of the ship towing the two boats after him, so that they performed a complete circuit.

Meantime, they hauled more and more upon their lines, till close flanking him on both sides, Stubb answered Flask with lance for lance; and thus round and round the Pequod the battle went, while the multitudes of sharks that had before swum round the Sperm Whale's body, rushed to the fresh blood that was spilled, thirstily drinking at every new gash, as the eager Israelites did at the new bursting fountains that poured from the smitten rock.

At last his spout grew thick, and with a frightful roll and vomit, he turned upon his back a corpse.

While the two headsmen were engaged in making fast cords to his flukes, and in other ways getting the mass in readiness for towing, some conversation ensued between them.

'I wonder what the old man wants with this lump of foul lard,' said Stubb, not without some disgust at the thought of having to do with so ignoble a leviathan.

'Wants with it?' said Flask, coiling some spare line in the boat's bow, 'did you ever hear that the ship which but once has a Sperm Whale's head hoisted on her starboard side, and at the same time a Right Whale's on the larboard; did you never hear, Stubb, that that ship can never afterwards capsize?'

'Why not?'

'I don't know, but I heard that gamboge ghost of a Fedallah saying so, and he seems to know all about ships' charms. But I sometimes think he'll charm the ship to no good at last. I don't half like that chap, Stubb. Did you ever notice how that tusk of his is a sort of carved into a snake's head, Stubb?'

'Sink him! I never look at him at all; but if ever I get a chance of a dark night, and he standing hard by the bulwarks, and no one by; look down there, Flask'—pointing into the sea with a peculiar motion of both hands—'Aye, will I! Flask, I take that Fedallah to be the devil in disguise. Do you believe that cock and bull story about his having been stowed away on board ship? He's the devil, I say. The reason why you don't see his tail, is because he tucks it up out of sight; he carries it coiled away in his pocket, I guess. Blast him! now that I think of it, he's always wanting oakum to stuff into the toes of his boots.'

'He sleeps in his boots, don't he? He hasn't got any hammock; but I've seen him lay of nights in a coil of rigging.'

'No doubt, and it's because of his cursed tail; he coils it down, do ye see, in the eye of the rigging.'

'What's the old man have so much to do with him for?'

'Striking up a swap or a bargain, I suppose.'

'Bargain?—about what?'

'Why, do ye see, the old man is hard bent after that White Whale, and the devil there is trying to come round him, and get him to swap away his silver watch, or his soul, or something of that sort, and then he'll surrender Moby Dick.'

'Pooh! Stubb, you are skylarking; how can Fedallah do that?'

'I don't know, Flask, but the devil is a curious chap, and a wicked one, I tell ye. Why, they say as how he went a sauntering into the old flag-ship once, switching his tail about devilish easy and gentlemanlike, and inquiring if the old governor was at home. Well, he was at home, and asked the devil what he wanted. The devil, switching his hoofs, up and says, "I want John." "What for?" said the old governor. "What business is that of yours," says the devil, getting mad,—"I want to use him." "Take him," says the governor—and by the Lord, Flask, if the devil didn't give John the Asiatic cholera before he got through with him, I'll eat this whale in one mouthful. But look sharp—aint you all ready there? Well, then, pull ahead, and let's get the whale alongside.'

'I think I remember some such story as you were telling,' said Flask, when at last the two boats were slowly advancing with their burden towards the ship, 'but I can't remember where.'

'Three Spaniards? Adventures of those three bloody-minded soldadoes? Did ye read it there, Flask? I guess ye did?'

'No: never saw such a book; heard of it, though. But now, tell me, Stubb, do you suppose that that devil you was speaking of just now, was the same you say is now on board the Pequod?'

'Am I the same man that helped kill this whale? Doesn't the devil live for ever; who ever heard that the devil was dead? Did you ever see any parson a wearing mourning for the devil? And if the devil has a latch-key to get into the admiral's cabin, don't you suppose he can crawl into a porthole? Tell me that, Mr Flask?'

'How old do you suppose Fedallah is, Stubb?'

'Do you see that mainmast there?' pointing to the ship; 'well, that's the figure one; now take all the hoops in the Pequod's hold, and string 'em along in a row with that mast, for oughts, do you see; well, that wouldn't begin to be Fedallah's age. Nor all the coopers in creation couldn't show hoops enough to make oughts enough.'

'But see here, Stubb, I though you a little boasted just now, that you meant to give Fedallah a sea-toss, if you got a good chance. Now, if he's so old as all those hoops of yours come to, and if he is going to live for ever, what good will it do to pitch him overboard—tell me that?'

'Give him a good ducking, anyhow.'

'But he'd crawl back.'

'Duck him again; and keep ducking him.'

'Suppose he should take it into his head to duck you, though—yes, and drown you—what then?'

'I should like to see him try it; I'd give him such a pair of black eyes that he wouldn't dare to show his face in the admiral's cabin again for a long while, let alone down in the orlop there, where he lives, and hereabouts on the upper decks where he sneaks so much. Damn the devil, Flask; do you suppose I'm afraid of the devil? Who's afraid of him, except the old governor who daresn't catch him and put him in double-darbies, as he deserves, but lets him go about kidnapping people; aye, and signed a bond with him, that all the people the devil kidnapped, he'd roast for him? There's a governor!'

'Do you suppose Fedallah wants to kidnap Captain Ahab?'

'Do I suppose it? You'll know it before long, Flask. But I am going now to keep a sharp look-out on him; and if I see anything very suspicious going on, I'll just take him by the nape of his neck, and say—Look here, Beelzebub, you don't do it! and if he makes any fuss, by the Lord I'll make a grab into his pocket for his tail, take it to the capstan, and give him such a wrenching and heaving, that his tail will come short off at the stump—do you see; and then, I rather guess when he finds himself docked in that queer fashion, he'll sneak off without the poor satisfaction of feeling his tail between his legs.'

'And what will you do with the tail, Stubb?'

'Do with it? Sell it for an ox whip when we get home;—what else?'

'Now, do you mean what you say, and have been saying all along, Stubb?'

'Mean or not mean, here we are at the ship.'

The boats were here hailed, to tow the whale on the larboard side, where fluke chains and other necessaries were already prepared for securing him.

'Didn't I tell you so?' said Flask; 'yes, you'll soon see this right whale's head hoisted up opposite that parmacetti's.'

In good time, Flask's saying proved true. As before, the Pequod steeply leaned over towards the sperm whale's head, now, by the counterpoise of both heads, she regained her even keel; though sorely strained, you may well believe. So, when on one side you hoist in Locke's head, you go over that way; but now, on the other side, hoist in Kant's and you come back again; but in very poor plight. Thus, some minds for ever keep trimming boat. Oh, ye foolish! throw all these thunder-heads overboard, and then you will float light and right.

In disposing of the body of a right whale, when brought alongside the ship, the same preliminary proceedings commonly take place as in the case of a sperm whale; only, in the latter instance, the head is cut off whole, but in the former the lips and tongue are separately removed and hoisted on deck, with all the well known black bone attached to what is called the crown-piece. But nothing like this, in the present case, had been done. The carcases of both whales had dropped astern; and the head-laden ship not a little resembled a mule carrying a pair of overburdening panniers.

Meantime, Fedallah was calmly eyeing the right whale's head, and ever and anon glancing from the deep wrinkles there to the lines in his own hand. And Ahab chanced so to stand, that the Parsee occupied his shadow; while, if the Parsee's shadow was there at all it seemed only to blend with, and lengthen Ahab's. As the crew toiled on, Laplandish speculations were bandied among them, concerning all these passing things.

CHAPTER LXXIV

THE SPERM WHALE'S HEAD—CONTRASTED VIEW

Here, now, are two great whales, laying their heads together; let us join them, and lay together our own.

Of the grand order of folio leviathans, the Sperm Whale and the Right Whale are by far the most noteworthy. They are the only whales regularly hunted by man. To the Nantucketer, they present the two extremes of all the known varieties of the whale. As the external difference between them is mainly observable in their heads; and as a head of each is this moment hanging from the Pequod's side; and as we may freely go from one to the other, by merely stepping across the deck:—where, I should like to know, will you obtain a better chance to study practical cetology than here?

In the first place, you are struck by the general contrast between these heads. Both are massive enough in all conscience; but there is a certain mathematical symmetry in the Sperm Whale's which the Right Whale's sadly lacks. There is more character in the Sperm Whale's head. As you behold it, you involuntarily yield the immense superiority to him, in point of pervading dignity. In the present instance, too, this dignity is heightened by the pepper and salt color of his head at the summit, giving token of advanced age and large experience. In short, he is what the fishermen technically call a 'grey-headed whale.'

Let us now note what is least dissimilar in these heads—namely, the two most important organs, the eye and the ear. Far back on the side of the head, and low down, near the angle of either whale's jaw, if you narrowly search, you will at last see a lashless eye, which you would fancy to be a young colt's eye; so out of all proportion is it to the magnitude of the head.

Now, from this peculiar sideway position of the whale's eyes, it is plain that he can never see an object which is exactly ahead, no more than he can one exactly astern. In a word, the position of the whale's eyes corresponds to that of a man's ears; and you may fancy, for yourself, how it would fare with you, did you sideways survey objects through your ears. You would find that you could only command some thirty degrees of vision in advance of the straight side-line of sight; and about thirty more behind it. If your bitterest foe were walking straight towards you, with dagger uplifted in broad day, you would not be able to see him, any more than if he were stealing upon you from behind. In a word, you would have two backs, so to speak; but, at the same time, also, two fronts (side fronts): for what is it that makes the front of a man—what, indeed, but his eyes?

Moreover, while in most other animals that I can now think of, the eyes are so planted as imperceptibly to blend their visual power, so as to produce one picture and not two to the brain; the peculiar position of the whale's eyes, effectually divided as they are by many cubic feet of solid head, which towers between them like a great mountain separating two lakes in valleys; this, of course, must wholly separate the impressions which each independent organ imparts. The whale, therefore, must see one distinct picture on this side, and another distinct picture on that side; while all between must be profound darkness and nothingness to him. Man may, in effect, be said to look out on the world from a sentry-box with two joined sashes for his window. But with the whale, these two sashes are separately inserted, making two distinct windows, but sadly impairing the view. This peculiarity of the whale's eyes is a thing always to be borne in mind in the fishery; and to be remembered by the reader in some subsequent scenes.

A curious and most puzzling question might be started concerning this visual matter as touching the Leviathan. But I must be content with a hint. So long as a man's eyes are open in the light, the act of seeing is involuntary; that is, he cannot then help mechanically seeing whatever objects are before him. Nevertheless, any one's experience will teach him, that though he can take in an undiscriminating sweep of things at one glance, it is quite impossible for him, attentively, and completely, to examine any two things—however large or however small—at one and the same instant of time; never mind if they lie side by side and touch each other. But if you now come to separate these two objects, and surround each by a circle of profound darkness; then, in order to see one of them, in such a manner as to bring your mind to bear on it, the other will be utterly excluded from your contemporary consciousness. How is it, then, with the whale? True, both his eyes, in themselves, must simultaneously act; but is his brain so much more comprehensive, combining, and subtle than man's, that he can at the same moment of time attentively examine two distinct prospects, one on one side of him, and the other in an exactly opposite direction? If he can, then is it as marvellous a thing in him, as if a man were able simultaneously to go through the demonstrations of two distinct problems in Euclid. Nor, strictly investigated, is there any incongruity in this comparison.

It may be but an idle whim, but it has always seemed to me, that the extraordinary vacillations of movement displayed by some whales when beset by three or four boats; the timidity and liability to queer frights, so common to such whales; I think that all this indirectly proceeds from the helpless perplexity of volition, in which their divided and diametrically opposite powers of vision must involve them.

But the ear of the whale is full as curious as the eye. If you are an entire stranger to their race, you might hunt over these two heads for hours, and never discover that organ. The ear has no external leaf whatever; and into the hole itself you can hardly insert a quill, so wondrously minute is it. It is lodged a little behind the eye. With respect to their ears, this important difference is to be observed between the sperm whale and the right. While the ear of the former has an external opening, that of the latter is entirely and evenly covered over with a membrane, so as to be quite imperceptible from without.

Is it not curious, that so vast a being as the whale should see the world through so small an eye, and hear the thunder through an ear which is smaller than a hare's? But if his eyes were broad as the lens of Herschel's great telescope; and his ears capacious as the porches of cathedrals; would that make him any longer of sight, or sharper of hearing? Not at all.—Why then do you try to 'enlarge' your mind? Subtilize it.

Let us now with whatever levers and steam-engines we have at hand, cant over the sperm whale's head, so that it may lie bottom up; then, ascending by a ladder to the summit, have a peep down the mouth; and were it not that the body is now completely separated from it, with a lantern we might descend into the great Kentucky Mammoth Cave of his stomach. But let us hold on here by this tooth, and look about us where we are. What a really beautiful and chaste-looking mouth! from floor to ceiling, lined, or rather papered with a glistening white membrane, glossy as bridal satins.

But come out now, and look at this portentous lower jaw, which seems like the long narrow lid of an immense snuff-box, with the hinge at one end, instead of one side. If you pry it up, so as to get it overhead, and expose its rows of teeth, it seems a terrific portcullis; and such, alas! it proves to many a poor wight in the fishery, upon whom these spikes fall with impaling force. But far more terrible is it to behold, when fathoms down in the sea, you see some sulky whale, floating there suspended, with his prodigious jaw, some fifteen feet long, hanging straight down at right-angles with his body, for all the world like a ship's jib-boom. This whale is not dead; he is only dispirited; out of sorts, perhaps; hypochondriac; and so supine, that the hinges of his jaw have relaxed, leaving him there in that ungainly sort of plight, a reproach to all his tribe, who must, no doubt, imprecate lock-jaws upon him.

In most cases this lower jaw—being easily unhinged by a practised artist—is disengaged and hoisted on deck for the purpose of extracting the ivory teeth, and furnishing a supply of that hard white whalebone with which the fishermen fashion all sorts of curious articles, including canes, umbrella-stocks, and handles to riding-whips.

With a long, weary hoist the jaw is dragged on board, as if it were an anchor; and when the proper time comes—some few days after the other work—

Queequeg, Daggoo, and Tashtego, being all accomplished dentists, are set to drawing teeth. With a keen cutting-spade, Queequeg lances the gums; then the jaw is lashed down to ringbolts, and a tackle being rigged from aloft, they drag out these teeth, as Michigan oxen drag stumps of old oaks out of wild wood-lands. There are generally forty-two teeth in all; in old whales, much worn down, but undecayed; nor filled after our artificial fashion. The jaw is afterwards sawn into slabs, and piled away like joists for building houses.

CHAPTER LXXV

THE RIGHT WHALE'S HEAD—CONTRASTED VIEW

Crossing the deck, let us now have a good long look at the Right Whale's head.

As in general shape the noble Sperm Whale's head may be compared to a Roman war-chariot (especially in front, where it is so broadly rounded); so, at a broad view, the Right Whale's head bears a rather inelegant resemblance to a gigantic galliot-toed shoe. Two hundred years ago an old Dutch voyager likened its shape to that of a shoemaker's last. And in this same last or shoe, that old woman of the nursery tale, with the swarming brood, might very comfortably be lodged, she and all her progeny.

But as you come nearer to this great head it begins to assume different aspects, according to your point of view. If you stand on its summit and look at these two *f*-shaped spout-holes, you would take the whole head for an enormous bass-viol, and these spiracles, the apertures in its sounding-board. Then, again, if you fix your eye upon this strange, crested, comb-like incrustation on the top of the mass—this green, barnacled thing, which the Greenlanders call the 'crown,' and the Southern fishers the 'bonnet' of the Right Whale; fixing your eyes solely on this, you would take the head for the trunk of some huge oak, with a bird's nest in its crotch. At any rate, when you watch those live crabs that nestle here on this bonnet, such an idea will be almost sure to occur to you; unless, indeed, your fancy has been fixed by the technical term 'crown' also bestowed upon it; in which case you will take great interest in thinking how this mighty monster is actually a diademed king of the sea, whose green crown has been put together for him in this marvellous manner. But if this whale be a king, he is a very sulky looking fellow to grace a diadem. Look at that hanging lower lip! what a huge sulk and pout is there! a sulk and pout, by carpenter's measurement, about twenty feet long and five feet deep; a sulk and pout that will yield you some 500 gallons of oil and more.

A great pity, now, that this unfortunate whale should be harelipped. The fissure is about a foot across. Probably the mother during an important interval was sailing down the Peruvian coast, when earthquakes caused the beach to gape. Over this lip, as over a slippery threshold, we now slide into the mouth. Upon my word were I at Mackinaw, I should take this to be the inside of an Indian wigwam. Good Lord! is this the road that Jonah went? The roof is about twelve feet high, and runs to a pretty sharp angle, as if there were a regular ridge-pole there; while these ribbed, arched, hairy sides, present us with those wondrous, half vertical, scimetar-shaped slats of whalebone, say three hundred on a side, which depending from the upper part of the head or crown bone, form those Venetian blinds which have elsewhere been cursorily mentioned. The edges of these bones are fringed with hairy fibres, through which the Right Whale strains the water, and in whose intricacies he retains the small fish, when open-mouthed he goes through the seas of brit in feeding time. In the central blinds of bone, as they stand in their natural order, there are certain curious marks, curves, hollows, and ridges, whereby some whalemen calculate the creature's age, as the age of an oak by its circular rings. Though the certainty of this criterion is far from demonstrable, yet it has the savor of analogical probability. At any rate, if we yield to it, we must grant a far greater age to the Right Whale than at first glance will seem reasonable.

In old times, there seem to have prevailed the most curious fancies concerning these blinds. One voyager in Purchas calls them the wondrous 'whiskers' inside of the whale's mouth;* another, 'hogs' bristles;' a third old gentleman in Hackluyt uses the following elegant language: 'There are about two hundred and fifty fins growing on each side of his upper *chop,* which arch over his tongue on each side of his mouth.'

As every one knows, these same 'hogs' bristles,' 'fins,' 'whiskers,' 'blinds,' or whatever you please, furnish to the ladies their busks and other stiffening contrivances. But in this particular, the demand has long been on the decline. It was in Queen Anne's time that the bone was in its glory, the farthingale being then all the fashion. And as those ancient dames moved about gaily, though in the jaws of the whale, as you may say; even so, in a shower, with the like thoughtlessness, do we nowadays fly under the same jaws for protection; the umbrella being a tent spread over the same bone.

But now forget all about blinds and whiskers for a moment, and, standing in the Right Whale's mouth, look around you afresh. Seeing all these colonnades of bone so methodically ranged about, would you not think you were inside of the great Haarlem organ, and gazing upon its thousand pipes? For a carpet to the organ we have a rug of the softest Turkey—the tongue, which is glued, as it were, to the floor of the mouth. It is very fat and tender, and apt to tear in pieces in hoisting it on deck. This particular tongue now before us; at a passing glance I should say it was a six-barreler; that is, it will yield you about that amount of oil.

Ere this, you must have plainly seen the truth of what I started with—that the Sperm Whale and the Right Whale have almost entirely different heads. To sum up, then: in the Right Whale's there is no great well of sperm; no ivory teeth at all; no long, slender mandible of a lower jaw, like the Sperm Whale's. Nor in the Sperm Whale are there any of those blinds of bone; no huge lower lip; and scarcely anything of a tongue. Again, the Right Whale has two external spout-holes, the Sperm Whale only one.

Look your last, now, on these venerable hooded heads, while they yet lie together; for one will soon sink, unrecorded, in the sea; the other will not be very long in following.

Can you catch the expression of the Sperm Whale's there? It is the same he died with, only some of the longer wrinkles in the forehead seem now faded away. I think his broad brow to be full of a prairie-like placidity, born of a speculative indifference as to death. But mark the other head's expression. See that amazing lower lip, pressed by accident against the vessel's side, so as firmly to embrace the

*This reminds us that the Right Whale really has a sort of whisker, or rather a moustache, consisting of a few scattered white hairs on the upper part of the outer end of the lower jaw. Sometimes these tufts impart a rather brigandish expression to his otherwise solemn countenance.

jaw. Does not this whole head seem to speak of an enormous practical resolution in facing death? This Right Whale I take to have been a Stoic; the Sperm Whale, a Platonian, who might have taken up Spinoza in his latter years.

CHAPTER LXXVI

THE BATTERING-RAM

Ere quitting, for the nonce, the Sperm Whale's head, I would have you, as a sensible physiologist, simply—particularly remark its front aspect, in all its compacted collectedness. I would have you investigate it now with the sole view of forming to yourself some unexaggerated, intelligent estimate of whatever battering-ram power may be lodged there. Here is a vital point; for you must either satisfactorily settle this matter with yourself, or for ever remain an infidel as to one of the most appalling, but not the less true events, perhaps anywhere to be found in all recorded history.

You observe that in the ordinary swimming position of the Sperm Whale, the front of his head presents an almost wholly vertical plane to the water; you observe that the lower part of that front slopes considerably backwards, so as to furnish more of a retreat for the long socket which receives the boom-like lower jaw; you observe that the mouth is entirely under the head, much in the same way, indeed, as though your own mouth were entirely under your chin. Moreover you observe that the whale has no external nose; and that what nose he has—his spout hole—is on the top of his head; you observe that his eyes and ears are at the sides of his head, nearly one third of his entire length from the front. Wherefore, you must now have perceived that the Sperm Whale's head is a dead, blind wall, without a single organ or tender prominence of any sort whatsoever. Furthermore, you are now to consider that only in the extreme, lower, backward sloping part of the front of the head, is there the slightest vestige of bone; and not till you get near twenty feet from the forehead do you come to the full cranial development. So that this whole enormous boneless mass is as one wad. Finally, though, as will soon be revealed, its contents partly comprise the most delicate oil; yet, you are now to be apprised of the nature of the substance which so impregnably invests all that apparent effeminacy. In some previous place I have described to you how the blubber wraps the body of the whale, as the rind wraps an orange. Just so with the head; but with this difference: about the head this envelope, though not so thick, is of a boneless toughness, inestimable by any man who has not handled it. The severest pointed harpoon, the sharpest lance darted by the strongest human arm, impotently rebounds from it. It is as though the forehead of the Sperm Whale were paved with horses' hoofs. I do not think that any sensation lurks in it.

Bethink yourself also of another thing. When two large loaded Indiamen chance to crowd and crush towards each other in the docks, what do the sailors do? They do not suspend between them, at the point of coming contact, any merely hard substance, like iron or wood. No, they hold there a large, round wad of tow and cork, enveloped in the thickest and toughest of ox-hide. That bravely and uninjured takes the jam which would have snapped all their oaken handspikes and iron crowbars. By itself this sufficiently illustrates the obvious fact I drive at. But supplementary to this, it has hypothetically occurred to me, that as ordinary fish possess what is called a swimming bladder in them, capable, at will, of distension or contraction; and as the Sperm Whale, as far as I know, has no such provision in him; considering, too, the otherwise inexplicable manner in which he now depresses his head altogether beneath the surface, and anon swims with it high elevated out of the water; considering the unobstructed elasticity of its envelope; considering the unique interior of his head; it has hypothetically occurred to me, I say, that those mystical lung-celled honeycombs there may possibly have some hitherto unknown and unsuspected connexion with the outer air, so as to be susceptible to atmospheric distension and contraction, If this be so, fancy the irresistibleness of that might, to which the most impalpable and destructive of all elements contributes.

Now, mark. Unerringly impelling this dead, impregnable, uninjurable wall, and this most buoyant thing within; there swims behind it all a mass of tremendous life, only to be adequately estimated as piled wood is—by the cord; and all obedient to one volition, as the smallest insect. So that when I shall hereafter detail to you all the specialties and concentrations of potency everywhere lurking in this expansive monster; when I shall show you some of his more inconsiderable braining feats; I trust you will have renounced all ignorant incredulity, and be ready to abide by this; that though the Sperm Whale stove a passage through the Isthmus of Darien, and mixed the Atlantic with the Pacific, you would not elevate one hair of your eye-brow. For unless you own the whale, you are but a provincial and sentimentalist in Truth. But clear Truth is a thing for salamander giants only to encounter; how small the chances for the provincials then? What befel the weakling youth lifting the dread goddess's veil at Sais?

CHAPTER LXXVII

THE GREAT HEIDELBURGH TUN

Now comes the Baling of the Case. But to comprehend it aright, you must know something of the curious internal structure of the thing operated upon.

Regarding the Sperm Whale's head as a solid oblong, you may, on an inclined plane, sideways divide it into two quoins,* whereof the lower is the bony structure, forming the cranium and jaws, and the upper an unctuous mass wholly free from bones; its broad forward end forming the expanded vertical apparent forehead of the whale. At the middle of the forehead horizontally subdivide this upper quoin, and then you have two almost equal parts, which before were naturally divided by an internal wall of a thick tendinous substance.

The lower subdivided part, called the junk, is one immense honeycomb of oil, formed by the crossing and recrossing, into ten thousand infiltrated cells, of tough elastic white fibres throughout its whole extent. The upper part, known as the Case, may be regarded as the great Heidelburgh Tun of the Sperm Whale. And as that famous great tierce is mystically carved in front, so the whales's vast plaited forehead forms innumerable strange devices for the emblematical adornment of

*Quoin is not a Euclidean term. It belongs to the pure nautical mathematics. I know not that it has been defined before. A quoin is a solid which differs from a wedge in having its sharp end formed by the steep inclination of one side, instead of the mutual tapering of both sides.

his wondrous tun. Moreover, as that of Heidelburgh was always replenished with the most excellent of the wines of the Rhenish valleys, so the tun of the whale contains by far the most precious of all his oily vintages; namely, the highly-prized spermaceti, in its absolutely pure, limpid, and odoriferous state. Nor is this precious substance found unalloyed in any other part of the creature. Though in life it remains perfectly fluid, yet, upon exposure to the air, after death, it soon begins to concrete; sending forth beautiful crystalline shoots, as when the first thin delicate ice is just forming in water. A large whale's case generally yields about five hundred gallons of sperm, though from unavoidable circumstances, considerable of it is spilled, leaks, and dribbles away, or is otherwise irrevocably lost in the ticklish business of securing what you can.

I know not with what fine and costly material the Heidelburgh Tun was coated within, but in superlative richness that coating could not possibly have compared with the silken pearl-colored membrane, like the lining of a fine pelisse, forming the inner surface of the Sperm Whale's case.

It will have been seen that the Heidelburgh Tun of the Sperm Whale embraces the entire length of the entire top of the head; and since—as has been elsewhere set forth—the head embraces one third of the whole length of the creature, then setting that length down at eighty feet for a good sized whale, you have more than twenty-six feet for the depth of the tun, when it is length-wise hoisted up and down against a ship's side.

As in decapitating the whale, the operator's instrument is brought close to the spot where an entrance is subsequently forced into the spermaceti magazine; he has, therefore, to be uncommonly heedful, lest a careless, untimely stroke should invade the sanctuary and wastingly let out its invaluable contents. It is this decapitated end of the head, also, which is at last elevated out of the water, and retained in that position by the enormous cutting tackles, whose hempen combinations, on one side, make quite a wilderness of ropes in that quarter.

Thus much being said, attend now, I pray you, to that marvellous and—in this particular instance—almost fatal operation whereby the Sperm Whale's great Heidelburgh Tun is tapped.

CHAPTER LXXVIII

CISTERN AND BUCKETS

Nimble as a cat, Tashtego mounts aloft; and without altering his erect posture, runs straight out upon the overhanging main-yard-arm, to the part where it exactly projects over the hoisted Tun. He has carried with him a light tackle called a whip, consisting of only two parts, travelling through a single-sheaved block. Securing this block, so that it hangs down from the yard-arm, he swings one end of the rope, till it is caught and firmly held by a hand on deck. Then, hand-over-hand, down the other part, the Indian drops through the air, till dexterously he lands on the summit of the head. There—still high elevated above the rest of the company, to whom he vivaciously cries—he seems some Turkish Muezzin calling the good people to prayers from the top of a tower. A short-handled sharp spade being sent up to him, he diligently searches for the proper place to begin breaking into the Tun. In this business he proceeds very heedfully, like a treasure-hunter in some old house, sounding the walls to find where the gold is masoned in. By the time this cautious search is over, a stout ironbound bucket, precisely like a well-bucket, has been attached to one end of the whip; while the other end, being stretched across the deck, is there held by two or three alert hands. These last now hoist the bucket within grasp of the Indian, to whom another person has reached up a very long pole. Inserting this pole into the bucket, Tashtego downward guides the bucket into the Tun, till it entirely disappears; then giving the word to the seamen at the whip, up comes the bucket again, all bubbling like a dairy-maid's pail of new milk. Carefully lowered from its height, the full-freighted vessel is caught by an appointed hand, and quickly emptied into a large tub. Then re-mounting aloft, it again goes through the same round until the deep cistern will yield no more. Towards the end, Tashtego has to ram his long pole harder and harder, and deeper and deeper into the Tun, until some twenty feet of the pole have gone down.

Now, the people of the Pequod had been baling some time in this way; several tubs had been filled with the fragrant sperm; when all at once a queer accident happened. Whether it was that Tashtego, that wild Indian, was so heedless and reckless as to let go for a moment his one-handed hold on the great cabled tackles suspending the head; or whether the place where he stood was so treacherous and oozy; or whether the Evil One himself would have it to fall out so, without stating his particular reasons; how it was exactly, there is no telling now; but, on a sudden, as the eightieth or ninetieth bucket came suckingly up—my God! poor Tashtego—like the twin reciprocating bucket in a veritable well, dropped head-foremost down into this great Tun of Heidelburgh, and with a horrible oily gurgling, went clean out of sight!

'Man overboard!' cried Daggoo, who amid the general consternation first came to his senses. 'Swing the bucket this way!' and putting one foot into it, so as the better to secure his slippery hand-hold on the whip itself, the hoisters ran him high up to the top of the head, almost before Tashtego could have reached its interior bottom. Meantime, there was a terrible tumult. Looking over the side, they saw the before lifeless head throbbing and heaving just below the surface of the sea, as if that moment seized with some momentous idea; whereas it was only the poor Indian unconsciously revealing by those struggles the perilous depth to which he had sunk.

At this instant, while Daggoo, on the summit of the head, was clearing the whip—which had somehow got foul of the great cutting tackles—a sharp cracking noise was heard; and to the unspeakable horror of all, one of the two enormous hooks suspending the head tore out, and with a vast vibration the enormous mass sideways swung, till the drunk ship reeled and shook as if smitten by an iceberg. The one remaining hook, upon which the entire strain now depended, seemed every instant to be on the point of giving way; an event still more likely from the violent motions of the head.

'Come down, come down!' yelled the seamen to Daggoo, but with one hand holding on to the heavy tackles, so that if the head should drop, he would remain suspended; the negro having cleared the foul line, rammed down the bucket into the now collapsed well, meaning that the buried harpooner should grasp it, and so be hoisted out.

'In heaven's name, man,' cried Stubb, 'are you ramming home a cartridge there?—Avast! How will that help him; jamming that iron-bound bucket on top of his head? Avast, will ye!'

'Stand clear of the tackle!' cried a voice like the bursting of a rocket.

Almost in the same instant, with a thunder-boom, the enormous mass dropped into the sea, like Niagara's Table-Rock into the whirlpool; the suddenly relieved hull rolled away from it, to far down her glittering copper; and all caught their breath, as half swinging—now over the sailors' heads, and now over the water—Daggoo, through a thick mist of spray, was dimly beheld clinging to the pendulous tackles, while poor, buried-alive Tashtego was sinking utterly down to the bottom of the sea! But hardly had the blinding vapor cleared away, when a naked figure with a boarding-sword in its hand, was for one swift moment seen hovering over the bulwarks. The next, a loud splash announced that my brave Queequeg had dived to the rescue. One packed rush was made to the side, and every eye counted every ripple, as moment followed moment, and no sign of either the sinker or the diver could be seen. Some hands now jumped into a boat alongside, and pushed a little off from the ship.

'Ha! ha!' cried Daggoo, all at once, from his now quiet, swinging perch overhead; and looking further off from the side, we saw an arm thrust upright from the blue waves; a sight strange to see, as an arm thrust forth from the grass over a grave.

'Both! both!—it is both!' cried Daggoo again with a joyful shout; and soon after, Queequeg was seen boldly striking out with one hand, and with the other clutching the long hair of the Indian. Drawn into the waiting boat, they were quickly brought to the deck; but Tashtego was long in coming to, and Queequeg did not look very brisk.

Now, how had this noble rescue been accomplished? Why, diving after the slowly descending head, Queequeg with his keen sword had made side lunges near its bottom, so as to scuttle a large hole there; then dropping his sword, had thrust his long arm far inwards and upwards, and so hauled out our poor Tash by the head. He averred, that upon first thrusting in for him, a leg was presented; but well knowing that that was not as it ought to be, and might occasion great trouble;—he had thrust back the leg, and by a dexterous heave and toss, had wrought a somerset upon the Indian; so that with the next trial, he came forth in the good old way—head foremost. As for the great head itself, that was doing as well as could be expected.

And thus, through the courage and great skill in obstetrics of Queequeg, the deliverance, or rather, delivery of Tashtego, was successfully accomplished, in the teeth, too, of the most untoward and apparently hopeless impediments; which is a lesson by no means to be forgotten. Midwifery should be taught in the same course with the fencing and boxing, riding and rowing.

I know that this queer adventure of the Gay-Header's will be sure to seem incredible to some landsmen, though they themselves may have either seen or heard of some one's falling into a cistern ashore; an accident which not seldom happens, and with much less reason too than the Indian's, considering the exceeding slipperiness of the curb of the Sperm Whale's well.

But, peradventure, it may be sagaciously urged, how is this? We thought the tissued, infiltrated head of the Sperm Whale, was the lightest and most corky part about him; and yet thou makest it sink in an element of a far greater specific gravity than itself. We have thee there. Not at all, but I have ye; for at the time poor Tash fell in, the case had been nearly emptied of its lighter contents, leaving little but the dense tendinous wall of the well—a double welded, hammered substance, as I have before said, much heavier than the sea water, and a lump of which sinks in it like lead almost. But the tendency to rapid sinking in this substance was in the present instance materially counteracted by the other parts of the head remaining undetached from it, so that it sank very slowly and deliberately indeed, affording Queequeg a fair chance for performing his agile obstetrics on the run, as you may say. Yes, it was a running delivery, so it was.

Now, had Tashtego perished in that head, it had been a very precious perishing; smothered in the very whitest and daintiest of fragrant spermaceti; coffined, hearsed, and tombed in the secret inner chamber and sanctum sanctorum of the whale. Only one sweeter end can readily be recalled—the delicious death of an Ohio honey-hunter, who seeking honey in the crotch of a hollow tree, found such exceeding store of it, that leaning too far over, it sucked him in, so that he died embalmed. How many, think ye, have likewise fallen into Plato's honey head, and sweetly perished there?

CHAPTER LXXIX

The Praire

To scan the lines of his face, or feel the bumps on the head of this Leviathan; this is a thing which no Physiognomist or Phrenologist has as yet undertaken. Such an enterprise would seem almost as hopeful as for Lavater to have scrutinized the wrinkles on the Rock of Gibraltar, or for Gall to have mounted a ladder and manipulated the Dome of the Pantheon. Still, in that famous work of his, Lavater not only treats of the various faces of men, but also attentively studies the faces of horses, birds, serpents, and fish; and dwells in detail upon the modifications of expression discernible therein. Nor have Gall and disciple Spurzheim failed to throw out some hints touching the phrenological characteristics of other beings than man. Therefore, though I am but ill qualified for a pioneer, in the application of these two semi-sciences to the whale, I will do my endeavor. I try all things; I achieve what I can.

Physiognomically regarded, the Sperm Whale is an anomalous creature. He has no proper nose. And since the nose is the central and most conspicuous of the features; and since it perhaps most modifies and finally controls their combined expression; hence it would seem that its entire absence, as an external appendage, must very largely affect the countenance of the whale. For as in landscape gardening, a spire, cupola, monument, or tower of some sort, is deemed almost indispensable to the completion of the scheme; so no face can be physiognomically in keeping without the elevated open-work belfry of the nose. Dash the nose from Phidias's marble Jove, and what a sorry remainder! Nevertheless, Leviathan is of so mighty a magnitude, all his proportions are so stately, that the same deficiency which in the sculptured Jove were hideous, in him is no blemish at all. Nay, it is an added grandeur. A nose to the whale would have been impertinent. As on your physiognomical voyage you sail round his vast head in your jollyboat, your noble conceptions of him are never insulted by the reflection that he has a nose to be pulled. A pestilent conceit, which so often will insist upon obtruding even when beholding the mightiest royal beadle on his throne.

In some particulars, perhaps the most imposing physiognomical view to be had of the Sperm Whale, is that of the full front of his head. This aspect is sublime.

In thought, a fine human brow is like the East when troubled with the morning. In the repose of the pasture, the curled brow of the bull has a touch of the grand in it. Pushing heavy cannon up mountain defiles, the elephant's brow is majestic.

Human or animal, the mystical brow is as that great golden seal affixed by the German emperors to their decrees. It signifies—'God: done this day by my hand.' But in most creatures, nay in man himself, very often the brow is but a mere strip of alpine land lying along the snow line. Few are the foreheads which like Shakespeare's or Melancthon's rise so high, and descend so low, that the eyes themselves seem clear, eternal, tideless mountain lakes; and all above them in the forehead's wrinkles, you seem to track the antlered thoughts descending there to drink, as the Highland hunters track the snow prints of the deer. But in the great Sperm Whale, this high and mighty god-like dignity inherent in the brow is so immensely amplified, that gazing on it, in that full front view, you feel the Deity and the dread powers more forcibly than in beholding any other object in living nature. For you see no one point precisely; not one distinct feature is revealed; no nose, eyes, ears, or mouth; no face; he has none, proper; nothing but that one broad firmament of a forehead, pleated with riddles; dumbly lowering with the doom of boats, and ships, and men. Nor, in profile, does this wondrous brow diminish; though that way viewed, its grandeur does not domineer upon you so. In profile, you plainly perceive that horizontal, semi-crescentic depression in the forehead's middle, which, in man, is Lavater's mark of genius.

But how? Genius in the Sperm Whale? Has the Sperm Whale ever written a book, spoken a speech? No, his great genius is declared in his doing nothing particular to prove it. It is moreover declared in his pyramidical silence. And this reminds me that had the great Sperm Whale been known to the young Orient World, he would have been deified by their child-magian thoughts. They deified the crocodile of the Nile, because the crocodile is tongueless; and the Sperm Whale has no tongue, or at least it is so exceedingly small, as to be incapable of protrusion. If hereafter any highly cultured, poetical nation shall lure back to their birthright, the merry May-day gods of old; and livingly enthrone them again in the now egotistical sky; on the now unhaunted hill; then be sure, exalted to Jove's high seat, the great Sperm Whale shall lord it.

Champollion deciphered the wrinkled granite hieroglyphics. But there is no Champollion to decipher the Egypt of every man's and every being's face. Physiognomy, like every other human science, is but a passing fable. If then, Sir William Jones, who read in thirty languages, could not read the simplest peasant's face in its profounder and more subtle meanings, how may unlettered Ishmael hope to read the awful Chaldee of the Sperm Whale's brow? I but put that brow before you. Read it if you can.

CHAPTER LXXX

THE NUT

If the Sperm Whale be physiognomically a Sphinx, to the phrenologist his brain seems that geometrical circle which it is impossible to square.

In the full-grown creature the skull will measure at least twenty feet in length. Unhinge the lower jar, and the side view of this skull is as the side view of a moderately inclined plane resting throughout on a level base. But in life—as we have elsewhere seen—this inclined plane is angularly filled up, and almost squared by the enormous superincumbent mass of the junk and sperm. At the high end the skull forms a crater to bed that part of the mass; while under the long floor of this crater—in another cavity seldom exceeding ten inches in length and as many in depth—reposes the mere handful of the monster's brain. The brain is at least twenty feet from the apparent forehead in life; it is hidden away behind its vast outworks, like the innermost citadel within the amplified fortifications of Quebec. So like a choice casket is it secreted in him, that I have known some whalemen who peremptorily deny that the Sperm Whale has any other brain than that palpable semblance of one formed by the cubic-yards of his sperm magazine. Lying in strange folds, courses, and convolutions, to their apprehensions, it seems more in keeping with the idea of his general might to regard that mystic part of him as the seat of his intelligence.

It is plain, then, that phrenologically the head of this Leviathan, in the creature's living intact state, is an entire delusion. As for his true brain, you can then see no indications of it, nor feel any. The whale, like all things that are mighty, wears a false brow to the common world.

If you unload his skull of its spermy heaps and then take a rear view of its rear end, which is the high end, you will be struck by its resemblance to the human skull, beheld in the same situation, and from the same point of view. Indeed, place this reversed skull (scaled down to the human magnitude) among a plate of men's skulls, and you would involuntarily confound it with them; and remarking the depressions on one part of its summit, in phrenological phrase you would say—This man had no self-esteem, and no veneration. And by those negations, considered along with the affirmative fact of his prodigious bulk and power, you can best form to yourself the truest, though not the most exhilarating conception of what the most exalted potency is.

But if from the comparative dimensions of the whale's proper brain, you deem it incapable of being adequately charted, then I have another idea for you. If you attentively regard almost any quadruped's spine, you will be struck with the resemblance of its vertebræ to a strung necklace of dwarfed skulls, all bearing rudimental resemblance to the skull proper. It is a German conceit, that the vertebræ are absolutely undeveloped skulls. But the curious external resemblance, I take it the Germans were not the first men to perceive. A foreign friend once pointed it out to me, in the skeleton of a foe he had slain, and with the vertebræ of which he was inlaying, in a sort of basso-relievo, the beaked prow of his canoe. Now, I consider that the phrenologists have omitted an important thing in not pushing their investigations from the cerebellum through the spinal canal. For I believe that much of a man's character will be found betokened in his backbone. I would rather feel your spine than your skull, whoever you are. A thin joist of a spine never yet upheld a full and noble soul. I rejoice in my spine, as in the firm audacious staff of that flag which I fling half out to the world.

Apply this spinal branch of phrenology to the Sperm Whale. His cranial cavity is continuous with the first neck-vertebra; and in that vertebra the bottom of the spinal canal will measure ten inches across, being eight in height, and of a triangular figure with the base downwards. As it passes through the remaining vertebræ the canal tapers in size, but for a considerable distance remains of large capacity. Now, of course, this canal is filled with much the same strangely fibrous substance—the spinal cord—as the brain; and directly communicates with the brain. And what is still more, for many feet after emerging from the brain's cavity, the spinal cord remains of an undecreasing girth, almost equal to that of the brain. Under all these circumstances, would it be unreasonable to survey and map out the whale's spine phrenologically? For, viewed in this light, the wonderful comparative smallness of his brain proper is more than compensated by the wonderful comparative magnitude of his spinal cord.

But leaving this hint to operate as it may with the phrenologists, I would merely assume the spinal theory for a moment, in reference to the Sperm Whale's hump. This august hump, if I mistake not, rises over one of the larger vertebræ, and is, therefore, in some sort, the outer convex mould of it. From its relative situation then, I should call this high hump the organ of firmness or indomitableness in the Sperm Whale. And that the great monster is indomitable, you will yet have reason to know.

CHAPTER LXXXI

THE PEQUOD MEETS THE VIRGIN

The predestinated day arrived, and we duly met the ship Jungfrau, Derick De Deer, master, of Bremen.

At one time the greatest whaling people in the world, the Dutch and Germans are now among the least; but here and there at very wide intervals of latitude and longitude, you still occasionally meet with their flag in the Pacific.

For some reason, the Jungfrau seemed quite eager to pay her respects. While yet some distance from the Pequod, she rounded to, and dropping a boat, her captain was impelled towards us, impatiently standing in the bows instead of the stern.

'What has he in his hand there?' cried Starbuck, pointing to something wavingly held by the German. 'Impossible!—a lamp-feeder!'

'Not that,' said Stubb, 'no, no, it's a coffee-pot, Mr Starbuck; he's coming off to make us our coffee, is the Yarman; don't you see that big tin can there alongside of him?—that's his boiling water. Oh! he's all right, is the Yarman.'

'Go along with you,' cried Flask, 'it's a lamp-feeder and an oil-can. He's out of oil, and has come a-begging.'

However curious it may seem for an oil-ship to be borrowing oil on the whale-ground, and however much it may invertedly contradict the old proverb about carrying coals to Newcastle, yet sometimes such a thing really happens; and in the present case Captain Derick De Deer did indubitably conduct a lamp-feeder as Flask did declare.

As he mounted the deck, Ahab abruptly accosted him, without at all heeding what he had in his hand; but in his broken lingo, the German soon evinced his complete ignorance of the White Whale; immediately turning the conversation to his lamp-feeder and oil-can, with some remarks touching his having to turn into his hammock at night in profound darkness—his last drop of Bremen oil being gone, and not a single flying-fish yet captured to supply the deficiency; concluding by hinting that his ship was indeed what in the Fishery is technically called a *clean* one (that is, an empty one), well deserving the name of Jungfrau or the Virgin.

His necessities supplied, Derick departed; but he had not gained his ship's side, when whales were almost simultaneously raised from the mast-heads of both vessels; and so eager for the chase was Derick, that without pausing to put his oil-can and lamp-feeder aboard, he slewed round his boat and made after the leviathan lamp-feeders.

Now, the game having risen to leeward, he and the other three German boats that soon followed him, had considerably the start of the Pequod's keels. There were eight whales, an average pod. Aware of their danger, they were going all abreast with great speed straight before the wind, rubbing their flanks as closely as so many spans of horses in harness. They left a great, wide wake, as though continually unrolling a great wide parchment upon the sea.

Full in this rapid wake, and many fathoms in the rear, swam a huge, humped old bull, which by his comparatively slow progress, as well as by the unusual yellowish incrustations overgrowing him, seemed afflicted with the jaundice, or some other infirmity. Whether this whale belonged to the pod in advance, seemed questionable; for it is not customary for such venerable leviathans to be at all social. Nevertheless, he stuck to their wake, though indeed their back water must have retarded him, because the white-bone or swell at his broad muzzle was a dashed one, like the swell formed when two hostile currents meet. His spout was short, slow, and laborious; coming forth with a choking sort of gush, and spending itself in torn shreds, followed by strange subterranean commotions in him, which seemed to have egress at his other buried extremity, causing the waters behind him to upbubble.

'Who's got some paregoric?' said Stubb, 'he has the stomach-ache, I'm afraid. Lord, think of having half an acre of a stomach-ache! Adverse winds are holding mad Christmas in him, boys. It's the first foul wind I ever knew to blow from astern; but look, did ever whale yaw so before? it must be, he's lost his tiller.'

As an overladen Indiaman bearing down the Hindostan coast with a deck load of frightened horses, careens, buries, rolls, and wallows on her way; so did this old whale heave his aged bulk, and now and then partly turning over on his cumbrous rib-ends, expose the cause of his devious wake in the unnatural stump of his starboard fin. Whether he had lost that fin in battle, or had been born without it, it were hard to say.

'Only wait a bit, old chap, and I'll give ye a sling for that wounded arm,' cried cruel Flask, pointing to the whale-line near him.

'Mind he don't sling thee with it,' cried Starbuck. 'Give way, or the German will have him.'

With one intent all the combined rival boats were pointed for this one fish, because not only was he the largest, and therefore the most valuable whale, but he was nearest to them, and the other whales were going with such great velocity, moreover, as almost to defy pursuit for the time. At this juncture, the Pequod's keels had shot by the three German boats last lowered; but from the great start he had had, Derick's boat still led the chase, though every moment neared by his foreign rivals. The only thing they feared, was, that from being already so nigh to his mark, he would be enabled to dart his iron before they could completely overtake and pass him. As for Derick, he seemed quite confident that this would be the case, and occasionally with a deriding gesture shook his lamp-feeder at the other boats.

'The ungracious and ungrateful dog!' cried Starbuck; 'he mocks and dares me with the very poor-box I filled for him not five minutes ago!'—then in his old intense whisper—'give way, greyhounds! Dog to it!'

'I tell ye what it is, men'—cried Stubb to his crew—'It's against my religion to get mad; but I'd like to eat that villanous Yarman—Pull—wont ye? Are you going to let that rascal beat ye? Do ye love brandy? A hogshead of brandy, then, to the best man. Come, why don't some of ye burst a blood-vessel? Who's that been dropping an anchor overboard—we don't budge an inch—we're becalmed. Halloo, here's grass growing in the boat's bottom—and by the Lord, the mast there's budding. This won't do, boys. Look at that Yarman! The short and long of it is, men, will ye spit fire or not?'

'Oh! see the suds he makes!' cried Flask, dancing up and down—'What a hump—Oh, *do* pile on the beef—lays like a log! Oh! my lads, *do* spring—slap-jacks and quohogs for supper, you know, my lads—baked clams and muffins—oh, *do, do,* spring—he's a hundred barreler—don't lose him now—don't oh, *don't!*—see that Yarman—Oh! won't ye pull for your duff, my lads—such a sog! such a sogger! Don't ye love sperm? There goes three thousand dollars, men!—a bank!—a whole bank! The bank of England!—Oh, *do, do, do!*—What's that Yarman about now?'

At this moment Derick was in the act of pitching his lamp-feeder at the advancing boats, and also his oil-can; perhaps with the double view of retarding his rivals' way, and at the same time economically accelerating his own by the momentary impetus of the backward toss.

'The unmannerly Dutch dogger!' cried Stubb. 'Pull now, men, like fifty thousand line-of-battle-ship loads of red-haired devils. What d'ye say, Tashtego; are you the man to snap your spine in two-and-twenty pieces for the honor of old Gay-head? What d'ye say?'

'I say, pull like god-dam,'—cried the Indian.

Fiercely but evenly, incited by the taunts of the German, the Pequod's three boats now began ranging almost abreast; and, so disposed, momentarily neared him. In that fine, loose, chivalrous attitude of the headsman when drawing near to his prey, the three mates stood up proudly, occasionally backing the after oarsman with an exhilarating cry of, 'There she slides, now! Hurrah for the white-ash breeze! Down with the Yarman! Sail over him!'

But so decided an original start had Derick had, that spite of all their gallantry, he would have proved the victor in this race, had not a righteous judgment descended upon him in a crab which caught the blade of his midship oarsman. While this clumsy lubber was striving to free his white-ash, and while, in consequence, Derick's boat was nigh to capsizing, and he thundering away at his men in a mighty rage; that was a good time for Starbuck, Stubb, and Flask. With a shout, they took a mortal start forwards, and slantingly ranged up on the German's quarter. An instant more, and all four boats were diagonally in the whale's immediate wake, while stretching from them, on both sides, was the foaming swell that he made.

It was a terrific, most pitiable, and maddening sight. The whale was now going head out, and sending his spout before him in a continual tormented jet; while his one poor fin beat his side in an agony of fright. Now to this hand, now to that, he yawed in his faltering flight, and still at every billow that he broke, he spasmodically sank in the sea, or sideways rolled towards the sky his one beating fin. So have I seen a bird with clipped wing, making affrighted broken circles in the air, vainly striving to escape the piratical hawks. But the bird has a voice, and with plaintive cries will make known her fear; but the fear of this vast dumb brute of the sea, was chained up and enchanted in him; he had no voice, save that choking respiration through his spiracle, and this made the sight of him unspeakably pitiable; while still, in his amazing bulk, portcullis jaw, and omnipotent tail, there was enough to appal the stoutest man who so pitied.

Seeing now that but a very few moments more would give the Pequod's boats the advantage, and rather than be thus foiled of his game, Derick chose to hazard what to him must have seemed a most unusually long dart, ere the last chance would for ever escape.

But no sooner did his harpooneer stand up for the stroke, than all three tigers—Queequeg, Tashtego, Daggoo—instinctively sprang to their feet, and standing in a diagonal row, simultaneously pointed their barbs; and, darted over the head of the German harpooneer, their three Nantucket irons entered the whale. Blinding vapors of foam and white-fire! The three boats, in the first fury of the whale's headlong rush, bumped the German's aside with such force, that both Derick and his baffled harpooneer were spilled out, and sailed over by the three flying keels.

'Don't be afraid, my butter-boxes,' cried Stubb, casting a passing glance upon them as he shot by; 'ye'll be picked up presently—all right—I saw some sharks astern—St Bernard's dogs, you know—relieve distressed travellers. Hurrah! this is the way to sail now. Every keel a sun-beam! Hurrah!—Here we go like three tin kettles at the tail of a mad cougar! This puts me in mind of fastening to an elephant in a tilbury on a plain—makes the wheel-spokes fly, boys, when you fasten to him that way; and there's a danger of being pitched out too, when you strike a hill. Hurrah! this is the way a fellow feels when he's going to Davy Jones—all a rush down an endless inclined plane! Hurrah! this whale carries the everlasting mail!'

But the monster's run was a brief one. Giving a sudden gasp, he tumultuously sounded. With a grating rush, the three lines flew round the loggerheads with such a force as to gouge deep grooves in them; while so fearful were the harpooneers that this rapid sounding would soon exhaust the lines, that using all their dexterous might, they caught repeated smoking turns with the rope to hold on; till at last—owing to the perpendicular strain from the lead-lined chocks of the boats, whence the three ropes went straight down into the blue—the gunwales of the bows were almost even with the water, while the three sterns tilted high in the air. And the whale soon ceasing to sound, for some time they remained in that attitude, fearful of expending more line, though the position was a little ticklish. But though boats have been taken down and lost in this way, yet it is this 'holding on', as it is called; this hooking up by the sharp barbs of his live flesh from the back; this it is that often torments the Leviathan into soon rising again to meet the sharp lance of his foes. Yet not to speak of the peril of the thing, it is to be doubted whether this course is always the best; for it is but reasonable to presume, that the longer the stricken whale stays under water, the more he is exhausted. Because, owing to the enormous surface of him—in a full grown sperm whale something less than 2000 square feet—the pressure of the water is immense. We all know what an astonishing atmospheric weight we ourselves stand up under; even here, above-ground, in the air; how vast, then, the burden of a whale, bearing on his back a column of two hundred fathoms of ocean! It must at least equal the weight of fifty atmospheres. One whaleman has estimated it at the weight of twenty line-of-battle ships, with all their guns, and stores, and men on board.

As the three boats lay there on that gently rolling sea, gazing down into its eternal blue noon; and as not a single groan or cry of any sort, nay, not so much as a ripple or a bubble came up from its depths; what landsman would have thought, that beneath all that silence and placidity, the utmost monster of the seas was writhing and wrenching in agony! Not eight inches of perpendicular rope were visible at the bows. Seems it credible that by three such thin threads the great Leviathan was suspended like the big weight to an eight day clock. Suspended? and to what? To three bits of board. Is this the creature of whom it was once so triumphantly said—'Canst thou fill his skin with barbed irons? or his head with fish-spears? The sword of him that layeth at him cannot hold, the spear, the dart, nor the habergeon: he esteemeth iron as straw; the arrow cannot make him flee; darts are counted as stubble; he laugheth at the shaking of a spear!' This the creature? this he? Oh! that unfulfilments should follow the prophets. For with the strength of a thousand thighs in his tail, Leviathan had run his head under the mountains of the sea, to hide him from the Pequod's fish-spears!

In that sloping afternoon sunlight, the shadows that the three boats sent down beneath the surface, must have been long enough and broad enough to shade half Xerxes' army. Who can tell how appalling to the wounded whale must have been such huge phantoms flitting over his head!

'Stand by, men; he stirs,' cried Starbuck, as the three lines suddenly vibrated in the water, distinctly conducting upwards to them, as by magnetic wires, the life and death throbs of the whale, so that every oarsman felt them in his seat. The next moment, relieved in great part from the downward strain at the bows, the boats gave a sudden bounce upwards, as a small ice-field will, when a dense herd of white bears are scared from it into the sea.

'Haul in! Haul in!' cried Starbuck again; 'he's rising.'

The lines, of which, hardly an instant before, not one hand's breadth could have been gained, were now in long quick coils flung back all dripping into the boats, and soon the whale broke water within two ship's lengths of the hunters.

His motions plainly denoted his extreme exhaustion. In most land animals there are certain valves or flood-gates in many of their veins, whereby when wounded, the blood is in some degree at least instantly shut off in certain directions. Not so with the whale; one of whose peculiarities it is, to have an entire non-valvular structure of the blood-vessels, so that when pierced even by so small a point as a harpoon, a deadly drain is at once begun upon his whole arterial system; and when this is heightened by the extraordinary pressure of water at a great distance below the surface, his life may be said to pour from him in incessant streams. Yet so vast is the quantity of blood in him, and so distant and numerous its interior fountains, that he will keep thus bleeding and bleeding for a considerable period; even as in a drought a river will flow, whose source is in the well-springs of far-off and undiscernible hills. Even now, when the boats pulled upon this whale, and perilously drew over his swaying flukes, and the lances were darted into him, they were followed by steady jets from the new made wound, which kept continually playing, while the natural spout-hole in his head was only at intervals, however rapid, sending its affrighted moisture into the air. From this last vent no blood yet came, because no vital part of him had thus far been struck. His life, as they significantly call it, was untouched.

As the boats now more closely surrounded him, the whole upper part of his form, with much of it that is ordinarily submerged, was plainly revealed. His eyes, or rather the places where his eyes had been, were beheld. As strange misgrown masses gather in the knot-holes of the noblest oaks when prostrate, so from the points which the whale's eyes had once occupied, now protruded blind bulbs, horribly pitiable to see. But pity there was none. For all his old age, and his one arm, and his blind eyes, he must die the death and be murdered, in order to light the gay bridals and other merry-makings of men and also to illuminate the solemn churches that preach unconditional inoffensiveness by all to all. Still rolling in his blood, at last he partially disclosed a strangely discolored bunch or protuberance, the size of a bushel, low down on the flank.

'A nice spot,' cried Flask; 'just let me prick him there once.'

'Avast!' cried Starbuck, 'there's no need of that!'

But humane Starbuck was too late. At the instant of the dart an ulcerous jet shot from this cruel wound, and goaded by it into more than sufferable anguish, the whale now spouting thick blood, with swift fury blindly darted at the craft, bespattering them and their glorying crews all over with showers of gore, capsizing Flask's boat and marring the bows. It was his death stroke. For, by this time, so spent was he by loss of blood, that he helplessly rolled away from the wreck he had made; lay panting on his side, impotently flapped with his stumped fin, then over and over slowly revolved like a waning world; turned up the white secrets of his belly; lay like a log, and died. It was most piteous, that last expiring spout. As when by unseen hands the water is gradually drawn off from some mighty fountain, and with half-stifled melancholy gurglings the spray-column lowers and lowers to the ground—so the last long dying spout of the whale.

Soon, while the crews were awaiting the arrival of the ship, the body showed symptoms of sinking with all its treasures unrifled. Immediately, by Starbuck's orders, lines were secured to it at different points, so that ere long every boat was a buoy; the sunken whale being suspended a few inches beneath them by the cords. By very heedful management, when the ship drew nigh, the whale was transferred to her side, and was strongly secured there by the stiffest fluke-chains, for it was plain that unless artificially upheld, the body would at once sink to the bottom.

It so chanced that almost upon first cutting into him with the spade, the entire length of a corroded harpoon was found imbedded in his flesh, on the lower part of the bunch before described. But as the stumps of harpoons are frequently found in the dead bodies of captured whales, with the flesh perfectly healed around them, and no prominence of any kind to denote their place; therefore, there must needs have been some other unknown reason in the present case fully to account for the ulceration alluded to. But still more curious was the fact of a lance-head of stone being found in him, not far from the buried iron, the flesh perfectly firm about them. Who had darted that stone lance? And when? It might have been darted by some Nor' West Indian long before America was discovered.

What other marvels might have been rummaged out of this monstrous cabinet there is no telling. But a sudden stop was put to further discoveries, by the ship's being unprecedentedly dragged over sideways to the sea, owing to the body's immensely increasing tendency to sink. However, Starbuck, who had the ordering of affairs, hung on to it to the last; hung on to it so resolutely, indeed, that when at length the ship would have been capsized, if still persisting in locking arms with the body; then, when the command was given to break clear from it, such was the immovable strain upon the timber-heads to which the fluke-chains and cables were fastened, that it was impossible to cast them off. Meantime everything in the Pequod was aslant. To cross to the other side of the deck was like walking up the steep gabled roof of a house. The ship groaned and gasped. Many of the ivory inlayings of her bulwarks and cabins were started from their places, by the unnatural dislocation. In vain handspikes and crows were brought to bear upon the immovable fluke-chains, to pry them adrift from the timber-heads; and so low had the whale now settled that the submerged ends could not be at all approached, while every moment whole tons of ponderosity seemed added to the sinking bulk, and the ship seemed on the point of going over.

'Hold on, hold on, won't ye?' cried Stubb to the body, 'don't be in such a devil of a hurry to sink! By thunder, men, we must do something or go for it. No use prying there; avast, I say with your handspikes, and run one of ye for a prayer book and a pen-knife, and cut the big chains.'

'Knife? Aye, aye,' cried Queequeg, and seizing the carpenter's heavy hatchet, he leaned out of a porthole, and steel to iron, began slashing at the largest fluke-chains. But a few strokes, full of sparks, were given, when the exceeding strain effected the rest. With a terrific snap, every fastening went adrift; the ship righted, the carcase sank.

Now, this occasional inevitable sinking of the recently killed Sperm Whale is a very curious thing; nor has any fisherman yet adequately accounted for it. Usually the dead Sperm Whale floats with great buoyancy, with its side or belly considerably elevated above the surface. If the only whales that thus sank were old, meagre, and broken-hearted creatures, their pads of lard diminished and all their bones heavy and rheumatic; then you might with some reason assert that this sinking is caused by an uncommon specific gravity in the fish so sinking, consequent upon this absence of buoyant matter in him. But it is not so. For young whales, in the highest health, and swelling with noble aspirations, prematurely cut off in the warm flush and May of life, with all their panting lard about them; even these brawny, buoyant heroes do sometimes sink.

Be it said, however, that the Sperm Whale is far less liable to this accident than any other species. Where one of that sort goes down, twenty Right Whales do. This difference in the species is no doubt imputable in no small degree to the greater quantity of bone in the Right Whale; his Venetian blinds alone sometimes weighing more than a ton; from this incumbrance the Sperm Whale is wholly free. But there are instances where, after the lapse of many hours or several days, the sunken whale again rises, more buoyant than in life. But the reason of this is obvious. Gases are generated in him; he swells to a prodigious magnitude; becomes a sort of animal balloon. A line-of-battle ship could hardly keep him under then. In the Shore Whaling, on soundings, among the Bays of New Zealand, when a Right Whale gives token of sinking, they fasten buoys to him, with plenty of rope; so that when the body has gone down, they know where to look for it when it shall have ascended again.

It was not long after the sinking of the body that a cry was heard from the Pequod's mast-heads, announcing that the Jungfrau was again lowering her boats; though the only spout in sight was that of a Fin-Back, belonging to the species of uncapturable whales, because of its incredible power of swimming. Nevertheless, the Fin-Back's spout is so similar to the Sperm Whale's, that by unskilful fishermen it is often mistaken for it. And consequently Derick and all his host were now in valiant chase of this unnearable brute. The Virgin crowding all sail, made after her four young keels, and thus they all disappeared far to leeward, still in bold, hopeful chase.

Oh! many are the Fin-Backs, and many are the Dericks, my friend.

CHAPTER LXXXII

THE HONOR AND GLORY OF WHALING

There are some enterprises in which a careful disorderliness is the true method.

The more I dive into this matter of whaling, and push my researches up to the very spring-head of it, so much the more am I impressed with its great honorableness and antiquity; and especially when I find so many great demigods and heroes, prophets of all sorts, who one way or other have shed distinction upon it, I am transported with the reflection that I myself belong, though but subordinately, to so emblazoned a fraternity.

The gallant Perseus, a son of Jupiter, was the first whaleman; and to the eternal honor of our calling be it said, that the first whale attacked by our brotherhood was not killed with any sordid intent. These were the knightly days of our profession, when we only bore arms to succor the distressed, and not to fill men's lamp-feeders. Every one knows the fine story of Perseus and Andromeda; how the lovely Andromeda, the daughter of a king, was tied to a rock on the sea-coast, and as Leviathan was in the very act of carrying her off, Perseus, the prince of whale-men, intrepidly advancing, harpooned the monster, and delivered and married the maid. It was an admirable artistic exploit, rarely achieved by the best harpooneers of the present day; inasmuch as this Leviathan was slain at the very first dart. And let no man doubt this Arkite story; for in the ancient Joppa, now Jaffa, on the Syrian coast, in one of the Pagan temples, there stood for many ages the vast skeleton of a whale, which the city's legends and all the inhabitants asserted to be the identical bones of the monster that Perseus slew. When the Romans took Joppa, the same skeleton was carried to Italy in triumph. What seems most singular and suggestively important in this story, is this: it was from Joppa that Jonah set sail.

Akin to the adventure of Perseus and Andromeda—indeed, by some supposed to be indirectly derived from it—is that famous story of St George and the Dragon; which dragon I maintain to have been a whale; for in many old chronicles whales and dragons are strangely jumbled together, and often stand for each other. 'Thou art as a lion of the waters, and as a dragon of the sea,' saith Ezekiel; hereby, plainly meaning a whale; in truth, some versions of the Bible use that word itself. Besides, it would much subtract from the glory of the exploit had St George but encountered a crawling reptile of the land, instead of doing battle with the great monster of the deep. Any man may kill a snake, but only a Perseus, a St George, a Coffin, have the heart in them to march boldly up to a whale.

Let not the modern paintings of this scene mislead us; for though the creature encountered by that valiant whaleman of old is vaguely represented of a griffin-like shape, and though the battle is depicted on land and the saint on horseback, yet considering the great ignorance of those times, when the true form of the whale was unknown to artists; and considering that as in Perseus' case, St George's whale might have crawled up out of the sea on the beach; and considering that the animal ridden by St George might have been only a large seal, or sea-horse; bearing all this in mind, it will not appear altogether incompatible with the sacred legend and the ancientest draughts of the scene, to hold this so-called dragon no other than the great Leviathan himself. In fact, placed before the strict and piercing truth, this whole story will fare like that fish, flesh, and fowl idol of the Philistines, Dagon by name; who being planted before the ark of Israel, his horse's head and both the palms of his hands fell off from him, and only the stump or fishy part of him remained. Thus, then, one of our own noble stamp, even a whaleman, is the tutelary guardian of England; and by good rights, we harpooneers of Nantucket should be enrolled in the most noble order of St George. And therefore, let not the knights of that honorable company (none of whom, I venture to say, have ever had to do with a whale like their great patron), let them never eye a Nantucketer with disdain, since even in our woollen frocks and tarred trowsers we are much better entitled to St George's decoration than they.

Whether to admit Hercules among us or not, concerning this I long remained dubious: for though according to the Greek mythologies, that antique Crockett and Kit Carson—that brawny doer of rejoicing good deeds, was swallowed down and thrown up by a whale; still, whether that strictly makes a whaleman of him, that might be mooted. It nowhere appears that he ever actually harpooned his fish, unless, indeed, from the inside. Nevertheless, he may be deemed a sort of involuntary whaleman; at any rate the whale caught him, if he did not the whale. I claim him for one of our clan.

But, by the best contradictory authorities, this Grecian story of Hercules and the whale is considered to be derived from the still more ancient Hebrew story of Jonah and the whale; and vice versa; certainly they are very similar. If I claim the demigod then, why not the prophet?

Nor do heroes, saints, demigods, and prophets alone comprise the whole roll of our order. Our grand master is still to be named; for like royal kings of old times, we find the head-waters of our fraternity in nothing short of the great gods themselves. That wondrous oriental story is now to be rehearsed from the Shaster, which gives us the dread Vishnoo, one of the three persons in the godhead of the Hindoos; gives us the divine Vishnoo himself for our Lord:—Vishnoo, who, by the first of his ten earthly incarnations, has for ever set apart and sanctified the whale. When Brahma, or the God of Gods, saith the Shaster, resolved to recreate the world after one of its periodical dissolutions, he gave birth to Vishnoo, to preside over the work; but the Vedas, or mystical books, whose perusal would seem to have been indispensable to Vishnoo before beginning the creation, and which therefore must have contained something in the shape of practical hints to young architects, these Vedas were lying at the bottom of the waters; so Vishnoo became incarnate in a whale, and sounding down in him to the uttermost depths, rescued the sacred volumes. Was not this Vishnoo a whaleman, then? even as a man who rides a horse is called a horseman?

Perseus, St George, Hercules, Jonah, and Vishnoo! there's a member-roll for you! What club but the whaleman's can head off like that?

CHAPTER LXXXIII

JONAH HISTORICALLY REGARDED

Reference was made to the historical story of Jonah and the whale in the preceding chapter. Now some Nantucketers rather distrust this historical story of Jonah and the whale. But then there were some sceptical Greeks and Romans, who, standing out from the orthodox pagans of their times, equally doubted the story of Hercules and the whale, and Arion and the dolphin; and yet their doubting those traditions did not make those traditions one whit the less facts, for all that.

One old Sag-Harbor whaleman's chief reason for questioning the Hebrew story was this:—He had one of those quaint old-fashioned Bibles, embellished with curious, unscientific plates; one of which represented Jonah's whale with two spouts in his head—a peculiarity only true with respect to a species of the Leviathan (the Right Whale, and the varieties of that order), concerning which the fishermen have this saying, 'A penny roll would choke him;' his swallow is so very small. But, to this, Bishop Jebb's anticipative answer is ready. It is not necessary, hints the Bishop, that we consider Jonah as tombed in the whale's belly, but as temporarily lodged in some part of his mouth. And this seems reasonable enough in the good Bishop. For truly, the Right Whale's mouth would accommodate a couple of whist-tables, and comfortably seat all the players. Possibly, too, Jonah might have ensconced himself in a hollow tooth; but, on second thoughts, the Right Whale is toothless.

Another reason which Sag-Harbor (he went by that name) urged for his want of faith in this matter of the prophet, was something obscurely in reference to his incarcerated body and the whale's gastric juices. But this objection likewise falls to the ground, because a German exegetist supposes that Jonah must have taken refuge in the floating body of a *dead* whale—even as the French soldiers in the Russian campaign turned their dead horses into tents, and crawled into them. Besides, it has been divined by other continental commentators, that when Jonah was thrown overboard from the Joppa ship, he straightway effected his escape to another vessel near by, some vessel with a whale for a figure-head; and, I would add, possibly called 'The Whale,' as some craft are nowadays christened the 'Shark,' the 'Gull,' the 'Eagle.' Nor have there been wanting learned exegetists who have opined that the whale mentioned in the book of Jonah merely meant a life-preserver—an inflated bag of wind—which the endangered prophet swam to, and so was saved from a watery doom. Poor Sag-Harbor, therefore, seems worsted all round. But he had still another reason for his want of faith. It was this, if I remember right: Jonah was swallowed by the whale in the Mediterranean Sea, and after three days he was vomited up somewhere within three days' journey of Nineveh, a city on the Tigris, very much more than three days' journey across from the nearest point of the Mediterranean coast. How is that?

But was there no other way for the whale to land the prophet within that short distance of Nineveh? Yes. He might have carried him round by the way of the Cape of Good Hope. But not to speak of the passage through the whole length of the Mediterranean, and another passage up the Persian Gulf and Red Sea, such a supposition would involve the complete circumnavigation of all Africa in three days, not to speak of the Tigris waters, near the site of Nineveh, being too shallow for any whale to swim in. Besides, this idea of Jonah's weathering the Cape of Good Hope at so early a day would wrest the honor of the discovery of that great headland from Bartholomew Diaz, its reputed discoverer, and so make modern history a liar.

But all these foolish arguments of old Sag-Harbor only evinced his foolish pride of reason—a thing still more reprehensible in him, seeing that he had but little learning except what he had picked up from the sun and the sea. I say it only shows his foolish, impious pride, and abominable, devilish rebellion against the reverend clergy. For by a Portuguese Catholic priest, this very idea of Jonah's going to Nineveh via the Cape of Good Hope was advanced as a signal magnification of the general miracle. And so it was. Besides, to this day, the highly enlightened Turks devoutly believe in the historical story of Jonah. And some three centuries ago, an English traveller in old Harris's Voyages, speaks of a Turkish Mosque built in honor of Jonah, in which mosque was a miraculous lamp that burnt without any oil.

CHAPTER LXXXIV

PITCHPOLING

To make them run easily and swiftly, the axles of carriages are anointed; and for much the same purpose, some whalers perform an analogous operation upon their boat; they grease the bottom. Nor is it to be doubted that as such a procedure can do no harm, it may possibly be of no contemptible advantage; considering that oil and water are hostile; that oil is a sliding thing, and that the object in view is to make the boat slide bravely. Queequeg believed strongly in anointing his boat, and one morning not long after the German ship Jungfrau disappeared, took more than customary pains in that occupation; crawling under its bottom, where it hung over the side, and rubbing in the unctuousness as though diligently seeking to insure a crop of hair from the craft's bald keel. He seemed to be working in obedience to some particular presentiment. Nor did it remain unwarranted by the event.

Towards noon whales were raised; but so soon as the ship sailed down to them, they turned and fled with swift precipitancy; a disordered flight, as of Cleopatra's barges from Actium.

Nevertheless, the boats pursued, and Stubb's was foremost. By great exertion, Tashtego at last succeeded in planting one iron; but the stricken whale, without at all sounding, still continued his horizontal flight, with added fleetness. Such unintermitted strainings upon the planted iron must sooner or later inevitably extract it. It became imperative to lance the flying whale, or be content to lose him. But to haul the boat up to his flank was impossible, he swam so fast and furious. What then remained?

Of all the wondrous devices and dexterities, the sleights of hand and countless subtleties, to which the veteran whaleman is so often forced, none exceed that fine manœuvre with the lance called pitchpoling. Small sword, or broad sword, in all its exercises boasts nothing like it. It is only indispensable with an inveterate running whale; its grand fact and feature is the wonderful distance to which the long lance is accurately darted from a violently rocking, jerking boat, under extreme headway. Steel and wood included, the entire spear is some ten or twelve feet in length; the staff is much slighter than that of the harpoon, and also of a lighter material—pine. It is furnished with a small rope called a warp, of considerable length, by which it can be hauled back to the hand after darting.

But before going further, it is important to mention here, that though the harpoon may be pitchpoled in the same way with the lance, yet it is seldom done; and when done, is still less frequently successful, on account of the greater weight and inferior length of the harpoon as compared with the lance, which in effect become serious drawbacks. As a general thing, therefore, you must first get fast to a whale, before any pitchpoling comes into play.

Look now at Stubb, a man who from his humorous, deliberate coolness and equanimity in the direst emergencies, was specially qualified to excel in pitchpoling. Look at him; he stands upright in the tossed bow of the flying boat; wrapt in fleecy foam, the towing whale is forty feet ahead. Handling the long lance lightly, glancing twice or thrice along its length to see if it be exactly straight, Stubb whistlingly gathers up the coil of the warp in one hand, so as to secure its free end in his grasp, leaving the rest unobstructed. Then holding the lance full before his waistband's middle, he levels it at the whale; when, covering him with it, he steadily depresses the butt-end in his hand, thereby elevating the point till the weapon stands fairly balanced upon his palm, fifteen feet in the air. He minds you somewhat of a juggler, balancing a long staff on his chin. Next moment with a rapid, nameless impulse, in a superb lofty arch the bright steel spans the foaming distance, and quivers in the life spot of the whale. Instead of sparkling water, he now spouts red blood.

'That drove the spigot out of him!' cries Stubb. ''Tis July's immortal Fourth; all fountains must run wine to-day! Would now, it were old Orleans whiskey, or old Ohio, or unspeakable old Monongahela! Then, Tashtego, lad, I'd have ye hold a canakin to the jet, and we'd drink round it! Yea, verily, hearts alive, we'd brew choice punch in the spread of his spout-hole there, and from that live punch-bowl quaff the living stuff!'

Again and again to such gamesome talk, the dexterous dart is repeated, the spear returning to its master like a greyhound held in skilful leash. The agonized whale goes into his flurry; the tow-line is slackened, and the pitchpoler dropping astern, folds his hands, and mutely watches the monster die.

CHAPTER LXXXV

The Fountain

That for six thousand years—and no one knows how many millions of ages before—the great whales should have been spouting all over the sea, and sprinkling and mistifying the gardens of the deep, as with so many sprinkling or mistifying pots; and that for some centuries back, thousands of hunters should have been close by the fountain of the whale, watching these sprinklings and spoutings—that all this should be, and yet, that down to this blessed minute (fifteen and a quarter minutes past one o'clock P.M. of this sixteenth day of December, A.D. 1850), it should still remain a problem, whether these spoutings are, after all, really water, or nothing but vapor—this is surely a noteworthy thing.

Let us, then, look at this matter, along with some interesting items contingent. Every one knows that by the peculiar cunning of their gills, the finny tribes in general breathe the air which at all times is combined with the element in which they swim hence, a herring or a cod might live a century, and never once raise its head above the surface. But owing to his marked internal structure which gives him regular lungs, like a human being's, the whale can only live by inhaling the disengaged air in the open atmosphere. Wherefore the necessity for his periodical visits to the upper world. But he cannot in any degree breathe through his mouth, for, in his ordinary attitude, the Sperm Whale's mouth is buried at least eight feet beneath the surface; and what is still more, his windpipe has no connexion with his mouth. No, he breathes through his spiracle alone; and this is on the top of his head.

If I say, that in any creature breathing is only a function indispensable to vitality, inasmuch as it withdraws from the air a certain element, which being subsequently brought into contact with the blood imparts to the blood its vivifying principle, I do not think I shall err; though I may possibly use some superfluous scientific words. Assume it, and it follows that if all the blood in a man could be aerated with one breath, he might then seal up his nostrils and not fetch another for a considerable time. That is to say, he would then live without breathing. Anomalous as it may seem, this is precisely the case with the whale, who systematically lives, by intervals, his full hour and more (when at the bottom) without drawing a single breath, or so much as in any way inhaling a particle of air; for, remember, he has no gills. How is this? Between his ribs and on each side of his spine he is supplied with a remarkable involved Cretan labyrinth of vermicelli-like vessels, which vessels, when he quits the surface, are completely distended with oxygenated blood. So that for an hour or more, a thousand fathoms in the sea, he carries a surplus stock of vitality in him, just as the camel crossing the waterless desert carries a surplus supply of drink for future use in its four supplementary stomachs. The anatomical fact of this labyrinth is indisputable; and that the supposition founded upon it is reasonable and true, seems the more cogent to me, when I consider the otherwise inexplicable obstinacy of that leviathan in *having his spoutings out,* as the fishermen phrase it. This is what I mean. If unmolested, upon rising to the surface, the Sperm Whale will continue there for a period of time exactly uniform with all his other unmolested risings. Say he stays eleven minutes, and jets seventy times, that is, respires seventy breaths; then whenever he rises again, he will be sure to have his seventy breaths over again, to a minute. Now, if after he fetches a few breaths you alarm him, so that he sounds, he will be always dodging up again to make good his regular allowance of air. And not till those seventy breaths are told, will he finally go down to stay out his full term below. Remark, however, that in different individuals these rates are different; but in any one they are alike. Now, why should the whale thus insist upon having his spoutings out, unless it be to replenish his reservoir of air, ere descending for good? How obvious is it, too, that this necessity for the whale's rising exposes him to all the fatal hazards of the chase. For not by hook or by net could this vast leviathan be caught, when sailing a thousand fathoms beneath the sunlight. Not so much thy skill, then, O hunter, as the great necessities, that strike the victory to thee!

In man, breathing is incessantly going on—one breath only serving for two or three pulsations; so that whatever other business he has to attend to, waking or sleeping, breathe he must, or die he will. But the Sperm Whale only breathes about one seventh or Sunday of his time.

It has been said that the whale only breathes through his spout-hole; if it could truthfully be added that his spouts are mixed with water, then I opine we should be furnished with the reason why his sense of smell seems obliterated in him; for the only thing about him that at all answers to his nose is that identical spout-hole; and being so clogged with two elements, it could not be expected to have the power of smelling. But owing to the mystery of the spout—whether it be water or whether it be vapor—no absolute certainty can as yet be arrived at on this head. Sure it is, nevertheless, that the Sperm Whale has no proper olfactories. But what does he want of them? No roses, no violets, no Cologne-water in the sea.

Furthermore, as his windpipe solely opens into the tube of his spouting canal, and as that long canal—like the grand Erie Canal—is furnished with a sort of locks (that open and shut) for the downward retention of air or the upward exclusion of water, therefore the whale has no voice, unless you insult him by saying, that when he so strangely rumbles, he talks through his nose. But then again, what has the whale to say? Seldom have I known any profound being that had anything to say to this world, unless forced to stammer out something by way of getting a living. Oh! happy that the world is such an excellent listener!

Now, the spouting canal of the Sperm Whale, chiefly intended as it is for the conveyance of air, and for several feet laid along, horizontally, just beneath the upper surface of his head, and a little to one side; this curious canal is very much like a gas-pipe laid down in a city on one side of a street. But the question returns whether this gas-pipe is also a water-pipe; in other words, whether the spout of the Sperm Whale is the mere vapor of the exhaled breath, or whether that exhaled breath is mixed with water taken in at the mouth, and discharged through the spiracle. It is certain that the mouth indirectly communicates with the spouting canal; but it cannot be proved that this is for the purpose of discharging water through the spiracle. Because the greatest necessity for so doing would seem to be, when in feeding he accidentally takes in water. But the Sperm Whale's food is far beneath the surface, and there he cannot spout even if he would. Besides, if you regard him very closely, and time him with your watch, you will find that when unmolested, there is an undeviating rhyme between the periods of his jets and the ordinary periods of respiration.

But why pester one with all this reasoning on the subject? Speak out! You have seen him spout; then declare what the spout is; can you not tell water from air? My dear sir, in this world it is not so easy to settle these plain things. I have ever found your plain things the knottiest of all. And as for this whale spout, you might almost stand in it, and yet be undecided as to what it is precisely.

The central body of it is hidden in the snowy sparkling mist enveloping it; and how can you certainly tell whether any water falls from it, when, always, when you are close enough to a whale to get a close view of his spout, he is in a prodigious commotion, the water cascading all around him. And if at such times you should think that you really perceived drops of moisture in the spout, how do you know that they are not merely condensed from its vapor; or how do you know that they are not those identical drops superficially lodged in the spout-hole fissure, which is counter-sunk into the summit of the whale's head? For even when tranquilly swimming through the mid-day sea in a calm, with his elevated hump sun-dried as a dromedary's in the desert; even then, the whale always carries a small basin of water on his head, as under a blazing sun you will sometimes see a cavity in a rock filled up with rain.

Nor is it at all prudent for the hunter to be over curious touching the precise nature of the whale spout. It will not do for him to be peering into it, and putting his face in it. You cannot go with your pitcher to this fountain and fill it, and bring it away. For even when coming into slight contact with the outer, vapory shreds of the jet, which will often happen, your skin will feverishly smart, from the acridness of the thing so touching it. And I know one, who coming into still closer contact with the spout, whether with some scientific object in view, or otherwise, I cannot say, the skin peeled off from his cheek and arm. Wherefore, among whalemen, the spout is deemed poisonous; they try to evade it. Another thing; I have heard it said, and I do not much doubt it, that if the jet is fairly spouted into your eyes, it will blind you. The wisest thing the investigator can do then, it seems to me, is to let this deadly spout alone.

Still, we can hypothesize, even if we cannot prove and establish. My hypothesis is this: that the spout is nothing but mist. And besides other reasons, to this conclusion I am impelled, by considerations touching the great inherent dignity and sublimity of the Sperm Whale; I account him no common, shallow being, inasmuch as it is an undisputed fact that he is never found on soundings, or near shores; all other whales sometimes are. He is both ponderous and profound. And I am convinced that from the heads of all ponderous profound beings, such as Plato, Pyrrho, the Devil, Jupiter, Dante, and so on, there always goes up a certain semi-visible steam, while in the act of thinking deep thoughts. While composing a little treatise on Eternity, I had the curiosity to place a mirror before me; and ere long saw reflected there, a curious involved worming and undulation in the atmosphere over my head. The invariable moisture of my hair, while plunged in deep thought, after six cups of hot tea in my thin shingled attic, of an August noon; this seems an additional argument for the above supposition.

And how nobly it raises our conceit of the mighty, misty monster, to behold him solemnly sailing through a calm tropical sea; his vast, mild head overhung by a canopy of vapor, engendered by his incommunicable contemplations, and that vapor—as you will sometimes see it—glorified by a rainbow, as if Heaven itself had put its seal upon his thoughts. For, d'ye see, rainbows do not visit the clear air; they only irradiate vapor. And so, through all the thick mists of the dim doubts in my mind, divine intuitions now and then shoot, enkindling my fog with a heavenly ray. And for this I thank God; for all have doubts; many deny; but doubts or denials, few along with them, have intuitions. Doubts of all things earthly, and intuitions of some things heavenly; this combination makes neither believer nor infidel, but makes a man who regards them both with equal eye.

CHAPTER LXXXVI

THE TAIL

Other poets have warbled the praises of the soft eye of the antelope, and the lovely plumage of the bird that never alights; less celestial, I celebrate a tail.

Reckoning the largest sized Sperm Whale's tail to begin at that point of the trunk where it tapers to about the girth of a man, it comprises upon its upper surface alone, an area of at least fifty square feet. The compact round body of its root expands into two broad, firm, flat palms or flukes, gradually shoaling away to less than an inch in thickness. At the crotch or junction, these flukes slightly overlap, then sideways recede from each other like wings, leaving a wide vacancy between. In no living thing are the lines of beauty more exquisitely defined than in the crescentic borders of these flukes. At its utmost expansion in the full grown whale, the tail will considerably exceed twenty feet across.

The entire member seems a dense webbed bed of welded sinews; but cut into it, and you find that three distinct strata compose it:—upper, middle, and lower. The fibres in the upper and lower layers, are long and horizontal; those of the middle one, very short, and running crosswise between the outside layers. This triune structure, as much as anything else, imparts power to the tail. To the student of old Roman walls, the middle layer will furnish a curious parallel to the thin course of tiles always alternating with the stone in those wonderful relics of the antique, and which undoubtedly contribute so much to the great strength of the masonry.

But as if this vast local power in the tendinous tail were not enough, the whole bulk of the leviathan is knit over with a warp and woof of muscular fibres and filaments, which passing on either side the loins and running down into the flukes, insensibly blend with them, and largely contribute to their might; so that in the tail the confluent measureless force of the whole whale seems concentrated to a point. Could annihilation occur to matter, this were the thing to do it.

Nor does this—its amazing strength, at all tend to cripple the graceful flexion of its motions; where infantileness of ease undulates through a Titanism of power. On the contrary, those motions derive their most appalling beauty from it. Real strength never impairs beauty or harmony, but it often bestows it; and in everything imposingly beautiful, strength has much to do with the magic. Take away the tied tendons that all over seem bursting from the marble in the carved Hercules, and its charm would be gone. As devout Eckerman lifted the linen sheet from the naked corpse of Goethe, he was overwhelmed with the massive chest of the man, that seemed as a Roman triumphal arch. When Angelo paints even God the Father in human form, mark what robustness is there. And whatever they may reveal of the divine love in the Son, the soft, curled, hermaphroditical Italian pictures, in which his idea has been most successfully embodied; these pictures, so destitute as they are of all brawniness, hint nothing of any power, but the mere negative, feminine one of submission and endurance, which on all hands it is conceded, form the peculiar practical virtues of his teachings.

Such is the subtle elasticity of the organ I treat of, that whether wielded in sport, or in earnest, or in anger, whatever be the mood it be in, its flexions are invariably marked by exceeding grace. Therein no fairy's arm can transcend it.

Five great motions are peculiar to it. First, when used as a fin for progression; Second, when used as a mace in battle; Third, in sweeping; Fourth, lobtailing; Fifth, in peaking flukes.

First: Being horizontal in its position, the Leviathan's tail acts in a different manner from the tails of all other sea creatures. It never wriggles. In man or fish, wriggling is a sign of inferiority. To the whale, his tail is the sole means of propulsion. Scroll-wise coiled forwards beneath the body, and then rapidly sprung backwards, it is this which gives that singular darting, leaping motion to the monster when furiously swimming. His side-fins only serve to steer by.

Second: It is a little significant, that while one sperm whale only fights another sperm whale with his head and jaw, nevertheless, in his conflicts with man, he chiefly and contemptuously uses his tail. In striking at a boat, he swiftly curves away his flukes from it, and the blow is only inflicted by the recoil. If it be made in the unobstructed air, especially if it descend to its mark, the stroke is then simply irresistible. No ribs of man or boat can withstand it. Your only salvation lies in eluding it; but if it comes sideways through the opposing water, then partly owing to the light buoyancy of the whale-boat, and the elasticity of its materials, a cracked rib or a dashed plank or two, a sort of stitch in the side, is generally the most serious result. These submerged side blows are so often received in the fishery, that they are accounted mere child's play. Some one strips off a frock, and the hole is stopped.

Third: I cannot demonstrate it, but it seems to me, that in the whale the sense of touch is concentrated in the tail; for in this respect there is a delicacy in it only equalled by the daintiness of the elephant's trunk. This delicacy is chiefly evinced in the action of sweeping, when in maidenly gentleness the whale with a certain soft slowness moves his immense flukes from side to side upon the surface of the sea; and if he feel but a sailor's whisker, woe to that sailor, whiskers and all. What tenderness there is in that preliminary touch! Had this tail any prehensile power, I should straightway bethink me of Darmonodes' elephant that so frequented the flower-market, and with low salutations presented nosegays to damsels, and then caressed their zones. On more accounts than one, a pity it is that the whale does not possess this prehensile virtue in his tail; for I have heard of yet another elephant, that when wounded in the fight, curved round his trunk and extracted the dart.

Fourth: Stealing unawares upon the whale in the fancied security of the middle of solitary seas, you find him unbent from the vast corpulence of his dignity, and kitten-like, he plays on the ocean as if it were a hearth. But still you see his power in his play. The broad palms of his tail are flirted high into the air; then smiting the surface, the thunderous concussion resounds for miles. You would almost think a great gun had been discharged; and if you noticed the light wreath of vapor from the spiracle at his other extremity, you would think that that was the smoke from the touch-hole.

Fifth: As in the ordinary floating posture of the leviathan the flukes lie considerably below the level of his back, they are then completely out of sight beneath the surface; but when he is about to plunge into the deeps, his entire flukes with at least thirty feet of his body are tossed erect in the air, and so remain vibrating a moment, till they downwards shoot out of view. Excepting the sublime *breach*—somewhere else to be described—this peaking of the whale's flukes is perhaps the grandest sight to be seen in all animated nature. Out of the bottomless profundities the gigantic tail seems spasmodically snatching at the highest heaven. So in dreams, have I seen majestic Satan thrusting forth his tormented colossal claw from the flame Baltic of Hell. But in gazing at such scenes, it is all in all what mood you are in; if in the Dantean, the devils will occur to you; if in that of Isaiah, the archangels. Standing at the mast-head of my ship during a sunrise that crimsoned sky and sea, I once saw a large herd of whales in the east, all heading towards the sun, and for a moment vibrating in concert with peaked flukes. As it seemed to me at the time, such a grand embodiment of adoration of the gods was never beheld, even in Persia, the home of the fire worshippers. As Ptolemy Philopater testified of the African elephant, I then testified of the whale, pronouncing him the most devout of all beings. For according to King Juba, the military elephants of antiquity often hailed the morning with their trunks uplifted in the profoundest silence.

The chance comparison in this chapter, between the whale and the elephant, so far as some aspects of the tail of the one and the trunk of the other are concerned, should not tend to place those two opposite organs on an equality, much less the creatures to which they respectively belong. For as the mightiest elephant is but a terrier to Leviathan, so, compared with Leviathan's tail, his trunk is but the stalk of a lily. The most direful blow from the elephant's trunk were as the playful tap of a fan, compared with the measureless crush and crash of the sperm whale's ponderous flukes, which in repeated instances have one after the other hurled entire boats with all their oars and crews into the air, very much as an Indian juggler tosses his balls.*

The more I consider this mighty tail, the more do I deplore my inability to express it. At times there are gestures in it, which, though they would well grace the hand of man, remain wholly inexplicable. In an extensive herd, so remarkable, occasionally, are these mystic gestures, that I have heard hunters who have declared them akin to Free-Mason signs and symbols; that the whale, indeed, by these methods intelligently conversed with the world. Nor are there wanting other motions of the whale in his general body, full of strangeness, and unaccountable to his most experienced assailant. Dissect him how I may, then, I but go skin deep; I know him not, and never will. But if I know not even the tail of this whale, how understand his head? much more, how comprehend his face, when face he has none? Thou shalt see my back parts, my tail, he seems to say, but my face shall not be seen. But I cannot completely make out his back parts; and hint what he will about his face, I say again he has no face.

CHAPTER LXXXVII

THE GRAND ARMADA

The long and narrow peninsula of Malacca, extending south-eastward from the territories of Birmah, forms the most southerly point of all Asia. In a continuous line from that peninsula stretch the long islands of Sumatra, Java, Bally, and Timor; which, with many others, form a vast mole, or rampart, lengthwise con-

*Though all comparison in the way of general bulk between the whale and the elephant is preposterous, inasmuch as in that particular the elephant stands in much the same respect to the whale that the dog does to the elephant; nevertheless, there are not wanting some points of curious similitude; among these is the spout. It is well known that the elephant will often draw up water or dust in his trunk, and then elevating it, jet it forth in a stream.

necting Asia with Australia, and dividing the long unbroken Indian ocean from the thickly studded oriental archipelagoes. This rampart is pierced by several sally-ports for the convenience of ships and whales; conspicuous among which are the straits of Sunda and Malacca. By the straits of Sunda, chiefly, vessels bound to China from the west, emerge into the China seas.

Those narrow straits of Sunda divide Sumatra from Java; and standing midway in that vast rampart of islands, buttressed by that bold green promontory, known to seamen as Java Head; they not a little correspond to the central gateway opening into some vast walled empire: and considering the inexhaustible wealth of spices, and silks, and jewels, and gold, and ivory, with which the thousand islands of that oriental sea are enriched, it seems a significant provision of nature, that such treasures, by the very formation of the land, should at least bear the appearance, however ineffectual, of being guarded from the all-grasping western world. The shores of the Straits of Sunda are unsupplied with those domineering fortresses which guard the entrances to the Mediterranean, the Baltic, and the Propontis. Unlike the Danes, these Orientals do not demand the obsequious homage of lowered top-sails from the endless procession of ships before the wind, which for centuries past, by night and by day, have passed between the islands of Sumatra and Java, freighted with the costliest cargoes of the east. But while they freely waive a ceremonial like this, they do by no means renounce their claim to more solid tribute.

Time out of mind the piratical proas of the Malays, lurking among the low shaded coves and islets of Sumatra, have sallied out upon the vessels sailing through the straits, fiercely demanding tribute at the point of their spears. Though by the repeated bloody chastisements, they have received at the hands of European cruisers, the audacity of these corsairs has of late been somewhat repressed; yet, even at the present day, we occasionally hear of English and American vessels, which, in those waters, have been remorselessly boarded and pillaged.

With a fair, fresh wind, the Pequod was now drawing nigh to these straits; Ahab purposing to pass through them into the Javan sea, and thence, cruising northwards, over waters known to be frequented here and there by the Sperm Whale, sweep inshore by the Philippine Islands, and gain the far coast of Japan, in time for the great whaling season there. By these means, the circumnavigating Pequod would sweep almost all the known Sperm Whale cruising grounds of the world, previous to descending upon the Line in the Pacific; where Ahab, though everywhere else foiled in his pursuit, firmly counted upon giving battle to Moby Dick, in the sea he was most known to frequent; and at a season when he might most reasonably be presumed to be haunting it.

But how now? in this zoned quest, does Ahab touch no land? does his crew drink air? Surely, he will stop for water. Nay. For a long time, now, the circus-running sun has raced within his fiery ring, and needs no sustenance but what's in himself. So Ahab. Mark this, too, in the whaler. While other hulls are loaded down with alien stuff, to be transferred to foreign wharves; the world-wandering whale-ship carries no cargo but herself and crew, their weapons and their wants. She has a whole lake's contents bottled in her ample hold. She is ballasted with utilities; not altogether with unusable pig-lead and kentledge. She carries years' water in her. Clear old prime Nantucket water; which, when three years afloat, the Nantucketer, in the Pacific, prefers to drink before the brackish fluid, but yesterday rafted off in casks, from the Peruvian or Indian streams. Hence it is, that, while other ships may have gone to China from New York, and back again, touching at a score of ports, the whale-ship, in all that interval, may not have sighted one grain of soil; her crew having seen no man but floating seamen like themselves. So that did you carry them the news that another flood had come; they would only answer—'Well, boys, here's the ark!'

Now, as many Sperm Whales had been captured off the western coast of Java, in the near vicinity of the Straits of Sunda; indeed, as most of the ground, roundabout, was generally recognized by the fishermen as an excellent spot for cruising; therefore, as the Pequod gained more and more upon Java Head, the look-outs were repeatedly hailed, and admonished to keep wide awake. But though the green palmy cliffs of the land soon loomed on the starboard bow, and with delighted nostrils the fresh cinnamon was snuffed in the air, yet not a single jet was descried. Almost renouncing all thought of falling in with any game hereabouts, the ship had well nigh entered the straits, when the customary cheering cry was heard from aloft, and ere long a spectacle of singular magnificence saluted us.

But here be it premised, that owing to the unwearied activity with which of late they have been hunted over all four oceans, the Sperm Whales, instead of almost invariably sailing in small detached companies, as in former times, are now frequently met with in extensive herds, sometimes embracing so great a multitude, that it would almost seem as if numerous nations of them had sworn solemn league and covenant for mutual assistance and protection. To this aggregation of the Sperm Whale into such immense caravans, may be imputed the circumstance that even in the best cruising grounds, you may now sometimes sail for weeks and months together, without being greeted by a single spout; and then be suddenly saluted by what sometimes seems thousands on thousands.

Broad on both bows, at the distance of some two or three miles, and forming a great semicircle, embracing one half of the level horizon, a continuous chain of whale-jets were up-playing and sparkling in the noon-day air. Unlike the straight perpendicular twin-jets of the Right Whale, which, dividing at top, fall over in two branches, like the cleft drooping boughs of a willow, the single forward-slanting spout of the Sperm Whale presents a thick curled bush of white mist, continually rising and falling away to leeward.

Seen from the Pequod's deck, then, as she would rise on a high hill of the sea, this host of vapory spouts, individually curling up into the air, and beheld through a blending atmosphere of bluish haze, showed like the thousand cheerful chimneys of some dense metropolis, descried of a balmy autumnal morning, by some horseman on a height.

As marching armies approaching an unfriendly defile in the mountains, accelerate their march, all eagerness to place that perilous passage in their rear, and once more expand in comparative security upon the plain; even so did this vast fleet of whales now seem hurrying forward through the straits; gradually contracting the wings of their semicircle, and swimming on, in one solid, but still crescentic centre.

Crowding all sail the Pequod pressed after them; the harpooneers handling their weapons, and loudly cheering from the heads of their yet suspended boats. If the wind only held, little doubt had they, that chased through these Straits of Sunda, the vast host would only deploy into the Oriental seas to witness the capture of not a few of their number. And who could tell whether, in that congregated caravan, Moby Dick himself might not temporarily be swimming, like the worshipped white-elephant in the coronation procession of the Siamese! So with stun-sail piled on stun-sail, we sailed along, driving these leviathans before us; when, of a sudden, the voice of Tashtego was heard, loudly directing attention to something in our wake.

Corresponding to the crescent in our van, we beheld another in our rear. It seemed formed of detached white vapors, rising and falling something like the spouts of the whales; only they did not so completely come and go; for they constantly hovered, without finally disappearing. Levelling his glass at this sight, Ahab quickly revolved in his pivot-hole, crying, 'Aloft there, and rig whips and buckets to wet the sails;—Malays, sir, and after us!'

As if too long lurking behind the headlands, till the Pequod should fairly have entered the straits, these rascally Asiatics were now in hot pursuit, to make up for their over-cautious delay. But when the swift Pequod, with a fresh leading wind, was herself in hot chase; how very kind of these tawny philanthropists to assist in speeding her on to her own chosen pursuit,—mere riding-whips and rowels to her, that they were. As with glass under arm, Ahab to-and-fro paced the deck; in his forward turn beholding the monsters he chased, and in the after one the bloodthirsty pirates chasing *him,* some such fancy as the above seemed his. And when he glanced upon the green walls of the watery defile in which the ship was then sailing, and bethought him that through that gate lay the route to his vengeance, and beheld, how that through that same gate he was now both chasing and being chased to his deadly end; and not only that, but a herd of remorseless wild pirates and inhuman atheistical devils were infernally cheering him on with their curses;—when all these conceits had passed through his brain, Ahab's brow was left gaunt and ribbed, like the black sand beach after some stormy tide has been gnawing it, without being able to drag the firm thing from its place.

But thoughts like these troubled very few of the reckless crew; and when, after steadily dropping and dropping the pirates astern, the Pequod at last shot by the vivid green Cockatoo Point on the Sumatra side, emerging at last upon the broad waters beyond; then, the harpooneers seemed more to grieve that the swift whales had been gaining upon the ship, than to rejoice that the ship had so victoriously gained upon the Malays. But still driving on in the wake of the whales, at length they seemed abating their speed; gradually the ship neared them; and the wind now dying away, word was passed to spring to the boats. But no sooner did the herd, by some presumed wonderful instinct of the Sperm Whale, become notified of the three keels that were after them,—though as yet a mile in their rear,—than they rallied again, and forming in close ranks and battalions, so that their spouts all looked like flashing lines of stacked bayonets, moved on with redoubled velocity.

Stripped to our shirts and drawers, we sprang to the white-ash, and after several hours' pulling were almost disposed to renounce the chase, when a general pausing commotion among the whales gave animating token that they were now at last under the influence of that strange perplexity of inert irresolution, which, when the fishermen perceive it in the whale, they say he is *gallied.** The compact martial columns in which they had been hitherto rapidly and steadily swimming, were

---

*To *gally,* or *gallow,* is to frighten excessively,—to confound with fright. It is an old Saxon word. It occurs once in Shakspere:—

> 'The wrathful skies
> *Gallow* the very wanderers of the dark,
> And make them keep their caves.'
> *Lear,* Act III. sc. ii.

To common land usages, the word is now completely obsolete. When the polite landman first hears it from the gaunt Nantucketer, he is apt to set it down as one of the whaleman's self-derived savageries. Much the same is it with many other sinewy Saxonisms of this sort, which emigrated to the New-England rocks with the noble brawn of the old English emigrants in the time of the Commonwealth. Thus, some of the best and furthest-descended English words—the etymological Howards and Percys—are now democratised, nay, plebeianised—so to speak—in the New World.

now broken up in one measureless rout; and like King Porus' elephants in the Indian battle with Alexander, they seemed going mad with consternation. In all directions expanding in vast irregular circles, and aimlessly swimming hither and thither, by their short thick spoutings, they plainly betrayed their distraction of panic. This was still more strangely evinced by those of their number, who, completely paralysed as it were, helplessly floated like water-logged dismantled ships on the sea. Had these leviathans been but a flock of simple sheep, pursued over the pasture by three fierce wolves, they could not possibly have evinced such excessive dismay. But this occasional timidity is characteristic of almost all herding creatures. Though banding together in tens of thousands, the lion-maned buffaloes of the West have fled before a solitary horseman. Witness, too, all human beings, how when herded together in the sheepfold of a theatre's pit, they will, at the slightest alarm of fire, rush helter-skelter for the outlets, crowding, trampling, jamming, and remorselessly dashing each other to death. Best, therefore, withhold any amazement at the strangely gallied whales before us, for there is no folly of the beasts of the earth which is not infinitely outdone by the madness of men.

Though many of the whales, as has been said, were in violent motion, yet it is to be observed that as a whole the herd neither advanced nor retreated, but collectively remained in one place. As is customary in those cases, the boats at once separated, each making for some one lone whale on the outskirts of the shoal. In about three minutes' time, Queequeg's harpoon was flung; the stricken fish darted blinding spray in our faces, and then running away with us like light, steered straight for the heart of the herd. Though such a movement on the part of the whale struck under such circumstances, is in no wise unprecedented; and indeed is almost always more or less anticipated; yet does it present one of the more perilous vicissitudes of the fishery. For as the swift monster drags you deeper and deeper into the frantic shoal, you bid adieu to circumspect life and only exist in a delirious throb.

As, blind and deaf, the whale plunged forward, as if by sheer power of speed to rid himself of the iron leech that had fastened to him; as we thus tore a white gash in the sea, on all sides menaced as we flew, by the crazed creatures to and fro rushing about us; our beset boat was like a ship mobbed by ice-isles in a tempest, and striving to steer through their complicated channels and straits, knowing not at what moment it may be locked in and crushed.

But not a bit daunted, Queequeg steered us manfully; now sheering off from this monster directly across our route in advance; now edging away from that, whose colossal flukes were suspended overhead, while all the time, Starbuck stood up in the bows, lance in hand, pricking out of our way whatever whales he could reach by short darts, for there was no time to make long ones. Nor were the oarsmen quite idle, though their wonted duty was now altogether dispensed with. They chiefly attended to the shouting part of the business. 'Out of the way, Commodore!' cried one, to a great dromedary that of a sudden rose bodily to the surface, and for an instant threatened to swamp us. 'Hard down with your tail, there!' cried a second to another, which, close to our gunwale, seemed calmly cooling himself with his own fan-like extremity.

All whaleboats carry certain curious contrivances, originally invented by the Nantucket Indians, called druggs. Two thick squares of wood of equal size are stoutly clenched together, so that they cross each other's grain at right angles; a line of considerable length is then attached to the middle of this block, and the other end of the line being looped, it can in a moment be fastened to a harpoon. It is chiefly among gallied whales that this drugg is used. For then, more whales are close round you than you can possibly chase at one time. But sperm whales are not every day encountered; while you may, then, you must kill all you can. And if you cannot kill them all at once, you must wing them, so that they can be afterwards killed at your leisure. Hence it is, that at times like these the drugg comes into requisition. Our boat was furnished with three of them. The first and second were successfully darted, and we saw the whales staggeringly running off, fettered by the enormous sidelong resistance of the towing drugg. They were cramped like malefactors with the chain and ball. But upon flinging the third, in the act of tossing overboard the clumsy wooden block, it caught under one of the seats of the boat, and in an instant tore it out and carried it away, dropping the oarsman in the boat's bottom as the seat slid from under him. On both sides the sea came in at the wounded planks, but we stuffed two or three drawers and shirts in, and so stopped the leaks for the time.

It had been next to impossible to dart these drugged-harpoons, were it not that as we advanced into the herd, our whale's way greatly diminished; moreover, that as we went still further and further from the circumference of commotion, the direful disorders seemed waning. So that when at last the jerking harpoon drew out, and the towing whale sideways vanished; then, with the tapering force of his parting momentum, we glided between two whales into the innermost heart of the shoal, as if from some mountain torrent we had slid into a serene valley lake. Here the storms in the roaring glens between the outermost whales, were heard but not felt. In this central expanse the sea presented that smooth satin-like surface, called a sleek, produced by the subtle moisture thrown off by the whale in his more quiet moods. Yes, we were now in that enchanted calm which they say lurks at the heart of every commotion. And still in the distracted distance we beheld the tumults of the outer concentric circles, and saw successive pods of whales, eight or ten in each, swiftly going round and round, like multiplied spans of horses in a ring; and so closely shoulder to shoulder, that a Titanic circus-rider might easily have over-arched the middle ones, and so have gone round on their backs. Owing to the density of the crowd of reposing whales, more immediately surrounding the embayed axis of the herd, no possible chance of escape was at present afforded us. We must watch for a breach in the living wall that hemmed us in; the wall that had only admitted us in order to shut us up. Keeping at the centre of the lake we were occasionally visited by small tame cows and calves; the women and children of this routed host.

Now, inclusive of the occasional wide intervals between the revolving outer circles, and inclusive of the spaces between the various pods in any one of those circles, the entire area at this juncture, embraced by the whole multitude, must have contained at least two or three square miles. At any rate—though indeed such a test at such a time might be deceptive—spoutings might be discovered from our low boat that seemed playing up almost from the rim of the horizon. I mention this circumstance, because, as if the cows and calves had been purposely locked up in this innermost fold; and as if the wide extent of the herd had hitherto prevented them from learning the precise cause of its stopping; or, possibly, being so young, unsophisticated, and every way innocent and inexperienced; however it may have been, these smaller whales—now and then visiting our becalmed boat from the margin of the lake—evinced a wondrous fearlessness and confidence, or else a still, becharmed panic which it was impossible not to marvel at. Like household dogs they came snuffling round us, right up to our gunwales, and touching them; till it almost seemed that some spell had suddenly domesticated them. Queequeg patted their foreheads; Starbuck scratched their backs with his lance; but fearful of the consequences, for the time refrained from darting it.

But far beneath this wondrous world upon the surface, another and still stranger world met our eyes as we gazed over the side. For, suspended in those watery vaults, floated the forms of the nursing mothers of the whales, and those that by their enormous girth seemed shortly to become mothers. The lake, as I have hinted, was to a considerable depth exceedingly transparent; and as human infants while suckling will calmly and fixedly gaze away from the breast, as if leading two different lives at the time; and while yet drawing mortal nourishment, be still spiritually feasting upon some unearthly reminiscence;—even so did the young of these whales seem looking up towards us, but not at us, as if we were but a bit of Gulf-weed in their new-born sight. Floating on their sides, the mothers also seemed quietly eyeing us. One of these little infants, that from certain queer tokens seemed hardly a day old, might have measured some fourteen feet in length, and some six feet in girth. He was a little frisky; though as yet his body seemed scarce yet recovered from that irksome position it had so lately occupied in the maternal reticule; where, tail to head, and all ready for the final spring, the unborn whale lies bent like a Tartar's bow. The delicate side-fins, and the palms of his flukes, still freshly retained the plaited crumpled appearance of a baby's ears newly arrived from foreign parts.

'Line! line!' cried Queequeg, looking over the gunwale; 'him fast! him fast!—Who line him! Who struck?—Two whale; one big, one little!'

'What ails ye, man?' cried Starbuck.

'Look-e here,' said Queequeg pointing down.

As when the stricken whale, that from the tub has reeled out hundreds of fathoms of rope; as, after deep sounding, he floats up again, and shows the slackened curling line buoyantly rising and spiralling towards the air; so now, Starbuck saw long coils of the umbilical cord of Madame Leviathan, by which the young cub seemed still tethered to its dam. Not seldom in the rapid vicissitudes of the chase, this natural line, with the maternal end loose, becomes entangled with the hempen one, so that the cub is thereby trapped. Some of the subtlest secrets of the seas seemed divulged to us in this enchanted pond. We saw young Leviathan amours in the deep.*

And thus, though surrounded by circle upon circle of consternations and affrights, did these inscrutable creatures at the centre freely and fearlessly indulge in all peaceful concernments; yea, serenely revelled in dalliance and delight. But even so, amid the tornadoed Atlantic of my being, do I myself still for ever centrally disport in mute calm; and while ponderous planets of unwaning woe revolve round me, deep down and deep inland there I still bathe me in eternal mildness of joy.

Meanwhile, as we thus lay entranced, the occasional sudden frantic spectacles in the distance evinced the activity of the other boats, still engaged in drugging the whales on the frontier of the host; or possibly carrying on the war within the first

*The sperm whale, as with all other species of the Leviathan, but unlike most other fish, breeds indifferently at all seasons; after a gestation which may probably be set down at nine months, producing but one at a time; though in some few known instances giving birth to an Esau and Jacob:—a contingency provided for in suckling by two teats, curiously situated, one on each side of the anus; but the breasts themselves extend upwards from that. When by chance these precious parts in a nursing whale are cut by the hunter's lance, the mother's pouring milk and blood rivallingly discolor the sea for rods. The milk is very sweet and rich; it has been tasted by man; it might do well with strawberries. When overflowing with mutual esteem, the whales salute *more hominum*.

circle, where abundance of room and some convenient retreats were afforded them. But the sight of the enraged drugged whales now and then blindly darting to and fro across the circles, was nothing to what at last met our eyes. It is sometimes the custom when fast to a whale more than commonly powerful and alert, to seek to hamstring him, as it were, by sundering or maiming his gigantic tail-tendon. It is done by darting a short-handled cutting-spade, to which is attached a rope for hauling it back again. A whale wounded (as we afterwards learned) in this part, but not effectually, as it seemed, had broken away from the boat, carrying along with him half of the harpoon line; and in the extraordinary agony of the wound, he was now dashing among the revolving circles like the lone mounted desperado Arnold, at the battle of Saratoga, carrying dismay wherever he went.

But agonizing as was the wound of this whale, and an appalling spectacle enough, any way; yet the peculiar horror with which he seemed to inspire the rest of the herd, was owing to a cause which at first the intervening distance obscured from us. But at length we perceived that by one of the unimaginable accidents of the fishery, this whale had become entangled in the harpoon-line that he towed; he had also run away with the cutting-spade in him; and while the free end of the rope attached to that weapon, had permanently caught in the coils of the harpoon-line round his tail, the cutting-spade itself had worked loose from his flesh. So that tormented to madness, he was now churning through the water, violently flailing with his flexible tail, and tossing the keen spade about him, wounding and murdering his own comrades.

This terrific object seemed to recall the whole herd from their stationary fright. First, the whales forming the margin of our lake began to crowd a little, and tumble against each other, as if lifted by half spent billows from afar; then the lake itself began faintly to heave and swell; the submarine bridal-chambers and nurseries vanished; in more and more contracting orbits the whales in the more central circles began to swim in thickening clusters. Yes, the long calm was departing. A low advancing hum was soon heard; and then like to the tumultuous masses of block-ice when the great river Hudson breaks up in Spring, the entire host of whales came tumbling upon their inner centre, as if to pile themselves up in one common mountain. Instantly Starbuck and Queequeg changed places; Starbuck taking the stern.

'Oars! Oars!' he intensely whispered, seizing the helm—'gripe your oars, and clutch your souls, now! My God, men, stand by! Shove him off, you Queequeg—the whale there!—prick him!—hit him! Stand up—stand up, and stay so! Spring, men—pull, men; never mind their backs—scrape them!—scrape away!'

The boat was now all but jammed between two vast black bulks, leaving a narrow Dardanelles between their long lengths. But by desperate endeavor we at last shot into a temporary opening; then giving way rapidly, and at the same time earnestly watching for another outlet. After many similar hair-breadth escapes, we at last swiftly glided into what had just been one of the outer circles, but now crossed by random whales, all violently making for one centre. This lucky salvation was cheaply purchased by the loss of Queequeg's hat, who, while standing in the bows to prick the fugitive whales, had his hat taken clean from his head by the air-eddy made by the sudden tossing of a pair of broad flukes close by.

Riotous and disordered as the universal commotion now was, it soon resolved itself into what seemed a systematic movement; for having clumped together at last in one dense body, they then renewed their onward flight with augmented fleetness. Further pursuit was useless; but the boats still lingered in their wake to pick up what drugged whales might be dropped astern, and likewise to secure one which Flask had killed and waifed. The waif is a pennoned pole, two or three of which are carried by every boat; and which, when additional game is at hand, are inserted upright into the floating body of a dead whale, both to mark its place on the sea, and also as token of prior possession, should the boats of any other ship draw near.

The result of this lowering was somewhat illustrative of that sagacious saying in the Fishery,—the more whales the less fish. Of all the drugged whales only one was captured. The rest contrived to escape for the time, but only to be taken, as will hereafter been seen, by some other craft than the Pequod.

CHAPTER LXXXVIII

SCHOOLS AND SCHOOLMASTERS

The previous chapter gave account of an immense body or herd of Sperm Whales, and there was also then given the probable cause inducing those vast aggregations.

Now, though such great bodies are at times encountered, yet, as must have been seen, even at the present day, small detached bands are occasionally observed, embracing from twenty to fifty individuals each. Such bands are known as schools. They generally are of two sorts; those composed almost entirely of females, and those mustering none but young vigorous males, or bulls, as they are familiarly designated.

In cavalier attendance upon the school of females, you invariably see a male of full grown magnitude, but not old; who, upon any alarm, evinces his gallantry by falling in the rear and covering the flight of his ladies. In truth, this gentleman is a luxurious Ottoman, swimming about over the watery world, surroundingly accompanied by all the solaces and endearments of the harem. The contrast between this Ottoman and his concubines is striking; because, while he is always of the largest leviathanic proportions, the ladies, even at full growth, are not more than one third of the bulk of an average-sized male. They are comparatively delicate, indeed; I dare say, not to exceed half a dozen yards round the waist. Nevertheless, it cannot be denied, that upon the whole they are hereditarily entitled to *en bon point*.

It is very curious to watch this harem and its lord in their indolent ramblings. Like fashionables, they are for ever on the move in leisurely search of variety. You meet them on the Line in time for the full flower of the Equatorial feeding season, having just returned, perhaps, from spending the summer in the Northern seas, and so cheating summer of all unpleasant weariness and warmth. By the time they have lounged up and down the promenade of the Equator awhile, they start for the Oriental waters in anticipation of the cool season there, and so evade the other excessive temperature of the year.

When serenely advancing on one of these journeys, if any strange suspicious sights are seen, my lord whale keeps a wary eye on his interesting family. Should any unwarrantably pert young Leviathan coming that way, presume to draw confidentially close to one of the ladies, with what prodigious fury the Bashaw assails him, and chases him away! High times, indeed, if unprincipled young rakes like him are to be permitted to invade the sanctity of domestic bliss; though do what the Bashaw will, he cannot keep the most notorious Lothario out of his bed; for, alas! all fish bed in common. As ashore, the ladies often cause the most terrible duels among their rival admirers; just so with the whales, who sometimes come to deadly battle, and all for love. They fence with their long lower jaws, sometimes locking them together, and so striving for the supremacy like elks that warringly interweave their antlers. Not a few are captured having the deep scars of these encounters,—furrowed heads, broken teeth, scolloped fins; and in some instances, wrenched and dislocated mouths.

But supposing the invader of domestic bliss to betake himself away at the first rush of the harem's lord, then is it very diverting to watch that lord. Gently he insinuates his vast bulk among them again and revels there awhile, still in tantalizing vicinity to young Lothario, like pious Solomon devoutly worshipping among his thousand concubines. Granting other whales to be in sight, the fishermen will seldom give chase to one of these Grand Turks; for these Grand Turks are too lavish of their strength, and hence their unctuousness is small. As for the sons and the daughters they beget, why, those sons and daughters must take care of themselves; at least, with only the maternal help. For like certain other omnivorous roving lovers that might be named, my Lord Whale has no taste for the nursery, however much for the bower; and so, being a great traveller, he leaves his anonymous babies all over the world; every baby an exotic. In good time, nevertheless, as the ardor of youth declines; as years and dumps increase; as reflection lends her solemn pauses; in short, as a general lassitude overtakes the sated Turk; then a love of ease and virtue supplants the love for maidens; our Ottoman enters upon the impotent, repentant, admonitory stage of life, forswears, disbands the harem, and grown to an exemplary, sulky old soul, goes about all alone among the meridians and parallels saying his prayers, and warning each young Leviathan from his amorous errors.

Now, as the harem of whales is called by the fishermen a school, so is the lord and master of that school technically known as the schoolmaster. It is therefore not in strict character, however admirably satirical, that after going to school himself, he should then go abroad inculcating not what he learned there, but the folly of it. His title, schoolmaster, would very naturally seem derived from the name bestowed upon the harem itself, but some have surmised that the man who first thus entitled this sort of Ottoman whale, must have read the memoirs of Vidocq, and informed himself what sort of a country-schoolmaster that famous Frenchman was in his younger days, and what was the nature of those occult lessons he inculcated into some of his pupils.

The same secludedness and isolation to which the schoolmaster whale betakes himself in his advancing years, is true of all aged Sperm Whales. Almost universally, a lone whale—as a solitary Leviathan is called—proves an ancient one. Like venerable moss-bearded Daniel Boone, he will have no one near him but Nature herself; and her he takes to wife in the wilderness of waters, and the best of wives she is, though she keeps so many moody secrets.

The schools composing none but young and vigorous males, previously mentioned, offer a strong contrast to the harem schools. For while those female whales are characteristically timid, the young males, or forty-barrel-bulls, as they call them, are by far the most pugnacious of all Leviathans, and proverbially the most dangerous to encounter; excepting those wondrous grey-headed, grizzled whales, sometimes met, and these will fight you like grim fiends exasperated by a penal gout.

The Forty-barrel-bull schools are larger than the harem schools. Like a mob of young collegians, they are full of fight, fun, and wickedness, tumbling round the world at such a reckless, rollicking rate, that no prudent underwriter would insure them any more than he would a riotous lad at Yale or Harvard. They soon relinquish this turbulence though, and when about three fourths grown, break up, and separately go about in quest of settlements, that is, harems.

Another point of difference between the male and female schools is still more characteristic of the sexes. Say you strike a Forty-barrel-bull—poor devil! all his comrades quit him. But strike a member of the harem school, and her companions swim around her with every token of concern, sometimes lingering so near her and so long, as themselves to fall a prey.

CHAPTER LXXXIX

FAST-FISH AND LOOSE-FISH

The allusion to the waifs and waif-poles in the last chapter but one, necessitates some accounts of the laws and regulations of the whale fishery, of which the waif may be deemed the grand symbol and badge.

It frequently happens that when several ships are cruising in company, a whale may be struck by one vessel, then escape, and be finally killed and captured by another vessel; and herein are indirectly comprised many minor contingencies, all partaking of this one grand feature. For example,—after a weary and perilous chase and capture of a whale, the body may get loose from the ship by reason of a violent storm; and drifting far away to leeward, be retaken by a second whaler, who, in a calm, snugly tows it alongside, without the risk of life or line. Thus the most vexatious and violent disputes would often arise between the fishermen, were there not some written or unwritten, universal, undisputed law applicable to all cases.

Perhaps the only formal whaling code authorized by legislative enactment, was that of Holland. It was decreed by the States-General in A.D. 1695. But though no other nation has ever had any written whaling law, yet the American fishermen have been their own legislators and lawyers in this matter. They have provided a system which for terse comprehensiveness surpasses Justinian's Pandects and the By-laws of the Chinese Society for the Suppression of Meddling with other People's Business. Yes; these laws might be engraven on a Queen Anne's farthing, or the barb of a harpoon, and worn round the neck, so small are they.

I. A Fast Fish belong to the party fast to it.

II. A Loose-Fish is fair game for anybody who can soonest catch it.

But what plays the mischief with this masterly code is the admirable brevity of it, which necessitates a vast volume of commentaries to expound it.

First: What is a Fast-Fish? Alive or dead a fish is technically fast, when it is connected with any occupied ship or boat, by any medium at all controllable by the occupant or occupants,—a mast, an oar, a nine-inch cable, a telegraph wire, or a strand of cobweb, it is all the same. Likewise a fish is technically fast when it bears a waif, or any other recognised symbol of possession; so long as the party waifing it plainly evince their ability at any time to take it alongside, as well as their intention so to do.

These are scientific commentaries; but the commentaries of the whalemen themselves consist in hard words and harder knocks—the Coke-upon-Littleton of the fist. True, among the more upright and honorable whalemen allowances are always made for peculiar cases, where it would be an outrageous moral injustice for one party to claim possession of a whale previously chased or killed by another party. But others are by no means so scrupulous.

Some fifty years ago there was a curious case of whale-trover litigated in England, wherein the plaintiffs set forth that after a hard chase of a whale in the Northern seas; and when indeed they (the plaintiffs) had succeeded in harpooning the fish; they were at last, through peril of their lives, obliged to forsake not only their lines, but their boat itself. Ultimately the defendants (the crew of another ship) came up with the whale, struck, killed, seized, and finally appropriated it before the very eyes of the plaintiffs. And when those defendants were remonstrated with, their captain snapped his fingers in the plaintiffs' teeth, and assured them that by way of doxology to the deed he had done, he would now retain their line, harpoons, and boat, which had remained attached to the whale at the time of the seizure. Wherefore the plaintiffs now sued for the recovery of the value of their whale, line, harpoons, and boat.

Mr Erskine was counsel for the defendants; Lord Ellenborough was the judge. In the course of the defence, the witty Erskine went on to illustrate his position, by alluding to a recent crim. con. case, wherein a gentleman, after in vain trying to bridle his wife's viciousness, had at last abandoned her upon the seas of life; but in the course of years, repenting of that step, he instituted an action to recover possession of her. Erskine was on the other side; and he then supported it by saying, that though the gentleman had originally harpooned the lady, and had once had her fast, and only by reason of the great stress of her plunging viciousness, had at last abandoned her; yet abandon her he did, so that she became a loose-fish; and therefore when a subsequent gentleman re-harpooned her, the lady then became that subsequent gentleman's property, along with whatever harpoon might have been found sticking in her.

Now in the present case Erskine contended that the examples of the whale and the lady were reciprocally illustrative of each other.

These pleadings, and the counter pleadings, being duly heard, the very learned judge in set terms decided, to wit,—That as for the boat, he awarded it to the plaintiffs, because they had merely abandoned it to save their lives; but that with regard to the controverted whale, harpoons, and line, they belonged to the defendants; the whale, because it was a Loose-Fish at the time of the final capture; and the harpoons and line because when the fish made off with them, it (the fish) acquired a property in those articles; and hence anybody who afterwards took the fish had a right to them. Now, the defendants afterwards took the fish; ergo, the aforesaid articles were theirs.

A common man looking at this decision of the very learned Judge, might possibly object to it. But ploughed up to the primary rock of the matter, the two great principles laid down in the twin whaling laws previously quoted, and applied and elucidated by Lord Ellenborough in the above cited case; these two laws touching Fast-Fish and Loose-Fish, I say, will, on reflection, be found the fundamentals of all human jurisprudence; for notwithstanding its complicated tracery of sculpture, the Temple of the Law, like the Temple of the Philistines, has but two props to stand on.

Is it not a saying in every one's mouth, Possession is half of the law: that is, regardless of how the thing came into possession? But often possession is the whole of the law. What are the sinews and souls of Russian serfs and Republican slaves but Fast-Fish, whereof possession is the whole of the law? What to the rapacious landlord is the widow's last mite but a Fast-Fish? What is yonder undetected villain's marble mansion with a door-plate for a waif; what is that but a Fast-Fish? What is the ruinous discount which Mordecai, the broker, gets from poor Woebegone, the bankrupt, on a loan to keep Woebegone's family from starvation; what is that ruinous discount but a Fast-Fish? What is the Archbishop of Savesoul's income of £100,000 seized from the scant bread and cheese of hundreds of thousands of broken-backed laborers (all sure of heaven without any of Savesoul's help) what is that globular 100,000 but a Fast-Fish? What are the Duke of Dunder's hereditary towns and hamlets but Fast-Fish? What to that redoubted harpooneer, John Bull, is poor Ireland, but a Fast-Fish? What to that apostolic lancer, Brother Jonathan, is Texas but a Fast-Fish? And concerning all these, is not Possession the whole of the law?

But if the doctrine of Fast-Fish be pretty generally applicable, the kindred doctrine of Loose-Fish is still more widely so. That is internationally and universally applicable.

What was America in 1492 but a Loose-Fish, in which Columbus struck the Spanish standard by way of waifing it for his royal master and mistress? What was Poland to the Czar? What Greece to the Turk? What India to England? What at last will Mexico be to the United States? All Loose-Fish.

What are the Rights of Man and the Liberties of the World but Loose-Fish? What all men's minds and opinions but Loose-Fish? What is the principle of religious belief in them but a Loose-Fish? What to the ostentatious smuggling verbalists are the thoughts of thinkers but Loose-Fish? What is the great globe itself but a Loose-Fish? And what are you, reader, but a Loose-Fish and a Fast-Fish, too?

CHAPTER XC

HEADS OR TAILS

'De balena vero sufficit, si rex habeat caput, et regina caudam.'
Bracton, l. 3, c. 3.

Latin from the books of the Laws of England, which taken along with the context, means, that of all whales captured by anybody on the coast of that land, the King, as Honorary Grand Harpooneer, must have the head, and the Queen be respectfully presented with the tail. A division which, in the whale, is much like halving an apple; there is no intermediate remainder. Now as this law, under a modified form, is to this day in force in England; and as it offers in various respects a strange anomaly touching the general law of Fast and Loose-Fish, it is here treated of in a separate chapter, on the same courteous principle that prompts the English railways to be at the expense of a separate car, specially reserved for the accommodation of royalty. In the first place, in curious proof of the fact that the above-mentioned law is still in force, I proceed to lay before you a circumstance that happened within the last two years.

It seems that some honest mariners of Dover, or Sandwich, or some one of the Cinque Ports, had after a hard chase succeeded in killing and beaching a fine whale which they had originally descried afar off from the shore. Now the Cinque Ports are partially or somehow under the jurisdiction of a sort of policeman or beadle, called a Lord Warden. Holding the office directly from the crown, I believe, all the royal emoluments incident to the Cinque Port territories become by assignment his. By some writers this office is called a sinecure. But not so. Because the Lord Warden is busily employed at times in fobbing his perquisites; which are his chiefly by virtue of that same fobbing of them.

Now when these poor sun-burnt mariners, bare-footed, and with their trowsers rolled up on their eely legs, had wearily hauled their fat fish high and dry, promising themselves a good £150 from the precious oil and bone; and in fantasy sipping rare tea with their wives, and good ale with their cronies, upon the strength of their respective shares; up steps a very learned and most Christian and charitable gentleman, with a copy of Blackstone under his arm; and laying it upon the whale's head, he says—'Hands off! this fish, my masters, is a Fast-Fish. I seize it as the Lord Warden's.' Upon this the poor mariners in their respectful consternation—so truly English—knowing not what to say, fall to vigorously scratching their heads all round; meanwhile ruefully glancing from the whale to the stranger. But that did in nowise mend the matter, or at all soften the hard heart of the learned gentleman with the copy of Blackstone. At length one of them, after long scratching about for his ideas, made bold to speak.

'Please, sir, who is the Lord Warden?'

'The Duke.'

'But the Duke had nothing to do with taking this fish?'

'It is his.'

'We have been at great trouble, and peril, and some expense, and is all that to go to the Duke's benefit; we getting nothing at all for our pains but our blisters?'

'It is his.''

'Is the Duke so very poor as to be forced to this desperate mode of getting a livelihood?'

'It is his.'

'I thought to relieve my old bed-ridden mother by part of my share of this whale.'

'It is his.'

'Won't the Duke be content with a quarter or a half?'

'It is his.'

In a word, the whale was seized and sold, and his Grace the Duke of Wellington received the money. Thinking that viewed in some particular lights, the case might by a bare possibility in some small degree be deemed, under the circumstances, a rather hard one, an honest clergyman of the town respectfully addressed a note to his Grace, begging him to take the case of those unfortunate mariners into full consideration. To which my Lord Duke in substance replied (both letters were published) that he had already done so, and received the money, and would be obliged to the reverend gentleman if for the future he (the reverend gentleman) would decline meddling with other people's business. Is this the still militant old man, standing at the corners of the three kingdoms, on all hands coercing alms of beggars?

It will readily be seen that in this case the alleged right of the Duke to the whale was a delegated one from the Sovereign. We must needs inquire then on what principle the Sovereign is originally invested with that right. The law itself has already been set forth. But Plowdon gives us the reason for it. Says Plowdon, the whale so caught belongs to the King and Queen, 'because of its superior excellence.' And by the soundest commentators this has ever been held a cogent argument in such matters.

But why should the King have the head, and the Queen the tail? A reason for that, ye lawyers!

In his treatise on 'Queen-Gold,' or Queen-pinmoney, an old King's Bench author, one William Prynne, thus discourseth: 'Y^e tail is ye Queen's, that ye Queen's wardrobe may be supplied with ye whalebone.' Now this was written at a time when the black limber bone of the Greenland or Right whale was largely used in ladies' bodices. But this same bone is not in the tail; it is in the head, which is a sad mistake for a sagacious lawyer like Prynne. But is the Queen a mermaid, to be presented with a tail? An allegorical meaning may lurk here.

There are two royal fish so styled by the English law writers—the whale and the sturgeon; both royal property under certain limitations, and nominally supplying the tenth branch of the crown's ordinary revenue. I know not that any other author has hinted of the matter; but by inference it seems to me that the sturgeon must be divided in the same way as the whale, the King receiving the highly dense and elastic head peculiar to that fish, which, symbolically regarded, may possibly be humorously grounded upon some presumed congeniality. And thus there seems a reason in all things, even in law.

CHAPTER XCI

The Pequod Meets the Rose-Bud

'In vain it was to rake for Ambergriese in the paunch of this Leviathan, insufferable fetor denying that inquiry.'
Sir T. Browne, V.E.

It was a week or two after the last whaling scene recounted, and when we were slowly sailing over a sleepy, vapory, midday sea, that the many noses on the Pequod's deck proved more vigilant discoverers than the three pairs of eyes aloft. A peculiar and not very pleasant smell was smelt in the sea.

'I will bet something now,' said Stubb, 'that somewhere hereabouts are some of those drugged whales we tickled the other day. I thought they would keel up before long.'

Presently, the vapors in advance slid aside; and there in the distance lay a ship, whose furled sails betokened that some sort of whale must be alongside. As we glided nearer, the stranger showed French colors from his peak; and by the eddying cloud of vulture sea-fowl that circled, and hovered, and swooped around him, it was plain that the whale alongside must be what the fishermen call a blasted whale, that is, a whale that has died unmolested on the sea, and so floated an unappropriated corpse. It may well be conceived, what an unsavory odor such a mass must exhale; worse than an Assyrian city in the plague, when the living are incompetent to bury the departed. So intolerable indeed is it regarded by some, that no cupidity could persuade them to moor alongside of it. Yet are there those who will still do it; notwithstanding the fact that the oil obtained from such subjects is of a very inferior quality, and by no means of the nature of attar-of-rose.

Coming still nearer with the expiring breeze, we saw that the Frenchmen had a second whale alongside; and this second whale seemed even more of a nosegay than the first. In truth, it turned out to be one of those problematical whales that seem to dry up and die with a sort of prodigious dyspepsia, or indigestion; leaving their defunct bodies almost entirely bankrupt of anything like oil. Nevertheless, in the proper place we shall see that no knowing fisherman will ever turn up his nose at such a whale as this, however much he may shun blasted whales in general.

The Pequod had now swept so nigh to the stranger, that Stubb vowed he recognized his cutting spade-pole entangled in the lines that were knotted round the tail of one of these whales.

'There's a pretty fellow, now,' he banteringly laughed, standing in the ship's bows, 'there's a jackal for ye! I well know that these Crappoes of Frenchmen are but poor devils in the fishery; sometimes lowering their boats for breakers, mistaking them for Sperm Whale spouts; yes, and sometimes sailing from their port with their hold full of boxes of tallow candles, and cases of snuffers, foreseeing that all the oil they will get won't be enough to dip the Captain's wick into; aye, we all know these things; but look ye, here's a Crappo that is content with our leavings, the drugged whale there, I mean; aye, and is content too with scraping the dry bones of that other precious fish he has there. Poor devil! I say, pass round a hat, some one, and let's make him a present of a little oil for dear charity's sake. For what oil he'll get from that drugged whale there, wouldn't be fit to burn in a jail; no, not in a condemned cell. And as for the other whale, why, I'll agree to get more oil by chopping up and trying out these three masts of ours, than he'll get from that bundle of bones; though, now that I think of it, it may contain something worth a good deal more than oil; yes, ambergris. I wonder now if our old man has thought of that. It's worth trying. Yes, I'm in for it;' and so saying he started for the quarter-deck.

By this time the faint air had become a complete calm; so that whether or no, the Pequod was now fairly entrapped in the smell, with no hope of escaping except by its breezing up again. Issuing from the cabin, Stubb now called his boat's crew, and pulled off for the stranger. Drawing across her bow, he perceived that in accordance with the fanciful French taste, the upper part of her stem-piece was carved in the likeness of a huge drooping stalk, was painted green, and for thorns had copper spikes projecting from it here and there; the whole terminating in a symmetrical folded bulb of a bright red color. Upon her head boards, in large gilt letters, he read 'Bouton de Rose,'—Rose-button, or Rose-bud; and this was the romantic name of this aromatic ship.

Though Stubb did not understand the *Bouton* part of the inscription, yet the word *rose,* and the bulbous figure-head put together, sufficiently explained the whole to him.

'A wooden rose-bud, eh?' he cried with his hand to his nose, 'that will do very well; but how like all creation it smells!'

Now in order to hold direct communication with the people on deck, he had to pull round the bows to the starboard side, and thus come close to the blasted whale; and so talk over it.

Arrived then at this spot, with one hand still to his nose, he bawled—'Bouton-de-Rose, ahoy! are there any of you Bouton-de-Roses that speak English?'

'Yes,' rejoined a Guernsey-man from the bulwarks, who turned out to be the chief-mate.

'Well, then, my Bouton-de-Rose-bud, have you seen the White Whale?'

'*What* whale?'

'The *White* Whale—a Sperm Whale—Moby Dick, have ye seen him?'

'Never heard of such a whale. Cachalot Blanche? White Whale—no.'

'Very good, then; good bye now, and I'll call again in a minute.'

Then rapidly pulling back towards the Pequod, and seeing Ahab leaning over the quarter-deck rail awaiting his report, he moulded his two hands into a trumpet and shouted—'No, Sir! No!' Upon which Ahab retired, and Stubb returned to the Frenchman.

He now perceived that the Guernsey-man, who had just got into the chains, and was using a cutting-spade, had slung his nose in a sort of bag.

'What's the matter with your nose, there?' said Stubb. 'Broke it?'

'I wish it was broken, or that I didn't have any nose at all!' answered the Guernsey-man, who did not seem to relish the job he was at very much. 'But what are you holding *yours* for?'

'Oh, nothing! It's a wax nose; I have to hold it on. Fine day, aint it? Air rather gardenny, I should say; throw us a bunch of posies, will ye, Bouton-de-Rose?'

'What in the devil's name do you want here?' roared the Guernsey-man, flying into a sudden passion.

'Oh! keep cool—cool? yes, that's the word; why don't you pack those whales in ice while you're working at 'em? But joking aside, though; do you know, Rose-bud, that it's all nonsense trying to get any oil out of such whales? As for that dried up one, there, he hasn't a gill in his whole carcase.'

'I know that well enough; but, d'ye see, the Captain here won't believe it; this is his first voyage; he was a Cologne manufacturer before. But come aboard, and mayhap he'll believe you, if he won't me; and so I'll get out of this dirty scrape.'

'Anything to oblige ye, my sweet and pleasant fellow,' rejoined Stubb, and with that he soon mounted to the deck. There a queer scene presented itself. The sailors, in tasselled caps of red worsted, were getting the heavy tackles in readiness for the whales. But they worked rather slow and talked very fast, and seemed in anything but a good humor. All their noses upwardly projected from their faces like so many jib-booms. Now and then pairs of them would drop their work, and run up to the mast-head to get some fresh air. Some thinking they would catch the plague, dipped oakum in coal-tar, and at intervals held it to their nostrils. Others having broken the stems of their pipes almost short off at the bowl, were vigorously puffing tobacco-smoke, so that it constantly filled their olfactories.

Stubb was struck by a shower of outcries and anathemas proceeding from the Captain's round-house abaft; and looking in that direction saw a fiery face thrust from behind the door, which was held ajar from within. This was the tormented surgeon, who, after in vain remonstrating against the proceedings of the day, had betaken himself to the Captain's round-house (*cabinet* he called it) to avoid the pest; but still, could not help yelling out his entreaties and indignations at times.

Marking all this, Stubb argued well for his scheme, and turning to the Guernsey-man had a little chat with him, during which the stranger mate expressed his detestation of his Captain as a conceited ignoramus, who had brought them all into so unsavory and unprofitable a pickle. Sounding him carefully, Stubb further perceived that the Guernsey-man had not the slightest suspicion concerning the ambergris. He therefore held his peace on that head, but otherwise was quite frank and confidential with him, so that the two quickly concocted a little plan for both circumventing and satirizing the Captain, without his at all dreaming of distrusting their sincerity. According to this little plan of theirs, the Guernsey-man, under cover of an interpreter's office, was to tell the Captain what he pleased, but as coming from Stubb; and as for Stubb, he was to utter any nonsense that should come uppermost in him during the interview.

By this time their destined victim appeared from his cabin. He was a small and dark, but rather delicate looking man for a sea-captain, with large whiskers and moustache, however; and wore a red cotton velvet vest with watch-seals at his side. To this gentleman, Stubb was now politely introduced by the Guernsey-man, who at once ostentatiously put on the aspect of interpreting between them.

'What shall I say to him first?' said he.

'Why,' said Stubb, eyeing the velvet vest and the watch and seals, 'you may as well begin by telling him that he looks a sort of babyish to me, though I don't pretend to be a judge.'

'He says, Monsieur,' said the Guernsey-man, in French, turning to his captain, 'that only yesterday his ship spoke a vessel, whose captain and chief-mate, with six sailors, had all died of a fever caught from a blasted whale they had brought alongside.'

Upon this the captain started, and eagerly desired to know more.

'What now?' said the Guernsey-man to Stubb.

'Why, since he takes it so easy, tell him that now I have eyed him carefully, I'm quite certain that he's no more fit to command a whale-ship than a St Jago monkey. In fact, tell him from me he's a baboon.'

'He vows and declares, Monsieur, that the other whale, the dried one, is far more deadly than the blasted one; in fine, Monsieur, he conjures us, as we value our lives, to cut loose from these fish.'

Instantly the captain ran forward, and in a loud voice commanded his crew to desist from hoisting the cutting-tackles, and at once cast loose the cables and chains confining the whales to the ship.

'What now?' said the Guernsey-man, when the captain had returned to them.

'Why, let me see; yes, you may as well tell him now that—that—in fact, tell him I've diddled him, and (aside to himself) perhaps somebody else.'

'He says, Monsieur, that he's very happy to have been of any service to us.'

Hearing this, the captain vowed that they were the grateful parties (meaning himself and mate) and concluded by inviting Stubb down into his cabin to drink a bottle of Bordeaux.

'He wants you to take a glass of wine with him,' said the interpreter.

'Thank him heartily; but tell him it's against my principles to drink with the man I've diddled. In fact, tell him I must go.'

'He says, Monsieur, that his principles won't admit of his drinking; but that if Monsieur wants to live another day to drink, then Monsieur had best drop all four boats, and pull the ship away from these whales, for it's so calm they won't drift.'

By this time Stubb was over the side, and getting into his boat, hailed the Guernsey-man to this effect,—that having a long tow-line in his boat, he would do what he could to help them, by pulling out the lighter whale of the two from the ship's side. While the Frenchman's boats, then, were engaged in towing the ship one way, Stubb benevolently towed away at his whale the other way, ostentatiously slacking out a most unusually long tow-line.

Presently a breeze sprang up; Stubb feigned to cast off from the whale; hoisting his boats, the Frenchman soon increased his distance, while the Pequod slid in between him and Stubb's whale. Whereupon Stubb quickly pulled to the floating body, and hailing the Pequod to give notice of his intentions, at once proceeded to reap the fruit of his unrighteous cunning. Seizing his sharp boat-spade, he commenced an excavation in the body, a little behind the side fin. You would almost have thought he was digging a cellar there in the sea; and when at length his spade struck against the gaunt ribs, it was like turning up old Roman tiles and pottery buried in fat English loam. His boat's crew were all in high excitement, eagerly helping their chief, and looking as anxious as gold-hunters.

And all the time numberless fowls were diving, and ducking, and screaming, and yelling, and fighting around them. Stubb was beginning to look disappointed, especially as the horrible nosegay increased, when suddenly from out of the very heart of this plague, there stole a faint stream of perfume, which flowed through the tide of bad smells without being absorbed by it, as one river will flow into and then along with another, without at all blending with it for a time.

'I have it, I have it,' cried Stubb, with delight, striking something in the subterranean regions, 'a purse! a purse!'

Dropping his spade, he thrust both hands in, and drew out handfuls of something that looked like ripe Windsor soap, or rich mottled old cheese, very unctuous and savory withal. You might easily dent it with your thumb; it is of a hue between yellow and ash color. And this, good friends, is ambergris, worth a gold guinea an ounce to any druggist. Some six handfuls were obtained; but more was unavoidably lost in the sea, and still more, perhaps, might have been secured were it not for impatient Ahab's loud command to Stubb to desist, and come on board, else the ship would bid them good bye.

CHAPTER XCII

AMBERGRIS

Now this ambergris is a very curious substance, and so important as an article of commerce, that in 1791 a certain Nantucket-born Captain Coffin was examined at the bar of the English house of Commons on that subject. For at that time, and indeed until a comparatively late day, the precise origin of ambergris remained, like amber itself, a problem to the learned. Though the word ambergris is but the French compound for grey amber, yet the two substances are quite distinct. For amber, though at times found on the sea-coast, is also dug up in some far inland soils, whereas ambergris is never found except upon the sea. Besides, amber is a hard, transparent, brittle, odorless substance, used for mouth-pieces to pipes, for beads and ornaments; but ambergris is soft, waxy, and so highly fragrant and spicy, that it is largely used in perfumery, in pastiles, precious candles, hair-powders, and pomatum. The Turks use it in cooking, and also carry it to Mecca, for the same purpose that frankincense is carried to St Peter's in Rome. Some wine merchants drop a few grains into claret, to flavor it.

Who would think, then, that such fine ladies and gentlemen should regale themselves with an essence found in the inglorious bowels of a sick whale! Yet so it is. By some, ambergris is supposed to be the cause, and by others the effect, of the dyspepsia in the whale. How to cure such a dyspepsia it were hard to say, unless by administering three or four boat loads of Brandreth's pills, and then running out of harm's way, as laborers do in blasting rocks.

I have forgotten to say that there were found in this ambergris, certain hard, round, bony plates, which at first Stubb thought might be sailors' trousers buttons; but it afterwards turned out that they were nothing more than pieces of small squid bones embalmed in that manner.

Now that the incorruption of this most fragrant ambergris should be found in the heart of such decay; is this nothing? Bethink thee of that saying of St Paul in Corinthians, about corruption and incorruption; how that we are sown in dishonor, but raised in glory. And likewise call to mind that saying of Paracelsus about what it is that maketh the best musk. Also forget not the strange fact that of all things of ill-savor, Cologne-water, in its rudimental manufacturing stages, is the worst.

I should like to conclude the chapter with the above appeal, but cannot, owing to my anxiety to repel a charge often made against whalemen, and which, in the estimation of some already biased minds, might be considered as indirectly substantiated by what has been said of the Frenchman's two whales. Elsewhere in this volume the slanderous aspersion has been disproved, that the vocation of whaling is throughout a slatternly, untidy business. But there is another thing to rebut. They hint that all whales always smell bad. Now how did this odious stigma originate?

I opine, that it is plainly traceable to the first arrival of the Greenland whaling ships in London, more than two centuries ago. Because those whalemen did not then, and do not now, try out their oil at sea as the Southern ships have always done; but cutting up the fresh blubber in small bits, thrust it through the bung holes of large casks, and carry it home in that manner; the shortness of the season in those Icy Seas, and the sudden and violent storms to which they are exposed, forbidding any other course. The consequence is, that upon breaking into the hold, and unloading one of these whale cemeteries, in the Greenland dock, a savor is given forth somewhat similar to that arising from excavating an old city graveyard, for the foundations of a Lying-in Hospital.

I partly surmise also, that this wicked charge against whalers may be likewise imputed to the existence on the coast of Greenland, in former times, of a Dutch village called Schmerenburgh or Smeerenberg, which latter name is the one used by the learned Fogo Von Slack, in his great work on Smells, a textbook on that subject. As its name imports (smeer, fat; berg, to put up), this village was founded in order to afford a place for the blubber of the Dutch whale fleet to be tried out, without being taken home to Holland for that purpose. It was a collection of furnaces, fat-kettles, and oil sheds; and when the works were in full operation certainly gave forth no very pleasant savor. But all this is quite different with a South Sea Sperm Whaler; which in a voyage of four years perhaps, after completely filling her hold with oil, does not, perhaps, consume fifty days in the business of boiling out; and in the state that it is casked, the oil is nearly scentless. The truth is, that living or dead, if but decently treated, whales as a species are by no means creatures of ill odor; nor can whalemen be recognised, as the people of the middle ages affected to detect a Jew in the company, by the nose. Nor indeed can the whale possibly be otherwise than fragrant, when, as a general thing, he enjoys such high health; taking abundance of exercise; always out of doors; though, it is true, seldom in the open air. I say, that the motion of a Sperm Whale's flukes above water dispenses a perfume, as when a musk-scented lady rustles her dress in a warm parlor. What then shall I liken the Sperm Whale to for fragrance, considering his magnitude? Must it not be to that famous elephant, with jewelled tusks, and redolent with myrrh, which was led out of an Indian town to do honor to Alexander the Great?

CHAPTER XCIII

THE CASTAWAY

It was but some few days after encountering the Frenchman, that a most significant event befell the most insignificant of the Pequod's crew; an event most lamentable; and which ended in providing the sometimes madly merry and predestinated craft with a living and ever accompanying prophecy of whatever shattered sequel might prove her own.

Now, in the whale ship, it is not every one that goes in the boats. Some few hands are reserved called ship-keepers, whose province it is to work the vessel while the boats are pursuing the whale. As a general thing, these ship-keepers are as hardy fellows as the men comprising the boats' crews. But if there happen to be an unduly slender, clumsy, or timorous wight in the ship, that wight is certain to be made a ship-keeper. It was so in the Pequod with our little negro Pippin by nick-name, Pip by abbreviation. Poor Pip! ye have heard of him before; ye must remember his tambourine on that dramatic midnight, so gloomy-jolly.

In outer aspect, Pip and Dough-Boy made a match, like a black pony and a white one, of equal developments, though of dissimilar color, driven by one eccentric span. But while hapless Dough-Boy was by nature dull and torpid in his intellects, Pip, though over tender-hearted, was at bottom very bright, with that pleasant, genial, jolly brightness peculiar to his tribe; a tribe, which ever enjoy all holidays and festivities with finer, freer relish than any other race. For blacks, the year's calendar should show naught but three hundred and sixty-five Fourth of Julys and New Year's Days. Nor smile so, while I write that this little black was brilliant, for even blackness has its brilliancy; behold yon lustrous ebony, panelled in kings' cabinets. But Pip loved life, and all life's peaceable securities; so that the panic-striking business in which he had somehow unaccountably become entrapped, had most sadly blurred his brightness; though, as ere long will be seen, what was thus temporarily subdued in him, in the end was destined to be luridly illumined by strange wild fires, that fictitiously showed him off to ten times the natural lustre with which in his native Tolland County in Connecticut, he had once enlivened many a fiddler's frolic on the green; and at melodious even-tide, with his gay ha-ha! had turned the round horizon into one star-belled tambourine. So, though in the clear air of day, suspended against a blue-veined neck, the pure-watered diamond drop will healthful glow; yet, when the cunning jeweller would show you the diamond in its most impressive lustre, he lays it against a gloomy ground, and then lights it up, not by the sun, but by some unnatural gases. Then come out those fiery effulgences, infernally superb; then the evil-blazing diamond, once the divinest symbol of the crystal skies, looks like some crown-jewel stolen from the King of Hell. But let us to the story.

It came to pass, that in the ambergris affair Stubb's after-oarsman chanced so to sprain his hand, as for a time to become quite maimed; and, temporarily, Pip was put into his place.

The first time Stubb lowered with him, Pip evinced much nervousness; but happily, for that time, escaped close contact with the whale; and therefore came off not altogether discreditably; though Stubb observing him, took care, afterwards, to exhort him to cherish his courageousness to the utmost, for he might often find it needful.

Now upon the second lowering, the boat paddled upon the whale; and as the fish received the darted iron, it gave its customary rap, which happened, in this instance, to be right under poor Pip's seat. The involuntary consternation of the moment caused him to leap, paddle in hand, out of the boat; and in such a way, that part of the slack whale line coming against his chest, he breasted it overboard with him, so as to become entangled in it, when at last plumping into the water. That instant the stricken whale started on a fierce run, the line swiftly straightened; and presto! poor Pip came all foaming up to the chocks of the boat, remorselessly dragged there by the line, which had taken several turns around his chest and neck.

Tashtego stood in the bows. He was full of the fire of the hunt. He hated Pip for a poltroon. Snatching the boat-knife from its sheath, he suspended its sharp edge over the line, and turning towards Stubb, exclaimed interrogatively, 'Cut?' Meantime Pip's blue, choked face plainly looked, Do, for God's sake! All passed in a flash. In less than half a minute, this entire thing happened.

'Damn him, cut!' roared Stubb; and so the whale was lost and Pip was saved.

So soon as he recovered himself, the poor little negro was assailed by yells and execrations from the crew. Tranquilly permitting these irregular cursings to evaporate, Stubb then in a plain, business-like, but still half humorous manner, cursed Pip officially; and that done, unofficially gave him much wholesome advice. The substance was, Never jump from a boat, Pip, except—but all the rest was indefinite, as the soundest advice ever is. Now, in general, *Stick to the boat,* is your true motto in whaling; but cases will sometimes happen when *Leap from the boat,* is still better. Moreover, as if perceiving at last that if he should give undiluted conscientious advice to Pip, he would be leaving him too wide a margin to jump in for the future; Stubb suddenly dropped all advice, and concluded with a peremptory command, 'Stick to the boat, Pip, or by the Lord, I wont pick you up if you jump; mind that. We can't afford to lose whales by the likes of you; a whale would sell for thirty times what you would, Pip, in Alabama. Bear that in mind, and don't jump any more.' Hereby perhaps Stubb indirectly hinted, that though man loves his fellow, yet man is a money-making animal, which propensity too often interferes with his benevolence.

But we are all in the hands of the Gods; and Pip jumped again. It was under very similar circumstances to the first performance; but this time he did not breast out the line; and hence, when the whale started to run, Pip was left behind on the sea, like a hurried traveller's trunk. Alas! Stubb was but too true to his word. It was a beautiful, bounteous, blue day; the spangled sea calm and cool, and flatly stretching away, all round, to the horizon, like gold-beater's skin hammered out to the extremest. Bobbing up and down in that sea, Pip's ebon head showed like a head of cloves. No boat-knife was lifted when he fell so rapidly astern. Stubb's inexorable back was turned upon him; and the whale was winged. In three minutes, a whole mile of shoreless ocean was between Pip and Stubb. Out from the centre of the sea, poor Pip turned his crisp, curling, black head to the sun, another lonely castaway, though the loftiest and the brightest.

Now, in calm weather, to swim in the open ocean is as easy to the practised swimmer as to ride in a spring-carriage ashore. But the awful lonesomeness is intolerable. The intense concentration of self in the middle of such a heartless immensity, my God! who can tell it? Mark, how when sailors in a dead calm bathe in the open sea—mark how closely they hug their ship and only coast along her sides.

But had Stubb really abandoned the poor little negro to his fate? No; he did not mean to, at least. Because there were two boats in his wake, and he supposed, no doubt, that they would of course come up to Pip very quickly, and pick him up; though, indeed, such considerateness towards oarsmen jeopardized through their own timidity, is not always manifested by the hunters in all similar instances; and such instances not unfrequently occur; almost invariably in the fishery, a coward, so called, is marked with the same ruthless detestation peculiar to military navies and armies.

But it so happened, that those boats, without seeing Pip, suddenly spying whales close to them on one side, turned, and gave chase; and Stubb's boat was now so far away, and he and all his crew so intent upon his fish, that Pip's ringed horizon began to expand around him miserably. By the merest chance the ship itself at last rescued him; but from that hour the little negro went about the deck an idiot; such, at least, they said he was. The sea had jeeringly kept his finite body up, but drowned the infinite of his soul. Not drowned entirely, though. Rather carried down alive to wondrous depths, where strange shapes of the unwarped primal world glided to and fro before his passive eyes; and the miser-merman, Wisdom, revealed his hoarded heaps; and among the joyous, heartless, ever-juvenile eternities, Pip saw the multitudinous, God-omnipresent, coral insects, that out of the firmament of waters heaved the colossal orbs. He saw God's foot upon the treadle of the loom, and spoke it; and therefore his shipmates called him mad. So man's insanity is heaven's sense; and wandering from all mortal reason, man comes at last to that celestial thought, which, to reason, is absurd and frantic; and weal or woe, feels then uncompromised, indifferent as his God.

For the rest, blame not Stubb too hardly. The thing is common in that fishery; and in the sequel of the narrative, it will then be seen what like abandonment befell myself.

CHAPTER XCIV

A SQUEEZE OF THE HAND

That whale of Stubb's so dearly purchased, was duly brought to the Pequod's side, where all those cutting and hoisting operations previously detailed, were regularly gone through, even to the baling of the Heidelburgh Tun, or Case.

While some were occupied with this latter duty, others were employed in dragging away the larger tubs, so soon as filled with the sperm; and when the proper time arrived, this same sperm was carefully manipulated ere going to the try-works, of which anon.

It had cooled and crystallized to such a degree, that when, with several others, I sat down before a large Constantine's bath of it, I found it strangely concreted into lumps, here and there rolling about in the liquid part. It was our business to squeeze these lumps back into fluid. A sweet and unctuous duty! No wonder that in old times this sperm was such a favorite cosmetic. Such a clearer! such a sweetener! such a softener! such a delicious mollifier! After having my hands in it for only a few minutes, my fingers felt like eels, and began, as it were, to serpentine and spiralize.

As I sat there at my ease, cross-legged on the deck; after the bitter exertion at the windlass; under a blue tranquil sky; the ship under indolent sail, and gliding so serenely along; as I bathed my hands among those soft, gentle globules of infiltrated tissues, woven almost within the hour; as they richly broke to my fingers, and discharged all their opulence, like fully ripe grapes their wine; as I snuffed up that uncontaminated aroma,—literally and truly, like the smell of spring violets; I declare to you, that for the time I lived as in a musky meadow; I forgot all about our horrible oath; in that inexpressible sperm, I washed my hands and my heart of it; I almost began to credit the old Paracelsan superstition that sperm is of rare virtue in allaying the heat of anger: while bathing in that bath, I felt divinely free from all ill-will, or petulance, or malice, of any sort whatsoever.

Squeeze! squeeze! squeeze! all the morning long; I squeezed that sperm till I myself almost melted into it; I squeezed that sperm till a strange sort of insanity came over me; and I found myself unwittingly squeezing my co-laborers' hands in it, mistaking their hands for the gentle globules. Such an abounding, affectionate, friendly, loving feeling did this avocation beget; that at last I was continually squeezing their hands, and looking up into their eyes sentimentally; as much as to say,—Oh! my dear fellow beings, why should we longer cherish any social acerbities, or know the slightest ill-humor or envy! Come; let us squeeze hands all round; nay, let us all squeeze ourselves into each other; let us squeeze ourselves universally into the very milk and sperm of kindness.

Would that I could keep squeezing that sperm for ever! For now, since by many prolonged, repeated experiences, I have perceived that in all cases man must eventually lower, or at least shift, his conceit of attainable felicity; not placing it anywhere in the intellect or the fancy; but in the wife, the heart, the bed, the table, the saddle, the fire-side, the country; now that I have perceived all this, I am ready to squeeze case eternally. In thoughts of the visions of the night, I saw long rows of angels in paradise, each with his hands in a jar of spermaceti.

* * * * * * *

Now, while discoursing of sperm, it behooves to speak of other things akin to it, in the business of preparing the sperm whale for the try-works.

First comes white-horse, so called, which is obtained from the tapering part of the fish, and also from the thicker portions of his flukes. It is tough with congealed tendons—a wad of muscle—but still contains some oil. After being severed from the whale, the white-horse is first cut into portable oblongs ere going to the mincer. They look much like blocks of Berkshire marble.

Plum-pudding is the term bestowed upon certain fragmentary parts of the whale's flesh, here and there adhering to the blanket of blubber, and often participating to a considerable degree in its unctuousness. It is a most refreshing, convivial, beautiful object to behold. As its name imports, it is of an exceedingly rich, mottled tint, with a bestreaked snowy and golden ground, dotted with spots of the deepest crimson and purple. It is plums of rubies, in pictures of citron. Spite of reason, it is hard to keep yourself from eating it. I confess, that once I stole behind the foremast to try it. It tasted something as I should conceive a royal cutlet from the thigh of Louis le Gros might have tasted, supposing him to have been killed the first day after the venison season, and that particular venison season contemporary with an unusually fine vintage of the vineyards of Champagne.

There is another substance, and a very singular one, which turns up in the course of this business, but which I feel it to be very puzzling adequately to describe. It is called slobgollion; an appellation original with the whalemen, and even so is the nature of the substance. It is an ineffably oozy, stringy affair, most frequently found in the tubs of sperm, after a prolonged squeezing, and subsequent decanting. I hold it to be the wondrously thin, ruptured membranes of the case, coalescing.

Gurry, so called, is a term properly belonging to right whalemen, but sometimes incidentally used by the sperm fishermen. It designates the dark, glutinous substance which is scraped off the back of the Greenland or right whale, and much of which covers the decks of those inferior souls who hunt that ignoble Leviathan.

Nippers. Strictly this word is not indigenous to the whale's vocabulary. But as applied by whalemen, it becomes so. A whaleman's nipper is a short firm strip of tendinous stuff cut from the tapering part of Leviathan's tail: it averages an inch in thickness, and for the rest, is about the size of the iron part of a hoe. Edgewise moved along the oily deck, it operates like a leathern squilgee; and by nameless blandishments, as of magic, allures along with it all impurities.

But to learn all about these recondite matters, your best way is at once to descend into the blubber-room, and have a long talk with its inmates. This place has previously been mentioned as the receptacle for the blanket-pieces, when stript and hoisted from the whale. When the proper time arrives for cutting up its contents, this apartment is a scene of terror to all tyros, especially by night. On one side, lit by a dull lantern, a space has been left clear for the workmen. They generally go in pairs,—a pike-and-gaff-man and a spade-man. The whaling-pike is similar to a frigate's boarding-weapon of the same name. The gaff is something like a boat-hook. With his gaff, the gaffman hooks on to a sheet of blubber, and strives to hold it from slipping, as the ship pitches and lurches about. Meanwhile, the spade-man stands on the sheet itself, perpendicularly chopping it into the portable horse-pieces. This spade is sharp as hone can make it; the spademan's feet are shoeless; the thing he stands on will sometimes irresistibly slide away from him, like a sledge. If he cuts off one of his own toes, or one of his assistant's, would you be very much astonished? Toes are scarce among veteran blubber-room men.

CHAPTER XCV

The Cassock

Had you stepped on board the Pequod at a certain juncture of this post-mortemizing of the whale; and had you strolled forward nigh the windlass, pretty sure am I that you would have scanned with no small curiosity a very strange, enigmatical object, which you would have seen there, lying along lengthwise in the lee scuppers. Not the wondrous cistern in the whale's huge head; not the prodigy of his unhinged lower jaw; not the miracle of his symmetrical tail; none of these would so surprise you, as half a glimpse of that unaccountable cone,—longer than a Kentuckian is tall, nigh a foot in diameter at the base, and jet-black as Yojo, the ebony idol of Queequeg. And an idol, indeed, it is; or, rather, in old times, its likeness was. Such an idol as that found in the secret groves of Queen Maachah in Judea; and for worshipping which, King Asa, her son, did depose her, and destroyed the idol, and burnt it for an abomination at the brook Kedron, as darkly set forth in the 15th chapter of the first book of Kings.

Look at the sailor, called the mincer, who now comes along, and assisted by two allies, heavily backs the grandissimus, as the mariners call it, and with bowed shoulders, staggers off with it as if he were a grenadier carrying a dead comrade from the field. Extending it upon the forecastle deck, he now proceeds cylindrically to remove its dark pelt, as an African hunter the pelt of a boa. This done he turns the pelt inside out, like a pantaloon leg; gives it a good stretching, so as almost to double its diameter; and at last hangs it, well spread, in the rigging, to dry. Ere long, it is taken down; when removing some three feet of it, towards the pointed extremity, and then cutting two slits for armholes at the other end, he lengthwise slips himself bodily into it. The mincer now stands before you invested in the full canonicals of his calling. Immemorial to all his order, this investiture alone will adequately protect him, while employed in the peculiar functions of his office.

That office consists in mincing the horse-pieces of blubber for the pots; an operation which is conducted at a curious wooden horse, planted endwise against the bulwarks, and with a capacious tub beneath it, into which the minced pieces drop, fast as the sheets from a rapt orator's desk. Arrayed in decent black; occupying a conspicuous pulpit; intent on bible leaves; what a candidate for an archbishoprick, what a lad for a Pope were this mincer!*

CHAPTER XCVI

The Try-Works

Besides her hoisted boats, an American whaler is outwardly distinguished by her try-works. She presents the curious anomaly of the most solid masonry joining with oak and hemp in constituting the completed ship. It is as if from the open field a brick-kiln were transported to her planks.

The try-works are planted between the foremast and main-mast, the most roomy part of the deck. The timbers beneath are of a peculiar strength, fitted to sustain the weight of an almost solid mass of brick and mortar, some ten feet by eight square, and five in height. The foundation does not penetrate the deck, but the masonry is firmly secured to the surface by ponderous knees of iron bracing it on all sides, and screwing it down to the timbers. On the flanks it is cased with wood, and at top completely covered by a large, sloping, battened hatchway. Removing this hatch we expose the great try-pots, two in number, and each of several barrels' capacity. When not in use, they are kept remarkably clean. Sometimes they are polished with soapstone and sand, till they shine within like silver punch-bowls. During the night-watches some cynical old sailors will crawl into them and coil themselves away there for a nap. While employed in polishing them—one man in each pot, side by side—many confidential communications are carried on, over the iron lips. It is a place also for profound mathematical meditation. It was in the left hand try-pot of the Pequod, with the soapstone diligently circling round me, that I was first indirectly struck by the remarkable fact, that in geometry all bodies gliding along

*Bible leaves! Bible leaves! This is the invariable cry from the mates to the mincer. It enjoins him to be careful, and cut his work into as thin slices as possible, inasmuch as by so doing the business of boiling out the oil is much accelerated, and its quantity considerably increased, besides perhaps improving it in quality.

the cycloid, my soapstone for example, will descend from any point in precisely the same time.

Removing the fire-board from the front of the try-works, the bare masonry of that side is exposed, penetrated by the two iron mouths of the furnaces, directly underneath the pots. These mouths are fitted with heavy doors of iron. The intense heat of the fire is prevented from communicating itself to the deck, by means of a shallow reservoir extending under the entire inclosed surface of the works. By a tunnel inserted at the rear, this reservoir is kept replenished with water as fast as it evaporates. There are no external chimneys; they open direct from the rear wall. And here let us go back for a moment.

It was about nine o'clock at night that the Pequod's try-works were first started on this present voyage. It belonged to Stubb to oversee the business.

'All ready there? Off hatch, then, and start her. You cook, fire the works.' This was an easy thing, for the carpenter had been thrusting his shavings into the furnace throughout the passage. Here be it said that in a whaling voyage the first fire in the try-works has to be fed for a time with wood. After that no wood is used, except as a means of quick ignition to the staple fuel. In a word, after being tried out, the crisp, shrivelled blubber, now called scraps or fritters, still contains considerable of its unctuous properties. These fritters feed the flames. Like a plethoric burning martyr, or a self-consuming misanthrope, once ignited, the whale supplies his own fuel and burns by his own body. Would that he consumed his own smoke! for his smoke is horrible to inhale, and inhale it you must, and not only that, but you must live in it for the time. It has an unspeakable, wild, Hindoo odor about it, such as may lurk in the vicinity of funereal pyres. It smells like the left wing of the day of judgment; it is an argument for the pit.

By midnight the works were in full operation. We were clear from the carcase; sail had been made; the wind was freshening; the wild ocean darkness was intense. But that darkness was licked up by the fierce flames, which at intervals forked forth from the sooty flues, and illuminated every lofty rope in the rigging, as with the famed Greek fire. The burning ship drove on, as if remorselessly commissioned to some vengeful deed. So the pitch and sulphur-freighted brigs of the bold Hydriote, Canaris, issuing from their midnight harbors, with broad sheets of flame for sails, bore down upon the Turkish frigates, and folded them in conflagrations.

The hatch, removed from the top of the works, now afforded a wide hearth in front of them. Standing on this were the Tartarean shapes of the pagan harpooneers, always the whale-ship's stokers. With huge pronged poles they pitched hissing masses of blubber into the scalding pots, or stirred up the fires beneath, till the snaky flames darted, curling, out of the doors to catch them by the feet. The smoke rolled away in sullen heaps. To every pitch of the ship there was a pitch of the boiling oil, which seemed all eagerness to leap into their faces. Opposite the mouth of the works, on the further side of the wide wooden hearth, was the windlass. This served for a sea-sofa. Here lounged the watch, when not otherwise employed, looking into the red heat of the fire, till their eyes felt scorched in their heads. Their tawny features, now all begrimed with smoke and sweat, their matted beards, and the contrasting barbaric brilliancy of their teeth, all these were strangely revealed in the capricious emblazonings of the works. As they narrated to each other their unholy adventures, their tales of terror told in words of mirth; as their uncivilized laughter forked upwards out of them, like the flames from the furnace; as to and fro, in their front, the harpooneers wildly gesticulated with their huge pronged forks and dippers; as the wind howled on, and the sea leaped, and the ship groaned and dived, and yet steadfastly shot her red hell further and further into the blackness of the sea and the night, and scornfully champed the white bone in her mouth, and viciously spat round her on all sides; then the rushing Pequod, freighted with savages, and laden with fire, and burning a corpse, and plunging into that blackness of darkness, seemed the material counterpart of her monomaniac commander's soul.

So seemed it to me, as I stood at her helm, and for long hours silently guided the way of this fire-ship on the sea. Wrapped, for that interval, in darkness myself, I but the better saw the redness, the madness, the ghastliness of others. The continual sight of the fiend shapes before me, capering half in smoke and half in fire, these at last begat kindred visions in my soul, so soon as I began to yield to that unaccountable drowsiness which ever would come over me at a midnight helm.

But that night, in particular, a strange (and ever since inexplicable) thing occurred to me. Starting from a brief standing sleep, I was horribly conscious of something fatally wrong. The jaw-bone tiller smote my side, which leaned against it; in my ears was the low hum of sails, just beginning to shake in the wind; I thought my eyes were open; I was half conscious of putting my fingers to the lids and mechanically stretching them still further apart. But, spite of all this, I could see no compass before me to steer by; though it seemed but a minute since I had been watching the card, by the steady binnacle lamp illuminating it. Nothing seemed before me but a jet gloom, now and then made ghastly by flashes of redness. Uppermost was the impression, that whatever swift, rushing thing I stood on was not so much bound to any haven ahead as rushing from all havens astern. A stark, bewildered feeling, as of death, came over me. Convulsively my hands grasped the tiller, but with the crazy conceit that the tiller was, somehow, in some enchanted way, inverted. My God! what is the matter with me? thought I. Lo! in my brief sleep I had turned myself about, and was fronting the ship's stern, with my back to her prow and the compass. In an instant I faced back, just in time to prevent the vessel from flying up into the wind, and very probably capsizing her. How glad and how grateful the relief from this unnatural hallucination of the night, and the fatal contingency of being brought by the lee!

Look not too long in the face of the fire, O man! Never dream with thy hand on the helm! Turn not thy back to the compass; accept the first hint of the hitching tiller; believe not the artificial fire, when its redness makes all things look ghastly. To-morrow, in the natural sun, the skies will be bright; those who glared like devils in the forking flames, the morn will show in far other, at least gentler, relief; the glorious, golden, glad sun, the only true lamp—all others but liars!

Nevertheless the sun hides not Virginia's Dismal Swamp, nor Rome's accursed Campagna, nor wide Sahara, nor all the millions of miles of deserts and of griefs beneath the moon. The sun hides not the ocean, which is the dark side of this earth, and which is two thirds of this earth. So, therefore, that mortal man who hath more of joy than sorrow in him, that mortal man cannot be true—not true, or undeveloped. With books the same. The truest of all men was the Man of Sorrows, and the truest of all books is Solomon's, and Ecclesiastes is the fine hammered steel of woe. 'All is vanity.' ALL. This wilful world hath not got hold of unchristian Solomon's wisdom yet. But he who dodges hospitals and jails, and walks fast crossing grave-yards, and would rather talk of operas than hell; calls Cowper, Young, Pascal, Rousseau, poor devils all of sick men; and throughout a care-free lifetime swears by Rabelais as passing wise, and therefore jolly;—not that man is fitted to sit down on tomb-stones, and break the green damp mould with unfathomably wondrous Solomon.

But even Solomon, he says, 'the man that wandereth out of the way of understanding shall remain' (*i.e.* even while living) 'in the congregation of the dead.' Give not thyself up, then, to fire, lest it invert thee, deaden thee; as for the time it did me. There is a wisdom that is woe; but there is a woe that is madness. And there is a Catskill eagle in some souls that can alike dive down into the blackest gorges, and soar out of them again and become invisible in the sunny spaces. And even if he for ever flies within the gorge, that gorge is in the mountains; so that even in his lowest swoop the mountain eagle is still higher than other birds upon the plain, even though they soar.

CHAPTER XCVII

The Lamp

Had you descended from the Pequod's try-works to the Pequod's forecastle, where the off duty watch were sleeping, for one single moment you would have almost thought you were standing in some illuminated shrine of canonized kings and counsellors. There they lay in their triangular oaken vaults, each mariner a chiselled muteness; a score of lamps flashing upon his hooded eyes.

In merchantmen, oil for the sailor is more scarce than the milk of queens. To dress in the dark, and eat in the dark, and stumble in darkness to his pallet, this is his usual lot. But the whaleman, as he seeks the food of light, so he lives in light. He makes his berth an Aladdin's lamp, and lays him down in it; so that in the pitchiest night the ship's black hull still houses an illumination.

See with what entire freedom the whaleman takes his handful of lamps—often but old bottles and vials, though—to the copper cooler at the try-works, and replenishes them there, as mugs of ale at a vat. He burns, too, the purest of oil, in its unmanufactured, and, therefore, unvitiated state; a fluid unknown to solar, lunar, or astral contrivances ashore. It is sweet as early grass butter in April. He goes and hunts for his oil, so as to be sure of its freshness and genuineness, even as the traveller on the prairie hunts up his own supper of game.

CHAPTER XCVIII

Stowing Down and Clearing Up

Already has it been related how the great leviathan is afar off descried from the mast-head; how he is chased over the watery moors, and slaughtered in the valleys of the deep; how he is then towed alongside and beheaded; and how (on the principle which entitled the headsman of old to the garments in which the beheaded was killed) his great padded surtout becomes the property of his executioner; how, in due time, he is condemned to the pots, and, like Shadrach, Meshach, and Abednego, his spermaceti, oil, and bone pass unscathed through the fire;—but now it remains to conclude the last chapter of this part of the description by rehearsing—singing, if I may—the romantic proceeding of decanting off his oil into the casks and striking them down into the hold, where once again leviathan returns to his native profundities, sliding along beneath the surface as before; but, alas! never more to rise and blow.

While still warm, the oil, like hot punch, is received into the six-barrel casks; and while, perhaps, the ship is pitching and rolling this way and that in the midnight sea, the enormous casks are slewed round and headed over, end for end, and sometimes perilously scoot across the slippery deck, like so many land slides, till at last man-handled and stayed in their course; and all round the hoops, rap, rap, go as many hammers as can play upon them, for now, *ex officio,* every sailor is a cooper.

At length, when the last pint is casked, and all is cool, then the great hatchways are unsealed, the bowels of the ship are thrown open, and down go the casks to their final rest in the sea. This done, the hatches are replaced, and hermetically closed, like a closet walled up.

In the sperm fishery, this is perhaps one of the most remarkable incidents in all the business of whaling. One day the planks stream with freshets of blood and oil; on the sacred quarter-deck enormous masses of the whale's head are profanely piled; great rusty casks lie about, as in a brewery yard; the smoke from the try-works has besooted all the bulwarks; the mariners go about suffused with unctuousness; the entire ship seems great leviathan himself; while on all hands the din is deafening.

But a day or two after, you look about you, and prick your ears in this self-same ship; and were it not for the tell-tale boats and try-works, you would all but swear you trod some silent merchant vessel, with a most scrupulously neat commander. The unmanufactured sperm oil possesses a singularly cleansing virtue. This is the reason why the decks never look so white as just after what they call an affair of oil. Besides, from the ashes of the burned scraps of the whale, a potent ley is readily made; and whenever any adhesiveness from the back of the whale remains clinging to the side, that ley quickly exterminates it. Hands go diligently along the bulwarks, and with buckets of water and rags restore them to their full tidiness. The soot is brushed from the lower rigging. All the numerous implements which have been in use are likewise faithfully cleansed and put away. The great hatch is scrubbed and placed upon the try-works, completely hiding the pots; every cask is out of sight; all tackles are coiled in unseen nooks; and when by the combined and simultaneous industry of almost the entire ship's company, the whole of this conscientious duty is at last concluded, then the crew themselves proceed to their own ablutions; shift themselves from top to toe; and finally issue to the immaculate deck, fresh and all aglow, as bridegrooms new-leaped from out the daintiest Holland.

Now, with elated step, they pace the planks in twos and threes, and humorously discourse of parlors, sofas, carpets, and fine cambrics; propose to mat the deck; think of having hangings to the top; object not to taking tea by moonlight on the piazza of the forecastle. To hint to such musked mariners of oil, and bone, and blubber, were little short of audacity. They know not the thing you distantly allude to. Away, and bring us napkins!

But mark: aloft there, at the three mast heads, stand three men intent on spying out more whales, which, if caught, infallibly will again soil the old oaken furniture, and drop at least one small grease-spot somewhere. Yes; and many is the time, when, after the severest uninterrupted labors, which know no night; continuing straight through for ninety-six hours; when from the boat, where they have swelled their wrists with all day rowing on the Line,—they only step to the deck to carry vast chains, and heave the heavy windlass, and cut and slash, yea, and in their very sweatings to be smoked and burned anew by the combined fires of the equatorial sun and the equatorial try-works; when, on the heel of all this, they have finally bestirred themselves to cleanse the ship, and make a spotless dairy room of it; many is the time the poor fellows, just buttoning the necks of their clean frocks, are startled by the cry of 'There she blows!' and away they fly to fight another whale, and go through the whole weary thing again. Oh! my friends, but this is man-killing! Yet this is life. For hardly have we mortals by long toilings extracted from this world's vast bulk its small but valuable sperm; and then, with weary patience, cleansed ourselves from its defilements, and learned to live here in clean tabernacles of the soul; hardly is this done, when—*There she blows!*—the ghost is spouted up, and away we sail to fight some other world, and go through young life's old routine again.

Oh! the metempsychosis! Oh! Pythagoras, that in bright Greece, two thousand years ago, did die, so good, so wise, so mild; I sailed with thee along the Peruvian coast last voyage—and, foolish as I am, taught thee, a green simple boy, how to splice a rope!

XCIX

THE DOUBLOON

Ere now it has been related how Ahab was wont to pace his quarter-deck, taking regular turns at either limit, the binnacle and mainmast; but in the multiplicity of other things requiring narration it has not been added how that sometimes in these walks, when most plunged in his mood, he was wont to pause in turn at each spot, and stand there strangely eyeing the particular object before him. When he halted before the binnacle, with his glance fastened on the pointed needle in the compass, that glance shot like a javelin with the pointed intensity of his purpose; and when resuming his walk he again paused before the mainmast, then, as the same riveted glance fastened upon the riveted gold coin there, he still wore the same aspect of nailed firmness, only dashed with a certain wild longing, if not hopefulness.

But one morning, turning to pass the doubloon, he seemed to be newly attracted by the strange figures and inscriptions stamped on it, as though now for the first time beginning to interpret for himself in some monomaniac way whatever significance might lurk in them. And some certain significance lurks in all things, else all things are little worth, and the round world itself but an empty cipher, except to sell by the cartload, as they do hills about Boston, to fill up some morass in the Milky Way.

Now this doubloon was of purest, virgin gold, raked somewhere out of the heart of gorgeous hills, whence, east and west, over golden sands, the head-waters of many a Pactolus flow. And though now nailed amidst all the rustiness of iron bolts and the verdigris of copper spikes, yet, untouchable and immaculate to any foulness, it still preserved its Quito glow. Nor, though placed amongst a ruthless crew and every hour passed by ruthless hands, and through the live-long nights shrouded with thick darkness which might cover any pilfering approach, nevertheless every sunrise found the doubloon where the sunset left it last. For it was set apart and sanctified to one awe-striking end; and however wanton in their sailor ways, one and all, the mariners revered it as the white whale's talisman. Sometimes they talked it over in the weary watch by night, wondering whose it was to be at last, and whether he would ever live to spend it.

Now these noble golden coins of South America are as medals of the sun and tropic token-pieces. Here palms, alpacas, and volcanoes; sun's disks and stars; ecliptics, horns-of-plenty, and rich banners waving, are in luxuriant profusion stamped; so that the precious gold seems almost to derive an added preciousness and enhancing glories, by passing through those fancy mints, so Spanishly poetic.

It so chanced that the doubloon of the Pequod was a most wealthy example of these things. On its round border it bore the letters, REPUBLICA DEL ECUADOR: QUITO. So this bright coin came from a country planted in the middle of the world, and beneath the great equator, and named after it; and it had been cast midway up the Andes, in the unwaning clime that knows no autumn. Zoned by those letters you saw the likeness of three Andes' summits; from one a flame; a tower on another; on the third a crowing cock; while arching over all was a segment of the partitioned zodiac, the signs all marked with their usual cabalistics, and the keystone sun entering the equinoctial point at Libra.

Before this equatorial coin, Ahab, not unobserved by others, was now pausing.

'There's something ever egotistical in mountain-tops and towers, and all other grand and lofty things; look here,—three peaks as proud as Lucifer. The firm tower, that is Ahab; the volcano, that is Ahab; the courageous, the undaunted, and victorious fowl, that, too, is Ahab; all are Ahab; and this round gold is but the image of the rounder globe, which, like a magician's glass, to each and every man in turn but mirrors back his own mysterious self. Great pains, small gains for those who ask the world to solve them; it cannot solve itself. Methinks now this coined sun wears a ruddy face; but see! aye, he enters the sign of storms, the equinox! and but six months before he wheeled out of a former equinox at Aries! From storm to storm! So be it, then. Born in throes, 'tis fit that man should live in pains and die in pangs! So be it, then! Here's stout stuff for woe to work on. So be it, then.'

'No fairy fingers can have pressed the gold, but devil's claws must have left their mouldings there since yesterday,' murmured Starbuck to himself, leaning against the bulwarks. 'The old man seems to read Belshazzar's awful writing. I have never marked the coin inspectingly. He goes below; let me read. A dark valley between three mighty, heaven-abiding peaks, that almost seem the Trinity, in some faint earthly symbol. So in this vale of Death, God girds us round; and over all our gloom, the sun of Righteousness still shines a beacon and a hope. If we bend down our eyes, the dark vale shows her mouldy soil; but if we lift them, the bright sun meets our glance half way, to cheer. Yet, oh, the great sun is no fixture; and if, at midnight, we would fain snatch some sweet solace from him, we gaze for him in vain! This coin speaks wisely, mildly, truly, but still sadly to me. I will quit it, lest Truth shake me falsely.'

'There now's the old Mogul,' soliloquized Stubb by the try-works, 'he's been twigging it; and there goes Starbuck from the same, and both with faces which I should say might be somewhere within nine fathoms long. And all from looking at a piece of gold, which did I have it now on Negro Hill or in Corlaer's Hook, I'd not look at it very long ere spending it. Humph! in my poor, insignificant opinion,

I regard this as queer. I have seen doubloons before now in my voyagings; your doubloons of old Spain, your doubloons of Peru, your doubloons of Chili, your doubloons of Bolivia, your doubloons of Popayan; with plenty of gold moidores and pistoles, and joes, and half joes, and quarter joes. What then should there be in this doubloon of the Equator that is so killing wonderful? By Golconda! let me read it once. Halloa! here's signs and wonders truly! That, now, is what old Bowditch in his Epitome calls the zodiac, and what my almanack below calls ditto. I'll get the almanack; and as I have heard devils can be raised with Daboll's arithmetic, I'll try my hand at raising a meaning out of these queer curvicues here with the Massachusetts calendar. Here's the book. Let's see now. Signs and wonders; and the sun, he's always among 'em. Hem, hem, hem; here they are—here they go—all alive:—Aries, or the Ram; Taurus, or the Bull;—and Jimini! here's Gemini himself, or the Twins. Well; the sun he wheels among 'em. Aye, here on the coin he's just crossing the threshold between two of twelve sitting-rooms all in a ring. Book! you lie there; the fact is, you books must know your places. You'll do to give us the bare words and facts, but we come in to supply the thoughts. That's my small experience, so far as the Massachusetts calendar, and Bowditch's navigator, and Daboll's arithmetic go. Signs and wonders, eh? Pity if there is nothing wonderful in signs, and significant in wonders! There's a clue somewhere; wait a bit; hist—hark! By Jove, I have it! Look you, Doubloon, your zodiac here is the life of man in one round chapter; and now I'll read it off, straight out of the book. Come, Almanack! To begin: there's Aries, or the Ram—lecherous dog, he begets us; then, Taurus, or the Bull—he bumps us the first thing; then Gemini, or the Twins—that is, Virtue and Vice; we try to reach Virtue, when lo! comes Cancer the Crab, and drags us back; and here, going from Virtue, Leo, a roaring Lion, lies in the path—he gives a few fierce bites and surly dabs with his paw; we escape, and hail Virgo, the Virgin! that's our first love; we marry and think to be happy for aye, when pop comes Libra, or the Scales—happiness weighed and found wanting; and while we are very sad about that, Lord! how we suddenly jump, as Scorpio, or the Scorpion, stings us in rear; we are curing the wound, when whang come the arrows all round; Sagittarius, or the Archer, is amusing himself. As we pluck out the shafts, stand aside! here's the battering-ram, Capricornus, or the Goat; full tilt, he comes rushing, and head-long we are tossed; when Aquarius, or the Water-bearer, pours out his whole deluge and drowns us; and to wind up with Pisces, or the Fishes, we sleep. There's a sermon now, writ in high heaven, and the sun goes through it every year, and yet comes out of it all alive and hearty. Jollily he, aloft there, wheels though toil and trouble; and so, alow here, does jolly Stubb. Oh, jolly's the word for aye! Adieu, Doubloon! But stop; here comes little King-Post; dodge round the try-works, now, and let's hear what he'll have to say. There; he's before it; he'll out with something presently. So, so; he's beginning.'

'I see nothing here, but a round thing made of gold, and whoever raises a certain whale, this round thing belongs to him. So, what's all this staring been about? It is worth sixteen dollars, that's true; and at two cents the cigar, that's nine hundred and sixty cigars. I wont smoke dirty pipes like Stubb, but I like cigars, and here's nine hundred and sixty of them; so here goes Flask aloft to spy 'em out.'

'Shall I call that wise or foolish, now; if it be really wise it has a foolish look to it; yet, if it be really foolish, then has it a sort of wiseish look to it. But, avast; here comes our old Manxman—the old hearse-driver, he must have been, that is, before he took to the sea. He luffs up before the doubloon; halloa, and goes round on the other side of the mast; why, there's a horse-shoe nailed on that side; and now he's back again; what does that mean? Hark! he's muttering—voice like an old worn-out coffee-mill. Prick ears, and listen!'

'If the White Whale be raised, it must be in a month and a day, when the sun stands in some one of these signs. I've studied signs, and know their marks; they were taught me two score years ago, by the old witch in Copenhagen. Now, in what sign will the sun then be? The horse-shoe sign; for there it is, right opposite the gold. And what's the horse-shoe sign? The lion is the horse-shoe sign—the roaring and devouring lion. Ship, old ship! my old head shakes to think of thee.'

'There's another rendering now; but still one text. All sorts of men in one kind of world, you see. Dodge again! here comes Queequeg—all tattooing—looks like the signs of the Zodiac himself. What says the Cannibal? As I live he's comparing notes; looking at his thigh bone; thinks the sun is in the thigh, or in the calf, or in the bowels, I suppose, as the old women talk Surgeon's Astronomy in the back country. And by Jove, he's found something there in the vicinity of his thigh—I guess it's Sagittarius, or the Archer. No: he don't know what to make of the doubloon; he takes it for an old button off some king's trowsers. But, aside again! here comes that ghost-devil, Fedallah; tail coiled out of sight as usual, oakum in the toes of his pumps as usual. What does he say, with that look of his? Ah, only makes a sign to the sign and bows himself; there is a sun on the coin—fire worshipper, depend upon it. Ho! more and more. This way comes Pip—poor boy! would he had died, or I; he's half horrible to me. He too has been watching all of these interpreters—myself included—and look now, he comes to read, with that unearthly idiot face. Stand away again and hear him. Hark!'

'I look, you look, he looks; we look, ye look, they look.'

'Upon my soul, he's been studying Murray's Grammar! Improving his mind, poor fellow! But what's that he says now—hist!'

'I look, you look, he looks; we look, ye look, they look.'

'Why, he's getting it by heart—hist! again.'

'I look, you look, he looks; we look, ye look, they look.'

'Well, that's funny.'

'And I, you, and he; and we, ye, and they, are all bats; and I'm a crow, especially when I stand a'top of this pine tree here. Caw! caw! caw! caw! caw! caw! Ain't I a crow? And where's the scare-crow? There he stands; two bones stuck into a pair of old trowsers, and two more poked into the sleeves of an old jacket.'

'Wonder if he means me?—complimentary!—poor lad!—I could go hang myself. Any way, for the present, I'll quit Pip's vicinity. I can stand the rest, for they have plain wits; but he's too crazy-witty for my sanity. So, so, I leave him muttering.'

'Here's the ship's navel, this doubloon here, and they are all on fire to unscrew it. But, unscrew your navel, and what's the consequence? Then again, if it stays here, that is ugly, too, for when aught's nailed to the mast it's a sign that things grow desperate. Ha, ha! old Ahab! the White Whale; he'll nail ye! This is a pine tree. My father, in old Tolland county, cut down a pine tree once, and found a silver ring grown over in it; some old darkey's wedding ring. How did it get there? And so they'll say in the resurrection, when they come to fish up this old mast, and find a doubloon lodged in it, with bedded oysters for the shaggy bark. Oh, the gold! the precious, precious gold!—the green miser 'll hoard ye soon! Hish! hish! God goes 'mong the worlds blackberrying. Cook! ho, cook! and cook us! Jenny! hey, hey, hey, hey, hey, Jenny, Jenny! and get your hoe-cake done!'

CHAPTER C

Leg and Arm

THE PEQUOD, OF NANTUCKET, MEETS THE SAMUEL ENDERBY, OF LONDON

'Ship, ahoy! Hast seen the White Whale?'

So cried Ahab, once more hailing a ship showing English colors, bearing down under the stern. Trumpet to mouth, the old man was standing in his hoisted quarter-boat, his ivory leg plainly revealed to the stranger captain, who was carelessly reclining in his own boat's bow. He was a darkly-tanned, burly, good-natured, fine-looking man, of sixty or thereabouts, dressed in a spacious roundabout, that hung round him in festoons of blue pilot-cloth; and one empty arm of this jacket streamed behind him like the broidered arm of a huzzar's surcoat.

'Hast seen the White Whale?'

'See you this?' and withdrawing it from the folds that had hidden it, he held up a white arm of sperm whale bone, terminating in a wooden head like a mallet.

'Man my boat!' cried Ahab, impetuously, and tossing about the oars near him—'Stand by to lower!'

In less than a minute, without quitting his little craft, he and his crew were dropped to the water, and were soon alongside of the stranger. But here a curious difficulty presented itself. In the excitement of the moment, Ahab had forgotten that since the loss of his leg he had never once stepped on board of any vessel at sea but his own, and then it was always by an ingenious and very handy mechanical contrivance peculiar to the Pequod, and a thing not to be rigged and shipped in any other vessel at a moment's warning. Now, it is no very easy matter for anybody—except those who are almost hourly used to it, like whalemen—to clamber up a ship's side from a boat on the open sea; for the great swells now lift the boat high up towards the bulwarks, and then instantaneously drop it half way down to the kelson. So, deprived of one leg, and the strange ship of course being altogether unsupplied with the kindly invention, Ahab now found himself abjectly reduced to a clumsy landsman again; hopelessly eyeing the uncertain changeful height he could hardly hope to attain.

It has before been hinted, perhaps, that every little untoward circumstance that befel him, and which indirectly sprang from his luckless mishap, almost invariably irritated or exasperated Ahab. And in the present instance, all this was heightened by the sight of the two officers of the strange ship, leaning over the side, by the perpendicular ladder of nailed cleets there, and swinging towards him a pair of tastefully-ornamented man-ropes; for at first they did not seem to bethink them that a one-legged man must be too much of a cripple to use their sea bannisters. But this awkwardness only lasted a minute, because the strange captain, observing at a glance how affairs stood, cried out, 'I see, I see!—avast heaving there! Jump, boys, and swing over the cutting-tackle.'

As good luck would have it, they had had a whale alongside a day or two previous, and the great tackles were still aloft, and the massive curved blubber-hook, now clean and dry, was still attached to the end. This was quickly lowered to Ahab, who at once comprehending it all, slid his solitary thigh into the curve of the hook (it was like sitting in the fluke of an anchor, or the crotch of an apple tree), and then giving the word, held himself fast, and at the same time also helped to hoist his own weight, by pulling hand-over-hand upon one of the running parts of the tackle. Soon he was carefully swung inside the high bulwarks, and gently landed upon the capstan head. With his ivory arm frankly thrust forth in welcome, the other captain advanced, and Ahab, putting out his ivory leg, and crossing the ivory arm (like two sword-fish blades) cried out in his walrus way, 'Aye, aye, hearty! let us shake bones together!—an arm and a leg!—an arm that never can shrink, d'ye see; and a leg that never can run. Where did'st thou see the White Whale?—how long ago?'

'The White Whale,' said the Englishman, pointing his ivory arm towards the East, and taking a rueful sight along it, as if it had been a telescope; 'There I saw him, on the Line, last season.'

'And he took that arm off, did he?' asked Ahab, now sliding down from the capstan, and resting on the Englishman's shoulder, as he did so.

'Aye, he was the cause of it, at least; and that leg, too?'

'Spin me the yarn,' said Ahab; 'how was it?'

'It was the first time in my life that I ever cruised on the Line,' began the Englishman. 'I was ignorant of the White Whale at that time. Well, one day we lowered for a pod of four or five whales, and my boat fastened to one of them; a regular circus horse he was, too, that went milling and milling round so, that my boat's crew could only trim dish, by sitting all their sterns on the outer gunwale. Presently up breaches from the bottom of the sea a bouncing great whale, with a milky-white head and hump, all crows' feet and wrinkles.'

'It was he, it was he!' cried Ahab, suddenly letting out his suspended breath.

'And harpoons sticking in near his starboard fin.'

'Aye, aye—they were mine—*my* irons,' cried Ahab, exultingly—'but on!'

'Give me a chance, then,' said the Englishman, good-humoredly. 'Well, this old great-grandfather, with the white head and hump, runs all afoam into the pod, and goes to snapping furiously at my fast-line.'

'Aye, I see!—wanted to part it; free the fast-fish—an old trick—I know him.'

'How it was exactly,' continued the one-armed commander, 'I do not know; but in biting the line, it got foul of his teeth, caught there somehow; but we didn't know it then; so that when we afterwards pulled on the line, bounce we came plump on to his hump! instead of the other whale's that went off to windward, all fluking. Seeing how matters stood, and what a noble great whale it was—the noblest and biggest I ever saw, sir, in my life—I resolved to capture him, spite of the boiling rage he seemed to be in. And thinking the hap-hazard line would get loose, or the tooth it was tangled to might draw (for I have a devil of a boat's crew for a pull on a whale-line); seeing all this, I say, I jumped into my first mate's boat—Mr Mounttop's here (by the way, Captain—Mounttop; Mounttop—the captain);—as I was saying, I jumped into Mounttop's boat, which, d'ye see, was gunwale and gunwale with mine, then; and snatching the first harpoon, let this old great-grandfather have it. But, Lord, look you, sir—hearts and souls alive, man—the next instant, in a jiff, I was blind as a bat—both eyes out—all befogged and bedeadened with black foam—the whale's tail looming straight up out of it, perpendicular in the air, like a marble steeple. No use sterning all, then; but as I was groping at midday, with a blinding sun, all crown-jewels; as I was groping, I say, after the second iron, to toss it overboard—down comes the tail like a Lima tower, cutting my boat in two, leaving each half in splinters; and, flukes first, the white hump backed through the wreck, as though it was all chips. We all struck out. To escape his terrible flailings, I seized hold of my harpoon-pole sticking in him, and for a moment clung to that like a sucking fish. But a combing sea dashed me off, and at the same instant, the fish, taking one good dart forwards, went down like a flash; and the barb of that cursed second iron towing along near me caught me here' (clapping his hand just below his shoulder); 'yes, caught me just here, I say, and bore me down to Hell's flames, I was thinking; when, when, all of a sudden, thank the good God, the barb ript its way along the flesh—clear along the whole length of my arm—came out nigh my wrist, and up I floated;—and that gentleman there will tell you the rest (by the way, captain—Dr Bunger, ship's surgeon: Bunger, my lad,—the captain). Now, Bunger boy, spin your part of the yarn.'

The professional gentleman thus familiarly pointed out, had been all the time standing near them, with nothing specific visible, to denote his gentlemanly rank on board. His face was an exceedingly round but sober one; he was dressed in a faded blue woollen frock or shirt, and patched trowsers; and had thus far been dividing his attention between a marlingspike he held in one hand, and a pill-box held in the other, occasionally casting a critical glance at the ivory limbs of the two crippled captains. But, at his superior's introduction of him to Ahab, he politely bowed, and straightway went on to do his captain's bidding.

'It was a shocking bad wound,' began the whale-surgeon; 'and, taking my advice, Captain Boomer here, stood our old Sammy—'

'Samuel Enderby is the name of my ship,' interrupted the one-armed captain, addressing Ahab; 'go on, boy.'

'Stood our old Sammy off to the northward, to get out of the blazing hot weather there on the Line. But it was no use—I did all I could; sat up with him nights; was very severe with him in the matter of diet—'

'Oh, very severe!' chimed in the patient himself; then suddenly altering his voice, 'Drinking hot rum toddies with me every night, till he couldn't see to put on the bandages; and sending me to bed, half seas over, about three o'clock in the morning. Oh, ye stars! he sat up with me indeed, and was very severe in my diet. Oh! a great watcher, and very dietetically severe, is Dr Bunger. (Bunger, you dog, laugh out! why don't ye? You know you're a precious jolly rascal.) But, heave ahead, boy, I'd rather be killed by you than kept alive by any other man.'

'My captain, you must have ere this perceived, respected sir'—said the imperturbable godly-looking Bunger, slightly bowing to Ahab—'is apt to be facetious at times; he spins us many clever things of that sort. But I may as well say—en passant, as the French remark—that I myself—that is to say, Jack Bunger, late of the reverend clergy—am a strict total abstinence man; I never drink—'

'Water!' cried the captain; 'he never drinks it; it's a sort of fits to him; fresh water throws him into the hydrophobia; but go on—go on with the arm story.'

'Yes, I may as well,' said the surgeon, coolly. 'I was about observing, sir, before Captain Boomer's facetious interruption, that spite of my best and severest endeavors, the wound kept getting worse and worse; the truth was, sir, it was as ugly gaping wound as surgeon ever saw; more than two feet and several inches long. I measured it with the lead line. In short, it grew black; I knew what was threatened, and off it came. But I had no hand in shipping that ivory arm there; that thing is against all rule'—pointing at it with the marlingspike—'that is the captain's work, not mine; he ordered the carpenter to make it; he had that club-hammer there put to the end, to knock some one's brains out with, I suppose, as he tried mine once. He flies into diabolical passions sometimes. Do ye see this dent, sir'—removing his hat, and brushing aside his hair, and exposing a bowl-like cavity in his skull, but which bore not the slightest scarry trace, or any token of ever having been a wound—'Well, the captain there will tell you how that came here; he knows.'

'No, I don't,' said the captain, 'but his mother did; he was born with it. Oh, you solemn rogue, you—you Bunger! was there ever such another Bunger in the watery world? Bunger, when you die, you ought to die in pickle, you dog; you should be preserved to future ages, you rascal.'

'What became of the White Whale?' now cried Ahab, who thus far had been impatiently listening to this bye-play between the two Englishmen.

'Oh!' cried the one-armed captain, 'Oh, yes! Well; after he sounded, we didn't see him again for some time; in fact, as I before hinted, I didn't then know what whale it was that had served me such a trick, till some time afterwards, when coming back to the Line, we heard about Moby Dick—as some call him—and then I knew it was he.'

'Did'st thou cross his wake again?'

'Twice.'

'But could not fasten?'

'Didn't want to try to: ain't one limb enough? What should I do without this other arm? And I'm thinking Moby Dick doesn't bite so much as he swallows.'

'Well, then,' interrupted Bunger, 'give him your left arm for bait to get the right. Do you know, gentlemen'—very gravely and mathematically bowing to each Captain in succession—'Do you know, gentlemen, that the digestive organs of the whale are so inscrutably constructed by Divine Providence, that it is quite impossible for him to completely digest even a man's arm? And he knows it too. So that what you take for the White Whale's malice is only his awkwardness. For he never means to swallow a single limb; he only thinks to terrify by feints. But sometimes he is like the old juggling fellow, formerly a patient of mine in Ceylon, that making believe swallow jack-knives, once upon a time let one drop into him in good earnest, and there it stayed for a twelvemonth or more; when I gave him an emetic, and he heaved it up in small tacks, d'ye see. No possible way for him to digest that jack-knife, and fully incorporate it into his general bodily system. Yes, Captain Boomer, if you are quick enough about it, and have a mind to pawn one arm for the sake of the privilege of giving decent burial to the other, why in that case the arm is yours; only let the whale have another chance at you shortly, that's all.'

'No, thank ye, Bunger,' said the English Captain, 'he's welcome to the arm he has, since I can't help it, and didn't know him then; but not to another one. No more White Whales for me; I've lowered for him once, and that has satisfied me. There would be great glory in killing him, I know that; and there is a ship-load of precious sperm in him, but, hark ye, he's best let alone; don't you think so, Captain?'—glancing at the ivory leg.

'He is. But he will still be hunted, for all that. What is best let alone, that accursed thing is not always what least allures. He's all a magnet! How long since thou saw'st him last? Which way heading?'

'Bless my soul, and curse the foul fiend's,' cried Bunger, stoopingly walking round Ahab, and like a dog, strangely snuffing; 'this man's blood—bring the thermometer;—it's at the boiling point!—his pulse makes these planks beat!—sir!'—taking a lancet from his pocket, and drawing near to Ahab's arm.

'Avast!' roared Ahab, dashing him against the bulwarks—'Man the boat! Which way heading?'

'Good God!' cried the English Captain, to whom the question was put. 'What's the matter? He was heading east, I think.—Is your Captain crazy?' whispering Fedallah.

But Fedallah, putting a finger on his lip, slid over the bulwarks to take the boat's steering oar, and Ahab, swinging the cutting-tackle towards him, commanded the ship's sailors to stand by to lower.

In a moment he was standing in the boat's stern, and the Manilla men were springing to their oars. In vain the English Captain hailed him. With back to the stranger ship, and face set like a flint to his own, Ahab stood upright till alongside of the Pequod.

CHAPTER CI

THE DECANTER

Ere the English ship fades from sight, be it set down here, that she hailed from London, and was named after the late Samuel Enderby, merchant of that city, the original of the famous whaling house of Enderby & Sons; a house which in my poor whaleman's opinion, comes not far behind the united royal houses of the Tudors and Bourbons, in point of real historical interest. How long, prior to the year of our Lord 1775, this great whaling house was in existence, my numerous fish-documents do not make plain; but in that year (1775) it fitted out the first English ships that ever regularly hunted the Sperm Whale; though for some score of years previous (ever since 1726) our valiant Coffins and Maceys of Nantucket and the Vineyard had in large fleets pursued that Leviathan, but only in the North and South Atlantic: not elsewhere. Be it distinctly recorded here, that the Nantucketers were the first among mankind to harpoon with civilized steel the great Sperm Whale; and that for half a century they were the only people of the whole globe who so harpooned him.

In 1778, a fine ship, the Amelia, fitted out for the express purpose, and at the sole charge of the vigorous Enderbys, boldly rounded Cape Horn, and was the first among the nations to lower a whale-boat of any sort in the great South Sea. The voyage was a skilful and lucky one; and returning to her berth with her hold full of the precious sperm, the Amelia's example was soon followed by other ships, English and American, and thus the vast Sperm Whale grounds of the Pacific were thrown open. But not content with this good deed, the indefatigable house again bestirred itself: Samuel and his Sons—how many, their mother only knows—and under their immediate auspices, and partly, I think, at their expense, the British government was induced to sent the sloop-of-war Rattler on a whaling voyage of discovery into the South Sea. Commanded by a naval Post-Captain, the Rattler made a rattling voyage of it, and did some service; how much does not appear. But this is not all. In 1819, the same house fitted out a discovery whale ship of their own, to go on a testing cruise to the remote waters of Japan. That ship—well called the 'Syren'—made a noble experimental cruise; and it was thus that the great Japanese Whaling Ground first became generally known. The Syren in this famous voyage was commanded by a Captain Coffin, a Nantucketer.

All honor to the Enderbies, therefore, whose house, I think, exists to the present day; though doubtless the original Samuel must long ago have slipped his cable for the great South Sea of the other world.

The ship named after him was worthy of the honor, being a very fast sailer and a noble craft every way. I boarded her once at midnight somewhere off the Patagonian coast, and drank good flip down in the forecastle. It was a fine gam we had, and they were all trumps—every soul on board. A short life to them, and a jolly death. And that fine gam I had—long, very long after old Ahab touched her planks with his ivory heel—it minds me of the noble, solid, Saxon hospitality of that ship; and may my parson forget me, and the devil remember me, if I ever lose sight of it. Flip? Did I say we had flip? Yes, and we flipped it at the rate of ten gallons the hour; and when the squall came (for it's squally off there by Patagonia), and all hands—visitors and all—were called to reef topsails, we were so top-heavy that we had to swing each other aloft in bowlines; and we ignorantly furled the skirts of our jackets into the sails, so that we hung there, reefed fast in the howling gale, a warning example to all drunken tars. However, the masts did not go overboard; and by and bye we scrambled down, so sober, that we had to pass the flip again, though the savage salt spray bursting down the forecastle scuttle, rather too much diluted and pickled it to my taste.

The beef was fine—tough, but with body in it. They said it was bull-beef; others, that it was dromedary beef; but I do not know, for certain, how that was. They had dumplings too; small, but substantial, symmetrically globular, and indestructible dumplings. I fancied that you could feel them, and roll them about in you after they were swallowed. If you stooped over too far forward, you risked their pitching out of you like billiard-balls. The bread—but that couldn't be helped; besides, it was an anti-scorbutic; in short, the bread contained the only fresh fare they had. But the forecastle was not very light, and it was very easy to step over into a dark corner when you ate it. But all in all, taking her from truck to helm, considering the dimensions of the cook's boilers, including his own live parchment boilers; fore and aft, I say, the Samuel Enderby was a jolly ship; of good fare and plenty; fine flip and strong; crack fellows all, and capital from boot heels to hat-band.

But why was it, think ye, that the Samuel Enderby, and some other English whalers I know of—not all though—were such famous, hospitable ships; that passed round the beef, and the bread, and the can, and the joke; and were not soon weary of eating, and drinking, and laughing? I will tell you. The abounding good cheer of these English whalers is matter for historical research. Nor have I been at all sparing of historical whale research, when it has seemed needed.

The English were preceded in the whale fishery by the Hollanders, Zealanders, and Danes; from whom they derived many terms still extant in the fishery; and what is yet more, their fat old fashions, touching plenty to eat and drink. For, as a general thing, the English merchant-ship scrimps her crew; but not so the English whaler. Hence, in the English, this thing of whaling good cheer is not normal and natural, but incidental and particular; and, therefore, must have some special origin, which is here pointed out, and will be still further elucidated.

During my researches in the Leviathanic histories, I stumbled upon an ancient Dutch volume, which, by the musty whaling smell of it, I knew must be about whalers. The title was, 'Dan Coopman,' wherefore I concluded that this must be the invaluable memoirs of some Amsterdam cooper in the fishery, as every whale ship must carry its cooper. I was reinforced in this opinion by seeing that it was the production of one 'Fitz Swackhammer.' But my friend Dr Snodhead, a very learned man, professor of Low Dutch and High German in the college of Santa Claus and St Pott's, to whom I handed the work for translation, giving him a box of sperm candles for his trouble—this same Dr Snodhead, so soon as he spied the book, assured me that 'Dan Coopman' did not mean 'The Cooper,' but 'The Merchant.' In short, this ancient and learned Low Dutch book treated of the commerce of Holland; and, among other subjects, contained a very interesting account of its whale fishery. And in this chapter it was, headed 'Smeer,' or 'Fat,' that I found a long detailed list of the outfits for the larders and cellars of 180 sail of Dutch whalemen; from which list, as translated by Dr Snodhead, I transcribe the following:

400,000 lbs. of beef.
60,000 lbs. Friesland pork.
150,000 lbs. of stock fish.
550,000 lbs. of biscuit.
72,000 lbs. of soft bread.
2,800 firkins of butter.
20,000 lbs. Texel & Leyden cheese.
144,000 lbs. cheese (probably an inferior article).
550 ankers of Geneva.
10,800 barrels of beer.

Most statistical tables are parchingly dry in the reading; not so in the present case, however, where the reader is flooded with whole pipes, barrels, quarts, and gills of good gin and good cheer.

At the time, I devoted three days to the studious digesting of all this beer, beef, and bread, during which many profound thoughts were incidentally suggested to me, capable of a transcendental and Platonic application; and, furthermore, I compiled supplementary tables of my own, touching the probable quantity of stock-fish, &c., consumed by every Low Dutch harpooneer in that ancient Greenland and Spitzbergen whale fishery. In the first place, the amount of butter, and Texel and Leyden cheese consumed, seems amazing. I impute it, though, to their naturally unctuous natures, being rendered still more unctuous by the nature of their vocation, and especially by their pursuing their game in those frigid Polar Seas, on the very coasts of that Esquimaux country where the convivial natives pledge each other in bumpers of train oil.

The quantity of beer, too, is very large, 10,800 barrels. Now, as those polar fisheries could only be prosecuted in the short summer of that climate, so that the whole cruise of one of these Dutch whalemen, including the short voyage to and from the Spitzbergen sea, did not much exceed three months, say, and reckoning 30 men to each of their fleet of 180 sail, we have 5,400 Low Dutch seamen in all; therefore, I say, we have precisely two barrels of beer per man, for a twelve weeks' allowance, exclusive of his fair proportion of that 550 ankers of gin. Now, whether these gin and beer harpooneers, so fuddled as one might fancy them to have been, were the right sort of men to stand up in a boat's head, and take good aim at flying whales; this would seem somewhat improbable. Yet they did aim at them, and hit them too. But this was very far North, be it remembered, where beer agrees well with the constitution; upon the Equator, in our southern fishery, beer would be apt to make the harpooneer sleepy at the mast-head and boozy in his boat; and grievous loss might ensue to Nantucket and New Bedford.

But no more; enough has been said to show that the old Dutch whalers of two or three centuries ago were high livers; and that the English whalers have not neglected so excellent an example. For, say they, when cruising in an empty ship, if you can get nothing better out of the world, get a good dinner out of it, at least. And this empties the decanter.

CHAPTER CII

A BOWER IN THE ARSACIDES

Hitherto, in descriptively treating of the Sperm Whale, I have chiefly dwelt upon the marvels of his outer aspect; or separately and in detail upon some few interior structural features. But to a large and thorough sweeping comprehension of him, it behoves me now to unbutton him still further, and untrussing the points of his hose, unbuckling his garters, and casting loose the hooks and the eyes of the joints of his innermost bones, set him before you in his ultimatum; that is to say, in his unconditional skeleton.

But how now, Ishmael? How is it, that you, a mere oarsman in the fishery, pretend to know aught about the subterranean parts of the whale? Did erudite Stubb, mounted upon your capstan, deliver lectures on the anatomy of the Cetacea; and by help of the windlass, hold up a specimen rib for exhibition? Explain thyself, Ishmael. Can you land a full-grown whale on your deck for examination, as a cook dishes a roast-pig? Surely not. A veritable witness have you hitherto been, Ishmael; but have a care how you seize the privilege of Jonah alone; the privilege of discoursing upon the joists and beams; the rafters, ridge-pole, sleepers, and under-pinnings, making up the frame-work of leviathan; and belike of the tallow-vats, dairy-rooms, butteries, and cheeseries in his bowels.

I confess, that since Jonah, few whalemen have penetrated very far beneath the skin of the adult whale; nevertheless, I have been blessed with an opportunity to dissect him in miniature. In a ship I belonged to, a small cub Sperm Whale was once bodily hoisted to the deck for his poke or bag, to make sheaths for the barbs of the harpoons, and for the heads of the lances. Think you I let that chance go, without using my boat-hatchet and jack-knife, and breaking the seal and reading all the contents of that young cub?

And as for my exact knowledge of the bones of the leviathan in their gigantic, full grown development, for that rare knowledge I am indebted to my late royal friend Tranquo, king of Tranque, one of the Arsacides. For being at Tranque, years ago, when attached to the trading-ship Dey of Algiers, I was invited to spend part of the Arsacidean holidays with the Lord of Tranque, at his retired palm villa at Pupella; a sea-side glen not very far distant from what our sailors called Bamboo-Town, his capital.

Among many other fine qualities, my royal friend Tranquo, being gifted with a devout love for all matters of barbaric vertù, had brought together in Pupella whatever rare things the more ingenious of his people could invent; chiefly carved woods of wonderful devices, chiselled shells, inlaid spears, costly paddles, aromatic canoes; and all these distributed among whatever natural wonders, the wonder-freighted, tribute-rendering waves had cast upon his shores.

Chief among these latter was a great Sperm Whale, which, after an unusually long raging gale, had been found dead and stranded, with his head against a cocoa-nut tree, whose plumage-like, tufted droopings seemed his verdant jet. When the vast body had at last been stripped of its fathom-deep enfoldings, and the bones become dust dry in the sun, then the skeleton was carefully transported up the Pupella glen, where a grand temple of lordly palms now sheltered it.

The ribs were hung with trophies; the vertebræ were carved with Arsacidean annals, in strange hieroglyphics; in the skull, the priests kept up an unextinguished aromatic flame, so that the mystic head again sent forth its vapory spout; while, suspended from a bough, the terrific lower jaw vibrated over all the devotees, like the hair-hung sword that so affrighted Damocles.

It was a wondrous sight. The wood was green as mosses of the Icy Glen; the trees stood high and haughty, feeling their living sap; the industrious earth beneath was as a weaver's loom, with a gorgeous carpet on it, whereof the ground-vine tendrils formed the warp and woof, and the living flowers the figures. All the trees, with all their laden branches; all the shrubs, and ferns, and grasses; the message-carrying air; all these unceasingly were active. Through the lacings of the leaves, the great sun seemed a flying shuttle weaving the unwearied verdure. Oh, busy weaver! unseen weaver!—pause!—one word!—whither flows the fabric? what palace may it deck? wherefore all these ceaseless toilings? Speak, weaver!—stay thy hand!—but one single word with thee! Nay—the shuttle flies—the figures float from forth the loom; the freshet-rushing carpet for ever slides away. The weaver-god, he weaves; and by that weaving is he deafened, that he hears no mortal voice; and by that humming, we, too, who look on the loom are deafened; and only when we escape it shall we hear the thousand voices that speak through it. For even so it is in all material factories. The spoken words that are inaudible among the flying spindles; those same words are plainly heard without the walls, bursting from the opened casements. Thereby have villanies been detected. Ah, mortal! then, be heedful; for so, in all this din of the great world's loom, thy subtlest thinkings may be overheard afar.

Now, amid the green, life-restless loom of that Arsacidean wood, the great, white, worshipped skeleton lay lounging—a gigantic idler! Yet, as the ever-woven verdant warp and woof intermixed and hummed around him, the mighty idler seemed the cunning weaver; himself all woven over with the vines; every month assuming greener, fresher verdure; but himself a skeleton. Life folded Death; Death trellised Life; the grim god wived with youthful Life, and begat him curly-headed glories.

Now, when with royal Tranquo I visited this wondrous whale, and saw the skull an altar, and the artificial smoke ascending from where the real jet had issued, I marvelled that the king should regard a chapel as an object of vertù. He laughed. But more I marvelled that the priests should swear that smoky jet of his was genuine. To and fro I paced before this skeleton—brushed the vines aside—broke through the ribs—and with a ball of Arsacidean twine, wandered, eddied long amid its many winding, shaded collonades and arbors. But soon my line was out; and following it back, I emerged from the opening where I entered. I saw no living thing within; naught was there but bones.

Cutting me a green measuring-rod, I once more dived within the skeleton. From their arrow-slit in the skull, the priests perceived me taking the altitude of the final rib. 'How now!' they shouted; 'Dar'st thou measure this our god! That's for us.' 'Aye, priests—well, how long do ye make him, then?' But hereupon a fierce contest rose among them, concerning feet and inches; they cracked each other's sconces with their yard-sticks—the great skull echoed—and seizing that lucky chance, I quickly concluded my own admeasurements.

These admeasurements I now propose to set before you. But first, be it recorded, that, in this matter, I am not free to utter any fancied measurement I please. Because there are skeleton authorities you can refer to, to test my accuracy. There is a Leviathanic Museum, they tell me, in Hull, England, one of the whaling ports of that country, where they have some fine specimens of fin-backs and other whales. Likewise, I have heard that in the museum of Manchester, in New Hampshire, they have what the proprietors call 'the only perfect specimen of a Greenland or River Whale in the United States.' Moreover, at a place in Yorkshire, England, Burton Constable by name, a certain Sir Clifford Constable has in his possession the skeleton of a Sperm Whale, but of moderate size, by no means of the full-grown magnitude of my friend King Tranquo's.

In both cases, the stranded whales to which these two skeletons belonged, were originally claimed by their proprietors upon similar grounds. King Tranquo seizing his because he wanted it; and Sir Clifford, because he was lord of the seignories of those parts. Sir Clifford's whale has been articulated throughout; so that, like a great chest of drawers, you can open and shut him, in all his bony cavities—spread out his ribs like a gigantic fan—and swing all day upon his lower jaw. Locks are to be put upon some of his trap-doors and shutters; and a footman will show round future visitors with a bunch of keys at his side. Sir Clifford thinks of charging twopence for a peep at the whispering gallery in the spinal column; threepence to hear the echo in the hollow of his cerebellum; and sixpence for the unrivalled view from his forehead.

The skeleton dimensions I shall now proceed to set down are copied verbatim from my right arm, where I had them tattooed; as in my wild wanderings at that period, there was no other secure way of preserving such valuable statistics. But as I was crowded for space, and wished the other parts of my body to remain a blank page for a poem I was then composing—at least, what untattooed parts might remain—I did not trouble myself with the odd inches; nor, indeed, should inches at all enter into a congenial admeasurement of the whale.

CHAPTER CIII

Measurement of the Whale's Skeleton

In the first place, I wish to lay before you a particular, plain statement, touching the living bulk of this leviathan, whose skeleton we are briefly to exhibit. Such a statement may prove useful here.

According to a careful calculation I have made, and which I partly base upon Captain Scoresby's estimate, of seventy tons for the largest sized Greenland whale of sixty feet in length; according to my careful calculation, I say, a Sperm Whale of the largest magnitude, between eighty-five and ninety feet in length, and something less than forty feet in its fullest circumference, such a whale will weigh at least ninety tons; so that, reckoning thirteen men to a ton, he would considerably outweigh the combined population of a whole village of one thousand one hundred inhabitants.

Think you not then that brains, like yoked cattle, should be put to this leviathan, to make him at all budge to any landsman's imagination?

Having already in various ways put before you his skull, spout-hole, jaw, teeth, tail, forehead, fins, and divers other parts, I shall now simply point out what is most interesting in the general bulk of his unobstructed bones. But as the colossal skull embraces so very large a proportion of the entire extent of the skeleton; as it is by far the most complicated part; and as nothing is to be repeated concerning it in this chapter, you must not fail to carry it in your mind, or under your arm, as we proceed, otherwise you will not gain a complete notion of the general structure we are about to view.

In length, the Sperm Whale's skeleton at Tranque measured seventy-two feet; so that when fully invested and extended in life, he must have been ninety feet long; for in the whale, the skeleton loses about one fifth in length compared with the living body. Of this seventy-two feet, his skull and jaw comprised some twenty feet, leaving some fifty feet of plain back-bone. Attached to this back-bone, for something less than a third of its length, was the mighty circular basket of ribs which once enclosed his vitals.

To me this vast ivory-ribbed chest, with the long, unrelieved spine, extending far away from it in a straight line, not a little resembled the embryo hull of a great ship new-laid upon the stocks, when only some twenty of her naked bow-ribs are inserted, and the keel is otherwise, for the time, but a long, disconnected timber.

The ribs were ten on a side. The first, to begin from the neck, was nearly six feet long; the second, third, and fourth were each successively longer, till you came to the climax of the fifth, or one of the middle ribs, which measured eight feet and some inches. From that part, the remaining ribs diminished, till the tenth and last only spanned five feet and some inches. In general thickness, they all bore a seemly correspondence to their length. The middle ribs were the most arched. In some of the Arsacides they are used for beams whereon to lay foot-path bridges over small streams.

In considering these ribs, I could not but be struck anew with the circumstance, so variously repeated in this book, that the skeleton of the whale is by no means the mould of his invested form. The largest of the Tranque ribs, one of the middle ones, occupied that part of the fish which, in life, is greatest in depth. Now, the greatest depth of the invested body of this particular whale must have been at least sixteen feet; whereas, the corresponding rib measured but little more than eight feet. So that this rib only conveyed half of the true notion of the living magnitude of that part. Besides, for some way, where I now saw but a naked spine, all that had been once wrapped round with tons of added bulk in flesh, muscle, blood, and bowels. Still more, for the ample fins, I here saw but a few disordered joints; and in place of the weighty and majestic, but boneless flukes, an utter blank!

How vain and foolish, then, thought I, for timid untravelled man to try to comprehend aright this wondrous whale, by merely poring over his dead attenuated skeleton, stretched in this peaceful wood. No. Only in the heart of quickest perils; only when within the eddyings of his angry flukes; only on the profound unbounded sea, can the fully invested whale be truly and livingly found out.

But the spine. For that, the best way we can consider it is, with a crane, to pile its bones high up on end. No speedy enterprise. But now it's done, it looks much like Pompey's Pillar.

There are forty and odd vertebræ in all, which in the skeleton are not locked together. They mostly lie like the great knobbed blocks on a Gothic spire, forming solid courses of heavy masonry. The largest, a middle one, is in width something less than three feet, and in depth more than four. The smallest, where the spine tapers away into the tail, is only two inches in width, and looks something like a white billiard-ball. I was told that there were still smaller ones, but they had been lost by some little cannibal urchins, the priest's children, who had stolen them to play marbles with. Thus we see how that the spine of even the hugest of living things tapers off at last into simple child's play.

CHAPTER CIV

THE FOSSIL WHALE

From his mighty bulk the whale affords a most congenial theme whereon to enlarge, amplify, and generally expatiate. Would you, you could not compress him. By good rights he should only be treated of in imperial folio. Not to tell over again his furlongs from spiracle to tail, and the yards he measures about the waist; only think of the gigantic involutions of his intestines, where they lie in him like great cables and hausers coiled away in the subterranean orlop-deck of a line-of-battle ship.

Since I have undertaken to manhandle this Leviathan, it behoves me to approve myself omnisciently exhaustive in the enterprise; not overlooking the minutest seminal germs of his blood, and spinning him out to the uttermost coil of his bowels. Having already described him in most of his present habitatory and anatomical peculiarities, it now remains to magnify him in an archæological, fossiliferous, and antediluvian point of view. Applied to any other creature than the Leviathan—to an ant or a flea—such portly terms might justly be deemed unwarrantably grandiloquent. But when Leviathan is the text, the case is altered. Fain am I to stagger to this emprise under the weightiest words of the dictionary. And here be it said, that whenever it has been convenient to consult one in the course of these dissertations, I have invariably used a huge quarto edition of Johnson, expressly purchased for that purpose; because that famous lexicographer's uncommon personal bulk more fitted him to compile a lexicon to be used by a whale author like me.

One often hears of writers that rise and swell with their subject, though it may seem but an ordinary one. How, then, with me, writing of this Leviathan? Unconsciously my chirography expands into placard capitals. Give me a condor's quill! Give me Vesuvius' crater for an inkstand! Friends, hold my arms! For in the mere act of penning my thoughts of this Leviathan, they weary me, and make me faint with their outreaching comprehensiveness of sweep, as if to include the whole circle of the sciences, and all the generations of whales, and men, and mastodons, past, present, and to come, with all the revolving panoramas of empire on earth, and throughout the whole universe, not excluding its suburbs. Such, and so magnifying, is the virtue of a large and liberal theme! We expand to its bulk. To produce a mighty book, you must choose a mighty theme. No great and enduring volume can ever be written on the flea, though many there be who have tried it.

Ere entering upon the subject of Fossil Whales, I present my credentials as a geologist, by stating that in my miscellaneous time I have been a stone-mason, and also a great digger of ditches, canals and wells, wine-vaults, cellars, and cisterns of all sorts. Likewise, by way of preliminary, I desire to remind the reader, that while in the earlier geological strata there are found the fossils of monsters now almost completely extinct; the subsequent relics discovered in what are called the Tertiary formations seem the connecting, or at any rate intercepted links, between the antechronical creatures, and those whose remote posterity are said to have entered the Ark; all the Fossil Whales hitherto discovered belong to the Tertiary period, which is the last preceding the superficial formations. And though none of them precisely answer to any known species of the present time, they are yet sufficiently akin to them in general respects, to justify their taking rank as Cetacean fossils.

Detached broken fossils of pre-adamite whales, fragments of their bones and skeletons, have within thirty years past, at various intervals, been found at the base of the Alps, in Lombardy, in France, in England, in Scotland, and in the States of Louisiana, Mississippi, and Alabama. Among the more curious of such remains is part of a skull, which in the year 1779 was disinterred in the Rue Dauphine in Paris, a short street opening almost directly upon the palace of the Tuileries; and bones disinterred in excavating the great docks of Antwerp, in Napoleon's time. Cuvier pronounced these fragments to have belonged to some utterly unknown Leviathanic species.

But by far the most wonderful of all cetacean relics was the almost complete vast skeleton of an extinct monster, found in the year 1842, on the plantation of Judge Creagh, in Alabama. The awe-stricken credulous slaves in the vicinity took it for the bones of one of the fallen angels. The Alabama doctors declared it a huge reptile, and bestowed upon it the name of Basilosaurus. But some specimen bones of it being taken across the sea to Owen, the English anatomist, it turned out that this alleged reptile was a whale, though of a departed species. A significant illustration of the fact, again and again repeated in this book, that the skeleton of the whale furnishes but little clue to the shape of his fully invested body. So Owen re-christened the monster Zeuglodon; and in his paper read before the London Geological Society, pronounced it, in substance, one of the most extraordinary creatures which the mutations of the globe have blotted out of existence.

When I stand among these mighty Leviathan skeletons, skulls, tusks, jaws, ribs, and vertebræ, all characterized by partial resemblances to the existing breeds of sea-monsters; but at the same time bearing on the other hand similar affinities to the annihilated ante-chronical Leviathans, their incalculable seniors; I am, by a flood, borne back to that wondrous period, ere time itself can be said to have begun; for time began with man. Here Saturn's grey chaos rolls over me, and I obtain dim, shuddering glimpses into those Polar eternities; when wedged bastions of ice pressed hard upon what are now the Tropics; and in all the 25,000 miles of this world's circumference, not an inhabitable hand's breadth of land was visible. Then the whole world was the whale's; and, king of creation, he left his wake along the present lines of the Andes and Himmalehs. Who can show a pedigree like Leviathan? Ahab's harpoon had shed older blood than the Pharaohs'. Methuselah seems a schoolboy. I look round to shake hands with Shem. I am horror-struck at this antemosaic, unsourced existence of the unspeakable terrors of the whale, which, having been before all time, must needs exist after all humane ages are over.

But not alone has this Leviathan left his pre-adamite traces in the stereotype plates of nature, and in limestone and marl bequeathed his ancient bust; but upon Egyptian tablets, whose antiquity seems to claim for them an almost fossiliferous character, we find the unmistakable print of his fin. In an apartment of the great temple of Denderah, some fifty years ago, there was discovered upon the granite ceiling a sculptured and painted planisphere, abounding in centaurs, griffins, and dolphins, similar to the grotesque figures on the celestial globe of the moderns. Gliding among them, old Leviathan swam as of yore; was there swimming in that planisphere, centuries before Solomon was cradled.

Nor must there be omitted another strange attestation of the antiquity of the whale, in his own osseous post-diluvian reality, as set down by the venerable John Leo, the old Barbary traveller.

'Not far from the Sea-side, they have a Temple, the Rafters and Beams of which are made of Whale-Bones; for Whales of a monstrous size are oftentimes cast up dead upon that shore. The Common People imagine, that by a secret Power bestowed by God upon the Temple, no Whale can pass it without immediate death. But the truth of the Matter is, that on either side of the Temple, there are Rocks that shoot two Miles into the Sea, and wound the Whales when they light upon 'em. They keep a Whale's Rib of an incredible length for a Miracle, which lying upon the Ground with its convex part uppermost, makes an Arch, the Head of which cannot be reached by a Man upon a Camel's Back. This Rib' (says John Leo) 'is said to have layn there a hundred Years before I saw it. Their Historians affirm, that a Prophet who prophesy'd of Mahomet, came from this Temple, and some do not stand to assert, that the Prophet Jonas was cast forth by the Whale at the Base of the Temple.'

In this Afric Temple of the Whale I leave you, reader, and if you be a Nantucketeer, and a whaleman, you will silently worship there.

CHAPTER CV

DOES THE WHALE'S MAGNITUDE DIMINISH?—WILL HE PERISH?

Inasmuch, then, as this Leviathan comes floundering down upon us from the head-waters of the Eternities, it may be fitly inquired, whether, in the long course of his generations, he has not degenerated from the original bulk of his sires.

But upon investigation we find, that not only are the whales of the present day superior in magnitude to those whose fossil remains are found in the Tertiary system (embracing a distinct geological period prior to man), but of the whales found in that Tertiary system, those belonging to its latter formations exceed in size those of its earlier ones.

Of all the pre-adamite whales yet exhumed, by far the largest is the Alabama one mentioned in the last chapter, and that was less than seventy feet in length in the skeleton. Whereas, we have already seen, that the tape-measure gives seventy-two feet for the skeleton of a large sized modern whale. And I have heard, on whalemen's authority, that Sperm Whales have been captured near a hundred feet long at the time of capture.

But may it not be, that while the whales of the present hour are an advance in magnitude upon those of all previous geological periods; may it not be, that since Adam's time they have degenerated?

Assuredly, we must conclude so, if we are to credit the accounts of such gentlemen as Pliny, and the ancient naturalists generally. For Pliny tells us of whales that embraced acres of living bulk, and Aldrovandus of others which measured eight hundred feet in length—Rope Walks and Thames Tunnels of Whales! And even in the days of Banks and Solander, Cooke's naturalists, we find a Danish member of the Academy of Sciences setting down certain Iceland Whales (reydan-siskur, or Wrinkled Bellies) at one hundred and twenty yards; that is, three hundred and sixty feet. And Lacépède, the French naturalist, in his elaborate history of whales, in the very beginning of his work (page 3), sets down the Right Whale at one hundred metres, three hundred and twenty-eight feet. And this work was published so late as A.D. 1825.

But will any whaleman believe these stories? No. The whale of to-day is as big as his ancestors in Pliny's time. And if ever I go where Pliny is, I, a whaleman (more than he was), will make bold to tell him so. Because I cannot understand how it is, that while the Egyptian mummies that were buried thousands of years before even Pliny was born, do not measure so much in their coffins as a modern Kentuckian in his socks; and while the cattle and other animals sculptured on the oldest Egyptian and Nineveh tablets, by the relative proportions in which they are drawn, just as plainly prove that the high-bred, stall-fed, prize cattle of Smithfield, not only equal, but far exceed in magnitude the fattest of Pharaoh's fat kine; in the face of all this, I will not admit that of all animals the whale alone should have degenerated.

But still another inquiry remains; one often agitated by the more recondite Nantucketers. Whether owing to the almost omniscient look-outs at the mast-heads of the whale-ships, now penetrating even through Behring's straits, and into the remotest secret drawers and lockers of the world; and the thousand harpoons and lances darted along all continental coasts; the moot point is, whether Leviathan can long endure so wide a chase, and so remorseless a havoc; whether he must not at last be exterminated from the waters, and the last whale, like the last man, smoke his last pipe, and then himself evaporate in the final puff.

Comparing the humped herds of whales with the humped herds of buffalo, which, not forty years ago, overspread by tens of thousands the prairies of Illinois and Missouri, and shook their iron manes and scowled with their thunder-clotted brows upon the sites of populous river capitals, where now the polite broker sells you land at a dollar an inch; in such a comparison an irresistible argument would seem furnished, to show that the hunted whale cannot now escape speedy extinction.

But you must look at this matter in every light. Though so short a period ago—not a good life-time—the census of the buffalo in Illinois exceeded the census of men now in London, and though at the present day not one horn or hoof of them remains in all that region; and though the cause of this wondrous extermination was the spear of man; yet the far different nature of the whale-hunt peremptorily forbids so inglorious an end to the Leviathan. Forty men in one ship hunting the Sperm Whale for forty-eight months think they have done extremely well, and thank God, if at last they carry home the oil of forty fish. Whereas, in the days of the old Canadian and Indian hunters and trappers of the West, when the far west (in whose sunset suns still rise) was a wilderness and a virgin, the same number of moccasined men, for the same number of months, mounted on horse instead of sailing in ships, would have slain not forty, but forty thousand and more buffaloes; a fact that, if need were, could be statistically stated.

Nor, considered aright, does it seem any argument in favor of the gradual extinction of the Sperm Whale, for example, that in former years (the latter part of the last century, say) these Leviathans, in small pods, were encountered much oftener than at present, and, in consequence, the voyages were not so prolonged, and were also much more remunerative. Because, as has been elsewhere noticed, those whales, influenced by some views to safety, now swim the seas in immense caravans, so that to a large degree the scattered solitaries, yokes, and pods, and schools of other days are now aggregated into vast but widely separated, unfrequent armies. That is all. And equally fallacious seems the conceit, that because the so-called whale-bone whales no longer haunt many grounds in former years abounding with them, hence that species also is declining. For they are only being driven from promontory to cape; and if one coast is no longer enlivened with their jets, then, be sure, some other and remoter strand has been very recently startled by the unfamiliar spectacle.

Furthermore: concerning these last mentioned Leviathans, they have two firm fortresses, which, in all human probability, will for ever remain impregnable. And as upon the invasion of their valleys, the frosty Swiss have retreated to their mountains; so, hunted from the savannas and glades of the middle seas, the whale-bone whales can at last resort to their Polar citadels, and diving under the ultimate glassy barriers and walls there, come up among icy fields and floes; and in a charmed circle of everlasting December, bid defiance to all pursuit from man.

But as perhaps fifty of these whale-bone whales are harpooned for one cachalot, some philosophers of the forecastle have concluded that this positive havoc has already very seriously diminished their battalions. But though for some time past a number of these whales, not less than 13,000, have been annually slain on the nor' west coast by the Americans alone; yet there are considerations which render even this circumstance of little or no account as an opposing argument in this matter.

Natural as it is to be somewhat incredulous concerning the populousness of the more enormous creatures of the globe, yet what shall we say to Harto, the historian of Goa, when he tells us that at one hunting the King of Siam took 4000 elephants; that in those regions elephants are numerous as droves of cattle in the temperate climes. And there seems no reason to doubt that if these elephants, which have now been hunted for thousands of years, by Semiramis, by Purus, by Hannibal, and by all the successive monarchs of the East—if they still survive there in great numbers, much more may the great whale outlast all hunting, since he has a pasture to expatiate in, which is precisely twice as large as all Asia, both Americas, Europe and Africa, New Holland, and all the Isles of the sea combined.

Moreover: we are to consider, that from the presumed great longevity of whales, their probably attaining the age of a century and more, therefore at any one period of time, several distinct adult generations must be contemporary. And what that is, we may soon gain some idea of, by imagining all the grave-yards, cemeteries, and family vaults of creation yielding up the live bodies of all the men, women, and children who were alive seventy-five years ago; and adding this countless host to the present human population of the globe.

Wherefore, for all these things, we account the whale immortal in his species, however perishable in his individuality. He swam the seas before the continents broke water; he once swam over the site of the Tuileries, and Windsor Castle, and the Kremlin. In Noah's flood he despised Noah's Ark; and if ever the world is to be again flooded, like the Netherlands, to kill off its rats, then the eternal whale will still survive, and rearing upon the topmost crest of the equatorial flood, spout his frothed defiance to the skies.

CHAPTER CVI

AHAB'S LEG

The precipitating manner in which Captain Ahab had quitted the Samuel Enderby of London, had not been unattended with some small violence to his own person. He had lighted with such energy upon a thwart of his boat that his ivory leg had received a half-splintering shock. And when after gaining his own deck, and his own pivot-hole there, he so vehemently wheeled round with an urgent command to the steersman (it was, as ever, something about his not steering inflexibly enough); then, the already shaken ivory received such an additional twist and wrench, that though it still remained entire, and to all appearances lusty, yet Ahab did not deem it entirely trustworthy.

And, indeed, it seemed small matter for wonder, that for all his pervading, mad recklessness, Ahab did at times give careful heed to the condition of that dead bone upon which he partly stood. For it had not been very long prior to the Pequod's sailing from Nantucket, that he had been found one night lying prone upon the ground, and insensible; by some unknown, and seemingly inexplicable, unimaginable casualty, his ivory limb having been so violently displaced, that it had stake-wise smitten, and all but pierced his groin; nor was it without extreme difficulty that the agonizing wound was entirely cured.

Nor, at the time, had it failed to enter his monomaniac mind, that all the anguish of that then present suffering was but the direct issue of a former woe; and he too plainly seemed to see, that as the most poisonous reptile of the marsh perpetuates his kind as inevitably as the sweetest songster of the grove; so, equally with every felicity, all miserable events do naturally beget their like. Yea, more than equally, thought Ahab; since both the ancestry and posterity of Grief go further than the ancestry and posterity of Joy. For, not to hint of this: that it is an inference from certain canonic teachings, that while some natural enjoyments here shall have no children born to them for the other world, but, on the contrary, shall be followed by the joy-childlessness of all hell's despair; whereas, some guilty mortal miseries shall still fertilely beget to themselves an eternally progressive progeny of griefs beyond the grave; not at all to hint of this, there still seems an inequality in the deeper analysis of the thing. For, thought Ahab, while even the highest earthly felicities ever have a certain unsignifying pettiness lurking in them, but, at bottom, all heart-woes, a mystic significance, and, in some men, an archangelic grandeur; so do their diligent tracings-out not belie the obvious deduction. To trail the genealogies of these high mortal miseries, carries us at last among the sourceless primogenitures of the gods; so that, in the face of all the glad, haymaking suns, and soft-cymballing, round harvest-moons, we must needs give in to this: that the gods themselves are not for ever glad. The ineffaceable, sad birthmark in the brow of man, is but the stamp of sorrow in the signers.

Unwittingly here a secret has been divulged, which perhaps might more properly, in set way, have been disclosed before. With many other particulars concerning Ahab, always had it remained a mystery to some, why it was, that for a certain period, both before and after the sailing of the Pequod, he had hidden himself away with such Grand-Lama-like exclusiveness; and, for that one interval, sought speechless refuge, as it were, among the marble senate of the dead. Captain Peleg's bruited reason for this thing appeared by no means adequate; though, indeed, as touching all Ahab's deeper part, every revelation partook more of significant darkness than of explanatory light. But, in the end, it all came out; this one matter did, at least. That direful mishap was at the bottom of his temporary recluseness. And not only this, but to that ever-contracting, dropping circle ashore, who, for any reason, possessed the privilege of a less banned approach to him; to that timid circle the above hinted casualty—remaining, as it did, moodily unaccounted for by Ahab—invested itself with terrors, not entirely underived from the land of spirits and of wails. So that, through their zeal for him, they had all conspired, so far as in them lay, to muffle up the knowledge of this thing from others; and hence it was, that not till a considerable interval had elapsed, did it transpire upon the Pequod's decks.

But be all this as it may; let the unseen, ambiguous synod in the air, or the vindictive princes and potentates of fire, have to do or not with earthly Ahab, yet, in this present matter of his leg, he took plain practical procedures;—he called the carpenter.

And when that functionary appeared before him, he bade him without delay set about making a new leg, and directed the mates to see him supplied with all the studs and joists of jaw-ivory (Sperm Whale) which had thus far been accumulated on the voyage, in order that a careful selection of the stoutest, clearest-grained stuff might be secured. This done, the carpenter received orders to have the leg completed that night; and to provide all the fittings for it, independent of those pertaining to the distrusted one in use. Moreover, the ship's forge was ordered to be hoisted out of its temporary idleness in the hold; and, to accelerate the affair, the blacksmith was commanded to proceed at once to the forging of whatever iron contrivances might be needed.

CHAPTER CVII

The Carpenter

Seat thyself sultanically among the moons of Saturn, and take high abstracted man alone; and he seems a wonder, a grandeur, and a woe. But from the same point, take mankind in mass, and for the most part, they seem a mob of unnecessary duplicates, both contemporary and hereditary. But most humble though he was, and far from furnishing an example of the high, humane abstraction; the Pequod's carpenter was no duplicate; hence, he now comes in person on this stage.

Like all sea-going ship carpenters, and more especially those belonging to whaling vessels, he was, to a certain off-handed, practical extent, alike experienced in numerous trades and callings collateral to his own; the carpenter's pursuit being the ancient and outbranching trunk of all those numerous handicrafts which more or less have to do with wood as an auxiliary material. But, besides the application to him of the generic remark above, this carpenter of the Pequod was singularly efficient in those thousand nameless mechanical emergencies continually recurring in a large ship, upon a three or four years' voyage, in uncivilized and far-distant seas. For not to speak of his readiness in ordinary duties:—repairing stove boats, sprung spars, reforming the shape of clumsy-bladed oars, inserting bull's eyes in the deck, or new tree-nails in the side planks, and other miscellaneous matters more directly pertaining to his special business; he was moreover unhesitatingly expert in all manner of conflicting aptitudes, both useful and capricious.

The one grand stage where he enacted all his various parts so manifold, was his vice-bench; a long rude ponderous table furnished with several vices, of different sizes, and both of iron and of wood. At all times except when whales were alongside, this bench was securely lashed athwartships against the rear of the Try-works.

A belaying pin is found too large to be easily inserted into its hole: the carpenter claps it into one of his ever-ready vices, and straightway files it smaller. A lost land-bird of strange plumage strays on board, and is made a captive: out of clean shaved rods of right-whale bone, and cross-beams of sperm whale ivory, the carpenter makes a pagoda-looking cage for it. An oarsman sprains his wrist: the carpenter concocts a soothing lotion. Stubb longs for vermillion stars to be painted upon the blade of his every oar: screwing each oar in his big vice of wood, the carpenter symmetrically supplies the constellation. A sailor takes a fancy to wear shark-bone ear-rings: the carpenter drills his ears. Another has the toothache: the carpenter out pincers, and clapping one hand upon his bench bids him be seated there; but the poor fellow unmanageably winces under the unconcluded operation; whirling round the handle of his wooden vice, the carpenter signs him to clap his jaw in that, if he would have him draw the tooth.

Thus, this carpenter was prepared at all points, and alike indifferent and without respect in all. Teeth he accounted bits of ivory; heads he deemed but top-blocks; men themselves he lightly held for capstans. But while now upon so wide a field thus variously accomplished, and with such liveliness of expertness in him, too; all this would seem to argue some uncommon vivacity of intelligence. But not precisely so. For nothing was this man more remarkable, than for a certain impersonal stolidity as it were; impersonal, I say; for it so shaded off into the surrounding infinite of things, that it seemed one with the general stolidity discernible in the whole visible world; which while pauselessly active in uncounted modes, still eternally holds its peace, and ignores you, though you dig foundations for cathedrals. Yet was this half-horrible stolidity in him, involving, too, as it appeared, an all-ramifying heartlessness;—yet was it oddly dashed at times, with an old, crutch-like, antediluvian, wheezing humorousness, not unstreaked now and then with a certain grizzled wittiness; such as might have served to pass the time during the midnight watch on the bearded forecastle of Noah's ark. Was it that this old carpenter had been a life-long wanderer, whose much rolling, to and fro, not only had gathered no moss; but what is more, had rubbed off whatever small outward clingings might have originally pertained to him? He was a stript abstract; an unfractioned integral; uncompromised as a new-born babe; living without premeditated reference to this world or the next. You might almost say, that this strange uncompromisedness of him involved a sort of unintelligence; for in his numerous trades, he did not seem to work so much by reason or by instinct, or simply because he had been tutored to it, or by any intermixture of all these, even or uneven; but merely by a kind of deaf and dumb, spontaneous literal process. He was a pure manipulator; his brain, if he had ever had one, must have early oozed along into the muscles of his fingers. He was like one of those unreasoning but still highly useful, *multum in parvo,* Sheffield contrivances, assuming the exterior—though a little swelled—of a common pocket knife; but containing, not only blades of various sizes, but also screw-drivers, cork-screws, tweezers, awls, pens, rulers, nail-filers, countersinkers. So, if his superiors wanted to use the carpenter for a screw-driver, all they had to do was to open that part of him, and the screw was fast: or if for tweezers, take him up by the legs, and there they were.

Yet, as previously hinted, this omnitooled, open-and-shut carpenter, was, after all, no mere machine of an automaton. If he did not have a common soul in him, he had a subtle something that somehow anomalously did its duty. What that was, whether essence of quicksilver, or a few drops of hartshorn, there is no telling. But there it was; and there it had abided for now some sixty years or more. And this it was, this same unaccountable, cunning life-principle in him; this it was, that kept him a great part of the time soliloquizing; but only like an unreasoning wheel, which also hummingly soliloquizes; or rather, his body was a sentry-box and this soliloquizer on guard there, and talking all the time to keep himself awake.

CHAPTER CVIII

AHAB AND THE CARPENTER

THE DECK—FIRST NIGHT WATCH

(Carpenter standing before his vice-bench, and by the light of two lanterns busily filing the ivory joist for the leg, which joist is firmly fixed in the vice. Slabs of ivory, leather straps, pads, screws, and various tools of all sorts lying about the bench. Forward, the red flame of the forge is seen, where the blacksmith is at work.)

Drat the file, and drat the bone! That is hard which should be soft, and that is soft which should be hard. So we go, who file old jaws and shinbones. Let's try another. Aye, now, this works better (*sneezes*). Halloa, this bone dust is (*sneezes*)—why it's (*sneezes*)—yes it's (*sneezes*)—bless my soul, it won't let me speak! This is what an old fellow gets now for working in dead lumber. Saw a live tree, and you don't get this dust; amputate a live bone, and you don't get it (*sneezes*). Come, come, you old Smut, there, bear a hand, and let's have that ferule and buckle-screw; I'll be ready for them presently. Lucky now (*sneezes*) there's no knee-joint to make; that might puzzle a little; but a mere shin-bone—why it's easy as making hop-poles; only I should like to put a good finish on. Time, time; if I but only had the time, I could turn him out as neat a leg now as ever (*sneezes*) scraped to a lady in a parlor. Those buckskin legs and calves of legs I've seen in shop windows wouldn't compare at all. They soak water, they do; and of course get rheumatic, and have to be doctored (*sneezes*) with washes and lotions, just like live legs. There; before I saw it off, now, I must call his old Mogulship, and see whether the length will be all right; too short, if anything, I guess. Ha! that's the heel; we are in luck; here he comes, or it's somebody else, that's certain.

AHAB (*advancing*).

(*During the ensuing scene, the carpenter continues sneezing at times.*)

Well, manmaker!

Just in time, sir. If the captain pleases, I will now mark the length. Let me measure, sir.

Measured for a leg! good. Well, it's not the first time. About it! There; keep thy finger on it. This is a cogent vice thou hast here, carpenter; let me feel its grip once. So, so; it does pinch some.

Oh, sir, it will break bones—beware, beware!

No fear; I like a good grip; I like to feel something in this slippery world that can hold, man. What's Prometheus about there?—the blacksmith, I mean—what's he about?

He must be forging the buckle-screw, sir, now.

Right. It's a partnership; he supplies the muscle part. He makes a fierce red flame there!

Aye, sir; he must have the white heat for this kind of fine work.

Um-m. So he must. I do deem it now a most meaning thing, that that old Greek, Prometheus, who made men, they say, should have been a blacksmith, and animated them with fire; for what's made in fire must properly belong to fire; and so hell's probable. How the soot flies! This must be the remainder the Greek made the Africans of. Carpenter, when he's through with that buckle, tell him to forge a pair of steel shoulder-blades; there's a pedlar aboard with a crushing pack.

Sir?

Hold; while Prometheus is about it, I'll order a complete man after a desirable pattern. Imprimis, fifty feet high in his socks; then, chest modelled after the Thames Tunnel; then, legs with roots to 'em, to stay in one place; then, arms three feet through the wrist; no heart at all, brass forehead, and about a quarter of an acre of fine brains; and let me see—shall I order eyes to see outwards? No, but put a sky-light on top of his head to illuminate inwards. There, take the order, and away.

Now, what's he speaking about, and who's he speaking to, I should like to know? Shall I keep standing here? (*aside*).

'Tis but indifferent architecture to make a blind dome; here's one. No, no, no; I must have a lantern.

Ho, ho! That's it, hey? Here are two, sir; one will serve my turn.

What art thou thrusting that thief-catcher into my face for, man? Thrusted light is worse than presented pistols.

I thought, sir, that you spoke to carpenter.

Carpenter? why that's—but no;—a very tidy, and, I may say, an extremely gentlemanlike sort of business thou art in here, carpenter;—or would'st thou rather work in clay?

Sir?—Clay? clay, sir? That's mud; we leave clay to ditchers, sir.

The fellow's impious! What art thou sneezing about?

Bone is rather dusty, sir.

Take the hint, then; and when thou art dead, never bury thyself under living people's noses.

Sir?—oh! ah!—I guess so;—yes—oh, dear!

Look ye, carpenter, I dare say thou callest thyself a right good workmanlike workman, eh? Well, then, will it speak thoroughly well for thy work, if, when I come to mount this leg thou makest, I shall nevertheless feel another leg in the same identical place with it; that is, carpenter, my old lost leg; the flesh and blood one, I mean. Canst thou not drive that old Adam away?

Truly, sir. I begin to understand somewhat now. Yes, I have heard something curious on that score, sir; how that a dismasted man never entirely loses the feeling of his old spar, but it will be still pricking him at times. May I humbly ask if it be really so, sir?

It is, man. Look, put thy live leg here in the place where mine once was; so, now, here is only one distinct leg to the eye, yet two to the soul. Where thou feelest tingling life; there, exactly there, there to a hair, do I. Is't a riddle?

I should humbly call it a poser, sir.

Hist, then. How dost thou know that some entire, living, thinking thing may not be invisibly and uninterpenetratingly standing precisely where thou now standest; aye, and standing there in thy spite? In thy most solitary hours, then, dost thou not fear eavesdroppers? Hold, don't speak! And if I still feel the smart of my crushed leg, though it be now so long dissolved; then, why mayst not thou, carpenter, feel the fiery pains of hell for ever, and without a body? Hah

Good Lord! Truly, sir, if it comes to that, I must calculate over again; I think I didn't carry a small figure, sir.

Look ye, pudding-heads should never grant premises.—How long before the leg is done?

Perhaps an hour, sir.

Bungle away at it then, and bring it to me (*turns to go*). Oh, Life! Here I am, proud as Greek god, and yet standing debtor to this blockhead for a bone to stand on! Cursed be that mortal inter-indebtedness which will not do away with ledgers. I would be free as air; and I'm down in the whole world's books. I am so rich, I could have given bid for bid with the wealthiest Prætorians at the auction of the Roman empire (which was the world's); and yet I owe for the flesh in the tongue I brag with. By heavens! I'll get a crucible, and into it, and dissolve myself down to one small, compendious vertebra. So.

CARPENTER (*resuming his work*).

Well, well, well! Stubb knows him best of all, and Stubb always says he's queer; says nothing but that one sufficient little word queer; he's queer, says Stubb; he's queer—queer, queer; and keeps dinning it into Mr Starbuck all the time—queer, sir—queer, queer, very queer. And here's his leg! Yes, now that I think of it, here's his bedfellow! has a stick of whale's jaw-bone for a wife! And this is his leg; he'll stand on this. What was that now about one leg standing in three places, and all three places standing in one hell—how was that? Oh! I don't wonder he looked so scornful at me! I'm a sort of strange-thoughted sometimes, they say; but that's only haphazard-like. Then, a short, little old body like me, should never undertake to wade out into deep waters with tall, heron-built captains; the water chucks you under the chin pretty quick, and there's a great cry for life-boats. And here's the heron's leg! long and slim, sure enough! Now, for most folks one pair of legs lasts a lifetime, and that must be because they use them mercifully, as a tender-hearted old lady uses her roly-poly old coach-horses. But Ahab; oh he's a hard driver. Look, driven one leg to death, and spavined the other for life, and now wears out bone legs by the cord. Halloa, there, you Smut! bear a hand there with those screws, and let's finish it before the resurrection fellow comes a-calling with his horn for all legs, true or false, as brewery-men go round collecting old beer barrels, to fill 'em up again. What a leg this is! It looks like a real live leg, filed down to nothing but the core; he'll be standing on this to-morrow; he'll be taking altitudes on it. Halloa! I almost forgot the little oval slate, smoothed ivory, where he figures up the latitude. So, so; chisel, file, and sandpaper, now!

CHAPTER CIX

AHAB AND STARBUCK IN THE CABIN

According to usage they were pumping the ship next morning; and lo! no inconsiderable oil came up with the water; the casks below must have sprung a bad leak. Much concern was shown; and Starbuck went down into the cabin to report this unfavorable affair.*

Now, from the South and West the Pequod was drawing nigh to Formosa and the Bashee Isles between which lies one of the tropical outlets from the China waters into the Pacific. And so Starbuck found Ahab with a general chart of the

*In Sperm-whalemen with any considerable quantity of oil on board, it is a regular semi-weekly duty to conduct a hose into the hold, and drench the casks with sea-water; which afterwards, at varying intervals, is removed by the ship's pumps. Hereby the casks are sought to be kept damply tight; while by the changed character of the withdrawn water, the mariners readily detect any serious leakage in the precious cargo.

oriental archipelagoes spread before him; and another separate one representing the long eastern coasts of the Japanese islands—Niphon, Matsmai, and Sikoke. With his snow-white new ivory leg braced against the screwed leg of his table, and with a long pruning-hook of a jack-knife in his hand, the wondrous old man, with his back to the gangway door, was wrinkling his brow, and tracing his old courses again.

'Who's there!' hearing the footstep at the door, but not turning round to it. 'On deck! Begone!'

'Captain Ahab mistakes; it is I. The oil in the hold is leaking, sir. We must up Burtons and break out.'

'Up Burtons and break out? Now that we are nearing Japan; heave-to here for a week to tinker a parcel of old hoops?'

'Either do that, sir, or waste in one day more oil than we may make good in a year. What we come twenty thousand miles to get is worth saving, sir.'

'So it is, so it is; if we get it.'

'I was speaking of the oil in the hold, sir.'

'And I was not speaking or thinking of that at all. Begone! Let it leak! I'm all aleak myself. Aye! leaks in leaks! not only full of leaky casks, but those leaky casks are in a leaky ship; and that's a far worse plight than the Pequod's, man. Yet I don't stop to plug my leak; for who can find it in the deep-loaded hull; or how hope to plug it, even if found, in this life's howling gale? Starbuck! I'll not have the Burtons hoisted.'

'What will the owners say, sir?'

'Let the owners stand on Nantucket beach and outyell the Typhoons. What cares Ahab? Owners, owners? Thou art always prating to me, Starbuck, about those miserly owners, as if the owners were my conscience. But look ye, the only real owner of anything is its commander; and hark ye, my conscience is in this ship's keel.—On deck!'

'Captain Ahab,' said the reddening mate, moving further into the cabin, with a daring so strangely respectful and cautious that it almost seemed not only every way seeking to avoid the slightest outward manifestation of itself, but within also seemed more than half distrustful of itself; 'A better man than I might well pass over in thee what he would quickly enough resent in a younger man; aye, and in a happier, Captain Ahab.'

'Devils! Dost thou then so much as dare to critically think of me?—On deck!'

'Nay, sir, not yet; I do entreat. And I do dare, sir—to be forbearing! Shall we not understand each other better than hitherto, Captain Ahab?'

Ahab seized a loaded musket from the rack (forming part of most South-Seamen's cabin furniture), and pointing it towards Starbuck, exclaimed: 'There is one God that is Lord over the earth, and one Captain that is lord over the Pequod.—On deck!'

For an instant in the flashing eyes of the mate, and his fiery cheeks, you would have almost thought that he had really received the blaze of the levelled tube. But, mastering his emotion, he half calmly rose, and as he quitted the cabin, paused for an instant and said: 'Thou hast outraged, not insulted me, sir; but for that I ask thee not to beware of Starbuck; thou wouldst but laugh; but let Ahab beware of Ahab; beware of thyself, old man.'

'He waxes brave, but nevertheless obeys; most careful bravery that!' murmured Ahab, as Starbuck disappeared. 'What's that he said—Ahab beware of Ahab—there's something there!' Then unconsciously using the musket for a staff, with an iron brow he paced to and fro in the little cabin; but presently the thick plaits of his forehead relaxed, and returning the gun to the rack, he went to the deck.

'Thou art but too good a fellow, Starbuck,' he said lowly to the mate; then raising his voice to the crew: 'Furl the t'gallant-sails and close-reef the top-sails, fore and aft; back the main-yard; up Burtons, and break out in the main-hold.'

It were perhaps vain to surmise exactly why it was, that as respecting Starbuck, Ahab thus acted. It may have been a flash of honesty in him; or mere prudential policy which, under the circumstance, imperiously forbade the slightest symptom of open disaffection, however transient, in the important chief officer of his ship. However it was, his orders were executed; and the Burtons were hoisted.

CHAPTER CX

QUEEQUEG IN HIS COFFIN

Upon searching, it was found that the casks last struck into the hold were perfectly sound, and that the leak must be further off. So, it being calm weather, they broke out deeper and deeper, disturbing the slumbers of the huge ground-tier butts; and from that black midnight sending those gigantic moles into the daylight above. So deep did they go; and so ancient, and corroded, and weedy the aspect of the lowermost puncheons, that you almost looked next for some mouldy corner-stone cask containing coins of Captain Noah, with copies of the posted placards, vainly warning the infatuated old world from the flood. Tierce after tierce, too, of water, and bread, and beef, and shooks of staves, and iron bundles of hoops, were hoisted out, till at last the piled decks were hard to get about; and the hollow hull echoed under foot, as if you were treading over empty catacombs, and reeled and rolled in the sea like an air-freighted demijohn. Top-heavy was the ship as a dinnerless student with all Aristotle in his head. Well was it that the Typhoons did not visit them then.

Now, at this time it was that my poor pagan companion, and fast bosom-friend, Queequeg, was seized with a fever, which brought him nigh to his endless end.

Be it said, that in this vocation of whaling, sinecures are unknown; dignity and danger go hand in hand; till you get to be Captain, the higher you rise the harder you toil. So with poor Queequeg, who, as harpooneer, must not only face all the rage of the living whale, but—as we have elsewhere seen—mount his dead back in a rolling sea; and finally descend into the gloom of the hold, and bitterly sweating all day in that subterraneous confinement, resolutely manhandle the clumsiest casks and see to their stowage. To be short, among whalemen, the harpooneers are the holders, so called.

Poor Queequeg! when the ship was about half disembowelled, you should have stooped over the hatchway, and peered down upon him there; where, stripped to his woollen drawers, the tattooed savage was crawling about amid that dampness and slime, like a green spotted lizard at the bottom of a well. And a well, or an ice-house, it somehow proved to him, poor pagan; where, strange to say, for all the heat of his sweatings, he caught a terrible chill which lapsed into a fever; and at last, after some days' suffering, laid him in his hammock, close to the very sill of the door of death. How he wasted and wasted away in those few long-lingering days, till there seemed but little left of him but his frame and tattooing. But as all else in him thinned, and his cheek-bones grew sharper, his eyes, nevertheless, seemed growing fuller and fuller; they became of a strange softness of lustre; and mildly but deeply looked out at you there from his sickness, a wondrous testimony to that immortal health in him which could not die, or be weakened. And like circles on the water, which, as they grow fainter, expand; so his eyes seemed rounding and rounding, like the rings of Eternity. An awe that cannot be named would steal over you as you sat by the side of this waning savage, and saw as strange things in his face, as any beheld who were bystanders when Zoroaster died. For whatever is truly wondrous and fearful in man, never yet was put into words or books. And the drawing near of Death, which alike levels all, alike impresses all with a last revelation, which only an author from the dead could adequately tell. So that—let us say it again—no dying Chaldee or Greek had higher and holier thoughts than those, whose mysterious shades you saw creeping over the face of poor Queequeg, as he quietly lay in his swaying hammock, and the rolling sea seemed gently rocking him to his final rest, and the ocean's invisible flood-tide lifted him higher and higher towards his destined heaven.

Not a man of the crew but gave him up; and, as for Queequeg himself, what he thought of his case was forcibly shown by a curious favor he asked. He called one to him in the grey morning watch, when the day was just breaking, and taking his hand, said that while in Nantucket he had chanced to see certain little canoes of dark wood, like the rich war-wood of his native isle; and upon inquiry, he had learned that all whalemen who died in Nantucket, were laid in those same dark canoes, and that the fancy of being so laid had much pleased him; for it was not unlike the custom of his own race, who, after embalming a dead warrior, stretched him out in his canoe, and so left him to be floated away to the starry archipelagoes; for not only do they believe that the stars are isles, but that far beyond all visible horizons, their own, mild, uncontinented seas, interflow with the blue heavens; and so form the white breakers of the milky way. He added, that he shuddered at the thought of being buried in his hammock, according to the usual sea-custom, tossed like something vile to the death-devouring sharks. No: he desired a canoe like those of Nantucket, all the more congenial to him, being a whaleman, that like a whale-boat these coffin-canoes were without a keel; though that involved but uncertain steering, and much lee-way adown the dim ages.

Now, when this strange circumstance was made known aft, the carpenter was at once commanded to do Queequeg's bidding, whatever it might include. There was some heathenish, coffin-colored old lumber aboard, which, upon a long previous voyage, had been cut from the aboriginal groves of the Lackaday islands, and from these dark planks the coffin was recommended to be made. No sooner was the carpenter apprised of the order, than taking his rule, he forthwith with all the indifferent promptitude of his character, proceeded into the forecastle and took Queequeg's measure with great accuracy, regularly chalking Queequeg's person as he shifted the rule.

'Ah! poor fellow! he'll have to die now,' ejaculated the Long Island sailor.

Going to his vice-bench, the carpenter for convenience' sake and general reference, now transferringly measured on it the exact length the coffin was to be, and then made the transfer permanent by cutting two notches at its extremities. This done, he marshalled the planks and his tools, and to work.

When the last nail was driven, and the lid duly planed and fitted, he lightly shouldered the coffin and went forward with it, inquiring whether they were ready for it yet in that direction.

Overhearing the indignant but half-humorous cries with which the people on deck began to drive the coffin away, Queequeg, to every one's consternation, commanded that the thing should be instantly brought to him, nor was there any denying him; seeing that, of all mortals, some dying men are the most tyrannical; and certainly, since they will shortly trouble us so little for evermore, the poor fellows ought to be indulged.

Leaning over in his hammock, Queequeg long regarded the coffin with an attentive eye. He then called for his harpoon, had the wooden stock drawn from it, and then had the iron part placed in the coffin along with one of the paddles of his boat. All by his own request, also, biscuits were then ranged round the sides within: a flask of fresh water was placed at the head, and a small bag of woody earth scraped up in the hold at the foot; and a piece of sailcloth being rolled up for a pillow, Queequeg now entreated to be lifted into his final bed, that he might make trial of its comforts, if any it had. He lay without moving a few minutes, then told one to go to his bag and bring out his little god, Yojo. Then crossing his arms on his breast with Yojo between, he called for the coffin lid (hatch he called it) to be placed over him. The head part turned over with a leather hinge, and there lay Queequeg in his coffin with little but his composed countenance in view. 'Rarmai' (it will do; it is easy), he murmured at last, and signed to be replaced in his hammock.

But ere this was done, Pip, who had been slily hovering near by all this while, drew nigh to him where he lay, and with soft sobbings, took him by the hand; in the other, holding his tambourine.

'Poor rover! will ye never have done with all this weary roving? where go ye now? But if the currents carry ye to those sweet Antilles where the beaches are only beat with water-lilies, will ye do one little errand for me? Seek out one Pip, who's now been missing long: I think he's in those far Antilles. If ye find him, then comfort him; for he must be very sad; for look! he's left his tambourine behind;—I found it. Rig-a-dig, dig, dig! Now, Queequeg, die; and I'll beat ye your dying march.'

'I have heard,' murmured Starbuck, gazing down the scuttle, 'that in violent fevers, men, all ignorance, have talked in ancient tongues; and that when the mystery is probed, it turns out always that in their wholly forgotten childhood those ancient tongues had been really spoken in their hearing by some lofty scholars. So, to my fond faith, poor Pip, in this strange sweetness of his lunacy, brings heavenly vouchers of all our heavenly homes. Where learned he that, but there?—Hark! he speaks again: but more wildly now.'

'Form two and two! Let's make a General of him! Ho, where's his harpoon? Lay it across here.—Rig-a-dig, dig, dig! huzza! Oh for a game cock now to sit upon his head and crow! Queequeg dies game!—mind ye that; Queequeg dies game!—take ye good heed of that; Queequeg dies game! I say; game, game, game! but base little Pip, he died a coward; died all a'shiver;—out upon Pip! Hark ye; if ye find Pip, tell all the Antilles he's a runaway; a coward, a coward, a coward! Tell them he jumped from a whale-boat! I'd never beat my tambourine over base Pip, and hail him General, if he were once more dying here. No, no! shame upon all cowards—shame upon them! Let 'em go drown like Pip, that jumped from a whale-boat. Shame! shame!'

During all this, Queequeg lay with closed eyes, as if in a dream. Pip was led away, and the sick man was replaced in his hammock.

But now that he had apparently made every preparation for death; now that his coffin was proved a good fit, Queequeg suddenly rallied; soon there seemed no need of the carpenter's box; and thereupon, when some expressed their delighted surprise, he, in substance, said, that the cause of his sudden convalescence was this;—at a critical moment, he had just recalled a little duty ashore, which he was leaving undone; and therefore had changed his mind about dying: he could not die yet, he averred. They asked him, then, whether to live or die was a matter of his own sovereign will and pleasure. He answered, certainly. In a word, it was Queequeg's conceit, that if a man made up his mind to live, mere sickness could not kill him: nothing but a whale, or a gale, or some violent, ungovernable, unintelligent destroyer of that sort.

Now, there is this noteworthy difference between savage and civilized! that while a sick, civilized man may be six months convalescing, generally speaking, a sick savage is almost half-well again in a day. So, in good time my Queequeg gained strength; and at length after sitting on the windlass for a few indolent days (but eating with a vigorous appetite) he suddenly leaped to his feet, threw out arms and legs, gave himself a good stretching, yawned a little bit, and then springing into the head of his hoisted boat, and poising a harpoon, pronounced himself fit for a fight.

With a wild whimsiness, he now used his coffin for a sea-chest; and emptying into it his canvas bag of clothes, set them in order there. Many spare hours he spent, in carving the lid with all manner of grotesque figures and drawings; and it seemed that hereby he was striving, in his rude way, to copy parts of the twisted tattooing on his body. And this tattooing, had been the work of a departed prophet and seer of his island, who, by those hieroglyphic marks, had written out on his body a complete theory of the heavens and the earth, and a mystical treatise on the art of attaining truth; so that Queequeg in his own proper person was a riddle to unfold; a wondrous work in one volume; but whose mysteries not even himself could read, though his own live heart beat against them; and these mysteries were therefore destined in the end to moulder away with the living parchment whereon they were inscribed, and so be unsolved to the last. And this thought it must have been which suggested to Ahab that wild exclamation of his, when one morning turning away from surveying poor Queequeg—'Oh, devilish tantalization of the gods!'

CHAPTER CXI

THE PACIFIC

When gliding by the Bashee isles we emerged at last upon the great South Sea; were it not for other things, I could have greeted my dear Pacific with uncounted thanks, for now the long supplication of my youth was answered; that serene ocean rolled eastwards from me a thousand leagues of blue.

There is, one knows not what sweet mystery about this sea, whose gently awful stirrings seem to speak of some hidden soul beneath; like those fabled undulations of the Ephesian sod over the buried Evangelist St John. And meet it is, that over these sea-pastures, wide-rolling watery prairies and Potters' Fields of all four continents, the waves should rise and fall, and ebb and flow unceasingly; for here, millions of mixed shades and shadows, drowned dreams, somnambulisms, reveries; all that we call lives and souls, lie dreaming, dreaming, still; tossing like slumberers in their beds; the ever-rolling waves but made so by their restlessness.

To any meditative Magian rover, this serene Pacific, once beheld, must ever after be the sea of his adoption. It rolls the midmost waters of the world, the Indian ocean and Atlantic being but its arms. The same waves wash the moles of the new-built Californian towns, but yesterday planted by the recentest race of men, and lave the faded but still gorgeous skirts of Asiatic lands, older than Abraham; while all between float milky-ways of coral isles, and low-lying, endless, unknown Archipelagoes, and impenetrable Japans. Thus this mysterious, divine Pacific zones the world's whole bulk about; makes all coasts one bay to it; seems the tide-beating heart of earth. Lifted by those eternal swells, you needs must own the seductive god, bowing your head to Pan.

But few thoughts of Pan stirred Ahab's brain, as standing like an iron statue at his accustomed place beside the mizen rigging, with one nostril he unthinkingly snuffed the sugary musk from the Bashee isles (in whose sweet woods mild lovers must be walking), and with the other consciously inhaled the salt breath of the new found sea; that sea in which the hated White Whale must even then be swimming. Launched at length upon these almost final waters, and gliding towards the Japanese cruising-ground, the old man's purpose intensified itself. His firm lips met like the lips of a vice; the Delta of his forehead's veins swelled like overladen brooks; in his very sleep, his ringing cry ran through the vaulted hull, 'Stern all! the White Whale spouts thick blood!'

CHAPTER CXII

THE BLACKSMITH

Availing himself of the mild, summer-cool weather that now reigned in these latitudes, and in preparation for the peculiarly active pursuits shortly to be anticipated, Perth, the begrimed, blistered old blacksmith, had not removed his portable forge to the hold again, after concluding his contributory work for Ahab's leg, but still retained it on deck, fast lashed to ringbolts by the foremast; being now almost incessantly invoked by the headsmen, and harpooneers, and bowsmen to do some little job for them; altering, or repairing, or new shaping their various weapons and boat furniture. Often he would be surrounded by an eager circle, all waiting to be served; holding boat-spades, pike-heads, harpoons, and lances, and jealously watching his every sooty movement, as he toiled. Nevertheless, this old man's was a patient hammer wielded by a patient arm. No murmur, no impatience, no petulance did come from him. Silent, slow, and solemn; bowing over still further his chronically broken back, he toiled away, as if toil were life itself, and the heavy beating of his hammer the heavy beating of his heart. And so it was.—Most miserable!

A peculiar walk in this old man, a certain slight but painful appearing yawing in his gait, had at an early period of the voyage excited the curiosity of the mariners. And to the importunity of their persisted questionings he had finally given in; and so it came to pass that every one now knew the shameful story of his wretched fate.

Belated, and not innocently, one bitter winter's midnight, on the road running between two country towns, the blacksmith half-stupidly felt the deadly numbness stealing over him, and sought refuge in a leaning, dilapidated barn. The issue was, the loss of the extremities of both feet. Out of this revelation, part by part, at last came out the four acts of the gladness, and the one long, and as yet uncatastrophied fifth act of the grief of his life's drama.

He was an old man, who at the age of nearly sixty, had postponedly encountered that thing in sorrow's technicals called ruin. He had been an artisan of famed excellence, and with plenty to do; owned a house and garden; embraced a youthful, daughter-like, loving wife, and three blithe, ruddy children; every Sunday went to a cheerful-looking church, planted in a grove. But one night, under cover of darkness, and further concealed in a most cunning disguisement, a desperate burglar slid into his happy home, and robbed them all of everything. And darker yet to tell, the blacksmith himself did ignorantly conduct this burglar into his family's heart. It was the Bottle Conjuror! Upon the opening of that fatal cork, forth flew the fiend, and shrivelled up his home. Now, for prudent, most wise, and economic reasons the blacksmith's shop was in the basement of his dwelling, but with a separate entrance to it; so that always had the young and loving healthy wife listened with no unhappy nervousness, but with vigorous pleasure, to the stout ringing of her young-armed old husband's hammer; whose reverberations, muffled by passing through the floors and walls, came up to her, not unsweetly, in her nursery; and so, to stout Labor's iron lullaby the blacksmith's infants were rocked to slumber.

Oh, woe on woe! Oh, Death, why canst thou not sometimes be timely? Hadst thou taken this old blacksmith to thyself ere his full ruin came upon him, then had the young widow had a delicious grief, and her orphans a truly venerable, legendary sire to dream of in their after years; and all of them a care-killing competency. But Death plucked down some virtuous elder brother, on whose whistling daily toil solely hung the responsibilities of some other family, and left the worse than useless old man standing, till the hideous rot of life should make him easier to harvest.

Why tell the whole? The blows of the basement hammer every day grew more and more between; and each blow every day grew fainter than the last; the wife sat frozen at the window, with tearless eyes, glitteringly gazing into the weeping faces of her children; the bellows fell; the forge choked up with cinders; the house was sold; the mother dived down into the long church-yard grass; her children twice followed her thither; and the houseless, familyless old man staggered off a vagabond in crape; his every woe unreverenced; his grey head a scorn to flaxen curls!

Death seems the only desirable sequel for a career like this; but Death is only a launching into the region of the strange Untried; it is but the first salutation to the possibilities of the immense Remote, the Wild, the Watery, the Unshored; therefore, to the death-longing eyes of such men, who still have left in them some interior compunctions against suicide, does the all-contributed and all-receptive ocean alluringly spread forth his whole plain of unimaginable, taking terrors, and wonderful, new-life adventures; and from the hearts of infinite Pacifics, the thousand mermaids sing to them—'Come hither, broken-hearted; here is another life without the guilt of intermediate death; here are wonders supernatural, without dying for them. Come hither! bury thyself in a life which, to your now equally abhorred and abhorring, landed world, is more oblivious than death. Come hither! put up *thy* grave-stone, too, within the churchyard, and come hither, till we marry thee!'

Hearkening to these voices, East and West, by early sunrise, and by fall of eve, the blacksmith's soul responded, Aye, I come! And so Perth went a-whaling.

CHAPTER CXIII

THE FORGE

With matted beard, and swathed in a bristling shark-skin apron, about mid-day, Perth was standing between his forge and anvil, the latter placed upon an iron-wood log, with one hand holding a pike-head in the coals, and with the other at his forge's lungs, when Captain Ahab came along, carrying in his hand a small rusty-looking leathern bag. While yet a little distance from the forge, moody Ahab paused; till at last, Perth, withdrawing his iron from the fire, began hammering it upon the anvil—the red mass sending off the sparks in thick hovering flights, some of which flew close to Ahab.

'Are these thy Mother Carey's chickens, Perth? they are always flying in thy wake; birds of good omen, too, but not to all;—look here, they burn; but thou—thou liv'st among them without a scorch.'

'Because I am scorched all over, Captain Ahab,' answered Perth, resting for a moment on his hammer; 'I am past scorching; not easily can'st thou scorch a scar.'

'Well, well; no more. Thy shrunk voice sounds too calmly, sanely woful to me. In no Paradise myself, I am impatient of all misery in others that is not mad. Thou should'st go mad, blacksmith; say, why dost thou not go mad? How can'st thou endure without being mad? Do the heavens yet hate thee, that thou can'st not go mad?—What wert thou making there?'

'Welding an old pike-head, sir; there were seams and dents in it.'

'And can'st thou make it all smooth again, blacksmith, after such hard usage as it had?'

'I think so, sir.'

'And I suppose thou can'st smoothe almost any seams and dents; never mind how hard the metal, blacksmith?'

'Aye, sir, I think I can; all seams and dents but one.'

'Look ye here, then,' cried Ahab, passionately advancing, and leaning with both hands on Perth's shoulders; 'look ye here—*here*—can you smoothe out a seam like this, blacksmith,' sweeping one hand across his ribbed brow; 'if thou could'st, blacksmith, glad enough would I lay my head upon thy anvil, and feel thy heaviest hammer between my eyes. Answer! Can'st thou smoothe this seam?'

'Oh! that is the one, sir! Said I not all seams and dents but one?'

'Aye, blacksmith, it is the one; aye, man, it is unsmoothable; for though thou only see'st it here in my flesh, it has worked down into the bone of my skull—*that* is all wrinkles! But, away with child's play; no more gaffs and pikes to-day. Look ye here!' jingling the leathern bag, as if it were full of gold coins. 'I, too, want a harpoon made; one that a thousand yoke of fiends could not part, Perth; something that will stick in a whale like his own fin-bone. There's the stuff,' flinging the pouch upon the anvil. 'Look ye, blacksmith, these are the gathered nail-stubbs of the steel shoes of racing horses.'

'Horse-shoe stubbs, sir? Why, Captain Ahab, thou hast here, then, the best and stubbornest stuff we blacksmiths ever work.'

'I know it, old man; these stubbs will weld together like glue from the melted bones of murderers. Quick! forge me the harpoon. And forge me first, twelve rods for its shank; then wind, and twist, and hammer these twelve together like the yarns and strands of a tow-line. Quick! I'll blow the fire.'

When at last the twelve rods were made, Ahab tried them, one by one, by spiralling them, with his own hand, round a long, heavy iron bolt. 'A flaw!' rejecting the last one. 'Work that over again, Perth.'

This done, Perth was about to begin welding the twelve into one, when Ahab stayed his hand, and said he would weld his own iron. As, then, with regular, gasping hems, he hammered on the anvil, Perth passing to him the glowing rods, one after the other, and the hard pressed forge shooting up its intense straight flame, the Parsee passed silently, and bowing over his head towards the fire, seemed invoking some curse or some blessing on the toil. But, as Ahab looked up, he slid aside.

'What's that bunch of lucifers dodging about there for?' muttered Stubb, looking on from the forecastle. 'That Parsee smells fire like a fusee; and smells of it himself, like a hot musket's powder-pan.'

At last the shank, in one complete rod, received its final heat; and as Perth, to temper it, plunged it all hissing into the cask of water near by, the scalding steam shot up into Ahab's bent face.

'Would'st thou brand me, Perth?' wincing for a moment with the pain; 'have I been but forging my own branding-iron, then?'

'Pray God, not that; yet I fear something, Captain Ahab. Is not this harpoon for the White Whale?'

'For the white fiend! But now for the barbs; thou must make them thyself, man. Here are my razors—the best of steel; here, and make the barbs sharp as the needle-sleet of the Icy Sea.'

For a moment, the old blacksmith eyed the razors as though he would fain not use them.

'Take them, man, I have no need for them; for I now neither shave, sup, nor pray till—but here—to work!'

Fashioned at last into an arrowy shape, and welded by Perth to the shank, the steel soon pointed the end of the iron; and as the blacksmith was about giving the barbs their final heat, prior to tempering them, he cried to Ahab to place the water-cask near.

'No, no—no water for that: I want it of the true death-temper. Ahoy, there! Tashtego, Queequeg, Daggoo! What say ye, pagans! Will ye give me as much blood as will cover this barb?' holding it high up. A cluster of dark nods replied, Yes. Three punctures were made in the heathen flesh, and the White Whale's barbs were then tempered.

'Ego non baptizo te in nomine patris, sed in nomine diaboli!' deliriously howled Ahab, as the malignant iron scorchingly devoured the baptismal blood.

Now, mustering the spare poles from below, and selecting one of hickory, with the bark still investing it, Ahab fitted the end to the socket of the iron. A coil of new tow-line was then unwound, and some fathoms of it taken to the windlass, and stretched to a great tension. Pressing his foot upon it, till the rope hummed like a harp-string, then eagerly bending over it, and seeing no strandings, Ahab exclaimed, 'Good! and now for the seizings.'

At one extremity the rope was unstranded, and the separate spread yarns were all braided and woven round the socket of the harpoon; the pole was then driven hard up into the socket; from the lower end the rope was traced half way along the pole's length, and firmly secured so, with intertwistings of twine. This done, pole, iron, and rope—like the Three Fates—remained inseparable, and Ahab moodily stalked away with the weapon; the sound of his ivory leg, and the sound of the hickory pole, both hollowly ringing along every plank. But ere he entered his cabin, a light, unnatural, half-bantering, yet most piteous sound was heard. Oh, Pip! thy wretched laugh, thy idle but unresting eye; all thy strange mummeries not unmeaningly blended with the black tragedy of the melancholy ship, and mocked it!

CHAPTER CXIV

The Gilder

Penetrating further and further into the heart of the Japanese cruising ground, the Pequod was soon all astir in the fishery. Often, in mild, pleasant weather, for twelve, fifteen, eighteen, and twenty hours on the stretch, they were engaged in the boats, steadily pulling, or sailing, or paddling after the whales, or for an interlude of sixty or seventy minutes calmly awaiting their uprising; though with but small success for their pains.

At such times, under an abated sun; afloat all day upon smooth, slow heaving swells; seated in his boat, light as a birch canoe; and so sociably mixing with the soft waves themselves, that like hearth-stone cats they purr against the gunwale; these are the times of dreamy quietude, when beholding the tranquil beauty and brilliancy of the ocean's skin, one forgets the tiger heart that pants beneath it; and would not willingly remember, that this velvet paw but conceals a remorseless fang.

These are the times, when in his whale-boat the rover softly feels a certain filial, confident, land-like feeling towards the sea; that he regards it as so much flowery earth; and the distant ship revealing only the tops of her masts, seems struggling forward, not through high rolling waves, but through the tall grass of a rolling prairie: as when the western emigrants' horses only show their erected ears, while their hidden bodies widely wade through the amazing verdure.

The long-drawn virgin vales; the mild blue hill-sides; as over these there steals the hush, the hum; you almost swear that play-wearied children lie sleeping in these solitudes, in some glad May-time, when the flowers of the woods are plucked. And all this mixes with your most mystic mood; so that fact and fancy, half-way meeting, interpenetrate, and form one seamless whole.

Nor did such soothing scenes, however temporary, fail of at least as temporary an effect on Ahab. But if these secret golden keys did seem to open in him his own secret golden treasuries, yet did his breath upon them prove but tarnishing.

Oh, grassy glades! oh, ever vernal endless landscapes in the soul; in ye—though long parched by the dead drought of the earthy life—in ye, men yet may roll, like young horses in new morning clover; and for some few fleeting moments, feel the cool dew of the life immortal on them. Would to God these blessed calms would last. But the mingled, mingling threads of life are woven by warp and woof: calms crossed by storms, a storm for every calm. There is no steady unretracing progress in this life; we do not advance through fixed gradations, and at the last one pause:—through infancy's unconscious spell, boyhood's thoughtless faith, adolescence' doubt (the common doom), then scepticism, then disbelief, resting at last in manhood's pondering repose of If. But once gone through, we trace the round again; and are infants, boys, and men, and Ifs eternally. Where lies the final harbor, whence we unmoor no more? In what rapt ether sails the world, of which the weariest will never weary? Where is the foundling's father hidden? Our souls are like those orphans whose unwedded mothers die in bearing them: the secret of our paternity lies in their grave, and we must there to learn it.

And that same day, too, gazing far down from his boat's side into that same golden sea, Starbuck lowly murmured:—

'Loveliness unfathomable, as ever lover saw in his young bride's eye!—Tell me not of thy teeth-tiered sharks, and thy kidnapping cannibal ways. Let faith oust fact; let fancy oust memory; I look deep down and do believe.'

And Stubb, fish-like, with sparkling scales, leaped up in that same golden light:—

'I am Stubb, and Stubb has his history; but here Stubb takes oaths that he has always been jolly!'

CHAPTER CXV

THE PEQUOD MEETS THE BACHELOR

And jolly enough were the sights and the sounds that came bearing down before the wind, some few weeks after Ahab's harpoon had been welded.

It was a Nantucket ship, the Bachelor, which had just wedged in her last cask of oil, and bolted down her bursting hatches; and now, in glad holiday apparel, was joyously, though somewhat vain-gloriously, sailing round among the widely-separated ships on the ground, previous to pointing her prow for home.

The three men at her mast-head wore long streamers of narrow red bunting at their hats; from the stern, a whaleboat was suspended, bottom down; and hanging captive from the bowsprit was seen the long lower jaw of the last whale they had slain. Signals, ensigns, and jacks of all colors were flying from her rigging, on every side. Sideways lashed in each of her three basketed tops were two barrels of sperm; above which, in her top-mast cross-trees, you saw slender breakers of the same precious fluid; and nailed to her main truck was a brazen lamp.

As was afterwards learned, the Bachelor had met with the most surprising success; all the more wonderful, for that while cruising in the same seas numerous other vessels had gone entire months without securing a single fish. Not only had barrels of beef and bread been given away to make room for the far more valuable sperm, but additional supplemental casks had been bartered for, from the ships she had met; and these were stowed along the deck, and in the captain's and officer's state-rooms. Even the cabin table itself had been knocked into kindling-wood; and the cabin mess dined off the broad head of an oil-butt, lashed down to the floor for a centrepiece. In the forecastle, the sailors had actually caulked and pitched their chests, and filled them; it was humorously added, that the cook had clapped a head on his largest boiler, and filled it; that the steward had plugged his spare coffee-pot and filled it; that the harpooneers had headed the sockets of their irons and filled them; that indeed everything was filled with sperm, except the captain's pantaloons pockets, and those he reserved to thrust his hands into, in self-complacent testimony of his entire satisfaction.

As this glad ship of good luck bore down upon the moody Pequod, the barbarian sound of enormous drums came from her forecastle; and drawing still nearer, a crowd of her men were seen standing round her huge try-pots, which, covered with the parchment-like *poke* or stomach skin of the black fish, gave forth a loud roar to every stroke of the clenched hands of the crew. On the quarter-deck, the mates and harpooneers were dancing with the olive-hued girls who had eloped with them from the Polynesian Isles; while suspended in an ornamented boat, firmly secured aloft between the foremast and mainmast, three Long Island negroes, with glittering fiddle-bows of whale ivory, were presiding over the hilarious jig. Meanwhile, others of the ship's company were tumultuously busy at the masonry of the try-works, from which the huge pots had been removed. You would have almost thought they were pulling down the cursed Bastile, such wild cries they raised, as the now useless brick and mortar were being hurled into the sea.

Lord and master over all this scene, the captain stood erect on the ship's elevated quarter-deck, so that the whole rejoicing drama was full before him, and seemed merely contrived for his own individual diversion.

And Ahab, he too was standing on his quarter-deck, shaggy and black, with a stubborn gloom; and as the two ships crossed each other's wakes—one all jubilations for things passed, the other all forebodings as to things to come—their two captains in themselves impersonated the whole striking contrast of the scene.

'Come aboard, come aboard!' cried the gay Bachelor's commander, lifting a glass and a bottle in the air.

'Hast seen the White Whale?' gritted Ahab in reply.

'No; only heard of him; but don't believe in him at all,' said the other good humoredly. 'Come aboard!'

'Thou art too damned jolly. Sail on. Hast lost any men?'

'Not enough to speak of—two islanders, that's all;—but come aboard, old hearty, come along. I'll soon take that black from your brow. Come along, will ye (merry's the play); a full ship and homeward-bound.'

'How wondrous familiar is a fool!' muttered Ahab; then aloud, 'Thou art a full ship and homeward bound, thou sayst; well, then, call me an empty ship, and outward-bound. So go thy ways, and I will mine. Forward there. Set all sail, and keep her to the wind!'

And thus, while the one ship went cheerily before the breeze, the other stubbornly fought against it; and so the two vessels parted; the crew of the Pequod looking with grave, lingering glances towards the receding Bachelor; but the Bachelor's men never heeding their gaze for the lively revelry they were in. And as Ahab, leaning over the taffrail, eyed the homeward-bound craft, he took from his pocket a small vial of sand, and then looking from the ship to the vial, seemed thereby bringing two remote associations together, for that vial was filled with Nantucket soundings.

CHAPTER CXVI

The Dying Whale

Not seldom in this life, when, on the right side, fortune's favorites sail close by us, we, though all adroop before, catch somewhat of the rushing breeze, and joyfully feel our bagging sails fill out. So seemed it with the Pequod. For next day after encountering the gay Bachelor, whales were seen and four were slain; and one of them by Ahab.

It was far down the afternoon; and when all the spearings of the crimson fight were done: and floating in the lovely sunset sea and sky, sun and whale both stilly died together; then, such a sweetness and such plaintiveness, such inwreathing orisons curled up on that rosy air, that it almost seemed as if far over from the deep green convent valleys of the Manilla isles, the Spanish land-breeze, wantonly turned sailor, had gone to sea, freighted with these vesper hymns.

Soothed again, but only soothed to deeper gloom, Ahab, who had sterned off from the whale, sat intently watching his final wanings from the now tranquil boat. For that strange spectacle observable in all sperm whales dying—the turning sunwards of the head, and so expiring—that strange spectacle, beheld of such a placid evening, somehow to Ahab conveyed a wondrousness unknown before.

'He turns and turns him to it,—how slowly, but how steadfastly, his homage-rendering and invoking brow, with his last dying motions. He too worships fire; most faithful, broad, baronial vassal of the sun!—Oh that these too-favoring eyes should see these too-favoring sights. Look! here, far water-locked; beyond all hum or human weal or woe; in these most candid and impartial seas; where to traditions no rocks furnish tablets; where for long Chinese ages, the billows have still rolled on speechless and unspoken to, as stars that shine upon the Niger's unknown source; here, too, life dies sunwards full of faith; but see! no sooner dead, than death whirls round the corpse, and it heads some other way.—

'Oh, thou dark Hindoo half of nature, who of drowned bones hast builded thy separate throne somewhere in the heart of these unverdured seas; thou art an infidel, thou queen, and too truly speakest to me in the wide-slaughtering Typhoon, and the hushed burial of its after calm. Nor has this thy whale sunwards turned his dying head, and then gone round again, without a lesson to me.

'Oh, trebly hooped and welded hip of power! Oh, high aspiring, rainbowed jet!—that one striveth, this one jetteth all in vain! In vain, oh whale, dost thou seek intercedings with yon all quickening sun, that only calls forth life, but gives it not again. Yet dost thou, darker half, rock me with a prouder, if a darker faith. All thy unnamable imminglings float beneath me here; I am buoyed by breaths of once living things, exhaled as air, but water now.

'Then hail, for ever hail, O sea, in whose eternal tossings the wild fowl finds his only rest. Born of earth, yet suckled by the sea; though hill and valley mothered me, ye billows are my foster-brothers!'

CHAPTER CXVII

THE WHALE WATCH

The four whales slain that evening had died wide apart; one, far to windward; one, less distant, to leeward; one ahead; one astern. These last three were brought alongside ere nightfall; but the windward one could not be reached till morning; and the boat that had killed it lay by its side all night; and that boat was Ahab's.

The waif-pole was thrust upright into the dead whale's spout hole; and the lantern hanging from its top, cast a troubled flickering glare upon the black, glossy back, and far out upon the midnight waves, which gently chafed the whale's broad flank, like soft surf upon a beach.

Ahab and all his boat's crew seemed asleep but the Parsee; who crouching in the bow, sat watching the sharks, that spectrally played round the whale, and tapped the light cedar planks with their tails. A sound like the moaning in squadrons over Asphaltites of unforgiven ghosts of Gomorrah, ran shuddering through the air.

Started from his slumbers, Ahab, face to face, saw the Parsee; and hooped round by the gloom of the night they seemed the last men in a flooded world. 'I have dreamed it again,' said he.

'Of the hearses? Have I not said, old man, that neither hearse nor coffin can be thine?'

'And who are hearsed that die on the sea?'

'But I said, old man, that ere thou couldst die on this voyage, two hearses must verily be seen by thee on the sea; the first not made by mortal hands; and the visible wood of the last one must be grown in America.'

'Aye, aye! a strange sight that, Parsee:—a hearse and its plumes floating over the ocean with the waves for the pall-bearers. Ha! Such a sight we shall not soon see.'

'Believe it or not, thou canst not die till it be seen, old man.'

'And what was that saying about thyself?'

'Though it come to the last, I shall still go before thee thy pilot.'

'And when thou are so gone before—if that ever befall—then ere I can follow, thou must still appear to me, to pilot me still?—Was it not so? Well, then, did I believe all ye say, oh my pilot! I have here two pledges that I shall yet slay Moby Dick and survive it.'

'Take another pledge, old man,' said the Parsee, as his eyes lighted up like fire-flies in the gloom—'Hemp only can kill thee.'

'The gallows, ye mean.—I am immortal then, on land and on sea,' cried Ahab with a laugh of derision;—'Immortal on land and on sea!'

Both were silent again, as one man. The grey dawn came on, and the slumbering crew arose from the boat's bottom, and ere noon the dead whale was brought to the ship.

CHAPTER CXVIII

The Quadrant

The season for the Line at length drew near; and every day when Ahab, coming from his cabin, cast his eyes aloft, the vigilant helmsman would ostentatiously handle his spokes, and the eager mariners quickly run to the braces, and would stand there with all their eyes centrally fixed on the nailed doubloon; impatient for the order to point the ship's prow for the equator. In good time the order came. It was hard upon high noon; and Ahab, seated in the bows of his high-hoisted boat, was about taking his wonted daily observation of the sun to determine his latitude.

Now, in that Japanese sea, the days in summer are as freshets of effulgences. That unblinkingly vivid Japanese sun seems the blazing focus of the glassy ocean's immeasurable burning-glass. The sky looks lacquered; clouds there are none; the horizon floats; and this nakedness of unrelieved radiance is as the insufferable splendors of God's throne. Well that Ahab's quadrant was furnished with colored glasses, through which to take sight of that solar fire. So, swinging his seated form to the roll of the ship, and with his astrological-looking instrument placed to his eye, he remained in that posture for some moments to catch the precise instant when the sun should gain its precise meridian. Meantime while his whole attention was absorbed, the Parsee was kneeling beneath him on the ship's deck, and with face thrown up like Ahab's, was eyeing the same sun with him; only the lids of his eyes half hooded their orbs, and his wild face was subdued to an unearthly passionlessness. At length the desired observation was taken; and with his pencil upon his ivory leg, Ahab soon calculated what his latitude must be at that precise instant. Then falling into a moment's revery, he again looked up towards the sun and murmured to himself: 'Thou sea-mark! thou high and mighty Pilot! thou tellest me truly where I *am*—but canst thou cast the least hint where I *shall* be? Or canst thou tell where some other thing besides me is this moment living? Where is Moby Dick? This instant thou must be eyeing him. These eyes of mine look into the very eye that is even now beholding him; aye, and into the eye that is even now equally beholding the objects on the unknown, thither side of thee, thou sun!'

Then gazing at his quadrant, and handling, one after the other, its numerous cabalistical contrivances, he pondered again, and muttered: 'Foolish toy! babies' plaything of haughty Admirals, and Commodores, and Captains; the world brags of thee, of thy cunning and might; but what after all canst thou do, but tell the poor, pitiful point, where thou thyself happenest to be on this wide planet, and the hand that holds thee: no! not one jot more! Thou canst not tell where one drop of water or one grain of sand will be to-morrow noon; and yet with thy impotence thou insultest the sun! Science! Curse thee, thou vain toy; and cursed be all the things that cast man's eyes aloft to that heaven, whose live vividness but scorches him, as these old eyes are even now scorched with thy light, O sun! Level by nature to this earth's horizon are the glances of man's eyes; not shot from the crown of his head, as if God had meant him to gaze on his firmament. Curse thee, thou quadrant!' dashing it to the deck, 'no longer will I guide my earthly way by thee; the level ship's compass, and the level dead-reckoning, by log and by line; *these* shall conduct me, and show me my place on the sea. Aye,' lighting from the boat to the deck, 'thus I trample on thee, thou paltry thing that feebly pointest on high; thus I split and destroy thee!'

As the frantic old man thus spoke and thus trampled with his live and dead feet, a sneering triumph that seemed meant for Ahab, and a fatalistic despair that seemed meant for himself—these passed over the mute, motionless Parsee's face. Unobserved he rose and glided away; while, awestruck by the aspect of their commander, the seamen clustered together on the forecastle, till Ahab, troubledly pacing the deck, shouted out—'To the braces! Up helm!—square in!'

In an instant the yards swung round; and as the ship half-wheeled upon her heel, her three firm-seated graceful masts erectly poised upon her long, ribbed hull, seemed as the three Horatii pirouetting on one sufficient steed.

Standing between the knight-heads, Starbuck watched the Pequod's tumultuous way, and Ahab's also, as he went lurching along the deck.

'I have sat before the dense coal fire and watched it all aglow, full of its tormented flaming life; and I have seen it wane at last, down, down, to dumbest dust. Old man of oceans! of all this fiery life of thine, what will at length remain but one little heap of ashes!'

'Aye,' cried Stubb, 'but sea-coal ashes—mind ye that, Mr Starbuck—sea-coal, not your common charcoal. Well, well; I heard Ahab mutter, "Here some one thrusts these cards into these old hands of mine; swears that I must play them, and no others." And damn me, Ahab, but thou actest right; live in the game, and die in it!'

CHAPTER CXIX

THE CANDLES

Warmest climes but nurse the cruellest fangs: the tiger of Bengal crouches in spiced groves of ceaseless verdure. Skies the most effulgent but basket the deadliest thunders: gorgeous Cuba knows tornadoes that never swept tame northern lands. So, too, it is, that in these resplendent Japanese seas the mariner encounters the direst of all storms, the Typhoon. It will sometimes burst from out that cloudless sky, like an exploding bomb upon a dazed and sleepy town.

Towards evening of that day, the Pequod was torn of her canvas, and bare-poled was left to fight a Typhoon which had struck her directly ahead. When darkness came on, sky and sea roared and split with the thunder, and blazed with the lightning, that showed the disabled masts fluttering here and there with the rags which the first fury of the tempest had left for its after sport.

Holding by a shroud, Starbuck was standing on the quarter-deck; at every flash of the lightning glancing aloft, to see what additional disaster might have befallen the intricate hamper there; while Stubb and Flask were directing the men in the higher hoisting and firmer lashing of the boats. But all their pains seemed naught. Though lifted to the very top of the cranes, the windward quarter boat (Ahab's) did not escape. A great rolling sea, dashing high up against the reeling ship's high tetering side, stove in the boat's bottom at the stern, and left it again, all dripping through like a sieve.

'Bad work, bad work! Mr Starbuck,' said Stubb, regarding the wreck, 'but the sea will have its way. Stubb, for one, can't fight it. You see, Mr Starbuck, a wave has such a great long start before it leaps, all round the world it runs, and then comes the spring! But as for me, all the start I have to meet it, is just across the deck here. But never mind; it's all in fun: so the old song says;'—*(sings.)*

Oh! jolly is the gale,
And a joker is the whale,
A'flourishing' his tail,—
Such a funny, sporty, gamy, jesty, joky, hoky-poky lad,
is the Ocean, oh!

The scud all aflying',
That's his flip only foamin';
When he stirs in the spicin',—
Such a funny, sporty, gamy, jesty, joky, hoky-poky lad,
is the Ocean, oh!

Thunder splits the ships,
But he only smacks his lips,
A tastin' of this flip,—
Such a funny, sporty, gamy, jesty, joky, hoky-poky lad,
is the Ocean, oh!

'Avast Stubb,' cried Starbuck 'let the Typhoon sing, and strike his harp here in our rigging; but if thou are a brave man thou wilt hold they peace.'

'But I am not a brave man; never said I was a brave men; I am a coward; and I sing to keep up my spirits. And I tell you what it is, Mr Starbuck, there's no way to stop my singing in this world but to cut my throat. And when that's done, ten to one I sing ye the doxology for a wind-up.'

'Madman! look through my eyes if thou has none of thine own.'

'What! how can you see better of a dark night than anybody else, never mind how foolish?'

'Here!' cried Starbuck seizing Stubb by the shoulder, and pointing his hand towards the weather bow, 'markest thou not that the gale comes from the eastward, the very course Ahab is to run for Moby Dick? the very course he swung to this day noon? now mark his boat there; where is that stove? In the stern-sheets, man; where he is wont to stand—his stand-point is stove, man! Now jump overboard, and sing away, if thou must!'

'I don't half understand ye: what's in the wind!'

'Yes, yes, round the Cape of Good Hope is the shortest way to Nantucket,' soliloquized Starbuck suddenly, heedless of Stubb's question. 'The gale that now hammers at us to stave us, we can turn it into a fair wind that will drive us towards home. Yonder, to windward, all is blackness of doom; but to leeward, homeward—I see it lightens up there; but not with the lightning.'

At that moment in one of the intervals of profound darkness, following the flashes, a voice was heard at his side; and almost at the same instant a volley of thunder peals rolled overhead.

'Who's there?'

'Old Thunder!' said Ahab, groping his way along the bulwarks to his pivot-hole; but suddenly finding his path made plain to him by elbowed lances of fire.

Now, as the lightning rod to a spire on shore is intended to carry off the perilous fluid into the soil; so the kindred rod which at sea some ships carry to each mast, is intended to conduct it into the water. But as this conductor must descend to considerable depth, that its end may avoid all contact with the hull; and as moreover, if kept constantly towing there, it would be liable to many mishaps, besides interfering not a little with some of the rigging, and more or less impeding the vessel's way in the water; because of all this, the lower parts of a ship's lightning-rods are not always overboard; but are generally made in long slender links, so as to be the more readily hauled up into the chains outside, or thrown down into the sea, as occasion may require.

'The rods! the rods!' cried Starbuck to the crew, suddenly admonished to vigilance by the vivid lightning that had just been darting flambeaux, to light Ahab to his post. 'Are they overboard? drop them over, fore and aft. Quick!'

'Avast!' cried Ahab; 'let's have fair play here, though we be the weaker side. Yet I'll contribute to raise rods on the Himmalehs and Andes, that all the world may be secured; but out on privileges! Let them be, sir.'

'Look aloft!' cried Starbuck. 'The corpusants! the corpusants!'

All the yard-arms were tipped with a pallid fire; and touched at each tri-pointed lightning-rod-end with three tapering white flames, each of the three tall masts was silently burning in that sulphurous air, like three gigantic wax tapers before an altar.

'Blast the boat! let it go!' cried Stubb at this instant, as a swashing sea heaved up under his own little craft, so that its gunwale violently jammed his hand, as he was passing a lashing. 'Blast it!'—but slipping backward on the deck, his uplifted eyes caught the flames; and immediately shifting his tone, he cried—'The corpusants have mercy on us all!'

To sailors, oaths are household words; they will swear in the trance of the calm, and in the teeth of the tempest; they will imprecate curses from the topsail-yard-arms, when most they teter over to a seething sea; but in all my voyagings, seldom have I heard a common oath when God's burning finger has been laid on the ship;

when His 'Mene, Mene, Tekel, Upharsin' has been woven into the shrouds and the cordage.

While this pallidness was burning aloft, few words were heard from the enchanted crew; who in one thick cluster stood on the forecastle, all their eyes gleaming in that pale phosphorescence, like a far away constellation of stars. Relieved against the ghostly light, the gigantic jet negro, Daggoo, loomed up to thrice his real stature, and seemed the black cloud from which the thunder had come. The parted mouth of Tashtego revealed his shark-white teeth, which strangely gleamed as if they too had been tipped by corpusants; while lit up by the preternatural light, Queequeg's tattooing burned like Satanic blue flames on his body.

The tableau all waned at last with the pallidness aloft; and once more the Pequod and every soul on her decks were wrapped in a pall. A moment or two passed, when Starbuck going forward, pushed against some one. It was Stubb. 'What thinkest thou now, man; I heard thy cry; it was not the same in the song.'

'No, no, it wasn't; I said the corpusants have mercy on us all; and I hope they will, still. But do they only have mercy on long faces?—have they no bowels for a laugh? And look ye, Mr Starbuck—but it's too dark to look. Hear me, then: I take that mast-head flame we saw for a sign of good luck; for those masts are rooted in a hold that is going to be chock a'block with sperm-oil, d'ye see; and so, all that sperm will work up into the masts, like sap in a tree. Yes, our three masts will yet be as three spermaceti candles—that's the good promise we saw.'

At that moment Starbuck caught sight of Stubb's face slowly beginning to glimmer into sight. Glancing upwards, he cried: 'See! see!' and once more the high tapering flames were beheld with what seemed redoubled supernaturalness in their pallor.

'The corpusants have mercy on us all,' cried Stubb, again.

At the base of the mainmast, full beneath the doubloon and the flame, the Parsee was kneeling in Ahab's front, but with his head bowed away from him; while near by, from the arched and overhanging rigging, where they had just been engaged securing a spar, a number of the seamen, arrested by the glare, now cohered together, and hung pendulous, like a knot of numbed wasps from a drooping, orchard twig. In various enchanted attitudes, like the standing, or stepping, or running skeletons in Herculaneum, others remained rooted to the deck; but all their eyes upcast.

'Aye, aye, men!' cried Ahab. 'Look up at it; mark it well; the white flame but lights the way to the White Whale! Hand me those main-masts links there; I would fain feel this pulse, and let mine beat against it; blood against fire! So.'

Then turning—the last link held fast in his left hand, he put his foot upon the Parsee; and with fixed upward eye, and high-flung right arm, he stood erect before the lofty tri-pointed trinity of flames.

'Oh! thou clear spirit of clear fire, whom on these seas I as Persian once did worship, till in the sacramental act so burned by thee, that to this hour I bear the scar; I now know thee, thou clear spirit, and I now know that thy right worship is defiance. To neither love nor reverence wilt thou be kind; and e'en for hate thou canst but kill; and all are killed. No fearless fool now fronts thee. I own thy speechless, placeless power; but to the last gasp of my earthquake life will dispute its unconditional, unintegral mastery in me. In the midst of the personified impersonal, a personality stands here. Though but a point at best; whencesoe'er I came; wheresoe'er I go; yet while I earthly live, the queenly personality lives in me, and feels her royal rights. But war is pain, and hate is woe. Come in thy lowest form of love, and I will kneel and kiss thee; but at thy highest, come as mere supernal power; and though thou launchest navies of full-freighted worlds, there's that in here that still remains indifferent. Oh, thou clear spirit, of thy fire thou madest me, and like a true child of fire, I breathe it back to thee.'

[*Sudden, repeated flashes of lightning; the nine flames leap lengthwise to thrice their previous height; Ahab, with the rest, closes his eyes, his right hand pressed hard upon them.*]

'I own thy speechless, placeless power; said I not so? Nor was it wrung from me; nor do I now drop these links. Thou canst blind; but I can then grope. Thou canst consume; but I can then be ashes. Take the homage of these poor eyes, and shutter-hands. I would not take it. The lightning flashes through my skull; mine eye-balls ache and ache; my whole beaten brain seems as beheaded, and rolling on some stunning ground. Oh, oh! Yet blindfold, yet will I talk to thee. Light though thou be, thou leapest out of darkness; but I am darkness leaping out of light, leaping out of thee! The javelins cease; open eyes; see, or not? There burn the flames! Oh, thou magnanimous! now I do glory in my genealogy. But thou are but my fiery father; my sweet mother, I know not, Oh, cruel! what hast thou done with her? There lies my puzzle; but thine is greater. Thou knowest not how came ye; hence callest thyself unbegotten; certainly knowest not thy beginning, hence callest thyself unbegun. I know that of me, which thou knowest not of thyself, oh, thou omnipotent. There is some unsuffusing thing beyond thee, thou clear spirit, to whom all thy eternity is but time, all thy creativeness mechanical. Through thee, thy flaming self, my scorched eyes do dimly see it. Oh, thou foundling fire, thou hermit immemorial, thou too hast thy incommunicable riddle, thy unparticipated grief. Here again with haughty agony, I read my sire. Leap! leap up, and lick the sky! I leap with thee; I burn with thee; would fain be welded with thee, defyingly I worship thee!'

'The boat! the boat!' cried Starbuck, 'look at thy boat, old man!'

Ahab's harpoon, the one forged at Perth's fire, remained firmly lashed in its conspicuous crotch, so that it projected beyond his whale-boat's bow; but the sea that had stove its bottom had caused the loose leather sheath to drop off; and from the keen steel barb there now came a levelled flame of pale, forked fire. As the silent harpoon burned there like a serpent's tongue, Starbuck grasped Ahab by the arm—'God, God is against thee, old man; forbear! 'tis an ill voyage! ill begun, ill continued; let me square the yards, while we may, old man, and make a fair wind of it homewards, to go on a better voyage than this.'

Overhearing Starbuck, the panic-stricken crew instantly ran to the braces—though not a sail was left aloft. For the moment all the aghast mate's thoughts seemed theirs; they raised a half mutinous cry. But dashing the rattling lightning links to the deck, and snatching the burning harpoon, Ahab waved it like a torch among them; swearing to transfix with it the first sailor that but cast loose a rope's end. Petrified by his aspect, and still more shrinking from the fiery dart that he held, the men fell back in dismay, and Ahab spoke again:—

'All your oaths to hunt the White Whale are as binding as mine; and heart, soul, and body, lungs and life, old Ahab is bound. And that ye may know to what tune this heart beats; look ye here; thus I blow out the last fear!' And with one blast of his breath he extinguished the flame.

As in the hurricane that sweeps the plain, men fly the neighborhood of some lone gigantic elm, whose very height and strength but render it so much the more unsafe, because so much the more a mark for thunderbolts; so at those last words of Ahab's many of the mariners did run from him in a terror of dismay.

CHAPTER CXX

THE DECK TOWARDS THE END OF THE FIRST NIGHT WATCH

Ahab standing by the helm. Starbuck approaching him.

'We must send down the main-top-sail yard, sir. The band is working loose, and the lee lift is half-stranded. Shall I strike it, sir?'

'Strike nothing; lash it. If I had sky-sail poles, I'd sway them up now.'

'Sir—in God's name!—sir?'

'Well.'

'The anchors are working, sir. Shall I get them inboard?'

'Strike nothing, and stir nothing, but lash everything. The wind rises, but it has not got up to my table-lands yet. Quick, and see to it.—By masts and keels! he takes me for the hunch-backed skipper of some coasting smack. Send down my main-top-sail yard! Ho, gluepots! Loftiest trucks were made for wildest winds, and this brain-truck of mine now sails amid the cloud-scud. Shall I strike that? Oh, none but cowards send down their brain-trucks in tempest time. What a hooroosh aloft there! I would e'en take it for sublime, did I not know that the colic is a noisy malady. Oh, take medicine, take medicine!'

CHAPTER CXXI

MIDNIGHT—THE FORECASTLE BULWARKS

Stubb and Flask mounted on them, and passing additional lashings over the anchors there hanging.

'No, Stubb; you may pound that knot there as much as you please, but you will never pound into me what you were just now saying. And how long ago is it since you said the very contrary? Didn't you once say that whatever ship Ahab sails in, that ship should pay something extra on its insurance policy, just as though it were loaded with powder barrels aft and boxes of lucifers forward? Stop, now; didn't you say so?'

'Well, suppose I did? What then? I've part changed my flesh since that time, why not my mind? Besides, supposing we *are* loaded with powder barrels aft and lucifers forward; how the devil could the lucifers get afire in this drenching spray here? Why, my little man, you have pretty red hair, but you couldn't get afire now. Shake yourself; you're Aquarius, or the water-bearer, Flask; might fill pitchers at your coat collar. Don't you see, then, that for these extra risks the Marine Insurance companies have extra guarantees? Here are hydrants, Flask. But hark, again, and I'll answer ye the other thing. First take your leg off from the crown of the anchor here, though, so I can pass the rope; now listen. What's the mighty difference between holding a mast's lightning-rod in the storm, and standing close by a mast that hasn't got any lightning-rod at all in a storm? Don't you see, you timber-head, that no harm can come to the holder of the rod, unless the mast is first struck? What are you talking about, then? Not one ship in a hundred carries rods, and Ahab,—aye, man, and all of us,—were in no more danger then, in my poor opinion, than all the crews in ten thousand ships now sailing the seas. Why, you

King-Post, you, I suppose you would have every man in the world go about with a small lightning-rod running up the corner of his hat, like a militia officer's skewered feather, and trailing behind like his sash. Why don't ye be sensible, Flask? it's easy to be sensible; why don't ye, then? any man with half an eye can be sensible.'

'I don't know that, Stubb. You sometimes find it rather hard.'

'Yes, when a fellow's soaked through, it's hard to be sensible, that's a fact. And I am about drenched with this spray. Never mind; catch the turn there, and pass it. Seems to me we are lashing down these anchors now as if they were never going to be used again. Tying these two anchors here, Flask, seems like tying a man's hands behind him. And what big generous hands they are, to be sure. These are your iron fists, hey? What a hold they have, too! I wonder, Flask, whether the world is anchored anywhere; if she is, she swings with an uncommon long cable, though. There, hammer that knot down, and we've done. So; next to touching land, lighting on deck is the most satisfactory. I say, just wring out my jacket skirts, will ye? Thank ye. They laugh at long-togs so, Flask; but seems to me a long tailed coat ought always to be worn in all storms afloat. The tails tapering down that way, serve to carry off the water, d'ye see. Same with cocked hats; the cocks form gable-end eave-troughs, Flask. No more monkey-jackets and tarpaulins for me; I must mount a swallow-tail, and drive down a beaver; so. Halloa? whew? there goes my tarpaulin overboard; Lord, Lord, that the winds that come from heaven should be so unmannerly! This is a nasty night, lad.'

CHAPTER CXXII

MIDNIGHT ALOFT—THUNDER AND LIGHTNING

The Main-top-sail yard.—Tashtego passing new lashings around it.

'Um, um, um. Stop that thunder! Plenty too much thunder up here. What's the use of thunder? Um, um, um. We don't want thunder; we want rum; give us a glass of rum. Um, um, um!'

CHAPTER CXXIII

THE MUSKET

During the most violent shocks of the Typhoon, the man at the Pequod's jaw-bone tiller had several times been reelingly hurled to the deck by its spasmodic motions, even though preventer tackles had been attached to it—for they were slack—because some play to the tiller was indispensable.

In a severe gale like this, while the ship is but a tossed shuttlecock to the blast, it is by no means uncommon to see the needles in the compasses, at intervals, go round and round. It was thus with the Pequod's; at almost every shock the helmsman had not failed to notice the whirling velocity with which they revolved upon the cards; it is a sight that hardly any one can behold without some sort of unwonted emotion.

Some hours after midnight, the Typhoon abated so much, that through the strenuous exertions of Starbuck and Stubb—one engaged forward and the other aft—the shivered remnants of the jib and fore and main-top-sails were cut adrift from the spars, and went eddying away to leeward, like the feathers of an albatross, which sometimes are cast to the winds when that storm-tossed bird is on the wing.

The three corresponding new sails were now bent and reefed, and a storm-trysail was set further aft; so that the ship soon went through the water with some precision again; and the course—for the present, East-south-east—which he was to steer, if practicable, was once more given to the helmsman. For during the violence of the gale, he had only steered according to its vicissitudes. But as he was now bringing the ship as near her course as possible, watching the compass meanwhile, lo! a good sign! the wind seemed coming round astern; aye, the foul breeze became fair!

Instantly the yards were squared, to the lively song of *'Ho! the fair wind! oh-he-yo, cheerly, men!'* the crew singing for joy, that so promising an event should so soon have falsified the evil portents preceding it.

In compliance with the standing order of his commander—to report immediately, and at any one of the twenty-four hours any decided change in the affairs of the deck,—Starbuck had no sooner trimmed the yards to the breeze—however reluctantly and gloomily,—than he mechanically went below to apprise Captain Ahab of the circumstance.

Ere knocking at his state-room, he involuntarily paused before it a moment. The cabin lamp—taking long swings this way and that—was burning fitfully, and casting fitful shadows upon the old man's bolted door,—a thin one, with fixed blinds inserted, in place of upper panels. The isolated subterraneousness of the cabin made a certain humming silence to reign there, though it was hooped round by all the roar of the elements. The loaded muskets in the rack were shiningly revealed, as they stood upright against the forward bulkhead. Starbuck was an honest, upright man; but out of Starbuck's heart, at that instant when he saw the muskets, there strangely evolved an evil thought; but so blent with its neutral or good accompaniments that for the instant he hardly knew it for itself.

'He would have shot me once,' he murmured, 'yes, there's the very musket that he pointed at me;—that one with the studded stock; let me touch it—lift it. Strange, that I, who have handled so many deadly lances, strange, that I should shake so now. Loaded? I must see. Aye, aye; and powder in the pan;—that's not good. Best spill it?—wait. I'll cure myself of this. I'll hold the musket boldly while I think.—I come to report a fair wind to him. But how fair? Fair for death and doom,—*that's* fair for Moby Dick. It's a fair wind that's only fair for that accursed fish.—The very tube he pointed at me!—the very one; *this* one—I hold it here; he would have killed me with the very thing I handle now.—Aye and he would fain kill all his crew. Does he not say he will not strike his spars to any gale? Has he not dashed his heavenly quadrant? and in these same perilous seas, gropes he not his way by mere dead reckoning of the error-abounding log? and in this very Typhoon, did he not swear that he would have no lightning-rods? But shall this crazed old man be tamely suffered to drag a whole ship's company down to doom with him?—Yes, it would make him the wilful murderer of thirty men and more, if this ship come to any deadly harm; and come to deadly harm, my soul swears this ship will, if Ahab have his way. If, then, he were this instant—put aside, that crime would not be his. Ha! is he muttering in his sleep? Yes, just there,—in there, he's sleeping. Sleeping? aye, but still alive, and soon awake again. I can't withstand thee, then, old man. Not reasoning; not remonstrance; not entreaty wilt thou hearken to; all this thou scornest. Flat obedience to thy own flat commands, this is all thou breathest. Aye, and say'st the men have vow'd thy vow; say'st all of us are Ahabs. Great God forbid!—But is there no other way? no lawful way?—Make him a prisoner to be taken home? What! hope to wrest this old man's living power from his own living hands? Only a fool would try it. Say he were pinioned even; knotted all over with ropes and hawsers; chained down to ring-bolts on this cabin floor; he would be more hideous than a caged tiger, then. I could not endure the sight; could not possibly fly his howlings; all comfort, sleep itself, inestimable reason would leave me on the long intolerable voyage. What, then, remains? The land is hundreds of leagues away, and locked Japan the nearest. I stand alone here upon an open sea, with two oceans and a whole continent between me and law.—Aye, aye, 'tis so.—Is heaven a murderer when its lightning strikes a would-be murderer in his bed, tindering sheets and skin together?—And would I be a murderer, then, if—' and slowly, stealthily, and half sideways looking, he placed the loaded musket's end against the door.

'On this level, Ahab's hammock swings within; his head this way. A touch, and Starbuck may survive to hug his wife and child again.—Oh Mary! Mary!—boy! boy! boy!—But if I wake thee not to death, old man, who can tell to what unsounded deeps Starbuck's body this day week may sink, with all the crew! Great God, where art thou? Shall I? shall I?—The wind has gone down and shifted, sir; the fore and main topsails are reefed and set; she heads her course.'

'Stern all! Oh Moby Dick, I clutch thy heart at last!'

Such were the sounds that now came hurtling from out the old man's tormented sleep, as if Starbuck's voice had caused the long dumb dream to speak.

The yet levelled musket shook like a drunkard's arm against the panel; Starbuck seemed wrestling with an angel; but turning from the door, he placed the death-tube in its rack and left the place.

'He's too sound asleep, Mr Stubb; go thou down, and wake him, and tell him. I must see to the deck here. Thou know'st what to say.'

CHAPTER CXXIV

THE NEEDLE

Next morning the not-yet-subsided sea rolled in long slow billows of mighty bulk, and striving in the Pequod's gurgling track, pushed her on like giants' palms outspread. The strong, unstaggering breeze abounded so, that sky and air seemed vast outbellying sails; the whole world boomed before the wind. Muffled in the full morning light, the invisible sun was only known by the spread intensity of his place; where his bayonet rays moved on in stacks. Emblazonings, as of crowned Babylonian kings and queens, reigned over everything. The sea was as a crucible of molten gold, that bubblingly leaps with light and heat.

Long maintaining an enchanted silence, Ahab stood apart; and every time the tetering ship loweringly pitched down her bowsprit, he turned to eye the bright sun's rays produced ahead; and when she profoundly settled by the stern, he turned behind, and saw the sun's rearward place, and how the same yellow rays were blending with his undeviating wake.

'Ha, ha, my ship! thou mightest well be taken now for the sea-chariot of the sun. Ho, ho! all ye nations before my prow, I bring the sun to ye! Yoke on the further billows; hallo! a tandem, I drive the sea!'

But suddenly reined back by some counter thought, he hurried towards the helm, huskily demanding how the ship was heading.

'East-sou-east, sir,' said the frightened steersman.

'Thou liest!' smiting him with his clenched fist. 'Heading East at this hour in the morning, and the sun astern?'

Upon this every soul was confounded; for the phenomenon just then observed by Ahab had unaccountably escaped every one else; but its very blinding palpableness must have been the cause.

Thrusting his head half way into the binnacle, Ahab caught one glimpse of the compasses; his uplifted arm slowly fell; for a moment he almost seemed to stagger. Standing behind him Starbuck looked, and lo! the two compasses pointed East, and the Pequod was as infallibly going West.

But ere the first wild alarm could get out abroad among the crew, the old man with a rigid laugh exclaimed, 'I have it! It has happened before. Mr Starbuck, last night's thunder turned our compasses—that's all. Thou hast before now heard of such a thing, I take it.'

'Aye; but never before has it happened to me, sir,' said the pale mate, gloomily.

Here, it must needs be said, that accidents like this have in more than one case occurred to ships in violent storms. The magnetic energy, as developed in the mariner's needle, is, as all know, essentially one with the electricity beheld in heaven; hence it is not to be much marvelled at, that such things should be. In instances where the lightning has actually struck the vessel, so as to smite down some of the spars and rigging, the effect upon the needle has at times been still more fatal; all its loadstone virtue being annihilated, so that the before magnetic steel was of no more use than an old wife's knitting needle. But in either case, the needle never again, of itself, recovers the original virtue thus marred or lost; and if the binnacle compasses be affected, the same fate reaches all the others that may be in the ship; even were the lowermost one inserted into the kelson.

Deliberately standing before the binnacle, and eyeing the transpointed compasses, the old man, with the sharp of his extended hand, now took the precise bearing of the sun, and satisfied that the needles were exactly inverted, shouted out his orders for the ship's course to be changed accordingly. The yards were braced hard up; and once more the Pequod thrust her undaunted bows into the opposing wind, for the supposed fair one had only been juggling her.

Meanwhile, whatever were his own secret thoughts, Starbuck said nothing, but quietly he issued all requisite orders; while Stubb and Flask—who in some small degree seemed then to be sharing his feelings—likewise unmurmuringly acquiesced. As for the men, though some of them lowly rumbled, their fear of Ahab was greater than their fear of Fate. But as ever before, the pagan harpooneers remained almost wholly unimpressed; or if impressed, it was only with a certain magnetism shot into their congenial hearts from inflexible Ahab's.

For a space the old man walked the deck in rolling reveries. But chancing to slip with his ivory heel, he saw the crushed copper sight-tubes of the quadrant he had the day before dashed to the deck.

'Thou poor, proud heaven-gazer and sun's pilot! yesterday I wrecked thee, and to-day the compasses would feign have wrecked me. So, so. But Ahab is lord over the level loadstone yet. Mr Starbuck—a lance without the pole; a top-maul, and the smallest of the sail-maker's needles. Quick!'

Accessory, perhaps, to the impulse dictating the thing he was now about to do, were certain prudential motives, whose object might have been to revive the spirits of his crew by a stroke of his subtle skill, in a matter so wondrous as that of the inverted compasses. Besides, the old man well knew that the steer by transpointed needles, though clumsily practicable, was not a thing to be passed over by superstitious sailors, without some shudderings and evil portents.

'Men,' said he, steadily turning upon the crew, as the mate handed him the things he had demanded, 'my men, the thunder turned old Ahab's needles; but out of this bit of steel Ahab can make one of his own, that will point as true as any.'

Abashed glances of servile wonder were exchanged by the sailors, as this was said; and with fascinated eyes they awaited whatever magic might follow. But Starbuck looked away.

With a blow from the top-maul Ahab knocked off the steel head of the lance, and then handing to the mate the long iron rod remaining, bade him hold it upright, without its touching the deck. Then, with the maul, after repeatedly smiting the upper end of this iron rod, he placed the blunted needle endwise on the top of it, and less strongly hammered that, several times, the mate still holding the rod as before. Then going through some small strange motions with it—whether indispensable to the magnetizing of the steel, or merely intended to augment the awe of the crew, is uncertain—he called for linen thread; and moving to the binnacle, slipped out the two reversed needles there, and horizontally suspended the sail-needle by its middle, over one of the compass-cards. At first, the steel went round and round, quivering and vibrating at either end; but at last it settled to its place, when Ahab, who had been intently watching for this result, stepped frankly back from the binnacle, and pointing his stretched arm towards it, exclaimed,—'Look ye, for yourselves, if Ahab be not lord of the level loadstone! The sun is East, and that compass swears it!'

One after another they peered in, for nothing but their own eyes could persuade such ignorance as theirs, and one after another they slunk away.

In his fiery eyes of scorn and triumph, you then saw Ahab in all his fatal pride.

CHAPTER CXXV

The Log and Line

While now the fated Pequod had been so long afloat this voyage, the log and line had but very seldom been in use. Owing to a confident reliance upon other means of determining the vessel's place, some merchantmen, and many whalemen, especially when cruising, wholly neglect to heave the log; though at the same time, and frequently more for form's sake than anything else, regularly putting down upon the customary slate the course steered by the ship, as well as the presumed average rate of progression every hour. It had been thus with the Pequod. The wooden reel and angular log attached hung, long untouched, just beneath the railing of the after bulwarks. Rains and spray had damped it; sun and wind had warped it; all the elements had combined to rot a thing that hung so idly. But heedless of all this, his mood seized Ahab, as he happened to glance upon the reel, not many hours after the magnet scene, and he remembered how his quadrant was no more, and recalled his frantic oath about the level log and line. The ship was sailing plungingly; astern the billows rolled in riots.

'Forward, there! Heave the log!'

Two seamen came. The golden-hued Tahitian and the grizzly Manxman. 'Take the reel, one of ye, I'll heave.'

They went towards the extreme stern, on the ship's lee side, where the deck, with the oblique energy of the wind, was now almost dipping into the creamy, sidelong-rushing sea.

The Manxman took the reel, and holding it high up, by the projecting handle-ends of the spindle, round which the spool of line revolved, so stood with the angular log hanging downwards, till Ahab advanced to him.

Ahab stood before him, and was lightly unwinding some thirty or forty turns to form a preliminary hand-coil to toss overboard, when the old Manxman, who was intently eyeing both him and the line, made bold to speak.

'Sir, I mistrust it; this line looks far gone, long heat and wet have spoiled it.'

''Twill hold, old gentleman. Long heat and wet, have they spoiled thee? Thou seem'st to hold. Or, truer perhaps, life holds thee; not thou it.'

'I hold the spool, sir. But just as my captain says. With these grey hairs of mine 'tis not worth while disputing, 'specially with a superior, who'll ne'er confess.'

'What's that? There now's a patched professor in Queen Nature's granite-founded College; but methinks he's too subservient. Where wert thou born?'

'In the little rocky Isle of Man, sir.'

'Excellent! Thou'st hit the world by that.'

'I know not, sir, but I was born there.'

'In the Isle of Man, hey? Well, the other way, it's good. Here's a man from Man; a man born in once independent Man, and now unmanned of Man; which is sucked in—by what? Up with the reel! The dead, blind wall butts all inquiring heads at last. Up with it! So.'

The log was heaved. The loose coils rapidly straightened out in a long dragging line astern, and then, instantly, the reel began to whirl. In turn, jerkingly raised and lowered by the rolling billows, the towing resistance of the log caused the old reelman to stagger strangely.

'Hold hard!'

Snap! the overstrained line sagged down in one long festoon; the tugging log was gone.

'I crush the quadrant, the thunder turns the needles, and now the mad sea parts the log-line. But Ahab can mend all. Haul in here, Tahitian; reel up, Manxman. And look ye, let the carpenter make another log, and mend thou the line. See to it.'

'There he goes now; to him nothing's happened; but to me, the skewer seems loosening out of the middle of the world. Haul in, haul in, Tahitian! These lines run whole, and whirling out: come in broken, and dragging slow. Ha, Pip? come to help; eh, Pip?'

'Pip? whom call ye Pip? Pip jumped from the whale-boat. Pip's missing. Let's see now if ye haven't fished him up here, fisherman. It drags hard; I guess he's holding on. Jerk him, Tahiti! Jerk him off; we haul in no cowards here. Ho! there's his arm just breaking water. A hatchet! a hatchet! cut it off—we haul in no cowards here. Captain Ahab! sir, sir! here's Pip, trying to get on board again.'

'Peace, thou crazy loon,' cried the Manxman, seizing him by the arm. 'Away from the quarter-deck!'

'The greater idiot ever scolds the lesser,' muttered Ahab, advancing. 'Hands off from that holiness! Where sayest thou Pip was, boy?'

'Astern there, sir, astern! Lo, lo!'

'And who art thou, boy? I see not my reflection in the vacant pupils of thy eyes. Oh God! that man should be a thing for immortal souls to sieve through! Who art thou, boy?'

'Bell-boy, sir; ship's-crier, ding, dong, ding! Pip! Pip! Pip! One hundred pounds of clay reward for Pip; five feet high—looks cowardly—quickest known by that! Ding, dong, ding! Who's seen Pip the coward?'

'There can be no hearts above the snow-line. Oh, ye frozen heavens! look down here. Ye did beget this luckless child, and have abandoned him, ye creative libertines. Here, boy; Ahab's cabin shall be Pip's home henceforth, while Ahab lives. Thou touchest my inmost centre, boy; thou art tied to me by cords woven of my heart-strings. Come, let's down.'

'What's this? here's velvet shark-skin,' intently gazing at Ahab's hand, and feeling it. 'Ah, now, had poor Pip but felt so kind a thing as this, perhaps he had ne'er been lost! This seems to me, sir, as a man-rope; something that weak souls may hold by. Oh, sir, let old Perth now come and rivet these two hands together; the black one with the white, for I will not let this go.'

'Oh, boy, nor will I thee, unless I should thereby drag thee to worse horrors than are here. Come, then, to my cabin. Lo! ye believers in gods all goodness, and in man all ill, lo you! see the omniscient gods oblivious of suffering man; and man, though idiotic, and knowing not what he does, yet full of the sweet things of love and gratitude. Come! I feel prouder leading thee by thy black hand, than though I grasped an Emperor's!'

'There go two daft ones now,' muttered the old Manxman. 'One daft with strength, the other daft with weakness. But here's the end of the rotten line—all dripping, too. Mend it, eh? I think we had best have a new line altogether. I'll see Mr Stubb about it.'

CHAPTER CXXVI

THE LIFE-BUOY

Steering now south-eastward by Ahab's levelled steel, and her progress solely determined by Ahab's level log and line; the Pequod held on her path towards the Equator. Making so long a passage through such unfrequented waters, descrying no ships, and ere long, sideways impelled by unvarying trade winds, over waves monotonously mild; all these seemed the strange calm things preluding some riotous and desperate scene.

At last, when the ship drew near to the outskirts, as it were, of the Equatorial fishing-ground, and in the deep darkness that goes before the dawn, was sailing by a cluster of rocky islets; the watch—then headed by Flask—was startled by a cry so plaintively wild and unearthly—like half-articulated wailings of the ghosts of all Herod's murdered Innocents—that one and all, they started from their reveries, and for the space of some moments stood, or sat, or leaned all transfixedly listening, like the carved Roman slave, while that wild cry remained within hearing. The Christian or civilized part of the crew said it was mermaids, and shuddered; but the pagan harpooneers remained unappalled. Yet the grey Manxman—the oldest mariner of all—declared that the wild thrilling sounds that were heard, were the voices of newly drowned men in the sea.

Below in his hammock, Ahab did not hear of this till grey dawn, when he came to the deck; it was then recounted to him by Flask, not unaccompanied with hinted dark meanings. He hollowly laughed, and thus explained the wonder.

Those rocky islands the ship had passed were the resort of great numbers of seals, and some young seals that had lost their dams, or some dams that had lost their cubs, must have risen nigh the ship and kept company with her, crying and sobbing with their human sort of wail. But this only the more affected some of them, because most mariners cherish a very superstitious feeling about seals, arising not only from their peculiar tones when in distress, but also from the human look of their round heads and semi-intelligent faces, seen peeringly uprising from the water alongside. In the sea, under certain circumstances, seals have more than once been mistaken for men.

But the bodings of the crew were destined to receive a most plausible confirmation in the fate of one of their number that morning. At sun-rise this man went from his hammock to his mast-head at the fore; and whether it was that he was not yet half waked from his sleep (for sailors sometimes go aloft in a transition state), whether it was thus with the man, there is now no telling; but, be that as it may, he had not been long at his perch, when a cry was heard—a cry and a rushing—and looking up, they saw a falling phantom in the air; and looking down, a little tossed heap of white bubbles in the blue of the sea.

The life-buoy—a long slender cask—was dropped from the stern, where it always hung obedient to a cunning spring; but no hand rose to seize it, and the sun having long beat upon this cask it had shrunken, so that it slowly filled, and the parched wood also filled at its every pore; and the studded iron-bound cask followed the sailor to the bottom, as if to yield him his pillow, though in sooth but a hard one.

And thus the first man of the Pequod that mounted the mast to look out for the White Whale, on the White Whale's own peculiar ground; that man was swallowed up in the deep. But few, perhaps, thought of that at the time. Indeed, in some sort, they were not grieved at this event, at least as a portent; for they regarded it, not as a foreshadowing of evil in the future, but as the fulfilment of an evil already presaged. They declared that now they knew the reason of those wild shrieks they had heard the night before. But again the old Manxman said nay.

The lost life-buoy was now to be replaced; Starbuck was directed to see to it; but as no cask of sufficient lightness could be found, and as in the feverish eagerness of what seemed the approaching crisis of the voyage, all hands were impatient of any toil but what was directly connected with its final end, whatever that might prove to be; therefore, they were going to leave the ship's stern unprovided with a buoy, when by certain strange signs and innuendoes Queequeg hinted a hint concerning his coffin.

'A life-buoy of a coffin!' cried Starbuck, starting.

'Rather queer, that, I should say,' said Stubb.

'It will make a good enough one,' said Flask, 'the carpenter here can arrange it easily.'

'Bring it up; there's nothing else for it,' said Starbuck, after a melancholy pause. 'Rig it, carpenter; do not look at me so—the coffin, I mean. Dost thou hear me? Rig it.'

'And shall I nail down the lid, sir?' moving his hand as with a hammer.

'Aye.'

'And shall I caulk the seams, sir?' moving his hand as with a caulking-iron.

'Aye.'

'And shall I then pay over the same with pitch, sir?' moving his hand as with a pitch-pot.

'Away! what possesses thee to this? Make a life-buoy of the coffin, and no more.—Mr Stubb, Mr Flask, come forward with me.'

'He goes off in a huff. The whole he can endure; at the parts he baulks. Now I don't like this. I make a leg for Captain Ahab, and he wears it like a gentleman; but I make a bandbox for Queequeg, and he wont put his head into it. Are all my pains to go for nothing with that coffin? And now I'm ordered to make a life-buoy of it. It's like turning an old coat; going to bring the flesh on the other side now. I don't like this cobbling sort of business—I don't like it at all; it's undignified; it's not my place. Let tinkers' brats do tinkerings; we are their betters. I like to take in hand none but clean, virgin, fair-and-square mathematical jobs, something that regularly begins at the beginning, and is at the middle when midway, and comes to an end at the conclusion; not a cobbler's job, that's at an end in the middle, and at the beginning at the end. It's the old woman's tricks to be giving cobbling jobs. Lord! what an affection all old women have for tinkers. I know an old woman of sixty-five who ran away with a bald-headed young tinker once. And that's the reason I never would work for lonely widow old women ashore, when I kept my job-shop in the Vineyard; they might have taken it into their lonely old heads to run off with me. But heigh-ho! there are no caps at sea but snow-caps. Let me see. Nail down the lid; caulk the seams; pay over the same with pitch; batten them down tight, and hang it with the snap-spring over the ship's stern. Were ever such things done before with a coffin? Some superstitious old carpenters, now, would be tied up in the rigging, ere they would do the job. But I'm made of knotty Aroostook hemlock; I don't budge. Cruppered with a coffin! Sailing about with a grave-yard tray! But never mind. We workers in woods make bridal-bedsteads, and card-tables, as well as coffins and hearses. We work by the month, or by the job, or by the profit; not for us to ask the why and wherefore of our work, unless it be too confounded cobbling, and then we stash it if we can. Hem! I'll do the job, now, tenderly. I'll have me—let's see—how many in the ship's company, all told? But I've forgotten. Any way, I'll have me thirty separate, Turk's-headed life-lines, each three feet long hanging all round to the coffin. Then, if the hull go down, there'll be thirty lively fellows all fighting for one coffin, a sight not seen very often beneath the sun! Come hammer, calking-iron, pitch-pot, and marling-spike! Let's to it.'

CHAPTER CXXVII

THE DECK

The coffin laid upon two line-tubs, between the vice-bench and the open hatchway; the Carpenter calking its seams; the string of twisted oakum slowly unwinding from a large roll of it placed in the bosom of his frock.—Ahab comes slowly from the cabin-gangway, and hears Pip following him.

'Back, lad; I will be with ye again presently. He goes! Not this hand complies with my humor more genially than that boy.—Middle aisle of a church! What's here?'

'Life-buoy, sir. Mr Starbuck's orders. Oh, look sir! beware the hatchway!'

'Thank ye, man. Thy coffin lies handy to the vault.'

'Sir? The hatchway? oh! So it does, sir, so it does.'

'Art not thou the leg-maker? Look, did not this stump come from thy shop?'

'I believe it did, sir; does the ferrule stand, sir?'

'Well enough. But art thou not also the undertaker?'

'Aye, sir; I patched up this thing here as a coffin for Queequeg; but they've set me now to turning it into something else.'

'Then tell me; art thou not an arrant, all-grasping, inter-meddling, monopolizing, heathenish old scamp, to be one day making legs, and the next day coffins to clap them in, and yet again life-buoys out of those same coffins? Thou art as unprincipled as the gods, and as much of a jack-of-all-trades.'

'But I do not mean anything, sir. I do as I do.'

'The gods again. Hark ye, dost thou not ever sing working about a coffin? The Titans, they say, hummed snatches when chipping out the craters for volcanoes; and the grave-digger in the play sings, spade in hand. Dost thou never?'

'Sing, sir? Do I sing? Oh, I'm indifferent enough, sir, for that; but the reason why the grave-digger made music must have been because there was none in his spade, sir. But the calking mallet is full of it. Hark to it.'

'Aye, and that's because the lid there's a sounding-board; and what in all things makes the sounding-board is this—there's naught beneath. And yet, a coffin with a body in it rings pretty much the same, Carpenter. Hast thou ever helped carry a bier, and heard the coffin knock against the churchyard gate, going in?'

'Faith, sir, I've—'

'Faith? What's that?'

'Why, faith, sir, it's only a sort of exclamation-like—that's all, sir.'

'Um, um; go on.'

'I was about to say, sir, that—'

'Art thou a silk-worm? Dost thou spin thy own shroud out of thyself? Look at thy bosom! Despatch! and get these traps out of sight.'

'He goes aft. That was sudden, now; but squalls come sudden in hot latitudes. I've heard that the Isle of Albemarle, one of the Gallipagos, is cut by the Equator right in the middle. Seems to me some sort of Equator cuts yon old man, too, right in his middle. He's always under the Line—fiery hot, I tell ye! He's looking this way—come, oakum; quick. Here we go again. This wooden mallet is the cork, and I'm the professor of musical glasses—tap, tap!'

(*Ahab to himself.*)

'There's a sight! There's a sound! The greyheaded woodpecker tapping the hollow tree! Blind and dumb might well be envied now. See! that thing rests on two line-tubs, full of tow-lines. A most malicious wag, that fellow. Rat-tat! So man's seconds tick! Oh! how immaterial are all materials! What things real are there, but imponderable thoughts? Here now's the very dreaded symbol of grim death, by a mere hap, made the expressive sign of the help and hope of most endangered life. A life-buoy of a coffin! Does it go further? Can it be that in some spiritual sense the coffin is, after all, but an immortality-preserver! I'll think of that. But no. So far gone am I in the dark side of earth, that its other side, the theoretic bright one, seems but uncertain twilight to me. Will ye never have done, Carpenter, with that accursed sound? I go below; let me not see that thing here when I return again. Now, then, Pip, we'll talk this over; I do suck most wondrous philosophies from thee! Some unknown conduits from the unknown worlds must empty into thee!'

CHAPTER CXXVIII

THE PEQUOD MEETS THE RACHEL

Next day, a large ship, the Rachel, was descried, bearing directly down upon the Pequod, all her spars thickly clustering with men. At the time the Pequod was making good speed through the water; but as the broad-winged windward stranger shot nigh to her, the boastful sails all fell together as blank bladders that are burst, and all life fled from the smitten hull.

'Bad news; she brings bad news,' muttered the old Manxman. But ere her commander, who, with trumpet to mouth, stood up in his boat; ere he could hopefully hail, Ahab's voice was heard.

'Hast seen the White Whale?'

'Aye, yesterday. Have ye seen a whale-boat adrift?'

Throttling his joy, Ahab negatively answered this unexpected question; and would then have fain boarded the stranger, when the stranger captain himself, having stopped his vessel's way, was seen descending her side. A few keen pulls, and his boat-hook soon clinched the Pequod's main-chains, and he sprang to the deck. Immediately he was recognized by Ahab for a Nantucketer he knew. But no formal salutation was exchanged.

'Where was he?—not killed!—not killed!' cried Ahab, closely advancing. 'How was it?'

It seemed that somewhat late on the afternoon of the day previous, while three of the stranger's boats were engaged with a shoal of whales, which had led them some four or five miles from the ship; and while they were yet in swift chase to windward, the white hump and head of Moby Dick had suddenly loomed up out of the blue water, not very far to leeward; whereupon, the fourth rigged boat—a reserved one—had been instantly lowered in chase. After a keen sail before the wind, this fourth boat—the swiftest keeled of all—seemed to have succeeded in fastening—at least, as well as the man at the mast-head could tell anything about it. In the distance he saw the diminished dotted boat; and then a swift gleam of bubbling white water; and after that nothing more; whence it was concluded that the stricken whale must have indefinitely run away with his pursuers, as often happens. There was some apprehension, but no positive alarm, as yet. The recall signals were placed in the rigging; darkness came on; and forced to pick up her three far to windward boats—ere going in quest of the fourth one in the precisely opposite direction—the ship had not only been necessitated to leave that boat to its fate till near midnight, but, for the time, to increase her distance from it. But the rest of her crew being at last safe aboard, she crowded all sail—stunsail on stunsail—after the missing boat; kindling a fire in her try-pots for a beacon; and every other man aloft on the look-out. But though when she had thus sailed a sufficient distance to gain the presumed place of the absent ones when last seen; though she then paused to lower her spare boats to pull all around her; and not finding anything, had again dashed on; again paused, and lowered her boats; and though she had thus continued doing till day light; yet not the least glimpse of the missing keel had been seen.

The story told, the stranger Captain immediately went on to reveal his object in boarding the Pequod. He desired that ship to unite with his own in the search; by sailing over the sea some four or five miles apart, on parallel lines, and so sweeping a double horizon, as it were.

'I will wager something now,' whispered Stubb to Flask, 'that some one in that missing boat wore off that Captain's best coat; mayhap, his watch—he's so cursed anxious to get it back. Who ever heard of two pious whale-ships cruising after one missing whale-boat in the height of the whaling season? See, Flask, only see how pale he looks—pale in the very buttons of his eyes—look—it wasn't the coat—it must have been the—'

'My boy, my own boy is among them. For God's sake—I beg, I conjure'—here exclaimed the stranger Captain to Ahab, who thus far had but icily received his petition. 'For eight-and-forty hours let me charter your ship—I will gladly pay for it, and roundly pay for it—if there be no other way—for eight-and-forty hours only—only that—you must, oh, you must, and you *shall* do this thing.'

'His son!' cried Stubb, 'oh, it's his son he's lost! I take back the coat and watch—what says Ahab? We must save that boy.'

'He's drowned with the rest on 'em, last night,' said the old Manx sailor standing behind them; 'I heard; all of ye heard their spirits.'

Now, as it shortly turned out, what made this incident of the Rachel's the more melancholy, was the circumstance, that not only was one of the Captain's sons among the number of the missing boat's crew; but among the number of the other boats' crews, at the same time, but on the other hand, separated from the ship during the dark vicissitudes of the chase, there had been still another son; as that for a time, the wretched father was plunged to the bottom of the cruellest perplexity; which was only solved for him by his chief mate's instinctively adopting the ordinary procedure of a whale-ship in such emergencies, that is, when placed between jeopardized but divided boats, always to pick up the majority first. But the captain, for some unknown constitutional reason, had refrained from mentioning all this, and not till forced to it by Ahab's iciness did he allude to his one yet missing boy; a little lad, but twelve years old, whose father with the earnest but unmisgiving hardihood of a Nantucketer's paternal love, had thus early sought to initiate him in the perils and wonders of a vocation almost immemorially the destiny of all his race. Nor does it unfrequently occur, that Nantucket captains will send a son of such tender age away from them, for a protracted three or four years' voyage in some other ship than their own; so that their first knowledge of a whaleman's career shall be unenervated by any chance display of a father's natural but untimely partiality, or undue apprehensiveness and concern.

Meantime, now the stranger was still beseeching his poor boon of Ahab; and Ahab still stood like an anvil, receiving every shock, but without the least quivering of his own.

'I will not go,' said the stranger, 'till you say *aye* to me. Do to me as you would have me do to you in the like case. For *you* too have a boy, Captain Ahab—though but a child, and nestling safely at home now—a child of your old age too—Yes, yes, you relent; I see it—run, run, men, now, and stand by to square in the yards.'

'Avast,' cried Ahab—'touch not a rope-yarn;' then in a voice that prolongingly moulded every word—'Captain Gardiner, I will not do it. Even now I lose time. Good bye, good bye. God bless ye, man, and may I forgive myself, but I must go. Mr Starbuck, look at the binnacle watch, and in three minutes from this present instant warn off all strangers: then brace forward again, and let the ship sail as before.'

Hurriedly turning, with averted face, he descended into his cabin, leaving the strange captain transfixed at this unconditional and utter rejection of his so earnest suit. But starting from his enchantment, Gardiner silently hurried to the side; more fell than stepped into his boat, and returned to his ship.

Soon the two ships diverged their wakes; and long as the strange vessel was in view, she was seen to yaw hither and thither at every dark spot, however small, on the sea. This way and that her yards were swung round; starboard and larboard, she continued to tack; now she beat against a head sea; and again it pushed her before it; while all the while, her masts and yards were thickly clustered with men, as three tall cherry trees, when the boys are cherrying among the boughs.

But by her still halting course and winding, woful way, you plainly saw that this ship that so wept with spray, still remained without comfort. She was Rachel, weeping for her children, because they were not.

CHAPTER CXXIX

THE CABIN

(*Ahab moving to go on deck; Pip catches him by the hand to follow.*)

'Lad, lad, I tell thee thou must not follow Ahab now. The hour is coming when Ahab would not scare thee from him, yet would not have thee by him. There is that in thee, poor lad, which I feel too curing to my malady. Like cures like; and for this hunt, my malady becomes my most desired health. Do thou abide below here, where they shall serve thee, as if thou wert the captain. Aye, lad, thou shalt sit here in my own screwed chair; another screw to it, thou must be.'

'No, no, no! ye have not a whole body, sir; do ye but use poor me for your one lost leg; only tread upon me, sir; I ask no more, so I remain a part of ye.'

'Oh! spite of million villains, this makes me a bigot in the fadeless fidelity of man!—and a black! and crazy!—but methinks like-cures-like applies to him too; he grows so sane again.'

'They tell me, sir, that Stubb did once desert poor little Pip, whose drowned bones now show white, for all the blackness of his living skin. But I will never desert ye, sir, as Stubb did him. Sir, I must go with ye.'

'If thou speakest thus to me much more, Ahab's purpose keels up in him. I tell thee no; it cannot be.'

'Oh good master, master, master!'

'Weep so, and I will murder thee! have a care, for Ahab too is mad. Listen, and thou wilt often hear my ivory foot upon the deck, and still know that I am there. And now I quit thee. Thy hand!—Met! True art thou, lad, as the circumference to its centre. So: God for ever bless thee; and if it come to that,—God for ever save thee, let what will befall.'

(*Ahab goes; Pip steps one step forward.*)

'Here he this instant stood; I stand in his air,—but I'm alone. Now were even poor Pip here I could endure it, but he's missing. Pip! Pip! Ding, dong, ding! Who's seen Pip? He must be up here; let's try the door. What? neither lock, nor bolt, nor bar; and yet there's no opening it. It must be the spell; he told me to stay here: Aye, and told me this screwed chair was mine. Here, then, I'll seat me, against the transom, in the ship's full middle, all her keel and her three masts before me. Here, our old sailors say, in their black seventy-fours great admirals sometimes sit at table, and lord it over rows of captains and lieutenants. Ha! what's this? epaulets! epaulets! the epaulets all come crowding! Pass round the decanters; glad to see ye; fill up, monsieurs! What an odd feeling, now, when a black boy's host to white men with gold lace upon their coats! Monsieurs, have ye seen one Pip?—a little negro lad, five feet high, hang-dog look, and cowardly! Jumped from a whale-boat once;—seen him? No! Well then, fill up again, captains, and let's drink shame upon all cowards! I name no names. Shame upon them! Put one foot upon the table. Shame upon all cowards.—Hist! above there, I hear ivory—Oh, master! master! I am indeed downhearted when you walk over me. But here I'll stay, though this stern strikes rocks; and they bulge through; and oysters come to join me.'

CHAPTER CXXX

THE HAT

And now that at the proper time and place, after so long and wide a preliminary cruise, Ahab,—all other whaling waters swept—seemed to have chased his foe into an ocean-fold, to slay him the more securely there; now, that he found himself hard by the very latitude and longitude where his tormenting wound had been inflicted; now that a vessel had been spoken which on the very day preceding had actually encountered Moby Dick;—and now that all his successive meetings with various ships contrastingly concurred to show the demoniac indifference with which the white whale tore his hunters, whether sinning or sinned against; now it was that there lurked a something in the old man's eyes, which it was hardly sufferable for feeble souls to see. As the unsetting polar star, which through the livelong, arctic, six months' night sustains its piercing, steady, central gaze; so Ahab's purpose now fixedly gleamed down upon the constant midnight of the gloomy crew. It domineered above them so, that all their bodings, doubts, misgivings, fears, were fain to hide beneath their souls, and not sprout forth a single spear or leaf.

In this foreshadowing interval too, all humor, forced or natural, vanished. Stubb no more strove to raise a smile; Starbuck no more strove to check one. Alike, joy and sorrow, hope and fear, seemed ground to finest dust, and powdered, for the time, in the clamped mortar of Ahab's iron soul. Like machines, they dumbly moved about the deck, ever conscious that the old man's despot eye was on them.

But did you deeply scan him in his more secret confidential hours; when he thought no glance but one was on him; then you would have seen that even as Ahab's eyes so awed the crew's, the inscrutable Parsee's glance awed his; or somehow, at least, in some wild way, at times affected it. Such an added, gliding strangeness began to invest the thin Fedallah now; such ceaseless shudderings shook him; that the men looked dubious at him; half uncertain, as it seemed, whether indeed he were a mortal substance, or else a tremulous shadow cast upon the deck by some unseen being's body. And that shadow was always hovering there. For not by night, even, had Fedallah ever certainly been known to slumber, or go below. He would stand still for hours: but never sat or leaned; his wan but wondrous eyes did plainly say—We two watchmen never rest.

Nor, at any time, by night or day could the mariners now step up the deck, unless Ahab was before them; either standing in his pivot-hole, or exactly pacing the planks between two undeviating limits,—the main-mast and the mizen; or else they saw him standing in the cabin-scuttle,—his living foot advanced upon the deck, as if to step; his hat slouched heavily over his eyes; so that however motionless he stood, however the days and nights were added on, that he had not swung in his hammock; yet hidden beneath that slouching hat, they could never tell unerringly whether, for all this, his eyes were really closed at times: or whether he was still intently scanning them; no matter, though he stood so in the scuttle for a whole long hour on the stretch, and the unheeded night-damp gathered in beads of dew upon that stone-carved coat and hat. The clothes that the night had wet, the next day's sunshine dried upon him; and so, day after day, and night after night; he went no more beneath the planks; whatever he wanted from the cabin that thing he sent for.

He ate in the same open air; that is, his two only meals,—breakfast and dinner: supper he never touched; nor reaped his beard; which darkly grew all gnarled, as unearthed roots of trees blown over, which still grow idly on at naked base, though perished in the upper verdure. But though his whole life was now become one watch on deck; and though the Parsee's mystic watch was without intermission as his own; yet these two never seemed to speak—one man to the other—unless at long intervals some passing unmomentous matter made it necessary. Though such a potent spell seemed secretly to join the twain; openly, and to the awe-struck crew, they seemed pole-like asunder. If by day they chanced to speak one word; by night, dumb men were both, so far as concerned the slightest verbal interchange. At times, for longest hours, without a single hail, they stood far parted in the starlight; Ahab in his scuttle, the Parsee by the main-mast; but still fixedly gazing upon each other, as if in the Parsee Ahab saw his forethrown shadow, in Ahab the Parsee his abandoned substance.

And yet, somehow, did Ahab—in his own proper self, as daily, hourly, and every instant, commandingly revealed to his subordinates,—Ahab seemed an independent lord; the Parsee but his slave. Still again both seemed yoked together, and an unseen tyrant driving them; the lean shade siding the solid rib. For be this Parsee what he may, all rib and keel was solid Ahab.

At the first faintest glimmering of the dawn, his iron voice was heard from aft—'Man the mast-heads!'—and all through the day, till after sunset and after twilight, the same voice every hour, at the striking of the helmsman's bell, was heard—'What d'ye see?—sharp! sharp!'

But when three or four days had slided by, after meeting the children-seeking Rachel; and no spout had yet been seen; the monomaniac old man seemed distrustful of his crew's fidelity; at least, of nearly all except the Pagan harpooneers; he seemed to doubt, even, whether Stubb and Flask might not willingly overlook the sight he sought. But if these suspicions were really his, he sagaciously refrained from verbally expressing them, however his actions might seem to hint them.

'I will have the first sight of the whale myself,'—he said. 'Aye! Ahab must have the doubloon!' and with his own hands he rigged a nest of basketed bowlines; and sending a hand aloft, with a single sheaved block, to secure to the main-mast head, he received the two ends of the downward-reeved rope; and attaching one to his basket prepared a pin for the other end, in order to fasten it at the rail. This done, with that end yet in his hand and standing beside the pin, he looked round upon his crew, sweeping from one to the other; pausing his glance long upon Daggoo, Queequeg, Tashtego; but shunning Fedallah; and then settling his firm relying eye upon the chief mate, said,—'Take the rope, sir—I give it into thy hands, Starbuck.' Then arranging his person in the basket, he gave the word for them to hoist him to his perch, Starbuck being the one who secured the rope at last; and afterwards stood near it. And thus, with one hand clinging round the royal mast, Ahab gazed abroad upon the sea for miles and miles,—ahead, astern, this side, and that,—within the wide expanded circle commanded at so great a height.

When in working with his hands at some lofty almost isolated place in the rigging, which chances to afford no foothold, the sailor at sea is hoisted up to that spot, and sustained there by the rope; under these circumstances, its fastened end on deck is always given in strict charge to some one man who has the special watch of it. Because in such a wilderness of running rigging, whose various different relations aloft cannot always be infallibly discerned by what is seen of them at the deck; and when the deck-ends of these ropes are being every few minutes cast down from the fastenings, it would be but a natural fatality, if, unprovided with a constant watchman, the hoisted sailor should by some carelessness of the crew be cast adrift and fall all swooping to the sea. So Ahab's proceedings in this matter were not unusual; the only strange thing about them seemed to be, that Starbuck, almost the one only man who had ever ventured to oppose him with anything in the slightest degree approaching to decision—one of those too, whose faithfulness on the look-out he had seemed to doubt somewhat;—it was strange, that this was the very man he should select for his watchman; freely giving his whole life into such an otherwise distrusted person's hands.

Now, the first time Ahab was perched aloft; ere he had been there ten minutes; one of those red-billed savage sea-hawks which so often fly incommodiously close round the manned mast-heads of whalemen in these latitudes; one of these birds came wheeling and screaming round his head in a maze of untrackably swift circlings. Then it darted a thousand feet straight up into the air; then spiralized downwards, and went eddying again round his head.

But with his gaze fixed upon the dim and distant horizon, Ahab seemed not to mark this wild bird; nor, indeed, would any one else have marked it much, it being no uncommon circumstance; only now almost the least heedful eye seemed to see some sort of cunning meaning in almost every sight.

'Your hat, your hat, sir!' suddenly cried the Sicilian sea-man, who being posted at the mizen-mast-head, stood directly behind Ahab, though somewhat lower than his level, and with a deep gulf of air dividing them.

But already the sable wing was before the old man's eyes; the long hooked bill at his head: with a scream, the black hawk darted away with his prize.

An eagle flew thrice round Tarquin's head, removing his cap to replace it, and thereupon Tanaquil, his wife, declared that Tarquin would be king of Rome. But only by the replacing of the cap was that omen accounted good. Ahab's hat was never restored; the wild hawk flew on and on with it; far in advance of the prow: and at last disappeared; while from the point of that disappearance, a minute black spot was dimly discerned, falling from that vast height into the sea.

CHAPTER CXXXI

The Pequod Meets the Delight

The intense Pequod sailed on; the rolling waves and days went by; the life-buoy-coffin still lightly swung; and another ship, most miserably misnamed the Delight, was descried. As she drew nigh, all eyes were fixed upon her broad beams, called shears, which, in some whaling-ships, cross the quarter-deck at the height of eight or nine feet; serving to carry the spare, unrigged, or disabled boats.

Upon the stranger's shears were beheld the shattered, white ribs, and some few splintered planks, of what had once been a whale-boat; but you now saw through this wreck, as plainly as you see through the peeled, half-unhinged, and bleaching skeleton of a horse.

'Hast seen the White Whale?'

'Look!' replied the hollow-cheeked captain from his taffrail; and with his trumpet he pointed to the wreck.

'Hast killed him?'

'The harpoon is not yet forged that will ever do that,' answered the other, sadly glancing upon a rounded hammock on the deck, whose gathered sides some noiseless sailors were busy in sewing together.

'Not forged!' and snatching Perth's levelled iron from the crotch, Ahab held it out, exclaiming—'Look ye, Nantucketer; here in this hand I hold his death! Tempered in blood, and tempered by lightning are these barbs; and I swear to temper them triply in that hot place behind the fin, where the White Whale most feels his accursed life!'

'Then God keep thee, old man—see'st thou that'—pointing to the hammock—'I bury but one of five stout men, who were alive only yesterday; but were dead ere night. Only *that* one I bury; the rest were buried before they died; you sail upon their tomb.' Then turning to his crew—'Are ye ready there? place the plank then on the rail, and lift the body; so, then—Oh! God'—advancing towards the hammock with uplifted hands—'may the resurrection and the life—'

'Brace forward! Up helm!' cried Ahab like lightning to his men.

But the suddenly started Pequod was not quick enough to escape the sound of the splash that the corpse soon made as it struck the sea; not so quick, indeed, but that some of the flying bubbles might have sprinkled her hull with their ghostly baptism.

As Ahab now glided from the dejected Delight, the strange life-buoy hanging at the Pequod's stern came into conspicuous relief.

'Ha! yonder! look yonder, men!' cried a foreboding voice in her wake. 'In vain, oh, ye strangers, ye fly our sad burial; ye but turn us your taffrail to show us your coffin!'

CHAPTER CXXXII

THE SYMPHONY

It was a clear steel-blue day. The firmaments of air and sea were hardly separable in that all-pervading azure; only, the pensive air was transparently pure and soft, with a woman's look and the robust and man-like sea heaved with long, strong, lingering swells, as Samson's chest in his sleep.

Hither, and thither, on high, glided the snow-white wings of small, unspeckled birds; these were the gentle thoughts of the feminine air; but to and fro in the deeps, far down in the bottomless blue, rushed mighty leviathans, sword-fish, and sharks; and these were the strong, troubled, murderous thinkings of the masculine sea.

But though thus contrasting within, the contrast was only in shades and shadows without; those two seemed one; it was only the sex, as it were, that distinguished them.

Aloft, like a royal czar and king, the sun seemed giving this gentle air to this bold and rolling sea; even as bride to groom. And at the girdling line of the horizon, a soft and tremulous motion—most seen here at the equator—denoted the fond, throbbing trust, the loving alarms, with which the poor bride gave her bosom away.

Tied up and twisted; gnarled and knotted with wrinkles; haggardly firm and unyielding; his eyes glowing like coals, that still glow in the ashes of ruin; untottering Ahab stood forth in the clearness of the morn; lifting his splintered helmet of a brow to the fair girl's forehead of heaven.

Oh, immortal infancy, and innocency of the azure! Invisible winged creatures that frolic all round us! Sweet childhood of air and sky! how oblivious were ye of old Ahab's close-coiled woe! But so have I seen little Miriam and Martha, laughing-eyed elves, heedlessly gambol around their old sire; sporting with the circle of singed locks which grew on the marge of that burnt-out crater of his brain.

Slowly crossing the deck from the scuttle, Ahab leaned over the side, and watched how his shadow in the water sank and sank to his gaze, the more and the more that he strove to pierce the profundity. But the lovely aromas in that enchanted air did at last seem to dispel, for a moment, the cankerous thing in his soul. That glad, happy air, that winsome sky, did at last stroke and caress him; the step-mother world, so long cruel—forbidding—now threw affectionate arms round his stubborn neck, and did seem to joyously sob over him, as if over one, that however wilful and erring, she could yet find it in her heart to save and to bless. From beneath his slouched hat Ahab dropped a tear into the sea; nor did all the Pacific contain such wealth as that one wee drop.

Starbuck saw the old man; saw him, how he heavily leaned over the side; and he seemed to hear in his own true heart the measureless sobbing that stole out of the centre of the serenity around. Careful not to touch him, or be noticed by him, he yet drew near to him, and stood there.

Ahab turned.

'Starbuck!'

'Sir.'

'Oh, Starbuck! it is a mild, mild wind, and a mild looking sky. On such a day—very much such a sweetness as this—I struck my first whale—a boy-harpooneer of eighteen! Forty—forty—forty years ago!—ago! Forty years of continual whaling! forty years of privation, and peril, and storm-time! forty years on the pitiless sea! for forty years has Ahab forsaken the peaceful land, for forty years to make war on the horrors of the deep! Aye and yes, Starbuck, out of those forty years I have not spent three ashore. When I think of this life I have led; the desolation of solitude it has been; the masoned, walled-town of a Captain's exclusiveness, which admits but small entrance to any sympathy from the green country without—oh, weariness! heaviness! Guinea-coast slavery of solitary command!—when I think of all this; only half-suspected, not so keenly known to me before—and how for forty years I have fed upon dry salted fare—fit emblem of the dry nourishment of my soul!—when the poorest landsman has had fresh fruit to his daily hand, and broken the world's fresh bread to my mouldy crusts—away, whole oceans away, from that young girl-wife I wedded past fifty, and sailed for Cape Horn the next day, leaving but one dent in my marriage pillow—wife? wife?—rather a widow with her husband alive! Aye, I widowed that poor girl when I married her, Starbuck; and then, the madness, the frenzy, the boiling blood and the smoking brow, with which, for a thousand lowerings old Ahab has furiously, foamingly chased his prey—more a demon than a man! aye, aye! what a forty years' fool—fool—old fool, has old Ahab been! Why this strife of the chase? why weary, and palsy the arm at the oar, and the iron, and the lance? how the richer or better is Ahab now? Behold. Oh, Starbuck! is it not hard, that with this weary load I bear, one poor leg should have been snatched from under me? Here, brush this old hair aside; it blinds me, that I seem to weep. Locks so grey did never grow but from out some ashes! But do I look very old, so very, very old, Starbuck? I feel deadly faint, bowed, and humped, as though I were Adam, staggering beneath the piled centuries since Paradise. God! God! God!—crack my heart!—stave my brain!—mockery! mockery! bitter, biting mockery of grey hairs, have I lived enough joy to wear ye; and seem and feel thus intolerably old? Close! stand close to me, Starbuck; let me look into a human eye; it is better than to gaze into sea or sky; better than to gaze upon God. By the green land; by the bright hearth-stone! this is the magic glass, man; I see my wife and my child in thine eye. No, no; stay on board, on board!—lower not when I do; when branded Ahab gives chase to Moby Dick. That hazard shall not be thine. No, no! not with the far away home I see in that eye!'

'Oh, my Captain! my Captain! noble soul! grand old heart, after all! why should any one give chase to that hated fish! Away with me! let us fly these deadly waters! let us home! Wife and child, too, are Starbuck's—wife and child of his brotherly, sisterly, play-fellow youth; even as thine, sir, are the wife and child of thy loving, longing, paternal old age! Away! let us away!—this instant let me alter the course! How cheerily, how hilariously, O my Captain, would we bowl on our way to see old Nantucket again! I think, sir, they have some such mild blue days, even as this, in Nantucket.'

'They have, they have. I have seen them—some summer days in the morning. About this time—yes, it is his noon nap now—the boy vivaciously wakes; sits up in bed; and his mother tells him of me, of cannibal old me; how I am abroad upon the deep, but will yet come back to dance him again.'

''Tis my Mary, my Mary herself! She promised that my boy, every morning, should be carried to the hill to catch the first glimpse of his father's sail! Yes, yes! no more! it is done! we head for Nantucket! Come, my Captain, study out the course, and let us away! See, see! the boy's face from the window! the boy's hand on the hill!'

But Ahab's glance was averted; like a blighted fruit tree he shook, and cast his last, cindered apple to the soil.

'What is it, what nameless, inscrutable, unearthly thing is it; what cozzening, hidden lord and master, and cruel, remorseless emperor commands me; that against all natural lovings and longings, I so keep pushing, and crowding, and jamming myself on all the time; recklessly making me ready to do what in my own proper, natural heart, I durst not so much as dare? Is Ahab, Ahab? Is it I, God, or who, that lifts this arm? But if the great sun move not of himself; but is as an errand-boy in heaven; nor one single star can revolve, but by some invisible power; how then can this one small heart beat; this one small brain think thoughts; unless God does that beating, does that thinking, does that living, and not I. By heaven, man, we are turned round and round in this world, like yonder windlass, and Fate is the handspike. And all the time, lo! that smiling sky, and this unsounded sea! Look! see yon Albicore! who put it into him to chase and fang that flying-fish? Where do murderers go, man! Who's to doom, when the judge himself is dragged to the bar? But it is a mild, mild wind, and a mild looking sky; and the air smells now, as if it blew from a far-away meadow; they have been making hay somewhere under the slopes of the Andes, Starbuck, and the mowers are sleeping among the new-mown hay. Sleeping? Aye, toil we how we may, we all sleep at last on the field. Sleep? Aye, and rust amid greenness; as last year's scythes flung down, and left in the half-cut swaths—Starbuck!'

But blanched to a corpse's hue with despair, the mate had stolen away.

Ahab crossed the deck to gaze over on the other side; but started at two reflected, fixed eyes in the water there. Fedallah was motionlessly leaning over the same rail.

CHAPTER CXXXIII

THE CHASE—FIRST DAY

That night, in the mid-watch, when the old man—as his wont at intervals—stepped forth from the scuttle in which he leaned, and went to his pivot-hole, he suddenly thrust out his face fiercely, snuffing up the sea air as a sagacious ship's dog will, in drawing nigh to some barbarous isle. He declared that a whale must be near. Soon that peculiar odor, sometimes to a great distance given forth by the living sperm whale, was palpable to all the watch; nor was any mariner surprised when, after inspecting the compass, and then the dog-vane, and then ascertaining the precise bearing of the odor as nearly as possible, Ahab rapidly ordered the ship's course to be slightly altered, and the sail to be shortened.

The acute policy dictating these movements was sufficiently vindicated at daybreak, by the sight of a long sleek on the sea directly and lengthwise ahead, smooth as oil, and resembling in the pleated watery wrinkles bordering it, the polished metallic-like marks of some swift tide-rip, at the mouth of a deep, rapid stream.

'Man the mast-heads! Call all hands!'

Thundering with the butts of three clubbed handspikes on the forecastle deck, Daggoo roused the sleepers with such judgment claps that they seemed to exhale from the scuttle, so instantaneously did they appear with their clothes in their hands.

'What d'ye see?' cried Ahab, flattening his face to the sky.

'Nothing, nothing, sir!' was the sound hailing down in reply.

'T'gallant sails!—stunsails! alow and aloft, and on both sides!'

All sail being set, he now cast loose the life-line, reserved for swaying him to the main royal-mast head; and in a few moments they were hoisting him thither, when, while but two thirds of the way aloft, and while peering ahead through the horizontal vacancy between the main-top-sail and top-gallant-sail, he raised a gull-like cry in the air, 'There she blows!—there she blows! A hump like a snow-hill! It is Moby Dick!'

Fired by the cry which seemed simultaneously taken up by the three look-outs, the men on deck rushed to the rigging to behold the famous whale they had so long been pursuing. Ahab had now gained his final perch, some feet above the other look-outs, Tashtego standing just beneath him on the cap of the top-gallant-mast, so that the Indian's head was almost on a level with Ahab's heel. From this height the whale was now seen some mile or so ahead, at every roll of the sea revealing his high sparkling hump, and regularly jetting his silent spout into the air. To the credulous mariners it seemed the same silent spout they had so long ago beheld in the moonlit Atlantic and Indian Oceans.

'And did none of ye see it before?' cried Ahab, hailing the perched men all around him.

'I saw him almost the same instant, sir, that Captain Ahab did, and I cried out,' said Tashtego.

'Not the same instant; not the same—no, the doubloon is mine, Fate reserved the doubloon for me. *I* only; none of ye could have raised the White Whale first. There she blows! there she blows!—there she blows! There again!—there again!' he cried, in long-drawn, lingering, methodic tones, attuned to the gradual prolongings of the whale's visible jets. 'He's going to sound! In stunsails! Down top-gallant-sails! Stand by three boats. Mr Starbuck, remember, stay on board, and keep the ship. Helm there! Luff, luff a point! So; steady, man, steady! There go flukes! No, no; only black water! All ready the boats there? Stand by, stand by! Lower me, Mr Starbuck; lower, lower,—quick, quicker!' and he slid through the air to the deck.

'He is heading straight to leeward, sir,' cried Stubb, 'right away from us; cannot have seen the ship yet.'

'Be dumb, man! Stand by the braces! Hard down the helm!—brace up! Shiver her!—shiver her! So; well that! Boats, boats!'

Soon all the boats but Starbuck's were dropped; all the boat-sails set—all the paddles plying; with rippling swiftness, shooting to leeward; and Ahab heading the onset. A pale, death-glimmer lit up Fedallah's sunken eyes; a hideous motion gnawed his mouth.

Like noiseless nautilus shells, their light prows sped through the sea; but only slowly they neared the foe. As they neared him, the ocean grew still more smooth; seemed drawing a carpet over its waves; seemed a noon-meadow, so serenely it spread. At length the breathless hunter came so nigh his seemingly unsuspecting prey, that his entire dazzling hump was distinctly visible, sliding along the sea as if an isolated thing, and continually set in a revolving ring of finest, fleecy, greenish foam. He saw the vast, involved wrinkles of the slightly projecting head beyond. Before it, far out on the soft Turkish-rugged waters, went the glistening white shadow from his broad, milky forehead, a musical rippling playfully accompanying the shade; and behind, the blue waters interchangeably flowed over into the moving valley of his steady wake; and on either hand bright bubbles arose and danced by his side. But these were broken again by the light toes of hundreds of gay fowl softly feathering the sea, alternate with their fitful flight; and like to some flagstaff rising from the painted hull of an argosy, the tall but shattered pole of a recent lance projected from the white whale's back; and at intervals one of the cloud of soft-toed fowls hovering, and to and fro skimming like a canopy over the fish, silently perched and rocked on this pole, the long tail feathers streaming like pennons.

A gentle joyousness—a mighty mildness of repose in swiftness, invested the gliding whale. Not the white bull Jupiter swimming away with ravished Europa clinging to his graceful horns; his lovely, leering eyes sideways intent upon the maid; with smooth bewitching fleetness, rippling straight for the nuptial bower in Crete; not Jove, not that great majesty Supreme! did surpass the glorified White Whale as he so divinely swam.

On each soft side—coincident with the parted swell, that but once laving him, then flowed so wide away—on each bright side, the whale shed off enticings. No wonder there had been some among the hunters who namelessly transported and allured by all this serenity, had ventured to assail it; but had fatally found that quietude but the vesture of tornadoes. Yet calm, enticing calm, oh, whale! thou glidest on, to all who for the first time eye thee, no matter how many in that same way thou may'st have bejuggled and destroyed before.

And thus, through the serene tranquilities of the tropical sea, among waves whose hand-clappings were suspended by exceeding rapture, Moby Dick moved on, still withholding from sight the full terrors of his submerged trunk, entirely hiding the wrenched hideousness of his jaw. But soon the fore part of him slowly rose from the water; for an instant his whole marbleized body formed a high arch, like Virginia's Natural Bridge, and warningly waving his bannered flukes in the air, the grand god revealed himself, sounded, and went out of sight. Hoveringly halting, and dipping on the wing, the white sea-fowls longingly lingered over the agitated pool that he left.

With oars apeak, and paddles down, the sheets of their sails adrift, the three boats now stilly floated, awaiting Moby Dick's reappearance.

'An hour,' said Ahab, standing rooted in his boat's stern; and he gazed beyond the whale's place, towards the dim blue spaces and wide wooing vacancies to leeward. It was only an instant; for again his eyes seemed whirling round in his head as he swept the watery circle. The breeze now freshened; the sea began to swell.

'The birds!—the birds!' cried Tashtego.

In long Indian file, as when herons take wing, the white birds were now all flying towards Ahab's boat; and when within a few yards began fluttering over the water there, wheeling round and round, with joyous, expectant cries. Their vision was keener than man's; Ahab could discover no sign in the sea. But suddenly as he peered down and down into its depths, he profoundly saw a white living spot no bigger than a white weasel, with wonderful celerity uprising, and magnifying as it rose, till it turned, and then there were plainly revealed two long crooked rows of white, glistening teeth, floating up from the undiscoverable bottom. It was Moby Dick's open mouth and scrolled jaw; his vast, shadowed bulk still half blending with the blue of the sea. The glittering mouth yawned beneath the boat like an open-doored marble tomb; and giving one sidelong sweep with his steering oar, Ahab whirled the craft aside from this tremendous apparition. Then, calling upon Fedallah to change places with him, went forward to the bows, and seizing Perth's harpoon, commanded his crew to grasp their oars and stand by to stern.

Now, by reason of this timely spinning round the boat upon its axis, its bow, by anticipation, was made to face the whale's head while yet under water. But as if perceiving this stratagem, Moby Dick, with that malicious intelligence ascribed to him, sidelingly transplanted himself, as it were, in an instant, shooting his pleated head lengthwise beneath the boat.

Through and through; through every plank and each rib, it thrilled for an instant, the whale obliquely lying on his back, in the manner of a biting shark, slowly and feelingly taking its bows full within his mouth, so that the long, narrow, scrolled lower jaw curled high up into the open air, and one of the teeth caught in a row-lock. The bluish pearl-white of the inside of the jaw was within six inches of Ahab's head, and reached higher than that. In this attitude the White Whale now shook the slight cedar as a mildly cruel cat her mouse. With unastonished eyes Fedallah gazed, and crossed his arms; but the tiger-yellow crew were tumbling over each other's heads to gain the uttermost stern.

And now, while both elastic gunwales were springing in and out, as the whale dallied with the doomed craft in this devilish way; and from his body being submerged beneath the boat, he could not be darted at from the bows, for the bows were almost inside of him, as it were; and while the other boats involuntarily paused, as before a quick crisis impossible to withstand, then it was the monomaniac Ahab, furious with this tantalizing vicinity of his foe, which placed him all alive and helpless in the very jaws he hated; frenzied with all this, he seized the long bone with his naked hands, and wildly strove to wrench it from its gripe. And now he thus vainly strove, the jaw slipped from him; the frail gunwales bent in, collapsed, and snapped, as both jaws, like an enormous shears, sliding further aft, bit the craft completely in twain, and locked themselves fast again in the sea, midway between the two floating wrecks. These floated aside, the broken ends drooping, the crew at the stern-wreck clinging to the gunwales, and striving to hold fast to the oars to lash them across.

At that preluding moment, ere the boat was yet snapped, Ahab, the first to perceive the whale's intent, by the crafty upraising of his head, a movement that loosed his hold for the time; at that moment his hand had made one final effort to push the boat out of the bite. But only slipping further into the whale's mouth, and tilting over sideways as it slipped, the boat had shaken off his hold on the jaw; spilled him out of it, as he leaned to the push; and so he fell flat-faced upon the sea.

Ripplingly withdrawing from his prey, Moby Dick now lay at a little distance, vertically thrusting his oblong white head up and down in the billows; and at the same time slowly revolving his whole spindled body; so that when his vast wrinkled forehead rose—some twenty or more feet out of the water—the now rising swells, with all their confluent waves, dazzlingly broke against it; vindictively tossing their shivered spray still higher into the air.* So, in a gale, the but half baffled Channel billows only recoil from the base of the Eddystone, triumphantly to overleap its summit with their scud.

But soon resuming his horizontal attitude, Moby Dick swam swiftly round and round the wrecked crew; sideways churning the water in his vengeful wake, as if lashing himself up to still another and more deadly assault. The sight of the splintered boat seemed to madden him, as the blood of grapes and mulberries cast before Antiochus's elephants in the book of Maccabees. Meanwhile Ahab half smothered in the foam of the whale's insolent tail, and too much of a cripple to swim,—though he could still keep afloat, even in the heart of such a whirlpool as that; helpless Ahab's head was seen, like a tossed bubble which the least chance shock might burst. From the boat's fragmentary stern, Fedallah incuriously and mildly eyed him; the clinging crew, at the other drifting end, could not succor him; more than enough was it for them to look to themselves. For so revolvingly appalling was the White Whale's aspect, and so planetarily swift the ever-contracting circles he made, that he seemed horizontally swooping upon them. And though the other boats, unharmed, still hovered hard by; still they dared not pull into the eddy to strike, lest that should be the signal for the instant destruction of the jeopardized castaways, Ahab and all; nor in that case could they themselves hope to escape. With straining eyes, then, they remained on the outer edge of the direful zone, whose centre had now become the old man's head.

---

*This motion is peculiar to the sperm whale. It receives its designation (pitchpoling) from its being likened to that preliminary up-and-down poise of the whale-lance, in the exercise called pitchpoling, previously described. By this motion the whale must best and most comprehensively view whatever objects may be encircling him.

Meantime, from the beginning all this had been descried from the ship's mast heads; and squaring her yards, she had borne down upon the scene; and was now so nigh, that Ahab in the water hailed her;—'Sail on the'—but that moment a breaking sea dashed on him from Moby Dick, and whelmed him for the time. But struggling out of it again, and chancing to rise on a towering crest, he shouted,—'Sail on the whale!—Drive him off!'

The Pequod's prow was pointed; and breaking up the charmed circle, she effectually parted the white whale from his victim. As he sullenly swam off, the boats flew to the rescue.

Dragged into Stubb's boat with blood-shot, blinded eyes, the white brine caking in his wrinkles; the long tension of Ahab's bodily strength did crack, and helplessly he yielded to his body's doom: for a time, lying all crushed in the bottom of Stubb's boat, like one trodden under foot of herds of elephants. Far inland, nameless wails came from him, as desolate sounds from our ravines.

But this intensity of his physical prostration did but so much the more abbreviate it. In an instant's compass, great hearts sometimes condense to one deep pang, the sum total of those shallow pains kindly diffused through feebler men's whole lives. And so, such hearts, though summary in each one suffering; still, if the gods decree it, in their life-time aggregate a whole age of woe, wholly made up of instantaneous intensities; for even in their pointless centres, those noble natures contain the entire circumferences of inferior souls.

'The harpoon,' said Ahab, half way rising, and draggingly leaning on one bended arm—'is it safe?'

'Aye, sir, for it was not darted; this is it,' said Stubb, showing it.

'Lay it before me;—any missing men?'

'One, two, three, four, five;—there were five oars, sir, and here are five men.'

'That's good.—Help me, man; I wish to stand. So, so, I see him! there! there! going to leeward still; what a leaping spout!—Hands off from me! The eternal sap runs up in Ahab's bones again! Set the sail; out oars; the helm!'

It is often the case that when a boat is stove, its crew, being picked up by another boat, help to work that second boat; and the chase is thus continued with what is called double-banked oars. It was thus now. But the added power of the boat did not equal the added power of the whale, for he seemed to have treble-banked his every fin; swimming with a velocity which plainly showed, that if now, under these circumstances, pushed on, the chase would prove an indefinitely prolonged, if not a hopeless one; nor could any crew endure for so long a period, such an unintermitted, intense straining at the oar; a thing barely tolerable only in some one brief vicissitude. The ship itself, then, as it sometimes happens, offered the most promising intermediate means of overtaking the chase. Accordingly, the boats now made for her, and were soon swayed up to their cranes—the two parts of the wrecked boat having been previously secured by her—and then hoisting everything to her side, and stacking her canvas high up, and sideways outstretching it with stun-sails, like the double-jointed wings of an albatross; the Pequod bore down in the leeward wake of Moby Dick. At the well known, methodic intervals, the whale's glittering spout was regularly announced from the manned mast-heads; and when he would be reported as just gone down, Ahab would take the time, and then pacing the deck, binnacle-watch in hand, so soon as the last second of the allotted hour expired, his voice was heard.—'Whose is the doubloon now? D'ye see him?' and if the reply was, No, sir! straightway he commanded them to lift him to his perch. In this way the day wore on; Ahab, now aloft and motionless; anon, unrestingly pacing the planks.

As he was thus walking, uttering no sound, except to hail the men aloft, or to bid them hoist a sail still higher, or to spread one to a still greater breadth—thus to and fro pacing, beneath his slouched hat, at every turn he passed his own wrecked boat, which had been dropped upon the quarter-deck, and lay there reversed; broken bow to shattered stern. At last he paused before it; and as in an already overclouded sky fresh troops of clouds will sometimes sail across, so over the old man's face there now stole some such added gloom as this.

Stubb saw him pause; and perhaps intending, not vainly, though, to evince his own unabated fortitude, and thus keep up a valiant place in his Captain's mind, he advanced, and eyeing the wreck exclaimed—'The thistle the ass refused; it pricked his mouth too keenly, sir; ha! ha!'

'What soulless thing is this that laughs before a wreck? Man, man! did I not know thee brave as fearless fire (and as mechanical) I could swear thou wert a poltroon. Groan nor laugh should be heard before a wreck.'

'Aye, sir,' said Starbuck drawing near, ''tis a solemn sight; an omen, and an ill one.'

'Omen? omen?—the dictionary! If the gods think to speak outright to man, they will honorably speak outright; not shake their heads, and give an old wives' darkling hint.—Begone! Ye two are the opposite poles of one thing; Starbuck is Stubb reversed, and Stubb is Starbuck; and ye two are all mankind; and Ahab stands alone among the millions of the peopled earth, nor gods nor men his neighbors! Cold, cold—I shiver!—How now? Aloft there? D'ye see him? Sing out for every spout, though he spout ten times a second!'

The day was nearly done; only the hem of his golden robe was rustling. Soon, it was almost dark, but the look-out men still remained unset.

'Can't see the spout now, sir;—too dark'—cried a voice from the air.

'How heading when last seen?'

'As before, sir,—straight to leeward.'

'Good! he will travel slower now 'tis night. Down royals and top-gallant stunsails, Mr Starbuck. We must not run over him before morning; he's making a passage now, and may heave-to a while. Helm there! keep her full before the wind!—Aloft! come down!—Mr Stubb, send a fresh hand to the fore-mast head, and see it manned till morning.'—Then advancing towards the doubloon in the main-mast—'Men, this gold is mine, for I earned it; but I shall let it abide here till the White Whale is dead; and then, whosoever of ye first raises him, upon the day he shall be killed, this gold is that man's; and if on that day I shall again raise him, then ten times its sum shall be divided among all of ye! Away now!—the deck is thine, sir.'

And so saying, he placed himself half way within the scuttle, and slouching his hat, stood there till dawn, except when at intervals rousing himself to see how the night wore on.

CHAPTER CXXXIV

THE CHASE—SECOND DAY

At day-break, the three mast-heads were punctually manned afresh.

'D'ye see him?' cried Ahab, after allowing a little space for the light to spread.

'See nothing, sir.'

'Turn up all hands and make sail! he travels faster than I thought for;—the top-gallant sails!—aye, they should have been kept on her all night. But no matter—'tis but resting for the rush.'

Here be it said, that this pertinacious pursuit of one particular whale, continued through day into night, and through night into day, is a thing by no means unprecedented in the South sea fishery. For such is the wonderful skill, prescience of experience, and invincible confidence acquired by some great natural geniuses among the Nantucket commanders; that from the simple observation of a whale when last descried, they will, under certain given circumstances, pretty accurately foretell both the direction in which he will continue to swim for a time, while out of sight, as well as his probable rate of progression during that period. And, in these cases, somewhat as a pilot, when about losing sight of a coast, whose general trending he well knows, and which he desires shortly to return to again, but at some further point; like as this pilot stands by his compass, and takes the precise bearing of the cape at present visible, in order the more certainly to hit aright the remote, unseen headland, eventually to be visited: so does the fisherman, at his compass, with the whale; for after being chased, and diligently marked, through several hours of daylight, then, when night obscures the fish, the creature's future wake through the darkness is almost as established to the sagacious mind of the hunter, as the pilot's coast is to him. So that to this hunter's wondrous skill, the proverbial evanescence of a thing writ in water, a wake, is to all desired purposes well nigh as reliable as the steadfast land. And as the mighty iron Leviathan of the modern railway is so familiarly known in its every pace, that, with watches in their hands, men time his rate as doctors that of a baby's pulse; and lightly say of it, the up train or the down train will reach such or such a spot, at such or such an hour; even so, almost, there are occasions when these Nantucketers time that other Leviathan of the deep, according to the observed humor of his speed; and say to themselves, so many hours hence this whale will have gone two hundred miles, will have about reached this or that degree of latitude or longitude. But to render this acuteness at all successful in the end, the wind and the sea must be the whale-man's allies; for of what present avail to the becalmed or windbound mariner is the skill that assures him he is exactly ninety-three leagues and a quarter from his port? Inferable from these statements, are many collateral subtile matters touching the chase of whales.

The ship tore on; leaving such a furrow in the sea as when a cannon-ball, missent, becomes a plough-share and turns up the level field.

'By salt and hemp!' cried Stubb, 'but this swift motion of the deck creeps up one's legs and tingles at the heart. This ship and I are two brave fellows!—Ha! ha! Some one take me up, and launch me, spine-wise, on the sea,—for by live-oaks! my spine's a keel. Ha, ha! we go the gait that leaves no dust behind!'

'There she blows—she blows!—she blows!—right ahead!' was now the mast-head cry.

'Aye, aye!' cried Stubb, 'I knew it—ye can't escape—blow on and split your spout, O whale! the mad fiend himself is after ye! blow your trump—blister your lungs!—Ahab will dam off your blood, as a miller shuts his water-gate upon the stream!'

And Stubb did but speak out for well nigh all that crew. The frenzies of the chase had by this time worked them bubblingly up, like old wine worked anew. Whatever pale fears and forebodings some of them might have felt before; these were not only now kept out of sight through the growing awe of Ahab, but they were broken up, and on all sides routed, as timid prairie hares that scatter before the bounding bison. The hand of Fate had snatched all their souls; and by the stirring perils of the previous day; the rack of the past night's suspense; the fixed, unfearing, blind, reckless way in which their wild craft went plunging towards its flying mark; by all these things, their hearts were bowled along. The wind that made great bellies of their sails, and rushed the vessel on by arms invisible as irresistible; this seemed the symbol of that unseen agency which so enslaved them to the race.

They were one man, not thirty. For as the one ship that held them all; though it was put together of all contrasting things—oak, and maple, and pine wood; iron, and pitch, and hemp—yet all these ran into each other in the one concrete hull, which shot on its way, both balanced and directed by the long central keel; even so, all the individualities of the crew, this man's valor, that man's fear; guilt and guiltiness, all varieties were welded into oneness, and were all directed to that fatal goal which Ahab their one lord and keel did point to.

The rigging lived. The mast-heads, like the tops of tall palms, were outspreadingly tufted with arms and legs. Clinging to a spar with one hand, some reached forth the other with impatient wavings; others, shading their eyes from the vivid sunlight, sat far out on the rocking yards; all the spars in full bearing of mortals, ready and ripe for their fate. Ah! how they still strove through that infinite blueness to seek out the thing that might destroy them!

'Why sing ye not out for him, if ye see him?' cried Ahab, when, after the lapse of some minutes since the first cry, no more had been heard. 'Sway me up, men; ye have been deceived; not Moby Dick casts one odd jet that way, and then disappears.'

It was even so; in their headlong eagerness, the men had mistaken some other thing for the whale-spout, as the event itself soon proved; for hardly had Ahab reached his perch; hardly was the rope belayed to its pin on deck, when he struck the key-note to an orchestra, that made the air vibrate as with the combined discharges of rifles. The triumphant halloo of thirty buckskin lungs was heard, as—much nearer to the ship than the place of the imaginary jet, less than a mile ahead—Moby Dick bodily burst into view! For not by any calm and indolent spoutings; not by the peaceable gush of that mystic fountain in his head, did the White Whale now reveal his vicinity; but by the far more wondrous phenomenon of breaching. Rising with his utmost velocity from the furthest depths, the Sperm Whale thus booms his entire bulk into the pure element of air, and piling up a mountain of dazzling foam, shows his place to the distance of seven miles and more. In those moments, the torn, enraged waves he shakes off, seem his mane; in some cases, this breaching is his act of defiance.

'There she breaches! there she breaches!' was the cry, as in his immeasurable bravadoes the White Whale tossed himself salmon-like to Heaven. So suddenly seen in the blue plain of the sea, and relieved against the still bluer margin of the sky, the spray that he raised, for the moment, intolerably glittered and glared like a glacier; and stood there gradually fading and fading away from its first sparkling intensity, to the dim mistiness of an advancing shower in a vale.

'Aye, breach your last to the sun, Moby Dick!' cried Ahab, 'thy hour and thy harpoon are at hand!—Down! down all of ye, but one man at the fore. The boats!—stand by!'

Unmindful of the tedious rope-ladders of the shrouds, the men, like shooting stars, slid to the deck, by the isolated backstays and halyards; while Ahab, less dartingly, but still rapidly was dropped from his perch.

'Lower away,' he cried, so soon as he had reached his boat—a spare one, rigged the afternoon previous. 'Mr Starbuck, the ship is thine—keep away from the boats, but keep near them. Lower, all!'

As if to strike a quick terror into them, by this time being the first assailant himself, Moby Dick had turned, and was now coming for the three crews. Ahab's boat was central; and cheering his men, he told them he would take the whale head-and-head,—that is, pull straight up to his forehead,—a not uncommon thing; for when within a certain limit, such a course excludes the coming onset from the whale's sidelong vision. But ere that close limit was gained, and while yet all three boats were plain as the ship's three masts to his eye; the White Whale churning himself into furious speed, almost in an instant as it were, rushing among the boats with open jaws, and a lashing tail, offered appalling battle on every side; and heedless of the irons darted at him from every boat, seemed only intent on annihilating each separate plank of which those boats were made. But skilfully manœuvred, incessantly wheeling like trained chargers in the field; the boats for a while eluded him; though, at times, but by a plank's breadth; while all the time, Ahab's unearthly slogan tore every other cry but his to shreds.

But at last in his untraceable evolutions, the White Whale so crossed and re-crossed, and in a thousand ways entangled the slack of the three lines now fast to him, that they foreshortened, and, of themselves, warped the devoted boats towards the planted irons in him; though now for a moment the whale drew aside a little, as if to rally for a more tremendous charge. Seizing that opportunity, Ahab first paid out more line: and then was rapidly hauling and jerking in upon it again—hoping that way to disencumber it of some snarls—when lo!—a sight more savage than the embattled teeth of sharks!

Caught and twisted—corkscrewed in the mazes of the line, loose harpoons and lances, with all their bristling barbs and points, came flashing and dripping up to the chocks in the bows of Ahab's boat. Only one thing could be done. Seizing the boat-knife, he critically reached within—through—and then, without—the rays of steel; dragged in the line beyond, passed it, inboard, to the bowsman, and then, twice sundering the rope near the chocks—dropped the intercepted fagot of steel into the sea; and was all fast again. That instant, the White Whale made a sudden rush among the remaining tangles of the other lines; by so doing, irresistibly dragged the more involved boats of Stubb and Flask towards his flukes; dashed them together like two rolling husks on a surf-beaten beach, and then, diving down into the sea, disappeared in a boiling maelstrom, in which, for a space, the odorous cedar chips of the wrecks danced round and round, like the grated nutmeg in a swiftly stirred bowl of punch.

While the two crews were yet circling in the waters, reaching out after the revolving line-tubs, oars, and other floating furniture, while aslope little Flask bobbed up an down like an empty vial, twitching his legs upwards to escape the dreaded jaws of sharks; and Stubb was lustily singing out for some one to ladle him up; and while the old man's line—now parting—admitted of his pulling into the creamy pool to rescue whom he could;—in that wild simultaneousness of a thousand concreted perils,—Ahab's yet unstricken boat seemed drawn up towards Heaven by invisible wires,—as, arrow-like, shooting perpendicularly from the sea, the White Whale dashed his broad forehead against its bottom, and sent it, turning over and over, into the air; till it fell again—gunwale downwards—and Ahab and his men struggled out from under it, like seals from a sea-side cave.

The first uprising momentum of the whale—modifying its direction as he struck the surface—involuntarily launched him along it, to a little distance from the centre of the destruction he had made; and with his back to it, he now lay for a moment slowly feeling with his flukes from side to side; and whenever a stray oar, bit of plank, the least chip or crumb of the boats touched his skin, his tail swiftly drew back, and came sideways smiting the sea. But soon, as if satisfied that his work for that time was done, he pushed his pleated forehead through the ocean, and trailing after him the intertangled lines, continued his leeward way at a traveller's methodic pace.

As before, the attentive ship having descried the whole fight, again came bearing down to the rescue, and dropping a boat, picked up the floating mariners, tubs, oars, and whatever else could be caught at, and safely landed them on her decks. Some sprained shoulders, wrists, and ankles; livid contusions; wrenched harpoons and lances; inextricable intricacies of rope; shattered oars and planks; all these were there; but no fatal or even serious ill seemed to have befallen any one. As with Fedallah the day before, so Ahab was now found grimly clinging to his boat's broken half, which afforded a comparatively easy float; nor did it so exhaust him as the previous day's mishap.

But when he was helped to the deck, all eyes were fastened upon him; as instead of standing by himself he still half-hung upon the shoulder of Starbuck, who had thus far been the foremost to assist him. His ivory leg had been snapped off, leaving but one short sharp splinter.

'Aye aye, Starbuck, 'tis sweet to lean sometimes, be the leaner who he will; and would old Ahab had leaned oftener than he has.'

'The ferrule has not stood, sir,' said the carpenter, now coming up; 'I put good work into that leg.'

'But no bones broken, sir, I hope,' said Stubb with true concern.

'Aye! and all splintered to pieces, Stubb!—d'ye see it.—But even with a broken bone, old Ahab is untouched; and I account no living bone of mine one jot more me, than this dead one that's lost. Nor white whale, nor man, nor fiend, can so much as graze old Ahab in his own proper and inaccessible being. Can any lead touch yonder floor, any mast scrape yonder roof?—Aloft there! which way?'

'Dead to leeward, sir.'

'Up helm, then; pile on the sail again, ship keepers! down the rest of the spare boats and rig them—Mr Starbuck away, and muster the boats' crews.'

'Let me first help thee towards the bulwarks, sir.'

'Oh, oh, oh! how this splinter gores me now! Accursed fate! that the unconquerable captain in the soul should have such a craven mate!'

'Sir?'

'My body, man, not thee. Give me something for a cane—there, that shivered lance will do. Muster the men. Surely I have not seen him yet. By heaven it cannot be!—missing?—quick! call them all.'

The old man's hinted thought was true. Upon mustering the company, the Parsee was not there.

'The Parsee!' cried Stubb—'he must have been caught in—'

'The black vomit wrench thee!—run all of ye above, alow, cabin, forecastle—find him—not gone—not gone!'

But quickly they returned to him with the tidings that the Parsee was nowhere to be found.

'Aye, sir,' said Stubb—'caught among the tangles of your line—I thought I saw him dragging under.'

'*My* line! *my* line? Gone?—gone? What means that little word?—What death-knell rings in it, that old Ahab shakes as if he were the belfry. The harpoon, too!—toss over the litter there,—d'ye see it?—the forged iron, men, the white whale's—no, no, no,—blistered fool! this hand did dart it!—'tis in the fish!—Aloft there! Keep him nailed—Quick!—all hands to the rigging of the boats—collect the oars—harpooneers! the irons, the irons!—hoist the royals higher—a pull on all the sheets!—helm there! steady, steady for your life! I'll ten times girdle the unmeasured globe; yea and dive straight through it, but I'll slay him yet!'

'Great God! but for one single instant show thyself,' cried Starbuck; 'never, never wilt thou capture him, old man—In Jesus' name no more of this, that's worse than devil's madness. Two days chased; twice stove to splinters; thy very leg once more snatched from under thee; thy evil shadow gone—all good angels mobbing thee with warnings:—what more wouldst thou have?—Shall we keep chasing this murderous fish till he swamps the last man? Shall we be dragged by him to the bottom of the sea? Shall we be towed by him to the infernal world? Oh, oh,—Impiety and blasphemy to hunt him more!'

'Starbuck, of late I've felt strangely moved to thee; ever since that hour we both saw—thou know'st what, in one another's eyes. But in this matter of the whale, be the front of thy face to me as the palm of this hand—a lipless, unfeatured blank. Ahab is for ever Ahab, man. This whole act's immutably decreed. 'Twas rehearsed by thee and me a billion years before this ocean rolled. Fool! I am the Fates' lieutenant; I act under orders. Look thou, underling! that thou obeyest mine.—Stand round me, men. Ye see an old man cut down to the stump; leaning on a shivered lance; propped up on a lonely foot. 'Tis Ahab—his body's part; but Ahab's soul's a centipede, that moves upon a hundred legs. I feel strained, half stranded, as ropes that tow dismasted frigates in a gale; and I may look so. But ere I break, ye'll hear me crack; and till ye hear *that,* know that Ahab's hawser tows his purpose yet. Believe ye, men, in the things called omens? Then laugh aloud, and cry encore! For ere they drown, drowning things will twice rise to the surface; then rise again, to sink for evermore. So with Moby Dick—two days he's floated—to-morrow will be the third. Aye, men, he'll rise once more,—but only to spout his last! D'ye feel brave, men, brave?'

'As fearless fire,' cried Stubb.

'And as mechanical,' muttered Ahab. Then as the men went forward, he muttered on:—'The things called omens! And yesterday I talked the same to Starbuck there, concerning my broken boat. Oh! how valiantly I seek to drive out of others' hearts what's clinched so fast in mine!—The Parsee—the Parsee!—gone, gone? and he was to go before:—but still was to be seen again ere I could perish—How's that?—There's a riddle now might baffle all the lawyers backed by the ghosts of the whole line of judges:—like a hawk's beak it pecks my brain. *I'll, I'll* solve it, though!'

When dusk descended, the whale was still in sight to leeward.

So once more the sail was shortened, and everything passed nearly as on the previous night; only, the sound of hammers, and the hum of the grindstone was heard till nearly daylight, as the men toiled by lanterns in the complete and careful rigging of the spare boats and sharpening their fresh weapons for the morrow. Meantime, of the broken keel of Ahab's wrecked craft the carpenter made him another leg; while still as on the night before, slouched Ahab stood fixed within his scuttle; his hid, heliotrope glance anticipatingly gone backward on its dial; set due eastward for the earliest sun.

CHAPTER CXXXV

The Chase—Third Day

The morning of the third day dawned fair and fresh, and once more the solitary night-man at the fore-mast-head was relieved by crowds of the daylight look-outs, who dotted every mast and almost every spar.

'D'ye see him?' cried Ahab; but the whale was not yet in sight.

'In his infallible wake, though; but follow that wake, that's all. Helm there; steady, as thou goest, and hast been going. What a lovely day again! were it a new-made world, and made for a summer-house to the angels, and this morning the first of its throwing open to them, a fairer day could not dawn upon that world. Here's food for thought, had Ahab time to think; but Ahab never thinks; he only feels, feels, feels; *that's* tingling enough for mortal man! to think's audacity. God only has that right and privilege. Thinking is, or ought to be, a coolness and a calmness; and our poor hearts throb, and our poor brains beat too much for that. And yet, I've sometimes thought my brain was very calm—frozen calm, this old skull cracks so, like a glass in which the contents turn to ice, and shiver it. And still this hair is growing now; this moment growing, and heat must breed it; but no, it's like that sort of common grass that will grow anywhere, between the earthly clefts of Greenland ice or in Vesuvius' lava. How the wild winds blow it; they whip it about me as the torn shreds of split sails lash the tossed ship they cling to. A vile wind that has no doubt blown ere this through prison corridors and cells, and wards of hospitals, and ventilated them, and now comes blowing hither as innocent as fleeces. Out upon it!—it's tainted. Were I the wind, I'd blow no more on such a wicked, miserable world. I'd crawl somewhere to a cave, and slink there. And yet, 'tis a noble and heroic thing, the wind! who ever conquered it? In every fight it has the last and bitterest blow. Run tilting at it, and you but run through it. Ha! a coward wind that strikes stark naked men, but will not stand to receive a single blow. Even Ahab is a braver thing—a nobler thing than *that.* Would now the wind but had a body; but all the things that most exasperate and outrage mortal man, all these things are bodiless, but only bodiless as objects, not as agents. There's a most special, a most cunning, oh, a most malicious difference! And yet, I say again, and swear it now, that there's something all glorious and gracious in the wind. These warm Trade Winds, at least, that in the clear heavens blow straight on, in strong and steadfast, vigorous mildness; and veer not from their mark, however the baser currents of the sea may turn and tack, and mightiest Mississippies of the land shift and swerve about, uncertain where to go at last. And by the eternal Poles! these same Trades that so directly blow my good ship on; these Trades, or something like them—something so unchangeable, and full as strong, blow my keeled soul along! To it! Aloft there! What d'ye see?'

'Nothing, sir.'

'Nothing! and noon at hand! The doubloon goes a-begging! See the sun! Aye, aye, it must be so. I've oversailed him. How, got the start? Aye, he's chasing *me* now; not I, *him*—that's bad; I might have known it, too. Fool! the lines—the harpoons he's towing. Aye, aye, I have run him by last night. About! about! Come down, all of ye, but the regular look outs! Man the braces!'

Steering as she had done, the wind had been somewhat on the Pequod's quarter, so that now being pointed in the reverse direction, the braced ship sailed hard upon the breeze as she rechurned the cream in her own white wake.

'Against the wind he now steers for the open jaw,' murmured Starbuck to himself, as he coiled the new-hauled main-brace upon the rail. 'God keep us, but already my bones feel damp within me, and from the inside wet my flesh. I misdoubt me that I disobey my God in obeying him!'

'Stand by to sway me up!' cried Ahab, advancing to the hempen basket. 'We should meet him soon.'

'Aye, aye, sir,' and straightway Starbuck did Ahab's bidding, and once more Ahab swung on high.

A whole hour now passed; gold-beaten out to ages. Time itself now held long breaths with keen suspense. But at last, some three points off the weather bow, Ahab descried the spout again, and instantly from the three mast-heads three shrieks went up as if the tongues of fire had voiced it.

'Forehead to forehead I meet thee, this third time, Moby Dick! On deck there!—brace sharper up; crowd her into the wind's eye. He's too far off to lower yet, Mr Starbuck. The sails shake! Stand over that helmsman with a top-maul! So, so; he travels fast, and I must down. But let me have one more good round look aloft here at the sea; there's time for that. An old, old sight, and yet somehow so young; aye, and not changed a wink since I first saw it, a boy, from the sand-hills of Nantucket! The same!—the same!—the same to Noah as to me. There's a soft shower to leeward. Such lovely leewardings! They must lead somewhere—to something else than common land, more palmy than the palms. Leeward! the white whale goes that way; to look to windward, then; the better if the bitterer quarter. But good bye, good bye, old mast-head! What's this?—green? aye, tiny mosses in these warped cracks. No such green weather stains on Ahab's head! There's the difference now between man's old age and matter's. But aye, old mast, we both grow old together; sound in our hulls, though, are we not, my ship? Aye, minus a leg, that's all. By heaven this dead wood has the better of my live flesh every way. I can't compare with it; and I've known some ships made of dead trees outlast the lives of men made of the most vital stuff of vital fathers. What's that he said? he should still go before me, my pilot; and yet to be seen again? But where? Will I have eyes at the bottom of the sea, supposing I descend those endless stairs? and all night I've been sailing from him, wherever he did sink to. Aye, aye, like many more thou told'st direful truth as touching thyself, O Parsee; but, Ahab, there thy shot fell short. Good by, mast-head—keep a good eye upon the whale, the while I'm gone. We'll talk to-morrow, nay, to-night, when the white whale lies down there, tied by head and tail.'

He gave the word; and still gazing round him, was steadily lowered through the cloven blue air to the deck.

In due time the boats were lowered; but as standing in his shallop's stern, Ahab just hovered upon the point of the descent, he waved to the mate,—who held one of the tackle-ropes on deck—and bade him pause.

'Starbuck!'

'Sir?'

'For the third time my soul's ship starts upon this voyage, Starbuck.'

'Aye, sir, thou wilt have it so.'

'Some ships sail from their ports, and ever afterwards are missing, Starbuck!'

'Truth, sir: saddest truth.'

'Some men die at ebb tide; some at low water; some at the full of the flood;—and I feel now like a billow that's all one crested comb, Starbuck. I am old;—shake hands with me, man.'

Their hands met; their eyes fastened; Starbuck's tears the glue.

'Oh, my captain, my captain!—noble heart—go not—go not!—see, it's a brave man that weeps; how great the agony of the persuasion then!'

'Lower away!—cried Ahab, tossing the mate's arm from him. 'Stand by the crew!'

In an instant the boat was pulling round close under the stern.

'The sharks! the sharks!' cried a voice from the low cabin-window there; 'O master, my master, come back!'

But Ahab heard nothing; for his own voice was high-lifted then; and the boat leaped on.

Yet the voice spake true; for scarce had he pushed from the ship, when numbers of sharks, seemingly rising from out the dark waters beneath the hull, maliciously snapped at the blades of the oars, every time they dipped in the water; and in this way accompanied the boat with their bites. It is a thing not uncommonly happening to the whaleboats in those swarming seas; the sharks at times apparently following them in the same prescient way that vultures hover over the banners of marching regiments in the east. But these were the first sharks that had been observed by the Pequod since the White Whale had been first descried; and whether it was that Ahab's crew were all such tiger-yellow barbarians, and therefore their flesh more musky to the senses of the sharks—a matter sometimes well known to affect them,—however it was, they seemed to follow that one boat without molesting the others.

'Heart of wrought steel!' murmured Starbuck gazing over the side, and following with his eyes the receding boat—'canst thou yet ring boldly to that sight—lowering thy keel among ravening sharks, and followed by them, openmouthed to the chase; and this the critical third day?—For when three days flow together in one continuous intense pursuit; be sure the first is the morning, the second the noon, and the third the evening and the end of that thing—be that end what it may. Oh! my god! what is this that shoots through me, and leaves me so deadly calm, yet expectant,—fixed at the top of a shudder! future things swim before me, as in empty outlines and skeletons; all the past is somehow grown dim. Mary, girl! thou fadest in pale glories behind me; boy! I seem to see but thy eyes grown wondrous blue. Strangest problems of life seem clearing; but clouds sweep between—Is my journey's end coming? My legs feel faint; like his who has footed it all day. Feel thy heart,—beats it yet?—Stir thyself, Starbuck!—stave it off—move, move! speak aloud!—Mast-head there! See ye my boy's hand on the hill?—Crazed; aloft there!—keep thy keenest eye upon the boats:—mark well the whale!—Ho! again!—drive off that hawk! see! he pecks—he tears the vane'—pointing to the red flag flying at the main-truck—'Ha! he soars away with it!—Where's the old man now? see'st thou that sight, oh Ahab!—shudder, shudder!'

The boats had not gone very far, when by a signal from the mast-heads—a downward pointed arm, Ahab knew that the whale had sounded; but intending to be near him at the next rising, he held on his way a little sideways from the vessel; the becharmed crew maintaining the profoundest silence, as the head-beat waves hammered and hammered against the opposing bow.

'Drive, drive in your nails, oh ye waves! to their uttermost heads drive them in! ye but strike a thing without a lid; and no coffin and no hearse can be mine:—and hemp only can kill me! Ha! ha!'

Suddenly the waters around them slowly swelled in broad circles; then quickly upheaved, as if sideways sliding from a submerged berg of ice, swiftly rising to the surface. A low rumbling sound was heard; a subterraneous hum; and then all held their breaths; as bedraggled with trailing ropes, and harpoons, and lances, a vast form shot lengthwise, but obliquely from the sea. Shrouded in a thin drooping veil of mist, it hovered for a moment in the rainbowed air; and then fell swamping back into the deep. Crushed thirty feet upwards, the waters flashed for an instant like heaps of fountains, then brokenly sank in a shower of flakes, leaving the circling surface creamed like new milk round the marble trunk of the whale.

'Give way!' cried Ahab to the oarsmen, and the boats darted forwards to the attack; but maddened by yesterday's fresh irons that corroded in him, Moby Dick seemed combinedly possessed by all the angels that fell from heaven. The wide tiers of welded tendons overspreading his broad white forehead, beneath the transparent skin, looked knitted together; as head on, he came churning his tail among the boats; and once more flailed them apart; spilling out the irons and lances from the two mates' boats, and dashing in one side of the upper part of their bows, but leaving Ahab's almost without a scar.

While Daggoo and Queequeg were stopping the strained planks; and as the whale swimming out from them, turned, and showed one entire flank as he shot by them again; at that moment a quick cry went up. Lashed round and round to the fish's back; pinioned in the turns upon turns in which, during the past night, the whale had reeled the involutions of the lines around him, the half torn body of the Parsee was seen; his sable raiment frayed to shreds; his distended eyes turned full upon old Ahab.

The harpoon dropped from his hand.

'Befooled, befooled!'—drawing in a long lean breath—'Aye, Parsee! I see thee again.—Aye, and thou goest before; and this, *this* then is the hearse that thou didst promise. But I hold thee to the last letter of thy word. Where is the second hearse? Away, mates, to the ship! those boats are useless now; repair them if ye can in time, and return to me; if not, Ahab is enough to die—Down, men! the first thing that but offers to jump from this boat I stand in, that thing I harpoon. Ye are not other men, but my arms and my legs; and so obey me. Where's the whale gone down again?'

But he looked too nigh the boat; for as if bent upon escaping with the corpse he bore, and as if the particular place of the last encounter had been but a stage in his leeward voyage, Moby Dick was now again steadily swimming forward; and had almost passed the ship,—which thus far had been sailing in the contrary direction to him, though for the present her headway had been stopped. He seemed swimming with his utmost velocity, and now only intent upon pursuing his own straight path in the sea.

'Oh! Ahab,' cried Starbuck, 'not too late is it, even now, the third day, to desist. See! Moby Dick seeks thee not. It is thou, thou, that madly seekest him!'

Setting sail to the rising wind, the lonely boat was swiftly impelled to leeward, by both oars and canvas. And at last when Ahab was sliding by the vessel, so near as plainly to distinguish Starbuck's face as he leaned over the rail, he hailed him to turn the vessel about, and follow him, not too swiftly, at a judicious interval. Glancing upwards, he saw Tashtego, Queequeg, and Daggoo, eagerly mounting to the three mast-heads; while the oarsmen were rocking in the two staved boats which had but just been hoisted to the side, and were busily at work in repairing them. One after the other, through the port-holes, as he sped, he also caught flying glimpses of Stubb and Flask, busying themselves on deck among bundles of new irons and lances. As he saw all this; as he heard the hammers in the broken boats; far other hammers seemed driving a nail into his heart. But he rallied. And now marking that the vane or flag was gone from the main-mast-head, he shouted to Tashtego, who had just gained that perch, to descend again for another flag, and a hammer and nails, and so nail it to the mast.

Whether fagged by the three days' running chase, and the resistance to his swimming in the knotted hamper he bore; or whether it was some latent deceitfulness and malice in him: whichever was true, the White Whale's way now began to abate, as it seemed, from the boat so rapidly nearing him once more; though indeed the whales's last start had not been so long a one as before. And still as Ahab glided over the waves the unpitying sharks accompanied him; and so pertinaciously stuck to the boat; and so continually bit at the plying oars, that the blades became jagged and crunched, and left small splinters in the sea, at almost every dip.

'Heed them not! those teeth but give new rowlocks to your oars. Pull on! 'tis the better rest, the shark's jaw than the yielding water.'

'But at every bite, sir, the thin blades grow smaller and smaller!'

'They will last long enough!—pull on!—But who can tell'—he muttered—'whether these sharks swim to feast on the whale or on Ahab?—But pull on! Aye, all alive, now—we near him. The helm! take the helm; let me pass,'—and so saying, two of the oarsmen helped him forward to the bows of the still flying boat.

At length as the craft was cast to one side, and ran ranging along with the White Whale's flank, he seemed strangely oblivious of its advance—as the whale sometimes will—and Ahab was fairly within the smoky mountain mist, which, thrown off from the whale's spout, curled round his great, Monadnock hump; he was even thus close to him; when, with body arched back, and both arms lengthwise high-lifted to the poise, he darted his fierce iron, and his far fiercer curse into the hated whale. As both steel and curse sank to the socket, as if sucked into a morass, Moby Dick sideways writhed; spasmodically rolled his nigh flank against the bow, and, without staving a hole in it, so suddenly canted the boat over, that had it not been for the elevated part of the gunwale to which he then clung, Ahab would once more have been tossed into the sea. As it was, three of the oarsmen—who foreknew not the precise instant of the dart, and were therefore unprepared for its effects—these were flung out; but so fell, that, in an instant two of them clutched the gunwale again, and rising to its level on a combing wave, hurled themselves bodily inboard again; the third man helplessly dropping astern, but still afloat and swimming.

Almost simultaneously, with a mighty volition of ungraduated, instantaneous, swiftness, the White Whale darted through the weltering sea. But when Ahab cried out to the steersman to take new turns with the line, and hold it so; and commanded the crew to turn round on their seats, and tow the boat up to the mark; the moment the treacherous line felt that double strain and tug, it snapped in the empty air!

'What breaks in me? Some sinew cracks!—'tis whole again; oars! oars! burst in upon him!'

Hearing the tremendous rush of the sea-crashing boat, the whale wheeled round to present his blank forehead at bay; but in that evolution, catching sight of the nearing black hull of the ship; seemingly seeing in it the source of all his persecutions; bethinking it—it may be—a larger and nobler foe; of a sudden, he bore down upon its advancing prow, smiting his jaws amid fiery showers of foam.

Ahab staggered; his hand smote his forehead. 'I grow blind; hands! stretch out before me that I may yet grope my way. Is't night?'

'The whale! The ship!' cried the cringing oarsmen.

'Oars! oars! Slope downwards to thy depths, O sea, that ere it be for ever too late, Ahab may slide this last, last time upon his mark! I see: the ship! the ship! Dash on, my men! Will ye not save my ship?'

But as the oarsmen violently forced their boat through the sledge-hammering seas, the before whale-smitten bow-ends of two planks burst through, and in an instant almost, the temporarily disabled boat lay nearly level with the waves; its half-wading, splashing crew, trying hard to stop the gap and bale out the pouring water.

Meantime, for that one beholding instant, Tashtego's mast-head hammer remained suspended in his hand; and the red flag, half-wrapping him as with a plaid, then streamed itself straight out from him, as his own forward-flowing heart; while Starbuck and Stubb, standing upon the bowsprit beneath, caught sight of the down-coming monster just as soon as he.

'The whale, the whale! Up helm, up helm! Oh, all ye sweet powers of air, now hug me close! Let not Starbuck die, if die he must, in a woman's fainting fit. Up helm, I say—ye fools, the jaw! the jaw! Is this the end of all my bursting prayers? all my life-long fidelities? Oh, Ahab, Ahab, lo, thy work. Steady! helmsman, steady. Nay, nay! Up helm again! He turns to meet us! Oh, his unappeasable brow drives on towards one, whose duty tells him he cannot depart. My God, stand by me now!'

'Stand not by me, but stand under me, whoever you are that will now help Stubb; for Stubb, too, sticks here. I grin at thee, thou grinning whale! Who ever helped Stubb, or kept Stubb awake, but Stubb's own unwinking eye? And now poor Stubb goes to bed upon a mattrass that is all too soft; would it were stuffed with brushwood! I grin at thee, thou grinning whale! Look ye, sun, moon, and stars! I call ye assassins of as good a fellow as ever spouted up his ghost. For all that, I would yet ring glasses with ye, would ye but hand the cup! Oh, oh! oh, oh! thou grinning whale, but there'll be plenty of gulping soon! Why fly ye not, O Ahab! For me, off shoes and jacket to it; let Stubb die in his drawers! A most mouldy and over salted death, though;—cherries! cherries! cherries! Oh, Flask, for one red cherry ere we die!'

'Cherries? I only wish that we were where they grow. Oh, Stubb, I hope my poor mother's drawn my part-pay ere this; if not, few coppers will now come to her, for the voyage is up.'

From the ship's bows, nearly all the seamen now hung inactive; hammers, bits of plank, lances, and harpoons, mechanically retained in their hands, just as they had darted from their various employments; all their enchanted eyes intent upon the whale, which from side to side strangely vibrating his predestinating head, sent a broad band of overspreading semicircular foam before him as he rushed. Retribution, swift vengeance, eternal malice were in his whole aspect, and spite of all that mortal man could do, the solid white buttress of his forehead smote the ship's starboard bow, till men and timbers reeled. Some fell flat upon their faces. Like dislodged trucks, the heads of the harpooneers aloft shook on their bull-like necks. Through the breach, they heard the waters pour, as mountain torrents down a flume.

'The ship! The hearse!—the second hearse!' cried Ahab from the boat; 'its wood could only be American!'

Diving beneath the settling ship, the whale ran quivering along its keel; but turning under water, swiftly shot to the surface again, far off the other bow, but within a few yards of Ahab's boat, where, for a time, he lay quiescent.

'I turn my body from the sun. What ho, Tashtego! let me hear thy hammer. Oh! ye three unsurrendered spires of mine; thou uncracked keel; and only god-bullied hull; thou firm deck, and haughty helm, and Pole-pointed prow,—death-glorious ship! must ye then perish, and without me? Am I cut off from the last fond pride of meanest shipwrecked captains? Oh, lonely death on lonely life! Oh, now I feel my topmost greatness lies in my topmost grief. Ho, ho! from all your furthest bounds, pour ye now in, ye bold billows of my whole foregone life, and top this one piled comber of my death! Towards thee I roll, thou all-destroying but unconquering whale; to the last I grapple with thee; from hell's heart I stab at thee; for hate's sake I spit my last breath at thee. Sink all coffins and all hearses to one common pool! and since neither can be mine, let me then tow to pieces, while still chasing thee, though tied to thee, thou damned whale! *Thus,* I give up the spear!'

The harpoon was darted; the stricken whale flew forward; with igniting velocity the line ran through the groove;—ran foul. Ahab stooped to clear it; he did clear it; but the flying turn caught him round the neck, and voicelessly as Turkish mutes bowstring their victim, he was shot out of the boat, ere the crew knew he was gone. Next instant, the heavy eye-splice in the rope's final end flew out of the stark-empty tub, knocked down an oarsman, and smiting the sea, disappeared in its depths.

For an instant, the tranced boat's crew stood still; then turned. 'The ship? Great God, where is the ship?' Soon they through dim, bewildering mediums saw her sidelong fading phantom, as in the gaseous Fata Morgana; only the uppermost masts out of water; while fixed by infatuation, or fidelity, or fate, to their once lofty perches, the pagan harpooneers still maintained their sinking lookouts on the sea. And now, concentric circles seized the lone boat itself, and all its crew, and each floating oar, and every lance-pole, and spinning, animate and inanimate, all round and round in one vortex, carried the smallest chip of the Pequod out of sight.

But as the last whelmings intermixingly poured themselves over the sunken head of the Indian at the mainmast, leaving a few inches of the erect spar yet visible, together with long streaming yards of the flag, which calmly undulated, with ironical coincidings, over the destroying billows they almost touched;—at that instant, a red arm and a hammer hovered backwardly uplifted in the open air, in the act of nailing the flag faster and yet faster to the subsiding spar. A sky-hawk that tauntingly had followed the main-truck downwards from its natural home among the stars, pecking at the flag, and incommoding Tashtego there; this bird now chanced to intercept its broad fluttering wing between the hammer and the wood; and simultaneously feeling that etherial thrill, the submerged savage beneath, in his death-gasp, kept his hammer frozen there; and so the bird of heaven, with archangelic shrieks, and his imperial beak thrust upwards, and his whole captive form folded in the flag of Ahab, went down with his ship, which, like Satan, would not sink to hell till she had dragged a living part of heaven along with her, and helmeted herself with it.

Now small fowls flew screaming over the yet yawning gulf; a sullen white surf beat against its steep sides; then all collapsed, and the great shroud of the sea rolled on as it rolled five thousand years ago.

EPILOGUE

'And I only am escaped alone to tell thee.'
Job.

The drama's done. Why then here does any step forth?—Because one did survive the wreck.

It so chanced, that after the Parsee's disappearance, I was he whom the Fates ordained to take the place of Ahab's bowsman, when that bowsman assumed the vacant post; the same, who, when on the last day the three men were tossed from out the rocking boat, was dropped astern. So, floating on the margin of the ensuing scene, and in full sight of it, when the half-spent suction of the sunk ship reached me, I was then, but slowly, drawn towards the closing vortex. When I reached it, it had subsided to a creamy pool. Round and round, then, and ever contracting towards the button-like black bubble at the axis of that slowly wheeling circle, like another Ixion I did revolve. Till, gaining that vital centre, the black bubble upward burst; and now, liberated by reason of its cunning spring, and, owing to its great buoyancy, rising with great force, the coffin life-buoy shot lengthwise from the sea, fell over, and floated by my side. Buoyed up by that coffin, for almost one whole day and night, I floated on a soft and dirge-like main. The unharming sharks, they glided by as if with padlocks on their mouths; the savage sea-hawks sailed with sheathed beaks. On the second day, a sail drew near, nearer, and picked me up at last. It was the devious-cruising Rachel, that in her retracing search after her missing children, only found another orphan.

FINIS.

MARK TWAIN
(Samuel Langhorne Clemens)
(1835–1910)

The Mississippi River flowed through the life of Sam Clemens and the writing of Mark Twain. He spent his idyllic Tom Sawyer-like childhood in Hannibal, Missouri, on the west bank; he spent his young manhood piloting a steamboat up and down the river. In his masterpiece, *The Adventures of Huckleberry Finn*, he captures the essence of both the village and the river experiences. Moving west or east of the river, he was always both a writer and a public entertainer in pursuit of the American dream of material success.

Samuel Clemens was born in Florida, Missouri, on November 30, 1835. His parents were Southerners who had migrated from Tennessee, and in 1839 they moved on to Hannibal. When Sam was twelve, his father died, having failed to achieve his dream of prosperity. With the moral support of his mother and the physical support of his brother, Sam went to work to contribute to the family income. After working several years in the printing offices of his brother's newspapers, he worked as a roving printer in St. Louis, New York, Philadelphia, and Cincinnati. In the spring of 1857, a boyhood dream came true. Horace Bixby apprenticed him as a pilot on the steamboat, the *Paul Jones*. When the Civil War broke out, he was a full-fledged pilot. He served in a Confederate militia in June of 1861, but his brother, a Unionist, lured him West where they hoped to strike it rich in silver. Sam finally settled for a job as reporter on a Virginia City, Nevada, newspaper, using the name "Mark Twain" for the first time in 1863. He spent the rest of the war as a journalist under Bret Harte's editorship in California. After a trip to the Hawaiian Islands, he gave his first lecture in October of 1866.

The first two works that brought Twain money and fame were *The Celebrated Jumping Frog of Calaveras County and Other Sketches* (1867) and *The Innocents Abroad, Or The New Pilgrim's Progress* (1869), based on his travels in Europe and the Holy Land. In these books, he subjects the cultural pretensions of the Old World to the savage wit of the New World frontier.

In the winter of 1870, Sam Clemens married Olivia Langdon, a coal heiress from upper New York state. They settled in Hartford, Connecticut. He was thirty-five. His days as a picaresque figure were over; before him were 40 years as Mark Twain in the realm of the spoken and written word, and 40 years of trying to make money. Twain's life-long dream of becoming a millionaire determined where he went, what he did, and what he chose to write about. He mined western American humor as if it were a vein of gold; there was a dollar value riding on his every observation. Ironically, he made more money in print and on the lecture circuit satirizing the American scramble for profit than in his own business ventures in the East.

Twain participated in and criticized major phases of the American experience: life in frontier villages, westward expansion and exploitation, the growth of political machines and big business. His fervent belief in democracy and simple justice led him to observe and satirically attack any abuse of political and economic power in American democracy, and any tyranny, past and present, in Europe. His own experience, combined with his observations of the American scene, made him see and then insinuate into his humorous tales the uglier enterprises of Americans: slavery, bigotry, hypocracy, greed, mendacity, and corruption.

From 1872 to 1884, Twain's writing alternates between his own past and the changing American scene. He romanticized his own past even as his acute observations of the present made him a severe realist. He became quite nostalgic, while at the same time he attacked the uncritical veneration of past cultures, especially English and European. He sketched his youthful adventures out West in *Roughing It* (1872). The next year, he so thoroughly satirized current American civilization in *The Gilded Age, A Tale of Today* that the title was popularly used to describe the era. Then he reached further into his past with the superb articles in the *Atlantic Monthly* called *Old Times on the Mississippi*, and even further in the following year with *The Adventures of Tom Sawyer* (1876). That was also the year he started *The Adventures of Huckleberry Finn*. Dropping the sunny, omniscient voice of *Tom Sawyer* to let Huck tell the darker tale was a transition so difficult for Twain that he had to quit working on it several times. He took time to go to Europe again, and wrote *A Tramp Abroad* (1880). He sunk his fortune in business ventures, wrote the satirical historical fantasy *The Prince and the Pauper* (1881), expanded the magazine articles to make a book, *Life on the Mississippi* (1883), and went again on the lecture circuit. Finally, the novel was published in 1884.

But *The Adventures of Huckleberry Finn*, his best novel, is, like all his work, flawed by contradictory intentions. There has been much debate about the ending, whether it descends into slap-stick showmanship or whether the shift in tone in some way harmonizes with the overall design. Contempt for all forms of pretentiousness in society and in art, especially as reverenced in Europe, led Twain to mistrust art as an element in his fiction, so that if a compulsion to entertain doesn't flaw his work, polemics do.

Americans, even those who don't read fiction much, have a clearer image of Mark Twain than of any other writer. They can easily picture Twain at the wheel of a steamboat, or Twain, the young journalist out West, gathering humorous material, or Twain giving public lectures all over the world. He was the first great American writer to acquire fame and fortune as a celebrity. He was the first to create his own legend, beginning with the colorful pseudonym and the studied wearing of white suits while smoking black cigars. As icon, he was always on stage, a showman, but also instructive: "Man is the only animal that blushes. Or needs to." The father of American black humor declared: "Everything human is pathetic. The secret source of Humor itself is not joy but sorrow. There is no humor in heaven." There is in him always a strain of Southern Gothic horror.

Superimposed over the Mark Twain icon, the public sees the lucid image of the even more world-famous Huck Finn and, less clearly, Tom Sawyer. Twain was a white-haired version of those two very different boys. *Huck Finn* is a kind of epic, comparable to Homer's in its rendering of the who, how, and where of a people, and in its effect on the young. *Tom Sawyer* is a children's book for children, but, as the saying goes, *Huck Finn* is a children's book for adults. *Tom Sawyer* is a fantasy of childhood, a nostalgic idyll. The popular image of *Huck Finn* is not much different. But readers are gradually coming to see that it is a realistic critique of the civilization it so faithfully depicts. "All right, then, I'll *go* to hell!" declares Huck, finally rejecting the code of a hypocritical, brutal, inhumane society. Ernest Hemingway tried to rescue *Huck Finn* from the realm of children's literature by declaring that, "All modern American literature comes from one book by Mark Twain called *Huckleberry Finn*."

Hemingway may have exaggerated, but others have argued that *Huck Finn* meets most criteria for choosing The Great American Novel. It has been a popular classic for generations. It dramatizes a conception of American character through representative types, male and female, black and white. The novel expresses religious and political aspects of American character, and it captures the American vernacular and frontier humor. It represents the American Land—the rural experience, the Westward movement, the frontier small-town era, and major phases of American growth. It deals with important themes in American history: race relations, violence, progress, innocence, and experience. Today, the novel is controversial. The extreme right charges it with being irreligious; the extreme left charges it with perpetuating racial stereotypes. Its appeal is to the broad majority between those extremes.

Cooper, Hawthorne, and Melville used a style derived from English and European models to present authentically American materials, subjects, images, and themes. Huck's voice as narrator is the first in a novel to be authentically American, in the vernacular, and in the tradition of oral American humor. "We . . . judged that we was free and safe once more. . . . We said there warn't no home like a raft, after all, other places do seem so cramped up and smothery, but a raft don't. You feel mighty free and easy and comfortable on a raft."

Twain attacked greed and devious means of obtaining money, while pursuing his own dream of material success all his life. He tried a number of get-rich-quick mining schemes out West and invention schemes in the East. He left the village of his childhood with the American Dream of Success and moved throughout his life toward the American nightmare of his last sixteen years. Having successfully published President Grant's memoirs, he plunged into debt when other schemes failed, and was forced into a lecture tour in South America, which did pay off in a way by providing material for *Following the Equator* (1897). His world grew much darker when his daughter Susy died in 1896, his wife died in 1904, and his daughter Jean died in 1909. Little wonder then that his works after *Huck Finn* grow progressively pessimistic. *A Connecticut Yankee in King Arthur's Court* (1889) is a satirical fantasy that criticizes anti-democratic conditions in the present by exposing the fraudulence of the ideals of the past. In *The Tragedy of Pudd'nhead Wilson* (1894), Twain turns to America's own past, the pre-Civil War era in Mississippi, to show the hideous face of racism. He makes another use of European history in the next book, *Personal Recollections of Joan of Arc* (1897). "The Mysterious Stranger," in which Satan visits an Austrian village, was written in 1898, but published posthumously. In *The Man That Corrupted Hadleyburg* (1900), another mysterious stranger takes advantage of the weaknesses of the citizens of an American village. This dark, almost black, pessimism about "the damned human race" did not discourage William Dean Howells, father of American realism, from calling Twain "the Lincoln of our literature." Mark Twain died at Redding, Connecticut, on April 21, 1910, at the age of seventy-five.

NOTICE

Persons attempting to find a motive in this narrative will be prosecuted; persons attempting to find a moral in it will be banished; persons attempting to find a plot in it will be shot.

By Order of the Author

Per G. G., Chief of Ordnance.

EXPLANATORY

In this book a number of dialects are used, to wit: the Missouri negro dialect; the extremest form of the backwoods South-Western dialect; the ordinary "Pike-County" dialect; and four modified varieties of this last. The shadings have not been done in a hap-hazard fashion, or by guess-work; but pains-takingly, and with the trustworthy guidance and support of personal familiarity with these several forms of speech.

I make this explanation for the reason that without it many readers would suppose that all these characters were trying to talk alike and not succeeding.

The Author

THE ADVENTURES OF HUCKLEBERRY FINN

Mark Twain

CHAPTER I

You don't know about me, without you have read a book by the name of "The Adventures of Tom Sawyer," but that ain't no matter. That book was made by Mr. Mark Twain, and he told the truth, mainly. There was things which he stretched, but mainly he told the truth. That is nothing. I never seen anybody but lied, one time or another, without it was Aunt Polly, or the widow, or maybe Mary. Aunt Polly—Tom's Aunt Polly, she is—and Mary, and the Widow Douglas, is all told about in that book—which is mostly a true book; with some stretchers, as I said before.

Now the way that the book winds up, is this: Tom and me found the money that the robbers hid in the cave, and it made us rich. We got six thousand dollars apiece—all gold. It was an awful sight of money when it was piled up. Well, Judge Thatcher, he took it and put it out at interest, and it fetched us a dollar a day apiece, all the year round—more than a body could tell what to do with. The Widow Douglas, she took me for her son, and allowed she would sivilize me; but it was rough living in the house all the time, considering how dismal regular and decent the widow was in all her ways; and so when I couldn't stand it no longer, I lit out. I got into my old rags, and my sugar-hogshead again, and was free and satisfied. But Tom Sawyer, he hunted me up and said he was going to start a band of robbers, and I might join if I would go back to the widow and be respectable. So I went back.

The widow she cried over me, and called me a poor lost lamb, and she called me a lot of other names, too, but she never meant no harm by it. She put me in them new clothes again, and I couldn't do nothing but sweat and sweat, and feel all cramped up. Well, then, the old thing commenced again. The widow rung a bell for supper, and you had to come to time. When you got to the table you couldn't go right to eating, but you had to wait for the widow to tuck down her head and grumble a little over the victuals, though there warn't really anything the matter with them. That is, nothing only everything was cooked by itself. In a barrel of odds and ends it is different; things get mixed up, and the juice kind of swaps around, and the things go better.

After supper she got out her book and learned me about Moses and the Bulrushers; and I was in a sweat to find out all about him; but by-and-by she let it out that Moses had been dead a considerable long time; so then I didn't care no more about him; because I don't take no stock in dead people.

Pretty soon I wanted to smoke, and asked the widow to let me. But she wouldn't. She said it was a mean practice and wasn't clean, and I must try to not do it any more. That is just the way with some people. They get down on a thing when they don't know nothing about it. Here she was a bothering about Moses, which was no kin to her, and no use to anybody, being gone, you see, yet finding a power of fault with me for doing a thing that had some good in it. And she took snuff too; of course that was all right, because she done it herself.

Her sister, Miss Watson, a tolerable slim old maid, with goggles on, had just come to live with her, and took a set at me now, with a spelling-book. She worked me middling hard for about an hour, and then the widow made her ease up. I couldn't stood it much longer. Then for an hour it was deadly dull, and I was fidgety. Miss Watson would say, "Don't put your feet up there, Huckleberry;" and "don't scrunch up like that, Huckleberry—set up straight;" and pretty soon she would say, "Don't gap and stretch like that, Huckleberry—why don't you try to behave?" Then she told me all about the bad place, and I said I wished I was there. She got mad, then, but I didn't mean no harm. All I wanted was to go somewheres; all I wanted was a change, I warn't particular. She said it was wicked to say what I said; said she wouldn't say it for the whole world; *she* was going to live so as to go to the good place. Well, I couldn't see no advantage in going where she was going, so I made up my mind I wouldn't try for it. But I never said so, because it would only make trouble, and wouldn't do no good.

Now she had got a start, and she went on and told me all about the good place. She said all a body would have to do there was to go around all day long with a harp and sing, forever and ever. So I didn't think much of it. But I never said so. I asked her if she reckoned Tom Sawyer would go there, and, she said, not by a considerable sight. I was glad about that, because I wanted him and me to be together.

Miss Watson she kept pecking at me, and it got tiresome and lonesome. By-and-by they fetched the niggers in and had prayers, and then everybody was off to bed. I went up to my room with a piece of candle and put it on the table. Then I set down in a chair by the window and tried to think of something cheerful, but it warn't no use. I felt so lonesome I most wished I was dead. The stars was shining, and the leaves rustled in the woods ever so mournful; and I heard an owl, away off, who-whooing about somebody that was dead, and a whippowill and a dog crying about somebody that was going to die; and the wind was trying to whisper something to me and I couldn't make out what it was, and so it made the cold shivers run over me. Then away out in the woods I heard that kind of a sound that a ghost makes when it wants to tell about something that's on its mind and can't make itself understood, and so can't rest easy in its grave and has to go about that way every night grieving. I got so down-hearted and scared, I did wish I had some company. Pretty soon a spider went crawling up my shoulder, and I flipped it off and it lit in the candle; and before I could budge it was all shriveled up. I didn't need anybody to tell me that that was an awful bad sign and would fetch me some bad luck, so I was scared and most shook the clothes off of me. I got up and turned around in my tracks three times and crossed my breast every time; and then I tied up a little lock of my hair with a thread to keep witches away. But I hadn't no confidence. You do that when you've lost a horse-shoe that you've found, instead of nailing it up over the door, but I hadn't ever heard anybody say it was any way to keep off bad luck when you'd killed a spider.

I set down again, a shaking all over, and got out my pipe for a smoke; for the house was all as still as death, now, and so the widow wouldn't know. Well, after a long time I heard the clock away off in the town go boom—boom—boom—twelve licks—and all still again—stiller than ever. Pretty soon I heard a twig snap, down in the dark amongst the trees—something was a stirring. I set still and listened. Directly I could just barely hear a "*me-yow! me-yow!*" down there. That was good! Says I, "*me-yow! me-yow!*" as soft as I could, and then I put out the light and scrambled out of the window onto the shed. Then I slipped down to the ground and crawled in amongst the trees, and sure enough there was Tom Sawyer waiting for me.

CHAPTER II

We went tip-toeing along a path amongst the trees back towards the end of the widow's garden, stooping down so as the branches wouldn't scrape our heads. When we was passing by the kitchen I fell over a root and made a noise. We scrouched down and laid still. Miss Watson's big nigger, named Jim, was setting in the kitchen door; we could see him pretty clear, because there was a light behind him. He got up and stretched his neck out about a minute, listening. Then he says,

"Who dah?"

He listened some more; then he come tip-toeing down and stood right between us; we could a touched him, nearly. Well, likely it was minutes and minutes that there warn't a sound, and we all there so close together. There was a place on my ankle that got to itching; but I dasn't scratch it; and then my ear begun to itch; and next my back, right between my shoulders. Seemed like I'd die if I couldn't scratch. Well, I've noticed that thing plenty of times since. If you are with the quality, or at a funeral, or trying to go to sleep when you ain't sleepy—if you are anywheres where it won't do for you to scratch, why you will itch all over in upwards of a thousand places. Pretty soon Jim says:

"Say—who is you? Whar is you? Dog my cats ef I didn't hear sumf'n. Well, I knows what I's gwyne to do. I's gwyne to set down here and listen tell I hears it agin."

So he set down on the ground betwixt me and Tom. He leaned his back up against a tree, and stretched his legs out till one of them most touched one of mine. My nose begun to itch. It itched till the tears come into my eyes. But I dasn't scratch. Then it begun to itch on the inside. Next I got to itching underneath. I didn't know how I was going to set still. This miserableness went on as much as six or seven minutes; but it seemed a sight longer than that. I was itching in eleven different places now. I reckoned I couldn't stand it more'n a minute longer, but I set my teeth hard and got ready to try. Just then Jim begun to breathe heavy; next he begun to snore—and then I was pretty soon comfortable again.

Tom he made a sign to me—kind of a little noise with his mouth—and we went creeping away on our hands and knees. When we was ten foot off, Tom whispered to me and wanted to tie Jim to the tree for fun; but I said no; he might wake and make a disturbance, and then they'd find out I warn't in. Then Tom said he hadn't got candles enough, and he would slip in the kitchen and get some more. I didn't want him to try. I said Jim might wake up and come. But Tom wanted to resk it; so we slid in there and got three candles, and Tom laid five cents on the table for pay. Then we got out, and I was in a sweat to get away; but nothing would do Tom but he must crawl to where Jim was, on his hands and knees, and play something on him. I waited, and it seemed a good while, everything was so still and lonesome.

As soon as Tom was back, we cut along the path, around the garden fence, and by-and-by fetched up on the steep top of the hill the other side of the house. Tom said he slipped Jim's hat off of his head and hung it on a limb right over him, and Jim stirred a little, but he didn't wake. Afterwards Jim said the witches bewitched him and put him in a trance, and rode him all over the State, and then set him under the trees again and hung his hat on a limb to show who done it. And next time Jim told it he said they rode him down to New Orleans: and after that, every time he told it he spread it more and more, till by-and-by he said they rode him all over the world, and tired him most to death, and his back was all over saddle-boils. Jim was monstrous proud about it, and he got so he wouldn't hardly notice the other niggers. Niggers would come miles to hear Jim tell about it, and he was more looked up to than any nigger in that country. Strange niggers would stand with their mouths open and look him all over, same as if he was a wonder. Niggers is always talking about witches in the dark by the kitchen fire; but whenever one was talking and letting on to know all about such things, Jim would happen in and say, "Hm! What you know 'bout witches?" and that nigger was corked up and had to take a back seat. Jim always kept that five-center piece around his neck with a string and said it was a charm the devil give to him with his own hands and told him he could cure anybody with it and fetch witches whenever he wanted to, just by saying something to it; but he never told what it was he said to it. Niggers would come from all around there and give Jim anything they had, just for a sight of that five-center piece; but they wouldn't touch it, because the devil had had his hands on it. Jim was most ruined, for a servant, because he got so stuck up on account of having seen the devil and been rode by witches.

Well, when Tom and me got to the edge of the hill-top, we looked away down into the village and could see three or four lights twinkling, where there was sick folks, may be; and the stars over us was sparkling ever so fine; and down by the village was the river, a whole mile broad, and awful still and grand. We went down the hill and found Jo Harper, and Ben Rogers, and two or three more of the boys, hid in the old tanyard. So we unhitched a skiff and pulled down the river two mile and a half, to the big scar on the hillside, and went ashore.

We went to a clump of bushes, and Tom made everybody swear to keep the secret, and then showed them a hole in the hill, right in the thickest part of the bushes. Then we lit the candles and crawled in on our hands and knees. We went about two hundred yards, and then the cave opened up. Tom poked about amongst the passages and pretty soon ducked under a wall where you wouldn't a noticed that there was a hole. We went along a narrow place and got into a kind of room, all damp and sweaty and cold, and there we stopped. Tom says:

"Now we'll start this band of robbers and call it Tom Sawyer's Gang. Everybody that wants to join has got to take an oath, and write his name in blood."

Everybody was willing. So Tom got out a sheet of paper that he had wrote the oath on, and read it. It swore every boy to stick to the band, and never tell any of the secrets; and if anybody done anything to any boy in the band, whichever boy was ordered to kill that person and his family must do it, and he mustn't eat and he mustn't sleep till he had killed them and hacked a cross in their breasts, which was the sign of the band. And nobody that didn't belong to the band could use that mark, and if he did he must be sued; and if he done it again he must be killed. And if anybody that belonged to the band told the secrets, he must have his throat cut, and then have his carcass burnt up and the ashes scattered all around, and his name blotted off of the list with blood and never mentioned again by the gang, but have a curse put on it and be forgot, forever.

Everybody said it was a real beautiful oath, and asked Tom if he got it out of his own head. He said, some of it, but the rest was out of pirate books, and robber books, and every gang that was high-toned had it.

Some thought it would be good to kill the *families* of boys that told the secrets. Tom said it was a good idea, so he took a pencil and wrote it in. Then Ben Rogers says:

"Here's Huck Finn, he hain't got no family—what you going to do 'bout him?"

"Well, hain't he got a father?" says Tom Sawyer.

"Yes, he's got a father, but you can't never find him, these days. He used to lay drunk with the hogs in the tanyard, but he hain't been seen in these parts for a year or more."

They talked it over, and they was going to rule me out, because they said every boy must have a family or somebody to kill, or else it wouldn't be fair and square for the others. Well, nobody could think of anything to do—everybody was stumped, and set still. I was most ready to cry; but all at once I thought of a way, and so I offered them Miss Watson—they could kill her. Everybody said:

"Oh, she'll do, she'll do. That's all right. Huck can come in."

Then they all stuck a pin in their fingers to get blood to sign with, and I made my mark on the paper.

"Now," says Ben Rogers, "what's the line of business of this Gang?"

"Nothing only robbery and murder," Tom said.

"But who are we going to rob? houses—or cattle—or—"

"Stuff! stealing cattle and such things ain't robbery, it's burglary," says Tom Sawyer. "We ain't burglars. That ain't no sort of style. We are highwaymen. We stop stages and carriages on the road, with masks on, and kill the people and take their watches and money."

"Must we always kill the people?"

"Oh, certainly. It's best. Some authorities think different, but mostly it's considered best to kill them. Except some that you bring to the cave here and keep them till they're ransomed."

"Ransomed? What's that?"

"I don't know. But that's what they do. I've seen it in books; and so of course that's what we've got to do."

"But how can we do it if we don't know what it is?"

"Why blame it all, we've *got* to do it. Don't I tell you it's in the books? Do you want to go to doing different from what's in the books, and get things all muddled up?"

"Oh, that's all very fine to *say*, Tom Sawyer, but how in the nation are these fellows going to be ransomed if we don't know how to do it to them? that's the thing *I* want to get at. Now what do you *reckon* it is?"

"Well I don't know. But per'aps if we keep them till they're ransomed, it means that we keep them till they're dead."

"Now, that's something *like*. That'll answer. Why couldn't you said that before? We'll keep them till they're ransomed to death—and a bothersome lot they'll be, too, eating up everything and always trying to get loose."

"How you talk, Ben Rogers. How can they get loose when there's a guard over them, ready to shoot them down if they move a peg?"

"A guard. Well, that *is* good. So somebody's got to set up all night and never get any sleep, just so as to watch them. I think that's foolishness. Why can't a body take a club and ransom them as soon as they get here?"

"Because it ain't in the books so—that's why. Now Ben Rogers, do you want to do things regular, or don't you?—that's the idea. Don't you reckon that the people that made the books knows what's the correct thing to do? Do you reckon *you* can learn 'em anything? Not by a good deal. No, sir, we'll just go on and ransom them in the regular way."

"All right. I don't mind; but I say it's a fool way, anyhow. Say—do we kill the women, too?"

"Well, Ben Rogers, if I was as ignorant as you I wouldn't let on. Kill the women? No—nobody ever saw anything in the books like that. You fetch them to the cave, and you're always as polite as pie to them; and by-and-by they fall in love with you and never want to go home any more."

"Well, if that's the way, I'm agreed, but I don't take no stock in it. Mighty soon we'll have the cave so cluttered up with women, and fellows waiting to be ransomed, that there won't be no place for the robbers. But go ahead, I ain't got nothing to say."

Little Tommy Barnes was asleep, now, and when they waked him up he was scared, and cried, and said he wanted to go home to his ma, and didn't want to be a robber any more.

So they all made fun of him, and called him cry-baby, and that made him mad, and he said he would go straight and tell all the secrets. But Tom give him five cents to keep quiet, and said we would all go home and meet next week and rob somebody and kill some people.

Ben Rogers said he couldn't get out much, only Sundays, and so he wanted to begin next Sunday; but all the boys said it would be wicked to do it on Sunday, and that settled the thing. They agreed to get together and fix a day as soon as they could, and then we elected Tom Sawyer first captain and Jo Harper second captain of the Gang, and so started home.

I clumb up the shed and crept into my window just before day was breaking. My new clothes was all greased up and clayey, and I was dog-tired.

CHAPTER III

Well, I got a good going-over in the morning, from old Miss Watson, on account of my clothes; but the widow she didn't scold, but only cleaned off the grease and clay and looked so sorry that I thought I would behave a while if I could. Then Miss Watson she took me in the closet and prayed, but nothing come of it. She told me to pray every day, and whatever I asked for I would get it. But it warn't so. I tried it. Once I got a fish-line, but no hooks. It warn't any good to me without hooks. I tried for the hooks three or four times, but somehow I couldn't make it work. By-and-by, one day, I asked Miss Watson to try for me, but she said I was a fool. She never told me why, and I couldn't make it out no way.

I set down, one time, back in the woods, and had a long think about it. I says to myself, if a body can get anything they pray for, why don't Deacon Winn get back the money he lost on pork? Why can't the widow get back her silver snuff-box that was stole? Why can't Miss Watson fat up? No, says I to myself, there ain't nothing in it. I went and told the widow about it, and she said the thing a body could get by praying for it was "spiritual gifts." This was too many for me, but she told me what she meant—I must help other people, and do everything I could for other people, and look out for them all the time, and never think about myself. This was including Miss Watson, as I took it. I went out in the woods and turned it over in my mind a long time, but I couldn't see no advantage about it—except for the other people—so at last I reckoned I wouldn't worry about it any more, but just let it go. Sometimes the widow would take me one side and talk about Providence in a way to make a body's mouth water; but maybe next day Miss Watson would take hold and knock it all down again. I judged I could see that there was two Providences, and a poor chap would stand considerable show with the widow's Providence, but if Miss Watson's got him there warn't no help for him any more. I thought it all out, and reckoned I would belong to the widow's, if he wanted me, though I couldn't make out how he was agoing to be any better off then than what he was before, seeing I was so ignorant and so kind of low-down and ornery.

Pap he hadn't been seen for more than a year, and that was comfortable for me; I didn't want to see him no more. He used to always whale me when he was sober and could get his hands on me; though I used to take to the woods most of the time when he was around. Well, about this time he was found in the river drowned, about twelve mile above town, so people said. They judged it was him, anyway; said this drowned man was just his size, and was ragged, and had uncommon long hair—which was all like pap—but they couldn't make nothing out of the face, because it had been in the water so long it warn't much like a face at all. They said he was floating on his back in the water. They took him and buried him on the bank. But I warn't comfortable long, because I happened to think of something. I knowed mighty well that a drownded man don't float on his back, but on his face. So I knowed, then, that this warn't pap, but a woman dressed up in man's clothes. So I was uncomfortable again. I judged the old man would turn up again by-and-by, though I wished he wouldn't.

We played robber now and then about a month, and then I resigned. All the boys did. We hadn't robbed nobody, we hadn't killed any people, but only just pretended. We used to hop out of the woods and go charging down on hog-drovers and women in carts taking garden stuff to market, but we never hived any of them. Tom Sawyer called the hogs "ingots," and he called the turnips and stuff "julery" and we would go to the cave and pow-wow over what we had done and how many people we had killed and marked. But I couldn't see no profit in it. One time Tom sent a boy to run about town with a blazing stick, which he called a slogan (which was the sign for the Gang to get together), and then he said he had got secret news by his spies that next day a whole parcel of Spanish merchants and rich A-rabs was going to camp in Cave Hollow with two hundred elephants, and six hundred camels, and over a thousand "sumter" mules, all loaded down with di'monds, and they didn't have only a guard of four hundred soldiers, and so we would lay in ambuscade, as he called it, and kill the lot and scoop the things. He said we must slick up our swords and guns, and get ready. He never could go after even a turnip-cart but he must have the swords and guns all scoured up for it; though they was only lath and broom-sticks, and you might scour at them till you rotted and then they warn't worth a mouthful of ashes more than what they was before. I didn't believe we could lick such a crowd of Spaniards and A-rabs, but I wanted to see the camels and elephants, so I was on hand next day, Saturday, in the ambuscade; and when we got the word, we rushed out of the woods and down the hill. But there warn't no Spaniards and A-rabs, and there warn't no camels nor no elephants. It warn't anything but a Sunday-school picnic, and only a primer-class at that. We busted it up, and chased the children up the hollow; but we never got anything but some doughnuts and jam, though Ben Rogers got a rag doll, and Jo Harper got a hymn-book and a tract; and then the teacher charged in and made us drop everything and cut. I didn't see no di'monds, and I told Tom Sawyer so. He said there was loads of them there, anyway; and he said there was A-rabs there, too, and elephants and things. I said, why couldn't we see them, then? He said if I warn't so ignorant, but had read a book called "Don Quixote," I would know without asking. He said it was all done by enchantment. He said there was hundreds of soldiers there, and elephants and treasure, and so on, but we had enemies which he called magicians, and they had turned the whole thing into an infant Sunday school, just out of spite. I said, all right, then the thing for us to do was to go for the magicians. Tom Sawyer said I was a numskull.

"Why," says he, "a magician could call up a lot of genies, and they would hash you up like nothing before you could say Jack Robinson. They are as tall as a tree and as big around as a church."

"Well," I says, "s'pose we got some genies to help *us*—can't we lick the other crowd then?"

"How you going to get them?"

"I don't know. How do *they* get them?"

"Why they rub an old tin lamp or an iron ring, and then the genies come tearing in, with the thunder and lightning a-ripping around and the smoke a-rolling, and everything they're told to do they up and do it. They don't think nothing of pulling a shot tower up by the roots, and belting a Sunday-school superintendent over the head with it—or any other man."

"Who makes them tear around so?"

"Why, whoever rubs the lamp or the ring. They belong to whoever rubs the lamp or the ring, and they've got to do whatever he says. If he tells them to build a palace forty miles long, out of di'monds, and fill it full of chewing gum, or whatever you want, and fetch an emperor's daughter from China for you to marry, they've got to do it—and they've got to do it before sun-up next morning, too. And more—they've got to waltz that palace around over the country wherever you want it, you understand."

"Well," says I, "I think they are a pack of flatheads for not keeping the palace themselves 'stead of fooling them away like that. And what's more—if I was one of them I would see a man in Jericho before I would drop my business and come to him for the rubbing of an old tin lamp."

"How you talk, Huck Finn. Why, you'd *have* to come when he rubbed it, whether you wanted to or not."

"What, and I as high as a tree and as big as a church? All right, then; I *would* come; but I lay I'd make that man climb the highest tree there was in the country."

"Shucks, it ain't no use to talk to you, Huck Finn. You don't seem to know anything, somehow—perfect sap-head."

I thought all this over for two or three days, and then I reckoned I would see if there was anything in it. I got an old tin lamp and an iron ring and went out in the woods and rubbed and rubbed till I sweat like an Injun, calculating to build a palace and sell it; but it warn't no use, none of the genies come. So then I judged that all that stuff was only just one of Tom Sawyer's lies. I reckoned he believed in the A-rabs and the elephants, but as for me I think different. It had all the marks of a Sunday school.

CHAPTER IV

Well, three or four months run along, and it was well into the winter, now. I had been to school most all the time, and could spell, and read, and write just a little, and could say the multiplication table up to six times seven is thirty-five, and I don't reckon I could ever get any further than that if I was to live forever. I don't take no stock in mathematics, anyway.

At first I hated the school, but by-and-by I got so I could stand it. Whenever I got uncommon tired I played hookey, and the hiding I got next day done me good and cheered me up. So the longer I went to school the easier it got to be. I was getting sort of used to the widow's ways, too, and they warn't so raspy on me. Living in a house, and sleeping in a bed, pulled on me pretty tight, mostly, but before the cold weather I used to slide out and sleep in the woods, sometimes, and so that was a rest to me. I liked the old ways best, but I was getting so I liked the new ones, too, a little bit. The widow said I was coming along slow but sure, and doing very satisfactory. She said she warn't ashamed of me.

One morning I happened to turn over the salt-cellar at breakfast. I reached for some of it as quick as I could, to throw over my left shoulder and keep off the bad luck, but Miss Watson was in ahead of me, and crossed me off. She says, "Take your hands away, Huckleberry—what a mess you are always making." The widow put in a good word for me, but that warn't going to keep off the bad luck, I knowed that well enough. I started out, after breakfast, feeling worried and shaky, and wondering where it was going to fall on me, and what it was going to be. There is ways to keep off some kinds of bad luck, but this wasn't one of them kind; so I never tried to do anything, but just poked along low-spirited and on the watch-out.

I went down the front garden and clumb over the stile, where you go through the high board fence. There was an inch of new snow on the ground, and I seen somebody's tracks. They had come up from the quarry and stood around the stile a while, and then went on around the garden fence. It was funny they hadn't come in, after standing around so. I couldn't make it out. It was very curious, somehow. I was going to follow around, but I stooped down to look at the tracks first. I didn't notice anything at first, but next I did. There was a cross in the left boot-heel made with big nails, to keep off the devil.

I was up in a second and shinning down the hill. I looked over my shoulder every now and then, but I didn't see nobody. I was at Judge Thatcher's as quick as I could get there. He said:

"Why, my boy, you are all out of breath. Did you come for your interest?"

"No sir," I says; "is there some for me?"

"Oh, yes, a half-yearly is in, last night. Over a hundred and fifty dollars. Quite a fortune for you. You better let me invest it along with your six thousand, because if you take it you'll spend it."

"No sir," I says, "I don't want to spend it. I don't want it at all—nor the six thousand, nuther. I want you to take it; I want to give it to you—the six thousand and all."

He looked surprised. He couldn't seem to make it out. He says:

"Why, what can you mean, my boy?"

I says, "Don't you ask me no questions about it, please. You'll take it—won't you?"

He says:

"Well I'm puzzled. Is something the matter?"

"Please take it," says I, "and don't ask me nothing—then I won't have to tell no lies."

He studied a while, and then he says:

"Oho-o. I think I see. You want to *sell* all your property to me—not give it. That's the correct idea."

Then he wrote something on a paper and read it over, and says:

"There—you see it says 'for a consideration.' That means I have bought it of you and paid you for it. Here's a dollar for you. Now, you sign it."

So I signed it, and left.

Miss Watson's nigger, Jim, had a hair-ball as big as your fist, which had been took out of the fourth stomach of an ox, and he used to do magic with it. He said there was a spirit inside of it, and it knowed everything. So I went to him that night and told him pap was here again, for I found his tracks in the snow. What I wanted to know, was, what he was going to do, and was he going to stay? Jim got out his hair-ball, and said something over it, and then he held it up and dropped it on the floor. It fell pretty solid, and only rolled about an inch. Jim tried it again, and then another time, and it acted just the same. Jim got down on his knees and put his ear against it and listened. But it warn't no use; he said it wouldn't talk. He said sometimes it wouldn't talk without money. I told him I had an old slick counterfeit quarter that warn't no good because the brass showed through the silver a little, and it wouldn't pass nohow, even if the brass didn't show, because it was so slick it felt greasy, and so that would tell on it every time. (I reckoned I wouldn't say nothing about the dollar I got from the judge.) I said it was pretty bad money, but maybe the hair-ball would take it, because maybe it wouldn't know the difference. Jim smelt it, and bit it, and rubbed it, and said he would manage so the hair-ball would think it was good. He said he would split open a raw Irish potato and stick the quarter in between and keep it there all night, and next morning you couldn't see no brass, and it wouldn't feel greasy no more, and so anybody in town would take it in a minute, let alone a hair-ball. Well, I knowed a potato would do that, before, but I had forgot it.

Jim put the quarter under the hair-ball and got down and listened again. This time he said the hair-ball was all right. He said it would tell my whole fortune if I wanted it to. I says, go on. So the hair-ball talked to Jim, and Jim told it to me. He says:

"Yo' ole father doan' know, yit, what he's a-gwyne to do. Sometimes he spec he'll go 'way, en den agin he spec he'll stay. De bes' way is to res' easy en let de ole man take his own way. Dey's two angels hoverin' roun' 'bout him. One uv 'em is white en shiny, en 'tother one is black. De white one gits him to go right, a little while, den de black one sail in en bust it all up. A body can't tell, yit, which one gwyne to fetch him at de las.' But you is all right. You gwyne to have considable trouble in yo' life, en considable joy. Sometimes you gwyne to git hurt, en sometimes you gwyne to git sick; but every time you's gwyne to git well agin. Dey's two gals flyin' 'bout you in yo' life. One uv 'em's light en 'tother one is dark. One is rich en 'tother is po'. You's gwyne to marry de po' one fust en de rich one by-en-by. You wants to keep 'way fum de water as much as you kin, en don't run no resk, 'kase it's down in de bills dat you's gwyne to git hung."

When I lit my candle and went up to my room that night, there set pap, his own self!

CHAPTER V

I had shut the door to. Then I turned around, and there he was. I used to be scared of him all the time, he tanned me so much. I reckoned I was scared now, too; but in a minute I see I was mistaken. That is, after the first jolt, as you may say, when my breath sort of hitched—he being so unexpected; but right away after, I see I warn't scared of him worth bothering about.

He was most fifty, and he looked it. His hair was long and tangled and greasy, and hung down, and you could see his eyes shining through like he was behind vines. It was all black, no gray; so was his long, mixed-up whiskers. There warn't no color in his face, where his face showed; it was white; not like another man's white, but a white to make a body sick, a white to make a body's flesh crawl—a tree-toad white, a fish-belly white. As for his clothes—just rags, that was all. He had one ankle resting on 'tother knee; the boot on that foot was busted, and two of his toes stuck through, and he worked them now and then. His hat was laying on the floor; an old black slouch with the top caved in, like a lid.

I stood a-looking at him; he set there a-looking at me, with his chair tilted back a little. I set the candle down. I noticed the window was up; so he had clumb in by the shed. He kept a-looking me all over. By-and-by he says:

"Starchy clothes—very. You think you're a good deal of a big-bug, *don't* you?"

"Maybe I am, maybe I ain't," I says.

"Don't you give me none o' your lip," says he. "You've put on considerble many frills since I been away. I'll take you down a peg before I get done with you. You're educated, too, they say; can read and write. You think you're better'n your father, now, don't you, because he can't? *I'll* take it out of you. Who told you you might meddle with such hifalut'n foolishness, hey?—who told you you could?"

"The widow. She told me."

"The widow, hey?—and who told the widow she could put in her shovel about a thing that ain't none of her business?

"Nobody never told her."

"Well, I'll learn her how to meddle. And looky here—you drop that school, you hear? I'll learn people to bring up a boy to put on airs over his own father and let on to be better'n what *he* is. You lemme catch you fooling around that school again, you hear? Your mother couldn't read, and she couldn't write, nuther, before she died. None of the family couldn't, before *they* died. *I* can't; and here you're a-swelling yourself up like this. I ain't the man to stand it—you hear? Say—lemme hear you read."

I took up a book and begun something about General Washington and the wars. When I'd read about a half a minute, he fetched the book a whack with his hand and knocked it across the house. He says:

"It's so. You can do it. I had my doubts when you told me. Now looky here; you stop that putting on frills. I won't have it. I'll lay for you, my smarty; and if I catch you about that school I'll tan you good. First you know you'll get religion, too. I never see such a son."

He took up a little blue and yaller picture of some cows and a boy, and says:

"What's this?"

"It's something they give me for learning my lessons good."

He tore it up, and says—

"I'll give you something better—I'll give you a cowhide."

He set there a-mumbling and a-growling a minute, and then he says—

"*Ain't* you a sweet-scented dandy, though? A bed; and bedclothes; and a look'n-glass; and a piece of carpet on the floor—and your own father got to sleep with the hogs in the tanyard. I never see such a son. I bet I'll take some o' these frills out o' you before I'm done with you. Why there ain't no end to your airs—they say you're rich. Hey?—how's that?"

"They lie—that's how."

"Looky here—mind how you talk to me; I'm a-standing about all I can stand, now—so don't gimme no sass. I've been in town two days, and I hain't heard nothing but about you bein' rich. I heard about it away down the river, too. That's why I come. You git me that money to-morrow—I want it."

"I hain't got no money."

"It's a lie. Judge Thatcher's got it. You git it. I want it."

"I hain't got no money, I tell you. You ask Judge Thatcher; he'll tell you the same."

"All right. I'll ask him; and I'll make him pungle, too, or I'll know the reason why. Say—how much you got in your pocket? I want it."

"I hain't got only a dollar, and I want that to—"

"It don't make no difference what you want it for—you just shell it out."

He took it and bit it to see if it was good, and then he said he was going down town to get some whisky; said he hadn't had a drink all day. When he had got out on the shed, he put his head in again, and cussed me for putting on frills and trying to be better than him; and when I reckoned he was gone, he come back and put his head in again, and told me to mind about that school, because he was going to lay for me and lick me if I didn't drop that.

Next day he was drunk, and he went to Judge Thatcher's and bullyragged him and tried to make him give up the money, but he couldn't, and then he swore he'd make the law force him.

The judge and the widow went to law to get the court to take me away from him and let one of them be my guardian; but it was a new judge that had just come, and he didn't know the old man; so he said courts mustn't interfere and separate families if they could help it; said he'd druther not take a child away from its father. So Judge Thatcher and the widow had to quit on the business.

That pleased the old man till he couldn't rest. He said he'd cowhide me till I was black and blue if I didn't raise some money for him. I borrowed three dollars from Judge Thatcher, and pap took it and got drunk and went a-blowing around and cussing and whooping and carrying on; and he kept it up all over town, with a tin pan, till most midnight; then they jailed him, and next day they had him before court, and jailed him again for a week. But he said *he* was satisfied; said he was boss of his son, and he'd make it warm for *him*.

When he got out the new judge said he was agoing to make a man of him. So he took him to his own house, and dressed him up clean and nice, and had him to breakfast and dinner and supper with the family, and was just old pie to him, so to speak. And after supper he talked to him about temperance and such things till the old man cried, and said he'd been a fool, and fooled away his life; but now he was agoing to turn over a new leaf and be a man nobody wouldn't be ashamed of, and he hoped the judge would help him and not look down on him. The judge said he could hug him for them words; so *he* cried, and his wife she cried again; pap said he'd been a man that had always been misunderstood before, and the judge said he believed it. The old man said that what a man wanted that was down, was sympathy; and the judge said it was so; so they cried again. And when it was bedtime, the old man rose up and held out his hand, and says:

"Look at it gentlemen, and ladies all; take ahold of it; shake it. There's a hand that was the hand of a hog; but it ain't so no more; it's the hand of a man that's started in on a new life, and 'll die before he'll go back. You mark them words—don't forget I said them. It's a clean hand now; shake it—don't be afeard."

So they shook it, one after the other, all around, and cried. The judge's wife she kissed it. Then the old man he signed a pledge—made his mark. The judge said it was the holiest time on record, or something like that. Then they tucked the old man into a beautiful room, which was the spare room, and in the night sometime he got powerful thirsty and clumb out onto the porch-roof and slid down a stanchion and traded his new coat for a jug of forty-rod, and clumb back again and had a good old time; and towards daylight he crawled out again, drunk as a fiddler, and rolled off the porch and broke his left arm in two places and was most froze to death when somebody found him after sun-up. And when they come to look at that spare room, they had to take soundings before they could navigate it.

The judge he felt kind of sore. He said he reckoned a body could reform the ole man with a shot-gun, maybe, but he didn't know no other way.

CHAPTER VI

Well, pretty soon the old man was up and around again, and then he went for Judge Thatcher in the courts to make him give up that money, and he went for me, too, for not stopping school. He catched me a couple of times and thrashed me, but I went to school just the same, and dodged him or out-run him most of the time. I didn't want to go to school much, before, but I reckoned I'd go now to spite pap. That law trial was a slow business; appeared like they warn't ever going to get started on it; so every now and then I'd borrow two or three dollars off of the judge for him, to keep from getting a cowhiding. Every time he got money he got drunk; and every time he got drunk he raised Cain around town; and every time he raised Cain he got jailed. He was just suited—this kind of thing was right in his line.

He got to hanging around the widow's too much, and so she told him at last, that if he didn't quit using around there she would make trouble for him. Well, *wasn't* he mad? He said he would show who was Huck Finn's boss. So he watched out for me one day in the spring, and catched me, and took me up the river about three mile, in a skiff, and crossed over to the Illinois shore where it was woody and there warn't no houses but an old log hut in a place where the timber was so thick you couldn't find it if you didn't know where it was.

He kept me with him all the time, and I never got a chance to run off. We lived in that old cabin, and he always locked the door and put the key under his head, nights. He had a gun which he had stole, I reckon, and we fished and hunted, and that was what we lived on. Every little while he locked me in and went down to the store, three miles, to the ferry, and traded fish and game for whisky and fetched it home and got drunk and had a good time, and licked me. The widow she found out where I was, by-and-by, and she sent a man over to try to get hold of me, but pap drove him off with the gun, and it warn't long after that till I was used to being where I was, and liked it, all but the cowhide part.

It was kind of lazy and jolly, laying off comfortable all day, smoking and fishing, and no books nor study. Two months or more run along, and my clothes got to be all rags and dirt, and I didn't see how I'd ever got to like it so well at the widow's, where you had to wash, and eat on a plate, and comb up, and go to bed and get up regular, and be forever bothering over a book and have old Miss Watson pecking at you all the time. I didn't want to go back no more. I had stopped cussing, because the widow didn't like it; but now I took to it again because pap hadn't no objections. It was pretty good times up in the woods there, take it all around.

But by-and-by pap got too handy with his hick'ry, and I couldn't stand it. I was all over welts. He got to going away so much, too, and locking me in. Once he locked me in and was gone three days. It was dreadful lonesome. I judged he had got drowned and I wasn't ever going to get out any more. I was scared. I made up my mind I would fix up some way to leave there. I had tried to get out of that cabin many a time, but I couldn't find no way. There warn't a window to it big enought for a dog to get through. I couldn't get up the chimbly, it was too narrow. The door was thick solid oak slabs. Pap was pretty careful not to leave a knife or anything in the cabin when he was away; I reckon I had hunted the place over as much as a hundred times; well, I was 'most all the time at it, because it was about the only way to put in the time. But this time I found something at last; I found an old rusty wood-saw without any handle; it was laid in between a rafter and the clapboards of the roof. I greased it up and went to work. There was an old horseblanket nailed against the logs at the far end of the cabin behind the table, to keep the wind from blowing through the chinks and putting the candle out. I got under the table and raised the blanket and went to work to saw a section of the big bottom log out, big enough to let me through. Well, it was a good long job, but I was getting towards the end of it when I heard pap's gun in the woods. I got rid of the signs of my work, and dropped the blanket and hid my saw, and pretty soon pap come in.

Pap warn't in a good humor—so he was his natural self. He said he was down to town, and everything was going wrong. His lawyer said he reckoned he would win his lawsuit and get the money, if they ever got started on the trial; but then there was ways to put it off a long time, and Judge Thatcher knowed how to do it. And he said people allowed there'd be another trial to get me away from him and give me to the widow for my guardian, and they guessed it would win, this time. This shook me up considerable, because I didn't want to go back to the widow's any more and be so cramped up and sivilized, as they called it. Then the old man got to cussing, and cussed everything and everybody he could think of, and then cussed them all over again to make sure he hadn't skipped any, and after that he polished off with a kind of a general cuss all round, including a considerable parcel of people which he didn't know the names of, and so called them what's-his-name, when he got to them, and went right along with his cussing.

He said he would like to see the widow get me. He said he would watch out, and if they tried to come any such game on him he knowed of a place six or seven mile off, to stow me in, where they might hunt till they dropped and they couldn't find me. That made me pretty uneasy again, but only for a minute; I reckoned I wouldn't stay on hand till he got that chance.

The old man made me go to the skiff and fetch the things he had got. There was a fifty-pound sack of corn meal, and a side of bacon, ammunition, and a four-gallon jug of whisky, and an old book and two newspapers for wadding, besides some tow. I toted up a load, and went back and set down on the bow of the skiff to rest. I thought it all over, and I reckoned I would walk off with the gun and some lines, and take to the woods when I run away. I guessed I wouldn't stay in one place, but just tramp right across the country, mostly night times, and hunt and fish to keep alive, and so get so far away that the old man nor the widow couldn't ever find me any more. I judged I would saw out and leave that night if pap got drunk enough, and I reckoned he would. I got so full of it I didn't notice how long I was staying, till the old man hollered and asked me whether I was asleep or drownded.

I got the things all up to the cabin, and then it was about dark. While I was cooking supper the old man took a swig or two and got sort of warmed up, and went to ripping again. He had been drunk over in town, and laid in the gutter all night, and he was a sight to look at. A body would a thought he was Adam, he was just all mud. Whenever his liquor begun to work, he most always went for the govment. This time he says:

"Call this a govment! why, just look at it and see what it's like. Here's the law a-standing ready to take a man's son away from him—a man's own son, which he has had all the trouble and all the anxiety and all the expense of raising. Yes, just as that man has got that son raised at last, and ready to go to work and begin to do suthin' for *him* and give him a rest, the law up and goes for him. And they call *that* govment! That ain't all, nuther. The law backs that old Judge Thatcher up and helps him to keep me out o' my property. Here's what the law does. The law takes a man worth six thousand dollars and upards, and jams him into an old trap of a cabin like this, and lets him go round in clothes that ain't fitten for a hog. They call that govment! A man can't get his rights in a govment like this. Sometimes I've a mighty notion to just leave the country for good and all. Yes, and I *told* 'em so; I told old Thatcher so to his face. Lots of 'em heard me, and can tell what I said. Says I, for two cents I'd leave the blamed country and never come anear it agin. Them's the very words. I says, look at my hat—if you call it a hat—but the lid raises up and the rest of it goes down till it's below my chin, and then it ain't rightly a hat at all, but more like my head was shoved up through a jint o' stovepipe. Look at it, says I—such a hat for me to wear—one of the wealthiest men in this town, if I could git my rights.

"Oh, yes, this is a wonderful govment, wonderful. Why, looky here. There was a free nigger there, from Ohio; a mulatter, most as white as a white man. He had the whitest shirt on you ever see, too, and the shiniest hat; and there ain't a man in that town that's got as fine clothes as what he had; and he had a gold watch and chain, and a silver-headed cane—the awfulest old gray-headed nabob in the State. And what do you think? they said he was a p'fessor in a college, and could talk all kinds of languages, and knowed everything. And that ain't the wust. They said he could *vote*, when he was at home. Well, that let me out. Thinks I, what is the country a-coming to? It was 'lection day, and I was just about to go and vote, myself, if I warn't too drunk to get there; but when they told me there was a State in this country where they'd let that nigger vote, I drawed out. I says I'll never vote agin. Them's the very words I said; they all heard me; and the country may rot for all me—I'll never vote agin as long as I live. And to see the cool way of that nigger—why, he wouldn't a give me the road if I hadn't shoved him out o' the way. I says to the people, why ain't this nigger put up at auction and sold?—that's what I want to know. And what do you reckon they said? Why, they said he couldn't be sold till he'd been in the State six months, and he hadn't been there that long yet. There, now—that's a specimen. They call that a govment that can't sell a free nigger till he's been in the State six months. Here's a govment that calls itself a govment, and lets on to be a govment, and thinks it is a govment, and yet's got to set stock-still for six whole months before it can take ahold of a prowling, thieving, infernal, white-shirted free nigger, and—"

Pap was agoing on so, he never noticed where his old limber legs was taking him to, so he went head over heels over the tub of salt pork, and barked both shins, and the rest of his speech was all the hottest kind of language—mostly hove at the nigger and the govment, though he give the tub some, too, all along, here and there. He hopped around the cabin considerable, first on one leg and then on the other, holding first one shin and then the other one, and at last he let out with his left foot all of a sudden and fetched the tub a rattling kick. But it warn't good judgment, because that was the boot that had a couple of his toes leaking out of the front end of it; so now he raised a howl that fairly made a body's hair raise, and down he went in the dirt, and rolled there, and held his toes; and the cussing he done then laid over anything he had ever done previous. He said so his own self, afterwards. He had heard old Sowberry Hagan in his best days, and he said it laid over him, too; but I reckon that was sort of piling it on, maybe.

After supper pap took the jug, and said he had enough whisky there for two drunks and one delirium tremens. That was always his word. I judged he would be blind drunk in about an hour, and then I would steal the key, or saw myself out, one or 'tother. He drank, and drank, and tumbled down on his blankets, by-and-by; but luck didn't run my way. He didn't go sound asleep, but was uneasy. He groaned, and moaned, and thrashed around this way and that, for a long time. At last I got so sleepy I couldn't keep my eyes open, all I could do, and so before I knowed what I was about I was sound asleep, and the candle burning.

I don't know how long I was asleep, but all of a sudden there was an awful scream and I was up. There was pap, looking wild and skipping around every which way and yelling about snakes. He said they was crawling up his legs; and then he would give a jump and scream, and say one had bit him on the cheek—but I couldn't see no snakes. He started and run round and round the cabin, hollering "take him off! take him off! he's biting me on the neck!" I never see a man look so wild in the eyes. Pretty soon he was all fagged out, and fell down panting; then he rolled over and over, wonderful fast, kicking things every which way, and striking and grabbing at the air with his hands, and screaming, and saying there was devils ahold of him. He wore out, by-and-by, and laid still a while, moaning. Then he laid stiller, and didn't make a sound. I could hear the owls and the wolves, away off in the woods, and it seemed terrible still. He was laying over by the corner. By-and-by he raised up, part way, and listened, with his head to one side. He says very low:

"Tramp—tramp—tramp; that's the dead; tramp—tramp—tramp; they're coming after me; but I won't go—Oh, they're here! don't touch me—don't! hands off—they're cold; let go—Oh, let a poor devil alone!"

Then he went down on all fours and crawled off begging them to let him alone, and he rolled himself up in his blanket and wallowed in under the old pine table, still a-begging; and then he went to crying. I could hear him through the blanket.

By-and-by he rolled out and jumped up on his feet looking wild and he see me and went for me. He chased me round and round the place, with a clasp-knife, calling me the Angel of Death and saying he would kill me and then I couldn't come for him no more. I begged, and told him I was only Huck, but he laughed *such* a screechy laugh, and roared and cussed, and kept on chasing me up. Once when I turned short and dodged under his arm he made a grab and got me by the jacket between my shoulders, and I thought I was gone; but I slid out of the jacket quick as lightning, and saved myself. Pretty soon he was all tired out, and dropped down with his back against the door, and said he would rest a minute and then kill me. He put his knife under him, and said he would sleep and get strong, and then he would see who was who.

So he dozed off, pretty soon. By-and-by I got the old split-bottom chair and clumb up, as easy as I could, not to make any noise, and got down the gun. I slipped the ramrod down it to make sure it was loaded, and then I laid it across the turnip barrel, pointing towards pap, and set down behind it to wait for him to stir. And how slow and still the time did drag along.

CHAPTER VII

"Git up! what you 'bout!"

I opened my eyes and looked around, trying to make out where I was. It was after sun-up, and I had been sound asleep. Pap was standing over me, looking sour—and sick, too. He says—

"What you doin' with this gun?"

I judged he didn't know nothing about what he had been doing, so I says:

"Somebody tried to get in, so I was laying for him."

"Why didn't you roust me out?"

"Well I tried to, but I couldn't; I couldn't budge you."

"Well, all right. Don't stand there palavering all day, but out with you and see if there's a fish on the lines for breakfast. I'll be along in a minute."

He unlocked the door and I cleared out, up the river bank. I noticed some pieces of limbs and such things floating down, and a sprinkling of bark; so I knowed the river had begun to rise. I reckoned I would have great times, now, if I was over at the town. The June rise used to be always luck for me; because as soon as that rise begins, here comes cord-wood floating down, and pieces of log rafts—sometimes a dozen logs together; so all you have to do is to catch them and sell them to the wood yards and the sawmill.

I went along up the bank with one eye out for pap and 'tother one out for what the rise might fetch along. Well, all at once, here comes a canoe; just a beauty, too, about thirteen or fourteen foot long, riding high like a duck. I shot head first off of the bank, like a frog, clothes and all on, and struck out for the canoe. I just expected there'd be somebody laying down in it, because people often done that to fool folks, and when a chap had pulled a skiff out most to it they'd raise up and laugh at him. But it warn't so this time. It was a drift-canoe, sure enough, and I clumb in and paddled her ashore. Thinks I, the old man will be glad when he sees this—she's worth ten dollars. But when I got to shore pap wasn't in sight yet, and as I was running her into a little creek like a gully, all hung over with vines and willows, I struck another idea; I judged I'd hide her good, and then, stead of taking to the woods when I run off, I'd go down the river about fifty mile and camp in one place for good, and not have such a rough time tramping on foot.

It was pretty close to the shanty, and I thought I heard the old man coming, all the time; but I got her hid; and then I out and looked around a bunch of willows, and there was the old man down the path apiece just drawing a bead on a bird with his gun. So he hadn't seen anything.

When he got along, I was hard at it taking up a "trot" line. He abused me a little for being so slow, but I told him I fell in the river and that was what made me so long. I knowed he would see I was wet, and then he would be asking questions. We got five cat-fish off of the lines and went home.

While we laid off, after breakfast, to sleep up, both of us being about wore out, I got to thinking that if I could fix up some way to keep pap and the widow from trying to follow me, it would be a certainer thing than trusting to luck to get far enough off before they missed me; you see, all kinds of things might happen. Well, I didn't see no way for a while, but by-and-by pap raised up a minute, to drink another barrel of water, and he says:

"Another time a man comes a-prowling round here, you roust me out, you hear? That man warn't here for no good. I'd a shot him. Next time, you roust me out, you hear?"

Then he dropped down and went to sleep again—but what he had been saying give me the very idea I wanted. I says to myself, I can fix it now so nobody won't think of following me.

About twelve o'clock we turned out and went along up the bank. The river was coming up pretty fast, and lots of drift-wood going by on the rise. By-and-by, along comes part of a log raft—nine logs fast together. We went out with the skiff and towed it ashore. Then we had dinner. Anybody but pap would a waited and seen the day through, so as to catch more stuff; but that warn't pap's style. Nine logs was enough for one time; he must shove right over to town and sell. So he locked me in and took the skiff and started off towing the raft about half-past three. I judged he wouldn't come back that night. I waited till I reckoned he had got a good start, then I out with my saw and went to work on that log again. Before he was 'tother side of the river I was out of the hole; him and his raft was just a speck on the water away off yonder.

I took the sack of corn meal and took it to where the canoe was hid, and shoved the vines and branches apart and put it in; then I done the same with the side of bacon; then the whisky jug; I took all the coffee and sugar there was, and all the ammunition; I took the wadding; I took the bucket and gourd, I took a dipper and a tin cup, and my old saw and two blankets, and the skillet and the coffee-pot. I took fish-lines and matches and other things—everything that was worth a cent. I cleaned out the place. I wanted an axe, but there wasn't any, only the one out at the wood pile, and I knowed why I was going to leave that. I fetched out the gun, and now I was done.

I had wore the ground a good deal, crawling out of the hole and dragging out so many things. So I fixed that as good as I could from the outside by scattering dust on the place, which covered up the smoothness and the sawdust. Then I fixed the piece of log back into its place, and put two rocks under it and one against it to hold it there,—for it was bent up at that place, and didn't quite touch ground. If you stood four or five foot away and didn't know it was sawed, you wouldn't ever notice it; and besides, this was the back of the cabin and it warn't likely anybody would go fooling around there.

It was all grass clear to the canoe; so I hadn't left a track. I followed around to see. I stood on the bank and looked out over the river. All safe. So I took the gun and went up a piece into the woods and was hunting around for some birds, when I see a wild pig; hogs soon went wild in them bottoms after they had got away from the prairie farms. I shot this fellow and took him into camp.

I took the axe and smashed in the door—I beat it and hacked it considerable, a-doing it. I fetched the pig in and took him back nearly to the table and hacked into his throat with the axe, and laid him down on the ground to bleed—I say ground, because it *was* ground—hard packed, and no boards. Well, next I took an old sack and put a lot of big rocks in it,—all I could drag—and I started it from the pig and dragged it to the door and through the woods down to the river and dumped it in, and down it sunk, out of sight. You could easy see that something had been dragged over the ground. I did wish Tom Sawyer was there, I knowed he would take an interest in this kind of business, and throw in the fancy touches. Nobody could spread himself like Tom Sawyer in such a thing as that.

Well, last I pulled out some of my hair, and bloodied the axe good, and stuck it on the back side, and slung the axe in the corner. Then I took up the pig and held him to my breast with my jacket (so he couldn't drip) till I got a good piece below the house and then dumped him into the river. Now I thought of something else. So I went and got the bag of meal and my old saw out of the canoe and fetched them to the house. I took the bag to where it used to stand, and ripped a hole in the bottom of it with the saw, for there warn't no knives and forks on the place—pap done everything with his clasp-knife, about the cooking. Then I carried the sack about a hundred yards across the grass and through the willows east of the house, to a shallow lake that was five mile wide and full of rushes—and ducks too, you might say, in the season. There was a slough or a creek leading out of it on the other side, that went miles away, I don't know where, but it didn't go to the river. The meal sifted out and made a little track all the way to the lake. I dropped pap's whetstone there too, so as to look like it had been done by accident. Then I tied up the rip in the meal sack with a string, so it wouldn't leak no more, and took it and my saw to the canoe again.

It was about dark, now; so I dropped the canoe down the river under some willows that hung over the bank, and waited for the moon to rise. I made fast to a willow; then I took a bite to eat, and by-and-by laid down in the canoe to smoke a pipe and lay out a plan. I says to myself, they'll follow the track of that sackful of rocks to the shore and then drag the river for me. And they'll follow that meal track to the lake and go browsing down the creek that leads out of it to find the robbers that killed me and took the things. They won't ever hunt the river for anything but my dead carcass. They'll soon get tired of that, and won't bother no more about me. All right; I can stop anywhere I want to. Jackson's Island is good enough for me; I know that island pretty well, and nobody ever comes there. And then I can paddle over to town, nights, and slink around and pick up things I want. Jackson's Island's the place.

I was pretty tired, and the first thing I knowed, I was asleep. When I woke up I didn't know where I was, for a minute. I set up and looked around, a little scared. Then I remembered. The river looked miles and miles across. The moon was so bright I could a counted the drift logs that went a slipping along, black and still, hundreds of yards out from shore. Everything was dead quiet, and it looked late, and *smelt* late. You know what I mean—I don't know the words to put it in.

I took a good gap and a stretch, and was just going to unhitch and start, when I heard a sound away over the water. I listened. Pretty soon I made it out. It was that dull kind of a regular sound that comes from oars working in rowlocks when it's a still night. I peeped out through the willow branches, and there it was—a skiff, away across the water. I couldn't tell how many was in it. It kept a-coming, and when it was abreast of me I see there warn't but one man in it. Thinks I, maybe it's pap, though I warn't expecting him. He dropped below me, with the current, and by-and-by he come a-swinging up shore in the easy water, and he went by so close I could a reached out the gun and touched him. Well, it *was* pap, sure enough—and sober, too, by the way he laid to his oars.

I didn't lose no time. The next minute I was a-spinning down stream soft but quick in the shade of the bank. I made two mile and a half, and then struck out a quarter of a mile or more towards the middle of the river, because pretty soon I would be passing the ferry landing and people might see me and hail me. I got out amongst the drift-wood and then laid down in the bottom of the canoe and let her float. I laid there and had a good rest and a smoke out of my pipe, looking away into the sky, not a cloud in it. The sky looks ever so deep when you lay down on your back in the moonshine; I never knowed it before. And how far a body can hear on the water such nights! I heard people talking at the ferry landing. I heard what they said, too, every word of it. One man said it was getting towards the long days and the short nights, now. 'Tother one said *this* warn't one of the short ones, he reckoned—and then they laughed, and he said it over again and they laughed again; then they waked up another fellow and told him, and laughed, but he didn't laugh; he ripped out something brisk and said let him alone. The first fellow said he 'lowed to tell it to his old woman—she would think it was pretty good; but he said that warn't nothing to some things he had said in his time. I heard one man say it was nearly three o'clock, and he hoped daylight wouldn't wait more than about a week longer. After that, the talk got further and further away, and I couldn't make out the words any more, but I could hear the mumble; and now and then a laugh, too, but it seemed a long ways off.

I was away below the ferry now. I rose up and there was Jackson's Island, about two mile and a half down stream, heavy-timbered and standing up out of the middle of the river, big and dark and solid, like a steamboat without any lights. There warn't any signs of the bar at the head—it was all under water, now.

It didn't take me long to get there. I shot past the head at a ripping rate, the current was so swift, and then I got into the dead water and landed on the side towards the Illinois shore. I run the canoe into a deep dent in the bank that I knowed about; I had to part the willow branches to get in; and when I made fast nobody could a seen the canoe from the outside.

I went up and set down on a log at the head of the island and looked out on the big river and the black driftwood, and away over to the town, three mile away, where there was three or four lights twinkling. A monstrous big lumber raft was about a mile up stream, coming along down, with a lantern in the middle of it. I watched it come creeping down, and when it was most abreast of where I stood I heard a man say, "Stern oars, there! heave her head to stabboard!" I heard that just as plain as if the man was by my side.

There was a little gray in the sky, now; so I stepped into the woods and laid down for a nap before breakfast.

CHAPTER VIII

The sun was up so high when I waked, that I judged it was after eight o'clock. I laid there in the grass and the cool shade, thinking about things and feeling rested and ruther comfortable and satisfied. I could see the sun out at one or two holes, but mostly it was big trees all about, and gloomy in there amongst them. There was freckled places on the ground where the light sifted down through the leaves, and the freckled places swapped about a little, showing there was a little breeze up there. A couple of squirrels set on a limb and jabbered at me very friendly.

I was powerful lazy and comfortable—didn't want to get up and cook breakfast. Well, I was dozing off again, when I thinks I hears a deep sound of "boom!" away up the river. I rouses up and rests on my elbow and listens; pretty soon I hears it again. I hopped up and went and looked out at a hole in the leaves, and I see a bunch of smoke laying on the water a long ways up—about abreast the ferry. And there was the ferry-boat full of people, floating along down. I knowed what was the matter, now. "Boom!" I see the white smoke squirt out of the ferry-boat's side. You see, they was firing cannon over the water, trying to make my carcass come to the top.

I was pretty hungry, but it warn't going to do for me to start a fire, because they might see the smoke. So I set there and watched the cannon-smoke and listened to the boom. The river was a mile wide, there, and it always looks pretty on a summer morning—so I was having a good enough time seeing them hunt for my remainders, if I only had a bite to eat. Well, then I happened to think how they always put quicksilver in loaves of bread and float them off because they always go right to the drownded carcass and stop there. So says I, I'll keep a lookout, and if any of them's floating around after me, I'll give them a show. I changed to the Illinois edge of the island to see what luck I could have, and I warn't disappointed. A big double loaf come along, and I most got it, with a long stick, but my foot slipped and she floated out further. Of course I was where the current set in the closest to the shore—I knowed enough for that. But by-and-by along comes another one, and this time I won. I took out the plug and shook out the little dab of quicksilver, and set my teeth in. It was "baker's bread"—what the quality eat—none of your low-down corn-pone.

I got a good place amongst the leaves, and set there on a log, munching the bread and watching the ferry-boat, and very well satisfied. And then something struck me. I says, now I reckon the widow or the parson or somebody prayed that this bread would find me, and here it has gone and done it. So there ain't no doubt but there is something in that thing. That is, there's something in it when a body like the widow or the parson prays, but it don't work for me, and I reckon it don't work for only just the right kind.

I lit a pipe and had a good long smoke and went on watching. The ferry-boat was floating with the current, and I allowed I'd have a chance to see who was aboard when she come along, because she would come in close, where the bread did. When she'd got pretty well along down towards me, I put out my pipe and went to where I fished out the bread, and laid down behind a log on the bank in a little open place. Where the log forked I could peep through.

By-and-by she come along, and she drifted in so close that they could a run out a plank and walked ashore. Most everybody was on the boat. Pap, and Judge Thatcher, and Bessie Thatcher, and Jo Harper, and Tom Sawyer, and his old Aunt Polly, and Sid and Mary, and plenty more. Everybody was talking about the murder, but the captain broke in and says:

"Look sharp, now; the current sets in the closest here, and maybe he's washed ashore and got tangled amongst the brush at the water's edge. I hope so, anyway."

I didn't hope so. They all crowded up and leaned over the rails, nearly in my face, and kept still, watching with all their might. I could see them first-rate, but they couldn't see me. Then the captain sung out:

"Stand away!" and the cannon let off such a blast right before me that it made me deef with the noise and pretty near blind with the smoke, and I judged I was gone. If they'd a had some bullets in, I reckon they'd a got the corpse they was after. Well, I see I warn't hurt, thanks to goodness. The boat floated on and went out of sight around the shoulder of the island. I could hear the booming, now and then, further and further off, and by-and-by after an hour, I didn't hear it no more. The island was three mile long. I judged they had got to the foot, and was giving it up. But they didn't yet a while. They turned around the foot of the island and started up the channel on the Missouri side, under steam, and booming once in a while as they went. I crossed over to that side and watched them. When they got abreast the head of the island they quit shooting and dropped over to the Missouri shore and went home to the town.

I knowed I was all right now. Nobody else would come a-hunting after me. I got my traps out of the canoe and made me a nice camp in the thick woods. I made a kind of a tent out of my blankets to put my things under so the rain couldn't get at them. I catched a cat-fish and haggled him open with my saw, and towards sundown I started my camp fire and had supper. Then I set out a line to catch some fish for breakfast.

When it was dark I set by my camp fire smoking, and feeling pretty satisfied; but by-and-by it got sort of lonesome, and so I went and set on the bank and listened to the currents washing along, and counted the stars and drift-logs and rafts that come down, and then went to bed; there ain't no better way to put in time when you are lonesome; you can't stay so, you soon get over it.

And so for three days and nights. No difference—just the same thing. But the next day I went exploring around down through the island. I was boss of it; it all belonged to me, so to say, and I wanted to know all about it; but mainly I wanted to put in the time. I found plenty strawberries, ripe and prime; and green summer-grapes, and green razberries; and the green blackberries was just beginning to show. They would all come handy by-and-by, I judged.

Well, I went fooling along in the deep woods till I judged I warn't far from the foot of the island. I had my gun along, but I hadn't shot nothing; it was for protection; thought I would kill some game nigh home. About this time I mighty near stepped on a good sized snake, and it went sliding off through the grass and flowers, and I after it, trying to get a shot at it. I clipped along, and all of a sudden I bounded right on to the ashes of a camp fire that was still smoking.

My heart jumped up amongst my lungs. I never waited for to look further, but uncocked my gun and went sneaking back on my tip-toes as fast as ever I could. Every now and then I stopped a second, amongst the thick leaves, and listened; but my breath come so hard I couldn't hear nothing else. I slunk along another piece further, then listened again; and so on, and so on; if I see a stump, I took it for a man; if I trod on a stick and broke it, it made me feel like a person had cut one of my breaths in two and I only got half, and the short half, too.

When I got to camp I warn't feeling very brash, there warn't much sand in my craw; but I says, this ain't no time to be fooling around. So I got all my traps into my canoe again so as to have them out of sight, and I put out the fire and scattered the ashes around to look like an old last year's camp, and then clumb a tree.

I reckon I was up in the tree two hours; but I didn't see nothing, I didn't hear nothing—I only *thought* I heard and seen as much as a thousand things. Well, I couldn't stay up there forever; so at last I got down, but I kept in the thick woods and on the lookout all the time. All I could get to eat was berries and what was left over from breakfast.

By the time it was night I was pretty hungry. So when it was good and dark, I slid out from shore before moonrise and paddled over to the Illinois bank—about a quarter of a mile. I went out in the woods and cooked a supper, and I had about made up my mind I would stay there all night, when I hear a *plunkety-plunk, plunkety-plunk*, and says to myself, horses coming; and next I hear people's voices. I got everything into the canoe as quick as I could, and then went creeping through the woods to see what I could find out. I hadn't got far when I hear a man say:

"We better camp here, if we can find a good place; the horses is about beat out. Let's look around."

I didn't wait, but shoved out and paddled away easy. I tied up in the old place, and reckoned I would sleep in the canoe.

I didn't sleep much. I couldn't somehow, for thinking. And every time I waked up I thought somebody had me by the neck. So the sleep didn't do me no good. By-and-by I says to myself, I can't live this way; I'm going to find out who it is that's here on the island with me; I'll find it out or bust. Well, I felt better, right off.

So I took my paddle and slid out from shore just a step or two, and then let the canoe drop along down amongst the shadows. The moon was shining, and outside of the shadows it made it most as light as day. I poked along well onto an hour, everything still as rocks and sound asleep. Well by this time I was most down to the foot of the island. A little ripply, cool breeze begun to blow, and that was as good as saying the night was about done. I give her a turn with the paddle and brung her nose to shore; then I got my gun and slipped out and into the edge of the woods. I set down there on a log and looked out through the leaves. I see the moon go off watch and the darkness begin to blanket the river. But in a little while I see a pale streak over the tree-tops, and knowed the day was coming. So I took my gun and slipped off towards where I had run across that camp fire, stopping every minute or two to listen. But I hadn't no luck, somehow; I couldn't seem to find the place. But by-and-by, sure enough, I catched a glimpse of fire, away through the trees. I went for it, cautious and slow. By-and-by I was close enough to have a look, and there laid a man on the ground. It most give me the fan-tods. He had a blanket around his head, and his head was nearly in the fire. I set there behind a clump of bushes, in about six foot of him, and kept my eyes on him steady. It was getting gray daylight, now. Pretty soon he gapped, and stretched himself, and hove off the blanket, and it was Miss Watson's Jim! I bet I was glad to see him. I says:

"Hello, Jim!" and skipped out.

He bounced up and stared at me wild. Then he drops down on his knees, and puts his hands together and says:

"Doan' hurt me—don't! I hain't ever done no harm to a ghos'. I awluz liked dead people, en done all I could for 'em. You go en git in de river agin, whah you b'longs, en doan' do nuffin to Ole Jim, 'at 'uz awluz yo' fren'."

Well, I warn't long making him understand I warn't dead. I was ever so glad to see Jim. I warn't lonesome, now. I told him I warn't afraid of *him* telling the people where I was. I talked along, but he only set there and looked at me; never said nothing. Then I says:

"It's good daylight. Let's get breakfast. Make up your camp fire good."

"What's de use er makin' up de camp fire to cook strawbries en sich truck? But you got a gun, hain't you? Den we kin git sumfn better den strawbries."

"Strawberries and such truck," I says. "Is that what you live on?"

"I couldn' git nuffn else," he says.

"Why, how long you been on the island, Jim?"

"I come heah de night arter you's killed."

"What, all that time?"

"Yes-indeedy."

"And ain't you had nothing but that kind of rubbage to eat?"

"No, sah—nuffn else."

"Well, you must be most starved, ain't you?"

"I reck'n I could eat a hoss. I think I could. How long you ben on de islan'?"

"Since the night I got killed."

"No! W'y, what has you lived on? But you got a gun. Oh, yes, you got a gun. Dat's good. Now you kill sumfn en I'll make up de fire."

So we went over to where the canoe was, and while he built a fire in a grassy open place amongst the trees, I fetched meal and bacon and coffee, and coffee-pot and frying-pan, and sugar and tin cups, and the nigger was set back considerable, because he reckoned it was all done with witchcraft. I catched a good big cat-fish, too, and Jim cleaned him with his knife, and fried him.

When breakfast was ready, we lolled on the grass and eat it smoking hot. Jim laid it in with all his might, for he was most about starved. Then when we had got pretty well stuffed, we laid off and lazied.

By-and-by Jim says:

"But looky here, Huck, who wuz it dat 'uz killed in dat shanty, ef it warn't you?"

Then I told him the whole thing, and he said it was smart. He said Tom Sawyer couldn't get up no better plan than what I had. Then I says:

"How do you come to be here, Jim, and how'd you get here?"

He looked pretty uneasy, and didn't say nothing for a minute. Then he says:

"Maybe I better not tell."

"Why, Jim?"

"Well, dey's reasons. But you wouldn' tell on me ef I 'uz to tell you, would you, Huck?"

"Blamed if I would, Jim."

"Well, I b'lieve you, Huck. I—I *run off*."

"Jim!"

"But mind, you said you wouldn't tell—you know you said you wouldn't tell, Huck."

"Well, I did. I said I wouldn't, and I'll stick to it. Honest *injun* I will. People would call me a low down Ablitionist and despise me for keeping mum—but that don't make no difference. I ain't agoing to tell, and I ain't agoing back there anyways. So now, le's know all about it."

"Well, you see, it 'uz dis way. Ole Missus—dat's Miss Watson—she pecks on me all de time, en treats me pooty rough, but she awluz said she wouldn' sell me down to Orleans. But I noticed dey wuz a nigger trader roun' de place considable, lately, en I begin to git oneasy. Well, one night I creeps to de do', pooty late, en de do' warn't quite shet, en I hear ole missus tell de widder she gwyne to sell me down to Orleans, but she didn' want to, but she could git eight hund'd dollars for me, en it 'uz sich a big stack o' money she couldn' resis'. De widder she try to git her to say she wouldn' do it, but I never waited to hear de res'. I lit out mighty quick, I tell you.

"I tuck out en shin down de hill en 'spec to steal a skift 'long de sho' som'ers 'bove de town, but dey wuz people a-stirrin' yit, so I hid in de ole tumble-down cooper shop on de bank to wait for everybody to go 'way. Well, I wuz dah all night. Dey wuz somebody roun' all de time. 'Long 'bout six in de mawnin', skifts begin to go by, en 'bout eight er nine every skift dat went 'long wuz talkin' 'bout how yo' pap come over to de town en say you's killed. Dese las' skifts wuz full o' ladies en genlmen agoin' over for to see de place. Sometimes dey'd pull up at de sho' en take a res' b'fo' dey started acrost, so by de talk I got to know all 'bout de killin'. I 'uz powerful sorry you's killed, Huck, but I ain't no mo', now.

"I laid dah under de shavins all day. I 'uz hungry, but I warn't afeard; bekase I knowed ole missus en de widder wuz goin' to start to de camp-meetn' right arter breakfas' en be gone all day, en dey knows I goes off wid de cattle 'bout daylight, so dey wouldn' 'spec to see me roun' de place, en so dey wouldn' miss me tell arter dark in de evenin'. De yuther servants wouldn' miss me, kase dey'd shin out en take holiday, soon as de ole folks 'uz out'n de way.

"Well, when it come dark I tuck out up de river road, en went 'bout two mile er more to whah dey warn't no houses. I'd made up my mine 'bout what I's agwyne to do. You see ef I kep' on tryin' to git away afoot, de dogs 'ud track me; ef I stole a skift to cross over, dey'd miss dat skift, you see, en dey'd know 'bout whah I'd lan' on de yuther side en whah to pick up my track. So I says, a raff is whah I's arter; it doan' *make* no track.

"I see a light a-comin' roun' de p'int, bymeby, so I wade' in en shove' a log ahead o' me, en swum more'n half-way acrost de river, en got in 'mongst de drift-wood, en kep' my head down low, en kinder swum agin de current tell de raff come along. Den I swum to de stern uv it, en tuck aholt. It clouded up en 'uz pooty dark for a little while. So I clumb up en laid down on de planks. De men 'uz all 'way yonder in de middle, whah de lantern wuz. De river wuz arisin' en dey wuz a good current; so I reck'n'd 'at by fo' in de mawnin' I'd be twenty-five mile down de river, en den I'd slip in, jis' b'fo' daylight, en swim asho' en take to de woods on de Illinoi side.

"But I didn' have no luck. When we 'uz mos' down to de head er de islan', a man begin to come aft wid de lantern. I see it warn't no use fer to wait, so I slid overboard, en struck out fer de islan'. Well, I had a notion I could lan' mos' anywhers, but I couldn't—bank too bluff. I 'uz mos' to de foot er de islan' b'fo' I foun' a good place. I went into de woods en jedged I wouldn' fool wid raffs no mo', long as dey move de lantern roun' so. I had my pipe en a plug er dog-leg, en some matches in my cap, en dey warn't wet, so I 'uz all right."

"And so you ain't had no meat nor bread to eat all this time? Why didn't you get mud-turkles?"

"How you gwyne to git'm? You can't slip up on um en grab um; en how's a body gwyne to hit um wid a rock? How could a body do it in de night? en I warn't gwyne to show mysef on de bank in de daytime."

"Well, that's so. You've had to keep in the woods all the time, of course. Did you hear 'em shooting the cannon?"

"Oh, yes. I knowed dey was arter you. I see um go by heah; watched um thoo de bushes."

Some young birds come along, flying a yard or two at a time and lighting. Jim said it was a sign it was going to rain. He said it was a sign when young chickens flew that way, and so he reckoned it was the same way when young birds done it. I was going to catch some of them, but Jim wouldn't let me. He said it was death. He said his father laid mighty sick once, and some of them catched a bird, and his old granny said his father would die, and he did.

And Jim said you musn't count the things you are going to cook for dinner, because that would bring bad luck. The same if you shook the table-cloth after sundown. And he said if a man owned a bee-hive, and that man died, the bees must be told about it before sun-up next morning, or else the bees would all weaken down and quit work and die. Jim said bees wouldn't sting idiots; but I didn't believe that, because I had tried them lots of times myself, and they wouldn't sting me.

I had heard about some of these things before, but not all of them. Jim knowed all kinds of signs. He said he knowed most everything. I said it looked to me like all the signs was about bad luck, and so I asked him if there warn't any good-luck signs. He says:

"Mighty few—an' *dey* ain' no use to a body. What you want to know when good luck's a-comin' for? want to keep it off?" And he said: "Ef you's got hairy arms en a hairy breas', it's a sign dat you's agwyne to be rich. Well, dey's some use in a sign like dat, 'kase it's so fur ahead. You see, maybe you's got to be po' a long time fust, en so you might git discourage' en kill yo'sef 'f you didn't know by de sign dat you gwyne to be rich bymeby."

"Have you got hairy arms and a hairy breast, Jim?"

"What's de use to ax dat question? don' you see I has?"

"Well, are you rich?"

"No, but I ben rich wunst, and gwyne to be rich agin. Wunst I had foteen dollars, but I tuck to specalat'n', en got busted out."

"What did you speculate in, Jim?"

"Well, fust I tackled stock."

"What kind of stock?"

"Why, live stock. Cattle, you know. I put ten dollars in a cow. But I ain' gwyne to resk no mo' money in stock. De cow up 'n' died on my han's."

"So you lost the ten dollars."

"No, I didn' lose it all. I on'y los' 'bout nine of it. I sole de hide en taller for a dollar en ten cents."

"You had five dollars and ten cents left. Did you speculate any more?"

"Yes. You know dat one-laigged nigger dat b'longs to old Misto Bradish? well, he sot up a bank, en say anybody dat put in a dollar would git fo' dollars mo' at de en' er de year. Well, all de niggers went in, but dey didn' have much. I wuz de on'y one dat had much. So I stuck out for mo' dan fo' dollars, en I said 'f I didn't git it I'd start a bank myself. Well o' course dat nigger want' to keep me out er de business, bekase he say dey warn't business 'nough for two banks, so he say I could put in my five dollars en he pay me thirty-five at de en' er de year.

"So I done it. Den I reck'n'd I'd inves' de thirty-five dollars right off en keep things a-movin'. Dey wuz a nigger name' Bob, dat had ketched a wood-flat, en his marster didn' know it; en I bought it off'n him en told him to take de thirty-five dollars when de en' er de year come; but somebody stole de wood-flat dat night, en nex' day de one-laigged nigger say de bank 's busted. So dey didn' none uv us git no money."

"What did you do with the ten cents, Jim?"

"Well, I 'uz gwyne to spen' it, but I had a dream, en de dream tole me to give it to a nigger name' Balum—Balum's Ass dey call him for short, he's one er dem chuckle-heads, you know. But he's lucky, dey say, en I see I warn't lucky. De dream say let Balum inves' de ten cents en he'd make a raise for me. Well, Balum he tuck de money, en when he wuz in church he hear de preacher say dat whoever give to de po' len' to de Lord, en boun' to git his money back a hund'd times. So Balum he tuck en give de ten cents to de po,' en laid low to see what wuz gwyne to come of it."

"Well, what did come of it, Jim?"

"Nuffn' never come of it. I couldn' manage to k'leck dat money no way; en Balum he couldn'. I ain' gwyne to len' no mo' money 'dout I see de security. Boun' to git yo' money back a hund'd times, de preacher says! Ef I could git de ten *cents* back, I'd call it squah, en be glad er de chanst."

"Well, it's all right, anyway, Jim, long as you're going to be rich again some time or other."

"Yes—en I's rich now, come to look at it. I owns mysef, en I's wuth eight hund'd dollars. I wisht I had de money, I wouldn' want no mo'."

CHAPTER IX

I wanted to go and look at a place right about the middle of the island, that I'd found when I was exploring; so we started, and soon got to it, because the island was only three miles long and a quarter of a mile wide.

This place was a tolerable long steep hill or ridge, about forty foot high. We had a rough time getting to the top, the sides was so steep and the bushes so thick. We tramped and clumb around all over it, and by-and-by found a good big cavern in the rock, most up to the top on the side towards Illinois. The cavern was as big as two or three rooms bunched together, and Jim could stand up straight in it. It was cool in there. Jim was for putting our traps in there, right away, but I said we didn't want to be climbing up and down there all the time.

Jim said if we had the canoe hid in a good place, and had all the traps in the cavern, we could rush there if anybody was to come to the island, and they would never find us without dogs. And besides, he said them little birds had said it was going to rain, and did I want the things to get wet?

So we went back and got the canoe and paddled up abreast the cavern, and lugged all the traps up there. Then we hunted up a place close by to hide the canoe in, amongst the thick willows. We took some fish off of the lines and set them again, and begun to get ready for dinner.

The door of the cavern was big enough to roll a hogshead in, and on one side of the door the floor stuck out a little bit and was flat and a good place to build a fire on. So we built it there and cooked dinner.

We spread the blankets inside for a carpet, and eat our dinner in there. We put all the other things handy at the back of the cavern. Pretty soon it darkened up and begun to thunder and lighten; so the birds was right about it. Directly it begun to rain, and it rained like all fury, too, and I never see the wind blow so. It was one of these regular summer storms. It would get so dark that it looked all blue-black outside, and lovely; and the rain would thrash along by so thick that the trees off a little ways looked dim and spider-webby; and here would come a blast of wind that would bend the trees down and turn up the pale underside of the leaves; and then a perfect ripper of a gust would follow along and set the branches to tossing their arms as if they was just wild; and next, when it was just about the bluest and blackest—*fst!* it was as bright as glory and you'd have a little glimpse of tree-tops a-plunging about, away off yonder in the storm, hundreds of yards further than you could see before; dark as sin again in a second, and now you'd hear the thunder let go with an awful crash and then go rumbling, grumbling, tumbling down the sky towards the under side of the world, like rolling empty barrels down stairs, where it's long stairs and they bounce a good deal, you know.

"Jim, this is nice," I says. "I wouldn't want to be nowhere else but here. Pass me along another hunk of fish and some hot cornbread."

"Well, you wouldn't a ben here, 'f it hadn't a ben for Jim. You'd a ben down dah in de woods widout any dinner, en gittin' mos' drownded, too, dat you would, honey. Chickens knows when its gwyne to rain, en so do de birds, chile."

The river went on raising and raising for ten or twelve days, till at last it was over the banks. The water was three or four foot deep on the island in the low places and on the Illinois bottom. On that side it was a good many miles wide; but on the Missouri side it was the same old distance across—a half a mile—because the Missouri shore was just a wall of high bluffs.

Daytimes we paddled all over the island in the canoe. It was mighty cool and shady in the deep woods even if the sun was blazing outside. We went winding in and out amongst the trees; and sometimes the vines hung so thick we had to back away and go some other way. Well, on every old broken-down tree, you could see rabbits, and snakes, and such things; and when the island had been overflowed a day or two, they got so tame, on account of being hungry, that you could paddle right up and put your hand on them if you wanted to; but not the snakes and turtles—they would slide off in the water. The ridge our cavern was in, was full of them. We could a had pets enough if we'd wanted them.

One night we catched a little section of a lumber raft—nice pine planks. It was twelve foot wide and about fifteen or sixteen foot long, and the top stood above water six or seven inches, a solid level floor. We could see saw-logs go by in the daylight, sometimes, but we let them go; we didn't show ourselves in daylight.

Another night, when we was up at the head of the island, just before daylight, here comes a frame house down, on the west side. She was a two-story, and tilted over, considerable. We paddled out and got aboard—clumb in at an up-stairs window. But it was too dark to see yet, so we made the canoe fast and set in her to wait for daylight.

The light begun to come before we got to the foot of the island. Then we looked in at the window. We could make out a bed, and a table, and two old chairs, and lots of things around about on the floor; and there was clothes hanging against the wall. There was something laying on the floor in the far corner that looked like a man. So Jim says:

"Hello, you!"

But it didn't budge. So I hollered again, and then Jim says:

"De man ain't asleep—he's dead. You hold still—I'll go en see."

He went and bent down and looked, and says:

"It's a dead man. Yes, indeedy; naked, too. He's ben shot in de back. I reck'n he's ben dead two er three days. Come in, Huck, but doan' look at his face—it's too gashly."

I didn't look at him at all. Jim throwed some old rags over him, but he needn't done it; I didn't want to see him. There was heaps of old greasy cards scattered around over the floor, and old whisky bottles, and a couple of masks made out of black cloth; and all over the walls was the ignorantest kind of words and pictures, made with charcoal. There was two old dirty calico dresses, and a sun-bonnet, and some women's underclothes, hanging against the wall, and some men's clothing, too. We put the lot into the canoe; it might come good. There was a boy's old speckled straw hat on the floor; I took that too. And there was a bottle that had had milk in it; and it had a rag stopper for a baby to suck. We would a took the bottle, but it was broke. There was a seedy old chest, and an old hair trunk with the hinges broke. They stood open, but there warn't nothing left in them that was any account. The way things was scattered about, we reckoned the people left in a hurry and warn't fixed so as to carry off most of their stuff.

We got an old tin lantern, and a butcher knife without any handle, and a bran-new Barlow knife worth two bits in any store, and a lot of tallow candles, and a tin candlestick, and a gourd, and a tin cup, and a ratty old bed-quilt off the bed, and a reticule with needles and pins and beeswax and buttons and thread and all such truck in it, and a hatchet and some nails, and a fish-line as thick as my little finger, with some monstrous hooks on it, and a roll of buckskin, and a leather dog-collar, and a horse-shoe, and some vials of medicine that didn't have no label on them; and just as we was leaving I found a tolerable good curry-comb, and Jim he found a ratty old fiddle-bow, and a wooden leg. The straps was broke off of it, but barring that, it was a good enough leg, though it was too long for me and not long enough for Jim, and we couldn't find the other one, though we hunted all around.

And so, take it all around, we made a good haul. When we was ready to shove off, we was a quarter of a mile below the island, and it was pretty broad day; so I made Jim lay down in the canoe and cover up with the quilt, because if he set up, people could tell he was a nigger a good ways off. I paddled over to the Illinois shore, and drifted down most a half a mile doing it. I crept up the dead water under the bank, and hadn't no accidents and didn't see nobody. We got home all safe.

CHAPTER X

After breakfast I wanted to talk about the dead man and guess out how he come to be killed, but Jim didn't want to. He said it would fetch bad luck; and besides, he said, he might come and ha'nt us; he said a man that warn't buried was more likely to go a-ha'nting around than one that was planted and comfortable. That sounded pretty reasonable, so I didn't say no more; but I couldn't keep from studying over it and wishing I knowed who shot the man, and what they done it for.

We rummaged the clothes we'd got, and found eight dollars in silver sewed up in the lining of an old blanket overcoat. Jim said he reckoned the people in that house stole the coat, because if they'd a knowed the money was there they wouldn't a left it. I said I reckoned they killed him, too; but Jim didn't want to talk about that. I says:

"Now you think it's bad luck; but what did you say when I fetched in the snake-skin that I found on the top of the ridge day before yesterday? You said it was the worst bad luck in the world to touch a snake-skin with my hands. Well, here's your bad luck! We've raked in all this truck and eight dollars besides. I wish we could have some bad luck like this every day, Jim."

"Never you mind, honey, never you mind. Don't you git too peart. It's a-comin'. Mind I tell you, it's a-comin'."

It did come, too. It was a Tuesday that we had that talk. Well, after dinner Friday, we was laying around in the grass at the upper end of the ridge, and got out of tobacco. I went to the cavern to get some, and found a rattlesnake in there. I killed him, and curled him up on the foot of Jim's blanket, ever so natural, thinking there'd be some fun when Jim found him there. Well, by night I forgot all about the snake, and when Jim flung himself down on the blanket while I struck a light, the snake's mate was there, and bit him.

He jumped up yelling, and the first thing the light showed was the varmint curled up and ready for another spring. I laid him out in a second with a stick, and Jim grabbed pap's whisky jug and begun to pour it down.

He was barefooted, and the snake bit him right on the heel. That all comes of my being such a fool as to not remember that wherever you leave a dead snake its mate always comes there and curls around it. Jim told me to chop off the snake's head and throw it away, and then skin the body and roast a piece of it. I done it, and he eat it and said it would help cure him. He made me take off the rattles and tie them around his wrist, too. He said that would help. Then I slid out quiet and throwed the snakes clear away amongst the bushes; for I warn't going to let Jim find out it was all my fault, not if I could help it.

Jim sucked and sucked at the jug, and now and then he got out of his head and pitched around and yelled; but every time he come to himself he went to sucking at the jug again. His foot swelled up pretty big, and so did his leg; but by-and-by the drunk begun to come, and so I judged he was all right; but I'd druther been bit with a snake than pap's whisky.

Jim was laid up for four days and nights. Then the swelling was all gone and he was around again. I made up my mind I wouldn't ever take aholt of a snake-skin again with my hands, now that I see what had come of it. Jim said he reckoned I would believe him next time. And he said that handling a snake-skin was such awful bad luck that maybe we hadn't got to the end of it yet. He said he druther see the new moon over his left shoulder as much as a thousand times than take up a snake-skin in his hand. Well, I was getting to feel that way myself, though I've always reckoned that looking at the new moon over your left shoulder is one of the carelessest and foolishest things a body can do. Old Hank Bunker done it once, and bragged about it; and in less than two years he got drunk and fell off of the shot tower and spread himself out so that he was just a kind of a layer, as you may say; and they slid him edgeways between two barn doors for a coffin, and buried him so, so they say, but I didn't see it. Pap told me. But anyway, it all come of looking at the moon that way, like a fool.

Well, the days went along, and the river went down between its banks again; and about the first thing we done was to bait one of the big hooks with a skinned rabbit and set it and catch a cat-fish that was as big as a man, being six foot two inches long, and weighed over two hundred pounds. We couldn't handle him, of course; he would a flung us into Illinois. We just set there and watched him rip and tear around till he drownded. We found a brass button in his stomach, and a round ball, and lots of rubbage. We split the ball open with the hatchet, and there was a spool in it. Jim said he'd had it there a long time, to coat it over so and make a ball of it. It was as big a fish as was ever catched in the Mississippi, I reckon. Jim said he hadn't ever seen a bigger one. He would a been worth a good deal over at the village. They peddle out such a fish as that by the pound in the market house there; everybody buys some of him; his meat's as white as snow and makes a good fry.

Next morning I said it was getting slow and dull, and I wanted to get a stirring up, some way. I said I reckoned I would slip over the river and find out what was going on. Jim liked that notion; but he said I must go in the dark and look sharp. Then he studied it over and said, couldn't I put on some of them old things and dress up like a girl? That was a good notion, too. So we shortened up one of the calico gowns and I turned up my trowser-legs to my knees and got into it. Jim hitched it behind with the hooks, and it was a fair fit. I put on the sun-bonnet and tied it under my chin, and then for a body to look in and see my face was like looking down a joint of stove-pipe. Jim said nobody would know me, even in the daytime, hardly. I practiced around all day to get the hang of things, and by-and-by I could do pretty well in them, only Jim said I didn't walk like a girl; and he said I must quit pulling up my gown to get at my britches pocket. I took notice, and done better.

I started up the Illinois shore in the canoe just after dark.

I started across to the town from a little below the ferry landing, and the drift of the current fetched me in at the bottom of the town. I tied up and started along the bank. There was a light burning in a little shanty that hadn't been lived in for a long time, and I wondered who had took up quarters there. I slipped up and peeped in at the window. There was a woman about forty year old in there, knitting by a candle that was on a pine table. I didn't know her face; she was a stranger, for you couldn't start a face in that town that I didn't know. Now this was lucky, because I was weakening; I was getting afraid I had come; people might know my voice and find me out. But if this woman had been in such a little town two days she could tell me all I wanted to know; so I knocked at the door, and made up my mind I wouldn't forget I was a girl.

CHAPTER XI

"Come in," says the woman, and I did. She says:

"Take a cheer."

I done it. She looked me all over with her little shiny eyes, and says:

"What might your name be?"

"Sarah Williams."

"Where 'bouts do you live? In this neighborhood?"

"No'm. In Hookerville, seven mile below. I've walked all the way and I'm all tired out."

"Hungry, too, I reckon. I'll find you something."

"No'm, I ain't hungry. I was so hungry I had to stop two mile below here at a farm; so I ain't hungry no more. It's what makes me so late. My mother's down sick, and out of money and everything, and I come to tell my uncle Abner Moore. He lives at the upper end of the town, she says. I hain't ever been here before. Do you know him?"

"No; but I don't know everybody yet. I haven't lived here quite two weeks. It's a considerable ways to the upper end of the town. You better stay here all night. Take off your bonnet."

"No," I says, "I'll rest a while, I reckon, and go on. I ain't afeard of the dark."

She said she wouldn't let me go by myself, but her husband would be in by-and-by, maybe in a hour and a half, and she'd send him along with me. Then she got to talking about her husband, and about her relations up the river, and her relations down the river, and about how much better off they used to was, and how they didn't know but they'd made a mistake coming to our town, instead of letting well alone—and so on and so on, till I was afeard *I* had made a mistake coming to her to find out what was going on in the town; but by-and-by she dropped onto pap and the murder, and then I was pretty willing to let her clatter right along. She told about me and Tom Sawyer finding the six thousand dollars (only she got it ten) and all about pap and what a hard lot he was, and what a hard lot I was, and at last she got down to where I was murdered. I says:

"Who done it? We've heard considerable about these goings on, down in Hookerville, but we don't know who 'twas that killed Huck Finn."

"Well, I reckon there's a right smart chance of people *here* that'd like to know who killed him. Some thinks old Finn done it himself."

"No—is that so?"

"Most everybody thought it at first. He'll never know how nigh he come to getting lynched. But before night they changed around and judged it was done by a runaway nigger named Jim."

"Why *he*—"

I stopped. I reckoned I better keep still. She run on, and never noticed I had put in at all.

"The nigger run off the very night Huck Finn was killed. So there's a reward out for him—three hundred dollars. And there's a reward out for old Finn too—two hundred dollars. You see, he come to town the morning after the murder, and told about it, and was out with 'em on the ferry-boat hunt, and right away after he up and left. Before night they wanted to lynch him, but he was gone, you see. Well, next day they found out the nigger was gone; they found out he hadn't ben seen sence ten o'clock the night the murder was done. So then they put it on him, you see, and while they was full of it, next day back comes old Finn and went boo-hooing to Judge Thatcher to get money to hunt for the nigger all over Illinois with. The judge give him some, and that evening he got drunk and was around till after midnight with a couple of mighty hard looking strangers, and then went off with them. Well, he hain't come back sence, and they ain't looking for him back till this thing blows over a little, for people thinks now that he killed his boy and fixed things so folks would think robbers done it, and then he'd get Huck's money without having to bother a long time with a lawsuit. People do say he warn't any too good to do it. Oh, he's sly, I reckon. If he don't come back for a year, he'll be all right. You can't prove anything on him, you know; everything will be quieted down then, and he'll walk into Huck's money as easy as nothing."

"Yes, I reckon so, 'm. I don't see nothing in the way of it. Has everybody quit thinking the nigger done it?"

"Oh, no, not everybody. A good many thinks he done it. But they'll get the nigger pretty soon, now, and maybe they can scare it out of him."

"Why, are they after him yet?"

"Well, you're innocent, ain't you! Does three hundred dollars lay round every day for people to pick up? Some folks thinks the nigger ain't far from here. I'm one of them—but I hain't talked it around. A few days ago I was talking with an old couple that lives next door in the log shanty, and they happened to say hardly anybody ever goes to that island over yonder that they call Jackson's Island. Don't anybody live there? says I. No, nobody, says they. I didn't say any more, but I done some thinking. I was pretty near certain I'd seen smoke over there, about the head of the island, a day or two before that, so I says to myself, like as not that nigger's hiding over there; anyway, says I, it's worth the trouble to give the place a hunt. I hain't seen any smoke sence, so I reckon maybe he's gone, if it was him; but husband's going over to see—him and another man. He was gone up the river; but he got back to-day and I told him as soon as he got here two hours ago."

I had got so uneasy I couldn't set still. I had to do something with my hands; so I took up a needle off of the table and went to threading it. My hands shook, and I was making a bad job of it. When the woman stopped talking, I looked up, and she was looking at me pretty curious, and smiling a little. I put down the needle and thread and let on to be interested—and I was, too—and says:

"Three hundred dollars is a power of money. I wish my mother could get it. Is your husband going over there to-night?"

"Oh, yes. He went up town with the man I was telling you of, to get a boat and see if they could borrow another gun. They'll go over after midnight."

"Couldn't they see better if they was to wait till daytime?"

"Yes. And couldn't the nigger see better, too? After midnight he'll likely be asleep, and they can slip around through the woods and hunt up his camp fire all the better for the dark, if he's got one."

"I didn't think of that."

The woman kept looking at me pretty curious, and I didn't feel a bit comfortable. Pretty soon she says:

"What did you say your name was, honey?"

"M—Mary Williams."

Somehow it didn't seem to me that I said it was Mary before, so I didn't look up; seemed to me I said it was Sarah; so I felt sort of cornered, and was afeared maybe I was looking it, too. I wished the woman would say something more; the longer she set still, the uneasier I was. But now she says:

"Honey, I thought you said it was Sarah when you first come in?"

"Oh, yes'm, I did. Sarah Mary Williams. Sarah's my first name. Some calls me Sarah, some calls me Mary."

"Oh, that's the way of it?"

"Yes'm."

I was feeling better, then, but I wished I was out of there, anyway. I couldn't look up yet.

Well, the woman fell to talking about how hard times was, and how poor they had to live, and how the rats was as free as if they owned the place, and so forth, and so on, and then I got easy again. She was right about the rats. You'd see one stick his nose out of a hole in the corner every little while. She said she had to have things handy to throw at them when she was alone, or they wouldn't give her no peace. She showed me a bar of lead, twisted up into a knot, and said she was a good shot with it generly, but she'd wrenched her arm a day or two ago, and didn't know whether she could throw true, now. But she watched for a chance, and directly she banged away at a rat, but she missed him wide, and said "Ouch!" it hurt her arm so. Then she told me to try for the next one. I wanted to be getting away before the old man got back, but of course I didn't let on. I got the thing, and the first rat that showed his nose I let drive, and if he'd a stayed where he was he'd a been a tolerable sick rat. She said that that was first-rate, and she reckoned I would hive the next one. She went and got the lump of lead and fetched it back and brought along a hank of yarn, which she wanted me to help her with. I held up my two hands and she put the hank over them and went on talking about her and her husband's matters. But she broke off to say:

"Keep your eye on the rats. You better have the lead in your lap, handy."

So she dropped the lump into my lap, just at that moment, and I clapped my legs together on it and she went on talking. But only about a minute. Then she took off the hank and looked me straight in the face, but very pleasant, and says:

"Come, now—what's your real name?"

"Wh-what, mum?"

"What's your real name? Is it Bill, or Tom, or Bob?—or what is it?"

I reckon I shook like a leaf, and I didn't know hardly what to do. But I says:

"Please to don't poke fun at a poor girl like me, mum. If I'm in the way, here. I'll—"

"No, you won't. Set down and stay where you are. I ain't going to hurt you, and I ain't going to tell on you, nuther. You just tell me your secret, and trust me. I'll keep it; and what's more, I'll help you. So'll my old man, if you want him to. You see, you're a runaway 'prentice—that's all. It ain't anything. There ain't any harm in it. You've been treated bad, and you made up your mind to cut. Bless you, child, I wouldn't tell on you. Tell me all about it, now—that's a good boy."

So I said it wouldn't be no use to try to play it any longer, and I would just make a clean breast and tell her everything, but she mustn't go back on her promise. Then I told her my father and mother was dead, and the law had bound me out to a mean old farmer in the country thirty mile back from the river, and he treated me so bad I couldn't stand it no longer; he went away to be gone a couple of days, and so I took my chance and stole some of his daughter's old clothes, and cleared out, and I had been three nights coming the thirty miles; I traveled nights, and hid day-times and slept, and the bag of bread and meat I carried from home lasted me all the way and I had a plenty. I said I believed my uncle Abner Moore would take care of me, and so that was why I struck out for this town of Goshen."

"Goshen, child? This ain't Goshen. This is St. Petersburg. Goshen's ten mile further up the river. Who told you this was Goshen?"

"Why, a man I met at day-break this morning, just as I was going to turn into the woods for my regular sleep. He told me when the roads forked I must take the right hand, and five mile would fetch me to Goshen."

"He was drunk I reckon. He told you just exactly wrong."

"Well, he did act like he was drunk, but it ain't no matter now. I got to be moving along. I'll fetch Goshen before daylight."

"Hold on a minute. I'll put you up a snack to eat. You might want it."

So she put me up a snack, and says:

"Say—when a cow's laying down, which end of her gets up first? Answer up prompt, now—don't stop to study over it. Which end gets up first?"

"The hind end, mum."

"Well, then a horse?"

"The for'rard end, mum."

"Which side of a tree does the most moss grow on?"

"North side."

"If fifteen cows is browsing on a hillside, how many of them eats with their heads pointed the same direction?"

"The whole fifteen, mum."

"Well, I reckon you *have* lived in the country. I thought maybe you was trying to hocus me again. What's your real name, now?"

"George Peters, mum."

"Well, try to remember it, George. Don't forget and tell me it's Elexander before you go, and then get out by saying it's George-Elexander when I catch you. And don't go about women in that old calico. You do a girl tolerable poor, but you might fool men, maybe. Bless you, child, when you set out to thread a needle, don't hold the thread still and fetch the needle up to it; hold the needle still and poke the thread at it—that's the way a woman most always does; but a man always does 'tother way. And when you throw at a rat or anything, hitch yourself up a tip-toe, and fetch your hand up over your head as awkard as you can, and miss your rat about six or seven foot. Throw stiff-armed from the shoulder, like there was a pivot there for it to turn on—like a girl; not from the wrist and elbow, with your arm out to one side, like a boy. And mind you, when a girl tries to catch anything in her lap, she throws her knees apart: she don't clap them together, the way you did when you catched the lump of lead. Why, I spotted you for a boy when you was threading the needle; and I contrived the other things just to make certain. Now trot along to your uncle, Sarah Mary Williams George Elexander Peters, and if you get into trouble you send word to Mrs. Judith Loftus, which is me, and I'll do what I can to get you out of it. Keep the river road, all the way, and next time you tramp, take shoes and socks with you. The river road's a rocky one, and your feet'll be in a condition when you get to Goshen, I reckon."

I went up the bank about fifty yards, and then I doubled on my tracks and slipped back to where my canoe was, a good piece below the house. I jumped in and was off in a hurry. I went up stream far enough to make the head of the island, and then started across. I took off the sun-bonnet, for I didn't want no blinders on, then. When I was about the middle, I hear the clock begin to strike; so I stops and listens; the sound come faint over the water, but clear—eleven. When I struck the head of the island I never waited to blow, though I was most winded, but I shoved right into the timber where my old camp used to be, and started a good fire there on a high-and-dry spot.

Then I jumped in the canoe and dug out for our place a mile and a half below, as hard as I could go. I landed, and slopped through the timber and up the ridge and into the cavern. There Jim laid, sound asleep on the ground. I roused him out and says:

"Git up and hump yourself, Jim! There ain't a minute to lose. They're after us!"

Jim never asked no questions, he never said a word; but the way he worked for the next half an hour showed about how he was scared. By that time everything we had in the world was on our raft and she was ready to be shoved out from the willow cove where she was hid. We put out the camp fire at the cavern the first thing, and didn't show a candle outside after that.

I took the canoe out from shore a little piece and took a look, but if there was a boat around I couldn't see it, for stars and shadows ain't good to see by. Then we got out the raft and slipped along down in the shade, past the foot of the island dead still, never saying a word.

CHAPTER XII

It must a been close onto one o'clock when we got below the island at last, and the raft did seem to go mighty slow. If a boat was to come along, we was going to take to the canoe and break for the Illinois shore; and it was well a boat didn't come, for we hadn't ever thought to put the gun into the canoe, or a fishing-line or anything to eat. We was in ruther too much of a sweat to think of so many things. It warn't good judgment to put *everything* on the raft.

If the men went to the island, I just expect they found the camp fire I built, and watched it all night for Jim to come. Anyways, they stayed away from us, and if my building the fire never fooled them it warn't no fault of mine. I played it as lowdown on them as I could.

When the first streak of day begun to show, we tied up to a tow-head in a big bend on the Illinois side, and hacked off cotton-wood branches with the hatchet and covered up the raft with them so she looked like there had been a cave-in in the bank there. A tow-head is a sand-bar that has cotton-woods on it as thick as harrow-teeth.

We had mountains on the Missouri shore and heavy timber on the Illinois side, and the channel was down the Missouri shore at that place, so we warn't afraid of anybody running across us. We laid there all day and watched the rafts and steamboats spin down the Missouri shore, and up-bound steamboats fight the big river in the middle. I told Jim all about the time I had jabbering with that woman; and Jim said she was a smart one, and if she was to start after us herself *she* wouldn't set down and watch a camp fire—no, sir, she'd fetch a dog. Well, then, I said, why couldn't she tell her husband to fetch a dog? Jim said he bet she did think of it by the time the men was ready to start, and he believed they must a gone up town to get a dog and so they lost all that time, or else we wouldn't be here on a tow-head sixteen or seventeen mile below the village—no, indeedy, we would be in that same old town again. So I said I didn't care what was the reason they didn't get us, as long as they didn't.

When it was beginning to come on dark, we poked our heads out of the cotton-wood thicket and looked up, and down, and across; nothing in sight; so Jim took up some of the top planks of the raft and built a snug wigwam to get under in blazing weather and rainy, and to keep the things dry. Jim made a floor for the wigwam, and raised it a foot or more above the level of the raft, so now the blankets and all the traps was out of the reach of steamboat waves. Right in the middle of the wigwam we made a layer of dirt about five or six inches deep with a frame around it for to hold it to its place; this was to build a fire on in sloppy weather or chilly; the wigwam would keep it from being seen. We made an extra steering oar, too, because one of the others might get broke, on a snag or something. We fixed up a short forked stick to hang the old lantern on; because we must always light the lantern whenever we see a steamboat coming down stream, to keep from getting run over; but we wouldn't have to light it for upstream boats unless we see we was in what they call a "crossing"; for the river was pretty high yet, very low banks being still a little under water; so up-bound boats didn't always run the channel, but hunted easy water.

This second night we run between seven and eight hours, with a current that was making over four mile an hour. We catched fish, and talked, and we took a swim now and then to keep off sleepiness. It was kind of solemn, drifting down the big still river, laying on our backs looking up at the stars, and we didn't ever feel like talking loud, and it warn't often that we laughed, only a little kind of a low chuckle. We had mighty good weather, as a general thing, and nothing ever happened to us at all, that night, nor the next, nor the next.

Every night we passed towns, some of them away up on black hillsides, nothing but just a shiny bed of lights, not a house could you see. The fifth night we passed St. Louis, and it was like the whole world lit up. In St. Petersburg they used to say there was twenty or thirty thousand people in St. Louis, but I never believed it till I see that wonderful spread of lights at two o'clock that still night. There warn't a sound there; everybody was asleep.

Every night, now, I used to slip ashore, towards ten o'clock, at some little village, and buy ten or fifteen cents' worth of meal or bacon or other stuff to eat; and sometimes I lifted a chicken that warn't roosting comfortable, and took him along. Pap always said, take a chicken when you get a chance, because if you don't want him yourself you can easy find somebody that does, and a good deed ain't ever forgot. I never see pap when he didn't want the chicken himself, but that is what he used to say, anyway.

Mornings, before daylight, I slipped into corn fields and borrowed a watermelon, or a mushmelon, or a punkin, or some new corn, or things of that kind. Pap always said it warn't no harm to borrow things, if you was meaning to pay them back, sometime; but the widow said it warn't anything but a soft name for stealing, and no decent body would do it. Jim said he reckoned the widow was partly right and pap was partly right; so the best way would be for us to pick out two or three things from the list and say we wouldn't borrow them any more—then he reckoned it wouldn't be no harm to borrow the others. So we talked it over all one night, drifting along down the river, trying to make up our minds whether to drop the watermelons, or the cantelopes, or the mushmelons, or what. But towards daylight we got it all settled satisfactory, and concluded to drop crabapples and p'simmons. We warn't feeling just right, before that, but it was all comfortable now. I was glad the way it come out, too, because crabapples ain't ever good, and the p'simmons wouldn't be ripe for two or three months yet.

We shot a water-fowl, now and then, that got up too early in the morning or didn't go to bed early enough in the evening. Take it all around, we lived pretty high.

The fifth night below St. Louis we had a big storm after midnight, with a power of thunder and lightning, and the rain poured down in a solid sheet. We stayed in the wigwam and let the raft take care of itself. When the lightning glared out we could see a big straight river ahead, and high rocky bluffs on both sides. By-and-by says I, "Hel-*lo*, Jim, looky yonder!" It was a steamboat that had killed herself on a rock. We was drifting straight down for her. The lightning showed her very distinct. She was leaning over, with part of her upper deck above water, and you could see every little chimbly-guy clean and clear, and a chair by the big bell, with an old slouch hat hanging on the back of it when the flashes come.

Well, it being away in the night, and stormy, and all so mysterious-like, I felt just the way any other boy would a felt when I see that wreck laying there so mournful and lonesome in the middle of the river. I wanted to get aboard of her and slink around a little, and see what there was there. So I says:

"Le's land on her, Jim."

But Jim was dead against it, at first. He says:

"I doan' want to go fool'n 'long er no wrack. We's doin' blame' well, en we better let blame' well alone, as de good book says. Like as not dey's a watchman on dat wrack."

"Watchman your grandmother," I says; "there ain't nothing to watch but the texas and the pilot-house; and do you reckon anybody's going to resk his life for a texas and a pilot-house such a night as this, when it's likely to break up and wash off down the river any minute?" Jim couldn't say nothing to that, so he didn't try. "And besides," I says, "we might borrow something worth having, out of the captain's stateroom. Seegars, *I* bet you—and cost five cents apiece, solid cash. Steamboat captains is always rich, and get sixty dollars a month, and *they* don't care a cent what a thing costs, you know, long as they want it. Stick a candle in your pocket; I can't rest, Jim, till we give her a rummaging. Do you reckon Tom Sawyer would ever go by this thing? Not for pie, he wouldn't. He'd call it an adventure—that's what he'd call it; and he'd land on that wreck if it was his last act. And wouldn't he throw style into it?—wouldn't he spread himself, nor nothing? Why, you'd think it was Christopher C'lumbus discovering Kingdom-Come. I wish Tom Sawyer *was* here."

Jim he grumbled a little, but give in. He said we mustn't talk any more than we could help, and then talk mighty low. The lightning showed us the wreck again, just in time, and we fetched the starboard derrick, and made fast there.

The deck was high out, here. We went sneaking down the slope of it to labboard, in the dark, towards the texas, feeling our way slow with our feet, and spreading our hands out to fend off the guys, for it was so dark we couldn't see no sign of them. Pretty soon we struck the forward end of the skylight, and clumb onto it; and the next step fetched us in front of the captain's door, which was open, and by Jimminy, away down through the texas-hall we see a light! and all in the same second we seem to hear low voices in yonder!

Jim whispered and said he was feeling powerful sick, and told me to come along. I says, all right; and was going to start for the raft; but just then I heard a voice wail out and say:

"Oh, please don't boys; I swear I won't ever tell!"

Another voice said, pretty loud:

"It's a lie, Jim Turner. You've acted this way before. You always want more'n your share of the truck, and you've always got it, too, because you've swore 't if you didn't you'd tell. But this time you've said it jest one time too many. You're the meanest, treacherousest hound in this country."

By this time Jim was gone for the raft. I was just a-biling with curiosity; and I says to myself, Tom Sawyer wouldn't back out now, and so I won't either; I'm agoing to see what's going on here. So I dropped on my hands and knees, in the little passage, and crept aft in the dark, till there warn't but about one stateroom betwixt me and the cross-hall of the texas. Then, in there I see a man stretched on the floor and tied hand and foot, and two men standing over him, and one of them had a dim lantern in his hand, and the other one had a pistol. This one kept pointing the pistol at the man's head on the floor and saying—

"I'd *like* to! And I orter, too, a mean skunk!"

The man on the floor would shrivel up, and say: "Oh, please don't, Bill—I hain't ever goin' to tell."

And every time he said that, the man with the lantern would laugh, and say: "'Deed you *ain't*! You never said no truer thing 'n that, you bet you." And once he said: "Hear him beg! and yit if we hadn't got the best of him and tied him, he'd a killed us both. And what *for*? Jist for noth'n. Jist because we stood on our *rights*—that's what for. But I lay you ain't agoin' to threaten nobody any more, Jim Turner. Put *up* that pistol, Bill."

Bill says:

"I don't want to, Jake Packard. I'm for killin' him—and didn't he kill old Hatfield jist the same way—and don't he deserve it?"

"But I don't *want* him killed, and I've got my reasons for it."

"Bless yo' heart for them words, Jake Packard! I'll never forgit you, long's I live!" says the man on the floor, sort of blubbering.

Packard didn't take no notice of that, but hung up his lantern on a nail, and started towards where I was, there in the dark, and motioned Bill to come. I crawfished as fast as I could, about two yards, but the boat slanted so that I couldn't make very good time; so to keep from getting run over and catched I crawled into a stateroom on the upper side. The man come a-pawing along in the dark, and when Packard got to my stateroom, he says:

"Here—come in here."

And in he come, and Bill after him. But before they got in, I was up in the upper berth, cornered, and sorry I come. Then they stood there, with their hands on the ledge of the berth, and talked. I couldn't see them, but I could tell where they was, by the whisky they'd been having. I was glad I didn't drink whisky; but it wouldn't made much difference, anyway, because most of the time they couldn't a treed me because I didn't breathe. I was too scared. And besides, a body *couldn't* breathe, and hear such talk. They talked low and earnest. Bill wanted to kill Turner. He says:

"He's said he'll tell, and he will. If we was to give both our shares to him *now*, it wouldn't make no difference after the row, and the way we've served him. Shore's you're born, he'll turn State's evidence; now you hear *me*. I'm for putting him out of his troubles."

"So'm I," says Packard, very quiet.

"Blame it, I'd sorter begun to think you wasn't. Well, then, that's all right. Les' go and do it."

"Hold on a minute; I hain't had my say yit. You listen to me. Shooting's good, but there's quieter ways if the thing's *got* to be done. But what *I* say, is this; it ain't good sense to go court'n around after a halter, if you can git at what you're up to in some way that's jist as good and at the same time don't bring you into no resks. Ain't that so?"

"You bet it is. But how you goin' to manage it this time?"

"Well, my idea is this: we'll rustle around and gether up whatever pickins we've overlooked in the staterooms, and shove for shore and hide the truck. Then we'll wait. Now I say it ain't agoin' to be more 'n two hours befo' this wrack breaks up and washes off down the river. See? He'll be drownded, and won't have nobody to blame for it but his own self. I reckon that's a considerble sight better'n killin' of him. I'm unfavorable to killin' a man as long as you can git around it; it ain't good sense, it ain't good morals. Ain't I right?"

"Yes—I reck'n you are. But s'pose she *don't* break up and wash off?"

"Well, we can wait the two hours anyway, and see, can't we?"

"All right, then; come along."

So they started, and I lit out, all in a cold sweat, and scrambled forward. It was dark as pitch there; but I said in a kind of a coarse whisper, "Jim!" and he answered up, right at my elbow, with a sort of a moan, and I says:

"Quick, Jim, it ain't no time for fooling around and moaning; there's a gang of murderers in yonder, and if we don't hunt up their boat and set her drifting down the river so these fellows can't get away from the wreck, there's one of 'em going to be in a bad fix. But if we find their boat we can put *all* of 'em in a bad fix—for the Sheriff 'll get 'em. Quick—hurry! I'll hunt the labboard side, you hunt the stabboard. You start at the raft, and—"

"Oh, my lordy, lordy! *Raf?* Dey ain' no raf' no mo', she done broke loose en gone!—'en here we is!"

CHAPTER XIII

Well, I catched my breath and most fainted. Shut up on a wreck with such a gang as that! But it warn't no time to be sentimentering. We'd *got* to find that boat, now—had to have it for ourselves. So we went a-quaking and shaking down the stabboard side, and slow work it was, too—seemed a week before we got to the stern. No sign of a boat. Jim said he didn't believe he could go any further—so scared he hadn't hardly any strength left, he said. But I said come on, if we get left on this wreck, we are in a fix, sure. So on we prowled, again. We struck for the stern of the texas, and found it, and then scrabbled along forwards on the skylight, hanging on from shutter to shutter, for the edge of the skylight was in the water. When we got pretty close to the cross-hall door, there was the skiff, sure enough! I could just barely see her. I felt ever so thankful. In another second I would a been aboard of her; but just then the door opened. One of the men stuck his head out, only about a couple of foot from me, and I thought I was gone; but he jerked it in again, and says:

"Heave that blame lantern out o'sight, Bill!"

He flung a bag of something into the boat, and then got in himself, and set down. It was Packard. Then Bill *he* come out and got in. Packard says, in a low voice:

"All ready—shove off!"

I couldn't hardly hang onto the shutters, I was so weak. But Bill says:

"Hold on—'d you go through him?"

"No. Didn't you?"

"No. So he's got his share o' the cash, yet."

"Well, then, come along—no use to take truck and leave money."

"Say—won't he suspicion what we're up to?"

"Maybe he won't. But we got to have it anyway. Come along."

So they got out and went in.

The door slammed to, because it was on the careened side; and in a half second I was in the boat, and Jim come a tumbling after me. I out with my knife and cut the rope, and away we went!

We didn't touch an oar, and we didn' speak nor whisper, nor hardly even breathe. We went gliding swift along, dead silent, past the tip of the paddle-box, and past the stern; then in a second or two more we was a hundred yards below the wreck, and the darkness soaked her up, every last sign of her, and we was safe, and knowed it.

When we was three or four hundred yards down stream, we see the lantern show like a little spark at the texas door, for a second, and we knowed by that that the rascals had missed their boat, and was beginning to understand that they was in just as much trouble, now, as Jim Turner was.

Then Jim manned the oars, and we took out after our raft. Now was the first time that I begun to worry about the men—I reckon I hadn't had time to before. I begun to think how dreadful it was, even for murderers, to be in such a fix. I says to myself, there ain't no telling but I might come to be a murderer myself, yet, and then how would *I* like it? So says I to Jim:

"The first light we see, we'll land a hundred yards below it or above it, in a place where it's a good hiding-place for you and the skiff, and then I'll go and fix up some kind of a yarn, and get somebody to go for that gang and get them out of their scrape, so they can be hung when their time comes."

But that idea was a failure; for pretty soon it begun to storm again, and this time worse than ever. The rain poured down, and never a light showed; everybody in bed, I reckon. We boomed along down the river, watching for lights and watching for our raft. After a long time the rain let up, but the clouds staid, and the lightning kept whimpering, and by-and-by a flash showed us a black thing ahead, floating, and we made for it.

It was the raft, and mighty glad was we to get aboard of it again. We seen a light, now, away down to the right, on shore. So I said I would go for it. The skiff was half full of plunder which that gang had stole, there on the wreck. We hustled it onto the raft in a pile, and I told Jim to float along down, and show a light when he judged he had gone about two mile, and keep it burning till I come; then I manned my oars and shoved for the light. As I got down towards it, three or four more showed—up on a hillside. It was a village. I closed in above the shore-light, and laid on my oars and floated. As I went by, I see it was a lantern hanging on the jackstaff of a double-hull ferry-boat. I skimmed around for the watchman, a-wondering whereabouts he slept; and by-and-by I found him roosting on the bitts, forward, with his head down between his knees. I give his shoulder two or three little shoves, and begun to cry.

He stirred up, in a kind of a startlish way; when he sees it was only me, he took a good gap and stretch, and then he says:

"Hello, what's up? Don't cry, bub. What's the trouble?"

I says:

"Pap, and mam, and sis, and—"

Then I broke down. He says:

"Oh, dang it, now, *don't* take on so, we all has to have our troubles and this'n 'll come out all right. What's the matter with 'em?"

"They're—they're—are you the watchman of the boat?"

"Yes," he says, kind of pretty-well-satisfied like. "I'm the captain and the owner, and the mate, and the pilot, and watchman, and head deck-hand; and sometimes I'm the freight and passengers. I ain't as rich as old Jim Hornback, and I can't be so blame' generous and good to Tom, Dick and Harry as what he is, and slam around money the way he does; but I've told him a many a time 't I wouldn't trade places with him; for, says I, a sailor's life's the life for me, and I'm derned if *I'd* live two mile out o' town, where there ain't nothing ever goin' on, not for all his spondulicks and as much more on top of it. Says I—"

I broke in and says:

"They're in an awful peck of trouble, and—"

"*Who* is?"

"Why, pap, and mam, and sis, and Miss Hooker; and if you'd take your ferry-boat and go up there—"

"Up where? Where are they?"

"On the wreck."

"What wreck?"

"Why, there ain't but one."

"What, you don't mean the *Walter Scott*?"

"Yes."

"Good land! what are they doin' *there*, for gracious sakes?"

"Well, they didn't go there a-purpose."

"I bet they didn't! Why, great goodness, there ain't no chance for 'em if they don't git off mighty quick! Why, how in the nation did they ever git into such a scrape?"

"Easy enough. Miss Hooker was a-visiting, up there to the town—"

"Yes, Booth's Landing—go on."

"She was a-visiting, there at Booth's Landing, and just in the edge of the evening she started over with her nigger woman in the horse-ferry, to stay all night at her friend's house, Miss What-you-may-call-her, I disremember her name, and they lost their steering-oar, and swung around and went a-floating down, stern-first, about two mile, and saddle-baggsed on the wreck, and the ferry man and the nigger woman and the horses was all lost, but Miss Hooker she made a grab and got aboard the wreck. Well, about an hour after dark, we come along down in our trading-scow, and it was so dark we didn't notice the wreck till we was right on it; and so *we* saddle-baggsed; but all of us was saved but Bill Whipple—and oh, he *was* the best cretur!—I most wish't it had been me, I do."

"My George! It's the beatenest thing I ever struck. And *then* what did you all do?"

"Well, we hollered and took on, but it's so wide there, we couldn't make nobody hear. So pap said somebody got to get ashore and get help somehow. I was the only one that could swim, so I made a dash for it, and Miss Hooker she said if I didn't strike help sooner, come here and hunt up her uncle, and he'd fix the thing. I made the land about a mile below, and been fooling along ever since, trying to get people to do something, but they said, 'What, in such a night and such a current? there ain't no sense in it; go for the steam-ferry.' Now if you'll go, and—"

"By Jackson, I'd *like* to, and blame it I don't know but I will; but who in the dingnation's agoin' to *pay* for it? Do you reckon your pap—"

"Why *that's* all right. Miss Hooker she told me, *particular*, that her uncle Hornback—"

"Great guns! is *he* her uncle? Looky here, you break for that light over yonder-way, and turn out west when you git there, and about a quarter of a mile out you'll come to the tavern; tell 'em to dart you out to Jim Hornback's and he'll foot the bill. And don't you fool around any, because he'll want to know the news. Tell him I'll have his niece all safe before he can get to town. Hump yourself, now; I'm agoing up around the corner here, to roust out my engineer."

I struck for the light, but as soon as he turned the corner I went back and got into my skiff and bailed her out and then pulled up shore in the easy water about six hundred yards, and tucked myself in among some woodboats; for I couldn't rest

float by in ten minutes. It had the big timber of a regular island; it might be five or six mile long and more than a half a mile wide.

I kept quiet, with my ears cocked, about fifteen minutes, I reckon. I was floating along, of course, four or five mile an hour; but you don't ever think of that. No, you *feel* like you are laying dead still on the water; and if a little glimpse of a snag slips by, you don't think to yourself how fast *you're* going, but you catch your breath and think, my! how that snag's tearing along. If you think it ain't dismal and lonesome out in a fog that way, by yourself, in the night, you try it once—you'll see.

Next, for about a half an hour, I whoops now and then; at last I hears the answer a long ways off, and tries to follow it, but I couldn't do it, and directly I judged I'd got into a nest of tow-heads, for I had little dim glimpses of them on both sides of me, sometimes just a narrow channel between; and some that I couldn't see, I knowed was there, because I'd hear the wash of the current against the old dead brush and trash that hung over the banks. Well, I warn't long losing the whoops, down amongst the tow-heads; and I only tried to chase them a little while, anyway, because it was worse than chasing a Jack-o-lantern. You never knowed a sound dodge around so, and swap places so quick and so much.

I had to claw away from the bank pretty lively, four or five times, to keep from knocking the islands out of the river; and so I judged the raft must be butting into the bank every now and then, or else it would get further ahead and clear out of hearing—it was floating a little faster than what I was.

Well, I seemed to be in the open river again, by-and-by, but I couldn't hear no sign of a whoop nowheres. I reckoned Jim had fetched up on a snag, maybe, and it was all up with him. I was good and tired, so I laid down in the canoe and said I wouldn't bother no more. I didn't want to go to sleep, of course; but I was so sleepy I couldn't help it; so I thought I would take just one little cat-nap.

But I reckon it was more than a cat-nap, for when I waked up the stars was shining bright, the fog was all gone, and I was spinning down a big bend stern first. First I didn't know where I was; I thought I was dreaming; and when things begun to come back to me, they seemed to come up dim out of last week.

It was a monstrous big river here, with the tallest and the thickest kind of timber on both banks; just a solid wall, as well as I could see, by the stars. I looked away down stream, and seen a black speck on the water. I took out after it; but when I got to it it warn't nothing but a couple of saw-logs made fast together. Then I see another speck, and chased that; then another, and this time I was right. It was the raft.

When I got to it Jim was setting there with his head down between his knees, asleep, with his right arm hanging over the steering oar. The other oar was smashed off, and the raft was littered up with leaves and branches and dirt. So she'd had a rough time.

I made fast and laid down under Jim's nose on the raft, and begun to gap, and stretch my fists out against Jim, and says:

"Hello, Jim, have I been asleep? Why didn't you stir me up?"

"Goodness gracious, is dat you, Huck? En you ain' dead—you ain' drownded—you's back agin? It's too good for true, honey, it's too good for true. Lemme look at you, chile, lemme feel o' you. No, you ain' dead! you's back agin, 'live en soun', jis de same ole Huck—de same ole Huck, thanks to goodness!"

"What's the matter with you, Jim? You been a drinking?"

"Drinkin'? Has I ben a drinkin'? Has I had a chance to be a drinkin'?"

"Well, then, what makes you talk so wild?"

"How does I talk wild?"

"*How*? why, hain't you been talking about my coming back, and all that stuff, as if I'd been gone away?"

"Huck—Huck Finn, you look me in de eye; look me in de eye. *Hain't* you been gone away?"

"Gone away? Why, what in the nation do you mean? *I* hain't been gone anywheres. Where would I go to?"

"Well, looky here, boss, dey's sumf'n wrong, dey is. Is I *me*, or who *is* I? Is I heah, or whah *is* I? Now dat's what I wants to know."

"Well, I think you're here, plain enough, but I think you're a tangle-headed old fool, Jim."

"I is, is I? Well you answer me dis. Didn't you tote out de line in de canoe, fer to make fas' to de tow-head?"

"No, I didn't. What tow-head? I hain't seen no tow-head."

"You hain't seen no tow-head? Looky here—didn't de line pull loose en de raf' go a hummin' down de river, en leave you en de canoe behine in de fog?"

"What fog?"

"Why *de* fog. De fog dat's ben aroun' all night. En didn't you whoop, en didn't I whoop, tell we got mix' up in de islands en one un us got los' en 'tother one was jis' as good as los', 'kase he didn't know whah he wuz? En didn't I bust up agin a lot er dem islands en have a turrible time en mos' git drownded? Now ain' dat so, boss—ain't it so? You answer me dat."

"Well, this is too many for me, Jim. I hain't seen no fog, nor no islands, nor no troubles, nor nothing. I been setting here talking with you all night till you went to sleep about ten minutes ago, and I reckon I done the same. You couldn't a got drunk in that time, so of course you've been dreaming."

"Dad fetch it, how is I gwyne to dream all dat in ten minutes?"

"Well, hang it all, you did dream it, because there didn't any of it happen."

"But Huck, it's all jis' as plain to me as—"

"It don't make no difference how plain it is, there ain't nothing in it. I know, because I've been here all the time."

Jim didn't say nothing for about five minutes, but set there studying over it. Then he says:

"Well, den, I reck'n I did dream it, Huck; but dog my cats ef it ain't de powerfullest dream I ever see. En I hain't ever had no dream b'fo' dat's tired me like dis one."

"Oh, well, that's all right, because a dream does tire a body like everything, sometimes. But this one was a staving dream—tell me all about it, Jim."

So Jim went to work and told me the whole thing right through, just as it happened, only he painted it up considerable. Then he said he must start in and "'terpret" it, because it was sent for a warning. He said the first tow-head stood for a man that would try to do us some good, but the current was another man that would get us away from him. The whoops was warnings that would come to us every now and then, and if we didn't try hard to make out to understand them they'd just take us into bad luck, 'stead of keeping us out of it. The lot of tow-heads was troubles we was going to get into with quarrelsome people and all kinds of mean folks, but if we minded our business and didn't talk back and aggravate them, we would pull through and get out of the fog and into the big clear river, which was the free States, and wouldn't have no more trouble.

It had clouded up pretty dark just after I got onto the raft, but it was clearing up again, now.

"Oh, well, that's all interpreted well enough, as far as it goes, Jim," I says; "but what does *these* things stand for?"

It was the leaves and rubbish on the raft, and the smashed oar. You could see them first rate, now.

Jim looked at the trash, and then looked at me, and back at the trash again. He had got the dream fixed so strong in his head that he couldn't seem to shake it loose and get the facts back into its place again, right away. But when he did get the thing straightened around, he looked at me steady, without ever smiling, and says:

"What do dey stan' for? I's gwyne to tell you. When I got all wore out wid work, en wid de callin' for you, en went to sleep, my heart wuz mos' broke bekase you wuz los', en I didn' k'yer no mo' what become er me en de raf'. En when I wake up en fine you back agin', all safe en soun', de tears come en I could a got down on my knees en kiss' yo' foot I's so thankful. En all you wuz thinkin 'bout wuz how you could make a fool uv ole Jim wid a lie. Dat truck dah is *trash*; en trash is what people is dat puts dirt on de head er dey fren's en makes 'em ashamed."

Then he got up slow, and walked to the wigwam, and went in there, without saying anything but that. But that was enough. It made me feel so mean I could almost kissed *his* foot to get him to take it back.

It was fifteen minutes before I could work myself up to go and humble myself to a nigger—but I done it, and I warn't ever sorry for it afterwards, neither. I didn't do him no more mean tricks, and I wouldn't done that one if I'd a knowed it would make him feel that way.

CHAPTER XVI

We slept most all day, and started out at night, a little ways behind a monstrous long raft that was as long going by as a procession. She had four long sweeps at each end, so we judged she carried as many as thirty men, likely. She had five big wigwams aboard, wide apart, and an open camp fire in the middle, and a tall flag-pole at each end. There was a power of style about her. It *amounted* to something being a raftsman on such a craft as that.

We went drifting down into a big bend, and the night clouded up and got hot. The river was very wide, and was walled with solid timber on both sides; you couldn't see a break in it hardly ever, or a light. We talked about Cairo, and wondered whether we would know it when we got to it. I said likely we wouldn't, because I had heard say there warn't but about a dozen houses there, and if they didn't happen to have them lit up, how was we going to know we was passing a town? Jim said if the two big rivers joined together there, that would show. But I said maybe we might think we was passing the foot of an island and coming into the same old river again. That disturbed Jim—and me too. So the question was, what to do? I said, paddle ashore the first time a light showed, and tell them pap was behind, coming along with a trading-scow, and was a green hand at the business, and wanted to know how far it was to Cairo. Jim thought it was a good idea, so we took a smoke on it and waited.

There warn't nothing to do, now, but to look out sharp for the town, and not pass it without seeing it. He said he'd be mighty sure to see it, because he'd be a free man the minute he seen it, but if he missed it he'd be in the slave country again and no more show for freedom. Every little while he jumps up and says:

"Dah she is!"

But it warn't. It was Jack-o-lanterns, or lightning-bugs; so he set down again, and went to watching, same as before. Jim said it made him all over trembly and feverish to be so close to freedom. Well, I can tell you it made me all over trembly and feverish, too, to hear him, because I begun to get it through my head that he *was* most free—and who was to blame for it? Why, *me*. I couldn't get that out of my conscience, no how nor no way. It got to troubling me so I couldn't rest; I couldn't stay still in one place. It hadn't ever come home to me before, what this thing was that I was doing. But now it did; and it staid with me, and scorched me more and more. I tried to make out to myself that *I* warn't to blame, because *I* didn't run Jim off from his rightful owner; but it warn't no use, conscience up and says, every time, "But you knowed he was running for his freedom, and you could a paddled ashore and told somebody." That was so—I couldn't get around that, noway. That was where it pinched. Conscience says to me, "What had poor Miss Watson done to you, that you could see her nigger go off right under your eyes and never say one single word? What did that poor old woman do to you, that you could treat her so mean? Why, she tried to learn you your book, she tried to learn you your manners, she tried to be good to you every way she knowed how. *That's* what she done."

I got to feeling so mean and so miserable I most wished I was dead. I fidgeted up and down the raft, abusing myself to myself, and Jim was fidgeting up and down past me. We neither of us could keep still. Every time he danced around and says, "Dah's Cairo!" it went through me like a shot, and I thought if it *was* Cairo I reckoned I would die of miserableness.

Jim talked out loud all the time while I was talking to myself. He was saying how the first thing he would do when he got to a free State he would go to saving up money and never spend a single cent, and when he got enough he would buy his wife, which was owned on a farm close to where Miss Watson lived; and then they would both work to buy the two children, and if their master wouldn't sell them, they'd get an Ab'litionist to go and steal them.

It most froze me to hear such talk. He wouldn't ever dared to talk such talk in his life before. Just see what a difference it made in him the minute he judged he was about free. It was according to the old saying, "give a nigger an inch and he'll take an ell." Thinks I, this is what comes of my not thinking. Here was this nigger which I had as good as helped to run away, coming right out flat-footed and saying he would steal his children—children that belonged to a man I didn't even know; a man that hadn't ever done me no harm.

I was sorry to hear Jim say that, it was such a lowering of him. My conscience got to stirring me up hotter than ever, until at last I says to it, "Let up on me—it ain't too late, yet—I'll paddle ashore at the first light, and tell." I felt easy, and happy, and light as a feather, right off. All my troubles was gone. I went to looking out sharp for a light, and sort of singing to myself. By-and-by one showed. Jim sings out:

"We's safe, Huck, we's safe! Jump up and crack yo' heels, dat's de good ole Cairo at las', I jis knows it!"

I says:

"I'll take the canoe and go see, Jim. It mightn't be, you know."

He jumped and got the canoe ready, and put his old coat in the bottom for me to set on, and give me the paddle; and as I shoved off, he says:

"Pooty soon I'll be a-shout'n for joy, en I'll say, it's all on accounts o' Huck; I's a free man, en I couldn't ever ben free ef it hadn' ben for Huck; Huck done it. Jim won't ever forgit you, Huck; you's de bes' fren' Jim's ever had; en you's de *only* fren' ole Jim's got now."

I was paddling off, all in a sweat to tell on him; but when he says this, it seemed to kind of take the tuck all out of me. I went along slow then, and I warn't right down certain whether I was glad I started or whether I warn't. When I was fifty yards off, Jim says:

"Dah you goes, de old true Huck; de on'y white genlman dat ever kep' his promise to ole Jim."

Well, I just felt sick. But I says, I *got* to do it—I can't get *out* of it. Right then, along comes a skiff with two men in it, with guns, and they stopped and I stopped. One of them says:

"What's that, yonder?"

"A piece of a raft," I says.

"Do you belong on it?"

"Yes, sir."

"Any men on it?"

"Only one, sir."

"Well, there's five niggers run off to-night, up yonder above the head of the bend. Is your man white or black?"

I didn't answer up prompt. I tried to, but the words wouldn't come. I tried, for a second or two, to brace up and out with it, but I warn't man enough—hadn't the spunk of a rabbit. I see I was weakening; so I just give up trying, and up and says—

"He's white."

"I reckon we'll go and see for ourselves."

"I wish you would," says I, "because it's pap that's there, and maybe you'd help me tow the raft ashore where the light is. He's sick—and so is mam and Mary Ann."

"Oh, the devil! we're in a hurry, boy. But I s'pose we've got to. Come—buckle to your paddle, and let's get along."

I buckled to my paddle and they laid to their oars. When we had made a stroke or two, I says:

"Pap'll be mighty much obleeged to you, I can tell you. Everybody goes away when I want them to help me tow the raft ashore, and I can't do it by myself."

"Well, that's infernal mean. Odd, too. Say, boy, what's the matter with your father?"

"It's the—a—the—well, it ain't anything much."

They stopped pulling. It warn't but a mighty little ways to the raft, now. One says:

"Boy, that's a lie. What *is* the matter with your pap? Answer up square, now, and it'll be the better for you."

"I will, sir, I will, honest—but don't leave us, please. It's the—the—gentlemen, if you'll only pull ahead, and let me heave you the head-line, you won't have to come a-near the raft—please do."

"Set her back, John, set her back!" says one. They backed water. "Keep away, boy—keep to looard. Confound it, I just expect the wind has blowed it to us. Your pap's got the small-pox, and you know it precious well. Why didn't you come out and say so? Do you want to spread it all over?"

"Well," says I, a-blubbering, "I've told everybody before, and then they just went away and left us."

"Poor devil, there's something in that. We are right down sorry for you, but we—well, hang it, we don't want the small-pox, you see. Look here, I'll tell you what to do. Don't you try to land by yourself, or you'll smash everything to pieces. You float along down about twenty miles and you'll come to a town on the left-hand side of the river. It will be long after sun-up, then, and when you ask for help, you tell them your folks are all down with chills and fever. Don't be a fool again, and let people guess what is the matter. Now we're trying to do you a kindness; so you just put twenty miles between us, that's a good boy. It wouldn't do any good to land yonder where the light is—it's only a wood-yard. Say—I reckon your father's poor, and I'm bound to say he's in pretty hard luck. Here—I'll put a twenty dollar gold piece on this board, and you get it when it floats by. I feel mighty mean to leave you, but my kingdom! it won't do to fool with small-pox, don't you see?"

"Hold on, Parker," says the other man, "here's a twenty to put on the board for me. Good-bye, boy, you do as Mr. Parker told you, and you'll be all right."

"That's so, my boy—good-bye, good-bye. If you see any runaway niggers, you get help and nab them, and you can make some money by it."

"Good-bye, sir," says I, "I won't let no runaway niggers get by me if I can help it."

They went off, and I got aboard the raft, feeling bad and low, because I knowed very well I had done wrong, and I see it warn't no use for me to try to learn to do right; a body that don't get *started* right when he's little, ain't got no show—when the pinch comes there ain't nothing to back him up and keep him to his work, and so he gets beat. Then I thought a minute, and says to myself, hold on,—s'pose you'd a done right and give Jim up; would you felt better than what you do now? No, says I, I'd feel bad—I'd feel just the same way I do now. Well, then, says I, what's the use you learning to do right, when it's troublesome to do right and ain't no trouble to do wrong, and the wages is just the same? I was stuck. I couldn't answer that. So I reckoned I wouldn't bother no more about it, but after this always do whichever come handiest at the time.

I went into the wigwam; Jim warn't there. I looked all around; he warn't anywhere. I says:

"Jim!"

"Here I is, Huck. Is dey out o' sight yit? Don't talk loud."

He was in the river, under the stern oar, with just his nose out. I told him they was out of sight, so he come aboard. He says:

"I was a-listenin' to all de talk, en I slips into de river en was gwyne to shove for sho' if dey come aboard. Den I was gwyne to swim to de raf' agin when dey was gone. But lawsy, how you did fool 'em, Huck! Dat *wuz* de smartes' dodge! I tell you, chile, I 'speck it save ole Jim—ole Jim ain't gwyne to forgit you for dat, honey."

Then we talked about the money. It was a pretty good raise, twenty dollars apiece. Jim said we could take deck passage on a steamboat now, and the money would last us as far as we wanted to go in the free States. He said twenty mile more warn't far for the raft to go, but he wished we was already there.

Towards daybreak we tied up, and Jim was mighty particular about hiding the raft good. Then he worked all day fixing things in bundles, and getting all ready to quit rafting.

That night about ten we hove in sight of the lights of a town away down in a left-hand bend.

I went off in the canoe, to ask about it. Pretty soon I found a man out in the river with a skiff, setting a trot-line. I ranged up and says:

"Mister, is that town Cairo?"

"Cairo? no. You must be a blame' fool."

"What town is it, mister?"

"If you want to know, go and find out. If you stay here botherin' around me for about a half a minute longer, you'll get something you won't want."

I paddled to the raft. Jim was awful disappointed, but I said never mind, Cairo would be the next place, I reckoned.

We passed another town before daylight, and I was going out again; but it was high ground, so I didn't go. No high ground about Cairo, Jim said. I had forgot it. We laid up for the day, on a tow-head tolerable close to the left-hand bank. I begun to suspicion something. So did Jim. I says:

"Maybe we went by Cairo in the fog that night."

He says:

"Doan' less' talk about it, Huck. Po' niggers can't have no luck. I awluz 'spected dat rattle-snake skin warn't done wid its work."

"I wish I'd never seen that snake-skin, Jim—I do wish I'd never laid eyes on it."

"It ain't yo' fault, Huck; you didn' know. Don't you blame yo'self 'bout it."

When it was daylight, here was the clear Ohio water in shore, sure enough, and outside was the old regular Muddy! So it was all up with Cairo.

We talked it all over. It wouldn't do to take to the shore; we couldn't take the raft up the stream, of course. There warn't no way but to wait for dark, and start back in the canoe and take the chances. So we slept all day amongst the cotton-wood thicket, so as to be fresh for the work, and when we went back to the raft about dark the canoe was gone!

We didn't say a word for a good while. There warn't anything to say. We both knowed well enough it was some more work of the rattle-snake skin; so what was the use to talk about it? It would only look like we was finding fault, and that would be bound to fetch more bad luck—and keep on fetching it, too, till we knowed enough to keep still.

By-and-by we talked about what we better do, and found there warn't no way but just to go along down with the raft till we got a chance to buy a canoe to go back in. We warn't going to borrow it when there warn't anybody around, the way pap would do, for that might set people after us.

So we shoved out, after dark, on the raft.

Anybody that don't believe yet, that it's foolishness to handle a snake-skin, after all that that snake-skin done for us, will believe it now, if they read on and see what more it done for us.

The place to buy canoes is off of rafts laying up at shore. But we didn't see no rafts laying up; so we went along during three hours and more. Well, the night got gray, and ruther thick, which is the next meanest thing to fog. You can't tell the shape of the river, and you can't see no distance. It got to be very late and still, and then along comes a steamboat up the river. We lit the lantern, and judged she would see it. Up-stream boats didn't generly come close to us; they go out and follow the bars and hunt for easy water under the reefs; but nights like this they bull right up the channel against the whole river.

We could hear her pounding along, but we didn't see her good till she was close. She aimed right for us. Often they do that and try to see how close they can come without touching; sometimes the wheel bites off a sweep, and then the pilot sticks his head out and laughs, and thinks he's mighty smart. Well, here she comes, and we said she was going to try to shave us; but she didn't seem to be sheering off a bit. She was a big one, and she was coming in a hurry, too, looking like a black cloud with rows of glow-worms around it; but all of a sudden she bulged out, big and scary, with a long row of wide-open furnace doors shining like red-hot teeth, and her monstrous bows and guards hanging right over us. There was a yell at us, and a jingling of bells to stop the engines, a pow-wow of cussing, and whistling of steam—and as Jim went overboard on one side and I on the other, she come smashing straight through the raft.

I dived—and I aimed to find the bottom, too, for a thirty-foot wheel had got to go over me, and I wanted it to have plenty of room. I could always stay under water a minute; this time I reckon I staid under water a minute and a half. Then I bounced for the top in a hurry, for I was nearly busting. I popped out to my armpits and blowed the water out of my nose, and puffed a bit. Of course there was a booming current; and of course that boat started her engines again ten seconds after she stopped them, for they never cared much for raftsmen; so now she was churning along up the river, out of sight in the thick weather, though I could hear her.

I sung out for Jim about a dozen times, but I didn't get any answer; so I grabbed a plank that touched me while I was "treading water," and struck out for shore, shoving it ahead of me. But I made out to see that the drift of the current was towards the left-hand shore, which meant that I was in a crossing; so I changed off and went that way.

It was one of these long, slanting, two-mile crossings; so I was a good long time in getting over. I made a safe landing, and clum up the bank. I couldn't see but a little ways, but I went poking along over rough ground for a quarter of a mile or more, and then I run across a big old-fashioned double log house, before I noticed it. I was going to rush by and get away, but a lot of dogs jumped out and went to howling and barking at me, and I knowed better than to move another peg.

CHAPTER XVII

In about half a minute somebody spoke out of a window, without putting his head out, and says:

"Be done, boys! Who's there?"

I says:

"It's me."

"Who's me?"

"George Jackson, sir."

"What do you want?"

"I don't want nothing, sir. I only want to go along by, but the dogs won't let me."

"What are you prowling around here this time of night, for—hey?"

"I warn't prowling around, sir; I fell overboard off of the steamboat."

"Oh, you did, did you? Strike a light there, somebody. What did you say your name was?"

"George Jackson, sir. I'm only a boy."

"Look here; if you're telling the truth, you needn't be afraid —nobody 'll hurt you. But don't try to budge; stand right where you are. Rouse out Bob and Tom, some of you, and fetch the guns. George Jackson, is there anybody with you?"

"No, sir, nobody."

I heard the people stirring around in the house, now, and see a light. The man sung out:

"Snatch that light away, Betsy, you old fool—ain't you got any sense? Put it on the floor behind the front door. Bob, if you and Tom are ready, take your places."

"All ready."

"Now, George Jackson, do you know the Shepherdsons?"

"No, sir—I never heard of them."

"Well, that may be so, and it mayn't. Now, all ready. Step forward, George Jackson. And mind, don't you hurry—come mighty slow. If there's anybody with you, let him keep back—if he shows himself he'll be shot. Come along, now. Come slow; push the door open, yourself—just enough to squeeze in, d' you hear?"

I didn't hurry, I couldn't if I'd a wanted to. I took one slow step at a time, and there warn't a sound, only I thought I could hear my heart. The dogs were as still as the humans, but they followed a little behind me. When I got to the three log doorsteps, I heard them unlocking and unbarring and unbolting. I put my hand on the door and pushed it a little and a little more, till somebody said, "There, that's enough—put your head in." I done it, but I judged they would take it off.

The candle was on the floor, and there they all was, looking at me, and me at them, for about a quarter of a minute. Three big men with guns pointed at me, which made me wince, I tell you; the oldest, gray and about sixty, the other two thirty or more—all of them fine and handsome—and the sweetest old gray-headed lady, and back of her two young women which I couldn't see right well. The old gentleman says:

"There—I reckon it's all right. Come in."

As soon as I was in, the old gentleman he locked the door and barred it and bolted it, and told the young men to come in with their guns, and they all went in a big parlor that had a new rag carpet on the floor, and got together in a corner that was out of range of the front windows—there warn't none on the side. They held the candle, and took a good look at me, and all said, "Why *he* ain't a Shepherdson—no, there ain't any Shepherdson about him." Then the old man said he hoped I wouldn't mind being searched for arms, because he didn't mean no harm by it—it was only to make sure. So he didn't pry into my pockets, but only felt outside with his hands, and said it was all right. He told me to make myself easy and at home, and tell all about myself; but the old lady says:

"Why bless you, Saul, the poor thing's as wet as he can be; and don't you reckon it may be he's hungry?"

"True for you, Rachel—I forgot."

So the old lady says:

"Betsy" (this was a nigger woman), "you fly around and get him something to eat, as quick as you can, poor thing; and one of you girls go and wake up Buck and tell him—Oh, here he is himself. Buck, take this little stranger and get the wet clothes off from him and dress him up in some of yours that's dry."

Buck looked about as old as me—thirteen or fourteen or along there, though he was a little bigger than me. He hadn't on anything but a shirt, and he was very frowsy-headed. He come in gaping and digging one fist into his eyes, and he was dragging a gun along with the other one. He says:

"Ain't they no Shepherdsons around?"

They said, no, 'twas a false alarm.

"Well," he says, "if they'd a been some, I reckon I'd a got one."

They all laughed, and Bob says:

"Why, Buck, they might have scalped us all, you've been so slow in coming."

"Well, nobody come after me, and it ain't right. I'm always kep' down; I don't get no show."

"Never mind, Buck, my boy," says the old man, "you'll have show enough, all in good time, don't you fret about that. Go 'long with you now, and do as your mother told you."

When we got up stairs to his room, he got me a coarse shirt and a roundabout and pants of his, and I put them on. While I was at it he asked me what my name was, but before I could tell him, he started to telling me about a blue jay and a young rabbit he had catched in the woods day before yesterday, and he asked me where Moses was when the candle went out. I said I didn't know; I hadn't heard about it before, no way.

"Well, guess," he says.

"How'm I going to guess," says I, "when I never heard tell about it before?"

"But you can guess, can't you? It's just as easy."

"*Which* candle?" I says.

"Why, any candle," he says.

"I don't know where he was," says I; "where was he?"

"Why he was in the *dark*! That's where he was!"

"Well, if you knowed where he was, what did you ask me for?"

"Why, blame it, it's a riddle, don't you see? Say, how long are you going to stay here? You got to stay always. We can just have booming times—they don't have no school now. Do you own a dog? I've got a dog—and he'll go in the river and bring out chips that you throw in. Do you like to comb up, Sundays, and all that kind of foolishness? You bet I don't, but ma she makes me. Confound these ole britches, I reckon I'd better put 'em on, but I'd ruther not, it's so warm. Are you all ready? All right—come along, old hoss."

Cold corn-pone, cold corn-beef, butter and butter-milk—that is what they had for me down there, and there ain't nothing better that ever I've come across yet. Buck and his ma and all of them smoked cob pipes, except the nigger woman, which was gone, and the two young women. They all smoked and talked, and I eat and talked. The young women had quilts around them, and their hair down their backs. They all asked me questions, and I told them how pap and me and all the family was living on a little farm down at the bottom of Arkansaw, and my sister Mary Ann run off and got married and never was heard of no more, and Bill went to hunt them and he warn't heard of no more, and Tom and Mort died, and then there warn't nobody but just me and pap left, and he was just trimmed down to nothing, on account of his troubles; so when he died I took what there was left, because the farm didn't belong to us, and started up the river, deck passage, and fell overboard; and that was how I come to be here. So they said I could have a home there as long as I wanted it. Then it was most daylight, and everybody went to bed, and I went to bed with Buck, and when I waked up in the morning, drat it all, I had forgot what my name was. So I laid there about an hour trying to think, and when Buck waked up, I says:

"Can you spell, Buck?"

"Yes," he says.

"I bet you can't spell my name," says I.

"I bet you what you dare I can," says he.

"All right," says I, "go ahead."

"G-o-r-g-e J-a-x-o-n—there now," he says.

"Well," says I, "you done it, but I didn't think you could. It ain't no slouch of a name to spell—right off without studying."

I set it down, private, because somebody might want *me* to spell it, next, and so I wanted to be handy with it and rattle it off like I was used to it.

It was a mighty nice family, and a mighty nice house, too. I hadn't seen no house out in the country before that was so nice and had so much style. It didn't have an iron latch on the front door, nor a wooden one with a buckskin string, but a brass knob to turn, the same as houses in a town. There warn't no bed in the parlor, not a sign of a bed; but heaps of parlors in towns has beds in them. There was a big fireplace that was bricked on the bottom, and the bricks was kept clean and red by pouring water on them and scrubbing them with another brick; sometimes they washed them over with red water-paint that they call Spanish-brown, same as they do in town. They had big brass dog-irons that could hold up a saw-log. There was a clock on the middle of the mantel-piece, with a picture of a town painted on the bottom half of the glass front, and a round place in the middle of it for the sun, and you could see the pendulum swing behind it. It was beautiful to hear that clock tick; and sometimes when one of these peddlers had been along and scoured her up and got her in good shape, she would start in and strike a hundred and fifty before she got tuckered out. They wouldn't took any money for her.

Well, there was a big outlandish parrot on each side of the clock, made out of something like chalk, and painted up gaudy. By one of the parrots was a cat made of crockery, and a crockery dog by the other; and when you pressed down on them they squeaked, but didn't open their mouths nor look different nor interested. They squeaked through underneath. There was a couple of big wild-turkey-wing fans spread out behind those things. On a table in the middle of the room was a kind of a lovely crockery basket that had apples and oranges and peaches and grapes piled up in it which was much redder and yellower and prettier than real ones is, but they warn't real because you could see where pieces had got chipped off and showed the white chalk or whatever it was, underneath.

This table had a cover made out of beautiful oil-cloth, with a red and blue spread-eagle painted on it, and a painted border all around. It come all the way from Philadelphia, they said. There was some books too, piled up perfectly exact, on each corner of the table. One was a big family Bible, full of pictures. One was "Pilgrim's Progress," about a man that left his family it didn't say why. I read considerable in it now and then. The statements was interesting, but tough. Another was "Friendship's Offering," full of beautiful stuff and poetry; but I didn't read the poetry. Another was Henry Clay's Speeches, and another was Dr. Gunn's Family Medicine, which told you all about what to do if a body was sick or dead. There was a Hymn Book, and a lot of other books. And there was nice split-bottom chairs, and perfectly sound, too—not bagged down in the middle and busted, like an old basket.

They had pictures hung on the walls—mainly Washingtons and Lafayettes, and battles, and Highland Marys, and one called "Signing the Declaration." There was some that they called crayons, which one of the daughters which was dead made her own self when she was only fifteen years old. They was different from any pictures I ever see before; blacker, mostly, than is common. One was a woman in a slim black dress, belted small under the arm-pits, with bulges like a cabbage in the middle of the sleeves, and a large black scoop-shovel bonnet with a black veil, and white slim ankles crossed about with black tape, and very wee black slippers, like a chisel, and she was leaning pensive on a tombstone on her right elbow, under a weeping willow, and her other hand hanging down her side holding a white handkerchief and a reticule, and underneath the picture it said "Shall I Never See Thee More Alas." Another one was a young lady with her hair all combed up straight to the top of her head, and knotted there in front of a comb like a chair-back, and she was crying into a handkerchief and had a dead bird laying on its back in her other hand with its heels up, and underneath the picture it said "I Shall Never Hear Thy Sweet Chirrup More Alas." There was one where a young lady was at a window looking up at the moon, and tears running down her cheeks; and she had an open letter in one hand with black sealing-wax showing on one edge of it, and she was mashing a locket with a chain to it against her mouth, and underneath the picture it said "And Art Thou Gone Yes Thou Art Gone Alas." These was all nice pictures, I reckon, but I didn't somehow seem to take to them, because if ever I was down a little, they always give me the fan-tods. Everybody was sorry she died, because she had laid out a lot more of these pictures to do, and a body could see by what she had done what they had lost. But I reckoned, that with her disposition, she was having a better time in the graveyard. She was at work on what they said was her greatest picture when she took sick, and every day and every night it was her prayer to be allowed to live till she got it done, but she never got the chance. It was a picture of a young woman in a long white gown, standing on the rail of a bridge all ready to jump off, with her hair all down her back, and looking up to the moon, with the tears running down her face, and she had two arms folded across her breast, and two arms stretched out in front, and two more reaching up towards the moon—and the idea was, to see which pair would look best and then scratch out all the other arms; but, as I was saying, she died before she got her mind made up, and now they kept this picture over the head of the bed in her room, and every time her birthday come they hung flowers on it. Other times it was hid with a little curtain. The young woman in the picture had a kind of a nice sweet face, but there was so many arms it made her look too spidery, seemed to me.

This young girl kept a scrap-book when she was alive, and used to paste obituaries and accidents and cases of patient suffering in it out of the *Presbyterian Observer*, and write poetry after them out of her own head. It was very good poetry. This is what she wrote about a boy by the name of Stephen Dowling Bots that fell down a well and was drownded:

ODE TO STEPHEN DOWLING BOTS, DEC'D.

And did young Stephen sicken,
And did young Stephen die?
And did the sad hearts thicken,
And did the mourners cry?

No; such was not the fate of
    Young Stephen Dowling Bots;
Though sad hearts round him thickened,
    'Twas not from sickness' shots.

No whooping-cough did rack his frame,
    Nor measles drear, with spots;
Not these impaired the sacred name
    Of Stephen Dowling Bots.

Despised love struck not with woe
    That head of curly knots,
Nor stomach troubles laid him low,
    Young Stephen Dowling Bots.

O no. Then list with tearful eye,
    Whilst I his fate do tell.
His soul did from this cold world fly,
    By falling down a well.

They got him out and emptied him;
    Alas it was too late;
His spirit was gone for to sport aloft
    In the realms of the good and great.

If Emmeline Grangerford could make poetry like that before she was fourteen, there ain't no telling what she could a done by-and-by. Buck said she could rattle off poetry like nothing. She didn't ever have to stop to think. He said she would slap down a line, and if she couldn't find anything to rhyme with it she would just scratch it out and slap down another one, and go ahead. She warn't particular, she could write about anything you choose to give her to write about, just so it was sadful. Every time a man died, or a woman died, or a child died, she would be on hand with her "tribute" before he was cold. She called them tributes. The neighbors said it was the doctor first, then Emmeline, then the undertaker—the undertaker never got in ahead of Emmeline but once, and then she hung fire on a rhyme for the dead person's name, which was Whistler. She warn't ever the same, after that; she never complained, but she kind of pined away and did not live long. Poor thing, many's the time I made myself go up to the little room that used to be hers and get out her poor old scrapbook and read in it when her pictures had been aggravating me and I had soured on her a little. I liked all that family, dead ones and all, and warn't going to let anything come between us. Poor Emmeline made poetry about all the dead people when she was alive, and it didn't seem right that there warn't nobody to make some about her, now she was gone; so I tried to sweat out a verse or two myself, but I couldn't seem to make it go, somehow. They kept Emmeline's room trim and nice and all the things fixed in it just the way she liked to have them when she was alive, and nobody ever slept there. The old lady took care of the room herself, though there was plenty of niggers, and she sewed there a good deal and read her Bible there, mostly.

Well, as I was saying about the parlor, there was beautiful curtains on the windows: white, with pictures painted on them, of castles with vines all down the walls, and cattle coming down to drink. There was a little old piano, too, that had tin pans in it, I reckon, and nothing was ever so lovely as to hear the young ladies sing, "The Last Link is Broken" and play "The Battle of Prague" on it. The walls of all the rooms was plastered, and most had carpets on the floors, and the whole house was whitewashed on the outside.

It was a double house, and the big open place betwixt them was roofed and floored, and sometimes the table was set there in the middle of the day, and it was a cool, comfortable place. Nothing couldn't be better. And warn't the cooking good, and just bushels of it too!

CHAPTER XVIII

Col. Grangerford was a gentleman, you see. He was a gentleman all over; and so was his family. He was well born, as the saying is, and that's worth as much in a man as it is in a horse, so the Widow Douglas said, and nobody ever denied that she was of the first aristocracy in our town; and pap he always said it, too, though he warn't no more quality than a mud-cat, himself. Col. Grangerford was very tall and very slim, and had a darkish-paly complexion, not a sign of red in it anywheres; he was clean-shaved every morning, all over his thin face, and he had the thinnest kind of lips, and the thinnest kind of nostrils, and a high nose, and heavy eyebrows, and the blackest kind of eyes, sunk so deep back that they seemed like they was looking out of caverns at you, as you may say. His forehead was high, and his hair was black and straight, and hung to his shoulders. His hands was long and thin, and every day of his life he put on a clean shirt and a full suit from head to foot made out of linen so white it hurt your eyes to look at it; and on Sundays he wore a blue tail-coat with brass buttons on it. He carried a mahogany cane with a silver head to it. There warn't no frivolishness about him, not a bit, and he warn't ever loud. He was as kind as he could be—you could feel that, you know, and so you had confidence. Sometimes he smiled, and it was good to see; but when he straightened himself up like a liberty-pole, and the lightning begun to flicker out from under his eyebrows you wanted to climb a tree first, and find out what the matter was afterwards. He didn't ever have to tell anybody to mind their manners—everybody was always good mannered where he was. Everybody loved to have him around, too; he was sunshine most always—I mean he made it seem like good weather. When he turned into a cloud-bank it was awful dark for a half a minute and that was enough; there wouldn't nothing go wrong again for a week.

When him and the old lady come down in the morning, all the family got up out of their chairs and give them good-day, and didn't set down again till they had set down. Then Tom and Bob went to the sideboard where the decanters was, and mixed a glass of bitters and handed it to him, and he held it in his hand and waited till Tom's and Bob's was mixed, and then they bowed and said "Our duty to you, sir, and madam"; and *they* bowed the least bit in the world and said thank you, and so they drank, all three, and Bob and Tom poured a spoonful of water on the sugar and the mite of whisky or apple brandy in the bottom of their tumblers, and give it to me and Buck, and we drank to the old people too.

Bob was the oldest, and Tom next. Tall, beautiful men with very broad shoulders and brown faces, and long black hair and black eyes. They dressed in white linen from head to foot, like the old gentleman, and wore broad Panama hats.

Then there was Miss Charlotte, she was twenty-five, and tall and proud and grand, but as good as she could be, when she warn't stirred up; but when she was, she had a look that would make you wilt in your tracks, like her father. She was beautiful.

So was her sister, Miss Sophia, but it was a different kind. She was gentle and sweet, like a dove, and she was only twenty.

Each person had their own nigger to wait on them—Buck, too. My nigger had a monstrous easy time, because I warn't used to having anybody do anything for me, but Buck's was on the jump most of the time.

This was all there was of the family, now; but there used to be more—three sons; they got killed; and Emmeline that died.

The old gentleman owned a lot of farms, and over a hundred niggers. Sometimes a stack of people would come there, horseback, from ten or fifteen mile around, and stay five or six days, and have such junketings round about and on the river, and dances and picnics in the woods, day-times, and balls at the house, nights. These people was mostly kin-folks of the family. The men brought their guns with them. It was a handsome lot of quality, I tell you.

There was another clan of aristocracy around there—five or six families—mostly of the name of Shepherdson. They was as high-toned, and well born, and rich and grand, as the tribe of Grangerfords. The Shepherdsons and the Grangerfords used the same steamboat landing, which was about two mile above our house; so sometimes when I went up there with a lot of our folks I used to see a lot of the Shepherdsons there, on their fine horses.

One day Buck and me was away out in the woods, hunting, and heard a horse coming. We was crossing the road. Buck says:

"Quick! Jump for the woods!"

We done it, and then peeped down the woods through the leaves. Pretty soon a splendid young man come galloping down the road, setting his horse easy and looking like a soldier. He had his gun across his pommel. I had seen him before. It was young Harney Shepherdson. I heard Buck's gun go off at my ear, and Harney's hat tumbled off from his head. He grabbed his gun and rode straight to the place where we was hid. But we didn't wait. We started through the woods on a run. The woods warn't thick, so I looked over my shoulder, to dodge the bullet, and twice I seen Harney cover Buck with his gun; and then he rode away the way he come—to get his hat, I reckon, but I couldn't see. We never stopped running till we got home. The old gentleman's eyes blazed a minute—'twas pleasure, mainly, I judged—then his face sort of smoothed down, and he says, kind of gentle:

"I don't like that shooting from behind a bush. Why didn't you step into the road, my boy?"

"The Shepherdsons don't, father. They always take advantage."

Miss Charlotte she held her head up like a queen while Buck was telling his tale, and her nostrils spread and her eyes snapped. The two young men looked dark, but never said nothing. Miss Sophia she turned pale, but the color come back when she found the man warn't hurt.

Soon as I could get Buck down by the corn-cribs under the trees by ourselves, I says:

"Did you want to kill him, Buck?"

"Well, I bet I did."

"What did he do to you?"

"Him? He never done nothing to me."

"Well, then, what did you want to kill him for?"

"Why nothing—only it's on account of the feud."

"What's a feud?"

"Why, where was you raised? Don't you know what a feud is?"

"Never heard of it before—tell me about it."

"Well," says Buck, "a feud is this way. A man has a quarrel with another man, and kills him; then that other man's brother kills *him*; then the other brothers, on both sides, goes for one another; then the *cousins* chip in—and by-and-by everybody's killed off, and there ain't no more feud. But it's kind of slow, and takes a long time."

"Has this one been going on long, Buck?"

"Well, I should *reckon!* it started thirty year ago, or som'ers along there. There was trouble 'bout something and then a lawsuit to settle it; and the suit went agin one of the men, and so he up and shot the man that won the suit—which he would naturally do, of course. Anybody would."

"What was the trouble about, Buck?—land?"

"I reckon maybe—I don't know."

"Well, who done the shooting?—was it a Grangerford or a Shepherdson?"

"Laws, how do *I* know? it was so long ago."

"Don't anybody know?"

"Oh, yes, pa knows, I reckon, and some of the other old folks; but they don't know, now, what the row was about in the first place."

"Has there been many killed, Buck?"

"Yes—right smart chance of funerals. But they don't always kill. Pa's got a few buck-shot in him; but he don't mind it 'cuz he don't weigh much anyway. Bob's been carved up some with a bowie, and Tom's been hurt once or twice."

"Has anybody been killed this year, Buck?"

"Yes, we got one and they got one. 'Bout three months ago my cousin Bud, fourteen year old, was riding through the woods on t'other side of the river, and didn't have no weapon with him, which was blame' foolishness, and in a lonesome place he hears a horse a-coming behind him, and sees old Baldy Shepherdson a-linkin' after him with his gun in his hand and his white hair a-flying in the wind; and 'stead of jumping off and taking to the brush, Bud 'lowed he could outrun him; so they had it, nip and tuck, for five mile or more, the old man a-gaining all the time; so at last Bud seen it warn't any use, so he stopped and faced around so as to have the bullet holes in front, you know, and the old man he rode up and shot him down. But he didn't git much chance to enjoy his luck, for inside of a week our folks laid *him* out."

"I reckon that old man was a coward, Buck."

"I reckon he *warn't* a coward. Not by a blame' sight. There ain't a coward amongst them Shepherdsons—not a one. And there ain't no cowards amongst the Grangerfords, either. Why, that old man kep' up his end in a fight one day, for a half an hour, against three Grangerfords, and come out winner. They was all a-horseback; he lit off of his horse and got behind a little wood-pile, and kep' his horse before him to stop the bullets; but the Grangerfords staid on their horses and capered around the old man, and peppered away at him, and he peppered away at them. Him and his horse both went home pretty leaky and crippled, but the Grangerfords had to be *fetched* home—and one of 'em was dead, and another died the next day. No, sir, if a body's out hunting for cowards, he don't want to fool away any time amongst them Shepherdsons, becuz they don't breed any of that *kind*."

Next Sunday we all went to church, about three mile, everybody a-horseback. The men took their guns along, so did Buck, and kept them between their knees or stood them handy against the wall. The Shepherdsons done the same. It was pretty ornery preaching—all about brotherly love, and such-like tiresomeness; but everybody said it was a good sermon, and they all talked it over going home, and had such a powerful lot to say about faith, and good works, and free grace, and preforeordestination, and I don't know what all, that it did seem to me to be one of the roughest Sundays I had run across yet.

About an hour after dinner everybody was dozing around, some in their chairs and some in their rooms, and it got to be pretty dull. Buck and a dog was stretched out on the grass in the sun, sound asleep. I went up to our room, and judged I would take a nap myself. I found that sweet Miss Sophia standing in her door, which was next to ours, and she took me in her room and shut the door very soft, and asked me if I liked her, and I said I did; and she asked me if I would do something for her and not tell anybody, and I said I would. Then she said she'd forgot her Testament, and left it in the seat at church, between two other books and would I slip out quiet and go there and fetch it to her, and not say nothing to nobody. I said I would. So I slid out and slipped off up the road, and there warn't anybody at the church, except maybe a hog or two, for there warn't any lock on the door, and hogs likes a puncheon floor in summer-time because it's cool. If you notice, most folks don't go to church only when they've got to; but a hog is different.

Says I to myself something's up—it ain't natural for a girl to be in such a sweat about a Testament; so I give it a shake, and out drops a little piece of paper with "*Half-past two*" wrote on it with a pencil. I ransacked it, but couldn't find anything else. I couldn't make anything out of that, so I put the paper in the book again, and when I got home and up stairs, there was Miss Sophia in her door waiting for me. She pulled me in and shut the door; then she looked in the Testament till she found the paper, and as soon as she read it she looked glad; and before a body could think, she grabbed me and give me a squeeze, and said I was the best boy in the world, and not to tell anybody. She was mighty red in the face, for a minute, and her eyes lighted up and made her powerful pretty. I was a good deal astonished, but when I got my breath I asked her what the paper was about, and she asked me if I had read it, and I said no, and she asked me if I could read writing, and I told her "no, only coarse-hand," and then she said the paper warn't anything but a book-mark to keep her place, and I might go and play now.

I went off down to the river, studying over this thing, and pretty soon I noticed that my nigger was following along behind. When we was out of sight of the house, he looked back and around a second, and then comes a-running, and says:

"Mars Jawge, if you'll come down into de swamp, I'll show you a whole stack o' water-moccasins."

Thinks I, that's mighty curious; he said that yesterday. He oughter know a body don't love water-moccasins enough to go around hunting for them. What is he up to anyway? So I says—

"All right, trot ahead."

I followed a half a mile, then he struck out over the swamp and waded ankle deep as much as another half mile. We come to a little flat piece of land which was dry and very thick with trees and bushes and vines, and he says—

"You shove right in dah, jist a few steps, Mars Jawge, dah's whah dey is. I's seed 'm befo', I don't k'yer to see 'em no mo'."

Then he slopped right along and went away, and pretty soon the trees hid him. I poked into the place a-ways, and come to a little open patch as big as a bedroom, all hung around with vines, and found a man laying there asleep—and by jings it was my old Jim!

I waked him up, and I reckoned it was going to be a grand surprise to him to see me again, but it warn't. He nearly cried, he was so glad, but he warn't surprised. He said he swum along behind me, that night, and heard me yell every time, but dasn't answer, because he didn't want nobody to pick *him* up, and take him into slavery again. Says he—

"I got hurt a little, en couldn't swim fas', so I wuz a considable ways behine you, towards de las'; when you landed I reck'ned I could ketch up wid you on de lan' 'dout havin' to shout at you, but when I see dat house I begin to go slow. I 'uz off too fur to hear what dey say to you—I wuz 'fraid o' de dogs—but when it 'uz all quiet agin, I knowed you's in de house, so I struck out for de woods to wait for day. Early in de mawnin' some er de niggers come along, gwyne to de fields, en dey tuck me en showed me dis place, whah de dogs can't track me on accounts o' de water, en dey brings me truck to eat every night, en tells me how you's a gitt'n along."

"Why didn't you tell my Jack to fetch me here sooner, Jim?"

"Well, 'twarn't no use to 'sturb you, Huck, tell we could do sumfn—but we's all right, now. I ben a-buyin' pots en pans en vittles, as I got a chanst, en a patchin' up de raf', nights, when—"

"*What* raft, Jim?"

"Our ole raf'."

"You mean to say our old raft warn't smashed to all flinders?"

"No, she warn't. She was tore up a good deal—one en' of her was—but dey warn't no great harm done, on'y our traps was mos' all los'. Ef we hadn' dive' so deep en swum so fur under water, en de night hadn' ben so dark, en we warn't so sk'yerd, en ben sich punkin-heads, as de sayin' is, we'd a seed de raf'. But it's jis' as well we didn't, 'kase now she's all fixed up agin mos' as good as new, en we's got a new lot o' stuff, too, in de place o' what 'uz los'."

"Why, how did you get hold of the raft again, Jim—did you catch her?"

"How I gwyne to ketch her, en I out in de woods? No, some er de niggers foun' her ketched on a snag, along heah in de ben', en dey hid her in a crick, 'mongst de willows, en dey wuz so much jawin' 'bout which un 'um she b'long to de mos', dat I come to heah 'bout it pooty soon, so I ups en settles de trouble by tellin' 'um she don't b'long to none uv um, but to you en me; en I ast 'm if dey gwyne to grab a young white genlman's propaty, en git a hid'n for it? Den I gin 'm ten cents apiece, en dey 'uz mighty well satisfied, en wisht some mo' raf's 'ud come along en make 'm rich agin. Dey's mighty good to me, dese niggers is, en whatever I wants 'm to do fur me, I doan' have to ast 'm twice, honey. Dat Jack's a good nigger, en pooty smart."

"Yes, he is. He ain't ever told me you was here; told me to come, and he'd show me a lot of water-moccasins. If anything happens, *he* ain't mixed up in it. He can say he never seen us together, and it'll be the truth."

I don't want to talk much about the next day. I reckon I'll cut it pretty short. I waked up about dawn, and was agoing to turn over and go to sleep again, when I noticed how still it was—didn't seem to be anybody stirring. That warn't usual. Next I noticed that Buck was up and gone. Well, I gets up, a-wondering, and goes down stairs—nobody around; everything as still as a mouse. Just the same outside; thinks I, what does it mean? Down by the wood-pile I comes across my Jack, and says:

"What's it all about?"

Says he:

"Don't you know, Mars Jawge?"

"No," says I, "I don't."

"Well, den, Miss Sophia's run off! 'deed she has. She run off in de night, sometime—nobody don't know jis' when—run off to git married to dat young Harney Shepherdson, you know—leastways, so dey 'spec. De fambly foun' it out, 'bout half an hour ago—maybe a little mo'—en' I *tell* you dey warn't no time los'. Sich another hurryin' up guns en hosses *you* never see! De women folks has gone for to stir up de relations, en ole Mars Saul en de boys tuck dey guns en rode up de river road for to try to ketch dat young man en kill him 'fo' he kin git acrost de river wid Miss Sophia. I reck'n dey's gwyne to be mighty rough times."

"Buck went off 'thout waking me up."

"Well, I reck'n he *did*! Dey warn't gwyne to mix you up in it. Mars Buck he loaded up his gun en 'lowed he's gwyne to fetch home a Shepherdson or bust. Well, dey'll be plenty un 'm dah, I reck'n, en you bet you he'll fetch one ef he gits a chanst."

I took up the river road as hard as I could put. By-and-by I begin to hear guns a good ways off. When I come in sight of the log store and the wood-pile where the steamboats lands, I worked along under the trees and brush till I got to a good place, and then I clumb up into the forks of a cotton-wood that was out of reach, and watched. There was a wood-rank four foot high, a little ways in front of the tree, and first I was going to hide behind that; but maybe it was luckier I didn't.

There was four or five men cavorting around on their horses in the open place before the log store, cussing and yelling, and trying to get at a couple of young chaps that was behind the wood-rank alongside of the steamboat landing—but they couldn't come it. Every time one of them showed himself on the river side of the wood-pile he got shot at. The two boys was squatting back to back behind the pile, so they could watch both ways.

By-and-by the men stopped cavorting around and yelling. They started riding towards the store; then up gets one of the boys, draws a steady bead over the wood-rank, and drops one of them out of his saddle. All the men jumped off of their horses and grabbed the hurt one and started to carry him to the store; and that minute the two boys started on the run. They got half-way to the tree I was in before the men noticed. Then the men see them, and jumped on their horses and took out after them. They gained on the boys, but it didn't do no good, the boys had too good a start; they got to the wood-pile that was in front of my tree, and slipped in behind it, and so they had the bulge on the men again. One of the boys was Buck, and the other was a slim young chap about nineteen years old.

The men ripped around awhile, and then rode away. As soon as they was out of sight, I sung out to Buck and told him. He didn't know what to make of my voice coming out of the tree, at first. He was awful surprised. He told me to watch out sharp and let him know when the men come in sight again; said they was up to some devilment or other—wouldn't be gone long. I wished I was out of that tree, but I dasn't come down. Buck begun to cry and rip, and 'lowed that him and his cousin Joe (that was the other young chap) would make up for this day, yet. He said his father and his two brothers was killed, and two or three of the enemy. Said the Shepherdsons laid for them, in ambush. Buck said his father and brothers ought to waited for their relations—the Shepherdsons was too strong for them. I asked him what was become of young Harney and Miss Sophia. He said they'd got across the river and was safe. I was glad of that; but the way Buck did take on because he didn't manage to kill Harney that day he shot at him—I hain't ever heard anything like it.

All of a sudden, bang! bang! bang! goes three or four guns—the men had slipped around through the woods and come in from behind without their horses! The boys jumped for the river—both of them hurt—and as they swum down the current the men run along the bank shooting at them and singing out, "Kill them, kill them!" It made me so sick I most fell out of the tree. I ain't agoing to tell *all* that happened—it would make me sick again if I was to do that. I wished I hadn't ever come ashore that night, to see such things. I ain't ever going to get shut of them—lots of times I dream about them.

I staid in the tree till it begun to get dark, afraid to come down. Sometimes I heard guns away off in the woods; and twice I seen little gangs of men gallop past the log store with guns; so I reckoned the trouble was still agoing on. I was mighty down-hearted; so I made up my mind I wouldn't ever go anear that house again, because I reckoned I was to blame, somehow. I judged that that piece of paper meant that Miss Sophia was to meet Harney somewheres at half-past two and run off; and I judged I ought to told her father about that paper and the curious way she acted, and then maybe he would a locked her up and this awful mess wouldn't ever happened.

When I got down out of the tree, I crept along down the river bank a piece, and found the two bodies laying in the edge of the water, and tugged at them till I got them ashore; then I covered up their faces, and got away as quick as I could. I cried a little when I was covering up Buck's face, for he was mighty good to me.

It was just dark, now. I never went near the house, but struck through the woods and made for the swamp. Jim warn't on his island, so I tramped off in a hurry for the crick, and crowded through the willows, red-hot to jump aboard and get out of that awful country—the raft was gone! My souls, but I was scared! I couldn't get my breath for most a minute. Then I raised a yell. A voice not twenty-five foot from me, says—

"Good lan'! is dat you, honey? Doan' make no noise."

It was Jim's voice—nothing ever sounded so good before. I run along the bank a piece and got aboard, and Jim he grabbed me and hugged me, he was so glad to see me. He says—

"Laws bless you, chile, I 'uz right down sho' you's dead agin. Jack's been heah, he say he reck'n you's ben shot, kase you didn' come home no mo'; so I's jes' dis minute a startin' de raf' down towards de mouf er de crick, so's to be all ready for to shove out en leave soon as Jack comes agin en tells me for certain you *is* dead. Lawsy, I's mighty glad to git you back agin, honey."

I says—

"All right—that's mighty good; they won't find me, and they'll think I've been killed, and floated down the river—there's something up there that'll help them to think so—so don't you lose no time, Jim, but just shove off for the big water as fast as ever you can."

I never felt easy till the raft was two mile below there and out in the middle of the Mississippi. Then we hung up our signal lantern, and judged that we was free and safe once more. I hadn't had a bite to eat since yesterday; so Jim he got out some corn-dodgers and buttermilk, and pork and cabbage, and greens—there ain't nothing in the world so good, when it's cooked right—and whilst I eat my supper we talked, and had a good time. I was powerful glad to get away from the feuds, and so was Jim to get away from the swamp. We said there warn't no home like a raft, after all. Other places do seem so cramped up and smothery, but a raft don't. You feel mighty free and easy and comfortable on a raft.

CHAPTER XIX

Two or three days and nights went by; I reckon I might say they swum by, they slid along so quiet and smooth and lovely. Here is the way we put in the time. It was a monstrous big river down there—sometimes a mile and a half wide; we run nights, and laid up and hid day-times; soon as night was most gone, we stopped navigating and tied up—nearly always in the dead water under a tow-head; and then cut young cottonwoods and willows and hid the raft with them. Then we set out the lines. Next we slid into the river and had a swim, so as to freshen up and cool off; then we set down on the sandy bottom where the water was about knee deep, and watched the daylight come. Not a sound, anywheres—perfectly still—just like the whole world was asleep, only sometimes the bull-frogs a-cluttering, maybe. The first thing to see, looking away over the water, was a kind of dull line—that was the woods on t'other side—you couldn't make nothing else out; then a pale place in the sky; then more paleness, spreading around; then the river softened up, away off, and warn't black any more, but gray; you could see little dark spots drifting along, ever so far away—trading scows, and such things; and long black streaks—rafts; sometimes you could hear a sweep screaking; or jumbled up voices, it was so still, and sounds come so far; and by-and-by you could see a streak on the water which you know by the look of the streak that there's a snag there in a swift current which breaks on it and makes that streak look that way; and you see the mist curl up off of the water, and the east reddens up, and the river, and you make out a log cabin in the edge of the woods, away on the bank on t'other side of the river, being a wood-yard, likely, and piled by them cheats so you can throw a dog through it anywheres; then the nice breeze springs up, and comes fanning you from over there, so cool and fresh, and sweet to smell, on account of the woods and the flowers; but sometimes not that way, because they've left dead fish laying around, gars, and such, and they do get pretty rank; and next you've got the full day, and everything smiling in the sun, and the song-birds just going it!

A little smoke couldn't be noticed, now, so we would take some fish off of the lines, and cook up a hot breakfast. And afterwards we would watch the lonesomeness of the river, and kind of lazy along, and by-and-by lazy off to sleep. Wake up, by-and-by, and look to see what done it, and maybe see a steamboat, coughing along up stream, so far off towards the other side you couldn't tell nothing about her only whether she was stern-wheel or side-wheel; then for about an hour there wouldn't be nothing to hear nor nothing to see—just solid lonesomeness. Next you'd see a raft sliding by, away off yonder, and maybe a galoot on it chopping, because they're most always doing it on a raft; you'd see the ax flash, and come down—you don't hear nothing; you see that ax go up again, and by the time it's above the man's head, then you hear the *k'chunk!*—it had took all that time to come over the water. So we would put in the day, lazying around, listening to the stillness. Once there was a thick fog, and the rafts and things that went by was beating tin pans so the steamboats wouldn't run over them. A scow or a raft went by so close we could hear them talking and cussing and laughing—heard them plain; but we couldn't see no sign of them; it made you feel crawly, it was like spirits carrying on that way in the air. Jim said he believed it was spirits; but I says:

"No, spirits wouldn't say, 'dern the dern fog.'"

Soon as it was night, out we shoved; when we got her out to about the middle, we let her alone, and let her float wherever the current wanted her to; then we lit the pipes, and dangled our legs in the water and talked about all kinds of things—we was always naked, day and night, whenever the mosquitoes would let us—the new clothes Buck's folks made for me was too good to be comfortable, and besides I didn't go much on clothes, nohow.

Sometimes we'd have that whole river all to ourselves for the longest time. Yonder was the banks and the islands, across the water; and maybe a spark—which was a candle in a cabin window—and sometimes on the water you could see a spark or two—on a raft or a scow, you know; and maybe you could hear a fiddle or a song coming over from one of them crafts. It's lovely to live on a raft. We had the sky, up there, all speckled with stars, and we used to lay on our backs and look up at them, and discuss about whether they was made, or only just happened—Jim he allowed they was made, but I allowed they happened; I judged it would have took too long to *make* so many. Jim said the moon could a *laid* them; well, that looked kind of reasonable, so I didn't say nothing against it, because I've seen a frog lay most as many, so of course it could be done. We used to watch the stars that fell, too, and see them streak down. Jim allowed they'd got spoiled and was hove out of the nest.

Once or twice of a night we would see a steamboat slipping along in the dark, and now and then she would belch a whole world of sparks up out of her chimbleys, and they would rain down in the river and look awful pretty; then she would turn a corner and her lights would wink out and her pow-wow shut off and leave the river still again; and by-and-by her waves would get to us, a long time after she was gone, and joggle the raft a bit, and after that you wouldn't hear nothing for you couldn't tell how long, except maybe frogs or something.

After midnight the people on shore went to bed, and then for two or three hours the shores was black—no more sparks in the cabin windows. These sparks was our clock—the first one that showed again meant morning was coming, so we hunted a place to hide and tie up, right away.

One morning about day-break, I found a canoe and crossed over a chute to the main shore—it was only two hundred yards—and paddled about a mile up a crick amongst the cypress woods, to see if I couldn't get some berries. Just as I was passing a place where a kind of a cow-path crossed the crick, here comes a couple of men tearing up the path as tight as they could foot it. I thought I was a goner, for whenever anybody was after anybody I judged it was *me*—or maybe Jim. I was about to dig out from there in a hurry, but they was pretty close to me then, and sung out and begged me to save their lives—said they hadn't been doing nothing, and was being chased for it—said there was men and dogs a-coming. They wanted to jump right in, but I says—

"Don't you do it. I don't hear the dogs and horses yet; you've got time to crowd through the brush and get up the crick a little ways; then you take to the water and wade down to me and get in—that'll throw the dogs off the scent."

They done it, and soon as they was aboard I lit out for our tow-head, and in about five or ten minutes we heard the dogs and the men away off, shouting. We heard them come along towards the crick, but couldn't see them; they seemed to stop and fool around a while; then, as we got further and further away all the time, we couldn't hardly hear them at all; by the time we had left a mile of woods behind us and struck the river, everything was quiet, and we paddled over to the tow-head and hid in the cotton-woods and was safe.

One of these fellows was about seventy, or upwards, and had a bald head and very gray whiskers. He had an old battered-up slouch hat on, and a greasy blue woolen shirt, and ragged old blue jeans britches stuffed into his boot tops, and home-knit galluses—no, he only had one. He had an old long-tailed blue jeans coat with slick brass buttons, flung over his arm, and both of them had big fat ratty-looking carpet-bags.

The other fellow was about thirty and dressed about as ornery. After breakfast we all laid off and talked, and the first thing that come out was that these chaps didn't know one another.

"What got you into trouble?" says the baldhead to t'other chap.

"Well, I'd been selling an article to take the tartar off the teeth—and it does take it off, too, and generly the enamel along with it—but I staid about one night longer than I ought to, and was just in the act of sliding out when I ran across you on the trail this side of town, and you told me they were coming, and begged me to help you to get off. So I told you I was expecting trouble myself and would scatter out *with* you. That's the whole yarn—what's yourn?"

"Well, I'd ben a-runnin' a little temperance revival thar, 'bout a week, and was the pet of the women-folks, big and little, for I was makin' it mighty warm for the rummies, I *tell* you, and takin' as much as five or six dollars a night—ten cents a head, children and niggers free—and business a growin' all the time; when somehow or another a little report got around, last night, that I had a way of puttin' in my time with a private jug, on the sly. A nigger rousted me out this mornin', and told me the people was getherin' on the quiet, with their dogs and horses, and they'd be along pretty soon and give me 'bout half an hour's start, and then run me down, if they could; and if they got me they'd tar and feather me and ride me on a rail, sure. I didn't wait for no breakfast—I warn't hungry."

"Old man," says the young one, "I reckon we might double-team it together; what do you think?"

"I ain't undisposed. What's your line—mainly?"

"Jour printer, by trade; do a little in patent medicines; theatre-actor—tragedy, you know; take a turn at mesmerism and phrenology when there's a chance; teach singing-geography school for a change; sling a lecture, sometimes—oh, I do lots of things—most anything that comes handy, so it ain't work. What's your lay?"

"I've done considerable in the doctoring way in my time. Layin' on o' hands is my best holt—for cancer, and paralysis, and sich things; and I k'n tell a fortune pretty good, when I've got somebody along to find out the facts for me. Preachin's my line, too; and workin' camp-meetin's; and missionaryin around."

Nobody never said anything for a while; then the young man hove a sigh and says—

"Alas!"

"What're you alassin' about?" says the baldhead.

"To think I should have lived to be leading such a life, and be degraded down into such company." And he begun to wipe the corner of his eye with a rag.

"Dern your skin, ain't the company good enough for you?" says the baldhead, pretty pert and uppish.

"Yes, it *is* good enough for me; it's as good as I deserve; for who fetched me so low, when I was so high? *I* did myself. I don't blame *you*, gentlemen—far from it; I don't blame anybody. I deserve it all. Let the cold world do its worst; one thing I know—there's a grave somewhere for me. The world may go on just as it's always done, and take everything from me—loved ones, property, everything—but it can't take that. Some day I'll lie down in it and forget it all, and my poor broken heart will be at rest." He went on a-wiping.

"Drot your pore broken heart," says the baldhead; "what are you heaving your pore broken heart at *us* f'r? *We* hain't done nothing."

"No, I know you haven't. I ain't blaming you, gentlemen. I brought myself down—yes, I did it myself. It's right I should suffer—perfectly right—I don't make any moan."

"Brought you down from whar? Whar was you brought down from?"

"Ah, you would not believe me; the world never believes—let it pass—'tis no matter. The secret of my birth—"

"The secret of your birth? Do you mean to say—"

"Gentlemen," says the young man, very solemn, "I will reveal it to you, for I feel I may have confidence in you. By rights I am a duke!"

Jim's eyes bugged out when he heard that; and I reckon mine did, too. Then the baldhead says: "No! you can't mean it?"

"Yes. My great-grandfather, eldest son of the Duke of Bridgewater, fled to this country about the end of the last century, to breathe the pure air of freedom; married here, and died, leaving a son, his own father dying about the same time. The second son of the late duke seized the title and estates—the infant real duke was ignored. I am the lineal descendant of that infant—I am the rightful Duke of Bridgewater; and here am I, forlorn, torn from my high estate, hunted of men, despised by the cold world, ragged, worn, heart-broken, and degraded to the companionship of felons on a raft!"

Jim pitied him ever so much, and so did I. We tried to comfort him, but he said it warn't much use, he couldn't be much comforted; said if we was a mind to acknowledge him, that would do him more good than most anything else; so we said we would, if he would tell us how. He said we ought to bow, when we spoke to him, and say "Your Grace," or "My Lord," or "Your Lordship"—and he wouldn't mind it if we called him plain "Bridgewater," which he said was a title, anyway, and not a name; and one of us ought to wait on him at dinner, and do any little thing for him he wanted done.

Well, that was all easy, so we done it. All through dinner Jim stood around and waited on him, and says, "Will yo' Grace have some o' dis, or some o' dat?" and so on, and a body could see it was mighty pleasing to him.

But the old man got pretty silent, by-and-by—didn't have much to say, and didn't look pretty comfortable over all that petting that was going on around that duke. He seemed to have something on his mind. So, along in the afternoon, he says:

"Looky here, Bilgewater," he says, "I'm nation sorry for you, but you ain't the only person that's had troubles like that."

"No?"

"No, you ain't. You ain't the only person that's ben snaked down wrongfully out'n a high place."

"Alas!"

"No, you ain't the only person that's had a secret of his birth." And by jing, *he* begins to cry.

"Hold! What do you mean?"

"Bilgewater, kin I trust you?" says the old man, still sort of sobbing.

"To the bitter death!" He took the old man by the hand and squeezed it, and says, "The secret of your being: speak!"

"Bilgewater, I am the late Dauphin!"

You bet you Jim and me stared, this time. Then the duke says:

"You are what?"

"Yes, my friend, it is too true—your eyes is lookin' at this very moment on the pore disappeared Dauphin, Looy the Seventeen, son of Looy the Sixteen and Marry Antonette."

"You! At your age! No! You mean you're the late Charlemagne; you must be six or seven hundred years old, at the very least."

"Trouble has done it, Bilgewater, trouble has done it; trouble has brung these gray hairs and this premature balditude. Yes, gentlemen, you see before you, in blue jeans and misery, the wanderin', exiled, trampled-on and sufferin' rightful King of France."

Well, he cried and took on so, that me and Jim didn't know hardly what to do, we was so sorry—and so glad and proud we'd got him with us, too. So we set in, like we done before with the duke, and tried to comfort *him*. But he said it warn't no use, nothing but to be dead and done with it all could do him any good; though he said it often made him feel easier and better for a while if people treated him according to his rights, and got down on one knee to speak to him, and always called him "Your Majesty," and waited on him first at meals, and didn't set down in his presence till he asked them. So Jim and me set to majestying him, and doing this and that and t'other for him, and standing up till he told us we might set down. This done him heaps of good, and so he got cheerful and comfortable. But the duke kind of soured on him, and didn't look a bit satisfied with the way things was going; still, the king acted real friendly towards him, and said the duke's great-grandfather and all the other Dukes of Bilgewater was a good deal thought of by *his* father and was allowed to come to the palace considerable; but the duke staid huffy a good while, till by-and-by the king says:

"Like as not we got to be together a blamed long time, on this h-yer raft, Bilgewater, and so what's the use o' your bein' sour? It'll only make things oncomfortable. It ain't my fault I warn't born a duke, it ain't your fault you warn't born a king—so what's the use to worry? Make the best o' things the way you find 'em, says I—that's my motto. This ain't no bad thing that we've struck here—plenty grub and an easy life—come, give us your hand, Duke, and less all be friends."

The duke done it, and Jim and me was pretty glad to see it. It took away all the uncomfortableness, and we felt mighty good over it, because it would a been a miserable business to have any unfriendliness on the raft; for what you want, above all things, on a raft, is for everybody to be satisfied, and feel right and kind towards the others.

It didn't take me long to make up my mind that these liars warn't no kings nor dukes, at all, but just low-down humbugs and frauds. But I never said nothing, never let on; kept it to myself; it's the best way; then you don't have no quarrels, and don't get into no trouble. If they wanted us to call them kings and dukes, I hadn't no objections, 'long as it would keep peace in the family; and it warn't no use to tell Jim, so I didn't tell him. If I never learnt nothing else out of pap, I learnt that the best way to get along with his kind of people is to let them have their own way.

CHAPTER XX

They asked us considerable many questions; wanted to know what we covered up the raft that way for, and laid by in the day-time insted of running—was Jim a runaway nigger? Says I—

"Goodness sakes, would a runaway nigger run *south*?"

No, they allowed he wouldn't. I had to account for things some way, so I says:

"My folks was living in Pike County, in Missouri, where I was born, and they all died off but me and pa and my brother Ike. Pa, he 'lowed he'd break up and go down and live with Uncle Ben, who's got a little one-horse place on the river, forty-four mile below Orleans. Pa was pretty poor, and had some debts; so when he'd squared up there warn't nothing left but sixteen dollars and our nigger, Jim. That warn't enough to take us fourteen hundred mile, deck passage nor no other way. Well, when the river rose, pa had a streak of luck one day; he ketched this piece of a raft; so we reckoned we'd go down to Orleans on it. Pa's luck didn't hold out; a steamboat run over the forrard corner of the raft, one night, and we all went overboard and dove under the wheel; Jim and me come up, all right, but pa was drunk, and Ike was only four years old, so they never come up no more. Well, for the next day or two we had considerable trouble, because people was always coming out in skiffs and trying to take Jim away from me, saying they believed he was a runaway nigger. We don't run day-times no more, now; nights they don't bother us."

The duke says—

"Leave me alone to cipher out a way so we can run in the day-time if we want to. I'll think the thing over—I'll invent a plan that'll fix it. We'll let it alone for to-day, because of course we don't want to go by that town yonder in daylight—it mightn't be healthy."

Towards night it begun to darken up and look like rain; the heat lightning was squirting around, low down in the sky, and the leaves was beginning to shiver—it was going to be pretty ugly, it was easy to see that. So the duke and the king went to overhauling our wigwam, to see what the beds was like. My bed was a straw tick—better than Jim's, which was a cornshuck tick; there's always cobs around about in a shuck tick, and they poke into you and hurt; and when you roll over, the dry shucks sound like you was rolling over in a pile of dead leaves; it makes such a rustling that you wake up. Well, the duke allowed he would take my bed; but the king allowed he wouldn't. He says—

"I should a reckoned the difference in rank would a sejested to you that a corn-shuck bed warn't just fitten for me to sleep on. Your Grace'll take the shuck bed yourself."

Jim and me was in a sweat again, for a minute, being afraid there was going to be some more trouble amongst them; so we was pretty glad when the duke says—

"'Tis my fate to be always ground into the mire under the iron heel of oppression. Misfortune has broken my once haughty spirit; I yield, I submit; 'tis my fate. I am alone in the world—let me suffer; I can bear it."

We got away as soon as it was good and dark. The king told us to stand well out towards the middle of the river, and not show a light till we got a long ways below the town. We come in sight of the little bunch of lights by-and-by—that was the town, you know—and slid by, about a half a mile out, all right. When we was three-quarters of a mile below, we hoisted up our signal lantern; and about ten o'clock it come on to rain and blow and thunder and lighten like everything; so the king told us to both stay on watch till the weather got better; then him and the duke crawled into the wigwam and turned in for the night. It was my watch below; till twelve, but I wouldn't a turned in, anyway, if I'd had a bed; because a body don't see such a storm as that every day in the week, not by a long sight. My souls, how the wind did scream along! And every second or two there'd come a glare that lit up the white-caps for a half a mile around, and you'd see the islands looking dusty through the rain, and the trees thrashing around in the wind; then comes a *h-wack!*—bum! bum! bumble-umble-um-bum-bum-bum-bum—and the thunder would go rumbling and grumbling away, and quit—and then *rip* comes another flash and another sockdolager. The waves most washed me off the raft, sometimes, but I hadn't any clothes on, and didn't mind. We didn't have no trouble about snags; the lightning was glaring and flittering around so constant that we could see them plenty soon enough to throw her head this way or that and miss them.

I had the middle watch, you know, but I was pretty sleepy by that time, so Jim he said he would stand the first half of it for me; he was always mighty good, that way, Jim was. I crawled into the wigwam, but the king and the duke had their legs sprawled around so there warn't no show for me; so I laid outside—I didn't mind the rain, because it was warm, and the waves warn't running so high, now. About two they come up again, though, and Jim was going to call me, but he changed his mind because he reckoned they warn't high enough yet to do any harm; but he was mistaken about that, for pretty soon all of a sudden along comes a regular ripper, and washed me overboard. It most killed Jim a-laughing. He was the easiest nigger to laugh that ever was, anyway.

I took the watch, and Jim he laid down and snored away; and by-and-by the storm let up for good and all; and the first cabin-light that showed, I rousted him out and we slid the raft into hiding-quarters for the day.

The king got out an old ratty deck of cards, after breakfast, and him and the duke played seven-up a while, five cents a game. Then they got tired of it, and allowed they would "lay out a campaign," as they called it. The duke went down into his carpet-bag and fetched up a lot of little printed bills, and read them out loud. One bill said "The celebrated Dr. Armand de Montalban of Paris," would "lecture on the Science of Phrenology" at such and such a place, on the blank day of blank, at ten cents admission, and "furnish charts of character at twenty-five cents apiece." The duke said that was *him*. In another bill he was the "world renowned Shakesperean tragedian, Garrick the Younger, of Drury Lane, London." In other bills he had a lot of other names and done other wonderful things, like finding water and gold with a "divining rod," "dissipating witch-spells," and so on. By-and-by he says—

"But the histrionic muse is the darling. Have you ever trod the boards, Royalty?"

"No," says the king.

"You shall, then, before you're three days older, Fallen Grandeur," says the duke. "The first good town we come to, we'll hire a hall and do the sword-fight in Richard III, and the balcony scene in Romeo and Juliet. How does that strike you?"

"I'm in, up to the hub, for anything that will pay, Bilgewater, but you see I don't know nothing about play-actn', and hain't ever seen much of it. I was too small when pap used to have 'em at the palace. Do you reckon you can learn me?"

"Easy!"

"All right. I'm jist a-freezn' for something fresh, anyway. Less commence, right away."

So the duke he told him all about who Romeo was, and who Juliet was, and said he was used to being Romeo, so the king could be Juliet.

"But if Juliet's such a young gal, Duke, my peeled head and my white whiskers is goin' to look oncommon odd on her, maybe."

"No, don't you worry—these country jakes won't ever think of that. Besides, you know, you'll be in costume, and that makes all the difference in the world; Juliet's in a balcony, enjoying the moonlight before she goes to bed, and she's got on her nightgown and her ruffled night-cap. Here are the costumes for the parts."

He got out two or three curtain-calico suits, which he said was meedyevil armor for Richard III, and t'other chap, and a long white cotton night-shirt and a ruffled night-cap to match. The king was satisfied; so the duke got out his book and read the parts over in the most splendid spread-eagle way, prancing around and acting at the same time, to show how it had got to be done; then he give the book to the king and told him to get his part by heart.

There was a little one-horse town about three mile down the bend, and after dinner the duke said he had ciphered out his idea about how to run in daylight without it being dangersome for Jim; so he allowed he would go down to the town and fix that thing. The king allowed he would go too, and see if he couldn't strike something. We was out of coffee, so Jim said I better go along with them in the canoe and get some.

When we got there, there warn't nobody stirring; streets empty, and perfectly dead and still, like Sunday. We found a sick nigger sunning himself in a back yard, and he said everybody that warn't too young or too sick or too old, was gone to camp-meeting, about two mile back in the woods. The king got the directions, and allowed he'd go and work that camp-meeting for all it was worth, and I might go, too.

The duke said what he was after was a printing office. We found it; a little bit of a concern, up over a carpenter shop—carpenters and printers all gone to the meeting, and no doors locked. It was a dirty, littered-up place, and had ink marks, and handbills with pictures of horses and runaway niggers on them, all over the walls. The duke shed his coat and said he was all right, now. So me and the king lit out for the camp-meeting.

We got there in about a half an hour, fairly dripping, for it was a most awful hot day. There was as much as a thousand people there, from twenty mile around. The woods was full of teams and wagons, hitched everywheres, feeding out of the wagon troughs and stomping to keep off the flies. There was sheds made out of poles and roofed over with branches, where they had lemonade and gingerbread to sell, and piles of watermelons and green corn and such-like truck.

The preaching was going on under the same kinds of sheds, only they was bigger and held crowds of people. The benches was made out of outside slabs of logs, with holes bored in the round side to drive sticks into for legs. They didn't have no backs. The preachers had high platforms to stand on, at one end of the sheds. The women had on sun-bonnets; and some had linsey-woolsey frocks, some gingham ones, and a few of the young ones had on calico. Some of the young men was barefooted, and some of the children didn't have on any clothes but just a tow-linen shirt. Some of the old women was knitting, and some of the young folks was courting on the sly.

The first shed we come to, the preacher was lining out a hymn. He lined out two lines, everybody sung it, and it was kind of grand to hear it, there was so many of them and they done it in such a rousing way; then he lined out two more for them to sing—and so on. The people woke up more and more, and sung louder and louder; and towards the end, some begun to groan, and some begun to shout. Then the preacher begun to preach; and begun in earnest, too; and went weaving first to one side of the platform and then the other, and then a leaning down over the front of it, with his arms and his body going all the time, and shouting his words out with all his might; and every now and then he would hold up his Bible and spread it open, and kind of pass it around this way and that, shouting, "It's the brazen serpent in the wilderness! Look upon it and live!" And people would shout out, "Glory!—A-a-*men*!" And so he went on, and the people groaning and crying and saying amen:

"Oh, come to the mourners' bench! come, black with sin! (*amen!*) come, sick and sore! (*amen!*) come, lame and halt, and blind! (*amen!*) come, pore and needy, sunk in shame! (*a-a-men!*) come all that's worn, and soiled, and suffering!—come with a broken spirit! come with a contrite heart! come in your rags and sin and dirt! the waters that cleanse is free, the door of heaven stands open—oh, enter in and be at rest!" (*a-a-men! glory, glory hallelujah!*)

And so on. You couldn't make out what the preacher said, any more, on account of the shouting and crying. Folks got up, everywheres in the crowd, and worked their way, just by main strength, to the mourners' bench, with the tears running down their faces; and when all the mourners had got up there to the front benches in a crowd, they sung, and shouted, and flung themselves down on the straw, just crazy and wild.

Well, the first I knowed, the king got agoing; and you could hear him over everybody; and next he went a-charging up on to the platform and the preacher he begged him to speak to the people, and he done it. He told them he was a pirate—been a pirate for thirty years, out in the Indian Ocean, and his crew was thinned out considerable, last spring, in a fight, and he was home now, to take out some fresh men, and thanks to goodness he'd been robbed last night, and put ashore off of a steamboat without a cent, and he was glad of it, it was the blessedest thing that ever happened to him, because he was a changed man now, and happy for the first time in his life; and poor as he was, he was going to start right off and work his way back to the Indian Ocean and put in the rest of his life trying to turn the pirates into the true path; for he could do it better than anybody else, being acquainted with all the pirate crews in that ocean; and though it would take him a long time to get there, without money, he would get there anyway, and every time he convinced a pirate he would say to him, "Don't you thank me, don't you give me no credit, it all belongs to them dear people in Pokeville camp-meeting, natural brothers and benefactors of the race—and that dear preacher there, the truest friend a pirate ever had!"

And then he busted into tears, and so did everybody. Then somebody sings out, "Take up a collection for him, take up a collection!" Well, a half a dozen made a jump to do it, but somebody sings out, "Let *him* pass the hat around!" Then everybody said it, the preacher too.

So the king went all through the crowd with his hat, swabbing his eyes, and blessing the people and praising them and thanking them for being so good to the poor pirates away off there; and every little while the prettiest kind of girls, with the tears running down their cheeks, would up and ask him would he let them kiss him, for to remember him by; and he always done it; and some of them he hugged and kissed as many as five or six times—and he was invited to stay a week; and everybody wanted him to live in their houses, and said they'd think it was an honor; but he said as this was the last day of the camp-meeting he couldn't do no good, and besides he was in a sweat to get to the Indian Ocean right off and go to work on the pirates.

When we got back to the raft and he come to count up, he found he had collected eighty-seven dollars and seventy-five cents. And then he had fetched away a three-gallon jug of whisky, too, that he found under a wagon when we was starting home through the woods. The king said, take it all around, it laid over any day he'd ever put in in the missionarying line. He said it warn't no use talking, heathens don't amount to shucks, alongside of pirates, to work a camp-meeting with.

The duke was thinking *he'd* been doing pretty well, till the king come to show up, but after that he didn't think so so much. He had set up and printed off two little jobs for farmers, in that printing office—horse bills—and took the money, four dollars. And he had got in ten dollars worth of advertisements for the paper, which he said he would put in for four dollars if they would pay in advance—so they done it. The price of the paper was two dollars a year, but he took in three subscriptions for half a dollar apiece on condition of them paying him in advance; they were going to pay in cord-wood and onions, as usual, but he said he had just bought the concern and knocked down the price as low as he could afford it, and was going to run it for cash. He set up a little piece of poetry, which he made, himself, out of his own head—three verses—kind of sweet and saddish—the name of it was, "Yes, crush, cold world, this breaking heart"—and he left that all set up and ready to print in the paper and didn't charge nothing for it. Well, he took in nine dollars and a half, and said he'd done a pretty square day's work for it.

Then he showed us another little job he'd printed and hadn't charged for, because it was for us. It had a picture of a runaway nigger, with a bundle on a stick, over his shoulder, and "$200 reward" under it. The reading was all about Jim, and just described him to a dot. It said he run away from St. Jacques' plantation, forty mile below New Orleans, last winter, and likely went north, and whoever would catch him and send him back, he could have the reward and expenses.

"Now," says the duke, "after to-night we can run in the daytime if we want to. Whenever we see anybody coming, we can tie Jim hand and foot with a rope, and lay him in the wigwam and show this handbill and say we captured him up the river, and were too poor to travel on a steamboat, so we got this little raft on credit from our friends and are going down to get the reward. Handcuffs and chains would look still better on Jim, but it wouldn't go well with the story of us being so poor. Too much like jewelry. Ropes are the correct thing—we must preserve the unities, as we say on the boards."

We all said the duke was pretty smart, and there couldn't be no trouble about running daytimes. We judged we could make miles enough that night to get out of the reach of the pow-wow we reckoned the duke's work in the printing office was going to make in that little town—then we could boom right along, if we wanted to.

We laid low and kept still, and never shoved out till nearly ten o'clock; then we slid by, pretty wide away from the town, and didn't hoist our lantern till we was clear out of sight of it.

When Jim called me to take the watch at four in the morning, he says—

"Huck, does you reck'n we gwyne to run acrost any mo' kings on dis trip?"

"No," I says, "I reckon not."

"Well," says he, "dat's all right, den. I doan' mine one er two kings, but dat's enough. Dis one's powerful drunk, en de duke ain' much better."

I found Jim had been trying to get him to talk French, so he could hear what it was like; but he said he had been in this country so long, and had so much trouble, he'd forgot it.

CHAPTER XXI

It was after sun-up, now, but we went right on, and didn't tie up. The king and the duke turned out, by-and-by, looking pretty rusty; but after they'd jumped overboard and took a swim, it chippered them up a good deal. After breakfast the king he took a seat on a corner of the raft, and pulled off his boots and rolled up his britches, and let his legs dangle in the water, so as to be comfortable, and lit his pipe, and went to getting his Romeo and Juliet by heart. When he had got it pretty good, him and the duke begun to practice it together. The duke had to learn him over and over again, how to say every speech; and he made him sigh, and put his hand on his heart, and after while he said he done it pretty well; "only," he says, "you mustn't bellow out *Romeo!* that way, like a bull—you must say it soft, and sick, and languishy, so—R-o-o-meo! that is the idea; for Juliet's a dear sweet mere child of a girl, you know, and she don't bray like a jackass."

Well, next they got out a couple of long swords that the duke made out of oak laths, and begun to practice the sword-fight—the duke called himself Richard III.; and the way they laid on, and pranced around the raft was grand to see. But by-and-by the king tripped and fell overboard, and after that they took a rest, and had a talk about all kinds of adventures they'd had in other times along the river.

After dinner, the duke says:

"Well, Capet, we'll want to make this a first-class show, you know, so I guess we'll add a little more to it. We want a little something to answer encores with, anyway."

"What's onkores, Bilgewater?"

The duke told him, and then says:

"I'll answer by doing the Highland fling or the sailor's hornpipe; and you—well, let me see—oh, I've got it—you can do Hamlet's soliloquy."

"Hamlet's which?"

"Hamlet's soliloquy, you know; the most celebrated thing in Shakespeare. Ah, it's sublime, sublime! Always fetches the house. I haven't got it in the book—I've only got one volume—but I reckon I can piece it out from memory. I'll just walk up and down a minute, and see if I can call it back from recollection's vaults."

So he went to marching up and down, thinking, and frowning horrible every now and then; then he would hoist up his eyebrows; next he would squeeze his hand on his forehead and stagger back and kind of moan; next he would sigh, and next he'd let on to drop a tear. It was beautiful to see him. By-and-by he got it. He told us to give attention. Then he strikes a most noble attitude, with one leg shoved forwards, and his arms stretched away up, and his head tilted back, looking up at the sky; and then he begins to rip and rave and grit his teeth; and after that, all through his speech he howled, and spread around, and swelled up his chest, and just knocked the spots out of any acting ever *I* see before. This is the speech—I learned it, easy enough, while he was learning it to the king:

To be, or not to be; that is the bare bodkin
That makes calamity of so long life;
For who would fardels bear, till Birnam Wood do come to Dunsinane,
But that the fear of something after death
Murders the innocent sleep,
Great nature's second course,
And makes us rather sling the arrows of outrageous fortune
Than fly to others that we know not of.
There's the respect must give us pause:
Wake Duncan with thy knocking! I would thou couldst;
For who would bear the whips and scorns of time,
The oppressor's wrong, the proud man's contumely,
The law's delay, and the quietus which his pangs might take,
In the dead waste and middle of the night, when churchyards yawn
In customary suits of solemn black,
But that the undiscovered country from whose bourne no traveler returns,
Breathes forth contagion on the world,
And thus the native hue of resolution, like the poor cat i' the adage,
Is sicklied o'er with care,
And all the clouds that lowered o'er our housetops,
With this regard their currents turn awry,
And lose the name of action.
'Tis a consummation devoutly to be wished. But soft you, the fair Ophelia:
Ope not thy ponderous and marble jaws,
But get thee to a nunnery—go!

Well, the old man he liked that speech, and he mighty soon got it so he could do it first rate. It seemed like he was just born for it; and when he had his hand in and was excited, it was perfectly lovely the way he would rip and tear and rair up behind when he was getting it off.

The first chance we got, the duke he had some show bills printed; and after that, for two or three days as we floated along, the raft was a most uncommon lively place, for there warn't nothing but sword-fighting and rehearsing—as the duke called it—going on all the time. One morning, when we was pretty well down the State of Arkansaw, we come in sight of a little one-horse town in a big bend; so we tied up about three-quarters of a mile above it, in the mouth of a crick which was shut in like a tunnel by the cypress trees, and all of us but Jim took the canoe and went down there to see if there was any chance in that place for our show.

We struck it mighty lucky; there was going to be a circus there that afternoon, and the country people was already beginning to come in, in all kinds of old shackly wagons, and on horses. The circus would leave before night, so our show would have a pretty good chance. The duke he hired the court house, and we went around and stuck up our bills. They read like this:

Shaksperean Revival ! ! !
Wonderful Attraction!
For One Night Only!
The world renowned tragedians,
David Garrick the younger, of Drury Lane Theatre, London,

and
Edmund Kean the elder, of the Royal Haymarket Theatre,
Whitechapel, Pudding Lane, Piccadilly, London, and the
Royal Continental Theatres, in their sublime
Shaksperean Spectacle entitled
The Balcony Scene
in
Romeo and Juliet ! ! !

Romeo . . . . Mr. Garrick.
Juliet . . . . Mr. Kean.

Assisted by the whole strength of the company!
New costumes, new scenery, new appointments!
Also:
The thrilling, masterly, and blood-curdling
Broad-sword conflict
In Richard III. ! ! !

Richard III . . . . Mr. Garrick.
Richmond . . . . Mr. Kean.

also:
(by special request,)
Hamlet's Immortal Soliloquy! !
By the Illustrious Kean!
Done by him 300 consecutive nights in Paris!
For One Night Only,
On account of imperative European engagements!
Admission 25 cents; children and servants, 10 cents.

Then we went loafing around the town. The stores and houses was most all old shackly dried-up frame concerns that hadn't ever been painted; they was set up three or four foot above ground on stilts, so as to be out of reach of the water when the river was overflowed. The houses had little gardens around them, but they didn't seem to raise hardly anything in them but jimpson weeds, and sunflowers, and ash-piles, and old curled-up boots and shoes, and pieces of bottles, and rags, and played-out tin-ware. The fences was made of different kinds of boards, nailed on at different times; and they leaned every which-way, and had gates that didn't generly have but one hinge—a leather one. Some of the fences had been white-washed, some time or another, but the duke said it was in Clumbus's time, like enough. There was generly hogs in the garden, and people driving them out.

All the stores was along one street. They had white-domestic awnings in front, and the country people hitched their horses to the awning-posts. There was empty dry-goods boxes under the awnings, and loafers roosting on them all day long, whittling them with their Barlow knives; and chawing tobacco, and gaping and yawning and stretching—a mighty ornery lot. They generly had on yellow straw hats most as wide as an umbrella, but didn't wear no coats nor waistcoats; they called one another Bill, and Buck, and Hank, and Joe, and Andy, and talked lazy and drawly, and used considerable many cuss-words. There was as many as one loafer leaning up against every awning-post, and he most always had his hands in his britches pockets, except when he fetched them out to lend a chaw of tobacco or scratch. What a body was hearing amongst them, all the time was—

"Gimme a chaw 'v tobacker, Hank."

"Cain't—I hain't got but one chaw left. Ask Bill."

Maybe Bill he gives him a chaw; maybe he lies and says he ain't got none. Some of them kinds of loafers never has a cent in the world, nor a chaw of tobacco of their own. They get all their chawing by borrowing—they say to a fellow, "I wisht you'd len' me a chaw, Jack, I jist this minute give Ben Thompson the last chaw I had"—which is a lie, pretty much every time; it don't fool nobody but a stranger; but Jack ain't no stranger, so he says—

"*You* give him a chaw, did you? so did your sister's cat's grandmother. You pay me back the chaws you've awready borry'd off'n me, Lafe Buckner, then I'll loan you one or two ton of it, and won't charge you no back intrust, nuther."

"Well, I *did* pay you back some of it wunst."

"Yes, you did—'bout six chaws. You borry'd store tobacker and paid back nigger-head."

Store tobacco is flat black plug, but these fellows mostly chaws the natural leaf twisted. When they borrow a chaw, they don't generly cut it off with a knife, but they set the plug in between their teeth, and gnaw with their teeth and tug at the plug with their hands till they get it in two—then sometimes the one that owns the tobacco looks mournful at it when it's handed back, and says, sarcastic—

"Here, gimme the *chaw*, and you take the *plug*."

All the streets and lanes was just mud, they warn't nothing else *but* mud—mud as black as tar, and nigh about a foot deep in some places; and two or three inches deep in *all* the places. The hogs loafed and grunted around, everywheres. You'd see a muddy sow and a litter of pigs come lazying along the street and whollop herself right down in the way, where folks had to walk around her, and she'd stretch out, and shut her eyes, and wave her ears, whilst the pigs was milking her, and look as happy as if she was on salary. And pretty soon you'd hear a loafer sing out, "Hi! *so* boy! sick him, Tige!" and away the sow would go, squealing most horrible, with a dog or two swinging to each ear, and three or four dozen more a-coming; and then you would see all the loafers get up and watch the thing out of sight, and laugh at the fun and look grateful for the noise. Then they'd settle back again till there was a dog-fight. There couldn't anything wake them up all over, and make them happy all over, like a dog-fight—unless it might be putting turpentine on a stray dog and setting fire to him, or tying a tin pan to his tail and see him run himself to death.

On the river front some of the houses was sticking out over the bank, and they was bowed and bent, and about ready to tumble in. The people had moved out of them. The bank was caved away under one corner of some others, and that corner was hanging over. People lived in them yet, but it was dangersome, because sometimes a strip of land as wide as a house caves in at a time. Sometimes a belt of land a quarter of a mile deep will start in and cave along and cave along till it all caves into the river in one summer. Such a town as that has to be always moving back, and back, and back, because the river's always gnawing at it.

The nearer it got to noon that day, the thicker and thicker was the wagons and horses in the streets, and more coming all the time. Families fetched their dinners with them, from the country, and eat them in the wagons. There was considerable whiskey drinking going on, and I seen three fights. By-and-by somebody sings out—

"Here comes old Boggs!—in from the country for his little old monthly drunk—here he comes, boys!"

All the loafers looked glad—I reckoned they was used to having fun out of Boggs. One of them says—

"Wonder who he's a gwyne to chaw up this time. If he'd a chawed up all the men he's ben a gwyne to chaw up in the last twenty year, he'd have a considerable ruputation, now."

Another one says, "I wisht old Boggs 'd threaten me, 'cuz then I'd know I warn't gwyne to die for a thousan' year."

Boggs comes a-tearing along on his horse, whooping and yelling like an Injun, and singing out—

"Cler the track, thar. I'm on the waw-path, and the price uv coffins is a gwyne to raise."

He was drunk, and weaving about in his saddle; he was over fifty year old, and had a very red face. Everybody yelled at him, and laughed at him, and sassed him, and he sassed back, and said he'd attend to them and lay them out in their regular turns, but he couldn't wait now, because he'd come to town to kill old Colonel Sherburn, and his motto was "meat first, and spoon vittles to top off on."

He see me, and rode up and says—

"Whar'd you come f'm, boy? You prepared to die?"

Then he rode on. I was scared; but a man says—

"He don't mean nothing; he's always a carryin' on like that, when he's drunk. He's the best-naturedest old fool in Arkansaw—never hurt nobody, drunk nor sober."

Boggs rode up before the biggest store in town and bent his head down so he could see under the curtain of the awning, and yells—

"Come out here, Sherburn! Come out and meet the man you've swindled. You're the houn' I'm after, and I'm a gwyne to have you, too!"

And so he went on, calling Sherburn everything he could lay his tongue to, and the whole street packed with people listening and laughing and going on. By-and-by a proud-looking man about fifty-five—and he was a heap the best dressed man in that town, too—steps out of the store, and the crowd drops back on each side to let him come. He says to Boggs, mighty ca'm and slow—he says:

"I'm tired of this; but I'll endure it till one o'clock. Till one o'clock, mind—no longer. If you open your mouth against me only once, after that time, you can't travel so far but I will find you."

Then he turns and goes in. The crowd looked mighty sober; nobody stirred, and there warn't no more laughing. Boggs rode off blackguarding Sherburn as loud as he could yell, all down the street; and pretty soon back he comes and stops before the store, still keeping it up. Some men crowded around him and tried to get him to shut up, but he wouldn't; they told him it would be one o'clock in about fifteen minutes, and so he *must* go home—he must go right away. But it didn't do no good. He cussed away, with all his might, and throwed his hat down in the mud and rode over it, and pretty soon away he went a-raging down the street again, with his gray hair a-flying. Everybody that could get a chance at him tried their best to coax him off of his horse so they could lock him up and get him sober; but it warn't no use—up the street he would tear again, and give Sherburn another cussing. By-and-by somebody says—

"Go for his daughter!—quick, go for his daughter; sometimes he'll listen to her. If anybody can persuade him, she can."

So somebody started on a run. I walked down street a ways, and stopped. In about five or ten minutes, here comes Boggs again—but not on his horse. He was a-reeling across the street towards me, bareheaded, with a friend on both sides of him aholt of his arms and hurrying him along. He was quiet, and looked uneasy; and he warn't hanging back any, but was doing some of the hurrying himself. Somebody sings out—

"Boggs!"

I looked over there to see who said it, and it was that Colonel Sherburn. He was standing perfectly still, in the street, and had a pistol raised in his right hand—

not aiming it, but holding it out with the barrel tilted up towards the sky. The same second I see a young girl coming on the run, and two men with her. Boggs and the men turned round, to see who called him, and when they see the pistol the men jumped to one side, and the pistol barrel come down slow and steady to a level—both barrels cocked. Boggs throws up both of his hands, and says, "O Lord, don't shoot!" Bang! goes the first shot, and he staggers back clawing at the air—bang! goes the second one, and he tumbles backwards onto the ground, heavy and solid, with his arms spread out. That young girl screamed out, and comes rushing, and down she throws herself on her father, crying, and saying, "Oh, he's killed him, he's killed him!" The crowd closed up around them, and shouldered and jammed one another, with their necks stretched, trying to see, and people on the inside trying to shove them back, and shouting, "Back, back! give him air, give him air!"

Colonel Sherburn he tossed his pistol onto the ground, and turned around on his heels and walked off.

They took Boggs to a little drug store, the crowd pressing around, just the same, and the whole town following, and I rushed and got a good place at the window, where I was close to him and could see in. They laid him on the floor, and put one large Bible under his head, and opened another one and spread it on his breast—but they tore open his shirt first, and I seen where one of the bullets went in. He made about a dozen long gasps, his breast lifting the Bible up when he drawed in his breath, and letting it down again when he breathed it out—and after that he laid still; he was dead. Then they pulled his daughter away from him, screaming and crying, and took her off. She was about sixteen, and very sweet and gentle-looking, but awful pale and scared.

Well, pretty soon the whole town was there, squirming and scrouging and pushing and shoving to get at the window and have a look, but people that had the places wouldn't give them up, and folks behind them was saying all the time, "Say, now, you've looked enough, you fellows; 'taint right and 'taint fair, for you to stay thar all the time, and never give nobody a chance; other folks has their rights as well as you."

There was considerable jawing back, so I slid out, thinking maybe there was going to be trouble. The streets was full, and everybody was excited. Everybody that seen the shooting was telling how it happened, and there was a big crowd packed around each one of these fellows, stretching their necks and listening. One long lanky man, with long hair and a big white fur stove-pipe hat on the back of his head, and a crooked-handled cane, marked out the places on the ground where Boggs stood, and where Sherburn stood, and the people following him around from one place to t'other and watching everything he done, and bobbing their heads to show they understood, and stooping a little and resting their hands on their thighs to watch him mark the places on the ground with his cane; and then he stood up straight and stiff where Sherburn had stood, frowning and having his hat-brim down over his eyes, and sung out, "Boggs!" and then fetched his cane down slow to a level, and says "Bang!" staggered backwards, says "Bang!" again, and fell down flat on his back. The people that had seen the thing said he done it perfect; said it was just exactly the way it all happened. Then as much as a dozen people got out their bottles and treated him.

Well, by-and-by somebody said Sherburn ought to be lynched. In about a minute everybody was saying it; so away they went, mad and yelling, and snatching down every clothes-line they come to, to do the hanging with.

The third night the house was crammed again—and they warn't new-comers, this time, but people that was at the show the other two nights. I stood by the duke at the door, and I see that every man that went in had his pockets bulging, or something muffled up under his coat—and I see it warn't no perfumery neither, not by a long sight. I smelt sickly eggs by the barrel, and rotten cabbages, and such things; and if I know the signs of a dead cat being around, and I bet I do, there was sixty-four of them went in. I shoved in there for a minute, but it was too various for me, I couldn't stand it. Well, when the place couldn't hold no more people, the duke he give a fellow a quarter and told him to tend door for him a minute, and then he started around for the stage door, I after him; but the minute we turned the corner and was in the dark, he says:

"Walk fast, now, till you get away from the houses, and then shin for the raft like the dickens was after you!"

I done it, and he done the same. We struck the raft at the same time, and in less than two seconds we was gliding down stream, all dark and still, and edging towards the middle of the river, nobody saying a word. I reckoned the poor king was in for a gaudy time of it with the audience; but nothing of the sort; pretty soon he crawls out from under the wigwam, and says:

"Well, how'd the old thing pan out this time, Duke?"

He hadn't been up town at all.

We never showed a light till we was about ten mile below that village. Then we lit up and had a supper, and the king and the duke fairly laughed their bones loose over the way they'd served them people. The duke says:

"Greenhorns, flatheads! *I* knew the first house would keep mum and let the rest of the town get roped in; and I knew they'd lay for us the third night, and consider it was *their* turn now. Well, it *is* their turn, and I'd give something to know how much they'd take for it. I *would* just like to know how they're putting in their opportunity. They can turn it into a picnic, if they want to—they brought plenty provisions."

Them rapscallions took in four hundred and sixty-five dollars in that three nights. I never see money hauled in by the wagonload like that, before.

By-and-by, when they was asleep and snoring, Jim says:

"Don't it 'sprise you, de way dem kings carries on, Huck?"

"No," I says, "it don't."

"Why don't it, Huck?"

"Well, it don't, because it's in the breed. I reckon they're all alike."

"But, Huck, dese kings o' ourn is regular rapscallions; dat's jist what dey is; dey's reglar rapscallions."

"Well, that's what I'm a-saying; all kings is mostly rapscallions, as fur as I can make out."

"Is dat so?"

"You read about them once—you'll see. Look at Henry the Eight; this'n 's a Sunday-School Superintendent to *him*. And look at Charles Second, and Louis Fourteen, and Louis Fifteen, and James Second, and Edward Second, and Richard Third, and forty more; besides all them Saxon heptarchies that used to rip around so in old times and raise Cain. My, you ought to seen old Henry the Eight when he was in bloom. He *was* a blossom. He used to marry a new wife every day, and chop off her head next morning. And he would do it just as indifferent as if he was ordering up eggs. 'Fetch up Nell Gwynn,' he says. They fetch her up. Next morning, 'Chop off her head!' And they chop it off. 'Fetch up Jane Shore,' he says; and up she comes. Next morning 'Chop off her head'—and they chop it off. 'Ring up Fair Rosamun.' Fair Rosamun answers the bell. Next morning, 'Chop off her head.' And he made every one of them tell him a tale every night; and he kept that up till he had hogged a thousand and one tales that way, and then he put them all in a book, and called it Domesday Book—which was a good name and stated the case. You don't know kings, Jim, but I know them; and this old rip of ourn is one of the cleanest I've struck in history. Well, Henry he takes a notion he wants to get up some trouble with this country. How does he go at it—give notice?—give the country a show? No. All of a sudden he heaves all the tea in Boston Harbor overboard, and whacks out a declaration of independence, and dares them to come on. That was *his* style—he never give anybody a chance. He had suspicions of his father, the Duke of Wellington. Well, what did he do?—ask him to show up? No—drownded him in a butt of mamsey, like a cat. Spose people left money laying around where he was—what did he do? He collared it. Spose he contracted to do a thing; and you paid him, and didn't set down there and see that he done it—what did he do? He always done the other thing. Spose he opened his mouth—what then? If he didn't shut it up powerful quick, he'd lose a lie, every time. That's the kind of a bug Henry was; and if we'd a had him along 'stead of our kings, he'd a fooled that town a heap worse than ourn done. I don't say that ourn is lambs, because they ain't, when you come right down to the cold facts; but they ain't nothing to *that* old ram, anyway. All I say is, kings is kings, and you got to make allowances. Take them all around, they're a mighty ornery lot. It's the way they're raised."

"But dis one do *smell* so like de nation, Huck."

"Well, they all do, Jim. *We* can't help the way a king smells; history don't tell no way."

"Now de duke, he's a tolerble likely man, in some ways."

"Yes, a duke's different. But not very different. This one's a middling hard lot, for a duke. When he's drunk, there ain't no near-sighted man could tell him from a king."

"Well, anyways, I doan' hanker for no mo' un um, Huck. Dese is all I kin stan'."

"It's the way I feel, too, Jim. But we've got them on our hands, and we got to remember what they are, and make allowances. Sometimes I wish we could hear of a country that's out of kings."

What was the use to tell Jim these warn't real kings and dukes? It wouldn't a done no good; and besides, it was just as I said; you couldn't tell them from the real kind.

I went to sleep, and Jim didn't call me when it was my turn. He often done that. When I waked up, just at day-break, he was setting there with his head down betwixt his knees, moaning and mourning to himself. I didn't take notice, nor let on. I knowed what it was about. He was thinking about his wife and his children, away up yonder, and he was low and homesick; because he hadn't ever been away from home before in his life; and I do believe he cared just as much for his people as white folks does for their'n. It don't seem natural, but I reckon it's so. He was often moaning and mourning that way, nights, when he judged I was asleep, and saying, "Po' little 'Lizabeth! po' little Johnny! It's mighty hard; I spec' I ain't ever gwyne to see you no mo', no mo'!" He was a mighty good nigger, Jim was.

But this time I somehow got to talking to him about his wife and young ones; and by-and-by he says:

"What makes me feel so bad dis time, 'uz bekase I hear sumpn over yonder on de bank like a whack, er a slam, while ago, en it mine me er de time I treat my little

'Lizabeth so ornery. She warn't on'y 'bout fo' year ole, en she tuck de sk'yarlet-fever, en had a powful rough spell; but she got well, en one day she was a-stannin' aroun', en I says to her, I says:

"Shet de do'."

"She never done it; jis' stood dah, kiner smilin' up at me. It make me mad; en I says agin, mighty loud, I says:

"'Doan' you hear me?—shet de do'!'

"She jis' stood de same way, kiner smilin' up. I was a-bilin'! I says:

"'I lay I *make* you mine!'

"En wid dat I fetch' her a slap side de head dat sont her a-sprawlin'. Den I went into de yuther room, en 'uz gone 'bout ten minutes; en when I come back, dah was dat do' a-stannin' open *yit*, en dat chile stannin' mos' right in it, a-lookin' down and mournin', en de tears runnin' down. My, but I *wuz* mad, I was agwyne for de chile, but jis' den—it was a do' dat open innerds—jis' den, 'long come de wind en slam it to, behine de chile, ker-*blam!*—en my lan', de chile never move'! My breff mos' hop outer me; en I feel so—so—I doan' know *how* I feel. I crope out, all a-tremblin', en crope aroun' en open de do' easy en slow, en poke my head in behine de chile, sof' en still, en all uv a sudden, I says *pow!* jis' as loud as I could yell: *She never budge!* Oh, Huck, I bust out a-cryin' en grab her up in my arms, en say, 'Oh, de po' little thing! de Lord God Amighty fogive po' ole Jim, kaze he never gwyne to fogive hisself as long's he live!' Oh, she was plumb deef en dumb, Huck, plumb deef en dumb—en I'd ben a-treat'n her so!"

CHAPTER XXIV

Next day, towards night, we laid up under a little willow tow-head out in the middle, where there was a village on each side of the river, and the duke and the king begun to lay out a plan for working them towns. Jim he spoke to the duke, and said he hoped it wouldn't take but a few hours, because it got mighty heavy and tiresome to him when he had to lay all day in the wigwam tied with the rope. You see, when we left him all alone we had to tie him, because if anybody happened on him all by himself and not tied, it wouldn't look much like he was a runaway nigger, you know. So the duke said it *was* kind of hard to have to lay roped all day, and he'd cipher out some way to get around it.

He was uncommon bright, the duke was, and he soon struck it. He dressed Jim up in King Lear's outfit—it was a long curtain-calico gown, and a white horse-hair wig and whiskers; and then he took his theatre-paint and painted Jim's face and hands and ears and neck all over a dead dull solid blue, like a man that's been drownded nine days. Blamed if he warn't the horriblest looking outrage I ever see. Then the duke took and wrote out a sign on a shingle so—

Sick Arab—but harmless when not out of his head.

And he nailed that shingle to a lath, and stood the lath up four or five foot in front of the wigwam. Jim was satisfied. He said it was a sight better than laying tied a couple of years every day and trembling all over every time there was a sound. The duke told him to make himself free and easy, and if anybody ever come meddling around, he must hop out of the wigwam, and carry on a little, and fetch a howl or two like a wild beast, and he reckoned they would light out and leave him alone. Which was sound enough judgment; but you take the average man, and he wouldn't wait for him to howl. Why, he didn't only look like he was dead, he looked considerable more than that.

These rapscallions wanted to try the Nonesuch again, because there was so much money in it, but they judged it wouldn't be safe, because maybe the news might a worked along down by this time. They couldn't hit no project that suited, exactly; so at last the duke said he reckoned he'd lay off and work his brains an hour or two and see if he couldn't put up something on the Arkansaw village; and the king he allowed he would drop over to t'other village, without any plan, but just trust in Providence to lead him the profitable way—meaning the devil, I reckon. We had all bought store clothes where we stopped last; and now the king put his'n on, and he told me to put mine on. I done it, of course. The king's duds was all black, and he did look real swell and starchy. I never knowed how clothes could change a body before. Why, before, he looked like the orneriest old rip that ever was; but now, when he'd take off his new white beaver and make a bow and do a smile, he looked that grand and good and pious that you'd say he had walked right out of the ark, and maybe was old Leviticus himself. Jim cleaned up the canoe, and I got my paddle ready. There was a big steamboat laying at the shore away up under the point, about three mile above town—been there a couple of hours, taking on freight. Says the king:

"Seein' how I'm dressed, I reckon maybe I better arrive down from St. Louis or Cincinnati, or some other big place. Go for the steamboat, Huckleberry; we'll come down to the village on her."

I didn't have to be ordered twice, to go and take a steamboat ride. I fetched the shore a half a mile above the village, and then went scooting along the bluff bank in the easy water. Pretty soon we come to a nice innocent-looking young country jake setting on a log swabbing the sweat off of his face, for it was powerful warm weather; and he had a couple of big carpet-bags by him.

"Run her nose in shore," says the king. I done it. "Wher' you bound for, young man?"

"For the steamboat; going to Orleans."

"Git aboard," says the king. "Hold on a minute, my servant 'll he'p you with them bags. Jump out and he'p the gentleman, Adolphus"—meaning me, I see.

I done so, and then we all three started on again. The young chap was mighty thankful; said it was tough work toting his baggage such weather. He asked the king where he was going, and the king told him he'd come down the river and landed at the other village this morning, and now he was going up a few mile to see an old friend on a farm up there. The young fellow says:

"When I first see you, I says to myself, 'It's Mr. Wilks, sure, and he come mighty near getting here in time.' But then I says again, 'No, I reckon it ain't him or else he wouldn't be paddling up the river.' You *ain't* him, are you?"

"No, my name's Blodgett—Elexander Blodgett—*Reverend* Elexander Blodgett, I spose I must say, as I'm one o' the Lord's poor servants. But still I'm jist as able to be sorry for Mr. Wilks for not arriving in time, all the same, if he's missed anything by it—which I hope he hasn't."

"Well, he don't miss any property by it, because he'll get that all right; but he's missed seeing his brother Peter die—which he mayn't mind, nobody can tell as to that—but his brother would a give anything in this world to see *him* before he died; never talked about nothing else all these three weeks; hadn't seen him since they was boys together—and hadn't ever seen his brother William at all—that's the deef and dumb one—William ain't more than thirty or thirty-five. Peter and George was the only ones that come out here; George was the married brother; him and his wife both died last year. Harvey and William's the only ones that's left now; and, as I was saying, they haven't got here in time."

"Did anybody send 'em word?"

"Oh, yes; a month or two ago, when Peter was first took; because Peter said then that he sorter felt like he warn't going to get well this time. You see, he was pretty old, and George's g'yirls was too young to be much company for him, except Mary Jane the red-headed one; and so he was kinder lonesome after George and his wife died, and didn't seem to care much to live. He most desperately wanted to see Harvey—and William too, for that matter—because he was one of them kind that can't bear to make a will. He left a letter behind for Harvey, and said he'd told in it where his money was hid, and how he wanted the rest of the property divided up so George's g'yirls would be all right—for George didn't leave nothing. And that letter was all they could get him to put a pen to."

"Why do you reckon Harvey don't come? Wher' does he live?"

"Oh, he lives in England—Sheffield—preaches there—hasn't ever been in this country. He hasn't had any too much time—and besides he mightn't a got the letter at all, you know."

"Too bad, too bad he couldn't a lived to see his brothers, poor soul. You going to Orleans, you say?"

"Yes, but that ain't only a part of it. I'm going in a ship, next Wednesday, for Ryo Janeero, where my uncle lives."

"It's a pretty long journey. But it'll be lovely; I wisht I was agoing. Is Mary Jane the oldest? How old is the others?"

"Mary Jane's nineteen, Susan's fifteen, and Joanna's about fourteen—that's the one that gives herself to good works and has a hare-lip."

"Poor things! to be left alone in the cold world so."

"Well, they could be worse off. Old Peter had friends, and they ain't going to let them come to no harm. There's Hobson, the Babtis' preacher; and Deacon Lot Hovey, and Ben Rucker, and Abner Shackleford, and Levi Bell, the lawyer; and Dr. Robinson, and their wives, and the widow Bartley, and—well, there's a lot of them; but these are the ones that Peter was thickest with, and used to write about sometimes, when he wrote home; so Harvey 'll know where to look for friends when he gets here."

Well, the old man he went on asking questions till he just fairly emptied that young fellow. Blamed if he didn't inquire about everybody and everything in that blessed town, and all about all the Wilkses; and about Peter's business—which was a tanner; and about George's—which was a carpenter; and about Harvey's—which was a dissentering minister; and so on, and so on. Then he says:

"What did you want to walk all the way up to the steamboat for?"

"Because she's a big Orleans boat, and I was afeard she mightn't stop there. When they're deep they won't stop for a hail. A Cincinnati boat will, but this is a St. Louis one."

"Was Peter Wilks well off?"

"Oh, yes, pretty well off. He had houses and land, and it's reckoned he left three or four thousand in cash hid up som'ers."

"When did you say he died?"

"I didn't say, but it was last night."

"Funeral to-morrow, likely?"

"Yes, 'bout the middle of the day."

"Well, it's all terrible sad; but we've all got to go, one time or another. So what we want to do is to be prepared; then we're all right."

"Yes, sir, it's the best way. Ma used to always say that."

When we struck the boat, she was about done loading, and pretty soon she got off. The king never said nothing about going aboard, so I lost my ride, after all. When the boat was gone, the king made me paddle up another mile to a lonesome place, and then he got ashore, and says:

"Now hustle back, right off, and fetch the duke up here, and the new carpet-bags. And if he's gone over to t'other side, go over there and git him. And tell him to git himself up regardless. Shove along, now."

I see what *he* was up to; but I never said nothing, of course. When I got back with the duke, we hid the canoe and then they set down on a log, and the king told him everything, just like the young fellow had said it—every last word of it. And all the time he was a doing it, he tried to talk like an Englishman; and he done it pretty well too, for a slouch. I can't imitate him, and so I ain't agoing to try to; but he really done it pretty good. Then he says:

"How are you on the deef and dumb, Bilgewater?"

The duke said, leave him alone for that; said he had played a deef and dumb person on the histrionic boards. So then they waited for a steamboat.

About the middle of the afternoon a couple of little boats come along, but they didn't come from high enough up the river; but at last there was a big one, and they hailed her. She sent out her yawl, and we went aboard, and she was from Cincinnati; and when they found we only wanted to go four or five mile, they was booming mad, and give us a cussing, and said they wouldn't land us. But the king was ca'm. He says:

"If gentlemen kin afford to pay a dollar a mile apiece, to be took on and put off in a yawl, a steamboat kin afford to carry 'em, can't it?"

So they softened down and said it was all right; and when we got to the village, they yawled us ashore. About two dozen men flocked down, when they see the yawl a coming; and when the king says—

"Kin any of you gentlemen tell me wher' Mr. Peter Wilks lives?" they give a glance at one another, and nodded their heads, as much as to say, "What d' I tell you?" Then one of them says, kind of soft and gentle:

"I'm sorry, sir, but the best we can do is to tell you where he *did* live yesterday evening."

Sudden as winking, the ornery old cretur went all to smash, and fell up against the man, and put his chin on his shoulder, and cried down his back, and says:

"Alas, alas, our poor brother—gone, and we never got to see him; oh, it's too, *too* hard!"

Then he turns around, blubbering, and makes a lot of idiotic signs to the duke on his hands, and blamed if *he* didn't drop a carpet-bag and bust out a-crying. If they warn't the beatenest lot, them two frauds, that ever I struck.

Well, the men gethered around, and sympathized with them, and said all sorts of kind things to them, and carried their carpet-bags up the hill for them, and let them lean on them and cry, and told the king all about his brother's last moments, and the king he told it all over again on his hands to the duke, and both of them took on about that dead tanner like they'd lost the twelve disciples. Well, if ever I struck anything like it, I'm a nigger. It was enough to make a body ashamed of the human race.

CHAPTER XXV

The news was all over town in two minutes, and you could see the people tearing down on the run, from every which way, some of them putting on their coats as they come. Pretty soon we was in the middle of a crowd, and the noise of the tramping was like a soldier-march. The windows and dooryards was full; and every minute somebody would say, over a fence:

"Is it *them*?"

And somebody trotting along with the gang would answer back and say,

"You bet it is."

When we got to the house, the street in front of it was packed, and the three girls was standing in the door. Mary Jane *was* red-headed, but that don't make no difference, she was most awful beautiful, and her face and her eyes was all lit up like glory, she was so glad her uncles was come. The king he spread his arms, and Mary Jane she jumped for them, and the hare-lip jumped for the duke, and there they *had* it! Everybody most, leastways women, cried for joy to see them meet again at last and have such good times.

Then the king he hunched the duke, private—I see him do it—and then he looked around and see the coffin, over in the corner on two chairs; so then, him and the duke, with a hand across each other's shoulder, and t'other hand to their eyes, walked slow and solemn over there, everybody dropping back to give them room, and all the talk and noise stopping, people saying "Sh!" and all the men taking their hats off and drooping their heads, so you could a heard a pin fall. And when they got there, they bent over and looked in the coffin, and took one sight, and then they bust out a crying so you could a heard them to Orleans, most; and then they put their arms around each other's necks, and hung their chins over each other's shoulders; and then for three minutes, or maybe four, I never see two men leak the way they done. And mind you, everybody was doing the same; and the place was that damp I never see anything like it. Then one of them got on one side of the coffin, and t'other on t'other side, and they kneeled down and rested their foreheads on the coffin, and let on to pray all to theirselves. Well, when it come to that, it worked the crowd like you never see anything like it, and so everybody broke down and went to sobbing right out loud—the poor girls, too; and every woman, nearly, went up to the girls, without saying a word, and kissed them, solemn, on the forehead, and then put their hand on their head, and looked up towards the sky, with the tears running down, and then busted out and went off sobbing and swabbing, and give the next woman a show. I never see anything so disgusting.

Well, by-and-by the king he gets up and comes forward a little, and works himself up and slobbers out a speech, all full of tears and flapdoodle about it's being a sore trial for him and his poor brother to lose the diseased, and to miss seeing diseased alive, after the long journey of four thousand mile, but it's a trial that's sweetened and sanctified to us by this dear sympathy and these holy tears, and so he thanks them out of his heart and out of his brother's heart, because out of their mouths they can't, words being too weak and cold, and all that kind of rot and slush, till it was just sickening; and then he blubbers out a pious goody-goody Amen, and turns himself loose and goes to crying fit to bust.

And the minute the words was out of his mouth somebody over in the crowd struck up the doxolojer, and everybody joined in with all their might, and it just warmed you up and made you feel as good as church letting out. Music *is* a good thing; and after all that soul-butter and hogwash, I never see it freshen up things so, and sound so honest and bully.

Then the king begins to work his jaw again, and says how him and his nieces would be glad if a few of the main principal friends of the family would take supper here with them this evening, and help set up with the ashes of the diseased; and says if his poor brother laying yonder could speak, he knows who he would name, for they was names that was very dear to him, and mentioned often in his letters; and so he will name the same, to-wit, as follows, vizz:—Rev. Mr. Hobson, and Deacon Lot Hovey, and Mr. Ben Rucker, and Abner Shackleford, and Levi Bell, and Dr. Robinson, and their wives, and the widow Bartley.

Rev. Hobson and Dr. Robinson was down to the end of the town, a-hunting together; that is, I mean the doctor was shipping a sick man to t'other world, and the preacher was pinting him right. Lawyer Bell was away up to Louisville on some business. But the rest was on hand, and so they all come and shook hands with the king and thanked him and talked to him; and then they shook hands with the duke, and didn't say nothing but just kept a-smiling and bobbing their heads like a passel of sapheads whilst he made all sorts of signs with his hands and said "Goo-goo—goo-goo-goo," all the time, like a baby that can't talk.

So the king he blatted along, and managed to inquire about pretty much everybody and dog in town, by his name, and mentioned all sorts of little things that happened one time or another in the town, or to George's family, or to Peter; and he always let on that Peter wrote him the things, but that was a lie, he got every blessed one of them out of that young flathead that we canoed up to the steamboat.

Then Mary Jane she fetched the letter her father left behind, and the king he read it out loud and cried over it. It give the dwelling-house and three thousand dollars, gold, to the girls; and it give the tanyard (which was doing a good business), along with some other houses and land (worth about seven thousand), and three thousand dollars in gold to Harvey and William, and told where the six thousand cash was hid, down cellar. So these two frauds said they'd go and fetch it up, and have everything square and above-board; and told me to come with a candle. We shut the cellar door behind us, and when they found the bag they spilt it out on the floor, and it was a lovely sight, all them yaller-boys. My, the way the king's eyes did shine! He slaps the duke on the shoulder, and says:

"Oh, *this* ain't bully, nor noth'n! Oh, no, I reckon not! Why, Biljy, it beats the Nonesuch, *don't* it!"

The duke allowed it did. They pawed the yaller-boys, and sifted them through their fingers and let them jingle down on the floor; and the king says:

"It ain't no use talkin'; bein' brothers to a rich dead man, and representatives of furrin heirs that's got left, is the line for you and me, Bilge. Thish-yer comes of trust'n to Providence. It's the best way, in the long run. I've tried 'em all, and ther' ain't no better way."

Most everybody would a been satisfied with the pile, and took it on trust; but no, they must count it. So they counts it, and it comes out four hundred and fifteen dollars short. Says the king:

"Dern him, I wonder what he done with that four hundred and fifteen dollars?"

They worried over that a while, and ransacked all around for it. Then the duke says:

"Well, he was a pretty sick man, and likely he made a mistake—I reckon that's the way of it. The best way's to let it go, and keep still about it. We can spare it."

"Oh, shucks, yes, we can *spare* it. I don't k'yer noth'n 'bout that—it's the *count* I'm thinkin' about. We want to be awful square and open and above-board, here, you know. We want to lug this h-yer money up stairs and count it before everybody—then ther' ain't noth'n suspicious. But when the dead man says ther's six thous'n dollars, you know, we don't want to—"

"Hold on," says the duke. "Less make up the deffisit"—and he begun to haul out yaller-boys out of his pocket.

"It's a most amaz'n' good idea, duke—you *have* got a rattlin' clever head on you," says the king. "Blest if the old Nonesuch ain't a heppin' us out agin"—and *he* begun to haul out yaller-jackets and stack them up.

It most busted them, but they made up the six thousand clean and clear.

"Say," says the duke, "I got another idea. Let's go up stairs and count this money, and then take and *give it to the girls*."

"Good land, duke, lemme hug you! It's the most dazzling idea 'at ever a man struck. You have cert'nly got the most astonishin' head I ever see. Oh, this is the boss dodge, ther' ain't no mistake 'bout it. Let 'em fetch along their suspicions now, if they want to—this'll lay 'em out."

When we got up stairs, everybody gethered around the table, and the king he counted it and stacked it up, three hundred dollars in a pile—twenty elegant little piles. Everybody looked hungry at it, and licked their chops. Then they raked it into the bag again, and I see the king begin to swell himself up for another speech. He says:

"Friends all, my poor brother that lays yonder, has done generous by them that's left behind in the vale of sorrers. He has done generous by these-'yer poor little lambs that he loved and sheltered, and that's left fatherless and motherless. Yes, and we that knowed him, knows that he would a done *more* generous by 'em if he hadn't ben afeard o' woundin' his dear William and me. Now, *wouldn't* he? Ther' ain't no question 'bout it, in *my* mind. Well, then—what kind o' brothers would it be, that 'd stand in his way at sech a time? And what kind o' uncles would it be that 'd rob—yes, *rob*—sech poor sweet lambs as these 'at he loved so, at sech a time? If I know William—and I *think* I do—he—well, I'll jest ask him." He turns around and begins to make a lot of signs to the duke with his hands; and the duke he looks at him stupid and leather-headed a while, then all of a sudden he seems to catch his meaning, and jumps for the king, goo-gooing with all his might for joy, and hugs him about fifteen times before he lets up. Then the king says, "I knowed it; I reckon *that* 'll convince anybody the way *he* feels about it. Here, Mary Jane, Susan, Joanner, take the money—take it *all*. It's the gift of him that lays yonder, cold but joyful."

Mary Jane she went for him, Susan and the hare-lip went for the duke, and then such another hugging and kissing I never see yet. And everybody crowded up with the tears in their eyes, and most shook the hands off of them frauds, saying all the time:

"You *dear* good souls!—how *lovely!*—how *could* you!"

Well, then, pretty soon all hands got to talking about the diseased again, and how good he was, and what a loss he was, and all that; and before long a big iron-jawed man worked himself in there from outside, and stood a listening and looking, and not saying anything; and nobody saying anything to him either, because the king was talking and they was all busy listening. The king was saying—in the middle of something he'd started in on—

"—they bein' partickler friends o' the diseased. That's why they're invited here this evenin'; but to-morrow we want *all* to come—everybody; for he respected everybody, he liked everybody, and so it's fitten that his funeral orgies sh'd be public."

And so he went a-mooning on and on, liking to hear himself talk, and every little while he fetched in his funeral orgies again, till the duke he couldn't stand it no more; so he writes on a little scrap of paper, "*obsequies*, you old fool," and folds it up and goes to goo-gooing and reaching it over people's heads to him. The king he reads it, and puts it in his pocket, and says:

"Poor William, afflicted as he is, his *heart's* aluz right. Asks me to invite everybody to come to the funeral—wants me to make 'em all welcome. But he needn't a worried—it was jest what I was at."

Then he weaves along again, perfectly ca'm, and goes to dropping in his funeral orgies again every now and then, just like he done before. And when he done it the third time, he says:

"I say orgies, not because it's the common term, because it ain't—obsequies bein' the common term—but because orgies is the right term. Obsequies ain't used in England no more, now—it's gone out. We say orgies now, in England. Orgies is better, because it means the thing you're after, more exact. It's a word that's made up out'n the Greek *orgo*, outside, open, abroad; and the Hebrew *jeesum*, to plant, cover up, hence in*ter*. So, you see, funeral orgies is an open er public funeral."

He was the *worst* I ever struck. Well, the iron-jawed man he laughed right in his face. Everybody was shocked. Everybody says, "Why *doctor!*" and Abner Shackleford says:

"Why, Robinson, hain't you heard the news? This is Harvey Wilks."

The king he smiled eager, and shoved out his flapper, and says:

"*Is* it my poor brother's dear good friend and physician? I—"

"Keep your hands off of me!" says the doctor. "*You* talk like an Englishman—*don't* you? It's the worse imitation I ever heard. *You* Peter Wilks's brother. You're a fraud, that's what you are!"

Well, how they all took on! They crowded around the doctor, and tried to quiet him down, and tried to explain to him, and tell him how Harvey'd showed in forty ways that he *was* Harvey, and knowed everybody by name, and the names of the very dogs, and begged and *begged* him not to hurt Harvey's feelings and the poor girls' feelings, and all that; but it warn't no use, he stormed right along, and said any man that pretended to be an Englishman and couldn't imitate the lingo no better than what he did, was a fraud and a liar. The poor girls was hanging to the king and crying; and all of a sudden the doctor ups and turns on *them*. He says:

"I was your father's friend, and I'm your friend; and I warn you *as* a friend, and an honest one, that wants to protect you and keep you out of harm and trouble, to turn your backs on that scoundrel, and have nothing to do with him, the ignorant tramp, with his idiotic Greek and Hebrew as he calls it. He is the thinnest kind of an impostor—has come here with a lot of empty names and facts which he has picked up somewheres, and you take them for *proofs*, and are helped to fool yourselves by these foolish friends here, who ought to know better. Mary Jane Wilks, you know me for your friend, and for your unselfish friend, too. Now listen to me; turn this pitiful rascal out—I *beg* you to do it. Will you?"

Mary Jane straightened herself up, and my, but she was handsome! She says:

"*Here* is my answer." She hove up the bag of money and put it in the king's hands, and says, "Take this six thousand dollars, and invest it for me and my sisters any way you want to, and don't give us no receipt for it."

Then she put her arm around the king on one side, and Susan and the hare-lip done the same on the other. Everybody clapped their hands and stomped on the floor like a perfect storm, whilst the king held up his head and smiled proud. The doctor says:

"All right, I wash *my* hands of the matter. But I warn you all that a time's coming when you're going to feel sick whenever you think of this day"—and away he went.

"All right, doctor," says the king, kinder mocking him, "we'll try and get 'em to send for you"—which made them all laugh, and they said it was a prime good hit.

CHAPTER XXVI

Well, when they was all gone, the king he asks Mary Jane how they was off for spare rooms, and she said she had one spare room, which would do for Uncle William, and she'd give her own room to Uncle Harvey, which was a little bigger, and she would turn into the room with her sisters and sleep on a cot; and up garret was a little cubby, with a pallet in it. The king said the cubby would do for his valley—meaning me.

So Mary Jane took us up, and she showed them their rooms, which was plain but nice. She said she'd have her frocks and a lot of other traps took out of her room if they was in Uncle Harvey's way, but he said they warn't. The frocks was hung along the wall, and before them was a curtain made out of calico that hung down to the floor. There was an old hair trunk in one corner, and a guitar box in another, and all sorts of little knick-knacks and jimcracks around, like girls brisken up a room with. The king said it was all the more homely and more pleasanter for these fixings, and so don't disturb them. The duke's room was pretty small, but plenty good enough, and so was my cubby.

That night they had a big supper, and all them men and women was there, and I stood behind the king and the duke's chairs and waited on them, and the niggers waited on the rest. Mary Jane she set at the head of the table, with Susan along side of her, and said how bad the biscuits was, and how mean the preserves was, and how ornery and tough the fried chickens was—and all that kind of rot, the way women always do for to force out compliments; and the people all knowed everything was tip-top, and said so—said "How *do* you get biscuits to brown so nice?" and "Where, for the land's sake *did* you get these amaz'n pickles?" and all that kind of humbug talky-talk, just the way people always does at a supper, you know.

And when it was all done, me and the hare-lip had supper in the kitchen off of the leavings, whilst the others was helping the niggers clean up the things. The hare-lip she got to pumping me about England, and blest if I didn't think the ice was getting mighty thin, sometimes. She says:

"Did you ever see the king?"

"Who? William Fourth? Well, I bet I have—he goes to our church." I knowed he was dead years ago, but I never let on. So when I says he goes to our church, she says:

"What—regular?"

"Yes—regular. His pew's right over opposite ourn—on 'tother side the pulpit."

"I thought he lived in London?"

"Well, he does. Where *would* he live?"

"But I thought *you* lived in Sheffield?"

I see I was up a stump. I had to let on to get choked with a chicken bone, so as to get time to think how to get down again. Then I says:

"I mean he goes to our church regular when he's in Sheffield. That's only in the summer-time, when he comes there to take the sea baths."

"Why, how you talk—Sheffield ain't on the sea."

"Well, who said it was?"

"Why, you did."

"I *didn't*, nuther."

"You did!"

"I didn't."

"You did."

"I never said nothing of the kind."

"Well, what *did* you say, then?"

"Said he come to take the sea *baths*—that's what I said."

"Well, then! how's he going to take the sea baths if it ain't on the sea?"

"Looky here," I says; "did you ever see any Congress water?"

"Yes."

"Well, did you have to go to Congress to get it?"

"Why, no."

"Well, neither does William Fourth have to go to the sea to get a sea bath."

"How does he get it, then?"

"Gets it the way people down here gets Congress water—in barrels. There in the palace at Sheffield they've got furnaces, and he wants his water hot. They can't bile that amount of water away off there at the sea. They haven't got no conveniences for it."

"Oh, I see, now. You might a said that in the first place and saved time."

When she said that, I see I was out of the woods again, and so I was comfortable and glad. Next, she says:

"Do you go to church, too?"

"Yes—regular."

"Where do you set?"

"Why, in our pew."

"*Whose* pew?"

"Why, *ourn*—your Uncle Harvey's."

"His'n? What does *he* want with a pew?"

"Wants it to set in. What did you *reckon* he wanted with it?"

"Why, I thought he'd be in the pulpit."

Rot him, I forgot he was a preacher. I see I was up a stump again, so I played another chicken bone and got another think. Then I says:

"Blame it, do you suppose there ain't but one preacher to a church?"

"Why, what do they want with more?"

"What!—to preach before a king? I never see such a girl as you. They don't have no less than seventeen."

"Seventeen! My land! Why, I wouldn't set out such a string as that, not if I *never* got to glory. It must take 'em a week."

"Shucks, they don't *all* of 'em preach the same day—only *one* of 'em."

"Well, then, what does the rest of 'em do?"

"Oh, nothing much. Loll around, pass the plate—and one thing or another. But mainly they don't do nothing."

"Well, then, what are they *for*?"

"Why, they're for *style*. Don't you know nothing?"

"Well, I don't *want* to know no such foolishness as that. How is servants treated in England? Do they treat 'em better 'n we treat our niggers?"

"*No*! A servant ain't nobody there. They treat them worse than dogs."

"Don't they give 'em holidays, the way we do, Christmas and New Year's week, and Fourth of July?"

"Oh, just listen! A body could tell *you* hain't ever been to England, by that. Why, Hare-l—why, Joanna, they never see a holiday from year's end to year's end; never go to the circus, nor theatre, nor nigger shows, nor nowheres."

"Nor church?"

"Nor church."

"But *you* always went to church."

Well, I was gone up again. I forgot I was the old man's servant. But next minute I whirled in on a kind of an explanation how a valley was different from a common servant, and *had* to go to church whether he wanted to or not, and set with the family, on account of it's being the law. But I didn't do it pretty good and when I got done I see she warn't satisfied. She says:

"Honest injun, now, hain't you been telling me a lot of lies?"

"Honest injun," says I.

"None of it at all?"

"None of it at all. Not a lie in it," says I.

"Lay your hand on this book and say it."

I see it warn't nothing but a dictionary, so I laid my hand on it and said it. So then she looked a little better satisfied, and says:

"Well, then, I'll believe some of it; but I hope to gracious if I'll believe the rest."

"What is it you won't believe, Joe?" says Mary Jane, stepping in with Susan behind her. "It ain't right nor kind for you to talk so to him, and him a stranger and so far from his people. How would you like to be treated so?"

"That's always your way, Maim—always sailing in to help somebody before they're hurt. I hain't done nothing to him. He's told some stretchers, I reckon; and I said I wouldn't swallow it all; and that's every bit and grain I *did* say. I reckon he can stand a little thing like that, can't he?"

"I don't care whether 'twas little or whether 'twas big, he's here in our house and a stranger, and it wasn't good of you to say it. If you was in his place, it would make you feel ashamed; and so you oughtn't to say a thing to another person that will make *them* feel ashamed."

"Why, Maim, he said—"

"It don't make no difference what he *said*—that ain't the thing. The thing is for you to treat him *kind*, and not be saying things to make him remember he ain't in his own country and amongst his own folks."

I says to myself, *this* is a girl that I'm letting that old reptle rob her of her money!

Then Susan *she* waltzed in; and if you'll believe me, she did give Hare-lip hark from the tomb!

Says I to myself, And this is *another* one that I'm letting him rob her of her money!

Then Mary Jane she took another inning, and went in sweet and lovely again—which was her way—but when she got done there warn't hardly anything left o' poor Hare-lip. So she hollered.

"All right, then," says the other girls, "you just ask his pardon."

She done it, too. And she done it beautiful. She done it so beautiful it was good to hear; and I wished I could tell her a thousand lies, so she could do it again.

I says to myself, this is *another* one that I'm letting him rob her of her money. And when she got through, they all jest laid theirselves out to make me feel at home and know I was amongst friends. I felt so ornery and low down and mean, that I says to myself, My mind's made up; I'll hive that money for them or bust.

So then I lit out—for bed, I said, meaning some time or another. When I got by myself, I went to thinking the thing over. I says to myself, shall I go to that doctor, private, and blow on these frauds? No—that won't do. He might tell who told him; then the king and the duke would make it warm for me. Shall I go, private, and tell Mary Jane? No—I dasn't do it. Her face would give them a hint, sure; they've got the money, and they'd slide right out and get away with it. If she was to fetch in help, I'd get mixed up in the business, before it was done with, I judge. No, there ain't no good way but one. I got to steal that money, somehow; and I got to steal it some way that they won't suspicion that I done it. They've got a good thing, here; and they ain't agoing to leave till they've played this family and this town for all they're worth, so I'll find a chance time enough. I'll steal it, and hide it; and by-and-by, when I'm away down the river, I'll write a letter and tell Mary Jane where it's hid. But I better hive it to-night, if I can, because the doctor maybe hasn't let up as much as he lets on he has; he might scare them out of here, yet.

So, thinks I, I'll go and search them rooms. Up stairs the hall was dark, but I found the duke's room, and started to paw around it with my hands; but I recollected it wouldn't be much like the king to let anybody else take care of that money but his own self; so then I went to his room and begun to paw around there. But I see I couldn't do nothing without a candle, and I dasn't light one, of course. So I judged I'd got to do the other thing—lay for them, and eavesdrop. About that time, I hears their footsteps coming, and was going to skip under the bed; I reached for it, but it wasn't where I thought it would be; but I touched the curtain that hid Mary Jane's frocks, so I jumped in behind that and snuggled in amongst the gowns, and stood there perfectly still.

They come in and shut the door; and the first thing the duke done was to get down and look under the bed. Then I was glad I hadn't found the bed when I wanted it. And yet, you know, it's kind of natural to hide under the bed when you are up to anything private. They sets down, then, and the king says:

"Well, what is it? and cut it middlin' short, because it's better for us to be down there a whoopin'-up the mournin', than up here givin' 'em a chance to talk us over."

"Well, this is it, Capet. I ain't easy; I ain't comfortable. That doctor lays on my mind. I wanted to know your plans. I've got a notion, and I think it's a sound one."

"What is it, duke?"

"That we better glide out of this, before three in the morning, and clip it down the river with what we've got. Specially, seeing we got it so easy—*given* back to us, flung at our heads, as you may say, when of course we allowed to have to steal it back. I'm for knocking off and lighting out."

That made me feel pretty bad. About an hour or two ago, it would a been a little different, but now it made me feel bad and disappointed. The king rips out and says:

"What! And not sell out the rest o' the property? March off like a passel o' fools and leave eight or nine thous'n' dollars' worth o' property layin' around jest sufferin' to be scooped in?—and all good salable stuff, too."

The duke he grumbled; said the bag of gold was enough, and he didn't want to go no deeper—didn't want to rob a lot of orphans of *everything* they had.

"Why, how you talk!" says the king. "We shan't rob 'em of nothing at all but jest this money. The people that *buys* the property is the suff'rers; because as soon's it's found out 'at we didn't own it—which won't be long after we've slid—the sale won't be valid, and it'll all go back to the estate. These-yer orphans 'll git their house back agin, and that's enough for *them*; they're young and spry, and k'n easy earn a livin'. *They* ain't agoing to suffer. Why, jest think—there's thous'n's and thous'n's that ain't nigh so well off. Bless you, *they* ain't got noth'n to complain of."

Well, the king he talked him blind; so at last he give in, and said all right, but said he believed it was blame foolishness to stay, and that doctor hanging over them. But the king says:

"Cuss the doctor! What do we k'yer for *him*? Hain't we got all the fools in town on our side? and ain't that a big enough majority in any town?"

So they got ready to go down stairs again. The duke says:

"I don't think we put that money in a good place."

That cheered me up. I'd begun to think I warn't going to get a hint of no kind to help me. The king says:

"Why?"

"Because Mary Jane 'll be in mourning from this out; and first you know the nigger that does up the rooms will get an order to box these duds up and put 'em away; and do you reckon a nigger can run across money and not borrow some of it?"

"Your head's level agin, duke," says the king; and he come a fumbling under the curtain two or three foot from where I was. I stuck tight to the wall, and kept mighty still, though quivery; and I wondered what them fellows would say to me if they catched me; and I tried to think what I'd better do if they did catch me. But the king he got the bag before I could think more than about a half a thought, and he never suspicioned I was around. They took and shoved the bag through a rip in the straw tick that was under the feather bed, and crammed it in a foot or two amongst the straw and said it was all right, now, because a nigger only makes up the feather bed, and don't turn over the straw tick only about twice a year, and so it warn't in no danger of getting stole, now.

But I knowed better. I had it out of there before they was half-way down stairs. I groped along up to my cubby, and hid it there till I could get a chance to do better. I judged I better hide it outside of the house somewheres, because if they missed it they would give the house a good ransacking. I knowed that very well. Then I turned in, with my clothes all on; but I couldn't a gone to sleep, if I'd a wanted to, I was in such a sweat to get through with the business. By-and-by I heard the king and the duke come up; so I rolled off of my pallet and laid with my chin at the top of my ladder and waited to see if anything was going to happen. But nothing did.

So I held on till all the late sounds had quit and the early ones hadn't begun, yet; and then I slipped down the ladder.

CHAPTER XXVII

I crept to their doors and listened; they was snoring, so I tiptoed along, and got down stairs all right. There warn't a sound anywheres. I peeped through a crack of the dining-room door, and see the men that was watching the corpse all sound asleep on their chairs. The door was open into the parlor, where the corpse was laying, and there was a candle in both rooms. I passed along, and the parlor door was open; but I see there warn't nobody in there but the remainders of Peter; so I shoved on by; but the front door was locked, and the key wasn't there. Just then I heard somebody coming down the stairs, back behind me. I run in the parlor, and took a swift look around, and the only place I see to hide the bag was in the coffin. The lid was shoved along about a foot, showing the dead man's face down in there, with a wet cloth over it, and his shroud on. I tucked the money-bag in under the lid, just down beyond where his hands was crossed, which made me creep, they was so cold, and then I run back across the room and in behind the door.

The person coming was Mary Jane. She went to the coffin, very soft, and kneeled down and looked in; then she put up her handkerchief and I see she begun to cry, though I couldn't hear her, and her back was to me. I slid out, and as I passed the dining-room I thought I'd make sure them watchers hadn't seen me; so I looked through the crack and everything was all right. They hadn't stirred.

I slipped up to bed, feeling ruther blue, on accounts of the thing playing out that way after I had took so much trouble and run so much resk about it. Says I, if it could stay where it is, all right; because when we get down the river a hundred mile or two, I could write back to Mary Jane, and she could dig him up again and get it; but that ain't the thing that's going to happen; the thing that's going to happen is, the money 'll be found when they come to screw on the lid. Then the king 'll get it again, and it 'll be a long day before he gives anybody another chance to smouch it from him. Of course I *wanted* to slide down and get it out of there, but I dasn't try it. Every minute it was getting earlier, now, and pretty soon some of them watchers would begin to stir, and I might get catched—catched with six thousand dollars in my hands that nobody hadn't hired me to take care of. I don't wish to be mixed up in no such business as that, I says to myself.

When I got down stairs in the morning, the parlor was shut up, and the watchers was gone. There warn't nobody around but the family and the widow Bartley and our tribe. I watched their faces to see if anything had been happening, but I couldn't tell.

Towards the middle of the day the undertaker come, with his man, and they set the coffin in the middle of the room on a couple of chairs, and then set all our chairs in rows, and borrowed more from the neighbors till the hall and the parlor and the dining-room was full. I see the coffin lid was the way it was before, but I dasn't go to look in under it, with folks around.

Then the people begun to flock in, and the beats and the girls took seats in the front row at the head of the coffin, and for a half an hour the people filed around slow, in single rank, and looked down at the dead man's face a minute, and some dropped in a tear, and it was all very still and solemn, only the girls and the beats holding handkerchiefs to their eyes and keeping their heads bent, and sobbing a little. There warn't no other sound but the scraping of the feet on the floor, and blowing noses—because people always blows them more at a funeral than they do at other places except church.

When the place was packed full, the undertaker he slid around in his black gloves with his softy soothering ways, putting on the last touches, and getting people and things all shipshape and comfortable, and making no more sound than a cat. He never spoke; he moved people around, he squeezed in late ones, he opened up passage-ways, and done it all with nods, and signs with his hands. Then he took his place over against the wall. He was the softest, glidingest, stealthiest man I ever see; and there warn't no more smile to him than there is to a ham.

They had borrowed a melodeum—a sick one; and when everything was ready, a young woman set down and worked it, and it was pretty skreeky and colicky, and everybody joined in and sung, and Peter was the only one that had a good thing, according to my notion. Then the Reverend Hobson opened up, slow and solemn, and begun to talk; and straight off the most outrageous row busted out in the cellar a body ever heard; it was only one dog, but he made a most powerful racket, and he kept it up, right along; the parson he had to stand there, over the coffin, and wait—you couldn't hear yourself think. It was right down awkward, and nobody didn't seem to know what to do. But pretty soon they see that long-legged undertaker make a sign to the preacher as much as to say, "Don't you worry—just depend on me." Then he stooped down and begun to glide along the wall, just his shoulders showing over the people's heads. So he glided along, and the pow-wow and racket getting more and more outrageous all the time; and at last, when he had gone around two sides of the room, he disappears down cellar. Then, in about two seconds we heard a whack, and the dog he finished up with a most amazing howl or two, and then everything was dead still, and the parson begun his solemn talk where he left off. In a minute or two here comes this undertaker's back and shoulders gliding along the wall again; and so he glided, and glided, around three sides of the room, and then rose up, and shaded his mouth with his hands, and stretched his neck out towards the preacher, over the people's heads, and says, in a kind of a coarse whisper, "*He had a rat!*" Then he drooped down and glided along the wall again to his place. You could see it was a great sastisfaction to the people, because naturally they wanted to know. A little thing like that don't cost nothing, and it's just the little things that makes a man to be looked up to and liked. There warn't no more popular man in town than what that undertaker was.

Well, the funeral sermon was very good, but pison long and tiresome; and then the king he shoved in and got off some of his usual rubbage, and at last the job was through, and the undertaker begun to sneak up on the coffin with his screw-driver. I was in a sweat then, and watched him pretty keen. But he never meddled at all; just slid the lid along, as soft as mush, and screwed it down tight and fast. So there I was! I didn't know whether the money was in there, or not. So, says I, spose somebody has hogged that bag on the sly?—now how do *I* know whether to write to Mary Jane or not? 'Spose she dug him up and didn't find nothing—what would she think of me? Blame it, I says, I might get hunted up and jailed; I'd better lay low and keep dark, and not write at all; the thing's awful mixed, now; trying to better it, I've worsened it a hundred times, and I wish to goodness I'd just let it alone, dad fetch the whole business!

They buried him, and we come back home, and I went to watching faces again—I couldn't help it, and I couldn't rest easy. But nothing come of it; the faces didn't tell me nothing.

The king he visited around, in the evening, and sweetened every body up, and made himself ever so friendly; and he give out the idea that his congregation over in England would be in a sweat about him, so he must hurry and settle up the estate right away, and leave for home. He was very sorry he was so pushed, and so was everybody; they wished he could stay longer, but they said they could see it couldn't be done. And he said of course him and William would take the girls home with them; and that pleased everybody too, because then the girls would be well fixed, and amongst their own relations; and it pleased the girls, too—tickled them so they clean forgot they ever had a trouble in the world; and told him to sell out as quick as he wanted to, they would be ready. Them poor things was that glad and happy it made my heart ache to see them getting fooled and lied to so, but I didn't see no safe way for me to chip in and change the general tune.

Well, blamed if the king didn't bill the house and the niggers and all the property for auction straight off—sale two days after the funeral; but anybody could buy private beforehand if they wanted to.

So the next day after the funeral, along about noontime, the girls' joy got the first jolt; a couple of nigger traders come along, and the king sold them the niggers reasonable, for three-day drafts as they called it, and away they went, the two sons up the river to Memphis, and their mother down the river to Orleans. I thought them poor girls and them niggers would break their hearts for grief; they cried around each other, and took on so it most made me down sick to see it. The girls said they hadn't ever dreamed of seeing the family separated or sold away from the town. I can't ever get it out of my memory, the sight of them poor miserable girls and niggers hanging around each other's necks and crying; and I reckon I couldn't a stood it all but would a had to bust out and tell on our gang if I hadn't knowed the sale warn't no account and the niggers would be back home in a week or two.

The thing made a big stir in the town, too, and a good many come out flatfooted and said it was scandalous to separate the mother and the children that way. It injured the frauds some; but the old fool he bulled right along, spite of all the duke could say or do, and I tell you the duke was powerful uneasy.

Next day was auction day. About broad-day in the morning, the king and the duke come up in the garret and woke me up, and I see by their look that there was trouble. The king says:

"Was you in my room night before last?"

"No, your majesty"—which was the way I always called him when nobody but our gang warn't around.

"Was you in there yisterday er last night?"

"No, your majesty."

"Honor bright, now—no lies."

"Honor bright, your majesty, I'm telling you the truth. I hain't been anear your room since Miss Mary Jane took you and the duke and showed it to you."

The duke says:

"Have you seen anybody else go in there?"

"No, your grace, not as I remember, I believe."

"Stop and think."

I studied a while, and see my chance, then I says:

"Well, I see the niggers go in there several times."

Both of them give a little jump; and looked like they hadn't ever expected it, and then like they *had*. Then the duke says:

"What, *all* of them?"

"No—leastways not all at once. That is, I don't think I ever see them all come *out* at once but just one time."

"Hello—when was that?"

"It was the day we had the funeral. In the morning. It wasn't early, because I overslept. I was just starting down the ladder, and I see them."

"Well, go on, *go* on—what did they do? How'd they act?"

"They didn't do nothing. And they didn't act anyway, much, as fur as I see. They tip-toed away; so I seen, easy enough, that they'd shoved in there to do up your majesty's room, or something, sposing you was up; and found you *warn't* up, and so they was hoping to slide out of the way of trouble without waking you up, if they hadn't already waked you up."

"Great guns, *this* is a go!" says the king; and both of them looked pretty sick, and tolerable silly. They stood there a thinking and scratching their heads, a minute, and then the duke he bust into a kind of a little raspy chuckle, and says:

"It does beat all, how neat the niggers played their hand. They let on to be *sorry* they was going out of this region! and I believed they *was* sorry. And so did you, and so did everybody. Don't ever tell *me* any more that a nigger ain't got any histrionic talent. Why, the way they played that thing, it would fool *anybody*. In my opinion there's a fortune in 'em. If I had capital and a theatre, I wouldn't want a better lay out than that—and here we've gone and sold 'em for a song. Yes, and ain't privileged to sing the song, yet. Say, where *is* that song?—that draft."

"In the bank for to be collected. Where *would* it be?"

"Well, *that's* all right then, thank goodness."

Says I, kind of timid-like:

"Is something gone wrong?"

The king whirls on me and rips out:

"None o' your business! You keep your head shet, and mind y'r own affairs—if you got any. Long as you're in this town, don't you forgit *that*, you hear?" Then he says to the duke, "We got to jest swaller it, and say noth'n: mum's the word for *us*."

As they was starting down the ladder, the duke he chuckles again, and says:

"Quick sales *and* small profits! It's a good business—yes."

The king snarls around on him and says,

"I was trying to do for the best, in sellin' 'm out so quick. If the profits has turned out to be none, lackin' considable, and none to carry, is it my fault any more'n it's yourn?"

"Well, *they'd* be in this house yet, and we *wouldn't* if I could a got my advice listened to."

The king sassed back, as much as was safe for him, and then swapped around and lit into *me* again. He give me down the banks for not coming and *telling* him I see the niggers come out of his room acting that way—said any fool would a *knowed* something was up. And then waltzed in and cussed *himself* a while; and said it all come of him not laying late and taking his natural rest that morning, and he'd be blamed if he'd ever do it again. So they went off a jawing; and I felt dreadful glad I'd worked it all off onto the niggers and yet hadn't done the niggers no harm by it.

CHAPTER XXVIII

By-and-by it was getting-up time; so I come down the ladder and started for down stairs, but as I come to the girls' room, the door was open, and I see Mary Jane setting by her old hair trunk, which was open and she'd been packing things in it—getting ready to go to England. But she had stopped now, with a folded gown in her lap, and had her face in her hands, crying. I felt awful bad to see it; of course anybody would. I went in there, and says:

"Miss Mary Jane, you can't abear to see people in trouble, and *I* can't—most always. Tell me about it."

So she done it. And it was the niggers—I just expected it. She said the beautiful trip to England was most about spoiled for her; she didn't know *how* she was ever going to be happy there, knowing the mother and the children warn't ever going to see each other no more—and then busted out bitterer than ever, and flung up her hands, and says:

"Oh, dear, dear, to think they ain't *ever* going to see each other any more!"

"But they *will*—and inside of two weeks—and I *know* it!" says I.

Laws it was out before I could think!—and before I could budge, she throws her arms around my neck, and told me to say it *again*, say it *again*, say it *again*!

I see I had spoke too sudden, and said too much, and was in a close place. I asked her to let me think a minute; and she set there, very impatient and excited, and handsome, but looking kind of happy and eased-up, like a person that's had a tooth pulled out. So I went to studying it out. I says to myself, I reckon a body that ups and tells the truth when he is in a tight place, is taking considerable many resks, though I ain't had no experience, and can't say for certain; but it looks so to me, anyway; and yet here's a case where I'm blest if it don't look to me like the truth is better, and actuly *safer*, than a lie. I must lay it by in my mind, and think it over some time or other, it's so kind of strange and unregular. I never see nothing like it. Well, I says to myself at last, I'm agoing to chance it; I'll up and tell the truth this time, though it does seem most like setting down on a kag of powder and touching it off just to see where you'll go to. Then I says:

"Miss Mary Jane, is there any place out of town a little ways, where you could go and stay three or four days?"

"Yes—Mr. Lothrop's. Why?"

"Never mind why, yet. If I'll tell you how I know the niggers will see each other again—inside of two weeks—here in this house—and *prove* how I know it—will you go to Mr. Lothrop's and stay four days?"

"Four days!" she says; "I'll stay a year!"

"All right," I says, "I don't want nothing more out of *you* than just your word—I druther have it than another man's kiss-the-Bible." She smiled, and reddened up very sweet, and I says, "If you don't mind it, I'll shut the door—and bolt it."

Then I come back and set down again, and says:

"Don't you holler. Just set still, and take it like a man. I got to tell the truth, and you want to brace up, Miss Mary, because it's a bad kind, and going to be hard to take, but there ain't no help for it. These uncles of yourn ain't no uncles at all—they're a couple of frauds—regular dead-beats. There, now we're over the worst of it—you can stand the rest middling easy."

It jolted her up like everything, of course; but I was over the shoal water now, so I went right along, her eyes a blazing higher and higher all the time, and told her every blame thing, from where we first struck that young fool going up to the steamboat, clear through to where she flung herself onto the king's breast at the front door and he kissed her sixteen or seventeen times—and then up she jumps, with her face afire like sunset, and says:

"The brute! Come—don't waste a minute—not a *second*—we'll have them tarred and feathered, and flung in the river!"

Says I:

"Cert'nly. But do you mean, *before* you go to Mr. Lothrop's, or—"

"Oh," she says, "what am I *thinking* about!" she says, and set right down again. "Don't mind what I said—please don't—you *won't*, now, *will* you?" Laying her silky hand on mind in that kind of a way that I said I would die first. "I never thought, I was so stirred up," she says; "now go on, and I won't do so any more. You tell me what to do, and whatever you say, I'll do it."

"Well," I says, "it's a rough gang, them two frauds, and I'm fixed so I got to travel with them a while longer, whether I want to or not—I druther not tell you why—and if you was to blow on them this town would get me out of their claws, and *I'd* be all right, but there'd be another person that you don't know about who'd be in big trouble. Well, we got to save *him*, hain't we? Of course. Well, then, we won't blow on them."

Saying them words put a good idea in my head. I see how maybe I could get me and Jim rid of the frauds; get them jailed here, and then leave. But I didn't want to run the raft in daytime, without anybody aboard to answer questions but me; so I didn't want the plan to begin working till pretty late to-night. I says:

"Miss Mary Jane, I'll tell you what we'll do—and you won't have to stay at Mr. Lothrop's so long, nuther. How fur is it?"

"A little short of four miles—right out in the country, back here."

"Well, that'll answer. Now you go along out there, and lay low till nine or half-past, to-night, and then get them to fetch you home again—tell them you've thought of something. If you get here before eleven, put a candle in this window, and if I don't turn up, wait *till* eleven, and *then* if I don't turn up it means I'm gone, and out of the way, and safe. Then you come out and spread the news around, and get these beats jailed."

"Good," she says, "I'll do it."

"And if it just happens so that I don't get away, but get took up along with them, you must up and say I told you the whole thing beforehand, and you must stand by me all you can."

"Stand by you, indeed I will. They sha'n't touch a hair of your head!" she says, and I see her nostrils spread and her eyes snap when she said it, too.

"If I get away, I sha'n't be here," I says, "to prove these rapscallions ain't your uncles, and I couldn't do it if I *was* here. I could swear they was beats and bummers, that's all; though that's worth something. Well, there's others can do that better than what I can—and they're people that ain't going to be doubted as quick as I'd be. I'll tell you how to find them. Gimme a pencil and a piece of paper. There—'*Royal Nonesuch, Bricksville.*' Put it away, and don't lose it. When the court wants to find out something about these two, let them send up to Bricksville and say they've got the men that played the Royal Nonesuch, and ask for some witnesses—why, you'll have that entire town down here before you can hardly wink, Miss Mary. And they'll come a-biling, too."

I judged we had got everything fixed about right, now. So I says:

"Just let the auction go right along, and don't worry. Nobody don't have to pay for the things they buy till a whole day after the auction, on accounts of the short notice, and they ain't going out of this till they get that money—and the way we've fixed it the sale ain't going to count, and they ain't going to *get* no money. It's just like the way it was with the niggers—it warn't no sale, and the niggers will be back before long. Why, they can't collect the money for the *niggers*, yet—they're in the worst kind of a fix, Miss Mary."

"Well," she says, "I'll run down to breakfast now, and then I'll start straight for Mr. Lothrop's."

"'Deed, *that* ain't the ticket, Miss Mary Jane," I says, "by no manner of means; go *before* breakfast."

"Why?"

"What did you reckon I wanted you to go at all for, Miss Mary?"

"Well, I never thought—and come to think, I don't know. What was it?"

"Why, it's because you ain't one of these leather-face people. I don't want no better book than what your face is. A body can set down and read it off like coarse print. Do you reckon you can go and face your uncles, when they come to kiss you good-morning, and never—"

"There, there, don't! Yes, I'll go before breakfast—I'll be glad to. And leave my sisters with them?"

"Yes—never mind about them. They've got to stand it yet a while. They might suspicion something if all of you was to go. I don't want you to see them, nor your sisters, nor nobody in this town—if a neighbor was to ask how is your uncles this morning, your face would tell something. No, you go right along, Miss Mary Jane, and I'll fix it with all of them. I'll tell Miss Susan to give your love to your uncles and say you've went away for a few hours for to get a little rest and change, or to see a friend, and you'll be back to-night or early in the morning."

"Gone to see a friend is all right, but I won't have my love given to them."

"Well, then, it sha'n't be." It was well enough to tell *her* so—no harm in it. It was only a little thing to do, and no trouble; and it's the little things that smoothes people's roads the most, down here below; it would make Mary Jane comfortable, and it wouldn't cost nothing. Then I says: "There's one more thing—that bag of money."

"Well, they've got that; and it makes me feel pretty silly to think *how* they got it."

"No, you're out, there. They hain't got it."

"Why, who's got it?"

"I wish I knowed, but I don't. I *had* it, because I stole it from them: and I stole it to give to you; and I know where I hid it, but I'm afraid it ain't there no more. I'm awful sorry, Miss Mary Jane, I'm just as sorry as I can be; but I done the best I could; I did, honest. I come nigh getting caught, and I had to shove it into the first place I come to, and run—and it warn't a good place."

"Oh, stop blaming yourself—it's too bad to do it, and I won't allow it—you couldn't help it; it wasn't your fault. Where did you hide it?"

I didn't want to set her to thinking about her troubles again; and I couldn't seem to get my mouth to tell her what would make her see that corpse laying in the coffin with that bag of money on his stomach. So for a minute I didn't say nothing—then I says:

"I'd ruther not *tell* you where I put it, Miss Mary Jane, if you don't mind letting me off; but I'll write it for you on a piece of paper, and you can read it along the road to Mr. Lothrop's, if you want to. Do you reckon that'll do?"

"Oh, yes."

So I wrote: "I put it in the coffin. It was in there when you was crying there, away in the night. I was behind the door, and I was mighty sorry for you, Miss Mary Jane."

It made my eyes water a little, to remember her crying there all by herself in the night, and them devils laying there right under her own roof, shaming her and robbing her; and when I folded it up and give it to her, I see the water come into her eyes, too; and she shook me by the hand, hard, and says:

"*Good*-bye—I'm going to do everything just as you've told me; and if I don't ever see you again, I sha'n't ever forget you, and I'll think of you a many and a many a time, and I'll *pray* for you, too!"—and she was gone.

Pray for me! I reckoned if she knowed me she'd take a job that was more nearer her size. But I bet she done it, just the same—she was just that kind. She had the grit to pray for Judus if she took the notion—there warn't no back-down to her, I judge. You may say what you want to, but in my opinion she had more sand in her than any girl I ever see; in my opinion she was just full of sand. It sounds like flattery, but it ain't no flattery. And when it comes to beauty—and goodness too—she lays over them all. I hain't ever seen her since that time that I see her go out of that door; no, I hain't ever seen her since, but I reckon I've thought of her a many and a many a million times, and of her saying she would pray for me; and if ever I'd a thought it would do any good for me to pray for *her*, blamed if I wouldn't a done it or bust.

Well, Mary Jane she lit out the back way, I reckon; because nobody see her go. When I struck Susan and the hare-lip, I says:

"What's the name of them people over on t'other side of the river that you all goes to see sometimes?"

They says:

"There's several; but it's the Proctors, mainly."

"That's the name," I says; "I most forgot it. Well, Miss Mary Jane she told me to tell you she's gone over there in a dreadful hurry—one of them's sick."

"Which one?"

"I don't know; leastways I kinder forget; but I think it's—"

"Sakes alive, I hope it ain't *Hanner*?"

"I'm sorry to say it," I says, "but Hanner's the very one."

"My goodness—and she so well only last week! Is she took bad?"

"It ain't no name for it. They set up with her all night, Miss Mary Jane said, and they don't think she'll last many hours."

"Only think of that, now! What's the matter with her?"

"I couldn't think of anything reasonable, right off that way, so I says:

"Mumps."

"Mumps your granny! They don't set up with people that's got the mumps."

"They don't, don't they? You better bet they do with *these* mumps. These mumps is different. It's a new kind, Miss Mary Jane said."

"How's it a new kind?"

"Because it's mixed up with other things."

"What other things?"

"Well, measles, and whooping-cough, and erysiplas, and consumption, and yaller janders, and brain fever, and I don't know what all."

"My land! And they call it the *mumps*?"

"That's what Miss Mary Jane said."

"Well, what in the nation do they call it the *mumps* for?"

"Why, because it *is* the mumps. That's what it starts with."

"Well, ther' ain't no sense in it. A body might stump his toe, and take pison, and fall down the well, and break his neck, and bust his brains out, and somebody come along and ask what killed him, and some numskull up and say, 'Why, he stumped his *toe*.' Would ther' be any sense in that? *No*. And ther' ain't no sense in *this*, nuther. Is it ketching?"

"Is it *ketching*? Why, how you talk. Is a *harrow* catching?—in the dark? If you don't hitch onto one tooth, you're bound to on another, ain't you? And you can't get away with that tooth without fetching the whole harrow along, can you? Well, these kind of mumps is a kind of a harrow, as you may say—and it ain't no slouch of a harrow, nuther, you come to get it hitched on good."

"Well, it's awful, *I* think," says the hare-lip. "I'll go to Uncle Harvey and—"

"Oh, yes," I says, "I *would*. Of *course* I would. I wouldn't lose no time."

"Well, why wouldn't you?"

"Just look at it a minute, and maybe you can see. Hain't your uncles obleeged to get along home to England as fast as they can? And do you reckon they'd be mean enough to go off and leave you to go all that journey by yourselves? *You* know they'll wait for you. So fur, so good. Your uncle Harvey's a preacher, ain't he? Very well, then; is a *preacher* going to deceive a steamboat clerk? is he going to deceive a *ship clerk*?—so as to get them to let Miss Mary Jane go aboard? Now *you* know he ain't. What *will* he do, then? Why, he'll say, 'It's a great pity, but my church matters has got to get along the best way they can; for my niece has been exposed to the dreadful pluribus-unum mumps, and so it's my bounden duty to set down here and wait the three months it takes to show on her if she's got it.' But never mind, if you think it's best to tell your uncle Harvey—"

"Shucks, and stay fooling around here when we could all be having good times in England whilst we was waiting to find out whether Mary Jane's got it or not? Why, you talk like a muggins."

"Well, anyway, maybe you better tell some of the neighbors."

"Listen at that, now. You do beat all, for natural stupidness. Can't you *see* that *they'd* go and tell? Ther' ain't no way but just to not tell anybody at *all*."

"Well, maybe you're right—yes, I judge you *are* right."

"But I reckon we ought to tell Uncle Harvey she's gone out a while, anyway, so he wont be uneasy about her?"

"Yes, Miss Mary Jane she wanted you to do that. She says, 'Tell them to give Uncle Harvey and William my love and a kiss, and say I've run over the river to see Mr.—Mr.—what *is* the name of that rich family your uncle Peter used to think so much of?—I mean the one that—"

"Why, you must mean the Apthorps, ain't it?"

"Of course; bother them kind of names, a body can't ever seem to remember them, half the time, somehow. Yes, she said, say she has run over for to ask the Apthorps to be sure and come to the auction and buy this house, because she allowed her uncle Peter would ruther they had it than anybody else; and she's going to stick to them till they say they'll come, and then, if she ain't too tired, she's coming home; and if she is, she'll be home in the morning anyway. She said, don't say nothing about the Proctors, but only about the Apthorps—which'll be perfectly true, because she *is* going there to speak about their buying the house; I know it, because she told me so, herself."

"All right," they said, and cleared out to lay for their uncles, and give them the love and the kisses, and tell them the message.

Everything was all right now. The girls wouldn't say nothing because they wanted to go to England; and the king and the duke would ruther Mary Jane was off working for the auction than around in reach of Doctor Robinson. I felt very good; I judged I had done it pretty neat—I reckoned Tom Sawyer couldn't a done it no neater himself. Of course he would a throwed more style into it, but I can't do that very handy, not being brung up to it.

Well, they held the auction in the public square, along towards the end of the afternoon, and it strung along, and strung along, and the old man he was on hand and looking his level piousest, up there longside of the auctioneer, and chipping in a little Scripture, now and then, or a little goody-goody saying, of some kind, and the duke he was around goo-gooing for sympathy all he knowed how, and just spreading himself generly.

But by-and-by the thing dragged through, and everything was sold. Everything but a little old trifling lot in the graveyard. So they'd got to work *that* off—I never see such a girafft as the king was for wanting to swallow *everything*. Well, whilst they was at it, a steamboat landed, and in about two minutes up comes a crowd a whooping and yelling and laughing and carrying on, and singing out:

"*Here's* your opposition line! here's your two sets o' heirs to old Peter Wilks—and you pays your money and you takes your choice!"

CHAPTER XXIX

They was fetching a very nice looking old gentleman along, and a nice looking younger one, with his right arm in a sling. And my souls, how the people yelled, and laughed, and kept it up. But I didn't see no joke about it, and I judged it would strain the duke and the king some to see any. I reckoned they'd turn pale. But no, nary a pale did *they* turn. The duke he never let on he suspicioned what was up, but just went a goo-gooing around, happy and satisfied, like a jug that's googling out buttermilk; and as for the king, he just gazed and gazed down sorrowful on them newcomers like it give him the stomach-ache in his very heart to think there could be such frauds and rascals in the world. Oh, he done it admirable. Lots of the principal people gethered around the king, to let him see they was on his side. That old gentleman that had just come looked all puzzled to death. Pretty soon he begun to speak, and I see, straight off, he pronounced *like* an Englishman, not the king's way, though the king's *was* pretty good, for an imitation. I can't give the old gent's words, nor I can't imitate him; but he turned around to the crowd, and says, about like this:

"This is a surprise to me which I wasn't looking for; and I'll acknowledge, candid and frank, I ain't very well fixed to meet it and answer it; for my brother and me has had misfortunes, he's broke his arm, and our baggage got put off at a town above here, last night in the night by a mistake. I am Peter Wilk's brother Harvey, and this is his brother William, which can't hear nor speak—and can't even make signs to amount to much, now 't he's only got one hand to work them with. We are who we say we are; and in a day or two, when I get the baggage, I can prove it. But, up till then, I won't say nothing more, but go to the hotel and wait."

So him and the new dummy started off; and the king he laughs, and blethers out:

"Broke his arm—*very* likely *ain't* it?—and very convenient, too, for a fraud that's got to make signs, and hain't learnt how. Lost their baggage! That's *mighty* good!—and mighty ingenious—under the *circumstances*!"

So he laughed again; and so did everybody else, except three or four, or maybe half a dozen. One of these was that doctor; another one was a sharp looking gentleman, with a carpet-bag of the old-fashioned kind made out of carpet-stuff, that had just come off of the steamboat and was talking to him in a low voice, and glancing towards the king now and then and nodding their heads—it was Levi Bell, the lawyer that was gone up to Louisville; and another one was a big rough husky that come along and listened to all the old gentleman said, and was listening to the king now. And when the king got done, this husky up and says:

"Say, looky here; if you are Harvey Wilks, when'd you come to this town?"

"The day before the funeral, friend," says the king.

"But what time o' day?"

"In the evenin'—'bout an hour er two before sundown."

"*How'd* you come?"

"I come down on the *Susan Powell*, from Cincinnati."

"Well, then, how'd you come to be up at the Pint in the *mornin'*—in a canoe?"

"I warn't up at the Pint in the mornin'."

"It's a lie."

Several of them jumped for him and begged him not to talk that way to an old man and a preacher.

"Preacher be hanged, he's a fraud and a liar. He was up at the Pint that mornin'. I live up there, don't I? Well, I was up there, and he was up there. I *see* him there. He come in a canoe, along with Tim Collins and a boy."

The doctor he up and says: "Would you know the boy again if you was to see him, Hines?"

"I reckon I would, but I don't know. Why, yonder he is, now. I know him perfectly easy."

It was me he pointed at. The doctor says:

"Neighbors, I don't know whether the new couple is frauds or not; but if *these* two ain't frauds, I am an idiot, that's all. I think it's our duty to see that they don't get away from here till we've looked into this thing. Come along, Hines; come along, the rest of you. We'll take these fellows to the tavern and affront them with t'other couple, and I reckon we'll find out *something* before we get through."

It was nuts for the crowd, though maybe not for the king's friends; so we all started. It was about sundown. The doctor he led me along by the hand, and was plenty kind enough, but he never let *go* my hand.

We all got in a big room in the hotel, and lit up some candles, and fetched in the new couple. First, the doctor says:

"I don't wish to be too hard on these two men, but *I* think they're frauds, and they may have complices that we don't know nothing about. If they have, won't the complices get away with that bag of gold Peter Wilks left? It ain't unlikely. If these men ain't frauds, they won't object to sending for that money and letting us keep it till they prove they're all right—ain't that so?"

Everybody agreed to that. So I judged they had our gang in a pretty tight place, right at the outstart. But the king he only looked sorrowful, and says:

"Gentlemen, I wish the money was there, for I ain't got no disposition to throw anything in the way of a fair, open, out-and-out investigation o' this misable business; but alas, the money ain't there; you k'n send and see, if you want to."

"Where is it, then?"

"Well, when my niece give it to me to keep for her, I took and hid it inside o' the straw tick o' my bed, not wishin' to bank it for the few days we'd be here, and considerin' the bed a safe place, we not bein' used to niggers, and suppos'n' 'em honest, like servants in England. The niggers stole it the very next mornin' after I had went down stairs; and when I sold 'em, I hadn't missed the money yit, so they got clean away with it. My servant here k'n tell you 'bout it gentlemen."

The doctor and several said "Shucks!" and I see nobody didn't altogether believe him. One man asked me if I see the niggers steal it. I said no, but I see them sneaking out of the room and hustling away, and I never thought nothing, only I reckoned they was afraid they had waked up my master and was trying to get away before he made trouble with them. That was all they asked me. Then the doctor whirls on me and says:

"Are *you* English too?"

I says yes; and him and some others laughed, and said, "Stuff!"

Well, then they sailed in on the general investigation, and there we had it, up and down, hour in, hour out, and nobody never said a word about supper, nor ever seemed to think about it—and so they kept it up, and kept it up; and it *was* the worst mixed-up thing you ever see. They made the king tell his yarn, and they made the old gentleman tell his'n; and anybody but a lot of prejudiced chuckleheads would a *seen* that the old gentleman was spinning truth and t'other one lies. And by-and-by they had me up to tell what I knowed. The king he give me a left-handed look out of the corner of his eye, and so I knowed enough to talk on the right side. I begun to tell about Sheffield, and how we lived there, and all about the English Wilkses, and so on; but I didn't get pretty fur till the doctor begun to laugh; and Levi Bell, the lawyer, says:

"Set down, my boy, I wouldn't strain myself, if I was you. I reckon you ain't used to lying, it don't seem to come handy; what you want is practice. You do it pretty awkward."

I didn't care nothing for the compliment, but I was glad to be let off, anyway.

The doctor he started to say something, and turns and says:

"If you'd been in town at first, Levi Bell—"

The king broke in and reached out his hand, and says:

"Why, is this my poor dead brother's old friend that he's wrote so often about?"

The lawyer and him shook hands, and the lawyer smiled and looked pleased, and they talked right along a while, and then got to one side and talked low; and at last the lawyer speaks up and says:

"That'll fix it. I'll take the order and send it, along with your brother's, and then they'll know it's all right."

So they got some paper and a pen, and the king he set down and twisted his head to one side, and chawed his tongue, and scrawled off something; and then they give the pen to the duke—and then for the first time, the duke looked sick. But he took the pen and wrote. So then the lawyer turns to the new old gentleman and says:

"You and your brother please write a line or two and sign your names."

The old gentleman wrote, but nobody couldn't read it. The lawyer looked powerful astonished, and says:

"Well, it beats *me*"—and snaked a lot of old letters out of his pocket, and examined them, and then examined the old man's writing, and then *them* again; and then says: "These old letters is from Harvey Wilks; and here's *these* two's handwritings, and anybody can see *they* didn't write them" (the king and the duke looked sold and foolish, I tell you, to see how the lawyer had took them in), "and here's *this* old gentleman's handwriting, and anybody can tell, easy enough, *he* didn't write them—fact is, the scratches he makes ain't properly *writing*, at all. Now here's some letters from—"

The new old gentleman says:

"If you please, let me explain. Nobody can read my hand but my brother there—so he copies for me. It's *his* hand you've got there, not mine."

"*Well!*" says the lawyer, "this *is* a state of things. I've got some of William's letters too; so if you'll get him to write a line or so we can com—"

"He *can't* write with his left hand," says the old gentleman. "If he could use his right hand, you would see that he wrote his own letters and mine too. Look at both, please—they're by the same hand."

The lawyer done it, and says:

"I believe it's so—and if it ain't so, there's a heap stronger resemblance than I'd noticed before, anyway. Well, well, well! I thought we was right on the track of a slution, but it's gone to grass, partly. But anyway, *one* thing is proved—*these* two ain't either of 'em Wilkses"—and he wagged his head towards the king and the duke.

Well, what do you think?—that muleheaded old fool wouldn't give in *then*! Indeed he wouldn't. Said it warn't no fair test. Said his brother William was the cussedest joker in the world, and hadn't *tried* to write—*he* see William was going to play one of his jokes the minute he put the pen to paper. And so he warmed up and went warbling and warbling right along, till he was actuly beginning to believe what he was saying, *himself*—but pretty soon the new old gentleman broke in, and says:

"I've thought of something. Is there anybody here that helped to lay out my br——helped to lay out the late Peter Wilks for burying?"

"Yes," says somebody, "me and Ab Turner done it. We're both here."

Then the old man turns towards the king, and says:

"Perhaps this gentleman can tell me what was tatooed on his breast?"

Blamed if the king didn't have to brace up mighty quick, or he'd a squshed down like a bluff bank that the river has cut under, it took him so sudden—and mind you, it was a thing that was calculated to make most *anybody* sqush to get fetched such a solid one as that without any notice—because how was *he* going to know what was tatooed on the man? He whitened a little; he couldn't help it; and it was mighty still in there, and everybody bending a little forwards and gazing at him. Says I to myself, *Now* he'll throw up the sponge—there ain't no more use. Well, did he? A body can't hardly believe it, but he didn't. I reckon he thought he'd keep the thing up till he tired them people out, so they'd thin out, and him and the duke could break loose and get away. Anyway, he set there, and pretty soon he begun to smile, and says:

"Mf! It's a *very* tough question, *ain't* it! *Yes*, sir, I k'n tell you what's tatooed on his breast. It's jest a small, thin, blue arrow—that's what it is; and if you don't look clost, you can't see it. *Now* what do you say—hey?"

Well, *I* never see anything like that old blister for clean out-and-out cheek.

The new old gentleman turns brisk towards Ab Turner and his pard, and his eye lights up like he judged he'd got the king *this* time, and says:

"There—you've heard what he said! Was there any such mark on Peter Wilks's breast?"

Both of them spoke up and says:

"We didn't see no such mark."

"Good!" says the old gentleman. "Now, what you *did* see on his breast was a small dim P, and a B (which is an initial he dropped when he was young), and a W, with dashes between them, so: P—B—W"—and he marked them that way on a piece of paper. "Come—ain't that what you saw?"

Both of them spoke up again, and says:

"No, we *didn't*. We never seen any marks at all."

Well, everybody *was* in a state of mind, now; and they sings out:

"The whole *bilin'* of 'm 's frauds! Le's duck 'em! le's drown 'em! le's ride 'em on a rail!" and everybody was whooping at once, and there was a rattling pow-wow. But the lawyer he jumps on the table and yells, and says:

"Gentlemen—gentle*men*! Hear me just a word—just a *single* word—if you PLEASE! There's one way yet—let's go and dig up the corpse and look."

That took them.

"Hooray!" they all shouted, and was starting right off; but the lawyer and the doctor sung out:

"Hold on, hold on! Collar all these four men and the boy, and fetch *them* along, too!"

"We'll do it!" they all shouted: "and if we don't find them marks we'll lynch the whole gang!"

I *was* scared, now, I tell you. But there warn't no getting away, you know. They gripped us all, and marched us right along, straight for the graveyard, which was a mile and half down the river, and the whole town at our heels, for we made noise enough, and it was only nine in the evening.

As we went by our house I wished I hadn't sent Mary Jane out of town; because now if I could tip her the wink, she'd light out and save me, and blow on our dead-beats.

Well, we swarmed along down the river road, just carrying on like wild-cats; and to make it more scary, the sky was darking up, and the lightning beginning to wink and flitter, and the wind to shiver amongst the leaves. This was the most awful trouble and most dangersome I ever was in; and I was kinder stunned; everything was going so different from what I had allowed for; stead of being fixed so I could take my own time, if I wanted to, and see all the fun, and have Mary Jane at my back to save me and set me free when the close-fit come, here was nothing in the world betwixt me and sudden death but just them tatoo-marks. If they didn't find them—

I couldn't bear to think about it; and yet, somehow, I couldn't think about nothing else. It got darker and darker, and it was a beautiful time to give the crowd the slip; but that big husky had me by the wrist—Hines—and a body might as well try to give Goliar the slip. He dragged me right along, he was so excited; and I had to run to keep up.

When they got there they swarmed into the graveyard and washed over it like an overflow. And when they got to the grave, they found they had about a hundred times as many shovels as they wanted, but nobody hadn't thought to fetch a lantern. But they sailed into digging, anyway, by the flicker of the lightning, and sent a man to the nearest house a half a mile off, to borrow one.

So they dug and dug, like everything; and it got awful dark, and the rain started, and the wind swished and swushed along, and the lightning come brisker and brisker, and the thunder boomed; but them people never took no notice of it, they was so full of this business; and one minute you could see everything and every face in that big crowd, and the shovelfuls of dirt sailing up out of the grave, and the next second the dark wiped it all out, and you couldn't see nothing at all.

At last they got out the coffin, and begun to unscrew the lid, and then such another crowding, and shouldering, and shoving as there was, to scrouge in and get a sight, you never see; and in the dark, that way, it was awful. Hines he hurt my wrist dreadful, pulling and tugging so, and I reckon he clean forgot I was in the world, he was so excited and panting.

All of a sudden the lightning let go a perfect sluice of white glare, and somebody sings out:

"By the living jingo, here's the bag of gold on his breast!"

Hines let out a whoop, like everybody else, and dropped my wrist and give a big surge to bust his way in and get a look, and the way I lit out and shinned for the road in the dark, there ain't nobody can tell.

I had the road all to myself, and I fairly flew—leastways I had it all to myself except the solid dark, and the now-and-then glares, and the buzzing of the rain, and the thrashing of the wind, and the splitting of the thunder; and sure as you are born I did clip it along!

When I struck the town, I see there warn't nobody out in the storm, so I never hunted for no back streets, but humped it straight through the main one; and when I begun to get towards our house I aimed my eye and set it. No light there; the house all dark—which made me feel sorry and disappointed, I didn't know why. But at last, just as I was sailing by, *flash* comes the light in Mary Jane's window! and my heart swelled up sudden, like to bust; and the same second the house and all was behind me in the dark, and wasn't ever going to be before me no more in this world. She *was* the best girl I ever see, and had the most sand.

The minute I was far enough above the town to see I could make the towhead, I begun to look sharp for a boat to borrow; and the first time the lightning showed me one that wasn't chained, I snatched it and shoved. It was a canoe, and warn't fastened with nothing but a rope. The towhead was a rattling big distance off, away out there in the middle of the river, but I didn't lose no time; and when I struck the raft at last, I was so fagged I would a just laid down to blow and gasp if I could afforded it. But I didn't. As I sprung aboard I sung out:

"Out with you Jim, and set her loose! Glory be to goodness, we're shut of them!"

Jim lit out, and was a coming for me with both arms spread, he was so full of joy; but when I glimpsed him in the lightning, my heart shot up in my mouth, and I went overboard backwards; for I forgot he was old King Lear and a drownded A-rab all in one, and it most scared the livers and lights out of me. But Jim fished me out, and was going to hug me and bless me, and so on, he was so glad I was back and we was shut of the king and the duke, but I says:

"Not now—have it for breakfast, have it for breakfast! Cut loose and let her slide!"

So, in two seconds, away we went, a sliding down the river, and it *did* seem so good to be free again and all by ourselves on the big river and nobody to bother us. I had to skip around a bit, and jump up and crack my heels a few times, I couldn't help it; but about the third crack, I noticed a sound that I knowed mighty well—and held my breath and listened and waited—and sure enough, when the next flash busted out over the water, here they come!—and just a laying to their oars and making their skiff hum! It was the king and the duke.

So I wilted right down onto the planks, then, and give up; and it was all I could do to keep from crying.

CHAPTER XXX

When they got aboard, the king went for me, and shook me by the collar, and says:

"Tryin' to give us the slip, was ye, you pup! Tired of our company—hey?"

I says:

"No, your majesty, we warn't—*please* don't, your majesty!"

"Quick, then, and tell us what *was* your idea, or I'll shake the insides out o' you!"

"Honest, I'll tell you everything, just as it happened, your majesty. The man that had aholt of me was very good to me, and kept saying he had a boy about as big as me that died last year, and he was sorry to see a boy in such a dangerous fix; and when they was all took by surprise by finding the gold, and made a rush for the coffin, he lets go of me and whispers, 'Heel it, now, or they'll hang ye, sure!' and I lit out. It didn't seem no good for *me* to stay—*I* couldn't do nothing, and I didn't want to be hung if I could get away. So I never stopped running till I found the canoe; and when I got here I told Jim to hurry, or they'd catch me and hang me yet, and said I was afeard you and the duke wasn't alive, now, and I was awful sorry, and so was Jim, and was awful glad when we see you coming, you may ask Jim if I didn't."

Jim said it was so; and the king told him to shut up, and said, "Oh, yes, it's *mighty* likely!" and shook me up again, and said he reckoned he'd drownd me. But the duke says:

"Leggo the boy, you old idiot! Would *you* a done any different? Did you inquire around for *him*, when you got loose? *I* don't remember it."

So the king let go of me, and begun to cuss that town and everybody in it. But the duke says:

"You better a blame sight give *yourself* a good cussing, for you're the one that's entitled to it most. You hain't done a thing, from the start, that had any sense in it, except coming out so cool and cheeky with that imaginary blue-arrow mark. That *was* bright—it was right down bully; and it was the thing that saved us. For if it hadn't been for that, they'd a jailed us till them Englishmen's baggage come—and then—the penitentiary, you bet! But that trick took 'em to the graveyard, and the gold done us a still bigger kindness; for if the excited fools hadn't let go all holts and made that rush to get a look, we'd a slept in our cravats to-night—cravats warranted to *wear*, too—longer than *we'd* need 'em."

They was still a minute—thinking—then the king says, kind of absent-minded like:

"Mf! And we reckoned the *niggers* stole it!"

That made me squirm!

"Yes," says the duke, kinder slow, and deliberate, and sarcastic. "*We* did."

After about a half a minute, the king drawls out:

"Leastways—*I* did."

The duke says, the same way:

"On the contrary—*I* did."

The king kind of ruffles up, and says:

"Looky here, Bilgewater, what'r you referrin' to?"

The duke says, pretty brisk:

"When it comes to that, maybe you'll let me ask, what was *you* referring to?"

"Shucks!" says the king, very sarcastic; "but *I* don't know—maybe you was asleep, and didn't know what you was about."

The duke bristles right up, now, and says:

"Oh, let *up* on this cussed nonsense—do you take me for a blame' fool? Don't you reckon *I* know who hid that money in that coffin?"

"*Yes*, sir! I know you *do* know—because you done it yourself!"

"It's a lie!"—and the duke went for him. The king sings out:

"Take y'r hands off!—leggo my throat!—I take it all back!"

The duke says:

"Well, you just own up, first, that you *did* hide that money there, intending to give me the slip one of these days, and come back and dig it up, and have it all to yourself."

"Wait jest a minute, duke—answer me this one question, honest and fair; if you didn't put the money there, say it, and I'll b'lieve you, and take back everything I said."

"You old scoundrel, I didn't, and you know I didn't. There, now!"

"Well, then, I b'lieve you. But answer me only jest this one more—now *don't* git mad; didn't you have it in your *mind* to hook the money and hide it?"

The duke never said nothing for a little bit; then he says:

"Well—I don't care if I *did*, I didn't *do* it, anyway. But you not only had it in mind to do it, but you *done* it."

"I wisht I may never die if I done it, duke, and that's honest. I won't say I warn't *goin'* to do it, because I *was*; but you—I mean somebody—got in ahead o' me."

"It's a lie! You done it, and you got to *say* you done it, or—"

The king begun to gurgle, and then he gasps out:

"'Nough!—*I own up*!"

I was very glad to hear him say that, it made me feel much more easier than what I was feeling before. So the duke took his hands off, and says:

"If you ever deny it again, I'll drown you. It's *well* for you to set there and blubber like a baby—it's fitten for you, after the way you've acted. I never see such an old ostrich for wanting to gobble everything—and I a trusting you all the time, like you was my own father. You ought to been ashamed of yourself to stand by and hear it saddled onto a lot of poor niggers and you never say a word for 'em. It makes me feel ridiculous to think I was soft enough to *believe* that rubbage. Cuss you, I can see, now, why you was so anxious to make up the deffersit—you wanted to get what money I'd got out of the Nonesuch and one thing or another, and scoop it *all*!"

The king says, timid, and still a snuffling:

"Why, duke, it was you that said make up the deffersit, it warn't me."

"Dry up! I don't want to hear no more *out* of you!" says the duke. "And *now* you see what you *got* by it. They've got all their own money back, and all of *ourn* but a shekel or two, *besides*. G'long to bed—and don't you deffersit *me* no more deffersits, long 's *you* live!"

So the king sneaked into the wigwam, and took to his bottle for comfort; and before long the duke tackled *his* bottle; and so in about a half an hour they was as thick as thieves again, and the tighter they got, the lovinger they got; and went off a snoring in each other's arms. They both got powerful mellow, but I noticed the king didn't get mellow enough to forget to remember to not deny about hiding the money-bag again. That made me feel easy and satisfied. Of course when they got to snoring, we had a long gabble, and I told Jim everything.

CHAPTER XXXI

We dasn't stop again at any town, for days and days; kept right along down the river. We was down south in the warm weather, now, and a mighty long ways from home. We begun to come to trees with Spanish moss on them, hanging down from the limbs like long gray beards. It was the first I ever see it growing, and it made the woods look solemn and dismal. So now the frauds reckoned they was out of danger, and they begun to work the villages again.

First they done a lecture on temperance; but they didn't make enough for them both to get drunk on. Then in another village they started a dancing school; but they didn't know no more how to dance than a kangaroo does; so the first prance they made, the general public jumped in and pranced them out of town. Another time they tried a go at yellocution; but they didn't yellocute long till the audience got up and give them a solid good cussing and made them skip out. They tackled missionarying, and mesmerizing, and doctoring, and telling fortunes, and a little of everything; but they couldn't seem to have no luck. So at last they got just about dead broke, and laid around the raft, as she floated along, thinking, and thinking, and never saying nothing, by the half a day at a time, and dreadful blue and desperate.

And at last they took a change, and begun to lay their heads together in the wigwam and talk low and confidential two or three hours at a time. Jim and me got uneasy. We didn't like the look of it. We judged they was studying up some kind of worse deviltry than ever. We turned it over and over, and at last we made up our minds they was going to break into somebody's house or store, or was going into the counterfeit-money business, or something. So then we was pretty scared, and made up an agreement that we wouldn't have nothing in the world to do with such actions, and if we ever got the least show we would give them the cold shake, and clear out and leave them behind. Well, early one morning we hid the raft in a good safe place about two mile below a little bit of a shabby village, named Pikesville, and the king he went ashore, and told us all to stay hid whilst he went up to town and smelt around to see if anybody had got any wind of the Royal Nonesuch there yet. ("House to rob, you *mean*," says I to myself; "and when you get through robbing it you'll come back here and wonder what's become of me and Jim and the raft—and you'll have to take it out in wondering.") And he said if he warn't back by midday, the duke and me would know it was all right, and we was to come along.

So we staid where we was. The duke he fretted and sweated around, and was in a mighty sour way. He scolded us for everything, and we couldn't seem to do nothing right; he found fault with every little thing. Something was a-brewing, sure. I was good and glad when midday come and no king; we could have a change, anyway—and maybe a chance for *the* change, on top of it. So me and the duke went up to the village, and hunted around there for the king, and by-and-by we found him in the back room of a little low doggery, very tight, and a lot of loafers bullyragging him for sport, and he a cussing and threatening with all his might, and so tight he couldn't walk, and couldn't do nothing to them. The duke he began to abuse him for an old fool, and the king begun to sass back; and the minute they was fairly at it, I lit out, and shook the reefs out of my hind legs, and spun down the river road like a deer—for I see our chance; and I made up my mind that it would be a long day before they ever see me and Jim again. I got down there all out of breath but loaded up with joy, and sung out—

"Set her loose, Jim, we're all right, now!"

But there warn't no answer, and nobody come out of the wigwam. Jim was gone! I set up a shout—and then another—and then another one; and run this way and that in the woods, whooping and screeching; but it warn't no use—old Jim was gone. Then I set down and cried; I couldn't help it. But I couldn't set still long. Pretty soon I went out on the road, trying to think what I better do, and I run across a boy walking, and asked him if he'd seen a strange nigger, dressed so and so, and he says:

"Yes."

"Whereabouts?" says I.

"Down to Silas Phelps's place, two mile below here. He's a runaway nigger, and they've got him. Was you looking for him?"

"You bet I ain't! I run across him in the woods about an hour or two ago, and he said if I hollered he'd cut my livers out—and told me to lay down and stay where I was; and I done it. Been there ever since; afeard to come out."

"Well," he says, "you needn't be afeard no more, becuz they've got him. He run off f'm down South, som'ers."

"It's a good job they got him."

"Well, I *reckon*! There's two hundred dollars reward on him. It's like picking up money out'n the road."

"Yes, it is—and *I* could a had it if I'd been big enough; I see him *first*. Who nailed him?"

"It was an old fellow—a stranger—and he sold out his chance in him for forty dollars, becuz he's got to go up the river and can't wait. Think o' that, now! You bet *I'd* wait, if it was seven year."

"That's me, every time," says I. "But maybe his chance ain't worth no more than that, if he'll sell it so cheap. Maybe there's something ain't straight about it."

"But it *is*, though—straight as a string. I see the handbill myself. It tells all about him, to a dot—paints him like a picture, and tells the plantation he's frum, below New*rleans*. No-sirree-*bob*, they ain't no trouble 'bout *that* speculation, you bet you. Say, gimme a chaw tobacker, won't ye?"

I didn't have none, so he left. I went to the raft, and set down in the wigwam to think. But I couldn't come to nothing. I thought till I wore my head sore, but I couldn't see no way out of the trouble. After all this long journey, and after all we'd done for them scoundrels, here was it all come to nothing, everything all busted up and ruined, because they could have the heart to serve Jim such a trick as that, and make him a slave again all his life, and amongst strangers, too, for forty dirty dollars.

Once I said to myself it would be a thousand times better for Jim to be a slave at home where his family was, as long as he'd *got* to be a slave, and so I'd better write a letter to Tom Sawyer and tell him to tell Miss Watson where he was. But I soon give up that notion, for two things: she'd be mad and disgusted at his rascality and ungratefulness for leaving her, and so she'd sell him straight down the river again; and if she didn't, everybody naturally despises an ungrateful nigger, and they'd make Jim feel it all the time, and so he'd feel ornery and disgraced. And then think of *me*! It would get all around, that Huck Finn helped a nigger to get his freedom; and if I was to ever see anybody from that town again, I'd be ready to get down and lick his boots for shame. That's just the way: a person does a low-down thing, and then he don't want to take no consequences of it. Thinks as long as he can hide it, it ain't no disgrace. That was my fix exactly. The more I studied about this, the more my conscience went to grinding me, and the more wicked and low-down and ornery I got to feeling. And at last, when it hit me all of a sudden that here was the plain hand of Providence slapping me in the face and letting me know my wickedness was being watched all the time from up there in heaven, whilst I was stealing a poor old woman's nigger that hadn't ever done me no harm, and now was showing me there's One that's always on the lookout, and ain't agoing to allow no such miserable doings to go only just so fur and no further, I most dropped in my tracks I was so scared. Well, I tried the best I could to kinder soften it up somehow for myself, by saying I was brung up wicked, and so I warn't so much to blame; but something inside of me kept saying, "There was the Sunday school, you could a gone to it; and if you'd a done it they'd a learnt you, there, that people that acts as I'd been acting about that nigger goes to everlasting fire."

It made me shiver. And I about made up my mind to pray; and see if I couldn't try to quit being the kind of a boy I was, and be better. So I kneeled down. But the words wouldn't come. Why wouldn't they? It warn't no use to try and hide it from Him. Nor from *me*, neither. I knowed very well why they wouldn't come. It was because my heart warn't right; it was because I warn't square; it was because I was playing double. I was letting *on* to give up sin, but away inside of me I was holding on to the biggest one of all. I was trying to make my mouth *say* I would do the right thing and the clean thing, and go and write to that nigger's owner and tell where he was; but deep down in me I knowed it was a lie—and He knowed it. You can't pray a lie—I found that out.

So I was full of trouble, full as I could be; and didn't know what to do. At last I had an idea; and I says, I'll go and write the letter—and *then* see if I can pray. Why, it was astonishing, the way I felt as light as a feather, right straight off, and my troubles all gone. So I got a piece of paper and a pencil, all glad and excited, and set down and wrote:

> Miss Watson your runaway nigger Jim is down here two mile below Pikesville and Mr. Phelps has got him and he will give him up for the reward if you send. HUCK FINN.

I felt good and all washed clean of sin for the first time I had ever felt so in my life, and I knowed I could pray now. But I didn't do it straight off, but laid the paper down and set there thinking—thinking how good it was all this happened so, and how near I come to being lost and going to hell. And went on thinking. And got to thinking over our trip down the river; and I see Jim before me, all the time, in the day, and in the night-time, sometimes moonlight, sometimes storms, and we a floating along, talking, and singing, and laughing. But somehow I couldn't seem to strike no places to harden me against him, but only the other kind. I'd see him standing my watch on top of his'n, stead of calling me, so I could go on sleeping; and see him how glad he was when I come back out of the fog; and when I come to him again in the swamp, up there where the feud was; and such-like times; and would always call me honey, and pet me, and do everything he could think of for me, and how good he always was; and at last I struck the time I saved him by telling the men we had small-pox aboard, and he was so grateful, and said I was the best friend old Jim ever had in the world, and the *only* one he's got now; and then I happened to look around, and see that paper.

It was a close place. I took it up, and held it in my hand. I was a trembling, because I'd got to decide, forever, betwixt two things, and I knowed it. I studied a minute, sort of holding my breath, and then says to myself:

"All right, then, I'll *go* to hell"—and tore it up.

It was awful thoughts, and awful words, but they was said. And I let them stay said; and never thought no more about reforming. I shoved the whole thing out of my head; and said I would take up wickedness again, which was in my line, being brung up to it, and the other warn't. And for a starter, I would go to work and steal

Jim out of slavery again; and if I could think up anything worse, I would do that, too; because as long as I was in, and in for good, I might as well go the whole hog.

Then I set to thinking over how to get at it, and turned over considerable many ways in my mind; and at last fixed up a plan that suited me. So then I took the bearings of a woody island that was down the river a piece, and as soon as it was fairly dark I crept out with my raft and went for it, and hid it there, and then turned in. I slept the night through, and got up before it was light, and had my breakfast, and put on my store clothes, and tied up some others and one thing or another in a bundle, and took the canoe and cleared for shore. I landed below where I judged was Phelps's place, and hid my bundle in the woods, and then filled up the canoe with water, and loaded rocks into her and sunk her where I could find her again when I wanted her, about a quarter of a mile below a little stream sawmill that was on the bank.

Then I struck up the road, and when I passed the mill I see a sign on it, "Phelps's Sawmill," and when I come to the farmhouses, two or three hundred yards further along, I kept my eyes peeled, but didn't see nobody around, though it was good daylight, now. But I didn't mind, because I didn't want to see nobody just yet—I only wanted to get the lay of the land. According to my plan, I was going to turn up there from the village, not from below. So I just took a look, and shoved along, straight for town. Well, the very first man I see, when I got there, was the duke. He was sticking up a bill for the Royal Nonesuch—three-night performance—like that other time. *They* had the cheek, them frauds! I was right on him, before I could shirk. He looked astonished, and says:

"Hel-*lo*! Where'd *you* come from?" Then he says, kind of glad and eager, "Where's the raft?—got her in a good place?"

I says:

"Why, that's just what I was a going to ask your grace."

Then he didn't look so joyful—and says:

"What was your idea for asking *me*?" he says.

"Well," I says, "when I see the king in that doggery yesterday, I says to myself, we can't get him home for hours, till he's soberer; so I went a loafing around town to put in the time, and wait. A man up and offered me ten cents to help him pull a skiff over the river and back to fetch a sheep, and so I went along; but when we was dragging him to the boat, and the man left me aholt of the rope and went behind him to shove him along, he was too strong for me, and jerked loose and run, and we after him. We didn't have no dog, and so we had to chase him all over the country till we tired him out. We never got him till dark, then we fetched him over, and I started down for the raft. When I got there and see it was gone, I says to myself, 'they've got into trouble and had to leave; and they've took my nigger, which is the only nigger I've got in the world, and now I'm in a strange country, and ain't got no property no more, nor nothing, and no way to make my living'; so I set down and cried. I slept in the woods all night. But what *did* become of the raft then?—and Jim, poor Jim!"

"Blamed if *I* know—that is, what's become of the raft. That old fool had made a trade and got forty dollars, and when we found him in the doggery the loafers had matched half dollars with him and got every cent but what he'd spent for whisky; and when I got him home late last night and found the raft gone, we said, 'That little rascal has stole our raft and shook us, and run off down the river.'"

"I wouldn't shake my *nigger*, would I?—the only nigger I had in the world, and the only property."

"We never thought of that. Fact is, I reckon we'd come to consider him *our* nigger; yes, we did consider him so—goodness knows we had trouble enough for him. So when we see the raft was gone, and we flat broke, there warn't anything for it but to try the Royal Nonesuch another shake. And I've pegged along ever since, dry as a powderhorn. Where's that ten cents? Give it here."

I had considerable money, so I give him ten cents, but begged him to spend it for something to eat, and give me some, because it was all the money I had, and I hadn't had nothing to eat since yesterday. He never said nothing. The next minute he whirls on me and says:

"Do you reckon that nigger would blow on us? We'd skin him if he done that!"

"How can he blow? Hain't he run off?"

"No! That old fool sold him, and never divided with me, and the money's gone."

"*Sold* him?" I says, and begun to cry; "why, he was *my* nigger, and that was my money. Where is he?—I want my nigger."

"Well, you can't *get* your nigger, that's all—so dry up your blubbering. Looky here—do you think *you'd* venture to blow on us? Blamed if I think I'd trust you. Why, if you *was* to blow on us—"

He stopped, but I never see the duke look so ugly out of his eyes before. I went on a-whimpering, and says:

"I don't want to blow on nobody; and I ain't got no time to blow, nohow. I got to turn out and find my nigger."

He looked kinder bothered, and stood there with his bills fluttering on his arm, thinking, and wrinkling up his forehead. At last he says:

"I'll tell you something. We got to be here three days. If you'll promise you won't blow, and won't let the nigger blow, I'll tell you where to find him."

So I promised, and he says:

"A farmer by the name of Silas Ph——" and then he stopped. You see he started to tell me the truth; but when he stopped, that way, and begun to study and think again, I reckoned he was changing his mind. And so he was. He wouldn't trust me; he wanted to make sure of having me out of the way the whole three days. So pretty soon he says: "The man that bought him is named Abram Foster—Abram G. Foster—and he lives forty mile back here in the country, on the road to Lafayette."

"All right," I says, "I can walk it in three days. And I'll start this very afternoon."

"No you won't, you'll start *now*; and don't you lose any time about it, neither, nor do any gabbling by the way. Just keep a tight tongue in your head and move right along, and then you won't get into trouble with *us*, d'ye hear?"

That was the order I wanted, and that was the one I played for. I wanted to be left free to work my plans.

"So clear out," he says; "and you can tell Mr. Foster whatever you want to. Maybe you can get him to believe that Jim *is* your nigger—some idiots don't require documents—leastways I've heard there's such down South here. And when you tell him the handbill and the reward's bogus, maybe he'll believe you when you explain to him what the idea was for getting 'em out. Go 'long, now, and tell him anything you want to; but mind you don't work your jaw any *between* here and there."

So I left, and struck for the back country. I didn't look around, but I kinder felt like he was watching me. But I knowed I could tire him out at that. I went straight out in the country as much as a mile, before I stopped; then I doubled back through the woods towards Phelps's. I reckoned I better start in on my plan straight off, without fooling around, because I wanted to stop Jim's mouth till these fellows could get away. I didn't want no trouble with their kind. I'd seen all I wanted to of them, and wanted to get entirely shut of them.

CHAPTER XXXII

When I got there it was all still and Sunday-like, and hot and sunshiny—the hands was gone to the fields; and there was them kind of faint dronings of bugs and flies in the air that makes it seem so lonesome and like everybody's dead and gone; and if a breeze fans along and quivers the leaves, it makes you feel mournful, because you feel like it's spirits whispering—spirits that's been dead ever so many years—and you always think they're talking about *you*. As a general thing it makes a body wish *he* was dead, too, and done with it all.

Phelps's was one of these little one-horse cotton plantations; and they all look alike. A rail fence round a two-acre yard; a stile, made out of logs sawed off and up-ended, in steps, like barrels of a different length, to climb over the fence with, and for the women to stand on when they are going to jump onto a horse; some sickly grass-patches in the big yard, but mostly it was bare and smooth, like an old hat with the nap rubbed off; big double log house for the white folks—hewed logs, with the chinks stopped up with mud or mortar, and these mud-stripes been whitewashed some time or another; round-log kitchen, with a big broad, open but roofed passage joining it to the house; log smoke-house back of the kitchen; three little log nigger-cabins in a row t'other side the smoke-house; one little hut all by itself away down against the back fence, and some out-buildings down a piece the other side; ash-hopper, and big kettle to bile soap in, by the little hut; bench by the kitchen door, with bucket of water and a gourd; hound asleep there, in the sun; more hounds asleep, round about; about three shade-trees away off in a corner; some currant bushes and gooseberry bushes in one place by the fence; outside of the fence a garden and a water-melon patch; then the cotton fields begins; and after the fields, the woods.

I went around and clumb over the back stile by the ash-hopper, and started for the kitchen. When I got a little ways, I heard the dim hum of a spinning-wheel wailing along up and sinking along down again; and then I knowed for certain I wished I was dead—for that *is* the lonesomest sound in the whole world.

I went right along, not fixing up any particular plan, but just trusting to Providence to put the right words in my mouth when the time come; for I'd noticed that Providence always did put the right words in my mouth, if I left it alone.

When I got half-way, first one hound and then another got up and went for me, and of course I stopped and faced them, and kept still. And such another pow-wow as they made! In a quarter of a minute I was a kind of a hub of a wheel, as you may say—spokes made out of dogs—circle of fifteen of them packed together around me, with their necks and noses stretched up towards me, a barking and howling; and more a coming; you could see them sailing over fences and around corners from everywheres.

A nigger woman come tearing out of the kitchen with a rolling-pin in her hand, singing out, "Begone! *you* Tige! you Spot! begone, sah!" and she fetched first one and then another of them a clip and sent him howling, and then the rest followed; and the next second, half of them come back, wagging their tails around me and making friends with me. There ain't no harm in a hound, nohow.

And behind the woman comes a little nigger girl and two little nigger boys, without anything on but tow-linen shirts, and they hung onto their mother's gown, and peeped out from behind her at me, bashful, the way they always do. And here comes the white woman running from the house, about forty-five or fifty year old, bareheaded, and her spinning-stick in her hand; and behind her comes her little white children, acting the same way the little niggers was doing. She was smiling all over so she could hardly stand—and says:

"It's *you*, at last!—*ain't* it?"

I out with a "Yes'm," before I thought.

She grabbed me and hugged me tight; and then gripped me by both hands and shook and shook; and the tears come in her eyes, and run down over; and she couldn't seem to hug and shake enough, and kept saying, "You don't look as much like your mother as I reckoned you would, but law sakes, I don't care for that, I'm *so* glad to see you! Dear, dear, it does seem like I could eat you up! Children, it's your cousin Tom!—tell him howdy."

But they ducked their heads, and put their fingers in their mouths, and hid behind her. So she run on:

"Lize, hurry up and get him a hot breakfast, right away—or did you get your breakfast on the boat?"

I said I had got it on the boat. So then she started for the house, leading me by the hand, and the children tagging after. When we got there, she set me down in a split-bottomed chair, and set herself down on a little low stool in front of me, holding both of my hands, and says:

"Now I can have a *good* look at you; and laws-a-me, I've been hungry for it a many and a many a time, all these long years, and it's come at last! We been expecting you a couple of days and more. What's kep' you?—boat get aground?"

"Yes'm—she—"

"Don't say yes'm—say Aunt Sally. Where'd she get aground?"

I didn't rightly know what to say, because I didn't know whether the boat would be coming up the river or down. But I go a good deal on instinct; and my instinct said she would be coming up—from down towards Orleans. That didn't help me much, though; for I didn't know the names of bars down that way. I see I'd got to invent a bar, or forget the name of the one we got aground on—or—Now I struck an idea, and fetched it out:

"It warn't the grounding—that didn't keep us back but a little. We blowed out a cylinder-head."

"Good gracious! Anybody hurt?"

"No'm. Killed a nigger."

"Well, it's lucky; because sometimes people do get hurt. Two years ago last Christmas, your uncle Silas was coming up from Newrleans on the old *Lally Rook*, and she blowed out a cylinder-head and crippled a man. And I think he died afterwards. He was a Babtist. Your uncle Silas knowed a family in Baton Rouge that knowed his people very well. Yes, I remember, now he *did* die. Mortification set in, and they had to amputate him. But it didn't save him. Yes, it was mortification—that was it. He turned blue all over, and died in the hope of a glorious resurrection. They say he was a sight to look at. Your uncle's been up to the town every day to fetch you. And he's gone again, not more'n an hour ago; he'll be back any minute, now. You must a met him on the road, didn't you?—oldish man, with a—"

"No, I didn't see nobody, Aunt Sally. The boat landed just at daylight, and I left my baggage on the wharf-boat and went looking around the town and out a piece in the country, to put in the time and not get here too soon; and so I come down the back way."

"Who'd you give the baggage to?"

"Nobody."

"Why, child, it'll be stole!"

"Not where *I* hid it I reckon it won't," I says.

"How'd you get your breakfast so early on the boat?"

It was kinder thin ice, but I says:

"The captain see me standing around, and told me I better have something to eat before I went ashore; so he took me in the texas to the officers' lunch, and give me all I wanted."

I was getting so uneasy I couldn't listen good. I had my mind on the children all the time; I wanted to get them out to one side, and pump them a little, and find out who I was. But I couldn't get no show, Mrs. Phelps kept it up and run on so. Pretty soon she made the cold chills streak all down my back, because she says:

"But here we're a running on this way, and you hain't told me a word about Sis, nor any of them. Now I'll rest my works a little, and you start up yourn; just tell me *everything*—tell me all about 'm all—every one of 'm; and how they are, and what they're doing, and what they told you to tell me; and every last thing you can think of."

Well, I see I was up a stump—and up it good. Providence had stood by me this fur, all right, but I was hard and tight aground, now. I see it warn't a bit of use to try to go ahead—I'd *got* to throw up my hand. So I says to myself, here's another place where I got to resk the truth. I opened my mouth to begin; but she grabbed me and hustled me in behind the bed, and says:

"Here he comes! stick your head down lower—there, that'll do; you can't be seen, now. Don't you let on you're here. I'll play a joke on him. Children, don't you say a word."

I see I was in a fix, now. But it warn't no use to worry; there warn't nothing to do but just hold still, and try and be ready to stand from under when the lightning struck.

I had just one little glimpse of the old gentleman when he come in, then the bed hid him. Mrs. Phelps she jumps for him and says:

"Has he come?"

"No," says her husband.

"Good-*ness* gracious!" she says, "what in the world *can* have become of him?"

"I can't imagine," says the old gentleman; "and I must say, it makes me dreadful uneasy."

"Uneasy!" she says, "I'm ready to go distracted! He *must* a come; and you've missed him along the road. I *know* it's so—something *tells* me so."

"Why Sally, I *couldn't* miss him along the road—*you* know that."

"But oh, dear, dear, what *will* Sis say? He must a come! You must a missed him. He—"

"Oh, don't distress me any more'n I'm already distressed. I don't know what in the world to make of it. I'm at my wit's end, and I don't mind acknowledging 't

I'm right down scared. But there's no hope that he's come; for he *couldn't* come and me miss him. Sally, it's terrible—just terrible—something's happened to the boat, sure!"

"Why, Silas! Look yonder!—up the road!—ain't that somebody coming?"

He sprung to the window at the head of the bed, and that give Mrs. Phelps the chance she wanted. She stooped down quick, at the foot of the bed, and give me a pull, and out I come; and when he turned back from the window, there she stood, a-beaming and a-smiling like a house afire, and I standing pretty meek and sweaty alongside. The old gentleman stared, and says:

"Why, who's that?"

"Who do you reckon 't is?"

"I hain't no idea. Who *is* it?"

"It's *Tom Sawyer*!"

By jings, I most slumped through the floor. But there warn't no time to swap knives; the old man grabbed me by the hand and shook, and kept on shaking; and all the time, how the woman did dance around and laugh and cry; and then how they both did fire off questions about Sid, and Mary, and the rest of the tribe.

But if they was joyful, it warn't nothing to what I was; for it was like being born again, I was so glad to find out who I was. Well, they froze to me for two hours; and at last when my chin was so tired it couldn't hardly go, any more, I had told them more about my family—I mean the Sawyer family—than ever happened to any six Sawyer families. And I explained all about how we blowed out a cylinder-head at the mouth of White River and it took us three days to fix it. Which was all right, and worked first rate; because *they* didn't know but what it would take three days to fix it. If I'd a called it a bolt-head it would a done just as well.

Now I was feeling pretty comfortable all down one side, and pretty uncomfortable all up the other. Being Tom Sawyer was easy and comfortable; and it stayed easy and comfortable till by-and-by I hear a steamboat coughing along down the river—then I says to myself, spose Tom Sawyer come down on that boat?—and spose he steps in here, any minute, and sings out my name before I can throw him a wink to keep quiet? Well, I couldn't *have* it that way—it wouldn't do at all. I must go up the road and waylay him. So I told the folks I reckoned I would go up to the town and fetch down my baggage. The old gentleman was for going along with me, but I said no, I could drive the horse myself, and I druther he wouldn't take no trouble about me.

CHAPTER XXXIII

So I started for town, in the wagon, and when I was half-way I see a wagon coming, and sure enough it was Tom Sawyer, and I stopped and waited till he come along. I says "Hold on!" and it stopped alongside, and his mouth opened up like a trunk, and staid so; and he swallowed two or three times like a person that's got a dry throat, and then says:

"I hain't ever done you no harm. You know that. So then, what you want to come back and ha'nt *me* for?"

I says:

"I hain't come back—I hain't been *gone*."

When he heard my voice, it righted him up some, but he warn't quite satisfied yet. He says:

"Don't you play nothing on me, because I wouldn't on you. Honest injun, now, you ain't a ghost?"

"Honest injun, I ain't," I says.

"Well—I—I—well, that ought to settle it, of course; but I can't somehow seem to understand it, no way. Looky here, warn't you ever murdered *at all*?"

"No. I warn't ever murdered at all—I played it on them. You come in here and feel of me if you don't believe me."

So he done it; and it satisfied him; and he was that glad to see me again, he didn't know what to do. And he wanted to know all about it right off; because it was a grand adventure, and mysterious, and so it hit him where he lived. But I said, leave it alone till by-and-by; and told his driver to wait, and we drove off a little piece, and I told him the kind of a fix I was in, and what did he reckon we better do? He said, let him alone a minute, and don't disturb him. So he thought and thought, and pretty soon he says:

"It's all right, I've got it. Take my trunk in your wagon, and let on it's your'n; and you turn back and fool along slow, so as to get to the house about the time you ought to; and I'll go towards town a piece, and take a fresh start, and get there a quarter or a half an hour after you; and you needn't let on to know me, at first."

I says:

"All right; but wait a minute. There's one more thing—a thing that *nobody* don't know but me. And that is, there's a nigger here that I'm a trying to steal out of slavery—and his name is *Jim*—old Miss Watson's Jim."

He says:

"What! Why Jim is—"

He stopped and went to studying. I says:

"*I* know what you'll say. You'll say it's dirty low-down business; but what if it is?—*I'm* low down; and I'm agoing to steal him, and I want you to keep mum and not let on. Will you?"

His eye lit up, and he says:

"I'll *help* you steal him!"

Well, I let go all holts then, like I was shot. It was the most astonishing speech I ever heard—and I'm bound to say Tom Sawyer fell, considerable, in my estimation. Only I couldn't believe it. Tom Sawyer a *nigger stealer!*

"Oh, shucks," I says, "you're joking."

"I ain't joking, either."

"Well, then," I says, "joking or no joking, if you hear anything said about a runaway nigger, don't forget to remember that *you* don't know nothing about him, and *I* don't know nothing about him."

Then we took the trunk and put it in my wagon, and he drove off his way, and I drove mine. But of course I forgot all about driving slow, on accounts of being glad and full of thinking; so I got home a heap too quick for that length of a trip. The old gentleman was at the door, and he says:

"Why, this is wonderful. Who ever would a thought it was in that mare to do it. I wish we'd a timed her. And she hain't sweated a hair—not a hair. It's wonderful. Why, I wouldn't take a hundred dollars for that horse now; I wouldn't, honest; and yet I'd a sold her for fifteen before, and thought 'twas all she was worth."

That's all he said. He was the innocentest, best old soul I ever see. But it warn't surprising; because he warn't only just a farmer, he was a preacher, too, and had a little one-horse log church down back of the plantation, which he built it himself at his own expense, for a church and school-house, and never charged nothing for his preaching, and it was worth it, too. There was plenty other farmer-preachers like that, and done the same way, down South.

In about half an hour Tom's wagon drove up to the front stile, and Aunt Sally she see it through the window because it was only about fifty yards, and says:

"Why, there's somebody come! I wonder who 'tis? Why, I do believe it's a stranger. Jimmy" (that's one of the children), "run and tell Lize to put on another plate for dinner."

Everybody made a rush for the front door, because, of course, a stranger don't come *every* year, and so he lays over the yaller fever, for interest, when he does come. Tom was over the stile and starting for the house; the wagon was spinning up the road for the village, and we was all bunched in the front door. Tom had his store clothes on, and an audience—and that was always nuts for Tom Sawyer. In them circumstances it warn't no trouble to him to throw in an amount of style that was suitable. He warn't a boy to meeky along up that yard like a sheep; no, he come ca'm and important, like the ram. When he got afront of us, he lifts his hat ever so gracious and dainty, like it was the lid of a box that had butterflies asleep in it and he didn't want to disturb them, and says:

"Mr. Archibald Nichols, I presume?"

"No, my boy," says the old gentleman, "I'm sorry to say 't your driver has deceived you; Nichols's place is down a matter of three mile more. Come in, come in."

Tom he took a look back over his shoulder, and says, "Too late—he's out of sight."

"Yes, he's gone, my son, and you must come in and eat your dinner with us; and then we'll hitch up and take you down to Nichols's."

"Oh, I *can't* make you so much trouble; I couldn't think of it. I'll walk—I don't mind the distance."

"But we won't *let* you walk—it wouldn't be Southern hospitality to do it. Come right in."

"Oh, *do*," says Aunt Sally; "it ain't a bit of trouble to us, not a bit in the world. You *must* stay. It's a long, dusty three mile, and we *can't* let you walk. And besides, I've already told 'em to put on another plate, when I see you coming; so you mustn't disappoint us. Come right in, and make yourself at home."

So Tom he thanked them very hearty and handsome, and let himself be persuaded, and come in; and when he was in, he said he was a stranger from Hicksville, Ohio, and his name was William Thompson—and he made another bow.

Well, he run on, and on, and on, making up stuff about Hicksville and everybody in it he could invent, and I getting a little nervious, and wondering how this was going to help me out of my scrape; and at last, still talking along, he reached over and kissed Aunt Sally right on the mouth, and then settled back again in his chair, comfortable, and was going on talking; but she jumped up and wiped it off with the back of her hand, and says:

"You owdacious puppy!"

He looked kind of hurt, and says:

"I'm surprised at you, m'am."

"You're s'rp—Why, what do you reckon *I* am? I've a good notion to take and—say, what do you mean by kissing me?"

He looked kind of humble, and says:

"I didn't mean nothing, m'am. I didn't mean no harm. I—I—thought you'd like it."

"Why, you born fool!" She took up the spinning-stick, and it looked like it was all she could do to keep from giving him a crack with it. "What made you think I'd like it?"

"Well, I don't know. Only, they—they—told me you would."

"*They* told you I would. Whoever told you's *another* lunatic. I never heard the beat of it. Who's *they*?"

"Why—everybody. They all said so, m'am."

It was all she could do to hold in; and her eyes snapped, and her fingers worked like she wanted to scratch him; and she says:

"Who's 'everybody?' Out with their names—or ther'll be an idiot short."

He got up and looked distressed, and fumbled his hat, and says:

"I'm sorry, and I warn't expecting it. They told me to. They all told me to. They all said kiss her; and said she'll like it. They all said it—every one of them. But I'm sorry, m'am, and I won't do it no more—I won't, honest."

"You won't, won't you? Well, I sh'd *reckon* you won't!"

"No'm, I'm honest about it; I won't ever do it again. Till you ask me."

"Till I *ask* you! Well, I never see the beat of it in my born days! I lay you'll be the Methusalem-numskull of creation before ever *I* ask you—or the likes of you."

"Well," he says, "it does surprise me so. I can't make it out, somehow. They said you would, and I thought you would. But—" He stopped and looked around slow, like he wished he could run across a friendly eye, somewhere's; and fetched up on the old gentleman's, and says, "Didn't *you* think she'd like me to kiss her, sir?"

"Why, no, I—I—well, no, I b'lieve I didn't."

Then he looks on around, the same way, to me—and says:

"Tom, didn't *you* think Aunt Sally 'd open out her arms and say, 'Sid Sawyer—'"

"My land!" she says, breaking in and jumping for him, "you impudent young rascal, to fool a body so—" and was going to hug him, but he fended her off, and says:

"No, not till you've asked me, first."

So she didn't lose no time, but asked him; and hugged him and kissed him, over and over again, and then turned him over to the old man, and he took what was left. And after they got a little quiet again, she says:

"Why, dear me, I never see such a surprise. We warn't looking for *you*, at all, but only Tom. Sis never wrote to me about anybody coming but him."

"It's because it warn't *intended* for any of us to come but Tom," he says; "but I begged and begged, and at the last minute she let me come, too; so, coming down the river, me and Tom thought it would be a first-rate surprise for him to come here to the house first, and for me to by-and-by tag along and drop in and let on to be a stranger. But it was a mistake, Aunt Sally. This ain't no healthy place for a stranger to come."

"No—not impudent whelps, Sid. You ought to had your jaws boxed; I hain't been so put out since I don't know when. But I don't care, I don't mind the terms—I'd be willing to stand a thousand such jokes to have you here. Well, to think of that performance! I don't deny it, I was most putrified with astonishment when you give me that smack."

We had dinner out in that broad open passage betwixt the house and the kitchen; and there was things enough on that table for seven families—and all hot, too; none of your flabby tough meat that's laid in a cupboard in a damp cellar all night and tastes like a hunk of old cold cannibal in the morning. Uncle Silas he asked a pretty long blessing over it, but it was worth it; and it didn't cool it a bit, neither, the way I've seen them kind of interruptions do, lots of times.

There was a considerable good deal of talk, all the afternoon, and me and Tom was on the lookout all the time, but it warn't no use, they didn't happen to say nothing about any runaway nigger, and we was afraid to try to work up to it. But at supper, at night, one of the little boys says:

"Pa, mayn't Tom and Sid and me go to the show?"

"No," says the old man, "I reckon there ain't going to be any; and you couldn't go if there was; because the runaway nigger told Burton and me all about that scandalous show, and Burton said he would tell the people; so I reckon they've drove the owdacious loafers out of town before this time."

So there it was!—but *I* couldn't help it. Tom and me was to sleep in the same room and bed; so, being tired, we bid good-night and went up to bed, right after supper, and clumb out of the window and down the lightning-rod, and shoved for the town; for I didn't believe anybody was going to give the king and the duke a hint, and so, if I didn't hurry up and give them one they'd get into trouble sure.

On the road Tom he told me all about how it was reckoned I was murdered, and how pap disappeared, pretty soon, and didn't come back no more, and what a stir there was when Jim run away; and I told Tom all about our Royal Nonesuch rapscallions, and as much of the raft-voyage as I had time to; and as we struck into the town and up through the middle of it—it was as much as half-after eight, then—here comes a raging rush of people, with torches, and an awful whooping and yelling, and banging tin pans and blowing horns; and we jumped to one side to let them go by; and as they went by, I see they had the king and the duke astraddle of a rail—that is, I knowed it *was* the king and the duke, though they was all over tar and feathers, and didn't look like nothing in the world that was human—just looked like a couple of monstrous big soldier-plumes. Well, it made me sick to see it; and I was sorry for them poor pitiful rascals, it seemed like I couldn't ever feel any hardness against them any more in the world. It was a dreadful thing to see. Human beings *can* be awful cruel to one another.

We see we was too late—couldn't do no good. We asked some stragglers about it, and they said everybody went to the show looking very innocent; and laid low and kept dark till the poor old king was in the middle of his cavortings on the stage; then somebody give a signal, and the house rose up and went for them.

So we poked along back home, and I warn't feeling so brash as I was before, but kind of ornery, and humble, and to blame, somehow—though *I* hadn't done nothing. But that's always the way; it don't make no difference whether you do right or wrong, a person's conscience ain't got no sense, and just goes for him *anyway*. If I had a yaller dog that didn't know no more than a person's conscience does, I would pison him. It takes up more room than all the rest of a person's insides, and yet ain't no good, nohow. Tom Sawyer he says the same.

CHAPTER XXXIV

We stopped talking, and got to thinking.

By-and-by Tom says:

"Looky here, Huck, what fools we are, to not think of it before! I bet I know where Jim is."

"No! Where?"

"In that hut down by the ash-hopper. Why, looky here. When we was at dinner, didn't you see a nigger man go in there with some vittles?"

"Yes."

"What did you think the vittles was for?"

"For a dog."

"So'd I. Well, it wasn't for a dog."

"Why?"

"Because part of it was watermelon."

"So it was—I noticed it. Well, it does beat all, that I never thought about a dog not eating watermelon. It shows how a body can see and don't see at the same time."

"Well, the nigger unlocked the padlock when he went in, and he locked it again when he come out. He fetched uncle a key, about the time we got up from table—same key, I bet. Watermelon shows man, lock shows prisoner; and it ain't likely there's two prisoners on such a little plantation, and where the people's all so kind and good. Jim's the prisoner. All right—I'm glad we found it out detective fashion; I wouldn't give shucks for any other way. Now you work your mind and study out a plan to steal Jim, and I will study out one, too; and we'll take the one we like the best."

What a head for just a boy to have! If I had Tom Sawyer's head, I wouldn't trade it off to be a duke, nor mate of a steamboat, nor clown in a circus, nor nothing I can think of. I went to thinking out a plan, but only just to be doing something; I knowed very well where the right plan was going to come from. Pretty soon, Tom says:

"Ready?"

"Yes," I says.

"All right—bring it out."

"My plan is this," I says. "We can easy find out if it's Jim in there. Then get up my canoe to-morrow night, and fetch my raft over from the island. Then the first dark night that comes, steal the key out of the old man's britches, after he goes to bed, and shove off down the river on the raft, with Jim, hiding daytimes and running nights, the way me and Jim used to do before. Wouldn't that plan work?"

"*Work*? Why cert'nly, it would work, like rats a fighting. But it's too blame' simple; there ain't nothing *to* it. What's the good of a plan that ain't no more trouble than that? It's as mild as goose-milk. Why, Huck, it wouldn't make no more talk than breaking into a soap factory."

I never said nothing, because I warn't expecting nothing different; but I knowed mighty well that whenever he got *his* plan ready it wouldn't have none of them objections to it.

And it didn't. He told me what it was, and I see in a minute it was worth fifteen of mine, for style, and would make Jim just as free a man as mine would, and maybe get us all killed besides. So I was satisfied, and said we would waltz in on it. I needn't tell what it was, here, because I knowed it wouldn't stay the way it was. I knowed he would be changing it around, every which way, as we went along, and heaving in new bullinesses wherever he got a chance. And that is what he done.

Well, one thing was dead sure; and that was, that Tom Sawyer was in earnest and was actuly going to help steal that nigger out of slavery. That was the thing that was too many for me. Here was a boy that was respectable, and well brung up; and had a character to lose; and folks at home that had characters; and he was bright and not leather-headed; and knowing and not ignorant; and not mean, but kind;

and yet here he was, without any more pride, or rightness, or feeling, than to stoop to this business, and make himself a shame, and his family a shame, before everybody. I *couldn't* understand it, no way at all. It was outrageous, and I knowed I ought to just up and tell him so; and so be his true friend, and let him quit the thing right where he was, and save himself. And I *did* start to tell him; but he shut me up, and says:

"Don't you reckon I know what I'm about? Don't I generly know what I'm about?"

"Yes."

"Didn't I *say* I was going to help steal the nigger?"

"Yes."

"*Well* then."

That's all he said, and that's all I said. It warn't no use to say any more; because when he said he'd do a thing, he always done it. But *I* couldn't make out how he was willing to go into this thing; so I just let it go, and never bothered no more about it. If he was bound to have it so, *I* couldn't help it.

When we got home, the house was all dark and still; so we went on down to the hut by the ash-hopper, for to examine it. We went through the yard, so as to see what the hounds would do. They knowed us, and didn't make no more noise than country dogs is always doing when anything comes by in the night. When we got to the cabin, we took a look at the front and the two sides; and on the side I warn't acquainted with—which was the north side—we found a square window-hole, up tolerable high, with just one stout board nailed across it. I says:

"Here's the ticket. This hole's big enough for Jim to get through, if we wrench off the board."

Tom says:

"It's as simple as tit-tat-toe, three-in-a-row, and as easy as playing hooky. I should *hope* we can find a way that's a little more complicated than *that*, Huck Finn."

"Well then," I says, "how'll it do to saw him out, the way I done before I was murdered, that time?"

"That's more *like*," he says. "It's real mysterious, and troublesome, and good," he says; "but I bet we can find a way that's twice as long. There ain't no hurry; le's keep on looking around."

Betwixt the hut and the fence, on the back side, was a lean-to, that joined the hut at the eaves, and was made out of plank. It was as long as the hut, but narrow—only about six foot wide. The door to it was at the south end, and was padlocked. Tom he went to the soap kettle, and searched around and fetched back the iron thing they lift the lid with; so he took it and prized out one of the staples. The chain fell down, and we opened the door and went in, and shut it, and struck a match, and see the shed was only built against the cabin and hadn't no connection with it; and there warn't no floor to the shed, nor nothing in it but some old rusty played-out hoes, and spades, and picks, and a crippled plow. The match went out, and so did we, and shoved in the staple again, and the door was locked as good as ever. Tom was joyful. He says:

"Now we're all right. We'll *dig* him out. It'll take about a week!"

Then we started for the house, and I went in the back door—you only have to pull a buckskin latch-string, they don't fasten the doors—but that warn't romantical enough for Tom Sawyer: no way would do him but he must climb up the lightning-rod. But after he got up half-way about three times, and missed fire and fell every time, and the last time most busted his brains out, he thought he'd got to give it up; but after he was rested, he allowed he would give her one more turn for luck, and this time he made the trip.

In the morning we was up at break of day, and down to the nigger cabins to pet the dogs and make friends with the nigger that fed Jim—if it *was* Jim that was being fed. The niggers was just getting through breakfast and starting for the fields; and Jim's nigger was piling up a tin pan with bread and meat and things; and whilst the others was leaving, the key come from the house.

This nigger had a good-natured, chuckle-headed face, and his wool was all tied up in little bunches with thread. That was to keep witches off. He said the witches was pestering him awful, these nights, and making him see all kinds of strange things, and hear all kinds of strange words and noises, and he didn't believe he was ever witched so long, before, in his life. He got so worked up, and got to running on so about his troubles, he forgot all about what he'd been agoing to do. So Tom says:

"What's the vittles for? Going to feed the dogs?"

The nigger kind of smiled around graduly over his face, like when you heave a brickbat in a mud puddle, and he says:

"Yes, Mars Sid, *a* dog. Cur'us dog, too. Does you want to go en look at 'im?"

"Yes."

I hunched Tom, and whispers:

"You going, right here in the day-break? *That* warn't the plan."

"No, it warn't—but it's the plan *now*."

So, drat him, we went along, but I didn't like it much. When we got in, we couldn't hardly see anything, it was so dark; but Jim was there, sure enough, and could see us; and he sings out:

"Why, *Huck!* En good *lan'!* ain' dat Misto Tom?"

I just knowed how it would be; I just expected it. *I* didn't know nothing to do; and if I had, I couldn't a done it; because that nigger busted in and says:

"Why, de gracious sakes! do he know you genlmen?"

We could see pretty well, now. Tom he looked at the nigger, steady and kind of wondering, and says:

"Does *who* know us?"

"Why, dish-yer runaway nigger."

"I don't reckon he does; but what put that into your head?"

"What *put* it dar? Didn' he jis' dis minute sing out like he knowed you?"

Tom says, in a puzzled-up kind of way:

"Well, that's mighty curious. *Who* sung out? *When* did he sing out? *What* did he sing out?" And turns to me, perfectly ca'm, and says, "Did *you* hear anybody sing out?"

Of course there warn't nothing to be said but the one thing; so I says:

"No; *I* ain't heard nobody say nothing."

Then he turns to Jim, and looks him over like he never see him before; and says:

"Did you sing out?"

"No, sah," says Jim; "*I* hain't said nothing, sah."

"Not a word?"

"No, sah, I hain't said a word."

"Did you ever see us before?"

"No, sah; not as *I* knows on."

So Tom turns to the nigger, which was looking wild and distressed, and says, kind of severe:

"What do you reckon's the matter with you, anyway? What made you think somebody sung out?"

"Oh, it's de dad-blame' witches, sah, en I wisht I was dead, I do. Dey's awluz at it, sah, en dey do mos' kill me, dey sk'yers me so. Please to don't tell nobody 'bout it sah, er ole Mars Silas he'll scole me; 'kase he say dey *ain't* no witches. I jis' wish to goodness he was heah now—*den* what would he say! I jis' bet he couldn' fine no way to git aroun' it *dis* time. But it's awluz jis' so; people dat's *sot*, stays sot; dey won't look into nothn' en fine it out f'r deyselves, en when *you* fine it out en tell um 'bout it, dey doan' b'lieve you."

Tom give him a dime, and said we wouldn't tell nobody; and told him to buy some more thread to tie up his wool with; and then looks at Jim, and says:

"I wonder if Uncle Silas is going to hang this nigger. If I was to catch a nigger that was ungrateful enough to run away, *I* wouldn't give him up, I'd hang him." And whilst the nigger stepped to the door to look at the dime and bite it to see if it was good, he whispers to Jim, and says:

"Don't ever let on to know us. And if you hear any digging going on nights, it's us: we're going to set you free."

Jim only had time to grab us by the hand and squeeze it, then the nigger come back, and we said we'd come again some time if the nigger wanted us to; and he said he would, more particular if it was dark, because the witches went for him mostly in the dark, and it was good to have folks around then.

CHAPTER XXXV

It would be most an hour, yet, till breakfast, so we left, and struck down into the woods; because Tom said we got to have *some* light to see how to dig by, and a lantern makes too much, and might get us into trouble; what we must have was a lot of them rotten chunks that's called fox-fire and just makes a soft kind of a glow when you lay them in a dark place. We fetched an armful and hid it in the weeds, and set down to rest, and Tom says, kind of dissatisfied:

"Blame it, this whole thing is just as easy and awkward as it can be. And so it makes it so rotten difficult to get up a difficult plan. There ain't no watchman to be drugged—now there *ought* to be a watchman. There ain't even a dog to give a sleeping-mixture to. And there's Jim chained by one leg, with a ten-foot chain, to the leg of his bed: why, all you got to do is to lift up the bedstead and slip off the chain. And Uncle Silas he trusts everybody; sends the key to the punkin-headed nigger, and don't send nobody to watch the nigger. Jim could a got out of that window hole before this, only there wouldn't be no use trying to travel with a ten-foot chain on his leg. Why, drat it, Huck, it's the stupidest arrangement I ever see. You got to invent *all* the difficulties. Well, we can't help it, we got to do the best we can with the materials we've got. Anyhow, there's one thing—there's more honor in getting him out through a lot of difficulties and dangers, where there warn't one of them furnished to you by the people who it was their duty to furnish them, and you had to contrive them all out of your own head. Now look at just that one thing of the lantern. When you come down to the cold facts, we simply got to *let on* that a lantern's resky. Why, we could work with a torchlight procession if we wanted to, *I* believe. Now, whilst I think of it, we got to hunt up something to make a saw out of, the first chance we get."

"What do we want of a saw?"

"What do we *want* of it? Hain't we got to saw the leg of Jim's bed off, so as to get the chain loose?"

"Why, you just said a body could lift up the bedstead and slip the chain off."

"Well, if that ain't just like you, Huck Finn. You *can* get up the infant-schooliest ways of going at a thing. Why, hain't you ever read any books at all?—Baron Trenck, nor Casanova, nor Benvenuto Chelleeny, nor Henri IV., nor none of them heroes? Whoever heard of getting a prisoner loose in such an old-maidy way as that? No; the way all the best authorities does, is to saw the bed-leg in two, and leave it just so, and swallow the sawdust, so it can't be found, and put some dirt and grease around the sawed place so the very keenest seneskal can't see no sign of it's being sawed, and thinks the bed-leg is perfectly sound. Then, the night you're ready, fetch the leg a kick, down she goes; slip off your chain, and there you are. Nothing to do but hitch your rope-ladder to the battlements, shin down it, break your leg in the moat—because a rope-ladder is nineteen foot too short, you know—and there's your horses and your trusty vassles, and they scoop you up and fling you across a saddle and away you go, to your native Langudoc, or Navarre, or wherever it is. It's gaudy, Huck. I wish there was a moat to this cabin. If we get time, the night of the escape, we'll dig one."

I says:

"What do we want of a moat, when we're going to snake him out from under the cabin?"

But he never heard me. He had forgot me and everything else. He had his chin in his hand, thinking. Pretty soon, he sighs, and shakes his head; then sighs again, and says:

"No, it wouldn't do—there ain't necessity enough for it."

"For what?" I says.

"Why, to saw Jim's leg off," he says.

"Good land!" I says, "why, there ain't *no* necessity for it. And what would you want to saw his leg off for, anyway?

"Well, some of the best authorities has done it. They couldn't get the chain off, so they just cut their hand off, and shoved. And a leg would be better still. But we got to let that go. There ain't necessity enough in this case; and besides, Jim's a nigger and wouldn't understand the reasons for it, and how it's the custom in Europe; so we'll let it go. But there's one thing—he can have a rope-ladder; we can tear up our sheets and make him a rope-ladder easy enough. And we can send it to him in a pie; it's mostly done that way. And I've et worse pies."

"Why, Tom Sawyer, how you talk," I says; "Jim ain't got no use for a rope-ladder."

"He *has* got use for it. How *you* talk, you better say; you don't know nothing about it. He's *got* to have a rope ladder; they all do."

"What in the nation can he *do* with it?"

"*Do* with it? He can hide it in his bed, can't he? That's what they all do; and *he's* got to, too. Huck, you don't ever seem to want to do anything that's regular; you want to be starting something fresh all the time. Spose he *don't* do nothing with it? ain't it there in his bed, for a clew, after he's gone? and don't you reckon they'll want clews? Of course they will. And you wouldn't leave them any? That would be a *pretty* howdy-do, *wouldn't* it! I never heard of such a thing."

"Well," I says, "If it's in the regulations, and he's got to have it, all right, let him have it; because I don't wish to go back on no regulations; but there's one thing,

Tom Sawyer—if we go to tearing up our sheets to make Jim a rope-ladder, we're going to get into trouble with Aunt Sally, just as sure as you're born. Now, the way I look at it, a hickry-bark ladder don't cost nothing, and don't waste nothing, and is just as good to load up a pie with, and hide in a straw tick, as any rag ladder you can start; and as for Jim, he ain't had no experience, and so *he* don't care what kind of a—"

"Oh, shucks, Huck Finn, if I was as ignorant as you, I'd keep still—that's what *I'd* do. Who ever heard of a state prisoner escaping by a hickry-bark ladder? Why, it's perfectly ridiculous."

"Well, all right, Tom, fix it your own way; but if you'll take my advice, you'll let me borrow a sheet off of the clothes-line."

He said that would do. And that give him another idea, and he says:

"Borrow a shirt, too."

"What do we want of a shirt, Tom?"

"Want it for Jim to keep a journal on."

"Journal your granny—*Jim* can't write."

"Spose he *can't* write—he can make marks on the shirt, can't he, if we make him a pen out of an old pewter spoon or a piece of an old iron barrel-hoop?"

"Why, Tom, we can pull a feather out of a goose and make him a better one; and quicker, too."

"*Prisoners* don't have geese running around the donjon-keep to pull pens out of, you muggins. They *always* make their pens out of the hardest, toughest, troublesomest piece of old brass candlestick or something like that they can get their hands on; and it takes them weeks and weeks, and months and months to file it out, too, because they've got to do it by rubbing it on the wall. *They* wouldn't use a goose-quill if they had it. It ain't regular."

"Well, then, what'll we make him the ink out of?"

"Many makes it out of iron-rust and tears; but that's the common sort and women; the best authorities uses their own blood. Jim can do that; and when he wants to send any little common ordinary mysterious message to let the world know where he's captivated, he can write it on the bottom of a tin plate with a fork and throw it out of the window. The Iron Mask always done that, and it's a blame' good way, too."

"Jim ain't got no tin plates. They feed him in a pan."

"That ain't anything; we can get him some."

"Can't nobody *read* his plates."

"That ain't got nothing to *do* with it, Huck Finn. All *he's* got to do is to write on the plate and throw it out. You don't *have* to be able to read it. Why, half the time you can't read anything a prisoner writes on a tin plate, or anywhere else."

"Well, then, what's the sense in wasting the plates?"

"Why, blame it all, it ain't the *prisoner's* plates."

"But it's *somebody's* plates, ain't it?"

"Well, spos'n it is? What does the *prisoner* care whose—"

He broke off there, because we heard the breakfast-horn blowing. So we cleared out for the house.

Along during that morning I borrowed a sheet and a white shirt off of the clothes-line; and I found an old sack and put them in it, and we went down and got the fox-fire, and put that in too. I called it borrowing, because that was what pap always called it; but Tom said it warn't borrowing, it was stealing. He said we was representing prisoners; and prisoners don't care how they get a thing so they get it, and nobody don't blame them for it, either. It ain't no crime in a prisoner to steal the thing he needs to get away with, Tom said; it's his right; and so, as long as we was representing a prisoner, we had a perfect right to steal anything on this place we had the least use for, to get ourselves out of prison with. He said if we warn't prisoners it would be a very different thing, and nobody but a mean ornery person would steal when he warn't a prisoner. So we allowed we would steal everything there was that come handy. And yet he made a mighty fuss, one day, after that, when I stole a watermelon out of the nigger patch and eat it; and he made me go and give the niggers a dime, without telling them what it was for. Tom said that what he meant was, we could steal anything we *needed*. Well, I says, I needed the watermelon. But he said I didn't need it to get out of prison with, there's where the difference was. He said if I'd a wanted it to hide a knife in, and smuggle it to Jim to kill the seneskal with, it would a been all right. So I let it go at that, though I couldn't see no advantage in my representing a prisoner, if I got to set down and chaw over a lot of gold-leaf distinctions like that, every time I see a chance to hog a watermelon.

Well, as I was saying, we waited that morning till everybody was settled down to business, and nobody in sight around the yard; then Tom he carried the sack into the lean-to whilst I stood off a piece to keep watch. By-and-by he come out, and we went and set down on the wood-pile, to talk. He says:

"Everything's all right, now, except tools; and that's easy fixed."

"Tools?" I says.

"Yes."

"Tools for what?"

"Why, to dig with. We ain't agoing to *gnaw* him out, are we?"

"Ain't them old crippled picks and things in there good enough to dig a nigger out with?" I says.

He turns on me looking pitying enough to make a body cry, and says:

"Huck Finn, did you *ever* hear of a prisoner having picks and shovels, and all the modern conveniences in his wardrobe to dig himself out with? Now I want to ask you—if you got any reasonableness in you at all—what kind of a show would *that* give him to be a hero? Why, they might as well lend him the key, and done with it. Picks and shovels—why they wouldn't furnish 'em to a king."

"Well, then," I says, "if we don't want the picks and shovels, what do we want?"

"A couple of case-knives."

"To dig the foundations out from under that cabin with?"

"Yes."

"Confound it, it's foolish, Tom."

"It don't make no difference how foolish it is, it's the *right* way—and it's the regular way. And there ain't no *other* way, that ever *I* heard of, and I've read all the books that gives any information about these things. They always dig out with a case-knife—and not through dirt, mind you; generly it's through solid rock. And it takes them weeks and weeks and weeks, and for ever and ever. Why, look at one of them prisoners in the bottom dungeon of the Castle Deef, in the harbor of Marseilles, that dug himself out that way; how long was *he* at it, you reckon?"

"I don't know."

"Well, guess."

"I don't know. A month and a half?"

"*Thirty-seven year*—and he come out in China. *That's* the kind. I wish the bottom of *this* fortress was solid rock."

"*Jim* don't know nobody in China."

"What's *that* got to do with it? Neither did that other fellow. But you're always a-wandering off on a side issue. Why can't you stick to the main point?"

"All right—I don't care where he comes out, so he *comes* out; and Jim don't, either, I reckon. But there's one thing, anyway—Jim's too old to be dug out with a case-knife. He won't last."

"Yes he will *last*, too. You don't reckon it's going to take thirty-seven years to dig out through a *dirt* foundation, do you?"

"How long will it take, Tom?"

"Well, we can't resk being as long as we ought to, because it mayn't take very long for Uncle Silas to hear from down there by New Orleans. He'll hear Jim ain't from there. Then his next move will be to advertise Jim, or something like that. So we can't resk being as long digging him out as we ought to. By rights I reckon we ought to be a couple of years; but we can't. Things being so uncertain, what I recommend is this: that we really dig right in, as quick as we can; and after that, we can *let on*, to ourselves, that we was at it thirty-seven years. Then we can snatch him out and rush him away the first time there's an alarm. Yes, I reckon that'll be the best way."

"Now, there's *sense* in that," I says. "Letting on don't cost nothing; letting on ain't no trouble; and if it's any object, I don't mind letting on we was at it a hundred and fifty year. It wouldn't strain me none, after I got my hand in. So I'll mosey along now, and smouch a couple of case-knives."

"Smouch three," he says; "we want one to make a saw out of."

"Tom, if it ain't unregular and irreligious to sejest it," I says, "there's an old rusty saw-blade around yonder sticking under the weatherboarding behind the smoke-house."

He looked kind of weary and discouraged-like, and says:

"It ain't no use to try to learn you nothing, Huck. Run along and smouch the knives—three of them." So I done it.

CHAPTER XXXVI

As soon as we reckoned everybody was asleep, that night, we went down the lightning-rod, and shut ourselves up in the lean-to, and got out our pile of fox-fire, and went to work. We cleared everything out of the way, about four or five foot along the middle of the bottom log. Tom said he was right behind Jim's bed now, and we'd dig in under it, and when we got through there couldn't nobody in the cabin ever know there was any hole there, because Jim's counterpin hung down most to the ground, and you'd have to raise it up and look under to see the hole. So we dug and dug, with the case-knives, till most midnight; and then we was dog-tired, and our hands was blistered, and yet you couldn't see we'd done anything, hardly. At last I says:

"This ain't no thirty-seven year job, this is a thirty-eight year job, Tom Sawyer."

He never said nothing. But he sighed, and pretty soon he stopped digging, and then for a good little while I knowed he was thinking. Then he says:

"It ain't no use, Huck, it ain't agoing to work. If we was prisoners it would, because then we'd have as many years as we wanted, and no hurry; and we wouldn't get but a few minutes to dig, every day, while they was changing watches, and so our hands wouldn't get blistered, and we could keep it up right along, year in and year out, and do it right, and the way it ought to be done. But *we* can't fool along, we got to rush; we ain't got no time to spare. If we was to put in another night this way, we'd have to knock off for a week to let our hands get well—couldn't touch a case-knife with them sooner."

"Well, then, what we going to do, Tom?"

"I'll tell you. It ain't right, and it ain't moral, and I wouldn't like it to get out—but there ain't only just the one way; we got to dig him out with the picks, and *let on* it's case-knives."

"*Now* you're *talking*!" I says; "your head gets leveler and leveler all the time, Tom Sawyer," I says. "Picks is the thing, moral or no moral; and as for me, I don't care shucks for the morality of it, nohow. When I start in to steal a nigger, or a watermelon, or a Sunday-school book, I ain't no ways particular how it's done so it's done. What I want is my nigger; or what I want is my watermelon; or what I want is my Sunday-school book; and if a pick's the handiest thing, that's the thing I'm agoing to dig that nigger or that watermelon or that Sunday-school book out with; and I don't give a dead rat what the authorities thinks about it nuther."

"Well," he says, "there's excuse for picks and letting-on in a case like this; if it warn't so, I wouldn't approve of it, nor I wouldn't stand by and see the rules broke—because right is right, and wrong is wrong, and a body ain't got no business doing wrong when he ain't ignorant and knows better. It might answer for *you* to dig Jim out with a pick, *without* any letting-on, because you don't know no better; but it wouldn't for me, because I do know better. Gimme a case-knife."

He had his own by him, but I handed him mine. He flung it down, and says:

"Gimme a *case-knife*."

I didn't know just what to do—but then I thought. I scratched around amongst the old tools, and got a pick-ax and give it to him, and he took it and went to work, and never said a word.

He was always just that particular. Full of principle.

So then I got a shovel, and then we picked and shoveled, turn about, and made the fur fly. We stuck to it about a half an hour, which was as long as we could stand up; but we had a good deal of a hole to show for it. When I got up stairs, I looked out at the window and see Tom doing his level best with the lightning-rod, but he couldn't come it, his hands was so sore. At last he says:

"It ain't no use, it can't be done. What you reckon I better do? Can't you think up no way?"

"Yes," I says, "but I reckon it ain't regular. Come up the stairs, and let on it's a lightning-rod."

So he done it.

Next day Tom stole a pewter spoon and a brass candlestick in the house, for to make some pens for Jim out of, and six tallow candles; and I hung around the nigger cabins, and laid for a chance, and stole three tin plates. Tom said it wasn't enough; but I said nobody wouldn't ever see the plates that Jim throwed out, because they'd fall in the dog-fennel and jimpson weeds under the window-hole—then we could tote them back and he could use them over again. So Tom was satisfied. Then he says:

"Now, the thing to study out is, how to get the things to Jim."

"Take them in through the hole," I says, "when we get it done."

He only just looked scornful, and said something about nobody ever heard of such an idiotic idea, and then he went to studying. By-and-by he said he had ciphered out two or three ways, but there warn't no need to decide on any of them yet. Said we'd got to post Jim first.

That night we went down the lightning-rod a little after ten, and took one of the candles along, and listened under the window-hole, and heard Jim snoring; so we pitched it in, and it didn't wake him. Then we whirled in with the pick and shovel, and in about two hours and a half the job was done. We crept in under Jim's bed and into the cabin, and pawed around and found the candle and lit it, and stood over Jim a while, and found him looking hearty and healthy, and then we woke him up gentle and gradual. He was so glad to see us he most cried; and called us honey, and all the pet names he could think of; and was for having us hunt up a cold chisel to cut the chain off of his leg with, right away, and clearing out without losing any time. But Tom he showed him how unregular it would be, and set down and told him all about our plans, and how we could alter them in a minute any time there was an alarm; and not to be the least afraid, because we would see he got away, *sure*. So Jim he said it was all right, and we set there and talked over old times a while, and then Tom asked a lot of questions, and when Jim told him Uncle Silas come in every day or two to pray with him, and Aunt Sally come in to see if he was comfortable and had plenty to eat, and both of them was kind as they could be, Tom says:

"*Now* I know how to fix it. We'll send you some things by them."

I said, "Don't do nothing of the kind; it's one of the most jackass ideas I ever struck;" but he never paid no attention to me; went right on. It was his way when he'd got his plans set.

So he told Jim how we'd have to smuggle in the rope-ladder pie, and other large things, by Nat, the nigger that fed him, and he must be on the lookout, and not be surprised, and not let Nat see him open them; and we would put small things in uncle's coat pockets and he must steal them out; and we would tie things to aunt's apron strings or put them in her apron pocket, if we got a chance; and told him what they would be and what they was for. And told him how to keep a journal on the shirt with his blood, and all that. He told him everything. Jim he couldn't see no sense in the most of it, but he allowed we was white folks and knowed better than him; so he was satisfied, and said he would do it all just as Tom said.

Jim had plenty corn-cob pipes and tobacco; so we had a right down good sociable time; then we crawled out through the hole, and so home to bed, with hands that looked like they'd been chawed. Tom was in high spirits. He said it was the best fun he ever had in his life, and the most intellectural; and said if he only could see his way to it we would keep it up all the rest of our lives and leave Jim to our children to get out; for he believed Jim would come to like it better and better the more he got used to it. He said that in that way it could be strung out to as much as eighty year, and would be the best time on record. And he said it would make us all celebrated that had a hand in it.

In the morning we went out to the wood-pile and chopped up the brass candlestick into handy sizes, and Tom put them and the pewter spoon in his pocket. Then we went to the nigger cabins, and while I got Nat's notice off, Tom shoved a piece of candlestick into the middle of a corn-pone that was in Jim's pan, and we went along with Nat to see how it would work, and it just worked noble; when Jim bit into it it most mashed all his teeth out; and there warn't ever anything could a worked better. Tom said so himself. Jim he never let on but what it was only just a piece of rock or something like that that's always getting into bread, you know; but after that he never bit into nothing but what he jabbed his fork into it in three or four places, first.

And whilst we was a standing there in the dimmish light, here comes a couple of the hounds bulging in, from under Jim's bed; and they kept on piling in till there was eleven of them, and there warn't hardly room in there to get your breath. By jings, we forgot to fasten that lean-to door. The nigger Nat he only just hollered "witches!" once, and keeled over onto the floor amongst the dogs, and begun to groan like he was dying. Tom jerked the door open and flung out a slab of Jim's meat, and the dogs went for it, and in two seconds he was out himself and back again and shut the door, and I knowed he'd fixed the other door too. Then he went to work on the nigger, coaxing him and petting him, and asking him if he'd been imagining he saw something again. He raised up, and blinked his eyes around, and says:

"Mars Sid, you'll say I's a fool, but if I didn't b'lieve I see most a million dogs, er devils, er some'n, I wisht I may die right heah in dese tracks. I did, mos' sholy. Mars Sid, I *felt* um—I *felt* um, sah; dey was all over me. Dad fetch it, I jis' wisht I could git my han's on one er dem witches jis' wunst—on'y jis' wunst—it's all *I'd* ast. But mos'ly I wisht dey'd lemme 'lone, I does."

Tom says:

"Well, I tell you what *I* think. What makes them come here just at this runaway nigger's breakfast-time? It's because they're hungry; that's the reason. You make them a witch pie; that's the thing for *you* to do."

"But my lan', Mars Sid, how's *I* gwyne to make 'm a witch pie? I doan' know how to make it. I hain't ever hearn er sich a thing b'fo'."

"Well, then, I'll have to make it myself."

"Will you do it, honey?—will you? I'll wusshup de groun' und' yo' foot, I will!"

"All right, I'll do it, seeing it's you, and you've been good to us and showed us the runaway nigger. But you got to be mighty careful. When we come around, you turn your back; and then whatever we've put in the pan, don't you let on you see it at all. And don't you look, when Jim unloads the pan—something might happen, I don't know what. And above all, don't you *handle* the witch-things."

"*Hannel*'m Mars Sid? What *is* you a talkin' 'bout? I wouldn' lay de weight er my finger on um, not f'r ten hund'd thous'n' billion dollars, I wouldn't."

CHAPTER XXXVII

That was all fixed. So then we went away and went to the rubbage-pile in the back yard where they keep the old boots, and rags, and pieces of bottles, and wore-out tin things, and all such truck, and scratched around and found an old tin washpan and stopped up the holes as well as we could, to bake the pie in, and took it down cellar and stole it full of flour, and started for breakfast and found a couple of shingle-nails that Tom said would be handy for a prisoner to scrabble his name and sorrows on the dungeon walls with, and dropped one of them in Aunt Sally's apron pocket which was hanging on a chair, and t'other we stuck in the band of Uncle Silas's hat, which was on the bureau, because we heard the children say their pa and ma was going to the runaway nigger's house this morning, and then went to breakfast, and Tom dropped the pewter spoon in Uncle Silas's coat pocket, and Aunt Sally wasn't come yet, so we had to wait a little while.

And when she come she was hot, and red, and cross, and couldn't hardly wait for the blessing; and then she went to sluicing out coffee with one hand and cracking the handiest child's head with her thimble with the other, and says:

"I've hunted high, and I've hunted low, and it does beat all, what *has* become of your other shirt."

My heart fell down amongst my lungs and livers and things, and a hard piece of corn-crust started down my throat after it and got met on the road with a cough and was shot across the table and took one of the children in the eye and curled him up like a fishing-worm, and let a cry out of him the size of a war-whoop, and Tom he turned kinder blue around the gills, and it all amounted to a considerable state of things for about a quarter of a minute or as much as that, and I would a sold out for half price if there was a bidder. But after that we was all right again—it was the sudden surprise of it that knocked us so kind of cold. Uncle Silas he says:

"It's most uncommon curious, I can't understand it. I know perfectly well I took it *off*, because—"

"Because you hain't got but one *on*. Just *listen* at the man! *I* know you took it off, and know it by a better way than your wool-gethering memory, too, because it was on the clo'es-line yesterday—I see it there myself. But it's gone—that's the long and the short of it, and you'll just have to change to a red flann'l one till I can get time to make a new one. And it'll be the third I've made in two years; it just keeps a body on the jump to keep you in shirts; and whatever you do manage to *do* with 'm all, is more'n *I* can make out. A body'd think you *would* learn to take some sort of care of 'em, at your time of life."

"I know it, Sally, and I do try all I can. But it oughtn't to be altogether my fault, because you know I don't see them nor have nothing to do with them except when they're on me; and I don't believe I've ever lost one of them *off* of me."

"Well, it ain't *your* fault if you haven't, Silas—you'd a done it if you could, I reckon. And the shirt ain't all that's gone, nuther. Ther's a spoon gone; and *that* ain't all. There was ten, and now ther's only nine. The calf got the shirt I reckon, but the calf never took the spoon, *that's* certain."

"Why, what else is gone, Sally?"

"Ther's six *candles* gone—that's what. The rats could a got the candles, and I reckon they did; I wonder they don't walk off with the whole place, the way you're always going to stop their holes and don't do it; and if they warn't fools they'd sleep in your hair, Silas—*you'd* never find it out; but you can't lay the *spoon* on the rats, and that I *know*."

"Well, Sally, I'm in fault, and I acknowledge it; I've been remiss; but I won't let to-morrow go by without stopping up them holes."

"Oh, I wouldn't hurry, next year'll do. Matilda Angelina Araminta *Phelps*!"

Whack comes the thimble, and the child snatches her claws out of the sugar-bowl without fooling around any. Just then, the nigger woman steps onto the passage, and says:

"Missus, dey's a sheet gone."

"A *sheet* gone! Well, for the land's sake!"

"I'll stop up them holes *to-day*," says Uncle Silas, looking sorrowful.

"Oh, *do* shet up!—spose the rats took the *sheet? Where's* it gone, Lize?"

"Clah to goodness I hain't no notion, Miss Sally. She wuz on de clo's-line yistiddy, but she done gone; she ain' dah no mo', now."

"I reckon the world *is* coming to an end. I *never* see the beat of it, in all my born days. A shirt, and a sheet, and a spoon, and six can—"

"Missus," comes a young yaller wench, "dey's a brass cannelstick miss'n."

"Cler out from here, you hussy, er I'll take a skillet to ye!"

Well, she was just a biling. I begun to lay for a chance; I reckoned I would sneak out and go for the woods till the weather moderated. She kept a raging right along, running her insurrection all by herself, and everybody else mighty meek and quiet; and at last Uncle Silas, looking kind of foolish, fishes up that spoon out of his pocket. She stopped, with her mouth open and her hands up; and as for me, I wished I was in Jeruslem or somewheres. But not long; because she says:

"It's *just* as I expected. So you had it in your pocket all the time; and like as not you've got the other things there, too. How'd it get there?"

"I reely don't know, Sally," he says, kind of apologizing, "or you know I would tell. I was a-studying over my text in Acts Seventeen, before breakfast, and I reckon I put it in there, not noticing, meaning to put my Testament in, and it must be so, because my Testament ain't in, but I'll go and see, and if the Testament is where I had it, I'll know I didn't put it in, and that will show that I laid the Testament down and took up the spoon, and—"

"Oh, for the land's sake! Give a body a rest! Go 'long now, the whole kit and biling of ye; and don't come nigh me again till I've got back my peace of mind."

I'd a heard her, if she'd a said it to herself, let alone speaking it out; and I'd a got up and obeyed her, if I'd a been dead. As we was passing through the setting-room, the old man he took up his hat, and the shingle-nail fell out on the floor, and he just merely picked it up and laid it on the mantel-shelf, and never said nothing, and went out. Tom see him do it, and remembered about the spoon, and says:

"Well, it ain't no use to send things by *him* no more, he ain't reliable." Then he says: "But he done us a good turn with the spoon, anyway, without knowing it, and so we'll go and do him one without *him* knowing it—stop up his rat-holes."

There was a noble good lot of them, down cellar, and it took us a whole hour, but we done the job tight and good, and shipshape. Then we heard steps on the stairs, and blowed out our light, and hid; and here comes the old man, with a candle in one hand and a bundle of stuff in t'other, looking as absentminded as year before last. He went a mooning around, first to one rat-hole and then another, till he'd been to them all. Then he stood about five minutes, picking tallow-drip off of his candle and thinking. Then he turns off slow and dreamy towards the stairs, saying:

"Well, for the life of me I can't remember when I done it. I could show her now that I warn't to blame on account of the rats. But never mind—let it go. I reckon it wouldn't do no good."

And so he went on a mumbling up stairs, and then we left. He was a mighty nice old man. And always is.

Tom was a good deal bothered about what to do for a spoon, but he said we'd got to have it; so he took a think. When he had ciphered it out, he told me how we was to do; then we went and waited around the spoon-basket till we see Aunt Sally coming, and then Tom went to counting the spoons and laying them out to one side, and I slid one of them up my sleeve, and Tom says:

"Why, Aunt Sally, there ain't but nine spoons, *yet*."

She says:

"Go 'long to your play, and don't bother me. I know better, I counted 'm myself."

"Well, I've counted them twice, Aunty, and *I* can't make but nine."

She looked out of all patience, but of course she come to count—anybody would.

"I declare to gracious ther' *ain't* but nine!" she says. "Why, what in the world—plague *take* the things, I'll count 'm again."

So I slipped back the one I had, and when she got done counting, she says:

"Hang the troublesome rubbage, ther's *ten* now!" and she looked huffy and bothered both. But Tom says:

"Why, Aunty, *I* don't think there's ten."

"You numskull, didn't you see me *count* 'm?"

"I know, but—"

"Well, I'll count 'm *again*."

So I smouched one, and they come out nine same as the other time. Well, she *was* in a tearing way—just a trembling all over, she was so mad. But she counted and counted, till she got that addled she'd start to count-in the *basket* for a spoon, sometimes; and so, three times they come out right, and three times they come out wrong. Then she grabbed up the basket and slammed it across the house and knocked the cat galley-west; and she said cle'r out and let her have some peace, and if we come bothering around her again betwixt that and dinner, she'd skin us. So we had the odd spoon; and dropped it in her apron pocket whilst she was a giving us our sailing-orders, and Jim got it all right, along with her shingle-nail, before noon. We was very well satisfied with this business, and Tom allowed it was worth twice the trouble it took, because he said *now* she couldn't ever count them spoons twice alike again to save her life; and wouldn't believe she'd counted them right, if she *did*; and said that after she'd about counted her head off, for the next three days, he judged she'd give it up and offer to kill anybody that wanted her to ever count them any more.

So we put the sheet back on the line, that night, and stole one out of her closet; and kept on putting it back and stealing it again, for a couple of days, till she didn't know how many sheets she had, any more, and said she didn't *care*, and warn't agoing to bullyrag the rest of her soul out about it, and wouldn't count them again not to save her life, she druther die first.

So we was all right now, as to the shirt and the sheet and the spoon and the candles, by the help of the calf and the rats and the mixed-up counting; and as to the candlestick, it warn't no consequence, it would blow over by-and-by.

But that pie was a job; we had no end of trouble with that pie. We fixed it up away down in the woods, and cooked it there; and we got it done at last, and very satisfactory, too; but not all in one day; and we had to use up three washpans full of flour, before we got through, and we got burnt pretty much all over, in places, and eyes put out with the smoke; because, you see, we didn't want nothing but a crust, and we couldn't prop it up right, and she would always cave in. But of course we thought of the right way at last; which was to cook the ladder, too, in the pie. So then we laid in with Jim, the second night, and tore up the sheet all in little strings, and twisted them together, and long before daylight we had a lovely rope, that you could a hung a person with. We let on it took nine months to make it.

And in the forenoon we took it down to the woods, but it wouldn't go in the pie. Being made of a whole sheet, that way, there was rope enough for forty pies, if we'd a wanted them, and plenty left over for soup, or sausage, or anything you choose. We could a had a whole dinner.

But we didn't need it. All we needed was just enough for the pie, and so we throwed the rest away. We didn't cook none of the pies in the washpan, afraid the solder would melt; but Uncle Silas he had a noble brass warming-pan which he thought considerable of, because it belonged to one of his ancesters with a long wooden handle that come over from England with William the Conqueror in the *Mayflower* or one of them early ships and was hid away up garret with a lot of other old pots and things that was valuable, not on account of being any account because they warn't, but on account of them being relicts, you know, and we snaked her out, private, and took her down there, but she failed on the first pies, because we didn't know how, but she come up smiling on the last one. We took and lined her with dough, and set her in the coals, and loaded her up with rag-rope, and put on a dough roof, and shut down the lid, and put hot embers on top, and stood off five foot, with the long handle, cool and comfortable, and in fifteen minutes she turned out a pie that was a satisfaction to look at. But the person that et it would want to fetch a couple of kags of toothpicks along, for if that rope-ladder wouldn't cramp him down to business, I don't know nothing what I'm talking about, and lay him in enough stomach-ache to last him till next time, too.

Nat didn't look, when we put the witch-pie in Jim's pan; and we put the three tin plates in the bottom of the pan under the vittles; and so Jim got everything all right, and as soon as he was by himself he busted into the pie and hid the rope-ladder inside of his straw tick, and scratched some marks on a tin plate and throwed it out of the window-hole.

CHAPTER XXXVIII

Making them pens was a distressid-tough job, and so was the saw; and Jim allowed the inscription was going to be the toughest of all. That's the one which the prisoner has to scrabble on the wall. But we had to have it; Tom said we'd *got* to; there warn't no case of a state prisoner not scrabbling his inscription to leave behind, and his coat of arms.

"Look at Lady Jane Grey," he says; "look at Gilford Dudley; look at old Northumberland! Why, Huck, spose it *is* considerble trouble?—what you going to do?—how you going to get around it? Jim's *got* to do his inscription and coat of arms. They all do."

Jim says:

"Why, Mars Tom, I hain't got no coat o' arms; I hain't got nuffn but dish-yer ole shirt, en you knows I got to keep de journal on dat."

"Oh, you don't understand, Jim; a coat of arms is very different."

"Well," I says, "Jim's right, anyway, when he says he hain't got no coat of arms, because he hain't."

"I reckon *I* knowed that," Tom says, "but you bet he'll have one before he goes out of this—because he's going out *right*, and there ain't going to be no flaws in his record."

So whilst me and Jim filed away at the pens on a brickbat apiece, Jim a making his'n out of the brass and I making mine out of the spoon, Tom set to work to think out the coat of arms. By-and-by he said he'd struck so many good ones he didn't hardly know which to take, but there was one which he reckoned he'd decide on. He says:

"On the scutcheon we'll have a bend *or* in the dexter base, a saltire *murrey* in the fess, with a dog, couchant, for common charge, and under his foot a chain embattled, for slavery, with a chevron *vert* in a chief engrailed, and three invected lines on a field *azure*, with the nombril points rampant on a dancette indented; crest, a runaway nigger, *sable*, with his bundle over his shoulder on a bar sinister: and a couple of gules for supporters, which is you and me; motto, *Maggiore fretta, minore atto*. Got it out of a book—means, the more haste, the less speed."

"Geewhillikins," I says, "but what does the rest of it mean?"

"We ain't got no time to bother over that," he says, "we got to dig in like all git-out."

"Well, anyway," I says, "what's *some* of it? What's a fess?"

"A fess—a fess is—*you* don't need to know what a fess is. I'll show him how to make it when he gets to it."

"Shucks, Tom," I says, "I think you might tell a person. What's a bar sinister?"

"Oh, *I* don't know. But he's got to have it. All the nobility does."

That was just his way. If it didn't suit him to explain a thing to you, he wouldn't do it. You might pump at him a week, it wouldn't make no difference.

He'd got all that coat of arms business fixed, so now he started in to finish up the rest of that part of the work, which was to plan out a mournful inscription—said Jim got to have one, like they all done. He made up a lot, and wrote them out on a paper, and read them off, so:

1. *Here a captive heart busted.*
2. *Here a poor prisoner, forsook by the world and friends, fretted out his sorrowful life.*
3. *Here a lonely heart broke, and a worn spirit went to its rest, after thirty-seven years of solitary captivity.*
4. *Here, homeless and friendless, after thirty-seven years of bitter captivity, perished a noble stranger, natural son of Louis XIV.*

Tom's voice trembled, whilst he was reading them, and he most broke down. When he got done, he couldn't no way make up his mind which one for Jim to scrabble onto the wall, they was all so good; but at last he allowed he would let him scrabble them all on. Jim said it would take him a year to scrabble such a lot of truck onto the logs with a nail, and he didn't know how to make letters, besides; but Tom said he would block them out for him, and then he wouldn't have nothing to do but just follow the lines. Then pretty soon he says:

"Come to think, the logs ain't agoing to do; they don't have log walls in a dungeon: we got to dig the inscriptions into a rock. We'll fetch a rock."

Jim said the rock was worse than the logs; he said it would take him such a pison long time to dig them into a rock, he wouldn't ever get out. But Tom said he would let me help him do it. Then he took a look to see how me and Jim was getting along with the pens. It was most pesky tedious hard work and slow, and didn't give my hands no show to get well of the sores, and we didn't seem to make no headway, hardly. So Tom says:

"I know how to fix it. We got to have a rock for the coat of arms and mournful inscriptions, and we can kill two birds with that same rock. There's a gaudy big grindstone down at the mill, and we'll smouch it, and carve the things on it, and file out the pens and the saw on it, too."

It warn't no slouch of an idea; and it warn't no slouch of a grindstone nuther; but we allowed we'd tackle it. It warn't quite midnight, yet, so we cleared out for the mill, leaving Jim at work. We smouched the grindstone, and set out to roll her home, but it was a most nation tough job. Sometimes, do what we could, we couldn't keep her from falling over, and she come mighty near mashing us, every time. Tom said she was going to get one of us, sure, before we got through. We got her half way; and then we was plumb played out, and most drownded with sweat. We see it warn't no use, we got to go and fetch Jim. So he raised up his bed and slid the chain off of the bed-leg, and wrapt it round and round his neck, and we crawled out through our hole and down there, and Jim and me laid into that grindstone and walked her along like nothing; and Tom superintended. He could out-superintend any boy I ever see. He knowed how to do everything.

Our hole was pretty big, but it warn't big enough to get the grindstone through; but Jim he took the pick and soon made it big enough. Then Tom marked out them things on it with the nail, and set Jim to work on them, with the nail for a chisel and an iron bolt from the rubbage in the lean-to for a hammer, and told him to work till the rest of his candle quit on him, and then he could go to bed, and hide the grindstone under his straw tick and sleep on it. Then we helped him fix his chain back on the bed-leg, and was ready for bed ourselves. But Tom thought of something, and says:

"You got any spiders in here, Jim?"

"No, sah, thanks to goodness I hain't, Mars Tom."

"All right, we'll get you some."

"But bless you, honey, I doan' *want* none. I's afeared un um. I jis' 's soon have rattlesnakes aroun'."

Tom thought a minute or two, and says:

"It's a good idea. And I reckon it's been done. It *must* a been done; it stands to reason. Yes, it's a prime good idea. Where could you keep it?"

"Keep what, Mars Tom?"

"Why, a rattlesnake."

"De goodness gracious alive, Mars Tom! Why, if dey was a rattlesnake to come in heah, I'd take en bust right out thoo dat log wall, I would, wid my head."

"Why, Jim, you wouldn't be afraid of it, after a little. You could tame it."

"*Tame* it!"

"Yes—easy enough. Every animal is grateful for kindness and petting, and they wouldn't *think* of hurting a person that pets them. Any book will tell you that. You try—that's all I ask; just try for two or three days. Why, you can get him so, in a little while, that he'll love you; and sleep with you; and won't stay away from you a minute; and will let you wrap him round your neck and put his head in your mouth."

"*Please*, Mars Tom—*doan'* talk so! I can't *stan'* it! He'd *let* me shove his head in my mouf—fer a favor, hain't it? I lay he'd wait a pow'ful long time 'fo' I *ast* him. En mo' en dat, I doan' *want* him to sleep wid me."

"Jim, don't act so foolish. A prisoner's *got* to have some kind of a dumb pet, and if a rattlesnake hain't ever been tried, why, there's more glory to be gained in your being the first to ever try it than any other way you could ever think of to save your life."

"Why, Mars Tom, I doan' *want* no sich glory. Snake take 'n bite Jim's chin off, den *whah* is de glory? No, sah, I doan' want no sich doin's."

"Blame it, can't you *try*? I only *want* you to try—you needn't keep it up if it don't work."

"But de trouble all *done*, ef de snake bite me while I's a tryin' him. Mars Tom, I's willin' to tackle mos' anything 'at ain't onreasonable, but ef you en Huck fetches a rattlesnake in heah for me to tame, I's gwyne to *leave*, dat's *shore*."

"Well, then, let it go, let it go, if you're so bullheaded about it. We can get you some garter-snakes and you can tie some buttons on their tails, and let on they're rattlesnakes, and I reckon that'll have to do."

"I k'n stan' *dem*, Mars Tom, but blame' 'f I couldn't get along widout um, I tell you dat. I never knowed b'fo', 't was so much bother and trouble to be a prisoner."

"Well, it *always* is, when it's done right. You got any rats around here?"

"No, sah, I hain't seed none."

"Well, we'll get you some rats."

"Why, Mars Tom, I doan' *want* no rats. Dey's de dad-blamedest creturs to sturb a body, en rustle roun' over 'im, en bite his feet, when he's tryin' to sleep, I ever see. No, sah, gimme g'yarter-snakes, 'f I's got to have 'm, but doan' gimme no rats, I ain' got no use f'r um, skasely."

"But Jim, you *got* to have 'em—they all do. So don't make no more fuss about it. Prisoners ain't ever without rats. There ain't no instance of it. And they train them, and pet them, and learn them tricks, and they get to be as sociable as flies. But you got to play music to them. You got anything to play music on?"

"I ain' got nuffn but a coase comb en a piece o' paper, en a juice-harp; but I reck'n dey wouldn' take no stock in a juice-harp."

"Yes they would. *They* don't care what kind of music 'tis. A jews-harp's plenty good enough for a rat. All animals likes music—in a prison they dote on it. Specially, painful music; and you can't get no other kind out of a jews-harp. It always interests them; they come out to see what's the matter with you. Yes, you're all right; you're fixed very well. You want to set on your bed, nights, before you go to sleep, and early in the mornings, and play your jews-harp; play The Last Link is Broken—that's the thing that'll scoop a rat, quicker'n anything else: and when you've played about two minutes, you'll see all the rats, and the snakes, and spiders, and things begin to feel worried about you, and come. And they'll just fairly swarm over you, and have a noble good time."

"Yes, *dey* will, I reck'n, Mars Tom, but what kine er time is *Jim* havin'? Blest if I kin see de pint. But I'll do it ef I got to. I reck'n I better keep de animals satisfied, en not have no trouble in de house."

Tom waited to think over, and see if there wasn't nothing else; and pretty soon he says:

"Oh—there's one thing I forgot. Could you raise a flower here, do you reckon?"

"I doan' know but maybe I could, Mars Tom; but it's tolable dark in heah, en I ain' got no use f'r no flower, nohow, en she'd be a pow'ful sight o' trouble."

"Well, you try it, anyway. Some other prisoners has done it."

"One er dem big cat-tail-lookin' mullen-stalks would grow in heah, Mars Tom, I reck'n, but she wouldn't be wuth half de trouble she'd coss."

"Don't you believe it. We'll fetch you a little one, and you plant it in the corner, over there, and raise it. And don't call it mullen, call it Pitchiola—that's its right name, when it's in a prison. And you want to water it with your tears."

"Why, I got plenty spring water, Mars Tom."

"You don't *want* spring water; you want to water it with your tears. It's the way they always do."

"Why, Mars Tom, I lay I kin raise one er dem mullen-stalks twyste wid spring water whiles another man's a *start'n* one wid tears."

"That ain't the idea. You *got* to do it with tears."

"She'll die on my han's, Mars Tom, she sholy will; kase I doan' skasely ever cry."

So Tom was stumped. But he studied it over, and then said Jim would have to worry along the best he could with an onion. He promised he would go to the nigger cabins and drop one, private, in Jim's coffee-pot, in the morning. Jim said he would "jis' 's soon have tobacker in his coffee;" and found so much fault with it, and with the work and bother of raising the mullen, and jews-harping the rats, and petting and flattering up the snakes and spiders and things, on top of all the other work he had to do on pens, and inscriptions, and journals, and things, which made it more trouble and worry and responsibility to be a prisoner than anything he ever undertook, that Tom most lost all patience with him; and said he was just loadened down with more gaudier chances than a prisoner ever had in the world to make a name for himself, and yet he didn't know enough to appreciate them, and they was just about wasted on him. So Jim he was sorry, and said he wouldn't behave so no more, and then me and Tom shoved for bed.

CHAPTER XXXIX

In the morning we went up to the village and bought a wire rat trap and fetched it down, and unstopped the best rat hole, and in about an hour we had fifteen of the bulliest kind of ones; and then we took it and put it in a safe place under Aunt Sally's bed. But while we was gone for spiders, little Thomas Franklin Benjamin Jefferson Elexander Phelps found it there, and opened the door of it to see if the rats would come out, and they did; and Aunt Sally she come in, and when we got back she was a standing on top of the bed raising Cain, and the rats was doing what they could to keep off the dull times for her. So she took and dusted us both with the hickry, and we was as much as two hours catching another fifteen or sixteen, drat that meddlesome cub, and they warn't the likeliest, nuther, because the first haul was the pick of the flock. I never see a likelier lot of rats than what that first haul was.

We got a splendid stock of sorted spiders, and bugs, and frogs, and caterpillars, and one thing or another; and we like-to got a hornet's nest, but we didn't. The family was at home. We didn't give it right up, but staid with them as long as we could; because we allowed we'd tire them out or they'd got to tire us out, and they done it. Then we got allycumpain and rubbed on the places, and was pretty near all right again, but couldn't set down convenient. And so we went for the snakes, and grabbed a couple of dozen garters and house-snakes, and put them in a bag, and put it in our room, and by that time it was supper time, and a rattling good honest day's work; and hungry?—oh, no, I reckon not! And there warn't a blessed snake up there, when we went back—we didn't half tie the sack, and they worked out, somehow, and left. But it didn't matter much, because they was still on the premises somewheres. So we judged we could get some of them again. No, there warn't no real scarcity of snakes about the house for a considerble spell. You'd see them dripping from the rafters and places, every now and then; and they generly landed in your plate, or down the back of your neck, and most of the time where you didn't want them. Well, they was handsome, and striped, and there warn't no harm in a million of them; but that never made no difference to Aunt Sally, she despised snakes, be the breed what they might, and she couldn't stand them no way you could fix it; and every time one of them flopped down on her, it didn't make no difference what she was doing, she would just lay that work down and light out. I never see such a woman. And you could hear her whoop to Jericho. You couldn't get her to take aholt of one of them with the tongs. And if she turned over and found one in bed, she would scramble out and lift a howl that you would think the house was afire. She disturbed the old man so, that he said he could most wish there hadn't ever been no snakes created. Why, after every last snake had been gone clear out of the house for as much as a week, Aunt Sally warn't over it yet; she warn't near over it; when she was setting thinking about something, you could touch her on the back of her neck with a feather and she would jump right out of her stockings. It was very curious. But Tom said all women was jut so. He said they was made that way; for some reason or other.

We got a licking every time one of our snakes come in her way; and she allowed these lickings warn't nothing to what she would do if we ever loaded up the place again with them. I didn't mind the lickings, because they didn't amount to nothing; but I minded the trouble we had, to lay in another lot. But we got them laid in, and all the other things; and you never see a cabin as blithesome as Jim's was when they'd all swarm out for music and go for him. Jim didn't like the spiders, and the spiders didn't like Jim; and so they'd lay for him and make it mighty warm for him. And he said that between the rats, and the snakes, and the grindstone, there warn't no room in bed for him, skasely; and when there was, a body couldn't sleep, it was so lively, and it was always lively, he said, because *they* never all slept at one time, but took turn about, so when the snakes was asleep the rats was on deck, and when the rats turned in the snakes come on watch, so he always had one gang under him, in his way, and t'other gang having a circus over him, and if he got up to hunt a new place, the spiders would take a chance at him as he crossed over. He said if he ever got out, this time, he wouldn't ever be a prisoner again, not for a salary.

Well, by the end of three weeks, everything was in pretty good shape. The shirt was sent in early, in a pie, and every time a rat bit Jim he would get up and write a little in his journal whilst the ink was fresh; the pens was made, the inscriptions and so on was all carved on the grindstone; the bed-leg was sawed in two, and we had et up the sawdust, and it give us a most amazing stomach-ache. We reckoned we was all going to die, but didn't. It was the most undigestible sawdust I ever see; and Tom said the same. But as I was saying, we'd got all the work done, now, at last; and we was all pretty much fagged out, too, but mainly Jim. The old man had wrote a couple of times to the plantation below Orleans to come and get their runaway nigger, but hadn't got no answer, because there warn't no such plantation; so he allowed he would advertise Jim in the St. Louis and New Orleans papers; and when he mentioned the St. Louis ones, it give me the cold shivers, and I see we hadn't no time to lose. So Tom said, now for the nonnamous letters.

"What's them?" I says.

"Warnings to the people that something is up. Sometimes it's done one way, sometimes another. But there's always somebody spying around, that gives notice to the governor of the castle. When Louis XVI. was going to light out of the Tooleries, a servant girl done it. It's a very good way, and so is the nonnamous letters. We'll use them both. And it's usual for the prisoner's mother to change clothes with him, and she stays in, and he slides out in her clothes. We'll do that too."

"But looky here, Tom, what do we want to *warn* anybody for, that something's up? Let them find it out for themselves—it's their lookout."

"Yes, I know; but you can't depend on them. It's the way they've acted from the very start—left us to do *everything*. They're so confiding and mullet-headed they don't take notice of nothing at all. So if we don't *give* them notice, there won't be nobody nor nothing to interfere with us, and so after all our hard work and trouble this escape 'll go off perfectly flat: won't amount to nothing—won't be nothing *to* it."

"Well, as for me, Tom, that's the way I'd like."

"Shucks," he says, and looked disgusted. So I says:

"But I ain't going to make no complaint. Anyway that suits you suits me. What you going to do about the servant-girl?"

"You'll be her. You slide in, in the middle of the night, and hook that yaller girl's frock."

"Why, Tom, that'll make trouble next morning; because of course she prob'bly hain't got any but that one."

"I know; but you don't want it but fifteen minutes, to carry the nonnamous letter and shove it under the front door."

"All right, then, I'll do it; but I could carry it just as handy in my own togs."

"You wouldn't look like a servant-girl *then*, would you?"

"No, but there won't be nobody to see what I look like, *anyway*."

"That ain't got nothing to do with it. The thing for us to do, is just to do our *duty*, and not worry about whether anybody *sees* us do it or not. Hain't you got no principle at all?"

"All right, I ain't saying nothing; I'm the servant-girl. Who's Jim's mother?"

"I'm his mother. I'll hook a gown from Aunt Sally."

"Well, then, you'll have to stay in the cabin when me and Jim leaves."

"Not much. I'll stuff Jim's clothes full of straw and lay it on his bed to represent his mother in disguise, and Jim 'll take the nigger woman's gown off of me and wear it, and we'll all evade together. When a prisoner of style escapes, it's called an evasion. It's always called so when a king escapes, f'rinstance. And the same with a king's son; it don't make no difference whether he's a natural one or an unnatural one."

So Tom he wrote the nonnamous letter, and I smouched the yaller wench's frock, that night, and put it on, and shoved it under the front door, the way Tom told me to. It said:

Beware. Trouble is brewing. Keep a sharp lookout.
UNKNOWN FRIEND.

Next night we stuck a picture which Tom drawed in blood, of a skull and crossbones, on the front door; and next night another one of a coffin, on the back door. I never see a family in such a sweat. They couldn't a been worse scared if the place had a been full of ghosts laying for them behind everything and under the beds and shivering through the air. If a door banged, Aunt Sally she jumped, and said "ouch!" if anything fell, she jumped and said "ouch!" if you happened to touch her, when she warn't noticing, she done the same; she couldn't face noway and be satisfied, because she allowed there was something behind her every time—so she was always a whirling around, sudden, and saying "ouch," and before she'd get two-thirds around, she'd whirl back again, and say it again; and she was afraid to go to bed, but she dasn't set up. So the thing was working very well, Tom said; he said he never see a thing work more satisfactory. He said it showed it was done right.

So he said, now for the grand bulge! So the very next morning at the streak of dawn we got another letter ready, and was wondering what we better do with it, because we heard them say at supper they was going to have a nigger on watch at both doors all night. Tom he went down the lightning-rod to spy around; and the nigger at the back door was asleep, and he stuck it in the back of his neck and come back. This letter said:

Don't betray me, I wish to be your friend. There is a desprate gang of cutthroats from over in the Ingean Territory going to steal your runaway nigger to-night, and they have been trying to scare you so as you will stay in the house and not bother them. I am one of the gang, but have got religgion and wish to quit it and lead a honest life again, and will betray the helish design. They will sneak down from northards, along the fence, at midnight exact, with a false key, and go in the nigger's cabin to get him. I am to be off a piece and blow a tin horn if I see any danger; but stead of that, I will BA *like a sheep soon as they get in and not blow at all; then whilst they are getting his chains loose, you slip there and lock them in, and can kill them at your leasure. Don't do anything but just the way I am telling you, if you do they will suspicion something and raise whoopjamboreehoo. I do not wish any reward but to know I have done the right thing.*

UNKNOWN FRIEND.

CHAPTER XL

We was feeling pretty good, after breakfast, and took my canoe and went over the river a fishing, with a lunch, and had a good time, and took a look at the raft and found her all right, and got home late to supper, and found them in such a sweat and worry they didn't know which end they was standing on, and made us go right off to bed the minute we was done supper, and wouldn't tell us what the trouble was, and never let on a word about the new letter, but didn't need to, because we knowed as much about it as anybody did, and as soon as we was half up stairs and her back was turned, we slid for the cellar cubboard and loaded up a good lunch and took it up to our room and went to bed, and got up about half-past eleven, and Tom put on Aunt Sally's dress that he stole and was going to start with the lunch, but says:

"Where's the butter?"

"I laid out a hunk of it," I says, "on a piece of a corn-pone."

"Well, you *left* it laid out, then—it ain't here."

"We can get along without it," I says.

"We can get along *with* it, too," he says; "just you slide down cellar and fetch it. And then mosey right down the lightning-rod and come along. I'll go and stuff the straw into Jim's clothes to represent his mother in disguise, and be ready to *ba* like a sheep and shove soon as you get there."

So out he went, and down cellar went I. The hunk of butter, big as a person's fist, was where I had left it, so I took up the slab of corn-pone with it on, and blowed out my light, and started up stairs, very stealthy, and got up to the main floor all right, but here comes Aunt Sally with a candle, and I clapped the truck in my hat, and clapped my hat on my head, and the next second she see me; and she says:

"You been down cellar?"

"Yes'm."

"What you been doing down there?"

"Noth'n."

"*Noth'n!*"

"No'm."

"Well, then, what possessed you to go down there, this time of night?"

"I don't know'm."

"You don't *know*? Don't answer me that way, Tom, I want to know what you been *doing* down there?"

"I hain't been doing a single thing, Aunt Sally, I hope to gracious if I have."

I reckoned she'd let me go, now, and as a generl thing she would; but I spose there was so many strange things going on she was just in a sweat about every little thing that warn't yard-stick straight; so she says, very decided:

"You just march into that setting-room and stay there till I come. You been up to something you no business to, and I lay I'll find out what it is before *I'm* done with you."

So she went away as I opened the door and walked into the setting-room. My, but there was a crowd there! Fifteen farmers, and every one of them had a gun. I was most powerful sick, and slunk to a chair and set down. They was setting around, some of them talking a little, in a low voice, and all of them fidgety and uneasy, but trying to look like they warn't; but I knowed they was, because they was always taking off their hats, and putting them on, and scratching their heads, and changing their seats, and fumbling with their buttons. I warn't easy myself, but I didn't take my hat off, all the same.

I did wish Aunt Sally would come, and get done with me, and lick me, if she wanted to, and let me get away and tell Tom how we'd overdone this thing, and what a thundering hornet's nest we'd got ourselves into, so we could stop fooling around, straight off, and clear out with Jim before these rips got out of patience and come for us.

At last she come, and begun to ask me questions, but I *couldn't* answer them straight, I didn't know which end of me was up; because these men was in such a fidget now, that some was wanting to start right *now* and lay for them desperadoes, and saying it warn't but a few minutes to midnight; and others was trying to get them to hold on and wait for the sheep-signal; and here was aunty pegging away at the questions, and me a shaking all over and ready to sink down in my tracks I was that scared; and the place getting hotter and hotter, and the butter beginning to melt and run down my neck and behind my ears: and pretty soon, when one of them says, "*I'm* for going and getting in the cabin *first*, and right *now*, and catching them when they come," I most dropped; and a streak of butter come a trickling down my forehead, and Aunt Sally she see it, and turns white as a sheet, and says:

"For the land's sake what *is* the matter with the child!—he's got the brain fever as shore as you're born, and they're oozing out!"

And everybody runs to see, and she snatches off my hat, and out comes the bread, and what was left of the butter, and she grabbed me, and hugged me, and says:

"Oh, what a turn you did give me! and how glad and grateful I am it ain't no worse; for luck's against us, and it never rains but it pours, and when I see that truck I thought we'd lost you, for I knowed by the color and all, it was just like your brains would be if—Dear, dear, whyd'nt you *tell* me that was what you'd been down there for, *I* wouldn't a cared. Now cler out to bed, and don't lemme see no more of you till morning!"

I was up stairs in a second, and down the lightning-rod in another one, and shinning through the dark for the lean-to. I couldn't hardly get my words out, I was so anxious; but I told Tom as quick as I could, we must jump for it, now, and not a minute to lose—the house full of men, yonder, with guns!

His eyes just blazed; and he says:

"No!—is that so? *Ain't* it bully! Why, Huck, if it was to do over again, I bet I could fetch two hundred! If we could put it off till—"

"Hurry! *hurry!*" I says. "Where's Jim?"

"Right at your elbow; if you reach out your arm you can touch him. He's dressed, and everything's ready. Now we'll slide out and give the sheep-signal."

But then we heard the tramp of men, coming to the door, and heard them begin to fumble with the padlock; and heard a man say:

"I *told* you we'd be too soon; they haven't come—the door is locked. Here, I'll lock some of you into the cabin and you lay for 'em in the dark and kill 'em when they come; and the rest scatter around a piece, and listen if you can hear 'em coming."

So in they come, but couldn't see us in the dark, and most trod on us whilst we was hustling to get under the bed. But we got under all right, and out through the hole, swift but soft—Jim first, me next, and Tom last, which was according to Tom's orders. Now we was in the lean-to, and heard trampings close by outside. So we crept to the door, and Tom stopped us there and put his eye to the crack, but couldn't make out nothing, it was so dark; and whispered and said he would listen for the steps to get further, and when he nudged us Jim must glide out first, and him last. So he set his ear to the crack and listened, and listened, and listened, and the steps a scraping around, out there, all the time; and at last he nudged us, and we slid out, and stooped down, not breathing, and not making the least noise, and slipped stealthy towards the fence, in Injun file, and got to it, all right, and me and Jim over it; but Tom's britches catched fast on a splinter on the top rail, and then he hear the steps coming, so he had to pull loose, which snapped the splinter and made a noise; and as he dropped in our tracks and started, somebody sings out:

"Who's that? Answer, or I'll shoot!"

But we didn't answer; we just unfurled our heels and shoved. Then there was a rush, and a *bang, bang, bang!* and the bullets fairly whizzed around us! We heard them sing out:

"Here they are! They've broke for the river! after 'em, boys! And turn loose the dogs!"

So here they come, full tilt. We could hear them, because they wore boots, and yelled, but we didn't wear no boots, and didn't yell. We was in the path to the mill; and when they got pretty close onto us, we dodged into the bush and let them go by, and then dropped in behind them. They'd had all the dogs shut up, so they wouldn't scare off the robbers; but by this time somebody had let them loose, and here they come, making pow-wow enough for a million; but they was our dogs; so we stopped in our tracks till they catched up; and when they see it warn't nobody but us, and no excitement to offer them, they only just said howdy, and tore right ahead towards the shouting and clattering; and then we up steam again and whizzed along after them till we was nearly to the mill, and then struck up through the bush to where my canoe was tied, and hopped in and pulled for dear life towards the middle of the river, but didn't make no more noise than we was obleeged to. Then we struck out, easy and comfortable, for the island where my raft was; and we could hear them yelling and barking at each other all up and down the bank, till we was so far away the sounds got dim and died out. And when we stepped onto the raft, I says:

"*Now*, old Jim, you're a free man *again*, and I bet you won't ever be a slave no more."

"En a mighty good job it wuz, too, Huck. It 'uz planned beautiful, en it 'uz *done* beautiful; en dey ain't *nobody* kin git up a plan dat's mo' mixed-up en splendid den what dat one wuz."

We was all as glad as we could be, but Tom was the gladdest of all, because he had a bullet in the calf of his leg.

When me and Jim heard that, we didn't feel so brash as what we did before. It was hurting him considerble, and bleeding; so we laid him in the wigwam and tore up one of the duke's shirts for to bandage him, but he says:

"Gimme the rags, I can do it myself. Don't stop, now; don't fool around here, and the evasion booming along so handsome; man the sweeps, and set her loose! Boys, we done it elegant!—'deed we did. I wish *we'd* a had the handling of Louis XVI., there wouldn't a been no 'Son of Saint Louis, ascend to heaven!' wrote down in *his* biography: no, sir, we'd a whooped him over the *border*—that's what we'd a done with *him*—and done it just as slick as nothing at all, too. Man the sweeps—man the sweeps!"

But me and Jim was consulting—and thinking. And after we'd thought a minute, I says:

"Say it, Jim."

So he says:

"Well, den, dis is de way it look to me, Huck. Ef it wuz *him* dat 'uz bein' sot free, en one er de boys wuz to git shot, would he say, 'Go on en save me, nemmine 'bout a doctor f'r to save dis one?' Is dat like Mars Tom Sawyer? Would he say dat? You *bet* he wouldn't! *Well*, den, is *Jim* gwyne to say it? No, sah—I doan' budge a step out'n dis place, 'dout a *doctor*; not if it's forty year!"

I knowed he was white inside, and I reckoned he'd say what he did say—so it was all right, now, and I told Tom I was agoing for a doctor. He raised considerble row about it, but me and Jim stuck to it and wouldn't budge; so he was for crawling out and setting the raft loose himself; but we wouldn't let him. Then he give us a piece of his mind—but it didn't do no good.

So when he see me getting the canoe ready, he says:

"Well, then, if you're bound to go, I'll tell you the way to do, when you get to the village. Shut the door, and blindfold the doctor tight and fast, and make him swear to be silent as the grave, and put a purse full of gold in his hand, and then take and lead him all around the back alleys and everywheres, in the dark, and then fetch him here in the canoe, in a roundabout way amongst the islands, and search him and take his chalk away from him, and don't give it back to him till you get him back to the village, or else he will chalk this raft so he can find it again. It's the way they all do."

So I said I would, and left, and Jim was to hide in the woods when he see the doctor coming, till he was gone again.

CHAPTER XLI

The doctor was an old man; a very nice, kind-looking old man, when I got him up. I told him me and my brother was over on Spanish Island hunting, yesterday afternoon, and camped on a piece of a raft we found, and about midnight he must a kicked his gun in his dreams, for it went off and shot him in the leg, and we wanted him to go over there and fix it and not say nothing about it, nor let anybody know, because we wanted to come home this evening, and surprise the folks.

"Who is your folks?" he says.

"The Phelpses, down yonder."

"Oh," he says. And after a minute, he says: "How'd you say he got shot?"

"He had a dream," I says, "and it shot him."

"Singular dream," he says.

So he lit up his lantern, and got his saddle-bags, and we started. But when he see the canoe, he didn't like the look of her—said she was big enough for one, but didn't look pretty safe for two. I says:

"Oh, you needn't be afeard, sir, she carried the three of us, easy enough."

"What three?"

"Why, me and Sid, and—and—and *the guns*; that's what I mean."

"Oh," he says.

But he put his foot on the gunnel, and rocked her; and shook his head, and said he reckoned he'd look around for a bigger one. But they was all locked and chained; so he took my canoe, and said for me to wait till he come back, or I could hunt around further, or maybe I better go down home and get them ready for the surprise, if I wanted to. But I said I didn't; so I told him just how to find the raft, and then he started.

I struck an idea, pretty soon. I says to myself, spos'n he can't fix that leg just in three shakes of a sheep's tail, as the saying is? spos'n it takes him three or four days? What are we going to do?—lay around there till he lets the cat out of the bag? No, sir, I know what *I'll* do. I'll wait, and when he comes back, if he says he's got to go any more, I'll get down there, too, if I swim; and we'll take and tie him, and keep him, and shove out down the river; and when Tom's done with him, we'll give him what it's worth, or all we got, and then let him get shore.

So then I crept into a lumber pile to get some sleep; and next time I waked up the sun was away up over my head! I shot out and went for the doctor's house, but they told me he'd gone away in the night, some time or other, and warn't back yet. Well, thinks I, that looks powerful bad for Tom, and I'll dig out for the island, right off. So away I shoved, and turned the corner, and nearly rammed my head into Uncle Silas's stomach! He says:

"Why, *Tom*! Where you been, all this time, you rascal?"

"*I* hain't been nowheres," I says, "only just hunting for the runaway nigger—me and Sid."

"Why, where ever did you go?" he says. "Your aunt's been mighty uneasy."

"She needn't," I says, "because we was all right. We followed the men and the dogs, but they out-run us, and we lost them; but we thought we heard them on the water, so we got a canoe and took out after them, and crossed over but couldn't find nothing of them; so we cruised along up-shore till we got kind of tired and beat out; and tied up the canoe and went to sleep, and never waked up till about an hour ago, then we paddled over here to hear the news, and Sid's at the post-office to see what he can hear, and I'm a branching out to get something to eat for us, and then we're going home."

So then we went to the post-office to get "Sid"; but just as I suspicioned, he warn't there; so the old man he got a letter out of the office, and we waited a while longer but Sid didn't come; so the old man said come along, let Sid foot it home, or canoe-it, when he got done fooling around—but we would ride. I couldn't get him to let me stay and wait for Sid; and he said there warn't no use in it, and I must come along, and let Aunt Sally see we was all right.

When we got home, Aunt Sally was that glad to see me she laughed and cried both, and hugged me, and give me one of them lickings of hern that don't amount to shucks, and said she'd serve Sid the same when he come.

And the place was plumb full of farmers and farmers' wives, to dinner; and such another clack a body never heard. Old Mrs. Hotchkiss was the worst; her tongue was agoing all the time. She says:

"Well, Sister Phelps, I've ransacked that-air cabin over an' I b'lieve the nigger was crazy. I says so to Sister Damrell—didn't I, Sister Damrell?—s'I, he's crazy, s'I—them's the very words I said. You all hearn me: he's crazy, s'I; everything show it, s'I. Look that-air grindstone s'I; want to tell *me*'t any cretur 'ts in his right mind 's agoin' to scrabble all them crazy things onto a grindstone, s'I? Here sich 'n' sich a person busted his heart; 'n' here so 'n' so pegged along for thirty-seven year, 'n' all that—natcherl son o' Louis somebody, 'n' sich everlast'n rubbage. He's plumb crazy, s'I; it's what I says in the fust place, it's what I says in the middle, 'n' it's what I says last 'n' all the time—the nigger's crazy—crazy 's Nebokoodneezer, s'I."

"An' look at that-air ladder made out'n rags, Sister Hotchkiss," says old Mrs. Damrell, "what in the name o' goodness *could* he ever want of—"

"The very words I was a-sayin' no longer ago th'n this minute to Sister Utterback, 'n' she'll tell you so herself. Sh-she, look at that-air rag ladder, sh-she; 'n' s'I, yes, *look* at it, s'I—what *could* he a wanted of it, s'I. Sh-she, Sister Hotchkiss, sh-she—"

"But how in the nation'd they ever *git* that grindstone *in* there, *any*-way? 'n' who dug that-air *hole*? 'n' who—"

"My very *words*, Brer Penrod! I was a-sayin'—pass that-air sasser o' m'lasses, won't ye?—I was a-sayin' to Sister Dunlap, jist this minute, how *did* they git that grindstone in there, s'I. Without *help*, mind you—'thout *help*! *Thar's* wher' 'tis. Don't tell *me*, s'I; there *wuz* help, s'I; 'n' ther' wuz a *plenty* help, too, s'I; ther's ben a *dozen* a-helpin' that nigger, 'n' I lay I'd skin every last nigger on this place, but *I'd* find out who done it, s'I; 'n' moreover, s'I—"

"A *dozen* says you!—*forty* couldn't a done everything that's been done. Look at them case-knife saws and things, how tedious they've been made; look at that bed-leg sawed off with 'm, a week's work for six men; look at that nigger made out'n straw on the bed; and look at—"

"You may *well* say it, Brer Hightower! It's jist as I was a-sayin' to Brer Phelps, his own self. S'e, what do *you* think of it, Sister Hotchkiss, s'e? think o' what, Brer Phelps, s'I? think o' that bed-leg sawed off that a way, s'e? *think* of it, s'I? I lay it never sawed *itself* off, s'I—somebody *sawed* it, s'I; that's my opinion, take it or leave it, it mayn't be no 'count, s'I, but sich as 't is, it's my opinion, s'I, 'n' if anybody k'n start a better one, s'I, let him *do* it, s'I, that's all. I says to Sister Dunlap, s'I—"

"Why, dog my cats, they must a ben a house-full o' niggers in there every night for four weeks, to a done all that work, Sister Phelps. Look at that shirt—every last inch of it kivered over with secret African writ'n done with blood! Must a ben a raft uv 'm at it right along, all the time, amost. Why, I'd give two dollars to have it read to me; 'n' as for the niggers that wrote it, I 'low I'd take 'n' lash 'm t'll—"

"People to *help* him, Brother Marples! Well, I reckon you'd *think* so, if you'd a been in this house for a while back. Why, they've stole everything they could lay their hands on—and we a watching, all the time, mind you. They stole that shirt right off o' the line! and as for that sheet they made the rag ladder out of ther' ain't no telling how many times they *didn't* steal that; and flour, and candles, and candlesticks, and spoons, and the old warming-pan, and most a thousand things that I disremember, now, and my new calico dress; and me, and Silas, and my Sid and Tom on the constant watch day *and* night, as I was a telling you, and not a one of us could catch hide nor hair, nor sight nor sound of them; and here at the last minute, lo and behold you, they slides right in under our noses, and fools us, and not only fools *us* but the Injun Territory robbers too, and actuly gets *away* with that nigger, safe and sound, and that with sixteen men and twenty-two dogs right on their very heels at that very time! I tell you, it just bangs anything I ever *heard* of. Why, *sperits* couldn't a done better, and been no smarter. And I reckon they must a *been* sperits—because, *you* know our dogs, and ther' ain't no better; well, them dogs never even got on the *track* of 'm once! You explain *that* to me, if you can!—*any* of you!"

"Well, it does beat—"

"Laws alive, I never—"

"So help me, I wouldn't a be—"

"*House*-thieves as well as—"

"Goodnessgracioussakes, I'd a ben afeard to *live* in sich a—"

"'Fraid to *live*!—why, I was that scared I dasn't hardly go to bed, or get up, or lay down, or *set* down, Sister Ridgeway. Why, they'd steal the very—why, goodness sakes, you can guess what kind of a fluster *I* was in by the time midnight come, last night. I hope to gracious if I warn't afraid they'd steal some o' the family! I was just to that pass, I didn't have no reasoning faculties no more. It looks foolish enough, *now*, in the day-time; but I says to myself, there's my two poor boys asleep, 'way up stairs in that lonesome room, and I declare to goodness I was that uneasy 't I crep' up there and locked 'em in! I *did*. And anybody would. Because, you know, when you get scared, that way, and it keeps running on, and getting worse and worse, all the time, and your wits gets to addling, and you get to doing all sorts o' wild things, and by-and-by you think to yourself, spos'n *I* was a boy, and was away up there, and the door ain't locked, and you—" She stopped, looking kind of wondering, and then she turned her head around slow, and when her eye lit on me—I got up and took a walk.

Says I to myself, I can explain better how we come to not be in that room this morning, if I go out to one side and study over it a little. So I done it. But I dasn't go fur, or she'd a sent for me. And when it was late in the day, the people all went, and then I come in and told her the noise and shooting waked up me and "Sid," and the door was locked, and we wanted to see the fun, so we went down the lightning-rod, and both of us got hurt a little, and we didn't never want to try *that* no more. And then I went on and told her all what I told Uncle Silas before; and then she said she'd forgive us, and maybe it was all right enough anyway, and about what a body might expect of boys, for all boys was a pretty harum-scarum lot, as fur as she could see; and so, as long as no harm hadn't come of it, she judged she better put in her time being grateful we was alive and well and she had us still, stead of fretting over what was past and done. So then she kissed me, and patted me on the head, and dropped into a kind of a brown study; and pretty soon jumps up, and says:

"Why, lawsamercy, it's most night, and Sid not come yet! What *has* become of that boy?"

I see my chance; so I skips up and says:

"I'll run right up to town and get him," I says.

"No you won't," she says. "You'll stay right wher' you are; *one's* enough to be lost at a time. If he ain't here to supper, your uncle 'll go."

Well, he warn't there to supper; so right after supper uncle went.

He come back about ten, a little bit uneasy; hadn't run across Tom's track. Aunt Sally was a good *deal* uneasy; but Uncle Silas he said there warn't no occasion to be—boys will be boys, he said, and you'll see this one turn up in the morning, all sound and right. So she had to be satisfied. But she said she'd set up for him a while, anyway, and keep a light burning, so he could see it.

And then when I went up to bed she come up with me and fetched her candle, and tucked me in, and mothered me so good I felt mean, and like I couldn't look her in the face; and she set down on the bed and talked with me a long time, and said what a splendid boy Sid was, and didn't seem to want to ever stop talking about him; and kept asking me every now and then, if I reckoned he could a got lost, or hurt, or maybe drownded, and might be laying at this minute, somewheres, suffering or dead, and she not by him to help him, and so the tears would drip down, silent, and I would tell her that Sid was all right, and would be home in the morning, sure; and she would squeeze my hand, or maybe kiss me, and tell me to say it again, and keep on saying it, because it done her good, and she was in so much trouble. And when she was going away, she looked down in my eyes, so steady and gentle, and says:

"The door ain't going to be locked, Tom; and there's the window and the rod; but you'll be good, *won't* you? And you won't go? For *my* sake?"

Laws knows I *wanted* to go, bad enough, to see about Tom, and was all intending to go; but after that, I wouldn't a went, not for kingdoms.

But she was on my mind, and Tom was on my mind; so I slept very restless. And twice I went down the rod, away in the night, and slipped around front, and see her setting there by her candle in the window with her eyes towards the road and the tears in them; and I wished I could do something for her, but I couldn't, only to swear that I wouldn't never do nothing to grieve her any more. And the third time, I waked up at dawn, and slid down, and she was there yet, and her candle was most out, and her old gray head was resting on her hand, and she was asleep.

CHAPTER XLII

The old man was up town again, before breakfast, but couldn't get no track of Tom; and both of them set at the table, thinking, and not saying nothing, and looking mournful, and their coffee getting cold, and not eating anything. And by-and-by the old man says:

"Did I give you the letter?"

"What letter?"

"The one I got yesterday out of the post-office."

"No, you didn't give me no letter."

"Well, I must a forgot it."

So he rummaged his pockets, and then went off somewheres where he had laid it down, and fetched it, and give it to her. She says:

"Why, it's from St. Petersburg—it's from Sis."

I allowed another walk would do me good; but I couldn't stir. But before she could break it open, she dropped it and run—for she see something. And so did I. It was Tom Sawyer on a mattress; and that old doctor; and Jim, in *her* calico dress, with his hands tied behind him; and a lot of people. I hid the letter behind the first thing that come handy, and rushed. She flung herself at Tom, crying, and says:

"Oh, he's dead, he's dead, I know he's dead!"

And Tom he turned his head a little, and muttered something or other, which showed he warn't in his right mind; then she flung up her hands, and says:

"He's alive, thank God! And that's enough!" and she snatched a kiss of him, and flew for the house to get the bed ready, and scattering orders right and left at the niggers and everybody else, as fast as her tongue could go, every jump of the way.

I followed the men to see what they was going to do with Jim; and the old doctor and Uncle Silas followed after Tom into the house. The men was very huffy, and some of them wanted to hang Jim, for an example to all the other niggers around there, so they wouldn't be trying to run away, like Jim done, and making such a raft of trouble, and keeping a whole family scared most to death for days and nights. But the others said, don't do it, it wouldn't answer at all, he ain't our nigger, and his owner would turn up and make us pay for him, sure. So that cooled them down a little, because the people that's always the most anxious for to hang a nigger that hain't done just right, is always the very ones that ain't the most anxious to pay for him when they've got their satisfaction out of him.

They cussed Jim considerble, though, and give him a cuff or two, side the head, once in a while, but Jim never said nothing, and he never let on to know me, and they took him to the same cabin, and put his own clothes on him, and chained him again, and not to no bed-leg, this time, but to a big staple drove into the bottom log, and chained his hands, too, and both legs, and said he warn't to have nothing but bread and water to eat, after this, till his owner come or he was sold at auction, because he didn't come in a certain length of time, and filled up our hole, and said a couple of farmers with guns must stand watch around about the cabin every night, and a bull-dog tied to the door in the day-time; and about this time they was through with the job and was tapering off with a kind of generl good-bye cussing, and then the old doctor comes and takes a look, and says:

"Don't be no rougher on him than you're obleeged to, because he ain't a bad nigger. When I got to where I found the boy, I see I couldn't cut the bullet out without some help, and he warn't in no condition for me to leave, to go and get help; and he got a little worse and a little worse, and after a long time he went out of his head, and wouldn't let me come enigh him, any more, and said if I chalked his raft he'd kill me, and no end of wild foolishness like that, and I see I couldn't do anything at all with him; so I says, I got to have *help*, somehow; and the minute I says it, out crawls this nigger from somewheres, and says he'll help, and he done it, too, and done it very well. Of course I judged he must be a runaway nigger, and there I *was!* and there I had to stick, right straight along all the rest of the day, and all night. It was a fix, I tell you! I had a couple of patients with the chills, and of course I'd of liked to run up to town and see them, but I dasn't, because the nigger might get away, and then I'd be to blame; and yet never a skiff come close enough for me to hail. So there I had to stick, plumb till daylight this morning; and I never see a nigger that was a better nuss or faithfuller, and yet he was resking his freedom to do it, and was all tired out, too, and I see plain enough he'd been worked main hard, lately. I liked the nigger for that; I tell you, gentlemen, a nigger like that is worth a thousand dollars—and kind treatment, too. I had everything I needed, and the boy was doing as well there as he would a done at home—better, maybe, because it was so quiet; but there I *was*, with both of 'm on my hands; and there I had to stick, till about dawn this morning; then some men in a skiff come by, and as good luck would have it, the nigger was setting by the pallet with his head propped on his knees, sound asleep; so I motioned them in, quiet, and they slipped up on him and grabbed him and tied him before he knowed what he was about, and we never had no trouble. And the boy being in a kind of a flighty sleep, too, we muffled the oars and hitched the raft on, and towed her over very nice and quiet, and the nigger never made the least row nor said a word, from the start. He ain't no bad nigger, gentlemen; that's what I think about him."

Somebody says:

"Well, it sounds very good, doctor, I'm obleeged to say."

Then the others softened up a little, too, and I was mighty thankful to that old doctor for doing Jim that good turn; and I was glad it was according to my judgment of him, too; because I thought he had a good heart in him and was a good man, the first time I see him. Then they all agreed that Jim had acted very well, and was deserving to have some notice took of it, and reward. So every one of them promised, right out and hearty, that they wouldn't cuss him no more.

Then they come out and locked him up. I hoped they was going to say he could have one or two of the chains took off, because they was rotten heavy, or could have meat and greens with his bread and water, but they didn't think of it, and I reckoned it warn't best for me to mix in, but I judged I'd get the doctor's yarn to Aunt Sally, somehow or other, as soon as I'd got through the breakers that was laying just ahead of me. Explanations, I mean, of how I forgot to mention about Sid being shot, when I was telling how him and me put in that dratted night paddling around hunting the runaway nigger.

But I had plenty time. Aunt Sally she stuck to the sick-room all day and all night; and every time I see Uncle Silas mooning around, I dodged him.

Next morning I heard Tom was a good deal better, and they said Aunt Sally was gone to get a nap. So I slips to the sick-room, and if I found him awake I reckoned we could put up a yarn for the family that would wash. But he was sleeping, and sleeping very peaceful, too; and pale, not fire-faced the way he was when he come. So I set down and laid for him to wake. In about a half an hour, Aunt Sally comes gliding in, and there I was, up a stump again! She motioned me to be still, and set down by me, and begun to whisper, and said we could all be joyful now, because all the symptoms was first rate, and he'd been sleeping like that for ever so long, and looking better and peacefuller all the time, and ten to one he'd wake up in his right mind.

So we set there watching, and by-and-by he stirs a bit, and opened his eyes very natural, and takes a look, and says:

"Hello, why I'm at *home*! How's that? Where's the raft?"

"It's all right," I says.

"And *Jim*?"

"The same," I says, but couldn't say it pretty brash. But he never noticed, but says:

"Good! Splendid! *Now* we're all right and safe! Did you tell Aunty?"

I was going to say yes; but she chipped in and says:

"About what, Sid?"

"Why, about the way the whole thing was done."

"What whole thing?"

"Why, *the* whole thing. There ain't but one; how we set the runaway nigger free—me and Tom."

"Good land! Set the run—What *is* the child talking about! Dear, dear, out of his head again!"

"*No*, I ain't out of my HEAD; I know all what I'm talking about. We *did* set him free—me and Tom. We laid out to do it, and we *done* it. And we done it elegant, too." He'd got a start, and she never checked him up, just set and stared and stared, and let him clip along, and I see it warn't no use for *me* to put in. "Why, Aunty, it cost us a power of work—weeks of it—hours and hours, every night, whilst you was all asleep. And we had to steal candles, and the sheet, and the shirt, and your dress, and spoons, and tin plates, and case-knives, and the warming-pan, and the grindstone, and flour, and just no end of things, and you can't think what work it was to make the saws, and pens, and inscriptions, and one thing or another, and you can't think *half* the fun it was. And we had to make up the pictures of coffins and things, and nonnamous letters from the robbers, and get up and down the lightning-rod, and dig the hole into the cabin, and make the rope-ladder and send it in cooked up in a pie, and send in spoons and things to work with, in your apron pocket"—

"Mercy sakes!"

—"and load up the cabin with rats and snakes and so on, for company for Jim; and then you kept Tom here so long with the butter in his hat that you come near spiling the whole business, because the men come before we was out of the cabin, and we had to rush, and they heard us and let drive at us, and I got my share, and we dodged out of the path and let them go by, and when the dogs come they warn't interested in us, but went for the most noise, and we got our canoe, and made for the raft, and was all safe, and Jim was a free man, and we done it all by ourselves, and *wasn't* it bully, Aunty!"

"Well, I never heard the likes of it in all my born days! So it was *you*, you little rapscallions, that's been making all this trouble, and turned everybody's wits clean inside out and scared us all most to death. I've as good a notion as ever I had in my life, to take it out o' you this very minute. To think, here I've been, night after night, a—*you* just get well once, you young scamp, and I lay I'll tan the Old Harry out o' both o' ye!"

But Tom, he *was* so proud and joyful, he just *couldn't* hold in, and his tongue just *went* it—she a-chipping in, and spitting fire all along, and both of them going it at once, like a cat-convention; and she says:

"*Well*, you get all the enjoyment you can out of it *now*, for mind I tell you if I catch you meddling with him again—"

"Meddling with *who*?" Tom says, dropping his smile and looking surprised.

"With *who*? Why, the runaway nigger, of course. Who'd you reckon?"

Tom looks at me very grave, and says:

"Tom, didn't you just tell me he was all right? Hasn't he got away?"

"*Him*?" says Aunt Sally; "the runaway nigger? 'Deed he hasn't. They've got him back, safe and sound, and he's in that cabin again, on bread and water, and loaded down with chains, till he's claimed or sold!"

Tom rose square up in bed, with his eye hot, and his nostrils opening and shutting like gills, and sings out to me:

"They hain't no *right* to shut him up! *Shove!*—and don't you lose a minute. Turn him loose! he ain't no slave; he's as free as any cretur that walks this earth!"

"What *does* the child mean?"

"I mean every word I *say*, Aunt Sally, and if somebody don't go, *I'll* go. I've knowed him all his life, and so has Tom, there. Old Miss Watson died two months ago, and she was ashamed she ever was going to sell him down the river, and *said* so; and she set him free in her will."

"Then what on earth did *you* want to set him free for, seeing he was already free?"

"Well, that *is* a question, I must say; and *just* like women! Why, I wanted the *adventure* of it; and I'd a waded neck-deep in blood to—goodness alive, AUNT POLLY!"

If she warn't standing right there, just inside the door, looking as sweet and contented as an angel half-full of pie, I wish I may never!

Aunt Sally jumped for her, and most hugged the head off of her, and cried over her, and I found a good enough place for me under the bed, for it was getting pretty sultry for *us*, seemed to me. And I peeped out, and in a little while Tom's Aunt Polly shook herself loose and stood there looking across at Tom over her spectacles—kind of grinding him into the earth, you know. And then she says:

"Yes, you *better* turn y'r head away—I would if I was you, Tom."

"Oh, deary me!" says Aunt Sally; "*is* he changed so? Why, that ain't *Tom* it's Sid; Tom's—Tom's—why, where is Tom? He was here a minute ago."

"You mean where's Huck *Finn*—that's what you mean! I reckon I hain't raised such a scamp as my Tom all these years, not to know him when I *see* him. That *would* be a pretty howdy-do. Come out from under that bed, Huck Finn."

So I done it. But not feeling brash.

Aunt Sally she was one of the mixed-upest looking persons I ever see; except one, and that was Uncle Silas, when he come in, and they told it all to him. It kind of made him drunk, as you may say, and he didn't know nothing at all the rest of the day, and preached a prayer-meeting sermon that night that give him a rattling ruputation, because the oldest man in the world couldn't a understood it. So Tom's Aunt Polly, she told all about who I was, and what; and I had to up and tell how I was in such a tight place that when Mrs. Phelps took me for Tom Sawyer—she chipped in and says, "Oh, go on and call me Aunt Sally, I'm used to it, now, and 'tain't no need to change"—that when Aunt Sally took me for Tom Sawyer, I had to stand it—there warn't no other way, and I knowed he wouldn't mind, because it would be nuts for him, being a mystery, and he'd make an adventure out of it and be perfectly satisfied. And so it turned out, and he let on to be Sid, and made things as soft as he could for me.

And his Aunt Polly she said Tom was right about old Miss Watson setting Jim free in her will; and so, sure enough, Tom Sawyer had gone and took all that trouble and bother to set a free nigger free! and I couldn't ever understand, before, until that minute and that talk, how he *could* help a body set a nigger free, with his bringing-up.

Well, Aunt Polly she said that when Aunt Sally wrote to her that Tom and *Sid* had come, all right and safe, she says to herself:

"Look at that, now! I might have expected it, letting him go off that way without anybody to watch him. So now I got to go and trapse all the way down the river, eleven hundred mile, and find out what that creetur's up to, *this* time; as long as I couldn't seem to get any answer out of you about it."

"Why, I never heard nothing from you," says Aunt Sally.

"Well, I wonder! Why, I wrote to you twice, to ask you what you could mean by Sid being here."

"Well, I never got 'em, Sis."

Aunt Polly, she turns around slow and severe, and says:

"You, Tom!"

"Well—*what*?" he says, kind of pettish.

"Don't you what *me*, you impudent thing—hand out them letters."

"What letters?"

"*Them* letters. I be bound, if I have to take aholt of you I'll—"

"They're in the trunk. There, now. And they're just the same as they was when I got them out of the office. I hain't looked into them, I hain't touched them. But I knowed they'd make trouble, and I thought if you warn't in no hurry, I'd—"

"Well, you *do* need skinning, there ain't no mistake about it. And I wrote another one to tell you I was coming; and I spose he—"

"No, it come yesterday; I hain't read it yet, but *it's* all right, I've got that one."

I wanted to offer to bet two dollars she hadn't, but I reckoned maybe it was just as safe to not to. So I never said nothing.

CHAPTER THE LAST

The first time I catched Tom, private, I asked him what was his idea, time of the evasion?—what it was he'd planned to do if the evasion worked all right and he managed to set a nigger free that was already free before? And he said, what he had planned in his head, from the start, if we got Jim out all safe, was for us to run him down the river, on the raft, and have adventures plumb to the mouth of the river, and then tell him about his being free, and take him back up home on a steamboat, in style, and pay him for his lost time, and write word ahead and get out all the niggers around, and have them waltz him into town with a torchlight procession and a brass band, and then he would be a hero, and so would we. But I reckoned it was about as well the way it was.

We had Jim out of the chains in no time, and when Aunt Polly and Uncle Silas and Aunt Sally found out how good he helped the doctor nurse Tom, they made a heap of fuss over him, and fixed him up prime, and give him all he wanted to eat, and a good time, and nothing to do. And we had him up to the sick-room; and had a high talk; and Tom give Jim forty dollars for being prisoner for us so patient, and doing it up so good, and Jim was pleased most to death, and busted out, and says:

"*Dah*, now, Huck, what I tell you?—what I tell you up dah on Jackson islan'? I *tole* you I got a hairy breas', en what's de sign un it; en I *tole* you I ben rich wunst, en gwineter to be rich *agin*; en it's come true, en heah she *is! Dah*, now! doan' talk to *me*—signs is *signs*, mine I tell you; en I knowed jis' 's well 'at I 'uz gwineter be rich agin as I's a stannin' heah dis minute!"

And then Tom he talked along, and talked along, and says, le's all three slide out of here, one of these nights, and get an outfit, and go for howling adventures amongst the Injuns, over in the Territory, for a couple of weeks or two; and I says, all right, that suits me, but I ain't got no money for to buy the outfit, and I reckon I couldn't get none from home, because it's likely pap's been back before now, and got it all away from Judge Thatcher and drunk it up.

"No he hain't," Tom says; "it's all there, yet—six thousand dollars and more; and your pap hain't ever been back since. Hadn't when I come away, anyhow."

Jim says, kind of solemn:

"He ain't a comin' back no mo', Huck."

I says:

"Why, Jim?"

"Nemmine why, Huck—but he ain't comin' back no mo'."

But I kept at him; so at last he says:

"Doan' you 'member de house dat was float'n down de river, en dey wuz a man in dah, kivered up, en I went in en unkivered him and didn' let you come in? Well, den, you k'n git yo' money when you wants it; kase dat wuz him."

Tom's most well, now, and got his bullet around his neck on a watch-guard for a watch, and is always seeing what time it is, and so there ain't nothing more to write about, and I am rotten glad of it, because if I'd a knowed what a trouble it was to make a book I wouldn't a tackled it and ain't agoing to no more. But I reckon I got to light out for the Territory ahead of the rest, because Aunt Sally she's going to adopt me and sivilize me and I can't stand it. I been there before.

THE END. YOURS TRULY, HUCK FINN.

STEPHEN CRANE
(1871–1900)

Stephen Crane's life story is quickly told. He died young, but his fiction has survived for almost a century. His 28 years were characterized by numerous ironies. Youngest of 14 children, he became an extreme individualist. Coming from a home shaped by a father who was a Methodist minister and a mother who was a temperance crusader, he declared himself an atheist when he was still a child. His family moved often, and he was constantly in motion himself until the day he died. Frail as a child, he excelled in boxing, horsemanship, and almost became a baseball player instead of a writer. Despite having malaria and tuberculosis, he actively sought adventure and danger in New York City slums, out West, in Mexico, and as a war correspondent. The life he observed in the slums made him not a reformer, but a cynic. While he pursued the bohemian lifestyle with a romantic robustness, part of him was always hoping to achieve an upper class status.

Crane's writing career was also full of ironies. He wrote an innovative novel about a prostitute, then later fell in love with one. He always wanted to become a soldier, and he wrote one of the greatest war novels before he even witnessed war as a correspondent. He wrote humorous and satirical sketches, but became internationally famous as a master of style, of realism, symbolism, and irony. Though he was an eyewitness to major social and historical events, Crane wrote only a few pieces of fiction in the first person. He hunted down the facts, but rendered them in profoundly personal impressions in a rich style. He began by writing local color sketches and ended writing from the perspective of cosmic determinism. He insisted on telling the bitter truth in fiction, but only as embodied in aesthetic innovations.

Born November 1, 1871, in Newark, New Jersey, he lived in various small towns in his native state and in New York. Hawthorne, Melville, Twain, and Crane had in common the lasting effect of the loss of their fathers; Crane was nine when his father died. When the family moved to Asbury Park, New York, Crane joined his mother and his brother in the newspaper business. He wrote his first short story when he was 14. Even as a teenager, Crane was always simultaneously seeking facts for newspaper stories and raw material for fiction.

At Syracuse University, at the age of 20, Crane decided to become a writer rather than a professional baseball player, and in the cupola of his fraternity house, he wrote the first draft of *Maggie: A Girl of the Streets.* Two years later, he published it in paperback under a pseudonym at his own expense, to his loss. Without rendering her thoughts, Crane objectively shows how a young woman's environment determines her struggle, how she becomes a prostitute in New York's Bowery, and how she ends her own life. The first naturalistic novel by an American, it paved the way for Frank Norris, Jack London, Theodore Dreiser, John Dos Passos, and James Farrell.

Crane left Syracuse after only one semester, and began a newspaper career in earnest. The next few years were rich in innovative literary achievement for Crane. His tales and sketches of the great metropolis and of small towns in Sullivan County in southwestern New York were published in the New York *Tribune.* He started *The Red Badge of Courage* and the somewhat autobiographical, naturalistic novella about a mother's domination of her youngest male child, "George's Mother" (1896). In December of 1894, *The Red Badge of Courage* appeared serially, abridged, in the Philadelphia *Press* and other papers. William Dean Howells and Hamlin Garland, the famous western regionalist, praised and promoted his writing.

During that same time, Crane was also writing poetry. His first love inspired his first poems, later collected in *The Black Riders* (1895). The poems of Emily Dickinson, recommended by American realist William Dean Howells, had an even greater impact than love, though. When, in the mid-1890s, Crane fell in love with a married woman, he was again inspired to write poetry. Using techniques he learned from Dickinson's poems, he wrote his "intrigue poems," collected in his second volume *War Is Kind* (1899).

Crane's last five years, while working as a newspaper man, were full of adventure. In 1895, a syndicate sent him out West. Out of that experience came two major works, the novella "The Blue Hotel," about a Swedish immigrant whose fear of Western violence inspires his own murder, and "The Bride Comes to Yellow Sky," a comic handling of fear in a duel. *The Red Badge of Courage* was published as a book that year. A bestseller, it was the first example of modern realism in American fiction to achieve popular success at home and in England.

Then came a rather sentimental, somewhat autobiographical story of a young painter, *The Third Violet* (1896). *The Little Regiment and Other Episodes of the American Civil War* (1896) includes stories that augmented the effect of his war novel. The now famous writer was able to get *Maggie* reprinted in hardcover. Near the end of 1896, he met Cora Taylor, an older woman, who owned the Hotel de Dream, a house of prostitution in Jacksonville, Florida. She was a contrast to the married woman who refused his proposal of marriage the year before.

Returning from Cuba in 1897, where he had reported on the insurrection against Spain, Crane experienced the shipwreck on which he based his most famous story, "The Open Boat." Crane excelled in short forms, and that novella was published, with other stories, the next year. Then, when he was sent to cover the Greco-Turkish War, Cora followed him. That war provided material for a minor work, *Active Service* (1899).

By then a legendary figure, Crane settled in England with Cora. He formed friendships with Henry James, Ford Madox Ford, Harold Frederick, H. G. Wells, and most closely with Joseph Conrad. During that time, he wrote three major works: "The Monster," "The Blue Hotel," and "The Bride Comes to Yellow Sky."

While covering the Spanish-American War in 1898, Crane was voted by his colleagues the best war correspondent of the year. He set an example for Hemingway, who covered three major wars. After lingering a while in Havana and New

York City, Crane rejoined Cora in England. High living put him in debt, so he began writing at a feverish pace. In 1899, he prepared *Wounds in the Rain* (1900), *Great Battles of the World* (1901), *Last Words* (1902), leaving *The O'Ruddy* (1903), a novel inspired by a trip to Ireland, unfinished (Robert Barr finished it). That year, he published *War Is Kind*, *Active Service*, and *The Monster and Other Stories*. "War Memories," about the Cuban experience, appeared in an English newspaper.

In 1900, he was covering yet another war, the Boer War, when he was forced to return to England because of tubercular hemorrhages. With Cora, he went to the Black Forest, seeking a rest cure. Soon after, on June 5, 1900, he died, in debt, leaving several works incomplete.

Crane called *The Red Badge of Courage, An Episode of the American Civil War* a potboiler aimed at the mass audience that had rejected *Maggie*. But readers today call it a major work of impressionistic realism, among other honorific terms. It is the first war novel to dispense with romantic heroics. It is also the first great modern novel of war by an American, and a masterpiece about the initiation and testing of youth, in all war, not just in the Civil War.

The novel is an early example of psychological realism under conditions of fear and violence. Using the omniscient point of view, Crane offers external, objective views of the uncertain, changing circumstances of battle, alternating with internal views of the youth's sensations and perceptions—a detailed process of stimulus and response. One of Crane's biographers argued that fear was the predominant emotion of Crane's life. Frequently, instinctive fear and crisis circumstances clash to produce violent resolutions in his characters' lives.

Many of Crane's own experiences were deliberate experiments, and so were the situations in which he entangled his characters. The techniques he used to depict them were also experiments, for he had no faith in literary conventions. The fallacies of human perception and illusion often prove fatal for Crane's characters, as they do for Ambrose Bierce's soldiers. As humans, his characters are mocked by natural and human forces. Reacting as animals, some fight savagely to survive. The moments of repose and joy are there only to sharpen the impact of violence and death. The youth in *Red Badge* is first a coward, then a kind of hero, but neither role means anything, as the stories "The Veteran" and "An Episode of War" demonstrate. Neither religion nor any other human institution offers any solace. Pessimistic determinism pervades Crane's fiction.

Superior to most fiction written by men who actually fought in the Civil War, *Red Badge* is an example of the supremacy of the imagination over actuality, a triumph of art over reportage. Paradoxically, an experiment in chaos is best rendered in a style that is very carefully controlled. Crane's patterning of words, his impressionistic use of sensory imagery, his counterpointing of characters and scenes, and the brevity of the novel create a unity of effect rarely found in fiction, except for Henry James'. No matter how negative a writer's vision, the creative process itself is celebratory.

THE RED BADGE OF COURAGE

Stephen Crane

CHAPTER I

The cold passed reluctantly from the earth, and the retiring fogs revealed an army stretched out on the hills, resting. As the landscape changed from brown to green, the army awakened, and began to tremble with eagerness at the noise of rumors. It cast its eyes upon the roads, which were growing from long troughs of liquid mud to proper thoroughfares. A river, amber-tinted in the shadow of its banks, purled at the army's feet; and at night, when the stream had become of a sorrowful blackness, one could see across it the red, eyelike gleam of hostile camp fires set in the low brows of distant hills.

Once a certain tall soldier developed virtues and went resolutely to wash a shirt. He came flying back from a brook waving his garment bannerlike. He was swelled with a tale he had heard from a reliable friend, who had heard it from a truthful cavalryman, who had heard it from his trustworthy brother, one of the orderlies at division headquarters. He adopted the important air of a herald in red and gold.

"We're goin' t' move t' morrah—sure," he said pompously to a group in the company street. "We're goin' 'way up the river, cut across, an' come around in behint 'em."

To his attentive audience he drew a loud and elaborate plan of a very brilliant campaign. When he had finished, the blue-clothed men scattered into small arguing groups between the rows of squat brown huts. A negro teamster who had been dancing upon a cracker box with the hilarious encouragement of two-score soldiers was deserted. He sat mournfully down. Smoke drifted lazily from a multitude of quaint chimneys.

"It's a lie! that's all it is—a thunderin' lie!" said another private loudly. His smooth face was flushed, and his hands were thrust sulkily into his trousers' pockets. He took the matter as an affront to him. "I don't believe the derned old army's ever going to move. We're set. I've got ready to move eight times in the last two weeks, and we ain't moved yet."

The tall soldier felt called upon to defend the truth of a rumor he himself had introduced. He and the loud one came near to fighting over it.

A corporal began to swear before the assemblage. He had just put a costly board floor in his house, he said. During the early spring he had refrained from adding extensively to the comfort of his environment because he had felt that the army might start on the march at any moment. Of late, however, he had been impressed that they were in a sort of eternal camp.

Many of the men engaged in a spirited debate. One outlined in a peculiarly lucid manner all the plans of the commanding general. He was opposed by men who advocated that there were other plans of campaign. They clamored at each other, numbers making futile bids for the popular attention. Meanwhile, the soldier who had fetched the rumor bustled about with much importance. He was continually assailed by questions.

"What's up, Jim?"

"Th' army's goin' t' move."

"Ah, what yeh talkin' about. How yeh know it is?"

"Well, yeh kin b'lieve me er not, jest as yeh like. I don't care a hang."

There was much food for thought in the manner in which he replied. He came near to convincing them by disdaining to produce proofs. They grew much excited over it.

There was a youthful private who listened with eager ears to the words of the tall soldier and to the varied comments of his comrades. After receiving a fill of discussions concerning marches and attacks, he went to his hut and crawled through an intricate hole that served it as a door. He wished to be alone with some new thoughts that had lately come to him.

He lay down on a wide bunk that stretched across the end of the room. In the other end, cracker boxes were made to serve as furniture. They were grouped about the fireplace. A picture from an illustrated weekly was upon the log walls, and three rifles were paralleled on pegs. Equipments hung on handy projections, and some tin dishes lay upon a small pile of firewood. A folded tent was serving as a roof. The sunlight, without, beating upon it, made it glow a light yellow shade. A small window shot an oblique square of whiter light upon the cluttered floor. The smoke from the fire at times neglected the clay chimney and wreathed into the room, and this flimsy chimney of clay and sticks made endless threats to set ablaze the whole establishment.

The youth was in a little trance of astonishment. So they were at last going to fight. On the morrow, perhaps, there would be a battle, and he would be in it. For a time he was obliged to labor to make himself believe. He could not accept with assurance an omen that he was about to mingle in one of those great affairs of the earth.

He had, of course, dreamed of battles all his life—of vague and bloody conflicts that had thrilled him with their sweep and fire. In visions he had seen himself in many struggles. He had imagined peoples secure in the shadow of his eagle-eyed prowess. But awake he had regarded battles as crimson blotches on the pages of the past. He had put them as things of the bygone with his thought-images of heavy crowns and high castles. There was a portion of the world's history which he had regarded as the time of wars, but it, he thought, had been long gone over the horizon and had disappeared forever.

From his home his youthful eyes had looked upon the war in his own country with distrust. It must be some sort of a play affair. He had long despaired of witnessing a Greeklike struggle. Such would be no more, he had said. Men were better, or more timid. Secular and religious education had effaced the throat-grappling instinct, or else firm finance held in check the passions.

He had burned several times to enlist. Tales of great movements shook the land. They might not be distinctly Homeric, but there seemed to be much glory in them. He had read of marches, sieges, conflicts, and he had longed to see it all. His busy mind had drawn for him large pictures extravagant in color, lurid with breathless deeds.

But his mother had discouraged him. She had affected to look with some contempt upon the quality of his war ardor and patriotism. She could calmly seat herself and with no apparent difficulty give him many hundreds of reasons why he was of vastly more importance on the farm than on the field of battle. She had had certain ways of expression that told him that her statements on the subject came from a deep conviction. Moreover, on her side, was his belief that her ethical motive in the argument was impregnable.

At last, however, he had made firm rebellion against this yellow light thrown upon the color of his ambitions. The newspapers, the gossip of the village, his own picturings, had aroused him to an uncheckable degree. They were in truth fighting finely down there. Almost every day the newspapers printed accounts of a decisive victory.

One night, as he lay in bed, the winds had carried to him the clangoring of the church bell as some enthusiast jerked the rope frantically to tell the twisted news of a great battle. This voice of the people rejoicing in the night had made him shiver in a prolonged ecstasy of excitement. Later, he had gone down to his mother's room and had spoken thus: "Ma, I'm going to enlist."

"Henry, don't you be a fool," his mother had replied. She had then covered her face with the quilt. There was an end to the matter for that night.

Nevertheless, the next morning he had gone to a town that was near his mother's farm and had enlisted in a company that was forming there. When he had returned home his mother was milking the brindle cow. Four others stood waiting. "Ma, I've enlisted," he had said to her diffidently. There was a short silence. "The Lord's will be done, Henry," she had finally replied, and had then continued to milk the brindle cow.

When he had stood in the doorway with his soldier's clothes on his back, and with the light of excitement and expectancy in his eyes almost defeating the glow of regret for the home bonds, he had seen two tears leaving their trails on his mother's scarred cheeks.

Still, she had disappointed him by saying nothing whatever about returning with his shield or on it. He had privately primed himself for a beautiful scene. He had prepared certain sentences which he thought could be used with touching effect. But her words destroyed his plans. She had doggedly peeled potatoes and addressed him as follows: "You watch out, Henry, an' take good care of yerself in this here fighting business—you watch out, an' take good care of yerself. Don't go a-thinkin' you can lick the hull rebel army at the start, because yeh can't. Yer jest one little feller amongst a hull lot of others, and yeh've got to keep quiet an' do what they tell yeh. I know how you are, Henry.

"I've knet yeh eight pair of socks, Henry, and I've put in all yer best shirts, because I want my boy to be jest as warm and comf'able as anybody in the army. Whenever they get holes in 'em, I want yeh to send 'em rightaway back to me, so's I kin dern 'em.

"An' allus be careful an' choose yer comp'ny. There's lots of bad men in the army, Henry. The army makes 'em wild, and they like nothing better than the job of leading off a young feller like you, as ain't never been away from home much and has allus had a mother, an' a-learning 'em to drink and swear. Keep clear of them folks, Henry. I don't want yeh to ever do anything, Henry, that yeh would be 'shamed to let me know about. Jest think as if I was a-watchin' yeh. If yeh keep that in yer mind allus, I guess yeh'll come out about right.

"Yeh must allus remember yer father, too, child, an' remember he never drunk a drop of licker in his life, and seldom swore a cross oath.

"I don't know what else to tell yeh, Henry, excepting that yeh must never do no shirking, child, on my account. If so be a time comes when yeh have to be kilt or do a mean thing, why, Henry, don't think of anything 'cept what's right, because there's many a woman has to bear up 'ginst sech things these times, and the Lord'll take keer of us all.

"Don't forgit about the socks and the shirts, child; and I've put a cup of blackberry jam with yer bundle, because I know yeh like it above all things. Good-by, Henry. Watch out, and be a good boy."

He had, of course, been impatient under the ordeal of this speech. It had not been quite what he expected, and he had borne it with an air of irritation. He departed feeling vague relief.

Still, when he had looked back from the gate, he had seen his mother kneeling among the potato parings. Her brown face, upraised, was stained with tears, and her spare form was quivering. He bowed his head and went on, feeling suddenly ashamed of his purposes.

From his home he had gone to the seminary to bid adieu to many schoolmates. They had thronged about him with wonder and admiration. He had felt the gulf now between them and had swelled with calm pride. He and some of his fellows who had donned blue were quite overwhelmed with privileges for all of one afternoon, and it had been a very delicious thing. They had strutted.

A certain light-haired girl had made vivacious fun at his martial spirit, but there was another and darker girl whom he had gazed at steadfastly, and he thought she grew demure and sad at sight of his blue and brass. As he had walked down the path between the rows of oaks, he had turned his head and detected her at a window watching his departure. As he perceived her, she had immediately begun to stare up through the high tree branches at the sky. He had seen a good deal of flurry and haste in her movement as she changed her attitude. He often thought of it.

On the way to Washington his spirit had soared. The regiment was fed and caressed at station after station until the youth had believed that he must be a hero. There was a lavish expenditure of bread and cold meats, coffee, and pickles and cheese. As he basked in the smiles of the girls and was patted and complimented by the old men, he had felt growing within him the strength to do mighty deeds of arms.

After complicated journeyings with many pauses, there had come months of monotonous life in a camp. He had had the belief that real war was a series of death struggles with small time in between for sleep and meals; but since his regiment had come to the field the army had done little but sit still and try to keep warm.

He was brought then gradually back to his old ideas. Greeklike struggles would be no more. Men were better, or more timid. Secular and religious education had effaced the throat-grappling instinct, or else firm finance held in check the passions.

He had grown to regard himself merely as a part of a vast blue demonstration. His province was to look out, as far as he could, for his personal comfort. For recreation he could twiddle his thumbs and speculate on the thoughts which must agitate the minds of the generals. Also, he was drilled and drilled and reviewed, and drilled and drilled and reviewed.

The only foes he had seen were some pickets along the river bank. They were a sun-tanned, philosophical lot, who sometimes shot reflectively at the blue pickets. When reproached for this afterward, they usually expressed sorrow, and swore by their gods that the guns had exploded without their permission. The youth, on guard duty one night, conversed across the stream with one of them. He was a slightly ragged man, who spat skillfully between his shoes and possessed a great fund of bland and infantile assurance. The youth liked him personally.

"Yank," the other had informed him, "yer a right dum good feller." This sentiment, floating to him upon the still air, had made him temporarily regret war.

Various veterans had told him tales. Some talked of gray, bewhiskered hordes who were advancing with relentless curses and chewing tobacco with unspeakable valor; tremendous bodies of fierce soldiery who were sweeping along like the Huns. Others spoke of tattered and eternally hungry men who fired despondent powders. "They'll charge through hell's fire an' brimstone t' git a holt on a haversack, an' sech stomachs ain't a-lastin' long," he was told. From the stories, the youth imagined the red, live bones, sticking out through slits in the faded uniforms.

Still, he could not put a whole faith in veterans' tales, for recruits were their prey. They talked much of smoke, fire, and blood, but he could not tell how much might be lies. They persistently yelled, "Fresh fish!" at him, and were in no wise to be trusted.

However, he perceived now that it did not greatly matter what kind of soldiers he was going to fight, so long as they fought, which fact no one disputed. There was a more serious problem. He lay in his bunk pondering upon it. He tried to mathematically prove to himself that he would not run from a battle.

Previously he had never felt obliged to wrestle too seriously with this question. In his life he had taken certain things for granted, never challenging his belief in ultimate success, and bothering little about means and roads. But here he was confronted with a thing of moment. It had suddenly appeared to him that perhaps in a battle he might run. He was forced to admit that as far as war was concerned he knew nothing of himself.

A sufficient time before he would have allowed the problem to kick its heels at the outer portals of his mind, but now he felt compelled to give serious attention to it.

A little panic-fear grew in his mind. As his imagination went forward to a fight, he saw hideous possibilities. He contemplated the lurking menaces of the future, and failed in an effort to see himself standing stoutly in the midst of them. He recalled his visions of broken-bladed glory, but in the shadow of the impending tumult he suspected them to be impossible pictures.

He sprang from the bunk and began to pace nervously to and fro. "Good Lord, what's th' matter with me?" he said aloud.

He felt that in this crisis his laws of life were useless. Whatever he had learned of himself was here of no avail. He was an unknown quantity. He saw that he would again be obliged to experiment as he had in early youth. He must accumulate information of himself, and meanwhile he resolved to remain close upon his guard lest those qualities of which he knew nothing should everlastingly disgrace him. "Good Lord!" he repeated in dismay.

After a time the tall soldier slid dexterously through the hole. The loud private followed. They were wrangling.

"That's all right," said the tall soldier as he entered. He waved his hand expressively. "You can believe me or not, jest as you like. All you got to do is to sit down and wait as quiet as you can. Then pretty soon you'll find out I was right."

His comrade grunted stubbornly. For a moment he seemed to be searching for a formidable reply. Finally he said: "Well, you don't know everything in the world, do you?"

"Didn't say I knew everything in the world," retorted the other sharply. He began to stow various articles snugly into his knapsack.

The youth, pausing in his nervous walk, looked down at the busy figure. "Going to be a battle, sure, is there, Jim?" he asked.

"Of course there is," replied the soldier. "Of course there is. You jest wait 'til tomorrow, and you'll see one of the biggest battles ever was. You jest wait."

"Thunder!" said the youth.

"Oh, you'll see fighting this time, my boy, what'll be regular out-and-out fighting," added the tall soldier, with the air of a man who is about to exhibit a battle for the benefit of his friends.

"Huh!" said the loud one from a corner.

"Well," remarked the youth, "like as not this story'll turn out jest like them others did."

"Not much it won't," replied the tall soldier, exasperated. "Not much it won't. Didn't the cavalry all start this morning?" He glared about him. No one denied his statement. "The cavalry started this morning," he continued. "They say there ain't hardly any cavalry left in camp. They're going to Richmond, or some place, while we fight all the Johnnies. It's some dodge like that. The regiment's got orders, too. A feller what seen 'em go to headquarters told me a little while ago. And they're raising blazes all over camp—anybody can see that."

"Shucks!" said the loud one.

The youth remained silent for a time. At last he spoke to the tall soldier. "Jim!"

"What?"

"How do you think the reg'ment'll do?"

"Oh, they'll fight all right, I guess, after they once get into it," said the other with cold judgment. He made a fine use of the third person. "There's been heaps of fun poked at 'em because they're new, of course, and all that; but they'll fight all right, I guess."

"Think any of the boys'll run?" persisted the youth.

"Oh, there may be a few of 'em run, but there's them kind in every regiment, 'specially when they first goes under fire," said the other in a tolerant way. "Of course it might happen that the hull kit-and-boodle might start and run, if some big fighting came first-off, and then again they might stay and fight like fun. But you can't bet on nothing. Of course they ain't never been under fire yet, and it ain't likely they'll lick the hull rebel army all-to-oncet the firs' time; but I think they'll fight better than some, if worse than others. That's the way I figger. They call the reg'ment 'Fresh fish' and everything; but the boys come of good stock, and most of 'em 'll fight like sin after they oncet git shootin'," he added, with a mighty emphasis on the last four words.

"Oh, you think you know—" began the loud soldier with scorn.

The other turned savagely upon him. They had a rapid altercation, in which they fastened upon each other various strange epithets.

The youth at last interrupted them. "Did you ever think you might run yourself, Jim?" he asked. On concluding the sentence he laughed as if he had meant to aim a joke. The loud soldier also giggled.

The tall private waved his hand. "Well," said he profoundly, "I've thought it might get too hot for Jim Conklin in some of them scrimmages, and if a whole lot of boys started and run, why, I s'pose I'd start and run. And if I once started to run, I'd run like the devil, and no mistake. But if everybody was a-standing and a-fighting, why, I'd stand and fight. Be jiminey, I would. I'll bet on it."

"Huh!" said the loud one.

The youth of this tale felt gratitude for these words of his comrade. He had feared that all of the untried men possessed a great and correct confidence. He now was in a measure reassured.

CHAPTER II

The next morning the youth discovered that his tall comrade had been the fast-flying messenger of a mistake. There was much scoffing at the latter by those who had yesterday been firm adherents of his views, and there was even a little sneering by men who had never believed the rumor. The tall one fought with a man from Chatfield Corners and beat him severely.

The youth felt, however, that his problem was in no wise lifted from him. There was, on the contrary, an irritating prolongation. The tale had created in him a great concern for himself. Now, with the newborn question in his mind, he was compelled to sink back into his old place as part of a blue demonstration.

For days he made ceaseless calculations, but they were all wondrously unsatisfactory. He found that he could establish nothing. He finally concluded that the only way to prove himself was to go into the blaze, and then figuratively to watch his legs to discover their merits and faults. He reluctantly admitted that he could not sit still and with a mental slate and pencil derive an answer. To gain it, he must have blaze, blood, and danger, even as a chemist requires this, that, and the other. So he fretted for an opportunity.

Meanwhile he continually tried to measure himself by his comrades. The tall soldier, for one, gave him some assurance. This man's serene unconcern dealt him a measure of confidence, for he had known him since childhood, and from his intimate knowledge he did not see how he could be capable of anything that was beyond him, the youth. Still, he thought that his comrade might be mistaken about himself. Or, on the other hand, he might be a man heretofore doomed to peace and obscurity, but, in reality, made to shine in war.

The youth would have liked to have discovered another who suspected himself. A sympathetic comparison of mental notes would have been a joy to him.

He occasionally tried to fathom a comrade with seductive sentences. He looked about to find men in the proper mood. All attempts failed to bring forth any statement which looked in any way like a confession to those doubts which he privately acknowledged in himself. He was afraid to make an open declaration of his concern, because he dreaded to place some unscrupulous confidant upon the high plane of the unconfessed from which elevation he could be derided.

In regard to his companions his mind wavered between two opinions, according to his mood. Sometimes he inclined to believing them all heroes. In fact, he usually admitted in secret the superior development of the higher qualities in others. He could conceive of men going very insignificantly about the world bearing a load of courage unseen, and although he had known many of his comrades through boyhood, he began to fear that his judgment of them had been blind. Then, in other moments, he flouted these theories, and assured himself that his fellows were all privately wondering and quaking.

His emotions made him feel strange in the presence of men who talked excitedly of a prospective battle as of a drama they were about to witness, with nothing but eagerness and curiosity apparent in their faces. It was often that he suspected them to be liars.

He did not pass such thoughts without severe condemnation of himself. He dinned reproaches at times. He was convicted by himself of many shameful crimes against the gods of traditions.

In his great anxiety his heart was continually clamoring at what he considered the intolerable slowness of the generals. They seemed content to perch tranquilly on the river bank, and leave him bowed down by the weight of a great problem. He wanted it settled forthwith. He could not long bear such a load, he said. Sometimes his anger at the commanders reached an acute stage, and he grumbled about the camp like a veteran.

One morning, however, he found himself in the ranks of his prepared regiment. The men were whispering speculations and recounting the old rumors. In the gloom before the break of the day their uniforms glowed a deep purple hue. From across the river the red eyes were still peering. In the eastern sky there was a yellow patch like a rug laid for the feet of the coming sun; and against it, black and patternlike, loomed the gigantic figure of the colonel on a gigantic horse.

From off in the darkness came the trampling of feet. The youth could occasionally see dark shadows that moved like monsters. The regiment stood at rest for what seemed a long time. The youth grew impatient. It was unendurable the way these affairs were managed. He wondered how long they were to be kept waiting.

As he looked all about him and pondered upon the mystic gloom, he began to believe that at any moment the ominous distance might be aflare, and the rolling crashes of an engagement come to his ears. Staring once at the red eyes across the river, he conceived them to be growing larger, as the orbs of a row of dragons advancing. He turned toward the colonel and saw him lift his gigantic arm and calmly stroke his mustache.

At last he heard from along the road at the foot of the hill the clatter of a horse's galloping hoofs. It must be the coming of orders. He bent forward, scarce breathing. The exciting clickety-click, as it grew louder and louder, seemed to be beating upon his soul. Presently a horseman with jangling equipment drew rein before the colonel of the regiment. The two held a short, sharp-worded conversation. The men in the foremost ranks craned their necks.

As the horseman wheeled his animal and galloped away he turned to shout over his shoulder, "Don't forget that box of cigars!" The colonel mumbled in reply. The youth wondered what a box of cigars had to do with war.

A moment later the regiment went swinging off into the darkness. It was now like one of those moving monsters wending with many feet. The air was heavy, and cold with dew. A mass of wet grass, marched upon, rustled like silk.

There was an occasional flash and glimmer of steel from the backs of all these huge crawling reptiles. From the road came creakings and rumblings as some surly guns were dragged away.

The men stumbled along still muttering speculations. There was a subdued debate. Once a man fell down, and as he reached for his rifle a comrade, unseeing, trod upon his hand. He of the injured fingers swore bitterly and aloud. A low tittering laugh went among his fellows.

Presently they passed into a roadway and marched forward with easy strides. A dark regiment moved before them, and from behind also came the tinkle of equipments on the bodies of marching men.

The rushing yellow of the developing day went on behind their backs. When the sunrays at last struck full and mellowingly upon the earth, the youth saw that the landscape was streaked with two long, thin, black columns which disappeared on the brow of a hill in front and rearward vanished in a wood. They were like two serpents crawling from the cavern of the night.

The river was not in view. The tall soldier burst into praises of what he thought to be his powers of perception.

Some of the tall one's companions cried with emphasis that they, too, had evolved the same thing, and they congratulated themselves upon it. But there were others who said that the tall one's plan was not the true one at all. They persisted with other theories. There was a vigorous discussion.

The youth took no part in them. As he walked along in careless line he was engaged with his own eternal debate. He could not hinder himself from dwelling upon it. He was despondent and sullen, and threw shifting glances about him. He looked ahead, often expecting to hear from the advance the rattle of firing.

But the long serpents crawled slowly from hill to hill without bluster of smoke. A dun-colored cloud of dust floated away to the right. The sky overhead was of a fairy blue.

The youth studied the faces of his companions, ever on the watch to detect kindred emotions. He suffered disappointment. Some ardor of the air which was causing the veteran commands to move with glee—almost with song—had infected the new regiment. The men began to speak of victory as of a thing they knew. Also, the tall soldier received his vindication. They were certainly going to come around in behind the enemy. They expressed commiseration for that part of the army which had been left upon the river bank, felicitating themselves upon being a part of a blasting host.

The youth, considering himself as separated from the others, was saddened by the blithe and merry speeches that went from rank to rank. The company wags all made their best endeavors. The regiment tramped to the tune of laughter.

The blatant soldier often convulsed whole files by his biting sarcasms aimed at the tall one.

And it was not long before all the men seemed to forget their mission. Whole brigades grinned in unison, and regiments laughed.

A rather fat soldier attempted to pilfer a horse from a dooryard. He planned to load his knapsack upon it. He was escaping with his prize when a young girl rushed from the house and grabbed the animal's mane. There followed a wrangle. The young girl, with pink cheeks and shining eyes, stood like a dauntless statue.

The observant regiment, standing at rest in the roadway, whooped at once, and entered whole-souled upon the side of the maiden. The men became so engrossed in this affair that they entirely ceased to remember their own large war. They jeered the piratical private, and called attention to various defects in his personal appearance; and they were wildly enthusiastic in support of the young girl.

To her, from some distance, came bold advice. "Hit him with a stick."

There were crows and catcalls showered upon him when he retreated without the horse. The regiment rejoiced at his downfall. Loud and vociferous congratulations were showered upon the maiden, who stood panting and regarding the troops with defiance.

At nightfall the column broke into regimental pieces, and the fragments went into the fields to camp. Tents sprang up like strange plants. Camp fires, like red, peculiar blossoms, dotted the night.

The youth kept from intercourse with his companions as much as circumstances would allow him. In the evening he wandered a few paces into the gloom. From this little distance the many fires, with the black forms of men passing to and fro before the crimson rays, made weird and satanic effects.

He lay down in the grass. The blades pressed tenderly against his cheek. The moon had been lighted and was hung in a treetop. The liquid stillness of the night enveloping him made him feel vast pity for himself. There was a caress in the soft winds; and the whole mood of the darkness, he thought, was one of sympathy for himself in his distress.

He wished, without reserve, that he was at home again making the endless rounds from the house to the barn, from the barn to the fields, from the fields to the barn, from the barn to the house. He remembered he had often cursed the brindle cow and her mates, and had sometimes flung milking stools. But, from his present point of view, there was a halo of happiness about each of their heads, and he would have sacrificed all the brass buttons on the continent to have been enabled to return to them. He told himself that he was not formed for a soldier. And he mused seriously upon the radical differences between himself and those men who were dodging implike around the fires.

As he mused thus he heard the rustle of grass, and, upon turning his head, discovered the loud soldier. He called out, "Oh, Wilson!"

The latter approached and looked down. "Why, hello, Henry; is it you? What you doing here?"

"Oh, thinking," said the youth.

The other sat down and carefully lighted his pipe. "You're getting blue, my boy. You're looking thundering peaked. What the dickens is wrong with you?"

"Oh, nothing," said the youth.

The loud soldier launched then into the subject of the anticipated fight. "Oh, we've got 'em now!" As he spoke his boyish face was wreathed in a gleeful smile, and his voice had an exultant ring. "We've got 'em now. At last, by the eternal thunders, we'll lick 'em good!

"If the truth was known," he added, more soberly, "*they've* licked *us* about every clip up to now; but this time—this time—we'll lick 'em good!"

"I thought you was objecting to this march a little while ago," said the youth coldly.

"Oh, it wasn't that," explained the other. "I don't mind marching, if there's going to be fighting at the end of it. What I hate is this getting moved here and moved there, with no good coming of it, as far as I can see, excepting sore feet and damned short rations."

"Well, Jim Conklin says we'll get a plenty of fighting this time."

"He's right for once, I guess, though I can't see how it come. This time we're in for a big battle, and we've got the best end of it, certain sure. Gee rod! how we will thump 'em!"

He arose and began to pace to and fro excitedly. The thrill of his enthusiasm made him walk with an elastic step. He was sprightly, vigorous, fiery in his belief in success. He looked into the future with clear, proud eye, and he swore with the air of an old soldier.

The youth watched him for a moment in silence. When he finally spoke his voice was as bitter as dregs. "Oh, you're going to do great things, I s'pose!"

The loud soldier blew a thoughtful cloud of smoke from his pipe. "Oh, I don't know," he remarked with dignity; "I don't know. I s'pose I'll do as well as the rest. I'm going to try like thunder." He evidently complimented himself upon the modesty of this statement.

"How do you know you won't run when the time comes?" asked the youth.

"Run?" said the loud one; "run?—of course not!" He laughed.

"Well," continued the youth, "lots of good-a-'nough men have thought they was going to do great things before the fight, but when the time come they skedaddled."

"Oh, that's all true, I s'pose," replied the other; "but I'm not going to skedaddle. The man that bets on my running will lose his money, that's all." He nodded confidently.

"Oh, shucks!" said the youth. "You ain't the bravest man in the world, are you?"

"No, I ain't," exclaimed the loud soldier indignantly; "and I didn't say I was the bravest man in the world, neither. I said I was going to do my share of fighting—that's what I said. And I am, too. Who are you, anyhow? You talk as if you thought you was Napoleon Bonaparte." He glared at the youth for a moment, and then strode away.

The youth called in a savage voice after his comrade: "Well, you needn't git mad about it!" But the other continued on his way and made no reply.

He felt alone in space when his injured comrade had disappeared. His failure to discover any mite of resemblance in their viewpoints made him more miserable than before. No one seemed to be wrestling with such a terrific personal problem. He was a mental outcast.

He went slowly to his tent and stretched himself on a blanket by the side of the snoring tall soldier. In the darkness he saw visions of a thousand-tongued fear that would babble at his back and cause him to flee, while others were going coolly about their country's business. He admitted that he would not be able to cope with this monster. He felt that every nerve in his body would be an ear to hear the voices, while other men would remain stolid and deaf.

And as he sweated with the pain of these thoughts, he could hear low, serene sentences. "I'll bid five." "Make it six." "Seven." "Seven goes."

He stared at the red, shivering reflection of a fire on the white wall of his tent until, exhausted and ill from the monotony of his suffering, he fell asleep.

CHAPTER III

When another night came the columns, changed to purple streaks, filed across two pontoon bridges. A glaring fire wine-tinted the waters of the river. Its rays, shining upon the moving masses of troops, brought forth here and there sudden gleams of silver or gold. Upon the other shore a dark and mysterious range of hills was curved against the sky. The insect voices of the night sang solemnly.

After this crossing the youth assured himself that at any moment they might be suddenly and fearfully assaulted from the caves of the lowering woods. He kept his eyes watchfully upon the darkness.

But his regiment went unmolested to a camping place, and its soldiers slept the brave sleep of wearied men. In the morning they were routed out with early energy, and hustled along a narrow road that led deep into the forest.

It was during this rapid march that the regiment lost many of the marks of a new command.

The men had begun to count the miles upon their fingers, and they grew tired. "Sore feet an' damned short rations, that's all," said the loud soldier. There were perspiration and grumblings. After a time they began to shed their knapsacks. Some tossed them unconcernedly down; others hid them carefully, asserting their plans to return for them at some convenient time. Men extricated themselves from thick shirts. Presently few carried anything but their necessary clothing, blankets, haversacks, canteens, and arms and ammunition. "You can now eat and shoot," said the tall soldier to the youth. "That's all you want to do."

There was sudden change from the ponderous infantry of theory to the light and speedy infantry of practice. The regiment, relieved of a burden, received a new impetus. But there was much loss of valuable knapsacks, and, on the whole, very good shirts.

But the regiment was not yet veteranlike in appearance. Veteran regiments in the army were likely to be very small aggregations of men. Once, when the command had first come to the field, some perambulating veterans, noting the length of their column, had accosted them thus: "Hey, fellers, what brigade is that?" And when the men had replied that they formed a regiment and not a brigade, the older soldiers had laughed, and said, "O Gawd!"

Also, there was too great a similarity in the hats. The hats of a regiment should properly represent the history of headgear for a period of years. And, moreover, there were no letters of faded gold speaking from the colors. They were new and beautiful, and the color bearer habitually oiled the pole.

Presently the army again sat down to think. The odor of the peaceful pines was in the men's nostrils. The sound of monotonous axe blows rang through the forest, and the insects, nodding upon their perches, crooned like old women. The youth returned to his theory of a blue demonstration.

One gray dawn, however, he was kicked in the leg by the tall soldier, and then, before he was entirely awake, he found himself running down a wood road in the midst of men who were panting from the first effects of speed. His canteen banged rhythmically upon his thigh, and his haversack bobbed softly. His musket bounced a trifle from his shoulder at each stride and made his cap feel uncertain upon his head.

He could hear the men whisper jerky sentences: "Say—what's all this—about?" "What th' thunder—we—skedaddlin' this way fer?" "Billie—keep off m' feet. Yeh run—like a cow." And the loud soldier's shrill voice could be heard: "What th' devil they in sich a hurry for?"

The youth thought the damp fog of early morning moved from the rush of a great body of troops. From the distance came a sudden spatter of firing.

He was bewildered. As he ran with his comrades he strenuously tried to think, but all he knew was that if he fell down those coming behind would tread upon him. All his faculties seemed to be needed to guide him over and past obstructions. He felt carried along by a mob.

The sun spread disclosing rays, and, one by one, regiments burst into view like armed men just born of the earth. The youth perceived that the time had come. He was about to be measured. For a moment he felt in the face of his great trial like a babe, and the flesh over his heart seemed very thin. He seized time to look about him calculatingly.

But he instantly saw that it would be impossible for him to escape from the regiment. It inclosed him. And there were iron laws of tradition and law on four sides. He was in a moving box.

As he perceived this fact it occurred to him that he had never wished to come to the war. He had not enlisted of his free will. He had been dragged by the merciless government. And now they were taking him out to be slaughtered.

The regiment slid down a bank and wallowed across a little stream. The mournful current moved slowly on, and from the water, shaded black, some white bubble eyes looked at the men.

As they climbed the hill on the farther side artillery began to boom. Here the youth forgot many things as he felt a sudden impulse of curiosity. He scrambled up the bank with a speed that could not be exceeded by a bloodthirsty man.

He expected a battle scene.

There were some little fields girted and squeezed by a forest. Spread over the grass and in among the tree trunks, he could see knots and waving lines of skirmishers who were running hither and thither and firing at the landscape. A dark battle line lay upon a sun-struck clearing that gleamed orange color. A flag fluttered.

Other regiments floundered up the bank. The brigade was formed in line of battle, and after a pause started slowly through the woods in the rear of the receding skirmishers, who were continually melting into the scene to appear again farther on. They were always busy as bees, deeply absorbed in their little combats.

The youth tried to observe everything. He did not use care to avoid trees and branches, and his forgotten feet were constantly knocking against stones or getting entangled in briers. He was aware that these battalions with their commotions were woven red and startling into the gentle fabric of softened greens and browns. It looked to be a wrong place for a battlefield.

The skirmishers in advance fascinated him. Their shots into thickets and at distant and prominent trees spoke to him of tragedies—hidden, mysterious, solemn.

Once the line encountered the body of a dead soldier. He lay upon his back staring at the sky. He was dressed in an awkward suit of yellowish brown. The youth could see that the soles of his shoes had been worn to the thinness of writing paper, and from a great rent in one the dead foot projected piteously. And it was as if fate had betrayed the soldier. In death it exposed to his enemies that poverty which in life he had perhaps concealed from his friends.

The ranks opened covertly to avoid the corpse. The invulnerable dead man forced a way for himself. The youth looked keenly at the ashen face. The wind raised the tawny beard. It moved as if a hand were stroking it. He vaguely desired to walk around and around the body and stare; the impulse of the living to try to read in dead eyes the answer to the Question.

During the march the ardor which the youth had acquired when out of view of the field rapidly faded to nothing. His curiosity was quite easily satisfied. If an intense scene had caught him with its wild swing as he came to the top of the bank, he might have gone roaring on. This advance upon Nature was too calm. He had opportunity to reflect. He had time in which to wonder about himself and to attempt to probe his sensations.

Absurd ideas took hold upon him. He thought that he did not relish the landscape. It threatened him. A coldness swept over his back, and it is true that his trousers felt to him that they were no fit for his legs at all.

A house standing placidly in distant fields had to him an ominous look. The shadows of the woods were formidable. He was certain that in this vista there lurked fierce-eyed hosts. The swift thought came to him that the generals did not know what they were about. It was all a trap. Suddenly those close forests would bristle with rifle barrels. Ironlike brigades would appear in the rear. They were all going to be sacrificed. The generals were stupids. The enemy would presently swallow the whole command. He glared about him, expecting to see the stealthy approach of his death.

He thought that he must break from the ranks and harangue his comrades. They must not all be killed like pigs; and he was sure it would come to pass unless they were informed of these dangers. The generals were idiots to send them marching into a regular pen. There was but one pair of eyes in the corps. He would step forth and make a speech. Shrill and passionate words came to his lips.

The line, broken into moving fragments by the ground, went calmly on through fields and woods. The youth looked at the men nearest him, and saw, for the most part, expressions of deep interest, as if they were investigating something that had fascinated them. One or two stepped with overvaliant airs as if they were already plunged into war. Others walked as upon thin ice. The greater part of the untested men appeared quiet and absorbed. They were going to look at war, the red animal—war, the blood-swollen god. And they were deeply engrossed in this march.

As he looked the youth gripped his outcry at his throat. He saw that even if the men were tottering with fear they would laugh at his warning. They would jeer him, and, if practicable, pelt him with missiles. Admitting that he might be wrong, a frenzied declamation of the kind would turn him into a worm.

He assumed, then, the demeanor of one who knows that he is doomed alone to unwritten responsibilities. He lagged, with tragic glances at the sky.

He was surprised presently by the young lieutenant of his company, who began heartily to beat him with a sword, calling out in a loud and insolent voice: "Come, young man, get up into ranks there. No skulking 'll do here." He mended his pace with suitable haste. And he hated the lieutenant, who had no appreciation of fine minds. He was a mere brute.

After a time the brigade was halted in the cathedral light of a forest. The busy skirmishers were still popping. Through the aisles of the wood could be seen the floating smoke from their rifles. Sometimes it went up in little balls, white and compact.

During this halt many men in the regiment began erecting tiny hills in front of them. They used stones, sticks, earth, and anything they thought might turn a bullet. Some built comparatively large ones, while others seemed content with little ones.

This procedure caused a discussion among the men. Some wished to fight like duelists, believing it to be correct to stand erect and be, from their feet to their foreheads, a mark. They said they scorned the devices of the cautious. But the others scoffed in reply, and pointed to the veterans on the flanks who were digging at the ground like terriers. In a short time there was quite a barricade along the regimental fronts. Directly, however, they were ordered to withdraw from that place.

This astounded the youth. He forgot his stewing over the advance movement. "Well, then, what did they march us out here for?" he demanded of the tall soldier. The latter with calm faith began a heavy explanation, although he had been compelled to leave a little protection of stones and dirt to which he had devoted much care and skill.

When the regiment was aligned in another position each man's regard for his safety caused another line of small intrenchments. They ate their noon meal behind a third one. They were moved from this one also. They were marched from place to place with apparent aimlessness.

The youth had been taught that a man became another thing in a battle. He saw his salvation in such a change. Hence this waiting was an ordeal to him. He was in a fever of impatience. He considered that there was denoted a lack of purpose on the part of the generals. He began to complain to the tall soldier. "I can't stand this much longer," he cried. "I don't see what good it does to make us wear out our legs for nothin'." He wished to return to camp, knowing that this affair was a blue demonstration; or else to go into a battle and discover that he had been a fool in his doubts, and was, in truth, a man of traditional courage. The strain of present circumstances he felt to be intolerable.

The philosophical tall soldier measured a sandwich of cracker and pork and swallowed it in a nonchalant manner. "Oh, I suppose we must go reconnoitering around the country jest to keep 'em from getting too close, or to develop 'em, or something."

"Huh!" cried the loud soldier.

"Well," cried the youth, still fidgeting, "I'd rather do anything 'most than go tramping 'round the country all day doing no good to nobody and jest tiring ourselves out."

"So would I," said the loud soldier. "It ain't right. I tell you if anybody with any sense was a-runnin' this army it—"

"Oh, shut up!" roared the tall private. "You little fool. You little damn' cuss. You ain't had that there coat and them pants on for six months, and yet you talk as if—"

"Well, I wanta do some fighting anyway," interrupted the other. "I didn't come here to walk. I could 'ave walked to home—'round an' 'round the barn, if I jest wanted to walk."

The tall one, red-faced, swallowed another sandwich as if taking poison in despair.

But gradually, as he chewed, his face became again quiet and contented. He could not rage in fierce argument in the presence of such sandwiches. During his meals he always wore an air of blissful contemplation of the food he had swallowed. His spirit seemed then to be communing with the viands.

He accepted new environment and circumstance with great coolness, eating from his haversack at every opportunity. On the march he went along with the stride of a hunter, objecting to neither gait nor distance. And he had not raised his voice when he had been ordered away from three little protective piles of earth and stone, each of which had been an engineering feat worthy of being made sacred to the name of his grandmother.

In the afternoon the regiment went out over the same ground it had taken in the morning. The landscape then ceased to threaten the youth. He had been close to it and become familiar with it.

When, however, they began to pass into a new region, his old fears of stupidity and incompetence reassailed him, but this time he doggedly let them babble. He was occupied with his problem, and in his desperation he concluded that the stupidity did not greatly matter.

Once he thought he had concluded that it would be better to get killed directly and end his troubles. Regarding death thus out of the corner of his eye, he conceived it to be nothing but rest, and he was filled with a momentary astonishment that he should have made an extraordinary commotion over the mere matter of getting killed. He would die; he would go to some place where he would be understood. It was useless to expect appreciation of his profound and fine senses from such men as the lieutenant. He must look to the grave for comprehension.

The skirmish fire increased to a long clattering sound. With it was mingled far-away cheering. A battery spoke.

Directly the youth would see the skirmishers running. They were pursued by the sound of musketry fire. After a time the hot, dangerous flashes of the rifles were visible. Smoke clouds went slowly and insolently across the fields like observant phantoms. The din became crescendo, like the roar of an oncoming train.

A brigade ahead of them and on the right went into action with a rending roar. It was as if it had exploded. And thereafter it lay stretched in the distance behind a long gray wall, that one was obliged to look twice at to make sure that it was smoke.

The youth, forgetting his neat plan of getting killed, gazed spellbound. His eyes grew wide and busy with the action of the scene. His mouth was a little ways open.

Of a sudden he felt a heavy and sad hand laid upon his shoulder. Awakening from his trance of observation he turned and beheld the loud soldier.

"It's my first and last battle, old boy," said the latter, with intense gloom. He was quite pale and his girlish lip was trembling.

"Eh?" murmured the youth in great astonishment.

"It's my first and last battle, old boy," continued the loud soldier. "Something tells me—"

"What?"

"I'm a gone coon this first time and—and I w-want you to take these here things—to—my—folks." He ended in a quavering sob of pity for himself. He handed the youth a little packet done up in a yellow envelope.

"Why, what the devil—" began the youth again.

But the other gave him a glance as from the depths of a tomb, and raised his limp hand in a prophetic manner and turned away.

CHAPTER IV

The brigade was halted in the fringe of a grove. The men crouched among the trees and pointed their restless guns out at the fields. They tried to look beyond the smoke.

Out of this haze they could see running men. Some shouted information and gestured as they hurried.

The men of the new regiment watched and listened eagerly, while their tongues ran on in gossip of the battle. They mouthed rumors that had flown like birds out of the unknown.

"They say Perry has been driven in with big loss."

"Yes, Carrott went t' th' hospital. He said he was sick. That smart lieutenant is commanding 'G' Company. Th' boys say they won't be under Carrott no more if they all have t' desert. They allus knew he was a—"

"Hannises' batt'ry is took."

"It ain't either. I saw Hannises' batt-ry off on th' left not more'n fifteen minutes ago."

"Well—"

"Th' general, he ses he is goin' t' take th' hull command of th' 304th when we go inteh action, an' then he ses we'll do sech fightin' as never another one reg'ment done."

"They say we're catchin' it over on th' left. They say th' enemy driv' our line inteh a devil of a swamp an' took Hannises' batt'ry."

"No sech thing. Hannises' batt-ry was 'long here 'bout a minute ago."

"That young Hasbrouck, he makes a good off'cer. He ain't afraid 'a nothin'."

"I met one of th' 148th Maine boys an' he ses his brigade fit th' hull rebel army fer four hours over on th' turnpike road an' killed about five thousand of 'em. He ses one more sech fight as that an' th' war 'll be over."

"Bill wasn't scared either. No, sir! It wasn't that. Bill ain't a-gettin' scared easy. He was jest mad, that's what he was. When that feller trod on his hand, he up an' sed that he was willin' t' give his hand t' his country, but he be dumbed if he was goin' t' have every dumb bushwacker in th' kentry walkin' 'round on it. So he went t' th' hospital disregardless of th' fight. Three fingers was crunched. Th' dern doctor wanted t' amputate 'm, an' Bill, he raised a heluva row, I hear. He's a funny feller."

The din in front swelled to a tremendous chorus. The youth and his fellows were frozen to silence. They could see a flag that tossed in the smoke angrily. Near it were the blurred and agitated forms of troops. There came a turbulent stream of men across the fields. A battery changing position at a frantic gallop scattered the stragglers right and left.

A shell screaming like a storm banshee went over the huddled heads of the reserves. It landed in the grove, and exploding redly flung the brown earth. There was a little shower of pine needles.

Bullets began to whistle among the branches and nip at the trees. Twigs and leaves came sailing down. It was as if a thousand axes, wee and invisible, were being wielded. Many of the men were constantly dodging and ducking their heads.

The lieutenant of the youth's company was shot in the hand. He began to swear so wondrously that a nervous laugh went along the regimental line. The officer's profanity sounded conventional. It relieved the tightened senses of the new men. It was as if he had hit his fingers with a tack hammer at home.

He held the wounded member carefully away from his side so that the blood would not drip upon his trousers.

The captain of the company, tucking his sword under his arm, produced a handkerchief and began to bind with it the lieutenant's wound. And they disputed as to how the binding should be done.

The battle flag in the distance jerked about madly. It seemed to be struggling to free itself from an agony. The billowing smoke was filled with horizontal flashes.

Men running swiftly emerged from it. They grew in numbers until it was seen that the whole command was fleeing. The flag suddenly sank down as if dying. Its motion as it fell was a gesture of despair.

Wild yells came from behind the walls of smoke. A sketch in gray and red dissolved into a moblike body of men who galloped like wild horses.

The veteran regiments on the right and left of the 304th immediately began to jeer. With the passionate song of the bullets and the banshee shrieks of shells were mingled loud cat-calls and bits of facetious advice concerning places of safety.

But the new regiment was breathless with horror. "Gawd! Saunders's got crushed!" whispered the man at the youth's elbow. They shrank back and crouched as if compelled to await a flood.

The youth shot a swift glance along the blue ranks of the regiment. The profiles were motionless, carven; and afterward he remembered that the color sergeant was standing with his legs apart, as if he expected to be pushed to the ground.

The following throng went whirling around the flank. Here and there were officers carried along on the stream like exasperated chips. They were striking about them with their swords and with their left fists, punching every head they could reach. They cursed like highwaymen.

A mounted officer displayed the furious anger of a spoiled child. He raged with his head, his arms, and his legs.

Another, the commander of the brigade, was galloping about bawling. His hat was gone and his clothes were awry. He resembled a man who had come from bed to go to a fire. The hoofs of his horse often threatened the heads of the running men, but they scampered with singular fortune. In this rush they were apparently all deaf and blind. They heeded not the largest and longest of the oaths that were thrown at them from all directions.

Frequently over this tumult could be heard the grim jokes of the critical veterans; but the retreating men apparently were not even conscious of the presence of an audience.

The battle reflection that shone for an instant in the faces on the mad current made the youth feel that forceful hands from heaven would not have been able to have held him in place if he could have got intelligent control of his legs.

There was an appalling imprint upon these faces. The struggle in the smoke had pictured an exaggeration of itself on the bleached cheeks and in the eyes wild with one desire.

The sight of this stampede exerted a floodlike force that seemed able to drag sticks and stones and men from the ground. They of the reserves had to hold on. They grew pale and firm, and red and quaking.

The youth achieved one little thought in the midst of this chaos. The composite monster which had caused the other troops to flee had not then appeared. He resolved to get a view of it, and then, he thought he might very likely run better than the best of them.

CHAPTER V

There were moments of waiting. The youth thought of the village street at home before the arrival of the circus parade on a day in the spring. He remembered how he had stood, a small, thrillful boy, prepared to follow the dingy lady upon the white horse, or the band in its faded chariot. He saw the yellow road, the lines of expectant people, and the sober houses. He particularly remembered an old fellow who used to sit upon a cracker box in front of the store and feign to despise such exhibitions. A thousand details of color and form surged in his mind. The old fellow upon the cracker box appeared in middle prominence.

Some one cried, "Here they come!"

There was rustling and muttering among the men. They displayed a feverish desire to have every possible cartridge ready to their hands. The boxes were pulled around into various positions, and adjusted with great care. It was as if seven hundred new bonnets were being tried on.

The tall soldier, having prepared his rifle, produced a red handkerchief of some kind. He was engaged in knitting it about his throat with exquisite attention to its position, when the cry was repeated up and down the line in a muffled roar of sound.

"Here they come! Here they come!" Gun locks clicked.

Across the smoke-infested fields came a brown swarm of running men who were giving shrill yells. They came on, stooping and swinging their rifles at all angles. A flag, tilted forward, sped near the front.

As he caught sight of them the youth was momentarily startled by a thought that perhaps his gun was not loaded. He stood trying to rally his faltering intellect so that he might recollect the moment when he had loaded, but he could not.

A hatless general pulled his dripping horse to a stand near the colonel of the 304th. He shook his fist in the other's face. "You've got to hold 'em back!" he shouted, savagely; "you've got to hold 'em back!"

In his agitation the colonel began to stammer. "A-all r-right, General, all right, by Gawd! We-we'll do our—we-we'll d-d-do—do our best, General." The general made a passionate gesture and galloped away. The colonel, perchance to relieve his feelings, began to scold like a wet parrot. The youth, turning swiftly to make sure that the rear was unmolested, saw the commander regarding his men in a highly resentful manner, as if he regretted above everything his association with them.

The man at the youth's elbow was mumbling, as if to himself: "Oh, we're in for it now! oh, we're in for it now!"

The captain of the company had been pacing excitedly to and fro in the rear. He coaxed in schoolmistress fashion, as to a congregation of boys with primers. His talk was an endless repetition. "Reserve your fire, boys—don't shoot till I tell you—save your fire—wait till they get close up—don't be damned fools—"

Perspiration streamed down the youth's face, which was soiled like that of a weeping urchin. He frequently, with a nervous movement, wiped his eyes with his coat sleeve. His mouth was still a little way open.

He got the one glance at the foe-swarming field in front of him, and instantly ceased to debate the question of his piece being loaded. Before he was ready to begin—before he had announced to himself that he was about to fight—he threw the obedient, well-balanced rifle into position and fired a first wild shot. Directly he was working at his weapon like an automatic affair.

He suddenly lost concern for himself, and forgot to look at a menacing fate. He became not a man but a member. He felt that something of which he was a part—a regiment, an army, a cause, or a country—was in a crisis. He was welded into a common personality which was dominated by a single desire. For some moments he could not flee, no more than a little finger can commit a revolution from a hand.

If he had thought the regiment was about to be annihilated perhaps he could have amputated himself from it. But its noise gave him assurance. The regiment was like a firework that, once ignited proceeds superior to circumstances until its blazing vitality fades. It wheezed and banged with a mighty power. He pictured the ground before it as strewn with the discomfited.

There was a consciousness always of the presence of his comrades about him. He felt the subtle battle brotherhood more potent even than the cause for which they were fighting. It was a mysterious fraternity born of the smoke and danger of death.

He was at a task. He was like a carpenter who has made many boxes, making still another box, only there was furious haste in his movements. He, in his thought, was careering off in other places, even as the carpenter who as he works whistles and thinks of his friend or his enemy, his home or a saloon. And these jolted dreams were never perfect to him afterward, but remained a mass of blurred shapes.

Presently he began to feel the effects of the war atmosphere—a blistering sweat, a sensation that his eyeballs were about to crack like hot stones. A burning roar filled his ears.

Following this came a red rage. He developed the acute exasperation of a pestered animal, a well-meaning cow worried by dogs. He had a mad feeling against his rifle, which could only be used against one life at a time. He wished to rush forward and strangle with his fingers. He craved a power that would enable him to make a world-sweeping gesture and brush all back. His impotency appeared to him, and made his rage into that of a driven beast.

Buried in the smoke of many rifles his anger was directed not so much against the men whom he knew were rushing toward him as against the swirling battle phantoms which were choking him, stuffing their smoke robes down his parched throat. He fought frantically for respite for his senses, for air, as a babe being smothered attacks the deadly blankets.

There was a blare of heated rage mingled with a certain expression of intentness on all faces. Many of the men were making low-toned noises with their mouths, and these subdued cheers, snarls, imprecations, prayers, made a wild, barbaric song that went as an undercurrent of sound, strange and chantlike with the resounding chords of the war march. The man at the youth's elbow was babbling. In it there was something soft and tender like the monologue of a babe. The tall soldier was swearing in a loud voice. From his lips came a black procession of curious oaths. Of a sudden another broke out in a querulous way like a man who has mislaid his hat. "Well, why don't they support us? Why don't they send supports? Do they think—"

The youth in his battle sleep heard this as one who dozes hears.

There was a singular absence of heroic poses. The men bending and surging in their haste and rage were in every impossible attitude. The steel ramrods clanked and clanged with incessant din as the men pounded them furiously into the hot rifle barrels. The flaps of the cartridge boxes were all unfastened, and bobbed idiotically with each movement. The rifles, once loaded, were jerked to the shoulder and fired without apparent aim into the smoke or at one of the blurred and shifting forms which, upon the field before the regiment, had been growing larger and larger like puppets under a magician's hand.

The officers, at their intervals, rearward, neglected to stand in picturesque attitudes. They were bobbing to and fro roaring directions and encouragements. The dimensions of their howls were extraordinary. They expended their lungs with prodigal wills. And often they nearly stood upon their heads in their anxiety to observe the enemy on the other side of the tumbling smoke.

The lieutenant of the youth's company had encountered a soldier who had fled screaming at the first volley of his comrades. Behind the lines these two were acting a little isolated scene. The man was blubbering and staring with sheeplike eyes at the lieutenant, who had seized him by the collar and was pommeling him. He drove him back into the ranks with many blows. The soldier went mechanically, dully, with his animal-like eyes upon the officer. Perhaps there was to him a divinity expressed in the voice of the other—stern, hard, with no reflection of fear in it. He tried to reload his gun, but his shaking hands prevented. The lieutenant was obliged to assist him.

The men dropped here and there like bundles. The captain of the youth's company had been killed in an early part of the action. His body lay stretched out in the position of a tired man resting, but upon his face there was an astonished and sorrowful look, as if he thought some friend had done him an ill turn. The babbling man was grazed by a shot that made the blood stream widely down his face. He clapped both hands to his head. "Oh!" he said, and ran. Another grunted suddenly as if he had been struck by a club in the stomach. He sat down and gazed ruefully. In his eyes there was mute, indefinite reproach. Farther up the line a man, standing behind a tree, had had his knee joint splintered by a ball. Immediately he had dropped his rifle and gripped the tree with both arms. And there he remained, clinging desperately and crying for assistance that he might withdraw his hold upon the tree.

At last an exultant yell went along the quivering line. The firing dwindled from an uproar to a last vindictive popping. As the smoke slowly eddied away, the youth saw that the charge had been repulsed. The enemy were scattered into reluctant groups. He saw a man climb to the top of the fence, straddle the rail, and fire a parting shot. The waves had receded, leaving bits of dark *débris* upon the ground.

Some in the regiment began to whoop frenziedly. Many were silent. Apparently they were trying to contemplate themselves.

After the fever had left his veins, the youth thought that at last he was going to suffocate. He became aware of the foul atmosphere in which he had been struggling. He was grimy and dripping like a laborer in a foundry. He grasped his canteen and took a long swallow of the warmed water.

A sentence with variations went up and down the line. "Well, we've helt 'em back. We've helt 'em back; derned if we haven't." The men said it blissfully, leering at each other with dirty smiles.

The youth turned to look behind him and off to the right and off to the left. He experienced the joy of a man who at last finds leisure in which to look about him.

Under foot there were a few ghastly forms motionless. They lay twisted in fantastic contortions. Arms were bent and heads were turned in incredible ways. It seemed that the dead men must have fallen from some great height to get into such positions. They looked to be dumped out upon the ground from the sky.

From a position in the rear of the grove a battery was throwing shells over it. The flash of the guns startled the youth at first. He thought they were aimed directly at him. Through the trees he watched the black figures of the gunners as they worked swiftly and intently. Their labor seemed a complicated thing. He wondered how they could remember its formula in the midst of confusion.

The guns squatted in a row like savage chiefs. They argued with abrupt violence. It was a grim pow-wow. Their busy servants ran hither and thither.

A small procession of wounded men were going drearily toward the rear. It was a flow of blood from the torn body of the brigade.

To the right and to the left were the dark lines of other troops. Far in front he thought he could see lighter masses protruding in points from the forest. They were suggestive of unnumbered thousands.

Once he saw a tiny battery go dashing along the line of the horizon. The tiny riders were beating the tiny horses.

From a sloping hill came the sound of cheerings and clashes. Smoke welled slowly through the leaves.

Batteries were speaking with thunderous oratorical effort. Here and there were flags, the red in the stripes dominating. They splashed bits of warm color upon the dark lines of troops.

The youth felt the old thrill at the sight of the emblem. They were like beautiful birds strangely undaunted in a storm.

As he listened to the din from the hillside, to a deep pulsating thunder that came from afar to the left, and to the lesser clamors which came from many directions, it occurred to him that they were fighting, too, over there, and over there, and over there. Heretofore he had supposed that all the battle was directly under his nose.

As he gazed around him the youth felt a flash of astonishment at the blue, pure sky and the sun gleaming on the trees and fields. It was surprising that Nature had gone tranquilly on with her golden process in the midst of so much devilment.

CHAPTER VI

The youth awakened slowly. He came gradually back to a position from which he could regard himself. For moments he had been scrutinizing his person in a dazed way as if he had never before seen himself. Then he picked up his cap from the ground. He wriggled in his jacket to make a more comfortable fit, and kneeling relaced his shoe. He thoughtfully mopped his reeking features.

So it was all over at last! The supreme trial had been passed. The red, formidable difficulties of war had been vanquished.

He went into an ecstasy of self-satisfaction. He had the most delightful sensations of his life. Standing as if apart from himself, he viewed that last scene. He perceived that the man who had fought thus was magnificent.

He felt that he was a fine fellow. He saw himself even with those ideals which he had considered as far beyond him. He smiled in deep gratification.

Upon his fellows he beamed tenderness and good will. "Gee! ain't it hot, hey?" he said affably to a man who was polishing his streaming face with his coat sleeves.

"You bet!" said the other, grinning sociably. "I never seen sech dumb hotness." He sprawled out luxuriously on the ground. "Gee, yes! An' I hope we don't have no more fightin' till a week from Monday."

There were some handshakings and deep speeches with men whose features were familiar, but with whom the youth now felt the bonds of tied hearts. He helped a cursing comrade to bind up a wound of the shin.

But, of a sudden, cries of amazement broke out along the ranks of the new regiment. "Here they come ag'in! Here they come ag'in!" The man who had sprawled upon the ground started up and said, "Gosh!"

The youth turned quick eyes upon the field. He discerned forms begin to swell in masses out of a distant wood. He again saw the tilted flag speeding forward.

The shells, which had ceased to trouble the regiment for a time, came swirling again, and exploded in the grass or among the leaves of the trees. They looked to be strange war flowers bursting into fierce bloom.

The men groaned. The luster faded from their eyes. Their smudged countenances now expressed a profound dejection. They moved their stiffened bodies slowly, and watched in sullen mood the frantic approach of the enemy. The slaves toiling in the temple of this god began to feel rebellion at his harsh tasks.

They fretted and complained each to each. "Oh, say, this is too much of a good thing! Why can't somebody send us supports?"

"We ain't never goin' to stand this second banging. I didn't come here to fight the hull damn' rebel army."

There was one who raised a doleful cry. "I wish Bill Smithers had trod on my hand, insteader me treddin' on his'n." The sore joints of the regiment creaked as it painfully floundered into position to repulse.

The youth stared. Surely, he thought, this impossible thing was not about to happen. He waited as if he expected the enemy to suddenly stop, apologize, and retire bowing. It was all a mistake.

But the firing began somewhere on the regimental line and ripped along in both directions. The level sheets of flame developed great clouds of smoke that tumbled and tossed in the mild wind near the ground for a moment, and then rolled through the ranks as through a gate. The clouds were tinged an earthlike yellow in the sunrays and in the shadow were a sorry blue. The flag was sometimes eaten and lost in this mass of vapor, but more often it projected, sun-touched, resplendent.

Into the youth's eyes there came a look that one can see in the orbs of a jaded horse. His neck was quivering with nervous weakness and the muscles of his arms felt numb and bloodless. His hands, too, seemed large and awkward as if he was wearing invisible mittens. And there was a great uncertainty about his knee joints.

The words that comrades had uttered previously to the firing began to recur to him. "Oh, say, this is too much of a good thing! What do they take us for—why don't they send supports? I didn't come here to fight the hull damned rebel army."

He began to exaggerate the endurance, the skill, and the valor of those who were coming. Himself reeling from exhaustion, he was astonished beyond measure at such persistency. They must be machines of steel. It was very gloomy struggling against such affairs, wound up perhaps to fight until sundown.

He slowly lifted his rifle and catching a glimpse of the thickspread field he blazed at a cantering cluster. He stopped then and began to peer as best he could through the smoke. He caught changing views of the ground covered with men who were all running like pursued imps, and yelling.

To the youth it was an onslaught of redoubtable dragons. He became like the man who lost his legs at the approach of the red and green monster. He waited in a sort of a horrified, listening attitude. He seemed to shut his eyes and wait to be gobbled.

A man near him who up to this time had been working feverishly at his rifle suddenly stopped and ran with howls. A lad whose face had borne an expression of exalted courage, the majesty of he who dares give his life, was, at an instant, smitten abject. He blanched like one who has come to the edge of a cliff at midnight and is suddenly made aware. There was a revelation. He, too, threw down his gun and fled. There was no shame in his face. He ran like a rabbit.

Others began to scamper away through the smoke. The youth turned his head, shaken from his trance by this movement as if the regiment was leaving him behind. He saw the few fleeting forms.

He yelled then with fright and swung about. For a moment, in the great clamor, he was like a proverbial chicken. He lost the direction of safety. Destruction threatened him from all points.

Directly he began to speed toward the rear in great leaps. His rifle and cap were gone. His unbuttoned coat bulged in the wind. The flap of his cartridge box bobbed wildly, and his canteen, by its slender cord, swung out behind. On his face was the horror of those things which he imagined.

The lieutenant sprang forward bawling. The youth saw his features wrathfully red, and saw him make a dab with his sword. His one thought of the incident was that the lieutenant was a peculiar creature to feel interested in such matters upon this occasion.

He ran like a blind man. Two or three times he fell down. Once he knocked his shoulder so heavily against a tree that he went headlong.

Since he had turned his back upon the fight his fears had been wondrously magnified. Death about to thrust him between the shoulder blades was far more dreadful than death about to smite him between the eyes. When he thought of it later, he conceived the impression that it is better to view the appalling than to be merely within hearing. The noises of the battle were like stones; he believed himself liable to be crushed.

As he ran on he mingled with others. He dimly saw men on his right and on his left, and he heard footsteps behind him. He thought that all the regiment was fleeing, pursued by these ominous crashes.

In his flight the sound of these following footsteps gave him his one meager relief. He felt vaguely that death must make a first choice of the men who were nearest; the initial morsels for the dragons would be then those who were following him. So he displayed the zeal of an insane sprinter in his purpose to keep them in the rear. There was a race.

As he, leading, went across a little field, he found himself in a region of shells. They hurtled over his head with long wild screams. As he listened he imagined them to have rows of cruel teeth that grinned at him. Once one lit before him and the livid lightning of the explosion effectually barred the way in his chosen direction. He groveled on the ground and then springing up went careering off through some bushes.

He experienced a thrill of amazement when he came within view of a battery in action. The men there seemed to be in conventional moods, altogether unaware of the impending annihilation. The battery was disputing with a distant antagonist and the gunners were wrapped in admiration of their shooting. They were continually bending in coaxing postures over the guns. They seemed to be patting them on the back and encouraging them with words. The guns, stolid and undaunted, spoke with dogged valor.

The precise gunners were coolly enthusiastic. They lifted their eyes every chance to the smoke-wreathed hillock from whence the hostile battery addressed them. The youth pitied them as he ran. Methodical idiots! Machinelike fools! The refined joy of planting shells in the midst of the other battery's formation would appear a little thing when the infantry came swooping out of the woods.

The face of a youthful rider, who was jerking his frantic horse with an abandon of temper he might display in a placid barnyard, was impressed deeply upon his mind. He knew that he looked upon a man who would presently be dead.

Too, he felt a pity for the guns, standing, six good comrades, in a bold row.

He saw a brigade going to the relief of its pestered fellows. He scrambled upon a wee hill and watched it sweeping finely, keeping formation in difficult places. The blue of the line was crusted with steel color, and the brilliant flags projected. Officers were shouting.

This sight also filled him with wonder. The brigade was hurrying briskly to be gulped into the infernal mouths of the war god. What manner of men were they, anyhow? Ah, it was some wondrous breed! Or else they didn't comprehend—the fools.

A furious order caused commotion in the artillery. An officer on a bounding horse made maniacal motions with his arms. The teams went swinging up from the rear, the guns were whirled about, and the battery scampered away. The cannon with their noses poked slantingly at the ground grunted and grumbled like stout men, brave but with objections to hurry.

The youth went on, moderating his pace since he had left the place of noises.

Later he came upon a general of division seated upon a horse that pricked its ears in an interested way at the battle. There was a great gleaming of yellow and patent leather about the saddle and bridle. The quiet man astride looked mouse-colored upon such a splendid charger.

A jingling staff was galloping hither and thither. Sometimes the general was surrounded by horsemen and at other times he was quite alone. He looked to be much harassed. He had the appearance of a business man whose market is swinging up and down.

The youth went slinking around this spot. He went as near as he dared trying to overhear words. Perhaps the general, unable to comprehend chaos, might call upon him for information. And he could tell him. He knew all concerning it. Of a surety the force was in a fix, and any fool could see that if they did not retreat while they had opportunity—why—

He felt that he would like to thrash the general, or at least approach and tell him in plain words exactly what he thought him to be. It was criminal to stay calmly in one spot and make no effort to stay destruction. He loitered in a fever of eagerness for the division commander to apply to him.

As he warily moved about, he heard the general call out irritably: "Tompkins, go over an' see Taylor, an' tell him not t' be in such an all-fired hurry; tell him t' halt his brigade in th' edge of th' woods; tell him t' detach a reg'ment—say I think th' center 'll break if we don't help it out some; tell him t' hurry up."

A slim youth on a fine chestnut horse caught these swift words from the mouth of his superior. He made his horse bound into a gallop almost from a walk in his haste to go upon his mission. There was a cloud of dust.

A moment later the youth saw the general bounce excitedly in his saddle.

"Yes, by heavens, they have!" The officer leaned forward. His face was aflame with excitement. "Yes, by heavens, they've held 'im! They've held 'im!"

He began to blithely roar at his staff: "We'll wallop 'im now. We'll wallop 'im now. We've got 'em sure." He turned suddenly upon an aide: "Here—you—Jones—quick—ride after Tompkins—see Taylor—tell him t' go in—everlastingly—like blazes—anything."

As another officer sped his horse after the first messenger, the general beamed upon the earth like a sun. In his eyes was a desire to chant a pæan. He kept repeating, "They've held 'em, by heavens!"

His excitement made his horse plunge, and he merrily kicked and swore at it. He held a little carnival of joy on horseback.

CHAPTER VII

The youth cringed as if discovered in a crime. By heavens, they had won after all! The imbecile line had remained and become victors. He could hear cheering.

He lifted himself upon his toes and looked in the direction of the fight. A yellow fog lay wallowing on the treetops. From beneath it came the clatter of musketry. Hoarse cries told of an advance.

He turned away amazed and angry. He felt that he had been wronged.

He had fled, he told himself, because annihilation approached. He had done a good part in saving himself, who was a little piece of the army. He had considered the time, he said, to be one in which it was the duty of every little piece to rescue itself if possible. Later the officers could fit the little pieces together again, and make a battle front. If none of the little pieces were wise enough to save themselves from the flurry of death at such a time, why, then, where would be the army? It was all plain that he had proceeded according to very correct and commendable rules. His actions had been sagacious things. They had been full of strategy. They were the work of a master's legs.

Thoughts of his comrades came to him. The brittle blue line had withstood the blows and won. He grew bitter over it. It seemed that the blind ignorance and stupidity of those little pieces had betrayed him. He had been overturned and crushed by their lack of sense in holding the position, when intelligent deliberation would have convinced them that it was impossible. He, the enlightened man who looks afar in the dark, had fled because of his superior perceptions and knowledge. He felt a great anger against his comrades. He knew it could be proved that they had been fools.

He wondered what they would remark when later he appeared in camp. His mind heard howls of derision. Their destiny would not enable them to understand his sharper point of view.

He began to pity himself acutely. He was ill used. He was trodden beneath the feet of an iron injustice. He had proceeded with wisdom and from the most righteous motives under heaven's blue only to be frustrated by hateful circumstances.

A dull, animal-like rebellion against his fellows, war in the abstract, and fate grew within him. He shambled along with bowed head, his brain in a tumult of agony and despair. When he looked loweringly up, quivering at each sound, his eyes had the expression of those of a criminal who thinks his guilt and his punishment great, and knows that he can find no words.

He went from the fields into a thick wood, as if resolved to bury himself. He wished to get out of hearing of the cracking shots which were to him like voices.

The ground was cluttered with vines and bushes, and the trees grew close and spread out like bouquets. He was obliged to force his way with much noise. The creepers, catching against his legs, cried out harshly as their sprays were torn from the barks of trees. The swishing saplings tried to make known his presence to the world. He could not conciliate the forest. As he made his way, it was always calling out protestations. When he separated embraces of trees and vines the disturbed foliages waved their arms and turned their face leaves toward him. He dreaded lest these noisy motions and cries should bring men to look at him. So he went far, seeking dark and intricate places.

After a time the sound of musketry grew faint and the cannon boomed in the distance. The sun, suddenly apparent, blazed among the trees. The insects were making rhythmical noises. They seemed to be grinding their teeth in unison. A woodpecker stuck his impudent head around the side of a tree. A bird flew on lighthearted wing.

Off was the rumble of death. It seemed now that Nature had no ears.

This landscape gave him assurance. A fair field holding life. It was the religion of peace. It would die if its timid eyes were compelled to see blood. He conceived Nature to be a woman with a deep aversion to tragedy.

He threw a pine cone at a jovial squirrel, and he ran with chattering fear. High in a treetop he stopped, and, poking his head cautiously from behind a branch, looked down with an air of trepidation.

The youth felt triumphant at this exhibition. There was the law, he said. Nature had given him a sign. The squirrel, immediately upon recognizing danger, had taken to his legs without ado. He did not stand stolidly baring his furry belly to the missile, and die with an upward glance at the sympathetic heavens. On the contrary, he had fled as fast as his legs could carry him; and he was but an ordinary squirrel, too—doubtless no philosopher of his race. The youth wended, feeling that Nature was of his mind. She re-enforced his argument with proofs that lived where the sun shone.

Once he found himself almost into a swamp. He was obliged to walk upon bog tufts and watch his feet to keep from the oily mire. Pausing at one time to look about him he saw, out at some black water, a small animal pounce in and emerge directly with a gleaming fish.

The youth went again into the deep thickets. The brushed branches made a noise that drowned the sounds of cannon. He walked on, going from obscurity into promises of a greater obscurity.

At length he reached a place where the high, arching boughs made a chapel. He softly pushed the green doors aside and entered. Pine needles were a gentle brown carpet. There was a religious half light.

Near the threshold he stopped, horror-stricken at the sight of a thing.

He was being looked at by a dead man who was seated with his back against a columnlike tree. The corpse was dressed in a uniform that once had been blue, but was now faded to a melancholy shade of green. The eyes, staring at the youth, had changed to the dull hue to be seen on the side of a dead fish. The mouth was open. Its red had changed to an appalling yellow. Over the gray skin of the face ran little ants. One was trundling some sort of a bundle along the upper lip.

The youth gave a shriek as he confronted the thing. He was for moments turned to stone before it. He remained staring into the liquid-looking eyes. The dead man and the living man exchanged a long look. Then the youth cautiously put one hand behind him and brought it against a tree. Leaning upon this he retreated, step by step, with his face still toward the thing. He feared that if he turned his back the body might spring up and stealthily pursue him.

The branches, pushing against him, threatened to throw him over upon it. His unguided feet, too, caught aggravatingly in brambles; and with it all he received a subtle suggestion to touch the corpse. As he thought of his hand upon it he shuddered profoundly.

At last he burst the bonds which has fastened him to the spot and fled, unheeding the underbrush. He was pursued by a sight of the black ants swarming greedily upon the gray face and venturing horribly near to the eyes.

After a time he paused, and, breathless and panting, listened. He imagined some strange voice would come from the dead throat and squawk after him in horrible menaces.

The trees about the portals of the chapel moved soughingly in a soft wind. A sad silence was upon the little guarding edifice.

CHAPTER VIII

The trees began softly to sing a hymn of twilight. The sun sank until slanted bronze rays struck the forest. There was a lull in the noises of insects as if they had bowed their beaks and were making a devotional pause. There was silence save for the chanted chorus of the trees.

Then, upon this stillness, there suddenly broke a tremendous clangor of sounds. A crimson roar came from the distance.

The youth stopped. He was transfixed by this terrific medley of all noises. It was as if worlds were being rended. There was the ripping sound of musketry and the breaking crash of artillery.

His mind flew in all directions. He conceived the two armies to be at each other panther fashion. He listened for a time. Then he began to run in the direction of the battle. He saw that it was an ironical thing for him to be running thus toward that which he had been at such pains to avoid. But he said, in substance, to himself that if the earth and the moon were about to clash, many persons would doubtless plan to get upon the roofs to witness the collision.

As he ran, he became aware that the forest had stopped its music, as if at last becoming capable of hearing the foreign sounds. The trees hushed and stood motionless. Everything seemed to be listening to the crackle and clatter and ear-shaking thunder. The chorus pealed over the still earth.

It suddenly occurred to the youth that the fight in which he had been was, after all, but perfunctory popping. In the hearing of this present din he was doubtful if he had seen real battle scenes. This uproar explained a celestial battle; it was tumbling hordes a-struggle in the air.

Reflecting, he saw a sort of humor in the point of view of himself and his fellows during the late encounter. They had taken themselves and the enemy very seriously and had imagined that they were deciding the war. Individuals must have supposed that they were cutting the letters of their names deep into everlasting tablets of brass, or enshrining their reputations forever in the hearts of their countrymen, while, as to fact, the affair would appear in printed reports under a meek and immaterial title. But he saw that it was good, else, he said, in battle every one would surely run save forlorn hopes and their ilk.

He went rapidly on. He wished to come to the edge of the forest that he might peer out.

As he hastened, there passed through his mind pictures of stupendous conflicts. His accumulated thought upon such subjects was used to form scenes. The noise was as the voice of an eloquent being, describing.

Sometimes the brambles formed chains and tried to hold him back. Trees, confronting him, stretched out their arms and forbade him to pass. After its previous hostility this new resistance of the forest filled him with a fine bitterness. It seemed that Nature could not be quite ready to kill him.

But he obstinately took roundabout ways, and presently he was where he could see long gray walls of vapor where lay battle lines. The voices of cannon shook him. The musketry sounded in long irregular surges that played havoc with his ears. He stood regardant for a moment. His eyes had an awestruck expression. He gawked in the direction of the fight.

Presently he proceeded again on his forward way. The battle was like the grinding of an immense and terrible machine to him. Its complexities and powers, its grim processes, fascinated him. He must go close and see it produce corpses.

He came to a fence and clambered over it. On the far side, the ground was littered with clothes and guns. A newspaper, folded up, lay in the dirt. A dead soldier was stretched with his face hidden in his arm. Farther off there was a group of four or five corpses keeping mournful company. A hot sun had blazed upon the spot.

In this place the youth felt that he was an invader. This forgotten part of the battleground was owned by the dead men, and he hurried, in the vague apprehension that one of the swollen forms would rise and tell him to begone.

He came finally to a road from which he could see in the distance dark and agitated bodies of troops, smoke-fringed. In the lane was a blood-stained crowd streaming to the rear. The wounded men were cursing, groaning, and wailing. In the air, always, was a mighty swell of sound that it seemed could sway the earth. With the courageous words of the artillery and the spiteful sentences of the musketry mingled red cheers. And from this region of noises came the steady current of the maimed.

One of the wounded men had a shoeful of blood. He hopped like a schoolboy in a game. He was laughing hysterically.

One was swearing that he had been shot in the arm through the commanding general's mismanagement of the army. One was marching with an air imitative of some sublime drum major. Upon his features was an unholy mixture of merriment and agony. As he marched he sang a bit of doggerel in a high and quavering voice:

"Sing a song 'a vic'try,
A pocketful 'a bullets,
Five an' twenty dead men
Baked in a—pie."

Parts of the procession limped and staggered to this tune.

Another had the gray seal of death already upon his face. His lips were curled in hard lines and his teeth were clinched. His hands were bloody from where he had passed them upon his wound. He seemed to be awaiting the moment when he should pitch headlong. He stalked like the specter of a soldier, his eyes burning with the power of a stare into the unknown.

There were some who proceeded sullenly, full of anger at their wounds, and ready to turn upon anything as an obscure cause.

An officer was carried along by two privates. He was peevish. "Don't joggle so, Johnson, yeh fool," he cried. "Think m' leg is made of iron? If yeh can't carry me decent, put me down an' let some one else do it."

He bellowed at the tottering crowd who blocked the quick march of his bearers. "Say, make way there, can't yeh? Make way, dickens take it all."

They sulkily parted and went to the roadsides. As he was carried past they made pert remarks to him. When he raged in reply and threatened them, they told him to be damned.

The shoulder of one of the tramping bearers knocked heavily against the spectral soldier who was staring into the unknown.

The youth joined this crowd and marched along with it. The torn bodies expressed the awful machinery in which the men had been entangled.

Orderlies and couriers occasionally broke through the throng in the roadway, scattering wounded men right and left, galloping on, followed by howls. The melancholy march was continually disturbed by the messengers, and sometimes by bustling batteries that came swinging and thumping down upon them, the officers shouting orders to clear the way.

There was a tattered man, fouled with dust, blood and powder stain from hair to shoes, who trudged quietly at the youth's side. He was listening with eagerness and much humility to the lurid descriptions of a bearded sergeant. His lean features wore an expression of awe and admiration. He was like a listener in a country store to wondrous tales told among the sugar barrels. He eyed the story-teller with unspeakable wonder. His mouth was agape in yokel fashion.

The sergeant, taking note of this, gave pause to his elaborate history while he administered a sardonic comment. "Be keerful, honey, you'll be a-ketchin' flies," he said.

The tattered man shrank back abashed.

After a time he began to sidle near to the youth, and in a different way try to make him a friend. His voice was gentle as a girl's voice and his eyes were pleading. The youth saw with surprise that the soldier had two wounds, one in the head, bound with a blood-soaked rag, and the other in the arm, making that member dangle like a broken bough.

After they had walked together for some time the tattered man mustered sufficient courage to speak. "Was pretty good fight, wasn't it?" he timidly said. The youth, deep in thought, glanced up at the bloody and grim figure with its lamblike eyes. "What?"

"Was pretty good fight, wa'n't it?"

"Yes," said the youth shortly. He quickened his pace.

But the other hobbled industriously after him. There was an air of apology in his manner, but he evidently thought that he needed only to talk for a time, and the youth would perceive that he was a good fellow.

"Was pretty good fight, wa'n't it?" he began in a small voice, and then he achieved the fortitude to continue. "Dern me if I ever see fellers fight so. Laws, how they did fight! I knowed th' boys 'd like it when they onct got square at it. Th' boys ain't had no fair chanct up t' now, but this time they showed what they was. I knowed it 'd turn out this way. Yeh can't lick them boys. No, sir! They're fighters, they be."

He breathed a deep breath of humble admiration. He had looked at the youth for encouragement several times. He received none, but gradually he seemed to get absorbed in his subject.

"I was talkin' 'cross pickets with a boy from Georgie, onct, an' that boy, he ses, 'Your fellers 'll all run like hell when they onct hearn a gun,' he ses. 'Mebbe they will,' I ses, 'but I don't b'lieve none of it,' I ses; 'an' b'jiminey,' I ses back t' 'um, 'mebbe your fellers 'll all run like hell when they onct hearn a gun,' I ses. He larfed. Well, they didn't run t'-day, did they, hey? No, sir! They fit, an' fit, an' fit."

His homely face was suffused with a light of love for the army which was to him all things beautiful and powerful.

After a time he turned to the youth. "Where yeh hit, ol' boy?" he asked in a brotherly tone.

The youth felt instant panic at this question, although at first its full import was not borne in upon him.

"What?" he asked.

"Where yeh hit?" repeated the tattered man.

"Why," began the youth, "I—I—that is—why—I—"

He turned away suddenly and slid through the crowd. His brow was heavily flushed, and his fingers were picking nervously at one of his buttons. He bent his head and fastened his eyes studiously upon the button as if it were a little problem.

The tattered man looked after him in astonishment.

CHAPTER IX

The youth fell back in the procession until the tattered soldier was not in sight. Then he started to walk on with the others.

But he was amid wounds. The mob of men was bleeding. Because of the tattered soldier's question he now felt that his shame could be viewed. He was continually casting sidelong glances to see if the men were contemplating the letters of guilt he felt burned into his brow.

At times he regarded the wounded soldiers in an envious way. He conceived persons with torn bodies to be peculiarly happy. He wished that he, too, had a wound, a red badge of courage.

The spectral soldier was at his side like a stalking reproach. The man's eyes were still fixed in a stare into the unknown. His gray, appalling face had attracted attention in the crowd, and men, slowing to his dreary pace, were walking with him. They were discussing his plight, questioning him and giving him advice. In a dogged way he repelled them, signing to them to go on and leave him alone. The shadows of his face were deepening and his tight lips seemed holding in check the moan of great despair. There could be seen a certain stiffness in the movements of his body, as if he were taking infinite care not to arouse the passion of his wounds. As he went on, he seemed always looking for a place, like one who goes to choose a grave.

Something in the gesture of the man as he waved the bloody and pitying soldiers away made the youth start as if bitten. He yelled in horror. Tottering forward he laid a quivering hand upon the man's arm. As the latter slowly turned his waxlike features toward him, the youth screamed:

"Gawd! Jim Conklin!"

The tall soldier made a little commonplace smile. "Hello, Henry," he said.

The youth swayed on his legs and glared strangely. He stuttered and stammered. "Oh, Jim—oh, Jim—oh, Jim—"

The tall soldier held out his gory hand. There was a curious red and black combination of new blood and old blood upon it. "Where yeh been, Henry?" he asked. He continued in a monotonous voice, "I thought mebbe yeh got keeled over. There's been thunder t' pay t'-day. I was worryin' about it a good deal."

The youth still lamented. "Oh, Jim—oh, Jim—oh, Jim—"

"Yeh know," said the tall soldier, "I was out there." He made a careful gesture. "An', Lord, what a circus! An', b'jiminey, I got shot—I got shot. Yes, b'jiminey, I got shot." He reiterated this fact in a bewildered way, as if he did not know how it came about.

The youth put forth anxious arms to assist him, but the tall soldier went firmly on as if propelled. Since the youth's arrival as a guardian for his friend, the other wounded men had ceased to display much interest. They occupied themselves again in dragging their own tragedies toward the rear.

Suddenly, as the two friends marched on, the tall soldier seemed to be overcome by a terror. His face turned to a semblance of gray paste. He clutched the youth's arm and looked all about him, as if dreading to be overheard. Then he began to speak in a shaking whisper:

"I tell yeh what I'm 'fraid of, Henry—I'll tell yeh what I'm 'fraid of. I'm 'fraid I'll fall down—an' then yeh know—them damned artillery wagons—they like as not 'll run over me. That's what I'm 'fraid of—"

The youth cried out to him hysterically: "I'll take care of yeh, Jim! I'll take care of yeh! I swear t' Gawd I will!"

"Sure—will yeh, Henry?" the tall soldier beseeched.

"Yes—yes—I tell yeh—I'll take care of yeh, Jim!" protested the youth. He could not speak accurately because of the gulpings in his throat.

But the tall soldier continued to beg in a lowly way. He now hung babelike to the youth's arm. His eyes rolled in the wildness of his terror. "I was allus a good friend t' yeh, wa'n't I, Henry? I've allus been a pretty good feller, ain't I? An' it ain't much t' ask, is it? Jest t' pull me along outer th' road? I'd do it fer you, wouldn't I, Henry?"

He paused in piteous anxiety to await his friend's reply.

The youth had reached an anguish where the sobs scorched him. He strove to express his loyalty, but he could only make fantastic gestures.

However, the tall soldier seemed suddenly to forget all those fears. He became again the grim, stalking specter of a soldier. He went stonily forward. The youth wished his friend to lean upon him, but the other always shook his head and strangely protested. "No—no—no—leave me be—leave me be—"

His look was fixed again upon the unknown. He moved with mysterious purpose, and all of the youth's offers he brushed aside. "No—no—leave me be—leave me be—"

The youth had to follow.

Presently the latter heard a voice talking softly near his shoulders. Turning he saw that it belonged to the tattered soldier. "Ye'd better take 'im outa th' road, pardner. There's a batt'ry comin' helitywhoop down th' road an' he'll git runned over. He's a goner anyhow in about five minutes—yeh kin see that. Ye'd better take 'im outa th' road. Where th' blazes does he git his stren'th from?"

"Lord knows!" cried the youth. He was shaking his hands helplessly.

He ran forward presently and grasped the tall soldier by the arm. "Jim! Jim!" he coaxed, "come with me."

The tall soldier weakly tried to wrench himself free. "Huh," he said vacantly. He stared at the youth for a moment. At last he spoke as if dimly comprehending. "Oh! Inteh th' fields? Oh!"

He started blindly through the grass.

The youth turned once to look at the lashing riders and jouncing guns of the battery. He was startled from this view by a shrill outcry from the tattered man.

"Gawd! He's runnin'!"

Turning his head swiftly, the youth saw his friend running in a staggering and stumbling way toward a little clump of bushes. His heart seemed to wrench itself almost free from his body at this sight. He made a noise of pain. He and the tattered man began a pursuit. There was a singular race.

When he overtook the tall soldier he began to plead with all the words he could find. "Jim—Jim—what are you doing—what makes you do this way—you'll hurt yerself."

The same purpose was in the tall soldier's face. He protested in a dulled way, keeping his eyes fastened on the mystic place of his intentions. "No—no—don't tech me—leave me be—leave me be—"

The youth, aghast and filled with wonder at the tall soldier, began quaveringly to question him. "Where yeh goin', Jim? What you thinking about? Where you going? Tell me, won't you, Jim?"

The tall soldier faced about as upon relentless pursuers. In his eyes there was a great appeal. "Leave me be, can't yeh? Leave me be fer a minnit."

The youth recoiled. "Why, Jim," he said, in a dazed way, "what's the matter with you?"

The tall soldier turned and, lurching dangerously, went on. The youth and the tattered soldier followed, sneaking as if whipped, feeling unable to face the stricken man if he should again confront them. They began to have thoughts of a solemn ceremony. There was something rite-like in these movements of the doomed soldier. And there was a resemblance in him to a devotee of a mad religion, blood-sucking, muscle-wrenching, bone-crushing. They were awed and afraid. They hung back lest he have at command a dreadful weapon.

At last, they saw him stop and stand motionless. Hastening up, they perceived that his face wore an expression telling that he had at last found the place for which he had struggled. His spare figure was erect; his bloody hands were quietly at his side. He was waiting with patience for something that he had come to meet. He was at the rendezvous. They paused and stood, expectant.

There was a silence.

Finally, the chest of the doomed soldier began to heave with a strained motion. It increased in violence until it was as if an animal was within and was kicking and tumbling furiously to be free.

This spectacle of gradual strangulation made the youth writhe, and once as his friend rolled his eyes, he saw something in them that made him sink wailing to the ground. He raised his voice in a last supreme call.

"Jim—Jim—Jim—"

The tall soldier opened his lips and spoke. He made a gesture. "Leave me be—don't tech me—leave me be—"

There was another silence while he waited.

Suddenly, his form stiffened and straightened. Then it was shaken by a prolonged ague. He stared into space. To the two watchers there was a curious and profound dignity in the firm lines of his awful face.

He was invaded by a creeping strangeness that slowly enveloped him. For a moment the tremor of his legs caused him to dance a sort of hideous hornpipe. His arms beat wildly about his head in expression of implike enthusiasm.

His tall figure stretched itself to its full height. There was a slight rending sound. Then it began to swing forward, slow and straight, in the manner of a falling tree. A swift muscular contortion made the left shoulder strike the ground first.

The body seemed to bounce a little way from the earth. "God!" said the tattered soldier.

The youth had watched, spellbound, this ceremony at the place of meeting. His face had been twisted into an expression of every agony he had imagined for his friend.

He now sprang to his feet and, going closer, gazed upon the pastelike face. The mouth was open and the teeth showed in a laugh.

As the flap of the blue jacket fell away from the body, he could see that the side looked as if it had been chewed by wolves.

The youth turned, with sudden, livid rage, toward the battlefield. He shook his fist. He seemed about to deliver a philippic.

"Hell—"

The red sun was pasted in the sky like a wafer.

CHAPTER X

The tattered man stood musing.

"Well, he was a reg'lar jim-dandy fer nerve, wa'n't he," said he finally in a little awe-struck voice. "A reg'lar jim-dandy." He thoughtfully poked one of the docile hands with his foot. "I wonner where he got 'is stren'th from? I never seen a man do like that before. It was a funny thing. Well, he was a reg'lar jim-dandy."

The youth desired to screech out his grief. He was stabbed, but his tongue lay dead in the tomb of his mouth. He threw himself again upon the ground and began to brood.

The tattered man stood musing.

"Look-a-here, pardner," he said, after a time. He regarded the corpse as he spoke. "He's up an' gone, ain't 'e, an' we might as well begin t' look out fer ol' number one. This here thing is all over. He's up an' gone, ain't 'e? An' he's all right here. Nobody won't bother 'im. An' I must say I ain't enjoying any great health m'self these days."

The youth, awakened by the tattered soldier's tone, looked quickly up. He saw that he was swinging uncertainly on his legs and that his face had turned to a shade of blue.

"Good Lord!" he cried, "you ain't goin' t'—not you, too."

The tattered man waved his hand. "Nary die," he said. "All I want is some pea soup an' a good bed. Some pea soup," he repeated dreamfully.

The youth arose from the ground. "I wonder where he came from. I left him over there." He pointed. "And now I find 'im here. And he was coming from over there, too." He indicated a new direction. They both turned toward the body as if to ask it a question.

"Well," at length spoke the tattered man, "there ain't no use in our stayin' here an' tryin' t' ask him anything."

The youth nodded an assent wearily. They both turned to gaze for a moment at the corpse.

The youth murmured something.

"Well, he was a jim-dandy, wa'n't 'e?" said the tattered man as if in response.

They turned their backs upon it and started away. For a time they stole softly, treading with their toes. It remained laughing there in the grass.

"I'm commencin' t' feel pretty bad," said the tattered man, suddenly breaking one of his little silences. "I'm commencin' t' feel pretty damn' bad."

The youth groaned. "O Lord!" He wondered if he was to be the tortured witness of another grim encounter.

But his companion waved his hand reassuringly. "Oh, I'm not goin' t' die yit! There's too much dependin' on me fer me t' die yit. No, sir! Nary die' I *can't*! Ye'd oughta see th' swad a' chil'ren I've got, an' all like that."

The youth glancing at his companion could see by the shadow of a smile that he was making some kind of fun.

As they plodded on the tattered soldier continued to talk. "Besides, if I died, I wouldn't die th' way that feller did. That was th' funniest thing. I'd jest flop down, I would. I never seen a feller die th' way that feller did.

"Yeh know Tom Jamison, he lives next door t' me up home. He's a nice feller, he is, an' we was allus good friends. Smart, too. Smart as a steel trap. Well, when we was a-fightin' this afternoon, all-of-a-sudden he begin t' rip up an' cuss an' beller at me. 'Yer shot, yeh blamed infernal!'—he swear horrible—he ses t' me. I put up m' hand t' m' head an' when I looked at m' fingers, I seen, sure 'nough, I was shot. I give a holler an' begin t' run, but b'fore I could git away another one hit me in th' arm an' whirl' me clean 'round. I got skeared when they was all a-shootin b'hind me an' I run t' beat all, but I cotch it pretty bad. I've an idee I'd a' been fightin' yit, if t'wasn't fer Tom Jamison."

Then he made a calm announcement: "There's two of 'em—little ones—but they're beginnin' t' have fun with me now. I don't b-lieve I kin walk much furder."

They went slowly on in silence. "Yeh look pretty peaked yerself," said the tattered man at last. "I bet yeh 've got a worser one than yeh think. Ye'd better take keer of yer hurt. It don't do t' let sech things go. It might be inside mostly, an' them plays thunder. Where is it located?" But he continued his harangue without waiting for a reply. "I see' a feller git hit plum in th' head when my reg'ment was a-standin' at ease onct. An' everybody yelled out to 'im: Hurt, John? Are yeh hurt much? 'No,' ses he. He looked kinder surprised, an' he went on tellin' 'em how he felt. He sed he didn't feel nothin'. But, by dad, th' first thing that feller knowed he was dead. Yes, he was dead—stone dead. So, yeh wanta watch out. Yeh might have some queer kind 'a hurt yerself. Yeh can't never tell. Where is your'n located?"

The youth had been wriggling since the introduction of this topic. He now gave a cry of exasperation and made a furious motion with his hand. "Oh, don't bother me!" he said. He was enraged against the tattered man, and could have strangled him. His companions seemed ever to play intolerable parts. They were ever upraising the ghost of shame on the stick of their curiosity. He turned toward the tattered man as one at bay. "Now, don't bother me," he repeated with desperate menace.

"Well, Lord knows I don't wanta bother anybody," said the other. There was a little accent of despair in his voice as he replied, "Lord knows I've gota 'nough m' own t' tend to."

The youth, who had been holding a bitter debate with himself and casting glances of hatred and contempt at the tattered man, here spoke in a hard voice. "Good-by," he said.

The tattered man looked at him in gaping amazement. "Why—why, pardner, where yeh goin'?" he asked unsteadily. The youth, looking at him, could see that he, too, like that other one, was beginning to act dumb and animallike. His thoughts seemed to be floundering about in his head. "Now—now—look—a—here, you Tom Jamison—now—I won't have this—this here won't do. Where—where yeh goin'?"

The youth pointed vaguely. "Over there," he replied.

"Well, now look—a—here—now," said the tattered man, rambling on in idiot fashion. His head was hanging forward and his words were slurred. "This thing won't do, now, Tom Jamison. It won't do. I know yeh, yeh pigheaded devil. Yeh wanta go trompin' off with a bad hurt. It ain't right—now—Tom Jamison—it ain't. Yeh wanta leave me take keer of yeh, Tom Jamison. It ain't—right—it ain't—fer yeh t' go—trompin' off—with a bad hurt—it ain't—ain't—ain't right—it ain't."

In reply the youth climbed a fence and started away. He could hear the tattered man bleating plaintively.

Once he faced about angrily. "What?"

"Look—a—here, now, Tom Jamison—now—it ain't—"

The youth went on. Turning at a distance he saw the tattered man wandering about helplessly in the field.

He now thought that he wished he was dead. He believed that he envied those men whose bodies lay strewn over the grass of the fields and on the fallen leaves of the forest.

The simple questions of the tattered man had been knife thrusts to him. They asserted a society that probes pitilessly at secrets until all is apparent. His late companion's chance persistency made him feel that he could not keep his crime concealed in his bosom. It was sure to be brought plain by one of those arrows which cloud the air and are constantly pricking, discovering, proclaiming those things which are willed to be forever hidden. He admitted that he could not defend himself against this agency. It was not within the power of vigilance.

CHAPTER XI

He became aware that the furnace roar of the battle was growing louder. Great brown clouds had floated to the still heights of air before him. The noise, too, was approaching. The woods filtered men and the fields became dotted.

As he rounded a hillock, he perceived that the roadway was now a crying mass of wagons, teams, and men. From the heaving tangle issued exhortations, commands, imprecations. Fear was sweeping it all along. The cracking whips bit and horses plunged and tugged. The white-topped wagons strained and stumbled in their exertions like fat sheep.

The youth felt comforted in a measure by this sight. They were all retreating. Perhaps, then, he was not so bad after all. He seated himself and watched the terror-stricken wagons. They fled like soft, ungainly animals. All the roarers and lashers served to help him to magnify the dangers and horrors of the engagement that he might try to prove to himself that the thing with which men could charge him was in truth a symmetrical act. There was an amount of pleasure to him in watching the wild march of this vindication.

Presently the calm head of a forward-going column of infantry appeared in the road. It came swiftly on. Avoiding the obstructions gave it the sinuous movement of a serpent. The men at the head butted mules with their musket stocks. They prodded teamsters indifferent to all howls. The men forced their way through parts of the dense mass by strength. The blunt head of the column pushed. The raving teamsters swore many strange oaths.

The commands to make way had the ring of a great importance in them. The men were going forward to the heart of the din. They were to confront the eager rush of the enemy. They felt the pride of their onward movement when the remainder of the army seemed trying to dribble down this road. They tumbled teams about with a fine feeling that it was no matter so long as their column got to the front in time. This importance made their faces grave and stern. And the backs of the officers were very rigid.

As the youth looked at them the black weight of his woe returned to him. He felt that he was regarding a procession of chosen beings. The separation was as great to him as if they had marched with weapons of flame and banners of sunlight. He could never be like them. He could have wept in his longings.

He searched about in his mind for an adequate malediction for the indefinite cause, the thing upon which men turn the words of final blame. It—whatever it was—was responsible for him, he said. There lay the fault.

The haste of the column to reach the battle seemed to the forlorn young man to be something much finer than stout fighting. Heroes, he thought, could find excuses in that long seething lane. They could retire with perfect self-respect and make excuses to the stars.

He wondered what those men had eaten that they could be in such haste to force their way to grim chances of death. As he watched, his envy grew until he thought that he wished to change lives with one of them. He would have liked to have used a tremendous force, he said, throw off himself and become a better. Swift pictures of himself, apart, yet in himself, came to him—a blue desperate figure leading lurid charges with one knee forward and a broken blade high—a blue, determined figure standing before a crimson and steel assault, getting calmly killed on a high place before the eyes of all. He thought of the magnificent pathos of his dead body.

These thoughts uplifted him. He felt the quiver of war desire. In his ears, he heard the ring of victory. He knew the frenzy of a rapid successful charge. The music of the trampling feet, the sharp voices, the clanking arms of the column near him made him soar on the red wings of war. For a few moments he was sublime.

He thought that he was about to start for the front. Indeed, he saw a picture of himself, dust-stained, haggard, panting, flying to the front at the proper moment to seize and throttle the dark, leering witch of calamity.

Then the difficulties of the thing began to drag at him. He hesitated, balancing awkwardly on one foot.

He had no rifle; he could not fight with his hands, said he resentfully to his plan. Well, rifles could be had for the picking. They were extraordinarily profuse.

Also, he continued, it would be a miracle if he found his regiment. Well, he could fight with any regiment.

He started forward slowly. He stepped as if he expected to tread upon some explosive thing. Doubts and he were struggling.

He would truly be a worm if any of his comrades should see him returning thus, the marks of his flight upon him. There was a reply that the intent fighters did not care for what happened rearward saving that no hostile bayonets appeared there. In the battle-blur his face would, in a way, be hidden, like the face of a cowled man.

But then he said that his tireless fate would bring forth, when the strife lulled for a moment, a man to ask of him an explanation. In imagination he felt the scrutiny of his companions as he painfully labored through some lies.

Eventually, his courage expended itself upon these objections. The debates drained him of his fire.

He was not cast down by this defeat of his plan, for, upon studying the affair carefully, he could not but admit that the objections were very formidable.

Furthermore, various ailments had begun to cry out. In their presence he could not persist in flying high with the wings of war; they rendered it almost impossible for him to see himself in a heroic light. He tumbled headlong.

He discovered that he had a scorching thirst. His face was so dry and grimy that he thought he could feel his skin crackle. Each bone of his body had an ache in it, and seemingly threatened to break with each movement. His feet were like two sores. Also, his body was calling for food. It was more powerful than a direct hunger. There was a dull, weight-like feeling in his stomach, and, when he tried to walk, his head swayed and he tottered. He could not see with distinctness. Small patches of green mist floated before his vision.

While he had been tossed by many emotions, he had not been aware of ailments. Now they beset him and made clamor. As he was at last compelled to pay attention to them, his capacity for self-hate was multiplied. In despair, he declared that he was not like those others. He now conceded it to be impossible that he should ever become a hero. He was a craven loon. Those pictures of glory were piteous things. He groaned from his heart and went staggering off.

A certain mothlike quality within him kept him in the vicinity of the battle. He had a great desire to see, and to get news. He wished to know who was winning.

He told himself that, despite his unprecedented suffering, he had never lost his greed for a victory, yet, he said, in a half-apologetic manner to his conscience, he could not but know that a defeat for the army this time might mean many favorable things for him. The blows of the enemy would splinter regiments into fragments. Thus, many men of courage, he considered, would be obliged to desert the colors and scurry like chickens. He would appear as one of them. They would be sullen brothers in distress, and he could then easily believe he had not run any farther or faster than they. And if he himself could believe in his virtuous perfection, he conceived that there would be small trouble in convincing all others.

He said, as if in excuse for this hope, that previously the army had encountered great defeats and in a few months had shaken off all blood and tradition of them, emerging as bright and valiant as a new one; thrusting out of sight the memory of disaster, and appearing with the valor and confidence of unconquered legions. The shrilling voices of the people at home would pipe dismally for a time, but various generals were usually compelled to listen to these ditties. He of course felt no compunctions for proposing a general as a sacrifice. He could not tell who the chosen for the barbs might be, so he could center no direct sympathy upon him. The people were afar and he did not conceive public opinion to be accurate at long range. It was quite probable they would hit the wrong man who, after he had recovered from his amazement, would perhaps spend the rest of his days in writing replies to the songs of his alleged failure. It would be very unfortunate, no doubt, but in this case a general was of no consequence to the youth.

In a defeat there would be a roundabout vindication of himself. He thought it would prove, in a manner, that he had fled early because of his superior powers of perception. A serious prophet upon predicting a flood should be the first man to climb a tree. This would demonstrate that he was indeed a seer.

A moral vindication was regarded by the youth as a very important thing. Without salve, he could not, he thought, wear the sore badge of his dishonor through life. With his heart continually assuring him that he was despicable, he could not exist without making it, through his actions, apparent to all men.

If the army had gone gloriously on he would be lost. If the din meant that now his army's flags were tilted forward he was a condemned wretch. He would be compelled to doom himself to isolation. If the men were advancing, their indifferent feet were trampling upon his chances for a successful life.

As these thoughts went rapidly through his mind, he turned upon them and tried to thrust them away. He denounced himself as a villain. He said that he was the most unutterably selfish man in existence. His mind pictured the soldiers who would place their defiant bodies before the spear of the yelling battle fiend, and as he saw their dripping corpses on an imagined field, he said that he was their murderer.

Again he thought that he wished he was dead. He believed that he envied a corpse. Thinking of the slain, he achieved a great contempt for some of them, as if they were guilty for thus becoming lifeless. They might have been killed by lucky chances, he said, before they had had opportunities to flee or before they had been really tested. Yet they would receive laurels from tradition. He cried out bitterly that their crowns were stolen and their robes of glorious memories were shams. However, he still said that it was a great pity he was not as they.

A defeat of the army had suggested itself to him as a means of escape from the consequences of his fall. He considered, now, however, that it was useless to think of such a possibility. His education had been that success for that mighty blue machine was certain; that it would make victories as a contrivance turns out buttons. He presently discarded all his speculations in the other direction. He returned to the creed of soldiers.

When he perceived again that it was not possible for the army to be defeated, he tried to bethink him of a fine tale which he could take back to his regiment, and with it turn the expected shafts of derision.

But, as he mortally feared these shafts, it became impossible for him to invent a tale he felt he could trust. He experimented with many schemes, but threw them aside one by one as flimsy. He was quick to see vulnerable places in them all.

Furthermore, he was much afraid that some arrow of scorn might lay him mentally low before he could raise his protecting tale.

He imagined the whole regiment saying: "Where's Henry Fleming? He run, didn't 'e? Oh, my!" He recalled various persons who would be quite sure to leave him no peace about it. They would doubtless question him with sneers, and laugh at his stammering hesitation. In the next engagement they would try to keep watch of him to discover when he would run.

Wherever he went in camp, he would encounter insolent and lingeringly cruel stares. As he imagined himself passing near a crowd of comrades, he could hear some one say, "There he goes!"

Then, as if the heads were moved by one muscle, all the faces were turned toward him with wide, derisive grins. He seemed to hear some one make a humorous remark in a low tone. At it the others all crowed and cackled. He was a slang phrase.

CHAPTER XII

The column that had butted stoutly at the obstacles in the roadway was barely out of the youth's sight before he saw dark waves of men come sweeping out of the woods and down through the fields. He knew at once that the steel fibers had been washed from their hearts. They were bursting from their coats and their equipments as from entanglements. They charged down upon him like terrified buffaloes.

Behind them blue smoke curled and clouded above the treetops, and through the thickets he could sometimes see a distant pink glare. The voices of the cannon were clamoring in interminable chorus.

The youth was horror-stricken. He stared in agony and amazement. He forgot that he was engaged in combating the universe. He threw aside his mental pamphlets on the philosophy of the retreated and rules for the guidance of the damned.

The fight was lost. The dragons were coming with invincible strides. The army, helpless in the matted thickets and blinded by the overhanging night, was going to be swallowed. War, the red animal, war, the blood-swollen god, would have bloated fill.

Within him some something bade to cry out. He had the impulse to make a rallying speech, to sing a battle hymn, but he could only get his tongue to call into the air: "Why—why—what—what's th' matter?"

Soon he was in the midst of them. They were leaping and scampering all about him. Their blanched faces shone in the dusk. They seemed, for the most part, to be very burly men. The youth turned from one to another of them as they galloped along. His incoherent questions were lost. They were heedless of his appeals. They did not seem to see him.

They sometimes gabbed insanely. One huge man was asking of the sky: "Say, where de plank road? Where de plank road!" It was as if he had lost a child. He wept in his pain and dismay.

Presently, men were running hither and thither in all ways. The artillery booming, forward, rearward, and on the flanks made jumble of ideas of direction. Landmarks had vanished into the gathered gloom. The youth began to imagine that he had got into the center of the tremendous quarrel, and he could perceive no way out of it. From the mouths of the fleeing men came a thousand wild questions, but no one made answers.

The youth, after rushing about and throwing interrogations at the heedless bands of retreating infantry, finally clutched a man by the arm. They swung around face to face.

"Why—why—" stammered the youth struggling with his balking tongue.

The man screamed: "Let go me! Let go me!" His face was livid and his eyes were rolling uncontrolled. He was heaving and panting. He still grasped his rifle, perhaps having forgotten to release his hold upon it. He tugged frantically, and the youth being compelled to lean forward was dragged several paces.

"Let go me! Let go me!"

"Why—why—" stuttered the youth.

"Well, then!" bawled the man in a lurid rage. He adroitly and fiercely swung his rifle. It crushed upon the youth's head. The man ran on.

The youth's fingers had turned to paste upon the other's arm. The energy was smitten from his muscles. He saw the flaming wings of lightning flash before his vision. There was a deafening rumble of thunder within his head.

Suddenly his legs seemed to die. He sank writhing to the ground. He tried to arise. In his efforts against the numbing pain he was like a man wrestling with a creature of the air.

There was a sinister struggle.

Sometimes he would achieve a position half erect, battle with the air for a moment, and then fall again, grabbing at the grass. His face was of a clammy pallor. Deep groans were wrenched from him.

At last, with a twisting movement, he got upon his hands and knees, and from thence, like a babe trying to walk, to his feet. Pressing his hands to his temples he went lurching over the grass.

He fought an intense battle with his body. His dulled senses wished him to swoon and he opposed them stubbornly, his mind portraying unknown dangers and mutilations if he should fall upon the field. He went tall soldier fashion. He imagined secluded spots where he could fall and be unmolested. To search for one he strove against the tide of his pain.

Once he put his hand to the top of his head and timidly touched the wound. The scratching pain of the contact made him draw a long breath through his clinched teeth. His fingers were dabbled with blood. He regarded them with a fixed stare.

Around him he could hear the grumble of jolted cannon as the scurrying horses were lashed toward the front. Once, a young officer on a besplashed charger nearly ran him down. He turned and watched the mass of guns, men, and horses sweeping in a wide curve toward a gap in a fence. The officer was making excited motions with a gauntleted hand. The guns followed the teams with an air of unwillingness, of being dragged by the heels.

Some officers of the scattered infantry were cursing and railing like fishwives. Their scolding voices could be heard above the din. Into the unspeakable jumble in the roadway rode a squadron of cavalry. The faded yellow of their facings shone bravely. There was a mighty altercation.

The artillery were assembling as if for a conference.

The blue haze of evening was upon the field. The lines of forest were long purple shadows. One cloud lay along the western sky partly smothering the red.

As the youth left the scene behind him, he heard the guns suddenly roar out. He imagined them shaking in black rage. They belched and howled like brass devils guarding a gate. The soft air was filled with the tremendous remonstrance. With it came the shattering peal of opposing infantry. Turning to look behind him he could see sheets of orange light illumine the shadowy distance. There were subtle and sudden lightnings in the far air. At times he thought he could see heaving masses of men.

He hurried on in the dusk. The day had faded until he could barely distinguish place for his feet. The purple darkness was filled with men who lectured and jabbered. Sometimes he could see them gesticulating against the blue and somber sky. There seemed to be a great ruck of men and munitions spread about in the forest and in the fields.

The little narrow roadway now lay lifeless. There were overturned wagons like sun-dried boulders. The bed of the former torrent was choked with the bodies of horses and splintered parts of war machines.

It had come to pass that his wound pained him but little. He was afraid to move rapidly, however, for a dread of disturbing it. He held his head very still and took many precautions against stumbling. He was filled with anxiety, and his face was pinched and drawn in anticipation of the pain of any sudden mistake of his feet in the gloom.

His thoughts, as he walked, fixed intently upon his hurt. There was a cool, liquid feeling about it and he imagined blood moving slowly down under his hair. His head seemed swollen to a size that made him think his neck to be inadequate.

The new silence of his wound made much worriment. The little blistering voices of pain that had called out from his scalp were, he thought, definite in their expression of danger. By them he believed that he could measure his plight. But when they remained ominously silent he became frightened and imagined terrible fingers that clutched into his brain.

Amid it he began to reflect upon various incidents and conditions of the past. He bethought him of certain meals his mother had cooked at home, in which those dishes of which he was particularly fond had occupied prominent positions. He saw the spread table. The pine walls of the kitchen were glowing in the warm light from the stove. Too, he remembered how he and his companions used to go from the schoolhouse to the bank of a shaded pool. He saw his clothes in disorderly array upon the grass of the bank. He felt the swash of the fragrant water upon his body. The leaves of the overhanging maple rustled with melody in the wind of youthful summer.

He was overcome presently by a dragging weariness. His head hung forward and his shoulders were stooped as if he were bearing a great bundle. His feet shuffled along the ground.

He held continuous arguments as to whether he should lie down and sleep at some near spot, or force himself on until he reached a certain haven. He often tried to dismiss the question, but his body persisted in rebellion and his senses nagged at him like pampered babies.

At last he heard a cheery voice near his shoulder: "Yeh seem t' be in a pretty bad way, boy?"

The youth did not look up, but he assented with thick tongue. "Uh!"

The owner of the cheery voice took him firmly by the arm. "Well," he said, with a round laugh, "I'm goin' your way. Th' hull gang is goin' your way. An' I guess I kin give yeh a lift." They began to walk like a drunken man and his friend.

As they went along, the man questioned the youth and assisted him with the replies like one manipulating the mind of a child. Sometimes he interjected anecdotes. "What reg'ment do yeh b'long teh? Eh? What's that? Th' 304th N' York? Why, what corps is that in? Oh, it is? Why, I thought they wasn't engaged t'-day—they're 'way over in th' center. Oh, they was, eh? Well, pretty nearly everybody got their share 'a fightin' t'-day. By dad, I give myself up fer dead any number 'a times. There was shootin' here an' shootin' there, an' hollerin' here an' hollerin' there, in th' damn' darkness, until I couldn't tell t' save m' soul which side I was on. Sometimes I thought I was sure 'nough from Ohier, an' other times I could a' swore I was from th' bitter end of Florida. It was th' most mixed up dern thing I ever see. An' these here hull woods is a reg'lar mess. It'll be a miracle if we find our reg'ments t'-night. Pretty soon, though, we'll meet a-plenty of guards an' provost-guards, an' one thing an' another. Ho! there they go with an off'cer, I guess. Look at his leg a-draggin'. He's got al th' war he wants, I bet. He won't be talkin' so big about his reputation an' all when they go t' sawin' off his leg. Poor feller! My brother's got whiskers jest like that. How did yeh git 'way over here, anyhow? Your reg'ment is a long way from here, ain't it? Well, I guess we can find it. Yeh know there was a boy killed in my comp'ny t'-day that I thought th' world an' all of. Jack was a nice feller. By ginger, it hurt like thunder t' see ol' Jack jest git knocked flat. We was a-standin' purty peaceable for a spell, 'though there was men runnin' ev'ry way all 'round us, an' while we was a-standin' like that, 'long come a big fat feller. He began t' peck at Jack's elbow, an' he ses: 'Say, where's th' road t' th' river?' An' Jack, he never paid no attention, an' th' feller kept on a-peckin' at his elbow an' sayin': 'Say, where's th' road t' th' river?' Jack was a-lookin' ahead all th' time tryin' t' see th' Johnnies comin' through th' woods, an' he never paid no attention t' this big fat feller fer a long time, but at last he turned 'round an' he ses: 'Ah, go t' hell an' find th' road t' th' river!' An' jest then a shot slapped him bang on th' side th' head. He was a sergeant, too. Them was his last words. Thunder, I wish we was sure 'a findin' our reg'ments t'-night. It's goin' t' be long huntin'. But I guess we kin do it."

In the search which followed, the man of the cheery voice seemed to the youth to possess a wand of a magic kind. He threaded the mazes of the tangled forest with a strange fortune. In encounter with guards and patrols he displayed the keenness of a detective and the valor of a gamin. Obstacles fell before him and became of assistance. The youth, with his chin still on his breast, stood woodenly by while his companion beat ways and means out of sullen things.

The forest seemed a vast hive of men buzzing about in frantic circles, but the cheery man conducted the youth without mistakes, until at last he began to chuckle with glee and self-satisfaction. "Ah, there yeh are! See that fire?"

The youth nodded stupidly.

"Well, there's where your reg'ment is. An' now, good-by, ol' boy, good luck t' yeh."

A warm and strong hand clasped the youth's languid fingers for an instant, and then he heard a cheerful and audacious whistling as the man strode away. As he who had so befriended him was thus passing out of his life, it suddenly occurred to the youth that he had not once seen his face.

CHAPTER XIII

The youth went slowly toward the fire indicated by his departed friend. As he reeled, he bethought him of the welcome his comrades would give him. He had a conviction that he would soon feel in his sore heart the barbed missiles of ridicule. He had no strength to invent a tale; he would be a soft target.

He made vague plans to go off into the deeper darkness and hide, but they were all destroyed by the voices of exhaustion and pain from his body. His ailments, clamoring, forced him to seek the place of food and rest, at whatever cost.

He swung unsteadily toward the fire. He could see the forms of men throwing black shadows in the red light, and as he went nearer it became known to him in some way that the ground was strewn with sleeping men.

Of a sudden he confronted a black and monstrous figure. A rifle barrel caught some glinting beams. "Halt! halt!" He was dismayed for a moment, but he presently thought that he recognized the nervous voice. As he stood tottering before the rifle barrel, he called out: "Why, hello, Wilson, you—you here?"

The rifle was lowered to a position of caution and the loud soldier came slowly forward. He peered into the youth's face. "That you, Henry?"

"Yes, it's—it's me."

"Well, well, ol' boy," said the other, "by ginger, I'm glad t' see yeh! I give yeh up fer a goner. I thought yeh was dead sure enough." There was husky emotion in his voice.

The youth found that now he could barely stand upon his feet. There was a sudden sinking of his forces. He thought he must hasten to produce his tale to protect him from the missiles already at the lips of his redoubtable comrades. So, staggering before the loud soldier, he began: "Yes, yes. I've—I've had an awful time. I've been all over. Way over on th' right. Ter'ble fightin' over there. I had an awful time. I got separated from th' reg'ment. Over on th' right, I got shot. In th' head. I never see sech fightin'. Awful time. I don't see how I could 'a' got separated from th' reg'ment. I got shot, too."

His friend had stepped forward quickly. "What? Got shot? Why didn't yeh say so first? Poor ol' boy, we must—hol' on a minnit; what am I doin'? I'll call Simpson."

Another figure at that moment loomed in the gloom. They could see that it was the corporal. "Who yeh talkin' to, Wilson?" he demanded. His voice was anger-toned. "Who yeh talkin' to? Yeh th' derndest sentinel—why—hello, Henry, you here? Why, I thought you was dead four hours ago! Great Jerusalem, they keep turnin' up every ten minutes or so! We thought we'd lost forty-two men by straight count, but if they keep on a-comin' this way, we'll git th' comp'ny all back by mornin' yit. Where was yeh?"

"Over on th' right. I got separated"—began the youth with considerable glibness.

But his friend had interrupted hastily. "Yes, an' he got shot in th' head an' he's in a fix, an' we must see t' him right away." He rested his rifle in the hollow of his left arm and his right around the youth's shoulder.

"Gee, it must hurt like thunder!" he said.

The youth leaned heavily upon his friend. "Yes, it hurts—hurts a good deal," he replied. There was a faltering in his voice.

"Oh," said the corporal. He linked his arm in the youth's and drew him forward. "Come on, Henry. I'll take keer 'a yeh."

As they went on together the loud private called out after them: "Put 'im t' sleep in my blanket, Simpson. An'—hol' on a minnit—here's my canteen. It's full 'a coffee. Look at his head by th' fire an' see how it looks. Maybe it's a pretty bad un. When I git relieved in a couple 'a minnits, I'll be over an' see t' him."

The youth's senses were so deadened that his friend's voice sounded from afar and he could scarcely feel the pressure of the corporal's arm. He submitted passively to the latter's directing strength. His head was in the old manner hanging forward upon his breast. His knees wobbled.

The corporal led him into the glare of the fire. "Now, Henry," he said, "let's have a look at yer ol' head."

The youth sat down obediently and the corporal, laying aside his rifle, began to fumble in the bushy hair of his comrade. He was obliged to turn the other's head so that the full flush of the fire light would beam upon it. He puckered his mouth with a critical air. He drew back his lips and whistled through his teeth when his fingers came in contact with the splashed blood and the rare wound.

"Ah, here we are!" he said. He awkwardly made further investigations. "Jest as I thought," he added, presently. "Yeh've been grazed by a ball. It's raised a queer lump jest as if some feller had lammed yeh on th' head with a club. It stopped a-bleedin' long time ago. Th' most about it is that in th' mornin' yeh'll feel that a number ten hat wouldn't fit yeh. An' your head 'll be all het up an' feel as dry as burnt pork. An' yeh may git a lot 'a other sicknesses, too, by mornin'. Yeh can't never tell. Still, I don't much think so. It's jest a damn' good belt on th' head, an' nothin' more. Now, you jest sit here an' don't move, while I go rout out th' relief. Then I'll send Wilson t' take keer 'a yeh."

The corporal went away. The youth remained on the ground like a parcel. He stared with a vacant look into the fire.

After a time he aroused, for some part, and the things about him began to take form. He saw that the ground in the deep shadows was cluttered with men, sprawling in every conceivable posture. Glancing narrowly into the more distant darkness, he caught occasional glimpses of visages that loomed pallid and ghostly, lit with a phosphorescent glow. These faces expressed in their lines the deep stupor of the tired soldiers. They made them appear like men drunk with wine. This bit of forest might have appeared to an ethereal wanderer as a scene of the result of some frightful debauch.

On the other side of the fire the youth observed an officer asleep, seated bolt upright, with his back against a tree. There was something perilous in his position. Badgered by dreams, perhaps, he swayed with little bounces and starts, like an old toddy-stricken grandfather in a chimney corner. Dust and stains were upon his face. His lower jaw hung down as if lacking strength to assume its normal position. He was the picture of an exhausted soldier after a feast of war.

He had evidently gone to sleep with his sword in his arms. These two had slumbered in an embrace, but the weapon had been allowed in time to fall unheeded to the ground. The brass-mounted hilt lay in contact with some parts of the fire.

Within the gleam of rose and orange light from the burning sticks were other soldiers, snoring and heaving, or lying deathlike in slumber. A few pairs of legs were stuck forth, rigid and straight. The shoes displayed the mud or dust of marches and bits of rounded trousers, protruding from the blankets, showed rents and tears from hurried pitchings through the dense brambles.

The fire crackled musically. From it swelled light smoke. Overhead the foliage moved softly. The leaves, with their faces turned toward the blaze, were colored shifting hues of silver, often edged with red. Far off to the right, through a window in the forest, could be seen a handful of stars lying, like glittering pebbles, on the black level of the night.

Occasionally, in this low-arched hall, a soldier would arouse and turn his body to a new position, the experience of his sleep having taught him of uneven and objectionable places upon the ground under him. Or, perhaps, he would lift himself to a sitting posture, blink at the fire for an unintelligent moment, throw a swift glance at his prostrate companion, and then cuddle down again with a grunt of sleepy content.

The youth sat in a forlorn heap until his friend, the loud young soldier, came, swinging two canteens by their light strings. "Well, now, Henry, ol' boy," said the latter, "we'll have yeh fixed up in jest about a minnit."

He had the bustling ways of an amateur nurse. He fussed around the fire and stirred the sticks to brilliant exertions. He made his patient drink largely from the canteen that contained the coffee. It was to the youth a delicious draught. He tilted his head afar back and held the canteen long to his lips. The cool mixture went caressingly down his blistered throat. Having finished, he sighed with comfortable delight.

The loud young soldier watched his comrade with an air of satisfaction. He later produced an extensive handkerchief from his pocket. He folded it into a manner of bandage and soused water from the other canteen upon the middle of it. This crude arrangement he bound over the youth's head, tying the ends in a queer knot at the back of the neck.

"There," he said, moving off and surveying his deed, "yeh look like th' devil, but I bet yeh feel better."

The youth contemplated his friend with grateful eyes. Upon his aching and swelling head the cold cloth was like a tender woman's hand.

"Yeh don't holler ner say nothin'," remarked his friend approvingly. "I know I'm a blacksmith at takin' keer 'a sick folks, an' yeh never squeaked. Yer a good un, Henry. Most 'a men would 'a been in th' hospital long ago. A shot in th' head ain't foolin' business."

The youth made no reply, but began to fumble with the buttons of his jacket.

"Well, come, now," continued his friend, "come on. I must put yeh t' bed an' see that yeh git a good night's rest."

The other got carefully erect, and the loud young soldier led him among the sleeping forms lying in groups and rows. Presently he stooped and picked up his blankets. He spread the rubber one upon the ground and placed the woolen one about the youth's shoulders.

"There now," he said, "lie down an' git some sleep."

The youth, with his manner of doglike obedience, got carefully down like a crone stooping. He stretched out with a murmur of relief and comfort. The ground felt like the softest couch.

But of a sudden he ejaculated: "Hol' on a minnit! Where you goin' t' sleep?"

His friend waved his hand impatiently. "Right down there by yeh."

"Well, but hol' on a minnit," continued the youth. "What yeh goin' t' sleep in? I've got your—"

The loud young soldier snarled: "Shet up an' go on t' sleep. Don't be makin' a damn' fool 'a yerself," he said severely.

After the reproof the youth said no more. An exquisite drowsiness had spread through him. The warm comfort of the blanket enveloped him and made a gentle languor. His head fell forward on his crooked arm and his weighted lids went slowly down over his eyes. Hearing a splatter of musketry from the distance, he wondered indifferently if those men sometimes slept. He gave a long sigh, snuggled down into his blanket, and in a moment was like his comrades.

CHAPTER XIV

When the youth awoke it seemed to him that he had been asleep for a thousand years, and he felt sure that he opened his eyes upon an unexpected world. Gray mists were slowly shifting before the first efforts of the sunrays. An impending splendor could be seen in the eastern sky. An icy dew had chilled his face, and immediately upon arousing he curled farther down into his blankets. He stared for a while at the leaves overhead, moving in a heraldic wind of the day.

The distance was splintering and blaring with the noise of fighting. There was in the sound an expression of a deadly persistency, as if it had not begun and was not to cease.

About him were the rows and groups of men that he had dimly seen the previous night. They were getting a last draught of sleep before the awakening. The gaunt, careworn features and dusty figures were made plain by this quaint light at the dawning, but it dressed the skin of the men in corpselike hues and made the tangled limbs appear pulseless and dead. The youth started up with a little cry when his eyes first swept over this motionless mass of men, thick-spread upon the ground, pallid, and in strange postures. His disordered mind interpreted the hall of the forest as a charnel place. He believed for an instant that he was in the house of the dead, and he did not dare to move lest these corpses start up, squalling and squawking. In a second, however, he achieved his proper mind. He swore a complicated oath at himself. He saw that this somber picture was not a fact of the present, but a mere prophecy.

He heard then the noise of a fire crackling briskly in the cold air, and, turning his head, he saw his friend pottering busily about a small blaze. A few other figures moved in the fog, and he heard the hard cracking of axe blows.

Suddenly there was a hollow rumble of drums. A distant bugle sang faintly. Similar sounds, varying in strength, came from near and far over the forest. The bugles called to each other like brazen gamecocks. The near thunder of the regimental drums rolled.

The body of men in the woods rustled. There was a general uplifting of heads. A murmuring of voices broke upon the air. In it there was much bass of grumbling oaths. Strange gods were addressed in condemnation of the early hours necessary to correct war. An officer's peremptory tenor rang out and quickened the stiffened movement of the men. The tangled limbs unraveled. The corpse-hued faces were hidden behind fists that twisted slowly in the eye sockets.

The youth sat up and gave vent to an enormous yawn. "Thunder!" he remarked petulantly. He rubbed his eyes, and then putting up his hand felt carefully of the bandage over his wound. His friend, perceiving him to be awake, came from the fire. "Well, Henry, ol' man, how do yeh feel this mornin'?" he demanded.

The youth yawned again. Then he puckered his mouth to a little pucker. His head, in truth, felt precisely like a melon, and there was an unpleasant sensation at his stomach.

"Oh, Lord, I feel pretty bad," he said.

"Thunder!" exclaimed the other. "I hoped ye'd feel all right this mornin'. Let's see th' bandage—I guess it's slipped." He began to tinker at the wound in rather a clumsy way until the youth exploded.

"Gosh-dern it!" he said in sharp irritation; "you're the hangdest man I ever saw! You wear muffs on your hands. Why in good thunderation can't you be more easy? I'd rather you'd stand off an' throw guns at it. Now, go slow, an' don't act as if you was nailing down carpet."

He glared with insolent command at his friend, but the latter answered soothingly. "Well, well, come now, an' git some grub," he said. "Then, maybe, yeh'll feel better."

At the fireside the loud young soldier watched over his comrade's wants with tenderness and care. He was very busy marshaling the little black vagabonds of tin cups and pouring into them the streaming, iron colored mixture from a small and sooty tin pail. He had some fresh meat, which he roasted hurriedly upon a stick. He sat down then and contemplated the youth's appetite with glee.

The youth took note of a remarkable change in his comrade since those days of camp life upon the river bank. He seemed no more to be continually regarding the proportions of his personal prowess. He was not furious at small words that pricked his conceits. He was no more a loud young soldier. There was about him now a fine reliance. He showed a quiet belief in his purposes and his abilities. And this inward confidence evidently enabled him to be indifferent to little words of other men aimed at him.

The youth reflected. He had been used to regarding his comrade as a blatant child with an audacity grown from his inexperience, thoughtless, headstrong, jealous, and filled with a tinsel courage. A swaggering babe accustomed to strut in his own dooryard. The youth wondered where had been born these new eyes; when his comrade had made the great discovery that there were many men who would refuse to be subjected by him. Apparently, the other had now climbed a peak of wisdom from which he could perceive himself as a very wee thing. And the youth saw that ever after it would be easier to live in his friend's neighborhood.

His comrade balanced his ebony coffee cup on his knee. "Well, Henry," he said, "what d'yeh think th' chances are? D'yeh think we'll wallop 'em?"

The youth considered for a moment. "Day-b'fore-yesterday," he finally replied, with boldness, "you would 'a' bet you'd lick the hull kit-an'-boodle all by yourself."

His friend looked a trifle amazed. "Would I?" he asked. He pondered. "Well, perhaps I would," he decided at last. He stared humbly at the fire.

The youth was quite disconcerted at this surprising reception of his remarks. "Oh, no, you wouldn't either," he said, hastily trying to retrace.

But the other made a deprecating gesture. "Oh, yeh needn't mind, Henry," he said. "I believe I was a pretty big fool in those days." He spoke as after a lapse of years.

There was a little pause.

"All th' officers say we've got th' rebs in a pretty tight box," said the friend, clearing his throat in a commonplace way. "They all seem t' think we've got 'em jest where we want 'em."

"I don't know about that," the youth replied. "What I seen over on th' right makes me think it was th' other way about. From where I was, it looked as if we was gettin' a good poundin' yestirday."

"D'yeh think so?" inquired the friend. "I thought we handled 'em pretty rough yestirday."

"Not a bit," said the youth. "Why, lord, man, you didn't see nothing of the fight. Why!" Then a sudden thought came to him. "Oh! Jim Conklin's dead."

His friend started. "What? Is he? Jim Conklin?"

The youth spoke slowly. "Yes. He's dead. Shot in th' side."

"Yeh don't say so. Jim Conklin . . . poor cuss!"

All about them were other small fires surrounded by men with their little black utensils. From one of these near came sudden sharp voices in a row. It appeared that two light-footed soldiers had been teasing a huge, bearded man, causing him to spill coffee upon his blue knees. The man had gone into a rage and had sworn comprehensively. Stung by his language, his tormentors had immediately bristled at him with a great show of resenting unjust oaths. Possibly there was going to be a fight.

The friend arose and went over to them, making pacific motions with his arms. "Oh, here, now, boys, what's th' use?" he said. "We'll be at th' rebs in less'n an hour. What's th' good fightin' 'mong ourselves?"

One of the light-footed soldiers turned upon him red-faced and violent. "Yeh needn't come around here with yer preachin'. I s'pose yeh don't approve 'a fightin' since Charley Morgan licked yeh; but I don't see what business this here is 'a yours or anybody else."

"Well, it ain't," said the friend mildly. "Still I hate t' see—"

That was a tangled argument.

"Well, he—," said the two, indicating their opponent with accusative forefingers.

The huge soldier was quite purple with rage. He pointed at the two soldiers with his great hand, extended clawlike. "Well, they—"

But during this argumentative time the desire to deal blows seemed to pass, although they said much to each other. Finally the friend returned to his old seat. In a short while the three antagonists could be seen together in an amiable bunch.

"Jimmie Rogers ses I'll have t' fight him after th' battle t'-day," announced the friend as he again seated himself. "He ses he don't allow no interferin' in his business. I hate t' see th' boys fightin' 'mong themselves."

The youth laughed. "Yer changed a good bit. Yeh ain't at all like yeh was. I remember when you an' that Irish feller—" He stopped and laughed again.

"No, I didn't use t' be that way," said his friend thoughtfully. "That's true 'nough."

"Well, I didn't mean—" began the youth.

The friend made another deprecatory gesture. "Oh, yeh needn't mind, Henry."

There was another little pause.

"Th' reg'ment lost over half th' men yestirday," remarked the friend eventually. "I thought 'a course they was all dead, but, laws, they kep' a-comin' back last night until it seems, after all, we didn't lose but a few. They'd been scattered all over, wanderin' around in th' woods, fightin' with other reg'ments, an' everything. Jest like you done."

"So?" said the youth.

CHAPTER XV

The regiment was standing at order arms at the side of a lane, waiting for the command to march, when suddenly the youth remembered the little packet enwrapped in a faded yellow envelope which the loud young soldier with lugubrious words had intrusted to him. It made him start. He uttered an exclamation and turned toward his comrade.

"Wilson!"

His friend, at his side in the ranks, was thoughtfully staring down the road. From some cause his expression was at that moment very meek. The youth, regarding him with sidelong glances, felt impelled to change his purpose. "Oh, nothing," he said.

His friend turned his head in some surprise. "Why, what was yeh goin' t' say?"

"Oh, nothing," repeated the youth.

He resolved not to deal the little blow. It was sufficient that the fact made him glad. It was not necessary to knock his friend on the head with the misguided packet.

He had been possessed of much fear of his friend, for he saw how easily questionings could make holes in his feelings. Lately, he had assured himself that the altered comrade would not tantalize him with a persistent curiosity, but he felt certain that during the first period of leisure his friend would ask him to relate his adventures of the previous day.

He now rejoiced in the possession of a small weapon with which he could prostrate his comrade at the first signs of a cross-examination. He was master. It would now be he who could laugh and shoot the shafts of derision.

The friend had, in a weak hour, spoken with sobs of his own death. He had delivered a melancholy oration previous to his funeral, and had doubtless, in the packet of letters, presented various keepsakes to relatives. But he had not died, and thus he had delivered himself into the hands of the youth.

The latter felt immensely superior to his friend, but he inclined to condescension. He adopted toward him an air of patronizing good humor.

His self-pride was now entirely restored. In the shade of its flourishing growth he stood with braced and self-confident legs, and since nothing could now be discovered he did not shrink from an encounter with the eyes of judges, and allowed no thoughts of his own to keep him from an attitude of manfulness. He had performed his mistakes in the dark, so he was still a man.

Indeed, when he remembered his fortunes of yesterday, and looked at them from a distance, he began to see something fine there. He had license to be pompous and veteran-like.

His panting agonies of the past he put out of his sight.

In the present, he declared to himself that it was only the doomed and the damned who roared with sincerity at circumstance. Few but they ever did it. A man with a full stomach and the respect of his fellows had no business to scold about anything that he might think to be wrong in the ways of the universe, or even with the ways of society. Let the unfortunates rail; the others may play marbles.

He did not give a great deal of thought to these battles that lay directly before him. It was not essential that he should plan his ways in regard to them. He had been taught that many obligations of a life were easily avoided. The lessons of yesterday had been that retribution was a laggard and blind. With these facts before him he did not deem it necessary that he should become feverish over the possibilities of the ensuing twenty-four hours. He could leave much to chance. Besides, a faith in himself had secretly blossomed. There was a little flower of confidence growing within him. He was now a man of experience. He had been out among the dragons, he said, and he assured himself that they were not so hideous as he had imagined them. Also, they were inaccurate; they did not sting with precision. A stout heart often defied, and, defying, escaped.

And, furthermore, how could they kill him who was the chosen of gods and doomed to greatness?

He remembered how some of the men had run from the battle. As he recalled their terror-struck faces he felt a scorn for them. They had surely been more fleet and more wild than was absolutely necessary. They were weak mortals. As for himself, he had fled with discretion and dignity.

He was aroused from this reverie by his friend, who, having hitched about nervously and blinked at the trees for a time, suddenly coughed in an introductory way, and spoke.

"Fleming!"

"What?"

The friend put his hand up to his mouth and coughed again. He fidgeted in his jacket.

"Well," he gulped, at last, "I guess yeh might as well give me back them letters." Dark, prickling blood had flushed into his cheeks and brow.

"All right, Wilson," said the youth. He loosened two buttons of his coat, thrust in his hand, and brought forth the packet. As he extended it to his friend the latter's face was turned from him.

He had been slow in the act of producing the packet because during it he had been trying to invent a remarkable comment upon the affair. He could conjure nothing of sufficient point. He was compelled to allow his friend to escape unmolested with his packet. And for this he took unto himself considerable credit. It was a generous thing.

His friend at his side seemed suffering great shame. As he contemplated him, the youth felt his heart grow more strong and stout. He had never been compelled to blush in such manner for his acts; he was an individual of extraordinary virtues.

He reflected, with condescending pity: "Too bad! Too bad! The poor devil, it makes him feel tough!"

After this incident, and as he reviewed the battle pictures he had seen, he felt quite competent to return home and make the hearts of the people glow with stories of war. He could see himself in a room of warm tints telling tales to listeners. He could exhibit laurels. They were insignificant; still, in a district where laurels were infrequent, they might shine.

He saw his gaping audience picturing him as the central figure in blazing scenes. And he imagined the consternation and the ejaculations of his mother and the young lady at the seminary as they drank his recitals. Their vague feminine formula for beloved ones doing brave deeds on the field of battle without risk of life would be destroyed.

CHAPTER XVI

A sputtering of musketry was always to be heard. Later, the cannon had entered the dispute. In the fog-filled air their voices made a thudding sound. The reverberations were continued. This part of the world led a strange, battleful existence.

The youth's regiment was marched to relieve a command that had lain long in some damp trenches. The men took positions behind a curving line of rifle pits that had been turned up, like a large furrow, along the line of woods. Before them was a level stretch, peopled with short, deformed stumps. From the woods beyond came the dull popping of the skirmishers and pickets, firing in the fog. From the right came the noise of a terrific fracas.

The men cuddled behind the small embankment and sat in easy attitudes awaiting their turn. Many had their backs to the firing. The youth's friend lay down, buried his face in his arms, and almost instantly, it seemed, he was in a deep sleep.

The youth leaned his breast against the brown dirt and peered over at the woods and up and down the line. Curtains of trees interfered with his ways of vision. He could see the low line of trenches but for a short distance. A few idle flags were perched on the dirt hills. Behind them were rows of dark bodies with a few heads sticking curiously over the top.

Always the noise of skirmishers came from the woods on the front and left, and the din on the right had grown to frightful proportions. The guns were roaring without an instant's pause for breath. It seemed that the cannon had come from all parts and were engaged in a stupendous wrangle. It became impossible to make a sentence heard.

The youth wished to launch a joke—a quotation from newspapers. He desired to say, "All quiet on the Rappahannock," but the guns refused to permit even a comment upon their uproar. He never successfully concluded the sentence. But at last the guns stopped, and among the men in the rifle pits rumors again flew, like birds, but they were now for the most part black creatures who flapped their wings drearily near to the ground and refused to rise on any wings of hope. The men's faces grew doleful from the interpreting of omens. Tales of hesitation and uncertainty on the part of those high in place and responsibility came to their ears. Stories of disaster were borne into their minds with many proofs. This din of musketry on the right, growing like a released genie of sound, expressed and emphasized the army's plight.

The men were disheartened and began to mutter. They made gestures expressive of the sentence: "Ah, what more can we do?" And it could always be seen that they were bewildered by the alleged news and could not fully comprehend a defeat.

Before the gray mists had been totally obliterated by the sun-rays, the regiment was marching in a spread column that was retiring carefully through the woods. The disordered, hurrying lines of the enemy could sometimes be seen down through the groves and little fields. They were yelling, shrill and exultant.

At this sight the youth forgot many personal matters and became greatly enraged. He exploded in loud sentences. "B'jiminey, we're generaled by a lot 'a lunkheads."

"More than one feller has said that t'-day," observed a man.

His friend, recently aroused, was still very drowsy. He looked behind him until his mind took in the meaning of the movement. Then he sighed. "Oh, well, I s'pose we got licked," he remarked sadly.

The youth had a thought that it would not be handsome for him to freely condemn other men. He made an attempt to restrain himself, but the words upon his tongue were too bitter. He presently began a long and intricate denunciation of the commander of the forces.

"Mebbe, it wa'n't all his fault—not all together. He did th' best he knowed. It's our luck t' git licked often," said his friend in a weary tone. He was trudging along with stooped shoulders and shifting eyes like a man who has been caned and kicked.

"Well, don't we fight like the devil? Don't we do all that men can?" demanded the youth loudly.

He was secretly dumbfounded at this sentiment when it came from his lips. For a moment his face lost its valor and he looked guiltily about him. But no one questioned his right to deal in such words, and presently he recovered his air of courage. He went on to repeat a statement he had heard going from group to group at the camp that morning. "The brigadier said he never saw a new reg'ment fight the way we fought yestirday, didn' he? And we didn't do better than any another reg'ment, did we? Well, then, you can't say it's th' army's fault, can you?"

In his reply, the friend's voice was stern. "'A course not," he said. "No man dare say we don't fight like th' devil. No man will ever dare say it. Th' boys fight like hell-roosters. But still—still, we don't have no luck."

"Well, then, if we fight like the devil an' don't ever whip, it must be the general's fault," said the youth grandly and decisively. "And I don't see any sense in fighting and fighting and fighting, yet always losing through some derned old lunkhead of a general."

A sarcastic man who was tramping at the youth's side then spoke lazily. "Mebbe yeh think yeh fit th' hull battle yestirday, Fleming," he remarked.

The speech pierced the youth. Inwardly he was reduced to an abject pulp by these chance words. His legs quaked privately. He cast a frightened glance at the sarcastic man.

"Why, no," he hastened to say in a conciliating voice, "I don't think I fought the whole battle yesterday."

But the other seemed innocent of any deeper meaning. Apparently, he had no information. It was merely his habit. "Oh!" he replied in the same tone of calm derision.

The youth, nevertheless, felt a threat. His mind shrank from going nearer to the danger, and thereafter he was silent. The significance of the sarcastic man's words took from him all loud moods that would make him appear prominent. He became suddenly a modest person.

There was low-toned talk among the troops. The officers were impatient and snappy, their countenances clouded with the tales of misfortune. The troops, sifting through the forest, were sullen. In the youth's company once a man's laugh rang out. A dozen soldiers turned their faces quickly toward him and frowned with vague displeasure.

The noise of firing dogged their footsteps. Sometimes, it seemed to be driven a little way, but it always returned again with increased insolence. The men muttered and cursed, throwing black looks in its direction.

In a clear space the troops were at last halted. Regiments and brigades, broken and detached through their encounters with thickets, grew together again and lines were faced toward the pursuing bark of the enemy's infantry.

This noise, following like the yellings of eager, metallic hounds, increased to a loud and joyous burst, and then, as the sun went serenely up the sky, throwing illuminating rays into the gloomy thickets, it broke forth into prolonged pealings. The woods began to crackle as if afire.

"Whoop-a-dadee," said a man, "here we are! Everybody fightin'. Blood an' destruction."

"I was willin' t' bet they'd attack as soon as th' sun got fairly up," savagely asserted the lieutenant who commanded the youth's company. He jerked without mercy at his little mustache. He strode to and fro with dark dignity in the rear of his men, who were lying down behind whatever protection they had collected.

A battery had trundled into position in the rear and was thoughtfully shelling the distance. The regiment, unmolested as yet, awaited the moment when the gray shadows of the woods before them should be slashed by the lines of flame. There was much growling and swearing.

"Good Gawd," the youth grumbled, "we're always being chased around like rats! It makes me sick. Nobody seems to know where we go or why we go. We just get fired around from pillar to post and get licked here and get licked there, and nobody knows what it's done for. It makes a man feel like a damn' kitten in a bag. Now, I'd like to know what the eternal thunders we was marched into these woods for anyhow, unless it was to give the rebs a regular pot shot at us. We came in here and got our legs all tangled up in these cussed briers, and then we begin to fight and the rebs had an easy time of it. Don't tell me it's just luck! I know better. It's this derned old—"

The friend seemed jaded, but he interrupted his comrade with a voice of calm confidence. "It'll turn out all right in th' end," he said.

"Oh, the devil it will! You always talk like a dog-hanged parson. Don't tell me! I know—"

At this time there was an interposition by the savage-minded lieutenant, who was obliged to vent some of his inward dissatisfaction upon his men. "You boys shut right up! There no need 'a your wastin' your breath in long-winded arguments about this an' that an' th' other. You've been jawin' like a lot 'a old hens. All you've got t' do is fight, an' you'll get plenty 'a that t' do in about ten minutes. Less talkin' an' more fightin' is what's best for you boys. I never saw sech gabbling jackasses."

He paused, ready to pounce upon any man who might have the temerity to reply. No words being said, he resumed his dignified pacing.

"There's too much chin music an' too little fightin' in this war, anyhow," he said to them, turning his head for a final remark.

The day had grown more white, until the sun shed its full radiance upon the thronged forest. A sort of a gust of battle came sweeping toward that part of the line where lay the youth's regiment. The front shifted a trifle to meet it squarely. There was a wait. In this part of the field there passed slowly the intense moments that precede the tempest.

A single rifle flashed in a thicket before the regiment. In an instant it was joined by many others. There was a mighty song of clashes and crashes that went sweeping through the woods. The guns in the rear, aroused and enraged by shells that had been thrown burr-like at them, suddenly involved themselves in a hideous altercation with another band of guns. The battle roar settled to a rolling thunder, which was a single long explosion.

In the regiment there was a peculiar kind of hesitation denoted in the attitudes of the men. They were worn, exhausted, having slept but little and labored much. They rolled their eyes toward the advancing battle as they stood awaiting the shock. Some shrank and flinched. They stood as men tied to stakes.

CHAPTER XVII

This advance of the enemy had seemed to the youth like a ruthless hunting. He began to fume with rage and exasperation. He beat his foot upon the ground, and scowled with hate at the swirling smoke that was approaching like a phantom flood. There was a maddening quality in this seeming resolution of the foe to give him no rest, to give him no time to sit down and think. Yesterday he had fought and had fled rapidly. There had been many adventures. For to-day he felt that he had earned opportunities for contemplative repose. He could have enjoyed portraying to uninitiated listeners various scenes at which he had been a witness or ably discussing the processes of war with other proved men. Too it was important that he should have time for physical recuperation. He was sore and stiff from his experiences. He had received his fill of all exertions, and he wished to rest.

But those other men seemed never to grow weary; they were fighting with their old speed. He had a wild hate for the relentless foe. Yesterday, when he had imagined the universe to be against him, he had hated it, little gods and big gods; to-day he hated the army of the foe with the same great hatred. He was not going to be badgered of his life, like a kitten chased by boys, he said. It was not well to drive men into final corners; at those moments they could all develop teeth and claws.

He leaned and spoke into his friend's ear. He menaced the woods with a gesture. "If they keep on chasing us, by Gawd, they'd better watch out. Can't stand *too* much."

The friend twisted his head and made a calm reply. "If they keep on a-chasin' us they'll drive us all inteh th' river."

The youth cried out savagely at this statement. He crouched behind a little tree, with his eyes burning hatefully and his teeth set in a curlike snarl. The awkward bandage was still about his head, and upon it, over his wound, there was a spot of dry blood. His hair was wondrously tousled, and some straggling, moving locks hung over the cloth of the bandage down toward his forehead. His jacket and shirt were open at the throat, and exposed his young bronzed neck. There could be seen spasmodic gulpings at his throat.

His fingers twined nervously about his rifle. He wished that it was an engine of annihilating power. He felt that he and his companions were being taunted and derided from sincere convictions that they were poor and puny. His knowledge of his inability to take vengeance for it made his rage into a dark and stormy specter, that possessed him and made him dream of abominable cruelties. The tormentors were flies sucking insolently at his blood, and he thought that he would have given his life for a revenge of seeing their faces in pitiful plights.

The winds of battle had swept all about the regiment, until the one rifle, instantly followed by others, flashed in its front. A moment later the regiment roared forth its sudden and valiant retort. A dense wall of smoke settled slowly down. It was furiously slit and slashed by the knifelike fire from the rifles.

To the youth the fighters resembled animals tossed for a death struggle into a dark pit. There was a sensation that he and his fellows, at bay, were pushing back, always pushing fierce onslaughts of creatures who were slippery. Their beams of crimson seemed to get no purchase upon the bodies of their foes; the latter seemed to evade them with ease, and come through, between, around, and about with unopposed skill.

When, in a dream, it occurred to the youth that his rifle was an impotent stick, he lost sense of everything but his hate, his desire to smash into pulp the glittering smile of victory which he could feel upon the faces of his enemies.

The blue smoke-swallowed line curled and writhed like a snake stepped upon. It swung its ends to and fro in an agony of fear and rage.

The youth was not conscious that he was erect upon his feet. He did not know the direction of the ground. Indeed, once he even lost the habit of balance and fell heavily. He was up again immediately. One thought went through the chaos of his brain at the time. He wondered if he had fallen because he had been shot. But the suspicion flew away at once. He did not think more of it.

He had taken up a first position behind the little tree, with a direct determination to hold it against the world. He had not deemed it possible that his army could that day succeed, and from this he felt the ability to fight harder. But the throng had surged in all ways, until he lost directions and locations, save that he knew where lay the enemy.

The flames bit him, and the hot smoke broiled his skin. His rifle barrel grew so hot that ordinarily he could not have borne it upon his palms; but he kept on stuffing cartridges into it, and pounding them with his clanking, bending ramrod. If he aimed at some changing form through the smoke, he pulled his trigger with a fierce grunt, as if he were dealing a blow of the fist with all his strength.

When the enemy seemed falling back before him and his fellows, he went instantly forward, like a dog who, seeing his foes lagging, turns and insists upon being pursued. And when he was compelled to retire again, he did it slowly, sullenly, taking steps of wrathful despair.

Once he, in his intent hate, was almost alone, and was firing, when all those near him had ceased. He was so engrossed in his occupation that he was not aware of a lull.

He was recalled by a hoarse laugh and a sentence that came to his ears in a voice of contempt and amazement. "Yeh infernal fool, don't yeh know enough t' quit when there ain't anything t' shoot at? Good Gawd!"

He turned then and, pausing with his rifle thrown half into position, looked at the blue line of his comrades. During this moment of leisure they seemed all to be engaged in staring with astonishment at him. They had become spectators. Turning to the front again he saw, under the lifted smoke, a deserted ground.

He looked bewildered for a moment. Then there appeared upon the glazed vacancy of his eyes a diamond point of intelligence. "Oh," he said, comprehending.

He returned to his comrades and threw himself upon the ground. He sprawled like a man who had been thrashed. His flesh seemed strangely on fire, and the sounds of the battle continued in his ears. He groped blindly for his canteen.

The lieutenant was crowing. He seemed drunk with fighting. He called out to the youth: "By heavens, if I had ten thousand wild cats like you I could tear th' stomach outa this war in less'n a week!" He puffed out his chest with large dignity as he said it.

Some of the men muttered and looked at the youth in awe-struck ways. It was plain that as he had gone on loading and firing and cursing without the proper intermission, they had found time to regard him. And they now looked upon him as a war devil.

The friend came staggering to him. There was some fright and dismay in his voice. "Are yeh all right, Fleming? Do yeh feel all right? There ain't nothin' th' matter with yeh, Henry, is there?"

"No," said the youth with difficulty. His throat seemed full of knobs and burrs.

These incidents made the youth ponder. It was revealed to him that he had been a barbarian, a beast. He had fought like a pagan who defends his religion. Regarding it, he saw that it was fine, wild, and, in some ways, easy. He had been a tremendous figure, no doubt. By this struggle he had overcome obstacles which he had admitted to be mountains. They had fallen like paper peaks, and he was now what he called a hero. And he had not been aware of the process. He had slept and, awakening, found himself a knight.

He lay and basked in the occasional stares of his comrades. Their faces were varied in degrees of blackness from the burned powder. Some were utterly smudged. They were reeking with perspiration, and their breaths came hard and wheezing. And from these soiled expanses they peered at him.

"Hot work! Hot work!" cried the lieutenant deliriously. He walked up and down, restless and eager. Sometimes his voice could be heard in a wild, incomprehensible laugh.

When he had a particularly profound thought upon the science of war he always unconsciously addressed himself to the youth.

There was some grim rejoicing by the men. "By thunder, I bet this army'll never see another new reg'ment like us!"

"You bet!

"A dog, a woman, an' a walnut tree,
Th' more yeh beat 'em, th' better they be!

That's like us."

"Lost a piler men, they did. If an ol' woman swep' up th' woods she'd git a dustpanful."

"Yes, an' if she'll come around ag'in in 'bout an hour she'll git a pile more."

The forest still bore its burden of clamor. From off under the trees came the rolling clatter of the musketry. Each distant thicket seemed a strange porcupine with quills of flame. A cloud of dark smoke, as from smoldering ruins, went up toward the sun now bright and gay in the blue-enameled sky.

CHAPTER XVIII

The ragged line had respite for some minutes, but during its pause the struggle in the forest became magnified until the trees seemed to quiver from the firing and the ground to shake from the rushing of the men. The voices of the cannon were mingled in a long and interminable row. It seemed difficult to live in such an atmosphere. The chests of the men strained for a bit of freshness, and their throats craved water.

There was one shot through the body, who raised a cry of bitter lamentation when came this lull. Perhaps he had been calling out during the fighting also, but at that time no one had heard him. But now the men turned at the woeful complaints of him upon the ground.

"Who is it? Who is it?"

"It's Jimmie Rogers. Jimmie Rogers."

When their eyes first encountered him there was a sudden halt, as if they feared to go near. He was thrashing about in the grass, twisting his shuddering body into many strange postures. He was screaming loudly. This instant's hesitation seemed to fill him with a tremendous, fantastic contempt, and he damned them in shrieked sentences.

The youth's friend had a geographical illusion concerning a stream, and he obtained permission to go for some water. Immediately canteens were showered upon him. "Fill mine, will yeh?" "Bring me some, too." "And me, too." He departed, laden. The youth went with his friend, feeling a desire to throw his heated body onto the stream and, soaking there, drink quarts.

They made a hurried search for the supposed stream but did not find it. "No water here," said the youth. They turned without delay and began to retrace their steps.

From their position as they again faced toward the place of the fighting, they could of course comprehend a greater amount of the battle than when their visions had been blurred by the hurling smoke of the line. They could see dark stretches winding along the land, and on one cleared space there was a row of guns making gray clouds, which were filled with large flashes of orange-colored flame. Over some foliage they could see the roof of a house. One window, glowing a deep murder red, shone squarely through the leaves. From the edifice a tall leaning tower of smoke went far into the sky.

Looking over their own troops, they saw mixed masses slowly getting into regular form. The sunlight made twinkling points of the bright steel. To the rear there was a glimpse of a distant roadway as it curved over a slope. It was crowded with retreating infantry. From all the interwoven forest arose the smoke and bluster of the battle. The air was always occupied by a blaring.

Near where they stood shells were flip-flapping and hooting. Occasional bullets buzzed in the air and spanged into tree trunks. Wounded men and other stragglers were slinking through the woods.

Looking down an aisle of the grove, the youth and his companion saw a jangling general and his staff almost ride upon a wounded man who was crawling on his hands and knees. The general reined strongly at his charger's opened and foamy mouth and guided it with dexterous horsemanship past the man. The latter scrambled in wild and torturing haste. His strength evidently failed him as he reached a place of safety. One of his arms suddenly weakened, and he fell, sliding over upon his back. He lay stretched out, breathing gently.

A moment later the small, creaking cavalcade was directly in front of the two soldiers. Another officer, riding with the skillful abandon of a cowboy, galloped his horse to a position directly before the general. The two unnoticed foot soldiers made a little show of going on, but they lingered near in the desire to overhear the conversation. Perhaps, they thought, some great inner historical things would be said.

The general, whom the boys knew as the commander of their division, looked at the other officer and spoke coolly, as if he were criticizing his clothes. "Th' enemy's formin' over there for another charge," he said. "It'll be directed against Whiterside, an' I fear they'll break through there unless we work like thunder t' stop them."

The other swore at his restive horse, and then cleared his throat. He made a gesture toward his cap. "It'll be hell t' pay stoppin' them," he said shortly.

"I presume so," remarked the general. Then he began to talk rapidly and in a lower tone. He frequently illustrated his words with a pointing finger. The two infantrymen could hear nothing until finally he asked: "What troops can you spare?"

The officer who rode like a cowboy reflected for an instant. "Well," he said, "I had to order in th' 12th to help th' 76th, an' I haven't really got any. But there's th' 304th. They fight like a lot 'a mule drivers. I can spare them best of any."

The youth and his friend exchanged glances of astonishment.

The general spoke sharply. "Get 'em ready, then. I'll watch developments from here, an' send you word when t' start them. It'll happen in five minutes."

As the other officer tossed his fingers toward his cap and, wheeling his horse, started away, the general called out to him in a sober voice: "I don't believe many of your mule drivers will get back."

The other shouted something in reply. He smiled.

With scared faces, the youth and his companion hurried back to the line.

These happenings had occupied an incredibly short time, yet the youth felt that in them he had been made aged. New eyes were given to him. And the most startling thing was to learn suddenly that he was very insignificant. The officer spoke of the regiment as if he referred to a broom. Some part of the woods needed sweeping, perhaps, and he merely indicated a broom in a tone properly indifferent to its fate. It was war, no doubt, but it appeared strange.

As the two boys approached the line, the lieutenant perceived them and swelled with wrath. "Fleming—Wilson—how long does it take yeh to git water, anyhow—where yeh been to?"

But his oration ceased as he saw their eyes, which were large with great tales. "We're goin' t' charge—we're goin' t' charge!" cried the youth's friend, hastening with his news.

"Charge?" said the lieutenant. "Charge? Well, b'Gawd! Now; this is real fightin'." Over his soiled countenance there went a boastful smile. "Charge? Well, b'Gawd!"

A little group of soldiers surrounded the two youths. "Are we, sure 'nough? Well, I'll be derned! Charge? What fer? What at? Wilson, you're lyin'."

"I hope to die," said the youth's friend, pitching his tones to the key of angry remonstrance. "Sure as shooting, I tell you."

And the youth spoke in re-enforcement. "Not by a blame sight, he ain't lyin'. We heard 'em talkin'."

They caught sight of two mounted figures a short distance from them. One was the colonel of the regiment and the other was the officer who had received orders from the commander of the division. They were gesticulating at each other. The soldier, pointing at them, interpreted the scene.

One man had a final objection: "How could yeh hear 'em talkin'?" But the men, for a large part, nodded, admitting that previously the two friends had spoken truth.

They settled back into reposeful attitudes with airs of having accepted the matter. And they mused upon it, with a hundred varieties of expression. It was an engrossing thing to think about. Many tightened their belts carefully and hitched at their trousers.

A moment later the officers began to bustle among the men, pushing them into a more compact mass and into a better alignment. They chased those that straggled and fumed at a few men who seemed to show by their attitudes that they had decided to remain at the spot. They were like critical shepherds struggling with sheep.

Presently, the regiment seemed to draw itself up and heave a deep breath. None of the men's faces were mirrors of large thoughts. The soldiers were bended and stooped like sprinters before a signal. Many pairs of glinting eyes peered from the grimy faces toward the curtains of the deeper woods. They seemed to be engaged in deep calculations of time and distance.

They were surrounded by the noises of the monstrous altercation between the two armies. The world was fully interested in other matters. Apparently, the regiment had its small affair to itself.

The youth, turning, shot a quick, inquiring glance at his friend. The latter returned to him the same manner of look. They were the only ones who possessed an inner knowledge. "Mule drivers—hell t' pay—don't believe many will get back." It was an ironical secret. Still, they saw no hesitation in each other's faces, and they nodded a mute and unprotesting assent when a shaggy man near them said in a meek voice: "We'll git swallowed."

CHAPTER XIX

The youth stared at the land in front of him. Its foliage now seemed to veil powers and horrors. He was unaware of the machinery of orders that started the charge, although from the corners of his eyes he saw an officer, who looked like a boy a-horseback, come galloping, waving his hat. Suddenly he felt a straining and heaving among the men. The line fell slowly forward like a toppling wall, and, with a convulsive gasp that was intended for a cheer, the regiment began its journey. The youth was pushed and jostled for a moment before he understood the movement at all, but directly he lunged ahead and began to run.

He fixed his eye upon a distant and prominent clump of trees where he had concluded the enemy were to be met, and he ran toward it as toward a goal. He had believed throughout that it was a mere question of getting over an unpleasant matter as quickly as possible, and he ran desperately, as if pursued for a murder. His face was drawn hard and tight with the stress of his endeavor. His eyes were fixed in a lurid glare. And with his soiled and disordered dress, his red and inflamed features surmounted by the dingy rag with its spot of blood, his wildly swinging rifle and banging accouterments, he looked to be an insane soldier.

As the regiment swung from its position out into a cleared space the woods and thickets before it awakened. Yellow flames leaped toward it from many directions. The forest made a tremendous objection.

The line lurched straight for a moment. Then the right wing swung forward; it in turn was surpassed by the left. Afterward the center careered to the front until the regiment was a wedge-shaped mass, but an instant later the opposition of the bushes, trees, and uneven places on the ground split the command and scattered it into detached clusters.

The youth, light-footed, was unconsciously in advance. His eyes still kept note of the clump of trees. From all places near it the clannish yell of the enemy could be heard. The little flames of rifles leaped from it. The song of the bullets was in the air and shells snarled among the tree-tops. One tumbled directly into the middle of a hurrying group and exploded in crimson fury. There was an instant's spectacle of a man, almost over it, throwing up his hands to shield his eyes.

Other men, punched by bullets, fell in grotesque agonies. The regiment left a coherent trail of bodies.

They had passed into a clearer atmosphere. There was an effect like a revelation in the new appearance of the landscape. Some men working madly at a battery were plain to them, and the opposing infantry's lines were defined by the gray walls and fringes of smoke.

It seemed to the youth that he saw everything. Each blade of the green grass was bold and clear. He thought that he was aware of every change in the thin, transparent vapor that floated idly in sheets. The brown or gray trunks of the trees showed each roughness of their surfaces. And the men of the regiment, with their starting eyes and sweating faces, running madly, or falling, as if thrown headlong, to queer, heaped-up corpses—all were comprehended. His mind took a mechanical but firm impression, so that afterward everything was pictured and explained to him, save why he himself was there.

But there was a frenzy made from this furious rush. The men, pitching forward insanely, had burst into cheerings, moblike and barbaric, but tuned in strange keys that can arouse the dullard and the stoic. It made a mad enthusiasm that, it seemed, would be incapable of checking itself before granite and brass. There was the delirium that encounters despair and death, and is heedless and blind to the odds. It is a temporary but sublime absence of selfishness. And because it was of this order was the reason, perhaps, why the youth wondered, afterward, what reasons he could have had for being there.

Presently the straining pace ate up the energies of the men. As if by agreement, the leaders began to slacken their speed. The volleys directed against them had had a seeming windlike effect. The regiment snorted and blew. Among some stolid trees it began to falter and hesitate. The men, staring intently, began to wait for some of the distant walls of smoke to move and disclose to them the scene. Since much of their strength and their breath had vanished, they returned to caution. They were become men again.

The youth had a vague belief that he had run miles, and he thought, in a way, that he was now in some new and unknown land.

The moment the regiment ceased its advance the protesting splutter of musketry became a steadied roar. Long and accurate fringes of smoke spread out. From the top of a small hill came level belchings of yellow flame that caused an inhuman whistling in the air.

The men halted, had opportunity to see some of their comrades dropping with moans and shrieks. A few lay under foot, still or wailing. And now for an instant the men stood, their rifles slack in their hands, and watched the regiment dwindle. They appeared dazed and stupid. This spectacle seemed to paralyze them, overcome them with a fatal fascination. They stared woodenly at the sights, and, lowering their eyes, looked from face to face. It was a strange pause, and a strange silence.

Then, above the sounds of the outside commotion, arose the roar of the lieutenant. He strode suddenly forth, his infantile features black with rage.

"Come on, yeh fools!" he bellowed. "Come on! Yeh can't stay here. Yeh must come on." He said more, but much of it could not be understood.

He started rapidly forward, with his head turned toward the men. "Come on," he was shouting. The men stared with blank and yokel-like eyes at him. He was obliged to halt and retrace his steps. He stood then with his back to the enemy and delivered gigantic curses into the faces of the men. His body vibrated from the weight and force of his imprecations. And he could string oaths with the facility of a maiden who strings beads.

The friend of the youth aroused. Lurching suddenly forward and dropping to his knees, he fired an angry shot at the persistent woods. This action awakened the men. They huddled no more like sheep. They seemed suddenly to bethink them of their weapons, and at once commenced firing. Belabored by their officers, they began to move forward. The regiment, involved like a cart involved in mud and muddle, started unevenly with many jolts and jerks. The men stopped now every few paces to fire and load, and in this manner moved slowly on from trees to trees.

The flaming opposition in their front grew with their advance until it seemed that all forward ways were barred by the thin leaping tongues, and off to the right an ominous demonstration could sometimes be dimly discerned. The smoke lately generated was in confusing clouds that made it difficult for the regiment to proceed with intelligence. As he passed through each curling mass the youth wondered what would confront him on the farther side.

The command went painfully forward until an open space interposed between them and the lurid lines. Here, crouching and cowering behind some trees, the men clung with desperation, as if threatened by a wave. They looked wild-eyed, and as if amazed at this furious disturbance they had stirred. In the storm there was an ironical expression of their importance. The faces of the men, too, showed a lack of a certain feeling of responsibility for being there. It was as if they had been driven. It was the dominant animal failing to remember in the supreme moments the forceful causes of various superficial qualities. The whole affair seemed incomprehensible to many of them.

As they halted thus the lieutenant again began to bellow profanely. Regardless of the vindictive threats of the bullets, he went about coaxing, berating, and bedamning. His lips, that were habitually in a soft and childlike curve, were now writhed into unholy contortions. He swore by all possible deities.

Once he grabbed the youth by the arm. "Come on, yeh lunkhead!" he roared. "Come on! We'll all git killed if we stay here. We've on'y got t' go across that lot. An' then"—the remainder of his idea disappeared in a blue haze of curses.

The youth stretched forth his arm. "Cross there?" His mouth was puckered in doubt and awe.

"Certainly. Jest 'cross th' lot! We can't stay here," screamed the lieutenant. He poked his face close to the youth and waved his bandaged hand. "Come on!" Presently he grappled with him as if for a wrestling bout. It was as if he planned to drag the youth by the ear on to the assault.

The private felt a sudden unspeakable indignation against his officer. He wrenched fiercely and shook him off.

"Come on yerself, then," he yelled. There was a bitter challenge in his voice.

They galloped together down the regimental front. The friend scrambled after them. In front of the colors the three men began to bawl: "Come on! come on!" They danced and gyrated like tortured savages.

The flag, obedient to these appeals, bended its glittering form and swept toward them. The men wavered in indecision for a moment, and then with a long, wailful cry the dilapidated regiment surged forward and began its new journey.

Over the field went the scurrying mass. It was a handful of men splattered into the faces of the enemy. Toward it instantly sprang the yellow tongues. A vast quantity of blue smoke hung before them. A mighty banging made ears valueless.

The youth ran like a madman to reach the woods before a bullet could discover him. He ducked his head low, like a football player. In his haste his eyes almost closed, and the scene was a wild blur. Pulsating saliva stood at the corners of his mouth.

Within him, as he hurled himself forward, was born a love, a despairing fondness for this flag which was near him. It was a creation of beauty and invulnerability. It was a goddess, radiant, that bended its form with an imperious gesture to him. It was a woman, red and white, hating and loving, that called him with the voice of his hopes. Because no harm could come to it he endowed it with power. He kept near, as if it could be a saver of lives, and an imploring cry went from his mind.

In the mad scramble he was aware that the color sergeant flinched suddenly, as if struck by a bludgeon. He faltered, and then became motionless, save for his quivering knees.

He made a spring and a clutch at the pole. At the same instant his friend grabbed it from the other side. They jerked at it, stout and furious, but the color sergeant was dead, and the corpse would not relinquish its trust. For a moment there was a grim encounter. The dead man, swinging with bended back, seemed to be obstinately tugging, in ludicrous and awful ways, for the possession of the flag.

It was past in an instant of time. They wrenched the flag furiously from the dead man, and, as they turned again, the corpse swayed forward with bowed head. One arm swung high, and the curved hand fell with heavy protest on the friend's unheeding shoulder.

CHAPTER XX

When the two youths turned with the flag they saw that much of the regiment had crumbled away, and the dejected remnant was coming back. The men, having hurled themselves in projectile fashion, had presently expended their forces. They slowly retreated, with their faces still toward the spluttering woods, and their hot rifles still replying to the din. Several officers were giving orders, their voices keyed to screams.

"Where in hell yeh goin'?" the lieutenant was asking in a sarcastic howl. And a red-bearded officer, whose voice of triple brass could plainly be heard, was commanding: "Shoot into 'em! Shoot into 'em, Gawd damn their souls!" There was a *mêlée* of screeches, in which the men were ordered to do conflicting and impossible things.

The youth and his friend had a small scuffle over the flag. "Give it t' me!" "No, let me keep it!" Each felt satisfied with the other's possession of it, but each felt bound to declare, by an offer to carry the emblem, his willingness to further risk himself. The youth roughly pushed his friend away.

The regiment fell back to the stolid trees. There it halted for a moment to blaze at some dark forms that had begun to steal upon its track. Presently it resumed its march again, curving among the tree trunks. By the time the depleted regiment had again reached the first open space they were receiving a fast and merciless fire. There seemed to be mobs all about them.

The greater part of the men, discouraged, their spirits worn by the turmoil acted as if stunned. They accepted the pelting of the bullets with bowed and weary heads. It was of no purpose to strive against walls. It was of no use to batter themselves against granite. And from this consciousness that they had attempted to conquer an unconquerable thing there seemed to arise a feeling that they had been betrayed. They glowered with bent brows, but dangerously, upon some of the officers, more particularly upon the red-bearded one with the voice of triple brass.

However, the rear of the regiment was fringed with men, who continued to shoot irritably at the advancing foes. They seemed resolved to make every trouble. The youthful lieutenant was perhaps the last man in the disordered mass. His forgotten back was toward the enemy. He had been shot in the arm. It hung straight and rigid. Occasionally he would cease to remember it, and be about to emphasize an oath with a sweeping gesture. The multiplied pain caused him to swear with incredible power.

The youth went along with slipping, uncertain feet. He kept watchful eyes rearward. A scowl of mortification and rage was upon his face. He had thought of a fine revenge upon the officer who had referred to him and his fellows as mule drivers. But he saw that it could not come to pass. His dreams had collapsed when the mule drivers, dwindling rapidly, had wavered and hesitated on the little clearing, and then had recoiled. And now the retreat of the mule drivers was a march of shame to him.

A dagger-pointed gaze from without his blackened face was held toward the enemy, but his greater hatred was riveted upon the man, who, not knowing him, had called him a mule driver.

When he knew that he and his comrades had failed to do anything in successful ways that might bring the little pangs of a kind of remorse upon the officer, the youth allowed the rage of the baffled to possess him. This cold officer upon a monument, who dropped epithets unconcernedly down, would be finer as a dead man, he thought. So grievous did he think it that he could never possess the secret right to taunt truly in answer.

He had pictured red letters of curious revenge. "We *are* mule drivers, are we?" And now he was compelled to throw them away.

He presently wrapped his head in the cloak of his pride and kept the flag erect. He harangued his fellows, pushing against their chests with his free hand. To those he knew well he made frantic appeals, beseeching them by name. Between him and the lieutenant, scolding and near to losing his mind with rage, there was felt a subtle fellowship and equality. They supported each other in all manner of hoarse, howling protests.

But the regiment was a machine run down. The two men babbled at a forceless thing. The soldiers who had heart to go slowly were continually shaken in their resolves by a knowledge that comrades were slipping with speed back to the lines. It was difficult to think of reputation when others were thinking of skins. Wounded men were left crying on this black journey.

The smoke fringes and flames blustered always. The youth, peering once through a sudden rift in a cloud, saw a brown mass of troops, interwoven and magnified until they appeared to be thousands. A fierce-hued flag flashed before his vision.

Immediately, as if the uplifting of the smoke had been prearranged, the discovered troops burst into a rasping yell, and a hundred flames jetted toward the retreating band. A rolling gray cloud again interposed as the regiment doggedly replied. The youth had to depend again upon his misused ears, which were trembling and buzzing from the *mêlée* of musketry and yells.

The way seemed eternal. In the clouded haze men became panicstricken with the thought that the regiment had lost its path, and was proceeding in a perilous direction. Once the men who headed the wild procession turned and came pushing back against their comrades, screaming that they were being fired upon from points which they had considered to be toward their own lines. At this cry a hysterical fear and dismay beset the troops. A soldier, who heretofore had been ambitious to make the regiment into a wise little band that would proceed calmly amid the huge-appearing difficulties, suddenly sank down and buried his face in his arms with an air of bowing to a doom. From another a shrill lamentation rang out filled with profane allusions to a general. Men ran hither and thither, seeking with their eyes roads of escape. With serene regularity, as if controlled by a schedule, bullets buffed into men.

The youth walked stolidly into the midst of the mob, and with his flag in his hands took a stand as if he expected an attempt to push him to the ground. He unconsciously assumed the attitude of the color bearer in the fight of the preceding day. He passed over his brow a hand that trembled. His breath did not come freely. He was choking during this small wait for the crisis.

His friend came to him. "Well, Henry, I guess this is good-by—John."

"Oh, shut up, you damned fool!" replied the youth, and he would not look at the other.

The officers labored like politicians to beat the mass into a proper circle to face the menaces. The ground was uneven and torn. The men curled into depressions and fitted themselves snugly behind whatever would frustrate a bullet.

The youth noted with vague surprise that the lieutenant was standing mutely with his legs far apart and his sword held in the manner of a cane. The youth wondered what had happened to his vocal organs that he no more cursed. There was something curious in this little intent pause of the lieutenant. He was like a babe which, having wept its fill, raises its eyes and fixes them upon a distant toy. He was engrossed in this contemplation, and the soft underlip quivered from self-whispered words.

Some lazy and ignorant smoke curled slowly. The men, hiding from the bullets, waited anxiously for it to lift and disclose the plight of the regiment.

The silent ranks were suddenly thrilled by the eager voice of the youthful lieutenant bawling out: "Here they come! Right on to us, b'Gawd!" His further words were lost in a roar of wicked thunder from the men's rifles.

The youth's eyes had instantly turned in the direction indicated by the awakened and agitated lieutenant, and he had seen the haze of treachery disclosing a body of soldiers of the enemy. They were so near that he could see their features. There was a recognition as he looked at the types of faces. Also he perceived with dim amazement that their uniforms were rather gay in effect, being light gray, accented with a brilliant-hued facing. Moreover, the clothes seemed new.

These troops had apparently been going forward with caution, their rifles held in readiness, when the youthful lieutenant had discovered them and their movement had been interrupted by the volley from the blue regiment. From the moment's glimpse, it was derived that they had been unaware of the proximity of their dark-suited foes or had mistaken the direction. Almost instantly they were shut utterly from the youth's sight by the smoke from the energetic rifles of his companions. He strained his vision to learn the accomplishment of the volley, but the smoke hung before him.

The two bodies of troops exchanged blows in the manner of a pair of boxers. The fast angry firings went back and forth. The men in blue were intent with the despair of their circumstances and they seized upon the revenge to be had at close range. Their thunder swelled loud and valiant. Their curving front bristled with flashes and the place resounded with the clangor of their ramrods. The youth ducked and dodged for a time and achieved a few unsatisfactory views of the enemy. There appeared to be many of them and they were replying swiftly. They seemed moving toward the blue regiment, step by step. He seated himself gloomily on the ground with his flag between his knees.

As he noted the vicious, wolflike temper of his comrades he had a sweet thought that if the enemy was about to swallow the regimental broom as a large prisoner, it could at least have the consolation of going down with bristles forward.

But the blows of the antagonist began to grow more weak. Fewer bullets ripped the air, and finally, when the men slackened to learn of the fight, they could see only dark, floating smoke. The regiment lay still and gazed. Presently some chance whim came to the pestering blur, and it began to coil heavily away. The men saw a ground vacant of fighters. It would have been an empty stage if it were not for a few corpses that lay thrown and twisted into fantastic shapes upon the sward.

At sight of this tableau, many of the men in blue sprang from behind their covers and made an ungainly dance of joy. Their eyes burned and a hoarse cheer of elation broke from their dry lips.

It had begun to seem to them that events were trying to prove that they were impotent. These little battles had evidently endeavored to demonstrate that the men could not fight well. When on the verge of submission to these opinions, the small duel had showed them that the proportions were not impossible, and by it they had revenged themselves upon their misgivings and upon the foe.

The impetus of enthusiasm was theirs again. They gazed about them with looks of uplifted pride, feeling new trust in the grim, always confident weapons in their hands. And they were men.

CHAPTER XXI

Presently they knew that no fighting threatened them. All ways seemed once more opened to them. The dusty blue lines of their friends were disclosed a short distance away. In the distance there were many colossal noises, but in all this part of the field there was a sudden stillness.

They perceived that they were free. The depleted band drew a long breath of relief and gathered itself into a bunch to complete its trip.

In this last length of journey the men began to show strange emotions. They hurried with nervous fear. Some who had been dark and unfaltering in the grimmest moments now could not conceal an anxiety that made them frantic. It was perhaps that they dreaded to be killed in insignificant ways after the times for proper military deaths had passed. Or, perhaps, they thought it would be too ironical to get killed at the portals of safety. With backward looks of perturbation, they hastened.

As they approached their own lines there was some sarcasm exhibited on the part of a gaunt and bronzed regiment that lay resting in the shade of trees. Questions were wafted to them.

"Where th' hell yeh been?"
"What yeh comin' back fer?"
"Why didn't yeh stay there?"
"Was it warm out there, sonny?"
"Goin' home now, boys?"

One shouted in taunting mimicry: "Oh, mother, come quick an' look at th' so'jers!"

There was no reply from the bruised and battered regiment, save that one man made broadcast challenges to fist fights and the red-bearded officer walked rather near and glared in great swashbuckler style at a tall captain in the other regiment. But the lieutenant suppressed the man who wished to fist fight, and the tall captain, flushing at the little fanfare of the red-bearded one, was obliged to look intently at some trees.

The youth's tender flesh was deeply stung by these remarks. From under his creased brows he glowered with hate at the mockers. He meditated upon a few revenges. Still, many in the regiment hung their heads in criminal fashion, so that it came to pass that the men trudged with sudden heaviness, as if they bore upon their bended shoulders the coffin of their honor. And the youthful lieutenant, recollecting himself, began to mutter softly in black curses.

They turned when they arrived at their old position to regard the ground over which they had charged.

The youth in this contemplation was smitten with a large astonishment. He discovered that the distances, as compared with the brilliant measurings of his mind, were trivial and ridiculous. The stolid trees, where much had taken place, seemed incredibly near. The time, too, now that he reflected, he saw to have been short. He wondered at the number of emotions and events that had been crowded into such little spaces. Elfin thoughts must have exaggerated and enlarged everything, he said.

It seemed, then, that there was bitter justice in the speeches of the gaunt and bronzed veterans. He veiled a glance of disdain at his fellows who strewed the ground, choking with dust, red from perspiration, misty-eyed, disheveled.

They were gulping at their canteens, fierce to wring every mite of water from them, and they polished at their swollen and watery features with coat sleeves and bunches of grass.

However, to the youth there was a considerable joy in musing upon his performances during the charge. He had had very little time previously in which to appreciate himself, so that there was now much satisfaction in quietly thinking of his actions. He recalled bits of color that in the flurry had stamped themselves unawares upon his engaged senses.

As the regiment lay heaving from its hot exertions the officer who had named them as mule drivers came galloping along the line. He had lost his cap. His tousled hair streamed wildly, and his face was dark with vexation and wrath. His temper was displayed with more clearness by the way in which he managed his horse. He jerked and wrenched savagely at his bridle, stopping the hard-breathing animal with a furious pull near the colonel of the regiment. He immediately exploded in reproaches which came unbidden to the ears of the men. They were suddenly alert, being always curious about black words between officers.

"Oh, thunder, MacChesnay, what an awful bull you made of this thing!" began the officer. He attempted low tones, but his indignation caused certain of the men to learn the sense of his words. "What an awful mess you made! Good Lord, man, you stopped a hundred feet this side of a very pretty success! If your men had gone a hundred feet farther you would have made a great charge, but as it is—what a lot of mud diggers you've got anyway!"

The men, listening with bated breath, now turned their curious eyes upon the colonel. They had a ragamuffin interest in this affair.

The colonel was seen to straighten his form and put one hand forth in oratorical fashion. He wore an injured air; it was as if a deacon had been accused of stealing. The men were wiggling in an ecstasy of excitement.

But of a sudden the colonel's manner changed from that of a deacon to that of a Frenchman. He shrugged his shoulders. "Oh, well, general, we went as far as we could," he said calmly.

"As far as you could? Did you, b'Gawd?" snorted the other. "Well, that wasn't very far, was it?" he added, with a glance of cold contempt into the other's eyes. "Not very far, I think. You were intended to make a diversion in favor of Whiterside. How well you succeeded your own ears can now tell you." He wheeled his horse and rode stiffly away.

The colonel, bidden to hear the jarring noises of an engagement in the woods to the left, broke out in vague damnations.

The lieutenant, who had listened with an air of impotent rage to the interview, spoke suddenly in firm and undaunted tones. "I don't care what a man is—whether he is a general or what—if he says th' boys didn't put up a good fight out there he's a damned fool."

"Lieutenant," began the colonel, severely, "this is my own affair, and I'll trouble you—"

The lieutenant made an obedient gesture. "All right, colonel, all right," he said. He sat down with an air of being content with himself.

The news that the regiment had been reproached went along the line. For a time the men were bewildered by it. "Good thunder!" they ejaculated, staring at the vanishing form of the general. They conceived it to be a huge mistake.

Presently, however, they began to believe that in truth their efforts had been called light. The youth could see this conviction weigh upon the entire regiment until the men were like cuffed and cursed animals, but withal rebellious.

The friend, with a grievance in his eye, went to the youth. "I wonder what he does want," he said. "He must think we went out there an' played marbles! I never see sech a man!"

The youth developed a tranquil philosophy for these moments of irritation. "Oh, well," he rejoined, "he probably didn't see nothing of it at all and got mad as blazes, and concluded we were a lot of sheep, just because we didn't do what he wanted done. It's a pity old Grandpa Henderson got killed yesterday—he'd have known that we did our best and fought good. It's just our awful luck, that's what."

"I should say so," replied the friend. He seemed to be deeply wounded at an injustice. "I should say we did have awful luck! There's no fun in fightin' fer people when everything yeh do—no matter what—ain't done right. I have a notion t' stay behind next time an' let 'em take their ol' charge an' go t' th' devil with it."

The youth spoke soothingly to his comrade. "Well, we both did good. I'd like to see the fool what'd say we both didn't do as good as we could!"

"Of course we did," declared the friend stoutly. "An' I'd break th' feller's neck if he was as big as a church. But we're all right, anyhow, for I heard one feller say that we two fit th' best in th' reg'ment, an' they had a great argument 'bout it. Another feller, 'a course, he had t' up an' say it was a lie—he seen all what was goin' on an' he never seen us from th' beginnin' t' th' end. An' a lot more struck in an' ses it wasn't a lie—we did fight like thunder, an' they give us quite a send-off. But this is what I can't stand—these everlastin' ol' soldiers, titterin' an' laughin', an' then that general, he's crazy."

The youth exclaimed with sudden exasperation: "He's a lunkhead! He makes me mad. I wish he'd come along next time. We'd show 'im what—"

He ceased because several men had come hurrying up. Their faces expressed a bringing of great news.

"O Flem, yeh jest oughta heard!" cried one, eagerly.

"Heard what?" said the youth.

"Yeh jest oughta heard!" replied the other, and he arranged himself to tell his tidings. The others made an excited circle. "Well, sir, th' colonel met your lieutenant right by us—it was damnedest thing I ever heard—an' he ses: 'Ahem! ahem!' he ses. 'Mr. Hasbrouck!' he ses, 'by th' way, who was that lad what carried th' flag?' he ses. There, Flemin', what d' yeh think 'a that? 'Who was th' lad what carried th' flag?' he ses, an' th' lieutenant, he speaks up right away: 'That's Flemin', an' he's a jimhickey,' he ses, right away. What? I say he did. 'A jimhickey,' he ses—those 'r his words. He did, too. I say he did. If you kin tell this story better than I kin, go ahead an' tell it. Well, then, keep yer mouth shet. Th' lieutenant, he ses: 'He's a jimhickey,' an' th' colonel, he ses: 'Ahem! ahem! he is, indeed, a very good man t' have, ahem! He kep' th' flag 'way t' th' front. I saw 'im. He's a good un,' ses th' colonel. 'You bet,' ses th' lieutenant, 'he an' a feller named Wilson was at th' head 'a th' charge, an' howlin' like Indians all th' time,' he ses. 'Head 'a th' charge all th' time,' he ses. 'A feller named Wilson,' he ses. There, Wilson, m'boy, put that in a letter an' send it hum t' yer mother, hay? 'A feller named Wilson,' he ses. An' th' colonel, he ses: 'Were they indeed? Ahem! ahem! My sakes!' he ses. 'At th' head 'a th' reg'ment?' he ses. 'They were,' ses th' lieutenant. 'My sakes!' ses th' colonel. He ses; 'Well, well, well,' he ses, 'those two babies?' 'They were,' ses th' lieutenant. 'Well, well,' ses th' colonel, 'they deserve t' be major generals,' he ses. 'They deserve t' be major generals.'"

The youth and his friend had said: "Huh!" "Yer lyin', Thompson." "Oh, go t' blazes!" "He never sed it." "Oh, what a lie!" "Huh!" But despite these youthful scoffings and embarrassments, they knew that their faces were deeply flushing from thrills of pleasure. They exchanged a secret glance of joy and congratulation.

They speedily forgot many things. The past held no pictures of error and disappointment. They were very happy, and their hearts swelled with grateful affection for the colonel and the youthful lieutenant.

CHAPTER XXII

When the woods again began to pour forth the dark-hued masses of the enemy the youth felt serene self-confidence. He smiled briefly when he saw men dodge and duck at the long screechings of shells that were thrown in giant handfuls over them. He stood, erect and tranquil, watching the attack begin against a part of the line that made a blue curve along the side of an adjacent hill. His vision being unmolested by smoke from the rifles of his companions, he had opportunities to see parts of the hard fight. It was a relief to perceive at last from whence came some of these noises which had been roared into his ears.

Off a short way he saw two regiments fighting a little separate battle with two other regiments. It was in a cleared space, wearing a set-apart look. They were blazing as if upon a wager, giving and taking tremendous blows. The firings were incredibly fierce and rapid. These intent regiments apparently were oblivious of all larger purposes of war, and were slugging each other as if at a matched game.

In another direction he saw a magnificent brigade going with the evident intention of driving the enemy from a wood. They passed in out of sight and presently there was a most awe-inspiring racket in the wood. The noise was unspeakable. Having stirred this prodigious uproar, and, apparently, finding it too prodigious, the brigade, after a little time, came marching airily out again with its fine formation in nowise disturbed. There were no traces of speed in its movements. The brigade was jaunty and seemed to point a proud thumb at the yelling wood.

On a slope to the left there was a long row of guns, gruff and maddened, denouncing the enemy, who, down through the woods, were forming for another attack in the pitiless monotony of conflicts. The round red discharges from the guns made a crimson flare and a high, thick smoke. Occasional glimpses could be caught of groups of the toiling artillerymen. In the rear of this row of guns stood a house, calm and white, amid bursting shells. A congregation of horses, tied to a long railing, were tugging frenziedly at their bridles. Men were running hither and thither.

The detached battle between the four regiments lasted for some time. There chanced to be no interference, and they settled their dispute by themselves. They struck savagely and powerfully at each other for a period of minutes, and then the lighter-hued regiments faltered and drew back, leaving the dark-blue lines shouting. The youth could see the two flags shaking with laughter amid the smoke remnants.

Presently there was a stillness, pregnant with meaning. The blue lines shifted and changed a trifle and stared expectantly at the silent woods and fields before them. The hush was solemn and churchlike, save for a distant battery that, evidently unable to remain quiet, sent a faint rolling thunder over the ground. It irritated, like the noises of unimpressed boys. The men imagined that it would prevent their perched ears from hearing the first words of the new battle.

Of a sudden the guns on the slope roared out a message of warning. A spluttering sound had begun in the woods. It swelled with amazing speed to a profound clamor that involved the earth in noises. The splitting crashes swept along the lines until an interminable roar was developed. To those in the midst of it it became a din fitted to the universe. It was the whirring and thumping of gigantic machinery, complications among the smaller stars. The youth's ears were filled up. They were incapable of hearing more.

On an incline over which a road wound he saw wild and desperate rushes of men perpetually backward and forward in riotous surges. These parts of the opposing armies were two long waves that pitched upon each other madly at dictated points. To and fro they swelled. Sometimes, one side by its yells and cheers would proclaim decisive blows, but a moment later the other side would be all yells and cheers. Once the youth saw a spray of light forms go in houndlike leaps toward the waving blue lines. There was much howling, and presently it went away with a vast mouthful of prisoners. Again, he saw a blue wave dash with such thunderous force against a gray obstruction that it seemed to clear the earth of it and leave nothing but trampled sod. And always in their swift and deadly rushes to and fro the men screamed and yelled like maniacs.

Particular pieces of fence or secure positions behind collections of trees were wrangled over, as gold thrones or pearl bedsteads. There were desperate lunges at these chosen spots seemingly every instant, and most of them were bandied like light toys between the contending forces. The youth could not tell from the battle flags flying like crimson foam in many directions which color of cloth was winning.

His emaciated regiment bustled forth with undiminished fierceness when its time came. When assaulted again by bullets, the men burst out in a barbaric cry of rage and pain. They bent their heads in aims of intent hatred behind the projected hammers of their guns. Their ramrods clanged loud with fury as their eager arms pounded the cartridges into the rifle barrels. The front of the regiment was a smoke-wall penetrated by the flashing points of yellow and red.

Wallowing in the fight, they were in an astonishingly short time resmudged. They surpassed in stain and dirt all their previous appearances. Moving to and fro with strained exertion, jabbering the while, they were, with their swaying bodies, black faces, and glowing eyes, like strange and ugly fiends jigging heavily in the smoke.

The lieutenant, returning from a tour after a bandage, produced from a hidden receptacle of his mind new and portentous oaths suited to the emergency. Strings of expletives he swung lashlike over the backs of his men, and it was evident that his previous efforts had in nowise impaired his resources.

The youth, still the bearer of the colors, did not feel his idleness. He was deeply absorbed as a spectator. The crash and swing of the great drama made him lean forward, intent-eyed, his face working in small contortions. Sometimes he prattled, words coming unconsciously from him in grotesque exclamations. He did not know that he breathed; that the flag hung silently over him, so absorbed was he.

A formidable line of the enemy came within dangerous range. They could be seen plainly—tall, gaunt men with excited faces running with long strides toward a wandering fence.

At sight of this danger the men suddenly ceased their cursing monotone. There was an instant of strained silence before they threw up their rifles and fired a plumping volley at the foes. There had been no order given; the men, upon recognizing the menace, had immediately let drive their flock of bullets without waiting for word of command.

But the enemy were quick to gain the protection of the wandering line of fence. They slid down behind it with remarkable celerity, and from this position they began briskly to slice up the blue men.

These latter braced their energies for a great struggle. Often, white clinched teeth shone from the dusky faces. Many heads surged to and fro, floating upon a pale sea of smoke. Those behind the fence frequently shouted and yelped in taunts and gibelike cries, but the regiment maintained a stressed silence. Perhaps, at this new assault the men recalled the fact that they had been named mud diggers, and it made their situation thrice bitter. They were breathlessly intent upon keeping the ground and thrusting away the rejoicing body of the enemy. They fought swiftly and with a despairing savageness denoted in their expressions.

The youth had resolved not to budge whatever should happen. Some arrows of scorn that had buried themselves in his heart had generated strange and unspeakable hatred. It was clear to him that his final and absolute revenge was to be achieved by his dead body lying, torn and gluttering, upon the field. This was to be a poignant retaliation upon the officer who had said "mule drivers," and later "mud diggers," for in all the wild graspings of his mind for a unit responsible for his sufferings and commotions he always seized upon the man who had dubbed him wrongly. And it was his idea, vaguely formulated, that his corpse would be for those eyes a great and salt reproach.

The regiment bled extravagantly. Grunting bundles of blue began to drop. The orderly sergeant of the youth's company was shot through the cheeks. Its supports being injured, his jaw hung afar down, disclosing in the wide cavern of his mouth a pulsing mass of blood and teeth. And with it all he made attempts to cry out. In his endeavor there was a dreadful earnestness, as if he conceived that one great shriek would make him well.

The youth saw him presently go rearward. His strength seemed in nowise impaired. He ran swiftly, casting wild glances for succor.

Others fell down about the feet of their companions. Some of the wounded crawled out and away, but many lay still, their bodies twisted into impossible shapes.

The youth looked once for his friend. He saw a vehement young man, powder-smeared and frowzled, whom he knew to be him. The lieutenant, also, was unscathed in his position at the rear. He had continued to curse, but it was now with the air of a man who was using his last box of oaths.

For the fire of the regiment had begun to wane and drip. The robust voice, that had come strangely from the thin ranks, was growing rapidly weak.

CHAPTER XXIII

The colonel came running along back of the line. There were other officers following him. "We must charge'm!" they shouted. "We must charge'm!" they cried with resentful voices, as if anticipating a rebellion against this plan by the men.

The youth, upon hearing the shouts, began to study the distance between him and the enemy. He made vague calculations. He saw that to be firm soldiers they must go forward. It would be death to stay in the present place, and with all the circumstances to go backward would exalt too many others. Their hope was to push the galling foes away from the fence.

He expected that his companions, weary and stiffened, would have to be driven to this assault, but as he turned toward them he perceived with a certain surprise that they were giving quick and unqualified expressions of assent. There was an ominous, clanging overture to the charge when the shafts of the bayonets rattled upon the rifle barrels. At the yelled words of command the soldiers sprang forward in eager leaps. There was new and unexpected force in the movement of the regiment. A knowledge of its faded and jaded condition made the charge appear like a paroxysm, a display of the strength that comes before a final feebleness. The men scampered in insane fever of haste, racing as if to achieve a sudden success before an exhilarating fluid should leave them. It was a blind and despairing rush by the collection of men in dusty and tattered blue, over a green sward and under a sapphire sky, toward a fence, dimly outlined in smoke, from behind which spluttered the fierce rifles of enemies.

The youth kept the bright colors to the front. He was waving his free arm in furious circles, the while shrieking mad calls and appeals, urging on those that did not need to be urged, for it seemed that the mob of blue men hurling themselves on the dangerous group of rifles were again grown suddenly wild with an enthusiasm of unselfishness. From the many firings starting toward them, it looked as if they would merely succeed in making a great sprinkling of corpses on the grass between their former position and the fence. But they were in a state of frenzy, perhaps because of forgotten vanities, and it made an exhibition of sublime recklessness. There was no obvious questioning, nor figurings, nor diagrams. There were, apparently, no considered loopholes. It appeared that the swift wings of their desires would have shattered against the iron gates of the impossible.

He himself felt the daring spirit of a savage religion-mad. He was capable of profound sacrifices, a tremendous death. He had no time for dissections, but he knew that he thought of the bullets only as things that could prevent him from reaching the place of his endeavor. There were subtle flashings of joy within him that thus should be his mind.

He strained all his strength. His eyesight was shaken and dazzled by the tension of thought and muscle. He did not see anything excepting the mist of smoke gashed by the little knives of fire, but he knew that in it lay the aged fence of a vanished farmer protecting the snuggled bodies of the gray men.

As he ran a thought of the shock of contact gleamed in his mind. He expected a great concussion when the two bodies of troops crashed together. This became a part of his wild battle madness. He could feel the onward swing of the regiment about him and he conceived of a thunderous, crushing blow that would prostrate the resistance and spread consternation and amazement for miles. The flying regiment was going to have a catapultian effect. This dream made him run faster among his comrades, who were giving vent to hoarse and frantic cheers.

But presently he could see that many of the men in gray did not intend to abide the blow. The smoke, rolling, disclosed men who ran, their faces still turned. These grew to a crowd, who retired stubbornly. Individuals wheeled frequently to send a bullet at the blue wave.

But at one part of the line there was a grim and obdurate group that made no movement. They were settled firmly down behind posts and rails. A flag, ruffled and fierce, waved over them and their rifles dinned fiercely.

The blue whirl of men got very near, until it seemed that in truth there would be a close and frightful scuffle. There was an expressed disdain in the opposition of the little group, that changed the meaning of the cheers of the men in blue. They became yells of wrath, directed, personal. The cries of the two parties were now in sound an interchange of scathing insults.

They in blue showed their teeth; their eyes shone all white. They launched themselves as at the throats of those who stood resisting. The space between dwindled to an insignificant distance.

The youth had centered the gaze of his soul upon that other flag. Its possession would be high pride. It would express bloody minglings, near blows. He had a gigantic hatred for those who made great difficulties and complications. They caused it to be as a craved treasure of mythology, hung amid tasks and contrivances of danger.

He plunged like a mad horse at it. He was resolved it should not escape if wild blows and darings of blows could seize it. His own emblem, quivering and aflare, was winging toward the other. It seemed there would shortly be an encounter of strange beaks and claws, as of eagles.

The swirling body of blue men came to a sudden halt at close and disastrous range and roared a swift volley. The group in gray was split and broken by this fire, but its riddled body still fought. The men in blue yelled again and rushed in upon it.

The youth, in his leapings, saw, as through a mist, a picture of four or five men stretched upon the ground or writhing upon their knees with bowed heads as if they had been stricken by bolts from the sky. Tottering among them was the rival color bearer, whom the youth saw had been bitten vitally by the bullets of the last formidable volley. He perceived this man fighting a last struggle, the struggle of one whose legs are grasped by demons. It was a ghastly battle. Over his face was the bleach of death, but set upon it were the dark and hard lines of desperate purpose. With this terrible grin of resolution he hugged his precious flag to him and was stumbling and staggering in his design to go the way that led to safety for it.

But his wounds always made it seem that his feet were retarded, held, and he fought a grim fight, as with invisible ghouls fastened greedily upon his limbs. Those in advance of the scampering blue men, howling cheers, leaped at the fence. The despair of the lost was in his eyes as he glanced back at them.

The youth's friend went over the obstruction in a tumbling heap and sprang at the flag as a panther at prey. He pulled at it and, wrenching it free, swung up its red brilliancy with a mad cry of exultation even as the color bearer, gasping, lurched over in a final throe and, stiffening convulsively, turned his dead face to the ground. There was much blood upon the grass blades.

At the place of success there began more wild clamorings of cheers. The men gesticulated and bellowed in an ecstasy. When they spoke it was as if they considered their listener to be a mile away. What hats and caps were left to them they often slung high in the air.

At one part of the line four men had been swooped upon, and they now sat as prisoners. Some blue men were about them in an eager and curious circle. The soldiers had trapped strange birds, and there was an examination. A flurry of fast questions was in the air.

One of the prisoners was nursing a superficial wound in the foot. He cuddled it, babywise, but he looked up from it often to curse with an astonishing utter abandon straight at the noses of his captors. He consigned them to red regions; he called upon the pestilential wrath of strange gods. And with it all he was singularly free from recognition of the finer points of the conduct of prisoners of war. It was as if a clumsy clod had trod upon his toe and he conceived it to be his privilege, his duty, to use deep, resentful oaths.

Another, who was a boy in years, took his plight with great calmness and apparent good nature. He conversed with the men in blue, studying their faces with his bright and keen eyes. They spoke of battles and conditions. There was an acute interest in all their faces during this exchange of viewpoints. It seemed a great satisfaction to hear voices from where all had been darkness and speculation.

The third captive sat with a morose countenance. He preserved a stoical and cold attitude. To all advances he made one reply without variation, "Ah, go t' hell!"

The last of the four was always silent and, for the most part, kept his face turned in unmolested directions. From the views the youth received he seemed to be in a state of absolute dejection. Shame was upon him, and with it profound regret that he was, perhaps, no more to be counted in the ranks of his fellows. The youth could detect no expression that would allow him to believe that the other was giving a thought to his narrowed future, the pictured dungeons, perhaps, and starvations and brutalities, liable to the imagination. All to be seen was shame for captivity and regret for the right to antagonize.

After the men had celebrated sufficiently they settled down behind the old rail fence, on the opposite side to the one from which their foes had been driven. A few shot perfunctorily at distant marks.

There was some long grass. The youth nestled in it and rested, making a convenient rail support the flag. His friend, jubilant and glorified, holding his treasure with vanity, came to him there. They sat side by side and congratulated each other.

CHAPTER XXIV

The roarings that had stretched in a long line of sound across the face of the forest began to grow intermittent and weaker. The stentorian speeches of the artillery continued in some distant encounter, but the crashes of the musketry had almost ceased. The youth and his friend of a sudden looked up, feeling a deadened form of distress at the waning of these noises, which had become a part of life. They could see changes going on among the troops. There were marchings this way and that way. A battery wheeled leisurely. On the crest of a small hill was the thick gleam of many departing muskets.

The youth arose. "Well, what now, I wonder?" he said. By his tone he seemed to be preparing to resent some new monstrosity in the way of dins and smashes. He shaded his eyes with his grimy hand and gazed over the field.

His friend also arose and stared. "I bet we're goin' t' git along out of this an' back over th' river," said he.

"Well, I swan!" said the youth.

They waited, watching. Within a little while the regiment received orders to retrace its way. The men got up grunting from the grass, regretting the soft repose. They jerked their stiffened legs, and stretched their arms over their heads. One man swore as he rubbed his eyes. They all groaned "O Lord!" They had as many objections to this change as they would have had to a proposal for a new battle.

They trampled slowly back over the field across which they had run in a mad scamper.

The regiment marched until it had joined its fellows. The reformed brigade, in column, aimed through a wood at the road. Directly they were in a mass of dust-covered troops, and were trudging along in a way parallel to the enemy's lines as these had been defined by the previous turmoil.

They passed within view of a stolid white house, and saw in front of it groups of their comrades lying in wait behind a neat breastwork. A row of guns were booming at a distant enemy. Shells thrown in reply were raising clouds of dust and splinters. Horsemen dashed along the line of intrenchments.

At this point of its march the division curved away from the field and went winding off in the direction of the river. When the significance of this movement had impressed itself upon the youth he turned his head and looked over his shoulder toward the trampled and *débris*-strewed ground. He breathed a breath of new satisfaction. He finally nudged his friend. "Well, it's all over," he said to him.

His friend gazed backward. "B'Gawd, it is," he assented. They mused.

For a time the youth was obliged to reflect in a puzzled and uncertain way. His mind was undergoing a subtle change. It took moments for it to cast off its battleful ways and resume its accustomed course of thought. Gradually his brain emerged from the clogged clouds, and at last he was enabled to more closely comprehend himself and circumstance.

He understood then that the existence of shot and countershot was in the past. He had dwelt in a land of strange, squalling upheavals and had come forth. He had been where there was red of blood and black of passion, and he was escaped. His first thoughts were given to rejoicings at this fact.

Later he began to study his deeds, his failures, and his achievements. Thus, fresh from scenes where many of his usual machines of reflection had been idle, from where he had proceeded sheeplike, he struggled to marshal all his acts.

At last they marched before him clearly. From this present viewpoint he was enabled to look upon them in spectator fashion and to criticize them with some correctness, for his new condition had already defeated certain sympathies.

Regarding his procession of memory he felt gleeful and unregretting, for in it his public deeds were paraded in great and shining prominence. Those performances which had been witnessed by his fellows marched now in wide purple and gold, having various deflections. They went gayly with music. It was pleasure to watch these things. He spent delightful minutes viewing the gilded images of memory.

He saw that he was good. He recalled with a thrill of joy the respectful comments of his fellows upon his conduct.

Nevertheless, the ghost of his flight from the first engagement appeared to him and danced. There were small shoutings in his brain about these matters. For a moment he blushed, and the light of his soul flickered with shame.

A specter of reproach came to him. There loomed the dogging memory of the tattered soldier—he who, gored by bullets and faint for blood, had fretted concerning an imagined wound in another; he who had loaned his last of strength and intellect for the tall soldier; he who, blind with weariness and pain, had been deserted in the field.

For an instant a wretched chill of sweat was upon him at the thought that he might be detected in the thing. As he stood persistently before his vision, he gave vent to a cry of sharp irritation and agony.

His friend turned. "What's the matter, Henry?" he demanded. The youth's reply was an outburst of crimson oaths.

As he marched along the little branch-hung roadway among his prattling companions this vision of cruelty brooded over him. It clung near him always and darkened his view of these deeds in purple and gold. Whichever way his thoughts turned they were followed by the somber phantom of the desertion in the fields. He looked stealthily at his companions, feeling sure that they must discern in his face evidences of this pursuit. But they were plodding in ragged array, discussing with quick tongues the accomplishments of the late battle.

"Oh, if a man should come up an' ask me, I'd say we got a dum good lickin'."

"Lickin'—in yer eye! We ain't licked, sonny. We're going down here aways, swing aroun', an' come in behint 'em."

"Oh, hush, with your comin' in behint 'em. I've seen all 'a that I wanta. Don't tell me about comin' in behint—"

"Bill Smithers, he ses he'd rather been in ten hundred battles than been in that heluva hospital. He ses they got shootin' in th' nighttime, an' shells dropped plum among 'em in th' hospital. He ses sech hollerin' he never see."

"Hasbrouck? He's th' best off'cer in this here reg'ment. He's a whale."

"Didn't I tell yeh we'd come aroun' in behint 'em? Didn't I tell yeh so? We—"

"Oh, shet yer mouth!"

For a time this pursuing recollection of the tattered man took all elation from the youth's veins. He saw his vivid error, and he was afraid that it would stand before him all his life. He took no share in the chatter of his comrades, nor did he look at them or know them, save when he felt sudden suspicion that they were seeing his thoughts and scrutinizing each detail of the scene with the tattered soldier.

Yet gradually he mustered force to put the sin at a distance. And at last his eyes seemed to open to some new ways. He found that he could look back upon the brass and bombast of his earlier gospels and see them truly. He was gleeful when he discovered that he now despised them.

With the conviction came a store of assurance. He felt a quiet manhood, nonassertive but of sturdy and strong blood. He knew that he would no more quail before his guides wherever they should point. He had been to touch the great death, and found that, after all, it was but the great death. He was a man.

So it came to pass that as he trudged from the place of blood and wrath his soul changed. He came from hot plowshares to prospects of clover tranquilly, and it was as if hot plowshares were not. Scars faded as flowers.

It rained. The procession of weary soldiers became a bedraggled train, despondent and muttering, marching with churning effort in a trough of liquid brown mud under a low, wretched sky. Yet the youth smiled, for he saw that the world was a world for him, though many discovered it to be made of oaths and walking sticks. He had rid himself of the red sickness of battle. The sultry nightmare was in the past. He had been an animal blistered and sweating in the heat and pain of war. He turned now with a lover's thirst to images of tranquil skies, fresh meadows, cool brooks—an existence of soft and eternal peace.

Over the river a golden ray of sun came through the hosts of leaden rain clouds.

KATE CHOPIN
(1851–1904)

Throughout her life, Kate Chopin struggled with the conflict between self-determination in a male-dominated world and conformity with the role of wife, mother, widow, and writer in that same world. Her fiction, consisting only of two novels and two collections of short stories, exhibits a parallel conflict. *The Awakening* (1899), "A Respectable Woman," "Athénaise," "The Story of an Hour," and "Désirée's Baby" all delineate struggles similar to Chopin's own. The other half of her work, including her first novel, *At Fault* (1890), and many of the stories in her two volumes, *Bayou Folk* (1894) and *A Night in Acadie* (1897), demonstrate her ability to comply with society's standards. They depict the traditional, conventional lives of Creoles (descendents of French and Spanish colonists), Acadians or Cajuns (French driven out of Acadia in Canada in the eighteenth century), Negroes, and half-breed Indians.

Katherine O'Flaherty was born on February 8, 1851, in St. Louis, Missouri, far from the locale of most of her fiction. Her mother, however, was aristocratic Creole French. Her father was a merchant, born in Ireland. During her convent education and her few years as a reluctant Southern belle, Kate rebelled in her reading, her own writing, and in her social behavior. But at nineteen, bowing to convention, she married a banker-cotton broker, Oscar Chopin (pronounced show-pan), who took her to live in New Orleans. Fluent in French, she participated in the social life there, spending summers at fashionable Grand Isle on the Gulf of Mexico. Nine years later, the Chopins moved to a small town in Northwestern Louisiana where Oscar managed a plantation and ran a store.

Kate Chopin was a good wife and mother of six children, but she always felt like an outsider pretending to conform. And her conformity had its limits. She remained open to the personal and literary influence of the "New Women" who fervently raised "the woman question," advocating women's rights, questioning the role of wife and mother, and posing other possibilities for self-realization and actualization. Ever curious, restless, and longing for solitude, she insisted on wearing unconventional clothes, smoking cigarettes, and taking long, exploratory walks and horseback rides by herself, or with male companions, into obscure quarters of New Orleans and back country areas.

The sudden death of her husband by swamp fever in 1883 compelled Chopin to attempt to run the plantation alone, but after a year she was forced to return to St. Louis. At age 35, influenced by French contemporary realists Emile Zola and Guy t, she ended her long silence and began writing. She had stories opular magazines, and she shocked the nation with her depiction of ıen making impulsive, often disastrous, leaps into freedom. But nd literary career ended too soon. She suffered a brain hemorrhage, and died on August 30, 1904. She was 53.

The Awakening was one of the first American novels to deal frankly with the sexual urges of a married woman. That, and the fact that it was written by a woman, created quite a stir in its day. It was even the target of censorship. But despite the initial attention, Chopin's fiction fell into obscurity, a fate that overtook several classic American writers—Melville and James, for instance—until some need in the culture revitalized interest in them. Although at least two critics as early as 1956 urged rediscovery, it was the publication in 1969 of *The Complete Works of Kate Chopin*, in two volumes, edited by Per Seyersted, and his *Kate Chopin: A Critical Biography* that gained the support of university programs focusing on feminist literature. *The Awakening* is now considered a major American novel that ranks with the earlier *Maggie* by Crane and the later *Sister Carrie* by Dreiser.

Chopin's lack of time for concentrated effort may have compelled her to be disdainful of revision. She put her faith in spontaneous writing. Working on a lapboard in her living room, often surrounded by her six children, she could finish a story in a single day. That may help explain the brevity of most of her 150 or so stories, and the fact that in some cases they are underdeveloped and contrived, as with the surprise ending of "Désirée's Baby." Relying heavily on the charm of exotic atmosphere and dialect, her stories are sometimes no more than anecdotal local color sketches, a genre much in vogue in the late nineteenth century. There is plenty of local color in *The Awakening*, but modern readers can readily see that the novel transcends to a more universal level, in the tradition of the stories of Sarah Orne Jewett and Mary Wilkins Freeman in New England; Mary N. Murfree, Joel Chandler Harris, George Washington Cable, and Chopin's contemporary New Orleanean Grace King in the South; and Bret Harte and Hamlin Garland in the West.

Edna Pontellier awakens in stages from the deep sleep of her marriage. Her body awakens to the effect of music, to the embrace of the sea, and to eroticism with Robert. Her spirit awakens to the desire for solitude ("A Solitary Soul" was an early title), to the drive for independence from others, and to the need for self-expression in painting. Chopin's use of the omniscient point of view enables her to offer contrasting attitudes held by the men and women of society toward Edna. In contrast to the moralistic attitude of one of Chopin's contemporary reviewers—"We are well satisfied when Mrs. Pontellier deliberately swims out to her death"—controversy today over the ending focuses on character motivation and artistic preparation. Questions, rather than judgements, arise, such as: Is the sea a medium in which Edna reconciles her contradictory impulses toward self-recreation and self-destruction? Or is the final irony that she awakens only to kill herself?

Chopin felt assaulted by the majority of her reviews, and by the censorship imposed upon her stories. A sampling of what she faced: "The purport of the story can hardly be described in language fit for publication"; "an essentially vulgar story"; "sex fiction"; "what an ugly, cruel, loathsome monster Passion can be"; "unhealthily introspective and morbid"; "should be labeled poison." Chopin's response was a hurt silence that filled her last years, just as the silence of postponement had filled her married years. Readers may regret that she was not more encouraged by Willa Cather's praise of the novel as a Creole version of Flaubert's masterpiece *Madame Bovary*.

THE AWAKENING

Kate Chopin

CHAPTER I

A green and yellow parrot, which hung in a cage outside the door, kept repeating over and over:

"*Allez vous-en! Allez vous-en! Sapristi!* That's all right!"

He could speak a little Spanish, and also a language which nobody understood, unless it was the mocking-bird that hung on the other side of the door, whistling his fluty notes out upon the breeze with maddening persistence.

Mr. Pontellier, unable to read his newspaper with any degree of comfort, arose with an expression and an exclamation of disgust. He walked down the gallery and across the narrow "bridges" which connected the Lebrun cottages one with the other. He had been seated before the door of the main house. The parrot and the mocking-bird were the property of Madame Lebrun, and they had the right to make all the noise they wished. Mr. Pontellier had the privilege of quitting their society when they ceased to be entertaining.

He stopped before the door of his own cottage, which was the fourth one from the main building and next to the last. Seating himself in a wicker rocker which was there, he once more applied himself to the task of reading the newspaper. The day was Sunday; the paper was a day old. The Sunday papers had not yet reached Grand Isle. He was already acquainted with the market reports, and he glanced restlessly over the editorials and bits of news which he had not had time to read before quitting New Orleans the day before.

Mr. Pontellier wore eye-glasses. He was a man of forty, of medium height and rather slender build; he stooped a little. His hair was brown and straight, parted on one side. His beard was neatly and closely trimmed.

Once in a while he withdrew his glance from the newspaper and looked about him. There was more noise than ever over at the house. The main building was called "the house," to distinguish it from the cottages. The chattering and whistling birds were still at it. Two young girls, the Farival twins, were playing a duet from "Zampa" upon the piano. Madame Lebrun was bustling in and out, giving orders in a high key to a yard-boy whenever she got inside the house, and directions in an equally high voice to a dining-room servant whenever she got outside. She was a fresh, pretty woman, clad always in white with elbow sleeves. Her starched skirts crinkled as she came and went. Farther down, before one of the cottages, a lady in black was walking demurely up and down, telling her beads. A good many persons of the *pension* had gone over to the *Chênière Caminada* in Beaudelet's lugger to hear mass. Some young people were out under the water-oaks playing croquet. Mr. Pontellier's two children were there—sturdy little fellows of four and five. A quadroon nurse followed them about with a far-away, meditative air.

Mr. Pontellier finally lit a cigar and began to smoke, letting the paper drag idly from his hand. He fixed his gaze upon a white sunshade that was advancing at snail's pace from the beach. He could see it plainly between the gaunt trunks of the water-oaks and across the stretch of yellow camomile. The gulf looked far away, melting hazily into the blue of the horizon. The sunshade continued to approach slowly. Beneath its pink-lined shelter were his wife, Mrs. Pontellier, and young Robert Lebrun. When they reached the cottage, the two seated themselves with some appearance of fatigue upon the upper step of the porch, facing each other, each leaning against a supporting post.

"What folly! to bathe at such an hour in such heat!" exclaimed Mr. Pontellier. He himself had taken a plunge at daylight. That was why the morning seemed long to him.

"You are burnt beyond recognition," he added, looking at his wife as one looks at a valuable piece of personal property which has suffered some damage. She held up her hands, strong, shapely hands, and surveyed them critically, drawing up her lawn sleeves above the wrists. Looking at them reminded her of her rings, which she had given to her husband before leaving for the beach. She silently reached out to him, and he, understanding, took the rings from his vest pocket and dropped them into her open palm. She slipped them upon her fingers; then clasping her knees, she looked across at Robert and began to laugh. The rings sparkled upon her fingers. He sent back an answering smile.

"What is it?" asked Pontellier, looking lazily and amused from one to the other. It was some utter nonsense; some adventure out there in the water, and they both tried to relate it at once. It did not seem half so amusing when told. They realized this, and so did Mr. Pontellier. He yawned and stretched himself. Then he got up, saying he had half a mind to go over to Klein's hotel and play a game of billiards.

"Come go along, Lebrun," he proposed to Robert. But Robert admitted quite frankly that he preferred to stay where he was and talk to Mrs. Pontellier.

"Well, send him about his business when he bores you, Edna," instructed her husband as he prepared to leave.

"Here, take the umbrella," she exclaimed, holding it out to him. He accepted the sunshade, and lifting it over his head descended the steps and walked away.

"Coming back to dinner?" his wife called after him. He halted a moment and shrugged his shoulders. He felt in his vest pocket; there was a ten-dollar bill there. He did not know; perhaps he would return for the early dinner and perhaps he would not. It all depended upon the company which he found over at Klein's and the size of "the game." He did not say this, but she understood it, and laughed, nodding good-by to him.

Both children wanted to follow their father when they saw him starting out. He kissed them and promised to bring them back bonbons and peanuts.

CHAPTER II

Mrs. Pontellier's eyes were quick and bright; they were a yellowish brown, about the color of her hair. She had a way of turning them swiftly upon an object and holding them there as if lost in some inward maze of contemplation or thought.

Her eyebrows were a shade darker than her hair. They were thick and almost horizontal, emphasizing the depth of her eyes. She was rather handsome than beautiful. Her face was captivating by reason of a certain frankness of expression and a contradictory subtle play of features. Her manner was engaging.

Robert rolled a cigarette. He smoked cigarettes because he could not afford cigars, he said. He had a cigar in his pocket which Mr. Pontellier had presented him with, and he was saving it for his after-dinner smoke.

This seemed quite proper and natural on his part. In coloring he was not unlike his companion. A clean-shaved face made the resemblance more pronounced than it would otherwise have been. There rested no shadow of care upon his open countenance. His eyes gathered in and reflected the light and languor of the summer day.

Mrs. Pontellier reached over for a palmleaf fan that lay on the porch and began to fan herself, while Robert sent between his lips light puffs from his cigarette. They chatted incessantly: about the things around them; their amusing adventure out in the water—it had again assumed its entertaining aspect; about the wind, the trees, the people who had gone to the *Chênière*; about the children playing croquet under the oaks, and the Farival twins, who were now performing the overture to "The Poet and the Peasant."

Robert talked a good deal about himself. He was very young, and did not know any better. Mrs. Pontellier talked a little about herself for the same reason. Each was interested in what the other said. Robert spoke of his intention to go to Mexico in the autumn, where fortune awaited him. He was always intending to go to Mexico, but some way never got there. Meanwhile he held on to his modest position in a mercantile house in New Orleans, where an equal familiarity with English, French and Spanish gave him no small value as a clerk and correspondent.

He was spending his summer vacation, as he always did, with his mother at Grand Isle. In former times, before Robert could remember, "the house" had been a summer luxury of the Lebruns. Now, flanked by its dozen or more cottages, which were always filled with exclusive visitors from the "*Quartier Français*," it enabled Madame Lebrun to maintain the easy and comfortable existence which appeared to be her birthright.

Mrs. Pontellier talked about her father's Mississippi plantation and her girlhood home in the old Kentucky blue-grass country. She was an American woman, with a small infusion of French which seemed to have been lost in dilution. She read a letter from her sister, who was away in the East, and who had engaged herself to be married. Robert was interested, and wanted to know what manner of girls the sisters were, what the father was like, and how long the mother had been dead.

When Mrs. Pontellier folded the letter it was time for her to dress for the early dinner.

"I see Léonce isn't coming back," she said, with a glance in the direction whence her husband had disappeared. Robert supposed he was not, as there were a good many New Orleans club men over at Klein's.

When Mrs. Pontellier left him to enter her room, the young man descended the steps and strolled over toward the croquet players, where, during the half-hour before dinner, he amused himself with the little Pontellier children, who were very fond of him.

CHAPTER III

It was eleven o'clock that night when Mr. Pontellier returned from Klein's hotel. He was in an excellent humor, in high spirits, and very talkative. His entrance awoke his wife, who was in bed and fast asleep when he came in. He talked to her while he undressed, telling her anecdotes and bits of news and gossip that he had gathered during the day. From his trousers pockets he took a fistful of crumpled bank notes and a good deal of silver coin, which he piled on the bureau indiscriminately with keys, knife, handkerchief, and whatever else happened to be in his pockets. She was overcome with sleep, and answered him with little half utterances.

He thought it very discouraging that his wife, who was the sole object of his existence, evinced so little interest in things which concerned him and valued so little his conversation.

Mr. Pontellier had forgotten the bonbons and peanuts for the boys. Notwithstanding he loved them very much, and went into the adjoining room where they slept to take a look at them and make sure that they were resting comfortably. The result of his investigation was far from satisfactory. He turned and shifted the youngsters about in bed. One of them began to kick and talk about a basket full of crabs.

Mr. Pontellier returned to his wife with the information that Raoul had a high fever and needed looking after. Then he lit a cigar and went and sat near the open door to smoke it.

Mrs. Pontellier was quite sure Raoul had no fever. He had gone to bed perfectly well, she said, and nothing had ailed him all day. Mr. Pontellier was too well acquainted with fever symptoms to be mistaken. He assured her the child was consuming at that moment in the next room.

He reproached his wife with her inattention, her habitual neglect of the children. If it was not a mother's place to look after children, whose on earth was it? He himself had his hands full with his brokerage business. He could not be in two places at once; making a living for his family on the street, and staying at home to see that no harm befell them. He talked in a monotonous, insistent way.

Mrs. Pontellier sprang out of bed and went into the next room. She soon came back and sat on the edge of the bed, leaning her head down on the pillow. She said nothing, and refused to answer her husband when he questioned her. When his cigar was smoked out he went to bed, and in half a minute he was fast asleep.

Mrs. Pontellier was by that time thoroughly awake. She began to cry a little, and wiped her eyes on the sleeve of her *peignoir.* Blowing out the candle, which her husband had left burning, she slipped her bare feet into a pair of satin *mules* at the foot of the bed and went out on the porch, where she sat down in the wicker chair and began to rock gently to and fro.

It was then past midnight. The cottages were all dark. A single faint light gleamed out from the hallway of the house. There was no sound abroad except the hooting of an old owl in the top of a water-oak, and the everlasting voice of the sea, that was not uplifted at that soft hour. It broke like a mournful lullaby upon the night.

The tears came so fast to Mrs. Pontellier's eyes that the damp sleeve of her *peignoir* no longer served to dry them. She was holding the back of her chair with one hand; her loose sleeve had slipped almost to the shoulder of her uplifted arm. Turning, she thrust her face, steaming and wet, into the bend of her arm, and she went on crying there, not caring any longer to dry her face, her eyes, her arms. She could not have told why she was crying. Such experiences as the foregoing were not uncommon in her married life. They seemed never before to have weighed much against the abundance of her husband's kindness and a uniform devotion which had come to be tacit and self-understood.

An indescribable oppression, which seemed to generate in some unfamiliar part of her consciousness, filled her whole being with a vague anguish. It was like a shadow, like a mist passing across her soul's summer day. It was strange and unfamiliar; it was a mood. She did not sit there inwardly upbraiding her husband, lamenting at Fate, which had directed her footsteps to the path which they had taken. She was just having a good cry all to herself. The mosquitoes made merry over her, biting her firm, round arms and nipping at her bare insteps.

The little stinging, buzzing imps succeeded in dispelling a mood which might have held her there in the darkness half a night longer.

The following morning Mr. Pontellier was up in good time to take the rockaway which was to convey him to the steamer at the wharf. He was returning to the city to his business, and they would not see him again at the Island till the coming Saturday. He had regained his composure, which seemed to have been somewhat impaired the night before. He was eager to be gone, as he looked forward to a lively week in Carondelet Street.

Mr. Pontellier gave his wife half the money which he had brought away from Klein's hotel the evening before. She liked money as well as most women, and accepted it with no little satisfaction.

"It will buy a handsome wedding present for Sister Janet!" she exclaimed, smoothing out the bills as she counted them one by one.

"Oh! we'll treat Sister Janet better than that, my dear," he laughed, as he prepared to kiss her good-by.

The boys were tumbling about, clinging to his legs, imploring that numerous things be brought back to them. Mr. Pontellier was a great favorite, and ladies, men, children, even nurses, were always on hand to say good-by to him. His wife stood smiling and waving, the boys shouting, as he disappeared in the old rockaway down the sandy road.

A few days later a box arrived for Mrs. Pontellier from New Orleans. It was from her husband. It was filled with *friandises*, with luscious and toothsome bits—

the finest of fruits, *patés*, a rare bottle or two, delicious syrups, and bonbons in abundance.

Mrs. Pontellier was always very generous with the contents of such a box; she was quite used to receiving them when away from home. The *patés* and fruit were brought to the dining-room; the bonbons were passed around. And the ladies, selecting with dainty and discriminating fingers and a little greedily, all declared that Mr. Pontellier was the best husband in the world. Mrs. Pontellier was forced to admit that she knew of none better.

CHAPTER IV

It would have been a difficult matter for Mr. Pontellier to define to his own satisfaction or any one else's wherein his wife failed in her duty toward their children. It was something which he felt rather than perceived, and he never voiced the feeling without subsequent regret and ample atonement.

If one of the little Pontellier boys took a tumble whilst at play, he was not apt to rush crying to his mother's arms for comfort; he would more likely pick himself up, wipe the water out of his eyes and the sand out of his mouth, and go on playing. Tots as they were, they pulled together and stood their ground in childish battles with doubled fists and uplifted voices, which usually prevailed against the other mother-tots. The quadroon nurse was looked upon as a huge encumbrance, only good to button up waists and panties and to brush and part hair; since it seemed to be a law of society that hair must be parted and brushed.

In short, Mrs. Pontellier was not a mother-woman. The mother-women seemed to prevail that summer at Grand Isle. It was easy to know them, fluttering about with extended, protecting wings when any harm, real or imaginary, threatened their precious brood. They were women who idolized their children, worshiped their husbands, and esteemed it a holy privilege to efface themselves as individuals and grow wings as ministering angels.

Many of them were delicious in the rôle; one of them was the embodiment of every womanly grace and charm. If her husband did not adore her, he was a brute, deserving of death by slow torture. Her name was Adèle Ratignolle. There are no words to describe her save the old ones that have served so often to picture the bygone heroine of romance and the fair lady of our dreams. There was nothing subtle or hidden about her charms; her beauty was all there, flaming and apparent: the spun-gold hair that comb nor confining pin could restrain; the blue eyes that were like nothing but sapphires; two lips that pouted, that were so red one could only think of cherries or some other delicious crimson fruit in looking at them. She was growing a little stout, but it did not seem to detract an iota from the grace of every step, pose, gesture. One would not have wanted her white neck a mite less full or her beautiful arms more slender. Never were hands more exquisite than hers, and it was a joy to look at them when she threaded her needle or adjusted her gold thimble to her taper middle finger as she sewed away on the little night-drawers or fashioned a bodice or a bib.

Madame Ratignolle was very fond of Mrs. Pontellier, and often she took her sewing and went over to sit with her in the afternoons. She was sitting there the afternoon of the day the box arrived from New Orleans. She had possession of the rocker, and she was busily engaged in sewing upon a diminutive pair of night-drawers.

She had brought the pattern of the drawers for Mrs. Pontellier to cut out—a marvel of construction, fashioned to enclose a baby's body so effectually that only two small eyes might look out from the garment, like an Eskimo's. They were designed for winter wear, when treacherous drafts came down chimneys and insidious currents of deadly cold found their way through key-holes.

Mrs. Pontellier's mind was quite at rest concerning the present material needs of her children, and she could not see the use of anticipating and making winter night garments the subject of her summer meditations. But she did not want to appear unamiable and uninterested, so she had brought forth newspapers which she spread upon the floor of the gallery, and under Madame Ratignolle's directions she had cut a pattern of the impervious garment.

Robert was there, seated as he had been the Sunday before, and Mrs. Pontellier also occupied her former position on the upper step, leaning listlessly against the post. Beside her was a box of bonbons, which she held out at intervals to Madame Ratignolle.

That lady seemed at a loss to make a selection, but finally settled upon a stick of nugat, wondering if it were not too rich; whether it could possibly hurt her. Madame Ratignolle had been married seven years. About every two years she had a baby. At that time she had three babies, and was beginning to think of a fourth one. She was always talking about her "condition." Her "condition" was in no way apparent, and no one would have known a thing about it but for her persistence in making it the subject of conversation.

Robert started to reassure her, asserting that he had known a lady who had subsisted upon nugat during the entire—but seeing the color mount into Mrs. Pontellier's face he checked himself and changed the subject.

Mrs. Pontellier, though she had married a Creole, was not thoroughly at home in the society of Creoles; never before had she been thrown so intimately among them. There were only Creoles that summer at Lebrun's. They all knew each other, and felt like one large family, among whom existed the most amicable relations. A characteristic which distinguished them and which impressed Mrs. Pontellier most forcibly was their entire absence of prudery. Their freedom of expression was at first incomprehensible to her, though she had no difficulty in reconciling it with a lofty chastity which in the Creole woman seems to be inborn and unmistakable.

Never would Edna Pontellier forget the shock with which she heard Madame Ratignolle relating to old Monsieur Farival the harrowing story of one of her *accouchements*, withholding no intimate detail. She was growing accustomed to like shocks, but she could not keep the mounting color back from her cheeks. Oftener than once her coming had interrupted the droll story with which Robert was entertaining some amused group of married women.

A book had gone the rounds of the *pension*. When it came her turn to read it, she did so with profound astonishment. She felt moved to read the book in secret and solitude, though none of the others had done so—to hide it from view at the sound of approaching footsteps. It was openly criticised and freely discussed at table. Mrs. Pontellier gave over being astonished, and concluded that wonders would never cease.

CHAPTER V

They formed a congenial group sitting there that summer afternoon—Madame Ratignolle sewing away, often stopping to relate a story or incident with much expressive gesture of her perfect hands; Robert and Mrs. Pontellier sitting idle, exchanging occasional words, glances or smiles which indicated a certain advanced stage of intimacy and *camaraderie*.

He had lived in her shadow during the past month. No one thought anything of it. Many had predicted that Robert would devote himself to Mrs. Pontellier when he arrived. Since the age of fifteen, which was eleven years before, Robert each summer at Grand Isle had constituted himself the devoted attendant of some fair dame or damsel. Sometimes it was a young girl, again a widow; but as often as not it was some interesting married woman.

For two consecutive seasons he lived in the sunlight of Mademoiselle Duvigné's presence. But she died between summers; then Robert posed as an inconsolable, prostrating himself at the feet of Madame Ratignolle for whatever crumbs of sympathy and comfort she might be pleased to vouchsafe.

Mrs. Pontellier liked to sit and gaze at her fair companion as she might look upon a faultless Madonna.

"Could any one fathom the cruelty beneath that fair exterior?" murmured Robert. "She knew that I adored her once, and she let me adore her. It was 'Robert, come; go; stand up; sit down; do this; do that; see if the baby sleeps; my thimble, please, that I left God knows where. Come and read Daudet to me while I sew.'"

"*Par exemple*! I never had to ask. You were always there under my feet, like a troublesome cat."

"You mean like an adoring dog. And just as soon as Ratignolle appeared on the scene, then it *was* like a dog. '*Passez! Adieu! Allez vous-en!*'"

"Perhaps I feared to make Alphonse jealous," she interjoined, with excessive naïveté. That made them all laugh. The right hand jealous of the left! The heart jealous of the soul! But for that matter, the Creole husband is never jealous; with him the gangrene passion is one which has become dwarfed by disuse.

Meanwhile Robert, addressing Mrs. Pontellier, continued to tell of his one time hopeless passion for Madame Ratignolle; of sleepless nights, of consuming flames till the very sea sizzled when he took his daily plunge. While the lady at the needle kept up a little running, contemptuous comment:

"*Blagueur—farceur—gros bête, va!*"

He never assumed this serio-comic tone when alone with Mrs. Pontellier. She never knew precisely what to make of it; at that moment it was impossible for her to guess how much of it was jest and what proportion was earnest. It was understood that he had often spoken words of love to Madame Ratignolle, without any thought of being taken seriously. Mrs. Pontellier was glad he had not assumed a similar rôle toward herself. It would have been unacceptable and annoying.

Mrs. Pontellier had brought her sketching materials, which she sometimes dabbled with in an unprofessional way. She liked the dabbling. She felt in it satisfaction of a kind which no other employment afforded her.

She had long wished to try herself on Madame Ratignolle. Never had that lady seemed a more tempting subject than at that moment, seated there like some sensuous Madonna, with the gleam of the fading day enriching her splendid color.

Robert crossed over and seated himself upon the step below Mrs. Pontellier, that he might watch her work. She handled her brushes with a certain ease and freedom which came, not from long and close acquaintance with them, but from a natural aptitude. Robert followed her work with close attention, giving forth little ejaculatory expressions of appreciation in French, which he addressed to Madame Ratignolle.

"*Mais ce n'est pas mal! Elle s'y connait, elle a de la force, oui.*"

During his oblivious attention he once quietly rested his head against Mrs. Pontellier's arm. As gently she repulsed him. Once again he repeated the offense. She could not but believe it to be thoughtlessness on his part; yet that was no reason she should submit to it. She did not remonstrate, except again to repulse him quietly but firmly. He offered no apology.

The picture completed bore no resemblance to Madame Ratignolle. She was greatly disappointed to find that it did not look like her. But it was a fair enough piece of work, and in many respects satisfying.

Mrs. Pontellier evidently did not think so. After surveying the sketch critically she drew a broad smudge of paint across its surface, and crumpled the paper between her hands.

The youngsters came tumbling up the steps, the quadroon following at the respectful distance which they required her to observe. Mrs. Pontellier made them carry her paints and things into the house. She sought to detain them for a little talk and some pleasantry. But they were greatly in earnest. They had only come to investigate the contents of the bonbon box. They accepted without murmuring what she chose to give them, each holding out two chubby hands scoop-like, in the vain hope that they might be filled; and then away they went.

The sun was low in the west, and the breeze soft and languorous that came up from the south, charged with the seductive odor of the sea. Children, freshly befurbelowed, were gathering for their games under the oaks. Their voices were high and penetrating.

Madame Ratignolle folded her sewing, placing thimble, scissors and thread all neatly together in the roll, which she pinned securely. She complained of faintness. Mrs. Pontellier flew for the cologne water and a fan. She bathed Madame Ratignolle's face with cologne, while Robert plied the fan with unnecessary vigor.

The spell was soon over, and Mrs. Pontellier could not help wondering if there were not a little imagination responsible for its origin, for the rose tint had never faded from her friend's face.

She stood watching the fair woman walk down the long line of galleries with the grace and majesty which queens are sometimes supposed to possess. Her little ones ran to meet her. Two of them clung about her white skirts, the third she took from its nurse and with a thousand endearments bore it along in her own fond, encircling arms. Though, as everybody well knew, the doctor had forbidden her to lift so much as a pin!

"Are you going bathing?" asked Robert of Mrs. Pontellier. It was not so much a question as a reminder.

"Oh, no," she answered, with a tone of indecision. "I'm tired; I think not." Her glance wandered from his face away toward the Gulf, whose sonorous murmur reached her like a loving but imperative entreaty.

"Oh, come!" he insisted. "You mustn't miss your bath. Come on. The water must be delicious; it will not hurt you. Come."

He reached up for her big, rough straw hat that hung on a peg outside the door, and put it on her head. They descended the steps, and walked away together toward the beach. The sun was low in the west and the breeze was soft and warm.

CHAPTER VI

Edna Pontellier could not have told why, wishing to go to the beach with Robert, she should in the first place have declined, and in the second place have followed in obedience to one of the two contradictory impulses which impelled her.

A certain light was beginning to dawn dimly within her,—the light which, showing the way, forbids it.

At that early period it served but to bewilder her. It moved her to dreams, to thoughtfulness, to the shadowy anguish which had overcome her the midnight when she had abandoned herself to tears.

In short, Mrs. Pontellier was beginning to realize her position in the universe as a human being, and to recognize her relations as an individual to the world within and about her. This may seem like a ponderous weight of wisdom to descend upon the soul of a young woman of twenty-eight—perhaps more wisdom than the Holy Ghost is usually pleased to vouchsafe to any woman.

But the beginning of things, of a world especially, is necessarily vague, tangled, chaotic, and exceedingly disturbing. How few of us ever emerge from such beginning! How many souls perish in its tumult!

The voice of the sea is seductive; never ceasing, whispering, clamoring, murmuring, inviting the soul to wander for a spell in abysses of solitude; to lose itself in mazes of inward contemplation.

The voice of the sea speaks to the soul. The touch of the sea is sensuous, enfolding the body in its soft, close embrace.

CHAPTER VII

Mrs. Pontellier was not a woman given to confidence, a characteristic hitherto contrary to her nature. Even as a child she had lived her own small life all within herself. At a very early period she had apprehended instinctively the dual life—that outward existence which conforms, the inward life which questions.

That summer at Grand Isle she began to loosen a little the mantle of reserve that had always enveloped her. There may have been—there must have been—influences, both subtle and apparent, working in their several ways to induce her to do this; but the most obvious was the influence of Adèle Ratignolle. The excessive physical charm of the Creole had first attracted her, for Edna had a sensuous susceptibility to beauty. Then the candor of the woman's whole existence, which every one might read, and which formed so striking a contrast to her own habitual reserve—this might have furnished a link. Who can tell what metals the gods use in forging the subtle bond which we call sympathy, which we might as well call love.

The two women went away one morning to the beach together, arm in arm, under the huge white sunshade. Edna had prevailed upon Madame Ratignolle to leave the children behind, though she could not induce her to relinquish a diminutive roll of needlework, which Adèle begged to be allowed to slip into the depths of her pocket. In some unaccountable way they had escaped from Robert.

The walk to the beach was no inconsiderable one, consisting as it did of a long, sandy path, upon which a sporadic and tangled growth that bordered it on either side made frequent and unexpected inroads. There were acres of yellow camomile reaching out on either hand. Further away still, vegetable gardens abounded, with frequent small plantations of orange or lemon trees intervening. The dark green clusters glistened from afar in the sun.

The women were both of goodly height, Madame Ratignolle possessing the more feminine and matronly figure. The charm of Edna Pontellier's physique stole insensibly upon you. The lines of her body were long, clean and symmetrical; it was a body which occasionally fell into splendid poses; there was no suggestion of the trim, stereotyped fashion-plate about it. A casual and indiscriminating observer, in passing, might not cast a second glance upon the figure. But with more feeling and discernment he would have recognized the noble beauty of its modeling, and the graceful severity of poise and movement, which made Edna Pontellier different from the crowd.

She wore a cool muslin that morning—white, with a waving vertical line of brown running through it; also a white linen collar and the big straw hat which she had taken from the peg outside the door. The hat rested any way on her yellow-brown hair, that waved a little, was heavy, and clung close to her head.

Madame Ratignolle, more careful of her complexion, had twined a gauze veil about her head. She wore dogskin gloves, with gauntlets that protected her wrists. She was dressed in pure white, with a fluffiness of ruffles that became her. The draperies and fluttering things which she wore suited her rich, luxuriant beauty as a greater severity of line could not have done.

There were a number of bath-houses along the beach, of rough but solid construction, built with small, protecting galleries facing the water. Each house consisted of two compartments, and each family at Lebrun's possessed a compartment for itself, fitted out with all the essential paraphernalia of the bath and whatever other conveniences the owners might desire. The two women had no intention of bathing; they had just strolled down to the beach for a walk and to be alone and near the water. The Pontellier and Ratignolle compartments adjoined one another under the same roof.

Mrs. Pontellier had brought down her key through force of habit. Unlocking the door of her bath-room she went inside, and soon emerged, bringing a rug, which she spread upon the floor of the gallery, and two huge hair pillows covered with crash, which she placed against the front of the building.

The two seated themselves there in the shade of the porch, side by side, with their backs against the pillows and their feet extended. Madame Ratignolle removed her veil, wiped her face with a rather delicate handkerchief, and fanned herself with the fan which she always carried suspended somewhere about her person by a long, narrow ribbon. Edna removed her collar and opened her dress at the throat. She took the fan from Madame Ratignolle and began to fan both herself and her companion. It was very warm, and for a while they did nothing but exchange remarks about the heat, the sun, the glare. But there was a breeze blowing, a choppy stiff wind that whipped the water into froth. It fluttered the skirts of the two women and kept them for a while engaged in adjusting, readjusting, tucking in, securing hair-pins and hat-pins. A few persons were sporting some distance away in the water. The beach was very still of human sound at that hour. The lady in black was reading her morning devotions on the porch of a neighboring bath-house. Two young lovers were exchanging their hearts' yearnings beneath the children's tent, which they had found unoccupied.

Edna Pontellier, casting her eyes about had finally kept them at rest upon the sea. The day was clear and carried the gaze out as far as the blue sky went; there were a few white clouds suspended idly over the horizon. A lateen sail was visible in the direction of Cat Island, and others to the south seemed almost motionless in the far distance.

"Of whom—of what are you thinking?" asked Adèle of her companion, whose countenance she had been watching with a little amused attention, arrested by the absorbed expression which seemed to have seized and fixed every feature into a statuesque repose.

"Nothing," returned Mrs. Pontellier, with a start, adding at once: "How stupid! But it seems to me it is the reply we make instinctively to such a question. Let me see," she went on, throwing back her head and narrowing her fine eyes till they shone like two vivid points of light. "Let me see. I was really not conscious of thinking of anything; but perhaps I can retrace my thoughts."

"Oh! never mind!" laughed Madame Ratignolle. "I am not quite so exacting. I will let you off this time. It is really too hot to think, especially to think about thinking."

"But for the fun of it," persisted Edna. "First of all, the sight of the water stretching so far away, those motionless sails against the blue sky, made a delicious picture that I just wanted to sit and look at. The hot wind beating in my face made me think—without any connection that I can trace—of a summer day in Kentucky, of a meadow that seemed as big as the ocean to the very little girl walking through the grass, which was higher than her waist. She threw out her arms as if swimming when she walked, beating the tall grass as one strikes out in the water. Oh, I see the connection now!"

"Where were you going that day in Kentucky, walking through the grass?"

"I don't remember now. I was just walking diagonally across a big field. My sun-bonnet obstructed the view. I could see only the stretch of green before me, and I felt as if I must walk on forever, without coming to the end of it. I don't remember whether I was frightened or pleased. I must have been entertained.

"Likely as not it was Sunday," she laughed; "and I was running away from prayers, from the Presbyterian service, read in a spirit of gloom by my father that chills me yet to think of."

"And have you been running away from prayers ever since, *ma chère*?" asked Madame Ratignolle, amused.

"No! oh, no!" Edna hastened to say. "I was a little unthinking child in those days, just following a misleading impulse without question. On the contrary, during one period of my life religion took a firm hold upon me; after I was twelve and until—until—why, I suppose until now, though I never thought much about it—just driven along by habit. But do you know," she broke off, turning her quick eyes upon Madame Ratignolle and leaning forward a little so as to bring her face quite close to that of her companion, "sometimes I feel this summer as if I were walking through the green meadow again; idly, aimlessly, unthinking and unguided."

Madame Ratignolle laid her hand over that of Mrs. Pontellier, which was near her. Seeing that the hand was not withdrawn, she clasped it firmly and warmly. She even stroked it a little, fondly, with the other hand, murmuring in an undertone, "*Pauvre chérie.*"

The action was at first a little confusing to Edna, but she soon lent herself readily to the Creole's gentle caress. She was not accustomed to an outward and spoken expression of affection, either in herself or in others. She and her younger sister, Janet, had quarreled a good deal through force of unfortunate habit. Her older sister, Margaret, was matronly and dignified, probably from having assumed matronly and house-wifely responsibilities too early in life, their mother having died when they were quite young. Margaret was not effusive; she was practical. Edna had had an occasional girl friend, but whether accidentally or not, they seemed to have been all of one type—the self-contained. She never realized that the reserve of her own character had much, perhaps everything, to do with this. Her most intimate friend at school had been one of rather exceptional intellectual gifts, who wrote fine-sounding essays, which Edna admired and strove to imitate; and with her she talked and glowed over the English classics, and sometimes held religious and political controversies.

Edna often wondered at one propensity which sometimes had inwardly disturbed her without causing any outward show or manifestation on her part. At a very early age—perhaps it was when she traversed the ocean of waving grass—she remembered that she had been passionately enamored of a dignified and sad-eyed cavalry officer who visited her father in Kentucky. She could not leave his presence when he was there, nor remove her eyes from his face, which was something like Napoleon's, with a lock of black hair falling across the forehead. But the cavalry officer melted imperceptibly out of her existence.

At another time her affections were deeply engaged by a young gentleman who visited a lady on a neighboring plantation. It was after they went to Mississippi to live. The young man was engaged to be married to the young lady, and they sometimes called upon Margaret, driving over of afternoons in a buggy. Edna was a little miss, just merging into her teens; and the realization that she herself was nothing, nothing, nothing to the engaged young man was a bitter affliction to her. But he, too, went the way of dreams.

She was a grown young woman when she was overtaken by what she supposed to be the climax of her fate. It was when the face and figure of a great tragedian began to haunt her imagination and stir her senses. The persistence of the infatuation lent it an aspect of genuineness. The hopelessness of it colored it with the lofty tones of a great passion.

The picture of the tragedian stood enframed upon her desk. Any one may possess the portrait of a tragedian without exciting suspicion or comment. (This was a sinister reflection which she cherished.) In the presence of others she expressed admiration for his exalted gifts, as she handed the photograph around and dwelt upon the fidelity of the likeness. When alone she sometimes picked it up and kissed the cold glass passionately.

Her marriage to Léonce Pontellier was purely an accident, in this respect resembling many other marriages which masquerade as the decrees of Fate. It was in the midst of her secret great passion that she met him. He fell in love, as men are in the habit of doing, and pressed his suit with an earnestness and an ardor which left nothing to be desired. He pleased her; his absolute devotion flattered her. She fancied there was a sympathy of thought and taste between them, in which fancy she was mistaken. Add to this the violent opposition of her father and her sister Margaret to her marriage with a Catholic, and we need seek no further for the motives which led her to accept Monsieur Pontellier for her husband.

The acme of bliss, which would have been a marriage with the tragedian, was not for her in this world. As the devoted wife of a man who worshiped her, she felt she would take her place with a certain dignity in the world of reality, closing the portals forever behind her upon the realm of romance and dreams.

But it was not long before the tragedian had gone to join the cavalry officer and the engaged young man and a few others; and Edna found herself face to face with the realities. She grew fond of her husband, realizing with some unaccountable satisfaction that no trace of passion or excessive and fictitious warmth colored her affection, thereby threatening its dissolution.

She was fond of her children in an uneven, impulsive way. She would sometimes gather them passionately to her heart; she would sometimes forget them. The year before they had spent part of the summer with their grandmother Pontellier in Iberville. Feeling secure regarding their happiness and welfare, she did not miss them except with an occasional intense longing. Their absence was a sort of relief, though she did not admit this, even to herself. It seemed to free her of a responsibility which she had blindly assumed and for which Fate had not fitted her.

Edna did not reveal so much as all this to Madame Ratignolle that summer day when they sat with faces turned to the sea. But a good part of it escaped her. She had put her head down on Madame Ratignolle's shoulder. She was flushed and felt intoxicated with the sound of her own voice and the unaccustomed taste of candor. It muddled her like wine, or like a first breath of freedom.

There was the sound of approaching voices. It was Robert, surrounded by a troop of children, searching for them. The two little Pontelliers were with him, and he carried Madame Ratignolle's little girl in his arms. There were other children beside, and two nursemaids followed, looking disagreeable and resigned.

The women at once rose and began to shake out their draperies and relax their muscles. Mrs. Pontellier threw the cushions and rug into the bath-house. The children all scampered off to the awning, and they stood there in a line, gazing upon the intruding lovers, still exchanging their vows and sighs. The lovers got up, with only a silent protest, and walked slowly away somewhere else.

The children possessed themselves of the tent, and Mrs. Pontellier went over to join them.

Madame Ratignolle begged Robert to accompany her to the house; she complained of cramp in her limbs and stiffness of the joints. She leaned draggingly upon his arm as they walked.

CHAPTER VIII

"Do me a favor, Robert," spoke the pretty woman at his side, almost as soon as she and Robert had started on their slow, homeward way. She looked up in his face, leaning on his arm beneath the encircling shadow of the umbrella which he had lifted.

"Granted; as many as you like," he returned, glancing down into her eyes that were full of thoughtfulness and some speculation.

"I only ask for one; let Mrs. Pontellier alone."

"*Tiens!*" he exclaimed, with a sudden, boyish laugh. "*Voilà que Madame Ratignolle est jalouse!*"

"Nonsense! I'm in earnest; I mean what I say. Let Mrs. Pontellier alone."

"Why?" he asked; himself growing serious at his companion's solicitation.

"She is not one of us; she is not like us. She might make the unfortunate blunder of taking you seriously."

His face flushed with annoyance, and taking off his soft hat he began to beat it impatiently against his leg as he walked. "Why shouldn't she take me seriously?" he demanded sharply. "Am I a comedian, a clown, a jack-in-the-box? Why shouldn't she? You Creoles! I have no patience with you! Am I always to be regarded as a feature of an amusing programme? I hope Mrs. Pontellier does take me seriously. I hope she has discernment enough to find in me something besides the *blagueur*. If I thought there was any doubt—"

"Oh, enough, Robert!" she broke into his heated outburst. "You are not thinking of what you are saying. You speak with about as little reflection as we might expect from one of those children down there playing in the sand. If your attentions to any married women here were ever offered with any intention of being convincing, you would not be the gentleman we all know you to be, and you would be unfit to associate with the wives and daughters of the people who trust you."

Madame Ratignolle had spoken what she believed to be the law and the gospel. The young man shrugged his shoulders impatiently.

"Oh! well! That isn't it," slamming his hat down vehemently upon his head. "You ought to feel that such things are not flattering to say to a fellow."

"Should our whole intercourse consist of an exchange of compliments? *Ma foi!*"

"It isn't pleasant to have a woman tell you—" he went on, unheedingly, but breaking off suddenly: "Now if I were like Arobin—you remember Alcée Arobin and that story of the consul's wife at Biloxi?" And he related the story of Alcée Arobin and the consul's wife; and another about the tenor of the French Opera, who received letters which should never have been written; and still other stories, grave and gay, till Mrs. Pontellier and her possible propensity for taking young men seriously was apparently forgotten.

Madame Ratignolle, when they had regained her cottage, went in to take the hour's rest which she considered helpful. Before leaving her, Robert begged her pardon for the impatience—he called it rudeness—with which he had received her well-meant caution.

"You made one mistake, Adèle," he said, with a light smile; "there is no earthly possibility of Mrs. Pontellier ever taking me seriously. You should have warned me against taking myself seriously. Your advice might then have carried some weight and given me subject for some reflection. *Au revoir*. But you look tired," he added, solicitously. "Would you like a cup of bouillon? Shall I stir you a toddy? Let me mix you a toddy with a drop of Angostura."

She acceded to the suggestion of bouillon, which was grateful and acceptable. He went himself to the kitchen, which was a building apart from the cottages and lying to the rear of the house. And he himself brought her the golden-brown bouillon, in a dainty Sèvres cup, with a flaky cracker or two on the saucer.

She thrust a bare, white arm from the curtain which shielded her open door, and received the cup from his hands. She told him he was a *bon garçon*, and she meant it. Robert thanked her and turned away toward "the house."

The lovers were just entering the grounds of the *pension*. They were leaning toward each other as the water-oaks bent from the sea. There was not a particle of earth beneath their feet. Their heads might have been turned upside-down, so absolutely did they tread upon blue ether. The lady in black, creeping behind them, looked a trifle paler and more jaded than usual. There was no sign of Mrs. Pontellier and the children. Robert scanned the distance for any such apparition. They would doubtless remain away till the dinner hour. The young man ascended to his mother's room. It was situated at the top of the house, made up of odd angles and a queer, sloping ceiling. Two broad dormer windows looked out toward the Gulf, and as far across it as a man's eye might reach. The furnishings of the room were light, cool, and practical.

Madame Lebrun was busily engaged at the sewing-machine. A little black girl sat on the floor, and with her hands worked the treadle of the machine. The Creole woman does not take any chances which may be avoided of imperiling her health.

Robert went over and seated himself on the broad sill of one of the dormer windows. He took a book from his pocket and began energetically to read it, judging by the precision and frequency with which he turned the leaves. The sewing-machine made a resounding clatter in the room; it was of a ponderous, by-gone make. In the lulls, Robert and his mother exchanged bits of desultory conversation.

"Where is Mrs. Pontellier?"

"Down at the beach with the children."

"I promised to lend her the Goncourt. Don't forget to take it down when you go; it's there on the bookshelf over the small table." Clatter, clatter, clatter, bang! for the next five or eight minutes.

"Where is Victor going with the rockaway?"

"The rockaway? Victor?"

"Yes; down there in front. He seems to be getting ready to drive away somewhere."

"Call him." Clatter, clatter!

Robert uttered a shrill, piercing whistle which might have been heard back at the wharf.

"He won't look up."

Madame Lebrun flew to the window. She called "Victor!" She waved a handkerchief and called again. The young fellow below got into the vehicle and started the horse off at a gallop.

Madame Lebrun went back to the machine, crimson with annoyance. Victor was the younger son and brother—a *tête montée*, with a temper which invited violence and a will which no ax could break.

"Whenever you say the word I'm ready to thrash any amount of reason into him that he's able to hold."

"If your father had only lived!" Clatter, clatter, clatter, clatter, bang! It was a fixed belief with Madame Lebrun that the conduct of the universe and all things pertaining thereto would have been manifestly of a more intelligent and higher order had not Monsieur Lebrun been removed to other spheres during the early years of their married life.

"What do you hear from Montel?" Montel was a middle-aged gentleman whose vain ambition and desire for the past twenty years had been to fill the void which Monsieur Lebrun's taking off had left in the Lebrun household. Clatter, clatter, bang, clatter!

"I have a letter somewhere," looking in the machine drawer and finding the letter in the bottom of the work-basket. "He says to tell you he will be in Vera Cruz the beginning of next month"—clatter, clatter!—"and if you still have the intention of joining him"—bang! clatter, clatter, bang!

"Why didn't you tell me so before, mother? You know I wanted—" Clatter, clatter, clatter!

"Do you see Mrs. Pontellier starting back with the children? She will be in late to luncheon again. She never starts to get ready for luncheon till the last minute." Clatter, clatter! "Where are you going?"

"Where did you say the Goncourt was?"

CHAPTER IX

Every light in the hall was ablaze; every lamp turned as high as it could be without smoking the chimney or threatening explosion. The lamps were fixed at intervals against the wall, encircling the whole room. Some one had gathered orange and lemon branches and with these fashioned graceful festoons between. The dark green of the branches stood out and glistened against the white muslin curtains which draped the windows, and which puffed, floated, and flapped at the capricious will of a stiff breeze that swept up from the Gulf.

It was Saturday night a few weeks after the intimate conversation held between Robert and Madame Ratignolle on their way from the beach. An unusual number of husbands, fathers, and friends had come down to stay over Sunday; and they were being suitably entertained by their families, with the material help of Madame Lebrun. The dining tables had all been removed to one end of the hall, and the chairs ranged about in rows and in clusters. Each little family group had had its say and exchanged its domestic gossip earlier in the evening. There was now an apparent disposition to relax; to widen the circle of confidences and give a more general tone to the conversation.

Many of the children had been permitted to sit up beyond their usual bedtime. A small band of them were lying on their stomachs on the floor looking at the colored sheets of the comic papers which Mr. Pontellier had brought down. The little Pontellier boys were permitting them to do so, and making their authority felt.

Music, dancing, and a recitation or two were the entertainments furnished, or rather, offered. But there was nothing systematic about the programme, no appearance of prearrangement nor even premeditation.

At an early hour in the evening the Farival twins were prevailed upon to play the piano. They were girls of fourteen, always clad in the Virgin's colors, blue and white, having been dedicated to the Blessed Virgin at their baptism. They played a duet from "Zampa," and at the earnest solicitation of every one present followed it with the overture to "The Poet and the Peasant."

"*Allez vous-en! Sapristi!*" shrieked the parrot outside the door. He was the only being present who possessed sufficient candor to admit that he was not listening to these gracious performances for the first time that summer. Old Monsieur Farival, grandfather of the twins, grew indignant over the interruption, and insisted upon having the bird removed and consigned to regions of darkness. Victor Lebrun objected; and his decrees were as immutable as those of Fate. The parrot fortunately offered no further interruption to the entertainment, the whole venom of his nature apparently having been cherished up and hurled against the twins in that one impetuous outburst.

Later a young brother and sister gave recitations, which every one present had heard many times at winter evening entertainments in the city.

A little girl performed a skirt dance in the center of the floor. The mother played her accompaniments and at the same time watched her daughter with greedy admiration and nervous apprehension. She need have had no apprehension. The child was mistress of the situation. She had been properly dressed for the occasion in black tulle and black silk tights. Her little neck and arms were bare, and her hair, artificially crimped, stood out like fluffy black plumes over her head. Her poses were full of grace, and her little black-shod toes twinkled as they shot out and upward with a rapidity and suddenness which were bewildering.

But there was no reason why every one should not dance. Madame Ratignolle could not, so it was she who gaily consented to play for the others. She played very well, keeping excellent waltz time and infusing an expression into the strains which was indeed inspiring. She was keeping up her music on account of the children, she said; because she and her husband both considered it a means of brightening the home and making it attractive.

Almost every one danced but the twins, who could not be induced to separate during the brief period when one or the other should be whirling around the room in the arms of a man. They might have danced together, but they did not think of it.

The children were sent to bed. Some went submissively; others with shrieks and protests as they were dragged away. They had been permitted to sit up till after the ice-cream, which naturally marked the limit of human indulgence.

The ice-cream was passed around with cake—gold and silver cake arranged on platters in alternate slices; it had been made and frozen during the afternoon back of the kitchen by two black women, under the supervision of Victor. It was pronounced a great success—excellent if it had only contained a little less vanilla or a little more sugar, if it had been frozen a degree harder, and if the salt might have been kept out of portions of it. Victor was proud of his achievement, and went about recommending it and urging every one to partake of it to excess.

After Mrs. Pontellier had danced twice with her husband, once with Robert, and once with Monsieur Ratignolle, who was thin and tall and swayed like a reed in the wind when he danced, she went out on the gallery and seated herself on the low window-sill, where she commanded a view of all that went on in the hall and could look out toward the Gulf. There was a soft effulgence in the east. The moon was coming up, and its mystic shimmer was casting a million lights across the distant, restless water.

"Would you like to hear Mademoiselle Reisz play?" asked Robert, coming out on the porch where she was. Of course Edna would like to hear Mademoiselle Reisz play; but she feared it would be useless to entreat her.

"I'll ask her," he said. "I'll tell her that you want to hear her. She likes you. She will come." He turned and hurried away to one of the far cottages, where Mademoiselle Reisz was shuffling away. She was dragging a chair in and out of her room, and at intervals objecting to the crying of a baby, which a nurse in the adjoining cottage was endeavoring to put to sleep. She was a disagreeable little woman, no longer young, who had quarreled with almost every one, owing to a temper which was self-assertive and a disposition to trample upon the rights of others. Robert prevailed upon her without any too great difficulty.

She entered the hall with him during a lull in the dance. She made an awkward, imperious little bow as she went in. She was a homely woman, with a small weazened face and body and eyes that glowed. She had absolutely no taste in dress, and wore a batch of rusty black lace with a bunch of artificial violets pinned to the side of her hair.

"Ask Mrs. Pontellier what she would like to hear me play," she requested of Robert. She sat perfectly still before the piano, not touching the keys, while Robert carried her message to Edna at the window. A general air of surprise and genuine satisfaction fell upon every one as they saw the pianist enter. There was a settling down, and a prevailing air of expectancy everywhere. Edna was a trifle embarrassed at being thus signaled out for the imperious little woman's favor. She would not dare to choose, and begged that Mademoiselle Reisz would please herself in her selections.

Edna was what she herself called very fond of music. Musical strains, well rendered, had a way of evoking pictures in her mind. She sometimes liked to sit in the room of mornings when Madame Ratignolle played or practiced. One piece which that lady played Edna had entitled "Solitude." It was a short, plaintive, minor strain. The name of the piece was something else, but she called it "Solitude." When she heard it there came before her imagination the figure of a man standing beside a desolate rock on the seashore. He was naked. His attitude was one of hopeless resignation as he looked toward a distant bird winging its flight away from him.

Another piece called to her mind a dainty young woman clad in an Empire gown, taking mincing dancing steps as she came down a long avenue between tall hedges. Again, another reminded her of children at play, and still another of nothing on earth but a demure lady stroking a cat.

The very first chords which Mademoiselle Reisz struck upon the piano sent a keen tremor down Mrs. Pontellier's spinal column. It was not the first time she had heard an artist at the piano. Perhaps it was the first time she was ready, perhaps the first time her being was tempered to take an impress of the abiding truth.

She waited for the material pictures which she thought would gather and blaze before her imagination. She waited in vain. She saw no pictures of solitude, of hope, of longing, or of despair. But the very passions themselves were aroused within her soul, swaying it, lashing it, as the waves daily beat upon her splendid body. She trembled, she was choking, and the tears blinded her.

Mademoiselle had finished. She arose, and bowing her stiff, lofty bow, she went away, stopping for neither thanks nor applause. As she passed along the gallery she patted Edna upon the shoulder.

"Well, how did you like my music?" she asked. The young woman was unable to answer; she pressed the hand of the pianist convulsively. Mademoiselle Reisz perceived her agitation and even her tears. She patted her again upon the shoulder as she said:

"You are the only one worth playing for. Those others? Bah!" and she went shuffling and sidling on down the gallery toward her room.

But she was mistaken about "those others." Her playing had aroused a fever of enthusiasm. "What passion!" "What an artist!" "I have always said no one could play Chopin like Mademoiselle Reisz!" "That last prelude! Bon Dieu! It shakes a man!"

It was growing late, and there was a general disposition to disband. But some one, perhaps it was Robert, thought of a bath at that mystic hour and under that mystic moon.

CHAPTER X

At all events Robert proposed it, and there was not a dissenting voice. There was not one but was ready to follow when he led the way. He did not lead the way, however, he directed the way; and he himself loitered behind with the lovers, who had betrayed a disposition to linger and hold themselves apart. He walked between them, whether with malicious or mischievous intent was not wholly clear, even to himself.

The Pontelliers and Ratignolles walked ahead; the women leaning upon the arms of their husbands. Edna could hear Robert's voice behind them, and could sometimes hear what he said. She wondered why he did not join them. It was unlike him not to. Of late he had sometimes held away from her for an entire day, redoubling his devotion upon the next and the next, as though to make up for hours that had been lost. She missed him the days when some pretext served to take him away from her, just as one misses the sun on a cloudy day without having thought much about the sun when it was shining.

The people walked in little groups toward the beach. They talked and laughed; some of them sang. There was a band playing down at Klein's hotel, and the strains reached them faintly, tempered by the distance. There were strange, rare odors abroad—a tangle of the sea smell and of weeds and damp, new-plowed earth, mingled with the heavy perfume of a field of white blossoms somewhere near. But the night sat lightly upon the sea and the land. There was no weight of darkness; there were no shadows. The white light of the moon had fallen upon the world like the mystery and the softness of sleep.

Most of them walked into the water as though into a native element. The sea was quiet now, and swelled lazily in broad billows that melted into one another and did not break except upon the beach in little foamy crests that coiled back like slow, white serpents.

Edna had attempted all summer to learn to swim. She had received instructions from both the men and women; in some instances from the children. Robert had pursued a system of lessons almost daily; and he was nearly at the point of discouragement in realizing the futility of his efforts. A certain ungovernable dread hung about her when in the water, unless there was a hand near by that might reach out and reassure her.

But that night she was like the little tottering, stumbling, clutching child, who of a sudden realizes its powers, and walks for the first time alone, boldly and with over-confidence. She could have shouted for joy. She did shout for joy, as with a sweeping stroke or two she lifted her body to the surface of the water.

A feeling of exultation overtook her, as if some power of significant import had been given her soul. She grew daring and reckless, overestimating her strength. She wanted to swim far out, where no woman had swum before.

Her unlooked-for achievement was the subject of wonder, applause, and admiration. Each one congratulated himself that his special teachings had accomplished this desired end.

"How easy it is!" she thought. "It is nothing," she said aloud; "why did I not discover before that it was nothing. Think of the time I have lost splashing about like a baby!" She would not join the groups in their sports and bouts, but intoxicated with her newly conquered power, she swam out alone.

She turned her face seaward to gather in an impression of space and solitude, which the vast expanse of water, meeting and melting with the moonlit sky, conveyed to her excited fancy. As she swam she seemed to be reaching out for the unlimited in which to lose herself.

Once she turned and looked toward the shore, toward the people she had left there. She had not gone any great distance—that is, what would have been a great distance for an experienced swimmer. But to her unaccustomed vision the stretch of water behind her assumed the aspect of a barrier which her unaided strength would never be able to overcome.

A quick vision of death smote her soul, and for a second of time appalled and enfeebled her senses. But by an effort she rallied her staggering faculties and managed to regain the land.

She made no mention of her encounter with death and her flash of terror, except to say to her husband, "I thought I should have perished out there alone."

"You were not so very far, my dear; I was watching you," he told her.

Edna went at once to the bath-house, and she had put on her dry clothes and was ready to return home before the others had left the water. She started to walk away alone. They all called to her and shouted to her. She waved a dissenting hand, and went on, paying no further heed to their renewed cries which sought to detain her.

"Sometimes I am tempted to think that Mrs. Pontellier is capricious," said Madame Lebrun, who was amusing herself immensely and feared that Edna's abrupt departure might put an end to the pleasure.

"I know she is," assented Mr. Pontellier; "sometimes, not often."

Edna had not traversed a quarter of the distance on her way home before she was overtaken by Robert.

"Did you think I was afraid?" she asked him, without a shade of annoyance.

"No; I knew you weren't afraid."

"Then why did you come? Why didn't you stay out there with the others?"

"I never thought of it."

"Thought of what?"

"Of anything. What difference does it make?"

"I'm very tired," she uttered, complainingly.

"I know you are."

"You don't know anything about it. Why should you know? I never was so exhausted in my life. But it isn't unpleasant. A thousand emotions have swept through me to-night. I don't comprehend half of them. Don't mind what I'm saying; I am just thinking aloud. I wonder if I shall ever be stirred again as Mademoiselle Reisz's playing moved me to-night. I wonder if any night on earth will ever again be like this one. It is like a night in a dream. The people about me are like some uncanny, half-human beings. There must be spirits abroad to-night."

"There are," whispered Robert. "Didn't you know this was the twenty-eighth of August?"

"The twenty-eighth of August?"

"Yes. On the twenty-eighth of August, at the hour of midnight, and if the moon is shining—the moon must be shining—a spirit that has haunted these shores for ages rises up from the Gulf. With its own penetrating vision the spirit seeks some one mortal worthy to hold him company, worthy of being exalted for a few hours into realms of the semi-celestials. His search has always hitherto been fruitless, and he has sunk back, disheartened, into the sea. But to-night he found Mrs. Pontellier. Perhaps he will never wholly release her from the spell. Perhaps she will never again suffer a poor, unworthy earthling to walk in the shadow of her divine presence."

"Don't banter me," she said, wounded at what appeared to be his flippancy. He did not mind the entreaty, but the tone with its delicate note of pathos was like a reproach. He could not explain; he could not tell her that he had penetrated her mood and understood. He said nothing except to offer her his arm, for, by her own admission, she was exhausted. She had been walking alone with her arms hanging limp, letting her white skirts trail along the dewy path. She took his arm, but she did not lean upon it. She let her hand lie listlessly, as though her thoughts were elsewhere—somewhere in advance of her body, and she was striving to overtake them.

Robert assisted her into the hammock which swung from the post before her door out to the trunk of a tree.

"Will you stay out here and wait for Mr. Pontellier?" he asked.

"I'll stay out here. Good-night."

"Shall I get you a pillow?"

"There's one here," she said, feeling about, for they were in the shadow.

"It must be soiled; the children have been tumbling it about."

"No matter." And having discovered the pillow, she adjusted it beneath her head. She extended herself in the hammock with a deep breath of relief. She was not a supercilious or an over-dainty woman. She was not much given to reclining in the hammock, and when she did so it was with no cat-like suggestion of voluptuous ease, but with a beneficent repose which seemed to invade her whole body.

"Shall I stay with you till Mr. Pontellier comes?" asked Robert, seating himself on the outer edge of one of the steps and taking hold of the hammock rope which was fastened to the post.

"If you wish. Don't swing the hammock. Will you get my white shawl which I left on the window-sill over at the house?"

"Are you chilly?"

"No; but I shall be presently."

"Presently?" he laughed. "Do you know what time it is? How long are you going to stay out here?"

"I don't know. Will you get the shawl?"

"Of course I will," he said, rising. He went over to the house, walking along the grass. She watched his figure pass in and out of the strips of moonlight. It was past midnight. It was very quiet.

When he returned with the shawl she took it and kept it in her hand. She did not put it around her.

"Did you say I should stay till Mr. Pontellier came back?"

"I said you might if you wished to."

He seated himself again and rolled a cigarette, which he smoked in silence. Neither did Mrs. Pontellier speak. No multitude of words could have been more significant than those moments of silence, or more pregnant with the first-felt throbbings of desire.

When the voices of the bathers were heard approaching, Robert said good-night. She did not answer him. He thought she was asleep. Again she watched his figure pass in and out of the strips of moonlight as he walked away.

CHAPTER XI

"What are you doing out here, Edna? I thought I should find you in bed," said her husband, when he discovered her lying there. He had walked up with Madame Lebrun and left her at the house. His wife did not reply.

"Are you asleep?" he asked, bending down close to look at her.

"No." Her eyes gleamed bright and intense, with no sleepy shadows, as they looked into his.

"Do you know it is past one o'clock? Come on," and he mounted the steps and went into their room.

"Edna!" called Mr. Pontellier from within, after a few moments had gone by.

"Don't wait for me," she answered. He thrust his head through the door.

"You will take cold out there," he said, irritably. "What folly is this? Why don't you come in?"

"It isn't cold; I have my shawl."

"The mosquitoes will devour you."

"There are no mosquitoes."

She heard him moving about the room; every sound indicating impatience and irritation. Another time she would have gone in at his request. She would, through habit, have yielded to his desire; not with any sense of submission or obedience to his compelling wishes, but unthinkingly, as we walk, move, sit, stand, go through the daily treadmill of the life which has been portioned out to us.

"Edna, dear, are you not coming in soon?" he asked again, this time fondly, with a note of entreaty.

"No; I am going to stay out here."

"This is more than folly," he blurted out. "I can't permit you to stay out there all night. You must come in the house instantly."

With a writhing motion she settled herself more securely in the hammock. She perceived that her will had blazed up, stubborn and resistant. She could not at that moment have done other than denied and resisted. She wondered if her husband had ever spoken to her like that before, and if she had submitted to his command. Of course she had; she remembered that she had. But she could not realize why or how she should have yielded, feeling as she then did.

"Léonce, go to bed," she said. "I mean to stay out here. I don't wish to go in, and I don't intend to. Don't speak to me like that again; I shall not answer you."

Mr. Pontellier had prepared for bed, but he slipped on an extra garment. He opened a bottle of wine, of which he kept a small and select supply in a buffet of his own. He drank a glass of the wine and went out on the gallery and offered a glass to his wife. She did not wish any. He drew up the rocker, hoisted his slippered feet on the rail, and proceeded to smoke a cigar. He smoked two cigars; then he went inside and drank another glass of wine. Mrs. Pontellier again declined to accept a glass when it was offered to her. Mr. Pontellier once more seated himself with elevated feet, and after a reasonable interval of time smoked some more cigars.

Edna began to feel like one who awakens gradually out of a dream, a delicious, grotesque, impossible dream, to feel again the realities pressing into her soul. The physical need for sleep began to overtake her; the exuberance which had sustained and exalted her spirit left her helpless and yielding to the conditions which crowded her in.

The stillest hour of the night had come, the hour before dawn, when the world seems to hold its breath. The moon hung low, and had turned from silver to copper in the sleeping sky. The old owl no longer hooted, and the water-oaks had ceased to moan as they bent their heads.

Edna arose, cramped from lying so long and still in the hammock. She tottered up the steps, clutching feebly at the post before passing into the house.

"Are you coming in, Léonce?" she asked, turning her face toward her husband.

"Yes, dear," he answered, with a glance following a misty puff of smoke. "Just as soon as I have finished my cigar."

CHAPTER XII

She slept but a few hours. They were troubled and feverish hours, disturbed with dreams that were intangible, that eluded her, leaving only an impression upon her half-awakened senses of something unattainable. She was up and dressed in the cool of the early morning. The air was invigorating and steadied somewhat her faculties. However, she was not seeking refreshment or help from any source, either external or from within. She was blindly following whatever impulse moved her, as if she had placed herself in alien hands for direction, and freed her soul of responsibility.

Most of the people at that early hour were still in bed and asleep. A few, who intended to go over to the *Chênière* for mass, were moving about. The lovers, who had laid their plans the night before, were already strolling toward the wharf. The lady in black, with her Sunday prayer book, velvet and gold-clasped, and her Sunday silver beads, was following them at no great distance. Old Monsieur Farival was up, and was more than half inclined to do anything that suggested itself. He put on his big straw hat, and taking his umbrella from the stand in the hall, followed the lady in black, never overtaking her.

The little negro girl who worked Madame Lebrun's sewing-machine was sweeping the galleries with long, absent-minded strokes of the broom. Edna sent her up into the house to awaken Robert.

"Tell him I am going to the *Chênière*. The boat is ready; tell him to hurry."

He had soon joined her. She had never sent for him before. She had never asked for him. She had never seemed to want him before. She did not appear conscious that she had done anything unusual in commanding his presence. He was apparently equally unconscious of anything extraordinary in the situation. But his face was suffused with a quiet glow when he met her.

They went together back to the kitchen to drink coffee. There was no time to wait for any nicety of service. They stood outside the window and the cook passed them their coffee and a roll, which they drank and ate from the window-sill. Edna said it tasted good. She had not thought of coffee nor of anything. He told her he had often noticed that she lacked forethought.

"Wasn't it enough to think of going to the *Chênière* and waking you up?" she laughed. "Do I have to think of everything?—as Léonce says when he's in a bad humor. I don't blame him; he'd never be in a bad humor if it weren't for me."

They took a short cut across the sands. At a distance they could see the curious procession moving toward the wharf—the lovers, shoulder to shoulder, creeping; the lady in black, gaining steadily upon them; old Monsieur Farival, losing ground inch by inch, and a young barefooted Spanish girl, with a red kerchief on her head and a basket on her arm, bringing up the rear.

Robert knew the girl, and he talked to her a little in the boat. No one present understood what they said. Her name was Mariequita. She had a round, sly, piquant face and pretty black eyes. Her hands were small, and she kept them folded over the handle of her basket. Her feet were broad and coarse. She did not strive to hide them. Edna looked at her feet, and noticed the sand and slime between her brown toes.

Beaudelet grumbled because Mariequita was there, taking up so much room. In reality he was annoyed at having old Monsieur Farival, who considered himself the better sailor of the two. But he would not quarrel with so old a man as

Monsieur Farival, so he quarreled with Mariequita. The girl was deprecatory at one moment, appealing to Robert. She was saucy the next, moving her head up and down, making "eyes" at Robert and making "mouths" at Beaudelet.

The lovers were all alone. They saw nothing, they heard nothing. The lady in black was counting her beads for the third time. Old Monsieur Farival talked incessantly of what he knew about handling a boat, and of what Beaudelet did not know on the same subject.

Edna liked it all. She looked Mariequita up and down, from her ugly brown toes to her pretty black eyes, and back again.

"Why does she look at me like that?" inquired the girl of Robert.

"Maybe she thinks you are pretty. Shall I ask her?"

"No. Is she your sweetheart?"

"She's a married lady, and has two children."

"Oh! well! Francisco ran away with Sylvano's wife, who had four children. They took all his money and one of the children and stole his boat."

"Shut up!"

"Does she understand?"

"Oh, hush!"

"Are those two married over there—leaning on each other?"

"Of course not," laughed Robert.

"Of course not," echoed Mariequita, with a serious, confirmatory bob of the head.

The sun was high up and beginning to bite. The swift breeze seemed to Edna to bury the sting of it into the pores of her face and hands. Robert held his umbrella over her.

As they went cutting sidewise through the water, the sails bellied taut, with the wind filling and overflowing them. Old Monsieur Farival laughed sardonically at something as he looked at the sails, and Beaudelet swore at the old man under his breath.

Sailing across the bay to the *Chênière Caminada*, Edna felt as if she were being borne away from some anchorage which had held her fast, whose chains had been loosening—had snapped the night before when the mystic spirit was abroad, leaving her free to drift whithersoever she chose to set her sails. Robert spoke to her incessantly; he no longer noticed Mariequita. The girl had shrimps in her bamboo basket. They were covered with Spanish moss. She beat the moss down impatiently, and muttered to herself sullenly.

"Let us go to Grande Terre to-morrow?" said Robert in a low voice.

"What shall we do there?"

"Climb up the hill to the old fort and look at the little wriggling gold snakes, and watch the lizards sun themselves."

She gazed away toward Grande Terre and thought she would like to be alone there with Robert, in the sun, listening to the ocean's roar and watching the slimy lizards writhe in and out among the ruins of the old fort.

"And the next day or the next we can sail to the Bayou Brulow," he went on.

"What shall we do there?"

"Anything—cast bait for fish."

"No; we'll go back to Grande Terre. Let the fish alone."

"We'll go wherever you like," he said. "I'll have Tonie come over and help me patch and trim my boat. We shall not need Beaudelet nor any one. Are you afraid of the pirogue?"

"Oh, no."

"Then I'll take you some night in the pirogue when the moon shines. Maybe your Gulf spirit will whisper to you in which of these islands the treasures are hidden—direct you to the very spot, perhaps."

"And in a day we should be rich!" she laughed. "I'd give it all to you, the pirate gold and every bit of treasure we could dig up. I think you would know how to spend it. Pirate gold isn't a thing to be hoarded or utilized. It is something to squander and throw to the four winds, for the fun of seeing the golden specks fly."

"We'd share it, and scatter it together," he said. His face flushed.

They all went together up to the quaint little Gothic church of Our Lady of Lourdes, gleaming all brown and yellow with paint in the sun's glare.

Only Beaudelet remained behind, tinkering at his boat, and Mariequita walked away with her basket of shrimps, casting a look of childish ill-humor and reproach at Robert from the corner of her eye.

CHAPTER XIII

A feeling of oppression and drowsiness overcame Edna during the service. Her head began to ache, and the lights on the altar swayed before her eyes. Another time she might have made an effort to regain her composure; but her one thought was to quit the stifling atmosphere of the church and reach the open air. She arose, climbing over Robert's feet with a muttered apology. Old Monsieur Farival, flurried, curious, stood up, but upon seeing that Robert had followed Mrs. Pontellier, he sank back into his seat. He whispered an anxious inquiry of the lady in black, who did not notice him or reply, but kept her eyes fastened upon the pages of her velvet prayer-book.

"I felt giddy and almost overcome," Edna said, lifting her hands instinctively to her head and pushing her straw hat up from her forehead. "I couldn't have stayed through the service." They were outside in the shadow of the church. Robert was full of solicitude.

"It was folly to have thought of going in the first place, let alone staying. Come over to Madame Antoine's; you can rest there." He took her arm and led her away, looking anxiously and continuously down into her face.

How still it was, with only the voice of the sea whispering through the reeds that grew in the salt-water pools! The long line of little gray, weather-beaten houses nestled peacefully among the orange trees. It must always have been God's day on that low, drowsy island, Edna thought. They stopped, leaning over a jagged fence made of sea-drift, to ask for water. A youth, a mild-faced Acadian, was drawing water from the cistern, which was nothing more than a rusty buoy, with an opening on one side, sunk in the ground. The water which the youth handed to them in a tin pail was not cold to taste, but it was cool to her heated face, and it greatly revived and refreshed her.

Madame Antoine's cot was at the far end of the village. She welcomed them with all the native hospitality, as she would have opened her door to let the sunlight in. She was fat, and walked heavily and clumsily across the floor. She could speak no English, but when Robert made her understand that the lady who accompanied him was ill and desired to rest, she was all eagerness to make Edna feel at home and to dispose of her comfortably.

The whole place was immaculately clean, and the big, four-posted bed, snow-white, invited one to repose. It stood in a small side room which looked out across a narrow grass plot toward the shed, where there was a disabled boat lying keel upward.

Madame Antoine had not gone to mass. Her son Tonie had, but she supposed he would soon be back, and she invited Robert to be seated and wait for him. But he went and sat outside the door and smoked. Madame Antoine busied herself in the large front room preparing dinner. She was boiling mullets over a few red coals in the huge fireplace.

Edna, left alone in the little side room, loosened her clothes, removing the greater part of them. She bathed her face, her neck and arms in the basin that stood between the windows. She took off her shoes and stockings and stretched herself in the very center of the high, white bed. How luxurious it felt to rest thus in a strange, quaint bed, with its sweet country odor of laurel lingering about the sheets and mattress! She stretched her strong limbs that ached a little. She ran her fingers through her loosened hair for a while. She looked at her round arms as she held them straight up and rubbed them one after the other, observing closely, as if it were something she saw for the first time, the fine, firm quality and texture of her flesh. She clasped her hands easily above her head, and it was thus she fell asleep.

She slept lightly at first, half awake and drowsily attentive to the things about her. She could hear Madame Antoine's heavy, scraping tread as she walked back and forth on the sanded floor. Some chickens were clucking outside the windows, scratching for bits of gravel in the grass. Later she half heard the voices of Robert and Tonie talking under the shed. She did not stir. Even her eyelids rested numb and heavily over her sleepy eyes. The voices went on—Tonie's slow, Acadian drawl, Robert's quick, soft, smooth French. She understood French imperfectly unless directly addressed, and the voices were only part of the other drowsy, muffled sounds lulling her senses.

When Edna awoke it was with the conviction that she had slept long and soundly. The voices were hushed under the shed. Madame Antoine's step was no longer to be heard in the adjoining room. Even the chickens had gone elsewhere to scratch and cluck. The mosquito bar was drawn over her; the old woman had come in while she slept and let down the bar. Edna arose quietly from the bed, and looking between the curtains of the window, she saw by the slanting rays of the sun that the afternoon was far advanced. Robert was out there under the shed, reclining in the shade against the sloping keel of the overturned boat. He was reading from a book. Tonie was no longer with him. She wondered what had become of the rest of the party. She peeped out at him two or three times as she stood washing herself in the little basin between the windows.

Madame Antoine had laid some coarse, clean towels upon a chair, and had placed a box of *poudre de riz* within easy reach. Edna dabbed the powder upon her nose and cheeks as she looked at herself closely in the little distorted mirror which hung on the wall above the basin. Her eyes were bright and wide awake and her face glowed.

When she had completed her toilet she walked into the adjoining room. She was very hungry. No one was there. But there was a cloth spread upon the table that stood against the wall, and a cover was laid for one, with a crusty brown loaf and a bottle of wine beside the plate. Edna bit a piece from the brown loaf, tearing it with her strong, white teeth. She poured some of the wine into the glass and drank it down. Then she went softly out of doors, and plucking an orange from the low-hanging bough of a tree, threw it at Robert, who did not know she was awake and up.

An illumination broke over his whole face when he saw her and joined her under the orange tree.

"How many years have I slept?" she inquired. "The whole island seems changed. A new race of beings must have sprung up, leaving only you and me as past relics. How many ages ago did Madame Antoine and Tonie die? and when did our people from Grand Isle disappear from the earth?"

He familiarly adjusted a ruffle upon her shoulder.

"You have slept precisely one hundred years. I was left here to guard your slumbers; and for one hundred years I have been out under the shed reading a book. The only evil I couldn't prevent was to keep a broiled fowl from drying up."

"If it had turned to stone, still will I eat it," said Edna, moving with him into the house. "But really, what has become of Monsieur Farival and the others?"

"Gone hours ago. When they found that you were sleeping they thought it best not to awake you. Any way, I wouldn't have let them. What was I here for?"

"I wonder if Léonce will be uneasy!" she speculated, as she seated herself at table.

"Of course not; he knows you are with me," Robert replied, as he busied himself among sundry pans and covered dishes which had been left standing on the hearth.

"Where are Madame Antoine and her son?" asked Edna.

"Gone to Vespers, and to visit some friends, I believe. I am to take you back in Tonie's boat whenever you are ready to go."

He stirred the smoldering ashes till the broiled fowl began to sizzle afresh. He served her with no mean repast, dripping the coffee anew and sharing it with her. Madame Antoine had cooked little else than the mullets, but while Edna slept Robert had foraged the island. He was childishly gratified to discover her appetite, and to see the relish with which she ate the food which he had procured for her.

"Shall we go right away?" she asked, after draining her glass and brushing together the crumbs of the crusty loaf.

"The sun isn't as low as it will be in two hours," he answered.

"The sun will be gone in two hours."

"Well, let it go; who cares!"

They waited a good while under the orange trees, till Madame Antoine came back, panting, waddling, with a thousand apologies to explain her absence. Tonie did not dare to return. He was shy, and would not willingly face any woman except his mother.

It was very pleasant to stay there under the orange trees, while the sun dipped lower and lower, turning the western sky to flaming copper and gold. The shadows lengthened and crept out like stealthy, grotesque monsters across the grass.

Edna and Robert both sat upon the ground—that is, he lay upon the ground beside her, occasionally picking at the hem of her muslin gown.

Madame Antoine seated her fat body, broad and squat, upon a bench beside the door. She had been talking all the afternoon, and had wound herself up to the story-telling pitch.

And what stories she told them! But twice in her life she had left the *Chênière Caminada*, and then for the briefest span. All her years she had squatted and waddled there upon the island, gathering legends of the Baratarians and the sea. The night came on, with the moon to lighten it. Edna could hear the whispering voices of dead men and the click of muffled gold.

When she and Robert stepped into Tonie's boat, with the red lateen sail, misty spirit forms were prowling in the shadows and among the reeds, and upon the water were phantom ships, speeding to cover.

CHAPTER XIV

The youngest boy, Etienne, had been very naughty, Madame Ratignolle said, as she delivered him into the hands of his mother. He had been unwilling to go to bed and had made a scene; whereupon she had taken charge of him and pacified him as well as she could. Raoul had been in bed and asleep for two hours.

The youngster was in his long white nightgown, that kept tripping him up as Madame Ratignolle led him along by the hand. With the other chubby fist he rubbed his eyes, which were heavy with sleep and ill humor. Edna took him in her arms, and seating herself in the rocker, began to coddle and caress him, calling him all manner of tender names, soothing him to sleep.

It was not more than nine o'clock. No one had yet gone to bed but the children.

Léonce had been very uneasy at first, Madame Ratignolle said, and had wanted to start at once for the *Chênière*. But Monsieur Farival had assured him that his wife was only overcome with sleep and fatigue, that Tonie would bring her safely back later in the day; and he had thus been dissuaded from crossing the bay. He had gone over to Klein's, looking up some cotton broker whom he wished to see in regard to securities, exchanges, stocks, bonds, or something of the sort, Madame Ratignolle did not remember what. He said he would not remain away late. She herself was suffering from heat and oppression, she said. She carried a bottle of salts and a large fan. She would not consent to remain with Edna, for Monsieur Ratignolle was alone, and he detested above all things to be left alone.

When Etienne had fallen asleep Edna bore him into the back room, and Robert went and lifted the mosquito bar that she might lay the child comfortably in his bed. The quadroon had vanished. When they emerged from the cottage Robert bade Edna good-night.

"Do you know we have been together the whole livelong day, Robert—since early this morning?" she said at parting.

"All but the hundred years when you were sleeping. Good-night."

He pressed her hand and went away in the direction of the beach. He did not join any of the others, but walked alone toward the Gulf.

Edna stayed outside, awaiting her husband's return. She had no desire to sleep or to retire; nor did she feel like going over to sit with the Ratignolles, or to join Madame Lebrun and a group whose animated voices reached her as they sat in conversation before the house. She let her mind wander back over her stay at Grand Isle; and she tried to discover wherein this summer had been different from any and every other summer of her life. She could only realize that she herself—her present self—was in some way different from the other self. That she was seeing with different eyes and making the acquaintance of new conditions in herself that colored and changed her environment, she did not yet suspect.

She wondered why Robert had gone away and left her. It did not occur to her to think he might have grown tired of being with her the livelong day. She was not tired, and she felt that he was not. She regretted that he had gone. It was so much more natural to have him stay, when he was not absolutely required to leave her.

As Edna waited for her husband she sang low a little song that Robert had sung as they crossed the bay. It began with "Ah! *Si tu savais*," and every verse ended with "*si tu savais*."

Robert's voice was not pretentious. It was musical and true. The voice, the notes, the whole refrain haunted her memory.

CHAPTER XV

When Edna entered the dining-room one evening a little late, as was her habit, an unusually animated conversation seemed to be going on. Several persons were talking at once, and Victor's voice was predominating, even over that of his mother. Edna had returned late from her bath, had dressed in some haste, and her face was flushed. Her head, set off by her dainty white gown, suggested a rich, rare blossom. She took her seat at table between old Monsieur Farival and Madame Ratignolle.

As she seated herself and was about to begin to eat her soup, which had been served when she entered the room, several persons informed her simultaneously that Robert was going to Mexico. She laid her spoon down and looked about her bewildered. He had been with her, reading to her all the morning, and had never even mentioned such a place as Mexico. She had not seen him during the afternoon; she had heard some one say he was at the house, upstairs with his mother. This she had thought nothing of, though she was surprised when he did not join her later in the afternoon, when she went down to the beach.

She looked across at him, where he sat beside Madame Lebrun, who presided. Edna's face was a blank picture of bewilderment, which she never thought of disguising. He lifted his eyebrows with the pretext of a smile as he returned her glance. He looked embarrassed and uneasy.

"When is he going?" she asked of everybody in general, as if Robert were not there to answer for himself.

"To-night!" "This very evening!" "Did you ever!" "What possesses him!" were some of the replies she gathered, uttered simultaneously in French and English.

"Impossible!" she exclaimed. "How can a person start off from Grand Isle to Mexico at a moment's notice, as if he were going over to Klein's or to the wharf or down to the beach?"

"I said all along I was going to Mexico; I've been saying so for years!" cried Robert, in an excited and irritable tone, with the air of a man defending himself against a swarm of stinging insects.

Madame Lebrun knocked on the table with her knife handle.

"Please let Robert explain why he is going, and why he is going to-night," she called out. "Really, this table is getting to be more and more like Bedlam every day, with everybody talking at once. Sometimes—I hope God will forgive me—but positively, sometimes I wish Victor would lose the power of speech."

Victor laughed sardonically as he thanked his mother for her holy wish, of which he failed to see the benefit to anybody, except that it might afford her a more ample opportunity and license to talk herself.

Monsieur Farival thought that Victor should have been taken out in mid-ocean in his earliest youth and drowned. Victor thought there would be more logic in thus disposing of old people with an established claim for making themselves universally obnoxious. Madame Lebrun grew a trifle hysterical; Robert called his brother some sharp, hard names.

"There's nothing much to explain, mother," he said; though he explained, nevertheless—looking chiefly at Edna—that he could only meet the gentleman whom he intended to join at Vera Cruz by taking such and such a steamer, which left New Orleans on such a day; that Beaudelet was going out with his lugger-load of vegetables that night, which gave him an opportunity of reaching the city and making his vessel in time.

"But when did you make up your mind to all this?" demanded Monsieur Farival.

"This afternoon," returned Robert, with a shade of annoyance.

"At what time this afternoon?" persisted the old gentleman, with nagging determination, as if he were cross-questioning a criminal in a court of justice.

"At four o'clock this afternoon, Monsieur Farival," Robert replied, in a high voice and with a lofty air, which reminded Edna of some gentleman on the stage.

She had forced herself to eat most of her soup, and now she was picking the flaky bits of a *court bouillon* with her fork.

The lovers were profiting by the general conversation on Mexico to speak in whispers of matters which they rightly considered were interesting to no one but themselves. The lady in black had once received a pair of prayer-beads of curious workmanship from Mexico, with very special indulgence attached to them, but she had never been able to ascertain whether the indulgence extended outside the Mexican border. Father Fochel of the Cathedral had attempted to explain it; but he had not done so to her satisfaction. And she begged that Robert would interest himself, and discover, if possible, whether she was entitled to the indulgence accompanying the remarkably curious Mexican prayer-beads.

Madame Ratignolle hoped that Robert would exercise extreme caution in dealing with the Mexicans, who, she considered, were a treacherous people, unscrupulous and revengeful. She trusted she did them no injustice in thus condemning them as a race. She had known personally but one Mexican, who made and sold excellent tamales, and whom she would have trusted implicitly, so soft-spoken was he. One day he was arrested for stabbing his wife. She never knew whether he had been hanged or not.

Victor had grown hilarious, and was attempting to tell an anecdote about a Mexican girl who served chocolate one winter in a restaurant in Dauphine Street. No one would listen to him but old Monsieur Farival, who went into convulsions over the droll story.

Edna wondered if they had all gone mad, to be talking and clamoring at that rate. She herself could think of nothing to say about Mexico or the Mexicans.

"At what time do you leave?" she asked Robert.

"At ten," he told her. "Beaudelet wants to wait for the moon."

"Are you all ready to go?"

"Quite ready. I shall only take a handbag, and shall pack my trunk in the city."

He turned to answer some question put to him by his mother, and Edna, having finished her black coffee, left the table.

She went directly to her room. The little cottage was close and stuffy after leaving the outer air. But she did not mind; there appeared to be a hundred different things demanding her attention indoors. She began to set the toilet-stand to rights, grumbling at the negligence of the quadroon, who was in the adjoining room putting the children to bed. She gathered together stray garments that were hanging on the backs of chairs, and put each where it belonged in closet or bureau drawer. She changed her gown for a more comfortable and commodious wrapper. She rearranged her hair, combing and brushing it with unusual energy. Then she went in and assisted the quadroon in getting the boys to bed.

They were very playful and inclined to talk—to do anything but lie quiet and go to sleep. Edna sent the quadroon away to her supper and told her she need not return. Then she sat and told the children a story. Instead of soothing it excited them, and added to their wakefulness. She left them in heated argument, speculating about the conclusion of the tale which their mother promised to finish the following night.

The little black girl came in to say that Madame Lebrun would like to have Mrs. Pontellier go and sit with them over at the house till Mr. Robert went away. Edna returned answer that she had already undressed, that she did not feel quite well, but perhaps she would go over to the house later. She started to dress again, and got as far advanced as to remove her *peignoir*. But changing her mind once more she resumed the *peignoir*, and went outside and sat down before her door. She was overheated and irritable, and fanned herself energetically for a while. Madame Ratignolle came down to discover what was the matter.

"All that noise and confusion at the table must have upset me," replied Edna, "and moreover, I hate shocks and surprises. The idea of Robert starting off in such a ridiculously sudden and dramatic way! As if it were a matter of life and death! Never saying a word about it all morning when he was with me."

"Yes," agreed Madame Ratignolle. "I think it was showing us all—you especially—very little consideration. It wouldn't have surprised me in any of the others; those Lebruns are all given to heroics. But I must say I should never have expected such a thing from Robert. Are you not coming down? Come on, dear; it doesn't look friendly."

"No," said Edna, a little sullenly. "I can't go to the trouble of dressing again; I don't feel like it."

"You needn't dress; you look all right; fasten a belt around your waist. Just look at me!"

"No," persisted Edna; "but you go on. Madame Lebrun might be offended if we both stayed away."

Madame Ratignolle kissed Edna good-night, and went away, being in truth rather desirous of joining in the general and animated conversation which was still in progress concerning Mexico and the Mexicans.

Somewhat later Robert came up, carrying his hand-bag.

"Aren't you feeling well?" he asked.

"Oh, well enough. Are you going right away?"

He lit a match and looked at his watch. "In twenty minutes," he said. The sudden and brief flare of the match emphasized the darkness for a while. He sat down upon a stool which the children had left out on the porch.

"Get a chair," said Edna.

"This will do," he replied. He put on his soft hat and nervously took it off again, and wiping his face with his handkerchief, complained of the heat.

"Take the fan," said Edna, offering it to him.

"Oh, no! Thank you. It does no good; you have to stop fanning some time, and feel all the more uncomfortable afterward."

"That's one of the ridiculous things which men always say. I have never known one to speak otherwise of fanning. How long will you be gone?"

"Forever, perhaps. I don't know. It depends upon a good many things."

"Well, in case it shouldn't be forever, how long will it be?"

"I don't know."

"This seems to me perfectly preposterous and uncalled for. I don't like it. I don't understand your motive for silence and mystery, never saying a word to me about it this morning." He remained silent, not offering to defend himself. He only said, after a moment:

"Don't part from me in an ill-humor. I never knew you to be out of patience with me before."

"I don't want to part in any ill-humor," she said. "But can't you understand? I've grown used to seeing you, to having you with me all the time, and your action seems unfriendly, even unkind. You don't even offer an excuse for it. Why, I was planning to be together, thinking of how pleasant it would be to see you in the city next winter."

"So was I," he blurted. "Perhaps that's the—" He stood up suddenly and held out his hand. "Good-by, my dear Mrs. Pontellier; good-by. You won't—I hope you won't completely forget me." She clung to his hand, striving to detain him.

"Write to me when you get there, won't you, Robert?" she entreated.

"I will, thank you. Good-by."

How unlike Robert! The merest acquaintance would have said something more emphatic than "I will, thank you; good-by," to such a request.

He had evidently already taken leave of the people over at the house, for he descended the steps and went to join Beaudelet, who was out there with an oar across his shoulder waiting for Robert. They walked away in the darkness. She could only hear Beaudelet's voice; Robert had apparently not even spoken a word of greeting to his companion.

Edna bit her handkerchief convulsively, striving to hold back and to hide, even from herself as she would have hidden from another, the emotion which was troubling—tearing—her. Her eyes were brimming with tears.

For the first time she recognized anew the symptoms of infatuation which she felt incipiently as a child, as a girl in her earliest teens, and later as a young woman. The recognition did not lessen the reality, the poignancy of the revelation by any suggestion or promise of instability. The past was nothing to her; offered no lesson which she was willing to heed. The future was a mystery which she never attempted to penetrate. The present alone was significant; was hers, to torture her as it was doing then with the biting conviction that she had lost that which she had held, that she had been denied that which her impassioned, newly awakened being demanded.

CHAPTER XVI

"Do you miss your friend greatly?" asked Mademoiselle Reisz one morning as she came creeping up behind Edna, who had just left her cottage on her way to the beach. She spent much of her time in the water since she had acquired finally the art of swimming. As their stay at Grand Isle drew near its close, she felt that she could not give too much time to a diversion which afforded her the only real pleasurable moments that she knew. When Mademoiselle Reisz came and touched her upon the shoulder and spoke to her, the woman seemed to echo the thought which was ever in Edna's mind; or, better, the feeling which constantly possessed her.

Robert's going had some way taken the brightness, the color, the meaning out of everything. The conditions of her life were in no way changed, but her whole existence was dulled, like a faded garment which seems to be no longer worth wearing. She sought him everywhere—in others whom she induced to talk about him. She went up in the mornings to Madame Lebrun's room, braving the clatter of the old sewing-machine. She sat there and chatted at intervals as Robert had done. She gazed around the room at the pictures and photographs hanging upon the wall, and discovered in some corner an old family album, which she examined with the keenest interest, appealing to Madame Lebrun for enlightenment concerning the many figures and faces which she discovered between its pages.

There was a picture of Madame Lebrun with Robert as a baby, seated in her lap, a round-faced infant with a fist in his mouth. The eyes alone in the baby suggested the man. And that was he also in kilts, at the age of five, wearing long curls and holding a whip in his hand. It made Edna laugh, and she laughed, too, at the portrait in his first long trousers; while another interested her, taken when he left for college, looking thin, long-faced, with eyes full of fire, ambition and great intentions. But there was no recent picture, none which suggested the Robert who had gone away five days ago, leaving a void and wilderness behind him.

"Oh, Robert stopped having his pictures taken when he had to pay for them himself! He found wiser use for his money, he says," explained Madame Lebrun. She had a letter from him, written before he left New Orleans. Edna wished to see the letter, and Madame Lebrun told her to look for it either on the table or the dresser, or perhaps it was on the mantelpiece.

The letter was on the bookshelf. It possessed the greatest interest and attraction for Edna; the envelope, its size and shape, the postmark, the handwriting. She examined every detail of the outside before opening it. There were only a few lines, setting forth that he would leave the city that afternoon, that he had packed his trunk in good shape, that he was well, and sent her his love and begged to be affectionately remembered to all. There was no special message to Edna except a postscript saying that if Mrs. Pontellier desired to finish the book which he had been reading to her, his mother would find it in his room, among other books there on the table. Edna experienced a pang of jealousy because he had written to his mother rather than to her.

Every one seemed to take for granted that she missed him. Even her husband, when he came down the Saturday following Robert's departure, expressed regret that he had gone.

"How do you get on without him, Edna?" he asked.

"It's very dull without him," she admitted. Mr. Pontellier had seen Robert in the city, and Edna asked him a dozen questions or more. Where had they met? On Carondelet Street, in the morning. They had gone "in" and had a drink and a cigar together. What had they talked about? Chiefly about his prospects in Mexico, which Mr. Pontellier thought were promising. How did he look? How did he seem—grave, or gay, or how? Quite cheerful, and wholly taken up with the idea of his trip, which Mr. Pontellier found altogether natural in a young fellow about to seek fortune and adventure in a strange, queer country.

Edna tapped her foot impatiently, and wondered why the children persisted in playing in the sun when they might be under the trees. She went down and led them out of the sun, scolding the quadroon for not being more attentive.

It did not strike her as in the least grotesque that she should be making of Robert the object of conversation and leading her husband to speak of him. The sentiment which she entertained for Robert in no way resembled that which she felt for her husband, or had ever felt, or ever expected to feel. She had all her life long been accustomed to harbor thoughts and emotions which never voiced themselves. They had never taken the form of struggles. They belonged to her and were her own, and she entertained the conviction that she had a right to them and that they concerned no one but herself. Edna had once told Madame Ratignolle that she would never sacrifice herself for her children, or for any one. Then had followed a rather heated argument; the two women did not appear to understand each other or to be talking the same language. Edna tried to appease her friend, to explain.

"I would give up the unessential; I would give my money, I would give my life for my children; but I wouldn't give myself. I can't make it more clear; it's only something which I am beginning to comprehend, which is revealing itself to me."

"I don't know what you would call the essential, or what you mean by the unessential," said Madame Ratignolle, cheerfully; "but a woman who would give her life for her children could do no more than that—your Bible tells you so. I'm sure I couldn't do more than that."

"Oh, yes you could!" laughed Edna.

She was not surprised at Mademoiselle Reisz's question the morning that lady, following her to the beach, tapped her on the shoulder and asked if she did not greatly miss her young friend.

"Oh, good morning, Mademoiselle; it is you? Why, of course I miss Robert. Are you going down to bathe?"

"Why should I go down to bathe at the very end of the season when I haven't been in the surf all summer?" replied the woman, disagreeably.

"I beg your pardon," offered Edna, in some embarrassment, for she should have remembered that Mademoiselle Reisz's avoidance of the water had furnished a theme for much pleasantry. Some among them thought it was on account of her false hair, or the dread of getting the violets wet, while others attributed it to the natural aversion for water sometimes believed to accompany the artistic temperament. Mademoiselle offered Edna some chocolates in a paper bag, which she took from her pocket, by way of showing that she bore no ill feeling. She habitually ate chocolates for their sustaining quality; they contained much nutriment in small compass, she said. They saved her from starvation, as Madame Lebrun's table was utterly impossible; and no one save so impertinent a woman as Madame Lebrun could think of offering such food to people and requiring them to pay for it.

"She must feel very lonely without her son," said Edna, desiring to change the subject. "Her favorite son, too. It must have been quite hard to let him go."

Mademoiselle laughed maliciously.

"Her favorite son! Oh, dear! Who could have been imposing such a tale upon you? Aline Lebrun lives for Victor, and for Victor alone. She has spoiled him into the worthless creature he is. She worships him and the ground he walks on. Robert is very well in a way, to give up all the money he can earn to the family, and keep the barest pittance for himself. Favorite son, indeed! I miss the poor fellow myself, my dear. I liked to see him and to hear him about the place—the only Lebrun who is worth a pinch of salt. He comes to see me often in the city. I like to play to him.

That Victor! hanging would be too good for him. It's a wonder Robert hasn't beaten him to death long ago."

"I thought he had great patience with his brother," offered Edna, glad to be talking about Robert, no matter what was said.

"Oh! he thrashed him well enough a year or two ago," said Mademoiselle. "It was about a Spanish girl, whom Victor considered that he had some sort of claim upon. He met Robert one day talking to the girl, or walking with her, or bathing with her, or carrying her basket—I don't remember what;—and he became so insulting and abusive that Robert gave him a thrashing on the spot that has kept him comparatively in order for a good while. It's about time he was getting another."

"Was her name Mariequita?" asked Edna.

"Mariequita—yes, that was it; Mariequita. I had forgotten. Oh, she's a sly one, and a bad one, that Mariequita!"

Edna looked down at Mademoiselle Reisz and wondered how she could have listened to her venom so long. For some reason she felt depressed, almost unhappy. She had not intended to go into the water; but she donned her bathing suit, and left Mademoiselle alone, seated under the shade of the children's tent. The water was growing cooler as the season advanced. Edna plunged and swam about with an abandon that thrilled and invigorated her. She remained a long time in the water, half hoping that Mademoiselle Reisz would not wait for her.

But Mademoiselle waited. She was very amiable during the walk back, and raved much over Edna's appearance in her bathing suit. She talked about music. She hoped that Edna would go to see her in the city, and wrote her address with the stub of a pencil on a piece of card which she found in her pocket.

"When do you leave?" asked Edna.

"Next Monday; and you?"

"The following week," answered Edna, adding, "It has been a pleasant summer, hasn't it, Mademoiselle?"

"Well," agreed Mademoiselle Reisz, with a shrug, "rather pleasant, if it hadn't been for the mosquitoes and the Farival twins."

CHAPTER XVII

The Pontelliers possessed a very charming home on Esplanade Street in New Orleans. It was a large, double cottage, with a broad front veranda, whose round, fluted columns supported the sloping roof. The house was painted a dazzling white; the outside shutters, or jalousies, were green. In the yard, which was kept scrupulously neat, were flowers and plants of every description which flourishes in South Louisiana. Within doors the appointments were perfect after the conventional type. The softest carpets and rugs covered the floors; rich and tasteful draperies hung at doors and windows. There were paintings, selected with judgment and discrimination, upon the walls. The cut glass, the silver, the heavy damask which daily appeared upon the table were the envy of many women whose husbands were less generous than Mr. Pontellier.

Mr. Pontellier was very fond of walking about his house examining its various appointments and details, to see that nothing was amiss. He greatly valued his possessions, chiefly because they were his, and derived genuine pleasure from contemplating a painting, a statuette, a rare lace curtain—no matter what—after he had bought it and placed it among his household gods.

On Tuesday afternoons—Tuesday being Mrs. Pontellier's reception day—there was a constant stream of callers—women who came in carriages or in the street cars, or walked when the air was soft and distance permitted. A light-colored mulatto boy, in dress coat and bearing a diminutive silver tray for the reception of cards, admitted them. A maid, in white fluted cap, offered the callers liqueur, coffee, or chocolate, as they might desire. Mrs. Pontellier, attired in a handsome reception gown, remained in the drawing-room the entire afternoon receiving her visitors. Men sometimes called in the evening with their wives.

This had been the programme which Mrs. Pontellier had religiously followed since her marriage, six years before. Certain evenings during the week she and her husband attended the opera or sometimes the play.

Mr. Pontellier left his home in the mornings between nine and ten o'clock, and rarely returned before half-past six or seven in the evening—dinner being served at half-past seven.

He and his wife seated themselves at table on Tuesday evening, a few weeks after their return from Grand Isle. They were alone together. The boys were being put to bed; the patter of their bare, escaping feet could be heard occasionally, as well as the pursuing voice of the quadroon, lifted in mild protest and entreaty. Mrs. Pontellier did not wear her usual Tuesday reception gown; she was in ordinary house dress. Mr. Pontellier, who was observant about such things, noticed it, as he served the soup and handed it to the boy in waiting.

"Tired out, Edna? Whom did you have? Many callers?" he asked. He tasted his soup and began to season it with pepper, salt, vinegar, mustard—everything within reach.

"There were a good many," replied Edna, who was eating her soup with evident satisfaction. "I found their cards when I got home; I was out."

"Out!" exclaimed her husband, with something like genuine consternation in his voice as he laid down the vinegar cruet and looked at her through his glasses. "Why, what could have taken you out on Tuesday? What did you have to do?"

"Nothing. I simply felt like going out, and I went out."

"Well, I hope you left some suitable excuse," said her husband, somewhat appeased, as he added a dash of cayenne pepper to the soup.

"No, I left no excuse. I told Joe to say I was out, that was all."

"Why, my dear, I should think you'd understand by this time that people don't do such things; we've got to observe *les convenances* if we ever expect to get on and keep up with the procession. If you felt that you had to leave home this afternoon, you should have left some suitable explanation for your absence.

"This soup is really impossible; it's strange that woman hasn't learned yet to make a decent soup. Any free-lunch stand in town serves a better one. Was Mrs. Belthrop here?"

"Bring the tray with the cards, Joe. I don't remember who was here."

The boy retired and returned after a moment, bringing the tiny silver tray, which was covered with ladies' visiting cards. He handed it to Mrs. Pontellier.

"Give it to Mr. Pontellier," she said.

Joe offered the tray to Mr. Pontellier, and removed the soup.

Mr. Pontellier scanned the names of his wife's callers, reading some of them aloud, with comments as he read.

"'The Misses Delasidas.' I worked a big deal in futures for their father this morning; nice girls; it's time they were getting married. 'Mrs. Belthrop.' I tell you what it is, Edna; you can't afford to snub Mrs. Belthrop. Why, Belthrop could buy and sell us ten times over. His business is worth a good, round sum to me. You'd better write her a note. 'Mrs. James Highcamp.' Hugh! the less you have to do with Mrs. Highcamp, the better. 'Madame Laforcé.' Came all the way from Carrolton, too, poor old soul. 'Miss Wiggs,' 'Mrs. Eleanor Boltons.'" He pushed the cards aside.

"Mercy!" exclaimed Edna, who had been fuming. "Why are you taking the thing so seriously and making such a fuss over it?"

"I'm not making any fuss over it. But it's just such seeming trifles that we've got to take seriously; such things count."

The fish was scorched. Mr. Pontellier would not touch it. Edna said she did not mind a little scorched taste. The roast was in some way not to his fancy, and he did not like the manner in which the vegetables were served.

"It seems to me," he said, "we spend money enough in this house to procure at least one meal a day which a man could eat and retain his self-respect."

"You used to think the cook was a treasure," returned Edna, indifferently.

"Perhaps she was when she first came; but cooks are only human. They need looking after, like any other class of persons that you employ. Suppose I didn't look after the clerks in my office, just let them run things their own way; they'd soon make a nice mess of me and my business."

"Where are you going?" asked Edna, seeing that her husband arose from table without having eaten a morsel except a taste of the highly-seasoned soup.

"I'm going to get my dinner at the club. Good night." He went into the hall, took his hat and stick from the stand, and left the house.

She was somewhat familiar with such scenes. They had often made her very unhappy. On a few previous occasions she had been completely deprived of any desire to finish her dinner. Sometimes she had gone into the kitchen to administer a tardy rebuke to the cook. Once she went to her room and studied the cookbook during an entire evening, finally writing out a menu for the week, which left her harassed with a feeling that, after all, she had accomplished no good that was worth the name.

But that evening Edna finished her dinner alone, with forced deliberation. Her face was flushed and her eyes flamed with some inward fire that lighted them. After finishing her dinner she went to her room, having instructed the boy to tell any other callers that she was indisposed.

It was a large, beautiful room, rich and picturesque in the soft, dim light which the maid had turned low. She went and stood at an open window and looked out upon the deep tangle of the garden below. All the mystery and witchery of the night seemed to have gathered there amid the perfumes and the dusky and tortuous outlines of flowers and foliage. She was seeking herself and finding herself in just such sweet, half-darkness which met her moods. But the voices were not soothing that came to her from the darkness and the sky above and the stars. They jeered and sounded mournful notes without promise, devoid even of hope. She turned back into the room and began to walk to and fro down its whole length, without stopping, without resting. She carried in her hands a thin handkerchief, which she tore into ribbons, rolled into a ball, and flung from her. Once she stopped, and taking off her wedding ring, flung it upon the carpet. When she saw it lying there, she stamped her heel upon it, striving to crush it. But her small boot heel did not make an indenture, not a mark upon the little glittering circlet.

In a sweeping passion she seized a glass vase from the table and flung it upon the tiles of the hearth. She wanted to destroy something. The crash and clatter were what she wanted to hear.

A maid, alarmed at the din of breaking glass, entered the room to discover what was the matter.

"A vase fell upon the hearth," said Edna. "Never mind; leave it till morning."

"Oh! you might get some of the glass in your feet, ma'am," insisted the young woman, picking up bits of the broken vase that were scattered upon the carpet. "And here's your ring, ma'am, under the chair."

Edna held out her hand, and taking the ring, slipped it upon her finger.

CHAPTER XVIII

The following morning Mr. Pontellier, upon leaving for his office, asked Edna if she would not meet him in town in order to look at some new fixtures for the library.

"I hardly think we need new fixtures, Léonce. Don't let us get anything new; you are too extravagant. I don't believe you ever think of saving or putting by."

"The way to become rich is to make money, my dear Edna, not to save it," he said. He regretted that she did not feel inclined to go with him and select new fixtures. He kissed her good-by, and told her she was not looking well and must take care of herself. She was unusually pale and very quiet.

She stood on the front veranda as he quitted the house, and absently picked a few sprays of jessamine that grew upon a trellis near by. She inhaled the odor of the blossoms and thrust them into the bosom of her white morning gown. The boys were dragging along the banquette a small "express wagon," which they had filled with blocks and sticks. The quadroon was following them with little quick steps, having assumed a fictitious animation and alacrity for the occasion. A fruit vender was crying his wares in the street.

Edna looked straight before her with a self-absorbed expression upon her face. She felt no interest in anything about her. The street, the children, the fruit vender, the flowers growing there under her eyes, were all part and parcel of an alien world which had suddenly become antagonistic.

She went back into the house. She had thought of speaking to the cook concerning her blunders of the previous night; but Mr. Pontellier had saved her that disagreeable mission, for which she was so poorly fitted. Mr. Pontellier's arguments were usually convincing with those whom he employed. He left home feeling quite sure that he and Edna would sit down that evening, and possibly a few subsequent evenings, to a dinner deserving of the name.

Edna spent an hour or two in looking over some of her old sketches. She could see their shortcomings and defects, which were glaring in her eyes. She tried to work a little, but found she was not in the humor. Finally she gathered together a few of the sketches—those which she considered the least discreditable; and she carried them with her when, a little later, she dressed and left the house. She looked handsome and distinguished in her street gown. The tan of the seashore had left her face, and her forehead was smooth, white, and polished beneath her heavy, yellow-brown hair. There were a few freckles on her face, and a small, dark mole near the under lip and one on the temple, half-hidden in her hair.

As Edna walked along the street she was thinking of Robert. She was still under the spell of her infatuation. She had tried to forget him, realizing the inutility of remembering. But the thought of him was like an obsession, ever pressing itself upon her. It was not that she dwelt upon details of their acquaintance, or recalled in any special or peculiar way his personality; it was his being, his existence, which dominated her thought, fading sometimes as if it would melt into the mist of the forgotten, reviving again with an intensity which filled her with an incomprehensible longing.

Edna was on her way to Madame Ratignolle's. Their intimacy, begun at Grand Isle, had not declined, and they had seen each other with some frequency since their return to the city. The Ratignolles lived at no great distance from Edna's home, on the corner of a side street, where Monsieur Ratignolle owned and conducted a drug store which enjoyed a steady and prosperous trade. His father had been in the business before him, and Monsieur Ratignolle stood well in the community and bore an enviable reputation for integrity and clear-headedness. His family lived in commodious apartments over the store, having an entrance on the side within the *porte cochère*. There was something which Edna thought very French, very foreign, about their whole manner of living. In the large and pleasant salon which extended across the width of the house, the Ratignolles entertained their friends once a fortnight with a *soirée musicale*, sometimes diversified by card-playing. There was a friend who played upon the 'cello. One brought his flute and another his violin, while there were some who sang and a number who performed upon the piano with various degrees of taste and agility. The Ratignolles' *soirées musicales* were widely known, and it was considered a privilege to be invited to them.

Edna found her friend engaged in assorting the clothes which had returned that morning from the laundry. She at once abandoned her occupation upon seeing Edna, who had been ushered without ceremony into her presence.

"'Cité can do it as well as I; it is really her business," she explained to Edna, who apologized for interrupting her. And she summoned a young black woman, whom she instructed, in French, to be very careful in checking off the list which she handed her. She told her to notice particularly if a fine linen handkerchief of Monsieur Ratignolle's, which was missing last week, had been returned; and to be sure to set to one side such pieces as required mending and darning.

Then placing an arm around Edna's waist, she led her to the front of the house, to the salon, where it was cool and sweet with the odor of great roses that stood upon the hearth in jars.

Madame Ratignolle looked more beautiful than ever there at home, in a negligé which left her arms almost wholly bare and exposed the rich, melting curves of her white throat.

"Perhaps I shall be able to paint your picture some day," said Edna with a smile when they were seated. She produced the roll of sketches and started to unfold them. "I believe I ought to work again. I feel as if I wanted to be doing something. What do you think of them? Do you think it worth while to take it up again and study some more? I might study for a while with Laidpore."

She knew that Madame Ratignolle's opinion in such a matter would be next to valueless, that she herself had not alone decided, but determined; but she sought the words and praise and encouragement that would help her to put heart into her venture.

"Your talent is immense, dear!"

"Nonsense!" protested Edna, well pleased.

"Immense, I tell you," persisted Madame Ratignolle, surveying the sketches one by one, at close range, then holding them at arm's length, narrowing her eyes, and dropping her head on one side. "Surely, this Bavarian peasant is worthy of framing; and this basket of apples! never have I seen anything more lifelike. One might almost be tempted to reach out a hand and take one."

Edna could not control a feeling which bordered upon complacency at her friend's praise, even realizing, as she did, its true worth. She retained a few of the sketches, and gave all the rest to Madame Ratignolle, who appreciated the gift far beyond its value and proudly exhibited the pictures to her husband when he came up from the store a little later for his midday dinner.

Mr. Ratignolle was one of those men who are called the salt of the earth. His cheerfulness was unbounded, and it was matched by his goodness of heart, his broad charity, and common sense. He and his wife spoke English with an accent which was only discernible through its un-English emphasis and a certain carefulness and deliberation. Edna's husband spoke English with no accent whatever. The Ratignolles understood each other perfectly. If ever the fusion of two human beings into one has been accomplished on this sphere it was surely in their union.

As Edna seated herself at table with them she thought, "Better a dinner of herbs," though it did not take her long to discover that was no dinner of herbs, but a delicious repast, simple, choice, and in every way satisfying.

Monsieur Ratignolle was delighted to see her, though he found her looking not so well as at Grand Isle, and he advised a tonic. He talked a good deal on various topics, a little politics, some city news and neighborhood gossip. He spoke with an animation and earnestness that gave an exaggerated importance to every syllable he uttered. His wife was keenly interested in everything he said, laying down her fork the better to listen, chiming in, taking the words out of his mouth.

Edna felt depressed rather than soothed after leaving them. The little glimpse of domestic harmony which had been offered her, gave her no regret, no longing. It was not a condition of life which fitted her, and she could see in it but an appalling and hopeless ennui. She was moved by a kind of commiseration for Madame Ratignolle,—a pity for that colorless existence which never uplifted its possessor beyond the region of blind contentment, in which no moment of anguish ever visited her soul, in which she would never have the taste of life's delirium. Edna vaguely wondered what she meant by "life's delirium." It had crossed her thought like some unsought, extraneous impression.

CHAPTER XIX

Edna could not help but think that it was very foolish, very childish, to have stamped upon her wedding ring and smashed the crystal vase upon the tiles. She was visited by no more outbursts, moving her to such futile expedients. She began to do as she liked and to feel as she liked. She completely abandoned her Tuesdays at home, and did not return the visits of those who had called upon her. She made no ineffectual efforts to conduct her household *en bonne ménagère*, going and coming as it suited her fancy, and, so far as she was able, lending herself to any passing caprice.

Mr. Pontellier had been a rather courteous husband so long as he met a certain tacit submissiveness in his wife. But her new and unexpected line of conduct completely bewildered him. It shocked him. Then her absolute disregard for her duties as a wife angered him. When Mr. Pontellier became rude, Edna grew insolent. She had resolved never to take another step backward.

"It seems to me the utmost folly for a woman at the head of a household, and the mother of children, to spend in an atelier days which would be better employed contriving for the comfort of her family."

"I feel like painting," answered Edna. "Perhaps I shan't always feel like it."

"Then in God's name paint! but don't let the family go to the devil. There's Madame Ratignolle; because she keeps up her music, she doesn't let everything else go to chaos. And she's more of a musician than you are a painter."

"She isn't a musician, and I'm not a painter. It isn't on account of painting that I let things go."

"On account of what, then?"

"Oh! I don't know. Let me alone; you bother me."

It sometimes entered Mr. Pontellier's mind to wonder if his wife were not growing a little unbalanced mentally. He could see plainly that she was not herself. That is, he could not see that she was becoming herself and daily casting aside that fictitious self which we assume like a garment with which to appear before the world.

Her husband let her alone as she requested, and went away to his office. Edna went up to her atelier—a bright room in the top of the house. She was working with great energy and interest, without accomplishing anything, however, which satisfied her even in the smallest degree. For a time she had the whole household enrolled in the service of art. The boys posed for her. They thought it amusing at first, but the occupation soon lost its attractiveness when they discovered that it was not a game arranged especially for their entertainment. The quadroon sat for hours before Edna's palette, patient as a savage, while the house-maid took charge of the children, and the drawing-room went undusted. But the house-maid, too, served her term as model when Edna perceived that the young woman's back and shoulders were molded on classic lines, and that her hair, loosened from its confining cap, became an inspiration. While Edna worked she sometimes sang low the little air, "*Ah! si tu savais!*"

It moved her with recollections. She could hear again the ripple of the water, the flapping sail. She could see the glint of the moon upon the bay, and could feel the soft, gusty beating of the hot south wind. A subtle current of desire passed through her body, weakening her hold upon the brushes and making her eyes burn.

There were days when she was very happy without knowing why. She was happy to be alive and breathing, when her whole being seemed to be one with the sunlight, the color, the odors, the luxuriant warmth of some perfect Southern day. She liked then to wander alone into strange and unfamiliar places. She discovered many a sunny, sleepy corner, fashioned to dream in. And she found it good to dream and to be alone and unmolested.

There were days when she was unhappy, she did not know why,—when it did not seem worth while to be glad or sorry, to be alive or dead; when life appeared to her like a grotesque pandemonium and humanity like worms struggling blindly toward inevitable annihilation. She could not work on such a day, nor weave fancies to stir her pulses and warm her blood.

CHAPTER XX

It was during such a mood that Edna hunted up Mademoiselle Reisz. She had not forgotten the rather disagreeable impression left upon her by their last interview; but she nevertheless felt a desire to see her—above all, to listen while she played upon the piano. Quite early in the afternoon she started upon her quest for the pianist. Unfortunately she had mislaid or lost Mademoiselle Reisz's card, and looking up her address in the city directory, she found that the woman lived on

Bienville Street, some distance away. The directory which fell into her hands was a a year or more old, however, and upon reaching the number indicated, Edna discovered that the house was occupied by a respectable family of mulattoes who had *chambres garnies* to let. They had been living there for six months, and knew absolutely nothing of a Mademoiselle Reisz. In fact, they knew nothing of any of their neighbors; their lodgers were all people of the highest distinction, they assured Edna. She did not linger to discuss class distinctions with Madame Pouponne, but hastened to a neighboring grocery store, feeling sure that Mademoiselle would have left her address with the proprietor.

He knew Mademoiselle Reisz a good deal better than he wanted to know her, he informed his questioner. In truth, he did not want to know her at all, anything concerning her—the most disagreeable and unpopular woman who ever lived in Bienville Street. He thanked heaven she had left the neighborhood, and was equally thankful that he did not know where she had gone.

Edna's desire to see Mademoiselle Reisz had increased tenfold since these unlooked-for obstacles had arisen to thwart it. She was wondering who could give her the information she sought, when it suddenly occurred to her that Madame Lebrun would be the one most likely to do so. She knew it was useless to ask Madame Ratignolle, who was on the most distant terms with the musician, and preferred to know nothing concerning her. She had once been almost as emphatic in expressing herself upon the subject as the corner grocer.

Edna knew that Madame Lebrun had returned to the city, for it was the middle of November. And she also knew where the Lebruns lived, on Chartres Street.

Their home from the outside looked like a prison, with iron bars before the door and lower windows. The iron bars were a relic of the old *régime*, and no one had ever thought of dislodging them. At the side was a high fence enclosing the garden. A gate or door opening upon the street was locked. Edna rang the bell at this side garden gate, and stood upon the banquette, waiting to be admitted.

It was Victor who opened the gate for her. A black woman, wiping her hands upon her apron, was close at his heels. Before she saw them Edna could hear them in altercation, the woman—plainly an anomaly—claiming the right to be allowed to perform her duties, one of which was to answer the bell.

Victor was surprised and delighted to see Mrs. Pontellier, and he made no attempt to conceal either his astonishment or his delight. He was a dark-browed, good-looking youngster of nineteen, greatly resembling his mother, but with ten times her impetuosity. He instructed the black woman to go at once and inform Madame Lebrun that Mrs. Pontellier desired to see her. The woman grumbled a refusal to do part of her duty when she had not been permitted to do it all, and started back to her interrupted task of weeding the garden. Whereupon Victor administered a rebuke in the form of a volley of abuse, which owing to its rapidity and incoherence, was all but incomprehensible to Edna. Whatever it was, the rebuke was convincing, for the woman dropped her hoe and went mumbling into the house.

Edna did not wish to enter. It was very pleasant there on the side porch, where there were chairs, a wicker lounge, and a small table. She seated herself, for she was tired from her long tramp; and she began to rock gently and smooth out the folds of her silk parasol. Victor drew up his chair beside her. He at once explained that the black woman's offensive conduct was all due to imperfect training, as he was not there to take her in hand. He had only come up from the island the morning before, and expected to return next day. He stayed all winter at the island; he lived there, and kept the place in order and got things ready for the summer visitors.

But a man needed occasional relaxation, he informed Mrs. Pontellier, and every now and again he drummed up a pretext to bring him to the city. My! but he had had a time of it the evening before! He wouldn't want his mother to know, and he began to talk in a whisper. He was scintillant with recollections. Of course, he couldn't think of telling Mrs. Pontellier all about it, she being a woman and not comprehending such things. But it all began with a girl peeping and smiling at him through the shutters as he passed by. Oh! but she was a beauty! Certainly he smiled back, and went up and talked to her. Mrs. Pontellier did not know him if she supposed he was one to let an opportunity like that escape him. Despite herself, the youngster amused her. She must have betrayed in her look some degree of interest or entertainment. The boy grew more daring, and Mrs. Pontellier might have found herself, in a little while, listening to a highly colored story but for the timely appearance of Madame Lebrun.

That lady was still clad in white, according to her custom of the summer. Her eyes beamed an effusive welcome. Would not Mrs. Pontellier go inside? Would she partake of some refreshment? Why had she not been there before? How was that dear Mr. Pontellier and how were those sweet children? Has Mrs. Pontellier ever known such a warm November?

Victor went and reclined on the wicker lounge behind his mother's chair, where he commanded a view of Edna's face. He had taken her parasol from her hands while he spoke to her, and he now lifted it and twirled it above him as he lay on his back. When Madame Lebrun complained that it was *so* dull coming back to the city; that she saw *so* few people now; that even Victor, when he came up from the island for a day or two, had *so* much to occupy him and engage his time; then it was that the youth went into contortions on the lounge and winked mischievously at Edna. She somehow felt like a confederate in crime, and tried to look severe and disapproving.

There had been but two letters from Robert, with little in them, they told her. Victor said it was really not worth while to go inside for the letters, when his mother entreated him to go in search of them. He remembered the contents, which in truth he rattled off very glibly when put to the test.

One letter was written from Vera Cruz and the other from the City of Mexico. He had met Montel, who was doing everything toward his advancement. So far, the financial situation was no improvement over the one he had left in New Orleans, but of course the prospects were vastly better. He wrote of the City of Mexico, the buildings, the people and their habits, the conditions of life which he found there. He sent his love to the family. He inclosed a check to his mother, and hoped she would affectionately remember him to all his friends. That was about the substance of the two letters. Edna felt that if there had been a message for her, she would have received it. The despondent frame of mind in which she had left home began again to overtake her, and she remembered that she wished to find Mademoiselle Reisz.

Madame Lebrun knew where Mademoiselle Reisz lived. She gave Edna the address, regretting that she would not consent to stay and spend the remainder of the afternoon, and pay a visit to Mademoiselle Reisz some other day. The afternoon was already well advanced.

Victor escorted her out upon the banquette, lifted her parasol, and held it over her while he walked to the car with her. He entreated her to bear in mind that the disclosures of the afternoon were strictly confidential. She laughed and bantered him a little, remembering too late that she should have been dignified and reserved.

"How handsome Mrs. Pontellier looked!" said Madame Lebrun to her son.

"Ravishing!" he admitted. "The city atmosphere has improved her. Some way she doesn't seem like the same woman."

CHAPTER XXI

Some people contended that the reason Mademoiselle Reisz always chose apartments up under the roof was to discourage the approach of beggars, peddlars and callers. There were plenty of windows in her little front room. They were for the most part dingy, but as they were nearly always open it did not make so much difference. They often admitted into the room a good deal of smoke and soot; but at the same time all the light and air that there was came through them. From her windows could be seen the crescent of the river, the masts of ships and the big chimneys of the Mississippi steamers. A magnificent piano crowded the apartment. In the next room she slept, and in the third and last she harbored a gasoline stove on which she cooked her meals when disinclined to descend to the neighboring restaurant. It was there also that she ate, keeping her belongings in a rare old buffet, dingy and battered from a hundred years of use.

When Edna knocked at Mademoiselle Reisz's front room door and entered, she discovered that person standing beside the window, engaged in mending or patching an old prunella gaiter. The little musician laughed all over when she saw Edna. Her laugh consisted of a contortion of the face and all the muscles of the body. She seemed strikingly homely, standing there in the afternoon light. She still wore the shabby lace and the artificial bunch of violets on the side of her head.

"So you remembered me at last," said Mademoiselle. "I had said to myself, 'Ah, bah! she will never come.'"

"Did you want me to come?" asked Edna with a smile.

"I had not thought much about it," answered Mademoiselle. The two had seated themselves on a little bumpy sofa which stood against the wall. "I am glad, however, that you came. I have the water boiling back there, and was just about to make some coffee. You will drink a cup with me. And how is *la belle dame*? Always handsome! always healthy! always contented!" She took Edna's hand between her strong wiry fingers, holding it loosely without warmth, and executing a sort of double theme upon the back and palm.

"Yes," she went on; "I sometimes thought: 'She will never come. She promised as those women in society always do, without meaning it. She will not come.' For I really don't believe you like me, Mrs. Pontellier."

"I don't know whether I like you or not," replied Edna, gazing down at the little woman with a quizzical look.

The candor of Mrs. Pontellier's admission greatly pleased Mademoiselle Reisz. She expressed her gratification by repairing forthwith to the region of the gasoline stove and rewarding her guest with the promised cup of coffee. The coffee and the biscuit accompanying it proved very acceptable to Edna, who had declined refreshment at Madame Lebrun's and was now beginning to feel hungry. Mademoiselle set the tray which she brought in upon a small table near at hand, and seated herself once again on the lumpy sofa.

"I have had a letter from your friend," she remarked, as she poured a little cream into Edna's cup and handed it to her.

"My friend?"

"Yes, your friend Robert. He wrote to me from the City of Mexico."

"Wrote to *you*?" repeated Edna in amazement, stirring her coffee absently.

"Yes, to me. Why not? Don't stir all the warmth out of your coffee; drink it. Though the letter might as well have been sent to you; it was nothing but Mrs. Pontellier from beginning to end."

"Let me see it," requested the young woman, entreatingly.

"No; a letter concerns no one but the person who writes it and the one to whom it is written."

"Haven't you just said it concerned me from beginning to end?"

"It was written about you, not to you. 'Have you seen Mrs. Pontellier? How is she looking?' he asks. 'As Mrs. Pontellier says,' or 'as Mrs. Pontellier once said.' 'If Mrs. Pontellier should call upon you, play for her that Impromptu of Chopin's, my favorite. I heard it here a day or two ago, but not as you play it. I should like to know how it affects her,' and so on, as if he supposed we were constantly in each other's society."

"Let me see the letter."

"Oh, no."

"Have you answered it?"

"No."

"Let me see the letter."

"No, and again, no."

"Then play the Impromptu for me."

"It is growing late; what time do you have to be home?"

"Time doesn't concern me. Your question seems a little rude. Play the Impromptu."

"But you have told me nothing of yourself. What are you doing?"

"Painting!" laughed Edna. "I am becoming an artist. Think of it!"

"Ah! an artist! You have pretensions, Madame."

"Why pretensions? Do you think I could not become an artist?"

"I do not know you well enough to say. I do not know your talent or your temperament. To be an artist includes much; one must possess many gifts—absolute gifts—which have not been acquired by one's own effort. And, moreover, to succeed, the artist must possess the courageous soul."

"What do you mean by the courageous soul?"

"Courageous, *ma foi!* The brave soul. The soul that dares and defies."

"Show me the letter and play for me the Impromptu. You see that I have persistence. Does that quality count for anything in art?"

"It counts with a foolish old woman whom you have captivated," replied Mademoiselle, with her wriggling laugh.

The letter was right there at hand in the drawer of the little table upon which Edna had just placed her coffee cup. Mademoiselle opened the drawer and drew forth the letter, the topmost one. She placed it in Edna's hands, and without further comment arose and went to the piano.

Mademoiselle played a soft interlude. It was an improvisation. She sat low at the instrument, and the lines of her body settled into ungraceful curves and angles that gave it an appearance of deformity. Gradually and imperceptibly the interlude melted into the soft opening minor chords of the Chopin Impromptu.

Edna did not know when the Impromptu began or ended. She sat in the sofa corner reading Robert's letter by the fading light. Mademoiselle had glided from the Chopin into the quivering love-notes of Isolde's song, and back again to the Impromptu with its soulful and poignant longing.

The shadows deepened in the little room. The music grew strange and fantastic—turbulent, insistent, plaintive and soft with entreaty. The shadows grew deeper. The music filled the room. It floated out upon the night, over the housetops, the crescent of the river, losing itself in the silence of the upper air.

Edna was sobbing, just as she had wept one midnight at Grand Isle when strange, new voices awoke in her. She arose in some agitation to take her departure. "May I come again, Mademoiselle?" she asked at the threshold.

"Come whenever you feel like it. Be careful; the stairs and landings are dark; don't stumble."

Mademoiselle reëntered and lit a candle. Robert's letter was on the floor. She stooped and picked it up. It was crumbled and damp with tears. Mademoiselle smoothed the letter out, restored it to the envelope, and replaced it in the table drawer.

CHAPTER XXII

One morning on his way into town Mr. Pontellier stopped at the house of his old friend and family physician, Doctor Mandelet. The Doctor was a semi-retired physician, resting, as the saying is, upon his laurels. He bore a reputation for wisdom rather than skill—leaving the active practice of medicine to his assistants and younger contemporaries—and was much sought for in matters of consultation. A few families, united to him by bonds of friendship, he still attended when they required the services of a physician. The Pontelliers were among these.

Mr. Pontellier found the Doctor reading at the open window of his study. His house stood rather far back from the street, in the center of a delightful garden, so that it was quiet and peaceful at the old gentleman's study window. He was a great reader. He stared up disapprovingly over his eye-glasses as Mr. Pontellier entered, wondering who had the temerity to disturb him at that hour of the morning.

"Ah, Pontellier! Not sick, I hope. Come and have a seat. What news do you bring this morning?" He was quite portly, with a profusion of gray hair, and small blue eyes which age had robbed of much of their brightness but none of their penetration.

"Oh! I'm never sick, Doctor. You know that I come of tough fiber—of that old Creole race of Pontelliers that dry up and finally blow away. I came to consult—no, not precisely to consult—to talk to you about Edna. I don't know what ails her."

"Madame Pontellier not well?" marveled the Doctor. "Why, I saw her—I think it was a week ago—walking along Canal Street, the picture of health, it seemed to me."

"Yes, yes; she seems quite well," said Mr. Pontellier, leaning forward and whirling his stick between his two hands; "but she doesn't act well. She's odd, she's not like herself. I can't make her out, and I thought perhaps you'd help me."

"How does she act?" inquired the doctor.

"Well, it isn't easy to explain," said Mr. Pontellier, throwing himself back in his chair. "She lets the housekeeping go to the dickens."

"Well, well; women are not all alike, my dear Pontellier. We've got to consider—"

"I know that; I told you I couldn't explain. Her whole attitude—toward me and everybody and everything—has changed. You know I have a quick temper, but I don't want to quarrel or be rude to a woman, especially my wife; yet I'm driven to it, and feel like ten thousand devils after I've made a fool of myself. She's making it devilishly uncomfortable for me," he went on nervously. "She's got some sort of notion in her head concerning the eternal rights of women; and—you understand—we meet in the morning at the breakfast table."

The old gentleman lifted his shaggy eyebrows, protruded his thick nether lip, and tapped the arms of his chair with his cushioned finger-tips.

"What have you been doing to her, Pontellier?"

"Doing! *Parbleu!*"

"Has she," asked the Doctor, with a smile, "has she been associating of late with a circle of pseudo-intellectual women—super-spiritual superior beings? My wife has been telling me about them."

"That's the trouble," broke in Mr. Pontellier, "she hasn't been associating with any one. She has abandoned her Tuesdays at home, has thrown over all her acquaintances, and goes tramping about by herself, moping in the street-cars, getting in after dark. I tell you she's peculiar. I don't like it; I feel a little worried over it."

This was a new aspect for the Doctor. "Nothing hereditary?" he asked, seriously. "Nothing peculiar about her family antecedents, is there?"

"Oh, no, indeed! She comes of sound old Presbyterian Kentucky stock. The old gentleman, her father, I have heard, used to atone for his week-day sins with his Sunday devotions. I know for a fact, that his race horses literally ran away with the prettiest bit of Kentucky farming land I ever laid eyes upon. Margaret—you know Margaret—she has all the Presbyterianism undiluted. And the youngest is something of a vixen. By the way, she gets married in a couple of weeks from now."

"Send your wife up to the wedding," exclaimed the Doctor, foreseeing a happy solution. "Let her stay among her own people for a while; it will do her good."

"That's what I want her to do. She won't go to the marriage. She says a wedding is one of the most lamentable spectacles on earth. Nice thing for a woman to say to her husband!" exclaimed Mr. Pontellier, fuming anew at the recollection.

"Pontellier," said the Doctor, after a moment's reflection, "let your wife alone for a while. Don't bother her, and don't let her bother you. Woman, my dear friend, is a very peculiar and delicate organism—a sensitive and highly organized woman, such as I know Mrs. Pontellier to be, is especially peculiar. It would require an inspired psychologist to deal successfully with them. And when ordinary fellows like you and me attempt to cope with their idiosyncrasies the result is bungling. Most women are moody and whimsical. This is some passing whim of your wife, due to some cause or causes which you and I needn't try to fathom. But it will pass happily over, especially if you let her alone. Send her around to see me."

"Oh! I couldn't do that; there'd be no reason for it," objected Mr. Pontellier.

"Then I'll go around and see her," said the Doctor. "I'll drop in to dinner some evening *en bon ami*."

"Do! by all means," urged Mr. Pontellier. "What evening will you come? Say Thursday. Will you come Thursday?" he asked, rising to take his leave.

"Very well; Thursday. My wife may possibly have some engagement for me Thursday. In case she has, I shall let you know. Otherwise, you may expect me."

Mr. Pontellier turned before leaving to say:

"I am going to New York on business very soon. I have a big scheme on hand, and want to be on the field proper to pull the ropes and handle the ribbons. We'll let you in on the inside if you say so, Doctor," he laughed.

"No, I thank you, my dear sir," returned the Doctor. "I leave such ventures to you younger men with the fever of life still in your blood."

"What I wanted to say," continued Mr. Pontellier, with his hand on the knob; "I may have to be absent a good while. Would you advise me to take Edna along?"

"By all means, if she wishes to go. If not, leave her here. Don't contradict her. The mood will pass, I assure you. It may take a month, two, three months—possibly longer, but it will pass; have patience."

"Well, good-by, *à jeudi*," said Mr. Pontellier, as he let himself out.

The Doctor would have liked during the course of conversation to ask, "Is there any man in the case?" but he knew his Creole too well to make such a blunder as that.

He did not resume his book immediately, but sat for a while meditatively looking out into the garden.

CHAPTER XXIII

Edna's father was in the city, and had been with them several days. She was not very warmly or deeply attached to him, but they had certain tastes in common, and when together they were companionable. His coming was in the nature of a welcome disturbance; it seemed to furnish a new direction for her emotions.

He had come to purchase a wedding gift for his daughter, Janet, and an outfit for himself in which he might make a creditable appearance at her marriage. Mr. Pontellier had selected the bridal gift, as every one immediately connected with him always deferred to his taste in such matters. And his suggestions on the question of dress—which too often assumes the nature of a problem—were of inestimable value to his father-in-law. But for the past few days the old gentleman had been upon Edna's hands, and in his society she was becoming acquainted with a new set of sensations. He had been a colonel in the Confederate army, and still maintained, with the title, the military bearing which had always accompanied it. His hair and mustache were white and silky, emphasizing the rugged bronze of his face. He was tall and thin, and wore his coats padded, which gave a fictitious breadth and depth to his shoulders and chest. Edna and her father looked very distinguished together, and excited a good deal of notice during their perambulations. Upon his arrival she began by introducing him to her atelier and making a sketch of him. He took the whole matter very seriously. If her talent had been tenfold greater than it was, it would not have surprised him, convinced as he was that he had bequeathed to all of his daughters the germs of a masterful capability, which only depended upon their own efforts to be directed toward successful achievement.

Before her pencil he sat rigid and unflinching, as he had faced the cannon's mouth in days gone by. He resented the intrusion of the children, who gaped with wondering eyes at him, sitting so stiff up there in their mother's bright atelier. When they drew near he motioned them away with an expressive action of the foot, loath to disturb the fixed lines of his countenance, his arms, or his rigid shoulders.

Edna, anxious to entertain him, invited Mademoiselle Reisz to meet him, having promised him a treat in her piano playing; but Mademoiselle declined the invitation. So together they attended a *soirée musicale* at the Ratignolles'. Monsieur and Madame Ratignolle made much of the Colonel, installing him as the guest of honor and engaging him at once to dine with them the following Sunday, or any day which he might select. Madame coquetted with him in the most captivating and naïve manner, with eyes, gestures, and a profusion of compliments, till the Colonel's old head felt thirty years younger on his padded shoulders. Edna marveled, not comprehending. She herself was almost devoid of coquetry.

There were one or two men whom she observed at the *soirée musicale*; but she would never have felt moved to any kittenish display to attract their notice—to any feline or feminine wiles to express herself toward them. Their personality attracted her in an agreeable way. Her fancy selected them, and she was glad when a lull in the music gave them an opportunity to meet her and talk with her. Often on the street the glance of strange eyes had lingered in her memory, and sometimes had disturbed her.

Mr. Pontellier did not attend these *soirées musicales*. He considered them *bourgeois*, and found more diversion at the club. To Madame Ratignolle he said the music dispensed at her *soirées* was too "heavy," too far beyond his untrained comprehension. His excuse flattered her. But she disapproved of Mr. Pontellier's club, and she was frank enough to tell Edna so.

"It's a pity Mr. Pontellier doesn't stay home more in the evenings. I think you would be more—well, if you don't mind my saying it—more united, if he did."

"Oh! dear no!" said Edna, with a blank look in her eyes. "What should I do if he stayed home? We wouldn't have anything to say to each other."

She had not much of anything to say to her father, for that matter; but he did not antagonize her. She discovered that he interested her, though she realized that he might not interest her long; and for the first time in her life she felt as if she were thoroughly acquainted with him. He kept her busy serving him and ministering to his wants. It amused her to do so. She would not permit a servant or one of the children to do anything for him which she might do herself. Her husband noticed, and thought it was the expression of a deep filial attachment which he had never suspected.

The Colonel drank numerous "toddies" during the course of the day, which left him, however, imperturbed. He was an expert at concocting strong drinks. He had even invented some, to which he had given fantastic names, and for whose manufacture he required diverse ingredients that it devolved upon Edna to procure for him.

When Doctor Mandelet dined with the Pontelliers on Thursday he could discern in Mrs. Pontellier no trace of that morbid condition which her husband had reported to him. She was excited and in a manner radiant. She and her father had been to the race course, and their thoughts when they seated themselves at table were still occupied with the events of the afternoon, and their talk was still of the track. The Doctor had not kept pace with turf affairs. He had certain recollections of racing in what he called "the good old times" when the Lecompte stables flourished, and he drew upon this fund of memories so that he might not be left out and seem wholly devoid of the modern spirit. But he failed to impose upon the Colonel, and was even far from impressing him with this trumped-up knowledge of bygone days. Edna had staked her father on his last venture, with the most gratifying results to both of them. Besides, they had met some very charming people, according to the Colonel's impressions. Mrs. Mortimer Merriman and Mrs. James Highcamp, who were there with Alcée Arobin, had joined them and had enlivened the hours in a fashion that warmed him to think of.

Mr. Pontellier himself had no particular leaning toward horse-racing, and was even rather inclined to discourage it as a pastime, especially when he considered the fate of that blue-grass farm in Kentucky. He endeavored, in a general way, to express a particular disapproval, and only succeeded in arousing the ire and opposition of his father-in-law. A pretty dispute followed, in which Edna warmly espoused her father's cause and the Doctor remained neutral.

He observed his hostess attentively from under his shaggy brows, and noted a subtle change which had transformed her from the listless woman he had known into a being who, for the moment, seemed palpitant with the forces of life. Her speech was warm and energetic. There was no repression in her glance or gesture. She reminded him of some beautiful, sleek animal waking up in the sun.

The dinner was excellent. The claret was warm and the champagne was cold, and under their beneficent influence the threatened unpleasantness melted and vanished with the fumes of the wine.

Mr. Pontellier warmed up and grew reminiscent. He told some amusing plantation experiences, recollections of old Iberville and his youth, when he hunted 'possum in company with some friendly darky; thrashed the pecan trees, shot the grosbec, and roamed the woods and fields in mischievous idleness.

The Colonel, with little sense of humor and of the fitness of things, related a somber episode of those dark and bitter days, in which he had acted a conspicuous part and always formed a central figure. Nor was the Doctor happier in his selection, when he told the old, ever new and curious story of the waning of a woman's love, seeking strange, new channels, only to return to its legitimate source after days of fierce unrest. It was one of the many little human documents which had been unfolded to him during his long career as a physician. The story did not seem especially to impress Edna. She had one of her own to tell, of a woman who paddled away with her lover one night in a pirogue and never came back. They were lost amid the Baratarian Islands, and no one ever heard of them or found trace of them from that day to this. It was a pure invention. She said that Madame Antoine had related it to her. That, also, was an invention. Perhaps it was a dream she had had. But every glowing word seemed real to those who listened. They could feel the hot breath of the Southern night; they could hear the long sweep of the pirogue through the glistening moonlit water, the beating of birds' wings, rising startled from among the reeds in the salt-water pools; they could see the faces of the lovers, pale, close together, rapt in oblivious forgetfulness, drifting into the unknown.

The champagne was cold, and its subtle fumes played fantastic tricks with Edna's memory that night.

Outside, away from the glow of the fire and the soft lamplight, the night was chill and murky. The Doctor doubled his old-fashioned cloak across his breast as he strode home through the darkness. He knew his fellow-creatures better than most men; knew that inner life which so seldom unfolds itself to unanointed eyes. He was sorry he had accepted Pontellier's invitation. He was growing old, and beginning to need rest and an imperturbed spirit. He did not want the secrets of other lives thrust upon him.

"I hope it isn't Arobin," he muttered to himself as he walked. "I hope to heaven it isn't Alcée Arobin."

CHAPTER XXIV

Edna and her father had a warm, and almost violent dispute upon the subject of her refusal to attend her sister's wedding. Mr. Pontellier declined to interfere, to interpose either his influence or his authority. He was following Doctor Mandelet's advice, and letting her do as she liked. The Colonel reproached his daughter for her lack of filial kindness and respect, her want of sisterly affection and womanly consideration. His arguments were labored and unconvincing. He doubted if Janet would accept any excuse—forgetting that Edna had offered none. He doubted if Janet would ever speak to her again, and he was sure Margaret would not.

Edna was glad to be rid of her father when he finally took himself off with his wedding garments and his bridal gifts, with his padded shoulders, his Bible reading, his "toddies" and ponderous oaths.

Mr. Pontellier followed him closely. He meant to stop at the wedding on his way to New York and endeavor by every means which money and love could devise to atone somewhat for Edna's incomprehensible action.

"You are too lenient, too lenient by far, Léonce," asserted the Colonel. "Authority, coercion are what is needed. Put your foot down good and hard; the only way to manage a wife. Take my word for it."

The Colonel was perhaps unaware that he had coerced his own wife into her grave. Mr. Pontellier had a vague suspicion of it which he thought it needless to mention at that late day.

Edna was not so consciously gratified at her husband's leaving home as she had been over the departure of her father. As the day approached when he was to leave her for a comparatively long stay, she grew melting and affectionate, remembering his many acts of consideration and his repeated expressions of an ardent attachment. She was solicitous about his health and his welfare. She bustled around, looking after his clothing, thinking about heavy underwear, quite as Madame Ratignolle would have done under similar circumstances. She cried when he went away, calling him her dear, good friend, and she was quite certain she would grow lonely before very long and go to join him in New York.

But after all, a radiant peace settled upon her when she at last found herself alone. Even the children were gone. Old Madame Pontellier had come herself and carried them off to Iberville with their quadroon. The old madame did not venture to say she was afraid they would be neglected during Léonce's absence; she hardly ventured to think so. She was hungry for them—even a little fierce in her attachment. She did not want them to be wholly "children of the pavement," she always said when begging to have them for a space. She wished them to know the country, with its streams, its fields, its woods, its freedom, so delicious to the young. She wished them to taste something of the life their father had lived and known and loved when he, too, was a little child.

When Edna was at last alone, she breathed a big, genuine sigh of relief. A feeling that was unfamiliar but very delicious came over her. She walked all through the house, from one room to another, as if inspecting it for the first time. She tried the various chairs and lounges, as if she had never sat and reclined upon them before. And she perambulated around the outside of the house, investigating, looking to see if windows and shutters were secure and in order. The flowers were like new acquaintances; she approached them in a familiar spirit, and made herself at home among them. The garden walks were damp, and Edna called to the maid to bring out her rubber sandals. And there she stayed, and stooped, digging around the plants, trimming, picking dead, dry leaves. The children's little dog came out, interfering, getting in her way. She scolded him, laughing at him, played with him. The garden smelled so good and looked so pretty in the afternoon sunlight. Edna plucked all the bright flowers she could find, and went into the house with them, she and the little dog.

Even the kitchen assumed a sudden interesting character which she had never before perceived. She went in to give directions to the cook, to say that the butcher would have to bring much less meat, that they would require only half their usual quantity of bread, of milk and groceries. She told the cook that she herself would be greatly occupied during Mr. Pontellier's absence, and she begged her to take all thought and responsibility of the larder upon her own shoulders.

That night Edna dined alone. The candelabra, with a few candles in the center of the table, gave all the light she needed. Outside the circle of light in which she sat, the large dining-room looked solemn and shadowy. The cook, placed upon her mettle, served a delicious repast—a luscious tenderloin broiled à point. The wine tasted good; the marron glacé seemed to be just what she wanted. It was so pleasant, too, to dine in a comfortable *peignoir.*

She thought a little sentimentally about Léonce and the children, and wondered what they were doing. As she gave a dainty scrap or two to the doggie, she talked intimately to him about Etienne and Raoul. He was beside himself with astonishment and delight over these companionable advances, and showed his appreciation by his little quick, snappy barks and a lively agitation.

Then Edna sat in the library after dinner and read Emerson until she grew sleepy. She realized that she had neglected her reading, and determined to start anew upon a course of improving studies, now that her time was completely her own to do with as she liked.

After a refreshing bath, Edna went to bed. And as she snuggled comfortably beneath the eiderdown a sense of restfulness invaded her, such as she had not known before.

CHAPTER XXV

When the weather was dark and cloudy Edna could not work. She needed the sun to mellow and temper her mood to the sticking point. She had reached a stage when she seemed to be no longer feeling her way, working, when in the humor, with sureness and ease. And being devoid of ambition, and striving not toward accomplishment, she drew satisfaction from the work in itself.

On rainy or melancholy days Edna went out and sought the society of the friends she had made at Grand Isle. Or else she stayed indoors and nursed a mood with which she was becoming too familiar for her own comfort and peace of mind. It was not despair; but it seemed to her as if life were passing by, leaving its promise broken and unfulfilled. Yet there were other days when she listened, was led on and deceived by fresh promises which her youth held out to her.

She went again to the races, and again. Alcée Arobin and Mrs. Highcamp called for her one bright afternoon in Arobin's drag. Mrs. Highcamp was a worldly but unaffected, intelligent, slim, tall blonde woman in the forties, with an indifferent manner and blue eyes that stared. She had a daughter who served her as a pretext for cultivating the society of young men of fashion. Alcée Arobin was one of

both

them. He was a familiar figure at the race course, the opera, the fashionable clubs. There was a perpetual smile in his eyes, which seldom failed to awaken a corresponding cheerfulness in any one who looked into them and listened to his good-humored voice. His manner was quiet, and at times a little insolent. He possessed a good figure, a pleasing face, not overburdened with depth of thought or feeling; and his dress was that of the conventional man of fashion.

He admired Edna extravagantly, after meeting her at the races with her father. He had met her before on other occasions, but she had seemed to him unapproachable until that day. It was at his instigation that Mrs. Highcamp called to ask her to go with them to the Jockey Club to witness the turf event of the season.

There were possibly a few track men out there who knew the race horse as well as Edna, but there was certainly none who knew it better. She sat between her two companions as one having authority to speak. She laughed at Arobin's pretensions, and deplored Mrs. Highcamp's ignorance. The race horse was a friend and intimate associate of her childhood. The atmosphere of the stables and the breath of the blue-grass paddock revived in her memory and lingered in her nostrils. She did not perceive that she was talking like her father as the sleek geldings ambled in review before them. She played for very high stakes, and fortune favored her. The fever of the game flamed in her cheeks and eyes, and it got into her blood and into her brain like an intoxicant. People turned their heads to look at her, and more than one lent an attentive ear to her utterances, hoping thereby to secure the elusive but ever-desired "tip." Arobin caught the contagion of excitement which drew him to Edna like a magnet. Mrs. Highcamp remained, as usual, unmoved, with her indifferent stare and uplifted eyebrows.

Edna stayed and dined with Mrs. Highcamp upon being urged to do so. Arobin also remained and sent away his drag.

The dinner was quiet and uninteresting, save for the cheerful efforts of Arobin to enliven things. Mrs. Highcamp deplored the absence of her daughter from the races, and tried to convey to her what she had missed by going to the "Dante reading" instead of joining them. The girl held a geranium leaf up to her nose and said nothing, but looked knowing and noncommittal. Mr. Highcamp was a plain, bald-headed man, who only talked under compulsion. He was unresponsive. Mrs. Highcamp was full of delicate courtesy and consideration toward her husband. She addressed most of her conversation to him at table. They sat in the library after dinner and read the evening papers together under the drop-light; while the younger people went into the drawing-room near by and talked. Miss Highcamp played some selections from Grieg upon the piano. She seemed to have apprehended all of the composer's coldness and none of his poetry. While Edna listened she could not help wondering if she had lost her taste for music.

When the time came for her to go home, Mr. Highcamp grunted a lame offer to escort her, looking down at his slippered feet with tactless concern. It was Arobin who took her home. The car ride was long, and it was late when they reached Esplanade Street. Arobin asked permission to enter for a second to light his cigarette—his match safe was empty. He filled his match safe, but did not light his cigarette until he left her, after she had expressed her willingness to go to the races with him again.

Edna was neither tired nor sleepy. She was hungry again, for the Highcamp dinner, though of excellent quality, had lacked abundance. She rummaged in the larder and brought forth a slice of "Gruyère" and some crackers. She opened a bottle of beer which she found in the ice-box. Edna felt extremely restless and excited. She vacantly hummed a fantastic tune as she poked at the wood embers on the hearth and munched a cracker.

She wanted something to happen—something, anything; she did not know what. She regretted that she had not made Arobin stay a half hour to talk over the horses with her. She counted the money she had won. But there was nothing else to do, so she went to bed, and tossed there for hours in a sort of monotonous agitation.

In the middle of the night she remembered that she had forgotten to write her regular letter to her husband; and she decided to do so next day and tell him about her afternoon at the Jockey Club. She lay wide awake composing a letter which was nothing like the one which she wrote next day. When the maid awoke her in the morning Edna was dreaming of Mr. Highcamp playing the piano at the entrance of a music store on Canal Street, while his wife was saying to Alcée Arobin, as they boarded an Esplanade Street car:

"What a pity that so much talent has been neglected! but I must go."

When, a few days later, Alcée Arobin again called for Edna in his drag, Mrs. Highcamp was not with him. He said they would pick her up. But as that lady had not been apprised of his intention of picking her up, she was not at home. The daughter was just leaving the house to attend the meeting of a branch Folk Lore Society, and regretted that she could not accompany them. Arobin appeared nonplused, and asked Edna if there were any one else she cared to ask.

She did not deem it worth while to go in search of any of the fashionable acquaintances from whom she had withdrawn herself. She thought of Madame Ratignolle, but knew that her fair friend did not leave the house, except to take a languid walk around the block with her husband after nightfall. Mademoiselle Reisz would have laughed at such a request from Edna. Madame Lebrun might have enjoyed the outing, but for some reason Edna did not want her. So they went alone, she and Arobin.

The afternon was intensely interesting to her. The excitement came back upon her like a remittent fever. Her talk grew familiar and confidential. It was no labor to become intimate with Arobin. His manner invited easy confidence. The preliminary stage of becoming acquainted was one which he always endeavored to ignore when a pretty and engaging woman was concerned.

He stayed and dined with Edna. He stayed and sat beside the wood fire. They laughed and talked; and before it was time to go he was telling her how different life might have been if he had known her years before. With ingenuous frankness he spoke of what a wicked, ill-disciplined boy he had been, and impulsively drew up his cuff to exhibit upon his wrist the scar from a saber cut which he had received in a duel outside of Paris when he was nineteen. She touched his hand as she scanned the red cicatrice on the inside of his white wrist. A quick impulse that was somewhat spasmodic impelled her fingers to close in a sort of clutch upon his hand. He felt the pressure of her pointed nails in the flesh of his palm.

She arose hastily and walked toward the mantel.

"The sight of a wound or scar always agitates and sickens me," she said. "I shouldn't have looked at it."

"I beg your pardon," he entreated, following her; "it never occurred to me that it might be repulsive."

He stood close to her, and the effrontery in his eyes repelled the old, vanishing self in her, yet drew all her awakening sensuousness. He saw enough in her face to impel him to take her hand and hold it while he said his lingering good night.

"Will you go to the races again?" he asked.

"No," she said. "I've had enough of the races. I don't want to lose all the money I've won, and I've got to work when the weather is bright, instead of—"

"Yes; work; to be sure. You promised to show me your work. What morning may I come up to your atelier? To-morrow?"

"No!"

"Day after?"

"No, no."

"Oh, please don't refuse me! I know something of such things. I might help you with a stray suggestion or two."

"No. Good night. Why don't you go after you have said good night? I don't like you," she went on in a high, excited pitch, attempting to draw away her hand. She felt that her words lacked dignity and sincerity, and she knew that he felt it.

"I'm sorry you don't like me. I'm sorry I offended you. How have I offended you? What have I done? Can't you forgive me?" And he bent and pressed his lips upon her hand as if he wished never more to withdraw them.

"Mr. Arobin," she complained, "I'm greatly upset by the excitement of the afternoon; I'm not myself. My manner must have misled you in some way. I wish you to go, please." She spoke in a monotonous, dull tone. He took his hat from the table, and stood with eyes turned from her, looking into the dying fire. For a moment or two he kept an impressive silence.

"Your manner has not misled me, Mrs. Pontellier," he said finally. "My own emotions have done that. I couldn't help it. When I'm near you, how could I help it? Don't think anything of it, don't bother, please. You see, I go when you command me. If you wish me to stay away, I shall do so. If you let me come back, I—oh! you will let me come back?"

He cast one appealing glance at her, to which she made no response. Alcée Arobin's manner was so genuine that it often deceived even himself.

Edna did not care or think whether it were genuine or not. When she was alone she looked mechanically at the back of her hand which he had kissed so warmly. Then she leaned her head down on the mantelpiece. She felt somewhat like a woman who in a moment of passion is betrayed into an act of infidelity, and realizes the significance of the act without being wholly awakened from its glamour. The thought was passing vaguely through her mind, "What would he think?"

She did not mean her husband; she was thinking of Robert Lebrun. Her husband seemed to her now like a person whom she had married without love as an excuse.

She lit a candle and went up to her room. Alcée Arobin was absolutely nothing to her. Yet his presence, his manners, the warmth of his glances, and above all the touch of his lips upon her hand had acted like a narcotic upon her.

She slept a languorous sleep, interwoven with vanishing dreams.

CHAPTER XXVI

Alcée Arobin wrote Edna an elaborate note of apology, palpitant with sincerity. It embarrassed her; for in a cooler, quieter moment it appeared to her absurd that she should have taken his action so seriously, so dramatically. She felt sure that the significance of the whole occurrence had lain in her own self-consciousness. If she ignored his note it would give undue importance to a trivial affair. If she replied to it in a serious spirit it would still leave in his mind the impression that she had in a susceptible moment yielded to his influence. After all, it was no great matter to have one's hand kissed. She was provoked at his having written the apology. She answered in as light and bantering a spirit as she fancied it deserved, and said she would be glad to have him look in upon her at work whenever he felt the inclination and his business gave him the opportunity.

He responded at once by presenting himself at her home with all his disarming naïveté. And then there was scarcely a day which followed that she did not see him or was not reminded of him. He was prolific in pretexts. His attitude became one of good-humored subservience and tacit adoration. He was ready at all times to submit to her moods, which were as often kind as they were cold. She grew accustomed to him. They became intimate and friendly by imperceptible degrees, and then by leaps. He sometimes talked in a way that astonished her at first and brought the crimson into her face; in a way that pleased her at last, appealing to the animalism that stirred impatiently within her.

There was nothing which so quieted the turmoil of Edna's senses as a visit to Mademoiselle Reisz. It was then, in the presence of that personality which was offensive to her, that the woman, by her divine art, seemed to reach Edna's spirit and set it free.

It was misty, with heavy, lowering atmosphere, one afternoon, when Edna climbed the stairs to the pianist's apartments under the roof. Her clothes were dripping with moisture. She felt chilled and pinched as she entered the room. Mademoiselle was poking at a rusty stove that smoked a little and warmed the room indifferently. She was endeavoring to heat a pot of chocolate on the stove. The room looked cheerless and dingy to Edna as she entered. A bust of Beethoven, covered with a hood of dust, scowled at her from the mantelpiece.

"Ah! here comes the sunlight!" exclaimed Mademoiselle, rising from her knees before the stove. "Now it will be warm and bright enough; I can let the fire alone."

She closed the stove door with a bang, and approaching, assisted in removing Edna's dripping mackintosh.

"You are cold; you look miserable. The chocolate will soon be hot. But would you rather have a taste of brandy? I have scarcely touched the bottle which you brought me for my cold." A piece of red flannel was wrapped around Mademoiselle's throat; a stiff neck compelled her to hold her head on one side.

"I will take some brandy," said Edna, shivering as she removed her gloves and overshoes. She drank the liquor from the glass as a man would have done. Then flinging herself upon the uncomfortable sofa she said, "Mademoiselle, I am going to move away from my house on Esplanade Street."

"Ah!" ejaculated the musician, neither surprised nor especially interested. Nothing ever seemed to astonish her very much. She was endeavoring to adjust the bunch of violets which had become loose from its fastening in her hair. Edna drew her down upon the sofa, and taking a pin from her own hair, secured the shabby artificial flowers in their accustomed place.

"Aren't you astonished?"

"Passably. Where are you going? To New York? to Iberville? to your father in Mississippi? where?"

"Just two steps away," laughed Edna, "in a little four-room house around the corner. It looks so cozy, so inviting and restful, whenever I pass by; and it's for rent. I'm tired looking after that big house. It never seemed like mine, anyway—

like home. It's too much trouble. I have to keep too many servants. I am tired bothering with them."

"That is not your true reason, *ma belle*. There is no use in telling me lies. I don't know your reason, but you have not told me the truth." Edna did not protest or endeavor to justify herself.

"The house, the money that provides for it, are not mine. Isn't that enough reason?"

"They are your husband's," returned Mademoiselle, with a shrug and a malicious elevation of the eyebrows.

"Oh! I see there is no deceiving you. Then let me tell you: It is a caprice. I have a little money of my own from my mother's estate, which my father sends me by driblets. I won a large sum this winter on the races, and I am beginning to sell my sketches. Laidpore is more and more pleased with my work; he says it grows in force and individuality. I cannot judge of that myself, but I feel that I have gained in ease and confidence. However, as I said, I have sold a good many through Laidpore. I can live in the tiny house for little or nothing, with one servant. Old Celestine, who works occasionally for me, says she will come stay with me and do my work. I know I shall like it, like the feeling of freedom and independence."

"What does your husband say?"

"I have not told him yet. I only thought of it this morning. He will think I am demented, no doubt. Perhaps you think so."

Mademoiselle shook her head slowly. "Your reason is not yet clear to me," she said.

Neither was it quite clear to Edna herself; but it unfolded itself as she sat for a while in silence. Instinct had prompted her to put away her husband's bounty in casting off her allegiance. She did not know how it would be when he returned. There would have to be an understanding, an explanation. Conditions would some way adjust themselves, she felt; but whatever came, she had resolved never again to belong to another than herself.

"I shall give a grand dinner before I leave the old house!" Edna exclaimed. "You will have to come to it, Mademoiselle. I will give you everything that you like to eat and to drink. We shall sing and laugh and be merry for once." And she uttered a sigh that came from the very depths of her being.

If Mademoiselle happened to have received a letter from Robert during the interval of Edna's visits, she would give her the letter unsolicited. And she would seat herself at the piano and play as her humor prompted her while the young woman read the letter.

The little stove was roaring; it was red-hot, and the chocolate in the tin sizzled and sputtered. Edna went forward and opened the stove door, and Mademoiselle rising, took a letter from under the bust of Beethoven and handed it to Edna.

"Another! so soon!" she exclaimed, her eyes filled with delight. "Tell me, Mademoiselle, does he know that I see his letters?"

"Never in the world! He would be angry and would never write to me again if he thought so. Does he write to you? Never a line. Does he send you a message? Never a word. It is because he loves you, poor fool, and is trying to forget you, since you are not free to listen to him or to belong to him."

"Why do you show me his letters, then?"

"Haven't you begged for them? Can I refuse you anything? Oh! you cannot deceive me," and Mademoiselle approached her beloved instrument and began to play. Edna did not at once read the letter. She sat holding it in her hand, while the music penetrated her whole being like an effulgence, warming and brightening the dark places of her soul. It prepared her for joy and exultation.

"Oh!" she exclaimed, letting the letter fall to the floor. "Why did you not tell me?" She went and grasped Mademoiselle's hands up from the keys. "Oh! unkind! malicious! Why did you not tell me?"

"That he was coming back? No great news, *ma foi*. I wonder he did not come long ago."

"But when, when?" cried Edna, impatiently. "He does not say when."

"He says 'very soon.' You know as much about it as I do; it is all in the letter."

"But why? Why is he coming? Oh, if I thought—" and she snatched the letter from the floor and turned the pages this way and that way, looking for the reason, which was left untold.

"If I were young and in love with a man," said Mademoiselle, turning on the stool and pressing her wiry hands between her knees as she looked down at Edna, who sat on the floor holding the letter, "it seems to me he would have to be some *grand esprit*; a man with lofty aims and ability to reach them; one who stood high enough to attract the notice of his fellow-men. It seems to me if I were young and in love I should never deem a man of ordinary caliber worthy of my devotion."

"Now it is you who are telling lies and seeking to deceive me, Mademoiselle; or else you have never been in love, and know nothing about it. Why," went on Edna, clasping her knees and looking up into Mademoiselle's twisted face, "do you suppose a woman knows why she loves? Does she select? Does she say to herself: 'Go to! Here is a distinguished statesman with presidential possibilities; I shall proceed to fall in love with him.' Or, 'I shall set my heart upon this musician, whose fame is on every tongue?' Or, 'This financier, who controls the world's money markets?'"

"You are purposely misunderstanding me, *ma reine*. Are you in love with Robert?"

"Yes," said Edna. It was the first time she had admitted it, and a glow overspread her face, blotching it with red spots.

"Why?" asked her companion. "Why do you love him when you ought not to?"

Edna, with a motion or two, dragged herself on her knees before Mademoiselle Reisz, who took the glowing face between her two hands.

"Why? Because his hair is brown and grows away from his temples; because he opens and shuts his eyes, and his nose is a little out of drawing; because he has two lips and a square chin, and a little finger which he can't straighten from having played baseball too energetically in his youth. Because—"

"Because you do, in short," laughed Mademoiselle. "What will you do when he comes back?" she asked.

"Do? Nothing, except feel glad and happy to be alive."

She was already glad and happy to be alive at the mere thought of his return. The murky, lowering sky, which had depressed her a few hours before, seemed bracing and invigorating as she splashed through the streets on her way home.

She stopped at a confectioner's and ordered a huge box of bon-bons for the children in Iberville. She slipped a card in the box, on which she scribbled a tender message and sent an abundance of kisses.

Before dinner in the evening Edna wrote a charming letter to her husband, telling him of her intention to move for a while into the little house around the block, and to give a farewell dinner before leaving, regretting that he was not there to share it, to help her out with the menu and assist her in entertaining the guests. Her letter was brilliant and brimming with cheerfulness.

CHAPTER XXVII

"What is the matter with you?" asked Arobin that evening. "I never found you in such a happy mood." Edna was tired by that time, and was reclining on the lounge before the fire.

"Don't you know the weather prophet has told us we shall see the sun pretty soon?"

"Well, that ought to be reason enough," he acquiesced. "You wouldn't give me another if I sat here all night imploring you." He sat close to her on a low tabouret, and as he spoke his fingers lightly touched the hair that fell a little over her forehead. She liked the touch of his fingers through her hair, and closed her eyes sensitively.

"One of these days," she said, "I'm going to pull myself together for a while and think—try to determine what character of a woman I am; for, candidly, I don't know. By all the codes which I am acquainted with, I am a devilishly wicked specimen of the sex. But some way I can't convince myself that I am. I must think about it."

"Don't. What's the use? Why should you bother thinking about it when I can tell you what manner of woman you are." His fingers strayed occasionally down to her warm, smooth cheeks and firm chin, which was growing a little full and double.

"Oh, yes! You will tell me that I am adorable; everything that is captivating. Spare yourself the effort."

"No; I shan't tell you anything of the sort, though I shouldn't be lying if I did."

"Do you know Mademoiselle Reisz?" she asked irrelevantly.

"The pianist? I know her by sight. I've heard her play."

"She says queer things sometimes in a bantering way that you don't notice at the time and you find yourself thinking about afterward."

"For instance?"

"Well, for instance, when I left her today, she put her arms around me and felt my shoulder blades, to see if my wings were strong, she said. 'The bird that would soar above the level plain of tradition and prejudice must have strong wings. It is a sad spectacle to see the weaklings bruised, exhausted, fluttering back to earth.'"

"Whither would you soar?"

"I'm not thinking of any extraordinary flights. I only half comprehend her."

"I've heard she's partially demented," said Arobin.

"She seems to me wonderfully sane," Edna replied.

"I'm told she's extremely disagreeable and unpleasant. Why have you introduced her at a moment when I desired to talk of you?"

"Oh! talk of me if you like," cried Edna, clasping her hands beneath her head; "but let me think of something else while you do."

"I'm jealous of your thoughts to-night. They're making you a little kinder than usual; but some way I feel as if they were wandering, as if they were not here with me." She only looked at him and smiled. His eyes were very near. He leaned upon the lounge with an arm extended across her, while the other hand still rested upon her hair. They continued silently to look into each other's eyes. When he leaned forward and kissed her, she clasped his head, holding his lips to hers.

It was the first kiss of her life to which her nature had really responded. It was a flaming torch that kindled desire.

CHAPTER XXVIII

Edna cried a little that night after Arobin left her. It was only one phase of the multitudinous emotions which had assailed her. There was with her an overwhelming feeling of irresponsibility. There was the shock of the unexpected and the unaccustomed. There was her husband's reproach looking at her from the external things around her which he had provided for her external existence. There was Robert's reproach making itself felt by a quicker, fiercer, more overpowering love, which had awakened within her toward him. Above all, there was understanding. She felt as if a mist had been lifted from her eyes, enabling her to look upon and comprehend the significance of life, that monster made up of beauty and brutality. But among the conflicting sensations which assailed her, there was neither shame nor remorse. There was a dull pang of regret because it was not the kiss of love which had inflamed her, because it was not love which had held this cup of life to her lips.

CHAPTER XXIX

Without even waiting for an answer from her husband regarding his opinion or wishes in the matter, Edna hastened her preparations for quitting her home on Esplanade Street and moving into the little house around the block. A feverish anxiety attended her every action in that direction. There was no moment of deliberation, no interval of repose between the thought and its fulfillment. Early upon the morning following those hours passed in Arobin's society, Edna set about securing her new abode and hurrying her arrangements for occupying it. Within the precincts of her home she felt like one who has entered and lingered within the portals of some forbidden temple in which a thousand muffled voices bade her begone.

Whatever was her own in the house, everything which she had acquired aside from her husband's bounty, she caused to be transported to the other house, supplying simple and meager deficiencies from her own resources.

Arobin found her with rolled sleeves, working in company with the housemaid when he looked in during the afternoon. She was splendid and robust, and had never appeared handsomer than in the old blue gown, with a red silk handkerchief knotted at random around her head to protect her hair from the dust. She was mounted upon a high step-ladder, unhooking a picture from the wall when he entered. He had found the front door open, and had followed his ring by walking in unceremoniously.

"Come down!" he said. "Do you want to kill yourself?" She greeted him with affected carelessness, and appeared absorbed in her occupation.

If he had expected to find her languishing, reproachful, or indulging in sentimental tears, he must have been greatly surprised.

He was no doubt prepared for any emergency, ready for any one of the foregoing attitudes, just as he bent himself easily and naturally to the situation which confronted him.

"Please come down," he insisted, holding the ladder and looking up at her.

"No," she answered; "Ellen is afraid to mount the ladder. Joe is working over at the 'pigeon house'—that's the name Ellen gives it, because it's so small and looks like a pigeon house—and some one has to do this."

Arobin pulled off his coat, and expressed himself ready and willing to tempt fate in her place. Ellen brought him one of her dust-caps, and went into contortions of mirth, which she found it impossible to control, when she saw him put it on before the mirror as grotesquely as he could. Edna herself could not refrain from smiling when she fastened it at his request. So it was he who in turn mounted the ladder, unhooking pictures and curtains, and dislodging ornaments as Edna directed. When he had finished he took off his dust-cap and went out to wash his hands.

Edna was sitting on the tabouret, idly brushing the tips of a feather duster along the carpet when he came in again.

"Is there anything more you will let me do?" he asked.

"That is all," she answered. "Ellen can manage the rest." She kept the young woman occupied in the drawing-room, unwilling to be left alone with Arobin.

"What about the dinner?" he asked; "the grand event, the *coup d'état*?"

"It will be day after to-morrow. Why do you call it the '*coup d'état*?' Oh! it will be very fine; all my best of everything—crystal, silver and gold, Sèvres, flowers, music, and champagne to swim in. I'll let Léonce pay the bills. I wonder what he'll say when he sees the bills."

"And you ask me why I call it a *coup d'état*?" Arobin had put on his coat, and he stood before her and asked if his cravat was plumb. She told him it was, looking no higher than the tip of his collar.

"When do you go to the 'pigeon house?'—with all due acknowledgment to Ellen."

"Day after to-morrow, after the dinner. I shall sleep there."

"Ellen, will you very kindly get me a glass of water?" asked Arobin. "The dust in the curtains, if you will pardon me for hinting such a thing, has parched my throat to a crisp."

"While Ellen gets the water," said Edna, rising, "I will say good-by and let you go. I must get rid of this grime, and I have a million things to do and think of."

"When shall I see you?" asked Arobin, seeking to detain her, the maid having left the room.

"At the dinner, of course. You are invited."

"Not before?—not to-night or to-morrow morning or to-morrow noon or night? or the day after morning or noon? Can't you see yourself, without my telling you, what an eternity it is?"

He had followed her into the hall and to the foot of the stairway, looking up at her as she mounted with her face half turned to him.

"Not an instant sooner," she said. But she laughed and looked at him with eyes that at once gave him courage to wait and made it torture to wait.

CHAPTER XXX

Though Edna had spoken of the dinner as a very grand affair, it was in truth a very small affair and very select, in so much as the guests invited were few and were selected with discrimination. She had counted upon an even dozen seating themselves at her round mahogany board, forgetting for the moment that Madame Ratignolle was to the last degree *souffrante* and unpresentable, and not foreseeing that Madame Lebrun would send a thousand regrets at the last moment. So there were only ten, after all, which made a cozy, comfortable number.

There were Mr. and Mrs. Merriman, a pretty, vivacious little woman in the thirties; her husband, a jovial fellow, something of a shallow-pate, who laughed a good deal at other people's witticisms, and had thereby made himself extremely popular. Mrs. Highcamp had accompanied them. Of course, there was Alcée Arobin; and Mademoiselle Reisz had consented to come. Edna had sent her a fresh bunch of violets with black lace trimmings for her hair. Monsieur Ratignolle brought himself and his wife's excuses. Victor Lebrun, who happened to be in the city, bent upon relaxation, had accepted with alacrity. There was a Miss Mayblunt, no longer in her teens, who looked at the world through lorgnettes and with the keenest interest. It was thought and said that she was intellectual; it was suspected of her that she wrote under a *nom de guerre*. She had come with a gentleman by the name of Gouvernail, connected with one of the daily papers, of whom nothing special could be said, except that he was observant and seemed quiet and inoffensive. Edna herself made the tenth, and at half-past eight they seated themselves at table, Arobin and Monsieur Ratignolle on either side of their hostess.

Mrs. Highcamp sat between Arobin and Victor Lebrun. Then came Mrs. Merriman, Mr. Gouvernail, Miss Mayblunt, Mr. Merriman, and Mademoiselle Reisz next to Monsieur Ratignolle.

There was something extremely gorgeous about the appearance of the table, an effect of splendor conveyed by a cover of pale yellow satin under strips of lacework. There were wax candles in massive brass candelabra, burning softly under yellow silk shades; full, fragrant roses, yellow and red, abounded. There were silver and gold, as she had said there would be, and crystal which glittered like the gems which the women wore.

The ordinary stiff dining chairs had been discarded for the occasion and replaced by the most commodious and luxurious which could be collected throughout the house. Mademoiselle Reisz, being exceedingly diminutive, was elevated upon cushions, as small children are sometimes hoisted at table upon bulky volumes.

"Something new, Edna?" exclaimed Miss Mayblunt, with lorgnette directed toward a magnificent cluster of diamonds that sparkled, that almost sputtered, in Edna's hair, just over the center of her forehead.

"Quite new; 'brand' new, in fact; a present from my husband. It arrived this morning from New York. I may as well admit that this is my birthday, and that I am twenty-nine. In good time I expect you to drink my health. Meanwhile, I shall ask you to begin with this cocktail, composed—would you say 'composed?'" with an appeal to Miss Mayblunt—"composed by my father in honor of Sister Janet's wedding."

Before each guest stood a tiny glass that looked and sparkled like a garnet gem.

"Then, all things considered," spoke Arobin, "it might not be amiss to start out by drinking the Colonel's health in the cocktail which he composed, on the birthday of the most charming of women—the daughter whom he invented."

Mr. Merriman's laugh at this sally was such a genuine outburst and so contagious that it started the dinner with an agreeable swing that never slackened.

Miss Mayblunt begged to be allowed to keep her cocktail untouched before her, just to look at it. The color was marvelous! She could compare it to nothing she had ever seen, and the garnet lights which it emitted were unspeakably rare. She pronounced the Colonel an artist, and stuck to it.

Monsieur Ratignolle was prepared to take things seriously; the *mets*, the *entremets*, the service, the decorations, even the people. He looked up from his pompono and inquired of Arobin if he were related to the gentleman of that name who formed one of the firm of Laitner and Arobin, lawyers. The young man admitted that Laitner was a warm personal friend, who permitted Arobin's name to decorate the firm's letterheads and to appear upon a shingle that graced Perdido Street.

"There are so many inquisitive people and institutions abounding," said Arobin, "that one is really forced as a matter of convenience these days to assume the virtue of an occupation if he has it not."

Monsieur Ratignolle stared a little, and turned to ask Mademoiselle Reisz if she considered the symphony concerts up to the standard which had been set the previous winter. Mademoiselle Reisz answered Monsieur Ratignolle in French, which Edna thought a little rude, under the circumstances, but characteristic. Mademoiselle had only disagreeable things to say of the symphony concerts, and insulting remarks to make of all the musicians of New Orleans, singly and collectively. All her interest seemed to be centered upon the delicacies placed before her.

Mr. Merriman said that Mr. Arobin's remark about inquisitive people reminded him of a man from Waco the other day at the St. Charles Hotel—but as Mr. Merriman's stories were always lame and lacking point, his wife seldom permitted him to complete them. She interrupted him to ask if he remembered the name of the author whose book she had bought the week before to send to a friend in Geneva. She was talking "books" with Mr. Gouvernail and trying to draw from him his opinion upon current literary topics. Her husband told the story of the Waco man privately to Miss Mayblunt, who pretended to be greatly amused and to think it extremely clever.

Mrs. Highcamp hung with languid but unaffected interest upon the warm and impetuous volubility of her left-hand neighbor, Victor Lebrun. Her attention was never for a moment withdrawn from him after seating herself at table; and when he turned to Mrs. Merriman, who was prettier and more vivacious than Mrs. Highcamp, she waited with easy indifference for an opportunity to reclaim his attention. There was the occasional sound of music, of mandolins, sufficiently removed to be an agreeable accompaniment rather than an interruption to the conversation. Outside the soft, monotonous splash of a fountain could be heard; the sound penetrated into the room with the heavy odor of jessamine that came through the open windows.

The golden shimmer of Edna's satin gown spread in rich folds on either side of her. There was a soft fall of lace encircling her shoulders. It was the color of her skin, without the glow, the myriad living tints that one may sometimes discover in vibrant flesh. There was something in her attitude, in her whole appearance when she leaned her head against the high-backed chair and spread her arms, which suggested the regal woman, the one who rules, who looks on, who stands alone.

But as she sat there amid her guests, she felt the old ennui overtaking her; the hopelessness which so often assailed her, which came upon her like an obsession, like something extraneous, independent of volition. It was something which announced itself; a chill breath that seemed to issue from some vast cavern wherein discords wailed. There came over her the acute longing which always summoned into her spiritual vision the presence of the beloved one, overpowering her at once with a sense of the unattainable.

The moments glided on, while a feeling of good fellowship passed around the circle like a mystic cord, holding and binding these people together with jest and laughter. Monsieur Ratignolle was the first to break the pleasant charm. At ten o'clock he excused himself. Madame Ratignolle was waiting for him at home. She was *bien souffrante*, and she was filled with vague dread, which only her husband's presence could allay.

Mademoiselle Reisz arose with Monsieur Ratignolle, who offered to escort her to the car. She had eaten well; she had tasted the good, rich wines, and they must have turned her head, for she bowed pleasantly to all as she withdrew from table. She kissed Edna upon the shoulder, and whispered: "*Bonne nuit, ma reine; soyez sage.*" She had been a little bewildered upon rising, or rather, descending from her cushions, and Monsieur Ratignolle gallantly took her arm and led her away.

Mrs. Highcamp was weaving a garland of roses, yellow and red. When she had finished the garland, she laid it lightly upon Victor's black curls. He was reclining far back in the luxurious chair, holding a glass of champagne to the light.

As if a magician's wand had touched him, the garland of roses transformed him into a vision of Oriental beauty. His cheeks were the color of crushed grapes, and his dusky eyes glowed with a languishing fire.

"*Sapristi!*" exclaimed Arobin.

But Mrs. Highcamp had one more touch to add to the picture. She took from the back of her chair a white silken scarf, with which she had covered her shoulders in the early part of the evening. She draped it across the boy in graceful folds, and in a way to conceal his black, conventional evening dress. He did not seem to mind what she did to him, only smiled, showing a faint gleam of white teeth, while he continued to gaze with narrowing eyes at the light through his glass of champagne.

"Oh! to be able to paint in color rather than in words!" exclaimed Miss Mayblunt, losing herself in a rhapsodic dream as she looked at him.

> "'There was a graven image of Desire
> Painted with red blood on a ground of gold.'"

murmured Gouvernail, under his breath.

The effect of the wine upon Victor was to change his accustomed volubility into ~~into~~ silence. He seemed to have abandoned himself to a reverie, and to be seeing pleasing visions in the amber bead.

"Sing," entreated Mrs. Highcamp. "Won't you sing to us?"

"Let him alone," said Arobin.

"He's posing," offered Mr. Merriman; "let him have it out."

"I believe he's paralyzed," laughed Mrs. Merriman. And leaning over the youth's chair, she took the glass from his hand and held it to his lips. He sipped the wine slowly, and when he had drained the glass she laid it upon the table and wiped his lips with her little filmy handkerchief.

"Yes, I'll sing for you," he said, turning in his chair toward Mrs. Highcamp. He clasped his hands behind his head, and looking up at the ceiling began to hum a little, trying his voice like a musician tuning an instrument. Then, looking at Edna, he began to sing:

> "Ah! si tu savais!"

"Stop!" she cried, "don't sing that. I don't want you to sing it," and she laid her glass so impetuously and blindly upon the table as to shatter it against a caraffe. The wine spilled over Arobin's legs and some of it trickled down upon Mrs. Highcamp's black gauze gown. Victor had lost all idea of courtesy, or else he thought his hostess was not in earnest, for he laughed and went on:

"Ah! si tu savais
Ce que tes yeux me disent"—

"Oh! you mustn't! you mustn't," exclaimed Edna, and pushing back her chair she got up, and going behind him placed her hand over his mouth. He kissed the soft palm that pressed upon his lips.

"No, no, I won't, Mrs. Pontellier. I didn't know you meant it," looking up at her with caressing eyes. The touch of his lips was like a pleasing sting to her hand. She lifted the garland of roses from his head and flung it across the room.

"Come, Victor; you've posed long enough. Give Mrs. Highcamp her scarf."

Mrs. Highcamp undraped the scarf from about him with her own hands. Miss Mayblunt and Mr. Gouvernail suddenly conceived the notion that it was time to say good night. And Mr. and Mrs. Merriman wondered how it could be so late.

Before parting from Victor, Mrs. Highcamp invited him to call upon her daughter, who she knew would be charmed to meet him and talk French and sing French songs with him. Victor expressed his desire and intention to call upon Miss Highcamp at the first opportunity which presented itself. He asked if Arobin were going his way. Arobin was not.

The mandolin players had long since stolen away. A profound stillness had fallen upon the broad, beautiful street. The voices of Edna's disbanding guests jarred like a discordant note upon the quiet harmony of the night.

CHAPTER XXXI

"Well?" questioned Arobin, who had remained with Edna after the others had departed.

"Well," she reiterated, and stood up, stretching her arms, and feeling the need to relax her muscles after having been so long seated.

"What next?" he asked.

"The servants are all gone. They left when the musicians did. I have dismissed them. The house has to be closed and locked, and I shall trot around to the pigeon house, and shall send Celestine over in the morning to straighten things up."

He looked around, and began to turn out some of the lights.

"What about upstairs?" he inquired.

"I think it is all right; but there may be a window or two unlatched. We had better look; you might take a candle and see. And bring me my wrap and hat on the foot of the bed in the middle room."

He went up with the light, and Edna began closing doors and windows. She hated to shut in the smoke and the fumes of the wine. Arobin found her cape and hat, which he brought down and helped her to put on.

When everything was secured and the lights put out, they left through the front door, Arobin locking it and taking the key, which he carried for Edna. He helped her down the steps.

"Will you have a spray of jessamine?" he asked, breaking off a few blossoms as he passed.

"No; I don't want anything."

She seemed disheartened, and had nothing to say. She took his arm, which he offered her, holding up the weight of her satin train with the other hand. She looked down, noticing the black line of his leg moving in and out so close to her against the yellow shimmer of her gown. There was the whistle of a railway train somewhere in the distance, and the midnight bells were ringing. They met no one in their short walk.

The "pigeon-house" stood behind a locked gate, and a shallow *parterre* that had been somewhat neglected. There was a small front porch, upon which a long window and the front door opened. The door opened directly into the parlor; there was no side entry. Back in the yard was a room for servants, in which old Celestine had been ensconced.

Edna had left a lamp burning low upon the table. She had succeeded in making the room look habitable and homelike. There were some books on the table and a lounge near at hand. On the floor was a fresh matting, covered with a rug or two; and on the walls hung a few tasteful pictures. But the room was filled with flowers. These were a surprise to her. Arobin had sent them, and had had Celestine distribute them during Edna's absence. Her bedroom was adjoining, and across a small passage were the dining-room and kitchen.

Edna seated herself with every appearance of discomfort.

"Are you tired?" he asked.

"Yes, and chilled, and miserable. I feel as if I had been wound up to a certain pitch—too tight—and something inside of me had snapped." She rested her head against the table upon her bare arm.

"You want to rest," he said, "and to be quiet. I'll go; I'll leave you and let you rest."

"Yes," she replied.

He stood up beside her and smoothed her hair with his soft, magnetic hand. His touch conveyed to her a certain physical comfort. She could have fallen quietly asleep there if he had continued to pass his hand over her hair. He brushed the hair upward from the nape of her neck.

"I hope you will feel better and happier in the morning," he said. "You have tried to do too much in the past few days. The dinner was the last straw; you might have dispensed with it."

"Yes," she admitted; "it was stupid."

"No, it was delightful; but it has worn you out." His hand had strayed to her beautiful shoulders, and he could feel the response of her flesh to his touch. He seated himself beside her and kissed her lightly upon the shoulder.

"I thought you were going away," she said, in an uneven voice.

"I am, after I have said good night."

"Good night," she murmured.

He did not answer, except to continue to caress her. He did not say good night until she had become supple to his gentle, seductive entreaties.

CHAPTER XXXII

When Mr. Pontellier learned of his wife's intention to abandon her home and take up her residence elsewhere, he immediately wrote her a letter of unqualified disapproval and remonstrance. She had given reasons which he was unwilling to acknowledge as adequate. He hoped she had not acted upon her rash impulse; and he begged her to consider first, foremost, and above all else, what people would say. He was not dreaming of scandal when he uttered this warning; that was a thing which would never have entered into his mind to consider in connection with his wife's name or his own. He was simply thinking of his financial integrity.

It might get noised about that the Pontelliers had met with reverses, and were forced to conduct their *ménage* on a humbler scale than heretofore. It might do incalculable mischief to his business prospects.

But remembering Edna's whimsical turn of mind of late, and foreseeing that she had immediately acted upon her impetuous determination, he grasped the situation with his usual promptness and handled it with his well-known business tact and cleverness.

The same mail which brought to Edna his letter of disapproval carried instructions—the most minute instructions—to a well-known architect concerning the remodeling of his home, changes which he had long contemplated, and which he desired carried forward during his temporary absence.

Expert and reliable packers and movers were engaged to convey the furniture, carpets, pictures—everything movable, in short—to places of security. And in an incredibly short time the Pontellier house was turned over to the artisans. There was to be an addition—a small snuggery; there was to be frescoing, and hardwood flooring was to be put into such rooms as had not yet been subjected to this improvement.

Furthermore, in one of the daily papers appeared a brief notice to the effect that Mr. and Mrs. Pontellier were contemplating a summer sojourn abroad, and that their handsome residence on Esplanade Street was undergoing sumptuous alterations, and would not be ready for occupancy until their return. Mr. Pontellier had saved appearances!

Edna admitted the skill of his maneuver, and avoided any occasion to balk his intentions. When the situation as set forth by Mr. Pontellier was accepted and taken for granted, she was apparently satisfied that it should be so.

The pigeon-house pleased her. It at once assumed the intimate character of a home, while she herself invested it with a charm which it reflected like a warm glow. There was with her a feeling of having descended in the social scale, with a corresponding sense of having risen in the spiritual. Every step which she took toward relieving herself from obligations added to her strength and expansion as an individual. She began to look with her own eyes; to see and to apprehend the deeper undercurrents of life. No longer was she content to "feed upon opinion" when her own soul had invited her.

After a little while, a few days, in fact, Edna went up and spent a week with her children in Iberville. They were delicious February days, with all the summer's promise hovering in the air.

How glad she was to see the children! She wept for very pleasure when she felt their little arms clasping her; their hard, ruddy cheeks pressed against her own glowing cheeks. She looked into their faces with hungry eyes that could not be satisfied with looking. And what stories they had to tell their mother! About the pigs, the cows, the mules! About riding to the mill behind Gluglu; fishing back in the lake with their Uncle Jasper; picking pecans with Lidie's little black brood, and hauling chips in their express wagon. It was a thousand times more fun to haul real chips for old lame Susie's real fire than to drag painted blocks along the banquette on Esplanade Street!

She went with them herself to see the pigs and the cows, to look at the darkies laying the cane, to thrash the pecan trees, and catch fish in the back lake. She lived with them a whole week long, giving them all of herself, and gathering and filling herself with their young existence. They listened, breathless, when she told them the house in Esplanade Street was crowded with workmen, hammering, nailing, sawing, and filling the place with clatter. They wanted to know where their bed was; what had been done with their rocking-horse; and where did Joe sleep, and where had Ellen gone, and the cook? But, above all, they were fired with a desire to see the little house around the block. Was there any place to play? Were there any boys next door? Raoul, with pessimistic foreboding, was convinced that there were only girls next door. Where would they sleep, and where would papa sleep? She told them the fairies would fix it all right.

The old Madame was charmed with Edna's visit, and showered all manner of delicate attentions upon her. She was delighted to know that the Esplanade Street house was in a dismantled condition. It gave her the promise and pretext to keep the children indefinitely.

It was with a wrench and a pang that Edna left her children. She carried away with her the sound of their voices and the touch of their cheeks. All along the journey homeward their presence lingered with her like the memory of a delicious song. But by the time she had regained the city the song no longer echoed in her soul. She was again alone.

CHAPTER XXXIII

It happened sometimes when Edna went to see Mademoiselle Reisz that the little musician was absent, giving a lesson or making some small necessary household purchase. The key was always left in a secret hiding-place in the entry, which Edna knew. If Mademoiselle happened to be away, Edna would usually enter and wait for her return.

When she knocked at Mademoiselle Reisz's door one afternoon there was no response; so unlocking the door, as usual, she entered and found the apartment deserted, as she had expected. Her day had been quite filled up, and it was for a rest, for a refuge, and to talk about Robert, that she sought out her friend.

She had worked at her canvas—a young Italian character study—all the morning, completing the work without the model; but there had been many interruptions, some incident to her modest housekeeping, and others of a social nature.

Madame Ratignolle had dragged herself over, avoiding the too public thoroughfares, she said. She complained that Edna had neglected her much of late. Besides, she was consumed with curiosity to see the little house and the manner in which it was conducted. She wanted to hear all about the dinner party; Monsieur Ratignolle had left *so* early. What had happened after he left? The champagne and grapes which Edna sent over were *too* delicious. She had so little appetite; they had refreshed and toned her stomach. Where on earth was she going to put Mr. Pontellier in that little house, and the boys? And then she made Edna promise to go to her when her hour of trial overtook her.

"At any time—any time of the day or night, dear," Edna assured her.

Before leaving Madame Ratignolle said:

"In some way you seem to me like a child, Edna. You seem to act without a certain amount of reflection which is necessary in this life. That is the reason I want to say you mustn't mind if I advise you to be a little careful while you are living here alone. Why don't you have some one come and stay with you? Wouldn't Mademoiselle Reisz come?"

"No; she wouldn't wish to come, and I shouldn't want her always with me."

"Well, the reason—you know how evil-minded the world is—some one was talking of Alcée Arobin visiting you. Of course, it wouldn't matter if Mr. Arobin had not such a dreadful reputation. Monsieur Ratignolle was telling me that his attentions alone are considered enough to ruin a woman's name."

"Does he boast of his successes?" asked Edna, indifferently, squinting at her picture.

"No, I think not. I believe he is a decent fellow as far as that goes. But his character is so well known among the men. I shan't be able to come back and see you; it was very, very imprudent to-day."

"Mind the step!" cried Edna.

"Don't neglect me," entreated Madame Ratignolle; "and don't mind what I said about Arobin, or having some one to stay with you."

"Of course not," Edna laughed. "You may say anything you like to me." They kissed each other good-by. Madame Ratignolle had not far to go, and Edna stood on the porch a while watching her walk down the street.

Then in the afternoon Mrs. Merriman and Mrs. Highcamp had made their "party call." Edna felt that they might have dispensed with the formality. They had also come to invite her to play *vingt-et-un* one evening at Mrs. Merriman's. She was asked to go early, to dinner, and Mr. Merriman or Mr. Arobin would take her home. Edna accepted in a half-hearted way. She sometimes felt very tired of Mrs. Highcamp and Mrs. Merriman.

Late in the afternoon she sought refuge with Mademoiselle Reisz, and stayed there alone, waiting for her, feeling a kind of repose invade her with the very atmosphere of the shabby, unpretentious little room.

Edna sat at the window, which looked out over the house-tops and across the river. The window frame was filled with pots of flowers, and she sat and picked the dry leaves from a rose geranium. The day was warm, and the breeze which blew from the river was very pleasant. She removed her hat and laid it on the piano. She went on picking the leaves and digging around the plants with her hat pin. Once she thought she heard Mademoiselle Reisz approaching. But it was a young black girl, who came in, bringing a small bundle of laundry, which she deposited in the adjoining room, and went away.

Edna seated herself at the piano, and softly picked out with one hand the bars of a piece of music which lay open before her. A half-hour went by. There was the occasional sound of people going and coming in the lower hall. She was growing interested in her occupation of picking out the aria, when there was a second rap at the door. She vaguely wondered what these people did when they found Mademoiselle's door locked.

"Come in," she called, turning her face toward the door. And this time it was Robert Lebrun who presented himself. She attempted to rise; she could not have done so without betraying the agitation which mastered her at sight of him, so she fell back upon the stool, only exclaiming, "Why, Robert!"

He came and clasped her hand, seemingly without knowing what he was saying or doing.

"Mrs. Pontellier! How do you happen—oh! how well you look! Is Mademoiselle Reisz not here? I never expected to see you."

"When did you come back?" asked Edna in an unsteady voice, wiping her face with her handkerchief. She seemed ill at ease on the piano stool, and he begged her to take the chair by the window. She did so, mechanically, while he seated himself on the stool.

"I returned day before yesterday," he answered, while he leaned his arm on the keys, bringing forth a crash of discordant sound.

"Day before yesterday!" she repeated, aloud; and went on thinking to herself, "day before yesterday," in a sort of an uncomprehending way. She had pictured him seeking her at the very first hour, and he had lived under the same sky since day before yesterday; while only by accident had he stumbled upon her. Mademoiselle must have lied when she said, "Poor fool, he loves you."

"Day before yesterday," she repeated, breaking off a spray of Mademoiselle's geranium; "then if you had not met me here to-day you wouldn't—when—that is, didn't you mean to come and see me?"

"Of course, I should have gone to see you. There have been so many things—" he turned the leaves of Mademoiselle's music nervously. "I started in at once yesterday with the old firm. After all there is as much chance for me here as there was there—that is, I might find it profitable some day. The Mexicans were not very congenial."

So he had come back because the Mexicans were not congenial; because business was as profitable here as there; because of any reason, and not because he cared to be near her. She remembered the day she sat on the floor, turning the pages of his letter, seeking the reason which was left untold.

She had not noticed how he looked—only feeling his presence; but she turned deliberately and observed him. After all, he had been absent but a few months, and was not changed. His hair—the color of hers—waved back from his temples in the same way as before. His skin was not more burned than it had been at Grand Isle. She found in his eyes, when he looked at her for one silent moment, the same tender caress, with an added warmth and entreaty which had not been there before—the same glance which had penetrated to the sleeping places of her soul and awakened them.

A hundred times Edna had pictured Robert's return, and imagined their first meeting. It was usually at her home, whither he had sought her out at once. She always fancied him expressing or betraying in some way his love for her. And here, the reality was that they sat ten feet apart, she at the window, crushing geranium leaves in her hand and smelling them, he twirling around on the piano stool, saying:

"I was very much surprised to hear of Mr. Pontellier's absence; it's a wonder Mademoiselle Reisz did not tell me; and your moving—mother told me yesterday. I should think you would have gone to New York with him, or to Iberville with the children, rather than be bothered here with housekeeping. And you are going abroad, too, I hear. We shan't have you at Grand Isle next summer; it won't seem—do you see much of Mademoiselle Reisz? She often spoke of you in the few letters she wrote."

"Do you remember that you promised to write to me when you went away?" A flush overspread his whole face.

"I couldn't believe that my letters would be of any interest to you."

"That is an excuse; it isn't the truth." Edna reached for her hat on the piano. She adjusted it, sticking the hat pin through the heavy coil of hair with some deliberation.

"Are you not going to wait for Mademoiselle Reisz?" asked Robert.

"No; I have found when she is absent this long, she is liable not to come back till late." She drew on her gloves, and Robert picked up his hat.

"Won't you wait for her?" asked Edna.

"Not if you think she will not be back till late," adding, as if suddenly aware of some discourtesy in his speech, "and I should miss the pleasure of walking home with you." Edna locked the door and put the key back in its hiding-place.

They went together, picking their way across muddy streets and sidewalks encumbered with the cheap display of small tradesmen. Part of the distance they rode in the car, and after disembarking, passed the Pontellier mansion, which looked broken and half torn asunder. Robert had never known the house, and looked at it with interest.

"I never knew you in your home," he remarked.

"I am glad you did not."

"Why?" She did not answer. They went on around the corner, and it seemed as if her dreams were coming true after all, when he followed her into the little house.

"You must stay and dine with me, Robert. You see I am all alone, and it is so long since I have seen you. There is so much I want to ask you."

She took off her hat and gloves. He stood irresolute, making some excuse about his mother who expected him; he even muttered something about an engagement. She struck a match and lit the lamp on the table; it was growing dusk. When he saw her face in the lamplight, looking pained, with all the soft lines gone out of it, he threw his hat aside and seated himself.

"Oh! you know I want to stay if you will let me!" he exclaimed. All the softness came back. She laughed, and went and put her hand on his shoulder.

"This is the first moment you have seemed like the old Robert. I'll go tell Celestine." She hurried away to tell Celestine to set an extra place. She even sent her off in search of some added delicacy which she had not thought of for herself. And she recommended great care in dripping the coffee and having the omelet done to a proper turn.

When she reëntered, Robert was turning over magazines, sketches, and things that lay upon the table in great disorder. He picked up a photograph, and exclaimed:

"Alcée Arobin! What on earth is his picture doing here?"

"I tried to make a sketch of his head one day," answered Edna, "and he thought the photograph might help me. It was at the other house. I thought it had been left there. I must have packed it up with my drawing materials."

"I should think you would give it back to him if you have finished with it."

"Oh! I have a great many such photographs. I never think of returning them. They don't amount to anything." Robert kept on looking at the picture.

"It seems to me—do you think his head worth drawing? Is he a friend of Mr. Pontellier's? You never said you knew him."

"He isn't a friend of Mr. Pontellier's; he's a friend of mine. I always knew him—that is, it is only of late that I know him pretty well. But I'd rather talk about you, and know what you have been seeing and doing and feeling out there in Mexico." Robert threw aside the picture.

"I've been seeing the waves and the white beach of Grand Isle; the quiet, grassy street of the *Chênière*; the old fort at Grande Terre. I've been working like a machine, and feeling like a lost soul. There was nothing interesting."

She leaned her head upon her hand to shade her eyes from the light.

"And what have you been seeing and doing and feeling all these days?" he asked.

"I've been seeing the waves and the white beach of Grand Isle; the quiet, grassy street of the *Chênière Caminada*; the old sunny fort at Grand Terre. I've been working with little more comprehension than a machine, and still feeling like a lost soul. There was nothing interesting."

"Mrs. Pontellier, you are cruel," he said, with feeling, closing his eyes and resting his head back in his chair. They remained in silence till old Celestine announced dinner.

CHAPTER XXXIV

The dining-room was very small. Edna's round mahogany would have almost filled it. As it was there was but a step or two from the little table to the kitchen, to the mantel, the small buffet, and the side door that opened out on the narrow brick-paved yard.

A certain degree of ceremony settled upon them with the announcement of dinner. There was no return to personalities. Robert related incidents of his sojourn in Mexico, and Edna talked of events likely to interest him, which had occurred during his absence. The dinner was of ordinary quality, except for the few delicacies which she had sent out to purchase. Old Celestine, with a bandana *tignon* twisted about her head, hobbled in and out, taking a personal interest in everything; and she lingered occasionally to talk patois with Robert, whom she had known as a boy.

He went out to a neighboring cigar stand to purchase cigarette papers, and when he came back he found that Celestine had served the black coffee in the parlor.

"Perhaps I shouldn't have come back," he said. "When you are tired of me, tell me to go."

"You never tire me. You must have forgotten the hours and hours at Grand Isle in which we grew accustomed to each other and used to being together."

"I have forgotten nothing at Grand Isle," he said, not looking at her, but rolling a cigarette. His tobacco pouch, which he laid upon the table, was a fantastic embroidered silk affair, evidently the handiwork of a woman.

"You used to carry your tobacco in a rubber pouch," said Edna, picking up the pouch and examining the needlework.

"Yes, it was lost."

"Where did you buy this one? In Mexico?"

"It was given to me by a Vera Cruz girl; they are very generous," he replied, striking a match and lighting his cigarette.

"They are very handsome, I suppose, those Mexican women; very picturesque, with their black eyes and their lace scarfs."

"Some are; others are hideous. Just as you find women everywhere."

"What was she like—the one who gave you the pouch? You must have known her very well."

"She was very ordinary. She wasn't of the slightest importance. I knew her well enough."

"Did you visit at her house? Was it interesting? I should like to know and hear about the people you met, and the impressions they made on you."

"There are some people who leave impressions not so lasting as the imprint of an oar upon the water."

"Was she such a one?"

"It would be ungenerous for me to admit that she was of that order and kind." He thrust the pouch back in his pocket, as if to put away the subject with the trifle which had brought it up.

Arobin dropped in with a message from Mrs. Merriman, to say that the card party was postponed on account of the illness of one of her children.

"How do you do, Arobin?" said Robert, rising from the obscurity.

"Oh! Lebrun. To be sure! I heard yesterday you were back. How did they treat you down in Mexique?"

"Fairly well."

"But not well enough to keep you there. Stunning girls, though, in Mexico. I thought I should never get away from Vera Cruz when I was down there a couple of years ago."

"Did they embroider slippers and tobacco pouches and hat-bands and things for you?" asked Edna.

"Oh! my! no! I didn't get so deep in their regard. I fear they made more impression on me than I made on them."

"You were less fortunate than Robert, then."

"I am always less fortunate than Robert. Has he been imparting tender confidences?"

"I've been imposing myself long enough," said Robert, rising, and shaking hands with Edna. "Please convey my regards to Mr. Pontellier when you write."

He shook hands with Arobin and went away.

"Fine fellow, that Lebrun," said Arobin when Robert had gone. "I never heard you speak of him."

"I knew him last summer at Grand Isle," she replied. "Here is that photograph of yours. Don't you want it?"

"What do I want with it? Throw it away." She threw it back on the table.

"I'm not going to Mrs. Merriman's," she said. "If you see her, tell her so. But perhaps I had better write. I think I shall write now, and say that I am sorry her child is sick, and tell her not to count on me."

"It would be a good scheme," acquiesced Arobin. "I don't blame you; stupid lot!"

Edna opened the blotter, and having procured paper and pen, began to write the note. Arobin lit a cigar and read the evening paper, which he had in his pocket.

"What is the date?" she asked. He told her.

"Will you mail this for me when you go out?"

"Certainly." He read to her little bits out of the newspaper, while she straightened things on the table.

"What do you want to do?" he asked, throwing aside the paper. "Do you want to go out for a walk or a drive or anything? It would be a fine night to drive."

"No; I don't want to do anything but just be quiet. You go away and amuse yourself. Don't stay."

"I'll go away if I must; but I shan't amuse myself. You know that I only live when I am near you."

He stood up to bid her good night.

"Is that one of the things you always say to women?"

"I have said it before, but I don't think I ever came so near meaning it," he answered with a smile. There were no warm lights in her eyes; only a dreamy, absent look.

"Good night. I adore you. Sleep well," he said, and he kissed her hand and went away.

She stayed alone in a kind of reverie—a sort of stupor. Step by step she lived over every instant of the time she had been with Robert after he had entered Mademoiselle Reisz's door. She recalled his words, his looks. How few and meager they had been for her hungry heart! A vision—a transcendently seductive vision of a Mexican girl arose before her. She writhed with a jealous pang. She wondered when he would come back. He had not said he would come back. She had been with him, had heard his voice and touched his hand. But some way he had seemed nearer to her off there in Mexico.

CHAPTER XXXV

The morning was full of sunlight and hope. Edna could see be denial—only the promise of excessive joy. She lay in bed awake, with bright eyes full of speculation. "He loves you, poor fool." If she could but get that conviction firmly fixed in her mind, what mattered about the rest? She felt she had been childish and unwise the night before in giving herself over to despondency. She recapitulated the motives which no doubt explained Robert's reserve. They were not insurmountable; they would not hold if he really loved her; they could not hold against her own passion, which he must come to realize in time. She pictured him going to his business that morning. She even saw how he was dressed; how he walked down one street, and turned the corner of another; saw him bending over his desk, talking to people who entered the office, going to his lunch, and perhaps watching for her on the street. He would come to her in the afternoon or evening, sit and roll his cigarette, talk a little, and go away as he had done the night before. But how delicious it would be to have him there with her! She would have no regrets, nor seek to penetrate his reserve if he still chose to wear it.

Edna ate her breakfast only half dressed. The maid brought her a delicious printed scrawl from Raoul, expressing his love, asking her to send him some bonbons, and telling her they had found that morning ten tiny white pigs all lying in a row beside Lidie's big white pig.

A letter also came from her husband, saying he hoped to be back early in March, and then they would get ready for that journey abroad which he had promised her so long, which he felt now fully able to afford; he felt able to travel as people should, without any thought of small economies—thanks to his recent speculations in Wall Street.

Much to her surprise she received a note from Arobin, written at midnight from the club. It was to say good morning to her, to hope that she had slept well, to assure her of his devotion, which he trusted she in some faintest manner returned.

All these letters were pleasing to her. She answered the children in a cheerful frame of mind, promising them bonbons, and congratulating them upon their happy find of the little pigs.

She answered her husband with friendly evasiveness,—not with any fixed design to mislead him, only because all sense of reality had gone out of her life; she had abandoned herself to Fate, and awaited the consequences with indifference.

To Arobin's note she made no reply. She put it under Celestine's stove-lid.

Edna worked several hours with much spirit. She saw no one but a picture dealer, who asked her if it were true that she was going abroad to study in Paris.

She said possibly she might, and he negotiated with her for some Parisian studies to reach him in time for the holiday trade in December.

Robert did not come that day. She was keenly disappointed. He did not come the following day, nor the next. Each morning she awoke with hope, and each night she was a prey to despondency. She was tempted to seek him out. But far from yielding to the impulse, she avoided any occasion which might throw her in his way. She did not go to Mademoiselle Reisz's nor pass by Madame Lebrun's, as she might have done if he had still been in Mexico.

When Arobin, one night, urged her to drive with him, she went—out to the lake, on the Shell Road. His horses were full of mettle, and even a little unmanageable. She liked the rapid gait at which they spun along, and the quick, sharp sound of the horses' hoofs on the hard road. They did not stop anywhere to eat or to drink. Arobin was not needlessly imprudent. But they ate and they drank when they regained Edna's little dining-room—which was comparatively early in the evening.

It was late when he left her. It was getting to be more than a passing whim with Arobin to see her and be with her. He had detected the latent sensuality, which unfolded under his delicate sense of her nature's requirements like a torpid, torrid, sensitive blossom.

There was no despondency when she fell asleep that night; nor was there hope when she awoke in the morning.

CHAPTER XXXVI

There was a garden out in the suburbs; a small, leafy corner, with a few green tables under the orange trees. An old cat slept all day on the stone step in the sun, and an old *mulatresse* slept her idle hours away in her chair at the open window, till some one happened to knock on one of the green tables. She had milk and cream cheese to sell, and bread and butter. There was no one who could make such excellent coffee or fry a chicken so golden brown as she.

The place was too modest to attract the attention of people of fashion, and so quiet as to have escaped the notice of those in search of pleasure and dissipation. Edna had discovered it accidentally one day when the high-board gate stood ajar. She caught sight of a little green table, blotched with the checkered sunlight that filtered through the quivering leaves overhead. Within she had found the slumbering *mulatresse*, the drowsy cat, and a glass of milk which reminded her of the milk she had tasted in Iberville.

She often stopped there during her perambulations; sometimes taking a book with her, and sitting an hour or two under the trees when she found the place deserted. Once or twice she took a quiet dinner there alone, having instructed Celestine beforehand to prepare no dinner at home. It was the last place in the city where she would have expected to meet any one she knew.

Still she was not astonished when, as she was partaking of a modest dinner late in the afternoon, looking into an open book, stroking the cat, which had made friends with her—she was not greatly astonished to see Robert come in at the tall garden gate.

"I am destined to see you only by accident," she said, shoving the cat off the chair beside her. He was surprised, ill at ease, almost embarrassed at meeting her thus so unexpectedly.

"Do you come here often?" he asked.

"I almost live here," she said.

"I used to drop in very often for a cup of Catiche's good coffee. This is the first time since I came back."

"She'll bring you a plate, and you will share my dinner. There's always enough for two—even three." Edna had intended to be indifferent and as reserved as he when she met him; she had reached the determination by a laborious train of reasoning, incident to one of her despondent moods. But her resolve melted when she saw him before her, seated there beside her in the little garden, as if a designing Providence had led him into her path.

"Why have you kept away from me, Robert?" she asked, closing the book that lay open upon the table.

"Why are you so personal, Mrs. Pontellier? Why do you force me to idiotic subterfuges?" he exclaimed with sudden warmth. "I suppose there's no use telling you I've been very busy, or that I've been sick, or that I've been to see you and not found you at home. Please let me off with any one of these excuses."

"You are the embodiment of selfishness," she said. "You save yourself something—I don't know what—but there is some selfish motive, and in sparing yourself you never consider for a moment what I think, or how I feel your neglect and indifference. I suppose this is what you would call unwomanly; but I have got into a habit of expressing myself. It doesn't matter to me, and you may think me unwomanly if you like."

"No; I only think you cruel, as I said the other day. Maybe not intentionally cruel; but you seem to be forcing me into disclosures which can result in nothing; as if you would have me bare a wound for the pleasure of looking at it, without the intention or power of healing it."

"I'm spoiling your dinner, Robert; never mind what I say. You haven't eaten a morsel."

"I only came in for a cup of coffee." His sensitive face was all disfigured with excitement.

"Isn't this a delightful place?" she remarked. "I am so glad it has never actually been discovered. It is so quiet, so sweet, here. Do you notice there is scarcely a sound to be heard? It's so out of the way; and a good walk from the car. However, I don't mind walking. I always feel so sorry for women who don't like to walk; they miss so much—so many rare little glimpses of life; and we women learn so little of life on the whole.

"Catiche's coffee is always hot. I don't know how she manages it, here in the open air. Celestine's coffee gets cold bringing it from the kitchen to the dining-room. Three lumps! How can you drink it so sweet? Take some of the cress with your chop; it's so biting and crisp. Then there's the advantage of being able to smoke with your coffee out here. Now, in the city—aren't you going to smoke?"

"After a while," he said, laying a cigar on the table.

"Who gave it to you?" she laughed.

"I bought it. I suppose I'm getting reckless; I bought a whole box." She was determined not to be personal again and make him uncomfortable.

The cat made friends with him, and climbed into his lap when he smoked his cigar. He stroked her silky fur, and talked a little about her. He looked at Edna's book, which he had read; and he told her the end, to save her the trouble of wading through it, he said.

Again he accompanied her back to her home; and it was after dusk when they reached the little "pigeon-house." She did not ask him to remain, which he was grateful for, as it permitted him to stay without the discomfort of blundering through an excuse which he had no intention of considering. He helped her to light the lamp; then she went into her room to take off her hat and to bathe her face and hands.

When she came back Robert was not examining the pictures and magazines as before; he sat off in the shadow, leaning his head back on the chair as if in a reverie. Edna lingered a moment beside the table, arranging the books there. Then she went across the room to where he sat. She bent over the arm of his chair and called his name.

"Robert," she said, "are you asleep?"

"No," he answered, looking up at her.

She leaned over and kissed him—a soft, cool, delicate kiss, whose voluptuous sting penetrated his whole being—then she moved away from him. He followed, and took her in his arms, just holding her close to him. She put her hand up to his face and pressed his cheek against her own. The action was full of love and tenderness. He sought her lips again. Then he drew her down upon the sofa beside him and held her hand in both of his.

"Now you know," he said, "now you know what I have been fighting against since last summer at Grand Isle; what drove me away and drove me back again."

"Why have you been fighting against it?" she asked. Her face glowed with soft lights.

"Why? Because you were not free; you were Léonce Pontellier's wife. I couldn't help loving you if you were ten times his wife; but so long as I went away from you and kept away I could help telling you so." She put her free hand up to his shoulder, and then against his cheek, rubbing it softly. He kissed her again. His face was warm and flushed.

"There in Mexico I was thinking of you all the time, and longing for you."

"But not writing to me," she interrupted.

"Something put into my head that you cared for me; and I lost my senses. I forgot everything but a wild dream of your some way becoming my wife."

"Your wife!"

"Religion, loyalty, everything would give way if only you cared."

"Then you must have forgotten that I was Léonce Pontellier's wife."

"Oh! I was demented, dreaming of wild, impossible things, recalling men who had set their wives free, we have heard of such things."

"Yes, we have heard of such things."

"I came back full of vague, mad intentions. And when I got here—"

"When you got here you never came near me!" She was still caressing his cheek.

"I realized what a cur I was to dream of such a thing, even if you had been willing."

She took his face between her hands and looked into it as if she would never withdraw her eyes more. She kissed him on the forehead, the eyes, the cheeks, and the lips.

"You have been a very, very foolish boy, wasting your time dreaming of impossible things when you speak of Mr. Pontellier setting me free! I am no longer one of Mr. Pontellier's possessions to dispose of or not. I give myself where I choose. If he were to say, 'Here, Robert, take her and be happy; she is yours,' I should laugh at you both."

His face grew a little white. "What do you mean?" he asked.

There was a knock at the door. Old Celestine came in to say that Madame Ratignolle's servant had come around the back way with a message that Madame had been taken sick and begged Mrs. Pontellier to go to her immediately.

"Yes, yes," said Edna, rising; "I promised. Tell her yes—to wait for me. I'll go back with her."

"Let me walk over with you," offered Robert.

"No," she said; "I will go with the servant." She went into her room to put on her hat, and when she came in again she sat once more upon the sofa beside him. He had not stirred. She put her arms about his neck.

"Good-by, my sweet Robert. Tell me good-by." He kissed her with a degree of passion which had not before entered into his caress, and strained her to him.

"I love you," she whispered, "only you; no one but you. It was you who awoke me last summer out of a life-long, stupid dream. Oh! you have made me so unhappy with your indifference. Oh! I have suffered, suffered! Now you are here we shall love each other, my Robert. We shall be everything to each other. Nothing else in the world is of any consequence. I must go to my friend; but you will wait for me? No matter how late; you will wait for me, Robert?"

"Don't go; don't go! Oh! Edna, stay with me," he pleaded. "Why should you go? Stay with me, stay with me."

"I shall come back as soon as I can; I shall find you here." She buried her face in his neck, and said good-by again. Her seductive voice, together with his great love for her, had enthralled his senses, had deprived him of every impulse but the longing to hold her and keep her.

CHAPTER XXXVII

Edna looked in at the drug store. Monsieur Ratignolle was putting up a mixture himself, very carefully, dropping a red liquid into a tiny glass. He was grateful to Edna for having come; her presence would be a comfort to his wife. Madame Ratignolle's sister, who had always been with her at such trying times, had not been able to come up from the plantation, and Adèle had been inconsolable until Mrs. Pontellier so kindly promised to come to her. The nurse had been with them at night for the past week, as she lived a great distance away. And Dr. Mandelet had been coming and going all the afternoon. They were then looking for him any moment.

Edna hastened upstairs by a private stairway that led from the rear of the store to the apartments above. The children were all sleeping in a back room. Madame Ratignolle was in the salon, whither she had strayed in her suffering impatience. She sat on the sofa, clad in an ample white *peignoir*, holding a handkerchief tight in her hand with a nervous clutch. Her face was drawn and pinched, her sweet blue eyes haggard and unnatural. All her beautiful hair had been drawn back and plaited. It lay in a long braid on the sofa pillow, coiled like a golden serpent. The nurse, a comfortable looking *Griffe* woman in white apron and cap, was urging her to return to her bedroom.

"There is no use, there is no use," she said at once to Edna. "We must get rid of Mandelet; he is getting too old and careless. He said he would be here at half-past seven; now it must be eight. See what time it is, Joséphine."

The woman was possessed of a cheerful nature, and refused to take any situation too seriously, especially a situation with which she was so familiar. She urged Madame to have courage and patience. But Madame only set her teeth hard into her under lip, and Edna saw the sweat gather in beads on her white forehead. After a moment or two she uttered a profound sigh and wiped her face with the handkerchief rolled in a ball. She appeared exhausted. The nurse gave her a fresh handkerchief, sprinkled with cologne water.

"This is too much!" she cried. "Mandelet ought to be killed! Where is Alphonse? Is it possible I am to be abandoned like this—neglected by every one?"

"Neglected, indeed!" exclaimed the nurse. Wasn't she there? And here was Mrs. Pontellier leaving, no doubt, a pleasant evening at home to devote to her? And wasn't Monsieur Ratignolle coming that very instant through the hall? And Joséphine was quite sure she had heard Doctor Mandelet's coupé. Yes, there it was, down at the door.

Adèle consented to go back to her room. She sat on the edge of a little low couch next to her bed.

Doctor Mandelet paid no attention to Madame Ratignolle's upbraidings. He was accustomed to them at such times, and was too well convinced of her loyalty to doubt it.

He was glad to see Edna, and wanted her to go with him into the salon and entertain him. But Madame Ratignolle would not consent that Edna should leave her for an instant. Between agonizing moments, she chatted a little, and said it took her mind off her sufferings.

Edna began to feel uneasy. She was seized with a vague dread. Her own like experiences seemed far away, unreal, and only half remembered. She recalled faintly an ecstasy of pain, the heavy odor of chloroform, a stupor which had deadened sensation, and an awakening to find a little new life to which she had given being, added to the great unnumbered multitude of souls that come and go.

She began to wish she had not come; her presence was not necessary. She might have invented a pretext for staying away; she might even invent a pretext now for going. But Edna did not go. With an inward agony, with a flaming, outspoken revolt against the ways of Nature, she witnessed the scene of torture.

She was still stunned and speechless with emotion when later she leaned over her friend to kiss her and softly say good-by. Adèle, pressing her cheek, whispered in an exhausted voice: "Think of the children, Edna. Oh think of the children! Remember them!"

CHAPTER XXXVIII

Edna still felt dazed when she got outside in the open air. The Doctor's coupé had returned for him and stood before the *porte cochère*. She did not wish to enter the coupé, and told Doctor Mandelet she would walk; she was not afraid, and would go alone. He directed his carriage to meet him at Mrs. Pontellier's, and he started to walk home with her.

Up—away up, over the narrow street between the tall houses, the stars were blazing. The air was mild and caressing, but cool with the breath of spring and the night. They walked slowly, the Doctor with a heavy, measured tread and his hands behind him; Edna, in an absent-minded way, as she had walked one night at Grand Isle, as if her thoughts had gone ahead of her and she was striving to overtake them.

"You shouldn't have been there, Mrs. Pontellier," he said. "That was no place for you. Adèle is full of whims at such times. There were a dozen women she might have had with her, unimpressionable women. I felt that it was cruel, cruel. You shouldn't have gone."

"Oh, well!" she answered, indifferently. "I don't know that it matters after all. One has to think of the children some time or other; the sooner the better."

"When is Léonce coming back?"

"Quite soon. Some time in March."

"And you are going abroad?"

"Perhaps—no, I am not going. I'm not going to be forced into doing things. I don't want to go abroad. I want to be let alone. Nobody has any right—except children, perhaps—and even then, it seems to me—or it did seem—" She felt that her speech was voicing the incoherency of her thoughts, and stopped abruptly.

"The trouble is," sighed the Doctor, grasping her meaning intuitively, "that youth is given up to illusions. It seems to be a provision of Nature; a decoy to secure mothers for the race. And Nature takes no account of moral consequences, of arbitrary conditions which we create, and which we feel obliged to maintain at any cost."

"Yes," she said. "The years that are gone seem like dreams—if one might go on sleeping and dreaming—but to wake up and find—oh! well! perhaps it is better to wake up after all, even to suffer, rather than to remain a dupe to illusions all one's life."

"It seems to me, my dear child," said the Doctor at parting, holding her hand, "you seem to me to be in trouble. I am not going to ask for your confidence. I will only say that if ever you feel moved to give it to me, perhaps I might help you. I know I would understand, and I tell you there are not many who would—not many, my dear."

"Some way I don't feel moved to speak of things that trouble me. Don't think I am ungrateful or that I don't appreciate your sympathy. There are periods of despondency and suffering which take possession of me. But I don't want anything but my own way. That is wanting a good deal, of course, when you have to trample upon the lives, the hearts, the prejudices of others—but no matter—still, I shouldn't want to trample upon the little lives. Oh! I don't know what I'm saying, Doctor. Good night. Don't blame me for anything."

"Yes, I will blame you if you don't come and see me soon. We will talk of things you never have dreamt of talking about before. It will do us both good. I don't want you to blame yourself, whatever comes. Good night, my child."

She let herself in at the gate, but instead of entering she sat upon the step of the porch. The night was quiet and soothing. All the tearing emotion of the last few hours seemed to fall away from her like a somber, uncomfortable garment, which she had but to loosen to be rid of. She went back to that hour before Adèle had sent for her; and her senses kindled afresh in thinking of Robert's words, the pressure of his arms, and the feeling of his lips upon her own. She could picture at that moment no greater bliss on earth than possession of the beloved one. His expression of love had already given him to her in part. When she thought that he was there at hand, waiting for her, she grew numb with the intoxication of expectancy. It was so late; he would be asleep perhaps. She would awaken him with a kiss. She hoped he would be asleep that she might arouse him with her caresses.

Still, she remembered Adèle's voice whispering, "Think of the children; think of them." She meant to think of them; that determination had driven into her soul like a death wound—but not to-night. To-morrow would be time to think of everything.

Robert was not waiting for her in the little parlor. He was nowhere at hand. The house was empty. But he had scrawled on a piece of paper that lay in the lamplight:

"I love you. Good-by—because I love you."

Edna grew faint when she read the words. She went and sat on the sofa. Then she stretched herself out there, never uttering a sound. She did not sleep. She did not go to bed. The lamp sputtered and went out. She was still awake in the morning, when Celestine unlocked the kitchen door and came in to light the fire.

CHAPTER XXXIX

Victor, with hammer and nails and scraps of scantling, was patching a corner of one of the galleries. Mariequita sat near by, dangling her legs, watching him work, and handing him nails from the tool-box. The sun was beating down upon them. The girl had covered her head with her apron folded into a square pad. They had been talking for an hour or more. She was never tired of hearing Victor describe the dinner at Mrs. Pontellier's. He exaggerated every detail, making it appear a veritable Lucillean feast. The flowers were in tubs, he said. The champagne was quaffed from huge golden goblets. Venus rising from the foam could have presented no more entrancing a spectacle than Mrs. Pontellier, blazing with beauty and diamonds at the head of the board, while the other women were all of them youthful houris possessed of incomparable charms.

She got it into her head that Victor was in love with Mrs. Pontellier, and he gave her evasive answers, framed so as to confirm her belief. She grew sullen and cried a little, threatening to go off and leave him to his fine ladies. There were a dozen men crazy about her at the *Chênière*; and since it was the fashion to be in love with married people, why, she could run away any time she liked to New Orleans with Célina's husband.

Célina's husband was a fool, a coward, and a pig, and to prove it to her, Victor intended to hammer his head into a jelly the next time he encountered him. This assurance was very consoling to Mariequita. She dried her eyes, and grew cheerful at the prospect.

They were still talking of the dinner and the allurements of city life when Mrs. Pontellier herself slipped around the corner of the house. The two youngsters stayed dumb with amazement before what they considered to be an apparition. But it was really she in flesh and blood, looking tired and a little travel-stained.

"I walked up from the wharf," she said, "and heard the hammering. I supposed it was you, mending the porch. It's a good thing. I was always tripping over those loose planks last summer. How dreary and deserted everything looks!"

It took Victor some little time to comprehend that she had come in Beaudelet's lugger, that she had come alone, and for no purpose but to rest.

"There's nothing fixed up yet, you see. I'll give you my room; it's the only place."

"Any corner will do," she assured him.

"And if you can stand Philomel's cooking," he went on, "though I might try to get her mother while you are here. Do you think she would come?" turning to Mariequita.

Mariequita thought that perhaps Philomel's mother might come for a few days, and money enough.

Beholding Mrs. Pontellier make her appearance, the girl had at once suspected a lovers' rendezvous. But Victor's astonishment was so genuine, and Mrs. Pontellier's indifference so apparent, that the disturbing notion did not lodge long in her brain. She contemplated with the greatest interest this woman who gave the most sumptuous dinners in America, and who had all the men in New Orleans at her feet.

"What time will you have dinner?" asked Edna. "I'm very hungry; but don't get anything extra."

"I'll have it ready in little or no time," he said, bustling and packing away his tools. "You may go to my room to brush up and rest yourself. Mariequita will show you."

"Thank you," said Edna. "But, do you know, I have a notion to go down to the beach and take a good wash and even a little swim, before dinner?"

"The water is too cold!" they both exclaimed. "Don't think of it."

"Well, I might go down and try—dip my toes in. Why, it seems to me the sun is hot enough to have warmed the very depths of the ocean. Could you get me a couple of towels? I'd better go right away, so as to be back in time. It would be a little too chilly if I waited till this afternoon."

Mariequita ran over to Victor's room, and returned with some towels, which she gave to Edna.

"I hope you have fish for dinner," said Edna, as she started to walk away; "but don't do anything extra if you haven't."

"Run and find Philomel's mother," Victor instructed the girl. "I'll go to the kitchen and see what I can do. By Gimminy! Women have no consideration! She might have sent me word."

Edna walked on down to the beach rather mechanically, not noticing anything special except that the sun was hot. She was not dwelling upon any particular train of thought. She had done all the thinking which was necessary after Robert went away, when she lay awake upon the sofa till morning.

She had said over and over to herself: "To-day it is Arobin; to-morrow it will be some one else. It makes no difference to me, it doesn't matter about Léonce Pontellier—but Raoul and Etienne!" She understood now clearly what she had meant long ago when she said to Adèle Ratignolle that she would give up the unessential, but she would never sacrifice herself for her children.

Despondency had come upon her there in the wakeful night, and had never lifted. There was no one thing in the world that she desired. There was no human being whom she wanted near her except Robert; and she even realized that the day would come when he, too, and the thought of him would melt out of her existence, leaving her alone. The children appeared before her like antagonists who had overcome her; who had overpowered and sought to drag her into the soul's slavery for the rest of her days. But she knew a way to elude them. She was not thinking of these things when she walked down to the beach.

The water of the Gulf stretched out before her, gleaming with the million lights of the sun. The voice of the sea is seductive, never ceasing, whispering, clamoring, murmuring, inviting the soul to wander in abysses of solitude. All along the white beach, up and down, there was no living thing in sight. A bird with a broken wing was beating the air above, reeling, fluttering, circling disabled down, down to the water.

Edna had found her old bathing suit still hanging, faded, upon its accustomed peg.

She put it on, leaving her clothing in the bath-house. But when she was there beside the sea, absolutely alone, she cast the unpleasant, pricking garments from her, and for the first time in her life she stood naked in the open air, at the mercy of the sun, the breeze that beat upon her, and the waves that invited her.

How strange and awful it seemed to stand naked under the sky! how delicious! She felt like some new-born creature, opening its eyes in a familiar world that it had never known.

The foamy wavelets curled up to her white feet, and coiled like serpents about her ankles. She walked out. The water was chill, but she walked on. The water was deep, but she lifted her white body and reached out with a long, sweeping stroke. The touch of the sea is sensuous, enfolding the body in its soft, close embrace.

n and on. She remembered the night she swam far out, and recalled seized her at the fear of being unable to regain the shore. She did not y, but went on and on, thinking of the blue-grass meadow that she when a little child, believing that it had no beginning and no end.

Her arms and legs were growing tired.

She thought of Léonce and the children. They were a part of her life. But they need not have thought that they could possess her, body and soul. How Mademoiselle Reisz would have laughed, perhaps sneered, if she knew! "And you call yourself an artist! What pretensions, Madame! The artist must possess the courageous soul that dares and defies."

Exhaustion was pressing upon and over-powering her.

"Good-by—because I love you." He did not know; he did not understand. He would never understand. Perhaps Doctor Mandelet would have understood if she had seen him—but it was too late; the shore was far behind her, and her strength was gone.

She looked into the distance, and the old terror flamed up for an instant, then sank again. Edna heard her father's voice and her sister Margaret's. She heard the barking of an old dog that was chained to the sycamore tree. The spurs of the cavalry officer clanged as he walked across the porch. There was the hum of bees, and the musky odor of pinks filled the air.

THEODORE DREISER
(1871–1945)

Within Theodore Dreiser's extensive body of work, both his own autobiography and the biography of American society at the turn of the century can be found. A victim of small town poverty, Dreiser escaped as a teenager to the big city in search of fame, fortune, and social status. Thirty years later, he could claim success. While his victory over his childhood circumstances was gratifying, Dreiser was never quite fulfilled. He always pushed ahead, searching out new territory. Like Twain and Crane, Dreiser was a newspaperman. He observed, participated in, and reported about the same deterministic world they saw. But there was a crucial difference. Dreiser did not distance himself from the plight of his characters with either Twain's satire or Crane's art. Having experienced emptiness in the face of triumph, Dreiser remained, like both his weak and his strong characters, a victim of forces over which control was impossible. That is why the omniscient voice of Dreiser, the creator, was always suffused with compassion, a quality rare in Twain and Crane.

The twelfth of thirteen children, Theodore Dreiser was born August 27, 1871, in Terre Haute, Indiana. His father was a German immigrant obsessed by religion; his mother was gentle and affectionate. Except for Paul, who became the famous songwriter, Paul Dresser, and who often helped support the family, Dreiser was humiliated by the sordid, sometimes criminal escapades of his wandering, shiftless brothers and sisters. He was the victim not only of severe poverty but of shyness and slow learning progress. The compassion he showed his hapless characters was also evident in his response to his own mother's illiteracy—he taught her to read and write.

With the help of a caring teacher, Dreiser was able to attend the University of Indiana after four years' entrapment in menial jobs in Chicago. But after a year, poverty cut him off from that avenue of escape, as well. He returned to the slums of Chicago, but two years later in 1892, he got his first job with a newspaper. He moved on to newspaper work in St. Louis, Cleveland, Pittsburgh, and New York, where he would live for the next four decades as a free-lance journalist and as the editor of popular women's and satirical magazines. In 1898, he married Sara White of St. Louis. At that time he had no thought of writing fiction, but within a year he was well into the composition of *Sister Carrie.*

Rejected as immoral by one publisher, *Sister Carrie* was not promoted by Doubleday. It sold less than 500 copies of the 1,000 first printing. Dreiser charged that Doubleday had suppressed it. Praise from naturalistic novelist Frank Norris and literary arbiter H. L. Mencken, who championed it as a landmark in American realism, was not enough for Dreiser. The fate of his novel and the failure of his marriage plunged Dreiser into a suicidal depression and a ten year silence. He concentrated on building a prosperous career as an editor. Then, partly encouraged by the republication of *Carrie* in 1907, he broke his silence with *Jennie Gerhardt* (1911). It was based, like *Sister Carrie*, on his sisters' efforts to survive in the city. But unlike Carrie, who becomes a success, Jennie—more gentle and more dependent, like Dreiser's mother—loses her long-time lover and surrenders to loneliness.

From 1911 until 1932, Dreiser's prodigious creative energy produced at least one or two books each year. On the average, his novels were 600 pages long. *The Financier* (1912; revised 1927) was the first of a massive "trilogy of desire," as he called it, about Frank Cowperwood, a ferociously motivated, amoral business magnate, modelled after Charles T. Yerkes, the Chicago financial wizard. Spanning American history from before the Civil War up to World War I, this trilogy occupied Dreiser to the end of his life. *The Titan* appeared two years later, but *The Stoic* (1947) was not finished until the year of his death. The canvas was broad enough to give full scope to Dreiser's romantic compulsion to gather the facts and render the sheer density of experience.

Dreiser indirectly dealt with his own life while writing about the travails of two women and the exploits of a rugged individualist typical of his era. And Dreiser examined with similar exactitude his own rise to power as an artist, using the story of a painter, rather than a writer. The story of an egocentric painter pursuing ideal beauty while battling the corruptive influence of commerce is told in *The "Genius"* (1915). It was banned and not released for sale until 1923. From 1913 to 1932, Dreiser dealt with many facets of his life in several nonfiction modes, always eager to capture the broader context of his changing times. *A Book About Myself* (1922; republished as *Newspaper Days*, 1931) and *Dawn: A History of Myself* (1931) were memoirs; his travel and social commentaries also projected his persona upon the panoramic screen of American history. They include: *A Traveler at Forty* (1913), *A Hoosier Holiday* (1916), *Twelve Men* (1919), *The Color of a Great City* (1923), *Dreiser Looks at Russia* (1928), and *Tragic America* (1932).

During the ten years between *The "Genius"* and his next novel, *An American Tragedy* (1925), the one that made him most famous and prosperous, Dreiser explored other genres and media. Although a dramatization later of *An American Tragedy* was very successful, Dreiser's *Plays of the Natural and Supernatural* (1916) and *The Hand of the Potter* (1918) did not do well in the theater. *Moods, Cadenced and Declaimed* (1922, 1926, 1928) did not earn him a reputation as a fine poet. Few of his short stories, collected in *Free and Other Stories* (1918), *Chains* (1927), and *A Gallery of Women* (1929), are distinguished achievements in the form. It was as a novelist that Dreiser excelled, and *An American Tragedy* is considered by many to be his best work. It is based on a true criminal case history. A young man, Clyde Griffiths, like most of Dreiser's characters, believes money brings potency. The American Dream encourages the belief that anyone can rise from the bottom to the top. But to marry the wealthy Sondra, Clyde must murder his pregnant girlfriend. In this novel, more than in any other, Dreiser indicts society for creating the environment that instills impossible dreams in dangerous weaklings like Clyde. Banned in Boston, yet another Dreiser novel proved offensive to a society that tolerated injustice while repressing natural emotions.

Between 1932 and 1946, no Dreiser books appeared. In 1939, Dreiser moved to Hollywood and supported himself by selling the movie rights to his novels. Dreiser turned to Oriental religious philosophy in his last years, after being a nonaffiliated communist most of his life. In his final two novels, *The Bulwark* (1946) and *The Stoic*, prepared just before his death, Dreiser shows how environment finally defeats two different kinds of powerful men. In 1944, Dreiser married Helen Richardson; he died a year later, at the age of 74.

All of Dreiser's strengths and weaknesses are as evident in *Sister Carrie*, his first novel, as they are in any of his others. That novel helped free American literature from the constraints of the genteel tradition. It launched Dreiser on his career as one of the most controversial writers in the history of American literature, and as America's greatest literary naturalist. Readers who praise him for successfully taking on the whole of America as his subject, and Darwinian determinism, leavened with compassion, as his theme, have triumphed over those who have charged him with employing the most graceless style of any important American writer. If Crane's short *Maggie* is a triumph of art over raw material, the massive *Sister Carrie* is the reverse. Even his defender Mencken said that Dreiser was "elephantine, doltish, coarse, dismal . . ." It is one of the great paradoxes of literature that his cliché-ridden, pseudo-literary, artificial style, which remained the same from the first novel to the last, somehow gives a powerful illusion of life.

SISTER CARRIE

Theodore Dreiser

CHAPTER I

THE MAGNET ATTRACTING: A WAIF AMID FORCES

When Caroline Meeber boarded the afternoon train for Chicago, her total outfit consisted of a small trunk, a cheap imitation alligator-skin satchel, a small lunch in a paper box, and a yellow leather snap purse, containing her ticket, a scrap of paper with her sister's address in Van Buren Street, and four dollars in money. It was in August, 1889. She was eighteen years of age, bright, timid, and full of the illusions of ignorance and youth. Whatever touch of regret at parting characterized her thoughts, it was certainly not for advantages now being given up. A gush of tears at her mother's farewell kiss, a touch in her throat when the cars clacked by the flour mill where her father worked by the day, a pathetic sigh as the familiar green environs of the village passed in review, and the threads which bound her so lightly to girlhood and home were irretrievably broken.

To be sure there was always the next station, where one might descend and return. There was the great city, bound more closely by these very trains which came up daily. Columbia City was not so very far away, even once she was in Chicago. What, pray, is a few hours—a few hundred miles? She looked at the little slip bearing her sister's address and wondered. She gazed at the green landscape, now passing in swift review, until her swifter thoughts replaced its impression with vague conjectures of what Chicago might be.

When a girl leaves her home at eighteen, she does one of two things. Either she falls into saving hands and becomes better, or she rapidly assumes the cosmopolitan standard of virtue and becomes worse. Of an intermediate balance, under the circumstances, there is no possibility. The city has its cunning wiles, no less than the infinitely smaller and more human tempter. There are large forces which allure with all the soulfulness of expression possible in the most cultured human. The gleam of a thousand lights is often as effective as the persuasive light in a wooing and fascinating eye. Half the undoing of the unsophisticated and natural mind is accomplished by forces wholly superhuman. A blare of sound, a roar of life, a vast array of human hives, appeal to the astonished senses in equivocal terms. Without a counselor at hand to whisper cautious interpretations, what falsehoods may not these things breathe into the unguarded ear? Unrecognized for what they are, their beauty, like music, too often relaxes, then weakens, then perverts the simpler human perceptions.

Caroline, or Sister Carrie, as she had been half affectionately termed by the family, was possessed of a mind rudimentary in its power of observation and analysis. Self-interest with her was high, but not strong. It was, nevertheless, her guiding characteristic. Warm with the fancies of youth, pretty with the insipid prettiness of the formative period, possessed of a figure promising eventual shapeliness and an eye alight with certain native intelligence, she was a fair example of the middle American class—two generations removed from the emigrant. Books were beyond her interest—knowledge a sealed book. In the intuitive graces she was still crude. She could scarcely toss her head gracefully. Her hands were almost ineffectual. The feet, though small, were set flatly. And yet she was interested in her charms, quick to understand the keener pleasures of life, ambitious to gain in material things. A half-equipped little knight she was, venturing to reconnoiter the mysterious city and dreaming wild dreams of some vague, far-off supremacy, which should make it prey and subject—the proper penitent, groveling at a woman's slipper.

"That," said a voice in her ear, "is one of the prettiest little resorts in Wisconsin."

"Is it?" she answered nervously.

The train was just pulling out of Waukesha. For some time she had been conscious of a man behind. She felt him observing her mass of hair. He had been fidgeting, and with natural intuition she felt a certain interest growing in that quarter. Her maidenly reserve, and a certain sense of what was conventional under the circumstances, called her to forestall and deny this familiarity, but the daring and magnetism of the individual, born of past experiences and triumphs, prevailed. She answered.

He leaned forward to put his elbows upon the back of her seat and proceeded to make himself volubly agreeable.

"Yes, that is a great resort for Chicago people. The hotels are swell. You are not familiar with this part of the country, are you?"

"Oh, yes, I am," answered Carrie. "That is, I live at Columbia City. I have never been through here, though."

"And so this is your first visit to Chicago," he observed.

All the time she was conscious of certain features out of the side of her eye. Flush, colorful cheeks, a light moustache, a gray fedora hat. She now turned and looked upon him in full, the instincts of self-protection and coquetry mingling confusedly in her brain.

"I didn't say that," she said.

"Oh," he answered, in a very pleasing way and with an assumed air of mistake, "I thought you did."

Here was a type of the traveling canvasser for a manufacturing house—a class which at that time was first being dubbed by the slang of the day "drummers." He came within the meaning of a still newer term, which had sprung into general use among Americans in 1880, and which concisely expressed the thought of one whose dress or manners are calculated to elicit the admiration of susceptible young women—a "masher." His suit was of a striped and crossed pattern of brown wool, new at that time, but since become familiar as a business suit. The low crotch of the vest revealed a stiff shirt bosom of white and pink stripes. From his coat sleeves protruded a pair of linen cuffs of the same pattern, fastened with large gold plate buttons, set with the common yellow agates known as "cat's-eyes." His fingers bore several rings—one, the ever-enduring heavy seal—and from his vest dangled a neat gold watch chain, from which was suspended the secret insignia of the Order of Elks. The whole suit was rather tight-fitting, and was finished off with heavy-soled tan shoes, highly polished, and the gray fedora hat. He was, for the order of intellect represented, attractive, and whatever he had to recommend him, you may be sure was not lost upon Carrie, in this, her first glance.

Lest this order of individual should permanently pass, let me put down some of the most striking characteristics of his most successful manner and method. Good clothes, of course, were the first essential, the things without which he was nothing. A strong physical nature, actuated by a keen desire for the feminine, was the next. A mind free of any consideration of the problems or forces of the world and actuated not by greed, but an insatiable love of variable pleasure. His method was always simple. Its principal element was daring, backed, of course, by an intense desire and admiration for the sex. Let him meet with a young woman once and he would approach her with an air of kindly familiarity, not unmixed with pleading, which would result in most cases in a tolerant acceptance. If she showed any tendency to coquetry he would be apt to straighten her tie, or if she "took up" with him at all, to call her by her first name. If he visited a department store it was to lounge familiarly over the counter and ask some leading questions. In more exclusive circles, on the train or in waiting stations, he went slower. If some seemingly vulnerable object appeared he was all attention—to pass the compliments of the day, to lead the way to the parlor car, carrying her grip, or, failing that, to take a seat next her with the hope of being able to court her to her destination. Pillows, books, a footstool, the shade lowered; all these figured in the things which he could do. If, when she reached her destination he did not alight and attend her baggage for her, it was because, in his own estimation, he had signally failed.

A woman should some day write the complete philosophy of clothes. No matter how young, it is one of the things she wholly comprehends. There is an indescribably faint line in the matter of a man's apparel which somehow divides for her those who are worth glancing at and those who are not. Once an individual has passed this faint line on the way downward he will get no glance from her. There is another line at which the dress of a man will cause her to study her own. This line the individual at her elbow now marked for Carrie. She became conscious of an inequality. Her own plain blue dress, with its black cotton tape trimmings, now seemed to her shabby. She felt the worn state of her shoes.

"Let's see," he went on, "I know quite a number of people in your town. Morgenroth the clothier and Gibson the dry goods man."

"Oh, do you?" she interrupted, aroused by memories of longings their show windows had cost her.

At last he had a clue to her interest, and followed it deftly. In a few minutes he had come about into her seat. He talked of sales of clothing, his travels, Chicago, and the amusements of that city.

"If you are going there, you will enjoy it immensely. Have you relatives?"

"I am going to visit my sister," she explained.

"You want to see Lincoln Park," he said, "and Michigan Boulevard. They are putting up great buildings there. It's a second New York—great. So much to see—theaters, crowds, fine houses—oh, you'll like that."

There was a little ache in her fancy of all he described. Her insignificance in the presence of so much magnificence faintly affected her. She realized that hers was not to be a round of pleasure, and yet there was something promising in all the material prospect he set forth. There was something satisfactory in the attention of this individual with his good clothes. She could not help smiling as he told her of some popular actress of whom she reminded him. She was not silly, and yet attention of this sort had its weight.

"You will be in Chicago some little time, won't you?" he observed at one turn of the now easy conversation.

"I don't know," said Carrie vaguely—a flash vision of the possibility of her not securing employment rising in her mind.

"Several weeks, anyhow," he said, looking steadily into her eyes.

There was much more passing now than the mere words indicated. He recognized the indescribable thing that made up for fascination and beauty in her. She realized that she was of interest to him from the one standpoint which a woman both delights in and fears. Her manner was simple, though for the very reason that she had not yet learned the many little affectations with which women conceal their true feelings. Some things she did appeared bold. A clever companion—had she ever had one—would have warned her never to look a man in the eyes so steadily.

"Why do you ask?" she said.

"Well, I'm going to be there several weeks. I'm going to study stock at our place and get new samples. I might show you 'round."

"I don't know whether you can or not. I mean I don't know whether I can. I shall be living with my sister, and—"

"Well, if she minds, we'll fix that." He took out his pencil and a little pocket note-book as if it were all settled. "What is your address there?"

She fumbled her purse which contained the address slip.

He reached down in his hip pocket and took out a fat purse. It was filled with slips of paper, some mileage books, a roll of greenbacks. It impressed her deeply. Such a purse had never been carried by any one attentive to her. Indeed, an experienced traveler, a brisk man of the world, had never come within such close range before. The purse, the shiny tan shoes, the smart new suit, and the *air* with which he did things, built up for her a dim world of fortune, of which he was the center. It disposed her pleasantly toward all he might do.

He took out a neat business card, on which was engraved Bartlett, Caryoe & Company, and down in the left-hand corner, Chas. H. Drouet.

"That's me," he said, putting the card in her hand and touching his name. "It's pronounced Drew-eh. Our family was French, on my father's side."

She looked at it while he put up his purse. Then he got out a letter from a bunch in his coat pocket. "This is the house I travel for," he went on, pointing to a picture on it, "corner of State and Lake." There was pride in his voice. He felt that it was something to be connected with such a place, and he made her feel that way.

"What is your address?" he began again, fixing his pencil to write.

She looked at his hand.

"Carrie Meeber," she said slowly. "Three hundred and fifty-four West Van Buren Street, care S. C. Hanson."

He wrote it carefully down and got out the purse again. "You'll be at home if I come around Monday night?" he said.

"I think so," she answered.

How true it is that words are but the vague shadows of the volumes we mean. Little audible links, they are, chaining together great inaudible feelings and purposes. Here were these two, bandying little phrases, drawing purses, looking at cards, and both unconscious of how inarticulate all their real feelings were. Neither was wise enough to be sure of the working of the mind of the other. He could not tell how his luring succeeded. She could not realize that she was drifting, until he secured her address. Now she felt that she had yielded something—he, that he had gained a victory. Already they felt that they were somehow associated. Already he took control in directing the conversation. His words were easy. Her manner was relaxed.

They were nearing Chicago. Signs were everywhere numerous. Trains flashed by them. Across wide stretches of flat, open prairie they could see lines of telegraph poles stalking across the fields toward the great city. Far away were indications of suburban towns, some big smoke-stacks towering high in the air.

Frequently there were two-story frame houses standing out in the open fields, without fence or trees, lone outposts of the approaching army of homes.

To the child, the genius with imagination, or the wholly untraveled, the approach to a great city for the first time is a wonderful thing. Particularly if it be evening—that mystic period between the glare and gloom of the world when life is changing from one sphere or condition to another. Ah, the promise of the night. What does it not hold for the weary! What old illusion of hope is not here forever repeated! Says the soul of the toiler to itself, "I shall soon be free. I shall be in the ways and the hosts of the merry. The streets, the lamps, the lighted chamber set for dining, are for me. The theater, the halls, the parties, the ways of rest and the paths of song—these are mine in the night." Though all humanity be still enclosed in the shops, the thrill runs abroad. It is in the air. The dullest feel something which they may not always express or describe. It is the lifting of the burden of toil.

Sister Carrie gazed out of the window. Her companion, affected by her wonder, so contagious are all things, felt anew some interest in the city and pointed out its marvels.

"This is northwest Chicago," said Drouet. "This is the Chicago River," and he pointed to a little muddy creek, crowded with the huge masted wanderers from far-off waters nosing the black-posted banks. With a puff, a clang, and a clatter of rails it was gone. "Chicago is getting to be a great town," he went on. "It's a wonder. You'll find lots to see here."

She did not hear this very well. Her heart was troubled by a kind of terror. The fact that she was alone, away from home, rushing into a great sea of life and endeavor, began to tell. She could not help but feel a little choked for breath—a little sick as her heart beat so fast. She half closed her eyes and tried to think it was nothing, that Columbia City was only a little way off.

"Chicago! Chicago!" called the brakeman, slamming open the door. They were rushing into a more crowded yard, alive with the clatter and clang of life. She began to gather up her poor little grip and closed her hand firmly upon her purse. Drouet arose, kicked his legs to straighten his trousers, and seized his clean yellow grip.

"I suppose your people will be here to meet you?" he said. "Let me carry your grip."

"Oh, no," she said. "I'd rather you wouldn't. I'd rather you wouldn't be with me when I meet my sister."

"All right," he said in all kindness. "I'll be near, though, in case she isn't here, and take you out there safely."

"You're so kind," said Carrie, feeling the goodness of such attention in her strange situation.

"Chicago!" called the brakeman, drawing the word out long. They were under a great shadowy train shed, where the lamps were already beginning to shine out, with passenger cars all about and the train moving at a snail's pace. The people in the car were all up and crowding about the door.

"Well, here we are," said Drouet, leading the way to the door. "Good-bye, till I see you Monday."

"Good-bye," she answered, taking his proffered hand.

"Remember, I'll be looking till you find your sister."

She smiled into his eyes.

They filed out, and he affected to take no notice of her. A lean-faced, rather commonplace woman recognized Carrie on the platform and hurried forward.

"Why, Sister Carrie!" she began, and there was a perfunctory embrace of welcome.

Carrie realized the change of affectional atmosphere at once. Amid all the maze, uproar, and novelty she felt cold reality taking her by the hand. No world of light and merriment. No round of amusement. Her sister carried with her most of the grimness of shift and toil.

"Why, how are all the folks at home?" she began; "how is father, and mother?"

Carrie answered, but was looking away. Down the aisle, toward the gate leading into the waiting-room and the street, stood Drouet. He was looking back. When he saw that she saw him and was safe with her sister he turned to go, sending back the shadow of a smile. Only Carrie saw it. She felt something lost to her when he moved away. When he disappeared she felt his absence thoroughly. With her sister she was much alone, a lone figure in a tossing, thoughtless sea.

CHAPTER II

What Poverty Threatened: Of Granite and Brass

Minnie's flat, as the one-floor resident apartments were then being called, was in a part of West Van Buren Street inhabited by families of laborers and clerks, men who had come, and were still coming, with the rush of population pouring in at the rate of 50,000 a year. It was on the third floor, the front windows looking down into the street, where, at night, the lights of grocery stores were shining and children were playing. To Carrie, the sound of the little bells upon the horse-cars, as they tinkled in and out of hearing, was as pleasing as it was novel. She gazed into the lighted street when Minnie brought her into the front room, and wondered at the sounds, the movement, the murmur of the vast city which stretched for miles and miles in every direction.

Mrs. Hanson, after the first greetings were over, gave Carrie the baby and proceeded to get supper. Her husband asked a few questions and sat down to read the evening paper. He was a silent man, American born, of a Swede father, and now employed as a cleaner of refrigerator cars at the stockyards. To him the presence or absence of his wife's sister was a matter of indifference. Her personal appearance did not affect him one way or the other. His one observation to the point was concerning the chances of work in Chicago.

"It's a big place," he said. "You can get in somewhere in a few days. Everybody does."

It had been tacitly understood beforehand that she was to get work and pay her board. He was of a clean, saving disposition, and had already paid a number of monthly installments on two lots far out on the West Side. His ambition was some day to build a house on them.

In the interval which marked the preparation of the meal Carrie found time to study the flat. She had some slight gift of observation and that sense, so rich in every woman—intuition.

She felt the drag of a lean and narrow life. The walls of the rooms were discordantly papered. The floors were covered with matting and the hall laid with a thin rag carpet. One could see that the furniture was of that poor, hurriedly patched together quality sold by the installment houses.

She sat with Minnie, in the kitchen, holding the baby until it began to cry. Then she walked and sang to it, until Hanson, disturbed in his reading, came and took it. A pleasant side to his nature came out here. He was patient. One could see that he was very much wrapped up in his offspring.

"Now, now," he said, walking. "There, there," and there was a certain Swedish accent noticeable in his voice.

"You'll want to see the city first, won't you?" said Minnie, when they were eating. "Well, we'll go out Sunday and see Lincoln Park."

Carrie noticed that Hanson had said nothing to this. He seemed to be thinking of something else.

"Well," she said, "I think I'll look around to-morrow. I've got Friday and Saturday, and it won't be any trouble. Which way is the business part?"

Minnie began to explain, but her husband took this part of the conversation to himself.

"It's that way," he said, pointing east. "That's east." Then he went off into the longest speech he had yet indulged in, concerning the lay of Chicago. "You'd better look in those big manufacturing houses along Franklin Street and just the other side of the river," he concluded. "Lots of girls work there. You could get home easy, too. It isn't very far."

Carrie nodded and asked her sister about the neighborhood. The latter talked in a subdued tone, telling the little she knew about it, while Hanson concerned himself with the baby. Finally he jumped up and handed the child to his wife.

"I've got to get up early in the morning, so I'll go to bed," and off he went, disappearing into the dark little bedroom off the hall, for the night.

"He works way down at the stock-yards," explained Minnie, "so he's got to get up at half-past five."

"What time do you get up to get breakfast?" asked Carrie.

"At about twenty minutes to five."

Together they finished the labor of the day, Carrie washing the dishes while Minnie undressed the baby and put it to bed. Minnie's manner was one of trained industry, and Carrie could see that it was a steady round of toil with her.

She began to see that her relations with Drouet would have to be abandoned. He could not come here. She read from the manner of Hanson, in the subdued air of Minnie, and, indeed, the whole atmosphere of the flat, a settled opposition to anything save a conservative round of toil. If Hanson sat every evening in the front room and read his paper, if he went to bed at nine, and Minnie a little later, what would they expect of her? She saw that she would first need to get work and establish herself on a paying basis before she could think of having company of any sort. Her little flirtation with Drouet seemed now an extraordinary thing.

"No," she said to herself, "he can't come here."

She asked Minnie for ink and paper, which were upon the mantel in the dining-room, and when the latter had gone to bed at ten, got out Drouet's card and wrote him.

"I cannot have you call on me here. You will have to wait until you hear from me again. My sister's place is so small."

She troubled herself over what else to put in the letter. She wanted to make some reference to their relations upon the train, but was too timid. She concluded by thanking him for his kindness in a crude way, then puzzled over the formality of signing her name, and finally decided upon the severe, winding up with a "Very truly," which she subsequently changed to "Sincerely." She sealed and addressed the letter, and going in the front room, the alcove of which contained her bed, drew the one small rocking-chair up to the open window, and sat looking out upon the night and streets in silent wonder. Finally, wearied by her own reflections, she began to grow dull in her chair, and feeling the need of sleep, arranged her clothing for the night and went to bed.

When she awoke at eight the next morning, Hanson had gone. Her sister was busy in the dining-room, which was also the sitting-room, sewing. She worked, after dressing, to arrange a little breakfast for herself, and then advised with Minnie as to which way to look. The latter had changed considerably since Carrie had seen her. She was now a thin, though rugged, woman of twenty-seven, with ideas of life colored by her husband's, and fast hardening into narrower conceptions of pleasure and duty than had ever been hers in a thoroughly circumscribed youth. She had invited Carrie, not because she longed for her presence, but because the latter was dissatisfied at home, and could probably get work and pay her board here. She was pleased to see her in a way but reflected her husband's point of view in the matter of work. Anything was good enough so long as it paid—say, five dollars a week to begin with. A shop girl was the destiny prefigured for the newcomer. She would get in one of the great shops and do well enough until—well, until something happened. Neither of them knew exactly what. They did not figure on promotion. They did not exactly count on marriage. Things would go on, though, in a dim kind of way until the better thing would eventuate, and Carrie would be rewarded for coming and toiling in the city. It was under such auspicious circumstances that she started out this morning to look for work.

Before following her in her round of seeking, let us look at the sphere in which her future was to lie. In 1889 Chicago had the peculiar qualifications of growth which made such adventuresome pilgrimages even on the part of young girls plausible. Its many and growing commercial opportunities gave it widespread fame, which made of it a giant magnet, drawing to itself, from all quarters, the hopeful and the hopeless—those who had their fortune yet to make and those whose fortunes and affairs had reached a disastrous climax elsewhere. It was a city of over 500,000, with the ambition, the daring, the activity of a metropolis of a million. Its streets and houses were already scattered over an area of seventy-five square miles. Its population was not so much thriving upon established commerce as upon the industries which prepared for the arrival of others. The sound of the hammer engaged upon the erection of new structures was everywhere heard. Great industries were moving in. The huge railroad corporations which had long before recognized the prospects of the place had seized upon vast tracts of land for transfer and shipping purposes. Street-car lines had been extended far out into the open country in anticipation of rapid growth. The city had laid miles and miles of streets and sewers through regions where, perhaps, one solitary house stood out alone—a pioneer of the populous ways to be. There were regions open to the sweeping winds and rain, which were yet lighted throughout the night with long, blinking lines of gas-lamps, fluttering in the wind. Narrow board walks extended out, passing here a house, and there a store, at far intervals, eventually ending on the open prairie.

In the central portion was the vast wholesale and shopping district, to which the uninformed seeker for work usually drifted. It was a characteristic of Chicago then, and one not generally shared by other cities, that individual firms of any pretension occupied individual buildings. The presence of ample ground made this possible. It gave an imposing appearance to most of the wholesale houses, whose offices were upon the ground floor and in plain view of the street. The large plate of window glass, now so common, was then rapidly coming into use, and gave to the ground floor offices a distinguished and prosperous look. The casual wanderer could see as he passed a polished array of office fixtures, much frosted glass, clerks hard at work, and genteel business men in "nobby" suits and clean linen lounging about or sitting in groups. Polished brass or nickel signs at the square stone entrances announced the firm and the nature of the business in rather neat and reserved terms. The entire metropolitan center possessed a high and mighty air calculated to overawe and abash the common applicant, and to make the gulf between poverty and success seem both wide and deep.

Into this important commercial region the timid Carrie went. She walked east along Van Buren Street through a region of lessening importance, until it deteriorated into a mass of shanties and coal-yards, and finally verged upon the river. She walked bravely forward, led by an honest desire to find employment and delayed at every step by the interest of the unfolding scene, and a sense of helplessness amid so much evidence of power and force which she did not understand. These vast buildings, what were they? These strange energies and huge interests, for what purposes were they there? She could have understood the meaning of a little stonecutter's yard at Columbia City, carving little pieces of marble for individual use, but when the yards of some huge stone corporation came into view, filled with spur tracks and flat cars, transpierced by docks from the river, and traversed overhead by immense trundling cranes of wood and steel, it lost all significance in her little world.

It was so with the vast railroad yards, with the crowded array of vessels she saw at the river, and the huge factories over the way, lining the water's edge. Through the open windows she could see the figures of men and women in working aprons, moving busily about. The great streets were wall-lined mysteries to her; the vast offices, strange mazes which concerned far-off individuals of importance. She could only think of people connected with them as counting money, dressing magnificently, and riding in carriages. What they dealt in, how they labored, to what end it all came, she had only the vaguest conception. It was all wonderful, all vast, all far removed, and she sank in spirit inwardly and fluttered feebly at the heart as she thought of entering any one of these mighty concerns and asking for something to do—something that she could do—anything.

CHAPTER III

WE QUESTION OF FORTUNE: FOUR-FIFTY A WEEK

Once across the river and into the wholesale district, she glanced about her for some likely door at which to apply. As she contemplated the wide windows and imposing signs, she became conscious of being gazed upon and understood for what she was—a wage-seeker. She had never done this thing before, and lacked courage. To avoid a certain indefinable shame she felt at being caught spying about for a position, she quickened her steps and assumed an air of indifference supposedly common to one upon an errand. In this way she passed many manufacturing and wholesale houses without once glancing in. At last, after several blocks of walking, she felt that this would not do, and began to look about again, though without relaxing her pace. A little way on she saw a great door which, for some reason, attracted her attention. It was ornamented by a small brass sign, and seemed to be the entrance to a vast hive of six or seven floors. "Perhaps," she thought, "they may want some one," and crossed over to enter. When she came within a score of feet of the desired goal, she saw through the window a young man in a gray checked suit. That he had anything to do with the concern, she could not tell, but because he happened to be looking in her direction her weakening heart misgave her and she hurried by, too overcome with shame to enter. Over the way stood a great six-story structure, labeled Storm and King, which she viewed with rising hope. It was a wholesale dry goods concern and employed women. She could see them moving about now and then upon the upper floors. This place she decided to enter, no matter what. She crossed over and walked directly toward the entrance. As she did so, two men came out and paused in the door. A telegraph messenger in blue dashed past her and up the few steps that led to the entrance and disappeared. Several pedestrians out of the hurrying throng which filled the sidewalks passed about her as she paused, hesitating. She looked helplessly around, and then, seeing herself observed, retreated. It was too difficult a task. She could not go past them.

So severe a defeat told sadly upon her nerves. Her feet carried her mechanically forward, every foot of her progress being a satisfactory portion of a flight which she gladly made. Block after block passed by. Upon street-lamps at the various corners she read names such as Madison, Monroe, La Salle, Clark, Dearborn, State, and still she went, her feet beginning to tire upon the broad stone flagging. She was pleased in part that the streets were bright and clean. The morning sun, shining down with steadily increasing warmth, made the shady side of the streets pleasantly cool. She looked at the blue sky overhead with more realization of its charm than had ever come to her before.

Her cowardice began to trouble her in a way. She turned back, resolving to hunt up Storm and King and enter. On the way she encountered a great wholesale shoe company, through the broad plate windows of which she saw an enclosed executive department, hidden by frosted glass. Without this enclosure, but just within the street entrance, sat a gray-haired gentleman at a small table, with a large open ledger before him. She walked by this institution several times hesitating, but, finding herself unobserved, faltered past the screen door and stood humbly waiting.

"Well, young lady," observed the old gentleman, looking at her somewhat kindly, "what is it you wish?"

"I am, that is, do you—I mean, do you need any help?" she stammered.

"Not just at present," he answered smiling. "Not just at present. Come in some time next week. Occasionally we need some one."

She received the answer in silence and backed awkwardly out. The pleasant nature of her reception rather astonished her. She had expected that it would be more difficult, that something cold and harsh would be said—she knew not what. That she had not been put to shame and made to feel her unfortunate position, seemed remarkable.

Somewhat encouraged, she ventured into another large structure. It was a clothing company, and more people were in evidence—well-dressed men of forty and more, surrounded by brass railings.

An office boy approached her.

"Who is it you wish to see?" he asked.

"I want to see the manager," she said.

He ran away and spoke to one of a group of three men who were conferring together. One of these came towards her.

"Well?" he said coldly. The greeting drove all courage from her at once.

"Do you need any help?" she stammered.

"No," he replied abruptly, and turned upon his heel.

She went foolishly out, the office boy deferentially swinging the door for her, and gladly sank into the obscuring crowd. It was a severe setback to her recently pleased mental state.

Now she walked quite aimlessly for a time, turning here and there, seeing one great company after another, but finding no courage to prosecute her single inquiry. High noon came, and with it hunger. She hunted out an unassuming restaurant and entered, but was disturbed to find that the prices were exorbitant for the size of her purse. A bowl of soup was all that she could afford, and, with this quickly eaten, she went out again. It restored her strength somewhat and made her moderately bold to pursue the search.

In walking a few blocks to fix upon some probable place, she again encountered the firm of Storm and King, and this time managed to get in. Some gentlemen were conferring close at hand, but took no notice of her. She was left standing, gazing nervously upon the floor. When the limit of her distress had been nearly reached, she was beckoned to by a man at one of the many desks within the near-by railing.

"Who is it you wish to see?" he inquired.

"Why, any one, if you please," she answered. "I am looking for something to do."

"Oh, you want to see Mr. McManus," he returned. "Sit down," and he pointed to a chair against the neighboring wall. He went on leisurely writing, until after a time a short, stout gentleman came in from the street.

"Mr. McManus," called the man at the desk, "this young woman wants to see you."

The short gentleman turned about towards Carrie, and she arose and came forward.

"What can I do for you, miss?" he inquired, surveying her curiously.

"I want to know if I can get a position," she inquired.

"As what?" he asked.

"Not as anything in particular," she faltered.

"Have you ever had any experience in the wholesale dry goods business?" he questioned.

"No, sir," she replied.

"Are you a stenographer or typewriter?"

"No, sir."

"Well, we haven't anything here," he said. "We employ only experienced help."

She began to step backward toward the door, when something about her plaintive face attracted him.

"Have you ever worked at anything before?" he inquired.

"No, sir," she said.

"Well, now, it's hardly possible that you would get anything to do in a wholesale house of this kind. Have you tried the department stores?"

She acknowledged that she had not.

"Well, if I were you," he said, looking at her rather genially, "I would try the department stores. They often need young women as clerks."

"Thank you," she said, her whole nature relieved by this spark of friendly interest.

"Yes," he said, as she moved toward the door, "you try the department stores," and off he went.

At that time the department store was in its earliest form of successful operation, and there were not many. The first three in the United States, established about 1884, were in Chicago. Carrie was familiar with the names of several through the advertisements in the "Daily News," and now proceeded to seek them. The words of Mr. McManus had somehow managed to restore her courage, which had fallen low, and she dared to hope that this new line would offer her something. Some time she spent in wandering up and down, thinking to encounter the buildings by chance, so readily is the mind, bent upon prosecuting a hard but needful errand, eased by that self-deception which the semblance of search, without the reality, gives. At last she inquired of a police officer, and was directed to proceed "two blocks up," where she would find "The Fair."

The nature of these vast retail combinations, should they ever permanently disappear, will form an interesting chapter in the commercial history of our nation. Such a flowering out of a modest trade principle the world had never witnessed up to that time. They were along the line of the most effective retail organization, with hundreds of stores coordinated into one and laid out upon the most imposing and economic basis. They were handsome, bustling, successful affairs, with a host of clerks and a swarm of patrons. Carrie passed along the busy aisles, much affected by the remarkable displays of trinkets, dress goods, stationery, and jewelry. Each separate counter was a show place of dazzling interest and attraction. She could not help feeling the claim of each trinket and valuable upon her personally, and yet she did not stop. There was nothing there which she could not have used—nothing which she did not long to own. The dainty slippers and stockings, the delicately frilled skirts and petticoats, the laces, ribbons, haircombs, purses, all touched her with individual desire, and she felt keenly the fact that not any of these things were in the range of her purchase. She was a work-seeker, an outcast without employment, one whom the average employee could tell at a glance was poor and in need of a situation.

It must not be thought that any one could have mistaken her for a nervous, sensitive, high-strung nature, cast unduly upon a cold, calculating, and unpoetic world. Such certainly she was not. But women are peculiarly sensitive to their adornment.

Not only did Carrie feel the drag of desire for all which was new and pleasing in apparel for women, but she noticed too, with a touch at the heart, the fine ladies who elbowed and ignored her, brushing past in utter disregard of her presence, themselves eagerly enlisted in the materials which the store contained. Carrie was not familiar with the appearance of her more fortunate sisters of the city. Neither had she before known the nature and appearance of the shop girls with whom she now compared poorly. They were pretty in the main, some even handsome, with an air of independence and indifference which added, in the case of the more favored, a certain piquancy. Their clothes were neat, in many instances fine, and wherever she encountered the eye of one it was only to recognize in it a keen analysis of her own position—her individual shortcomings of dress and that shadow of *manner* which she thought must hang about her and make clear to all who and what she was. A flame of envy lighted in her heart. She realized in a dim way how much the city held—wealth, fashion, ease—every adornment for women, and she longed for dress and beauty with a whole heart.

On the second floor were the managerial offices, to which, after some inquiry, she was now directed. There she found other girls ahead of her, applicants like herself, but with more of that self-satisfied and independent air which experience of the city lends; girls who scrutinized her in a painful manner. After a wait of perhaps three-quarters of an hour, she was called in turn.

"Now," said a sharp, quick-mannered Jew, who was sitting at a roll-top desk near the window, "have you ever worked in any other store?"

"No, sir," said Carrie.

"Oh, you haven't," he said, eyeing her keenly.

"No, sir," she replied.

"Well, we prefer young women just now with some experience. I guess we can't use you."

Carrie stood waiting a moment, hardly certain whether the interview had terminated.

"Don't wait!" he exclaimed. "Remember we are very busy here."

Carrie began to move quickly to the door.

"Hold on," he said, calling her back. "Give me your name and address. We want girls occasionally."

When she had gotten safely into the street, she could scarcely restrain the tears. It was not so much the particular rebuff which she had just experienced, but the whole abashing trend of the day. She was tired and nervous. She abandoned the thought of appealing to the other department stores and now wandered on, feeling a certain safety and relief in mingling with the crowd.

In her indifferent wandering she turned into Jackson Street, not far from the river, and was keeping her way along the south side of that imposing thoroughfare, when a piece of wrapping paper, written on with marking ink and tacked up on the door, attracted her attention. It read, "Girls wanted—wrappers & stitchers." She hesitated a moment, then entered.

The firm of Speigelheim & Co., makers of boys caps, occupied one floor of the building, fifty feet in width and some eighty feet in depth. It was a place rather dingily lighted, the darkest portions having incandescent lights, filled with machines and work benches. At the latter labored quite a company of girls and some men. The former were drabby-looking creatures, stained in face with oil and dust, clad in thin, shapeless, cotton dresses and shod with more or less worn shoes. Many of them had their sleeves rolled up, revealing bare arms, and in some cases, owing to the heat, their dresses were open at the neck. They were a fair type of nearly the lowest order of shop-girls—careless, slouchy, and more or less pale from confinement. They were not timid, however; were rich in curiosity, and strong in daring and slang.

Carrie looked about her, very much disturbed and quite sure that she did not want to work here. Aside from making her uncomfortable by sidelong glances, no one paid her the least attention. She waited until the whole department was aware of her presence. Then some word was sent around, and a foreman, in an apron and shirt sleeves, the latter rolled up to his shoulders, approached.

"Do you want to see me?" he asked.

"Do you need any help?" said Carrie, already learning directness of address.

"Do you know how to stitch caps?" he returned.

"No, sir," she replied.

"Have you ever had any experience at this kind of work?" he inquired.

She answered that she had not.

"Well," said the foreman, scratching his ear meditatively, "we do need a stitcher. We like experienced help, though. We've hardly got time to break people in." He paused and looked away out of the window. "We might, though, put you at finishing," he concluded reflectively.

"How much do you pay a week?" ventured Carrie, emboldened by a certain softness in the man's manner and his simplicity of address.

"Three and a half," he answered.

"Oh," she was about to exclaim, but checked herself and allowed her thoughts to die without expression.

"We're not exactly in need of anybody," he went on vaguely, looking her over as one would a package. "You can come on Monday morning, though," he added, "and I'll put you to work."

"Thank you," said Carrie weakly.

"If you come, bring an apron," he added.

He walked away and left her standing by the elevator, never so much as inquiring her name.

While the appearance of the shop and the announcement of the price paid per week operated very much as a blow to Carrie's fancy, the fact that work of any kind was offered after so rude a round of experience was gratifying. She could not begin to believe that she would take the place, modest as her aspirations were. She had been used to better than that. Her mere experience and the free out-of-door life of the country caused her nature to revolt at such confinement. Dirt had never been her share. Her sister's flat was clean. This place was grimy and low, the girls were careless and hardened. They must be bad-minded and hearted, she imagined. Still, a place had been offered her. Surely Chicago was not so bad if she could find one place in one day. She might find another and better later.

Her subsequent experiences were not of a reassuring nature, however. From all the more pleasing or imposing places she was turned away abruptly with the most chilling formality. In others where she applied only the experienced were required. She met with painful rebuffs, the most trying of which had been in a manufacturing cloak house, where she had gone to the fourth floor to inquire.

"No, no," said the foreman, a rough, heavily built individual, who looked after a miserably lighted workshop, "we don't want any one. Don't come here."

With the wane of the afternoon went her hopes, her courage, and her strength. She had been astonishingly persistent. So earnest an effort was well deserving of a better reward. On every hand, to her fatigued senses, the great business portion grew larger, harder, more stolid in its indifference. It seemed as if it was all closed to her, that the struggle was too fierce for her to hope to do anything at all. Men and women hurried by in long, shifting lines. She felt the flow of the tide of effort and interest—felt her own helplessness without quite realizing the wisp on the tide that she was. She cast about vainly for some possible place to apply, but found no door which she had the courage to enter. It would be the same thing all over. The old humiliation of her plea, rewarded by curt denial. Sick at heart and in body, she turned to the west, the direction of Minnie's flat, which she had now fixed in mind, and began that wearisome, baffled retreat which the seeker for employment at nightfall too often makes. In passing through Fifth Avenue, south towards Van Buren Street, where she intended to take a car, she passed the door of a large wholesale shoe house, through the plate-glass window of which she could see a middle-aged gentleman sitting at a small desk. One of those forlorn impulses which often grow out of a fixed sense of defeat, the last sprouting of a baffled and uprooted growth of ideas, seized upon her. She walked deliberately through the door and up to the gentleman, who looked at her weary face with partially awakened interest.

"What is it?" he said.

"Can you give me something to do?" said Carrie.

"Now, I really don't know," he said kindly. "What kind of work is it you want—you're not a typewriter, are you?"

"Oh, no," answered Carrie.

"Well, we only employ book-keepers and typewriters here. You might go around to the side and inquire upstairs. They did want some help upstairs a few days ago. Ask for Mr. Brown."

She hastened around to the side entrance and was taken up by the elevator to the fourth floor.

"Call Mr. Brown, Willie," said the elevator man to a boy near by.

Willie went off and presently returned with the information that Mr. Brown said she should sit down and that he would be around in a little while.

It was a portion of the stock room which gave no idea of the general character of the place, and Carrie could form no opinion of the nature of the work.

"So you want something to do," said Mr. Brown, after he inquired concerning the nature of her errand. "Have you ever been employed in a shoe factory before?"

"No, sir," said Carrie.

"What is your name?" he inquired, and being informed, "Well, I don't know as I have anything for you. Would you work for four and a half a week?"

Carrie was too worn by defeat not to feel that it was considerable. She had not expected that he would offer her less than six. She acquiesced, however, and he took her name and address.

"Well," he said, finally, "you report here at eight o'clock Monday morning. I think I can find something for you to do."

He left her revived by the possibilities, sure that she had found something at last. Instantly the blood crept warmly over her body. Her nervous tension relaxed. She walked out into the busy street and discovered a new atmosphere. Behold, the throng was moving with a lightsome step. She noticed that men and women were smiling. Scraps of conversation and notes of laughter floated to her. The air was light. People were already pouring out of the buildings, their labor ended for the day. She noticed that they were pleased, and thoughts of her sister's home and the meal that would be awaiting her quickened her steps. She hurried on, tired perhaps, but no longer weary of foot. What would not Minnie say! Ah, the long winter in Chicago—the lights, the crowd, the amusement! This was a great, pleasing metropolis after all. Her new firm was a goodly institution. Its windows were of huge plate glass. She could probably do well there. Thoughts of Drouet returned—of the things he had told her. She now felt that life was better, that it was livelier, sprightlier. She boarded a car in the best of spirits, feeling her blood still flowing pleasantly. She would live in Chicago, her mind kept saying to itself. She would have a better time than she had ever had before—she would be happy.

CHAPTER IV

THE SPENDINGS OF FANCY: FACTS ANSWER WITH SNEERS

For the next two days Carrie indulged in the most highflown speculations.

Her fancy plunged recklessly into privileges and amusements which would have been much more becoming had she been cradled a child of fortune. With ready will and quick mental selection she scattered her meager four-fifty per week with a swift and graceful hand. Indeed, as she sat in her rocking-chair these several evenings before going to bed and looked out upon the pleasantly lighted street, this money cleared for its prospective possessor the way to every joy and every bauble which the heart of woman may desire. "I will have a fine time," she thought.

Her sister Minnie knew nothing of these rather wild cerebrations, though they exhausted the markets of delight. She was too busy scrubbing the kitchen woodwork and calculating the purchasing power of eighty cents for Sunday's dinner. When Carrie had returned home, flushed with her first success and ready, for all her weariness, to discuss the now interesting events which led up to her achievement, the former had merely smiled approvingly and inquired whether she would have to spend any of it for car fare. This consideration had not entered in before, and it did not now for long affect the glow of Carrie's enthusiasm. Disposed as she then was to calculate upon that vague basis which allows the subtraction of one sum from another without any perceptible diminution, she was happy.

When Hanson came home at seven o'clock, he was inclined to be a little crusty—his usual demeanor before supper. This never showed so much in anything he said as in a certain solemnity of countenance and the silent manner in which he slopped about. He had a pair of yellow carpet slippers which he enjoyed wearing, and these he would immediately substitute for his solid pair of shoes. This, and washing his face with the aid of common washing soap until it glowed a shiny red, constituted his only preparation for his evening meal. He would then get his evening paper and read in silence.

For a young man, this was rather a morbid turn of character, and so affected Carrie. Indeed, it affected the entire atmosphere of the flat, as such things are inclined to do, and gave to his wife's mind its subdued and tactful turn, anxious to avoid taciturn replies. Under the influence of Carrie's announcement he brightened up somewhat.

"You didn't lose any time, did you?" he remarked, smiling a little.

"No," returned Carrie with a touch of pride.

He asked her one or two more questions and then turned to play with the baby, leaving the subject until it was brought up again by Minnie at the table.

Carrie, however, was not to be reduced to the common level of observation which prevailed in the flat.

"It seems to be such a large company," she said, at one place. "Great big plate-glass windows and lots of clerks. The man I saw said they hired ever so many people."

"It's not very hard to get work now," put in Hanson, "if you look right."

Minnie, under the warming influence of Carrie's good spirits and her husband's somewhat conversational mood, began to tell Carrie of some of the well-known things to see—things the enjoyment of which cost nothing.

"You'd like to see Michigan Avenue. There are such fine houses. It is such a fine street."

"Where is 'H. R. Jacob's'?" interrupted Carrie, mentioning one of the theaters devoted to melodrama which went by that name at the time.

"Oh, it's not very far from here," answered Minnie. "It's in Halstead Street, right up here."

"How I'd like to go there. I crossed Halstead Street today, didn't I?"

At this there was a slight halt in the natural reply. Thoughts are a strangely permeating factor. At her suggestion of going to the theater, the unspoken shade of disapproval to the doing of those things which involved the expenditure of money—shades of feeling which arose in the mind of Hanson and then in Minnie—slightly affected the atmosphere of the table. Minnie answered "yes," but Carrie could feel that going to the theater was poorly advocated here. The subject was put off for a little while until Hanson, through with his meal, took his paper and went into the front room.

When they were alone, the two sisters began a somewhat freer conversation, Carrie interrupting it to hum a little, as they worked at the dishes.

"I should like to walk up and see Halstead Street, if it isn't too far," said Carrie, after a time. "Why don't we go to the theater to-night?"

"Oh, I don't think Sven would want to go to-night," returned Minnie. "He has to get up so early."

"He wouldn't mind—he'd enjoy it," said Carrie.

"No, he doesn't go very often," returned Minnie.

"Well, I'd like to go," rejoined Carrie. "Let's you and me go."

Minnie pondered a while, not upon whether she could or would go—for that point was already negatively settled with her—but upon some means of diverting the thoughts of her sister to some other topic.

"We'll go some other time," she said at last, finding no ready means of escape.

Carrie sensed the root of the opposition at once.

"I have some money," she said. "You go with me."

Minnie shook her head.

"He could go along," said Carrie.

"No," returned Minnie softly, and rattling the dishes to drown the conversation. "He wouldn't."

It had been several years since Minnie had seen Carrie, and in that time the latter's character had developed a few shades. Naturally timid in all things that related to her own advancement, and especially so when without power or resource, her craving for pleasure was so strong that it was the one stay of her nature. She would speak for that when silent on all else.

"Ask him," she pleaded softly.

Minnie was thinking of the resource which Carrie's board would add. It would pay the rent and would make the subject of expenditure a little less difficult to talk about with her husband. But if Carrie was going to think of running around in the beginning there would be a hitch somewhere. Unless Carrie submitted to a solemn round of industry and saw the need of hard work without longing for play, how was her coming to the city to profit them? These thoughts were not those of a cold, hard nature at all. They were the serious reflections of a mind which invariably adjusted itself, without much complaining, to such surroundings as its industry could make for it.

At last she yielded enough to ask Hanson. It was a halfhearted procedure without a shade of desire on her part.

"Carrie wants us to go to the theater," she said, looking in upon her husband. Hanson looked up from his paper, and they exchanged a mild look, which said as plainly as anything: "This isn't what we expected."

"I don't care to go," he returned. "What does she want to see?"

"H. R. Jacob's," said Minnie.

He looked down at his paper and shook his head negatively.

When Carrie saw how they looked upon her proposition, she gained a still clearer feeling of their way of life. It weighed on her, but took no definite form of opposition.

"I think I'll go down and stand at the foot of the stairs," she said, after a time.

Minnie made no objection to this, and Carrie put on her hat and went below.

"Where has Carrie gone?" asked Hanson, coming back into the dining-room when he heard the door close.

"She said she was going down to the foot of the stairs," answered Minnie. "I guess she just wants to look out a while."

"She oughtn't to be thinking about spending her money on theaters already, do you think?" he said.

"She just feels a little curious, I guess," ventured Minnie. "Everything is so new."

"I don't know," said Hanson, and went over to the baby, his forehead slightly wrinkled.

He was thinking of a full career of vanity and wastefulness which a young girl might indulge in, and wondering how Carrie could contemplate such a course when she had so little, as yet, with which to do.

On Saturday Carrie went out by herself—first toward the river, which interested her, and then back along Jackson Street, which was then lined by the pretty houses and fine lawns which subsequently caused it to be made into a boulevard. She was struck with the evidences of wealth, although there was, perhaps, not a person on the street worth more than a hundred thousand dollars. She was glad to be out of the flat, because already she felt that it was a narrow, humdrum place, and that interest and joy lay elsewhere. Her thoughts now were of a more liberal character, and she punctuated them with speculations as to the whereabouts of Drouet. She was not sure but that he might call anyhow Monday night, and, while she felt a little disturbed at the possibility, there was, nevertheless, just the shade of a wish that he would.

On Monday she arose early and prepared to go to work. She dressed herself in a worn shirt-waist of dotted blue percale, a skirt of light-brown serge rather faded, and a small straw hat which she had worn all summer at Columbia City. Her shoes were old, and her necktie was in that crumpled, flattened state which time and much wearing impart. She made a very average looking shop-girl with the exception of her features. These were slightly more even than common, and gave her a sweet, reserved, and pleasing appearance.

It is no easy thing to get up early in the morning when one is used to sleeping until seven and eight, as Carrie had been at home. She gained some inkling of the character of Hanson's life when, half asleep, she looked out into the dining-room at six o'clock and saw him silently finishing his breakfast. By the time she was dressed he was gone, and she, Minnie, and the baby ate together, the latter being just old enough to sit in a high chair and disturb the dishes with a spoon. Her spirits were greatly subdued now when the fact of entering upon strange and untried duties confronted her. Only the ashes of all her fine fancies were remaining—ashes still concealing, nevertheless, a few red embers of hope. So subdued was she by her weakening nerves, that she ate quite in silence, going over imaginary conceptions of the character of the shoe company, the nature of the work, her employer's attitude. She was vaguely feeling that she would come in contact with the great owners, that her work would be where grave, stylishly dressed men occasionally look on.

"Well, good luck," said Minnie, when she was ready to go. They had agreed it was best to walk, that morning at least, to see if she could do it every day—sixty cents a week for car fare being quite an item under the circumstances.

"I'll tell you how it goes to-night," said Carrie.

Once in the sunlit street, with laborers tramping by in either direction, the horse-cars passing crowded to the rails with the small clerks and floor help in the great wholesale houses, and men and women generally coming out of doors and passing about the neighborhood, Carrie felt slightly reassured. In the sunshine of the morning, beneath the wide, blue heavens, with a fresh wind astir, what fears, except the most desperate, can find a harborage? In the night, or the gloomy chambers of the day, fears and misgivings wax strong, but out in the sunlight there is, for a time, cessation even of the terror of death.

Carrie went straight forward until she crossed the river, and then turned into Fifth Avenue. The thoroughfare, in this part, was like a walled cañon of brown stone and dark red brick. The big windows looked shiny and clean. Trucks were rumbling in increasing numbers; men and women, girls and boys were moving onward in all directions. She met girls of her own age, who looked at her as if with contempt for her diffidence. She wondered at the magnitude of this life and at the importance of knowing much in order to do anything in it at all. Dread at her own inefficiency crept upon her. She would not know how, she would not be quick enough. Had not all the other places refused her because she did not know something or other? She would be scolded, abused, ignominiously discharged.

It was with weak knees and a slight catch in her breathing that she came up to the great shoe company at Adams and Fifth Avenue and entered the elevator. When she stepped out on the fourth floor there was no one at hand, only great aisles of boxes piled to the ceiling. She stood, very much frightened, awaiting some one.

Presently Mr. Brown came up. He did not seem to recognize her.

"What is it you want?" he inquired.

Carrie's heart sank.

"You said I should come this morning to see about work—"

"Oh," he interrupted. "Um—yes. What is your name?"

"Carrie Meeber."

"Yes," said he. "You come with me."

He led the way through dark, box-lined aisles which had the smell of new shoes, until they came to an iron door which opened into the factory proper. There was a large, low-ceiled room, with clacking, rattling machines at which men in white shirt sleeves and blue gingham aprons were working. She followed him diffidently through the clattering automatons, keeping her eyes straight before her, and flushing slightly. They crossed to a far corner and took an elevator to the sixth floor. Out of the array of machines and benches, Mr. Brown signaled a foreman.

"This is the girl," he said, and turning to Carrie. "You go with him." He then returned, and Carrie followed her new superior to a little desk in a corner, which he used as a kind of official center.

"You've never worked at anything like this before, have you?" he questioned, rather sternly.

"No, sir," she answered.

He seemed rather annoyed at having to bother with such help, but put down her name and then led her across to where a line of girls occupied stools in front of clacking machines. On the shoulder of one of the girls who was punching eyeholes in one piece of the upper, by the aid of the machine, he put his hand.

"You," he said, "show this girl how to do what you're doing. When you get through, come to me."

The girl so addressed rose promptly and gave Carrie her place.

"It isn't hard to do," she said, bending over. "You just take this so, fasten it with this clamp, and start the machine."

She suited action to word, fastened the piece of leather, which was eventually to form the right half of the upper of a man's shoe, by little adjustable clamps, and pushed a small steel rod at the side of the machine. The latter jumped to the task of punching, with sharp, snapping clicks, cutting circular bits of leather out of the side of the upper, leaving the holes which were to hold the laces. After observing a few times, the girl let her work at it alone. Seeing that it was fairly well done, she went away.

The pieces of leather came from the girl at the machine to her right, and were passed on to the girl at her left. Carrie saw at once that an average speed was necessary or the work would pile up on her and all those below would be delayed. She had no time to look about, and bent anxiously to her task. The girls at her left and right realized her predicament and feelings, and, in a way, tried to aid her, as much as they dared, by working slower.

At this task she labored incessantly for some time, finding relief from her own nervous fears and imaginings in the humdrum, mechanical movement of the machine. She felt, as the minutes passed, that the room was not very light. It had a thick odor of fresh leather, but that did not worry her. She felt the eyes of the other help upon her, and troubled lest she was not working fast enough.

Once, when she was fumbling at the little clamp, having made a slight error in setting in the leather, a great hand appeared before her eyes and fastened the clamp for her. It was the foreman. Her heart thumped so that she could scarcely see to go on.

"Start your machine," he said, "start your machine. Don't keep the line waiting."

This recovered her sufficiently and she went excitedly on, hardly breathing until the shadow moved away from behind her. Then she heaved a great breath.

As the morning wore on the room became hotter. She felt the need of a breath of fresh air and a drink of water but did not venture to stir. The stool she sat on was without a back or foot-rest, and she began to feel uncomfortable. She found, after a time, that her back was beginning to ache. She twisted and turned from one position to another slightly different, but it did not ease her for long. She was beginning to weary.

"Stand up, why don't you?" said the girl at her right, without any form of introduction. "They won't care."

Carrie looked at her gratefully. "I guess I will," she said.

She stood up from her stool and worked that way for a while, but it was a more difficult position. Her neck and shoulders ached in bending over.

The spirit of the place impressed itself on her in a rough way. She did not venture to look around, but above the clack of the machine she could hear an occasional remark. She could also note a thing or two out of the side of her eye.

"Did you see Harry last night?" said the girl at her left, addressing her neighbor.

"No."

"You ought to have seen the tie he had on. Gee, but he was a mark."

"S-s-t," said the other girl, bending over her work. The first, silenced, instantly assumed a solemn face. The foreman passed slowly along, eyeing each worker distinctly. The moment he was gone, the conversation was resumed again.

"Say," began the girl at her left, "what jeh think he said?"

"I don't know."

"He said he saw us with Eddie Harris at Martin's last night."

"No!" They both giggled.

A youth with tan-colored hair, that needed clipping very badly, came shuffling along between the machines, bearing a basket of leather findings under his left arm, and pressed against his stomach. When near Carrie, he stretched out his right hand and gripped one girl under the arm.

"Aw, let me go," she exclaimed angrily. "Duffer."

He only grinned broadly in return.

"Rubber!" he called back as she looked after him. There was nothing of the gallant in him.

Carrie at last could scarcely sit still. Her legs began to tire and she wanted to get up and stretch. Would noon never come? It seemed as if she had worked an entire day. She was not hungry at all, but weak, and her eyes were tired, straining at the one point where the eye-punch came down. The girl at the right noticed her squirmings and felt sorry for her. She was concentrating herself too thoroughly—what she did really required less mental and physical strain. There was nothing to be done, however. The halves of the uppers came piling steadily down. Her hands began to ache at the wrists and then in the fingers, and towards the last she seemed one mass of dull, complaining muscles, fixed in an eternal position and performing a single mechanical movement which became more and more distasteful, until at last it was absolutely nauseating. When she was wondering whether the strain would ever cease, a dull-sounding bell clanged somewhere down an elevator shaft, and the end came. In an instant there was a buzz of action and conversation. All the girls instantly left their stools and hurried away in an adjoining room, men passed through, coming from some department which opened on the right. The whirling wheels began to sing in a steadily modifying key, until at last they died away in a low buzz. There was an audible stillness, in which the common voice sounded strange.

Carrie got up and sought her lunch box. She was stiff, a little dizzy, and very thirsty. On the way to the small space portioned off by wood, where all the wraps and lunches were kept, she encountered the foreman, who stared at her hard.

"Well," he said, "did you get along all right?"

"I think so," she replied, very respectfully.

"Um," he replied, for want of something better, and walked on.

Under better material conditions, this kind of work would not have been so bad, but the new socialism which involves pleasant working conditions for employees had not then taken hold upon manufacturing companies.

The place smelled of the oil of the machines and the new leather—a combination which, added to the stale odors of the building, was not pleasant even in cold weather. The floor, though regularly swept every evening, presented a littered surface. Not the slightest provision had been made for the comfort of the employees, the idea being that something was gained by giving them as little and making the work as hard and unremunerative as possible. What we know of footrests, swivel-back chairs, dining-rooms for the girls, clean aprons and curling irons supplied free, and a decent cloak room, were unthought of. The washrooms were disagreeable, crude, if not foul places, and the whole atmosphere was sordid.

Carrie looked about her, after she had drunk a tinful of water from a bucket in one corner, for a place to sit and eat. The other girls had ranged themselves about the windows or the work-benches of those of the men who had gone out. She saw no place which did not hold a couple or a group of girls, and being too timid to think of intruding herself, she sought out her machine and, seated upon her stool, opened her lunch on her lap. There she sat listening to the chatter and comment about her. It was, for the most part, silly and graced by the current slang. Several of the men in the room exchanged compliments with the girls at long range.

"Say, Kitty," called one to a girl who was doing a waltz step in a few feet of space near one of the windows, "are you going to the ball with me?"

"Look out, Kitty," called another, "you'll jar your back hair."

"Go on, Rubber," was her only comment.

As Carrie listened to this and much more of similar familiar badinage among the men and girls, she instinctively withdrew into herself. She was not used to this type, and felt that there was something hard and low about it all. She feared that the young boys about would address such remarks to her—boys who, beside Drouet, seemed uncouth and ridiculous. She made the average feminine distinction between clothes, putting worth, goodness, and distinction in a dress suit, and leaving all the unlovely qualities and those beneath notice in overalls and jumper.

She was glad when the short half hour was over and the wheels began to whirr again. Though wearied, she would be inconspicuous. This illusion ended when another young man passed along the aisle and poked her indifferently in the ribs with his thumb. She turned about, indignation leaping to her eyes, but he had gone on and only once turned to grin. She found it difficult to conquer an inclination to cry.

The girl next to her noticed her state of mind. "Don't you mind," she said. "He's too fresh."

Carrie said nothing, but bent over her work. She felt as though she could hardly endure such a life. Her idea of work had been so entirely different. All during the long afternoon she thought of the city outside and its imposing show, crowds, and fine buildings. Columbia City and the better side of her home life came back. By three o'clock she was sure it must be six, and by four it seemed as if they had forgotten to note the hour and were letting all work overtime. The foreman became a true ogre, prowling constantly about, keeping her tied down to her miserable task. What she heard of the conversation about her only made her feel sure that she did not want to make friends with any of these. When six o'clock came she hurried eagerly away, her arms aching and her limbs stiff from sitting in one position.

As she passed out along the hall after getting her hat, a young machine hand, attracted by her looks, made bold to jest with her.

"Say, Maggie," he called, "if you wait, I'll walk with you."

It was thrown so straight in her direction that she knew who was meant, but never turned to look.

In the crowded elevator, another dusty, toil-stained youth tried to make an impression on her by leering in her face.

One young man, waiting on the walk outside for the appearance of another, grinned at her as she passed.

"Ain't going my way, are you?" he called jocosely.

Carrie turned her face to the west with a subdued heart. As she turned the corner, she saw through the great shiny window the small desk at which she had applied. There were the crowds, hurrying with the same buzz and energy-yielding enthusiasm. She felt a slight relief, but it was only at her escape. She felt ashamed in the face of better dressed girls who went by. She felt as though she should be better served, and her heart revolted.

CHAPTER V

A GLITTERING NIGHT FLOWER: THE USE OF A NAME

Drouet did not call that evening. After receiving the letter, he had laid aside all thought of Carrie for the time being and was floating around having what he considered a gay time. On this particular evening he dined at "Rector's," a restaurant of some local fame, which occupied a basement at Clark and Monroe Streets. Thereafter he visited the resort of Fitzgerald and Moy's in Adams Street, opposite the imposing Federal Building. There he leaned over the splendid bar and swallowed a glass of plain whiskey and purchased a couple of cigars, one of which he lighted. This to him represented in part high life—a fair sample of what the whole must be.

Drouet was not a drinker in excess. He was not a moneyed man. He only craved the best, as his mind conceived it, and such doings seemed to him a part of the best. Rector's, with its polished marble walls and floor, its profusion of lights, its show of china and silverware, and, above all, its reputation as a resort for actors and professional men, seemed to him the proper place for a successful man to go. He loved fine clothes, good eating, and particularly the company and acquaintanceship of successful men. When dining, it was a source of keen satisfaction to him to know that Joseph Jefferson was wont to come to this same place, or that Henry E. Dixie, a well-known performer of the day, was then only a few tables off. At Rector's he could always obtain this satisfaction, for there one could encounter politicians, brokers, actors, some rich young "rounders" of the town, all eating and drinking amid a buzz of popular commonplace conversation.

"That's So-and-so over there," was a common remark of these gentlemen among themselves, particularly among those who had not yet reached, but hoped to do so, the dazzling height which money to dine here lavishly represented.

You don't say so," would be the reply.

"Why, yes, didn't you know that? Why, he's manager of the Grand Opera House."

When these things would fall upon Drouet's ears, he would straighten himself a little more stiffly and eat with solid comfort. If he had any vanity, this augmented it, and if he had any ambition, this stirred it. He would be able to flash a roll of greenbacks too some day. As it was, he could eat where *they* did.

His preference for Fitzgerald and Moy's Adams Street place was another yard off the same cloth. This was really a gorgeous saloon from a Chicago standpoint. Like Rector's, it was also ornamented with a blaze of incandescent lights, held in handsome chandeliers. The floors were of brightly colored tiles, the walls a composition of rich, dark, polished wood, which reflected the light, and colored stucco-work, which gave the place a very sumptuous appearance. The long bar was a blaze of lights, polished wood-work, colored and cut glassware, and many fancy bottles. It was a truly swell saloon, with rich screens, fancy wines, and a line of bar goods unsurpassed in the country.

At Rector's, Drouet had met Mr. G. W. Hurstwood, manager of Fitzgerald and Moy's. He had been pointed out as a very successful and well-known man about town. Hurstwood looked the part, for, besides being slightly under forty, he had a good, stout constitution, an active manner, and a solid, substantial air, which was composed in part of his fine clothes, his clean linen, his jewels, and, above all, his own sense of his importance. Drouet immediately conceived a notion of him as being some one worth knowing, and was glad not only to meet him, but to visit the Adams Street bar thereafter whenever he wanted a drink or a cigar.

Hurstwood was an interesting character after his kind. He was shrewd and clever in many little things, and capable of creating a good impression. His managerial position was fairly important—a kind of stewardship which was imposing, but lacked financial control. He had risen by perseverance and industry, through long years of service, from the position of barkeeper in a commonplace saloon to his present altitude. He had a little office in the place, set off in polished cherry and grill-work, where he kept, in a roll-top desk, the rather simple accounts of the place—supplies ordered and needed. The chief executive and financial functions devolved upon the owners—Messrs. Fitzgerald and Moy—and upon a cashier who looked after the money taken in.

For the most part he lounged about, dressed in excellent tailored suits of imported goods, a solitaire ring, a fine blue diamond in his tie, a striking vest of some new pattern, and a watch-chain of solid gold, which held a charm of rich design, and a watch of the latest make and engraving. He knew by name, and could greet personally with a "Well, old fellow," hundreds of actors, merchants, politicians, and the general run of successful characters about town, and it was part of his success to do so. He had a finely graduated scale of informality and friendship, which improved from the "How do you do?" addressed to the fifteen-dollar-a-week clerks and office attachés, who, by long frequenting of the place, became aware of his position, to the "Why, old man, how are you?" which he addressed to those noted or rich individuals who knew him and were inclined to be friendly. There was a class, however, too rich, too famous, or too successful, with whom he could not attempt any familiarity of address, and with these he was professionally tactful, assuming a grave and dignified attitude, paying them the deference which would win their good feeling without in the least compromising his own bearing and opinions. There were, in the last place, a few good followers, neither rich nor poor, famous, nor yet remarkably successful, with whom he was friendly on the score of good-fellowship. These were the kind of men with whom he would converse longest and most seriously. He loved to go out and have a good time once in a while—to go to the races, the theaters, the sporting entertainments at some of the clubs. He kept a horse and neat trap, had his wife and two children, who were well established in a neat house on the North Side near Lincoln Park, and was altogether a very acceptable individual of our great American upper class—the first grade below the luxuriously rich.

Hurstwood liked Drouet. The latter's genial nature and dressy appearance pleased him. He knew that Drouet was only a traveling salesman—and not one of many years at that—but the firm of Bartlett, Caryoe & Company was a large and prosperous house, and Drouet stood well. Hurstwood knew Caryoe quite well, having drunk a glass now and then with him, in company with several others, when the conversation was general. Drouet had what was a help in his business, a moderate sense of humor, and could tell a good story when the occasion required. He could talk races with Hurstwood, tell interesting incidents concerning himself and his experiences with women, and report the state of trade in the cities which he visited, and so managed to make himself almost invariably agreeable. To-night he was particularly so, since his report to the company had been favorably commented upon, his new samples had been satisfactorily selected, and his trip marked out for the next six weeks.

"Why, hello, Charlie, old man," said Hurstwood, as Drouet came in that evening about eight o'clock. "How goes it?" The room was crowded.

Drouet shook hands, beaming good nature, and they strolled towards the bar.

"Oh, all right."

"I haven't seen you in six weeks. When did you get in?"

"Friday," said Drouet. "Had a fine trip."

"Glad of it," said Hurstwood, his black eyes lit with a warmth which half displaced the cold make-believe that usually dwelt in them. "What are you going to take?" he added, as the barkeeper, in snowy jacket and tie, leaned toward them from behind the bar.

"Old Pepper," said Drouet.

"A little of the same for me," put in Hurstwood.

"How long are you in town this time?" inquired Hurstwood.

"Only until Wednesday. I'm going up to St. Paul."

"George Evans was in here Saturday and said he saw you in Milwaukee last week."

"Yes, I saw George," returned Drouet. "Great old boy, isn't he? We had quite a time there together."

The barkeeper was setting out the glasses and bottle before them, and they now poured out the draught as they talked, Drouet filling his to within a third of full, as was considered proper, and Hurstwood taking the barest suggestion of whiskey and modifying it with seltzer.

"What's become of Caryoe?" remarked Hurstwood. "I haven't seen him around here in two weeks."

"Laid up, they say," exclaimed Drouet. "Say, he's a gouty old boy!"

"Made a lot of money in his time, though, hasn't he?"

"Yes, wads of it," returned Drouet. "He won't live much longer. Barely comes down to the office now."

"Just one boy, hasn't he?" asked Hurstwood.

"Yes, and a swift-pacer," laughed Drouet.

"I guess he can't hurt the business very much, though, with the other members all there."

"No, he can't injure that any, I guess."

Hurstwood was standing, his coat open, his thumbs in his pockets, the light on his jewels and rings relieving them with agreeable distinctness. He was the picture of fastidious comfort.

To one not inclined to drink, and gifted with a more serious turn of mind, such a bubbling, chattering, glittering chamber must ever seem an anomaly, a strange commentary on nature and life. Here come the moths, in endless procession, to bask in the light of the flame. Such conversation as one may hear would not warrant a commendation of the scene upon intellectual grounds. It seems plain that schemers would choose more sequestered quarters to arrange their plans, that politicians would not gather here in company to discuss anything save formalities, where the sharp-eared may hear, and it would scarcely be justified on the score of thirst, for the majority of those who frequent these more gorgeous places have no craving for liquor. Nevertheless, the fact that here men gather, here chatter, here love to pass and rub elbows, must be explained upon some grounds. It must be that a strange bundle of passions and vague desires give rise to such a curious social institution or it would not be.

Drouet, for one, was lured as much by his longing for pleasure as by his desire to shine among his betters. The many friends he met here dropped in because they craved, without, perhaps, consciously analyzing it, the company, the glow, the atmosphere which they found. One might take it, after all, as an augur of the better social order, for the things which they satisfied here, though sensory, were not evil. No evil could come out of the contemplation of an expensively decorated chamber. The worst effect of such a thing would be, perhaps, to stir up in the material-minded an ambition to arrange their lives upon a similarly splendid basis. In the last analysis, that would scarcely be called the fault of the decorations, but rather of the innate trend of the mind. That such a scene might stir the less expensively dressed to emulate the more expensively dressed could scarcely be laid at the door of anything save the false ambition of the minds of those so affected. Remove the element so thoroughly and solely complained of—liquor—and there would not be one to gainsay the qualities of beauty and enthusiasm which would remain. The pleased eye with which our modern restaurants of fashion are looked upon is proof of this assertion.

Yet, here is the fact of the lighted chamber, the dressy, greedy company, the small, self-interested palaver, the disorganized, aimless, wandering mental action which it represents—the love of light and show and finery which, to one outside, under the serene light of the eternal stars, must seem a strange and shiny thing. Under the stars and sweeping night winds, what a lamp-flower it must bloom; a strange, glittering night-flower, odor-yielding, insect-drawing, insect-infested rose of pleasure.

"See that fellow coming in there?" said Hurstwood, glancing at a gentleman just entering, arrayed in a high hat and Prince Albert coat, his fat cheeks puffed and red as with good eating.

"No, where?" said Drouet.

"There," said Hurstwood, indicating the direction by a cast of his eye, "the man with the silk hat."

"Oh, yes," said Drouet, now affecting not to see. "Who is he?"

"That's Jules Wallace, the spiritualist."

Drouet followed him with his eyes, much interested.

"Doesn't look much like a man who sees spirits, does he?" said Drouet.

"Oh, I don't know," returned Hurstwood. "He's got the money, all right," and a little twinkle passed over his eyes.

"I don't go much on those things, do you?" asked Drouet.

"Well, you never can tell," said Hurstwood. "There may be something to it. I wouldn't bother about it myself, though. By the way," he added, "are you going anywhere to-night?"

"'The Hole in the Ground,'" said Drouet, mentioning the popular farce of the time.

"Well, you'd better be going. It's half after eight already," and he drew out his watch.

The crowd was already thinning out considerably—some bound for the theaters, some to their clubs, and some to that most fascinating of all the pleasures—for the type of man there represented, at least—the ladies.

"Yes, I will," said Drouet.

"Come around after the show. I have something I want to show you," said Hurstwood.

"Sure," said Drouet, elated.

"You haven't anything on hand for the night, have you?" added Hurstwood.

"Not a thing."

"Well, come round, then."

"I struck a little peach coming in on the train Friday," remarked Drouet, by way of parting. "By George, that's so, I must go and call on her before I go away."

"Oh, never mind her," Hurstwood remarked.

"Say, she was a little dandy, I tell you," went on Drouet confidentially, and trying to impress his friend.

"Twelve o'clock," said Hurstwood.

"That's right," said Drouet, going out.

Thus was Carrie's name bandied about in the most frivolous and gay of places, and that also when the little toiler was bemoaning her narrow lot, which was almost inseparable from the early stages of this, her unfolding fate.

CHAPTER VI

THE MACHINE AND THE MAIDEN: A KNIGHT OF TO-DAY

At the flat that evening Carrie felt a new phase of its atmosphere. The fact that it was unchanged, while her feelings were different, increased her knowledge of its character. Minnie, after the good spirits Carrie manifested at first, expected a fair report. Hanson supposed that Carrie would be satisfied.

"Well," he said, as he came in from the hall in his working clothes, and looked at Carrie through the dining-room door, "how did you make out?"

"Oh," said Carrie, "it's pretty hard. I don't like it."

There was an air about her which showed plainer than any words that she was both weary and disappointed.

"What sort of work is it?" he asked, lingering a moment as he turned upon his heel to go into the bathroom.

"Running a machine," answered Carrie.

It was very evident that it did not concern him much, save from the side of the flat's success. He was irritated a shade because it could not have come about in the throw of fortune for Carrie to be pleased.

Minnie worked with less elation than she had just before Carrie arrived. The sizzle of the meat frying did not sound quite so pleasing now that Carrie had reported her discontent. To Carrie, the one relief of the whole day would have been a jolly home, a sympathetic reception, a bright supper table, and some one to say: "Oh, well, stand it a little while. You will get something better," but now this was ashes. She began to see that they looked upon her complaint as unwarranted, and that she was supposed to work on and say nothing. She knew that she was to pay four dollars for her board and room, and now she felt that it would be an exceedingly gloomy round, living with these people.

Minnie was no companion for her sister—she was too old. Her thoughts were staid and solemnly adapted to a condition. If Hanson had any pleasant thoughts or happy feelings he concealed them. He seemed to do all his mental operations without the aid of physical expression. He was as still as a deserted chamber. Carrie, on the other hand, had the blood of youth and some imagination. Her day of love and the mysteries of courtship were still ahead. She could think of things she would like to do, of clothes she would like to wear, and of places she would like to visit. These were the things upon which her mind ran, and it was like meeting with opposition at every turn to find no one here to call forth or respond to her feelings.

She had forgotten, in considering and explaining the result of her day, that Drouet might come. Now, when she saw how unreceptive these two people were, she hoped he would not. She did not know exactly what she would do or how she would explain to Drouet, if he came. After supper she changed her clothes. When she was trimly dressed she was rather a sweet little being, with large eyes and a sad mouth. Her face expressed the mingled expectancy, dissatisfaction, and depression she felt. She wandered about after the dishes were put away, talked a little with Minnie, and then decided to go down and stand in the door at the foot of the stairs. If Drouet came, she could meet him there. Her face took on the semblance of a look of happiness as she put on her hat to go below.

"Carrie doesn't seem to like her place very well," said Minnie to her husband when the latter came out, paper in hand, to sit in the dining-room a few minutes.

"She ought to keep it for a time, anyhow," said Hanson. "Has she gone downstairs?"

"Yes," said Minnie.

"I'd tell her to keep it if I were you. She might be here weeks without getting another one."

Minnie said she would, and Hanson read his paper.

"If I were you," he said a little later, "I wouldn't let her stand in the door down there. It don't look good."

"I'll tell her," said Minnie.

The life of the streets continued for a long time to interest Carrie. She never wearied of wondering where the people in the cars were going or what their enjoyments were. Her imagination trod a very narrow round, always winding up at points which concerned money, looks, clothes, or enjoyment. She would have a far-off thought of Columbia City now and then, or an irritating rush of feeling concerning her experiences of the present day, but, on the whole, the little world about her enlisted her whole attention.

The first floor of the building, of which Hanson's flat was the third, was occupied by a bakery, and to this, while she was standing there, Hanson came down to buy a loaf of bread. She was not aware of his presence until he was quite near her.

"I'm after bread," was all he said as he passed.

The contagion of thought here demonstrated itself. While Hanson really came for bread, the thought dwelt with him that now he would see what Carrie was doing. No sooner did he draw near her with that in mind than she felt it. Of course, she had no understanding of what put it into her head, but, nevertheless, it aroused in her the first shade of real antipathy to him. She knew now that she did not like him. He was suspicious.

A thought will color a world for us. The flow of Carrie's meditations had been disturbed, and Hanson had not long gone upstairs before she followed. She had realized with the lapse of the quarter hours that Drouet was not coming, and somehow she felt a little resentful, a little as if she had been forsaken—was not good enough. She went upstairs, where everything was silent. Minnie was sewing by a lamp at the table. Hanson had already turned in for the night. In her weariness and disappointment Carrie did no more than announce that she was going to bed.

"Yes, you'd better," returned Minnie. "You've got to get up early, you know."

The morning was no better. Hanson was just going out the door as Carrie came from her room. Minnie tried to talk with her during breakfast, but there was not much of interest which they could mutually discuss. As on the previous morning, Carrie walked down town, for she began to realize now that her four-fifty would not even allow her car fare after she paid her board. This seemed a miserable arrangement. But the morning light swept away the first misgivings of the day, as morning light is ever wont to do.

At the shoe factory she put in a long day, scarcely so wearisome as the preceding, but considerably less novel. The head foreman, in his round, stopped by her machine.

"Where did you come from?" he inquired.

"Mr. Brown hired me," she replied.

"Oh, he did, eh!" and then, "See that you keep things going."

The machine girls impressed her even less favorably. They seemed satisfied with their lot, and were in a sense "common." Carrie had more imagination than they. She was not used to slang. Her instinct in the matter of dress was naturally better. She disliked to listen to the girl next to her, who was rather hardened by experience.

"I'm going to quit this," she heard her remark to her neighbor. "What with the stipend and being up late, it's too much for me health."

They were free with the fellows, young and old, about the place, and exchanged banter in rude phrases, which at first shocked her. She saw that she was taken to be of the same sort and addressed accordingly.

"Hello," remarked one of the stout-wristed sole-workers to her at noon. "You're a daisy." He really expected to hear the common "Aw! go chase yourself!" in return, and was sufficiently abashed, by Carrie's silently moving away, to retreat, awkwardly grinning.

That night at the flat she was even more lonely—the dull situation was becoming harder to endure. She could see that the Hansons seldom or never had any company. Standing at the street door looking out, she ventured to walk out a little way. Her easy gait and idle manner attracted attention of an offensive but common sort. She was slightly taken back at the overtures of a well-dressed man of thirty, who in passing looked at her, reduced his pace, turned back, and said:

"Out for a little stroll, are you, this evening?"

Carrie looked at him in amazement, and then summoned sufficient thought to reply: "Why, I don't know you," backing away as she did so.

"Oh, that don't matter," said the other affably.

She bandied no more words with him, but hurried away, reaching her own door quite out of breath. There was something in the man's look which frightened her.

During the remainder of the week it was very much the same. One or two nights she found herself too tired to walk home, and expended car fare. She was not very strong, and sitting all day affected her back. She went to bed one night before Hanson.

Transplantation is not always successful in the matter of flowers or maidens. It requires sometimes a richer soil, a better atmosphere to continue even a natural growth. It would have been better if her acclimatization had been more gradual—less rigid. She would have done better if she had not secured a position so quickly, and had seen more of the city which she constantly troubled to know about.

On the first morning it rained she found that she had no umbrella. Minnie loaned her one of hers, which was worn and faded. There was the kind of vanity in Carrie that troubled at this. She went to one of the great department stores and bought herself one, using a dollar and a quarter of her small store to pay for it.

"What did you do that for, Carrie?" asked Minnie, when she saw it.

"Oh, I need one," said Carrie.

"You foolish girl."

Carrie resented this, though she did not reply. She was not going to be a common shop-girl, she thought; they need not think it, either.

On the first Saturday night Carrie paid her board, four dollars. Minnie had a quaver of conscience as she took it, but did not know how to explain to Hanson if she took less. That worthy gave up just four dollars less toward the household expenses with a smile of satisfaction. He contemplated increasing his Building and Loan payments. As for Carrie, she studied over the problem of finding clothes and amusement on fifty cents a week. She brooded over this until she was in a state of mental rebellion.

"I'm going up the street for a walk," she said after supper.

"Not alone, are you?" asked Hanson.

"Yes," returned Carrie.

"I wouldn't," said Minnie.

"I want to see *something*," said Carrie, and by the tone she put into the last word they realized for the first time she was not pleased with them.

"What's the matter with her?" asked Hanson, when she went into the front room to get her hat.

"I don't know," said Minnie.

"Well, she ought to know better than to want to go out alone."

Carrie did not go very far, after all. She returned and stood in the door. The next day they went out to Garfield Park, but it did not please her. She did not look well enough. In the shop next day she heard the highly colored reports which girls give of their trivial amusements. They had been happy. On several days it rained and she used up car fare. One night she got thoroughly soaked, going to catch the car at Van Buren Street. All that evening she sat alone in the front room looking out upon the street, where the lights were reflected on the wet pavements, thinking. She had imagination enough to be moody.

On Saturday she paid another four dollars and pocketed her fifty cents in despair. The speaking acquaintanceship which she formed with some of the girls at the shop discovered to her the fact that they had more of their earnings to use for themselves than she did. They had young men of the kind whom she, since her experience with Drouet, felt above, who took them about. She came to thoroughly dislike the light-headed young fellows of the shop. Not one of them had a show of refinement. She saw only their workday side.

There came a day when the first premonitory blast of winter swept over the city. It scudded the fleecy clouds in the heavens, trailed long, thin streamers of smoke from the tall stacks, and raced about the streets and corners in sharp and sudden puffs. Carrie now felt the problem of winter clothes. What was she to do? She had no winter jacket, no hat, no shoes. It was difficult to speak to Minnie about this, but at last she summoned the courage.

"I don't know what I'm going to do about clothes," she said one evening when they were together. "I need a hat."

Minnie looked serious.

"Why don't you keep part of your money and buy yourself one?" she suggested, worried over the situation which the withholding of Carrie's money would create.

"I'd like to for a week or so, if you don't mind," ventured Carrie.

"Could you pay two dollars?" asked Minnie.

Carrie readily acquiesced, glad to escape the trying situation, and liberal now that she saw a way out. She was elated and began figuring at once. She needed a hat first of all. How Minnie explained to Hanson she never knew. He said nothing at all, but there were thoughts in the air which left disagreeable impressions.

The new arrangement might have worked if sickness had not intervened. It blew up cold after a rain one afternoon when Carrie was still without a jacket. She came out of the warm shop at six and shivered as the wind struck her. In the morning she was sneezing, and going down town made it worse. That day her bones ached and she felt light-headed. Towards evening she felt very ill, and when she reached home was not hungry. Minnie noticed her drooping actions and asked her about herself.

"I don't know," said Carrie. "I feel real bad."

She hung about the stove, suffered a chattering chill, and went to bed sick. The next morning she was thoroughly feverish.

Minnie was truly distressed at this, but maintained a kindly demeanor. Hanson said perhaps she had better go back home for a while. When she got up after three days, it was taken for granted that her position was lost. The winter was near at hand, she had no clothes, and now she was out of work.

"I don't know," said Carrie; "I'll go down Monday and see if I can't get something."

If anything, her efforts were more poorly rewarded on this trial than the last. Her clothes were nothing suitable for fall wearing. Her last money she had spent for a hat. For three days she wandered about, utterly dispirited. The attitude of the flat was fast becoming unbearable. She hated to think of going back there each evening. Hanson was so cold. She knew it could not last much longer. Shortly she would have to give up and go home.

On the fourth day she was down town all day, having borrowed ten cents for lunch from Minnie. She had applied in the cheapest kind of places without success. She even answered for a waitress in a small restaurant where she saw a card in the window, but they wanted an experienced girl. She moved through the thick throng of strangers, utterly subdued in spirit. Suddenly a hand pulled her arm and turned her about.

"Well, well!" said a voice. In the first glance she beheld Drouet. He was not only rosy-cheeked, but radiant. He was the essence of sunshine and good-humor. "Why, how are you, Carrie?" he said. "You're a daisy. Where have you been?"

Carrie smiled under his irresistible flood of geniality.

"I've been out home," she said.

"Well," he said, "I saw you across the street there. I thought it was you. I was just coming out to your place. How are you, anyhow?"

"I'm all right," said Carrie, smiling.

Drouet looked her over and saw something different.

"Well," he said, "I want to talk to you. You're not going anywhere in particular, are you?"

"Not just now," said Carrie.

"Let's go up here and have something to eat. George! but I'm glad to see you again."

She felt so relieved in his radiant presence, so much looked after and cared for, that she assented gladly, though with the slightest air of holding back.

"Well," he said, as he took her arm—and there was an exuberance of good-fellowship in the word which fairly warmed the cockles of her heart.

They went through Monroe Street to the old Windsor dining-room, which was then a large, comfortable place, with an excellent cuisine and substantial service. Drouet selected a table close by the window, where the busy rout of the street could be seen. He loved the changing panorama of the street—to see and be seen as he dined.

"Now," he said, getting Carrie and himself comfortably settled, "what will you have?"

Carrie looked over the large bill of fare which the waiter handed her without really considering it. She was very hungry, and the things she saw there awakened her desires, but the high prices held her attention. "Half broiled spring chicken—seventy-five. Sirloin steak with mushrooms—one twenty-five." She had dimly heard of these things, but it seemed strange to be called to order from the list.

"I'll fix this," exclaimed Drouet. "Sst! Waiter."

That officer of the board, a full-chested, round-faced Negro, approached, and inclined his ear.

"Sirloin with mushrooms," said Drouet. "Stuffed tomatoes."

"Yassah," assented the Negro, nodding his head.

"Hashed brown potatoes."

"Yassah."

"Asparagus."

"Yassah."

"And a pot of coffee."

Drouet turned to Carrie. "I haven't had a thing since breakfast. Just got in from Rock Island. I was going off to dine when I saw you."

Carrie smiled and smiled.

"What have you been doing?" he went on. "Tell me all about yourself. How is your sister?"

"She's well," returned Carrie, answering the last query.

He looked at her hard.

"Say," he said, "you haven't been sick, have you?"

Carrie nodded.

"Well, now, that's a blooming shame, isn't it? You don't look very well. I thought you looked a little pale. What have you been doing?"

"Working," said Carrie.

"You don't say so! At what?"

She told him.

"Rhodes, Morgenthau and Scott—why, I know that house. Over here on Fifth Avenue, isn't it? They're a close-fisted concern. What made you go there?"

"I couldn't get anything else," said Carrie frankly.

"Well, that's an outrage," said Drouet. "You oughtn't to be working for those people. Have the factory right back of the store, don't they?"

"Yes," said Carrie.

"That isn't a good house," said Drouet. "You don't want to work at anything like that, anyhow."

He chattered on at a great rate, asking questions, explaining things about himself, telling her what a good restaurant it was, until the waiter returned with an immense tray, bearing the hot savory dishes which had been ordered. Drouet fairly shone in the matter of serving. He appeared to great advantage behind the white napery and silver platters of the table and displaying his arms with a knife and fork. As he cut the meat his rings almost spoke. His new suit creaked as he stretched to reach the plates, break the bread, and pour the coffee. He helped Carrie to a rousing plateful and contributed the warmth of his spirit to her body until she was a new girl. He was a splendid fellow in the true popular understanding of the term, and captivated Carrie completely.

That little soldier of fortune took her good turn in an easy way. She felt a little out of place, but the great room soothed her and the view of the well-dressed throng outside seemed a splendid thing. Ah, what was it not to have money! What a thing it was to be able to come in here and dine! Drouet must be fortunate. He rode on trains, dressed in such nice clothes, was so strong, and ate in these fine places. He seemed quite a figure of a man, and she wondered at his friendship and regard for her.

"So you lost your place because you got sick, eh?" he said. "What are you going to do now?"

"Look around," she said, a thought of the need that hung outside this fine restaurant like a hungry dog at her heels passing into her eyes.

"Oh, no," said Drouet, "that won't do. How long have you been looking?"

"Four days," she answered.

"Think of that!" he said, addressing some problematical individual. "You oughtn't to be doing anything like that. These girls," and he waved an inclusion of all shop and factory girls, "don't get anything. Why, you can't live on it, can you?"

He was a brotherly sort of creature in his demeanor. When he had scouted the idea of that kind of toil, he took another tack. Carrie was really very pretty. Even then, in her commonplace garb, her figure was evidently not bad, and her eyes were large and gentle. Drouet looked at her and his thoughts reached home. She felt his admiration. It was powerfully backed by his liberality and good-humor. She felt that she liked him—that she could continue to like him ever so much. There was something even richer than that, running as a hidden strain, in her mind. Every little while her eyes would meet his, and by that means the interchanging current of feeling would be fully connected.

"Why don't you stay down town and go to the theater with me?" he said, hitching his chair closer. The table was not very wide.

"Oh, I can't," she said.

"What are you going to do to-night?"

"Nothing," she answered, a little drearily.

"You don't like out there where you are, do you?"

"Oh, I don't know."

"What are you going to do if you don't get work?"

"Go back home, I guess."

There was the least quaver in her voice as she said this. Somehow, the influence he was exerting was powerful. They came to an understanding of each other without words—he of her situation, she of the fact that he realized it.

"No," he said, "you can't make it!" genuine sympathy filling his mind for the time. "Let me help you. You take some of my money."

"Oh, no!" she said, leaning back.

"What are you going to do?" he said.

She sat meditating, merely shaking her head.

He looked at her quite tenderly for his kind. There were some loose bills in his vest pocket—greenbacks. They were soft and noiseless, and he got his fingers about them and crumpled them up in his hand.

"Come on," he said, "I'll see you through all right. Get yourself some clothes."

It was the first reference he had made to that subject, and now she realized how bad off she was. In his crude way he had struck the key-note. Her lips trembled a little.

She had her hand out on the table before her. They were quite alone in their corner, and he put his larger, warmer hand over it.

"Aw, come, Carrie," he said, "what can you do alone? Let me help you."

He pressed her hand gently and she tried to withdraw it. At this he held it fast, and she no longer protested. Then he slipped the greenbacks he had into her palm, and when she began to protest, he whispered:

"I'll loan it to you—that's all right. I'll loan it to you."

He made her take it. She felt bound to him by a strange tie of affection now. They went out, and he walked with her far out south toward Polk Street, talking.

"You don't want to live with those people?" he said in one place, abstractedly. Carrie heard it, but it made only a slight impression.

"Come down and meet me to-morrow," he said, "and we'll go to the matinee. Will you?"

Carrie protested a while, but acquiesced.

"You're not doing anything. Get yourself a nice pair of shoes and a jacket."

She scarcely gave a thought to the complication which would trouble her when he was gone. In his presence, she was of his own hopeful, easy-way-out mood.

"Don't you bother about those people out there," he said at parting. "I'll help you."

Carrie left him, feeling as though a great arm had slipped out before her to draw off trouble. The money she had accepted was two soft, green, handsome ten-dollar bills.

CHAPTER VII

The Lure of the Material: Beauty Speaks for Itself

The true meaning of money yet remains to be popularly explained and comprehended. When each individual realizes for himself that this thing primarily stands for and should only be accepted as a moral due—that it should be paid out as honestly stored energy, and not as a usurped privilege—many of our social, religious, and political troubles will have permanently passed. As for Carrie, her understanding of the moral significance of money was the popular understanding, nothing more. The old definition: "Money: something everybody else has and I must get," would have expressed her understanding of it thoroughly. Some of it she now held in her hand—two soft, green ten-dollar bills—and she felt that she was immensely better off for the having of them. It was something that was power in itself. One of her order of mind would have been content to be cast away upon a desert island with a bundle of money, and only the long strain of starvation would have taught her that in some cases it could have no value. Even then she would have had no conception of the relative value of the thing; her one thought would, undoubtedly, have concerned the pity of having so much power and the inability to use it.

The poor girl thrilled as she walked away from Drouet. She felt ashamed in part because she had been weak enough to take it, but her need was so dire, she was still glad. Now she would have a nice new jacket! Now she would buy a nice pair of pretty button shoes. She would get stockings, too, and a skirt, and, and—until already, as in the matter of her prospective salary, she had got beyond, in her desires, twice the purchasing power of her bills.

She conceived a true estimate of Drouet. To her, and indeed to all the world, he was a nice, good-hearted man. There was nothing evil in the fellow. He gave her the money out of a good heart—out of a realization of her want. He would not have given the same amount to a poor young man, but we must not forget that a poor young man could not, in the nature of things, have appealed to him like a poor young girl. Femininity affected his feelings. He was the creature of an inborn desire. Yet no beggar could have caught his eye and said, "My God, mister, I'm starving," but he would gladly have handed out what was considered the proper portion to give beggars and thought no more about it. There would have been no speculation, no philosophizing. He had no mental process in him worthy the dignity of either of those terms. In his good clothes and fine health, he was a merry, unthinking moth of the lamp. Deprived of his position, and struck by a few of the involved and baffling forces which sometimes play upon man, he would have been as helpless as Carrie—as helpless, as nonunderstanding, as pitiable, if you will, as she.

Now, in regard to his pursuit of women, he meant them no harm, because he did not conceive of the relation which he hoped to hold with them as being harmful. He loved to make advances to women, to have them succumb to his charms, not because he was a cold-blooded, dark, scheming villain, but because his inborn desire urged him to that as a chief delight. He was vain, he was boastful, he was as deluded by fine clothes as any silly-headed girl. A truly deep-eyed villain could have hornswaggled him as readily as he could have flattered a pretty shop-girl. His fine success as a salesman lay in his geniality and the thoroughly reputable standing of his house. He bobbed about among men, a veritable bundle of enthusiasm—no power worthy the name of intellect, no thoughts worthy the adjective noble, no feelings long continued in one strain. A Madame Sappho would have called him a pig; a Shakespeare would have said "my merry child;" old, drinking Caryoe thought him a clever, successful businessman. In short, he was as good as his intellect conceived.

The best proof that there was something open and commendable about the man was the fact that Carrie took the money. No deep, sinister soul with ulterior motives could have given her fifteen cents under the guise of friendship. The unintellectual are not so helpless. Nature has taught the beasts of the field to fly when some unheralded danger threatens. She has put into the small, unwise head of the chipmunk the untutored fear of poisons. "He keepeth His creatures whole," was not written of beasts alone. Carrie was unwise, and, therefore, like the sheep in its unwisdom, strong in feeling. The instinct of self-protection, strong in all such natures, was roused but feebly, if at all, by the overtures of Drouet.

When Carrie had gone, he felicitated himself upon her good opinion. By George, it was a shame young girls had to be knocked around like that. Cold weather coming on and no clothes. Tough. He would go around to Fitzgerald and Moy's and get a cigar. It made him feel light of foot as he thought about her.

Carrie reached home in high good spirits, which she could scarcely conceal. The possession of the money involved a number of points which perplexed her seriously. How should she buy any clothes when Minnie knew that she had no money? She had no sooner entered the flat than this point was settled for her. It could not be done. She could think of no way of explaining.

"How did you come out?" asked Minnie, referring to the day.

Carrie had none of the small deception which could feel one thing and say something directly opposed. She would prevaricate, but it would be in the line of her feelings at least. So instead of complaining when she felt so good, she said:

"I have the promise of something."

"Where?"

"At the Boston Store."

"Is it sure promised?" questioned Minnie.

"Well, I'm to find out to-morrow," returned Carrie, disliking to draw out a lie any longer than was necessary.

Minnie felt the atmosphere of good feeling which Carrie brought with her. She felt now was the time to express to Carrie the state of Hanson's feeling about her entire Chicago venture.

"If you shouldn't get it—" she paused, troubled for an easy way.

"If I don't get something pretty soon, I think I'll go home."

Minnie saw her chance.

"Sven thinks it might be best for the winter, anyhow."

The situation flashed on Carrie at once. They were unwilling to keep her any longer, out of work. She did not blame Minnie, she did not blame Hanson very much. Now, as she sat there digesting the remark, she was glad she had Drouet's money.

"Yes," she said after a few moments, "I thought of doing that."

She did not explain that the thought, however, had aroused all the antagonism of her nature. Columbia City, what was there for her? She knew its dull, little round by heart. Here was the great, mysterious city which was still a magnet for her. What she had seen only suggested its possibilities. Now to turn back on it and live the little old life out there—she almost exclaimed against the thought.

She had reached home early and went in the front room to think. What could she do? She could not buy new shoes and wear them here. She would need to save part of the twenty to pay her fare home. She did not want to borrow of Minnie for that. And yet, how could she explain where she even got that money? If she could only get enough to let her out easy.

She went over the tangle again and again. Here, in the morning, Drouet would expect to see her in a new jacket, and that couldn't be. The Hansons expected her to go home, and she wanted to get away, and yet she did not want to go home. In the light of the way they would look on her getting money without work, the taking of it now seemed dreadful. She began to be ashamed. The whole situation depressed her. It was all so clear when she was with Drouet. Now it was all so tangled, so hopeless—much worse than it was before, because she had the semblance of aid in her hand which she could not use.

Her spirits sank so that at supper Minnie felt that she must have had another hard day. Carrie finally decided that she would give the money back. It was wrong to take it. She would go down in the morning and hunt for work. At noon she would meet Drouet as agreed and tell him. At this decision her heart sank, until she was the old Carrie of distress.

Curiously, she could not hold the money in her hand without feeling some relief. Even after all her depressing conclusions, she could sweep away all thought about the matter and then the twenty dollars seemed a wonderful and delightful thing. Ah, money, money, money! What a thing it was to have. How plenty of it would clear away all these troubles.

In the morning she got up and started out a little early. Her decision to hunt for work was moderately strong, but the money in her pocket, after all her troubling over it, made the work question the least shade less terrible. She walked into the wholesale district, but as the thought of applying came with each passing concern, her heart shrank. What a coward she was, she thought to herself. Yet she had applied so often. It would be the same old story. She walked on and on, and finally did go into one place, with the old result. She came out feeling that luck was against her. It was no use.

Without much thinking, she reached Dearborn Street. Here was the great Fair store with its multitude of delivery wagons about, its long window display, its crowd of shoppers. It readily changed her thoughts, she who was so weary of them. It was here that she had intended to come and get her new things. Now for relief from distress; she thought she would go in and see. She would look at the jackets.

There is nothing in this world more delightful than that middle state in which we mentally balance at times, possessed of the means, lured by desire, and yet deterred by conscience or want of decision. When Carrie began wandering around the store amid the fine displays she was in this mood. Her original experience in this same place had given her a high opinion of its merits. Now she paused at each individual bit of finery, where before she had hurried on. Her woman's heart was warm with desire for them. How would she look in this, how charming that would make her! She came upon the corset counter and paused in rich reverie as she noted the dainty concoctions of color and lace there displayed. If she would only make up her mind, she could have one of those now. She lingered in the jewelry department. She saw the earrings, the bracelets, the pins, the chains. What would she not have given if she could have had them all! She would look fine too, if only she had some of these things.

The jackets were the greatest attraction. When she entered the store, she already had her heart fixed upon the peculiar little tan jacket with large mother-of-pearl buttons which was all the rage that fall. Still she delighted to convince herself that there was nothing she would like better. She went about among the glass cases and racks where these things were displayed, and satisfied herself that the one she thought of was the proper one. All the time she wavered in mind, now persuading herself that she could buy it right away if she chose, now recalling to herself the actual condition. At last the noon hour was dangerously near, and she had done nothing. She must go now and return the money.

Drouet was on the corner when she came up.

"Hello," he said, "where is the jacket and"—looking down—"the shoes?"

Carrie had thought to lead up to her decision in some intelligent way, but this swept the whole fore-schemed situation by the board.

"I came to tell you that—that I can't take the money."

"Oh, that's it, is it?" he returned. "Well, you come on with me. Let's go over here to Partridge's."

Carrie walked with him. Behold, the whole fabric of doubt and impossibility had slipped from her mind. She could not get at the points that were so serious, the things she was going to make plain to him.

"Have you had lunch yet? Of course you haven't. Let's go in here," and Drouet turned into one of the very nicely furnished restaurants off State Street, in Monroe.

"I mustn't take the money," said Carrie, after they were settled in a cosy corner, and Drouet had ordered the lunch. "I can't wear those things out there. They—they wouldn't know where I got them."

"What do you want to do," he smiled, "go without them?"

"I think I'll go home," she said, wearily.

"Oh, come," he said, "you've been thinking it over too long. I'll tell you what you do. You say you can't wear them out there. Why don't you rent a furnished room and leave them in that for a week?"

Carrie shook her head. Like all women, she was there to object and be convinced. It was for him to brush the doubts away and clear the path if he could.

"Why are you going home?" he asked.

"Oh, I can't get anything here."

"They won't keep you?" he remarked, intuitively.

"They can't," said Carrie.

"I'll tell you what you do," he said. "You come with me. I'll take care of you."

Carrie heard this passively. The peculiar state which she was in made it sound like the welcome breath of an open door. Drouet seemed of her own spirit and pleasing. He was clean, handsome, well-dressed, and sympathetic. His voice was the voice of a friend.

"What can you do back at Columbia City?" he went on, rousing by the words in Carrie's mind a picture of the dull world she had left. "There isn't anything down there. Chicago's the place. You can get a nice room here and some clothes, and then you can do something."

Carrie looked out through the window into the busy street. There it was, the admirable, great city, so fine when you are not poor. An elegant coach, with a prancing pair of bays, passed by, carrying in its upholstered depths a young lady.

"What will you have if you go back?" asked Drouet. There was no subtle undercurrent to the question. He imagined that she would have nothing at all of the things he thought worth while.

Carrie sat still, looking out. She was wondering what she could do. They would be expecting her to go home this week.

Drouet turned to the subject of the clothes she was going to buy.

"Why not get yourself a nice little jacket? You've got to have it. I'll loan you the money. You needn't worry about taking it. You can get yourself a nice room by yourself. I won't hurt you."

Carrie saw the drift, but could not express her thoughts. She felt more than ever the helplessness of her case.

"If I could only get something to do," she said.

"Maybe you can," went on Drouet, "if you stay here. You can't if you go away. They won't let you stay out there. Now, why not let me get you a nice room? I won't bother you—you needn't be afraid. Then, when you get fixed up, maybe you could get something."

He looked at her pretty face and it vivified his mental resources. She was a sweet little mortal to him—there was no doubt of that. She seemed to have some power back of her actions. She was not like the common run of store-girls. She wasn't silly.

In reality, Carrie had more imagination than he—more taste. It was a finer mental strain in her that made possible her depression and loneliness. Her poor clothes were neat, and she held her head unconsciously in a dainty way.

"Do you think I could get something?" she asked.

"Sure," he said, reaching over and filling her cup with tea. "I'll help you."

She looked at him, and he laughed reassuringly.

"Now I'll tell you what we'll do. We'll go over here to Partridge's and you pick out what you want. Then we'll look around for a room for you. You can leave the things there. Then we'll go to the show to-night."

Carrie shook her head.

"Well, you can go out to the flat then, that's all right. You don't need to stay in the room. Just take it and leave your things there."

She hung in doubt about this until the dinner was over.

"Let's go over and look at the jackets," he said.

Together they went. In the store they found that shine and rustle of new things which immediately laid hold of Carrie's heart. Under the influence of a good dinner and Drouet's radiating presence, the scheme proposed seemed feasible. She looked about and picked a jacket like the one which she had admired at The Fair. When she got it in her hand it seemed so much nicer. The saleswoman helped her on with it, and, by accident, it fitted perfectly. Drouet's face lightened as he saw the improvement. She looked quite smart.

"That's the thing," he said.

Carrie turned before the glass. She could not help feeling pleased as she looked at herself. A warm glow crept into her cheeks.

"That's the thing," said Drouet. "Now pay for it."

"It's nine dollars," said Carrie.

"That's all right—take it," said Drouet.

She reached in her purse and took out one of the bills. The woman asked if she would wear the coat and went off. In a few minutes she was back and the purchase was closed.

From Partridge's they went to a shoe store, where Carrie was fitted for shoes. Drouet stood by, and when he saw how nice they looked, said, "Wear them." Carrie shook her head, however. She was thinking of returning to the flat. He bought her a purse for one thing, and a pair of gloves for another, and let her buy the stockings.

"To-morrow," he said, "you come down here and buy yourself a skirt."

In all of Carrie's actions there was a touch of misgiving. The deeper she sank into the entanglement, the more she imagined that the thing hung upon the few remaining things she had not done. Since she had not done these, there was a way out.

Drouet knew a place in Wabash Avenue where there were rooms. He showed Carrie the outside of these, and said: "Now, you're my sister." He carried the arrangement off with an easy hand when it came to the selection, looking around, criticizing, opining. "Her trunk will be here in a day or so," he observed to the landlady, who was very pleased.

When they were alone, Drouet did not change in the least. He talked in the same general way as if they were out in the street. Carrie left her things.

"Now," said Drouet, "why don't you move to-night?"

"Oh, I can't," said Carrie.

"Why not?"

"I don't want to leave them so."

He took that up as they walked along the avenue. It was a warm afternoon. The sun had come out and the wind had died down. As he talked with Carrie, he secured an accurate detail of the atmosphere of the flat.

"Come out of it," he said, "they won't care. I'll help you get along."

She listened until her misgivings vanished. He would show her about a little and then help her get something. He really imagined that he would. He would be out on the road and she could be working.

"Now, I'll tell you what you do," he said, "you go out there and get whatever you want and come away."

She thought a long time about this. Finally she agreed. He would come out as far as Peoria Street and wait for her. She was to meet him at half-past eight. At half-past five she reached home, and at six her determination was hardened.

"So you didn't get it?" said Minnie, referring to Carrie's story of the Boston Store.

Carrie looked at her out of the corner of her eye. "No," she answered.

"I don't think you'd better try any more this fall," said Minnie.

Carrie said nothing.

When Hanson came home he wore the same inscrutable demeanor. He washed in silence and went off to read his paper. At dinner Carrie felt a little nervous. The strain of her own plans was considerable, and the feeling that she was not welcome here was strong.

"Didn't find anything, eh?" said Hanson.

"No."

He turned to his eating again, the thought that it was a burden to have her here dwelling in his mind. She would have to go home, that was all. Once she was away, there would be no more coming back in the spring.

Carrie was afraid of what she was going to do, but she was relieved to know that this condition was ending. They would not care. Hanson particularly would be glad when she went. He would not care what became of her.

After dinner she went into the bathroom, where they could not disturb her, and wrote a little note.

"Good-bye, Minnie," it read. "I'm not going home. I'm going to stay in Chicago a little while and look for work. Don't worry. I'll be all right."

In the front room Hanson was reading his paper. As usual, she helped Minnie clear away the dishes and straighten up. Then she said:

"I guess I'll stand down at the door a little while." She could scarcely prevent her voice from trembling.

Minnie remembered Hanson's remonstrance.

"Sven doesn't think it looks good to stand down there," she said.

"Doesn't he?" said Carrie. "I won't do it any more after this."

She put on her hat and fidgeted around the table in the little bedroom, wondering where to slip the note. Finally she put it under Minnie's hair-brush.

When she had closed the hall-door, she paused a moment and wondered what they would think. Some thought of the queerness of her deed affected her. She went slowly down the stairs. She looked back up the lighted step, and then affected to stroll up the street. When she reached the corner she quickened her pace.

As she was hurrying away, Hanson came back to his wife.

"Is Carrie down at the door again?" he asked.

"Yes," said Minnie; "she said she wasn't going to do it any more."

He went over to the baby where it was playing on the floor and began to poke his finger at it.

Drouet was on the corner waiting, in good spirits.

"Hello, Carrie," he said, as a sprightly figure of a girl drew near him. "Got here safe, did you? Well, we'll take a car."

CHAPTER VIII

Intimations by Winter: An Ambassador Summoned

Among the forces which sweep and play throughout the universe, untutored man is but a wisp in the wind. Our civilization is still in a middle stage, scarcely beast, in that it is no longer wholly guided by instinct; scarcely human, in that it is not yet wholly guided by reason. On the tiger no responsibility rests. We see him aligned by nature with the forces of life—he is born into their keeping and without thought he is protected. We see man far removed from the lairs of the jungles, his innate instincts dulled by too near an approach to free-will, his free-will not sufficiently developed to replace his instincts and afford him perfect guidance. He is becoming too wise to hearken always to instincts and desires; he is still too weak to always prevail against them. As a beast, the forces of life aligned him with them; as a man, he has not yet wholly learned to align himself with the forces. In this intermediate stage he wavers—neither drawn in harmony with nature by his instincts nor yet wisely putting himself into harmony by his own free-will. He is even as a wisp in the wind, moved by every breath of passion, acting now by his will and now by his instincts, erring with one, only to retrieve by the other, falling by one, only to rise by the other—a creature of incalculable variability. We have the consolation of knowing that evolution is ever in action, that the ideal is a light that cannot fail. He will not forever balance thus between good and evil. Where this jangle of free-will and instinct shall have been adjusted, when perfect understanding has given the former the power to replace the latter entirely, man will no longer vary. The needle of understanding will yet point steadfast and unwavering to the distant pole of truth.

In Carrie—as in how many of our worldlings do they not?—instinct and reason, desire and understanding, were at war for the mastery. She followed whither her craving led. She was as yet more drawn than she drew.

When Minnie found the note next morning, after a night of mingled wonder and anxiety, which was not exactly touched by yearning, sorrow, or love, she exclaimed: "Well, what do you think of that?"

"What?" said Hanson.

"Sister Carrie has gone to live somewhere else."

Hanson jumped out of bed with more celerity than he usually displayed and looked at the note. The only indication of his thoughts came in the form of a little clicking sound made by his tongue; the sound some people make when they wish to urge on a horse.

"Where do you suppose she's gone to?" said Minnie, thoroughly aroused.

"I don't know," a touch of cynicism lighting his eye. "Now she has gone and done it."

Minnie moved her head in a puzzled way.

"Oh, oh," she said, "she doesn't know what she has done."

"Well," said Hanson, after a while, sticking his hands out before him, "what can you do?"

Minnie's womanly nature was higher than this. She figured the possibilities in such cases.

"Oh," she said at last, "poor Sister Carrie!"

At the time of this particular conversation, which occurred at 5 A. M., that little soldier of fortune was sleeping a rather troubled sleep in her new room, alone.

Carrie's new state was remarkable in that she saw possibilities in it. She was no sensualist, longing to drowse sleepily in the lap of luxury. She turned about, troubled by her daring, glad of her release, wondering whether she would get something to do, wondering what Drouet would do. That worthy had his future fixed for him beyond a peradventure. He could not help what he was going to do. He could not see clearly enough to wish to do differently. He was drawn by his innate desire to act the old pursuing part. He would need to delight himself with Carrie as surely as he would need to eat his heavy breakfast. He might suffer the least rudimentary twinge of conscience in whatever he did, and in just so far he was evil and sinning. But whatever twinges of conscience he might have would be rudimentary, you may be sure.

The next day he called upon Carrie, and she saw him in her chamber. He was the same jolly, enlivening soul.

"Aw," he said, "what are you looking so blue about? Come on out to breakfast. You want to get your other clothes to-day."

Carrie looked at him with the hue of shifting thought in her large eyes.

"I wish I could get something to do," she said.

"You'll get that all right," said Drouet. "What's the use worrying right now? Get yourself fixed up. See the city. I won't hurt you."

"I know you won't," she remarked, half truthfully.

"Got on the new shoes, haven't you? Stick 'em out. George, they look fine. Put on your jacket."

Carrie obeyed.

"Say, that fits like a T, don't it?" he remarked, feeling the set of it at the waist and eyeing it from a few paces with real pleasure. "What you need now is a new skirt. Let's go to breakfast."

Carrie put on her hat.

"Where are the gloves?" he inquired.

"Here," she said, taking them out of the bureau drawer.

"Now, come on," he said.

Thus the first hour of misgiving was swept away.

It went this way on every occasion. Drouet did not leave her much alone. She had time for some lone wanderings, but mostly he filled her hours with sightseeing. At Carson, Pirie's he bought her a nice skirt and a shirt waist. With his money she purchased the little necessaries of toilet, until at last she looked quite another maiden. The mirror convinced her of a few things which she had long believed. She was pretty, yes, indeed! How nice her hat set, and weren't her eyes pretty. She caught her little red lip with her teeth and felt her first thrill of power. Drouet was so good.

They went to see "The Mikado" one evening, an opera which was hilariously popular at that time. Before going, they made off for the Windsor dining-room, which was in Dearborn Street, a considerable distance from Carrie's room. It was blowing up cold, and out of her window Carrie could see the western sky, still pink with the fading light, but steely blue at the top where it met the darkness. A long, thin cloud of pink hung in midair, shaped like some island in a far-off sea. Somehow the swaying of some dead branches of trees across the way brought back the picture with which she was familiar when she looked from their front window in December days at home.

She paused and wrung her little hands.

"What's the matter?" said Drouet.

"Oh, I don't know," she said, her lip trembling.

He sensed something, and slipped his arm over her shoulder, patting her arm.

"Come on," he said gently, "you're all right."

She turned to slip on her jacket.

"Better wear that boa about your throat to-night."

They walked north on Wabash to Adams Street and then west. The lights in the stores were already shining out in gushes of golden hue. The arc lights were sputtering overhead, and high up were the lighted windows of the tall office buildings. The chill wind whipped in and out in gusty breaths. Homeward bound, the six o'clock throng bumped and jostled. Light overcoats were turned up about the ears, hats were pulled down. Little shop-girls went fluttering by in pairs and fours, chattering, laughing. It was a spectacle of warm-blooded humanity.

Suddenly a pair of eyes met Carrie's in recognition. They were looking out from a group of poorly dressed girls. Their clothes were faded and loose-hanging, their jackets old, their general make-up shabby.

Carrie recognized the glance and the girl. She was one of those who worked at the machines in the shoe factory. The latter looked, not quite sure, and then turned her head and looked. Carrie felt as if some great tide had rolled between them. The old dress and the old machine came back. She actually started. Drouet didn't notice until Carrie bumped into a pedestrian.

"You must be thinking," he said.

They dined and went to the theater. That spectacle pleased Carrie immensely. The color and grace of it caught her eye. She had vain imaginings about place and power, about far-off lands and magnificent people. When it was over, the clatter of coaches and the throng of fine ladies made her stare.

"Wait a minute," said Drouet, holding her back in the showy foyer where ladies and gentlemen were moving in a social crush, skirts rustling, lace-covered heads nodding, white teeth showing through parted lips. "Let's see."

"Sixty-seven," the coach-caller was saying, his voice lifted in a sort of euphonious cry. "Sixty-seven."

"Isn't it fine?" said Carrie.

"Great," said Drouet. He was as much affected by this show of finery and gaiety as she. He pressed her arm warmly. Once she looked up, her even teeth glistening through her smiling lips, her eyes alight. As they were moving out he whispered down to her, "You look lovely!" They were right where the coach-caller was swinging open a coach-door and ushering in two ladies.

"You stick to me and we'll have a coach," laughed Drouet.

Carrie scarcely heard, her head was so full of the swirl of life.

They stopped in at a restaurant for a little after-theater lunch. Just a shade of a thought of the hour entered Carrie's head, but there was no household law to govern her now. If any habits ever had time to fix upon her, they would have operated here. Habits are peculiar things. They will drive the really non-religious mind out of bed to say prayers that are only a custom and not a devotion. The victim of habit, when he has neglected the thing which it was his custom to do, feels a little scratching in the brain, a little irritating something which comes of being out of the rut, and imagines it to be the prick of conscience, the still, small voice that is urging him ever to righteousness. If the digression is unusual enough, the drag of habit will be heavy enough to cause the unreasoning victim to return and perform the perfunctory thing. "Now, bless me," says such a mind, "I have done my duty," when, as a matter of fact, it has merely done its old, unbreakable trick once again.

Carrie had no excellent home principles fixed upon her. If she had, she would have been more consciously distressed. Now the lunch went off with considerable warmth. Under the influence of the varied occurrences, the fine, invisible passion which was emanating from Drouet, the food, the still unusual luxury, she relaxed and heard with open ears. She was again the victim of the city's hypnotic influence.

"Well," said Drouet at last, "we had better be going."

They had been dawdling over the dishes, and their eyes had frequently met. Carrie could not help but feel the vibration of force which followed, which, indeed, was his gaze. He had a way of touching her hand in explanation, as if to impress a fact upon her. He touched it now as he spoke of going.

They arose and went out into the street. The down-town section was now bare, save for a few whistling strollers, a few *owl* cars, a few open resorts whose windows were still bright. Out Wabash Avenue they strolled, Drouet still pouring forth his volume of small information. He had Carrie's arm in his, and held it closely as he explained. Once in a while, after some witticism, he would look down, and his eyes would meet hers. At last they came to the steps, and Carrie stood up on the first one, her head now coming even with his own. He took her hand and held it genially. He looked steadily at her as she glanced about, warmly musing.

At about that hour, Minnie was soundly sleeping, after a long evening of troubled thought. She had her elbow in an awkward position under her side. The muscles so held irritated a few nerves, and now a vague scene floated in on the drowsy mind. She fancied she and Carrie were somewhere beside an old coal-mine. She could see the tall runway and the heap of earth and coal cast out. There was a deep pit, into which they were looking; they could see the curious wet stones far down where the wall disappeared in vague shadows. An old basket, used for descending, was hanging there, fastened by a worn rope.

"Let's get in," said Carrie.

"Oh, no," said Minnie.

"Yes, come on," said Carrie.

She began to pull the basket over, and now, in spite of all protest, she had swung over and was going down.

"Carrie," she called, "Carrie, come back;" but Carrie was far down now and the shadow had swallowed her completely.

She moved her arm.

Now the mystic scenery merged queerly and the place was by waters she had never seen. They were upon some board or ground or something that reached far out, and at the end of this was Carrie. They looked about, and now the thing was sinking, and Minnie heard the low sip of the encroaching water.

"Come on, Carrie," she called, but Carrie was reaching farther out. She seemed to recede, and now it was difficult to call to her.

"Carrie," she called, "Carrie," but her own voice sounded far away, and the strange waters were blurring everything. She came away suffering as though she had lost something. She was more inexpressibly sad than she had ever been in life.

It was this way through many shifts of the tired brain, those curious phantoms of the spirit slipping in, blurring strange scenes, one with the other. The last one made her cry out, for Carrie was slipping away somewhere over a rock, and her fingers had let loose and she had seen her falling.

"Minnie! What's the matter? Here, wake up," said Hanson, disturbed, and shaking her by the shoulder.

"Wha—what's the matter?" said Minnie, drowsily.

"Wake up," he said, "and turn over. You're talking in your sleep."

A week or so later Drouet strolled into Fitzgerald and Moy's, spruce in dress and manner.

"Hello, Charlie," said Hurstwood, looking out from his office door.

Drouet strolled over and looked in upon the manager at his desk.

"When do you go out on the road again?" he inquired.

"Pretty soon," said Drouet.

"Haven't seen much of you this trip," said Hurstwood.

"Well, I've been busy," said Drouet.

They talked some few minutes on general topics.

"Say," said Drouet, as if struck by a sudden idea, "I want you to come out some evening."

"Out where?" inquired Hurstwood.

"Out to my house, of course," said Drouet, smiling.

Hurstwood looked up quizzically, the least suggestion of a smile hovering about his lips. He studied the face of Drouet in his wise way, and then with the demeanor of a gentleman, said: "Certainly; glad to."

"We'll have a nice game of euchre."

"May I bring a nice little bottle of Sec?" asked Hurstwood.

"Certainly," said Drouet. "I'll introduce you."

CHAPTER IX

CONVENTION'S OWN TINDER-BOX: THE EYE THAT IS GREEN

Hurstwood's residence on the North Side, near Lincoln Park, was a brick building of a very popular type then, a three-story affair with the first floor sunk a very little below the level of the street. It had a large bay window bulging out from the second floor, and was graced in front by a small grassy plot, twenty-five feet wide and ten feet deep. There was also a small rear yard, walled in by the fences of the neighbors and holding a stable where he kept his horse and trap.

The ten rooms of the house were occupied by himself, his wife Julia, and his son and daughter, George, Jr., and Jessica. There were besides these a maid-servant, represented from time to time by girls of various extraction, for Mrs. Hurstwood was not always easy to please.

"George, I let Mary go yesterday," was not an unfrequent salutation at the dinner table.

"All right," was his only reply. He had long since wearied of discussing the rancorous subject.

A lovely home atmosphere is one of the flowers of the world, than which there is nothing more tender, nothing more delicate, nothing more calculated to make strong and just the natures cradled and nourished within it. Those who have never experienced such a beneficent influence will not understand wherefore the tear springs glistening to the eyelids at some strange breath in lovely music. The mystic chords which bind and thrill the heart of the nation, they will never know.

Hurstwood's residence could scarcely be said to be infused with this home spirit. It lacked that toleration and regard without which the home is nothing. There was fine furniture, arranged as soothingly as the artistic perception of the occupants warranted. There were soft rugs, rich, upholstered chairs and divans, a grand piano, a marble carving of some unknown Venus by some unknown artist, and a number of small bronzes gathered from heaven knows where, but generally sold by the large furniture houses along with everything else which goes to make the "perfectly appointed house."

In the dining-room stood a sideboard laden with glistening decanters and other utilities and ornaments in glass, the arrangement of which could not be questioned. Here was something Hurstwood knew about. He had studied the subject for years in his business. He took no little satisfaction in telling each Mary, shortly after she arrived, something of what the art of the thing required. He was not garrulous by any means. On the contrary, there was a fine reserve in his manner toward the entire domestic economy of his life which was all that is comprehended by the popular term, gentlemanly. He would not argue, he would not talk freely. In his manner was something of the dogmatist. What he could not correct, he would ignore. There was a tendency in him to walk away from the impossible thing.

There was a time when he had been considerably enamored of his Jessica, especially when he was younger and more confined in his success. Now, however, in her seventeenth year, Jessica had developed a certain amount of reserve and independence which was not inviting to the richest form of parental devotion. She was in the high school, and had notions of life which were decidedly those of a patrician. She liked nice clothes and urged for them constantly. Thoughts of love and elegant individual establishments were running in her head. She met girls at the high school whose parents were truly rich and whose fathers had standing locally as partners or owners of solid businesses. These girls gave themselves the airs befitting the thriving domestic establishments from whence they issued. They were the only ones of the school about whom Jessica concerned herself.

Young Hurstwood, Jr., was in his twentieth year, and was already connected in a promising capacity with a large real estate firm. He contributed nothing for the domestic expenses of the family, but was thought to be saving his money to invest in real estate. He had some ability, considerable vanity, and a love of pleasure that had not, as yet, infringed upon his duties, whatever they were. He came in and went out, pursuing his own plans and fancies, addressing a few words to his mother occasionally, relating some little incident to his father, but for the most part confining himself to those generalities with which most conversation concerns itself. He was not laying bare his desires for any one to see. He did not find any one in the house who particularly cared to see.

Mrs. Hurstwood was the type of the woman who has ever endeavored to shine and has been more or less chagrined at the evidences of superior capability in this direction elsewhere. Her knowledge of life extended to that little conventional round of society of which she was not—but longed to be—a member. She was not without realization already that this thing was impossible, so far as she was concerned. For her daughter, she hoped better things. Through Jessica she might rise a little. Through George, Jr's., possible success she might draw to herself the privilege of pointing proudly. Even Hurstwood was doing well enough, and she was anxious that his small real estate adventures should prosper. His property holdings, as yet, were rather small, but his income was pleasing and his position with Fitzgerald and Moy was fixed. Both those gentlemen were on pleasant and rather informal terms with him.

The atmosphere which such personalities would create must be apparent to all. It worked out in a thousand little conversations, all of which were of the same caliber.

"I'm going up to Fox Lake to-morrow," announced George, Jr., at the dinner table one Friday evening.

"What's going on up there?" queried Mrs. Hurstwood.

"Eddie Fahrway's got a new steam launch, and he wants me to come up and see how it works."

"How much did it cost him?" asked his mother.

"Oh, over two thousand dollars. He says it's a dandy."

"Old Fahrway must be making money," put in Hurstwood.

"He is, I guess. Jack told me they were shipping Vegacura to Australia now—said they sent a whole box to Cape Town last week."

"Just think of that!" said Mrs. Hurstwood, "and only four years ago they had that basement in Madison Street."

"Jack told me they were going to put up a six-story building next spring in Robey Street."

"Just think of that!" said Jessica.

On this particular occasion Hurstwood wished to leave early.

"I guess I'll be going down town," he remarked, rising.

"Are we going to McVicker's Monday?" questioned Mrs. Hurstwood, without rising.

"Yes," he said indifferently.

They went on dining, while he went upstairs, for his hat and coat. Presently the door clicked.

"I guess papa's gone," said Jessica.

The latter's school news was of a particular stripe.

"They're going to give a performance in the Lyceum, upstairs," she reported one day, "and I'm going to be in it."

"Are you?" said her mother.

"Yes, and I'll have to have a new dress. Some of the nicest girls in the school are going to be in it. Miss Palmer is going to take the part of Portia."

"Is she?" said Mrs. Hurstwood.

"They've got that Martha Griswold in it again. She thinks she can act."

"Her family doesn't amount to anything, does it?" said Mrs. Hurstwood sympathetically. "They haven't anything, have they?"

"No," returned Jessica, "they're poor as church mice."

She distinguished very carefully between the young boys of the school, many of whom were attracted by her beauty.

"What do you think?" she remarked to her mother one evening; "that Herbert Crane tried to make friends with me."

"Who is he, my dear?" inquired Mrs. Hurstwood.

"Oh, no one," said Jessica, pursing her pretty lips. "He's just a student there. He hasn't anything."

The other half of this picture came when young Blyford, son of Blyford, the soap manufacturer, walked home with her. Mrs. Hurstwood was on the third floor, sitting in a rocking-chair reading, and happened to look out at the time.

"Who was that with you, Jessica?" she inquired, as Jessica came upstairs.

"It's Mr. Blyford, mamma," she replied.

"Is it?" said Mrs. Hurstwood.

"Yes, and he wants me to stroll over into the park with him," explained Jessica, a little flushed with running up the stairs.

"All right, my dear," said Mrs. Hurstwood. "Don't be gone long."

As the two went down the street, she glanced interestedly out of the window. It was a most satisfactory spectacle indeed, most satisfactory.

In this atmosphere Hurstwood had moved for a number of years, not thinking deeply concerning it. His was not the order of nature to trouble for something better, unless the better was immediately and sharply contrasted. As it was, he received and gave, irritated sometimes by the little displays of selfish indifference, pleased at times by some show of finery which supposedly made for dignity and social distinction. The life of the resort which he managed was his life. There he spent most of his time. When he went home evenings the house looked nice. With rare exceptions the meals were acceptable, being the kind that an ordinary servant can arrange. In part, he was interested in the talk of his son and daughter, who always looked well. The vanity of Mrs. Hurstwood caused her to keep her person rather showily arrayed, but to Hurstwood this was much better than plainness. There was no love lost between them. There was no great feeling of dissatisfaction. Her opinion on any subject was not startling. They did not talk enough together to come to the argument of any one point. In the accepted and popular phrase, she had her ideas and he had his. Once in a while he would meet a woman whose youth, sprightliness, and humor would make his wife seem rather deficient by contrast, but the temporary dissatisfaction which such an encounter might arouse would be counterbalanced by his social position and a certain matter of policy. He could not complicate his home life, because it might affect his relations with his employers. They wanted no scandals. A man, to hold his position, must have a dignified manner, a clean record, a respectable home anchorage. Therefore he was circumspect in all he did, and whenever he appeared in the public ways in the afternoon, or on Sunday, it was with his wife, and sometimes his children. He would visit the local resorts, or those near by in Wisconsin, and spend a few stiff, polished days strolling about conventional places doing conventional things. He knew the need of it.

When some one of the many middle-class individuals whom he knew, who had money, would get into trouble, he would shake his head. It didn't do to talk about those things. If it came up for discussion among such friends as with him passed for close, he would deprecate the folly of the thing. "It was all right to do it—all men do those things—but why wasn't he careful? A man can't be too careful." He lost sympathy for the man that made a mistake and was found out.

On this account he still devoted some time to showing his wife about—time which would have been wearisome indeed if it had not been for the people he would meet and the little enjoyments which did not depend upon her presence or absence. He watched her with considerable curiosity at times, for she was still attractive in a way and men looked at her. She was affable, vain, subject to flattery, and this combination, he knew quite well, might produce a tragedy in a woman of her home position. Owing to his order of mind, his confidence in the sex was not great. His wife never possessed the virtues which would win the confidence and admiration of a man of his nature. As long as she loved him vigorously he could see how confidence could be, but when that was no longer the binding chain—well, something might happen.

During the last year or two the expenses of the family seemed a large thing. Jessica wanted fine clothes, and Mrs. Hurstwood, not to be outshone by her daughter, also frequently enlivened her apparel. Hurstwood had said nothing in the past, but one day he murmured.

"Jessica must have a new dress this month," said Mrs. Hurstwood one morning.

Hurstwood was arraying himself in one of his perfection vests before the glass at the time.

"I thought she just bought one," he said.

"That was just something for evening wear," returned his wife complacently.

"It seems to me," returned Hurstwood, "that she's spending a good deal for dresses of late."

"Well, she's going out more," concluded his wife, but the tone of his voice impressed her as containing something she had not heard there before.

He was not a man who traveled much, but when he did, he had been accustomed to take her along. On one occasion recently a local aldermanic junket had been arranged to visit Philadelphia—a junket that was to last ten days. Hurstwood had been invited.

"Nobody knows us down there," said one, a gentleman whose face was a slight improvement over gross ignorance and sensuality. He always wore a silk hat of most imposing proportions. "We can have a good time." His left eye moved with just the semblance of a wink. "You want to come along, George."

The next day Hurstwood announced his intention to his wife.

"I'm going away, Julia," he said, "for a few days."

"Where?" she asked, looking up.

"To Philadelphia, on business."

She looked at him consciously, expecting something else.

"I'll have to leave you behind this time."

"All right," she replied, but he could see that she was thinking that it was a curious thing. Before he went she asked him a few more questions, and that irritated him. He began to feel that she was a disagreeable attachment.

On this trip he enjoyed himself thoroughly, and when it was over he was sorry to get back. He was not willingly a prevaricator, and hated thoroughly to make explanations concerning it. The whole incident was glossed over with general remarks, but Mrs. Hurstwood gave the subject considerable thought. She drove out more, dressed better, and attended theaters freely to make up for it.

Such an atmosphere could hardly come under the category of home life. It ran along by force of habit, by force of conventional opinion. With the lapse of time it must necessarily become dryer and dryer—must eventually be tinder, easily lighted and destroyed.

CHAPTER X

THE COUNSEL OF WINTER: FORTUNE'S AMBASSADOR CALLS

In the light of the world's attitude toward woman and her duties, the nature of Carrie's mental state deserves consideration. Actions such as hers are measured by an arbitrary scale. Society possesses a conventional standard whereby it judges all things. All men should be good, all women virtuous. Wherefore, villain, hast thou failed?

For all the liberal analysis of Spencer and our modern naturalistic philosophers, we have but an infantile perception of morals. There is more in the subject than mere conformity to a law of evolution. It is yet deeper than conformity to things of earth alone. It is more involved than we, as yet, perceive. Answer, first, why the heart thrills; explain wherefore some plaintive note goes wandering about the world, undying; make clear the rose's subtle alchemy evolving its ruddy lamp in light and rain. In the essence of these facts lie the first principles of morals.

"Oh," thought Drouet, "how delicious is my conquest."

"Ah," thought Carrie, with mournful misgivings, "what is it I have lost?"

Before this world-old proposition we stand, serious, interested, confused; endeavoring to evolve the true theory of morals—the true answer to what is right.

In the view of a certain stratum of society, Carrie was comfortably established—in the eyes of the starveling, beaten by every wind and gusty sheet of rain, she was safe in a halcyon harbor. Drouet had taken three rooms, furnished, in Ogden Place, facing Union Park, on the West Side. That was a little, green-carpeted breathing spot, than which, to-day, there is nothing more beautiful in Chicago. It afforded a vista pleasant to contemplate. The best room looked out upon the lawn of the park, now sear and brown, where a little lake lay sheltered. Over the bare limbs of the trees, which now swayed in the wintry wind, rose the steeple of the Union Park Congregational Church, and far off the towers of several others.

The rooms were comfortably enough furnished. There was a good Brussels carpet on the floor, rich in dull red and lemon shades, and representing large jardinières filled with gorgeous, impossible flowers. There was a large pier-glass mirror between the two windows. A large, soft, green, plush-covered couch occupied one corner, and several rocking-chairs were set about. Some pictures, several rugs, a few small pieces of bric-a-brac, and the tale of contents is told.

In the bedroom, off the front room, was Carrie's trunk, bought by Drouet, and in the wardrobe built into the wall quite an array of clothing—more than she had ever possessed before, and of very becoming designs. There was a third room for possible use as a kitchen, where Drouet had Carrie establish a little portable gas stove for the preparation of small lunches, oysters, Welsh rarebits, and the like, of which he was exceedingly fond; and, lastly, a bath. The whole place was cosy, in that it was lighted by gas and heated by furnace registers, possessing also a small grate, set with an asbestos back, a method of cheerful warming which was then first coming into use. By her industry and natural love of order, which now developed, the place maintained an air pleasing in the extreme.

Here, then, was Carrie, established in a pleasant fashion, free of certain difficulties, which most ominously confronted her, laden with many new ones which were of a mental order, and altogether so turned about in all of her earthly relationships that she might well have been a new and different individual. She looked into her glass and saw a prettier Carrie than she had seen before; she looked into her mind, a mirror prepared of her own and the world's opinions, and saw a worse. Between these two images she wavered, hesitating which to believe.

"My, but you're a little beauty," Drouet was wont to exclaim to her.

She would look at him with large, pleased eyes.

"You know it, don't you?" he would continue.

"Oh, I don't know," she would reply, feeling delight in the fact that one should think so, hesitating to believe, though she really did, that she was vain enough to think so much of herself.

Her conscience, however, was not a Drouet, interested to praise. There she heard a different voice, with which she argued, pleaded, excused. It was no just and sapient counselor, in its last analysis. It was only an average little conscience, a thing which represented the world, her past environment, habit, convention, in a confused way. With it, the voice of the people was truly the voice of God.

"Oh, thou failure!" said the voice.

"Why?" she questioned.

"Look at those about," came the whispered answer. "Look at those who are good. How would they scorn to do what you have done. Look at the good girls; how will they draw away from such as you when they know you have been weak. You had not tried before you failed."

It was when Carrie was alone, looking out across the park, that she would be listening to this. It would come infrequently—when something else did not interfere, when the pleasant side was not too apparent, when Drouet was not there. It was somewhat clear in utterance at first, but never wholly convincing. There was always an answer, always the December days threatened. She was alone; she was desireful; she was fearful of the whistling wind. The voice of want made answer for her.

Once the bright days of summer pass by, a city takes on that somber garb of gray, wrapt in which it goes about its labors during the long winter. Its endless buildings look gray, its sky and its streets assume a somber hue; the scattered, leafless trees and wind-blown dust and paper but add to the general solemnity of color. There seems to be something in the chill breezes which scurry through the long, narrow thoroughfares productive of rueful thoughts. Not poets alone, nor artists, nor that superior order of mind which arrogates to itself all refinement, feel this, but dogs and all men. These feel as much as the poet, though they have not the same power of expression. The sparrow upon the wire, the cat in the doorway, the dray horse tugging his weary load, feel the long, keen breaths of winter. It strikes to the heart of all life, animate and inanimate. If it were not for the artificial fires of merriment, the rush of profit-seeking trade, and pleasure-selling amusements; if the various merchants failed to make the customary display within and without their establishments; if our streets were not strung with signs of gorgeous hues and thronged with hurrying purchasers, we would quickly discover how firmly the chill hand of winter lays upon the heart; how dispiriting are the days during which the sun withholds a portion of our allowance of light and warmth. We are more dependent upon these things than is often thought. We are insects produced by heat, and pass without it.

In the drag of such a gray day the secret voice would reassert itself, feebly and more feebly.

Such mental conflict was not always uppermost. Carrie was not by any means a gloomy soul. More, she had not the mind to get firm hold upon a definite truth. When she could not find her way out of the labyrinth of ill-logic which thought upon the subject created, she would turn away entirely.

Drouet, all the time, was conducting himself in a model way for one of his sort. He took her about a great deal, spent money upon her, and when he traveled took her with him. There were times when she would be alone for two or three days, while he made the shorter circuits of his business, but, as a rule, she saw a great deal of him.

"Say, Carrie," he said one morning, shortly after they had so established themselves, "I've invited my friend Hurstwood to come out some day and spend the evening with us."

"Who is he?" asked Carrie, doubtfully.

"Oh, he's a nice man. He's manager of Fitzgerald and Moy's."

"What's that?" said Carrie.

"The finest resort in town. It's a way-up, swell place."

Carrie puzzled a moment. She was wondering what Drouet had told him, what her attitude would be.

"That's all right," said Drouet, feeling her thought. "He doesn't know anything. You're Mrs. Drouet now."

There was something about this which struck Carrie as slightly inconsiderate. She could see that Drouet did not have the keenest sensibilities.

"Why don't we get married?" she inquired, thinking of the voluble promises he had made.

"Well, we will," he said, "just as soon as I get this little deal of mine closed up."

He was referring to some property which he said he had, and which required so much attention, adjustment, and what not, that somehow or other it interfered with his free moral, personal actions.

"Just as soon as I get back from my Denver trip in January we'll do it."

Carrie accepted this as basis for hope—it was a sort of salve to her conscience, a pleasant way out. Under the circumstances, things would be righted. Her actions would be justified.

She really was not enamored of Drouet. She was more clever than he. In a dim way, she was beginning to see where he lacked. If it had not been for this, if she had not been able to measure and judge him in a way, she would have been worse off than she was. She would have adored him. She would have been utterly wretched in her fear of not gaining his affection, of losing his interest, of being swept away and left without an anchorage. As it was, she wavered a little, slightly anxious, at first, to gain him completely, but later feeling at ease in waiting. She was not exactly sure what she thought of him—what she wanted to do.

When Hurstwood called, she met a man who was more clever than Drouet in a hundred ways. He paid that peculiar deference to women which every member of the sex appreciates. He was not overawed, he was not overbold. His great charm was attentiveness. Schooled in winning those birds of fine feather among his own sex, the merchants and professionals who visited his resort, he could use even greater tact when endeavoring to prove agreeable to some one who charmed him.

In a pretty woman of any refinement of feeling whatsoever he found his greatest incentive. He was mild, placid, assured, giving the impression that he wished to be of service only—to do something which would make the lady more pleased.

Drouet had ability in this line himself when the game was worth the candle, but he was too much the egotist to reach the polish which Hurstwood possessed. He was too buoyant, too full of ruddy life, too assured. He succeeded with many who were not quite schooled in the art of love. He failed dismally where the woman was slightly experienced and possessed innate refinement. In the case of Carrie he found a woman who was all of the latter, but none of the former. He was lucky in the fact that opportunity tumbled into his lap, as it were. A few years later, with a little more experience, the slightest tide of success, and he had not been able to approach Carrie at all.

"You ought to have a piano here, Drouet," said Hurstwood, smiling at Carrie, on the evening in question, "so that your wife could play."

Drouet had not thought of that.

"So we ought," he observed readily.

"Oh, I don't play," ventured Carrie.

"It isn't very difficult," returned Hurstwood. "You could do very well in a few weeks."

He was in the best form for entertaining this evening. His clothes were particularly new and rich in appearance. The coat lapels stood out with that medium stiffness which excellent cloth possesses. The vest was of a rich Scotch plaid, set with a double row of round mother-of-pearl buttons. His cravat was a shiny combination of silken threads, not loud, not inconspicuous. What he wore did not strike the eye so forcibly as that which Drouet had on, but Carrie could see the elegance of the material. Hurstwood's shoes were of soft, black calf, polished only to a dull shine. Drouet wore patent leather, but Carrie could not help feeling that there was a distinction in favor of the soft leather, where all else was so rich. She noticed these things almost unconsciously. They were things which would naturally flow from the situation. She was used to Drouet's appearance.

"Suppose we have a little game of euchre?" suggested Hurstwood, after a light round of conversation. He was rather dexterous in avoiding everything that would suggest that he knew anything of Carrie's past. He kept away from personalities altogether, and confined himself to those things which did not concern individuals at all. By his manner, he put Carrie at her ease, and by his deference and pleasantries he amused her. He pretended to be seriously interested in all she said.

"I don't know how to play," said Carrie.

"Charlie, you are neglecting a part of your duty," he observed to Drouet most affably. "Between us, though," he went on, "we can show you."

By his tact he made Drouet feel that he admired his choice. There was something in his manner that showed that he was pleased to be there. Drouet felt really closer to him than ever before. It gave him more respect for Carrie. Her appearance came into a new light, under Hurstwood's appreciation. The situation livened considerably.

"Now, let me see," said Hurstwood, looking over Carrie's shoulder very deferentially. "What have you?" He studied for a moment. "That's rather good," he said.

"You're lucky. Now, I'll show you how to trounce your husband. You take my advice."

"Here," said Drouet, "if you two are going to scheme together, I won't stand a ghost of a show. Hurstwood's a regular sharp."

"No, it's your wife. She brings me luck. Why shouldn't she win?"

Carrie looked gratefully at Hurstwood, and smiled at Drouet. The former took the air of a mere friend. He was simply there to enjoy himself. Anything that Carrie did was pleasing to him, nothing more.

"There," he said, holding back one of his own good cards, and giving Carrie a chance to take a trick. "I count that clever playing for a beginner."

The latter laughed gleefully as she saw the hand coming her way. It was as if she were invincible when Hurstwood helped her.

He did not look at her often. When he did, it was with a mild light in his eye. Not a shade was there of anything save geniality and kindness. He took back the shifty, clever gleam, and replaced it with one of innocence. Carrie could not guess but that it was pleasure with him in the immediate thing. She felt that he considered she was doing a great deal.

"It's unfair to let such playing go without earning something," he said after a time, slipping his finger into the little coin pocket of his coat. "Let's play for dimes."

"All right," said Drouet, fishing for bills.

Hurstwood was quicker. His fingers were full of new ten-cent pieces. "Here we are," he said, supplying each one with a little stack.

"Oh, this is gambling," smiled Carrie. "It's bad."

"No," said Drouet, "only fun. If you never play for more than that, you will go to Heaven."

"Don't you moralize," said Hurstwood to Carrie gently, "until you see what becomes of the money."

Drouet smiled.

"If your husband gets them, he'll tell you how bad it is."

Drouet laughed loud.

There was such an ingratiating tone about Hurstwood's voice, the insinuation was so perceptible that even Carrie got the humor of it.

"When do you leave?" said Hurstwood to Drouet.

"On Wednesday," he replied.

"It's rather hard to have your husband running about like that, isn't it?" said Hurstwood, addressing Carrie.

"She's going along with me this time," said Drouet.

"You must both go with me to the theater before you go."

"Certainly," said Drouet. "Eh, Carrie?"

"I'd like it ever so much," she replied.

Hurstwood did his best to see that Carrie won the money. He rejoiced in her success, kept counting her winnings, and finally gathered and put them in her extended hand. They spread a little lunch, at which he served the wine, and afterwards he used fine tact in going.

"Now," he said, addressing first Carrie and then Drouet with his eyes, "you must be ready at 7:30. I'll come and get you."

They went with him to the door and there was his cab waiting, its red lamps gleaming cheerfully in the shadow.

"Now," he observed to Drouet, with a tone of good-fellowship, "when you leave your wife alone, you must let me show her around a little. It will break up her loneliness."

"Sure," said Drouet, quite pleased at the attention shown.

"You're so kind," observed Carrie.

"Not at all," said Hurstwood, "I would want your husband to do as much for me."

He smiled and went lightly away. Carrie was thoroughly impressed. She had never come in contact with such grace. As for Drouet, he was equally pleased.

"There's a nice man," he remarked to Carrie, as they returned to their cozy chamber. "A good friend of mine, too."

"He seems to be," said Carrie.

CHAPTER XI

The Persuasion of Fashion: Feeling Guards O'er Its Own

Carrie was an apt student of fortune's ways—of fortune's superficialities. Seeing a thing, she would immediately set to inquiring how she would look, properly related to it. Be it known that this is not fine feeling, it is not wisdom. The greatest minds are not so afflicted; and, on the contrary, the lowest order of mind is not so disturbed. Fine clothes to her were a vast persuasion; they spoke tenderly and Jesuitically for themselves. When she came within earshot of their pleading, desire in her bent a willing ear. The voice of the so-called inanimate! Who shall translate for us the language of the stones?

"My dear," said the lace collar she secured from Partridge's, "I fit you beautifully; don't give me up."

"Ah, such little feet," said the leather of the soft new shoes; "how effectively I cover them. What a pity they should ever want my aid."

Once these things were in her hand, on her person, she might dream of giving them up; the method by which they came might intrude itself so forcibly that she would ache to be rid of the thought of it, but she would not give them up. "Put on the old clothes—that torn pair of shoes," was called to her by her conscience in vain. She could possibly have conquered the fear of hunger and gone back; the thought of hard work and a narrow round of suffering would, under the last pressure of conscience, have yielded, but spoil her appearance?—be old-clothed and poor-appearing?—never!

Drouet heightened her opinion on this and allied subjects in such a manner as to weaken her power of resisting their influence. It is so easy to do this when the thing opined is in the line of what we desire. In his hearty way, he insisted upon her good looks. He looked at her admiringly, and she took it at its full value. Under the circumstances, she did not need to carry herself as pretty women do. She picked that knowledge up fast enough for herself. Drouet had a habit, characteristic of his kind, of looking after stylishly dressed or pretty women on the street and remarking upon them. He had just enough of the feminine love of dress to be a good judge—not of intellect, but of clothes. He saw how they set their little feet, how they carried their chins, with what grace and sinuosity they swung their bodies. A dainty, self-conscious swaying of the hips by a woman was to him as alluring as the glint of rare wine to a toper. He would turn and follow the disappearing vision with his eyes. He would thrill as a child with the unhindered passion that was in him. He loved the thing that women love in themselves, grace. At this, their own shrine, he knelt with them, an ardent devotee.

"Did you see that woman who went by just now?" he said to Carrie on the first day they took a walk together. "Fine stepper, wasn't she?"

Carrie looked, and observed the grace commended.

"Yes, she is," she returned, cheerfully, a little suggestion of possible defect in herself awakening in her mind. If that was so fine, she must look at it more closely. Instinctively, she felt a desire to imitate it. Surely she could do that too.

When one of her mind sees many things emphasized and reemphasized and admired, she gathers the logic of it and applies accordingly. Drouet was not shrewd enough to see that this was not tactful. He could not see that it would be better to make her feel that she was competing with herself, not others better than herself. He would not have done it with an older, wiser woman, but in Carrie he saw only the novice. Less clever than she, he was naturally unable to comprehend her sensibility. He went on educating and wounding her, a thing rather foolish in one whose admiration for his pupil and victim was apt to grow.

Carrie took the instructions affably. She saw what Drouet liked; in a vague way she saw where he was weak. It lessens a woman's opinion of a man when she learns that his admiration is so pointedly and generously distributed. She sees but one object of supreme compliment in this world, and that is herself. If a man is to succeed with many women, he must be all in all to each.

In her own apartments Carrie saw things which were lessons in the same school.

In the same house with her lived an official of one of the theaters, Mr. Frank A. Hale, manager of the Standard, and his wife, a pleasing-looking brunette of thirty-five. They were people of a sort very common in America today, who live respectably from hand to mouth. Hale received a salary of forty-five dollars a week. His wife, quite attractive, affected the feeling of youth, and objected to that sort of home life which means the care of a house and the raising of a family. Like Drouet and Carrie, they also occupied three rooms on the floor above.

Not long after she arrived Mrs. Hale established social relations with her, and together they went about. For a long time this was her only companionship, and the gossip of the manager's wife formed the medium through which she saw the world. Such trivialities, such praises of wealth, such conventional expression of morals as sifted through this passive creature's mind, fell upon Carrie and for the while confused her.

On the other hand, her own feelings were a corrective influence. The constant drag to something better was not to be denied. By those things which address the heart was she steadily recalled. In the apartments across the hall were a young girl and her mother. They were from Evansville, Indiana, the wife and daughter of a railroad treasurer. The daughter was here to study music, the mother to keep her company.

Carrie did not make their acquaintance, but she saw the daughter coming in and going out. A few times she had seen her at the piano in the parlor, and not infrequently had heard her play. This young woman was particularly dressy for her station, and wore a jeweled ring or two which flashed upon her white fingers as she played.

Now Carrie was affected by music. Her nervous composition responded to certain strains, much as certain strings of a harp vibrate when a corresponding key of a piano is struck. She was delicately molded in sentiment, and answered with vague ruminations to certain wistful chords. They awoke longings for those things which she did not have. They caused her to cling closer to things she possessed. One short song the young lady played in a most soulful and tender mood. Carrie heard it through the open door from the parlor below. It was at that hour between afternoon and night when, for the idle, the wanderer, things are apt to take on a wistful aspect. The mind wanders forth on far journeys and returns with sheaves of withered and departed joys. Carrie sat at her window looking out.

Drouet had been away since ten in the morning. She had amused herself with a walk, a book by Bertha M. Clay which Drouet had left there, though she did not wholly enjoy the latter, and by changing her dress for the evening. Now she sat looking out across the park as wistful and depressed as the nature which craves variety and life can be under such circumstances. As she contemplated her new state, the strain from the parlor below stole upward. With it her thoughts became colored and enmeshed. She reverted to the things which were best and saddest within the small limit of her experience. She became for the moment a repentant.

While she was in this mood Drouet came in, bringing with him an entirely different atmosphere. It was dusk and Carrie had neglected to light the lamp. The fire in the grate, too, had burned low.

"Where are you, Cad?" he said, using a pet name he had given her.

"Here," she answered.

There was something delicate and lonely in her voice, but he could not hear it. He had not the poetry in him that would seek a woman out under such circumstances and console her for the tragedy of life. Instead, he struck a match and lighted the gas.

"Hello," he exclaimed, "you've been crying."

Her eyes were still wet with a few vague tears.

"Pshaw," he said, "you don't want to do that."

He took her hand, feeling in his good-natured egotism that it was probably lack of his presence which had made her lonely.

"Come on, now," he went on; "it's all right. Let's waltz a little to that music."

He could not have introduced a more incongruous proposition. It made clear to Carrie that he could not sympathize with her. She could not have framed thoughts which would have expressed his defect or made clear the difference between them, but she felt it. It was his first great mistake.

What Drouet said about the girl's grace, as she tripped out evenings accompanied by her mother, caused Carrie to perceive the nature and value of those little modish ways which women adopt when they would presume to be something. She looked in the mirror and pursed up her lips, accompanying it with a little toss of the head, as she had seen the railroad treasurer's daughter do. She caught up her skirts with an easy swing, for had not Drouet remarked that in her and several others, and Carrie was naturally imitative. She began to get the hang of those little things which the pretty woman who has vanity invariably adopts. In short, her knowledge of grace doubled, and with it her appearance changed. She became a girl of considerable taste.

Drouet noticed this. He saw the new bow in her hair and the new way of arranging her locks which she affected one morning.

"You look fine that way, Cad," he said.

"Do I?" she replied, sweetly. It made her try for other effects that selfsame day.

She used her feet less heavily, a thing that was brought about by her attempting to imitate the treasurer's daughter's graceful carriage. How much influence the presence of that young woman in the same house had upon her it would be difficult to say. But, because of all these things, when Hurstwood called he had found a young woman who was much more than the Carrie to whom Drouet had first spoken. The primary defects of dress and manner had passed. She was pretty, graceful, rich in the timidity born of uncertainty, and with a something childlike in her large eyes which captured the fancy of this starched and conventional poser among men. It was the ancient attraction of the fresh for the stale. If there was a touch of appreciation left in him for the bloom and unsophistication which is the charm of youth, it rekindled now. He looked into her pretty face and felt the subtle waves of young life radiating therefrom. In that large clear eye he could see nothing that his *blasé* nature could understand as guile. The little vanity, if he could have perceived it there, would have touched him as a pleasant thing.

"I wonder," he said, as he rode away in his cab, "how Drouet came to win her."

He gave her credit for feelings superior to Drouet at the first glance.

The cab plopped along between the far-receding lines of gas lamps on either hand. He folded his gloved hands and saw only the lighted chamber and Carrie's face. He was pondering over the delight of youthful beauty.

"I'll have a bouquet for her," he thought. "Drouet won't mind."

He never for a moment concealed the fact of her attraction for himself. He troubled himself not at all about Drouet's priority. He was merely floating those gossamer threads of thought which, like the spider's, he hoped would lay hold somewhere. He did not know, he could not guess, what the result would be.

A few weeks later Drouet, in his peregrinations, encountered one of his well-dressed lady acquaintances in Chicago on his return from a short trip to Omaha. He had intended to hurry out to Ogden Place and surprise Carrie, but now he fell into an interesting conversation and soon modified his original intention.

"Let's go to dinner," he said, little recking any chance meeting which might trouble his way.

"Certainly," said his companion.

They visited one of the better restaurants for a social chat. It was five in the afternoon when they met; it was seven-thirty before the last bone was picked.

Drouet was just finishing a little incident he was relating, and his face was expanding into a smile, when Hurstwood's eye caught his own. The latter had come in with several friends, and, seeing Drouet and some woman, not Carrie, drew his own conclusion.

"Ah, the rascal," he thought, and then, with a touch of righteous sympathy, "that's pretty hard on the little girl."

Drouet jumped from one easy thought to another as he caught Hurstwood's eye. He felt but very little misgiving, until he saw that Hurstwood was cautiously pretending not to see. Then some of the latter's impression forced itself upon him. He thought of Carrie and their last meeting. By George, he would have to explain this to Hurstwood. Such a chance half-hour with an old friend must not have anything more attached to it than it really warranted.

For the first time he was troubled. Here was a moral complication of which he could not possibly get the ends. Hurstwood would laugh at him for being a fickle boy. He would laugh with Hurstwood. Carrie would never hear, his present companion at table would never know, and yet he could not help feeling that he was getting the worst of it—there was some faint stigma attached, and he was not guilty. He broke up the dinner by becoming dull, and saw his companion on her car. Then he went home.

"He hasn't talked to me about any of these later flames," thought Hurstwood to himself. "He thinks I think he cares for the girl out there."

"He ought not to think I'm knocking around, since I have just introduced him out there," thought Drouet.

"I saw you," Hurstwood said, genially, the next time Drouet drifted in to his polished resort, from which he could not stay away. He raised his forefinger indicatively, as parents do to children.

"An old acquaintance of mine that I ran into just as I was coming up from the station," explained Drouet. "She used to be quite a beauty."

"Still attracts a little, eh?" returned the other, affecting to jest.

"Oh, no," said Drouet, "just couldn't escape her this time."

"How long are you here?" asked Hurstwood.

"Only a few days."

"You must bring the girl down and take dinner with me," he said. "I'm afraid you keep her cooped up out there. I'll get a box for Joe Jefferson."

"Not me," answered the drummer. "Sure I'll come."

This pleased Hurstwood immensely. He gave Drouet no credit for any feelings toward Carrie whatever. He envied him, and now, as he looked at the well-dressed jolly salesman, whom he so much liked, the gleam of the rival glowed in his eye. He began to "size up" Drouet from the standpoints of wit and fascination. He began to look to see where he was weak. There was no disputing that, whatever he might think of him as a good fellow, he felt a certain amount of contempt for him as a lover. He could hoodwink him all right. Why, if he would just let Carrie see one such little incident as that of Thursday, it would settle the matter. He ran on in thought, almost exulting, the while he laughed and chatted, and Drouet felt nothing. He had no power of analyzing the glance and the atmosphere of a man like Hurstwood. He stood and smiled and accepted the invitation while his friend examined him with the eye of a hawk.

The object of this peculiarly involved comedy was not thinking of either. She was busy adjusting her thoughts and feelings to newer conditions, and was not in danger of suffering disturbing pangs from either quarter.

One evening Drouet found her dressing herself before the glass.

"Cad," said he, catching her, "I believe you're getting vain."

"Nothing of the kind," she returned, smiling.

"Well, you're mighty pretty," he went on, slipping his arm around her. "Put on that navy-blue dress of yours and I'll take you to the show."

"Oh, I've promised Mrs. Hale to go with her to the Exposition to-night," she returned, apologetically.

"You did, eh?" he said, studying the situation abstractedly. "I wouldn't care to go to that myself."

"Well, I don't know," answered Carrie, puzzling, but not offering to break her promise in his favor.

Just then a knock came at their door and the maid-servant handed a letter in.

"He says there's an answer expected," she explained.

"It's from Hurstwood," said Drouet, noting the superscription as he tore it open.

"You are to come down and see Joe Jefferson with me to-night," it ran in part. "It's my turn, as we agreed the other day. All other bets are off."

"Well, what do you say to this?" asked Drouet, innocently, while Carrie's mind bubbled with favorable replies.

"You had better decide, Charlie," she said, reservedly.

"I guess we had better go, if you can break that engagement upstairs," said Drouet.

"Oh, I can," returned Carrie without thinking.

Drouet selected writing paper while Carrie went to change her dress. She hardly explained to herself why this latest invitation appealed to her most.

"Shall I wear my hair as I did yesterday?" she asked, as she came out with several articles of apparel pending.

"Sure," he returned, pleasantly.

She was relieved to see that he felt nothing. She did not credit her willingness to go to any fascination Hurstwood held for her. It seemed that the combination of Hurstwood, Drouet, and herself was more agreeable than anything else that had been suggested. She arrayed herself most carefully and they started off, extending excuses upstairs.

"I say," said Hurstwood, as they came up the theater lobby, "we are exceedingly charming this evening."

Carrie fluttered under his approving glance.

"Now, then," he said, leading the way up the foyer into the theater.

If ever there was dressiness it was here. It was the personification of the old term spick and span.

"Did you ever see Jefferson?" he questioned, as he leaned toward Carrie in the box.

"I never did," she returned.

"He's delightful, delightful," he went on, giving the commonplace rendition of approval which such men know. He sent Drouet after a program, and then discoursed to Carrie concerning Jefferson as he had heard of him. The former was pleased beyond expression, and was really hypnotized by the environment, the trappings of the box, the elegance of her companion. Several times their eyes accidentally met, and then there poured into hers such a flood of feeling as she had never before experienced. She could not for the moment explain it, for in the next glance or the next move of the hand there was seeming indifference, mingled only with the kindest attention.

Drouet shared in the conversation, but he was almost dull in comparison. Hurstwood entertained them both, and now it was driven into Carrie's mind that here was the superior man. She instinctively felt that he was stronger and higher, and yet withal so simple. By the end of the third act she was sure that Drouet was only a kindly soul, but otherwise defective. He sank every moment in her estimation by the strong comparison.

"I have had such a nice time," said Carrie, when it was all over and they were coming out.

"Yes, indeed," added Drouet, who was not in the least aware that a battle had been fought and his defenses weakened. He was like the Emperor of China, who sat glorying in himself, unaware that his fairest provinces were being wrested from him.

"Well, you have saved me a dreary evening," returned Hurstwood. "Good-night."

He took Carrie's little hand, and a current of feeling swept from one to the other.

"I'm so tired," said Carrie, leaning back in the car when Drouet began to talk.

"Well, you rest a little while I smoke," he said, rising, and then he foolishly went to the forward platform of the car and left the game as it stood.

CHAPTER XII

Of the Lamps of the Mansions: The Ambassador Plea

Mrs. Hurstwood was not aware of any of her husband's moral defections, though she might readily have suspected his tendencies, which she well understood. She was a woman upon whose action under provocation you could never count. Hurstwood, for one, had not the slightest idea of what she would do under certain circumstances. He had never seen her thoroughly aroused. In fact, she was not a woman who would fly into a passion. She had too little faith in mankind not to know that they were erring. She was too calculating to jeopardize any advantage she might gain in the way of information by fruitless clamor. Her wrath would never wreak itself in one fell blow. She would wait and brood, studying the details and adding to them until her power might be commensurate with her desire for revenge. At the same time, she would not delay to inflict any injury, big or little, which would wound the object of her revenge and still leave him uncertain as to the source of the evil. She was a cold, self-centered woman, with many a thought of her own which never found expression, not even by so much as the glint of an eye.

Hurstwood felt some of this in her nature, though he did not actually perceive it. He dwelt with her in peace and some satisfaction. He did not fear her in the least—there was no cause for it. She still took a faint pride in him, which was augmented by her desire to have her social integrity maintained. She was secretly somewhat pleased by the fact that much of her husband's property was in her name, a precaution which Hurstwood had taken when his home interests were somewhat more alluring than at present. His wife had not the slightest reason to feel that anything would ever go amiss with their household, and yet the shadows which run before gave her a thought of the good of it now and then. She was in a position to become refractory with considerable advantage, and Hurstwood conducted himself circumspectly because he felt that he could not be sure of anything once she became dissatisfied.

It so happened that on the night when Hurstwood, Carrie, and Drouet were in the box at McVickar's, George, Jr., was in the sixth row of the parquet with the daughter of H. B. Carmichael, the third partner of a wholesale dry-goods house of that city. Hurstwood did not see his son, for he sat, as was his wont, as far back as possible, leaving himself just partially visible, when he bent forward, to those within the first six rows in question. It was his wont to sit this way in every theater—to make his personality as inconspicuous as possible where it would be no advantage to him to have it otherwise.

He never moved but what, if there was any danger of his conduct being misconstrued or ill-reported, he looked carefully about him and counted the cost of every inch of conspicuity.

The next morning at breakfast his son said:

"I saw you, Governor, last night."

"Were you at McVickar's?" said Hurstwood, with the best grace in the world.

"Yes," said young George.

"Who with?"

"Miss Carmichael."

Mrs. Hurstwood directed an inquiring glance at her husband, but could not judge from his appearance whether it was any more than a casual look into the theater which was referred to.

"How was the play?" she inquired.

"Very good," returned Hurstwood, "only it's the same old thing, 'Rip Van Winkle.'"

"Whom did you go with?" queried his wife, with assumed indifference.

"Charlie Drouet and his wife. They are friends of Moy's, visiting here."

Owing to the peculiar nature of his position, such a disclosure as this would ordinarily create no difficulty. His wife took it for granted that his situation called for certain social movements in which she might not be included. But of late he had pleaded office duty on several occasions when his wife asked for his company to an evening entertainment. He had done so in regard to the very evening in question only the morning before.

"I thought you were going to be busy," she remarked, very carefully.

"So I was," he exclaimed. "I couldn't help the interruption, but I made up for it afterward by working until two."

This settled the discussion for the time being, but there was a residue of opinion which was not satisfactory. There was no time at which the claims of his wife could have been more unsatisfactorily pushed. For years he had been steadily modifying his matrimonial devotion, and found her company dull. Now that a new light shone upon the horizon, this older luminary paled in the west. He was satisfied to turn his face away entirely, and any call to look back was irksome.

She, on the contrary, was not at all inclined to accept anything less than a complete fulfillment of the letter of their relationship, though the spirit might be wanting.

"We are coming down town this afternoon," she remarked, a few days later. "I want you to come over to Kinsley's and meet Mr. Phillips and his wife. They're stopping at the Tremont, and we're going to show them around a little."

After the occurrence of Wednesday, he could not refuse, though the Phillips were about as uninteresting as vanity and ignorance could make them. He agreed, but it was with short grace. He was angry when he left the house.

"I'll put a stop to this," he thought. "I'm not going to be bothered fooling around with visitors when I have work to do."

Not long after this Mrs. Hurstwood came with a similar proposition, only it was to a matinee this time.

"My dear," he returned, "I haven't time. I'm too busy."

"You find time to go with other people, though," she replied, with considerable irritation.

"Nothing of the kind," he answered. "I can't avoid business relations, and that's all there is to it."

"Well, never mind," she exclaimed. Her lips tightened. The feeling of mutual antagonism was increased.

On the other hand, his interest in Drouet's little shop-girl grew in an almost evenly balanced proportion. That young lady, under the stress of her situation and the tutelage of her new friend, changed effectively. She had the aptitude of the struggler who seeks emancipation. The glow of a more showy life was not lost upon her. She did not grow in knowledge so much as she awakened in the matter of desire. Mrs. Hale's extended harangues upon the subjects of wealth and position taught her to distinguish between degrees of wealth.

Mrs. Hale loved to drive in the afternoon in the sun when it was fine, and to satisfy her soul with a sight of those mansions and lawns which she could not afford. On the North Side had been erected a number of elegant mansions along what is now known as the North Shore Drive. The present lake wall of stone and granitoid was not then in place, but the road had been well laid out, the intermediate spaces of lawn were lovely to look upon, and the houses were thoroughly new and imposing. When the winter season had passed and the first fine days of the early spring appeared, Mrs. Hale secured a buggy for an afternoon and invited Carrie. They rode first through Lincoln Park and on far out towards Evanston, turning back at four and arriving at the north end of the Shore Drive at about five o'clock. At this time of year the days are still comparatively short, and the shadows of the evening were beginning to settle down upon the great city. Lamps were beginning to burn with that mellow radiance which seems almost watery and translucent to the eye. There was a softness in the air which speaks with an infinite delicacy of feeling to the flesh as well as to the soul. Carrie felt that it was a lovely day. She was ripened by it in spirit for many suggestions. As they drove along the smooth pavement an occasional carriage passed. She saw one stop and the footman dismount, opening the door for a gentleman who seemed to be leisurely returning from some afternoon pleasure. Across the broad lawns, now first freshening into green, she saw lamps faintly glowing upon rich interiors. Now it was but a chair, now a table, now an ornate corner, which met her eye, but it appealed to her as almost nothing else could. Such childish fancies as she had had of fairy palaces and kingly quarters now came back. She imagined that across these richly carved entrance-ways, where the globed and crystalled lamps shone upon paneled doors set with stained and designed panes of glass, was neither care nor unsatisfied desire. She was perfectly certain that here was happiness. If she could but stroll up yon broad walk, cross that rich entrance-way, which to her was of the beauty of a jewel, and sweep in grace and luxury to possession and command—oh! how quickly would sadness flee; how, in an instant, would the heartache end. She gazed and gazed, wondering, delighting, longing, and all the while the siren voice of the unrestful was whispering in her ear.

"If we could have such a home as that," said Mrs. Hale sadly, "how delightful it would be."

"And yet they do say," said Carrie, "that no one is ever happy."

She had heard so much of the canting philosophy of the grapeless fox.

"I notice," said Mrs. Hale, "that they all try mighty hard, though, to take their misery in a mansion."

When she came to her own rooms, Carrie saw their comparative insignificance. She was not so dull but that she could perceive they were but three small rooms in a moderately well-furnished boarding-house. She was not contrasting it now with what she had had, but what she had so recently seen. The glow of the palatial doors was still in her eye, the roll of cushioned carriages still in her ears. What, after all, was Drouet? What was she? At her window, she thought it over, rocking to and fro, and gazing out across the lamp-lit park toward the lamp-lit houses on Warren and Ashland avenues. She was too wrought up to care to go down to eat, too pensive to do aught but rock and sing. Some old tunes crept to her lips, and, as she sang them, her heart sank. She longed and longed and longed. It was now for the old cottage room in Columbia City, now the mansion upon the Shore Drive, now the fine dress of some lady, now the elegance of some scene. She was sad beyond measure, and yet uncertain, wishing, fancying. Finally, it seemed as if all her state was one of loneliness and forsakenness, and she could scarce refrain from trembling at the lip. She hummed and hummed as the moments went by, sitting in the shadow by the window, and was therein as happy though she did not perceive it, as she ever would be.

While Carrie was still in this frame of mind, the house-servant brought up the intelligence that Mr. Hurstwood was in the parlor asking to see Mr. and Mrs. Drouet.

"I guess he doesn't know that Charlie is out of town," thought Carrie.

She had seen comparatively little of the manager during the winter, but had been kept constantly in mind of him by one thing and another, principally by the strong impression he had made. She was quite disturbed for the moment as to her appearance, but soon satisfied herself by the aid of the mirror, and went below.

Hurstwood was in his best form, as usual. He hadn't heard that Drouet was out of town. He was but slightly affected by the intelligence, and devoted himself to the more general topics which would interest Carrie. It was surprising—the ease with which he conducted a conversation. He was like every man who has had the advantage of practice and knows he has sympathy. He knew that Carrie listened to him pleasurably, and, without the least effort, he fell into a train of observation which absorbed her fancy. He drew up his chair and modulated his voice to such a degree that what he said seemed wholly confidential. He confined himself almost exclusively to his observation of men and pleasures. He had been here and there, he had seen this and that. Somehow he made Carrie wish to see similar things, and all the while kept her aware of himself. She could not shut out the consciousness of his individuality and presence for a moment. He would raise his eyes slowly in smiling emphasis of something, and she was fixed by their magnetism. He would draw out, with the easiest grace, her approval. Once he touched her hand for emphasis and she only smiled. He seemed to radiate an atmosphere which suffused her being. He was never dull for a minute, and seemed to make her clever. At least, she brightened under his influence until all her best side was exhibited. She felt that she was more clever with him than with others. At least, he seemed to find so much in her to applaud. There was not the slightest tough of patronage. Drouet was full of it.

There had been something so personal, so subtle, in each meeting between them, both when Drouet was present and when he was absent, that Carrie could not speak of it without feeling a sense of difficulty. She was no talker. She could never arrange her thoughts in fluent order. It was always a matter of feeling with her, strong and deep. Each time there had been no sentence of importance which she could relate, and as for the glances and sensations, what woman would reveal them? Such things had never been between her and Drouet. As a matter of fact, they could never be. She had been dominated by distress and the enthusiastic forces of relief which Drouet represented at an opportune moment when she yielded to him. Now she was persuaded by secret current feelings which Drouet had never understood. Hurstwood's glance was as effective as the spoken words of a lover, and more. They called for no immediate decision, and could not be answered.

People in general attach too much importance to words. They are under the illusion that talking effects great results. As a matter of fact, words are, as a rule, the shallowest portion of all the argument. They but dimly represent the great surging feelings and desires which lie behind. When the distraction of the tongue is removed, the heart listens.

In this conversation she heard, instead of his words, the voices of the things which he represented. How suave was the counsel of his appearance! How feelingly did his superior state speak for itself! The growing desire he felt for her lay upon her spirit as a gentle hand. She did not need to tremble at all, because it was invisible; she did not need to worry over what other people would say—what she herself would say—because it had no tangibility. She was being pleaded with, persuaded, led into denying old rights and assuming new ones, and yet there were no words to prove it. Such conversation as was indulged in held the same relationship to the actual mental enactments of the twain that the low music of the orchestra does to the dramatic incident which it is used to cover.

"Have you ever seen the houses along the Lake Shore on the North Side?" asked Hurstwood.

"Why, I was just over there this afternoon—Mrs. Hale and I. Aren't they beautiful?"

"They're very fine," he answered.

"Oh, me," said Carrie, pensively. "I wish I could live in such a place."

"You're not happy," said Hurstwood, slowly, after a slight pause.

He had raised his eyes solemnly and was looking into her own. He assumed that he had struck a deep chord. Now was a slight chance to say a word in his own behalf. He leaned over quietly and continued his steady gaze. He felt the critical character of the period. She endeavored to stir, but it was useless. The whole strength of a man's nature was working. He had good cause to urge him on. He looked and looked, and the longer the situation lasted the more difficult it became. The little shop-girl was getting into deep water. She was letting her few supports float away from her.

"Oh," she said at last, "you mustn't look at me like that."

"I can't help it," he answered.

She relaxed a little and let the situation endure, giving him strength.

"You are not satisfied with life, are you?"

"No," she answered, weakly.

He saw he was the master of the situation—he felt it. He reached over and touched her hand.

"You mustn't," she exclaimed, jumping up.

"I didn't intend to," he answered, easily.

She did not run away, as she might have done. She did not terminate the interview, but he drifted off into a pleasant field of thought with the readiest grace. Not long after he rose to go, and she felt that he was in power.

"You mustn't feel bad," he said kindly; "things will straighten out in the course of time."

She made no answer, because she could think of nothing to say.

"We are good friends, aren't we?" he said, extending his hand.

"Yes," she answered.

"Not a word, then, until I see you again."

He retained a hold on her hand.

"I can't promise," she said, doubtfully.

"You must be more generous than that," he said, in such a simple way that she was touched.

"Let's not talk about it any more," she returned.

"All right," he said, brightening.

He went down the steps and into his cab. Carrie closed the door and ascended into her room. She undid her broad lace collar before the mirror and unfastened her pretty alligator belt which she had recently bought.

"I'm getting terrible," she said, honestly affected by a feeling of trouble and shame. "I don't seem to do anything right."

She unloosed her hair after a time, and let it hang in loose brown waves. Her mind was going over the events of the evening.

"I don't know," she murmured at last, "what I can do."

"Well," said Hurstwood as he rode away, "she likes me all right; that I know."

The aroused manager whistled merrily for a good four miles to his office an old melody that he had not recalled for fifteen years.

CHAPTER XIII

His Credentials Accepted: A Babel of Tongues

It was not quite two days after the scene between Carrie and Hurstwood in the Ogden Place parlor before he again put in his appearance. He had been thinking almost uninterruptedly of her. Her leniency had, in a way, inflamed his regard. He felt that he must succeed with her, and that speedily.

The reason for his interest, not to say fascination, was deeper than mere desire. It was a flowering out of feelings which had been withering in dry and almost barren soil for many years. It is probable that Carrie represented a better order of woman than had ever attracted him before. He had had no love affair since that which culminated in his marriage, and since then time and the world had taught him how raw and erroneous was his original judgment. Whenever he thought of it, he told himself that, if he had it to do over again, he would never marry such a woman. At the same time, his experience with women in general had lessened his respect for the sex. He maintained a cynical attitude, well grounded on numerous experiences. Such women as he had known were of nearly one type, selfish, ignorant, flashy. The wives of his friends were not inspiring to look upon. His own wife had developed a cold, commonplace nature which to him was anything but pleasing. What he knew of that under-world where grovel the beast-men of society (and he knew a great deal) had hardened his nature. He looked upon most women with suspicion—a single eye to the utility of beauty and dress. He followed them with a keen, suggestive glance. At the same time, he was not so dull but that a good woman commanded his respect. Personally, he did not attempt to analyze the marvel of a saintly woman. He would take off his hat, and would silence the light-tongued and the vicious in her presence—much as the Irish keeper of a Bowery hall will humble himself before a Sister of Mercy, and pay toll to charity with a willing and reverent hand. But he would not think much upon the question of why he did so.

A man in his situation who comes, after a long round of worthless or hardening experiences, upon a young, unsophisticated, innocent soul, is apt either to hold aloof, out of a sense of his own remoteness, or to draw near and become fascinated and elated by his discovery. It is only by a round-about process that such men ever do draw near such a girl. They have no method, no understanding of how to ingratiate themselves in youthful favor, save when they find virtue in the toils. If, unfortunately, the fly has got caught in the net, the spider can come forth and talk business upon its own terms. So when maidenhood has wandered into the moil of the city, when it is brought within the circle of the "rounder" and the roué, even though it be at the outermost rim, they can come forth and use their alluring arts.

Hurstwood had gone, at Drouet's invitation, to meet a new baggage of fine clothes and pretty features. He entered, expecting to indulge in an evening of lightsome frolic, and then lose track of the newcomer forever. Instead he found a woman whose youth and beauty attracted him. In the mild light of Carrie's eye was nothing of the calculation of the mistress. In the diffident manner was nothing of the art of the courtesan. He saw at once that a mistake had been made, that some difficult conditions had pushed this troubled creature into his presence, and his interest was enlisted. Here sympathy sprang to the rescue, but it was not unmixed with selfishness. He wanted to win Carrie because he thought her fate mingled with his was better than if it were united with Drouet's. He envied the drummer his conquest as he had never envied any man in all the course of his experience.

Carrie was certainly better than this man, as she was superior, mentally, to Drouet. She came fresh from the air of the village, the light of the country still in her eye. Here was neither guile nor rapacity. There were slight inherited traits of both in her, but they were rudimentary. She was too full of wonder and desire to be greedy. She still looked about her upon the great maze of the city without understanding. Hurstwood felt the bloom and the youth. He picked her as he would the fresh fruit of a tree. He felt as fresh in her presence as one who is taken out of the flash of summer to the first cool breath of spring.

Carrie, let alone since the scene in question, and having no one with whom to counsel, had at first wandered from one strange mental conclusion to another, until at last, tired out, she gave it up. She owed something to Drouet, she thought. It did not seem more than yesterday that he had aided her when she was worried and distressed. She had the kindliest feelings for him in every way. She gave him credit for his good looks, his generous feelings, and even, in fact, failed to recollect his egotism when he was absent; but she could not feel any binding influence keeping her for him as against all others. In fact, such a thought had never had any grounding, even in Drouet's desires.

The truth is, that this goodly drummer carried the doom of all enduring relationships in his own lightsome manner and unstable fancy. He went merrily on, assured that he was alluring all, that affection followed tenderly in his wake, that things would endure unchangingly for his pleasure. When he missed some old face, or found some door finally shut to him, it did not grieve him deeply. He was too young, too successful. He would remain thus young in spirit until he was dead.

As for Hurstwood, he was alive with thoughts and feelings concerning Carrie. He had no definite plans regarding her, but he was determined to make her confess an affection for him. He thought he saw in her drooping eye, her unstable glance, her wavering manner, the symptoms of a budding passion. He wanted to stand near her and make her lay her hand in his—he wanted to find out what her next step would be—what the next sign of feeling for him would be. Such anxiety and enthusiasm had not affected him for years. He was a youth again in feeling—a cavalier in action.

In his position opportunity for taking his evenings out was excellent. He was a most faithful worker in general, and a man who commanded the confidence of his employers in so far as the distribution of his time was concerned. He could take such hours off as he chose, for it was well known that he fulfilled his managerial duties successfully, whatever time he might take. His grace, tact, and ornate appearance gave the place an air which was most essential, while at the same time his long experience made him a most excellent judge of its stock necessities. Bartenders and assistants might come and go, singly or in groups, but, so long as he was present, the host of old-time customers would barely notice the change. He gave the place the atmosphere to which they were used. Consequently, he arranged his hours very much to suit himself, taking now an afternoon, now an evening, but invariably returning between eleven and twelve to witness the last hour or two of the day's business and look after the closing details.

"You see that things are safe and all the employees are out when you go home, George," Moy had once remarked to him, and he never once, in all the period of his long service, neglected to do this. Neither of the owners had for years been in the resort after five in the afternoon, and yet their manager as faithfully fulfilled this request as if they had been there regularly to observe.

On this Friday afternoon, scarcely two days after his previous visit, he made up his mind to see Carrie. He could not stay away longer.

"Evans," he said, addressing the head barkeeper, "if any one calls, I will be back between four and five."

He hurried to Madison Street and boarded a horse-car, which carried him to Ogden Place in half an hour.

Carrie had thought of going for a walk, and had put on a light gray woollen dress with a jaunty double-breasted jacket. She had out her hat and gloves, and was fastening a white lace tie about her throat when the housemaid brought up the information that Mr. Hurstwood wished to see her.

She started slightly at the announcement, but told the girl to say that she would come down in a moment, and proceeded to hasten her dressing.

Carrie could not have told herself at this moment whether she was glad or sorry that the impressive manager was awaiting her presence. She was slightly flurried and tingling in the cheeks, but it was more nervousness than either fear or favor. She did not try to conjecture what the drift of the conversation would be. She only felt that she must be careful, and that Hurstwood had an indefinable fascination for her. Then she gave her tie its last touch with her fingers and went below.

The deep-feeling manager was himself a little strained in the nerves by the thorough consciousness of his mission. He felt that he must make a strong play on this occasion, but now that the hour was come, and he heard Carrie's feet upon the stair, his nerve failed him. He sank a little in determination, for he was not so sure, after all, what her opinion might be.

When she entered the room, however, her appearance gave him courage. She looked simple and charming enough to strengthen the daring of any lover. Her apparent nervousness dispelled his own.

"How are you?" he said, easily. "I could not resist the temptation to come out this afternoon, it was so pleasant."

"Yes," said Carrie, halting before him, "I was just preparing to go for a walk myself."

"Oh, were you?" he said. "Supposing, then, you get your hat and we both go?"

They crossed the park and went west along Washington Boulevard, beautiful with its broad macadamized road, and large frame houses set back from the sidewalks. It was a street where many of the more prosperous residents of the West Side lived, and Hurstwood could not help feeling nervous over the publicity of it. They had gone but a few blocks when a livery stable sign in one of the side streets solved the difficulty for him. He would take her to drive along the new Boulevard.

The Boulevard at that time was little more than a country road. The part he intended showing her was much farther out on this same West Side, where there was scarcely a house. It connected Douglas Park with Washington or South Park, and was nothing more than a neatly *made* road, running due south for some five miles over an open, grassy prairie, and then due east over the same kind of prairie for the same distance. There was not a house to be encountered anywhere along the larger part of the route, and any conversation would be pleasantly free of interruption.

At the stable he picked a gentle horse, and they were soon out of range of either public observation or hearing.

"Can you drive?" he said, after a time.

"I never tried," said Carrie.

He put the reins in her hand, and folded his arms.

"You see there's nothing to it much," he said, smilingly.

"Not when you have a gentle horse," said Carrie.

"You can handle a horse as well as any one, after a little practice," he added, encouragingly.

He had been looking for some time for a break in the conversation when he could give it a serious turn. Once or twice he had held his peace, hoping that in silence her thoughts would take the color of his own, but she had lightly continued the subject. Presently, however, his silence controlled the situation. The drift of his thoughts began to tell. He gazed fixedly at nothing in particular, as if he were thinking of something which concerned her not at all. His thoughts, however, spoke for themselves. She was very much aware that a climax was pending.

"Do you know," he said, "I have spent the happiest evenings in years since I have known you?"

"Have you?" she said, with assumed airiness, but still excited by the conviction which the tone of his voice carried.

"I was going to tell you the other evening," he added, "but somehow the opportunity slipped away."

Carrie was listening without attempting to reply. She could think of nothing worth while to say. Despite all the ideas concerning right which had troubled her vaguely since she had last seen him, she was now influenced again strongly in his favor.

"I came out here to-day," he went on, solemnly, "to tell you just how I feel—to see if you wouldn't listen to me."

Hurstwood was something of a romanticist after his kind. He was capable of strong feelings—often poetic ones—and under a stress of desire, such as the present, he waxed eloquent. That is, his feelings and his voice were colored with that seeming repression and pathos which is the essence of eloquence.

"You know," he said, putting his hand on her arm, and keeping a strange silence while he formulated words, "that I love you?"

Carrie did not stir at the words. She was bound up completely in the man's atmosphere. He would have churchlike silence in order to express his feelings, and she kept it. She did not move her eyes from the flat, open scene before her. Hurstwood waited for a few moments, and then repeated the words.

"You must not say that," she weakly.

Her words were not convincing at all. They were the result of a feeble thought that something ought to be said. He paid no attention to them whatever.

"Carrie," he said, using her first name with sympathetic familiarity, "I want you to love me. You don't know how much I need some one to waste a little affection on me. I am practically alone. There is nothing in my life that is pleasant or delightful. It's all work and worry with people who are nothing to me."

As he said this, Hurstwood really imagined that his state was pitiful. He had the ability to get off at a distance and view himself objectively—of seeing what he wanted to see in the things which made up his existence. Now, as he spoke, his voice trembled with that peculiar vibration which is the result of tensity. It went ringing home to his companion's heart.

"Why, I should think," she said, turning upon him large eyes which were full of sympathy and feeling, "that you would be very happy. You know so much of the world."

"That is it," he said, his voice dropping to a soft minor, "I know too much of the world."

It was an important thing to her to hear one so well-positioned and powerful speaking in this manner. She could not help feeling the strangeness of her situation. How was it that, in so little a while, the narrow life of the country had fallen from her as a garment, and the city, with all its mystery, taken its place? Here was this greatest mystery, the man of money and affairs sitting beside her, appealing to her. Behold, he had ease and comfort, his strength was great, his position high, his clothing rich, and yet he was appealing to her. She could formulate no thought which would be just and right. She troubled herself no more upon the matter. She only basked in the warmth of his feeling, which was as a grateful blaze to one who is cold. Hurstwood glowed with his own intensity, and the heat of his passion was already melting the wax of his companion's scruples.

"You think," he said, "I am happy; that I ought not to complain? If you were to meet all day with people who care absolutely nothing about you, if you went day after day to a place where there was nothing but show and indifference, if there was not one person in all those you knew to whom you could appeal for sympathy or talk to with pleasure, perhaps you would be unhappy too."

He was striking a chord now which found sympathetic response to her own situation. She knew what it was to meet with people who were indifferent, to walk alone amid so many who cared absolutely nothing about you. Had not she? Was not she at this very moment quite alone? Who was there among all whom she knew to whom she could appeal for sympathy? Not one. She was left to herself to brood and wonder.

"I could be content," went on Hurstwood, "if I had you to love me. If I had you to go to; you for a companion. As it is, I simply move about from place to place without any satisfaction. Time hangs heavily on my hands. Before you came I did nothing but idle and drift into anything that offered itself. Since you came—well, I've had you to think about."

The old illusion that here was some one who needed her aid began to grow in Carrie's mind. She truly pitied this sad, lonely figure. To think that all his fine state should be so barren for want of her; that he needed to make such an appeal when she herself was lonely and without anchor. Surely, this was too bad.

"I am not very bad," he said, apologetically, as if he owed it to her to explain on this score. "You think, probably, that I roam around, and get into all sorts of evil? I have been rather reckless, but I could easily come out of that. I need you to draw me back, if my life ever amounts to anything."

Carrie looked at him with the tenderness which virtue ever feels in its hope of reclaiming vice. How could such a man need reclaiming? His errors, what were they, that she could correct? Small they must be, where all was so fine. At worst, they were gilded affairs, and with what leniency are gilded errors viewed.

He put himself in such a lonely light that she was deeply moved.

"Is it that way?" she mused.

He slipped his arm about her waist, and she could not find the heart to draw away. With his free hand he seized upon her fingers. A breath of soft spring wind went bounding over the road, rolling some brown twigs of the previous autumn before it. The horse paced leisurely on, unguided.

"Tell me," he said, softly, "that you love me."

Her eyes fell consciously.

"Own to it, dear," he said, feelingly; "you do, don't you?"

She made no answer, but he felt his victory.

"Tell me," he said, richly, drawing her so close that their lips were near together. He pressed her hand warmly, and then released it to touch her cheek.

"You do?" he said, pressing his lips to her own.

For answer, her lips replied.

"Now," he said joyously, his fine eyes ablaze, "you're my own girl, aren't you?"

By way of further conclusion, her head lay softly upon his shoulder.

CHAPTER XIV

WITH EYES AND NOT SEEING: ONE INFLUENCE WANES

Carrie in her rooms that evening was in a fine glow, physically and mentally. She was deeply rejoicing in her affection for Hurstwood and his love, and looked forward with fine fancy to their next meeting Sunday night. They had agreed, without any feeling of enforced secrecy, that she should come down town and meet him, though, after all, the need of it was the cause.

Mrs. Hale, from her upper window, saw her come in.

"Um," she thought to herself, "she goes riding with another man when her husband is out of the city. He had better keep an eye on her."

The truth is that Mrs. Hale was not the only one who had a thought on this score. The house-maid who had welcomed Hurstwood had her opinion also. She had no particular regard for Carrie, whom she took to be cold and disagreeable. At the same time, she had a fancy for the merry and easy-mannered Drouet, who threw her a pleasant remark now and then, and in other ways extended her the evidence of that regard which he had for all members of the sex. Hurstwood was more reserved and critical in his manner. He did not appeal to this bodiced functionary in the same pleasant way. She wondered that he came so frequently, that Mrs. Drouet should go out with him this afternoon when Mr. Drouet was absent. She gave vent to her opinions in the kitchen where the cook was. As a result, a hum of gossip was set going which moved about the house in that secret manner common to gossip.

Carrie, now that she had yielded sufficiently to Hurstwood to confess her affection, no longer troubled about her attitude towards him. Temporarily she gave little thought to Drouet, thinking only of the dignity and grace of her lover and of his consuming affection for her. On the first evening, she did little but go over the details of the afternoon. It was the first time her sympathies had ever been thoroughly aroused, and they threw a new light on her character. She had some power of initiative, latent before, which now began to exert itself. She looked more practically upon her state and began to see glimmerings of a way out. Hurstwood seemed a drag in the direction of honor. Her feelings were exceedingly creditable, in that they constructed out of these recent developments something which conquered freedom from dishonor. She had no idea what Hurstwood's next word would be. She only took his affection to be a fine thing, and appended better, more generous results accordingly.

As yet, Hurstwood had only a thought of pleasure without responsibility. He did not feel that he was doing anything to complicate his life. His position was secure, his home-life, if not satisfactory, was at least undisturbed, his personal liberty rather untrammeled. Carrie's love represented only so much added pleasure. He would enjoy this new gift over and above his ordinary allowance of pleasure. He would be happy with her and his own affairs would go on as they had, undisturbed.

On Sunday evening Carrie dined with him at a place he had selected in East Adams Street, and thereafter they took a cab to what was then a pleasant evening resort out on Cottage Grove Avenue near 39th Street. In the process of his declaration he soon realized that Carrie took his love upon a higher basis than he had anticipated. She kept him at a distance in a rather earnest way, and submitted only to those tender tokens of affection which better become the inexperienced lover. Hurstwood saw that she was not to be possessed for the asking, and deferred pressing his suit too warmly.

Since he feigned to believe in her married state he found that he had to carry out the part. His triumph, he saw, was still at a little distance. How far he could not guess.

They were returning to Ogden Place in the cab, when he asked:

"When will I see you again?"

"I don't know," she answered, wondering herself.

"Why not come down to The Fair," he suggested, "next Tuesday?"

She shook her head.

"Not so soon," she answered.

"I'll tell you what I'll do," he added. "I'll write you, care of this West Side Post-office. Could you call next Tuesday?"

Carrie assented.

The cab stopped one door out of the way according to his call.

"Good-night," he whispered, as the cab rolled away.

Unfortunately for the smooth progression of this affair, Drouet returned. Hurstwood was sitting in his imposing little office the next afternoon when he saw Drouet enter.

"Why, hello, Charles," he called affably; "back again?"

"Yes," smiled Drouet, approaching and looking in at the door.

Hurstwood arose.

"Well," he said, looking the drummer over, "rosy as ever, eh?"

They began talking of the people they knew and things that had happened.

"Been home yet?" finally asked Hurstwood.

"No, I am going, though," said Drouet.

"I remembered the little girl out there," said Hurstwood, "and called once. Thought you wouldn't want her left quite alone."

"Right you are," agreed Drouet. "How is she?"

"Very well," said Hurstwood. "Rather anxious about you, though. You'd better go out now and cheer her up."

"I will," said Drouet, smilingly.

"Like to have you both come down and go to the show with me Wednesday," concluded Hurstwood at parting.

"Thanks, old man," said his friend, "I'll see what the girl says and let you know."

They separated in the most cordial manner.

"There's a nice fellow," Drouet thought to himself as he turned the corner towards Madison.

"Drouet is a good fellow," Hurstwood thought to himself as he went back into his office, "but he's no man for Carrie."

The thought of the latter turned his mind into a most pleasant vein, and he wondered how he would get ahead of the drummer.

When Drouet entered Carrie's presence, he caught her in his arms as usual, but she responded to his kiss with a tremor of opposition.

"Well," he said, "I had a great trip."

"Did you? How did you come out with that La Crosse man you were telling me about?"

"Oh, fine; sold him a complete line. There was another fellow there, representing Burnstein, a regular hook-nosed sheeny, but he wasn't in it. I made him look like nothing at all."

As he undid his collar and unfastened his studs, preparatory to washing his face and changing his clothes, he dilated upon his trip. Carrie could not help listening with amusement to his animated descriptions.

"I tell you," he said, "I surprised the people at the office. I've sold more goods this last quarter than any other man of our house on the road. I sold three thousand dollars' worth in La Crosse."

He plunged his face in a basin of water, and puffed and blew as he rubbed his neck and ears with his hands, while Carrie gazed upon him with mingled thoughts of recollection and present judgment. He was still wiping his face, when he continued:

"I'm going to strike for a raise in June. They can afford to pay it, as much business as I turn in. I'll get it too, don't you forget."

"I hope you do," said Carrie.

"And then if that little real estate deal I've got on goes through, we'll get married," he said, with a great show of earnestness, the while he took his place before the mirror and began brushing his hair.

"I don't believe you ever intend to marry me, Charlie," Carrie said ruefully. The recent protestations of Hurstwood had given her courage to say this.

"Oh, yes I do—course I do—what put that into your head?"

He had stopped his trifling before the mirror now and crossed over to her. For the first time Carrie felt as if she must move away from him.

"But you've been saying that so long," she said, looking with her pretty face upturned into his.

"Well, and I mean it too, but it takes money to live as I want to. Now, when I get this increase, I can come pretty near fixing things all right, and I'll do it. Now, don't you worry, girlie."

He patted her reassuringly upon the shoulder, but Carrie felt how really futile had been her hopes. She could clearly see that this easy-going soul intended no move in her behalf. He was simply letting things drift because he preferred the free round of his present state to any legal trammelings.

In contrast, Hurstwood appeared strong and sincere. He had no easy manner of putting her off. He sympathized with her and showed her what her true value was. He needed her, while Drouet did not care.

"Oh, no," she said remorsefully, her tone reflecting some of her own success and more of her helplessness, "you never will."

"Well, you wait a little while and see," he concluded. "I'll marry you all right."

Carrie looked at him and felt justified. She was looking for something which would calm her conscience, and here it was, a light, airy disregard of her claims upon his justice. He had faithfully promised to marry her, and this was the way he fulfilled his promise.

"Say," he said, after he had, as he thought, pleasantly disposed of the marriage question, "I saw Hurstwood to-day, and he wants us to go to the theater with him."

Carrie started at the name, but recovered quickly enough to avoid notice.

"When?" she asked, with assumed indifference.

"Wednesday. We'll go, won't we?"

"If you think so," she answered, her manner being so enforcedly reserved as to almost excite suspicion. Drouet noticed something, but he thought it was due to her feelings concerning their talk about marriage.

"He called once, he said."

"Yes," said Carrie, "he was out here Sunday evening."

"Was he?" said Drouet. "I thought from what he said that he had called a week or so ago."

"So he did," answered Carrie, who was wholly unaware of what conversation her lovers might have held. She was all at sea mentally, and fearful of some entanglement which might ensue from what she would answer.

"Oh, then he called twice?" said Drouet, the first shade of misunderstanding showing in his face.

"Yes," said Carrie innocently, feeling now that Hurstwood must have mentioned but one call.

Drouet imagined that he must have misunderstood his friend. He did not attach particular importance to the information, after all.

"What did he have to say?" he queried, with slightly increased curiosity.

"He said he came because he thought I might be lonely. You hadn't been in there so long he wondered what had become of you."

"George is a fine fellow," said Drouet, rather gratified by his conception of the manager's interest. "Come on and we'll go out to dinner."

When Hurstwood saw that Drouet was back he wrote at once to Carrie, saying:

"I told him I called on you, dearest, when he was away. I did not say how often, but he probably thought once. Let me know of anything you may have said. Answer by special messenger when you get this, and, darling, I must see you. Let me know if you can't meet me at Jackson and Throop Streets Wednesday afternoon at two o'clock. I want to speak with you before we meet at the theater."

Carrie received this Tuesday morning when she called at the West Side branch of the post-office, and answered at once.

"I said you called twice," she wrote. "He didn't seem to mind. I will try and be at Throop Street if nothing interferes. I seem to be getting very bad. It's wrong to act as I do, I know."

Hurstwood, when he met her as agreed, reassured her on this score.

"You mustn't worry, sweetheart," he said. "Just as soon as he goes on the road again we will arrange something. We'll fix it so that you won't have to deceive any one."

Carrie imagined that he would marry her at once, though he had not directly said so, and her spirits rose. She proposed to make the best of the situation until Drouet left again.

"Don't show any more interest in me than you ever have," Hurstwood counseled concerning the evening at the theater.

"You mustn't look at me steadily then," she answered, mindful of the power of his eyes.

"I won't," he said, squeezing her hand at parting and giving the glance she had just cautioned against.

"There," she said playfully, pointing a finger at him.

"The show hasn't begun yet," he returned.

He watched her walk from him with tender solicitation. Such youth and prettiness reacted upon him more subtly than wine.

At the theater things passed as they had in Hurstwood's favor. If he had been pleasing to Carrie before, how much more so was he now. His grace was more permeating because it found a readier medium. Carrie watched his every movement with pleasure. She almost forgot poor Drouet, who babbled on as if he were the host.

Hurstwood was too clever to give the slightest indication of a change. He paid, if anything, more attention to his old friend than usual, and yet in no way held him up to that subtle ridicule which a lover in favor may so secretly practice before the mistress of his heart. If anything, he felt the injustice of the game as it stood, and was not cheap enough to add to it the slightest mental taunt.

Only the play produced an ironical situation, and this was due to Drouet alone.

The scene was one in "The Covenant," in which the wife listened to the seductive voice of a lover in the absence of her husband.

"Served him right," said Drouet afterward, even in view of her keen expiation of her error. "I haven't any pity for a man who would be such a chump as that."

"Well, you never can tell," returned Hurstwood gently. "He probably thought he was right."

"Well, a man ought to be more attentive than that to his wife if he wants to keep her."

They had come out of the lobby and made their way through the showy crush about the entrance way.

"Say, mister," said a voice at Hurstwood's side, "would you mind giving me the price of a bed?"

Hurstwood was interestedly remarking to Carrie.

"Honest to God, mister, I'm without a place to sleep."

The plea was that of a gaunt-faced man of about thirty, who looked the picture of privation and wretchedness. Drouet was the first to see. He handed over a dime with an upwelling feeling of pity in his heart. Hurstwood scarcely noticed the incident. Carrie quickly forgot.

CHAPTER XV

THE IRK OF THE OLD TIES: THE MAGIC OF YOUTH

The complete ignoring by Hurstwood of his own home came with the growth of his affection for Carrie. His actions, in all that related to his family, were of the most perfunctory kind. He sat at breakfast with his wife and children, absorbed in his own fancies, which reached far without the realm of their interests. He read his paper, which was heightened in interest by the shallowness of the themes discussed by his son and daughter. Between himself and his wife ran a river of indifference.

Now that Carrie had come, he was in a fair way to be blissful again. There was delight in going down town evenings. When he walked forth in the short days, the street lamps had a merry twinkle. He began to experience the almost forgotten feeling which hastens the lover's feet. When he looked at his fine clothes, he saw them with her eyes—and her eyes were young.

When in the flush of such feelings he heard his wife's voice, when the insistent demands of matrimony recalled him from dreams to a stale practice, how it grated. He then knew that this was a chain which bound his feet.

"George," said Mrs. Hurstwood, in that tone of voice which had long since come to be associated in his mind with demands, "we want you to get us a season ticket to the races."

"Do you want to go to all of them?" he said with a rising inflection.

"Yes," she answered.

The races in question were soon to open at Washington Park, on the South Side, and were considered quite society affairs among those who did not affect religious rectitude and conservatism. Mrs. Hurstwood had never asked for a whole season ticket before, but this year certain considerations decided her to get a box. For one thing, one of her neighbors, a certain Mr. and Mrs. Ramsey, who were possessors of money, made out of the coal business, had done so. In the next place, her favorite physician, Dr. Beale, a gentleman inclined to horses and betting, had talked with her concerning his intention to enter a two-year-old in the Derby. In the third place, she wished to exhibit Jessica, who was gaining in maturity and beauty, and whom she hoped to marry to a man of means. Her own desire to be about in such things and parade among her acquaintances and the common throng was as much an incentive as anything.

Hurstwood thought over the proposition a few moments without answering. They were in the sitting-room on the second floor, waiting for supper. It was the evening of his engagement with Carrie and Drouet to see "The Covenant," which had brought him home to make some alterations in his dress.

"You're sure separate tickets wouldn't do as well?" he asked, hesitating to say anything more rugged.

"No," she replied impatiently.

"Well," he said, taking offense at her manner, "you needn't get mad about it. I'm just asking you."

"I'm not mad," she snapped. "I'm merely asking you for a season ticket."

"And I'm telling you," he returned, fixing a clear, steady eye on her, "that it's no easy thing to get. I'm not sure whether the manager will give it to me."

He had been thinking all the time of his "pull" with the race-track magnates.

"We can buy it then," she exclaimed sharply.

"You talk easy," he said. "A season family ticket costs one hundred and fifty dollars."

"I'll not argue with you," she replied with determination. "I want the ticket and that's all there is to it."

She had risen, and now walked angrily out of the room.

"Well, you get it then," he said grimly, though in a modified tone of voice.

As usual, the table was one short that evening.

The next morning he had cooled down considerably, and later the ticket was duly secured, though it did not heal matters. He did not mind giving his family a fair share of all that he earned, but he did not like to be forced to provide against his will.

"Did you know, mother," said Jessica another day, "the Spencers are getting ready to go away?"

"No. Where, I wonder?"

"Europe," said Jessica. "I met Georgine yesterday and she told me. She just put on more airs about it."

"Did she say when?"

"Monday, I think. They'll get a notice in the papers again—they always do."

"Never mind," said Mrs. Hurstwood consolingly, "we'll go one of these days."

Hurstwood moved his eyes over the paper slowly, but said nothing.

"'We sail for Liverpool from New York,'" Jessica exclaimed, mocking her acquaintance. "'Expect to spend most of the "summah" in France,'—vain thing. As if it was anything to go to Europe."

"It must be if you envy her so much," put in Hurstwood.

It grated upon him to see the feeling his daughter displayed.

"Don't worry over them, my dear," said Mrs. Hurstwood.

"Did George get off?" asked Jessica of her mother another day, thus revealing something that Hurstwood had heard nothing about.

"Where has he gone?" he asked, looking up. He had never before been kept in ignorance concerning departures.

"He was going to Wheaton," said Jessica, not noticing the slight put upon her father.

"What's out there?" he asked, secretly irritated and chagrined to think that he should be made to pump for information in this manner.

"A tennis match," said Jessica.

"He didn't say anything to me," Hurstwood concluded, finding it difficult to refrain from a bitter tone.

"I guess he must have forgotten," exclaimed his wife blandly.

In the past he had always commanded a certain amount of respect, which was a compound of appreciation and awe. The familiarity which in part still existed between himself and his daughter he had courted. As it was, it did not go beyond the light assumption of words. The *tone* was always modest. Whatever had been, however, had lacked affection and now he saw that he was losing track of their doings. His knowledge was no longer intimate. He sometimes saw them at table, and sometimes did not. He heard of their doings occasionally, more often not. Some days he found that he was all at sea as to what they were talking about—things they had arranged to do or that they had done in his absence. More affecting was the feeling that there were little things going on of which he no longer heard. Jessica was beginning to feel that her affairs were her own. George, Jr., flourished about as if he were a man entirely and must needs have private matters. All this Hurstwood could see, and it left a trace of feeling, for he was used to being considered—in his official position, at least—and felt that his importance should not begin to wane here. To darken it all, he saw the same indifference and independence growing in his wife, while he looked on and paid the bills.

He consoled himself with the thought, however, that, after all, he was not without affection. Things might go as they would at his house, but he had Carrie outside of it. With his mind's eye, he looked into her comfortable room in Ogden Place, where he had spent several such delightful evenings, and thought how charming it would be when Drouet was disposed of entirely and she was waiting evenings in cosy little quarters for him. That no cause would come up whereby Drouet would be led to inform Carrie concerning his married state, he felt hopeful. Things were going so smoothly that he believed they would not change. Shortly now he would persuade Carrie and all would be satisfactory.

The day after their theater visit he began writing her regularly—a letter every morning, and begging her to do as much for him. He was not literary by any means, but experience of the world and his growing affection gave him somewhat of a style. This he exercised at his office desk with perfect deliberation. He purchased a box of delicately colored and scented writing paper in monogram, which he kept locked in one of the drawers. His friends now wondered at the cleric and very official-looking nature of his position. The five bartenders viewed with respect the duties which could call a man to do so much deskwork and penmanship.

Hurstwood surprised himself with his fluency. By the natural law which governs all effort, what he wrote reacted upon him. He began to feel those subtleties which he could find words to express. With every expression came increased conception. Those inmost breathings which there found words took hold upon him. He thought Carrie worthy of all the affection he could there express.

Carrie was indeed worth loving if ever youth and grace are to command that token of acknowledgment from life in their bloom. Experience had not yet taken away that freshness of the spirit which is the charm of the body. Her soft eyes contained in their liquid luster no suggestion of the knowledge of disappointment. She had been troubled in a way by doubt and longing, but these had made no deeper impression than could be traced in a certain open wistfulness of glance and speech. The mouth had the expression at times, in talking and in repose, of one who might be upon the verge of tears. It was not that grief was thus ever present. The pronunciation of certain syllables gave to her lips this peculiarity of formation—a formation as suggestive and moving as pathos itself.

There was nothing bold in her manner. Life had not taught her domination—superciliousness of grace, which is the lordly power of some women. Her longing for consideration was not sufficiently powerful to move her to demand it. Even now she lacked self-assurance, but there was that in what she had already experienced which left her a little less than timid. She wanted pleasure, she wanted position, and yet she was confused as to what these things might be. Every hour the kaleidoscope of human affairs threw a new luster upon something, and therewith it became for her the desired—the all. Another shift of the box, and some other had become the beautiful, the perfect.

On her spiritual side, also, she was rich in feeling, as such a nature well might be. Sorrow in her was aroused by many a spectacle—an uncritical upwelling of grief for the weak and the helpless. She was constantly pained by the sight of the whitefaced, ragged men who slopped desperately by her in a sort of wretched mental stupor. The poorly clad girls who went blowing by her window evenings, hurrying home from some of the shops of the West Side, she pitied from the depths of her heart. She would stand and bite her lips as they passed, shaking her little head and wondering. They had so little, she thought. It was so sad to be ragged and poor. The hang of faded clothes pained her eyes.

"And they have to work so hard!" was her only comment.

On the street sometimes she would see men working—Irishmen with picks, coal-heavers with great loads to shovel, Americans busy about some work which was a mere matter of strength—and they touched her fancy. Toil, now that she was free of it, seemed even a more desolate thing than when she was part of it. She saw it through a mist of fancy—a pale, somber half-light, which was the essence of poetic feeling. Her old father, in his flour-dusted miller's suit, sometimes returned to her in memory, revived by a face in a window. A shoemaker pegging at his last, a blastman seen through a narrow window in some basement where iron was being melted, a bench-worker seen high aloft in some window, his coat off, his sleeves rolled up; these took her back in fancy to the details of the mill. She felt, though she seldom expressed them, sad thoughts upon this score. Her sympathies were ever with that under-world of toil from which she had so recently sprung, and which she best understood.

Though Hurstwood did not know it, he was dealing with one whose feelings were as tender and as delicate as this. He did not know, but it was this in her, after all, which attracted him. He never attempted to analyze the nature of his affection. It was sufficient that there was tenderness in her eye, weakness in her manner, good-nature and hope in her thoughts. He drew near this lily, which had sucked its waxen beauty and perfume from below a depth of waters which he had never penetrated, and out of ooze and mould which he could not understand. He drew near because it was waxen and fresh. It lightened his feelings for him. It made the morning worth while.

In a material way, she was considerably improved. Her awkwardness had all but passed, leaving, if anything, a quaint residue which was as pleasing as perfect grace. Her little shoes now fitted her smartly and had high heels. She had learned much about laces and those little neckpieces which add so much to a woman's appearance. Her form had filled out until it was admirably plump and well-rounded.

Hurstwood wrote her one morning, asking her to meet him in Jefferson Park, Monroe Street. He did not consider it policy to call any more, even when Drouet was at home.

The next afternoon he was in the pretty little park by one, and had found a rustic bench beneath the green leaves of a lilac bush which bordered one of the paths. It was at that season of the year when the fulness of spring had not yet worn quite away. At a little pond near by some cleanly dressed children were sailing white canvas boats. In the shade of a green pagoda a bebuttoned officer of the law was resting, his arms folded, his club at rest in his belt. An old gardener was upon the lawn, with a pair of pruning shears, looking after some bushes. High overhead was the clear blue sky of the new summer, and in the thickness of the shiny green leaves of the trees hopped and twittered the busy sparrows.

Hurstwood had come out of his own home that morning feeling much of the same old annoyance. At his store he had idled, there being no need to write. He had come away to this place with the lightness of heart which characterizes those who put weariness behind. Now, in the shade of this cool, green bush, he looked about him with the fancy of the lover. He heard the carts go lumbering by upon the neighboring streets, but they were far off, and only buzzed upon his ear. The hum of the surrounding city was faint, the clang of an occasional bell was as music. He looked and dreamed a new dream of pleasure which concerned his present fixed condition not at all. He got back in fancy to the old Hurstwood, who was neither married nor fixed in a solid position for life. He remembered the light spirit in which he once looked after the girls—how he had danced, escorted them home, hung over their gates. He almost wished he was back there again—here in this pleasant scene he felt as if he were wholly free.

At two Carrie came tripping along the walk toward him, rosy and clean. She had just recently donned a sailor hat for the season with a band of pretty white-dotted blue silk. Her skirt was of a rich blue material, and her shirt waist matched it, with a thin stripe of blue upon a snow-white ground—stripes that were as fine as hairs. Her brown shoes peeped occasionally from beneath her skirt. She carried her gloves in her hand.

Hurstwood looked up at her with delight.

"You came, dearest," he said eagerly, standing to meet her and taking her hand.

"Of course," she said, smiling; "did you think I wouldn't?"

"I didn't know," he replied.

He looked at her forehead, which was moist from her brisk walk. Then he took out one of his own soft, scented silk handkerchiefs and touched her face here and there.

"Now," he said affectionately, "you're all right."

They were happy in being near one another—in looking into each other's eyes. Finally, when the long flush of delight had subsided, he said:

"When is Charlie going away again?"

"I don't know," she answered. "He says he has some things to do for the house here now."

Hurstwood grew serious, and he lapsed into quiet thought. He looked up after a time to say:

"Come away and leave him."

He turned his eyes to the boys with the boats, as if the request were of little importance.

"Where would we go?" she asked in much the same manner, rolling her gloves, and looking into a neighboring tree.

"Where do you want to go?" he enquired.

There was something in the tone in which he said this which made her feel as if she must record her feelings against any local habitation.

"We can't stay in Chicago," she replied.

He had no thought that this was in her mind—that any removal would be suggested.

"Why not?" he asked softly.

"Oh, because," she said, "I wouldn't want to."

He listened to this with the dull perception of what it meant. It had no serious ring to it. The question was not up for immediate decision.

"I would have to give up my position," he said.

The tone he used made it seem as if the matter deserved only slight consideration. Carrie thought a little, the while enjoying the pretty scene.

"I wouldn't like to live in Chicago and him here," she said, thinking of Drouet.

"It's a big town, dearest," Hurstwood answered. "It would be as good as moving to another part of the country to move to the South Side."

He had fixed upon that region as an objective point.

"Anyhow," said Carrie, "I shouldn't want to get married as long as he is here. I wouldn't want to run away."

The suggestion of marriage struck Hurstwood forcibly. He saw clearly that this was her idea—he felt that it was not to be gotten over easily. Bigamy lightened the horizon of his shadowy thoughts for a moment. He wondered for the life of him how it would all come out. He could not see that he was making any progress save in her regard. When he looked at her now, he thought her beautiful. What a thing it was to have her love him, even if it be entangling! She increased in value in his eyes because of her objection. She was something to struggle for, and that was everything. How different from the women who yielded willingly! He swept the thought of them from his mind.

"And you don't know when he'll go away?" asked Hurstwood, quietly.

She shook her head.

He sighed.

"You're a determined little miss, aren't you?" he said, after a few moments, looking up into her eyes.

She felt a wave of feeling sweep over her at this. It was pride at what seemed his admiration—affection for the man who could feel this concerning her.

"No," she said coyly, "but what can I do?"

Again he folded his hands and looked away over the lawn into the street.

"I wish," he said pathetically, "you would come to me. I don't like to be away from you this way. What good is there in waiting? You're not any happier, are you?"

"Happier!" she exclaimed softly, "you know better than that."

"Here we are then," he went on in the same tone, "wasting our days. If you are not happy, do you think I am? I sit and write to you the biggest part of the time. I'll tell you what, Carrie," he exclaimed, throwing sudden force of expression into his voice and fixing her with his eyes, "I can't live without you, and that's all there is to it. Now," he concluded, showing the palm of one of his white hands in a sort of at-an-end, helpless expression, "what shall I do?"

This shifting of the burden to her appealed to Carrie. The semblance of the load without the weight touched the woman's heart.

"Can't you wait a little while yet?" she said tenderly. "I'll try and find out when he's going."

"What good will it do?" he asked, holding the same strain of feeling.

"Well, perhaps we can arrange to go somewhere."

She really did not see anything clearer than before, but she was getting into that frame of mind where, out of sympathy, a woman yields.

Hurstwood did not understand. He was wondering how she was to be persuaded—what appeal would move her to forsake Drouet. He began to wonder how far her affections for him would carry her. He was thinking of some question which would make her tell.

Finally he hit upon one of those problematical propositions which often disguise our own desires while leading us to an understanding of the difficulties which others make for us, and so discover for us a way. It had not the slightest connection with anything intended on his part, and was spoken at random before he had given it a moment's serious thought.

"Carrie," he said, looking into her face and assuming a serious look which he did not feel, "suppose I were to come to you next week, or this week for that matter—to-night say—and tell you I had to go away—that I couldn't stay another minute and wasn't coming back any more—would you come with me?"

His sweetheart viewed him with the most affectionate glance, her answer ready before the words were out of his mouth.

"Yes," she said.

"You wouldn't stop to argue or arrange?"

"Not if you couldn't wait."

He smiled when he saw that she took him seriously, and he thought what a chance it would afford for a possible junket of a week or two. He had a notion to tell her that he was joking and so brush away her sweet seriousness, but the effect of it was too delightful. He let it stand.

"Suppose we didn't have time to get married here?" he added, an afterthought striking him.

"If we got married as soon as we got to the other end of the journey it would be all right."

"I meant that," he said.

"Yes."

The morning seemed peculiarly bright to him now. He wondered whatever could have put such a thought into his head. Impossible as it was, he could not help smiling at its cleverness. It showed how she loved him. There was no doubt in his mind now, and he would find a way to win her.

"Well," he said, jokingly, "I'll come and get you one of these evenings," and then he laughed.

"I wouldn't stay with you, though, if you didn't marry me," Carrie added reflectively.

"I don't want you to," he said tenderly, taking her hand.

She was extremely happy now that she understood. She loved him the more for thinking that he would rescue her so. As for him, the marriage clause did not dwell in his mind. He was thinking that with such affection there could be no bar to his eventual happiness.

"Let's stroll about," he said gaily, rising and surveying all the lovely park.

"All right," said Carrie.

They passed the young Irishman, who looked after them with envious eyes.

"'Tis a foine couple," he observed to himself. "They must be rich."

CHAPTER XVI

A WITLESS ALADDIN: THE GATE TO THE WORLD

In the course of his present stay in Chicago, Drouet paid some slight attention to the secret order to which he belonged. During his last trip he had received a new light on its importance.

"I tell you," said another drummer to him, "it's a great thing. Look at Hazenstab. He isn't so deuced clever. Of course he's got a good house behind him, but that won't do alone. I tell you it's his degree. He's a way-up Mason, and that goes a long way. He's got a secret sign that stands for something."

Drouet resolved then and there that he would take more interest in such matters. So when he got back to Chicago he repaired to his local lodge headquarters.

"I say, Drouet," said Mr. Harry Quincel, an individual who was very prominent in this local branch of the Elks, "you're the man that can help us out."

It was after the business meeting and things were going socially with a hum. Drouet was bobbing around chatting and joking with a score of individuals whom he knew.

"What are you up to?" he inquired genially, turning a smiling face upon his secret brother.

"We're trying to get up some theatricals for two weeks from to-day, and we want to know if you don't know some young lady who could take a part—it's an easy part."

"Sure," said Drouet, "what is it?" He did not trouble to remember that he knew no one to whom he could appeal on this score. His innate good-nature, however, dictated a favorable reply.

"Well, now, I'll tell you what we are trying to do," went on Mr. Quincel. "We are trying to get a new set of furniture for the lodge. There isn't enough money in the treasury at the present time, and we thought we would raise it by a little entertainment."

"Sure," interrupted Drouet, "that's a good idea."

"Several of the boys around here have got talent. There's Harry Burbeck, he does a fine black-face turn. Mac Lewis is all right at heavy dramatics. Did you ever hear him recite 'Over the Hills'?"

"Never did."

"Well, I tell you, he does it fine."

"And you want me to get some woman to take a part?" questioned Drouet, anxious to terminate the subject and get on to something else. "What are you going to play?"

"'Under the Gaslight,'" said Mr. Quincel, mentioning Augustin Daly's famous production, which had worn from a great public success down to an amateur theatrical favorite, with many of the troublesome accessories cut out and the *dramatis personæ* reduced to the smallest possible number.

Drouet had seen this play some time in the past.

"That's it," he said; "that's a fine play. It will go all right. You ought to make a lot of money out of that."

"We think we'll do very well," Mr. Quincel replied. "Don't you forget now," he concluded, Drouet showing signs of restlessness; "some young woman to take the part of Laura."

"Sure, I'll attend to it."

He moved away, forgetting almost all about it the moment Mr. Quincel had ceased talking. He had not even thought to ask the time or place.

Drouet was reminded of his promise a day or two later by the receipt of a letter announcing that the first rehearsal was set for the following Friday evening, and urging him to kindly forward the young lady's address at once, in order that the part might be delivered to her.

"Now, who the deuce do I know?" asked the drummer reflectively, scratching his rosy ear. "I don't know anyone that knows anything about amateur theatricals."

He went over in memory the names of a number of women he knew, and finally fixed on one, largely because of the convenient location of her home on the West Side, and promised himself that as he came out that evening he would see her. When, however, he started west on the car he forgot, and was only reminded of his delinquency by an item in the "Evening News"—a small three-line affair under the head of Secret Society Notes—which stated the Custer Lodge of the Order of Elks would give a theatrical performance in Avery Hall on the 16th, when "Under the Gaslight" would be produced.

"George!" exclaimed Drouet, "I forgot that."

"What?" inquired Carrie.

They were at their little table in the room which might have been used for a kitchen, where Carrie occasionally served a meal. To-night the fancy had caught her, and the little table was spread with a pleasing repast.

"Why, my lodge entertainment. They're going to give a play, and they wanted me to get them some young lady to take a part."

"What is it they're going to play?"

"'Under the Gaslight.'"

"When?"

"On the 16th."

"Well, why don't you?" asked Carrie.

"I don't know anyone," he replied.

Suddenly he looked up.

"Say," he said, "how would you like to take the part?"

"Me?" said Carrie. "I can't act."

"How do you know?" questioned Drouet reflectively.

"Because," answered Carrie, "I never did."

Nevertheless, she was pleased to think he would ask. Her eyes brightened, for if there was anything that enlisted her sympathies it was the art of the stage.

True to his nature, Drouet clung to this idea as an easy way out.

"That's nothing. You can act all you have to down there."

"No, I can't," said Carrie weakly, very much drawn toward the proposition and yet fearful.

"Yes, you can. Now, why don't you do it? They need some one, and it will be lots of fun for you."

"Oh, no, it won't," said Carrie seriously.

"You'd like that. I know you would. I've seen you dancing around here and giving imitations and that's why I asked you. You're clever enough, all right."

"No, I'm not," said Carrie shyly.

"Now, I'll tell you what you do. You go down and see about it. It'll be fun for you. The rest of the company isn't going to be any good. They haven't any experience. What do they know about theatricals?"

He frowned as he thought of their ignorance.

"Hand me the coffee," he added.

"I don't believe I could act, Charlie," Carrie went on pettishly. "You don't think I could, do you?"

"Sure. Out o' sight. I bet you make a hit. Now you want to go. I know you do. I knew it when I came home. That's why I asked you."

"What is the play, did you say?"

"'Under the Gaslight.'"

"What part would they want me to take?"

"Oh, one of the heroines—I don't know."

"What sort of a play is it?"

"Well," said Drouet, whose memory for such things was not the best, "it's about a girl who gets kidnapped by a couple of crooks—a man and a woman that live in the slums. She had some money or something and they wanted to get it. I don't know now how it did go exactly."

"Don't you know what part I would have to take?"

"No, I don't, to tell the truth." He thought a moment. "Yes, I do, too. Laura, that's the thing—you're to be Laura."

"And you can't remember what the part is like?"

"To save me, Cad, I can't," he answered. "I ought to, too; I've seen the play enough. There's a girl in it that was stolen when she was an infant—was picked off the street or something—and she's the one that's hounded by the two old criminals I was telling you about." He stopped with a mouthful of pie poised on a fork before her face. "She comes very near getting drowned—no, that's not it. I'll tell you what I'll do," he concluded hopelessly, "I'll get you the book. I can't remember now for the life of me."

"Well, I don't know," said Carrie, when he had concluded, her interest and desire to shine dramatically struggling with her timidity for the mastery. "I might go if you thought I'd do all right."

"Of course, you'll do," said Drouet, who, in his efforts to enthuse Carrie, had interested himself. "Do you think I'd come home here and urge you to do something that I didn't think you would make a success of? You can act all right. It'll be good for you."

"When must I go?" said Carrie, reflectively.

"The first rehearsal is Friday night. I'll get the part for you to-night."

"All right," said Carrie resignedly, "I'll do it, but if I make a failure now it's your fault."

"You won't fail," assured Drouet. "Just act as you do around here. Be natural. You're all right. I've often thought you'd make a corking good actress."

"Did you really?" asked Carrie.

"That's right," said the drummer.

He little knew as he went out of the door that night what a secret flame he had kindled in the bosom of the girl he left behind. Carrie was possessed of that sympathetic, impressionable nature which, ever in the most developed form, has been the glory of the drama. She was created with that passivity of soul which is always the mirror of the active world. She possessed an innate taste for imitation and no small ability. Even without practice, she could sometimes restore dramatic situations she had witnessed by re-creating, before her mirror, the expressions of the various faces taking part in the scene. She loved to modulate her voice after the conventional manner of the distressed heroine, and repeat such pathetic fragments as appealed most to her sympathies. Of late, seeing the airy grace of the ingenue in several well-constructed plays, she had been moved to secretly imitate it, and many were the little movements and expressions of the body in which she indulged from time to time in the privacy of her chamber. On several occasions, when Drouet had caught her admiring herself, as he imagined, in the mirror, she was doing nothing more than recalling some little grace of the mouth or the eyes which she had witnessed in another. Under his airy accusation she mistook this for vanity and accepted the blame with a faint sense of error, though, as a matter of fact, it was nothing more than the first subtle outcroppings of an artistic nature, endeavoring to re-create the perfect likeness of some phase of beauty which appealed to her. In such feeble tendencies, be it known, such outworking of desire to reproduce life, lies the basis of all dramatic art.

Now, when Carrie heard Drouet's laudatory opinion of her dramatic ability, her body tingled with satisfaction. Like the flame which welds the loosened particles into a solid mass, his words united those floating wisps of feeling which she had felt, but never believed, concerning her possible ability, and made them into a gaudy shred of hope. Like all human beings, she had a touch of vanity. She felt that she could do things if she only had a chance. How often had she looked at the well-dressed actresses on the stage and wondered how she would look, how delightful she would feel if only she were in their place. The glamor, the tense situation, the fine clothes, the applause, these had lured her until she felt that she, too, could act—that she, too, could compel acknowledgment of power. Now she was told that she really could—that little things she had done about the house had made even him feel her power. It was a delightful sensation while it lasted.

When Drouet was gone, she sat down in her rocking-chair by the window to think about it. As usual, imagination exaggerated the possibilities for her. It was as if he had put fifty cents in her hand and she had exercised the thoughts of a thousand dollars. She saw herself in a score of pathetic situations in which she assumed a tremulous voice and suffering manner. Her mind delighted itself with scenes of luxury and refinement, situations in which she was the cynosure of all eyes, the arbiter of all fates. As she rocked to and fro she felt the tensity of woe in abandonment, the magnificence of wrath after deception, the languor of sorrow after defeat. Thoughts of all the charming women she had seen in plays—every fancy, every illusion which she had concerning the stage—now came back as a returning tide after the ebb. She built up feelings and a determination which the occasion did not warrant.

Drouet dropped in at the lodge when he went down town, and swashed around with a great *air,* as Quincel met him.

"Where is that young lady you were going to get for us?" asked the latter.

"I've got her," said Drouet.

"Have you?" said Quincel, rather surprised by his promptness; "that's good.

What's her address?" and he pulled out his note-book in order to be able to send her part to her.

"You want to send her her part?" asked the drummer.

"Yes."

"Well, I'll take it. I'm going right by her house in the morning."

"What did you say her address was? We only want it in case we have any information to send her."

"Twenty-nine Ogden Place."

"And her name?"

"Carrie Madenda," said the drummer, firing at random. The lodge members knew him to be single.

"That sounds like somebody that can act, doesn't it?" said Quincel.

"Yes, it does."

He took the part home to Carrie and handed it to her with the manner of one who does a favor.

"He says that's the best part. Do you think you can do it?"

"I don't know until I look it over. You know I'm afraid, now that I've said I would."

"Oh, go on. What have you got to be afraid of? It's a cheap company. The rest of them aren't as good as you are."

"Well, I'll see," said Carrie, pleased to have the part for all her misgivings.

He sidled around, dressing and fidgeting before he arranged to make his next remark.

"They were getting ready to print the programs," he said, "and I gave them the name of Carrie Madenda. Was that all right?"

"Yes, I guess so," said his companion, looking up at him. She was thinking it was slightly strange.

"If you didn't make a hit, you know," he went on.

"Oh, yes," she answered, rather pleased now with his caution. It was clever for Drouet.

"I didn't want to introduce you as my wife, because you'd feel worse then if you didn't *go*. They all know me so well. But you'll *go* all right. Anyhow, you'll probably never meet any of them again."

"Oh, I don't care," said Carrie desperately. She was determined now to have a try at the fascinating game.

Drouet breathed a sigh of relief. He had been afraid that he was about to precipitate another conversation upon the marriage question.

The part of Laura, as Carrie found out when she began to examine it, was one of suffering and tears. As delineated by Mr. Daly, it was true to the most sacred traditions of melodrama as he found it when he began his career. The sorrowful demeanor, the tremolo music, the long, explanatory, cumulative addresses, all were there.

"Poor fellow," read Carrie, consulting the text and drawing her voice out pathetically. "Martin, be sure and give him a glass of wine before he goes."

She was surprised at the briefness of the entire part, not knowing that she must be on the stage while others were talking, and not only be there, but also keep herself in harmony with the dramatic movement of the scenes.

"I think I can do that, though," she concluded.

When Drouet came the next night, she was very much satisfied with her day's study.

"Well, how goes it, Caddie?" he said.

"All right," she laughed. "I think I have it memorized nearly."

"That's good," he said. "Let's hear some of it."

"Oh, I don't know whether I can get up and say it off here," she said bashfully.

"Well, I don't know why you shouldn't. It'll be easier here than it will there."

"I don't know about that," she answered.

Eventually she took off the ball-room episode with considerable feeling, forgetting, as she got deeper in the scene, all about Drouet, and letting herself rise to a fine state of feeling.

"Good," said Drouet; "fine; out o' sight! You're all right, Caddie, I tell you."

He was really moved by her excellent representation and the general appearance of the pathetic little figure as it swayed and finally fainted to the floor. He had bounded up to catch her, and now held her laughing in his arms.

"Ain't you afraid you'll hurt yourself?" he asked.

"Not a bit."

"Well, you're a wonder. Say, I never knew you could do anything like that."

"I never did, either," said Carrie merrily, her face flushed with delight.

"Well, you can bet that you're all right," said Drouet. "You can take my word for that. You won't fail."

CHAPTER XVII

A GLIMPSE THROUGH THE GATEWAY: HOPE LIGHTENS THE EYE

The, to Carrie, very important theatrical performance was to take place at the Avery on conditions which were to make it more noteworthy than was at first anticipated. The little dramatic student had written to Hurstwood the very morning her part was brought her that she was going to take part in a play.

"I really am," she wrote, feeling that he might take it as a jest; "I have my part now, honest, truly."

Hurstwood smiled in an indulgent way as he read this.

"I wonder what it is going to be? I must see that."

He answered at once, making a pleasant reference to her ability. "I haven't the slightest doubt you will make a success. You must come to the park to-morrow morning and tell me all about it."

Carrie gladly complied, and revealed all the details of the undertaking as she understood it.

"Well," he said, "that's fine. I'm glad to hear it. Of course, you will do well, you're so clever."

He had truly never seen so much spirit in the girl before. Her tendency to discover a touch of sadness had for the nonce disappeared. As she spoke her eyes were bright, her cheeks red. She radiated much of the pleasure which her undertakings gave her. For all her misgivings—and they were as plentiful as the moments of the day—she was still happy. She could not repress her delight in doing this little thing which, to an ordinary observer, had no importance at all.

Hurstwood was charmed by the development of the fact that the girl had capabilities. There is nothing so inspiring in life as the sight of a legitimate ambition, no matter how incipient. It gives color, force, and beauty to the possessor.

Carrie was now lightened by a touch of this divine afflatus. She drew to herself commendation from her two admirers which she had not earned. Their affection for her naturally heightened their perception of what she was trying to do and their approval of what she did. Her inexperience conserved her own exuberant fancy, which ran riot with every straw of opportunity, making of it a golden divining rod whereby the treasure of life was to be discovered.

"Let's see," said Hurstwood, "I ought to know some of the boys in the lodge. I'm an Elk myself."

"Oh, you mustn't let him know I told you."

"That's so," said the manager.

"I'd like for you to be there, if you want to come, but I don't see how you can unless he asks you."

"I'll be there," said Hurstwood affectionately. "I can fix it so he won't know you told me. You leave it to me."

This interest of the manager was a large thing in itself for the performance, for his standing among the Elks was something worth talking about. Already he was thinking of a box with some friends, and flowers for Carrie. He would make it a dress-suit affair and give the little girl a chance.

Within a day or two, Drouet dropped into the Adams Street resort, and he was at once spied by Hurstwood. It was at five in the afternoon and the place was crowded with merchants, actors, managers, politicians, a goodly company of rotund, rosy figures, silk-hatted, starchy-bosomed, beringed and bescarfpinned to the queen's taste. John L. Sullivan, the pugilist, was at one end of the glittering bar, surrounded by a company of loudly dressed sports, who were holding a most animated conversation. Drouet came across the floor with a festive stride, a new pair of tan shoes squeaking audibly at his progress.

"Well, sir," said Hurstwood, "I was wondering what had become of you. I thought you had gone out of town again."

Drouet laughed.

"If you don't report more regularly we'll have to cut you off the list."

"Couldn't help it," said the drummer, "I've been busy."

They strolled over toward the bar amid the noisy, shifting company of notables. The dressy manager was shaken by the hand three times in as many minutes.

"I hear your lodge is going to give a performance," observed Hurstwood, in the most offhand manner.

"Yes, who told you?"

"No one," said Hurstwood. "They just sent me a couple of tickets, which I can have for two dollars. Is it going to be any good?"

"I don't know," replied the drummer. "They've been trying to get me to get some woman to take a part."

"I wasn't intending to go," said the manager easily. "I'll subscribe, of course. How are things over there?"

"All right. They're going to fit things up out of the proceeds."

"Well," said the manager, "I hope they make a success of it. Have another?"

He did not intend to say any more. Now, if he should appear on the scene with a few friends, he could say that he had been urged to come along. Drouet had a desire to wipe out the possibility of confusion.

"I think the girl is going to take a part in it," he said abruptly, after thinking it over.

"You don't say so! How did that happen?"

"Well, they were short and wanted me to find them some one. I told Carrie, and she seems to want to try."

"Good for her," said the manager. "It'll be a real nice affair. Do her good, too. Has she ever had any experience?"

"Not a bit."

"Oh, well, it isn't anything very serious."

"She's clever, though," said Drouet, casting off any imputation against Carrie's ability. "She picks up her part quick enough."

"You don't say so!" said the manager.

"Yes, sir; she surprised me the other night. By George, if she didn't."

"We must give her a nice little send-off," said the manager. "I'll look after the flowers."

Drouet smiled at his good-nature.

"After the show you must come with me and we'll have a little supper."

"I think she'll do all right," said Drouet.

"I want to see her. She's got to do all right. We'll make her," and the manager gave one of his quick, steely half-smiles, which was a compound of good-nature and shrewdness.

Carrie, meanwhile, attended the first rehearsal. At this performance Mr. Quincel presided, aided by Mr. Millice, a young man who had some qualifications of past experience, which were not exactly understood by anyone. He was so experienced and so business-like, however, that he came very near being rude—failing to remember, as he did, that the individuals he was trying to instruct were volunteer players and not salaried underlings.

"Now, Miss Madenda," he said, addressing Carrie, who stood in one part uncertain as to what move to make, "you don't want to stand like that. Put expression in your face. Remember, you are troubled over the intrusion of the stranger. Walk so," and he struck out across the Avery stage in almost drooping manner.

Carrie did not exactly fancy the suggestion, but the novelty of the situation, the presence of strangers, all more or less nervous, and the desire to do anything rather than make a failure, made her timid. She walked in imitation of her mentor as requested, inwardly feeling that there was something strangely lacking.

"Now, Mrs. Morgan," said the director to one young married woman who was to take the part of Pearl, "you sit here. Now, Mr. Bamberger, you stand here, so. Now, what is it you say?"

"Explain," said Mr. Bamberger feebly. He had the part of Ray, Laura's lover, the society individual who was to waver in his thoughts of marrying her, upon finding that she was a waif and a nobody by birth.

"How is that—what does your text say?"

"Explain," repeated Mr. Bamberger, looking intently at his part.

"Yes, but it also says," the director remarked, "that you are to look shocked. Now, say it again, and see if you can't look shocked."

"Explain!" demanded Mr. Bamberger vigorously.

"No, no, that won't do! Say it this way—*explain*."

"Explain," said Mr. Bamberger, giving a modified imitation.

"That's better. Now go on."

"One night," resumed Mrs. Morgan, whose lines came next, "father and mother were going to the opera. When they were crossing Broadway, the usual crowd of children accosted them for alms—"

"Hold on," said the director, rushing forward, his arm extended. "Put more feeling into what you are saying."

Mrs. Morgan looked at him as if she feared a personal assault. Her eye lightened with resentment.

"Remember, Mrs. Morgan," he added, ignoring the gleam, but modifying his manner, "that you're detailing a pathetic story. You are now supposed to be telling something that is a grief to you. It requires feeling, repression, thus: 'The usual crowd of children accosted them for alms.'"

"All right," said Mrs. Morgan.

"Now, go on."

"As mother felt in her pocket for some change, her fingers touched a cold and trembling hand which had clutched her purse."

"Very good," interrupted the director, nodding his head significantly.

"A pickpocket! Well!" exclaimed Mr. Bamberger, speaking the lines that here fell to him.

"No, no, Mr. Bamberger," said the director, approaching, "not that way. 'A pickpocket—well?' so. That's the idea."

"Don't you think," said Carrie weakly, noticing that it had not been proved yet whether the members of the company knew their lines, let alone the details of expression, "that it would be better if we just went through our lines once to see if we know them? We might pick up some points."

"A very good idea, Miss Madenda," said Mr. Quincel, who sat at the side of the stage, looking serenely on and volunteering opinions which the director did not heed.

"All right," said the latter, somewhat abashed, "it might be well to do it." Then brightening, with a show of authority, "Suppose we run right through, putting in as much expression as we can."

"Good," said Mr. Quincel.

"This hand," resumed Mrs. Morgan, glancing up at Mr. Bamberger and down at her book, as the lines proceeded, "my mother grasped in her own, and so tight that a small, feeble voice uttered an exclamation of pain. Mother looked down, and there beside her was a little ragged girl."

"Very good," observed the director, now hopelessly idle.

"The thief!" exclaimed Mr. Bamberger.

"Louder," put in the director, finding it almost impossible to keep his hands off.

"The thief!" roared poor Bamberger.

"Yes, but a thief hardly six years old, with a face like an angel's. 'Stop,' said my mother. 'What are you doing?'

"'Trying to steal,' said the child.

"'Don't you know that it is wicked to do so?' asked my father.

"'No,' said the girl, 'but it is dreadful to be hungry.'

"'Who told you to steal?' asked my mother.

"'She—there,' said the child, pointing to a squalid woman in a doorway opposite, who fled suddenly down the street. 'That is old Judas,' said the girl."

Mrs. Morgan read this rather flatly, and the director was in despair. He fidgeted around, and then went over to Mr. Quincel.

"What do you think of them?" he asked.

"Oh, I guess we'll be able to whip them into shape," said the latter, with an air of strength under difficulties.

"I don't know," said the director. "That fellow Bamberger strikes me as being a pretty poor shift for a lover."

"He's all we've got," said Quincel, rolling up his eyes. "Harrison went back on me at the last minute. Who else can we get?"

"I don't know," said the director. "I'm afraid he'll never pick up."

At this moment Bamberger was exclaiming, "Pearl, you are joking with me."

"Look at that now," said the director, whispering behind his hand. "My Lord! what can you do with a man who drawls out a sentence like that?"

"Do the best you can," said Quincel consolingly.

The rendition ran on in this wise until it came to where Carrie, as Laura, comes into the room to explain to Ray, who, after hearing Pearl's statement about her birth, had written the letter repudiating her, which, however, he did not deliver. Bamberger was just concluding the words of Ray, "I must go before she returns. Her step! Too late," and was cramming the letter in his pocket, when she began sweetly with:

"Ray!"

"Miss—Miss Courtland," Bamberger faltered weakly.

Carrie looked at him a moment and forgot all about the company present. She began to feel the part, and summoned an indifferent smile to her lips, turning as the lines directed and going to a window, as if he were not present. She did it with a grace which was fascinating to look upon.

"Who is that woman?" asked the director, watching Carrie in her little scene with Bamberger.

"Miss Madenda," said Quincel.

"I know her name," said the director. "But what does she do?"

"I don't know," said Quincel. "She's a friend of one of our members."

"Well, she's got more gumption than any one I've seen here so far—seems to take an interest in what she's doing."

"Pretty, too, isn't she?" said Quincel.

The director strolled away without answering.

In the second scene, where she was supposed to face the company in the ballroom, she did even better, winning the smile of the director, who volunteered, because of her fascination for him, to come over and speak with her.

"Were you ever on the stage?" he asked insinuatingly.

"No," said Carrie.

"You do so well, I thought you might have had some experience."

Carrie only smiled consciously.

He walked away to listen to Bamberger, who was feebly spouting some ardent line.

Mrs. Morgan saw the drift of things and gleamed at Carrie with envious and snapping black eyes.

"She's some cheap professional," she gave herself the satisfaction of thinking, and scorned and hated her accordingly.

The rehearsal ended for one day, and Carrie went home feeling that she had acquitted herself satisfactorily. The words of the director were ringing in her ears, and she longed for an opportunity to tell Hurstwood. She wanted him to know just how well she was doing. Drouet, too, was an object for her confidences. She could hardly wait until he should ask her, and yet she did not have the vanity to bring it up. The drummer, however, had another line of thought to-night, and her little experience did not appeal to him as important. He let the conversation drop, save for what she chose to recite without solicitation, and Carrie was not good at that. He took it for granted that she was doing very well and he was relieved of further worry. Consequently he threw Carrie into repression, which was irritating. She felt his indifference keenly and longed to see Hurstwood. It was as if he were now the only friend she had on earth. The next morning Drouet was interested again, but the damage had been done.

She got a pretty letter from the manager, saying that by the time she got it he would be waiting for her in the park. When she came, he shone upon her as the morning sun.

"Well, my dear," he asked, "how did you come out?"

"Well enough," she said, still somewhat reduced after Drouet.

"Now, tell me just what you did. Was it pleasant?"

Carrie related the incidents of the rehearsal, warming up as she proceeded.

"Well, that's delightful," said Hurstwood. "I'm so glad. I must get over there to see you. When is the next rehearsal?"

"Tuesday," said Carrie, "but they don't allow visitors."

"I imagine I could get in," said Hurstwood significantly.

She was completely restored and delighted by his consideration, but she made him promise not to come around.

"Now, you must do your best to please me," he said encouragingly. "Just remember that I want you to succeed. We will make the performance worth while. You do that now."

"I'll try," said Carrie, brimming with affection and enthusiasm.

"That's the girl," said Hurstwood fondly. "Now, remember," shaking an affectionate finger at her, "your best."

"I will," she answered, looking back.

The whole earth was brimming sunshine that morning. She tripped along, the clear sky pouring liquid blue into her soul. Oh, blessed are the children of endeavor in this, that they try and are hopeful. And blessed also are they who, knowing, smile and approve.

CHAPTER XVIII

JUST OVER THE BORDER: A HAIL AND FAREWELL

By the evening of the 16th the subtle hand of Hurstwood had made itself apparent. He had given the word among his friends—and they were many and influential—that here was something which they ought to attend, and, as a consequence, the sale of tickets by Mr. Quincel, acting for the lodge, had been large. Small four-line notes had appeared in all of the daily newspapers. These he had arranged for by the aid of one of his newspaper friends on the "Times," Mr. Harry McGarren, the managing editor.

"Say, Harry," Hurstwood said to him one evening, as the latter stood at the bar drinking before wending his belated way homeward, "you can help the boys out, I guess."

"What is it?" said McGarren, pleased to be consulted by the opulent manager.

"The Custer Lodge is getting up a little entertainment for their own good, and they'd like a little newspaper notice. You know what I mean—a squib or two saying that it's going to take place."

"Certainly," said McGarren, "I can fix that for you, George."

At the same time Hurstwood kept himself wholly in the background. The members of Custer Lodge could scarcely understand why their little affair was taking so well. Mr. Harry Quincel was looked upon as quite a star for this sort of work.

By the time the 16th had arived Hurstwood's friends had rallied like Romans to a senator's call. A well-dressed, good-natured, flatteringly-inclined audience was assured from the moment he thought of assisting Carrie.

That little student had mastered her part to her own satisfaction, much as she trembled for her fate when she should once face the gathered throng, behind the glare of the footlights. She tried to console herself with the thought that a score of other persons, men and women, were equally tremulous concerning the outcome of their efforts, but she could not disassociate the general danger from her own individual liability. She feared that she would forget her lines, that she might be unable to master the feeling which she now felt concerning her own movements in the play. At times she wished that she had never gone into the affair; at others, she trembled lest she should be paralyzed with fear and stand white and gasping, not knowing what to say and spoiling the entire performance.

In the matter of the company, Mr. Bamberger had disappeared. That hopeless example had fallen under the lance of the director's criticism. Mrs. Morgan was still present, but envious and determined, if for nothing more than spite, to do as well as Carrie at least. A loafing professional had been called in to assume the role of Ray, and, while he was a poor stick of his kind, he was not troubled by any of those qualms which attack the spirit of those who have never faced an audience. He swashed about (cautioned though he was to maintain silence concerning his past theatrical relationships) in such a self-confident manner that he was like to convince everyone of his identity by mere matter of circumstantial evidence.

"It is so easy," he said to Mrs. Morgan, in the usual affected stage voice. "An audience would be the last thing to trouble me. It's the spirit of the part, you know, that is difficult."

Carrie disliked his appearance, but she was too much the actress not to swallow his qualities with complaisance, seeing that she must suffer his fictitious love for the evening.

At six she was ready to go. Theatrical paraphernalia had been provided over and above her care. She had practiced her make-up in the morning, had rehearsed and arranged her material for the evening by one o'clock, and had gone home to have a final look at her part, waiting for the evening to come.

On this occasion the lodge sent a carriage. Drouet rode with her as far as the door, and then went about the neighboring stores, looking for some good cigars. The little actress marched nervously into her dressing-room and began that painfully anticipated matter of make-up which was to transform her, a simple maiden, to Laura, The Belle of Society.

The flare of the gas-jets, the open trunks, suggestive of travel and display, the scattered contents of the make-up box—rouge, pearl powder, whiting, burnt cork, India ink, pencils for the eyelids, wigs, scissors, looking-glasses, drapery—in short, all the nameless paraphernalia of disguise, have a remarkable atmosphere of their own. Since her arrival in the city many things had influenced her, but always in a far-removed manner. This new atmosphere was more friendly. It was wholly unlike the great brilliant mansions which waved her coldly away, permitting her only awe and distant wonder. This took her by the hand kindly, as one who says, "My dear, come in." It opened for her as if for its own. She had wondered at the greatness of the names upon the bill-boards, the marvel of the long notices in the papers, the beauty of the dresses upon the stage, the atmosphere of carriages, flowers, refinement. Here was no illusion. Here was an open door to see all of that. She had come upon it as one who stumbles upon a secret passage, and behold, she was in the chamber of diamonds and delight!

As she dressed with a flutter, in her little stage room, hearing the voices outside, seeing Mr. Quincel hurrying here and there, noting Mrs. Morgan and Mrs. Hoagland at their nervous work of preparation, seeing all the twenty members of the cast moving about and worrying over what the result would be, she could not help thinking what a delight this would be if it would endure; how perfect a state, if she could only do well now, and then some time get a place as a real actress. The thought had taken a mighty hold upon her. It hummed in her ears as the melody of an old song.

Outside in the little lobby another scene was being enacted. Without the interest of Hurstwood, the little hall would probably have been comfortably filled, for the members of the lodge were moderately interested in its welfare. Hurstwood's word, however, had gone the rounds. It was to be a full-dress affair. The four boxes had been taken. Dr. Norman McNeill Hale and his wife were to occupy one. This was quite a card. C. R. Walker, dry-goods merchant and possessor of at least two hundred thousand dollars, had taken another; a well-known coal merchant had been induced to take the third, and Hurstwood and his friends the fourth. Among the latter was Drouet. The people who were now pouring here were not celebrities, nor even local notabilities, in a general sense. They were the lights of a certain circle—the circle of small fortunes and secret order distinctions. These gentlemen Elks knew the standing of one another. They had regard for the ability which could amass a small fortune, own a nice home, keep a barouche or carriage, perhaps, wear fine clothes, and maintain a good mercantile position. Naturally, Hurstwood, who was a little above the order of mind which accepted this standard as perfect, who had shrewdness and much assumption of dignity, who held an imposing and authoritative position, and commanded friendship by intuitive tact in handling people was quite a figure. He was more generally known than most others in the same circle, and was looked upon as someone whose reserve covered a mine of influence and solid financial prosperity.

To-night he was in his element. He came with several friends directly from Rector's in a carriage. In the lobby he met Drouet, who was just returning from a trip for more cigars. All five now joined in an animated conversation concerning the company present and the general drift of lodge affairs.

"Who's here?" said Hurstwood, passing into the theater proper, where the lights were turned up and a company of gentlemen were laughing and talking in the open space back of the seats.

"Why, how do you do, Mr. Hurstwood?" came from the first individual recognized.

"Glad to see you," said the latter, grasping his hand lightly.

"Looks quite an affair, doesn't it?"

"Yes, indeed," said the manager.

"Custer seems to have the backing of its members," observed the friend.

"So it should," said the knowing manager. "I'm glad to see it."

"Well, George," said another rotund citizen, whose avoirdupois made necessary an almost alarming display of starched shirt bosom, "how goes it with you?"

"Excellent," said the manager.

"What brings you over here? You're not a member of Custer."

"Good-nature," returned the manager. "Like to see the boys, you know."

"Wife here?"

"She couldn't come to-night. She's not well."

"Sorry to hear it—nothing serious, I hope."

"No, just feeling a little ill."

"I remember Mrs. Hurstwood when she was traveling once with you over to St. Joe—" and here the newcomer launched off in a trivial recollection, which was terminated by the arrival of more friends.

"Why, George, how are you?" said another genial West Side politician and lodge member. "My, but I'm glad to see you again; how are things, anyhow?"

"Very well; I see you got that nomination for alderman."

"Yes, we whipped them out over there without much trouble."

"What do you suppose Hennessy will do now?"

"Oh, he'll go back to hs brick business. He has a brickyard, you know."

"I didn't know that," said the manager. "Felt pretty sore, I suppose, over his defeat."

"Perhaps," said the other, winking shrewdly.

Some of the more favored of his friends whom he had invited began to roll up in carriages now. They came shuffling in with a great show of finery and much evident feeling of content and importance.

"Here we are," said Hurstwood, turning to one from a group with whom he was talking.

"That's right," returned the newcomer, a gentleman of about forty-five.

"And say," he whispered, jovially, pulling Hurstwood over by the shoulder so that he might whisper in his ear, "if this isn't a good show, I'll punch your head."

"You ought to pay for seeing your old friends. Bother the show!"

To another who inquired, "Is it something really good?" the manager replied:

"I don't know. I don't suppose so." Then, lifting his hand graciously, "For the lodge."

"Lots of boys out, eh?"

"Yes, look up Shanahan. He was just asking for you a moment ago."

It was thus that the little theater resounded to a babble of successful voices, the creak of fine clothes, the commonplace of good-nature, and all largely because of this man's bidding. Look at him any time within the half hour before the curtain was up, he was a member of an eminent group—a rounded company of five or more whose stout figures, large white bosoms, and shining pins bespoke the character of their success. The gentlemen who brought their wives called him out to shake hands. Seats clicked, ushers bowed while he looked blandly on. He was evidently a light among them, reflecting in his personality the ambitions of those who greeted him. He was acknowledged, fawned upon, in a way lionized. Through it all one could see the standing of the man. It was greatness in a way, small as it was.

CHAPTER XIX

AN HOUR IN ELFLAND: A CLAMOR HALF HEARD

At last the curtain was ready to go up. All the details of the make-up had been completed, and the company settled down as the leader of the small, hired orchestra tapped significantly upon his music rack with his baton and began the soft curtain-raising strain. Hurstwood ceased talking, and went with Drouet and his friend Sagar Morrison around to the box.

"Now, we'll see how the little girl does," he said to Drouet, in a tone which no one else could hear.

On the stage, six of the characters had already appeared in the opening parlor scene. Drouet and Hurstwood saw at a glance that Carrie was not among them, and went on talking in a whisper. Mrs. Morgan, Mrs. Hoagland, and the actor who had taken Bamberger's part were representing the principal roles in this scene. The professional, whose name was Patton, had little to recommend him outside of his assurance, but this at the present moment was most palpably needed. Mrs. Morgan, as Pearl, was stiff with fright. Mrs. Hoagland was husky in the throat. The whole company was so weak-kneed that the lines were merely spoken, and nothing more. It took all the hope and uncritical good-nature of the audience to keep from manifesting pity by that unrest which is the agony of failure.

Hurstwood was perfectly indifferent. He took it for granted that it would be worthless. All he cared for was to have it endurable enough to allow for pretension and congratulation afterward.

After the first rush of fright, however, the players got over the danger of collapse. They rambled weakly forward, losing nearly all the expression which was intended, and making the thing dull in the extreme, when Carrie came in.

One glance at her, and both Hurstwood and Drouet saw plainly that she also was weak-kneed. She came faintly across the stage, saying:

"And you, sir; we have been looking for you since eight o'clock," but with so little color and in such a feeble voice that it was positively painful.

"She's frightened," whispered Drouet to Hurstwood.

The manager made no answer.

She had a line presently which was supposed to be funny.

"Well, that's as much as to say that I'm a sort of life pill."

It came out so flat, however, that it was a deathly thing, Drouet fidgeted. Hurstwood moved his toe the least bit.

There was another place in which Laura was to rise and, with a sense of impending disaster, say, sadly:

"I wish you hadn't said that, Pearl. You know the old proverb, 'Call a maid by a married name.'"

The lack of feeling in the thing was ridiculous. Carrie did not get it at all. She seemed to be talking in her sleep. It looked as if she were certain to be a wretched failure. She was more hopeless than Mrs. Morgan, who had recovered somewhat, and was now saying her lines clearly at least. Drouet looked away from the stage at the audience. The latter held out silently, hoping for a general change, of course. Hurstwood fixed his eye on Carrie, as if to hypnotize her into doing better. He was pouring determination of his own in her direction. He felt sorry for her.

In a few more minutes it fell to her to read the letter sent in by the strange villain. The audience had been slightly diverted by a conversation between the professional actor and a character called Snorky, impersonated by a short little American, who really developed some humor as a half-crazed, one-armed soldier, turned messenger for a living. He bawled his lines out with such defiance that, while they really did not partake of the humor intended, they were funny. Now he was off, however, and it was back to pathos, with Carrie as the chief figure. She did not recover. She wandered through the whole scene between herself and the intruding villain, straining the patience of the audience, and finally exiting, much to their relief.

"She's too nervous," said Drouet, feeling in the mildness of the remark that he was lying for once.

"Better go back and say a word to her."

Drouet was glad to do anything for relief. He fairly hustled around to the side entrance, and was let in by the friendly doorkeeper. Carrie was standing in the wings, weakly waiting her next cue, all the snap and nerve gone out of her.

"Say, Cad," he said, looking at her, "you mustn't be nervous. Wake up. Those guys out there don't amount to anything. What are you afraid of?"

"I don't know," said Carrie. "I just don't seem to be able to do it."

She was grateful for the drummer's presence, though. She had found the company so nervous that her own strength had gone.

"Come on," said Drouet. "Brace up. What are you afraid of? Go on out there now, and do the trick. What do you care?"

Carrie revived a little under the drummer's electrical, nervous condition.

"Did I do so very bad?"

"Not a bit. All you need is a little more ginger. Do it as you showed me. Get that toss of your head you had the other night."

Carrie remembered her triumph in the room. She tried to think she could do it.

"What's next?" he said, looking at her part, which she had been studying.

"Why, the scene between Ray and me when I refuse him."

"Well, now you do that lively," said the drummer. "Put in snap, that's the thing. Act as if you didn't care."

"Your turn next, Miss Madenda," said the prompter.

"Oh, dear," said Carrie.

"Well, you're a chump for being afraid," said Drouet. "Come on now, brace up. I'll watch you from right here."

"Will you?" said Carrie.

"Yes, now go on. Don't be afraid."

The prompter signaled her.

She started out, weak as ever, but suddenly her nerve partially returned. She thought of Drouet looking.

"Ray," she said, gently, using a tone of voice much more calm than when she had last appeared. It was the scene which had pleased the director at the rehearsal.

"She's easier," thought Hurstwood to himself.

She did not do the part as she had at rehearsal, but she was better. The audience was at least not irritated. The improvement of the work of the entire company took away direct observation from her. They were making very fair progress, and now it looked as if the play would be passable, in the less trying parts at least.

Carrie came off warm and nervous.

"Well," she said, looking at him, "was it any better?"

"Well, I should say so. That's the way. Put life into it. You did that about a thousand per cent. better than you did the other scene. Now go on and fire up. You can do it. Knock 'em."

"Was it really better?"

"Better, I should say so. What comes next?"

"That ballroom scene."

"Well, you can do that all right," he said.

"I don't know," answered Carrie.

"Why, woman," he exclaimed, "you did it for me! Now you go out there and do it. It'll be fun for you. Just do as you did in the room. If you'll reel it off that way, I'll bet you make a hit. Now, what'll you bet? You do it."

The drummer usually allowed his ardent good-nature to get the better of his speech. He really did think that Carrie had acted this particular scene very well, and he wanted her to repeat it in public. His enthusiasm was due to the mere spirit of the occasion.

When the time came, he buoyed Carrie up most effectually. He began to make her feel as if she had done very well. The old melancholy of desire began to come back as he talked to her, and by the time the situation rolled around she was running high in feeling.

"I think I can do this."

"Sure you can. Now you go ahead and see."

On the stage, Mrs. Van Dam was making her cruel insinuation against Laura.

Carrie listened, and caught the infection of something—she did not know what. Her nostrils sniffed thinly.

"It means," the professional actor began, speaking as Ray, "that society is a terrible avenger of insult. Have you ever heard of the Siberian wolves? When one of the pack falls through weakness, the others devour him. It is not an elegant comparison, but there is something wolfish in society. Laura has mocked it with a pretence, and society, which is made up of pretence, will bitterly resent the mockery."

At the sound of her stage name Carrie started. She began to feel the bitterness of the situation. The feelings of the outcast descended upon her. She hung at the wing's edge, wrapt in her own mounting thoughts. She hardly heard anything more, save her own rumbling blood.

"Come, girls," said Mrs. Van Dam, solemnly, "let us look after our things. They are no longer safe when such an accomplished thief enters."

"Cue," said the prompter, close to her side, but she did not hear. Already she was moving forward with a steady grace, born of inspiration. She dawned upon the audience, handsome and proud, shifting, with the necessity of the situation, to a cold, white, helpless object, as the social pack moved away from her scornfully.

Hurstwood blinked his eyes and caught the infection. The radiating waves of feeling and sincerity were already breaking against the farthest walls of the chamber. The magic of passion, which will yet dissolve the world, was here at work.

There was a drawing, too, of attention, a riveting of feeling, heretofore wandering.

"Ray! Ray! Why do you not come back to her?" was the cry of Pearl.

Every eye was fixed on Carrie, still proud and scornful. They moved as she moved. Their eyes were with her eyes.

Mrs. Morgan, as Pearl, approached her.

"Let us go home," she said.

"No," answered Carrie, her voice assuming for the first time a penetrating quality which it had never known. "Stay with him!"

She pointed an almost accusing hand toward her lover. Then, with a pathos which struck home because of its utter simplicity, "He shall not suffer long."

Hurstwood realized that he was seeing something extraordinarily good. It was heightened for him by the applause of the audience as the curtain descended and the fact that it was Carrie. He thought now that she was beautiful. She had done something which was above his sphere. He felt a keen delight in realizing that she was his.

"Fine," he said, and then, seized by a sudden impulse, arose and went about to the stage door.

When he came in upon Carrie she was still with Drouet. His feelings for her were most exuberant. He was almost swept away by the strength and feeling she exhibited. His desire was to pour forth his praise with the unbounded feelings of a lover, but here was Drouet, whose affection was also rapidly reviving. The latter was more fascinated, if anything, than Hurstwood. At least, in the nature of things, it took a more ruddy form.

"Well, well," said Drouet, "you did out of sight. That was simply great. I knew you could do it. Oh, but you're a little daisy!"

Carrie's eyes flamed with the light of achievement.

"Did I do all right?"

"Did you? Well, I guess. Didn't you hear the applause?"

There was some faint sound of clapping yet.

"I thought I got it something like—I felt it."

Just then Hurstwood came in. Instinctively he felt the change in Drouet. He saw that the drummer was near to Carrie, and jealousy leaped alight in his bosom. In a flash of thought, he reproached himself for having sent him back. Also, he hated him as an intruder. He could scarcely pull himself down to the level where he would have to congratulate Carrie as a friend. Nevertheless, the man mastered himself, and it was a triumph. He almost jerked the old subtle light to his eyes.

"I thought," he said, looking at Carrie, "I would come around and tell you how well you did, Mrs. Drouet. It was delightful."

Carrie took the cue, and replied:

"Oh, thank you."

"I was just telling her," put in Drouet, now delighted with his possession, "that I thought she did fine."

"Indeed you did," said Hurstwood, turning upon Carrie eyes in which she read more than the words.

Carrie laughed luxuriantly.

"If you do as well in the rest of the play, you will make us all think you are a born actress."

Carrie smiled again. She felt the acuteness of Hurstwood's position, and wished deeply that she could be alone with him, but she did not understand the change in Drouet. Hurstwood found that he could not talk, repressed as he was, and grudging Drouet every moment of his presence, he bowed himself out with the elegance of a Faust. Outside he set his teeth with envy.

"Damn it!" he said, "is he always going to be in the way?" He was moody when he got back to the box, and could not talk for thinking of his wretched situation.

As the curtain for the next act arose, Drouet came back. He was very much enlivened in temper and inclined to whisper, but Hurstwood pretended interest. He fixed his eyes on the stage, although Carrie was not there, a short bit of melodramatic comedy preceding her entrance. He did not see what was going on, however. He was thinking his own thoughts, and they were wretched.

The progress of the play did not improve matters for him. Carrie, from now on, was easily the center of interest. The audience, which had been inclined to feel that nothing could be good after the first gloomy impression, now went to the other extreme and saw power where it was not. The general feeling reacted on Carrie. She presented her part with some felicity, though nothing like the intensity which had aroused the feeling at the end of the long first act.

Both Hurstwood and Drouet viewed her pretty figure with rising feelings. The fact that such ability should reveal itself in her, that they should see it set forth under such effective circumstances, framed almost in massy gold and shone upon by the appropriate lights of sentiment and personality, heightened her charm for them. She was more than the old Carrie to Drouet. He longed to be at home with her until he could tell her. He awaited impatiently the end, when they should go home alone.

Hurstwood, on the contrary, saw in the strength of her new attractiveness his miserable predicament. He could have cursed the man beside him. By the Lord, he could not even applaud feelingly as he would. For once he must simulate when it left a taste in his mouth.

It was in the last act that Carrie's fascination for her lovers assumed its most effective character.

Hurstwood listened to its progress, wondering when Carrie would come on. He had not long to wait. The author had used the artifice of sending all the merry company for a drive, and now Carrie came in alone. It was the first time that Hurstwood had had a chance to see her facing the audience quite alone, for nowhere else had she been without a foil of some sort. He suddenly felt, as she entered, that her old strength—the power that had grasped him at the end of the first act—had come back. She seemed to be gaining feeling, now that the play was drawing to a close and the opportunity for great action was passing.

"Poor Pearl," she said, speaking with natural pathos. "It is a sad thing to want for happiness, but it is a terrible thing to see another groping about blindly for it, when it is almost within the grasp."

She was gazing now sadly out upon the open sea, her arm resting listlessly upon the polished door-post.

Hurstwood began to feel a deep sympathy for her and for himself. He could almost feel that she was talking to him. He was, by a combination of feelings and entanglements, almost deluded by that quality of voice and manner which, like a pathetic strain of music, seems ever a personal and intimate thing. Pathos has this quality, that it seems ever addressed to one alone.

"And yet, she can be very happy with him," went on the little actress. "Her sunny temper, her joyous face will brighten any home."

She turned slowly toward the audience without seeing. There was so much simplicity in her movements that she seemed wholly alone. Then she found a seat by a table, and turned over some books, devoting a thought to them.

"With no longings for what I may not have," she breathed in conclusion—and it was almost a sigh—"my existence hidden from all save two in the wide world, and making my joy out of the joy of that innocent girl who will soon be his wife."

Hurstwood was sorry when a character, known as Peach Blossom, interrupted her. He stirred irritably, for he wished her to go on. He was charmed by the pale face, the lissome figure, draped in pearl gray, with a coiled string of pearls at her throat. Carrie had the air of one who was weary and in need of protection, and, under the fascinating make-believe of the moment, he rose in feeling until he was ready in spirit to go to her and ease her out of her misery by adding to his own delight.

In a moment Carrie was alone again, and was saying, with animation:

"I must return to the city, no matter what dangers may lurk here. I must go, secretly if I can; openly, if I must."

There was a sound of horses' hoofs outside, and then Ray's voice saying:

"No, I shall not ride again. Put him up."

He entered, and then began a scene which had as much to do with the creation of the tragedy of affection in Hurstwood as anything in his peculiar and involved career. For Carrie had resolved to make something of this scene, and, now that the cue had come, it began to take a feeling hold upon her. Both Hurstwood and Drouet noted the rising sentiment as she proceeded.

"I thought you had gone with Pearl," she said to her lover.

"I did go part of the way, but I left the party a mile down the road."

"You and Pearl had no disagreement?"

"No—yes; that is, we always have. Our social barometers always stand at 'cloudy and overcast.'"

"And whose fault is that?" she said, easily.

"Not mine," he answered, pettishly. "I know I do all I can—I say all I can—but she—"

This was rather awkwardly put by Patton, but Carrie redeemed it with a grace which was inspiring.

"But she is your wife," she said, fixing her whole attention upon the stilled actor, and softening the quality of her voice until it was again low and musical. "Ray, my friend, courtship is the text from which the whole sermon of married life takes its theme. Do not let yours be discontented and unhappy."

She put her two little hands together and pressed them appealingly.

Hurstwood gazed with slightly parted lips. Drouet was fidgeting with satisfaction.

"To be my wife, yes," went on the actor in a manner which was weak by comparison, but which could not now spoil the tender atmosphere which Carrie had created and maintained. She did not seem to feel that he was wretched. She would have done nearly as well with a block of wood. The accessories she needed were within her own imagination. The acting of others could not affect them.

"And you repent already?" she said, slowly.

"I lost you," he said, seizing her little hand, "and I was at the mercy of any flirt who chose to give me an inviting look. It was your fault—you know it was—why did you leave me?"

Carrie turned slowly away, and seemed to be mastering some impulse in silence. Then she turned back.

"Ray," she said, "the greatest happiness I have ever felt has been the thought that all your affection was forever bestowed upon a virtuous woman, your equal in family, fortune, and accomplishments. What a revelation do you make to me now! What is it makes you continually war with your happiness?"

The last question was asked so simply that it came to the audience and the lover as a personal thing.

At last it came to the part where the lover exclaimed, "Be to me as you used to be."

Carrie answered, with affecting sweetness, "I cannot be that to you, but I can speak in the spirit of the Laura who is dead to you forever."

"Be it as you will," said Patton.

Hurstwood leaned forward. The whole audience was silent and intent.

"Let the woman you look upon be wise or vain," said Carrie, her eyes bent sadly upon the lover, who had sunk into a seat, "beautiful or homely, rich or poor, she has but one thing she can really give or refuse—her heart."

Drouet felt a scratch in his throat.

"Her beauty, her wit, her accomplishments, she may sell to you; but her love is the treasure without money and without price."

The manager suffered this as a personal appeal. It came to him as if they were alone, and he could hardly restrain the tears for sorrow over the hopeless, pathetic, and yet dainty and appealing woman whom he loved. Drouet also was beside himself. He was resolving that he would be to Carrie what he had never been before. He would marry her, by George! She was worth it.

"She asks only in return," said Carrie, scarcely hearing the small, scheduled reply of her lover, and putting herself even more in harmony with the plaintive melody now issuing from the orchestra, "that when you look upon her your eyes shall speak devotion; that when you address her your voice shall be gentle, loving, and kind; that you shall not despise her because she cannot understand all at once your vigorous thoughts and ambitious designs; for, when misfortune and evil have defeated your greatest purposes, her love remains to console you. You look to the trees," she continued, while Hurstwood restrained his feelings only by the grimmest repression, "for strength and grandeur; do not despise the flowers because their fragrance is all they have to give. Remember," she concluded, tenderly, "love is all a woman has to give," and she laid a strange, sweet accent on the all, "but it is the only thing which God permits us to carry beyond the grave."

The two men were in the most harrowed state of affection. They scarcely heard the few remaining words with which the scene concluded. They only saw their idol, moving about with appealing grace, continuing a power which to them was a revelation.

Hurstwood resolved a thousand things, Drouet as well. They joined equally in the burst of applause which called Carrie out. Drouet pounded his hands until they ached. Then he jumped up again and started out. As he went, Carrie came out, and, seeing an immense basket of flowers being hurried down the aisle toward her, she waited. They were Hurstwood's. She looked toward the manager's box for a moment, caught his eye, and smiled. He could have leaped out of the box to enfold her. He forgot the need of circumspectness which his married state enforced. He almost forgot that he had with him in the box those who knew him. By the Lord, he would have that lovely girl if it took his all. He would act at once. This should be the end of Drouet, and don't you forget it. He would not wait another day. The drummer should not have her.

He was so excited that he could not stay in the box. He went into the lobby, and then into the street, thinking. Drouet did not return. In a few minutes the last act was over, and he was crazy to have Carrie alone. He cursed the luck that could keep him smiling, bowing, shamming, when he wanted to tell her that he loved her, when he wanted to whisper to her alone. He groaned as he saw that his hopes were futile. He must even take her to supper, shamming. He finally went about and asked how she was getting along. The actors were all dressing, talking, hurrying about. Drouet was palavering himself with the looseness of excitement and passion. The manager mastered himself only by a great effort.

"We are going to supper, of course," he said, with a voice that was a mockery of his heart.

"Oh, yes," said Carrie, smiling.

The little actress was in fine feather. She was realizing now what it was to be petted. For once she was the admired, the sought-for. The independence of success now made its first faint showing. With the tables turned, she was looking down, rather than up, to her lover. She did not fully realize that this was so, but there was something in condescension coming from her which was infinitely sweet. When she was ready they climbed into the waiting coach and drove downtown; once, only, did she find an opportunity to express her feeling, and that was when the manager preceded Drouet in the coach and sat beside her. Before Drouet was fully in she had squeezed Hurstwood's hand in a gentle, impulsive manner. The manager was beside himself with affection. He could have sold his soul to be with her alone. "Ah," he thought, "the agony of it."

Drouet hung on, thinking he was all in all. The dinner was spoiled by his enthusiasm. Hurstwood went home feeling as if he should die if he did not find affectionate relief. He whispered "to-morrow" passionately to Carrie, and she understood. He walked away from the drummer and his prize at parting feeling as if he could slay him and not regret. Carrie also felt the misery of it.

"Good-night," he said, simulating an easy friendliness.

"Good-night," said the little actress, tenderly.

"The fool!" he said, now hating Drouet. "The idiot! I'll do him yet, and that quick! We'll see to-morrow."

"Well, if you aren't a wonder," Drouet was saying, complacently, squeezing Carrie's arm. "You are the dandiest little girl on earth."

CHAPTER XX

THE LURE OF THE SPIRIT: THE FLESH IN PURSUIT

Passion in a man of Hurstwood's nature takes a vigorous form. It is no musing, dreamy thing. There is none of the tendency to sing outside of my lady's window—to languish and repine in the face of difficulties. In the night he was long getting to sleep because of too much thinking, and in the morning he was early awake, seizing with alacrity upon the same dear subject and pursuing it with vigor. He was out of sorts physically, as well as disordered mentally, for did he not delight in a new manner in his Carrie, and was not Drouet in the way? Never was man more harassed than he by the thoughts of his love being held by the elated, flush-mannered drummer. He would have given anything, it seemed to him, to have the complication ended—to have Carrie acquiesce to an arrangement which would dispose of Drouet effectually and forever.

What to do. He dressed thinking. He moved about in the same chamber with his wife, unmindful of her presence.

At breakfast he found himself without an appetite. The meat to which he helped himself remained on his plate untouched. His coffee grew cold, while he scanned the paper indifferently. Here and there he read a little thing, but remembered nothing. Jessica had not yet come down. His wife sat at one end of the table revolving thoughts of her own in silence. A new servant had been recently installed and had forgot the napkins. On this account the silence was irritably broken by a reproof.

"I've told you about this before, Maggie," said Mrs. Hurstwood. "I'm not going to tell you again."

Hurstwood took a glance at his wife. She was frowning. Just now her manner irritated him excessively. Her next remark was addressed to him.

"Have you made up your mind, George, when you will take your vacation?"

It was customary for them to discuss the regular summer outing at this season of the year.

"Not yet," he said, "I'm very busy just now."

"Well, you'll want to make up your mind pretty soon, won't you, if we're going?" she returned.

"I guess we have a few days yet," he said.

"Hmff," she returned. "Don't wait until the season's over."

She stirred in aggravation as she said this.

"There you go again," he observed. "One would think I never did anything, the way you begin."

"Well, I want to know about it," she reiterated.

"You've got a few days yet," he insisted. "You'll not want to start before the races are over."

He was irritated to think that this should come up when he wished to have his thoughts for other purposes.

"Well, we may. Jessica doesn't want to stay until the end of the races."

"What did you want with a season ticket, then?"

"Uh!" she said, using the sound as an exclamation of disgust, "I'll not argue with you," and therewith arose to leave the table.

"Say," he said, rising, putting a note of determination in his voice which caused her to delay her departure. "What's the matter with you of late? Can't I talk with you any more?"

"Certainly you can *talk* with me," she replied, laying emphasis on the word.

"Well, you wouldn't think so by the way you act. Now, you want to know when I'll be ready—not for a month yet. Maybe not then."

"We'll go without you."

"You will, eh?" he sneered.

"Yes, we will."

He was astonished at the woman's determination, but it only irritated him the more.

"Well, we'll see about that. It seems to me you're trying to run things with a pretty high hand of late. You talk as though you settled my affairs for me. Well, you don't. You don't regulate anything that's connected with me. If you want to go, go, but you won't hurry me by any such talk as that."

He was thoroughly aroused now. His dark eyes snapped, and he crunched his paper as he laid it down. Mrs. Hurstwood said nothing more. He was just finishing when she turned on her heel and went out into the hall and upstairs. He paused for a moment, as if hesitating, then sat down and drank a little coffee, and thereafter arose and went for his hat and gloves upon the main floor.

His wife had really not anticipated a row of this character. She had come down to the breakfast table feeling a little out of sorts with herself and revolving a scheme which she had in her mind. Jessica had called her attention to the fact that the races were not what they were supposed to be. The social opportunities were not what they had thought they would be this year. The beautiful girl found going every day a dull thing. There was an earlier exodus this year of people who were anybody to the watering places and Europe. In her own circle of acquaintances several young men in whom she was interested had gone to Waukesha. She began to feel that she would like to go too, and her mother agreed with her.

Accordingly, Mrs. Hurstwood decided to broach the subject. She was thinking this over when she came down to the table, but for some reason the atmosphere was wrong. She was not sure, after it was all over, just how the trouble had begun. She was determined now, however, that her husband was a brute, and that, under no circumstances, would she let this go by unsettled. She would have more ladylike treatment or she would know why.

For his part, the manager was loaded with the care of this new argument until he reached his office and started from there to meet Carrie. Then the other complications of love, desire, and opposition possessed him. His thoughts fled on before him upon eagles' wings. He could hardly wait until he should meet Carrie face to face. What was the night, after all, without her—what the day? She must and should be his.

For her part, Carrie had experienced a world of fancy and feeling since she had left him, the night before. She had listened to Drouet's enthusiastic maunderings with much regard for that part which concerned herself, with very little for that which affected his own gain. She kept him at such lengths as she could, because her thoughts were with her own triumph. She felt Hurstwood's passion as a delightful background to her own achievement, and she wondered what he would have to say. She was sorry for him, too, with that peculiar sorrow which finds something complimentary to itself in the misery of another. She was now experiencing the first shades of feeling of that subtle change which removes one out of the ranks of the suppliants into the lines of the dispensers of charity. She was, all in all, exceedingly happy.

On the morrow, however, there was nothing in the papers concerning the event, and, in view of the flow of common, everyday things about, it now lost a shade of the glow of the previous evening. Drouet himself was not talking so much *of* as *for* her. He felt instinctively that, for some reason or other, he needed reconstruction in her regard.

"I think," he said, as he spruced around their chambers the next morning, preparatory to going downtown, "that I'll straighten out that little deal of mine this month and then we'll get married. I was talking with Mosher about that yesterday."

"No, you won't," said Carrie, who was coming to feel a certain faint power to jest with the drummer.

"Yes, I will," he exclaimed, more feelingly than usual, adding, with the tone of one who pleads, "Don't you believe what I've told you?"

Carrie laughed a little.

"Of course I do," she answered.

Drouet's assurance now misgave him. Shallow as was his mental observation, there was that in the things which had happened which made his little power of analysis useless. Carrie was still with him, but not helpless and pleading. There was a lilt in her voice which was new. She did not study him with eyes expressive of dependence. The drummer was feeling the shadow of something which was coming. It colored his feelings and made him develop those little attentions and say those little words which were mere forefendations against danger.

Shortly afterward he departed, and Carrie prepared for her meeting with Hurstwood. She hurried at her toilet, which was soon made, and hastened down the stairs. At the corner she passed Drouet, but they did not see each other.

The drummer had forgotten some bills which he wished to turn into his house. He hastened up the stairs and burst into the room, but found only the chambermaid, who was cleaning up.

"Hello," he exclaimed, half to himself, "has Carrie gone?"

"Your wife? Yes, she went out just a few minutes ago."

"That's strange," thought Drouet. "She didn't say a word to me. I wonder where she went?"

He hastened about, rummaging in his valise for what he wanted, and finally pocketing it. Then he turned his attention to his fair neighbor, who was good-looking and kindly disposed towards him.

"What are you up to?" he said, smiling.

"Just cleaning," she replied, stopping and winding a dusting towel about her hand.

"Tired of it?"

"Not so very."

"Let me show you something," he said, affably, coming over and taking out of his pocket a little lithographed card which had been issued by a wholesale tobacco company. On this was printed a picture of a pretty girl, holding a striped parasol, the colors of which could be changed by means of a revolving disk in the back, which showed red, yellow, green, and blue through little interstices made in the ground occupied by the umbrella top.

"Isn't that clever?" he said, handing it to her and showing her how it worked. "You never saw anything like that before."

"Isn't it nice?" she answered.

"You can have it if you want it," he remarked.

"That's a pretty ring you have," he said, touching a commonplace setting which adorned the hand holding the card he had given her.

"Do you think so?"

"That's right," he answered, making use of a pretence at examinations to secure her finger. "That's fine."

The ice being thus broken, he launched into further observation, pretending to forget that her fingers were still retained by his. She soon withdrew them, however, and retreated a few feet to rest against the window-sill.

"I didn't see you for a long time," she said, coquettishly, repulsing one of his exuberant approaches. "You must have been away."

"I was," said Drouet.

"Do you travel far?"

"Pretty far—yes."

"Do you like it?"

"Oh, not very well. You get tired of it after a while."

"I wish I could travel," said the girl, gazing idly out of the window.

"What has become of your friend, Mr. Hurstwood?" she suddenly asked, bethinking herself of the manager, who, from her own observation, seemed to contain promising material.

"He's here in town. What makes you ask about him?"

"Oh, nothing, only he hasn't been here since you got back."

"How did you come to know him?"

"Didn't I take up his name a dozen times in the last month?"

"Get out," said the drummer, lightly. "He hasn't called more than half a dozen times since we've been here."

"He hasn't, eh?" said the girl, smiling. "That's all you know about it."

Drouet took on a slightly more serious tone. He was uncertain as to whether she was joking or not.

"Tease," he said, "what makes you smile that way?"

"Oh, nothing."

"Have you seen him recently?"

"Not since you came back," she laughed.

"Before?"

"Certainly."

"How often?"

"Why, nearly every day."

She was a mischievous newsmonger, and was keenly wondering what the effect of her words would be.

"Who did he come to see?" asked the drummer, incredulously.

"Mrs. Drouet."

He looked rather foolish at this answer, and then attempted to correct himself so as not to appear a dupe.

"Well," he said, "what of it?"

"Nothing," replied the girl, her head cocked coquettishly on one side.

"He's an old friend," he went on, getting deeper into the mire.

He would have gone on further with his little flirtation, but the taste for it was temporarily removed. He was quite relieved when the girl's name was called from below.

"I've got to go," she said, moving away from him airily.

"I'll see you later," he said, with a pretence of disturbance at being interrupted.

When she was gone, he gave freer play to his feelings. His face, never easily controlled by him, expressed all the perplexity and disturbance which he felt. Could it be that Carrie had received so many visits and yet said nothing about them? Was Hurstwood lying? What did the chambermaid mean by it, anyway? He had thought there was something odd about Carrie's manner at the time. Why did she look so disturbed when he had asked her how many times Hurstwood had called? By George! he remembered now. There was something strange about the whole thing.

He sat down in a rocking-chair to think the better, drawing up one leg on his knee and frowning mightily. His mind ran on at a great rate.

And yet Carrie hadn't acted out of the ordinary. It couldn't be, by George, that she was deceiving him. She hadn't acted that way. Why, even last night she had been as friendly toward him as could be, and Hurstwood too. Look how they acted! He could hardly believe they would try to deceive him.

His thoughts burst into words.

"She did act sort of funny at times. Here she had dressed and gone out this morning and never said a word."

He scratched his head and prepared to go downtown. He was still frowning. As he came into the hall he encountered the girl, who was now looking after another chamber. She had on a white dusting cap, beneath which her chubby face shone goodnaturedly. Drouet almost forgot his worry in the fact that she was smiling on him. He put his hand familiarly on her shoulder, as if only to greet her in passing.

"Got over being mad?" she said, still mischievously inclined.

"I'm not mad," he answered.

"I thought you were," she said, smiling.

"Quit your fooling about that," he said, in an offhand way. "Were you serious?"

"Certainly," she answered. Then, with an air of one who did not intentionally mean to create trouble, "He came lots of times. I thought you knew."

The game of deception was up with Drouet. He did not try to simulate indifference further.

"Did he spend the evenings here?" he asked.

"Sometimes. Sometimes they went out."

"In the evening?"

"Yes. You mustn't look so mad, though."

"I'm not," he said. "Did any one else see him?"

"Of course," said the girl, as if, after all, it were nothing in particular.

"How long ago was this?"

"Just before you came back."

The drummer pinched his lip nervously.

"Don't say anything, will you?" he asked, giving the girl's arm a gentle squeeze.

"Certainly not," she returned. "I wouldn't worry over it."

"All right," he said, passing on, seriously brooding for once, and yet not wholly unconscious of the fact that he was making a most excellent impression upon the chambermaid.

"I'll see her about that," he said to himself, passionately, feeling that he had been unduly wronged. "I'll find out, b'George, whether she'll act that way or not."

CHAPTER XXI

THE LURE OF THE SPIRIT: THE FLESH IN PURSUIT

When Carrie came Hurstwood had been waiting many minutes. His blood was warm; his nerves wrought up. He was anxious to see the woman who had stirred him so profoundly the night before.

"Here you are," he said, repressedly, feeling a spring in his limbs and an elation which was tragic in itself.

"Yes," said Carrie.

They walked on as if bound for some objective point, while Hurstwood drank in the radiance of her presence. The rustle of her pretty skirt was like music to him.

"Are you satisfied?" he asked, thinking of how well she did the night before.

"Are you?"

He tightened his fingers as he saw the smile she gave him.

"It was wonderful."

Carrie laughed ecstatically.

"That was one of the best things I've seen in a long time," he added.

He was dwelling on her attractiveness as he had felt it the evening before, and mingling it with the feeling her presence inspired now.

Carrie was dwelling in the atmosphere which this man created for her. Already she was enlivened and suffused with a glow. She felt his drawing toward her in every sound of his voice.

"Those were such nice flowers you sent me," she said, after a moment or two. "They were beautiful."

"Glad you liked them," he answered, simply.

He was thinking all the time that the subject of his desire was being delayed. He was anxious to turn the talk to his own feelings. All was ripe for it. His Carrie was beside him. He wanted to plunge in and expostulate with her, and yet he found himself fishing for words and feeling for a way.

"You got home all right," he said, gloomily, of a sudden, his tone modifying itself to one of self-commiseration.

"Yes," said Carrie, easily.

He looked at her steadily for a moment, slowing his pace and fixing her with his eye.

She felt the flood of feeling.

"How about me?" he asked.

This confused Carrie considerably, for she realized the floodgates were open. She didn't know exactly what to answer.

"I don't know," she answered.

He took his lower lip between his teeth for a moment, and then let it go. He stopped by the walk side and kicked the grass with his toe. He searched her face with a tender, appealing glance.

"Won't you come away from him?" he asked, intensely.

"I don't know," returned Carrie, still illogically drifting and finding nothing at which to catch.

As a matter of fact, she was in a most hopeless quandary. Here was a man whom she thoroughly liked, who exercised an influence over her, sufficient almost to delude her into the belief that she was possessed of a lively passion for him. She was still the victim of his keen eyes, his suave manners, his fine clothes. She looked and saw before her a man who was most gracious and sympathetic, who leaned toward her with a feeling that was a delight to observe. She could not resist the glow of his temperament, the light of his eye. She could hardly keep from feeling what he felt.

And yet she was not without thoughts which were disturbing. What did he know? What had Drouet told him? Was she a wife in his eyes, or what? Would he marry her? Even while he talked, and she softened, and her eyes were lighted with a tender glow, she was asking herself if Drouet had told him they were not married. There was never anything at all convincing about what Drouet said.

And yet she was not grieved at Hurstwood's love. No strain of bitterness was in it for her, whatever he knew. He was evidently sincere. His passion was real and warm. There was power in what he said. What should she do? She went on thinking this, answering vaguely, languishing affectionately, and altogether drifting, until she was on a borderless sea of speculation.

"Why don't you come away?" he said, tenderly. "I will arrange for you whatever—"

"Oh, don't," said Carrie.

"Don't what?" he asked. "What do you mean?"

There was a look of confusion and pain in her face. She was wondering why that miserable thought must be brought in. She was struck as by a blade with the miserable provision which was outside the pale of marriage.

He himself realized that it was a wretched thing to have dragged in. He wanted to weigh the effects of it, and yet he could not see. He went beating on, flushed by her presence, clearly awakened, intensely enlisted in his plan.

"Won't you come?" he said, beginning over and with a more reverent feeling. "You know I can't do without you—you know it—it can't go on this way—can it?"

"I know," said Carrie.

"I wouldn't ask if I—I wouldn't argue with you if I could help it. Look at me, Carrie. Put yourself in my place. You don't want to stay away from me, do you?"

She shook her head as if in deep thought.

"Then why not settle the whole thing, once and for all?"

"I don't know," said Carrie.

"Don't know! Ah, Carrie, what makes you say that? Don't torment me. Be serious."

"I am," said Carrie, softly.

"You can't be, dearest, and say that. Not when you know how I love you. Look at last night."

His manner as he said this was the most quiet imaginable. His face and body retained utter composure. Only his eyes moved, and they flashed a subtle, dissolving fire. In them the whole intensity of the man's nature was distilling itself.

Carrie made no answer.

"How can you act this way, dearest?" he inquired, after a time. "You love me, don't you?"

He turned on her such a storm of feeling that she was overwhelmed. For the moment all doubts were cleared away.

"Yes," she answered, frankly and tenderly.

"Well, then you'll come, won't you—come to-night?"

Carrie shook her head in spite of her distress.

"I can't wait any longer," urged Hurstwood. "If that is too soon, come Saturday."

"When will we be married?" she asked, diffidently, forgetting in her difficult situation that she had hoped he took her to be Drouet's wife.

The manager started, hit as he was by a problem which was more difficult than hers. He gave no sign of the thoughts that flashed like messages to his mind.

"Any time you say," he said, with ease, refusing to discolor his present delight with this miserable problem.

"Saturday?" asked Carrie.

He nodded his head.

"Well, if you will marry me then," she said, "I'll go."

The manager looked at his lovely prize, so beautiful, so winsome, so difficult to be won, and made strange resolutions. His passion had gotten to that stage now where it was no longer colored with reason. He did not trouble over little barriers of this sort in the face of so much loveliness. He would accept the situation with all its difficulties; he would not try to answer the objections which cold truth thrust upon him. He would promise anything, everything, and trust to fortune to disentangle him. He would make a try for Paradise, whatever might be the result. He would be happy, by the Lord, if it cost all honesty of statement, all abandonment of truth.

Carrie looked at him tenderly. She could have laid her head upon his shoulder, so delightful did it all seem.

"Well," she said, "I'll try and get ready then."

Hurstwood looked into her pretty face, crossed with little shadows of wonder and misgiving, and thought he had never seen anything more lovely.

"I'll see you again to-morrow," he said, joyously, "and we'll talk over the plans."

He walked on with her, elated beyond words, so delightful had been the result. He impressed a long story of joy and affection upon her, though there was but here and there a word. After a half-hour he began to realize that the meeting must come to an end, so exacting is the world.

"To-morrow," he said at parting, a gaiety of manner adding wonderfully to his brave demeanor.

"Yes," said Carrie, tripping elatedly away.

There had been so much enthusiasm engendered that she was believing herself deeply in love. She sighed as she thought of her handsome adorer. Yes, she would get ready by Saturday. She would go, and they would be happy.

CHAPTER XXII

THE BLAZE OF THE TINDER: FLESH WARS WITH THE FLESH

The misfortune of the Hurstwood household was due to the fact that jealousy, having been born of love, did not perish with it. Mrs. Hurstwood retained this in such form that subsequent influences could transform it into hate. Hurstwood was still worthy, in a physical sense, of the affection his wife had once bestowed upon him, but in a social sense he fell short. With his regard died his power to be attentive to her, and this, to a woman, is much greater than outright crime toward another. Our self-love dictates our appreciation of the good or evil in another. In Mrs. Hurstwood it discolored the very hue of her husband's indifferent nature. She saw design in deeds and phrases which sprung only from a faded appreciation of her presence.

As a consequence, she was resentful and suspicious. The jealousy that prompted her to observe every falling away from the little amenities of the married relation on his part served to give her notice of the airy grace with which he still took the world. She could see from the scrupulous care which he exercised in the matter of his personal appearance that his interest in life had abated not a jot. Every motion, every glance had something in it of the pleasure he felt in Carrie, of the zest this new pursuit of pleasure lent to his days. Mrs. Hurstwood felt something, sniffing change, as animals do danger, afar off.

This feeling was strengthened by actions of a direct and more potent nature on the part of Hurstwood. We have seen with what irritation he shirked those little duties which no longer contained any amusement or satisfaction for him, and the open snarls with which, more recently, he resented her irritating goads. These little rows were really precipitated by an atmosphere which was surcharged with dissension. That it would shower, with a sky so full of blackening thunderclouds, would scarcely be thought worthy of comment. Thus, after leaving the breakfast table this morning, raging inwardly at his blank declaration of indifference at her plans, Mrs. Hurstwood encountered Jessica in her dressing-room, very leisurely arranging her hair. Hurstwood had already left the house.

"I wish you wouldn't be so late coming down to breakfast," she said, addressing Jessica, while making for her crochet basket. "Now here the things are quite cold, and you haven't eaten."

Her natural composure was sadly ruffled, and Jessica was doomed to feel the fag end of the storm.

"I'm not hungry," she answered.

"Then why don't you say so, and let the girl put away the things, instead of keeping her waiting all morning?"

"She doesn't mind," answered Jessica, coolly.

"Well, I do, if she doesn't," returned the mother, "and, anyhow, I don't like you to talk that way to me. You're too young to put on such an air with your mother."

"Oh, mamma, don't row," answered Jessica. "What's the matter this morning, anyway?"

"Nothing's the matter, and I'm not rowing. You mustn't think because I indulge you in some things that you can keep everybody waiting. I won't have it."

"I'm not keeping anybody waiting," returned Jessica, sharply, stirred out of a cynical indifference to a sharp defense. "I said I wasn't hungry. I don't want any breakfast."

"Mind how you address me, missy. I'll not have it. Hear me now; I'll not have it!"

Jessica heard this last while walking out of the room, with a toss of her head and a flick of her pretty skirts indicative of the independence and indifference she felt. She did not propose to be quarreled with.

Such little arguments were all too frequent, the result of a growth of natures which were largely independent and selfish. George, Jr., manifested even greater touchiness and exaggeration in the matter of his individual rights, and attempted to make all feel that he was a man with a man's privileges—an assumption which, of all things, is most groundless and pointless in a youth of nineteen.

Hurstwood was a man of authority and some fine feeling, and it irritated him excessively to find himself surrounded more and more by a world upon which he had no hold, and of which he had a lessening understanding.

Now, when such little things, such as the proposed earlier start to Waukesha, came up, they made clear to him his position. He was being made to follow, was not leading. When, in addition, a sharp temper was manifested, and to the process of shouldering him out of his authority was added a rousing intellectual kick, such as a sneer or a cynical laugh, he was unable to keep his temper. He flew into hardly repressed passion, and wished himself clear of the whole household. It seemed a most irritating drag upon all his desires and opportunities.

For all this, he still retained the semblance of leadership and control, even though his wife was straining to revolt. Her display of temper and open assertion of opposition were based upon nothing more than the feeling that she could do it. She had no special evidence wherewith to justify herself—the knowledge of something which would give her both authority and excuse. The latter was all that was lacking, however, to give a solid foundation to what, in a way, seemed groundless discontent. The clear proof of one overt deed was the cold breath needed to convert the lowering clouds of suspicion into a rain of wrath.

An inkling of untoward deeds on the part of Hurstwood had come. Doctor Beale, the handsome resident physician of the neighborhood, met Mrs. Hurstwood at her own doorstep some days after Hurstwood and Carrie had taken the drive west on Washington Boulevard. Dr. Beale, coming east on the same drive, had recognized Hurstwood, but not before he was quite past him. He was not so sure of Carrie—did not know whether it was Hurstwood's wife or daughter.

"You don't speak to your friends when you meet them out driving, do you?" he said, jocosely, to Mrs. Hurstwood.

"If I see them, I do. Where was I?"

"On Washington Boulevard," he answered, expecting her eye to light with immediate remembrance.

She shook her head.

"Yes, out near Hoyne Avenue. You were with your husband."

"I guess you're mistaken," she answered. Then, remembering her husband's part in the affair, she immediately fell a prey to a host of young suspicions, of which, however, she gave no sign.

"I know I saw your husband," he went on. "I wasn't so sure about you. Perhaps it was your daughter."

"Perhaps it was," said Mrs. Hurstwood, knowing full well that such was not the case, as Jessica had been her companion for weeks. She had recovered herself sufficiently to wish to know more of the details.

"Was it in the afternoon?" she asked, artfully, assuming an air of acquaintanceship with the matter.

"Yes, about two or three."

"It must have been Jessica," said Mrs. Hurstwood, not wishing to seem to attach any importance to the incident.

The physician had a thought or two of his own, but dismissed the matter as worthy of no further discussion on his part at least.

Mrs. Hurstwood gave this bit of information considerable thought during the next few hours, and even days. She took it for granted that the doctor had really seen her husband, and that he had been riding, most likely, with some other woman, after announcing himself as *busy* to her. As a consequence, she recalled, with rising feeling, how often he had refused to go to places with her, to share in little visits, or, indeed, take part in any of the social amenities which furnished the diversion of her existence. He had been seen at the theater with people whom he called Moy's friends; now he was seen driving, and, most likely, would have an excuse for that. Perhaps there were others of whom she did not hear, or why should he be so busy, so indifferent, of late? In the last six weeks he had become strangely irritable—strangely satisfied to pick up and go out, whether things were right or wrong in the house. Why?

She recalled, with more subtle emotions, that he did not look at her now with any of the old light of satisfaction or approval in his eye. Evidently, along with other things, he was taking her to be getting old and uninteresting. He saw her wrinkles, perhaps. She was fading, while he was still preening himself in his elegance and youth. He was still an interested factor in the merry-makings of the world, while she—but she did not pursue the thought. She only found the whole situation bitter, and hated him for it thoroughly.

Nothing came of this incident at the time, for the truth is it did not seem conclusive enough to warrant any discussion. Only the atmosphere of distrust and ill-feeling was strengthened, precipitating every now and then little sprinklings of irritable conversation, enlivened by flashes of wrath. The matter of the Waukesha outing was merely a continuation of other things of the same nature.

The day after Carrie's appearance on the Avery stage, Mrs. Hurstwood visited the races with Jessica and a youth of her acquaintance, Mr. Bart Taylor, the son of the owner of a local house-furnishing establishment. They had driven out early, and, as it chanced, encountered several friends of Hurstwood, all Elks, and two of whom had attended the performance the evening before. A thousand chances the subject of the performance had never been brought up had Jessica not been so engaged by the attentions of her young companion, who usurped as much time as possible. This left Mrs. Hurstwood in the mood to extend the perfunctory greetings of some who knew her into short conversations, and the short conversations of friends into long ones. It was from one who meant but to greet her perfunctorily that this interesting intelligence came.

"I see," said this individual, who wore sporting clothes of the most attractive pattern, and had a field-glass strung over his shoulder, "that you did not get over to our little entertainment last evening."

"No?" said Mrs. Hurstwood, inquiringly, and wondering why he should be using the tone he did in noting the fact that she had not been to something she knew nothing about. It was on her lips to say, "What was it?" when he added, "I saw your husband."

Her wonder was at once replaced by the more subtle quality of suspicion.

"Yes," she said, cautiously, "was it pleasant? He did not tell me much about it."

"Very. Really one of the best private theatricals I ever attended. There was one actress who surprised us all."

"Indeed," said Mrs. Hurstwood.

"It's too bad you couldn't have been there, really. I was sorry to hear you weren't feeling well."

Feeling well! Mrs. Hurstwood could have echoed the words after him open-mouthed. As it was, she extricated herself from her mingled impulse to deny and question, and said, almost raspingly:

"Yes, it is too bad."

"Looks like there will be quite a crowd here to-day, doesn't it?" the acquaintance observed, drifting off upon another topic.

The manager's wife would have questioned farther, but she saw no opportunity. She was for the moment wholly at sea, anxious to think for herself, and wondering what new deception was this which caused him to give out that she was ill when she was not. Another case of her company not wanted, and excuses being made. She resolved to find out more.

"Were you at the performance last evening?" she asked of the next of Hurstwood's friends who greeted her, as she sat in her box.

"Yes. You didn't get around."

"No," she answered, "I was not feeling very well."

"So your husband told me," he answered. "Well, it was really very enjoyable. Turned out much better than I expected."

"Were there many there?"

"The house was full. It was quite an Elk night. I saw quite a number of your friends—Mrs. Harrison, Mrs. Barnes, Mrs. Collins."

"Quite a social gathering."

"Indeed it was. My wife enjoyed it very much."

Mrs. Hurstwood bit her lip.

"So," she thought, "that's the way he does. Tells my friends I am sick and cannot come."

She wondered what could induce him to go alone. There was something back of this. She rummaged her brain for a reason.

By evening, when Hurstwood reached home, she had brooded herself into a state of sullen desire for explanation and revenge. She wanted to know what this peculiar action of his imported. She was certain there was more behind it all than what she had heard, and evil curiosity mingled well with distrust and the remnants of her wrath of the morning. She, impending disaster itself, walked about with gathered shadow at the eyes and the rudimentary muscles of savagery fixing the hard lines of her mouth.

On the other hand, as we may well believe, the manager came home in the sunniest mood. His conversation and agreement with Carrie had raised his spirits until he was in the frame of mind of one who sings joyously. He was proud of himself, proud of his success, proud of Carrie. He could have been genial to all the world, and he bore no grudge against his wife. He meant to be pleasant, to forget her presence, to live in the atmosphere of youth and pleasure which had been restored to him.

So now, the house, to his mind, had a most pleasing and comfortable appearance. In the hall he found an evening paper, laid there by the maid and forgotten by Mrs. Hurstwood. In the dining-room the table was clean laid with linen and napery and shiny with glasses and decorated china. Through an open door he saw into the kitchen, where the fire was crackling in the stove and the evening meal already well under way. Out in the small back yard was George, Jr., frolicking with a young dog he had recently purchased, and in the parlor Jessica was playing at the piano, the sounds of a merry waltz filling every nook and corner of the comfortable home. Every one, like himself, seemed to have regained his good spirits, to be in sympathy with youth and beauty, to be inclined to joy and merry-making. He felt as if he could say a good word all around himself, and took a most genial glance at the spread table and polished sideboard before going upstairs to read his paper in the comfortable arm-chair of the sitting-room which looked through the open windows into the street. When he entered there, however, he found his wife brushing her hair and musing to herself the while.

He came lightly in, thinking to smooth over any feeling that might still exist by a kindly word and a ready promise, but Mrs. Hurstwood said nothing. He seated himself in the large chair, stirred lightly in making himself comfortable, opened his paper, and began to read. In a few moments he was smiling merrily over a very comical account of a baseball game which had taken place between the Chicago and Detroit teams.

The while he was doing this Mrs. Hurstwood was observing him casually through the medium of the mirror which was before her. She noticed his pleasant and contented manner, his airy grace and smiling humor, and it merely aggravated her the more. She wondered how he could think to carry himself so in her presence after the cynicism, indifference, and neglect he had heretofore manifested and would continue to manifest so long as she would endure it. She thought how she should like to tell him—what stress and emphasis she would lend her assertions, how she should drive over this whole affair until satisfaction should be rendered her. Indeed, the shining sword of her wrath was but weakly suspended by a thread of thought.

In the meanwhile Hurstwood encountered a humorous item concerning a stranger who had arrived in the city and became entangled with a bunco-steerer. It amused him immensely, and at last he stirred and chuckled to himself. He wished that he might enlist his wife's attention and read it to her.

"Ha, ha," he exclaimed softly, as if to himself, "that's funny."

Mrs. Hurstwood kept on arranging her hair, not so much as deigning a glance.

He stirred again and went on to another subject. At last he felt as if his good-humor must find some outlet. Julia was probably still out of humor over that affair of this morning, but that could easily be straightened. As a matter of fact, she was in the wrong, but he didn't care. She could go to Waukesha right away if she wanted to. The sooner the better. He would tell her that as soon as he got a chance, and the whole thing would blow over.

"Did you notice," he said, at last, breaking forth concerning another item which he had found, "that they have entered suit to compel the Illinois Central to get off the lake front, Julia?" he asked.

She could scarcely force herself to answer, but managed to say "No," sharply.

Hurstwood pricked up his ears. There was a note in her voice which vibrated keenly.

"It would be a good thing if they did," he went on, half to himself, half to her, though he felt that something was amiss in that quarter. He withdrew his attention to his paper very circumspectly, listening mentally for the little sounds which should show him what was on foot.

As a matter of fact, no man as clever as Hurstwood—as observant and sensitive to atmospheres of many sorts, particularly upon his own plane of thought—would have made the mistake which he did in regard to his wife, wrought up as she was, had he not been occupied mentally with a very different train of thought. Had not the influence of Carrie's regard for him, the elation which her promise aroused in him, lasted over, he would not have seen the house in so pleasant a mood. It was not extraordinarily bright and merry this evening. He was merely very much mistaken, and would have been much more fitted to cope with it had he come home in his normal state.

After he had studied his paper a few moments longer, he felt that he ought to modify matters in some way or other. Evidently his wife was not going to patch up peace at a word. So he said:

"Where did George get the dog he has there in the yard?"

"I don't know," she snapped.

He put his paper down on his knees and gazed idly out of the window. He did not propose to lose his temper, but merely to be persistent and agreeable, and by a few questions bring around a mild understanding of some sort.

"Why do you feel so bad about that affair of this morning?" he said, at last. "We needn't quarrel about that. You know you can go to Waukesha if you want to."

"So you can stay here and trifle around with someone else?" she exclaimed, turning to him a determined countenance upon which was drawn a sharp and wrathful sneer.

He stopped as if slapped in the face. In an instant his persuasive, conciliatory manner fled. He was on the defensive at a wink and puzzled for a word to reply.

"What do you mean?" he said at last, straightening himself and gazing at the cold, determined figure before him, who paid no attention, but went on arranging herself before the mirror.

"You know what I mean," she said, finally, as if there were a world of information which she held in reserve—which she did not need to tell.

"Well, I don't," he said, stubbornly, yet nervous and alert for what should come next. The finality of the woman's manner took away his feeling of superiority in battle.

She made no answer.

"Hmph!" he murmured, with a movement of his head to one side. It was the weakest thing he had ever done. It was totally unassured.

Mrs. Hurstwood noticed the lack of color in it. She turned upon him, animal-like, able to strike an effectual second blow.

"I want the Waukesha money to-morrow morning," she said.

He looked at her in amazement. Never before had he seen such a cold, steely determination in her eye—such a cruel look of indifference. She seemed a thorough master of her mood—thoroughly confident and determined to wrest all control from him. He felt that all his resources could not defend him. He must attack.

"What do you mean?" he said, jumping up. "*You* want! I'd like to know what's got into you to-night."

"Nothing's *got* into me," she said, flaming. "I want that money. You can do your swaggering afterwards."

"Swaggering, eh! What! You'll get nothing from me. What do you mean by your insinuations, anyhow?"

"Where were you last night?" she answered. The words were hot as they came. "Who were you driving with on Washington Boulevard? Who were you with at the theater when George saw you? Do you think I'm a fool to be duped by you? Do you think I'll sit at home here and take your 'too busy' and 'can't come,' while you parade around and make out that I'm unable to come? I want you to know that lordly airs have come to an end so far as I am concerned. You can't dictate to me nor my children. I'm through with you entirely."

"It's a lie," he said, driven to a corner and knowing no other excuse.

"Lie, eh!" she said, fiercely, but with returning reserve; "you may call it a lie if you want to, but I know."

"It's a lie, I tell you," he said, in a low, sharp voice. "You've been searching around for some cheap accusation for months, and now you think you have it. You think you'll spring something and get the upper hand. Well, I tell you, you can't. As long as I'm in this house I'm master of it, and you or any one else won't dictate to me—do you hear?"

He crept toward her with a light in his eye that was ominous. Something in the woman's cool, cynical, upper-handish manner, as if she were already master, caused him to feel for the moment as if he could strangle her.

She gazed at him—a pythoness in humor.

"I'm not dictating to you," she returned; "I'm telling you what I want."

The answer was so cool, so rich in bravado, that somehow it took the wind out of his sails. He could not attack her, he could not ask her for proofs. Somehow he felt evidence, law, the remembrance of all his property which she held in her name, to be shining in her glance. He was like a vessel, powerful and dangerous, but rolling and floundering without sail.

"And I'm telling you," he said in the end, slightly recovering himself, "what you'll not get."

"We'll see about it," she said. "I'll find out what my rights are. Perhaps you'll talk to a lawyer, if you won't talk to me."

It was magnificent play, and had its effect. Hurstwood fell back beaten. He knew now that he had more than mere bluff to contend with. He felt that he was face to face with a dull proposition. What to say he hardly knew. All the merriment had gone out of the day. He was disturbed, resentful. What should he do?

"Do as you please," he said, at last. "I'll have nothing more to do with you," and out he strode.

CHAPTER XXIII

A SPIRIT IN TRAVAIL: ONE RUNG PUT BEHIND

When Carrie reached her own room she had already fallen a prey to those doubts and misgivings which are ever the result of a lack of decision. She could not persuade herself as to the advisability of her promise, or that now, having given her word, she ought to keep it. She went over the whole ground in Hurstwood's absence, and discovered little objections that had not occurred to her in the warmth of the manager's argument. She saw where she had put herself in a peculiar light, namely, that of agreeing to marry when she was already supposedly married. She remembered a few things Drouet had done, and now that it came to walking away from him without a word, she felt as if she were doing wrong. Now, she was comfortably situated, and to one who is more or less afraid of the world, this is an urgent matter, and one which puts up strange, uncanny arguments. "You do not know what will come. There are miserable things outside. People go a-begging. Women are wretched. You never can tell what will happen. Remember the time you were hungry. Stick to what you have."

Curiously, for all her leaning towards Hurstwood, he had not taken a firm hold on her understanding. She was listening, smiling, approving, and yet not finally agreeing. This was due to a lack of power on his part, a lack of that majesty of passion that sweeps the mind from its seat, fuses and melts all arguments and theories into a tangled mass, and destroys for the time being the reasoning power. The majesty of passion is possessed by nearly every man once in his life, but it is usually an attribute of youth and conduces to the first successful mating.

Hurstwood, being an older man, could scarcely be said to retain the fire of youth, though he did possess a passion warm and unreasoning. It was strong enough to induce the leaning toward him which, on Carrie's part, we have seen. She might have been said to be imagining herself in love, when she was not. Women frequently do this. It flows from the fact that in each exists a bias toward affection, a craving for the pleasure of being loved. The longing to be shielded, bettered, sympathized with, is one of the attributes of the sex. This, coupled with sentiment and a natural tendency to emotion, often makes refusing difficult. It persuades them that they are in love.

Once at home, she changed her clothes and straightened the rooms for herself. In the matter of the arrangement of the furniture she never took the house-maid's opinion. That young woman invariably put one of the rocking-chairs in the corner, and Carrie as regularly moved it out. To-day she hardly noticed that it was in the wrong place, so absorbed was she in her own thoughts. She worked about the room until Drouet put in appearance at five o'clock. The drummer was flushed and excited and full of determination to know all about her relations with Hurstwood. Nevertheless, after going over the subject in his mind the livelong day, he was rather weary of it and wished it over with. He did not foresee serious consequences of any sort, and yet he rather hesitated to begin. Carrie was sitting by the window when he came in, rocking and looking out.

"Well," she said innocently, weary of her own mental discussion and wondering at his haste and ill-concealed excitement, "what makes you hurry so?"

Drouet hesitated, now that he was in her presence, uncertain as to what course to pursue. He was no diplomat. He could neither read nor see.

"When did you get home?" he asked foolishly.

"Oh, an hour or so ago. What makes you ask that?"

"You weren't here," he said, "when I came back this morning, and I thought you had gone out."

"So I did," said Carrie simply. "I went for a walk."

Drouet looked at her wonderingly. For all his lack of dignity in such matters he did not know how to begin. He stared at her in the most flagrant manner until at last she said:

"What makes you stare at me so? What's the matter?"

"Nothing," he answered. "I was just thinking."

"Just thinking what?" she returned smilingly, puzzled by his attitude.

"Oh, nothing—nothing much."

"Well, then, what makes you look so?"

Drouet was standing by the dresser, gazing at her in a comic manner. He had laid off his hat and gloves and was now fidgeting with the little toilet pieces which were nearest him. He hesitated to believe that the pretty woman before him was involved in anything so unsatisfactory to himself. He was very much inclined to feel that it was all right, after all. Yet the knowledge imparted to him by the chambermaid was rankling in his mind. He wanted to plunge in with a straight remark of some sort, but he knew not what.

"Where did you go this morning?" he finally asked weakly.

"Why, I went for a walk," said Carrie.

"Sure you did?" he asked.

"Yes, what makes you ask?"

She was beginning to see now that he knew something. Instantly she drew herself into a more reserved position. Her cheeks blanched slightly.

"I thought maybe you didn't," he said, beating about the bush in the most useless manner.

Carrie gazed at him, and as she did so her ebbing courage halted. She saw that he himself was hesitating, and with a woman's intuition realized that there was no occasion for great alarm.

"What makes you talk like that?" she asked, wrinkling her pretty forehead. "You act so funny to-night."

"I feel funny," he answered.

They looked at one another for a moment, and then Drouet plunged desperately into his subject.

"What's this about you and Hurstwood?" he asked.

"Me and Hurstwood—what do you mean?"

"Didn't he come here a dozen times while I was away?"

"A dozen times," repeated Carrie, guiltily. "No, but what do you mean?"

"Somebody said that you went out riding with him and that he came here every night."

"No such thing," answered Carrie. "It isn't true. Who told you that?"

She was flushing scarlet to the roots of her hair, but Drouet did not catch the full hue of her face, owing to the modified light of the room. He was regaining much confidence as Carrie defended herself with denials.

"Well, some one," he said. "You're sure you didn't?"

"Certainly," said Carrie. "You know how often he came."

Drouet paused for a moment and thought.

"I know what you told me," he said finally.

He moved nervously about, while Carrie looked at him confusedly.

"Well, I know that I didn't tell you any such thing as that," said Carrie, recovering herself.

"If I were you," went on Drouet, ignoring her last remark, "I wouldn't have anything to do with him. He's a married man, you know."

"Who—who is?" said Carrie, stumbling at the word.

"Why, Hurstwood," said Drouet, noting the effect and feeling that he was delivering a telling blow.

"Hurstwood!" exclaimed Carrie, rising. Her face had changed several shades since this announcement was made. She looked within and without herself in a half-dazed way.

"Who told you this?" she asked, forgetting that her interest was out of order and exceedingly incriminating.

"Why, I know it. I've always known it," said Drouet.

Carrie was feeling about for a right thought. She was making a most miserable showing, and yet feelings were generating within her which were anything but crumbling cowardice.

"I thought I told you," he added.

"No, you didn't," she contradicted, suddenly recovering her voice. "You didn't do anything of the kind."

Drouet listened to her in astonishment. This was something new.

"I thought I did," he said.

Carrie looked around her very solemnly, and then went over to the window.

"You oughtn't to have had anything to do with him," said Drouet in an injured tone, "after all I've done for you."

"You," said Carrie, "you! What have you done for me?"

Her little brain had been surging with contradictory feelings—shame at exposure, shame at Hurstwood's perfidy, anger at Drouet's deception, the mockery he had made of her. Now one clear idea came into her head. He was at fault. There was no doubt about it. Why did he bring Hurstwood out—Hurstwood, a married man, and never say a word to her? Never mind now about Hurstwood's perfidy—why had he done this? Why hadn't he warned her? There he stood now, guilty of this miserable breach of confidence and talking about what he had done for her!

"Well, I like that," exclaimed Drouet, little realizing the fire his remark had generated. "I think I've done a good deal."

"You have, eh?" she answered. "You've deceived me—that's what you've done. You've brought your old friends out here under false pretences. You've made me out to be—Oh," and with this her voice broke and she pressed her two little hands together tragically.

"I don't see what that's got to do with it," said the drummer quaintly.

"No," she answered, recovering herself and shutting her teeth. "No, of course you don't see. There isn't anything you see. You couldn't have told me in the first place, could you? You had to make me out wrong until it was too late. Now you come sneaking around with your information and your talk about what you have done."

Drouet had never suspected this side of Carrie's nature. She was alive with feeling, her eyes snapping, her lips quivering, her whole body sensible of the injury she felt, and partaking of her wrath.

"Who's sneaking?" he asked, mildly conscious of error on his part, but certain that he was wronged.

"You are," stamped Carrie. "You're a horrid, conceited coward, that's what you are. If you had any sense of manhood in you, you wouldn't have thought of doing any such thing."

The drummer stared.

"I'm not a coward," he said. "What do you mean by going with other men, anyway?"

"Other men!" exclaimed Carrie. "Other men—you know better than that. I did go with Mr. Hurstwood, but whose fault was it? Didn't you bring him here? You told him yourself that he should come out here and take me out. Now, after it's all over, you come and tell me that I oughtn't to go with him and that he's a married man."

She paused at the sound of the last two words and wrung her hands. The knowledge of Hurstwood's perfidy wounded her like a knife.

"Oh," she sobbed, repressing herself wonderfully and keeping her eyes dry. "Oh, oh!"

"Well, I didn't think you'd be running around with him when I was away," insisted Drouet.

"Didn't think!" said Carrie, now angered to the core by the man's peculiar attitude. "Of course not. You thought only of what would be to your satisfaction. You thought you'd make a toy of me—a plaything. Well, I'll show you that you won't. I'll have nothing more to do with you at all. You can take your old things and keep them," and unfastening a little pin he had given her, she flung it vigorously upon the floor and began to move about as if to gather up the things which belonged to her.

By this Drouet was not only irritated but fascinated the more. He looked at her in amazement, and finally said:

"I don't see where your wrath comes in. I've got the right of this thing. You oughtn't to have done anything that wasn't right after all I did for you."

"What have you done for me?" asked Carrie blazing, her head thrown back and her lips parted.

"I think I've done a good deal," said the drummer, looking around. "I've given you all the clothes you wanted, haven't I? I've taken you everywhere you wanted to go. You've had as much as I've had, and more too."

Carrie was not ungrateful, whatever else might be said of her. In so far as her mind could construe, she acknowledged benefits received. She hardly knew how to answer this, and yet her wrath was not placated. She felt that the drummer had injured her irreparably.

"Did I ask you to?" she returned.

"Well, I did it," said Drouet, "and you took it!"

"You talk as though I had persuaded you," answered Carrie. "You stand there and throw up what you've done. I don't want your old things. I'll not have them. You take them to-night and do what you please with them. I'll not stay here another minute."

"That's nice!" he answered, becoming angered now at the sense of his own approaching loss. "Use everything and abuse me and then walk off. That's just like a woman. I take you when you haven't got anything, and then when some one else comes along, why I'm no good. I always thought it'd come out that way."

He felt really hurt as he thought of his treatment, and looked as if he saw no way of obtaining justice.

"It's not so," said Carrie, "and I'm not going with anybody else. You have been as miserable and inconsiderate as you can be. I hate you, I tell you, and I wouldn't live with you another minute. You're a big, insulting"—here she hesitated and used no word at all—"or you wouldn't talk that way."

She had secured her hat and jacket and slipped the latter on over her little evening dress. Some wisps of wavy hair had loosened from the bands at the side of her head and were straggling over her hot, red cheeks. She was angry, mortified, grief-stricken. Her large eyes were full of the anguish of tears, but her lids were not yet wet. She was distracted and uncertain, deciding and doing things without an aim or conclusion, and she had not the slightest conception of how the whole difficulty would end.

"Well, that's a fine finish," said Drouet. "Pack up and pull out, eh? You take the cake. I bet you were knocking around with Hurstwood or you wouldn't act like that. I don't want the old rooms. You needn't pull out for me. You can have them for all I care, but b'George, you haven't done me right."

"I'll not live with you," said Carrie. "I don't want to live with you. You've done nothing but brag around ever since you've been here."

"Aw, I haven't anything of the kind," he answered.

Carrie walked over to the door.

"Where are you going?" he said, stepping over and heading her off.

"Let me out," she said.

"Where are you going?" he repeated.

He was, above all, sympathetic, and the sight of Carrie wandering out, he knew not where, affected him, despite his grievance.

Carrie merely pulled at the door.

The strain of the situation was too much for her, however. She made one more vain effort and then burst into tears.

"Now, be reasonable, Cad," said Drouet gently. "What do you want to rush out for this way? You haven't any place to go. Why not stay here now and be quiet? I'll not bother you. I don't want to stay here any longer."

Carrie had gone sobbing from the door to the window. She was so overcome she could not speak.

"Be reasonable now," he said. "I don't want to hold you. You can go if you want to, but why don't you think it over? Lord knows, I don't want to stop you."

He received no answer. Carrie was quieting, however, under the influence of his plea.

"You stay here now, and I'll go," he added at last.

Carrie listened to this with mingled feelings. Her mind was shaken loose from the little mooring of logic that it had. She was stirred by this thought, angered by that—her own injustice, Hurstwood's, Drouet's their respective qualities of kindness and favor, the threat of the world outside, in which she had failed once before, the impossibility of this state inside, where the chambers were no longer justly hers, the effect of the argument upon her nerves, all combined to make her a mass of jangling fibers—an anchorless, storm-beaten little craft which could do absolutely nothing but drift.

"Say," said Drouet, coming over to her after a few moments, with a new idea, and putting his hand upon her.

"Don't!" said Carrie, drawing away, but not removing her handkerchief from her eyes.

"Never mind about this quarrel now. Let it go. You stay here until the month's out, anyhow, and then you can tell better what you want to do. Eh?"

Carrie made no answer.

"You'd better do that," he said. "There's no use your packing up now. You can't go anywhere."

Still he got nothing for his words.

"If you'll do that, we'll call it off for the present and I'll get out."

Carrie lowered her handkerchief slightly and looked out of the window.

"Will you do that?" he asked.

Still no answer.

"Will you?" he repeated.

She only looked vaguely into the street.

"Aw! come on," he said, "tell me. Will you?"

"I don't know," said Carrie softly, forced to answer.

"Promise me you'll do that," he said, "and we'll quit talking about it. It'll be the best thing for you."

Carrie heard him, but she could not bring herself to answer reasonably. She felt that the man was gentle, and that his interest in her had not abated, and it made her suffer a pang of regret. She was in a most helpless plight.

As for Drouet, his attitude had been that of the jealous lover. Now his feelings were a mixture of anger at deception, sorrow at losing Carrie, misery at being defeated. He wanted his rights in some way or other, and yet his rights included the retaining of Carrie, the making her feel her error.

"Will you?" he urged.

"Well, I'll see," said Carrie.

This left the matter as open as before, but it was something. It looked as if the quarrel would blow over, if they could only get some way of talking to one another. Carrie was ashamed, and Drouet aggrieved. He pretended to take up the task of packing some things in a valise.

Now, as Carrie watched him out of the corner of her eye, certain sound thoughts came into her head. He had erred, true, but what had she done? He was kindly and good-natured for all his egotism. Throughout this argument he had said nothing very harsh. On the other hand, there was Hurstwood—a greater deceiver than he. He had pretended all this affection, all this passion, and he was lying to her all the while. Oh, the perfidy of men! And she had loved him. There could be nothing more in that quarter. She would see Hurstwood no more. She would write him and let him know what she thought. Thereupon what would she do? Here were these rooms. Here was Drouet, pleading for her to remain. Evidently things could go on here somewhat as before, if all were arranged. It would be better than the street, without a place to lay her head.

All this she thought of as Drouet rummaged the drawers for collars and labored long and painstakingly at finding a shirt-stud. He was in no hurry to rush this matter. He felt an attraction to Carrie which would not down. He could not think that the thing would end by his walking out of the room. There must be some way round, some way to make her own up that he was right and she was wrong—to patch up a peace and shut out Hurstwood for ever. Mercy, how he turned at the man's shameless duplicity.

"Do you think," he said, after a few moments' silence, "that you'll try and get on the stage?"

He was wondering what she was intending.

"I don't know what I'll do yet," said Carrie.

"If you do, maybe I can help you. I've got a lot of friends in that line."

She made no answer to this.

"Don't go and try to knock around now without any money. Let me help you," he said. "It's no easy thing to go on your own hook here."

Carrie only rocked back and forth in her chair.

"I don't want you to go up against a hard game that way."

He bestirred himself about some other details and Carrie rocked on.

"Why don't you tell me all about this thing," he said, after a time, "and let's call it off? You don't really care for Hurstwood, do you?"

"Why do you want to start on that again?" said Carrie. "You were to blame."

"No, I wasn't," he answered.

"Yes, you were, too," said Carrie. "You shouldn't have ever told me such a story as that."

"But you didn't have much to do with him, did you?" went on Drouet, anxious for his own peace of mind to get some direct denial from her.

"I won't talk about it," said Carrie, pained at the quizzical turn the peace arrangement had taken.

"What's the use of acting like that now, Cad?" insisted the drummer, stopping in his work and putting up a hand expressively. "You might let me know where I stand, at least."

"I won't," said Carrie, feeling no refuge but in anger. "Whatever has happened is your own fault."

"Then you do care for him?" said Drouet, stopping completely and experiencing a rush of feeling.

"Oh, stop!" said Carrie.

"Well, I'll not be made a fool of," exclaimed Drouet. "You may trifle around with him if you want to, but you can't lead me. You can tell me or not, just as you want to, but I won't fool any longer!"

He shoved the last few remaining things he had laid out into the valise and snapped it with vengeance. Then he grabbed his coat, which he had laid off to work, picked up his gloves, and started out.

"You can go to the deuce as far as I am concerned," he said, as he reached the door. "I'm no sucker," and with that he opened it with a jerk and closed it equally vigorously.

Carrie listened at her window view, more astonished than anything else at this sudden rise of passion in the drummer. She could hardly believe her senses—so good-natured and tractable had he invariably been. It was not for her to see the wellspring of human passion. A real flame of love is a subtle thing. It burns as a will-o'-the-wisp, dancing onward to fairylands of delight. It roars as a furnace. Too often jealousy is the quality upon which it feeds.

CHAPTER XXIV

Ashes of Tinder: A Face at the Window

That night Hurstwood remained downtown entirely, going to the Palmer House for a bed after his work was through. He was in a fevered state of mind, owing to the blight his wife's action threatened to cast upon his entire future. While he was not sure how much significance might be attached to the threat she had made, he was sure that her attitude, if long continued, would cause him no end of trouble. She was determined, and had worsted him in a very important contest. How would it be from now on? He walked the floor of his little office, and later that of his room, putting one thing and another together to no avail.

Mrs. Hurstwood, on the contrary, had decided not to lose her advantage by inaction. Now that she had practically cowed him, she would follow up her work with demands, the acknowledgment of which would make her word *law* in the future. He would have to pay her the money which she would now regularly demand or there would be trouble. It did not matter what he did. She really did not care whether he came home any more or not. The household would move along much more pleasantly without him, and she could do as she wished without consulting any one. Now she proposed to consult a lawyer and hire a detective. She would find out at once just what advantages she could gain.

Hurstwood walked the floor, mentally arranging the chief points of his situation. "She has that property in her name," he kept saying to himself. "What a fool trick that was. Curse it! What a fool move that was."

He also thought of his managerial position. "If she raises a row now I'll lose this thing. They won't have me around if my name gets in the papers. My friends, too!" He grew more angry as he thought of the talk any action on her part would create. How would the papers talk about it? Every man he knew would be wondering. He would have to explain and deny and make a general mark of himself. Then Moy would come and confer with him and there would be the devil to pay.

Many little wrinkles gathered between his eyes as he contemplated this, and his brow moistened. He saw no solution of anything—not a loophole left.

Through all this thoughts of Carrie flashed upon him, and the approaching affair of Saturday. Tangled as all his matters were, he did not worry over that. It was the one pleasing thing in this whole rout of trouble. He could arrange that satisfactorily, for Carrie would be glad to wait, if necessary. He would see how things turned out to-morrow, and then he would talk to her. They were going to meet as usual. He saw only her pretty face and neat figure and wondered why life was not arranged so that such joy as he found with her could be steadily maintained. How much more pleasant it would be. Then he would take up his wife's threat again, and the wrinkles and moisture would return.

In the morning he came over from the hotel and opened his mail, but there was nothing in it outside the ordinary run. For some reason he felt as if something might come that way, and was relieved when all the envelopes had been scanned and nothing suspicious noticed. He began to feel the appetite that had been wanting before he had reached the office, and decided before going out to the park to meet Carrie to drop in at the Grand Pacific and have a pot of coffee and some rolls. While the danger had not lessened, it had not as yet materialized, and with him no news was good news. If he could only get plenty of time to think, perhaps something would turn up. Surely, surely, this thing would not drift along to catastrophe and he not find a way out.

His spirits fell, however, when, upon reaching the park, he waited and waited and Carrie did not come. He held his favorite post for an hour or more, then arose and began to walk about restlessly. Could something have happened out there to keep her away? Could she have been reached by his wife? Surely not. So little did he consider Drouet that it never once occurred to him to worry about his finding out. He grew restless as he ruminated, and then decided that perhaps it was nothing. She had not been able to get away this morning. That was why no letter notifying him had come. He would get one today. It would probably be on his desk when he got back. He would look for it at once.

After a time he gave up waiting and drearily headed for the Madison car. To add to his distress, the bright blue sky became overcast with little fleecy clouds which shut out the sun. The wind veered to the east, and by the time he reached his office it was threatening to drizzle all afternoon.

He went in and examined his letters, but there was nothing from Carrie. Fortunately, there was nothing from his wife either. He thanked his stars that he did not have to confront that proposition just now when he needed to think so much. He walked the floor again, pretending to be in an ordinary mood, but secretly troubled beyond the expression of words.

At one-thirty he went to Rector's for lunch, and when he returned a messenger was waiting for him. He looked at the little chap with a feeling of doubt.

"I'm to bring an answer," said the boy.

Hurstwood recognized his wife's writing. He tore it open and read without a show of feeling. It began in the most formal manner and was sharply and coldly worded throughout.

"I want you to send the money I asked for at once. I need it to carry out my plans. You can stay away if you want to. It doesn't matter in the least. But I must have some money. So don't delay, but send it by the boy."

When he had finished it, he stood holding it in his hands. The audacity of the thing took his breath. It roused his ire also—the deepest element of revolt in him. His first impulse was to write but four words in reply—"Go to the devil!"—but he compromised by telling the boy that there would be no reply. Then he sat down in his chair and gazed without seeing, contemplating the result of his work. What would she do about that? The confounded wretch! Was she going to try to bulldoze him into submission? He would go up there and have it out with her, that's what he would do. She was carrying things with too high a hand. These were his first thoughts.

Later, however, his old discretion asserted itself. Something had to be done. A climax was near and she would not sit idle. He knew her well enough to know that when she had decided upon a plan she would follow it up. Possibly matters would go into a lawyer's hands at once.

"Damn her!" he said softly, with his teeth firmly set, "I'll make it hot for her if she causes me trouble. I'll make her change her tone if I have to use force to do it!"

He arose from his chair and went and looked out into the street. The long drizzle had begun. Pedestrians had turned up collars, and trousers at the bottom. Hands were hidden in the pockets of the umbrellaless; umbrellas were up. The street looked like a sea of round black cloth roofs, twisting, bobbing, moving. Trucks and vans were rattling in a noisy line and everywhere men were shielding themselves as best they could. He scarcely noticed the picture. He was forever confronting his wife, demanding of her to change her attitude toward him before he worked her bodily harm.

At four o'clock another note came, which simply said that if the money was not forthcoming that evening the matter would be laid before Fitzgerald and Moy on the morrow, and other steps would be taken to get it.

Hurstwood almost exclaimed out loud at the insistency of this thing. Yes, he would send her the money. He'd take it to her—he would go up there and have a talk with her, and that at once.

He put on his hat and looked around for his umbrella. He would have some arrangement of this thing.

He called a cab and was driven through the dreary rain to the North Side. On the way his temper cooled as he thought of the details of the case. What did she know? What had she done? Maybe she'd got hold of Carrie, who knows—or—or Drouet. Perhaps she really had evidence, and was prepared to fell him as a man does another from secret ambush. She was shrewd. Why should she taunt him this way unless she had good grounds?

He began to wish that he had compromised in some way or other—that he had sent the money. Perhaps he could do it up here. He would go in and see, anyhow. He would have no row.

By the time he reached his own street he was keenly alive to the difficulties of his situation and wished over and over that some solution would offer itself, that he could see his way out. He alighted and went up the steps to the front door, but it was with a nervous palpitation of the heart. He pulled out his key and tried to insert it, but another key was on the inside. He shook at the knob, but the door was locked. Then he rang the bell. No answer. He rang again—this time harder. Still no answer. He jangled it fiercely several times in succession, but without avail. Then he went below.

There was a door which opened under the steps into the kitchen, protected by an iron grating, intended as a safeguard against burglars. When he reached this he noticed that it also was bolted and that the kitchen windows were down. What could it mean? He rang the bell and then waited. Finally, seeing that no one was coming, he turned and went back to his cab.

"I guess they've gone out," he said apologetically to the individual who was hiding his red face in a loose tarpaulin raincoat.

"I saw a young girl up in that winder," returned the cabby.

Hurstwood looked, but there was no face there now. He climbed moodily into the cab, relieved and distressed.

So this was the game, was it? Shut him out and make him pay. Well, by the Lord, that did beat all!

CHAPTER XXV

ASHES OF TINDER: THE LOOSING OF STAYS

When Hurstwood got back to his office again he was in a greater quandary than ever. Lord, Lord, he thought, what had he got into? How could things have taken such a violent turn, and so quickly? He could hardly realize how it had all come about. It seemed a monstrous, unnatural, unwarranted condition which had suddenly descended upon him without his let or hindrance.

Meanwhile he gave a thought now and then to Carrie. What could be the trouble in that quarter? No letter had come, no word of any kind, and yet here it was late in the evening and she had agreed to meet him that morning. To-morrow they were to have met and gone off—where? He saw that in the excitement of recent events he had not formulated a plan upon that score. He was desperately in love, and would have taken great chances to win her under ordinary circumstances, but now—now what? Supposing she had found out something? Supposing she, too, wrote him and told him that she knew all—that she would have nothing more to do with him? It would be just like this to happen as things were going now. Meanwhile he had not sent the money.

He strolled up and down the polished floor of the resort, his hands in his pockets, his brow wrinkled, his mouth set. He was getting some vague comfort out of a good cigar, but it was no panacea for the ill which affected him. Every once in a while he would clinch his fingers and tap his foot—signs of the stirring mental process he was undergoing. His whole nature was vigorously and powerfully shaken up, and he was finding what limits the mind has to endurance. He drank more brandy and soda than he had any evening in months. He was altogether a fine example of great mental perturbation.

For all his study nothing came of the evening except this—he sent the money. It was with great opposition, after two or three hours of the most urgent mental affirmation and denial, that at last he got an envelope, placed in it the requested amount, and slowly sealed it up.

Then he called Harry, the boy of all work around the place.

"You take this to this address," he said, handing him the envelope, "and give it to Mrs. Hurstwood."

"Yes, sir," said the boy.

"If she isn't there bring it back."

"Yes, sir."

"You've seen my wife?" he asked as a precautionary measure as the boy turned to go.

"Oh, yes, sir. I know her."

"All right, now. Hurry right back."

"Any answer?"

"I guess not."

The boy hastened away and the manager fell to his musings. Now he had done it. There was no use speculating over that. He was beaten for to-night and he might just as well make the best of it. But, oh, the wretchedness of being forced this way! He could see her meeting the boy at the door and smiling sardonically. She would take the envelope and know that she had triumphed. If he only had that letter back he wouldn't send it. He breathed heavily and wiped the moisture from his face.

For relief, he arose and joined in the conversation with a few friends who were drinking. He tried to get the interest of things about him, but it was not to be. All the time his thoughts would run out to his home and see the scene being therein enacted. All the time he was wondering what she would say when the boy handed her the envelope.

In about an hour and three-quarters the boy returned. He had evidently delivered the package, for, as he came up, he made no sign of taking anything out of his pocket.

"Well?" said Hurstwood.

"I gave it to her."

"My wife?"

"Yes, sir."

"Any answer?"

"She said it was high time."

Hurstwood scowled fiercely.

There was no more to be done upon that score that night. He went on brooding over his situation until midnight, when he repaired again to the Palmer House. He wondered what the morning would bring forth, and slept anything but soundly upon it.

Next day he went again to the office and opened his mail, suspicious and hopeful of its contents. No word from Carrie. Nothing from his wife, which was pleasant.

The fact that he had sent the money and that she had received it worked to the ease of his mind, for, as the thought that he had done it receded, his chagrin at it grew less and his hope of peace more. He fancied, as he sat at his desk, that nothing would be done for a week or two. Meanwhile, he would have time to think.

This process of *thinking* began by a reversion to Carrie and the arrangement by which he was to get her away from Drouet. How about that now? His pain at her failure to meet or write him rapidly increased as he devoted himself to this subject. He decided to write her care of the West Side Post-office and ask for an explanation, as well as to have her meet him. The thought that this letter would probably not reach her until Monday chafed him exceedingly. He must get some speedier method—but how?

He thought upon it for a half-hour, not contemplating a messenger or a cab direct to the house, owing to the exposure of it, but finding that time was slipping away to no purpose, he wrote the letter and then began to think again.

The hours slipped by, and with them the possibility of the union he had contemplated. He had thought to be joyously aiding Carrie by now in the task of joining her interests to his, and here it was afternoon and nothing done. Three o'clock came, four, five, six, and no letter. The helpless manager paced the floor and grimly endured the gloom of defeat. He saw a busy Saturday ushered out, the Sabbath in, and nothing done. All day, the bar being closed, he brooded alone, shut out from home, from the excitement of his resort, from Carrie, and without the ability to alter his condition one iota. It was the worst Sunday he had spent in his life.

In Monday's second mail he encountered a very legal-looking letter, which held his interest for some time. It bore the imprint of the law offices of McGregor, James and Hay, and with a very formal "Dear Sir," and "We beg to state," went on to inform him briefly that they had been retained by Mrs. Julia Hurstwood to adjust certain matters which related to her sustenance and property rights, and would he kindly call and see them about the matter at once.

He read it through carefully several times, and then merely shook his head. It seemed as if his family troubles were just beginning.

"Well!" he said after a time, quite audibly. "I don't know."

Then he folded it up and put it in his pocket.

To add to his misery there was no word from Carrie. He was quite certain now that she knew he was married and was angered at his perfidy. His loss seemed all the more bitter now that he needed her most. He thought he would go out and insist on seeing her if she did not send him word of some sort soon. He was really affected most miserably of all by this desertion. He had loved her earnestly enough, but now that the possibility of losing her stared him in the face she seemed much more attractive. He really pined for a word, and looked out upon her with his mind's eye in the most wistful manner. He did not propose to lose her, whatever she might think. Come what might, he would adjust this matter, and soon. He would go to her and tell her all his family complications. He would explain to her just where he stood and how much he needed her. Surely she couldn't go back on him now? It wasn't possible. He would plead until her anger would melt—until she would forgive him.

Suddenly he thought: "Supposing she isn't out there—suppose she has gone?"

He was forced to take to his feet. It was too much to think of and sit still.

Nevertheless, his rousing availed him nothing.

On Tuesday it was the same way. He did manage to bring himself into the mood to go out to Carrie, but when he got in Ogden Place he thought he saw a man watching him and went away. He did not go within a block of the house.

One of the galling incidents of this visit was that he came back on a Randolph Street car, and without noticing arrived almost opposite the building of the concern with which his son was connected. This sent a pang through his heart. He had called on his boy there several times. Now the lad had not sent him a word. His absence did not seem to be noticed by either of his children. Well, well, fortune plays a man queer tricks. He got back to his office and joined in a conversation with friends. It was as if idle chatter deadened the sense of misery.

That night he dined at Rector's and returned at once to his office. In the bustle and show of the latter was his only relief. He troubled over many little details and talked perfunctorily to everybody. He stayed at his desk long after all others had gone, and only quitted it when the night watchman on his round pulled at the front door to see if it was safely locked.

On Wednesday he received another polite note from McGregor, James and Hay. It read:

> "*Dear Sir:* We beg to inform you that we are instructed to wait until to-morrow (Thursday) at one o'clock, before filing suit against you, on behalf of Mrs. Julia Hurstwood, for divorce and alimony. If we do not hear from you before that time we shall consider that you do not wish to compromise the matter in any way and act accordingly.
>
> "Very truly yours, etc."

"Compromise!" exclaimed Hurstwood bitterly. "Compromise!"

Again he shook his head.

So here it was spread out clear before him, and now he knew what to expect. If he didn't go and see them they would sue him promptly. If he did, he would be offered terms that would make his blood boil. He folded the letter and put it with the other one. Then he put on his hat and went for a turn about the block.

CHAPTER XXVI

THE AMBASSADOR FALLEN: A SEARCH FOR THE GATE

Carrie, left alone by Drouet, listened to his retreating steps, scarcely realizing what had happened. She knew that he had stormed out. It was some moments before she questioned whether he would return, not now exactly, but ever. She looked around her upon the rooms, out of which the evening light was dying, and wondered why she did not feel quite the same towards them. She went over to the dresser and struck a match, lighting the gas. Then she went back to the rocker to think.

It was some time before she could collect her thoughts, but when she did, this truth began to take on importance. She was quite alone. Suppose Drouet did not come back? Suppose she should never hear anything more of him? This fine arrangement of chambers would not last long. She would have to quit them.

To her credit, be it said, she never once counted on Hurstwood. She could only approach that subject with a pang of sorrow and regret. For a truth, she was rather shocked and frightened by this evidence of human depravity. He would have tricked her without turning an eyelash. She would have been led into a newer and worse situation. And yet she could not keep out the pictures of his looks and manners. Only this one deed seemed strange and miserable. It contrasted sharply with all she felt and knew concerning the man.

But she was alone. That was the greater thought just at present. How about that? Would she go out to work again? Would she begin to look around in the business district? The stage! Oh, yes. Drouet had spoken about that. Was there any hope there? She moved to and fro, in deep and varied thoughts, while the minutes slipped away and night fell completely. She had had nothing to eat, and yet there she sat, thinking it over.

She remembered that she was hungry and went to the little cupboard in the rear room where were the remains of one of their breakfasts. She looked at these things with certain misgivings. The contemplation of food had more significance than usual.

While she was eating she began to wonder how much money she had. It struck her as exceedingly important, and without ado she went to look for her purse. It was on the dresser, and in it were seven dollars in bills and some change. She quailed as she thought of the insignificance of the amount and rejoiced because the rent was paid until the end of the month. She began also to think what she would have done if she had gone out into the street when she first started. By the side of that situation, as she looked at it now, the present seemed agreeable. She had a little time at least, and then, perhaps everything would come out all right, after all.

Drouet had gone, but what of it? He did not seem seriously angry. He only acted as if he were huffy. He would come back—of course he would. There was his cane in the corner. Here was one of his collars. He had left his light overcoat in the wardrobe. She looked about and tried to assure herself with the sight of a dozen such details, but, alas, the secondary thought arrived. Supposing he did come back. Then what?

Here was another proposition nearly, if not quite, as disturbing. She would have to talk with and explain to him. He would want her to admit that he was right. It would be impossible for her to live with him.

On Friday Carrie remembered her appointment with Hurstwood, and the passing of the hour when she should, by all right of promise, have been in his company served to keep the calamity which had befallen her exceedingly fresh and clear. In her nervousness and stress of mind she felt it necessary to act, and consequently put on a brown street dress, and at eleven o'clock started to visit the business portion once again. She must look for work.

The rain, which threatened at twelve and began at one, served equally well to cause her to retrace her steps and remain within doors as it did to reduce Hurstwood's spirits and give him a wretched day.

The morrow was Saturday, a half-holiday in many business quarters, and besides it was a balmy, radiant day, with the trees and grass shining exceedingly green after the rain of the night before. When she went out the sparrows were twittering merrily in joyous choruses. She could not help feeling, as she looked across the lovely park, that life was a joyous thing for those who did not need to worry, and she wished over and over that something might interfere now to preserve for her the comfortable state which she had occupied. She did not want Drouet or his money when she thought of it, nor anything more to do with Hurstwood, but only the content and ease of mind she had experienced, for, after all, she had been happy—happier, at least, than she was now when confronted by the necessity of making her way alone.

When she arrived in the business part it was quite eleven o'clock, and the business had little longer to run. She did not realize this at first, being affected by some of the old distress which was a result of her earlier adventure into this strenuous and exacting quarter. She wandered about, assuring herself that she was making up her mind to look for something, and at the same time feeling that perhaps it was not necessary to be in such haste about it. The thing was difficult to encounter, and she had a few days. Besides, she was not sure that she was really face to face again with the bitter problem of self-sustenance. Anyhow, there was one change for the better. She knew that she had improved in appearance. Her manner had vastly changed. Her clothes were becoming, and men—well-dressed men, some of the kind who before had gazed at her indifferently from behind their polished railings and imposing office partitions—now gazed into her face with a soft light in their eyes. In a way, she felt the power and satisfaction of the thing, but it did not wholly reassure her. She looked for nothing save what might come legitimately and without the appearance of special favor. She wanted something, but no man should buy her by false protestations or favor. She proposed to earn her living honestly.

"This store closes at one on Saturdays," was a pleasing and satisfactory legend to see upon doors which she felt she ought to enter and inquire for work. It gave her an excuse, and after encountering quite a number of them, and noting that the clock registered 12:15, she decided that it would be no use to seek further to-day, so she got on a car and went to Lincoln Park. There was always something to see there—the flowers, the animals, the lake—and she flattered herself that on Monday she would be up betimes and searching. Besides, many things might happen between now and Monday.

Sunday passed with equal doubts, worries, assurances, and heaven knows what vagaries of mind and spirit. Every half-hour in the day the thought would come to her most sharply, like the tail of a swishing whip, that action—immediate action—was imperative. At other times she would look about her and assure herself that things were not so bad—that certainly she would come out safe and sound. At such times she would think of Drouet's advice about going on the stage, and saw some chance for herself in that quarter. She decided to take up that opportunity on the morrow.

Accordingly, she arose early Monday morning and dressed herself carefully. She did not know just how such applications were made, but she took it to be a matter which related more directly to the theater buildings. All you had to do was to inquire of some one about the theater for the manager and ask for a position. If there was anything, you might get it, or, at least, he could tell you how.

She had had no experience with this class of individuals whatsoever, and did not know the salacity and humor of the theatrical tribe. She only knew of the position which Mr. Hale occupied, but, of all things, she did not wish to encounter that personage, on account of her intimacy with his wife.

There was, however, at this time, one theater, the Chicago Opera House, which was considerably in the public eye, and its manager, David A. Henderson, had a fair local reputation. Carrie had seen one or two elaborate performances there and had heard of several others. She knew nothing of Henderson nor of the methods of applying, but she instinctively felt that this would be a likely place, and accordingly strolled about in that neighborhood. She came bravely enough to the showy entrance way, with the polished and begilded lobby, set with framed pictures out of the current attraction, leading up to the quiet box-office, but she could get no further. A noted comic opera comedian was holding forth that week, and the air of distinction and prosperity overawed her. She could not imagine that there would be anything in such a lofty sphere for her. She almost trembled at the audacity which might have carried her on to a terrible rebuff. She could find heart only to look at the pictures which were showy and then walk out. It seemed to her as if she had made a splendid escape and that it would be foolhardy to think of applying in that quarter again.

This little experience settled her hunting for one day. She looked around elsewhere, but it was from the outside. She got the location of several playhouses fixed in her mind—notably the Grand Opera House and McVickar's, both of which were leading in attractions—and then came away. Her spirits were materially reduced, owing to the newly restored sense of magnitude of the great interests and the insignificance of her claims upon society, such as she understood them to be.

That night she was visited by Mrs. Hale, whose chatter and protracted stay made it impossible to dwell upon her predicament or the fortune of the day. Before retiring, however, she sat down to think, and gave herself up to the most gloomy forebodings. Drouet had not put in an appearance. She had had no word from any quarter, she had spent a dollar of her precious sum in procuring food and paying car fare. It was evident that she would not endure long. Besides, she had discovered no resource.

In this situation her thoughts went out to her sister in Van Buren Street, whom she had not seen since the night of her flight, and to her home at Columbia City, which seemed now a part of something that could not be again. She looked for no refuge in that direction. Nothing but sorrow was brought her by thoughts of Hurstwood, which would return. That he could have chosen to dupe her in so ready a manner seemed a cruel thing.

Tuesday came, and with it appropriate indecision and speculation. She was in no mood, after her failure of the day before, to hasten forth upon her work-seeking errand, and yet she rebuked herself for what she considered her weakness the day before. Accordingly she started out to revisit the Chicago Opera House, but possessed scarcely enough courage to approach.

She did manage to inquire at the box-office, however.

"Manager of the company or the house?" asked the smartly dressed individual who took care of the tickets. He was favorably impressed by Carrie's looks.

"I don't know," said Carrie, taken back by the question.

"You couldn't see the manager of the house to-day, anyhow," volunteered the young man. "He's out of town."

He noted her puzzled look, and then added: "What is it you wish to see about?"

"I want to see about getting a position," she answered.

"You'd better see the manager of the company," he returned, "but he isn't here now."

"When will he be in?" asked Carrie, somewhat relieved by this information.

"Well, you might find him in between eleven and twelve. He's here after two o'clock."

Carrie thanked him and walked briskly out, while the young man gazed after her through one of the side windows of his gilded coop.

"Good-looking," he said to himself, and proceeded to visions of condescensions on her part which were exceedingly flattering to himself.

One of the principal comedy companies of the day was playing an engagement at the Grand Opera House. Here Carrie asked to see the manager of the company. She little knew the trivial authority of this individual, or that had there been a vacancy an actor would have been sent on from New York to fill it.

"His office is upstairs," said a man in the box-office.

Several persons were in the manager's office, two lounging near a window, another talking to an individual sitting at a roll-top desk—the manager. Carrie glanced nervously about, and began to fear that she should have to make her appeal before the assembled company, two of whom—the occupants of the window—were already observing her carefully.

"I can't do it," the manager was saying; "it's a rule of Mr. Frohman's never to allow visitors back of the stage. No, no!"

Carrie timidly waited, standing. There were chairs, but no one motioned her to be seated. The individual to whom the manager had been talking went away quite crestfallen. That luminary gazed earnestly at some papers before him, as if they were of the greatest concern.

"Did you see that in the 'Herald' this morning about Nat Goodwin, Harris?"

"No," said the person addressed. "What was it?"

"Made quite a curtain address at Hooley's last night. Better look it up."

Harris reached over to a table and began to look for the "Herald."

"What is it?" said the manager to Carrie, apparently noticing her for the first time. He thought he was going to be held up for free tickets.

Carrie summoned up all her courage, which was little at best. She realized that she was a novice, and felt as if a rebuff were certain. Of this she was so sure that she only wished now to pretend she had called for advice.

"Can you tell me how to go about getting on the stage?"

It was the best way after all to have gone about the matter. She was interesting, in a manner, to the occupant of the chair, and the simplicity of her request and attitude took his fancy. He smiled, as did the others in the room, who, however, made some slight effort to conceal their humor.

"I don't know," he answered, looking her brazenly over. "Have you ever had any experience upon the stage?"

"A little," answered Carrie. "I have taken part in amateur performances."

She thought she had to make some sort of showing in order to retain his interest.

"Never studied for the stage?" he said, putting on an air intended as much to impress his friends with his discretion as Carrie.

"No, sir."

"Well, I don't know," he answered, tipping lazily back in his chair while she stood before him. "What makes you want to get on the stage?"

She felt abashed at the man's daring, but could only smile in answer to his engaging smirk, and say:

"I need to make a living."

"Oh," he answered, rather taken by her trim appearance, and feeling as if he might scrape up an acquaintance with her. "That's a good reason, isn't it? Well, Chicago is not a good place for what you want to do. You ought to be in New York. There's more chance there. You could hardly expect to get started out here."

Carrie smiled genially, grateful that he should condescend to advise her even so much. He noticed the smile, and put a slightly different construction on it. He thought he saw an easy chance for a little flirtation.

"Sit down," he said, pulling a chair forward from the side of his desk and dropping his voice so that the two men in the room should not hear. Those two gave each other the suggestion of a wink.

"Well, I'll be going, Barney," said one, breaking away and so addressing the manager. "See you this afternoon."

"All right," said the manager.

The remaining individual took up a paper as if to read.

"Did you have any idea what sort of part you would like to get?" asked the manager softly.

"Oh, no," said Carrie. "I would take anything to begin with."

"I see," he said. "Do you live here in the city?"

"Yes, sir."

The manager smiled most blandly.

"Have you ever tried to get in as a chorus girl?" he asked, assuming a more confidential air.

Carrie began to feel that there was something exuberant and unnatural in his manner.

"No," she said.

"That's the way most girls begin," he went on, "who go on the stage. It's a good way to get experience."

He was turning on her a glance of the companionable and persuasive manner.

"I didn't know that," said Carrie.

"It's a difficult thing," he went on, "but there's always a chance, you know." Then, as if he suddenly remembered, he pulled out his watch and consulted it. "I've an appointment at two," he said, "and I've got to go to lunch now. Would you care to come and dine with me? We can talk it over there."

"Oh, no," said Carrie, the whole motive of the man flashing on her at once. "I have an engagement myself."

"That's too bad," he said, realizing that he had been a little beforehand in his offer and that Carrie was about to go away. "Come in later. I may know of something."

"Thank you," she answered, with some trepidation, and went out.

"She was good-looking, wasn't she?" said the manager's companion, who had not caught all the details of the game he had played.

"Yes, in a way," said the other, sore to think the game had been lost. "She'd never make an actress, though. Just another chorus girl—that's all."

This little experience nearly destroyed her ambition to call upon the manager at the Chicago Opera House, but she decided to do so after a time. He was of a more sedate turn of mind. He said at once that there was no opening of any sort, and seemed to consider her search foolish.

"Chicago is no place to get a start," he said. "You ought to be in New York."

Still she persisted, and went to McVickar's, where she could not find any one. "The Old Homestead" was running there, but the person to whom she was referred was not to be found.

These little expeditions took up her time until quite four o'clock, when she was weary enough to go home. She felt as if she ought to continue and inquire elsewhere, but the results so far were too dispiriting. She took the car and arrived at Ogden Place in three-quarters of an hour, but decided to ride on to the West Side branch of the Post-office, where she was accustomed to receive Hurstwood's letters. There was one there now, written Saturday, which she tore open and read with mingled feelings. There was so much warmth in it and such tense complaint at her having failed to meet him, and her subsequent silence, that she rather pitied the man. That he loved her was evident enough. That he had wished and dared to do so, married as he was, was the evil. She felt as if the thing deserved an answer, and consequently decided that she would write and let him kow that she knew of his married state and was justly incensed at his deception. She would tell him that it was all over between them.

At her room, the wording of this missive occupied her for some time, for she fell to the task at once. It was most difficult.

"You do not need to have me explain why I did not meet you," she wrote in part. "How could you deceive me so? You cannot expect me to have anything more to do with you. I wouldn't under any circumstances. Oh, how could you act so?" she added in a burst of feeling. "You have caused me more misery than you can think. I hope you will get over your infatuation for me. We must not meet any more. Good-bye."

She took the letter the next morning, and at the corner dropped it reluctantly into the letter-box, still uncertain as to whether she should do so or not. Then she took the car and went downtown.

This was the dull season with the department stores, but she was listened to with more consideration than was usually accorded to young women applicants, owing to her neat and attractive appearance. She was asked the same old questions with which she was already familiar.

"What can you do? Have you ever worked in a retail store before? Are you experienced?"

At The Fair, See and Company's, and all the great stores it was much the same. It was the dull season, she might come in a little later, possibly they would like to have her.

When she arrived at the house at the end of the day, weary and disheartened, she discovered that Drouet had been there. His umbrella and light overcoat were gone. She thought she missed other things, but could not be sure. Everything had not been taken.

So his going was crystallizing into staying. What was she to do now? Evidently she would be facing the world in the same old way within a day or two. Her clothes would get poor. She put her two hands together in her customary expressive way and pressed her fingers. Large tears gathered in her eyes and broke hot across her cheeks. She was alone, very much alone.

Drouet really had called, but it was with a very different mind from that which Carrie had imagined. He expected to find her, to justify his return by claiming that he came to get the remaining portion of his wardrobe, and before he got away again to patch up a peace.

Accordingly, when he arrived, he was disappointed to find Carrie out. He trifled about, hoping that she was somewhere in the neighborhood and would soon return. He constantly listened, expecting to hear her foot on the stair.

When he did so, it was his intention to make believe that he had just come in and was disturbed at being caught. Then he would explain his need of his clothes and find out how things stood.

Wait as he did, however, Carrie did not come. From pottering around among the drawers, in momentary expectation of her arrival, he changed to looking out of the window, and from that to resting himself in the rocking-chair. Still no Carrie. He began to grow restless and lit a cigar. After that he walked the floor. Then he looked out of the window and saw clouds gathering. He remembered an appointment at three. He began to think that it would be useless to wait, and got hold of his umbrella and light coat, intending to take these things, anyway. It would scare her, he hoped. To-morrow he would come back for the others. He would find out how things stood.

As he started to go he felt truly sorry that he had missed her. There was a little picture of her on the wall, showing her arrayed in the little jacket he had first bought her—her face a little more wistful than he had seen it lately. He was really touched by it, and looked into the eyes of it with a rather rare feeling for him.

"You didn't do me right, Cad," he said, as if he were addressing her in the flesh.

Then he went to the door, took a good look around, and went out.

CHAPTER XXVII

When Waters Engulf Us We Reach for a Star

It was when he returned from his disturbed stroll about the streets, after receiving the decisive note from McGregor, James and Hay, that Hurstwood found the letter Carrie had written him that morning. He thrilled intensely as he noted the handwriting, and rapidly tore it open.

"Then," he thought, "she loves me or she would not have written to me at all."

He was slightly depressed at the tenor of the note for the first few minutes, but soon recovered. "She wouldn't write at all if she didn't care for me."

This was his one resource against the depression which held him. He could extract little from the wording of the letter, but the spirit he thought he knew.

There was really something exceedingly human—if not pathetic—in his being thus relieved by a clearly worded reproof. He who had for so long remained satisfied with himself now looked outside of himself for comfort—and to such a source. The mystic cords of affection! How they bind us all.

The color came to his cheeks. For the moment he forgot the letter from McGregor, James and Hay. If he could only have Carrie, perhaps he could get out of the whole entanglement—perhaps it would not matter. He wouldn't care what his wife did with herself if only he might not lose Carrie. He stood up and walked about, dreaming his delightful dream of a life continued with this lovely possessor of his heart.

It was not long, however, before the old worry was back for consideration, and with it what weariness! He thought of the morrow and the suit. He had done nothing, and here was the afternoon slipping away. It was now a quarter of four. At five the attorneys would have gone home. He still had the morrow until noon. Even as he thought, the last fifteen minutes passed away and it was five. Then he abandoned the thought of seeing them any more that day and turned to Carrie.

It is to be observed that the man did not justify himself to himself. He was not troubling about that. His whole thought was the possibility of persuading Carrie. Nothing was wrong in that. He loved her dearly. Their mutual happiness depended upon it. Would that Drouet were only away!

While he was thinking thus elatedly, he remembered that he wanted some clean linen in the morning.

This he purchased, together with a half-dozen ties, and went to the Palmer House. As he entered he thought he saw Drouet ascending the stairs with a key. Surely not Drouet! Then he thought, perhaps they had changed their abode temporarily. He went straight up to the desk.

"Is Mr. Drouet stopping here?" he asked of the clerk.

"I think he is," said the latter, consulting his private registry list. "Yes."

"Is that so?" exclaimed Hurstwood, otherwise concealing his astonishment. "Alone?" he added.

"Yes," said the clerk.

Hurstwood turned away and set his lips so as best to express and conceal his feelings.

"How's that?" he thought. "They've had a row."

He hastened to his room with rising spirits and changed his linen. As he did so, he made up his mind that if Carrie was alone, or if she had gone to another place, it behooved him to find out. He decided to call at once.

"I know what I'll do," he thought. "I'll go to the door and ask if Mr. Drouet is at home. That will bring out whether he is there or not and where Carrie is."

He was almost moved to some muscular display as he thought of it. He decided to go immediately after supper.

On coming down from his room at six, he looked carefully about to see if Drouet was present and then went out to lunch. He could scarcely eat, however, he was so anxious to be about his errand. Before starting he thought it well to discover where Drouet would be, and returned to his hotel.

"Has Mr. Drouet gone out?" he asked of the clerk.

"No," answered the latter, "he's in his room. Do you wish to send up a card?"

"No, I'll call around later," answered Hurstwood, and strolled out.

He took a Madison car and went direct to Ogden Place, this time walking boldly up to the door. The chambermaid answered his knock.

"Is Mr. Drouet in?" said Hurstwood blandly.

"He is out of the city," said the girl, who had heard Carrie tell this to Mrs. Hale.

"Is Mrs. Drouet in?"

"No, she has gone to the theater."

"Is that so?" said Hurstwood, considerably taken back; then, as if burdened with something important, "You don't know to which theater?"

The girl really had no idea where she had gone, but not liking Hurstwood, and wishing to cause him trouble, answered: "Yes, Hooley's."

"Thank you," returned the manager, and, tipping his hat slightly, went away.

"I'll look in at Hooley's," thought he, but as a matter of fact he did not. Before he had reached the central portion of the city he thought the whole matter over and decided it would be useless. As much as he longed to see Carrie, he knew she would be with some one and did not wish to intrude with his plea there. A little later he might do so—in the morning. Only in the morning he had the lawyer question before him.

This little pilgrimage threw quite a wet blanket upon his rising spirits. He was soon down again to his old worry, and reached the resort anxious to find relief. Quite a company of gentlemen were making the place lively with their conversation. A group of Cook County politicians were conferring about a round cherry-wood table in the rear portion of the room. Several young merry-makers were chattering at the bar before making a belated visit to the theater. A shabbily-genteel individual, with a red nose and an old high hat, was sipping a quiet glass of ale alone at one end of the bar. Hurstwood nodded to the politicians and went into his office.

About ten o'clock a friend of his, Mr. Frank L. Taintor, a local sport and racing man, dropped in, and seeing Hurstwood alone in his office came to the door.

"Hello, George!" he exclaimed.

"How are you, Frank?" said Hurstwood, somewhat relieved by the sight of him. "Sit down," and he motioned him to one of the chairs in the little room.

"What's the matter, George?" asked Taintor. "You look a little glum. Haven't lost at the track, have you?"

"I'm not feeling very well to-night. I had a slight cold the other day."

"Take a whiskey, George," said Taintor. "You ought to know that."

Hurstwood smiled.

While they were still conferring there, several other of Hurstwood's friends entered, and not long after eleven, the theaters being out, some actors began to drop in—among them some notabilities.

Then began one of those pointless social conversations so common in American resorts where the would-be *gilded* attempt to rub off gilt from those who have it in abundance. If Hurstwood had one leaning, it was toward notabilities. He considered that, if anywhere, he belonged among them. He was too proud to toady, too keen not to strictly observe the plane he occupied when there were those present who did not appreciate him, but, in situations like the present, where he could shine as a gentleman and be received without equivocation as a friend and equal among men of known ability, he was most delighted. It was on such occasions, if ever, that he would "take something." When the social flavor was strong enough he would even unbend to the extent of drinking glass for glass with his associates, punctiliously observing his turn to pay as if he were an outsider like the others. If he ever approached intoxication—or rather that ruddy warmth and comfortableness which precedes the more sloven state—it was when individuals such as these were gathered about him, when he was one of a circle of chatting celebrities. To-night, disturbed as was his state, he was rather relieved to find company, and now that notabilities were gathered, he laid aside his troubles for the nonce, and joined in right heartily.

It was not long before the imbibing began to tell. Stories began to crop up—those ever-enduring, droll stories which form the major portion of the conversation among American men under such circumstances.

Twelve o'clock arrived, the hour for closing, and with it the company took leave. Hurstwood shook hands with them most cordially. He was very roseate physically. He had arrived at that state where his mind, though clear, was, nevertheless, warm in its fancies. He felt as if his troubles were not very serious. Going into his office, he began to turn over certain accounts, awaiting the departure of the bartenders and the cashier, who soon left.

It was the manager's duty, as well as his custom, after all were gone to see that everything was safely closed up for the night. As a rule, no money except the cash taken in after banking hours was kept about the place, and that was locked in the safe by the cashier, who, with the owners, was joint keeper of the secret combination, but, nevertheless, Hurstwood nightly took the precaution to try the cash drawers and the safe in order to see that they were tightly closed. Then he would lock his own little office and set the proper light burning near the safe, after which he would take his departure.

Never in his experience had he found anything out of order, but to-night, after shutting down his desk, he came out and tried the safe. His way was to give a sharp pull. This time the door responded. He was slightly surprised at that, and looking in found the money cases as left for the day, apparently unprotected. His first thought was, of course, to inspect the drawers and shut the door.

"I'll speak to Mayhew about this to-morrow," he thought.

The latter had certainly imagined upon going out a half-hour before that he had turned the knob on the door so as to spring the lock. He had never failed to do so before. But to-night Mayhew had other thoughts. He had been revolving the problem of a business of his own.

"I'll look in here," thought the manager, pulling out the money drawers. He did not know why he wished to look in there. It was quite a superfluous action, which another time might not have happened at all.

As he did so, a layer of bills, in parcels of a thousand, such as banks issue, caught his eye. He could not tell how much they represented, but paused to view them. Then he pulled out the second of the cash drawers. In that were the receipts of the day.

"I didn't know Fitzgerald and Moy ever left any money this way," his mind said to itself. "They must have forgotten it."

He looked at the other drawer and paused again.

"Count them," said a voice in his ear.

He put his hand into the first of the boxes and lifted the stack, letting the separate parcels fall. They were bills of fifty and one hundred dollars done in packages of a thousand. He thought he counted ten such.

"Why don't I shut the safe?" his mind said to itself, lingering. "What makes me pause here?"

For an answer there came the strangest words:

"Did you ever have ten thousand dollars in ready money?"

Lo, the manager remembered that he had never had so much. All his property had been slowly accumulated, and now his wife owned that. He was worth more than forty thousand, all told—but she would get that.

He puzzled as he thought of these things, then pushed in the drawers and closed the door, pausing with his hand upon the knob, which might so easily lock it all beyond temptation. Still he paused. Finally he went to the windows and pulled down the curtains. Then he tried the door, which he had previously locked. What was this thing, making him suspicious? Why did he wish to move about so quietly? He came back to the end of the counter as if to rest his arm and think. Then he went and unlocked his little office door and turned on the light. He also opened his desk, sitting down before it, only to think strange thoughts.

"The safe is open," said a voice. "There is just the least little crack in it. The lock has not been sprung."

The manager floundered among a jumble of thoughts. Now all the entanglement of the day came back. Also the thought that here was a solution. That money would do it. If he had that and Carrie. He rose up and stood stock-still, looking at the floor.

"What about it?" his mind asked, and for answer he put his hand slowly up and scratched his head.

The manager was no fool to be led blindly away by such an errant proposition as this, but his situation was peculiar. Wine was in his veins. It had crept up into his head and given him a warm view of the situation. It also colored the possibilities of ten thousand for him. He could see great opportunities with that. He could get Carrie. Oh, yes, he could! He could get rid of his wife. That letter, too, was waiting discussion to-morrow morning. He would not need to answer that. He went back to the safe and put his hand on the knob. Then he pulled the door open and took the drawer with the money quite out.

With it once out and before him, it seemed a foolish thing to think about leaving it. Certainly it would. Why, he could live quietly with Carrie for years.

Lord! what was that? For the first time he was tense, as if a stern hand had been laid upon his shoulder. He looked fearfully around. Not a soul was present. Not a sound. Some one was shuffling by on the sidewalk. He took the box and the money and put it back in the safe. Then he partly closed the door again.

To those who have never wavered in conscience, the predicament of the individual whose mind is less strongly constituted and who trembles in the balance between duty and desire is scarcely appreciable, unless graphically portrayed. Those who have never heard that solemn voice of the ghostly clock which ticks with awful distinctness, "thou shalt," "thou shalt not," "thou shalt," "thou shalt not," are in no position to judge. Not alone in sensitive, highly organized natures is such a mental conflict possible. The dullest specimen of humanity, when drawn by desire toward evil, is recalled by a sense of right, which is proportionate in power and strength to his evil tendency. We must remember that it may not be a knowledge of right, for no knowledge of right is predicated of the animal's instinctive recoil at evil. Men are still led by instinct before they are regulated by knowledge. It is instinct which recalls the criminal—it is instinct (where highly organized reasoning is absent) which gives the criminal his feeling of danger, his fear of wrong.

At every first adventure, then, into some untried evil, the mind wavers. The clock of thought ticks out its wish and its denial. To those who have never experienced such a mental dilemma, the following will appeal on the simple ground of revelation.

When Hurstwood put the money back, his nature again resumed its ease and daring. No one had observed him. He was quite alone. No one could tell what he wished to do. He could work this thing out for himself.

The imbibation of the evening had not yet worn off. Moist as was his brow, tremble as did his hand once after the nameless fright, he was still flushed with the fumes of liquor. He scarcely noticed that the time was passing. He went over his situation once again, his eye always seeing the money in a lump, his mind always seeing what it would do. He strolled into his little room, then to the door, then to the safe again. He put his hand on the knob and opened it. There was the money! Surely no harm could come from looking at it!

He took out the drawer again and lifted the bills. They were so smooth, so compact, so portable. How little they made, after all. He decided he would take them. Yes, he would. He would put them in his pocket. Then he looked at that and saw they would not go there. His hand satchel! To be sure, his hand satchel. They would go in that—all of it would. No one would think anything of it either. He went into the little office and took it from the shelf in the corner. Now he set it upon his desk and went out toward the safe. For some reason he did not want to fill it out in the big room.

First he brought the bills and then the loose receipts of the day. He would take it all. He put the empty drawers back and pushed the iron door almost to, then stood beside it meditating.

The wavering of a mind under such circumstances is an almost inexplicable thing, and yet it is absolutely true. Hurstwood could not bring himself to act definitely. He wanted to think about it—to ponder over it, to decide whether it were best. He was drawn by such a keen desire for Carrie, driven by such a state of turmoil in his own affairs that he thought constantly it would be best, and yet he wavered. He did not know what evil might result from it to him—how soon he might come to grief. The true ethics of the situation never once occurred to him, and never would have, under any circumstances.

After he had all the money in the hand bag, a revulsion of feeling seized him. He would not do it—no! Think of what a scandal it would make. The police! They would be after him. He would have to fly, and where? Oh, the terror of being a fugitive from justice! He took out the two boxes and put all the money back. In his excitement he forgot what he was doing, and put the sums in the wrong boxes. As he pushed the door to, he thought he remembered doing it wrong and opened the door again. There were the two boxes mixed.

He took them out and straightened the matter, but now the terror had gone. Why be afraid?

While the money was in his hand the lock clicked. It had sprung! Did he do it? He grabbed at the knob and pulled vigorously. It had closed. Heavens! he was in for it now, sure enough.

The moment he realized that the safe was locked for a surety, the sweat burst out upon his brow and he trembled violently. He looked about him and decided instantly. There was no delaying now.

"Supposing I do lay it on the top," he said, "and go away, they'll know who took it. I'm the last to close up. Besides, other things will happen."

At once he became the man of action.

"I must get out of this," he thought.

He hurried into his little room, took down his light overcoat and hat, locked his desk, and grabbed the satchel. Then he turned out all but one light and opened the door. He tried to put on his old assured air, but it was almost gone. He was repenting rapidly.

"I wish I hadn't done that," he said. "That was a mistake."

He walked steadily down the street, greeting a night watchman whom he knew who was trying doors. He must get out of the city, and that quickly.

"I wonder how the trains run?" he thought.

Instantly he pulled out his watch and looked. It was nearly half-past one.

At the first drug store he stopped, seeing a long-distance telephone both inside. It was a famous drug store, and contained one of the first private telephone booths ever erected.

"I want to use your 'phone a minute," he said to the night clerk.

The latter nodded.

"Give me 1643," he called to Central, after looking up the Michigan Central depot number. Soon he got the ticket agent.

"How do the trains leave here for Detroit?" he asked.

The man explained the hours.

"No more to-night?"

"Nothing with a sleeper. Yes, there is, too," he added. "There is a mail train out of here at three o'clock."

"All right," said Hurstwood. "What time does that get to Detroit?"

He was thinking if he could only get there and cross the river into Canada, he could take his time about getting to Montreal. He was relieved to learn that it would reach there by noon.

"Mayhew won't open the safe till nine," he thought. "They can't get on my track before noon."

Then he thought of Carrie. With what speed must he get her, if he got her at all. She would have to come along. He jumped into the nearest cab standing by.

"To Ogden Place," he said sharply. "I'll give you a dollar more if you make good time."

The cabby beat his horse into a sort of imitation gallop, which was fairly fast, however. On the way Hurstwood thought what to do. Reaching the number, he hurried up the steps and did not spare the bell in waking the servant.

"Is Mrs. Drouet in?" he asked.

"Yes," said the astonished girl.

"Tell her to dress and come to the door at once. Her husband is in the hospital, injured, and wants to see her."

The servant girl hurried upstairs, convinced by the man's strained and emphatic manner.

"What!" said Carrie, lighting the gas and searching for her clothes.

"Mr. Drouet is hurt and in the hospital. He wants to see you. The cab's downstairs."

Carrie dressed very rapidly, and soon appeared below, forgetting everything save the necessities.

"Drouet is hurt," said Hurstwood quickly. "He wants to see you. Come quickly."

Carrie was so bewildered that she swallowed the whole story.

"Get in," said Hurstwood, helping her and jumping after.

The cabby began to turn the horse around.

"Michigan Central depot," he said, standing up and speaking so low that Carrie could not hear, "as fast as you can go."

CHAPTER XXVIII

A PILGRIM, AN OUTLAW: THE SPIRIT DETAINED

The cab had not traveled a short block before Carrie, settling herself and thoroughly waking in the night atmosphere asked:

"What's the matter with him? Is he hurt badly?"

"It isn't anything very serious," Hurstwood said solemnly. He was very much disturbed over his own situation, and now that he had Carrie with him, he only wanted to get safely out of reach of the law. Therefore he was in no mood for anything save such words as would further his plans distinctly.

Carrie did not forget that there was something to be settled between her and Hurstwood, but the thought was ignored in her agitation. The one thing was to finish this strange pilgrimage.

"Where is he?"

"Way out on the South Side," said Hurstwood. "We'll have to take the train. It's the quickest way."

Carrie said nothing, and the horse gamboled on. The weirdness of the city by night held her attention. She looked at the long receding rows of lamps and studied the dark, silent houses.

"How did he hurt himself?" she asked—meaning what was the nature of his injuries. Hurstwood understood. He hated to lie any more than necessary, and yet he wanted no protests until he was out of danger.

"I don't know exactly," he said. "They just called me up to go and get you and bring you out. They said there wasn't any need for alarm, but that I shouldn't fail to bring you."

The man's serious manner convinced Carrie, and she became silent, wondering.

Hurstwood examined his watch and urged the man to hurry. For one in so delicate a position he was exceedingly cool. He could only think of how needful it was to make the train and get quietly away. Carrie seemed quite tractable, and he congratulated himself.

In due time they reached the depot, and after helping her out he handed the man a five-dollar bill and hurried on.

"You wait here," he said to Carrie, when they reached the waiting-room, "while I get the tickets."

"Have I much time to catch that train for Detroit?" he asked of the agent.

"Four minutes," said the latter.

He paid for two tickets as circumspectly as possible.

"Is it far?" said Carrie, as he hurried back.

"Not very," he said. "We must get right in."

He pushed her before him at the gate, stood between her and the ticket man while the latter punched their tickets, so that she could not see, and then hurried after.

There was a long line of express and passenger cars and one or two common day coaches. As the train had only recently been made up and few passengers were expected, there were only one or two brakemen waiting. They entered the rear day coach and sat down. Almost immediately, "All aboard," resounded faintly from the outside, and the train started.

Carrie began to think it was a little bit curious—this going to a depot—but said nothing. The whole incident was so out of the natural that she did not attach too much weight to anything she imagined.

"How have you been?" asked Hurstwood gently, for he now breathed easier.

"Very well," said Carrie, who was so disturbed that she could not bring a proper attitude to bear in the matter. She was still nervous to reach Drouet and see what could be the matter. Hurstwood contemplated her and felt this. He was not disturbed that it should be so. He did not trouble because she was moved sympathetically in the matter. It was one of the qualities in her which pleased him exceedingly. He was only thinking how he should explain. Even this was not the most serious thing in his mind, however. His own deed and present flight were the great shadows which weighed upon him.

"What a fool I was to do that," he said over and over. "What a mistake!"

In his sober senses, he could scarcely realize that the thing had been done. He could not begin to feel that he was a fugitive from justice. He had often read of such things, and had thought they must be terrible, but now that the thing was upon him, he only sat and looked into the past. The future was a thing which concerned the Canadian line. He wanted to reach that. As for the rest, he surveyed his actions for the evening, and counted them parts of a great mistake.

"Still," he said, "what could I have done?"

Then he would decide to make the best of it, and would begin to do so by starting the whole inquiry over again. It was a fruitless, harassing round, and left him in a queer mood to deal with the proposition he had in the presence of Carrie.

The train clacked through the yards along the lake front, and ran rather slowly to Twenty-fourth Street. Brakes and signals were visible without. The engine gave short calls with its whistle, and frequently the bell rang. Several brakemen came through, bearing lanterns. They were locking the vestibules and putting the cars in order for a long run.

Presently it began to gain speed, and Carrie saw the silent streets flashing by in rapid succession. The engine also began its whistle-calls of four parts, with which it signaled danger to important crossings.

"Is it very far?" asked Carrie.

"Not so very," said Hurstwood. He could hardly repress a smile at her simplicity. He wanted to explain and conciliate her, but he also wanted to be well out of Chicago.

In the lapse of another half-hour it became apparent to Carrie that it was quite a run to wherever he was taking her, anyhow.

"Is it in Chicago?" she asked nervously. They were now far beyond the city limits, and the train was scudding across the Indiana line at a great rate.

"No," he said, "not where we are going."

There was something in the way he said this which aroused her in an instant.

Her pretty brow began to contract.

"We are going to see Charlie, aren't we?" she asked.

He felt that the time was up. An explanation might as well come now as later. Therefore, he shook his head in the most gentle negative.

"What?" said Carrie. She was nonplussed at the possibility of the errand being different from what she had thought.

He only looked at her in the most kindly and mollifying way.

"Well, where are you taking me, then?" she asked, her voice showing the quality of fright.

"I'll tell you, Carrie, if you'll be quiet. I want you to come along with me to another city."

"Oh," said Carrie, her voice rising into a weak cry. "Let me off. I don't want to go with you."

She was quite appalled at the man's audacity. This was something which had never for a moment entered her head. Her one thought now was to get off and away. If only the flying train could be stopped, the terrible trick would be amended.

She arose and tried to push out into the aisle—anywhere. She knew she had to do something. Hurstwood laid a gentle hand on her.

"Sit still, Carrie," he said. "Sit still. It won't do you any good to get up here. Listen to me and I'll tell you what I'll do. Wait a moment."

She was pushing at his knees, but he only pulled her back. No one saw this little altercation, for very few persons were in the car, and they were attempting to doze.

"I won't," said Carrie, who was, nevertheless, complying against her will. "Let me go," she said. "How dare you?" and large tears began to gather in her eyes.

Hurstwood was now fully aroused to the immediate difficulty, and ceased to think of his own situation. He must do something with this girl, or she would cause him trouble. He tried the art of persuasion with all his powers aroused.

"Look here now, Carrie," he said, "you mustn't act this way. I didn't mean to hurt your feelings. I don't want to do anything to make you feel bad."

"Oh," sobbed Carrie, "oh, oh—oo—o!"

"There, there," he said, "you mustn't cry. Won't you listen to me? Listen to me a minute, and I'll tell you why I came to do this thing. I couldn't help it. I assure you I couldn't. Won't you listen?"

Her sobs disturbed him so that he was quite sure she did not hear a word he said.

"Won't you listen?" he asked.

"No, I won't," said Carrie, flashing up. "I want you to take me out of this, or I'll tell the conductor. I won't go with you. It's a shame," and again sobs of fright cut off her desire for expression.

Hurstwood listened with some astonishment. He felt that she had just cause for feeling as she did, and yet he wished that he could straighten this thing out quickly. Shortly the conductor would come through for the tickets. He wanted no noise, no trouble of any kind. Before everything he must make her quiet.

"You couldn't get out until the train stops again," said Hurstwood. "It won't be very long until we reach another station. You can get out then if you want to. I won't stop you. All I want you to do is to listen a moment. You'll let me tell you, won't you?"

Carrie seemed not to listen. She only turned her head toward the window, where outside all was black. The train was speeding with steady grace across the fields and through patches of wood. The long whistles came with sad, musical effect as the lonely woodland crossings were approached.

Now the conductor entered the car and took up the one or two fares that had been added at Chicago. He approached Hurstwood, who handed out the tickets. Poised as she was to act, Carrie made no move. She did not look about.

When the conductor had gone again Hurstwood felt relieved.

"You're angry at me because I deceived you," he said. "I didn't mean to, Carrie. As I live I didn't. I couldn't help it. I couldn't stay away from you after the first time I saw you."

He was ignoring the last deception as something that might go by the board. He wanted to convince her that his wife could no longer be a factor in their relationship. The money he had stolen he tried to shut out of his mind.

"Don't talk to me," said Carrie, "I hate you. I want you to go away from me. I am going to get out at the very next station."

She was in a tremble of excitement and opposition as she spoke.

"All right," he said, "but you'll hear me out, won't you? After all you have said about loving me, you might hear me. I don't want to do you any harm. I'll give you the money to go back with when you go. I merely want to tell you, Carrie. You can't stop me from loving you, whatever you may think."

He looked at her tenderly, but received no reply.

"You think I have deceived you badly, but I haven't. I didn't do it willingly. I'm through with my wife. She hasn't any claims on me. I'll never see her any more. That's why I'm here to-night. That's why I came and got you."

"You said Charlie was hurt," said Carrie, savagely. "You deceived me. You've been deceiving me all the time, and now you want to force me to run away with you."

She was so excited that she got up and tried to get by him again. He let her, and she took another seat. Then he followed.

"Don't run away from me, Carrie," he said gently. "Let me explain. If you will only hear me out you will see where I stand. I tell you my wife is nothing to me. She hasn't been anything for years or I wouldn't have ever come near you. I'm going to get a divorce just as soon as I can. I'll never see her again. I'm done with all that. You're the only person I want. If I can have you I won't ever think of another woman again."

Carrie heard all this in a very ruffled state. It sounded sincere enough, however, despite all he had done. There was a tenseness in Hurstwood's voice and manner which could but have some effect. She did not want anything to do with him. He was married, he had deceived her once, and now again, and she thought him terrible. Still there is something in such daring and power which is fascinating to a woman, especially if she can be made to feel that it is all prompted by love of her.

The progress of the train was having a great deal to do with the solution of this difficult situation. The speeding wheels and disappearing country put Chicago farther and farther behind. Carrie could feel that she was being borne a long distance off—that the engine was making an almost through run to some distant city. She felt at times as if she could cry out and make such a row that someone would come to her aid; at other times it seemed an almost useless thing—so far was she from any aid, no matter what she did. All the while Hurstwood was endeavoring to formulate his plea in such a way that it should strike home and bring her into sympathy with him.

"I was simply put where I didn't know what else to do."

Carrie deigned no suggestion of hearing this.

"When I saw you wouldn't come unless I could marry you, I decided to put everything else behind me and get you to come away with me. I'm going off now to another city. I want to go to Montreal for a while, and then anywhere you want to. We'll go and live in New York, if you say."

"I'll not have anything to do with you," said Carrie. "I want to get off this train. Where are we going?"

"To Detroit," said Hurstwood.

"Oh!" said Carrie, in a burst of anguish. So distant and definite a point seemed to increase the difficulty.

"Won't you come along with me?" he said, as if there was great danger that she would not. "You won't need to do anything but travel with me. I'll not trouble you in any way. You can see Montreal and New York, and then if you don't want to stay you can go back. It will be better than trying to go back to-night."

The first gleam of fairness shone in this proposition for Carrie. It seemed a plausible thing to do, much as she feared his opposition if she tried to carry it out. Montreal and New York! Even now she was speeding toward those great, strange lands, and could see them if she liked. She thought, but made no sign.

Hurstwood thought he saw a shade of compliance in this. He redoubled his ardor.

"Think," he said, "what I've given up. I can't go back to Chicago any more. I've got to stay away and live alone now, if you don't come with me. You won't go back on me entirely, will you, Carrie?"

"I don't want you to talk to me," she answered forcibly.

Hurstwood kept silent for a while.

Carrie felt the train to be slowing down. It was the moment to act if she was to act at all. She stirred uneasily.

"Don't think of going, Carrie," he said. "If you ever cared for me at all, come along and let's start right. I'll do whatever you say. I'll marry you, or I'll let you go back. Give yourself time to think it over. I wouldn't have wanted you to come if I hadn't loved you. I tell you, Carrie, before God, I can't live without you. I won't!"

There was the tensity of fierceness in the man's plea which appealed deeply to her sympathies. It was a dissolving fire which was actuating him now. He was loving her too intensely to think of giving her up in this, his hour of distress. He clutched her hand nervously and pressed it with all the force of an appeal.

The train was now all but stopped. It was running by some cars on a side track. Everything outside was dark and dreary. A few sprinkles on the window began to indicate that it was raining. Carrie hung in a quandary, balancing between decision and helplessness. Now the train stopped, and she was listening to his plea. The engine backed a few feet and all was still.

She wavered, totally unable to make a move. Minute after minute slipped by and still she hesitated, he pleading.

"Will you let me come back if I want to?" she asked, as if she now had the upper hand and her companion was utterly subdued.

"Of course," he answered, "you know I will."

Carrie only listened as one who has granted a temporary amnesty. She began to feel as if the matter were in her hands entirely.

The train was again in rapid motion. Hurstwood changed the subject.

"Aren't you very tired?" he said.

"No," she answered.

"Won't you let me get you a berth in the sleeper?"

She shook her head, though for all her distress and his trickery she was beginning to notice what she had always felt—his thoughtfulness.

"Oh, yes," he said, "you will feel so much better."

She shook her head.

"Let me fix my coat for you, anyway," and he arose and arranged his light coat in a comfortable position to receive her head.

"There," he said tenderly, "now see if you can't rest a little." He could have kissed her for her compliance. He took his seat beside her and thought a moment.

"I believe we're in for a heavy rain," he said.

"So it looks," said Carrie, whose nerves were quieting under the sound of the rain drops, driven by a gusty wind, as the train swept on frantically through the shadow to a newer world.

The fact that he had in a measure mollified Carrie was a source of satisfaction to Hurstwood, but it furnished only the most temporary relief, now that her opposition was out of the way, he had all of his time to devote to the consideration of his own error.

His condition was bitter in the extreme, for he did not want the miserable sum he had stolen. He did not want to be a thief. That sum or any other could never compensate for the state which he had thus foolishly doffed. It could not give him back his host of friends, his name, his house and family, nor Carrie, as he had meant to have her. He was shut out from Chicago—from his easy, comfortable state. He had robbed himself of his dignity, his merry meetings, his pleasant evenings. And for what? The more he thought of it the more unbearable it became. He began to think that he would try and restore himself to his old state. He would return the miserable thievings of the night and explain. Perhaps Moy would understand. Perhaps they would forgive him and let him come back.

By noontime the train rolled into Detroit and he began to feel exceedingly nervous. The police must be on his track by now. They had probably notified all the police of the big cities, and detectives would be watching for him. He remembered instances in which defaulters had been captured. Consequently, he breathed heavily and paled somewhat. His hands felt as if they must have something to do. He simulated interest in several scenes without which he did not feel. He repeatedly beat his foot upon the floor.

Carrie noticed his agitation, but said nothing. She had no idea what it meant or that it was important.

He wondered now why he had not asked whether this train went on through to Montreal or some Canadian point. Perhaps he could have saved time. He jumped up and sought the conductor.

"Does any part of this train go to Montreal?" he asked.

"Yes, the next sleeper back does."

He would have asked more, but it did not seem wise, so he decided to inquire at the depot.

The train rolled into the yards, clanging and puffing.

"I think we had better go right on through to Montreal," he said to Carrie. "I'll see what the connections are when we get off."

He was exceedingly nervous, but did his best to put on a calm exterior. Carrie only looked at him with large, troubled eyes. She was drifting mentally, unable to say to herself what to do.

The train stopped and Hurstwood led the way out. He looked warily around him, pretending to look after Carrie. Seeing nothing that indicated studied observation, he made his way to the ticket office.

"The next train for Montreal leaves when?" he asked.

"In twenty minutes," said the man.

He bought two tickets and Pullman berths. Then he hastened back to Carrie.

"We go right out again," he said, scarcely noticing that Carrie looked tired and weary.

"I wish I was out of all this," she exclaimed gloomily.

"You'll feel better when we reach Montreal," he said.

"I haven't an earthly thing with me," said Carrie; "not even a handkerchief."

"You can buy all you want as soon as you get there, dearest," he explained. "You can call in a dressmaker."

Now the crier called the train ready and they got on. Hurstwood breathed a sigh of relief as it started. There was a short run to the river, and there they were ferried over. They had barely pulled the train off the ferry-boat when he settled back with a sigh.

"It won't be so very long now," he said, remembering her in his relief. "We get there the first thing in the morning."

Carrie scarcely deigned to reply.

"I'll see if there is a dining-car," he added. "I'm hungry."

CHAPTER XXIX

The Solace of Travel: The Boats of the Sea

To the untraveled, territory other than their own familiar hearth is invariably fascinating. Next to love, it is the one thing which solaces and delights. Things new are too important to be neglected, and mind, which is a mere reflection of sensory impressions, succumbs to the flood of objects. Thus lovers are forgotten, sorrow laid aside, death hidden from view. There is a world of accumulated feeling back of the trite dramatic expression—"I am going away."

As Carrie looked out upon the flying scenery she almost forgot that she had been tricked into this long journey against her will and that she was without the necessary apparel for traveling. She quite forgot Hurstwood's presence at times, and looked away to homely farmhouses and cosy cottages in villages with wondering eyes. It was an interesting world to her. Her life had just begun. She did not feel herself defeated at all. Neither was she blasted in hope. The great city held much. Possibly she would come out of bondage into freedom—who knows? Perhaps she would be happy. These thoughts raised her above the level of erring. She was saved in that she was hopeful.

The following morning the train pulled safely into Montreal and they stepped down, Hurstwood glad to be out of danger, Carrie wondering at the novel atmosphere of the northern city. Long before Hurstwood had been here, and now he remembered the name of the hotel at which he had stopped. As they came out of the main entrance of the depot he heard it called anew by a busman.

"We'll go right up and get rooms," he said.

At the clerk's office Hurstwood swung the register about while the clerk came forward. He was thinking what name he would put down. With the latter before him he found no time for hesitation. A name he had seen out of the car window came swiftly to him. It was pleasing enough. With an easy hand he wrote, "G. W. Murdock and wife." It was the largest concession to necessity he felt like making. His initials he could not spare.

When they were shown their room Carrie saw at once that he had secured her a lovely chamber.

"You have a bath there," said he. "Now you can clean up when you get ready."

Carrie went over and looked out the window, while Hurstwood looked at himself in the glass. He felt dusty and unclean. He had no trunk, no change of linen, not even a hairbrush.

"I'll ring for soap and towels," he said, "and send you up a hairbrush. Then you can bathe and get ready for breakfast. I'll go for a shave and come back and get you, and then we'll go out and look for some clothes for you."

He smiled good-naturedly as he said this.

"All right," said Carrie.

She sat down in one of the rocking-chairs, while Hurstwood waited for the boy, who soon knocked.

"Soap, towels, and a pitcher of ice-water."

"Yes, sir."

"I'll go now," he said to Carrie, coming toward her and holding out his hands, but she did not move to take them.

"You're not mad at me, are you?" he asked softly.

"Oh, no!" she answered, rather indifferently.

"Don't you care for me at all?"

She made no answer, but looked steadily toward the window.

"Don't you think you could love me a little?" he pleaded, taking one of her hands, which she endeavored to draw away. "You once said you did."

"What made you deceive me so?" asked Carrie.

"I couldn't help it," he said, "I wanted you too much."

"You didn't have any right to want me," she answered, striking cleanly home.

"Oh, well, Carrie," he answered, "here I am. It's too late now. Won't you try and care for me a little?"

He looked rather worsted in thought as he stood before her.

She shook her head negatively.

"Let me start all over again. Be my wife from today on."

Carrie rose up as if to step away, he holding her hand. Now he slipped his arm about her and she struggled, but in vain. He held her quite close. Instantly there flamed up in his body the all-compelling desire. His affection took an ardent form.

"Let me go," said Carrie, who was folded close to him.

"Won't you love me?" he said. "Won't you be mine from now on?"

Carrie had never been ill-disposed toward him. Only a moment before she had been listening with some complacency, remembering her old affection for him. He was so handsome, so daring!

Now, however, this feeling had changed to one of opposition, which rose feebly. It mastered her for a moment, and then, held close as she was, began to wane. Something else in her spoke. This man, to whose bosom she was being pressed, was strong; he was passionate, he loved her, and she was alone. If she did not turn to him—accept of his love—where else might she go? Her resistance half dissolved in the flood of his strong feeling.

She found him lifting her head and looking into her eyes. What magnetism there was she could never know. His many sins, however, were for the moment all forgotten.

He pressed her closer and kissed her, and she felt that further opposition was useless.

"Will you marry me?" she asked, forgetting *how*.

"This very day," he said, with all delight.

Now the hall-boy pounded on the door and he released his hold upon her regretfully.

"You get ready now, will you," he said, "at once?"

"Yes," she answered.

"I'll be back in three-quarters of an hour."

Carrie, flushed and excited, moved away as he admitted the boy.

Below stairs, he halted in the lobby to look for a barber shop. For the moment, he was in fine feather. His recent victory over Carrie seemed to atone for much he had endured during the last few days. Life seemed worth fighting for. This eastward flight from all things customary and attached seemed as if it might have happiness in store. The storm showed a rainbow at the end of which might be a pot of gold.

He was about to cross to a little red-and-white striped bar which was fastened up beside a door when a voice greeted him familiarly. Instantly his heart sank.

"Why, hello, George, old man!" said the voice. "What are you doing down here?"

Hurstwood was already confronted, and recognized his friend Kenny, the stock-broker.

"Just attending to a little private matter," he answered, his mind working like a key-board of a telephone station. This man evidently did not know—he had not read the papers.

"Well, it seems strange to see you way up here," said Mr. Kenny genially. "Stopping here?"

"Yes," said Hurstwood uneasily, thinking of his handwriting on the register.

"Going to be in town long?"

"No, only a day or so."

"Is that so? Had your breakfast?"

"Yes," said Hurstwood, lying blandly. "I'm just going for a shave."

"Won't you come have a drink?"

"Not until afterwards," said the ex-manager. "I'll see you later. Are you stopping here?"

"Yes," said Mr. Kenny, and then, turning the word again, added: "How are things out in Chicago?"

"About the same as usual," said Hurstwood, smiling genially.

"Wife with you?"

"No."

"Well, I must see more of you to-day. I'm just going in here for breakfast. Come in when you're through."

"I will," said Hurstwood, moving away. The whole conversation was a trial to him. It seemed to add complications with every word. This man called up a thousand memories. He represented everything he had left. Chicago, his wife, the elegant resort—all these were in his greeting and inquiries. And here he was in this same hotel expecting to confer with him, unquestionably waiting to have a good time with him. All at once the Chicago papers would arrive. The local papers would have accounts in them this very day. He forgot his triumph with Carrie in the possibility of soon being known for what he was, in this man's eyes, a safe-breaker. He could have groaned as he went into the barber shop. He decided to escape and seek a more secluded hotel.

Accordingly, when he came out he was glad to see the lobby clear, and hastened toward the stairs. He would get Carrie and go out by the ladies' entrance. They would have breakfast in some more inconspicuous place.

Across the lobby, however, another individual was surveying him. He was of a commonplace Irish type, small of stature, cheaply dressed, and with a head that seemed a smaller edition of some huge ward politician's. This individual had been evidently talking with the clerk, but now he surveyed the ex-manager keenly.

Hurstwood felt the long-range examination and recognized the type. Instinctively he felt that the man was a detective—that he was being watched. He hurried across, pretending not to notice, but in his mind was a world of thoughts. What would happen now? What could these people do? He began to trouble concerning the extradition laws. He did not understand them absolutely. Perhaps he could be arrested. Oh, if Carrie should find out! Montreal was too warm for him. He began to long to be out of it.

Carrie had bathed and was waiting when he arrived. She looked refreshed—more delightful than ever, but reserved. Since he had gone she had resumed somewhat of her cold attitude towards him. Love was not blazing in her heart. He felt it, and his troubles seemed increased. He could not take her in his arms; he did not even try. Something about her forbade it. In part his opinion was the result of his own experiences and reflections below stairs.

"You're ready, are you?" he said kindly.

"Yes," she answered.

"We'll go out for breakfast. This place down here doesn't appeal to me very much."

"All right," said Carrie.

They went out, and at the corner the commonplace Irish individual was standing, eyeing him. Hurstwood could scarcely refrain from showing that he knew of this chap's presence. The insolence in the fellow's eye was galling. Still they passed, and he explained to Carrie concerning the city. Another restaurant was not long in showing itself, and here they entered.

"What a queer town this is," said Carrie, who marveled at it solely because it was not like Chicago.

"It isn't as lively as Chicago," said Hurstwood. "Don't you like it?"

"No," said Carrie, whose feelings were already localized in the great Western city.

"Well, it isn't as interesting," said Hurstwood.

"What's here?" asked Carrie, wondering at his choosing to visit this town.

"Nothing much," returned Hurstwood. "It's quite a resort. There's some pretty scenery about here."

Carrie listened, but with a feeling of unrest. There was much about her situation which destroyed the possibility of appreciation.

"We won't stay here long," said Hurstwood, who was now really glad to note her dissatisfaction. "You pick out your clothes as soon as breakfast is over and we'll run down to New York soon. You'll like that. It's a lot more like a city than any place outside Chicago."

He was really planning to slip out and away. He would see what these detectives would do—what move his employers at Chicago would make—then he would slip away—down to New York, where it was easy to hide. He knew enough about that city to know that its mysteries and possibilities of mystification were infinite.

The more he thought, however, the more wretched his situation became. He saw that getting here did not exactly clear up the ground. The firm would probably employ detectives to watch him—Pinkerton men or agents of Mooney and Boland. They might arrest him the moment he tried to leave Canada. So he might be compelled to remain here months, and in what a state!

Back at the hotel Hurstwood was anxious and yet fearful to see the morning papers. He wanted to know how far the news of his criminal deed had spread. So he told Carrie he would be up in a few moments, and went to secure and scan the dailies. No familiar or suspicious faces were about, and yet he did not like reading in the lobby, so he sought the main parlor on the floor above and, seated by a window there, looked them over. Very little was given to his crime, but it was there, several "sticks" in all, among all the riffraff of telegraphed murders, accidents, marriages, and other news. He wished, half sadly, that he could undo it all. Every moment of his time in this far-off abode of safety but added to his feeling that he had made a great mistake. There could have been an easier way out if he had only known.

He left the papers before going to the room, thinking thus to keep them out of the hands of Carrie.

"Well, how are you feeling?" he asked of her. She was engaged in looking out of the window.

"Oh, all right," she answered.

He came over, and was about to begin a conversation with her, when a knock came at their door.

"Maybe it's one of my parcels," said Carrie.

Hurstwood opened the door, outside of which stood the individual whom he had so thoroughly suspected.

"You're Mr. Hurstwood, are you?" said the latter, with a volume of affected shrewdness and assurance.

"Yes," said Hurstwood calmly. He knew the type so thoroughly that some of his old familiar indifference to it returned. Such men as these were of the lowest stratum welcomed at the resort. He stepped out and closed the door.

"Well, you know what I am here for, don't you?" said the man confidentially.

"I can guess," said Hurstwood softly.

"Well, do you intend to try and keep the money?"

"That's my affair," said Hurstwood grimly.

"You can't do it, you know," said the detective, eyeing him coolly.

"Look here, my man," said Hurstwood authoritatively, "you don't understand anything about this case, and I can't explain to you. Whatever I intend to do I'll do without advice from the outside. You'll have to excuse me."

"Well, now, there's no use of your talking that way," said the man, "when you're in the hands of the police. We can make a lot of trouble for you if we want to. You're not registered right in this house, you haven't got your wife with you, and the newspapers don't know you're here yet. You might as well be reasonable."

"What do you want to know?" asked Hurstwood.

"Whether you're going to send back that money or not."

Hurstwood paused and studied the floor.

"There's no use explaining to you about this," he said at last. "There's no use of your asking me. I'm no fool, you know. I know just what you can do and what you can't. You can create a lot of trouble if you want to. I know that all right, but it won't help you to get the money. Now, I've made up my mind what to do. I've already written Fitzgerald and Moy, so there's nothing I can say. You wait until you hear more from them."

All the time he had been talking he had been moving away from the door, down the corridor, out of the hearing of Carrie. They were now near the end where the corridor opened into the large general parlor.

"You won't give it up?" said the man.

The words irritated Hurstwood greatly. Hot blood poured into his brain. Many thoughts formulated themselves. He was no thief. He didn't want the money. If he could only explain to Fitzgerald and Moy, maybe it would be all right again.

"See here," he said, "there's no use my talking about this at all. I respect your power all right, but I'll have to deal with the people who know."

"Well, you can't get out of Canada with it," said the man.

"I don't want to get out," said Hurstwood. "When I get ready there'll be nothing to stop me for."

He turned back, and the detective watched him closely. It seemed an intolerable thing. Still he went on and into the room.

"Who was it?" asked Carrie.

"A friend of mine from Chicago."

The whole of this conversation was such a shock that, coming as it did after all the other worry of the past week, it sufficed to induce a deep gloom and moral revulsion in Hurstwood. What hurt him most was the fact that he was being pursued as a thief. He began to see the nature of that social injustice which sees but one side—often but a single point in a long tragedy. All the newspapers noted but one thing, his taking the money. How and wherefore were but indifferently dealt with. All the complications which led up to it were unknown. He was accused without being understood.

Sitting in his room with Carrie the same day, he decided to send the money back. He would write Fitzgerald and Moy, explain all, and then send it by express. Maybe they would forgive him. Perhaps they would ask him back. He would make good the false statement he had made about writing them. Then he would leave this peculiar town.

For an hour he thought over this plausible statement of the tangle. He wanted to tell them about his wife, but couldn't. He finally narrowed it down to an assertion that he was lightheaded from entertaining friends, had found the safe open, and having gone so far as to take the money out, had accidentally closed it. This act he regretted very much. He was sorry he had put them to so much trouble. He would undo what he could by sending the money back—the major portion of it. The remainder he would pay up as soon as he could. Was there any possibility of his being restored? This he only hinted at.

The troubled state of the man's mind may be judged by the very construction of this letter. For the nonce he forgot what a painful thing it would be to resume his old place, even if it were given him. He forgot that he had severed himself from the past as by a sword, and that if he did manage to in some way reunite himself with it, the jagged line of separation and reunion would always show. He was always forgetting something—his wife, Carrie, his need of money, present situation, or something—and so did not reason clearly. Nevertheless, he sent the letter, waiting a reply before sending the money.

Meanwhile, he accepted his present situation with Carrie, getting what joy out of it he could.

Out came the sun by noon, and poured a golden flood through their open windows. Sparrows were twittering. There were laughter and song in the air. Hurstwood could not keep his eyes from Carrie. She seemed the one ray of sunshine in all his trouble. Oh, if she would only love him wholly—only throw her arms around him in the blissful spirit in which he had seen her in the little park in Chicago—how happy he would be! It would repay him; it would show him that he had not lost all. He would not care.

"Carrie," he said, getting up once and coming over to her, "are you going to stay with me from now on?"

She looked at him quizzically, but melted with sympathy as the value of the look upon his face forced itself upon her. It was love now, keen and strong—love enhanced by difficulty and worry. She could not help smiling.

"Let me be everything to you from now on," he said. "Don't make me worry any more. I'll be true to you. We'll go to New York and get a nice flat. I'll go into business again, and we'll be happy. Won't you be mine?"

Carrie listened quite solemnly. There was no great passion in her, but the drift of things and this man's proximity created a semblance of affection. She felt rather sorry for him—a sorrow born of what had only recently been a great admiration. True love she had never felt for him. She would have known as much if she could have analyzed her feelings, but this thing which she now felt aroused by his great feeling broke down the barriers between them.

"You'll stay with me, won't you?" he asked.

"Yes," she said, nodding her head.

He gathered her to himself, imprinting kisses upon her lips and cheeks.

"You must marry me, though," she said.

"I'll get a license to-day," he answered.

"How?" she asked.

"Under a new name," he answered. "I'll take a new name and live a new life. From now on I'm Murdock."

"Oh, don't take that name," said Carrie.

"Why not?" he said.

"I don't like it."

"Well, what shall I take?" he asked.

"Oh, anything, only don't take that."

He thought a while, still keeping his arms about her, and then said:

"How would Wheeler do?"

"That's all right," said Carrie.

"Well, then, Wheeler," he said. "I'll get the license this afternoon."

They were married by a Baptist minister, the first divine they found convenient.

At last the Chicago firm answered. It was by Mr. Moy's dictation. He was astonished that Hurstwood had done this; very sorry that it had come about as it had. If the money were returned, they would not trouble to prosecute him, as they really bore him no ill-will. As for his returning, or their restoring him to his former position, they had not quite decided what the effect of it would be. They would think it over and correspond with him later, possibly, after a little time, and so on.

The sum and substance of it was that there was no hope, and they wanted the money with the least trouble possible. Hurstwood read his doom. He decided to pay $9,500 to the agent whom they said they would send, keeping $1,300 for his own use. He telegraphed his acquiescence, explained to the representative who called at the hotel the same day, took a certificate of payment, and told Carrie to pack her trunk. He was slightly depressed over this newest move at the time he began to make it, but eventually restored himself. He feared that even yet he might be seized and taken back, so he tried to conceal his movements, but it was scarcely possible. He ordered Carrie's trunk sent to the depot, where he had it sent by express to New York. No one seemed to be observing him, but he left at night. He was greatly agitated lest at the first station across the border or at the depot in New York there should be waiting for him an officer of the law.

Carrie, ignorant of his theft and his fears, enjoyed the entry into the latter city in the morning. The round green hills sentineling the broad, expansive bosom of the Hudson held her attention by their beauty as the train followed the line of the stream. She had heard of the Hudson River, the great city of New York, and now she looked out, filling her mind with the wonder of it.

As the train turned east at Spuyten Duyvil and followed the east bank of the Harlem River, Hurstwood nervously called her attention to the fact that they were on the edge of the city. After her experience with Chicago, she expected long lines of cars—a great highway of tracks—and noted the difference. The sight of a few boats in the Harlem and more in the East River tickled her young heart. It was the first sign of the great sea. Next came a plain street with five-story brick flats, and then the train plunged into the tunnel.

"Grand Central Station!" called the trainman, as, after a few minutes of darkness and smoke, daylight reappeared. Hurstwood arose and gathered up his small grip. He was screwed up to the highest tension. With Carrie he waited at the door and then dismounted. No one approached him, but he glanced furtively to and fro as he made for the street entrance. So excited was he that he forgot all about Carrie, who fell behind, wondering at his self-absorption. As he passed through the depot proper the strain reached its climax and began to wane. All at once he was on the sidewalk, and none but cabmen hailed him. He heaved a great breath and turned, remembering Carrie.

"I thought you were going to run off and leave me," she said.

"I was trying to remember which car takes us to the Gilsey," he answered.

Carrie hardly heard him, so interested was she in the busy scene.

"How large is New York?" she asked.

"Oh, a million or more," said Hurstwood.

He looked around and hailed a cab, but he did so in a changed way.

For the first time in years the thought that he must count these little expenses flashed through his mind. It was a disagreeable thing.

He decided he would lose no time living in hotels but would rent a flat. Accordingly he told Carrie, and she agreed.

"We'll look to-day, if you want to," she said.

Suddenly he thought of his experience in Montreal. At the more important hotels he would be certain to meet Chicagoans whom he knew. He stood up and spoke to the driver.

"Take me to the Belford," he said, knowing it to be less frequented by those whom he knew. Then he sat down.

"Where is the residence part?" asked Carrie, who did not take the tall five-story walls on either hand to be the abodes of families.

"Everywhere," said Hurstwood, who knew the city fairly well. "There are no lawns in New York. All these are houses."

"Well, then, I don't like it," said Carrie, who was coming to have a few opinions of her own.

CHAPTER XXX

THE KINGDOM OF GREATNESS: THE PILGRIM ADREAM

Whatever a man like Hurstwood could be in Chicago, it is very evident that he would be but an inconspicuous drop in an ocean like New York. In Chicago, whose population still ranged about 500,000, millionaires were not numerous. The rich had not become so conspicuously rich as to drown all moderate incomes in obscurity. The attention of the inhabitants was not so distracted by local celebrities in the dramatic, artistic, social, and religious fields as to shut the well-positioned man from view. In Chicago the two roads to distinction were politics and trade. In New York the roads were any one of a half-hundred, and each had been diligently pursued by hundreds, so that celebrities were numerous. The sea was already full of whales. A common fish must needs disappear wholly from view—remain unseen. In other words, Hurstwood was nothing.

There is a more subtle result of such a situation as this, which, though not always taken into account, produces the tragedies of the world. The great create an atmosphere which reacts badly upon the small. This atmosphere is easily and quickly felt. Walk among the magnificent residences, the splendid equipages, the gilded shops, restaurants, resorts of all kinds; scent the flowers, the silks, the wines; drink of the laughter springing from the soul of luxurious content, of the glances which gleam like light from defiant spears; feel the quality of the smiles which cut like glistening swords and of strides born of place, and you shall know of what is the atmosphere of the high and mighty. Little use to argue that of such is not the kingdom of greatness, but so long as the world is attracted by this and the human heart views this as the one desirable realm which it must attain, so long, to that heart, will this remain the realm of greatness. So long, also, will the atmosphere of this realm work its desperate results in the soul of man. It is like a chemical reagent. One day of it, like one drop of the other, will so affect and discolor the views, the aims, the desire of the mind, that it will thereafter remain forever dyed. A day of it to the untried mind is like opium to the untried body. A craving is set up which, if gratified, shall eternally result in dreams and death. Aye! dreams unfulfilled—gnawing, luring, idle phantoms which beckon and lead, beckon and lead, until death and dissolution dissolve their power and restore us blind to nature's heart.

A man of Hurstwood's age and temperament is not subject to the illusions and burning desires of youth, but neither has he the strength of hope which gushes as a fountain in the heart of youth. Such an atmosphere could not incite in him the cravings of a boy of eighteen, but in so far as they were excited, the lack of hope made them proportionately bitter. He could not fail to notice the signs of affluence and luxury on every hand. He had been to New York before and knew the resources of its folly. In part it was an awesome place to him, for here gathered all that he most respected on this earth—wealth, place, and fame. The majority of the celebrities with whom he had tipped glasses in his day as manager hailed from this self-centered and populous spot. The most inviting stories of pleasure and luxury had been told of places and individuals here. He knew it to be true that unconsciously he was brushing elbows with fortune the livelong day; that a hundred or five hundred thousand gave no one the privilege of living more than comfortably in so wealthy a place. Fashion and pomp required more ample sums, so that the poor man was nowhere. All this he realized, now quite sharply, as he faced the city, cut off from his friends, despoiled of his modest fortune, and even his name, and forced to begin the battle for place and comfort all over again. He was not old, but he was not so dull but that he could feel he soon would be. Of a sudden, then, this show of fine clothes, place, and power took on peculiar significance. It was emphasized by contrast with his own distressing state.

And it was distressing. He soon found that freedom from fear of arrest was not the *sine qua non* of his existence. That danger dissolved, the next necessity became the grievous thing. The paltry sum of thirteen hundred and some odd dollars set against the need of rent, clothing, food, and pleasure for years to come was a spectacle little calculated to induce peace of mind in one who had been accustomed to spend five times that sum in the course of a year. He thought upon the subject rather actively the first few days he was in New York, and decided that he must act quickly. As a consequence, he consulted the business opportunities advertised in the morning papers and began investigations on his own account.

That was not before he had become settled, however. Carrie and he went looking for a flat, as arranged, and found one in Seventy-eighth Street near Amsterdam Avenue. It was a five-story building, and their flat was on the third floor. Owing to the fact that the street was not yet built up solidly, it was possible to see east to the green tops of the trees in Central Park and west to the broad waters of the Hudson, a glimpse of which was to be had out of the west windows. For the privilege of six rooms and a bath, running in a straight line, they were compelled to pay thirty-five dollars a month—an average, and yet exorbitant, rent for a home at the time. Carrie noticed the difference between the size of the rooms here and in Chicago and mentioned it.

"You'll not find anything better, dear," said Hurstwood, "unless you go into one of the old-fashioned houses, and then you won't have any of these conveniences."

Carrie picked out the new abode because of its newness and bright wood-work. It was one of the very new ones supplied with steam heat, which was a great advantage. The stationary range, hot and cold water, dumb-waiter, speaking tubes, and call-bell for the janitor pleased her very much. She had enough of the instincts of a housewife to take great satisfaction in these things.

Hurstwood made arrangement with one of the instalment houses whereby they furnished the flat complete and accepted fifty dollars down and ten dollars a month. He then had a little plate, bearing the name G. W. Wheeler, made, which he placed on his letter-box in the hall. It sounded exceedingly odd to Carrie to be called Mrs. Wheeler by the janitor, but in time she became used to it and looked upon the name as her own.

These house details settled, Hurstwood visited some of the advertised opportunities to purchase an interest in some flourishing down-town bar. After the palatial resort in Adams Street, he could not stomach the commonplace saloons which he found advertised. He lost a number of days looking up three and finding them disagreeable. He did, however, gain considerable knowledge by talking, for he discovered the influence of Tammany Hall and the value of standing in with the police. The most profitable and flourishing places he found to be those which conducted anything but a legitimate business, such as that controlled by Fitzgerald and Moy. Elegant back rooms and private drinking booths on the second floor were usually adjuncts of very profitable places. He saw by portly keepers, whose shirt fronts shone with large diamonds, and whose clothes were properly cut, that the liquor business here, as elsewhere, yielded the same golden profit.

At last he found an individual who had a resort in Warren Street, which seemed an excellent venture. It was fairly well-appearing and susceptible of improvement. The owner claimed the business to be excellent, and it certainly looked so.

"We deal with a very good class of people," he told Hurstwood. "Merchants, salesmen, and professionals. It's a well-dressed class. No bums. We don't allow 'em in the place."

Hurstwood listened to the cash-register ring, and watched the trade for a while.

"It's profitable enough for two, is it?" he asked.

"You can see for yourself if you're any judge of the liquor trade," said the owner. "This is only one of the two places I have. The other is down in Nassau Street. I can't tend to them both alone. If I had some one who knew the business thoroughly I wouldn't mind sharing with him in this one and letting him manage it."

"I've had experience enough," said Hurstwood blandly, but he felt a little diffident about referring to Fitzgerald and Moy.

"Well, you can suit yourself, Mr. Wheeler," said the proprietor.

He only offered a third interest in the stock, fixtures, and good-will, and this in return for a thousand dollars and managerial ability on the part of the one who should come in. There was no property involved, because the owner of the saloon merely rented from an estate.

The offer was genuine enough, but it was a question with Hurstwood whether a third interest in that locality could be made to yield one hundred and fifty dollars a month, which he figured he must have in order to meet the ordinary family expenses and be comfortable. It was not the time, however, after many failures to find what he wanted, to hesitate. It looked as though a third would pay a hundred a month now. By judicious management and improvement, it might be made to pay more. Accordingly he agreed to enter into partnership, and made over his thousand dollars, preparing to enter the next day.

His first inclination was to be elated, and he confided to Carrie that he thought he had made an excellent arrangement. Time, however, introduced food for reflection. He found his partner to be very disagreeable. Frequently he was the worse for liquor, which made him surly. This was the last thing which Hurstwood was used to in business. Besides, the business varied. It was nothing like the class of patronage which he had enjoyed in Chicago. He found that it would take a long time to make friends. These people hurried in and out without seeking the pleasures of friendship. It was no gathering or lounging place. Whole days and weeks passed without one such hearty greeting as he had been wont to enjoy every day in Chicago.

For another thing, Hurstwood missed the celebrities—those well-dressed, *élite* individuals who lend grace to the average bars and bring news from far-off and exclusive circles. He did not see one such in a month. Evenings, when still at his post, he would occasionally read in the evening papers incidents concerning celebrities whom he knew—whom he had drunk a glass with many a time. They would visit a bar like Fitzgerald and Moy's in Chicago, or the Hoffman House, uptown, but he knew that he would never see them down here.

Again, the business did not pay as well as he thought. It increased a little, but he found he would have to watch his household expenses, which was humiliating.

In the very beginning it was a delight to go home late at night, as he did, and find Carrie. He managed to run up and take dinner with her between six and seven, and to remain home until nine o'clock in the morning, but the novelty of this waned after a time, and he began to feel the drag of his duties.

The first month had scarcely passed before Carrie said in a very natural way: "I think I'll go down this week and buy a dress."

"What kind?" said Hurstwood.

"Oh, something for street wear."

"All right," he answered, smiling, although he noted mentally that it would be more agreeable to his finances if she didn't. Nothing was said about it the next day but the following morning he asked:

"Have you done anything about your dress?"

"Not yet," said Carrie.

He paused a few moments, as if in thought, and then said:

"Would you mind putting it off a few days?"

"No," replied Carrie, who did not catch the drift of his remarks. She had never thought of him in connection with money troubles before. "Why?"

"Well, I'll tell you," said Hurstwood. "This investment of mine is taking a lot of money just now. I expect to get it all back shortly, but just at present I am running close."

"Oh!" answered Carrie. "Why, certainly dear. Why didn't you tell me before?"

"It wasn't necessary," said Hurstwood.

For all her acquiescence, there was something about the way Hurstwood spoke which reminded Carrie of Drouet and his little deal which he was always about to put through. It was only the thought of a second, but it was a beginning. It was something new in her thinking of Hurstwood.

Other things followed from time to time, little things of the same sort, which in their cumulative effect were eventually equal to a full revelation. Carrie was not dull by any means. Two persons cannot long dwell together without coming to an understanding of one another. The mental difficulties of an individual reveal themselves whether he voluntarily confesses them or not. Trouble gets in the air and contributes gloom, which speaks for itself. Hurstwood dressed as nicely as usual, but they were the same clothes he had in Canada. Carrie noticed that he did not install a large wardrobe, though his own was anything but large. She noticed, also, that he did not suggest many amusements, said nothing about the food, seemed concerned about his business. This was not the easy Hurstwood of Chicago—not the liberal, opulent Hurstwood she had known. The change was too obvious to escape detection.

In time she began to feel that a change had come about, and that she was not in his confidence. He was evidently secretive and kept his own counsel. She found herself asking him questions about little things. This is a disagreeable state to a woman. Great love makes it seem reasonable, sometimes plausible, but never satisfactory. Where great love is not, a more definite and less satisfactory conclusion is reached.

As for Hurstwood, he was making a great fight against the difficulties of a changed condition. He was too shrewd not to realize the tremendous mistake he had made, and appreciate that he had done well in getting where he was, and yet he could not help contrasting his present state with his former, hour after hour, and day after day.

Besides, he had the disagreeable fear of meeting old-time friends, ever since one such encounter which he made shortly after his arrival in the city. It was in Broadway that he saw a man approaching him whom he knew. There was no time for simulating non-recognition. The exchange of glances had been too sharp, the knowledge of each other too apparent. So the friend, a buyer for one of the Chicago wholesale houses, felt, perforce, the necessity of stopping.

"How are you?" he said, extending his hand with an evident mixture of feeling and a lack of plausible interest.

"Very well," said Hurstwood, equally embarrassed. "How is it with you?"

"All right; I'm down here doing a little buying. Are you located here now?"

"Yes," said Hurstwood, "I have a place down in Warren Street."

"Is that so?" said the friend. "Glad to hear it. I'll come down and see you."

"Do," said Hurstwood.

"So long," said the other, smiling affably and going on.

"He never asked for my number," thought Hurstwood; "he wouldn't think of coming." He wiped his forehead, which had grown damp, and hoped sincerely he would meet no one else.

These things told upon his good-nature, such as it was. His one hope was that things would change for the better in a money way. He had Carrie. His furniture was being paid for. He was maintaining his position. As for Carrie, the amusements he could give her would have to do for the present. He could probably keep up his pretensions sufficiently long without exposure to make good, and then all would be well. He failed therein to take account of the frailties of human nature—the difficulties of matrimonial life. Carrie was young. With him and with her varying mental states were common. At any moment the extremes of feeling might be anti-polarized at the dinner table. This often happens in the best regulated families. Little things brought out on such occasions need great love to obliterate them afterward. Where that is not, both parties count two and two and make a problem after a while.

CHAPTER XXXI

A Pet of Good Fortune: Broadway Flaunts Its Joys

The effect of the city and his own situation on Hurstwood was paralleled in the case of Carrie, who accepted the things which fortune provided with the most genial good-nature. New York, despite her first expression of disapproval, soon interested her exceedingly. Its clear atmosphere, more populous thoroughfares, and peculiar indifference struck her forcibly. She had never seen such a little flat as hers, and yet it soon enlisted her affection. The new furniture made an excellent showing, the sideboard which Hurstwood himself arranged gleamed brightly. The furniture for each room was appropriate, and in the so-called parlor, or front room, was installed a piano, because Carrie said she would like to learn to play. She kept a servant and developed rapidly in household tactics and information. For the first time in her life she felt settled, and somewhat justified in the eyes of society as she conceived of it. Her thoughts were merry and innocent enough. For a long while she concerned herself over the arrangement of New York flats, and wondered at ten families living in one building and all remaining strange and indifferent to each other. She also marveled at the whistles of the hundreds of vessels in the harbor—the long, low cries of the Sound steamers and ferry-boats when fog was on. The mere fact that these things spoke from the sea made them wonderful. She looked much at what she could see of the Hudson from her west windows and of the great city building up rapidly on either hand. It was much to ponder over, and sufficed to entertain her for more than a year without becoming stale.

For another thing, Hurstwood was exceedingly interesting in his affection for her. Troubled as he was, he never exposed his difficulties to her. He carried himself with the same self-important air, took his new state with easy familiarity, and rejoiced in Carrie's proclivities and successes. Each evening he arrived promptly to dinner, and found the little dining-room a most inviting spectacle. In a way, the smallness of the room added to its luxury. It looked full and replete. The white-covered table was arrayed with pretty dishes and lighted with a four-armed candelabra, each light of which was topped with a red shade. Between Carrie and the girl the steaks and chops came out all right, and canned goods did the rest for a while. Carrie studied the art of making biscuit, and soon reached the stage where she could show a plate of light, palatable morsels for her labor.

In this manner the second, third, and fourth months passed. Winter came, and with it a feeling that indoors was best, so that the attending of theaters was not much talked of. Hurstwood made great efforts to meet all expenditures without a show of feeling one way or the other. He pretended that he was reinvesting his money in strengthening the business for greater ends in the future. He contented himself with a very moderate allowance of personal apparel, and rarely suggested anything for Carrie. Thus the first winter passed.

In the second year, the business which Hurstwood managed did increase somewhat. He got out of it regularly the $150 per month which he had anticipated. Unfortunately, by this time Carrie had reached certain conclusions, and he had scraped up a few acquaintances.

Being of a passive and receptive rather than an active and aggressive nature, Carrie accepted the situation. Her state seemed satisfactory enough. Once in a while they would go to a theater together, occasionally in season to the beaches and different points about the city, but they picked up no acquaintances. Hurstwood naturally abandoned his show of fine manners with her and modified his attitude to one of easy familiarity. There were no misunderstandings, no apparent differences of opinion. In fact, without money or visiting friends, he led a life which could neither arouse jealousy nor comment. Carrie rather sympathized with his efforts and thought nothing upon her lack of entertainment such as she had enjoyed in Chicago. New York as a corporate entity and her flat temporarily seemed sufficient.

However, as Hurstwood's business increased, he, as stated, began to pick up acquaintances. He also began to allow himself more clothes. He convinced himself that his home life was very precious to him, but allowed that he could occasionally stay away from dinner. The first time he did this he sent a message saying that he would be detained. Carrie ate alone, and wished that it might not happen again. The second time, also, he sent word, but at the last moment. The third time he forgot entirely and explained afterwards. These events were months apart, each.

"Where were you, George?" asked Carrie, after the first absence.

"Tied up at the office," he said genially. "There were some accounts I had to straighten."

"I'm sorry you couldn't get home," she said kindly. "I was fixing to have such a nice dinner."

The second time he gave a similar excuse, but the third time the feeling about it in Carrie's mind was a little bit out of the ordinary.

"I couldn't get home," he said, when he came in later in the evening, "I was so busy."

"Couldn't you have sent me word?" asked Carrie.

"I meant to," he said, "but you know I forgot it until it was too late to do any good."

"And I had such a good dinner!" said Carrie.

Now, it so happened that from his observations of Carrie he began to imagine that she was of the thoroughly domestic type of mind. He really thought, after a year, that her chief expression in life was finding its natural channel in household duties. Notwithstanding the fact that he had observed her act in Chicago, and that during the past year he had only seen her limited in her relations to her flat and him by conditions which he made, and that she had not gained any friends or associates, he drew this peculiar conclusion. With it came a feeling of satisfaction in having a wife who could thus be content, and this satisfaction worked its natural result. That is, since he imagined he saw her satisfied, he felt called upon to give only that which contributed to such satisfaction. He supplied the furniture, the decorations, the food, and the necessary clothing. Thoughts of entertaining her, leading her out into the shine and show of life, grew less and less. He felt attracted to the outer world, but did not think she would care to go along. Once he went to the theater alone. Another time he joined a couple of his new friends at an evening game of poker. Since his money-feathers were beginning to grow again he felt like sprucing about. All this, however, in a much less imposing way than had been his wont in Chicago. He avoided the gay places where he would be apt to meet those who had known him.

Now, Carrie began to feel this in various sensory ways. She was not the kind to be seriously disturbed by his actions. Not loving him greatly, she could not be jealous in a disturbing way. In fact, she was not jealous at all. Hurstwood was pleased with her placid manner, when he should have duly considered it. When he did not come home it did not seem anything like a terrible thing to her. She gave him credit for having the usual allurements of men—people to talk to, places to stop, friends to consult with. She was perfectly willing that he should enjoy himself in his way, but she did not care to be neglected herself. Her state still seemed fairly reasonable, however. All she did observe was that Hurstwood was somewhat different.

Some time in the second year of their residence in Seventy-eighth Street the flat across the hall from Carrie became vacant, and into it moved a very handsome young woman and her husband, with both of whom Carrie afterwards became acquainted. This was brought about solely by the arrangement of the flats, which were united in one place, as it were, by the dumbwaiter. This useful elevator, by which fuel, groceries, and the like were sent up from the basement, and garbage and waste went down, was used by both residents of one floor; that is, a small door opened into it from each flat.

If the occupants of both flats answered to the whistle of the janitor at the same time they would stand face to face when they opened the dumb-waiter doors. One morning, when Carrie went to remove her paper, the newcomer, a handsome brunette of perhaps twenty-three years of age, was there for a like purpose. She was in a night-robe and dressing-gown, with her hair very much tousled, but she looked so pretty and good-natured that Carrie instantly conceived a liking for her. The newcomer did no more than smile shamefacedly, but it was sufficient. Carrie felt that she would like to know her, and a similar feeling stirred in the mind of the other, who admired Carrie's innocent face.

"That's a real pretty woman who has moved in next door," said Carrie to Hurstwood at the breakfast table.

"Who are they?" asked Hurstwood.

"I don't know," said Carrie. "The name on the bell is Vance. Some one over there plays beautifully. I guess it must be she."

"Well, you never can tell what sort of people you're living next to in this town, can you?" said Hurstwood, expressing the customary New York opinion about neighbors.

"Just think," said Carrie, "I have been in this house with nine other families for over a year and I don't know a soul. These people have been here over a month and I haven't seen any one before this morning."

"It's just as well," said Hurstwood. "You never know who you're going to get in with. Some of these people are pretty bad company."

"I expect so," said Carrie, agreeably.

The conversation turned to other things, and Carrie thought no more upon the subject until a day or two later, when, going out to market, she encountered Mrs. Vance coming in. The latter recognized her and nodded, for which Carrie returned a smile. This settled the probability of acquaintanceship. If there had been no faint recognition on this occasion, there would have been no future association.

Carrie saw no more of Mrs. Vance for several weeks, but she heard her play through the thin walls which divided the front rooms of the flats, and was pleased by the merry selection of pieces and the brilliance of their rendition. She could play only moderately herself, and such variety as Mrs. Vance exercised bordered, for Carrie, upon the verge of great art. Everything she had seen and heard thus far—the merest scraps and shadows—indicated that these people were, in a measure, refined and in comfortable circumstances. So Carrie was ready for any extension of the friendship which might follow.

One day Carrie's bell rang and the servant, who was in the kitchen, pressed the button which caused the front door of the general entrance on the ground floor to be electrically unlatched. When Carrie waited at her own door on the third floor to see who it might be coming up to call on her, Mrs. Vance appeared.

"I hope you'll excuse me," she said. "I went out a while ago and forgot my outside key, so I thought I'd ring your bell."

This was a common trick of other residents of the building, whenever they had forgotten their outside keys. They did not apologize for it, however.

"Certainly," said Carrie. "I'm glad you did. I do the same thing sometimes."

"Isn't it just delightful weather?" said Mrs. Vance, pausing for a moment.

Thus, after a few more preliminaries, this visiting acquaintance was well launched, and in the young Mrs. Vance Carrie found an agreeable companion.

On several occasions Carrie visited her and was visited. Both flats were good to look upon, though that of the Vances tended somewhat more to the luxurious.

"I want you to come over this evening and meet my husband," said Mrs. Vance, not long after their intimacy began. "He wants to meet you. You play cards, don't you?"

"A little," said Carrie.

"Well, we'll have a game of cards. If your husband comes home bring him over."

"He's not coming to dinner to-night," said Carrie.

"Well, when he does come we'll call him in."

Carrie acquiesced, and that evening met the portly Vance, an individual a few years younger than Hurstwood, and who owed his seemingly comfortable matrimonial state much more to his money than to his good looks. He thought well of Carrie upon the first glance and laid himself out to be genial, teaching her a new game of cards and talking to her about New York and its pleasures. Mrs. Vance played some upon the piano, and at last Hurstwood came.

"I am very glad to meet you," he said to Mrs. Vance when Carrie introduced him, showing much of the old grace which had captivated Carrie.

"Did you think your wife had run away?" said Mr. Vance, extending his hand upon introduction.

"I didn't know but what she might have found a better husband," said Hurstwood.

He now turned his attention to Mrs. Vance, and in a flash Carrie saw again what she for some time had sub-consciously missed in Hurstwood—the adroitness and flattery of which he was capable. She also saw that she was not well dressed—not nearly as well dressed—as Mrs. Vance. These were not vague ideas any longer. Her situation was cleared up for her. She felt that her life was becoming stale, and therein she felt cause for gloom. The old helpful, urging melancholy was restored. The desirous Carrie was whispered to concerning her possibilities.

There were no immediate results to this awakening, for Carrie had little power of initiative; but, nevertheless, she seemed ever capable of getting herself into the tide of change where she would be easily borne along. Hurstwood noticed nothing. He had been unconscious of the marked contrasts which Carrie had observed. He did not even detect the shade of melancholy which settled in her eyes. Worst of all, she now began to feel the loneliness of the flat and seek the company of Mrs. Vance, who liked her exceedingly.

"Let's go to the matinee this afternoon," said Mrs. Vance, who had stepped across into Carrie's flat one morning, still arrayed in a soft pink dressing-gown, which she had donned upon rising. Hurstwood and Vance had gone their separate ways nearly an hour before.

"All right," said Carrie, noticing the air of the petted and well-groomed woman in Mrs. Vance's general appearance. She looked as though she was dearly loved and her every wish gratified. "What shall we see?"

"Oh, I do want to see Nat Goodwin," said Mrs. Vance. "I do think he is the jolliest actor. The papers say this is such a good play."

"What time will we have to start?" asked Carrie.

"Let's go at once and walk down Broadway from Thirty-fourth Street," said Mrs. Vance. "It's such an interesting walk. He's at the Madison Square."

"I'll be glad to go," said Carrie. "How much will we have to pay for seats?"

"Not more than a dollar," said Mrs. Vance.

The latter departed, and at one o'clock reappeared, stunningly arrayed in a dark-blue walking dress, with a nobby hat to match. Carrie had gotten herself up charmingly enough, but this woman pained her by contrast. She seemed to have so many dainty little things which Carrie had not. There were trinkets of gold, an elegant green leather purse set with her initials, a fancy handkerchief, exceedingly rich in design, and the like. Carrie felt that she needed more and better clothes to compare with this woman, and that any one looking at the two would pick Mrs. Vance for her raiment alone. It was a trying, though rather unjust thought, for Carrie had now developed an equally pleasing figure, and had grown in comeliness until she was a thoroughly attractive type of her color of beauty. There was some difference in the clothing of the two, both of quality and age, but this difference was not especially noticeable. It served, however, to augment Carrie's dissatisfaction with her state.

The walk down Broadway, then as now, was one of the remarkable features of the city. There gathered, before the matinee and afterwards, not only all the pretty women who love a showy parade, but the men who love to gaze upon and admire them. It was a very imposing procession of pretty faces and fine clothes. Women appeared in their very best hats, shoes, and gloves, and walked arm in arm on their way to the fine shops or theaters strung along from Fourteenth to Thirty-fourth streets. Equally the men paraded with the very latest they could afford. A tailor might have secured hints on suit measurements, a shoemaker on proper lasts and colors, a hatter on hats. It was literally true that if a lover of fine clothes secured a new suit, it was sure to have its first airing on Broadway. So true and well understood was this fact, that several years later a popular song, detailing this and other facts concerning the afternoon parade on matinee days, and entitled "What Right Has He on Broadway?" was published, and had quite a vogue about the music-halls of the city.

In all her stay in the city, Carrie had never heard of this showy parade; had never even been on Broadway when it was taking place. On the other hand, it was a familiar thing to Mrs. Vance, who not only knew of it as an entity, but had often been in it, going purposely to see and be seen, to create a stir with her beauty and dispel any tendency to fall short in dressiness by contrasting herself with the beauty and fashion of the town.

Carrie stepped along easily enough after they got out of the car at Thirty-fourth Street, but soon fixed her eyes upon the lovely company which swarmed by and with them as they proceeded. She noticed suddenly that Mrs. Vance's manner had rather stiffened under the gaze of handsome men and elegantly dressed ladies, whose glances were not modified by any rules of propriety. To stare seemed the proper and natural thing. Carrie found herself stared at and ogled. Men in flawless top-coats, high hats, and silver-headed walking sticks elbowed near and looked too often into conscious eyes. Ladies rustled by in dresses of stiff cloth, shedding affected smiles and perfume. Carrie noticed among them the sprinkling of goodness and the heavy percentage of vice. The rouged and powdered cheeks and lips, the scented hair, the large, misty, and languorous eye, were common enough. With a start she awoke to find that she was in fashion's crowd, on parade in a show place—and such a show place! Jewelers' windows gleamed along the path with remarkable frequency. Florist shops, furriers, haberdashers, confectioners—all followed in rapid succession. The street was full of coaches. Pompous doormen in immense coats, shiny brass belts and buttons, waited in front of expensive salesrooms. Coachmen in tan boots, white tights, and blue jackets waited obsequiously for the mistresses of carriages who were shopping inside. The whole street bore the flavor of riches and show, and Carrie felt that she was not of it. She could not, for the life of her, assume the attitude and smartness of Mrs. Vance, who, in her beauty, was all assurance. She could only imagine that it must be evident to many that she was the less handsomely dressed of the two. It cut her to the quick, and she resolved that she would not come here again until she looked better. At the same time she longed to feel the delight of parading here as an equal. Ah, then she would be happy!

CHAPTER XXXII

THE FEAST OF BELSHAZZAR: A SEER TO TRANSLATE

Such feelings as were generated in Carrie by this walk put her in an exceedingly receptive mood for the pathos which followed in the play. The actor whom they had gone to see had achieved his popularity by presenting a mellow type of comedy, in which sufficient sorrow was introduced to lend contrast and relief to humor. For Carrie, as we well know, the stage had a great attraction. She had never forgotten her one histrionic achievement in Chicago. It dwelt in her mind and occupied her consciousness during many long afternoons in which her rocking-chair and her latest novel contributed the only pleasures of her state. Never could she witness a play without having her own ability vividly brought to consciousness. Some scenes made her long to be a part of them—to give expression to the feelings which she, in the place of the character represented, would feel. Almost invariably she would carry the vivid imaginations away with her and brood over them the next day alone. She lived as much in these things as in the realities which made up her daily life.

It was not often that she came to the play stirred to her heart's core by actualities. To-day a low song of longing had been set singing in her heart by the finery, the merriment, the beauty she had seen. Oh, these women who had passed her by, hundreds and hundreds strong, who were they? Whence came the rich, elegant dresses, the astonishingly colored buttons, the knick-knacks of silver and gold? Where were these lovely creatures housed? Amid what elegancies of carved furniture, decorated walls, elaborate tapestries did they move? Where were their rich apartments, loaded with all that money could provide? In what stables champed these sleek, nervous horses and rested the gorgeous carriages? Where lounged the richly groomed footmen? Oh, the mansions, the lights, the perfume, the loaded boudoirs and tables! New York must be filled with such bowers, or the beautiful, insolent, supercilious creatures could not be. Some hothouses held them. It ached her to know that she was not one of them—that, alas, she had dreamed a dream and it had not come true. She wondered at her own solitude these two years past—her indifference to the fact that she had never achieved what she had expected.

The play was one of those drawing-room concoctions in which charmingly overdressed ladies and gentlemen suffer the pangs of love and jealousy amid gilded surroundings. Such bon-mots are ever enticing to those who have all their days longed for such material surroundings and have never had them gratified. They have the charm of showing suffering under ideal conditions. Who would not grieve upon a gilded chair? Who would not suffer amid perfumed tapestries, cushioned furniture, and liveried servants? Grief under such circumstances becomes an enticing thing. Carrie longed to be of it. She wanted to take her sufferings, whatever they were, in such a world, or failing that, at least to simulate them under such charming conditions upon the stage. So affected was her mind by what she had seen, that the play now seemed an extraordinarily beautiful thing. She was soon lost in the world it represented, and wished that she might never return. Between the acts she studied the galaxy of matinee attendants in front rows and boxes, and conceived a new idea of the possibilities of New York. She was sure she had not seen it all—that the city was one whirl of pleasure and delight.

Going out, the same Broadway taught her a sharper lesson. The scene she had witnessed coming down was now augmented and at its height. Such a crush of finery and folly she had never seen. It clinched her convictions concerning her state. She had not lived, could not lay claim to having lived, until something of this had come into her own life. Women were spending money like water; she could see that in every elegant shop she passed. Flowers, candy, jewelry, seemed the principal things in which the elegant dames were interested. And she—she had scarcely enough pin money to indulge in such outings as this a few times a month.

That night the pretty little flat seemed a commonplace thing. It was not what the rest of the world was enjoying. She saw the servant working at dinner with an indifferent eye. In her mind were running scenes of the play. Particularly she remembered one beautiful actress—the sweetheart who had been wooed and won. The grace of this woman had won Carrie's heart. Her dresses had been all that art could suggest, her sufferings had been so real. The anguish which she had portrayed Carrie could feel. It was done as she was sure she could do it. There were places in which she could even do better. Hence she repeated the lines to herself. Oh, if she could only have such a part, how broad would be her life! She, too, could act appealingly.

When Hurstwood came, Carrie was moody. She was sitting, rocking and thinking, and did not care to have her enticing imaginations broken in upon; so she said little or nothing.

"What's the matter, Carrie?" said Hurstwood after a time, noticing her quiet, almost moody state.

"Nothing," said Carrie. "I don't feel very well tonight."

"Not sick, are you?" he asked, approaching very close.

"Oh, no," she said, almost pettishly, "I just don't feel very good."

"That's too bad," he said, stepping away and adjusting his vest after his slight bending over. "I was thinking we might go to a show to-night."

"I don't want to go," said Carrie, annoyed that her fine visions should have thus been broken into and driven out of her mind. "I've been to the matinee this afternoon."

"Oh, you have?" said Hurstwood. "What was it?"

"A Gold Mine."

"How was it?"

"Pretty good," said Carrie.

"And you don't want to go again to-night?"

"I don't think I do," she said.

Nevertheless, wakened out of her melancholia and called to the dinner table, she changed her mind. A little food in the stomach does wonders. She went again, and in so doing temporarily recovered her equanimity. The great awakening blow had, however, been delivered. As often as she might recover from these discontented thoughts now, they would occur again. Time and repetition—ah, the wonder of it! The dropping water and the solid stone—how utterly it yields at last!

Not long after this matinee experience—perhaps a month—Mrs. Vance invited Carrie to an evening at the theater with them. She heard Carrie say that Hurstwood was not coming home to dinner.

"Why don't you come with us? Don't get dinner for yourself. We're going down to Sherry's for dinner and then over to the Lyceum. Come along with us."

"I think I will," answered Carrie.

She began to dress at three o'clock for her departure at half-past five for the noted dining-room which was then crowding Delmonico's for position in society. In this dressing Carrie showed the influence of her association with the dashing Mrs. Vance. She had constantly had her attention called by the latter to novelties in everything which pertains to a woman's apparel.

"Are you going to get such and such a hat?" or, "Have you seen the new gloves with the oval pearl buttons?" were but sample phrases out of a large selection.

"The next time you get a pair of shoes, dearie," said Mrs. Vance, "get button, with thick soles and patent-leather tips. They're all the rage this fall."

"I will," said Carrie.

"Oh, dear, have you seen the new shirtwaists at Altman's? They have some of the loveliest patterns. I saw one there that I know would look stunning on you. I said so when I saw it."

Carrie listened to these things with considerable interest, for they were suggested with more of friendliness than is usually common between pretty women. Mrs. Vance liked Carrie's stable good-nature so well that she really took pleasure in suggesting to her the latest things.

"Why don't you get yourself one of those nice serge skirts they're selling at Lord & Taylor's?" she said one day. "They're the circular style, and they're going to be worn from now on. A dark blue one would look so nice on you."

Carrie listened with eager ears. These things never came up between her and Hurstwood. Nevertheless, she began to suggest one thing and another, which Hurstwood agreed to without any expression of opinion. He noticed the new tendency on Carrie's part, and finally, hearing much of Mrs. Vance and her delightful ways, suspected whence the change came. He was not inclined to offer the slightest objection so soon, but he felt that Carrie's wants were expanding. This did not appeal to him exactly, but he cared for her in his own way, and so the thing stood. Still, there was something in the details of the transactions which caused Carrie to feel that her requests were not a delight to him. He did not enthuse over the purchases. This led her to believe that neglect was creeping in, and so another small wedge was entered.

Nevertheless, one of the results of Mrs. Vance's suggestions was the fact that on this occasion Carrie was dressed somewhat to her own satisfaction. She had on her best, but there was comfort in the thought that if she must confine herself to a *best,* it was neat and fitting. She looked the well-groomed woman of twenty-one, and Mrs. Vance praised her, which brought color to her plump cheeks and a noticeable brightness into her large eyes. It was threatening rain, and Mr. Vance, at his wife's request, had called a coach.

"Your husband isn't coming?" suggested Mr. Vance, as he met Carrie in his little parlor.

"No; he said he wouldn't be home for dinner."

"Better leave a little note for him, telling him where we are. He might turn up."

"I will," said Carrie who had not thought of it before.

"Tell him we'll be at Sherry's until eight o'clock. He knows, though, I guess."

Carrie crossed the hall with rustling skirts, and scrawled the note, gloves on. When she returned a newcomer was in the Vance flat.

"Mrs. Wheeler, let me introduce Mr. Ames, a cousin of mine," said Mrs. Vance. "He's going along with us, aren't you, Bob?"

"I'm very glad to meet you," said Ames, bowing politely to Carrie.

The latter caught in a glance the dimensions of a very stalwart figure. She also noticed that he was smooth-shaven, good looking, and young but nothing more.

"Mr. Ames is just down in New York for a few days," put in Vance, "and we're trying to show him around a little."

"Oh, are you?" said Carrie, taking another glance at the newcomer.

"Yes; I am just on here from Indianapolis for a week or so," said young Ames, seating himself on the edge of a chair to wait while Mrs. Vance completed the last touches of her toilet.

"I guess you find New York quite a thing to see, don't you?" said Carrie, venturing something to avoid a possible deadly silence.

"It is rather large to get around in a week," answered Ames, pleasantly.

He was an exceedingly genial soul, this young man, and wholly free of affectation. It seemed to Carrie he was as yet only overcoming the last traces of the bashfulness of youth. He did not seem apt at conversation but he had the merit of being well dressed and wholly courageous. Carrie felt as if it were not going to be hard to talk to him.

"Well, I guess we're ready now. The coach is outside."

"Come on, people," said Mrs. Vance, coming in smiling. "Bob, you'll have to look after Mrs. Wheeler."

"I'll try to," said Bob smiling, and edging closer to Carrie. "You won't need much watching, will you?" he volunteered, in a sort of ingratiating and help-me-out kind of way.

"Not very, I hope," said Carrie.

They descended the stairs, Mrs. Vance offering suggestions, and climbed into the open coach.

"All right," said Vance, slamming the coach door, and the conveyance rolled away.

"What is it we're going to see?" asked Ames.

"Sothern," said Vance, "in 'Lord Chumley.'"

"Oh, he is so good!" said Mrs. Vance. "He's just the funniest man."

"I notice the papers praise it," said Ames.

"I haven't any doubt," put in Vance, "but we'll enjoy it very much."

Ames had taken a seat beside Carrie, and accordingly he felt it his bounden duty to pay her some attention. He was interested to find her so young a wife, and so pretty, though it was only a respectful interest. There was nothing of the dashing lady's man about him. He had respect for the married state, and thought only of some pretty marriageable girls in Indianapolis.

"Are you a born New Yorker?" asked Ames of Carrie.

"Oh, no; I've only been here for two years."

"Oh, well, you've had time to see a great deal of it, anyhow."

"I don't seem to have," answered Carrie. "It's about as strange to me as when I first came here."

"You're not from the West, are you?"

"Yes. I'm from Wisconsin," she answered.

"Well, it does seem as if most people in this town haven't been here so very long. I hear of lots of Indiana people in my line who are here."

"What is your line?" asked Carrie.

"I'm connected with an electric company," said the youth.

Carrie followed up this desultory conversation with occasional interruptions from the Vances. Several times it became general and partially humorous, and in that manner the restaurant was reached.

Carrie had noticed the appearance of gaiety and pleasure-seeking in the streets which they were following. Coaches were numerous, pedestrians many, and in Fifty-ninth Street the street cars were crowded. At Fifty-ninth Street and Fifth Avenue a blaze of lights from several new hotels which bordered the Plaza Square gave a suggestion of sumptuous hotel life. Fifth Avenue, the home of the wealthy, was noticeably crowded with carriages, and gentlemen in evening dress. At Sherry's an imposing doorman opened the coach door and helped them out. Young Ames held Carrie's elbow as he helped her up the steps. They entered the lobby already swarming with patrons, and then, after divesting themselves of their wraps, went into a sumptuous dining-room.

In all Carrie's experience she had never seen anything like this. In the whole time she had been in New York Hurstwood's modified state had not permitted his bringing her to such a place. There was an almost indescribable atmosphere about it which convinced the newcomer that this was the proper thing. Here was the place where the matter of expense limited the patrons to the moneyed or pleasure-loving class. Carrie had read of it often in the "Morning" and "Evening World." She had seen notices of dances, parties, balls, and suppers at Sherry's. The Misses So-and-so would give a party on Wednesday evening at Sherry's. Young Mr. So-and-so would entertain a party of friends at a private luncheon on the sixteenth, at Sherry's. The common run of conventional, perfunctory notices of the doings of society, which she could scarcely refrain from scanning each day, had given her a distinct idea of the gorgeousness and luxury of this wonderful temple of gastronomy. Now, at last, she was really in it. She had come up the imposing steps, guarded by the large and portly doorman. She had seen the lobby, guarded by another large and portly gentleman, and been waited upon by uniformed youths who took care of canes, overcoats, and the like. Here was the splendid dining-chamber, all decorated and aglow, where the wealthy ate. Ah, how fortunate was Mrs. Vance; young, beautiful, and well off—at least, sufficiently so to come here in a coach. What a wonderful thing it was to be rich.

Vance led the way through lanes of shining tables, at which were seated parties of two, three, four, five or six. The air of assurance and dignity about it all was exceedingly noticeable to the novitiate. Incandescent lights, the reflection of their glow in polished glasses, and the shine of gilt upon the walls, combined into one tone of light which it requires minutes of complacent observation to separate and take particular note of. The white shirt fronts of the gentlemen, the bright costumes of the ladies, diamonds, jewels, fine feathers—all were exceedingly noticeable.

Carrie walked with an air equal to that of Mrs. Vance, and accepted the seat which the head waiter provided for her. She was keenly aware of all the little things that were done—the little genuflections and attentions of the waiters and head waiter which Americans pay for. The air with which the latter pulled out each chair, and the wave of the hand with which he motioned them to be seated, were worth several dollars in themselves.

Once seated, there began that exhibition of showy, wasteful, and unwholesome gastronomy as practiced by wealthy Americans, which is the wonder and astonishment of true culture and dignity the world over. The large bill of fare held an array of dishes sufficient to feed an army, sidelined with prices which made reasonable expenditure a ridiculous impossibility—an order of soup at fifty cents or a dollar, with a dozen kinds to choose from; oysters in forty styles and at sixty cents the half-dozen; entrées, fish, and meats at prices which would house one overnight in an average hotel. One dollar fifty and two dollars seemed to be the most common figures upon this most tastefully printed bill of fare.

Carrie noticed this, and in scanning it the price of spring chicken carried her back to that other bill of fare and far different occasion when, for the first time, she sat with Drouet in a good restaurant in Chicago. It was only momentary—a sad note as out of an old song—and then it was gone. But in that flash was seen the other Carrie—poor, hungry, drifting at her wits' ends, and all Chicago a cold and closed world, from which she only wandered because she could not find work.

On the walls were designs in color, square spots of robin's-egg blue, set in ornate frames of gilt, whose corners were elaborate moldings of fruit and flowers, with fat cupids hovering in angelic comfort. On the ceilings were colored traceries with more gilt, leading to a center where spread a cluster of lights—incandescent globes mingled with glittering prisms and stucco tendrils of gilt. The floor was of a reddish hue, waxed and polished, and in every direction were mirrors—tall, brilliant, bevel-edged mirrors—reflecting and re-reflecting forms, faces, and candelabra a score and a hundred times.

The tables were not so remarkable in themselves, and yet the imprint of Sherry upon the napery, the name of Tiffany upon the silverware, the name of Haviland upon the china, and over all the glow of the small, red-shaded candelabra and the reflected tints of the walls on garments and faces, made them seem remarkable. Each waiter added an air of exclusiveness and elegance by the manner in which he bowed, scraped, touched, and trifled with things. The exclusively personal attention which he devoted to each one, standing half bent, ear to one side, elbows akimbo, saying: "Soup—green turtle, yes. One portion, yes. Oysters—certainly—half-dozen—yes. Asparagus. Olives—yes."

It would be the same with each one, only Vance essayed to order for all, inviting counsel and suggestions. Carrie studied the company with open eyes. So this was high life in New York. It was so that the rich spent their days and evenings. Her poor little mind could not rise above applying each scene to all society. Every fine lady must be in the crowd on Broadway in the afternoon, in the theater at the matinee, in the coaches and dining-halls at night. It must be glow and shine everywhere, with coaches waiting, and footmen attending, and she was out of it all. In two long years she had never even been in such a place as this.

Vance was in his element here, as Hurstwood would have been in former days. He ordered freely of soup, oysters, roast meats, and side dishes, and had several bottles of wine brought, which were set down beside the table in a wicker basket.

Ames was looking away rather abstractedly at the crowd and showed an interesting profile to Carrie. His forehead was high, his nose rather large and strong, his chin moderately pleasing. He had a good, wide, well-shaped mouth, and his dark-brown hair was parted slightly on one side. He seemed to have the least touch of boyishness to Carrie, and yet he was a man full grown.

"Do you know," he said, turning back to Carrie, after his reflection, "I sometimes think it is a shame for people to spend so much money this way."

Carrie looked at him a moment with the faintest touch of surprise at his seriousness. He seemed to be thinking about something over which she had never pondered.

"Do you?" she answered, interestedly.

"Yes," he said, "they pay so much more than these things are worth. They put on so much show."

"I don't know why people shouldn't spend when they have it," said Mrs. Vance.

"It doesn't do any harm," said Vance, who was still studying the bill of fare, though he had ordered.

Ames was looking away again, and Carrie was again looking at his forehead. To her he seemed to be thinking about strange things. As he studied the crowd his eye was mild.

"Look at that woman's dress over there," he said, again turning to Carrie, and nodding in a direction.

"Where?" said Carrie, following his eyes.

"Over there in the corner—way over. Do you see that brooch?"

"Isn't it large?" said Carrie.

"One of the largest clusters of jewels I have ever seen," said Ames.

"It is, isn't it?" said Carrie. She felt as if she would like to be agreeable to this young man, and also there came with it, or perhaps preceded it, the slightest shade of a feeling that he was better educated than she was—that his mind was better. He seemed to look it, and the saving grace in Carrie was that she could understand that people could be wiser. She had seen a number of people in her life who reminded her of what she had vaguely come to think of as scholars. This strong young man beside her, with his clear, natural look, seemed to get a hold of things which she did not quite understand, but approved of. It was fine to be so, as a man, she thought.

The conversation changed to a book that was having its vogue at the time—"Moulding a Maiden," by Albert Ross. Mrs. Vance had read it. Vance had seen it discussed in some of the papers.

"A man can make quite a strike writing a book," said Vance. "I notice this fellow Ross is very much talked about." He was looking at Carrie as he spoke.

"I hadn't heard of him," said Carrie, honestly.

"Oh, I have," said Mrs. Vance. "He's written lots of things. This last story is pretty good."

"He doesn't amount to much," said Ames.

Carrie turned her eyes toward him as to an oracle.

"His stuff is nearly as bad as 'Dora Thorne,'" concluded Ames.

Carrie felt this as a personal reproof. She read "Dora Thorne," or had a great deal in the past. It seemed only fair to her, but she supposed that people thought it very fine. Now this clear-eyed, fine-headed youth, who looked something like a student to her, made fun of it. It was poor to him, not worth reading. She looked down, and for the first time felt the pain of not understanding.

Yet there was nothing sarcastic or supercilious in the way Ames spoke. He had very little of that in him. Carrie felt that it was just kindly thought of a high order—the right thing to think, and wondered what else was right, according to him. He seemed to notice that she listened and rather sympathized with him, and from now on he talked mostly to her.

As the waiter bowed and scraped about, felt the dishes to see if they were hot enough, brought spoons and forks, and did all those little attentive things calculated to impress the luxury of the situation upon the diner, Ames also leaned slightly to one side and told her of Indianapolis in an intelligent way. He really had a very bright mind, which was finding its chief development in electrical knowledge. His sympathies for other forms of information, however, and for types of people, were quick and warm. The red glow on his head gave it a sandy tinge and put a bright glint in his eye. Carrie noticed all these things as he leaned toward her and felt exceedingly young. This man was far ahead of her. He seemed wiser than Hurstwood, saner and brighter than Drouet. He seemed innocent and clean, and she thought that he was exceedingly pleasant. She noticed, also, that his interest in her was a far-off one. She was not in his life, nor any of the things that touched his life, and yet now, as he spoke of these things, they appealed to her.

"I shouldn't care to be rich," he told her, as the dinner proceeded and the supply of food warmed up his sympathies; "not rich enough to spend my money this way."

"Oh, wouldn't you?" said Carrie, the, to her, new attitude forcing itself distinctly upon her for the first time.

"No," he said. "What good would it do? A man doesn't need this sort of thing to be happy."

Carrie thought of this doubtfully; but, coming from him, it had weight with her.

"He probably could be happy," she thought to herself, "all alone. He's so strong."

Mr. and Mrs. Vance kept up a running fire of interruptions, and these impressive things by Ames came at odd moments. They were sufficient, however, for the atmosphere that went with this youth impressed itself upon Carrie without words. There was something in him, or the world he moved in, which appealed to her. He reminded her of scenes she had seen on the stage—the sorrows and sacrifices that always went with she knew not what. He had taken away some of the bitterness of the contrast between this life and her life, and all by a certain calm indifference which concerned only him.

As they went out, he took her arm and helped her into the coach, and then they were off again, and so to the show.

During the acts Carrie found herself listening to him very attentively. He mentioned things in the play which she most approved of—things which swayed her deeply.

"Don't you think it rather fine to be an actor?" she asked once.

"Yes, I do," he said, "to be a good one. I think the theater a great thing."

Just this little approval set Carrie's heart bounding. Ah, if she could only be an actress—a good one! This man was wise—he knew—and he approved of it. If she were a fine actress, such men as he would approve of her. She felt that he was good to speak as he had, although it did not concern her at all. She did not know why she felt this way.

At the close of the show it suddenly developed that he was not going back with them.

"Oh, aren't you?" said Carrie, with an unwarrantable feeling.

"Oh, no," he said; "I'm stopping right around here in Thirty-third Street."

Carrie could not say anything else, but somehow this development shocked her. She had been regretting the wane of a pleasant evening, but she had thought there was a half-hour more. Oh, the half-hours, the minutes of the world; what miseries and griefs are crowded into them!

She said good-bye with feigned indifference. What matter could it make? Still, the coach seemed lorn.

When she went into her own flat she had this to think about. She did not know whether she would ever see this man any more. What difference could it make—what difference could it make?

Hurstwood had returned, and was already in bed. His clothes were scattered loosely about. Carrie came to the door and saw him, then retreated. She did not want to go in yet a while. She wanted to think. It was disagreeable to her.

Back in the dining-room she sat in her chair and rocked. Her little hands were folded tightly as she thought. Through a fog of longing and conflicting desires she was beginning to see. Oh, ye legions of hope and pity—of sorrow and pain! She was rocking, and beginning to see.

CHAPTER XXXIII

WITHOUT THE WALLED CITY: THE SLOPE OF THE YEARS

The immediate result of this was nothing. Results from such things are usually long in growing. Morning brings a change of feeling. The existent condition invariably pleads for itself. It is only at odd moments that we get glimpses of the misery of things. The heart understands when it is confronted with contrasts. Take them away and the ache subsides.

Carrie went on, leading much this same life for six months thereafter or more. She did not see Ames any more. He called once upon the Vances, but she only heard about it through the young wife. Then he went West, and there was a gradual subsidence of whatever personal attraction had existed. The mental effect of the thing had not gone, however, and never would entirely. She had an ideal to contrast men by—particularly men close to her.

During all this time—a period rapidly approaching three years—Hurstwood had been moving along in an even path. There was no apparent slope downward, and distinctly none upward, so far as the casual observer might have seen. But psychologically there was a change, which was marked enough to suggest the future very distinctly indeed. This was in the mere matter of the halt his career had received when he departed from Chicago. A man's fortune or material progress is very much the same as his bodily growth. Either he is growing stronger, healthier, wiser, as the youth approaching manhood, or he is growing weaker, older, less incisive mentally, as the man approaching old age. There are no other states. Frequently there is a period between the cessation of youthful accretion and the setting in, in the case of the middle-aged man, of the tendency toward decay when the two processes are almost perfectly balanced and there is little doing in either direction. Given time enough, however, the balance becomes a sagging to the grave side. Slowly at first, then with a modest momentum, and at last the graveward process is in the full swing. So it is frequently with man's fortune. If its process of accretion is never halted, if the balancing stage is never reached, there will be no toppling. Rich men are, frequently, in these days, saved from this dissolution of their fortune by their ability to hire younger brains. These younger brains look upon the interests of the fortune as their own, and so steady and direct its progress. If each individual were left absolutely to the care of his own interests, and were given time enough in which to grow exceedingly old, his fortune would pass as his strength and will. He and his would be utterly dissolved and scattered unto the four winds of the heavens.

But now see wherein the parallel changes. A fortune, like a man, is an organism which draws to itself other minds and other strength than that inherent in the founder. Beside the young minds drawn to it by salaries, it becomes allied with young forces, which make for its existence even when the strength and wisdom of the founder are fading. It may be conserved by the growth of a community or of a state. It may be involved in providing something for which there is a growing demand. This removes it at once beyond the special care of the founder. It needs not so much foresight now as direction. The man wanes, the need continues or grows, and the fortune, fallen into whose hands it may, continues. Hence, some men never recognize the turning in the tide of their abilities. It is only in chance cases, where a fortune or a state of success is wrested from them, that the lack of ability to do as they did formerly becomes apparent. Hurstwood, set down under new conditions, was in a position to see that he was no longer young. If he did not, it was due wholly to the fact that his state was so well balanced that an absolute change for the worse did not show.

Not trained to reason or introspect himself, he could not analyze the change that was taking place in his mind, and hence his body, but he felt the depression of it. Constant comparison between his old state and his new showed a balance for the worse, which produced a constant state of gloom or, at least, depression. Now, it has been shown experimentally that a constantly subdued frame of mind produces certain poisons in the blood, called katastates, just as virtuous feelings of pleasure and delight produce helpful chemicals called anastates. The poisons generated by remorse inveigh against the system, and eventually produce marked physical deterioration. To these Hurstwood was subject.

In the course of time it told upon his temper. His eye no longer possessed that buoyant, searching shrewdness which had characterized it in Adams Street. His step was not as sharp and firm. He was given to thinking, thinking, thinking. The new friends he made were not celebrities. They were of a cheaper, a slightly more sensual and cruder, grade. He could not possibly take the pleasure in this company that he had in that of those fine frequenters of the Chicago resort. He was left to brood.

Slowly, exceedingly slowly, his desire to greet, conciliate, and make at home these people who visited the Warren Street place passed from him. More and more slowly the significance of the realm he had left began to be clear. It did not seem so wonderful to be in it when he was in it. It had seemed very easy for any one to get up there and have ample raiment and money to spend, but now that he was out of it, how far off it became. He began to see as one sees a city with a wall about it. Men were posted at the gates. You could not get in. Those inside did not care to come out to see who you were. They were so merry inside there that all those outside were forgotten, and he was on the outside.

Each day he could read in the evening papers of the doings within this walled city. In the notices of passengers for Europe he read the names of eminent frequenters of his old resort. In the theatrical column appeared, from time to time, announcements of the latest successes of men he had known. He knew that they were at their old gaieties. Pullmans were hauling them to and fro about the land, papers were greeting them with interesting mentions, the elegant lobbies of hotels and the glow of polished dining-rooms were keeping them close within the walled city. Men whom he had known, men whom he had tipped glasses with—rich men, and he was forgotten! Who was Mr. Wheeler? What was the Warren Street resort? Bah!

If one thinks that such thoughts do not come to so common a type of mind—that such feelings require a higher mental development—I would urge for their consideration the fact that it is the higher mental development that does away with such thoughts. It is the higher mental development which induces philosophy and that fortitude which refuses to dwell upon such things—refuses to be made to suffer by their consideration. The common type of mind is exceedingly keen on all matters which relate to its physical welfare—exceedingly keen. It is the unintellectual miser who sweats blood at the loss of a hundred dollars. It is the Epictetus who smiles when the last vestige of physical welfare is removed.

The time came, in the third year, when this thinking began to produce results in the Warren Street place. The tide of patronage dropped a little below what it had been at its best since he had been there. This irritated and worried him.

There came a night when he confessed to Carrie that the business was not doing as well this month as it had the month before. This was in lieu of certain suggestions she had made concerning little things she wanted to buy. She had not failed to notice that he did not seem to consult her about buying clothes for himself. For the first time, it struck her as a ruse, or that he said it so that she would not think of asking for things. Her reply was mild enough, but her thoughts were rebellious. He was not looking after her at all. She was depending for her enjoyment upon the Vances.

And now the latter announced that they were going away. It was approaching spring, and they were going North.

"Oh, yes," said Mrs. Vance to Carrie, "we think we might as well give up the flat and store our things. We'll be gone for the summer, and it would be a useless expense. I think we'll settle a little farther down town when we come back."

Carrie heard this with genuine sorrow. She had enjoyed Mrs. Vance's companionship so much. There was no one else in the house whom she knew. Again she would be all alone.

Hurstwood's gloom over the slight decrease in profits and the departure of the Vances came together. So Carrie had loneliness and this mood of her husband to enjoy at the same time. It was a grievous thing. She became restless and dissatisfied, not exactly, as she thought, with Hurstwood, but with life. What was it? A very dull round indeed. What did she have? Nothing but this narrow, little flat. The Vances could travel, they could do the things worth doing, and here she was. For what was she made, anyhow? More thought followed, and then tears—tears seemed justified, and the only relief in the world.

For another period this state continued, the twain leading a rather monotonous life, and then there was a slight change for the worse. One evening, Hurstwood, after thinking about a way to modify Carrie's desire for clothes and the general strain upon his ability to provide, said:

"I don't think I'll ever be able to do much with Shaughnessy."

"What's the matter?" said Carrie.

"Oh, he's a slow, greedy 'mick'! He won't agree to anything to improve the place, and it won't ever pay without it."

"Can't you make him?" said Carrie.

"No; I've tried. The only thing I can see, if I want to improve, is to get hold of a place of my own."

"Why don't you?" said Carrie.

"Well, all I have is tied up there just now. If I had a chance to save awhile I think I could open a place that would give up plenty of money."

"Can't we save?" said Carrie.

"We might try it," he suggested. "I've been thinking that if we'd take a smaller flat down town and live economically for a year, I would have enough, with what I have invested, to open a good place. Then we could arrange to live as you want to."

"It would suit me all right," said Carrie, who, nevertheless, felt badly to think it had come to this. Talk of a smaller flat sounded like poverty.

"There are lots of nice little flats down around Sixth Avenue, below Fourteenth Street. We might get one down there."

"I'll look at them if you say so," said Carrie.

"I think I could break away from this fellow inside of a year," said Hurstwood. "Nothing will ever come of this arrangement as it's going on now."

"I'll look around," said Carrie, observing that the proposed change seemed to be a serious thing with him.

The upshot of this was that the change was eventually effected; not without great gloom on the part of Carrie. It really affected her more seriously than anything that had yet happened. She began to look upon Hurstwood wholly as a man, and not as a lover or husband. She felt thoroughly bound to him as a wife, and that her lot was cast with his, whatever it might be; but she began to see that he was gloomy and taciturn, not a young, strong, and buoyant man. He looked a little bit old to her about the eyes and mouth now, and there were other things which placed him in his true rank, so far as her estimation was concerned. She began to feel that she had made a mistake. Incidentally, she also began to recall the fact that he had practically forced her to flee with him.

The new flat was located in Thirteenth Street, a half block west of Sixth Avenue, and contained only four rooms. The new neighborhood did not appeal to Carrie as much. There were no trees here, no west view of the river. The street was solidly built up. There were twelve families here, respectable enough, but nothing like the Vances. Richer people required more space.

Being left alone in this little place, Carrie did without a girl. She made it charming enough, but could not make it delight her. Hurstwood was not inwardly pleased to think that they should have to modify their state, but he argued that he could do nothing. He must put the best face on it, and let it go at that.

He tried to show Carrie that there was no cause for financial alarm, but only congratulation over the chance he would have at the end of the year by taking her rather more frequently to the theater and by providing a liberal table. This was for the time only. He was getting in the frame of mind where he wanted principally to be alone and to be allowed to think. The disease of brooding was beginning to claim him as a victim. Only the newspapers and his own thoughts were worth while. The delight of love had again slipped away. It was a case of live, now, making the best you can out of a very commonplace station in life.

The road downward has but few landings and level places. The very state of his mind, superinduced by his condition, caused the breach to widen between him and his partner. At last that individual began to wish that Hurstwood was out of it. It so happened, however, that a real estate deal on the part of the owner of the land arranged things even more effectually than ill-will could have schemed.

"Did you see that?" said Shaughnessy one morning to Hurstwood, pointing to the real estate column in a copy of the "Herald," which he held.

"No, what is it?" said Hurstwood, looking down the items of news.

"The man who owns this ground has sold it."

"You don't say so?" said Hurstwood.

He looked, and there was the notice. Mr. August Viele had yesterday registered the transfer of the lot, 25 x 75 feet, at the corner of Warren and Hudson streets, to J. F. Slawson for the sum of $57,000.

"Our lease expires when?" asked Hurstwood, thinking. "Next February, isn't it?"

"That's right," said Shaughnessy.

"It doesn't say what the new man's going to do with it," remarked Hurstwood, looking back to the paper.

"We'll hear, I guess, soon enough," said Shaughnessy.

Sure enough, it did develop. Mr. Slawson owned the property adjoining, and was going to put up a modern office building. The present one was to be torn down. It would take probably a year and a half to complete the other one.

All these things developed by degrees, and Hurstwood began to ponder over what would become of the saloon. One day he spoke about it to his partner.

"Do you think it would be worth while to open up somewhere else in the neighborhood?"

"What would be the use?" said Shaughnessy. "We couldn't get another corner around here."

"It wouldn't pay anywhere else, do you think?"

"I wouldn't try it," said the other.

The approaching change now took on a most serious aspect to Hurstwood. Dissolution meant the loss of his thousand dollars, and he could not save another thousand in the time. He understood that Shaughnessy was merely tired of the arrangement, and would probably lease the new corner, when completed, alone. He began to worry about the necessity of a new connection and to see impending serious financial straits unless something turned up. This left him in no mood to enjoy his flat or Carrie, and consequently the depression invaded that quarter.

Meanwhile, he took such time as he could to look about, but opportunities were not numerous. More, he had not the same impressive personality which he had when he first came to New York. Bad thoughts had put a shade into his eyes which did not impress others favorably. Neither had he thirteen hundred dollars in hand to talk with. About a month later, finding that he had not made any progress, Shaughnessy reported definitely that Slawson would not extend the lease.

"I guess this thing's got to come to an end," he said, affecting an air of concern.

"Well, if it has, it has," answered Hurstwood, grimly. He would not give the other a key to his opinions, whatever they were. He should not have the satisfaction.

A day or two later he saw that he must say something to Carrie.

"You know," he said, "I think I'm going to get the worst of my deal down there."

"How is that?" asked Carrie in astonishment.

"Well, the man who owns the ground has sold it, and the new owner won't re-lease it to us. The business may come to an end."

"Can't you start somewhere else?"

"There doesn't seem to be any place. Shaughnessy doesn't want to."

"Do you lose what you put in?"

"Yes," said Hurstwood, whose face was a study.

"Oh, isn't that too bad?" said Carrie.

"It's a trick," said Hurstwood. "That's all. They'll start another place there all right."

Carrie looked at him, and gathered from his whole demeanor what it meant. It was serious, very serious.

"Do you think you can get something else?" she ventured, timidly.

Hurstwood thought a while. It was all up with the bluff about money and investment. She could see now that he was "broke."

"I don't know," he said solemnly; "I can try."

CHAPTER XXXIV

THE GRIND OF THE MILLSTONES: A SAMPLE OF CHAFF

Carrie pondered over this situation as consistently as Hurstwood, once she got the facts adjusted in her mind. It took several days for her to fully realize that the approach of the dissolution of her husband's business meant commonplace struggle and privation. Her mind went back to her early venture in Chicago, the Hansons and their flat, and her heart revolted. That was terrible! Everything about poverty was terrible. She wished she knew a way out. Her recent experiences with the Vances had wholly unfitted her to view her own state with complacence. The glamor of the high life of the city had, in the few experiences afforded her by the former, seized her completely. She had been taught how to dress and where to go without having ample means to do either. Now, these things—ever-present realities as they were—filled her eyes and mind. The more circumscribed became her state, the more entrancing seemed this other. And now poverty threatened to seize her entirely and to remove this other world far upward like a heaven to which any Lazarus might extend, appealingly, his hands.

So, too, the ideal brought into her life by Ames remained. He had gone, but here was his word that riches were not everything; that there was a great deal more in the world than she knew; that the stage was good, and the literature she read poor. He was a strong man and clean—how much stronger and better than Hurstwood and Drouet she only half formulated to herself, but the difference was painful. It was something to which she voluntarily closed her eyes.

During the last three months of the Warren Street connection, Hurstwood took parts of days off and hunted, tracking the business advertisements. It was a more or less depressing business, wholly because of the thought that he must soon get something or he would begin to live on the few hundred dollars he was saving, and then he would have nothing to invest—he would have to hire out as a clerk.

Everything he discovered in his line advertised as an opportunity, was either too expensive or too wretched for him. Besides, winter was coming, the papers were announcing hardships, and there was a general feeling of hard times in the air, or, at least, he thought so. In his worry, other people's worries became apparent. No item about a firm failing, a family starving, or a man dying upon the streets, supposedly of starvation, but arrested his eye as he scanned the morning papers. Once the "World" came out with a flaring announcement about "80,000 people out of employment in New York this winter," which struck as a knife at his heart.

"Eighty thousand!" he thought. "What an awful thing that is."

This was new reasoning for Hurstwood. In the old days the world had seemed to be getting along well enough. He had been wont to see similar things in the "Daily News," in Chicago, but they did not hold his attention. Now, these things were like gray clouds hovering along the horizon of a clear day. They threatened to cover and obscure his life with chilly grayness. He tried to shake them off, to forget and brace up. Sometimes he said to himself, mentally:

"What's the use worrying? I'm not out yet. I've got six weeks more. Even if worst comes to worst, I've got enough to live on for six months."

Curiously, as he troubled over his future, his thoughts occasionally reverted to his wife and family. He had avoided such thoughts for the first three years as much as possible. He hated her, and he could get along without her. Let her go. He would do well enough. Now, however, when he was not doing well enough, he began to wonder what she was doing, how his children were getting along. He could see them living as nicely as ever, occupying the comfortable house and using his property.

"By George! it's a shame they should have it all," he vaguely thought to himself on several occasions. "I didn't do anything."

As he looked back now and analyzed the situation which led up to his taking the money, he began mildly to justify himself. What had he done—what in the world—that should bar him out this way and heap such difficulties upon him? It seemed only yesterday to him since he was comfortable and well-to-do. But now it was all wrested from him.

"She didn't deserve what she got out of me, that is sure. I didn't do so much, if everybody could just know."

There was no thought that the facts ought to be advertised. It was only a mental justification he was seeking from himself—something that would enable him to bear his state as a righteous man.

One afternoon, five weeks before the Warren Street place closed up, he left the saloon to visit three or four places he saw advertised in the "Herald." One was down in Gold Street, and he visited that, but did not enter. It was such a cheap looking place he felt that he could not abide it. Another was on the Bowery, which he knew contained many showy resorts. It was near Grand Street, and turned out to be very handsomely fitted up. He talked around about investments for fully three-quarters of an hour with the proprietor, who maintained that his health was poor, and that was the reason he wished a partner.

"Well, now, just how much money would it take to buy a half interest here?" said Hurstwood, who saw seven hundred dollars as his limit.

"Three thousand," said the man.

Hurstwood's jaw fell.

"Cash?" he said.

"Cash."

He tried to put on an air of deliberation, as one who might really buy; but his eyes showed gloom. He wound up by saying he would think it over, and came away. The man he had been talking to sensed his condition in a vague way.

"I don't think he wants to buy," he said to himself. "He doesn't talk right."

The afternoon was as gray as lead and cold. It was blowing up a disagreeable winter wind. He visited a place far up on the east side, near Sixty-ninth Street, and it was five o'clock, and growing dim, when he reached there. A portly German kept this place.

"How about this ad. of yours?" asked Hurstwood, who rather objected to the looks of the place.

"Oh, dat iss all over," said the German. "I vill not sell now."

"Oh, is that so?"

"Yes; dere is nothing to dat. It iss all over."

"Very well," said Hurstwood, turning around.

The German paid no more attention to him, and it made him angry.

"The crazy ass!" he said to himself. "What does he want to advertise for?"

Wholly depressed, he started for Thirteenth Street. The flat had only a light in the kitchen, where Carrie was working. He struck a match and, lighting the gas, sat down in the dining-room without even greeting her. She came to the door and looked in.

"It's you, is it?" she said, and went back.

"Yes," he said, without even looking up from the evening paper he had bought.

Carrie saw things were wrong with him. He was not so handsome when gloomy. The lines at the sides of the eyes were deepened. Naturally dark of skin, gloom made him look slightly sinister. He was quite a disagreeable figure.

Carrie set the table and brought in the meal.

"Dinner's ready," she said, passing him for something.

He did not answer, reading on.

She came in and sat down at her place, feeling exceedingly wretched.

"Won't you eat now?" she asked.

He folded his paper and drew near, silence holding for a time, except for the "Pass me's."

"It's been gloomy to-day, hasn't it?" ventured Carrie, after a time.

"Yes," he said.

He only picked at his food.

"Are you still sure to close up?" said Carrie, venturing to take up the subject which they had discussed often enough.

"Of course we are," he said, with the slightest modification of sharpness.

This retort angered Carrie. She had had a dreary day of it herself.

"You needn't talk like that," she said.

"Oh!" he exclaimed, pushing back from the table, as if to say more, but letting it go at that. Then he picked up his paper. Carrie left her seat, containing herself with difficulty. He saw she was hurt.

"Don't go 'way," he said, as she started back into the kitchen. "Eat your dinner."

She passed, not answering.

He looked at the paper a few moments, and then rose up and put on his coat.

"I'm going downtown, Carrie," he said, coming out. "I'm out of sorts to-night."

She did not answer.

"Don't be angry," he said. "It will be all right to-morrow."

He looked at her, but she paid no attention to him, working at her dishes.

"Good-bye!" he said finally, and went out.

This was the first strong result of the situation between them, but with the nearing of the last day of the business the gloom became almost a permanent thing. Hurstwood could not conceal his feelings about the matter. Carrie could not help wondering where she was drifting. It got so that they talked even less than usual, and yet it was not Hurstwood who felt any objection to Carrie. It was Carrie who shied away from him. This he noticed. It aroused an objection to her becoming indifferent to him. He made the possibility of friendly intercourse almost a giant task, and then noticed with discontent that Carrie added to it by her manner and made it more impossible.

At last the final day came. When it actually arrived, Hurstwood, who had got his mind into such a state where a thunder-clap and raging storm would have seemed highly appropriate, was rather relieved to find that it was a plain, ordinary day. The sun shone, the temperature was pleasant. He felt, as he came to the breakfast table, that it wasn't so terrible, after all.

"Well," he said to Carrie, "to-day's my last day on earth."

Carrie smiled in answer to his humor.

Hurstwood glanced over his paper rather gaily. He seemed to have lost a load.

"I'll go down for a little while," he said after breakfast, "and then I'll look around. To-morrow I'll spend the whole day looking about. I think I can get something, now this thing's off my hands."

He went out smiling and visited the place. Shaughnessy was there. They had made all arrangements to share according to their interests. When, however, he had been there several hours, gone out three more, and returned, his elation had departed. As much as he had objected to the place, now that it was no longer to exist, he felt sorry. He wished that things were different.

Shaughnessy was coolly business-like.

"Well," he said at five o'clock, "we might as well count the change and divide."

They did so. The fixtures had already been sold and the sum divided.

"Good-night," said Hurstwood at the final moment, in a last effort to be genial.

"So long," said Shaughnessy, scarcely deigning a notice.

Thus the Warren Street arrangement was permanently concluded.

Carrie had prepared a good dinner at the flat, but after his ride up, Hurstwood was in a solemn and reflective mood.

"Well?" said Carrie, inquisitively.

"I'm out of that," he answered, taking off his coat.

As she looked at him, she wondered what his financial state was now. They ate and talked a little.

"Will you have enough to buy in anywhere else?" asked Carrie.

"No," he said. "I'll have to get something else and save up."

"It would be nice if you could get some place," said Carrie, prompted by anxiety and hope.

"I guess I will," he said reflectively.

For some days thereafter he put on his overcoat regularly in the morning and sallied forth. On these ventures he first consoled himself with the thought that with the seven hundred dollars he had he could still make some advantageous arrangement. He thought about going to some brewery, which, as he knew, frequently controlled saloons which they leased, and get them to help him. Then he remembered that he would have to pay out several hundred anyway for fixtures and that he would have nothing left for his monthly expenses. It was costing him nearly eighty dollars a month to live.

"No," he said, in his sanest moments, "I can't do it. I'll get something else and save up."

This getting-something proposition complicated itself the moment he began to think of what it was he wanted to do. Manage a place? Where should he get such a position? The papers contained no requests for managers. Such positions, he knew well enough, were either secured by long years of service or were bought with a half or third interest. Into a place important enough to need such a manager he had not money enough to buy.

Nevertheless, he started out. His clothes were very good and his appearance still excellent, but it involved the trouble of deluding. People, looking at him, imagined instantly that a man of his age, stout and well dressed, must be well off. He appeared a comfortable owner of something, a man from whom the common run of mortals could well expect gratuities. Being now forty-three years of age, and comfortably built, walking was not easy. He had not been used to exercise for many years. His legs tired, his shoulders ached, and his feet pained him at the close of the day, even when he took street cars in almost every direction. The mere getting up and down, if long continued, produced this result.

The fact that people took him to be better off than he was, he well understood. It was so painfully clear to him that it retarded his search. Not that he wished to be less well-appearing, but that he was ashamed to belie his appearance by incongruous appeals. So he hesitated, wondering what to do.

He thought of the hotels, but instantly he remembered that he had had no experience as a clerk, and, what was more important, no acquaintances or friends in that line to whom he could go. He did know some hotel owners in several cities, including New York, but they knew of his dealings with Fitzgerald and Moy. He could not apply to them. He thought of other lines suggested by large buildings or businesses which he knew of—wholesale groceries, hardware, insurance concerns, and the like—but he had had no experience.

How to go about getting anything was a bitter thought. Would he have to go personally and ask; wait outside an office door, and, then, distinguished and affluent looking, announce that he was looking for something to do? He strained painfully at the thought. No, he could not do that.

He really strolled about, thinking, and then, the weather being cold, stepped into a hotel. He knew hotels well enough to know that any decent looking individual was welcome to a chair in the lobby. This was in the Broadway Central, which was then one of the most important hotels in the city. Taking a chair here was a painful thing to him. To think he should come to this! He had heard loungers about hotels called chair-warmers. He had called them that himself in his day. But here he was, despite the possibility of meeting some one who knew him, shielding himself from cold and the weariness of the streets in a hotel lobby.

"I can't do this way," he said to himself. "There's no use of my starting out mornings without first thinking up some place to go. I'll think of some places and then look them up."

It occurred to him that the positions of bartenders were sometimes open, but he put this out of his mind. Bartender—he, the ex-manager!

It grew awfully dull sitting in the hotel lobby, and so at four he went home. He tried to put on a business air as he went in, but it was a feeble imitation. The rocking-chair in the dining-room was comfortable. He sank into it gladly, with several papers he had bought, and began to read.

As she was going through the room to begin preparing dinner, Carrie said:

"The man was here for the rent to-day."

"Oh, was he?" said Hurstwood.

The least wrinkle crept into his brow as he remembered that this was February 2d, the time the man always called. He fished down in his pocket for his purse, getting the first taste of paying out when nothing is coming in. He looked at the fat, green roll as a sick man looks at the one possible saving cure. Then he counted off twenty-eight dollars.

"Here you are," he said to Carrie, when she came through again.

He buried himself in his papers and read. Oh, the rest of it—the relief from walking and thinking! What Lethean waters were these floods of telegraphed intelligence! He forgot his troubles, in part. Here was a young, handsome woman, if you might believe the newspaper drawing, suing a rich, fat, candy-making husband in Brooklyn for divorce. Here was another item detailing the wrecking of a vessel in ice and snow off Prince's Bay on Staten Island. A long, bright column told of the doings in the theatrical world—the plays produced, the actors appearing, the managers making announcements. Fannie Davenport was just opening at the Fifth Avenue. Daly was producing "King Lear." He read of the early departure for the season of a party composed of the Vanderbilts and their friends for Florida. An interesting shooting affray was on in the mountains of Kentucky. So he read, read, read, rocking in the warm room near the radiator and waiting for dinner to be served.

CHAPTER XXXV

THE PASSING OF EFFORT: THE VISAGE OF CARE

The next morning he looked over the papers and waded through a long list of advertisements, making a few notes. Then he turned to the male-help-wanted column, but with disagreeable feelings. The day was before him—a long day in which to discover something—and this was how he must begin to discover. He scanned the long column, which mostly concerned bakers, bushelmen, cooks, compositors, drivers, and the like, finding two things only which arrested his eye. One was a cashier wanted in a wholesale furniture house, and the other a salesman for a whiskey house. He had never thought of the latter. At once he decided to look that up.

The firm in question was Alsbery & Co., whiskey brokers.

He was admitted almost at once to the manager on his appearance.

"Good-morning, sir," said the latter, thinking at first that he was encountering one of his out-of-town customers.

"Good-morning," said Hurstwood. "You advertised, I believe, for a salesman?"

"Oh," said the man, showing plainly the enlightenment which had come to him. "Yes. Yes, I did."

"I thought I'd drop in," said Hurstwood, with dignity. "I've had some experience in that line myself."

"Oh, have you?" said the man. "What experience have you had?"

"Well, I've managed several liquor houses in my time. Recently I owned a third-interest in a saloon at Warren and Hudson streets."

"I see," said the man.

Hurstwood ceased, waiting for some suggestion.

"We did want a salesman," said the man. "I don't know as it's anything you'd care to take hold of though."

"I see," said Hurstwood. "Well, I'm in no position to choose, just at present. If it were open, I should be glad to get it."

The man did not take kindly at all to his "No position to choose." He wanted someone who wasn't thinking of a choice or something better. Especially not an old man. He wanted some one young, active, and glad to work actively for a moderate sum. Hurstwood did not please him at all. He had more of an air than his employers.

"Well," he said in answer, "we'd be glad to consider your application. We shan't decide for a few days yet. Suppose you send us your references."

"I will," said Hurstwood.

He nodded good-morning and came away. At the corner he looked at the furniture company's address, and saw that it was in West Twenty-third Street. Accordingly, he went up there. The place was not large enough, however. It looked moderate, the men in it idle and small salaried. He walked by, glancing in and then decided not to go in there.

"They want a girl, probably, at ten a week," he said.

At one o'clock he thought of eating, and went to a restaurant in Madison Square. There he pondered over places which he might look up. He was tired. It was blowing up gray again. Across the way, through Madison Square Park, stood the great hotels, looking down upon the busy scene. He decided to go over to the lobby of one and sit a while. It was warm in there and bright. He had seen no one he knew at the Broadway Central. In all likelihood he would encounter no one here. Finding a seat on one of the red plush divans close to the great windows which look out on Broadway's busy rout, he sat musing. His state did not seem so bad in here. Sitting still and looking out, he could take some slight consolation in the few hundred dollars he had in his purse. He could forget, in a measure, the weariness of the street and his tiresome searches. Still, it was only escape from a severe to a less severe state. He was still gloomy and disheartened. There, minutes seemed to go very slowly. An hour was a long, long time in passing. It was filled for him with observations and mental comments concerning the actual guests of the hotel, who passed in and out, and those more prosperous pedestrians whose good fortune showed in their clothes and spirits as they passed along Broadway, outside. It was nearly the first time since he had arrived in the city that his leisure afforded him ample opportunity to contemplate this spectacle. Now, being, perforce, idle himself, he wondered at the activity of others. How gay were the youths he saw, how pretty the women. Such fine clothes they all wore. They were so intent upon getting somewhere. He saw coquettish glances cast by magnificent girls. Ah, the money it required to train with such—how well he knew! How long it had been since he had had the opportunity to do so!

The clock outside registered four. It was a little early, but he thought he would go back to the flat.

This going back to the flat was coupled with the thought that Carrie would think he was sitting around too much if he came home early. He hoped he wouldn't have to, but the day hung heavily on his hands. Over there he was on his own ground. He could sit in his rocking-chair and read. This busy, distracting, suggestive scene was shut out. He could read his papers. Accordingly, he went home. Carrie was reading, quite alone. It was rather dark in the flat, shut in as it was.

"You'll hurt your eyes," he said when he saw her.

After taking off his coat, he felt it incumbent upon him to make some little report of his day.

"I've been talking with a wholesale liquor company," he said. "I may go out on the road."

"Wouldn't that be nice!" said Carrie.

"It wouldn't be such a bad thing," he answered.

Always from the man at the corner now he bought two papers—the "Evening World" and "Evening Sun." So now he merely picked his papers up, as he came by, without stopping.

He drew up his chair near the radiator and lighted the gas. Then it was as the evening before. His difficulties vanished in the items he so well loved to read.

The next day was even worse than the one before, because now he could not think of where to go. Nothing he saw in the papers he studied—till ten o'clock—appealed to him. He felt that he ought to go out, and yet he sickened at the thought. Where to, where to?

"You mustn't forget to leave me my money for this week," said Carrie, quietly.

They had an arrangement by which he placed twelve dollars a week in her hands, out of which to pay current expenses. He heaved a little sigh as she said this, and drew out his purse. Again he felt the dread of the thing. Here he was taking off, taking off, and nothing coming in.

"Lord!" he said, in his own thoughts, "this can't go on."

To Carrie he said nothing whatsoever. She could feel that her request disturbed him. To pay her would soon become a distressing thing.

"Yet, what have I got to do with it?" she thought. "Oh, why should I be made to worry?"

Hurstwood went out and made for Broadway. He wanted to think up some place. Before long, though, he reached the Grand Hotel at Thirty-first Street. He knew of its comfortable lobby. He was cold after his twenty blocks' walk.

"I'll go in their barber shop and get a shave," he thought.

Thus he justified himself in sitting down in here after his tonsorial treatment.

Again, time hanging heavily on his hands, he went home early, and this continued for several days, each day the need to hunt paining him, and each day disgust, depression, shamefacedness driving him into lobby idleness.

At last three days came in which a storm prevailed, and he did not go out at all. The snow began to fall late one afternoon. It was a regular flurry of large, soft, white flakes. In the morning it was still coming down with a high wind, and the papers announced a blizzard. From out the front windows one could see a deep, soft bedding.

"I guess I'll not try to go out to-day," he said to Carrie at breakfast. "It's going to be awful bad, so the papers say."

"The man hasn't brought my coal, either," said Carrie, who ordered by the bushel.

"I'll go over and see about it," said Hurstwood. This was the first time he had ever suggested doing an errand, but, somehow, the wish to sit about the house prompted it as a sort of compensation for the privilege.

All day and all night it snowed, and the city began to suffer from a general blockade of traffic. Great attention was given to the details of the storm by the newspapers, which played up the distress of the poor in large type.

Hurstwood sat and read by his radiator in the corner. He did not try to think about his need of work. This storm being so terrific, and tying up all things, robbed him of the need. He made himself wholly comfortable and toasted his feet.

Carrie observed his ease with some misgiving. For all the fury of the storm she doubted his comfort. He took his situation too philosophically.

Hurstwood, however, read on and on. He did not pay much attention to Carrie. She fulfilled her household duties and said little to disturb him.

The next day it was still snowing, and the next, bitter cold. Hurstwood took the alarm of the paper and sat still. Now he volunteered to do a few other little things. One was to go to the butcher, another to the grocery. He really thought nothing of these little services in connection with their true significance. He felt as if he were not wholly useless—indeed, in such a stress of weather, quite worth while about the house.

On the fourth day, however, it cleared, and he read that the storm was over. Now, however, he idled, thinking how sloppy the streets would be.

It was noon before he finally abandoned his papers and got under way. Owing to the slightly warmer temperature the streets were bad. He went across Fourteenth Street on the car and got a transfer south on Broadway. One little advertisement he had, relating to a saloon down in Pearl Street. When he reached the Broadway Central, however, he changed his mind.

"What's the use?" he thought, looking out upon the slop and snow. "I couldn't buy into it. It's a thousand to one nothing comes of it. I guess I'll get off," and off he got. In the lobby he took a seat and waited again, wondering what he could do.

While he was idly pondering, satisfied to be inside, a well-dressed man passed up the lobby, stopped, looked sharply, as if not sure of his memory, and then approached. Hurstwood recognized Cargill, the owner of the large stables in Chicago of the same name, whom he had last seen at Avery Hall, the night Carrie appeared there. The remembrance of how this individual brought up his wife to shake hands on that occasion was also on the instant clear.

Hurstwood was greatly abashed. His eyes expressed the difficulty he felt.

"Why, it's Hurstwood!" said Cargill, remembering now, and sorry that he had not recognized him quickly enough in the beginning to have avoided this meeting.

"Yes," said Hurstwood. "How are you?"

"Very well," said Cargill, troubled for something to talk about. "Stopping here?"

"No," said Hurstwood, "just keeping an appointment."

"I knew you had left Chicago. I was wondering what had become of you."

"Oh, I'm here now," answered Hurstwood, anxious to get away.

"Doing well, I suppose?"

"Excellent."

"Glad to hear it."

They looked at one another, rather embarrassed.

"Well, I have an engagement with a friend upstairs. I'll leave you. So long."

Hurstwood nodded his head.

"Damn it all," he murmured, turning toward the door. "I knew that would happen."

He walked several blocks up the street. His watch only registered 1.30. He tried to think of some place to go or something to do. The day was so bad he wanted only to be inside. Finally his feet began to feel wet and cold, and he boarded a car. This took him to Fifty-ninth Street, which was as good as anywhere else. Landed here, he turned to walk back along Seventh Avenue, but the slush was too much. The misery of lounging about with nowhere to go became intolerable. He felt as if he were catching cold.

Stopping at a corner, he waited for a car south bound. This was no day to be out; he would go home.

Carrie was surprised to see him at a quarter of three.

"It's a miserable day out," was all he said. Then he took off his coat and changed his shoes.

That night he felt a cold coming on and took quinine. He was feverish until morning, and sat about the next day while Carrie waited on him. He was a helpless creature in sickness, not very handsome in a dull-colored bath gown and his hair uncombed. He looked haggard about the eyes and quite old. Carrie noticed this, and it did not appeal to her. She wanted to be good-natured and sympathetic, but something about the man held her aloof.

Toward evening he looked so badly in the weak light that she suggested he go to bed.

"You'd better sleep alone," she said, "you'll feel better. I'll open your bed for you now."

"All right," he said.

As she did all these things, she was in a most despondent state.

"What a life! What a life!" was her one thought.

Once during the day, when he sat near the radiator, hunched up and reading, she passed through, and seeing him, wrinkled her brows. In the front room, where it was not so warm, she sat by the window and cried. This was the life cut out for her, was it? To live cooped up in a small flat with some one who was out of work, idle, and indifferent to her. She was merely a servant to him now, nothing more.

This crying made her eyes red, and when, in preparing his bed, she lighted the gas, and, having prepared it, called him in, he noticed the fact.

"What's the matter with you?" he asked, looking into her face. His voice was hoarse and his unkempt head only added to its gruesome quality.

"Nothing," said Carrie, weakly.

"You've been crying," he said.

"I haven't, either," she answered.

It was not for love of him, that he knew.

"You needn't cry," he said, getting into bed. "Things will come out all right."

In a day or two he was up again, but rough weather holding, he stayed in. The Italian newsdealer now delivered the morning papers, and these he read assiduously. A few times after that he ventured out, but meeting another of his old-time friends, he began to feel uneasy sitting about hotel corridors.

Every day he came home early, and at last made no pretence of going anywhere. Winter was no time to look for anything.

Naturally, being about the house, he noticed the way Carrie did things. She was far from perfect in household methods and economy, and her little deviations on this score first caught his eye. Not, however, before her regular demand for her allowance became a grievous thing. Sitting around as he did, the weeks seemed to pass very quickly. Every Tuesday Carrie asked for her money.

"Do you think we live as cheaply as we might?" he asked one Tuesday morning.

"I do the best I can," said Carrie.

Nothing was added to this at the moment, but the next day he said:

"Do you ever go to the Gansevoort Market over here?"

"I didn't know there was such a market," said Carrie.

"They say you can get things lots cheaper there."

Carrie was very indifferent to the suggestion. These were things which she did not like at all.

"How much do you pay for a pound of meat?" he asked one day.

"Oh, there are different prices," said Carrie. "Sirloin steak is twenty-two cents."

"That's steep, isn't it?" he answered.

So he asked about other things, until finally, with the passing days, it seemed to become a mania with him. He learned the prices and remembered them.

His errand-running capacity also improved. It began in a small way, of course. Carrie, going to get her hat one morning, was stopped by him.

"Where are you going, Carrie?" he asked.

"Over to the baker's," she answered.

"I'd just as leave go for you," he said.

She acquiesced, and he went. Each afternoon he would go to the corner for the papers.

"Is there anything you want?" he would say.

By degrees she began to use him. Doing this, however, she lost the weekly payment of twelve dollars.

"You want to pay me to-day," she said one Tuesday, about this time.

"How much?" he asked.

She understood well enough what it meant.

"Well, about five dollars," she answered. "I owe the coal man."

The same day he said:

"I think this Italian up here on the corner sells coal at twenty-five cents a bushel. I'll trade with him."

Carrie heard this with indifference.

"All right," she said.

Then it came to be:

"George, I must have some coal to-day," or, "You must get some meat of some kind for dinner."

He would find out what she needed and order.

Accompanying this plan came skimpiness.

"I only got a half-pound of steak," he said, coming in one afternoon with his papers. "We never seem to eat very much."

These miserable details ate the heart out of Carrie. They blackened her days and grieved her soul. Oh, how this man had changed! All day and all day, here he sat, reading his papers. The world seemed to have no attraction. Once in a while he would go out, in fine weather, it might be four or five hours, between eleven and four. She could do nothing but view him with gnawing contempt.

It was apathy with Hurstwood, resulting from his inability to see his way out. Each month drew from his small store. Now, he had only five hundred dollars left, and this he hugged, half feeling as if he could stave off absolute necessity for an indefinite period. Sitting around the house, he decided to wear some old clothes he had. This came first with the bad days. Only once he apologized in the very beginning:

"It's so bad to-day, I'll just wear these around."

Eventually these became the permanent thing.

Also, he had been wont to pay fifteen cents for a shave, and a tip of ten cents. In his first distress, he cut down the tip to five, then to nothing. Later, he tried a ten-cent barber shop, and, finding that the shave was satisfactory, patronized regularly. Later still, he put off shaving to every other day, then to every third, and so on, until once a week became the rule. On Saturday he was a sight to see.

Of course, as his own self-respect vanished, it perished for him in Carrie. She could not understand what had gotten into the man. He had some money, he had a decent suit remaining, he was not bad looking when dressed up. She did not forget her own difficult struggle in Chicago, but she did not forget either that she had never ceased trying. He never tried. He did not even consult the ads. in the paper any more.

Finally, a distinct impression escaped from her.

"What makes you put so much butter on the steak?" he asked her one evening, standing around in the kitchen.

"To make it good, of course," she answered.

"Butter is awful dear these days," he suggested.

"You wouldn't mind it if you were working," she answered.

He shut up after this, and went in to his paper, but the retort rankled in his mind. It was the first cutting remark that had come from her.

That same evening, Carrie, after reading, went off to the front room to bed. This was unusual. When Hurstwood decided to go, he retired, as usual, without a light. It was then that he discovered Carrie's absence.

"That's funny," he said: "maybe she's sitting up."

He gave the matter no more thought, but slept. In the morning she was not beside him. Strange to say, this passed without comment.

Night approaching, and a slightly more conversational feeling prevailing, Carrie said:

"I think I'll sleep alone to-night. I have a headache."

"All right," said Hurstwood.

The third night she went to her front bed without apologies.

This was a grim blow to Hurstwood, but he never mentioned it.

"All right," he said to himself, with an irrepressible frown, "let her sleep alone."

CHAPTER XXXVI

A GRIM RETROGRESSION: THE PHANTOM OF CHANCE

The Vances, who had been back in the city ever since Christmas, had not forgotten Carrie; but they, or rather Mrs. Vance, had never called on her, for the very simple reason that Carrie had never sent her address. True to her nature, she corresponded with Mrs. Vance as long as she still lived in Seventy-eighth Street, but when she was compelled to move into Thirteenth, her fear that the latter would take it as an indication of reduced circumstances caused her to study some way of avoiding the necessity of giving her address. Not finding any convenient method, she sorrowfully resigned the privilege of writing to her friend entirely. The latter wondered at this strange silence, thought Carrie must have left the city, and in the end gave her up as lost. So she was thoroughly surprised to encounter her in Fourteenth Street, where she had gone shopping. Carrie was there for the same purpose.

"Why, Mrs. Wheeler," said Mrs. Vance, looking Carrie over in a glance, "where have you been? Why haven't you been to see me? I've been wondering all this time what had become of you. Really, I—"

"I'm so glad to see you," said Carrie, pleased and yet nonplussed. Of all times, this was the worst to encounter Mrs. Vance. "Why, I'm living downtown here. I've been intending to come and see you. Where are you living now?"

"In Fifty-eight Street," said Mrs. Vance, "just off Seventh Avenue—218. Why don't you come and see me?"

"I will," said Carrie. "Really, I've been wanting to come. I know I ought to. It's a shame. But you know—"

"What's your number?" said Mrs. Vance.

"Thirteenth Street," said Carrie, reluctantly. "112 West."

"Oh," said Mrs. Vance, "that's right near here, isn't it?"

"Yes," said Carrie. "You must come down and see me some time."

"Well, you're a fine one," said Mrs. Vance, laughing, the while noting that Carrie's appearance had modified somewhat. "The address, too," she added to herself. "They must be hard up."

Still she liked Carrie well enough to take her in tow.

"Come with me in here a minute," she exclaimed, turning into a store.

When Carrie returned home, there was Hurstwood, reading as usual. He seemed to take his condition with the utmost nonchalance. His beard was at least four days old.

"Oh," thought Carrie, "if she were to come here and see him?"

She shook her head in absolute misery. It looked as if her situation was becoming unbearable.

Driven to desperation, she asked at dinner:

"Did you ever hear any more from that wholesale house?"

"No," he said. "They don't want an inexperienced man."

Carrie dropped the subject, feeling unable to say more.

"I met Mrs. Vance this afternoon," she said, after a time.

"Did, eh?" he answered.

"They're back in New York now," Carrie went on. "She did look so nice."

"Well, she can afford it as long as he puts up for it," returned Hurstwood. "He's got a soft job."

Hurstwood was looking into the paper. He could not see the look of infinite weariness and discontent Carrie gave him.

"She said she thought she'd call here some day."

"She's been long getting round to it, hasn't she?" said Hurstwood, with a kind of sarcasm.

The woman didn't appeal to him from her spending side.

"Oh, I don't know," said Carrie, angered by the man's attitude. "Perhaps I didn't want her to come."

"She's too gay," said Hurstwood, significantly. "No one can keep up with her pace unless they've got a lot of money."

"Mr. Vance doesn't seem to find it very hard."

"He may not now," answered Hurstwood, doggedly, well understanding the inference, "but his life isn't done yet. You can't tell what'll happen. He may get down like anybody else."

There was something quite knavish in the man's attitude. His eye seemed to be cocked with a twinkle upon the fortunate, expecting their defeat. His own state seemed a thing apart—not considered.

This thing was the remains of his old-time cocksureness and independence. Sitting in his flat, and reading of the doings of other people, sometimes this independent, undefeated mood came upon him. Forgetting the weariness of the streets and the degradation of search, he would sometimes prick up his ears. It was as if he said:

"I can do something. I'm not down yet. There's a lot of things coming to me if I want to go after them."

It was in this mood that he would occasionally dress up, go for a shave, and, putting on his gloves, sally forth quite actively. Not with any definite aim. It was more a barometric condition. He felt just right for being outside and doing something.

On such occasions, his money went also. He knew of several poker rooms downtown. A few acquaintances he had in downtown resorts and about the City Hall. It was a change to see them and exchange a few friendly commonplaces.

He had once been accustomed to hold a pretty fair hand at poker. Many a friendly game had netted him a hundred dollars or more at the time when that sum was merely sauce to the dish of the game—not the all in all. Now, he thought of playing.

"I might win a couple of hundred. I'm not out of practice."

It is but fair to say that this thought had occurred to him several times before he acted upon it.

The poker room which he first invaded was over a saloon in West Street, near one of the ferries. He had been there before. Several games were going. These he watched for a time and noticed that the pots were quite large for the ante involved.

"Deal me a hand," he said at the beginning of a new shuffle. He pulled up a chair and studied his cards. Those playing made that quiet study of him which is so unapparent, and yet invariably so searching.

Poor fortune was with him at first. He received a mixed collection without progression or pairs. The pot was opened.

"I pass," he said.

On the strength of this, he was content to lose his ante. The deals did fairly by him in the long run, causing him to come away with a few dollars to the good.

The next afternoon he was back again, seeking amusement and profit. This time he followed up three of a kind to his doom. There was a better hand across the table, held by a pugnacious Irish youth, who was a political hanger-on of the Tammany district in which they were located. Hurstwood was surprised at the persistence of this individual, whose bets came with a *sangfroid* which, if a bluff, was excellent art. Hurstwood began to doubt, but kept, or thought to keep, at least, the cool demeanor with which, in olden times, he deceived those psychic students of the gaming table, who seem to read thoughts and moods, rather than exterior evidences, however subtle. He could not down the cowardly thought that this man had something better and would stay to the end, drawing his last dollar into the pot, should he choose to go so far. Still, he hoped to win much—his hand was excellent. Why not raise it five more?

"I raise you three," said the youth.

"Make it five," said Hurstwood, pushing out his chips.

"Come again," said the youth, pushing out a small pile of reds.

"Let me have some more chips," said Hurstwood to the keeper in charge, taking out a bill.

A cynical grin lit up the face of his youthful opponent. When the chips were laid out, Hurstwood met the raise.

"Five again," said the youth.

Hurstwood's brow was wet. He was deep in now—very deep for him. Sixty dollars of his good money was up. He was ordinarily no coward, but the thought of losing so much weakened him. Finally he gave way. He would not trust to this fine hand any longer.

"I call," he said.

"A full house!" said the youth, spreading out his cards.

Hurstwood's hand dropped.

"I thought I had you," he said, weakly.

The youth raked in his chips, and Hurstwood came away, not without first stopping to count his remaining cash on the stair.

"Three hundred and forty dollars," he said.

With this loss and ordinary expenses, so much had already gone.

Back in the flat, he decided he would play no more.

Remembering Mrs. Vance's promise to call, Carrie made one other mild protest. It was concerning Hurstwood's appearance. This very day, coming home, he changed his clothes to the old togs he sat around in.

"What makes you always put on those old clothes?" asked Carrie.

"What's the use wearing my good ones around here?" he asked.

"Well, I should think you'd feel better." Then she added: "Some one might call."

"Who?" he said.

"Well, Mrs. Vance," said Carrie.

"She needn't see me," he answered, sullenly.

This lack of pride and interest made Carrie almost hate him.

"Oh," she thought, "there he sits. 'She needn't see me.' I should think he would be ashamed of himself."

The real bitterness of this thing was added when Mrs. Vance did call. It was on one of her shopping rounds. Making her way up the commonplace hall, she knocked at Carrie's door. To her subsequent and agonizing distress, Carrie was out. Hurstwood opened the door, half-thinking that the knock was Carrie's. For once, he was taken honestly aback. The lost voice of youth and pride spoke in him.

"Why," he said, actually stammering, "how do you do?"

"How do you do?" said Mrs. Vance, who could scarcely believe her eyes. His great confusion she instantly perceived. He did not know whether to invite her in or not.

"Is your wife at home?" she inquired.

"No," he said, "Carrie's out; but won't you step in? She'll be back shortly."

"No-o," said Mrs. Vance, realizing the change of it all. "I'm really very much in a hurry. I thought I'd just run up and look in, but I couldn't stay. Just tell your wife she must come and see me."

"I will," said Hurstwood, standing back, and feeling intense relief at her going. He was so ashamed that he folded his hands weakly, as he sat in the chair afterwards, and thought.

Carrie, coming in from another direction, thought she saw Mrs. Vance going away. She strained her eyes, but could not make sure.

"Was anybody here just now?" she asked of Hurstwood.

"Yes," he said guiltily; "Mrs. Vance."

"Did she see you?" she asked, expressing her full despair.

This cut Hurstwood like a whip, and made him sullen.

"If she had eyes, she did. I opened the door."

"Oh," said Carrie, closing one hand tightly out of sheer nervousness. "What did she have to say?"

"Nothing," he answered. "She couldn't stay."

"And you looking like that!" said Carrie, throwing aside a long reserve.

"What of it?" he said, angering. "I didn't know she was coming, did I?"

"You knew she might," said Carrie. "I told you she said she was coming. I've asked you a dozen times to wear your other clothes. Oh, I think this is just terrible."

"Oh, let up," he answered. "What difference does it make? You couldn't associate with her, anyway. They've got too much money."

"Who said I wanted to?" said Carrie, fiercely.

"Well, you act like it, rowing around over my looks. You'd think I'd committed—"

Carrie interrupted:

"It's true," she said. "I couldn't if I wanted to, but whose fault is it? You're very free to sit and talk about who I could associate with. Why don't you get out and look for work?"

This was a thunderbolt in camp.

"What's it to you?" he said, rising, almost fiercely. "I pay the rent, don't I? I furnish the—"

"Yes, you pay the rent," said Carrie. "You talk as if there was nothing else in the world but a flat to sit around in. You haven't done a thing for three months except sit around and interfere here. I'd like to know what you married me for?"

"I didn't marry you," he said, in a snarling tone.

"I'd like to know what you did, then, in Montreal?" she answered.

"Well, I didn't marry you," he answered. "You can get that out of your head. You talk as though you didn't know."

Carrie looked at him a moment, her eyes distending. She had believed it was all legal and binding enough.

"What did you lie to me for, then?" she asked, fiercely. "What did you force me to run away with you for?"

Her voice became almost a sob.

"Force!" he said, with curled lip. "A lot of forcing I did."

"Oh!" said Carrie, breaking under the strain, and turning. "Oh, oh!" and she hurried into the front room.

Hurstwood was now hot and waked up. It was a great shaking up for him, both mental and moral. He wiped his brow as he looked around, and then went for his clothes and dressed. Not a sound came from Carrie; she ceased sobbing when she heard him dressing. She thought, at first, with the faintest alarm, of being left without money—not of losing him, though he might be going away permanently. She heard him open the top of the wardrobe and take out his hat. Then the dining-room door closed, and she knew he had gone.

After a few moments of silence, she stood up, dry-eyed, and looked out the window. Hurstwood was just strolling up the street, from the flat, toward Sixth Avenue.

The latter made progress along Thirteenth and across Fourteenth Street to Union Square.

"Look for work!" he said to himself. "Look for work! She tells me to get out and look for work."

He tried to shield himself from his own mental accusation, which told him that she was right.

"What a cursed thing that Mrs. Vance's call was, anyhow," he thought. "Stood right there, and looked me over. I know what she was thinking."

He remembered the few times he had seen her in Seventy-eighth Street. She was always a swell-looker, and he had tried to put on the air of being worthy of such as she, in front of her. Now, to think she had caught him looking this way. He wrinkled his forehead in his distress.

"The devil!" he said a dozen times in an hour.

It was a quarter after four when he left the house. Carrie was in tears. There would be no dinner that night.

"What the deuce," he said, swaggering mentally to hide his own shame from himself. "I'm not so bad. I'm not down yet."

He looked around the square, and seeing the several large hotels, decided to go to one for dinner. He would get his papers and make himself comfortable there.

He ascended into the fine parlor of the Morton House, then one of the best New York hotels, and, finding a cushioned seat, read. It did not trouble him much that his decreasing sum of money did not allow of such extravagance. Like the morphine fiend, he was becoming addicted to his ease. Anything to relieve his mental distress, to satisfy his craving for comfort. He must do it. No thoughts for the morrow—he could not stand to think of it any more than he could of any other calamity. Like the certainty of death, he tried to shut the certainty of soon being without a dollar completely out of his mind, and he came very near doing it.

Well-dressed guests moving to and fro over the thick carpets carried him back to the old days. A young lady, a guest of the house, playing a piano in an alcove pleased him. He sat there reading.

His dinner cost him $1.50. By eight o'clock he was through, and then, seeing guests leaving and the crowd of pleasure-seekers thickening outside wondered where he should go. Not home. Carrie would be up. No, he would not go back there this evening. He would stay out and knock around as a man who was independent—not broke—well might. He bought a cigar, and went outside on the corner where other individuals were lounging—brokers, racing people, thespians—his own flesh and blood. As he stood there, he thought of the old evenings in Chicago, and how he used to dispose of them. Many's the game he had had. This took him to poker.

"I didn't do that thing right the other day," he thought, referring to his loss of sixty dollars. "I shouldn't have weakened. I could have bluffed that fellow down. I wasn't in form, that's what ailed me."

Then he studied the possibilities of the game as it had been played, and began to figure how he might have won, in several instances, by bluffing a little harder.

"I'm old enough to play poker and do something with it. I'll try my hand tonight."

Visions of a big stake floated before him. Supposing he did win a couple of hundred, wouldn't he be in it? Lots of sports he knew made their living at this game, and a good living, too.

"They always had as much as I had," he thought.

So off he went to a poker room in the neighborhood, feeling much as he had in the old days. In this period of self-forgetfulness, aroused first by the shock of argument and perfected by a dinner in the hotel, with cocktails and cigars, he was as nearly like the old Hurstwood as he would ever be again. It was not the old Hurstwood—only a man arguing with a divided conscience and lured by a phantom.

This poker room was much like the other one, only it was a back room in a better drinking resort. Hurstwood watched a while, and then, seeing an interesting game, joined in. As before, it went easy for a while, he winning a few times and cheering up, losing a few pots and growing more interested and determined on that account. At last the fascinating game took a strong hold on him. He enjoyed its risks and ventured, on a trifling hand, to bluff the company and secure a fair stake. To his self-satisfaction intense and strong, he did it.

In the height of this feeling he began to think his luck was with him. No one else had done so well. Now came another moderate hand, and again he tried to open the jack-pot on it. There were others there who were almost reading his heart, so close was their observation.

"I have three of a kind," said one of the players to himself. "I'll just stay with that fellow to the finish."

The result was that bidding began.

"I raise you ten."

"Good."

"Ten more."

"Good."

"Ten again."

"Right you are."

It got to where Hurstwood had seventy-five dollars up. The other man really became serious. Perhaps this individual (Hurstwood) really did have a stiff hand.

"I call," he said.

Hurstwood showed his hand. He was done. The bitter fact that he had lost seventy-five dollars made him desperate.

"Let's have another pot," he said, grimly.

"All right," said the man.

Some of the other players quit, but observant loungers took their places. Time passed, and it came to twelve o'clock. Hurstwood held on, neither winning nor losing much. Then he grew weary, and on a last hand lost twenty more. He was sick at heart.

At a quarter after one in the morning he came out of the place. The chill, bare streets seemed a mockery of his state. He walked slowly west, little thinking of his row with Carrie. He ascended the stairs and went into his room as if there had been no trouble. It was his loss that occupied his mind. Sitting down on the bedside he counted his money. There was now but a hundred and ninety dollars and some change. He put it up and began to undress.

"I wonder what's getting into me, anyhow?" he said.

In the morning Carrie scarcely spoke and he felt as if he must go out again. He had treated her badly, but he could not afford to make up. Now desperation seized him, and for a day or two, going out thus, he lived like a gentleman—or what he conceived to be a gentleman—which took money. For his escapades he was soon poorer in mind and body, to say nothing of his purse, which had lost thirty by the process. Then he came down to cold, bitter sense again.

"The rent man comes to-day," said Carrie, greeting him thus indifferently three mornings later.

"He does?"

"Yes; this is the second," answered Carrie.

Hurstwood frowned. Then in despair he got out his purse.

"It seems an awful lot to pay for rent," he said.

He was nearing his last hundred dollars.

CHAPTER XXXVII

THE SPIRIT AWAKENS: NEW SEARCH FOR THE GATE

It would be useless to explain how in due time the last fifty dollars was in sight. The seven hundred, by his process of handling, had only carried them into June. Before the final hundred mark was reached he began to indicate that a calamity was approaching.

"I don't know," he said one day, taking a trivial expenditure for meat as a text, "it seems to take an awful lot for us to live."

"It doesn't seem to me," said Carrie, "that we spend very much."

"My money is nearly gone," he said, "and I hardly know where it's gone to."

"All that seven hundred dollars?" asked Carrie.

"All but a hundred."

He looked so disconsolate that it scared her. She began to see that she herself had been drifting. She had felt it all the time.

"Well, George," she exclaimed, "why don't you get out and look for something? You could find something."

"I have looked," he said. "You can't make people give you a place."

She gazed weakly at him and said: "Well, what do you think you will do? A hundred dollars won't last long."

"I don't know," he said. "I can't do any more than look."

Carrie became frightened over this announcement. She thought desperately upon the subject. Frequently she had considered the stage as a door through which she might enter that gilded state which she had so much craved. Now, as in Chicago, it came as a last resource in distress. Something must be done if he did not get work soon. Perhaps she would have to go out and battle again alone.

She began to wonder how one would go about getting a place. Her experience in Chicago proved that she had not tried the right way. There must be people who would listen to and try you—men who would give you an opportunity.

They were talking at the breakfast table, a morning or two later, when she brought up the dramatic subject by saying that she saw that Sarah Bernhardt was coming to this country. Hurstwood had seen it, too.

"How do people get on the stage, George?" she finally asked, innocently.

"I don't know," he said. "There must be dramatic agents."

Carrie was sipping coffee, and did not look up.

"Regular people who get you a place?"

"Yes, I think so," he answered.

Suddenly the air with which she asked attracted his attention.

"You're not still thinking about being an actress, are you?" he asked.

"No," she answered, "I was just wondering."

Without being clear, there was something in the thought which he objected to. He did not believe any more, after three years of observation, that Carrie would ever do anything great in that line. She seemed too simple, too yielding. His idea of the art was that it involved something more pompous. If she tried to get on the stage she would fall into the hands of some cheap manager and become like the rest of them. He had a good idea of what he meant by *them*. Carrie was pretty. She would get along all right, but where would he be?

"I'd get that idea out of my head, if I were you. It's a lot more difficult than you think."

Carrie felt this to contain, in some way, an aspersion upon her ability.

"You said I did real well in Chicago," she rejoined.

"You did," he answered, seeing that he was arousing opposition, "but Chicago isn't New York, by a big jump."

Carrie did not answer this at all. It hurt her.

"The stage," he went on, "is all right if you can be one of the big guns, but there's nothing to the rest of it. It takes a long while to get up."

"Oh, I don't know," said Carrie, slightly aroused.

In a flash, he thought he foresaw the result of this thing. Now, when the worst of his situation was approaching, she would get on the stage in some cheap way and forsake him. Strangely, he had not conceived well of her mental ability. That was because he did not understand the nature of emotional greatness. He had never learned that a person might be emotionally—instead of intellectually—great. Avery Hall was too far away for him to look back and sharply remember. He had lived with this woman too long.

"Well, I do," he answered. "If I were you I wouldn't think of it. It's not much of a profession for a woman."

"It's better than going hungry," said Carrie. "If you don't want me to do that, why don't you get work yourself?"

There was no answer ready for this. He had got used to the suggestion.

"Oh, let up," he answered.

The result of this was that she secretly resolved to try. It didn't matter about him. She was not going to be dragged into poverty and something worse to suit him. She could act. She could get something and then work up. What would he say then? She pictured herself already appearing in some fine performance on Broadway; of going every evening to her dressing-room and making up. Then she would come out at eleven o'clock and see the carriages ranged about, waiting for the people. It did not matter whether she was the star or not. If she were only once in, getting a decent salary, wearing the kind of clothes she liked, having the money to do with, going here and there as she pleased, how delightful it would all be. Her mind ran over this picture all the day long. Hurstwood's dreary state made its beauty become more and more vivid.

Curiously this idea soon took hold of Hurstwood. His vanishing sum suggested that he would need sustenance. Why could not Carrie assist him a little until he could get something?

He came in one day with something of this idea in his mind.

"I met John B. Drake to-day," he said. "He's going to open a hotel here in the fall. He says that he can make a place for me then."

"Who is he?" asked Carrie.

"He's the man that runs the Grand Pacific in Chicago."

"Oh," said Carrie.

"I'd get about fourteen hundred a year out of that."

"That would be good, wouldn't it?" she said, sympathetically.

"If I can only get over this summer," he added, "I think I'll be all right. I'm hearing from some of my friends again."

Carrie swallowed this story in all its pristine beauty. She sincerely wished he could get through the summer. He looked so hopeless.

"How much money have you left?"

"Only fifty dollars."

"Oh, mercy," she exclaimed, "what will we do? It's only twenty days until the rent will be due again."

Hurstwood rested his head on his hands and looked blankly at the floor.

"Maybe you could get something in the stage line?" he blandly suggested.

"Maybe I could," said Carrie, glad that some one approved of the idea.

"I'll lay my hand to whatever I can get," he said, now that he saw her brighten up. "I can get something."

She cleaned up the things one morning after he had gone, dressed as neatly as her wardrobe permitted, and set out for Broadway. She did not know that thoroughfare very well. To her it was a wonderful conglomeration of everything great and mighty. The theaters were there—these agencies must be somewhere about.

She decided to stop in at the Madison Square Theater and ask how to find the theatrical agents. This seemed the sensible way. Accordingly, when she reached that theater she applied to the clerk at the box office.

"Eh?" he said, looking out. "Dramatic agents? I don't know. You'll find them in the 'Clipper,' though. They all advertise in that."

"Is that a paper?" said Carrie.

"Yes," said the clerk, marveling at such ignorance of a common fact. "You can get it at the news-stands," he added politely, seeing how pretty the inquirer was.

Carrie proceeded to get the "Clipper," and tried to find the agents by looking over it as she stood beside the stand. This could not be done so easily. Thirteenth street was a number of blocks off, but she went back, carrying the precious paper and regretting the waste of time.

Hurstwood was already there, sitting in his place.

"Where were you?" he asked.

"I've been trying to find some dramatic agents."

He felt a little difficult about asking concerning her success. The paper she began to scan attracted his attention.

"What have you got there?" he asked.

"The 'Clipper.' The man said I'd find their addresses in here."

"Have you been all the way over to Broadway to find that out? I could have told you."

"Why didn't you?" she asked, without looking up.

"You never asked me," he returned.

She went hunting aimlessly through the crowded columns. Her mind was distracted by this man's indifference. The difficulty of the situation she was facing was only added to by all he did. Self-commiseration brewed in her heart. Tears trembled along her eyelids but did not fall. Hurstwood noticed something.

"Let me look."

To recover herself she went into the front room while he searched. Presently she returned. He had a pencil, and was writing upon an envelope.

"Here're three," he said.

Carrie took it and found that one was Mrs. Bermudez, another Marcus Jenks, a third Percy Weil. She paused only a moment, and then moved toward the door.

"I might as well go right away," she said, without looking back.

Hurstwood saw her depart with some faint stirrings of shame, which were the expression of a manhood rapidly becoming stultified. He sat a while, and then it became too much. He got up and put on his hat.

"I guess I'll go out," he said to himself, and went, strolling nowhere in particular, but feeling somehow that he must go.

Carrie's first call was upon Mrs. Bermudez, whose address was quite the nearest. It was an old-fashioned residence turned into offices. Mrs. Bermudez's offices consisted of what formerly had been a back chamber and a hall bedroom, marked "Private."

As Carrie entered she noticed several persons lounging about—men, who said nothing and did nothing.

While she was waiting to be noticed, the door of the hall bedroom opened and from it issued two very mannish-looking women, very tightly dressed, and wearing white collars and cuffs. After them came a portly lady of about forty-five, lighthaired, sharp-eyed, and evidently good-natured. At least she was smiling.

"Now, don't forget about that," said one of the mannish women.

"I won't," said the portly woman. "Let's see," she added, "where are you the first week in February?"

"Pittsburgh," said the woman.

"I'll write you there."

"All right," said the other, and the two passed out.

Instantly the portly lady's face became exceedingly sober and shrewd. She turned about and fixed on Carrie a very searching eye.

"Well," she said, "young woman, what can I do for you?"

"Are you Mrs. Bermudez?"

"Yes."

"Well," said Carrie, hesitating how to begin, "do you get places for persons upon the stage?"

"Yes."

"Could you get me one?"

"Have you ever had any experience?"

"A very little," said Carrie.

"Whom did you play with?"

"Oh, with no one," said Carrie. "It was just a show gotten—"

"Oh, I see," said the woman, interrupting her. "No, I don't know of anything now."

Carrie's countenance fell.

"You want to get some New York experience," concluded the affable Mrs. Bermudez. "We'll take your name, though."

Carrie stood looking while the lady retired to her office.

"What is your address?" inquired a young lady behind the counter, taking up the curtailed conversation.

"Mrs. George Wheeler," said Carrie, moving over to where she was writing. The woman wrote her address in full and then allowed her to depart at her leisure.

She encountered a very similar experience in the office of Mr. Jenks, only he varied it by saying at the close: "If you could play at some local house, or had a program with your name on it, I might do something."

In the third place the individual asked:

"What sort of work do you want to do?"

"What do you mean?" said Carrie.

"Well, do you want to get in a comedy or on the vaudeville stage or in the chorus?"

"Oh, I'd like to get a part in a play," said Carrie.

"Well," said the man, "it'll cost you something to do that."

"How much?" said Carrie, who, ridiculous as it may seem, had not thought of this before.

"Well, that's for you to say," he answered shrewdly.

Carrie looked at him curiously. She hardly knew how to continue the inquiry.

"Could you get me a part if I paid?"

"If we didn't you'd get your money back."

"Oh," she said.

The agent saw he was dealing with an inexperienced soul, and continued accordingly.

"You'd want to deposit fifty dollars, any way. No agent would trouble about you for less than that."

Carrie saw a light.

"Thank you," she said. "I'll think about it."

She started to go, and then bethought herself.

"How soon would I get a place?" she asked.

"Well, that's hard to say," said the man. "You might get one in a week, or it might be a month. You'd get the first thing that we thought you could do."

"I see," said Carrie, and then, half-smiling to be agreeable, she walked out.

The agent studied a moment, and then said to himself:

"It's funny how anxious these women are to get on the stage."

Carrie found ample food for reflection in the fifty-dollar proposition. "Maybe they'd take my money and not give me anything," she thought. She had some jewelry—a diamond ring and pin and several other pieces. She could get fifty dollars for those if she went to a pawnbroker.

Hurstwood was home before her. He had not thought she would be so long seeking.

"Well?" he said, not venturing to ask what news.

"I didn't find out anything to-day," said Carrie, taking off her gloves. "They all want money to get you a place."

"How much?" asked Hurstwood.

"Fifty dollars."

"They don't want anything, do they?"

"Oh, they're like everybody else. You can't tell whether they'd ever get you anything after you did pay them."

"Well, I wouldn't put up fifty on that basis," said Hurstwood, as if he were deciding, money in hand.

"I don't know," said Carrie. "I think I'll try some of the managers."

Hurstwood heard this, dead to the horror of it. He rocked a little to and fro, and chewed at his finger. It seemed all very natural in such extreme states. He would do better later on.

CHAPTER XXXVIII

IN ELFLAND DISPORTING: THE GRIM WORLD WITHOUT

When Carrie renewed her search, as she did the next day, going to the Casino, she found that in the opera chorus, as in other fields, employment is difficult to secure. Girls who can stand in line and look pretty are as numerous as laborers who can swing a pick. She found there was no discrimination between one and the other of applicants, save as regards a conventional standard of prettiness and form. Their own opinion or knowledge of their ability went for nothing.

"Where shall I find Mr. Gray?" she asked of a sulky doorman at the stage entrance of the Casino.

"You can't see him now; he's busy."

"Do you know when I can see him?"

"Got an appointment with him?"

"No."

"Well, you'll have to call at his office."

"Oh, dear!" exclaimed Carrie. "Where is his office?"

He gave her the number.

She knew there was no need of calling there now. He would not be in. Nothing remained but to employ the intermediate hours in search.

The dismal story of ventures in other places is quickly told. Mr. Daly saw no one save by appointment. Carrie waited an hour in a dingy office, quite in spite of obstacles, to learn this fact of the placid, indifferent Mr. Dorney.

"You will have to write and ask him to see you."

So she went away.

At the Empire Theatre she found a hive of peculiarly listless and indifferent individuals. Everything ornately upholstered, everything carefully finished, everything remarkably reserved.

At the Lyceum she entered one of those secluded, under-stairway closets, berugged and bepanneled, which causes one to feel the greatness of all positions of authority. Here was reserve itself done into a box-office clerk, a doorman, and an assistant, glorying in their fine positions.

"Ah, be very humble now—very humble indeed. Tell us what it is you require. Tell it quickly, nervously, and without a vestige of self-respect. If no trouble to us in any way, we may see what we can do."

This was the atmosphere of the Lyceum—the attitude, for that matter, of every managerial office in the city. These little proprietors of businesses are lords indeed on their own ground.

Carrie came away wearily, somewhat more abashed for her pains.

Hurstwood heard the details of the weary and unavailing search that evening.

"I didn't get to see any one," said Carrie. "I just walked, and walked, and waited around."

Hurstwood only looked at her.

"I suppose you have to have some friends before you can get in," she added, disconsolately.

Hurstwood saw the difficulty of this thing, and yet it did not seem so terrible. Carrie was tired and dispirited, but now she could rest. Viewing the world from his rocking-chair, its bitterness did not seem to approach so rapidly. To-morrow was another day.

To-morrow came, and the next, and the next.

Carrie saw the manager at the Casino once.

"Come around," he said, "the first of next week. I may make some changes then."

He was a large and corpulent individual, surfeited with good clothes and good eating, who judged women as another would horseflesh. Carrie was pretty and graceful. She might be put in even if she did not have any experience. One of the proprietors had suggested that the chorus was a little weak on looks.

The first of next week was some days off yet. The first of the month was drawing near. Carrie began to worry as she had never worried before.

"Do you really look for anything when you go out?" she asked Hurstwood one morning as a climax to some painful thoughts of her own.

"Of course I do," he said pettishly, troubling only a little over the disgrace of the insinuation.

"I'd take anything," she said, "for the present. It will soon be the first of the month again."

She looked the picture of despair.

Hurstwood quit reading his paper and changed his clothes.

"He would look for something," he thought. "He would go and see if some brewery couldn't get him in somewhere. Yes, he would take a position as bartender, if he could get it."

It was the same sort of pilgrimage he had made before. One or two slight rebuffs, and the bravado disappeared.

"No use," he thought. "I might as well go on back home."

Now that his money was so low, he began to observe his clothes and feel that even his best ones were beginning to look commonplace. This was a bitter thought.

Carrie came in after he did.

"I went to see some of the variety managers," she said, aimlessly. "You have to have an act. They don't want anybody that hasn't."

"I saw some of the brewery people to-day," said Hurstwood. "One man told me he'd try to make a place for me in two or three weeks."

In the face of so much distress on Carrie's part, he had to make some showing, and it was thus he did so. It was lassitude's apology to energy.

Monday Carrie went again to the Casino.

"Did I tell you to come around to-day?" said the manager, looking her over as she stood before him.

"You said the first of the week," said Carrie, greatly abashed.

"Ever had any experience?" he asked again, almost severely.

Carrie owned to ignorance.

He looked her over again as he stirred among some papers. He was secretly pleased with this pretty, disturbed-looking young woman. "Come around to the theater to-morrow morning."

Carrie's heart bounded to her throat.

"I will," she said with difficulty. She could see he wanted her, and turned to go.

"Would he really put her to work? Oh, blessed fortune, could it be?"

Already the hard rumble of the city through the open windows became pleasant.

A sharp voice answered her mental interrogation, driving away all immediate fears on that score.

"Be sure you're there promptly," the manager said roughly. "You'll be dropped if you're not."

Carrie hastened away. She did not quarrel now with Hurstwood's idleness. She had a place—she had a place! This sang in her ears.

In her delight she was almost anxious to tell Hurstwood. But, as she walked homeward, and her survey of the facts of the case became larger, she began to think of the anomaly of her finding work in several weeks and his lounging in idleness for a number of months.

"Why don't he get something?" she openly said to herself. "If I can he surely ought to. It wasn't very hard for me."

She forgot her youth and her beauty. The handicap of age she did not, in her enthusiasm, perceive.

Thus, ever, the voice of success.

Still, she could not keep her secret. She tried to be calm and indifferent, but it was a palpable sham.

"Well?" he said, seeing her relieved face.

"I have a place."

"You have?" he said, breathing a better breath.

"Yes."

"What sort of a place is it?" he asked, feeling in his veins as if now he might get something good also.

"In the chorus," she answered.

"Is it the Casino show you told me about?"

"Yes," she answered. "I begin rehearsing tomorrow."

There was more explanation volunteered by Carrie, because she was happy. At last Hurstwood said:

"Do you know how much you'll get?"

"No, I didn't want to ask," said Carrie. "I guess they pay twelve or fourteen dollars a week."

"About that, I guess," said Hurstwood.

There was a good dinner in the flat that evening, owing to the mere lifting of the terrible strain. Hurstwood went out for a shave, and returned with a fair-sized sirloin steak.

"Now, to-morrow," he thought, "I'll look around myself," and with renewed hope he lifted his eyes from the ground.

On the morrow Carrie reported promptly and was given a place in the line. She saw a large, empty, shadowy playhouse, still redolent of the perfumes and blazonry of the night, and notable for its rich, oriental appearance. The wonder of it awed and delighted her. Blessed be its wondrous reality. How hard she would try to be worthy of it. It was above the common mass, above idleness, above want, above insignificance. People came to it in finery and carriages to see. It was ever a center of light and mirth. And here she was of it. Oh, if she could only remain, how happy would be her days!

"What is your name?" said the manager, who was conducting the drill.

"Madenda," she replied, instantly mindful of the name Drouet had selected in Chicago, "Carrie Madenda."

"Well, now, Miss Madenda," he said, very affably, as Carrie thought, "you go over there."

Then he called to a young woman who was already of the company:

"Miss Clark, you pair with Miss Madenda."

This young lady stepped forward, so that Carrie saw where to go, and the rehearsal began.

Carrie soon found that while this drilling had some slight resemblance to the rehearsals as conducted at Avery Hall, the attitude of the manager was much more pronounced. She had marveled at the insistence and superior airs of Mr. Millice, but the individual conducting here had the same insistence, coupled with almost brutal roughness. As the drilling proceeded, he seemed to wax exceedingly wroth over trifles, and to increase his lung power in proportion. It was very evident that he had a great contempt for any assumption of dignity or innocence on the part of these young women.

"Clark," he would call—meaning, of course, Miss Clark—"why don't you catch step there?"

"By fours, right! Right, I said, right! For Heaven's sake, get on to yourself! Right!" and in saying this he would lift the last sounds into a vehement roar.

"Maitland! Maitland!" he called once.

A nervous, comely-dressed little girl stepped out. Carrie trembled for her out of the fulness of her own sympathies and fear.

"Yes, sir," said Miss Maitland.

"Is there anything the matter with your ears?"

"No, sir."

"Do you know what 'column left' means?"

"Yes, sir."

"Well, what are you stumbling around the right for? Want to break up the line?"

"I was just—"

"Never mind what you were just. Keep your ears open."

Carrie pitied, and trembled for her turn.

Yet another suffered the pain of personal rebuke.

"Hold on a minute," cried the manager, throwing up his hands, as if in despair. His demeanor was fierce.

"Elvers," he shouted, "what have you got in your mouth?"

"Nothing," said Miss Elvers, while some smiled and stood nervously by.

"Well, are you talking?"

"No, sir."

"Well, keep your mouth still then. Now, all together again."

At last Carrie's turn came. It was because of her extreme anxiety to do all that was required that brought on the trouble.

She heard some one called.

"Mason," said the voice. "Miss Mason."

She looked around to see who it could be. A girl behind shoved her a little, but she did not understand.

"You, you!" said the manager. "Can't you hear?"

"Oh," said Carrie, collapsing, and blushing fiercely.

"Isn't your name Mason?" asked the manager.

"No, sir," said Carrie, "it's Madenda."

"Well, what's the matter with your feet? Can't you dance?"

"Yes, sir," said Carrie, who had long since learned this art.

"Why don't you do it then? Don't go shuffling along as if you were dead. I've got to have people with life in them."

Carrie's cheek burned with a crimson heat. Her lips trembled a little.

"Yes, sir," she said.

It was this constant urging, coupled with irascibility and energy, for three long hours. Carrie came away worn enough in body, but too excited in mind to notice it. She meant to go home and practice her evolutions as prescribed. She would not err in any way, if she could help it.

When she reached the flat Hurstwood was not there. For a wonder he was out looking for work, as she supposed. She took only a mouthful to eat and then practiced on, sustained by visions of freedom from financial distress—"The sound of glory ringing in her ears."

When Hurstwood returned he was not so elated as when he went away, and now she was obliged to drop practice and get dinner. Here was an early irritation. She would have her work and this. Was she going to act and keep house?

"I'll not do it," she said, "after I get started. He can take his meals out."

Each day thereafter brought its cares. She found it was not such a wonderful thing to be in the chorus, and she also learned that her salary would be twelve dollars a week. After a few days she had her first sight of those high and mighties—the leading ladies and gentlemen. She saw that they were privileged and deferred to. She was nothing—absolutely nothing at all.

At home was Hurstwood, daily giving her cause for thought. He seemed to get nothing to do, and yet he made bold to inquire how she was getting along. The regularity with which he did this smacked of some one who was waiting to live upon her labor. Now that she had a visible means of support, this irritated her. He seemed to be depending upon her little twelve dollars.

"How are you getting along?" he would blandly inquire.

"Oh, all right," she would reply.

"Find it easy?"

"It will be all right when I get used to it."

His paper would then engross his thoughts.

"I got some lard," he would add, as an afterthought. "I thought maybe you might want to make some biscuit."

The calm suggestion of the man astonished her a little, especially in the light of recent developments. Her dawning independence gave her more courage to observe, and she felt as if she wanted to say things. Still she could not talk to him as she had to Drouet. There was something in the man's manner of which she had always stood in awe. He seemed to have some invisible strength in reserve.

One day, after her first week's rehearsal, what she expected came openly to the surface.

"We'll have to be rather saving," he said, laying down some meat he had purchased. "You won't get any money for a week or so yet."

"No," said Carrie, who was stirring a pan at the stove.

"I've only got the rent and thirteen dollars more," he added.

"That's it," she said to herself. "I'm to use my money now."

Instantly she remembered that she had hoped to buy a few things for herself. She needed clothes. Her hat was not nice.

"What will twelve dollars do towards keeping up this flat?" she thought. "I can't do it. Why doesn't he get something to do?"

The important night of the first real performance came. She did not suggest to Hurstwood that he come and see. He did not think of going. It would only be money wasted. She had such a small part.

The advertisements were already in the papers; the posters upon the bill-boards. The leading lady and many members were cited. Carrie was nothing.

As in Chicago, she was seized with stage fright as the very first entrance of the ballet approached, but later she recovered. The apparent and painful insignificance of the part took fear away from her. She felt that she was so obscure it did not matter. Fortunately, she did not have to wear tights. A group of twelve were assigned pretty golden-hued skirts which came only to a line about an inch above the knee. Carrie happened to be one of the twelve.

In standing about the stage, marching, and occasionally lifting up her voice in the general chorus, she had a chance to observe the audience and to see the inauguration of a great hit. There was plenty of applause, but she could not help noting how poorly some of the women of alleged ability did.

"I could do better than that," Carrie ventured to herself, in several instances. To do her justice, she was right.

After it was over she dressed quickly, and as the manager had scolded some others and passed her, she imagined she must have proved satisfactory. She wanted to get out quickly, because she knew but few, and the stars were gossiping. Outside were carriages and some correct youths in attractive clothing, waiting. Carrie saw that she was scanned closely. The flutter of an eyelash would have brought her a companion. That she did not give.

One experienced youth volunteered, anyhow.

"Not going home alone, are you?" he said.

Carrie merely hastened her steps and took the Sixth Avenue car. Her head was so full of the wonder of it that she had time for nothing else.

"Did you hear any more from the brewery?" she asked at the end of the week, hoping by the question to stir him on to action.

"No," he answered, "they're not quite ready yet. I think something will come of that, though."

She said nothing more then, objecting to giving up her own money, and yet feeling that such would have to be the case. Hurstwood felt the crisis, and artfully decided to appeal to Carrie. He had long since realized how good-natured she was, how much she would stand. There was some little shame in him at the thought of doing so, but he justified himself with the thought that he really would get something. Rent day gave him his opportunity.

"Well," he said, as he counted it out, "that's about the last of my money. I'll have to get something pretty soon."

Carrie looked at him askance, half-suspicious of an appeal.

"If I could only hold out a little longer I think I could get something. Drake is sure to open a hotel here in September."

"Is he?" said Carrie, thinking of the short month that still remained until that time.

"Would you mind helping me out until then?" he said appealingly. "I think I'll be all right after that time."

"No," said Carrie, feeling sadly handicapped by fate.

"We can get along if we economize. I'll pay you back all right."

"Oh, I'll help you," said Carrie, feeling quite hard-hearted at thus forcing him to humbly appeal, and yet her desire for the benefit of her earnings wrung a faint protest from her.

"Why don't you take anything, George, temporarily?" she said. "What difference does it make? Maybe, after a while, you'll get something better."

"I will take anything," he said, relieved, and wincing under reproof. "I'd just as leave dig on the streets. Nobody knows me here."

"Oh, you needn't do that," said Carrie, hurt by the pity of it. "But there must be other things."

"I'll get something!" he said, assuming determination.

Then he went back to his paper.

CHAPTER XXXIX

Of Lights and of Shadows: The Parting of Worlds

What Hurstwood got as the result of this determination was more self-assurance that each particular day was not the day. At the same time, Carrie passed through thirty days of mental distress.

Her need of clothes—to say nothing of her desire for ornaments—grew rapidly as the fact developed that for all her work she was not to have them. The sympathy she felt for Hurstwood, at the time he asked her to tide him over, vanished with these newer urgings of decency. He was not always renewing his request, but this love of good appearance was. It insisted, and Carrie wished to satisfy it, wished more and more that Hurstwood was not in the way.

Hurstwood reasoned, when he neared the last ten dollars, that he had better keep a little pocket change and not become wholly dependent for car-fare, shaves, and the like; so when this sum was still in his hand he announced himself as penniless.

"I'm clear out," he said to Carrie one afternoon. "I paid for some coal this morning, and that took all but ten or fifteen cents."

"I've got some money there in my purse."

Hurstwood went to get it, starting for a can of tomatoes. Carrie scarcely noticed that this was the beginning of the new order. He took out fifteen cents and bought the can with it. Thereafter it was dribs and drabs of this sort, until one morning Carrie suddenly remembered that she would not be back until close to dinner time.

"We're all out of flour," she said; "you'd better get some this afternoon. We haven't any meat, either. How would it do if we had liver and bacon?"

"Suits me," said Hurstwood.

"Better get a half or three-quarters of a pound of that."

"Half'll be enough," volunteered Hurstwood.

She opened her purse and laid down a half dollar. He pretended not to notice it.

Hurstwood bought the flour—which all grocers sold in 3½-pound packages—for thirteen cents and paid fifteen cents for a half-pound of liver and bacon. He left the packages, together with the balance of twenty-two cents, upon the kitchen table, where Carrie found it. It did not escape her that the change was accurate. There was something sad in realizing that, after all, all that he wanted of her was something to eat. She felt that hard thoughts were unjust. Maybe he would get something yet. He had no vices.

That very evening, however, on going into the theater, one of the chorus girls passed her all newly arrayed in a pretty mottled tweed suit, which took Carrie's eye. The young woman wore a fine bunch of violets and seemed in high spirits. She smiled at Carrie good-naturedly as she passed, showing pretty, even teeth, and Carrie smiled back.

"She can afford to dress well," thought Carrie, "and so could I, if I could only keep my money. I haven't a decent tie of any kind to wear."

She put out her foot and looked at her shoe reflectively.

"I'll get a pair of shoes Saturday, anyhow; I don't care what happens."

One of the sweetest and most sympathetic little chorus girls in the company made friends with her because in Carrie she found nothing to frighten her away. She was a gay little Manon, unwitting of society's fierce conception of morality, but, nevertheless, good to her neighbor and charitable. Little license was allowed the chorus in the matter of conversation, but, nevertheless, some was indulged in.

"It's warm to-night, isn't it?" said this girl, arrayed in pink fleshings and an imitation golden helmet. She also carried a shining shield.

"Yes, it is," said Carrie, pleased that someone should talk to her.

"I'm almost roasting," said the girl.

Carrie looked into her pretty face, with its large blue eyes, and saw little beads of moisture.

"There's more marching in this opera than ever I did before," added the girl.

"Have you been in others?" asked Carrie, surprised at her experience.

"Lots of them," said the girl; "haven't you?"

"This is my first experience."

"Oh, is it? I thought I saw you the time they ran 'The Queen's Mate' here."

"No," said Carrie, shaking her head; "not me."

This conversation was interrupted by the blare of the orchestra and the sputtering of the calcium lights in the wings as the line was called to form for a new entrance. No further opportunity for conversation occurred, but the next evening, when they were getting ready for the stage, this girl appeared anew at her side.

"They say this show is going on the road next month."

"Is it?" said Carrie.

"Yes; do you think you'll go?"

"I don't know; I guess so, if they'll take me."

"Oh, they'll take you. I wouldn't go. They won't give you any more, and it will cost you everything you make to live. I never leave New York. There are too many shows going on here."

"Can you always get in another show?"

"I always have. There's one going on up at the Broadway this month. I'm going to try and get in that if this one really goes."

Carrie heard this with aroused intelligence. Evidently it wasn't so very difficult to get on. Maybe she also could get a place if this show went away.

"Do they all pay about the same?" she asked.

"Yes. Sometimes you get a little more. This show doesn't pay very much."

"I get twelve," said Carrie.

"Do you?" said the girl. "They pay me fifteen, and you do more work than I do. I wouldn't stand it if I were you. They're just giving you less because they think you don't know. You ought to be making fifteen."

"Well, I'm not," said Carrie.

"Well, you'll get more at the next place if you want it," went on the girl, who admired Carrie very much. "You do fine, and the manager knows it."

To say the truth, Carrie did unconsciously move about with an air pleasing and somewhat distinctive. It was due wholly to her natural manner and total lack of self-consciousness.

"Do you suppose I could get more up at the Broadway?"

"Of course you can," answered the girl. "You come with me when I go. I'll do the talking."

Carrie heard this, flushing with thankfulness. She liked this little gaslight soldier. She seemed so experienced and self-reliant in her tinsel helmet and military accoutrements.

"My future must be assured if I can always get work this way," thought Carrie.

Still, in the morning, when her household duties would infringe upon her and Hurstwood sat there, a perfect load to contemplate, her fate seemed dismal and unrelieved. It did not take so very much to feed them under Hurstwood's close-measured buying, and there would possibly be enough for rent, but it left nothing else. Carrie bought the shoes and some other things, which complicated the rent problem very seriously. Suddenly, a week from the fatal day, Carrie realized that they were going to run short.

"I don't believe," she exclaimed, looking into her purse at breakfast, "that I'll have enough to pay the rent."

"How much have you?" inquired Hurstwood.

"Well, I've got twenty-two dollars, but there's everything to be paid for this week yet, and if I use all I get Saturday to pay this, there won't be any left for next week. Do you think your hotel man will open his hotel this month?"

"I think so," returned Hurstwood. "He said he would."

After a while, Hurstwood said:

"Don't worry about it. Maybe the grocer will wait. He can do that. We've traded there long enough to make him trust us for a week or two."

"Do you think he will?" she asked.

"I think so."

On this account, Hurstwood, this very day, looked grocer Oeslogge clearly in the eye as he ordered a pound of coffee, and said:

"Do you mind carrying my account until the end of every week?"

"No, no, Mr. Wheeler," said Mr. Oeslogge. "Dat iss all right."

Hurstwood, still tactful in distress, added nothing to this. It seemed an easy thing. He looked out of the door, and then gathered up his coffee when ready and came away. The game of a desperate man had begun.

Rent was paid, and now came the grocer. Hurstwood managed by paying out of his own ten and collecting from Carrie at the end of the week. Then he delayed a day next time settling with the grocer, and so soon had his ten back, with Oeslogge getting his pay on this Thursday or Friday for last Saturday's bill.

This entanglement made Carrie anxious for a change of some sort. Hurstwood did not seem to realize that she had a right to anything. He schemed to make what she earned cover all expenses, but seemed not to trouble over adding anything himself.

"He talks about worrying," thought Carrie. "If he worried enough he couldn't sit there and wait for me. He'd get something to do. No man could go seven months without finding something if he tried."

The sight of him always around in his untidy clothes and gloomy appearance drove Carrie to seek relief in other places. Twice a week there were matinees, and then Hurstwood ate a cold snack, which he prepared himself. Two other days there were rehearsals beginning at ten in the morning and lasting usually until one. Now, to this Carrie added a few visits to one or two chorus girls, including the blue-eyed soldier of the golden helmet. She did it because it was pleasant and a relief from dullness of the home over which her husband brooded.

The blue-eyed soldier's name was Osborne—Lola Osborne. Her room was in Nineteenth Street near Fourth Avenue, a block now given up wholly to office buildings. Here she had a comfortable back room, looking over a collection of back yards in which grew a number of shade trees pleasant to see.

"Isn't your home in New York?" she asked of Lola one day.

"Yes; but I can't get along with my people. They always want me to do what they want. Do you live here?"

"Yes," said Carrie.

"With your family?"

Carrie was ashamed to say that she was married. She had talked so much about getting more salary and confessed to so much anxiety about her future, that now, when the direct question of fact was waiting, she could not tell this girl.

"With some relatives," she answered.

Miss Osborne took it for granted that, like herself, Carrie's time was her own. She invariably asked her to stay, proposing little outings and other things of that sort until Carrie began neglecting her dinner hours. Hurstwood noticed it, but felt in no position to quarrel with her. Several times she came so late as scarcely to have an hour in which to patch up a meal and start for the theater.

"Do you rehearse in the afternoons?" Hurstwood once asked, concealing almost completely the cynical protest and regret which prompted it.

"No; I was looking around for another place," said Carrie.

As a matter of fact she was, but only in such a way as furnished the least straw of an excuse. Miss Osborne and she had gone to the office of the manager who was to produce the new opera at the Broadway and returned straight to the former's room, where they had been since three o'clock.

Carrie felt this question to be an infringement on her liberty. She did not take into account how much liberty she was securing. Only the latest step, the newest freedom, must not be questioned.

Hurstwood saw it all clearly enough. He was shrewd after his kind, and yet there was enough decency in the man to stop him from making any effectual protest. In his almost inexplicable apathy he was content to droop supinely while Carrie drifted out of his life, just as he was willing supinely to see opportunity pass beyond his control. He could not help clinging and protesting in a mild, irritating, and ineffectual way, however—a way that simply widened the breach by slow degrees.

A further enlargement of this chasm between them came when the manager, looking between the wings upon the brightly lighted stage where the chorus was going through some of its glittering evolutions, said to the master of the ballet:

"Who is that fourth girl there on the right—the one coming around at the end now?"

"Oh," said the ballet-master, "that's Miss Madenda."

"She's good looking. Why don't you let her head that line?"

"I will," said the man.

"Just do that. She'll look better there than the woman you've got."

"All right. I will do that," said the master.

The next evening Carrie was called out, much as if for an error.

"You lead your company to-night," said the master.

"Yes, sir," said Carrie.

"Put snap into it," he added. "We must have snap."

"Yes, sir," replied Carrie.

Astonished at this change, she thought that the heretofore leader must be ill; but when she saw her in the line, with a distinct expression of something unfavorable in her eye, she began to think that perhaps it was merit.

She had a chic way of tossing her head to one side, and holding her arms as if for action—not listlessly. In front of the line this showed up even more effectually.

"That girl knows how to carry herself," said the manager, another evening. He began to think that he should like to talk with her. If he hadn't made it a rule to have nothing to do with the members of the chorus, he would have approached her most unbendingly.

"Put that girl at the head of the white column," he suggested to the man in charge of the ballet.

This white column consisted of some twenty girls, all in snow-white flannel trimmed with silver and blue. Its leader was most stunningly arrayed in the same colors, elaborated, however, with epaulets and a belt of silver, with a short sword dangling at one side. Carrie was fitted for this costume, and a few days later appeared, proud of her new laurels. She was especially gratified to find that her salary was now eighteen instead of twelve.

Hurstwood heard nothing about this.

"I'll not give him the rest of my money," said Carrie. "I do enough. I am going to get me something to wear."

As a matter of fact, during this second month she had been buying for herself as recklessly as she dared, regardless of the consequences. There were impending more complications rent day, and more extension of the credit system in the neighborhood. Now, however, she proposed to do better by herself.

Her first move was to buy a shirt waist, and in studying these she found how little her money would buy—how much, if she could only use all. She forgot that if she were alone she would have to pay for a room and board, and imagined that every cent of her eighteen could be spent for clothes and things that she liked.

At last she picked upon something, which not only used up all her surplus above twelve, but invaded that sum. She knew she was going too far, but her feminine love of finery prevailed. The next day Hurstwood said:

"We owe the grocer five dollars and forty cents this week."

"Do we?" said Carrie, frowning a little.

She looked in her purse to leave it.

"I've only got eight dollars and twenty cents altogether."

"We owe the milkman sixty cents," added Hurstwood.

"Yes, and there's the coal man," said Carrie.

Hurstwood said nothing. He had seen the new things she was buying; the way she was neglecting household duties; the readiness with which she was slipping out afternoons and staying. He felt that something was going to happen. All at once she spoke:

"I don't know," she said; "I can't do it all. I don't earn enough."

This was a direct challenge. Hurstwood had to take it up. He tried to be calm.

"I don't want you to do it all," he said. "I only want a little help until I can get something to do."

"Oh, yes," answered Carrie. "That's always the way. It takes more than I can earn to pay for things. I don't see what I'm going to do."

"Well, I've tried to get something," he exclaimed. "What do you want me to do?"

"You couldn't have tried so very hard," said Carrie. "I got something."

"Well, I did," he said, angered almost to harsh words. "You needn't throw up your success to me. All I asked was a little help until I could get something. I'm not down yet. I'll come up all right."

He tried to speak steadily, but his voice trembled a little.

Carrie's anger melted on the instant. She felt ashamed.

"Well," she said, "here's the money," and emptied it out on the table. "I haven't got quite enough to pay it all. If they can wait until Saturday, though, I'll have some more."

"You keep it," said Hurstwood, sadly. "I only want enough to pay the grocer."

She put it back, and proceeded to get dinner early and in good time. Her little bravado made her feel as if she ought to make amends.

In a little while their old thoughts returned to both.

"She's making more than she says," thought Hurstwood. "She says she's making twelve, but that wouldn't buy all those things. I don't care. Let her keep her money. I'll get something again one of these days. Then she can go to the deuce."

He only said this in his anger, but it prefigured a possible course of action and attitude well enough.

"I don't care," thought Carrie. "He ought to be told to get out and do something. It isn't right that I should support him."

In these days Carrie was introduced to several youths, friends of Miss Osborne, who were of the kind most aptly described as gay and festive. They called once to get Miss Osborne for an afternoon drive. Carrie was with her at the time.

"Come and go along," said Lola.

"No, I can't," said Carrie.

"Oh, yes, come and go. What have you got to do?"

"I have to be home by five," said Carrie.

"What for?"

"Oh, dinner."

"They'll take us to dinner," said Lola.

"Oh, no," said Carrie. "I won't go. I can't."

"Oh, do come. They're awful nice boys. We'll get you back in time. We're only going for a drive in Central Park."

Carrie thought a while, and at last yielded.

"Now, I must be back by half-past four," she said.

The information went in one ear of Lola and out the other.

After Drouet and Hurstwood, there was the least touch of cynicism in her attitude toward young men—especially of the gay and frivolous sort. She felt a little older than they. Some of their pretty compliments seemed silly. Still, she was young in heart and body and youth appealed to her.

"Oh, we'll be right back, Miss Madenda," said one of the chaps, bowing. "You wouldn't think we'd keep you over time, now, would you?"

"Well, I don't know," said Carrie, smiling.

They were off for a drive—she, looking about and noticing fine clothing, the young men voicing those silly pleasantries and weak quips which pass for humor in coy circles. Carrie saw the great park parade of carriages, beginning at the Fifty-ninth Street entrance and winding past the Museum of Art to the exit at One Hundred and Tenth Street and Seventh Avenue. Her eye was once more taken by the show of wealth—the elaborate costumes, elegant harnesses, spirited horses, and, above all, the beauty. Once more the plague of poverty galled her, but now she forgot in a measure her own troubles so far as to forget Hurstwood. He waited until four, five, and even six. It was getting dark when he got up out of his chair.

"I guess she isn't coming home," he said, grimly.

"That's the way," he thought. "She's getting a start now. I'm out of it."

Carrie had really discovered her neglect, but only at a quarter after five, and the open carriage was now far up Seventh Avenue, near the Harlem River.

"What time is it?" she inquired. "I must be getting back."

"A quarter after five," said her companion, consulting an elegant, open-faced watch.

"Oh, dear me!" exclaimed Carrie. Then she settled back with a sigh. "There's no use crying over spilt milk," she said. "It's too late."

"Of course it is," said the youth, who saw visions of a fine dinner now, and such invigorating talk as would result in a reunion after the show. He was greatly taken with Carrie. "We'll drive down to Delmonico's now and have something there, won't we, Orrin?"

"To be sure," replied Orrin, gaily.

Carrie thought of Hurstwood. Never before had she neglected dinner without an excuse.

They drove back, and at 6:15 sat down to dine. It was the Sherry incident over again, the remembrance of which came painfully back to Carrie. She remembered Mrs. Vance, who had never called again after Hurstwood's reception, and Ames.

At this figure her mind halted. It was a strong, clean vision. He liked better books than she read, better people than she associated with. His ideals burned in her heart.

"It's fine to be a good actress," came distinctly back.

What sort of an actress was she?

"What are you thinking about, Miss Madenda?" inquired her merry companion. "Come, now, let's see if I can guess."

"Oh, no," said Carrie. "Don't try."

She shook it off and ate. She forgot, in part, and was merry.

When it came to the after-theater proposition, however, she shook her head.

"No," she said. "I can't. I have a previous engagement."

"Oh, now, Miss Madenda," pleaded the youth.

"No," said Carrie, "I can't. You've been so kind but you'll have to excuse me."

The youth looked exceedingly crestfallen.

"Cheer up, old man," whispered his companion. "We'll go around, anyhow. She may change her mind."

CHAPTER XL

A Public Dissension: A Final Appeal

There was no after-theater lark, however, so far as Carrie was concerned. She made her way homeward, thinking about her absence. Hurstwood was asleep, but roused up to look as she passed through to her own bed.

"Is that you?" he said.

"Yes," she answered.

The next morning at breakfast she felt like apologizing.

"I couldn't get home last evening," she said.

"Ah, Carrie," he answered, "what's the use saying that? I don't care. You needn't tell me that, though."

"I couldn't," said Carrie, her color rising. Then, seeing that he looked as if he said "I know," she exclaimed: "Oh, all right. I don't care."

From now on, her indifference to the flat was even greater. There seemed no common ground on which they could talk to one another. She let herself be asked for expenses. It became so with him that he hated to do it. He preferred standing off the butcher and baker. He ran up a grocery bill of sixteen dollars with Oeslogge, laying in a supply of staple articles, so that they would not have to buy any of those things for some time to come. Then he changed his grocery. It was the same with the butcher and several others. Carrie never heard anything of this directly from him. He asked for such as he could expect, drifting farther and farther into a situation which could have but one ending.

In this fashion, September went by.

"Isn't Mr. Drake going to open his hotel?" Carrie asked several times.

"Yes. He won't do it before October, though, now."

Carrie became disgusted. "Such a man," she said to herself frequently. More and more she visited. She put most of her spare money in clothes, which, after all, was not an astonishing amount. At last the opera she was with announced its departure within four weeks. "Last two weeks of the Great Comic Opera success—The—," etc., was upon all billboards and in the newspapers, before she acted.

"I'm not going out on the road," said Miss Osborne.

Carrie went with her to apply to another manager.

"Ever had any experience?" was one of his questions.

"I'm with the company at the Casino now."

"Oh, you are?" he said.

The end of this was another engagement at twenty per week.

Carrie was delighted. She began to feel that she had a place in the world. People recognized ability.

So changed was her state that the home atmosphere became intolerable. It was all poverty and trouble there, or seemed to be, because it was a load to bear. It became a place to keep away from. Still she slept there, and did a fair amount of work, keeping it in order. It was a sitting place for Hurstwood. He sat and rocked, rocked and read, enveloped in the gloom of his own fate. October went by, and November. It was the dead of winter almost before he knew it, and there he sat.

Carrie was doing better, that he knew. Her clothes were improved now, even fine. He saw her coming and going, sometimes picturing to himself her rise. Little eating had thinned him somewhat. He had no appetite. His clothes, too, were a poor man's clothes. Talk about getting something had become even too threadbare and ridiculous for him. So he folded his hands and waited—for what, he could not anticipate.

At last, however, troubles became too thick. The hounding of creditors, the indifference of Carrie, the silence of the flat, and presence of winter, all joined to produce a climax. It was effected by the arrival of Oeslogge personally, when Carrie was there.

"I call about my bill," said Mr. Oeslogge.

Carrie was only faintly surprised.

"How much is it?" she asked.

"Sixteen dollars," he replied.

"Oh, that much?" said Carrie. "Is this right?" she asked, turning to Hurstwood.

"Yes," he said.

"Well, I never heard anything about it."

She looked as if she thought he had been contracting some needless expense.

"Well, we had it all right," he answered. Then he went to the door. "I can't pay you anything on that to-day," he said, mildly.

"Well, when can you?" said the grocer.

"Not before Saturday, anyhow." said Hurstwood.

"Huh!" returned the grocer. "This is fine. I must have that. I need the money."

Carrie was standing farther back in the room, hearing it all. She was greatly distressed. It was so bad and commonplace. Hurstwood was annoyed also.

"Well," he said, "there's no use talking about it now. If you'll come in Saturday, I'll pay you something on it."

The grocery man went away.

"How are we going to pay it?" asked Carrie, astonished by the bill. "I can't do it."

"Well, you don't have to," he said. "He can't get what he can't get. He'll have to wait."

"I don't see how we ran up such a bill as that," said Carrie.

"Well, we ate it," said Hurstwood.

"It's funny," she replied, still doubting.

"What's the use of your standing there and talking like that, now?" he asked. "Do you think I've had it alone? You talk as if I'd taken something."

"Well, it's too much, anyhow," said Carrie. "I oughtn't to be made to pay for it. I've got more than I can pay for now."

"All right," replied Hurstwood, sitting down in silence. He was sick of the grind of this thing.

Carrie went out, and there he sat, determining to do something.

There had been appearing in the papers about this time rumors and notices of an approaching strike on the trolley lines in Brooklyn. There was general dissatisfaction as to the hours of labor required and the wages paid. As usual—and for some inexplicable reason—the men chose the winter for the forcing of the hand of their employers and the settlement of their difficulties.

Hurstwood had been reading of this thing, and wondering concerning the huge tie-up which would follow. A day or two before this trouble with Carrie, it came. On a cold afternoon, when everything was gray and it threatened to snow, the papers announced that the men had been called out on all the lines.

Being so utterly idle, and his mind filled with the numerous predictions which had been made concerning the scarcity of labor this winter and the panicky state of the financial market, Hurstwood read this with interest. He noted the claims of the striking motormen and conductors, who said that they had been wont to receive two dollars a day in times past, but that for a year or more "trippers" had been introduced, which cut down their chance of livelihood one-half, and increased their hours of servitude from ten to twelve, and even fourteen. These "trippers" were men put on during the busy and rush hours, to take a car out for one trip. The compensation paid for such a trip was only twenty-five cents. When the rush or busy hours were over, they were laid off. Worst of all, no man might know when he was going to get a car. He must come to the barns in the morning and wait around in fair and foul weather until such time as he was needed. Two trips were an average reward for so much waiting—a little over three hours' work for fifty cents. The work of waiting was not counted.

The men complained that this system was extending, and that the time was not far off when but a few out of 7,000 employees would have regular two-dollar-a-day work at all. They demanded that the system be abolished, and that ten hours be considered a day's work, barring unavoidable delays, with $2.25 pay. They demanded immediate acceptance of these terms, which the various trolley companies refused.

Hurstwood at first sympathized with the demands of these men—indeed, it is a question whether he did not always sympathize with them to the end, belie him as his actions might. Reading nearly all the news, he was attracted first by the scare-heads with which the trouble was noted in the "World." He read it fully—the names of the seven companies involved, the number of men.

"They're foolish to strike in this sort of weather," he thought to himself. "Let 'em win if they can, though."

The next day there was even a larger notice of it. "Brooklynites Walk," said the "World." "Knights of Labor Tie up the Trolley Lines Across the Bridge." "About Seven Thousand Men Out."

Hurstwood read this, formulating to himself his own idea of what would be the outcome. He was a great believer in the strength of corporations.

"They can't win," he said, concerning the men. "They haven't any money. The police will protect the companies. They've got to. The public has to have its cars."

He didn't sympathize with the corporations, but strength was with them. So was property and public utility.

"Those fellows can't win," he thought.

Among other things, he noticed a circular issued by one of the companies, which read:

ATLANTIC AVENUE RAILROAD.

SPECIAL NOTICE.

The motormen and conductors and other employees of this company having abruptly left its service, an opportunity is now given to all loyal men who have struck against their will to be reinstated, providing they will make their applications by twelve o'clock noon on Wednesday, January 16th. Such men will be given employment (with guaranteed protection) in the order in which such applications are received, and runs and positions assigned them accordingly. Otherwise, they will be considered discharged, and every vacancy will be filled by a new man as soon as his services can be secured.

(Signed)
BENJAMIN NORTON,
President,

He also noted among the want ads, one which read:

WANTED.—50 skilled motormen, accustomed to Westinghouse system, to run U. S. mail cars only, in the City of Brooklyn; protection guaranteed.

He noted particularly in each the "protection guaranteed." It signified to him the unassailable power of the companies.

"They've got the militia on their side," he thought. "There isn't anything those men can do."

While this was still in his mind, the incident with Oeslogge and Carrie occurred. There had been a good deal to irritate him, but this seemed much the worst. Never before had she accused him of stealing—or very near that. She doubted the naturalness of so large a bill. And he had worked so hard to make expenses seem light. He had been "doing" butcher and baker in order not to call on her. He had eaten very little—almost nothing.

"Damn it all!" he said. "I can get something. I'm not down yet."

He thought that he really must do something now. It was too cheap to sit around after such an insinuation as this. Why, after a little, he would be standing anything.

He got up and looked out the window into the chilly street. It came gradually into his mind, as he stood there, to go to Brooklyn.

"Why not?" his mind said. "Any one can get work over there. You'll get two a day."

"How about accidents?" said a voice. "You might get hurt."

"Oh, there won't be much of that," he answered. "They've called out the police. Any one who wants to run a car will be protected all right."

"You don't know how to run a car," rejoined the voice.

"I won't apply as a motorman," he answered. "I can ring up fares all right."

"They'll want motormen mostly."

"They'll take anybody; that I know."

For several hours he argued pro and con with this mental counselor, feeling no need to act at once in a matter so sure of profit.

In the morning he put on his best clothes, which were poor enough, and began stirring about, putting some bread and meat into a page of a newspaper. Carrie watched him, interested in this new move.

"Where are you going?" she asked.

"Over to Brooklyn," he answered. Then, seeing her still inquisitive, he added: "I think I can get on over there."

"On the trolley lines?" said Carrie, astonished.

"Yes," he rejoined.

"Aren't you afraid?" she asked.

"What of?" he answered. "The police are protecting them."

"The paper said four men were hurt yesterday."

"Yes," he returned; "but you can't go by what the papers say. They'll run the cars all right."

He looked rather determined now, in a desolate sort of way, and Carrie felt very sorry. Something of the old Hurstwood was here—the least shadow of what was once shrewd and pleasant strength. Outside, it was cloudy and blowing a few flakes of snow.

"What a day to go over there," thought Carrie.

Now he left before she did, which was a remarkable thing, and tramped eastward to Fourteenth Street and Sixth Avenue, where he took the car. He had read that scores of applicants were applying at the office of the Brooklyn City Railroad building and were being received. He made his way there by horse-car and ferry—a dark, silent man—to the offices in question. It was a long way, for no cars were running, and the day was cold; but he trudged along grimly. Once in Brooklyn, he could clearly see and feel that a strike was on. People showed it in their manner. Along the routes of certain tracks not a car was running. About certain corners and nearby saloons small groups of men were lounging. Several spring wagons passed him, equipped with plain wooden chairs, and labeled "Flatbush" or "Prospect

Park. Fare, Ten Cents." He noticed cold and even gloomy faces. Labor was having its little war.

When he came near the office in question, he saw a few men standing about, and some policemen. On the far corners were other men—whom he took to be strikers—watching. All the houses were small and wooden, the streets poorly paved. After New York, Brooklyn looked actually poor and hard-up.

He made his way into the heart of the small group, eyed by policemen and the men already there. One of the officers addressed him.

"What are you looking for?"

"I want to see if I can get a place."

"The offices are up those steps," said the bluecoat. His face was a very neutral thing to contemplate. In his heart of hearts, he sympathized with the strikers and hated this "scab." In his heart of hearts, also, he felt the dignity and use of the police force, which commanded order. Of its true social significance, he never once dreamed. His was not the mind for that. The two feelings blended in him—neutralized one another and him. He would have fought for this man as determinedly as for himself, and yet only so far as commanded. Strip him of his uniform, and he would have soon picked his side.

Hurstwood ascended a dusty flight of steps and entered a small, dust-colored office, in which were a railing, a long desk, and several clerks.

"Well, sir?" said a middle-aged man, looking up at him from the long desk.

"Do you want to hire any men?" inquired Hurstwood.

"What are you—a motorman?"

"No; I'm not anything," said Hurstwood.

He was not at all abashed by his position. He knew these people needed men. If one didn't take him, another would. This man could take him or leave him, just as he chose.

"Well, we prefer experienced men, of course," said the man. He paused, while Hurstwood smiled indifferently. Then he added: "Still, I guess you can learn. What is your name?"

"Wheeler," said Hurstwood.

The man wrote an order on a small card. "Take that to our barns," he said, "and give it to the foreman. He'll show you what to do."

Hurstwood went down and out. He walked straight away in the direction indicated, while the policemen looked after.

"There's another wants to try it," said Officer Kiely to Officer Macey.

"I have my mind he'll get his fill," returned the latter, quietly.

They had been in strikes before.

CHAPTER XLI

The Strike

The barn at which Hurstwood applied was exceedingly short-handed, and was being operated practically by three men as directors. There were a lot of green hands around—queer, hungry-looking men, who looked as if want had driven them to desperate means. They tried to be lively and willing, but there was an air of hang-dog diffidence about the place.

Hurstwood went back through the barns and out into a large, enclosed lot, where were a series of tracks and loops. A half-dozen cars were there, manned by instructors, each with a pupil at the lever. More pupils were waiting at one of the rear doors of the barn.

In silence Hurstwood viewed this scene, and waited. His companions took his eye for a while, though they did not interest him much more than the cars. They were an uncomfortable-looking gang, however. One or two were very thin and lean. Several were quite stout. Several others were raw-boned and sallow, as if they had been beaten upon by all sorts of rough weather.

"Did you see by the paper they are going to call out the militia?" Hurstwood heard one of them remark.

"Oh, they'll do that," returned the other. "They always do."

"Think we're liable to have much trouble?" said another, whom Hurstwood did not see.

"Not very."

"That Scotchman that went out on the last car," put in a voice, "told me that they hit him in the ear with a cinder."

A small, nervous laugh accompanied this.

"One of those fellows on the Fifth Avenue line must have had a hell of a time, according to the papers," drawled another. "They broke his car windows and pulled him off into the street 'fore the police could stop 'em."

"Yes; but there are more police around to-day," was added by another.

Hurstwood hearkened without much mental comment. These talkers seemed scared to him. Their gabbling was feverish—things said to quiet their own minds. He looked out into the yard and waited.

Two of the men got around quite near him, but behind his back. They were rather social, and he listened to what they said.

"Are you a railroad man?" said one.

"Me? No. I've always worked in a paper factory."

"I had a job in Newark until last October," returned the other, with reciprocal feeling.

There were some words which passed too low to hear. Then the conversation became strong again.

"I don't blame these fellers for striking," said one. "They've got the right of it, all right, but I had to get something to do."

"Same here," said the other. "If I had any job in Newark I wouldn't be over here takin' chances like these."

"It's hell these days, ain't it?" said the man. "A poor man ain't nowhere. You could starve, by God, right in the streets, and there ain't most no one would help you."

"Right you are," said the other. "The job I had I lost 'cause they shut down. They run all summer and lay up a big stock, and then shut down."

Hurstwood paid some little attention to this. Somehow, he felt a little superior to these two—a little better off. To him these were ignorant and commonplace, poor sheep in a driver's hand.

"Poor devils," he thought, speaking out of the thoughts and feelings of a bygone period of success.

"Next," said one of the instructors.

"You're next," said a neighbor, touching him.

He went out and climbed on the platform. The instructor took it for granted that no preliminaries were needed.

"You see this handle," he said, reaching up to an electric cut-off, which was fastened to the roof. "This throws the current off or on. If you want to reverse the car you turn it over here. If you want to send it forward, you put it over here. If you want to cut off the power, you keep it in the middle."

Hurstwood smiled at the simple information.

"Now, this handle here regulates your speed. To here," he said, pointing with his finger, "gives you about four miles an hour. This is eight. When it's full on, you make about fourteen miles an hour."

Hurstwood watched him calmly. He had seen motormen work before. He knew just about how they did it, and was sure he could do as well, with a very little practice.

The instructor explained a few more details, and then said:

"Now, we'll back her up."

Hurstwood stood placidly by, while the car rolled back into the yard.

"One thing you want to be careful about, and that is to start easy. Give one degree time to act before you start another. The one fault of most men is that they always want to throw her wide open. That's bad. It's dangerous, too. Wears out the motor. You don't want to do that."

"I see," said Hurstwood.

He waited and waited, while the man talked on.

"Now you take it," he said, finally.

The ex-manager laid hand to the lever and pushed it gently, as he thought. It worked much easier than he imagined, however, with the result that the car jerked quickly forward, throwing him back against the door. He straightened up sheepishly, while the instructor stopped the car with the brake.

"You want to be careful about that," was all he said.

Hurstwood found, however, that handling a brake and regulating speed were not so instantly mastered as he had imagined. Once or twice he would have ploughed through the rear fence if it had not been for the hand and word of his companion. The latter was rather patient with him, but he never smiled.

"You've got to get the knack of working both arms at once," he said. "It takes a little practice."

One o'clock came while he was still on the car practicing, and he began to feel hungry. The day set in snowing, and he was cold. He grew weary of running to and fro on the short track.

They ran the car to the end and both got off. Hurstwood went into the barn and sought a car step, pulling out his paper-wrapped lunch from his pocket. There was no water and the bread was dry, but he enjoyed it. There was no ceremony about dining. He swallowed and looked about, contemplating the dull, homely labor of the thing. It was disagreeable—miserably disagreeable—in all its phases. Not because it was bitter, but because it was hard. It would be hard to any one, he thought.

After eating, he stood about as before, waiting until his turn came.

The intention was to give him an afternoon of practice, but the greater part of the time was spent in waiting about.

At last evening came, and with it hunger and a debate with himself as to how he should spend the night. It was half-past five. He must soon eat. If he tried to go home, it would take him two hours and a half of cold walking and riding. Besides, he had orders to report at seven the next morning, and going home would necessitate his rising at an unholy and disagreeable hour. He had only something like a dollar and fifteen cents of Carrie's money, with which he had intended to pay the two weeks' coal bill before the present idea struck him.

"They must have some place around here," he thought. "Where does that fellow from Newark stay?"

Finally he decided to ask. There was a young fellow standing near one of the doors in the cold, waiting a last turn. He was a mere boy in years—twenty-one about—but with a body lank and long, because of privation. A little good living would have made this youth plump and swaggering.

"How do they arrange this, if a man hasn't any money?" inquired Hurstwood, discreetly.

The fellow turned a keen, watchful face on the inquirer.

"You mean eat?" he replied.

"Yes, and sleep. I can't go back to New York tonight."

"The foreman'll fix that if you ask him, I guess. He did me."

"That so?"

"Yes. I just told him I didn't have anything. Gee, I couldn't go home. I live way over in Hoboken."

Hurstwood only cleared his throat by way of acknowledgment.

"They've got a place upstairs here, I understand. I don't know what sort of a thing it is. Purty tough, I guess. He gave me a meal ticket this noon. I know that wasn't much."

Hurstwood smiled grimly, and the boy laughed.

"It ain't no fun, is it?" he inquired, wishing vainly for a cheery reply.

"Not much," answered Hurstwood.

"I'd tackle him now," volunteered the youth. "He may go 'way."

Hurstwood did so.

"Isn't there some place I can stay around here to-night?" he inquired. "If I have to go back to New York, I'm afraid I won't—"

"There're some cots upstairs," interrupted the man, "if you want one of them."

"That'll do," he assented.

He meant to ask for a meal ticket, but the seemingly proper moment never came, and he decided to pay himself that night.

"I'll ask him in the morning."

He ate in a cheap restaurant in the vicinity, and, being cold and lonely, went straight off to seek the loft in question. The company was not attempting to run cars after nightfall. It was so advised by the police.

The room seemed to have been a lounging place for night workers. There were some nine cots in the place, two or three wooden chairs, a soap box, and a small, round-bellied stove, in which a fire was blazing. Early as he was, another man was there before him. The latter was sitting beside the stove warming his hands.

Hurstwood approached and held out his own toward the fire. He was sick of the bareness and privation of all things connected with his venture, but was steeling himself to hold out. He fancied he could for a while.

"Cold, isn't it?" said the early guest.

"Rather."

A long silence.

"Not much of a place to sleep in, is it?" said the man.

"Better than nothing," replied Hurstwood.

Another silence.

"I believe I'll turn in," said the man.

Rising, he went to one of the cots and stretched himself, removing only his shoes, and pulling the one blanket and dirty old comforter over him in a sort of bundle. The sight disgusted Hurstwood, but he did not dwell on it, choosing to gaze into the stove and think of something else. Presently he decided to retire, and picked a cot, also removing his shoes.

While he was doing so, the youth who had advised him to come here entered, and, seeing Hurstwood, tried to be genial.

"Better'n nothin'," he observed, looking around.

Hurstwood did not take this to himself. He thought it to be an expression of individual satisfaction, and so did not answer. The youth imagined he was out of sorts, and set to whistling softly. Seeing another man asleep, he quit that and lapsed into silence.

Hurstwood made the best of a bad lot by keeping on his clothes and pushing away the dirty covering from his head, but at last he dozed in sheer weariness. The covering became more and more comfortable, its character was forgotten, and he pulled it about his neck and slept.

In the morning he was aroused out of a pleasant dream by several men stirring about in the cold, cheerless room. He had been back in Chicago in fancy, in his own comfortable home. Jessica had been arranging to go somewhere, and he had been talking with her about it. This was so clear in his mind, that he was startled now by the contrast of this room. He raised his head, and the cold, bitter reality jarred him into wakefulness.

"Guess I'd better get up," he said.

There was no water on this floor. He put on his shoes in the cold and stood up, shaking himself in his stiffness. His clothes felt disagreeable, his hair bad.

"Hell!" he muttered, as he put on his hat.

Downstairs things were stirring again.

He found a hydrant, with a trough which had once been used for horses, but there was no towel here, and his handkerchief was soiled from yesterday. He contented himself with wetting his eyes with the ice-cold water. Then he sought the foreman, who was already on the ground.

"Had your breakfast yet?" inquired that worthy.

"No," said Hurstwood.

"Better get it, then; your car won't be ready for a little while."

Hurstwood hesitated.

"Could you let me have a meal ticket?" he asked with an effort.

"Here you are," said the man, handing him one.

He breakfasted as poorly as the night before on some fried steak and bad coffee. Then he went back.

"Here," said the foreman, motioning him, when he came in. "You take this car out in a few minutes."

Hurstwood climbed up on the platform in the gloomy barn and waited for a signal. He was nervous, and yet the thing was a relief. Anything was better than the barn.

On this the fourth day of the strike, the situation had taken a turn for the worse. The strikers, following the counsel of their leaders and the newspapers, had struggled peaceably enough. There had been no great violence done. Cars had been stopped, it is true, and the men argued with. Some crews had been won over and led away, some windows broken, some jeering and yelling done; but in no more than five or six instances had men been seriously injured. These by crowds whose acts the leaders disclaimed.

Idleness, however, and the sight of the company, backed by the police, triumphing, angered the men. They saw that each day more cars were going on, each day more declarations were being made by the company officials that the effective opposition of the strikers was broken. This put desperate thoughts in the minds of the men. Peaceful methods meant, they saw, that the companies would soon run all their cars and those who had complained would be forgotten. There was nothing so helpful to the companies as peaceful methods.

All at once they blazed forth, and for a week there was storm and stress. Cars were assailed, men attacked, policemen struggled with, tracks torn up, and shots fired, until at last street fights and mob movements became frequent, and the city was invested with militia.

Hurstwood knew nothing of the change of temper.

"Run your car out," called the foreman, waving a vigorous hand at him. A green conductor jumped up behind and rang the bell twice as a signal to start. Hurstwood turned the lever and ran the car out through the door into the street in front of the barn. Here two brawny policemen got up beside him on the platform—one on either hand.

At the sound of a gong near the barn door, two bells were given by the conductor and Hurstwood opened his lever.

The two policemen looked about them calmly.

"'Tis cold, all right, this morning," said the one on the left, who possessed a rich brogue.

"I had enough of it yesterday," said the other. "I wouldn't want a steady job of this."

"Nor I."

Neither paid the slightest attention to Hurstwood, who stood facing the cold wind, which was chilling him completely, and thinking of his orders.

"Keep a steady gait," the foreman had said. "Don't stop for any one who doesn't look like a real passenger. Whatever you do, don't stop for a crowd."

The two officers kept silent for a few moments.

"The last man must have gone through all right," said the officer on the left. "I don't see his car anywhere."

"Who's on there?" asked the second officer, referring, of course, to its complement of policemen.

"Schaeffer and Ryan."

There was another silence, in which the car ran smoothly along. There were not so many houses along this part of the way. Hurstwood did not see many people either. The situation was not wholly disagreeable to him. If he were not so cold, he thought he would do well enough.

He was brought out of this feeling by the sudden appearance of a curve ahead, which he had not expected. He shut off the current and did an energetic turn at the brake, but not in time to avoid an unnaturally quick turn. It shook him up and made him feel like making some apologetic remarks, but he refrained.

"You want to look out for them things," said the officer on the left, condescendingly.

"That's right," agreed Hurstwood, shamefacedly.

"There's lots of them on this line," said the officer on the right.

Around the corner a more populated way appeared. One or two pedestrians were in view ahead. A boy coming out of a gate with a tin milk bucket gave Hurstwood his first objectionable greeting.

"Scab!" he yelled. "Scab!"

Hurstwood heard it, but tried to make no comment, even to himself. He knew he would get that, and much more of the same sort, probably.

At a corner farther up a man stood by the track and signaled the car to stop.

"Never mind him," said one of the officers. "He's up to some game."

Hurstwood obeyed. At the corner he saw the wisdom of it. No sooner did the man perceive the intention to ignore him, than he shook his fist.

"Ah, you bloody coward!" he yelled.

Some half dozen men, standing on the corner, flung taunts and jeers after the speeding car.

Hurstwood winced the least bit. The real thing was slightly worse than the thoughts of it had been.

Now came in sight, three or four blocks farther on, a heap of something on the track.

"They've been at work, here, all right," said one of the policemen.

"We'll have an argument, maybe," said the other.

Hurstwood ran the car close and stopped. He had not done so wholly, however, before a crowd gathered about. It was composed of ex-motormen and conductors in part, with a sprinkling of friends and sympathizers.

"Come off the car, pardner," said one of the men in a voice meant to be conciliatory. "You don't want to take the bread out of another man's mouth, do you?"

Hurstwood held to his brake and lever, pale and very uncertain what to do.

"Stand back," yelled one of the officers, leaning over the platform railing. "Clear out of this, now. Give the man a chance to do his work."

"Listen, pardner," said the leader, ignoring the policeman and addressing Hurstwood. "We're all working men, like yourself. If you were a regular motorman, and had been treated as we've been, you wouldn't want any one to come in and take your place, would you? You wouldn't want any one to do you out of your chance to get your rights, would you?"

"Shut her off! shut her off!" urged the other of the policemen, roughly. "Get out of this, now," and he jumped the railing and landed before the crowd and began shoving. Instantly the other officer was down beside him.

"Stand back, now," they yelled. "Get out of this. What the hell do you mean? Out, now."

It was like a small swarm of bees.

"Don't shove me," said one the strikers, determinedly. "I'm not doing anything."

"Get out of this!" cried the officer, swinging his club. "I'll give ye a bat on the sconce. Back, now."

"What the hell!" cried another of the strikers, pushing the other way, adding at the same time some lusty oaths.

Crack came an officer's club on his forehead. He blinked his eyes blindly a few times, wabbled on his legs, threw up his hands, and staggered back. In return, a swift fist landed on the officer's neck.

Infuriated by this, the latter plunged left and right, laying about madly with his club. He was ably assisted by his brother of the blue, who poured ponderous oaths upon the troubled waters. No severe damage was done, owing to the agility of the strikers in keeping out of reach. They stood about the sidewalk now and jeered.

"Where is the conductor?" yelled one of the officers, getting his eye on that individual, who had come nervously forward to stand by Hurstwood. The latter had stood gazing upon the scene with more astonishment than fear.

"Why don't you come down here and get these stones off the track?" inquired the officer. "What you standing there for? Do you want to stay here all day? Get down."

Hurstwood breathed heavily in excitement and jumped down with the nervous conductor as if he had been called.

"Hurry up, now," said the other policeman.

Cold as it was, these officers were hot and mad. Hurstwood worked with the conductor, lifting stone after stone and warming himself by the work.

"Ah, you scab, you!" yelled the crowd. "You coward! Steal a man's job, will you? Rob the poor, will you, you thief. We'll get you yet, now. Wait."

Not all of this was delivered by one man. It came from here and there, incorporated with much more of the same sort and curses.

"Work, you blackguards," yelled a voice. "Do the dirty work. You're the suckers that keep the poor people down!"

"May God starve ye yet," yelled an old Irish woman, who now threw open a nearby window and stuck out her head.

"Yes, and you," she added, catching the eye of one of the policemen. "You bloody, murtherin' thafe! Crack my son over the head, will you, you hardhearted, murtherin' devil? Ah, ye—"

But the officer turned a deaf ear.

"Go to the devil, you old hag," he half muttered as he stared round upon the scattered company.

Now the stones were off, and Hurstwood took his place again amid a continued chorus of epithets. Both officers got up beside him and the conductor rang the bell, when, bang! bang! through window and door came rocks and stones. One narrowly grazed Hurstwood's head. Another shattered the window behind.

"Throw open your lever," yelled one of the officers, grabbing at the handle himself.

Hurstwood complied and the car shot away, followed by a rattle of stones and a rain of curses.

"That ——— hit me in the neck," said one of the officers. "I gave him a good crack for it, though."

"I think I must have left spots on some of them," said the other.

"I know that big guy that called us a ———," said the first. "I'll get him yet for that."

"I thought we were in for it sure, once there," said the second.

Hurstwood, warmed and excited, gazed steadily ahead. It was an astonishing experience for him. He had read of these things, but the reality seemed something altogether new. He was no coward in spirit. The fact that he had suffered this much now rather operated to arouse a stolid determination to stick it out. He did not recur in thought to New York or the flat. This one trip seemed a consuming thing.

They now ran into the business heart of Brooklyn uninterrupted. People gazed at the broken windows of the car and at Hurstwood in his plain clothes. Voices called "scab" now and then, as well as other epithets, but no crowd attacked the car. At the downtown end of the line, one of the officers went to call up his station and report the trouble.

"There's a gang out there," he said, "laying for us yet. Better send some one over there and clean them out."

The car ran back more quietly—hooted, watched, flung at, but not attacked. Hurstwood breathed freely when he saw the barns.

"Well," he observed to himself, "I came out of that all right."

The car was turned in and he was allowed to loaf a while, but later he was again called. This time a new team of officers was aboard. Slightly more confident, he sped the car along the commonplace streets and felt somewhat less fearful. On one side, however, he suffered intensely. The day was raw, with a sprinkling of snow and a gusty wind, made all the more intolerable by the speed of the car. His clothing was not intended for this sort of work. He shivered, stamped his feet, and beat his arms as he had seen other motormen do in the past, but said nothing. The novelty and danger of the situation modified in a way his disgust and distress at being compelled to be here, but not enough to prevent him from feeling grim and sour. This was a dog's life, he thought. It was a tough thing to have to come to.

The one thought that strengthened him was the insult offered by Carrie. He was not down so low as to take all that, he thought. He could do something—this, even—for a while. It would get better. He would save a little.

A boy threw a clod of mud while he was thus reflecting and hit him upon the arm. It hurt sharply and angered him more than he had been any time since morning.

"The little cur!" he muttered.

"Hurt you?" asked one of the policemen.

"No," he answered.

At one of the corners, where the car slowed up because of a turn, an ex-motorman, standing on the sidewalk, called to him:

"Won't you come out, pardner, and be a man? Remember we're fighting for a decent day's wages, that's all. We've got families to support." The man seemed most peaceably inclined.

Hurstwood pretended not to see him. He kept his eyes straight on before and opened the lever wide. The voice had something appealing in it.

All morning this went on and long into the afternoon. He made three such trips. The dinner he had was no stay for such work and the cold was telling on him. At each end of the line he stopped to thaw out, but he could have groaned at the anguish of it. One of the barnmen, out of pity, loaned him a heavy cap and a pair of sheepskin gloves, and for once he was extremely thankful.

On the second trip of the afternoon he ran into a crowd about half way along the line, that had blocked the car's progress with an old telegraph pole.

"Get that thing off the track," shouted the two policemen.

"Yah, yah, yah!" yelled the crowd. "Get it off yourself."

The two policemen got down and Hurstwood started to follow.

"You stay there," one called. "Some one will run away with your car."

Amid the babel of voices, Hurstwood heard one close beside him.

"Come down, pardner, and be a man. Don't fight the poor. Leave that to the corporations."

He saw the same fellow who had called to him from the corner. Now, as before, he pretended not to hear him.

"Come down," the man repeated gently. "You don't want to fight poor men. Don't fight at all." It was a most philosophic and jesuitical motorman.

A third policeman joined the other two from somewhere and someone ran to telephone for more officers. Hurstwood gazed about, determined but fearful.

A man grabbed him by the coat.

"Come off of that," he exclaimed, jerking at him and trying to pull him over the railing.

"Let go," said Hurstwood, savagely.

"I'll show you—you scab!" cried a young Irishman, jumping up on the car and aiming a blow at Hurstwood. The latter ducked and caught it on the shoulder instead of the jaw.

"Away from here," shouted an officer, hastening to the rescue, and adding, of course, the usual oaths.

Hurstwood recovered himself, pale and trembling. It was becoming serious with him now. People were looking up and jeering at him. One girl was making faces.

He began to waver in his resolution, when a patrol wagon rolled up and more officers dismounted. Now the track was quickly cleared and the release effected.

"Let her go now, quick," said the officer, and again he was off.

The end came with a real mob, which met the car on its return trip a mile or two from the barns. It was an exceedingly poor-looking neighborhood. He wanted to run fast through it, but again the track was blocked. He saw men carrying something out to it when he was yet a half-dozen blocks away.

"There they are again!" exclaimed one policeman.

"I'll give them something this time," said the second officer, whose patience was becoming worn. Hurstwood suffered a qualm of body as the car rolled up. As before, the crowd began hooting, but now, rather than come near, they threw things. One or two windows were smashed and Hurstwood dodged a stone.

Both policemen ran out toward the crowd, but the latter replied by running toward the car. A woman—a mere girl in appearance—was among these, bearing a rough stick. She was exceedingly wrathful and struck at Hurstwood, who dodged. Thereupon, her companions, duly encouraged, jumped on the car and pulled Hurstwood over. He had hardly time to speak or shout before he fell.

"Let go of me," he said, falling on his side.

"Ah, you sucker," he heard someone say. Kicks and blows rained on him. He seemed to be suffocating. Then two men seemed to be dragging him off and he wrestled for freedom.

"Let up," said a voice, "you're all right. Stand up."

He was let loose and recovered himself. Now he recognized two officers. He felt as if he would faint from exhaustion. Something was wet on his chin. He put up his hand and felt, then looked. It was red.

"They cut me," he said, foolishly, fishing for his handkerchief.

"Now, now," said one of the officers. "It's only a scratch."

His senses became cleared now and he looked around. He was standing in a little store, where they left him for the moment. Outside, he could see, as he stood wiping his chin, the car and the excited crowd. A patrol wagon was there, and another.

He walked over and looked out. It was an ambulance, backing in.

He saw some energetic charging by the police and arrests being made.

"Come on, now, if you want to take your car," said an officer, opening the door and looking in.

He walked out, feeling rather uncertain of himself. He was very cold and frightened.

"Where's the conductor?" he asked.

"Oh, he's not here now," said the policeman.

Hurstwood went toward the car and stepped nervously on. As he did so there was a pistol shot. Something stung his shoulder.

"Who fired that?" he heard an officer exclaim. "By God! who did that?" Both left him, running toward a certain building. He paused a moment and then got down.

"George!" exclaimed Hurstwood, weakly, "this is too much for me."

He walked nervously to the corner and hurried down a side street.

"Whew!" he said, drawing in his breath.

A half block away, a small girl gazed at him.

"You'd better sneak," she called.

He walked homeward in a blinding snowstorm, reaching the ferry by dusk. The cabins were filled with comfortable souls, who studied him curiously. His head was still in such a whirl that he felt confused. All the wonder of the twinkling lights of the river in a white storm passed for nothing. He trudged doggedly on until he reached the flat. There he entered and found the room warm. Carrie was gone. A couple of evening papers were lying on the table where she left them. He lit the gas and sat down. Then he got up and stripped to examine his shoulder. It was a mere scratch. He washed his hands and face, still in a brown study, apparently, and combed his hair. Then he looked for something to eat, and finally, his hunger gone, sat down in his comfortable rocking-chair. It was a wonderful relief.

He put his hand to his chin, forgetting, for the moment, the papers.

"Well," he said, after a time, his nature recovering itself, "that's a pretty tough game over there."

Then he turned and saw the papers. With half a sigh he picked up the "World."

"Strike Spreading in Brooklyn," he read. "Rioting Breaks Out in all Parts of the City."

He adjusted his paper very comfortably and continued. It was the one thing he read with absorbing interest.

CHAPTER XLII

A TOUCH OF SPRING: THE EMPTY SHELL

Those who look upon Hurstwood's Brooklyn venture as an error of judgment will nonetheless realize the negative influence on him of the fact that he had tried and failed. Carrie got a wrong idea of it. He said so little that she imagined he had encountered nothing worse than the ordinary roughness—quitting so soon in the face of this seemed trifling. He did not want to work.

She was now one of a group of oriental beauties who, in the second act of the comic opera, were paraded by the vizier before the new potentate as the treasures of his harem. There was no word assigned to any of them, but on the evening when Hurstwood was housing himself in the loft of the street-car barn, the leading comedian and star, feeling exceedingly facetious, said in a profound voice, which created a ripple of laughter:

"Well, who are you?"

It merely happened to be Carrie who was curtsying before him. It might as well have been any of the others, so far as he was concerned. He expected no answer and a dull one would have been reproved. But Carrie, whose experience and belief in herself gave her daring, curtsied sweetly again and answered:

"I am yours truly."

It was a trivial thing to say, and yet something in the way she did it caught the audience, which laughed heartily at the mock-fierce potentate towering before the young woman. The comedian also liked it, hearing the laughter.

"I thought your name was Smith," he returned, endeavoring to get the last laugh.

Carrie almost trembled for her daring after she had said this. All members of the company had been warned that to interpolate lines or "business" meant a fine or worse. She did not know what to think.

As she was standing in her proper position in the wings, awaiting another entry, the great comedian made his exit past her and paused in recognition.

"You can just leave that in hereafter," he remarked, seeing how intelligent she appeared. "Don't add any more, though."

"Thank you," said Carrie, humbly. When he went on she found herself trembling violently.

"Well, you're in luck," remarked another member of the chorus. "There isn't another one of us has got a line."

There was no gainsaying the value of this. Everybody in the company realized that she had got a start. Carrie hugged herself when next evening the lines got the same applause. She went home rejoicing, knowing that soon something must come of it. It was Hurstwood who, by his presence, caused her merry thoughts to flee and replaced them with sharp longings for an end of distress.

The next day she asked him about his venture.

"They're not trying to run any cars except with police. They don't want anybody just now—not before next week."

Next week came, but Carrie saw no change. Hurstwood seemed more apathetic than ever. He saw her off mornings to rehearsals and the like with the utmost calm. He read and read. Several times he found himself staring at an item, but thinking of something else. The first of these lapses that he sharply noticed concerned a hilarious party he had once attended at a driving club, of which he had been a member. He sat, gazing downward, and gradually thought he heard the old voices and the clink of glasses.

"You're a dandy, Hurstwood," his friend Walker said. He was standing again well dressed, smiling, good-natured, the recipient of encores for a good story.

All at once he looked up. The room was so still it seemed ghostlike. He heard the clock ticking audibly and half suspected that he had been dozing. The paper was so straight in his hands, however, and the items he had been reading so directly before him, that he rid himself of the doze idea. Still, it seemed peculiar. When it occurred a second time, however, it did not seem quite so strange.

Butcher and grocery man, baker and coal man—not the group with whom he was then dealing, but those who had trusted him to the limit—called. He met them all blandly, becoming deft in excuse. At last he became bold, pretended to be out, or waved them off.

"They can't get blood out of a turnip," he said. "If I had it I'd pay them."

Carrie's little soldier friend, Miss Osborne, seeing her succeeding, had become a sort of satellite. Little Osborne could never of herself amount to anything. She seemed to realize it in a sort of pussy-like way and instinctively concluded to cling with her soft little claws to Carrie.

"Oh, you'll get up," she kept telling Carrie with admiration. "You're so good."

Timid as Carrie was, she was strong in capability. The reliance of others made her feel as if she must, and when she must she dared. Experience of the world and of necessity was in her favor. No longer the lightest word of a man made her head dizzy. She had learned that men could change and fail. Flattery in its most palpable form had lost its force with her. It required superiority—kindly superiority—to move her—the superiority of a genius like Ames.

"I don't like the actors in our company," she told Lola one day. "They're all so stuck on themselves."

"Don't you think Mr. Barclay's pretty nice?" inquired Lola, who had received a condescending smile or two from that quarter.

"Oh, he's nice enough," answered Carrie; "but he isn't sincere. He assumes such an air."

Lola felt for her first hold upon Carrie in the following manner:

"Are you paying room-rent where you are?"

"Certainly," answered Carrie. "Why?"

"I know where I could get the loveliest room and bath, cheap. It's too big for me, but it would be just right for two, and the rent is only six dollars a week for both."

"Where?" said Carrie.

"In Seventeenth Street."

"Well, I don't know as I'd care to change," said Carrie, who was already turning over the three-dollar rate in her mind. She was thinking if she had only herself to support this would leave her seventeen for herself.

Nothing came of this until after the Brooklyn adventure of Hurstwood's and her success with the speaking part. Then she began to feel as if she must be free. She thought of leaving Hurstwood and thus making him act for himself, but he had developed such peculiar traits she feared he might resist any effort to throw him off. He might hunt her out at the show and hound her in that way. She did not wholly believe that he would, but he might. This, she knew, would be an embarrassing thing if he made himself conspicuous in any way. It troubled her greatly.

Things were precipitated by the offer of a better part. One of the actresses playing the part of a modest sweetheart gave notice of leaving and Carrie was selected.

"How much are you going to get?" asked Miss Osborne, on hearing the good news.

"I didn't ask him," said Carrie.

"Well, find out. Goodness, you'll never get anything if you don't ask. Tell them you must have forty dollars, anyhow."

"Oh, no," said Carrie.

"Certainly!" exclaimed Lola. "Ask 'em, anyway."

Carrie succumbed to this prompting, waiting, however, until the manager gave her notice of what clothing she must have to fit the part.

"How much do I get?" she inquired.

"Thirty-five dollars," he replied.

Carrie was too much astonished and delighted to think of mentioning forty. She was nearly beside herself, and almost hugged Lola, who clung to her at the news.

"It isn't as much as you ought to get," said the latter, "especially when you've got to buy clothes."

Carrie remembered this with a start. Where to get the money? She had none laid up for such an emergency. Rent day was drawing near.

"I'll not do it," she said, remembering her necessity. "I don't use the flat. I'm not going to give up my money this time. I'll move."

Fitting into this came another appeal from Miss Osborne, more urgent than ever.

"Come live with me, won't you?" she pleaded. "We can have the loveliest room. It won't cost you hardly anything that way."

"I'd like to," said Carrie, frankly.

"Oh, do," said Lola. "We'll have such a good time."

Carrie thought a while.

"I believe I will," she said, and then added: "I'll have to see first, though."

With the idea thus grounded, rent day approaching, and clothes calling for instant purchase, she soon found excuse in Hurstwood's lassitude. He said less and drooped more than ever.

As rent day approached, an idea grew in him. It was fostered by the demands of creditors and the impossibility of holding up many more. Twenty-eight dollars was too much rent. "It's hard on her," he thought. "We could get a cheaper place."

Stirred with this idea, he spoke at the breakfast table.

"Don't you think we pay too much rent here?" he asked.

"Indeed I do," said Carrie, not catching his drift.

"I should think we could get a smaller place," he suggested. "We don't need four rooms."

Her countenance, had he been scrutinizing her, would have exhibited the disturbance she felt at this evidence of his determination to stay by her. He saw nothing remarkable in asking her to come down lower.

"Oh, I don't know," she answered, growing wary.

"There must be places around here where we could get a couple of rooms, which would do just as well."

Her heart revolted. "Never!" she thought. Who would furnish the money to move? To think of being in two rooms with him! She resolved to spend her money for clothes quickly, before something terrible happened. That very day she did it. Having done so, there was but one other thing to do.

"Lola," she said, visiting her friend, "I think I'll come."

"Oh, jolly!" cried the latter.

"Can we get it right away?" she asked, meaning the room.

"Certainly," cried Lola.

They went to look at it. Carrie had saved ten dollars from her expenditures—enough for this and her board beside. Her enlarged salary would not begin for ten days yet—would not reach her for seventeen. She paid half of the six dollars with her friend.

"Now, I've just enough to get on to the end of the week," she confided.

"Oh, I've got some," said Lola. "I've got twenty-five dollars, if you need it."

"No," said Carrie. "I guess I'll get along."

They decided to move Friday, which was two days away. Now that the thing was settled, Carrie's heart misgave her. She felt very much like a criminal in the matter. Each day looking at Hurstwood, she had realized that, along with the disagreeableness of his attitude, there was something pathetic.

She looked at him the same evening she made up her mind to go, and now he seemed not so shiftless and worthless, but run down and beaten upon by chance. His eyes were not keen, his face marked, his hands flabby. She thought his hair had a touch of gray. All unconscious of his doom, he rocked and read his paper, while she glanced at him.

Knowing that the end was so near, she became rather solicitous.

"Will you go over and get some canned peaches?" she asked Hurstwood, laying down a two-dollar bill.

"Certainly," he said, looking in wonder at the money.

"See if you can get some nice asparagus," she added. "I'll cook it for dinner."

Hurstwood rose and took the money, slipping on his overcoat and getting his hat. Carrie noticed that both of these articles of apparel were old and poor looking in appearance. It was plain enough before, but now it came home with peculiar force. Perhaps he couldn't help it, after all. He had done well in Chicago. She remembered his fine appearance the days he had met her in the park. Then he was so sprightly, so clean. Had it been all his fault?

He came back and laid the change down with the food.

"You'd better keep it," she observed. "We'll need other things."

"No," he said, with a sort of pride; "you keep it."

"Oh, go on and keep it," she replied, rather unnerved. "There'll be other things."

He wondered at this, not knowing the pathetic figure he had become in her eyes. She restrained herself with difficulty from showing a quaver in her voice.

To say truly, this would have been Carrie's attitude in any case. She had looked back at times upon her parting from Drouet and had regretted that she had served him so badly. She hoped she would never meet him again, but she was ashamed of her conduct. Not that she had any choice in the final separation. She had gone willingly to seek him, with sympathy in her heart, when Hurstwood had reported him ill. There was something cruel somewhere, and not being able to track it mentally to its logical lair, she concluded with feeling that he would never understand what Hurstwood had done and would see hard-hearted decision in her deed; hence her shame. Not that she cared for him. She did not want to make any one who had been good to her feel badly.

She did not realize what she was doing by allowing these feelings to possess her. Hurstwood, noticing the kindness, conceived better of her. "Carrie's good-natured, anyhow," he thought.

Going to Miss Osborne's that afternoon, she found that little lady packing and singing.

"Why don't you come over with me to-day?" she asked.

"Oh, I can't," said Carrie. "I'll be there Friday. Would you mind lending me the twenty-five dollars you spoke of?"

"Why, no," said Lola, going for her purse.

"I want to get some other things," said Carrie.

"Oh, that's all right," answered the little girl, good-naturedly, glad to be of service.

It had been days since Hurstwood had done more than go to the grocery or to the news-stand. Now the weariness of indoors was upon him—had been for two days—but chill, gray weather had held him back. Friday broke fair and warm. It was one of those lovely harbingers of spring, given as a sign in dreary winter that earth is not forsaken of warmth and beauty. The blue heaven, holding its one golden orb, poured down a crystal wash of warm light. It was plain, from the voice of the sparrows, that all was halcyon outside. Carrie raised the front windows, and felt the south wind blowing.

"It's lovely out to-day," she remarked.

"Is it?" said Hurstwood.

After breakfast, he immediately got his other clothes.

"Will you be back for lunch?" asked Carrie, nervously.

"No," he said.

He went out into the streets and tramped north, along Seventh Avenue, idly fixing upon the Harlem River as an objective point. He had seen some ships up there, the time he had called upon the brewers. He wondered how the territory thereabouts was growing.

Passing Fifty-ninth Street, he took the west side of Central Park, which he followed to Seventy-eighth Street. Then he remembered the neighborhood and turned over to look at the mass of buildings erected. It was very much improved. The great open spaces were filling up. Coming back, he kept to the Park until 110th Street, and then turned into Seventh Avenue again, reaching the pretty river by one o'clock.

There it ran winding before his gaze, shining brightly in the clear light, between the undulating banks on the right and the tall, tree-covered heights on the left. The spring-like atmosphere woke him to a sense of its loveliness, and for a few moments he stood looking at it, folding his hands behind his back. Then he turned and followed it toward the east side, idly seeking the ships he had seen. It was four o'clock before the waning day, with its suggestion of a cooler evening, caused him to return. He was hungry and would enjoy eating in the warm room.

When he reached the flat by half-past five, it was still dark. He knew that Carrie was not there, not only because there was no light showing through the transom, but because the evening papers were stuck between the outside knob and the door. He opened with his key and went in. Everything was still dark. Lighting the gas, he sat down, preparing to wait a little while. Even if Carrie did come now, dinner would be late. He read until six, then got up to fix something for himself.

As he did so, he noticed that the room seemed a little queer. What was it? He looked around, as if he missed something, and then saw an envelope near where he had been sitting. It spoke for itself, almost without further action on his part.

Reaching over, he took it, a sort of chill settling upon him even while he reached. The crackle of the envelope in his hands was loud. Green paper money lay soft within the note.

"Dear George," he read, crunching the money in one hand. "I'm going away. I'm not coming back any more. It's no use trying to keep up the flat; I can't do it. I wouldn't mind helping you, if I could, but I can't support us both, and pay the rent. I need what little I make to pay for my clothes. I'm leaving twenty dollars. It's all I have just now. You can do whatever you like with the furniture. I won't want it.—Carrie."

He dropped the note and looked quietly round. Now he knew what he missed. It was the little ornamental clock, which was hers. It had gone from the mantelpiece. He went into the front room, his bedroom, the parlor, lighting the gas as he went. From the chiffonier had gone the knick-knacks of silver and plate. From the table-top, the lace coverings. He opened the wardrobe—no clothes of hers. He opened the drawers—nothing of hers. Her trunk was gone from its accustomed place. Back in his own room hung his old clothes, just as he had left them. Nothing else was gone.

He stepped into the parlor and stood for a few moments looking vacantly at the floor. The silence grew oppressive. The little flat seemed wonderfully deserted. He wholly forgot that he was hungry, that it was only dinner-time. It seemed later in the night.

Suddenly, he found that the money was still in his hands. There were twenty dollars in all, as she had said. Now he walked back, leaving the lights ablaze, and feeling as if the flat were empty.

"I'll get out of this," he said to himself.

Then the sheer loneliness of his situation rushed upon him in full.

"Left me!" he muttered, and repeated, "left me!"

The place that had been so comfortable, where he had spent so many days of warmth, was now a memory. Something colder and chillier confronted him. He sank down in his chair, resting his chin in his hand—mere sensation, without thought, holding him.

Then something like a bereaved affection and self-pity swept over him.

"She needn't have gone away," he said. "I'd have got something."

He sat a long while without rocking, and added quite clearly, out loud:

"I tried, didn't I?"

At midnight he was still rocking, staring at the floor.

CHAPTER XLIII

THE WORLD TURNS FLATTER: AN EYE IN THE DARK

Installed in her comfortable room, Carrie wondered how Hurstwood had taken her departure. She arranged a few things hastily and then left for the theater, half expecting to encounter him at the door. Not finding him, her dread lifted, and she felt more kindly toward him. She quite forgot him until about to come out, after the show, when the chance of his being there frightened her. As day after day passed and she heard nothing at all, the thought of being bothered by him passed. In a little while she was, except for occasional thoughts, wholly free of the gloom with which her life had been weighed in the flat.

It is curious to note how quickly a profession absorbs one. Carrie became wise in theatrical lore, hearing the gossip of little Lola. She learned what the theatrical papers were, which ones published items about actresses and the like. She began to read the newspaper notices, not only of the opera in which she had so small a part, but of others. Gradually the desire for notice took hold of her. She longed to be renowned like others, and read with avidity all the complimentary or critical comments made concerning others high in her profession. The showy world in which her interest lay completely absorbed her.

It was about this time that the newspapers and magazines were beginning to pay that illustrative attention to the beauties of the stage which has since become fervid. The newspapers, and particularly the Sunday newspapers, indulged in large decorative theatrical pages, in which the faces and forms of well-known theatrical celebrities appeared, enclosed with artistic scrolls. The magazines also—or at least one or two of the newer ones—published occasional portraits of pretty stars, and now and again photos of scenes from various plays. Carrie watched these with growing interest. When would a scene from her opera appear? When would some paper think her photo worth while?

The Sunday before taking her new part she scanned the theatrical pages for some little notice. It would have accorded with her expectations if nothing had been said, but there in the squibs, tailing off several more substantial items, was a wee notice. Carrie read it with a tingling body:

> "The part of Katisha, the country maid, in 'The Wives of Abdul' at the Broadway, heretofore played by Inez Carew, will be hereafter filled by Carrie Madenda, one of the cleverest members of the chorus."

Carrie hugged herself with delight. Oh, wasn't it just fine! At last! The first, the long-hoped for, the delightful notice! And they called her clever. She could hardly restrain herself from laughing loudly. Had Lola seen it?

"They've got a notice here of the part I'm going to play to-morrow night," said Carrie to her friend.

"Oh, jolly! Have they?" cried Lola, running to her. "That's all right," she said, looking. "You'll get more now, if you do well. I had my picture in the 'World' once."

"Did you?" asked Carrie.

"Did I? Well, I should say," returned the little girl. "They had a frame around it."

Carrie laughed.

"They've never published my picture."

"But they will," said Lola. "You'll see. You do better than most that get theirs in now."

Carrie felt deeply grateful for this. She almost loved Lola for the sympathy and praise she extended. It was so helpful to her—so almost necessary.

Fulfilling her part capably brought another notice in the papers that she was doing her work acceptably. This pleased her immensely. She began to think the world was taking note of her.

The first week she got her thirty-five dollars, it seemed an enormous sum. Paying only three dollars for room rent seemed ridiculous. After giving Lola her twenty-five, she still had seven dollars left. With four left over from previous earnings, she had eleven. Five of this went to pay the regular installment on the clothes she had to buy. The next week she was even in greater feather. Now, only three dollars need be paid for room rent and five on her clothes. The rest she had for food and her own whims.

"You'd better save a little for summer," cautioned Lola. "We'll probably close in May."

"I intend to," said Carrie.

The regular entrance of thirty-five dollars a week to one who has endured scant allowances for several years is a demoralizing thing. Carrie found her purse bursting with good green bills of comfortable denominations. Having no one dependent upon her, she began to buy pretty clothes and pleasing trinkets, to eat well, and to ornament her room. Friends were not long in gathering about. She met a few young men who belonged to Lola's staff. The members of the opera company made her acquaintance without the formality of introduction. One of these discovered a fancy for her. On several occasions he strolled home with her.

"Let's stop in and have a rarebit," he suggested one midnight.

"Very well," said Carrie.

In the rosy restaurant, filled with the merry lovers of late hours, she found herself criticizing this man. He was too stilted, too self-opinionated. He did not talk of anything that lifted her above the common run of clothes and material success. When it was all over, he smiled most graciously.

"Got to go straight home, have you?" he said.

"Yes," she answered, with an air of quiet understanding.

"She's not so inexperienced as she looks," he thought, and thereafter his respect and ardor were increased.

She could not help sharing in Lola's love for a good time. There were days when they went carriage riding, nights when after the show they dined, afternoons when they strolled along Broadway, tastefully dressed. She was getting in the metropolitan whirl of pleasure.

At last her picture appeared in one of the weeklies. She had not known of it, and it took her breath. "Miss Carrie Madenda," it was labeled. "One of the favorites of 'The Wives of Abdul' company." At Lola's advice she had had some pictures taken by Sarony. They had got one there. She thought of going down and buying a few copies of the paper, but remembered that there was no one she knew well enough to send them to. Only Lola, apparently, in all the world was interested.

The metropolis is a cold place socially, and Carrie soon found that a little money brought her nothing. The world of wealth and distinction was quite as far away as ever. She could feel that there was no warm, sympathetic friendship back of the easy merriment with which many approached her. All seemed to be seeking their own amusement, regardless of the possible sad consequences to others. So much for the lessons of Hurstwood and Drouet.

In April she learned that the opera would probably last until the middle or the end of May, according to the size of the audiences. Next season it would go on the road. She wondered if she would be with it. As usual, Miss Osborne, owing to her moderate salary, was for securing a home engagement.

"They're putting on a summer play at the Casino," she announced, after figuratively putting her ear to the ground. "Let's try and get in that."

"I'm willing," said Carrie.

They tried in time and were apprised of the proper date to apply again. That was May 16th. Meanwhile their own show closed May 5th.

"Those that want to go with the show next season," said the manager, "will have to sign this week."

"Don't you sign," advised Lola. "I wouldn't go."

"I know," said Carrie, "but maybe I can't get anything else."

"Well, I won't," said the little girl, who had a resource in her admirers. "I went once and I didn't have anything at the end of the season."

Carrie thought this over. She had never been on the road.

"We can get along," added Lola. "I always have."

Carrie did not sign.

The manager who was putting on the summer skit at the Casino had never heard of Carrie, but the several notices she had received, her published picture, and the program bearing her name had some little weight with him. He gave her a silent part at thirty dollars a week.

"Didn't I tell you?" said Lola. "It doesn't do you any good to go away from New York. They forget all about you if you do."

Now, because Carrie was pretty, the gentlemen who made up the advance illustrations of shows about to appear for the Sunday papers selected Carrie's photo along with others to illustrate the announcement. Because she was very pretty, they gave it excellent space and drew scrolls about it. Carrie was delighted. Still, the management did not seem to have seen anything of it. At least, no more attention was paid to her than before. At the same time there seemed very little in her part. It consisted of standing around in all sorts of scenes, a silent little Quakeress. The author of the skit had fancied that a great deal could be made of such a part, given to the right actress, but now, since it had been doled out to Carrie, he would as leave have had it cut out.

"Don't kick, old man," remarked the manager. "If it don't go the first week we will cut it out."

Carrie had no warning of this halcyon intention. She practiced her part ruefully, feeling that she was effectually shelved. At the dress rehearsal she was disconsolate.

"That isn't so bad," said the author, the manager noting the curious effect which Carrie's blues had upon the part. "Tell her to frown a little more when Sparks dances."

Carrie did not know it, but there was the least show of wrinkles between her eyes and her mouth was puckered quaintly.

"Frown a little more, Miss Madenda," said the stage manager.

Carrie instantly brightened up, thinking he had meant it as a rebuke.

"No; frown," he said. "Frown as you did before."

Carrie looked at him in astonishment.

"I mean it," he said. "Frown hard when Mr. Sparks dances. I want to see how it looks."

It was easy enough to do. Carrie scowled. The effect was something so quaint and droll it caught even the manager.

"That *is* good," he said. "If she'll do that all through, I think it will take."

Going over to Carrie, he said:

"Suppose you try frowning all through. Do it hard. Look mad. It'll make the part really funny."

On the opening night it looked to Carrie as if there were nothing to her part, after all. The happy, sweltering audience did not seem to see her in the first act. She frowned and frowned, but to no effect. Eyes were riveted upon the more elaborate efforts of the stars.

In the second act, the crowd, wearied by a dull conversation, roved with its eyes about the stage and sighted her. There she was, gray-suited, sweet-faced, demure, but scowling. At first the general idea was that she was temporarily irritated, that the look was genuine and not fun at all. As she went on frowning, looking now at one principal and now at the other, the audience began to smile. The portly gentlemen in the front rows began to feel that she was a delicious little morsel. It was the kind of frown they would have loved to force away with kisses. All the gentlemen yearned toward her. She was capital.

At last, the chief comedian, singing in the center of the stage, noticed a giggle where it was not expected. Then another and another. When the place came for loud applause it was only moderate. What could be the trouble? He realized that something was up.

All at once, after an exit, he caught sight of Carrie. She was frowning alone on the stage and the audience was giggling and laughing.

"By George, I won't stand that!" thought the thespian. "I'm not going to have my work cut up by someone else. Either she quits that when I do my turn or I quit."

"Why, that's all right," said the manager, when the kick came. "That's what she's supposed to do. You needn't pay any attention to that."

"But she ruins my work."

"No, she don't," returned the former, soothingly. "It's only a little fun on the side."

"It is, eh?" exclaimed the big comedian. "She killed my hand all right. I'm not going to stand that."

"Well, wait until after the show. Wait until tomorrow. We'll see what we can do."

The next act, however, settled what was to be done. Carrie was the chief feature of the play. The audience, the more it studied her, the more it indicated its delight. Every other feature paled beside the quaint, teasing, delightful atmosphere which Carrie contributed while on the stage. Manager and company realized she had made a hit.

The critics of the daily papers completed her triumph. There were long notices in praise of the quality of the burlesque, touched with recurrent references to Carrie. The contagious mirth of the thing was repeatedly emphasized.

> "Miss Madenda presents one of the most delightful bits of character work ever seen on the Casino stage," observed the sage critic of the "Sun." "It is a bit of quiet, unassuming drollery which warms like good wine. Evidently the part was not intended to take precedence, as Miss Madenda is not often on the stage, but the audience, with

the characteristic perversity of such bodies, selected for itself. The little Quakeress was marked for a favorite the moment she appeared, and thereafter easily held attention and applause. The vagaries of fortune are indeed curious."

The critic of the "Evening World," seeking as usual to establish a catch phrase which should "go" with the town, wound up by advising: "If you wish to be merry, see Carrie frown."

The result was miraculous so far as Carrie's fortune was concerned. Even during the morning she received a congratulatory message from the manager.

"You seem to have taken the town by storm," he wrote. "This is delightful. I am as glad for your sake as for my own."

The author also sent word.

That evening when she entered the theater the manager had a most pleasant greeting for her.

"Mr. Stevens," he said, referring to the author, "is preparing a little song, which he would like you to sing next week."

"Oh, I can't sing," returned Carrie.

"It isn't anything difficult. 'It's something that is very simple,' he says, 'and would suit you exactly.'"

"Of course, I wouldn't mind trying," said Carrie, archly.

"Would you mind coming to the box-office a few moments before you dress?" observed the manager, in addition. "There's a little matter I want to speak to you about."

"Certainly," replied Carrie.

In that latter place the manager produced a paper.

"Now, of course," he said, "we want to be fair with you in the matter of salary. Your contract here only calls for thirty dollars a week for the next three months. How would it do to make it, say, one hundred and fifty a week and extend it for twelve months?"

"Oh, very well," said Carrie, scarcely believing her ears.

"Supposing, then, you just sign this."

Carrie looked and beheld a new contract made out like the other one, with the exception of the new figures of salary and time. With a hand trembling from excitement she affixed her name.

"One hundred and fifty a week!" she murmured, when she was again alone. She found, after all—as what millionaire has not?—that there was no realizing, in consciousness, the meaning of large sums. It was only a shimmering, glittering phrase in which lay a world of possibilities.

Down in a third-rate Bleecker Street hotel, the brooding Hurstwood read the dramatic item covering Carrie's success, without at first realizing who was meant. Then suddenly it came to him and he read the whole thing over again.

"That's her, all right, I guess," he said.

Then he looked about upon a dingy, moth-eaten hotel lobby.

"I guess she's struck it," he thought, a picture of the old shiny, plush-covered world coming back, with its lights, its ornaments, its carriages, and flowers. Ah, she was in the walled city now! Its splendid gates had opened, admitting her from a cold, dreary outside. She seemed a creature afar off—like every other celebrity he had known.

"Well, let her have it," he said. "I won't bother her."

It was the grim resolution of a bent, bedraggled, but unbroken pride.

CHAPTER XLIV

AND THIS IS NOT ELFLAND: WHAT GOLD WILL NOT BUY

When Carrie got back on the stage, she found that over night her dressing-room had been changed.

"You are to use this room, Miss Madenda," said one of the stage lackeys.

No longer any need of climbing several flights of steps to a small coop shared with another. Instead, a comparatively large and commodious chamber with conveniences not enjoyed by the small fry overhead. She breathed deeply and with delight. Her sensations were more physical than mental. In fact, she was scarcely thinking at all. Heart and body were having their say.

Gradually the deference and congratulation gave her a mental appreciation of her state. She was no longer ordered, but requested, and that politely. The other members of the cast looked at her enviously as she came out arrayed in her simple habit, which she wore all through the play. All those who had supposedly been her equals and superiors now smiled the smile of sociability, as much as to say: "How friendly we have always been." Only the star comedian whose part had been so deeply injured stalked by himself. Figuratively, he could not kiss the hand that smote him.

Doing her simple part, Carrie gradually realized the meaning of the applause which was for her, and it was sweet. She felt mildly guilty of something—perhaps unworthiness. When her associates addressed her in the wings she only smiled weakly. The pride and daring of place were not for her. It never once crossed her mind to be reserved or haughty—to be other than she had been. After the performances she rode to her room with Lola, in a carriage provided.

Then came a week in which the first fruits of success were offered to her lips—bowl after bowl. It did not matter that her splendid salary had not begun. The world seemed satisfied with the promise. She began to get letters and cards. A Mr. Withers—whom she did not know from Adam—having learned by some hook or crook where she resided, bowed himself politely in.

"You will excuse me for intruding," he said; "but have you been thinking of changing your apartments?"

"I hadn't thought of it," returned Carrie.

"Well, I am connected with the Wellington—the new hotel on Broadway. You have probably seen notices of it in the papers."

Carrie recognized the name as standing for one of the newest and most imposing hostelries. She had heard it spoken of as having a splendid restaurant.

"Just so," went on Mr. Withers, accepting her acknowledgment of familiarity. "We have some very elegant rooms at present which we would like to have you look at, if you have not made up your mind where you intend to reside for the summer. Our apartments are perfect in every detail—hot and cold water, private baths, special hall service for every floor, elevators, and all that. You know what our restaurant is."

Carrie looked at him quietly. She was wondering whether he took her to be a millionaire.

"What are your rates?" she inquired.

"Well, now, that is what I came to talk with you privately about. Our regular rates are anywhere from three to fifty dollars a day."

"Mercy!" interrupted Carrie. "I couldn't pay any such rate as that."

"I know how you feel about it," exclaimed Mr. Withers, halting. "But just let me explain. I said those are our regular rates. Like every other hotel we make special ones, however. Possibly you have not thought about it, but your name is worth something to us."

"Oh!" ejaculated Carrie, seeing at a glance.

"Of course. Every hotel depends upon the repute of its patrons. A well-known actress like yourself," and he bowed politely, while Carrie flushed, "draws attention to the hotel, and—although you may not believe it—patrons."

"Oh, yes," returned Carrie, vacantly, trying to arrange this curious proposition in her mind.

"Now," continued Mr. Withers, swaying his derby hat softly and beating one of his polished shoes upon the floor, "I want to arrange, if possible, to have you come and stop at the Wellington. You need not trouble about terms. In fact, we need hardly discuss them. Anything will do for the summer—a mere figure—anything that you think you could afford to pay."

Carrie was about to interrupt, but he gave her no chance.

"You can come to-day or to-morrow—the earlier the better—and we will give you your choice of nice, light, outside rooms—the very best we have."

"You're very kind," said Carrie, touched by the agent's extreme affability. "I should like to come very much. I would want to pay what is right, however. I shouldn't want to—"

"You need not trouble about that at all," interrupted Mr. Withers. "We can arrange that to your entire satisfaction at any time. If three dollars a day is satisfactory to you, it will be so to us. All you have to do is to pay that sum to the clerk at the end of the week or month, just as you wish, and he will give you a receipt for what the rooms would cost if charged for at our regular rates."

The speaker paused.

"Suppose you come and look at the rooms," he added.

"I'd be glad to," said Carrie, "but I have a rehearsal this morning."

"I did not mean at once," he returned. "Any time will do. Would this afternoon be inconvenient?"

"Not at all," said Carrie.

Suddenly she remembered Lola, who was out at the time.

"I have a room-mate," she added, "who will have to go wherever I do. I forgot about that."

"Oh, very well," said Mr. Withers, blandly. "It is for you to say whom you want with you. As I say, all that can be arranged to suit yourself."

He bowed and backed toward the door.

"At four, then, we may expect you?"

"Yes," said Carrie.

"I will be there to show you," and so Mr. Withers withdrew.

After rehearsal Carrie informed Lola.

"Did they really?" exclaimed the latter, thinking of the Wellington as a group of managers. "Isn't that fine? Oh, jolly! It's so swell. That's where we dined that night we went with those two Cushing boys. Don't you know?"

"I remember," said Carrie.

"Oh, it's as fine as it can be."

"We'd better be going up there," observed Carrie later in the afternoon.

The rooms which Mr. Withers displayed to Carrie and Lola were three and bath—a suite on the parlor floor. They were done in chocolate and dark red, with rugs and hangings to match. Three windows looked down into busy Broadway on the east, three into a side street which crossed there. There were two lovely bedrooms, set with brass and white enamel beds, white, ribbon-trimmed chairs and chiffoniers to match. In the third room, or parlor, was a piano, a heavy piano lamp, with a shade of gorgeous pattern, a library table, several huge easy rockers, some dado book shelves, and a gilt curio case, filled with oddities. Pictures were upon the walls, soft Turkish pillows upon the divan, footstools of brown plush upon the floor. Such accommodations would ordinarily cost a hundred dollars a week.

"Oh, lovely!" exclaimed Lola, walking about.

"It is comfortable," said Carrie, who was lifting a lace curtain and looking down into crowded Broadway.

The bath was a handsome affair, done in white enamel, with a large, blue-bordered stone tub and nickel trimmings. It was bright and commodious, with a beveled mirror set in the wall at one end and incandescent lights arranged in three places.

"Do you find these satisfactory?" observed Mr. Withers.

"Oh, very," answered Carrie.

"Well, then, any time you find it convenient to move in, they are ready. The boy will bring you the keys at the door."

Carrie noted the elegantly carpeted and decorated hall, the marbled lobby, and showy waiting-room. It was such a place as she had often dreamed of occupying.

"I guess we'd better move right away, don't you think so?" she observed to Lola, thinking of the commonplace chamber in Seventeenth Street.

"Oh, by all means," said the latter.

The next day her trunks left for the new abode.

Dressing, after the matinee on Wednesday, a knock came at her dressing-room door.

Carrie looked at the card handed by the boy and suffered a shock of surprise.

"Tell her I'll be right out," she said softly. Then, looking at the card, added: "Mrs. Vance."

"Why, you little sinner," the latter exclaimed, as she saw Carrie coming toward her across the now vacant stage. "How in the world did this happen?"

Carrie laughed merrily. There was no trace of embarrassment in her friend's manner. You would have thought that the long separation had come about accidentally.

"I don't know," returned Carrie, warming, in spite of her first troubled feelings, toward this handsome, good-natured young matron.

"Well, you know, I saw your picture in the Sunday paper, but your name threw me off. I thought it must be you or somebody that looked just like you, and I said: 'Well, now, I will go right down there and see.' I was never more surprised in my life. How are you, anyway?"

"Oh, very well," returned Carrie. "How have you been?"

"Fine. But aren't you a success! Dear, oh! All the papers talking about you. I should think you would be just too proud to breathe. I was almost afraid to come back here this afternoon."

"Oh, nonsense," said Carrie, blushing. "You know I'd be glad to see you."

"Well, anyhow, here you are. Can't you come up and take dinner with me now? Where are you stopping?"

"At the Wellington," said Carrie, who permitted herself a touch of pride in the acknowledgment.

"Oh, are you?" exclaimed the other, upon whom the name was not without its proper effect.

Tactfully, Mrs. Vance avoided the subject of Hurstwood, of whom she could not help thinking. No doubt Carrie had left him. That much she surmised.

"Oh, I don't think I can," said Carrie, "to-night. I have so little time. I must be back here by 7:30. Won't you come and dine with me?"

"I'd be delighted, but I can't to-night," said Mrs. Vance, studying Carrie's fine appearance. The latter's good fortune made her seem more than ever worthy and delightful in the other's eyes. "I promised faithfully to be home at six." Glancing at the small gold watch pinned to her bosom, she added: "I must be going, too. Tell me when you're coming up, if at all."

"Why, any time you like," said Carrie.

"Well, to-morrow then. I'm living at the Chelsea now."

"Moved again?" exclaimed Carrie, laughing.

"Yes. You know I can't stay six months in one place. I just have to move. Remember now—half-past five."

"I won't forget," said Carrie, casting a glance at her as she went away. Then it came to her that she was as good as this woman now—perhaps better. Something in the other's solicitude and interest made her feel as if she were the one to condescend.

Now, as on each preceding day, letters were handed her by the doorman at the Casino. This was a feature which had rapidly developed since Monday. What they contained she well knew. *Mash notes* were old affairs in their mildest form. She remembered having received her first one far back in Columbia City. Since then, as a chorus girl, she had received others—gentlemen who prayed for an engagement. They were common sport between her and Lola, who received some also. They both frequently made light of them.

Now, however, they came thick and fast. Gentlemen with fortunes did not hesitate to note, as an addition to their own amiable collection of virtues, that they had their horses and carriages. Thus one:

> "I have a million in my own right. I could give you every luxury. There isn't anything you could ask for that you couldn't have. I say this, not because I want to speak of my money, but because I love you and wish to gratify your every desire. It is love that prompts me to write. Will you not give me one half-hour in which to plead my cause?"

Such of these letters as came while Carrie was still in the Seventeenth Street place were read with more interest—though never delight—than those which arrived after she was installed in her luxurious quarters at the Wellington. Even there her vanity—or that self-appreciation which, in its more rabid form, is called vanity—was not sufficiently cloyed to make these things wearisome. Adulation, being new in any form, pleased her. Only she was sufficiently wise to distinguish between her old condition and her new one. She had not had fame or money before. Now they had come. She had not had adulation and affectionate propositions before. Now they had come. Wherefore? She smiled to think that men should suddenly find her so much more attractive. In the least way it incited her to coolness and indifference.

"Do look here," she remarked to Lola. "See what this man says: 'If you will only deign to grant me one half-hour,'" she repeated, with an imitation of languor. "The idea. Aren't men silly?"

"He must have lots of money, the way he talks," observed Lola.

"That's what they all say," said Carrie, innocently.

"Why don't you see him," suggested Lola, "and hear what he has to say?"

"Indeed I won't," said Carrie. "I know what he'd say. I don't want to meet anybody that way."

Lola looked at her with big, merry eyes.

"He couldn't hurt you," she returned. "You might have some fun with him."

Carrie shook her head.

"You're awfully queer," returned the little, blue-eyed soldier.

Thus crowded fortune. For this whole week, though her large salary had not yet arrived, it was as if the world understood and trusted her. Without money—or the requisite sum, at least—she enjoyed the luxuries which money could buy. For her the doors of fine places seemed to open quite without the asking. These palatial chambers, how marvelously they came to her. The elegant apartments of Mrs. Vance in the Chelsea—these were hers. Men sent flowers, love notes, offers of fortune. And still her dreams ran riot. The one hundred and fifty! the one hundred and fifty! What a door to an Aladdin's cave it seemed to be. Each day, her head almost turned by developments, her fancies of what her fortune must be, with ample money, grew and multiplied. She conceived of delights which were not—saw lights of joy that never were on land or sea. Then, at last, after a world of anticipation, came her first installment of one hundred and fifty dollars.

It was paid to her in greenbacks—three twenties, six tens, and six fives. Thus collected it made a very convenient roll. It was accompanied by a smile and a salutation from the cashier who paid it.

"Ah, yes," said the latter, when she applied; "Miss Madenda—one hundred and fifty dollars. Quite a success the show seems to have made."

"Yes, indeed," returned Carrie.

Right after came one of the insignificant members of the company, and she heard the changed tone of address.

"How much?" said the same cashier, sharply. One, such as she had only recently been, was waiting for her modest salary. It took her back to the few weeks in which she had collected—or rather had received—almost with the air of a domestic, four-fifty per week from a lordly foreman in a shoe factory—a man who, in distributing the envelopes, had the manner of a prince doling out favors to a servile group of petitioners. She knew that out in Chicago this very day the same factory chamber was full of poor homely-clad girls working in long lines at clattering machines; that at noon they would eat a miserable lunch in a half-hour; that Saturday they would gather, as they had when she was one of them, and accept the small pay for work a hundred times harder than she was now doing. Oh, it was so easy now! The world was so rosy and bright. She felt so thrilled that she must needs walk back to the hotel to think, wondering what she should do.

It does not take money long to make plain its impotence, providing the desires are in the realm of affection. With her one hundred and fifty in hand, Carrie could think of nothing particularly to do. In itself, as a tangible, apparent thing which she could touch and look upon, it was a diverting thing for a few days, but this soon passed. Her hotel bill did not require its use. Her clothes had for some time been wholly satisfactory. Another day or two and she would receive another hundred and fifty. It began to appear as if this were not so startlingly necessary to maintain her present state. If she wanted to do anything better or move higher she must have more—a great deal more.

Now a critic called to get up one of those tinsel interviews which shine with clever observations, show up the wit of critics, display the folly of celebrities, and divert the public. He liked Carrie, and said so, publicly—adding, however, that she was merely pretty, good-natured, and lucky. This cut like a knife. The

"Herald," getting up an entertainment for the benefit of its free ice fund, did her the honor to beg her to appear along with celebrities for nothing. She was visited by a young author, who had a play which he thought she could produce. Alas, she could not judge. It hurt her to think it. Then she found she must put her money in the bank for safety, and so moving, finally reached the place where it struck her that the door to life's perfect enjoyment was not open.

Gradually she began to think it was because it was summer. Nothing was going on much save such entertainments as the one in which she was the star. Fifth Avenue was boarded up where the rich had deserted their mansions. Madison Avenue was little better. Broadway was full of loafing thespians in search of next season's engagements. The whole city was quiet and her nights were taken up with her work. Hence the feeling that there was little to do.

"I don't know," she said to Lola one day, sitting at one of the windows which looked down into Broadway, "I get lonely; don't you?"

"No," said Lola, "not very often. You won't go anywhere. That's what's the matter with you."

"Where can I go?"

"Why, there're lots of places," returned Lola, who was thinking of her own lightsome tourneys with the gay youths. "You won't go with anybody."

"I don't want to go with these people who write to me. I know what kind they are."

"You oughtn't to be lonely," said Lola, thinking of Carrie's success. "There're lots would give their ears to be in your shoes."

Carrie looked out again at the passing crowd.

"I don't know," she said.

Unconsciously her idle hands were beginning to weary.

CHAPTER XLV

CURIOUS SHIFTS OF THE POOR

The gloomy Hurstwood, sitting in his cheap hotel, where he had taken refuge with seventy dollars—the price of his furniture—between him and nothing, saw a hot summer out and a cool fall in, reading. He was not wholly indifferent to the fact that his money was slipping away. As fifty cents after fifty cents were paid out for a day's lodging he became uneasy, and finally took a cheaper room—thirty-five cents a day—to make his money last longer. Frequently he saw notices of Carrie. Her picture was in the "World" once or twice, and an old "Herald" he found in a chair informed him that she had recently appeared with some others at a benefit for something or other. He read these things with mingled feelings. Each one seemed to put her farther and farther away into a realm which became more imposing as it receded from him. On the bill-boards, too, he saw a pretty poster, showing her as the Quaker Maid, demure and dainty. More than once he stopped and looked at these, gazing at the pretty face in a sullen sort of way. His clothes were shabby, and he presented a marked contrast to all that she now seemed to be.

Somehow, so long as he knew she was at the Casino, though he had never any intention of going near her, there was a sub-conscious comfort for him—he was not quite alone. The show seemed such a fixture that, after a month or two, he began to take it for granted that it was still running. In September it went on the road and he did not notice it. When all but twenty dollars of his money was gone, he moved to a fifteen-cent lodging-house in the Bowery, where there was a bare lounging-room filled with tables and benches as well as some chairs. Here his preference was to close his eyes and dream of other days, a habit which grew upon him. It was not sleep at first, but a mental hearkening back to scenes and incidents in his Chicago life. As the present became darker, the past grew brighter, and all that concerned it stood in relief.

He was unconscious of just how much this habit had hold of him until one day he found his lips repeating an old answer he had made to one of his friends. They were in Fitzgerald and Moy's. It was as if he stood in the door of his elegant little office, comfortably dressed, talking to Sagar Morrison about the value of South Chicago real estate in which the latter was about to invest.

"How would you like to come in on that with me?" he heard Morrison say.

"Not me," he answered, just as he had years before. "I have my hands full now."

The movement of his lips aroused him. He wondered whether he had really spoken. The next time he noticed anything of the sort he really did talk.

"Why don't you jump, you bloody fool?" he was saying. "Jump!"

It was a funny English story he was telling to a company of actors. Even as his voice recalled him, he was smiling. A crusty old codger, sitting near by, seemed disturbed; at least, he stared in a most pointed way. Hurstwood straightened up. The humor of the memory fled in an instant and he felt ashamed. For relief, he left his chair and strolled out into the streets.

One day, looking down the ad. columns of the "Evening World," he saw where a new play was at the Casino. Instantly, he came to a mental halt. Carrie had gone! He remembered seeing a poster of her only yesterday, but no doubt it was one left uncovered by the new signs. Curiously, this fact shook him up. He had almost to admit that somehow he was dependent upon her being in the city. Now she was gone. He wondered how this important fact had skipped him. Goodness knows when she would be back now. Impelled by a nervous fear, he rose and went into the dingy hall, where he counted his remaining money, unseen. There were but ten dollars in all.

He wondered how all these other lodging-house people around him got along. They didn't seem to do anything. Perhaps they begged—unquestionably they did. Many was the dime he had given to such as they in his day. He had seen other men asking for money on the streets. Maybe he could get some that way. There was horror in this thought.

Sitting in the lodging-house room, he came to his last fifty cents. He had saved and counted until his health was affected. His stoutness had gone. With it, even the semblance of a fit in his clothes. Now he decided he must do something, and, walking about, saw another day go by, bringing him down to his last twenty cents—not enough to eat for the morrow.

Summoning all his courage, he crossed to Broadway and up to the Broadway Central Hotel. Within a block he halted, undecided. A big, heavy-faced porter was standing at one of the side entrances, looking out. Hurstwood purposed to appeal to him. Walking straight up, he was upon him before he could turn away.

"My friend," he said, recognizing even in his plight the man's inferiority, "is there anything about this hotel that I could get to do?"

The porter stared at him the while he continued to talk.

"I'm out of work and out of money and I've got to get something—it doesn't matter what. I don't care to talk about what I've been, but if you'd tell me how to get something to do, I'd be much obliged to you. It wouldn't matter if it only lasted a few days just now. I've got to have something."

The porter still gazed, trying to look indifferent. Then, seeing that Hurstwood was about to go on, he said:

"I've nothing to do with it. You'll have to ask inside."

Curiously, this stirred Hurstwood to further effort.

"I thought you might tell me."

The fellow shook his head irritably.

Inside went the ex-manager and straight to an office off the clerk's desk. One of the managers of the hotel happened to be there. Hurstwood looked him straight in the eye.

"Could you give me something to do for a few days?" he said. "I'm in a position where I have to get something at once."

The comfortable manager looked at him, as much as to say: "Well, I should judge so."

"I came here," explained Hurstwood, nervously, "because I've been a manager myself in my day. I've had bad luck in a way, but I'm not here to tell you that. I want something to do, if only for a week."

The man imagined he saw a feverish gleam in the applicant's eye.

"What hotel did you manage?" he inquired.

"It wasn't a hotel," said Hurstwood. "I was manager of Fitzgerald and Moy's place in Chicago for fifteen years."

"Is that so?" said the hotel man. "How did you come to get out of that?"

The figure of Hurstwood was rather surprising in contrast to the fact.

"Well, by foolishness of my own. It isn't anything to talk about now. You could find out if you wanted to. I'm 'broke' now and, if you will believe me, I haven't eaten anything to-day."

The hotel man was slightly interested in this story. He could hardly tell what to do with such a figure, and yet Hurstwood's earnestness made him wish to do something.

"Call Olsen," he said, turning to the clerk.

In reply to a bell and a disappearing hall-boy, Olsen, the head porter, appeared.

"Olsen," said the manager, "is there anything downstairs you could find for this man to do? I'd like to give him something."

"I don't know, sir," said Olsen. "We have about all the help we need. I think I could find something, sir, though, if you like."

"Do. Take him to the kitchen and tell Wilson to give him something to eat."

"All right, sir," said Olsen.

Hurstwood followed. Out of the manager's sight, the head porter's manner changed.

"I don't know what the devil there is to do," he observed.

Hurstwood said nothing. To him the big trunk hustler was a subject for private contempt.

"You're to give this man something to eat," he observed to the cook.

The latter looked Hurstwood over, and seeing something keen and intellectual in his eyes, said:

"Well, sit down over there."

Thus was Hurstwood installed in the Broadway Central, but not for long. He was in no shape or mood to do the scrub work that exists about the foundation of every hotel. Nothing better offering, he was set to aid the fireman, to work about the basement, to do anything and everything that might offer. Porters, cooks, firemen, clerks—all were over him. Moreover his appearance did not please these individuals—his temper was too lonely—and they made it disagreeable for him.

With the stolidity and indifference of despair, however, he endured it all, sleeping in an attic at the roof of the house, eating what the cook gave him, accepting a few dollars a week, which he tried to save. His constitution was in no shape to endure.

One day the following February he was sent on an errand to a large coal company's office. It had been snowing and thawing and the streets were sloppy. He soaked his shoes in his progress and came back feeling dull and weary. All the next day he felt unusually depressed and sat about as much as possible, to the irritation of those who admired energy in others.

In the afternoon some boxes were to be moved to make room for new culinary supplies. He was ordered to handle a truck. Encountering a big box, he could not lift it.

"What's the matter there?" said the head porter. "Can't you handle it?"

He was straining hard to lift it, but now he quit.

"No," he said, weakly.

The man looked at him and saw that he was deathly pale.

"Not sick, are you?" he asked.

"I think I am," returned Hurstwood.

"Well, you'd better go sit down, then."

This he did, but soon grew rapidly worse. It seemed all he could do to crawl to his room, where he remained for a day.

"That man Wheeler's sick," reported one of the lackeys to the night clerk.

"What's the matter with him?"

"I don't know. He's got a high fever."

The hotel physician looked at him.

"Better send him to Bellevue," he recommended. "He's got pneumonia."

Accordingly, he was carted away.

In three weeks the worst was over, but it was nearly the first of May before his strength permitted him to be turned out. Then he was discharged.

No more weakly looking object ever strolled out into the spring sunshine than the once hale, lusty manager. All his corpulency had fled. His face was thin and pale, his hands white, his body flabby. Clothes and all, he weighed but one hundred and thirty-five pounds. Some old garments had been given him—a cheap brown coat and misfit pair of trousers. Also some change and advice. He was told to apply to the charities.

Again he resorted to the Bowery lodging-house, brooding over where to look. From this it was but a step to beggary.

"What can a man do?" he said. "I can't starve."

His first application was in sunny Second Avenue. A well-dressed man came leisurely strolling toward him out of Stuyvesant Park. Hurstwood nerved himself and sidled near.

"Would you mind giving me ten cents?" he said, directly. "I'm in a position where I must ask some one."

The man scarcely looked at him, but fished in his vest pocket and took out a dime.

"There you are," he said.

"Much obliged," said Hurstwood, softly, but the other paid no more attention to him.

Satisfied with his success and yet ashamed of his situation, he decided that he would only ask for twenty-five cents more, since that would be sufficient. He strolled about sizing up people, but it was long before just the right face and situation arrived. When he asked, he was refused. Shocked by this result, he took an hour to recover and then asked again. This time a nickel was given him. By the most watchful effort he did get twenty cents more, but it was painful.

The next day he resorted to the same effort, experiencing a variety of rebuffs and one or two generous receptions. At last it crossed his mind that there was a science of faces, and that a man could pick the liberal countenance if he tried.

It was no pleasure to him, however, this stopping of passersby. He saw one man taken up for it and now troubled lest he should be arrested. Nevertheless, he went on, vaguely anticipating that indefinite something which is always better.

It was with a sense of satisfaction, then, that he saw announced one morning the return of the Casino Company, "with Miss Carrie Madenda." He had thought of her often enough in days past. How successful she was—how much money she must have! Even now, however, it took a severe run of ill-luck to decide him to appeal to her. He was truly hungry before he said:

"I'll ask her. She won't refuse me a few dollars."

Accordingly, he headed for the Casino one afternoon, passing it several times in an effort to locate the stage entrance. Then he sat in Bryant Park, a block away, waiting. "She can't refuse to help me a little," he kept saying to himself.

Beginning with half-past six, he hovered like a shadow about the Thirty-ninth Street entrance, pretending always to be a hurrying pedestrian and yet fearful lest he should miss his object. He was slightly nervous, too, now that the eventful hour had arrived; but being weak and hungry, his ability to suffer was modified. At last he saw that the actors were beginning to arrive, and his nervous tension increased, until it seemed as if he could not stand much more.

Once he thought he saw Carrie coming and moved forward, only to see that he was mistaken.

"She can't be long, now," he said to himself, half fearing to encounter her and equally depressed at the thought that she might have gone in by another way. His stomach was so empty that it ached.

Individual after individual passed him, nearly all well dressed, almost all indifferent. He saw coaches rolling by, gentlemen passing with ladies—the evening's merriment was beginning in this region of theaters and hotels.

Suddenly a coach rolled up and the driver jumped down to open the door. Before Hurstwood could act, two ladies flounced across the broad walk and disappeared in the stage door. He thought he saw Carrie, but it was so unexpected, so elegant and far away, he could hardly tell. He waited a while longer, growing feverish with want, and then seeing that the stage door no longer opened, and that a merry audience was arriving, he concluded it must have been Carrie and turned away.

"Lord," he said, hastening out of the street into which the more fortunate were pouring. "I've got to get something."

At that hour, when Broadway is wont to assume its most interesting aspect, a peculiar individual invariably took his stand at the corner of Twenty-sixth Street and Broadway—a spot which is also intersected by Fifth Avenue. This was the hour when the theaters were just beginning to receive their patrons. Fire signs announcing the night's amusements blazed on every hand. Cabs and carriages, their lamps gleaming like yellow eyes, pattered by. Couples and parties of three and four freely mingled in the common crowd, which poured by in a thick stream, laughing and jesting. On Fifth Avenue were loungers—a few wealthy strollers, a gentleman in evening dress with his lady on his arm, some clubmen passing from one smoking-room to another. Across the way the great hotels showed a hundred gleaming windows, their cafés and billiard-rooms filled with a comfortable, well-dressed, and pleasure-loving throng. All about was the night, pulsating with the thoughts of pleasure and exhilaration—the curious enthusiasm of a great city bent upon finding joy in a thousand different ways.

This unique individual was no less than an ex-soldier turned religionist, who, having suffered the whips and privations of our peculiar social system, had concluded that his duty to the God which he conceived lay in aiding his fellow man. The form of aid which he chose to administer was entirely original with himself. It consisted of securing a bed for all such homeless wayfarers as should apply to him at this particular spot, though he had scarcely the wherewithal to provide a comfortable habitation for himself.

Taking his place amid this lightsome atmosphere, he would stand, his stocky figure cloaked in a great cape overcoat, his head protected by a broad slouch hat, awaiting the applicants who had in various ways learned the nature of his charity. For a while he would stand alone, gazing like any idler upon an ever-fascinating scene. On the evening in question, a policeman passing saluted him as "captain," in a friendly way. An urchin who had frequently seen him before, stopped to gaze. All others took him for nothing out of the ordinary, save in the matter of dress, and conceived of him as a stranger whistling and idling for his own amusement.

As the first half-hour waned, certain characters appeared. Here and there in the passing crowds one might see, now and then, a loiterer edging interestedly near. A slouchy figure crossed the opposite corner and glanced furtively in his direction. Another came down Fifth Avenue to the corner of Twenty-sixth Street, took a general survey, and hobbled off again. Two or three noticeable Bowery types edged along the Fifth Avenue side of Madison Square, but did not venture over. The soldier, in his cape overcoat, walked a short line of ten feet at his corner, to and fro, indifferently whistling.

As nine o'clock approached, some of the hubbub of the earlier hour passed. The atmosphere of the hotels was not so youthful. The air, too, was colder. On every hand curious figures were moving—watchers and peepers, without an imaginary circle, which they seemed afraid to enter—a dozen in all. Presently, with the arrival of a keener sense of cold, one figure came forward. It crossed Broadway from out of the shadow of Twenty-sixth Street, and, in a halting, circuitous way, arrived close to the waiting figure. There was something shamefaced or diffident about the movement, as if the intention were to conceal any idea of stopping until the very last moment. Then suddenly, close to the soldier, came the halt.

The captain looked in recognition, but there was no especial greeting. The newcomer nodded slightly and murmured something like one who waits for gifts. The other simply motioned toward the edge of the walk.

"Stand over there," he said.

By this the spell was broken. Even while the soldier resumed his short, solemn walk, other figures shuffled forward. They did not so much as greet the leader, but joined the one, sniffling and hitching and scraping their feet.

"Cold, ain't it?"

"I'm glad winter's over."

"Looks as though it might rain."

The motley company had increased to ten. One or two knew each other and conversed. Others stood off a few feet, not wishing to be in the crowd and yet not counted out. They were peevish, crusty, silent, eying nothing in particular and moving their feet.

There would have been talking soon, but the soldier gave them no chance. Counting sufficient to begin, he came forward.

"Beds, eh, all of you?"

There was a general shuffle and murmur of approval.

"Well, line up here. I'll see what I can do. I haven't a cent myself."

They fell into a sort of broken, ragged line. One might see, now, some of the chief characteristics by contrast. There was a wooden leg in the line. Hats were all drooping, a group that would ill become a second-hand Hester Street basement collection. Trousers were all warped and frayed at the bottom and coats worn and faded. In the glare of the store lights, some of the faces looked dry and chalky; others were red with blotches and puffed in the cheeks and under the eyes; one or two were rawboned and reminded one of railroad hands. A few spectators came near, drawn by the seemingly conferring group, then more and more, and quickly there was a pushing, gaping crowd. Some one in the line began to talk.

"Silence!" exclaimed the captain. "Now, then, gentlemen, these men are without beds. They have to have some place to sleep to-night. They can't lie out in the streets. I need twelve cents to put one of them to bed. Who will give it to me?"

No reply.

"Well, we'll have to wait here, boys, until some one does. Twelve cents isn't so very much for one man."

"Here's fifteen," exclaimed a young man, peering forward with strained eyes. "It's all I can afford."

"All right. Now I have fifteen. Step out of the line," and seizing one by the shoulder, the captain marched him off a little way and stood him up alone.

Coming back, he resumed his place and began again.

"I have three cents left. These men must be put to bed somehow. There are"—counting—"one, two, three, four, five, six, seven, eight, nine, ten, eleven, twelve men. Nine cents more will put the next man to bed; give him a good, comfortable bed for the night. I go right along and look after that myself. Who will give me nine cents?"

One of the watchers, this time a middle-aged man, handed him a five-cent piece.

"Now, I have eight cents. Four more will give this man a bed. Come, gentlemen. We are going very slow this evening. You all have good beds. How about these?"

"Here you are," remarked a bystander, putting a coin into his hand.

"That," said the captain, looking at the coin, "pays for two beds for two men gives me five on the next one. Who will give me seven cents more?"

"I will," said a voice.

Coming down Sixth Avenue this evening, Hurstwood chanced to cross east through Twenty-sixth Street toward Third Avenue. He was wholly disconsolate in spirit, hungry to what he deemed an almost mortal extent, weary, and defeated. How should he get at Carrie now? It would be eleven before the show was over. If she came in a coach, she would go away in one. He would need to interrupt under most trying circumstances. Worst of all, he was hungry and weary, and at best a whole day must intervene, for he had not heart to try again to-night. He had no food and no bed.

When he neared Broadway, he noticed the captain's gathering of wanderers, but thinking it to be the result of a street preacher or some patent medicine fakir, was about to pass on. However, in crossing the street toward Madison Square Park, he noticed the line of men whose beds were already secured, stretching out from the main body of the crowd. In the glare of the neighboring electric light he recognized a type of his own kind—the figures whom he saw about the streets and in the lodging-houses, drifting in mind and body like himself. He wondered what it could be and turned back.

There was the captain curtly pleading as before. He heard with astonishment and sense of relief the oft-repeated words: "These men must have a bed." Before him was the line of unfortunates whose beds were yet to be had, and seeing a newcomer quietly edge up and take a position at the end of the line, he decided to do likewise. What use to contend? He was weary to-night. It was a simple way out of one difficulty, at least. To-morrow, maybe, he would do better.

Back of him, where some of those were whose beds were safe, a relaxed air was apparent. The strain of uncertainty being removed, he heard them talking with moderate freedom and some leaning toward sociability. Politics, religion, the state of the government, some newspaper sensations, and the more notorious facts the world over, found mouthpieces and auditors there. Cracked and husky voices pronounced forcibly upon odd matters. Vague and rambling observations were made in reply.

There were squints, and leers, and some dull, ox-like stares from those who were too dull or too weary to converse.

Standing tells. Hurstwood became more weary waiting. He thought he should drop soon and shifted restlessly from one foot to the other. At last his turn came. The man ahead had been paid for and gone to the blessed line of success. He was now first, and already the captain was talking for him.

"Twelve cents, gentlemen—twelve cents puts this man to bed. He wouldn't stand here in the cold if he had any place to go."

Hurstwood swallowed something that rose to his throat. Hunger and weakness had made a coward of him.

"Here you are," said a stranger, handing money to the captain.

Now the latter put a kindly hand on the ex-manager's shoulder.

"Line up over there," he said.

Once there, Hurstwood breathed easier. He felt as if the world were not quite so bad with such a good man in it. Others seemed to feel like himself about this.

"Captain's a great feller, ain't he?" said the man ahead—a little, woe-begone, helpless-looking sort of individual, who looked as though he had ever been the sport and care of fortune.

"Yes," said Hurstwood, indifferently.

"Huh! there's a lot back there yet," said a man farther up, leaning out and looking back at the applicants for whom the captain was pleading.

"Yes. Must be over a hundred to-night," said another.

"Look at the guy in the cab," observed a third.

A cab had stopped. Some gentleman in evening dress reached out a bill to the captain, who took it with simple thanks and turned away to the line. There was a general craning of necks as the jewel in the white shirt front sparkled and the cab moved off. Even the crowd gaped in awe.

"That fixes up nine men for the night," said the captain, counting out as many of the line near him. "Line up over there. Now, then, there are only seven. I need twelve cents."

Money came slowly. In the course of time the crowd thinned out to a meager handful. Fifth Avenue, save for an occasional cab or foot passenger, was bare. Broadway was thinly peopled with pedestrians. Only now and then a stranger passing noticed the small group, handed out a coin, and went away, unheeding.

The captain remained stolid and determined. He talked on, very slowly, uttering the fewest words and with a certain assurance, as though he could not fail.

"Come; I can't stay out here all night. These men are getting tired and cold. Some one give me four cents."

There came a time when he said nothing at all. Money was handed him, and for each twelve cents he singled out a man and put him in the other line. Then he walked up and down as before, looking at the ground.

The theaters let out. Fire signs disappeared. A clock struck eleven. Another half-hour and he was down to the last two men.

"Come now," he exclaimed to several curious observers; "eighteen cents will fix us all up for the night. Eighteen cents. I have six. Somebody give me the money. Remember, I have to go over to Brooklyn yet to-night. Before that I have to take these men down and put them to bed. Eighteen cents."

No one responded. He walked to and fro, looking down for several minutes, occasionally saying softly: "Eighteen cents." It seemed as if this paltry sum would delay the desired culmination longer than all the rest had. Hurstwood, buoyed up slightly by the long line of which he was a part, refrained with an effort from groaning, he was so weak.

At last a lady in opera cape and rustling skirts came down Fifth Avenue, accompanied by her escort. Hurstwood gazed wearily, reminded by her both of Carrie in her new world and of the time when he had escorted his own wife in like manner.

While he was gazing, she turned and, looking at the remarkable company, sent her escort over. He came, holding a bill in his fingers, all elegant and graceful.

"Here you are," he said.

"Thanks," said the captain, turning to the two remaining applicants. "Now we have some for to-morrow night," he added.

Therewith he lined up the last two and proceeded to the head, counting as he went.

"One hundred and thirty-seven," he announced. "Now, boys, line up. Right dress there. We won't be much longer about this. Steady, now."

He placed himself at the head and called out "Forward." Hurstwood moved with the line. Across Fifth Avenue, through Madison Square by the winding paths, east on Twenty-third Street, and down Third Avenue wound the long, serpentine company. Midnight pedestrians and loiterers stopped and stared as the company passed. Chatting policemen, at various corners, stared indifferently or nodded to the leader, whom they had seen before. On Third Avenue they marched, a seemingly weary way, to Eighth Street, where there was a lodging-house, closed, apparently, for the night. They were expected, however.

Outside in the gloom they stood, while the leader parleyed within. Then doors swung open and they were invited in with a "Steady, now."

Someone was at the head showing rooms, so that there was no delays for keys. Toiling up the creaky stairs, Hurstwood looked back and saw the captain, watching; the last one of the line being included in his broad solicitude. Then he gathered his cloak about him and strolled out into the night.

"I can't stand much of this," said Hurstwood, whose legs ached him painfully, as he sat down upon the miserable bunk in the small, lightless chamber allotted to him. "I've got to eat, or I'll die."

CHAPTER XLVI

STIRRING TROUBLED WATERS

Playing in New York one evening on this her return, Carrie was putting the finishing touches to her toilet before leaving for the night, when a commotion near the stage door caught her ear. It included a familiar voice.

"Never mind, now. I want to see Miss Madenda."

"You'll have to send in your card."

"Oh, come off! Here."

A half-dollar was passed over, and now a knock came at her dressing-room door.

Carrie opened it.

"Well, well!" said Drouet. "I do swear! Why, how are you? I knew that was you the moment I saw you."

Carrie fell back a pace, expecting a most embarrassing conversation.

"Aren't you going to shake hands with me? Well, you're a dandy! That's all right, shake hands."

Carrie put out her hand, smiling, if for nothing more than the man's exuberant good-nature. Though older, he was but slightly changed. The same fine clothes, the same stocky body, the same rosy countenance.

"That fellow at the door there didn't want to let me in, until I paid him. I knew it was you, all right. Say, you've got a great show. You do your part fine. I knew you would. I just happened to be passing tonight and thought I'd drop in for a few minutes. I saw your name on the program, but I didn't remember it until you came on the stage. Then it struck me all at once. Say, you could have knocked me down with a feather. That's the same name you used out there in Chicago, isn't it?"

"Yes," answered Carrie, mildly, overwhelmed by the man's assurance.

"I knew it was, the moment I saw you. Well, how have you been, anyhow?"

"Oh, very well," said Carrie, lingering in her dressing-room. She was rather dazed by the assault. "How have you been?"

"Me? Oh, fine. I'm here now."

"Is that so?" said Carrie.

"Yes. I've been here for six months. I've got charge of a branch here."

"How nice!"

"Well, when did you go on the stage, anyhow?" inquired Drouet.

"About three years ago," said Carrie.

"You don't say so! Well, sir, this is the first I've heard of it. I knew you would, though. I always said you could act—didn't I?"

Carrie smiled.

"Yes, you did," she said.

"Well, you do look great," he said. "I never saw anybody improve so. You're taller, aren't you?"

"Me? Oh, a little, maybe."

He gazed at her dress, then at her hair, where a becoming hat was set jauntily, then into her eyes, which she took all occasion to avert. Evidently he expected to restore their old friendship at once and without modification.

"Well," he said, seeing her gather up her purse, handkerchief, and the like, preparatory to departing. "I want you to come out to dinner with me; won't you? I've got a friend out here."

"Oh, I can't," said Carrie. "Not to-night. I have an early engagement to-morrow."

"Aw, let the engagement go. Come on. I can get rid of him. I want to have a good talk with you."

"No, no," said Carrie; "I can't. You mustn't ask me any more. I don't care for a late dinner."

"Well, come on and have a talk, then, anyhow."

"Not to-night," she said, shaking her head. "We'll have a talk some other time."

As a result of this, she noticed a shade of thought pass over his face, as if he were beginning to realize that things were changed. Good-nature dictated something better than this for one who had always liked her.

"You come around to the hotel to-morrow," she said, as sort of penance for error. "You can take dinner with me."

"All right," said Drouet, brightening. "Where are you stopping?"

"At the Waldorf," she answered, mentioning the fashionable hostelry then but newly erected.

"What time?"

"Well, come at three," said Carrie, pleasantly.

The next day Drouet called, but it was with no especial delight that Carrie remembered her appointment. However, seeing him, handsome as ever, after his kind, and most genially disposed, her doubts as to whether the dinner would be disagreeable were swept away. He talked as volubly as ever.

"They put on a lot of lugs here, don't they?" was his first remark.

"Yes; they do," said Carrie.

Genial egotist that he was, he went at once into a detailed account of his own career.

"I'm going to have a business of my own pretty soon," he observed in one place. "I can get backing for two hundred thousand dollars."

Carrie listened most good-naturedly.

"Say," he said, suddenly; "where is Hurstwood now?"

Carrie flushed a little.

"He's here in New York, I guess," she said. "I haven't seen him for some time."

Drouet mused for a moment. He had not been sure until now that the ex-manager was not an influential figure in the background. He imagined not; but this assurance relieved him. It must be that Carrie had got rid of him—as well she ought, he thought.

"A man always makes a mistake when he does anything like that," he observed.

"Like what?" said Carrie, unwitting of what was coming.

"Oh, you know," and Drouet waved her intelligence, as it were, with his hand.

"No, I don't," she answered. "What do you mean?"

"Why that affair in Chicago—the time he left."

"I don't know what you are talking about," said Carrie. Could it be he would refer so rudely to Hurstwood's flight with her?

"Oho!" said Drouet, incredulously. "You knew he took ten thousand dollars with him when he left, didn't you?"

"What!" said Carrie. "You don't mean to say he stole money, do you?"

"Why," said Drouet, puzzled at her tone, "you knew that, didn't you?"

"Why, no," said Carrie. "Of course I didn't."

"Well, that's funny," said Drouet. "He did, you know. It was in all the papers."

"How much did you say he took?" said Carrie.

"Ten thousand dollars. I heard he sent most of it back afterwards, though."

Carrie looked vacantly at the richly carpeted floor. A new light was shining upon all the years since her enforced flight. She remembered now a hundred things that indicated as much. She also imagined that he took it on her account. Instead of hatred springing up there was a kind of sorrow generated. Poor fellow! What a thing to have had hanging over his head all the time.

At dinner Drouet, warmed up by eating and drinking and softened in mood, fancied he was winning Carrie to her oldtime good-natured regard for him. He began to imagine it would not be so difficult to enter into her life again, high as she was. Ah, what a prize! he thought. How beautiful, how elegant, how famous! In her theatrical and Waldorf setting, Carrie was to him the all-desirable.

"Do you remember how nervous you were that night at the Avery?" he asked.

Carrie smiled to think of it.

"I never saw anybody do better than you did then, Cad," he added ruefully, as he leaned an elbow on the table; "I thought you and I were going to get along fine those days."

"You mustn't talk that way," said Carrie, bringing in the least touch of coldness.

"Won't you let me tell you—"

"No," she answered, rising. "Besides, it's time I was getting ready for the theater. I'll have to leave you. Come, now."

"Oh, stay a minute," pleaded Drouet. "You've got plenty of time."

"No," said Carrie, gently.

Reluctantly Drouet gave up the bright table and followed. He saw her to the elevator and, standing there, said:

"When do I see you again?"

"Oh, some time, possibly," said Carrie. "I'll be here all summer. Good-night!"

The elevator door was open.

"Good-night!" said Drouet, as she rustled in.

Then he strolled sadly down the hall, all his old longing revived, because she was now so far off. The merry frou-frou of the place spoke all of her. He thought himself hardly dealt with. Carrie, however, had other thoughts.

That night it was that she passed Hurstwood, waiting at the Casino, without observing him.

The next night, walking to the theater, she encountered him face to face. He was waiting, more gaunt than ever, determined to see her, if he had to send in word. At first she did not recognize the shabby, baggy figure. He frightened her, edging so close, a seemingly hungry stranger.

"Carrie," he half whispered, "can I have a few words with you?"

She turned and recognized him on the instant. If there ever had lurked any feeling in her heart against him, it deserted her now. Still, she remembered what Drouet said about his having stolen the money.

"Why, George," she said: "what's the matter with you?"

"I've been sick," he answered. "I've just got out of the hospital. For God's sake, let me have a little money, will you?"

"Of course," said Carrie, her lip trembling in a strong effort to maintain her composure. "But what's the matter with you, anyhow?"

She was opening her purse, and now pulled out all the bills in it—a five and two twos.

"I've been sick, I told you," he said, peevishly, almost resenting her excessive pity. It came hard to him to receive it from such a source.

"Here," she said. "It's all I have with me."

"All right," he answered, softly. "I'll give it back to you some day."

Carrie looked at him, while pedestrians stared at her. She felt the strain of publicity. So did Hurstwood.

"Why don't you tell me what's the matter with you?" she asked, hardly knowing what to do. "Where are you living?"

"Oh, I've got a room down in the Bowery," he answered. "There's no use trying to tell you here. I'm all right now."

He seemed in a way to resent her kindly inquiries—so much better had fate dealt with her.

"Better go on in," he said. "I'm much obliged, but I won't bother you any more."

She tried to answer, but he turned away and shuffled off toward the east.

For days this apparition was a drag on her soul before it began to wear partially away. Drouet called again, but now he was not even seen by her. His attentions seemed out of place.

"I'm out," was her reply to the boy.

So peculiar, indeed, was her lonely, self-withdrawing temper, that she was becoming an interesting figure in the public eye—she was so quiet and reserved.

Not long after the management decided to transfer the show to London. A second summer season did not seem to promise well here.

"How would you like to try subduing London?" asked her manager, one afternoon.

"It might be just the other way," said Carrie.

"I think we'll go in June," he answered.

In the hurry of departure, Hurstwood was forgotten. Both he and Drouet were left to discover that she was gone. The latter called once, and exclaimed at the news. Then he stood in the lobby, chewing the ends of his moustache. At last he reached a conclusion—the old days had gone for good.

"She isn't so much," he said; but in his heart of hearts he did not believe this.

Hurstwood shifted by curious means through a long summer and fall. A small job as janitor of a dance hall helped him for a month. Begging, sometimes going hungry, sometimes sleeping in the park, carried him over more days. Resorting to those peculiar charities, several of which, in the press of hungry search, he accidentally stumbled upon, did the rest. Toward the dead of winter, Carrie came back, appearing on Broadway in a new play; but he was not aware of it. For weeks he wandered about the city, begging, while the fire sign, announcing her engagement, blazed nightly upon the crowded street of amusements. Drouet saw it, but did not venture in.

About this time Ames returned to New York. He had made a little success in the West, and now opened a laboratory in Wooster Street. Of course, he encountered Carrie through Mrs. Vance; but there was nothing responsive between them. He thought she was still united to Hurstwood, until otherwise informed. Not knowing the facts then, he did not profess to understand, and refrained from comment.

With Mrs. Vance, he saw the new play, and expressed himself accordingly.

"She ought not to be in comedy," he said. "I think she could do better than that."

One afternoon they met at the Vances' accidentally, and began a very friendly conversation. She could hardly tell why the one-time keen interest in him was no longer with her. Unquestionably, it was because at that time he had represented something which she did not have; but this she did not understand. Success had given her the momentary feeling that she was now blessed with much of which he would approve. As a matter of fact, her little newspaper fame was nothing at all to him. He thought she could have done better, by far.

"You didn't go into comedy-drama, after all?" he said, remembering her interest in that form of art.

"No," she answered; "I haven't, so far."

He looked at her in such a peculiar way that she realized she had failed. It moved her to add: "I want to, though."

"I should think you would," he said. "You have the sort of disposition that would do well in comedy-drama."

It surprised her that he should speak of disposition. Was she, then, so clearly in his mind?

"Why?" she asked.

"Well," he said. "I should judge you were rather sympathetic in your nature."

Carrie smiled and colored slightly. He was so innocently frank with her that she drew nearer in friendship. The old call of the ideal was sounding.

"I don't know," she answered, pleased, nevertheless, beyond all concealment.

"I saw your play," he remarked. "It's very good."

"I'm glad you liked it."

"Very good, indeed," he said, "for a comedy."

This is all that was said at the time, owing to an interruption, but later they met again. He was sitting in a corner after dinner, staring at the floor, when Carrie came up with another of the guests. Hard work had given his face the look of one who is weary. It was not for Carrie to know the thing in it which appealed to her.

"All alone?" she said.

"I was listening to the music."

"I'll be back in a moment," said her companion, who saw nothing in the inventor.

Now he looked up in her face, for she was standing a moment, while he sat.

"Isn't that a pathetic strain?" he inquired, listening.

"Oh, very," she returned, also catching it, now that her attention was called.

"Sit down," he added, offering her the chair beside him.

They listened a few moments in silence, touched by the same feeling, only hers reached her through the heart. Music still charmed her as in the old days.

"I don't know what it is about music," she started to say, moved by the inexplicable longings which surged through her; "but it always makes me feel as if I wanted something—I—"

"Yes," he replied; "I know how you feel."

Suddenly he turned to considering the peculiarity of her disposition, expressing her feelings so frankly.

"You ought not to be melancholy," he said.

He thought a while, and then went off into a seemingly alien observation which, however, accorded with their feelings.

"The world is full of desirable situations, but, unfortunately, we can occupy but one at a time. It doesn't do us any good to wring our hands over the far-off things."

The music ceased and he arose, taking a standing position before her, as if to rest himself.

"Why don't you get into some good, strong comedy-drama?" he said. He was looking directly at her now, studying her face. Her large, sympathetic eyes and pain-touched mouth appealed to him as proofs of his judgment.

"Perhaps I shall," she returned.

"That's your field," he added.

"Do you think so?"

"Yes," he said; "I do. I don't suppose you're aware of it, but there is something about your eyes and mouth which fits you for that sort of work."

Carrie thrilled to be taken so seriously. For the moment, loneliness deserted her. Here was praise which was keen and analytical.

"It's in your eyes and mouth," he went on abstractedly. "I remember thinking, the first time I saw you, that there was something peculiar about your mouth. I thought you were about to cry."

"How odd," said Carrie, warm with delight. This was what her heart craved.

"Then I noticed that that was your natural look, and to-night I saw it again. There's a shadow about your eyes, too, which gives your face much this same character. It's in the depth of them, I think."

Carrie looked straight into his face, wholly aroused.

"You probably are not aware of it," he added.

She looked away, pleased that he should speak thus, longing to be equal to this feeling written upon her countenance. It unlocked the door to a new desire.

She had cause to ponder over this until they met again—several weeks or more. It showed her she was drifting away from the old ideal which had filled her in the dressing-rooms of the Avery stage and thereafter, for a long time. Why had she lost it?

"I know why you should be a success," he said, another time, "if you had a more dramatic part. I've studied it out—"

"What is it?" said Carrie.

"Well," he said, as one pleased with a puzzle, "the expression in your face is one that comes out in different things. You get the same thing in a pathetic song, or any picture which moves you deeply. It's a thing the world likes to see, because it's a natural expression of its longing."

Carrie gazed without exactly getting the import of what he meant.

"The world is always struggling to express itself," he went on. "Most people are not capable of voicing their feelings. They depend upon others. That is what genius is for. One man expresses their desires for them in music; another one in poetry; another one in a play. Sometimes nature does it in a face—it makes the face representative of all desire. That's what has happened in your case."

He looked at her with so much of the import of the thing in his eyes that she caught it. At least, she got the idea that her look was something which represented the world's longing. She took it to heart as a creditable thing, until he added:

"That puts a burden of duty on you. It so happens that you have this thing. It is no credit to you—that is, I mean, you might not have had it. You paid nothing to get it. But now that you have it, you must do something with it."

"What?" asked Carrie.

"I should say, turn to the dramatic field. You have so much sympathy and such a melodious voice. Make them valuable to others. It will make your powers endure."

Carrie did not understand this last. All the rest showed her that her comedy success was little or nothing.

"What do you mean?" she asked.

"Why, just this. You have this quality in your eyes and mouth and in your nature. You can lose it, you know. If you turn away from it and live to satisfy yourself alone, it will go fast enough. The look will leave your eyes. Your mouth will change. Your power to act will disappear. You may think they won't, but they will. Nature takes care of that."

He was so interested in forwarding all good causes that he sometimes became enthusiastic, giving vent to these preachments. Something in Carrie appealed to him. He wanted to stir her up.

"I know," she said, absently, feeling slightly guilty of neglect.

"If I were you," he said, "I'd change."

The effect of this was like roiling helpless waters. Carrie troubled over it in her rocking-chair for days.

"I don't believe I'll stay in comedy so very much longer," she eventually remarked to Lola.

"Oh, why not?" said the latter.

"I think," she said, "I can do better in a serious play."

"What put that idea in your head?"

"Oh, nothing," she answered; "I've always thought so."

Still, she did nothing—grieving. It was a long way to this better thing—or seemed so—and comfort was about her; hence the inactivity and longing.

CHAPTER XLVII

THE WAY OF THE BEATEN: A HARP IN THE WIND

In the city, at that time, there were a number of charities similar in nature to that of the captain's, which Hurstwood now patronized in a like unfortunate way. One was a convent mission-house of the Sisters of Mercy in Fifteenth Street—a row of red brick family dwellings, before the door of which hung a plain wooden contribution box, on which was painted the statement that every noon a meal was given free to all those who might apply and ask for aid. This simple announcement was modest in the extreme, covering, as it did, a charity so broad. Institutions and charities are so large and so numerous in New York that such things as this are not often noticed by the more comfortably situated. But to one whose mind is upon the matter, they grow exceedingly under inspection. Unless one were looking up this matter in particular, he could have stood at Sixth Avenue and Fifteenth Street for days around the noon hour and never have noticed that out of the vast crowd that surged along that busy thoroughfare there turned out, every few seconds, some weather-beaten, heavy-footed specimen of humanity, gaunt in countenance and dilapidated in the matter of clothes. The fact is none the less true, however, and the colder the day the more apparent it became. Space and a lack of culinary room in the mission-house, compelled an arrangement which permitted of only twenty-five or thirty eating at one time, so that a line had to be formed outside and an orderly entrance effected. This caused a daily spectacle which, however, had become so common by repetition during a number of years that now nothing was thought of it. The men waited patiently, like cattle, in the coldest weather—waited for several hours before they could be admitted. No questions were asked and no service rendered. They ate and went away again, some of them returning regularly day after day the winter through.

A big, motherly looking woman invariably stood guard at the door during the entire operation and counted the admissible number. The men moved up in solemn order. There was no haste and no eagerness displayed. It was almost a dumb procession. In the bitterest weather this line was to be found here. Under an icy wind there was a prodigious slapping of hands and a dancing of feet. Fingers and the features of the face looked as if severely nipped by the cold. A study of these men in broad light proved them to be nearly all of a type. They belonged to the class that sit on the park benches during the endurable days and sleep upon them during the summer nights. They frequent the Bowery and those down-at-the-heels East Side streets where poor clothes and shrunken features are not singled out as curious. They are the men who are in the lodging-house sitting-rooms during bleak and bitter weather and who swarm about the cheaper shelters which only open at six in a number of the lower East Side streets. Miserable food, ill-timed and greedily eaten, had played havoc with bone and muscle. They were all pale, flabby, sunken-eyed, hollow-chested, with eyes that glinted and shone and lips that were a sickly red by contrast. Their hair was but half attended to, their ears anemic in hue, and their shoes broken in leather and run down at heel and toe. They were of the class which simply floats and drifts, every wave of people washing up one, as breakers do driftwood upon a stormy shore.

For nearly a quarter of a century, in another section of the city, Fleischmann, the baker, had given a loaf of bread to any one who would come for it to the side door of his restaurant at the corner of Broadway and Tenth Street, at midnight. Every night during twenty years about three hundred men had formed in line and at the appointed time marched past the doorway, picked their loaf from a great box placed just outside, and vanished again into the night. From the beginning to the present time there had been little change in the character or number of these men. There were two or three figures that had grown familiar to those who had seen this little procession pass year after year. Two of them had missed scarcely a night in fifteen years. There were about forty, more or less, regular callers. The remainder of the line was formed of strangers. In times of panic and unusual hardships there were seldom more than three hundred. In times of prosperity, when little is heard of the unemployed, there were seldom less. The same number, winter and summer, in storm or calm, in good times and bad, held this melancholy midnight rendezvous at Fleischmann's bread box.

At both of these two charities, during the severe winter which was now on, Hurstwood was a frequent visitor. On one occasion it was peculiarly cold, and finding no comfort in begging about the streets, he waited until noon before seeking his free offering to the poor. Already, at eleven o'clock of this morning, several such as he had shambled forward out of Sixth Avenue, their thin clothes flapping and fluttering in the wind. They leaned against the iron railing which protects the walls of the Ninth Regiment Armory, which fronts upon that section of Fifteenth Street, having come early in order to be first in. Having an hour to wait, they at first lingered at a respectful distance; but others coming up, they moved closer in order to protect their right of precedence. To this collection Hurstwood came up from the west out of Seventh Avenue and stopped close to the door, nearer than all the others. Those who had been waiting before him, but farther away, now drew near, and by a certain stolidity of demeanor, no words being spoken, indicated that they were first.

Seeing the opposition to his action, he looked sullenly along the line, then moved out, taking his place at the foot. When order had been restored, the animal feeling of opposition relaxed.

"Must be pretty near noon," ventured one.

"It is," said another. "I've been waiting nearly an hour."

"Gee, but it's cold!"

They peered eagerly at the door, where all must enter. A grocery man drove up and carried in several baskets of eatables. This started some words upon grocery men and the cost of food in general.

"I see meat's gone up," said one.

"If there wuz war, it would help this country a lot."

The line was growing rapidly. Already there were fifty or more, and those at the head, by their demeanor, evidently congratulated themselves upon not having so long to wait as those at the foot. There was much jerking of heads, and looking down the line.

"It don't matter how near you get to the front, so long as you're in the first twenty-five," commented one of the first twenty-five. "You all go in together."

"Humph!" ejaculated Hurstwood, who had been so sturdily displaced.

"This here Single Tax is the thing," said another. "There ain't going to be no order till it comes."

For the most part there was silence; gaunt men shuffling, glancing, and beating their arms.

At last the door opened and the motherly-looking sister appeared. She only looked an order. Slowly the line moved up and, one by one, passed in, until twenty-five were counted. Then she interposed a stout arm, and the line halted, with six men on the steps. Of these the ex-manager was one. Waiting thus, some talked, some ejaculated concerning the misery of it; some brooded, as did Hurstwood. At last he was admitted, and, having eaten, came away, almost angered because of his pains in getting it.

At eleven o'clock of another evening, perhaps two weeks later, he was at the midnight offering of a loaf—waiting patiently. It had been an unfortunate day with him, but now he took his fate with a touch of philosophy. If he could secure no supper, or was hungry late in the evening, here was a place he could come. A few minutes before twelve, a great box of bread was pushed out, and exactly on the hour a portly, round-faced German took position by it, calling "Ready." The whole line at once moved forward, each taking his loaf in turn and going his separate way. On this occasion, the ex-manager ate his as he went plodding the dark streets in silence to his bed.

By January he had about concluded that the game was up with him. Life had always seemed a precious thing, but now constant want and weakened vitality had made the charms of earth rather dull and inconspicuous. Several times, when fortune pressed most harshly, he thought he would end his troubles; but with a change of weather, or the arrival of a quarter or a dime, his mood would change, and he would wait. Each day he would find some old paper lying about and look into it, to see if there was any trace of Carrie, but all summer and fall he had looked in vain. Then he noticed that his eyes were beginning to hurt him, and this ailment rapidly increased until, in the dark chambers of the lodgings he frequented, he did not attempt to read. Bad and irregular eating was weakening every function of his body. The one recourse left him was to doze when a place offered and he could get the money to occupy it.

He was beginning to find, in his wretched clothing and meager state of body, that people took him for a chronic type of bum and beggar. Police hustled him along, restaurant and lodging-house keepers turned him out promptly the moment he had his due; pedestrians waved him off. He found it more and more difficult to get anything from anybody.

At last he admitted to himself that the game was up. It was after a long series of appeals to pedestrians, in which he had been refused and refused—every one hastening from contact.

"Give me a little something, will you, mister?" he said to the last one. "For God's sake do; I'm starving."

"Aw, get out," said the man, who happened to be a common type himself. "You're no good. I'll give you nawthin'."

Hurstwood put his hands, red from cold, down in his pockets. Tears came into his eyes.

"That's right," he said; "I'm no good now. I was all right. I had money. I'm going to quit this," and, with death in his heart, he started down toward the Bowery. People had turned on the gas before and died; why shouldn't he? He remembered a lodging-house where there were little, close rooms, with gas-jets in them, almost pre-arranged, he thought, for what he wanted to do, which rented for fifteen cents. Then he remembered that he had no fifteen cents.

On the way he met a comfortable-looking gentleman, coming, clean-shaven, out of a fine barber shop.

"Would you mind giving me a little something?" he asked this man boldly.

The gentleman looked him over and fished for a dime. Nothing but quarters were in his pocket.

"Here," he said, handing him one, to be rid of him. "Be off, now."

Hurstwood moved on, wondering. The sight of the large, bright coin pleased him a little. He remembered that he was hungry and that he could get a bed for ten cents. With this, the idea of death passed, for the time being, out of his mind. It was only when he could get nothing but insults that death seemed worth while.

One day, in the middle of the winter, the sharpest spell of the season set in. It broke gray and cold in the first day, and on the second snowed. Poor luck pursuing him, he had secured but ten cents by nightfall, and this he had spent for food. At evening he found himself at the Boulevard and Sixty-seventh Street, where he finally turned his face Bowery-ward. Especially fatigued because of the wandering propensity which had seized him in the morning, he now half dragged his wet feet, shuffling the soles upon the sidewalk. An old, thin coat was turned up about his red ears—his cracked derby hat was pulled down until it turned them outward. His hands were in his pockets.

"I'll just go down Broadway," he said to himself.

When he reached Forty-second Street, the fire signs were already blazing brightly. Crowds were hastening to dine. Through bright windows, at every corner, might be seen gay companies in luxuriant restaurants. There were coaches and crowded cable cars.

In his weary and hungry state, he should never have come here. The contrast was too sharp. Even he was recalled keenly to better things.

"What's the use?" he thought. "It's all up with me. I'll quit this."

People turned to look after him, so uncouth was his shambling figure. Several officers followed him with their eyes, to see that he did not beg of anybody.

Once he paused in an aimless, incoherent sort of way and looked through the windows of an imposing restaurant, before which blazed a fire sign, and through the large, plate windows of which could be seen the red and gold decorations, the palms, the white napery, and shining glassware, and, above all, the comfortable crowd. Weak as his mind had become, his hunger was sharp enough to show the importance of this. He stopped stock still, his frayed trousers soaking in the slush, and peered foolishly in.

"Eat," he mumbled. "That's right, eat. Nobody else wants any."

Then his voice dropped even lower, and his mind half lost the fancy it had.

"It's mighty cold," he said. "Awful cold."

At Broadway and Thirty-ninth Street was blazing, in incandescent fire, Carrie's name. "Carrie Madenda," it read, "and the Casino Company." All the wet, snowy sidewalk was bright with this radiated fire. It was so bright that it attracted Hurstwood's gaze. He looked up, and then at a large, gilt-framed posterboard, on which was a fine lithograph of Carrie, life-size.

Hurstwood gazed at it a moment, snuffling and hunching one shoulder, as if something were scratching him. He was so run down, however, that his mind was not exactly clear.

"That's you," he said at last, addressing her. "Wasn't good enough for you, was I? Huh!"

He lingered, trying to think logically. This was no longer possible with him.

"She's got it," he said, incoherently, thinking of money. "Let her give me some."

He started around to the side door. Then he forgot what he was going for and paused, pushing his hands deeper to warm the wrists. Suddenly it returned. The stage door! That was it.

He approached the entrance and went in.

"Well?" said the attendant, staring at him. Seeing him pause, he went over and shoved him. "Get out of here," he said.

"I want to see Miss Madenda," he said.

"You do, eh?" the other said, almost tickled at the spectacle. "Get out of here," and he shoved him again. Hurstwood had no strength to resist.

"I want to see Miss Madenda," he tried to explain, even as he was being hustled away. "I'm all right. I—"

The man gave him a last push and closed the door. As he did so, Hurstwood slipped and fell in the snow. It hurt him, and some vague sense of shame returned. He began to cry and swear foolishly.

"God damned dog!" he said. "Damned old cur," wiping the slush from his worthless coat. "I—I hired such people as you once."

Now a fierce feeling against Carrie welled up—just one fierce, angry thought before the whole thing slipped out of his mind.

"She owes me something to eat," he said. "She owes it to me."

Hopelessly he turned back into Broadway again and slopped onward and away, begging, crying, losing track of his thoughts, one after another, as a mind decayed and disjointed is wont to do.

It was truly a wintry evening, a few days later, when his one distinct mental decision was reached. Already, at four o'clock, the somber hue of night was thickening the air. A heavy snow was falling—a fine picking, whipping snow, borne forward by a swift wind in long, thin lines. The streets were bedded with it—six inches of cold, soft carpet, churned to a dirty brown by the crush of teams and the feet of men. Along Broadway men picked their way in ulsters and umbrellas. Along the Bowery, men slouched through it with collars and hats pulled over their ears. In the former thoroughfare businessmen and travelers were making for comfortable hotels. In the latter, crowds on cold errands shifted past dingy stores, in the deep recesses of which lights were already gleaming. There were early lights in the cable cars, whose usual clatter was reduced by the mantle about the wheels. The whole city was muffled by this fast-thickening mantle.

In her comfortable chambers at the Waldorf, Carrie was reading at this time "Père Goriot," which Ames had recommended to her. It was so strong, and

Ames's mere recommendation had so aroused her interest, that she caught nearly the full sympathetic significance of it. For the first time, it was being borne in upon her how silly and worthless had been her earlier reading, as a whole. Becoming wearied however, she yawned and came to the window, looking out upon the old winding procession of carriages rolling up Fifth Avenue.

"Isn't it bad?" she observed to Lola.

"Terrible!" said that little lady, joining her. "I hope it snows enough to go sleigh riding."

"Oh, dear," said Carrie, with whom the sufferings of Father Goriot were still keen. "That's all you think of. Aren't you sorry for the people who haven't anything tonight?"

"Of course I am," said Lola; "but what can I do? I haven't anything."

Carrie smiled.

"You wouldn't care, if you had," she returned.

"I would, too," said Lola. "But people never gave me anything when I was hard up."

"Isn't it just awful?" said Carrie, studying the winter's storm.

"Look at that man over there," laughed Lola, who had caught sight of someone falling down. "How sheepish men look when they fall, don't they?"

"We'll have to take a coach to-night," answered Carrie absently.

In the lobby of the Imperial, Mr. Charles Drouet was just arriving, shaking the snow from a very handsome ulster. Bad weather had driven him home early and stirred his desire for those pleasures which shut out the snow and gloom of life. A good dinner, the company of a young woman, and an evening at the theater were the chief things for him.

"Why, hello, Harry!" he said, addressing a lounger in one of the comfortable lobby chairs. "How are you?"

"Oh, about six and six," said the other.

"Rotten weather, isn't it?"

"Well, I should say," said the other. "I've been just sitting here thinking where I'd go to-night."

"Come along with me," said Drouet. "I can introduce you to something dead swell."

"Who is it?" said the other.

"Oh, a couple of girls over here in Fortieth Street. We could have a dandy time. I was just looking for you."

"Supposing we get 'em and take 'em out to dinner?"

"Sure," said Drouet. "Wait'll I go upstairs and change my clothes."

"Well, I'll be in the barber shop," said the other. "I want to get a shave."

"All right," said Drouet, creaking off in his good shoes toward the elevator. The old butterfly was as light on the wing as ever.

On an incoming vestibuled Pullman, speeding at forty miles an hour through the snow of the evening, were three others, all related.

"First call for dinner in the dining-car," a Pullman servitor was announcing, as he hastened through the aisle in snow-white apron and jacket.

"I don't believe I want to play any more," said the youngest, a black-haired beauty, turned supercilious by fortune, as she pushed a euchre hand away from her.

"Shall we go into dinner?" inquired her husband, who was all that fine raiment can make.

"Oh, not yet," she answered. "I don't want to play any more, though."

"Jessica," said her mother, who was also a study in what good clothing can do for age, "push that pin down in your tie—it's coming up."

Jessica obeyed, incidentally touching at her lovely hair and looking at a little jewel-faced watch. Her husband studied her, for beauty, even cold, is fascinating from one point of view.

"Well, we won't have much more of this weather," he said. "It only takes two weeks to get to Rome."

Mrs. Hurstwood nestled comfortably in her corner and smiled. It was so nice to be the mother-in-law of a rich young man—one whose financial state had borne her personal inspection.

"Do you suppose the boat will sail promptly?" asked Jessica, "if it keeps up like this?"

"Oh, yes," answered her husband. "This won't make any difference."

Passing down the aisle came a very fair-haired banker's son, also of Chicago, who had long eyed this supercilious beauty. Even now he did not hesitate to glance at her, and she was conscious of it. With a specially conjured show of indifference, she turned her pretty face wholly away. It was not wifely modesty at all. By so much was her pride satisfied.

At this moment Hurstwood stood before a dirty four-story building in a side street quite near the Bowery, whose one-time coat of buff had been changed by soot and rain. He mingled with a crowd of men—a crowd which had been, and was still, gathering by degrees.

It began with the approach of two or three, who hung about the closed wooden doors and beat their feet to keep them warm. They had on faded derby hats with dents in them. Their misfit coats were heavy with melted snow and turned up at the collars. Their trousers were mere bags, frayed at the bottom and wobbling over big, soppy shoes, torn at the sides and worn almost to shreds. They made no effort to go in, but shifted ruefully about, digging their hands deep in their pockets and leering at the crowd and the increasing lamps. With the minutes, increased the number. There were old men with grizzled beards and sunken eyes, men who were comparatively young but shrunken by diseases, men who were middle-aged. None were fat. There was a face in the thick of the collection which was as white as drained veal. There was another red as brick. Some came with thin, rounded shoulders, others with wooden legs, still others with frames so lean that clothes only flapped about them. There were great ears, swollen noses, thick lips, and, above all, red, blood-shot eyes. Not a normal, healthy face in the whole mass; not a straight figure; not a straight-forward, steady glance.

In the drive of the wind and sleet they pushed in on one another. There were wrists, unprotected by coat or pocket, which were red with cold. There were ears, half covered by every conceivable semblance of a hat, which still looked stiff and bitten. In the snow they shifted, now one foot, now another, almost rocking in unison.

With the growth of the crowd about the door came a murmur. It was not conversation, but a running comment directed at any one in general. It contained oaths and slang phrases.

"By damn, I wish they'd hurry up."

"Look at the copper watchin'."

"Maybe it ain't winter, nuther!"

"I wisht I was in Sing Sing."

Now a sharper lash of wind cut down and they huddled closer. It was an edging, shifting, pushing throng. There was no anger, no pleading, no threatening words. It was all sullen endurance, unlightened by either wit or good fellowship.

A carriage went jingling by with some reclining figure in it. One of the men nearest the door saw it.

"Look at the bloke ridin'."

"He ain't so cold."

"Eh, eh, eh!" yelled another, the carriage having long since passed out of hearing.

Little by little the night crept on. Along the walk a crowd turned out on its way home. Men and shop-girls went by with quick steps. The cross-town cars began to be crowded. The gas lamps were blazing, and every window bloomed ruddy with a steady flame. Still the crowd hung about the door, unwavering.

"Ain't they ever goin' to open up?" queried a hoarse voice, suggestively.

This seemed to renew the general interest in the closed door, and many gazed in that direction. They looked at it as dumb brutes look, as dogs paw and whine and study the knob. They shifted and blinked and muttered, now a curse, now a comment. Still they waited and still the snow whirled and cut them with biting flakes. On the old hats and peaked shoulders it was piling. It gathered in little heaps and curves and no one brushed it off. In the center of the crowd the warmth and steam melted it, and water trickled off hat rims and down noses, which the owners could not reach to scratch. On the outer rim the piles remained unmelted. Hurstwood, who could not get in the center, stood with head lowered to the weather and bent his form.

A light appeared through the transom overhead. It sent a thrill of possibility through the watchers. There was a murmur of recognition. At last the bars grated inside and the crowd pricked up its ears. Footsteps shuffled within and it murmured again. Some one called: "Slow up there, now," and then the door opened. It was push and jam for a minute, with grim, beast silence to prove its quality, and then it melted inward, like logs floating, and disappeared. There were wet hats and wet shoulders, a cold, shrunken, disgruntled mass, pouring in between bleak walls. It was just six o'clock and there was supper in every hurrying pedestrian's face. And yet no supper was provided here—nothing but beds.

Hurstwood laid down his fifteen cents and crept off with weary steps to his allotted room. It was a dingy affair—wooden, dusty, hard. A small gas-jet furnished sufficient light for so rueful a corner.

"Hm!" he said, clearing his throat and locking the door.

Now he began leisurely to take off his clothes, but stopped first with his coat, and tucked it along the crack under the door. His vest he arranged in the same place. His old wet, cracked hat he laid softly upon the table. Then he pulled off his shoes and lay down.

It seemed as if he thought a while, for now he arose and turned the gas out, standing calmly in the blackness, hidden from view. After a few moments, in which he reviewed nothing, but merely hesitated, he turned the gas on again, but applied no match. Even then he stood there, hidden wholly in that kindness which is night, while the uprising fumes filled the room. When the odor reached his nostrils, he quit his attitude and fumbled for the bed.

"What's the use?" he said, weakly, as he stretched himself to rest.

And now Carrie had attained that which in the beginning seemed life's object, or, at least, such fraction of it as human beings ever attain of their original desires. She could look about on her gowns and carriage, her furniture and bank account.

Friends there were, as the world takes it—those who would bow and smile in acknowledgment of her success. For these she had once craved. Applause there was, and publicity—once far off, essential things, but now grown trivial and indifferent. Beauty also—her type of loveliness—and yet she was lonely. In her rocking-chair she sat, when not otherwise engaged—singing and dreaming.

Thus in life there is ever the intellectual and the emotional nature—the mind that reasons, and the mind that feels. Of one come the men of action—generals and statesmen; of the other, the poets and dreamers—artists all.

As harps in the wind, the latter respond to every breath of fancy, voicing in their moods all the ebb and flow of the ideal.

Man has not yet comprehended the dreamer any more than he has the ideal. For him the laws and morals of the world are unduly severe. Ever hearkening to the sound of beauty, straining for the flash of its distant wings, he watches to follow, wearying his feet in traveling. So watched Carrie, so followed, rocking and singing.

And it must be remembered that reason had little part in this. Chicago dawning, she saw the city offering more of loveliness than she had ever known, and instinctively, by force of her moods alone, clung to it. In fine raiment and elegant surroundings, men seemed to be contented. Hence, she drew near these things, Chicago, New York; Drouet, Hurstwood; the world of fashion and the world of stage—these were but incidents. Not them, but that which they represented, she longed for. Time proved the representation false.

Oh, the tangle of human life! How dimly as yet we see. Here was Carrie, in the beginning poor, unsophisticated, emotional; responding with desire to everything most lovely in life, yet finding herself turned as by a wall. Laws to say: "Be allured, if you will, by everything lovely, but draw not nigh unless by righteousness." Convention to say: "You shall not better your situation save by honest labor." If honest labor be unremunerative and difficult to endure; if it be the long, long road which never reaches beauty, but wearies the feet and the heart; if the drag to follow beauty be such that one abandons the admired way, taking rather the despised path leading to her dreams quickly, who shall cast the first stone? Not evil, but longing for that which is better, more often directs the steps of the erring. Not evil, but goodness more often allures the feeling mind unused to reason.

Amid the tinsel and shine of her state walked Carrie, unhappy. As when Drouet took her, she had thought: "Now I am lifted into that which is best"; as when Hurstwood seemingly offered her the better way: "Now am I happy." But since the world goes its way past all who will not partake of its folly, she now found herself alone. Her purse was open to him whose need was greatest. In her walks on Broadway, she no longer thought of the elegance of the creatures who passed her. Had they more of that peace and beauty which glimmered afar off, then were they to be envied.

Drouet abandoned his claim and was seen no more. Of Hurstwood's death she was not even aware. A slow, black boat setting out from the pier at Twenty-seventh Street upon its weekly errand bore, with many others, his nameless body to the Potter's Field.

Thus passed all that was of interest concerning these twain in their relation to her. Their influence upon her life is explicable alone by the nature of her longings. Time was when both represented for her all that was most potent in earthly success. They were the personal representatives of a state most blessed to attain—the titled ambassadors of comfort and peace, aglow with their credentials. It is but natural that when the world which they represented no longer allured her, its ambassadors should be discredited. Even had Hurstwood returned in his original beauty and glory, he could not now have allured her. She had learned that in his world, as in her own present state, was not happiness.

Sitting alone, she was now an illustration of the devious ways by which one who feels, rather than reasons, may be led in the pursuit of beauty. Though often disillusioned, she was still waiting for that halcyon day when she should be led forth among dreams become real. Ames had pointed out a farther step, but on and on beyond that, if accomplished, would lie others for her. It was forever to be the pursuit of that radiance of delight which tints the distant hill-tops of the world.

Oh, Carrie, Carrie! Oh, blind strivings of the human heart! Onward, onward, it saith, and where beauty leads, there it follows. Whether it be the tinkle of a lone sheep bell o'er some quiet landscape, or the glimmer of beauty in sylvan places, or the show of soul in some passing eye, the heart knows and makes answer, following. It is when the feet weary and hope seems vain that the heartaches and the longings arise. Know, then, that for you is neither surfeit nor content. In your rocking-chair, by your window dreaming, shall you long, alone. In your rocking-chair, by your window, shall you dream such happiness as you may never feel.

HENRY JAMES
(1843–1916)

On the narrative level, Henry James' characters visit each other, at home or abroad. And not much else. They don't fight Indians, wear scarlet letters in the public square, pursue whales, raft rivers, fight battles, commit suicide, or clash in city streets. The drama of events did not interest James. With a consummately artful control of point of view and style, he convinced his rather limited audience of readers that there is more than enough drama in episodes of perception, conflicts of temperaments and motives, and revelations of consciousness.

A life concentrated upon the ongoing drama of consciousness does not reveal much of itself in events. What is sufficient to know about James may be readily found within the body of his work, much of it in the configurations of *The Ambassadors*. But some of the specifics may be illuminating. He was born April 15, 1843, in New York City, to Henry James, Sr., a prosperous Irish Protestant and Mary Robertson Walsh. There was a great deal of intelligence and talent in the James family. Older brother William became one of America's first great philosophers and psychologists. There has been speculation that Alice might have realized her potential had she not lived in the intimidating shadow of her two famous older brothers. James' two younger brothers served in the Union Army during the Civil War. Illness kept Henry from joining them. He studied law at Harvard briefly. In 1865, his first tale, "The Story of a Year," appeared in print. Two years after his family settled in Cambridge, Massachusetts, he began a series of trips abroad. He was 33 when his first novel, *Roderick Hudson*, appeared. It dealt with the dilemma of the modern artist on the American cultural scene.

Like Cooper, Hawthorne, Melville, Twain, and Crane, James travelled in Europe. But perhaps a childhood spent there had determined that he would become more of an American expatriate than the others. Many of his most famous works deal with various dilemmas of upper class Americans as they encounter the Old World as travellers, such as: *The American* (1877), *Daisy Miller* (1879), and *The Portrait of a Lady* (1881) from what has been called his early period; *The Wings of the Dove* (1902) and *The Ambassadors* (1903) from his mature years. The masterwork of the middle period, *The Bostonians* (1886), was set in America and was a deliberate effort "to write a very American tale," dealing with "the situation of women . . . the agitation in their behalf." He returned to the United States for the last time in 1905. *The American Scene* (1907), an account of his travels then, is full of distinctive insights. A long nervous illness began in 1909. Facing death in 1915, the year he became a naturalized British citizen, he exclaimed, "So here it is at last, the distinguished thing!" Death itself came February 28, 1916, in the midst of World War I, when James was 72.

James published in every genre except poetry, including short story, tale, novella, novel, play, autobiography, theater and literary criticism, and essay. One of his most famous tales, "The Turn of the Screw" (1891), is as much a study of the narrator's neurosis as it is a tale of the supernatural. Two other studies in the effect of adult psychology upon children and adolescents are *What Maisie Knew* (1897) and *The Awkward Age* (1899), an experiment in extended use of dialog. Several years earlier, James wrote a number of plays. Ironically, the American writer whose style has proven most difficult is most adaptable to the stage and screen and thus accessible to mass audiences.

"It is art," wrote James, "that *makes* life." Because of James' belief in the primacy of art and because of the nature of his fiction, products of "an inexhaustible sensibility," James' works will never lure a great many readers. "Live all you can," Strether tells little Bilham in *The Ambassadors*. But to James, "experience consists of impressions . . .impressions *are* experience." It is "the power to guess the unseen from the seen, to trace the implications of things, to judge the whole piece by the pattern. . . ." He exhorted young writers to "try to be one of the people on whom nothing is lost." To James, "few things" were "more exciting than a psychological reason." Few readers bring such attitudes and expectations to fiction, and so they fail to experience with Strether "the terrible *fluidity* of self-revelation."

The creative process was endlessly fascinating to James. He was "the great reviser." In 1906, he started revising once again all his works for the definitive New York Edition. Prefaces to each of the novels describing the inception, gestation, and writing problems for each are collected in *The Art of the Novel* (1934). In one of them he stated that life is "all inclusion and confusion" and art is "all discrimination and selection." His essays on technique are collected in *The Art of Fiction* (1948).

Major differences between Henry James and other classic American writers lie in the realms of temperament and technique. His emotions, imagination, and intellect were stimulated by daily interactions with members of English and European high society within the constraints of convention. The gathering of raw material from observation of the rapidly changing American experience did not appeal to him. The techniques of allegory, symbolism, realism, and naturalism were less useful for the effect he wanted his reader to experience than the creation of elaborate psychological contexts that generate multiple implications. He sought opportunities to gather impressions, not raw material, and he said he would "go to the stake" for his impressions. To convey that subtle, nuanced kind of experience, he developed a new technique that characterized his best work and that influenced many writers: everything was experienced by a single consciousness. The effect of this focus was a more intense experience for the reader. James' own third person style caught the rhythm of consciousness of his upperclass, sophisticated characters. James filters the story of Chad Newsome in *The Ambassadors* through the consciousness of Lambert Strether in such a way that the development of Strether's responses are more dramatic for the reader than Chad's story. Formerly restricted to either first person or omniscient narration, writers now had the option of employing the Jamesian third person, central intelligence point-of-view technique. Consciousness itself became a rich new subject matter and its quality a new moral consideration.

THE AMBASSADORS

Henry James

BOOK FIRST

I

Strether's first question, when he reached the hotel, was about his friend; yet on his learning that Waymarsh was apparently not to arrive till evening he was not wholly disconcerted. A telegram from him bespeaking a room "only if not noisy," reply paid, was produced for the enquirer at the office, so that the understanding they should meet at Chester rather than at Liverpool remained to that extent sound. The same secret principle, however, that had prompted Strether not absolutely to desire Waymarsh's presence at the dock, that had led him thus to postpone for a few hours his enjoyment of it, now operated to make him feel he could still wait without disappointment. They would dine together at the worst, and, with all respect to dear old Waymarsh—if not even, for that matter, to himself—there was little fear that in the sequel they shouldn't see enough of each other. The principle I have just mentioned as operating had been, with the most newly disembarked of the two men, wholly instinctive—the fruit of a sharp sense that, delightful as it would be to find himself looking, after so much separation, into his comrade's face, his business would be a trifle bungled should he simply arrange for this countenance to present itself to the nearing steamer as the first "note" of Europe. Mixed with everything was the apprehension, already, on Strether's part, that it would, at best, throughout, prove the note of Europe in quite a sufficient degree.

That note had been meanwhile—since the previous afternoon, thanks to this happier device—such a consciousness of personal freedom as he hadn't known for years; such a deep taste of change and of having above all for the moment nobody and nothing to consider, as promised already, if headlong hope were not too foolish, to colour his adventure with cool success. There were people on the ship with whom he had easily consorted—so far as ease could up to now be imputed to him—and who for the most part plunged straight into the current that set from the landing-stage to London; there were others who had invited him to a tryst at the inn and had even invoked his aid for a "look round" at the beauties of Liverpool; but he had stolen away from every one alike, had kept no appointment and renewed no acquaintance, had been indifferently aware of the number of persons who esteemed themselves fortunate in being, unlike himself, "met," and had even independently, unsociably, alone, without encounter or relapse and by mere quiet evasion, given his afternoon and evening to the immediate and the sensible. They formed a qualified draught of Europe, an afternoon and an evening on the banks of the Mersey, but such as it was he took his potion at least undiluted. He winced a little, truly, at the thought that Waymarsh might be already at Chester; he reflected that, should he have to describe himself there as having "got in" so early, it would be difficult to make the interval look particularly eager; but he was like a man who, elatedly finding in his pocket more money than usual, handles it a while and idly and pleasantly chinks it before addressing himself to the business of spending. That he was prepared to be vague to Waymarsh about the hour of the ship's touching, and that he both wanted extremely to see him and enjoyed extremely the duration of delay—these things, it is to be conceived, were early signs in him that his relation to his actual errand might prove none of the simplest. He was burdened, poor Strether—it had better be confessed at the outset—with the oddity of a double consciousness. There was detachment in his zeal and curiosity in his indifference.

After the young woman in the glass cage had held up to him across her counter the pale-pink leaflet bearing his friend's name, which she neatly pronounced, he turned away to find himself, in the hall, facing a lady who met his eyes as with an intention suddenly determined, and whose features—not freshly young, not markedly fine, but on happy terms with each other—came back to him as from a recent vision. For a moment they stood confronted; then the moment placed her: he had noticed her the day before, noticed her at his previous inn, where—again in the hall—she had been briefly engaged with some people of his own ship's company. Nothing had actually passed between them, and he would as little have been able to say what had been the sign of her face for him on the first occasion as to name the ground of his present recognition. Recognition at any rate appeared to prevail on her own side as well—which would only have added to the mystery. All she now began by saying to him nevertheless was that, having chanced to catch his enquiry, she was moved to ask, by his leave, if it were possibly a question of Mr. Waymarsh of Milrose, Connecticut—Mr. Waymarsh the American lawyer.

"Oh yes," he replied, "my very well-known friend. He's to meet me here, coming up from Malvern, and I supposed he'd already have arrived. But he doesn't come till later, and I'm relieved not to have kept him. Do you know him?" Strether wound up.

It wasn't till after he had spoken that he became aware of how much there had been in him of response; when the tone of her own rejoinder, as well as the play of something more in her face—something more, that is, than its apparently usual restless light—seemed to notify him. "I've met him at Milrose—where I used sometimes, a good while ago, to stay; I had friends there who were friends of his, and I've been at his house. I won't answer for it that he would know me," Strether's new acquaintance pursued; "but I should be delighted to see him. Perhaps," she added, "I shall—for I'm staying over." She paused while our friend took in these things, and it was as if a good deal of talk had already passed. They even vaguely smiled at it, and Strether presently observed that Mr. Waymarsh would, no doubt, be easily to be seen. This, however, appeared to affect the lady as if she might have advanced too far. She appeared to have no reserves about anything. "Oh," she said, "he won't care!"—and she immediately thereupon remarked that she believed Strether knew the Munsters; the Munsters being the people he had seen her with at Liverpool.

But he didn't, it happened, know the Munsters well enough to give the case much of a lift; so that they were left together as if over the mere laid table of conversation. Her qualification of the mentioned connexion had rather removed than placed a dish, and there seemed nothing else to serve. Their attitude remained, none the less, that of not forsaking the board; and the effect of this in turn was to give them the appearance of having accepted each other with an absence of preliminaries practically complete. They moved along the hall together, and Strether's companion threw off that the hotel had the advantage of a garden. He was aware by this time of his strange inconsequence: he had shirked the intimacies of the steamer and had muffled the shock of Waymarsh only to find himself forsaken, in this sudden case, both of avoidance and of caution. He passed, under this unsought protection and before he had so much as gone up to his room, into the garden of the hotel, and at the end of ten minutes had agreed to meet there again, as soon as he should have made himself tidy, the dispenser of such good assurances. He wanted to look at the town, and they would forthwith look together. It was almost as if she had been in possession and received him as a guest. Her acquaintance with the place presented her in a manner as a hostess, and Strether had a rueful glance for the lady in the glass cage. It was as if this personage had seen herself instantly superseded.

When in a quarter of an hour he came down, what his hostess saw, what she might have taken in with a vision kindly adjusted, was the lean, the slightly loose figure of a man of the middle height and something more perhaps than the middle age—a man of five-and-fifty, whose most immediate signs were a marked bloodless brownness of face, a thick dark moustache, of characteristically American cut, growing strong and falling low, a head of hair still abundant but irregularly streaked with grey, and a nose of bold free prominence, the even line, the high finish, as it might have been called, of which had a certain effect of mitigation. A perpetual pair of glasses astride of this fine ridge, and a line, unusually deep and drawn, the prolonged pen-stroke of time, accompanying the curve of the moustache from nostril to chin, did something to complete the facial furniture that an attentive observer would have seen catalogued, on the spot, in the vision of the other party to Strether's appointment. She waited for him in the garden, the other party, drawing on a pair of singularly fresh soft and elastic light gloves and presenting herself with a superficial readiness which, as he approached her over the small smooth lawn and in the watery English sunshine, he might, with his rougher preparation, have marked as the model for such an occasion. She had, this lady, a perfect plain propriety, an expensive subdued suitability, that her companion was not free to analyse, but that struck him, so that his consciousness of it was instantly acute, as a quality quite new to him. Before reaching her he stopped on the grass and went through the form of feeling for something, possibly forgotten, in the light overcoat he carried on his arm; yet the essence of the act was no more than the impulse to gain time. Nothing could have been odder than Strether's sense of himself as at that moment launched in something of which the sense would be quite disconnected from the sense of his past and which was literally beginning there and then. It had begun in fact already upstairs and before the dressing-glass that struck him as blocking further, so strangely, the dimness of the window of his dull bedroom; begun with a sharper survey of the elements of Appearance than he had for a long time been moved to make. He had during those moments felt these elements to be not so much to his hand as he should have liked, and then had fallen back on the thought that they were precisely a matter as to which help was supposed to come from what he was about to do. He was about to go up to London, so that hat and necktie might wait. What had come as straight to him as a ball in a well-played game—and caught moreover not less neatly—was just the air, in the person of his friend, of having seen and chosen, the air of achieved possession of those vague qualities and quantities that collectively figured to him as the advantage snatched from lucky chances. Without pomp or circumstance, certainly, as her original address to him, equally with his own response, had been, he would have sketched to himself his impression of her as: "Well, she's more thoroughly civilized—!" If "More thoroughly than *whom*?" would not have been for him a sequel to this remark, that was just by reason of his deep consciousness of the bearing of his comparison.

The amusement, at all events, of a civilization intenser was what—familiar compatriot as she was, with the full tone of the compatriot and the rattling link not with mystery but only with dear dyspeptic Waymarsh—she appeared distinctly to promise. His pause while he felt in his overcoat was positively the pause of confidence, and it enabled his eyes to make out as much of a case for her, in proportion, as her own made out for himself. She affected him as almost insolently young; but an easily carried five-and-thirty could still do that. She was, however, like himself, marked and wan; only it naturally couldn't have been known to him how much a spectator looking from one to the other might have discerned that they had in common. It wouldn't for such a spectator have been altogether insupposable that, each so finely brown and so sharply spare, each confessing so to dents of surface and aids to sight, to a disproportionate nose and a head delicately or grossly grizzled, they might have been brother and sister. On this ground indeed there would have been a residuum of difference; such a sister having surely known in respect to such a brother the extremity of separation, and such a brother now feeling in respect to such a sister the extremity of surprise. Surprise, it was true, was not on the other hand what the eyes of Strether's friend most showed him while she gave him, stroking her gloves smoother, the time he appreciated. They had taken hold of him straightway, measuring him up and down as if they knew how; as if he were human material they had already in some sort handled. Their possessor was in truth, it may be communicated, the mistress of a hundred cases or categories, receptacles of the mind, subdivisions for convenience, in which, from a full experience, she pigeon-holed her fellow mortals with a hand as free as that of a compositor scattering type. She was as equipped in this particular as Strether was the reverse, and it made an opposition between them which he might well have shrunk from submitting to if he had fully suspected it. So far as he did suspect it he was on the contrary, after a short shake of his consciousness, as pleasantly passive as might be. He really had a sort of sense of what she knew. He had quite the sense that she knew things he didn't, and though this was a concession that in general he found not easy to make to women, he made it now as good-humouredly as if it lifted a burden. His eyes were so quiet behind his eternal nippers that they might almost have been absent without changing his face, which took its expression mainly, and not least its stamp of sensibility from other sources, surface and grain and form. He joined his guide in an instant, and then felt she had profited still better than he by his having been, for the moments just mentioned, so at the disposal of her intelligence. She knew even intimate things about him that he hadn't yet told her and perhaps never would. He wasn't unaware that he had told her rather remarkably many for the time, but these were not the real ones. Some of the real ones however, precisely, were what she knew.

They were to pass again through the hall of the inn to get into the street, and it was here she presently checked him with a question. "Have you looked up my name?"

He could only stop with a laugh. "Have you looked up mine?"

"Oh dear, yes—as soon as you left me. I went to the office and asked. Hadn't *you* better do the same?"

He wondered. "Find out who you are?—after the uplifted young woman there has seen us thus scrape acquaintance!"

She laughed on her side now at the shade of alarm in his amusement. "Isn't it a reason the more? If what you're afraid of is the injury for me—my being seen to walk off with a gentleman who has to ask who I am—I assure you I don't in the least mind. Here, however," she continued, "is my card, and as I find there's something else again I have to say at the office, you can just study it during the moment I leave you."

She left him after he had taken from her the small pasteboard she had extracted from her pocket-book, and he had extracted another from his own, to exchange with it, before she came back. He read thus the simple designation "Maria Gostrey," to which was attached, in a corner of the card, with a number, the name of a street, presumably in Paris, without other appreciable identity than its foreignness. He put the card into his waistcoat pocket, keeping his own meanwhile in evidence; and as he leaned against the door-post he met with the smile of a straying thought what the expanse before the hotel offered to his view. It was positively droll to him that he should already have Maria Gostrey, whoever she was—of which he hadn't really the least idea—in a place of safe keeping. He had somehow an assurance that he should carefully preserve the little token he had just tucked in. He gazed with unseeing lingering eyes as he followed some of the implications of his act, asking himself if he really felt admonished to qualify it as disloyal. It was prompt, it was possibly even premature, and there was little doubt of the expression of face the sight of it would have produced in a certain person. But if it were "wrong"—why then he had better not have come out at all. At this, poor man, had he already—and even before meeting Waymarsh—arrived. He had believed he had a limit, but the limit had been transcended within thirty-six hours. By how long a space on the plane of manners, or even of morals, moreover, he felt still more sharply after Maria Gostrey had come back to him and with a gay decisive "So now—!" led him forth into the world. This counted, it struck him as he walked beside her with his overcoat on an arm, his umbrella under another and his personal pasteboard a little stiffly retained between forefinger and thumb, this struck him as really, in comparison, his introduction to things. It hadn't been "Europe" at Liverpool, no—not even in the dreadful delightful impressive streets the night before—to the extent his present companion made it so. She hadn't yet done that so much as when after their walk had lasted a few minutes and he had had time to wonder if a couple of sidelong glances from her meant that he had best have put on gloves, she almost pulled him up with an amused challenge. "But why—fondly as it's so easy to imagine your clinging to it—don't you put it away? Or if it's an inconvenience to you to carry it, one's often glad to have one's card back. The fortune one spends in them!"

Then he saw both that his way of marching with his own prepared tribute had affected her as a deviation in one of those directions he couldn't yet measure, and that she supposed this emblem to be still the one he had received from her. He accordingly handed her the card as if in restitution, but as soon as she had it she felt the difference and, with her eyes on it, stopped short for apology. "I like," she observed, "your name."

"Oh," he answered, "you won't have heard of it!" Yet he had his reasons for not being sure but that she perhaps might.

Ah it was but too visible! She read it over again as one who had never seen it. "Mr. Lewis Lambert Strether"—she sounded it almost as freely as for any stranger. She repeated, however, that she liked it—"Particularly the Lewis Lambert. It's the name of a novel of Balzac's."

"Oh I know that!" said Strether.

"But the novel's an awfully bad one."

"I know that too," Strether smiled. To which he added with an irrelevance that was only superficial: "I come from Woollett, Massachusetts." It made her for some reason—the irrelevance or whatever—laugh. Balzac had described many cities, but hadn't described Woollett, Massachusetts. "You say that," she returned, "as if you wanted one immediately to know the worst."

"Oh I think it's a thing," he said, "that you must already have made out. I feel it so that I certainly must look it, speak it, and, as people say there, 'act' it. It sticks out of me, and you knew surely for yourself as soon as you looked at me."

"The worst, you mean?"

"Well, the fact of where I come from. There at any rate it *is*; so that you won't be able, if anything happens, to say that I've not been straight with you."

"I see"—and Miss Gostrey looked really interested in the point he had made. "But what do you think of as happening?"

Though he wasn't shy—which was rather anomalous—Strether gazed about without meeting her eyes; a motion that was frequent with him in talk, yet of which his words often seemed not at all the effect. "Why that you should find me too hopeless." With which they walked on again together while she answered, as they went, that the most "hopeless" of her countryfolk were in general precisely those she liked best. All sorts of other pleasant small things—small things that were yet large for him—flowered in the air of the occasion; but the bearing of the occasion itself on matters still remote concerns us too closely to permit us to multiply our illustrations. Two or three, however, in truth, we should perhaps regret to lose. The tortuous wall—girdle, long since snapped, of the little swollen city, half held in place by careful civic hands—wanders in narrow file between parapets smoothed by peaceful generations, pausing here and there for a dismantled gate or a bridged gap, with rises and drops, steps up and steps down, queer twists, queer contacts, peeps into homely streets and under the brows of gables, views of cathedral tower and waterside fields, of huddled English town and ordered English country. Too deep almost for words was the delight of these things to Strether; yet as deeply mixed with it were certain images of his inward picture. He had trod this walk in the far-off time, at twenty-five; but that, instead of spoiling it, only enriched it for present feeling and marked his renewal as a thing substantial enough to share. It was with Waymarsh he should have shared it, and he was now accordingly taking from him something that was his due. He looked repeatedly at his watch, and when he had done so for the fifth time Miss Gostrey took him up.

"You're doing something that you think not right."

It so touched the place that he quite changed colour and his laugh grew almost awkward. "Am I enjoying it as much as *that*?"

"You're not enjoying it, I think, so much as you ought."

"I see"—he appeared thoughtfully to agree. "Great is my privilege."

"Oh it's not your privilege! It has nothing to do with *me*. It has to do with yourself. Your failure's general."

"Ah there you are!" he laughed. "It's the failure of Woollett. *That's* general."

"The failure to enjoy," Miss Gostrey explained, "is what I mean."

"Precisely. Woollett isn't sure it ought to enjoy. If it were it would. But it hasn't, poor thing," Strether continued, "any one to show it how. It's not like me. I have somebody."

They had stopped, in the afternoon sunshine—constantly pausing, in their stroll, for the sharper sense of what they saw—and Strether rested on one of the high sides of the old stony groove of the little rampart. He leaned back on this support with his face to the tower of the cathedral, now admirably commanded by their station, the high red-brown mass, square and subordinately spired and crocketed, retouched and restored, but charming to his long-sealed eyes and with the first swallows of the year weaving their flight all round it. Miss Gostrey lingered near him, full of an air, to which she more and more justified her right, of understanding and effect of things. She quite concurred. "You've indeed somebody." And she added: "I wish you *would* let me show you how!"

"Oh I'm afraid of you!" he cheerfully pleaded.

She kept on him a moment, through her glasses and through his own, a certain pleasant pointedness. "Ah no, you're not! You're not in the least, thank goodness! If you had been we shouldn't so soon have found ourselves here together. I think," she comfortably concluded, "you trust me."

"I think I do!—but that's exactly what I'm afraid of. I shouldn't mind if I didn't. It's falling thus in twenty minutes so utterly into your hands. I daresay," Strether continued, "it's a sort of thing you're thoroughly familiar with; but nothing more extraordinary has ever happened to me."

She watched him with all her kindness. "That means simply that you've recognised me—which *is* rather beautiful and rare. You see what I am." As on this, however, he protested, with a good-humoured headshake, a resignation of any such a claim, she had a moment of explanation. "If you'll only come on further as you *have* come you'll at any rate make out. My own fate has been too many for me, and I've succumbed to it. I'm a general guide—to 'Europe,' don't you know? I wait for people—I put them through. I pick them up—I set them down. I'm a sort of superior 'courier-maid.' I'm a companion at large. I take people, as I've told you, about. I never sought it—it has come to me. It has been my fate, and one's fate one accepts. It's a dreadful thing to have to say, in so wicked a world, but I verily believe that, such as you see me, there's nothing I don't know. I know all the shops and the prices—but I know worse things still. I bear on my back the huge load of our national consciousness, or, in other words—for it comes to that—of our nation itself. Of what is our nation composed but of the men and women individually on my shoulders? I don't do it, you know, for any particular advantage. I don't do it, for instance—some people do, you know—for money."

Strether could only listen and wonder and weigh his chance. "And yet, affected as you are then to so many of your clients, you can scarcely be said to do it for love." He waited a moment. "How do we reward you?"

She had her own hesitation, but "You don't!" she finally returned, setting him again in motion. They went on, but in a few minutes, though while still thinking over what she had said, he once more took out his watch; mechanically, unconsciously and as if made nervous by the mere exhilaration of what struck him as her strange and cynical wit. He looked at the hour without seeing it, and then, on something again said by his companion, had another pause. "You're really in terror of him."

He smiled a smile that he almost felt to be sickly. "Now you can see why I'm afraid of you."

"Because I've such illuminations? Why, they're all for your help! It's what I told you," she added, "just now. You feel as if this were wrong."

He fell back once more, settling himself against the parapet as if to hear more about it. "Then get me out!"

Her face fairly brightened for the joy of the appeal, but, as if it were a question of immediate action, she visibly considered. "Out of waiting for him?—of seeing him at all?"

"Oh no—not that," said poor Strether, looking grave. "I've got to wait for him—and I want very much to see him. But out of the terror. You did put your finger on it a few minutes ago. It's general, but it avails itself of particular occasions. That's what it's doing for me now. I'm always considering something else; something else, I mean, than the thing of the moment. The obsession of the other thing is the terror. I'm considering at present for instance something else than *you*."

She listened with charming earnestness. "Oh you oughtn't to do that!"

"It's what I admit. Make it then impossible."

She continued to think. "Is it really an 'order' from you?—that I shall take the job? *Will* you give yourself up?"

Poor Strether heaved his sigh. "If I only could! But that's the deuce of it—that I never can. No—I can't."

She wasn't, however, discouraged. "But you want to at least?"

"Oh unspeakably!"

"Ah then, if you'll try!"—and she took over the job, as she had called it, on the spot. "Trust me!" she exclaimed; and the action of this, as they retraced their steps, was presently to make him pass his hand into her arm in the manner of a benign dependent paternal old person who wishes to be "nice" to a younger one. If he drew it out again indeed as they approached the inn this may have been because, after more talk had passed between them, the relation of age, or at least of experience—which, for that matter, had already played to and fro with some freedom—affected him as incurring a readjustment. It was at all events perhaps lucky that they arrived in sufficiently separate fashion within range of the hotel-door. The young lady they had left in the glass cage watched as if she had come to await them on the threshold. At her side stood a person equally interested, by his attitude, in their return, and the effect of the sight of whom was instantly to determine for Strether another of those responsive arrests that we have had so repeatedly to note. He left it to Miss Gostrey to name, with the fine full bravado, as it almost struck him, of her "Mr. Waymarsh!" what was to have been, what—he more than ever felt as his short stare of suspended welcome took things in—would have been, but for herself, his doom. It was already upon him even at that distance—Mr. Waymarsh was for *his* part joyless.

II

He had none the less to confess to this friend that evening that he knew almost nothing about her, and it was a deficiency that Waymarsh, even with his memory refreshed by contact, by her own prompt and lucid allusions and enquiries, by their having publicly partaken of dinner in her company, and by another stroll, to which she was not a stranger, out into the town to look at the cathedral by moonlight—it was a blank that the resident of Milrose, though admitting acquaintance with the Munsters, professed himself unable to fill. He had no recollection of Miss Gostrey, and two or three questions that she put to him about those members of his circle had, to Strether's observation, the same effect he himself had already more directly felt—the effect of appearing to place all knowledge, for the time, on this original woman's side. It interested him indeed to mark the limits of any such relation for her with his friend as there could possibly be a question of, and it particularly struck him that they were to be marked altogether in Waymarsh's quarter. This added to his own sense of having gone far with her—gave him an early illustration of a much shorter course. There was a certitude he immediately grasped—a conviction that Waymarsh would quite fail, as it were, and on whatever degree of acquaintance, to profit by her.

There had been after the first interchange among the three a talk of some five minutes in the hall, and then the two men had adjourned to the garden, Miss Gostrey for the time disappearing. Strether in due course accompanied his friend to the room he had bespoken and had, before going out, scrupulously visited; where at the end of another half-hour he had no less discreetly left him. On leaving him he repaired straight to his own room, but with the prompt effect of feeling the compass of that chamber resented by his condition. There he enjoyed at once the first consequence of their reunion. A place was too small for him after it that had seemed large enough before. He had awaited it with something he would have been sorry, have been almost ashamed not to recognise as emotion, yet with a tacit assumption at the same time that emotion would in the event find itself relieved. The actual oddity was that he was only more excited; and his excitement—to which indeed he would have found it difficult instantly to give a name—brought him once more downstairs and caused him for some minutes vaguely to wander. He went once more to the garden; he looked into the public room, found Miss Gostrey writing letters and backed out; he roamed, fidgeted and wasted time; but he was to have his more intimate session with his friend before the evening closed.

It was late—not till Strether had spent an hour upstairs with him—that this subject consented to betake himself to doubtful rest. Dinner and the subsequent stroll by moonlight—a dream, on Strether's part, of romantic effects rather prosaically merged in a mere missing of thicker coats—had measurably intervened, and this midnight conference was the result of Waymarsh's having (when they were free, as he put it, of their fashionable friend) found the smoking-room not quite what he wanted, and yet bed what he wanted less. His most frequent form of words was that he knew himself, and they were applied on this occasion to his certainty of not sleeping. He knew himself well enough to know that he should have a night of prowling unless he should succeed, as a preliminary, in getting prodigiously tired. If the effort directed to this end involved till a late hour the presence of Strether—consisted, that is, in the detention of the latter for full discourse—there was yet an impression of minor discipline involved for our friend in the picture Waymarsh made as he sat in trousers and shirt on the edge of his couch. With his long legs extended and his large back much bent, he nursed, alternately, for an almost incredible time, his elbows and his beard. He struck his visitor as extremely, as almost wilfully uncomfortable; yet what had this been for Strether, from that first glimpse of him disconcerted in the porch of the hotel, but the predominant note? The discomfort was in a manner contagious, as well as also in a manner inconsequent and unfounded; the visitor felt that unless he should get used to it—or unless Waymarsh himself should—it would constitute a menace for his own prepared, his own already confirmed, consciousness of the agreeable. On their first going up together to the room Strether had selected for him Waymarsh had looked it over in silence with a sigh that represented for his companion, if not the habit of disapprobation, at least the despair of felicity; and this look had recurred to Strether as the key of much he had since observed. "Europe," he had begun to gather from these things, had up to now rather failed of its message to him; he hadn't got into tune with it and had at the end of three months almost renounced any such expectation.

He really appeared at present to insist on that by just perching there with the gas in his eyes. This of itself somehow conveyed the futility of single rectifications in a multiform failure. He had a large handsome head and a large sallow seamed face—a striking significant physiognomic total, the upper range of which, the great political brow, the thick loose hair, the dark fuliginous eyes, recalled even to a generation whose standard had dreadfully deviated the impressive image, familiar by engravings and busts, of some great national worthy of the earlier part of the mid-century. He was of the personal type—and it was an element in the power and promise that in their early time Strether had found in him—of the American statesman, the statesman trained in "Congressional halls," of an elder day. The legend had been in later years that as the lower part of his face, which was weak and slightly crooked, spoiled the likeness, this was the real reason for the growth of his beard, which might have seemed to spoil it for those not in the secret. He shook his mane; he fixed, with his admirable eyes, his auditor or his observer; he wore no glasses and had a way, partly formidable, yet also partly encouraging, as from a representative to a constituent, of looking very hard at those who approached him. He met you as if you had knocked and he had bidden you enter. Strether, who hadn't seen him for so long an interval, apprehended him now with a freshness of taste, and had perhaps never done him such ideal justice. The head was bigger, the eyes finer, than they need have been for the career; but that only meant, after all, that the career was itself expressive. What it expressed at midnight in the gas-glaring bedroom at Chester was that the subject of it had, at the end of years, barely escaped, by flight in time, a general nervous collapse. But this very proof of the full life, as the full life was understood at Milrose, would have made to Strether's imagination an element in which Waymarsh could have floated easily had he only consented to float. Alas nothing so little resembled floating as the rigour with which, on the edge of his bed, he hugged his posture of prolonged impermanence. It suggested to his comrade something that always, when kept up, worried him—a person established in a railway coach with a forward inclination.

It represented the angle at which poor Waymarsh was to sit through the ordeal of Europe.

Thanks to the stress of occupation, the strain of professions, the absorption and embarrassment of each, they had not, at home, during years before this sudden brief and almost bewildering reign of comparative ease, found so much as a day for a meeting; a fact that was in some degree an explanation of the sharpness with which most of his friend's features stood out to Strether. Those he had lost sight of since the early time came back to him; others that it was never possible to forget struck him now as sitting, clustered and expectant, like a somewhat defiant family-group, on the door-step of their residence. The room was narrow for its length, and the occupant of the bed thrust so far a pair of slippered feet that the visitor had almost to step over them in his recurrent rebounds from his chair to fidget back and forth. There were marks the friends made on things to talk about, and on things not to, and one of the latter in particular fell like the tap of chalk on the blackboard. Married at thirty, Waymarsh had not lived with his wife for fifteen years, and it came up vividly between them in the glare of the gas that Strether wasn't to ask about her. He knew they were still separate and that she lived at hotels, travelled in Europe, painted her face and wrote her husband abusive letters, of not one of which, to a certainty, that sufferer spared himself the perusal; but he respected without difficulty the cold twilight that had settled on this side of his companion's life. It was a province in which mystery reigned and as to which Waymarsh had never spoken the informing word. Strether, who wanted to do him the highest justice wherever he *could* do it, singularly admired him for the dignity of this reserve, and even counted it as one of the grounds—grounds all handled and numbered—for ranking him, in the range of their acquaintance, as a success. He *was* a success, Waymarsh, in spite of overwork, of prostration, of sensible shrinkage, of his wife's letters and of his not liking Europe. Strether would have reckoned his own career less futile had he been able to put into it anything so handsome as so much fine silence. One might one's self easily have left Mrs. Waymarsh; and one would assuredly have paid one's tribute to the ideal in covering with that attitude the derision of having been left by her. Her husband had held his tongue and had made a large income; and these were in especial the achievements as to which Strether envied him. Our friend had had indeed on his side too, a subject for silence, which he fully appreciated; but it was a matter of a different sort and the figure of the income he had arrived at had never been high enough to look any one in the face.

"I don't know as I quite see what you require it for. You don't appear sick to speak of." It was of Europe that Waymarsh thus finally spoke.

"Well," said Strether, who fell as much as possible into step, "I guess I don't *feel* sick now that I've started. But I had pretty well run down before I did start."

Waymarsh raised his melancholy look. "Ain't you about up to your usual average?"

It was not quite pointedly sceptical, but it seemed somehow a plea for the purest veracity, and it thereby affected our friend as the very voice of Milrose. He had long since made a mental distinction—though never in truth daring to betray it—between the voice of Milrose and the voice even of Woollett. It was the former, he felt, that was most in the real tradition. There had been occasions in his past when the sound of it had reduced him to temporary confusion, and the present, for some reason, suddenly became such another. It was nevertheless no light matter that the very effect of his confusion should be to make him again prevaricate. "That description hardly does justice to a man to whom it has done such a lot of good to see *you*."

Waymarsh fixed on his washing-stand the silent detached stare with which Milrose in person, as it were, might have marked the unexpectedness of a compliment from Woollett; and Strether, for his part, felt once more like Woollett in person. "I mean," his friend presently continued, "that your appearance isn't as bad as I've seen it: it compares favourably with what it was when I last noticed it." On this appearance Waymarsh's eyes yet failed to rest; it was almost as if they obeyed an instinct of propriety, and the effect was still stronger when, always considering the basin and jug, he added, "You've filled out some since then."

"I'm afraid I have," Strether laughed: "one does fill some with all one takes in, and I've taken in, I dare say, more than I've natural room for. I was dog-tired when I sailed." It had the oddest sound of cheerfulness.

"*I* was dog-tired," his companion returned, "when I arrived, and it's this wild hunt for rest that takes all the life out of me. The fact is, Strether—and it's a comfort to have you here at last to say it to; though I don't know, after all, that I've really waited; I've told it to people I've met in the cars—the fact is, such a country as this ain't my *kind* of country anyway. There ain't a country I've seen over here that *does* seem my kind. Oh I don't say but what there are plenty of pretty places and remarkable old things; but the trouble is that I don't seem to feel anywhere in tune. That's one of the reasons why I suppose I've gained so little. I haven't had the first sign of that lift I was led to expect." With this he broke out more earnestly. "Look here—I want to go back."

His eyes were all attached to Strether's now, for he was one of the men who fully face you when they talk of themselves. This enabled his friend to look at him hard and immediately to appear to the highest advantage in his own eyes by doing so. "That's a genial thing to say to a fellow who has come out on purpose to meet you!"

Nothing could have been finer, on this, than Waymarsh's sombre glow. "*Have* you come out on purpose?"

"Well—very largely."

"I thought from the way you wrote there was something back of it."

Strether hesitated. "Back of my desire to be with you?"

"Back of your prostration."

Strether, with a smile made more dim by a certain consciousness, shook his head. "There are all the causes of it!"

"And no particular cause that seemed most to drive you?"

Our friend could at last conscientiously answer. "Yes. One. There *is* a matter that has had much to do with my coming out."

Waymarsh waited a little. "Too private to mention?"

"No, not too private—for *you*. Only rather complicated."

"Well," said Waymarsh, who had waited again. "I *may* lose my mind over here, but I don't know as I've done so yet."

"Oh you shall have the whole thing. But not to-night."

Waymarsh seemed to sit stiffer and to hold his elbows tighter. "Why not—if I can't sleep?"

"Because, my dear man, I *can*!"

"Then where's your prostration?"

"Just in that—that I can put in eight hours." And Strether brought it out that if Waymarsh didn't "gain" it was because he didn't go to bed: the result of which was, in its order, that, to do the latter justice, he permitted his friend to insist on his really getting settled. Strether, with a kind coercive hand for it, assisted him to this consummation, and again found his own part in their relation auspiciously enlarged by the smaller touches of lowering the lamp and seeing to a sufficiency of blanket. It somehow ministered for him to indulgence to feel Waymarsh, who looked unnaturally big and black in bed, as much tucked in as a patient in a hospital and, with this covering up to his chin, as much simplified by it. He hovered in vague pity, to be brief, while his companion challenged him out of the bedclothes. "Is she really after you? Is that what's behind?"

Strether felt an uneasiness at the direction taken by his companion's insight, but he played a little at uncertainty. "Behind my coming out?"

"Behind your prostration or whatever. It's generally felt, you know, that she follows you up pretty close."

Strether's candour was never very far off. "Oh it has occurred to you that I'm literally running away from Mrs. Newsome?"

"Well, I haven't *known* but what you are. You're a very attractive man, Strether. You've seen for yourself," said Waymarsh, "what that lady downstairs makes of it. Unless indeed," he rambled on with an effect between the ironic and the anxious, "it's you that are after *her*. Is Mrs. Newsome *over* here?" He spoke as with a droll dread of her.

It made his friend—though rather dimly—smile. "Dear no; she's safe, thank goodness—as I think I more and more feel—at home. She thought of coming, but she gave it up. I've come in a manner instead of her; and come to that extent—for you're right in your inference—on her business. So you see there *is* plenty of connexion."

Waymarsh continued to see at least all there was. "Involving accordingly the particular one I've referred to?"

Strether took another turn about the room, giving a twitch to his companion's blanket and finally gaining the door. His feeling was that of a nurse who had earned personal rest by having made everything straight. "Involving more things than I can think of breaking ground on now. But don't be afraid—you shall have them from me: you'll probably find yourself having quite as much of them as you can do with. I shall—if we keep together—very much depend on your impression of some of them."

Waymarsh's acknowledgement of this tribute was characteristically indirect. "You mean to say you don't believe we *will* keep together?"

"I only glance at the danger," Strether paternally said, "because when I hear you wail to go back I seem to see you open up such possibilities of folly."

Waymarsh took it—silent a little—like a large snubbed child. "What are you going to do with me?"

It was the very question Strether himself had put to Miss Gostrey, and he wondered if he had sounded like that. But *he* at least could be more definite. "I'm going to take you right down to London."

"Oh I've *been* down to London!" Waymarsh more softly moaned. "I've no use, Strether, for anything down there."

"Well," said Strether good-humouredly, "I guess you've some use for *me*."

"So I've got to go?"

"Oh you've got to go further yet."

"Well," Waymarsh sighed, "do your damnedest! Only you *will* tell me before you lead me on all the way—?"

Our friend had again so lost himself, both for amusement and for contrition, in the wonder of whether he had made, in his own challenge that afternoon, such another figure, that he for an instant missed the thread. "Tell you—?"

"Why what you've got on hand."

Strether hesitated. "Why it's such a matter as that even if I positively wanted I shouldn't be able to keep it from you."

Waymarsh gloomily gazed. "What does that mean then but that your trip is just *for* her?"

"For Mrs. Newsome? Oh it certainly is, as I say. Very much."

"Then why do you also say it's for me?"

Strether, in impatience, violently played with his latch.

"It's simple enough. It's for both of you."

Waymarsh at last turned over with a groan. "Well, *I* won't marry you!"

"Neither, when it comes to that—!" But the visitor had already laughed and escaped.

III

He had told Miss Gostrey that he should probably take, for departure with Waymarsh, some afternoon train, and it thereupon in the morning appeared that this lady had made her own plan for an earlier one. She had breakfasted when Strether came into the coffee-room; but, Waymarsh not having yet emerged, he was in time to recall her to the terms of their understanding and to pronounce her discretion overdone. She was surely not to break away at the very moment she had created a want. He had met her as she rose from her little table in a window, where, with the morning papers beside her, she reminded him, as he let her know, of Major Pendennis breakfasting at his club—a compliment of which she professed a deep appreciation; and he detained her as pleadingly as if he had already—and notably under pressure of the visions of the night—learned to be unable to do without her. She must teach him at all events, before she went, to order breakfast as breakfast was ordered in Europe, and she must especially sustain him in the problem of ordering for Waymarsh. The latter had laid upon his friend, by desperate sounds through the door of his room, dreadful divined responsibilities in respect to beefsteak and oranges—responsibilities which Miss Gostrey took over with an alertness of action that matched her quick intelligence. She had before this weaned the expatriated from traditions compared with which the matutinal beefsteak was but the creature of an hour, and it was not for her, with some of her memories, to falter in the path; though she freely enough declared, on reflexion, that there was always in such cases a choice of opposed policies. "There are times when to give them their head, you know—!"

They had gone to wait together in the garden for the dressing of the meal, and Strether found her more suggestive than ever. "Well, what?"

"Is to bring about for them such a complexity of relations—unless indeed we call it a simplicity!—that the situation *has* to wind itself up. They want to go back."

"And you want them to go!" Strether gaily concluded.

"I always want them to go, and I send them as fast as I can."

"Oh I know—you take them to Liverpool."

"Any port will serve in a storm. I'm—with all my other functions—an agent for repatriation. I want to re-people our stricken country. What will become of it else? I want to discourage others."

The ordered English garden, in the freshness of the day, was delightful to Strether, who liked the sound, under his feet, of the tight fine gravel, packed with the chronic damp, and who had the idlest eye for the deep smoothness of turf and the clean curves of paths. "Other people?"

"Other countries. Other people—yes. I want to encourage our own."

Strether wondered. "Not to come? Why then do you 'meet' them?—since it doesn't appear to be to stop them?"

"Oh that they shouldn't come is as yet too much to ask. What I attend to is that they come quickly and return still more so. I meet them to help it to be over as soon as possible, and though I don't stop them I've my way of putting them through. That's my little system; and, if you want to know," said Maria Gostrey, "it's my real secret, my innermost mission and use. I only seem, you see, to beguile and approve; but I've thought it all out and I'm working all the while underground. I can't perhaps quite give you my formula, but I think that practically I succeed. I send you back spent. So you stay back. Passed through my hands—"

"We don't turn up again?" The further she went the further he always saw himself able to follow. "I don't want your formula—I feel quite enough, as I hinted yesterday, your abysses. Spent!" he echoed. "If that's how you're arranging so subtly to send me I thank you for the warning."

For a minute, amid the pleasantness—poetry in tariffed items, but all the more, for guests already convicted, a challenge to consumption—they smiled at each other in confirmed fellowship. "Do you call it subtly? It's a plain poor tale. Besides, you're a special case."

"Oh special cases—that's weak!" She was weak enough, further still, to defer her journey and agree to accompany the gentlemen on their own, might a separate carriage mark her independence; though it was in spite of this to befall after luncheon that she went off alone and that, with a tryst taken for a day of her company in London, they lingered another night. She had, during the morning—spent in a way that he was to remember later on as the very climax of his foretaste, as warm with presentiments, with what he would have called collapses—had all sorts of things out with Strether; and among them the fact that though there was never a moment of her life when she wasn't "due" somewhere, there was yet scarce a perfidy to others of which she wasn't capable for his sake. She explained moreover that wherever she happened to be she found a dropped thread to pick up, a ragged edge to repair, some familiar appetite in ambush, jumping out as she approached, yet appeasable with a temporary biscuit. It became, on her taking the risk of the deviation imposed on him by her insidious arrangement of his morning meal, a point of honour for her not to fail with Waymarsh of the larger success too; and her subsequent boast to Strether was that she had made their friend fare—and quite without his knowing what was the matter—as Major Pendennis would have fared at the Megatherium. She had made him breakfast like a gentleman, and it was nothing, she forcibly asserted, to what she would yet make him do. She made him participate in the slow reiterated ramble with which, for Strether, the new day amply filled itself; and it was by her art that he somehow had the air, on the ramparts and in the Rows, of carrying a point of his own.

The three strolled and stared and gossiped, or at least the two did; the case really yielding for their comrade, if analysed, but the element of stricken silence. This element indeed affected Strether as charged with audible rumblings, but he was conscious of the care of taking it explicitly as a sign of pleasant peace. He wouldn't appeal too much, for that provoked stiffness; yet he wouldn't be too freely tacit, for that suggested giving up. Waymarsh himself adhered to an ambiguous dumbness that might have represented either the growth of a perception or the despair of one; and at times and in places—where the low-browed galleries were darkest, the opposite gables queerest, the solicitations of every kind densest—the others caught him fixing hard some object of minor interest, fixing even at moments nothing discernible, as if he were indulging it with a truce. When he met Strether's eye on such occasions he looked guilty and furtive, fell the next minute into some attitude of retraction. Our friend couldn't show him the right things for fear of provoking some total renouncement, and was tempted even to show him the wrong in order to make him differ with triumph. There were moments when he himself felt shy of professing the full sweetness of the taste of leisure, and there were others when he found himself feeling as if his passages of interchange with the lady at his side might fall upon the third member of their party very much as Mr. Burchell, at Dr. Primrose's fireside, was influenced by the high flights of the visitors from London. The smallest things so arrested and amused him that he repeatedly almost apologised—brought up afresh in explanation his plea of a previous grind. He was aware at the same time that his grind had been as nothing to Waymarsh's, and he repeatedly confessed that, to cover his frivolity, he was doing his best for his previous virtue. Do what he might, in any case, his previous virtue was still there, and it seemed fairly to stare at him out of the windows of shops that were not as the shops of Woollett, fairly to make him want things that he shouldn't know what to do with. It was by the oddest, the least admissible of laws demoralising him now; and the way it boldly took was to make him want more wants. These first walks in Europe were in fact a kind of finely lurid intimation of what one might find at the end of that process. Had he come back after long years, in something already so like the evening of life, only to be exposed to it? It was at all events over the shop-windows that he made, with Waymarsh, most free; though it would have been easier had not the latter most sensibly yielded to the appeal of the merely useful trades. He pierced with his sombre detachment the plate-glass of ironmongers and saddlers, while Strether flaunted an affinity with the dealers in stamped letter-paper and in smart neckties. Strether was in fact recurrently shameless in the presence of the tailors, though it was just over the heads of the tailors that his countryman most loftily looked. This gave Miss Gostrey a grasped opportunity to back up Waymarsh at his expense. The weary lawyer—it was unmistakable—had a conception of dress; but that, in view of some of the features of the effect produced, was just what made the danger of insistence on it. Strether wondered if he by this time thought Miss Gostrey less fashionable or Lambert Strether more so; and it appeared probable that most of the remarks exchanged between this latter pair about passers, figures, faces, personal types, exemplified in their degree the disposition to talk as "society" talked.

Was what was happening to himself then, was what already *had* happened, really that a woman of fashion was floating him into society and that an old friend deserted on the brink was watching the force of the current? When the woman of fashion permitted Strether—as she permitted him at the most—the purchase of a pair of gloves, the terms she made about it, the prohibition of neckties and other items till she should be able to guide him through the Burlington Arcade, were such as to fall upon a sensitive ear as a challenge to unjust imputations. Miss Gostrey was such a woman of fashion as could make without a symptom of vulgar blinking an appointment for the Burlington Arcade. Mere discriminations about a pair of gloves could thus at any rate represent—always for such sensitive ears as were in question—possibilities of something that Strether could make a mark against only as the peril of apparent wantonness. He had quite the consciousness of his new friend, for their companion, that he might have had of a Jesuit in petticoats, a representative of the recruiting interests of the Catholic Church. The Catholic Church for Waymarsh—that was to say the enemy, the monster of bulging eyes and far-reaching quivering groping tentacles—was exactly society, exactly the multiplication of shibboleths, exactly the discrimination of types and tones, exactly the wicked old Rows of Chester, rank with feudalism; exactly in short Europe.

There was light for observation, however, in an incident that occurred just before they turned back to luncheon. Waymarsh had been for a quarter of an hour exceptionally mute and distant, and something, or other—Strether was never to make out exactly what—proved, as it were, too much for him after his comrades had stood for three minutes taking in, while they leaned on an old balustrade that guarded the edge of the Row, a particularly crooked and huddled street-view. "He thinks us sophisticated, he thinks us worldly, he thinks us wicked, he thinks us all sorts of queer things," Strether reflected; for wondrous were the vague quantities our friend had within a couple of short days acquired the habit of conveniently and conclusively lumping together. There seemed moreover a direct connexion between some such inference and a sudden grim dash taken by Waymarsh to the opposite side. This movement was startingly sudden, and his companions at first supposed him to have espied, to be pursuing, the glimpse of an acquaintance. They next made out, however, that an open door had instantly received him, and they then recognised him as engulfed in the establishment of a jeweller, behind whose glittering front he was lost to view. The act had somehow the note of a demonstration, and it left each of the others to show a face almost of fear. But Miss Gostrey broke into a laugh. "What's the matter with him?"

"Well," said Strether, "he can't stand it."

"But can't stand what?"

"Anything. Europe."

"Then how will that jeweller help him?"

Strether seemed to make it out, from their position, between the interstices of arrayed watches, of close-hung dangling gewgaws. "You'll see."

"Ah that's just what—if he buys anything—I'm afraid of: that I shall see something rather dreadful."

Strether studied the finer appearances. "He may buy everything."

"Then don't you think we ought to follow him?"

"Not for worlds. Besides we can't. We're paralysed. We exchange a long scared look, we publicly tremble. The thing is, you see, we 'realise.' He has struck for freedom."

She wondered but she laughed. "Ah what a price to pay! And I was preparing some for him so cheap."

"No, no," Strether went on, frankly amused now; "don't call it that: the kind of freedom *you* deal in is dear." Then as to justify himself: "Am I not in *my* way trying it? It's this."

"Being here, you mean, with me?"

"Yes, and talking to you as I do. I've known you a few hours and I've known *him* all my life; so that if the ease I thus take with you about him isn't magnificent"—and the thought of it held him a moment—"why, it's rather base."

"It's magnificent!" said Miss Gostrey to make an end of it. "And you should hear," she added, "the ease *I* take—and I above all intend to take—with Mr. Waymarsh."

Strether thought. "About *me*? Ah that's no equivalent. The equivalent would be Waymarsh's himself serving me up—his remorseless analysis of me. And he'll never do that"—he was sadly clear. "He'll never remorselessly analyse me." He quite held her with the authority of this. "He'll never say a word to you about me."

She took it in; she did it justice; yet after an instant her reason, her restless irony, disposed of it. "Of course he won't. For what do you take people, that they're able to say words about anything, able remorselessly to analyse? There are not many like you and me. It will be only because he's too stupid."

It stirred in her friend a sceptical echo which was at the same time the protest of the faith of years. "Waymarsh stupid?"

"Compared with you."

Strether had still his eyes on the jeweller's front, and he waited a moment to answer. "He's a success of a kind that I haven't approached."

"Do you mean he has made money?"

"He makes it—to my belief. And I," said Strether, "though with a back quite as bent, have never made anything. I'm a perfectly equipped failure."

He feared an instant she'd ask him if he meant he was poor; and he was glad she didn't, for he really didn't know to what the truth on this unpleasant point mightn't have prompted her. She only, however, confirmed his assertion. "Thank goodness you're a failure—it's why I so distinguish you! Anything else to-day is too hideous. Look about you—look at the successes. Would you *be* one, on your honour? Look, moreover," she continued, "at me."

For a little accordingly their eyes met. "I see," Strether returned. "You too are out of it."

"The superiority you discern in me," she concurred, "announces my futility. If you knew," she sighed, "the dreams of my youth! But our realities are what has brought us together. We're beaten brothers in arms."

He smiled at her kindly enough, but he shook his head. "It doesn't alter the fact that you're expensive. You've cost me already—!"

But he had hung fire. "Cost you what?"

"Well, my past—in one great lump. But no matter," he laughed; "I'll pay with my last penny."

Her attention had unfortunately now been engaged by their comrade's return, for Waymarsh met their view as he came out of his shop. "I hope he hasn't paid," she said, "with *his* last; though I'm convinced he has been splendid, and has been so for you."

"Ah no—not that!"

"Then for me?"

"Quite as little." Waymarsh was by this time near enough to show signs his friends could read, though he seemed to look almost carefully at nothing in particular.

"Then for himself?"

"For nobody. For nothing. For freedom."

"But what has freedom to do with it?"

Strether's answer was indirect. "To be as good as you and me. But different."

She had had time to take in their companion's face; and with it, as such things were easy for her, she took in all. "Different—yes. But better!"

If Waymarsh was sombre he was also indeed almost sublime. He told them nothing, left his absence unexplained, and though they were convinced he had made some extraordinary purchase they were never to learn its nature. He only glowered grandly at the tops of the old gables. "It's the sacred rage," Strether had had further time to say; and this sacred rage was to become between them, for convenient comprehension, the description of one of his periodical necessities. It was Strether who eventually contended that it did make him better than they. But by that time Miss Gostrey was convinced that she didn't want to be better than Strether.

BOOK SECOND

I

Those occasions on which Strether was, in association with the exile from Milrose, to see the sacred rage glimmer through would doubtless have their due periodicity; but our friend had meanwhile to find names for many other matters. On no evening of his life perhaps, as he reflected, had he had to supply so many as on the third of his short stay in London; an evening spent by Miss Gostrey's side at one of the theatres, to which he had found himself transported, without his own hand raised, on the mere expression of a conscientious wonder. She knew her theatre, she knew her play, as she had triumphantly known, three days running, everything else, and the moment filled to the brim, for her companion, that apprehension of the interesting which, whether or no the interesting happened to filter through his guide, strained now to its limits his brief opportunity. Waymarsh hadn't come with them; he had seen plays enough, he signified, before Strether had joined him—an affirmation that had its full force when his friend ascertained by questions that he had seen two and a circus. Questions as to what he had seen had on him indeed an effect only less favourable than questions as to what he hadn't. He liked the former to be discriminated; but how could it be done, Strether asked of their constant counsellor, without discriminating the latter?

Miss Gostrey had dined with him at his hotel, face to face over a small table on which the lighted candles had rose-coloured shades; and the rose-coloured shades and the small table and the soft fragrance of the lady—had anything to his mere sense ever been so soft?—were so many touches in he scarce knew what positive high picture. He had been to the theatre, even to the opera, in Boston, with Mrs. Newsome, more than once acting as her only escort; but there had been no little confronted dinner, no pink lights, no whiff of vague sweetness, as a preliminary: one of the results of which was that at present, mildly rueful, though with a sharpish accent, he actually asked himself *why* there hadn't. There was much the same difference in his impression of the noticed state of his companion, whose dress was "cut down," as he believed the term to be, in respect to shoulders and bosom, in a manner quite other than Mrs. Newsome's, and who wore round her throat a broad red velvet band with an antique jewel—he was rather complacently sure it was antique—attached to it in front. Mrs. Newsome's dress was never in any degree "cut down," and she never wore round her throat a broad red velvet band: if she had, moreover, would it ever have served so to carry on and complicate, as he now almost felt, his vision?

It would have been absurd of him to trace into ramifications the effect of the ribbon from which Miss Gostrey's trinket depended, had he not for the hour, at the best, been so given over to uncontrolled perceptions. What was it but an uncontrolled perception that his friend's velvet band somehow added, in her appearance to the value of every other item—to that of her smile and of the way she carried her head, to that of her complexion, of her lips, her teeth, her eyes, her hair? What certainty, had a man conscious of a man's work in the world to do with red velvet bands? He wouldn't for anything have so exposed himself as to tell Miss Gostrey how much he liked hers, yet he *had* none the less not only caught himself in the act—frivolous, no doubt, idiotic, and above all unexpected—of liking it: he had in addition taken it as a starting-point for fresh backward, fresh forward, fresh lateral flights. The manner in which Mrs. Newsome's throat *was* encircled suddenly represented for him, in an alien order, almost as many things as the manner in which Miss Gostrey's was. Mrs. Newsome wore, at operatic hours, a black silk dress—very handsome, he knew it was "handsome"—and an ornament that his memory was able further to identify as a ruche. He had his association indeed with the ruche, but it was rather imperfectly romantic. He had once said to the wearer—and it was as "free" a remark as he had ever made to her—that she looked, with her ruff and other matters, like Queen Elizabeth; and it had after this in truth been his fancy that, as a consequence of that tenderness and an acceptance of the idea, the form of this special tribute to the "frill" had grown slightly more marked. The connexion, as he sat there and let his imagination roam, was to strike him as vaguely pathetic; but there it all was, and pathetic was doubtless in the conditions the best thing it could possibly be. It had assuredly existed at any rate; for it seemed now to come over him that no gentleman of his age at Woollett could ever, to a lady of Mrs. Newsome's, which was not much less than his, have embarked on such a simile.

All sorts of things in fact now seemed to come over him, comparatively few of which his chronicler can hope for space to mention. It came over him for instance that Miss Gostrey looked perhaps like Mary Stuart: Lambert Strether had a candour of fancy which could rest for an instant gratified in such an antithesis. It came over him that never before—no, literally never—had a lady dined with him at a public place before going to the play. The publicity of the place was just, in the matter, for Strether, the rare strange thing; it affected him almost as the achievement of privacy might have affected a man of a different experience. He had married, in the far-away years, so young as to have missed the natural time in Boston for taking girls to the Museum; and it was absolutely true of him that—even after the close of the period of conscious detachment occupying the centre of his life, the grey middle desert of the two deaths, that of his wife and that, ten years later, of his boy—he had never taken any one anywhere. It came over him in especial—though the monition had, as happened, already sounded, fitfully gleamed, in other forms—that the business he had come out on hadn't yet been so brought home to him as by the sight of the people about him. She gave him the impression, his friend, at first, more straight than he got it for himself—gave it simply by saying with off-hand illumination, "Oh yes, they're types!"—but after he had taken it he made to the full his own use of it; both while he kept silence for the four acts and while he talked in the intervals. It was an evening, it was a world of types, and this was a connexion above all in which the figures and faces in the stalls were interchangeable with those on the stage.

He felt as if the play itself penetrated him with the naked elbow of his neighbour, a great stripped handsome red-haired lady who conversed with a gentleman on her other side in stray dissyllables which had for his ear, in the oddest way in the world, so much sound that he wondered they hadn't more sense; and he recognized by the same law, beyond the footlights, what he was pleased to take for the very flush of English life. He had distracted drops in which he couldn't have said if it were actors or auditors who were most true, and the upshot of which, each time, was the consciousness of new contracts. However he viewed his job it was "types" he should have to tackle. Those before him and around him were not as the types of Woollett, where, for that matter, it had begun to seem to him that there must only have been the male and the female. These made two exactly, even with the individual varieties. Here, on the other hand, apart from the personal and the sexual range—which might be greater or less—a series of strong stamps had been applied, as it were, from without; stamps that his observation played with as, before a glass case on a table, it might have passed from medal to medal and from copper to gold. It befell that in the drama precisely there was a bad woman in a yellow frock who made a pleasant weak good-looking young man in perpetual evening dress do the most dreadful things. Strether felt himself on the whole not afraid of the yellow frock, but he was vaguely anxious over a certain kindness into which he found himself drifting for its victim. He hadn't come out, he reminded himself, to be too kind, or indeed to be kind at all, to Chadwick Newsome. Would Chad also be in perpetual evening dress? He somehow rather hoped it—it seemed so to add to *this* young man's general amenability; though he wondered too if, to fight him with his own weapons, he himself (a thought almost startling) would have likewise to be. This young man furthermore would have been much more easy to handle—at least for *him*—than appeared probable in respect to Chad.

It came up for him with Miss Gostrey that there were things of which she would really perhaps after all have heard; and she admitted when a little pressed that she was never quite sure of what she heard as distinguished from things such as, on occasions like the present, she only extravagantly guessed. "I seem with this freedom, you see, to have guessed Mr. Chad. He's a young man on whose head high hopes are placed at Woollett; a young man a wicked woman has got hold of and whom his family over there have sent you out to rescue. You've accepted the mission of separating him from the wicked woman. Are you quite sure she's very bad for him?"

Something in his manner showed it as quite pulling him up. "Of course we are. Wouldn't *you* be?"

"Oh I don't know. One never does—does one?—beforehand. One can only judge on the facts. Yours are quite new to me; I'm really not in the least, as you see, in possession of them: so it will be awfully interesting to have them from you. If you're satisfied, that's all that's required. I mean if you're sure you *are* sure: sure it won't do."

"That he should lead such a life? Rather!"

"Oh but I don't know, you see, about his life; you've not told me about his life. She may be charming—his life!"

"Charming?"—Strether stared before him. "She's base, venal—out of the streets."

"I see. And *he*—?"

"Chad, wretched boy?"

"Of what type and temper is he?" she went on as Strether had lapsed.

"Well—the obstinate." It was as if for a moment he had been going to say more and had then controlled himself.

That was scarce what she wished. "Do you like him?"

This time he was prompt. "No. How *can* I?"

"Do you mean because of your being so saddled with him?"

"I'm thinking of his mother," said Strether after a moment. "He has darkened her admirable life." He spoke with austerity. "He has worried her half to death."

"Oh that's of course odious." She had a pause as if for renewed emphasis of this truth, but it ended on another note. "Is her life very admirable?"

"Extraordinarily."

There was so much in the tone that Miss Gostrey had to devote another pause to the appreciation of it. "And has he only *her*? I don't mean the bad woman in Paris," she quickly added—"for I assure you I shouldn't even at the best be disposed to allow him more than one. But has he only his mother?"

"He has also a sister, older than himself and married; and they're both remarkably fine women."

"Very handsome, you mean?"

This promptitude—almost, as he might have thought, this precipitation, gave him a brief drop; but he came up again. "Mrs. Newsome, I think, is handsome, though she's not of course, with a son of twenty-eight and a daughter of thirty, in her very first youth. She married, however, extremely young."

"And is wonderful," Miss Gostrey asked, "for her age?"

Strether seemed to feel with a certain disquiet the pressure of it. "I don't say she's wonderful. Or rather," he went on to the next moment, "I do say it. It's exactly what she *is*—wonderful. But I wasn't thinking of her appearance," he explained—"striking as that doubtless is. I was thinking—well, of many other things." He seemed to look at these as if to mention some of them; then took, pulling himself up, another turn. "About Mrs. Pocock people may differ."

"Is that the daughter's name—'Pocock'?"

"That's the daughter's name," Strether sturdily confessed.

"And people may differ, you mean, about *her* beauty?"

"About everything."

"But *you* admire her?"

He gave his friend a glance as to show how he could bear this. "I'm perhaps a little afraid of her."

"Oh," said Miss Gostrey, "I see her from here! You may say then I see her very fast and very far, but I've already shown you I do. The young man and the two ladies," she went on, "are at any rate all the family?"

"Quite all. His father has been dead ten years, and there's no brother, nor any other sister. They'd do," said Strether, "anything in the world for him."

"And you'd do anything in the world for *them*?"

He shifted again; she had made it perhaps just a shade too affirmative for his nerves. "Oh I don't know!"

"You'd do at any rate this, and the 'anything' they'd do is represented by their *making* you do it."

"Ah they couldn't have come—either of them. They're very busy people and Mrs. Newsome in particular has a large full life. She's moreover highly nervous—and not at all strong."

"You mean she's an American invalid?"

He carefully distinguished. "There's nothing she likes less than to be called one, but she would consent to be one of those things, I think," he laughed, "if it were the only way to be the other."

"Consent to be an American in order to be an invalid?"

"No," said Strether, "the other way round. She's at any rate delicate sensitive high-strung. She puts so much of herself into everything—"

Ah Maria knew these things! "That she has nothing left for anything else? Of course she hasn't. To whom do you say it? High-strung? Don't I spend my life, for them, jamming down the pedal? I see moreover how it has told on you."

Strether took this more lightly. "Oh I jam down the pedal too!"

"Well," she lucidly returned, "we must from this moment bear on it together with all our might." And she forged ahead. "Have they money?"

But it was as if, while her energetic image still held him, her enquiry fell short. "Mrs. Newsome," he wished further to explain, "hasn't moreover your courage on the question of contact. If she had come it would have been to see the person herself."

"The woman? Ah but that's courage."

"No—it's exaltation, which is a very different thing. Courage," he, however, accommodatingly threw out, "is what *you* have."

She shook her head. "You say that only to patch me up—to cover the nudity of my want of exaltation. I've neither the one nor the other. I've mere battered indifference. I see that what you mean," Miss Gostrey pursued, "is that if your friend *had* come she would take great views, and the great views, to put it simply, would be too much for her."

Strether looked amused at her notion of the simple, but he adopted her formula. "Everything's too much for her."

"Ah then such a service as this of yours—"

"Is more for her than anything else? Yes—far more. But so long as it isn't too much for *me*—!"

"Her condition doesn't matter? Surely not; we leave her condition out; we take it, that is, for granted. I see it, her condition, as behind and beneath you; yet at the same time I see it as bearing you up."

"Oh it does bear me up!" Strether laughed.

"Well then as yours bears *me* nothing more's needed." With which she put again her question. "Has Mrs. Newsome money?"

This time he heeded. "Oh plenty. That's the root of the evil. There's money, to very large amounts, in the concern. Chad has had the free use of a great deal. But if he'll pull himself together and come home, all the same, he'll find his account in it."

She had listened with all her interest. "And I hope to goodness you'll find yours!"

"He'll take up his definite material reward," said Strether without acknowledgement of this. "He's at the parting of the ways. He can come into the business now—he can't come later."

"Is there a business?"

"Lord, yes—a big brave bouncing business. A roaring trade."

"A great shop?"

"Yes—a workshop; a great production, a great industry. The concern's a manufacture—and a manufacture that, if it's only properly looked after, may well be on the way to become a monopoly. It's a little thing they make—make better, it appears, than other people can, or than other people, at any rate, do. Mr. Newsome, being a man of ideas, at least in that particular line," Strether explained, "put them on it with great effect, and gave the place altogether, in his time, an immense lift."

"It's a place in itself?"

"Well, quite a number of buildings; almost a little industrial colony. But above all it's a thing. The article produced."

"And what *is* the article produced?"

Strether looked about him as in slight reluctance to say; then the curtain, which he saw about to rise, came to his aid. "I'll tell you next time." But when the next time came he only said he'd tell her later on—after they should have left the theatre; for she had immediately reverted to their topic, and even for himself the picture of the stage was now overlaid with another image. His postponements, however, made her wonder—wonder if the article referred to were anything bad. And she explained that she meant improper or ridiculous or wrong. But Strether, so far as that went, could satisfy her. "Unmentionable? Oh no, we constantly talk of it; we are quite familiar and brazen about it. Only, as a small, trivial, rather ridiculous object of the commonest domestic use, it's just wanting in—what shall I say? Well, dignity, or the least approach to distinction. Right here, therefore, with everything about us so grand—!" In short he shrank.

"It's a false note?"

"Sadly. It's vulgar."

"But surely not vulgarer than this." Then on his wondering as she herself had done: "Than everything about us." She seemed a trifle irritated. "What do you take this for?"

"Why for—comparatively—divine!"

"This dreadful London theatre? It's impossible, if you really want to know."

"Oh then," laughed Strether, "I *don't* really want to know!"

It made between them a pause, which she, however, still fascinated by the mystery of the production at Woollett, presently broke. "'Rather ridiculous'? Clothes-pins? Saleratus? Shoe-polish?"

It brought him round. "No—you don't even 'burn.' I don't think, you know, you'll guess it."

"How then can I judge how vulgar it is?"

"You'll judge when I do tell you"—and he persuaded her to patience. But it may even now frankly be mentioned that he in the sequel never *was* to tell her. He actually never did so, and it moreover oddly occurred that by the law, within her, of the incalculable, her desire for the information dropped and her attitude to the question converted itself into a positive cultivation of ignorance. In ignorance she could humour her fancy, and that proved a useful freedom. She could treat the little nameless object as indeed unnamable—she could make their abstention enormously definite. There might indeed have been for Strether the portent of this in what she next said.

"Is it perhaps then because it's so bad—because your industry, as you call it, *is* so vulgar—that Mr. Chad won't come back? Does he feel the taint? Is he staying away not to be mixed up in it?"

"Oh," Strether laughed, "it wouldn't appear—would it?—that he feels 'taints'! He's glad enough of the money from it, and the money's his whole basis. There's appreciation in that—I mean as to the allowance his mother has hitherto made him. She has of course the resource of cutting this allowance off; but even then he has unfortunately, and on no small scale, his independent supply—money left him by his grandfather, her own father."

"Wouldn't the fact you mention then," Miss Gostrey asked, "make it just more easy for him to be particular? Isn't he conceivable as fastidious about the source—the apparent and public source—of his income?"

Strether was able quite good-humouredly to entertain the proposition. "The source of his grandfather's wealth—and thereby of his own share in it—was not particularly noble."

"And what source was it?"

Strether cast about. "Well—practices."

"In business? Infamies? He was an old swindler?"

"Oh," he said with more emphasis than spirit, "I shan't describe *him* nor narrate his exploits."

"Lord, what abysses! And the late Mr. Newsome then?"

"Well, what about him?"

"Was he like the grandfather?"

"No—he was on the other side of the house. And he was different."

Miss Gostrey kept it up. "Better?"

Her friend for a moment hung fire. "No."

Her comment on his hesitation was scarce the less marked for being mute. "Thank you. *Now* don't you see," she went on, "why the boy doesn't come home? He's drowning his shame."

"His shame? What shame?"

"What shame? *Comment donc? The* shame."

"But where and when," Strether asked, "is '*the* shame'—where is any shame—to-day? The men I speak of—they did as every one does; and (besides being ancient history) it was all a matter of appreciation."

She showed how she understood. "Mrs. Newsome has appreciated?"

"Ah I can't speak for *her*!"

"In the midst of such doings—and as I understand you, profiting by them, she at least has remained exquisite?"

"Oh I can't talk of her!" Strether said.

"I thought she was just what you *could* talk of. You *don't* trust me," Miss Gostrey after a moment declared.

It had its effect. "Well, her money is spent, her life conceived and carried on with a large beneficence—"

"That's a kind of expiation of wrongs? Gracious," she added before he could speak, "how intensely you make me see her!"

"If you see her," Strether dropped, "it's all that's necessary."

She really seemed to have her. "I feel that. She *is*, in spite of everything, handsome."

This at least enlivened him. "What do you mean by everything?"

"Well, I mean *you*." With which she had one of her swift changes of ground. "You say the concern needs looking after; but doesn't Mrs. Newsome look after it?"

"So far as possible. She's wonderfully able, but it's not her affair, and her life's a good deal overcharged. She has many, many things."

"And you also?"

"Oh yes—I've many too, if you will."

"I see. But what I mean is," Miss Gostrey amended, "do you also look after the business?"

"Oh no, I don't touch the business."

"Only everything else?"

"Well, yes—some things."

"As for instance—?"

Strether obligingly thought. "Well, the Review."

"The Review?—you have a Review?"

"Certainly, Woollett has a Review—which Mrs. Newsome, for the most part, magnificently pays for and which I, not at all magnificently, edit. My name's on the cover," Strether pursued, "and I'm really rather disappointed and hurt that you seem never to have heard of it."

She neglected for a moment this grievance. "And what kind of a Review is it?"

His serenity was not completely restored. "Well, it's green."

"Do you mean in political colour as they say here—in thought?"

"No; I mean the cover's green—of the most lovely shade."

"And with Mrs. Newsome's name on it too?"

He waited a little. "Oh as for that you must judge if she peeps out. She's behind the whole thing; but she's of a delicacy and discretion—!"

Miss Gostrey took it all. "I'm sure. She *would* be. I don't underrate her. She must be rather a swell."

"Oh yes, she's rather a swell!"

"A Woollett swell—*bon*! I like the idea of a Woollett swell. And you must be rather one too, to be so mixed up with her."

"Ah no," said Strether, "that's not the way it works."

But she had already taken him up. "The way it works—you needn't tell me!—is of course that you efface yourself."

"With my name on the cover?" he lucidly objected.

"Ah but you don't put it on for yourself."

"I beg your pardon—that's exactly what I do put it on for. It's exactly the thing that I'm reduced to doing for myself. It seems to rescue a little, you see, from the wreck of hopes and ambitions, the refuse heap of disappointments and failures, my one presentable little scrap of an identity."

On this she looked at him as to say many things, but what she at last simply said was: "She likes to see it there. You're the bigger swell of the two," she immediately continued, "because you think you're not one. She thinks she *is* one. However," Miss Gostrey added, "she thinks you're one too. You're at all events the biggest she can get hold of." She embroidered, she abounded. "I don't say it to interfere between you, but on the day she gets hold of a bigger one—!" Strether had thrown back his head as in silent mirth over something that struck him in her audacity or felicity, and her flight meanwhile was already higher. "Therefore close with her—!"

"Close with her?" he asked, as she seemed to hang poised.

"Before you lose your chance."

Their eyes met over it. "What do you mean by closing?"

"And what do I mean by your chance? I'll tell when you tell me all the things *you* don't. Is it her *greatest* fad?" she briskly pursued.

"The Review?" He seemed to wonder how he could best describe it. This resulted however but in a sketch. "It's her tribute to the ideal."

"I see. You go in for tremendous things."

"We go in for the unpopular side—that is so far as we dare."

"And how far *do* you dare?"

"Well, she very far. I much less. I don't begin to have her faith. She provides," said Strether, "three-fourths of that. And she provides, as I've confided to you, *all* the money."

It evoked somehow a vision of gold that held for a little Miss Gostrey's eyes, and she looked as if she heard the bright dollars shovelled in. "I hope then you make a good thing—"

"I *never* make a good thing!" he at once returned.

She just waited. "Don't you call it a good thing to be loved?"

"Oh we're not loved. We're not even hated. We're only just sweetly ignored."

She had another pause. "You don't trust me!" she once more repeated.

"Don't I when I lift the last veil?—tell you the very secret of the prison-house?"

Again she met his eyes, but to the result that after an instant her own turned away with impatience. "You don't sell? Oh, I'm glad of *that*!" After which however, and before he could protest, she was off again. "She's just a *moral* swell."

He accepted gaily enough the definition. "Yes—I really think that describes her."

But it had for his friend the oddest connexion. "How does she do her hair?"

He laughed out. "Beautifully!"

"Ah that doesn't tell me. However, it doesn't matter—I know. It's tremendously neat—a real reproach; quite remarkably thick and without, as yet, a single strand of white. There!"

He blushed for her realism, but he gaped at her truth. "You're the very deuce."

"What else *should* I be? It was as the very deuce I pounced upon you. But don't let it trouble you, for everything but the very deuce—at our age—is a bore and a delusion, and even he himself, after all, but half a joy." With which, on a single sweep of her wing, she resumed. "You assist her to expiate—which is rather hard when you've yourself not sinned."

"It's she who hasn't sinned," Strether replied. "I've sinned the most."

"Ah," Miss Gostrey cynically laughed, "what a picture of *her*! Have you robbed the widow and the orphan?"

"I've sinned enough," said Strether.

"Enough for whom? Enough for what?"

"Well, to be where I am."

"Thank you!" They were disturbed at this moment by the passage between their knees and the back of the seats before them of a gentleman who had been absent during a part of the performance and who now returned for the close; but the interruption left Miss Gostrey time, before the subsequent hush, to express as a sharp finality her sense of the moral of all their talk. "I knew you had something up your sleeve!" This finality, however, left them in its turn, at the end of the play, as disposed to hang back as if they had still much to say; so that they easily agreed to let every one go before them—they found an interest in waiting. They made out from the lobby that the night had turned to rain; yet Miss Gostrey let her friend know that he wasn't to see her home. He was simply to put her, by herself, into a four-wheeler; she liked so in London, of wet nights after wild pleasures, thinking things over, on the return, in lonely four-wheelers. This was her great time, she intimated, for pulling herself together. The delays caused by the weather, the struggle for vehicles at the door, gave them occasion to subside on a divan at the back of the vestibule and just beyond the reach of the fresh damp gusts from the street. Here Strether's comrade resumed that free handling of the subject to which his own imagination of it already owed so much. "Does your young friend in Paris like you?"

It had almost, after the interval, startled him. "Oh, I hope not! Why *should* he?"

"Why shouldn't he?" Miss Gostrey asked. "That you're coming down on him need have nothing to do with it."

"You see more in it," he presently returned, "than I."

"Of course I see *you* in it."

"Well then you see more in 'me.'"

"Than you see yourself? Very likely. That's always one's right. What I was thinking of," she explained, "is the possible particular effect on him of his *milieu*."

"Oh his *milieu*—!" Strether really felt that he could imagine it better now than three hours before.

"Do you mean it can only have been so lowering?"

"Why that's my very starting-point."

"Yes, but you start so far back. What do his letters say?"

"Nothing. He practically ignores us—or spares us. He doesn't write."

"I see. But there are all the same," she went on, "two quite distinct things that—given the wonderful place he's in—may have happened to him. One is that he may have got brutalised. The other is that he may have got refined."

Strether stared—this *was* a novelty. "Refined?"

"Oh," she said quietly, "there are refinements."

The way of it made him, after looking at her, break into a laugh. "*You* have them!"

"As one of the signs," she continued in the same tone, "they constitute perhaps the worst."

He thought it over and his gravity returned. "Is it a refinement not to answer his mother's letters?"

She appeared to have a scruple, but she brought it out. "Oh I should say the greatest of all."

"Well," said Strether, "*I*'m quite content to let it, as one of the signs, pass for the worst that I know he believes he can do what he likes with me."

This appeared to strike her. "How do you know it?"

"Oh I'm sure of it. I feel it in my bones."

"Feel he *can* do it?"

"Feel that he believes he can. It may come to the same thing!" Strether laughed.

She wouldn't, however, have this. "Nothing for you will ever come to the same thing as anything else." And she understood what she meant, it seemed, sufficiently to go straight on. "You say that if he does break he'll come in for things at home?"

"Quite positively. He'll come in for a particular chance—a chance that any properly constituted young man would jump at. The business has so developed that an opening scarcely apparent three years ago, but which his father's will took account of as in certain conditions possible and which, under that will, attaches to Chad's availing himself of it a large contingent advantage—this opening, the conditions having come about, now simply awaits him. His mother has kept it for him, holding out against strong pressure, till the last possible moment. It requires, naturally, as it carries with it a handsome 'part,' a large share in profits, his being on the spot and making a big effort for a big result. That's what I mean by his chance. If he misses it he comes in, as you say, for nothing. And to see that he doesn't miss it is, in a word, what I've come out for."

She let it all sink in. "What you've come out for then is simply to render him an immense service."

Well, poor Strether was willing to take it so. "Ah if you like."

"He stands, as they say, if you succeed with him, to gain—"

"Oh a lot of advantages." Strether had them clearly at his fingers' ends.

"By which you mean of course a lot of money."

"Well, not only. I'm acting with a sense for him of other things too. Consideration and comfort and security—the general safety of being anchored by a strong chain. He wants, as I see him, to be protected. Protected I mean from life."

"Ah voilà!"—her thought fitted with a click. "From life. What you *really* want to get him home for is to marry him."

"Well, that's about the size of it."

"Of course," she said, "it's rudimentary. But to anyone in particular?"

He smiled at this, looking a little more conscious. "You get everything out."

For a moment again their eyes met. "You put everything in!"

He acknowledged the tribute by telling her. "To Mamie Pocock."

She wondered; then gravely, even exquisitely, as if to make the oddity also fit: "His own niece?"

"Oh you must yourself find a new name for the relation. His brother-in-law's sister. Mrs. Jim's sister-in-law."

It seemed to have on Miss Gostrey a certain hardening effect. "And who in the world's Mrs. Jim?"

"Chad's sister—who was Sarah Newsome. She's married—didn't I mention it?—to Jim Pocock."

"Ah yes," she tacitly replied; but he had mentioned things—! Then, however, with all the sound it could have, "Who in the world's Jim Pocock?" she asked.

"Why Sally's husband. That's the only way we distinguish people at Woollett," he good-humouredly explained.

"And it is a great distinction—being Sally's husband?"

He considered. "I think there can be scarcely a greater—unless it may become one, in the future, to be Chad's wife."

"Then how do they distinguish *you*?"

"They *don't*—except, as I've told you, by the green cover."

Once more their eyes met on it, and she held him an instant. "The green cover won't—nor will *any* cover—avail you with *me*. You're of a depth of duplicity!" Still she could in her own large grasp of the real condone it. "Is Mamie a great *parti*?"

"Oh the greatest we have—our prettiest brightest girl."

Miss Gostrey seemed to fix the poor child. "I know what they *can* be. And with money?"

"Not perhaps with a great deal of that—but with so much of everything else that we don't miss it. We *don't* miss money much, you know," Strether added, "in general, in America, in pretty girls."

"No," she conceded; "but I know also what you do sometimes miss. And do you," she asked, "yourself admire her?"

It was a question, he indicated, that there might be several ways of taking; but he decided after an instant for the humorous. "Haven't I sufficiently showed you how I admire *any* pretty girl?"

Her interest in his problem was by this time such that it scarce left her freedom, and she kept close to the facts. "I supposed that at Woollett you wanted them—what shall I call it?—blameless. I mean your young men for your pretty girls."

"So did I," Strether confessed. "But you strike there a curious fact—the fact that Woollett too accommodates itself to the spirit of the age and the increasing mildness of manners. Everything changes, and I hold that our situation precisely marks a date. We *should* prefer them blameless, but we have to make the best of them as we find them. Since the spirit of the age and the increasing mildness send them so much more to Paris—"

"You've to take them back as they come. When they *do* come. *Bon!*" Once more she embraced it all, but she had a moment of thought. "Poor Chad!"

"Ah," said Strether cheerfully, "Mamie will save him!"

She was looking away, still in her vision, and she spoke with impatience and almost as if he hadn't understood her. "*You'll* save him. That's who'll save him."

"Oh but with Mamie's aid. Unless indeed you mean," he added, "that I shall effect so much more with yours!"

It made her at last again look at him. "You'll do more—as you're so much better—than all of us put together."

"I think I'm only better since I've known *you*!" Strether bravely returned.

The depletion of the place, the shrinkage of the crowd and now comparatively quiet withdrawal of its last elements had already brought them nearer the door and put them in relation with a messenger of whom he bespoke Miss Gostrey's cab.

But this left them a few minutes more, which she was clearly in no mood not to use. "You've spoken to me of what—by your success—Mr. Chad stands to gain. But you've not spoken to me of what you do."

"Oh I've nothing more to gain," said Strether very simply.

She took it as even quite too simple. "You mean you've got it all 'down'? You've been paid in advance?"

"Ah don't talk about payment!" he groaned.

Something in the tone of it pulled her up, but as their messenger still delayed she had another chance and she put it another way. "What—by failure—do you stand to lose?"

He still, however, wouldn't have it. "Nothing!" he exclaimed, and on the messenger's at this instant reappearing he was able to sink the subject in their responsive advance. When, a few steps up the street, under a lamp, he had put her into her four-wheeler and she had asked him if the man had called for him no second conveyance, he replied before the door was closed. "You won't take me with you?"

"Not for the world."

"Then I shall walk."

"In the rain?"

"I like the rain," said Strether. "Good night!"

She kept him a moment, while his hand was on the door, by not answering; after which she answered by repeating her question. "What do you stand to lose?"

Why the question now affected him as other he couldn't have said; he could only this time meet it otherwise. "Everything."

"So I thought. Then you shall succeed. And to that end I'm yours—"

"Ah, dear lady!" he kindly breathed.

"Till death!" said Maria Gostrey. "Good night."

II

Strether called, his second morning in Paris, on the bankers of the Rue Scribe to whom his letter of credit was addressed, and he made this visit attended by Waymarsh, in whose company he had crossed from London two days before. They had hastened to the Rue Scribe on the morrow of their arrival, but Strether had not then found the letters the hope of which prompted this errand. He had had as yet none at all; hadn't expected them in London, but had counted on several in Paris, and, disconcerted now, had presently strolled back to the boulevard with a sense of injury that he felt himself taking for as good a start as any other. It would serve, this spur to his spirit, he reflected, as, pausing at the top of the street, he looked up and down the great foreign avenue, it would serve to begin business with. His idea was to begin business immediately, and it did much for him the rest of his day that the beginning of business awaited him. He did little else till night but ask himself what he should do if he hadn't fortunately had so much to do; but he put himself the question in many different situations and connexions. What carried him hither and yon was an admirable theory that nothing he could do wouldn't be in some manner related to what he fundamentally had on hand, or *would* be—should he happen to have a scruple—wasted for it. He did happen to have a scruple—a scruple about taking no definite step till he should get letters; but this reasoning carried it off. A single day to feel his feet—he had felt them as yet only at Chester and in London—was, he could consider, none too much; and having, as he had often privately expressed it, Paris to reckon with, he threw these hours of freshness consciously into the reckoning. They made it continually greater, but that was what it had best be if it was to be anything at all, and he gave himself up till far into the evening, at the theatre and on the return, after the theatre, along the bright congested Boulevard, to feeling it grow. Waymarsh had accompanied him this time to the play, and the two men had walked together, as a first stage, from the Gymnase to the Café Riche, into the crowded "terrace" of which establishment—the night, or rather the morning, for midnight had struck, being bland and populous—they had wedged themselves for refreshment. Waymarsh, as a result of some discussion with his friend, had made a marked virtue of his having now let himself go and there had been elements of impression in their half-hour over their watered beer-glasses that gave him his occasion for conveying that he held this compromise with his stiffer self to have become extreme. He conveyed it—for it was still, after all, his stiffer self who gloomed out of the glare of the terrace—in solemn silence; and there was indeed a great deal of critical silence, every way, between the companions, even till they gained the Place de l'Opéra, as to the character of their nocturnal progress.

This morning there *were* letters—letters which had reached London, apparently all together, the day of Strether's journey, and had taken their time to follow him; so that, after a controlled impulse to go into them in the reception-room of the bank, which, reminding him of the post office at Woollett, affected him as the abutment of some transatlantic bridge, he slipped them into the pocket of his loose grey overcoat with a sense of the felicity of carrying them off. Waymarsh, who had had letters yesterday, had had them again to-day, and Waymarsh suggested in this particular no controlled impulses. The last one he was at all events likely to be observed to struggle with was clearly that of bringing to a premature close any visit to the Rue Scribe. Strether had left him there yesterday; he wanted to see the papers, and he had spent, by what his friend could make out, a succession of hours with the papers. He spoke of the establishment, with emphasis, as a post of superior observation; just as he spoke generally of his actual damnable doom as a device for hiding from him what was going on. Europe was best described, to his mind, as an elaborate engine for dissociating the confined American from that indispensable knowledge, and was accordingly only rendered bearable by these occasional stations of relief, traps for the arrest of wandering western airs. Strether, on his side, set himself to walk again—he had his relief in his pocket; and indeed, much as he had desired his budget, the growth of restlessness might have been marked in him from the moment he had assured himself of the superscription of most of the missives it contained. This restlessness became therefore his temporary law; he knew he should recognize as soon as see it the best place of all for settling down with his chief correspondent. He had for the next hour an accidental air of looking for it in the windows of shops: he came down the Rue de la Paix in the sun and, passing across the Tuileries and the river, indulged more than once—as if on finding himself determined—in a sudden pause before the book-stalls of the opposite quay. In the garden of the Tuileries he had lingered, on two or three spots, to look; it was as if the wonderful Paris spring had stayed him as he roamed. The prompt Paris morning struck its cheerful notes—in a soft breeze and a sprinkled smell, in the light flit, over the garden-floor, of bareheaded girls with the buckled strap of oblong boxes, in the type of ancient thrifty persons basking betimes where terrace-walls were warm, in the blue-frocked brass-labelled officialism of humble rakers and scrapers, in the deep references of a straight-pacing priest or the sharp ones of a white-gaitered red-legged soldier. He watched little brisk figures, figures whose movement was as the tick of the great Paris clock, take their smooth diagonal from point to point; the air had a taste of something mixed with art, something that presented nature as a whitecapped master-chef. The palace was gone, Strether remembered the palace; and when he gazed into the irremediable void of its site the historic sense in him might have been freely at play—the play under which in Paris indeed it so often winces like a touched nerve. He filled out spaces with dim symbols of scenes; he caught the gleam of white statues at the base of which, with his letters out, he could tilt back a straw-bottomed chair. But his drift was, for reasons, to the other side, and it floated him unspent up the Rue de Seine and as far as the Luxembourg.

In the Luxembourg Gardens he pulled up; here at last he found his nook, and here, on a penny chair from which terraces, alleys, vistas, fountains, little trees in green tubs, little women in white caps and shrill little girls at play all sunnily "composed" together, he passed an hour in which the cup of his impressions seemed truly to overflow. But a week had elapsed since he quitted the ship, and there were more things in his mind than so few days could account for. More than once, during the time, he had regarded himself as admonished; but the admonition, this morning, was formidably sharp. It took as it hadn't done yet the form of a question—the question of what he was doing with such an extraordinary sense of escape. This sense was sharpest after he had read his letters, but that was also precisely why the question pressed. Four of the letters were from Mrs. Newsome and none of them short; she had lost no time, had followed on his heels while he moved, so expressing herself that he now could measure the probable frequency with which he should hear. They would arrive, it would seem, her communications, at the rate of several a week; he should be able to count, it might even prove, on more than one by each mail. If he had begun yesterday with a small grievance he had therefore an opportunity to begin to-day with its opposite. He read the letters successively and slowly, putting others back into his pocket but keeping these for a long time afterwards gathered in his lap. He held them there, lost in thought, as if to prolong the presence of what they gave him; or as if at the least to assure them their part in the constitution of some lucidity. His friend wrote admirably, and her tone was even more in her style than in her voice—he might almost, for the hour, have had to come this distance to get its full carrying quality; yet the plentitude of his consciousness of difference consorted perfectly with the deepened intensity of the connexion. It was the difference, the difference of being just where he was and *as* he was, that formed the escape—this difference was so much greater than he had dreamed it would be; and what finally he sat there turning over was the strange logic of his finding himself so free. He felt it in a manner his duty to think out his state, to approve the process, and when he came in fact to trace the steps and add up the items they sufficiently accounted for the sum. He had never expected—that was the truth of it—again to find himself young, and all the years and other things it had taken to make him so were exactly his present arithmetic. He had to make sure of them to put his scruple to rest.

It all sprang at bottom from the beauty of Mrs. Newsome's desire that he should be worried with nothing that was not of the essence of his task; by insisting that he should thoroughly intermit and break she had so provided for his freedom that she would, as it were, have only herself to thank. Strether could not at this point indeed have completed his thought by the image of what she might have to thank herself *for*: the image, at best, of his own likeness—poor Lambert Strether washed up on the sunny strand by the waves of a single day, poor Lambert Strether thankful for breathing-time and stiffening himself while he gasped. There he was, and with nothing in his aspect or his posture to scandalize: it was only true that if he had seen Mrs. Newsome coming he would instinctively have jumped up to walk away a little. He would have come round and back to her bravely, but he would have had first to pull himself together. She abounded in news of the situation at home, proved to him how perfectly she was arranging for his absence, told him who would take up this and who take up that exactly where he had left it, gave him in fact chapter and verse for the moral that nothing would suffer. It filled for him, this tone of hers, all the air; yet it struck him at the same time as the hum of vain things. This latter effect was what he tried to justify—and with the success that, grave though the appearance, he at last lighted on a form that was happy. He arrived at it by the inevitable recognition of his having been a fortnight before one of the weariest of men. If ever a man had come off tired Lambert Strether was that man; and hadn't it been distinctly on the ground of his fatigue that his wonderful friend at home had so felt for him and so contrived? It seemed to him somehow at these instants that, could he only maintain with sufficient firmness his grasp of that truth, it might become in a manner his compass and his helm. What he wanted most was some idea that would simplify, and nothing would do this so much as the fact that he was done for and finished. If it had been in such a light that he had just detected in his cup the dregs of youth, that was a mere flaw of the surface of his scheme. He was so distinctly fagged-out that it must serve precisely as his convenience, and if he could but consistently be good for little enough he might do everything he wanted.

Everything he wanted was comprised moreover in a single boon—the common unattainable art of taking things as they came. He appeared to himself to have given his best years to an active appreciation of the way they didn't come; but perhaps—as they would seemingly here be things quite other—this long ache might at last drop to rest. He could easily see that from the moment he should accept the notion of his foredoomed collapse the last thing he would lack would be reasons and memories. Oh if he *should* do the sum no slate would hold the figures! The fact that he had failed, as he considered, in everything, in each relation and in half a dozen trades, as he liked luxuriously to put it, might have made, might still make, for an empty present; but it stood solidly for a crowded past. It had not been, so much achievement missed, a light yoke nor a short load. It was at present as if the backward picture had hung there, the long crooked course, grey in the shadow of his solitude. It had been a dreadful cheerful sociable solitude, a solitude of life or choice, of community; but though there had been people enough all round it there had been but three or four persons *in* it. Waymarsh was one of these, and the fact struck him just now as marking the record. Mrs. Newsome was another, and Miss Gostrey had of a sudden shown signs of becoming a third. Beyond, behind them was the pale figure of his real youth, which held against its breast the two presences paler than itself—the young wife he had early lost and the young son he had stupidly sacrificed. He had again and again made out for himself that he might have kept his little boy, his little dull boy, who had died at school of rapid diphtheria, if he had not in those years so insanely given himself to merely missing the mother. It was the soreness of his remorse that the child had in all likelihood not really been dull—had been dull, as he had been banished and neglected, mainly because the father had been unwittingly selfish. This was doubtless but the secret habit of sorrow, which had slowly given way to time; yet there remained an ache sharp enough to make the spirit, at the sight now and again of some fair young man just growing up, wince with the thought of an opportunity lost. Had ever a man, he had finally fallen into the way of asking himself, lost so much and even done so much for so little? There had been particular reasons why all yesterday, beyond other days, he should have had in one ear this cold inquiry. His name on the green cover, where he had put it for Mrs. Newsome, expressed him doubtless just enough to make the world—the world as distinguished, both for more and for less, from Woollett—ask who he was. He had incurred the ridicule of having to have his explanation explained. He was Lambert Strether because he was on the cover, whereas it should have been, for anything like glory, that he was on the cover because he was Lambert Strether. He would have done anything for Mrs. Newsome, have been still more ridiculous—as he might, for that matter, have occasion to be yet; which came to saying that this acceptance of fate was all he had to show at fifty-five.

He judged the quantity as small because it *was* small, and all the more egregiously since it couldn't, as he saw the case, so much as thinkably have been larger. He hadn't had the gift of making the most of what he tried, and if he had tried and tried again—no one but himself knew how often—it appeared to have been that he might demonstrate what else, in default of that, *could* be made. Old ghosts of experiments came back to him, old drudgeries and delusions, and disgusts, old recoveries with their relapses, old fevers with their chills, broken moments of good faith, others of still better doubt; adventures, for the most part, of the sort qualified as lessons. The special spring that had constantly played for him the day before was the recognition—frequent enough to surprise him—of the promises to himself that he had after his other visit never kept. The reminiscence to-day most quickened for him was that of the vow taken in the course of the pilgrimage that, newly-married, with the War just over, and helplessly young in spite of it, he had recklessly made with the creature who was so much younger still. It had been a bold dash, for which they had taken money set apart for necessities, but kept sacred at the moment in a hundred ways, and in none more so than by this private pledge of his own to treat the occasion as a relation formed with the higher culture and see that, as they said at Woollett, it should bear a good harvest. He had believed, sailing home again, that he had gained something great, and his theory—with an elaborate innocent plan of reading, digesting, coming back even, every few years—had then been to preserve, cherish and extend it. As such plans as these had come to nothing, however, in respect to acquisitions still more precious, it was doubtless little enough of a marvel that he should have lost account of that handful of seed. Buried for long years in dark corners at any rate these few germs had sprouted again under forty-eight hours of Paris. The process of yesterday had really been the process of feeling the general stirred life of connexions long since individually dropped. Strether had become acquainted even on this ground with short gusts of speculation—sudden flights of fancy in Louvre galleries, hungry gazes through clear plates behind which lemon-coloured volumes were as fresh as fruit on the tree.

These were instants at which he could ask whether, since there had been fundamentally so little question of his keeping anything, the fate after all decreed for him hadn't been only to *be* kept. Kept for something, in that event, that he didn't pretend, didn't possibly dare as yet to divine; something that made him hover and wonder and laugh and sigh, made him advance and retreat, feeling half ashamed of his impulse to plunge and more than half afraid of his impulse to wait. He remembered for instance how he had gone back in the sixties with lemon-coloured volumes in general on the brain as with a dozen—selected for his wife too—in his trunk; and nothing had at the moment shown more confidence than this invocation of the finer taste. They were still somewhere at home, the dozen—stale and soiled and never sent to the binder; but what had become of the sharp initiation they represented? They represented now the mere sallow paint on the door of the temple of taste that he had dreamed of raising up—a structure he had practically never carried further. Strether's present highest flights were perhaps those in which this particular lapse figured to him as a symbol, a symbol of his long grind and his want of odd moments, his want moreover of money, of opportunity, of positive dignity. That the memory of the vow of his youth should, in order to throb again, have had to wait for this last, as he felt it, of all his accidents—that was surely proof enough of how his conscience had been encumbered. If any further proof were needed it would have been to be found in the fact that, as he perfectly now saw, he had ceased even to measure his meagreness, a meagreness that sprawled, in this retrospect, vague and comprehensive, stretching back like some unmapped Hinterland from a rough coast-settlement. His conscience had been amusing itself for the forty-eight hours by forbidding him the purchase of a book; he held off from that, held off from everything; from the moment he didn't yet call on Chad he wouldn't for the world have taken any other step. On this evidence, however, of the way they actually affected him he glared at the lemon-coloured covers in confession of the subconsciousness that, all the same, in the great desert of the years, he must have had of them. The green covers at home comprised, by the law of their purpose, no tribute to letters; it was of a mere rich kernel of economics, politics, ethics that, glazed and, as Mrs. Newsome maintained, rather against *his* view, pre-eminently pleasant to touch, they formed the specious shell. Without therefore any needed instinctive knowledge of what was coming out, in Paris, on the bright highway, he struck himself at present as having more than once flushed with a suspicion: he couldn't otherwise at present be feeling so many fears confirmed. There were "movements" he was too late for: weren't they, with the fun of them, already spent? There were sequences he had missed and great gaps in the procession: he might have been watching it all recede in a golden cloud of dust. If the playhouse wasn't closed his seat had at least fallen to somebody else. He had had an uneasy feeling the night before that if he was at the theatre at all—though he indeed justified the theatre, in the specific sense, and with a grotesqueness to which his imagination did all honour, as something he owed poor Waymarsh—he should have been there with, and as might have been said, *for* Chad.

This suggested the question of whether he could properly have taken him to such a play, and what effect—it was a point that suddenly rose—his peculiar responsibility might be held in general to have on his choice of entertainment. It had literally been present to him at the Gymnase—where one was held moreover comparatively safe—that having his young friend at his side would have been an odd feature of the work of redemption; and this quite in spite of the fact that the picture presented might well, confronted with Chad's own private stage, have seemed the pattern of propriety. He clearly hadn't come out in the name of propriety only to visit unattended equivocal performances; yet still less had he done so to undermine his authority by sharing them with the graceless youth. Was he to renounce all amusement for the sweet sake of that authority? and *would* such renouncement give him for Chad a moral glamour? The little problem bristled the more by reason of poor Strether's fairly open sense of the irony of things. Were there then sides on which his predicament threatened to look rather droll to him? Should he have to pretend to believe—either to himself or the wretched boy—that there was anything that could make the latter worse? Wasn't some such pretence on the other hand involved in the assumption of possible processes that would make him better? His greatest uneasiness seemed to peep at him out of the imminent impression that almost any acceptance of Paris might give one's authority away. It hung before him this morning, the vast bright Babylon, like some huge iridescent object, a jewel brilliant and hard, in which parts were not to be discriminated nor differences comfortably marked. It twinkled and trembled and melted together, and what seemed all surface one moment seemed all depth the next. It was a place of which, unmistakably, Chad was fond; wherefore if he, Strether, should like it too much, what on earth, with such a bond, would become of either of them? It all depended of course—which was a gleam of light—on how the "too much" was measured; though indeed our friend fairly felt, while he prolonged the meditation I describe, that for himself even already a certain measure had been reached. It will have been sufficiently seen that he was not a man to neglect any good chance for reflexion. Was it at all possible for instance to like Paris enough without liking it too much? He luckily however hadn't promised Mrs. Newsome not to like it at all. He was ready to recognise at this stage that such an engagement *would* have tied his hands. The Luxembourg Gardens were incontestably just so adorable at this hour by reason—in addition to their intrinsic charm—of his not having taken it. The only engagement he had taken, when he looked the thing in the face, was to do what he reasonably could.

It upset him a little none the less and after a while to find himself at last remembering on what current of association he had been floated so far. Old imaginations of the Latin Quarter had played their part for him, and he had duly recalled its having been with this scene of rather ominous legend that, like so many young men in fiction as well as in fact, Chad had begun. He was now quite out of it, with his "home" as Strether figured the place, in the Boulevard Malesherbes; which was perhaps why, repairing, not to fail of justice either, to the elder neighbourhood, our friend had felt he could allow for the element of the usual, the immemorial, without courting perturbation. He was not at least in danger of seeing the youth and the particular Person flaunt by together; and yet he was in the very air of which—just to feel what the early natural note must have been—he wished most to take counsel. It became at once vivid to him that he had originally had, for a few days, an almost envious vision of the boy's romantic privilege. Melancholy Mürger, with Francine and Musette and Rodolphe, at home, in the company of the tattered, one—if not in his single self two or three—of the unbound, the paper-covered dozen on the shelf; and when Chad had written, five years ago, after a sojourn then already prolonged to six months, that he had decided to go in for economy and the real thing, Strether's fancy had quite fondly accompanied him in this migration, which was to convey him, as they somewhat confusedly learned at Woollett, across the bridges and up the Montagne Sainte-Geneviève. This was the region—Chad had been quite distinct about it—in which the best French, and many other things, were to be learned at least cost, and in which all sorts of clever fellows, compatriots there for a purpose, formed an awfully pleasant set. The clever fellows, the friendly countrymen were mainly young painters, sculptors, architects, medical students; but they were, Chad sagely opined, a much more profitable lot to be with—even on the footing of not being quite one of them—than the "terrible toughs" (Strether remembered the edifying discrimination) of the American bars and banks roundabout the Opéra. Chad had thrown out, in the communications following this one—for at that time he did once in a while communicate—that several members of a band of earnest workers under one of the great artists had taken him right in, making him dine every night, almost for nothing, at their place, and even pressing him not to neglect the hypothesis of there being as much "in him" as in any of them. There had been literally a moment at which it appeared there might be something in him; there had been at any rate a moment at which he had written that he didn't know but what a month or two more might see him enrolled in some atelier. The season had been one at which Mrs. Newsome was moved to gratitude for small mercies; it had broken on them all as a blessing that their absentee *had* perhaps a conscience—that he was sated in fine with idleness, was ambitious of variety. The exhibition was doubtless as yet not brilliant, but Strether himself, even by that time much enlisted and immersed, had determined, on the part of the two ladies, a temperate approval and in fact, as he now recollected, a certain austere enthusiasm.

But the very next thing that happened had been a dark drop of the curtain. The son and brother had not browsed long on the Montagne Sainte-Geneviève—his effective little use of the name of which, like his allusion to the best French, appeared to have been but one of the notes of his rough cunning. The light refreshment of these vain appearances had not accordingly carried any of them very far. On the other hand it had gained Chad time; it had given him a chance, unchecked, to strike his roots, had paved the way for initiations more direct and more deep. It was Strether's belief that he had been comparatively innocent before this first migration, and even that the first effects of the migration would not have been, without some particular bad accident, to have been deplored. There had been three months—he had sufficiently figured it out—in which Chad had wanted to try. He *had* tried, though not very hard—he had had his little hour of good faith. The weakness of this principle in him was that almost any accident attestedly bad enough was stronger. Such had at any rate markedly been the case for the precipitation of a special series of impressions. They had proved, successively, these impressions—all of Musette and Francine, but Musette and Francine vulgarised by the larger evolution of the type—irresistibly sharp: he had "taken up," by what was at the time to be shrinkingly gathered, as it was scantily mentioned, with one ferociously "interested" little person after another. Strether had read somewhere of a Latin motto, a description of the hours, observed on a clock by a traveller in Spain; and he had been led to apply it in thought to Chad's number one, number two, number three. *Omnes vulnerant, ultima necat*—they had all morally wounded, the last had morally killed. The last had been longest in possession—in possession, that is, of whatever was left of the poor boy's finer mortality. And it hadn't been she, it had been one of her early predecessors, who had determined the second migration, the expensive return and relapse, the exchange again, as was fairly to be presumed, of the vaunted best French for some special variety of the worst.

He pulled himself then at last together for his own progress back; not with the feeling that he had taken his walk in vain. He prolonged it a little, in the immediate neighbourhood, after he had quitted his chair; and the upshot of the whole morning for him was that his campaign had begun. He had wanted to put himself in relation, and he would be hanged if he were *not* in relation. He was that at no moment so much as while, under the old arches of the Odéon, he lingered before the charming open-air array of literature classic and casual. He found the effect of tone and tint, in the long charged tables and shelves, delicate and appetising;

the impression—substituting one kind of low-priced *consommation* for another—might have been that of one of the pleasant cafés that overlapped, under an awning, to the pavement; but he edged along, grazing the tables, with his hands firmly behind him. He wasn't there to dip, to consume—he was there to reconstruct. He wasn't there for his own profit—not, that is, the direct; he was there on some chance of feeling the brush of the wing of the stray spirit of youth. He felt it in fact, he had it beside him; the old arcade indeed, as his inner sense listened, gave out the faint sound, as from far off, of the wild waving of wings. They were folded now over the breasts of buried generations; but a flutter or two lived again in the turned page of shock-headed, slouch-hatted loiterers whose young intensity of type, in the direction of pale acuteness, deepened his vision, and even his appreciation, of racial differences, and whose manipulation of the uncut volume was too often, however, but a listening at closed doors. He reconstructed a possible groping Chad of three or four years before, a Chad who had after all, simply—for that was the only way to see it—been too vulgar for his privilege. Surely it *was* a privilege to have been young and happy just there. Well, the best thing Strether knew of him was that he had had such a dream.

But his own actual business half an hour later was with a third floor on the Boulevard Malesherbes—so much as that was definite; and the fact of the enjoyment by the third-floor windows of a continuous balcony, to which he was helped by this knowledge, had perhaps something to do with his lingering for five minutes on the opposite side of the street. There were points as to which he had quite made up his mind, and one of these bore precisely on the wisdom of the abruptness to which events had finally committed him, a policy that he was pleased to find not at all shaken as he now looked at his watch and wondered. He *had* announced himself—six months before; had written out at least that Chad wasn't to be surprised should he see him some day turn up. Chad had thereupon, in a few words of rather carefully colourless answer, offered him a general welcome; and Strether, ruefully reflecting that he might have understood the warning as a hint to hospitality, a bid for an invitation, had fallen back upon silence as the corrective most to his own taste. He had asked Mrs. Newsome moreover not to announce him again; he had so distinct an opinion on attacking his job, should he attack it at all, in his own way. Not the least of this lady's high merits for him was that he could absolutely rest on her word. She was the only woman he had known, even at Woollett, as to whom his conviction was positive that to lie was beyond her art. Sarah Pocock, for instance, her own daughter, though with social ideals, as they said, in some respects different—Sarah who *was*, in her way, esthetic, had never refused to human commerce that mitigation of rigour; there were occasions when he had distinctly seen her apply it. Since, accordingly, at all events, he had had it from Mrs. Newsome that she had, at whatever cost to her more strenuous view, conformed, in the matter of preparing Chad, wholly to his restrictions, he now looked up at the fine continuous balcony with a safe sense that if the case had been bungled the mistake was at least his property. Was there perhaps just a suspicion of that in his present pause on the edge of the boulevard and well in the pleasant light?

Many things came over him here, and one of them was that he should doubtless presently know whether he had been shallow or sharp. Another was that the balcony in question didn't somehow show as a convenience easy to surrender. Poor Strether had at this very moment to recognise the truth that wherever one paused in Paris the imagination reacted before one could stop it. This perpetual reaction put a price, if one would, on pauses; but it piled up consequences till there was scarce room to pick one's steps among them. What call had he, at such a juncture, for example, to like Chad's very house? High broad clear—he was expert enough to make out in a moment that it was admirably built—it fairly embarrassed our friend by the quality that, as he would have said, it "sprang" on him. He had struck off the fancy that it might, as a preliminary, be of service to him to be seen, by a happy accident, from the third-story windows, which took all the March sun, but of what service was it to find himself making out after a moment that the quality "sprung," the quality produced by measure and balance, the fine relation of part to part and space to space, was probably—aided by the presence of ornament as positive as it was discreet, and by the complexion of the stone, a cold, fair grey, warmed and polished a little by life—neither more nor less than a case of distinction, such a case as he could only feel unexpectedly as a sort of delivered challenge? Meanwhile, however, the chance he had allowed for—the chance of being seen in time from the balcony—had become a fact. Two or three of the windows stood open to the violet air; and, before Strether had cut the knot by crossing, a young man had come out and looked about him, had lighted a cigarette and tossed the match over, and then resting on the rail, had given himself up to watching the life below while he smoked. His arrival contributed, in its order, to keeping Strether in position; the result of which in turn was that Strether soon felt himself noticed. The young man began to look at him as in acknowledgment of his being himself in observation.

This was interesting so far as it went, but the interest was affected by the young man's not being Chad. Strether wondered at first if he were perhaps Chad altered, and then saw that this was asking too much of alteration. The young man was light bright and alert—with an air too pleasant to have been arrived at by patching. Strether had conceived Chad as patched, but not beyond recognition. He was in presence, he felt, of amendments enough as they stood; it was a sufficient amendment that the gentleman up there should be Chad's friend. He was young too then, the gentleman up there—he was very young; young enough apparently to be amused at an elderly watcher, to be curious even to see what the elderly watcher would do on finding himself watched. There was youth in that, there was youth in the surrender to the balcony, there was youth for Strether at this moment in everything but his own business; and Chad's thus pronounced association with youth had given the next instant an extraordinary quick lift to the issue. The balcony, the distinguished front testified suddenly, for Strether's fancy, to something that was up and up; they placed the whole case materially, and as by an admirable image, on a level that he found himself at the end of another moment rejoicing to think he might reach. The young man looked at him still, he looked at the young man; and the issue, by a rapid process, was that this knowledge of a perched privacy appeared to him the last of luxuries. To him too the perched privacy was open, and he saw it now but in one light—that of the only domicile, the only fireside, in the great ironic city, on which he had the shadow of a claim. Miss Gostrey had a fireside; she had told him of it, and it was something that doubtless awaited him; but Miss Gostrey hadn't yet arrived—she mightn't arrive for days; and the sole attenuation of his excluded state was his vision of the small, the admittedly secondary hotel in the bye-street from the Rue de la Paix, in which her solicitude for his purse had placed him, which affected him somehow as all indoor chill, glass-roofed court and slippery staircase, and which, by the same token, expressed the presence of Waymarsh even at times when Waymarsh might have been certain to be round at the bank. It came to pass before he moved that Waymarsh, and Waymarsh alone, Waymarsh not only undiluted but positively strengthened, struck him as the present alternative to the young man in the balcony. When he did move it was fairly to escape that alternative. Taking his way over the street at last and passing through the *porte cochère* of the house was like consciously leaving Waymarsh out. However, he would tell him all about it.

BOOK THIRD

I

Strether told Waymarsh all about it that very evening, on their dining together at the hotel; which needn't have happened, he was all the while aware, hadn't he chosen to sacrifice to this occasion a rarer opportunity. The mention to his companion of the sacrifice was moreover exactly what introduced his recital—or, as he would have called it with more confidence in his interlocutor, his confession. His confession was that he had been captured and that one of the features of the affair had just failed to be his engaging himself on the spot to dinner. As by such a freedom Waymarsh would have lost him he had obeyed his scruple; and he had likewise obeyed another scruple—which bore on the question of his himself bringing a guest.

Waymarsh looked gravely ardent, over the finished soup, at this array of scruples; Strether hadn't yet got quite used to being so unprepared for the consequences of the impression he produced. It was comparatively easy to explain, however, that he hadn't felt sure his guest would please. The person was a young man whose acquaintance he had made but that afternoon in the course of rather a hindered enquiry for another person—an enquiry that his new friend had just prevented in fact from being vain. "Oh," said Strether, "I've all sorts of things to tell you!"—and he put it in a way that was a virtual hint to Waymarsh to help him to enjoy the telling. He waited for his fish, he drank of his wine, he wiped his long moustache, he leaned back in his chair, he took in the two English ladies who had just creaked past them and whom he would even have articulately greeted if they hadn't rather chilled the impulse; so that all he could do was—by way of doing something—to say "Merci, François!" out quite loud when his fish was brought. Everything was there that he wanted, everything that could make the moment an occasion, that would do beautifully—everything but what Waymarsh might give. The little waxed salle-à-manger was sallow and sociable; François, dancing over it, all smiles, was a man and a brother; the high-shouldered *patronne*, with her high-held, much-rubbed hands, seemed always assenting exuberantly to something unsaid; the Paris evening in short was, for Strether, in the very taste of the soup, in the goodness, as he was innocently pleased to think, of the wine, in the pleasant coarse texture of the napkin and the crunch of the thick-crusted bread. These all were things congruous with his confession, and his confession was that he *had*—it would come out properly just there if Waymarsh would only take it properly—agreed to breakfast out, at twelve literally, the next day. He didn't quite know where; the delicacy of the case came straight up in the remembrance of his new friend's "We'll see; I'll take you somewhere!"—for it had required little more than that, after all, to let him right in. He was affected after a minute, face to face with his actual comrade, with the impulse to over-colour. There had already been things in respect to which he knew himself tempted by this perversity. If Waymarsh thought them bad he should at least have his reason for his discomfort; so Strether showed them as worse. Still, he was now, in his way, sincerely perplexed.

Chad had been absent from the Boulevard Malesherbes—was absent from Paris altogether; he had learned that from the concierge, but had nevertheless gone up, and gone up—there were no two ways about it—from an uncontrollable, a really, if one would, depraved curiosity. The concierge had mentioned to him that a friend of the tenant of the troisième was for the time in possession; and this had been Strether's pretext for a further inquiry, an experiment carried on, under Chad's roof, without his knowledge. "I found his friend in fact there keeping the place warm, as he called it, for him; Chad himself being, as appears, in the south. He went a month ago to Cannes and though his return begins to be looked for it can't be for some days. I might you see, perfectly have waited a week; might have beaten a retreat as soon as I got this essential knowledge. But I beat no retreat; I did the opposite; I stayed, I dawdled, I trifled; above all I looked round. I saw, in fine; and—I don't know what to call it—I sniffed. It's a detail, but it's as if there were something—something very good—*to* sniff."

Waymarsh's face had shown his friend an attention apparently so remote that the latter was slightly surprised to find it at this point abreast with him. "Do you mean a smell? What of?"

"A charming scent. But I don't know."

Waymarsh gave an inferential grunt. "Does he live there with a woman?"

"I don't know."

Waymarsh waited an instant for more, then resumed: "Has he taken her off with him?"

"And will he bring her back?"—Strether fell into the inquiry. But he wound it up as before. "I don't know."

The way he wound it up, accompanied as this was with another drop back, another degustation of the Léoville, another wipe of his moustache and another good word for François, seemed to produce in his companion a slight irritation. "Then what the devil *do* you know?"

"Well," said Strether almost gaily, "I guess I don't know anything!" His gaiety might have been a tribute to the fact that the state he had been reduced to did for him again what had been done by his talk of the matter with Miss Gostrey at the London theatre. It was somehow enlarging; and the air of that amplitude was now doubtless more or less—and all for Waymarsh to feel—in his further response. "That's what I found out from the young man."

"But I thought you said you found out nothing."

"Nothing but that—that I don't know anything."

"And what good does that do you?"

"It's just," said Strether, "what I've come to you to help me to discover. I mean anything about anything over here. I *felt* that, up there. It regularly rose before me in its might. The young man moreover—Chad's friend—as good as told me so."

"As good as told you you know nothing about anything?" Waymarsh appeared to look at some one who might have as good as told *him*. "How old is he?"

"Well, I guess not thirty."

"Yet you had to take that from him?"

"Oh I took a good deal more—since, as I tell you, I took an invitation to déjeuner."

"And are you *going* to that unholy meal?"

"If you'll come with me. He wants you too, you know. I told him about you. He gave me his card," Strether pursued, "and his name's rather funny. It's John Little Bilham, and he says his two surnames are, on account of his being small, inevitably used together."

"Well," Waymarsh asked with due detachment from these details, "what's he doing up there?"

"His account of himself is that he's 'only a little artist-man.' That seemed to me perfectly to describe him. But he's yet in the phase of study; this, you know, is the great art-school—to pass a certain number of years in which he came over. And he's a great friend of Chad's, and occupying Chad's rooms just now because they're so pleasant. *He's* very pleasant and curious too," Strether added—"though he's not from Boston."

Waymarsh looked already rather sick of him. "Where *is* he from?"

Strether thought. "I don't know that, either. But he's 'notoriously,' as he put it himself, not from Boston."

"Well," Waymarsh moralised from dry depths, "every one can't notoriously *be* from Boston. "Why," he continued, "is he curious?"

"Perhaps just for *that*—for one thing! But really," Strether added, "for everything. When you meet him you'll see."

"Oh I don't want to meet him," Waymarsh impatiently growled. "Why don't he go home?"

Strether hesitated. "Well, because he likes it over here."

This appeared in particular more than Waymarsh could bear. "He ought then to be ashamed of himself, and as you admit that you think so too, why drag him in?"

Strether's reply again took time. "Perhaps I do think so myself—though I don't quite yet admit it. I'm not a bit sure—it's again one of the things I want to find out. I liked him, and *can* you like people—? But no matter." He pulled himself up. "There's no doubt I want you to come down on me and squash me."

Waymarsh helped himself to the next course, which, however, proving not the dish he had just noted as supplied to the English ladies, had the effect of causing his imagination temporarily to wander. But it presently broke out at a softer spot. "Have they got a handsome place up there?"

"Oh a charming place; full of beautiful and valuable things. I never saw such a place"—and Strether's thought went back to it. "For a little artist-man—!" He could in fact scarce express it.

But his companion, who appeared now to have a view, insisted. "Well?"

"Well, life can hold nothing better. Besides, they're things of which he's in charge."

"So that he does door-keeper for your precious pair? Can life," Waymarsh inquired, "hold nothing better than *that*?" Then as Strether, silent, seemed even yet to wonder, "Doesn't he know what *she* is?" he went on.

"*I* don't know. I didn't ask him. I couldn't. It was impossible. You wouldn't either. Besides I didn't want to. No more would you." Strether in short explained it at a stroke. "You can't make out over here what people do know."

"Then what did you come over for?"

"Well, I suppose exactly to see for myself—without their aid."

"Then what do you want mine for?"

"Oh," Strether laughed, "you're not one of *them*! I do know what *you* know."

As, however, this last assertion caused Waymarsh again to look at him hard—such being the latter's doubt of its implications—he felt his justification lame. Which was still more the case when Waymarsh presently said: "Look here, Strether. Quit this."

Our friend smiled with a doubt of his own. "Do you mean my tone?"

"No—damn your tone. I mean you nosing round. Quit the whole job. Let them stew in their juice. You're being used for a thing you ain't fit for. People don't take a fine-tooth comb to groom a horse."

"Am I a fine-tooth comb?" Strether laughed. "It's something I never called myself!"

"It's what you are, all the same. You ain't so young as you were, but you've kept your teeth."

He acknowledged his friend's humour. "Take care I don't get them into *you*! You'd like them, my friends at home, Waymarsh," he declared; "you'd really particularly like them. And I know"—it was slightly irrelevant, but he gave it sudden and singular force—"I know they'd like you!"

"Oh don't work them off on *me*!" Waymarsh groaned.

Yet Strether still lingered with his hands in his pockets. "It's really quite as indispensable as I say that Chad should be got back."

"Indispensable to whom? To you?"

"Yes," Strether presently said.

"Because if you get him you also get Mrs. Newsome?"

Strether faced it. "Yes."

"And if you don't get him you don't get her?"

It might be merciless, but he continued not to flinch. "I think it might have some effect on our personal understanding. Chad's of real importance—or can easily become so if he will—to the business."

"And the business is of real importance to his mother's husband?"

"Well, I naturally want what my future wife wants. And the thing will be much better if we have our own man in it."

"If you have your own man in it, in other words," Waymarsh said, "you'll marry—you personally—more money. She's already rich, as I understand you, but she'll be richer still if the business can be made to boom on certain lines that you've laid down."

"*I* haven't laid them down," Strether promptly returned. "Mr. Newsome—who knew extraordinarily well what he was about—laid them down ten years ago."

Oh well, Waymarsh seemed to indicate with a shake of his mane, *that* didn't matter! "You're fierce for the boom anyway."

His friend weighed a moment in silence the justice of the charge. "I can scarcely be called fierce, I think, when I so freely take my chance of the possibility, the danger, of being influenced in a sense counter to Mrs. Newsome's own feelings."

Waymarsh gave this proposition a long hard look. "I see. You're afraid yourself of being squared. But you're a humbug," he added, "all the same."

"Oh!" Strether quickly protested.

"Yes, you ask me for protection—which makes you very interesting; and then you won't take it. You say you want to be squashed—"

"Ah but not so easily! Don't you see," Strether demanded, "where my interest, as already shown you, lies? It lies in my not being squared. If I'm squared where's my marriage? If I miss my errand I miss that; and if I miss that I miss everything—I'm nowhere."

Waymarsh—but all relentlessly—took this in. "What do I care where you are if you're spoiled?"

Their eyes met on it an instant. "Thank you awfully," Strether at last said. "But don't you think *her* judgment of that—?"

"Ought to content me? No."

It kept them again face to face, and the end of this was that Strether again laughed. "You do her injustice. You really *must* know her. Good night."

He breakfasted with Mr. Bilham on the morrow, and, as inconsequently befell, with Waymarsh massively of the party. The latter announced, at the eleventh hour and much to his friend's surprise, that, damn it, he would as soon join him as do anything else; on which they proceeded together, strolling in a state of detachment practically luxurious for them, to the Boulevard Malesherbes, a couple engaged that day with the sharp spell of Paris as confessedly, it might have been seen, as any couple among the daily thousands so compromised. They walked, wandered, wondered and, a little, lost themselves; Strether hadn't had for years so rich a consciousness of time—a bag of gold into which he constantly dipped for a handful. It was present to him that when the little business with Mr. Bilham should be over he would still have shining hours to use absolutely as he liked. There was no great pulse of haste yet in this process of saving Chad; nor was that effect a bit more marked as he sat, half an hour later, with his legs under Chad's mahogany, with Mr. Bilham on one side, with a friend of Mr. Bilham's on the other, with Waymarsh stupendously opposite, and with the great hum of Paris coming up in softness, vagueness—for Strether himself indeed already positive sweetness—through the sunny windows towards which, the day before, his curiosity had raised its wings from below. The feeling strongest with him at that moment had borne fruit almost faster than he could taste it, and Strether literally felt at the present moment that there was a precipitation in his fate. He had known nothing and nobody as he stood in the street; but hadn't his view now taken a bound in the direction of every one and of every thing?

"What's he up to, what's he up to?"—something like that was at the back of his head all the while in respect to little Bilham; but meanwhile, till he should make out, every one and every thing were as good as represented for him by the combination of his host and the lady on his left. The lady on his left, the lady thus promptly and ingeniously invited to "meet" Mr. Strether and Mr. Waymarsh—it was the way she herself expressed her case—was a very marked person, a person who had much to do with our friend's asking himself if the occasion weren't in its essence the most baited, the most gilded of traps. Baited it could properly be called when the repast was of so wise a savour, and gilded surrounding objects seemed inevitably to need to be when Miss Barrace—which was the lady's name—looked at them with convex Parisian eyes and through a glass with a remarkably long tortoise-shell handle. Why Miss Barrace, mature meagre erect and eminently gay, highly adorned, perfectly familiar, freely contradictious, and reminding him of some last-century portrait of a clever head without powder—why Miss Barrace should have been in particular the note of a "trap" Strether couldn't on the spot have explained; he blinked in the light of a conviction that he should know later on, and know well—as it came over him, for that matter, with force, that he should need to. He wondered what he was to think exactly of either of his new friends; since the young man, Chad's intimate and deputy, had, in thus constituting the scene, practised so much more subtly than he had been prepared for, and since in especial Miss Barrace, surrounded clearly by every consideration, hadn't scrupled to figure as a familiar object. It was interesting to him to feel that he was in the presence of new measures, other standards, a different scale of relations, and that evidently here were a happy pair who didn't think of things at all as he and Waymarsh thought. Nothing was less to have been calculated in the business than that it should now be for him as if he and Waymarsh were comparatively quite at one.

The latter was magnificent—this at least was an assurance privately given him by Miss Barrace. "Oh your friend's a type, the grand old American—what shall one call it? The Hebrew prophet, Ezekiel, Jeremiah, who used when I was a little girl in the Rue Montaigne to come to see my father and who was usually the American Minister to the Tuileries or some other court. I haven't seen one of these ever so many years; the sight of it warms my poor old chilled heart; this specimen is wonderful; in the right quarter, you know, he'll have a *succès fou*." Strether hadn't failed to ask what the right quarter might be, much as he required his presence of mind to meet such a change in their scheme. "Oh the artist-quarter and that kind of thing; *here* already, for instance, as you see." He had been on the point of echoing "'Here'?—is *this* the artist-quarter?" but she had already disposed of the question with a wave of all her tortoise-shell and an easy "Bring him to *me*!" He knew on the spot how little he should be able to bring him, for the very air was by this time, to his sense, thick and hot with poor Waymarsh's judgment of it. He was in the trap still more than his companion and, unlike his companion, not making the best of it; which was precisely what doubtless gave him his admirable sombre glow. Little did Miss Barrace know that what was behind it was his grave estimate of her own laxity. The general assumption with which our two friends had arrived had been that of finding Mr. Bilham ready to conduct them to one or other of those resorts of the earnest, the esthetic fraternity which were shown among the sights of Paris. In this character it would have justified them in a proper insistence on discharging their score. Waymarsh's only proviso at the last had been that nobody should pay for him; but he found himself, as the occasion developed, paid for on a scale as to which Strether privately made out that he already nursed retribution. Strether was conscious across the table of what worked in him, conscious when they passed back to the small salon to which, the previous evening, he himself had made so rich a reference; conscious most of all as they stepped out to the balcony in which one would have had to be an ogre not to recognise the perfect place for easy aftertastes. These things were enhanced for Miss Barrace by a succession of excellent cigarettes—acknowledged, acclaimed, as a part of the wonderful supply left behind him by Chad—in an almost equal absorption of which Strether found himself blindly, almost wildly pushing forward. He might perish by the sword as well as by famine, and he knew that his having abetted the lady by an excess that was rare with him would count for little in the sum—as Waymarsh might so easily add it up—of her licence. Waymarsh had smoked of old, smoked hugely; but Waymarsh did nothing now, and that gave him his advantage over people who took things up lightly just when others had laid them heavily down. Strether had never smoked, and he felt as if he flaunted at his friend that this had been only because of a reason. The reason, it now began to appear even to himself, was that he had never had a lady to smoke with.

It was this lady's being there at all, however, that was the strange free thing; perhaps, since she *was* there, her smoking was the least of her freedoms. If Strether had been sure at each juncture of what—with Bilham in especial—she talked about, he might have traced others and winced at them and felt Waymarsh wince; but he was in fact so often at sea that his sense of the range of reference was merely general and that he on several different occasions guessed and interpreted only to doubt. He wondered what they meant, but there were things he scarce thought they could be supposed to mean, and "Oh no—not *that*!" was at the end of most of his ventures. This was the very beginning with him of a condition as to which, later on, as will be seen, he found cause to pull himself up; and he was to remember the moment duly as the first step in a process. The central fact of the place was neither more or less, when analysed—and a pressure superficial sufficed—than the fundamental impropriety of Chad's situation, round about which they thus seemed cynically clustered. Accordingly, since they took it for granted, they took for granted all that was in connexion with it taken for granted at Woollett—matters as to which, verily, he had been reduced with Mrs. Newsome to the last intensity of silence. That was the consequence of their being too bad to be talked about, and was the accompaniment, by the same token, of a deep conception of their badness. It befell therefore that when poor Strether put it to himself that the badness was ultimately, or perhaps even insolently, what such a scene as the one before him was, so to speak, built upon, he could scarce shirk the dilemma of reading a roundabout echo of them into almost anything that came up. This, he was well aware, was a dreadful necessity; but such was the stern logic, he could only gather, of a relation to the irregular life.

It was the way the irregular life sat upon Bilham and Miss Barrace that was the insidious, the delicate marvel. He was eager to concede that their relation to it was all indirect, for anything else in him would have shown the grossness of bad manners; but the indirectness was none the less consonant—*that* was striking—with a grateful enjoyment of everything that was Chad's. They spoke of him repeatedly, invoking his good name and good nature, and the worst confusion of mind for Strether was that all their mention of him was of a kind to do him honour. They commended his munificence and approved his taste, and in doing so sat down, as it seemed to Strether, in the very soil out of which these things flowered. Our friend's final predicament was that he himself was sitting down, for the time, *with* them, and there was a supreme moment at which, compared with his collapse, Waymarsh's erectness affected him as really high. One thing was certain—he saw he must make up his mind. He must approach Chad, must wait for him, deal with him, master him, but he mustn't dispossess himself of the faculty of seeing things as they were. He must bring him to *him*—not go himself, as it were, so much of the way. He must at any rate be clearer as to what—should he continue to do that for convenience—he was still condoning. It was on the detail of this quantity—and what could the fact be but mystifying?—that Bilham and Miss Barrace threw so little light. So there they were.

II

When Miss Gostrey arrived, at the end of a week, she made him a sign; he went immediately to see her, and it wasn't till then that he could again close his grasp on the idea of a corrective. This idea however was luckily all before him again from the moment he crossed the threshold of the little entresol of the Quartier Marbœuf into which she had gathered, as she said, picking them up in a thousand flights and funny little passionate pounces, the makings of a final nest. He recognised in an instant that there really, there only, he should find the boon with the vision of which he had first mounted Chad's stairs. He might have been a little scared at the picture of how much more, in this place, he should know himself "in" hadn't his friend been on the spot to measure the amount to his appetite. Her compact and crowded little chambers, almost dusky, as they at first struck him, with accumulations, represented a supreme general adjustment to opportunities and conditions. Wherever he looked he saw an old ivory or an old brocade, and he scarce knew where to sit for fear of a misappliance. The life of the occupant struck him of a sudden as more charged with possession even than Chad's or than Miss Barrace's; wide as his glimpse had lately become of the empire of "things," what was before him still enlarged it; the lust of the eyes and the pride of life had indeed thus their temple. It was the innermost nook of the shrine—as brown as a pirate's cave. In the brownness were glints of gold; patches of purple were in the gloom; objects all that caught, through the muslin, with their high rarity, the light of the low windows. Nothing was clear about them but that they were precious, and they brushed his ignorance with their contempt as a flower, in a liberty taken with him, might have been whisked under his nose. But after a full look at his hostess he knew none the less what most concerned him. The circle in which they stood together was warm with life, and every question between them would live there as nowhere else. A question came up as soon as they had spoken, for his answer with a laugh, was quickly: "Well, they've got hold of me!" Much of their talk on this first occasion was his development of that truth. He was extraordinarily glad to see her, expressing to her frankly what she most showed him, that one might live for years without a blessing unsuspected, but that to know it at last for no more than three days was to need it or miss it for ever. She was the blessing that had now become his need, and what could prove it better than that without her he had lost himself?

"What do you mean?" she asked with an absence of alarm that, correcting him as if he had mistaken the "period" of one of her pieces, gave him afresh a sense of her easy movement through the maze he had but begun to tread. "What in the name of all the Pococks have you managed to do?"

"Why exactly the wrong thing. I've made a frantic friend of little Bilham."

"Ah that sort of thing was the essence of your case and to have been allowed for from the first." And it was only after this that, quite as a minor matter, she asked who in the world little Bilham might be. When she learned that he was a friend of Chad's and living for the time in Chad's rooms in Chad's absence, quite as if acting in Chad's spirit and serving Chad's cause, she showed, however, more interest. "Should you mind my seeing him? Only once, you know," she added.

"Oh the oftener the better: he's amusing—he's original."

"He doesn't shock you?" Miss Gostrey threw out.

"Never in the world! We escape that with a perfection—! I feel it to be largely, no doubt, because I don't half understand him; but our *modus vivendi* isn't spoiled even by that. You must dine with me to meet him," Strether went on. "Then you'll see."

"Are you giving dinners?"

"Yes—there I am. That's what I mean."

All her kindness wondered. "That you're spending too much money?"

"Dear no—they seem to cost so little. But that I do it to *them*. I ought to hold off."

She thought again—she laughed. "The money you must be spending to think it cheap! But I must be out of it—to the naked eye."

He looked for a moment as if she were really failing him. "Then you won't meet them?" It was almost as if she had developed an unexpected personal prudence.

She hesitated. "Who are they—first?"

"Why little Bilham to begin with." He kept back for the moment Miss Barrace. "And Chad—when he comes—you must absolutely see."

"When then does he come?"

"When Bilham has had time to write him, and hear from him, about me. Bilham, however," he pursued, "will report favourably—favourably for Chad. That will make him not afraid to come. I want you the more therefore, you see, for my bluff."

"Oh you'll do yourself for your bluff." She was perfectly easy. "At the rate you've gone I'm quiet."

"Ah but I haven't," said Strether, "made one protest."

She turned it over. "Haven't you been seeing what there's to protest about?"

He let her, with this, however ruefully, have the whole truth.

"I haven't yet found a single thing."

"Isn't there any one *with* him then?"

"Of the sort I came out about?" Strether took a moment. "How do I know? And what do I care?"

"Oh oh!"—and her laughter spread. He was struck in fact by the effect on her of his joke. He saw now how he meant it as a joke. *She* saw, however, still other things, though in an instant she had hidden them. "You've got at no facts at all?"

He tried to muster them. "Well, he has a lovely home."

"Ah that, in Paris," she quickly returned, "proves nothing. That is rather it *dis*proves nothing. They may very well, you see, the people your mission is concerned with, have done it *for* him."

"Exactly. And it was on the scene of their doings then that Waymarsh and I sat guzzling."

"Oh if you forbore to guzzle here on scenes of doings," she replied, "you might easily die of starvation." With which she smiled at him. "You've worse before you."

"Ah I've *everything* before me. But on your hypothesis, you know, they must be wonderful."

"They *are*!" said Miss Gostrey. "You're not therefore, you see," she added, "wholly without facts. They've *been*, in effect, wonderful."

To have got at something comparatively definite appeared at last a little to help—a wave by which, moreover, the next moment, recollection was washed. "My young man does admit furthermore that they're our friend's great interest."

"Is that the expression he uses?"

Strether more exactly recalled. "No—not quite."

"Something more vivid? Less?"

He had bent, with neared glasses, over a group of articles on a small stand; and at this he came up. "It was a mere allusion, but, on the lookout as I was, it struck me. 'Awful, you know, as Chad is'—those were Bilham's words."

"'Awful, you know—'? Oh!"—and Miss Gostrey turned them over. She seemed, however, satisfied. "Well, what more do you want?"

He glanced once more at a *bibelot* or two, but everything sent him back. "But it *is* all the same as if they wished to let me have it between the eyes."

She wondered. "Quoi donc?"

"Why what I speak of. The amenity. They can stun you with that as well as with anything else."

"Oh," she answered, "you'll come round! I must see them each," she went on, "for myself. I mean Mr. Bilham and Mr. Newsome—Mr. Bilham naturally first. Once only—once for each; that will do. But face to face—for half an hour. What's

Mr. Chad," she immediately pursued, "doing at Cannes? Decent men don't go to Cannes with the—well, with the kind of ladies you mean."

"Don't they?" Strether asked with an interest in decent men that amused her.

"No; elsewhere, but not to Cannes. Cannes is different. Cannes is better. Cannes is best. I mean it's all people you know—when you do know them. And if *he* does, why that's different too. He must have gone alone. She can't be with him."

"I haven't," Strether confessed in his weakness, "the least idea." There seemed much in what she said, but he was able after a little to help her to a nearer impression. The meeting with little Bilham took place, by easy arrangement, in the great gallery of the Louvre; and when, standing with his fellow visitor before one of the splendid Titians—the overwhelming portrait of the young man with the strangely-shaped glove and the blue-grey eyes—he turned to see the third member of their party advance from the end of the waxed and gilded vista, he had a sense of having at last taken hold. He had agreed with Miss Gostrey—it dated even from Chester—for a morning at the Louvre, and he had embraced independently the same idea as thrown out by little Bilham, whom he had already accompanied to the museum of the Luxembourg. The fusion of these schemes presented no difficulty, and it was to strike him again that in little Bilham's company contrarieties in general dropped.

"Oh he's all right—he's one of *us*!" Miss Gostrey, after the first exchange soon found a chance to murmur to her companion; and Strether, as they proceeded and paused and while a quick unanimity between the two appeared to have phrased itself in half a dozen remarks—Strether knew that he knew almost immediately what she meant, and took it as still another sign that he had got his job in hand. This was the more grateful to him that he could think of the intelligence now serving him as an acquisition positively new. He wouldn't have known even the day before what she meant—that is if she meant, what he assumed, that they were intense Americans together. He had just worked round—and with a sharper turn of the screw than any yet—to the conception of an American intense as little Bilham was intense. The young man was his first specimen; the specimen had profoundly perplexed him; at present however there was light. It was by little Bilham's amazing serenity that he had at first been affected, but he had inevitably, in his circumspection, felt it as the trail of the serpent, the corruption, as he might conveniently have said, of Europe; whereas the promptness with which it came up for Miss Gostrey but as a special little form of the oldest thing they knew justified it at once to his own vision as well. He wanted to be able to like his specimen with a clear good conscience, and this fully permitted it. What had muddled him was precisely the small artistman's way—it was so complete—of being more American than anybody. But it now for the time put Strether vastly at his ease to have this view of a new way.

The amiable youth then looked out, as it had first struck Strether, at a world in respect to which he hadn't a prejudice. The one our friend most instantly missed was the usual one in favour of an occupation accepted. Little Bilham had an occupation, but it was only an occupation declined; and it was by his general exemption from alarm, anxiety or remorse on this score that the impression of his serenity was made. He had come out to Paris to paint—to fathom, that is, at large, that mystery; but study had been fatal to him so far as anything *could* be fatal, and his productive power faltered in proportion as his knowledge grew. Strether had gathered from him that at the moment of his finding him in Chad's rooms he hadn't saved from his shipwreck a scrap of anything but his beautiful intelligence and his confirmed habit of Paris. He referred to these things with an equal fond familiarity, and it was sufficiently clear that, as an outfit, they still served him. They were charming to Strether through the hour spent at the Louvre, where indeed they figured for him as an unseparated part of the charged iridescent air, the glamour of the name, the splendour of the space, the colour of the masters. Yet they were present too wherever the young man led, and the day after the visit to the Louvre they hung, in a different walk, about the steps of our party. He had invited his companions to cross the river with him, offering to show them his own poor place; and his own poor place, which was very poor, gave to his idiosyncrasies, for Strether—the small sublime indifferences and independences that had struck the latter as fresh—an odd and engaging dignity. He lived at the end of an alley that went out of an old short cobbled street, a street that went in turn out of a new long smooth avenue—street and avenue and alley having, however, in common a sort of social shabbiness; and he introduced them to the rather cold and blank little studio which he had lent to a comrade for the term of his elegant absence. The comrade was another ingenuous compatriot, to whom he had wired that tea was to await them "regardless," and this reckless repast, and the second ingenuous compatriot, and the faraway makeshift life, with its jokes and its gaps, its delicate daubs and its three or four chairs, its overflow of taste and conviction and its lack of nearly all else—these things wove round the occasion a spell to which our hero unreservedly surrendered.

He liked the ingenuous compatriots—for two or three others soon gathered; he liked the delicate daubs and the free discriminations—involving references indeed, involving enthusiasms and execrations that made him, as they said, sit up; he liked above all the legend of good-humoured poverty, of mutual accommodation fairly raised to the romantic, that he soon read into the scene. The ingenuous compatriots showed a candour, he thought, surpassing even the candour of Woollett; they were red-haired and long-legged, they were quaint and queer and dear and droll; they made the place resound with the vernacular, which he had never known so marked as when figuring for the chosen language, he must suppose, of contemporary art. They twanged with a vengeance the aesthetic lyre—they drew from it wonderful airs. This aspect of their life had an admirable innocence; and he looked on occasion at Maria Gostrey to see to what extent that element reached her. She gave him however for the hour, as she had given him the previous day, no further sign than to show how she dealt with boys; meeting them with the air of old Parisian practice that she had for every one, for everything, in turn. Wonderful about the delicate daubs, masterful about the way to make tea, trustful about the legs of chairs and familiarly reminiscent of those, in the other time, the named, the numbered or the caricatured, who had flourished or failed, disappeared or arrived, she had accepted with the best grace her second course of little Bilham, and had said to Strether, the previous afternoon, on his leaving them, that, since her impression was to be renewed, she would reserve judgement till after the new evidence.

The new evidence was to come, as it proved, in a day or two. He soon had from Maria a message to the effect that an excellent box at the Français had been lent her for the following night; it seeming on such occasions not the least of her merits that she was subject to such approaches. The sense of how she was always paying for something in advance was equalled on Strether's part only by the sense of how she was always being paid; all of which made for his consciousness, in the larger air, of a lively bustling traffic, the exchange of such values as were not for him to handle. She hated, he knew, at the French play, anything but a box—just as she hated at the

English anything but a stall; and a box was what he was already in this phase girding himself to press upon her. But she had for that matter her community with little Bilham: she too always, on the great issues, showed as having known in time. It made her constantly beforehand with him and gave him mainly the chance to ask himself how on the day of their settlement their account would stand. He endeavoured even now to keep it a little straight by arranging that if he accepted her invitation she should dine with him first; but the upshot of this scruple was that at eight o'clock on the morrow he awaited her with Waymarsh under the pillared portico. She hadn't dined with him, and it was characteristic of their relation that she had made him embrace her refusal without in the least understanding it. She ever caused her rearrangements to affect him as her tenderest touches. It was on that principle for instance that, giving him the opportunity to be amiable again to little Bilham, she had suggested his offering the young man a seat in their box. Strether had despatched for this purpose a small blue missive to the Boulevard Malesherbes, but up to the moment of their passing into the theatre he had received no response to his message. He held, however, even after they had been for some time conveniently seated, that their friend, who knew his way about, would come in at his own right moment. His temporary absence moreover seemed, as never yet, to make the right moment for Miss Gostrey. Strether had been waiting till to-night to get back from her in some mirrored form her impressions and conclusions. She had elected, as they said, to see little Bilham once; but now she had seen him twice and had nevertheless not said more than a word.

Waymarsh meanwhile sat opposite him with their hostess between; and Miss Gostrey spoke of herself as an instructor of youth introducing her little charges to a work that was one of the glories of literature. The glory was happily unobjectionable, and the little charges were candid; for herself she had travelled that road and she merely waited on their innocence. But she referred in due time to their absent friend, whom it was clear they should have to give up. "He either won't have got your note," she said, "or you won't have got his: he has had some kind of hindrance, and, of course, for that matter, you know, a man never writes about coming to a box." She spoke as if, with her look, it might have been Waymarsh who had written to the youth, and the latter's face showed a mixture of austerity and anguish. She went on however as if to meet this. "He's far and away, you know, the best of them."

"The best of whom, ma'am?"

"Why of all the long procession—the boys, the girls, or the old men and old women as they sometimes really are; the hope, as one may say, of our country. They've all passed, year after year; but there has been no one in particular I've ever wanted to stop. I feel—don't *you*?—that I want to stop little Bilham; he's so exactly right as he is." She continued to talk to Waymarsh. "He's too delightful. If he'll only not spoil it! But they always *will*; they always do; they always have."

"I don't think Waymarsh knows," Strether said after a moment, "quite what it's open to Bilham to spoil."

"It can't be a good American," Waymarsh lucidly enough replied, "for it didn't strike me the young man had developed much in *that* shape."

"Ah," Miss Gostrey sighed, "the name of the good American is as easily given as taken away! What *is* it, to begin with, to *be* one, and what's the extraordinary hurry? Surely nothing that's so pressing was ever so little defined. It's such an order, really, that before we cook you the dish we must at least have your receipt. Besides, the poor chicks have time! What I've seen so often spoiled," she pursued, "is the happy attitude itself, the state of faith and—what shall I call it?—the sense of beauty. You're right about him"—she now took in Strether—"little Bilham has them to a charm; we must keep little Bilham along." Then she was all again for Waymarsh. "The others have all wanted so dreadfully to do something, and they've gone and done it in too many cases indeed. It leaves them never the same afterwards; the charm's always somehow broken. Now *he*, I think, you know, really won't. He won't do the least dreadful little thing. We shall continue to enjoy him just as he is. No—he's quite beautiful. He sees everything. He isn't a bit ashamed. He has every scrap of the courage of it that one could ask. Only think what he *might* do. One wants really—for fear of some accident—to keep him in view. At this very moment perhaps what mayn't he be up to? I've had my disappointments—the poor things are never really safe; or only at least when you have them under your eye. One can never completely trust them. One's uneasy, and I think that's why I most miss him now."

She had wound up with a laugh of enjoyment over her embroidery of her idea—an enjoyment that her face communicated to Strether, who almost wished none the less at this moment that she would let poor Waymarsh alone. *He* knew more or less what she meant; but the fact wasn't a reason for her not pretending to Waymarsh that he didn't. It was craven of him perhaps, but he would, for the high amenity of the occasion, have liked Waymarsh not to be so sure of his wit. Her recognition of it gave him away and, before she had done with him or with that article, would give him worse. What was he, all the same, to do? He looked across the box at his friend; their eyes met; something queer and stiff, something that bore on the situation but that it was better not to touch, passed in silence between them. Well, the effect of it for Strether was an abrupt reaction, a final impatience of his own tendency to temporise. Where was that taking him anyway? It was one of the quiet instants that sometimes settle more matters than the outbreaks dear to the historic muse. The only qualification of the quietness was the synthetic "Oh hang it!" into which Strether's share of the silence soundlessly flowered. It represented, this mute ejaculation, a final impulse to burn his ships. These ships, to the historic muse, may seem of course mere cockles, but when he presently spoke to Miss Gostrey it was with the sense at least of applying the torch. "Is it then a conspiracy?"

"Between the two young men? Well, I don't pretend to be a seer or a prophetess," she presently replied; "but if I'm simply a woman of sense he's working for you to-night. I don't quite know how—but it's in my bones." And she looked at him at last as if, little material as she yet gave him, he'd really understand. "For an opinion *that's* my opinion. He makes you out too well not to."

"Not to work for me to-night?" Strether wondered. "Then I hope he isn't doing anything bad."

"They've got you," she portentously answered.

"Do you mean he *is*—?"

"They've got you," she merely repeated. Though she disclaimed the prophetic vision she was at this instant the nearest approach he had ever met to the priestess of the oracle. The light was in her eyes. "You must face it now."

He faced it on the spot. "They *had* arranged—?"

"Every move in the game. And they've been arranging ever since. He has had every day his little telegram from Cannes."

It made Strether open his eyes. "Do you *know* that?"

"I do better. I see it. This was, before I met him, what I wondered whether I *was* to see. But as soon as I met him I ceased to wonder, and our second meeting made me sure. I took him all in. He was acting—he is still—on his daily instructions."

"So that Chad has done the whole thing?"

"Oh no—not the whole. *We've* done some of it. You and I and 'Europe.'"

"Europe—yes," Strether mused.

"Dear old Paris," she seemed to explain. But there was more, and with one of her turns, she risked it. "And dear old Waymarsh. You," she declared, "have been a good bit of it."

He sat massive. "A good bit of what, ma'am?"

"Why of the wonderful consciousness of our friend here. You've helped too in your way to float him to where he is."

"And where the devil *is* he?"

She passed it on with a laugh. "Where the devil, Strether, are you?"

He spoke as if he had just been thinking it out. "Well, quite already in Chad's hands, it would seem." And he had had with this another thought. "Will that be—just all through Bilham—the way he's going to work it? It would be for him, you know, an idea. And Chad with an idea—!"

"Well?" she asked while the image held him.

"Well, is Chad—what shall I say?—monstrous?"

"Oh as much as you like! But the idea you speak of," she said, "won't have been his best. He'll have a better. It won't be all through little Bilham that he'll work it."

This already sounded almost like a hope destroyed. "Through whom else then?"

"That's what we shall see!" But quite as she spoke she turned, and Strether turned; for the door of the box had opened, with the click of the *ouvreuse*, from the lobby, and a gentleman, a stranger to them, had come in with a quick step. The door closed behind him, and, though their faces showed him his mistake, his air, which was striking, was all good confidence. The curtain had just again risen, and, in the hush of the general attention, Strether's challenge was tacit, as was also the greeting, with a quickly-deprecating hand and smile, of the unannounced visitor. He discreetly signed that he would wait, would stand, and these things and his face, one look from which she had caught, had suddenly worked for Miss Gostrey. She fitted to them all an answer for Strether's last question. The solid stranger was simply the answer—as she now, turning to her friend, indicated. She brought it straight out for him—it presented the intruder. "Why, through this gentleman!" The gentleman indeed, at the same time, though sounding for Strether a very short name, did practically as much to explain. Strether gasped the name back—then only had he seen. Miss Gostrey had said more than she knew. They were in presence of Chad himself.

Our friend was to go over it afterwards again and again—he was going over it much of the time that they were together, and they were together constantly for three or four days: the note had been so strongly struck during that first half-hour that everything happening since was comparatively a minor development. The fact was that his perception of the young man's identity—so absolutely checked for a minute—had been quite one of the sensations that count in life; he certainly had never known one that had acted, as he might have said, with more of a crowded rush. And the rush, though both vague and multitudinous, had lasted a long time, protected, as it were, yet at the same time aggravated, by the circumstance of its coinciding with a stretch of decorous silence. They couldn't talk without disturbing the spectators in the part of the balcony just below them; and it, for that matter, came to Strether—being a thing of the sort that did come to him—that these were the accidents of a high civilization; the imposed tribute to propriety, the frequent exposure to conditions, usually brilliant, in which relief has to await its time. Relief was never quite near at hand for kings, queens, comedians and other such people, and though you might be yourself not exactly one of those, you could yet, in leading the life of high pressure, guess a little how they sometimes felt. It was truly the life of high pressure that Strether had seemed to feel himself lead while he sat there, close to Chad, during the long tension of the act. He was in presence of a fact that occupied his whole mind, that occupied for the half-hour his senses themselves all together; but he couldn't without inconvenience show anything—which moreover might count really as luck. What he might have shown, had he shown at all, was exactly the kind of emotion—the emotion of bewilderment—that he had proposed to himself from the first, whatever should occur, to show least. The phenomenon that had suddenly sat down there with him was a phenomenon of change so complete that his imagination, which had worked so beforehand, felt itself, in the connexion, without margin or allowance. It had faced every contingency but that Chad should not *be* Chad, and this was what it now had to face with a mere strained smile and an uncomfortable flush.

He asked himself if, by any chance, before he should have in some way to commit himself, he might feel his mind settled to the new vision, might habituate it, so to speak, to the remarkable truth. But oh it was too remarkable, the truth; for what could be more remarkable than this sharp rupture of an identity? You could deal with a man as himself—you couldn't deal with him as somebody else. It was a small source of peace moreover to be reduced to wondering how little he might know in such an event what a sum he was setting you. He couldn't absolutely not know, for you couldn't absolutely not let him. It was a *case* then simply, a strong case, as people nowadays called such things, a case of transformation unsurpassed, and the hope was but in the general law that strong cases were liable to control from without. Perhaps he, Strether himself, was the only person after all aware of it. Even Miss Gostrey, with all her science, wouldn't be, would she?—and he had never seen any one less aware of anything than Waymarsh as he glowered at Chad. The social sightlessness of his old friend's survey marked for him afresh, and almost in a humiliating way, the inevitable limits of direct aid from this source. He was not certain, however, of not drawing a shade of compensation from the privilege, as yet untasted, of knowing more about something in particular than Miss Gostrey did. His situation too was a case, for that matter, and he was now sc interested, quite so privately agog, about it, that he had already an eye to the fun it would be to open up to her afterwards. He derived during his half-hour no assistance from her, and just this fact of her not meeting his eyes played a little, it must be confessed, into his predicament.

He had introduced Chad, in the first minutes, under his breath, and there was never the primness in her of the person unacquainted; but she had none the less betrayed at first no vision but of the stage, where she occasionally found a pretext for an appreciative moment that she invited Waymarsh to share. The latter's faculty of participation had never had, all round, such an assault to meet; the pressure on him being the sharper for this chosen attitude in her, as Strether judged it, of isolating, for their natural intercourse, Chad and himself. This intercourse was meanwhile restricted to a frank friendly look from the young man, something markedly like a smile, but falling far short of a grin, and to the vivacity of Strether's private speculation as to whether *he* carried himself like a fool. He didn't quite see how he could so feel as one without somehow showing as one. The worst of that question moreover was that he knew it as a symptom the sense of which annoyed him. "If I'm going to be odiously conscious of how I may strike the fellow," he reflected, "it was so little what I came out for that I may as well stop before I begin." This sage consideration too, distinctly, seemed to leave untouched the fact that he *was* going to be conscious. He was conscious of everything but of what would have served him.

He was to know afterwards, in the watches of the night, that nothing would have been more open to him than after a minute or two to propose to Chad to seek with him the refuge of the lobby. He hadn't only not proposed it, but had lacked even the presence of mind to see it as possible. He had stuck there like a schoolboy wishing not to miss a minute of the show; though for that portion of the show then presented he hadn't had an instant's real attention. He couldn't when the curtain fell have given the slightest account of what had happened. He had therefore, further, not at that moment acknowledged the amenity added by this acceptance of his awkwardness to Chad's general patience. Hadn't he none the less known at the very time—known it stupidly and without reaction—that the boy was accepting something? He was modestly benevolent, the boy—that was at least what he had been capable of the superiority of making out his chance to be; and one had one's self literally not had the gumption to get in ahead of him. If we should go into all that occupied our friend in the watches of the night we should have to mend our pen; but an instance or two may mark for us the vividness with which he could remember. He remembered the two absurdities that, if his presence of mind *had* failed, were the things that had had most to do with it. He had never in his life seen a young man come into a box at ten o'clock at night, and would, if challenged on the question in advance, scarce have been ready to pronounce as to different ways of doing so. But it was in spite of this definite to him that Chad had had a way that was wonderful: a fact carrying with it an implication that, as one might imagine it, he knew, he had learned, how.

Here already then were abounding results; he had on the spot and without the least trouble of intention taught Strether that even in so small a thing as that there were different ways. He had done in the same line still more than this; had by a mere shake or two of the head made his old friend observe that the change in him was perhaps more than anything else, for the eye, a matter of the marked streaks of grey, extraordinary at his age, in his thick black hair; as well as that this new feature was curiously becoming to him, did something for him, as characterisation, also even—of all things in the world—as refinement, that had been a good deal wanted. Strether felt, however, he would have had to confess, that it wouldn't have been easy just now, on this and other counts, in the presence of what had been supplied, to be quite clear as to what had been missed. A reflexion a candid critic might have made of old, for instance, was that it would have been much happier for the son to look more like the mother; but this was a reflexion that at present would never occur. The ground had quite fallen away from it, yet no resemblance whatever to the mother had supervened. It would have been hard for a young man's face and air to disconnect themselves more completely than Chad's at this juncture from any discerned, from any imaginable aspect of a New England female parent. That of course was no more than had been on the cards; but it produced in Strether none the less one of those frequent phenomena of mental reference with which all judgement in him was actually beset.

Again and again as the days passed he had had a sense of the pertinence of communicating quickly with Woollett—communicating with a quickness with which telegraphy alone would rhyme; the fruit really of a fine fancy in him for keeping things straight, for the happy forestalment of error. No one could explain better when needful, nor put more conscience into an account or a report; which burden of conscience is perhaps exactly the reason why his heart always sank when the clouds of explanation gathered. His highest ingenuity was in keeping the sky of life clear of them. Whether or no he had a grand idea of the lucid, he held that nothing ever was in fact—for any one else—explained. One went through the vain motions, but it was mostly a waste of life. A personal relation was a relation only so long as people either perfectly understood or, better still, didn't care if they didn't. From the moment they cared if they didn't it was living by the sweat of one's brow; and the sweat of one's brow was just what one might buy one's self off from by keeping the ground free of the wild weed of delusion. It easily grew too fast, and the Atlantic cable now alone could race with it. That agency would each day have testified for him to something that was not what Woollett had argued. He was not at this moment absolutely sure that the effect of the morrow's—or rather of the night's—appreciation of the crisis wouldn't be to determine some brief missive. "Have at last seen him, but oh dear!"—some temporary relief of that sort seemed to hover before him. It hovered somehow as preparing them all—yet preparing them for what? If he might do so more luminously and cheaply he would tick out in four words: "Awfully old—grey hair." To this particular item in Chad's appearance he constantly, during their mute half-hour, reverted; as if so very much more than he could have said had been involved in it. The most he could have said would have been: "If he's going to make me feel young—!" which indeed, however, carried with it quite enough. If Strether was to feel young, that is, it would be because Chad was to feel old; and an aged and hoary sinner had been no part of the scheme.

The question of Chadwick's true time of life was, doubtless, what came up quickest after the adjournment of the two, when the play was over, to a café in the Avenue de l'Opéra. Miss Gostrey had in due course been perfect for such a step; she had known exactly what they wanted—to go straight somewhere and talk; and Strether had even felt that she had known what he wished to say and that he was arranging immediately to begin. She hadn't pretended this, as she *had* pretended, on the other hand, to have divined Waymarsh's wish to extend to her an independent protection homeward; but Strether nevertheless found how, after he had Chad opposite to him at a small table in the brilliant halls that his companion straightway selected, sharply and easily discriminated from others, it was quite, to his mind, as if she heard him speak; as if, sitting up, a mile away, in the little apartment he knew, she would listen hard enough to catch. He found too that he liked that idea, and he wished that, by the same token, Mrs. Newsome might have caught as well. For what had above all been determined in him as a necessity of the first order was not to lose another hour, nor a fraction of one; was to advance, to overwhelm, with a rush. This was how he would anticipate—by a night-attack, as might be—any forced maturity that a crammed consciousness of Paris was likely to take upon itself to assert on behalf of the boy. He knew to the full, on what he had just extracted from Miss Gostrey, Chad's marks of alertness; but they were a reason the more for not dawdling. If he was himself moreover to be treated as young he wouldn't at all events be so treated before he should have struck out at least once. His arms might be pinioned afterwards, but it would have been left on record that he was fifty. The importance of this he had indeed begun to feel before they left the theatre; it had become a wild unrest, urging him to seize his chance. He could scarcely wait for it as they went; he was on the verge of the indecency of bringing up the question in the street; he fairly caught himself going on—so he afterwards invidiously named it—as if there would be for him no second chance should the present be lost. Not till, on the purple divan before the perfunctory *bock*, he had brought out the words themselves, was he sure, for that matter, that the present would be saved.

BOOK FOURTH

I

"I've come, you know, to make you break with everything, neither more nor less, and take you straight home; so you'll be so good as immediately and favourably to consider it!"—Strether, face to face with Chad after the play, had sounded these words almost breathlessly, and with an effect at first positively disconcerting to himself alone. For Chad's receptive attitude was that of a person who had been gracefully quiet while the messenger at last reaching him has run a mile through the dust. During some seconds after he had spoken Strether felt as if *he* had made some such exertion; he was not even certain that the perspiration wasn't on his brow. It was the kind of consciousness for which he had to thank the look that, while the strain lasted, the young man's eyes gave him. They reflected—and the deuce of the thing was that they reflected really with a sort of shyness of kindness—his momentarily disordered state; which fact brought on in its turn for our friend the dawn of a fear that Chad might simply "take it out"—take everything out—in being sorry for him. Such a fear, any fear, was unpleasant. But everything was unpleasant; it was odd how everything had suddenly turned so. This, however, was no reason for letting the least thing go. Strether had the next minute proceeded as roundly as if with an advantage to follow up. "Of course I'm a busybody, if you want to fight the case to the death; but after all mainly in the sense of having known you and having given you such attention as you kindly permitted when you were in jackets and knickerbockers. Yes—it was knickerbockers, I'm busybody enough to remember that; and that you had, for your age—I speak of the first far-away time—tremendously stout legs. Well, we want you to break. Your mother's heart's passionately set upon it, but she has above and beyond that excellent arguments and reasons. I've not put them into her head—I needn't remind you how little she's a person who needs that. But they exist—you must take it from me as a friend both of hers and yours—for myself as well. I didn't invent them, I didn't originally work them out; but I understand them, I think I can explain them—by which I mean make you actively do them justice; and that's why you see me here. You had better know the worst at once. It's a question of an immediate rupture and an immediate return. I've been conceited enough to dream I can sugar that pill. I take at any rate the greatest interest in the question. I took it already before I left home; and I don't mind telling you that, altered as you are, I take it still more now that I've seen you. You're older and—I don't know what to call it!—more of a handful; but you're by so much the more, I seem to make out, to our purpose."

"Do I strike you as improved?" Strether was to recall that Chad had at this point inquired.

He was likewise to recall—and it had to count for some time as his greatest comfort—that it had been "given" him, as they said at Woollett, to reply with some presence of mind: "I haven't the least idea." He was really for a while to like thinking he had been positively hard. On the point of conceding that Chad had improved in appearance, but that to the question of appearance the remark must be confined, he checked even that compromise and left his reservation bare. Not only his moral, but also, as it were, his aesthetic sense had a little to pay for this, Chad being unmistakably—and wasn't it a matter of the confounded grey hair again?—handsomer than he had ever promised. That, however, fell in perfectly with what Strether had said. They had no desire to keep down his proper expansion, and he wouldn't be less to their purpose for not looking, as he had too often done of old, only bold and wild. There was indeed a signal particular in which he would distinctly be more so. Strether didn't as he talked, absolutely follow himself; he only knew he was clutching his thread and that he held it from moment to moment a little tighter; his mere uninterruptedness during the few minutes helped him to do that. He had frequently, for a month, turned over what he should say on this very occasion, and he seemed at last to have said nothing he had thought of—everything was so totally different.

But in spite of that he had put the flag at the window. This was what he had done, and there was a minute during which he affected himself as having shaken it hard, flapped it with a mighty flutter, straight in front of his companion's nose. It gave him really almost the sense of having already acted his part. The momentary relief—as if from the knowledge that nothing of *that* at least could be undone—sprang from a particular cause, the cause that had flashed into operation, in Miss Gostrey's box, with direct apprehension, with amazed recognition, and that had been concerned since then in every throb of his consciousness. What it came to was that with an absolutely *new* quantity to deal with one simply couldn't know. The new quantity was represented by the fact that Chad had been made over. That was all; whatever it was it was everything. Strether had never seen the thing so done before—it was perhaps a specialty of Paris. If one had been present at the process one might little by little have mastered the result; but he was face to face, as matters stood, with the finished business. It had freely been noted for him that he might be received as a dog among skittles; but that was on the basis of the old quantity. He had originally thought of lines and tones as things to be taken, but these possibilities had now quite melted away. There was no computing at all what the young man before him would think or feel or say on any subject whatever. This intelligence Strether had afterwards, to account for his nervousness, reconstituted as he might, just as he had also reconstituted the promptness with which Chad had corrected his uncertainty. An extraordinarily short time had been required for the correction, and there had ceased to be anything negative in his companion's face and air as soon as it was made. "Your engagement to my mother has become then what they call here a *fait accompli*?"—it had consisted, the determinant touch, in nothing more than that.

Well, that was enough, Strether had felt while his answer hung fire. He had felt at the same time, however, that nothing could less become him than that it should hang fire too long. "Yes," he said brightly, "it was on the happy settlement of the question that I started. You see therefore to what tune I'm in your family. Moreover," he added, "I've been supposing you'd suppose it."

"Oh I've been supposing it for a long time, and what you tell me helps me to understand that you should want to do something. To do something, I mean," said Chad, "to commemorate an event so—what do they call it?—so auspicious. I see you make out, and not unnaturally," he continued, "that bringing me home in triumph as a sort of wedding-present to Mother would commemorate it better than anything else. You want to make a bonfire in fact," he laughed, "and you pitch me on. Thank you, thank you!" he laughed again.

He was altogether easy about it, and this made Strether now see how at bottom, and in spite of the shade of shyness that really cost him nothing, he had from the first moment been easy about everything. The shade of shyness was mere good taste. People with manners formed could apparently have, as one of their best cards, the shade of shyness too. He had leaned a little forward to speak; his elbows were on the table; and the inscrutable new face that he had got somewhere and somehow was brought by the movement nearer to his critic's. There was a fascination for that critic in its not being, this ripe physiognomy, the face that, under observation at least, he had originally carried away from Woollett. Strether found a certain freedom on his own side in defining it as that of a man of the world—a formula that indeed seemed to come now in some degree to his relief; that of a man to whom things had happened and were variously known. In gleams, in glances, the past did perhaps peep out of it; but such lights were faint and instantly merged. Chad was brown and thick and strong; and of old Chad had been rough. Was all the difference therefore that he was actually smooth? Possibly; for that he *was* smooth was as marked as in the taste of a sauce or in the rub of a hand. The effect of it was general—it had retouched his features, drawn them with a cleaner line. It had cleared his eyes and settled his colour and polished his fine square teeth—the main ornament of his face; and at the same time that it had given him a form and a surface, almost a design, it had toned his voice, established his accent, encouraged his smile to more play and his other motions to less. He had formerly, with a great deal of action, expressed very little; and he now expressed whatever was necessary with almost none at all. It was as if in short he had really, copious perhaps but shapeless, been put into a firm mould and turned successfully out. The phenomenon—Strether kept eyeing it as a phenomenon, an eminent case—was marked enough to be touched by the finger. He finally put his hand across the table and laid it on Chad's arm. "If you'll promise me—here on the spot and giving me your word of honour—to break straight off, you'll make the future the real right thing for all of us alike. You'll ease off the strain of this decent but none the less acute suspense in which I've for so many days been waiting for you, and let me turn in to rest. I shall leave you with my blessing and go to bed in peace."

Chad again fell back at this and, his hands pocketed, settled himself a little; in which posture he looked, though he rather anxiously smiled, only the more earnest. Then Strether seemed to see that he was really nervous, and he took that as what he would have called a wholesome sign. The only mark of it hitherto had been his more than once taking off and putting on his wide-brimmed crush hat. He had at this moment made the motion again to remove it, then had only pushed it back, so that it hung informally on his strong young grizzled crop. It was a touch that gave the note of the familiar—the intimate and the belated—to their quiet colloquy; and it was indeed by some such trivial aid that Strether became aware at the same moment of something else. The observation was at any rate determined in him by some light too fine to distinguish from so many others, but it was none the less sharply determined. Chad looked unmistakably during these instants—well, as Strether put it to himself, all he was worth. Our friend had a sudden apprehension of what that would on certain sides be. He saw him in a flash as the young man marked out by women; and for a concentrated minute the dignity, the comparative austerity, as he funnily fancied it, of this character affected him almost with awe. There was an experience on his interlocutor's part that looked out at him from under the displaced hat, and that looked out moreover by a force of its own, the deep fact of its quantity and quality, and not through Chad's intending bravado or swagger. That was then the way men marked out by women *were*—and also the men by whom the women were doubtless in turn sufficiently distinguished. It affected Strether for thirty seconds as a relevant truth; a truth which, however, the next minute, had fallen into its relation. "Can't you imagine there being some questions," Chad asked, "that a fellow—however much impressed by your charming way of stating things—would like to put to you first?"

"Oh yes—easily. I'm here to answer everything. I think I can even tell you things, of the greatest interest to you, that you won't know enough to ask me. We'll take as many days to it as you like. But I want," Strether wound up, "to go to bed now."

"Really?"

Chad had spoken in such surprise that he was amused. "Can't you believe it?—with what you put me through?"

The young man seemed to consider. "Oh I haven't put you through much—yet."

"Do you mean there's so much more to come?" Strether laughed. "All the more reason then that I should gird myself." And as if to mark what he felt he could by this time count on he was already on his feet.

Chad, still seated, stayed him, with a hand against him, as he passed him between their table and the next. "Oh we shall get on!"

The tone was, as who should say, everything Strether could have desired; and quite as good the expression of face with which the speaker had looked up at him and kindly held him. All these things lacked was their not showing quite so much as the fruit of experience. Yes, experience was what Chad did play on him, if he didn't play any grossness of defiance. Of course experience was in a manner defiance; but it wasn't, at any rate—rather indeed quite the contrary—grossness; which was so much gained. He fairly grew older, Strether thought, while he himself so reasoned. Then with his mature pat of his visitor's arm he also got up; and there had been enough of it all by this time to make the visitor feel that something *was* settled. Wasn't it settled that he had at least the testimony of Chad's own belief in a settlement? Strether found himself treating Chad's profession that they would get on as a sufficient basis for going to bed. He hadn't nevertheless after this gone to bed directly; for when they had again passed out together into the mild bright night a check had virtually sprung from nothing more than a small circumstance which might have acted only as confirming quiescence. There were people, expressive sound, projected light, still abroad, and after they had taken in for a moment, through everything, the great clear architectural street, they turned off in tacit union to the quarter of Strether's hotel. "Of course," Chad here abruptly began, "of course Mother's making things out with you about me has been natural—and of course also you've had a good deal to go upon. Still, you must have filled out."

He had stopped, leaving his friend to wonder a little what point he wished to make; and this it was that enabled Strether meanwhile to make one. "Oh we've never pretended to go into detail. We weren't in the least bound to *that*. It was 'filling out' enough to miss you as we did."

But Chad rather oddly insisted, though under the high lamp at their corner, where they paused, he had at first looked as if touched by Strether's allusion to the long sense, at home, of his absence. "What I mean is you must have imagined."

"Imagined what?"

"Well—horrors."

It affected Strether: horrors were so little—superficially at least—in this robust and reasoning image. But he was none the less there to be veracious. "Yes, I daresay we *have* imagined horrors. But where's the harm if we haven't been wrong?"

Chad raised his face to the lamp, and it was one of the moments at which he had, in his extraordinary way, most his air of designedly showing himself. It was as if at these instants he just presented himself, his identity so rounded off, his palpable presence and his massive young manhood, as such a link in the chain as might practically amount to a kind of demonstration. It was as if—and how but anomalously?—he couldn't after all help thinking sufficiently well of these things to let them go for what they were worth. What could there be in this for Strether but the hint of some self-respect, some sense of power, oddly perverted; something latent and beyond access, ominous and perhaps enviable? The intimation had the next thing, in a flash, taken on a name—a name on which our friend seized as he asked himself if he weren't perhaps really dealing with an irreducible young Pagan. This description—he quite jumped at it—had a sound that gratified his mental ear, so that of a sudden he had already adopted it. Pagan—yes, that was, wasn't it? what Chad *would* logically be. It was what he must be. It was what he was. The idea was a clue and, instead of darkening the prospect, projected a certain clearness. Strether made out in this quick ray that a Pagan was perhaps, at the pass they had come to, the thing most wanted at Woollett. They'd be able to do with one—a good one; he'd find an opening—yes; and Strether's imagination even now prefigured and accompanied the first appearance there of the rousing personage. He had only the slight discomfort of feeling, as the young man turned away from the lamp, that his thought had in the momentary silence possibly been guessed. "Well, I've no doubt," said Chad, "you've come near enough. The details, as you say, don't matter. It *has* been generally the case that I've let myself go. But I'm coming round—I'm not so bad now." With which they walked on again to Strether's hotel.

"Do you mean," the latter asked as they approached the door, "that there isn't any woman with you now?"

"But pray what has that to do with it?"

"Why it's the whole question."

"Of my going home?" Chad was clearly surprised. "Oh not much! Do you think that when I want to go any one will have any power—"

"To keep you"—Strether took him straight up—"from carrying out your wish? Well, our idea has been that somebody had hitherto—or a good many persons perhaps—kept you pretty well from 'wanting.' That's what—if you're in anybody's hands—may again happen. You don't answer my question"—he kept it up; "but if you aren't in anybody's hands so much the better. There's nothing then but what makes for your going."

Chad turned this over. "I don't answer your question?" He spoke quite without resenting it. "Well, such questions have always a rather exaggerated side. One doesn't know quite what you mean by being in women's 'hands.' It's all so vague. One is when one isn't. One isn't when one is. And then one can't quite give people away." He seemed kindly to explain. "I've *never* got stuck—so very hard; and, as against anything at any time really better, I don't think I've ever been afraid." There was something in it that held Strether to wonder, and this gave him time to go on. He broke out as with a more helpful thought. "Don't you know how I like Paris itself?"

The upshot was indeed to make our friend marvel. "Oh if *that's* all that's the matter with you—!" It was *he* who almost showed resentment.

Chad's smile of a truth more than met it. "But isn't that enough?"

Strether hesitated, but it came out. "Not enough for your mother!" Spoken, however, it sounded a trifle odd—the effect of which was that Chad broke into a laugh. Strether, at this, succumbed as well, though with extreme brevity. "Permit us to have still our theory. But if you *are* so free and so strong you're inexcusable. I'll write in the morning," he added with decision. "I'll say I've got you."

This appeared to open for Chad a new interest. "How often do you write?"

"Oh perpetually."

"And at great length?"

Strether had become a little impatient. "I hope it's not found too great."

"Oh, I'm sure not. And you hear as often?"

Again Strether paused. "As often as I deserve."

"Mother writes," said Chad, "a lovely letter."

Strether, before the closed porte cochère, fixed him a moment. "It's more, my boy, than *you* do! But our suppositions don't matter," he added, "if you're actually not entangled."

Chad's pride seemed none the less a little touched. "I never *was* that—let me insist. I always had my own way." With which he pursued: "And I have it at present."

"Then what are you here for? What has kept you," Strether asked, "if you *have* been able to leave?"

It made Chad, after a stare, throw himself back. "Do you think one's kept only by women?" His surprise and his verbal emphasis rang out so clear in the still street that Strether winced till he remembered the safety of their English speech. "Is that," the young man demanded, "what they think at Woollett?" At the good faith in the question Strether had changed colour, feeling that, as he would have said, he had put his foot in it. He had appeared stupidly to misrepresent what they thought at Woollett; but before he had time to rectify Chad again was upon him. "I must say then you show a low mind!"

It so fell in, unhappily for Strether, with that reflexion of his own prompted in him by the pleasant air of the Boulevard Malesherbes, that its disconcerting force was rather unfairly great. It was a dig that, administered by himself—and administered even to poor Mrs. Newsome—was no more than salutary; but administered by Chad—and quite logically—it came nearer drawing blood. They *hadn't* a low mind—nor any approach to one; yet incontestably they had worked, and with a certain smugness, on a basis that might be turned against them. Chad had at any rate pulled his visitor up; he had even pulled up his admirable mother; he had absolutely, by a turn of the wrist and a jerk of the far-flung noose, pulled up, in a bunch, Woollett browsing in its pride. There was no doubt Woollett *had* insisted on his coarseness; and what he at present stood there for in the sleeping street was, by his manner of striking the other note, to make of such insistence a preoccupation compromising to the insisters. It was exactly as if they had imputed to him a vulgarity which he had by a mere gesture caused to fall from him. The devil of the case was that Strether felt it, by the same stroke, as falling straight upon himself. He had been wondering a minute ago if the boy weren't a Pagan, and he found himself wondering now if he weren't by chance a gentleman. It didn't in the least, on the spot, spring up helpfully for him that a person couldn't at the same time be both. There was nothing at this moment in the air to challenge the combination; there was everything to give it on the contrary something of a flourish. It struck Strether into the bargain as doing something to meet the most difficult of the questions; though perhaps indeed only by substituting another. Wouldn't it be precisely by having learned to be a gentleman that he had mastered the consequent trick of looking so well that one could scarce speak to him straight? But what in the world was the clue to such a prime producing cause? There were too many clues then that Strether still lacked, and these clues to clues were among them. What it accordingly amounted to for him was that he had to take full in the face a fresh attribution of ignorance. He had grown used by this time to reminders, especially from his own lips, of what he didn't know; but he had borne them because in the first place they were private and because in the second they practically conveyed a tribute. He didn't know what was bad, and—as others didn't know how little he knew it—he could put up with his state. But if he didn't know, in so important a particular, what was good, Chad at least was now aware he didn't; and that, for some reason, affected our friend as curiously public. It was in fact an exposed condition that the young man left him in long enough for him to feel its chill—till he saw fit, in a word, generously again to cover him. This last was in truth what Chad quite gracefully did. But he did it as with a simple thought that met the whole of the case. "Oh I'm all right!" It was what Strether had rather bewilderedly to go to bed on.

II

It really looked true moreover from the way Chad was to behave after this. He was full of attentions to his mother's ambassador; in spite of which, all the while, the latter's other relations rather remarkably contrived to assert themselves. Strether's sittings pen in hand with Mrs. Newsome up in his own room were broken, yet they were richer; and they were more than ever interspersed with the hours in which he reported himself, in a different fashion, but with scarce less earnestness and fullness, to Maria Gostrey. Now that, as he would have expressed it, he had really something to talk about he found himself, in respect to any oddity that might reside for him in the double connexion, at once more aware and more indifferent. He had been fine to Mrs. Newsome about his useful friend, but it had begun to haunt his imagination that Chad, taking up again for her benefit a pen too long disused, might possibly be finer. It wouldn't at all do, he saw, that anything should come up for him at Chad's hands but what specifically *was* to have come; the greatest divergence from which would be precisely the element of any lubrication of their intercourse by levity. It was accordingly to forestall such an accident that he frankly put before the young man the several facts, just as they had occurred, of his funny alliance. He spoke of these facts, pleasantly and obligingly, as "the whole story," and felt that he might qualify the alliance as funny if he remained sufficiently grave about it. He flattered himself that he even exaggerated the wild freedom of his original encounter with the wonderful lady; he was scrupulously definite about the absurd conditions in which they had made acquaintance—their having picked each other up almost in the street; and he had (finest inspiration of all!) a conception of carrying the war into the enemy's country by showing surprise at the enemy's ignorance.

He had always had a notion that this last was the grand style of fighting; the greater therefore the reason for it, as he couldn't remember that he had ever before fought in the grand style. Every one, according to this, knew Miss Gostrey: how came it Chad didn't know her? The difficulty, the impossibility, was really to escape it; Strether put on him, by what he took for granted, the burden of proof of the contrary. This tone was so far successful as that Chad quite appeared to recognise her as a person whose fame had reached him, but against his acquaintance with whom much mischance had worked. He made the point at the same time that his social relations, such as they could be called, were perhaps not to the extent Strether supposed with the rising flood of their compatriots. He hinted at his having more and more given way to a different principle of selection; the moral of which seemed to be that he went about little in the "colony." For the moment certainly he had quite another interest. It was deep, what he understood; and Strether, for himself, could only so observe it. He couldn't see as yet how deep. Might he not all too soon! For there was really too much of their question that Chad had already committed himself to liking. He liked, to begin with, his prospective stepfather; which was distinctly what had not been on the cards. His hating him was the untowardness for which Strether had been best prepared; he hadn't expected the boy's actual form to give him more to do than his imputed. It gave him more through suggesting that he must somehow make up to himself for not being sure he was sufficiently disagreeable. That had really been present to him as his only way to be sure he was sufficiently thorough. The point was that if Chad's tolerance of his thoroughness were insincere, were but the best of devices for gaining time, it none the less did treat everything as tacitly concluded.

That seemed at the end of ten days the upshot of the abundant, the recurrent talk through which Strether poured into him all it concerned him to know, put him in full possession of facts and figures. Never cutting these colloquies short by a minute, Chad behaved, looked and spoke as if he were rather heavily, perhaps even a trifle gloomily, but none the less fundamentally and comfortably free. He made no crude profession of eagerness to yield, but he asked the most intelligent questions, probed, at moments, abruptly, even deeper than his friend's layer of information, justified by these touches the native estimate of his latent stuff, and had in every way the air of trying to live, reflectively, into the square bright picture. He walked up and down in front of this production, sociably took Strether's arm at the points at which he stopped, surveyed it repeatedly from the right and from the left, inclined a critical head to either quarter, and, while he puffed a still more critical cigarette, animadverted to his companion on this passage and that. Strether sought relief—there were hours when he required it—in repeating himself; it was in truth not to be blinked that Chad had a way. The main question as yet was of what it was a way *to*. It made vulgar questions no more easy; but that was unimportant when all questions save those of his own asking had dropped. That he was free was answer enough, and it wasn't quite ridiculous that this freedom should end by presenting itself as what was difficult to move. His changed state, his lovely home, his beautiful things, his easy talk, his very appetite for Strether, insatiable and, when all was said, flattering—what were such marked matters all but the notes of his freedom? He had the effect of making a sacrifice of it just in these handsome forms to his visitor; which was mainly the reason the visitor was privately, for the time, a little out of countenance. Strether was at this period again and again thrown back on a felt need to remodel somehow his plan. He fairly caught himself shooting rueful glances, shy looks of pursuit, toward the embodied influence, the definite adversary, who had by a stroke of her own failed him and on a fond theory of whose palpable presence he had, under Mrs. Newsome's inspiration, altogether proceeded. He had once or twice, in secret, literally expressed the irritated wish that *she* would come out and find her.

He couldn't quite yet force it upon Woollett that such a career, such a perverted young life, showed after all a certain plausible side, *did* in the case before them flaunt something like an impunity for the social man; but he could at least treat himself to the statement that would prepare him for the sharpest echo. This echo—as distinct over there in the dry thin air as some shrill "heading" above a column of print—seemed to reach him even as he wrote. "He says there's no woman," he could hear Mrs. Newsome report, in capitals almost of newspaper size, to Mrs. Pocock; and he could focus in Mrs. Pocock the response of the reader of the journal. He could see in the younger lady's face the earnestness of her attention and catch the full scepticism of her but slightly delayed "What is there then?" Just so he could again as little miss the mother's clear decision: "There's plenty of disposition, no doubt, to pretend there isn't." Strether had, after posting his letter, the whole scene out; and it was a scene during which, coming and going, as befell, he kept his eye not least upon the daughter. He had his fine sense of the conviction Mrs. Pocock would take occasion to reaffirm—a conviction bearing, as he had from the first deeply divined it to bear, on Mr. Strether's essential inaptitude. She had looked him in his conscious eyes even before he sailed, and that she didn't believe *he* would find the woman had been written in her book. Hadn't she at the best but a scant faith in his ability to find women? It wasn't even as if he had found her mother—so much more, to her discrimination, had her mother performed the finding. Her mother had, in a case her private judgment of which remained educative of Mrs. Pocock's critical sense, found the man. The man owed his unchallenged state, in general, to the fact that Mrs. Newsome's discoveries were accepted at Woollett; but he knew in his bones, our friend did, how almost irresistibly Mrs. Pocock would now be moved to show what she thought of his own. Give *her* a free hand, would be the moral, and the woman would soon be found.

His impression of Miss Gostrey after her introduction to Chad was meanwhile an impression of a person almost unnaturally on her guard. He struck himself as at first unable to extract from her what he wished; though indeed *of* what he wished at this special juncture he would doubtless have contrived to make but a crude statement. It sifted and settled nothing to put to her, *tout bêtement*, as she often said, "Do you like him, eh?"—thanks to his feeling it actually the least of his needs to heap up the evidence in the young man's favour. He repeatedly knocked at her door to let her have it afresh that Chad's case—whatever else of minor interest it might yield—was first and foremost a miracle almost monstrous. It was the alteration of the entire man, and was so signal an instance that nothing else, for the intelligent observer, could—*could* it?—signify. "It's a plot," he declared—"there's more in it than meets the eye." He gave the rein to his fancy. "It's a plant!"

His fancy seemed to please her. "Whose then?"

"Well, the party responsible is, I suppose, the fate that waits for one, the dark doom that rides. What I mean is that with such elements one can't count. I've but my poor individual, my modest human means. It isn't playing the game to turn on the uncanny. All one's energy goes to facing it, to tracking it. One wants, confound it, don't you see?" he confessed with a queer face—"one wants to enjoy anything so rare. Call it then life"—he puzzled it out—"call it poor dear old life simply that springs the surprise. Nothing alters the fact that the surprise is paralysing, or at any rate engrossing—all, practically, hang it, that one sees, that one *can* see."

Her silences were never barren, nor even dull. "Is that what you've written home?"

He tossed it off. "Oh dear, yes!"

She had another pause while, across her carpets, he had another walk. "If you don't look out you'll have them straight over."

"Oh but I've said he'll go back."

"And *will* he?" Miss Gostrey asked.

The special tone of it made him, pulling up, look at her long. "What's that but just the question I've spent treasures of patience and ingenuity in giving *you*, by the sight of him—after everything had led up—every facility to answer? What is it but just the thing I came here to-day to get out of you? Will he?"

"No—he won't," she said at last. "He's not free."

The air of it held him. "Then you've all the while known—?"

"I've known nothing but what I've seen; and I wonder," she declared with some impatience, "that you didn't see as much. It was enough to be with him there—"

"In the box? Yes," he rather blankly urged.

"Well—to feel sure."

"Sure of what?"

She got up from her chair, at this, with a nearer approach than she had ever yet shown to dismay at his dimness. She even, fairly pausing for it, spoke with a shade of pity. "Guess!"

It was a shade, fairly, that brought a flush into his face; so that for a moment, as they waited together, their difference was between them. "You mean that just your hour with him told you so much of his story? Very good; I'm not such a fool, on my side, as that I don't understand you, or as that I didn't in some degree understand *him*. That he has done what he liked most isn't, among any of us, a matter the least in dispute. There's equally little question at this time of day of what it is he does like most. But I'm not talking," he reasonably explained, "of any mere wretch he may still pick up. I'm talking of some person who in his present situation may have held her own, may really have counted."

"That's exactly what *I* am!" said Miss Gostrey. But she as quickly made her point. "I thought you thought—or that they think at Woollett—that that's what mere wretches necessarily do. Mere wretches necessarily *don't!*" she declared with spirit. "There must, behind every appearance to the contrary, still be somebody—somebody who's not a mere wretch, since we accept the miracle. What else but such a somebody can such a miracle be?"

He took it in. "Because the fact itself *is* the woman?"

"*A* woman. Some woman or other. It's one of the things that *have* to be."

"But you mean then at least a good one."

"A good woman?" She threw up her arms with a laugh. "I should call her excellent!"

"Then why does he deny her?"

Miss Gostrey thought a moment. "Because she's too good to admit! Don't you see," she went on, "how she accounts for him?"

Strether clearly, more and more, did see; yet it made him also see other things. "But isn't what we want that he shall account for *her*?"

"Well, he does. What you have before you is his way. You must forgive him if it isn't quite outspoken. In Paris such debts are tacit."

Strether could imagine; but still—! "Even when the woman's good?"

Again she laughed out. "Yes, and even when the man is! There's always a caution in such cases," she more seriously explained—"for what it may seem to show. There's nothing that's taken as showing so much here as sudden unnatural goodness."

"Ah then you're speaking now," Strether said, "of people who are *not* nice."

"I delight," she replied, "in your classifications. But do you want me," she asked, "to give you in the matter, on this ground, the wisest advice I'm capable of?

Don't consider her, don't judge her at all in herself. Consider her and judge her only in Chad."

He had the courage at least of his companion's logic. "Because then I shall like her?" He almost looked, with his quick imagination, as if he already did, though seeing at once also the full extent of how little it would suit his book. "But is that what I came out for?"

She had to confess indeed that it wasn't. But there was something else. "Don't make up your mind. There are all sorts of things. You haven't seen him all."

This on his side Strether recognised; but his acuteness none the less showed him the danger. "Yes, but if the more I see the better he seems?"

Well, she found something. "That may be—but his disavowal of her isn't, all the same, pure consideration. There's a hitch." She made it out. "It's the effort to sink her."

Strether winced at the image. "To 'sink'—?"

"Well, I mean there's a struggle, and a part of it is just what he hides. Take time—that's the only way not to make some mistake that you'll regret. Then you'll see. He really does want to shake her off."

Our friend had by this time so got into the vision that he almost gasped. "After all she has done for him?"

Miss Gostrey gave him a look which broke the next moment into a wonderful smile. "He's not so good as you think!"

They remained with him, these words, promising him, in their character of warning, considerable help; but the support he tried to draw from them found itself on each renewal of contact with Chad defeated by something else. What could it be, this disconcerting force, he asked himself, but the sense, constantly renewed, that Chad *was*—quite in fact insisted on being—as good as he thought? It seemed somehow as if he couldn't *but* be as good from the moment he wasn't as bad. There was a succession of days at all events when contact with him—and in its immediate effect, as if it could produce no other—elbowed out of Strether's consciousness everything but itself. Little Bilham once more pervaded the scene, but little Bilham became even in a higher degree than he had originally been one of the numerous forms of the inclusive relation; a consequence promoted, to our friend's sense, by two or three incidents with which we have yet to make acquaintance. Waymarsh himself, for the occasion, was drawn into the eddy; it absolutely, though but temporarily, swallowed him down, and there were days when Strether seemed to bump against him as a sinking swimmer might brush a submarine object. The fathomless medium held them—Chad's manner was the fathomless medium; and our friend felt as if they passed each other, in their deep immersion, with the round impersonal eye of silent fish. It was practically produced between them that Waymarsh was giving him then his chance; and the shade of discomfort that Strether drew from the allowance resembled not a little the embarrassment he had known at school, as a boy, when members of his family had been present at exhibitions. He could perform before strangers, but relatives were fatal, and it was now as if, comparatively, Waymarsh were a relative. He seemed to hear him say "Strike up then!" and to enjoy a foretaste of conscientious domestic criticism. He *had* struck up, so far as he actually could; Chad knew by this time in profusion what he wanted; and what vulgar violence did his fellow pilgrim expect of him when he had really emptied his mind? It went somehow to and fro that what poor Waymarsh meant was "I told you so—that you'd lose your immortal soul!" but it was also fairly explicit that Strether had his own challenge and that, since they must go to the bottom of things, he wasted no more virtue in watching Chad than Chad wasted in watching him. His dip for duty's sake—where was it worse than Waymarsh's own? For *he* needn't have stopped resisting and refusing, needn't have parleyed, at that rate, with the foe.

The strolls over Paris to see something or call somewhere were accordingly inevitable and natural, and the late sessions in the wondrous troisième, the lovely home, when men dropped in and the picture composed more suggestively through the haze of tobacco, of music more or less good and of talk more or less polyglot, were on a principle not to be distinguished from that of the mornings and the afternoons. Nothing, Strether had to recognise as he leaned back and smoked, could well less resemble a scene of violence than even the liveliest of these occasions. They were occasions of discussion, none the less, and Strether had never in his life heard so many opinions on so many subjects. There were opinions at Woollett, but only on three or four. The differences were there to match; if they were doubtless deep, though few, they were quiet—they were, as might be said, almost as shy as if people had been ashamed of them. People showed little diffidence about such things, on the other hand, in the Boulevard Malesherbes, and were so far from being ashamed of them—or indeed of anything else—that they often seemed to have invented them to avert those agreements that destroy the taste of talk. No one had ever done that at Woollett, though Strether could remember times when he himself had been tempted to it without quite knowing why. He saw why at present—he had but wanted to promote intercourse.

These, however, were but parenthetic memories; and the turn taken by his affair on the whole was positively that if his nerves were on the stretch it was because he missed violence. When he asked himself if none would then, in connexion with it, ever come at all, he might almost have passed as wondering how to provoke it. It would be too absurd if such a vision as *that* should have to be invoked for relief; it was already marked enough as absurd that he should actually have begun with flutters and dignities on the score of a single accepted meal. What sort of a brute had he expected Chad to be, anyway?—Strether had occasion to make the enquiry but was careful to make it in private. He could himself, comparatively recent as it was—it was truly but the fact of a few days since—focus his primal crudity; but he would on the approach of an observer, as if handling an illicit possession, have slipped the reminiscence out of sight. There were echoes of it still in Mrs. Newsome's letters, and there were moments when these echoes made him exclaim on her want of tact. He blushed, of course, at once, still more for the explanation than for the ground of it: it came to him in time to save his manners that she couldn't at the best become tactful as quickly as he. Her tact had to reckon with the Atlantic Ocean, the General Post-Office and the extravagant curve of the globe.

Chad had one day offered tea at the Boulevard Malesherbes to a chosen few, a group again including the unobscured Miss Barrace; and Strether had on coming out walked away with the acquaintance whom in his letters to Mrs. Newsome he always spoke of as the little artistman. He had had full occasion to mention him as the other party, so oddly, to the only close personal alliance observation had as yet detected in Chad's existence. Little Bilham's way this afternoon was not Strether's, but he had none the less kindly come with him, and it was somehow a part of his kindness that as it had sadly begun to rain they suddenly found themselves seated for conversation at a café in which they had taken refuge. He had passed no more crowded hour in Chad's society than the one just ended; he had talked with Miss Barrace, who had reproached him with not having come to see her, and he had above all hit on a happy thought for causing Waymarsh's tension to relax. Something might possibly be extracted for the latter from the idea of his success with that lady, whose quick apprehension of what might amuse her had given Strether a free hand. What had she meant if not to ask whether she couldn't help him with his splendid encumbrance, and mightn't the sacred rage at any rate be kept a little in abeyance by thus creating for his comrade's mind even in a world of irrelevance the possibility of a relation? What was it but a relation to be regarded as so decorative and, in especial, on the strength of it, to be whirled away, amid flounces and feathers, in a coupé lined, by what Strether could make out, with dark blue brocade? He himself had never been whirled away—never at least in a coupé and behind a footman; he had driven with Miss Gostrey in cabs, with Mrs. Pocock, a few times, in an open buggy, with Mrs. Newsome in a four-seated cart and, occasionally up at the mountains, on a buckboard; but his friend's actual adventure transcended his personal experience. He now showed his companion soon enough indeed how inadequate, as a general monitor, this last queer quantity could once more feel itself.

"What game under the sun is he playing?" He signified the next moment that his allusion was not to the fat gentleman immersed in dominoes on whom his eyes had begun by resting, but to their host of the previous hour, as to whom, there on the velvet bench, with a final collapse of all consistency, he treated himself to the comfort of indiscretion. "Where do you see him come out?"

Little Bilham, in meditation, looked at him with a kindness almost paternal. "Don't you like it over here?"

Strether laughed out—for the tone was indeed droll; he let himself go. "What has that to do with it? The only thing I've any business to like is to feel that I'm moving him. That's why I ask you whether you believe I *am*. Is the creature"—and he did his best to show that he simply wished to ascertain—"honest?"

His companion looked responsible, but looked it through a small dim smile. "What creature do you mean?"

It was on this that they did have for a little a mute interchange. "Is it true that he's free? How then," Strether asked wondering, "does he arrange his life?"

"Is the creature you mean Chad himself?" little Bilham said.

Strether here, with a rising hope, just thought, "We must take one of them at a time." But his coherence lapsed, "*Is* there some woman? Of whom he's really afraid of course I mean—or who does with him what she likes."

"It's awfully charming of you," Bilham presently remarked, "not to have asked me that before."

"Oh I'm not fit for my job!"

The exclamation had escaped our friend, but it made little Bilham more deliberate. "Chad's a rare case!" he luminously observed. "He's awfully changed," he added.

"Then you see it too?"

"The way he has improved? Oh yes—I think every one must see it. But I'm not sure," said little Bilham, "that I didn't like him about as well in his other state."

"Then this *is* really a new state altogether?"

"Well," the young man after a moment returned, "I'm not sure he was really meant by nature to be quite so good. It's like the new edition of an old book that one has been fond of—revised and amended, brought up to date, but not quite the thing that one knew and loved. However that may be at all events," he pursued, "I don't think, you know, that he's really playing, as you call it, any game. I believe he really wants to go back and take up a career. He's capable of one, you know, that will improve and enlarge him still more. He won't then," little Bilham continued to remark, "be my pleasant well-rubbed old-fashioned volume at all. But of course

I'm beastly immoral. I'm afraid it would be a funny world altogether—a world with things the way I like them. I ought, I dare say, to go home and go into business myself. Only I'd simply rather die—simply. And I've not the least difficulty in making up my mind not to, and in knowing exactly why, and in defending my ground against all comers. All the same," he wound up, "I assure you I don't say a word against it—for himself, I mean—to Chad. I seem to see it as much the best thing for him. You see he's not happy."

"*Do* I?"—Strether stared. "I've been supposing I see just the opposite—an extraordinary case of the equilibrium arrived at and assured."

"Oh there's a lot behind it."

"Ah there you are!" Strether exclaimed. "That's just what I want to get at. You speak of your familiar volume altered out of recognition. Well, who's the editor?"

Little Bilham looked before him a minute in silence. "He ought to get married. *That* would do it. And he wants to."

"Wants to marry her?"

Again little Bilham waited, and, with a sense that he had information, Strether scarce knew what was coming. "He wants to be free. He isn't used, you see," the young man explained in his lucid way, "to being so good."

Strether hesitated. "Then I may take it from you that he *is* good?"

His companion matched his pause, but making it up with a quiet fullness. "*Do* take it from me."

"Well then why isn't he free? He swears to me he is, but meanwhile does nothing—except of course that he's so kind to me—to prove it; and couldn't really act much otherwise if he weren't. My question to you just now was exactly on this queer impression of his diplomacy; as if instead of really giving ground his line were to keep me on here and set me a bad example."

As the half-hour meanwhile had ebbed Strether paid his score, and the waiter was presently in the act of counting out change. Our friend pushed back to him a fraction of it, with which, after an emphatic recognition, the personage in question retreated. "You give too much," little Bilham permitted himself benevolently to observe.

"Oh I always give too much!" Strether helplessly sighed. "But you don't," he went on as if to get quickly away from the contemplation of that doom, "answer my question. Why isn't he free?"

Little Bilham had got up as if the transaction with the waiter had been a signal, and had already edged out between the table and the divan. The effect of this was that a minute later they had quitted the place, the gratified waiter alert again at the open door. Strether had found himself deferring to his companion's abruptness as to a hint that he should be answered as soon as they were more isolated. This happened when after a few steps in the outer air they had turned the next corner. There our friend had kept it up. "Why isn't he free if he's good?"

Little Bilham looked him full in the face. "Because it's a virtuous attachment."

This had settled the question so effectually for the time—that is for the next few days—that it had given Strether almost a new lease on life. It must be added however that, thanks to his constant habit of shaking the bottle in which life handed him the wine of experience, he presently found the taste of the lees rising as usual into his draught. His imagination had in other words already dealt with his young friend's assertion; of which it had made something that sufficiently came out on the very next occasion of his seeing Maria Gostrey. This occasion moreover had been determined promptly by a new circumstance—a circumstance he was the last man to leave her for a day in ignorance of. "When I said to him last night," he immediately began, "that without some definite word from him now that will enable me to speak to them over there of our sailing—or at least of mine, giving them some sort of date—my responsibility becomes uncomfortable and my situation awkward; when I said that to him what do you think was his reply?" And then as she this time gave it up: "Why that he had two particular friends, two ladies, mother and daughter, about to arrive in Paris—coming back from an absence; and that he wants me so furiously to meet them, know them and like them, that I shall oblige him by kindly not bringing our business to a crisis till he has had a chance to see them again himself. Is that," Strether inquired, "the way he's going to try to get off? These are the people," he explained, "that he must have gone down to see before I arrived. They're the best friends he has in the world, and they take more interest than any one else in what concerns him. As I'm his next best he sees a thousand reasons why we should comfortably meet. He hasn't broached the question sooner because their return was uncertain—seemed in fact for the present impossible. But he more than intimates that—if you can believe it—their desire to make my acquaintance has had to do with their surmounting difficulties."

"They're dying to see you?" Miss Gostrey asked.

"Dying. Of course," said Strether, "they're the virtuous attachment." He had already told her about that—had seen her the day after his talk with little Bilham; and they had then threshed out together the bearing of the revelation. She had helped him to put into it the logic in which little Bilham had left it slightly deficient. Strether hadn't pressed him as to the object of the preference so unexpectedly described; feeling in the presence of it, with one of his irrepressible scruples, a delicacy from which he had in the quest of the quite other article worked himself sufficiently free. He had held off, as on a small principle of pride, from permitting his young friend to mention a name; wishing to make with this the great point that Chad's virtuous attachments were none of his business. He had wanted from the first not to think too much of his dignity, but that was no reason for not allowing it any little benefit that might turn up. He had often enough wondered to what degree his interference might pass for interested; so that there was no want of luxury in letting it be seen whenever he could that he didn't interfere. That had of course at the same time not deprived him of the further luxury of much private astonishment; which however he had reduced to some order before communicating his knowledge. When he had done this at last it was with the remark that surprised as Miss Gostrey might, like himself, at first be, she would probably agree with him on reflexion that such an account of the matter did after all fit the confirmed appearances. Nothing certainly, on all the indications, could have been a greater change for him than a virtuous attachment, and since they had been in search of the "word," as the French called it, of that change, little Bilham's announcement—though so long and so oddly delayed—would serve as well as another. She had assured Strether in fact after a pause that the more she thought of it the more it did serve; and yet her assurance hadn't so weighed with him as that before they parted he hadn't ventured to challenge her sincerity. Didn't she believe the attachment *was* virtuous?—he had made sure of her again with the aid of that question. The tidings he brought her on this second occasion were moreover such as would help him to make surer still.

She showed at first none the less as only amused. "You say there are two? An attachment to them both then would, I suppose, almost necessarily be innocent."

Our friend took the point, but he had his clue. "Mayn't he be still in the stage of not quite knowing which of them, mother or daughter, he likes best?"

She gave it more thought. "Oh it must be the daughter—at his age."

"Possibly. Yet what do we know," Strether asked, "about hers? She may be old enough."

"Old enough for what?"

"Why to marry Chad. That may be, you know, what they want. And if Chad wants it too, and little Bilham wants it, and even *we*, at a pinch, could do with it—that is if she doesn't prevent repatriation—why it may be plain sailing yet."

It was always the case for him in these counsels that each of her remarks, as it came, seemed to drop into a deeper well. He had at all events to wait a moment to hear the slight splash of this one. "I don't see why if Mr. Newsome wants to marry the young lady he hasn't already done it or hasn't been prepared with some statement to you about it. And if he both wants to marry her and is on good terms with them why isn't he 'free'?"

Strether, responsively, wondered indeed. "Perhaps the girl herself doesn't like him."

"Then why does he speak of them to you as he does?"

Strether's mind echoed the question, but also again met it. "Perhaps it's with the mother he's on good terms."

"As against the daughter?"

"Well, if she's trying to persuade the daughter to consent to him, what could make him like the mother more? Only," Strether threw out, "why shouldn't the daughter consent to him?"

"Oh," said Miss Gostrey, "mayn't it be that every one else isn't quite so struck with him as you?"

"Doesn't regard him you mean as such an 'eligible' young man? *Is* that what I've come to?" he audibly and rather gravely sought to know. "However," he went on, "his marriage is what his mother most desires—that is if it will help. And oughtn't *any* marriage to help? They must want him"—he had already worked it out—"to be better off. Almost any girl he may marry will have a direct interest in his taking up his chances. It won't suit *her* at least that he shall miss them."

Miss Gostrey cast about. "No—you reason well! But of course on the other hand there's always dear old Woollett itself."

"Oh yes," he mused—"there's always dear old Woollett itself."

She waited a moment. "The young lady mayn't find herself able to swallow *that* quantity. She may think it's paying too much; she may weigh one thing against another."

Strether, ever restless in such debates, took a vague turn. "It will all depend on who she is. That of course—the proved ability to deal with dear old Woollett, since I'm sure she does deal with it—is what makes so strongly for Mamie."

"Mamie?"

He stopped short, at her tone, before her; then, though seeing that it represented not vagueness, but a momentary embarrassed fullness, he let his exclamations come. "You surely haven't forgotten about Mamie!"

"No, I haven't forgotten about Mamie," she smiled. "There's no doubt whatever that there's ever so much to be said for her. Mamie's *my* girl!" she roundly declared.

Strether resumed for a minute his walk. "She's really perfectly lovely, you know. Far prettier than any girl I've seen over here yet."

"That's precisely on what I perhaps most build." And she mused a moment in her friend's way. "I should positively like to take her in hand!"

He humoured the fancy, though indeed finally to deprecate it. "Oh but don't, in your zeal, go over to her! I need you most and can't, you know, be left."

But she kept it up. "I wish they'd send her out to me!"

"If they knew you," he returned, "they would."

"Ah but don't they?—after all that, as I've understood you, you've told them about me?"

He had paused before her again, but he continued his course. "They *will*—before, as you say, I've done." Then he came out with the point he had wished after all most to make. "It seems to give away now his game. This is what he has been doing—keeping me along for. He has been waiting for them."

Miss Gostrey drew in her lips. "You see a good deal in it!"

"I doubt if I see as much as you. Do you pretend," he went on, "that you don't see—?"

"Well, what?"—she pressed him as he paused.

"Why that there must be a lot between them—and that it has been going on from the first; even from before I came."

She took a minute to answer. "Who are they then—if it's so grave?"

"It mayn't be grave—it may be gay. But at any rate it's marked. Only I don't know," Strether had to confess, "anything about them. Their name for instance was a thing that, after little Bilham's information, I found it a kind of refreshment not to feel obliged to follow up."

"Oh," she returned, "if you think you've got off—!"

Her laugh produced in him a momentary gloom. "I don't think I've got off. I only think I'm breathing for about five minutes. I daresay I *shall* have, at the best, still to get on." A look, over it all, passed between them, and the next minute he had come back to good humour. "I don't meanwhile take the smallest interest in their name."

"Nor in their nationality?—American, French, English, Polish?"

"I don't care the least little 'hang,'" he smiled, "for their nationality. It would be nice if they're Polish!" he almost immediately added.

"Very nice indeed." The transition kept up her spirits. "So you see you do care."

He did this contention a modified justice. "I think I should if they *were* Polish. Yes," he thought—"there might be joy in *that*."

"Let us then hope for it." But she came after this nearer to the question. "If the girl's of the right age of course the mother can't be. I mean for the virtuous attachment. If the girl's twenty—and she can't be less—the mother must be at least forty. So it puts the mother out. *She's* too old for him."

Strether, arrested again, considered and demurred. "Do you think so? Do you think any one would be too old for him? *I'm* eighty, and I'm too young. But perhaps the girl," he continued, "*isn't* twenty. Perhaps she's only ten—but such a little dear that Chad finds himself counting her in as an attraction of the acquaintance. Perhaps she's only five. Perhaps the mother's but five-and-twenty—a charming young widow."

Miss Gostrey entertained the suggestion. "She *is* a widow then?"

"I haven't the least idea!" They once more, in spite of this vagueness, exchanged a look—a look that was perhaps the longest yet. It seemed in fact, the next thing, to require to explain itself; which it did as it could. "I only feel what I've told you—that he has some reason."

Miss Gostrey's imagination had taken its own flight. "Perhaps she's *not* a widow."

Strether seemed to accept the possibility with reserve. Still he accepted it. "Then that's why the attachment—if it's to her—is virtuous."

But she looked as if she scarce followed. "Why is it virtuous if—since she's free—there's nothing to impose on it any condition?"

He laughed at her question. "Oh I perhaps don't mean as virtuous as *that*! Your idea is that it can be virtuous—in any sense worthy of the name—only if she's *not* free? But what does it become then," he asked, "for *her*?"

"Ah that's another matter." He said nothing for a moment, and she soon went on. "I dare say you're right, at any rate, about Mr. Newsome's little plan. He *has* been trying you—has been reporting on you to these friends."

Strether meanwhile had had time to think more. "Then where's his straightness?"

"Well, as we say, it's struggling up, breaking out, asserting itself as it can. We can be on the side, you see, of his straightness. We can help him. But he has made out," said Miss Gostrey, "that you'll do."

"Do for what?"

"Why, for *them*—for *ces dames*. He has watched you, studied you, liked you—and recognised that *they* must. It's a great compliment to you, my dear man; for I'm sure they're particular. You came out for a success. Well," she gaily declared, "you're having it!"

He took it from her with momentary patience and then turned abruptly away. It was always convenient to him that there were so many fine things in her room to look at. But the examination of two or three of them appeared soon to have determined a speech that had little to do with them. "You don't believe in it!"

"In what?"

"In the character of the attachment. In its innocence."

But she defended herself. "I don't pretend to know anything about it. Everything's possible. We must see."

"See?" he echoed with a groan. "Haven't we seen enough?"

"*I* haven't," she smiled.

"But do you suppose then little Bilham has lied?"

"You must find out."

It made him almost turn pale. "Find out any *more*?"

He had dropped on a sofa for dismay; but she seemed, as she stood over him, to have the last word. "Wasn't what you came out for to find out *all*?"

BOOK FIFTH

I

The Sunday of the next week was a wonderful day, and Chad Newsome had let his friend know in advance that he had provided for it. There had already been a question of his taking him to see the great Gloriani, who was at home on Sunday afternoons and at whose house, for the most part, fewer bores were to be met than elsewhere; but the project, through some accident, had not had instant effect, and now revived in happier conditions. Chad had made the point that the celebrated sculptor had a queer old garden, for which the weather—spring at last frank and fair—was propitious; and two or three of his other allusions had confirmed for Strether the expectation of something special. He had by this time, for all introductions and adventures, let himself recklessly go, cherishing the sense that whatever the young man showed him he was showing at least himself. He could have wished indeed, so far as this went, that Chad were less of a mere cicerone; for he was not without the impression—now that the vision of his game, his plan, his deep diplomacy, did recurrently assert itself—of his taking refuge from the realities of their intercourse in profusely dispensing, as our friend mentally phrased it, *panem et circenses*. Our friend continued to feel rather smothered in flowers, though he made in his other moments the almost angry inference that this was only because of his odious ascetic suspicion of any form of beauty. He periodically assured himself—for his reactions were sharp—that he shouldn't reach the truth of anything till he had at least got rid of that.

He had known beforehand that Mme. de Vionnet and her daughter would probably be on view, an intimation to that effect having constituted the only reference again made by Chad to his good friends from the south. The effect of Strether's talk about them with Miss Gostrey had been quite to consecrate his reluctance to pry; something in the very air of Chad's silence—judged in the light of that talk—offered it to him as a reserve he could markedly match. It shrouded them about with he scarce knew what, a consideration, a distinction; he was in presence at any rate—so far as it placed him there—of ladies; and the one thing that was definite for him was that they themselves should be, to the extent of his responsibility, in presence of a gentleman. Was it because they were very beautiful, very clever, or even very good—was it for one of these reasons that Chad was, so to speak, nursing his effect? Did he wish to spring them, in the Woollett phrase, with a fuller force—to confound his critic, slight though as yet the criticism, with some form of merit exquisitely incalculable? The most the critic had at all events asked was whether the persons in question were French; and that enquiry had been but a proper comment on the sound of their name. "Yes. That is no!" had been Chad's reply; but he had immediately added that their English was the most charming in the world, so that if Strether were wanting an excuse for not getting on with them he wouldn't in the least find one. Never in fact had Strether—in the mood into which the place had quickly launched him—felt, for himself, less the need of an excuse. Those he might have found would have been, at the worst, all for the others, the people before him, in whose liberty to be as they were he was aware that he positively rejoiced. His fellow guests were multiplying, and these things, their liberty, their intensity, their variety, their conditions at large, were in fusion in the admirable medium of the scene.

The place itself was a great impression—a small pavilion, clear-faced and sequestered, an effect of polished parquet, of fine white panel and spare sallow gilt, of decoration delicate and rare, in the heart of the Faubourg Saint-Germain and on the edge of a cluster of gardens attached to old noble houses. Far back from streets and unsuspected by crowds, reached by a long passage and a quiet court, it was as striking to the unprepared mind, he immediately saw, as a treasure dug up; giving him too, more than anything yet, the note of the range of the immeasurable town and sweeping away, as by a last brave brush, his usual landmarks and terms. It was in the garden, a spacious cherished remnant, out to which a dozen persons had already passed, that Chad's host presently met them; while the tall bird-haunted trees, all of a twitter with the spring and the weather, and the high party-walls, on the other side of which grave *hôtels* stood off for privacy, spoke of survival, transmission, association, a strong indifferent persistent order. The day was so soft that the little party had practically adjourned to the open air, but the open air was in such conditions all a chamber of state. Strether had presently the sense of a great convent, a convent of missions, famous for he scarce knew what, a nursery of young priests, of scattered shade, of straight alleys and chapel-bells, that spread its mass in one quarter; he had the sense of names in the air, of ghosts at the windows, of signs and tokens, a whole range of expression, all about him, too thick for prompt discrimination.

This assault of images became for a moment, in the address of the distinguished sculptor, almost formidable: Gloriani showed him, in such perfect confidence, on Chad's introduction of him, a fine worn handsome face, a face that was like an open letter in a foreign tongue. With his genius in his eyes, his manners on his lips, his long career behind him and his honours and rewards all round, the great artist, in the course of a single sustained look and a few words of delight at receiving him, affected our friend as a dazzling prodigy of type. Strether had seen in museums—in the Luxembourg as well as, more reverently, later on, in the New York of the billionaires—the work of his hand; knowing too that after an earlier time in his native Rome he had migrated, in mid-career, to Paris, where, with a personal lustre almost violent, he shone in a constellation: all of which was more than enough to crown him, for his guest, with the light, with the romance, of glory. Strether, in contact with that element as he had never yet so intimately been, had the consciousness of opening to it, for the happy instant, all the windows of his mind, of letting this rather grey interior drink in for once the sun of a clime not marked in his old geography. He was to remember again repeatedly the medal-like Italian face, in which every line was an artist's own, in which time told only as tone and consecration; and he was to recall in especial, as the penetrating radiance, as the communication of the illustrious spirit itself, the manner in which, while they stood briefly, in welcome and response, face to face, he was held by the sculptor's eyes. He wasn't soon to forget them, was to think of them, all unconscious, unintending, preoccupied though they were, as the source of the deepest intellectual sounding to which he had ever been exposed. He was in fact quite to cherish his vision of it, to play with it in idle hours; only speaking of it to no one and quite aware he couldn't have spoken without appearing to talk nonsense. Was what it had told him or what it had asked him the greater of the mysteries? Was it the most special flare, unequalled, supreme, of the aesthetic torch, lighting that wondrous world for ever, or was it above all the long straight shaft sunk by a personal acuteness that life had seasoned to steel? Nothing on earth could have been stranger and no one doubtless more surprised than the artist himself, but it was for all the world to Strether just then as if in the matter of his accepted duty he had positively been on trial. The deep human expertness in Gloriani's charming smile—oh the terrible life behind it!—was flashed upon him as a test of his stuff.

Chad meanwhile, after having easily named his companion, had still more easily turned away and was already greeting other persons present. He was as easy, clever Chad, with the great artist as with his obscure compatriot, and as easy with every one else as with either: this fell into its place for Strether and made almost a new light, giving him, as a concatenation, something more he could enjoy. He liked Gloriani, but should never see him again; of that he was sufficiently sure. Chad accordingly, who was wonderful with both of them, was a kind of link for hopeless fancy, an implication of possibilities—oh if everything had been different! Strether noted at all events that he was thus on terms with illustrious spirits, and also that—yes, distinctly—he hadn't in the least swaggered about it. Our friend hadn't come there only for this figure of Abel Newsome's son, but that presence threatened to affect the observant mind as positively central. Gloriani indeed, remembering something and excusing himself, pursued Chad to speak to him, and Strether was left musing on many things. One of them was the question of whether, since he had been tested, he had passed. Did the artist drop him from having made out that he wouldn't do? He really felt just to-day that he might do better than usual. Hadn't he done well enough, so far as that went, in being exactly so dazzled? and in not having too, as he almost believed, wholly hidden from his host that he felt the latter's plummet? Suddenly, across the garden, he saw little Bilham approach, and it was a part of the fit that was on him that as their eyes met he guessed also *his* knowledge. If he had said to him on the instant what was uppermost he would have said: "*Have* I passed?—for of course I know one has to pass here." Little Bilham would have reassured him, have told him that he exaggerated, and have adduced happily enough the argument of little Bilham's own very presence; which, in truth, he could see, was as easy a one as Gloriani's own or as Chad's. He himself would perhaps then after a while cease to be frightened, would get the point of view for some of the faces—types tremendously alien, alien to Woollett—that he had already begun to take in. Who were they all, the dispersed groups and couples, the ladies even more unlike those of Woollett than the gentlemen?—this was the inquiry that, when his young friend had greeted him, he did find himself making.

"Oh they're every one—all sorts and sizes; of course I mean within limits, though limits down perhaps rather more than limits up. There are always artists—he's beautiful and inimitable to the *cher confrère*; and then *gros bonnets* of many kinds—ambassadors, cabinet ministers, bankers, generals, what do I know? even Jews. Above all always some awfully nice women—and not too many; sometimes an actress, an artist, a great performer—but only when they're not monsters; and in particular the right *femmes du monde*. You can fancy his history on that side—I believe it's fabulous: they *never* give him up. Yet he keeps them down: no one knows how he manages; it's too beautiful and bland. Never too many—and a mighty good thing too; just a perfect choice. But there are not in any way many bores; it has always been so; he has some secret. It's extraordinary. And you don't find it out. He's the same to every one. He doesn't ask questions."

"Ah doesn't he?" Strether laughed.

Bilham met it with all his candour. "How then should *I* be here?"

"Oh for what you tell me. You're part of the perfect choice."

Well, the young man took in the scene. "It seems rather good to-day."

Strether followed the direction of his eyes. "Are they all, this time, *femmes du monde*?"

Little Bilham showed his competence. "Pretty well."

This was a category our friend had a feeling for; a light, romantic and mysterious, on the feminine element, in which he enjoyed for a little watching it. "Are there any Poles?"

His companion considered. "I think I made out a 'Portuguee.' But I've seen Turks."

Strether wondered, desiring justice. "They seem—all the women—very harmonious."

"Oh in closer quarters they come out!" And then, while Strether was aware of fearing closer quarters, though giving himself again to the harmonies, "Well," little Bilham went on, "it *is* at the worst rather good, you know. If you like it, you feel it, this way, that shows you're not in the least out. But you always know things," he handsomely added, "immediately."

Strether liked it and felt it only too much; so "I say, don't lay traps for me!" he rather helplessly murmured.

"Well," his companion returned, "he's wonderfully kind to *us*."

"To us Americans you mean?"

"Oh no—he doesn't know anything about *that*. That's half the battle here—that you can never hear politics. We don't talk them. I mean to poor young wretches of all sorts. And yet it's always as charming as this; it's as if, by something in the air, our squalor didn't show. It puts us all back—into the last century."

"I'm afraid," Strether said, amused, "that it puts me rather forward: oh ever so far!"

"Into the next? But isn't that only," little Bilham asked, "because you're really of the century before?"

"The century before the last? Thank you!" Strether laughed. "If I ask you about some of the ladies it can't be then that I may hope, as such a specimen of the rococo, to please them."

"On the contrary they adore—we all adore here—the rococo, and where is there a better setting for it than the whole thing, the pavilion and the garden, together? There are lots of people with collections," little Bilham smiled as he glanced round. "You'll be secured!"

It made Strether for a moment give himself again to contemplation. There were faces he scarce knew what to make of. Were they charming or were they only strange? He mightn't talk politics, yet he suspected a Pole or two. The upshot was the question at the back of his head from the moment his friend had joined him. "Have Madame de Vionnet and her daughter arrived?"

"I haven't seen them yet, but Miss Gostrey has come. She's in the pavilion looking at objects. One can see *she's* a collector," little Bilham added without offence.

"Oh yes, she's a collector, and I knew she was to come. Is Madame de Vionnet a collector?" Strether went on.

"Rather, I believe; almost celebrated." The young man met, on it, a little, his friend's eyes. "I happen to know—from Chad, whom I saw last night—that they've come back; but only yesterday. He wasn't sure—up to the last. This, accordingly," little Bilham went on, "will be—if they *are* here—their first appearance after their return."

Strether, very quickly, turned these things over. "Chad told you last night? To me, on our way here, he said nothing about it."

"But did you ask him?"

Strether did him the justice. "I dare say not."

"Well," said little Bilham, "you're not a person to whom it's easy to tell things you don't want to know. Though it *is* easy, I admit—it's quite beautiful," he benevolently added, "when you do want to."

Strether looked at him with an indulgence that matched his intelligence. "Is that the deep reasoning on which—about these ladies—you've been yourself so silent?"

Little Bilham considered the depth of the reasoning. "I haven't been silent. I spoke of them to you the other day, the day we sat together after Chad's tea-party."

Strether came round to it. "They then are the virtuous attachment?"

"I can only tell you that it's what they pass for. But isn't that enough? What more than a vain appearance does the wisest of us know? I commend you," the young man declared with a pleasant emphasis, "the vain appearance."

Strether looked more widely round, and what he saw, from face to face, deepened the effect of his young friend's words. "Is it so good?"

"Magnificent."

Strether had a pause. "The husband's dead?"

"Dear no. Alive."

"Oh!" said Strether. After which, as his companion laughed: "How then can it be so good?"

"You'll see for yourself. One does see."

"Chad's in love with the daughter?"

"That's what I mean."

Strether wondered. "Then where's the difficulty?"

"Why, aren't you and I—with our grander bolder ideas?"

"Oh mine—!" Strether said rather strangely. But then as if to attenuate: "You mean they won't hear of Woollett?"

Little Bilham smiled. "Isn't that just what you must see about?"

It had brought them, as she caught the last words, into relation with Miss Barrace, whom Strether had already observed—as he had never before seen a lady at a party—moving about alone. Coming within sound of them she had already spoken, and she took again, through her long-handled glass, all her amused and amusing possession. "How much, poor Mr. Strether, you seem to have to see about! But you can't say," she gaily declared, "that I don't do what I can to help you. Mr. Waymarsh is placed. I've left him in the house with Miss Gostrey."

"The way," little Bilham exclaimed, "Mr. Strether gets the ladies to work for him! He's just preparing to draw in another; to pounce—don't you see him?—on Madame de Vionnet."

"Madame de Vionnet? Oh, oh, oh!" Miss Barrace cried in a wonderful crescendo. There was more in it, our friend made out, than met the ear. Was it after all a joke that he should be serious about anything? He envied Miss Barrace at any rate her power of not being. She seemed, with little cries and protests and quick recognitions, movements like the darts of some fine high-feathered free-pecking bird, to stand before life as before some full shop-window. You could fairly hear, as she selected and pointed, the tap of her tortoise-shell against the glass. "It's certain that we do need seeing about; only I'm glad it's not I who have to do it. One does, no doubt, begin that way; then suddenly one finds that one has given it up. It's too much, it's too difficult. You're wonderful, you people," she continued to Strether, "for not feeling those things—by which I mean impossibilities. You never feel them. You face them with a fortitude that makes it a lesson to watch you."

"Ah but"—little Bilham put it with discouragement—"what do we achieve after all? We see about you and report—when we even go so far as reporting. But nothing's done."

"Oh you, Mr. Bilham," she replied as with an impatient rap on the glass, "you're not worth sixpence! You come over to convert the savages—for I know you verily did, I remember you—and the savages simply convert *you*."

"Not even!" the young man woefully confessed: "they haven't gone through that form. They've simply—the cannibals!—eaten me; converted me if you like, but converted me into food. I'm but the bleached bones of a Christian."

"Well then there we are! Only"—and Miss Barrace appealed again to Strether—"don't let it discourage you. You'll break down soon enough, but you'll meanwhile have had your moments. *Il faut en avoir.* I always like to see you while you last. And I'll tell you who *will* last."

"Waymarsh?"—he had already taken her up.

She laughed out as at the alarm of it. "He'll resist even Miss Gostrey: so grand is it not to understand. He's wonderful."

"He is indeed," Strether conceded. "He wouldn't tell me of this affair—only said he had an engagement; but with such a gloom, you must let me insist, as if it had been an engagement to be hanged. Then silently and secretly he turns up here with you. Do you call *that* 'lasting'?"

"Oh I hope it's lasting!" Miss Barrace said. "But he only, at the best, bears with me. He doesn't understand—not one little scrap. He's delightful. He's wonderful," she repeated.

"Michelangelesque!"—little Bilham completed her meaning. "He *is* a success. Moses, on the ceiling, brought down to the floor; overwhelming, colossal, but somehow portable."

"Certainly, if you mean by portable," she returned, "looking so well in one's carriage. He's too funny beside me in his corner; he looks like somebody, somebody foreign and famous, *en exil*; so that people wonder—it's very amusing—whom I'm taking about. I show him Paris, show him everything, and he never turns a hair. He's like the Indian chief one reads about, who, when he comes up to Washington to see the Great Father, stands wrapt in his blanket and gives no sign. *I* might be the Great Father from the way he takes everything." She was delighted at this hit of her identity with that personage—it fitted so her character; she declared it was the title she meant henceforth to adopt. "And the way he sits, too, in the corner of my room, only looking at my visitors very hard and as if he wanted to start something! They wonder what he does want to start. But he's wonderful," Miss Barrace once more insisted. "He has never started anything yet."

It presented him none the less, in truth, to her actual friends, who looked at each other in intelligence, with frank amusement on Bilham's part and a shade of sadness on Strether's. Strether's sadness sprang—for the image had its grandeur—from his thinking how little he himself was wrapt in his blanket, how little, in marble halls, all too oblivious of the Great Father, he resembled a really majestic aboriginal. But he had also another reflexion. "You've all of you here so much visual sense that you've somehow all 'run' to it. There are moments when it strikes one that you haven't any other."

"Any moral," little Bilham explained, watching serenely, across the garden, the several *femmes du monde*. "But Miss Barrace has a moral distinction," he kindly continued; speaking as if for Strether's benefit not less than for her own.

"*Have* you?" Strether, scarce knowing what he was about, asked of her almost eagerly.

"Oh not a distinction"—she was mightily amused at his tone—"Mr. Bilham's too good. But I think I may say a sufficiency. Yes, a sufficiency. Have you supposed strange things of me?"—and she fixed him again, through all her tortoise-shell, with the droll interest of it. "You *are* all indeed wonderful. I should awfully disappoint you. I do take my stand on my sufficiency. But I know, I confess," she went on, "strange people. I don't know how it happens; I don't do it on purpose; it seems to be my doom—as if I were always one of their habits: it's wonderful! I dare say, moreover," she pursued with an interested gravity, "that I do, that we all do here, run too much to mere eye. But how can it be helped? We're all looking at each other—and in the light of Paris one sees what things resemble. That's what the light of Paris seems always to show. It's the fault of the light of Paris—dear old light!"

"Dear old Paris!" little Bilham echoed.

"Everything, every one shows," Miss Barrace went on.

"But for what they really are?" Strether asked.

"Oh, I like your Boston 'reallys'! But sometimes—yes."

"Dear old Paris then!" Strether resignedly sighed while for a moment they looked at each other. Then he broke out: "Does Madame de Vionnet do that? I mean really show for what she is?"

Her answer was prompt. "She's charming. She's perfect."

"Then why did you a minute ago say, 'Oh, oh, oh!' at her name?"

She easily remembered. "Why, just because—! She's wonderful."

"Ah she too?"—Strether had almost a groan.

But Miss Barrace had meanwhile perceived relief. "Why not put your question straight to the person who can answer it best?"

"No," said little Bilham; "don't put any question; wait, rather—it will be much more fun—to judge for yourself. He has come to take you to her."

II

On which Strether saw that Chad was again at hand, and he afterwards scarce knew, absurd as it may seem, what had then quickly occurred. The moment concerned him, he felt, more deeply than he could have explained, and he had a subsequent passage of speculation as to whether, on walking off with Chad, he hadn't looked either pale or red. The only thing he was clear about was that, luckily, nothing indiscreet had in fact been said, and that Chad himself was more than ever, in Miss Barrace's great sense, wonderful. It was one of the connexions—though really why it should be, after all, was none so apparent—in which the whole change in him came out as most striking. Strether recalled as they approached the house that he had impressed him that first night as knowing how to enter a box. Well, he impressed him scarce less now as knowing how to make a presentation. It did something for Strether's own quality—marked it as estimated; so that our poor friend, conscious and passive, really seemed to feel himself quite handed over and delivered; absolutely, as he would have said, made a present of, given away. As they reached the house a young woman, about to come forth, appeared, unaccompanied, on the steps; at the exchange with whom of a word on Chad's part Strether immediately perceived that, obligingly, kindly, she was there to meet them. Chad had left her in the house, but she had afterwards come half way and then the next moment had joined them in the garden. Her air of youth, for Strether, was at first almost disconcerting, while, his second impression was, not less sharply, a degree of relief at there not having just been, with the others, any freedom used about her. It was upon him at a touch that she was no subject for that, and meanwhile, on Chad's introducing him, she had spoken to him, very simply and gently, in an English clearly of the easiest to her, yet unlike any other he had ever heard. It wasn't as if she tried; nothing, he could see after they had been a few minutes together, was as if she tried; but her speech, charming correct and odd, was like a precaution against her passing for a Pole. There were precautions, he seemed indeed to see, only when there were really dangers.

Later on he was to feel many more of them, but by that time he was to feel other things besides. She was dressed in black, but in black that struck him as light and transparent; she was exceedingly fair, and, though she was as markedly slim, her face had a roundness, with eyes far apart and a little strange. Her smile was natural and dim; her hat not extravagant; he had only perhaps a sense of the clink, beneath her fine black sleeves, of more gold bracelets and bangles than he had ever seen a lady wear. Chad was excellently free and light about their encounter; it was one of the occasions on which Strether most wished he himself might have arrived at such ease and such humour: "Here you are then, face to face at last; you're made for each other—*vous allez voir*; and I bless your union." It was indeed, after he had gone off, as if he had been partly serious too. This latter motion had been determined by an enquiry from him about "Jeanne"; to which her mother had replied that she was probably still in the house with Miss Gostrey, to whom she had lately committed her. "Ah but you know," the young man had rejoined, "he must see her"; with which, while Strether pricked up his ears, he had started as if to bring her, leaving the other objects of his interest together. Strether wondered to find Miss Gostrey already involved, feeling that he missed a link; but feeling also, with small delay, how much he should like to talk with her of Madame de Vionnet on this basis of evidence.

The evidence as yet in truth was meagre; which, for that matter, was perhaps a little why his expectation had had a drop. There was somehow not quite a wealth in her; and a wealth was all that, in his simplicity, he had definitely prefigured. Still, it was too much to be sure already that there was but a poverty. They moved away from the house, and, with eyes on a bench at some distance, he proposed that they should sit down. "I've heard a great deal about you," she said as they went; but he had an answer to it that made her stop short. "Well, about *you*, Madame de Vionnet, I've heard, I'm bound to say, almost nothing"—those struck him as the only words he himself could utter with any lucidity; conscious as he was, and as with more reason, of the determination to be in respect to the rest of his business perfectly plain and go perfectly straight. It hadn't at any rate been in the least his idea to spy on Chad's proper freedom. It was possibly, however, at this very instant and under the impression of Madame de Vionnet's pause, that going straight began to announce itself as a matter for care. She had only after all to smile at him ever so gently in order to make him ask himself if he weren't already going crooked. It might be going crooked to find it of a sudden just only clear that she intended very definitely to be what he would have called nice to him. This was what passed between them while, for another instant, they stood still; he couldn't at least remember afterwards what else it might have been. The thing indeed really unmistakeable was that it rolled over him as a wave that he had been, in conditions incalculable and unimaginable, a subject of discussion. He had been, on some ground that concerned her, answered for; which gave her an advantage he should never be able to match.

"Hasn't Miss Gostrey," she asked, "said a good word for me?"

What had struck him first was the way he was bracketed with that lady; and he wondered what account Chad would have given of their acquaintance. Something not as yet traceable, at all events, had obviously happened. "I didn't even know of her knowing you."

"Well, now she'll tell you all. I'm so glad you're in relation with her."

This was one of the things—the "all" Miss Gostrey would now tell him—that, with every deference to present preoccupation, was uppermost for Strether after they had taken their seat. One of the others was, at the end of five minutes, that she—oh, incontestably, yes—*differed* less; differed, that is, scarcely at all—well, superficially speaking, from Mrs. Newsome or even from Mrs. Pocock. She was ever so much younger than the one and not so young as the other; but what *was* there in her, if anything, that would have made it impossible he should meet her at Woollett? And wherein was her talk during their moments on the bench together not the same as would have been found adequate for a Woollett garden-party?—

unless perhaps truly in not being quite so bright. She observed to him that Mr. Newsome had, to her knowledge, taken extraordinary pleasure in his visit; but there was no good lady at Woollett who wouldn't have been at least up to that. Was there in Chad, by chance, after all, deep down, a principle of aboriginal loyalty that had made him, for sentimental ends, attach himself to elements, happily encountered, that would remind him most of the old air and the old soil? Why accordingly be in a flutter—Strether could even put it that way—about this unfamiliar phenomenon of the *femme du monde*? On these terms Mrs. Newsome herself was as much of one. Little Bilham verily had testified that they came out, the ladies of the type, in close quarters; but it was just in these quarters—now comparatively close—that he felt Madame de Vionnet's common humanity. She did come out, and certainly to his relief, but she came out as the usual thing. There might be motives behind, but so could there often be even at Woollett. The only thing was that if she showed him she wished to like him—as the motives behind might conceivably prompt—it would possibly have been more thrilling for him that she should have shown as more vividly alien. Ah she was neither Turk nor Pole!—which would be indeed flat once more for Mrs. Newsome and Mrs. Pocock. A lady and two gentlemen had meanwhile, however, approached their bench, and this accident stayed for the time further developments.

They presently addressed his companion, the brilliant strangers; she rose to speak to them, and Strether noted how the escorted lady, though mature and by no means beautiful, had more of the bold high look, the range of expensive reference, that he had, as might have been said, made his plans for. Madame de Vionnet greeted her as "Duchesse" and was greeted in turn, while talk started in French, as "Ma toute-belle"; little facts that had their due, their vivid interest for Strether. Madame de Vionnet didn't, none the less, introduce him—a note he was conscious of as false to the Woollett scale and the Woollett humanity; though it didn't prevent the duchess, who struck him as confident and free, very much what he had obscurely supposed duchesses, from looking at him as straight and as hard—for it *was* hard—as if she would have liked, all the same, to know him. "Oh yes, my dear, it's all right, it's *me*; and who are *you*, with your interesting wrinkles and your most effective (is it the handsomest, is it the ugliest?) of noses?"—some such loose handful of bright flowers she seemed, fragrantly enough, to fling at him. Strether almost wondered—at such a pace was he going—if some divination of the influence of either party were what determined Madame de Vionnet's abstention. One of the gentlemen, in any case, succeeded in placing himself in close relation with our friend's companion; a gentleman rather stout and importantly short, in a hat with a wonderful wide curl to its brim and a frock coat buttoned with an effect of superlative decision. His French had quickly turned to equal English, and it occurred to Strether that he might well be one of the ambassadors. His design was evidently to assert a claim to Madame de Vionnet's undivided countenance, and he made it good in the course of a minute—led her away with a trick of three words; a trick played with a social art of which Strether, looking after them as the four, whose backs were now all turned, moved off, felt himself no master.

He sank again upon his bench and, while his eyes followed the party, reflected, as he had done before, on Chad's strange communities. He sat there alone for five minutes, with plenty to think of; above all with his sense of having suddenly been dropped by a charming woman overlaid now by other impressions and in fact quite cleared and indifferent. He hadn't yet had so quiet a surrender; he didn't in the least care if nobody spoke to him more. He might have been, by his attitude, in for something of a march so broad that the want of ceremony with which he had just been used could fall into its place as but a minor incident of the procession. Besides, there would be incidents enough, as he felt when this term of contemplation was closed by the reappearance of little Bilham, who stood before him a moment with a suggestive "Well?" in which he saw himself reflected as disorganised, as possibly floored. He replied with a "Well!" intended to show that he wasn't floored in the least. No indeed; he gave it out, as the young man sat down beside him, that if, at the worst, he had been overturned at all, he had been overturned into the upper air, the sublimer element with which he had an affinity and in which he might be trusted a while to float. It wasn't a descent to earth to say after an instant in sustained response to the reference: "You're quite sure her husband's living?"

"Oh dear, yes."

"Ah then—!"

"Ah then what?"

Strether had after all to think. "Well, I'm sorry for them." But it didn't for the moment matter more than that. He assured his young friend he was quite content. They wouldn't stir; were all right as they were. He didn't want to be introduced; had been introduced already about as far as he could go. He had seen, moreover, an immensity; liked Gloriani, who, as Miss Barrace kept saying, was wonderful; had made out, he was sure, the half-dozen other men who were distinguished, the artists, the critics and oh the great dramatist—*him* it was easy to spot; but wanted—no, thanks, really—to talk with none of them; having nothing at all to say and finding it would do beautifully as it was; do beautifully because what it was—well, was just simply too late. And when after this little Bilham, submissive and responsive, but with an eye to the consolation nearest, easily threw off some "Better late than never!" all he got in return for it was a sharp "Better early than late!" This note indeed the next thing overflowed for Strether into a quiet stream of demonstration that as soon as he had let himself go he felt as the real relief. It had consciously gathered to a head, but the reservoir had filled sooner than he knew, and his companion's touch was to make the waters spread. There were some things that had to come in time if they were to come at all. If they didn't come in time they were lost for ever. It was the general sense of them that had overwhelmed him with its long slow rush.

"It's not too late for *you*, on any side, and you don't strike me as in danger of missing the train; besides which people can be in general pretty well trusted, of course—with the clock of their freedom ticking as loud as it seems to do here—to keep an eye on the fleeting hour. All the same don't forget that you're young—blessedly young; be glad of it on the contrary and live up to it. Live all you can; it's a mistake not to. It doesn't so much matter what you do in particular, so long as you have your life. If you haven't had that what *have* you had? This place and these impressions—mild as you may find them to wind a man up so; all my impressions of Chad and of people I've seen at *his* place—well, have had their abundant message for me, have just dropped *that* into my mind. I see it now. I haven't done so enough before—and now I'm old; too old at any rate for what I see. Oh, I *do* see, at least; and more than you'd believe or I can express. It's too late. And it's as if the train had fairly waited at the station for me without my having had the gumption to know it was there. Now I hear its faint receding whistle miles and miles down the line. What one loses one loses; make no mistake about that. The affair—I mean the affair of life—couldn't, no doubt, have been different for me; for it's at the best a tin mould, either fluted and embossed, with ornamental excrescences, or else smooth and dreadfully plain, into which, a helpless jelly, one's consciousness is poured—so that one 'takes' the form, as the great cook says, and is more or less compactly held by it; one lives in fine as one can. Still, one has the illusion of freedom; therefore don't be, like me, without the memory of that illusion. I was either, at the right time, too stupid or too intelligent to have it; I don't quite know which. Of course at present I'm a case of reaction against the mistake; and the voice of reaction should, no doubt, always be taken with an allowance. But that doesn't affect the point that the right time is now yours. The right time is *any* time that one is still so lucky as to have. You've plenty; that's the great thing; you're, as I say, damn you, so happily and hatefully young. Don't at any rate miss things out of stupidity. Of course I don't take you for a fool, or I shouldn't be addressing you thus awfully. Do what you like so long as you don't make *my* mistake. For it was a mistake. Live!" . . . Slowly and sociably, with full pauses and straight dashes, Strether had so delivered himself; holding little Bilham from step to step deeply and gravely attentive. The end of all was that the young man had turned quite solemn, and that this was a contradiction of the innocent gaiety the speaker had wished to promote. He watched for a moment the consequence of his words, and then, laying a hand on his listener's knee and as if to end with the proper joke: "And now for the eye I shall keep on you!"

"Oh but I don't know that I want to be, at your age, too different from you!"

"Ah prepare while you're about it," said Strether, "to be more amusing."

Little Bilham continued to think, but at last had a smile. "Well, you *are* amusing—to *me*."

"*Impayable*, as you say, no doubt. But what am I to myself?" Strether had risen with this, giving his attention now to an encounter that, in the middle of the garden, was in the act of taking place between their host and the lady at whose side Madame de Vionnet had quitted him. This lady, who appeared within a few minutes to have left her friends, awaited Gloriani's eager approach with words on her lips that Strether couldn't catch, but of which her interesting, witty face seemed to give him the echo. He was sure she was prompt and fine, but also that she had met her match, and he liked—in the light of what he was quite sure was the Duchess's latent insolence—the good humour with which the great artist asserted equal resources. Were they, this pair, of the "great world"?—and was he himself, for the moment and thus related to them by his observation, *in* it? Then there was something in the great world covertly tigerish, which came to him across the lawn and in the charming air, as a waft from the jungle. Yet it made him admire most of the two, made him envy, the glossy male tiger, magnificently marked. These absurdities of the stirred sense, fruits of suggestion ripening on the instant, were all reflected in his next words to little Bilham. "I know—if we talk of that—whom *I* should enjoy being like!"

Little Bilham followed his eyes; but then as with a shade of knowing surprise: "Gloriani?"

Our friend had in fact already hesitated, though not on the hint of his companion's doubt, in which there were depths of critical reserve. He had just made out, in the now full picture, something and somebody else; another impression had been superimposed. A young girl in a white dress and a softly plumed white hat had suddenly come into view, and what was presently clear was that her course was toward them. What was clearer still was that the handsome young man at her side was Chad Newsome, and what was clearest of all was that she was therefore Mademoiselle de Vionnet, that she was unmistakeably pretty—bright gentle shy happy wonderful—and that Chad now, with a consummate calculation of effect, was about to present her to his old friend's vision. What was clearest of all indeed was something much more than this, something at the single stroke of which—and wasn't it simply juxtaposition?—all vagueness vanished. It was the click of a spring—he saw the truth. He had by this time also met Chad's look; there was more of it in that; and the truth, accordingly, so far as Bilham's enquiry was concerned, had thrust in the answer. "Oh, Chad!"—it was that rare youth he should have enjoyed being "like." The virtuous attachment would be all there before him; the virtuous attachment would be in the very act of appeal for his blessing; Jeanne de Vionnet, this charming creature, would be—exquisitely, intensely now—the object of it. Chad brought her straight up to him, and Chad was, oh yes, at this moment—for the glory of Woollett or whatever—better still even than Gloriani. He had plucked this blossom; he had kept it overnight in water; and at last as he held it up to wonder he did enjoy his effect. That was why Strether had felt at first the breath of calculation—and why moreover, as he now knew, his look at the girl would be, for the young man, a sign of the latter's success. What young man had ever paraded about that way, without a reason, a maiden in her flower? And there was nothing in his reason at present obscure. Her type sufficiently told of it—they wouldn't, they couldn't, want her to go to Woollett. Poor Woollett, and what it might miss!—though brave Chad indeed too, and what it might gain! Brave Chad however had just excellently spoken. "This is a good little friend of mine who knows all about you and has, moreover a message for you. And this, my dear"—he had turned to the child herself—"is the best man in the world, who has it in his power to do a great deal for us and whom I want you to like and revere as nearly as possible as much as I do."

She stood there quite pink, a little frightened, prettier and prettier and not a bit like her mother. There was in this last particular no resemblance but that of youth to youth; and here was in fact suddenly Strether's sharpest impression. It went wondering, dazed, embarrassed, back to the woman he had just been talking with; it was revelation in the light of which he already saw she would become more interesting. So slim and fresh and fair, she had yet put forth this perfection; so that for really believing it of her, for seeing her to any such developed degree as a mother, comparison would be urgent. Well, what was it now but fairly thrust upon him? "Mamma wishes me to tell you before we go," the girl said, "that she hopes very much you'll come to see us very soon. She has something important to say to you."

"She quite reproaches herself," Chad helpfully explained: "you were interesting her so much when she accidentally suffered you to be interrupted."

"Ah don't mention it!" Strether murmured, looking kindly from one to the other and wondering at many things.

"And I'm to ask you for myself," Jeanne continued with her hands clasped together as if in some small learnt prayer—"I'm to ask you for myself if you won't positively come."

"Leave it to me, dear—I'll take care of it!" Chad genially declared in answer to this, while Strether himself almost held his breath. What was in the girl was indeed too soft, too unknown for direct dealing; so that one could only gaze at it as at a picture, quite staying one's own hand. But with Chad he was now on ground—Chad he could meet; so pleasant a confidence in that and in everything did the young man freely exhale. There was the whole of a story in his tone to his companion, and he spoke indeed as if already of the family. It made Strether guess the more quickly what it might be about which Madame de Vionnet was so urgent. Having seen him then she had found him easy; she wished to have it out with him that some way for the young people must be discovered, some way that would not impose as a condition the transplantation of her daughter. He already saw himself discussing with this lady the attractions of Woollett as a residence for Chad's companion. Was that youth going now to trust her with the affair—so that it would be after all with one of his "lady-friends" that his mother's missionary should be condemned to deal? It was quite as if for an instant the two men looked at each other on this question. But there was no mistaking at last Chad's pride in the display of such a connexion. This was what had made him so carry himself while, three mintues before, he was bringing it into view; what had caused his friend, first catching sight of him, to be so struck with his air. It was, in a word, just when he thus finally felt Chad putting things straight off on him that he envied him, as he had mentioned to little Bilham, most. The whole exhibition however was but a matter of three or four minutes, and the author of it had soon explained that, as Madame de Vionnet was immediately going "on," this could be for Jeanne but a snatch. They would all meet again soon, and Strether was meanwhile to stay and amuse himself—"I'll pick you up again in plenty of time." He took the girl off as he had brought her, and Strether, with the faint sweet foreignness of her "Au revoir, monsieur!" in his ears as a note almost unprecedented, watched them recede side by side and felt how, once more, her companion's relation to her got an accent from it. They disappeared among the others and apparently into the house; whereupon our friend turned round to give out to little Bilham the conviction of which he was full. But there was no little Bilham any more; little Bilham had within the few moments, for reasons of his own, proceeded further: a circumstance by which, in its order, Strether was also sensibly affected.

III

Chad was not in fact on this occasion to keep his promise of coming back; but Miss Gostrey had soon presented herself with an explanation of his failure. There had been reasons at the last for his going off with *ces dames*; and he had asked her with much instance to come out and take charge of their friend. She did so, Strether felt as she took her place beside him, in a manner that left nothing to desire. He had dropped back on his bench, alone again for a time, and the more conscious for little Bilham's defection of his unexpressed thought; in respect to which, however, this next converser was a still more capacious vessel. "It's the child!" he had exclaimed to her almost as soon as she appeared; and though her direct response was for some time delayed he could feel in her meanwhile the working of this truth. It might have been simply, as she waited, that they were now in presence altogether of truth spreading like a flood and not for the moment to be offered her in the mere cupful; inasmuch as who should *ces dames* prove to be but persons about whom—once thus face to face with them—she found she might from the first have told him almost everything? This would have freely come had he taken the simple precaution of giving her their name. There could be no better example—and she appeared to note it with high amusement—than the way, making things out already so much for himself, if he was at last throwing precautions to the winds. They were neither more nor less, she and the child's mother, than old school-friends—friends who had scarcely met for years but whom this unlooked-for chance had brought together with a rush. It was a relief, Miss Gostrey hinted, to feel herself no longer groping; she was unaccustomed to grope and as a general thing, he might well have seen, made straight enough for her clue. With the one she had now picked up in her hands there need be at least no waste of wonder. "She's coming to see me—that's for *you*," Strether's counsellor continued; "but I don't require it to know where I am."

The waste of wonder might be proscribed; but Strether, characteristically, was even by this time in the immensity of space. "By which you mean that you know where *she* is?"

She just hesitated. "I mean that if she comes to see me I shall—now that I've pulled myself round a bit after the shock—not be at home."

Strether hung poised. "You call it—your recognition—a shock?"

She gave one of her rare flickers of impatience. "It was a surprise, an emotion. Don't be so literal. I wash my hands of her."

Poor Strether's face lengthened. "She's impossible—?"

"She's even more charming than I remembered her."

"Then what's the matter?"

She had to think how to put it. "Well, *I'm* impossible. It's impossible. Everything's impossible."

He looked at her an instant. "I see where you're coming out. Everything's possible." Their eyes had on it in fact an exchange of some duration; after which he pursued: "Isn't it that beautiful child?" Then as she still said nothing: "Why don't you mean to receive her?"

Her answer in an instant rang clear. "Because I wish to keep out of the business."

It provoked in him a weak wail. "You're going to abandon me *now*?"

"No, I'm only going to abandon *her*. She'll want me to help her with you. And I won't."

"You'll only help me with her? Well, then—!"

Most of the persons previously gathered had, in the interest of tea, passed into the house, and they had the gardens mainly to themselves. The shadows were long, the last call of the birds, who had made a home of their own in the noble interspaced quarter, sounded from the high trees in the other gardens as well, those of the old convent and of the old *hôtels*; it was as if our friends had waited for the full charm to come out. Strether's impressions were still present; it was as if something had happened that "nailed" them, made them more intense; but he was to ask himself soon afterwards, that evening, what really *had* happened—conscious as he could after all remain that for a gentleman taken, and taken for the first time, into the "great world," the world of ambassadors and duchesses, the items made a meagre total. It was nothing new to him, however, as we know, that a man might have—at all events such a man as he—an amount of experience out of any proportion to his adventures; so that, though it was doubtless no great adventure to sit on there with Miss Gostrey and hear about Madame de Vionnet, the hour, the picture, the immediate, the recent, the possible—as well as the communication itself, not a note of which failed to reverberate—only gave the moments more of the taste of history.

It was history, to begin with, that Jeanne's mother had been three-and-twenty years before, at Geneva, schoolmate and good girl-friend to Maria Gostrey, who had moreover enjoyed since then, though interruptedly and above all with a long recent drop, other glimpses of her. Twenty-three years put them both on, no doubt; and Madame de Vionnet—though she had married straight after school—couldn't be to-day an hour less than thirty-eight. This made her ten years older than Chad—though ten years, also, if Strether liked, older than she looked; the least, at any rate, that a prospective mother-in-law could be expected to do with. She would be of all mothers-in-law the most charming; unless indeed, through some perversity as yet insupposable, she should utterly belie herself in that relation. There was none surely in which, as Maria remembered her, she mustn't be charming; and this frankly in spite of the stigma of failure in the tie where failure always most showed. It was no test there—when indeed *was* it a test there?—for Monsieur de Vionnet had been a brute. She had lived for years apart from him—which was of course always a horrid position; but Miss Gostrey's impression of the matter had been that she could scarce have made a better thing of it had she done it on purpose to show she was amiable. She was so amiable that nobody had had a word to say; which was luckily not the case for her husband. He was so impossible that she had the advantage of all her merits.

It was still history for Strether that the Comte de Vionnet—it being also history that the lady in question was a Countess—should now, under Miss Gostrey's sharp touch, rise before him as a high distinguished polished impertinent reprobate, the product of a mysterious order; it was history, further, that the charming girl so freely sketched by his companion should have been married out of hand by a mother, another figure of striking outline, full of dark personal motive; it was perhaps history most of all that this company was, as a matter of course, governed by such considerations as put divorce out of the question. "*Ces gens-là* don't divorce, you know, any more than they emigrate or abjure—they think it impious and vulgar"; a fact in the light of which they seemed but the more richly special. It was all special; it was all, for Strether's imagination, more or less rich. The girl at the Genevese school, an isolated interesting attaching creature, then both sensitive and violent, audacious but always forgiven, was the daughter of a French father and an English mother who, early left a widow, had married again—tried afresh with a foreigner; in her career with whom she had apparently given her child no example of comfort. All these people—the people of the English mother's side—had been of condition more or less eminent; yet with oddities and disparities that had often since made Maria, thinking them over, wonder what they really quite rhymed to. It was in any case her belief that the mother, interested and prone to adventure, had been without conscience, had only thought of ridding herself most quickly of a possible, an actual encumbrance. The father, by her impression, a Frenchman with a name one knew, had been a different matter, leaving his child, she clearly recalled, a memory all fondness, as well as an assured little fortune which was unluckily to make her more or less of a prey later on. She had been in particular, at school, dazzlingly, though quite booklessly, clever; as polyglot as a little Jewess (which she wasn't, oh no!) and chattering French, English, German, Italian, anything one would, in a way that made a clean sweep, if not of prizes and parchments, at least of every "part," whether memorized or improvised, in the curtained costumed school repertory, and in especial of all mysteries of race and vagueness of reference, all swagger about "home," among their variegated mates.

It would doubtless be difficult to-day, as between French and English, to name her and place her; she would certainly show, on knowledge, Miss Gostrey felt, as one of those convenient types who don't keep you explaining—minds with doors as numerous as the many-tongued cluster of confessionals at Saint Peter's. You might confess to her with confidence in Roumelian, and even Roumelian sins. Therefore—! But Strether's narrator covered her implication with a laugh; a laugh by which his betrayal of a sense of the lurid in the picture was also perhaps sufficiently protected. He had a moment of wondering, while his friend went on, what sins might be especially Roumelian. She went on at all events to the mention of her having met the young thing—again by some Swiss lake—in her first married state, which had appeared for the few intermediate years not at least violently disturbed. She had been lovely at that moment, delightful to *her*, full of responsive emotion, of amused recognitions and amusing reminders; and then, once more, much later, after a long interval, equally but differently charming—touching and rather mystifying for the five minutes of an encounter at a railway-station *en province*, during which it had come out that her life was all changed. Miss Gostrey had understood enough to see, essentially, what had happened, and yet had beautifully dreamed that she was herself faultless. There were doubtless depths in her, but she was all right; Strether would see if she wasn't. She was another person, however—that had been promptly marked—from the small child of nature at the Geneva school; a little person quite made over (as foreign women *were*, compared with American) by marriage. Her situation too had evidently cleared itself up; there would have been—all that was possible—a judicial separation. She had settled in Paris, brought up her daughter, steered her boat. It was no very pleasant boat—especially there—to be in; but Marie de Vionnet would have headed straight. She would have friends, certainly—and very good ones. There she was at all events—and it was very interesting. Her knowing Mr. Chad didn't in the least prove she hadn't friends; what it proved was what good ones *he* had. "I saw that," said Miss Gostrey, "that night at the Français; it came out for me in three minutes. I saw *her*—or somebody like her. And so," she immediately added, "did you."

"Oh no—not anybody like her!" Strether laughed. "But you mean," he as promptly went on, "that she has had such an influence on him?"

Miss Gostrey was on her feet; it was time for them to go. "She has brought him up for her daughter."

Their eyes, as so often, in candid conference, through their settled glasses, met over it long; after which Strether's again took in the whole place. They were quite alone there now. "Mustn't she rather—in the time then—have rushed it?"

"Ah she won't of course have lost an hour. But that's just the good mother—the good French one. You must remember that of her—that as a mother she's French, and that for them there's a special providence. It precisely, however—that she mayn't have been able to begin as far back as she'd have liked—makes her grateful for aid."

Strether took this in as they slowly moved to the house on their way out. "She counts on me then to put the thing through?"

"Yes—she counts on you. Oh and first of all of course," Miss Gostrey added, "on her—well, convincing you."

"Ah," her friend returned, "she caught Chad young!"

"Yes, but there are women who are for all your 'times of life.' They're the most wonderful sort."

She had laughed the words out, but they brought her companion, the next thing, to a stand. "Is what you mean that she'll try to make a fool of me?"

"Well, I'm wondering what she *will*—with an opportunity—make."

"What do you call," Strether asked, "an opportunity? My going to see her?"

"Ah you must go to see her"—Miss Gostrey was a trifle evasive. "You can't not do that. You'd have gone to see the other woman. I mean if there had been one—a different sort. It's what you came out for."

It might be; but Strether distinguished. "I didn't come out to see *this* sort."

She had a wonderful look at him now. "Are you disappointed she isn't worse?"

He for a moment entertained the question, then found for it the frankest of answers. "Yes. If she were worse she'd be better for our purpose. It would be simpler."

"Perhaps," she admitted. "But won't this be pleasanter?"

"Ah you know," he promptly replied, "I didn't come out—wasn't that just what you originally reproached me with?—for the pleasant."

"Precisely. Therefore I say again what I said at first. You must take things as they come. Besides," Miss Gostrey added, "I'm not afraid for myself."

"For yourself—?"

"Of your seeing her. I trust her. There's nothing she'll say about me. In fact there's nothing she *can*."

Strether wondered—little as he had thought of this. Then he broke out. "Oh you women!"

There was something in it at which she flushed. "Yes—there we are. We're abysses." At last she smiled. "But I risk her!"

He gave himself a shake. "Well then so do I!" But he added as they passed into the house that he would see Chad the first thing in the morning.

This was the next day the more easily effected that the young man, as it happened, even before he was down, turned up at his hotel. Strether took his coffee, by habit, in the public room; but on his descending for this purpose Chad instantly proposed an adjournment to what he called greater privacy. He had himself as yet had nothing—they would sit down somewhere together; and when after a few steps and a turn into the Boulevard they had, for their greater privacy, sat down among twenty others, our friend saw in his companion's move a fear of the advent of Waymarsh. It was the first time Chad had to that extent given this personage "away"; and Strether found himself wondering of what it was symptomatic. He made out in a moment that the youth was in earnest as he hadn't yet seen him; which in its turn threw a ray perhaps a trifle startling on what they had each up to that time been treating as earnestness. It was sufficiently flattering, however, that the real thing—if this *was* at last the real thing—should have been determined, as appeared, precisely by an accretion of Strether's importance. For this was what it quickly enough came to—that Chad, rising with the lark, had rushed down to let him know while his morning consciousness was yet young that he had literally made the afternoon before a tremendous impression. Madame de Vionnet wouldn't, couldn't rest till she should have some assurance from him that he *would* consent again to see her. The announcement was made, across their marble-topped table, while the foam of the hot milk was in their cups and its plash still in the air, with the smile of Chad's easiest urbanity; and this expression of his face caused our friend's doubts to gather on the spot into a challenge of the lips. "See here"—that was all; he only for the moment said again "See here." Chad met it with all his air of straight intelligence, while Strether remembered again that fancy of the first impression of him, the happy young Pagan, handsome and hard but oddly indulgent whose mysterious measure he had under the street-lamp tried mentally to take. The young Pagan, while a long look passed between them, sufficiently understood. Strether scarce needed at last to say the rest—"I want to know where I am." But he said it, adding before any answer, something more. "Are you engaged to be married—is that your secret?—to the young lady?"

Chad shook his head with the slow amenity that was one of his ways of conveying that there was time for everything. "I have no secret—though I may have secrets! I haven't at any rate that one. We're not engaged. No."

"Then where's the hitch?"

"Do you mean why I haven't already started with you?" Chad, beginning his coffee and buttering his roll, was quite ready to explain. "Nothing would have induced me—nothing will still induce me—not to try to keep you here as long as you can be made to stay. It's too visibly good for you." Strether had himself plenty to say about this, but it was amusing also to measure the march of Chad's tone. He had never been more a man of the world, and it was always in his company present to our friend that one was seeing how in successive connexions a man of the world acquitted himself. Chad kept it up beautifully. "My idea—*voyons!*—is simply that you should let Madame de Vionnet know you, simply that you should consent to know *her*. I don't in the least mind telling you that, clever and charming as she is, she's ever so much in my confidence. All I ask of you is to let her talk to you. You've asked me about what you call my hitch, and so far as it goes she'll explain it to you. She's herself my hitch, hang it—if you must really have it all out. But in a sense," he hastened in the most wonderful manner to add, "that you'll quite make out for yourself. She's too good a friend, confound her. Too good, I mean, for me to leave without—without—" It was his first hesitation.

"Without what?"

"Well, without my arranging somehow or other the damnable terms of my sacrifice."

"It *will* be a sacrifice then?"

"It will be the greatest loss I ever suffered. I owe her so much."

It was beautiful, the way Chad said these things, and his plea was now confessedly—oh quite flagrantly and publicly—interesting. The moment really took on for Strether an intensity. Chad owed Madame de Vionnet so much? What *did* that do then but clear up the whole mystery? He was indebted for alterations, and she was thereby in a position to have sent in her bill for expenses incurred in reconstruction. What was this at bottom but what had been to be arrived at? Strether sat there arriving at it while he munched toast and stirred his second cup. To do this with the aid of Chad's pleasant earnest face was also to do more besides. No, never before had he been so ready to take him as he was. What was it that had suddenly so cleared up? It was just everybody's character; that is everybody's but—in a measure—his own. Strether felt *his* character receive for the instant a smutch from all the wrong things he had suspected or believed. The person to whom Chad owed it that he could positively turn out such comfort to other persons—such a person was sufficiently raised above any "breath" by the nature of her work and the young man's steady light. All of which was vivid enough to come and go quickly; though indeed in the midst of it Strether could utter a question. "Have I your word of honour that if I surrender myself to Madame de Vionnet you'll surrender yourself to *me*?"

Chad laid his hand firmly on his friend's. "My dear man, you have it."

There was finally something in his felicity almost embarrassing and oppressive—Strether had begun to fidget under it for the open air and the erect posture. He had signed to the waiter that he wished to pay, and this transaction took some moments, during which he thoroughly felt, while he put down money and pretended—it was quite hollow—to estimate change, that Chad's higher spirit, his youth, his practice, his paganism, his felicity, his assurance, his impudence, whatever it might be, had consciously scored a success. Well, that was all right so far as it went; his sense of the thing in question covered our friend for a minute like a veil through which—as if he had been muffled—he heard his interlocutor ask him if he mightn't take him over about five. "Over" was over the river, and over the river was where Madame de Vionnet lived, and five was that very afternoon. They got at last out of the place—got out before he answered. He lighted in the street, a cigarette, which again gave him more time. But it was already sharp for him that there was no use in time. "What does she propose to do to me?" he had presently demanded.

Chad had no delays. "Are you afraid of her?"

"Oh immensely. Don't you see it?"

"Well," said Chad, "she won't do anything worse to you than make you like her."

"It's just of that I'm afraid."

"Then it's not fair to me."

Strether cast about. "It's fair to your mother."

"Oh," said Chad, "are you afraid of *her*?"

"Scarcely less. Or perhaps even more. But is this lady against your interests at home?" Strether went on.

"Not directly, no doubt; but she's greatly in favour of them here."

"And what—'here'—does she consider them to be?"

"Well, good relations!"

"With herself?"

"With herself."

"And what is it that makes them so good?"

"What? Well, that's exactly what you'll make out if you'll only go, as I'm supplicating you, to see her."

Strether stared at him with a little of the wanness, no doubt, that the vision of more to "make out" could scarce help producing. "I mean *how* good are they?"

"Oh awfully good."

Again Strether had faltered, but it was brief. It was all very well, but there was nothing now he wouldn't risk. "Excuse me, but I must really—as I began by telling you—know where I am. Is she bad?"

"'Bad'?"—Chad echoed it, but without a shock. "Is that what's implied—?"

"When relations are good?" Strether felt a little silly, and was even conscious of a foolish laugh, at having it imposed on him to have appeared to speak so. What indeed was he talking about? His stare had relaxed; he looked now all round him. But something in him brought him back, though he still didn't know quite how to turn it. The two or three ways he thought of, and one of them in particular, were, even with scruples dismissed, too ugly. He none the less at last found something. "Is her life without reproach?"

It struck him, directly he had found it, as pompous and priggish; so much so that he was thankful to Chad for taking it only in the right spirit. The young man spoke so immensely to the point that the effect was practically of positive blandness. "Absolutely without reproach. A beautiful life. *Allez donc voir!*"

These last words were, in the liberality of their confidence, so imperative that Strether went through no form of assent; but before they separated it had been confirmed that he should be picked up at a quarter to five.

BOOK SIXTH

I

It was quite by half-past five—after the two men had been together in Madame de Vionnet's drawing-room not more than a dozen minutes—that Chad, with a look at his watch and then another at their hostess, said genially, gaily, "I've an engagement, and I know you won't complain if I leave him with you. He'll interest you immensely; and as for her," he declared to Strether, "I assure you, if you're at all nervous, she's perfectly safe."

He had left them to be embarrassed or not by this guarantee, as they could best manage, and embarrassment was a thing that Strether wasn't at first sure Madame de Vionnet escaped. He escaped it himself, to his surprise; but he had grown used by this time to thinking of himself as brazen. She occupied, his hostess, in the Rue de Bellechasse, the first floor of an old house to which our visitors had had access from an old clean court. The court was large and open, full of revelations, for our friend, of the habit of privacy, the peace of intervals, the dignity of distances and approaches; the house, to his restless sense, was in the high homely style of an elder day, and the ancient Paris that he was always looking for—sometimes intensely felt, sometimes more acutely missed—was in the immemorial polish of the wide waxed staircase and in the fine *boiseries*, the medallions, mouldings, mirrors, great clear spaces, of the greyish-white salon into which he had been shown. He seemed at the very outset to see her, in the midst of possessions not vulgarly numerous, but hereditary cherished charming. While his eyes turned after a little from those of his hostess and Chad freely talked—not in the least about *him*, but about other people, people he didn't know, and quite as if he did know them—he found himself making out, as a background of the occupant, some glory, some prosperity of the First Empire, some Napoleonic glamour, some dim lustre of the great legend; elements clinging still to all the consular chairs and mythological brasses and sphinxes' heads and faded surfaces of satin striped with alternate silk.

The place itself went further back—that he guessed, and how old Paris continued in a manner to echo there; but the post-revolutionary period, the world he vaguely thought of as the world of Chateaubriand, of Madame de Staël, even of the young Lamartine, had left its stamp of harps and urns and torches, a stamp impressed on sundry small objects, ornaments and relics. He had never before, to his knowledge, had present to him relics, of any special dignity, of a private order—little old miniatures, medallions, pictures, books; books in leather bindings, pinkish and greenish, with gilt garlands on the back, ranged, together with other promiscuous properties, under the glass of brass-mounted cabinets. His attention took them all tenderly into account. They were among the matters that marked Madame de Vionnet's apartment as something quite different from Miss Gostrey's little museum of bargains and from Chad's lovely home; he recognised it as founded much more on old accumulations that had possibly from time to time shrunken than on any contemporary method of acquisition or form of curiosity. Chad and Miss Gostrey had rummaged and purchased and picked up and exchanged, sifting, selecting, comparing; whereas the mistress of the scene before him, beautifully passive under the spell of transmission—transmission from her father's line, he quite made up his mind—had only received, accepted and been quiet. When she hadn't been quiet she had been moved at the most to some occult charity for some fallen fortune. There had been objects she or her predecessors might even conceivably have parted with under need; but Strether couldn't suspect them of having sold old pieces to get "better" ones. They would have felt no difference as to better or worse. He could but imagine their having felt—perhaps in emigration, in proscription, for his sketch was slight and confused—the pressure of want or the obligation of sacrifice.

The pressure of want—whatever might be the case with the other force—was, however, presumably not active now, for the tokens of a chastened ease still abounded after all, many marks of a taste whose discriminations might perhaps have been called eccentric. He guessed at intense little preferences and sharp little exclusions, a deep suspicion of the vulgar and a personal view of the right. The general result of this was something for which he had no name on the spot quite ready, but something he would have come nearest to naming in speaking of it as the air of supreme respectability, the consciousness, small, still, reserved, but none the less distinct and diffused, of private honour. The air of supreme respectability—that was a strange blank wall for his adventure to have brought him to break his nose against. It had in fact, as he was now aware, filled all the approaches, hovered in the court as he passed, hung on the staircase as he mounted, sounded in the grave rumble of the old bell, as little electric as possible, of which Chad, at the door, had pulled the ancient but neatly-kept tassel; it formed in short the clearest medium of its particular kind that he had ever breathed. He would have answered for it at the end of a quarter of an hour that some of the glass cases contained swords and epaulettes of ancient colonels and generals; medals and orders once pinned over hearts that had long since ceased to beat; snuff-boxes bestowed on ministers and envoys; copies of works presented, with inscriptions, by authors now classic. At bottom of it all for him was the sense of her rare unlikeness to the women he had known. This sense had grown, since the day before, the more he recalled her, and had been above all singularly fed by his talk with Chad in the morning. Everything in fine made her immeasurably new, and nothing so new as the old house and the old objects. There were books, two or three, on a small table near his chair, but they hadn't the lemon-coloured covers with which his eye had begun to dally from the hour of his arrival and to the opportunity of a further acquaintance with which he had for a fortnight now altogether succumbed. On another table, across the room, he made out the great *Revue*; but even that familiar face, conspicuous in Mrs. Newsome's parlours, scarce counted here as a modern note. He was sure on the spot—and he afterwards knew he was right—that this was a touch of Chad's own hand. What would Mrs. Newsome say to the circumstance that Chad's interested "influence" kept her paper-knife in the *Revue*? The interested influence at any rate had, as we say, gone straight to the point—had in fact soon left it quite behind.

She was seated, near the fire, on a small stuffed and fringed chair, one of the few modern articles in the room; and she leaned back in it with her hands clasped in her lap and no movement, in all her person, but the fine prompt play of her deep young face. The fire, under the low white marble, undraped and academic, had burnt down to the silver ashes of light wood; one of the windows, at a distance, stood open to the mildness and stillness, out of which, in the short pauses, came the faint sound, pleasant and homely, almost rustic, of a plash and a clatter of *sabots* from some coach-house on the other side of the court. Madame de Vionnet, while Strether was there, wasn't to shift her posture by an inch. "I don't think you seriously believe in what you're doing," she said; "but all the same, you know, I'm going to treat you quite as if I did."

"By which you mean," Strether directly replied, "quite as if you didn't! I assure you it won't make the least difference with me how you treat me."

"Well," she said, taking that menace bravely and philosophically enough, "the only thing that really matters is that you shall get on with me."

"Ah but I don't!" he immediately returned.

It gave her another pause; which, however, she happily enough shook off. "Will you consent to go on with me a little—provisionally—as if you did?"

Then it was that he saw how she had decidedly come all the way; and there accompanied it an extraordinary sense of her raising from somewhere below him her beautiful suppliant eyes. He might have been perched at his door-step or at his window and she standing in the road. For a moment he let her stand and couldn't moreover have spoken. It had been sad, of a sudden, with a sadness that was like a cold breath in his face. "What can I do," he finally asked, "but listen to you as I promised Chadwick?"

"Ah but what I'm asking you," she quickly said, "isn't what Mr. Newsome had in mind." She spoke at present, he saw, as if to take courageously *all* her risk. "This is my own idea and a different thing."

It gave poor Strether in truth—uneasy as it made him too—something of the thrill of a bold perception justified. "Well," he answered kindly enough, "I was sure a moment since that some idea of your own had come to you."

She seemed still to look up at him, but now more serenely. "I made out you were sure—and that helped it to come. So you see," she continued, "we do get on."

"Oh but it appears to me I don't at all meet your request. How can I when I don't understand it?"

"It isn't at all necessary you should understand; it will do quite well enough if you simply remember it. Only feel I trust you—and for nothing so tremendous after all. Just," she said with a wonderful smile, "for common civility."

Strether had a long pause while they sat again face to face, as they had sat, scarce less conscious, before the poor lady had crossed the stream. She was the poor lady for Strether now because clearly she had some trouble, and her appeal to him could only mean that her trouble was deep. He couldn't help it; it wasn't his fault; he had done nothing; but by a turn of the hand she had somehow made their encounter a relation. And the relation profited by a mass of things that were not strictly in it or of it; by the very air in which they sat, by the high cold delicate room, by the world outside and the little plash in the court, by the First Empire and the relics in the stiff cabinets, by matters as far off as those and by others as near as the unbroken clasp of her hands in her lap and the look her expression had of being most natural when her eyes were most fixed. "You count upon me of course for something really much greater than it sounds."

"Oh it sounds great enough too!" she laughed at this.

He found himself in time on the point of telling her that she was, as Miss Barrace called it, wonderful; but, catching himself up, he said something else instead. "What was it Chad's idea then that you should say to me?"

"Ah his idea was simply what a man's idea always is—to put every effort off on the woman."

"The 'woman'—?" Strether slowly echoed.

"The woman he likes—and just in proportion as he likes her. In proportion too—for shifting the trouble—as she likes *him*."

Strether followed it; then with an abruptness of his own: "How much do you like Chad?"

"Just as much as *that*—to take all, with you, on myself." But she got at once again away from this. "I've been trembling as if we were to stand or fall by what you think of me; and I'm even now," she went on wonderfully, "drawing a long breath—and, yes, truly taking a great courage—from the hope that I don't in fact strike you as impossible."

"That's at all events, clearly," he observed after an instant, "the way I don't strike *you*."

"Well," she so far assented, "as you haven't yet said you *won't* have the little patience with me I ask for—"

"You draw splendid conclusions? Perfectly. But I don't understand them." Strether pursued. "You seem to me to ask for much more than you need. What, at the worst for you, what at the best for myself, can I after all do? I can use no pressure that I haven't used. You come really late with your request. I've already done all that for myself the case admits of. I've said my say, and here I am."

"Yes, here you are, fortunately!" Madame de Vionnet laughed. "Mrs. Newsome," she added in another tone, "didn't think you can do so little."

He had an hesitation, but he brought the words out. "Well, she thinks so now."

"Do you mean by that—?" But she also hung fire.

"Do I mean what?"

She still rather faltered. "Pardon me if I touch on it, but if I'm saying extraordinary things, why, perhaps, mayn't I? Besides, doesn't it properly concern us to know?"

"To know what?" he insisted as after thus beating about the bush she had again dropped.

She made the effort. "Has she given you up?"

He was amazed afterwards to think how simply and quietly he had met it. "Not yet." It was almost as if he were a trifle disappointed—had expected still more of her freedom. But he went straight on. "Is that what Chad has told you will happen to me?"

She was evidently charmed with the way he took it. "If you mean if we've talked of it—most certainly. And the question's not what has had least to do with my wishing to see you."

"To judge if I'm the sort of man a woman *can*—?"

"Precisely," she exclaimed—"you wonderful gentleman! I do judge—*I have* judged. A woman can't. You're safe—with every right to be. You'd be much happier if you'd only believe it."

Strether was silent a little; then he found himself speaking with a cynicism of confidence of which even at the moment the sources were strange to him. "I try to believe it. But it's a marvel," he exclaimed, "how *you* already get at it!"

Oh she was able to say. "Remember how much I was on the way to it through Mr. Newsome—before I saw you. He thinks everything of your strength."

"Well, I can bear almost anything!" our friend briskly interrupted. Deep and beautiful on this her smile came back, and with the effect of making him hear what he had said just as she had heard it. He easily enough felt that it gave him away, but what in truth had everything done but that? It had been all very well to think at moments that he was holding her nose down and that he had coerced her: what had he by this time done but let her practically see that he accepted their relation? What was their relation moreover—though light and brief enough in form as yet—but whatever she might choose to make it? Nothing could prevent her—certainly he couldn't—from making it pleasant. At the back of his head, behind everything, was the sense that she was—there, before him, close to him, in vivid imperative form—one of the rare women he had so often heard of, read of, thought of, but never met, whose very presence, look, voice, the mere contemporaneous *fact* of whom, from the moment it was at all presented, made a relation of mere recognition. That was not the kind of woman he had ever found Mrs. Newsome, a contemporaneous fact who had been distinctly slow to establish herself; and at present, confronted with Madame de Vionnet, he felt the simplicity of his original impression of Miss Gostrey. She certainly had been a fact of rapid growth; but the world was wide, each day was more and more a new lesson. There were at any rate even among the stranger ones relations and relations. "Of course I suit Chad's grand way," he quickly added. "He hasn't had much difficulty in working me in."

She seemed to deny a little, on the young man's behalf, by the rise of her eyebrows, an intention of any process at all inconsiderate. "You must know how grieved he'd be if you were to lose anything. He believes you can keep his mother patient."

Strether wondered with his eyes on her. "I see. *That's* then what you really want of me. And how am I to do it? Perhaps you'll tell me that."

"Simply tell her the truth."

"And what do you call the truth?"

"Well, *any* truth—about us all—that you see yourself. I leave it to you."

"Thank you very much. I like," Strether laughed with a slight harshness, "the way you leave things!"

But she insisted kindly, gently, as if it wasn't so bad. "Be perfectly honest. Tell her all."

"All?" he oddly echoed.

"Tell her the simple truth," Madame de Vionnet again pleaded.

"But what *is* the simple truth? The simple truth is exactly what I'm trying to discover."

She looked about a while, but presently she came back to him. "Tell her, fully and clearly, about *us*."

Strether meanwhile had been staring. "You and your daughter?"

"Yes—little Jeanne and me. Tell her," she just slightly quavered, "you like us."

"And what good will that do me? Or rather"—he caught himself up—"what good will it do *you*?"

She looked graver. "None, you believe, really?"

Strether debated. "She didn't send me out to 'like' you."

"Oh," she charmingly contended, "she sent you out to face the facts."

He admitted after an instant that there was something in that. "But how can I face them till I know what they are? Do you want him," he then braced himself to ask, "to marry your daughter?"

She gave a headshake as noble as it was prompt. "No—not that."

"And he really doesn't want to himself?"

She repeated the movement, but now with a strange light in her face. "He likes her too much."

Strether wondered. "To be willing to consider, you mean, the question of taking her to America?"

"To be willing to do anything with her but be immensely kind and nice—really tender of her. We watch over her, and you must help us. You must see her again."

Strether felt awkward. "Ah with pleasure—she's so remarkably attractive."

The mother's eagerness with which Madame de Vionnet jumped at this was to come back to him later as beautiful in its grace. "The dear thing *did* please you?" Then as he met it with the largest "Oh!" of enthusiasm: "She's perfect. She's my joy."

"Well, I'm sure that—if one were near her and saw more of her—she'd be mine."

"Then," said Madame de Vionnet, "tell Mrs. Newsome that!"

He wondered the more. "What good will that do you?" As she appeared unable at once to say, however, he brought out something else. "Is your daughter in love with our friend?"

"Ah," she rather startlingly answered, "I wish you'd find out!"

He showed his surprise. "I? A stranger?"

"Oh you won't be a stranger—presently. You shall see her quite, I assure you, as if you weren't."

It remained for him none the less an extraordinary notion. "It seems to me surely that if her mother can't—"

"Ah little girls and their mothers to-day!" she rather inconsequently broke in. But she checked herself with something she seemed to give out as after all more to the point. "Tell her I've been good for him. Don't you think I have?"

It had its effect on him—more than at the moment he quite measured. Yet he was consciously enough touched. "Oh, if it's all *you*—!"

"Well, it may not be 'all,'" she interrupted, "but it's to a great extent. Really and truly," she added in a tone that was to take its place with him among things remembered.

"Then it's very wonderful." He smiled at her from a face that he felt as strained, and her own face for a moment kept him so. At last she also got up. "Well, don't you think that for that—"

"I ought to save you?" So it was that the way to meet her—and the way, as well, in a manner, to get off—came over him. He heard himself use the exorbitant word, the very sound of which helped to determine his flight. "I'll save you if I can."

II

In Chad's lovely home, however, one evening ten days later, he felt himself present at the collapse of the question of Jeanne de Vionnet's shy secret. He had been dining there in the company of that young lady and her mother, as well as of other persons, and he had gone into the *petit salon*, at Chad's request, on purpose to talk with her. The young man had put this to him as a favour—"I should like so awfully to know what you think of her. It will really be a chance for you," he had said, "to see the *jeune fille*—I mean the type—as she actually is, and I don't think that, as an observer of manners, it's a thing you ought to miss. It will be an impression that—whatever else you take—you can carry home with you, where you'll find again so much to compare it with."

Strether knew well enough with what Chad wished him to compare it, and though he entirely assented he hadn't yet somehow been so deeply reminded that he was being, as he constantly though mutely expressed it, used. He was as far as ever from making out exactly to what end; but he was none the less constantly accompanied by a sense of the service he rendered. He conceived only that this service was highly agreeable to those who profited by it; and he was indeed still waiting for the moment at which he should catch it in the act of proving disagreeable, proving in some degree intolerable, to himself. He failed quite to see how his situation could clear up at all logically except by some turn of events that would give him the pretext of disgust. He was building from day to day on the possibility of disgust, but each day brought forth meanwhile a new and more engaging bend of the road. That possibility was now ever so much further from sight than on the eve of his arrival, and he perfectly felt that, should it come at all, it would have to be at best inconsequent and violent. He struck himself as a little nearer to it only when he asked himself what service, in such a life of utility, he was after all rendering Mrs. Newsome. When he wished to help himself to believe that he was still all right he reflected—and in fact with wonder—on the unimpaired frequency of their correspondence; in relation to which what was after all more natural than that it should become more frequent just in proportion as their problem became more complicated?

Certain it is at any rate that he now often brought himself balm by the question, with the rich consciousness of yesterday's letter, "Well, what can I do more than that—what can I do more than tell her everything?" To persuade himself that he did tell her, had told her, everything, he used to try to think of particular things he hadn't told her. When at rare moments and in the watches of the night he pounced on one it generally showed itself to be—to a deeper scrutiny—not quite truly of the essence. When anything new struck him as coming up, or anything already noted as reappearing, he always immediately wrote, as if for fear that if he didn't he would miss something; and also that he might be able to say to himself from time to time, "She knows it *now*, even while I worry." It was a great comfort to him in general not to have left past things to be dragged to light and explained; not to have to produce at so late a stage anything not produced, or anything even veiled and attenuated, at the moment. She knew it now: that was what he said to himself to-night in relation to the fresh fact of Chad's acquaintance with the two ladies—not to speak of the fresher one of his own. Mrs. Newsome knew in other words that very night at Woollett that he himself knew Madame de Vionnet and that he had conscientiously been to see her; also that he had found her remarkably attractive and that there would probably be a good deal more to tell. But she further knew, or would know very soon, that, again conscientiously, he hadn't repeated his visit; and that when Chad had asked him on the Countess's behalf—Strether made her out vividly, with a thought at the back of his head, a Countess—if he wouldn't name a day for dining with her, he had replied lucidly: "Thank you very much—impossible." He had begged the young man would present his excuses and had trusted him to understand that it couldn't really strike one as quite the straight thing. He hadn't reported to Mrs. Newsome that he had promised to "save" Madame de Vionnet; but, so far as he was concerned with that reminiscence, he hadn't at any rate promised to haunt her house. What Chad had understood could only, in truth, be inferred from Chad's behaviour, which had been in this connexion as easy as in every other. He was easy, always, when he understood; he was easier still, if possible, when he didn't; he had replied that he would make it right; and he had proceeded to do this by substituting the present occasion—as he was ready to substitute others—for any, for every occasion as to which his old friend should have a funny scruple.

"Oh but I'm not a little foreign girl; I'm just as English as I can be," Jeanne de Vionnet had said to him as soon as, in the *petit salon*, he sank, shyly enough on his own side, into the place near her vacated by Madame Gloriani at his approach. Madame Gloriani, who was in black velvet, with white lace and powdered hair, and whose somewhat massive majesty melted, at any contact, into the graciousness of some incomprehensible tongue, moved away to make room for the vague gentleman, after benevolent greetings to him which embodied, as he believed, in baffling accents, some recognition of his face from a couple of Sundays before. Then he had remarked—making the most of the advantage of his years—that it frightened him quite enough to find himself dedicated to the entertainment of a little foreign girl. There were girls he wasn't afraid of—he was quite bold with little Americans. Thus it was that she had defended herself to the end—"Oh but I'm almost American too. That's what mamma has wanted me to be—I mean *like* that; for she has wanted me to have lots of freedom. She has known such good results from it."

She was fairly beautiful to him—a faint pastel in an oval frame: he thought of her already as of some lurking image in a long gallery, the portrait of a small old-time princess of whom nothing was known but that she had died young. Little Jeanne wasn't, doubtless, to die young, but one couldn't, all the same, bear on her lightly enough. It was bearing hard, it was bearing as *he*, in any case, wouldn't bear, to concern himself, in relation to her, with the question of a young man. Odious really the question of a young man; one didn't treat such a person as a maidservant suspected of a "follower." And then young men, young men—well, the thing was their business simply, or was at all events hers. She was fluttered, fairly fevered—to the point of a little glitter that came and went in her eyes and a pair of pink spots that stayed in her cheeks—with the great adventure of dining out and with the greater one still, possibly, of finding a gentleman whom she must think of as very, very old, a gentleman with eyeglasses, wrinkles, a long grizzled moustache. She spoke the prettiest English, our friend thought, that he had ever heard spoken, just as he had believed her a few minutes before to be speaking the prettiest French. He wondered almost wistfully if such a sweep of the lyre didn't react on the spirit itself; and his fancy had in fact, before he knew it, begun so to stray and embroider that he finally found himself, absent and extravagant, sitting with the child in a friendly silence. Only by this time he felt her flutter to have fortunately dropped and that she was more at her ease. She trusted him, liked him, and it was to come back to him afterwards that she had told him things. She had dipped into the waiting medium at last and found neither surge nor chill—nothing but the small splash she could herself make in the pleasant warmth, nothing but the safety of dipping and dipping again. At the end of the ten minutes he was to spend with her his impression—with all it had thrown off and all it had taken in—was complete. She had been free, as she knew freedom, partly to show him that, unlike other little persons she knew, she had imbibed that ideal. She was delightfully quaint about herself, but the vision of what she had imbibed was what most held him. It really consisted, he was soon enough to feel, in just one great little matter, the fact that, whatever her nature, she was thoroughly—he had to cast about for the word, but it came—bred. He couldn't of course on so short an acquaintance speak for her nature, but the idea of breeding was what she had meanwhile dropped into his mind. He had never yet known it so sharply presented. Her mother gave it, no doubt; but her mother, to make that less sensible, gave so much else besides, and on neither of the two previous occasions, extraordinary woman, Strether felt, anything like what she was giving to-night. Little Jeanne was a case, an exquisite case of education; whereas the Countess, whom it so amused him to think of by that denomination, was a case, also exquisite, of—well, he didn't know what.

"He has wonderful taste, *notre jeune homme*": this was what Gloriani said to him on turning away from the inspection of a small picture suspended near the door of the room. The high celebrity in question had just come in, apparently in search of Mademoiselle de Vionnet, but while Strether had got up from beside her their fellow guest, with his eye sharply caught, had paused for a long look. The thing was a landscape, of no size, but of the French school, as our friend was glad to feel he knew, and also of a quality—which he liked to think he should also have guessed; its frame was large out of proportion to the canvas, and he had never seen a person look at anything, he thought, just as Gloriani, with his nose very near and quick movements of the head from side to side and bottom to top, examined this feature of Chad's collection. The artist used that word the next moment, smiling courteously, wiping his nippers and looking round him further—paying the place in short by the very manner of his presence and by something Strether fancied he could make out in this particular glance, such a tribute as, to the latter's sense, settled many things once for all. Strether was conscious at this instant, for that matter, as he hadn't yet been, of how, round about him, quite without him, they *were* consistently settled. Gloriani's smile, deeply Italian, he considered, and finely inscrutable, had had for him, during dinner, at which they were not neighbours, an indefinite greeting; but the quality in it was gone that had appeared on the other occasion to turn him inside out; it was as if even the momentary link supplied by the doubt between them had snapped. He was conscious now of the final reality, which was that there wasn't so much a doubt as a difference altogether; all the more that over the difference the famous sculptor seemed to signal almost condolingly, yet oh how vacantly! as across some great flat sheet of water. He threw out the bridge of a charming hollow civility in which Strether wouldn't have trusted his own full weight a moment. That idea, even though but transient and perhaps belated, had performed the office of putting Strether more at his ease, and the blurred picture had already dropped—dropped with the sound of something else said and with his becoming aware, by another quick turn, that Gloriani was now on the sofa talking with Jeanne, while he himself had in his ears again the familiar friendliness and the elusive meaning of the "Oh, oh, oh!" that had made him, a fortnight before, challenge Miss Barrace in vain. She had always the air, this picturesque and original lady, who struck him, so oddly, as both antique and modern—she had always the air of taking up some joke that one had already had out with her. The point itself, no doubt, was what was antique, and the use she made of it what was modern. He felt just now that her good-natured irony did bear on something, and it troubled him a little that she wouldn't be more explicit, only assuring him, with the pleasure of observation so visible in her, that she wouldn't tell him more for the world.

He could take refuge but in asking her what she had done with Waymarsh, though it must be added that he felt himself a little on the way to a clue after she had answered that this personage was, in the other room, engaged in conversation with Madame de Vionnet. He stared a moment at the image of such a conjunction; then, for Miss Barrace's benefit, he wondered. "Is she too then under the charm—?"

"No, not a bit"—Miss Barrace was prompt. "She makes nothing of him. She's bored. She won't help you with him."

"Oh," Strether laughed, "she can't do everything."

"Of course not—wonderful as she is. Besides, he makes nothing of *her*. She won't take him from me—though she wouldn't, no doubt, having other affairs in hand, even if she could. I've never," said Miss Barrace, "seen her fail with any one before. And to-night, when she's so magnificent, it would seem to her strange—if she minded. So at any rate I have him all. *Je suis tranquille!*"

Strether understood, so far as that went; but he was feeling for his clue. "She strikes you to-night as particularly magnificent?"

"Surely. Almost as I've never seen her. Doesn't she you? Why, it's *for* you."

He persisted in his candour. "'For' me—?"

"Oh, oh, oh!" cried Miss Barrace, who persisted in the opposite of that quality.

"Well," he acutely admitted, "she *is* different. She's gay."

"She's gay!" Miss Barrace laughed. "And she has beautiful shoulders—though there's nothing different in that."

"No," said Strether, "one was sure of her shoulders. It isn't her shoulders."

His companion, with renewed mirth and the finest sense, between the puffs of her cigarette, of the drollery of things, appeared to find their conversation highly delightful. "Yes, it isn't her shoulders."

"What then is it?" Strether earnestly inquired.

"Why, it's *she*—simply. It's her mood. It's her charm."

"Of course it's her charm, but we're speaking of the difference."

"Well," Miss Barrace explained, "she's just brilliant, as we used to say. That's all. She's various. She's fifty women."

"Ah but only one"—Strether kept it clear—"at a time."

"Perhaps. But in fifty times—!"

"Oh we shan't come to that," our friend declared; and the next moment he had moved in another direction. "Will you answer me a plain question? Will she ever divorce?"

Miss Barrace looked at him through all her tortoise-shell. "Why should she?"

It wasn't what he had asked for, he signified; but he met it well enough. "To marry Chad."

"Why should she marry Chad?"

"Because I'm convinced she's very fond of him. She has done wonders for him."

"Well then, how could she do more? Marrying a man, or a woman either," Miss Barrace sagely went on, "is never the wonder, for any Jack and Jill can bring *that* off. The wonder is their doing such things without marrying."

Strether considered a moment this proposition. "You mean it's so beautiful for our friends simply to go on so?"

But whatever he said made her laugh. "Beautiful."

He nevertheless insisted. "And *that* because it's disinterested?"

She was now, however, suddenly tired of the question. "Yes, then—call it that. Besides, she'll never divorce. Don't, moreover," she added, "believe everything you hear about her husband."

"He's not then," Strether asked, "a wretch?"

"Oh yes. But charming."

"Do you know him?"

"I've met him. He's *bien aimable*."

"To every one but his wife?"

"Oh for all I know, to her too—to any, to every woman. I hope you at any rate," she pursued with a quick change, "appreciate the care I take of Mr. Waymarsh."

"Oh immensely." But Strether was not yet in line. "At all events," he roundly brought out, "the attachment's an innocent one."

"Mine and his? Ah," she laughed, "don't rob it of *all* interest!"

"I mean our friend's here—to the lady we've been speaking of." That was what he had settled to as an indirect but none the less closely involved consequence of his impression of Jeanne. That was where he meant to stay. "It's innocent," he repeated—"I see the whole thing."

Mystified by his abrupt declaration, she had glanced over at Gloriani as at the unnamed subject of his allusion, but the next moment she had understood; though indeed not before Strether had noticed her momentary mistake and wondered what might possibly be behind that too. He already knew that the sculptor admired Madame de Vionnet; but did this admiration also represent an attachment of which the innocence was discussable? He was moving verily in a strange air and on ground not of the firmest. He looked hard for an instant at Miss Barrace, but she had already gone on. "All right with Mr. Newsome? Why of course she is!"—and she got gaily back to the question of her own good friend. "I daresay you're surprised that I'm not worn out with all I see—it being so much!—of Sitting Bull. But I'm not, you know—I don't mind him; I bear up, and we get on beautifully. I'm very strange; I'm like that; and often I can't explain. There are people who are supposed interesting or remarkable or whatever, and who bore me to death; and then there are others as to whom nobody can understand what anybody sees in them—in whom I see no end of things." Then after she had smoked a moment, "He's touching, you know," she said.

"'Know'?" Strether echoed—"don't I, indeed? We must move you almost to tears."

"Oh but I don't mean *you*!" she laughed.

"You ought to then, for the worst sign of all—as I must have it for you—is that you can't help me. That's when a woman pities."

"Ah but I do help you!" she cheerfully insisted.

Again he looked at her hard, and then after a pause: "No you don't!"

Her tortoise-shell, on its long chain, rattled down. "I help you with Sitting Bull. That's a good deal."

"Oh that, yes." But Strether hesitated. "Do you mean he talks of me?"

"So that I have to defend you? No, never."

"I see," Strether mused. "It's too deep."

"That's his only fault," she returned—"that everything, with him, is too deep. He has depths of silence—which he breaks only at the longest intervals by a remark. And when the remark comes it's always something he has seen or felt for himself—never a bit banal. *That* would be what one might have feared and what would kill me. But never." She smoked again as she thus, with amused complacency, appreciated her acquisition. "And never about you. We keep clear of you. We're wonderful. But I'll tell you what he does do," she continued: "he tries to make me presents."

"Presents?" poor Strether echoed, conscious with a pang that *he* hadn't yet tried that in any quarter.

"Why you see," she explained, "he's as fine as ever in the victoria; so that when I leave him, as I often do almost for hours—he likes it so—at the doors of shops, the sight of him there helps me, when I come out, to know my carriage away off in the rank. But sometimes, for a change, he goes with me into the shops, and then I've all I can do to prevent his buying me things."

"He wants to 'treat' you?" Strether almost gasped at all he himself hadn't thought of. He had a sense of admiration. "Oh he's much more in the real tradition than I. Yes," he mused; "it's the sacred rage."

"The sacred rage, exactly!"—and Miss Barrace, who hadn't before heard this term applied, recognised its bearing with a clap of her gemmed hands. "Now I do know why he's not banal. But I do prevent him all the same—and if you saw what he sometimes selects—from buying. I save him hundreds and hundreds. I only take flowers."

"Flowers?" Strether echoed again with a rueful reflexion. How many nosegays had her present converser sent?

"Innocent flowers," she pursued, "as much as he likes. And he sends me splendours; he knows all the best places—he has found them for himself; he's wonderful."

"He hasn't told them to *me*," her friend smiled; "he has a life of his own." But Strether had swung back to the consciousness that for himself after all it never would have done. Waymarsh hadn't Mrs. Waymarsh in the least to consider, whereas Lambert Strether had constantly, in the inmost honour of his thoughts, to consider Mrs. Newsome. He liked moreover to feel how much his friend was in the real tradition. Yet he had his conclusion. "*What* a rage it is!" He had worked it out. "It's an opposition."

She followed, but at a distance. "That's what I feel. Yet to what?"

"Well, he thinks, you know, that *I've* a life of my own. And I haven't!"

"You haven't?" She showed doubt, and her laugh confirmed it. "Oh, oh, oh!"

"No—not for myself. I seem to have a life only for other people."

"Ah for them and *with* them! Just now for instance with—"

"Well, with whom?" he asked before she had had time to say.

His tone had the effect of making her hesitate and even, as he guessed, speak with a difference. "Say with Miss Gostrey. What do you do for *her*?"

It really made him wonder. "Nothing at all!"

III

Madame de Vionnet, having meanwhile come in, was at present close to them, and Miss Barrace hereupon, instead of risking a rejoinder, became again with a look that measured her from top to toe all mere long-handled appreciative tortoise-shell. She had struck our friend, from the first of her appearing, as dressed for a great occasion, and she met still more than on either of the others the conception reawakened in him at their garden-party, the idea of the *femme du monde* in her habit as she lived. Her bare shoulders and arms were white and beautiful; the materials of her dress, a mixture, as he supposed, of silk and crape, were of a silvery grey so artfully composed as to give an impression of warm splendour; and round her neck she wore a collar of large old emeralds, the green note of which was more dimly repeated, at other points of her apparel, in embroidery, in enamel, in satin, in substances and textures vaguely rich. Her head, extremely fair and exquisitely festal, was like a happy fancy, a notion of the antique, of an old precious medal, some silver coin of the Renaissance; while her slim lightness and brightness, her gaiety, her expression, her decision, contributed to an effect that might have been felt by a poet as half mythological and half conventional. He could have compared her to a goddess still partly engaged in a morning cloud, or to a sea-nymph waist-high in the summer surge. Above all she suggested to him the reflexion that the *femme du monde*—in these finest developments of the type—was, like Cleopatra in the play, indeed various and multifold. She had aspects, characters, days, nights—or had them at least, showed them by a mysterious law of her own, when in addition to everything she happened also to be a woman of genius. She was an obscure person, a muffled person one day, and a showy person, an uncovered person the next. He thought of Madame de Vionnet to-night as showy and uncovered, though he felt the formula rough, because, thanks to one of the short-cuts of genius, she had taken all his categories by surprise. Twice during dinner he had met Chad's eyes in a longish look; but these communications had in truth only stirred up again old ambiguities—so little was it clear from them whether they were an appeal or an admonition. "You see how I'm fixed" was what they appeared to convey; yet how he was fixed was exactly what Strether didn't see. However, perhaps he should see now.

"Are you capable of the very great kindness of going to relieve Newsome, for a few minutes, of the rather crushing responsibility of Madame Gloriani, while I say a word, if he'll allow me, to Mr. Strether, of whom I've a question to ask? Our host ought to talk a bit to those other ladies, and I'll come back in a minute to your rescue." She made this proposal to Miss Barrace as if her consciousness of a special duty had just flickered up, but that lady's recognition of Strether's little start at it—as at a betrayal on the speaker's part of a domesticated state—was as mute as his own comment; and after an instant, when their fellow guest had good-naturedly left them, he had been given something else to think of. "Why has Maria so suddenly gone? Do you know?" That was the question Madame de Vionnet had brought with her.

"I'm afraid I've no reason to give you but the simple reason I've had from her in a note—the sudden obligation to join in the south a sick friend who has got worse."

"Ah then she had been writing you?"

"Not since she went—I had only a brief explanatory word before she started. I went to see her," Strether explained—"it was the day after I called on you—but she was already on her way, and her concierge told me that in case of my coming I was to be informed she had written to me. I found her note when I got home."

Madame de Vionnet listened with interest and with her eyes on Strether's face; then her delicately decorated head had a small melancholy motion. "She didn't write to *me*. I went to see her," she added, "almost immediately after I had seen you, and as I assured her I would do when I met her at Gloriani's. She hadn't then told me she was to be absent, and I felt at her door as if I understood. She's absent—with all respect to her sick friend, though I know indeed she has plenty—so that I may not see her. She doesn't want to meet me again. Well," she continued with a beautiful conscious mildness, "I liked and admired her beyond every one in the old time, and she knew it—perhaps that's precisely what has made her go—and I dare say I haven't lost her for ever." Strether still said nothing; he had a horror, as he now thought of himself, of being in question between women—was in fact already quite enough on his way to that; and there was, moreover, as it came to him, perceptibly, something behind these allusions and professions that, should he take it in, would square but ill with his present resolve to simplify. It was as if, for him, all the same, her softness and sadness were sincere. He felt that not less when she soon went on: "I'm extremely glad of her happiness." But it also left him mute—sharp and fine though the imputation it conveyed. What it conveyed was that *he* was Maria Gostrey's happiness, and for the least little instant he had the impulse to challenge the thought. He could have done so however only by saying, "What then do you suppose to be between us?" and he was wonderfully glad a moment later not to have spoken. He would rather seem stupid any day than fatuous, and he drew back as well, with a smothered inward shudder, from the consideration of what women—of highly-developed type in particular—might think of each other. Whatever he had come out for he hadn't come to go into that; so that he absolutely took up nothing his interlocutress had now let drop. Yet, though he had kept away from her for days, had laid wholly on herself the burden of their meeting again, she hadn't a gleam of irritation to show him. "Well, about Jeanne now?" she smiled—it had the gaiety with which she had originally come in. He felt it on the instant to represent her motive and real errand. But he had been schooling her of a truth to say much in proportion to his little. "*Do* you make out that she has a sentiment? I mean for Mr. Newsome?"

Almost resentful, Strether could at last be prompt. "How can I make out such things?"

She remained perfectly good-natured. "Ah but they're beautiful little things, and you make out—don't pretend!—everything in the world. Haven't you," she asked, "been talking with her?"

"Yes, but not about Chad. At least not much."

"Oh you don't require 'much'!" she reassuringly declared. But she immediately changed her ground. "I hope you remember your promise of the other day."

"To 'save' you, as you called it?"

"I call it so still. You *will*?" she insisted. "You haven't repented?"

He wondered. "No—but I've been thinking what I meant."

She kept it up. "And not, a little, what *I* did?"

"No—that's not necessary. It will be enough if I know what I meant myself."

"And don't you know," she asked, "by this time?"

Again he had a pause. "I think you ought to leave it to me. But how long," he added, "do you give me?"

"It seems to me much more a question of how long you give *me*. Doesn't our friend here himself, at any rate," she went on, "perpetually make me present to you?"

"Not," Strether replied, "by ever speaking of you to me."

"He never does that?"

"Never."

She considered, and, if the fact was disconcerting to her, effectually concealed it. The next minute indeed she had recovered. "No, he wouldn't. But do you *need* that?"

Her emphasis was wonderful, and though his eyes had been wandering he looked at her longer now. "I see what you mean."

"Of course you see what I mean."

Her triumph was gentle, and she really had tones to make justice weep. "I've before me what he owes you."

"Admit then that that's something," she said, yet still with the same discretion in her pride.

He took in this note but went straight on. "You've made of him what I see, but what I don't see is how in the world you've done it."

"Ah that's another question!" she smiled. "The point is of what use is your declining to know me when to know Mr. Newsome—as you do me the honour to find him—*is* just to know me."

"I see," he mused, still with his eyes on her. "I shouldn't have met you to-night."

She raised and dropped her linked hands. "It doesn't matter. If I trust you why can't you a little trust me too? And why can't you also," she asked in another tone, "trust yourself?" But she gave him no time to reply. "Oh I shall be so easy for you! And I'm glad at any rate you've seen my child."

"I'm glad too," he said; "but she does you no good."

"No good?"—Madame de Vionnet had a clear stare. "Why, she's an angel of light."

"That's precisely the reason. Leave her alone. Don't try to find out. I mean," he explained, "about what you spoke to me of—the way she feels."

His companion wondered. "Because one really won't?"

"Well, because I ask you, as a favour to myself, not to. She's the most charming creature I've ever seen. Therefore don't touch her. Don't know—don't want to know. And moreover—yes—you *won't*."

It was an appeal, of a sudden, and she took it in. "As a favour to you?"

"Well—since you ask me."

"Anything, everything you ask," she smiled. "I shan't know then—never. Thank you," she added with peculiar gentleness as she turned away.

The sound of it lingered with him, making him fairly feel as if he had been tripped up and had a fall. In the very act of arranging with her for his independence he had, under pressure from a particular perception, inconsistently, quite stupidly, committed himself, and, with her subtlety sensitive on the spot to an advantage, she had driven in by a single word a little golden nail, the sharp intention of which he signally felt. He hadn't detached, he had more closely connected himself, and his eyes, as he considered with some intensity this circumstance, met another pair which had just come within their range and which struck him as reflecting his sense of what he had done. He recognised them at the same moment as those of little Bilham, who had apparently drawn near on purpose to speak to him, and little Bilham wasn't, in the conditions, the person to whom his heart would be most closed. They were seated together a minute later at the angle of the room obliquely opposite the corner in which Gloriani was still engaged with Jeanne de Vionnet, to whom at first and in silence their attention had been benevolently given. "I can't see for my life," Strether had then observed, "how a young fellow of any spirit—such a one as you for instance—can be admitted to the sight of that young lady without being hard hit. Why don't you go in, little Bilham?" He remembered the tone into which he had been betrayed on the garden-bench at the sculptor's reception, and this might make up for that by being much more the right sort of thing to say to a young man worthy of any advice at all. "There *would* be some reason."

"Some reason for what?"

"Why for hanging on here."

"To offer my hand and fortune to Mademoiselle de Vionnet?"

"Well," Strether asked, "to what lovelier apparition *could* you offer them? She's the sweetest little thing I've ever seen."

"She's certainly immense. I mean she's the real thing. I believe the pale pink petals are folded up there for some wondrous efflorescence in time; to open, that is, to some great golden sun. *I'm* unfortunately but a small farthing candle. What chance in such a field for a poor little painter-man?"

"Oh you're good enough," Strether threw out.

"Certainly I'm good enough. We're good enough, I consider, *nous autres*, for anything. But she's *too* good. There's the difference. They wouldn't look at me."

Strether, lounging on his divan and still charmed by the young girl, whose eyes had consciously strayed to him, he fancied, with a vague smile—Strether, enjoying the whole occasion as with dormant pulses at last awake and in spite of new material thrust upon him, thought over his companion's words. "Whom do you mean by 'they'? She and her mother?"

"She and her mother. And she had a father too, who, whatever else he may be, certainly can't be indifferent to the possibilities she represents. Besides, there's Chad."

Strether was silent a little. "Ah but he doesn't care for her—not, I mean, it appears, after all, in the sense I'm speaking of. He's *not* in love with her."

"No—but he's her best friend; after her mother. He's very fond of her. He has his ideas about what can be done for her."

"Well, it's very strange!" Strether presently remarked with a sighing sense of fullness.

"Very strange indeed. That's just the beauty of it. Isn't it very much the kind of beauty you had in mind," little Bilham went on, "when you were so wonderful and so inspiring to me the other day? Didn't you adjure me, in accents I shall never forget, to see, while I've a chance, everything I can?—and *really* to see, for it must have been that only you meant. Well, you did me no end of good, and I'm doing my best. I *do* make it out a situation."

"So do I!" Strether went on after a moment. But he had the next minute an inconsequent question. "How comes Chad so mixed up, anyway?"

"Ah, ah, ah!"—and little Bilham fell back on his cushions.

It reminded our friend of Miss Barrace, and he felt again the brush of his sense of moving in a maze of mystic closed allusions. Yet he kept hold of his thread. "Of course I understand really; only the general transformation makes me occasionally gasp. Chad with such a voice in the settlement of the future of a little countess—no," he declared, "it takes more time! You say, moreover," he resumed, "that we're inevitably, people like you and me, out of the running. The curious fact remains that Chad himself isn't. The situation doesn't make for it, but in a different one he could have her if he would."

"Yes, but that's only because he's rich and because there's a possibility of his being richer. They won't think of anything but a great name or a great fortune."

"Well," said Strether, "he'll have no great fortune on *these* lines. He must stir his stumps."

"Is that," little Bilham inquired, "what you were saying to Madame de Vionnet?"

"No—I don't say much to her. Of course, however," Strether continued, "he can make sacrifices if he likes."

Little Bilham had a pause. "Oh he's not keen for sacrifices; or thinks, that is, possibly, that he has made enough."

"Well, it *is* virtuous," his companion observed with some decision.

"That's exactly," the young man dropped after a moment, "what I mean."

It kept Strether himself silent a little. "I've made it out for myself," he then went on; "I've really, within the last half hour, got hold of it. I understand it in short at last; which at first—when you originally spoke to me—I didn't. Nor when Chad originally spoke to me either."

"Oh," said little Bilham, "I don't think that at that time you believed me."

"Yes—I did; and I believed Chad too. It would have been odious and unmannerly—as well as quite perverse—if I hadn't. What interest have you in deceiving me?"

The young man cast about. "What interest have *I*?"

"Yes. Chad *might* have. But you?"

"Ah, ah, ah!" little Bilham exclaimed.

It might, on repetition, as a mystification, have irritated our friend a little; but he knew, once more, as we have seen, where he was, and his being proof against everything was only another attestation that he meant to stay there. "I couldn't, without my own impression, realise. She's a tremendously clever brilliant capable woman, and with an extraordinary charm on top of it all—the charm we surely all of us this evening know what to think of. It isn't every clever brilliant capable woman that has it. In fact it's rare with any woman. So there you are," Strether proceeded as if not for little Bilham's benefit alone. "I understand what a relation with such a woman—what such a high fine friendship—may be. It can't be vulgar or coarse, anyway—and that's the point."

"Yes, that's the point," said little Bilham. "It can't be vulgar or coarse. And, bless us and save us, it *isn't*! It's, upon my word, the very finest thing I ever saw in my life, and the most distinguished."

Strether, from beside him and leaning back with him as he leaned, dropped on him a momentary look which filled a short interval and of which he took no notice. He only gazed before him with intent participation. "Of course what it has done for him," Strether at all events presently pursued, "of course what it has done for him—that is as to *how* it has so wonderfully worked—isn't a thing I pretend to understand. I've to take it as I find it. There he is."

"There he is!" little Bilham echoed. "And it's really and truly she. I don't understand either, even with my longer and closer opportunity. But I'm like you," he added; "I can admire and rejoice even when I'm a little in the dark. You see I've watched it for some three years, and especially for this last. He wasn't so bad before it as I seem to have made out that you think—"

"Oh I don't think anything now!" Strether impatiently broke in: "that is but what I *do* think! I mean that originally, for her to have cared for him—"

"There must have been stuff in him? Oh yes, there was stuff indeed, and much more of it than ever showed, I daresay, at home. Still, you know," the young man in all fairness developed, "there was room for her, and that's where she came in. She saw her chance and took it. That's what strikes me as having been so fine. But of course," he wound up, "he liked her first."

"Naturally," said Strether.

"I mean that they first met somehow and somewhere—I believe in some American house—and she, without in the least then intending it, made her impression. Then with time and opportunity he made his; and after *that* she was as bad as he."

Strether vaguely took it up. "As 'bad'?"

"She began, that is, to care—to care very much. Alone, and in her horrid position, she found it, when once she had started, an interest. It was, it is, an interest; and it did—it continues to do—a lot for herself as well. So she still cares. She cares in fact," said little Bilham thoughtfully, "more."

Strether's theory that it was none of his business was somehow not damaged by the way he took this. "More, you mean, than he?" On which his companion looked round at him, and now for an instant their eyes met. "More than he?" he repeated.

Little Bilham, for as long, hung fire. "Will you never tell any one?"

Strether thought. "Whom should I tell?"

"Why I supposed you reported regularly—"

"To people at home?"—Strether took him up. "Well, I won't tell them this."

The young man at last looked away. "Then she does now care more than he."

"Oh!" Strether oddly exclaimed.

But his companion immediately met it. "Haven't you after all had your impression of it? That's how you've got hold of him."

"Ah but I haven't got hold of him!"

"Oh I say!" But it was all little Bilham said.

"It's at any rate none of my business. I mean," Strether explained, "nothing else than getting hold of him is." It appeared, however, to strike him as his business to add: "The fact remains nevertheless that she has saved him."

Little Bilham just waited. "I thought that was what *you* were to do."

But Strether had his answer ready. "I'm speaking—in connexion with her—of his manners and morals, his character and life. I'm speaking of him as a person to deal with and talk with and live with—speaking of him as a social animal."

"And isn't it as a social animal that you also want him?"

"Certainly; so that it's as if she had saved him *for* us."

"It strikes you accordingly then," the young man threw out, "as for you all to save *her*?"

"Oh for us 'all'—!" Strether could but laugh at that. It brought him back, however, to the point he had really wished to make. "They've accepted their situation—hard as it is. They're not free—at least, she's not; but they take what's left to them. It's a friendship, of a beautiful sort; and that's what makes them so strong. They're straight, they feel; and they keep each other up. It's doubtless she, however, who, as you yourself have hinted, feels it most."

Little Bilham appeared to wonder what he had hinted. "Feels most that they're straight?"

"Well, feels that *she* is, and the strength that comes from it. She keeps *him* up—she keeps the whole thing up. When people are able to it's fine. She's wonderful, wonderful, as Miss Barrace says; and he is, in his way, too; however, as a mere man, he may sometimes rebel and not feel that he finds his account in it. She has simply given him an immense moral lift, and what that can explain is prodigious. That's why I speak of it as a situation. It *is* one, if there ever was." And Strether, with his head back and his eyes on the ceiling, seemed to lose himself in the vision of it.

His companion attended deeply. "You state it much better than I could."

"Oh you see it doesn't concern you."

Little Bilham considered. "I thought you said just now that it doesn't concern you either."

"Well, it doesn't a bit, as Madame de Vionnet's affair. But as we were again saying just now, what did I come out for but to save him?"

"Yes—to remove him."

"To save him *by* removal; to win him over to *himself* thinking it best he shall take up business—thinking he must immediately do therefore what is necessary to that end."

"Well," said little Bilham after a moment, "you *have* won him over. He does think it best. He has within a day or two again said to me as much."

"And that," Strether asked, "is why you considered that he cares less than she?"

"Cares less for her than she for him? Yes, that's one of the reasons. But other things too have given me the impression. A man, don't you think?" little Bilham presently pursued, "*can't*, in such conditions, care so much as a woman. It takes different conditions to make him, and then perhaps he cares more. Chad," he wound up, "has his possible future before him."

"Are you speaking of his business future?"

"No—on the contrary; of the other, the future of what you so justly call their situation. Monsieur de Vionnet may live for ever."

"So that they can't marry?"

The young man waited a moment. "Not being able to marry is all they've with any confidence to look forward to. A woman—a particular woman—may stand that strain. But can a man?" he propounded.

Strether's answer was as prompt as if he had already, for himself, worked it out. "Not without a very high ideal of conduct. But that's just what we're attributing to Chad. And how, for that matter," he mused, "does his going to America diminish the particular strain? Wouldn't it seem rather to add to it?"

"Out of sight out of mind!" his companion laughed. Then more bravely: "Wouldn't distance lessen the torment?" But before Strether could reply, "The thing is, you see, Chad ought to marry!" he wound up.

Strether, for a little, appeared to think of it. "If you talk of torments you don't diminish mine!" he then broke out. The next moment he was on his feet with a question. "He ought to marry whom?"

Little Bilham rose more slowly. "Well, some one he *can*—some thoroughly nice girl."

Strether's eyes, as they stood together, turned again to Jeanne. "Do you mean *her*?"

His friend made a sudden strange face. "After being in love with her mother? No."

"But isn't it exactly your idea that he *isn't* in love with her mother?"

His friend once more had a pause. "Well, he isn't at any rate with Jeanne."

"I daresay not."

"How *can* he be with any other woman?"

"Oh that I admit. But being in love isn't, you know, here"—little Bilham spoke in friendly reminder—"thought necessary, in strictness, for marriage."

"And what torment—to call a torment—can there ever possibly be with a woman like that?" As if from the interest of his own question Strether had gone on without hearing. "Is it for her to have turned a man out so wonderfully, too, only for somebody else?" He appeared to make a point of this, and little Bilham looked at him now. "When it's for each other that people give things up they don't miss them." Then he threw off as with an extravagance of which he was conscious: "Let them face the future together!"

Little Bilham looked at him indeed. "You mean that after all he shouldn't go back?"

"I mean that if he gives her up—!"

"Yes?"

"Well, he ought to be ashamed of himself." But Strether spoke with a sound that might have passed for a laugh.

BOOK SEVENTH

I

It wasn't the first time Strether had sat alone in the great dim church—still less was it the first of his giving himself up, so far as conditions permitted, to its beneficent action on his nerves. He had been to Notre Dame with Waymarsh, he had been there with Miss Gostrey, he had been there with Chad Newsome, and had found the place, even in company, such a refuge from the obsession of his problem that, with renewed pressure from that source, he had not unnaturally recurred to a remedy meeting the case, for the moment, so indirectly, no doubt, but so relievingly. He was conscious enough that it was only for the moment, but good moments—if he could call them good—still had their value for a man who by this time struck himself as living almost disgracefully from hand to mouth. Having so well learnt the way, he had lately made the pilgrimage more than once by himself—had quite stolen off, taking an unnoticed chance and making no point of speaking of the adventure when restored to his friends.

His great friend, for that matter, was still absent, as well as remarkably silent; even at the end of three weeks Miss Gostrey hadn't come back. She wrote to him from Mentone, admitting that he must judge her grossly inconsequent—perhaps in fact for the time odiously faithless; but asking for patience, for a deferred sentence throwing herself in short on his generosity. For her too, she could assure him, life was complicated—more complicated than he could have guessed; she had moreover made certain of him—certain of not wholly missing him on her return—before her disappearance. If furthermore she didn't burden him with letters it was frankly because of her sense of the other great commerce he had to carry on. He himself, at the end of a fortnight, had written twice, to show how his generosity could be trusted; but he reminded himself in each case of Mrs. Newsome's epistolary manner at the times when Mrs. Newsome kept off delicate ground. He sank his problem, he talked of Waymarsh and Miss Barrace, of little Bilham and the set over the river, with whom he had again had tea, and he was easy, for convenience, about Chad and Madame de Vionnet and Jeanne. He admitted that he continued to see them, he was decidedly so confirmed a haunter of Chad's premises, and that young man's practical intimacy with them was so undeniably great; but he had his reason for not attempting to render for Miss Gostrey's benefit the impression of these last days. That would be to tell her too much about himself—it being at present just from himself he was trying to escape.

This small struggle sprang not a little, in its way, from the same impulse that had now carried him across to Notre Dame; the impulse to let things be, to give them time to justify themselves or at least to pass. He was aware of having no errand in such a place but the desire not to be, for the hour, in certain other places; a sense of safety, of simplification, which each time he yielded to it he amused himself by thinking of as a private concession to cowardice. The great church had no altar for his worship, no direct voice for his soul; but it was none the less soothing even to sanctity; for he could feel while there what he couldn't elsewhere, that he was a plain tired man taking the holiday he had earned. He was tired, but he wasn't plain—that was the pity and the trouble of it; he was able, however, to drop his problem at the door very much as if it had been the copper piece that he deposited, on the threshold, in the receptacle of the inveterate blind beggar. He trod the long dim nave, sat in the splendid choir, paused before the clustered chapels of the east end, and the mighty monument laid upon him its spell. He might have been a student under the charm of a museum—which was exactly what, in a foreign town, in the afternoon of life, he would have liked to be free to be. This form of sacrifice did at any rate for the occasion as well as another; it made him quite sufficiently understand how, within the precinct, for the real refugee, the things of the world could fall into abeyance. That was the cowardice, probably—to dodge them, to beg the question, not to deal with it in the hard outer light; but his own oblivions were too brief, too vain, to hurt any one but himself, and he had a vague and fanciful kindness for certain persons whom he met, figures of mystery and anxiety, and whom, with observation for his pastime, he ranked as those who were fleeing from justice. Justice was outside, in the hard light, and injustice too; but one was as absent as the other from the air of the long aisles and the brightness of the many altars.

Thus it was, at all events that, one morning some dozen days after the dinner in the Boulevard Malesherbes at which Madame de Vionnet had been present with her daughter, he was called upon to play his part in an encounter that deeply stirred his imagination. He had the habit, in these contemplations, of watching a fellow visitant, here and there, from a respectable distance, remarking some note of behaviour, of penitence, of prostration, of the absolved, relieved state; this was the manner in which his vague tenderness took its course, the degree of demonstration to which it naturally had to confine itself. It hadn't indeed so felt its responsibility as when on this occasion he suddenly measured the suggestive effect of a lady whose supreme stillness, in the shade of one of the chapels, he had two or three times noticed as he made, and made once more, his slow circuit. She wasn't prostrate—not in any degree bowed, but she was strangely fixed, and her prolonged immobility showed her, while he passed, and paused, as wholly given up to the need, whatever it was, that had brought her there. She only sat and gazed before her, as he himself often sat; but she had placed herself, as he never did, within the focus of the shrine, and she had lost herself, he could easily see, as he would only have liked to do. She was not a wandering alien, keeping back more than she gave, but one of the familiar, the intimate, the fortunate, for whom these dealings had a method and a meaning. She reminded our friend—since it was the way of nine-tenths of his current impressions to act as recalls of things imagined—of some fine firm concentrated heroine of an old story, something he had heard, read, something that, had he had a hand for drama, he might himself have written, renewing her courage, renewing her clearness, in splendidly-protected meditation. Her back, as she sat, was turned to him, but his impression absolutely required that she should be young and interesting, and she carried her head moreover, even in the sacred shade, with a discernible faith in herself, a kind of implied conviction of consistency, security, impunity. But what had such a woman come for if she hadn't come to pray? Strether's reading of such matters was, it must be owned, confused; but he wondered if her attitude were some congruous fruit of absolution, of "indulgence." He knew but dimly what indulgence, in such a place, might mean; yet he had, as with a soft sweep, a vision of how it might indeed add to the zest of active rites. All this was a good deal to have been denoted by a mere lurking figure who was nothing to him; but, the last thing before leaving the church, he had the surprise of a still deeper quickening.

He had dropped upon a seat halfway down the nave and, again in the museum mood, was trying with head thrown back and eyes aloft, to reconstitute a past, to reduce it in fact to the convenient terms of Victor Hugo, whom, a few days before, giving the rein for once in a way to the joy of life, he had purchased in seventy bound volumes, a miracle of cheapness, parted with, he was assured by the shopman, at the price of the red-and-gold alone. He looked, doubtless, while he played his eternal nippers over Gothic glooms, sufficiently rapt in reverence; but what his thought had finally bumped against was the question of where, among packed accumulations, so multiform a wedge would be able to enter. Were seventy volumes in red-and-gold to be perhaps what he should most substantially have to show at Woollett as the fruit of his mission? It was a possibility that held him a minute—held him till he happened to feel that some one, unnoticed, had approached him and paused. Turning, he saw that a lady stood there as for a greeting, and he sprang up as he next took her, securely, for Madame de Vionnet, who appeared to have recognised him as she passed near him on her way to the door. She checked, quickly and gaily, a certain confusion in him, came to meet it, turned it back, by an art of her own; the confusion having threatened him as he knew her for the person he had lately been observing. She was the lurking figure of the dim chapel; she had occupied him more than she guessed; but it came to him in time, luckily, that he needn't tell her and that no harm, after all, had been done. She herself, for that matter, straightway showed she felt their encounter as the happiest of accidents, had for him a "You come here too?" that despoiled surprise of every awkwardness.

"I come often," she said; "I love this place, but I'm terrible, in general, for churches. The old women who live in them all know me; in fact I'm already myself one of the old women. It's like that, at all events, that I foresee I shall end." Looking about for a chair, so that he instantly pulled one nearer, she sat down with him again to the sound of an "Oh, I like so much your also being fond—!"

He confessed the extent of his feeling, though she left the object vague; and he was struck with the tact, the taste of her vagueness, which simply took for granted in him a sense of beautiful things. He was conscious of how much it was affected, this sense, by something subdued and discreet in the way she had arranged herself for her special object and her morning walk—he believed her to have come on foot; the way her slightly thicker veil was drawn—a mere touch, but everything; the composed gravity of her dress, in which, here and there, a dull wine-colour seemed to gleam faintly through black; the charming discretion of her small compact head; the quiet note, as she sat, of her folded, grey-gloved hands. It was, to Strether's mind, as if she sat on her own ground, the light honours of which, at an open gate, she thus easily did him, while all the vastness and mystery of the domain stretched off behind. When people were so completely in possession they could be extraordinarily civil; and our friend had indeed at this hour a kind of revelation of her heritage. She was romantic for him far beyond what she could have guessed, and again he found his small comfort in the conviction that, subtle though she was, his impression must remain a secret from her. The thing that, once more, made him uneasy for secrets in general was this particular patience she could have with his own want of colour; albeit that on the other hand his uneasiness pretty well dropped after he had been for ten minutes as colourless as possible and at the same time as responsive.

The moments had already, for that matter, drawn their deepest tinge from the special interest excited in him by his vision of his companion's identity with the person whose attitude before the glimmering altar had so impressed him. This attitude fitted admirably into the stand he had privately taken about her connexion with Chad on the last occasion of his seeing them together. It helped him to stick fast at the point he had then reached; it was there he had resolved that he *would* stick, and at no moment since had it seemed as easy to do so. Unassailably innocent was a relation that could make one of the parties to it so carry herself. If it wasn't innocent why did she haunt the churches?—into which, given the woman he could believe he made out, she would never have come to flaunt an insolence of guilt. She haunted them for continued help, for strength, for peace—sublime support which, if one were able to look at it so, she found from day to day. They talked in low easy tones and with lifted lingering looks, about the great monument and its history and its beauty—all of which, Madame de Vionnet professed, came to her most in the other, the outer view. "We'll presently, after we go," she said, "walk round it again if you like. I'm not in a particular hurry, and it will be pleasant to look at it well with you." He had spoken of the great romancer and the great romance, and of what, to his imagination, they had done for the whole, mentioning to her moreover the exorbitance of his purchase, the seventy blazing volumes that were so out of proportion.

"Out of proportion to what?"

"Well, to any other plunge." Yet he felt even as he spoke how at that instant he was plunging. He had made up his mind and was impatient to get into the air; for his purpose was a purpose to be uttered outside, and he had a fear that it might with delay still slip away from him. She however took her time; she drew out their quiet gossip as if she had wished to profit by their meeting, and this confirmed precisely an interpretation of her manner, of her mystery. While she rose, as he would have called it, to the question of Victor Hugo, her voice itself, the light low quaver of her deference to the solemnity about them, seemed to make her words mean something that they didn't mean openly. Help, strength, peace, a sublime support—she hadn't found so much of these things as that the amount wouldn't be sensibly greater for any scrap his appearance of faith in her might enable her to feel in her hand. Every little, in a long strain, helped, and if he happened to affect her as a firm object she could hold on by, he wouldn't jerk himself out of her reach. People in difficulties held on by what was nearest, and he was perhaps after all not further off than sources of comfort more abstract. It was as to this he had made up his mind; he had made it up, that is, to give her a sign. The sign would be that—though it was her own affair—he understood; the sign would be that—though it was her own affair—she was free to clutch. Since she took him for a firm object—much as he might to his own sense appear at times to rock—he would do his best to *be* one.

The end of it was that half an hour later they were seated together for an early luncheon at a wonderful, a delightful house of entertainment on the left bank—a place of pilgrimage for the knowing, they were both aware, the knowing who came, for its great renown, the homage of restless days, from the other end of the town. Strether had already been there three times—first with Miss Gostrey, then with Chad, then with Chad again and with Waymarsh and little Bilham, all of whom he had himself sagaciously entertained; and his pleasure was deep now on learning that Madame de Vionnet hadn't yet been initiated. When he had said, as they strolled round the church, by the river, acting at last on what, within, he had made up his mind to, "Will you, if you have time, come to déjeuner with me somewhere? For instance, if you know it, over there on the other side, which is so easy a walk"—and then had named the place; when he had done this she stopped short as for quick intensity, and yet deep difficulty, of response. She took in the proposal as if it were almost too charming to be true; and there had perhaps never yet been for her companion so unexpected a moment of pride—so fine, so odd a case, at any rate, as his finding himself thus able to offer to a person in such universal possession a new, a rare amusement. She had heard of the happy spot, but she asked him in reply to a further question how in the world he could suppose her to have been there. He supposed himself to have supposed that Chad might have taken her, and she guessed this the next moment, to his no small discomfort.

"Ah, let me explain," she smiled, "that I don't go about with him in public; I never have such chances—not having them otherwise—and it's just the sort of thing that, as a quiet creature living in my hole, I adore." It was more than kind of him to have thought of it—though, frankly, if he asked whether she had time she hadn't a single minute. That however made no difference—she'd throw everything over. Every duty at home, domestic, maternal, social, awaited her; but it was a case for a high line. Her affairs would go to smash, but hadn't one a right to one's snatch of scandal when one was prepared to pay? It was on this pleasant basis of costly disorder, consequently, that they eventually seated themselves, on either side of a small table, at a window adjusted to the busy quay and the shining barge-burdened Seine; where, for an hour, in the matter of letting himself go, of diving deep, Strether was to feel that he had touched bottom. He was to feel many things on this occasion, and one of the first of them was that he had travelled far since that evening in London, before the theatre, when his dinner with Maria Gostrey, between the pink-shaded candles, had struck him as requiring so many explanations. He had at that time gathered them in, the explanations—he had stored them up; but it was at present as if he had either soared above or sunk below them—he couldn't tell which; he could somehow think of none that didn't seem to leave the appearance of collapse and cynicism easier for him than lucidity. How could he wish it to be lucid for others, for any one, that he, for the hour, saw reasons enough in the mere way the bright clean ordered waterside life came in at the open window?—the mere way Madame de Vionnet, opposite him over their intensely white table-linen, their *omelette aux tomates*, their bottle of straw-coloured Chablis, thanked him for everything almost with the smile of a child, while her grey eyes moved in and out of their talk, back to the quarter of the warm spring air, in which early summer had already begun to throb, and then back again to his face and their human questions.

Their human questions became many before they had done—many more, as one after the other came up, than our friend's free fancy had at all foreseen. The sense he had had before, the sense he had had repeatedly, the sense that the situation was running away with him, had never been so sharp as now; and all the more that he could perfectly put his finger on the moment it had taken the bit in its teeth. That accident had definitely occurred, the other evening, after Chad's dinner; it had occurred, as he fully knew, at the moment when he interposed between this lady and her child, when he suffered himself so to discuss with her a matter closely concerning them that her own subtlety, marked by its significant "Thank you!" instantly sealed the occasion in her favour. Again he had held off for ten days, but the situation had continued out of hand in spite of that; the fact that it was running so fast being indeed just *why* he had held off. What had come over him as he recognised her in the nave of the church was that holding off could be but a losing game from the instant she was worked for not only by her subtlety, but by the hand of fate itself. If all the accidents were to fight on her side—and by the actual showing they loomed large—he could only give himself up. This was what he had done in privately deciding then and there to propose she should breakfast with him. What did the success of his proposal in fact resemble but the smash in which a regular runaway probably ends? The smash was their walk, their déjeuner, their omelette, the Chablis, the place, the view, their present talk and his present pleasure in it—to say nothing, wonders of wonders, of her own. To this tune and nothing less, accordingly, was his surrender made good. It sufficiently lighted up at least the folly of holding off. Ancient proverbs sounded, for his memory, in the tone of their words and the clink of their glasses, in the hum of the town and the plash of the river. It *was* clearly better to suffer as a sheep than as a lamb. One might as well perish by the sword as by famine.

"Maria's still away?"—that was the first thing she had asked him; and when he had found the frankness to be cheerful about it in spite of the meaning he knew her to attach to Miss Gostrey's absence, she had gone on to inquire if he didn't tremendously miss her. There were reasons that made him by no means sure, yet he nevertheless answered "Tremendously"; which she took in as if it were all she had wished to prove. Then, "A man in trouble *must* be possessed somehow of a woman," she said; "if she doesn't come in one way she comes in another."

"Why do you call me a man in trouble?"

"Ah because that's the way you strike me." She spoke ever so gently and as with all fear of wounding him while she sat partaking of his bounty. "*Aren't* you in trouble?"

He felt himself colour at the question, and then he hated that—hated to pass for anything so idiotic as woundable. Woundable by Chad's lady, in respect to whom he had come out with such a fund of indifference—was he already at that point? Perversely, none the less, his pause gave a strange air of truth to her supposition; and what was he in fact but disconcerted at having struck her just in the way he had most dreamed of not doing? "I'm not in trouble yet," he at last smiled. "I'm not in trouble now."

"Well, I'm always so. But that you sufficiently know." She was a woman who, between courses, could be graceful with her elbows on the table. It was a posture unknown to Mrs. Newsome, but it was easy for a *femme du monde*. "Yes—I am 'now'!"

"There was a question you put to me," he presently returned, "the night of Chad's dinner. I didn't answer it then, and it has been very handsome of you not to have sought an occasion for pressing me about it since."

She was instantly all there. "Of course I know what you allude to. I asked you what you had meant by saying, the day you came to see me, just before you left me, that you'd save me. And you then said—at our friend's—that you'd have really to wait to see, for yourself, what you did mean."

"Yes, I asked for time," said Strether. "And it sounds now, as you put it, like a very ridiculous speech."

"Oh!" she murmured—she was full of attenuation. But she had another thought. "If it does sound ridiculous why do you deny that you're in trouble?"

"Ah if I were," he replied, "it wouldn't be the trouble of fearing ridicule. I don't fear it."

"What then do you?"

"Nothing—now." And he leaned back in his chair.

"I like your 'now'!" she laughed across at him.

"Well, it's precisely that it fully comes to me at present that I've kept you long enough. I know by this time, at any rate, what I meant by my speech; and I really knew it the night of Chad's dinner."

"Then why didn't you tell me?"

"Because it was difficult at the moment. I had already at that moment done something for you, in the sense of what I had said the day I went to see you; but I wasn't then sure of the importance I might represent this as having."

She was all eagerness. "And you're sure now?"

"Yes; I see that, practically, I've done for you—had done for you when you put me your question—all that it's as yet possible to me to do. I feel now," he went on, "that it may go further than I thought. What I did after my visit to you," he explained, "was to write straight off to Mrs. Newsome about you, and I'm at last, from one day to the other, expecting her answer. It's this answer that will represent, as I believe, the consequences."

Patient and beautiful was her interest. "I see—the consequences of your speaking for me." And she waited as if not to hustle him.

He acknowledged it by immediately going on. "The question, you understand, was *how* I should save you. Well, I'm trying it by thus letting her know that I consider you worth saving."

"I see—I see." Her eagerness broke through.

"How can I thank you enough?" He couldn't tell her that, however, and she quickly pursued. "You do really, for yourself, consider it?"

His only answer at first was to help her to the dish that had been freshly put before them. "I've written to her again since then—I've left her in no doubt of what I think. I've told her all about you."

"Thanks—not so much. 'All about' me," she went on—"yes."

"All it seems to me you've done for him."

"Ah and you might have added all it seems to *me*!" She laughed again, while she took up her knife and fork, as in the cheer of these assurances. "But you're not sure how she'll take it."

"No, I'll not pretend I'm sure."

"Voilà." And she waited a moment. "I wish you'd tell me about her."

"Oh," said Strether with a slightly strained smile, "all that need concern you about her is that she's really a grand person."

Madame de Vionnet seemed to demur. "Is that all that need concern me about her?"

But Strether neglected the question. "Hasn't Chad talked to you?"

"Of his mother? Yes a great deal—immensely. But not from your point of view."

"He can't," our friend returned, "have said any ill of her."

"Not the least bit. He has given me, like you, the assurance that she's really grand. But her being really grand is somehow just what hasn't seemed to simplify our case. Nothing," she continued, "is further from me than to wish to say a word against her; but of course I feel how little she can like being told of her owing me anything. No woman ever enjoys such an obligation to another woman."

This was a proposition Strether couldn't contradict. "And yet what other way could I have expressed to her what I felt? It's what there was most to say about you."

"Do you mean then that she *will* be good to me?"

"It's what I'm waiting to see. But I've little doubt she would," he added, "if she could comfortably see you."

It seemed to strike her as a happy, a beneficent thought. "Oh then couldn't that be managed? Wouldn't she come out? Wouldn't she if you so put it to her? *Did* you by any possibility?" she faintly quavered.

"Oh no"—he was prompt. "Not that. It would be, much more, to give an account of you that—since there's no question of *your* paying the visit—I should go home first."

It instantly made her graver. "And are you thinking of that?"

"Oh all the while, naturally."

"Stay with us—stay with us!" she exclaimed on this. "That's your only way to make sure."

"To make sure of what?"

"Why that he doesn't break up. You didn't come out to do that to him."

"Doesn't it depend," Strether returned after a moment, "on what you mean by breaking up?"

"Oh you know well enough what I mean!"

His silence seemed again for a little to denote an understanding. "You take for granted remarkable things."

"Yes, I do—to the extent that I don't take for granted vulgar ones. You're perfectly capable of seeing that what you came out for wasn't really at all to do what you'd now have to do."

"Ah it's perfectly simple," Strether good-humouredly pleaded. "I've had but one thing to do—to put our case before him. To put it as it could only be put here on the spot—by personal pressure. My dear lady," he lucidly pursued, "my work, you see, is really done, and my reasons for staying on even another day are none of the best. Chad's in possession of our case and professes to do it full justice. What remains is with himself. I've had my rest, my amusement, and refreshment; I've had, as we say at Woollett, a lovely time. Nothing in it has been more lovely than this happy meeting with you—in these fantastic conditions to which you've so delightfully consented. I've a sense of success. It's what I wanted. My getting all this good is what Chad has waited for, and I gather that if I'm ready to go he's the same."

She shook her head with a finer deeper wisdom. "You're not ready. If you're ready why did you write to Mrs. Newsome in the sense you've mentioned to me?"

Strether considered. "I shan't go before I hear from her. You're too much afraid of her," he added.

It produced between them a long look from which neither shrank. "I don't think you believe that—believe I've not really reason to fear her."

"She's capable of great generosity," Strether presently declared.

"Well then let her trust me a little. That's all I ask. Let her recognise in spite of everything what I've done."

"Ah remember," our friend replied, "that she can't effectually recognise it without seeing it for herself. Let Chad go over and show her what you've done, and let him plead with her there for it and, as it were, for *you*."

She measured the depth of this suggestion. "Do you give your word of honour that if she once has him there she won't do her best to marry him?"

It made her companion, this inquiry, look again a while out at the view; after which he spoke without sharpness. "When she sees for herself what he is—"

But she had already broken in. "It's when she sees for herself what he is that she'll want to marry him most."

Strether's attitude, that of due deference to what she said, permitted him to attend for a minute to his luncheon. "I doubt if that will come off. It won't be easy to make it."

"It will be easy if he remains there—and he'll remain for the money. The money appears to be, as a probability, so hideously much."

"Well," Strether presently concluded, "nothing *could* really hurt you but his marrying."

She gave a strange light laugh. "Putting aside what may really hurt *him*."

But her friend looked at her as if he had thought of that too. "The question will come up, of course, of the future that you yourself offer him."

She was leaning back now, but she fully faced him. "Well, let it come up!"

"The point is that it's for Chad to make of it what he can. His being proof against marriage will show what he does make."

"If he *is* proof, yes"—she accepted the proposition. "But for myself," she added, "the question is what *you* make."

"Ah I make nothing. It's not my affair."

"I beg your pardon. It's just there that, since you've taken it up and are committed to it, it most intensely becomes yours. You're not saving me, I take it, for your interest in myself, but for your interest in our friend. The one's at any rate wholly dependent on the other. You can't in honour not see me through," she wound up, "because you can't in honour not see *him*."

Strange and beautiful to him was her quiet soft acuteness. The thing that most moved him was really that she was so deeply serious. She had none of the portentous forms of it, but he had never come in contact, it struck him, with a force brought to so fine a head. Mrs. Newsome, goodness knew, was serious; but it was nothing to this. He took it all in, he saw it all together. "No," he mused, "I can't in honour not see him."

Her face affected him as with an exquisite light. "You *will* then?"

"I will."

At this she pushed back her chair and was the next moment on her feet. "Thank you!" she said with her hand held out to him across the table and with no less a meaning in the words than her lips had so particularly given them after Chad's dinner. The golden nail she had then driven in pierced a good inch deeper. Yet he reflected that he himself had only meanwhile done what he had made up his mind to on the same occasion. So far as the essence of the matter went he had simply stood fast on the spot on which he had then planted his feet.

II

He received three days after this a communication from America, in the form of a scrap of blue paper folded and gummed, not reaching him through his bankers, but delivered at his hotel by a small boy in uniform, who, under instructions from the concierge, approached him as he slowly paced the little court. It was the evening hour, but daylight was long now and Paris more than ever penetrating. The scent of flowers was in the streets, he had the whiff of violets perpetually in his nose; and he had attached himself to sounds and suggestions, vibrations of the air, human and dramatic, he imagined, as they were not in other places, that came out for him more and more as the mild afternoons deepened—a far-off hum, a sharp near click on the asphalt, a voice calling, replying, somewhere and as full of tone as an actor's in a play. He was to dine at home, as usual, with Waymarsh—they had settled to that for thrift and simplicity; and he now hung about before his friend came down.

He read his telegram in the court, standing still a long time where he had opened it and giving five minutes afterwards to the renewed study of it. At last, quickly, he crumpled it up as if to get it out of the way; in spite of which, however, he kept it there—still kept it when, at the end of another turn, he had dropped into a chair placed near a small table. Here, with his scrap of paper compressed in his fist and further concealed by his folding his arms tight, he sat for some time in thought, gazed before him so straight that Waymarsh appeared and approached him without catching his eye. The latter in fact, struck with his appearance, looked at him hard for a single instant and then, as if determined to that course by some special vividness in it, dropped back into the *salon de lecture* without addressing him. But the pilgrim from Milrose permitted himself still to observe the scene from behind the clear glass plate of that retreat. Strether ended, as he sat, by a fresh scrutiny of his compressed missive, which he smoothed out carefully again as he placed it on his table. There it remained for some minutes, until, at last looking up, he saw Waymarsh watching him from within. It was on this that their eyes met—met for a moment during which neither moved. But Strether then got up, folding his telegram more carefully and putting it into his waistcoat pocket.

A few minutes later the friends were seated together at dinner; but Strether had meanwhile said nothing about it, and they eventually parted, after coffee in the court, with nothing said on either side. Our friend had moreover the consciousness that even less than usual was on this occasion said between them, so that it was almost as if each had been waiting for something from the other. Waymarsh had always more or less the air of sitting at the door of his tent, and silence, after so many weeks, had come to play its part in their concert. This note indeed, to Strether's sense, had lately taken a fuller tone, and it was his fancy to-night that they had never quite so drawn it out. Yet it befell, none the less, that he closed the door to confidence when his companion finally asked him if there were anything particular the matter with him. "Nothing," he replied, "more than usual."

On the morrow, however, at an early hour, he found occasion to give an answer more in consonance with the facts. What was the matter had continued to be so all the previous evening, the first hours of which, after dinner, in his room, he had devoted to the copious composition of a letter. He had quitted Waymarsh for this purpose, leaving him to his own resources with less ceremony than their wont, but finally coming down again with his letter unconcluded and going forth into the streets without inquiry for his comrade. He had taken a long vague walk, and one o'clock had struck before his return and his re-ascent to his room by the aid of the glimmering candle-end left for him on the shelf outside the porter's lodge. He had possessed himself, on closing his door, of the numerous loose sheets of his unfinished composition, and then, without reading them over, had torn them into small pieces. He had thereupon slept—as if it had been in some measure thanks to that sacrifice—the sleep of the just, and had prolonged his rest considerably beyond his custom. Thus it was that when between nine and ten, the tap of the knob of a walking-stick sounded on his door, he had not yet made himself altogether presentable. Chad Newsome's bright deep voice determined quickly enough none the less the admission of the visitor. The little blue paper of the evening before, plainly an object the more precious for its escape from premature destruction, now lay on the sill of the open window, smoothed out afresh and kept from blowing away by the superincumbent weight of his watch. Chad, looking about with careless and competent criticism, as he looked wherever he went, immediately espied it and permitted himself to fix it for a moment rather hard. After which he turned his eyes to his host. "It has come then at last?"

Strether paused in the act of pinning his necktie. "Then you know—? You have had one too?"

"No, I've had nothing, and I only know what I see. I see that thing and I guess. Well," he added, "it comes as pat as in a play, for I've precisely turned up this morning—as I would have done yesterday, but it was impossible—to take you."

"To take me?" Strether had turned again to his glass.

"Back, at last, as I promised. I'm ready—I've really been ready this month. I've only been waiting for you—as was perfectly right. But you're better now; you're safe—I see that for myself; you've got all your good. You're looking, this morning, as fit as a flea."

Strether, at his glass, finished dressing; consulting that witness moreover on this last question. *Was* he looking preternaturally fit? There was something in it perhaps for Chad's wonderful eye, but he had felt himself for hours rather in pieces. Such a judgement, however, was after all but a contribution to his resolve; it testified unwittingly to his wisdom. He was still firmer, apparently—since it shone in him as a light—than he had flattered himself. His firmness indeed was slightly compromised, as he faced about to his friend, by the way this very personage looked—though the case would of course have been worse hadn't the secret of personal magnificence been at every hour Chad's unfailing possession. There he was in all the pleasant morning freshness of it—strong and sleek and gay, easy and fragrant and fathomless, with happy health in his colour, and pleasant silver in his thick young hair, and the right word for everything on the lips that his clear brownness caused to show as red. He had never struck Strether as personally such a success; it was as if now, for his definite surrender, he had gathered himself vividly together. This, sharply and rather strangely, was the form in which he was to be presented to Woollett. Our friend took him in again—he was always taking him in and yet finding that parts of him still remained out; though even thus his image showed through a mist of other things. "I've had a cable," Strether said, "from your mother."

"I dare say, my dear man. I hope she's well."

Strether hesitated. "No—she's not well, I'm sorry to have to tell you."

"Ah," said Chad, "I must have had the instinct of it. All the more reason then that we should start straight off."

Strether had now got together hat, gloves and stick, but Chad had dropped on the sofa as if to show where he wished to make his point. He kept observing his companion's things; he might have been judging how quickly they could be packed. He might even have wished to hint that he'd send his own servant to assist. "What do you mean," Strether inquired, "by 'straight off'?"

"Oh by one of next week's boats. Everything at this season goes out so light that berths will be easy anywhere."

Strether had in his hand his telegram, which he had kept there after attaching his watch, and he now offered it to Chad, who, however, with an odd movement, declined to take it. "Thanks, I'd rather not. Your correspondence with Mother's your own affair. I'm only *with* you both on it, whatever it is." Strether, at this, while their eyes met, slowly folded the missive and put it in his pocket; after which, before he had spoken again, Chad broke fresh ground. "Has Miss Gostrey come back?"

But when Strether presently spoke it wasn't in answer. "It's not, I gather, that your mother's physically ill; her health, on the whole, this spring, seems to have been better than usual. But she's worried, she's anxious, and it appears to have risen within the last few days to a climax. We've tired out, between us, her patience."

"Oh it isn't *you*!" Chad generously protested.

"I beg your pardon—it *is* me." Strether was mild and melancholy, but firm. He saw it far away and over his companion's head. "It's very particularly me."

"Well then all the more reason. *Marchons, marchons!*" said the young man gaily. His host, however, at this, but continued to stand agaze; and he had the next thing repeated his question of a moment before. "Has Miss Gostrey come back?"

"Yes, two days ago."

"Then you've seen her?"

"No—I'm to see her to-day." But Strether wouldn't linger now on Miss Gostrey. "Your mother sends me an ultimatum. If I can't bring you I'm to leave you; I'm to come at any rate myself."

"Ah but you *can* bring me now," Chad, from his sofa, reassuringly replied.

Strether had a pause. "I don't think I understand you. Why was it that, more than a month ago, you put it to me so urgently to let Madame de Vionnet speak for you?"

"'Why'?" Chad considered, but he had it at his fingers' ends. "Why but because I knew how well she'd do it? It was the way to keep you quiet and, to that extent, do you good. Besides," he happily and comfortably explained, "I wanted you really to know her and to get the impression of her—and you see the good that *has* done you."

"Well," said Strether, "the way she has spoken for you, all the same—so far as I've given her a chance—has only made me feel how much she wishes to keep you. If you make nothing of that I don't see why you wanted me to listen to her."

"Why my dear man," Chad explained, "I make everything of it! How can you doubt—?"

"I doubt only because you come to me this morning with your signal to start."

Chad stared, then gave a laugh. "And isn't my signal to start just what you've been waiting for?"

Strether debated; he took another turn. "This last month I've been awaiting, I think, more than anything else, the message I have here."

"You mean you've been afraid of it?"

"Well, I was doing my business in my own way. And I suppose your present announcement," Strether went on, "isn't merely the result of your sense of what I've expected. Otherwise you wouldn't have put me in relation—" But he paused, pulling up.

At this Chad rose. "Ah, *her* wanting me to not go has nothing to do with it! It's only because she's afraid—afraid of the way that, over there, I may get caught. But her fear's groundless."

He had met again his companion's sufficiently searching look. "Are you tired of her?"

Chad gave him in reply to this, with a movement of the head, the strangest slow smile he had ever had from him. "Never."

It had immediately, on Strether's imagination, so deep and soft an effect that our friend could only for the moment keep it before him. "Never?"

"Never," Chad obligingly and serenely repeated.

It made his companion take several more steps. "Then *you're* not afraid?"

"Afraid to go?"

Strether pulled up again. "Afraid to stay."

The young man looked brightly amazed. "You want me now to 'stay'?"

"If I don't immediately sail the Pococks will immediately come out. That's what I mean," said Strether, "by your mother's ultimatum."

Chad showed a still livelier, but not an alarmed interest. "She has turned on Sarah and Jim?"

Strether joined him for an instant in the vision. "Oh and you may be sure Mamie. *That's* whom she's turning on."

This also Chad saw—he laughed out. "Mamie—to corrupt me?"

"Ah," said Strether, "she's very charming."

"So you've already more than once told me. I should like to see her."

Something happy and easy, something above all unconscious, in the way he said this, brought home again to his companion the facility of his attitude and the enviability of his state. "See her then by all means. And consider too," Strether went on, "that you really give your sister a lift in letting her come to you. You give her a couple of months of Paris, which she hasn't seen, if I'm not mistaken, since just after she was married, and which I'm sure she wants but the pretext to visit."

Chad listened, but with all his own knowledge of the world. "She has had it, the pretext, these several years, yet she has never taken it."

"Do you mean *you*?" Strether after an instant inquired.

"Certainly—the lone exile. And whom do you mean?" said Chad.

"Oh I mean *me*. I'm her pretext. That is—for it comes to the same thing—I'm your mother's."

"Then why," Chad asked, "doesn't Mother come herself?"

His friend gave him a long look. "Should you like her to?" And as he for the moment said nothing: "It's perfectly open to you to cable for her."

Chad continued to think. "Will she come if I do?"

"Quite possibly. But try, and you'll see."

"Why don't *you* try?" Chad after a moment asked.

"Because I don't want to."

Chad thought. "Don't desire her presence here?"

Strether faced the question, and his answer was the more emphatic. "Don't put it off, my dear boy, on *me*!"

"Well—I see what you mean. I'm sure you'd behave beautifully, but you *don't* want to see her. So I won't play you that trick."

"Ah," Strether declared, "I shouldn't call it a trick. You've a perfect right, and it would be perfectly straight of you." Then he added in a different tone: "You'd have moreover, in the person of Madame de Vionnet, a very interesting relation prepared for her."

Their eyes, on this proposition, continued to meet, but Chad's pleasant and bold, never flinched for a moment. He got up at last and he said something with which Strether was struck. "She wouldn't understand her, but that makes no difference. Madame de Vionnet would like to see her. She'd like to be charming to her. She believes she could work it."

Strether thought a moment, affected by this, but finally turning away. "She couldn't!"

"You're quite sure?" Chad asked.

"Well, risk it if you like!"

Strether, who uttered this with serenity, had urged a plea for their now getting into the air; but the young man still waited. "Have you sent your answer?"

"No, I've done nothing yet."

"Were you waiting to see me?"

"No, not that."

"Only waiting"—and Chad, with this, had a smile for him—"to see Miss Gostrey?"

"No—not even Miss Gostrey. I wasn't waiting to see any one. I had only waited, till now, to make up my mind—in complete solitude; and, since I of course absolutely owe you the information, was on the point of going out with it quite made up. Have therefore a little more patience with me. Remember," Strether went on, "that that's what you originally asked *me* to have. I've had it, you see, and you see what has come of it. Stay on with me."

Chad looked grave. "How much longer?"

"Well, till I make you a sign. I can't myself, you know, at the best, or the worst, stay for ever. Let the Pococks come," Strether repeated.

"Because it gains you time?"

"Yes—it gains me time."

Chad, as if it still puzzled him, waited a minute. "You don't want to get back to Mother?"

"Not just yet. I'm not ready."

"You feel," Chad asked in a tone of his own, "the charm of life over here?"

"Immensely." Strether faced it. "You've helped me so to feel it that that surely needn't surprise you."

"No, it doesn't surprise me, and I'm delighted. But what, my dear man," Chad went on with conscious queerness, "does it all lead to for you?"

The change of position and of relation, for each, was as oddly betrayed in the question that Chad laughed out as soon as he had uttered it—which made Strether also laugh. "Well, to my having a certitude that has been tested—that has passed through the fire. But oh," he couldn't help breaking out, "if within my first month here you had been willing to move with me—!"

"Well?" said Chad, while he broke down as for weight of thought.

"Well, we should have been over there by now."

"Ah but you wouldn't have had your fun!"

"I should have had a month of it; and I'm having now, if you want to know," Strether continued, "enough to last me for the rest of my days."

Chad looked amused and interested, yet still somewhat in the dark; partly perhaps because Strether's estimate of fun had required of him from the first a good deal of elucidation. "It wouldn't do if I left you—?"

"Left me?" Strether remained blank.

"Only for a month or two—time to go and come. Madame de Vionnet," Chad smiled, "would look after you in the interval."

"To go back by yourself, I remaining here?" Again for an instant their eyes had the question out; after which Strether said: "Grotesque!"

"But I want to see Mother," Chad presently returned. "Remember how long it is since I've seen Mother."

"Long indeed; and that's exactly why I was originally so keen for moving you. Hadn't you shown us enough how beautifully you could do without it?"

"Oh but," said Chad wonderfully, "I'm better now."

There was an easy triumph in it that made his friend laugh out again. "Oh if you were worse I *should* know what to do with you. In that case I believe I'd have you gagged and strapped down, carried on board resisting, kicking. How *much*," Strether asked, "do you want to see Mother?"

"How much?" Chad seemed to find it in fact difficult to say.

"How much."

"Why as much as you've made me. I'd give anything to see her. And you've left me," Chad went on, "in little enough doubt as to how much *she* wants it."

Strether thought a minute. "Well then if those things are really your motive catch the French steamer and sail to-morrow. Of course, when it comes to that, you're absolutely free to do as you choose. From the moment you can't hold yourself I can only accept your flight."

"I'll fly in a minute then," said Chad, "if you'll stay here."

"I'll stay here till the next steamer—then I'll follow you."

"And do you call that," Chad asked, "accepting my flight?"

"Certainly—it's the only thing to call it. The only way to keep me here, accordingly," Strether explained, "is by staying yourself."

Chad took it in. "All the more that I've really dished you, eh?"

"Dished me?" Strether echoed as inexpressibly as possible.

"Why if she sends out the Pococks it will be that she doesn't trust you, and if she doesn't trust you, that bears upon—well you know what."

Strether decided after a moment that he did know what and in consonance with this he spoke. "You see then all the more what you owe me."

"Well, if I do see, how can I pay?"

"By not deserting me. By standing by me."

"Oh I say—!" But Chad, as they went downstairs, clapped a firm hand, in the manner of a pledge, upon his shoulder. They descended slowly together and had, in the court of the hotel, some further talk, of which the upshot was that they presently separated. Chad Newsome departed, and Strether, left alone, looked about, superficially, for Waymarsh. But Waymarsh hadn't yet, it appeared, come down, and our friend finally went forth without a sight of him.

III

At four o'clock that afternoon he had still not seen him, but he was then, as to make up for this, engaged in talk about him with Miss Gostrey. Strether had kept away from home all day, given himself up to the town and to his thoughts, wandered and mused, been at once restless and absorbed—and all with the present climax of a rich little welcome to the Quartier Marboeuf. "Waymarsh has been, 'unbeknown' to me, I'm convinced"—for Miss Gostrey had enquired—"in communication with Woollett: the consequence of which was, last night, the loudest possible call for me."

"Do you mean a letter to bring you home?"

"No—a cable, which I have at this moment in my pocket: a 'Come back by the first ship.'"

Strether's hostess, it might have been made out, just escaped changing colour. Reflexion arrived but in time and established a provisional serenity. It was perhaps exactly this that enabled her to say with duplicity: "And you're going—?"

"You almost deserve it when you abandon me so."

She shook her head as if this were not worth taking up. "My absence has helped you—as I've only to look at you to see. It was my calculation, and I'm justified. You're not where you were. And the thing," she smiled, "was for me not to be there either. You can go of yourself."

"Oh but I feel to-day," he comfortably declared, "that I shall want you yet."

She took him all in again. "Well, I promise you not again to leave you, but it will only be to follow you. You've got your momentum and can toddle alone."

He intelligently accepted it. "Yes—I suppose I can toddle. It's the sight of that in fact that has upset Waymarsh. He can bear it—the way I strike him as going—no longer. That's only the climax of his original feeling. He wants me to quit; and he must have written to Woollett that I'm in peril of perdition."

"Ah good!" she murmured. "But is it only your supposition?"

"I make it out—it explains."

"Then he denies?—or haven't you asked him?"

"I've not had time," Strether said. "I made it out but last night, putting various things together, and I've not been since then face to face with him."

She wondered. "Because you're too disgusted? You can't trust yourself?"

He settled his glasses on his nose. "Do I look in a great rage?"

"You look divine!"

"There's nothing," he went on, "to be angry about. He has done me on the contrary a service."

She made it out. "By bringing things to a head?"

"How well you understand!" he almost groaned. "Waymarsh won't in the least, at any rate, when I have it out with him, deny or extenuate. He has acted from the deepest conviction, with the best conscience and after wakeful nights. He'll recognize that he's fully responsible, and will consider that he has been highly successful; so that any discussion we may have will bring us quite together again—bridge the dark stream that has kept us so thoroughly apart. We shall have at last, in the consequences of his act, something we can definitely talk about."

She was silent a little. "How wonderfully you take it! But you're always wonderful."

He had a pause that matched her own; then he had, with an adequate spirit, a complete admission. "It's quite true. I'm extremely wonderful just now. I daresay in fact I'm quite fantastic, and I shouldn't be at all surprised if I were mad."

"Then tell me!" she earnestly pressed. As he, however, for the time answered nothing, only returning the look with which she watched him, she presented herself where it was easier to meet her. "What will Mr. Waymarsh exactly have done?"

"Simply have written a letter. One will have been quite enough. He has told them I want looking after."

"And *do* you?"—she was all interest.

"Immensely. And I shall get it."

"By which you mean you don't budge?"

"I don't budge."

"You've cabled?"

"No. I've made Chad do it."

"That you decline to come?"

"That *he* declines. We had it out this morning and I brought him round. He had come in, before I was down, to tell me he was ready—ready, I mean, to return. And he went off, after ten minutes with me, to say he wouldn't."

Miss Gostrey followed with intensity. "Then you've *stopped* him?"

Strether settled himself afresh in his chair. "I've stopped him. That is for the time. That"—he gave it to her more vividly—"is where I am."

"I see, I see. But where's Mr. Newsome? He was ready," she asked, "to go?"

"All ready."

"And sincerely—believing *you'd* be?"

"Perfectly, I think; so that he was amazed to find the hand I had laid on him to pull him over suddenly converted into an engine for keeping him still."

It was an account of the matter Miss Gostrey could weigh. "Does he think the conversion sudden?"

"Well," said Strether, "I'm not altogether sure what he thinks. I'm not sure of anything that concerns him, except that the more I've seen of him the less I've found him what I originally expected. He's obscure, and that's why I'm waiting."

She wondered. "But for what in particular?"

"For the answer to his cable."

"And what was his cable?"

"I don't know," Strether replied; "it was to be, when he left me, according to his own taste. I simply said to him: 'I want to stay, and the only way for me to do so is for *you* to.' That I wanted to stay seemed to interest him, and he acted on that."

Miss Gostrey turned it over. "He wants then himself to stay?"

"He half wants it. That is he half wants to go. My original appeal has to that extent worked in him. Nevertheless," Strether pursued, "he won't go. Not, at least, so long as I'm here."

"But you can't," his companion suggested, "stay here always. I wish you could."

"By no means. Still, I want to see him a little further. He's not in the least the case I supposed; he's quite another case. And it's as such that he interests me." It was almost as if for his own intelligence that, deliberate and lucid, our friend thus expressed the matter. "I don't want to give him up."

Miss Gostrey but desired to help his lucidity. She had, however, to be light and tactful. "Up, you mean—a—to his mother?"

"Well, I'm not thinking of his mother now. I'm thinking of the plan of which I was the mouthpiece, which, as soon as we met, I put before him as persuasively as I knew how, and which was drawn up, as it were, in complete ignorance of all that, in this last long period, has been happening to him. It took no account whatever of the impressions I was here on the spot immediately to begin to receive from him—impressions of which I feel sure I'm far from having had the last."

Miss Gostrey had a smile of the most genial criticism. "So your idea is—more or less—to stay out of curiosity?"

"Call it what you like! I don't care what it's called—"

"So long as you do stay? Certainly not then. I call it, all the same, immense fun," Maria Gostrey declared; "and to see you work it out will be one of the sensations of my life. It *is* clear you can toddle alone!"

He received this tribute without elation. "I shan't be alone when the Pococks have come."

Her eyebrows went up. "The Pococks are coming?"

"That, I mean, is what will happen—and happen as quickly as possible—in consequence of Chad's cable. They'll simply embark. Sarah will come to speak for her mother—with an effect different from *my* muddle."

Miss Gostrey more gravely wondered. "*She* then will take him back?"

"Very possibly—and we shall see. She must at any rate have the chance, and she may be trusted to do all she can."

"And do you *want* that?"

"Of course," said Strether, "I want it. I want to play fair."

But she had lost for a moment the thread. "If it devolves on the Pococks why do you stay?"

"Just to see that I *do* play fair—and a little also, no doubt, that they do." Strether was luminous as he had never been. "I came out to find myself in presence of new facts—facts that have kept striking me as less and less met by our old reasons. The matter's perfectly simple. New reasons—reasons as new as the facts themselves—are wanted; and of this our friends at Woollett—Chad's and mine—were at the earliest moment definitely notified. If any are producible Mrs. Pocock will produce them; she'll bring over the whole collection. They'll be," he added with a pensive smile, "a part of the 'fun' you speak of."

She was quite in the current now and floating by his side. "It's Mamie—so far as I've had it from you—who'll be their great card." And then as his contemplative silence wasn't a denial she significantly added: "I think I'm sorry for her."

"I think *I* am!"—and Strether sprang up, moving about a little as her eyes followed him. "But it can't be helped."

"You mean her coming out can't be?"

He explained after another turn what he meant. "The only way for her not to come is for me to go home—as I believe that on the spot I could prevent it. But the difficulty as to that is that if I do go home—"

"I see, I see,"—she had easily understood. "Mr. Newsome will do the same, and that's not"—she laughed out now—"to be thought of."

Strether had no laugh; he had only a quiet comparatively placid look that might have shown him as proof against ridicule. "Strange, isn't it?"

They had, in the matter that had so much interested them, come so far as this without sounding another name—to which however their present momentary silence was full of a conscious reference. Strether's question was a sufficient implication of the weight it had gained with him during the absence of his hostess; and just for that reason a single gesture from her could pass for him as a vivid answer. Yet he was answered still better when she said in a moment: "Will Mr. Newsome introduce his sister—?"

"To Madame de Vionnet?" Strether spoke the name at last. "I shall be greatly surprised if he doesn't."

She seemed to gaze at the possibility. "You mean you've thought of it, and you're prepared."

"I've thought of it and I'm prepared."

It was to her visitor now that she applied her consideration. "Bon! You *are* magnificent!"

"Well," he answered after a pause and a little wearily, but still standing there before her—"well, that's what, just once in all my dull days, I think I shall like to have been!"

Two days later he had news from Chad of a communication from Woollett in response to their determinant telegram, this missive being addressed to Chad himself and announcing the immediate departure for France of Sarah and Jim and Mamie. Strether had meanwhile on his own side cabled; he had but delayed that act till after his visit to Miss Gostrey, an interview by which, as so often before, he felt his sense of things cleared up and settled. His message to Mrs. Newsome, in answer to her own, had consisted of the words: "Judge best to take another month, but with full appreciation of all re-enforcements." He had added that he was writing, but he was of course always writing; it was a practice that continued, oddly enough, to relieve him, to make him come nearer than anything else to the consciousness of doing something: so that he often wondered if he hadn't really, under his recent stress, acquired some hollow trick, one of the specious arts of make-believe. Wouldn't the pages he still so frequently dispatched by the American post have been worthy of a showy journalist, some master of the great new science of beating the sense out of words? Wasn't he writing against time, and mainly to show he was kind?—since it had become quite his habit not to like to read himself over. On those lines he could still be liberal, yet it was at best a sort of whistling in the dark. It was unmistakable moreover that the sense of being in the dark now pressed on him more sharply—creating thereby the need for a louder and livelier whistle. He whistled long and hard after sending his message; he whistled again and again in celebration of Chad's news; there was an interval of a fortnight in which this exercise helped him. He had no great notion of what, on the spot, Sarah Pocock would have to say, though he had indeed confused premonitions; but it shouldn't be in her power to say—it shouldn't be in any one's anywhere to say—that he was neglecting her mother. He might have written before more freely, but he had never written more copiously; and he frankly gave for a reason at Woollett that he wished to fill the void created by Sarah's departure.

The increase of his darkness, however, and the quickening, as I have called it, of his tune, resided in the fact that he was hearing almost nothing. He had for some time been aware that he was hearing less than before, but he was now clearly following a process by which Mrs. Newsome's letters could but logically stop. He hadn't had a line for many days, and he needed no proof—though he was, in time, to have plenty—that she wouldn't have put pen to paper after receiving the hint that had determined her telegram. She wouldn't write till Sarah should have seen him and reported on him. It was strange, though it might well be less so than his own behaviour appeared at Woollett. It was at any rate significant, and what *was* remarkable was the way his friend's nature and manner put on for him, through this very drop of demonstration, a greater intensity. It struck him really that he had never so lived with her as during this period of her silence; the silence was a sacred hush, a finer clearer medium, in which her idiosyncrasies showed. He walked about with her, sat with her, drove with her and dined face-to-face with her—a rare treat "in his life," as he could perhaps have scarce escaped phrasing it; and if he had never seen her so soundless he had never, on the other hand, felt her so highly, so almost austerely, herself: pure and by the vulgar estimate "cold," but deep devoted delicate sensitive noble. Her vividness in these respects became for him, in the special conditions, almost an obsession; and though the obsession sharpened his pulses, adding really to the excitement of life, there were hours at which, to be less on the stretch, he directly sought forgetfulness. He knew it for the queerest of adventures—a circumstance capable of playing such a part only for Lambert Strether—that in Paris itself, of all places, he should find this ghost of the lady of Woollett more importunate than any other presence.

When he went back to Maria Gostrey it was for the change to something else. And yet after all the change scarcely operated, for he talked to her of Mrs. Newsome in these days as he had never talked before. He had hitherto observed in that particular a discretion and a law; considerations that at present broke down quite as if relations had altered. They hadn't *really* altered, he said to himself, so much as that came to; for if what had occurred was of course that Mrs. Newsome had ceased to trust him, there was nothing on the other hand to prove that he shouldn't win back her confidence. It was quite his present theory that he would leave no stone unturned to do so; and in fact if he now told Maria things about her that he had never told before this was largely because it kept before him the idea of the honour of such a woman's esteem. His relation with Maria as well was, strangely enough, no longer quite the same; this truth—though not too disconcertingly—had come up between them on the renewal of their meetings. It was all contained in what she had then almost immediately said to him; it was represented by the remark she had needed but ten minutes to make and that he hadn't been disposed to gainsay. He could toddle alone, and the difference that showed was extraordinary. The turn taken by their walk had promptly confirmed this difference; his larger confidence on the score of Mrs. Newsome did the rest; and the time seemed already far off when he had held out his small thirsty cup to the spout of her pail. Her pail was scarce touched now, and other fountains had flowed for him; she fell into her place as but one of his tributaries; and there was a strange sweetness—a melancholy mildness that touched him—in her acceptance of the altered order.

It marked for himself the flight of time, or at any rate what he was pleased to think of with irony and pity as the rush of experience; it having been but the day before yesterday that he sat at her feet and held on by her garment and was fed by her hand. It was the proportions that were changed, and the proportions were at all times, he philosophised, the very conditions of perception, the terms of thought. It was as if, with her effective little entresol and her wide acquaintance, her activities, varieties, promiscuities, the duties and devotions that took nine tenths of her time and of which he got, guardedly, but the side-wind—it was as if she had shrunk to a secondary element and had consented to the shrinkage with the perfection of tact. This perfection had never failed her; it had originally been greater than his prime measure for it; it had kept him quite apart, kept him out of the shop, as she called her huge general acquaintance, made their commerce as quiet, as much a thing of the home alone—the opposite of the shop—as if she had never another customer. She had been wonderful to him at first, with the memory of her little entresol, the image to which, on most mornings at that time, his eyes directly opened; but now she mainly figured for him as but part of the bristling total—though of course always as a person to whom he should never cease to be indebted. It would never be given to him certainly to inspire a greater kindness. She had decked him out for others, and he saw at this point at least nothing she would ever ask for. She only wondered and questioned and listened, rendering him the homage of a wistful speculation. She expressed it repeatedly; he was already far beyond her, and she must prepare herself to lose him. There was but one little chance for her.

Often as she had said it he met it—for it was a touch he liked—each time the same way. "My coming to grief?"

"Yes—then I might patch you up."

"Oh for my real smash, if it takes place, there will be no patching."

"But you surely don't mean it will kill you."

"No—worse. It will make me old."

"Ah nothing can do that! The wonderful and special thing about you is that you *are*, at this time of day, youth." Then she always made, further, one of those remarks that she had completely ceased to adorn with hesitations or apologies, and that had, by the same token, in spite of their extreme straightness, ceased to produce in Strether the least embarrassment. She made him believe them, and they became thereby as impersonal as truth itself. "It's just your particular charm."

His answer too was always the same. "Of course I'm youth—youth for the trip to Europe. I began to be young, or at least to get the benefit of it, the moment I met you at Chester, and that's what has been taking place ever since. I never had the benefit at the proper time—which comes to saying that I never had the thing itself. I'm having the benefit at this moment; I had it the other day when I said to Chad 'Wait'; I shall have it still again when Sarah Pocock arrives. It's a benefit that would make a poor show for many people; and I don't know who else but you and I, frankly, could begin to see in it what I feel. I don't get drunk; I don't pursue the ladies; I don't spend money; I don't even write sonnets. But nevertheless I'm making up late for what I didn't have early. I cultivate my little benefit in my own little way. It amuses me more than anything that has happened to me in all my life. They may say what they like—it's my surrender, it's my tribute, to youth. One puts that in where one can—it has to come in somewhere, if only out of the lives, the conditions, the feelings of other persons. Chad gives me the sense of it, for all his grey hairs, which merely make it solid in him and safe and serene; and *she* does the same, for all her being older than he, for all her marriageable daughter, her separated husband, her agitated history. Though they're young enough, my pair, I don't say they're, in the freshest way, their *own* absolutely prime adolescence; for that has nothing to do with it. The point is that they're mine. Yes, they're my youth; since somehow at the right time nothing else ever was. What I meant just now therefore is that it would all go—go before doing its work—if they were to fail me."

On which, just here, Miss Gostrey inveterately questioned. "What do you, in particular, call its work?"

"Well, to see me through."

"But through what?"—she liked to get it all out of him.

"Why through this experience." That was all that would come.

It regularly gave her none the less the last word. "Don't you remember how in those first days of our meeting it was *I* who was to see you through?"

"Remember? Tenderly, deeply"—he always rose to it. "You're just doing your part in letting me maunder to you thus."

"Ah don't speak as if my part were small; since whatever else fails you—"

"*You* won't, ever, ever, ever?"—he thus took her up. "Oh I beg your pardon; you necessarily, you inevitably *will*. Your conditions—that's what I mean—won't allow me anything to do for you."

"Let alone—I see what you mean—that I'm drearily, dreadfully old. I *am*, but there's a service—possible for you to render—that I know, all the same, I shall think of."

"And what will it be?"

This, in fine, however, she would never tell him. "You shall hear only if your smash takes place. As that's really out of the question, I won't expose myself"—a point at which, for reasons of his own, Strether ceased to press.

He came round, for publicity—it was the easiest thing—to the idea that his smash *was* out of the question, and this rendered idle the discussion of what might follow it. He attached an added importance, as the days elapsed, to the arrival of the Pococks; he had even a shameful sense of waiting for it insincerely and incorrectly. He accused himself of making believe to his own mind that Sarah's presence, her impression, her judgement would simplify and harmonise; he accused himself of being so afraid of what they *might* do that he sought refuge, to beg the whole question, in a vain fury. He had abundantly seen at home what they were in the habit of doing, and he had not at present the smallest ground. His clearest vision was when he made out that what he most desired was an account more full and free of Mrs. Newsome's state of mind than any he felt he could now expect from herself; that calculation at least went hand in hand with the sharp consciousness of wishing to prove to himself that he was not afraid to look his behaviour in the face. If he was by an inexorable logic to pay for it he was literally impatient to know the cost, and he held himself ready to pay in instalments. The first instalment would be precisely this entertainment of Sarah; as a consequence of which, moreover, he should know vastly better how he stood.

BOOK EIGHTH

I

Strether rambled largely alone during these few days, the effect of the incident of the previous week having been to simplify in a marked fashion his mixed relations with Waymarsh. Nothing had passed between them in reference to Mrs. Newsome's summons but that our friend had mentioned to his own the departure of the deputation actually at sea—giving him thus an opportunity to confess to the occult intervention he imputed to him. Waymarsh however in the event confessed to nothing; and though this falsified in some degree Strether's forecast the latter amusedly saw in it the same depth of good conscience out of which the dear man's impertinence had originally sprung. He was patient with the dear man now and delighted to observe how unmistakeably he had put on flesh; he felt his own holiday so successfully large and free that he was full of allowances and charities in respect to those cabined and confined: his instinct toward a spirit so strapped down as Waymarsh's was to walk round it on tiptoe for fear of waking it up to a sense of losses by this time irretrievable. It was all very funny, he knew, and but the difference, as he often said to himself, of tweedledum and tweedledee—an emancipation so purely comparative that it was like the advance of the door-mat on the scraper; yet the present crisis was happily to profit by it and the pilgrim from Milrose to know himself more than ever in the right.

Strether felt that when he heard of the approach of the Pococks the impulse of pity quite sprang up in him beside the impulse of triumph. That was exactly why Waymarsh had looked at him with eyes in which the heat of justice was measured and shaded. He had looked very hard, as if affectionately sorry for the friend—the friend of fifty-five—whose frivolity had had thus to be recorded; becoming however, but obscurely sententious and leaving his companion to formulate a charge. It was in this general attitude that he had of late altogether taken refuge; with the drop of discussion they were solemnly sadly superficial; Strether recognised in him the mere portentous rumination to which Miss Barrace had so good-humouredly described herself as assigning a corner of her salon. It was quite as if he knew his surreptitious step had been divined, and it was also as if he missed the chance to explain the purity of his motive; but this privation of relief should be precisely his small penance: it was not amiss for Strether that he should find himself to that degree uneasy. If he had been challenged or accused, rebuked for meddling or otherwise pulled up, he would probably have shown, on his own system, all the height of his consistency, all the depth of his good faith. Explicit resentment of his course would have made him take the floor, and the thump of his fist on the table would have affirmed him as consciously incorruptible. Had what now really prevailed with Strether been but a dread of that thump—a dread of wincing a little painfully at what it might invidiously demonstrate? However this might be, at any rate, one of the marks of the crisis was a visible, a studied lapse, in Waymarsh, of betrayed concern. As if to make up to his comrade for the stroke by which he had played providence he now conspicuously ignored his movements, withdrew himself from the pretension to share them, stiffened up his sensibility to neglect, and, clasping his large empty hands and swinging his large restless foot, clearly looked to another quarter for justice.

This made for independence on Strether's part, and he had in truth at no moment of his stay been so free to go and come. The early summer brushed the picture over and blurred everything but the near; it made a vast warm fragrant medium in which the elements floated together on the best of terms, in which rewards were immediate and reckonings postponed. Chad was out of town again, for the first time since his visitor's first view of him; he had explained this necessity—without detail, yet also without embarrassment; the circumstance was one of those which, in the young man's life, testified to the variety of his ties. Strether wasn't otherwise concerned with it than for its so testifying—a pleasant multitudinous image in which he took comfort. He took comfort, by the same stroke, in the swing of Chad's pendulum back from that other swing, the sharp jerk towards Woollett, so stayed by his own hand. He had the entertainment of thinking that if he had for that moment stopped the clock it was to promote the next minute this still livelier action. He himself did what he hadn't done before; he took two or three times whole days off—irrespective of others, of two or three taken with Miss Gostrey, two or three taken with little Bilham: he went to Chartres and cultivated, before the front of the cathedral, a general easy beatitude; he went to Fontainbleau and imagined himself on the way to Italy; he went to Rouen with a little handbag and inordinately spent the night.

One afternoon he did something quite different; finding himself in the neighbourhood of a fine old house across the river, he passed under the great arch of its doorway and asked at the porter's lodge for Madame de Vionnet. He had already hovered more than once about that possibility, been aware of it, in the course of ostensible strolls, as lurking but round the corner. Only it had perversely happened, after his morning at Notre Dame, that his consistency, as he considered and intended it, had come back to him; whereby he had reflected that the encounter in question had been none of his making, clinging again intensely to the strength of his position, which was precisely that there was nothing in it for himself. From the moment he actively pursued the charming associate of his adventure, from that moment his position weakened, for he was then acting in an interested way. It was only within a few days that he had fixed himself a limit: he promised himself his consistency should end with Sarah's arrival. It was arguing correctly to feel the title to a free hand conferred on him by this event. If he wasn't to be let alone he should be merely a dupe to act with delicacy. If he wasn't to be trusted he could at least take his ease. If he was to be placed under control he gained leave to try what his position *might* agreeably give him. An ideal rigour would perhaps postpone the trial till after the Pococks had shown their spirit; and it was to an ideal rigour that he had quite promised himself to conform.

Suddenly, however, on this particular day, he felt a particular fear under which everything collapsed. He knew abruptly that he was afraid of himself—and yet not in relation to the effect on his sensibilities of another hour of Madame de Vionnet. What he dreaded was the effect of a single hour of Sarah Pocock, as to whom he was visited, in troubled nights, with fantastic waking dreams. She loomed at him larger than life; she increased in volume as she drew nearer; she so met his eyes that, his imagination taking, after the first step, all, and more than all, the strides, he already felt her come down on him, already burned, under her reprobation, with the blush of guilt, already consented by way of penance, to the instant forfeiture of everything. He saw himself, under her direction, recommitted to Woollett as juvenile offenders are committed to reformatories. It wasn't of course that Woollett was really a place of discipline; but he knew in advance that Sarah's salon at the hotel would be. His danger, at any rate in such moods of alarm, was some concession, on this ground, that would involve a sharp rupture with the actual; therefore if he waited to take leave of that actual he might wholly miss his chance. It was represented with supreme vividness by Madame de Vionnet, and that is why, in a word, he waited no longer. He had seen in a flash that he must anticipate Mrs. Pocock. He was accordingly much disappointed on now learning from the portress that the lady of his quest was not in Paris. She had gone for some days to the country. There was nothing in this accident but what was natural; yet it produced for poor Strether a drop of all confidence. It was suddenly as if he should never see her again and as if moreover he had brought it on himself by not having been quite kind to her.

It was the advantage of his having let his fancy lose itself for a little in the gloom that, as by reaction, the prospect began really to brighten from the moment the deputation from Woollett alighted on the platform of the station. They had come straight from Havre, having sailed from New York to that port, and having also, thanks to a happy voyage, made land with a promptitude that left Chad Newsome, who had meant to meet them at the dock, belated. He had received their telegram, with the announcement of their immediate further advance, just as he was taking the train for Havre, so that nothing had remained for him but to await them in Paris. He hastily picked up Strether, at the hotel, for this purpose, and he even, with easy pleasantry, suggested the attendance of Waymarsh as well—Waymarsh, at the moment his cab rattled up, being engaged, under Strether's contemplative range, in a grave perambulation of the familiar court. Waymarsh had learned from his companion, who had already had a note, delivered by hand, from Chad, that the Pococks were due, and had ambiguously, though, as always, impressively, glowered at him over the circumstance; carrying himself in a manner in which Strether was now expert enough to recognise his uncertainty, in the premises, as to the best tone. The only tone he aimed at with confidence was a full tone—which was necessarily difficult in the absence of a full knowledge. The Pococks were a quantity as yet unmeasured, and, as he had practically brought them over, so this witness had to that extent exposed himself. He wanted to feel right about it, but could only, at the best, for the time, feel vague. "I shall look to you, you know, immensely," and our friend had said, "to help me with them," and he had been quite conscious of the effect of the remark, and of others of the same sort, on his comrade's sombre sensibility. He had insisted on the fact that Waymarsh would quite like Mrs. Pocock—one could be certain he would: he would be with her about everything, and she would also be with *him*, and Miss Barrace's nose, in short, would find itself out of joint.

Strether had woven this web of cheerfulness while they waited in the court for Chad; he had sat smoking cigarettes to keep himself quiet while, caged and leonine, his fellow traveller paced and turned before him. Chad Newsome was doubtless to be struck, when he arrived, with the sharpness of their opposition at this particular hour; he was to remember, as a part of it, how Waymarsh came with him and with Strether to the street and stood there with a face half-wistful and half-rueful. They talked of him, the two others, as they drove, and Strether put Chad in possession of much of his own strained sense of things. He had already, a few days before, named to him the wire he was convinced their friend had pulled—a confidence that had made on the young man's part quite hugely for curiosity and diversion. The action of the matter, moreover, Strether could see, was to penetrate; he saw, that is, how Chad judged a system of influence in which Waymarsh had served as a determinant—an impression just now quickened again; with the whole bearing of such a fact on the youth's view of his relatives. As it came up between them that they might now take their friend for a feature of the control of these latter now sought to be exerted from Woollett, Strether felt indeed that it would be stamped all over him, half an hour later, for Sarah Pocock's eyes, that he was as much on Chad's "side" as Waymarsh had probably described him. He was letting himself, at present, go; there was no denying it; it might be desperation, it might be confidence; he should offer himself to the arriving travellers bristling with all the lucidity he had cultivated.

He repeated to Chad what he had been saying in the court to Waymarsh; how there was no doubt whatever that his sister would find the latter a kindred spirit, no doubt of the alliance, based on an exchange of views, that the pair would successfully strike up. They would become as thick as thieves—which moreover was but a development of what Strether remembered to have said in one of his first discussions with his mate, struck as he had then already been with the elements of affinity between that personage and Mrs. Newsome herself. "I told him, one day, when he had questioned me on your mother, that she was a person who, when he should know her, would rouse in him, I was sure, a special enthusiasm; and that hangs together with the conviction we now feel—this certitude that Mrs. Pocock will take him into her boat. For it's your mother's own boat that she's pulling."

"Ah," said Chad, "Mother's worth fifty of Sally!"

"A thousand; but when you presently meet her, all the same, you'll be meeting your mother's representative—just as I shall. I feel like the outgoing ambassador," said Strether, "doing honour to his appointed successor." A moment after speaking as he had just done he felt that he had inadvertently rather cheapened Mrs. Newsome to her son; an impression audibly reflected, as at first seen, in Chad's prompt protest. He had recently rather failed of apprehension of the young man's attitude and temper—remaining principally conscious of how little worry, at the worst, he wasted; and he studied him at this critical hour with renewed interest. Chad had done exactly what he had promised him a fortnight previous—had accepted without another question his plea for delay. He was waiting cheerfully and handsomely, but also inscrutably and with a slight increase perhaps of the hardness originally involved in his acquired high polish. He was neither excited nor depressed; was easy and acute and deliberate—unhurried unflurried unworried, only at most a little less amused than usual. Strether felt him more than ever a justification of the extraordinary process of which his own absurd spirit had been the arena; he knew as their cab rolled along, knew as he hadn't even yet known, that nothing else than what Chad had done and had been would have led to his present showing. They had made him, these things, what he was, and the business hadn't been easy; it had taken time and trouble, it had cost, above all, a price. The result at any rate was now to be offered to Sally; which Strether, so far as that was concerned, was glad to be there to witness. Would she in the least make it out or take it in, the result, or would she in the least care for it if she did? He scratched his chin as he asked himself by what name, when challenged—as he was sure he should be—he could call it for her. Oh those were determinations she must herself arrive at; since she wanted so much to see, let her see then and welcome. She had come out in the pride of her competence, yet it hummed in Strether's inner sense that she practically wouldn't see.

That this was moreover what Chad shrewdly suspected was clear from a word that next dropped from him. "They're children; they play at life!"—and the exclamation was significant and reassuring. It implied that he hadn't then, for his companion's sensibility, appeared to give Mrs. Newsome away; and it facilitated our friend's presently asking him if it were his idea that Mrs. Pocock and Madame de Vionnet should become acquainted. Strether was still more sharply struck, hereupon, with Chad's lucidity. "Why, isn't that exactly—to get a sight of the company I keep—what she has come out for?"

"Yes—I'm afraid it is," Strether unguardedly replied.

Chad's quick rejoinder lighted his precipitation. "Why do you say you're afraid?"

"Well, because I feel a certain responsibility. It's my testimony, I imagine, that will have been at the bottom of Mrs. Pocock's curiosity. My letters, as I've supposed you to understand from the beginning, have spoken freely. I've certainly said my little say about Madame de Vionnet."

All that, for Chad, was beautifully obvious. "Yes, but you've only spoken handsomely."

"Never more handsomely of any woman. But it's just that tone—!"

"That tone," said Chad, "that has fetched her? I daresay; but I've no quarrel with you about it. And no more has Madame de Vionnet. Don't you know by this time how she likes you?"

"Oh!"—and Strether had, with his groan, a real pang of melancholy. "For all I've done for her!"

"And you've done a great deal."

Chad's urbanity fairly shamed him, and he was at this moment absolutely impatient to see the face Sarah Pocock would present to a sort of thing, as he synthetically phrased it to himself, with no adequate forecast of which, despite his admonitions, she would certainly arrive. "I've done *this*!"

"Well, this is all right. She likes," Chad comfortably remarked, "to be liked."

It gave his companion a moment's thought. "And she's sure Mrs. Pocock *will*—?"

"No, I say that for you. She likes your liking her; it's so much, as it were," Chad laughed, "to the good. However, she doesn't despair of Sarah either, and is prepared, on her own side, to go all lengths."

"In the way of appreciation?"

"Yes, and of everything else. In the way of general amiability, hospitality and welcome. She's under arms," Chad laughed again; "she's prepared."

Strether took it in; then, as if an echo of Miss Barrace were in the air: "She's wonderful."

"You don't begin to know *how* wonderful!"

There was a depth in it, to Strether's ear, of confirmed luxury—almost a kind of unconscious insolence of proprietorship; but the effect of this glimpse was not at this moment to foster speculation: there was something so conclusive in so much graceful and generous assurance. It was in fact a fresh evocation; and the evocation had before many minutes another consequence. "Well, I shall see her oftener now. I shall see her as much as I like—by your leave; which is what I hitherto haven't done."

"It has been," said Chad, but without reproach, "only your own fault. I tried to bring you together, and *she*, my dear fellow—I never saw her more charming to any man. But you've got your extraordinary ideas."

"Well, I *did* have," Strether murmured; while he felt both how they had possessed him and how they had now lost their authority. He couldn't have traced the sequence to the end, but it was all because of Mrs. Pocock. Mrs. Pocock might be because of Mrs. Newsome, but that was still to be proved. What came over him was the sense of having stupidly failed to profit where profit would have been precious. It had been open to him to see so much more of her, and he had but let the good days pass. Fierce in him almost was the resolve to lose no more of them, and he whimsically reflected, while at Chad's side he drew nearer to his destination, that it was after all Sarah who would have quickened his chance. What her visit of inquisition might achieve in other directions was as yet all obscure—only not obscure that it would do supremely much to bring two earnest persons together. He had only to listen to Chad at this moment to feel it; for Chad was in the act of remarking to him that they of course both counted on him—he himself and the other earnest person—for cheer and support. It was brave to Strether to hear him talk as if the line of wisdom they had struck out was to make things ravishing to the Pococks. No, if Madame de Vionnet compassed *that*, compassed the ravishment of the Pococks, Madame de Vionnet would be prodigious. It would be a beautiful plan if it succeeded, and it all came to the question of Sarah's being really bribeable. The precedent of his own case helped Strether perhaps but little to consider she might prove so; it being distinct that her character would rather make for every possible difference. This idea of his own bribeability set him apart for himself; with the further mark in fact that his case was absolutely proved. He liked always, where Lambert Strether was concerned, to know the worst, and what he now seemed to know was not only that he was bribeable, but that he had been effectually bribed. The only difficulty was that he couldn't quite have said with what. It was as if he had sold himself, but hadn't somehow got the cash. That, however, was what, characteristically, *would* happen to him. It would naturally be his kind of traffic. While he thought of these things he reminded Chad of the truth they mustn't lose sight of—the truth that, with all deference to her susceptibility to new interests, Sarah would have come out with a high firm definite purpose. "She hasn't come out, you know, to be bamboozled. We may all be ravishing—nothing perhaps can be more easy for us; but she hasn't come out to be ravished. She has come out just simply to take you home."

"Oh well, with *her* I'll go!" said Chad good-humouredly. "I suppose you'll allow *that*." And then as for a minute Strether said nothing: "Or is your idea that when I've seen her I shan't want to go?" As this question, however, again left his friend silent he presently went on: "My own idea at any rate is that they shall have while they're here the best sort of time."

It was at this that Strether spoke. "Ah there you are! I think if you really wanted to go—!"

"Well?" said Chad to bring it out.

"Well, you wouldn't trouble about our good time. You wouldn't care what sort of a time we have."

Chad could always take in the easiest way in the world, an ingenious suggestion. "I see. But can I help it? I'm too decent."

"Yes, you're too decent!" Strether heavily sighed. And he felt for the moment as if it were the preposterous end of his mission.

It ministered for the time to this temporary effect that Chad made no rejoinder. But he spoke again as they came in sight of the station. "Do you mean to introduce her to Miss Gostrey?"

As to this Strether was ready. "No."

"But haven't you told me they know about her?"

"I think I've told you your mother knows."

"And won't she have told Sally?"

"That's one of the things I want to see."

"And if you find she *has*—?"

"Will I then, you mean, bring them together?"

"Yes," said Chad with his pleasant promptness: "to show her there's nothing in it."

Strether hesitated. "I don't know that I care very much what she may think there's in it."

"Not if it represents what Mother thinks?"

"Ah what *does* your mother think?" There was in this some sound of bewilderment.

But they were just driving up, and help, of a sort, might after all be quite at hand. "Isn't that, my dear man, what we're both just going to make out?"

II

Strether quitted the station half an hour later in different company. Chad had taken charge, for the journey to the hotel, of Sarah, Mamie, the maid and the luggage, all spaciously installed and conveyed; and it was only after the four had rolled away that his companion got into a cab with Jim. A strange new feeling had come over Strether, in consequence of which his spirits had risen; it was as if what had occurred on the alighting of his critics had been something other than his fear, though his fear had yet not been of an instant scene of violence. His impression had been nothing but what was inevitable—he said that to himself; yet relief and reassurance had softly dropped upon him. Nothing could be so odd as to be indebted for these things to the look of faces and the sound of voices that had been with him to satiety, as he might have said, for years; but he now knew, all the same, how uneasy he had felt; that was brought home to him by his present sense of a respite. It had come moreover in a flash of an eye; it had come in the smile with which Sarah, whom, at the window of her compartment, they had effusively greeted from the platform, rustled down to them a moment later, fresh and handsome from her cool June progress through the charming land. It was only a sign, but enough: she was going to be gracious and unallusive, she was going to play the larger game—which was still more apparent, after she had emerged from Chad's arms, in her direct greeting to the valued friend of her family.

Strether *was* then as much as ever the valued friend of her family; it was something he could at all events go on with; and the manner of his response to it expressed even for himself how little he had enjoyed the prospect of ceasing to figure in that likeness. He had always seen Sarah gracious—had in fact rarely seen her shy or dry; her marked thin-lipped smile, intense without brightness and as prompt to act as the scrape of a safety-match; the protrusion of her rather remarkably long chin, which in her case represented invitation and urbanity, and not, as in most others, pugnacity and defiance; the penetration of her voice to a distance, the general encouragement and approval of her manner, were all elements with which intercourse had made him familiar, but which he noted to-day almost as if she had been a new acquaintance. This first glimpse of her had given a brief but vivid accent to her resemblance to her mother; he could have taken her for Mrs. Newsome while she met his eyes as the train rolled into the station. It was an impression that quickly dropped; Mrs. Newsome was much handsomer, and while Sarah inclined to the massive her mother had, at an age, still the girdle of a maid; also the latter's chin was rather short, than long, and her smile, by good fortune, much more, oh ever so much more, mercifully vague. Strether had seen Mrs. Newsome reserved; he had literally heard her silent, though he had never known her unpleasant. It was the case with Mrs. Pocock that he had known *her* unpleasant, even though he had never known her not affable. She had forms of affability that were in a high degree assertive; nothing for instance had ever been more striking than that she was affable to Jim.

What had told in any case at the window of the train was her high clear forehead, that forehead which her friends, for some reason, always thought of as a "brow"; the long reach of her eyes—it came out at this juncture in such a manner as to remind him, oddly enough, also of that of Waymarsh's; and the unusual gloss of her dark hair, dressed and hatted, after her mother's refined example, with such an avoidance of extremes that it was always spoken of at Woollett as "their own." Though this analogy dropped as soon as she was on the platform it had lasted long enough to make him feel all the advantage, as it were, of his relief. The woman at home, the woman to whom he was attached, was before him just long enough to give him again the measure of the wretchedness, in fact really of the shame, of their having to recognise the formation, between them, of a "split." He had taken this measure in solitude and meditation; but the catastrophe, as Sarah steamed up, looked for its few seconds unprecedently dreadful—or proved, more exactly, altogether unthinkable; so that his finding something free and familiar to respond to brought with it in an instant renewal of his loyalty. He had suddenly sounded the whole depth, had gasped at what he might have lost.

Well, he could now, for the quarter of an hour of their detention, hover about the travellers as soothingly as if their direct message to him was that he had lost nothing. He wasn't going to have Sarah write to her mother that night that he was in any way altered or strange. There had been times enough for a month when it had seemed to him that he was strange, that he was altered, in every way; but that was a matter for himself; he knew at least whose business it was *not*; it was not at all events such a circumstance as Sarah's own unaided lights would help her to. Even if she had come out to flash those lights more than yet appeared she wouldn't make much headway against mere pleasantness. He counted on being able to be merely pleasant to the end, and if only from incapacity moreover to formulate anything different. He couldn't even formulate to himself his being changed and queer; it had taken place, the process, somewhere deep down; Maria Gostrey had caught glimpses of it; but how was he to fish it up, even if he desired, for Mrs. Pocock? This was then the spirit in which he hovered, and with the easier throb in it much indebted furthermore to the impression of high and established adequacy as a pretty girl promptly produced in him by Mamie. He had wondered vaguely—turning over many things in the fidget of his thoughts—if Mamie *were* as pretty as Woollett published her; as to which issue seeing her now again was to be so swept away by Woollett's opinion that this consequence really let loose for the imagination an avalanche of others. There were positively five minutes in which the last word seemed of necessity to abide with a Woollett represented by a Mamie. This was the sort of truth the place itself would feel; it would send her forth in confidence; it would point to her with triumph; it would take its stand on her with assurance; it would be conscious of no requirement she didn't meet, of no question she couldn't answer.

Well, it was right, Strether slipped smoothly enough into the cheerfulness of saying: granted that a community *might* be best represented by a young lady of twenty-two, Mamie perfectly played the part, played it as if she were used to it, and looked and spoke and dressed the character. He wondered if she mightn't, in the high light of Paris, a cool full studio-light, becoming yet treacherous, show as too conscious of these matters; but the next moment he felt satisfied that her consciousness was after all empty for its size, rather too simple than too mixed, and that the kind way with her would be not to take many things out of it, but to put as many as possible in. She was robust and conveniently tall; just a trifle too bloodlessly fair perhaps, but with a pleasant public familiar radiance that affirmed her vitality. She might have been "receiving" for Woollett, wherever she found herself, and there was something in her manner, her tone, her motion, her pretty blue eyes, her pretty perfect teeth and her very small, too small, nose, that immediately placed her, to the fancy, between the windows of a hot bright room in which voices were high—up at that end to which people were brought to be "presented." They were there to congratulate, these images, and Strether's renewed vision, on this hint, completed the idea. What Mamie was like was the happy bride, the bride after the church and just before going away. She wasn't the mere maiden, and yet was only as much married as that quantity came to. She was in the brilliant acclaimed festal stage. Well, might it last her long!

Strether rejoiced in these things for Chad, who was all genial attention to the needs of his friends, besides having arranged that his servant should re-enforce him; the ladies were certainly pleasant to see, and Mamie would be at any time and anywhere pleasant to exhibit. She would look extraordinarily like his young wife—the wife of a honeymoon, should he go about with her; but that was his own affair—or perhaps it was hers; it was at any rate something she couldn't help. Strether remembered how he had seen him come up with Jeanne de Vionnet in Gloriani's garden, and the fancy he had had about that—the fancy obscured now, thickly overlaid with others; the recollection was during these minutes his only note of trouble. He had often, in spite of himself, wondered if Chad but too probably were not with Jeanne the object of a still and shaded flame. It was on the cards that the child *might* be tremulously in love, and this conviction now flickered up not a bit the less for his disliking to think of it, for its being, in a complicated situation, a complication the more, and for something indescribable in Mamie, something at all events straightway lent her by his own mind, something that gave her value, gave her intensity and purpose, as the symbol of an opposition. Little Jeanne wasn't really at all in question—how *could* she be?—yet from the moment Miss Pocock had shaken her skirts on the platform, touched up the immense bows of her hat and settled properly over her shoulder the strap of her morocco-and-gilt travelling-satchel, from that moment little Jeanne was opposed.

It was in the cab with Jim that impressions really crowded on Strether, giving him the strangest sense of length of absence from people among whom he had lived for years. Having them thus come out to him was as if he had returned to find them; and the droll promptitude of Jim's mental reaction threw his own initiation far back into the past. Whoever might or mightn't be suited by what was going on among them, Jim, for one, would certainly be: his instant recognition—frank and whimsical—of what the affair was for *him* gave Strether a glow of pleasure. "I say, you know, this *is* about my shape, and if it hadn't been for *you*—!" so he broke out as the charming streets met his healthy appetite; and he wound up, after an expressive nudge, with a clap of his companion's knee and an "Oh you, you—you *are* doing it!" that was charged with rich meaning. Strether felt in it the intention of homage, but, with a curiosity otherwise occupied, postponed taking it up. What he was asking himself for the time was how Sarah Pocock, in the opportunity already given her, had judged her brother—from whom he himself, as they finally, at the station, separated for their different conveyances, had had a look into which he could read more than one message. However Sarah was judging her brother, Chad's conclusion about his sister, and about her husband and her husband's sister, was at the least on the way not to fail of confidence. Strether felt the confidence, and that, as the look between them was an exchange, what he himself gave back was relatively vague. This comparison of notes however could wait; everything struck him as depending on the effect produced by Chad. Neither Sarah nor Mamie had in any way, at the station—where they had had after all ample time—broken out about it; which, to make up for this, was what our friend had expected of Jim as soon as they should find themselves together.

It was queer to him that he had that noiseless brush with Chad; an ironic intelligence with this youth on the subject of his relatives, an intelligence carried on under their nose and, as might be said at their expense—such a matter marked again for him strongly the number of stages he had come; albeit that if the number seemed great the time taken for the final one was but the turn of a hand. He had before this had many moments of wondering if he himself weren't perhaps changed even as Chad was changed. Only what in Chad was conspicuous improvement—well, he had no name ready for the working, in his own organism, of his own more timid dose. He should have to see first what this action would amount to. And for his occult passage with the young man, after all, the directness of it had no greater oddity than the fact that the young man's way with the three travellers should have been so happy a manifestation. Strether liked him for it, on the spot, as he hadn't yet liked him; it affected him while it lasted as he might have been affected by some light pleasant perfect work of art: to that degree that he wondered if they were really worthy of it, took it in and did it justice; to that degree that it would have been scarce a miracle if, there in the luggage-room, while they waited for their things, Sarah had pulled his sleeve and drawn him aside. "You're right; we haven't quite known what you mean, Mother and I, but now we see. Chad's magnificent; what can one want more? If *this* is the kind of thing—!" On which they might, as it were, have embraced and begun to work together.

Ah how much, as it was, for all her bridling brightness—which was merely general and noticed nothing—*would* they work together? Strether knew he was unreasonable; he set it down to his being nervous: people couldn't notice everything and speak of everything in a quarter of an hour. Possibly, no doubt, also, he made too much of Chad's display. Yet, none the less, when, at the end of five minutes, in the cab, Jim Pocock had said nothing either—hadn't said, that is, what Strether wanted, though he had said much else—it all suddenly bounced back to their being either stupid or wilful. It was more probably on the whole the former; so that that would be the drawback of the bridling brightness. Yes, they would bridle and be bright; they would make the best of what was before them, but their observation would fail; it would be beyond them; they simply wouldn't understand. Of what use would it be then that they had come?—if they weren't to be intelligent up to *that* point: unless indeed he himself were utterly deluded and extravagant? Was he, on this question of Chad's improvement, fantastic and away from the truth? Did he live in a false world, a world that had grown simply to suit him, and was his present slight irritation—in the face now of Jim's silence in particular—but the alarm of the vain thing menaced by the touch of the real? Was this contribution of the real possibly the mission of the Pococks?—had they come to make the work of observation, as *he* had practised observation, crack and crumble, and to reduce Chad to the plain terms in which honest minds could deal with him? Had they come in short to be sane where Strether was destined to feel that he himself had only been silly?

He glanced at such a contingency, but it failed to hold him long when once he had reflected that he would have been silly, in this case, with Maria Gostrey and little Bilham, with Madame de Vionnet and little Jeanne, with Lambert Strether, in fine, and above all with Chad Newsome himself. Wouldn't it be found to have made more for reality to be silly with these persons than sane with Sarah and Jim? Jim in fact, he presently made up his mind, was individually out of it; Jim didn't care; Jim hadn't come out either for Chad or for him; Jim in short left the moral side to Sally and indeed simply availed himself now, for the sense of recreation, of the fact that he left almost everything to Sally. He was nothing compared to Sally, and not so much by reason of Sally's temper and will as by that of her more developed type and greater acquaintance with the world. He quite frankly and serenely confessed, as he sat there with Strether, that he felt his type hang far in the rear of his wife's and still further, if possible, in the rear of his sister's. Their types, he well knew, were recognised and acclaimed; whereas the most a leading Woollett business-man could hope to achieve socially, and for that matter industrially, was a certain freedom to play into this general glamour.

The impression he made on our friend was another of the things that marked our friend's road. It was a strange impression, especially as so soon produced; Strether had received it, he judged, all in the twenty minutes; it struck him at least as but in a minor degree the work of the long Woollett years. Pocock was normally and consentingly though not quite wittingly out of the question. It was despite his being normal; it was despite his being cheerful; it was despite his being a leading Woollett business-man; and the determination of his fate left him thus perfectly usual—as everything else about it was clearly, to his sense, not less so. He seemed to say that there was a whole side of life on which the perfectly usual *was* for leading Woollett business-men to be out of the question. He made no more of it than that, and Strether, so far as Jim was concerned, desired to make no more. Only Strether's imagination, as always, worked, and he asked himself if this side of life were not somehow connected, for those who figured on it, with the fact of marriage. Would *his* relation to it, had he married ten years before, have become now the same as Pocock's? Might it even become the same should he marry in a few months? Should he ever know himself as much out of the question for Mrs. Newsome as Jim knew himself—in a dim way—for Mrs. Jim?

To turn his eyes in that direction was to be personally reassured; he was different from Pocock; he had affirmed himself differently and he was held after all in a higher esteem. What none the less came home to him, however, at this hour, was that the society over there, of which Sarah and Mamie—and in a more eminent way, Mrs. Newsome herself—were specimens, was essentially a society of women, and that poor Jim wasn't in it. He himself, Lambert Strether, *was* as yet in some degree—which was an odd situation for a man; but it kept coming back to him in a whimsical way that he should perhaps find his marriage had cost him his place. This occasion indeed, whatever that fancy represented, was not a time of sensible exclusion for Jim, who was in a state of manifest response to the charm of his adventure. Small and fat and constantly facetious, straw-coloured and destitute of marks, he would have been practically indistinguishable hadn't this constant preference for light-grey clothes, for white hats, for very big cigars and very little stories, done what it could for his identity. There were signs in him, though none of them plaintive, of always paying for others; and the principal one perhaps was just this failure of type. It was with this that he paid, rather than with fatigue or waste; and also doubtless a little with the effort of humour—never irrelevant to the conditions, to the relations, with which he was acquainted.

He gurgled his joy as they rolled through the happy streets; he declared that his trip was a regular windfall, and that he wasn't there, he was eager to remark, to hang back from anything; he didn't know quite what Sally had come for, but *he* had come for a good time. Strether indulged him even while wondering if what Sally wanted her brother to go back for was to become like her husband. He trusted that a good time was to be, out and out, the programme for all of them; and he assented liberally to Jim's proposal that, disencumbered and irresponsible—his things were in the omnibus with those of the others—they should take a further turn round before going to the hotel. It wasn't for *him* to tackle Chad—it was Sally's job; and as it would be like her, he felt, to open fire on the spot, it wouldn't be amiss of them to hold off and give her time. Strether, on his side, only asked to give her time; so he jogged with his companion along boulevards and avenues, trying to extract from meagre material some forecast of his catastrophe. He was quick enough to see that Jim Pocock declined judgement, had hovered quite round the outer edge of discussion and anxiety, leaving all analysis of their question to the ladies alone and now only feeling his way toward some small droll cynicism. It broke out afresh, the cynicism—it had already shown a flicker—in a but slightly deferred "Well, hanged if I would if *I* were he!"

"You mean you wouldn't in Chad's place—?"

"Give up this to go back and boss the advertising!" Poor Jim, with his arms folded and his little legs out in the open fiacre, drank in the sparkling Paris noon and carried his eyes from one side of their vista to the other. "Why I want to come right out here and live myself. And I want to live while I *am* here too. I feel with *you*—oh you've been grand, old man, and I've twigged—that it ain't right to worry Chad. *I* don't mean to persecute him; I couldn't in conscience. It's thanks to you at any rate that I'm here, and I'm sure I'm much obliged. You're a lovely pair."

There were things in this speech that Strether let pass for the time. "Don't you then think it important the advertising should be thoroughly taken in hand? Chad *will* be, so far as capacity is concerned," he went on, "the man to do it."

"Where did he get his capacity," Jim asked, "over here?"

"He didn't get it over here, and the wonderful thing is that over here he hasn't inevitably lost it. He has a natural turn for business, an extraordinary head. He comes by that," Strether explained, "honestly enough. He's in that respect his father's son, and also—for she's wonderful in her way too—his mother's. He has other tastes and other tendencies; but Mrs. Newsome and your wife are quite right about his having that. He's very remarkable."

"Well, I guess he is," Jim Pocock comfortably sighed. "But if you've believed so in his making us hum, why have you so prolonged the discussion? Don't you know we've been quite anxious about you?"

These questions were not informed with earnestness, but Strether saw he must none the less make a choice and take a line. "Because, you see, I've greatly liked it. I've liked my Paris. I dare say I've liked it too much."

"Oh you old wretch!" Jim gaily exclaimed.

"But nothing's concluded," Strether went on. "The case is more complex than it looks from Woollett."

"Oh well, it looks bad enough from Woollett!" Jim declared.

"Even after all I've written?"

Jim bethought himself. "Isn't it what you've written that has made Mrs. Newsome pack us off? That at least and Chad's not turning up?"

Strether made a reflexion of his own. "I see. That she should do something was, no doubt, inevitable, and your wife has therefore of course come out to act."

"Oh yes," Jim concurred—"to act. But Sally comes out to act, you know," he lucidly added, "every time she leaves the house. She never comes out but she *does* act. She's acting moreover now for her mother, and that fixes the scale." Then he wound up, opening all his senses to it, with a renewed embrace of pleasant Paris. "We haven't all the same at Woollett got anything like this."

Strether continued to consider. "I'm bound to say for you all that you strike me as having arrived in a very mild and reasonable frame of mind. You don't show your claws. I felt just now in Mrs. Pocock no sympton of that. She isn't fierce," he went on. "I'm such a nervous idiot that I thought she might be."

"Oh don't you know her well enough," Pocock asked, "to have noticed that she never gives herself away, any more than her mother ever does? They ain't fierce, either of 'em; they let you come quite close. They wear their fur smooth side out—

the warm side in. Do you know what they are?" Jim pursued as he looked about him, giving the question, as Strether felt, but half his care—"do you know what they are? They're about as intense as they can live."

"Yes"—and Strether's concurrence had a positive precipitation; "they're about as intense as they can live."

"They don't lash about and shake the cage," said Jim, who seemed pleased with his analogy; "and it's at feeding-time that they're quietest. But they always get there."

"They do indeed—they always get there!" Strether replied with a laugh that justified his confession of nervousness. He disliked to be talking sincerely of Mrs. Newsome with Pocock; he could have talked insincerely. But there was something he wanted to know, a need created in him by her recent intermission, by his having given from the first so much, as now more than ever appeared to him, and got so little. It was as if a queer truth in his companion's metaphor had rolled over him with a rush. She *had* been quiet at feeding-time; she had fed, and Sarah had fed with her, out of the big bowl of all his recent free communication, his vividness and pleasantness, his ingenuity and even his eloquence, while the current of her response had steadily run thin. Jim meanwhile however, it was true, slipped characteristically into shallowness from the moment he ceased to speak out of the experience of a husband.

"But of course Chad has now the advantage of being there before her. If he doesn't work that for all it's worth—!" He sighed with contingent pity at his brother-in-law's possible want of resource. "He has worked it on *you*, pretty well, eh?" and he asked the next moment if there were anything new at the Varieties, which he pronounced in the American manner. They talked about the Varieties—Strether confessing to a knowledge which produced again on Pocock's part a play of innuendo as vague as a nursery rhyme, yet as aggressive as an elbow in his side; and they finished their drive under the protection of easy themes. Strether waited to the end, but still in vain, for any show that Jim had seen Chad as different; and he could scarce have explained the discouragement he drew from the absence of this testimony. It was what he had taken his own stand on, so far as he had taken a stand; and if they were all going to see nothing he had only wasted his time. He gave his friend till the very last moment, till they had come into sight of the hotel; and when poor Pocock only continued cheerful and envious and funny he fairly grew to dislike him, to feel him extravagantly common. If they were *all* going to see nothing! Strether knew, as this came back to him, that he was also letting Pocock represent for him what Mrs. Newsome wouldn't see. He went on disliking, in the light of Jim's commonness, to talk to him about that lady; yet just before the cab pulled up he knew the extent of his desire for the real word from Woollett.

"Has Mrs. Newsome at all given way—?"

"'Given way'?"—Jim echoed it with the practical derision of his sense of a long past.

"Under the strain, I mean, of hope deferred, of disappointment repeated and thereby intensified."

"Oh is she prostrate, you mean?"—he had his categories in hand. "Why yes, she's prostrate—just as Sally is. But they're never so lively, you know, as when they're prostrate."

"Ah Sarah's prostrate?" Strether vaguely murmured.

"It's when they're prostrate that they most sit up."

"And Mrs. Newsome's sitting up?"

"All night, my boy—for *you*!" And Jim fetched him, with a vulgar little guffaw, a thrust that gave relief to the picture. But he had got what he wanted. He felt on the spot that this *was* the real word from Woollett. "So don't you go home!" Jim added while he alighted and while his friend, letting him profusely pay the cabman, sat on in a momentary muse. Strether wondered if that were the real word too.

III

As the door of Mrs. Pocock's salon was pushed open for him, the next day, well before noon, he was reached by a voice with a charming sound that made him just falter before crossing the threshold. Madame de Vionnet was already on the field, and this gave the drama a quicker pace than he felt it as yet—though his suspense had increased—in the power of any act of his own to do. He had spent the previous evening with all his old friends together; yet he would still have described himself as quite in the dark in respect to a forecast of their influence on his situation. It was strange now, none the less, that in the light of this unexpected note of her presence he felt Madame de Vionnet a part of that situation as she hadn't even yet been. She was alone, he found himself assuming, with Sarah, and there was a bearing in that—somehow beyond his control—on his personal fate. Yet she was only saying something quite easy and independent—the thing she had come, as a good friend of Chad's, on purpose to say. "There isn't anything at all—? I should be so delighted."

It was clear enough, when they were there before him, how she had been received. He saw this, as Sarah got up to greet him, from something fairly hectic in Sarah's face. He saw furthermore that they weren't, as had first come to him, alone together; he was at no loss as to the identity of the broad high back presented to him in the embrasure of the window furthest from the door. Waymarsh, whom he had to-day not yet seen, whom he only knew to have left the hotel before him, and who had taken part, the night previous, on Mrs. Pocock's kind invitation, conveyed by Chad, in the entertainment, informal but cordial, promptly offered by that lady—Waymarsh had anticipated him even as Madame de Vionnet had done, and, with his hands in his pockets and his attitude unaffected by Strether's entrance, was looking out, in marked detachment, at the Rue de Rivoli. The latter felt it in the air—it was immense how Waymarsh could mark things—that he had remained deeply dissociated from the overture to their hostess that we have recorded on Madame de Vionnet's side. He had, conspicuously, tact, besides a stiff general view; and this was why he had left Mrs. Pocock to struggle alone. He would outstay the visitor; he would unmistakeably wait; to what had he been doomed for months past but waiting? Therefore she was to feel that she had him in reserve. What support she drew from this was still to be seen, for, although Sarah was vividly bright, she had given herself up for the moment to an ambiguous flushed formalism. She had had to reckon more quickly than she expected; but it concerned her first of all to signify that she was not to be taken unawares. Strether arrived precisely in time for her showing it. "Oh you're too good; but I don't think I feel quite helpless. I have my brother—and these American friends. And then you know I've been to Paris. I *know* Paris," said Sally Pocock in a tone that breathed a certain chill on Strether's heart.

"Ah but a woman, in this tiresome place where everything's always changing, a woman of good will," Madame de Vionnet threw off, "can always help a woman. I'm sure you 'know'—but we know perhaps different things." She too, visibly, wished to make no mistake; but it was a fear of a different order and more kept out of sight. She smiled in welcome at Strether; she greeted him more familiarly than Mrs. Pocock; she put out her hand to him without moving from her place; and it came to him in the course of a minute and in the oddest way—yes, positively—she was giving him over to ruin. She was all kindness and ease, but she couldn't help so giving him; she was exquisite, and her being just as she was poured for Sarah a sudden rush of meaning into his own equivocations. How could she know how she was hurting him? She wanted to show as simple and humble—in the degree compatible with operative charm; but it was just this that seemed to put him on her side. She struck him as dressed, as arranged, as prepared infinitely to conciliate—with the very poetry of good taste in her view of the conditions of her early call. She was ready to advise about dressmakers and shops; she held herself wholly at the disposition of Chad's family. Strether noticed her card on the table—her coronet and her "Comtesse"—and the imagination was sharp in him of certain private adjustments in Sarah's mind. She had never, he was sure, sat with a "Comtesse" before, and such was the specimen of that class he had been keeping to play on her. She had crossed the sea very particularly for a look at her; but he read in Madame de Vionnet's own eyes that this curiosity hadn't been so successfully met as that she herself wouldn't now have more than ever need of him. She looked much as she had looked to him that morning at Notre Dame; he noted in fact the suggestive sameness of her discreet and delicate dress. It seemed to speak—perhaps a little prematurely or too finely—of the sense in which she would help Mrs. Pocock with the shops. The way that lady took her in, moreover, added depth to his impression of what Miss Gostrey, by their common wisdom, had escaped. He winced as he saw himself but for that timely prudence ushering in Maria as a guide and an example. There was however a touch of relief for him in his glimpse, so far as he had got it, of Sarah's line. She "knew Paris." Madame de Vionnet had, for that matter, lightly taken this up. "Ah then you've a turn for that, an affinity that belongs to your family. Your brother, though his long experience makes a difference, I admit, has become one of us in a marvellous way." And she appealed to Strether in the manner of a woman who could always glide off with smoothness into another subject. Wasn't *he* struck with the way Mr. Newsome had made the place his own, and hadn't he been in a position to profit by his friend's wondrous expertness?

Strether felt the bravery, at the least, of her presenting herself so promptly to sound that note, and yet asked himself what other note, after all, she *could* strike from the moment she presented herself at all. She could meet Mrs. Pocock only on the ground of the obvious, and what feature of Chad's situation was more eminent than the fact that he had created for himself a new set of circumstances? Unless she hid herself altogether she could show but as one of these, an illustration of his domiciled and indeed of his confirmed condition. And the consciousness of all this in her charming eyes was so clear and fine that as she thus publicly drew him into her boat she produced in him such a silent agitation as he was not to fail afterwards to denounce as pusillanimous. "Ah don't be so charming to me!—for it makes us intimate, and after all what *is* between us when I've been so tremendously on my guard and have seen you but half a dozen times?" He recognised once more the perverse law that so inveterately governed his poor personal aspects: it would be exactly *like* the way things always turned out for him that he should affect Mrs. Pocock and Waymarsh as launched in a relation in which he had never been launched at all. They were at this very moment—they could only be—attributing to him the full licence of it, and all by the operation of her own tone with him;

whereas his sole licence had been to cling with intensity to the brink, not to dip so much as a toe into the flood. But the flicker of his fear on this occasion was not, as may be added, to repeat itself; it sprang up, for its moment, only to die down and then go out for ever. To meet his fellow visitor's invocation and, with Sarah's brilliant eyes on him, answer, *was* quite sufficiently to step into her boat. During the rest of the time her visit lasted he felt himself proceed to each of the proper offices, successively, for helping to keep the adventurous skiff afloat. It rocked beneath him, but he settled himself in his place. He took up an oar and, since he was to have the credit of pulling, pulled.

"That will make it all the pleasanter if it so happens that we *do* meet," Madame de Vionnet had further observed in reference to Mrs. Pocock's mention of her initiated state; and she had immediately added that, after all, her hostess couldn't be in need with the good offices of Mr. Strether so close at hand. "It's he, I gather, who has learned to know his Paris, and to love it, better than any one ever before in so short a time; so that between him and your brother, when it comes to the point, how can you possibly want for good guidance? The great thing, Mr. Strether will show you," she smiled, "is just to let one's self go."

"Oh I've not let myself go very far," Strether answered, feeling quite as if he had been called upon to hint to Mrs. Pocock how Parisians could talk. "I'm only afraid of showing I haven't let myself go far enough. I've taken a good deal of time, but I must quite have had the air of not budging from one spot." He looked at Sarah in a manner that he thought she might take as engaging, and he made, under Madame de Vionnet's protection, as it were, his first personal point. "What has really happened has been that, all the while, I've done what I came out for."

Yet it only at first gave Madame de Vionnet a chance immediately to take him up. "You've renewed acquaintance with your friend—you've learned to know him again." She spoke with such cheerful helpfulness that they might, in a common cause, have been calling together and pledged to mutual aid.

Waymarsh, at this, as if he had been in question, straightway turned from the window. "Oh yes, Countess—he has renewed acquaintance with *me*, and he *has*, I guess, learnt something about me, though I don't know how much he has liked it. It's for Strether himself to say whether he has felt it justifies his course."

"Oh but *you*," said the Countess gaily, "are not in the least what he came out for—is he really, Strether?—and I hadn't you at all in my mind. I was thinking of Mr. Newsome, of whom we think so much and with whom, precisely, Mrs. Pocock has given herself the opportunity to take up threads. What a pleasure for you both!" Madame de Vionnet, with her eyes on Sarah, bravely continued.

Mrs. Pocock met her handsomely, but Strether quickly saw she meant to accept no version of her movements or plans from any other lips. She required no patronage and no support, which were but other names for a false position; she would show in her own way what she chose to show, and this she expressed with a dry glitter that recalled to him a fine Woollett wintry morning. "I've never wanted for opportunities to see my brother. We've many things to think of at home, and great responsibilities and occupations, and our home's not an impossible place. We've plenty of reasons," Sarah continued a little piercingly, "for everything we do"—and in short she wouldn't give herself the least little scrap away. But she added as one who was always bland and who could afford a concession: "I've come because—well, because we do come."

"Ah then fortunately!"—Madame de Vionnet breathed it to the air. Five minutes later they were on their feet for her to take leave, standing together in an affability that had succeeded in surviving a further exchange of remarks; only with the emphasised appearance on Waymarsh's part of a tendency to revert, in a ruminating manner and as with an instinctive or a precautionary lightening of his tread, to an open window and his point of vantage. The glazed and gilded room, all red damask, ormolu, mirrors, clocks, looked south, and the shutters were bowed upon the summer morning; but the Tuileries garden and what was beyond it, over which the whole place hung, were things visible through gaps; so that the far-spreading presence of Paris came up in coolness, dimness and invitation, in the twinkle of gilt-tipped palings, the crunch of gravel, the click of hoofs, the crack of whips, things that suggested some parade of the circus. "I think it probable," said Mrs. Pocock, "that I shall have the opportunity of going to my brother's. I've no doubt it's very pleasant indeed." She spoke as to Strether, but her face was turned with an intensity of brightness to Madame de Vionnet, and there was a moment during which, while she thus fronted her, our friend expected to hear her add: "I'm much obliged to you, I'm sure, for inviting me there." He guessed that for five seconds these words were on the point of coming; he heard them as clearly as if they had been spoken; but he presently knew they had just failed—knew it by a glance, quick and fine, from Madame de Vionnet, which told him that she too had felt them in the air, but that the point had luckily not been made in any manner requiring notice. This left her free to reply only to what had been said.

"That the Boulevard Malesherbes may be common ground for us offers me the best prospect I see for the pleasure of meeting you again."

"Oh I shall come to see you, since you've been so good": and Mrs. Pocock looked her invader well in the eyes. The flush in Sarah's cheeks had by this time settled to a small definite crimson spot that was not without its own bravery; she held her head a good deal up, and it came to Strether that of the two, at this moment, she was the one who most carried out the idea of a Countess. He quite took in, however, that she would really return her visitor's civility: she wouldn't report again at Woollett without at least so much producible history as that in her pocket.

"I want extremely to be able to show you my little daughter," Madame de Vionnet went on; "and I should have brought her with me if I hadn't wished first to ask your leave. I was in hopes I should perhaps find Miss Pocock, of whose being with you I've heard from Mr. Newsome and whose acquaintance I should so much like my child to make. If I have the pleasure of seeing her and you do permit it I shall venture to ask her to be kind to Jeanne. Mr. Strether will tell you"—she beautifully kept it up—"that my poor girl is gentle and good and rather lonely. They've made friends, he and she, ever so happily, and he doesn't, I believe, think ill of her. As for Jeanne herself he has had the same success with her that I know he has had here wherever he has turned." She seemed to ask him for permission to say these things, or seemed rather to take it, softly and happily, with the ease of intimacy, for granted, and he had quite the consciousness now that not to meet her at any point more than half way would be odiously, basely to abandon her. Yes, he was *with* her, and, opposed even in this covert, this semi-safe fashion to those who were not, he felt, strangely and confusedly, but excitedly, inspiringly, how much and how far. It was as if he had positively waited in suspense for something from her that would let him in deeper, so that he might show her how he could take it. And what did in fact come as she drew out a little her farewell served sufficiently the purpose. "As his success is a matter that I'm sure he'll never mention for himself, I feel, you see, the less scruple; which it's very good of me to say, you know, by the way," she added as she addressed herself to him; "considering how little direct advantage I've gained from your triumphs with *me*. When does one ever see you? I wait at home and I languish. You'll have rendered me the service, Mrs. Pocock, at least," she wound up, "of giving me one of my much-too-rare glimpses of this gentleman."

"I certainly should be sorry to deprive you of anything that seems so much, as you describe it, your natural due. Mr. Strether and I are very old friends," Sarah allowed, "but the privilege of his society isn't a thing I shall quarrel about with any one."

"And yet, dear Sarah," he freely broke in, "I feel, when I hear you say that, that you don't quite do justice to the important truth of the extent to which—as you're also mine—I'm *your* natural due. I should like much better," he laughed, "to see you fight for me."

She met him, Mrs. Pocock, on this, with an arrest of speech—with a certain breathlessness, as he immediately fancied, on the score of a freedom for which she wasn't quite prepared. It had flared up—for all the harm he had intended by it—because, confoundedly, he didn't want any more to be afraid about her than he wanted to be afraid about Madame de Vionnet. He had never, naturally, called her anything but Sarah at home, and though he had perhaps never quite so markedly invoked her as his "dear," that was somehow partly because no occasion had hitherto laid so effective a trap for it. But something admonished him now that it was too late—unless indeed it were possibly too early; and that he at any rate shouldn't have pleased Mrs. Pocock the more by it. "Well, Mr. Strether—!" she murmured with vagueness, yet with sharpness, while her crimson spots burned a trifle brighter and he was aware that this must be for the present the limit of her response. Madame de Vionnet had already, however, come to his aid, and Waymarsh, as if for further participation, moved again back to them. It was true that the aid rendered by Madame de Vionnet was questionable; it was a sign that, for all one might confess to with her, and for all she might complain of not enjoying, she could still insidiously show how much of the material of conversation had accumulated between them.

"The real truth is, you know, that you sacrifice one without mercy to dear old Maria. She leaves no room in your life for anybody else. Do you know," she inquired of Mrs. Pocock, "about dear old Maria? The worst is that Miss Gostrey is really a wonderful woman."

"Oh yes indeed," Strether answered for her, "Mrs. Pocock knows about Miss Gostrey. Your mother, Sarah, must have told you about her; your mother knows everything," he sturdily pursued. "And I cordially admit," he added with his conscious gaiety of courage, "that she's as wonderful a woman as you like."

"Ah it isn't *I* who 'like,' dear Mr. Strether, anything to do with the matter!" Sarah Pocock promptly protested; "and I'm by no means sure I have—from my mother or from any one else—a notion of whom you're talking about."

"Well, he won't let you see her, you know," Madame de Vionnet sympathetically threw in. "He never lets *me*—old friends as we are: I mean as I am with Maria. He reserves her for his best hours; keeps her consummately to himself; only gives us others the crumbs of the feast."

"Well, Countess, *I've* had some of the crumbs," Waymarsh observed with weight and covering her with his large look; which led her to break in before he could go on.

"*Comment donc*, he shares her with *you*?" she exclaimed in droll stupefaction. "Take care you don't have, before you go much further, rather more of all *ces dames* than you may know what to do with!"

But he only continued in his massive way. "I can post you about the lady, Mrs. Pocock, so far as you may care to hear. I've seen her quite a number of times, and I was practically present when they made acquaintance. I've kept my eye on her right along, but I don't know as there's any real harm in her."

"'Harm'?" Madame de Vionnet quickly echoed. "Why she's the dearest and cleverest of all the clever and dear."

"Well, you run her pretty close, Countess," Waymarsh returned with spirit; "though there's no doubt she's pretty well up in things. She knows her way round Europe. Above all there's no doubt she does love Strether."

"Ah but we all do that—we all love Strether: it isn't a merit!" their fellow visitor laughed, keeping to her idea with a good conscience at which our friend was aware that he marvelled, though he trusted also for it, as he met her exquisitely expressive eyes, to some later light.

The prime effect of her tone, however—and it was a truth which his own eyes gave back to her in sad ironic play—could only be to make him feel that, to say such things to a man in public, a woman must practically think of him as ninety years old. He had turned awkwardly, responsibly red, he knew, at her mention of Maria Gostrey; Sarah Pocock's presence—the particular quality of it—had made this inevitable; and then he had grown still redder in proportion as he hated to have shown anything at all. He felt indeed that he was showing much, as, uncomfortably and almost in pain, he offered up his redness to Waymarsh, who, strangely enough, seemed now to be looking at him with a certain explanatory yearning. Something deep—something built on their old old relation—passed, in this complexity, between them; he got the side-wind of a loyalty that stood behind all actual queer questions. Waymarsh's dry bare humour—as it gave itself to be taken—gloomed out to demand justice. "Well, if you talk of Miss Barrace I've *my* chance too," it appeared stiffly to nod, and it granted that it was giving him away, but struggled to add that it did so only to save him. The sombre glow stared it at him till it fairly sounded out "to save you, poor old man, to save you; to save you in spite of yourself." Yet it was somehow just this communication that showed him to himself as more than ever lost. Still another result of it was to put before him as never yet that between his comrade and the interest represented by Sarah there was already a basis. Beyond all question now, yes: Waymarsh had been in occult relation with Mrs. Newsome—out, out it all came in the very effort of his face. "Yes, you're feeling my hand"—he as good as proclaimed it: "but only because this at least I *shall* have got out of the damned Old World: that I shall have picked up the pieces into which it has caused you to crumble." It was as if in short, after an instant, Strether had not only had it from him, but had recognised that so far as this went the instant had cleared the air. Our friend understood and approved; he had the sense that they wouldn't otherwise speak of it. This would be all, and it would mark in himself a kind of intelligent generosity. It was with grim Sarah then—Sarah grim for all her grace—that Waymarsh had begun at ten o'clock in the morning to save him. Well—if he *could*, poor dear man, with his big bleak kindness! The upshot of which crowded perception was that Strether, on his own side, still showed no more than he absolutely had to. He showed the least possible by saying to Mrs. Pocock after an interval much briefer than our glance at the picture reflected in him: "Oh it's as true as they please!—There's no Miss Gostrey for any one but me—not the least little peep. I keep her to myself."

"Well, it's very good of you to notify me," Sarah replied without looking at him and thrown for a moment by this discrimination, as the direction of her eyes showed, upon a dimly desperate little community with Madame de Vionnet. "But I hope I shan't miss her too much."

Madame de Vionnet instantly rallied. "And you know—though it might occur to one—it isn't in the least that he's ashamed of her. She's really—in a way—extremely good-looking."

"Ah but extremely!" Strether laughed while he wondered at the odd part he had found thus imposed on him.

It continued to be so by every touch from Madame de Vionnet. "Well, as I say, you know, I wish you would keep *me* a little more to yourself. Couldn't you name some day for me, some hour—and better soon than late? I'll be at home whenever it best suits you. There—I can't say fairer."

Strether thought a moment while Waymarsh and Mrs. Pocock affected him as standing attentive. "I did lately call on you. Last week—while Chad was out of town."

"Yes—and I was away, as it happened, too. You choose your moments well. But don't wait for my next absence, for I shan't make another," Madame de Vionnet declared, "while Mrs. Pocock's here."

"That vow needn't keep you long, fortunately," Sarah observed with reasserted suavity. "I shall be at present but a short time in Paris. I have my plans for other countries. I meet a number of charming friends"—and her voice seemed to caress that description of these persons.

"Ah then," her visitor cheerfully replied, "all the more reason! To-morrow, for instance, or next day?" she continued to Strether. "Tuesday would do for me beautifully."

"Tuesday then with pleasure."

"And at half-past five—or at six?"

It was ridiculous, but Mrs. Pocock and Waymarsh struck him as fairly waiting for his answer. It was indeed as if they were arranged, gathered for a performance, the performance of "Europe" by his confederate and himself. Well, the performance could only go on. "Say five forty-five."

"Five forty-five—good." And now at last Madame de Vionnet must leave them, though it carried, for herself, the performance a little further. "I *did* hope so much also to see Miss Pocock. Mayn't I still?"

Sarah hesitated, but she rose equal. "She'll return your visit with me. She's at present out with Mr. Pocock and my brother."

"I see—of course Mr. Newsome has everything to show them. He has told me of much about her. My great desire's to give my daughter the opportunity of making her acquaintance. I'm always on the look-out for such chances for her. If I didn't bring her to-day it was only to make sure first that you'd let me." After which the charming woman risked a more intense appeal. "It wouldn't suit *you* also to mention some near time, so that we shall be sure not to lose you?" Strether on his side waited, for Sarah likewise had, after all, to perform; and it occupied him to have been thus reminded that she had stayed at home—and on her first morning of Paris—while Chad led the others forth. Oh she was up to her eyes; if she had stayed at home she had stayed by an understanding, arrived at the evening before, that Waymarsh would come and find her alone. This was beginning well—for a first day in Paris; and the thing might be amusing yet. But Madame de Vionnet's earnestness was meanwhile beautiful. "You may think me indiscreet, but I've *such* a desire my Jeanne shall know an American girl of the really delightful kind. You see I throw myself for it on your charity."

The manner of this speech gave Strether such a sense of depths below it and behind it as he hadn't yet had—ministered in a way that almost frightened him to his dim divinations of reasons; but if Sarah still, in spite of it, faltered, this was why he had time for a sign of sympathy with her petitioner. "Let me say then, dear lady, to back your plea, that Miss Mamie is of the most delightful kind of all—is charming among the charming."

Even Waymarsh, though with more to produce on the subject, could get into motion in time. "Yes, Countess, the American girl's a thing that your country must at least allow ours the privilege to say we *can* show you. But her full beauty is only for those who know how to make use of her."

"Ah then," smiled Madame de Vionnet, "that's exactly what I want to do. I'm sure she has much to teach us."

It was wonderful, but what was scarce less so was that Strether found himself, by the quick effect of it, moved another way. "Oh that may be! But don't speak of your own exquisite daughter, you know, as if she weren't pure perfection. *I* at least won't take that from you. Mademoiselle de Vionnet," he explained, in considerable form, to Mrs. Pocock, "*is* pure perfection. Mademoiselle de Vionnet *is* exquisite."

It had been perhaps a little portentous, but "Ah?" Sarah simply glittered.

Waymarsh himself, for that matter, apparently recognised, in respect to the facts, the need of a larger justice, and he had with it an inclination to Sarah. "Miss Jane's strikingly handsome—in the regular French style."

It somehow made both Strether and Madame de Vionnet laugh out, though at the very moment he caught in Sarah's eyes, as glancing at the speaker, a vague but unmistakeable "You too?" It made Waymarsh in fact look consciously over her head. Madame de Vionnet meanwhile, however, made her point in her own way. "I wish indeed I could offer you my poor child as a dazzling attraction: it would make one's position simple enough! She's as good as she can be, but of course she's different, and the question is now—in the light of the way things seem to go—if she isn't after all *too* different: too different I mean from the splendid type every one is so agreed that your wonderful country produces. On the other hand of course Mr. Newsome, who knows it so well, has, as a good friend, dear kind man that he is, done everything he can—to keep us from fatal benightedness—for my small shy creature. Well," she wound up after Mrs. Pocock had signified, in a murmur still a little stiff, that she would speak to her own young charge on the question—"well, we shall sit, my child and I, and wait and wait and wait for you." But her last fine turn was for Strether. "Do speak of us in such a way—!"

"As that something can't but come of it? Oh something *shall* come of it! I take a great interest!" he further declared; and in proof of it, the next moment, he had gone with her down to her carriage.

BOOK NINTH

I

"The difficulty is," Strether said to Madame de Vionnet a couple of days later, "that I can't surprise them into the smallest sign of his not being the same old Chad they've been for the last three years glowering at across the sea. They simply won't give any, and as a policy, you know—what you call a *parti pris*, a deep game—that's positively remarkable."

It was so remarkable that our friend had pulled up before his hostess with the vision of it; he had risen from his chair at the end of ten minutes and begun, as a help not to worry, to move about her quite as he moved before Maria. He had kept his appointment with her to the minute and had been intensely impatient, though divided in truth between the sense of having everything to tell her and the sense of having nothing at all. The short interval had, in the face of their complication, multiplied his impressions—it being meanwhile to be noted, moreover, that he already frankly, already most publicly, viewed the complication as common to them. If Madame de Vionnet, under Sarah's eyes, had pulled him into her boat, there was by this time no doubt whatever that he had remained in it and that what he had really most been conscious of for many hours together was the movement of the vessel itself. They were in it together this moment as they hadn't yet been, and he hadn't at present uttered the least of the words of alarm or remonstrance that had died on his lips at the hotel. He had other things to say to her than that she had put him in a position; so quickly had his position grown to affect him as quite excitingly, altogether richly, inevitable. That the outlook, however—given the point of exposure—hadn't cleared up half so much as he had reckoned was the first warning she received from him on his arrival. She had replied with indulgence that he was in too great a hurry, and had remarked soothingly that if she knew how to be patient surely *he* might be. He felt her presence, on the spot, he felt her tone and everything about her, as an aid to that effort; and it was perhaps one of the proofs of her success with him that he seemed so much to take his ease while they talked. By the time he had explained to her why his impressions, though multiplied, still baffled him, it was as if he had been familiarly talking for hours. They baffled him because Sarah—well, Sarah was deep; deeper than she had ever yet had a chance to show herself. He didn't say that this was partly the effect of her opening so straight down, as it were, into her mother, and that, given Mrs. Newsome's profundity, the shaft thus sunk might well have a reach; but he wasn't without a resigned apprehension that, at such a rate of confidence between the two women, he was likely soon to be moved to show how already, at moments, it had been for him as if he were dealing directly with Mrs. Newsome. Sarah, to a certainty, would have begun herself to feel it in him—and this naturally put it in her power to torment him the more. From the moment she knew he *could* be tormented—!

"But *why* can you be?"—his companion was surprised at his use of the word.

"Because I'm made so—I think of everything."

"Ah one must never do that," she smiled. "One must think of as few things as possible."

"Then," he answered, "one must pick them out right. But all I mean is—for I express myself with violence—that she's in a position to watch me. There's an element of suspense for me, and she can see me wriggle. But my wriggling doesn't matter," he pursued. "I can bear it. Besides, I shall wriggle out."

The picture at any rate stirred in her an appreciation that he felt to be sincere. "I don't see how a man can be kinder to a woman than you are to me."

Well, kind was what he wanted to be; yet even while her charming eyes rested on him with the truth of this he none the less had his humour of honesty. "When I say suspense I mean, you know," he laughed, "suspense about my own case too!"

"Oh yes—about your own case too!" It diminished his magnanimity, but she only looked at him the more tenderly.

"Not, however," he went on, "that I want to talk to you about that. It's my own little affair, and I mentioned it simply as part of Mrs. Pocock's advantage." No, no; though there was a queer present temptation in it, and his suspense was so real that to fidget was a relief, he wouldn't talk to her about Mrs. Newsome, wouldn't work off on her the anxiety produced in him by Sarah's calculated omissions of reference. The effect she produced of representing her mother had been produced—and that was just the immense, the uncanny part of it—without her having so much as mentioned that lady. She had brought no message, had alluded to no question, had only answered his inquiries with hopeless limited propriety. She had invented a way of meeting them—as if he had been a polite perfunctory poor relation, of distant degree—that made them almost ridiculous in him. He couldn't, moreover, on his own side ask much without appearing to publish how he had lately lacked news; a circumstance of which it was Sarah's profound policy not to betray a suspicion. These things, all the same, he wouldn't breathe to Madame de Vionnet—much as they might make him walk up and down. And what he didn't say—as well as what *she* didn't, for she had also her high decencies—enhanced the effect of his being there with her at the end of ten minutes more intimately on the basis of saving her than he had yet had occasion to be. It ended in fact by being quite beautiful between them, the number of things they had a manifest consciousness of not saying. He would have liked to turn her, critically, to the subject of Mrs. Pocock, but he so stuck to the line he felt to be the point of honour and of delicacy that he scarce even asked her what her personal impression had been. He knew it, for that matter, without putting her to trouble: that she wondered how, with such elements, Sarah could still have no charm, was one of the principal things she held her tongue about. Strether would have been interested in her estimate of the elements—indubitably there, some of them, and to be appraised according to taste—but he denied himself even the luxury of this diversion. The way Madame de Vionnet affected him to-day was in itself a kind of demonstration of the happy employment of gifts. How could a woman think Sarah had charm who struck one as having arrived at it herself by such different roads? On the other hand of course Sarah wasn't obliged to have it. He felt as if somehow Madame de Vionnet *was*. The great question meanwhile was what Chad thought of his sister; which was naturally ushered in by that of Sarah's apprehension of Chad. *That* they could talk of, and with a freedom purchased by their discretion in other directions. The difficulty however was that they were reduced as yet to conjecture. He had given them in the day or two as little of a lead as Sarah, and Madame de Vionnet mentioned that she hadn't seen him since his sister's arrival.

"And does that strike you as such an age?"

She met it in all honesty. "Oh I won't pretend I don't miss him. Sometimes I see him every day. Our friendship's like that. Make what you will of it!" she whimsically smiled; a little flicker of the kind, occasional in her, that had more than once moved him to wonder what he might best make of *her*. "But he's perfectly right," she hastened to add, "and I wouldn't have him fail in any way at present for the world. I'd sooner not see him for three months. I begged him to be beautiful to them, and he fully feels it for himself."

Strether turned away under his quick perception; she was so odd a mixture of lucidity and mystery. She fell in at moments with the theory about her he most cherished, and she seemed at others to blow it into air. She spoke now as if her art were all an innocence, and then again as if her innocence were all an art. "Oh he's giving himself up, and he'll do so to the end. How can he but want, now that it's within reach, his full impression?—which is much more important, you know, than either yours or mine. But he's just soaking," Strether said as he came back; "he's going in conscientiously for a saturation. I'm bound to say he *is* very good."

"Ah," she quietly replied, "to whom do you say it?" And then more quietly still: "He's capable of anything."

Strether more than reaffirmed—"Oh he's excellent. I more and more like," he insisted, "to see him with them"; though the oddity of this tone between them grew sharper for him even while they spoke. It placed the young man so before them as the result of her interest and the product of her genius, acknowledged so her part in the phenomenon and made the phenomenon so rare, that more than ever yet he might have been on the very point of asking her for some more detailed account of the whole business than he had yet received from her. The occasion almost forced upon him some question as to how she had managed and as to the appearance such miracles presented from her own singularly close place of survey. The moment in fact however passed, giving way to more present history, and he continued simply to mark his appreciation of the happy truth. "It's a tremendous comfort to feel how one can trust him." And then again while for a little she said nothing—as if after all to *her* trust there might be a special limit: "I mean for making a good show to them."

"Yes," she thoughtfully returned—"but if they shut their eyes to it!"

Strether for an instant had his own thought. "Well, perhaps that won't matter!"

"You mean because he probably—do what they will—won't like them?"

"Oh 'do what they will'—! They won't do much; especially if Sarah hasn't more—well, more than one has yet made out—to give."

Madame de Vionnet weighed it. "Ah she has all her grace!" It was a statement over which, for a little, they could look at each other sufficiently straight, and though it produced no protest from Strether the effect was somehow as if he had treated it as a joke. "She may be persuasive and caressing with him; she may be eloquent beyond words. She may get hold of him," she wound up—"well, as neither you nor I have."

"Yes, she *may*"—and now Strether smiled. "But he has spent all his time each day with Jim. He's still showing Jim round."

She visibly wondered. "Then how about Jim?"

Strether took a turn before he answered. "Hasn't he given you Jim? Hasn't he before this 'done' him for you?" He was a little at a loss. "Doesn't he tell you things?"

She hesitated. "No"—and their eyes once more gave and took. "Not as you do. You somehow make me see them—or at least feel them. And I haven't asked too much," she added; "I've of late wanted so not to worry him."

"Ah for that, so have I," he said with encouraging assent; so that—as if she had answered everything—they were briefly sociable on it. It threw him back on his other thought, with which he took another turn; stopping again, however, presently with something of a glow. "You see Jim's really immense. I think it will be Jim who'll do it."

She wondered. "Get hold of him?"

"No—just the other thing. Counteract Sarah's spell." And he showed now, our friend, how far he had worked it out. "Jim's intensely cynical."

"Oh dear Jim!" Madame de Vionnet vaguely smiled.

"Yes, literally—dear Jim! He's awful. What *he* wants, heaven forgive him, is to help us."

"You mean"—she was eager—"help *me*?"

"Well, Chad and me in the first place. But he throws you in too, though without as yet seeing you much. Only, so far as he does see you—if you don't mind—he sees you as awful."

"'Awful'?"—she wanted it all.

"A regular bad one—though of course of a tremendously superior kind. Dreadful, delightful, irresistible."

"Ah dear Jim! I should like to know him. I *must*."

"Yes, naturally. But will it do? You may, you know," Strether suggested, "disappoint him."

She was droll and humble about it. "I can but try. But my wickedness then," she went on, "is my recommendation for him?"

"Your wickedness and the charms with which, in such a degree as yours, he associates it. He understands, you see, that Chad and I have above all wanted to have a good time, and his view is simple and sharp. Nothing will persuade him—in the light, that is, of my behaviour—that I really didn't, quite as much as Chad, come over to have one before it was too late. He wouldn't have expected it of me; but men of my age, at Woollett—and especially the least likely ones—have been noted as liable to strange outbreaks, belated uncanny clutches at the unusual, the ideal. It's an effect that a lifetime of Woollett has quite been observed as having; and I thus give it to you, in Jim's view, for what it's worth. Now his wife and his mother-in-law," Strether continued to explain, "have, as in honour bound, no patience with such phenomena, late or early—which puts Jim, as against his relatives, on the other side. Besides," he added, "I don't think he really wants Chad back. If Chad doesn't come—"

"He'll have"—Madame de Vionnet quite apprehended—"more of the free hand?"

"Well, Chad's the bigger man."

"So he'll work now *en dessous*, to keep him quiet?"

"No—he won't 'work' at all, and he won't do anything *en dessous*. He's very decent and won't be a traitor in the camp. But he'll be amused with his own little view of our duplicity, he'll sniff up what he supposes to be Paris from morning till night, and he'll be, as to the rest, for Chad—well, just what he is."

She thought it over. "A warning?"

He met it almost with glee. "You *are* as wonderful as everybody says!" And then to explain all he meant: "I drove him about for his first hour, and do you know what—all beautifully unconscious—he most put before me? Why that something like *that* is at bottom, as an improvement to his present state, as in fact the real redemption of it, what they think it may not be too late to make of our friend." With which, as, taking it in, she seemed, in her recurrent alarm, bravely to gaze at the possibility, he completed his statement. "But it *is* too late. Thanks to you!"

It drew from her again one of her indefinite reflexions. "Oh 'me'—after all!"

He stood before her so exhilarated by his demonstration that he could fairly be jocular. "Everything's comparative. You're better than *that*."

"You"—she could but answer him—"are better than anything." But she had another thought. "*Will* Mrs. Pocock come to me?"

"Oh yes—she'll do that. As soon, that is, as my friend Waymarsh—*her* friend now—leaves her leisure."

She showed an interest. "Is he so much her friend as that?"

"Why, didn't you see it all at the hotel?"

"Oh"—she was amused—"'all' is a good deal to say. I don't know—I forget. I lost myself in *her*."

"You were splendid," Strether returned—"but 'all' isn't a good deal to say: it's only a little. Yet it's charming so far as it goes. She wants a man to herself."

"And hasn't she got *you*?"

"Do you think she looked at me—or even at you—as if she had?" Strether easily dismissed that irony. "Every one, you see, must strike her as having somebody. You've got Chad—and Chad has got you."

"I see"—she made of it what she could. "And you've got Maria."

Well, he on his side accepted that. "I've got Maria. And Maria has got me. So it goes."

"But Mr. Jim—whom has he got?"

"Oh he has got—or it's as *if* he had—the whole place."

"But for Mr. Waymarsh"—she recalled—"isn't Miss Barrace before any one else?"

He shook his head. "Miss Barrace is a *raffinée*, and her amusement won't lose by Mrs. Pocock. It will gain rather—especially if Sarah triumphs and she comes in for a view of it."

"How well you know us!" Madame de Vionnet, at this, frankly sighed.

"No—it seems to me it's we that I know. I know Sarah—it's perhaps on that ground only that my feet are firm. Waymarsh will take her round while Chad takes Jim—and I shall be, I assure you, delighted for both of them. Sarah will have had what she requires—she will have paid her tribute to the ideal; and he will have done about the same. In Paris it's in the air—so what can one do less? If there's a point that, beyond any other, Sarah wants to make, it's that she didn't come out to be narrow. We shall feel at least that."

"Oh," she sighed, "the quantity we seem likely to 'feel'! But what becomes, in these conditions, of the girl?"

"Of Mamie—if we're all provided? Ah for that," said Strether, "you can trust Chad."

"To be, you mean, all right to her?"

"To pay her every attention as soon as he has polished off Jim. He wants what Jim can give him—and what Jim really won't—though he has had it all, and more than all, from me. He wants in short his own personal impression, and he'll get it—strong. But as soon as he has got it Mamie won't suffer."

"Oh, Mamie mustn't *suffer*!" Madame de Vionnet soothingly emphasized.

But Strether could reassure her. "Don't fear. As soon as he has done with Jim, Jim will fall to me. And then you'll see."

It was as if in a moment she saw already; yet she still waited. Then, "Is she really quite charming?" she asked.

He had got up with his last words and gathered in his hat and gloves. "I don't know; I'm watching. I'm studying the case, as it were—and I daresay I shall be able to tell you."

She wondered. "Is it a case?"

"Yes—I think so. At any rate I shall see."

"But haven't you known her before?"

"Yes," he smiled—"but somehow at home she wasn't a case. She has become one since." It was as if he made it out for himself. "She has become one here."

"So very very soon?"

He measured it, laughing. "Not sooner than I did."

"And you became one—?"

"Very very soon. The day I arrived."

Her intelligent eyes showed her thought of it. "Ah but the day you arrived you met Maria. Whom has Miss Pocock met?"

He paused again, but he brought it out. "Hasn't she met Chad?"

"Certainly—but not for the first time. He's an old friend." At which Strether had a slow amused significant headshake that made her go on: "You mean that for *her* at least he's a new person—that she sees him as different?"

"She sees him as different."

"And how does she see him?"

Strether gave it up. "How can one tell how a deep little girl sees a deep young man?"

"Is every one so deep? Is she too?"

"So it strikes me—deeper than I thought. But wait a little—between us we'll make it out. You'll judge for that matter yourself."

Madame de Vionnet looked for the moment fairly bent on the chance. "Then she *will* come with her?—I mean Mamie with Mrs. Pocock?"

"Certainly. Her curiosity, if nothing else, will in any case work that. But leave it all to Chad."

"Ah," wailed Madame de Vionnet, turning away a little wearily, "the things I leave to Chad!"

The tone of it made him look at her with a kindness that showed his vision of her suspense. But he fell back on his confidence. "Oh well—trust him. Trust him all the way." He had indeed no sooner so spoken than the queer displacement of his point of view appeared again to come up for him in the very sound, which drew from him a short laugh, immediately checked. He became still more advisory. "When they do come give them plenty of Miss Jeanne. Let Mamie see her well."

She looked for a moment as if she placed them face to face. "For Mamie to hate her?"

He had another of his corrective headshakes. "Mamie won't. Trust *them*."

She looked at him hard, and then as if it were what she must always come back to: "It's *you* I trust. But I was sincere," she said, "at the hotel. I did, I do, want my child—"

"Well?" Strether waited with deference while she appeared to hesitate as to how to put it.

"Well, to do what she can for me."

Strether for a little met her eyes on it; after which something that might have been unexpected to her came from him. "Poor little duck!"

Not more expected for himself indeed might well have been her echo of it. "Poor little duck! But she immensely wants herself," she said, "to see our friend's cousin."

"Is that what she thinks her?"

"It's what we call the young lady."

He thought again; then with a laugh: "Well, your daughter will help you."

And now at last he took leave of her, as he had been intending for five minutes. But she went part of the way with him, accompanying him out of the room and into the next and the next. Her noble old apartment offered a succession of three, the first two of which indeed, on entering, smaller than the last, but each with its faded and formal air, enlarged the office of the antechamber and enriched the sense of approach. Strether fancied them, liked them, and, passing through them with her more slowly now, met a sharp renewal of his original impression. He stopped, he looked back; the whole thing made a vista, which he found high melancholy and sweet—full, once more, of dim historic shades, of the faint far-away cannon-roar of the great Empire. It was doubtless half the projection of his mind, but his mind was a thing that, among old waxed parquets, pale shades of pink and green, pseudo-classic candelabra, he had always needfully to reckon with. They could easily make him irrelevant. The oddity, the originality, the poetry—he didn't know what to call it—of Chad's connexion reaffirmed for him its romantic side. "They ought to see this, you know. They *must*."

"The Pococks?"—she looked about in deprecation; she seemed to see gaps he didn't.

"Mamie and Sarah—Mamie in particular."

"My shabby old place? But *their* things—!"

"Oh their things! You were talking of what will do something for you—"

"So that it strikes you," she broke in, "that my poor place may? Oh," she ruefully mused, "that *would* be desperate!"

"Do you know what I wish?" he went on. "I wish Mrs. Newsome herself could have a look."

She stared, missing a little his logic. "It would make a difference?"

Her voice was so earnest that as he continued to look about he laughed. "It might!"

"But you've told her, you tell me—"

"All about you? Yes, a wonderful story. But there's all the indescribable—what one gets only on the spot."

"Thank you!" she charmingly and sadly smiled.

"It's all about me here," he freely continued. "Mrs. Newsome feels things."

But she seemed doomed always to come back to doubt. "No one feels so much as *you*. No—not any one."

"So much the worse then for every one. It's very easy."

They were by this time in the antechamber, still alone together, as she hadn't rung for a servant. The antechamber was high and square, grave and suggestive too, a little cold and slippery even in summer, and with a few old prints that were precious, Strether divined, on the walls. He stood in the middle, slightly lingering, vaguely directing his glasses, while, leaning against the door-post of the room, she gently pressed her cheek to the side of the recess. "*You* would have been a friend."

"I?"—it started him a little.

"For the reason you say. You're not stupid." And then abruptly, as if bringing it out were somehow founded on that fact, "We're marrying Jeanne."

It affected him on the spot as a move in a game, and he was even then not without the sense that that wasn't the way Jeanne should be married. But he quickly showed his interest, though—as quickly afterwards struck him—with an absurd confusion of mind. "'You'? and—a—not Chad?" Of course it was the child's father who made the 'we,' but to the child's father it would have cost him an effort to allude. Yet didn't it seem the next minute that Monsieur de Vionnet was after all not in the question?—since she had gone on to say that it was indeed to Chad she referred and that he had been in the whole matter kindness itself.

"If I must tell you all, it is he himself who has put us in the way. I mean in the way of an opportunity that, so far as I can yet see, is all I could possibly have dreamed of. For all the trouble Monsieur de Vionnet will ever take!" It was the first time she had spoken to him of her husband, and he couldn't have expressed how much more intimate with her it suddenly made him feel. It wasn't much, in truth—there were other things in what she was saying that were far more; but it was as if, while they stood there together so easily in these cold chambers of the past, the single touch had shown the reach of her confidence. "But our friend," she asked, "hasn't then told you?"

"He has told me nothing."

"Well, it has come with rather a rush—all in a very few days; and hasn't moreover yet taken a form that permits an announcement. It's only for you—absolutely you alone—that I speak; I so want you to know." The sense he had so often had, since the first hour of his disembarkment, of being further and further "in," treated him again at this moment to another twinge; but in this wonderful way of her putting him in there continued to be something exquisitely remorseless. "Monsieur de Vionnet will accept what he *must* accept. He has proposed half a dozen things—each one more impossible than the other; and he wouldn't have found this if he lives to a hundred. Chad found it," she continued with her lighted, faintly flushed, her conscious confidential face, "in the quietest way in the world. Or rather it found *him*—for everything finds him; I mean finds him right. You'll think we do such things strangely—but at my age," she smiled, "one has to accept one's conditions. Our young man's people had seen her; one of his sisters, a charming woman—we know all about them—had observed her somewhere with me. She had spoken to her brother—turned him on; and we were again observed, poor Jeanne and I, without our in the least knowing it. It was at the beginning of the winter; it went on for some time; it outlasted our absence; it began again on our return; and it luckily seems all right. The young man had met Chad, and he got a friend to approach him—as having a decent interest in us. Mr. Newsome looked well before he leaped; he kept beautifully quiet and satisfied himself fully; then only he spoke. It's what has for some time past occupied us. It seems as if it were what would do; really, really all one could wish. There are only two or three points to be settled—they depend on her father. But this time I think we're safe."

Strether, consciously gaping a little, had fairly hung upon her lips. "I hope so with all my heart." And then he permitted himself: "Does nothing depend on *her*?"

"Ah naturally; everything did. But she's pleased *comme tout*. She has been perfectly free; and he—our young friend—is really a combination. I quite adore him."

Strether just made sure. "You mean your future son-in-law?"

"Future if we all bring it off."

"Ah well," said Strether, decorously, "I heartily hope you may." There seemed little else for him to say, though her communication had the oddest effect on him. Vaguely and confusedly he was troubled by it; feeling as if he had even himself been concerned in something deep and dim. He had allowed for depths, but these were greater: and it was as if, oppressively—indeed absurdly—he was responsible for what they had now thrown up to the surface. It was—through something ancient and cold in it—what he would have called the real thing. In short his hostess's news, though he couldn't have explained why, was a sensible shock, and his oppression a weight he felt he must somehow or other immediately get rid of. There were too many connexions missing to make it tolerable he should do anything else. He was prepared to suffer—before his own inner tribunal—for Chad; he was prepared to suffer even for Madame de Vionnet. But he wasn't prepared to suffer for the little girl. So now having said the proper thing, he wanted to get away. She held him an instant, however, with another appeal.

"Do I seem to you very awful?"

"Awful? Why so?" But he called it to himself, even as he spoke, his biggest insincerity yet.

"Our arrangements are so different from yours."

"Mine?" Oh he could dismiss that too! "I haven't any arrangements."

"Then you must accept mine; all the more that they're excellent. They're founded on a *vieille sagesse*. There will be much more, if all goes well, for you to hear and to know, and everything, believe me, for you to like. Don't be afraid; you'll be satisfied." Thus she could talk to him of what, of her innermost life—for that was what it came to—he must "accept"; thus she could extraordinarily speak as if in such an affair his being satisfied had an importance. It was all a wonder and made the whole case larger. He had struck himself at the hotel, before Sarah and Waymarsh, as being in her boat; but where on earth was he now? This question was in the air till her own lips quenched it with another. "And do you suppose *he*—who loves her so—would do anything reckless or cruel?"

He wondered what he supposed. "Do you mean your young man—?"

"I mean yours. I mean Mr. Newsome." It flashed for Strether the next moment a finer light, and the light deepened as she went on. "He takes, thank God, the truest tenderest interest in her."

It deepened indeed. "Oh I'm sure of that!"

"You were talking," she said, "about one's trusting him. You see then how I do."

He wanted a moment—it all came. "I see—I see." He felt he really did see.

"He wouldn't hurt her for the world, nor—assuming she marries at all—risk anything that might make against her happiness. And—willingly, at least—he would never hurt *me*."

Her face, with what he had by this time grasped, told him more than her words; whether something had come into it, or whether he only read clearer, her whole story—what at least he then took for such—reached out to him from it. With the initiative she now attributed to Chad it all made a sense, and this sense—a light, a lead, was what had abruptly risen before him. He wanted, once more, to get off with these things; which was at last made easy, a servant having, for his assistance, on hearing voices in the hall, just come forward. All that Strether had made out was, while the man opened the door and impersonally waited, summed up in his last word. "I don't think, you know, Chad will tell me anything."

"No—perhaps not yet."

"And I won't as yet speak to him."

"Ah that's as you'll think best. You must judge."

She had finally given him her hand, which he held a moment. "How *much* I have to judge!"

"Everything," said Madame de Vionnet: a remark that was indeed—with the refined disguised suppressed passion of her face—what he most carried away.

II

So far as a direct approach was concerned Sarah had neglected him, for the week now about to end, with a civil consistency of chill that, giving him a higher idea of her social resource, threw him back on the general reflexion that a woman could always be amazing. It indeed helped a little to console him that he felt sure she had for the same period also left Chad's curiosity hanging; though on the other hand, for his personal relief, Chad could at least go through the various motions—and he made them extraordinarily numerous—of seeing she had a good time. There wasn't a motion on which, in her presence, poor Strether could so much as venture, and all he could do when he was out of it was to walk over for a talk with Maria. He walked over of course much less than usual, but he found a special compensation in a certain half-hour during which, toward the close of a crowded empty expensive day, his several companions seemed to him so disposed of as to give his forms and usages a rest. He had been with them in the morning and had nevertheless called on the Pococks in the afternoon; but their whole group, he then found, had dispersed after a fashion of which it would amuse Miss Gostrey to hear. He was sorry again, gratefully sorry she was so out of it—she who had really put him in; but she had fortunately always her appetite for news. The pure flame of the disinterested burned in her cave of treasures as a lamp in a Byzantine vault. It was just now, as happened, that for so fine a sense as hers a near view would have begun to pay. Within three days, precisely, the situation on which he was to report had shown signs of an equilibrium; the effect of his look in at the hotel was to confirm this appearance. If the equilibrium might only prevail! Sarah was out with Waymarsh, Mamie was out with Chad, and Jim was out alone. Later on indeed he himself was booked to Jim, was to take him that evening to the Varieties—which Strether was careful to pronounce as Jim pronounced them.

Miss Gostrey drank it in. "What then to-night do the others do?"

"Well, it has been arranged. Waymarsh takes Sarah to dine at Bignon's."

She wondered. "And what do they do after? They can't come straight home."

"No, they can't come straight home—at least Sarah can't. It's their secret, but I think I've guessed it." Then as she waited: "The circus."

It made her stare a moment longer, then laugh almost to extravagance. "There's no one like you!"

"Like *me*?"—he only wanted to understand.

"Like all of you together—like all of us: Woollett, Milrose and their products. We're abysmal—but may we never be less so! Mr. Newsome," she continued, "meanwhile takes Miss Pocock—?"

"Precisely—to the Français: to see what *you* took Waymarsh and me to, a family-bill."

"Ah then may Mr. Chad enjoy it as I did!" But she saw so much in things. "Do they spend their evenings, your young people, like that, alone together?"

"Well, they're young people—but they're old friends."

"I see, I see. And do *they* dine—for a difference—at Brébant's?"

"Oh where they dine is their secret, too. But I've my idea that it will be, very quietly, at Chad's own place."

"She'll come to him there alone?"

They looked at each other a moment. "He has known her from a child. Besides," said Strether with emphasis, "Mamie's remarkable. She's splendid."

She wondered. "Do you mean she expects to bring it off?"

"Getting hold of him? No—I think not."

"She doesn't want him enough?—or doesn't believe in her power?" On which as he said nothing she continued: "She finds she doesn't care for him?"

"No—I think she finds she does. But that's what I mean by so describing her. It's *if* she does that she's splendid. But we'll see," he wound up, "where she comes out."

"You seem to show me sufficiently," Miss Gostrey laughed, "where she goes in! But is her childhood's friend," she asked, "permitting himself recklessly to flirt with her?"

"No—not that. Chad's also splendid. They're *all* splendid!" he declared with a sudden strange sound of wistfulness and envy. "They're at least *happy*."

"Happy?—it appeared, with their various difficulties, to surprise her.

"Well—I seem to myself among them the only one who isn't."

She demurred. "With your constant tribute to the ideal?"

He had a laugh at his tribute to the ideal, but he explained after a moment his impression. "I mean they're living. They're rushing about. I've already had my rushing. I'm waiting."

"But aren't you," she asked by way of cheer, "waiting with *me*?"

He looked at her in all kindness. "Yes—if it weren't for that!"

"And you help me to wait," she said. "However," she went on, "I've really something for you that will help you to wait and which you shall have in a minute. Only there's something more I want from you first. I revel in Sarah."

"So do I. If it weren't," he again amusedly sighed. "for *that*—!"

"Well, you owe more to women than any man I ever saw. We do seem to keep you going. Yet Sarah, as I see her, must be great."

"She *is*"—Strether fully assented: "great! Whatever happens, she won't, with these unforgettable days, have lived in vain."

Miss Gostrey had a pause. "You mean she has fallen in love?"

"I mean she wonders if she hasn't—and it serves all her purpose."

"It has indeed," Maria laughed, "served women's purposes before!"

"Yes—for giving in. But I doubt if the idea—as an idea—had ever up to now answered so well for holding out. That's *her* tribute to the ideal—we each have our own. It's her romance—and it seems to me better on the whole than mine. To have it in Paris too," he explained—"on this classic ground, in this charged infectious air, with so sudden an intensity: well, it's more than she expected. She has had in short to recognize the breaking out for her of a real affinity—and with everything to enhance the drama."

Miss Gostrey followed. "Jim, for instance?"

"Jim. Jim hugely enhances. Jim was made to enhance. And then Mrs. Waymarsh. It's the crowning touch—it supplies the colour. He's positively separated."

"And she herself unfortunately isn't—that supplies the colour too." Miss Gostrey was all there. But somehow—! "Is *he* in love?"

Strether looked at her a long time; then looked all about the room; then came a little nearer. "Will you never tell any one in the world as long as ever you live?"

"Never." It was charming.

"He thinks Sarah really is. But he has no fear," Strether hastened to add.

"Of her being affected by it?"

"Of *his* being. He likes it, but he knows she can hold out. He's helping her, he's floating her over, by kindness."

Maria rather funnily considered it. "Floating her over in champagne? The kindness of dining her, nose to nose, at the hour when all Paris is crowding to profane delights, and in the—well, in the great temple, as one hears of it, of pleasure?"

"That's just *it,* for both of them," Strether insisted—"and all of a supreme innocence. The Parisian place, the feverish hour, the putting before her of a hundred francs' worth of food and drink, which they'll scarcely touch—all that's the dear man's own romance; the expensive kind, expensive in francs and centimes, in which he abounds. And the circus afterwards—which is cheaper, but which he'll find some means of making as dear as possible—that's also *his* tribute to the ideal. It does for him. He'll see her through. They won't talk of anything worse than you and me."

"Well, we're bad enough perhaps, thank heaven," she laughed, "to upset them! Mr. Waymarsh at any rate is a hideous old coquette." And the next moment she had dropped everything for a different pursuit. "What you don't appear to know is that Jeanne de Vionnet has become engaged. She's to marry—it has been definitely arranged—young Monsieur de Montbron."

He fairly blushed. "Then—if you know it—it's 'out'?"

"Don't I often know things that are *not* out? However," she said, "this will be out to-morrow. But I see I've counted too much on your possible ignorance. You've been before me, and I don't make you jump as I hoped."

He gave a gasp at her insight. "You never fail! I've *had* my jump. I had it when I first heard."

"Then if you knew why didn't you tell me as soon as you came in?"

"Because I had it from her as a thing not yet to be spoken of."

Miss Gostrey wondered. "From Madame de Vionnet herself?"

"As a probability—not quite a certainty: a good cause in which Chad has been working. So I've waited."

"You need wait no longer," she returned. "It reached me yesterday—roundabout and accidental, but by a person who had had it from one of the young man's own people—as a thing quite settled. I was only keeping it for you."

"You thought Chad wouldn't have told me?"

She hesitated. "Well, if he hasn't—"

"He hasn't. And yet the thing appears to have been practically his doing. So there we are."

"There we are!" Maria candidly echoed.

"That's why I jumped. I jumped," he continued to explain, "because it means, this disposition of the daughter, that there's now nothing else: nothing else but him and the mother."

"Still—it simplifies."

"It simplifies"—he fully concurred. "But that's precisely where we are. It marks a stage in his relation. The act is his answer to Mrs. Newsome's demonstration."

"It tells," Maria asked, "the worst?"

"The worst."

"But is the worst what he wants Sarah to know?"

"He doesn't care for Sarah."

At which Miss Gostrey's eyebrows went up. "You mean she has already dished herself?"

Strether took a turn about; he had thought it out again and again before this, to the end; but the vista seemed each time longer. "He wants his good friend to know the best. I mean the measure of his attachment. She asked for a sign, and he thought of that one. There it is."

"A concession to her jealousy?"

Strether pulled up. "Yes—call it that. Make it lurid—for that makes my problem richer."

"Certainly, let us have it lurid—for I quite agree with you that we want none of our problems poor. But let us also have it clear. Can he, in the midst of such a preoccupation, or on the heels of it, have seriously cared for Jeanne?—cared, I mean, as a young man at liberty would have cared?"

Well, Strether had mastered it. "I think he can have thought it would be charming if he *could* care. It would be nicer."

"Nicer than being tied up to Marie?"

"Yes—than the discomfort of an attachment to a person he can never hope, short of a catastrophe, to marry. And he was quite right," said Strether. "It would certainly have been nicer. Even when a thing's already nice there mostly *is* some other thing that would have been nicer—or as to which we wonder if it wouldn't. But his question was all the same a dream. He *couldn't* care in that way. He *is* tied up to Marie. The relation is too special and has gone too far. It's the very basis, and his recent lively contribution toward establishing Jeanne in life has been his definite and final acknowledgement to Madame de Vionnet that he has ceased squirming. I doubt meanwhile," he went on, "if Sarah has at all directly attacked him."

His companion brooded. "But won't he wish for his own satisfaction to make his ground good to her?"

"No—he'll leave it to me, he'll leave everything to me. I 'sort of' feel"—he worked it out—"that the whole thing will come upon me. Yes, I shall have every inch and every ounce of it. I shall be *used* for it—!" And Strether lost himself in the prospect. Then he fancifully expressed the issue. "To the last drop of my blood."

Maria, however, roundly protested. "Ah you'll please keep a drop for *me*. *I* shall have a use for it!"—which she didn't however follow up. She had come back the next moment to another matter. "Mrs. Pocock, with her brother, is trusting only to her general charm?"

"So it would seem."

"And the charm's not working?"

Well, Strether put it otherwise, "She's sounding the note of home—which is the very best thing she can do."

"The best for Madame de Vionnet?"

"The best for home itself. The natural one; the right one."

"Right," Maria asked, "when it fails?"

Strether had a pause. "The difficulty's Jim. Jim's the note of home."

She debated. "Ah surely not the note of Mrs. Newsome."

But he had it all. "The note of the home for which Mrs. Newsome wants him—the home of the business. Jim stands, with his little legs apart, at the door of *that* tent; and Jim *is*, frankly speaking, extremely awful."

Maria stared. "And you in, you poor thing, for your evening with him?"

"Oh he's all right for *me*!" Strether laughed. "Any one's good enough for *me*. But Sarah shouldn't, all the same, have brought him. She doesn't appreciate him."

His friend was amused with this statement of it. "Doesn't know, you mean, how bad he is?"

Strether shook his head with decision. "Not really."

She wondered. "Then doesn't Mrs. Newsome?"

It made him frankly do the same. "Well, no—since you ask me."

Maria rubbed it in. "Not really either?"

"Not at all. She rates him rather high." With which indeed, immediately, he himself took up. "Well, he *is* good too, in his way. It depends on what you want him for."

Miss Gostrey, however, wouldn't let it depend on anything—wouldn't have it, and wouldn't want him, at any price. "It suits my book," she said, "that he should be impossible; and it suits it still better," she more imaginatively added, "that Mrs. Newsome doesn't know he is."

Strether, in consequence, had to take it from her, but he fell back on something else. "I'll tell you who does really know."

"Mr. Waymarsh? Never!"

"Never indeed. I'm not *always* thinking of Mr. Waymarsh; in fact I find now I never am." Then he mentioned the person as if there were a good deal in it. "Mamie."

"His own sister?" Oddly enough it but let her down. "What good will that do?"

"None perhaps. But there—as usual—we are!"

III

There they were yet again, accordingly, for two days more; when Strether, on being, at Mrs. Pocock's hotel, ushered into that lady's salon, found himself at first assuming a mistake on the part of the servant, who had introduced him and retired. The occupants hadn't come in, for the room looked empty as only a room can look in Paris, of a fine afternoon, when the faint murmur of the huge collective life, carried on out of doors, strays among scattered objects even as a summer air idles in a lonely garden. Our friend looked about and hesitated; observed, on the evidence of a table charged with purchases and other matters, that Sarah had become possessed—by no aid from *him*—of the last number of the salmon-coloured Revue; noted further that Mamie appeared to have received a present of Fromentin's "Maîtres d'Autrefois" from Chad, who had written her name on the cover; and pulled up at the sight of a heavy letter addressed in a hand he knew. This letter, forwarded by a banker and arriving in Mrs. Pocock's absence, had been placed in evidence, and it drew from the fact of its being unopened a sudden queer power to intensify the reach of its author. It brought home to him the scale on which Mrs. Newsome—for she had been copious indeed this time—was writing to her daughter while she kept *him* in durance; and it had altogether such an effect upon him as made him for a few minutes stand still and breathe low. In his own room, at his own hotel, he had dozens of well-filled envelopes superscribed in that character; and there was actually something in the renewal of his interrupted vision of the character that played straight into the so frequent question of whether he weren't already disinherited beyond appeal. It was such an assurance as the sharp downstrokes of her pen hadn't yet had occasion to give him; but they somehow at the present crisis stood for a probable absoluteness in any decree of the writer. He looked at Sarah's name and address, in short, as if he had been looking hard into her mother's face, and then turned from it as if the face had declined to relax. But since it was in a manner as if Mrs. Newsome were thereby all the more, instead of the less, in the room, and were conscious, sharply and solely conscious, of himself, so he felt both held and hushed, summoned to stay at least and take his punishment. By staying, accordingly, he took it—creeping softly and vaguely about and waiting for Sarah to come in. She *would* come in if he stayed long enough, and he had now more than ever the sense of her success in leaving him a prey to anxiety. It wasn't to be denied that she had had a happy instinct, from the point of view of Woollett, in placing him thus at the mercy of her own initiative. It was very well to try to say he didn't care—that she might break ground when she would, might never break it at all if she wouldn't, and that he had no confession whatever to wait upon her with: he breathed from day to day an air that damnably required clearing, and there were moments when he quite ached to precipitate that process. He couldn't doubt that, should she only oblige him by surprising him just as he then was, a clarifying scene of some sort would result from the concussion.

He humbly circulated in this spirit till he suddenly had a fresh arrest. Both the windows of the room stood open to the balcony, but it was only now that, in the glass of the leaf of one of them, folded back, he caught a reflexion quickly recognized as the colour of a lady's dress. Somebody had been then all the while on the balcony, and the person, whoever it might be, was so placed between the windows as to be hidden from him; while on the other hand the many sounds of the street had covered his own entrance and movements. If the person were Sarah he might on the spot therefore be served to his taste. He might lead her by a move or two up to the remedy for his vain tension; as to which, should he get nothing else from it, he would at least have the relief of pulling down the roof on their heads. There was fortunately no one at hand to observe—in respect to his valour—that even on this completed reasoning he still hung fire. He had been waiting for Mrs. Pocock and the sound of the oracle; but he had to gird himself afresh—which he did in the embrasure of the window, neither advancing nor retreating—before provoking the revelation. It was apparently for Sarah to come more into view; he was in that case there at her service. She did, however, as meanwhile happened, come more into view; only she luckily came at the last minute as a contradiction of Sarah. The occupant of the balcony was after all quite another person, a person presented, on a second look, by a charming back and a slight shift of her position, as beautiful brilliant unconscious Mamie—Mamie alone at home, Mamie passing her time in her own innocent way, Mamie in short rather shabbily used, but Mamie absorbed interested and interesting. With her arms on the balustrade and her attention dropped to the street she allowed Strether to watch her, to consider several things, without her turning round.

But the oddity was that when he *had* so watched and considered he simply stepped back into the room without following up his advantage. He revolved there again for several minutes, quite as with something new to think of and as if the bearings of the possibility of Sarah had been superseded. For frankly, yes, it *had* bearings thus to find the girl in solitary possession. There was something in it that touched him to a point not to have been reckoned beforehand, something that softly but quite pressingly spoke to him, and that spoke the more each time he paused again at the edge of the balcony and saw her still unaware. Her companions were plainly scattered; Sarah would be off somewhere with Waymarsh and Chad off somewhere with Jim. Strether didn't at all mentally impute to Chad that he was with his "good friend"; he gave him the benefit of supposing him involved in appearances that, had he had to describe them—for instance to Maria—he would have conveniently qualified as more subtle. It came to him indeed the next thing that there was perhaps almost an excess of refinement in having left Mamie in such weather up there alone, however she might in fact have extemporised, under the charm of the Rue de Rivoli, a little makeshift Paris of wonder and fancy. Our friend in any case now recognised—and it was as if at the recognition Mrs. Newsome's fixed intensity had suddenly, with a deep audible gasp, grown thin and vague—that day after day he had been conscious in respect to his young lady of something odd and ambiguous, yet something into which he could at last read a meaning. It had been at the most, this mystery, an obsession—oh an obsession agreeable; and it had just now fallen into its place as at the touch of a spring. It had represented the possibility between them of some communication baffled by accident and delay—the possibility even of some relation as yet unacknowledged.

There was always their old relation, the fruit of the Woollett years; but that—and it was what was strangest—had nothing whatever in common with what was now in the air. As a child, as a "bud," and then again as a flower of expansion, Mamie had bloomed for him, freely, in the almost incessantly open doorways of home; where he remembered her as first very forward, as then very backward—for he had carried on at one period, in Mrs. Newsome's parlours (oh Mrs. Newsome's phases and his own!) a course of English Literature reenforced by exams and teas—and once more, finally, as very much in advance. But he had kept no great sense of points of contact; it not being in the nature of things at Woollett that the freshest of the buds should find herself in the same basket with the most withered of the winter apples. The child had given sharpness, above all, to his sense of the flight of time; it was but the day before yesterday that he had tripped up on her hoop, yet his experience of remarkable women—destined, it would seem, remarkably to grow—felt itself ready this afternoon, quite braced itself, to include her. She had in fine more to say to him than he had ever dreamed the pretty girl of the moment *could* have; and the proof of the circumstance was that, visibly, unmistakeably, she had been able to say it to no one else. It was something she could mention neither to her brother, to her sister-in-law nor to Chad; though he could just imagine that had she still been at home she might have brought it out, as a supreme tribute to age, authority and attitude, for Mrs. Newsome. It was moreover something in which they all took an interest; the strength of their interest was in truth just the reason of her prudence. All this then, for five minutes, was vivid to Strether, and it put before him that, poor child, she had now but her prudence to amuse her. That, for a pretty girl in Paris, struck him, with a rush, as a sorry state; so that under the impression he went out to her with a step as hypocritically alert, he was well aware, as if he had just come into the room. She turned with a start at his voice; preoccupied with him though she might be, she was just a scrap disappointed. "Oh I thought you were Mr. Bilham!"

The remark had been at first surprising and our friend's private thought, under the influence of it, temporarily blighted; yet we are able to add that he presently recovered his inward tone and that many a fresh flower of fancy was to bloom in the same air. Little Bilham—since little Bilham was, somewhat incongruously, expected—appeared behindhand; a circumstance by which Strether was to profit. They came back into the room together after a little, the couple on the balcony, and amid its crimson-and-gold elegance, with the others still absent, Strether passed forty minutes that he appraised even at the time as far, in the whole queer connexion, from his idlest. Yes indeed, since he had the other day so agreed with Maria about the inspiration of the lurid, here was something for his problem that surely didn't make it shrink and that was floated in upon him as part of a sudden flood. He was doubtless not to know till afterwards, on turning them over in thought, of how many elements his impression was composed; but he none the less felt, as he sat with the charming girl, the signal growth of a confidence. For she *was* charming, when all was said—and none the less so for the visible habit and practice of freedom and fluency. She was charming, he was aware, in spite of the fact that if he hadn't found her so he would have found her something he should have been in peril of expressing as "funny." Yes, she was funny, wonderful Mamie, and without dreaming it; she was bland, she was bridal—with never, that he could make out as yet, a bridegroom to support it; she was handsome and portly and easy and chatty, soft and sweet and almost disconcertingly reassuring. She was dressed, if we might so far discriminate, less as a young lady than as an old one—had an old one been supposable to Strether as so committed to vanity; the complexities of her hair missed moreover also the looseness of youth; and she had a mature manner of bending a little, as to encourage and reward, while she held neatly together in front of her a pair of strikingly polished hands: the combination of all of which kept up about her the glamour of her "receiving," placed her again perpetually between the windows and within sound of the ice-cream plates, suggested the enumeration of all the names, all the Mr. Brookses and Mr. Snookses, gregarious specimens of a single type, she was happy to "meet."

But if all this was where she was funny, and if what was funnier than the rest was the contrast between her beautiful benevolent patronage—such a hint of the polysyllabic as might make her something of a bore toward middle age—and her rather flat little voice, the voice, naturally, unaffectedly yet, of a girl of fifteen; so Strether, none the less, at the end of ten minutes, felt in her a quiet dignity that pulled things bravely together. If quiet dignity, almost more than matronly, with voluminous, too voluminous clothes, was the effect she proposed to produce, that was an ideal one could like in her when once one had got into relation. The great thing now for her visitor was that this was exactly what he had done; it made so extraordinary a mixture of the brief and crowded hour. It was the mark of a relation that he had begun so quickly to find himself sure she was, of all people, as might have been said, on the side and of the party of Mrs. Newsome's original ambassador. She was in *his* interest and not in Sarah's; and some sign of that was precisely what he had been feeling in her, these last days, as imminent. Finally placed, in Paris, in immediate presence of the situation and of the hero of it—by whom Strether was incapable of meaning any one but Chad—she had accomplished, and really in a manner all unexpected to herself, a change of base; deep still things had come to pass within her, and by the time she had grown sure of them Strether had become aware of the little drama. When she knew where she was, in short, he had made it out; and he made it out at present still better; though with never a direct word passing between them all the while on the subject of his own predicament. There had been at first, as he sat there with her, a moment during which he wondered if she meant to break ground in respect to his prime undertaking. That door stood so strangely ajar that he was half-prepared to be conscious, at any juncture, of her having, of any one's having, quite bounced in. But, friendly, familiar, light of touch and happy of tact, she exquisitely stayed out, so that it was for all the world as if to show she could deal with him without being reduced to—well, scarcely anything.

It fully came up for them then, by means of their talking of everything *but* Chad, that Mamie, unlike Sarah, unlike Jim, knew perfectly what had become of him. It fully came up that she had taken to the last fraction of an inch the measure of the change in him, and that she wanted Strether to know what a secret she proposed to make of it. They talked most conveniently—as if they had had no chance yet—about Woollett; and that had virtually the effect of their keeping the secret more close. The hour took on for Strether, little by little, a queer sad sweetness of quality; he had such a revulsion in Mamie's favour and on behalf of her social value as might have come from remorse at some early injustice. She made him, as under the breath of some vague western whiff, homesick and freshly restless; he could really for the time have fancied himself stranded with her on a far shore, during an ominous calm, in a quaint community of shipwreck. Their little interview was like a picnic on a coral strand; they passed each other, with melancholy smiles and looks sufficiently allusive, such cupfuls of water as they had saved. Especially sharp in Strether meanwhile was the conviction that his companion really knew, as we have hinted, where she had come out. It was at a very particular place—only *that* she would never tell him; it would be above all what he should have to puzzle for himself. This was what he hoped for, because his interest in the girl wouldn't be complete without it. No more would the appreciation to which she was entitled—so assured was he that the more he saw of her process the more he should see of her pride. She saw, herself, everything; but she knew what she didn't want, and that it was that had helped her. What didn't she want?—there was a pleasure lost for her old friend in not yet knowing, as there would doubtless be a thrill in getting a glimpse. Gently and sociably she kept that dark to him, and it was as if she soothed and beguiled him in other ways to make up for it. She came out with her impression of Madame de Vionnet—of whom she had "heard so much"; she came out with her impression of Jeanne, whom she had been "dying to see": she brought it out with a blandness by which her auditor was really stirred that she had been with Sarah early that very afternoon, and after dreadful delays caused by all sorts of things, mainly, eternally, by the purchase of clothes—clothes that unfortunately wouldn't be themselves eternal—to call in the Rue de Bellechasse.

At the sound of these names Strether almost blushed to feel that he couldn't have sounded them first—and yet couldn't either have justified his squeamishness. Mamie made them easy as he couldn't have begun to do, and yet it could only have cost her more than he should ever have had to spend. It was as friends of Chad's, friends special, distinguished, desirable, enviable, that she spoke of them, and she beautifully carried it off that much as she had heard of them—though she didn't say how or where, which was a touch of her own—she had found them beyond her supposition. She abounded in praise of them, and after the manner of Woollett—which made the manner of Woollett a lovable thing again to Strether. He had never so felt the true inwardness of it as when his blooming companion pronounced the elder of the ladies of the Rue de Bellechasse too fascinating for words and declared of the younger that she was perfectly ideal, a real little monster of charm. "Nothing," she said of Jeanne, "ought ever to happen to her—she's so awfully right as she is. Another touch will spoil her—so she oughtn't to *be* touched."

"Ah but things, here in Paris," Strether observed, "do happen to little girls." And then for the joke's and the occasion's sake: "Haven't you found that yourself?"

"That things happen—? Oh I'm not a little girl. I'm a big battered blowsy one. *I* don't care," Mamie laughed, "*what* happens."

Strether had a pause while he wondered if it mightn't happen that he should give her the pleasure of learning that he found her nicer than he had really dreamed—a pause that ended when he had said to himself that, so far as it at all mattered for her, she had in fact perhaps already made this out. He risked accordingly a different question—though conscious, as soon as he had spoken, that he seemed to place it in relation to her last speech. "But that Mademoiselle de Vionnet is to be married—I suppose you've heard of *that*."

For all, he then found, he need fear! "Dear, yes; the gentleman was there: Monsieur de Montbron, whom Madame de Vionnet presented to us."

"And was he nice?"

Mamie bloomed and bridled with her best reception manner. "Any man's nice when he's in love."

It made Strether laugh. "But is Monsieur de Montbron in love—already—with *you*?"

"Oh that's not necessary—it's so much better he should be so with *her:* which, thank goodness, I lost no time in discovering for myself. He's perfectly gone—and I couldn't have borne it for her if he hadn't been. She's just too sweet."

Strether hesitated. "And through being in love too?"

On which with a smile that struck him as wonderful Mamie had a wonderful answer. "She doesn't know if she is or not."

It made him again laugh out. "Oh but *you* do?"

She was willing to take it that way. "Oh yes, I know everything." And as she sat there rubbing her polished hands and making the best of it—only holding her elbows perhaps a little too much out—the momentary effect for Strether was that every one else, in all their affair, seemed stupid.

"Know that poor little Jeanne doesn't know what's the matter with her?"

It was as near as they came to saying that she was probably in love with Chad; but it was quite near enough for what Strether wanted; which was to be confirmed in his certitude that, whether in love or not, she appealed to something large and easy in the girl before him. Mamie would be fat, too fat, at thirty; but she would always be the person who, at the present sharp hour, had been disinterestedly tender. "If I see a little more of her, as I hope I shall, I think she'll like me enough—for she seemed to like me to-day—to want me to tell her."

"And *shall* you?"

"Perfectly. I shall tell her the matter with her is that she wants only too much to do right. To do right for her, naturally," said Mamie "is to please."

"Her mother, do you mean?"

"Her mother first."

Strether waited. "And then?"

"Well, 'then'—Mr. Newsome."

There was something really grand for him in the serenity of this reference. "And last only Monsieur de Montbron?"

"Last only"—she good-humouredly kept it up.

Strether considered. "So that every one after all then will be suited?"

She had one of her few hesitations, but it was a question only of a moment; and it was her nearest approach to being explicit with him about what was between them. "I think I can speak for myself. *I* shall be."

It said indeed so much, told such a story of her being ready to help him, so committed to him that truth, in short, for such use as he might make of it toward those ends of his own with which, patiently and trustfully, she had nothing to do—it so fully achieved all this that he appeared to himself simply to meet it in his own spirit by the last frankness of admiration. Admiration was of itself almost accusatory, but nothing less would serve to show her how nearly he understood. He put out his hand for good-bye with a "Splendid, splendid, splendid!" And he left her, in her splendour, still waiting for little Bilham.

BOOK TENTH

I

Strether occupied beside little Bilham, three evenings after his interview with Mamie Pocock, the same deep divan they had enjoyed together on the first occasion of our friend's meeting Madame de Vionnet and her daughter in the apartment of the Boulevard Malesherbes, where his position affirmed itself again as ministering to an easy exchange of impressions. The present evening had a different stamp; if the company was much more numerous, so, inevitably, were the ideas set in motion. It was on the other hand, however, now strongly marked that the talkers moved, in respect to such matters, round an inner, a protected circle. They knew at any rate what really concerned them to-night, and Strether had begun by keeping his companion close to it. Only a few of Chad's guests had dined—that is fifteen or twenty, a few compared with the large concourse offered to sight by eleven o'clock; but number and mass, quantity and quality, light, fragrance, sound, the overflow of hospitality meeting the high tide of response, had all from the first pressed upon Strether's consciousness, and he felt himself somehow part and parcel of the most festive scene, as the term was, in which he had ever in his life been engaged. He had perhaps seen, on Fourths of July and on dear old domestic Commencements, more people assembled, but he had never seen so many in proportion to the space, or had at all events never known so great a promiscuity to show so markedly as picked. Numerous as was the company, it had still been made so by selection, and what was above all rare for Strether was that, by no fault of his own, he was in the secret of the principle that had worked. He hadn't inquired, he had averted his head, but Chad put him a pair of questions that themselves smoothed the ground. He hadn't answered the questions, he had replied that they were the young man's own affair; and he had then seen perfectly that the latter's direction was already settled.

Chad had applied for counsel only by way of intimating that he knew what to do; and he had clearly never known it better than in now presenting to his sister the whole circle of his society. This was all in the sense and the spirit of the note struck by him on that lady's arrival; he had taken at the station itself a line that led him without a break, and that enabled him to lead the Pococks—though dazed a little, no doubt, breathless, no doubt, and bewildered—to the uttermost end of the passage accepted by them perforce as pleasant. He had made it for them violently pleasant and mercilessly full; the upshot of which was, to Strether's vision, that they had come all the way without discovering it to be really no passage at all. It was a brave blind alley, where to pass was impossible and where, unless they stuck fast, they would have—which was always awkward—publicly to back out. They were touching bottom assuredly to-night; the whole scene represented the terminus of the *cul-de-sac*. So could things go when there was a hand to keep them consistent—a hand that pulled the wire with a skill at which the elder man more and more marvelled. The elder man felt responsible, but he also felt successful, since what had taken place was simply the issue of his own contention, six weeks before, that they properly should wait to see what their friends would have really to say. He had determined Chad to wait, he had determined him to see; he was therefore not to quarrel with the time given up to the business. As much as ever, accordingly, now that a fortnight had elapsed, the situation created for Sarah, and against which she had raised no protest, was that of her having accommodated herself to her adventure as to a pleasure-party surrendered perhaps even somewhat in excess to bustle and to "pace." If her brother had been at any point the least bit open to criticism it might have been on the ground of his spicing the draught too highly and pouring the cup too full. Frankly treating the whole occasion of the presence of his relatives as an opportunity for amusement, he left it, no doubt, but scant margin as an opportunity for anything else. He suggested, invented, abounded—yet all the while with the loosest easiest rein. Strether, during his own weeks, had gained a sense of knowing Paris; but he saw it afresh, and with fresh emotion, in the form of the knowledge offered to his colleague.

A thousand unuttered thoughts hummed for him in the air of these observations; not the least frequent of which was that Sarah might well of a truth not quite know whither she was drifting. She was in no position not to appear to expect that Chad should treat her handsomely; yet she struck our friend as privately stiffening a little each time she missed the chance of marking the great *nuance*. The great *nuance* was in brief that of course her brother must treat her handsomely—she should like to see him not; but that treating her handsomely, none the less, wasn't all in all—treating her handsomely buttered no parsnips; and that in fine there were moments when she felt the fixed eyes of their admirable absent mother fairly screw into the flat of her back. Strether, watching, after his habit, and overscoring with thought, positively had moments of his own in which he found himself sorry for her—occasions on which she affected him as a person seated in a runaway vehicle and turning over the question of a possible jump. *Would* she jump, could she, would *that* be a safe place?—this question, at such instants, sat for him in her lapse into pallor, her tight lips, her conscious eyes. It came back to the main point at issue; would she be, after all, to be squared? He believed on the whole she would jump; yet his alternations on this subject were the more especial stuff of his suspense. One thing remained well before him—a conviction that was in fact to gain sharpness from the impressions of this evening: that if she *should* gather in her skirts, close her eyes and quit the carriage while in motion, he would promptly enough become aware. She would alight from her headlong course more or less directly upon him; it would be appointed to him, unquestionably, to receive her entire weight. Signs and portents of the experience thus in reserve for him had, as it happened, multiplied even through the dazzle of Chad's party. It was partly under the nervous consciousness of such a prospect that, leaving almost every one in the two other rooms, leaving those of the guests already known to him as well as a mass of brilliant strangers of both sexes and of several varieties of speech, he had desired five quiet minutes with little Bilham, whom he always found soothing and even a little inspiring, and to whom he had actually, moreover, something distinct and important to say.

He had felt of old—for it already seemed long ago—rather humiliated at discovering he could learn in talk with a personage so much his junior the lesson of a certain moral ease; but he had now got used to that—whether or no the mixture of the fact with other humiliations had made it indistinct, whether or no directly from little Bilham's example, the example of his being contentedly just the obscure and acute little Bilham he was. It worked so for him, Strether seemed to see; and our friend had at private hours a wan smile over the fact that he himself, after so many more years, was still in search of something that would work. However, as we have said, it worked just now for them equally to have found a corner a little apart. What particularly kept it apart was the circumstance that the music in the salon was admirable, with two or three such singers as it was a privilege to hear in private. Their presence gave a distinction to Chad's entertainment, and the interest of calculating their effect on Sarah was actually so sharp as to be almost painful. Unmistakeably, in her single person, the motive of the composition and dressed in a splendour of crimson which affected Strether as the sound of a fall through a skylight, she would now be in the forefront of the listening circle and committed by it up to her eyes. Those eyes during the wonderful dinner itself he hadn't once met; having confessedly—perhaps a little pusillanimously—arranged with Chad that he should be on the same side of the table. But there was no use in having arrived now with little Bilham at an unprecedented point of intimacy unless he could pitch everything into the pot. "You who sat where you could see her, what does she make of it all? By which I mean on what terms does she take it?"

"Oh she takes it, I judge, as proving that the claim of his family is more than ever justified."

"She isn't then pleased with what he has to show?"

"On the contrary; she's pleased with it as with his capacity to do this kind of thing—more than she has been pleased with anything for a long time. But she wants him to show it *there*. He has no right to waste it on the likes of us."

Strether wondered. "She wants him to move the whole thing over?"

"The whole thing—with an important exception. Everything he has 'picked up'—and the way he knows how. She sees no difficulty in that. She'd run the whole show herself, and she'll make the handsome concession that Woollett would be on the whole in some ways the better for it. Not that it wouldn't be also in some ways the better for Woollett. The people there are just as good."

"Just as good as you and these others? Ah that may be. But such an occasion as this, whether or no," Strether said "isn't the people. It's what has made the people possible."

"Well then," his friend replied, "there you are; I give you my impression for what it's worth. Mrs. Pocock has *seen,* and that's to-night how she sits there. If you were to have a glimpse of her face you'd understand me. She has made up her mind—to the sound of expensive music."

Strether took it freely in. "Ah then I shall have news of her."

"I don't want to frighten you, but I think that likely. However," little Bilham continued, "if I'm of the least use to you to hold on by—!"

"You're not of the least!"—and Strether laid an appreciative hand on him to say it. "No one's of the least." With which, to mark how gaily he could take it, he patted his companion's knee. "I must meet my fate alone, and I *shall*—oh you'll see! And yet," he pursued the next moment, "you *can* help me too. You once said to me"—he followed this further—"that you held Chad should marry. I didn't see then so well as I know now that you meant he should marry Miss Pocock. Do you still consider that he should? Because if you do"—he kept it up—"I want you immediately to change your mind. You can help me that way."

"Help you by thinking he should *not* marry?"

"Not marry at all events Mamie."

"And who then?"

"Ah," Strether returned, "that I'm not obliged to say. But Madame de Vionnet—I suggest—when he can."

"Oh!" said little Bilham with some sharpness.

"Oh precisely! But he needn't marry at all—I'm at any rate not obliged to provide for it. Whereas in your case I rather feel that I *am*."

Little Bilham was amused. "Obliged to provide for my marrying?"

"Yes—after all I've done to you!"

The young man weighed it. "Have you done as much as that?"

"Well," said Strether, thus challenged, "of course I must remember what you've also done to *me*. We may perhaps call it square. But all the same," he went on, "I wish awfully you'd marry Mamie Pocock yourself."

Little Bilham laughed out. "Why it was only the other night, in this very place, that you were proposing to me a different union altogether."

"Mademoiselle de Vionnet?" Well, Strether easily confessed it. "That, I admit, was a vain image. *This* is practical politics. I want to do something good for both of you—I wish you each so well; and you can see in a moment the trouble it will save me to polish you off by the same stroke. She likes you, you know. You console her. And she's splendid."

Little Bilham stared as a delicate appetite stares at an overheaped plate. "What do I console her for?"

It just made his friend impatient. "Oh, come, you know!"

"And what proves for you that she likes me?"

"Why the fact that I found her three days ago stopping at home alone all the golden afternoon on the mere chance that you'd come to her, and hanging over her balcony on that of seeing your cab drive up. I don't know what you want more."

Little Bilham after a moment found it. "Only just to know what proves to you that I like *her*."

"Oh if what I've just mentioned isn't enough to make you do it, you're a stony-hearted little fiend. Besides"—Strether encouraged his fancy's flight—"you showed your inclination in the way you kept her waiting, kept her on purpose to see if she cared enough for you."

His companion paid his ingenuity the deference of a pause. "I didn't keep her waiting. I came at the hour. I wouldn't have kept her waiting for the world," the young man honourably declared.

"Better still—then there you are!" And Strether, charmed, held him the faster. "Even if you didn't do her justice, moreover," he continued, "I should insist on your immediately coming round to it. I want awfully to have worked it. I want"—and our friend spoke now with a yearning that was really earnest—"at least to have done *that*."

"To have married me off—without a penny?"

"Well, I shan't live long; and I give you my word, now and here, that I'll leave you every penny of my own. I haven't many, unfortunately, but you shall have them all. And Miss Pocock, I think, has a few. I want," Strether went on, "to have been at least to that extent constructive—even expiatory. I've been sacrificing so to strange gods that I feel I want to put on record somehow, my fidelity—fundamentally unchanged after all—to our own. I feel as if my hands were embrued with the blood of monstrous alien altars—of another faith altogether. There it is—it's done." And then he further explained. "It took hold of me because the idea of getting her quite out of the way for Chad helps to clear my ground."

The young man, at this, bounced about, and it brought them face to face in admitted amusement. "You want me to marry as a convenience to Chad?"

"No," Strether debated—"*he* doesn't care whether you marry or not. It's as a convenience simply to my own plan *for* him."

"'Simply'!"—and little Bilham's concurrence was in itself a lively comment. "Thank you. But I thought," he continued, "you had exactly *no* plan 'for' him."

"Well then call it my plan for myself—which may be well, as you say, to have none. His situation, don't you see? is reduced now to the bare facts one has to recognise. Mamie doesn't want him, and he doesn't want Mamie: so much as that these days have made clear. It's a thread we can wind up and tuck in."

But dear little Bilham still questioned. "*You* can—since you seem so much to want to. But why should I?"

Poor Strether thought it over, but was obliged of course to admit that his demonstration did superficially fail. "Seriously, there *is* no reason. It's my affair—I must do it alone. I've only my fantastic need of making my dose stiff."

Little Bilham wondered. "What do you call your dose."

"Why what I have to swallow. I want my conditions unmitigated."

He had spoken in the tone of talk for talk's sake, and yet with an obscure truth lurking in the loose folds; a circumstance presently not without its effect on his young friend. Little Bilham's eyes rested on him a moment with some intensity; then suddenly, as if everything had cleared up, he gave a happy laugh. It seemed to say that if pretending, or even trying, or still even hoping, to be able to care for

Mamie would be of use, he was all there for the job. "I'll do anything in the world for you!"

"Well," Strether smiled, "anything in the world is all I want. I don't know anything that pleased me in her more," he went on, "than the way that, on my finding her up there all alone, coming on her unawares and feeling greatly for her being so out of it, she knocked down my tall house of cards with her instant and cheerful allusion to the next young man. It was somehow so the note I needed—her staying at home to receive him."

"It was Chad of course," said little Bilham, "who asked the next young man—I like your name for me!—to call."

"So I supposed—all of which, thank God, is in our innocent and natural manners. But do you know," Strether asked, "if Chad knows—?" And then as his interlocutor seemed at a loss: "Why where she has come out."

Little Bilham, at this, met his face with a conscious look; it was as if, more than anything yet, the allusion had penetrated. "Do you know yourself?"

Strether lightly shook his head. "There I stop. Oh, odd as it may appear to you, there *are* things I don't know. I only got the sense from her of something very sharp, and yet very deep down, that she was keeping all to herself. That is I had begun with the belief that she *had* kept it to herself; but face to face with her there I soon made out that there was a person with whom she would have shared it. I had thought she possibly might with *me*—but I saw then that I was only half in her confidence. When, turning to me to greet me—for she was on the balcony and I had come in without her knowing it—she showed me she had been expecting *you* and was proportionately disappointed, I got hold of the tail of my conviction. Half an hour later I was in possession of all the rest of it. You know what has happened." He looked at his young friend hard—then he felt sure. "For all you say, you're up to your eyes. So there you are."

Little Bilham after an instant pulled half round. "I assure you she hasn't told me anything."

"Of course she hasn't. For what do you suggest that I suppose her to take you? But you've been with her every day, you've seen her freely, you've liked her greatly—I stick to that—and you've made your profit of it. You know what she has been through as well as you know that she has dined here to-night—which must have put her, by the way, through a good deal more."

The young man faced this blast; after which he pulled round the rest of the way. "I haven't in the least said she hasn't been nice to me. But she's proud."

"And quite properly. But not too proud for that."

"It's just her pride that has made her. Chad," little Bilham loyally went on, "has really been as kind to her as possible. It's awkward for a man when a girl's in love with him."

"Ah but she isn't—now."

Little Bilham sat staring before him; then he sprang up as if his friend's penetration, recurrent and insistent, made him really after all too nervous. "No—she isn't now. It isn't in the least," he went on, "Chad's fault. He's really all right. I mean he would have been willing. But she came over with ideas. Those she had got at home. They had been her motive and support in joining her brother and his wife. She was to *save* our friend."

"Ah like me, poor thing?" Strether also got to his feet.

"Exactly—she had a bad moment. It was very soon distinct to her, to pull her up, to let her down, that, alas, he was, he *is,* saved. There's nothing left for her to do."

"Not even to love him?"

"She would have loved him better as she originally believed him."

Strether wondered. "Of course one asks one's self what notion a little girl forms, where a young man's in question, of such a history and such a state."

"Well, this little girl saw them, no doubt, as obscure, but she saw them practically as wrong. The wrong for her *was* the obscure. Chad turns out at any rate right and good and disconcerting, while what she was all prepared for, primed and girded and wound up for, was to deal with him as the general opposite."

"Yet wasn't her whole point"—Strether weighted it—"that he was able to be, that he *could* be, made better, redeemed?"

Little Bilham fixed it all a moment, and then with a small headshake that diffused a tenderness: "She's too late. Too late for the miracle."

"Yes"—his companion saw enough. "Still, if the worst fault of his condition is that it may be all there for her to profit by—?"

"Oh she doesn't want to 'profit,' in that flat way. She doesn't want to profit by another woman's work—she wants the miracle to have been her own miracle. *That's* what she's too late for."

Strether quite felt how it all fitted, yet there seemed one loose piece. "I'm bound to say, you know, that she strikes one, on these lines, as fastidious—what you call here *difficile*."

Little Bilham tossed up his chin. "Of course she's *difficile*—on any lines! What else in the world *are* our Mamies—the real, the right ones?"

"I see, I see," our friend repeated, charmed by the responsive wisdom he had ended by so richly extracting. "Mamie is one of the real and the right."

"The very thing itself."

"And what it comes to then," Strether went on, "is that poor awful Chad is simply too good for her."

"Ah too good was what he was after all to be; but it was she herself, and she herself only, who was to have made him so."

It hung beautifully together, but with still a loose end. "Wouldn't he do for her even if he should after all break—"

"With his actual influence?" Oh little Bilham had for this enquiry the sharpest of all his controls. "How can he 'do'—on any terms whatever—when he's flagrantly spoiled?"

Strether could only meet the question with his passive, his receptive pleasure. "Well, thank goodness, *you're* not! *You* remain for her to save, and I come back, on so beautiful and full a demonstration, to my contention of just now—that of your showing distinct signs of her having already begun."

The most he could further say to himself—as his young friend turned away—was that the charge encountered for the moment no renewed denial. Little Bilham, taking his course back to the music, only shook his good-natured ears an instant, in the manner of a terrier who has got wet; while Strether relapsed into the sense—which had for him in these days most of comfort—that he was free to believe in anything that from hour to hour kept him going. He had positively motions and flutters of this conscious hour-to-hour kind, temporary surrenders to irony, to fancy, frequent instinctive snatches at the growing rose of observation, constantly stronger for him, as he felt, in scent and colour, and in which he could bury his nose even to wantonness. This last resource was offered him, for that matter, in the very form of his next clear perception—the vision of a prompt meeting, in the doorway of the room, between little Bilham and brilliant Miss Barrace, who was entering as Bilham withdrew. She had apparently put him a question, to which he had replied by turning to indicate his late interlocutor; toward whom, after an interrogation further aided by a resort to the optical machinery that seemed, like her other ornaments, curious and archaic, the genial lady, suggesting more than ever for her fellow guest the old French print, the historic portrait, directed herself with an intention that Strether instantly met. He knew in advance the first note she would sound, and took in as she approached all her need of sounding it. Nothing yet had been so "wonderful" between them as the present occasion; and it was her special sense of this quality in occasions that she was there, as she was in most places, to feed. That sense had already been so well fed by the situation about them that she had quitted the other room, forsaken the music, dropped out of the play, abandoned, in a word, the stage itself, that she might stand a minute behind the scenes with Strether and so perhaps figure as one of the famous augurs replying, behind the oracle, to the wink of the other. Seated near him presently where little Bilham had sat she replied in truth to many things; beginning as soon as he had said to her—what he hoped he said without fatuity—"All you ladies are extraordinarily kind to me."

She played her long handle, which shifted her observation; she saw in an instant all the absences that left them free. "How can we be anything else? But isn't that exactly your plight? 'We ladies'—oh, we're nice, and you must be having enough of us! As one of us, you know, I don't pretend I'm crazy about us! But Miss Gostrey at least to-night has left you alone, hasn't she?" With which she again looked about as if Maria might still lurk.

"Oh yes," said Strether; "She's only sitting up for me at home." And then as this elicited from his companion her gay "Oh, oh, oh!" he explained that he meant sitting up in suspense and prayer. "We thought it on the whole better she shouldn't be present; and either way of course it's a terrible worry for her." He abounded in the sense of his appeal to the ladies, and they might take their choice of his doing so from humility or from pride. "Yet she inclines to believe I shall come out."

"Oh I incline to believe too you'll come out!"—Miss Barrace, with her laugh, was not to be behind. "Only the question's about *where,* isn't it? However," she happily continued, "if it's anywhere at all it must be very far on, mustn't it? To do us justice, I think, you know," she laughed, "we do, among us all, want you rather far on. Yes, yes," she repeated in her quick droll way; "we want you very *very* far on!" After which she wished to know why he had thought it better Maria shouldn't be present.

"Oh," he replied, "it was really her own idea. I should have wished it. But she dreads responsibility."

"And isn't that a new thing for her?"

"To dread it? No doubt—no doubt. But her nerve has given way."

Miss Barrace looked at him a moment. "She has too much at stake." Then less gravely: "Mine, luckily for me, holds out."

"Luckily for me too"—Strether came back to that. "My own isn't so firm, *my* appetite for responsibility isn't so sharp, as that I haven't felt the very principle of this occasion to be 'the more the merrier.' If we *are* so merry it's because Chad has understood so well."

"He has understood amazingly," said Miss Barrace.

"It's wonderful!"—Strether anticipated for her.

"It's wonderful!" she, to meet it, intensified; so that, face to face over it, they largely and recklessly laughed. But she presently added: "Oh I see the principle. If one didn't one would be lost. But when once one has got hold of it—"

"It's as simple as twice two! From the moment he had to do something—"

"A crowd"—she took him straight up—"was the only thing? Rather, rather: a rumpus of sound," she laughed, "or nothing. Mrs. Pocock's built in, or built out—whichever you call it; she's packed so tight she can't move. She's in splendid isolation"—Miss Barrace embroidered the theme.

Strether followed, but scrupulous of justice. "Yet with every one in the place successively introduced to her."

"Wonderfully—but just so that it does build her out. She's bricked up, she's buried alive!"

Strether seemed for a moment to look at it; but it brought him to a sigh. "Oh but she's not dead! It will take more than this to kill her."

His companion had a pause that might have been for pity. "No, I can't pretend I think she's finished—or that it's for more than to-night." She remained pensive as if with the same compunction. "It's only up to her chin." Then again for the fun of it: "She can breathe."

"She can breathe!"—he echoed it in the same spirit. "And do you know," he went on, "what's really all this time happening to me?—through the beauty of music, the gaiety of voices, the uproar in short of our revel and the felicity of your wit? The sound of Mrs. Pocock's respiration drowns for me, I assure you, every other. It's literally all I hear."

She focused him with her clink of chains. "Well—!" she breathed ever so kindly.

"Well, what?"

"She *is* free from her chin up," she mused; "and that *will* be enough for her."

"It will be enough for me!" Strether ruefully laughed. "Waymarsh has really," he then asked, "brought her to see you?"

"Yes—but that's the worst of it. I could do you no good. And yet I tried hard."

Strether wondered. "And how did you try?"

"Why I didn't speak of you."

"I see. That was better."

"Then what would have been worse? For speaking or silent," she lightly wailed, "I somehow 'compromise.' And it has never been any one but you."

"That shows"—he was magnanimous—"that it's something not in you, but in one's self. It's *my* fault."

She was silent a little. "No, it's Mr. Waymarsh's. It's the fault of his having brought her."

"Ah then," said Strether good-naturedly, why *did* he bring her?"

"He couldn't afford not to."

"Oh you were a trophy—one of the spoils of conquest? But why in that case since you do 'compromise'—"

"Don't I compromise *him* as well? I do compromise him as well," Miss Barrace smiled. "I compromise him as hard as I can. But for Mr. Waymarsh it isn't fatal. It's—so far as his wonderful relation with Mrs. Pocock is concerned—favourable." And then, as he still seemed slightly at sea: "The man who had succeeded with *me,* don't you see? For her to get him from me was such an added incentive."

Strether saw, but as if his path was still strewn with surprises. "It's 'from' you then that she had got him?"

She was amused at his momentary muddle. "You can fancy my fight! She believes in her triumph. I think it has been part of her joy."

"Oh her joy!" Strether sceptically murmured.

"Well, she thinks she has had her own way. And what's to-night for her but a kind of apotheosis? Her frock's really good."

"Good enough to go to heaven in? For after a real apotheosis," Strether went on, "there's nothing *but* heaven. For Sarah there's only to-morrow."

"And you mean that she won't find to-morrow heavenly?"

"Well, I mean that I somehow feel to-night—on her behalf—too good to be true. She has had her cake; that is she's in the act now of having it, of swallowing the largest and sweetest piece. There won't be another left for her. Certainly *I* haven't one. It can only, at the best, be Chad." He continued to make it out as for their common entertainment. "He may have one, as it were, up his sleeve; yet it's borne in upon me that if he had—"

"He wouldn't"—she quite understood—"have taken all *this* trouble? I dare say not, and, if I may be quite free and dreadful, I very much hope he won't take any more. Of course I won't pretend now," she added, "not to know what it's a question of."

"Oh every one must know now," poor Strether thoughtfully admitted; "and it's strange enough and funny enough that one should feel everybody here at this very moment to be knowing and watching and waiting."

"Yes—isn't it indeed funny?" Miss Barrace quite rose to it. "That's the way we *are* in Paris." She was always pleased with a new contribution to that queerness. "It's wonderful! But, you know," she declared, "it all depends on you. I don't want to turn the knife in your vitals, but that's naturally what you just now meant by our being on top of you. We know you as the hero of the drama, and we're gathered to see what you'll do."

Strether looked at her a moment with a light perhaps slightly obscured. "I think that must be why the hero has taken refuge in this corner. He's scared at his heroism—he shrinks from his part."

"Ah but we nevertheless believe he'll play it. That's why," Miss Barrace kindly went on, "we take such an interest in you. We feel that you'll come up to the scratch." And then as he seemed perhaps not quite to take fire: "Don't let him do it."

"Don't let Chad go?"

"Yes, keep hold of him. With all this"—and she indicated the general tribute—"he has done enough. We love him here—he's charming."

"It's beautiful," said Strether, "the way you all can simplify when you will."

But she gave it to him back. "It's nothing to the way *you* will when you must."

He winced at it as at the very voice of prophecy, and it kept him a moment quiet. He detained her, however, on her appearing about to leave him alone in the rather cold clearance their talk had made. "There positively isn't a sign of a hero to-night; the hero's dodging and shirking, the hero's ashamed. Therefore, you know, I think, what you must all *really* be occupied with is the heroine."

Miss Barrace took a minute. "The heroine?"

"The heroine. I've treated her," said Strether, "not a bit like a hero. Oh," he sighed, "I don't do it well!"

She eased him off. "You do it as you can." And then after another hesitation: "I think she's satisfied."

But he remained compunctious. "I haven't been near her. I haven't looked at her."

"Ah then you've lost a good deal!"

He showed that he knew it. "She's more wonderful than ever?"

"Than ever. With Mr. Pocock."

Strether wondered. "Madame de Vionnet—with Jim?"

"Madame de Vionnet—with 'Jim.'" Miss Barrace was historic.

"And what's she doing with him?"

"Ah you must ask *him*!"

Strether's face lighted again at the prospect. "It *will* be amusing to do so." Yet he continued to wonder. "But she must have some idea."

"Of course she has—she has twenty ideas. She has in the first place," said Miss Barrace, swinging a little her tortoise-shell, "that of doing her part. Her part is to help *you*."

It came out as nothing had come yet; links were missing and connexions unnamed, but it was suddenly as if they were at the heart of their subject. "Yes; how much more she does it," Strether gravely reflected, "than I help *her*!" It all came over him as with the near presence of the beauty, the grace, the intense, dissimulated spirit with which he had, as he said, been putting off contact. "*She* has courage."

"Ah she has courage!" Miss Barrace quite agreed; and it was as if for a moment they saw the quantity in each other's face.

But indeed the whole thing was present. "How much she must care!"

"Ah there it is. She does care. But it isn't, is it," Miss Barrace considerately added, "as if you had ever had any doubt of that?"

Strether seemed suddenly to like to feel that he really never had. "Why of course it's the whole point."

"*Voilà!*" Miss Barrace smiled.

"It's why one came out," Strether went on. "And it's why one has stayed so long. And it's also"—he abounded—"why one's going home. It's why, it's why—"

"It's why everything!" she concurred. "It's why she might be tonight—for all she looks and shows, and for all your friend 'Jim' does—about twenty years old. That's another of her ideas; to be for him, and to be quite easily and charmingly, as young as a little girl."

Strether assisted at his distance. "'For him'? For Chad—?"

"For Chad, in a manner, naturally, always. But in particular to-night for Mr. Pocock." And then as her friend still stared: "Yes, it *is* of a bravery! But that's what she has: her high sense of duty." It was more than sufficiently before them. "When Mr. Newsome has his hands so embarrassed with his sister—"

"It's quite the least"—Strether filled it out—"that she should take his sister's husband? Certainly—quite the least. So she has taken him."

"She has taken him." It was all Miss Barrace had meant.

Still it remained enough. "It must be funny."

"Oh it *is* funny." That of course essentially went with it.

But it brought them back. "How indeed then she must care!" In answer to which Strether's entertainer dropped a comprehensive "Ah!" expressive perhaps of some impatience for the time he took to get used to it. She herself had got used to it long before.

II

When one morning within the week he perceived the whole thing to be really at last upon him Strether's immediate feeling was all relief. He had known this morning that something was about to happen—known it, in a moment, by Waymarsh's manner when Waymarsh appeared before him during his brief consumption of coffee and a roll in the small slippery *salle-à-manger* so associated now with rich rumination. Strether had taken there of late various lonely and absent-minded meals; he communed there, even at the end of June, with a suspected chill, the air of old shivers mixed with old savours, the air in which so many of his impressions had perversely matured; the place meanwhile renewing its message to him by the very circumstance of his single state. He now sat there, for the most part, to sigh, softly, while he vaguely tilted his carafe, over the vision of how much better Waymarsh was occupied. That was really his success by the common measure—to have led his companion so on and on. He remembered how at first there had been scarce a squatting-place he could beguile him into passing; the actual outcome of which at last was that there was scarce one that could arrest him in his rush. His rush—as Strether vividly and amusedly figured it—continued to be all with Sarah, and contained perhaps moreover the word of the whole enigma, whipping up in its fine full-flavoured froth the very principle, for good or for ill, of his own, of Strether's destiny. It might after all, to the end, only be that they had united to save him, and indeed, so far as Waymarsh was concerned, that *had* to be the spring of action. Strether was glad at all events, in connexion with the case, that the saving he required was not more scant; so constituted a luxury was it in certain lights just to lurk there out of the full glare. He had moments of quite seriously wondering whether Waymarsh wouldn't in fact, thanks to old friendship and a conceivable indulgence, make about as good terms for him as he might make for himself. They wouldn't be the same terms of course; but they might have the advantage that he himself probably should be able to make none at all.

He was never in the morning very late, but Waymarsh had already been out, and, after a peep into the dim refectory, he presented himself there with much less than usual of his large looseness. He had made sure, through the expanse of glass exposed to the court, that they would be alone; and there was now in fact that about him that pretty well took up the room. He was dressed in the garments of summer; and save that his white waistcoat was redundant and bulging these things favoured, they determined, his expression. He wore a straw hat such as his friend hadn't yet seen in Paris, and he showed a buttonhole freshly adorned with a magnificent rose. Strether read on the instant his story—how, astir for the previous hour, the sprinkled newness of the day, so pleasant at that season in Paris, he was fairly panting with the pulse of adventure and had been with Mrs. Pocock, unmistakeably, to the Marchè aux Fleurs. Strether really knew in this vision of him a joy that was akin to envy; so reversed as he stood there did their old positions seem; so comparatively doleful now showed, by the sharp turn of the wheel, the posture of the pilgrim from Woollett. He wondered, this pilgrim, if he had originally looked to Waymarsh so brave and well, so remarkably launched, as it was at present the latter's privilege to appear. He recalled that his friend had remarked to him even at Chester that his aspect belied his plea of prostration; but there certainly couldn't have been, for an issue, an aspect less concerned than Waymarsh's with the menace of decay. Strether had at any rate never resembled a Southern planter of the great days—which was the image picturesquely suggested by the happy relation between the fuliginous face and the wide panama of his visitor. This type, it further amused him to guess, had been, on Waymarsh's part, the object of Sarah's care; he was convinced that her taste had not been a stranger to the conception and purchase of the hat, any more than her fine fingers had been guiltless of the bestowal of the rose. It came to him in the current of thought, as things so oddly did come, that *he* had never risen with the lark to attend a brilliant woman to the Marchè aux Fleurs; this could be fastened on him in connexion neither with Miss Gostrey nor with Madame de Vionnet; the practice of getting up early for adventures could indeed in no manner be fastened on him. It came to him in fact that just here was his usual case: he was for ever missing things through his general genius for missing them, while others were for ever picking them up through a contrary bent. And it was others who looked abstemious and he who looked greedy; it was he somehow who finally paid, and it was others who mainly partook. Yes, he should go to the scaffold yet for he wouldn't know quite whom. He almost, for that matter, felt on the scaffold now and really quite enjoying it. It worked out as *because* he was anxious there—it worked out as for this reason that Waymarsh was so blooming. It was *his* trip for health, for a change, that proved the success—which was just what Strether, planning and exerting himself, had desired it should be. That truth already sat full-blown on his companion's lips; benevolence breathed from them as with the warmth of active exercise, and also a little as with the bustle of haste.

"Mrs. Pocock, whom I left a quarter of an hour ago at her hotel, has asked me to mention to you that she would like to find you at home here in about another hour. She wants to see you; she has something to say—or considers, I believe, that you may have: so that I asked her myself why she shouldn't come right round. She hasn't *been* round yet—to see our place; and I took upon myself to say that I was sure you'd be glad to have her. The thing's therefore, you see, to keep right here till she comes."

The announcement was sociably, even though, after Waymarsh's wont, somewhat solemnly made; but Strether quickly felt other things in it than these light features. It was the first approach, from that quarter, to admitted consciousness; it quickened his pulse; it simply meant at last that he should have but himself to thank if he didn't know where he was. He had finished his breakfast; he pushed it away and was on his feet. There were plenty of elements of surprise, but only one of doubt. "The thing's for *you* to keep here too?" Waymarsh had been slightly ambiguous.

He wasn't ambiguous, however, after this inquiry; and Strether's understanding had probably never before opened so wide and effective a mouth as it was to open during the next five minutes. It was no part of his friend's wish, as appeared, to help to receive Mrs. Pocock; he quite understood the spirit in which she was to present herself, but his connexion with her visit was limited to his having—well, as he might say—perhaps a little promoted it. He had thought, and had let her know it, that Strether possibly would think she might have been round before. At any rate, as turned out, she had been wanting herself, quite a while, to come. "I told her," said Waymarsh, "that it would have been a bright idea if she had only carried it out before."

Strether pronounced it so bright as to be almost dazzling. "But why *hasn't* she carried it out before? She has seen me every day—she had only to name her hour. I've been waiting and waiting."

"Well, I told her you had. And she has been waiting too." It was, in the oddest way in the world, on the showing of this tone, a genial new pressing coaxing Waymarsh; a Waymarsh conscious with a different consciousness from any he had yet betrayed, and actually rendered by it almost insinuating. He lacked only time for full persuasion, and Strether was to see in a moment why. Meantime, however, our friend perceived, he was announcing a step of some magnanimity on Mrs. Pocock's part, so that he could deprecate a sharp question. It was his own high purpose in fact to have smoothed sharp questions to rest. He looked his old comrade very straight in the eyes, and he had never conveyed to him in so mute a manner so much kind confidence and so much good advice. Everything that was between them was again in his face, but matured and shelved and finally disposed of. "At any rate," he added, "she's coming now."

Considering how many pieces had to fit themselves, it all fell, in Strether's brain, into a close rapid order. He saw on the spot what had happened, and what probably would yet; and it was all funny enough. It was perhaps just this freedom of appreciation that wound him up to his flare of high spirits. "What is she coming *for*?—to kill me?"

"She's coming to be very *very* kind to you, and you must let me say that I greatly hope you'll not be less so to herself."

This was spoken by Waymarsh with much gravity of admonition, and as Strether stood there he knew he had but to make a movement to take the attitude of a man gracefully receiving a present. The present was that of the opportunity dear old Waymarsh had flattered himself he had divined in him the slight soreness of not having yet thoroughly enjoyed; so he had brought it to him thus, as on a little silver breakfast-tray, familiarly though delicately—without oppressive pomp; and he was to bend and smile and acknowledge, was to take and use and be grateful. He was not—that was the beauty of it—to be asked to deflect too much from his dignity. No wonder the old boy bloomed in this bland air of his own distillation. Strether felt for a moment as if Sarah were actually walking up and down outside. Wasn't she hanging about the porte-cochère while her friend thus summarily opened a way? Strether would meet her but to take it, and everything would be for the best in the best of possible worlds. He had never so much known what any one meant as, in the light of this demonstration, he knew what Mrs. Newsome did. It had reached Waymarsh from Sarah, but it had reached Sarah from her mother, and there was no break in the chain by which it reached *him*. "Has anything particular happened," he asked after a minute—"so suddenly to determine her? Has she heard anything unexpected from home?"

Waymarsh, on this, it seemed to him, looked at him harder than ever. "'Unexpected'?" He had a brief hesitation; then, however, he was firm. "We're leaving Paris."

"Leaving? That *is* sudden."

Waymarsh showed a different opinion. "Less so than it may seem. The purpose of Mrs. Pocock's visit is to explain to you in fact that it's *not*."

Strether didn't at all know if he had really an advantage—anything that would practically count as one; but he enjoyed for the moment—as for the first time in his life—the sense of so carrying it off. He wondered—it was amusing—if he felt as the impudent feel. "I shall take great pleasure, I assure you, in any explanation. I shall be delighted to receive Sarah."

The sombre glow just darkened in his comrade's eyes; but he was struck with the way it died out again. It was too mixed with another consciousness—it was too smothered, as might be said, in flowers. He really for the time regretted it—poor dear old sombre glow! Something straight and simple, something heavy and empty, had been eclipsed in its company; something by which he had best known his friend. Waymarsh wouldn't *be* his friend, somehow, without the occasional ornament of the sacred rage, and the right to the sacred rage—inestimably precious for Strether's charity—he also seemed in a manner, and at Mrs. Pocock's elbow, to have forfeited. Strether remembered the occasion early in their stay when on that very spot he had come out with his earnest, his ominous "Quit it!"—and, so remembering, felt it hang by a hair that he didn't himself now utter the same note. Waymarsh was having a good time—this was the truth that was embarrassing for him, and he was having it then and there, he was having it in Europe, he was having it under the very protection of circumstances of which he didn't in the least approve; all of which placed him in a false position, with no issue possible—none at least by the grand manner. It was practically in the manner of any one—it was all but in poor Strether's own—that instead of taking anything up he merely made the most of having to be himself explanatory. "I'm not leaving for the United States direct. Mr. and Mrs. Pocock and Miss Mamie are thinking of a little trip before their own return, and we've been talking for some days past of our joining forces. We've settled it that we do join and that we sail together the end of next month. But we start tomorrow for Switzerland. Mrs. Pocock wants some scenery. She hasn't had much yet."

He was brave in his way too, keeping nothing back, confessing all there was, and only leaving Strether to make certain connexions. "Is what Mrs. Newsome had cabled her daughter an injunction to break off short?"

The grand manner indeed at this just raised its head a little. "I know nothing about Mrs. Newsome's cables."

Their eyes met on it with some intensity—during the few seconds of which something happened quite out of proportion to the time. It happened that Strether, looking thus at his friend, didn't take his answer for truth—and that something more again occurred in consequence of *that*. Yes—Waymarsh just *did* know about Mrs. Newsome's cables: to what other end than that had they dined together at Bignon's? Strether almost felt for the instant that it was to Mrs. Newsome herself the dinner had been given; and, for that matter, quite felt how she must have known about it and, as he might think, protected and consecrated it. He had a quick blurred view of daily cables, questions, answers, signals: clear enough was his vision of the expense that, when so wound up, the lady at home was prepared to incur. Vivid not less was his memory of what, during his long observation of her, some of her attainments of that high pitch had cost her. Distinctly she was at the highest now, and Waymarsh, who imagined himself an independent performer, was really, forcing his fine old natural voice, an overstrained accompanist. The whole reference of his errand seemed to mark her for Strether as by this time consentingly familiar to him, and nothing yet had so despoiled her of a special shade of consideration. "You don't know," he asked, "whether Sarah has been directed from home to try me on the matter of my also going to Switzerland?"

"I know," said Waymarsh as manfully as possible, "nothing whatever about her private affairs; though I believe her to be acting in conformity with things that have my highest respect." It was as manful as possible, but it was still the false note—as it had to be to convey so sorry a statement. He knew everything, Strether more and more felt, that he thus disclaimed, and his little punishment was just in this doom to a second fib. What falser position—given the man—could the most vindictive mind impose? He ended by squeezing through a passage in which three months before he would certainly have stuck fast. "Mrs. Pocock will probably be ready herself to answer any inquiry you may put to her. But," he continued, "*but—!*" He faltered on it.

"But what? Don't put her too many?"

Waymarsh looked large, but the harm was done; he couldn't, do what he would, help looking rosy. "Don't do anything you'll be sorry for."

It was an attenuation, Strether guessed, of something else that had been on his lips; it was a sudden drop to directness, and was thereby the voice of sincerity. He had fallen to the supplicating note, and that immediately, for our friend, made a difference and reinstated him. They were in communication as they had been, that first morning, in Sarah's salon and in her presence and Madame de Vionnet's; and the same recognition of a great goodwill was again, after all, possible. Only the amount of response Waymarsh had then taken for granted was doubled, decupled now. This came out when he presently said: "Of course I needn't assure you *I* hope you'll come with us." Then it was that his implications and expectations loomed up for Strether as almost pathetically gross.

The latter patted his shoulder while he thanked him, giving the go-by to the question of joining the Pococks; he expressed the joy he felt at seeing him go forth again so brave and free, and he in fact almost took leave of him on the spot. "I shall see you again of course before you go; but I'm meanwhile much obliged to you for arranging so conveniently for what you've told me. I shall walk up and down in the court—dear little old court which we've each bepaced so, this last couple of months, to the tune of our flights and our drops, our hesitations and our plunges: I shall hang about there, all impatience and excitement, please let Sarah know, till she graciously presents herself. Leave me with her without fear," he laughed; "I assure you I shan't hurt her. I don't think either she'll hurt *me:* I'm in a situation in which damage was some time ago discounted. Besides, *that* isn't what worries you—but don't, don't explain! We're all right as we are: which was the degree of success our adventure was pledged to for each of us. We weren't, it seemed, all right as we were before; and we've got over the ground, all things considered, quickly. I hope you'll have a lovely time in the Alps."

Waymarsh fairly looked up at him as from the foot of them. "I don't know as I *ought* really to go."

It was the conscience of Milrose in the very voice of Milrose, but, oh it was feeble and flat! Strether suddenly felt quite ashamed for him; he breathed a greater boldness. "*Let* yourself, on the contrary, go—in all agreeable directions. These are precious hours—at our age they mayn't recur. Don't have it to say to yourself at Milrose, next winter, that you hadn't courage for them." And then as his comrade queerly stared: "Live up to Mrs. Pocock."

"Live up to her?"

"You're a great help to her."

Waymarsh looked at it as at one of the uncomfortable things that were certainly true and that it was yet ironical to say. "It's more then than you are."

"That's exactly your own chance and advantage. Besides," said Strether, "I do in my way contribute. I know what I'm about."

Waymarsh had kept on his great panama, and, as he now stood nearer the door, his last look beneath the shade of it had turned again to darkness and warning. "So do I! See here, Strether."

"I know what you're going to say. Quit this!"

"Quit this!" But it lacked its old intensity; nothing of it remained; it went out of the room with him.

III

Almost the first thing, strangely enough, that, about an hour later, Strether found himself doing in Sarah's presence was to remark articulately on this failure, in their friend, of what had been superficially his great distinction. It was as if—he alluded of course to the grand manner—the dear man had sacrificed it to some other advantage; which would be of course only for himself to measure. It might be simply that he was physically so much more sound than on his first coming out; this was all prosaic, comparatively cheerful and vulgar. And fortunately, if one came to that, his improvement in health was really itself grander than any manner it could be conceived as having cost him. "You yourself alone, dear Sarah"—

Strether took the plunge—"have done him, it strikes me, in these three weeks, as much good as all the rest of his time together."

It was a plunge because somehow the range of reference was, in the conditions, "funny," and made funnier still by Sarah's attitude, by the turn the occasion had, with her appearance, so sensibly taken. Her appearance was really indeed funnier than anything else—the spirit in which he felt her to be there as soon as she *was* there, the shade of obscurity that cleared up for him as soon as he was seated with her in the small *salon de lecture* that had, for the most part, in all the weeks, witnessed the wane of his early vivacity of discussion with Waymarsh. It was an immense thing, quite a tremendous thing, for her to have come: this truth opened out to him in spite of his having already arrived for himself at a fairly vivid view of it. He had done exactly what he had given Waymarsh his word for—had walked and re-walked the court while he awaited her advent; acquiring in this exercise an amount of light that affected him at the time as flooding the scene. She had decided upon the step in order to give him the benefit of a doubt, in order to be able to say to her mother that she had, even to abjectness, smoothed the way for him. The doubt had been as to whether he mightn't take her as not having smoothed it—and the admonition had possibly come from Waymarsh's more detached spirit. Waymarsh had at any rate, certainly, thrown his weight into the scale—he had pointed to the importance of depriving their friend of a grievance. She had done justice to the plea, and it was to set herself right with a high ideal that she actually sat there in her state. Her calculation was sharp in the immobility with which she held her tall parasol-stick upright and at arm's length, quite as if she had struck the place to plant her flag; in the separate precautions she took not to show as nervous; in the aggressive repose in which she did quite nothing but wait for him. Doubt ceased to be possible from the moment he had taken in that she had arrived with no proposal whatever; that her concern was simply to show what she had come to receive. She had come to receive his submission, and Waymarsh was to have made it plain to him that she would expect nothing less. He saw fifty things, her host, at this convenient stage; but one of those he most saw was that their anxious friend hadn't quite had the hand required of him. Waymarsh *had,* however, uttered the request that she might find him mild, and while hanging about the court before her arrival he had turned over with zeal the different ways in which he could be so. The difficulty was that if he was mild he wasn't, for her purpose, conscious. If she wished him conscious—as everything about her cried aloud that she did—she must accordingly be at costs to make him so. Conscious he *was,* for himself—but only of too many things; so she must choose the one she required.

Practically, however, it at last got itself named, and when once that had happened they were quite at the centre of their situation. One thing had really done as well as another; when Strether had spoken of Waymarsh's leaving him, and that had necessarily brought on a reference to Mrs. Pocock's similar intention, the jump was but short to supreme lucidity. Light became indeed after that so intense that Strether would doubtless have but half made out, in the prodigious glare, by which of the two the issue had been in fact precipitated. It was, in their contracted quarters, as much there between them as if it had been something suddenly spilled with a crash and a splash on the floor. The form of his submission was to be an engagement to acquit himself within the twenty-four hours. "He'll go in a moment if you give him the word—he assures me on his honour he'll do that": this came in its order, out of its order, in respect to Chad, after the crash had occurred.

It came repeatedly during the time taken by Strether to feel that he was even more fixed in his rigour than he had supposed—the time he was not above adding to a little by telling her that such a way of putting it on her brother's part left him sufficiently surprised. She wasn't at all funny at last—she was really fine; and he felt easily where she was strong—strong for herself. It hadn't yet so come home to him that she was nobly and appointedly officious. She was acting in interests grander and clearer than that of her poor little personal, poor little Parisian equilibrium, and all his consciousness of her mother's moral pressure profited by this proof of its sustaining force. She would be held up; she would be strengthened; he needn't in the least be anxious for her. What would once more have been distinct to him had he tried he make it so was that, as Mrs. Newsome was essentially all moral pressure, the presence of this element was almost identical with her own presence. It wasn't perhaps that he felt he was dealing with her straight, but it was certainly as if she had been straight with *him*. She was reaching him somehow by the lengthened arm of the spirit, and he was having to that extent to take her into account; but he wasn't reaching her in turn, not making her take *him*; he was only reaching Sarah, who appeared to take so little of him. "Something has clearly passed between you and Chad," he presently said, "that I think I ought to know something more about. Does he put it all," he smiled, "on me?"

"Did you come out," she asked, "to put it all on *him*?"

But he replied to this no further than, after an instant, by saying, "Oh it's all right. Chad I mean's all right in having said to you—well anything he may have said. I'll *take* it all—what he does put on me. Only I must see him before I see you again."

She hesitated, but she brought it out. "Is it absolutely necessary you should see me again?"

"Certainly, if I'm to give you any definite word about anything."

"Is it your idea then," she returned, "that I shall keep on meeting you only to be exposed to fresh humiliation?"

He fixed her a longer time. "Are your instructions from Mrs. Newsome that you shall, even at the worst, absolutely and irretrievably break with me?"

"My instructions from Mrs. Newsome are, if you please, my affair. You know perfectly what your own were, and you can judge for yourself of what it can do for you to have made what you have of them. You can perfectly see, at any rate, I'll go so far as to say, that if I wish not to expose myself I must wish still less to expose *her*." She had already said more than she had quite expected; but, though she had also pulled up, the colour in her face showed him he should from one moment to the other have it all. He now indeed felt the high importance of his having it. "What is your conduct but an outrage to women like *us*? I mean your acting as if there can be a doubt—as between us and such another—of his duty?"

He thought a moment. It was rather much to deal with at once; not only the question itself, but the sore abysses it revealed. "Of course they're totally different kinds of duty."

"And do you pretend that he has any at all—to such another?"

"Do you mean to Madame de Vionnet?" He uttered the name not to affront her, but yet again to gain time—time that he needed for taking in something still other and larger than her demand of a moment before. It wasn't at once that he could see all that was in her actual challenge; but when he did he found himself just checking a low vague sound, a sound which was perhaps the nearest approach his vocal chords had ever known to a growl. Everything Mrs. Pocock had failed to give a sign of recognising in Chad as a particular part of a transformation—everything that had lent intention to this particular failure—affected him as gathered into a large loose bundle and thrown, in her words, into his face. The missile made him to that extent catch his breath; which however he presently recovered. "Why when a woman's at once so charming and so beneficent—"

"You can sacrifice mothers and sisters to her without a blush, and can make them cross the ocean on purpose to feel the more, and take from you the straighter, *how* you do it?"

Yes, she had taken him up as short and as sharply as that; but he tried not to flounder in her grasp. "I don't think there's anything I've done in any such calculated way as you describe. Everything has come as a sort of indistinguishable part of everything else. Your coming out belonged closely to my having come before you, and my having come was a result of our general state of mind. Our general state of mind had proceeded, on its side, from our queer ignorance, our queer misconceptions and confusions—from which, since then, an inexorable tide of light seems to have floated us into our perhaps still queerer knowledge. Don't you *like* your brother as he is," he went on, "and haven't you given your mother an intelligible account of all that that comes to?"

It put to her also, doubtless, his own tone, too many things; this at least would have been the case hadn't his final challenge directly helped her. Everything, at the stage they had reached, directly helped her, because everything betrayed in him such a basis of intention. He saw—the odd way things came out!—that he would have been held less monstrous had he only been a little wilder. What exposed him was just his poor old trick of quiet inwardness, what exposed him was his *thinking* such offence. He hadn't in the least however the desire to irritate that Sarah imputed to him, and he could only at last temporise, for the moment, with her indignant view. She was altogether more inflamed than he had expected, and he would probably understand this better when he should learn what had occurred for her with Chad. Till then her view of his particular blackness, her clear surprise at his not clutching the pole she held out, must pass as extravagant. "I leave you to flatter yourself," she returned, "that what you speak of is what *you've* beautifully done. When a thing has been already described in such a lovely way—!" But she caught herself up, and her comment on his description rang out sufficiently loud. "Do you consider her even an apology for a decent woman?"

Ah there it was at last! She put the matter more crudely than, for his own mixed purposes, he had yet had to do; but essentially it was all one matter. It was so much—so much; and she treated it, poor lady, as so little. He grew conscious, as he was now apt to do, of a strange smile, and the next moment he found himself talking like Miss Barrace. "She has struck me from the first as wonderful. I've been thinking too moreover that, after all, she would probably have represented even for yourself something rather new and rather good."

He was to have given Mrs. Pocock with this, however, but her best opportunity for a sound of derision. "Rather new? I hope so with all my heart!"

"I mean," he explained, "that she might have affected you by her exquisite amiability—a real revelation, it has seemed to myself; her high rarity, her distinction of every sort."

He had been, with these words, consciously a little "precious"; but he had had to be—he couldn't give her the truth of the case without them; and it seemed to him moreover now that he didn't care. He had at all events not served his cause, for she sprang at its exposed side. "A 'revelation'—to *me*: I've come to such a woman for a revelation? You talk to me about 'distinction'—*you*, you who've had your privilege?—when the most distinguished woman we shall either of us have seen in this world sits there insulted, in her loneliness, by your incredible comparison!"

Strether forbore, with an effort, from straying; but he looked all about him. "Does your mother herself make the point that she sits insulted?"

Sarah's answer came so straight, so "pat," as might have been said, that he felt on the instant its origin. "She has confided to my judgement and my tenderness the expression of her personal sense of everything, and the assertion of her personal dignity."

They were the very words of the lady of Woollett—he would have known them in a thousand; her parting charge to her child. Mrs. Pocock accordingly spoke to this extent by book, and the fact immensely moved him. "If she does really feel as you say it's of course very very dreadful. I've given sufficient proof, one would have thought," he added, "of my deep admiration for Mrs. Newsome."

"And pray what proof would one have thought you'd *call* sufficient? That of thinking this person here so far superior to her?"

He wondered again; he waited. "Ah dear Sarah, you must *leave* me this person here!"

In his desire to avoid all vulgar retorts, to show how, even perversely, he clung to his rag of reason, he had softly almost wailed this plea. Yet he knew it to be perhaps the most positive declaration he had ever made in his life, and his visitor's reception of it virtually gave it that importance. "That's exactly what I'm delighted to do. God knows *we* don't want her! You take good care not to meet," she observed in a still higher key, "my question about their life. If you do consider it a thing one can even *speak* of, I congratulate you on your taste!"

The life she alluded to was of course Chad's and Madame de Vionnet's, which she thus bracketed together in a way that made him wince a little; there being nothing for him but to take home her full intention. It was none the less his inconsequence that while he had himself been enjoying for weeks the view of the brilliant woman's specific action, he just suffered from any characterisation of it by other lips. "I think tremendously well of her, at the same time that I seem to feel her 'life' to be really none of my business. It's my business, that is, only so far as Chad's own life is affected by it; and what has happened, don't you see? is that Chad's has been affected so beautifully. The proof of the pudding's in the eating."—he tried, with no great success, to help it out with a touch of pleasantry, while she let him go on as if to sink and sink. He went on however well enough, as well as he could do without fresh counsel; he indeed shouldn't stand quite firm, he felt, till he should have re-established his communications with Chad. Still, he could always speak for the woman he had so definitely promised to "save." This wasn't quite for her the air of salvation; but as that chill fairly deepened what did it become but a reminder that one might at the worst perish *with* her? And it was simple enough—it was rudimentary: not, not to give her away. "I find in her more merits than you would probably have patience with my counting over. And do you know," he inquired, "the effect you produce on me by alluding to her in such terms? It's as if you had some motive in not recognising all she has done for your brother, and so shut your eyes to each side of the matter, in order, whichever side comes up, to get rid of the other. I don't, you must allow me to say, see how you can with any pretence to candour get rid of the side nearest you."

"Near me—*that* sort of thing?" And Sarah gave a jerk back of her head that well might have nullified any active proximity.

It kept her friend himself at his distance, and he respected for a moment the interval. Then with a last persuasive effort he bridged it. "You don't, on your honour, appreciate Chad's fortunate development?"

"Fortunate?" she echoed again. And indeed she was prepared. "I call it hideous."

Her departure had been for some minutes marked as imminent, and she was already at the door that stood open to the court, from the threshold of which she delivered herself of this judgement. It rang out so loud as to produce for the time the hush of everything else. Strether quite, as an effect of it, breathed less bravely; he could acknowledge it, but simply enough. "Oh if you think *that*—!"

"Then all's at an end? So much the better. I do think that!" She passed out as she spoke and took her way straight across the court, beyond which, separated from them by the deep arch of the porte-cochère, the low victoria that had conveyed her from her own hotel was drawn up. She made for it with decision, and the manner of her break, the sharp shaft of her rejoinder, had an intensity by which Strether was at first kept in arrest. She had let fly at him as from a stretched cord, and it took him a minute to recover from the sense of being pierced. It was not the penetration of surprise; it was that, much more, of certainty; his case being put for him as he had as yet only put it to himself. She was away at any rate; she had distanced him—with rather a grand spring, an effect of pride and ease, after all; she had got into her carriage before he could overtake her, and the vehicle was already in motion. He stopped half way; he stood there in the court only seeing her go and noting that she gave him no other look. The way he had put it to himself was that all quite *might* be at an end. Each of her movements, in this resolute rupture, reaffirmed, re-enforced that idea. Sarah passed out of sight in the sunny street while, planted there in the centre of the comparatively grey court, he continued merely to look before him. It probably *was* all at an end.

BOOK ELEVENTH

I

He went late that evening to the Boulevard Malesherbes, having his impression that it would be vain to go early, and having also, more than once in the course of the day, made enquiries of the concierge. Chad hadn't come in and had left no intimation; he had affairs, apparently, at this juncture as it occurred to Strether he so well might have—that kept him long abroad. Our friend asked once for him at the hotel in the Rue de Rivoli, but the only contribution offered there was the fact that every one was out. It was with the idea that he would have to come home to sleep that Strether went up to his rooms, from which however he was still absent, though, from the balcony, a few moments later, his visitor heard eleven o'clock strike. Chad's servant had by this time, answered for his reappearance; he *had*, the visitor learned, come quickly in to dress for dinner and vanish again. Strether spent an hour in waiting for him—an hour full of strange suggestions, persuasions, recognitions; one of those that he was to recall, at the end of his adventure, as the particular handful that most had counted. The mellowest lamplight and the easiest chair had been placed at his disposal by Baptiste, subtlest of servants; the novel half uncut, the novel lemon-coloured and tender, with the ivory knife athwart it like a dagger in a contadina's hair, had been pushed within the soft circle—a circle which, for some reason, affected Strether as softer still after the same Baptiste had remarked that in the absence of a further need of anything by Monsieur he would betake himself to bed. The night was hot and heavy and the single lamp sufficient; the great flare of the lighted city, rising high, spending itself afar, played up from the Boulevard and, through the vague vista of the successive rooms, brought objects into view and added to their dignity. Strether found himself in possession as he never yet had been; he had been there alone, had turned over books and prints, had invoked, in Chad's absence, the spirit of the place, but never at the witching hour and never with a relish quite so like a pang.

He spent a long time on the balcony; he hung over it as he had seen little Bilham hang the day of his first approach, as he had seen Mamie hang over her own the day little Bilham himself might have seen her from below; he passed back into the rooms, the three that occupied the front and that communicated by wide doors; and, while he circulated and rested, tried to recover the impression that they had made on him three months before, to catch again the voice in which they had seemed then to speak to him. That voice, he had to note, failed audibly to sound; which he took as the proof of all the change in himself. He had heard, of old, only what he *could* then hear; what he could do now was to think of three months ago as a point in the far past. All voices had grown thicker and meant more things; they crowded on him as he moved about—it was the way they sounded together that wouldn't let him be still. He felt, strangely, as sad as if he had come for some wrong, and yet as excited as if he had come for some freedom. But the freedom was what was most in the place and the hour; it was the freedom that most brought him round again to the youth of his own that he had long ago missed. He could have explained little enough to-day either why he had missed it or why, after years and years, he should care that he had; the main truth of the actual appeal of everything was none the less that everything represented the substance of his loss, put it within reach, within touch, made it, to a degree it had never been, an affair of the senses. That was what it became for him at this singular time, the youth he had long ago missed—a queer concrete presence, full of mystery, yet full of reality, which he could handle, taste, smell, the deep breathing of which he could positively hear. It was in the outside air as well as within; it was in the long watch, from the balcony, in the summer night, of the wide late life of Paris, the unceasing soft quick rumble, below, of the little lighted carriages that, in the press, always suggested the gamblers he had seen of old at Monte Carlo pushing up to the tables. This image was before him when he at last became aware that Chad was behind.

"She tells me you put it all on *me*"—he had arrived after this promptly enough at that information; which expressed the case however quite as the young man appeared willing for the moment to leave it. Other things, with this advantage of their virtually having the night before them, came up for them, and had, as well, the odd effect of making the occasion, instead of hurried and feverish, one of the largest, loosest and easiest to which Strether's whole adventure was to have treated him. He had been pursuing Chad from an early hour and had overtaken him only now; but now the delay was repaired by their being so exceptionally confronted. They had foregathered enough of course in all the various times; they had again and again, since that first night at the theatre, been face to face over their question; but they had never been so alone together as they were actually alone—their talk hadn't been so supremely for themselves. And if many things moreover passed before them, none passed more distinctly for Strether than that striking truth about Chad of which he had been so often moved to take note: the truth that everything came happily back with him to his knowing how to live. It had been seated in his pleased smile—a smile that pleased exactly in the right degree—as his visitor turned round, on the balcony, to greet his advent; his visitor in fact felt on the spot that there was nothing their meeting would so much do as bear witness to that facility. He surrendered himself accordingly to so approved a gift; for what was the meaning of the facility but that others *did* surrender themselves? He didn't want, luckily, to prevent Chad from living; but he was quite aware that even if he had he would himself have thoroughly gone to pieces. It was in truth essentially by bringing down his personal life to a function all subsidiary to the young man's own that he held together. And the great point, above all, the sign of how completely Chad possessed the knowledge in question, was that one thus became, not only with a proper cheerfulness, but with wild native impulses, the feeder of his stream. Their talk had accordingly not lasted three minutes without Strether's feeling basis enough for the excitement in which he had waited. This overflow fairly deepened, wastefully abounded, as he observed the smallness of anything corresponding to it on the part of his friend. That was exactly this friend's happy case; he "put out" his excitement, or whatever other emotion the matter involved, as he put out his washing; than which no arrangement could make more for domestic order. It was quite for Strether himself in short to feel a personal analogy with the laundress bringing home the triumphs of the mangle.

When he had reported on Sarah's visit, which he did very fully, Chad answered his question with perfect candour. "I positively referred her to you—told her she must absolutely see you. This was last night, and it all took place in ten minutes. It was our first free talk—really the first time she had tackled me. She knew I also knew what her line had been with yourself; knew moreover how little you had been doing to make anything difficult for her. So I spoke for you frankly—assured her you were all at her service. I assured her *I* was too," the young man continued; "and I pointed out how she could perfectly, at any time, have got at me. Her difficulty has been simply her not finding the moment she fancied."

"Her difficulty," Strether returned, "has been simply that she finds she's afraid of you. She's not afraid of me, Sarah, one little scrap; and it was just because she has seen how I can fidget when I give my mind to it that she has felt her best chance, rightly enough, to be in making me as uneasy as possible. I think she's at bottom as pleased to *have* you put it on me as you yourself can possibly be to put it."

"But what in the world, my dear man," Chad enquired in objection to this luminosity, "have I done to make Sally afraid?"

"You've been 'wonderful, wonderful,' as we say—we poor people who watch the play from the pit; and that's what has, admirably, made her. Made her all the more effectually that she could see you didn't set about it on purpose—I mean set about affecting her as with fear."

Chad cast a pleasant backward glance over his possibilities of motive. "I've only wanted to be kind and friendly, to be decent and attentive—and I still only want to be."

Strether smiled at his comfortable clearness. "Well, there can certainly be no way for it better than by my taking the onus. It reduces your personal friction and your personal offence to almost nothing."

Ah but Chad, with his completer conception of the friendly, wouldn't quite have this! They had remained on the balcony, where, after their day of great and premature heat, the midnight air was delicious; and they leaned back in turn against the balustrade, all in harmony with the chairs and the flower-pots, the cigarettes and the starlight. "The onus isn't *really* yours—after our agreeing so to wait together and judge together. That was all my answer to Sally," Chad pursued—"that we have been, that we are, just judging together."

"I'm not afraid of the burden," Strether explained; "I haven't come in the least that you should take it off me. I've come very much, it seems to me, to double up my fore legs in the manner of the camel when he gets down on his knees to make his back convenient. But I've supposed you all this while to have been doing a lot of special and private judging—about which I haven't troubled you; and I've only wished to have your conclusion first from you. I don't ask more than that; I'm quite ready to take it as it has come."

Chad turned up his face to the sky with a slow puff of his smoke. "Well, I've seen."

Strether waited a little. "I've left you wholly alone; haven't, I think I may say, since the first hour or two—when I merely preached patience—so much as breathed on you."

"Oh you've been awfully good!"

"We've both been good then—we've played the game. We've given them the most liberal conditions."

"Ah," said Chad, "splendid conditions! It was open to them, open to them"—he seemed to make it out, as he smoked, with his eyes still on the stars. He might in quiet sport have been reading their horoscope. Strether wondered meanwhile what had been open to them, and he finally let him have it. "It was open to them simply to let me alone; to have made up their minds, on really seeing me for themselves, that I could go on well enough as I was."

Strether assented to this proposition with full lucidity, his companion's plural pronoun, which stood all for Mrs. Newsome and her daughter, having no ambiguity for him. There was nothing, apparently, to stand for Mamie and Jim; and this added to our friend's sense of Chad's knowing what he thought. "But they've made up their minds to the opposite—that you *can't* go on as you are."

"No," Chad continued in the same way; "they won't have it for a minute."

Strether on his side also reflectively smoked. It was as if their high place really represented some moral elevation from which they could look down on their recent past. "There never was the smallest chance, do you know, that they *would* have it for a moment."

"Of course not—no real chance. But if they were willing to think that there was—!"

"They weren't willing." Strether had worked it all out. "It wasn't for you they came out, but for me. It wasn't to see for themselves what you're doing, but what I'm doing. The first branch of their curiosity was inevitably destined, under my culpable delay, to give way to the second; and it's on the second that, if I may use the expression and you don't mind my marking the invidious fact, they've been of late exclusively perched. When Sarah sailed it was me, in other words, they were after."

Chad took it in both with intelligence and with indulgence. "It *is* rather a business then—what I've let you in for!"

Strether had again a brief pause; which ended in a reply that seemed to dispose once and for all of this element of compunction. Chad was to treat it, at any rate, so far as they were again together, as having done so. "I was 'in' when you found me."

"Ah but it was you," the young man laughed, "who found *me*."

"I only found you out. It was you who found me in. It was all in the day's work for them, at all events, that they should come. And they greatly enjoyed it," Strether declared.

"Well, I've tried to make them," said Chad.

His companion did himself presently the same justice. "So have I. I tried even this very morning—while Mrs. Pocock was with me. She enjoys for instance, almost as much as anything else, not being, as I've said, afraid of me; and I think I gave her help in that."

Chad took a deeper interest. "Was she very very nasty?"

Strether debated. "Well, she was the important thing—she was definite. She was—at last—crystalline. And I felt no remorse. I saw that they must have come."

"Oh I wanted to see them for myself; so that if it were only for *that*—!" Chad's own remorse was as small.

This appeared almost all Strether wanted. "Isn't your having seen them for yourself then *the* thing, beyond all others, that has come of their visit?"

Chad looked as if he thought it nice of his old friend to put it so. "Don't you count it as anything that you're dished—if you *are* dished? Are you, my dear man, dished?"

It sounded as if he were asking if he had caught cold or hurt his foot, and Strether for a minute but smoked and smoked. "I want to see her again. I must see her."

"Of course you must." Then Chad hesitated. "Do you mean—a—Mother herself?"

"Oh your mother—that will depend."

It was as if Mrs. Newsome had somehow been placed by the words very far off. Chad however endeavoured in spite of this to reach the place. "What do you mean it will depend on?"

Strether, for all answer, gave him a longish look. "I was speaking of Sarah. I must positively—though she quite cast me off—see *her* again. I can't part with her that way."

"Then she was awfully unpleasant?"

Again Strether exhaled. "She was what she had to be. I mean that from the moment they're not delighted they can only be—well what I admit she was. We gave them," he went on, "their chance to be delighted, and they've walked up to it, and looked all round it, and not taken it."

"You can bring a horse to water—!" Chad suggested.

"Precisely. And the tune to which this morning Sarah wasn't delighted—the tune to which, to adopt your metaphor, she refused to drink—leaves us on that side nothing more to hope."

Chad had a pause, and then as if consolingly: "It was never of course really the least on the cards that they would be 'delighted.'"

"Well, I don't know, after all," Strether mused. "I've had to come as far round. However"—he shook it off—"it's doubtless *my* performance that's absurd."

"There are certainly moments," said Chad, "when you seem to me too good to be true. Yet if you are true," he added, "that seems to be all that need concern me."

"I'm true, but I'm incredible. I'm fantastic and ridiculous—I don't explain myself even *to* myself. How can they then," Strether asked, "understand me? So I don't quarrel with them."

"I see. They quarrel," said Chad rather comfortably, "with *us*." Strether noted once more the comfort, but his young friend had already gone on. "I should feel greatly ashamed, all the same, if I didn't put it before you again that you ought to think, after all, tremendously well. I mean before giving up beyond recall—" With which insistence, as from a certain delicacy, dropped.

Ah but Strether wanted it. "Say it all, say it all."

"Well, at your age, and with what—when all's said and done—Mother might do for you and be for you."

Chad had said it all, from his natural scruple, only to that extent; so that Strether after an instant himself took a hand. "My absence of an assured future. The little I have to show toward the power to take care of myself. The way, the wonderful way, she would certainly take care of me. Her fortune, her kindness, and the constant miracle of her having been disposed to go even so far. Of course, of course,"—he summed it up. "There are those sharp facts."

Chad had meanwhile thought of another still. "And don't you really care—?"

His friend slowly turned round to him. "Will you go?"

"I'll go if you say you now consider I should. You know," he went on, "I was ready six weeks ago."

"Ah," said Strether, "that was when you didn't know *I* wasn't! You're ready at present because you do know it."

"That may be," Chad returned; "but all the same I'm sincere. You talk about taking the whole thing on your shoulders, but in what light do you regard me that you think me capable of letting you pay?" Strether patted his arm, as they stood together against the parapet, reassuringly—seeming to wish to contend that he *had* the wherewithal; but it was again round this question of purchase and price that the young man's sense of fairness continued to hover. "What it literally comes to for you, if you'll pardon my putting it so, is that you give up money. Possibly a good deal of money."

"Oh," Strether laughed, "if it were only just enough you'd still be justified in putting it so! But I've on my side to remind you too that *you* give up money; and more than 'possibly'—quite certainly, as I should suppose—a good deal."

"True enough; but I've got a certain quantity," Chad returned after a moment. "Whereas you, my dear man, you—"

"I can't be at all said"—Strether took him up—"to have a 'quantity' certain or uncertain? Very true. Still, I shan't starve."

"Oh you mustn't *starve!*" Chad pacifically emphasised; and so, in the pleasant conditions, they continued to talk; though there was, for that matter, a pause in which the younger companion might have been taken as weighing against the delicacy of his then and there promising the elder some provision against the possibility just mentioned. This, however, he presumably thought best not to do, for at the end of another minute they had moved in quite a different direction. Strether had broken in by returning to the subject of Chad's passage with Sarah and enquiring if they had arrived, in the event, at anything in the nature of a "scene." To this Chad replied that they had on the contrary kept tremendously polite; adding moreover that Sally was after all not the woman to have made the mistake of not being. "Her hands are a good deal tied, you see. I got so, from the first," he sagaciously observed, "the start of her."

"You mean she has taken so much from you?"

"Well, I couldn't of course in common decency give less; only she hadn't expected, I think, that I'd give her nearly so much. And she began to take it before she knew it."

"And she began to like it," said Strether, "as soon as she began to take it!"

"Yes, she has liked it—also more than she expected." After which Chad observed: "But she doesn't like *me*. In fact she hates me."

Strether's interest grew. "Then why does she want you at home?"

"Because when you hate you want to triumph, and if she should get me neatly stuck there she *would* triumph."

Strether followed afresh, but looking as he went. "Certainly—in a manner. But it would scarce be a triumph worth having if, once entangled, feeling her dislike and possibly conscious in time of a certain quantity of your own, you should on the spot make yourself unpleasant to her."

"Ah," said Chad, "she can bear *me*—could bear me at least at home. It's my being there that would be her triumph. She hates me in Paris."

"She hates in other words—"

"Yes, *that's* it!"—Chad had quickly understood this understanding; which formed on the part of each as near an approach as they had yet made to naming Madame de Vionnet. The limitations of their distinctness didn't, however, prevent its fairly lingering in the air that it was this lady Mrs. Pocock hated. It added one more touch moreover to their established recognition of the rare intimacy of Chad's association with her. He had never yet more twitched away the last veil from this phenomenon than in presenting himself as confounded and submerged in the feeling she had created at Woollett. "And I'll tell you who hates me too," he immediately went on.

Strether knew as immediately whom he meant, but with as prompt a protest. "Ah no! Mamie doesn't hate—well," he caught himself in time—"anybody at all. Mamie's beautiful."

Chad shook his head. "That's just why I mind it. She certainly doesn't like me."

"How much do you mind it? What would you do for her?"

"Well, I'd like her if she'd like me. Really, really," Chad declared.

It gave his companion a moment's pause. "You asked me just now if I don't, as you said, 'care' about a certain person. You rather tempt me therefore to put the question in my turn. Don't *you* care about a certain other person?"

Chad looked at him hard in the lamplight of the window. "The difference is that I don't want to."

Strether wondered. "'Don't want to'?"

"I try not to—that is, I *have* tried. I've done my best. You can't be surprised," the young man easily went on, "when you yourself set me on it. I was indeed," he added, "already on it a little; but you set me harder. It was six weeks ago that I thought I had come out."

Strether took it well in. "But you haven't come out!"

"I don't know—it's what I *want* to know," said Chad. "And if I could have sufficiently wanted—by myself—to go back, I think I might have found out."

"Possibly"—Strether considered. "But all you were able to achieve was to want to want to! And even then," he pursued, "only till our friends there came. Do you want to sit still?" As with a sound half-dolorous, half-droll and all vague and equivocal, Chad buried his face for a little in his hands, rubbing it in a whimsical way that amounted to an evasion, he brought it out more sharply: "*Do* you?"

Chad kept for a time his attitude, but at last he looked up, and then, abruptly, "Jim *is* a damned dose!" he declared.

"Oh I don't ask you to abuse or describe or in any way pronounce on your relatives; I simply put it to you once more whether you're *now* ready. You say you've 'seen.' Is what you've seen that you can't resist?"

Chad gave him a strange smile—the nearest approach he had ever shown to a troubled one. "Can't you make me *not* resist?"

"What it comes to," Strether went on very gravely now and as if he hadn't heard him, "what it comes to is that more has been done for you, I think, than I've ever seen done—attempted perhaps, but never so successfully done—by one human being for another."

"Oh an immense deal certainly"—Chad did it full justice. "And you yourself are adding to it."

It was without heeding this either that his visitor continued. "And our friends there won't have it."

"No, they simply won't."

"They demand you on the basis, as it were, of repudiation and ingratitude; and what has been the matter with me," Strether went on, "is that I haven't seen my way to working with you for repudiation."

Chad appreciated this. "Then as you haven't seen yours you naturally haven't seen mine. There it is." After which he proceeded, with a certain abruptness, to a sharp interrogation. "*Now* do you say she doesn't hate me?"

Strether hesitated. "'She'—?"

"Yes—Mother. We called it Sarah, but it comes to the same thing."

"Ah," Strether objected, "not to the same thing as her hating *you*."

On which—though as if for an instant it had hung fire—Chad remarkably replied: "Well, if they hate my good friend, *that* comes to the same thing." It had a note of inevitable truth that made Strether take it as enough, feel he wanted nothing more. The young man spoke in it for his "good friend" more than he had ever yet directly spoken, confessed to such deep identities between them as he might play with the idea of working free from, but which at a given moment could still draw him down like a whirlpool. And meanwhile he had gone on. "Their hating you too moreover—that also comes to a good deal."

"Ah," said Strether, "your mother doesn't."

Chad, however, loyally stuck to it—loyally, that is, to Strether. "She will if you don't look out."

"Well, I do look out. I am, after all, looking out. That's just why," our friend explained, "I want to see her again."

It drew from Chad again the same question. "To see Mother?"

"To see—for the present—Sarah."

"Ah then there you are! And what I don't for the life of me make out," Chad pursued with resigned perplexity, "is what you *gain* by it."

Oh it would have taken his companion too long to say! "That's because you have, I verily believe, no imagination. You've other qualities. But no imagination, don't you see? at all."

"I dare say. I do see." It was an idea in which Chad showed interest. "But haven't you yourself rather too much?"

"Oh, *rather*—!" So that after an instant under this reproach and as if it were at last a fact really to escape from, Strether made his move for departure.

II

One of the features of the restless afternoon passed by him after Mrs. Pocock's visit was an hour spent, shortly before dinner, with Maria Gostrey, whom of late, in spite of so sustained a call on his attention from other quarters, he had by no means neglected. And that he was still not neglecting her will appear from the fact that he was with her again at the same hour on the very morrow—with no less fine a consciousness moreover of being able to hold her ear. It continued inveterately to occur, for that matter, that whenever he had taken one of his greater turns he came back to where she so faithfully awaited him. None of these excursions had on the whole been livelier than the pair of incidents—the fruit of the short interval since his previous visit—on which he had now to report to her. He had seen Chad Newsome late the night before, and he had had that morning, as a sequel to this conversation, a second interview with Sarah. "But they're all off," he said, "at last."

It puzzled her a moment. "All?—Mr. Newsome with them?"

"Ah not yet! Sarah and Jim and Mamie. But Waymarsh with them—for Sarah. It's too beautiful," Strether continued; "I find I don't get over that—it's always a fresh joy. But it's a fresh joy too," he added, "that—well what do you think? Little Bilham also goes. But he of course goes for Mamie."

Miss Gostrey wondered. "'For' her? Do you mean they're already engaged?"

"Well," said Strether, "say then for *me*. He'll do anything for me; just as I will, for that matter—anything I can—for him. Or for Mamie either. *She'll* do anything for me."

Miss Gostrey gave a comprehensive sigh. "The way you reduce people to subjection!"

"It's certainly, on one side, wonderful. But it's quite equalled, on another, by the way I don't. I haven't reduced Sarah, since yesterday; though I've succeeded in seeing her again, as I'll presently tell you. The others, however, are all right. Mamie, by that blessed law of ours, absolutely must have a young man."

"But what must poor Mr. Bilham have? Do you mean they'll *marry* for you?"

"I mean that, by the same blessed law, it won't matter a grain if they don't—I shan't have in the least to worry."

She saw as usual what he meant. "And Mr. Jim?—who goes for him?"

"Oh," Strether had to admit, "I couldn't manage *that*. He's thrown, as usual, on the world; the world which, after all, by his account—for he had prodigious adventures—seems very good to him. He fortunately—'over here,' as he says—finds the world everywhere; and his most prodigious adventure of all," he went on, "has been of course of the last few days."

Miss Gostrey, already knowing, instantly made the connexion. "He has seen Marie de Vionnet again?"

"He went, all by himself, the day after Chad's party—didn't I tell you?—to tea with her. By her invitation—all alone."

"Quite like yourself!" Maria smiled.

"Oh but he's more wonderful about her than I am!" And then as his friend showed how she could believe it, filling it out, fitting it on to old memories of the wonderful woman: "What I should have liked to manage would have been *her* going."

"To Switzerland with the party?"

"For Jim and for symmetry. If it had been workable moreover for a fortnight she'd have gone. She's ready"—he followed up his renewed vision of her—"for anything."

Miss Gostrey went with him a minute. "She's too perfect!"

"She *will*, I think," he pursued, "go to-night to the station."

"To see him off?"

"With Chad—marvellously—as part of their general attention. And she does it"—it kept before him—"with a light, light grace, a free, free gaiety, that may well softly bewilder Mr. Pocock."

It kept so before him that his companion had after an instant a friendly comment. "As in short it has softly bewildered a saner man. Are you really in love with her?" Maria threw off.

"It's of no importance I should know," he replied. "It matters so little—had nothing to do, practically, with either of us."

"All the same"—Maria continued to smile—"they go, the five, as I understand you, and you and Madame de Vionnet stay."

"Oh and Chad." To which Strether added: "And you."

"Ah 'me'!"—she gave a small impatient wail again, in which something of the unreconciled seemed suddenly to break out. "*I* don't stay, it somehow seems to me, much to my advantage. In the presence of all you cause to pass before me I've a tremendous sense of privation."

Strether hesitated. "But your privation, your keeping out of everything, has been—hasn't it?—by your own choice."

"Oh yes; it has been necessary—that is it has been better for you. What I mean is only that I seem to have ceased to serve you."

"How can you tell that?" he asked. "You don't know how you serve me. When you cease—"

"Well?" she said as he dropped.

"Well, I'll *let* you know. Be quiet till then."

She thought a moment. "Then you positively like me to stay?"

"Don't I treat you as if I did?"

"You're certainly very kind to me. But that," said Maria "is for myself. It's getting late, as you see, and Paris turning rather hot and dusty. People are scattering, and some of them, in other places, want me. But if you want me here—!"

She had spoken as resigned to his word, but he had of a sudden a still sharper sense than he would have expected of desiring not to lose her. "I want you here."

She took it as if the words were all she had wished; as if they brought her, gave her something that was the compensation of her case. "Thank you," she simply answered. And then as he looked at her a little harder, "Thank you very much," she repeated.

It had broken as with a slight arrest into the current of their talk, and it held him a moment longer. "Why, two months, or whatever the time was, ago, did you suddenly dash off? The reason you afterwards gave me for keeping away three weeks wasn't the real one."

She recalled. "I never supposed you believed it was. Yet," she continued, "if you didn't guess it that was just what helped you."

He looked away from her on this; he indulged, so far as space permitted, in one of his slow absences. "I've often thought of it, but never to feel that I could guess it. And you see the consideration with which I've treated you in never asking till now."

"Now then why *do* you ask?"

"To show you how I miss you when you're not here, and what it does for me."

"It doesn't seem to have done," she laughed, "all it might! However," she added, "if you've really never guessed the truth I'll tell you."

"I've never guessed it," Strether declared.

"Never?"

"Never."

"Well then I dashed off, as you say, so as not to have the confusion of being there if Marie de Vionnet should tell you anything to my detriment."

He looked as if he considerably doubted. "You even then would have had to face it on your return."

"Oh if I had found reason to believe it something very bad I'd have left you altogether."

"So then," he continued, "it was only on guessing she had been on the whole merciful that you ventured back?"

Maria kept it together. "I owe her thanks. Whatever her temptation she didn't separate us. That's one of my reasons," she went on, "for admiring her so."

"Let it pass then," said Strether, "for one of mine as well. But what would have been her temptation?"

"What are ever the temptations of women?"

He thought—but hadn't, naturally, to think too long. "Men?"

"She would have had you, with it, more for herself. But she saw she could have you without it."

"Oh 'have' me!" Strether a trifle ambiguously sighed. "*You,*" he handsomely declared, "would have had me at any rate *with* it."

"Oh 'have' you!"—she echoed it as he had done. "I do have you, however," she less ironically said, "from the moment you express a wish."

He stopped before her, full of the disposition. "I'll express fifty."

Which indeed begot in her, with a certain inconsequence, a return of her small wail. "Ah there you are!"

There, if it were so, he continued for the rest of the time to be, and it was as if to show her how she could still serve him that, coming back to the departure of the Pococks, he gave her the view, vivid with a hundred more touches than we can reproduce, of what had happened for him that morning. He had had ten minutes with Sarah at her hotel, ten minutes reconquered, by irresistible pressure, from the time over which he had already described her to Miss Gostrey as having, at the end of their interview on his own premises, passed the great sponge of the future. He had caught her by not announcing himself, had found her in her sitting-room with a dressmaker and a *lingère* whose accounts she appeared to have been more or less ingenuously settling and who soon withdrew. Then he had explained to her how he had succeeded, late the night before, in keeping his promise of seeing Chad. "I told her I'd take it all."

"You'd 'take' it?"

"Why if he doesn't go."

Maria waited. "And who takes it if he does?" she enquired with a certain grimness of gaiety.

"Well," said Strether, "I think I take, in any event, everything."

"By which I suppose you mean," his companion brought out after a moment, "that you definitely understand you now lose everything."

He stood before her again. "It does come perhaps to the same thing. But Chad, now that he has seen, doesn't really want it."

She could believe that, but she made, as always, for clearness. "Still, what, after all, *has* he seen?"

"What they want of him. And it's enough."

"It contrasts so unfavourably with what Madame de Vionnet wants?"

"It contrasts—just so; all round, and tremendously."

"Therefore, perhaps, most of all with what *you* want?"

"Oh," said Strether, "what I want is a thing I've ceased to measure or even to understand."

But his friend none the less went on. "Do you want Mrs. Newsome—after such a way of treating you?"

It was a straighter mode of dealing with this lady than they had as yet—such was their high form—permitted themselves; but it seemed not wholly for this that he delayed a moment. "I dare say it has been, after all, the only way she could have imagined."

"And does that make you want her any more?"

"I've tremendously disappointed her," Strether thought it worth while to mention.

"Of course you have. That's rudimentary; that was plain to us long ago. But isn't it almost as plain," Maria went on, "that you've even yet your straight remedy? Really drag him away, as I believe you still can, and you'd cease to have to count with her disappointment."

"Ah then," he laughed, "I should have to count with yours!"

But this barely struck her now. "What, in that case, should you call counting? You haven't come out where you are, I think, to please *me*."

"Oh," he insisted, "that too, you know, has been part of it. I can't separate—it's all one; and that's perhaps why, as I say, I don't understand." But he was ready to declare again that this didn't in the least matter; all the more that, as he affirmed, he *hadn't* really as yet "come out." "She gives me after all, on its coming to the pinch, a last mercy, another chance. They don't sail, you see, for five or six weeks more, and they haven't—she admits that—expected Chad would take part in their tour. It's still open to him to join them, at the last, at Liverpool."

Miss Gostrey considered. "How in the world is it 'open' unless you open it? How can he join them at Liverpool if he but sinks deeper into his situation here?"

"He has given her—as I explained to you that she let me know yesterday—his word of honour to do as I say."

Maria stared. "But if you say nothing!"

Well, he as usual walked about on it. "I did say something this morning. I gave her my answer—the word I had promised her after hearing from himself what *he* had promised. What she demanded of me yesterday, you'll remember, was the engagement then and there to make him take up this vow."

"Well then," Miss Gostrey inquired, "was the purpose of your visit to her only to decline?"

"No; it was to ask, odd as that may seem to you, for another delay."

"Ah that's weak!"

"Precisely!" She had spoken with impatience, but, so far as that at least, he knew where he was. "If I *am* weak I want to find it out. If I don't find it out I shall have the comfort, the little glory, of thinking I'm strong."

"It's all the comfort, I judge," she returned, "that you *will* have!"

"At any rate," he said, "it will have been a month more. Paris may grow, from day to day, hot and dusty, as you say; but there are other things that are hotter and dustier. I'm not afraid to stay on; the summer here must be amusing in a wild—if it isn't a tame—way of its own; the place at no time more picturesque. I think I shall like it. And then," he benevolently smiled for her, "there will be always you."

"Oh," she objected, "it won't be as a part of the picturesqueness that I shall stay, for I shall be the plainest thing about you. You may, you see, at any rate," she pursued, "have nobody else. Madame de Vionnet may very well be going off, mayn't she?—and Mr. Newsome by the same stroke; unless indeed you've had an assurance from them to the contrary. So that if your idea's to stay for them"—it was her duty to suggest it—"you may be left in the lurch. Of course if they do stay"—she kept it up—"they would be part of the picturesqueness. Or else indeed you might join them somewhere."

Strether seemed to face it as if it were a happy thought; but the next moment he spoke more critically. "Do you mean that they'll probably go off together?"

She just considered. "I think it will be treating you quite without ceremony if they do; though after all," she added, "it would be difficult to see now quite what degree of ceremony properly meets your case."

"Of course," Strether conceded, "my attitude toward them is extraordinary."

"Just so; so that one may ask one's self what style of proceeding on their own part can altogether match it. The attitude of their own that won't pale in its light they've doubtless still to work out. The really handsome thing perhaps," she presently threw off, "*would* be for them to withdraw into more secluded conditions, offering at the same time to share them with you." He looked at her, on this, as if some generous irritation—all in his interest—had suddenly again flickered in her; and what she next said indeed half explained it. "Don't really be afraid to tell me if what now holds you *is* the pleasant prospect of the empty town, with plenty of seats in the shade, cool drinks, deserted museums, drives to the Bois in the evening, and our wonderful woman all to yourself." And she kept it up still more. "The handsomest thing of *all*, when one makes it out, would, I dare say, be that Mr. Chad should for a while go off by himself. It's a pity, from that point of view," she wound up, "that he doesn't pay his mother a visit. It would at least occupy your interval." The thought in fact held her a moment. "Why doesn't he pay his mother a visit? Even a week, at this good moment, would do."

"My dear lady," Strether replied—and he had it even to himself surprisingly ready—"my dear lady, his mother has paid *him* a visit. Mrs. Newsome has been with him, this month, with an intensity that I'm sure he has thoroughly felt; he has lavishly entertained her, and she has let him have her thanks. Do you suggest he shall go back for more of them?"

Well, she succeeded after a little in shaking it off. "I see. It's what you don't suggest—what you haven't suggested. And you know."

"So would you, my dear," he kindly said, "if you had so much as seen her."

"As seen Mrs. Newsome?"

"No, Sarah—which, both for Chad and for myself, has served all the purpose."

"And served it in a manner," she responsively mused, "so extraordinary!"

"Well, you see," he partly explained, "what it comes to is that she's all cold thought—which Sarah could serve to us cold without its really losing anything. So it is that we know what she thinks of us."

Maria had followed, but she had an arrest. "What I've never made out, if you come to that, is what you think—I mean personally—of *her*. Don't you so much, when all's said, as care a little?"

"That," he answered with no loss of promptness, "is what even Chad himself asked me last night. He asked me if I don't mind the loss—well, the loss of an opulent future. Which moreover," he hastened to add, "was a perfectly natural question."

"I call your attention, all the same," said Miss Gostrey, "to the fact that I don't ask it. What I venture to ask is whether it's to Mrs. Newsome herself that you're indifferent."

"I haven't been so"—he spoke with all assurance. "I've been the very opposite. I've been, from the first moment, preoccupied with the impression everything might be making on her—quite oppressed, haunted, tormented by it. I've been interested *only* in her seeing what I've seen. And I've been as disappointed in her refusal to see it as she has been in what has appeared to her the perversity of my insistence."

"Do you mean that she has shocked you as you've shocked her?"

Strether weighed it. "I'm probably not so shockable. But on the other hand I've gone much further to meet her. She, on her side, hasn't budged an inch."

"So that you're now at last"—Maria pointed the moral—"in the sad stage of recriminations."

"No—it's only to you I speak. I've been like a lamb to Sarah. I've only put my back to the wall. It's to *that* one naturally staggers when one has been violently pushed there."

She watched him a moment. "Thrown over?"

"Well, as I feel so I've landed somewhere I think I must have been thrown."

She turned it over, but as hoping to clarify much rather than to harmonise. "The thing is that I suppose you've been disappointing—"

"Quite from the very first of my arrival? I dare say. I admit I was surprising even to myself."

"And then of course," Maria went on, "I had much to do with it."

"With my being surprising—?"

"That will do," she laughed, "if you're too delicate to call it *my* being! Naturally," she added, "you came over more or less for surprises."

"Naturally!"—he valued the reminder.

"But they were to have been all for you"—she continued to piece it out—"and none of them for *her*."

Once more he stopped before her as if she had touched the point. "That's just her difficulty—that she doesn't admit surprises. It's a fact that, I think, describes and represents her; and it falls in with what I tell you—that she's all, as I've called it, fine cold thought. She had, to her own mind, worked the whole thing out in advance, and worked it out for me as well as for herself. Whenever she has done that, you see, there's no room left; no margin, as it were, for any alteration. She's filled as full, packed as tight, as she'll hold, and if you wish to get anything more or different either out or in—"

"You've got to make over altogether the woman herself?"

"What it comes to," said Strether, "is that you've got morally and intellectually to get rid of her."

"Which would appear," Maria returned, "to be practically what you've done."

But her friend threw back his head. "I haven't touched her. She won't *be* touched. I see it now as I've never done; and she hangs together with a perfection of her own," he went on, "that does suggest a kind of wrong in *any* change of her composition. It was at any rate," he wound up, "the woman herself, as you call her, the whole moral and intellectual being or block, that Sarah brought me over to take or to leave."

It turned Miss Gostrey to deeper thought. "Fancy having to take at the point of the bayonet a whole moral and intellectual being or block!"

"It was in fact," said Strether, "what, at home, I *had* done. But somehow over there I didn't quite know it."

"One never does, I suppose," Miss Gostrey concurred, "realise in advance, in such a case, the size, as you may say, of the block. Little by little it looms up. It has been looming for you more and more till at last you see it all."

"I see it all," he absently echoed, while his eyes might have been fixing some particularly large iceberg in a cool blue northern sea. "It's magnificent!" he then rather oddly exclaimed.

But his friend, who was used to this kind of inconsequence in him, kept the thread. "There's nothing so magnificent—for making others feel you—as to have no imagination."

It brought him straight round. "Ah there you are! It's what I said last night to Chad. That he himself, I mean, has none."

"Then it would appear," Maria suggested, "that he has, after all, something in common with his mother."

"He has in common that he makes one, as you say, 'feel' him. And yet," he added, as if the question were interesting, "one feels others too, even when they have plenty."

Miss Gostrey continued suggestive. "Madame de Vionnet?"

"*She* has plenty."

"Certainly—she had quantities of old. But there are different ways of making one's self felt."

"Yes, it comes, no doubt, to that. You now—"

He was benevolently going on, but she wouldn't have it. "Oh I *don't* make myself felt; so my quantity needn't be settled. Yours, you know," she said, "is monstrous. No one has ever had so much."

It struck him for a moment. "That's what Chad also thinks."

"There *you* are then—though it isn't for him to complain of it!"

"Oh he doesn't complain of it," said Strether.

"That's all that would be wanting! But apropos of what," Maria went on, "did the question come up?"

"Well, of his asking me what it is I gain."

She had a pause. "Then as I've asked you too it settles *my* case. Oh you *have*," she repeated, "treasures of imagination."

But he had been for an instant thinking away from this, and he came up in another place. "And yet Mrs. Newsome—it's a thing to remember—*has* imagined, did, that is, imagine, and apparently still does, horrors about what I should have found. I was booked, by her vision—extraordinarily intense, after all—to find them; and that I didn't, that I couldn't, that, as she evidently felt, I wouldn't—this evidently didn't at all, as they say, 'suit' her book. It was more than she could bear. That was her disappointment."

"You mean you were to have found Chad himself horrible?"

"I was to have found the woman."

"Horrible?"

"Found her as she imagined her." And Strether paused as if for his own expression of it he could add no touch to that picture.

His companion had meanwhile thought. "She imagined stupidly—so it comes to the same thing."

"Stupidly? Oh!" said Strether.

But she insisted. "She imagined meanly."

He had it, however, better. "It couldn't but be ignorantly."

"Well, intensity with ignorance—what do you want worse?"

This question might have held him, but he let it pass. "Sarah isn't ignorant—now; she keeps up the theory of the horrible."

"Ah but she's intense—and that by itself will do sometimes as well. If it doesn't do, in this case, at any rate, to deny that Marie's charming, it will do at least to deny that she's good."

"What I claim is that she's good for Chad."

"You don't claim"—she seemed to like it clear—"that she's good for *you*."

But he continued without heeding. "That's what I wanted them to come out for—to see for themselves if she's bad for him."

"And now that they've done so they won't admit that she's good even for anything?"

"They do think," Strether presently admitted, "that she's on the whole about as bad for me. But they're consistent of course, inasmuch as they've their clear view of what's good for both of us."

"For you, to begin with"—Maria, all responsive, confined the question for the moment—"to eliminate from your existence and if possible even from your memory the dreadful creature that *I* must gruesomely shadow forth for them, even more than to eliminate the distincter evil—thereby a little less portentous—of the person whose confederate you've suffered yourself to become. However, that's comparatively simple. You can easily, at the worst, after all, give me up."

"I can easily at the worst, after all, give you up." The irony was so obvious that it needed no care. "I can easily at the worst, after all, even forget you."

"Call that then workable. But Mr. Newsome has much more to forget. How can *he* do it?"

"Ah there again we are! That's just what I was to have made him do; just where I was to have worked with him and helped."

She took it in silence and without attenuation—as if perhaps from very familiarity with the facts; and her thought made a connexion without showing the links. "Do you remember how we used to talk at Chester and in London about my seeing you through?" She spoke as of far-off things and as if they had spent weeks at the places she named.

"It's just what you *are* doing."

"Ah but the worst—since you've left such a margin—may be still to come. You may yet break down."

"Yes, I may yet break down. But will you take me—?"

He had hesitated, and she waited. "Take you—?"

"For as long as I can bear it."

She also debated. "Mr. Newsome and Madame de Vionnet may, as we were saying, leave town. How long do you think you can bear it without them?"

Strether's reply to this was at first another question. "Do you mean in order to get away from me?"

Her answer had an abruptness. "Don't find me rude if I say I should think they'd want to!"

He looked at her hard again—seemed even for an instant to have an intensity of thought under which his colour changed. But he smiled. "You mean after what they've done to me?"

"After what *she* has."

At this, however, with a laugh, he was all right again. "Ah but she hasn't done it yet!"

III

He had taken the train a few days after this from a station—as well as *to* a station—selected almost at random; such days, whatever should happen, were numbered, and he had gone forth under the impulse—artless enough, no doubt—to give the whole of one of them to that French ruralism, with its cool special green, into which he had hitherto looked only through the little oblong window of the picture-frame. It had been as yet for the most part but a land of fancy for him—the background of fiction, the medium of art, the nursery of letters; practically as distant as Greece, but practically also well-nigh as consecrated. Romance could weave itself, for Strether's sense, out of elements mild enough; and even after what he had, as he felt, lately "been through," he could thrill a little at the chance of seeing something somewhere that would remind him of a certain small Lambinet that had charmed him, long years before, at a Boston dealer's and that he had quite absurdly never forgotten. It had been offered, he remembered, at a price he had been instructed to believe the lowest ever named for a Lambinet, a price he had never felt so poor as on having to recognise, all the same, as beyond a dream of possibility. He had dreamed—had turned and twisted possibilities for an hour: it had been the only adventure of his life in connexion with the purchase of a work of art. The adventure, it will be perceived, was modest; but the memory, beyond all reason and by some accident of association, was sweet. The little Lambinet abode with him as the picture he *would* have bought—the particular production that had made him for the moment overstep the modesty of nature. He was quite aware that if he were to see it again he should perhaps have a drop or a shock, and he never found himself wishing that the wheel of time would turn it up again, just as he had seen it in the maroon-coloured, sky-lighted inner shrine of Tremont Street. It would be a different thing, however, to see the remembered mixture resolved back into its elements—to assist at the restoration to nature of the whole far-away hour: the dusty day in Boston, the background of the Fitchburg Depot, of the maroon-coloured sanctum, the special-green vision, the ridiculous price, the poplars, the willows, the rushes, the river, the sunny silvery sky, the shady woody horizon.

He observed in respect to his train almost no condition save that it should stop few times after getting out of the *banlieue;* he threw himself on the general amiability of the day for the hint of where to alight. His theory of his excursion was that he could alight anywhere—not nearer Paris than an hour's run—on catching a suggestion of the particular note required. It made its sign, the suggestion—weather, air, light, colour and his mood all favouring—at the end of some eighty minutes; the train pulled up just at the right spot, and he found himself getting out as securely as if to keep an appointment. It will be felt of him that he could amuse himself, at his age, with very small things if it be again noted that his appointment was only with a superseded Boston fashion. He hadn't gone far without the quick confidence that it would be quite sufficiently kept. The oblong gilt frame disposed its enclosing lines; the poplars and willows, the reeds and river—a river of which he didn't know, and didn't want to know, the name—fell into a composition, full of felicity, within them; the sky was silver and turquoise and varnish; the village on the left was white and the church on the right was grey; it was all there, in short—it was what he wanted: it was Tremont Street, it was France, it was Lambinet. Moreover he was freely walking about in it. He did this last, for an hour, to his heart's content, making for the shady woody horizon and boring so deep into his impression and his idleness that he might fairly have got through them again and reached the maroon-coloured wall. It was a wonder, no doubt, that the taste of idleness for him shouldn't need more time to sweeten; but it had in fact taken the few previous days; it had been sweetening in truth ever since the retreat of the Pococks. He walked and walked as if to show himself how little he had now to do; he had nothing to do but turn off to some hillside where he might stretch himself and hear the poplars rustle, and whence—in the course of an afternoon so spent, an afternoon richly suffused too with the sense of a book in his pocket—he should sufficiently command the scene to be able to pick out just the right little rustic inn for an experiment in respect to dinner. There was a train back to Paris at 9.20, and he saw himself partaking, at the close of the day, with the enhancements of a coarse white cloth and a sanded floor, of something fried and felicitous, washed down with authentic wine; after which he might, as he liked, either stroll back to his station in the gloaming or propose for the local *carriole* and converse with his driver, a driver who naturally wouldn't fail of a stiff clean blouse, of a knitted nightcap and of the genius of response—who, in fine, would sit on the shafts, tell him what the French people were thinking, and remind him, as indeed the whole episode would incidentally do, of Maupassant. Strether heard his lips, for the first time in French air, as this vision assumed consistency, emit sounds of expressive intention without fear of his company. He had been afraid of Chad and of Maria and of Madame de Vionnet; he had been most of all afraid of Waymarsh, in whose presence, so far as they had mixed together in the light of the town, he had never without somehow paying for it aired either his vocabulary or his accent. He usually paid for it by meeting immediately afterwards Waymarsh's eye.

Such were the liberties with which his fancy played after he had turned off to the hillside that did really and truly, as well as most amiably, await him beneath the poplars, the hillside that made him feel, for a murmurous couple of hours, how happy had been his thought. He had the sense of success, of a finer harmony in things; nothing but what had turned out as yet according to his plan. It most of all came home to him, as he lay on his back on the grass, that Sarah had really gone, that his tension was really relaxed; the peace diffused in these ideas might be delusive, but it hung about him none the less for the time. It fairly, for half an hour, sent him to sleep; he pulled his straw hat over his eyes—he had bought it the day before with a reminiscence of Waymarsh's—and lost himself anew in Lambinet. It was as if he had found out he was tired—tired not from his walk, but from that inward exercise which had known, on the whole, for three months, so little intermission. That was it—when once they were off he had dropped; this moreover was what he had dropped to, and now he was touching bottom. He was kept luxuriously quiet, soothed and amused by the consciousness of what he had found at the end of his descent. It was very much what he had told Maria Gostrey he should like to stay on for, the hugely-distributed Paris of summer, alternately dazzling and dusky, with a weight lifted for him off its columns and cornices and with shade and air in the flutter of awnings as wide as avenues. It was present to him without attenuation that, reaching out, the day after making the remark, for some proof of his freedom, he had gone that very afternoon to see Madame de Vionnet. He had gone again the next day but one, and the effect of the two visits, the after-sense of the couple of hours spent with her, was almost that of fullness and frequency. The brave intention of frequency, so great with him from the moment of his finding himself unjustly suspected at Woollett, had remained rather theoretic, and one of the things he could muse about under his poplars was the source of the special shyness that had still made him careful. He had surely got rid of it now, this special shyness; what had become of it if it hadn't precisely, within the week, rubbed off?

It struck him now in fact as sufficiently plain that if he had still been careful he had been so for a reason. He had really feared, in his behaviour, a lapse from good faith; if there was a danger of one's liking such a woman too much one's best safety was in waiting at least till one had the right to do so. In the light of the last few days the danger was fairly vivid; so that it was proportionately fortunate that the right was likewise established. It seemed to our friend that he had on each occasion profited to the utmost by the latter: how could he have done so more, he at all events asked himself, than in having immediately let her know that, if it was all the same to her, he preferred not to talk about anything tiresome? He had never in his life so sacrificed an armful of high interests as in that remark; he had never so prepared the way for the comparatively frivolous as in addressing it to Madame de Vionnet's intelligence. It hadn't been till later that he quite recalled how in conjuring away everything but the pleasant he had conjured away almost all they had hitherto talked about; it was not till later even that he remembered how, with their new tone, they hadn't so much as mentioned the name of Chad himself. One of the things that most lingered with him on his hillside was this delightful facility, with such a woman, of arriving at a new tone; he thought, as he lay on his back, of all the tones she might make possible if one were to try her, and at any rate of the probability that one could trust her to fit them to occasions. He had wanted her to feel that, as he was disinterested now, so she herself should be, and she had showed she felt it, and he had showed he was grateful, and it had been for all the world as if he were calling for the first time. They had had other, but irrelevant, meetings; it was quite as if, had they sooner known how much they *really* had in common, there were quantities of comparatively dull matters they might have skipped. Well, they were skipping them now, even to graceful gratitude, even to handsome "Don't mention it!"—and it was amazing what could still come up without reference to what had been going on between them. It might have been, on analysis, nothing more than Shakespeare and the musical glasses; but it had served all the purpose of his appearing to have said to her: "Don't like me, if it's a question of liking me, for anything obvious and clumsy that I've, as they call it, 'done' for you: like me—well, like me, hang it, for anything else you choose. So, by the same propriety, don't be for me simply the person I've come to know through my awkward connexion with Chad—was ever anything, by the way, *more* awkward? Be for me, please, with all your admirable tact and trust, just whatever I may show you it's a present pleasure to me to think you." It had been a large indication to meet; but if she hadn't met it what *had* she done, and how had their time together slipped along so smoothly, mild but now slow, and melting, liquefying, into his happy illusion of idleness? He could recognise on the other hand that he had probably not been without reason, in his prior, his restricted state, for keeping an eye on his liability to lapse from good faith.

He really continued in the picture—that being for himself his situation—all the rest of this rambling day; so that the charm was still, was indeed more than ever upon him when, towards six o'clock, he found himself amicably engaged with a stout white-capped deep-voiced woman at the door of the *auberge* of the biggest village, a village that affected him as a thing of whiteness, blueness and crookedness, set in coppery green, and that had the river flowing behind or before it—one couldn't say which; at the bottom, in particular, of the inn-garden. He had had other adventures before this; had kept along the height, after shaking off slumber; had admired, had almost coveted, another small old church, all steep roof and dim slate colour without and all whitewash and paper flowers within; had lost his way and had found it again; had conversed with rustics who struck him perhaps a little more as men of the world than he had expected; had acquired at a bound a fearless facility in French; had had, as the afternoon waned, a watery *bock*, all pale and Parisian, in the café of the furthest village, which was not the biggest; and had meanwhile not once overstepped the oblong gilt frame. The frame had drawn itself out for him, as much as you please; but that was just his luck. He had finally come down again to the valley, to keep within touch of stations and trains, turning his face to the quarter from which he had started; and thus it was that he had at last pulled up before the hostess of the Cheval Blanc, who met him, with a rough readiness that was like the clatter of sabots over stones, on their common ground of a *côtelette de veau à l'oseille* and a subsequent lift. He had walked many miles and didn't know he was tired; but he still knew he was amused, and even that, though he had been alone all day, he had never yet so struck himself as engaged with others and in midstream of his drama. It might have passed for finished, his drama, with its catastrophe all but reached; it had, however, none the less been vivid again for him as he thus gave it its fullest chance. He had only had to be at last well out of it to feel it, oddly enough, still going on.

For this had been all day at bottom the spell of the picture—that it was essentially more than anything else a scene and a stage, that the very air of the play was in the rustle of the willows and the tone of the sky. The play and the characters had, without his knowing it till now, peopled all his space for him, and it seemed somehow quite happy that they should offer themselves, in the conditions so supplied, with a kind of inevitability. It was as if the conditions made them not only inevitable, but so much more nearly natural and right as that they were at least easier, pleasanter, to put up with. The conditions had nowhere so asserted their difference from those of Woollett as they appeared to him to assert it in the little court of the Cheval Blanc while he arranged with his hostess for a comfortable climax. They were few and simple, scant and humble, but they were *the thing*, as he would have called it, even to a greater degree than Madame de Vionnet's old high salon where the ghost of the Empire walked. "The" thing was the thing that implied the greatest number of other things of the sort he had had to tackle; and it was queer of course, but so it was—the implication here was complete. Not a single one of his observations but somehow fell into a place in it; not a breath of the cooler evening that wasn't somehow a syllable of the text. The text was simply, when condensed, that in *these* places such things were, and that if it was in them one elected to move about one had to make one's account with what one lighted on. Meanwhile at all events it was enough that they did affect one—so far as the village aspect was concerned—as whiteness, crookedness and blueness set in coppery green; there being positively, for that matter, an outer wall of the White Horse that was painted the most improbable shade. That was part of the amusement—as if to show that the fun was harmless; just as it was enough, further, that the picture and the play seemed supremely to melt together in the good woman's broad sketch of what she could do for her visitor's appetite. He felt in short a confidence, and it was general, and it was all he wanted to feel. It suffered no shock even on her mentioning that she had in fact just laid the cloth for two persons who, unlike Monsieur, had arrived by the river—in a boat of their own; who had asked her, half an hour before, what she could do for them, and had then paddled away to look at something a little further up—from which promenade they would presently return. Monsieur might meanwhile, if he liked, pass into the garden, such as it was, where she would serve him, should he wish it—for there were tables and benches in plenty—a "bitter" before his repast. Here she would also report to him on the possibility of a conveyance to his station, and here at any rate he would have the *agrément* of the river.

It may be mentioned without delay that Monsieur had the *agrément* of everything, and in particular, for the next twenty minutes, of a small and primitive pavilion, that, at the garden's edge, almost overhung the water, testifying, in its somewhat battered state, to much fond frequentation. It consisted of little more than a platform, slightly raised, with a couple of benches and a table, a protecting rail and a projecting roof; but it raked the full grey-blue stream, which, taking a turn a short distance above, passed out of sight to reappear much higher up; and it was clearly in esteemed requisition for Sundays and other feasts. Strether sat there and, though hungry, felt at peace; the confidence that had so gathered for him deepened with the lap of the water, the ripple of the surface, the rustle of the reeds on the opposite bank, the faint diffused coolness and the slight rock of a couple of small boats attached to a rough landing-place hard by. The valley on the further side was all copper-green level and glazed pearly sky, a sky hatched across with screens of trimmed trees, which looked flat, like espaliers; and though the rest of the village straggled away in the near quarter the view had an emptiness that made one of the boats suggestive. Such a river set one afloat almost before one could take up the oars—the idle play of which would be moreover the aid to the full impression. This perception went so far as to bring him to his feet; but that movement, in turn, made him feel afresh that he was tired, and while he leaned against a post and continued to look out he saw something that gave him a sharper arrest.

IV

What he saw was exactly the right thing—a boat advancing round the bend and containing a man who held the paddles and a lady, at the stern, with a pink parasol. It was suddenly as if these figures, or something like them, had been wanted in the picture, had been wanted more or less all day, and had now drifted into sight, with the slow current, on purpose to fill up the measure. They came slowly, floating down, evidently directed to the landing-place near their spectator and presenting themselves to him not less clearly as the two persons for whom his hostess was already preparing a meal. For two very happy persons he found himself straightway taking them—a young man in shirt-sleeves, a young woman easy and fair, who had pulled pleasantly up from some other place and, being acquainted with the neighbourhood, had known what this particular retreat could offer them. The air quite thickened, at their approach, with further intimations; the intimation that they were expert, familiar, frequent—that this wouldn't at all events be the first time. They knew how to do it, he vaguely felt—and it made them but the more idyllic, though at the very moment of the impression, as happened, their boat seemed to have begun to drift wide, the oarsman letting it go. It had by this time none the less come much nearer—near enough for Strether to dream the lady in the stern had for some reason taken account of his being there to watch them. She had remarked on it sharply, yet her companion hadn't turned round; it was in fact almost as if our friend had felt her bid him keep still. She had taken in something as a result of which their course had wavered, and it continued to waver while they just stood off. This little effect was sudden and rapid, so rapid that Strether's sense of it was separate only for an instant from a sharp start of his own. He too had within the minute taken in something, taken in that he knew the lady whose parasol, shifting as if to hide her face, made so fine a pink point in the shining scene. It was too prodigious, a chance in a million, but, if he knew the lady, the gentleman, who still presented his back and kept off, the gentleman, the coatless hero of the idyll, who had responded to her start, was, to match the marvel, none other than Chad.

Chad and Madame de Vionnet were then like himself taking a day in the country—though it was as queer as fiction, as farce, that their country could happen to be exactly his; and she had been the first at recognition, the first to feel, across the water, the shock—for it appeared to come to that—of their wonderful accident. Strether became aware, with this, of what was taking place—that her recognition had been even stranger for the pair in the boat, that her immediate impulse had been to control it, and that she was quickly and intensely debating with Chad the risk of betrayal. He saw they would show nothing if they could feel sure he hadn't made them out; so that he had before him for a few seconds his own hesitation. It was a sharp fantastic crisis that had popped up as if in a dream, and it had had only to last the few seconds to make him feel it as quite horrible. They were thus, on either side, *trying* the other side, and all for some reason that broke the stillness like some unprovoked harsh note. It seemed to him again, within the limit, that he had but one thing to do—to settle their common question by some sign of surprise and joy. He hereupon gave large play to these things, agitating his hat and his stick and loudly calling out—a demonstration that brought him relief as soon as he had seen it answered. The boat, in midstream, still went a little wild—which seemed natural, however, while Chad turned round, half springing up; and his good friend, after blankness and wonder, began gaily to wave her parasol. Chad dropped afresh to his paddles and the boat headed round, amazement and pleasantry filling the air meanwhile, and relief, as Strether continued to fancy, superseding mere violence. Our friend went down to the water under this odd impression as of violence averted—the violence of their having "cut" him, out there in the eye of nature, on the assumption that he wouldn't know it. He awaited them with a face from which he was conscious of not being able quite to banish this idea that they would have gone on, not seeing and not knowing, missing their dinner and disappointing their hostess, had he himself taken a line to match. That at least was what darkened his vision for the moment. Afterwards, after they had bumped at the landing-place and he had assisted their getting ashore, everything found itself sponged over by the mere miracle of the encounter.

They could so much better at last, on either side, treat it as a wild extravagance of hazard, that the situation was made elastic by the amount of explanation called into play. Why indeed—apart from oddity—the situation should have been really stiff was a question naturally not practical at the moment, and in fact, so far as we are concerned, a question tackled, later on and in private, only by Strether himself. He was to reflect later on and in private that it was mainly *he* who had explained—as he had had moreover comparatively little difficulty in doing. He was to have at all events meanwhile the worrying thought of their perhaps secretly suspecting him of having plotted this coincidence, taking such pains as might be to give it the semblance of an accident. That possibility—as their imputation—didn't of course bear looking into for an instant; yet the whole incident was so manifestly, arrange it as they would, an awkward one, that he could scarce keep disclaimers in respect to his own presence from rising to his lips. Disclaimers of intention would have been as tactless as his presence was practically gross; and the narrowest escape they either of them had was his lucky escape, in the event, from making any. Nothing of the sort, so far as surface and sound were involved, was even in question; surface and sound all made for their common ridiculous good fortune, for the general *invraisemblance* of the occasion, for the charming chance that they had, the others, in passing, ordered some food to be ready, the charming chance that he had himself not eaten, the charming chance, even more, that their little plans, their hours, their train, in short, from *là-bas,* would all match for their return together to Paris.

The chance that was most charming of all, the chance that drew from Madame de Vionnet her clearest, gayest "*Comme cela se trouve!*" was the announcement made to Strether after they were seated at table, the word given him by their hostess in respect to his carriage for the station, on which he might now count. It settled the matter for his friends as well; the conveyance—it *was* all too lucky!—would serve for them; and nothing was more delightful than his being in a position to make the train so definite. It might have been, for themselves—to hear Madame de Vionnet—almost unnaturally vague, a detail left to be fixed; though Strether indeed was afterwards to remember that Chad had promptly enough intervened to forestall this appearance, laughing at his companion's flightiness and making the point that he had, after all, in spite of the bedazzlement of a day out with her, known what he was about.

Strether was to remember afterwards further that this had had for him the effect of forming Chad's almost sole intervention; and indeed he was to remember further still, in subsequent meditation, many things that, as it were, fitted together. Another of them was for instance that the wonderful woman's overflow of surprise and amusement was wholly in French, which she struck him as speaking with an unprecedented command of idiomatic turns, but in which she got, as he might have said, somewhat away from him, taking all at once little brilliant jumps that he could but lamely match. The question of his own French had never come up for them; it was the one thing she wouldn't have permitted—it belonged, for a person who had been through much, to mere boredom; but the present result was odd, fairly veiling her identity, shifting her back into a mere voluble class or race to the intense audibility of which he was by this time inured. When she spoke the charming slightly strange English he best knew her by he seemed to feel her as a creature, among all the millions, with a language quite to herself, the real monopoly of a special shade of speech, beautifully easy for her, yet of a colour and a cadence that were both inimitable and matters of accident. She came back to these things after they had shaken down in the inn-parlour and knew, as it were, what was to become of them; it was inevitable that loud ejaculation over the prodigy of their convergence should at last wear itself out. Then it was that his impression took fuller form—the impression, destined only to deepen, to complete itself, that they had something to put a face upon, to carry off and make the best of, and that it was she who, admirably on the whole, was doing this. It was familiar to him of course that they had something to put a face upon; their friendship, their connexion, took any amount of explaining—that would have been made familiar by his twenty minutes with Mrs. Pocock if it hadn't already been so. Yet his theory, as we know, had bountifully been that the facts were specifically none of his business, and were, over and above, so far as one had to do with them, intrinsically beautiful; and this might have prepared him for anything, as well as rendered him proof against mystification. When he reached home that night, however, he knew he had been, at bottom, neither prepared nor proof; and since we have spoken of what he was, after his return, to recall and interpret, it may as well immediately be said that his real experience of these few hours put on, in that belated vision—for he scarce went to bed till morning—the aspect that is most to our purpose.

He then knew more or less how he had been affected—he but half knew at the time. There had been plenty to affect him even after, as has been said, they had shaken down; for his consciousness, though muffled, had its sharpest moments during this passage, a marked drop into innocent friendly Bohemia. They then had put their elbows on the table, deploring the premature end of their two or three dishes; which they had tried to make up with another bottle while Chad joked a little spasmodically, perhaps even a little irrelevantly, with the hostess. What it all came to had been that fiction and fable *were,* inevitably, in the air, and not as a simple term of comparison, but as a result of things said; also that they were blinking it, all round, and that they yet needn't, so much as that, have blinked it—though indeed if they hadn't Strether didn't quite see what else they could have done. Strether didn't quite see *that* even at an hour or two past midnight, even when he had, at his hotel, for a long time, without a light and without undressing, sat back on his bedroom sofa and stared straight before him. He was, at that point of vantage, in full possession, to make of it all what he could. He kept making of it that there had been simply a *lie* in the charming affair—a lie on which one could now, detached and deliberate, perfectly put one's finger. It was with the lie that they had eaten and drunk and talked and laughed, that they had waited for their *carriole* rather impatiently, and had then got into the vehicle and, sensibly subsiding, driven their three or four miles through the darkening summer night. The eating and drinking, which had been a resource, had had the effect of having served its turn; the talk and laughter had done as much; and it was during their somewhat tedious progress to the station, during the waits there, the further delays, their submission to fatigue, their silences in the dim compartment of the much-stopping train, that he prepared himself for reflexions to come. It had been a performance, Madame de Vionnet's manner, and though it had to that degree faltered toward the end, as though her ceasing to believe in it, as if she had asked herself, or Chad had found a moment surreptitiously to ask her, what after all was the use, a performance it had none the less quite handsomely remained, with the final fact about it that it was on the whole easier to keep up than to abandon.

From the point of view of presence of mind it had been very wonderful indeed, wonderful for readiness, for beautiful assurance, for the way her decision was taken on the spot, without time to confer with Chad, without time for anything. Their only conference could have been the brief instants in the boat before they confessed to recognising the spectator on the bank, for they hadn't been alone together a moment since and must have communicated all in silence. It was a part of the deep impression for Strether, and not the least of the deep interest, that they *could* so communicate—that Chad in particular could let her know he left it to her. He habitually left things to others, as Strether was so well aware, and it in fact came over our friend in these meditations that there had been as yet no such vivid illustration of his famous knowing how to live. It was as if he had humoured her to the extent of letting her lie without correction—almost as if, really, he would be coming round in the morning to set the matter, as between Strether and himself, right. Of course he couldn't quite come; it was a case in which a man was obliged to accept the woman's version, even when fantastic; if she had, with more flurry than she cared to show, elected, as the phrase was, to represent that they had left Paris that morning, and with no design but of getting back within the day—if she had so sized-up, in the Woollett phrase, their necessity, she knew best her own measure. There were things, all the same, it was impossible to blink and which made this measure an odd one—the too evident fact for instance that she hadn't started out for the day dressed and hatted and shod, and even, for that matter, pink parasol'd, as she had been in the boat. From what did the drop in her assurance proceed as the tension increased—from what did this slightly baffled ingenuity spring but from her consciousness of not presenting, as night closed in, with not so much as a shawl to wrap her round, an appearance that matched her story? She admitted that she was cold, but only to blame her imprudence, which Chad suffered her to give such account of as she might. Her shawl and Chad's overcoat and her other garments, and his, those they had each worn the day before, were at the place, best known to themselves—a quiet retreat enough, no doubt—at which they had been spending the twenty-four hours, to which they had fully meant to return that evening, from which they had so remarkably swum into Strether's ken, and the tacit repudiation of which had been thus the essence of her comedy. Strether saw how she had perceived in a flash that they couldn't quite look to going back there under his nose; though, honestly, as he gouged deeper into the matter, he was somewhat surprised, as Chad likewise had perhaps been, at the uprising of this scruple. He seemed even to divine that she had entertained it rather for Chad than for herself, and that, as the young man had lacked the chance to enlighten her, she had had to go on with it, he meanwhile mistaking her motive.

He was rather glad, none the less, that they had in point of fact not parted at the Cheval Blanc, that he hadn't been reduced to giving them his blessing for an idyllic retreat down the river. He had had in the actual case to make-believe more than he liked, but this was nothing, it struck him, to what the other event would have required. Could he, literally, quite have faced the other event? Would he have been capable of making the best of it with them? This was what he was trying to do now; but with the advantage of his being able to give more time to it a good deal counteracted by his sense of what, over and above the central fact itself, he had to swallow. It was the quantity of make-believe involved and so vividly exemplified that most disagreed with his spiritual stomach. He moved, however, from the consideration of that quantity—to say nothing of the consciousness of that organ—back to the other feature of the show, the deep, deep truth of the intimacy revealed. That was what, in his vain vigil, he oftenest reverted to: intimacy, at such a point, was *like* that—and what in the world else would one have wished it to be like? It was all very well for him to feel the pity of its being so much like lying; he almost blushed, in the dark, for the way he had dressed the possibility in vagueness, as a little girl might have dressed her doll. He had made them—and by no fault of their own—momentarily pull it for him, the possibility, out of this vagueness; and must he not therefore take it now as they had had simply, with whatever thin attenuations, to give it to him? The very question, it may be added, made him feel lonely and cold. There was the element of the awkward all round, but Chad and Madame de Vionnet had at least the comfort that they could talk it over together. With whom could *he* talk of such things?—unless indeed always, at almost any stage, with Maria? He foresaw that Miss Gostrey would come again into requisition on the morrow; though it wasn't to be denied that he was already a little afraid of her "What on earth—that's what I want to know now—had you then supposed?" He recognised at last that he had really been trying all along to suppose nothing. Verily, verily, his labour had been lost. He found himself supposing innumerable and wonderful things.

BOOK TWELFTH

I

Strether couldn't have said he had during the previous hours definitely expected it; yet when, later on, that morning—though no later indeed than for his coming forth at ten o'clock—he saw the concierge produce, on his approach, a *petit bleu* delivered since his letters had been sent up, he recognised the appearance as the first symptom of a sequel. He then knew he had been thinking of some early sign from Chad as more likely, after all, than not; and this would be precisely the early sign. He took it so for granted that he opened the *petit bleu* just where he had stopped, in the pleasant cool draught of the porte-cochère—only curious to see where the young man would, at such a juncture, break out. His curiosity, however, was more than gratified; the small missive, whose gummed edge he had detached without attention to the address, not being from the young man at all, but from the person whom the case gave him on the spot as still more worth while. Worth while or not, he went round to the nearest telegraph-office, the big one on the Boulevard, with a directness that almost confessed to a fear of the danger of delay. He might have been thinking that if he didn't go before he could think he wouldn't perhaps go at all. He at any rate kept, in the lower side-pocket of his morning-coat, a very deliberate hand on his blue missive, crumpling it up rather tenderly than harshly. He wrote a reply, on the Boulevard, also in the form of a *petit bleu*—which was quickly done, under pressure of the place, inasmuch as, like Madame de Vionnet's own communication, it consisted of the fewest words. She had asked him if he could do her the very great kindness of coming to see her that evening at half-past nine, and he answered, as if nothing were easier, that he would present himself at the hour she named. She had added a line of postscript, to the effect that she would come to him elsewhere and at his own hour if he preferred; but he took no notice of this, feeling that if he saw her at all half the value of it would be in seeing her where he had already seen her best. He mightn't see her at all; that was one of the reflexions he made after writing and before he dropped his closed card into the box; he mightn't see any one at all any more at all; he might make an end as well now as ever, leaving things as they were, since he was doubtless not to leave them better, and taking his way home so far as should appear that a home remained to him. This alternative was for a few minutes so sharp that if he at last did deposit his missive it was perhaps because the pressure of the place had an effect.

There was none other, however, than the common and constant pressure, familiar to our friend under the rubric of *Postes et Télégraphes*—the something in the air of these establishments; the vibration of the vast strange life of the town, the influence of the types, the performers concocting their messages; the little prompt Paris women, arranging, pretexting goodness knew what, driving the dreadful needle-pointed public pen at the dreadful sand-strewn public table: implements that symbolised for Strether's too interpretative innocence something more acute in manners, more sinister in morals, more fierce in the national life. After he had put in his paper he had ranged himself, he was really amused to think, on the side of the fierce, the sinister, the acute. He was carrying on a correspondence, across the great city, quite in the key of the *Postes et Télégraphes* in general; and it was fairly as if the acceptance of that fact had come from something in his state that sorted with the occupation of his neighbours. He was mixed up with the typical tale of Paris, and so were they, poor things—how could they altogether help being? They were no worse than he, in short, and he no worse than they—if, queerly enough, no better; and at all events he had settled his hash, so that he went out to begin, from that moment, his day of waiting. The great settlement was, as he felt, in his preference for seeing his correspondent in her own best conditions. *That* was part of the typical tale, the part most significant in respect to himself. He liked the place she lived in, the picture that each time squared itself, large and high and clear, around her: every occasion of seeing it was a pleasure of a different shade. Yet what precisely was he doing with shades of pleasure now, and why hadn't he properly and logically compelled her to commit herself to whatever of disadvantage and penalty the situation might throw up? He might have proposed, as for Sarah Pocock, the cold hospitality of his own *salon de lecture,* in which the chill of Sarah's visit seemed still to abide and shades of pleasure were dim; he might have suggested a stone bench in the dusty Tuileries or a penny chair at the back part of the Champs Élysées. These things would have been a trifle stern, and sternness alone now wouldn't be sinister. An instinct in him cast about for some form of discipline in which they might meet—some awkwardness they would suffer from, some danger, or at least some grave inconvenience, they would incur. This would give a sense—which the spirit required, rather ached and sighed in the absence of—that somebody was paying something somewhere and somehow, that they were at least not all floating together on the silver stream of impunity. Just instead of that to go and see her late in the evening, as if, for all the world—well, as if he were as much in the swim as anybody else: this had as little as possible in common with the penal form.

Even when he had felt that objection melt away, however, the practical difference was small; the long stretch of his interval took the colour it would, and if he lived on thus with the sinister from hour to hour it proved an easier thing than one might have supposed in advance. He reverted in thought to his old tradition, the one he had been brought up on and which even so many years of life had but little worn away; the notion that the state of the wrongdoer, or at least this person's happiness, presented some special difficulty. What struck him now rather was the ease of it—for nothing in truth appeared easier. It was an ease he himself fairly tasted of for the rest of the day; giving himself quite up; not so much as trying to dress it out, in any particular whatever, as a difficulty; not after all going to see Maria—which would have been in a manner a result of such dressing; only idling, lounging, smoking, sitting in the shade, drinking lemonade and consuming ices. The day had turned to heat and eventual thunder, and he now and again went back to his hotel to find that Chad hadn't been there. He hadn't yet struck himself, since leaving Woollett, so much as a loafer, though there had been times when he believed himself touching bottom. This was a deeper depth than any, and with no foresight, scarcely with a care, as to what he should bring up. He almost wondered if he didn't *look* demoralized and disreputable; he had the fanciful vision, as he sat and smoked, of some accidental, some motived, return of the Pococks, who would be passing along the Boulevard and would catch this view of him. They would have distinctly, on his appearance, every ground for scandal. But fate failed to administer even that sternness; the Pococks never passed and Chad made no sign. Strether meanwhile continued to hold off from Miss Gostrey, keeping her till to-morrow; so that by evening his irresponsibility, his impunity, his luxury, had become—there was no other word for them—immense.

Between nine and ten, at last, in the high clear picture—he was moving in these days, as in a gallery, from clever canvas to clever canvas—he drew a long breath: it was so presented to him from the first that the spell of his luxury wouldn't be broken. He wouldn't have, that is, to become responsible—this was admirably in the air: she had sent for him precisely to let him feel it, so that he might go on with the comfort (comfort already established, hadn't it been?) of regarding his ordeal, the ordeal of the weeks of Sarah's stay and of their climax, as safely traversed and left behind him. Didn't she just wish to assure him that *she* now took it all and so kept it; that he was absolutely not to worry any more, was only to rest on his laurels and continue generously to help her? The light in her beautiful, formal room was dim, though it would do, as everything would always do; the hot night had kept out lamps, but there was a pair of clusters of candles that glimmered over the chimney-piece like the tall tapers of an altar. The windows were all open, their redundant hangings swaying a little, and he heard once more, from the empty court, the small plash of the fountain. From beyond this, and as from a great distance—beyond the court, beyond the *corps de logis* forming the front—came, as if excited and exciting, the vague voice of Paris. Strether had all along been subject to sudden gusts of fancy in connexion with such matters as these—odd starts of the historic sense, suppositions and divinations with no warrant but their intensity. Thus and so, on the eve of the great recorded dates, the days and nights of revolution, the sounds had come in, the omens, the beginnings broken out. They were the smell of revolution, the smell of the public temper—or perhaps simply the smell of blood.

It was at present queer beyond words, "subtle," he would have risked saying, that such suggestions should keep crossing the scene; but it was doubtless the effect of the thunder in the air, which had hung about all day without release. His hostess was dressed as for thunderous times, and it fell in with the kind of imagination we have just attributed to him that she should be in simplest coolest white, of a character so old-fashioned, if he were not mistaken, that Madame Roland must on the scaffold have worn something like it. This effect was enhanced by a small black fichu or scarf, of crape or gauze, disposed quaintly round her bosom and now completing as by a mystic touch the pathetic, the noble analogy. Poor Strether in fact scarce knew what analogy was evoked for him as the charming woman, receiving him and making him, as she could do such things, at once familiarly and gravely welcome, moved over her great room with her image almost repeated in its polished floor, which had been fully bared for summer. The associations of the place, all felt again; the gleam here and there, in the subdued light, of glass and gilt and parquet, with the quietness of her own note as the centre—these things were at first as delicate as if they had been ghostly, and he was sure in a moment that, whatever he should find he had come for, it wouldn't be for an impression that had previously failed him. That conviction held him from the outset, and, seeming singularly to simplify, certified to him that the objects about would help him, would really help them both. No, he might never see them again—this was only too probably the last time; and he should certainly see nothing in the least degree like them. He should soon be going to where such things were not, and it would be a small mercy for memory, for fancy, to have, in that stress, a loaf on the shelf. He knew in advance he should look back on the perception actually sharpest with him as on the view of something old, old, old, the oldest thing he had ever personally touched; and he also knew, even while he took his companion in as the feature among features, that memory and fancy couldn't help being enlisted for her. She might intend what she would, but this was beyond anything she could intend, with things from far back—tyrannies of history, facts of type, values, as the painters said, of expression—all working for her and giving her the supreme chance, the chance of the happy, the really luxurious few, the chance, on a great occasion, to be natural and simple. She had never, with him, been more so; or if it was the perfection of art it would never—and that came to the same thing—be proved against her.

What was truly wonderful was her way of differing so from time to time without detriment to her simplicity. Caprices, he was sure she felt, were before anything else bad manners, and that judgement in her was by itself a thing making more for safety of intercourse than anything that in his various own past intercourses he had had to reckon on. If therefore her presence was now quite other than the one she had shown him the night before, there was nothing of violence in the change—it was all harmony and reason. It gave him a mild deep person, whereas he had had on the occasion to which their interview was a direct reference a person committed to movement and surface and abounding in them; but she was in either character more remarkable for nothing than for her bridging of intervals, and this now fell in with what he understood he was to leave to her. The only thing was that, if he was to leave it *all* to her, why exactly had she sent for him? He had had, vaguely, in advance, his explanation, his view of the probability of her wishing to set something right, to deal in some way with the fraud so lately practised on his presumed credulity. Would she attempt to carry it further or would she blot it out? Would she throw over it some more or less happy colour; or would she do nothing about it at all? He perceived soon enough at least that, however reasonable she might be, she wasn't vulgarly confused, and it herewith pressed upon him that their eminent "lie," Chad's and hers, was simply after all such an inevitable tribute to good taste as he couldn't have wished them not to render. Away from them, during his vigil, he had seemed to wince at the amount of comedy involved; whereas in his present posture he could only ask himself how he should enjoy any attempt from her to take the comedy back. He shouldn't enjoy it at all; but, once more and yet once more, he could trust her. That is he could trust her to make deception right. As she presented things the ugliness—goodness knew why—went out of them; none the less too that she could present them, with an art of her own, by not so much as touching them. She let the matter, at all events, lie where it was—where the previous twenty-four hours had placed it; appearing merely to circle about it respectfully, tenderly, almost piously, while she took up another question.

She knew she hadn't really thrown dust in his eyes; this, the previous night, before they separated, had practically passed between them; and, as she had sent for him to see what the difference thus made for him might amount to, so he was conscious at the end of five minutes that he had been tried and tested. She had settled with Chad after he left them that she would, for her satisfaction, assure herself of this quantity, and Chad had, as usual, let her have her way. Chad was always letting people have their way when he felt that it would somehow turn his wheel for him; it somehow always did turn his wheel. Strether felt, oddly enough, before these facts, freshly and consentingly passive; they again so rubbed it into him that the couple thus fixing his attention were intimate, that his intervention had absolutely aided and intensified their intimacy, and that in fine he must accept the consequence of that. He had absolutely become, himself, with his perceptions and his mistakes, his concessions and his reserves, the droll mixture, as it must seem to them, of his braveries and his fears, the general spectacle of his art and his innocence, almost an added link and certainly a common priceless ground for them to meet upon. It was as if he had been hearing their very tone when she brought out a reference that was comparatively straight. "The last twice that you've been here, you know, I never asked you," she said with an abrupt transition—they had been pretending before this to talk simply of the charm of yesterday and of the interest of the country they had seen. The effort was confessedly vain; not for such talk had she invited him; and her impatient reminder was of their having done for it all the needful on his coming to her after Sarah's flight. What she hadn't asked him then was to state to her where and how he stood for her: she had been resting on Chad's report of their midnight hour together in the Boulevard Malesherbes. The thing therefore she at present desired was ushered in by this recall of the two occasions on which, disinterested and merciful, she hadn't worried him. To-night truly she *would* worry him, and this was her appeal to him to let her risk it. He wasn't to mind if she bored him a little: she had behaved, after all—hadn't she?—so awfully, awfully well.

II

"Oh, you're all right, you're all right," he almost impatiently declared; his impatience being moreover not for her pressure, but for her scruple. More and more distinct to him was the tune to which she would have had the matter out with Chad; more and more vivid for him the idea that she had been nervous as to what he might be able to "stand." Yes, it had been a question if he had "stood" what the scene on the river had given him, and, though the young man had doubtless opined in favour of his recuperation, her own last word must have been that she should feel easier in seeing for herself. That was it, unmistakeably; she *was* seeing for herself. What he could stand was thus, in these moments, in the balance for Strether, who reflected, as he became fully aware of it, that he must properly brace himself. He wanted fully to appear to stand all he might; and there was a certain command of the situation for him in this very wish not to look too much to sea. She was ready with everything, but so, sufficiently, was he; that is he was at one point the more prepared of the two, inasmuch as, for all her cleverness, she couldn't produce on the spot—and it was surprising—an account of the motive of her note. He had the advantage that his pronouncing her "all right" gave him for an enquiry. "May I ask, delighted as I've been to come, if you've wished to say something special?" He spoke as if she might have seen he had been waiting for it—not indeed with discomfort, but with natural interest. Then he saw that she was a little taken aback, was even surprised herself at the detail she had neglected—the only one ever yet; having somehow assumed he would know, would recognise, would leave some things not to be said. She looked at him, however, an instant as if to convey that if he wanted them *all*—!

"Selfish and vulgar—that's what I must seem to you. You've done everything for me, and here I am as if I were asking for more. But it isn't," she went on, "because I'm afraid—though I *am* of course afraid, as a woman in my position always is. I mean it isn't because one lives in terror—it isn't because of that one is selfish, for I'm ready to give you my word to-night that I don't care; don't care what still may happen and what I may lose. I don't ask you to raise your little finger for me again, nor do I wish so much as to mention to you what we've talked of before, either my danger or my safety, or his mother, or his sister, or the girl he may marry, or the fortune he may make or miss, or the right or the wrong, of any kind, he may do. If after the help one has had from you one can't either take care of one's self or simply hold one's tongue, one must renounce all claim to be an object of interest. It's in the name of what I *do* care about that I've tried still to keep hold of you. How can I be indifferent," she asked, "to how I appear to you?" And as he found himself unable immediately to say: "Why, if you're going, *need* you, after all? Is it impossible you should stay on—so that one mayn't lose you?"

"Impossible I should live with you here instead of going home?"

"Not 'with' us, if you object to that, but near enough to us, somewhere, for us to see you—well," she beautifully brought out, "when we feel we *must*. How shall we not sometimes feel it? I've wanted to see you often when I couldn't," she pursued, "all these last weeks. How shan't I then miss you now, with the sense of your being gone for ever?" Then as if the straightness of this appeal, taking him unprepared, had visibly left him wondering: "Where *is* your 'home' moreover now—what has become of it? I've made a change in your life, I know I have; I've upset everything in your mind as well; in your sense of—what shall I call it?—all the decencies and possibilities. It gives me a kind of detestation—." She pulled up short.

Oh but he wanted to hear. "Detestation of what?"

"Of everything—of life."

"Ah that's too much," he laughed—"or too little!"

"Too little, precisely"—she was eager. "What I hate is myself—when I think that one has to take so much, to be happy, out of the lives of others, and that one isn't happy even then. One does it to cheat one's self and to stop one's mouth—but that's only at the best for a little. The wretched self is always there, always making one somehow a fresh anxiety. What it comes to is that it's not, that it's never, a happiness, any happiness at all, to *take*. The only safe thing is to give. It's what plays you least false." Interesting, touching, strikingly sincere as she let these things come from her, she yet puzzled and troubled him—so fine was the quaver of her quietness. He felt what he had felt before with her, that there was always more behind what she showed, and more and more again behind that. "You know so, at least," she added, "where you are!"

"*You* ought to know it indeed then; for isn't what you've been giving exactly what has brought us together this way? You've been making, as I've so fully let you know I've felt," Strether said, "the most precious present I've ever seen made, and if you can't sit down peacefully on that performance you *are,* no doubt, born to torment yourself. But you ought," he wound up, "to be easy."

"And not trouble you any more, no doubt—not thrust on you even the wonder and the beauty of what I've done; only let you regard our business as over, and well over, and see you depart in a peace that matches my own! No doubt, no doubt, no doubt," she nervously repeated—"all the more that I don't really pretend I believe you couldn't, for yourself, *not* have done what you have. I don't pretend you feel yourself victimised, for this evidently is the way you live, and it's what—we're agreed—is the best way. Yes, as you say," she continued after a moment, "I ought to be easy and rest on my work. Well then here I am doing so. I *am* easy. You'll have it for your last impression. When is it you say you go?" she asked with a quick change.

He took some time to reply—his last impression was more and more so mixed a one. It produced in him a vague disappointment, a drop that was deeper even than the fall of his elation the previous night. The good of what he had done, if he had done so much, wasn't there to enliven him quite to the point that would have been ideal for a grand gay finale. Women were thus endlessly absorbent, and to deal with them was to walk on water. What was at bottom the matter with her, embroider as she might and disclaim as she might—what was at bottom the matter with her was simply Chad himself. It was of Chad she was after all renewedly afraid; the strange strength of her passion was the very strength of her fear; she clung to *him,* Lambert Strether, as to a source of safety she had tested, and, generous graceful truthful as she might try to be, exquisite as she was, she dreaded the term of his being within reach. With this sharpest perception yet, it was like a chill in the air to him, it was almost appalling, that a creature so fine could be, by mysterious forces, a creature so exploited. For at the end of all things they *were* mysterious: she had but made Chad what he was—so why could she think she had made him infinite? She had made him better, she had made him best, she had made him anything one would; but it came to our friend with supreme queerness that he was none the less only Chad. Strether had the sense that *he,* a little, had made him too; his high appreciation had, as it were, consecrated her work. The work, however admirable, was nevertheless of the strict human order, and in short it was marvellous that the companion of mere earthly joys, of comforts, aberrations (however one classed them) within the common experience, should be so transcendently prized. It might have made Strether hot or shy, as such secrets of others brought home sometimes do make us; but he was held there by something so hard that it was fairly grim. This was not the discomposure of last night; that had quite passed—such discomposures were a detail; the real coercion was to see a man ineffably adored. There it was again—it took women, it took women; if to deal with them was to walk on water, what wonder that the water rose? And it had never surely risen higher than round this woman. He presently found himself taking a long look from her, and the next thing he knew he had uttered all his thought. "You're afraid for your life!"

It drew out her long look, and he soon enough saw why. A spasm came into her face, the tears she had already been unable to hide overflowed at first in silence, and then, as the sound suddenly comes from a child, quickened to gasps, to sobs. She sat and covered her face with her hands, giving up all attempt at a manner. "It's how you see me, it's how you see me"—she caught her breath with it—"and it's as I *am,* and as I must take myself, and of course it's no matter." Her emotion was at first so incoherent that he could only stand there at a loss, stand with his sense of having upset her, though of having done it by the truth. He had to listen to her in a silence that he made no immediate effort to attenuate, feeling her doubly woeful amid all her dim diffused elegance; consenting to it as he had consented to the rest, and even conscious of some vague inward irony in the presence of such a fine free range of bliss and bale. He couldn't say it was *not* no matter; for he was serving her to the end, he now knew, anyway—quite as if what he thought of her had nothing to do with it. It was actually moreover as if he didn't think of her at all, as if he could think of nothing but the passion, mature, abysmal, pitiful, she represented, and the possibilities she betrayed. She was older for him to-night, visibly less exempt from the touch of time; but she was as much as ever the finest and subtlest creature, the happiest apparition, it had been given him, in all his years, to meet; and yet he could see her there as vulgarly troubled, in very truth, as a maidservant crying for her young man. The only thing was that she judged herself as the maidservant wouldn't; the weakness of which wisdom too, the dishonour of which judgment, seemed but to sink her lower. Her collapse, however, no doubt, was briefer and she had in a manner recovered herself before he intervened. "Of course I'm afraid for my life. But that's nothing. It isn't that."

He was silent a little while longer, as if thinking what it might be. "There's something I have in mind that I can still do."

But she threw off at last, with a sharp sad headshake, drying her eyes, what he could still do. "I don't care for that. Of course, as I've said, you're acting, in your wonderful way, for yourself; and what's for yourself is no more my business—though I may reach out unholy hands so clumsily to touch it—than if it were something in Timbuctoo. It's only that you don't snub me, as you've had fifty chances to do—it's only your beautiful patience that makes one forget one's manners. In spite of your patience, all the same," she went on, "you'd do anything rather than be with us here, even if that were possible. You'd do everything for us but be mixed up with us—which is a statement you can easily answer to the advantage of your own manners. You can say 'What's the use of talking of things that at the best are impossible?' What *is,* of course, the use? It's only my little madness. You'd talk if you were tormented. And I don't mean now about *him*. Oh for him—!" Positively, strangely, bitterly, as it seemed to Strether, she gave "him," for the moment, away. "You don't care what I think of you; but I happen to care what you think of me. And what you *might,*" she added. "What you perhaps even did."

He gained time. "What I did?"

"Did think before. Before this. *Didn't* you think—?"

But he had already stopped her. "I didn't think anything. I never think a step further than I'm obliged to."

"That's perfectly false, I believe," she returned—"except that you may, no doubt, often pull up when things become *too* ugly; or even, I'll say, to save you a protest, too beautiful. At any rate, even so far as it's true, we've thrust on you appearances that you've had to take in and that have therefore made your obligation. Ugly or beautiful—it doesn't matter what we call them—you were getting on without them, and that's where we're detestable. We bore you—that's where we are. And we may well—for what we've cost you. All you can do *now* is not to think at all. And I who should have liked to seem to you—well, sublime!"

He could only after a moment, re-echo Miss Barrace. "You're wonderful!"

"I'm old and abject and hideous"—she went on as without hearing him. "Abject above all. Or old above all. It's when one's old that it's worst. I don't care what becomes of it—let what *will*; there it is. It's a doom—I know it; you can't see it more than I do myself. Things have to happen as they will." With which she came back again to what, face to face with him, had so quite broken down. "Of course you wouldn't, even if possible, and no matter what may happen to you, be near us. But think of me, think of me—!" She exhaled it into air.

He took refuge in repeating something he had already said and that she had made nothing of. "There's something I believe I can still do." And he put out his hand for good-bye.

She again made nothing of it; she went on with her insistence. "That won't help you. There's nothing to help you."

"Well, it may help *you,*" he said.

She shook her head. "There's not a grain of certainty in my future—for the only certainty is that I shall be the loser in the end."

She hadn't taken his hand, but she moved with him to the door. "That's cheerful," he laughed, "for your benefactor!"

"What's cheerful for *me,*" she replied, "is that we might, you and I, have been friends. That's it—that's it. You see how, as I say, I want everything. I've wanted you too."

"Ah but you've *had* me!" he declared, at the door, with an emphasis that made an end.

III

His purpose had been to see Chad the next day, and he had prefigured seeing him by an early call; having in general never stood on ceremony in respect to visits in the Boulevard Malesherbes. It had been more often natural for him to go there than for Chad to come to the small hotel, the attractions of which were scant; yet it nevertheless, just now, at the eleventh hour, did suggest itself to Strether to begin by giving the young man a chance. It struck him that, in the inevitable course, Chad would be "round," as Waymarsh used to say—Waymarsh who already, somehow, seemed long ago. He hadn't come the day before, because it had been arranged between them that Madame de Vionnet should see their friend first; but now that this passage had taken place he would present himself, and their friend wouldn't have long to wait. Strether assumed, he became aware, on this reasoning, that the interesting parties to the arrangement would have met betimes, and that the more interesting of the two—as she was after all—would have communicated to the other the issue of her appeal. Chad would know without delay that his mother's messenger had been with her, and, though it was perhaps not quite easy to see how she could qualify what had occurred, he would at least have been sufficiently advised to feel he could go on. The day, however, brought, early or late, no word from him, and Strether felt, as a result of this, that a change had practically come over their intercourse. It was perhaps a premature judgement; or it only meant perhaps—how could he tell?—that the wonderful pair he protected had taken up again together the excursion he had accidentally checked. They might have gone back to the country, and gone back but with a long breath drawn; that indeed would best mark Chad's sense that reprobation hadn't rewarded Madame de Vionnet's request for an interview. At the end of the twenty-four hours, at the end of the forty-eight, there was still no overture; so that Strether filled up the time, as he had so often filled it before, by going to see Miss Gostrey.

He proposed amusements to her; he felt expert now in proposing amusements; and he had thus, for several days, an odd sense of leading her about Paris, of driving her in the Bois, of showing her the penny steamboats—those from which the breeze of the Seine was to be best enjoyed—that might have belonged to a kindly uncle doing the honours of the capital to an intelligent niece from the country. He found means even to take her to shops she didn't know, or that she pretended she didn't; while she, on her side, was, like the country maiden, all passive modest and grateful—going in fact so far as to emulate rusticity in occasional fatigues and bewilderments. Strether described these vague proceedings to himself, described them even to her, as a happy interlude; the sign of which was that the companions said for the time no further word about the matter they had talked of to satiety. He proclaimed satiety at the outset, and she quickly took the hint; as docile both in this and in everything else as the intelligent obedient niece. He told her as yet nothing of his late adventure—for as an adventure it now ranked with him; he pushed the whole business temporarily aside and found his interest in the fact of her beautiful assent. She left questions unasked—she who for so long had been all questions; she gave herself up to him with an understanding of which mere mute gentleness might have seemed the sufficient expression. She knew his sense of his situation had taken still another step—of that he was quite aware; but she conveyed that, whatever had thus happened for him, it was thrown into the shade by what was happening for herself. This—though it mightn't to a detached spirit have seemed much—was the major interest, and she met it with a new directness of response, measuring it from hour to hour with her grave hush of acceptance. Touched as he had so often been by her before, he was, for his part too, touched afresh; all the more that though he could be duly aware of the principle of his own mood he couldn't be equally so of the principle of hers. He knew, that is, in a manner—knew roughly and resignedly—what he himself was hatching; whereas he had to take the chance of what he called to himself Maria's calculations. It was all he needed that she liked him enough for what they were doing, and even should they do a good deal more would still like him enough for that; the essential freshness of a relation so simple was a cool bath to the soreness produced by other relations. These others appeared to him now horribly complex; they bristled with fine points, points all unimaginable beforehand, points that pricked and drew blood; a fact that gave to an hour with his present friend on a *bateau-mouche,* or in the afternoon shade of the Champs Élysées, something of the innocent pleasure of handling rounded ivory. His relation with Chad personally—from the moment he had got his point of view—had been of the simplest; yet this also struck him as bristling, after a third and a fourth blank day had passed. It was as if at last however his care for such indications had dropped; there came a fifth blank day and he ceased to inquire or to heed.

They now took on to his fancy, Miss Gostrey and he, the image of the Babes in the Wood; they could trust the merciful elements to let them continue at peace. He had been great already, as he knew, at postponements; but he had only to get afresh into the rhythm of one to feel its fine attraction. It amused him to say to himself that he might for all the world have been going to die—die resignedly; the scene was filled for him with so deep a death-bed hush, so melancholy a charm. That meant the postponement of everything else—which made so for the quiet lapse of life; and the postponement in especial of the reckoning to come—unless indeed the reckoning to come were to be one and the same thing with extinction. It faced him, the reckoning, over the shoulder of much interposing experience—which also faced him; and one would float to it doubtless duly through these caverns of Kubla Khan. It was really behind everything; it hadn't merged in what he had done; his final appreciation of what he had done—his appreciation on the spot—would provide it with its main sharpness. The spot so focused was of course Woollett, and he was to see, at the best, what Woollett would be with everything there changed for him. Wouldn't *that* revelation practically amount to the wind-up of his career? Well, the summer's end would show; his suspense had meanwhile exactly the sweetness of vain delay; and he had with it, we should mention, other pastimes than Maria's company—plenty of separate musings in which his luxury failed him but at one point. He was well in port, the outer sea behind him, and it was only a matter of getting ashore. There was a question that came and went for him, however, as he rested against the side of his ship, and it was a little to get rid of the obsession that he prolonged his hours with Miss Gostrey. It was a question about himself, but it could only be settled by seeing Chad again; it was indeed his principal reason for wanting to see Chad. After that it wouldn't signify—it was a ghost that certain words would easily lay to rest. Only the young man must be there to take the words. Once they were taken he wouldn't have a question left; none, that is, in connexion with this particular affair. It wouldn't then matter even to himself that he might now have been guilty of speaking *because* of what he had forfeited. That was the refinement of his supreme scruple—he wished so to leave what he had forfeited out of account. He wished not to do anything because he had missed something else, because he was sore or sorry or impoverished, because he was maltreated or desperate; he wished to do everything because he was lucid and quiet, just the same for himself on all essential points as he had ever been. Thus it was that while he virtually hung about for Chad he kept mutely putting it: "You've been chucked, old boy; but what has that to do with it?" It would have sickened him to feel vindictive.

These tints of feeling indeed were doubtless but the iridescence of his idleness, and they were presently lost in new light from Maria. She had a fresh fact for him before the week was out, and she practically met him with it on his appearing one night. He hadn't on this day seen her, but had planned presenting himself in due course to ask her to dine with him somewhere out of doors, on one of the terraces, in one of the gardens, of which the Paris of summer was profuse. It had then come on to rain, so that, disconcerted, he changed his mind; dining alone at home, a little stuffily and stupidly, and waiting on her afterwards to make up his loss. He was sure within a minute that something had happened; it was so in the air of the rich little room that he had scarcely to name his thought. Softly lighted, the whole colour of the place, with its vague values, was in cool fusion—an effect that made the visitor stand for a little agaze. It was as if in doing so now he had felt a recent presence—his recognition of the passage of which his hostess in turn divined. She had scarcely to say it—"Yes, she has been here, and this time I received her." It wasn't till a minute later that she added: "There being, as I understand you, no reason *now*—!"

"None for your refusing?"

"No—if you've done what you've had to do."

"I've certainly so far done it," Strether said, "as that you needn't fear the effect, or the appearance of coming between us. There's nothing between us now but what we ourselves have put there, and not an inch of room for anything else whatever. Therefore you're only beautifully *with* us as always—though doubtless now, if she has talked to you, rather more with us than less. Of course if she came," he added, "it was to talk to you."

"It was to talk to me," Maria returned; on which he was further sure that she was practically in possession of what he himself hadn't yet told her. He was even sure she was in possession of things he himself couldn't have told; for the consciousness of them was now all in her face and accompanied there with a shade of sadness that marked in her the close of all uncertainties. It came out for him more than ever yet that she had had from the first a knowledge she believed him not to have had, a knowledge the sharp acquisition of which might be destined to make a difference for him. The difference for him might not inconceivably be an arrest of his independence and a change in his attitude—in other words a revulsion in favour of the principles of Woollett. She had really prefigured the possibility of a shock that would send him swinging back to Mrs. Newsome. He hadn't, it was true, week after week, shown signs of receiving it, but the possibility had been none the less in the air. What Maria accordingly had had now to take in was that the shock had descended and that he hadn't, all the same, swung back. He had grown clear, in a flash, on a point long since settled for himself; but no reapproximation to Mrs. Newsome had occurred in consequence. Madame de Vionnet had by her visit held up the torch to these truths, and what now lingered in poor Maria's face was the somewhat smoky light of the scene between them. If the light however wasn't, as we have hinted, the glow of joy, the reasons for this also were perhaps discernible to Strether even through the blur cast over them by his natural modesty. She had held herself for months with a firm hand; she hadn't interfered on any chance—and chances were specious enough—that she might interfere to her profit. She had turned her back on the dream that Mrs. Newsome's rupture, their friend's forfeiture—the engagement, the relation itself, broken beyond all mending—might furnish forth her advantage; and, to stay her hand from promoting these things, she had, on private, difficult, but rigid, lines, played strictly fair. She couldn't therefore but feel that, though, as the end of all, the facts in question had been stoutly confirmed, her ground for personal, for what might have been called interested, elation remained rather vague. Strether might easily have made out that she had been asking herself, in the hours she had just sat through, if there were still for her, or were only not, a fair shade of uncertainty. Let us hasten to add, however, that what he at first made out on this occasion he also at first kept to himself. He only asked what in particular Madame de Vionnet had come for; and as to this his companion was ready.

"She wants tidings of Mr. Newsome, whom she appears not to have seen for some days."

"Then she hasn't been away with him again?"

"She seemed to think," Maria answered, "that he might have gone away with *you*."

"And did you tell her I know nothing of him?"

She had her indulgent headshake. "I've known nothing of what you know. I could only tell her I'd ask you."

"Then I've not seen him for a week—and of course I've wondered." His wonderment showed at this moment as sharper, but he presently went on. "Still, I dare say I can put my hand on him. Did she strike you," he asked, "as anxious?"

"She's always anxious."

"After all I've done for her?" And he had one of the last flickers of his occasional mild mirth. "To think that that was just what I came out to prevent!"

She took it up but to reply. "You don't regard him then as safe?"

"I was just going to ask you how in that respect you regard Madame de Vionnet."

She looked at him a little. "What woman was *ever* safe? She told me," she added—and it was as if at the touch of the connexion—"of your extraordinary meeting in the country. After that *à quoi se fier*?"

"It was, as an accident, in all the possible or impossible chapter," Strether conceded, "amazing enough. But still, but still—!"

"But still she didn't mind?"

"She doesn't mind anything."

"Well, then, as you don't either, we may all sink to rest!"

He appeared to agree with her, but he had his resrvation. "I do mind Chad's disappearance."

"Oh you'll get him back. But now you know," she said, "why I went to Mentone." He had sufficiently let her see that he had by this time gathered things together, but there was nature in her wish to make them clearer still. "I didn't want you to put it to me."

"To put it to you—?"

"The question of what you were at last—a week ago—to see for yourself. I didn't want to have to lie for her. I felt that to be too much for me. A man of course is always expected to do it—to do it, I mean, for a woman; but not a woman for another woman; unless perhaps on the tit-for-tat principle, as an indirect way of protecting herself. I don't need protection, so that I was free to 'funk' you—simply to dodge your test. The responsibility was too much for me. I gained time, and when I came back the need of a test had blown over."

Strether thought of it serenely. "Yes; when you came back little Bilham had shown me what's expected of a gentleman. Little Bilham had lied like one."

"And like what you believed him?"

"Well," said Strether, "it was but a technical lie—he classed the attachment as virtuous. That was a view for which there was much to be said—and the virtue came out for me hugely. There was of course a great deal of it. I got it full in the face, and I haven't, you see, done with it yet."

"What I see, what I saw," Maria returned, "is that you dressed up even the virtue. You were wonderful—you were beautiful, as I've had the honour of telling you before; but, if you wish really to know," she sadly confessed, "I never quite knew *where* you were. There were moments," she explained, "when you struck me as grandly cynical; there were others when you struck me as grandly vague."

Her friend considered. "I had phases. I had flights."

"Yes, but things must have a basis."

"A basis seemed to me just what her beauty supplied."

"Her beauty of person?"

"Well, her beauty of everything. The impression she makes. She has such variety and yet such harmony."

She considered him with one of her deep returns of indulgence—returns out of all proportion to the irritations they flooded over. "You're complete."

"You're always too personal," he good-humouredly said; "but that's precisely how I wondered and wandered."

"If you mean," she went on, "that she was from the first for you the most charming woman in the world, nothing's more simple. Only that was an odd foundation."

"For what I reared on it?"

"For what you didn't!"

"Well, it was all not a fixed quantity. And it had for me—it has still—such elements of strangeness. Her greater age than his, her different world, traditions, associations; her other opportunities, liabilities, standards."

His friend listened with respect to his enumeration of these disparities; then she disposed of them at a stroke. "Those things are nothing when a woman's hit. It's very awful. She was hit."

Strether, on his side, did justice to that plea. "Oh of course I saw she was hit. That she was hit was what we were busy with; that she was hit was our great affair. But somehow I couldn't think of her as down in the dust. And as put there by *our* little Chad!"

"Yet wasn't 'your' little Chad just your miracle?"

Strether admitted it. "Of course I moved among miracles. It was all phantasmagoric. But the great fact was that so much of it was none of my business—as I saw my business. It isn't even now."

His companion turned away on this, and it might well have been yet again with the sharpness of a fear of how little his philosophy could bring her personally. "I wish *she* could hear you!"

"Mrs. Newsome?"

"No—not Mrs. Newsome; since I understand you that it doesn't matter now what Mrs. Newsome hears. Hasn't she heard everything?"

"Practically—yes." He had thought a moment, but he went on. "You wish Madame de Vionnet could hear me?"

"Madame de Vionnet." She had come back to him. "She thinks just the contrary of what you say. That you distinctly judge her."

He turned over the scene as the two women thus placed together for him seemed to give it. "She might have known—!"

"Might have known you don't?" Miss Gostrey asked as he let it drop. "She was sure of it at first," she pursued as he said nothing; "she took it for granted, at least, as any woman in her position would. But after that she changed her mind; she believed you believed—"

"Well?"—he was curious.

"Why in her sublimity. And that belief had remained with her, I make out, till the accident of the other day opened your eyes. For that it did," said Maria, "open them—"

"She can't help"—he had taken it up—"being aware? No," he mused; "I suppose she thinks of that even yet."

"Then they *were* closed? There you are! However, if you see her as the most charming woman in the world it comes to the same thing. And if you'd like me to tell her that you do still so see her—!" Miss Gostrey, in short, offered herself for service to the end.

It was an offer he could temporarily entertain; but he decided. "She knows perfectly how I see her."

"Not favourably enough, she mentioned to me, to wish ever to see her again. She told me you had taken a final leave of her. She says you've done with her."

"So I have."

Maria had a pause; then she spoke as if for conscience. "She wouldn't have done with *you*. She feels she has lost you—yet that she might have been better for you."

"Oh she has been quite good enough!" Strether laughed.

"She thinks you and she might at any rate have been friends."

"We might certainly. That's just"—he continued to laugh—"why I'm going."

It was as if Maria could feel with this then at last that she had done her best for each. But she had still an idea. "Shall I tell her that?"

"No. Tell her nothing."

"Very well then." To which in the next breath Miss Gostrey added: "Poor dear thing!"

Her friend wondered; then with raised eyebrows: "Me?"

"Oh no. Marie de Vionnet."

He accepted the correction, but he wondered still. "Are you so sorry for her as that?"

It made her think a moment—made her even speak with a smile. But she didn't really retract. "I'm sorry for us all!"

IV

He was to delay no longer to re-establish communication with Chad, and we have just seen that he had spoken to Miss Gostrey of this intention on hearing from her of the young man's absence. It was not moreover only the assurance so given that prompted him; it was the need of causing his conduct to square with another profession still—the motive he had described to her as his sharpest for now getting away. If he was to get away because of some of the relations involved in staying, the cold attitude toward them might look pedantic in the light of lingering on. He must do both things; he must see Chad, but he must go. The more he thought of the former of these duties the more he felt himself make a subject of insistence of the latter. They were alike intensely present to him as he sat in front of a quiet little café into which he had dropped on quitting Maria's entresol. The rain that had spoiled his evening with her was over; for it was still to him as if his evening *had* been spoiled—though it mightn't have been wholly the rain. It was late when he left the café, yet not too late; he couldn't in any case go straight to bed, and he would walk round by the Boulevard Malesherbes—rather far round—on his way home. Present enough always was the small circumstance that had originally pressed for him the spring of so big a difference—the accident of little Bilham's appearance on the balcony of the mystic troisième at the moment of his first visit, and the effect of it on his sense of what was there before him. He recalled his watch, his wait, and the recognition that had proceeded from the young stranger, that had played frankly into the air and had presently brought him up—things smoothing the way for his first straight step. He had since had occasion, a few times, to pass the house without going in; but had never passed it without again feeling how it had then spoken to him. He stopped short to-night on coming to sight of it: it was as if his last day were oddly copying his first. The windows of Chad's apartment were open to the balcony—a pair of them lighted; and a figure that had come out and taken up little Bilham's attitude, a figure whose cigarette spark he could see leaned on the rail and looked down at him. It denoted, however, no reappearance of his younger friend; it quickly defined itself in the tempered darkness as Chad's more solid shape; so that Chad's was the attention that, after he had stepped forward into the street and signalled, he easily engaged; Chad's was the voice that, sounding into the night with promptness and seemingly with joy, greeted him and called him up.

That the young man had been visible there just in this position expressed somehow for Strether that, as Maria Gostrey had reported, he had been absent and silent; and our friend drew breath on each landing—the lift, at that hour, having ceased to work—before the implications of the fact. He had been for a week intensely away, away to a distance and alone; but he was more back than ever, and the attitude in which Strether had surprised him was something more than a return—it was clearly a conscious surrender. He had arrived but an hour before, from London, from Lucerne, from Homburg, from no matter where—though the visitor's fancy, on the staircase, liked to fill it out; and after a bath, a talk with Baptiste and a supper of light cold clever French things, which one could see the remains of there in the circle of the lamp, pretty and ultra-Parisian, he had come into the air again for a smoke, was occupied at the moment of Strether's aproach in what might have been called taking up his life afresh. His life, his life!—Strether paused anew, on the last flight, at this final rather breathless sense of what Chad's life was doing with Chad's mother's emissary. It was dragging him, at strange hours, up the staircases of the rich; it was keeping him out of bed at the end of long hot days; it was transforming beyond recognition the simple, subtle, conveniently uniform thing that had anciently passed with him for a life of his own. Why should it concern him that Chad was to be fortified in the pleasant practice of smoking on balconies, of supping on salads, of feeling his special conditions agreeably reaffirm themselves, of finding reassurance in comparisons and contrasts? There was no answer to such a question but that he was still practically committed—he had perhaps never yet so much known it. It made him feel old, and he would buy his railway ticket—feeling, no doubt, older—the next day; but he had meanwhile come up four flights, counting the entresol, at midnight and without a lift, for Chad's life. The young man, hearing him by this time, and with Baptiste sent to rest, was already at the door; so that Strether had before him in full visibility the cause in which he was labouring and even, with the troisième fairly gained, panting a little.

Chad offered him, as always, a welcome in which the cordial and the formal—so far as the formal was the respectful—handsomely met; and after he had expressed a hope that he would let him put him up for the night Strether was in full possession of the key, as it might have been called, to what had lately happened. If he had just thought of himself as old Chad was at sight of him thinking of him as older; he wanted to put him up for the night just because he was ancient and weary. It could never be said the tenant of these quarters wasn't nice to him; a tenant who, if he might indeed now keep him, was probably prepared to work it all still more thoroughly. Our friend had in fact the impression that with the minimum of encouragement Chad would propose to keep him indefinitely; an impression in the lap of which one of his own possibilities seemed to sit. Madame de Vionnet had wished him to stay—so why didn't that happily fit? He could enshrine himself for the rest of his days in his young host's *chambre d'ami* and draw out these days at his young host's expense: there could scarce be greater logical expression of the countenance he had been moved to give. There was literally a minute—it was strange enough—during which he grasped the idea that as he *was* acting, as he could only act, he was inconsistent. The sign that the inward forces he had obeyed really hung together would be that—in default always of another career—he should promote the good cause by mounting guard on it. These things, during his first minutes, came and went; but they were after all practically disposed of as soon as he had mentioned his errand. He had come to say good-bye—yet that was only a part; so that from the moment Chad accepted his farewell the question of a more ideal affirmation gave way to something else. He proceeded with the rest of his business. "You'll be a brute, you know—you'll be guilty of the last infamy—if you ever forsake her."

That, uttered there at the solemn hour, uttered in the place that was full of her influence, was the rest of his business; and when once he had heard himself say it he felt that his message had never before been spoken. It placed his present call immediately on solid ground, and the effect of it was to enable him quite to play with what we have called the key. Chad showed no shade of embarrassment, but had none the less been troubled for him after their meeting in the country; had had fears and doubts on the subject of his comfort. He was disturbed, as it were, only *for* him, and had positively gone away to ease him off, to let him down—if it wasn't indeed rather to screw him up—the more gently. Seeing him now fairly jaded he had come, with characteristic good humour, all the way to meet him, and what Strether thereupon supremely made out was that he would abound for him to the end in conscientious assurances. This was what was between them while the visitor remained; so far from having to go over old ground he found his entertainer keen to agree to everything. It couldn't be put too strongly for him that he'd be a brute. "Oh rather!—if I should do anything of *that* sort. I hope you believe I really feel it."

"I want it," said Strether, "to be my last word of all to you. I can't say more, you know; and I don't see how I can do more, in every way, than I've done."

Chad took this, almost artlessly, as a direct allusion. "You've seen her?"

"Oh yes—to say good-bye. And if I had doubted the truth of what I tell you—"

"She'd have cleared up your doubt?" Chad understood—"rather"—again! It even kept him briefly silent. But he made that up. "She must have been wonderful."

"She *was*," Strether candidly admitted—all of which practically told as a reference to the conditions created by the accident of the previous week.

They appeared for a little to be looking back at it; and that came out still more in what Chad next said. "I don't know what you've really thought, all along; I never did know—for anything, with you, seemed to be possible. But of course—of course—" Without confusion, quite with nothing but indulgence, he broke down, he pulled up. "After all, you understand. I spoke to you originally only as I *had* to speak. There's only one way—isn't there?—about such things. However," he smiled with a final philosophy, "I see it's all right."

Strether met his eyes with a sense of multiplying thoughts. What was it that made him at present, late at night and after journeys, so renewedly, so substantially young? Strether saw in a moment what it was—it was that he was younger again than Madame de Vionnet. He himself said immediately none of the things that he was thinking; he said something quite different. "You *have* really been to a distance?"

"I've been to England." Chad spoke cheerfully and promptly, but gave no further account of it than to say: "One must sometimes get off."

Strether wanted no more facts—he only wanted to justify, as it were, his question. "Of course you do as you're free to do. But I hope, this time, that you didn't go for *me*."

"For very shame at bothering you really too much? My dear man," Chad laughed, "what *wouldn't* I do for you?"

Strether's easy answer for this was that it was a disposition he had exactly come to profit by. "Even at the risk of being in your way I've waited on, you know, for a definite reason."

Chad took it in. "Oh yes—for us to make if possible a still better impression." And he stood there happily exhaling his full general consciousness. "I'm delighted to gather that you feel we've made it."

There was a pleasant irony in the words, which his guest, preoccupied and keeping to the point, didn't take up. "If I had my sense of wanting the rest of the time—the time of their being still on this side," he continued to explain—"I know now why I wanted it."

He was as grave, as distinct, as a demonstrator before a blackboard, and Chad continued to face him like an intelligent pupil. "You wanted to have been put through the whole thing."

Strether again, for a moment, said nothing; he turned his eyes away, and they lost themselves, through the open window, in the dusky outer air. "I shall learn from the Bank here where they're now having their letters, and my last word, which I shall write in the morning and which they're expecting as my ultimatum, will so immediately reach them." The light of his plural pronoun was sufficiently reflected in his companion's face as he again met it; and he completed his demonstration. He pursued indeed as if for himself. "Of course I've first to justify what I shall do."

"You're justifying it beautifully!" Chad declared.

"It's not a question of advising you not to go," Strether said, "but of absolutely preventing you, if possible, from so much as thinking of it. Let me accordingly appeal to you by all you hold sacred."

Chad showed a surprise. "What makes you think me capable—?"

"You'd not only be, as I say, a brute; you'd be," his companion went on in the same way, "a criminal of the deepest dye."

Chad gave a sharper look, as if to gauge a possible suspicion. "I don't know what should make you think I'm tired of her."

Strether didn't quite know either, and such impressions, for the imaginative mind, were always too fine, too floating, to produce on the spot their warrant. There was none the less for him, in the very manner of his host's allusion to satiety as a thinkable motive, a slight breath of the ominous. "I feel how much more she can do for you. She hasn't done it all yet. Stay with her at least till she has."

"And leave her *then*?"

Chad had kept smiling, but its effect in Strether was a shade of dryness. "Don't leave her *before*. When you've got all that can be got—I don't say," he added a trifle grimly. "That will be the proper time. But as, for you, from such a woman, there will always be something to be got, my remark's not a wrong to her." Chad let him go on, showing every decent deference, showing perhaps also a candid curiosity for this sharper accent. "I remember you, you know, as you were."

"An awful ass, wasn't I?"

The response was as prompt as if he had pressed a spring; it had a ready abundance at which he even winced; so that he took a moment to meet it. "You certainly then wouldn't have seemed worth all you've let me in for. You've defined yourself better. Your value has quintupled."

"Well then, wouldn't that be enough—?"

Chad had risked it jocosely, but Strether remained blank. "Enough?"

"If one *should* wish to live on one's accumulations?" After which, however, as his friend appeared cold to the joke, the young man as easily dropped it. "Of course I really never forget, night or day, what I owe her. I owe her everything. I give you my word of honour," he frankly rang out, "that I'm not a bit tired of her." Strether at this only gave him a stare: the way youth could express itself was again and again a wonder. He meant no harm, though he might after all be capable of much; yet he spoke of being "tired" of her almost as he might have spoken of being tired of roast mutton for dinner. "She has never for a moment yet bored me—never been wanting, as the cleverest women sometimes are, in tact. She has never talked about her tact—as even they too sometimes talk; but she has always had it. She has never had it more"—he handsomely made the point—"than just lately." And he scrupulously went further. "She has never been anything I could call a burden."

Strether for a moment said nothing; then he spoke gravely, with his shade of dryness deepened. "Oh if you didn't do her justice—!"

"I *should* be a beast, eh?"

Strether devoted no time to saying what he would be; *that,* visibly, would take them far. If there was nothing for it but to repeat, however, repetition was no mistake. "You owe her everything—very much more than she can ever owe you. You've in other words duties to her, of the most positive sort; and I don't see what other duties—as the others are presented to you—can be held to go before them."

Chad looked at him with a smile. "And you know of course about the others, eh?—since it's you yourself who have done the presenting."

"Much of it—yes—and to the best of my ability. But not all—from the moment your sister took my place."

"She didn't," Chad returned. "Sally took a place, certainly; but it was never, I saw from the first moment, to be yours. No one—with us—will ever take yours. It wouldn't be possible."

"Ah of course," sighed Strether, "I knew it. I believe you're right. No one in the world, I imagine, was ever so portentously solemn. There I am," he added with another sigh, as if weary enough, on occasion, of this truth. "I was made so."

Chad appeared for a little to consider the way he was made; he might for this purpose have measured him up and down. His conclusion favoured the fact. "*You* have never needed any one to make you better. There has never been any one good enough. They couldn't," the young man declared.

His friend hesitated. "I beg your pardon. They *have*."

Chad showed, not without amusement, his doubt. "Who then?"

Strether—though a little dimly—smiled at him. "Women—too."

"'Two'?"—Chad stared and laughed. "Oh I don't believe, for such work, in any more than one! So you're proving too much. And what *is* beastly, at all events," he added, "is losing you."

Strether had set himself in motion for departure, but at this he paused. "Are you afraid?"

"Afraid—?"

"Of doing wrong. I mean away from my eye." Before Chad could speak, however, he had taken himself up. "I *am* certainly," he laughed, "prodigious."

"Yes, you spoil us for all the stupid—!" This might have been, on Chad's part, in its extreme emphasis, almost too freely extravagant; but it was full, plainly enough, of the intention of comfort, it carried with it a protest against doubt and a promise, positively, of performance. Picking up a hat in the vestibule he came out with his friend, came downstairs, took his arm, affectionately, as to help and guide him, treating him if not exactly as aged and infirm, yet as a noble eccentric who appealed to tenderness, and keeping on with him, while they walked, to the next corner and the next. "You needn't tell me, you needn't tell me!"—this again, as they proceeded, he wished to make Strether feel. What he needn't tell him was now at last, in the geniality of separation, anything at all it concerned him to know. He knew, up to the hilt—that really came over Chad; he understood, felt, recorded his vow; and they lingered on it as they had lingered in their walk to Strether's hotel the night of their first meeting. The latter took, at this hour, all he could get, he had given all he had had to give; he was as depleted as if he had spent his last sou. But there was just one thing for which, before they broke off, Chad seemed disposed slightly to bargain. His companion needn't, as he said, tell him, but he might himself mention that he had been getting some news of the art of advertisement. He came out quite suddenly with his announcement, while Strether wondered if his revived interest were what had taken him, with strange inconsequence, over to London. He appeared at all events to have been looking into the question and had encountered a revelation. Advertising scientifically worked presented itself thus as the great new force. "It really does the thing, you know."

They were face to face under the street-lamp as they had been the first night, and Strether, no doubt, looked blank. "Affects, you mean, the sale of the object advertised?"

"Yes—but affects it extraordinarily; really beyond what one had supposed. I mean of course when it's done as one makes out that, in our roaring age, it *can* be done. I've been finding out a little; though it doubtless doesn't amount to much more than what you originally, so awfully vividly—and all, very nearly, that first night—put before me. It's an art like another, and infinite like all the arts." He went on as if for the joke of it—almost as if his friend's face amused him. "In the hands, naturally, of a master. The right man must take hold. With the right man to work it *c'est un monde*."

Strether had watched him quite as if, there on the pavement, without a pretext, he had begun to dance a fancy step. "Is what you're thinking of that you yourself, in the case you have in mind, would be the right man?"

Chad had thrown back his light coat and thrust each of his thumbs into an armhole of his waistcoat; in which position his fingers played up and down. "Why, what is he but what you yourself, as I say, took me for when you first came out?"

Strether felt a little faint, but he coerced his attention. "Oh yes, and there's no doubt that, with your natural parts, you'd have much in common with him. Advertising is clearly at this time of day the secret of trade. It's quite possible it will be open to you—giving the whole of your mind to it—to make the whole place hum with you. Your mother's appeal is to the whole of your mind, and that's exactly the strength of her case."

Chad's fingers continued to twiddle, but he had something of a drop. "Ah we've been through my mother's case!"

"So I thought. Why then do you speak of the matter?"

"Only because it was a part of our original discussion. To wind up where we began, my interest's purely platonic. There at any rate the fact is—the fact of the possible. I mean the money in it."

"Oh damn the money in it!" said Strether. And then as the young man's fixed smile seemed to shine out more strange: "Shall you give your friend up for the money in it?"

Chad preserved his handsome grimace as well as the rest of his attitude. "You're not altogether—in your so great 'solemnity'—kind. Haven't I been drinking you in—showing you all I feel you're worth to me? What have I done, what am I doing, but cleave to her to the death? The only thing is," he good-humouredly explained, "that one can't but have it before one, in the cleaving—the point where the death comes in. Don't be afraid for *that*. It's pleasant to a fellow's feelings," he developed, "to 'size-up' the bribe he applies his foot to."

"Oh then if all you want's a kickable surface the bribe's enormous."

"Good. Then there it goes!" Chad administered his kick with fantastic force and sent an imaginary object flying. It was accordingly as if they were once more rid of the question and could come back to what really concerned them. "Of course I shall see you to-morrow."

But Strether scarce heeded the plan proposed for this; he had still the impression—not the slighter for the simulated kick—of an irrelevant hornpipe or jig. "You're restless."

"Ah," returned Chad as they parted, "you're exciting."

V

He had, however, within two days, another separation to face. He had sent Maria Gostrey a word early, by hand, to ask if he might come to breakfast; in consequence of which, at noon, she awaited him in the cool shade of her little Dutch-looking dining-room. This retreat was at the back of the house, with a view of a scrap of old garden that had been saved from modern ravage; and though he had on more than one other occasion had his legs under its small and peculiarly polished table of hospitality, the place had never before struck him as so sacred to pleasant knowledge, to intimate charm, to antique order, to a neatness that was almost august. To sit there was, as he had told his hostess before, to see life reflected for the time in ideally kept pewter; which was somehow becoming, improving to life, so that one's eyes were held and comforted. Strether's were comforted at all events now—and the more that it was the last time—with the charming effect, on the board bare of a cloth and proud of its perfect surface, of the small old crockery and old silver, matched by the more substantial pieces happily disposed about the room. The specimens of vivid Delf, in particular, had the dignity of family portraits; and it was in the midst of them that our friend resignedly expressed himself. He spoke even with a certain philosophic humour. "There's nothing more to wait for; I seem to have done a good day's work. I've let them have it all round. I've seen Chad, who has been to London and come back. He tells me I'm 'exciting,' and I seem indeed pretty well to have upset every one. I've at any rate excited *him*. He's distinctly restless."

"You've excited *me*," Miss Gostrey smiled. "*I'm* distinctly restless."

"Oh you were that when I found you. It seems to me I've rather got you out of it. What's this," he asked as he looked about him, "but a haunt of ancient peace?"

"I wish with all my heart," she presently replied, "I could make you treat it as a haven of rest." On which they fronted each other across the table, as if things unuttered were in the air.

Strether seemed, in his way, when he next spoke, to take some of them up. "It wouldn't give me—that would be the trouble—what it will, no doubt, still give you. I'm not," he explained, leaning back in his chair, but with his eyes on a small ripe round melon—"in real harmony with what surrounds me. You *are*. I take it too hard. You *don't*. It makes—that's what it comes to in the end—a fool of me." Then at a tangent, "What has he been doing in London?" he demanded.

"Ah one may go to London," Maria laughed. "You know *I* did."

Yes—he took the reminder. "And you brought *me* back." He brooded there opposite to her, but without gloom. "Whom has Chad brought? He's full of ideas. And I wrote to Sarah," he added, "the first thing this morning. So I'm square. I'm ready for them."

She neglected certain parts of this speech in the interest of others. "Marie said to me the other day that she felt him to have the makings of an immense man of business."

"There it is. He's the son of his father!"

"But *such* a father!"

"Ah, just the right one from that point of view! But it isn't his father in him," Strether added, "that troubles me."

"What is it then?" He came back to his breakfast; he partook presently of the charming melon, which she liberally cut for him; and it was only after this that he met her question. Then moreover it was but to remark that he'd answer her presently. She waited, she watched, she served him and amused him, and it was perhaps with this last idea that she soon reminded him of his having never yet named to her the article produced at Woollett. "Do you remember our talking of it in London—that night at the play?" Before he could say yes, however, she had put it to him for other matters. Did he remember, did he remember—this and that of their first days? He remembered everything, bringing up with humour even things of which she professed no recollection, things she vehemently denied; and falling back above all on the great interest of their early time, the curiosity felt by both of them as to where he could "come out." They had so assumed it was to be in some wonderful place—they had thought of it as so very *much* out. Well, that was doubtless what it had been—since he had come out just there. He was out, in truth, as far as it was possible to be, and must now rather bethink himself of getting in again. He found on the spot the image of his recent history; he was like one of the figures of the old clock at Berne. *They* came out, on one side, at their hour, jigged along their little course in the public eye, and went in on the other side. He too had jigged his little course—him too a modest retreat awaited. He offered now, should she really like to know, to name the great product of Woollett. It would be a great commentary on everything. At this she stopped him off; she not only had no wish to know, but she wouldn't know for the world. She had done with the products of Woollett—for all the good she had got from them. She desired no further news of them, and she mentioned that Madame de Vionnet herself had, to her knowledge, lived exempt from the information he was ready to supply. She had never consented to receive it, though she would have taken it, under stress, from Mrs. Pocock. But it was a matter about which Mrs. Pocock appeared to have had little to say—never sounding the word—and it didn't signify now. There was nothing clearly for Maria Gostrey that signified now—save one sharp point, that is, to which she came in time. "I don't know whether it's before you as a possibility that, left to himself, Mr. Chad may after all go back. I judge that it *is* more or less so before you, from what you just now said of him."

Her guest had his eyes on her, kindly but attentively, as if foreseeing what was to follow this. "I don't think it will be for the money." And then as she seemed uncertain: "I mean I don't believe it will be for that he'll give her up."

"Then he *will* give her up?"

Strether waited a moment, rather slow and deliberate now, drawing out a little this last soft stage, pleading with her in various suggestive and unspoken ways for patience and understanding. "What were you just about to ask me?"

"Is there anything he can do that would make you patch it up?"

"With Mrs. Newsome?"

Her assent, as if she had had a delicacy about sounding the name, was only in her face; but she added with it: "Or is there anything he can do that would make *her* try it?"

"To patch it up with me?" His answer came at last in a conclusive headshake. "There's nothing any one can do. It's over. Over for both of us."

Maria wondered, seemed a little to doubt. "Are you so sure for her?"

"Oh yes—sure now. Too much has happened. I'm different for her."

She took it in then, drawing a deeper breath. "I see. So that as she's different for *you*—"

"Ah but," he interrupted, "she's not." And as Miss Gostrey wondered again: "She's the same. She's more than ever the same. But I do what I didn't before—I *see* her."

He spoke gravely and as if responsibly—since he had to pronounce; and the effect of it was slightly solemn, so that she simply exclaimed "Oh!" Satisfied and grateful, however, she showed in her own next words an acceptance of his statement. "What then do you go home to?"

He had pushed his plate a little away, occupied with another side of the matter; taking refuge verily in that side and feeling so moved that he soon found himself on his feet. He was affected in advance by what he believed might come from her, and he would have liked to forestall it and deal with it tenderly; yet in the presence of it he wished still more to be—though as smoothly as possible—deterrent and conclusive. He put the question by for the moment; he told her more about Chad. "It would have been impossible to meet me more than he did last night on the question of the infamy of not sticking to her."

"Is that what you called it for him—'infamy'?"

"Oh rather! I described to him in detail the base creature he'd be, and he quite agrees with me about it."

"So that it's really as if you had nailed him?"

"Quite really as if—! I told him I should curse him."

"Oh," she smiled, "you *have* done it." And then having thought again: "You *can't* after that propose—!" Yet she scanned his face.

"Propose again to Mrs. Newsome?"

She hesitated afresh, but she brought it out. "I've never believed, you know, that you did propose. I always believed it was really she—and, so far as that goes, I can understand it. What I mean is," she explained, "that with such a spirit—the spirit of curses!—your breach is past mending. She has only to know what you've done to him never again to raise a finger."

"I've done," said Strether, "what I could—one can't do more. He protests his devotion and his horror. But I'm not sure I've saved him. He protests too much. He asks how one can dream of his being tired. But he has all life before him."

Maria saw what he meant. "He's formed to please."

"And it's our friend who has formed him." Strether felt in it the strange irony.

"So it's scarcely his fault!"

"It's at any rate his danger. I mean," said Strether, "It's hers. But she knows it."

"Yes, she knows it. And is your idea," Miss Gostrey asked, "that there was some other woman in London?"

"Yes. No. That is, I *have* no ideas. I'm afraid of them. I've done with them." And he put out his hand to her. "Good-bye."

It brought her back to her unanswered question. "To what do you go home?"

"I don't know. There will always be something."

"To a great difference," she said as she kept his hand.

"A great difference—no doubt. Yet I shall see what I can make of it."

"Shall you make anything so good—?" But, as if remembering what Mrs. Newsome had done, it was as far as she went.

He had sufficiently understood. "So good as this place at this moment? So good as what *you* make of everything you touch?" He took a minute to say, for, really and truly, what stood about him there in her offer—which was as the offer of exquisite service, of lightened care, for the rest of his days—might well have tempted. It built him softly round, it roofed him warmly over, it rested, all so firm, on selection. And what ruled selection was beauty and knowledge. It was awkward, it was almost stupid, not to seem to prize such things; yet, none the less, so far as they made his opportunity they made it only for a moment. She would moreover understand—she always understood.

That indeed might be, but meanwhile she was going on. "There's nothing, you know, I wouldn't do for you."

"Oh yes—I know."

"There's nothing," she repeated, "in all the world."

"I know. I know. But all the same I must go." He had got it at last. "To be right."

"To be right?"

She had echoed it in vague deprecation, but he felt it already clear for her. 'That, you see, is my only logic. Not, out of the whole affair, to have got anything for myself."

She thought. "But with your wonderful impressions you'll have got a great deal."

"A great deal"—he agreed. "But nothing like *you*. It's you who would make me wrong!"

Honest and fine, she couldn't greatly pretend she didn't see it. Still, she could pretend just a little. "But why should you be so dreadfully right?"

"That's the way that—if I must go—you yourself would be the first to want me. And I can't do anything else."

So then she had to take it, though still with her defeated protest. "It isn't so much your *being* 'right'—it's your horrible sharp eye for what makes you so."

"Oh but you're just as bad yourself. You can't resist me when I point that out."

She sighed it at last all comically, all tragically, away. "I can't indeed resist you."

"Then there we are!" said Strether.

FURTHER READINGS

COOPER

Mary E. Cunningham, ed., *James Fenimore Cooper: A Re-appraisal*, 1954;
Blake Nevius, *Cooper's Landscapes*, 1976;
Thomas L. Philbrick, *James Fenimore Cooper and the Development of American Sea Fiction*, 1961;
Stephen Railton, *Fenimore Cooper*, 1978;
Robert E. Spiller, *Fenimore Cooper: Critic of His Times*, 1931;
Robert E. Spiller, ed., *James Fenimore Cooper: Representative Selections*, 1936;
Warren S. Walker, *Leather-stocking and the Critics*, 1965.

HAWTHORNE

Newton Arvin, *Nathaniel Hawthorne*, 1929;
Nina Baym, *The Shape of Hawthorne's Career*, 1976;
Frederick Crews, *The Sins of the Fathers: Hawthorne's Psychological Themes*, 1966;
Kenneth Dauber, *Rediscovering Hawthorne*, 1977;
Charles Feidelson, Jr., "The Scarlet Letter," in *Hawthorne Centenary Essays*, Roy Harvey Pearce, ed., 1964;
R. H. Fogle, *Hawthorne's Fiction: The Light and the Dark*, 1952;
Henry James, *Hawthorne*, 1879;
Anne Marie McNamara, "The Character of Flame: The Function of Pearl in *The Scarlet Letter*," *American Literature*, 27 (January, 1956), pp. 537–53;
F. O. Matthiessen, *American Renaissance*, 1941;
Hyatt Waggoner, *Hawthorne: A Critical Study*, rev. 1963.

MELVILLE

Newton Arvin, *Herman Melville*, 1950;
Richard Chase, *Herman Melville: A Critical Study*, 1949;

Richard Chase, "Melville and Moby-Dick," *The American Novel and Its Tradition*, 1957;
Bainard Cowan, *Exiled Waters: Moby-Dick and the Crisis of Allegory*, 1982;
Leon Howard, *Herman Melville: A Biography*, 1951;
James E. Miller, *A Reader's Guide to Herman Melville*, 1962, 1973;
Lewis Mumford, *Herman Melville*, rev. 1962;
Charles Olson, *Call Me Ishmael*, 1947;
Hershel Parker, ed., *The Recognition of Herman Melville: Selected Criticism Since 1846*, 1967;
Howard P. Vincent, *Studies in Moby-Dick*, 1969;
Raymond Weaver, *Herman Melville: Mariner and Mystic*, 1921;
Nathalia Wright in *Eight American Authors*, James Woodress, ed., rev. 1971.

TWAIN

Gladys Carmen Bellamy, *Mark Twain as a Literary Artist*, 1950;
Walter Blair, *Mark Twain and Huck Finn*, 1960;
Van Wyck Brooks, *The Ordeal of Mark Twain*, rev. 1933;
Clara Clemens, *My Father, Mark Twain*, 1931;
Bernard De Voto, *Mark Twain's America*, 1932;
De Lancey Furguson, *Mark Twain: Man and Legend*, 1943;
William M. Gibson, *The Art of Mark Twain*, 1976;
Justin Kaplan, *Mr. Clemens and Mark Twain, A Biography*, 1966;
Kenneth S. Lynn, *Mark Twain and Southwestern Humor*, 1960;
Henry Nash Smith, *Mark Twain: The Development of a Writer*, 1962;
Dixon Wecter, *Sam Clemens of Hannibal*, 1952.

CRANE

Thomas Beer, *Stephen Crane: A Study in American Letters*, with an introduction by Joseph Conrad, 1923;
Frank Bergon, *Stephen Crane's Artistry*, 1975;
John Berryman, *Stephen Crane*, 1950;
Edwin Cady, *Stephen Crane*, 1962;
Jean Cazemajou, *Stephen Crane*, 1969;
Lillian Gilkes, *Cora Crane*, 1960;
Matthew Josephson, *Portrait of the Artist as American*, 1930;
R. W. Stallman, *Stephen Crane*, 1968.

CHOPIN

Robert Cantwell, "*The Awakening* by Kate Chopin," *Georgia Reveiw*, 10 (Winter, 1956), pp. 489–94;
Kenneth Eble, "A Forgotten Novel: Kate Chopin's *The Awakening*," *Western Humanities Review*, 10 (Summer, 1956), pp. 261–69;

John R. May, "Local Color in *The Awakening*," *Southern Review*, 6 (Fall, 1970), pp. 1031–40;
Emily Toth, "The Independent Woman and 'Free Love,'" *Massachusetts Review*, 16 (Autumn, 1975), pp. 647–64;
Emily Toth, *Kate Chopin*, 1990;
Nancy Walker, "Feminist or Naturalist: The Social Context of Kate Chopin's *The Awakening*," *Southern Quarterly*, 17 (1979), pp. 95–103;
Cynthia Griffin Wolff, "Thanatos and Eros: Kate Chopin's *The Awakening*," *American Quarterly*, 25 (October, 1973), pp. 449–71.

DREISER

Helen Dreiser, *My Life with Dreiser*, 1951;
Dorothy Dudley, *Forgotten Frontiers: Dreiser and the Land of the Free*, 1932;
William J. Handy, "A Re-examination of Dreiser's *Sister Carrie*," *Texas Studies in Literature and Language*, 1 (1959), pp. 380–93;
Richard Lehan, *Theodore Dreiser: His World and His Novels*, 1970;
F. O. Matthiessen, *Theodore Dreiser*, 1951;
Ellen Moers, *Two Dreisers: The Man and the Novelist*, 1970;
Donald Pizer, *The Novels of Theodore Dreiser*, 1976;
W. A. Swanberg, *Dreiser*, 1965;
Robert Penn Warren, *Homage to Theodore Dreiser*, 1971.

JAMES

Louis Auchincloss, *Reading Henry James*, 1975;
Joseph Warren Beach, *The Method of Henry James*, 1918;
R. P. Blackmur, ed., *The Art of Henry James: Critical Prefaces*, 1934;
Theodora Bosanquet, *Henry James at Work*, 1924;
Van Wyck Brooks, *The Pilgrimage of Henry James*, 1925;
Richard Chase, "James' Ambassadors," *Twelve Original Essays on Great American Novels*, ed. by Charles Shapiro, 1958;
F. W. Dupee, *Henry James*, 1951;
Leon Edel, *Henry James*, 5 vols., 1953–72;
Daniel Mark Fogel, *Henry James and the Structure of the Romantic Imagination*, 1981;
Kenneth Graham, *Henry James: The Drama of Fulfillment*, 1976;
Dorothea Krook, *The Ordeal of Consciousness in Henry James*, 1962;
Percy Lubbock, *The Craft of Fiction*, 1931;
Bruce McElderry, *Henry James*, 1965;
F. O. Matthiessen, *Henry James: The Major Phase*, 1944;
F. O. Matthiessen, *The James Family*, 1947;
Richard Poirier, *The Comic Sense in Henry James*, 1960;
Sallie Sears, *The Negative Imagination*, 1968;
Elizabeth Stevenson, *The Crooked Corridor*, 1949;
Tony Tanner, *Henry James: Modern Comments*, 1968.

SOME ELEMENTS FOR DISCUSSION AND WRITING

These alphabetical lists are an innovative teaching, reading, discussion, and writing aid, suggested several years ago by McKenzie Professor of English David Kirby, Florida State University. Students often make notes in the margins as they read or study. To organize such notes alphabetically for quick reference or review struck us as a worthwhile innovation. Each of the following lists has been prepared by a teacher who has written extensively on the novel in question or has taught it frequently. Because of the newness and diversity of this concept, no attempt has been made to make the lists conform to a single pattern. The elements listed have been chosen, however, on the assumption that students and teachers are likely to want to locate them before or during discussion and writing. Not every instance of a given topic has been cited, only those considered most likely to be of use. Readers may want to add their own entries or page numbers.

THE LAST OF THE MOHICANS:
Some Elements for Discussion and Writing

PREPARED BY WARREN S. WALKER, TEXAS TECH UNIVERSITY

THE SCARLET LETTER: Some Elements for Discussion and Writing

PREPARED BY JOHN ALLISON, EASTERN ILLINOIS UNIVERSITY

The Custom-House

The Scarlet Letter

MOBY DICK: Some Elements for Discussion and Writing

Prepared by Bainard Cowan, Louisiana State University

THE ADVENTURES OF HUCKLEBERRY FINN: Some Elements for Discussion and Writing

PREPARED BY ROBERT MERRILL, UNIVERSITY OF NEVADA, RENO

THE RED BADGE OF COURAGE: Some Elements for Discussion and Writing

PREPARED BY SCOTT F. STODDART, MOUNT ST. CLARE COLLEGE

THE AWAKENING: Some Elements for Discussion and Writing

Prepared by David Madden, Louisiana State University

SISTER CARRIE:
Some Elements for Discussion and Writing

PREPARED BY J. GERALD KENNEDY, LOUISIANA STATE UNIVERSITY

THE AMBASSADORS:
Some Elements for Discussion and Writing

PREPARED BY DANIEL MARK FOGEL, LOUISIANA STATE UNIVERSITY

A 9
B 0
C 1
D 2
E 3
F 4
G 5
H 6
I 7
J 8